The Seconde

Chapter. Fo. iiii.

¶When Jesus was borne in beth
lehem a towne of iury/in the tyme of kynge Here
de/beholde/there cam wyse men fro the est to Je
rusalem sayinge : where is he that is borne kynge
of the iewes? we have sene his starre in the est/and are co
me to worshippe hym.

When Herode the kynge/after he hadde herde this/was tro
bled/and all Jerusalem with hym, and he sent for all the chefe
prestes and scribes of the people/and demaunded of them
where Christ shulde be borne. And they sayde vnto him : in beth
lehem in iury, For thus is it written by the prophet:

And thou bethlehem in the londe of iury/shalt not be the leest
as pertaynynge to the princes of iuda. For out of the shall come
the captayne that shall governe my people israel.

Then Herode previly called the wyse men/and dyligently
enquyred of them the tyme of the starre that appered. And
he sent them to bethlehem sayinge: when ye be come thyder se
arch diligently for the chylde. And when ye have founde hym
brynge me worde that I maye come and worshippe hym also.

When they had herde the kynge/they departed and lo the star
re which they sawe in the est went before them/tyll it came
and stode over the place where the chylde was. When they sa
we the starre, they were marveilously glad. And entred in
to the house/and fonde the chylde with Mary hys mother, and
kneled doune and worshipped hym/and opened there treas
ures, and offered vnto him gyftes/gold frank sence/and
myrre. And after they were warned in there slepe/that they
shulde not goo agayne to Herode/they returned into there awne

See page xxiv

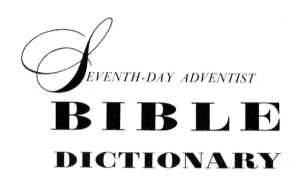

*S*EVENTH-DAY ADVENTIST
BIBLE
DICTIONARY

SEVENTH-DAY ADVENTIST
BIBLE DICTIONARY

Editor

DON F. NEUFELD

Associate Editor

JULIA NEUFFER

Assistant Editor

THOMAS A. DAVIS

Associate Writers

Ernest S. Booth

Raymond F. Cottrell

James J. Cox

Robert L. Cunningham

Thomas A. Davis

Alger F. Johns

Richard L. Litke

Norval F. Pease

Walter F. Specht

F. Donald Yost

COMMENTARY REFERENCE SERIES

Volume 8

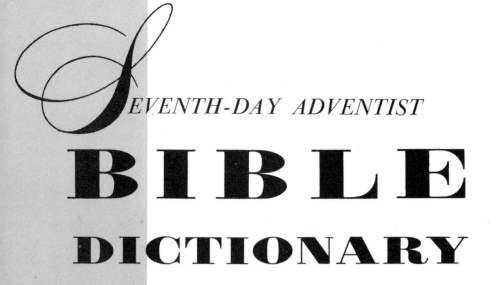

*S*EVENTH-DAY ADVENTIST

BIBLE

DICTIONARY

By SIEGFRIED H. HORN, Ph.D.

Professor of Archeology and History of Antiquity
Andrews University

With contributions by other writers

With Atlas

REVIEW AND HERALD

PUBLISHING ASSOCIATION

WASHINGTON, D.C.

1960

Library of Congress Catalog Card Number: 60-12204

(OFFSET IN U.S.A.)

Table of Contents

List of Illustrations

vi

LIST OF ILLUSTRATIONS

LIST OF ILLUSTRATIONS

LIST OF ILLUSTRATIONS

LIST OF ILLUSTRATIONS

LIST OF ILLUSTRATIONS

LIST OF ILLUSTRATIONS

LIST OF ILLUSTRATIONS

LIST OF ILLUSTRATIONS

LIST OF ILLUSTRATIONS

Preface

A Bible dictionary is one of the indispensable tools of every student of the Bible, and many such works have been produced in the past. The need for a new dictionary, embodying the results of the latest archeological finds, and free from certain doctrinal and philosophical peculiarities, was especially expressed during the quadrennial convention of Bible teachers held at La Sierra College, Arlington, California, in June 1954. During this convention, which was attended by Bible teachers from all the Seventh-day Adventist colleges in North America and by some from overseas colleges, an official action was taken requesting the production of a new Bible dictionary. It was observed that the publication of *The Seventh-day Adventist Bible Commentary* by the Review and Herald Publishing Association, two volumes of which were then in circulation, had demonstrated that the necessary scholarship, editorial competency, and financial backing were available within the Seventh-day Adventist denomination for such undertakings. In response to this appeal the Executive Committee of the Review and Herald Publishing Association took an action in its meeting of January 30, 1957, to publish an illustrated, one-volume Bible dictionary, matching in size one of the volumes of the *Bible Commentary* and containing an atlas of historical maps pertaining to Bible times.

Don F. Neufeld, one of the associate editors of the *Bible Commentary,* was appointed as editor, and Julia Neuffer, also of the editorial staff of the *Bible Commentary,* was asked to be associate editor. Later, Thomas A. Davis joined the *Dictionary* staff as an assistant editor.

Siegfried H. Horn, professor of archeology and history of antiquity (of Andrews University), was asked to write the geographical, historical, and most of the biographical articles, as well as certain other articles in which archeology played a major role, an assignment that covered more than half of the material in the volume. A heavy writing assignment was accepted also by Raymond F. Cottrell, former associate editor of the *Bible Commentary,* who now serves as associate editor of the weekly journal *The Review and Herald.* He wrote the articles on the books of the Bible, the biographic articles on the apostles, many prophets, and certain other Bible characters, besides many of the theological articles. The remaining articles were furnished by nine other contributors, who were teachers of either Bible or Biblical languages in Seventh-day Adventist colleges or were men who through specialized studies or interest were qualified to write articles in certain areas of Biblical knowledge. Their names appear as contributors facing the title page.

Help was also obtained from several experts in the fields of linguistics, Old and New Testament studies, theology, et cetera, through their critical reading of those articles that fell within the realm of their specialties. The galley proofs were submitted for criticism to a group of general readers. For the hundreds of helpful suggestions and corrections made and for the constructive criticism of these readers the editors wish to record their deep-felt gratitude. To them are due many of the merits this dictionary may possess, but they should not be blamed for any mistakes that may remain. For these the contributors and editors accept full responsibility. The names of the various readers are: Walter R. Beach, Maynard V. Campbell, Theodore Carcich, Earle Hilgert, Alger F. Johns, Lewis E. Lenheim, Richard L. Litke, William G. C. Murdoch, Merwin R. Thurber, Kenneth H. Wood, Jr.

Purpose. The purpose of a Bible dictionary is to present in a concise but clear way all Biblical and pertinent extra-Biblical information available concerning individuals, countries, places, objects, and concepts mentioned in the Bible, and to convey to English Bible readers the meaning of the underlying Hebrew, Aramaic, or Greek terms.

Some Bible dictionaries discuss only important Biblical names and expressions, leaving out subjects, places, and persons about whom little or nothing is known except their names. Other Bible dictionaries are complete, but the individual articles are so lengthy that the whole work consists of several large volumes, hence addresses itself to a select and small group of readers. From the outset it has been the aim of the producers of this Bible dictionary to attain completeness, and to discuss every proper name and significant word found in the Bible, without creating a Biblical encyclopedia. Since the whole work had to be limited to about 1,200 pages, certain restraints with regard to the length of all articles had to be exercised. However, the user of this dictionary may be assured that it contains helpful information on every Bible name and important word. No proper name has been left out, even if nothing could be said to explain it, except to record its occurrence in a certain text. The reader is thus enabled to evaluate the relative importance of any individual or place.

Form of Headings. Proper names appear in the spelling of the Revised Standard Version (RSV), published by Thomas Nelson & Sons, New York, because names are transliterated more uniformly in that version than in the King James Version (KJV). However, names as spelled in the KJV are also listed, and are followed by a cross reference to the pertinent material. For example, the personal name occurring in the KJV as Lakum and in the RSV as Lakkum (Heb. *Laqqûm*) is discussed in this dictionary under the form **Lakkum.** However, under the entry **Lakum** the notation is found: *See* Lakkum. Since millions of copies of the Revised Standard Version are now in the hands of English-speaking Bible readers, significant words in that version have also been incorporated into this dictionary.

Pronunciation. Every proper name is followed in parentheses ( ) by its phonetic spelling according to the system employed in Webster's *New International Dictionary of the English Language.* The list of phonetic symbols employed appears on page xxxii. Thus the entry **Phicol** has the phonetic spelling fī′kŏl, which means that the "i" should be pronounced like the "i" in "sight," and the "o" as the "o" in "not"; the accent is on the first syllable, "fi."

Use of Brackets, Parentheses, and Asterisks. Brackets [ ] are used for four purposes: (1) to enclose the linguistic sections at the beginning of many articles; (2) to take the place of parentheses if the words enclosed occur within a section already inside parentheses; for example: (*BASOR* 100 [1945], 14); (3) to indicate the interpolation of words not in the original into a quotation from the Bible or some other book; (4) to indicate, in the case of an ancient text (such as a tablet, papyrus, or stone inscription), a sentence, section, word, or letter that has been broken off or otherwise lost. For example, certain words or letters now illegible on the Moabite Stone have been restored by the modern editors and translators of these texts and have been put in brackets (*see* Moabite Stone). Likewise, part of the inscription on a Hebrew seal impression found at Lachish is broken off so that one Hebrew letter is lacking at each end of the lower line. Hence, this inscription, which is quoted in the article on Gedaliah, reads, " (Belonging) to Gedaliah [w]ho is over the hou[se]," for the letter *'aleph* of the Heb. *'shr,* "who," and the letter *t* in the Heb. *hbyt,* "the house," are now lacking.

Parentheses ( ) are used to enclose phonetically spelled proper names. They also enclose explanatory remarks such as references to Bible texts, to extra-Biblical sources, to the maps of the atlas, to other articles in this dictionary, et cetera. If parentheses occur in translated ancient texts, or in the translation of proper names, they supply information needed by the English reader for a correct understanding of the translation, although the words thus enclosed are no part of the texts translated. See, for example, the entry Lebanon, the translation of which is given as "white (mountain)." The word "mountain" is supplied to clarify what the ancients meant, although the word "Lebanon" literally means no more than "white."

PREFACE

An asterisk * before a word indicates that the word is the heading of another article in which additional information on the topic may be found. A *see* followed by a name or term tells the reader that additional or related information is available in the article referred to under that particular word.

Abbreviations. A list of abbreviations used for the books of the Bible, for the titles of frequently quoted periodicals, of certain reference works such as *The Seventh-day Adventist Bible Commentary,* and of certain general terms appears on pages xxvii-xxxi.

Non-Biblical Subjects. Although this work is not a Biblical encyclopedia, a few articles on non-Biblical subjects are nevertheless included. This has been done because frequent references are made to such subjects as the Amarna Letters and the Moabite Stone, terms meaningless to the average reader of the Bible unless explained. Also articles on the Bible, writing, writing materials, the Apocrypha, and on other related subjects have been included in this dictionary because of their importance for the Bible reader.

Source Material and Bibliographies. A list of the titles of all the books, reference works, and periodical articles consulted by the contributors and editors of this Bible dictionary would fill many pages. Practically all standard Bible dictionaries and encyclopedias, as well as dictionaries of Biblical Hebrew and Greek, were frequently consulted, also dictionaries on Akkadian, Egyptian, Ugaritic, Phoenician, South Arabic, and other ancient languages, encyclopedias of Egyptian, Assyrian, classical, and other early historical antiquities. In most cases no credit is given for the information obtained from the many works consulted, and bibliographies appear only sporadically at the end of certain articles. Exceptions are made in cases where the information is not readily available, or where views are presented that are not generally accepted. Where no sources are given for views expressed the reader can in most cases find help for further study by going to the larger encyclopedias.

A studious effort has been made to guarantee that the interpretations presented in this dictionary are in harmony with sound conservative scholarship. At the same time they are in accord with the teachings held by Seventh-day Adventists. Where controversies on certain subjects exist and space did not permit extended discussions, references were made to such discussions in the seven-volume *Seventh-day Adventist Bible Commentary (SDA Com).* The reader will also notice that references to the writings of Ellen G. White do not appear, although her books were frequently consulted. The omission of such references is due to the same limitations of space that prevented other works from being quoted, and also to the fact that the *SDACom* contains a rather complete cross reference system to these writings.

Illustrations. This Bible dictionary contains 536 photographs, line drawings, and charts, and an end sheet portraying an ancient wall painting in color. Most of the illustrations were secured by S. H. Horn. Many were taken during travels in the Bible lands and are published in this work for the first time. The illustrations were not chosen to serve merely as an embellishment to this book or for their aesthetic value, but rather to acquaint the reader with the topography of the Bible lands, with Biblical sites, with archeological objects that illustrate events recorded in the Bible, and with the appearance of ancient objects, such as tools, weapons, or musical instruments. Many private and public institutions and numerous scholars in several countries have contributed pictures and have given permission to use them. Their names and their contributions appear on pages vi-xviii, and a word of deep-felt gratitude is due to each one of them. The task of collecting pictures was a major one, and it is the hope of the contributors and editors that their inclusion in this dictionary may serve to further the understanding of the Scriptures by means of visual aids.

Maps. A Bible dictionary in which the location of hundreds of geographical sites is discussed would be incomplete without appropriate maps. Therefore it was planned to include in this dictionary an accurate atlas of Biblical maps in color, produced by the latest processes of map making. At the time when the first steps were taken to produce this dictionary, the firm of Rand McNally, a well-known publisher of maps and atlases, had recently published a new *Bible Atlas,* edited by Emil G. Kraeling. It was decided that the full set of maps of the *Rand McNally Bible Atlas* be included in this new Bible dictionary. Professor Kraeling and the firm of Rand McNally have been extremely helpful, and in cooperation with the editorial staff of this dictionary have eliminated certain inaccuracies and mistakes that occurred on the maps of that work. The new maps printed for this dictionary are therefore superior.

The reader may occasionally notice minor differences in the spelling of Arabic names as presented in the text and on the maps. The reason is that in the text Arabic names are spelled according to the system used in *The Westminster Historical Atlas to the Bible,* from which the system of transliteration that was used by Professor Kraeling differs slightly. In a few instances this dictionary proposes the identification of a Biblical locality with a site different from that proposed by Professor Kraeling, in which case the reader is informed of this in the respective geographical articles. In one case the news of the discovery of the true site of an ancient city came too late to the notice of the engravers to make the change on the plates (*see* Derbe). On Map V various theories of the route of the Exodus are presented, some of which vary from the traditional route, and are based on hypotheses not accepted in this dictionary.

History and Chronology. In no field of Biblical studies have the archeological discoveries·of the past century been more instructive and enlightening than in the reconstruction of ancient history and its ancillary science, chronology. The historical background of the Bible is now well known—of some periods only in general outline, of others in great detail. Also the ancient chronology has been stabilized and the unusually early dates for the beginnings of Mesopotamian and Egyptian history found in older books have been reduced by several millenniums in some instances and by centuries in others. Yet there are no·exact dates in Egyptian history for events preceding 1991 B.C., and the exact chronology in Mesopotamia does not begin until the ninth century B.C. All earlier dates are only approximate and may represent small or large errors.

Biblical chronology has profited by the stabilization of secular chronology. Differences among scholars for dated events of the first millennium B.C. are therefore insignificant, and dates presented in this dictionary for that period hardly ever differ more than one or two years from those found in other recent works. Dates for the patriarchal period, the Exodus, and the period of the judges show greater differences, because of different interpretations of Biblical data and the lack of extra-Biblical references to Biblical·events and persons during the second millennium B.C. The reader may be assured, however, that the contributors and editors are aware of the latest chronological theories discussed in the scholarly world, have taken account of the best available historical and archeological evidence, and have adopted a scheme based on this and on the Biblical data. However, it is readily admitted that this scheme is only tentative and may undergo adjustments through future discoveries. The reader of this dictionary should keep this in mind when using any of the dates presented in it. Some dates may be absolutely accurate, others may be off by not more than one year, whereas some, especially the earlier ones, could be in error to a much greater degree. *See* Chronology IX, notes to tables.

Linguistic explanations. Every proper name and its phonetic spelling is followed by a linguistic statement enclosed in brackets [ ]. Readers who are not interested in this matter may skip this section and continue with the reading of the other factual information that follows the bracket closing the linguistic explanation. In the bracketed sections appear Biblical Hebrew, (or) Aramaic, and (or) Greek forms of the words under discussion transliterated according to the systems explained on pages xxv, xxvi.

If possible, the meaning of each proper name is given, and the lack of such information indicates that the meaning of the name is unknown. Many times the phrase "meaning uncertain" follows the transliterated name, showing that the meanings given such names in certain Bible dictionaries are hypothetical and that no real linguistic basis for them exists. Even where meanings appear, the reader should remember that there is not always certainty regarding the accuracy of such translations. In most cases where there is some question the word "possibly" or "probably" is inserted to alert the reader to the absence of absolute certainty with regard to the meaning.

Many Hebrew personal names contain as one of their elements an abbreviated form of God's name; for example, in the name Hezekiah (Heb. *Chizqîyah* or *Chizqîyahû*) the ending "-iah" (Heb. *-yah* or *-yahû*) is an abbreviation of the divine name *YHWH*. For this the transliterated form "Yahweh" is given because it more correctly represents the original pronunciation than the popular form "Jehovah." Hence, the spelling "Yahweh" is used in the linguistic section, but the terms "Lord" and "God" are used in the main sections of the articles.

The Hebrew verbal system, unlike the English, does not express past, present, and future tenses, but its inflected forms indicate whether an action is complete or incomplete. Where a verb occurs in a textual context its meaning is usually clear and can easily be rendered into English so that its meaning is accurately conveyed. Proper names, however, are so short that in most cases it is difficult to ascertain the exact verbal form. It is for this reason that the present tense is used in the translation of most names, although a rendering into the past tense could as easily be defended on linguistic grounds. For example, Nathanael can mean "God has given" or "God gives."

If a proper name occurs in inscriptions and other texts of the ancient world, such as in Assyrian cuneiform texts, in Egyptian inscriptions, on Hebrew seals or in Aramaic papyri, this fact is noted, together with the spelling of such names in transliteration. This information with regard to personal names is presented to show how widely some names were used in the ancient world; otherwise the impression might be gained that Bible names were confined only to the people mentioned in the Scriptures. It should be remembered, however, that where extra-Biblical sources contain such personal names, their bearers are in most cases not the individuals mentioned in the Bible. Wherever extra-Biblical sources actually mention persons known from the Bible this fact is discussed in the main section of the biographical articles, but not in the linguistic section.

If, on the other hand, geographical or ethnic names are quoted as being mentioned in ancient literature, the reader can in almost all cases be sure that they refer to sites, countries, or peoples named in the Bible. The reason for the difference is that while the same personal names were borne by many people, there were not many cities, countries, or nations that had identical names.

Description of End Sheet

A wall painting showing the arrival of a group of Palestinians in Egypt

Against a background of ancient Bible manuscripts and early printings the end sheet reproduces a color mural of the 19th cent. B.C. depicting a group of Palestinian men, women, and children being introduced to the nomarch Khnem-hotep (not reproduced here), a nobleman of central Egypt and a contemporary of Abraham. This mural painting is one of a series found on the walls of a rock-cut tomb of Khnem-hotep at *Beni-hasan*, about 150 miles south of Cairo, on the right bank of the Nile.

Before the nobleman stands his scribe (at the extreme right), an Egyptian, as his dark skin and his dress show. He holds in his hand a document with a text saying that in the 6th year of King Sen-Usert (Sesostris) II (1892 B.C.) 37 Asiatics arrived bringing eye paint. Underneath this document is a short hieroglyphic inscription that reads: "The royal scribe Nefer-hotep." This scribe is followed by the chief hunter, also an Egyptian, of whom the hieroglyphic inscription says: "The chief hunter Khety."

The upper hieroglyphic inscription, read from right to left, says: "The arrival, bringing eye paint, which 37 Asiatics bring to him."

Of the 37 Asiatics the mural depicts only 15, including four women and three children (three men are left out in the reproduction presented here). The first Asiatic is a prince called "a ruler of a foreign country" by the name of Abishar (meaning "my father is king"), as indicated by the inscription painted above and below the head of the antelope that he leads. He and the following man were probably the only ones of the whole group admitted into the presence of the nomarch, since only they and the Egyptian officials are shown barefooted, while all others are shown wearing either sandals or moccasin-type shoes. Abishar, the prince, wears a garb much more colorful than the dress of his followers, with which may be compared the coat Joseph received from his father (Gen 37:3). The Asiatics are distinguished by their relatively light skin, Semitic noses, pointed beards, and black, cropped hair. In his left hand the prince holds a boomerang, a weapon so common among the Canaanites that the Egyptians adopted it as a hieroglyph meaning "Asiatic" (see the red hieroglyph in front of the bound kneeling man in the top inscription). The second Asiatic, leading a gazelle, wears a three-colored loincloth. The third man carries a bow, and the three who follow (not depicted in this reproduction) carry two spears, two boomerangs, and a skin water bottle. Two of them wear white garments.

Then follows a donkey carrying two children in a pack saddle, and an instrument explained as being a bellows. If this interpretation is correct, the traveling Asiatics may have been not only traders but also itinerating smiths. The four women wear long garments. The garments of three of them are fastened on the left shoulder, leaving the right shoulder bare, but that of the fourth (the third woman from the right) covers both shoulders. A second donkey carries a spear and bellows, and is followed by two more men. The first carries a skin water bottle and a lyre (the earliest extant picture of a Palestinian musical instrument); the second, a bow, a quiver, and a battle-ax.

This mural is our only contemporary pictorial representation of inhabitants of Canaan in the patriarchal period, and is therefore extremely important as a source for our knowledge of the appearance of these people, their dress, weapons, and other objects.

The picture was first copied by artists of the Lepsius expedition (1842-1845), and is reproduced from R. Lepsius' *Denkmäler aus Aegypten und Aethiopien* (Berlin, 1849-1859).

Guide to Transliteration

1. *Biblical Hebrew, Aramaic, and Greek.* In adopting systems of transliterating Hebrew, Aramaic, and Greek words the editors kept in mind those who do not know these ancient languages—doubtless the majority of the readers of this Bible dictionary. It is for this reason that the Hebrew שׁ (*shin*) is not transliterated as *š* but as *sh*, and ח (*cheth*) not as *ḥ*, but as *ch* (to be pronounced as the "ch" in the Scotch "loch" or the German "Loch"). The two laryngals א (*'aleph*) and ע (*'ayin*), for which our script has no characters, are expressed by the conventional signs ' for *'aleph* and ' for *'ayin*. No difference is made in the transliteration of בּ and ב, גּ and ג, דּ and ד, כּ and כ, unless the dot in the character is a *dagesh* and thus calls for a doubling of the letter, because a transliteration of *bh, gh, dh,* or *kh* for the letters without the *dagesh* would not convey the correct pronunciation to the English reader. However, a difference is made between פּ = *p* and פ = *ph*, and between תּ = *t* and ת = *th*. To indicate the use of a י (*yod*) after the vowels *e* or *i*, and of a ו (*waw*) in connection with *o* or *u*, these vowels are given a circumflex (*ê, î, ô, û*). No attempt has been made to indicate the length of Hebrew and Aramaic vowels or the place of accentuation. The systems are kept simple, so that words can easily be pronounced without the knowledge of ancient languages; at the same time they provide enough information to students of ancient languages to enable them to recognize such words and look them up in Hebrew, Aramaic, or Greek dictionaries.

The following list gives the transliteration of the Hebrew and Aramaic alphabet according to the system employed in this dictionary:

Consonants

א = '	ו = *w*	כ, ך = *k*	ע = '	ר = *r*
בּ, ב = *b*	ז = *z*	ל = *l*	פּ = *p*	שׂ = *ś*
גּ, ג = *g*	ח = *ch*	מ = *m*	פ = *ph*	שׁ = *sh*
דּ, ד = *d*	ט = *ṭ*	נ = *n*	צ = *ṣ*	תּ = *t*
ה = *h*	י = *y*	ס = *s*	ק = *q*	ת = *th*

Masoretic Vowel Pointings

ָ ַ ֳ = *a*		ֹ ָ = *o*	
(vocal shewa) = *e*		וֹ = *ô*	
ֵ ֶ = *ê*		ֻ = *u*	
ִ = *i*		וּ = *û*	
ִי = *î*			

The following list presents the transliteration of the Greek alphabet as used in this Bible dictionary. No accents are indicated, but a difference is made between long and short vowels. The rough breathing (') is transliterated as *h;* the smooth breathing (') is not transliterated, since it is not pronounced.

Α α = *A a*	Ζ ζ = *Z z*	Λ λ = *L l*	Π π = *P p*	Φ φ = *Ph ph*
Β β = *B b*	Η η = *Ē ē*	Μ μ = *M m*	Ρ ϱ = *R r*	Χ χ = *Ch ch*
Γ γ = *G g*	Θ θ = *Th th*	Ν ν = *N n*	Σ σ = *S s*	Ψ ψ = *Ps ps*
Δ δ = *D d*	Ι ι = *I i*	Ξ ξ = *X x*	Τ τ = *T t*	Ω ω = *Ō ō*
Ε ε = *E e*	Κ ϰ = *K k*	Ο ο = *O o*	Υ υ = *U u*	' = *H h*

The first letter in a transliterated proper name is always expressed by a capital letter, although Hebrew and Aramaic scripts make no differences between capital and small letters; examples are Heb. *Chizqîyahû,* "Hezekiah," and Gr. *Paulos,* "Paul." Common words are expressed without the capital; for example, Heb. *nephesh,* "soul," and Gr. *pneuma,* "spirit."

If a name is spelled in two different ways in Hebrew as, for examples, *Chizqîyah* and *Chizqîyahû* (Hezekiah), both spellings are given, but only one spelling if the difference pertains to the presence or absence of a *yod* in connection with an *i* or *e,* or of a *waw* in connection with an *o* or *u.* In all such cases only the spelling given first in L. Koehler and W. Baumgartner's *Lexicon in Veteris Testamenti Libros* (2d ed.; Leiden, 1958) is adopted; hence only the spelling *'Ôphîr* is given under the entry Ophir, although the spelling *'Ophîr* also occurs in the Hebrew Bible.

2. *Phoenician, Ugaritic, South Arabic, Nabataean, Palmyrene, and extra-Biblical Aramaic.* Texts and inscriptions using these languages contain no vowels (for a partial exception in Ugaritic, see below), and their vocalization is therefore known only in part. It is for this reason that no attempt has been made to furnish vowels to any words quoted from those languages. If vowels were supplied many readers might forget their hypothetical value. Such words are mainly given for students interested in ancient languages, and to indicate the wide range of Biblical terms in other ancient cognate languages. The transliteration of the consonants follows closely the system adopted for Biblical Hebrew and Aramaic, but for Ugaritic (fig. 531) *h* and *ḥ* are used, since two different characters are found in that script which in Hebrew had coalesced to the one letter *cheth.* Ugaritic also expresses the vowels *a, i,* and *u* if they are connected with the consonant ' *('aleph);* consequently they appear in transliterated Ugaritic words as *'a, 'i,* and *'u.*

3. *Egyptian.* For the transliteration of Egyptian words a generally accepted system is used. Since ancient Egyptian does not express vowels, they are not given in the transliteration. Egyptian has two *'alephs,* represented by the symbols ꜣ and *i̓,* four *h*'s, represented by the letter *h* pronounced as "h" in English, *ḥ* spoken as an emphatic "h," *ḫ* pronounced like "ch" in Scotch "loch," and *ẖ* pronounced like "ch" in German "ich." It has two *t*'s, of which *t* corresponds to English "t" and *ṱ* to "tj," and two *d*'s, of which *d* is pronounced as English "d" and *ḏ* as "dj." Egyptologists by common consent pronounce one *'aleph* (ꜣ) and the *'ayin* (') like the English "a" in "asterisk," but pronounce a second *'aleph* (*i̓*) usually as a consonantal "y", the *w* as a "u." Elsewhere the letter *e* is put between consonants. Hence the word *R'mśś* is pronounced Rameses, and the word *Ḏd-p3-nṯr-iwf-'nḥ* would have to be pronounced Djed-pa-netjer-yuf-anch (Joseph's name Zaphenath-paneah).

4. *Akkadian, Assyrian, and Babylonian.* The Assyrian and Babylonian languages are both dialects of Akkadian. If a word is common to both dialects the term Akkadian is used, if it occurs only in Assyrian or in Babylonian texts these respective terms are employed. Since Akkadian texts are written in the syllabic cuneiform script in which vowels are expressed, transliterated Akkadian words contain vowels. The many proper names occurring in the *Amarna Letters, written in the Babylonian language and script, are therefore also presented in a vocalized transliteration. The generally accepted system of transliteration is used, except that *sh* is used for *š,* an unfamiliar sign to most readers, and *y* is substituted for *i* if it stands before another vowel.

5. *Arabic.* Arabic words occur almost exclusively in the form of place names or geographical terms. Systems of transliterations vary widely among scholars. In this dictionary the spelling of Arabic proper names is followed as given in G. E. Wright and F. V. Filson's *Westminster Historical Atlas to the Bible* (rev. ed.; Philadelphia, 1956). Names that do not occur in this work are spelled as they appear in the *Bulletins* or *Annuals of the American Schools of Oriental Research,* or if not found there, are spelled, as far as possible, according to the system adopted in these works.

List of Abbreviations

1. Books of the Bible

Gen Ex Lev Num Deut Jos Jgs Ruth 1 Sa 2 Sa 1 Ki 2 Ki 1 Chr 2 Chr Ezr
Neh Est Job Ps Prov Ec Song Is Jer Lam Eze Dan Hos Joel Amos
Ob Jon Mic Nah Hab Zep Hag Zec Mal
Mt Mk Lk Jn Acts Rom 1 Cor 2 Cor Gal Eph Php Col 1 Th 2 Th 1 Ti
2 Ti Tit Phm Heb Jas 1 Pe 2 Pe 1 Jn 2 Jn 3 Jn Jude Rev

2. Other Abbreviations

1QIs^a	The complete Isaiah scroll from Qumran Cave 1, published by Millar Burrows *et al., The Dead Sea Scrolls of St. Mark's Monastery*, vol. 1 (New Haven, Conn., 1950)
1QIs^b	A somewhat poorly preserved Isaiah scroll from Cave 1. E. L. Sukenik, *The Dead Sea Scrolls of the Hebrew University* (Jerusalem, 1955)
1 QS	"A Sectarian Rule," also called "Manual of Discipline," published by Millar Burrows *et al., The Dead Sea Scrolls of St. Mark's Monastery*, vol. 2 (New Haven, Conn., 1951)
AASOR.	*Annual of the American Schools of Oriental Research* (New Haven, Conn., 1920-)
Abel, *Géographie*	F.-M. Abel, *Géographie de la Palestine* (2 vols.; Paris, 1933, 1938)
AfO	*Archiv für Orientforschung* (Graz, 1923-)
Against Apion	see Apion
AJA	*American Journal of Archaeology* (Princeton, N.J., 1897-)
AJSL	*American Journal of Semitic Languages and Literatures,* vols. 12-58 (Chicago, 1895-1941)
Anab.	Xenophon, *The Anabasis of Cyrus,* translated by C. L. Brownson, Loeb Classical Library (London, 1921-1922)
ANEP	J. B. Pritchard, *The Ancient Near East in Pictures Relating to the Old Testament* (Princeton, N.J., 1954)
ANET	J. B. Pritchard, ed., *Ancient Near Eastern Texts Relating to the Old Testament* (Princeton, N.J., 1st ed. 1950; 2d ed. 1955)
ANF	*The Ante-Nicene Fathers,* edited by Alexander Roberts and James Donaldson (10 vols.; New York, 1885-1896)
Ann.	Tacitus, *Annals*
Ant.	see Jos. *Ant.*
AO	*Der Alte Orient,* vols. 1-43 (Leipzig, 1900-1945)
Apion	Flavius Josephus, *Against Apion,* translated by H. St. J. Thackeray, Loeb Classical Library (London, 1956)
AR	*Ancient Records,* see Breasted, *AR,* see also Luckenbill, *AR*
art.	article
ASV	The Holy Bible. The Standard American Edition of the Revised Version of the Bible (New York, 1901)

av.	avoirdupois
BA	*The Biblical Archaeologist* (New Haven, Conn., 1938-)
BASOR	*Bulletin of the American Schools of Oriental Research* (New Haven, 1919-)
Bibl. Reallexikon	Kurt Galling, *Biblisches Reallexikon* (Tübingen, 1937)
BiOr	*Bibliotheca Orientalis* (Leiden, 1943-)
BR	see *Bibl. Reallexikon*
Breasted, *AR*	James H. Breasted, *Ancient Records of Egypt* (5 vols.; Chicago, 1906-1907)
bu.	bushel, bushels
c.	*circa*, "about"
cent.	century, centuries
cf.	*confer*, "compare"
ch	chapter
chs	chapters
Cicero, *Pro Flacco*	Cicero, *The Speeches, Pro Flacco*, translated by Louis E. Lord, Loeb Classical Library (London, 1937)
CIL	*Corpus Inscriptionum Latinarum* (Vienna, 1862-1909)
cm.	centimeter, centimeters
col.	column
Cowley, *Aramaic Papyri*	A. Cowley, *Aramaic Papyri of the Fifth Century B.C.* (Oxford, 1923)
cu.	cubit, cubits
d.	died
Diodorus	Diodorus Siculus, translated by C. H. Oldfather and Russel M. Geer, Loeb Classical Library (10 vols.; London, 1933-1957 [vols. 8 and 12 forthcoming])
Diringer, *Iscrizioni*	David Diringer, *Le iscrizioni antico-ebraiche palestinesi* (Florence, 1934)
DSS	Dead Sea scrolls. *See* Scrolls, Dead Sea
Dussaud, *Topographie*	René Dussaud, *Topographie historique de la Syrie antique et médiévale* (Paris, 1927)
Ecclus	Ecclesiasticus, a book of the Apocrypha
ed.	edited, edition, editor
et al.	*et alii*, "and others"
Eusebius, *Hist. Eccl.*	Eusebius, *The Church History, The Nicene and Post-Nicene Fathers*, 2d series, vol. 1 (New York, 1890)
fig.	figure
figs.	figures
fl.	flourished
ft.	foot, feet
gal.	gallon, gallons
Gr.	Greek
Heb.	Hebrew
Heb. Gr.	Hebrew Grammar
Herod.	Herodotus, translated by A. D. Godley, Loeb Classical Library (4 vols.; London, 1920-1925)
Hist.	History, Histories
Hist. Eccl.	See Eusebius, *Hist. Eccl.*
Hist. Nat.	See Pliny, *Hist. Nat.*
ibid.	*ibidem*, "in the same place"
IEJ	*Israel Exploration Journal* (Jerusalem, 1950-)

in.	inch, inches
JAOS	*Journal of the American Oriental Society* (New Haven, 1849-)
JBL	*Journal of Biblical Literature* (Philadelphia, 1881-)
JEA	*The Journal of Egyptian Archaeology* (London, 1914-)
JEOL	*Jaarbericht "Ex Oriente Lux"* (Leiden, 1933-)
JNES	*Journal of Near Eastern Studies* (Chicago, 1942-)
Jos. *Ant.*	Flavius Josephus, *Jewish Antiquities,* books i-xiv translated by H. St. J. Thackeray and Ralph Marcus, Loeb Classical Library (4 vols.; London, 1930-1943). For books xv-xx see the older translation of William Whiston
Jos. *War*	Flavius Josephus, *The Jewish War,* translated by H. St. J. Thackeray, Loeb Classical Library (2 vols.; London, 1927-1928)
JPOS	*Journal of the Palestine Oriental Society,* vols. 1-21 (Jerusalem, 1920-1948)
JSS	*Journal of Semitic Studies* (Manchester, 1956-)
JTS	*The Journal of Theological Studies* (Oxford, 1900-)
K	*Kethib,* "written," indicating the reading of a certain Hebrew term in its pre-Masoretic form, before being corrected. See also Q
kilogr.	kilogram, kilograms
KJV	The Holy Bible. The King James Version
Lat.	Latin
lb.	pound, pounds
Lidzbarski, *Ephemeris*	Mark Lidzbarski, *Ephemeris für semitische Epigraphik* (3 vols.; Giessen, 1902-1915)
Life	Flavius Josephus, *The Life,* translated by H. St. J. Thackeray, Loeb Classical Library (London, 1926)
Lit.	Literature
Livy	Livy, translated by B. O. Foster and A. C. Schlesinger, Loeb Classical Library (14 vols.; London, 1919-1951)
Luckenbill, *AR*	D. D. Luckenbill, *Ancient Records of Assyria and Babylonia* (2 vols.; Chicago, 1926-1927)
LVTL	L. Koehler and W. Baumgartner, *Lexicon in Veteris Testamenti Libros* (Leiden, 1st ed. 1953; 2d ed. with *Supplementum,* 1958)
LXX	Septuagint. A. Rahlfs, editor, *Septuaginta* (2 vols.; Stuttgart, 1935)
m.	meter, meters
Macc	Maccabees, two books of the Apocrypha, 1 Maccabees and 2 Maccabees
mi.	mile, miles
Mishnah	*The Mishnah,* translated by Herbert Danby, London, 1954; also the Mishnah section of the Talmud as published in *The Babylonian Talmud,* Soncino ed. (London, 1948-1952)
MNDPV	*Mittheilungen und Nachrichten des Deutschen Palästina-Vereins,* vols. 1-18 (Leipzig, 1895-1912)
MS, Ms	Manuscript
MSS, Mss	Manuscripts
n.	note
n. d.	no date (of publication given)
NT	New Testament
OLZ	*Orientalistische Literaturzeitung* (Berlin, 1898-)
Onomasticon	Eusebius, *Onomasticon.* E. Klostermann, *Eusebius Werke,* III. Band, 1. Hälfte: *Das Onomastikon der biblischen Ortsnamen* (Leipzig, 1904)
op. cit.	*opere citato,* "in the work cited"
opp.	opposite
Or.	Manuscript code used by British Museum
OT	Old Testament

oz.	ounce, ounces
p.	page
P⁴⁵	A third-century payrus containing fragments of the Gospels and Acts. Frederic G. Kenyon, editor, *The Chester Beatty Biblical Papyri*, fascicle ii (2 vols.; London, 1933, 1934)
P⁴⁶	A third-century papyrus of the Pauline Epistles. Frederic G. Kenyon, editor, *The Chester Beatty Biblical Papyri*, fascicle iii and Supplement (3 vols.; London, 1934-1937)
P⁴⁷	A third-century papyrus of Revelation. Frederic G. Kenyon, editor, *The Chester Beatty Biblical Papyri*, fascicle iii (2 vols.; London, 1934, 1936)
P⁵²	A papyrus fragment of the Gospel of John of the early second century. C. H. Roberts, editor, *An Unpublished Fragment of the Fourth Gospel in the John Rylands Library* (Manchester, 1935)
P⁶⁶	A second-century papyrus containing the Gospel of John. Victor Martin, editor, *Papyrus Bodmer II* (2 vols.; Cologny-Genève, 1956, 1958)
P⁷²	A third-century papyrus containing Jude, 1 and 2 Peter. Michel Testuz, editor, *Papyrus Bodmer VII-IX* (Cologny-Genève, 1959)
para.	paragraph
PEFQS	*Palestine Exploration Fund, Quarterly Statement,* vols. 1-69 (London, 1869-1937)
PEQ	*Palestine Exploration Quarterly,* vols. 70- (London, 1938-)
PJB	*Palästinajahrbuch,* vols. 1-37 (Berlin, 1905-1941)
pl.	plate, plural
Pliny, *Hist. Nat.*	Pliny, *Natural History,* translated by H. Rackham and W. H. S. Jones, Loeb Classical Library (9 vols.; London, 1938-1952)
Polybius	Polybius, *The Histories,* translated by W. R. Paton, Loeb Classical Library (6 vols.; London, 1922-1927)
pp.	pages
pt.	pint, pints
Ptol.	Ptolemy of Alexandria (Claudius Ptolemaeus). References refer either to his Canon (an appendix to his *Almagest*) or to his *Geography*
publ.	published
P-W	*Paulys Real-Encyclopädie der classischen Altertumswissenschaft,* Georg Wissowa, editor (Stuttgart, 1893-)
Q	*Qerê,* "to be read," the Hebrew form of a certain OT term as corrected by the Masoretes. See also K
QDAP	*The Quarterly of the Department of Antiquities in Palestine,* vols. 1-14 (Jerusalem, 1932-1950)
QSPEF	see *PEFQS*
qt.	quart, quarts
RB	*Revue Biblique* (Paris, 1892-)
Reallexikon der Vorgesch.	*Reallexikon der Vorgeschichte,* Max Ebert, editor (15 vols.; Berlin, 1924-1932)
RLA	*Reallexikon der Assyriologie,* Erich Ebeling and Bruno Meissner, editors (Berlin, 1932-)
RSV	The Holy Bible. Revised Standard Version (New York, 1952)
SDACom	*The Seventh-day Adventist Bible Commentary,* F. D. Nichol *et al.,* editors (7 vols.; Washington, D.C., 1953-1957)
sec.	section
sing.	singular
Strabo	see Strabo, *Geogr.*
Strabo, *Geogr.*	*The Geography of Strabo,* translated by Horace L. Jones, Loeb Classical Library (8 vols.; London, 1917-1932)

Suetonius, *Claud.*	Suetonius, *The Lives of the Caesars,* book v, *The Deified Claudius,* translated by J. C. Rolfe, Loeb Classical Library (London, 1914)
Suetonius, *Div. Julius*	Suetonius, *The Lives of the Caesars,* book i, *The Deified Julius,* translated by J. C. Rolfe, Loeb Classical Library (London, 1914)
Talmud	*The Babylonian Talmud,* Soncino ed., translated under the editorship of I. Epstein (35 vols.; London, 1948-1952)
TR	*Textus Receptus,* the designation for a printed Greek NT text, in common use up to the middle of the 19th century
tr.	translated
transl.	translated, translation
v	verse
vol.	volume
vols.	volumes
vs	verses
VT	*Vetus Testamentum* (Leiden, 1951-)
War	see Jos. *War*
WHAB	*The Westminster Historical Atlas to the Bible,* G. Ernest Wright and Floyd V. Filson, editors (Philadelphia, 1st ed. 1945; 2d rev. ed. 1956)
WO	*Die Welt des Orients* (Göttingen, 1947-)
Xenophon, *Cyrop.*	Xenophon, *Cyropaedia,* translated by Walter Miller, Loeb Classical Library (2 vols.; London, 1914)
YHWH	The divine name of God, in vocalized Hebrew *Yahweh, see* Yahweh
ZAW	*Zeitschrift für die alttestamentliche Wissenschaft* (Berlin, 1881-)
ZDPV	*Zeitschrift des Deutschen Palästina-Vereins* (Wiesbaden, 1878-)

Key to Pronunciation

The following diacritical marks found in Webster's *New International Dictionary of the English Language* are used in the phonetic spellings appearing in this dictionary.

ā	as in labor	ē	as in he	ō	as in note	ū	as in cube
ȧ	" " chaotic	ê	" " create	ȯ	" " obey	ů	" " unite
â	" " care	ĕ	" " end	ô	" " lord	û	" " urn
ă	" " fat	ĕ	" " silent	ŏ	" " not	ŭ	" " up
ă̄	" " infant	ē̄	" " maker	ŏ	" " connect	ŭ	" " circus
ä	" " far	ī	" " sight	o͞o	" " food		
à	" " ask	ĭ	" " ill	o͝o	" " foot		
a̍	" " sofa	ĭ	" " charity				

A

Aaron (âr'ŭn). [Heb. *'Aharôn,* meaning uncertain; Gr. *Aarōn.*] Son of Amram and Jochebed (Ex 6:20), and descendant of Levi (1 Chr 6:1-3). He had an older sister, Miriam (Ex 7:7; cf. ch 2:4), and a younger brother, Moses (ch 7:7). He married Elisheba, a daughter of Amminadab, of the tribe of Judah, who bore him four sons, Nadab, Abihu, Eleazar, and Ithamar (ch 6:23).

Aaron enters the Bible narrative when the Lord commissioned him to go from Egypt to meet his brother Moses at Mount Horeb (Ex 4:27). There the two conferred together about returning to Egypt to effect the release of their people from bondage (v 28). The Lord had already appeared to Moses, and had indicated to him that Aaron was to be his spokesman in the new assignment (vs 14-16). From that time forth the two brothers labored side by side to secure freedom for their oppressed kinsmen (vs 29, 30; etc.). Even after the departure from Egypt Aaron continued, at least at times, as Moses' spokesman to the children of Israel (ch 16:9, 10). At Rephidim, a short distance from the Wilderness of Sin, Aaron and Hur sustained the uplifted arms of Moses in the successful battle with a band of Amalekites (ch 17:12).

During the encampment at Mount Sinai, Aaron and his sons Nadab and Abihu, together with 70 of the elders of Israel, were accorded the special privilege of accompanying Moses beyond the bounds at the foot of the mountain which the people generally might not pass (Ex 24:1-11). During Moses' prolonged absence from camp, Aaron acquiesced in the demand of the people for visible "gods" by making a golden calf and leading in its worship (ch 32). While the Israelites were still encamped at Sinai, Aaron and his sons were appointed and consecrated to serve as priests in the sanctuary (Ex 28:40 to 29:37; 40:13-16; Lev 8). Aaron served as high priest for 38 years, until within a few months of the entry into Canaan (Num 20:22-29).

Soon after the departure from Sinai, Aaron and Miriam united in opposing Moses as supreme commander of Israel, under God, and claimed for themselves a voice in the administration of the nation. God decisively silenced the two who had presumed to challenge the one whom He had appointed leader (Num 12:1-15). Somewhat later a group of disaffected Levites united forces with certain men of the tribe of Reuben, and others, in revolt against the leadership of Moses and Aaron, and once more God vindicated His chosen leaders (ch 16). Lest there should be any lingering doubt concerning the fact that it was God who had appointed Aaron to have charge of the religious life of the nation, God gave dramatic proof by causing Aaron's rod to bud, blossom, and bear almonds overnight (ch 17). Toward the close of the 40 years in the wilderness, almost on the borders of Canaan, Aaron joined with Moses in a demonstration of impatience at Kadesh, where the latter impetuously struck the rock from which water was to flow forth for the people. As a result, the two brothers were barred from entering the Land of Promise (ch 20:7-13).

Not long after the experience at Kadesh the people of Israel broke camp and journeyed around the borders of Edom, having been refused permission to take a more direct route through that country. On the way the Lord directed Moses and Aaron that the latter should prepare to lay down his duties and to die (Num 20:22-24; cf. Deut 10:6). By divine order the high-priestly robes were taken from Aaron and placed on his son Eleazar, in token of his succession to Aaron as high priest (Num 20:25-28). Aaron died at the age of 123 (cf. Ex 7:7; Deut 34:7), and was mourned by Israel for a period of 30 days (Num 20:29).

Aaronites (âr'ŭn-īts). [Heb. *'Aharôn,* "Aaron."] The descendants of Aaron the priest (1 Chr 12:27; 27:17). The Hebrew word is the same as that for "Aaron," but in these verses is used collectively.

Aaron's Rod. The staff used by Aaron as a symbol of his commission of authority. It was probably similar to a shepherd's rod, a stout stick or club, perhaps 3 ft. long, used both to drive away predators and to direct and control the flock, hence its appropriateness as a symbol of authority. Aaron's rod symbolized God's will and authority in conflict with the will and authority of Pharaoh (Ex 7:10, 12, 19, 20; 8:5, 16). The incident of the budding of Aaron's rod (Num 16; 17) stands out as a significant OT miracle whereby God vindicated His choice of leadership in a time of crisis and rebellion. After the miracle, Moses was directed to place the rod "before the testimony" where it was to be kept as a "token against the rebels" (ch 17:10) and to serve as a witness to later generations of Israelites. In the NT Aaron's rod is mentioned once (Heb 9:4), simply to note that it was one of the items preserved in the ark of the ancient tabernacle.

Abaddon (á-băd'ŭn). [Heb. *'Abaddôn,* "destruction," "ruin"; Gr. *Abaddōn,* a transliteration of the Hebrew.] A word designating destruction. It occurs in the KJV only in Rev 9:11, where in a symbolic vision it is the name given to the king of an army of locusts. In the RSV it appears also in Job 26:6; 28:22; 31:12; Ps 88:11; Prov 15:11; 27:20, where in each case the KJV reads "destruction." In these latter occurrences *'Abaddôn* is paralleled with Sheol, the grave, and death, and seems to describe a place of destruction, or, more generally, the realm of the dead.

Abagtha (á-băg'thá). [Heb. *'Abagtha',* a name of Persian origin, and of uncertain meaning.] One of the 7 chamberlains, literally, "eunuchs," serving the Persian king Ahasuerus (Xerxes). See Est 1:10.

Abana (ăb'á-ná). [Heb. *'Abanah,* possibly "the stony one." A variant form is *'Amanah,* perhaps meaning "constant."] One of the two rivers of Damascus, which the Syrian Naaman considered to be superior to the Jordan (2 Ki 5:12). Because the writer of Kings mentions this river first, it has been thought to be the main river that reaches Damascus, and has therefore been identified with the *Chrusorrhoas* of classical writers, now called *Nahr Baradá,* meaning "the cold stream." Its source is a large pool of great depth on a high plain south of Zebedany in the Anti-Lebanon Mountains, 23 mi. northwest of Damascus. After making a rapid descent down the mountains the stream

1. The Abana River in modern Damascus

divides itself into several branches in the vicinity of Damascus. After leaving Damascus, whose fertility it provides, it flows sluggishly through the desert for about 20 mi. and then loses itself in one of 3 swampy lakes. Map IX, A-5.

Abarim (ăb'á-rĭm). [Heb. *'Abarim,* "regions beyond."] The region east of Jordan, or perhaps specifically the mountain range in that region. Jeremiah (Jer 22:20) mentions three regions in the following sequence going from north to south: Lebanon, Bashan, and Abarim (KJV "passages"). The children of Israel encamped in the "mountains of Abarim" before they moved down to Shittim (Num 33:47, 48), and Mount Nebo is mentioned as part of Abarim (Num 27:12; Deut 32:49). The mountain range of Abarim rises about 600 ft. above the high plateau of Moab and overlooks the northern part of the Dead Sea, which lies some 4,000 ft. below its peaks. The Arabs call this range *esh-Shefa.*

Abba (ăb'á). [Gr. *abba,* a transliteration of the Aramaic *'abba',* the form of *'ab,* "father," used in direct address.] A title meaning "father," used for God in early Christian prayers (Rom 8:15; Gal 4:6), after the example of our Lord (Mk 14:36).

Abda (ăb'dá). [Heb. *'Abda',* a shortened form of *'Obadyah,* Obadiah, meaning "servant of Yahweh." The name is attested in cuneiform records and in Phoenician and Nabataean documents.]

1. An Israelite whose son Adoniram (1 Ki 4:6) was Solomon's officer handling revenue.

2. A Levite of Nehemiah's time (Neh 11:17).

Abdeel (ăb'dê-ĕl). [Heb. *'Abde'el,* "servant of God."] An Israelite whose son Shelemiah was commissioned to arrest Jeremiah (Jer 36:26).

Abdi (ăb'dī). [Heb. *'Abdi,* "my servant." The name is attested on a seal impression from an ancient Hebrew jar handle and in Akkadian cuneiform records.]

1. A Levite (1 Chr 6:44), probably identical with the Levite mentioned in 2 Chr 29:12. Some make the Abdi of 2 Chr 29:12 a contemporary of King Hezekiah.

2. A man from the family of Elam who was married to a foreign wife in Ezra's time (Ezr 10:26).

Abdiel (ăb′dĭ-ĕl). [Heb. *'Abdî'el*, "servant of God." The name is attested in Akkadian cuneiform texts from Mesopotamia and Ugarit.] A Gadite (1 Chr 5:15).

Abdon (ăb′dŏn). [Heb. *'Abdôn*, possibly "servile."]

1. A man from Pirathon in Ephraim, who judged Israel 8 years. Nothing concerning his judgeship is recorded, but the fact is mentioned that he had 40 sons and 30 grandsons who rode on ass colts (Jgs 12:13-15). Horses were not yet common in Israel.

2. A chieftain of the tribe of Benjamin who lived in Jerusalem (1 Chr 8:23, 28).

3. A Benjamite of Gibeon and a relative, possibly a great-uncle, of King Saul (1 Chr 8:30; 9:35, 36).

4. Son of Micah; an official of Josiah (2 Chr 34:20).

5. A town in Asher assigned to the Levites (Jos 21:30; 1 Chr 6:74), identified with *Khirbet 'Abdeh*, about 10 mi. northeast of Accho.

Abednego (á-bĕd′nĕ-gō). [Heb. *'Abed Negô;* Aramaic once *'Abed Negô'*, Dan. 3:29. Since the name is inexplicable in this form it is generally agreed that it stands for *'Ebed Nebo,* meaning "a servant of (the Babylonian god) Nabu," a name attested by an Aramaic papyrus from Egypt. Nabu was the Babylonian god of wisdom, the son of Marduk, and had his seat in Borsippa.] The name the Babylonians gave to Azariah, one of Daniel's friends (Dan 1:7; 2:49; 3:12-30).

Abel, I (ā′bĕl). [Heb. *Hebel,* a word of uncertain meaning, possibly "breath," "transitoriness"; Gr. *Abel.* Compare the Akkadian *aplu* and Sumerian *ibila,* "son." If *Hebel* means "breath," the name would be appropriate as a reference to the shortness of Abel's life. The Bible gives no indication as to when such a name would have been given.] The second son of Adam and Eve (Gen 4:2; etc.). The one incident of his life that Scripture records is his offering of a more acceptable sacrifice than that of his brother Cain (vs 3-5). Abel's offering was noteworthy in that, being of the flock, it bespoke his faith in the promised Deliverer, the true Lamb of God, who was to bruise the serpent's head (Gen 3:

15; Jn 1:29). The shedding of its blood was an acknowledgment on the part of Abel that he was a sinner in need of divine mercy and forgiveness (see Lev 17:11; Heb 9:22). Furthermore, Abel's offering was of the choicest of the flock—a "firstling," and "of the fat thereof"—and as such, an evidence of his readiness to give the Lord the best he had. Abel's faithfulness won for his name a place of honor among the worthies of Heb 11.

Abel, II (ā′bĕl). [Heb. *'Abel,* "stream," "brook," or "meadow."] A shortened form of **Abel-beth-maacah (2 Sa 20:14, 15, 18). In 1 Sa 6:18 *'abel* is probably an erroneous reading for *'eben,* "stone" (see RSV). Several Hebrew MSS actually read *'eben.*

Abel-beth-maacah (ā′bĕl-bĕth-mā′á-ká), or **Abel of Beth-maacah** (ā-bĕl of bĕth-mā′á-ká). [Heb. *'Abel Beth (ham) Ma'akah,* "meadow of the house of Maacah." The last element is spelled "maachah" in the KJV. The place was also called Abel-maim (ā′bĕl-mā′ĭm; Heb. *'Abel-mayim,* "meadow of waters") because it lay in a well-watered plain (2 Chr 16:4).] A city about 20 mi. east of Tyre overlooking the upper Jordan Valley. It was besieged by Joab when Sheba fled to it after his unsuccessful rebellion against David (2 Sa 20:14-22). It was smitten by Ben-hadad of Syria in the time of Baasha (1 Ki 15:20; 2 Chr 16:4), and finally conquered by Tiglath-pileser III, who incorporated it into an Assyrian province (2 Ki 15:29). The site is now called *Tell Abil.* Map VIII, B-4.

Abel-keramim (ā′bĕl-kĕr′á-mĭm). [Heb. *'Abel-Keramîm,* "meadow of vineyards." The KJV translates this term as "the plain of the vineyards."] A place in Transjordan where Jephthah defeated the Ammonites (Jgs 11:33). Its site is unknown but is believed to be near the present city of Amman. Map VI, E-4.

Abel-maim. *See* Abel-beth-maacah.

Abel-meholah (ā′bĕl-mĕ-hō′lá). [Heb. *'Abel Mechôlah,* "meadow of dancing."] A town, presumably in the Jordan Valley, where Elisha lived (Jgs 7:22; 1 Ki 4:12; 19:16). Its exact site is uncertain. Some identify it with *Tell el-Hammi,* 9 mi. south of Beth-shan, others with either *Tell 'Abil* or *Tell el-Maqlûb,* both lying about 13 mi. southeast of Beth-shan (Nelson Glueck, *BASOR* 91 [1943], 15, 16). Map VI, D-4, gives 2 possible locations.

Abel-mizraim (ā′bĕl-mĭz′rá-im). [Heb. *'Abel Miṣrayim,* "meadow of the Egyptians."] An unknown site in Transjordan, where Joseph and his company mourned for

Jacob 7 days on their way to Hebron to bury the body of the patriarch (Gen 50: 9-13). Earlier the place was known as the "[threshing] floor of Atad (ā'tăd)," but following the ceremony the Canaanites called it *'Abel Miṣrayim,* "meadow of the Egyptians." There is a possible play on words, *'abel* with different vowels (*'ebel*) meaning "mourning."

Abel-shittim. *See* Shittim.

Abez. *See* Ebez.

Abi. *See* Abijah, 7.

Abia. *See* Abijah, 6.

Abiah. *See* Abijah, 1, 3, 4.

Abi-albon (ā'bĭ-ăl'bŏn). [Heb. *'Abî-'albôn.*] One of David's "mighty men" (2 Sa 23: 31). He is called Abiel in 1 Chr 11:32.

Abiasaph (a-bī'a-săf), or **Ebiasaph** (ĕ-bī'a-săf). [Heb. *'Abî'asaph* and *'Ebyasaph,* "my father has gathered (or added)."] A Korahite Levite (Ex 6:24; 1 Chr 6:23, 37; 9:19).

Abiathar (a-bī'a-thar). [Heb. *'Ebyathar,* "the father of abundance" or "the father is pre-eminent." The name occurs in Old-Babylonian as *Abiyatar.* Gr. *Abiathar.*] The priest who escaped Saul's massacre of the priests at Nob for their alleged assistance of David. His father was Ahimelech, the high priest at Nob, of the house of Ithamar. Abiathar carried an *ephod in his flight and joined David, whose priest he became and for whom he consulted the Lord (1 Sa 22:20-23; 23:6-9; 30:7, 8). Later he shared the office of the high priesthood with Zadok of the house · of Eleazar (2 Sa 15:24, 29, 35; 17:15; 19:11; 20:25). He remained priest when Solomon ascended the throne (1 Ki 4:4), but was soon removed from office and banished to Anathoth for being involved in Adonijah's attempt to gain the throne (chs 2:26; 1:7). With his demotion the rule of the line of Eli ended, and the prophecy of 1 Sa 2:27-36 was fulfilled.

Abib (ā'bĭb). [Heb. *'Abîb,* "month of the ears."] The first month of the Hebrew religious *year, called Nisan after the Babylonian exile. It was at the time of the Exodus that God appointed it as the first month and the month of the Passover (Deut 16:1; cf. Ex 12:2). It began at the new moon of our March or April.

Abida (a-bī'da), KJV once **Abidah** (a-bī'da). [Heb. *'Abîda',* "my father knows." The name occurs in Akkadian as *Abi-yadi'.*] A descendant of Abraham through Midian (Gen 25:4; 1 Chr 1:33).

Abidah. *See* Abida.

Abidan (a-bī'dăn). [Heb. *'Abîdan,* "my fa-

ther is judge." The name occurs in Assyrian as *Abi-dâna.*] The prince of the Benjamites appointed at Sinai (Num 1:11; 2:22; 7:60, 65; 10:24).

Abiel (ā'bĭ-ĕl). [Heb. *'Abî'el,* "God is my father." The name occurs in Akkadian as *Abi-ili,* and in ancient South Arabic as *'b'l.*]

1. An ancestor of Saul. According to 1 Sa 9:1 he appears to be the grandfather of Saul, but according to 1 Sa 14:50, 51, if Abner is taken as the one referred to as Saul's uncle, the great-grandfather. The simplest solution to the apparent discrepancy is to interpret the phrase "son of Abiel" (ch 9:1) as "grandson of Abiel." *See* Son.

2. One of David's "mighty men" from Beth-arabah (1 Chr 11:32), also called Abi-albon (2 Sa 23:31).

Abiezer (ā'bĭ-ē'zẽr). [Heb. *'Abî'ezer,* "my father is a help," or "father of help."]

1. A Manassite, founder of the family of the Abiezrites to which Gideon belonged (Jos 17:2; Jgs 6:11, 24, 34; 8:2; 1 Chr 7:18). In Num 26:30 are found the contracted forms Jeezer (jĕ-ē'zẽr) [Heb. *'I'ezer*], in RSV "Iezer" (ī-ē'zẽr); and Jeezerites (jĕ-ē'zẽr-īts) [Heb. *'I'ezrî*], in RSV Iezerites (ī-ē'zẽr-īts).

2. One of David's "mighty men" (2 Sa 23:27; 1 Chr 11:28; 27:12).

Abiezrite (ā'bĭ-ĕz'rīt). [Heb. *'Abî 'Ezrî.* The contracted form *'I'ezrî,* Jeezerite (jĕ-ē'zẽr-īt) or Iezerite (ī-ē'zẽr-īt), is found in Num 26:30.] A member of the family of *Abiezer (Jgs 6:11, 24; 8:32).

Abigail (ăb'ĭ-gāl), RSV once **Abigal** (ăb'ĭ-găl). [Heb. *'Abîgayil* and *'Abîgal,* probably "my father rejoices."]

1. The wife of Nabal, a wealthy shepherd at Carmel in southern Judea, a beautiful and prudent woman who after Nabal's death became David's wife (1 Sa 25: 2-42). She accompanied David to Gath (ch 27:3), to Ziklag (ch 30:5), and to Hebron (2 Sa 2:2). She bore him Chileab, a son (ch 3:3), also called Daniel (1 Chr 3:1).

2. A sister, most likely a half sister, of David, and mother of Amasa (1 Chr 2:16; 2 Sa 17:25).

Abigal. *See* Abigail, 2.

Abihail, I (ăb'ĭ-hāl). [Heb. *'Abîchayil,* "my father is strong."]

1. A Merarite Levite (Num 3:35).

2. A Gadite (1 Chr 5:14).

3. Queen Esther's father (Est 2:15).

Abihail, II (ăb'ĭ-hāl). [Heb. *'Abihayil,* meaning unknown. In 1 Chr 2:29 a number of

Hebrew manuscripts, the Syriac, and the Targums support the reading *'Abichayil.*]

1. A descendant of David's brother Eliab, and wife of King Rehoboam (2 Chr 11:18).

2. The wife of Abishur (1 Chr 2:29).

Abihu (*à-bī′hū*). [Heb. *'Abīhû'*, "my father is he."] One of Aaron's sons, appointed priest at Sinai (Ex 6:23; 28:1). He and his brother Nadab died childless before the Lord for offering strange fire (Lev 10: 1-7; Num 3:2-4; 26:60, 61). The context (Lev 10:8-11) suggests that Abihu and Nadab were intoxicated when they committed their offense.

Abihud (*à-bī′hŭd*). [Heb. *'Abīhûd,* "my father is majesty."] A Benjamite (1 Chr 8:3).

Abijah (*à-bī′jà*), KJV of OT 4 times **Abiah** (*à-bī′à*), once **Abia** (*à-bī′à*); KJV of NT **Abia** (*à-bī′à*). [Heb. *'Abîyah* and *'Abîyahû,* "Yahweh is a father"; Gr. *Abia.*]

1. The wife of Hezron, a famous ancestor in the line of Judah (1 Chr 2:24, Abiah in the KJV).

2. A descendant of Aaron, head of one of the 24 courses into which the priests were divided in the time of David (1 Chr 24:10).

3. A descendant of Benjamin (1 Chr 7:8, Abiah in the KJV).

4. The younger son of Samuel; he was appointed judge in Beer-sheba, when his father was old. His judgeship was corrupt (1 Sa 8:2, 3; 1 Chr 6:28; Abiah in the KJV).

5. A son of Jeroboam I. When he was a young child he became ill and his father sent his wife to the prophet Ahijah for help. She appeared in disguise, but was recognized by the prophet, who predicted the child's death, which occurred shortly afterward (I Ki 14:1-18).

6. The second king of Judah after Solomon, called Abijam (*à-bī′jăm*) [Heb. *'Abîyam,* of obscure meaning], by the author of Kings. He was the son of Rehoboam and ruled Judah 3 years (*c.* 913-*c.* 911 B.C.). Through his mother he was a descendant of Absalom (1 Ki 15:2). He followed his father in wickedness, and also continued the war with Jeroboam I (vs 3, 6, 7). In a certain battle, because he "relied upon the Lord God" he was able to inflict a crushing defeat upon Israel (2 Chr 13:3-20). He had 14 wives, 22 sons, and 16 daughters (v 21). His biography was written by the prophet Iddo (v 22).

The apparent discrepancy in the maternity of Abijah (1 Ki 15:2; cf. 2 Chr 13:2)

is generally explained as follows: "Maachah, the daughter of Abishalom," or Absalom, was really the granddaughter, not daughter, of Absalom. The Hebrew word for daughter may refer to any female descendant no matter how remote. *See* Son.

7. The mother of Hezekiah (2 Chr 29: 1), called Abi (*ā′bī*) [Heb. *'Abî*] in 2 Ki 18:2.

8. One of the chief of the priests who returned from Babylon in Zerubbabel's time (Neh 12:4). A priestly family was called after him in Nehemiah's time (v 17). The father of John the Baptist may have belonged to this family (Lk 1:5).

9. A priest who signed the covenant in the days of Nehemiah (Neh 10:7). He may have belonged to the family described under Abijah, 8.

Abijam. *See* Abijah, 6.

Abilene (*ăb′ī-lē′nē*). [Gr. *Abilēnē.*] A territory that received its name from the city of Abila about 18 mi. northwest of Damascus in the Anti-Lebanon Mountains, near the village of *es-Suk* in the depression of *Wâdī Baradā,* the ancient Abana River. Abilene was part of the territory of Ituraea, which was dismembered about 34 B.C. From that time until the territory was given to Agrippa I in A.D. 37, nothing is known of Abilene, except that under Tiberius it was ruled by the tetrarch Lysanias (Lk 3:1). After Agrippa's death in A.D. 44 it was administered by Roman procurators until A.D. 53, when it was given to Agrippa II, the last of the Herodian kings. Map XVI, B-5.

Abimael (*à-bīm′å-ĕl*). [Heb. *'Abîma'el,* "God is my father." A similar name, *Ili-ma-abi,* occurs in Akkadian.] One of the descendants of Joktan (Gen 10:28).

Abimelech (*à-bīm′ĕ-lĕk*). [Heb. *'Abimelek,* "my father is king." The name occurs in the Amarna Letters as *Abi-milki,* and in ancient South Arabic as *'bmlk.*]

1 and 2. The name or the official title of two kings of Gerar with whom Abraham, as well as Isaac, had dealings (Gen 20:1-18; 21:22-34; 26:1-33).

3. The son of Gideon through a concubine from Shechem. With the help of the Shechemites, after the death of his father, he killed 70 of his brothers on a stone at Ophrah, Jotham only escaping. Abimelech was then made king, and ruled "Israel" 3 years, at the end of which the Shechemites under the leadership of Gaal became dissatisfied and rebelled against him. The rebellion was suppressed and

the city with its outer fortification (tower) destroyed. Soon afterward Abimelech met his end during the siege of Thebez, which had joined the rebellion. A millstone that a woman threw from the besieged city wall fell on his head, wounding him severely. Lest anyone should say that a woman had slain him, Abimelech had his attendant slay him (Jgs 9; 2 Sa 11:21).

4. A name appearing in the superscription of Ps 34, probably to be identified with Achish, the king of the Philistines to whom David fled before Saul (1 Sa 21:10-15).

5. A priest, son of Abiathar (1 Chr 18:16). It is generally agreed that the reading here should be Ahimelech, as the son of Abiathar is called in ch 24:6. The LXX reads "Ahimelech."

Abinadab (*a*-bin′*a*-dăb). [Heb. *'Abînadab,* "my father is generous."]

1. A man of Kiriath-jearim, in whose house the ark remained for 20 years after the Philistines sent it back (1 Sa 7:1, 2; 2 Sa 6:3; 1 Chr 13:7).

2. One of David's older brothers (1 Sa 16:8; 17:13; 1 Chr 2:13).

3. One of King Saul's sons, killed in battle (1 Sa 31:2; 1 Chr 8:33; 9:39; 10:2).

4. One of Solomon's sons-in-law, the father of one of his district commissioners (1 Ki 4:11).

Abinoam (*a*-bǐn′ō-ăm). [Heb. *'Abinoʻam,* "my father is pleasant." The name is found also in ancient South Arabic inscriptions.] The father of Barak (Jgs 4:6, 12; 5:1, 12).

Abiram (*a*-bī′răm). [Heb. *'Abîram,* "my father is high."]

1. A Reubenite who with Korah and Dathan conspired against Moses in the wilderness and was destroyed (Num 16:1-35; Deut 11:6; Ps 106:17).

2. The son who presumably perished when his father, Hiel, began to rebuild Jericho in Ahab's time. His death was a fulfillment of Joshua's curse (1 Ki 16:34; cf. Jos 6:26).

Abishag (ăb′ĭ-shăg). [Heb. *'Abîshag,* meaning uncertain.] A beautiful maiden from Shunem, who served David as nurse during his old age (1 Ki 1:3, 15). After David's death Adonijah requested to marry her. According to Oriental laws this would be regarded as an attempt to seize the throne (cf. 2 Sa 16:21, 22), so Adonijah was executed as one guilty of high treason (1 Ki 2:17-25).

Abishai (*a*-bǐsh′*a*-ī). [Heb. *'Abîshay,* once *'Abshay,* meaning uncertain.] A nephew of David and brother of Joab and Asahel

(1 Chr 2:16), one of David's outstanding warriors. He stood loyally by David against Saul (1 Sa 26:7-12), against Abner (2 Sa 2:18-25), and against the Philistines (ch 21:16, 17). He took part in the assassination of Abner to gain blood revenge, for which he was cursed by David (ch 3:28-30). He fought with Joab against the Ammonites (ch 10:6-14) and against Absalom (ch 18:2, 5, 12). Abishai held a leading position in the fight against the rebel Sheba (ch 20:6) and against the Edomites in the Valley of Salt (1 Chr 18:12, 13).

Abishalom. *See* Absalom.

Abishua (*a*-bǐsh′ū-*a*). [Heb. *'Abîshûʻa,* probably "my father saves." The name appears in Babylonian texts as *Abi-eshuʻa.*]

1. A Benjamite (1 Chr 8:4).

2. Son of Phinehas, the priest (1 Chr 6:4, 5, 50; Ezr 7:5).

Abishur (*a*-bī′shẽr). [Heb. *'Abîshûr,* "my father is a wall." The name appears also in ancient South Arabic inscriptions.] A man of the family of Hezron of the tribe of Judah (1 Chr 2:28, 29).

Abital (*a*-bī′tăl). [Heb. *'Abîtal,* "my father is dew."] One of David's wives, the mother of Shephatiah (2 Sa 3:4; 1 Chr 3:3).

Abitub (*a*-bī′tŭb). [Heb. *'Abîtûb,* "my father is good." The name occurs in Akkadian as *Abi-ṭābu.*] A man of the tribe of Benjamin (1 Chr 8:8-11).

Abiud (*a*-bī′ŭd). [Gr. *Abioud,* probably a transliteration of the Heb. *'Abîhûd.*] One mentioned in Matthew's genealogy of Jesus Christ (Mt 1:13).

Abject. A term appearing as a noun in Ps 35:15, KJV, as a rendering of the Heb. *nekeh,* a word of uncertain meaning. The RSV renders *nekeh* "cripple."

Ablutions. A term appearing twice in the RSV (Heb 6:2; 9:10). The Greek word thus translated (*baptismoi*) signifies acts of washing or of immersing in water. The "washings" of Heb 9:10 are done as a religious rite; hence "ablutions" is a suitable translation. However, many commentators believe that in ch 6:2 the reference is to Christian baptism, and hence prefer to render *baptismoi* "baptisms." True, the general word for Christian baptism is *baptisma,* but it is possible that *baptismoi* refers to this rite also.

Abner (ăb′nẽr). [Heb. *'Abner,* once *'Abiner,* 1 Sa 14:50, "the father is a lamp," or "my father is a lamp." The name appears in Akkadian texts down to the Neo-Babylonian period as *Abu-nûri,* and is found on an ancient seal impression discovered at Gezer.] A son of Ner of the tribe of Benjamin, and relative of King Saul (1 Sa 14:50, 51; 1 Chr 9:35, 36), under whom he served as commander in chief of the army (1 Sa 17:55). From his victories in war he dedicated some of the spoil for a fund to be used for the upkeep of the house of the Lord (1 Chr 26:27, 28). He was engaged in Saul's fight against David (1 Sa 26:5, 7, 14, 15), and after Saul's death made Ish-bosheth, the son of Saul, king over the northern tribes, with the capital in Mahanaim in Transjordan (2 Sa 2:8 to 3:1). In the war that followed he lost against the forces of David. In his retreat he slew Asahel, one of Joab's brothers, in self-defense (ch 2:12-32).

Later, when Ish-bosheth accused Abner for having had relations with Rizpah, Saul's concubine, Abner offered to turn the northern kingdom over to David. David received him and completed arrangements of transfer with him, but Joab assassinated Abner following the negotiations (2 Sa 3:6-27). David composed a beautiful lamentation for Abner (ch 3:28-39) and mourned for him so sincerely that the people were convinced that the king was innocent with regard to his murder. The revenge for Abner's blood David committed to Solomon, who ordered Joab executed (1 Ki 2:5, 28-34). The Abner mentioned in 1 Chr 27:21 as the father of Jaasiel, chief of the tribe of Benjamin, is probably to be identified with Saul's commander in chief.

Abomination of Desolation. [Gr. *bdelugma tēs erēmōseōs*, a translation of the Heb. *shiqqûṣ shomem* (Dan 12:11), literally "an abomination that desolates" or "an abomination that appalls," thus an abominable, detestable thing that results in desolation and that appalls those who behold it.] An expression occurring in the KJV of Mt 24:15 (RSV "desolating sacrilege"), and in slightly varying form in Dan 11:31; 12:11. Context implies that the expression "transgression of desolation" (Heb. *pesha' shomem*) of ch 8:13 refers to the same thing. In Daniel this abominable thing that causes appalling desolation is mentioned in connection with the "daily sacrifice" (*see* Daily), and apparently applies to a rival religious system that takes a position of avowed hostility to the worship of the true God centering in the services of the sanctuary, or Temple. The two systems are mutually exclusive, since the setting up of the abomination of desolation is accompanied by the trampling down of the

sanctuary (ch 8:13) and by the taking away of the "daily" (chs 11: 31; 12:11).

This substitute system of worship is abominable, or detestable, because it stands in implacable opposition to that of the true God. It desolates the sanctuary by replacing its services with its own. This turn of events naturally appalls worshipers of the true God. In the symbolic prophecy of Dan 8 it is the power represented by the *"little horn" that terminates the worship of the true God in His sanctuary and institutes a false system of worship in its place (vs 9-12). At the end of "two thousand and three hundred days" the sanctuary was to be cleansed (v 14) by the restoration of the worship of the true God.

Various interpretations have been given of the "abomination of desolation." Writing about A.D. 70, the Jewish historian Josephus applies the prophecies of Daniel relating to the "abomination of desolation" to Antiochus IV Epiphanes, who set out to obliterate every trace of the Jewish religion and who in the year 168 B.C. plundered the Temple, suspended its services, and desecrated the altar of burnt offering by erecting an idol altar upon it whereon he caused swine to be offered. This state of affairs continued for at least three full years, until Judas Maccabeus rallied his fellow Jews and repulsed the forces of Antiochus. Thereupon the Temple was "cleansed" —the idol altar removed, a new altar erected in its place, and the "daily sacrifice" reinstituted (Jos. *Ant.* x. 11. 7; xii. 5. 3, 4; 7. 6, 7; *War* i. 1. 1, 2). The writer of 1 Macc (probably *c.* 100 B.C.), who records the attempts of Antiochus to Hellenize the Jews and the valorous exploits of Judas Maccabeus and his successors (1 Macc 1:20-64; 4:36-60; 6:7), was apparently familiar with the book of Daniel. He does not state that these events are fulfillments of Daniel's prophecies, nor does he apparently apply any of the time periods to the persecution by Antiochus, for he stresses the duration as exactly 3 years. However, he uses the same Greek words for "abomination," "desolation," "cleansed," "daily," and other key expressions as appear in the LXX of Daniel, which is thought to have been translated *c.* 150 B.C., about the time these events occurred.

Our Lord used the expression "abomination of desolation" with reference to the impending destruction of Jerusalem and the Temple (Mt 24:15-20; cf. Lk 21: 20-24). Numerous Protestant interpreters, understanding these prophecies of Daniel to refer to the opposition of papal Rome to true Christians as well as that of pagan Rome toward the Jews, have applied the "abomination of desolation" to such papal practices as the confessional and the sacrifice of the mass (see *SDACom* 4:842, 843, 873-877).

Abraham (ā′brȧ-hăm), or **Abram** (ā′brăm). [Heb. *'Abraham* and *'Abram,* the former meaning "the father is exalted," the latter possibly "the father of a multitude," as the Arabic *ruha'm,* "multitude," suggests. The name occurs in Old Babylonian as *Abraḥam,* in Egyptian texts of the 19th cent. B.C. (as the name of a prince in Palestine) as *'Ibwrhni',* in ancient South Arabic as *'brhn,* in Pharaoh Shishak's list of conquered Palestinian places as *'Ibrm,* on a Ugaritic inscription as *'Abrm,* and on an ancient Hebrew seal as *'brm.* Gr. *Abraam.*]

The world in which Abraham lived. According to the Biblical chronology adopted in this dictionary Abraham was born in 1950 B.C., left Haran for Canaan after the death of his father in 1875 B.C., visited Egypt between 1875 and 1864 B.C.,

2. Ancient painting of Abraham receiving the promise, found in the 3d cent. synagogue at Dura Europus (Map XIII, C-5)

and died in 1775 B.C. after having lived in Canaan for 100 years. He was born in Ur in southern Mesopotamia during the Neo-Sumerian period. In about 1960 B.C., according to the so-called Low Chronology, shortly before his birth, the strong 3d dynasty of Ur, which had ruled for more than 100 years, came to an end, and was replaced by the rival dynasties of Isin and Larsa, under which Ur declined somewhat in importance as a political center in the Mesopotamian valley. During the 75 years that Abraham lived in Ur and Haran the country was under the domination of Sumerian rulers, although the Amorites, who had already taken over most of Syria and Palestine, were already pouring into Mesopotamia. By 1830 B.C. they founded the powerful 1st dynasty of Babylon, whose 6th king, Hammurabi (*c.* 1728-1686 B.C.), became the strongest ruler.

When Abraham entered Canaan he found the country for the greater part in the hands of the Amorites. The country was not a unified state, however, but consisted of numerous city-states of various sizes with kings and kinglets of Amorite stock forming the ruling class. Egypt, on the other hand, was at that time ruled by the powerful kings of the 12th dynasty (1991 to *c.* 1780 B.C.). If Abraham was in Egypt between 1875 and 1864 B.C. (see Gen 12) he must have met Sesostris III as king of Egypt who ruled from 1878 to 1840 B.C. According to ancient records this king conducted a military campaign into Palestine, directing it against *Škmm,* which is probably Shechem, but did not occupy the country. It seems that the campaign was a punitive raid, and that its object was not conquest.

During Abraham's time occurred the military campaigns described in Gen 14. None of the kings mentioned in the narrative can be identified with monarchs known from secular sources (*see* Chedorlaomer; Amraphel; Arioch; Tidal); however, archeological evidence confirms the narrative. The explorations of Albright and Glueck have brought to light evidence that a flourishing culture and many cities in Transjordan were destroyed in the 20th or 19th cent. B.C., and that the country remained almost entirely uninhabited for several centuries afterward. There is also some evidence that Sodom and Gomorrah, which presumably lay at the southern end of the Dead Sea, were destroyed at that time (*see* Sodom).

The life of Abraham may be considered

under four major periods: (1) His life prior to his journeying to Canaan, at the age of 75. (2) His early sojourn in Canaan to the birth of Isaac, a period of 25 years. (3) His life from the birth of Isaac to the death of Sarah and the marriage of Isaac to Rebekah, about 40 years. (4) His later life, old age, and death, about 35 years.

His life prior to arrival in Canaan. Abraham was born in or near the city of Ur in lower Mesopotamia. Abraham's father Terah had 2 other sons, Nahor and Haran the father of Lot (Gen 11:27). The family worshiped heathen deities as well as the true God (Jos 24:2). The Genesis record says nothing about God appearing to Abraham prior to the departure from Ur, but Acts 7:2-4 clearly applies the command of Gen 12:1-3 to the time when the family still lived in Ur. The original destination of the family caravan of Abraham, Terah, Nahor, and Lot, as it set out from the lower Mesopotamian valley, was Canaan (ch 11:31). They settled first at Haran in northern Mesopotamia, but how long they remained there is not known, nor is the reason for the sojourn there given. They may have planned to stay only long enough to rest the flocks and herds, or perhaps Terah's advanced age made it impossible for the group to journey farther (cf. v 32). The fact that Nahor did not accompany Abraham to Canaan after the death of their father may imply, also, that opinion was divided about the wisdom of leaving the lush grazing lands of Haran. In time, however, the call to Abraham was repeated, and taking his nephew Lot with him he left Haran and went to the land of Canaan. Apparently the two had accumulated considerable "substance" —primarily flocks and herds—and were accompanied by slaves and retainers (ch 12:1-5).

Early sojourn in Canaan. During the 25 years that elapsed between Abraham's entrance into the land of Canaan and the birth of Isaac, the patriarchal family moved intermittently from place to place. From Shechem, their first place of sojourn (Gen 12:6), they journeyed southward to Bethel (v 8), and thence toward the Negeb, or south country (v 9), and eventually to Egypt (v 10). Returning to the Negeb (ch 13:1) and to Bethel (v 3), they finally settled at Mamre, near Hebron, where they remained for a major portion of the period of early sojourn (chs 13:18 to 19:38). Not long before the birth of Isaac, Abraham again journeyed

3. Entrance to the *Ḥaram* at Hebron, the site of the Cave of Machpelah

toward the Negeb and "sojourned in Gerar" (ch 20:1).

The journey into Egypt was apparently made not long after Abraham entered Canaan. Drought and famine, which intermittently brought suffering to Palestinian dwellers, impelled him to seek food in a land where there was usually plenty in spite of the fact that there is practically no rainfall (Gen 12:10). While in Egypt, fear for his personal safety led the patriarch to represent Sarah as only his sister. This manifest lack of faith in God to protect His servants resulted in embarrassment and in Abraham's expulsion from the land (vs 11-20). When Abraham returned to Canaan he is described as being "very rich in cattle, in silver, and in gold" (ch 13:1, 2). Lot also "had flocks, and herds, and tents" (v 5). Insufficient pasturage and water for these large herds led the patriarch and his nephew to separate. Lot settled first in the luxuriant Jordan Valley and later "pitched his tent toward Sodom," whereas Abraham returned to Mamre, near Hebron (vs 6-18), where he remained for approximately 20 years.

9

During this residence at Mamre a number of important events occurred. The first of these was an invasion of Canaan by a confederacy of four kings from Mesopotamia under the leadership of Chedorlaomer (Gen 14:1-10). Five kings in the vicinity of Sodom banded together against the invaders, but were defeated, with the result that their peoples and property were lost (vs 11, 12). Upon learning that his nephew was in the hands of the invading army, Abraham pursued the Mesopotamian kings with his own private army of 318 men and rescued the captives from the vicinity of Sodom, together with their possessions (vs 13-16). It was upon his return from this expedition that Abraham met, and paid "tithes of all" to, Melchizedek, ruler of Salem, or Jerusalem as the city was then known (vs 17-24). Soon after this experience the Lord entered into solemn covenant with the patriarch, assuring him that, eventually, his descendants would possess Canaan as their own (ch 15). As the years went by at Mamre without the birth of an heir, Abraham took matters into his own hand and married Hagar, his wife's Egyptian maid, who presented him with his first son, Ishmael (ch 16:1-4). This ill-advised marriage brought discord into the home which culminated in the eventual banishment of Hagar and Ishmael from the home (chs 16:5-16; 21:9-21).

During this residence at Mamre the Lord renewed His covenant with Abraham, and instructed him to institute the rite of circumcision as a token of the covenant (Gen 17). Later, the Lord appeared in the form of a wayfarer and renewed the promise of a son and heir, and upon the same occasion warned Abraham of the imminent destruction of Sodom and its sister cities, which took place the following day (chs 18; 19). Soon after this event the patriarchal family moved to Gerar, where Abraham again pretended that Sarah was not his wife (ch 20), but only his sister.

With Isaac in the southland. Not long after the move to Gerar, Isaac was born (Gen 21:1-7). Soon friction arose between Sarah and Hagar, doubtless over the matter of whose son should be heir to Abraham, with the result that Hagar and her son were banished from the home forever (vs 8-21). Abraham remained in the vicinity of Gerar and Beer-sheba until Isaac reached manhood (vs 22-34). It was while the patriarchal home was at Beer-sheba that God tested Abraham's faith by calling

upon him to offer his son as a sacrifice. God's promises that the land was to belong to him and to his descendants were as yet unfulfilled after nearly half a century of residence in the land of Canaan, yet, with repeated tests to his faith, that faith now rose in majesty to the supreme test and triumphed (ch 22). The writer of Hebrews devotes nearly a third of his comment on evidences of faithfulness, in the lives of the ancient worthies' to incidents in the life of Abraham that tested and proved his faith (Heb 11:8-19). Toward the close of this period of his sojourn in Canaan, Abraham apparently returned to Hebron, where, at the age of 127 years, Sarah died (Gen 23:1, 2). By purchase from the Hittites then occupying that part of the land, Abraham came into possession of the first portion of Canaan that he could call his own—the Cave of Machpelah, and the field in which it was located—and it was there he buried his beloved wife (vs 3-20). See figs. 3, 216, 311.

Later life and old age. With the passing of Sarah, Abraham realized that his own life might soon end. Though Isaac was nearly 40 years of age he was yet unmarried, and the patriarch felt constrained to make provision for the perpetuation of the family line concerning which the promises had been made. Accordingly, he sent his trusted servant Eliezer to Mesopotamia, where his kinsmen (Gen 22:20-24) lived, to arrange for a wife for Isaac who might be expected to understand and appreciate the covenant privileges and responsibilities (ch 24:1-9). The mission was successful, and in due time Eliezer returned to Canaan with Rebekah, a daughter of Bethuel, Abraham's nephew, a son of his brother Nahor (vs 10-67). Love cemented the union thus arranged, and some 20 years later the first children were born (ch 25:20-26). For about 35 years after his marriage, Isaac shared the ancestral home with his father Abraham, who married again and reared several children born to him by his wife Keturah (vs 1-4).

Prior to his death, at the age of 175 years, Abraham arranged for the transfer of all his property, with the rights and privileges appertaining to it, to Isaac as heir to the covenant promises (Gen 25:5), while to his other sons he gave substantial gifts—consisting doubtless of cattle and herds—and sent them away to the eastward (v 6). Ishmael and Isaac buried their father in the Cave of Machpelah, the place where Sarah had been buried some time earlier (vs 8-10).

In spite of the frailties that are common to man, Abraham persevered in his lifelong purpose to follow wherever God should lead, whether it be on the long trek from Ur to Canaan or to Mount Moriah to offer his only son, the son of the promise. Through the fires of trial, delay, and disappointment, his faith was perfected, so that he became "the Friend of God" (Jas 2:23). The high esteem in which his descendants rightfully held him eventually degenerated almost to the point where they honored him above God. But the luster of his faith and long life of devotion to the will of God shine forth undimmed for all generations.

Abraham's Bosom. A figurative expression based possibly on the picture of a mother fondling and nourishing a child on her breast (cf. Jn 1:18), a symbol of the friendly communion that was thought to exist between Abraham and his blessed descendants in Hades; or possibly on the ancient custom of reclining at meals in which the head of one participant could lie on the breast of one next to him (see ch 13:23), an indication that the blessed would have the privilege of being next to Abraham in the other world (see Mt 8: 11). The figure appears but rarely in Jewish literature. One reference (4 Macc 13:17) speaks of 7 brethren expecting to be received, when they died, by Abraham, Isaac, and Jacob. The Talmud speaks of Adda b. Ahabah sitting "in Abraham's lap" (*Kiddushin* 72a, Soncino ed., p. 369). In his *Discourse to the Greeks Concerning Hades* Josephus describes the "Bosom of Abraham" as follows:

"For there is one descent into this region, at whose gate we believe there stands an archangel with an host; which gate when those pass through that are conducted down by the angels appointed over souls, they do not go the same way; but the just are guided to the right hand, and are led with hymns, sung by the angels appointed over that place, unto a region of light, in which the just have dwelt from the beginning of the world; not constrained by necessity, but ever enjoying the prospect of the good things they see, and rejoice in the expectation of those new enjoyments which will be peculiar to every one of them, and esteeming those things beyond what we have here; with whom there is no place of toil, no burning heat, no piercing cold, nor are any briers

there; but the countenance of the fathers and of the just, which they see, always smiles upon them, while they wait for that rest and eternal new life in heaven, which is to succeed this region. This place we call *The Bosom of Abraham.*"

Jesus' use of the term "Abraham's bosom" in His parable of the rich man and Lazarus (Lk 16:22), must not be construed as His endorsement of Jewish eschatological concepts concerning the rewards of the righteous. To do so would make Him contradict His literal statements elsewhere concerning the condition of man in death (*see* Death). He was simply drawing upon contemporary concepts for an illustration.

Abram. *See* Abraham.

Abronah (à-brō′nà), KJV **Ebronah** (ĕ-brō′nà). [Heb. *'Abronah,* either "a passage" or "opposite place."] A station near Eziongeber where the Israelites camped (Num 33:34, 35); not identified.

Absalom (ăb′sà-lŏm), or **Abishalom** (à-bĭsh′à-lŏm). [Heb. *'Abshalôm* and *'Abîshalôm,* "my father is peace." The name occurs in secular sources as *Abisalamu,* of a ruler of Gozan in upper Mesopotamia in the 10th-9th cent. B.C.] Third son of David by his wife Maacah, daughter of Talmai, the king of Geshur (2 Sa 3:3). He was known for his handsome appearance (2 Sa 14: 25, 26). To avenge the crime committed by his half brother Amnon against his sister Tamar, he killed Amnon and then fled to his grandfather, Talmai, king of Geshur, to escape possible reprisal from David (ch 13). About three years later, by engaging the services of a wise woman from Tekoa, Joab succeeded in obtaining permission for him to return to Jerusalem. Two years later he reconciled father and son (ch 14).

Shortly after this Absalom began to scheme against his father to obtain the kingship, and had himself proclaimed king at Hebron (2 Sa 15:1-12). Marching against Jerusalem, he forced David to flee the capital and took possession of the royal palace and of the harem. He disregarded the counsel of Ahithophel and did not immediately pursue the small forces of David, but followed, instead, the advice of David's friend Hushai, who counseled him to mobilize all of Israel's army before continuing the pursuit. This gave David time to reorganize his forces and get ready for the decisive encounter (chs 15:13 to 17:23). The battle took place in the "wood of Ephraim," somewhere in

4. The so-called Tomb of Absalom in the Kidron Valley of Jerusalem

Gilead, probably near Mahanaim. The forces of Absalom were severely beaten and in the confusion of battle Absalom was caught by the head in the branches of a tree, and left hanging helpless. While thus suspended he was killed by Joab against the explicit command of David. He was buried like a criminal in a large pit in the wood, and a big heap of stones was erected over his grave (2 Sa 17:24 to 18:17). During his life Absalom had erected for himself a monument, which

Acco (ăk′ō), KJV **Accho** (ăk′ō). [Heb. *'Akkô.*] An old Canaanite city mentioned first in Egyptian records of the 19th cent. B.C. as *'ky.* It lay about 25 mi. south of Tyre on the Bay of Acco and thus possessed the best natural harbor of Palestine, a circumstance responsible for its importance. It is mentioned in the *Amarna Letters as *Akkâ* and in Assyrian inscriptions as *Akkû.* Joshua assigned it to the tribe of Asher, if the "Ummah" in Jos 19:30 is to be read Acco (as the LXX has it) as is thought by some commentators. However, the city was not occupied by Israel (Jgs 1:31), and probably never became part of Israelite territory. In the time of Shalmaneser V (727-722 B.C.) Acco came under Assyrian domination (Jos. *Ant.* ix. 14. 2), and again submitted to Sennacherib in 701 B.C. (*ANET* 287). Ashurbanipal conquered the city *c.* 640 B.C. and deported much of its population to Assyria (*ANET* 300). In the 3d cent. B.C. its name was changed to *Ptolemais, and it appears under this name in the NT. Its modern name is Acre, but the site of the ancient city is *Tell el-Fukhkhâr.* Map VI, C-3.

Aceldama. *See* Akeldama.

Achaia (ȧ-kā′yȧ). [Gr. *Achaia.*] In NT times a Roman province. In the time of Homer, Achaia designated all of Greece as inhabited by the Achaeans, then for a time it designated only a coastal strip along the south of the Gulf of Corinth. When Greece fell to the Romans in the 2d cent. B.C. the territory was added (146 B.C.) to the province of Macedonia, but in 27 B.C. it was organized as a separate province. In A.D. 15 it was again united with neighboring Macedonia, and was under an imperial administrator until Claudius in A.D. 44 restored the province to the Senate. It was then administered separately by a proconsul who had his seat in Corinth (cf. Acts 18:12). Within its boundary was all of Greece south of Thessaly (Map XIX, D-10). Paul came to Achaia for the first time in about A.D. 51 during his 2d Missionary Journey, and visited the cities of Athens, Corinth, and Cenchreae (Acts 17:16 to 18:18). He revisited the province about the winter of A.D. 57/58 during his 3d Missionary Journey (ch 19:21). Apollos also conducted gospel work in that province (Acts 18:24, 27; cf. 1 Cor. 3:4-7; 16:12).

Achaicus (ȧ-kā′ĭ-kŭs). [Gr. *Achaïkos,* "belonging to Achaia."] A Christian from Corinth who with Stephanas and Fortunatus visited Paul at Ephesus (1 Cor 16:17; cf. v 8). The name appears in secular literature as the surname of Mummius, who conquered Corinth in 146 B.C. It was also borne by members and freedmen of his family. It is possible that the Christian from Corinth was a descendant of one of these freedmen.

Achan (ā′kăn), or **Achar** (ā′kär). [Heb. *'Akan,* meaning uncertain, and *'Akar,* "troubler."] A Judahite who, against the explicit command of God that all of Jericho was to be devoted to God, appropriated to himself a Babylonian garment, a piece of gold, and a quantity of silver from the spoil of the city. His act brought a curse upon the whole nation and caused the defeat of the Israelites at Ai. As punishment he and his family were stoned to death and all his property was destroyed (Jos 7:1-26; 22:20).

Achar. *See* Achan.

Achaz. *See* Ahaz, 2.

Achbor (ăk′bôr). [Heb. *'Akbôr,* "mouse"; the name is found in Phoenician and Aramaic inscriptions as *'kbr* and in Akkadian texts as *Agaburu, Agbur,* and *Akbar(u).*]
1. An Edomite whose son Baal-hanan was one of the kings of Edom (Gen 36:38; 1 Chr 1:49).
2. An officer at Josiah's court (2 Ki 22:12, 14; cf. Jer 26:22; 36:12).

Achim (ā′-kĭm). [Gr. *Achim,* a transliteration of an uncertain Hebrew name.] One named in Matthew's genealogy of Jesus (Mt 1:14).

Achish (ā′kĭsh). [Heb. *'Akîsh,* apparently a Philistine name. It appears in cuneiform records of the time of Esarhaddon, 7th cent. B.C., for a Philistine king of Ekron, in the form of *Ikausu* (*ANET* 291).] A Philistine king, or more likely two Philistine kings, in the time of David and Solomon (1 Sa 21:11; 1 Ki 2:39). It seems unlikely that the Achish of Solomon's time was the Achish of David's time. If he was he would have been quite aged when the incident recorded in 1 Ki 2:39 took place. David's first flight to Achish (1 Sa 21:10) occurred nearly 50 years earlier; and his second flight (ch 27:1-12) came only a few years after the first. Furthermore, the Achish of 1 Sa 27:2 is described as the son of Maoch, and the one of 1 Ki 2:39 as the son of Maachah. It is possible, of course, that Maoch may be a variant spelling of Maachah, but on the other hand it is more probable that the Achish of David's time was the grandfather of the Achish living in Solomon's time.

Achmetha. *See* Ecbatana.

Achor (ā′kôr). [Heb. *'Akôr*, "trouble."] The valley in which Achan and his family were stoned to death for taking some of the spoils of Jericho, which were devoted to God (Jos 7:24-26; cf. Is 65:10; Hos 2:15). It lay near Jericho and formed part of the northern boundary of Judah (Jos 15:7). M. Noth has now conclusively identified this valley with the plain *el-Buqê'ah* beginning about 3 mi. southwest of *Khirbet Qumrân* (for which see Map XVI, E-3), in the northeastern part of the wilderness of Judea. The plain is about 5 by 2 mi. (*ZDPV* 71 [1955], 42-55; *BASOR* 142 [1956], 5-17).

Achsa. *See* Achsah.

Achsah (ăk′sà), KJV once **Achsa** (ăk′sà). [Heb. *'Aksah*, "anklet."] A daughter of Caleb, given in marriage to Caleb's younger brother (or nephew) Othniel as a reward for his capture of Kiriath-sepher (Jos 15:16-19; Jgs 1:12-15; 1 Chr 2:49).

Achshaph (ăk′shăf). [Heb. *'Akshaph*, possibly "place of sorcery," if it is a Semitic name, or "indestructible place," if the name is of Indo-European origin.] An old Canaanite city captured by Joshua (Jos 11:1; 12:20). After the division of the land it lay on the border of Asher (ch 19:25). The city is mentioned in Egyptian texts as early as the 18th cent. B.C. as *'Ikspî*, and in the Amarna Letters as *Akshapa*. It was conquered by Thutmose III. Map VI, C-3.

Achzib (ăk′zĭb). [Heb. *'Akzîb*, possibly "treacherous," "deceitful."]

1. A town in southwestern Judah (Jos 15:44; Mic 1:14), probably the same as Chezib (kē′zĭb) [Heb. *Kezib*] (Gen 38:5). It has been identified with *Tell el-Beidā* southwest of Adullam. It seems also to be mentioned in one of the *Lachish Letters (No. 8).

2. A town on the seacoast of Asher (Jos 19:29), from which the Canaanites were not expelled (Jgs 1:31). It was taken by Sennacherib in 701 B.C. (*ANET* 287). In NT times it was known as Ekdippa (Jos. *War* i. 13. 4). It has been identified with *ez-Zîb*, about 8 mi. north of Acre. Map VI, B-3.

Acrabbim. *See* Akrabbim.

Acre. [Heb. *ṣemed*, "yoke."] Ṣemed indicates the amount of land that a yoke of cattle could plow in a day. It is impossible today to ascertain this accurately. The Roman "yoke" was about ⅔ of an English acre, and for lack of a more accurate measure commentators generally adopt this. The word appears twice (1 Sa 14:14; Is 5:10).

Acts of the Apostles, The. The earliest extant copy of this book of the NT appears in a document known as Papyrus 45, a manuscript written during the 3d cent. In this manuscript, which contains portions of 14 chapters of the book, the title is given simply as *Praxeis*, "Acts." The same brief title appears in the Sinaiticus a century later. Other ancient titles are "The Acts" and "Acts of the Apostles." The writer himself seems not to have provided his work with a title, but was content to indicate only that he had addressed a "former treatise" to his friend Theophilus in addition to the one he now proceeded to write. The narrative of his "former treatise"—the Gospel of Luke (Acts 1:1, 2; cf. Lk 1:1-4; 24:50-52)—closes with the ascension of our Lord, the point at which this latter "treatise" takes up the narrative (Acts 1:4-11). The book of Acts is not an exhaustive record of the postascension ministry of any of the apostles, and mentions only a few of them by name. It seems not to have circulated among the early Christian communities at quite as early a period as the Gospels and the Epistles, but it was, nevertheless, in general use by the middle of the 2d cent., as writings such as those of Justin Martyr testify. Toward the close of the same century Irenaeus (*Against Heresies* i. 23. 1; ii. 20. 2; etc.) cites the book as Scripture, and its title appears in the first known list of NT books, the Muratorian Fragment, dated about the same time.

Although the writer of the book of Acts does not identify himself directly, he does provide at least three indirect clues which leave no doubt that he was none other than Luke, the writer of the third Gospel: (1) He is the same person who wrote a "former treatise" on the life of Christ and addressed it to a certain Theophilus (Acts 1:1, 2; cf. Lk 1:1-4; 24:50-52). (2) In certain passages (Acts 16:10-17; 20:6-16; 21; 27; 28) known as the "we" sections the author was a member of Paul's evangelistic company. Paul repeatedly mentions Luke as one of his companions during the later part of his ministry (Col 4:14; 2 Ti 4:11; Phm 24). (3) The language, diction, and style of the Acts corresponds closely with that of the Gospel of Luke. From the very earliest times Christian writers speak of Luke as the author.

The book of Acts was, in all probability, written by Luke at Rome during the two years of Paul's first imprisonment there, A.D. 61-63. Of this, the way in which the narrative breaks off abruptly soon after the arrival of Paul in Rome is almost conclusive evidence. The author having followed the labors of the great apostle to the Gentiles from the very beginning, often in great detail, it would be strange indeed if he said nothing of the outcome of Paul's first trial before Caesar, of his later ministry, second arrest and imprisonment, and execution—if these events had already occurred. Apparently Luke told no more in the book of Acts because, at the time he wrote, there was no more to tell. As to his reliability as a historian this has been fully vindicated at every important point.

In his introduction the author of the book of Acts implies that his objective is to provide a continuation of his earlier narrative, the Gospel, in order that the two treatises, taken together, might constitute a rather complete historical account of the origin and growth of the Christian religion. He proposes to relate how the gospel found its way from Jerusalem to Judea and Samaria, and eventually "unto the uttermost part" of the then-known world (Acts 1:8). To begin with, there were no more than about 120 members of the church (v 15), all loyal adherents of Judaism. But the infant church grew rapidly, at times almost explosively, in membership, and, hesitatingly at first, accepted proselytes and then Gentiles into its fellowship. Like the ever-widening ripples from a pebble cast into a quiet pond, the church reached out to a waiting world, first to nearby regions and then to lands afar. The story of how all this came about—how an insignificant Jewish sect became a world religion—forms the theme of the book of Acts.

The book naturally falls into two major divisions: (1) chapters 1-12, in which Peter is the leading character, and (2) chapters 13-28, where Paul is the focus of attention. The first section records the development of the church at Jerusalem (chs 1-7), its expansion into the neighboring regions of Judea and Samaria (ch 8), the conversion of Saul (ch 9) and of Cornelius (ch 10), the acceptance of the first non-Jewish converts by the church at Jerusalem (ch 11:1-18), and the establishment of the first Gentile church, at Antioch in Syria (vs 19-30). The second section covers the ministry of Paul to the heathen of the Roman world—his 1st Missionary Journey, to Cyprus and Asia Minor (chs 13:1 to 15:35), his 2d Missionary Journey, that took him into Macedonia

and Greece (chs 15:36 to 18:22), his 3d Journey, much of which was devoted to Ephesus and the Roman province of Asia (chs 18:23 to 20:3), his return to Jerusalem and arrest there (chs 20:4 to 23:30), his imprisonment at Caesarea, appeal to Caesar, and journey to Rome (chs 23:31 to 28:31).

Adadah (ă'dà-dà). [Heb. '*Ad'adah,* possibly "festival."] A city in the south of Judah (Jos 15:22); not identified. Many think that Adadah is a misreading for Aroer (see 1 Sa 30:28). *See* Aroer, 3.

Adah (ā'dà). [Heb. '*Adah,* "ornament."]
1. One of Lamech's wives, the mother of Jabal and Jubal (Gen 4:19-21, 23).
2. The daughter of Elon the Hittite, one of Esau's wives (Gen 36:2, 4, 10, 12, 16), also called Basemath (ch 26:34).

Adaiah (à-dā'yà). [Heb. '*Adayah* and '*Adayahù,* "Yahweh has adorned." The name occurs on six jar stamps from Ophel and Gezer. In Assyrian inscriptions it appears as *Adiya.*]
1. The maternal grandfather of Josiah (2 Ki 22:1).
2. A Levite from the family of Gershom (1 Chr 6:41-43).
3. A priest of Nehemiah's time (1 Chr 9:12; Neh 11:12).
4. A Benjamite (1 Chr 8:21).
5 and 6. Two men who were married to foreign wives in Ezra's time (Ezr 10:29, 39).
7. The father of Hazaiah (Neh 11:5).
8. The father of Maaseiah (2 Chr 23:1).

Adalia (à-dā'lĭ-à). [Heb. '*Adalya',* meaning uncertain.] One of Haman's ten sons (Est 9:8).

Adam (ăd'ăm). [Heb. '*Adam,* "man," etymology uncertain. There is a possible connection with the verb '*adam,* "to be ruddy," and thus a reference to the clay from which man was formed (Gen 2:7). In the cognate languages, Phoenician and Ugaritic, '*dm* also means "man," but in ancient South Arabic it means "servant," and in Akkadian *admu* means "child." Gr. *Adam.*]
1. The first member of the human family, created by God from the dust of the earth (Gen 2:7). His wife, Eve, was formed out of a rib from his side (vs 21, 22). Adam was given authority over the earth and all living creatures (ch 1:26); and was commanded to populate the world (v 28). He and his wife were placed in a "garden eastward in Eden," and were given the task of caring for it (ch 2:

5. The flow of the Jordan stopped by landslides near Adam during the earthquake of July 11, 1927

8, 15). The product of plant and tree was to be their food (ch 1:29).

Adam and Eve were created perfect (Gen 1:31), and thus sinless. But they were also created with the power of choice, and thus had the freedom to disobey God. They were tested by means of "the tree of the knowledge of good and evil," the fruit of which God forbade them to taste or even to touch (chs 2:17; 3:3). Eve was beguiled by the serpent to eat of the tree, and then persuaded Adam to eat also (ch 3:1-7). By this act of disobedience they brought the curse of sin upon themselves and their children, and were expelled from the garden (vs 8-24). After the expulsion from the Garden of Eden, Adam and Eve became the parents of Cain, Abel, Seth, and "sons and daughters" (chs 4:1, 2, 25; 5:4). Adam was 930 years of age at his death (ch 5:5). It is not known how long he lived in Eden, although it was only a comparatively short period, for he was only 130 years old when Seth was born (v 3), which was evidently some time after the expulsion (cf. 4:1-25).

Through the sin of Adam death came upon the entire human family (Rom 5: 12-14; Eph 2:12). However, Christ, the second Adam (1 Cor 15:45-47) overcame where the first Adam failed (cf. Mt 4:1-10), and by His sacrifice made our redemption from the results of Adam's sin possible (Heb 5:9; 9:28).

2. A city in the Jordan Valley (Jos 3: 16), now *Tell ed-Dâmiyeh*, about 1 mi. from the eastern bank of the Jordan near the junction of the Jabbok (Map VI, D-4). Several times in the past 700 years, notably in 1267 and 1927, the Jordan has become dammed up at this place. Some think God may have used a similar damming up to dry up the river for the children of Israel to cross dry-shod (see *SDACom* 2:41).

Adamah (ăd′à-mà). [Heb. *'Adamah.*] A fenced city in Naphtali (Jos 19:36) in northeastern Galilee; not identified.

Adamant. [Heb. *shamîr.*] An extremely hard metallic or mineral substance, possibly emery or a related corundum. *Shamîr* appears three times in the OT and is translated "adamant" twice and "diamond" once. It cannot have been the diamond, however, since this mineral was unknown in OT times. The word is used to illustrate the steadfastness Jehovah would give the prophet to deal with a stubbornly rebellious people (Eze 3:9), as well as the hardness of the people's hearts (Zec 7:12). The point of the engraving tool that figuratively records the sin of Judah is made of *shamir* (Jer 17:1).

Adami. See Adami-nekeb.

Adami-nekeb (ăd'á-mī-nē'kĕb). [Heb. *'Adami Hanneqeb,* perhaps "Adam of the pass."] A town in Naphtali (Jos 19:33). The KJV lists Adami-nekeb as two separate towns, Adami and Nekeb, but the Hebrew favors combining the words. The term *nekeb,* "defile" or "pass," is probably used to distinguish this town from Adam in the Jordan Valley (Jos 3:16), about 23 mi. north of the mouth of the Jordan River (*see* Adam, 2). Adami-nekeb has been identified with *Khirbet ed-Dâmiyeh* lying close to a spring at the head of a pass about 5 mi. northeast of Mount Tabor on the Hauran-Acco caravan route.

Adar, I (á-där'). [Heb. and Aramaic *'Adar; Akkadian Addaru.*] The 12th month of the Jewish religious year (Est 3:7); it began at the new moon of February or March. *See* Year.

Adar, II. See Addar, 1.

Adbeel (ăd'bĕ-ĕl). [Heb. *'Adbe'el,* meaning uncertain. The name occurs in Assyrian inscriptions of Tiglath-pileser III as *Idibi'lu,* the name of an Arabian, and of an Arabian tribe living near the border of Egypt (see Luckenbill, *Ancient Records of Assyria and Babylon,* Vol. I, pp. 279, 280, 287, 293).] A son of Ishmael (Gen 25:13; 1 Chr 1:29), probably the ancestor of the tribe by this name mentioned in the Assyrian records of Tiglath-pileser III.

Addan (ăd'ăn), or **Addon** (ăd'ŏn). [Heb. *'Addan* and *'Addón.*] A place in Babylonia from which Israelite exiles "went up" in the time of Zerubbabel (Ezr 2:59; Neh 7:61); not identified.

Addar (ăd'är), KJV once **Adar** (á'där). [Heb. *'Addar.*]

1. A town in Judah (Jos 15:3), also called *Hazar-addar (Num 34:4).

2. A Benjamite (1 Chr 8:3), probably to be identified with Ard (Gen 46:21).

Adder. *See* Serpent.

Addi (ăd'ī). [Gr. *Addi,* probaby a transliteration of the Heb. *'Iddô.*] A Judahite listed in Luke's genealogy of Jesus (Lk 3:28).

Addon. *See* Addan.

Ader. *See* Eder, 3.

Adiel (ā'dĭ-ĕl). [Heb. *'Adi'el,* "God is an ornament." The name occurs on ancient Hebrew seals as *'d'l.*]

1. A Simeonite (1 Chr 4:36).

2. A priest (1 Chr 9:12).

3. The father of David's treasurer Azmaveth (1 Chr 27:25).

Adin (ā'-dĭn). [Heb. *'Adîn,* "voluptuous."] Head of a family of which, according to Ezr 2:15, 454 male members returned from Babylon with Zerubbabel. The number is given as 655 in Neh 7:20, but this total is probably arrived at from a later list brought up to date. According to Ezr 8:6, 51 males of the family of Adin came with Ezra to Jerusalem. One of the family signed Nehemiah's covenant (Neh 10:16).

Adina (ăd'ĭ-na). [Heb. *'Adina',* "voluptuous."] A Reubenite officer (1 Chr. 11:42).

Adino (ăd'ĭ-nō). [Heb. *'Adinô.*] According to the KJV one of David's "mighty men" (2 Sa 23:8). However, it is generally believed that the text is in disorder and that instead of "Adino the Eznite (ĕz'nīt)" we should read as in 1 Chr 11:11: "he lifted up his spear" (see RSV).

Adithaim (ăd'-ĭ-thā'ĭm). [Heb. *'Adîthayim.*] A place in the *Shephelah near Bethshemesh (Jos 15:36); not identified.

Adlai (ăd'lá-ī). [Heb. *'Adlay,* possibly, "Yahweh is just."] Father of David's herdsman Shaphat (1 Chr 27:29).

Admah (ăd'má). [Heb. *'Admah.*] One of the cities of the plain that rebelled against Chedorlaomer and his confederates (Gen 10:19; 14:2, 8). Later, like * Sodom, it was destroyed for its wickedness (Deut 29:23; Hos 11:8). It was probably situated in the valley that is now covered by the southern part of the Dead Sea.

Admatha (ăd'má-thá). [Heb. *'Admatha',* of Indo-European origin, meaning uncertain.] One of the 7 princes of the Persian kingdom under Ahasuerus (Est 1:14).

Admin (ăd'mĭn). [Gr. *Admin.*] A Judahite named in Luke's genealogy of Jesus (ch 3:33, RSV).

Adna (ăd'ná). [Heb. *'Adna',* "delight."]

1. An Israelite of the family of Pahath-moab. He was married to a foreign wife (Ezr 10:30).

2. A priest who headed the house of Harim after the Exile (Neh 12:15).

Adnah, I (ăd'ná). [Heb. *'Adnah,* "delight."] A military officer under King Jehoshaphat (2 Chr 17:14).

Adnah, II (ăd'ná). [Heb. *'Adnach,* meaning uncertain.] A Manassite who joined David at Ziklag (1 Chr 12:20).

Adoni-bezek (*à-dō'nĭ-bē'zĕk*). [Heb. *'Adoni Bezeq*, "lord of Bezek," or "my lord is (the god) Bezek." Since a god Bezek is not known, but the city Bezek is attested, the former meaning is preferable.] A Canaanite or Perizzite king captured and mutilated by men of the tribe of Judah (Jgs 1:4-7).

Adonijah (*ăd'ô-nī'jà*). [Heb. *'Adoniyah* and *'Adoniyahû*, "my Lord is Yahweh."]

1. Fourth son of David, born at Hebron of Haggith (2 Sa 3:2, 4). When David was old, Adonijah, apparently now the eldest surviving royal prince, made an attempt to seize the throne, doubtless knowing that his father, following divine directions, planned to make Solomon king. With the support of Joab, the commander in chief, and of Abiathar, one of the chief priests, Adonijah had himself proclaimed king at a feast at the well En-rogel, south of Jerusalem. However, he lacked the support of Zadok, the other chief priest, of Benaiah, commander of the royal bodyguard, and of Nathan, the prophet. These informed David of Adonijah's treacherous activity and reminded him of his promises to Solomon. David then gave orders to crown Solomon at once at the Gihon, a spring in the Kidron Valley. When Adonijah heard of this he fled to the sanctuary, laying hold of the horns of the altar, thereby conceding his guilt. Solomon pardoned him but under certain conditions (1 Ki 1:5-53). When Adonijah later requested permission to marry Abishag, David's nurse, the suspicion fastened upon him that he was scheming to obtain a legal title to the throne. As a result Solomon ordered Benaiah to put Adonijah to death (ch 2:13-25).

2. A Levite who instructed the people under Jehoshaphat (2 Chr 17:8).

3. An Israelite who signed Nehemiah's covenant (Neh 10:16).

Adonikam (*ăd'ô-nī'kăm*). [Heb. *'Adoniqam*, "my Lord is risen."] Founder of a family of which 666 male members returned from exile with Zerubbabel (Ezr 2:13; Neh 7:18 [667]), and again 63 males with Ezra (Ezr 8:13).

Adoniram (*ăd'ô-nī'răm*). [Heb. *'Adoniram*, "my lord is exalted." The name appears twice in the shortened form Adoram (*à-dō'răm*) [Heb. *'Adoram*] (2 Sa 20:24; 1 Ki 12:18) and once in the form *Hadoram* [Heb. *Hadoram*] (2 Chr 10:18). An officer of David and Solomon in charge of the levy. When the ten tribes revolted, Rehoboam sent him to confer with the

rebels, who, when they saw the king's officer, stoned him (1 Ki 4:6; 12:18).

Adoni-zedec. *See* Adoni-zedek.

Adoni-zedek (*à-dō'nĭ-zē'dĕk*), KJV **Adoni-zedec.** [Heb. *'Adoni-ṣedeq*, "my Lord is righteous."] A Canaanite king of Jerusalem. When the Gibeonites entered into a treaty with the Israelites, he with his confederates besieged the city of Gibeon. Joshua defeated him at Makkedah, slew him, and hanged his body on a tree (Jos 10:1-27).

Adoption. [Gr. *huiothesia*, "adoption," "adoption as sons," "a placing in the condition of a son."] A NT term used to describe the process by which the believer in Christ enters into sonship to the Father (Rom 8:15, 23; Gal 4:5; Eph 1:5). The figure was doubtless drawn from Roman law, according to which an adopted son participated in the full privileges enjoyed by a natural son. The term emphasizes God's desire to bestow tender love upon His children. In Rom 9:4 God's special calling of the Jewish nation as His representatives and sons by faith is termed "adoption." In Rom 8:23 the word describes "the redemption of our body" from sin, pain, and death at the second advent of Christ. Though the word is not found in the OT the practice of adoption was known. For example, Moses was adopted by Pharaoh's daughter (Ex 2:8-10), and Esther by Mordecai (Est 2:7).

Adoraim (*ăd'ô-rā'ĭm*). [Heb. *'Adôrayim*.] A city of Judah, which Rehoboam fortified (2 Chr 11:9). In Pharaoh *Shishak's hieroglyphic list of Palestinian cities conquered, the city is called *'Idrm*. It was probably originally a Canaanite city, and may have been the one mentioned in the *Amarna Letters as *Aduri*. The site is now called *Dûrā* and lies about 5 mi. west of Hebron. Map IX, F-3.

Adoram. *See* Adoniram.

Adrammelech (*à-drăm'ĕ-lĕk*). [Heb. *'Adrammelek*, "Adar is king." The name *'Drmlk* occurs in Phoenician inscriptions as a personal name. However, in the case of Adrammelech, 1, the better reading is generally considered to be *'Adadmelek*, "(the god) Adad is king." In Hebrew the letters *d* and *r* are similar and easily confused.]

1. A deity introduced into Samaria by the settlers from Sepharvaim whom Sargon II transplanted from northern Mesopotamia into Palestine after the fall of Samaria. To this deity children were sacrificed in fire (2 Ki 17:31). Cuneiform

records from *Tell Ḥalâf*, the Biblical Gozan, in northern Mesopotamia, mention this god by the name *Adad-milki* (Pohl, *Biblica* 22 [1941], 35).

2. A son of Sennacherib. He and his brother Sharezer assassinated their father and escaped to Armenia (2 Ki 19:37; Is 37:38).

Adramyttium (ăd′rȧ-mĭt′ĭ-ŭm). [Gr. *Adramutteion*.] A small port city of Mysia in the Roman province of Asia, situated at the head of the Gulf of Adramyttium and at the base of Mount Ida (Map XX, B-4). It obtained the rank of metropolis under the Romans. The village *Edremit* near the ancient site perpetuates the old name. The ship that was used to transport Paul as a prisoner from Caesarea to Myra in Lycia apparently had Adramyttium as its home port (Acts 27:2).

Adria (ā′drĭ-ȧ). [Gr. *Adrias*.] The sea between Crete and Sicily (Acts 27:27). The name was probably derived from Adria, an Etruscan colony at the mouth of the Po River in Italy. Originally *Adrias* referred only to the Adriatic or Ionian Sea, lying between the Balkan peninsula and Italy. But Strabo, Ptolemy, and Pausanias used the name in the same sense as Luke. Map XX, B-2.

Adriel (ā′drĭ-ĕl). [Heb. *'Adrî'el*, "God is my help." The name occurs on an ancient seal from Damascus as *'dr'l*, and in Akkadian inscriptions with the following spellings: *Iddiriya-el, Adarri-el,* and *Idrili*.] A man from Meholah to whom Saul gave his daughter Merab as wife after having promised her to David (1 Sa 18:19; 2 Sa 21:8).

Adullam (ȧ-dŭl′ăm). [Heb. *'Adullam*.] An old Canaanite city (Gen 38:1, 2) mentioned in connection with Jarmuth and Socoh (Jos 15:35). Joshua defeated its king (ch 12:15) and assigned the city to Judah (ch 15:35). David hid himself from Saul in a cave near Adullam (1 Sa 22:1; 2 Sa 23:13; 1 Chr 11:15). Rehoboam fortified the city (2 Chr 11:7), and Micah mentions it (Mic 1:15). It was reinhabited after the Exile (Neh 11:30). The site has been identified with *Khirbet esh-Sheikh Madhkûr,* 10 mi. northwest of Hebron, and just south of *Khirbet 'id el-Miyeh,* in which the old name of Adullam has been preserved. Map VI, E-2.

Adullamite (ȧ-dŭl′ăm-īt). [Heb. *'Adullami*.] A native of Adullam (Gen 38:1, 12, 20).

Adultery. The Hebrew and Greek words thus translated describe specifically sexual intercourse of a married person with one who is not a lawful spouse. Under the Levitical law such an act was punishable by death (Lev 20:10). However, the seventh commandment (Ex 20:14) seems to comprehend sexual impurity of any kind, whether in act or thought. Traditional accretions to the commandment obscured the idea of spotless moral purity and provided loopholes for conduct patterns neither sincere nor guiltless, but in His Sermon on the Mount Jesus clarified the intent of the commandment (Mt 5: 27, 28, 32).

The term "adultery" is frequently used figuratively. Whereas marital faithfulness symbolizes undivided loyalty to the Creator, adultery is the symbol of man's breach of covenant with God, whether by idolatry or by other forms of apostasy (Jer 3:8, 9; Eze 23:37; Hos 2:2; Mt 12:39; Rev 2:22).

Adummim (ȧ-dŭm′ĭm). [Heb. *'Adummîm,* "red things."] The Ascent of Adummim is a pass on the road from Jericho to Jerusalem. It was near the boundary between Benjamin and Judah (Jos 15:7; 18:17). Its name was probably derived from the red-colored stone in the pass, though Jerome believes that the pass got its name from the blood that had been spilled there by robbers (cf. Lk 10:30). Its present Arabic name is *Ṭal'at ed-Damm,* which means "ascent of blood."

Adversary. This word occurs frequently in the general sense of an opponent, an enemy (Deut 32:27; Jos 5:13; etc.). It is used in a specialized sense in the KJV of Mt 5:25; Lk 12:58, where the word thus translated (*antidikos*) and the context indicate that the "adversary" is an opponent in a lawsuit (RSV "accuser"). This may be the meaning of *antidikos* also in Lk 18:3 and in 1 Pe 5:8, but then, again, the general meaning of "enemy," "opponent," may apply. In several OT passages (Num 22:22; 1 Sa 29:4; 2 Sa 19: 22; etc.) "adversary" is the translation of the Heb. *śaṭan,* the word sometimes transliterated as Satan (Job 1:6; etc.). Satan is the adversary par excellence.

Advocate. [Gr. *paraklētos,* a person called to one's side to give assistance or counsel, hence "helper," "intercessor," "counselor."] A term appearing once in the Bible, used of Christ in His ministry on behalf of repentant sinners (1 Jn 2:1). *Paraklētos* in its other occurrences in the NT (Jn 14:16, 26; 15:26; 16:7) refers to the Holy Spirit and is rendered "Comforter" (KJV) and "Counselor" (RSV). Designation of the Holy Spirit as "another

Comforter" in Jn 14:16 implies that Christ had been serving His disciples in the same role—that of a "Comforter." It is difficult to find a single English word that conveys adequately the various offices suggested by *paraklētos*. In 1 Jn 2:1 the functions of "intercessor," "mediator," "helper," were probably in the author's mind.

Aeneas (ė-nē'ăs). [Gr. *Aineas*, the name of a Trojan leader in Homer's *Iliad*, the hero of Vergil's *Aeneid*, also of a Greek general of the 4th cent. B.C.] A paralytic of Lydda, healed by Peter (Acts 9:33, 34).

Aenon (ē'nŏn). [Gr. *Ainōn*, probably a transliteration of the Aramaic *'enawan*, "springs."] A place near Salim where John baptized because there was much water there (Jn 3:23). The site has not yet been identified. Tradition places it in the Jordan Valley. According to Jerome it was 8 Roman mi. south of Scythopolis, that is, Beth-shean (Map XVI, D-3), but no site preserving the ancient name of Aenon or Salim is found in this area. W. F. Albright identifies Aenon with the modern village of *'Ainûn* near the headwaters of the *Wâdī Fâr'ah* (Map XVI, D-3), where there are numerous springs (in *Studies in Honor of C. H. Dodd*, p. 159).

Agabus (ăg'à-bŭs). [Gr. *Agabos*.] A Christian prophet who predicted the famine that occurred in the reign of the emperor Claudius (Acts 11:28). He also predicted Paul's imprisonment (ch 21:10, 11).

Agag (ā'găg). [Heb. *'Agag*. The word appears in Phoenician inscriptions as a personal name in the form of *'gg*. Referring to Amalekite kings as in the Scripture references below it is either a personal name or a title (like Pharaoh).]

1. A king of Amalek in the time of Moses, mentioned by Balaam (Num 24:7).

2. The king of Amalek whom Saul captured and Samuel slew (1 Sa 15:9-33).

Agagite (ăg'à-gīt). [Heb. *'Agagî*.] An epithet of Haman, the great enemy of Mordecai and of the Jews in general (Est 3:1, 10; 8:3-5). Some scholars think that it is a Persian appellative, but a satisfactory interpretation in that direction has not yet been found. Later Jewish tradition connects Agagite with Agag, the name or title of the Amalekite kings of the OT (Num 24:7; 1 Sa 15:9). Josephus holds that Haman was an Amalekite (Jos. *Ant.* xi. 6. 5).

Agar. *See* Hagar.

Agate. [Heb. *kadkod*, and *shebô;* Gr.

chalkēdōn.] A precious stone. However, there is uncertainty as to the identity of the Hebrew and Greek words rendered "agate." The modern agate is a variegated chalcedony, with its colors arranged in stripes or clouds. Some scholars suggest the identification "ruby" for *kadkod*. In the high priest's breastplate *shebô* was the middle stone of the third row (Ex 28:19; 39:12). In the restoration of His faithful people, the Lord promised to make their windows (RSV "pinnacles") of *kadkod* (Is 54:12). In Ezekiel's lamentation for Tyre the same gem is depicted as an item of trade with Edom (Eze 27:16, RSV). The RSV lists agate as the third stone in the foundation of the New Jerusalem. However, it is uncertain what is meant by the term thus translated (*chalkēdōn*).

Age.

1. The measure, as in years, of the duration of one's life at any given time. Age is generally stated in whole numbers and, in modern Western usage, in terms of years elapsed from the date of birth. That is, a man 30 years old has already passed the 30th anniversary of his birth and entered his 31st year; he will become 31 years of age on the completion of his 31st year. However, in the Far East today age is counted inclusively, so that a person in his 31st year is reckoned as being 31 years old. His years are counted, not from the date of his birth, but from the calendar year in which he was born. Thus in China and Japan a child is reckoned to be 1 year old from the time he is born until the end of the calendar year. On New Year's Day his 2d year begins, and his age is reckoned as 2 even though he may have been born but a few days before the new year began. A year later, when he has lived one full year and a part of another year (and thus in Western reckoning would be one year old), his recorded age would be 3 years, because he has entered his third calendar year.

The Bible does not give sufficient information on the system of reckoning to enable us to discover how Biblical characters counted their age, whether their method was exactly that of the modern Far East. Certainly Noah was "600 years old," literally "a son of 600 years," *in* his 600th year rather than at the end of it (Gen 7:6, 11). But we do not know whether Noah's years were counted by anniversaries of his birth or by calendar years. Nor do we know that the Jews reckoned age by the same method used in Genesis. However, since inclusive reckoning was commonly employed in various countries in Bible times, it is probable that age was counted similarly, at least that a person was reckoned 30 years old as soon as he entered his 30th year. There are references in the Bible to two birthdays, both royal celebrations (Gen 40:20; Mt 14:6 and Mk 6:21), one, that of an Egyptian Pharaoh and the other, that of Herod Antipas, who was of Idumaean and Samaritan descent and was brought up in Rome. Neither reference proves that age was reckoned by birthday anniversaries (see Birthday). In China the birthdays of the emperor and empress were festivals, yet a Chinese, to this day, becomes a year older on New Year's Day.

The age of the patriarchs as given in Gen 5 is much greater than the life span of man in later generations. This may be accounted for by the changed conditions produced by the Flood, which, by affecting the atmosphere, climate, land, and food supply, reduced the average age suddenly and drastically (ch 11). Attempts to reckon these ages by shorter units, such as months, result in the absurdity of making some patriarchs fathers at the age of 3 or less. Ps 90 mentions 70 or 80 as the expected life span (v 10).

2. A period of time, or in the history of the world. See World.

Agee (ā'gē). [Heb. *'Age'*. The name occurs in Babylonian records as *Aga'*, as the name of a king of Ashkelon, and in ancient South Arabic as *'g'*.] A Hararite whose son was one of David's "mighty men" (2 Sa 23:11).

Agrippa (à-grĭp'à). [Gr. *Agrippas*.] Historically, the name of two kings in the 1st cent. A.D. In the Bible only one is named Agrippa (Acts 25; 26), the other being called "Herod the king" (Acts 12:1). See Herod, 6, 7.

Agur (ā'gûr). [Heb. *'Agûr*, "gatherer," "collector." The name occurs also in ancient South Arabic and in Ugaritic texts.] The author of part or all of Prov 30 (Prov 30:1).

Ahab (ā'hăb). [Heb. *'Ach'ab,* "father's brother." The name occurs also on a Hebrew seal. In cuneiform records it is spelled *Ahabbu* and *Ahi-abi*.]

1. The 8th king (if Tibni is included in the count) of the northern kingdom of Israel, son and successor of Omri. He reigned 22 years, from 874 to 853 B.C. He was married to Jezebel, the daughter of Ethbaal, "king of the Zidonians" (1 Ki 16:31). He was a strong military leader, keeping the Moabites in subjection (2 Ki

3:4, 5; *Moabite Stone, line 8). He lived on friendly terms with the Phoenicians and kept peace with Judah, whose crown prince married Ahab's daughter Athaliah (2 Ki 8:18, 26). He defeated the Syrians twice in battle, and possessed the largest army of any nation lying between Assyria and Egypt. When Benhadad II of Damascus with 32 allies besieged Samaria, Ahab drove him back (1 Ki 20:1-21) and a year later inflicted an even more severe defeat on him in the battle of Aphek (vs 22-30), and captured him. Ahab, however, showed himself foolishly magnanimous and spared Benhadad's life, even released him. Benhadad promised to return certain cities which his father had conquered from Ahab's father Omri, or possibly, as some think, Baasha (see ch 15:18-22), and also made economic concessions by allowing Israelite merchants to open shops in the bazaars of Damascus (ch 20:31-34, RSV).

When the Assyrians under Shalmaneser III threatened to end the independence of the small states in Syria and Palestine, a coalition of 12 nations was formed under the leadership of Damascus to meet the common enemy. Shalmaneser's inscriptions show that of the allied armies Ahab (called *Ahabbu* ^mat *Sir'ilâ,* "Ahab the Israelite") had the largest chariot force, 2,000 out of a total of 3,940, and a formidable infantry of 10,000 foot soldiers out of a total of about 60,000. The battle (which is not mentioned in the Bible) took place at Qarqar on the Orontes in central Syria in Shalmaneser's 6th year, which can be dated, with a great degree of certainty, in 853 B.C. The record of Ahab's participation in this battle helps to provide the earliest synchronism between Biblical and secular history (see Chronology, V, 3). While the allies won no decisive victory, the Assyrians were forced to retreat and leave Syria temporarily unconquered. As soon as the common threat was averted, the alliance broke up, and the old feuds between the various small nations in Syria and Palestine were continued. Ahab also set out at once to take the city of Ramoth-gilead from the Aramaeans of Syria, who had occupied it for some time. In a battle for this city Ahab was mortally wounded (1 Ki 22:2-36). His body was taken to Samaria for burial, and, as the Lord had predicted through Elijah (ch 21:19), the dogs licked Ahab's blood, which had stained the chariot (ch 22:38).

The prosperous reign of Ahab and his

friendly connections with Phoenicia brought much wealth into the country, enabling the king to engage in extensive building activities, attested in the Bible by only a brief word (1 Ki 22:39), but corroborated by the excavation of Samaria. Ruins of the city indicate that Ahab built his palace next to and partly on that of Omri, and that he had his residence decorated with beautifully carved ivory plaques (see Ivory; Samaria), from which it evidently became known as Ahab's ivory palace. According to ch 21:1 there was also a royal palace at the city of Jezreel.

Though enjoying great military and political success, Ahab was weak in religious matters. He "did evil in the sight of the Lord above all that were before him" (1 Ki 16:30). He permitted his pagan wife to introduce the worship of Baal and Asherah, and to persecute the worshipers of Israel's God. Personally Ahab seems to have considered himself a worshiper of Yahweh, for he consulted Yahweh's prophets repeatedly (chs 20:13, 14, 22, 28; 22:8, 16), and gave to at least three of his children names incorporating the divine name Yahweh: Ahaziah, Joram (Jehoram), and Athaliah. He also cooperated in making possible the contest between Elijah and the Baal priests, and did not interfere when Elijah ordered these priests slain (ch 18:16-45). He tolerated a prophet's rebuke for his foolish magnanimity toward Benhadad (ch 20:35-43) and showed sorrow for the murder of Naboth, which was instigated by Jezebel (ch 21:27-29), and for which the prophet held him accountable.

Lit.: J. W. Jack, *Samaria in Ahab's Time* (Edinburgh, 1929).

2. A false and immoral prophet among the exiles in Babylon. He would, Jeremiah predicted, be roasted in the fire by Nebuchadnezzar (Jer 29:21-23).

Aharah (à-hăr′à). [Heb. *'Achrach.*] A descendant of Benjamin and founder of a family (1 Chr 8:1); probably identical with Ehi (ē′hī; Gen 46:21) and Ahiram (Num 26:38).

Aharhel (à-här′hĕl). [Heb. *'Acharchel,* possibly "anguish," or "feverish heat."] A founder of a family in the tribe of Judah (1 Chr 4:8).

Ahasai. See Ahzai.

Ahasbai (à-hăs′bī). [Heb. *'Achasbay,* possibly "refuge is in Yahweh."] A Maacathite, whose son was one of David's "mighty men" (2 Sa 23:34).

6. Relief showing Darius I seated, with his son Xerxes (Biblical Ahasuerus) standing behind. From Persepolis (Map XII, E-9)

Ahasuerus (à-hăz′û-ē′rŭs). [Heb. *'Achashwerôsh.* The name is spelled *Khashayârshâ* in Old Persian, and *Aḥshiyarshu* in Babylonian. However, these are only representative spellings, the name being spelled variously in these ancient languages.]

1. The father of Darius the Mede (Dan 9:1). See Darius, 1.

2. A son and successor of Darius I on the Persian throne (486-465 B.C.), known in secular history as Xerxes. Shortly after taking the throne he successfully put down a serious rebellion in Egypt that had broken out before his father's death. He also quenched a serious Babylonian revolt and largely destroyed the city of Babylon, especially its fortifications, palaces, and temples. His military campaigns against the Greeks, however, ended in failures, so that the battles at Salamis, Plataea, Mycale, and the Eurymedon are known for the defeats the Persians suffered. Yet Xerxes was not perturbed by these misfortunes, and lived the carefree life of an Oriental despot. The description of his character by contemporary historians agrees well with the impression one gains from reading the story of Esther, his queen (Est 2:16, 17). He was a weak character and was easily influenced by his courtiers and wives. Ezr 4:6 tells how the Samaritans attempted to influence "Ahasuerus," identified by many with Xerxes, against the Jews. Whether this effort succeeded or failed is not known.

Ahava (à-hā′và). [Heb. *'Ahawa'.*] A canal in Babylonia at which Ezra gathered the company of exiles who were to return with him to Jerusalem (Ezr 8:15, 21, 31); not identified.

Ahaz (ā′hăz), KJV of NT **Achaz** (ā′kăz).

[Heb. *'Achaz,* "he has seized"; Gr. *Achaz.*
The name occurs also on an ancient Hebrew
seal. In the cuneiform inscriptions
of Tiglath-pileser III the name of Ahaz
of Judah is given as *Iaúḥazi (ANET*
282), i.e. Jehoahaz, "Yahweh has seized."]
1. A descendant of Saul through Jonathan
(1 Chr 8:35; 9:42).
2. The 12th occupant of the throne of
the kingdom of Judah, who reigned approximately
20 years (*c.* 735 - *c.* 715 B.C.), if
the years of his presumable coregencies,
with his father, *Jotham, and with his son
*Hezekiah are included. After his father's
death he reigned 16 years (2 Ki 16:2;
2 Chr 28:1). Ahaz was an idolater, had his
son pass through the fire (*see* Molech),
and worshiped strange gods on high
places, on hills, and under trees (2 Ki 16:
3, 4; 2 Chr 28:2-4, 23-25). Early in his
reign, while. his father was still alive,
Pekah of Israel and Rezin of Damascus
began to invade Judah (2 Ki 15:37; 16:
5). The pretext for this military action
was probably a refusal on the part of
Ahaz to join these two kings in an alliance
against Assyria. It was in connection with
this crisis that the prophet Isaiah was
sent to Ahaz to assure him of God's help
in his struggle with Israel and the Syrians,
and evidently also to warn him against
calling for foreign aid (Is 7). Ahaz, however,
did not appreciate this counsel and
turned to Tiglath-pileser III of Assyria
for help, sending him a large gift of
money taken from the treasures of the
Temple and palace. Tiglath-pileser responded
by invading Israel and besieging
Damascus (2 Ki 16:5-9; 2 Chr 28:6-21).
Damascus was captured and Rezin killed,
and much territory of Israel was taken
from Pekah and made into an Assyrian
province (see 2 Ki 15:29). It was probably
with the connivance of Tiglath-
pileser that Pekah was assassinated by
Hoshea, who usurped the throne for himself
and was confirmed in his office by the
Assyrian king. While Tiglath-pileser was
at Damascus Ahaz went up to meet him,
apparently to pay homage as a vassal
along with the Syrians. He sent home a
model of a foreign altar that he had seen
in Damascus, with an order to have a
similar one built for the Temple at Jerusalem.
This was probably an Assyrian
altar to be used to worship Assyrian national
gods. It replaced Solomon's altar of
burnt offerings (2 Ki 16:10-16). Hosea,
Micah, and Isaiah all prophesied during
Ahaz' reign (Hos 1:1; Mic 1:1; Is 1:1;
7:1-16). Ahaz is listed in the genealogy

of Jesus Christ (Mt 1:9; KJV "Achaz").
Ahaziah (ā'hȧ-zī'ȧ). [Heb. *'Achazyah* and
'Achazyahû, "Yahweh has grasped (my
hand)."]
1. The 9th king of Israel, the northern
kingdom (if Tibni is included in the
count). Ahaziah followed his father Ahab
on the throne and reigned less than
2 years (*c.* 853-852 B.C.). It is unusual that
his mother, probably Jezebel, is not mentioned
by name. True to the family tradition
he "did evil in the sight of the Lord"
and served Baal (1 Ki 22:40, 51-53). He
joined Jehoshaphat of Judah in building
a fleet of ships to be sent out to Ophir for
gold. The ships were wrecked at Ezion-
geber on the Gulf of Aqabah, probably in
one of the dangerous storms that come up
very suddenly there. Ahaziah apparently
proposed a second attempt, but Jehoshaphat
declined after being warned by a
prophet against joining the wicked king
of Israel (1 Ki 22:48, 49; 2 Chr 20:35-37).
The rebellion of Moab seems to have occurred
during his reign, but nothing
was done to force that country back into
subjection (2 Ki 1:1). Ahaziah was seriously
injured when he "fell down through
a lattice" in his palace. When he sent messengers
to Baal-zebub, god of Ekron, to
request healing, his men were intercepted
by Elijah, who sent them back with word
that the king would die of his injuries
(vs 2-4). Since he died without a son,
the throne passed to his brother *Jehoram,
or Joram (v 17).
2. The 6th king of. the southern kingdom
of Judah, who reigned for less than
one year (*c.* 841 B.C.). In 2 Chr 21:17 he is
called Jehoahaz, a name in which the two
component parts of Ahaziah are simply
reversed, leaving the meaning unchanged.
"Azariah" in 2 Chr 22:6 should doubtless
be read "Ahaziah," in harmony with the
LXX, the Syriac, and 15 Hebrew manuscripts.
Ahaziah was the youngest son of
Jehoram and Athaliah, and followed his
father in wickedness. He came to the
throne at the age of 22 (2 Ki 8:26; 2 Chr
22:1-4; for the apparent discrepancy in
the ages given in these texts see *SDACom*
3:269). He joined his uncle Joram (or
Jehoram) of Israel to fight against Hazael
of Damascus at Ramoth-gilead. Jehoram
was wounded in this battle and retired to
Jezreel to recover from his wounds. While
he was there Ahaziah paid him a visit (2
Ki 8:28, 29; 2 Chr 22:5, 6), and it was during
their stay in Jezreel that Jehu revolted.
Upon arriving at Jezreel this new aspirant
to the throne slew Jehoram. Ahaziah fled

but was fatally wounded. His body was taken to Jerusalem for burial (2 Ki 9:27-29; 2 Chr 22:7-9). After his death his mother Athaliah slew his heirs (except the infant Joash, who was hidden away) and took the throne (2 Ki 11:1-3).

Ahban (ä'băn). [Heb. *'Achban,* "the brother understands."] A Judahite (1 Chr 2:29).

Aher (ā'hēr). [Heb. *'Acher,* "another one," perhaps signifying that Aher was a substitute for a deceased earlier child.] A Benjamite (1 Chr 7:12).

Ahi (ā'hī). [Heb. *'Achi,* "my brother." However, it is possibly an abbreviated form of Ahijah, in which case the meaning would be "my brother is Yahweh."]
1. A chief of the Gadites in Gilead (1 Chr 5:15).
2. An Asherite (1 Chr 7:34), if a proper name. The RSV, assuming that a proper name is not intended, translates the Hebrew term as "his brother."

Ahiah. *See* Ahijah, 2, 3, 6, 9.

Ahiam (á-hī'ăm). [Heb. *'Achi'am,* meaning unknown.] One of the "mighty men" of David (2 Sa 23:33).

Ahian (á-hī'ăn). [Heb. *'Achyan,* probably "little brother."] A Manassite (1 Chr 7:19).

Ahiezer (ā'-hī-ē'zēr). [Heb. *'Achi'ezer,* "my brother is a help."]
1. Head of the tribe of Dan during the wilderness wandering (Num 1:12; 2:25; 7:66).
2. A man of Gibeah who joined David at Ziklag (1 Chr 12:3).

Ahihud, I (á-hī'hŭd). [Heb. *'Achihud,* "my brother is majesty."] A chief of the tribe of Asher, one of those appointed to assist in dividing the land of Canaan among the tribes (Num 34:27).

Ahihud, II (á-hī'hŭd). [Heb. *'Achichud,* "my brother is a riddle."] A chief of the Benjamites (1 Chr 8:7).

Ahijah (á-hī'já), KJV 4 times and RSV once **Ahiah** (á-hī'á). [Heb. *'Achiyah,* 5 times *'Achiyahu,* "my brother is Yahweh." The name occurs on an ancient ostracon found in the excavations of Jerusalem, and in Babylonian documents, as *Ahi-'au.*]
1. A descendant of Judah through Jerahmeel (1 Chr 2:25).
2. A Benjamite (1 Chr 8:7).
3. A son of Ahitub, and great-grandson of Eli; priest at Gibeah during the reign of Saul (1 Sa 14:3, 18).
4. A Pelonite, one of David's "mighty men" (1 Chr 11:36).
5. A Levite appointed by David as treasurer in the sanctuary (1 Chr 26:20).

6. A high official under Solomon (1 Ki 4:3).
7. A prophet from Shiloh who predicted that Jeroboam would become king over ten tribes of Israel (1 Ki 11:29-39). Later he informed Jeroboam's wife, who had come disguised to seek his counsel, that her stricken child would die (ch 14: 2-16). His prophecies in written form were apparently available to the author of Chronicles (2 Chr 9:29).
8. The father of King Baasha of Israel (1 Ki 15:27, 33).
9. A man who set his seal to Nehemiah's covenant (Neh 10:26).

Ahikam (á-hī'kăm). [Heb. *'Achiqam,* "my brother rises."] One of the princes of Judah whom Josiah sent to consult the prophetess Huldah (2 Ki 22:12-14), and who protected Jeremiah when the priests and false prophets demanded that the prophet die (Jer 26:24). He was the father of Gedaliah (2 Ki 25:22; Jer 39: 14; etc.).

Ahilud (á-hī'lŭd). [Heb. *'Achilud,* "a child's brother."]
1. Father of David's recorder, Jehoshaphat (2 Sa 8:16; 20:24; 1 Ki 4:3; 1 Chr 18:15).
2. The father of Solomon's officer Baana (1 Ki 4:12), possibly identical with Ahilud, 1.

Ahimaaz (á-hĭm'á-ăz). [Heb. *'Achima'as,* "my brother is wrath."]
1. Father-in-law of Saul (1 Sa 14:50).
2. Son of Zadok the priest; a messenger to David during Absalom's rebellion (2 Sa 15:27, 36; 17:20), and the first to reach David's headquarters with the news of the victory over Absalom (ch 18:19-30).
3. An official of Solomon (1 Ki 4:15); possibly identical with Ahimaaz, 2.

Ahiman (á-hī'măn). [Heb. *'Achiman,* meaning uncertain; the name occurs in Phoenician texts as *'chmn,* and in Ugaritic texts as *'hmn.* It occurs also on an ancient Hebrew seal.]
1. A son or descendant of Anak, possibly a clan name of a family of the Anakim at Hebron (Num 13:22), who were driven out by Caleb (Jos 15:14; Jgs 1:10).
2. A Levite gatekeeper (1 Chr 9:17).

Ahimelech (á-hĭm'ĕ-lĕk). [Heb. *'Achimelek,* "my brother is king." The name occurs in Assyrian records as *Ahimilki,* repeatedly on the ostraca excavated at Samaria, and on ancient Hebrew seals, etc.]
1. A descendant of Eli and a high priest in the tabernacle at Nob in the time of

7. Seal bearing the name Ahimelech
(actual size)

Saul. Not knowing that David was a fugitive, he assisted him and his men by giving them from the showbread and by offering David the sword that had been taken from Goliath. When *Doeg informed Saul of this act of assistance, Saul ordered the slaughter of Ahimelech, his fellow priests, and all the population of Nob (1 Sa 21:1-9; 22:7-19; Title of Ps 52). Only Abiathar, Ahimelech's son, who was already performing the functions of a high priest (see Mk 2:26), escaped (1 Sa 22:20).

2. Son of Abiathar, and grandson of Ahimelech, 1. He was joint high priest with Zadok during David's reign (2 Sa 8:17; 1 Chr 24:3, 6, 31). In 1 Chr 18:16 "Ahimelech" should probably be read instead of "Abimelech."

3. A Hittite follower of David during the reign of Saul (1 Sa 26:6).

Ahimoth (ȧ-hī′mŏth). [Heb. '*Achîmôth,* "my brother is death," but if derived from the Akkadian *Aḫi-imitti,* "my brother is my support."] A Levite (1 Chr 6:25).

Ahinadab (ȧ-hĭn′ȧ-dăb). [Heb. '*Achînadab,* "my brother is generous." The name occurs in Akkadian inscriptions as *Aḫi-nadbi.*] Solomon's supply officer in Mahanaim (1 Ki 4:14).

Ahinoam (ȧ-hĭn′ō-ăm). [Heb. '*Achîno'am,* "my brother is pleasant." The name occurs also on one of the ancient Hebrew ostraca from Samaria.]

1. Saul's wife (1 Sa 14:50).

2. One of David's wives (1 Sa 25:43; 27:3; 30:5; 2 Sa 2:2), mother of Amnon (2 Sa 3:2; 1 Chr 3:1).

Ahio (ȧ-hī′ō). [Heb. '*Achyô,* probably "little brother." The name occurs in the Aramaic Elephantine texts.]

1. Brother of Uzzah, and one of the drivers of the cart that brought the ark to Jerusalem (2 Sa 6:3, 4; 1 Chr 13:7).

2. A Benjamite (1 Chr 8:14).

3. Another Benjamite (1 Chr 8:31; 9:37).

Ahira (ȧ-hī′rȧ). [Heb. '*Achîra',* "my brother is (the Egyptian sun-god) Ra."] A chieftain of the tribe of Naphtali in the wilderness wandering (Num 1:15; 2:29; 7:78, 83; 10:27). Like many other Israelites who left Egypt with Moses, Ahira had been given a name one element of which was an Egyptian word.

Ahiram (ȧ-hī′răm). [Heb. '*Achîram,* "the brother is exalted." The name occurs in Assyrian inscriptions as *Aḫi-râmu* and *Aḫi-râme.*] A son of Benjamin and founder of a family (Num 26:38). Ehi (ē′hī) [Heb. '*Echî*] in Gen 46:21 is probably an abbreviation of Ahiram, or the last 2 consonants, *r* and *m,* may have been lost from the vowelless Hebrew script. Also *Aharah (Heb. '*Achrach*) in 1 Chr 8:1 may be a variant spelling or a misspelling of Ahiram.

Ahiramites (ȧ-hī′răm-īts). [Heb. '*Achirami.*] The family of Ahiram (Num 26:38).

Ahisamach (ȧ-hĭs′ȧ-măk). [Heb. '*Achîsamak,* "my brother is a support." The name occurs in an ancient Hebrew seal impression from Lachish as '*chsmk.*] A Danite whose son Aholiab was one of the skilled craftsmen employed for building the tabernacle (Ex 31:6).

Ahishahar (ȧ-hĭsh′ȧ-här). [Heb. '*Achîshachar,* "my brother is the dawn."] A Benjamite (1 Chr 7:10).

Ahishar (ȧ-hī′shär). [Heb. '*Achîshar,* "my brother is a singer," or with a change in vowel pointing, "the brother is upright."] One of Solomon's officials (1 Ki 4:6).

Ahithophel (ȧ-hĭth′ō-fĕl). [Heb. '*Achithophel,* meaning unknown.] A man of Giloh in southwestern Judah who was one of David's counselors (2 Sa 15:12). His son was one of David's "mighty men" and seems to have been Bathsheba's father (chs 23:34; 11:3). Ahithophel's wisdom was so great that the people considered it divine (ch 16:23). He chose Absalom's side in the rebellion against David, but when he saw that his counsel was rejected for that of Hushai he committed suicide, possibly in order to avoid further disgrace, recognizing that the rebellion was doomed to certain failure (chs 15:12, 31-34; 16:15; 17:23).

Ahitub (ȧ-hī′tŭb). [Heb. '*Achîṭûb,* "my brother is good." The name occurs in Akkadian texts as *Aḫu-ṭâb.*]

1. A priest of the line of Eli (1 Sa 14:3), and father of Ahimelech, the priest (ch 22:9), who is identified as of the line of Ithamar (1 Chr 24:3).

2. A priest of the line of Eleazar (1 Chr 6:7, 8, 52), and father of David's priest Zadok (2 Sa 8:17).

3. Another priest, a descendant of Ahitub, 2 (1 Chr 6:11, 12; Neh 11:11).

Ahlab (ä′lăb). [Heb. '*Achlab.*] A town assigned to the tribe of Asher, but from which the Canaanites were not driven (Jgs 1:31). It is doubtless the city referred to in Assyrian inscriptions as *Mahaliba*, now *Khirbet el-Mahâlib*, about 4 mi. northeast of Tyre. Map VI, B-3. *See* Helbah; Mahalab.

Ahlai (ä′lī). [Heb. *'Achlay*, "the brother of my God," as the Akkadian equivalent *Ah-iliya* shows.]

1. A descendant of Hezron (1 Chr 2:31; cf. v 25), probably a woman (see v 34).

2. Father of one of David's "mighty men" (1 Chr 11:41).

Ahoah (à-hō′à). [Heb. *'Achôach*, meaning unknown.] A Benjamite (1 Chr 8:4).

Ahohi (à-hō′hī). [Heb. *'Achôchi*.] According to the RSV, an ancestor of one of David's "mighty men" (2 Sa 23:9).

Ahohite (à-hō′hīt). [Heb. *'Achôchi*.] A member of the family of Ahoah (2 Sa 23:9, 28; 1 Chr 11:12, 29).

Aholah. *See* Oholah.

Aholiab. *See* Oholiab.

Aholibah. *See* Oholibah.

Aholibamah. *See* Oholibamah.

Ahumai (à-hū′mī). [Heb. *'Achûmay*, meaning unknown. The name occurs in Akkadian as *Ahumma*.] A Judahite (1 Chr 4:2).

Ahuzam. *See* Ahuzzam.

Ahuzzam (à-hŭz′ăm), KJV **Ahuzam** (à-hŭz′ăm). [Heb. *'Achuzzam*, "grasp."] A Judahite (1 Chr 4:6).

Ahuzzath (à-hŭz′ăth). [Heb. *'Achuzzath*, "grasp."] A friend of Abimelech of Gerar in Isaac's time (Gen 26:26).

Ahzai (ä′zī), KJV **Ahasai** (à-hā′sī). [Heb. *'Achzay*, a contraction of *'Achazyah*, meaning "Yahweh has seized."] A priest descended from Immer (Neh 11:13); probably the Jahzerah of 1 Chr 9:12.

Ai (ä′ī), KJV twice **Hai** (hā′ī). [Heb. *'Ay*, "heap of stones." The place is also known as **Aija** (à-ī′jà), Heb. *'Ayya'* (Neh 11:31), and **Aiath** (à-ī′ăth), Heb. *'Ayyath* (Is 10:28).]

1. A Canaanite city in the vicinity of Bethel (Jos 7:2; 12:9). Abraham pitched his tent between Bethel and Ai (Gen 12:8; 13:3). Its army smote an Israelite detachment sent against the place from Jericho, the defeat being the result of the curse of Achan resting upon the people (Jos 7:2-5). After the curse was removed a new attack was made and the town and its inhabitants were completely destroyed (ch 8:1-29). On the basis of the Biblical data and of the meaning of the name the site has been identified with *et-Tell*, 1½ mi. southeast of Bethel (Map VI, E-3).

Excavations were carried out at *et-Tell* under the direction of Judith Marquet-Krause from 1933 to 1935. It was found that the city, possessing a wall 20 ft. thick, had flourished in the 3d millennium B.C., and that it had been destroyed about 2000 B.C. After that it lay in ruins until it was rebuilt on a modest scale in the 10th cent. B.C. Those who hold that the site is correctly identified with Ai believe that the city Joshua attacked consisted of perhaps only ruins, and was therefore called Ai, "a heap of stones." They believe that its population consisted of a small number (Jos 7:3) of squatters living on the ancient ruins. However, some scholars are not convinced that Ai is to be identified with *et-Tell*, and maintain that its correct site has not yet been discovered. The postexilic Ai of Ezr 2:28; Neh 7:32; 11:31, should perhaps be located at *Khirbet Haiyân*, immediately to the south of *et-Tell*.

2. A city in Ammon, perhaps near Heshbon (Jer 49:3); not identified.

Aiah (ä-ī′à), KJV once **Ajah** (ä′jà). [Heb. *'Ayyah*, "falcon." Since Aiah, 1, is a Hurrian, the name should be compared with the Hurrian *Aya*.]

1. A Horite or Hurrian of Mount Seir (Gen 36:24; 1 Chr 1:40).

2. The father of Saul's concubine Rizpah (2 Sa 3:7; 21:8, 10, 11).

Aiath. *See* Ai.

Aija. *See* Ai.

Aijalon (ä′jà-lŏn), KJV 3 times **Ajalon** (ăj′à-lŏn). [Heb. *'Ayyalôn*.]

1. An Amorite city, mentioned in the *Amarna Letters as *Ayaluna*. It was assigned to the tribe of Dan, but the Israelites did not occupy it until much later (Jgs 1:34, 35). It was also designated as a Levitical city for the Kohathites (Jos 21:20, 24; 1 Chr 6:69). After the ten tribes seceded, it came under the possession of

8. The Valley of Aijalon

Benjamin and was fortified by Rehoboam (1 Chr 8:13; 2 Chr 11:10). It was later captured by Shishak, who mentions it in his list of conquered cities as *'Iyrn*. The Philistines captured it again in the time of Ahaz (2 Chr 28:18). The site is now called *Yâlō*, a village 14 mi. northwest of Jerusalem (Map VI, E-3). The Valley of Aijalon (Jos 10:12) has been identified with the *Wâdî Selmân*, which runs in a northwesterly direction from Aijalon toward Lod (Lydda).

2. A place in Zebulun, in which the judge Elon was buried (Jgs 12:12); not identified.

Aijeleth Shahar (ā'jĕ-lĕth shā'här). [Heb. *'Ayyeleth Hashshachar*, "hind of the dawn."] A title appearing in the superscription of Ps 22, probably suggesting the melody according to which the psalm was to be sung.

Ain (ā'ĭn). [Heb. *'Ayin*, "a spring."]

1. A locality west of Riblah on the northeastern boundary of Palestine (Num 34:11); not identified.

2. A city in the south of Judah near Rimmon (Jos 15:32). It was transferred to Simeon and assigned to the priests residing in the territory of that tribe (Jos 19:7; 21:16; 1 Chr 4:32). Some suggest that the name should be combined with Rimmon into the compound name Ain-rimmon or En-rimmon (Neh 11:29), and that Ain was an abbreviated form of the longer name. En-rimmon is identified with *Khirbet Umm er-Ramâmîn*, about 11 mi. northeast of Beer-sheba.

3. The 16th letter of the Hebrew alphabet, written ע, appearing as the title to the 16th section of Ps 119 in the KJV. *See* Aleph.

Ajah. *See* Aiah.

Ajalon. *See* Aijalon.

Akan. *See* Jaakan.

Akeldama (á-kĕl'dá-má), KJV **Aceldama** (á-sĕl'dá-má). [Gr. *Akeldamach*, a transliteration of the Aramaic *Chaqel dema'*, "field of blood."] A piece of land originally designated a potter's field, but given the name "field of blood" after Jewish officials bought it with the blood money that Judas in remorse of soul returned to them. The newly acquired field was devoted to the burial of strangers (Mt 27: 6-9). The transliterated form "Akeldama" appears in Acts 1:19, followed immediately by its definition. A local tradition reaching back to the 4th cent. locates this spot on the southern slope of the Valley of Hinnom, where there is red clay and

where the potters in Jeremiah's day probably had workshops (Jer 18:2; 19:2, 11).

Akkub (ăk'ŭb). [Heb. *'Aqqûb*, "a guard." The name occurs in Akkadian as *Aqubu* and *Aqqubu*.]

1. A descendant of David (1 Chr 3:24).

2. A Levite who became the head of a family of Temple porters (1 Chr 9:17; Ezr 2:42; Neh 11:19; 12:25).

3. The family head of the Nethinim (Ezr 2:45).

4. A Levite who taught the law with Ezra (Neh 8:7).

Akrabbim (ăk-răb'ĭm), KJV once **Acrabbim** (ăk-răb'ĭm). [Heb. *'Aqrabbîm*, "scorpions."] The name of an ascent on the southeastern border of Judah which gave access to the Wilderness of Zin (Num 34:4; Jos 15:3, RSV; Jgs 1:36). It is generally identified with the *Naqb eṣ-Ṣafā*. Its northern end begins about 17 mi. west of the southwestern tip of the Dead Sea and winds for about 15 mi. through the mountains in a south-southeasterly direction. Map VI, G-3. See M. Harel, *IEJ* 9 (1959), 175-179.

Alabaster. [Heb. *shesh*; Gr. *alabastros*.] In ancient times, probably any soft stone suitable to be turned on a lathe or carved into household containers or ornaments. Archeological findings reveal such utensils and ornaments to be of a translucent limestone. In the Song of Solomon (ch 5: 15, RSV) the bridegroom's legs are compared to alabaster columns. In the gospel narrative a woman brought an alabaster box containing an expensive unguent and anointed the feet of Jesus shortly before His crucifixion (Mt 26:7; Mk 14:3; Lk 7:37, 38; see *SDACom* 5:764-767).

Alameth. *See* Alemeth, 1.

Alammelech. *See* Allammelech.

Alamoth (ăl'á-mŏth). [Heb. *'alamôth*, an unexplained musical term.] This term appears only in 1 Chr 15:20 and in the title of Ps 46, and appears to refer to a particular style of musical composition or to the manner in which it was to be performed.

Alarm. [Heb. *terû'ah*.] A term describing the battle cry for war (Jer 4:19; 49:2; Zep 1:16), which accompanied the rushing of the host against the enemy forces, or the signal given for the moving of the camp in the wilderness (Num 10:5, 6). In other passages *terû'ah* is variously rendered, "blowing of trumpets" (Lev 23: 24), "shout" (Jos 6:5); etc.

Alemeth (ăl'ĕ-mĕth), KJV once **Alameth** (ăl'á-mĕth). [Heb. *'Alemeth*, "concealment."]

1. A Benjamite (1 Chr 7:8).

2. A descendant of King Saul (1 Chr 8:36; 9:42).

3. A city (1 Chr 6:60). *See* Almon.

Aleph. [Heb. *'aleph.*] The first letter of the Hebrew alphabet, written א. This Hebrew letter and its English transliteration appear as a title to the first section of Ps 119 in the KJV, which includes vs 1-8. In the Hebrew Ps 119 is in the form of an acrostic. Each of the 8 verses of the first section begins with a word whose first letter is *'aleph*. Each of the verses of the second section, also consisting of 8 verses, begins with a word whose first letter is *bêth* (ב), the second letter in the Hebrew alphabet. This pattern follows through the 22 letters of the Hebrew alphabet, so that the psalm contains $8 \times 22 = 176$ verses.

Alexander (ăl'ĕg-zăn'dẽr. [Gr. *Alexandros*, "defender of man," a common Greek name since the time of Alexander the Great, borne not only by Greeks but also by many non-Greeks.]

1. A son of Simon, 6 (Mk 15:21).

2. A member of the high-priestly family during apostolic times (Acts 4:6).

3. A Jew in Ephesus involved in the riot against Paul (Acts 19:33); possibly identical with Alexander, 5.

4. An apostate Christian (1 Ti 1:19, 20).

5. A coppersmith who did Paul great harm (2 Ti 4:14, 15); possibly identical with Alexander, 3.

Alexandria (ăl'ĕg-zăn'drĭ-á). [Gr. *Alexandria*. The NT has only the forms *Alexandreus*, "an Alexandrian," and *Alexandrinos*, "Alexandrian."] The largest city in Hellenistic Egypt. It was founded by Alexander the Great in 332/331 B.C. on the northwestern coast of the Delta, about 15 mi. west of the Canopic Mouth of the Nile, on a strip of land 2 mi. wide lying between the Mediterranean and Lake Mareotis (Map XX, C-4). It was connected by a causeway with the Isle of Pharos, famous for its lighthouse. A reconstruction of the layout of the ancient city is difficult since ruins of ancient buildings do not exist, and the present city of *Iskanderîyeh* stands on the debris of the earlier city. Whether Alexander had planned to make it the capital of Egypt is not known, but Ptolemy I moved the capital from Memphis to Alexandria soon after establishing himself as ruler over Egypt. The city, thoroughly Hellenistic, became famous for its temples, theaters, and other magnificent buildings, and the royal palace. Most famous of all was the Museum with its library containing perhaps hundreds of thousands of scrolls.

In Roman times Alexandria was the second city of the empire, and the most important city in the East. It was famous for its Museum, which developed into a great university, making the city a center of Hellenistic learning and culture, and also for its economic significance as the main port supplying grain for Rome. Of the three ships which Paul used to take him to Rome in c. A.D. 60/61, two were probably grain ships from Alexandria (Acts 27:6; 28:11). The population of Alexandria during Roman times is not known, and estimates range from 600,000 to a much higher figure, but the lower estimate is probably correct. The city was divided into 5 districts, of which one, in the northeast, was occupied by Jews, who enjoyed special privileges and lived under their own ethnarch as administrator (Jos. *Ant.* xix. 5. 2; *War* ii. 18. 7). Philo's claim that the Jewish population counted one million is probably an exaggeration. The Greek translation of the Hebrew OT, named the Septuagint (abbreviated LXX), was either made or begun in Alexandria. The Jews of Alexandria, along with the "Libertines" (literally, "freedmen") and Cyrenians, had a synagogue in Jerusalem, whose members took part in the accusation against Stephen (Acts 6: 9). The teachings of John the Baptist had probably found their way to Alexandria and gained followers there. At least one such convert, Apollos, a native of Alexandria, is mentioned in the NT (ch 18: 24, 25). There is a tradition that Christianity came to Alexandria through Mark. In later centuries Alexandria became a famous seat of Christian philosophy. It was the home of Clement of Alexandria (c. A.D. 150 - c. 220) and Origen (c. A.D. 185 - c. 254). An allegorical method of Bible interpretation was developed by Christian scholars of that city.

Alexandrian (ăl'ĕg-zăn'drĭ-ăn). [Gr. *Alexandreus.*] An inhabitant of *Alexandria (Acts 6:9).

Algum. *See* Almug.

Aliah (á-lī'á), or **Alvah** (ăl'vá). [Heb. *'Alyah*, "tall," and *'Alwah*, "height."] One of the chiefs who descended from Esau. He probably bore the name of the district he controlled (1 Chr 1:51; Gen 36:40).

Alian (ăl'ĭ-ăn), or **Alvan** (ăl'văn). [Heb. *'Alyan* and *'Alwan*, probably a Hurrian name.] A Horite, a descendant of Seir (1 Chr 1:40; Gen 36:23).

Allammelech (ăl-lăm′ĕ-lĕk), KJV **Alam-melech** (á-lăm′ĕ-lĕk). [Heb. *'Allammelek,* perhaps originally pronounced *'Almelek* with the meaning "oak of the king" or "royal oak."] A town in Asher (Jos 19:26); not identified.

Allegory. [Heb. *mashal,* "a proverbial saying," "a prophetic figurative discourse," from the root *mashal,* "to be like." The NT term is from the Gr. *allēgoreō,* "to speak allegorically," from two Greek words meaning "otherwise" and "to speak."] A form of literary expression in which one truth is presented under the image of another and in which the words and the narrative itself are clothed with a meaning other than that which they naturally convey, which secondary meaning is implied but not explicitly stated. In the RSV of the OT, "allegory" is used for two of Ezekiel's figurative prophetic discourses (Eze 17:2; 24:3). In the NT, "allegory" is used to introduce and describe a section of Paul's argument in Galatians (ch 4:21-31).

Alleluia. *See* Hallelujah.

Allon, I (ăl′ŏn). [Heb. *'Allôn,* "strong tree."] A Simeonite (1 Chr 4:37).

Allon, II (ăl′ŏn). [Heb. *'Elôn.*] A town in Naphtali (Jos 19:33), according to the KJV. However, some prefer to render the phrase translated "Allon to Zaanannim" as "the oak in Zaanannim" (RSV) or "the big tree of Bezaanannim." *See* Zaanannim.

Allon-bachuth. *See* Allon-bacuth.

Allon-bacuth (ăl′ŏn-băk′ŭth), KJV **Allon-bachuth** (ăl′ŏn-băk′ŭth). [Heb. *'Allôn Bakûth,* "strong tree of weeping."] A place near Bethel where Deborah, Rebekah's nurse, was buried (Gen 35:8); not identified.

Almighty. [Heb. *shadday,* meaning uncertain; Gr. *pantokratōr,* "universal sovereign."] A descriptive title of God that appears in combination with "God" (as in Gen 17:1) or alone (as in Job 5:17) altogether 48 times in the OT, and 10 times in the NT. (The KJV translates *pantokratōr* once "omnipotent," Rev 19:6.) In the LXX *shadday* is often, though not always, translated *pantokratōr.*

Almodad (ăl-mō′dăd). [Heb. *'Almôdad.*] A son of Joktan, descendant of Shem, and probably also the ancestor of an unidentified Arabic tribe (Gen 10:26; 1 Chr 1:20).

Almon (ăl′mŏn). [Heb. *'Almôn,* "way-mark."] A town in Benjamin, assigned to the priests (Jos 21:18), called Alemeth in 1 Chr 6:60. The site has been identified with *Khirbet 'Almît,* about 2 mi. northeast of Anathoth.

Almond. [Heb. *shaqed,* from a root meaning "to be wakeful," "to watch"; *lûz.*] The flowering nut tree, *Amygdalus communis,* a member of the peach family. Its white or delicately pink blossoms appear as early as January, long before other trees flower. As a harbinger of spring, it became known as the "wakeful tree" or

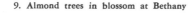
9. Almond trees in blossom at Bethany

"wake-tree." The tree attains a height of from 12 to 16 ft. and is valued for its delicate oil. The leaves, which appear some time after the blossoms, are long and ovate, with serrated edges and an acute apex. The familiar kernel is incased in a hard shell, within a downy succulent covering. Although the tree closely resembles the peach tree in form and blossoms, the fruit lacks the pulpy flesh of the peach. Possibly this tree was not found in Egypt in patriarchal times, for Jacob sent its fruit there as a gift (Gen 43:11). God directed Moses to have the seven-branched candlestick and its bowls fashioned after the almond branch and flower (Ex 25:33, 34; 37:19, 20). The rod of Aaron budded, blossomed, and produced ripe almonds (Num 17:8). The "almond tree" of Ec 12:5 is believed to represent the hoary head of a patriarch, for the blossoms, seen from a distance, have a snowy-white appearance. The Lord used this tree as a symbol of His watchcare over His word in Jeremiah's first vision (ch 1:11). In Gen 30:37, KJV *lûz* is translated "hazel," but this rendering is without support.

Almon-diblathaim (ăl'mŏn-dĭb'lá-thā'ĭm). [Heb. *'Almon Diblathayim*.] A stopping place of the Israelites during the Exodus, situated in Transjordan between Dibon-Gad and Nebo (Num 33:46, 47). Some have identified it with the *Khirbet Deleilât esh-Sherqîyeh*, about halfway between Dibon and Medeba, considering it as probably identical with Beth-diblathaim in Jer 48:22 and Beth-diblathen on the Moabite Stone, line 30. On Map VI, E-4, it is called Almon, on the interpretation that the name means "the Almon in the bailiwick of Diblathaim," that is, of Beth-diblathaim, and that Almon may be located at *'Ain ed Dib.*

Alms. Works of mercy or relief to the poor; the money or other substance so given. The word is not mentioned in the OT, but consideration "for the stranger, for the fatherless, and for the widow" (Deut 24:19) was enjoined upon God's people (Lev 25:35; Deut 15:7, 8, 11; 26:12), and to some extent practiced. Christ approved the practice of almsgiving, but taught that it should not be done out of selfish or insincere motives (Mt 6:2-4). He set forth generosity toward the poor, even to the extent of real personal sacrifice, as a test of Christian character and integrity (Mt 19:16-22; Lk 12:33). The practice in the apostolic period is illustrated in the narrative of the healing of the lame man who was laid daily at the gate of the Temple to ask alms of the Temple visitors (Acts 3:1-10). The Gentile Cornelius was described as a "devout man" and one who "gave much alms" (ch 10:2, 4, 31). Paul carried a burden for the physical needs of his people (ch 24:17).

Almug or **Algum.** [Heb. *'almuggîm* and *'algûmmîm;* Ugaritic *'lmg*. It is generally believed that the two Hebrew terms refer to the same tree, the variant forms having resulted from a transposition of characters.] A tree of Ophir, the wood of which was used in quantity as supporting timber in Solomon's Temple and in his house, and for musical instruments (1 Ki 10:11, 12; 2 Chr 9:10, 11). Certain identification is not possible. Some scholars suppose it to be red sandalwood, a tree of heavy, fine-grained timber which grows to a height of 20 ft. The wood itself, black on the outside and ruby inside, possesses an odor repellent to insects but pleasing to human beings. However, the sandalwood is not found in Lebanon, and in his initial order for Temple materials to be shipped by the king of Tyre, Solomon requested "algum trees, out of Lebanon" (2 Chr 2:8; cf. ch 9:10, 11). Consequently other scholars suggest either Eastern savin or Grecian juniper.

Aloes. [Heb. *'ahalîm* and *'ahalôth;* Gr. *aloē*.] Probably the eaglewood tree (*Aquilaria agallocha*) of southeast Asia, the wood of which provided valuable perfume and an embalming ingredient. Some believe the NT aloes to be the true or bitter aloes (*Aloe succotrina*), but others hold that in all cases "aloes" represents the eaglewood. This large tree, indigenous to the Malay Peninsula and northern India, attains a height of 100 to 120 ft. The perfume is produced by burning the wood. In Balaam's prophecy (Num 24:6) "aloes" (KJV "lign aloes") represents the lofty and abiding position accorded the people of God. The delightful fragrance of the tree's perfume is poetically employed to describe the bridegroom in the psalmist's marriage hymn (Ps 45:8), and the tree itself is given as a symbol of attractiveness in Song 4:14, but the harlot of Prov 7:17 uses this same perfume in her evil enticements. Nicodemus brought aloes mixed with myrrh to embalm the body of Jesus (Jn 19:39).

Aloth (ā'lŏth). [Heb. *'Alôth.*] According to the KJV, a place in the north of Palestine from which Solomon received provisions (1 Ki 4:16). However, more likely the term translated "in Aloth" should be rendered *Bealoth as in the RSV.

10. Great Canaanite altar at Megiddo

Alpha and Omega. [Gr. A (*alpha*) and Ω (*ōmega*), the first and last letters of the Greek alphabet.] A title for God the Father and for Christ that occurs 4 times (chs 1:8, 11; 21:6; 22:13) in the book of Revelation (3 times, RSV, the expression being omitted in v 11 on the basis of strong textual evidence). As John himself explains, this expression means "the beginning and the ending" (ch 1:8). It implies that God is eternal—He always was, He always will be. In chs 1:8 (cf. v 4); 21: 6 (cf. chs 20:11; 21:3, 5) the title is probably descriptive of God the Father, whereas in ch 22:13 (cf. v 16) it clearly refers to Christ.

Alphabet. *See* Writing.

Alphaeus (ăl-fē'ŭs). [Gr. *Halphaios,* a transliteration of the Heb. *Chalpay,* meaning uncertain.]

　　1. Father of Levi (Matthew) (Mk 2:14; cf. Mt 9:9).

　　2. Father of the second James in the lists of the 12 apostles (Mt 10:3; Mk 3:18; Lk 6:15; Acts 1:13).

Altar. [Heb. generally *mizbeach,* from *zabach,* "to slaughter"; Gr. *thusiastērion,* from *thuō,* "to slaughter," "to sacrifice."] A structure on which sacrifices or incense is offered to a deity. Altars were used by almost every ancient nation, not only in temples but also in open-air sanctuaries. Some of them were made of stones heaped up to form a cubical platform on which the sacrifices were offered, with steps leading up to it if the altar was high. Others were made of earth, with stone enclosures. Still others were made of one piece, and cut out of the rock, either left attached to the rock, as in Petra, or detached from it and of small dimensions so that they could be moved. In Stratum XVI (20th cent. b.c.) of the Megiddo excavations archeologists discovered a large circular altar about 30 ft. in diameter at the base, but somewhat smaller at the top, and 6½ ft. high, with a flight of 8 steps on its east side (see fig. 10). Animal bones found at the base showed that the altar had served for burnt offerings. The altar on the great high place of Petra is cut out of the living rock, as is everything else at that site, and is 9 ft. long and 6 ft. wide, with 4 steps leading up to it at the east side. Assyrian temple altars are usually cut of one block of stone with three legs and a round tablelike top. These apparently were considered tables of the gods, at which they sat to partake of the offerings brought to them. Palestinian house altars found at Megiddo and Shechem are of a different kind, one interesting feature being that they have rims and the horns at the four corners, items mentioned in descriptions of Biblical altars (see fig. 11).

　　The first altar mentioned in the Bible is that on which Noah offered his sacrifices after the Flood (Gen 8:20). However, altars may have been erected much earlier, since burnt offerings were offered from the time of Cain and Abel (ch 4:3-5). The patriarchs are reported to have erected their altars either under large trees (chs 12:6-8; 13:18; RSV) or on top of a hill or mountain (chs 22:2, 9; 31:54). Altars were not always used to offer sacrifices; they served also as memorials (Jos 22:22-29). Almost never does the Bible call the altar "a table" (Mal 1:7, 12). Possibly the term was avoided because the

11. Small limestone altar found at Megiddo

12. Altar with the emblem of a sun-god found in a Canaanite temple at Hazor

pagan altars were always considered to be tables of the gods.

The tabernacle Moses erected in the wilderness had two altars, the altar of burnt offering (Ex 27:1-8; 38:1, 2) and the altar of incense (ch 30:1-10). The altar of burnt offering, made of acacia wood and overlaid with *bronze, was 3 cu. (about 5 ft. 2 in.) high and 5 cu. (about 8 ft. 7 in.) square (*see* Cubit). Bronze horns extended from each top corner, and a grating of the same metal was fitted inside the altar. Rings were attached to two sides, through which poles might be placed for the purpose of transportation as the Israelites moved from place to place. The altar stood in the outer court, near the door of the tabernacle leading to the first apartment (ch 40:29). The Mosaic law forbade local altars after a central place of worship should be chosen (Deut 12:10-14), yet they were apparently permitted before the Temple was built (see 1 Sa 7:10; 9:12, 13; 14:35; 1 Chr 21:26). The altar of burnt offering in the Temple built by Solomon was made of *bronze. It was 10 cu. (about 17 ft. 2 in.) high and 20 cu. (about 34 ft. 4 in.) square (2 Chr 4:1). These measurements are given in terms of Egyptian cubits.

Little is known of the altar of the post-exilic Temple (Ezr 3:2, 3). Josephus records a description of the altar at Jerusalem by Hecateus, a contemporary of Alexander the Great, according to which the altar was composed of white stones and was 20 cu. square and 10 cu. high (*Against Apion* i. 22). The writer of 1 Macc mentions that the altar defiled by Antiochus IV (Epiphanes) was made of stone, as was the one replacing it (1 Macc 4:44-49). Josephus records the dimensions of the later altar as 15 cu. high and 50 cu. square (*War* v. 5. 6).

The altar of Ezekiel's temple vision is described in considerable detail (Eze 43:13-18). It was to be an elaborate structure, set upon a base 1 cu. high, or about 20 in., according to Ezekiel's cubit, which was a handbreadth longer (v 13) than the ordinary cubit. The cubit of Ezekiel's day, about 17½ in. plus a handbreadth, would almost equal the Egyptian cubit of the Exodus period. This base was to be surmounted by successive ledges; the topmost, reached by steps, being a hearth 12 cu. (about 20 ft.) square (see *SDACom* 4:715-717).

The altar of incense, or golden altar, was placed inside the holy place, directly in front of the veil separating the holy place from the Most Holy (Ex 30:1, 6). The altar of the Mosaic tabernacle was made of acacia wood, and was plated with gold. It measured 2 cu. (about 3 ft. 5 in.) high and 1 cu. (about 1 ft. 9 in.) square (ch 30:1-3). A "crown," or molding, of gold bordered it, which projected into horns at the corners (cf. Lev 4:7). Two golden rings, fastened to opposite sides of the altar, were provided for the insertion of poles when transportation was necessary (Ex 30:4). An incense of specified ingredients was to be burned upon it twice daily as a "perpetual incense," implying a constantly ascending fragrance (vs 7, 8, 34-38).

The altar of incense of Solomon's Temple was made of cedarwood, and was overlaid with gold (1 Ki 6:20, 22).

A golden altar was seen by John the revelator in vision, and was represented as standing before the throne of Deity. Upon it an angel was burning incense, which mingled with the prayers of saints (Rev 8:3). This can be taken as symbolizing the ministration of Christ.

An altar "to an unknown god" provided the "text" for Paul's sermon to the polytheistic Athenians (Acts 17:23). They had perhaps built it to avoid offending any god.

Altaschith. [Heb. *'al-tashcheth,* literally, "destroy not."] A word occurring in the titles of Ps 57, 58, 59, 75, in the KJV. The RSV renders the Hebrew literally as "Do Not Destroy." The significance of the Hebrew term is uncertain. Some think the expression specifies the tune to which the words of the psalm are to be sung.

Alush (ā'lŭsh). [Heb. *'Alûsh.*] A place where the Israelites camped in their desert wanderings (Num 33:13, 14).

Alvah. *See* Aliah.

Alvan. *See* Alian.

Amad (ā'măd). [Heb. *'Am'ad,* "people of duration."] A town in the territory of Asher (Jos 19:26); not identified.

Amal (ā'măl). [Heb. *'Amal,* "trouble"; the name occurs as a component part of the Edomite name *Qaus-'amal,* found in a seal impression at Ezion-geber.] An Asherite (1 Chr 7:35).

Amalek (ăm'à-lĕk) and **Amalekites** (ăm'à-lĕk-īts). [Heb. *'Amaleq* and *'Amaleqî.*] Amalek was a son of Esau's son Eliphaz and Eliphaz' concubine Timna (Gen 36:12, 16; 1 Chr 1:36). The word is also used frequently in the collective sense and then means Amalekites (Ex 17:8; Num 13:29; 24:20; etc.). The reference of Gen 14:7 to "all the country of the Amalekites" as smitten by Chedorlaomer and his confederates does not mean that they already existed at that time, but designates the territory as it was known to the author of the narrative and to his readers.

The main territory of the Amalekites was the desert between Sinai and the southern part of Palestine (Map V, B-6), but some seem to have dwelt also in the area known later as the Ephraim mountains, which retained their name for some time (Jgs 5:14; 12:15). Throughout their history they were involved in fighting with Israel. The first encounter took place shortly after the Exodus when the Amalekites attacked the rear of the Israelites, but then were defeated by Joshua at Rephidim (Ex 17:8-13; Deut 25:17, 18). They were then cursed and their annihilation predicted, first by Moses (Ex 17:14-16; Deut 25:19) and later by Balaam (Num 24:20). They oppressed Israel in the period of the judges twice, once with the Moabites (Jgs 3:12, 13), and again with the Midianites (chs 6:3; 7:12). Saul carried out a systematic military campaign against them, and captured their king, who was slain by Samuel (1 Sa 15). Yet there remained some powerful Amalekite groups, against whom David fought repeatedly (chs 27:8; 30:1, 17, 18). David's last encounter seems to have broken their power; with one exception they are not mentioned again. The last remnants of them were annihilated by the Simeonites in the time of King Hezekiah (1 Chr 4:42, 43).

Amalekites. *See* Amalek.

Amam (ā'măm). [Heb. *'Amam.*] A place in the south of Judah near Beer-sheba (Jos 15:26); not identified.

Amana (à-mā'nà). [Heb. *'Amanah;* in Akkadian inscriptions *Umânum, Ammana,* and *Ammun.*] A designation for the Anti-Lebanon Mountains (Song 4:8; Map XIV, A-5). Sargon II obtained alabaster from there.

Amariah (ăm'à-rī'à). [Heb. *'Amaryah* and *'Amaryahû,* "Yahweh has spoken." The name occurs in ancient Hebrew inscriptions found at Gibeon.]
1. A high priest late in the period of the judges (1 Chr 6:7).
2. A Levitical head of a family (1 Chr 23:19; 24:23).
3. A high priest in Solomon's and Rehoboam's time (1 Chr 6:11; Ezr 7:3).
4. A chief priest in Jehoshaphat's time (2 Chr 19:11).
5. A distributor of the freewill offerings in Hezekiah's time (2 Chr 31:14, 15).
6. A son of Hizkiah (probably King Hezekiah) and an ancestor of the prophet Zephaniah (Zep 1:1).
7. A chief of the priests who returned from Babylon with Zerubbabel (Neh 12:2, 13).
8. A man who was married to a foreign wife in Ezra's time (Ezr 10:42).
9. A priest who set his seal to Nehemiah's covenant (Neh 10:3).
10. A citizen of Jerusalem in Nehemiah's time (Neh 11:4).

Amarna (*Tell el-'Amârna*). The site of the ancient capital of Egypt during the reign of Ikhnaton (Amenhotep IV, *c.* 1387-1366 B.C.), situated about 200 mi. south of Cairo on the right bank of the Nile (see Map III, D-3). When Ikhnaton initiated the monotheistic sun worship of Aten (Aton) he found so much opposition in Thebes, the royal residence and center of the old religion, that he moved the capital to a new site, which he called Akhetaton, "Horizon of Aton." The movement collapsed soon after his death, and the capital was moved back to Thebes. Ikhnaton and his short-lived capital were forgotten until its ruins were rediscovered in modern times.

In 1887 a local woman, while digging in the ruins for waste to be used as fertilizer, accidentally discovered the official archive of the kings Amenhotep III (*c.* 1412 - *c.* 1375 B.C.) and Ikhnaton. It contained more than 350 letters written on clay tablets in Babylonian cuneiform script comprising the correspondence between the Egyptian court and the kings of Babylonia, Assyria, Mitanni, Arzawa, Cyprus, and the Hittites, and of many vassal princes of Syria and Palestine. After many vicissitudes the tablets finally came into the hands of scholars. A few additional ones were later discovered in regular excavations at Amarna. Nearly 300 of these tablets are now in the Berlin Museum, and others are in the museums of London, Cairo, Oxford, Paris, and Brussels.

13. Two of the Amarna Letters sent to the Pharaoh. Upper: from Labaia of Shechem (Map VI, D-3). Lower: from the king of Arzawa (Map III, B-3)

These documents, usually referred to as the Amarna Letters, are first-rate sources for the political and cultural history of Western Asia and Egypt during the 14th cent. B.C., and their discovery was a major event in the history of Near Eastern and Biblical archeology. They reveal that the Babylonian script and language were universally used in the Near East for diplomatic correspondence, even between the Egyptian overlord and his Asiatic vassals, thus showing the great influence of Babylonian culture on Syria and Palestine. These letters show that the kings of Babylon, of Assyria, and of Mitanni dealt with the Egyptian Pharaoh on a basis of equality. They reveal Egypt, which a generation earlier was the greatest world power, in an acute state of political inactivity and weakness, doing virtually nothing to retain her Asiatic empire built up by Thutmose III and his successors. They show the Hittites revealing themselves as a menace in the north by encroaching on Egyptian possessions in Syria through direct aggression and intrigue. Syria and Palestine, nominally Egyptian protectorates, are found to be in a state of anarchy and extreme weakness, split up into many little kingdoms. Their rulers, who call themselves kings, claim to be loyal to the Egyptian crown, but fight against one another, some in open warfare, others by denunciation and intrigue. Several of these princes take advantage of Egyptian political inactivity during this period to become independent and to enlarge their territory at the expense of their neighbors. Another cause of political unrest is the appearance of the 'Apiru (written Ḫabiru in syllabic spelling or SA.GAZ in ideographic script), in whom the invading Hebrews can be recognized (see Hebrews). 'Abdu-Heba, the king of Jerusalem, complains especially bitterly about the intrusion of the 'Apiru and claims that already large parts of the country have fallen into their hands by conquest and treason. Other well-known Palestinian and Syrian cities from whose rulers letters are preserved are Ashkelon, Lachish, Gezer, Megiddo, Acco, Tyre, Sidon, Beirut, and Byblos.

Lit.: S. A. B. Mercer, The Tell el-Amarna Tablets (2 vols.; Toronto, 1939); ANET 483-490 (contains many letters translated by W. F. Albright).

Amasa (ăm'ȧ-sȧ). [Heb. 'Amaśa', usually considered to be a shortened form of 'Amaśay, meaning "Yahweh has borne." The name occurs also on an ancient Hebrew seal.]

1. A son of the Ishmaelite Jether and David's (half) sister Abigail (1 Chr 2:17), and thus Joab's cousin (2 Sa 17:25). Deserting David, he joined Absalom's rebellion and was appointed captain in

Absalom's forces (2 Sa 17:25). After Absalom's defeat David not only forgave Amasa for his desertion but also honored him by giving him Joab's office, probably because Joab had just killed Absalom, against David's orders (ch 19:13). Joab, angered by this demotion, assassinated Amasa at Gibeon (ch 20:1-13). Amasa is possibly identical with *Amasai, 2.

2. An Ephraimite who aided in securing the release of captives from Judah who were being carried away by the army of King Pekah of Israel (2 Chr 28:12).

Amasai (*à-măs′â-ī*). [Heb. *'Amaśay,* "Yahweh has borne." The name occurs in Babylonian texts as *Ammashi'.*]

1. A Kohathite Levite, ancestor of Heman the singer (1 Chr 6:35). Whether the Amasai of v 25 is the same Levite is uncertain.

2. Onè of David's captains (1 Chr 12: 18). Possibly the same as Amasa, 1.

3. A priest in the time of David (1 Chr 15:24).

4. A Kohathite Levite in Hezekiah's time (2 Chr 29:12).

Amashai. *See* Amashsai.

Amashsai (*à-măsh′sâ-ī*), KJV **Amashai** (*à-măsh′â-ī*). [Heb. *'Amashsay,* meaning unknown.] A priest in Nehemiah's time (Neh 11:13); probably identical with Maasai (1 Chr 9:12).

Amasiah (*ăm′à-sī′à*). [Heb. *'Amasyah,* "Yahweh has borne." The name occurs in Assyrian inscriptions as *Amsi,* and in Phoenician texts as *'ms.*] A military officer serving King Jehoshaphat (2 Chr 17:16).

Amaw (*à-mä′*). [Heb. *'Ammô,* in cuneiform *Amae,* and in an Egyptian inscription *'m3w.*] The name of the homeland of the renegade prophet Balaam (Num 22:5, RSV), identified as lying in the *Sâjûr* Valley between Aleppo and Carchemish. The translators of the KJV mistook the Hebrew word and thought that it meant "his people." Its true significance was discovered by W. F. Albright after the publication of the cuneiform inscription of Idri-mi's statue found at ancient Alalakh, which dates from Moses' time, about 1480 B.C. (*BASOR* 118 [1950], 14-20).

Amaziah (*ăm′à-zī′à*). [Heb. *'Amasyah* and *'Amasyahû,* "Yahweh is strong."]

1. The 9th king of Judah, the southern kingdom, who reigned for 29 years (*c.* 796 - *c.* 767 B.C.). He succeeded his father Joash, who had been slain for the murder of the priest Zechariah. When Amaziah felt himself securely established on the throne he put his father's murderers to death but spared their children in harmony with the principles laid down by Moses in the Law (2 Ki 14:1-6; 2 Chr 24: 23-26; 25:1-4; cf. Deut 24:16). He planned a military campaign against Edom, and to assist him hired 100,000 troops from Israel, but on the advice of a man of God he dismissed them. Bitterly disappointed, these rejected men plundered the cities of Judah north of Beth-horon on their way home. Amaziah meanwhile attacked the Edomites and defeated them thoroughly in the Valley of Salt. He also took *Sela, their capital. In view of the supposedly impregnable position of Sela this victory was a major military feat (2 Ki 14:7; 2 Chr 25:5-12). Although Amaziah had been faithful to God in his early reign (2 Ki 14:3; 2 Chr 25:2), after his victory over Edom he began to worship Edomite gods that he had brought back to Jerusalem. As a prophet had forewarned (2 Chr 25:14-16), this act of idolatry caused his downfall. Following certain advice, he challenged Jehoash (Joash) of Israel to battle, but was badly defeated at Beth-shemesh. Jehoash thereupon took Amaziah to Jerusalem, despoiled his treasures, took hostages, and broke down a portion of the defenses of the capital city of Judah (2 Ki 14:8-14; 2 Chr 25:17-24). Later a conspiracy was formed against Amaziah. He fled to Lachish, but was murdered there. He was buried at Jerusalem in a royal tomb (2 Ki 14:19, 20; 2 Chr 25:27, 28).

2. A Simeonite (1 Chr 4:34).

3. A Levite of the family of Merari (1 Chr 6:45).

4. The leading priest of the calf temple at Bethel in the time of Jeroboam II. When Amos predicted the fall of Jeroboam and the captivity of Israel, Amaziah tried to silence him, whereupon Amos turned his prophecy against this idolatrous priest and forecast a tragic future for him (Amos 7:10-17).

Ambassage. An archaic word meaning "embassy," occurring in Lk 14:32, KJV.

Amber. [Heb. *chashmal.*] A term appearing in the KJV for a substance to which Ezekiel compared a certain appearance in his visions (Eze 1:4, 27; 8:2). *Chashmal* is of uncertain origin and of unknown meaning. The various translations of the term in the versions are simply conjectural. The LXX reads *elektron,* a whitish yellow alloy of gold and silver. The RSV reads "gleaming bronze."

Amen. [Heb. *'amen,* "surely," "indeed," "truly," from *'aman,* "to be faithful," "to be firmly established"; Gr. *amēn,* a transliteration of the Hebrew.] In the OT, "Amen" appears as an affirmation assenting to a proclamation (as in Deut 27:15-26), and as a response, perhaps by an audience, to psalms chanted in the Temple service (as in Ps 41:13). In Is 65:16 *'amen* is translated "truth," in the expression "God of truth," literally, "God of Amen," stressing the faithfulness and reliability of God. In the NT, "Amen" commonly follows a doxology, or ascription of praise to God, whether long (as in 1 Ti 1:17) or short (as in Rom 11:36). It is used also as the closing word of most of the epistles (as in Jude 25), though in some instances manuscript evidence is divided as to whether the word occurred in the original autographs (see Php 4:23, KJV and RSV). In some instances the Gr. *amēn* is translated as "verily" ("truly," RSV), instead of being transliterated. This is the case when *amēn* prefixes our Lord's most solemn affirmations of truth, as in Mt 5:18. In the Gospel of John (ch 1:51; etc.) the term is doubled in each instance, doubtless for emphasis.

Amethyst. [Heb. *'achlamah;* Gr. *amethustos.*] The Hebrew term is of uncertain identification. Some scholars suggest red or brown jasper, others, amethyst. The Greek term is generally identified with the modern amethyst, a transparent quartz given a purple or bluish cast by the presence of manganese. It is known to have been used in necklaces and bracelets in ancient times. The *'achlamah* was used in the third row of precious stones composing the high priest's breastplate (Ex 28:19; 39:12), and the *amethustos* formed the twelfth foundation of the New Jerusalem (Rev 21:20).

Ami. *See* Amon, 3.

Aminadab. *See* Amminadab, 1.

Amittai (ă-mĭt'ī). [Heb. *'Amittay,* "truthful."] The father of the prophet Jonah (2 Ki 14:25; Jon 1:1).

Ammah (ăm'ă). [Heb. *'Ammah,* probably "dwarf" (W. F. Albright *IEJ* 4 [1954], 3, 4).] The name of a hill between Gibeon and the Jordan Valley where the forces of Joab defeated those of Abner (2 Sa 2:24); not identified.

Ammi (ăm'ī). [Heb. *'Ammi,* "my people."] A figurative name signifying "my people," typifying Israel as God's own people, within the bond of the covenant relationship (Hos 2:1; cf. Rom 9:25). Compare

the name Lo-ammi, "not my people," in Hos 1:9.

Ammiel (ăm'ĭ-ĕl). [Heb. *'Ammi'el,* "God is my kinsman."]
1. One of the twelve spies, a Danite (Num 13:12).
2. The father of Machir of Lo-debar (2 Sa 9:4, 5; 17:27).
3. The father of Bath-shua or Bath-sheba (1 Chr 3:5); he is called Eliam in 2 Sa 11:3.
4. A Levite (1 Chr 26:5).

Ammihud (ă-mī'hŭd). [Heb. *'Ammihud,* "my (divine) kinsman is majesty."]
1. An Ephraimite (Num 1:10; 1 Chr 7:26).
2. A Simeonite (Num 34:20).
3. A Naphtalite (Num 34:28).
4. Father of Talmai, king of Geshur (2 Sa 13:37).
5. A Judahite (1 Chr 9:4).

Amminadab (ă-mĭn'ă-dăb), KJV of NT **Aminadab** (ă-mĭn'ă-dăb). [Heb. *'Amminadab,* "the (divine) kinsman is generous." The name occurs on two ancient Ammonite seals and in an inscription of Ashurbanipal, where it is the name of the king of Ammon and is spelled *Amminadbi* (*ANET* 294). Gr. *Aminadab.*]
1. A descendant of Judah through Hezron (1 Chr 2:10). He was father of Nahshon, the prince of Judah in Moses' time (Num 1:7), and father-in-law of Aaron, the high priest (Ex 6:23), also an ancestor of David (Ruth 4:19; Mt 1:4; Lk 3:33).
2. A Kohathite Levite (1 Chr 6:22) otherwise called Izhar in the genealogies listing the descendants of Kohath (1 Chr 6:18-38; Ex 6:18, 21).
3. A Kohathite Levite in David's time (1 Chr 15:10, 11).

Amminadib (ă-mĭn'ă-dĭb). [Heb. *'Amminadib.*] A personal name in the KJV of unknown identity (Song 6:12). The meaning of the Hebrew term is uncertain. The RSV reads "my prince."

Ammishaddai (ăm'ĭ-shăd'ī). [Heb. *'Ammishadday,* "the Almighty is my kinsman." The name occurs in Egypt in the late 14th cent. B.C. as that of a petty official spelled *śd'my.*] A Danite (Num 1:12; 2:25).

Ammizabad (ă-mĭz'ă-băd). [Heb. *'Ammizabad,* "my (divine) kinsman has presented (me a gift)."] A son of one of David's "mighty men" (1 Chr 27:6).

Ammon (ăm'ŏn) and **Ammonites** (ăm'ŏn-īts). [Heb. *'Ammôn* and *'Ammonim,* possibly meaning "people," "kinsman," or "paternal uncle."] The people descended from Ben-Ammi, son of Lot by his own younger daughter (Gen 19:38). By the time of Moses the Ammonites had displaced the aboriginal Rephaim (KJV "giants"), called Zamzummim by the Ammonites (Deut 2:20, 21), from the headwaters of the Jabbok. Their capital was Rabbah, also called Rabbath-ammon, now 'Ammân. Map VI, D, E-4/5.

The Ammonites began hostile actions against the Israelites in the time of the judges when, as confederates of Eglon of Moab and of the Amalekites, they attacked Israel (Jgs 3:12-14). During the late 12th cent. b.c. they oppressed the Israelites in Transjordan, while the Philistines oppressed those living in the west, but were defeated and pushed back to their original home area (chs 10:6-9; 11:1-33). Later Nahash, the king of the Ammonites, attacked Jabesh-gilead, but was defeated by the newly chosen king Saul, who came to the help of the besieged city (1 Sa 11:1-11). When David's envoys were humiliated at the court of Hanun, the successor of Nahash, war ensued between the two nations. The Ammonites, although assisted by several Aramaean city-states, were defeated by the armies of David commanded by Joab and Abishai (2 Sa 10; 1 Chr 19). A later campaign against the Ammonites ended with the capture of the capital city, Rabbah (2 Sa 11; 12; 1 Chr 20:1-3). The Ammonites, tributary to David, seem however under Solomon to have enjoyed a measure of independence, as suggested by the fact that Solomon took wives from the princesses of the Ammonites (1 Ki 11:1). They attempted another invasion of Judah in the time of Jehoshaphat (2 Chr 20:1-30), but were again made tributary. The payment of tribute by the Ammonites to the kingdom of Judah is recorded for the times of Uzziah, or Azariah (ch 26:8), and Jotham (ch 27:5). After that they came under the full dominance of Assyria.

Assyrian texts mention the Ammonites (Bit-Ammânu) as early as the time of Shalmaneser III, who tells us that their king Ba'sa, son of Ruhubi, took part with his forces in the battle of Qarqar in 853 b.c. (ANET 279). Tiglath-pileser III (745-727 b.c.) received tribute from Sanipu of the house of Ammon (ibid. 282), Esarhaddon (681-669 b.c.) from Puduil (ibid. 291), and Ashurbanipal (669-627 b.c.) from Amminadbi (ibid. 294). The name Amminadbi occurs also on two Ammonite seals written in the vowelless Phoenician characters 'mndb (Diringer, Iscrizioni, pp. 253-255).

After the fall of the Assyrian Empire the Ammonites became vassals of the Babylonian king, and when Jehoiakim of Judah rebelled against Nebuchadnezzar, the Ammonites were allowed to harass their western neighbors (2 Ki 24:2). After Jerusalem's destruction the Ammonite king Baalis hired Ishmael, one of the former army commanders of Judah, to assassinate Gedaliah, who had been appointed by the Babylonians as the new governor over the province of Judah (2 Ki 25:23; Jer 40:14; 41:1, 2). The reasons for this act are not clear. In the time of the Persian Empire the territory of Ammon was, like Judea and Samaria, a province belonging to the satrapy of "Beyond the River." The old enmity against Israel was still alive, as is evident from the opposition of the Ammonites, along with others, to the rebuilding of the wall of Jerusalem (Neh 4:3, 7). At the same time there were intermarriages between the two nations, which displeased leaders like Nehemiah and Ezra (Ezr 9:1, 2; Neh 13:23-31). Military encounters occurred between the Ammonites and the Israelites as late as the time of the Maccabees (1 Macc 5:1-8). In 64 b.c. their territory was put under Roman control.

The OT prophets directed many of their prophecies against the Ammonites (Jer 9:25, 26; 49:1-6; Eze 21:20; 25:1-7; Amos 1:13-15; Zep 2:8-11).

Ammonites. See Ammon.

Amnon (ăm'nŏn). [Heb. 'Amnôn and 'Amînôn, "trustworthy."]

1. The eldest son of David and Ahinoam of Jezreel, born in Hebron (2 Sa 3:2; 1 Chr 3:1). He raped and then rejected Tamar, his half sister, for which crime he was assassinated by her brother Absalom (2 Sa 13:1-29).

2. A descendant of Judah (1 Chr 4:20).

Amok (ā'mŏk). [Heb. 'Amôq, "capable."] A chief priest who returned with Zerubbabel from Babylon, and after whom a family was named (Neh 12:7, 20).

Amon (ā'mŏn). [Heb. 'Amôn. In personal names of Hebrew origin 'Amôn means "faithful," but when representing the Egyptian deity it is a transliteration of the Egyptian 'Imn, which means "the hidden one." Gr. Amôn.]

1. The governor of Samaria in Ahab's time (1 Ki 22:26; 2 Chr 18:25).

2. The 15th king of Judah, the southern kingdom, who reigned 2 years (c. 641-

639 B.C.). He was the son of Manasseh and followed his father's evil example. His life ended in a palace revolution (2 Ki 21:19-26; 2 Chr 33:21-25). His name (RSV "Amos") appears in Matthew's genealogy of Jesus (ch 1:10).

3. An ancestral name for one group of "Solomon's servants," who returned with Zerubbabel from the Babylonian exile (Neh 7:57-59; called sons of Ami (*ā'mī*) [Heb. *'ami*] in Ezr 2:57).

4. An Egyptian god, also called Amen, originally the local god of Thebes, the city of Upper Egypt called No in the KJV of Jer 46:25 and Nah 3:8. The word translated "multitude" (Jer 46:25) and "populous" (Nah 3:8) is *'Amon,* so that Thebes is called literally "Amon of No" or "No Amon," showing that the name of the god is part of the name of the city. Amon became the chief god of Egypt during the Middle Kingdom (*c.* 2025 - *c.* 1780 B.C.), and from the 18th dynasty on (beginning *c.* 1570 B.C.) was identified with the sungod Ra, and thenceforth was called Amon-Ra, and regarded as the king of gods. Amon, with his consort Mut (meaning "mother") and his son Khonsu, a moongod, formed a Theban triad. Since the animal sacred to Amon was the ram, the deity is depicted either as a god with a ram's head or in the form of a man wearing a disk with two long feathers as a crown. Amon was also worshiped at Siwa in North Africa, west of Egypt, and was known to the Greeks as Zeus Ammon.

Amorites (ăm'ŏ-rīts). [Heb. *'Emorî;* Akkadian *Amurru.*] A people frequently mentioned in the early books of the Bible. The history of the Amorites is somewhat obscure, since they have left us no historical records in their own language, and what they left us in Akkadian covers only short periods, such as the reigns of a few individual rulers like Hammurabi of Babylon or Zimri-Lim of Mari. The first mention of Amorites comes from Mesopotamia, where Shu-Sin, one of the last kings of the 3d dynasty of Ur, says that he has built a wall against them. This shows that an Amorite migration posed a menace for Mesopotamia. At that time all of Syria and Palestine was simply called *Amurru* (Map III, C-4) by the Babylonians, which may be an indication that the Amorites came from there into Mesopotamia. During the period of the dynasties of Isin and Larsa two kings of Larsa appear with Amorite names. Although the rule of these kings was brief, it was a foretaste of things to come, and toward the end of the

19th cent. we find Amorites entrenched as kings and rulers throughout Mesopotamia. They founded, for example, the 1st dynasty of Babylon, whose famous ruler, Hammurabi, built an empire that reached from the Persian Gulf to the Mediterranean Sea. Also of Amorite origin was the powerful kingdom of Mari. Recent French excavations have discovered a large palace archive in the city of Mari. The kingdom was in turn conquered by Hammurabi in his 33d regnal year. The rule of the Amorites in Mesopotamia was brought to an end partly by the Hittites in the 16th cent., when Mursilis I captured and destroyed Babylon, and partly by the invasion of the Kassites, who took over the administration of most of the country at about the same time. Even before the Amorites, coming probably from the Arabian Desert or Syria, began to invade Mesopotamia, they had poured into Palestine and Syria, and by the time of the powerful 12th dynasty of Egypt the majority of cities in Palestine and Syria were in the hands of Amorite rulers. Many of their names are mentioned in the Egyptian execration texts, which the Egyptians used in an attempt to curb the power of these dangerous chieftains. In the Amarna period (14th cent. B.C.), *Amurru,* a kingdom in inland Syria (Map III, C-4), a vassal state of Egypt, took advantage of Egypt's weakness under the rule of Amenhotep III and Ikhnaton by conniving with the Hittites and by conquering many Syrian and Phoenician cities whose rulers, like the kings of *Amurru,* were vassals of Egypt.

Most of our information about the Amorites in Palestine comes from the Bible. They were apparently in possession of a considerable part of the country during the time of the patriarchs and before the Israelite invasion. They are mentioned as living at Hebron and as confederates of Abraham (Gen 14:13), and at times their name was used as representative of the entire population of the country (ch 15:16). Jacob said that he had taken a certain section of Canaan by sword and bow from the Amorites (ch 48:22). They are also generally mentioned in the lists of nations whom the Israelites were commanded to destroy (Gen 15:21; Ex 3:8; Deut 7:1, 2; etc.). At the time of the Exodus the Amorites were still in possession of the hill country of western Palestine and also controlled certain areas in Transjordan (Num 13:29; 21:26-30; Deut 1:7, 19, 20, 44). The Israelites defeated the Amorites on several occasions and took much of their territory (Num 21:25, 31, 32; Jos 10:5, 6, 28-43), yet strong remnants of these people remained (Jgs 1:35; 3:5). In Samuel's time they lived at peace with the Israelites and did not side with the hostile Philistines (1 Sa 7:14). Solomon incorporated all remaining Amorites in his kingdom into his forced labor corps (1 Ki 9:20, 21; 2 Chr 8:7, 8).

One problem remains to be mentioned, and that is the racial affinity of the Amorites. Little is known of the Amorite language. The few Amorite phrases found in Akkadian texts and the personal names of these people show that the Amorites spoke a Semitic language. Consequently many scholars classify them among the Semites. Yet the Bible lists the Amorites along with the Hittites and Phoenicians, concerning whom the same problem exists, as descendants of Ham through Canaan. The only reasonable solution to this problem is to assume that the Hamitic Amorites at an early stage of their history had taken over a Semitic language through close association with Semites, and through an active intermarriage with Semites had also lost some of their Hamitic features, and therefore had become in appearance and speech largely Semites.

Amos (ā'mŏs). [Heb. *'Amôs,* "burden," "burden bearer," from *'amas,* "to lift (a load)," "to carry (a load)"; Gr. *Amôs.*]

1. A prophet of the town of Tekoa, in Judah, whom God sent with a message to the northern kingdom, Israel. The book of Amos is a record of that message and of his experience in delivering it. Our knowledge concerning the prophet is meager and must be gleaned from his book. His home was in *Tekoa, a small town at the edge of the barren Wilderness of Judah that falls away in undulating hills to the Dead Sea, some 12 mi. distant. Prior to his call to the prophetic office Amos was a shepherd who devoted a part of his time to tending sycamore trees and gathering their fruit, which resembles figs (ch 7:14). Although from one of the humbler walks of life, Amos was a man of natural intelligence, of a deeply religious bent, and with shrewd powers of observance. He was unassuming, but bold and fearless when called to bear witness against the evils of his day. The message he bore was graphic and powerful. Some have concluded from his mention of 5 of the neighboring nations that he may have traveled as far as Damascus and Egypt (ch 1).

2. For Mt 1:10, RSV, *see* Amon, 2.

3. A Judahite listed in Luke's genealogy of Christ (Lk 3:25).

Amos, Book of. The 3d of the so-called Minor Prophets. Amos bore his message while Jeroboam II was king of Israel and Uzziah was king of Judah (ch 1:1). The fact that these two monarchs reigned concurrently, each as sole ruler of his realm, only between *c.* 767 and 753 B.C. probably limits Amos' prophetic ministry to this brief period, and 760 may therefore be taken as an approximate date for his book. During the 2 centuries that had intervened since the splendor of Solomon's reign, Israel and Judah had fallen on evil times, both morally and politically. But Jeroboam II and Uzziah had been successful in restoring their respective domains until combined they reached approximately the extent of the empire under David and Solomon. As a result a deceptive wave of prosperity filled the land. At the same time, idolatry flourished and the moral state of society sank to a new low, with the rich oppressing the poor and officialdom dispensing justice to the highest bidder (see chs 2:6, 7; 3:10, 15; 4:1; 5:7-13; 6:4-6; 8:4-6). Neither rulers nor people of the northern kingdom realized that their nation was actually tottering on the brink of catastrophe, and that in about 40 years the nation would cease to exist and its people be led away into Assyrian captivity. It was under these circumstances that the Lord commissioned Amos, and a little later Hosea, as prophets to warn the northern kingdom of its impending doom and offer them a final opportunity to amend their evil ways. When Amos said, "I was no prophet, neither was I a prophet's son" (ch 7:14), he meant that he had not been formally trained for the prophetic office in the schools of the prophets, nor was he the son of one so trained. Yet he measures up in every respect to the qualifications of a prophet. He carried his message into the very center of apostate worship, to Bethel, the religious capital of the northern kingdom. Here Amaziah, the high priest of Bethel, sought to intimidate him and make him leave the country (vs 10-17).

The theme of the book is divine judgment (ch 1:2), and its aim is to effect repentance and reformation in view of the inevitability of impending judgments unless the people amended their ways (ch 5:4). The message of the book logically divides into four major parts: (1) a denunciation of evil coupled with a warning of judgment (chs 1:1 to 2:16); (2) an appeal to return to the Lord (chs 3:1 to

6:14); (3) an emphatic warning of the finality of this appeal (chs 7:1 to 9:10); (4) a promise of national blessing and restoration in the event of repentance and reformation (ch 9:11-15). The 1st of these 4 parts consists of an enumeration of the sins of 6 neighboring nations, and Judah, with the purpose of highlighting the enormity of the sins of Israel. The 2d part consists of a series of 3 sermons, each beginning with the proclamation, "Hear [ye] this word!" The 3d is composed of 5 symbolic visions, with a short historical interlude inserted between visions 3 and 4 in which the official reaction of the northern kingdom becomes apparent. In a few deft strokes, part 4 paints a glowing picture of the bright future in store for Israel if the nation returns to the Lord in wholehearted repentance and reformation, and accepts her divinely appointed role.

In part 1 the prophet, with consummate skill, seeks to lead his hearers at Bethel to acknowledge that national sin deserves, and is certain to encounter, divine punishment. He accomplishes this, his first objective, by enumerating the crimes of Israel's neighbor nations, which are well known to his hearers. Israel has suffered at their hands, and by declaring the judgments of the Lord upon those nations because of their criminal conduct, Amos is certain to elicit the response "Amen!" Damascus (Syria) has invaded Gilead and laid it desolate (ch 1:3), Gaza (Philistia) has taken Israelites captive and turned them over to Edom (v 6), Tyrus (Phoenicia) has done the same (v 9), Edom has treated Israel with unwonted cruelty (v 11), Ammon has done likewise (v 13), and Moab also (ch 2:1). In order to leave his Israelite hearers without any avenue of self-justification when he finally takes up their evil course of action, and also in order to preclude any accusation that, as a prophet from the land of Judah, he is prompted by national pride, Amos first excoriates his own nation of Judah for rejecting the revealed will of God (v 4). Thus, when he mentions what God has done for Israel and enumerates some of the grosser forms of injustice rampant in the land, his hearers are left speechless and must admit, to themselves at least, that if the 7 neighboring nations are deserving of the judgments of God, they themselves cannot expect to escape (vs 6-16). They cannot deny the prophet's evaluation of conditions in Israel or his declaration that they deserve punishment.

Having anchored these two solemn facts in the minds of his audience, Amos proceeds in part 2 to make clear to the people that they have, indeed, forsaken the God whom they still profess to worship, that they will soon have to reckon accounts with Him, and that they will do well to seek reconciliation with Him before He hales them into court. The theme of the 1st sermon is, "Can two walk together, except they be agreed?" (ch 3:3). Obviously not. But Israel, as evidenced by her conduct, has come to be in utter disagreement with God, and unless a change takes place God must abandon her people forever to their evil course of action. The theme of the 2d sermon is, "Prepare to meet thy God, O Israel" (ch 4:12). God has suffered long with them and sought by many lesser judgments to bring them to their senses, but to no avail. As a last resort He must bring them to judgment and sentence them as a nation to death, and they should ponder the matter now before they meet their Judge face to face. The 3d sermon comes to a focus in the tender appeal, "Seek ye me, and ye shall live" (ch 5:4). And how shall they seek the Lord? The question is answered in the admonition: "Seek good, and not evil, that ye may live" (v 14).

Lest the people think they can deceive or bribe God, as if He were one of their own venal judges, Amos in part 3 relates a series of 5 symbolic visions from the Lord that emphasize the finality of His appeal to the men of that generation. The first 2 visions look to the past, when God has repeatedly relented when asked to pass by their transgressions, but in the 3d vision God announces that He will no longer "pass by" (ch 7:8), or continue to deal leniently with them. An attempt at this point on the part of Amaziah, priest of Bethel, to frighten the prophet into silence elicits the bold declaration, "Now therefore hear thou the word of the Lord: . . . Israel shall surely go into captivity" (vs 16, 17). The theme of the 4th vision, which follows immediately, is, "The end is come upon my people of Israel; I will not again pass by them any more" (ch 8:2). In the 5th vision the Lord appears in person, to "slay the last of them with the sword" (ch 9:1).

However bleak the prospect in case Israel chooses to persist in her impenitent course, the prophet Amos, in part 4 of his message, holds up once more before the nation that is soon to meet its fate a picture of the glorious purpose of God for His people if they will but repent and turn again to Him. He will "build" the nation as "in the days of old" (ch 9:11)— He will restore it to the glory of its golden age under David and Solomon. One noteworthy characteristic of the OT prophets is that practically every warning of doom is accompanied by an offer of hope, and it is on such a note that Amos concludes his impassioned message.

Amoz (ā'mŏz). [Heb. *'Amôṣ*, "strong."] The father of the prophet Isaiah (2 Ki 19:2, 20; Is 1:1; etc.).

Amphipolis (ăm-fĭp'ô-lĭs). [Gr. *Amphipolis*, "surrounded city."] A city in eastern Macedonia colonized by Athenians in the 5th cent. B.C., and named Amphipolis because it was almost surrounded by the river Strymon (now called Struma). It lay about 30 mi. southwest of Philippi (Map XX, A-3). When the Romans came into control of Macedonia in 168 B.C. and divided it into four republics (before annexing it in 146 B.C. as the province of Macedonia), Amphipolis became the capital of the first of these four protectorates. Located on the Via Egnatia, it was an important trading center. Paul passed through the city during his 2d Missionary Journey on his way from Philippi to Thessalonica (Acts 17:1). The city may not have had a Jewish community, a possible reason why he did not stop there. He must have passed through the city again on later visits to Macedonia (ch 20:1, 6), although this fact is not specifically recorded.

Amplias. *See* Ampliatus.

Ampliatus (ăm'plĭ-ā'tŭs), KJV **Amplias** (ăm'-plĭ-ăs). [Gr. *Ampliatos;* textual variant *Amplias.* The transliteration of a Latin name meaning "enlarged." The name appears frequently in the inscriptions as borne by slaves.] A Christian of Rome to whom Paul sent greetings in his epistle to the Romans (Rom 16:8).

Amram, I (ăm'răm). [Heb. *'Amram,* probably "the kinsman is exalted." The name occurs in Assyrian as *Amramu.*]

    1. A descendant of Levi; father of Miriam, Aaron, and Moses, and ancestor of the Amramites (Ex 6:18, 20; Num 3:19; 1 Chr 6:2, 3; cf. 1 Chr 26:23).

    2. A Jew in Ezra's time (Ezr 10:34).

Amram, II (ăm'răm). [Heb. *Chamran.*] For the Amram of 1 Chr 1:41 (KJV) *see* Hemdan.

Amramites (ăm'răm-īts). [Heb. *'Amrami.*] The descendants of Amram, I, 1 (Num 3:27; 1 Chr 26:23).

Amraphel (ăm'rá-fĕl). [Heb. *'Amraphel.*] King of Shinar, who with the confederate kings invaded and subjugated Transjordan during the time of Abraham (Gen 14: 1, 9). This king has not yet been identified. Since "Shinar" in all other OT passages is used as a designation for Babylonia, it has been thought that Amraphel must have been a king of that region; therefore in the past the great King Hammurabi has been identified with Amraphel. There are grave objections to this identification. Biblical chronology places the events of Gen 14 in the 19th cent. B.C., but Hammurabi cannot have ruled over Babylonia until the 18th cent. B.C. Another difficulty is the transliteration of the name. In Hebrew, Amraphel's name begins with an *'aleph,* whereas in Babylonian, Hammurabi's name begins with *ḥ,* but the Hebrew *'aleph* (') is never used for the Babylonian *ḥ,* which is regularly represented by the Hebrew *'ayin* ('). Furthermore, the final *l* in *'Amraphel* is difficult to explain. Even if the name Hammurabi could be identified with that of Amraphel, there is still the difficulty of identifying the particular Hammurabi, for three kings bore that name: Hammurabi of Ugarit, Hammurabi of Aleppo, and Hammurabi of an unidentified city. R. de Vaux suggests that Amraphel represents the Akkadian name *Amur-pi-el,* meaning "the mouth of god has spoken" (*RB* 55 [1948], 331-337). F. M. Th. Böhl compares the name to that of a king of Qatna, *Amut-pi-el* (*Opera Minora* [Leiden, 1953], 45). These and all other proposed identifications are uncertain.

Amulet. The rendering in the RSV of Is 3:20 of the Heb. *lachash,* the exact meaning of which is uncertain. It is believed to describe some band, gem, or package containing a potent object or inscription, believed to ward off evil when worn on the person. The KJV conjecturally renders this *lachash* "earrings."

Amzi (ăm'zī). [Heb. *'Amṣî,* "my strength." However, the name is possibly a shortened form of *'Amaṣyah,* "Amaziah," meaning "Yahweh is strong."]

    1. A Levite (1 Chr 6:46).

    2. A priest (Neh 11:12).

Anab (ā'năb). [Heb. *'Anab,* "grape."] A town in southwestern Judah 13 mi. southwest of Hebron (Jos 11:21; 15:50), now called *'Anāb* (Map VI, F-2). The city is repeatedly mentioned in the Egyptian hieroglyphic texts of Seti I and Ramses II and III as *Qrt-'nb,* corresponding to the Heb. *Qiryath 'Anab,* "city of Anab."

Anah (ā'nȧ). [Heb. *'Anah,* a Horite name, attested in Old Assyrian texts as *Ana,* the name of a divinity, and in Akkadian as *Ânâ,* a personal name.] A Horite (Hivite), chief of a Horite, or Hurrian, clan (Gen 36:2, 14, 18, 20, 24, 25, 29; 1 Chr 1:38-41). The Masoretic text makes the Anah of Gen 36:2, 14 a daughter of Zibeon, but the LXX, the Samaritan Pentateuch, and the Syriac read "son" for "daughter." The Masoretic *bt,* "daughter," in vs 2, 14 is probably a mistake for *bn,* "son," since according to vs 20, 24, 29 Anah is obviously a man.

Anaharath (ȧ-nā'hȧ-răth). [Heb. *'Anacharath.*] A town on the border of Issachar (Jos 19:19), now *en-Na'ûrah,* 5 mi. northeast of Jezreel. The place is mentioned in a list of Palestinian towns of Thutmose III as *'Inhṛt.*

Anaiah (ȧ-nī'ȧ). [Heb. *'Anayah,* "Yahweh has answered."]
1. An assistant of Ezra (Neh 8:4); possibly identical with Anaiah, 2.
2. An Israelite who set his seal to Nehemiah's covenant (Neh 10:22); possibly identical with Anaiah, 1.

Anak (ā'năk) and **Anakim** (ăn'ȧ-kĭm), KJV **Anakims** (ăn'ȧ-kĭmz). [Heb. *'Anaq* and *'Anaqîm.* The name is possibly attested in the Egyptian execration texts of the 19th and 18th cent. B.C. as *'Iy'nk* and *Y'nkî,* which probably mean "coastland of the Anakim."] Anak was the ancestor of the Anakim (Num 13:22), a tribe of giants in southern Palestine (Deut 2:10, 11; Jos 15:12, 13; Jgs 1:20; etc.), especially in the vicinity of Hebron at the time of the Israelite invasion of the country. The three Anakite personal names Ahiman, Sheshai, and Talmai are Aramaic. Caleb drove the Anakim from Hebron (Jos 14: 6-15; 15:13-19; 21:11, 12). However, Anakim remained in the cities of Gath, Gaza, and Ashdod (ch 11:21, 22).

Anakim. See Anak.

Anamim (ăn'ȧ-mĭm). [Heb. *'Anamîm.*] An Egyptian tribe or country (Gen 10:13; 1 Chr 1:11), which has been identified with the great Egyptian oasis *Kenemet.* Albright, however, points out that in an Assyrian text the name *Anami* appears with *Kaptara* (Caphtor=Crete), and he identifies this *Anami* with Cyrene (*JPOS* 1 [1920], 191, 192). Map IV, B-4.

Anammelech (ȧ-năm'ĕ-lĕk). [Heb. *'Anammelek.*] A deity of the north-Syrian city of Sepharvaim (2 Ki 17:31). The name has not yet been found in secular sources. It has been suggested that the first part contains the name of Anu, one of the principal Babylonian gods, the personified ·sky or heaven, and that the second part is the West Semitic *malku, melek,* "king," "prince." According to these derivations the name of the god would be "Anu is king."

Anan (ā'năn). [Heb. *'Anan,* "cloud." The name occurs also in Phoenician texts.] An Israelite who set his seal to Nehemiah's covenant (Neh 10:26).

Anani (ȧ-nā'nĭ). [Heb. *'Ananî,* a shorter form of *'Ananyah,* meaning "Yahweh has appeared."] A descendant of David (1 Chr 3:24).

Ananiah (ăn'ȧ-nī'ȧ). [Heb. *'Ananyah,* "Yahweh has appeared."]
1. The grandfather of one of the builders of Jerusalem's wall in Nehemiah's time (Neh 3:23).
2. A town in Benjamin (Neh 11:32), better known by its NT name of *Bethany. See Bethany, 1.

Ananias (ăn'ȧ-nī'ăs). [Gr. *Ananias,* a transliteration of the Heb. *Chananyah* (Jer 28:1; Dan 1:6; etc.), "Yahweh is gracious."]
1. A Christian of the church at Jerusalem who pledged to sell a piece of property and give the proceeds for the indigent believers in that city. However, with the knowledge and agreement of his wife (see Sapphira) he later decided to retain part of the price, but to pretend that he was contributing the entire proceeds. His desire was doubtless to gain the approbation of the church by appearing to be generous. Upon bringing part of the money to the church leaders he was questioned as to whether it was the full amount, to which he replied that it was. At this, Peter accused him of lying to the Holy Ghost, whereupon Ananias immediately collapsed and died (Acts 5:1-11). This sobering event served as a warning and deterrent to all who by insincerity or greed would endeavor to take advantage of the infant church to further their own selfish ends. See Covetousness; Hypocrite.
2. A Christian living at Damascus at the time of Paul's conversion, who was declared to be "a devout man according to the law, having a good report of all the Jews" in that city (Acts 9:10; 22:12). In vision he was informed that Saul of Tarsus, now blind, had received a vision in which he saw one Ananias place his hands upon him and restore his sight (ch 9:12). He was directed to inquire for Saul

at the home of a man named Judas, who lived on the street called Straight (v 11). Ananias hesitated because of Paul's previous course in persecuting the Christians, but was assured that God had chosen Paul for a special work (vs 13-16). After this, Ananias found Paul and carried out the instructions God had given him (vs 17, 18).

3. The Jewish high priest mentioned in Acts 23:2; 24:1, who was in office at the time of Paul's arrest in Jerusalem. According to Josephus (*Ant.* xx. 5. 2), he was the son of Nebedeus (or Nedebeus), and was made high priest by Herod, king of Chalcis. When examined by the Sanhedrin, Paul made a statement that angered Ananias, whereupon the priest commanded that Paul be struck upon the mouth. Paul, apparently not recognizing him as the high priest, rebuked him strongly for his actions, but apologized upon learning who he was (Acts 23:1-5). In ch 24:1 Ananias is mentioned as being among the group of Jewish leaders who journeyed to Caesarea to accuse Paul before the Roman governor, Felix. Ananias was assassinated when the Roman war began (Jos. *War* ii. 17. 6, 9), probably in A.D. 66.

Anath (āʹnăth). [Heb. *'Anath;* Ugaritic *'nt;* Akkadian *Anata;* Egyptian *'nt.*]

1. A Canaanite goddess not mentioned in the OT, though the name Anath appears in Palestinian place names like Bethanath (Jos 19:38; etc.) and Anathoth (ch 21:18; etc.). Anath, as the goddess of war and sex, appears in the Ugaritic mythology as an extremely bloodthirsty deity who, although raped by her brother Baal, retained her title "virgin." In the Baal myths she is represented as the one who killed Mot, the god of heat and drought, and was the instrument of Baal's resurrection to a new life before each rainy season began in the autumn. *See also* Asherah; Ashtoreth.

2. Father of the judge Shamgar (Jgs 3:31; 5:6).

Anathema. [Gr. *anathema,* literally, "something placed," "something set up," then "something set apart," as a votive gift at a temple, "something accursed." In the LXX, *anathema* commonly translates the Heb. *cherem,* "(a thing) devoted," "(a thing) accursed."] A term used in the KJV of 1 Cor 16:22 to pronounce a curse on the one who deliberately spurns the love of Christ. More commonly, *anathema* is translated "accursed" (Rom 9:3; 1 Cor 12:3; Gal 1:8). This is also the rendering of *anathema* in the RSV of 1 Cor 16:22.

14. The village of Anathoth, the home of the prophet Jeremiah

Anathoth (ănʹá-thŏth). [Heb. *'Anathôth.* Literally the plural form of the name Anath, the famous goddess of the Canaanites; but it is strange to see this plural as the name of an individual. Hence the derivation must be considered uncertain.]

1. A Benjamite (1 Chr 7:8).

2. An Israelite who signed Nehemiah's covenant (Neh 10:19).

3. A town in Benjamin assigned to the priests (Jos 21:18; 1 Chr 6:60). It was the home town of the high priest Abiathar (1 Ki 2:26) and of Jeremiah, the prophet (Jer 1:1; 11:21). There were 128 exiles from Anathoth among those who returned with Zerubbabel from Babylon (Ezr 2:23; Neh 7:27). The ancient name has been perpetuated in modern *'Anāta,* a village of recent origin, about 3 mi. north of Jerusalem. The ancient city lay about ½ mi. to the southwest of *'Anāta,* and is now called *Râs el-Kharrûbeh.* From the ancient site, about 150 ft. higher than *'Anāta,* it is possible to overlook the Jordan Valley.

Anathothite (ănʹá-thŏth-īt), KJV **Anethothite** (ănʹĕ-thŏth-īt), **Anetothite** (ănʹĕ-tŏth-īt), and **Antothite** (ănʹtŏth-īt). [Heb. *'Annethothî.*] A man originating from or living in Anathoth (2 Sa 23:27; 1 Chr 11:28; 12:3; 27:12).

Anchor. An iron instrument, usually with two hooks, used in shallow water to hold a ship secure (Acts 27:29, 30, 40). Used allegorically, it refers to that which provides security and that in which one can trust for safety (Heb 6:19). The anchor is also a symbol of hope in pagan Greek literature, and appears on both pagan and Christian graves, probably as an indication of hope in afterlife.

Ancient of Days. [Aramaic *'attîq yômîn.*] A term found in Dan 7:9, 13, 22, where it is descriptive of God the Father as He was presented in vision sitting in judgment. The term does not refer so much to the eternal existence of God, though such might be implied, as to His appearance as Daniel saw Him in vision. To an ancient Oriental such an appearance would command supreme awe, reverence, and respect.

Ancients. A term describing those members of a society considered wise and venerable by virtue of their age and experience. The term occurs only in the OT, 9 times in the KJV and once in the RSV. The RSV generally substitutes the readings "aged" or "elders." See 1 Sa 24:13, RSV; Is 3:2, 5, KJV; etc.

Ancles. A variant spelling of "ankles" in certain editions of the KJV (Eze 47:3; Acts 3:7).

Andrew (ăn′drōō). [Gr. *Andreas*, "manly," from *anēr*, "man." One of the Twelve, a brother of Simon Peter. In two lists of the Twelve appearing in the Gospels his name is second, following that of Peter (Mt 10:2; Lk 6:14), and in two others it follows those of Peter, James, and John, the inner circle of disciples (Mk 3:18; Acts 1:13). Andrew came from Bethsaida (Jn 1:44) on the northern shore of the Lake of Galilee, and was a fisherman by occupation, in partnership with his brother Peter (Mt 4:18). Andrew was one of the two disciples to whom John the Baptist pointed out Jesus as "the Lamb of God" at the Jordan (Jn 1:35-40). Apparently Andrew was in the group of disciples who then followed Jesus into Galilee and attended the marriage feast at Cana (chs 1:43; 2:1, 2). He is next mentioned as one of the four called to permanent, full-time discipleship more than a year later (Mt 4:18-22). During the time of Jesus' ministry in Galilee, Andrew and Peter lived together in their own house at Capernaum (Mk 1: 21, 29). A few months later Andrew and 11 others were selected from a larger group of disciples and ordained to be apostles (Lk 6:13-16), and as one of the Twelve he went out the following winter, paired presumably with his brother (Mt 10:1-5). With Philip, he introduced a group of Greek proselytes to Jesus in the outer court of the Temple during Passion Week, and was one of the four disciples to whom Jesus divulged the signs of His coming on the Mount of Olives a few hours later (Jn 12:20-22; Mk 13:1-4). After the resurrection he was associated with the other disciples in Jerusalem (Acts 1:13, 14). Nothing is known with certainty of his later life and ministry, though tradition asserts that he was once in Scotland and that he was martyred in Greece.

Andronicus (ăn′drō-nī′kŭs). [Gr. *Andronikos*, "victorious man." The name occurs frequently in Greek inscriptions.] A Christian in Rome to whom Paul sent greetings (Rom 16:7).

Anem (ā′nĕm). [Heb. *'Anem*.] A town in Issachar assigned to the descendants of Gershom (1 Chr 6:73). Some commentators see in the name a contraction of *En-gannim. Others see no connection. Conder identified it with *'Anin*, southwest of Taanach, but Abel rejects this identification and suggests *Khirbet 'Anīn*, about 5 mi. southwest of the southern tip of the Sea of Galilee (Abel, *Géographie* II, 244). Wright suggests, with some hesitation, *'Olam*, 1 mi. southwest of Abel's Anem (*WHAB* 121).

Aner (ā′nēr). [Heb. *'Aner*.]
1. An Amorite neighbor and confederate of Abraham when the patriarch lived at Mamre near Hebron (Gen 14:13, 24).
2. A town in western Manasseh assigned to the Kohathite Levites (1 Chr 6:70). Many believe on the basis of Jos 21:25 that instead of "Aner" the text should read "Taanach" (KJV "Tanach").

Anethothite and **Anetothite.** *See* Anathothite.

Angel. [Heb. *mal'ak*, "messenger"; Gr. *aggelos*, "messenger."] A supernatural being, created by God, superior to man, and acting as a representative or messenger of God. There are Bible passages where *mal'ak* and *aggelos* do not refer to supernatural beings, but to prophets and others fulfilling the function of "messenger" (2 Sa 3:14; Eze 23:16; Hag 1:13; Mt 11:10; Lk 7:24; etc.). There are other passages where the terms seem to apply to Christ Himself (Ex 23:20; Mal 3:1b; Acts 7:35). The specific references in any case must be found by a study of the context.

The existence and activity of angels is taken for granted throughout the OT and NT. The word "angel" occurs first in the OT in Gen 16:7-12, which describes the ministry of "the angel of the Lord" to the fugitive Hagar. Angels had a part in the warning of Lot before the destruction of Sodom (ch 19:1). Jacob saw "angels of God" ascending and descending between earth and heaven (ch 28:12), and in his old age reminisced about "the Angel which redeemed me from all evil" (ch 48:16). Angels appeared to Moses (Ex 3:2), led Israel (chs 14:19; 23:23), frustrated Balaam (Num 22:22), commissioned Gideon (Jgs 6:11), promised a son to Manoah (ch 13:3), threatened to destroy David's people (2 Sa 24:16), ministered to

Elijah (1 Ki 19:5), destroyed the Assyrian army (2 Ki 19:35), saved Daniel from the lions (Dan 6:22), gave prophetic messages to Zechariah and other prophets (Zec 1:9). In some cases it is hard to distinguish between the direct intervention of God, of Christ, and of angels. This problem emphasizes the unity that exists among the heavenly beings.

The references to angels in connection with the life of Jesus are many. Angels directed the parents of Jesus (Mt 1:20; 2:13, 19), sang in chorus on the night of His birth (Lk 2:13), ministered to Him on the Mount of Temptation (Mt 4:11), rolled away the stone from the tomb (ch 28:2), and proclaimed the resurrected Christ (vs 5-7). The teachings of Jesus often referred to angels (Mt 13:41; 18: 10; 22:30; 25:41; Lk 15:10). Jesus made clear that angels are a higher and different order of being from man (Mt 22:30; Mk 12:25). He also taught the existence of evil angels (Mt 25:41).

Angels ministered to the early Christian church. They opened prison doors (Acts 5:19; 12:7-11), guided in missionary endeavor (ch 8:26), impressed non-Christians to inquire about the gospel (ch 10:1-7), appeared to Paul during a storm at sea (ch 27:23), stood by the side of John during his apocalyptic visions (Rev 1:1).

The book of Revelation mentions angels more than seventy times. The author saw angels surrounding God's throne (Rev 5:11), blowing trumpets (ch 8:2, 6), carrying messages (ch 7:2, 3), executing judgment (ch 16), and reaping earth's harvest at the last day (ch 14:19). A large number of the actors in the drama of the Apocalypse are angels.

Perhaps the most definitive text regarding angels is Heb 1:14. From man's standpoint, angels' ministry to man is most significant. Eternity will reveal the breadth of the functions of these beings in relation to the universe. Man will in eternity be "equal unto the angels" (Lk 20:36; cf. Mt 22:30). The relationship between angels and men in the plan of redemption indicates the possibility of a unique relationship throughout eternity. *See* Angel of the Lord.

Angel of the Lord. This and the expression "angel of God" are common expressions in both OT and NT designating a supernatural being sent by God to men, to counsel, warn, comfort, direct, and assist them. The Hebrew and Greek terms translated "angel" (*mal'ak* and *aggelos*) mean simply "messenger" and are applied to men as well as to angels. An "angel of the Lord" is thus a messenger of the Lord not only in the sense that he belongs to the Lord and is faithful to Him, but more particularly in the sense that he comes as a messenger sent by God with a message from God. It seems that Christ is sometimes referred to as the "angel of the Lord" (Ex 3:2, 4; Zec 3:1, 2; cf. Gen 32: 24, 30; Ex 23:20, 21; 32:34; 33:14; Jos 5:13-15; 1 Cor 10:4).

Angle. (1) In the KJV (Is 19:8; Hab 1:15) the translation of the Heb. *chakkah,* a hook, or angular piece of metal used in catching fish. *Chakkah* is translated "hook" in Job 41:1, and in the RSV in Is 19:8 and Hab 1:15 also. (2) In the RSV (2 Chr 26:9; Neh 3:24, 25) the translation of the Heb. *pinnah,* "corner," "angle," in these verses designating a certain corner in the wall of Jerusalem, probably somewhere in the eastern wall of the southern sector.

Aniam (á-nī′ăm). [Heb. *'Ani'am,* meaning uncertain.] A descendant of Manasseh (1 Chr 7:19).

Anim (ā′nĭm). [Heb. *'Anim.*] A town of Judah (Jos 15:50). Because it is listed immediately after Eshtemoh it has been identified with *Khirbet Ghuwein et-Tahtā,* in the vicinity (3 mi. south) of *es-Semū‘* (Eshtemoh or Eshtemoa), and about 11 mi. south of Hebron (Abel, *Géographie* II, 244).

Animals. *See* Flora and Fauna; also names of specific animals.

Anise. *See* Dill.

Anklets. [Heb. *'akasim,* "anklets," "bangles."] Ornaments of metal or glass worn about the ankle as are bracelets about the wrist. The word occurs in the RSV of Is 3:18, where the KJV reads "tinkling ornaments about their feet." Isaiah lists anklets among the ornaments of which the daughters of Zion were to be deprived in the day of Jerusalem's fall.

Anna (ăn′á). [Gr. *Anna,* a transliteration of the Heb. *Channah,* meaning "grace."] An aged prophetess, of the tribe of Asher, who hailed the infant Jesus as the Messiah when He was brought into the Temple (Lk 2:36-38).

Annas (ăn′ăs). [Gr. *Hannas,* in Josephus, *Ananos,* a Greek form of the Heb. *Chananyah,* "Yahweh is gracious."] A son of Seth, appointed high priest about A.D. 6 by Quirinius, Roman legate of Syria. In about A.D. 15 he was deposed by the procurator of Judea, Valerius Gratus, and replaced by Ismael, son of Phiabi. In the course of time 5 of his sons, and also Caiaphas, his son-in-law, became high priest (Jos. *Ant.* xviii. 2. 1, 2; 4. 3; 5. 3; xx. 9. 1). He, with Caiaphas, the officiating high priest, is mentioned in connection with the ministries of John the Baptist (Lk 3:2), Jesus (Jn 18:13, 24), and the apostles Peter and John (Acts 4:6). Although officially no longer in office, he retained his title and position of importance. It was in deference to him that Jesus after His arrest was taken to Annas before being taken to Caiaphas (Jn 18:13, 14, 24). The family had a bad name even among the Jews. The Talmud declares concerning it: "Woe is me because of the house of Ḥanin [i.e., Annas], woe is me because of their whisperings!" (*Pesaḥim* 57a).

Anoint. A word occurring frequently in the Bible meaning "to smear or pour oil or other unctuous substance upon." It is the rendering of different Hebrew and Greek words, all apparently closely related in meaning. At least three uses of anointing were understood by the Jews: (1) Ordinary anointing, which served to facilitate personal cleanliness and freshness and was often performed upon guests as a matter of conventional courtesy. This sense generally uses the Heb. *suk* or the Gr. *aleiphō* (2 Sa 12:20; Dan 10:3; Mt 6:17; Lk 7:46). (2) Official anointing, which prophets, priests, and kings received at (or before) their accession to office. In this sense Elijah anointed Elisha (1 Ki 19:16), Aaron and his sons were approved for the priesthood (Ex 30:30), the tabernacle was prepared for its role in Israel's worship of God (ch 40:9). Thus Saul (1 Sa 9:16), David (ch 16:12), Solomon (1 Ki 1:34), and Hazael of Syria (ch 19:15) were all anointed as kings. The Hebrew word generally used for official anointings is *mashach,* from which *mashiach,* "an anointed one," or "Messiah," is derived. Christ was anointed (Gr. *chriō,* the equivalent of *mashach,* hence *Christos,* Christ, "the anointed one") for His ministry (Lk 4:18; Heb 1:9). (3) Anointing as an adjunct to healing—sometimes in a medicinal sense, and sometimes in a symbolic sense. Examples are found in Mk 6:13; Jas 5:14, 15 (Gr. *aleiphō*); Jn 9:6 (Gr. *epichriō,* "to rub on"); and Rev. 3:18 (Gr. *egchriō,* "to rub in"). The spiritual meaning stems from the use of oil in physical healing. The Gr. *murizō,* "to anoint with aromatics," is used of Mary who Christ said had come to anoint His body aforehand (Mk 14:8).

Anon. An archaic term meaning "immediately" (Mt 13:20; Mk 1:30; KJV).

Ant. [Heb. *nemalah.*] An insect of the family Formicidae, mentioned twice in the Bible. In Prov 6:6-8 it is held up to the sluggard as an example of industry because it prepares for winter by storing up food during harvesttime (cf. ch 30:25). Although none of the 31 kinds of ants now known in Palestine actually has this habit, it is known that certain species of ants do store up food. An interesting proverb about the ant is quoted in one of the *Amarna Letters of the 14th cent. B.C. in which the Canaanite word for ant, *na-am-lu,* the equivalent of the Heb. *nemalah,* is used: "If ants are smitten, they do not receive (the smiting passively) but they bite the hand of the man who smites them!" (W. F. Albright, *BASOR* 89 [1943], 31).

Antelope. [Heb. *te'ô.*] An animal mentioned twice in the Bible (RSV), in Deut 14:5 as one of the clean animals fit for food, and in Is 51:20 as an animal caught in a net. The exact identity of *te'ô* is uncertain, but many believe that the Hebrew word refers to an antelope found in Egypt, Arabia, and Syria, called the oryx (*Antilope leucoryx*), which is the reading of the LXX and the Vulgate of the *te'ô* of Deut 14:5. The animal is white, with a black tuft of hair under the throat, and has long conical horns. Others identify *te'ô* with a wild sheep ("wild ox," Deut 14:5; "wild bull," Is 51:20; KJV).

Anthothijah (ăn'thô-thī'jȧ), KJV **Antothijah** (ăn'tô-thī'jȧ). [Heb. *'Anethothiyah,* meaning unknown.] A Benjamite (1 Chr 8:24).

Antichrist (ăn'tĭ-krīst'). [Gr. *antichristos,* from *anti,* "against," or "instead of," and *Christos,* Christ.] A term that may mean one who is opposed to Christ, or one who assumes the place of Christ, or one who combines both of these roles by assuming the prerogatives of Christ in such a way as actually to militate against the spirit, principles, and person of Christ. The term appears in the NT only in the writings of John (1 Jn 2:18, 22; 4:3; 2 Jn 7). The apostle takes for granted that his readers have already been taught concerning antichrist, and that they believe that antichrist's full manifestation will be in connection with the last days. As a result, he does not specifically identify antichrist as a particular person or organization. He speaks, in fact, of many antichrists and of their being active in his day (1 Jn 2:18). However, he does note that they are characterized by a denial that Jesus is the Christ and the Incarnate Son of God (1 Jn 2:22; 4:3; 2 Jn 7).

Although John alone uses the term "antichrist," the doctrine of an antichrist appears in other NT passages. In the Revelation the same author under the figure of a leopard beast depicts a great power that would oppose Christ and His people (ch 13:1-18). See *SDACom* 7:816-824. Particularly has the power described by Paul in 2 Th 2:2-12 been termed "antichrist." This passage predicts a developing apostasy in the church culminating in the revelation of the "man of sin" or "man of lawlessness (RSV)," who would sit in the temple of God and declare himself to be God. This revelation would be followed by the second coming of Christ, which would destroy the antichrist. This passage seems to have a dual application, describing first the developing apostasy in the Christian church, and second, the deceptive work of Satan, the antichrist par excellence.

Satan has opposed Christ through various human agencies. He has introduced various heresies through the centuries, all suited to deceive. In John's day Docetism and Gnosticism were doubtless considered anti-Christian. Through the centuries many have identified the Papacy as Antichrist. It appears that in the end Satan will play a more personal role in world affairs (2 Th 2:9), but his "coming" (Gr. *parousia*) in this special role will be followed quickly by his destruction.

Antimony. An element tin-white in color and metallic in appearance. The ancients are believed to have used powdered antimony compounds as a cosmetic with which to paint their eyebrows and eyelashes (*see* Paint). The term "antimony" appears only twice (1 Chr 29:2; Is 54:11; RSV), a rendering of the Heb. *pûk*, which, however, in these passages may refer to a hard mortar.

Antioch (ăn′tĭ-ŏk). [Gr. *Antiocheia*.] Two cities by this name appear in the NT.

1. Antioch in Syria. This city lay on the southern bank of the Orontes River, some 15 mi. from the Mediterranean, near the Amanus Mountains and Mount Casius (Map XX, B-6). It was founded by Seleucus I Nicator about 300 B.C. and called Antioch in honor of his father, Antiochus. One part of the city was settled with Athenians and Macedonians, the other with natives. Later Seleucus II and Antiochus IV enlarged the city and brought in new settlers, among whom were many

15. Antioch on the Orontes, with Mount Silpius in the background

Jews. The city experienced rapid growth, and as residence of the Seleucids became a wealthy merchant city and an important center of Hellenistic culture in the East. In 64 B.C., after more than two centuries as a capital of the Seleucid Empire, and after a short interlude of Armenian rule, Antioch passed into the hands of the Romans when Pompey annexed Syria. Pompey made Antioch the capital of this new senatorial province and the seat of the Roman legate. In this way the city lost nothing of its importance. It was known as "The Queen of the East," and became the third metropolis of the empire, being next to Rome and Alexandria in size. Its population in NT times is estimated at 250,000 to 800,000.

The Christian religion was carried to Antioch first by members of the Jerusalem church who fled there during the persecution that followed the stoning of Stephen. When news about their work reached the leaders in Jerusalem, they dispatched Barnabas to foster the new interests. Barnabas, seeing that more help was needed, brought Paul from Tarsus, and the two, working together for a whole year, seem to have built up a strong Christian center in Antioch. The city was also the place where the followers of Jesus Christ were first called "Christians" (Acts 11:19-26). Further re-enforcements came to the church in the person of prophets (v 27). The next important step in the history of this church was taken when the Antiochian Christians sponsored organized mission work in foreign countries, sending out Paul and Barnabas on a missionary journey (ch 13:1-3). Paul considered Antioch his headquarters, and began also his 2d and 3d Missionary Journeys from this city (chs 15:35-41; 18:22, 23). Yet the Christians at Antioch felt their dependence on the church leaders of Jerusalem and sought their counsel (ch 15:1, 2). They also accepted the responsibility of aiding the mother church in Judea with a financial contribution in a time of need (ch 11:27-30). In later periods Antioch was the scene of several church councils.

The city was destroyed by Chosroes, king of Persia, in A.D. 538, and never recovered from this blow. After its conquest by the Arabs a century later it rapidly lost what importance it still had. It now belongs to Turkey, and has finally become a mere town of about 30,000, now called *Anṭâkiyeh.* Excavations were conducted by an American-French expedition during the 1930's.

2. "Antioch in Pisidia." This city was actually located in Phrygia, but near the borders of Pisidia. To distinguish it from another Antioch on the Maeander secular historians often call it "Pisidian Antioch." However, confusion of the two cities is found in ancient and modern literature on the subject.

Antioch in Pisidia was founded by Seleucus I Nicator (301-280 B.C.), who named it Antioch in honor of Antiochus, his father, and settled colonists there from

16. The aqueduct of Antioch of Pisidia

Magnesia-on-the-Maeander. After the defeat of the Seleucids by the Romans in 190 B.C., Antioch was made a free city, but 150 years later was given to Amyntas, king of Pisidia, Phrygia-toward-Pisidia, and Galatia. When the Galatian kingdom became a Roman province in 25 B.C., Antioch became part of it. Some years later the city was made a colony by Augustus and was given the additional name of Caesarea. It was linked by military roads to other colony cities of Pisidia in order to control this area. Near the city stood a large temple, which has recently been excavated, dedicated to the Phrygian moon-god *Mên,* to whom healing power was attributed. Wide estates and numerous serfs belonged to this temple. Paul and Barnabas preached in the city during their 1st Missionary Journey and founded a Christian church there (Acts 13:14-50; 2 Ti 3:11). They were later expelled from the city, but returned to it on their return journey to Syria (Acts 14:21). Arundel identified the ancient city (1833) as being adjacent to the Turkish town of *Yalvaç.* Map XX, B-5.

Antipas (ăn′tĭ-păs). [Gr. *Antipas,* probably a contraction of *Antipatēr,* "Antipater," "father's image."] A Christian martyr who lost his life at Pergamum (Rev 2:13). An old tradition claims that he was the bishop of Pergamum at the time of his death. (For Herod Antipas, one of several Herods mentioned in the NT, *see* Herod, 3.)

Antipatris (ăn-tĭp′ȧ-trĭs). [Gr. *Antipatris.*] A city between Jerusalem and Caesarea, founded by Herod the Great at the site of Aphek, about 39 mi. from Jerusalem and 24 mi. from Caesarea (Map XVI, D-2). It was named in honor of Herod's father, Antipater (Jos. *Ant.* xiii. 15. 1; xvi. 5. 2; *War* i. 4. 7; 21. 9). Its name lives on in *Nahr abu-fûtrûs,* a river northeast of Jaffa. The site is now called *Râs el-'Ain* (*see* Aphek, 1). Paul passed through this place when he was transported as a prisoner from Jerusalem to Caesarea (Acts 23:31).

Antothijah. *See* Anthothijah.

Antothite. *See* Anathothite.

Anub (ā′nŭb). [Heb. *'Anûb,* meaning uncertain.] A man of Judah (1 Chr 4:8).

Ape. [Heb. *qôph,* related to the Sanscrit *kapi,* the Egyptian *gîf,* and the Akkadian *uqupu,* all meaning the long-tailed monkey.] An animal mentioned in two OT texts (1 Ki 10:22; 2 Chr 9:21), which list the articles that were brought to Palestine by Solomon's Ophir expeditions. Since linguistically the long-tailed monkey is indicated, the translation "ape" is misleading, for "ape" properly describes tailless types. W. F. Albright has shown that the Hebrew word *tuki* found in the same two texts and usually translated "peacock" is derived from the Egyptian *kyw*, or *t3-kyw*, and describes another kind of monkey, a female, since *t3* is a feminine article. The Egyptian story "The Shipwrecked Sailor" mentions, among the articles that he received on the Red Sea island where he had suffered shipwreck, two kinds of monkeys, *gif* and *kyw*. These terms, so parallel to the Biblical *qóph* and *tuki*, favor an African origin of the animals as well as an African location for Ophir (W. F. Albright, *AJSL* 37 [1920-21], 144; also his *Archeology and the Religion of Israel* [4th ed., Baltimore, 1956], p. 212, n. 16). There are no monkeys native to Palestine, and those imported by Solomon were probably of the long-tailed kind, whether they came from India, as was formerly believed, or from Somaliland in Eastern Africa, as is now held by many scholars.

Apelles (*à-pĕl'ēz*). [Gr. *Apellēs*, a name frequently borne by Greeks and Jews according to inscriptional evidence.] A Christian of Rome to whom Paul sent greetings (Rom 16:10).

Apharsachites (*à-fär'săk-īts*), or **Apharsathchites** (*ăf'är-săth'kīts*). [Aramaic *'Apharsekaye'*, and *'Apharsathkaye'*.] Probably an Aramaic or Persian term designating a certain class of officers (Ezr 4:9; 5:6; RSV "governors"). Exact equivalents in secular sources have not yet been found.

Apharsathchites. See Apharsachites.

Apharsites (*à-fär'sīts*). [Aramaic *'Apharsaye'*.] Either a class of officers whose identity is not now known, or a term meaning "Persians." The latter definition requires a different vocalization (Ezr 4:9).

Aphek (*ā'fĕk*). [Heb. *'Apheq*, "fortress."]
1. An important town of the Canaanites, already mentioned by Thutmose III, who calls it *'Ipk,* and speaks of it as lying between Ono and Socoh. Joshua defeated its king (Jos 12:18), but the Israelites apparently did not take the city, for we find it later in the hands of the Philistines and used as a base for military activities against the Israelites. During the first battle of Aphek the ark was lost to the Philistines (1 Sa 4:1, 11). From this

17. **Air view of an old caravansary standing at the site of Antipatris**

city the Philistines directed their war that ended with the defeat and death of Saul (ch 29:1). The city is also mentioned in an Aramaic papyrus of Nebuchadnezzar's time (fig. 22). The site has been identified with *Râs el-'Ain* at the source of the *'Aujah* River (Map VI, D-2). Archeological evidence shows that it was inhabited from about 2000 B.C. to Arabic times (Albright, *BASOR* 11 [Oct. 1923], 6, 7). In Hellenistic times the town was called Pegae. Herod the Great rebuilt it and called it *Antipatris after his father.
2. A town in the territory of Asher (Jos 19:30), perhaps the same as Aphik (*ā'fĭk*) [Heb. *'Aphîq*], mentioned in Jgs 1:31 as a town from which the Canaanites were not expelled. The site has been identified with *Tell Kurdâneh,* 6 mi. southeast of Acco (Map VI, C-3), but this identification is not certain. Some identify Aphik with Aphek, 3.
3. A city probably north of Sidon (Jos 13:4), generally identified with *Afqâ,* 14 mi. east of Byblos, near the source of the *Nahr Ibrâhîm,* the Adonis River of the ancients. For a possible identification with Aphik *see* Aphek, 2.
4. A city in Transjordan, where the Syrians suffered a defeat in Ahab's time (1 Ki 20:26-30), and again in Joash's time (2 Ki 13:14-19). It has been identified with *Fîq,* about 3 mi. east of the Sea of Galilee (Map IX, C-4).

Aphekah (*à-fē'kà*). [Heb. *'Apheqah*, "fortress."] A town in the southern part of Judah (Jos 15:53). The site has not been identified with certainty. Alt locates it at *Khirbet ed-Darrâme* southwest of Hebron (*PJB* 28 [1932], 16, 17).

Aphiah (*à-fī'à*). [Heb. *'Aphîach*, "skull fontanel."] A Benjamite, an ancestor of King Saul (1 Sa 9:1).

Aphik. *See* Aphek, 2.

Aphrah. *See* Beth-le-aphrah.

Aphses. *See* Happizzez.

Apis (ā′pĭs). The sacred bull worshiped by the ancient Egyptians at Memphis. He was considered the earthly representative of the god Ptah. In 1850 A. Mariette discovered at Saqqara (Map V, C-3) the Serapeum, the subterranean burial vaults containing many huge sarcophagi of the sacred bulls. The name for Apis does not appear in the Hebrew Bible, except by emendation, and is not found in the KJV. However, Apis does appear in the RSV in Jer 46:15 on the basis of the LXX.

Apocrypha. [Gr. *apokruphos*, "hidden," which, when the Gr. *biblia*, "books" or "scrolls," is understood, means "hidden books."] A term that has been used variously from time to time, and by different groups and individuals. Some ancient writers applied it to books of esoteric, or otherwise mysterious, wisdom, which were too complicated for the ordinary man and which could be understood only by the initiated. Hence they were "secret books," hidden from the general reading public. Others used the term in the disparaging sense of "false," "spurious," "heretical," and "extracanonical," hence, hidden or withdrawn from circulation. Even in ecclesiastical circles there has been, and is, a variety of usage. Some in these circles use it to apply to all religious literature of ancient times that is outside the canon of Holy Scripture. Among Protestants it is generally used to specify those books that were included in copies of the Greek Septuagint and the Latin Vulgate, but which were excluded from the Hebrew canon of Scriptures. Catholics designate at least 12 of these books as "deuterocanonical," and use "apocrypha" to apply to other extracanonical literature which Protestants have come to call "pseudepigrapha," meaning "falsely entitled." In this article "Apocrypha" is used, as in the Reformed churches, to designate the 15 documents found in some Greek and Latin manuscripts of the OT, but which were not included in the canon of the Hebrew Scriptures.

These Apocryphal books were produced, for the most part, during the last 2 centuries B.C., though one or two probably came from the 1st cent. A.D. These books have been variously classified: chronologically, by language, by literary type, and by place of origin. They represent a great variety of literary forms, including history, romance, poetry, apocalypse, wisdom, and devotion. They are listed and briefly described below in the order in which they appear in the RSV of the Apocrypha, published in 1957:

1. *The First Book of Esdras,* sometimes called the "Greek Esdras," and 3 Esdras in the Latin Vulgate, where Ezr and Neh are called I and II Esdras, respectively. It was composed in Greek probably by an Egyptian Jew about the middle of the 2d cent. B.C. This historical book gives an independent account of the general period covered by portions of 2 Chr, Ezr, and Neh, beginning with the celebration of the Passover in the reign of Josiah (621 B.C.) and extending to the reading of the Law by Ezra, the scribe (444 B.C.); yet it is frequently inconsistent with the canonical sources and with itself as well. Hence it is often described as historical fiction. Neither Catholics nor Protestants accept it as canonical. It is best known for its account of a trial of wits among 3 young bodyguards of King Darius I, who sought the best answer to the question, What is the strongest thing in the world? (1 Esdras 3:5 to 4:63). The first affirmed, "Wine is strongest." The 2d said, "The king is strongest." But the 3d, who is supposed to have been Zerubbabel, declared, "Women are strongest, but truth is victor over all things." At the answer of the 3d the people applauded and cried, "Great is truth, and strongest of all" (ch 4:41). The narrative describes this event as furnishing the opportunity for Zerubbabel to obtain from Darius the command to resume the building of the Temple in Jerusalem (vs 43-57).

2. *The Second Book of Esdras.* An apocalyptic work, also known as 4 Esdras, or even 3 Esdras when, as in the Greek, Ezr and Neh are reckoned as 1 book. It has had a complicated literary history. The Oriental versions in which it has come down to us (Syriac, Ethiopic, Armenian, Georgian, and 2 Arabic) recognize only chs 3 to 14. Only the Latin versions contain the preface, chs 1 and 2, and the conclusion, chs 15 and 16, and are believed by scholars today to be of Christian origin, probably from the 2d and 3d cent. A.D., respectively. Chapter 1:30, for example, clearly appears to be borrowed from Mt 23:37, and ch 1:37 is to be compared with Jn 20:29. The concept of the rejection of the Jews as God's people and the calling of the Gentiles definitely reflects a Christian viewpoint (chs 1:24, 25, 35-40; 2:10, 11, 34). Chapters 3-14 consist of

the alleged apocalypse of Salathiel, who is identified with Ezra. It is believed that this part of the book was written probably in Hebrew, that it dates from some time near the end of the 1st cent. A.D., and that it was named Esdras (Ezra) to commend it to the rabbinic Judaism of that period. The apocalypse is composed of 7 visions that attempt to unveil the future, and to answer certain aspects of the problem of God's dealings with His people. The writer uses an involved symbolism, especially in the visions of the mourning woman (chs 9:26 to 10:59), the eagle with 3 heads, 12 wings, and 8 smaller wings (chs 11:1 to 12:39), and the man rising from the sea (ch 13:1-56). Chapter 14 has the fictitious account of the restoration of the sacred books which Nebuchadnezzar is said to have burned, and of Ezra's dictating to 5 secretaries the contents of 24 OT books, and 70 apocalypses. In the Oriental versions the story culminates in the assumption of Ezra (see footnote of ch 14:48, RSV). The unusual numbering in ch 7 in the RSV is to be explained on the basis of a further complication in the book's history. A section of some 70 verses was left out in most Latin manuscripts, probably for dogmatic reasons, since it contained an emphatic denial of the value of prayers for the dead (v 105). The lost section was recovered in a Latin manuscript, and is now inserted after v 35 as vs 36-105. The rest of the chapter contains a double enumeration in the RSV, the old as found in the KJV and an additional one from vs 106-140. 2 Esdras is not accepted as canonical by either Catholics or Protestants.

3. *Tobit.* A piece of pious fiction, written possibly in Aramaic by a Diaspora Jew *c.* 200 B.C. It is an adventure story, built around Tobit, a supposed Jewish captive in Assyria, and his son Tobias, written with the object of setting forth elevated principles of morality. Although Tobit was a devout man who helped the poor, he suffered reproach from his countrymen and was stricken with blindness (chs 1; 2). A quarrel with his wife so discouraged him that he prayed that he might die. At the same time at Ecbatana in Media, a virgin-widow named Sarah, who had married 7 husbands successively, each of whom had been slain on the wedding night by a demon named Asmodeus, prayed that she, too, might die or be given respite from reproach and false accusations. The prayer of both was heard and the angel Raphael was sent to bring

relief (ch 3). Pretending to be a man named Azarias, Raphael became Tobias' guide to take him to Media to secure 10 talents of silver left there by Tobit (chs 4; 5). Arriving at the Tigris River, Tobias at Raphael's direction caught a huge fish (ch 6), the entrails of which proved effective later in banishing the demon Asmodeus and in curing Tobit's blindness. The journey was successful. Tobias acquired the money and married Sarah, who, according to the angel, was destined for him from eternity (chs 7-9). The return to Nineveh was a joyful event for the entire family and for the inhabitants of Nineveh. Tobit was cured of his blindness, and welcomed his daughter-in-law, offering praise and blessing to God (chs 10-14).

4. *Judith.* A thrilling religious romance deriving its name from a devout, wealthy, and beautiful Jewish widow heroine. It was originally written in Hebrew *c.* 150 B.C. The Assyrian king, Nebuchadnezzar, who is said to have ruled from Nineveh, defeated Arphaxad, king of the Medes in Ecbatana. He then sent his commander in chief, Holofernes, to punish the nations to the west, including the Jews, who had refused to assist him in his conquest of the Medes. The only people in the west who dared defy him were the Jews who, according to the book, had but recently returned from captivity. Holofernes besieged the city of Bethulia. Through her enticement, trickery, and bravery, Judith rescued her people by cutting off the head of Holofernes with his own sword while he slept in a drunken stupor.

5. *The Additions to the Book of Esther.* Six passages totaling 107 verses interpolated in the canonical book of Esther at various places during the 1st cent. B.C. by pious Jews of Egypt. Since the canonical book of Esther does not contain the name of God, it is thought that the motive for the additions was the desire to supply this name, but these additions have introduced discrepancies and contradictions into the account.

6. *The Wisdom of Solomon.* A religio-political treatise combining OT theological concepts with Alexandrian philosophical ideas derived from Platonism and Stoicism. It was composed in Greek during the 1st cent. B.C., probably at Alexandria. The author, purporting to be Solomon, explains how, after he was divinely chosen as king (ch 9:7), he was endowed with wisdom in answer to prayer

(ch 7:7-14). The book encourages the Jews to uphold wisdom and righteousness, and shows the folly of heathenism. The 2d half of the book is a religio-philosophical sketch of the history of Pentateuchal times. It attributes the preservation of God's servants from Adam to Moses, and onward, to wisdom (chs 10; 11), and shows the folly of idolatry (chs 13-15). The histories of Israel and Egypt are a special demonstration of the results of wisdom on the one hand and of folly on the other (chs 16-19).

7. *The Wisdom of Jesus the Son of Sirach,* or *Ecclesiasticus.* A book of wisdom, which is the longest and the most highly esteemed of all the Apocryphal books. Its alternative name, Ecclesiasticus, "churchly [book]," is usually taken to mean that it was of a quality suitable for reading in the church and for the instruction of catechumens. This is the only Apocryphal work of which the author can be identified. Jesus the son of Sirach was evidently a teacher, and it has been suggested that his book contains many of his classroom lectures (see Pfeiffer, *History of New Testament Times,* pp. 353, 354). It was written originally in Hebrew *c.* 180 B.C. and was translated into Greek *c.* 132 B.C. by the author's grandson. It sets forth the nature of true wisdom in its application to practical life and human conduct. It is patterned after such wisdom books as Proverbs, and contains instruction on morality and practical godliness. The subject matter is not set forth systematically. It covers a variety of aspects of life, such as filial and marital duties, friendship, correctness of speech, self-control, hypocrisy, slander, table conduct, rules of etiquette, almsgiving, and mourning for the dead. In spite of the length of the work the writer affirms: "I have yet more to say, which I have thought upon, and I am filled, like the moon at the full" (ch 39:12). One of its most famous sections is its recital of the stories of the heroes of old (chs 44-50), beginning with the familiar words, "Let us now praise famous men. . . ."

8. *Baruch.* This book is patterned after the prophetic writings of the OT and was purportedly written by Baruch, the friend and secretary of Jeremiah (Jer 36:4), during the Babylonian exile. Many scholars regard it as a composite work by 2 or more writers. In its final Greek form the book is believed by many to have been published in the 1st cent. A.D., with the object of interpreting the terrible calamity that befell the Jews in A.D. 70. The prose section, possibly originally written in Hebrew (chs 1:1 to 3:8), depicts the Hebrew exiles as being so profoundly affected by the message read them that they repented of their sins and sent a sum of money to Jerusalem to be used for offerings on the altar of God. The prayer of confession and the plea for divine mercy that follows is placed in the mouth of all Israel. The 2d half of the book (chs 3:9 to 5:9) is in a poetic pattern strongly reminiscent of portions of Isaiah. Israel has forsaken God, the fountain of wisdom (chs 3:9 to 4:4), hence, the calamities of the Exile have come. The final section (chs 4:5 to 5:9) promises restoration to Israel and predicts the humbling of her oppressors.

9. *The Letter of Jeremiah.* This is not a letter at all, nor was it written by Jeremiah. It is a fervent dissertation based on Jer 10:11, urging the Jews to cling to the God of their fathers and not to become fascinated with the idols of the lands of their captivity, which are but insensible metal and wood. Although the Latin Vulgate and other versions, ancient and modern, attach it to the Apocryphal book of Baruch as ch 6, it is an independent composition and is printed as a separate book in the RSV, which in this follows manuscripts of the LXX. It was written probably between the 4th and 2d cent. B.C., and probably in Greek.

10. *The Prayer of Azariah and the Song of the Three Young Men.* This is the 1st of 3 unauthentic additions to the book of Daniel, and is inserted between vs 23 and 24 of ch 3. It was composed probably in Hebrew about the 1st cent. B.C. It professes to record the prayer of Azariah (Abednego), one of the 3 Hebrew worthies, while he and his companions are walking in the midst of the burning fiery furnace (vs 1-22). The angel of the Lord then miraculously changes the terrific flames of the superheated furnace into "a moist whistling wind" (vs 23-28). The 3 Hebrews are then pictured as joining in a hymn of praise for deliverance (vs 29-68) that is reminiscent of Ps 148.

11. *Susanna.* In the Vulgate this religious romance follows the last chapter of Daniel and is numbered as ch 13. It was composed probably in Hebrew about the 1st cent. B.C. Susanna, the beautiful and pious wife of Joakim, a prominent Babylonian Jew, was unlawfully approached by two Jewish elders who had been ap-

pointed as judges. When she resisted their lustful suggestions they falsely accused her of committing adultery, and as a result she was convicted and sentenced to death. She was saved by Daniel, who cross-examined the accusers separately and thereby proved their testimony to be contradictory and thus false and malicious.

12. *Bel and the Dragon.* Two stories, written probably in Hebrew during the 1st cent. B.C. In the Vulgate they appear as ch 14 of Daniel. The first story is, like Susanna, one of the world's oldest detective stories. In a contest with Babylonian priests regarding Bel (Marduk), Daniel, by sprinkling ashes on the floor, demonstrated that it was not this heathen idol that was devouring food placed in his temple, but the 70 priests with their families, who entered the temple by a secret door. The 2d story tells how Daniel killed a great dragon, who was an object of worship, by feeding him a concoction of pitch, fat, and hair, boiled together. Then Daniel was cast into the lions' den where he remained 6 days, but was miraculously fed by Habakkuk the prophet, who was transported by an angel from Judea to Babylon.

13. *The Prayer of Manasseh.* The prayer purported to be uttered by Manasseh while in Assyrian captivity. It was written probably in Hebrew c. 100-50 B.C. According to the Biblical account, Manasseh became one of Judah's most wicked kings (2 Ki 21:1-18; 2 Chr 33:1-20). However, when one of the Assyrian kings (probably either Esarhaddon or Ashurbanipal) took him captive to Babylon, he came to his senses and "besought the Lord his God and humbled himself greatly before the God of his fathers" (2 Chr 33:12). This prayer, which led to his restoration to Judah and his throne, is said to have been recorded in the "book of the kings of Israel" (v 18). The Apocryphal Prayer of Manasseh purports to be this missing entreaty. Its 15 verses emanate a spirit of sincere penitence and deep religious feeling, although they certainly are not the actual prayer of Judah's king, and are not considered to be of canonical status even by Catholics.

14. *The First Book of the Maccabees.* This is a work of historical importance, recording the struggles of the Jews for religious and political liberty in the 2d cent. B.C. The name of 1 and 2 Macc is derived from Judas Maccabeus, the 3d son of Mattathias, a priest. The designation "Maccabeus" is usually derived from the Heb. *maqqebeth* and interpreted as meaning "hammer." The name is thought to imply that he, as no other, caused the enemies of Israel and of God to feel hammer blows, although Zeitlin thinks that the name indicates that Judas was hammer-headed. 1 Maccabees was written in Hebrew by a Palestinian Jew, c. 100 B.C., and is our best source for the history of the first 40 years of the Maccabean wars. It gives a reasonably dependable account of the period from Antiochus Epiphanes (175 B.C.), to John Hyrcanus (c. 135 B.C.). Its emphasis, however, is chiefly on military activity and it tends to neglect the social, economic, and religious aspects of the period. After giving an account of the events leading up to the Maccabean rebellion (chs 1:1 to 2:70), the main part of the book centers about the military exploits of Judas (chs 3:1 to 9:22) and his brothers, Jonathan (chs 9:23 to 12:53) and Simon (chs 13:1 to 16:24), who succeeded him in the struggle first for religious, and then for political, freedom.

15. *The Second Book of the Maccabees.* This is an independent, divergent, and more elaborate account of the events portrayed in 1 Macc 1-7, written from the viewpoint of a moralizing theologian. It was composed by a Diaspora Jew in Greek, about the 1st cent. B.C. The greater part of the book, which covers the first 15 years of the Maccabean wars, is admitted to be a condensation of the 5-volume historical work of Jason of Cyrene (ch 2:19-32). The Hasidim, "the pious" or "the godly ones," zealous devotees of the Torah and legalistic orthodoxy, are described as resisting the forcible Hellenization of the Jews. The book lays stress on the supernatural interpositions of God in behalf of the faithful. The writer purposes to show "the appearances which came from heaven to those who strove zealously on behalf of Judaism" (ch 2:21), and thus to give instruction and encouragement to the Jews. The book opens with 2 letters allegedly from the Jews in Palestine to the Jews in Egypt describing the rededication of the Temple and inviting the Jews in Egypt to join in the celebration of the annual Feast of Lights (chs 1:1 to 2:18). The author proceeds to recall the history that led to the Maccabean revolt (chs 3-7), and in the remainder of the book portrays the successes of the Maccabean revolt, victories in battles (ch 8), the death of Antiochus Epiphanes (ch 9), the purification and rededication of

the Temple, and subsequent military victories won for the Jews by Judas Maccabeus (chs 10-15).

The Apocryphal books were included in the 1st complete English Bible, the Wycliffe Bible of *c.* 1382, and in all the English Bibles of the 16th cent., as well as in the King James, or so-called Authorized, Version of 1611. At first they were interspersed among the various books of the OT. In his German translation Martin Luther segregated these books and placed them, with the exception of 1 and 2 Esdras, as a separate group at the end of the OT, prefaced by the statement: "Apocrypha—that is books which are not held equal to the Holy Scriptures, yet are profitable and good to read." Coverdale's English Bible of 1535 followed Luther in segregating these books, but added 1 and 2 Esdras to them. The preface to the Geneva Bible said of them: "As books proceeding from godly men [they] were received to be read for the advancement and furtherance of the knowledge of history and for the instruction of godly manners." One of the translators of the King James Version, George Abbot, as Archbishop of Canterbury, issued a decree in 1615 that any printer daring to bind and sell a copy of the English Bible without the Apocrypha would be liable to a whole year's imprisonment. However, doctrinal problems caused the Apocrypha to be excluded more and more from Bibles in following years. Finally, early in the 19th cent. the British and Foreign Bible Society decided to deny any support to the publication or circulation of these disputed books.

With reference to the relation of these books to the canon of the OT 3 main positions have been taken by Christian denominations.

a. The Roman Catholic Church has given 12 of these books a full canonical status. The 4th Session of the Council of Trent on April 8, 1546, decreed that, with the exception of 1 and 2 Esdras and the Prayer of Manasseh, the Apocryphal books "entire and with all their parts" are "sacred and canonical." An anathema is further pronounced on anyone who "knowingly and deliberately" rejects them. Though denied canonicity and authority, 1 and 2 Esdras and the Prayer of Manasseh are included in Latin manuscripts of the Vulgate, and in later printed editions they were placed in an appendix to the Bible.

b. The Church of England, the Lutheran, and Zurich Reformed churches hold that these books are useful but not canonical. Article VI of the famous 39 articles of the Church of England (1562) states that these books are read "for example of life and instruction of manners," but the church does not use them "to establish any doctrine." The Swiss Reformer Oecolampadius stated in 1530: "We do not despise Judith, Tobit, Ecclesiasticus, Baruch, the last two books of Esdras, the three books of Maccabees, the additions to Daniel; but we do not allow them divine authority with the other."

c. The Calvinistic and other Reformed churches have plainly set forth their position in the Westminster Confession of Faith (1647): "The books, commonly called Apocrypha, not being of divine inspiration, are no part of the Canon of Scripture; and therefore are of no authority in the Church of God, nor to be any otherwise approved, or made use of, than other human writings."

The Greek Orthodox Church has never made a decision relative to the canon which has been accepted by all of its communion. The LXX, which includes the Apocrypha, is accepted as the authentic text of the OT. The synod of Jerusalem (1672) placed the Apocrypha in coordination with the canonical books, while the Synod of Constantinople of the same year took the position that these books are not equal to the canonical, but since they are "good and worthy of praise" they are not to be rejected altogether. In actual practice, however, this communion has moved toward an almost complete acceptance of the Apocrypha.

Protestants, on the basis of internal and external evidence, deny divine authority for, and thus the canonicity of, the Apocrypha. Their English Bibles generally contain the same books as the Hebrews accepted as inspired Scripture. Although the Apocrypha, as well as the canonical books, were produced by Jews, they were not accepted by the Jewish people as a part of the official Hebrew canon. The Jews of the intertestamental period seem, in fact, to have been aware of the absence of the spiritual gift which alone qualified men to write sacred Scripture. The 1st-cent. Jewish historian, Josephus, expressed it thus: "Our history hath been written since Artaxerxes very particularly, but hath not been esteemed of the like authority with the former by our forefathers, because there hath not been an exact succession of prophets" (*Against Apion* 1. 8).

Furthermore, persistent uncertainty regarding the Apocryphal books is found throughout the history of the church. From Jerome (*c.* 340-420) to the Reformation learned Fathers and theologians are found who insisted upon the basic differences between the canonical books of the OT and the Apocrypha.

Perhaps even more important is the internal character of the books themselves. Actually they do not add essentially to the story of redemption. They teach doctrines and foster practices that are out of harmony with the accepted books of the canon. The idea of making prayers and offerings for the dead, for example, is taught in 2 Macc (ch 12:41-45; cf. Baruch 3:4). There is a tendency in the apocryphal books to magnify the externals of religion. Almsgiving and works, they declare, will atone for sin and bring a reward (2 Esdras 8:33; Tobit 12:9; Ecclus 3:14). The book of Tobit presents an admixture of piety, folklore, and magic. The demon Asmodeus is represented as a jealous murderer of a young woman's 7 successive bridegrooms, but is finally exorcized by the burning entrails of a fish (Tobit 6:1-8; 8:1-9). A potent medicine derived from the gall of the same fish cures a father's blindness which had been caused by bird droppings (chs 2:9, 10; 6:8; 11:7-15). Judith's language and conduct, characterized by double-dealing and falsehood, are represented as meeting with God's approval and assistance (Judith 9:10, 13; etc.). The Wisdom of Solomon teaches the Platonic doctrine that man's soul is inherently immortal, and that his body is a mere hindrance to the soul (ch 9:15), a view foreign to both the OT and the NT. The author has also borrowed Plato's doctrine of the pre-existence of souls (ch 8:19, 20).

However, although the Apocryphal books cannot claim canonicity, they are still of value to the Bible student. They provide a knowledge of the 400-year gap between the OT and the NT. They help us to understand the social, political, and religious climate of the NT. The books of the Maccabees, particularly 1 Macc, trace the struggles of the Jews for political and religious freedom against the tyranny of Greek paganism. They help us to understand the rise of such sects as the Pharisees and the Sadducees. They throw light on the growth of institutions and beliefs among the Jews of NT times and thus on the background of the early church.

Apocryphal Books (NT). The NT apocryphal books have never maintained a position of esteem among Christians equal to that held by the OT Apocrypha. Few of them have ever been seriously considered by the church as candidates for canonicity. As Montague Rhodes James has pointed out in his Preface to *The Apocryphal New Testament* (Oxford, 1955), the reader can satisfy himself as to the wise judgment in this matter by reading this literature: "It will very quickly be seen that there is no question of any one's having excluded them from the New Testament: they have done that for themselves" (pp. xi, xii; his is the standard collection and English translation of these works).

None of the books usually classified among the NT Apocrypha are earlier than the 2d cent. A.D. None of them can justly claim apostolic authorship or apostolic authority, which was one of the tests of canonicity used by the early church. Their literary and spiritual quality marks them as definitely on a secondary level.

I. Apocryphal Gospels. The scattered references to, and quotations from, extra-Biblical gospels in patristic writings, combined with ancient lists of noncanonical works and fragments of actual manuscripts from Egypt, furnish evidence of the existence of some 50 apocryphal gospels. Of a large number of these, little or nothing more than the name is known. Only a few of the more prominent ones can be mentioned here.

1. *The Gospel According to the Egyptians.* Originating in Egypt in Greek shortly before the middle of the 2d cent., this work heads Origen's list of heretical gospels. Our chief source of information regarding it is Clement of Alexandria (*c.* 150 - *c.* 220), who has preserved a few quotations from it, and who tells us that it was read and accepted by the ascetic Encratites. Reference to it is also made by 2 Clement, Hippolytus' *Refutation of All Heresies,* and Epiphanius' *Panarion.* These writers claim that, besides being strongly ascetic in its teachings, it supports Sabellianism (a heresy that makes the Father, Son, and Holy Spirit mere successive aspects of an eternal unity) and the idea of the fluidity of the soul.

2. *The Gospel According to the Hebrews.* This work is so named either because it was used by Jewish Christians in Egypt or because of its strongly Jewish tendencies. It is made up largely of material borrowed from the canonical Gospel of Matthew. It is known from a few quotations of early Christian writers, principally Jerome. With reference to the

temptation, this gospel pictures Jesus as saying: "Even now did my mother the Holy Spirit take me by one of mine hairs, and carried me away unto the great mountain Thabor." Jerome refers to two interesting resurrection incidents found in this gospel. In one of these Jesus is quoted as saying to Peter and those with him: "Lo, feel me and see that I am not a bodiless spirit (demon)." In the other the statement is made: "Now the Lord, when he had given the linen cloth unto the servant of the priest, went unto James and appeared to him (for James had sworn that he would not eat bread from that hour wherein he had drunk the Lord's cup until he should see him risen again from among them that sleep)."

3. *The Gospel of Peter.* A 2d cent. pseudonymous work characterized by anti-Judaism and by Docetism—a view that denied Jesus' real humanity (by attributing to Him only a phantom body) and consequently denied the reality of His suffering. A fragment of this gospel was discovered in a tomb at Akhmim in Upper Egypt in 1884 and was published in 1892. Its Docetic character is clearly revealed by two statements: "And they brought two malefactors, and crucified the Lord betwixt them. But he kept silence, as one feeling no pain." "And the Lord cried out aloud saying: 'My power, my power, thou hast forsaken me.' And when he had so said, he was taken up."

4. *The Gospel of the Ebionites.* A work written probably in Greek, toward the end of the 2d cent., to promote the schismatic views of the Ebionites, Jewish Christians affected by Gnosticism; known by Origen as the Gospel of the Twelve Apostles. It is known chiefly through quotations from it in Epiphanius' *Panarion.* These Ebionites were vegetarians, and their gospel pictures John's diet as composed of wild honey and cakes dipped in oil.

5. *The Gospels of Thomas.* (1) A work pretending to be "the stories of Thomas the Israelite, the Philosopher, concerning the works of the childhood of the Lord." It is concerned largely with a group of supposed miracles performed by Jesus while a child between the ages of 5 and 12. According to these accounts, Jesus as a child possessed supernatural powers, but those powers were often used in destructive and vengeful ways. People even complained to Joseph, "Thou that hast such a child canst not dwell with us in the village: or do thou teach him to bless and not to curse: for he slayeth our children" (ch IV). (2) Another work, also called Gospel of Thomas, a collection of more than 100 sayings *(logia)* of Jesus, referred to in patristic literature. Some of these sayings were known from papyri found at Oxyrhynchus. The complete collection in a Coptic translation was discovered at Chenoboskion, in Egypt, in 1946.

6. *The Book of James.* One of a number of infancy gospels that attempted to glorify the childhood of Jesus. This gospel aims to promote the sanctity and veneration of the virgin Mary. Following the pattern of the story of the birth of Samuel, it tells of the angelic announcement of Mary's birth to Joachim and Anna, her parents, in answer to their earnest prayers, and of how Mary, like Samuel, was presented to the Lord and trained in the Temple. It pictures her miraculous conception of Jesus, and her life in the home of Joseph, an old widower. It declares that Zacharias the father of John the Baptist was slain by Herod for refusing to disclose the hiding place of Elizabeth and John when the infants were slain. Concerning this gospel, which claims to be the work of James, the Lord's brother, Dr. E. J. Goodspeed has said, "No gospel is more completely fiction."

7. *The Gospel of Nicodemus.* One of several passion gospels, also called Acts of Pilate. It dates from about the middle of the 4th cent. and is composed of 2 distinct parts: (1) the story of the trial, passion, and resurrection, featuring particularly the parts played by Pilate and Nicodemus; (2) an account of the supposed Descent into Hell. The alleged documents of Pilate regarding Jesus are purely imaginary fabrications.

II. Apocryphal Acts. A number of fanciful travel romances concerning the great apostolic leaders arose in the early church to supplement the brief account given in our canonical book of Acts. The NT book of Acts centers about Peter (Acts 1-12) and Paul (chs 13-28) and although the names of the apostles are given in ch 1, nothing is said of the work or the fate of most of them in the book. Even the narrative of the apostle Paul breaks off suddenly, without giving us information concerning the outcome of his trial.

The apocryphal Acts purport to answer the inquiries that spring naturally from this silence, but the accounts are of a purely legendary character. They exalt the apostles above the level of reality and make of them fanciful characters.

While there may be some substratum of fact in some of the items related, they are for the most part devoid of historical value. They revel in wonder tales of a miraculous nature. They are strongly ascetic in character. Marriage relations are regarded as evil. Most of them present the theologically heretical view of Jesus known as Docetism, and some of them teach a naive form of Modalism, a doctrine that makes no clear distinction between the Father and the Son. However, they contain passages of fervent piety and sincere devotion. Only the 5 most prominent of these apocryphal Acts are here discussed.

1. *The Acts of John.* A fictitious travel narrative of the apostle John produced in the 2d cent. It contains fanciful tales of John's miracles and discourses. It is especially noteworthy for its exposition of a Docetic view of our Lord (*see* I, 3). In these Acts of John, Jesus appears in varying and changing forms—as a youth, and as an old man, as immaterial, and as having a solid body (chs 88-93). He could do without food and sleep (ch 89). He left no discernible footprints as He walked (ch 93). His sufferings were unreal and the crucifixion was a phantasm (chs 97-101). Thus the Acts of John pictures the apostle John as teaching the very doctrines which his Gospel and Epistles show evidence of being designed to refute and to oppose.

2. *The Acts of Paul.* According to Tertullian, an apostolic novel produced by a presbyter in Asia before A.D. 190 and after the martyrdom of Polycarp, which occurred *c.* A.D. 155. Only fragments of it remain. It is noteworthy for its famous description of Paul as a man of small stature, with a bald head, bowed legs, meeting eyebrows, and a prominent nose. It also contains the well-known story of Paul and Thecla, the latter a betrothed virgin who broke off her engagement to Thamyris, after listening to Paul's teaching extolling the virtues of virginity, and followed Paul. The work also contains some supposed correspondence with the Corinthian church (sometimes designated as 3 Corinthians), and an account of Paul's martyrdom. The work expresses a strong aversion to marriage and contains several supposed beatitudes of Paul on chastity, including the famous saying: "Blessed are they that possess their wives as though they had them not, for they shall inherit God." The Acts of Paul was highly regarded in the East for a time.

3. *The Acts of Peter.* A book of the wonders and words of Peter, produced about the close of the 2d or the early part of the 3d cent. A.D. About two thirds of the text has been recovered from various sources. It purports to relate how Peter came to Rome and tells of his doings and teachings there, particularly as the opponent of Simon Magus, who had misled a large part of the church in Rome. In confuting this magician, Peter did all sorts of wonders, such as causing a dog to speak, a dead herring to swim, a baby to speak as an adult, and several people to rise from the dead. According to the narrative Peter's teaching on asceticism and chastity caused a number of women to separate from their husbands, which eventually got Peter into trouble with the authorities, who were determined to put him to death. At first he yielded to the entreaty of friends and fled from Rome. But on the way he met the Lord Jesus entering Rome in the famous *Quo vadis* legend. Peter asked Jesus, "Lord, whither goest thou?" The reply was, "I go into Rome to be crucified." Peter then turned around and returned to Rome, where he was crucified—with his head downward, at his own request. The Acts of Peter is of interest to students of the history of Sabbath- and Sunday-keeping, since this book specifically designates the first day of the week as the "Lord's day."

4. *The Acts of Andrew.* A book telling of the travels and marvelous deeds of the apostle Andrew in Pontus, Bithynia, Macedonia, and Greece, dated by scholars about the middle of the 3d cent., possibly as late as A.D. 260. Like the Acts of Peter and Paul, these Acts regard marriage relations as evil and encourage celibacy and continency. Andrew persuades Maximilla, the wife of Aegetes, the proconsul of Greece, to leave her husband, and as a result the apostle suffers martyrdom. He is crucified but lingers on the cross for 3 days, and after refusing release, finally succumbs.

5. *The Acts of Thomas.* A travel-romance of "Judas" Thomas, produced probably around the end of the 2d cent. A.D. It has been completely preserved. Scholars are divided on the question of its original language, some holding that it was Syriac, others that it was Greek, and others that the book was produced in both languages. It strongly echoes Gnostic ideas, uses Manichaean phraseology, and teaches asceticism. Thomas' abstemious life is thus described: "He fasteth con-

tinually and prayeth, and eateth bread only, with salt, and his drink is water, and he weareth but one garment alike in fair weather and in winter, and receiveth naught of any man, and that he hath he giveth unto others" (ch 20). The book sets forth one indispensable condition for salvation—abstinence from sexual relations, which it designates as "foul intercourse" (ch 12). It consists of 13 "acts" of Thomas, followed by an account of his martyrdom. The story begins with a meeting of the apostles in Jerusalem to divide the regions of the world for missionary service. Thomas receives India by lot, but refuses to accept this charge even after Jesus appears to him and tries to dispel his fears. Jesus then sells him as a carpenter slave to a merchant (Abbanes) sent by the king of India. In India the ministry of Thomas is filled with the miraculous and the supernatural. The colt of an ass is made to speak. A serpent is made to suck out the poison from the body of a slain youth, thus restoring him to life. A murdered young woman is raised to life and relates the horrors of her experiences in hell. Four wild asses are called as substitutes for exhausted beasts of burden. One of these exorcises a demon from a woman and her daughter. Thomas is freed from prison to baptize some converts, and after he returns, the seal on the doors of the prison appears to be unbroken. The whole book is devoid of historical value, though the author made use of historical figures.

6. *Secondary Acts.* Of secondary importance are the Acts of Philip, of Andrew and Matthew, of Peter and Andrew, and of Andrew and Paul.

III. Apocryphal Epistles. Apocryphal writings of this type are not numerous, and certainly not impressive. The epistles of the NT are more difficult to imitate than the gospels or apocalypses, and it is therefore easier to detect forgeries in letters.

Two spurious letters purport to be the correspondence between Jesus and Abgarus, the king of Edessa. The Clementine Homilies begin with a supposed letter of Peter to James. Works attributed to Paul include the Epistle to the Laodiceans, which purport to be the Laodicean letter mentioned in Col 4:16; the Lost Epistle to the Corinthians (cf. 1 Cor 5:9), which is part of the apocryphal Acts of Paul; and the forged correspondence of Paul with Seneca—14 letters, 6 attributed to Paul and 8 to Seneca. Finally, there is the Epistle of the Apostles, written about the middle of the 2d cent. "for all men" in the name of Christ's apostles. None of these can justly claim any place in the canon of the NT.

IV. Apostolic Fathers. More important than the apocryphal epistles are the so-called Apostolic Fathers, which are usually not reckoned among NT apocryphal literature, but some of which made a rather strong claim for a time to canonicity. Several of these writings are in the form of epistles or letters.

1. *1 Clement.* A letter from the church in Rome to the church in Corinth, written between A.D. 75 and 110, and most probably about A.D. 95. The actual writer of the letter, according to the tradition of the early church, was Clement, the head of the church in Rome. The main theme of the letter is an appeal to the church in Corinth to harmonize their differences and to submit to the authority of their elders, some of whom had been deposed. The letter contains the earliest clear statement of the principle of apostolic succession (ch 44). It contains also the earliest noncanonical references to Peter and Paul and is of value in the study of the NT canon for its quotations from, and allusions and references to, NT books. It was apparently accepted as canonical by Clement of Alexandria (d. *c.* A.D. 220). The 5th-cent. Bible manuscript, Codex Alexandrinus, included it, and a 12th-cent. manuscript of a Syriac version placed it between the letters of Paul and the Catholic Epistles. It was mentioned as a part of the NT in the Apostolic canons of *c.* A.D. 350.

2. *2 Clement.* This work is not really a letter, nor is it by Clement. It is a sermon, produced about the middle of the 2d cent., which came to be associated with 1 Clement. It is an appeal for repentance, for pure and godly living, and for a belief in Christ and in the resurrection.

3. *The Epistle of Barnabas.* This is an anonymous work coming probably from the 1st half of the 2d cent. A.D., which tradition has erroneously ascribed to Barnabas, the friend of Paul.

4. *The Shepherd of Hermas.* A 2d-cent. homily attributed to one Hermas of Rome, who claimed the gift of prophecy. This book consists largely of allegory and represents an attempt to re-establish the waning authority of the prophetic gift in the church. Some regarded it as canonical; it was included in the NT in the Codex Sinaiticus.

5. *The Didache* (*The Teaching of the Twelve Apostles*). A pseudo-apostolic book dating from the 2d cent. It is divided into 2 parts, the first possibly a Jewish work called The Two Ways, and the second a sort of manual of church organization.

A large number of early apocryphal works of a Gnostic nature in Coptic translations have recently been discovered at Chenoboskion, Egypt. When published, these works will shed great light on the religious tendencies of the Christian church in the period of the 2d and 3d centuries A.D.

Apollonia (ăp'ŏ-lō'nĭ-à). [Gr. *Apollōnia*, "belonging to Apollo."] A city of Macedonia, about 30 mi. west of Amphipolis, on the famous Roman highway Via Egnatia. Paul passed through the city on his 2d Missionary Journey, on the way from Philippi and Amphipolis to Thessalonica (Acts 17:1). Map XX, A-3.

Apollos (à-pŏl'ŏs). [Gr. *Apollōs*, a contraction of *Apollōnios*.] A Jewish convert to the message of John the Baptist, described as being diligent, fervent, and "an eloquent man, and mighty in the scriptures" (Acts 18:24, 25). He was born at the Egyptian city of *Alexandria. After his conversion he became an itinerant evangelist (chs 18:24, 27; 19:1). While preaching at Ephesus he met Aquila and Priscilla, Christian Jews, who instructed him in the tenets of Christianity (ch 18:26, 28). After this Apollos went to the Roman province of *Achaia, taking with him a letter of recommendation from the church at Ephesus (v 27). While in Achaia he preached with success in the city of Corinth (chs 18:28; 19:1), and because of his abilities became popular with a certain faction that began to exalt him, as opposed to other groups which exalted Paul, Peter, or Christ (1 Cor 1:12). This condition received no encouragement from Apollos, and it was doubtless because of it that he refused to return to Corinth when Paul asked him to do so (ch 16:12). In his rebuke to the church for their factious spirit Paul stated that he and Apollos were "one," and "labourers together" (ch 3:6-9).

In his letter to Titus, Paul exhorted him to do all in his power to help Apollos and "Zenas the lawyer," Apollos' traveling companion, in their preparation for a projected journey (Tit 3:13).

Apollyon (à-pŏl'yŭn). [Gr. *Apolluōn*, "destroyer," from *apollumi*, "to destroy," equivalent to the Heb. *'abaddôn*, "destruc-

tion."] The name given to the "angel" of the "bottomless pit," or *"abyss," who was "king" over the "locusts" in the symbolic prophecy of Rev 9:1-11.

Apostle. [Gr. *apostolos*, from *apo*, "off," "away," and *stello*, "to send," "to dispatch"; thus literally, "one sent forth," and by extension, "a messenger," "an ambassador." In classical Greek *apostolos* is frequently used of a ship or fleet dispatched on a merchant or naval expedition; of the captain of a ship or the commander of a naval squadron; of a representative in the sense of an ambassador or envoy. In Koine Greek, the Greek in which the NT was written, *apostolos* is also used with these 2 general applications: (1) to things, and (2) to persons. It appears with the connotations of a ship sent, a cargo dispatched; of the documents that represent the ship and its cargo, the bill of lading, or, perhaps, the export license. It is used of persons in the sense of ambassador, envoy, delegate. Josephus uses this word when speaking of the ambassadors whom the Jews sent as their representatives to Rome (*Ant.* xvii. 11. 1).]

In NT usage *apostolos* carries the ideas of mission and representation. The term appears in the record of Jesus' ordaining and sending forth His disciples on an evangelistic mission (Mt 10:2-6). It is probable that Jesus on this occasion used the Aramaic *shelucha'*, the equivalent of the Hebrew participle *shaluach*, "sent." This Semitic term of which *apostolos* is the Greek equivalent appears to have had a technical use among the Jews. In rabbinical literature it appears with reference to authoritative messengers and representatives, such as those responsible for gathering offerings from among the Diaspora Jews. It seems apparent that *apostolos* is used in the NT, in the main, with a similar technical significance.

The term *apostolos* is used in the Gospels, with one exception (Lk 11:49), only with reference to the Twelve whom Jesus called and sent out. These 12 were Andrew and his brother Simon, later known as Simon Peter (Mt 4:18-20; Mk 1:16-18; Lk 6:14; Jn 1:35-42); James and his brother John, sons of Zebedee (Mt 4:21, 22; Mk 1:19, 20; Lk 6:14); Philip (Jn 1:43, 44); Nathanael, also named Bartholomew (Jn 1:45-51); Matthew, also called Levi (Mt 9:9; Mk 2:14; Lk 5:27, 28); Thomas; James the son of Alphaeus; Simon the Zealot or Cananaean; Judas, brother of James; and Judas Iscariot. There are 3 complete listings of the 12 apostles in the NT (Mt 10:2-4; Mk 3:14-19; Lk 6:13-16). A 4th listing (Acts 1:13) omits the name of Judas Iscariot. A comparison of the order of the names in these listings shows that the names are apparently given in no particular order, with the exception of Simon Peter, Philip, and James the son of Alphaeus, whose names appear 1st, 5th, and 9th, respectively, in each list. This has led to the suggestion that there were 3 groups of 4, headed by these 3 men. *See* names of individual apostles. Of the Twelve, Peter, James, and John seem to have been singled out for special privileges. They were present at the raising from death of the daughter of Jairus (Mk 5:37-42); at the transfiguration of Jesus (Mt 17:1, 2); and in the Garden of Gethsemane during the agony (Mk 14:32, 33). This was no doubt due to the fact that these 3 had a clearer comprehension of, and a deeper sympathy with, the work and teachings of Jesus. One of the Twelve, Judas Iscariot, became a traitor, and later Matthias was elected to fill his office and thus to preserve the original number of the 12 apostles (Acts 1:15-26).

The term *apostolos*, however, is not restricted to the Twelve. When Paul, in defending himself against those who challenged his ministry, laid claim to being an apostle, he used the word in its technical sense, giving as proof of his apostleship the fact that he had seen the Lord (1 Cor 9:1, 2; cf. Acts 1:21, 22, 25) and had received a direct commission (Gal 2:8, 9; cf. Rom 1:1). The term "apostle" is applied also to Barnabas (Acts 14:14); to Apollos, whom Paul includes among the apostles who have become "a spectacle unto the world, and to angels, and to men" (1 Cor 4:6, 9); and to Silvanus and Timothy, who are described as "apostles of Christ" (1 Th 1:1; 2:6).

Apothecary. Perfumer or compounder of incense and anointing oils. The Hebrew word thus translated is derived from *raqach*, "to mix," "to compound," "to perfume." Apothecaries also prepared flavoring extracts and medicinal herbs. In 2 Chr 16:14 they are mentioned as preparing embalming spices, oils, or ointments. The medical arts were developed early; thus the art, the work, and the ointment of the apothecary are mentioned early in the OT (Ex 30:25; 37:29; cf. Ec 10:1). The apothecaries helped restore the walls of Jerusalem (Neh 3:8). For "apothecary" the RSV consistently reads "perfumer."

Appaim (ăp′å-ĭm). [Heb. *'Appayim,* "little nose."] A Judahite (1 Chr 2:30, 31).

Apparel. *See* Clothing.

Apphia (ăf′ĭ-á). [Gr. *Apphia,* a female name common in western Asia Minor, as inscriptions show.] A Christian woman in Colossae, probably the wife of Philemon (Phm 2).

Appii Forum. *See* Forum of Appius.

Apple. [Heb. *tappuach,* a term describing a certain kind of fruit, as well as the tree producing the fruit. *'Îshôn,* "little man," *bath,* "daughter," and *babah,* "little child," occur in expressions translated "apple of the eye."] There has been considerable difference of opinion as to the identity of *tappuach.* The term has been variously identified with the apple, apricot, citron, orange, and quince, with the apricot favored by many. However, insufficient reasons have been set forth to rule out the apple as at least a strong possibility. In Solomon's love song the tree is compared to the bridegroom (Song 2:3) and recalled as a trysting place (ch 8:5). The fruit is refreshing (ch 2:5) and its fragrance a delight (ch 7:8). Joel (ch 1:12) mentions the apple trees as sharing the fate of all other trees in a terrible drought.

In the expression "apple of the eye," apple refers to the pupil or the eyeball. *'Îshôn,* "little man," probably refers to the tiny image a man sees of himself in the pupil of another person's eye (Deut 32:10; Ps 17:8; Prov 7:2).

Apron. In the OT (Gen 3:7) a translation of the Heb. *chagôrah,* generally translated "girdle" (2 Sa 18:11; 1 Ki 2:5; etc.). *Chagôrah* comes from *chagar,* "to gird oneself [or "someone"] with a girdle or belt." Adam and Eve are spoken of as making "aprons" of fig leaves (Gen 3:7) to hide their nakedness after the Fall. The exact form of these "aprons" or "girdles" is a matter of conjecture. In the NT "apron" is the translation of the Gr. *simikinthion,* apparently a transliteration of the Latin *semicinctium.* At Ephesus, "aprons" were carried from Paul to the sick (Acts 19:12), and "the diseases departed." Again the exact form of these "aprons" is uncertain. Some think they were aprons such as are worn by workmen, others, undergarments worn next to the skin, still others, bands or bandages.

Aquila (ăk′wĭ-lå). [Gr. *Akulas,* a transliteration of the Latin *Aquila,* meaning "eagle." The name is attested by inscriptions, one of them actually found at Sinope in Pontus, the homeland of the NT Aquila.] A

Jew from Pontus, who, with his wife Priscilla, had lived in Rome, but had moved to Corinth after Claudius (about A.D. 49) expelled the Jews from Rome. They may already have been Christians when Paul met them in Corinth and worked with them as a tentmaker (Acts 18:1-3). When the apostle returned to Palestine, probably in the fall of A.D. 52, the couple accompanied him as far as Ephesus. There they met Apollos and helped him to see the full light of Christianity (vs 18, 19, 24-26). They were still at Ephesus when Paul wrote 1 Cor from there, for he sent greetings from the church using their home for meetings (1 Cor 16:19). They must have returned to Rome about the time Paul left Ephesus (spring, A.D. 57); in his letter to the Romans (Rom 16:3, 4), perhaps written the winter of A.D. 57/58, Paul sent greetings to them. At the time of Paul's 2d Roman imprisonment the couple seem to have been at Ephesus again, as the greetings sent to Timothy indicate (2 Ti 4:19). Paul's repeated mention of them in several letters shows that they must have been extremely valuable lay workers in the Christian churches to which they belonged.

Ar (är). [Heb. *'Ar,* "city."] An important city on the border of Moab (Num 21:15; Deut 2:18), also called "Ar of Moab" (Is 15:1, KJV). In Greek and Roman times Ar was called Areopolis, "The City of Ares," by a transfer of the Semitic word *'Ar,* "city," to the Gr. *Ares,* "Mars." In the Christian period it bore the name Rabbath Moab, now identified with *Khirbet er-Rabbah.* The ancient name of Ar persists in *el-'Eyr,* a place in the vicinity of *Khirbet er-Rabbah.* One suggested site for the OT Ar is *el-Miṣna',* 2 mi. northeast of *Khirbet er-Rabbah* and about 13 mi. south of the Arnon (Abel, *Géographie* II, 248). The difficulty with this identification is that this does not place Ar at the border of Moab. Some identify Ar with Kerioth (Jer 48:24, 41). *See* Kerioth, 2. The Rand McNally maps incorporated into this volume place it on the south bank of the Arnon (Map VI, F-4), but this is only a conjecture, as indicated by the question mark.

Ara (ā'rà). [Heb. *'Ara'.*] An Asherite (1 Chr 7:38).

Arab, I (ā'răb). [Heb. *'Arab.*] A town in southern Judah (Jos 15:52), identified with modern *er-Rābiyeh,* 7 mi. southwest of Hebron.

Arab, II. *See* Arabia, Arab, and Arabians.

18. The Wadi Arabah, south of the Dead Sea

Arabah (ăr'à-bà). [Heb. *'Arabah,* "desert."] The designation for the whole geographical depression between the Sea of Galilee and the Gulf of Aqabah (Deut 1:1, 7; 3:17; Jos 3:16; 11:2; 12:3; 2 Ki 25:4; etc.), which today is called *el-Ghôr* north of the Dead Sea and *Wâdi el-'Arabah* south of the Dead Sea (*see* Palestine). The name appears frequently in the RSV, but only twice in the KJV (Jos 18:18), which generally renders the Hebrew term "plain." *'Arabah* is also frequently used in the general sense of "desert," "wilderness," or "plain."

Arabia (à-rā'bĭ-à), **Arab** (ăr'ăb), and **Arabians** (à-rā'bĭ-ănz). [Heb. *'Arab* and *'Ereb* for the country, and *'Arabî* and *'Arebî* for the people. In Akkadian the name of the people occurs as *Aribu* and *Arubu.*] The name Arabs (KJV "Arabians") was used mainly as a designation for the nomadic people (cf. Is 13:20; Jer 3:2) of the Syrian and Arabian deserts (2 Chr 17:11; 26:7), to which the name of Arabia was applied (1 Ki 10:15; 2 Chr 9:14; Is 21:13; Jer 25:24; Eze 27:21). In later OT times, that is, in the postexilic period, Arabia designates the (partly Edomite) province of "Arabia" (cf. Neh 2:19), which, like Judea and Samaria, formed part of the Persian satrapy of *Abar Nahara,* "Beyond the River" (Map XII, D-6).

Arabs in the modern sense of the term —the inhabitants of the Arab countries of the Near East, including many who are Arab only in language and culture— were unknown to the writers of the OT. For the inhabitants of the Arabian peninsula, which consisted of the fertile coastal regions and the great central desert, tribal names were used. These, according to the Bible, were descendants of the Hamitic Cush (Gen 10:7), of the Semitic Joktan (vs 26-29), of Abraham by Keturah (ch 25:1-4), and of Ishmael (vs 12:16).

The various specific tribal groups descended from these four are included in the following tabulation:

LISTS OF ARABIC TRIBES IN THE OT

The sons of Cush Gen 10:7	*The sons of Joktan* Gen 10:26-29	*The sons of Keturah* Gen 25:1-4	*The sons of Ishmael* Gen 25:12-16
1. Seba	1. Almodad	1. Zimran	1. Nebaioth
2. Havilah	2. Sheleph	2. Jokshan	2. Kedar
3. Sabtah	3. Hazarmaveth	(1) Sheba	3. Adbeel
4. Raamah	4. Jerah	(2) Dedan	4. Mibsam
(1) Sheba	5. Hadoram	(a) Asshurim	5. Mishma
(2) Dedan	6. Uzal	(b) Letushim	6. Dumah
5. Sabteca	7. Diklah	(c) Leummim	7. Massa
	8. Obal	3. Medan	8. Hadad
	9. Abimael	4. Midian	9. Tema
	10. Sheba	(1) Ephah	10. Jetur
	11. Ophir	(2) Epher	11. Naphish
	12. Havilah	(3) Hanoch	12. Kedemah
	13. Jobab	(4) Abida	
		(5) Eldaah	

Arab tribes were among the enemies of Israel in the time of the judges (Jgs 6-8). Contacts with Arabs whose tribal connections remain undefined were made by Solomon, who obtained from them gold, silver, and spices (1 Ki 10:15; 2 Chr 9:14), and who was visited by the queen of Sheba from southwest Arabia. Jehoshaphat received sheep and goats from Arabs as tribute (2 Chr 17:11). During the reign of Jehoram, Judah suffered an invasion of Arabs who even plundered Jerusalem (ch 21:16), but Uzziah defeated them (ch 26:7). They were denounced by the prophets Isaiah (ch 21:12-17) and Jeremiah (ch 25:24, 27).

In the time of Nehemiah an Arab ruler, *Geshem, was an opponent of the rebuilding of Jerusalem's wall (Neh 2:19; 6:1-6). He was probably the ruler of Dedan mentioned in the inscriptions of the Lihyanites, an Arabic people who displaced the Edomites in the 5th cent. B.C. The Arabs also fought against the Jews in the Maccabean period (1 Macc 5:39).

The Arabians at Jerusalem at the time of Pentecost (Acts 2:11) were probably Jews or proselytes who lived in the Naba-

19. Assyrian stone relief depicting Ashurbanipal's war against the Arabs

taean kingdom of Aretas, which extended along the east and south of Palestine. The Arabia in which Paul spent some time after his conversion (Gal 1:17) is usually believed to be this same Nabataean kingdom, of which Petra was the capital. Gal 4:25 refers to the same country, since the Peninsula of Sinai was included in the area controlled by the Nabataeans. There were many Christians as well as Jews in Arabia and Nabataea. The Christian Arabs of today are descendants of the Christians of the early church period.

See Dedan; Kedar; People of the East; Queen of Sheba; Tadmor.

Arad (āʹrăd). [Heb. *ʹArad,* "wild ass."]

1. A Benjamite (1 Chr 8:15).

2. A Canaanite city whose king fought against the Israelites when they were at Mount Hor (Num 21:1; 33:40). Joshua later vanquished its king (Jos 12:14). Arad is mentioned again in Jgs 1:16 as a city on the border of the Wilderness of Judah, near the region where the Kenites settled. The site has been identified as *Tell ʹArâd,* about 17 mi. south of Hebron (Map VI, F-3).

Arah (āʹrä). [Heb. *ʹArach,* "traveler."]

1. An Asherite (1 Chr 7:39).

2. A family of which 775 male members returned from Babylon with Zerubbabel (Ezr 2:5; Neh 7:10 [652]); possibly identical with Arah, 3.

3. An Israelite whose granddaughter was married to the Ammonite Tobiah in Nehemiah's time (Neh 6:18). Possibly Arah is a family name, that is, Arah, 2.

Aram (āʹrăm). [Heb. *ʹAram;* Akkadian *Aramu, Arumu,* and *Arimu.*]

1. A son of Shem, the ancestor of the Aramaeans (Gen 10:22, 23; 1 Chr 1:17). *See* Aram, 5.

2. Son of Kemuel (Gen 22:21).

3. An Asherite (1 Chr 7:34).

4. Son of Esrom (Mt 1:3, 4; Lk 3:33; KJV). *See* Ram, II.

5. A country north of Palestine stretching from the Mediterranean eastward perhaps as far as the Habur River (Maps IV, B-5; VI, A-5). When referring to this country the Heb. *ʹAram* is usually translated "Syria," and *ʹArammî,* "Syrian." The RSV occasionally translates *ʹArammî,* "Aramean" (Gen 25:20; 28:5; etc.), also spelled "Aramaean" (ărʹá-mēʹăn). The Aramaeans were descendants of Aram, Semites probably originally from the area inside the great bend of the Euphrates in northern Mesopotamia, the land called *ʹAram-Naharayim* in the Hebrew OT,

20. Assyrian stone relief of an Arabian camp

translated "Mesopotamia" (Gen 24:10; Deut 23:4; Jgs 3:8), and once "Aram-naharaim" (āʹrăm-naʹhá-rāʹĭm) in Ps 60: Title, meaning "Aram of the two rivers." This name is found in cuneiform records as *Naḥrima* and in Egyptian hieroglyphic inscriptions as *Nhrn.* The term *"Paddan-aram" in Gen 28:5 and elsewhere is either another name of Aram-naharaim or the name of a part of that country. Aramaean tribes were also found at the Persian Gulf (*see* Chaldeans). The early history of the Aramaeans is still obscure. Laban, living in the area of the Aramaeans in the early 2d millennium B.C., is called an Aramaean (Gen 25:20, RSV), as was even Jacob (Deut 26:5, RSV). A place name *Arami* appears in a cuneiform document of the Ur III period (*c.* 2070-*c.* 1960 B.C.), but the first clear inscriptional evidence for the existence of the Aramaeans comes from the time of Tiglath-pileser I (1113-1074 B.C.). For the earlier occurrence of Aramaic words *see* Aramaic. From the 12th cent. B.C. on we find the Aramaeans constantly fighting against the Assyrians, being called *Aramu* and also *Aḥlame.* They never formed great kingdoms unless the short-lived Neo-Babylonian Empire of the Chaldeans may be considered Aramaean, but they organized numerous city-states, the strongest being Damascus.

The following Aramaean states are mentioned in the OT:

a. Aram of Beth-rehob, an Aramaean state hired by the Ammonites in their war against David (2 Sa 10:6), apparently small. Beth-rehob is mentioned in Jgs 18:28 as lying in the same valley in which Dan was located, and in Num 13:21 as lying on the way to Hamath, but the exact site has not yet been identified. Some would consider the Aramaean state that helped Ammon against David to be different from the Beth-rehob near Dan, and they place it in Transjordan, near *Rihab* (Map VI, D-5).

b. *Aram of Damascus,* the strongest city-state of the Aramaeans (Map VIII, A-5). It appears as such first in the time of David, when it was subjugated (2 Sa 8: 5, 6). In Solomon's time Damascus seems to have been lost to Israel. According to the record, Rezon, an officer of Hadadezer of Zobah, took Damascus and became "an adversary to Israel all the days of Solomon" (1 Ki 11:23-25). From that time on, Damascus took the lead among the Aramaean states, and through the centuries was involved in hostilities with the kingdom of Israel. In 732 B.C. it was conquered by Tiglath-pileser III, who made it into an Assyrian province. Assyria thus became the political victor over the Aramaeans, but the Aramaeans became the cultural victors over the Assyrians. The Aramaeans spread their language and culture throughout the Assyrian Empire, and in the course of time Aramaic became an international language, which long held its supremacy. *See* Damascus.

c. *Aram of Geshur* (gēshĕr), close to Bashan (Deut 3:14). It was not subdued by Israel (Jos 13:13), and in the time of the judges it occupied some Israelite territory in Gilead, but Jair reconquered it (1 Chr 2:22, 23). A princess from the court of Talmai, king of Geshur, was a wife of David and the mother of Absalom (2 Sa 3:3). Geshur is generally believed to be east of the Jordan, near Mount Hermon, exact location unknown. Map VIII, C-4.

d. *Aram of *Maacah,* a state near Geshur, which remained independent of Israel (Deut 3:14; Jos 13:13). This state joined other Aramaeans of that area to help the Ammonites in their war against David, and like them were defeated (2 Sa 10:6-8, 19). This state is called Aram-maacah in 1 Chr 19:6, RSV.

e. *Aram of Zobah* (zō'bä) [Heb. *Ṣôba'* and *Ṣobah,* appearing in cuneiform documents as *Ṣubatu*], next to Damascus, the largest and most powerful Aramaean state of Syria (Map XI, C-4). It apparently took in part of *Beqa',* the plain lying between the Lebanon and the Anti-Lebanon, also the Anti-Lebanon and the area

east of the mountains and north of Damascus. Saul fought against it (1 Sa 14:47), and David defeated it twice, once while it was engaged in a military campaign toward the Euphrates (2 Sa 8:3-5) and again when it was allied to the Ammonites (2 Sa 10:6-19; 1 Chr 19:6-19). David obtained much bronze from there (1 Chr 18:8), which came from the copper mines in the Lebanon Mountains. The wealth of this metal had probably given the name Zobah to the country, since the Aramaic *ṣohaba'* means "red." Its later Greek name *Chalkis* means "of copper." On King Hadadezer of Zobah *see* Hadadezer. This state is called Aram-zobah in the superscription of Ps 60. The spelling "Zoba" appears in 2 Sa 10:8.

Aramaic (ăr'á-mā'ĭk). [Heb. *'Aramîth,* rendered "Syriack" or "Syrian" in the KJV, but correctly translated "Aramaic" in the RSV (2 Ki 18:26; Ezr 4:7; Is 36:11). Since in the narrative of Dan 2 it was the Chaldeans who addressed the king in the Aramaic, the language has sometimes

21. Aramaic stone inscription from Nerab

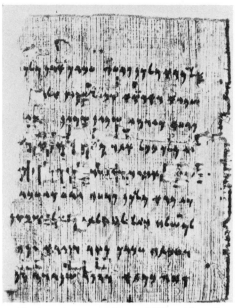

22. Aramaic papyrus letter of King Adon of
Ashkelon(?)

been called Chaldee or Chaldaic, although there is no ancient justification for this name. Jerome seems to be the first to use the term Chaldee thus. The name "Syriac" is properly reserved for the dialect of Edessa, and the term "Aramaic" is the proper designation for the language spoken by the Aramaeans.]

Aramaic was spoken as early as the 17th cent. B.C. by Laban, who called the stone monument that he and Jacob erected as a symbol of their agreement by the Aramaic term *Yegar Šahadûtha'*, "Jegarsahadutha," meaning "stone heap of witness," whereas Jacob gave to it the Hebrew name *Galʻed*, "Galeed," which has the same meaning (Gen 31:47). The earliest non-Biblical evidence for the existence of Aramaic comes from the 15th cent. B.C. It consists of certain Aramaic words in Ugaritic texts written in alphabetic cuneiform script. The oldest Aramaic inscriptions written in alphabetic script (also known as Phoenician) come from the 9th cent. B.C. They consist of an altar inscription from *Tell Ḥalaf,* and inscriptions of King Kilamuwa and King Bar-Rekub from Senjirli, of King Bar-Hadad of Damascus, and of King Zakir from Hamath.

Aramaic was first spoken only by the Aramaeans, who lived mainly in northern Mesopotamia and Syria, a strategi-

cally important area. The language spread to other areas when the Assyrians came into contact with the Aramaeans, and especially after they deported the Aramaeans to various parts of the Assyrian Empire. Their simple language and script were widely adopted by Assyrian officials and merchants. Hence we find that in 701 B.C. the officials of King Hezekiah of Judah understood Aramaic, and asked the Assyrian envoys to employ it (2 Ki 18:26).

The widespread use of Aramaic is attested also by the discovery of an Aramaic letter in Asshur written by an Assyrian officer, and by Aramaic inscriptions on Assyrian weights and dockets of the 7th cent. B.C. During the Neo-Babylonian period, when the ruling class belonged to the Chaldean tribe of the house of *Yakin,* a tribe closely related to the Aramaeans, the process of Aramaization continued even more rapidly. Hence we find the courtiers of Nebuchadnezzar speaking to the king in Aramaic (Dan 2:4). There are also many Aramaic inscriptions on clay tablets. Even a letter written by the Palestinian king Adon (probably of Ashkelon) to Pharaoh Hophra of Egypt during that period is in the Aramaic script and language (*BASOR* 111 [Oct. 1948], 24-27). See fig. 22. Thus it is not strange to find Daniel using this language in his book (Dan 2:4b to 7:28). Most officials seem to have been bilingual, or even trilingual, at that time.

When the Persians established their rule over the Near East, they found Aramaic widely used and wisely refrained from forcing their new subjects to use Persian. Instead, they made Aramaic the official language of the empire, in which decrees were issued and letters between officials were written. This is attested by the Elephantine papyri, the recently published Aramaic leather documents of the dossier of Arsham, and the Aramaic sections in the book of Ezra (chs 4:8 to 6:18; 7:12-26). When Aramaic became a popular language throughout the Persian Empire, several dialects were developed with provincial peculiarities of which the following are the most important:

I. Western Aramaic:

1. Nabataean, spoken and written in the Nabataean kingdom, of which Perta was the capital.

2. Palmyrene, spoken and written in Palmyra, that is, Tadmor, in the Syrian Desert.

3. Jewish-Egyptian Aramaic found in the Elephantine papyri (see fig. 47).

4. Palestinian Aramaic of the time of Christ, attested by quotations in the NT (Mt 27:46; Mk 7:34; etc.).

5. The Aramaic found in the Jewish Targums (paraphrastic translations of the OT).

6. The Aramaic of the Palestinian Talmud.

7. The Samaritan dialect written in an archaic script.

II. Eastern Aramaic:

1. The Aramaic of the Babylonian Talmud.

2. The Aramaic of the Mandaean and Manichaean literature.

3. Syriac, spoken first in Edessa, which became the language of the Christian Syrians. Nestorian missionaries spread this language as far as India and China. A dialectic (Jacobite) Syriac is still spoken by Christian communities in the Anti-Lebanon and near Lake Urmia in Iran, and by communities in Iraq, and is the liturgical language of the Syrian Christian church.

Lit.: F. Rosenthal, *Die aramaistische Forschung seit Th. Nöldeke's Veröffentlichungen* (Leiden, 1939); J. J. Koopmans, *"De literatuur over het Aramees na 1940," JEOL* 15 (1957-1958), 125-132.

Aramean. *See* Aram, 5.

Aramitess (ăr′á-mīt′ĕs). [Heb. *'Arammîyah.*] An Aramaean woman (1 Chr 7:14, KJV). *See* Aram, 5.

Aram-maacah. *See* Aram, 5, d.

Aram-naharaim. *See* Aram, 5.

Aram-Zobah. *See* Aram, 5, e.

Aran (ā′răn). [Heb. *'Aran,* possibly "mountain goat," if a Semitic name. The name occurs in Akkadian as *Aranu.*] A descendant of Seir, the Horite, or Hurrian (Gen 36:28; 1 Chr 1:42).

Ararat (ăr′á-răt). [Heb. *'Ararat;* Akkadian *Urartu,* and in the Dead Sea scroll 1QIsª, in harmony with Babylonian spelling, correctly *'wrrṭ* (Is 37:38).] In the OT, not the name of a mountain, but of a country, now called Armenia. A powerful kingdom, called Urartu by the Assyrians, existed in

23. Mount Ararat

this area from the 9th to the 7th cent. B.C. (Map XI, B-5) against which the Assyrians waged many wars before they were able to subjugate it completely. The language spoken in this area was not Semitic but Asiatic. Its texts were written in cuneiform script. Ararat is mentioned in the Bible first as the country in which the ark of Noah settled (Gen 8:4). Traditions have designated several mountains in that area as the one on which the ark landed. The name Mount Ararat is now given to one lofty mountain lying about halfway between the Black Sea and the Caspian Sea (Map III, B-5). It has two peaks, perennially snowclad, the higher of which rises 16,916 ft. above sea level. Ararat is also mentioned in the Bible as the land to which Sennacherib's sons fled after they had murdered their father (2 Ki 19:37; Is 37:38; KJV "Armenia," är-mē′nĭ-á). In Jer. 51:27 it is designated a kingdom.

Araunah (á-rô′ná), or **Ornan** (ôr′năn). [Heb. *'Arawnah, 'Awarnah, 'Aranyah,* and *'Ornan.* The name has not yet been fully explained, but it is almost certain that it is related to Hurrian. The Hurrian *ewirni,* meaning "lord," and the Hurrian divine name *Varuna* have been compared with Araunah. Similar personal names have been found in widely separated places: A king of northern Syria bore the name *Ari-wa-na;* Ugaritic texts (14th cent. B.C.) contain the name TUR-*shu-wa-ar-ni,* and in an Egyptian papyrus of the time of Ramses III (12th cent. B.C.) a non-Egyptian is mentioned by the name *w3rn3.*] The Jebusite whose threshing floor David purchased. The floor later became the site of Solomon's Temple (2 Sa 24:16-25; 1 Chr 21:15-28; 2 Chr 3:1).

Arba (är′bá), KJV once **Arbah** (är′bá). [Heb. *'Arba‘,* "four," if a Semitic name, which is doubtful. If it is not, the meaning is uncertain.] The father or chief of the Anakim, who seems to have been also the founder of *Kiriath-arba, later called Hebron (Jos 14:15; 15:13; 21:11; Jgs 1:10).

Arbah. *See* Arba.

Arbathite (är′bá-thīt). [Heb. *'Arbathî.*] A native of *Beth-arabah (2 Sa 23:31; 1 Chr 11:32).

Arbite (är′bīt). [Heb. *'Arbî.*] Possibly a native of *Arab, a town in Judah (2 Sa 23:35; cf. Jos 15:52).

Archangel. *See* Michael.

Archelaus. *See* Herod, 2.

Archer. *See* Arrow; Bow.

Archevites (är′kē-vīts). [Aramaic *'Arkewaye* Q *'Arkewaye').*] Natives of the Babylonian city of Erech mentioned in Gen 10:10, called *Uruk* in cuneiform records. After the deportation of the ten tribes, men from Erech (Ezr 4:9) were settled in Samaria by Osnappar (KJV "Asnapper"), or Ashurbanipal.

Archi. *See* Archite.

Archippus (är-kĭp′ŭs). [Gr. *Archippos,* "master of the horse." A frequently occurring Greek personal name, attested also in the inscriptions of western Asia Minor.] A prominent Christian of Colossae, who was closely associated with Philemon, being, possibly, his son (Col 4:17; Phm 2).

Archite (är′kīt), KJV once **Archi** (är′kī). [Heb. *'Arkî.*] A native of a Canaanite tribe or of a place known as Erech, on the border between Ephraim and Benjamin (Jos 16:2). Hushai, a friend of David, whose loyalty became especially manifest during Absalom's rebellion, was an Archite (2 Sa 15:32; 16:16; 17:5, 14; 1 Chr 27:33).

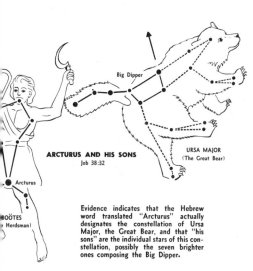

24. The constellations Boötes, the Herdsman (in which Arcturus is the brightest star), and Ursa Major, the Great Bear

Evidence indicates that the Hebrew word translated "Arcturus" actually designates the constellation of Ursa Major, the Great Bear, and that "his sons" are the individual stars of this constellation, possibly the seven brighter ones composing the Big Dipper.

Arcturus (ärk-tū′rŭs). [Heb. *'ash* and *'ayish.*] An astronomical term occurring in Job 9:9; 38:32; KJV. The Hebrew words cannot be identified with certainty. Some think they represent the Great Bear (see RSV), others, Leo the Lion. "Arcturus" is a Latinized word borrowed from the Greek *Arktouros,* "Bear Keeper," the first-magnitude star that appears to follow the con-

25. Athens: The Areopagus in the left center foreground, with the Acropolis behind

stellation known as the Great Bear in its daily circuit of the northern heavens.

Ard (ärd), and **Ardites** (är′dīts). [Heb. *'Ard* and *'Ardî. 'Ard* means "humpbacked."] Ard was a grandson of Benjamin, and founder of the Benjamite family, the Ardites (Gen 46:21; Num 26:40). The *Addar of 1 Chr 8:3 is probably identical with Ard, the difference in spelling possibly resulting from a transposition of the *r* and *d,* very similar in postexilic Hebrew.

Ardites. *See* Ard.

Ardon (är′dŏn). [Heb. *'Ardôn,* possibly "humpbacked." The name occurs in Akkadian as *Urdanu.*] A man of Judah (1 Chr 2:18).

Areli (à-rē′lī). [Heb. *'Ar'elî,* meaning uncertain. The name appears on line 13 of the *Moabite Stone (*BASOR* 89 [1943], 16, note 55).] A son of Gad and founder of a clan (Gen 46:16; Num 26:17).

Arelites (à-rē′līts). [Heb. *'Ar'elî,* meaning uncertain.] Members of the clan founded by *Areli (Num 26:17).

Areopagite (ăr′ē-ŏp′à-jīt). [Gr. *Areopagitēs.*] A member of the council, or court, of the *Areopagus at Athens. Its members, elected for life, were chosen from the wealthiest and most aristocratic families, and from early times included ex-archons. Hence any Areopagite (like Dionysius in Acts 17:34, a convert of Paul at Athens) is known to have been a highly respected person, belonging to the elite of the city.

Areopagus (ăr′ē-ŏp′à-gŭs). [*Areios pagos,* from *Arēs,* "Mars," and *pagos,* "hill."] The name of a barren, rocky hill northwest of the Acropolis of ancient Athens, indicating that the hill was dedicated to Ares, the god of war (called Mars by the Romans), hence the translation "Mars' hill" (Acts 17:22). The limestone ridge, rising 50 to 60 ft. above the valley that lies be-

26. The Areopagus as seen from the Acropolis, with the agora in the right center

tween it and the Acropolis, has an elevation of 370 ft. above sea level. From the time of the kingdom it was the seat of a high court of justice which had jurisdiction over certain crimes, including religious offenses. The status and authority of this council of the Areopagus was not always the same during the history of Athens, but under the Roman administration it was more powerful than it had been before for some time. Among its powers was that of licensing teachers and the control of education. It remained in existence until about A.D. 400. The court conducted trials in the Stoa Basileios in the agora, the "marketplace." This was its official seat, and in it were its administrative offices. Sentences, however, were pronounced from the hill, to which the court for that purpose adjourned. (On the members of this court *see* Areopagite.)

Commentators have variously understood Luke's statement that the apostle Paul was taken "unto Areopagus" (Acts 17:19) to defend his teachings. It has been held: (1) that Paul was taken to the hill so that from its elevated position he could better be understood by a greater number of people than in the crowded agora; (2) that Paul was taken to the council of the Areopagus in the Stoa Basileios since the philosophers wanted to attribute a greater significance to Paul's speech than would have been given to it if it had been delivered in the open market place (this view was first propounded by E. Curtius, "Paulus in Athen," *Sitzungsberichte der Akademie* [Berlin, 1893], part 2, pp. 925-938); (3) that Paul had to appear for examination before this body in the Stoa Basileios in order to receive a license as a foreign professor. This last view was held by Sir William Ramsay (*St. Paul the Traveller and the Roman Citizen* [London, 1896], pp. 243-247). Al-

though it is not easy to account for the change of locality from the agora to the Areopagus, Curtius' and Ramsay's views have not found wide support, because the scene is not a judicial procedure, and the philosophers of his day were not much impressed by him. The strongest argument in favor of Paul's actually delivering his speech on the hill below the Acropolis, and not in the council chamber in the agora, is the statement in v 19 that they brought him *"epi ton Areion pagon,"* the *epi* having more the meaning "upon" than "into" or "unto." Hence, the first of the three views listed above may be considered as the most plausible.

Aretas (ăr'ĕ-tăs). [Gr. *Haretas,* a transliteration of the Aramaic *Chârithath,* a name appearing in Nabataean inscriptions.] The 4th of 4 Nabataean kings of that name. His capital was Petra, south of the Dead Sea. The 4 were Aretas I (*c.* 170 B.C.), Aretas II (*c.* 96 B.C.), Aretas III (*c.* 18 B.C.), and Aretas IV (9 B.C. to A.D. 40). The daughter of Aretas IV was married to Herod Antipas, who sent her away when he fell in love with Herodias. Aretas thereupon fought a war of revenge against Antipas, and occupied sections of Perea, east of the Jordan. Upon Antipas' appeal to Tiberius for help, the emperor sent Vitellius, the governor of Syria, to punish Aretas. But Tiberius died and the expedition was not carried out. Caligula seems to have been friendly toward Aretas, and to have given him control of Damascus, which was then administered by an ethnarch in Aretas' name (2 Cor 11:32). The period of Nabataean occupation of Damascus was doubtless between Tiberius' death in A.D. 37 and the death of Aretas in A.D. 40.

Argob (är'gŏb). [Heb. *'Argob,* meaning unknown.]

1. According to the KJV of 2 Ki 15:25 either a fellow conspirator of Pekah against King Pekahiah or one slain along with Pekahiah. However, the Hebrew text is not clear and it is possible that Argob is the name of an area (*see* Argob, 2), and that the name really belongs in v 29.

2. A region in Bashan in northern Transjordan. According to Deut 3:14 it bordered on Geshur and Maacah, and had 60 walled cities within its boundaries (v 4). It was taken from Og, the king of Bashan, in Moses' time (vs 4, 13, 14), and in Solomon's time formed a subdistrict of one of the 12 administrative areas into which the kingdom was divided for tax purposes (1 Ki 4:13). The identifica-

tion of this area is still uncertain. The Targum puts it in Trachonitis, which places it too far to the northeast; Josephus indicates that a portion of Argob was Gaulonitis (*Ant.* viii. 2. 3). Many divergent modern identifications have been suggested, but none is conclusive. It is safe to say only that the area lay somewhere near the river Yarmuk (Map VI, C-4/5).

Lit.: Dussaud, *Topographie*, 324; Abel, *Géographie* I, 275; Noth, *PJB* 37 [1941], 97, 98.

Aridai (á-rĭd'á-ī). [Heb. *'Ariday,* meaning uncertain, probably a Persian name.] One of Haman's ten sons (Est 9:9).

Aridatha (á-rĭd'á-thá). [Heb. *'Arîdatha',* meaning uncertain, probably a Persian name.] One of Haman's ten sons (Est 9:8).

Arieh (á-rī'ĕ). [Heb. *Ha-'aryeh,* "the lion."] According to the KJV of 2 Ki 15:25 either a fellow conspirator of Pekah against King Pekahiah or one slain along with Pekahiah. However, the Hebrew text is not clear, and it is possible that Arieh is the name of an area, and that the name really belongs in v 29.

Ariel (ár'ĭ-ĕl). [Heb. *'Arî'el,* meaning uncertain. The definitions "lion of God" and "altar hearth" have been proposed. Some see in the word a derivation of the Akkadian *arallu,* which means "underworld" as well as "mountain of the gods." It appears on the *Moabite Stone (line 12) as the personal name of an Israelite chieftain who was captured by King Mesha of Moab and dragged before his god Chemosh (*ANET* 320).]

1. A transliteration of the Heb. *'arî'el* (2 Sa 23:20, RSV), a word of uncertain meaning. The KJV translates the term "lionlike man."

2. A chief of the Jews who assisted Ezra in soliciting Levites and other lower Temple personnel to join those returning from Babylon to Jerusalem (Ezr 8:16).

3. An otherwise unknown name, apparently of a part of Jerusalem (Is 29:1, 2, 7). The Dead Sea scroll 1QIsᵃ, however, reads *'rw'l,* which can be pronounced *'Uru'el,* and therefore has been explained as another form of the name Jerusalem (*BiOr* 14 [1957], 43).

Arimathea (ár'ĭ-má-thē'á). [Gr. *Arimathaia.*] A Palestinian town or village, the home of a certain Joseph in whose tomb Jesus was buried (Mt 27:57-60; Mk 15:43; Lk 23:50-53; Jn 19:38). The site cannot be identified with certainty. The following names are suggested as possible OT equivalents: Ramah, Ramath, Ramathaim, or Ramathaim-zophim. See Map XVI, D-2.

Arioch (ăr'ĭ-ŏk). [Heb. and Aramaic *'Aryôk.*]

1. King of Ellasar, who under Chedorlaomer invaded Transjordan in Abraham's time (Gen 14:1, 9). As long as *Amraphel was identified with Hammurabi, it was thought that Arioch could be identified with Warad-Sin, king of Larsa (see Map III, C-6). This was done on the basis that the Akkadian of the name Warad-Sin means "servant of (the moon-god) Sin." It was thought that the name Arioch could be explained to consist of the Sumerian word *eri,* "servant," and the Elamite word *aku,* "moon," so that Arioch, like Warad-Sin, would mean also "servant of the Moon (god)." This identification has been given up by most scholars, since Warad-Sin's name is never attested in this hybrid Sumerian-Elamite combination Eri-Aku, and also because Warad-Sin was not even a contemporary of Hammurabi. In view of these objections some suggested that Arioch be identified with Rim-Sin. Although Rim-Sin was a contemporary of Hammurabi, it is even more difficult to equate his name with Arioch. The name Arioch has now been found in the cuneiform texts from Mari on the Euphrates (see Map III, C-5) in the form of *Arriwuk,* as the name of the fifth son of Zimri-Lim, king of Mari in the 18th cent. B.C. However, *Arriwuk* lived at least a century after the events recorded in Gen 14, and so cannot be identified with the Biblical Arioch. But the occurrence of that name in inscriptions from. the patriarchal period is significant.

2. Captain of Nebuchadnezzar's guard, whom the king ordered to slay all the wise men of Babylon (Dan 2:14, 15, 24).

Arisai (á-rĭs'á-ī). [Heb. *'Arîsay,* meaning uncertain, probably a Persian name.] One of Haman's sons (Est 9:9).

Aristarchus (ăr'ĭs-tär'kŭs). [Gr. *Aristarchos,* "best ruling," a widely occurring Greek personal name as attested by inscriptional evidence.] A Christian companion of Paul, from Thessalonica in Macedonia. He was in Ephesus when the riot against Paul broke out, and was dragged by the mob into the theater (Acts 19:29), but apparently was not seriously hurt. We find him again in Paul's 3d Missionary Tour traveling from Greece to Jerusalem (ch 20:4). He also went with Paul to Rome (ch 27:2), probably as a personal servant of the apostle, since a political prisoner who was a Roman citizen, like Paul, had the right to be accompanied by a servant in addition to a personal physician, which place was taken by Luke. Hence we find Aristarchus mentioned in the prison epistles (Phm 24; Col 4:10) as being with the apostle as a "fellowlabourer" and a "fellow-prisoner."

Aristobulus (*à-rĭs′tö-bū′lŭs*). [Gr. *Aristoboulos,* meaning "well advised." The name is widely attested and was borne by many Greeks and Jews, among whom were 3 Maccabeans.] An inhabitant of Rome to whose household Paul sent greetings (Rom 16:10). It has been suggested that he may have been Herod the Great's grandson who lived in Rome as a friend of the emperor Claudius, and in whose household there may have been some Christians.

Ark, I. [Heb. *'arón,* "ark," "chest," "box"; Gr. *kibōtos,* "ark."] The chest or ornate box that served as the depository for the tables of stone on which were engraved the Ten Commandments. It was housed in the Most Holy Place of the sanctuary of ancient Israel's tabernacle (Ex 26:34; 30:6) and, later, of the Temple (1 Ki 8:6). It was 2½ cu. long, 1½ cu. wide, and 1½ cu. high (Ex 25:10), or, if measured by the Egyptian cubit, about 4 ft. 4 in. long and 2 ft. 7 in. in breadth and height. The ark was constructed of acacia wood and overlaid, inside and out, with pure gold (Ex 25:10-22). Two golden rings on each side at the bottom enabled the ark to be carried on two poles borne on the shoulders of the Kohathite Levites when Israel moved (Num 3:29-31; 4:5-15; Jos 3:3) and on certain solemn occasions (Jos 8:33; 1 Ki 8:2, 3). On the solid gold lid, which has been called the mercy seat, stood two golden cherubim, one on either end, looking down at the place where Jehovah dwelt when He spoke to His people (Num 7:89; Ex 25:22).

The ark was the central object of all the furnishings of the sanctuary. At first it contained only the stone tablets of the Ten Commandments (Ex 25:21; Deut 10:3, 5); but later Aaron's rod that budded, a pot of manna, and the "book of the law" were placed "before the testimony" or "in the side of" the ark (Ex 16:33, 34; Num 17:10; Deut 31:24-26). The first two items may actually have been preserved inside of the ark (Heb 9:4), but were apparently removed at a later period in the troubled history of Israel, as the author of Kings indicates (1 Ki 8:9).

As Israel journeyed from Sinai toward the Promised Land, the ark "went before them" (Num 10:33). Its bearers stood in the midst of Jordan's parted waters while

the people passed over (Jos 4:9-11). The ark was carried 7 days around Jericho in the march that preceded the city's fall (ch 6:1-20). After the conquest of Canaan it remained in the tabernacle in Shiloh (ch 18:1), apparently until captured in the time of Eli. In the hope that the ark's presence would turn the tide of war against the Philistines, Eli's sons, neglecting to consider the conditions under which God cooperates with men, carried it into battle, only to have it captured by the enemy (1 Sa 4:1-11). It was returned to Hebrew territory (chs 5:1 to 6:15) and resided successively at Bethshemesh (ch 6:15-21), Kiriath-jearim (ch 7:1, 2), and in the house of Obed-edom at Perez-uzzah (2 Sa 6:1-11; 1 Chr 13:5-14). David finally removed the ark to Jerusalem (2 Sa 6:12-17; 1 Chr 15:25 to 16:1), where it was placed "in the midst of the tabernacle that David had pitched for it" (2 Sa 6:17; 7:1, 2; 1 Chr 16:1, 4-6). Later it was placed in the Most Holy Place of Solomon's Temple (1 Ki 8:1-9), where it remained until the destruction of Jerusalem by Nebuchadnezzar. The Scriptures are silent concerning its fate at that time or its subsequent history.

Ark, II. [Heb. *tebah,* "ark," "boat," "vessel," "chest," a loan word from Egyptian *ḏb3t. Tebah* is used only in Moses' writings. Gr. *kibōtos,* "ark."]

1. In the narrative of Gen 6:14 to 9:18 the boat or vessel built by Noah under divine direction, to house his family and preserve alive pairs of the animal species during the Deluge that overwhelmed the world. The ark was 300 cu. long, 50 cu. broad, and 30 cu. high (ch 6:15), built of *gopher wood, and was made watertight with pitch or bitumen (v 14). There were 3 stories, or decks, of rooms, and the entrance was by way of a door in the side (v 16). The ark's "window" (Heb. *sohar*) was probably its roof. Its "covering" (Heb. *mikseh*), which after the Flood was removed to facilitate a better view of the receding waters (ch 8:13), was probably a portion of the roof. *Mikseh* is used in Ex 26:14 to designate the roof of the tabernacle, and in Num 4:10-12 to designate the covers placed over the sanctuary furniture while it was being transported. Since these coverings were made of skins, some have suggested that the covering of the ark was also of the same material.

2. The basket, made of bulrushes or papyrus and smeared with pitch for watertightness, in which the infant Moses

was hidden along the Nile by his mother (Ex 2:3-6).

Arkites (är′kīts), KJV **Arkite** (är′kīt). [Heb. *'Arqî*.] Descendants of Canaan (Gen 10: 17; 1 Chr 1:15), and natives of a Syrian coast city (Map IV, B-5). Their city is mentioned as early as the Egyptian execration texts of the 19th and 18th cents. B.C. as *'3ktm* and *'3ktî*, and in the annals of Thutmose III as a conquered Phoenician coast city, spelled *'rkt*. The *Amarna Letters call this city *Irqata*, and Tiglath-pileser III of Assyria speaks of it as a captured city, calling it *Arqa* (*ANET* 283). It has been identified with the present *Tell 'Arqah* north of Tripoli, in the plain of the mouth of the *Nahr el-Kebîr* (the Eleutherus). Archeological remains show that the city was inhabited in the 3d and 2d millenniums B.C.

Armageddon (är′má-gĕd′ŭn). [Gr. *Harmagedōn*, variant *Harmageddōn*, a composite transliteration from the Hebrew. Opinions differ as to what Hebrew words the Greek transliteration represents. The first component, *Har-*, means "mountain." The second component, *-magedōn*, may be from the Heb. *Megiddô* or *Megiddôn* (1 Ki 9:15; 2 Chr 35:22; Zec 12:11), the city of Megiddo, or possibly, though improbably, from *mô'ed*, the word commonly used throughout the OT for "congregation" (Ex 27:21; etc.), "assembly," or "place of assembly" (Lam 1:15; 2:6). In Is 14:13 *Har-mo'ed* is translated "mount of the congregation" or "mount of assembly," and designates the hill on which the "king of Babylon" aspired to sit. Megiddo would be reminiscent of Israel's dramatic victory over the Canaanites at the waters of Megiddo (Jgs 5:19).]

The cryptic designation of the battlefield to which the kings of earth are gathered for "the battle of that great day of God Almighty" (Rev 16:14, 16). In popular modern usage "Armageddon" designates any great military conflict involving the nations of earth, usually without reference to the setting of the term in Bible prophecy. The drying up of the "Euphrates" and the gathering of the nations to "Armageddon" both take place under the 6th of the 7 last plagues (vs 12, 16; cf. ch 17:16), as the result of the outpouring of the 6th vial and the miracle-working activities of the "three unclean spirits like frogs" representing the dragon, the beast, and the false prophet (ch 16: 12-14). The fact that no mention is made of the fighting of the "battle of that great day of God Almighty" under the 6th

plague implies that the battle itself takes place later—during the 7th plague—under which "great Babylon" receives "the cup of the wine of the fierceness of his [God's] wrath" (v 19). The additional fact that ancient Babylon was situated on the river Euphrates implies a close relationship, in the symbolism of the Revelation, between the Euphrates of the 6th plague and the city Babylon of the 7th plague. In context, vs 16 and 17 imply further that as soon as the nations have been gathered to "Armageddon" the 7th angel pours out his vial, and the decree, "It is done," issues from God's throne (v 17). With the gathering of the nations at Armageddon, rebellion on earth reaches its climax and God intervenes to execute "the fierceness of his wrath" upon apostate Babylon and to bring deliverance to His own people (chs 16:19; 17:14; 18:20; 19:2).

The great battle of the day of God is described in greater detail in Rev 17:11-18 and 19:11-21. In ch 17 the kings of the earth are represented as allied with Babylon the great in her work of persecuting the saints (vs 1-6, 12, 13), by doing which they "make war with the Lamb" in His role as "Lord of lords, and King of kings" (v 14; cf. ch 19:16). In this role He overcomes the coalition of kings who, realizing that they have suffered defeat (ch 17: 14), turn upon Babylon and destroy her (vs 16, 17). John presents a highly figurative description of this event in ch 18: 4-24. A song of victory over Babylon occupies the opening verses of ch 19. Christ then takes His kingdom and the figurative "marriage of the Lamb" is consummated (vs 7-10). In vs 11-21, Christ's role in this last great battle—as "King of kings, and Lord of lords" (v 16)—is set forth. He comes forth from heaven to "smite the nations . . . with a rod of iron" and to tread "the winepress of the fierceness and wrath of Almighty God" (v 15). In v 19—as in chs 16:13-16 and 17:12-14—the kings of the earth are "gathered together to make war" against Christ, but suffer defeat (ch 19:19-21). The utter terror of these "kings" upon finding themselves face to face with "him that sitteth on the throne" is graphically described in ch 6:15-17, where Christ is again referred to as "the Lamb," and the occasion as "the great day of his wrath." See Babylon.

As with symbols generally throughout the book of Revelation, the figurative language associated with the "battle of that great day of God Almighty" of Rev

16:12-16 is based on OT historical parallels that depict ancient Babylon as preeminently the great oppressor of God's chosen people (see Jer 50:11; etc.). *See* Babylon; *SDACom* 7:828-830, 866-869. As in ancient times the literal city of Babylon "sat" upon the waters of the river Euphrates (Jer 51:12, 13, 63, 64), so mystical Babylon, "that great city," sits "upon many waters" (Rev 17:1), which are identified in v 15 as "peoples, and multitudes, and nations, and tongues" (see vs 1, 2, 18; cf. ch 16:12, 19). As ancient Babylon persecuted God's people, so mystical "Babylon the great" is pictured as "drunken with the blood of the saints, and with the blood of the martyrs of Jesus" (ch 17:6). As anciently "the Lord of hosts" mustered the nations of earth as "the weapons of his indignation, to destroy the whole land" of Babylon upon "the day of the Lord" (Is 13:4-22; cf. Jer 25:32-38), and raised "up against Babylon an assembly of great nations" that "set themselves in array against her" (Jer 50:9), so in the book of Revelation it is the nations of earth that carry out God's decree of vengeance against mystical Babylon (Rev 16:13-16; cf. chs 17:12-17; 19: 2; cf. vs 18-21). Similarly, the figurative drying up of the river Euphrates (ch 16: 12) is doubtless based on Isaiah's prophetic description of Cyrus—as God's "servant"—drying up the literal river Euphrates in order to take the city of Babylon and to release God's people from captivity (see Is 44:26 to 45:13). See further *SDACom* 7:842-848.

Armenia. *See* Ararat.

Armlet. A rendering of: (1) The Heb. *ṣeʻadah,* "an ornamental bracelet or chain" (Is 3:20, RSV). It is uncertain whether this was worn on the arm or the ankle. Some suggest it was a chain worn between the ankles designed to compel the wearer to take short steps. The article taken from Saul's body was probably a bracelet (2 Sa 1:10). (2) The Heb. *kûmaz,* a female ornament. Some suggest breastplates, others a bracelet probably worn higher on the arm than the wrist (Ex 35:22, KJV "tablets"; Num 31:50, KJV "chains").

Armoni (är-mō′nī). [Heb. *'Armoni,* "palace man."] A son of Saul and his concubine Rizpah. He was hanged by the Gibeonites, with the consent of David (2 Sa 21:8, 9), in revenge for the cruelties committed by Saul upon the Gibeonites.

Armor. Equipment worn to defend its wearer against offensive weapons. The OT does not have a collective word like the Gr. *hoplon* covering all kinds of armor and weapons, although it sometimes uses the word *kelim* in the sense of weapons. The Biblical writers represent God as destroying the weapons of men (Ps 46:9). He is even represented as a fully armed warrior (Is 42:13), although the weapons He employs for the benefit of His children are spiritual and not material (Is 59:17; Ps 7:12, 13; 91:4). Paul compares missionary work to military service, and speaks of having a defensive armor which he uses to good effect (2 Cor 6:7; 10:4). He encourages every Christian to put on this kind of armor (Rom 13:12-14; Eph 6: 10-17).

For the different parts of armor, *see* Boot; Coat of Mail; Greaves; Helmet; Shield.

Armoury. *See* Arsenal.

Army. Israel had no standing army before the time of the kings. During the wilderness wanderings all able-bodied men, except the Levites, at the age of 20 years and above were automatically members of the citizen army (Num 1:2, 3), consisting at that time only of foot soldiers (ch 11:21). The Levites, though exempt from military service (ch 1:45-50), were assigned armed duties on special occasions (1 Chr 12:23, 26-28). The soldiers were usually divided into spearmen, slingers, and archers (*see* Arrow; Bow; Sling; Spear) according to the weapons they handled. The army was organized on the basis of the political divisions of Israel, of which the largest unit below the tribe was "the thousand" or a "father's house," or the "clan," these larger units being subdivided into hundreds, fifties, and tens (see Ex 18:25; Num 1:2, 16; Deut 1:15; etc.). We find similar military divisions later (Num 31:5; 2 Sa 18:1) in Israelite history.

The same organization was probably continued during the period of the judges. In times of national peril the recognized leaders of the people, the judges, sent messengers through the country and called up the men of war from the various tribes (Jgs 6:34, 35; 19:29 to 20:2; 1 Sa 11:7). As soon as the danger was past or the victory gained and the invading enemy expelled, all the people dispersed again and returned to their homes. Apparently the army had no supply corps during that time; every soldier carried his own equipment and secured his own provisions by foraging or as occasion offered (cf. 1 Sa 17:17, 18).

27. Ancient model of an Egyptian army corps consisting of Sudanese soldiers

What was apparently the first standing army, a force of 3,000 men, was organized by Saul (1 Sa 13:2), although for special occasions he called up the whole nation (ch 11:7). His regular army seems to have been composed of men of marked valor pressed into the service (ch 14:52). During his reign and that of David there was no chariotry, such as the Canaanites and other surrounding nations had used for centuries. The army remained purely an infantry force. This is evident from the fact that David lamed the captured horses of defeated enemies (2 Sa 8:4), apparently having no use for these animals himself. Solomon, however, organized the army according to the pattern of the Egyptians, by adding a large force of chariots (see Chariot), for which garrison cities were built throughout his kingdom (1 Ki 9:19; 10:26; 2 Chr 9:25). When Ahab joined several Syrian armies fighting against Shalmaneser at Qarqar in 853 B.C., the northern kingdom could muster 2,000 chariots and 10,000 foot soldiers (ANET 279a). Later, cavalry units seem to have been organized after the Assyrian pattern (2 Ki 13:7). Some of the Hebrew kings made special efforts to maintain a large army for defensive and offensive purposes, as, for example, Jehoshaphat (2 Chr 17:13-19), Amaziah (ch 25:5, 6), and Uzziah (ch 26:11-15). During the period of the kings there was also a well-trained officer corps. Several brilliant generals such as Abner, Saul's general, and Joab, the general of David, are known by name. There were secretaries who took care of the conscription of soldiers (2 Ki 25:19; 2 Chr 26:11) and probably also the record of booty.

Some of the kings employed a bodyguard, mainly composed of foreign mercenaries (2 Sa 8:18; 1 Ki 1:38; 2 Ki 11:4, 7, 8, 19, RSV). In doing this they followed a practice of the Egyptian kings of the later dynasties. See Carites; Cherethites; Pelethites.

Much of what has been said about the organization of the Hebrew army during the period of the kings applies also to the armies of other nations mentioned in the OT. The Egyptian army was composed of professionals from the beginning of the 18th dynasty (c. 1570 B.C.), when it consisted of large forces of infantry and chariotry, organized into divisions. Engineers and a quartermaster corps were attached to each unit. The Assyrians created large units of cavalry and invented special techniques to storm fortified cities by means of battering rams and other war machines. Their army became the most perfectly organized instrument of warfare ever conceived in ancient times. The Babylonian army probably continued the Assyrian organization, traditions, and methods of warfare. For the Roman armies see Centurion; Cohort; Legion.

Arnan (är′năn). [Heb. *'Arnan,* meaning uncertain.] A descendant of David (1 Chr 3:21).

Arni (är′nĭ). [Gr. *Arni.* The Greek text on which the KJV is based reads *Aram,* hence the KJV reading Aram.] The NT equivalent of the OT Ram in the genealogy of Jesus (Lk 3:33).

Arnon (är′nŏn). [Heb. *'Arnôn.* The name is probably connected with *'oren,* "laurel," and may mean " (The river) bordered by laurel bushes."] One of the main rivers of Transjordan, formed by several smaller tributaries, mentioned as "the brooks of Arnon" (Num 21:14, KJV). It flows through a tremendous canyon into the Dead Sea (Map VI, F-4). The valley is now called the *Wâdī el-Môjib.* In pre-Mosaic times it formed the boundary between the Moabites in the south and the Amorites in the north (Num 21:13), and during the early history of Israel the boundary between Moab and the tribe of

28. The canyon of the river Arnon as seen from the northern rim

29. Sunset over the Dead Sea from the canyon of the Arnon

74

Reuben (Deut 3:16; Jos 13:16). Later, according to the *Moabite Stone, the Moabites established themselves north of the Arnon and occupied Israelite territory.

Arod (ā'rŏd), or **Arodi** (ăr'ŏ-dī). [Heb. *'Arôd,* "humpbacked" and *'Arôdî.*] A son of Gad, and founder of the family of Arodites (Gen 46:16; Num 26:17).

Arodi. *See* Arod.

Arodites (ăr'ŏ-dīts). [Heb. *'Arôdî.*] Descendants of Arod (Num 26:17).

Aroer (à-rō'ēr). [Heb. *'Arô'er,* "juniper."]
1. A town on the northern bank of the Arnon, which in Moses' time was the southern border of the Amorite kingdom of Sihon of Heshbon (Deut 2:36; Jos 12: 2; Jgs 11:26). After its conquest by the Israelites it was assigned to the tribe of Reuben (Jos 13:15, 16), but the people of Gad rebuilt and occupied it (Num 32: 34). Mesha of Moab wrested it from Israel and fortified it (*Moabite Stone, line 26). Hazael of Damascus conquered it a little later (2 Ki 10:32, 33), but it reverted to Moab according to Jeremiah (Jer 48:19, 20). The site is now called *'Arâ'ir,* and lies a short distance south of Dibon, to the east of the old Roman road (Map VI, F-4).
2. A town in Gilead on the frontier of Gad near Rabbah, by which probably Rabbath Ammon is meant (Jos 13:25; Jgs 11:33). The site has not been identified.
3. One of the places in southern Judah to whose inhabitants David sent spoil from his victory over the Amalekites after they had destroyed Ziklag during his absence (1 Sa 30:28). This place has been identified at *'Ar'arah,* 12 mi. southeast of Beer-sheba (Map VIII, F-2).
4. A city apparently in the country of the kingdom of Damascus, according to the Hebrew text of Is 17:2. The LXX translators did not take *'arô'er* as a proper noun, but probably read *'areha,* which means "her [that is, Damascus'] cities," instead of *'aro'er.* A city by the name of Aroer in the area of Damascus is otherwise unknown.

Aroerite (à-rō'ēr-īt). [Heb. *'Aro'erî.*] A native of Aroer (1 Chr 11:44), probably *Aroer, 3.

Arpachshad (är-păk'shăd), NT **Arphaxad** (är-făk'săd). [Heb. *'Arpakshad;* Gr. *Arphaxad.*] Son of Shem and ancestor of Abraham; born two years after the Flood (Gen 10:22-24; 11:10-26; Lk 3:36; see Map IV, B-6). The country of *Arrapachitis* (Ptol. vi. 1. 2), between Lake Urmiah and Lake Van, was probably named after him.

Arpad (är'păd), KJV twice **Arphad** (är'făd). [Heb. *'Arpad,* spelled *'rpd* in an Aramaic inscription, and *Arpadda* in Akkadian records.] An important Aramaean city-state, 30 mi. north of Aleppo, now *Tell Erfâd* (Map XI, B-4). It is mentioned in the OT most often in connection with its destruction by the Assyrians (2 Ki 18:34; 19:13; Is 10:9; 36:19; 37:13; Jer 49:23). At first the Assyrians punished the state (Adad-ninari III in 806 B.C. and Ashurdan III in 754 B.C.), then Tiglath-pileser III in 740 B.C. conquered it and made it into an Assyrian province. In 720 B.C. Arpad rebelled against its overlords, but Sargon II quenched the uprising.

Arphad. *See* Arpad.

Arphaxad. *See* Arpachshad.

Array. Many passages (Jgs 20:20, 22, 33; 2 Sa 10:8, 9; etc.) speak of armies being put "in array." The Hebrew word employed is *'arak,* "to draw up in battle order." From *'arak* is derived the noun *ma'arakah,* "battle order" or "battle line" (1 Sa 4: 12; 17:20; etc.; RSV). Nothing is known about the battle formations of the ancient Hebrews or of the disposition of army groups for a battle.

Arrow. Ancient arrows consisted of (1) a point or head, in early times made of flint, later of bronze, and in Roman times of iron; (2) a shaft, mostly of cane, occasionally of polished wood; and (3) a feather at the end to hold the arrow on a straight course. The arrowhead was either inserted into the end of the shaft or socketed to receive the shaft. The earlier arrowheads were flat, but the later ones show triangular sections. The Assyrians invented the barbed arrows, a type difficult to remove from wounds. Soldiers carried their arrows in quivers of leather.

Arrows were sometimes dipped in poison (Job 6:4). Burning arrows were also used to set on fire the war equipment, the camp, or the city of the enemy. Heads from these incendiary arrows have been found and show holes through which tow saturated with oil was threaded.

30. Four arrowheads found in Palestine

The Bible frequently uses the term "arrows" in a figurative sense. God shoots the godless with His arrows (Deut 32:23, 42; Ps 7:13; 64:7). The servant of God compares himself with a polished arrow shaft (Is 49:2). Lightnings are called the Lord's arrows (Ps 144:6), and the "arrow that flieth by day" is possibly a figure for sunstroke (Ps 91:5). The NT mentions the fiery darts of Satan, which can be quenched with the "shield of faith" (Eph 6:16).

Arsenal. The translation in the RSV of the Heb. *talpîyôth* in Song 4:4 ("armoury," KJV). The Hebrew term is of uncertain meaning. A. M. Honeyman interprets it to mean "courses" (*JTS* 50 [1949], 51,

52), and B. S. J. Isserlin, agreeing with Honeyman, illustrates its meaning by referring to a sculpture of Arsos of Cyprus that shows a necklace of several layers (*PEQ* 90 [1958], 59, 60).

Artaxerxes (är'tăg-zûrk'sēz). [Heb. *'Artachshaste'*; Aramaic *'Artachshaste'* and *'Artachshaste'*; Old Persian *Artakhshatrâ*; Babylonian *Artakshatsu*. The name is spelled variously in these ancient languages, and the foregoing are only representative spellings. Best known is the Greek form *Artaxerxes*.] Artaxerxes I Longimanus (465-423 B.C.), king of Persia, 3d son and successor of Xerxes. Three kings bore the name Artaxerxes in Persian history, but only the 1st is men-

31. Tombs of Persian kings Artaxerxes I (left) and Darius I at *Naqsh-i-Rustam*, near Persepolis

tioned in Biblical history. Like his father, he was a weak ruler, easily influenced by courtiers and women, and spent most of his life in his various palace cities while the empire was ruled by trusted friends and relatives, and his military campaigns were carried out by his generals. According to Ezr 4:7-23, Artaxerxes once prohibited the rebuilding of Jerusalem. For a discussion of the problems involved in this narrative, and whether Artaxerxes I Longimanus is referred to, see *SDACom* 3:347-351. According to ch 7, Artaxerxes in his 7th regnal year (457 B.C. according to the Jewish civil year running 6 months later than the Persian) sent the Jewish scribe Ezra back to Jerusalem with extensive privileges to reorganize Judah's judicial and administrative structure as a Jewish state within the Persian Empire—in harmony with the Laws of Moses. Ezra also received generous financial support from the king, and a permit to lead back to Palestine all Jews who desired to return to their homeland. Several thousand exiles made use of this opportunity. Artaxerxes later appointed his Jewish cupbearer, Nehemiah, as governor of the province of Judah, and sent him to Jerusalem to complete the city wall, the rebuilding of which had run into difficulties because of the antagonism of Judah's neighboring nations (Neh 1; 2). This permit was given in the 20th year of Artaxerxes (444 B.C. by the same Jewish calendar). After Nehemiah had served as governor of Judea for 12 years he was recalled to the Persian court but later was allowed to serve a second term (chs 5:14; 13:6, 7). The arguments in favor of identifying the Artaxerxes of Ezr 7 and Neh 1 and 2 with Artaxerxes I are discussed in *SDACom* 3:369-374, 399, 400.

Artemas (är′tĕ-măs). [Gr. *Artemas,* a contracted form of *Artemidōros,* "gift of Artemis," a name attested by inscriptions.] A Christian worker whom Paul desired to send to Titus (Tit 3:12).

Artemis (är′tĕ-mĭs), KJV **Diana** (dī-ăn′á). [Gr. *Artemis,* named Diana by the Romans.] A goddess worshiped at Ephesus (Acts 19:24, 27, 28, 34, 35), more or less equivalent to Cybele, or to Magna Mater, the Great Mother, one of the many forms of the mother goddess of the Orient. As a goddess of fertility she was depicted as a woman whose upper body was covered with many breasts. Ancient replicas of her image have been found, and she is also depicted on coins. However, silver models of her temple, such as those made by Demetrius the silversmith and his fellow

32. Life-size statue of Artemis discovered at Ephesus

craftsmen (Acts 19:24), have not yet been discovered in excavations. The cult statue that originally stood in the temple dedicated to the goddess Artemis in Ephesus was made either of black olivewood, as some sources seem to indicate, or of a meteoric iron, as the city clerk seems to have believed, who said that her image had fallen from heaven (v 35). This goddess must not be confused with the Artemis of Greek mythology, the goddess of hunting, and the symbol of chastity and virginity, the twin sister of Apollo. Statues show the Greek goddess as a youthful, beautiful girl with a quiver on her shoulder, and a bow or a spear in her right hand, often accompanied by deer.

Artificer. A word used in the KJV to describe an artisan, skilled craftsman, deviser, or inventor. Tubal-cain was "an instructor of every artificer in brass and iron" (Gen 4:22). The people gave gold and silver in response to David's plea, that it might be fashioned by artisans for use in the Temple (1 Chr 29:5). In 2 Chr 34:11 the allusion to "timber for couplings" suggests that the artisans were carpenters. The "cunning artificer" was among those taken away from Jerusalem and Judah as part of the fruits of Judah's sins (Is 3:3).

Artillery. [Heb. *kelîm*.] A word occurring once in the KJV (1 Sa 20:40), in the sense of weapons of war. The word must not be construed in the sense of modern artillery. In this particular passage a bow and arrows are meant.

Artisans. Persons skilled in various handicrafts. The word does not occur in the KJV, and only once in the RSV (Jer 52:15), but the concept is implicit in many places in Scripture. Ancient Hebrew tradition decreed that every boy learn a trade. Adam was instructed as a gardener; Jesus was a carpenter; Paul, a tentmaker. Society in Bible times had its boatbuilders (2 Chr 9:21), brickmakers (Gen 11:3; Ex 5; Is 9:10), carpenters (2 Ki 22:6; Ezr 3:7; Is 41:7; Mk 6:3), fullers (Mal 3:2; Mk 9:3), masons (2 Sa 5:11; 2 Ki 12:12; 2 Chr 24:12), metal workers (Ex 25:31-39; 26:37), miners (Job 28:1, 2), potters (Jer 18:6), tanners (Acts 9:43), tentmakers (Acts 18:3), timber cutters (1 Ki 5:6, 15), weavers (Ex 36:8), etc. The social backgrounds of Bible narrative implied artisans of many other sorts, though not all are named—for example, harness makers, shoemakers, designers and builders of roads, aqueducts, etc.

Arubboth (*a-rŭb'ŏth*), KJV **Aruboth** (*a-rōō'-bŏth*). [Heb. *'Arubbôth*, "windows."] The city of residence of one of Solomon's supply officers to whose territory Socoh and Hepher belonged (1 Ki 4:10). The site has not been identified with certainty. Some seek it at *'Arrâbeh,* 2 mi. southwest of Dothan. Alt identifies it hesitatingly with *Bâqa el-Gharbîyeh* (*PJB* 28 [1932], 31, 32), with whom Kraeling agrees (*Rand McNally Bible Atlas,* p. 214; Map VIII, D-2).

Aruboth. *See* Arubboth.

Arumah (*a-rōō'má*). [Heb. *'Arûmah,* meaning uncertain.] A place near Shechem, for some time the residence of King Abimelech (Jgs 9:41). Some scholars believe it was identical with Rumah (2 Ki 23:36). The site has been identified with *el-'Ormeh,* about 6 mi. to the southeast of Shechem.

Arvad (*är'văd*) and **Arvadites** (*är'văd-īts*). [Heb. *'Arwad* and *'Arwadi.*] Arvad (classical Aradus, modern Ruad or Arwad) was a port city of northern Phoenicia, located on the island of *Ruad,* about 2 mi. off the mainland, about 30 mi. north of Tripolis and 125 mi. north of Tyre (Map III, C-4). The city is mentioned in the *Amarna Letters as *Arwada,* and in Assyrian inscriptions with various spellings: *Armada, Aruda, Aruadi,* etc. It is also depicted on the Assyrian bronze gates of Balawat. Its ancient history can be reconstructed from the Assyrian and Babylonian records. Ezekiel mentions the mariners and soldiers of Arvad as helping Tyre in its defense (Eze 27:8, 11). The Arvadites are listed in Gen 10:18 and 1 Chr 1:16 as descendants of Canaan.

Arvadites. *See* Arvad.

Arza (*är'zà*). [Heb. *'Arṣa',* possibly "delight."] Steward of King Elah's house in Tirzah. It was in this house that Zimri killed the intoxicated Elah (1 Ki 16:9, 10).

Asa (*ā'sà*). [Heb. *'Asa',* meaning uncertain. "Myrtle," "physician," and " (Yahweh) has healed," are conjectural definitions. Gr. *Asaph,* variant reading *Asa.*]

1. A Levite, son of Elkanah. He lived in a Netophathite village (1 Chr 9:16).

2. The 3d king of Judah, the southern kingdom, who reigned for 41 years (*c.* 911-*c.* 869 B.C.). He was a good king, and made strong efforts to purify the religion of his people. He removed his "mother" (actually grandmother), Maachah, the daughter of Absalom, from the powerful office of queen mother, because she had made an image to Asherah. Asa destroyed not only this image but also the idols of his predecessors and all strange altars and sun images. He cleared the country of its male cult prostitutes (*sodomites) and of many high places. The people continued to use the remaining high places for worship (1 Ki 15:9-14; 2 Chr 14:1-5; 15:16, 17). The first 10 years of his reign were peaceful, and were used to strengthen the country's fortifications and the army (2 Chr 14:1, 6-8). Hence he was ready for, and able to repulse, the invasion of Zerah and his great host of Africans (vs 9-15). In his 15th regnal year, with the help of the prophet Azariah, the son of Oded, he

carried out a great religious reformation. He rededicated the altar of burnt offering in the Temple and caused the people to renew their covenant with God (ch 15: 1-15). In the 36th year (probably the 36th year after the division of the kingdom) Baasha of Israel invaded Benjamin and began to fortify Ramah on the main road from Jerusalem to the north, thus blocking Judah's northern exit. Feeling that he was not strong enough to meet Baasha's threat by force, Asa offered Ben-hadad I of Damascus a heavy tribute as an inducement to attack Israel. Ben-hadad accepted the offer and forced Baasha to withdraw from Ramah. Asa then took the building material left by Baasha at Ramah and with it built Geba and Mizpah (1 Ki 15:16-22; 2 Chr 16:1-6). Asa's act of seeking foreign aid displeased God, who sent His prophet Hanani to reprove the king. Asa rejected this message and jailed Hanani. He also mistreated other well-meaning subjects during the latter part of his reign (2 Chr 16:7-10). The last years of his reign were marked by severe suffering through disease in his feet. During this time he apparently let his son Jehoshaphat act as coregent and take care of administrative duties. Asa was buried in a tomb that he had prepared for himself in Jerusalem (1 Ki 15: 23; 2 Chr 16:12-14).

Asahel (ăs'á-hĕl). [Heb. *'Asah'el*, "God has made."]

1. A son of David's sister Zeruiah, and a brother of Joab and Abishai (1 Chr 2: 16), a brave warrior and a swift runner (2 Sa 2:18; 23:24). He fell near Gibeon at the hand of Abner, who slew him in self-defense. His brothers nevertheless avenged his death (chs 2:12-23; 3:27-30). The statement that in the organization of David's army the 4th corps was put under "Asahel the brother of Joab, and Zebadiah his son after him" probably indicates that as an act of honor this corps was put under Asahel's name, and that his son Zebadiah acted for his dead father (1 Chr 27:7, KJV). It is also possible that the text refers to an arrangement that had been made before Asahel's death, and before the reorganization of the army recorded in 1 Chr 27.

2. A Levite who taught the people the law in Jehoshaphat's time (2 Chr 17:8).

3. An overseer in the Temple in the time of Hezekiah (2 Chr 31:13).

4. The father of one of Ezra's assistants named Jonathan (Ezr 10:15).

Asahiah. *See* Asaiah.

Asaiah (á-sā'yá), KJV twice **Asahiah** (ăs'á-hī'á). [Heb. *'Asayah*, "Yahweh has made."]

1. A Simeonite (1 Chr 4:36).

2. A Merarite Levite in David's time (1 Chr 6:30; 15:6, 11).

3. A high officer whom Josiah sent to the prophetess Huldah (2 Ki 22:12, 14; 2 Chr 34:20-22).

4. A Shilonite (1 Chr 9:5), believed to be identical with Maaseiah (Neh 11:5).

Asaph (ā'săf). [Heb. *'Asaph*, "gatherer," "collector," from the root *'asaph*, "to gather," "to collect." The name occurs on a Hebrew seal found at Megiddo.]

1. The son of Berachiah, a descendant of Gershom, a son of Levi (1 Chr 6:39, 43). Soon after David moved the ark of the covenant to Jerusalem, early in his reign over all Israel, he established that

33. Seal bearing the name Asaph, found at Megiddo (one and a half times actual size)

city as the center of the worship of Jehovah and reorganized Levitical and priestly ministries. In this reorganization certain of the Levites were assigned to provide vocal and instrumental music for the sacred services conducted in front of the sacred tent in which the ark was kept. Among them was Asaph, spoken of as both a singer and a player of cymbals (chs 15:19; 16:4-7). Asaph's sons and their descendants perpetuated the assignment made to their father (ch 25:1-9), and 128 of them returned to Jerusalem from Babylonian captivity (Ezr 2:41) to participate in the re-establishment of worship in the second Temple (ch 3:10). The superscriptions to 11 (Ps 73 to 83) of the 17 psalms in Book Three of the Psalms (Ps 73 to 89) contain the phrase "of Asaph" (see *SDACom* 3:616, 617, 626) as does Ps 50 in Book Two. In 2 Chr 29:30 Asaph is spoken of as a "seer."

2. The father of Hezekiah's recorder, Joah (2 Ki 18:18).

3. An official in charge of the royal forest in Palestine maintained by the Persian king Artaxerxes (Neh 2:8).

4. A son of Korah, elsewhere called Ebiasaph (1 Chr 26:1; cf. 6:37; 9:19).

Asareel. *See* Asarel.

Asarel (ăs′à-rĕl), KJV **Asareel** (à-sā′rĕ-ĕl). [Heb. *'Aśar'el,* meaning uncertain.] A Judahite (1 Chr 4:16).

Asarelah. *See* Asharelah.

Ascension. A technical term for the ascension of our Lord, which took place 40 days after the resurrection. By inclusive reckoning 40 days from a Sunday would end on a Thursday, which for centuries Christians have taken as the day of the ascension (Acts 1:3-11). The place from which Jesus ascended was the Mount of Olives (v 12), a spot in the vicinity of Bethany (Lk 24:50). The event was witnessed by the Eleven (Acts 1:12, 13) and possibly others. The ascension marks the close of our Lord's earthly ministry and the beginning of His ministry in heaven on our behalf (Heb 4:14-16; 9:24). As a historical event the ascension stands as an assurance that Christ will return to receive us (Acts 1:11; cf. Jn 14:1-3).

Ascent. The way by means of which one ascends. The word is used chiefly in a geographical sense such as in the phrases the "ascent of Akrabbim" (Num 34:4), the "ascent of Beth-horon" (Jos 10:10, RSV), meaning in modern terminology "the pass of Akrabbim," the "pass of Beth-horon." In two instances where the KJV reads "ascent" (1 Ki 10:5; 2 Chr 9:4) the reading should be "burnt offerings," as the Hebrew of 1 Ki 10:5 shows. *See* Ascents.

Ascents. [Heb. *ma'alôth,* "ascents," "steps," "goings up."] A term occurring in the titles "A Song of Ascents" appearing in the superscriptions to Psalms 120 to 134 (the KJV reads "A Song of degrees"). There is considerable uncertainty regarding the meaning of these titles. The Heb. *ma'alôth* literally means "ascents," "goings up," but its meaning in this passage is obscure. According to a certain tradition the Levites sang these psalms during the all-night feast of the first night of Tabernacles, on the 15 steps between the court of Israel and the court of the women. According to another, Levites stood with harps upon the 15 steps which go down from the court of Israel to the court of the women, corresponding in number with the 15 songs of Maaloth which are in the book of Psalms, while holy men repeated songs and praises.

Perhaps most plausible is the view that these psalms were sung by pilgrims on their ascent to Jerusalem (cf. Ps 122:4).

Asenath (ăs′ĕ-năth). [Heb. *'Asenath,* a transliteration of the Egyptian female name *Ns-Nît* or *'Iws-Nît,* both meaning "the one belonging to (the goddess) Neith."] The wife of Joseph, daughter of Potiphera, priest of On, or Heliopolis (Gen 41:45). She was the mother of Manasseh and Ephraim (chs 41:50-52; 46:20), the ancestors of two important Israelite tribes.

Aser. *See* Asher.

Ash. [Heb. *'oren.*] A tree used, among other things, to make household gods (Is 44:14). As the name of a tree *'oren* occurs only once in the OT and its identity is a matter of considerable doubt. Fir tree, pine, cedar, and laurel are some of the identifications that have been suggested.

Ashan (ā′shăn). [Heb. *'Ashan,* "smoke."] A Levitical town in the Shephelah, belonging to Judah, later assigned to Simeon (Jos 15:42; 19:7; 1 Chr 4:32). The site has been identified with *Khirbet 'Asan,* about 5 mi. northwest of Beer-sheba. It is not certain whether the Ashan of 1 Chr 6:59 is the same town or one called Ain as in Jos 21:16. If the reading Ashan in 1 Chr 6:59 is correct, then Ain in Jos 21:16 should be corrected to read Ashan. It is generally believed that the Bor-ashan (bôr′ăsh′ăn) [Heb. *Bôr-'ashan*] (KJV "Chor-ashan," kôr′ăsh′ăn) of 1 Sa 30:30 is the same town as Ashan.

Asharelah (ăsh′à-rē′là), KJV **Asarelah** (ăs′à-rē′là). [Heb. *'Aśar'elah,* meaning uncertain.] A son of the singer Asaph (1 Chr 25:2), also called Jesharelah (v 14).

Ashbea (ăsh′bĕ-à). [Heb. *'Ashbea',* "plenty."] According to the KJV the head of a family of the tribe of Judah (1 Chr 4:21). Members of this family were weavers of fine linen. Instead of "house of Ashbea" the RSV reads the place name "Beth-ashbea."

Ashbel (ăsh′bĕl). [Heb. *'Ashbel,* "(possessor of) a long upper lip."] A son of Benjamin and founder of a family (Gen 46:21; Num 26:38; 1 Chr 8:1). Apparently he was also called Jediael (1 Chr 7:6).

Ashbelite (ăsh′bĕl-īt). [Heb. *'Ashbeli.*] A family descended from *Ashbel.

Ashchenaz. *See* Ashkenaz.

Ashdod (ăsh′dŏd), NT **Azotus** (à-zō′tŭs). [Heb. *'Ashdôd;* Gr. *Azōtos.*] One of the famous 5 cities of the Philistines, situated about 3 mi. from the sea, about halfway between Joppa and Gaza (Map VI, E-2). It was an old Canaanite city, which in the time of Joshua was inhabited by the remnants of the Anakim, men of great stature (Jos 11:22). Although it was assigned to Judah, it was held by that tribe only briefly, the conquest of Ashdod by Uzziah being only a momentary success (2 Chr 26:6). As a Philistine city it was denounced by the prophets (Jer 25:20; Amos 1:8; Zep 2:4; Zec 9:6). Sargon II took the city in 711 B.C. (Is 20:1; *ANET* 285, 286), and made Ashdod the capital of the Assyrian province of *Asdudu*. Herodotus (ii. 157) claims that Psamtik I (663-609 B.C.) took Ashdod after a siege of 29 years. Only remnants of the population survived. Jer 25:20 may refer to this situation. During the Persian period the city once more gained in importance, and in Nehemiah's time took part in a coalition against the Jews (Neh 4:7, 8). Many Jews were attracted by the Ashdodites and married wives from among them (ch 13:23). The "speech of Ashdod" (v 24, KJV) was probably a local Aramaic dialect spoken in that city, although it is possible that the Philistinian language was still used. Judas Maccabeus and his brother Jonathan attacked the city and John Hyrcanus conquered it (1 Macc 5:68; 10:84; 11:4, 5; 16:10). Pompey made it a free city in 63 B.C. It is mentioned in Acts 8:40 by its Greek name *Azōtos*, as a city where the evangelist Philip was found after meeting the eunuch. The place is now called *Esdûd*.

Ashdodite (ăsh'dŏd-īt), KJV once **Ashdothite** (ăsh'dŏth-īt). [Heb. *'Ashdôdî*.] A native of Ashdod (Jos 13:3; Neh 4:7). In Jos 13:3 the RSV translates *'Ashdôdî* "those of . . . Ashdod."

Ashdothite. *See* Ashdodite.

Ashdoth-pisgah (ăsh'dŏth-pĭz'gà). [Heb. *'Ashdôth Happisgah*.] This phrase, found in three texts in the KJV (Deut 3:17; Jos 12:3; 13:20), should rather be rendered the "slopes of *Pisgah" as in the RSV.

Asher (ăsh'ẽr), KJV of NT **Aser** (ā'sẽr). [Heb. *'Asher*, "happy"; Gr. *Asēr*.]

1. The eighth son of Jacob by Zilpah, the maidservant of Leah (Gen 30:12, 13; 35:26). He had 4 sons and a daughter (Gen 46:17; 1 Chr 7:30), and became the founder of a tribe. *See* Asher, 2.

2. The tribe descended from Asher, 1. In the distribution of Palestine among the 12 tribes, Asher received the fertile strip of coastland north of Mount Carmel to the north of Sidon (Jos 19:24-31; Map VI, B, C-3). However, the tribe conquered and occupied its territory only partially, and was never able to drive out the inhabitants of Acco, Tyre, Sidon, and other

34. Ruins at Ashdod

Phoenician or Canaanite cities (Jgs 1:31). Its land was well adapted to olive culture, which seems to be referred to in the prophetic blessing Moses bestowed upon this tribe (Deut 33:24). Asher did not join the other tribes in their fight against Hazor in the time of the judges (Jgs 5:17).

Late-Egyptian texts and inscriptions from the time of Seti I (1319-1299 B.C.) and Ramses II (1299-1232 B.C.) speak of the hinterland of Phoenicia as *'Isr*, which may refer to Asher. It formed one of the districts in the time of Solomon into which the country was divided for tax purposes (1 Ki 4:16). The NT Anna, the prophetess in the Temple of Jerusalem, who recognized the infant Jesus as the redeemer of mankind, was of the tribe of Asher (Lk 2:36). Ezekiel included Asher among other tribes in his prophecy of Israel's restoration (ch 48). In vision John saw 12,000 Asherites sealed (Rev 7:6).

3. Possibly a town near Shechem (Jos 17:7); not identified. Some commentators take this Asher to be a reference to the territory of the tribe.

Asherah (à-shē'rà), plurals **Asherahs, Asherim** (à-shē'rĭm), and **Asheroth** (à-shē'rŏth), KJV **Grove, Groves.** [Heb. *'Asherah*, plurals *'Asherîm* and *'Asherôth;* Ugaritic *'Atrt.*]

1. A Phoenician goddess of vegetation, called "*'Atrt* of the Tyrians" in a Ugaritic text. Ugaritic literature refers to her also as the "Lady of the gods," the "Mistress of the gods," and as the mother of 70 deities, but her most distinctive title is "Asherat,

Lady of the Sea." In the *Amarna Letters she appears by the name '*Ashirtu* and '*Ashratu.* A Canaanite temple of the 18th or 17th cent. B.C. thought to have been dedicated to her was excavated at *Nahariya,* about 5 mi. north of Accho, close to the seashore. Here were found many figurines of doves, a silver figurine of a goddess, small offering vessels, and fragments of incense burners, all of which revealed the character of the cult practices in Asherah worship.

Asherah was the female counterpart of Baal, and her worship seems to have been especially attractive to the Hebrews. Her cult image was set up and worshiped in Jerusalem (1 Ki 15:13, RSV), as well as in Samaria (1 Ki 16:33; 2 Ki 13:6; 21:3), probably in the temple of Baal (2 Ki 10: 25). Under King Manasseh her image stood in the Temple of Jerusalem itself (ch 21:3, 7). Prophets were installed to serve her (1 Ki 18:19), and vessels needed for her cult are mentioned (2 Ki 23:4), while women were engaged to weave curtains for this goddess (v 7). Some passages mention the existence of more than one Asherah image besides Baal images (Jgs 3:7; 2 Ki 17:10; 2 Chr 19:3; 24:18; 33:3).
2. A cult object symbolizing Asherah.

35. The Mediterranean Sea viewed through the ruins of Ashkelon

When the goddess or her cult image is not meant, the word Asherah refers to a wooden pole or tree trunk which stood in Canaanite sanctuaries (Ex 34:13), dedicated to the goddess as a symbol of vegetation. The cult object was made (1 Ki 14:15), planted (Deut 16:21), or set up (2 Ki 17:10), could be burned (Deut 12:3; 2 Ki 23:6, 15), cut down (Ex 34:13; Deut 7:5; etc.), plucked up (Mic 5:14), or broken into pieces (2 Chr 34:4). See the tree trunks on the Elamite model of an open-air sanctuary, fig. 228.

Lit.: William L. Reed, *The Asherah in the Old Testament* (Fort Worth, Texas, 1949); I. Ben-Dor, "A Middle Bronze-Age Temple at Nahariya," *QDAP* 14 (1950), 1-41.

Asherim. *See* Asherah.

Asherite (ăsh'ĕr-īt). [Heb. '*Asheri.*] A descendant of Asher (Jgs 1:32).

Asheroth. *See* Asherah.

Ashes. Among the ancient Hebrews, to put on sackcloth and ashes, or to lie in them, or to sprinkle ashes on the head was a token of grief and mourning (2 Sa 13:19; Est 4:1, 3; Job 2:8; Neh 9:1). To sit in ashes was also a sign of penitence (Jon 3:6; cf. Job 42:6).

Ashhur (ăsh'ĕr), KJV **Ashur** (ăsh'ĕr). [Heb. '*Ashchur,* meaning uncertain.] A Calebite ancestor of the inhabitants of Tekoa (1 Chr 2:24; 4:5-7). It seems evident that he is the "father" of the town of Tekoa in the sense of the "founder" (cf. ch 2:50, 51). No Tekoa is listed as being among the sons of Ashhur (cf. ch 4:5-7). The Hebrews often used such terms as *"father," *"brother," *"son," or *"daughter" in a number of various meanings.

Ashima (à-shī'mà). [Heb. '*Ashima'.*] One of the gods of Hamath, introduced into Samaria by the Assyrian colonists (2 Ki 17: 30) upon their transplantation into the former territory of Israel by Sargon II. Attested (in Greek inscriptions) is a Syrian god *Semios* and a Syrian goddess *Sima* or *Sēmea* (Lidzbarski, *Ephemeris* II. 323; III. 247, 260-265), and in the Aramaic papyri from the Jewish colony of Elephantine a god '*shmbyt'l* appears (Cowley, *Aramaic Papyri,* No. 22, line 124), which may be pronounced *Ashim bethel.*

Ashimah (à-shī'mà). [Heb. '*Ashmah,* "guilt," emended to '*Ashima'.*] Variant spelling of *Ashima (Amos 8:14, RSV).

Ashkelon (ash'kĕ-lŏn), KJV sometimes **Askelon** (ăs'kĕ-lŏn). [Heb. '*Ashqelón.* The name appears in the Egyptian execration

texts as early as the 12th dynasty, spelled
'Iskȝnw. In the *Amarna Letters it appears
as *Ashqaluna,* and in Akkadian inscriptions as *Isqaluna.*] One of the 5 important cities of the Philistines, now *Khirbet
Asqalân,* about 12 mi. north of Gaza
(Map VI, E-2). It was conquered by the
tribe of Judah soon after the initial Hebrew conquest of Canaan (Jgs 1:18), but
the Israelites apparently did not hold
the city (see v 19). About 1280 B.C. Ramses II took the city, as shown on a relief
(see fig. 36). Later the Philistines took
the city at the time of the invasion of the
Sea Peoples. They held possession of it
(cf. Jos 13:3; Jgs 3:3; 14:19; 1 Sa 6:17;
2 Sa 1:20) until Tiglath-pileser III in
734 B.C. conquered the city, calling it
Isqaluna. In 701 B.C. Sennacherib subdued the city. Later it fell to Tyre, and in
the Maccabean period was hostile to the
Jews, but submitted to Jonathan (1 Macc
10:86; 11:60; 12:33). In 104 B.C. it became
a free city under the Roman Empire and
started its own era. Brief English excavations carried out in 1921 uncovered only
parts of the city of Roman times (John
Garstang, *QSPEF* 54 [1922], 112-119).
The Hebrew prophets spoke repeatedly
against the city (Jer 25:20; 47:5, 7; Amos
1:8; Zep 2:7; Zec 9:5).

Ashkenaz (ăsh′kĕ-năz), KJV twice **Ashchenaz**
(ăsh′kĕ-năz). [Heb. *'Ashkenaz.*] The eldest
son of Gomer, and grandson of Japheth
(Gen 10:3; 1 Chr 1:6). He was the ancestor of the *Ashkuza,* an Indo-European
people who lived southeast of Lake Urmiah in the time of Esarhaddon (681-
669 B.C.). See Map IV, B-7. The Ashkenian Lake in Phrygia is named for
them. Their king Bartatua married the
daughter of Esarhaddon, after Esarhaddon had received assurance from his sungod that the *Ashkuza* would remain loyal
to him. They joined the Assyrians in military campaigns against the Cimmerians
and the Medes. It is also recorded that
they unsuccessfully tried to bring relief
to Nineveh when it was besieged by the
Babylonians and the Medes in 612. After
the fall of Assyria the *Ashkuza* became
subject to Media. Jeremiah called on
them and on the kingdoms of Ararat,
Minni, and Media to destroy Babylon
(Jer 51:27, 28).

Ashnah (ăsh′nȧ). [Heb. *'Ashnah.*]
1. A place in Judah near Zorah in the
Shephelah (Jos 15:33), tentatively identified with *'Aslin,* a village between Zorah
and Eshtaol.

36. Egyptian temple relief showing the conquest of
Ashkelon by Pharaoh Ramses II

2. Another place in Judah (Jos 15:43),
identified with *Idhna,* 6 mi. from Hebron
on the way to Mareshah.

Ashpenaz (ăsh′pĕ-năz). [Heb. *'Ashpenaz.* The
name appears in the Aramaic incantation
texts from Nippur as *'spnz,* and is probably attested in cuneiform records as
Ashpazanda.] The chief of King Nebuchadnezzar's eunuchs (Dan 1:3).

Ashriel. *See* Asriel.

Ashtaroth (ăsh′tȧ-rŏth), KJV once **Astaroth**
(ăs′tȧ-rŏth). [Heb. *'Ashtarôth,* the plural
form of *'Ashtoreth,* the Canaanite goddess
Ashtoreth, or Astarte. The name (as that
of a city) appears first in the Egyptian
execration texts of the 18th cent. as
's[t]ȝtm. In the *Amarna Letters of the
14th cent. it appears as *Astarte,* and in the
inscription accompanying a stone relief
of Tiglath-pileser III (745-727 B.C.) as
Ashtartu (*ANEP* 128).] See fig. 37.
1. An ancient city of Bashan, the residence of King Og of Bashan. Though inhabited by giants, it was defeated by the
Israelites in Móses' time (Deut 1:4; Jos
9:10; 12:4; 13:12). The city was assigned
to Machir, a son of Manasseh (Jos 13:
31), and became a city of the Gershonite
Levites (1 Chr 6:71). Uzzia, one of David's
"mighty men," was a native of Ashtaroth
(ch 11:44). Ashteroth-karnaim, the city
smitten by Chedorlaomer and his confederates in the time of Abraham (Gen 14:5),

37. Stone relief of Tiglath-pileser III, depicting the city of Ashtaroth and the deportation of its citizens

is probably identical with Ashtaroth. The city has been identified with *Tell 'Ashtarah,* 21 mi. east of the Lake of Galilee (Map VI, C-5). Archeological remains show that the city was inhabited from before 2000 B.C. to the 1st millennium B.C.

2. The plural form of Ashtoreth, the Canaanite goddess. *See* Ashtoreth.

Ashterathite (ăsh'tĕ-răth-īt). [Heb. *'Ashterathî.*] A native of Ashtaroth (1 Chr 11:44).

Ashteroth-karnaim (ăsh'tĕ-rŏth-kär-nā'ĭm). [Heb. *'Ashterôth Qarnayim,* which some define as "the two-horned Ashtaroth," others, probably more correctly, as "Ashtaroth (which lies near) Karnaim."] A city conquered by Chedorlaomer and his confederates (Gen 14:5); probably identical with *Ashtaroth. *See* Karnaim.

Ashtoreth (ăsh'tô-rĕth). [Heb. *'Ashtoreth;* Phoenician *'Shtrt;* Moabitic *'Shtr;* Ugaritic *'Ttrt;* Akkadian *Ishtar;* and Egyptian *'Strt.*] A Semitic fertility goddess who was worshiped throughout the ancient East. In the OT she appears as the chief goddess of the Sidonians (1 Ki 11:5, 33; 2 Ki 23:13). She was the patron goddess of sexual love, maternity, and fertility. Images dedicated to her show her as a nude woman with the sex features grossly accentuated. Many figurines of the goddess have been found in Palestinian excavations, suggesting that they must have been carried by many people, presumably women, as charms or amulets. Prostitution as a religious rite was widely practiced in the service of this goddess.

The Greeks identified Ashtoreth with Aphrodite, clear evidence of her sexual character. In Assyria and Babylonia, Ishtar functioned also as goddess of war. The Philistines may also have considered Ashtoreth a war deity, as suggested by the removal of Saul's armor to her temple (1 Sa 31:10).

Her cult was already established in Transjordan in the days of Abraham, as the city name Asheroth-karnaim proves (Gen 14:5). By the time of the judges, Ashtoreth worship had been adopted by the Hebrews (Jgs 2:13; 10:6), and even Solomon fell to the charms of this goddess (1 Ki 11:5; 2 Ki 23:13).

The Hebrew pronunciation of the name represented by Ashtoreth varies from what is believed to be a correct pronunciation, Ashtareth. This has been explained by assuming that the Masoretes applied to the name the vowels of the Hebrew word *bosheth,* meaning "shame," to express their loathing for idolatry.

In his excavations of Bethel, W. F. Albright found a seal from the period of the judges with the name of the goddess *'Astart* engraved in Egyptian hieroglyphs

38. Cylinder seal found at Bethel, and its impression. The inscription reads *'Astart.* Approximate size

84

between two deities. '*Astart* stood at the right, and a horned god, probably Baal, at the left.

It is evident that the goddesses *Anath, *Asherah, and Ashtoreth were frequently confused, since in character and by nature they had much in common.

Lit.: J. B. Pritchard, *Palestinian Figurines in Relation to Certain Goddesses Known Through Literature* (New Haven, 1943); *ANEP* 468.

Ashur. *See* Ashhur.

Ashurites (ăsh′ẽr-īts). [Heb. *'Ashûrî.* The Syriac and Vulgate read "Geshurites" but probably incorrectly (cf. 2 Sa 3:3). Some scholars suggest a vocalization that gives the reading "Asherites," that is, men of the tribe of Asher.] A people who belonged to the kingdom of Ishbosheth (ch 2:9).

Ashvath (ăsh′văth). [Heb. *'Ashwath,* meaning uncertain.] An Asherite (1 Chr 7:33).

Asia (ā′zhȧ). [Gr. *Asia.*] The name of the western territory of Asia Minor. This territory was taken by Rome from the Seleucid Empire in 190 B.C. and given mostly to the Attalid kingdom of Pergamum, which used Asia as a designation for its territory. When by his will Attalus III bequeathed his kingdom to the Romans in 133 B.C., the region was organized as the province of Asia. It consisted of the areas of Mysia, Caria, Lydia, western Phrygia, and some islands lying off the Asia Minor coast (Map XX, B-4). In NT times it was ruled as a senatorial province by a proconsul, with its capital in Pergamum. Later it was an imperial province administered from Ephesus. Some ancient writers make a distinction between Phrygia and Asia, as if the former were still a separate unit. Luke and Paul did this also (Acts 2:9, 10; 16:6). Also Mysia was sometimes distinguished from Asia (ch 16:6, 7), showing that occasionally the term Asia was not used in the strict sense of a political province, but rather as the name of the western coastal region of Asia Minor. In the other NT references the term Asia appears to apply to the Roman province (Acts 6:9; 19:10, 22, 26, 27, 31; 20:4, 18; 21:27; 24:18; 27:2; 1 Cor 16:19; 2 Cor 1:8; 2 Ti 1:15; 1 Pe 1:1; Rev 1:4, 11). Paul traveled through the province of Asia during his 2d Missionary Journey (Acts 16:6-9; 18:19-21), and labored in that province for 3 years during his 3d Missionary Journey (ch 20:31). It is probable that at this time in addition to Ephesus several of the strong city churches were founded which are addressed in the seven letters of John (Rev 2; 3). For centuries this area remained a stronghold of Christianity.

Asiarch (ā′shĭ-ärk). [Gr. *Asiarchēs,* "chief of Asia."] The title of a certain official in the province of Asia. Although this title is encountered frequently in inscriptions of western Asia Minor, the real function of its bearers is not sufficiently clear. Two views prevail: (1) The Asiarch was the high priest of Asia, who presided over religious feasts, games, and political assemblies of the provincial government. He was appointed for one year, but then retained his title without occupying an office. This shows how there could be several living Asiarchs. (2) The Asiarchs were municipal delegates of the individual cities of Asia to the provincial assembly. Being men of dignity and wealth, they are frequently mentioned in inscriptions. Whatever the meaning of the term Asiarch, it is surprising that Paul had friends among these influential people (Acts 19:31, RSV)—officials who, if the first definition is accepted, were leaders in pagan rites that were an abomination to Jews and Christians alike.

Asiel (ā′sĭ-ĕl). [Heb. *'Asî'el,* "God is my maker."] A Simeonite (1 Chr 4:35).

Askelon. *See* Ashkelon.

Asnah (ăs′nȧ). [Heb. *'Asnah,* meaning uncertain.] Head of a family of *Nethinim. Some of his descendants returned from Babylon with Zerubbabel (Ezr 2:50).

Asnapper. *See* Osnappar.

Asp. *See* Serpent.

Aspatha (ăs-pā′thȧ). [Heb. *'Aspatha',* probably a Persian name, but the meaning is uncertain.] One of Haman's sons (Est 9:7).

Asriel (ăs′rĭ-ĕl), KJV once **Ashriel** (ăsh′rĭ-ĕl). [Heb. *'Asrî'el,* meaning uncertain.] A Manassite founder of a family (Num 26:31; Jos 17:2).

Asrielite (ăs′rĭ-ĕl-īt). [Heb. *'Asrî'eli.*] A member of the family of *Asriel.

Ass. The Bible mentions two asses, the wild and the domestic.

1. *The wild ass* [Heb. *pere';* Aramaic *'arad* (*'arôd* in Job 39:5).] The Asiatic onager, a swift and strong animal that lives in large herds in the steppe countries that surround Palestine. It is mentioned almost exclusively in the poetic and prophetic literature of the Bible (Job 6:5; 11:12; 24:5; Ps 104:11; Is 32:14; etc.).

2. *The domestic ass.* [Heb. *'athôn, chamôr, 'ayir;* Gr. *onos, hupozugion, onarion.*] One of the most valuable of the domestic animals of the ancient world (Is 1:3; Lk 13:15). It is more handsome than

its European fellow; its ears are erect and it carries its head high. Its coat is smooth and usually reddish brown.

The ass was used as a beast of burden (Gen 42:26; 1 Sa 25:18). Thus, in the blessings of Jacob, Issachar is compared to a "strong ass couching down between two burdens" (Gen 49:14). The ass was also used to pull the plow, but the Mosaic law did not permit it to be yoked with the slower but stronger ox (Deut 22:10; Is 30:24; see fig. 500). It was widely used for riding purposes. Thus Abraham, Balaam, sons of judges and prophets, and women rode on asses (Gen 22:3; Num 22:21; Jgs 10:4; 1 Sa 25:20; 1 Ki 13:13; 2 Ki 4:24). The saddle in most cases was simply a blanket (Gen 22:3), and the garments of the disciples served this purpose when Jesus entered Jerusalem riding on an ass (Mt 21:7). Asses were also used by military forces (Is 21:7; 2 Ki 7:7, 10; Zec 14:15), either as beasts of burden or as riding animals. They had the advantage of being more sure-footed on difficult terrain than horses.

Since the ass belonged to the unclean animals, it was not used in Jewish sacrifices, nor was it permitted to be eaten. However, in an extremely severe famine the people paid as much as 80 shekels for the head of an ass (2 Ki 6:25). Because of its uncleanness, no one would wish to touch its carcass, much less to bury it. This situation gives point to Jeremiah's prediction concerning Jehoiakim that he was to be buried with the burial of an ass (Jer 22:19).

Assassins. [Gr. *sikarioi,* literally, "dagger men."] An extremist organization of Jews who conducted a reign of terror in Judea *c.* A.D. 50-70. Their avowed purpose was to secure freedom from the Romans. These men carried a small dagger concealed beneath the cloak and, as they mingled with the crowd, often stabbed the persons marked for that fate by the organization. They also decimated small Roman garrisons where sneak attacks could be carried out. Jews who refused to support their aims were often their victims. The Roman captain who rescued Paul from a mob in Jerusalem suspected him of belonging to the *sikarioi,* or assassins (Acts 21:38).

Assayer. A term appearing in the RSV of Jer 6:27 translating the Heb. *bachôn,* "one who tests," or "one who examines," probably particular metals. The translation "tower" in the KJV apparently resulted from an incorrect association of *bachôn*

with *bachîn,* the plural of which is translated "towers" in the KJV of Is 23:13. However, the word *bachîn* is of uncertain meaning.

Asshur (ăs'shoōr), KJV twice **Assur** (ăs'ẽr). [Heb. *'Ashshûr.*]
1. A son of Shem (Gen 10:22), from whom the Assyrians descended.
2. The land of *Assyria (Num 24:22, 24; Ezr 4:2, KJV; Eze 27:23). Maps III, B-5; IV, B-6. The Assyrian city of that name (Map XI, B-5) is not mentioned in the Bible.

Asshurim (ă-shoō'rĭm). [Heb. *'Ashshûrîm.*] An Arabic tribe descended from Abraham through his wife Keturah (Gen 25:3). It is probably this tribe that is mentioned in a South Arabic text as residing in northwestern Arabia (Montgomery, *Arabia and the Bible* [1934], p. 44).

Assir (ăs'ẽr). [Heb. *'Assîr,* either "captive," or "Osiris," the Egyptian god. Possibly in 1 and 2 the latter definition applies, and in 3 the former.]
1. A descendant of Levi through Korah, born in Egypt (Ex 6:24; 1 Chr 6:22).
2. A great-grandson of Assir, 1 (1 Chr 6:23, 37).
3. A son of King Jeconiah (Jehoiachin) according to the KJV of 1 Chr 3:17. The translators of the RSV have taken the word *'assîr* not as a proper name but as a term descriptive of the king and render it "the captive." However, the absence of the article before *'assîr* makes the rendering of the RSV doubtful. Assir, with the meaning "a captive," would certainly be an appropriate name for a son of the young king, if he was born in captivity.

Assos (ăs'ŏs). [Gr. *Assos.*] A port city in the Troad, 20 mi. southeast of Troas, where Paul embarked on his voyage to Jerusalem when returning from his 3d Missionary Journey (Acts 20:13, 14). The site is now called *Behramköy,* and contains extensive ruins from this ancient city. Map XX, B-4.

Assur. *See* Asshur, 2.

Assyria (ă-sĭr'ĭ-à). [Heb. *'Ashshûr;* Akkadian *Ashshur;* Egyptian *'Iswr;* and Phoenician *'Shr.* The English spelling is a transliteration of the Gr. *Assuria.*] A country on the upper Tigris in Mesopotamia, also the empire ruled by the Assyrians (Map XI). The name became so much a synonym of imperial rule over that region that the Babylonians, and later the Persians, who succeeded Assyria as world powers, were occasionally called "Assyrians" (Lam 5:6; Ezr 6:22). It is in the same sense that the Seleucid rulers are called Assyrians in a document belonging to the famous Dead Sea scrolls.

The homeland of the Assyrians had its southern border at the Little Zab (Lesser Zab, or Lower Zab), a tributary of the Tigris. In the vicinity of the mouth of the Little Zab, and on the right (west) bank of the Tigris, lay Asshur (Ashur, or Assur), the earliest capital of Assyria (the city of Asshur must not be confused with the term *Asshur used in the Bible to refer to the country of Assyria or the Assyrians). From there the homeland of Assyria extended in a northwesterly direction for about 80 mi. along the river Tigris. Its most important cities were located along the left bank of this river: Kar-Tukulti-Ninurta, not far north of Asshur, Calah, Nineveh, and Dur-Sharrukin. The country was not very large, because to the west of the river was a desert area, and the strip of agricultural land lying between the river and the mountains on the east was narrow and much less fertile than the soil of southern Mesopotamia.

The scarcity of land may have been responsible for some of the national characteristics of the Assyrians. They were an enterprising commercial people, daring adventurers, brave warriors, and talented organizers. Rigidly disciplined themselves, they were cruel to others. They were not a scientific or literary people, as were their southern kinsmen, the Babylonians, yet they were not void of artistic talents. Their sculptures reveal a mastery of the handling of stone, which was furnished by the mountains nearby. See figs. 19, 105, 284, 301, etc.

The Assyrians were Semites like the Babylonians and Aramaeans (Gen 10:22), and spoke a language closely related to Babylonian. They also used the cuneiform script of the Babylonians with some local modifications in the shape of the characters. By the 1st millennium B.C., when the Assyrians came into close contact with the Hebrews in Palestine, they had lost their racial purity, because in ruling over a whole empire they had absorbed many subjugated peoples, such as the Hurrians, and therefore showed much mixture in their appearance and characteristics.

The Religion of the Assyrians. Being Semites, the Assyrians had many gods in common with other Semitic nations, notably with the Babylonians. They worshiped the great Babylonian deities, such as the sun-god Shamash; Sin, the moon-god; Ea,

39. An Assyrian city gate (a modern reconstruction) at Baghdad

the god of waters; and Ishtar, the great goddess of fertility. They also honored Anu, Marduk (*Bel), and his son Nabu (*Nebo). However, the principal god of the Assyrians, throughout their history, was Ashur, who did not belong to the Babylonian pantheon. Ashur was depicted as a winged sun that protected and guided the king, his principal servant (see fig. 255, center). He was also symbolized by a tree, representative of fertility. Yet he was first and foremost a war god, and war became part of the national religion of the Assyrians. Every military campaign was thought to be carried out in response to the direct orders of Ashur. Hence participation in warfare was an act of worship. This association of Ashur with Assyrian military campaigns accounts for the fact that the cult of Ashur vanished with the destruction of the Assyrian Empire, in contrast to the cults of the gods of other nations, which survived the destruction of their people. For example, the Babylonian patron god Marduk remained the chief deity of the Mesopotamian valley under the Persians, who captured Babylon, but Ashur never reappeared in the ancient world after the capture and destruction of Nineveh.

The Pre-Empire Period. A brief statement in Gen 10:11, 12 shows that the Assyrian cities owed their existence to an extension of the power of early Babylonia. Mic 5:6 calls Assyria simply the land of Nimrod, who was the first empire builder operating from Lower Mesopotamia. In secular history Assyria appears first in the 19th cent. B.C. as a vassal kingdom of southern Mesopotamian kings. From that time on it was engaged in a continual struggle for independence, for supremacy, and sometimes for imperial power over other nations. Its most ambitious rulers during its early history were Sargon I (c. 1780 B.C.), and Shamshi-Adad I (c. 1749-1717 B.C.), an Amorite, both of whom extended their economic or military influence into Anatolia and Syria.

Then followed a struggle against the Hurrians of Mitanni and the Hittites, out of which, after several setbacks, Assyria emerged a survivor.

During the latter part of the 2d millennium B.C. several strong and ambitious Assyrian rulers tried to establish an empire, and succeeded briefly. Of these the following may be named: Adad-nirari I (c. 1306 - c. 1274 B.C.), who defeated Babylonia and campaigned in the east and north with great success; Tukulti-Ninurta I (c. 1244-1207 B.C.), who defeated the Babylonians again and captured their capital, and also won victories over Elam, the Aramaeans, and Urartians; and Tiglath-pileser I (1113-1074 B.C.), who established his rule over an area that reached from the Persian Gulf to the Mediterranean Sea. Then followed several weak rulers, whose power hardly reached beyond the boundaries of their homeland.

The Empire Period. Beginning, however, about 150 years after Tiglath-pileser's death, Assyria was for about 300 years (from 933 until shortly before 612 B.C.) the most powerful nation on earth. It established an empire that covered all of Mesopotamia and most of its neighboring countries, large stretches of Anatolia, all of Syria and Palestine, and even, for a short time, Egypt (Map XI). It was during this period that Assyria came into close contact with the Hebrews, and eventually destroyed the northern kingdom of Israel. Hence we find several Assyrian kings mentioned in the Bible and ten Hebrew kings named in Assyrian records (Omri, Ahab, Jehu, Menahem, Pekah, Hoshea of Israel, and Azariah, Ahaz, Hezekiah, Manasseh of Judah).

The first strong ruler of this new period was Ashur-dan II (933-910 B.C.), who conquered northern Mesopotamia. From his time on the Assyrian armies were on the march into foreign countries practically every year, and continued this for centuries. Streams of blood were shed, and corpses were piled up like mountains, to use the language of the Assyrians. The first of these cruel Assyrian kings of the empire period to come into repeated contact with Israel was Shalmaneser III (859-824 B.C.). In fighting against an alliance of Syrian kings at Qarqar in 853 B.C. he encountered King Ahab, who had brought into the battle 2,000 chariots and 10,000 foot soldiers. The same Assyrian king records that 12 years later he received tribute from King Jehu of Israel, and his carved Black Obelisk shows Jehu kneeling

before him (see fig. 255). During his long reign of 35 years this Assyrian king campaigned in practically all the countries surrounding his homeland, and established his overlordship in their territories. He was followed by several weak rulers, and during the next 80 years the empire lost much of its hold on the subjugated nations. This does not mean that Assyria was powerless during this period, for military campaigns occasionally reached as far as Damascus, which Adad-nirari III (810-782 B.C.) conquered from Hazael; but the Assyrian military successes were not permanent. It must have been in this period, probably under Adad-nirari III, that Jonah carried out his mission to Nineveh. This period of comparative weakness in Assyria was taken advantage of by Jeroboam II, a strong ruler of Israel, who restored control over territories that had been lost since the time of Solomon.

However, the Assyrians made a marvelous comeback when *Tiglath-pileser III occupied the throne (745-727 B.C.). He was a great monarch and an empire builder, and sought remedies for all the ills of his country by systematically reestablishing Assyrian power over the neighboring countries. Babylon had been conquered many times and brought as a vassal kingdom under Assyrian overlordship, but it had always been lost again. To prevent an additional loss Tiglath-pileser united it firmly with Assyria by crowning himself as king of Babylon under the throne name of *Pul. This was the first time an Assyrian king attempted this. He also established firm control over the area of Syria and parts of Palestine and destroyed many city-states like Damascus, reorganizing the conquered areas as Assyrian provinces. Their populations were transplanted to other areas of the empire, and their territories were resettled with peoples from other subjugated countries. The northern part of the defeated kingdom of Israel was detached and made into the Assyrian province of Megiddo, and captives were deported from its territory east of the Jordan. The remainder, with Samaria as capital, was allowed to survive as a vassal state. Ahaz, the king of Judah, voluntarily bowed to the king of Assyria and became his vassal. Tiglath-pileser gained another major success when he permanently broke the power of the northern state of Urartu, which had troubled Assyria so much in the past.

Shalmaneser V (727-722 B.C.), successor

of Tiglath-pileser III, ruled only briefly, but copied his predecessor's methods of warfare and rulership. He assumed the kingship of Babylon under the name of Ululai, and with strength and determination met a coalition of western kings (to whom Israel belonged) who had ceased to pay tribute. Samaria was besieged for 3 years (inclusive) and was captured, probably shortly before the king's death, although the task of deporting the Israelites and resettling their territory by people from other areas fell on the shoulders of Sargon II, his successor. Sargon II claimed that he conquered Samaria during the first year of his reign. *See* Shalmaneser, 2.

Sargon II (722-705 B.C.) was probably a usurper, although he called himself "son of Tiglath-pileser." A strong king, he surmounted great difficulties during his reign. In his numerous campaigns he defeated the Elamites in the east, Marduk-apal-iddina (the Biblical Merodach-baladan) of Babylon in the south, and the Urarteans and Aramaeans in the north and northwest. He also built a new capital, Dur-Sharrukin, now called Khorsabad (see fig. 364), a few miles north of Nineveh. This was the first Assyrian palace city that revealed its ancient treasures to the modern excavator. *See* Sargon.

Sennacherib (705-681 B.C.), son of Sargon II, took great interest in technical improvements of his war machinery. He rebuilt Nineveh, and made it the most glorious city of its time, introducing new building methods. Ruthless and uncompromising, Sennacherib made some far-reaching political blunders, such as his senseless destruction of Babylon in 689 B.C. in order to end the continual rebellions of that city. Because of his policies he became the most hated man of that era. Also in his dealings with the West he was not always successful. In 701 B.C. he crushed a rebellion of Syrian and Palestinian princes, and then moved against the kingdom of Hezekiah, who may have been the leader in the revolt. He destroyed many cities of Judah, including the strong fortress city of Lachish, whose siege and capture are depicted in a whole series of Assyrian palace reliefs now in the British Museum (see fig. 284). Jerusalem was saved when Sennacherib had to break up his campaign because his army was urgently needed elsewhere. Later, after the Nubian Tirhakah (Taharka) had come to the throne of Egypt, Sennacherib came back with the intention of destroying Hezekiah's kingdom. This campaign ended in disaster —a circumstance that accounts for its omission from the king's annals. However, the Bible mentions the campaign (2 Ki 19; 2 Chr 32; Is 37), and some memory of it seems to have been preserved in a story told to Herodotus in Egypt more than 2 centuries later (ii. 141). The king was murdered by his own sons, an event recorded both in the Bible and in Babylonian and Assyrian inscriptions. *See* Sennacherib.

Esarhaddon (681-669 B.C.), a son of Sennacherib who had not been involved in the murder of his father, took the throne. The great achievement of his reign was a successful military campaign against Egypt, which pushed the Assyrian Empire to its greatest extent. However, troubles against the empire rose in the border regions, where barbaric nations such as the Scythians, Cimmerians, and Medes attempted to overrun sections of the Assyrian territory in order to obtain some of its wealth. Esarhaddon was able to hold these nations back, but not to eliminate the threat. Under his son Ashurbanipal (669-627? B.C.) the empire was at its height in glory and extent, but definite signs of weakness, which foreshadowed the rapid decline and destruction of the empire, were apparent. Egypt, which had revolted in the last years of his father's reign, was subjugated once more, and Thebes, probably the largest city of the world at that time, was sacked. Babylon, led by Shamash-shum-ukin, Ashurbanipal's brother, also revolted but the revolt was quelled. But above all his military successes Ashurbanipal is known as the founder of his great palace library at Nineveh. This library, consisting of thousands of clay tablets, which are now in the British Museum, has been the greatest single source of information for the reconstruction of Assyrian literature, history, and civilization.

Details of the last years of the Assyrian Empire are meager for lack of clear historical records. Two of Ashurbanipal's sons ruled for a few years over Assyria, but were unable to cope with the forces that were gathering against the Assyrian Empire, especially the Babylonians and the Medes. The former, who had proclaimed their independence under Nabopolassar in 626 B.C., were subsequently at almost continual war with the Assyrians. In 614 B.C. the Medes under Cyaxares destroyed the city of Asshur, and Nineveh shared the same fate 2 years later (612 B.C.) when it fell to the combined armies of Cyaxares and Nabopolassar. The last king of Assyria, a certain Ashur-uballit II, was able to rally some of the remnant Assyrian forces around him and retreat to Haran, which he made the capital for a short time. However, the Babylonians soon evicted him from the city, and with his eviction the Assyrians vanished from history (c. 609 B.C.).

Assyrian (ă-sĭr'ĭ-ăn). [Heb. *'Ashshûr.*] An inhabitant of *Assyria.

Astaroth. See Ashtaroth.

Astrologers. In the KJV the translation of two distinct expressions: (1) Heb. *'ashshaphîm,* Aramaic *'ashephîn* (Dan 1:20; 2:2, 10, 27; 4:7; 5:7, 11, 15), practitioners of magic arts. But the particular branch or branches of magic in which these men engaged is not known. The RSV always renders the Hebrew and Aramaic terms "enchanters." (2) Heb. *hobrê shamayim* (Is 47:13), "dividers of the heavens." This class is mentioned with "stargazers" and "monthly prognosticators," and clearly seems to represent astrologers, men who attempt to foretell earthly events by noting the positions and aspects of the planets, the sun, and the moon in the various signs of the zodiac at particular moments of time. In the RSV "astrologers" is the translation of the Aramaic *gazerîn,* "determiners of destiny," whether by astrology, or by other means, such as consulting the liver, cannot be determined with certainty. See *SDACom* 4:763.

Asuppim. [Heb. *'asuppîm,* literally, "gatherings," hence "stores," from *'asaph,* "to gather in."] A transliterated term that appears as a proper name in the KJV of 1 Chr 26:15, 17. However, the Hebrew term should be translated instead and should be rendered "stores," or "storehouses" (RSV).

Asyncritus (ă-sĭng'krĭ-tŭs). [Gr. *Asugkritos,* "incomparable."] The name occurs in ancient Greek and Latin inscriptions.] A Christian of Rome to whom Paul sent greetings (Rom 16:14).

Atad. See Abel-mizraim.

Atarah (ăt'ă-rä). [Heb. *'Aṭarah,* "diadem."] One of the wives of Jerahmeel of Judah (1 Chr 2:26).

Ataroth (ăt'ă-rŏth). [Heb. *'Aṭarôth,* "folds," "crowns."]

1. A town in Transjordan that Moses took from the king of Heshbon and the Gadites rebuilt (Num 32:3, 34). Mesha, king of Moab, claims to have taken it from Gad (*Moabite Stone, lines 10, 11). It has been identified with *Khirbet 'Aṭṭârûs* (Map VI, E-4), 2½ mi. north-

east of Machaerus and about 6 mi. north-west of Dibon.

2. A town (Jos 16:2), most probably *Ataroth-addar.

3. A border town of Ephraim toward the Jordan (Jos 16:7), which has been tentatively identified with *Tell Sheik ed-Dhiab,* about 2 mi. northeast of Phasaelis in the foothills of Mount Ephraim in the Jordan Valley.

4. A place in Judah (1 Chr 2:54, KJV) which should be read *Atroth-beth-joab (RSV).

Ataroth-addar (ăt'ă-rŏth-ă'där), KJV once **Ataroth-adar** (ăt'ă-rŏth-ă'där). [Heb. *'Aṭrôth 'Addar,* "the fold of Addar."] A place on the border of Ephraim and Benjamin (Jos 16:5), south of Bethel, and not far from the nether Beth-horon (ch 18:13). It has not been identified. If *Tell en-Naṣbeh,* 7 mi. north of Jerusalem, is not Mizpah, it could be Ataroth-addar.

Ater (ā'tẽr). [Heb. *'Aṭer,* "crooked."]

1. The ancestor of a family. He is called "Ater of Hezekiah," and may possibly have been related to the royal family. Of this family 98 male members returned with Zerubbabel from Babylonia (Ezr 2:16; Neh 7:21). A man by that name, probably representing the same family, signed Nehemiah's covenant (Neh 10:17).

2. The head of a family of porters that returned with Zerubbabel from Babylonia (Ezr 2:42; Neh 7:45).

Athach (ā'thăk). [Heb. *'Athak.*] A place in southern Judah. When in Ziklag, David sent some of the spoil of his raids to the inhabitants of Athach (1 Sa 30:30). Some identify the site with *Ether, 1.

Athaiah (ă-thā'yă). [Heb. *'Athayah,* possibly "Yahweh is superior."] A man of Judah who lived in Jerusalem in Nehemiah's time (Neh 11:4).

Athaliah (ăth'ă-lī'ă). [Heb. *'Athalyah* and *'Athalyahû,* "Yahweh is exalted."]

1. A Benjamite (1 Chr 8:26).

2. The wife of King Jehoram of Judah, a daughter of Ahab and granddaughter of Omri (2 Ki 8:18, 26; 2 Chr 21:6; 22:2), the only reigning queen in OT Hebrew history. She usurped the throne when Jehu of Israel slew her son Ahaziah. To secure her position she ordered all her son's offspring killed. However, without her knowledge, Joash, an infant son of Ahaziah, escaped the massacre, and was hidden by Jehosheba, the wife of the high priest Jehoiada (2 Ki 11:1, 2; 2 Chr 22:10, 11). Having been reared in the idolatrous house of Ahab and Jezebel, Athaliah

introduced the worship of Baal into Judah (2 Ki 11:18; 2 Chr 23:17). In her 7th regnal year (c. 841-835 B.C.), in an insurrection against her rule, Athaliah was slain and the child Joash crowned (2 Ki 11:3-16; 2 Chr 22:12; 23:1-16).

3. A man of the house of Elam whose son returned with Ezra from Babylonia (Ezr 8:7).

Atharim (ăth'á-rĭm). [Heb. *'Atharim.*] A topographical name in the RSV, but rendered "spies" in the KJV (Num 21:1). If it is a place, its identity is not known.

Athenian (á-thē'nǐ-ăn). [Gr. *Athēnaios.*] An inhabitant of *Athens (Acts 17:21).

Athens (ăth'ĕnz). [Gr. *Athēnai.*] The most illustrious city of ancient Greece, and its present capital. It was named after Athena, the patron goddess of the city. According to tradition it was founded in the 16th cent. B.C. It lay about 4 mi. from the sea, and at one time was connected by long walls with its harbor, Piraeus. Map XX, B-3. See figs. 25, 26, 40, 41.

During the first centuries of its history the city was governed by kings. When these were deposed Athens became an oligarchy, a rule of the aristocracy. From that time on its chief magistrates were *archons* (rulers). Draco codified Athens' stern laws about 621 B.C., but Solon, the second wise lawgiver of Athens, modified them about 594 B.C., making them more humane. Athens became a democracy, that is, it was ruled by its citizens (though citizens constituted a minority of the total population). During the 6th cent., and especially in the 5th, the city became a center of Greek art and literature, which fame it retained even during periods of political insignificance. Its most glorious period began with the Persian wars, in the 5th cent., when it led the Greeks in a series of victories over the imperial forces of the Persians. The first victory at Marathon (490 B.C.) over Darius I proved to the astonished world that the armies of the little Greek city-states were vastly superior to the mammoth army of the Persian Empire. Ten years later Darius' successor, Xerxes,

41. View of the agora (market place) and the temple of Hephaestus at Athens, with the columns of the reconstructed Stoa of Attalus in the foreground

attacked Greece. He was victorious at Thermopylae, and burned Athens, which had been forsaken by its inhabitants, but Xerxes was defeated in the naval battle at Salamis (480 B.C.), and at Plataea and Mycale in 479 B.C.

Later Athens became the head of the Greek confederacy, and under the able leadership of Pericles experienced its golden age. The city rose from its ashes more beautiful than it had ever been. On the Acropolis, the steep central hill of the city, was built the immortal Parthenon, the pearl of all classical temples; also the charming Erechtheum and the magnificent Propylaea. After the period of Athenian leadership there followed a ruinous struggle with Sparta and the loss of Greek supremacy to Thebes. In 338 B.C. Philip of Macedon conquered both Athens and Thebes in the battle of Chaeronea. From then on it was a pawn of Macedonia, of Alexander, and of Alexander's successors. In 146 B.C. the Romans organized Greece as the province of *Achaia. Thenceforth Athens was under Roman rule, but enjoyed considerable local independence. When Sulla plundered it in 86 B.C., it experienced only a brief setback, the Romans embellishing it lavishly with buildings. Because of its fame as the mother of Western culture, which included art, literature, architecture, and philosophy, it remained an important city in Roman times, although it had neither the economic nor the political importance of Corinth, the capital of the province. It was especially famous as a seat of learning, and its university was considered the best in the world. All the main schools of philosophy—Platonic, *Stoic, *Epicurean, and Peripatetic—were developed in Athens.

The apostle Paul came to Athens in the course of his 2d Missionary Journey, probably in A.D. 51. In dealing with the

40. The Acropolis of Athens

people and speaking with them in the agora, he found the Athenians inquisitive (Acts 17:21) and religious (v 22, RSV). That they were religious was obvious to every observer, since there were about 3,000 statues in Athens—most of them probably objects of worship, also many temples and altars. Among the altars was one dedicated to "an unknown god" (v 23). No altar with such an inscription has been found so far in the excavations of Athens, but one discovered at Pergamum bears the broken inscription "To the unk[nown] gods" (A. Deissmann, *St. Paul* [London, 1912], pp. 261-266). Such altars are also mentioned by ancient writers (for example, by Pausanias, *Descriptio Graeciae* I. 1. 4) as having been erected to avert public calamities that could not be ascribed to known gods. It is possible that the altar that Paul saw at Athens belonged to a mystery cult (*see* Mystery). There was also a Jewish community in Athens with a synagogue in which Paul preached, according to his custom of beginning his work in a new city among the Jews (v 17). His discussions with the Athenians in the agora opened the way for his *Areopagus discourse (vs 22-31). Although his immediate success was not great, he left a group of Christians at Athens, among whom are listed a high official and a woman of high repute (vs 32-34). There can be little doubt that Paul revisited Athens during his 3d Missionary Journey (ch 20:2, 3), although this fact is not specifically recorded by Luke.

Athlai (ăth′lȧ-ī). [Heb. *'Athlay*, probably a shortened form of *'Athalyah*, "Yahweh is exalted."] A man who was married to a foreign wife in Ezra's time (Ezr 10:28).

Atonement. [Heb. *kippurîm*, "a covering," literally, "coverings," from the verb *kaphar*, "to cover," "to make atonement"; Gr. *katallagē*, "reconciliation."] A term appearing in the OT, usually in connection with various sacrifices and services of the ceremonial system. The term appears in the NT but once and only in the KJV (Rom 5:11), where it describes the state of reconciliation the sinner attains through the sacrifice and priestly ministry of Christ. The English word "atonement" originally meant "at-one-ment," that is, a state of being "at one," or in agreement. Accordingly, "atonement" denoted harmony of relationship, and when there had been estrangement this harmony would be the result of a process of reconcil-

iation. Understood in terms of its original meaning, "atonement" properly denotes a state of reconciliation that terminated a state of estrangement, and was thus reasonably close in meaning to the Biblical terms it was used to translate.

However, the word "atonement" has acquired the special, technical theological meaning of "propitiation" or "expiation," and when so used implies that the sacrifice of Christ on the cross constituted reparation to an offended God. This concept reflects the pagan idea of propitiating an offended deity in order to avert his anger and vengeance, and assumes that God must be reconciled to us. Thus, today, the word "atonement" does not properly convey either its own original meaning—the state of being "at one"—or the sense of the Hebrew and Greek terms thus translated.

As noted, the root ideas of *kaphar* and *kippurîm*, the Hebrew words translated "to make atonement" and "atonement," are "to cover" and "covering." When using these words in connection with the ceremonial system, the Bible writer assumes that the persons or things for which a "covering" is made—the persons or things "covered"—were common, "unclean," or sinful in the sight of a righteous God, and thus not acceptable to Him. By reason of sin in general, and at times because of specific sins in particular, men are assumed to be in a state of estrangement from God. But the Bible writers present God as anxious that there shall be a reconciliation and show that He has provided the means by which it may be accomplished. No change is necessary on His part in order to effect the reconciliation, but man in his natural state is a sinner who does not even desire to be reconciled, and a change is therefore necessary on his part. It is the sinner who must be "covered," or reconciled to God, not God with respect to the sinner.

The ritual system provided an objective illustration of how men may become reconciled to God. The blood of the sacrificial animals provided the objective covering (Lev 17:11), but this blood could not, in and of itself, actually cover the sinner (Heb 10:1, 4, 6, 8, 11). Only as by faith he saw in it a type of the blood of Christ and accepted the promise of divine grace thus represented, was he actually "covered" and so reconciled to God (vs 10, 12, 14-18). Forgiveness of sin and acceptance with God always accompanied the "covering" thus provided (Lev 4:20;

Num 15:25; etc.). God was satisfied with the sincerity of purpose of the person or persons on whose behalf the "covering" was made, and entertained no further claims against them so long as they remained in accord with Him.

A few illustrations of the use of the word "atonement" in the OT will suffice to clarify its meaning. The sanctuary and its equipment were made out of common materials, and it was necessary to "cover," or "make an atonement" for them, before they could be put to holy use (Ex 29:36, 37; 30:10; Lev 8:15; etc.). Aaron and his sons were common people, and they likewise had to be "covered" when set apart for the priesthood (Ex 29:35; Lev 8: 34). A blood covering was also prescribed for the sins of the entire congregation (Lev 4:20; Num 15:25), for those of individuals (Lev 4:27-35; Num 15:28), and for various forms of ritual uncleanness (Lev 12:7, 8; 14:18, 20, 53; 15:28). At the close of the annual round of ceremonial services, on a special "day of atonement" (Lev 16:21-28; Heb 10:1-3), a final "covering" for the accumulated uncleanness of the year was made for Aaron and his sons, the priests (Lev 16:6, 11, 24), for the sanctuary and its furnishings (vs 16-20, 33, 34), and for the people of Israel (vs 30, 34). This typified the final and complete removal of sin from God's universe.

In the NT, where the word "atonement" occurs only once (Rom 5:11) and that only in the KJV, the experience represented by *kaphar* and *kippurîm* is probably most closely described in the word "reconciliation." The true "covering" has been provided by the precious blood of our Saviour, and reconciliation with God is possible through faith in Him (Rom 5:8-11; 2 Cor 5:17-19). *See* Mercy Seat.

Atonement, Day of. The 10th day of the 7th month (*Ethanim, or Tishri), the most solemn day of the year. On it all were not only to refrain from work but also to afflict their souls (Lev 23:27-32). This probably included fasting, since in NT times it is evidently this day that is referred to as "the fast" (Acts 27:9). On this day all the sins of the preceding year were finally disposed of in the ceremony of cleansing the sanctuary (Lev 16). All who did not afflict their souls on that day were cut off from Israel (ch 23:29). The Day of Atonement was to the Jews a day of judgment. As their tradition later describes it, all are judged on New Year's Day, but those who are not outstandingly good or hopelessly wicked have 9 days more, until

the Day of Atonement, before their doom is finally sealed (Talmud *Rosh Hashanah* 16a).

Another important event connected with the Day of Atonement was the blowing of the trumpet on that day to announce the 50th year of the sabbatical year cycle, the year of jubilee (Lev 25: 9, 10). Presumably, then, the sabbatical years, running in the same series with the jubilee years, also began at that time. The Day of Atonement services represented cleansing from sin and reconciliation to God (ch 16:16, 33, 34). The ritual began with the high priest bathing his body and putting on the holy linen garments (v 4). For himself and his house he offered a bull for a sin offering (v 6). After this personal preparation a goat designated "for the Lord," previously chosen by lot from two acquired for the service (vs 5, 7, 8), was sacrificed (v 9). Then, amid clouds of incense ascending from the altar before the second veil (vs 12, 13) the high priest entered the Most Holy Place and sprinkled the blood first of the bull, then of the goat, upon and before the mercy seat (v 15), which covered the ark containing, among other things, the tables of the Decalogue (Heb 9:4). In this manner the holy place was cleansed, and atonement made for the sins of the people (Lev 16:16). In a similar manner the altar was cleansed (vs 18, 19). Later, but not until the work of reconciliation for the holy place, the altar, and the people was ended (v 20), the transgressions of the people were transferred ritually to the goat, described as being "for *Azazel," (v 10, RSV). This goat was then led into the wilderness (vs 20-22).

The high priest was a type of Christ, the high priest in the heavenly sanctuary (Heb 8:1). The earthly priest performed his services "unto the example and shadow of heavenly things" (v 5). The author of Hebrews explains that by the high priest's entering only once a year into the second apartment the Holy Spirit signified that "the way into the holiest of all was not yet made manifest, while as the first tabernacle was yet standing" (ch 9:8). See *SDACom* 1:772-780; 4:844, 845; 7:450, 451, 455, 456.

Atroth. *See* Atroth-Shophan.

Atroth-beth-joab (ăt′rŏth-bĕth-jō′ăb). [Heb. *'Aṭrôth Bêth Yô'ab,* "the wreath of the house of Joab."] A place in Judah (1 Chr 2:54, RSV), now unidentified. The KJV separates the name and renders it "Ataroth, the house of Joab."

Atroth-Shophan (ăt′rŏth-shō′făn). [Heb. *'Aṭrôth Shôphan,* "the wreath of Shophan."] A place in the territory of Gad (Num 32:35). Instead of the compound name the KJV incorrectly reads "Atroth, Shophan," on the assumption that two towns are represented. The place has not been identified.

Attai (ăt′ă-ī). [Heb. *'Attay,* possibly "timely."]
1. A man whose mother was an Israelite, but whose father was an Egyptian slave (1 Chr 2:34-36).
2. A Gadite who joined David at Ziklag (1 Chr 12:11).
3. A son of King Rehoboam by Maacah, the queen (2 Chr 11:20).

Attalia (ăt′á-lī′á). [Gr. *Attaleia.*] A port city of Pamphylia, at the mouth of the Catarrhactes River. It was founded by King Attalus II (159-138 B.C.) of Pergamum (Map XX, B-5). Its name is now *Adalia.* Paul and Barnabas sailed from this port city en route to Syria at the end of their 1st Missionary Journey (Acts 14:25).

Augury. This word occurs three times in the RSV in the sense of "to practice augury" (Lev 19:26; 2 Ki 21:6; 2 Chr 33:6). In all three instances the KJV uses the term "enchantment." The Hebrew word thus translated (*nachash*) is general in its meaning, including all forms of augury, enchantment, divination. The Scriptures forbid the use of augury or enchantments in any form (Lev 19:26). *See* Divination.

Augustan Cohort. *See* Cohort, b.

Augustus (ô-gŭs′tŭs). [Gr. *Augoustos,* a transliteration of Latin *Augustus,* "majestic."]
1. The title conferred in 27 B.C. upon Gaius Octavius, and by which as the first Roman emperor he is known. He was born in 63 B.C., a grandnephew of Julius Caesar. When Julius Caesar died, Octavius, having been adopted as his son and heir, took the name Gaius Julius Caesar Octavianus. This is the reason he is referred to as Octavian in his preimperial period. Shortly after Julius Caesar's death (44 B.C.) Octavian became consul (43 B.C.), and then formed the Second Triumvirate with Antony and Lepidus. The next 12 years were filled with administrative and military activities, during which time he gained the supremacy over his competitors. Lepidus was eliminated from the triumvirate in 36 B.C., and Antony, who tried to build an eastern empire with Cleopatra, was defeated in 31 B.C. in the famous battle of Actium. From that time until his death 44 years later Octavian was sole master of the empire. This

42. Statue of Augustus from Via Labinica in the Museo delle Terme, Rome

period was considered the golden age of Rome. His standing army consisted of 25 legions, which, together with about an equal number of auxiliary troops, totaled about 250,000 to 300,000 men. The frontiers of the empire were extended by him and his generals in Spain, western Germany, and western Parthia. In A.D. 4 he adopted Tiberius, who succeeded him after his death at 76 in A.D. 14. His biography is extant in a long Greek and Latin inscription found at Ankara, Turkey.

Octavian appears in the NT under the title "Caesar Augustus" (Lk 2:1) in connection with the Palestinian census that brought Joseph and Mary to Bethlehem at the time of Christ's birth. Although Augustus was not a friend of the Jews, he favored them for expediency's sake, seeking to hold their loyalty because of the geographical location of their homeland on the eastern border of the empire. He valued the loyalty and friendship of Herod who in turn honored the emperor by naming his capital Caesarea after him, and giving the city of Samaria the new name Sebaste (from *Sebastos,* the Greek equivalent of the Latin word *Augustus*). Augustus had daily sacrifices offered in his name and at his own expense in the Temple at Jerusalem.

2. A term appearing in the KJV of Acts 25:21, 25 designating the emperor. The Greek word thus translated is *Sebastos*, which means "revered," "reverend."

Augustus' Band. *See* Cohort, b.

Aul. *See* Awl.

Ava. *See* Avva.

Aven (ā'vĕn). [Heb. *'Awen*, "wickedness."]

1. A city of Egypt, according to the Masoretic text of Eze 30:17. The consonants *'wn* are the same as those in the word *'On* in Gen 41:45, 50; 46:20, which stands for the Egyptian city of Heliopolis. The Masoretes supplied a pointing to the vowelless text of Eze 30:17 that changed the city's name to *'Awen*, "wickedness," doubtless for its idolatry. *See* On, 2.

2. A designation of Bethel used by Hosea, because Bethel, which means "house of God," had become a place of wicked idolatry (Hos 10:8). *See* Beth-Aven, 2.

3. The designation of a plain or valley (Amos 1:5) in the kingdom of Damascus, possibly *el-Biqa'*, where Baalbek, a center of pagan worship, was located. This center doubtless gave rise to the symbolic name given to the plain by Amos.

Avenger of Blood. A person (usually the nearest blood relative or next heir of one who had been murdered) who assumed the responsibility of punishing the murderer. The Hebrew word translated "avenger" (KJV frequently "revenger") is *go'el*, which has the basic meaning of "redeemer." When coupled with "blood" it has the idea of redeeming the guilt of the murder by putting to death the murderer (see Num 35:19, 21, 24, 27; etc.). In a well-regulated civil society, courts of justice and police departments dispense justice and punish offenders, but in ancient Semitic societies the family unit carried functions later assigned to the state. The avenger apparently was generally more zealous for revenge than for justice, hence provision was made for establishment of "cities of refuge"—Hebron, Shechem, and Kedesh west of Jordan (Jos 20:7), and Bezer, Ramoth-gilead, and Golan east of the river (Deut 4:41-43). To these one guilty of manslaughter might flee, and here he could remain until granted a fair trial. Such persons would then not be put to death unless the homicide was intentional (Ex 21:13; Num 35:19, 21, 24, 27). God did not institute the custom of private vengeance. He sought to regulate it so as to prevent abuses. He leads men only as rapidly as

they are able to advance, adapting His directions to prevailing conditions.

Avim. *See* Avvim.

Avims. *See* Avvim.

Avites. *See* Avvim; Avvites.

Avith (ā'vĭth). [Heb. *'Awîth*.] An Edomite or Moabite city, the royal city of the Edomite king Hadad (Gen 36:35; 1 Chr 1:46); not certainly identified.

Avva (ăv'à), KJV **Ava** (ā'và). [Heb. *'Awwa'*.] A city from which the Assyrians brought people to colonize Samaria, after the Israelite population had been deported (2 Ki 17:24), probably identical with Ivvah (Heb. *'Iwwah*) mentioned in chs 18:34; 19:13. The site has not been identified with certainty. Sachau suggests *'Imm* between Antioch and Aleppo; Šanda prefers the city of *Ammia* near Byblos mentioned in the *Amarna Letters; and Dhorme and Abel, *Tell Kafr 'Aya* on the Orontes River, southwest of Homs.

Avvim (ăv'ĭm), KJV **Avims** (ā'vĭmz), **Avites** (ā'vĭts), and **Avim** (ā'vĭm). [Heb. *'Awwîm*.]

1. Aborigines of the coastal area of southern Palestine who were destroyed by the Caphtorim (Cretans) at the time of the invasion of the Peoples of the Sea. The Israelites encountered only small remnants of them (Deut 2:23; Jos 13:3).

2. A place in the territory of Benjamin (Jos 18:23); not identified.

Avvites (ăv'ĭts), KJV **Avites** (ā'vĭts). [Heb. *'Awwîm*.] Inhabitants of *Avva (2 Ki 17:31).

Awl, KJV **Aul.** A sharp-pointed instrument for piercing small holes. In its two occurrences in Scripture the word describes the instrument used to bore through the ear of a Hebrew slave if after seven years of bondage he chose perpetual servitude in place of proffered freedom (Ex 21:6; Deut 15:17).

Awning. This word appears only in Eze 27:7 (RSV) and is a translation of the Heb. *mekasseh*, "a covering." The context suggests that in this instance it probably describes a cloth covering spread as protection from the sun.

Ax, Axe. A tool with a blade of metal (2 Ki 6:5, 6) or stone at the end of a wooden handle fastened with thongs or by some other means. Conventional axes were used for cutting and splitting wood (Deut 20:19) and for shaping timbers. The *battle-ax, used in warfare to do violence to men's bodies, was little used by the Israelites. In the NT the word occurs twice (Mt 3:10; Lk 3:9) as a symbol of divine judgment.

Axletree. [Heb. *yad,* "hand."] The transverse nonrotating beam or shaft connecting the wheels of a chariot (1 Ki 7:32, 33; RSV "axle").

Ayyah (ăy'ȧ). [Heb. *'Ayyah,* "heap" or "ruin."] A town mentioned in a list of Ephraimite possessions (1 Chr 7:28, RSV), possibly to be identified with *Khirbet Ḥaiyān,* 3 mi. southeast of Bethel. The KJV, following a different reading of the Hebrew text, represented by many Hebrew manuscripts, has "Gaza."

Azal (ā'zăl). [Heb. *'Aṣal.*] According to the KJV a place near Jerusalem (Zec 14:5), but the identity is not known. The LXX reads *Iasol,* which suggests identification with the *Wâdī Yaṣūl,* a tributary of the Kidron. Some scholars do not believe a locality is represented and read *'eṣel,* "the side (of it)" (see RSV).

Azaliah (ăz'ȧ-lī'ȧ). [Heb. *'Aṣalyahû,* "Yahweh keeps in reserve."] Father of the Shaphan who was a scribe in King Josiah's time (2 Ki 22:3; 2 Chr 34:8).

Azaniah (ăz'ȧ-nī'ȧ). [Heb. *'Azanyah,* "Yahweh has given ear."] A Levite in Nehemiah's time (Neh 10:9).

Azarael. *See* Azarel.

Azareel. *See* Azarel.

Azarel (ăz'ȧ-rĕl), KJV **Azareel** (à-zā'rē-ĕl), once **Azarael** (à-zā'rā-ĕl). [Heb. *'Azar'el,* "God has helped."]

1. A Levite who joined David at Ziklag (1 Chr 12:6).

2. A musician in David's time (1 Chr 25:18). Some commentators identify the Uzziel of v 4 with this man.

3. A prince of the tribe of Dan (1 Chr 27:22).

4. A man who was married to a foreign wife in Ezra's time (Ezr 10:41).

5. A priest of the family of Immer in Nehemiah's time (Neh 11:13), possibly the same as Azarel, 6.

6. A priestly musician in Nehemiah's time (Neh 12:36), possibly identical with Azarel, 5.

Azariah (ăz'ȧ-rī'ȧ). [Heb. and Aramaic *'Azaryahû* and *'Azaryah,* "Yahweh has helped." The name occurs in several ancient Hebrew inscriptions.]

1. A descendant of Judah, of the family of Zerah (1 Chr 2:8).

2. A Kohathite Levite, an ancestor of the prophet Samuel as well as of the singer Heman (1 Chr 6:36), possibly also the ancestor of Joel, a Levite of Hezekiah's time (2 Chr 29:12). *See* Azariah, 15.

3. Son of the high priest Zadok in Solomon's time (1 Ki 4:2).

4. A grandson of Zadok (1 Chr 6:9).

5. Son of Nathan; a chief officer of Solomon, possibly the king's nephew (1 Ki 4:5; see 2 Sa 5:14).

6. Son of Oded; a prophet who advised King Asa of Judah to carry out a religious reformation (2 Chr 15:1-8).

7 and 8. Two sons of King Jehoshaphat of Judah (2 Chr 21:2). The assignment of the same name to two sons of Jehoshaphat can be explained by assuming that they had different mothers, and therefore were half brothers. In Hebrew there is also a slight difference in the spelling of the two names, the first one being written *'Azaryah,* and the second one *'Azaryahû.*

9. A descendant of Judah of the family of Hezron (1 Chr 2:38, 39). Since he was the grandson of Obed, some have identified him with Azariah, 11.

10. Son of Jeroham; an army officer who helped to overthrow Athaliah and put Joash on the throne of Judah (2 Chr 23:1).

11. Son of Obed; another army officer who helped to overthrow Athaliah (2 Chr 23:1), possibly identical with Azariah, 9.

12. Son of Johanan; a prince of Ephraim who with others persuaded the soldiers of Pekah's army to release the prisoners taken in Judah (2 Chr 28:12).

13. The 10th king of Judah, who took the throne name Uzziah. *See* Uzziah, 3.

14. A high priest, son of Jonathan (1 Chr 6:10). He was probably the officiating priest who with 80 others withstood Uzziah when the king desired to enter the Temple to offer incense in the holy place (2 Chr 26:17-20). Some believe that he is identical with the high priest of the same name in Hezekiah's time (*see* Azariah, 15).

15. A high priest of King Hezekiah's time (2 Chr 31:10, 13), possibly identical with Azariah, 14.

16. A Levite of the family of Kohath, the father or ancestor of Joel (2 Chr 29:12), perhaps identical with Azariah, 2.

17. Son of Jehalelel of the family of Merari; a Levite. He assisted in the cleansing of the Temple in Hezekiah's time (2 Chr 29:12).

18. Son of Hilkiah and father of Seraiah; a high priest, who seems to have lived shortly before the Exile (1 Chr 6: 13, 14), perhaps identical with Azariah, 21.

19. Son of Hoshaiah; an opponent of the prophet Jeremiah (Jer 43:2).

20. One of the three companions of Daniel (Dan 1:7). His Babylonian name was Abednego.

21. Son (or descendant) of Hilkiah; a priest possibly after the Exile (1 Chr 9: 11), although he may have lived before the Exile and may have been identical with Azariah, 18.

22. Son of Maaseiah; owner of a house at Jerusalem in Nehemiah's time, who repaired a section of the wall in its vicinity (Neh 3:23, 24); perhaps identical with Azariah, 23 and (or) Azariah, 25.

23. One of the prominent leaders in Nehemiah's time who marched in the procession at the dedication of the wall of Jerusalem (Neh 12:33), perhaps the same as Azariah, 22.

24. One of the Levites who assisted Ezra in explaining the Law of God (Neh 8:7), perhaps identical with Azariah, 25.

25. A priest who signed the covenant in Nehemiah's time (Neh 10:2), perhaps identical with Azariah, 24.

In 2 Chr 22:6 "Azariah the son of Jehoram" must be considered a scribal mistake for Ahaziah, as indicated by v 7 and the parallel text in 2 Ki 8:29.

Azaz (ā'zăz). [Heb. *'Azaz*, "strong," probably a shortened form of *'Azazyahû*, "Azaziah."] A Reubenite (1 Chr 5:8).

Azazel (*a*-zā'zĕl), KJV **Scapegoat**. [Heb. *'aza'zel*, a word of uncertain derivation and meaning.] A term occurring in Lev 16:8, 10, 26. The form "Azazel" is a transliteration of the Hebrew. The translation "scapegoat" (escape-goat) came from the Vulgate *caper emissarius*, "goat sent away," and *caper emissarius* in turn was apparently based on Symmachus' revision of the LXX. It is not certainly known whether *'aza'zel* is the name of a personal being, or whether it refers to the act of sending away, or to the place to which the goat was sent. The KJV considers *'aza'zel* in the impersonal sense, while the RSV takes it to be the name of a personal being. Two facts lend weight to the argument that it should be considered a personal noun: (1) the parallel Hebrew construction "for Yahweh . . . for Azazel" implies that Azazel is a personal being, even as Yahweh (the Lord) is; (2) certain Jewish expositors and writers so considered the term. The pseudepigraphical Book of Enoch, for instance, characterizes Azazel as the one who "hath taught all unrighteousness on earth" (ch 9:6), and adds that "the whole earth has been corrupted through the works that were taught by Azazel: to him ascribe all sin" (ch 10:8). Azazel is also pictured as being bound hand and foot and being cast into an abyss somewhere in the desert, awaiting "the

day of the great judgment" when "he shall be cast into the fire" (ch 10:4, 6; cf. 54:1-5).

On the Day of Atonement two goats were brought into the court of the sanctuary, where lots were cast to select one of them "for the Lord" and the other "for Azazel" (Lev 16:5-10). With the blood of the goat on which the lot fell "for the Lord" the high priest made atonement for the Most Holy Place, the holy place, and the altar of burnt offering, because of the sins of Israel (vs 16-19). It is important to note that the goat selected "for Azazel" had no part whatever in the services of the Day of Atonement until this work of atonement had been made with the goat "for the Lord" (v 20). Only then did the high priest figuratively transfer the accumulated sins of the year to the goat "for Azazel" and send it away into the wilderness (vs 21, 22). It was the blood of the Lord's goat that atoned, in figure, for the sins of the people (vs 15-17). The blood of the goat "for Azazel" was not shed (vs 10, 20). His removal represented the final and complete removal of sin from the universe.

Azaziah (ăz'*a*-zī'*a*). [Heb. *'Azazyahû*, "Yahweh is strong."]

1. A Temple musician in the time of David (1 Chr 15:21).

2. The father of a prince of Ephraim in David's time (1 Chr 27:20).

3. An overseer of the Temple in the days of Hezekiah (2 Chr 31:13).

Azbuk (ăz'bŭk). [Heb. *'Azbúq*, meaning unknown.] Father of a certain Nehemiah who repaired the wall of Jerusalem in the time of his great contemporary and namesake (Neh 3:16).

Azekah (*a*-zē'k*a*). [Heb. *'Azeqah*, "a hacked-up (place)"; Assyrian *Azaqa*.] One of the cities of the Shephelah assigned to Judah (Jos 15:35). The city is first mentioned as the terminal point to which Joshua drove his enemies after the battle at Gibeon (ch 10:10, 11). The Philistines with Goliath as their champion encamped between Socoh and Azekah (1 Sa 17:1). Rehoboam fortified the city (2 Chr 11:9). It was one of the last cities taken by Nebuchadnezzar before Jerusalem was captured (Jer 34:7). A remark found in one of the Lachish Letters refers to this event. A Jewish army officer, stationed at a place from which he could watch the (fire) signals of Azekah and Lachish, reported to the commanding officer at Lachish: "And let (my lord) know that we are watching for the signals of Lachish, according to all the indications which my lord hath given, for we cannot see Azekah" (*ANET* 322). It seems that Azekah had already fallen and thus could not send out more signals. The city was reoccupied by Jews after the Exile (Neh 11:30). It has been identified with *Tell ez-Zakarîyeh* in the *Wâdî es-Sant*, about 16 mi. west of Bethlehem (Map VI, E-2). Excavations at the site were conducted by F. J. Bliss and R. A. S. Macalister in 1898 and 1899, when Palestinian archeology was in its infancy.

Azel (ā'zĕl). [Heb. *'Asel*, "noble."] A descendant of Saul through Jonathan (1 Chr 8:37, 38; 9:43, 44).

Azem. *See* Ezem.

Azgad (ăz'găd). [Heb. *'Azgad*, probably a name of Persian origin, meaning "messenger." It occurs also in the Aramaic papyri from the Jewish colony of Elephantine in Egypt.] The founder of a family of whom 1,222 male members returned to Palestine with Zerubbabel (Ezr 2:12; Neh 7:17 [2,322]), and again 110 male members with Ezra (Ezr 8:12). A representative of the family set his seal to Nehemiah's covenant (Neh 10:15).

Aziel (ā'zĭ-ĕl). [Heb. *'Azî'el*, "my strength is God."] A Levite musician of the second degree in the time of David (1 Chr 15:20). Many commentators identify him with the Jaaziel of v 18 and the Jeiel of ch 16:5.

Aziza (á-zī'zá). [Heb. *'Azîza'*, "strong." The name occurs in Assyrian texts as *Azizu*.] An Israelite married to a foreign wife in the time of Ezra's campaign of reform (Ezr 10:27).

Azmaveth (ăz-mā'vĕth). [Heb. *'Azmaweth*, "death is strong." It is also the name of a plant that grows in Arabia and is widely used as camel fodder.]
1. One of David's "mighty men" (2 Sa 23:31).
2. A Benjamite whose sons joined David at Ziklag (1 Chr 12:3).
3. A royal treasurer (1 Chr 27:25).
4. A descendant of King Saul through Jonathan (1 Chr 8:33, 36).
5. A place in the neighborhood of Jerusalem to which 42 Jews whose ancestors had lived there returned with Zerubbabel from the exile in Babylon (Ezr 2:24). In Neh 7:28 it is called Beth-azmaveth. Some of the Temple singers made their homes there (ch 12:29). It has been identified with *Ḥizmeh*, between Geba and Anathoth, situated about 5 mi. northeast of Jerusalem.

Azmon (ăz'mŏn). [Heb. *'Asmôn*.] A place on the southern border of Palestine, west of Kadesh-barnea (Num 34:4, 5; Jos 15:4). It has been identified with *Qoseimeh* (Map V, B-6), approximately 60 mi. south of Gaza.

Aznoth-tabor (ăz'nŏth-tā'bôr). [Heb. *'Aznôth Tabôr*, literally, "the ears of Tabor."] A place near the southern border of Naphtali (Jos 19:34). The site has been identified with *Umm Jebeil* in the vicinity of Mt. Tabor.

Azor (ā'zôr). [Gr. *Azōr*.] A postexilic Judahite appearing in Matthew's genealogy of Jesus. (Mt 1:13).

Azotus. *See* Ashdod.

Azriel (ăz'rĭ-ĕl). [Heb. *'Azrî'el*, "God is my help."]
1. Head of a Manassite family (1 Chr 5:24).
2. A Naphtalite, a contemporary of David (1 Chr 27:19).
3. Father of a royal courtier in Jeremiah's time (Jer 36:26).

Azrikam (ăz'rĭ-kăm). [Heb. *'Azrîqam*, "my help has risen."]
1. A descendant of Saul through Jonathan (1 Chr 8:38; 9:44).
2. A descendant of David (1 Chr 3:23).
3. A Levite of the house of Merari (1 Chr 9:14), perhaps identical with Azrikam, 5.
4. The governor of the palace in King Ahaz' time (2 Chr 28:7).
5. A Levite whose descendant lived in the time of Nehemiah (Neh 11:15), perhaps identical with Azrikam, 3.

Azubah (á-zū'bá). [Heb. *'Azûbah*, "forsaken."]
1. Wife of Caleb (1 Chr 2:18, 19).
2. Mother of King Jehoshaphat (1 Ki 22:42).

Azur. *See* Azzur, 1, 2.

Azzah. *See* Gaza.

Azzan (ăz'ăn). [Heb. *'Azzan*, "strong." The name occurs also in the Ugaritic texts of the 2d millennium B.C.] Father of a prince of Issachar in the days of Moses (Num 34:26).

Azzur (ăz'ēr), KJV twice **Azur** (ā'zēr). [Heb. *'Azzur*, "helped." The name occurs also in the Aramaic texts of a Jewish colony at Elephantine in Egypt, in the 5th cent. B.C.]
1. Father of the false prophet Hananiah who prophesied in Jeremiah's time (Jer 28:1).
2. Father of a prince in Jerusalem in Zedekiah's time (Eze 11:1).
3. A signer of Nehemiah's covenant (Neh 10:17).

B

Baal (bā'ăl). [Heb. *Ba'al,* "lord," "possessor," "husband." The name is found in Akkadian as *Bêlu,* in Ugaritic as *b'l,* in Egyptian (13th cent. B.C. on) as *b'r.* Gr. *Baal.*]

1. A Semitic god. The name Baal was (1) a designation for a local god in the sense of "lord," as in Baal-gad, Baal-peor, Baal-hermon; (2) the name of a Canaanite god. The Canaanites believed that Baals dwelt in holy trees, springs, mountain summits, rocks, etc., and spoke of each of these local gods as the Baal, i.e., "lord," of that particular locality. These local gods are often referred to in the OT, where Baal appears in its plural form Baalim (Jgs 2:11; 3:7; 8:33; etc.). These Baalim were considered nature deities who took care of the vegetation and the increase of cattle and flocks. Where the name appears in the singular it generally refers to the chief national god of the Canaanites.

In the *Ras Shamra texts the word Baal sometimes applies to gods as possessors of particular places and sanctuaries, but more generally it is the name of the highest of the gods. As head of the Canaanite pantheon he seems to have been a latecomer, for El had possessed prominence long before Baal arrived, and a temple was dedicated to Dagon before one was built for Baal. But when Baal emerged from the struggle for supremacy among the gods as the chief god, he held his position for many centuries. He was the storm god, and was therefore frequently identified with Adad (Hadad). Bringing the winter rains with storms and lightnings, he was held responsible for the fertility of the country. His sister and wife was Anath, the ferocious goddess of bloodshed and war, and his antagonist was Mot, the god of drought and of the scorching heat. When Baal was killed (whether by Mot is not clear, since the text is broken), Anath implored Mot to raise him to life again, but when all her efforts failed, she became furious and in her rage overpowered and killed Mot, took her dead brother, and carried him to the mountain of the gods, where he was resurrected to a new life. After that Baal's death and resurrection were supposed to occur annually, and resulted, the Canaanites believed, in the two main seasons of Syria-Palestine, summer and winter. Baal's death at the hand of evil Mot at the end of each rainy season was observed by bitter mourning, and his annual resurrection at the end of the long, dry summer months when the rainy season began, bringing new life to fields and vineyards, was celebrated with joyous and licentious feasting. Baal worship, universal throughout Syria and Palestine, seems to have held a great attraction for the Israelites. They repeatedly turned to it from the time they entered the land of Canaan until they were carried into exile. The first time that Baal is mentioned in the history of Israel is shortly before Moses' death, when the Israelites encamped in the fields of Moab near a high place of Baal (Num 22:41, KJV; RSV "Bamoth-baal"). The

43. **Baal as the Canaanite god of storm and thunder on a stele from Ugarit**

44. Six columns of the temple of Zeus (Jupiter) built in Roman times at Baalbek (Syrian Heliopolis)

'*Abiba'al*, "Baal is my father," *Ba'alzamar*, "Baal sings," *Ba'ala'zakar*, "Baal remembers (?)," *Ba'alma'anî*, "Baal is my answer," *Meriba'al*, "My lord is Baal [if the name is Aramaic]," and *Ba'ala*. These names prove that there were many followers of Baal among the common people during the generations living shortly after Ahab's reign. In the southern kingdom this cult was especially encouraged by Ahaz of Judah, who made images to the Baalim (2 Chr 28:2). These idols were removed during the reign of his good son Hezekiah, but altars to Baal were again erected by Manasseh, the next king (2 Ki 21:3). Good King Josiah in turn destroyed the vessels that had been used in the cult of Baal (ch 23:4, 5). The worship of Baal was one of the principal causes for the desolation of Judah (Jer 19:5).

The OT testifies also that the cult of Baal was accompanied by the burning of children in the fire (Jer 19:5) and the kissing of the image (1 Ki 19:18). It was probably also accompanied by gross lasciviousness. Associated frequently with Baal is the goddess *Ashtoreth (Jgs 2:13), and on the high places dedicated to Baal was usually found an *Asherah (Jgs 6:30; 1 Ki 16:32, 33; RSV).

In various places Baal came to be identified with Helios (the sun), with Hercules, or with the chief Greek god, *Zeus (the Roman Jupiter). See fig. 44.

Lit.: Arvid S. Kapelrud, *Baal in the Ras Shamra Texts* (Copenhagen, 1952); W. F. Albright, *Archaeology and the Religion of Israel* (4th ed; Baltimore, 1956).

2. A village in the territory of Simeon otherwise known as *Baalath-beer.

3. A Reubenite (1 Chr 5:5, 6).

4. A Benjamite, son of King Saul's ancestor Jehiel (1 Chr 8:30; 9:36).

Baalah (bā'á-lá). [Heb. *Ba'alah*, "mistress."]
1. A town about 5 mi. northwest of Jerusalem (Jos 15:9), more commonly known as *Kiriath-jearim. Map VI, E-3.

2. A mountain in Judah, between Shikkeron and Jabneel (Jos 15:11); unknown.

3. A town in southern Judah (Jos 15:29), apparently later assigned to Simeon (ch 19:3, contracted to Balah, bā'lá). In 1 Chr 4:29 it is called Bilhah. All suggested identifications are uncertain.

Baalath (bā'ál-ăth). [Heb. *Ba'alath*, "mistress."] A place in the southern (earlier) territory of Dan (Jos 19:44), fortified by Solomon (1 Ki 9:18; 2 Chr 8:6). According to Josephus it lay near Gezer (*Ant.* viii. 6. 1), but its exact site has not yet been identified with certainty. Y. Aharoni

"gods" to which the Israelites bowed down (Num 25:2) probably included Baal. Baal was worshiped again by the Israelites in the time of the judges (Jgs 2:13; 6: 28-32) and frequently during the period of the kings of Judah and Israel. Baal almost supplanted Yahweh in the kingdom of Israel in the time of Ahab, when Jezebel, Ahab's headstrong Tyrian wife, attempted to establish the religion of Baal as the only legitimate mode of worship. The story of Elijah's fight against this cult and his contest with the Baal priests on Mount Carmel is well known (1 Ki 16: 31, 32; 18:17-40). But his victory for Yahweh was short-lived. Even King Jehu's ruthless crushing of Baal worship at his accession to the throne (2 Ki 10:18-28) resulted in only temporary reform. Baal worship thrived also for a time in Judah, where Athaliah, Ahab's wicked daughter, had introduced it (ch 11:18).

The existence of Baal worship in the northern kingdom is attested by the ostraca found during the Harvard University excavations of Samaria, dated either in the late 9th or early 8th cent. B.C. Among the many personal names of citizens of that kingdom in these texts there were found several Baal names, such as identifies it with *Qaṭrā* in the *Wâdī eṣ-Ṣarar* (*PEQ* 90 [1958], 30).

Baalath-beer (bā´ȧ-lăth-bē´ẽr). [Heb. *Ba‘alath Be’er,* "mistress of the well."] A place on the border of the territory of Simeon (Jos 19:8), apparently the same as Baal, 2 (1 Chr 4:33). Many scholars think that it is identical with "Ramath of the south" (Jos 19:8; RSV "Ramah of the Negeb"). The site has not been identified.

Baal-berith (bā´ăl-bē´rĭth), or **El-berith** (ĕl-bē´rĭth). [Heb. *Ba‘al berîth,* "lord of a covenant," and *’El Berîth,* "god of a covenant."] A deity worshiped by the Israelites in the period of the judges (Jgs 8:33; 9:4, 46), called "the god Berith" in the KJV of Jgs 9:46. A temple dedicated to this god was situated in Shechem and, like most temples, was a storehouse of treasures (v 4). It is not known how this god received its name or to which covenant reference is made. The following suggestion has been made: The Shechemites traced their origin back to Hamor (Jgs 9:28; cf. Gen 34:20; etc.). Hamor literally means "ass." The Mari documents show that among the Amorites the expression "killing an ass" was synonymous with "making a treaty." Hence, the "sons of Hamor" or "sons of an ass" may mean "members of a confederacy," and Baal-berith may have been the god called to witness the treaty (see Albright, *Archaeology and the Religion of Israel* [1942], p. 113).

Baale (of Judah). *See* Baale-judah.

Baale-judah (bā´ȧ-lĕ-jōō´dȧ), KJV **Baale** (bā´ȧ-lē) **Judah.** [Heb. *Ba‘alê Yehûdah,* probably Baalah of Judah.] A. town in Judah (2 Sa 6:2), usually identified with Kiriath-baal or *Kiriath-jearim, whence David brought the sacred ark to Jerusalem.

Baal-gad (bā´ăl-găd). [Heb. *Ba‘al-gad,* "Gad is Baal."] A place in the valley of Lebanon below Mount *Hermon, where, presumably, Gad, the Phoenician god of fortune, was worshiped. It represented the northernmost limits of Joshua's conquests (Jos 11:17; 12:7; 13:5). Attempts have been made to identify the place with Baalbek, but not many scholars accept this identification.

Baal-hamon (bā´ăl-hā´mŏn). [Heb. *Ba‘al Hamôn,* "Baal of a multitude."] A place where Solomon had a vineyard (Song 8:11); not identified.

Baal-hanan (bā´ăl-hā´năn). [Heb. *Ba‘al Chanan,* "Baal is gracious." The name occurs on ancient Hebrew seal inscriptions;

in cuneiform records as that of the prince of Arwad, *Ba‘alhanûnu;* and, with its component parts reversed, as Hannibal (Punic *Chnb‘l*), the name of a famous Carthaginian general.]

1. A king of Edom (Gen 36:38; 1 Chr 1:49).

2. A Gederite in charge of David's olive and sycamore trees in the *Shephelah (1 Chr 27:28).

Baal-hazor (bā´ăl-hā´zôr). [Heb. *Ba‘al Chaṣôr,* "Baal of an enclosure."] A place near Ephraim (2 Sa 13:23), probably *Jebel ‘Aṣûr* 5 mi. northeast of Bethel.

Baal-hermon (bā´ăl-hûr´mŏn). [Heb. *Ba‘al Chermôn,* "Baal of Hermon."] A place near or on Mount Hermon, probably an old sanctuary devoted to Baal. It formed the northern boundary of Manasseh in Transjordan (Jgs 3:3; 1 Chr 5:23).

Baali (bā´ȧ-lī). [Heb. *Ba‘lî,* "my lord," "my Baal" (RSV).] A name Israel applied to the Lord during the time of her unfaithfulness to Him (Hos 2:16). Before her apostasy her relationship to God is described as that of a wife to her husband (v 7). An attempt to blend the worship of Baal with that of the true God had so confused the thinking of Israel that she addressed God as if He had become identified with Baal. In His appeal to His wayward people God set before them the prospect of having the former relationship restored. Israel would then call God Ishi, "my husband," and no longer Baali, "my lord," or "my Baal."

Baalim. *See* Baal.

Baalis (bā´ȧ-lĭs). [Heb. *Ba‘alîs,* meaning unknown. The name occurs in Ugarit as *B‘ls.*] A king of the Ammonites (Jer 40:14).

Baal-meon (bā´ăl-mē´ŏn). [Heb. *Ba‘al Me‘ôn,* "Baal of the habitation."] An ancient Amorite city (Num 32:38; *Moabite Stone, line 9) about 4 mi. southwest of Medeba. It was also called Beth-baal-meon (bĕth´bā´ăl-mē´ŏn) (Jos 13:17; *Moabite Stone, line 30), Beth-meon (bĕth´mē´ŏn) (Jer 48:23), and Beon, a contracted form (Num 32:3). It was assigned to the Transjordan Reubenites, and was rebuilt by them (Num 32:38). Later (9th cent. B.C.), according to the *Moabite Stone, the Moabites occupied it. In the 6th cent. B.C., according to Jeremiah (ch 48:23) and Ezekiel (ch 25:9), it was still in their hands. The site is now called *Ma‘în.* Map VI, E-4.

Baal-peor (bā´ăl-pē´ôr). [Heb. *Ba‘al Pe‘ôr,* "Baal of Peor."] A Moabite god worshiped on Mount *Peor. During their stay at Shittim the Israelites, seduced by Moabite women, were led into idolatrous worship of him. As a result a plague broke out among the Israelites, during the course of which many died (Num 25:1-9; Ps 106:28; Hos 9:10). The deity is usually identified with Chemosh, but such an identity cannot be proved.

Baal-perazim (bā'ăl-pĕ-rā'zĭm). [Heb. *Ba'al Peraṣîm*, "Baal (or lord) of breakings forth."] A place in or near the valley of Rephaim, where David gained a signal victory over the Philistines (2 Sa 5:18-20; 1 Chr 14:9-11). Some scholars believe it lay on the ridge 3 mi. south of Jerusalem on which the monastery of Mars Eliãs now stands. Other sites have been suggested, but identification remains uncertain.

Baal-shalisha. See Baal-shalishah.

Baal-shalishah (bā'ăl-shăl'ĭ-shá), KJV **Baal-shalisha** (bā'ăl-shăl'ĭ-shá). [Heb. *Ba'al Shalishah.*] A place in Ephraim from which a man brought bread and corn to the prophet Elisha at Gilgal (2 Ki 4:42-44). Its site has not been identified with certainty.

Baal-tamar (bā'ăl-tā'mär). [Heb. *Ba'al Tamar*, "Baal of the date palm."] A place near Gibeah and Geba, from which the Israelites began their attack on Gibeah (Jgs 20:33). Its location is uncertain.

Baal-zebub (bā'ăl-zē'bŭb). [Heb. *Ba'al Zebûb*, "Baal (or lord) of the fly."] The god of Ekron. He was probably worshiped to appease the flies, which were doubtless bothersome then as now. The numerous golden images of flies found in the excavations of Philistine sites were probably dedicated to this god. King Ahaziah of Israel sent messengers to this deity to seek counsel concerning his health (2 Ki 1:6, 16). See Beelzebul; also fig. 185.

Baal-zephon (bā'ăl-zē'fŏn). [Heb. *Ba'al Ṣephôn*, "Baal of the North."] A place at the eastern border of Egypt mentioned in the Exodus story (Ex 14:2, 9; Num 33:7). The name is attested in an Aramaic papyrus from Egypt as that of a god in or near Tahpanhes. It has therefore been thought that the site of Baal-zephon was at Tahpanhes (Map V, B-4), now *Tell Defneh*, southeast of Tanis (*BASOR* 109 [1948], 15, 16). Yet, this place is rather far north if the Israelites crossed the Red Sea somewhere near Suez, as is generally thought. It is possible that the god Baal-zephon of Tahpanhes has nothing more in common with the place Baal-zephon than its name. Map V shows Baal-zephon, with question marks, at two places: one

at Tahpanhes (B-4) and the other (according to another theory, which does not accept the Red Sea as the place of the crossing) on the Mediterranean coast (B-5).

Baana (bā'à-nà), KJV once **Baanah** (bā'à-nà). [Heb. *Ba'ana'*, meaning uncertain.]
1. One of Solomon's supply officers whose district lay in the Plain of Esdraelon and reached from Megiddo to the Jordan (1 Ki 4:12).
2. Another of Solomon's supply officers, whose territory lay in Asher. His father was Hushai, probably the famous counselor of David (1 Ki 4:16). His name is spelled Baanah in the KJV.
3. Father of one of the builders of Jerusalem's wall in Nehemiah's time (Neh 3:4).

Baanah (bā'à-nà). [Heb. *Ba'anah*, meaning uncertain.]
1. A Benjamite captain of a band in Ish-bosheth's kingdom. He and his brother Rechab assassinated Ish-bosheth and took his head to David at Hebron, expecting a reward for their deed. David, however, had them executed as criminals (2 Sa 4:2-12).
2. The father of one of David's "mighty men" from Netophah (1 Chr 11:30).
3. A misspelling of Baana. See Baana, 2.
4. One of the leaders of the exiles returning with Zerubbabel from Babylonia (Ezr 2:2; Neh 7:7). The Baanah in Neh 10:27 who signed Nehemiah's covenant was probably a representative of the family of this leader.

Baara (bā'à-rà). [Heb. *Ba'ara'*. The name appears also on the ostraca from Samaria.] The wife of a Benjamite who lived in Moab (1 Chr 8:8).

Baaseiah (bā'à-sē'yá). [Heb. *Ba'aśeyah*, thought to stand for *Ma'aśeyah* (Maaseiah), "work of Yahweh," as several Hebrew manuscripts have it, and in accordance with the LXX, which reads *Maasia* instead of *Baasia*.] A Gershonite Levite who was an ancestor of the singer Asaph (1 Chr 6:40).

Baasha (bā'à-shà). [Heb. *Ba'esha'*, meaning obscure, although the name occurs in cuneiform records as *Ba'sa*, a king of Ammon.] The son of Ahijah, of the tribe of Issachar, the 3d king of the northern kingdom of Israel. He acquired the throne by slaying King Nadab during a siege of the Philistine city of Gibbethon (1 Ki 15:27, 28). One of the first acts of his reign was to exterminate all remaining relatives of Jeroboam I, thus fulfilling the prophet Ahijah's prediction (vs 29, 30; ch 14:10,

11). The 24 years of Baasha's reign (*c*. 909 - *c*. 886 B.C.) were marked by wickedness (1 Ki 15:34) and by continual warfare with the southern kingdom (v 32). His attempt to build up Ramah as a military fortress within the border of Judah failed when Asa of Judah hired Ben-hadad I of Damascus against him (1 Ki 15:16-21; 2 Chr 16:1-6). The prophet Jehu predicted the extermination of Baasha's dynasty (1 Ki 16:1-4).

Babel (bā'bĕl). [Heb. *Babel*. According to Gen 11:9 the name means "confusion," based, evidently, on the fact that the Hebrew verb *balal* means "to confuse." The Babylonians, however, explained the name of their city, which they called *Bâbilu*, to mean "gate of god" or *Bâbi-ilâni*, "gate of the gods" (*RLA* 1:333). Possibly the name was originally derived from the Babylonian verb *babalu*, "to scatter," or "to disappear"; but the Babylonians may not have been proud of the original meaning of their city, hence their explanation of it as a compound of the names *babu*, "gate," and *ilu*, "god."] A city dating from the earliest inhabitants of Mesopotamia, the beginning of Nimrod's kingdom, being probably the seat of his power (Gen 10:10). Outside of Gen 10:10; 11:9 the city of Babel is always called Babylon in the Bible. *See* Babylon.

The Tower of Babel. A term not found in the OT, but it is the name generally given to the structure that the early inhabitants of Shinar began to build, the progress of which was halted by divine intervention bringing confusion of tongues (Gen 11:1-8). The builders used bricks, because their country was completely void

46. The temple tower of Babylon as reconstructed by Th. Dombart

of stones. "Slime," or asphalt, as mortar has been found in many Babylonian public buildings (see fig. 388). It was obtained from open pitch wells at *Hît*, 120 mi. north of Babylon (see Map III, C-5). Of the Biblical tower nothing remains, but the idea of erecting towers was popular among the early Mesopotamians. Practically every city of importance had at least one. These towers were called ziggurats, and were usually built in progressively smaller stages, and had on the top a shrine dedicated to the principal god of the city or of the land. The ruins of some of the ziggurats are still standing; the best preserved are those of Ur in southern Iraq and of *Choga Zambil* near Susa in Iran, but even the remains of the ziggurats at *Nimrûd*, *Qal'a Sherqat*, *'Aqarquf*, *Birs Nimrûd*, and *Warka* (see Map XXI, B/C-5) are impressive ruins. The temple tower of Babylon, mentioned in historical records from the beginning of the 2d millennium B.C., which was the highest and largest of all such structures which stood in historical times in Mesopotamia, has completely vanished. Excavators found no more of it than its foundations and a few steps of its stairway. However, an ancient cuneiform tablet describes this tower, and Herodotus mentions it; hence it is possible to get a fairly accurate picture of this famous structure. We know that it was about 300 ft. square at its base, and more than 300 ft. high, and that it was built in 7 stages, having on top of the 7th stage a shrine dedicated to the god Marduk.

The tower was repaired from time to time, the last time by Nebuchadnezzar, who said that he received a command from his god Marduk to build it so that

45. Air picture of the site where the temple tower of the city of Babylon stood. Remains of the core of the ancient tower protrude from the water-filled hole. It is the probable site of the Tower of Babel

BABYLON AND ITS ENVIRONS

SIXTH CENTURY B.C.

ACCORDING TO ECKHARD UNGER,

BABYLON; DIE HEILIGE STADT

SCALE IN ENGLISH MILES

0   ¼   ½   ¾   1 mi.

SCALE IN ENGLISH MILES
0 2 4 6 8 10

WESTERN BRANCH OF EUPHRATES R.
EASTERN BRANCH OF EUPHRATES R.

Babil   Kish
Modern Irrigation Canals

BABYLON
Hilla

Borsippa
(Birs Nimrud)

The Euphrates is shown in its present be[d] having changed its course near Baby[lon] and Borsippa. Lines extending from t[he] river are modern irrigation canals, dou[bt]less similar to ancient canals

Key to Temples

A Temple of the New Year's Feast
B Temple of Ninmach
C Temple of Belit Ninâ
D Temple of Adad
E Temple of Shamash
F Temple of Ishtar of Akkad
G Etemenanki (temple tower)
H Temple of Marduk
I Temple of Gula
J Temple of Ninurta

Nebuchadnezzar's Summer Palace

River Road to Akkad
Road to Bit Habban
NEBUCHADNEZZAR'S
Old Cuthah Canal
Road to Cuthah

NEBUCHADNEZZAR'S OUTER CITY

OUTER WALL

North Citadel
MOAT
A
Sin Gate
Ishtar Gate
Central Palace
B
Hanging Gardens
Southern Palace
Citadel
Sin Street
Marduk Gate
Cuthah Canal
INNER CITY
MOAT
Lugal Girra Gate
Shamash Street
Procession Street
E F
Marduk Street
Central Canal
Enlil Street
Road to Kish
C
Esagila
Street
Ninurta Gate
D
Canal
Adad Street
H
Nabu Street
J
Zababa Street
Adad Gate
NEW CITY
Enlil Gate
NEBUCHADNEZZAR'S
New Canal
OUTER WALL
MOAT
E
Urash Gate
Road to Nippur
Shamash Gate
MOAT
Road to Borsippa
MOAT
Borsippa Canal

EUPHRATES R. (PRESENT BED)
RIVER (OLD BED)

47. Map of ancient Babylon

"its top might rival heaven." He called his temple tower, which stood in the sacred compound of the Marduk temple, *Etemenanki,* meaning "the foundation stone of heaven and earth." It was destroyed by Xerxes. Alexander the Great planned to rebuild it; in fact, he had most of the debris removed, preparatory to its reconstruction, when death took him. Since practically nothing of the old temple tower remained above ground, men of later generations questioned its existence. A tradition also arose that connected the ruined but impressive tower at Borsippa, now *Birs Nimrûd,* with the Tower of Babel. However, excavations have now proved this tradition to be erroneous.

When Assyriology was in its infancy, a badly broken cuneiform tablet in the British Museum was interpreted to refer to the story of the Tower of Babel. More careful reading has shown this view to be erroneous. See L. W. King, *The Seven Tablets of Creation* (London, 1902), vol. 1, pp. 219, 220.

Babylon (băb′ĭ-lŏn). [Heb. and Aramaic *Babel (see* Babel); Gr. *Babulōn.*] A city in the Mesopotamian valley (see Map III, C-5; also fig. 47), one of the first cities founded *(see* Babel). Little of its history and features from the pre-empire period are known, since excavations have uncovered only the highest levels, which include that of the Neo-Babylonian kingdom. Since the water table is higher now than in ancient times, the remains of earlier cities on this site lie below the water level. The city experienced its first rise to importance as the capital of the 1st dynasty of Babylon (called the Amorite dynasty), to which the famous Hammurabi belonged. This political importance was lost after the fall of that dynasty, but Babylon continued to be highly respected as a cultural and religious center of the ancient world. During the time of the Assyrian Empire it became a vassal kingdom of that empire but frequently rebelled against the yoke of its overlords. Sennacherib became so incensed at these frequent rebellions that he systematically and thoroughly destroyed the city in 689 B.C., intending that it should not be rebuilt. However, public opinion even in his homeland was against so rash a deed, and the rebuilding of the city began immediately after Sennacherib's death.

When in 626 B.C. Nabopolassar founded the independent Babylonian kingdom, Babylon became the capital of the new monarchy and soon that of a widespread empire. It is the Babylon of this period that R. Koldewey from 1899 to 1917 excavated for the German Orient Society. These excavations showed that the old, or inner, city, that is, the original portion of the city, lay on the east bank of the Euphrates and had a size of about one square mi. In its northwestern corner lay the royal palace, and south of that the sacred precinct of *Esagila,* in which area stood *Etemenanki,* the 300-foot temple tower (see fig. 46 for its probable appearance; see fig. 47 for its location), and the famous temple of Marduk. Nebuchadnezzar rebuilt and extended the palace, adding among other things a vaulted structure with a roof garden on it, called the Hanging Gardens of Babylon, known in the ancient world as one of the Seven Wonders of the World. He also added a New City on the western bank of the river and connected it by means of a permanent bridge with the old city (later called the Inner City). A mile and a half to the north of the city he erected a new palace, the so-called Summer Palace, and built a double

48. Ruins of the Ishtar Gate of Babylon through which the Procession Street led toward the main temple of Marduk

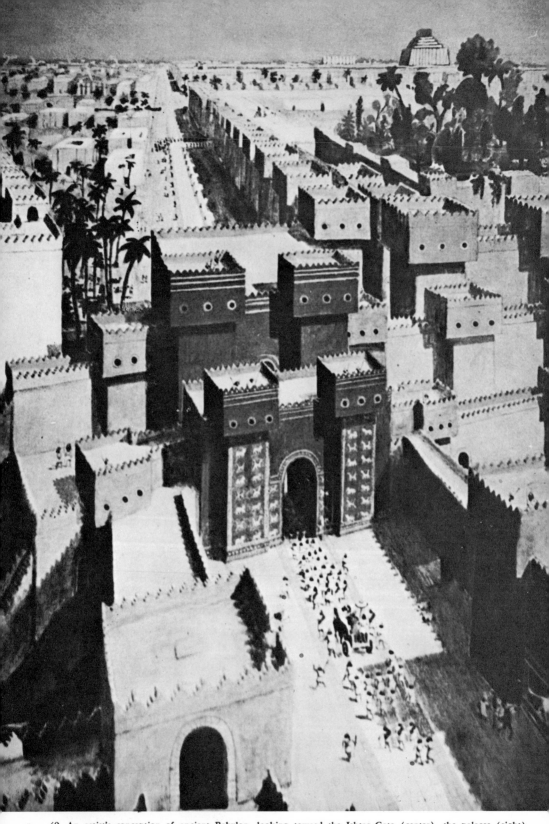

49. An artist's conception of ancient Babylon, looking toward the Ishtar Gate (center), the palaces (right), and the Procession Street, with the temple tower of Babylon in the distance (J. Bardin, artist)

wall that included this palace and the suburbs within its confines. He also surrounded the New City with a double wall and a moat that met the wall and moat that protected the Inner City. See fig. 47. With a total circumference of about 10 mi., Babylon was probably the largest city of antiquity, with the possible exception of Egyptian Thebes.

The city was built of bricks, since the alluvial soil of that area contains no stone. Ordinary bricks were unbaked, but the public buildings were faced with baked or glazed wall bricks in different colors, which gave to this metropolis a beauty that was hardly equaled by any other city of comparable size. The bricks of the outer walls of the city were yellow, the gates blue, the palaces rose-red, and the temples white. Furthermore, city gates had decorations of bulls in relief alternating with dragonlike figures in various colors. The walls of the Procession Street, which led from the north to the Marduk temple, showed varicolored lions in glazed brick reliefs (see figs. 49, 137 for these decorations). No wonder that the builder of this marvelous city became proud and overbearing. This fact is testified to not only by the book of Dan (ch 4:30) but also by the building inscriptions that Nebuchadnezzar left for posterity, to proclaim his name and fame.

A number of prophecies were directed against Babylon, predicting that the city would be destroyed and become an uninhabited place (Is 13; 14:1-23; Jer 50; 51). This prophecy has gradually been fulfilled. When Cyrus the Great took the city in 539 B.C. it suffered no violence and was taken over intact by the Persians, who made it one of the capitals of the new empire. However, several rebellions against Persian rule under Darius I and Xerxes led the latter king to punish the rebellious city by destroying its palaces, temples, and walls c. 480 B.C. He also abolished the title "king of Babylon," which he with his precursors had borne up to that time, and made Babylon a mere province. A century and a half later, Alexander the Great planned to make Babylon the capital of his empire, but he died before he could even begin to carry out his ambitious plans. None of his successors chose Babylon as a capital; Seleucus I Nicator in 312 B.C. built Seleucia as his new capital on the banks of the Tigris (Map XIII, C-5), using much building material from old Babylon. From that time on until modern times the city has

served as a quarry of bricks. The river dam of Hindiya was built with the ancient bricks of Babylon. So was the city of Hilla, lying 3½ mi. to the south of Babylon, and many of the villages surrounding the ancient city ruins. The great metropolis of former times is thus completely forsaken.

Tremendous hills of debris mark the former sections of Babylon. In the north is *Tell Babil,* covering up the miserable remains of Nebuchadnezzar's magnificent Summer Palace; farther to the south is the *Kasr,* under which lie the confusing foundations and ruined walls of the main city palace area, largely excavated now. To the south of the *Kasr* are the mounds of *Amran,* the site of the sacred precinct of Marduk, with its temple of *Esagila* buried under many feet of debris and sand. The foundations of the temple tower *Etemenanki* are now covered by water in the excavation pit. The old city walls can be traced in most places and are clearly visible as low parallel running mounds, which in shape and height hardly differ from the banks of ancient canals.

Babylon is also mentioned in the NT. Peter sent greetings from the church in "Babylon" (1 Pe 5:13), by which, commentators generally agree, he meant Rome, not the unimportant village that was all that remained of literal Babylon. In the Revelation, Babylon stands as a symbol of opposition against Christ and His followers (Rev 14:8; 16:19; 17:18).

Babylonia (băb'ĭ-lō'nĭ-å). [Heb. *Babel.* For etymology *see* Babel. *Babel* is rendered Babylonia 8 times in the RSV (Ezr 1:11; 2:1; etc.).] A name usually given to southern Mesopotamia from the Persian Gulf to about latitude 34° (see Map XII, D-7/8). This whole country is formed of alluvial deposits and was extremely fertile, but since the region lacked rainfall, irrigation was required. In ancient times a whole network of canals brought water to all parts of that area and made the whole region a virtual garden of God. Early inscriptions refer to this country as Sumer and Akkad, Sumer being the southern section from the Persian Gulf to about latitude 32°, and Akkad the section north of it. Both sections were dotted with numerous cities both large and small. The most important of these in Sumer were Ur, Uruk (Biblical Erech), Eridu, Nippur, Lagash, Larsa, and Isin, and in Akkad: Babylon, Kish, Cuthah, Borsippa, and Sippar (see Maps III, XI, C-5/6). Akkad is called Shinar in certain Bible texts (Gen 10:10; 11:2; Is 11:11), and the land of the Chaldeans in others (Jer 24:5; 25:12; Eze 12:13).

The first recorded inhabitants of the southern part of this region were the Sumerians, who spoke a language that shows no affinities with any other known language, ancient or modern. The Sumerians developed a high form of civilization, invented the art of writing, and two systems of calculating, the sexagesimal and decimal systems. They divided their country into many city-states. Their chief divinities were Anu, the sky-god; Enlil, god of the atmosphere; Dingirmah, goddess of the earth and fertility; and Ea, god of the waters. According to the so-called "low chronology," the first Sumerian period was replaced by the dynasty of Akkad in the 24th cent. B.C., when Semitic rulers defeated the Sumerians and took over the whole country. The great king Sargon of Akkad created an empire that reached from the Persian Gulf to the interior of Asia Minor. After a rule of a century this dynasty was brought to an end by an invasion of mountain people, the Guti. They ruled over all of Mesopotamia, although some cities seem to have enjoyed a kind of autonomy, such as prosperous Lagash (*Telloh*, Map XXI, C-6) under its able ruler Gudea. The Guti were driven out, after slightly more than a century of rule, by the Sumerians, who had experienced a renascence of power. They established the strong 3d dynasty of Ur, which ruled over Lower Mesopotamia from c. 2070 to c. 1960 B.C. The kings of this dynasty codified laws and built up a strong and prosperous economic empire. After the fall of Ur the power shifted to the two cities of Isin and Larsa, where it remained for more than a hundred years. In the 19th cent. B.C. the country was twice invaded, once by the Elamites from the eastern mountains, and once by the Amorites from the Syrian Desert. The latter succeeded in founding the strong 1st dynasty of Babylon c. 1830 B.C., of which the 6th king was the famous Hammurabi (1728-1686 B.C.). He defeated the last king of Larsa and ruled over practically the whole Mesopotamian valley. During this period Babylon came into its own as the capital of the empire. Hammurabi is best known as a great lawgiver (see fig. 291), but he was more than that. He was also a wise administrator and a sponsor of literature and art. His dynasty came to an end c. 1550 B.C. through a raid of the Hittites under Mur-

silis I. These invaders sacked Babylon, captured its king, and carried away the golden statue of its chief god, Marduk. During this same time the Kassites from the northeast overran the country and ruled over Lower Mesopotamia for several centuries. Their capital was Dûr Kurigalzu, now 'Aqarquf, a few miles west of Baghdad (Map III, C-5). The correspondence of one of the Kassite kings with the kings of Egypt has been preserved among the *Amarna Letters.

In the 13th cent. B.C. the Assyrians, then ruled by Tukulti-Ninurta I, invaded Babylonia. They, too, carried away the golden statue of Marduk. For 6 centuries Babylonia was more or less an Assyrian dependency. Rebellions against the foreign yoke were frequent, but regularly suppressed. *Tiglath-pileser III (745-727 B.C.), who introduced several military and political innovations, made himself king of Babylon under the name of Pul. Sargon II also ruled as king of Babylon, but Sennacherib, tired of the constant rebellions, in 689 B.C. thoroughly destroyed the city of Babylon. Esarhaddon rebuilt it, after which the city experienced its most flourishing period. In 626 B.C. Nabopolassar, a Chaldean official subject to the Assyrians, declared himself king of Babylon, as one of his tribal relatives, Marduk-apaliddina, the Biblical Merodach-baladan, had done a century earlier. Merodachbaladan's bid for independence lasted only 18 years, but the new kingdom became a success, and developed into an empire that soon succeeded that of the Assyrians. After Nabopolassar had fought against the Assyrians for several years with uneven success, he joined the Medes, and with their help after a siege of 3 months conquered Nineveh in 612 B.C. When the conquerors divided the Assyrian Empire, the Babylonian king inherited all of Mesopotamia, Syria, and Palestine. It was necessary for him to fight remnants of Assyrian resistance in Upper Mesopotamia for a few more years, and also the Egyptians, who had helped the Assyrians and who tried to become the masters of Syria and Palestine. In 605 B.C. Nebuchadnezzar, still crown prince, defeated Necho of Egypt, first at Carchemish and then at Hamath. Late in the same summer his father died and he succeeded to the throne. Annual campaigns in Syria and Palestine followed. Jerusalem was taken several times, and after its third capture in 586 B.C. the rebellious city was destroyed and its population deported to Babylonia.

Nebuchadnezzar was a strong king and a great builder. He practically rebuilt the city of Babylon, and erected many structures in other cities. After a successful rule of more than 40 years, he was followed by several weak rulers under whose inefficient government the empire deteriorated rapidly. His son Amel-Marduk, the Biblical Evil-merodach, reigned for only 2 years (562-560 B.C.), and was then assassinated and succeeded by his brother-in-law Nergal-shar-usur, who ruled in Babylon for 4 years (560-556 B.C.). He was followed by his son Labashi-Marduk, who was murdered after a reign of less than 2 months. The murderers put one of the conspirators, Nabonidus, on the throne. Nabonidus saw danger from Persia and made an alliance against it with Egypt, Lydia, and Sparta. He also campaigned in Arabia and made Tema in northwestern Arabia his residence for a number of years, while his eldest son, Belshazzar, to whom he entrusted the kingship as coregent, ruled in Babylon. In October, 539 B.C., only 23 years after Nebuchadnezzar's death, the empire fell into the hands of Cyrus the Persian, almost without a fight. Cyrus had forced an entrance into the Mesopotamian valley in the battle of Opis, and a few days later the capital city fell to the Persians without a battle, and with its fall ended the history of Babylon as an independent power. The kingdom became part of the Persian Empire and later was reduced to a province. The territory then fell to Alexander the Great and belonged successively to the Seleucids, Parthians, Sassanids, and others; now it is part of the country of Iraq.

Babylonians (băb′ĭ-lō′nĭ-ănz). [Heb. *Benê-babel;* Aramaic *Babelaye'.*] The inhabitants of Babylon (Ezr 4:9; Eze 23:15).

Babylonish Garment. *See* Mantle from Shinar.

Baca (bā′kà). [Heb. *Baka',* possibly "balsam tree."] The name of a valley in Palestine (Ps 84:6), possibly so named because balsam trees grew there. Some have thought that it is another name for the Valley of Rephaim, where trees of that species were found (2 Sa 5:22, 23, RSV), but this is pure conjecture. There were doubtless many valleys in which balsam trees grew. Another interpretation names it the valley of "weeping" from the Heb. *bakah,* "to weep," a word that differs only slightly from *baka'.* However, neither interpretation helps to identify this place.

Bachrites. *See* Becherites.

Badger. [Heb. *tachash,* meaning uncertain; it has long been recognized that the rendering "badger" is erroneous. On the basis of Arabic it was thought for awhile that the seal or the dolphin, both inhabitants of the Red Sea, were meant. K. Galling suggested that "badgers' skins" may have come from the town of *Taḥshi,* north of Damascus (*Bibl. Reallexikon* 357). A more plausible explanation is that *tachash* is a loan word from the Egyptian, where *tḥś* describes a thin leather that was used for furniture (Thomsen, *Reallexikon der Vorgesch.,* vol. vii, pp. 265, 266).] A word appearing in the expression "badgers' skins" (Ex 25:5; 26:14; 35:7; etc.; KJV). Instead of "badgers' skins" the RSV reads "goatskins," but the exact meaning of the Hebrew expression remains uncertain (see etymology given above). *See* Rock Badger.

Bag. The translation of various Hebrew and Greek words. In some instances it refers to a leather purse for carrying or keeping money and other valuables (2 Ki 5:23; 12:10; Job 14:17; Hag 1:6; Lk 12:33; etc.). Again, it may refer to the bag in which a merchant kept his weights (Deut 25:13; Prov 16:11; Mic 6:11; etc.), and at times money also (Is 46:6, RSV "purse"). Another leather bag was the type used by shepherds and travelers, probably a knapsack or a haversack that was slung over the shoulders (1 Sa 17:40, 49; Mt 10:10; KJV "scrip"). There was, as well, a case or container of the sort used for carrying the mouthpieces of wind instruments, also for carrying money and other things (Jn 12:6; 13:29; RSV "money box").

Bagpipe. [Aramaic *sûmponyah* and *sûmponya',* a loan word from the Gr. *sumphōnia,* a musical term and also the name of a musical instrument that might be described as a bagpipe.] An instrument mentioned in Dan 3:5, 10, 15 (KJV "dulcimer"), where the musical instruments in Nebuchadnezzar's band are listed. Greek musicians employed at the Babylonian court may have introduced this instrument and its name into Babylonia. That Greeks were employed by Nebuchadnezzar is attested by cuneiform records. The bagpipe is also mentioned by Polybius, a 2d cent. B.C. Greek historian (xxvi. 10; xxxi. 4), who describes it as an instrument played at the court of King Antiochus IV. That it is an extremely ancient musical instrument is shown by a Hittite relief of Eyuk in central Anatolia. The relief is dated the middle of the

2d millennium B.C., and seems to indicate that, as in later times, the bagpipe was made of the skin of a dog. Modern bagpipes used in the Orient consist of a leather bag in which two pipes have been inserted. One is used to inflate the bag, the other produces the tones. The pitch is controlled by the fingers of the player covering up various holes on this pipe.

Baharum (bȧ-hā'rŭm). [Derived from the Heb. *Bacharûmî,* "Baharumite."] A variant spelling of *Bahurim. The RSV reads "Baharum" in 1 Chr 11:33 as the place from which Azmaveth came. The KJV reads, "Azmaveth the Baharumite."

Baharumite (bȧ-hā'rŭm-īt). [Heb. *Bacharûmi.*] An inhabitant of Bahurim (1 Chr 11:33, KJV), called "Barhumite" (bär-hū'mīt) [Heb. *Barchumi*] in 2 Sa 23:31, KJV. *See* Baharum.

Bahurim (bȧ-hū'rĭm). [Heb. *Bachurîm,* "young men."] A place in Benjamin (1 Ki 2:8) on the way from Jerusalem to the Jordan, near the Mount of Olives (2 Sa 16:5; cf. 15:30, 32). Shimei, David's enemy, came from there (ch 19:16), and Jonathan and Ahimaaz hid in one of its cisterns (ch 17:18-21). It has been identified with *Râs eṭ-Ṭmîm,* a short distance east of Mount Scopus.

Bajith (bā'jĭth). [Heb. *Bayith,* "house" or "temple."] According to the KJV a town or a temple in Moab (Is 15:2). A textual problem in the Hebrew makes exact identification impossible. The translators of the RSV consider the Hebrew text in disorder, and correct it to read *bath,* "daughter."

Bakbakkar (băk-băk'ẽr). [Heb. *Baqbaqqar,* meaning uncertain.] A Levite (1 Chr 9:15).

Bakbuk (băk'bŭk). [Heb. *Baqbûq,* "bottle."] The founder of a family of Nethinim, or temple servants, some members of which returned from Babylon with Zerubbabel (Ezr 2:51; Neh 7:53).

Bakbukiah (băk'bû-kī'ȧ). [Heb. *Baqbuqyah,* "bottle of Yahweh."]

1. A high Levite officer in Jerusalem in Nehemiah's time (Neh 11:17).

2. A Levite, gatekeeper of the Temple in Nehemiah's time (Neh 12:25).

Balaam (bā'lăm). [Heb. *Bil'am,* probably "glutton," or "devourer," from *bala',* "to swallow," "to devour"; Gr. *Balaam.*] An Aramaean prophet or soothsayer bribed by the Moabite king Balak for the purpose of imposing a curse, or evil spell, over the Hebrew people encamped at Shittim on the eve of their crossing the Jordan River into Canaan (Num 22:1-6).

Balaam's home was in the city of *Pethor in the region of *Amaw (v 5, RSV) on the Euphrates River. Balaam was noted for possessing unusual powers (v 6), and his reputation must have been widely known. The account in chs 22 to 24 leaves no doubt that he knew the true God and that God communicated with him. Certainly the gift of prophecy rested upon him as he delivered his several oracles concerning the Hebrew people, though the Bible writers nowhere call him a prophet (ch 24:4, 16).

The utter consternation of the heathen nations of Palestine and Transjordan because of the Israelites is reflected in the admission of Rahab of Jericho: "Your terror is fallen upon us" and "all the inhabitants of the land faint because of you" (Jos 2:9). Reports of the miraculous crossing of the Red Sea and of Hebrew victories over the powerful Amorites east of the Jordan (v 10) terrified the inhabitants of the land. They feared that they would be next to fall before the apparently invincible Hebrew forces (v 11). The royal bribe Balak offered Balaam (Num 22:7, 17; 24:11) testifies to the king's abject fear of the Israelites, as well as his faith in Balaam's occult powers.

The first messengers Balak sent were "elders" (Num 22:5-7) or "princes" (vs 13, 14). When Balaam, as instructed by the Lord, refused to return with them, Balak dispatched a second delegation composed of "princes" of higher rank and offered a higher bribe (vs 15-17). Although he now knew the Lord's will in the matter, Balaam presumed to inquire again for permission to go with the messengers (vs 18, 19). The Lord permitted him to accompany them, if called, but bade him speak only what would be given him (v 20). Bent on acquiring the honors and reward Balak had offered, Balaam set out with the princes, seemingly forgetful of the fact that the restrictions placed on him would defeat the purpose of the journey (vs 20-22). On the way Balaam received signal evidence that he was proceeding contrary to the Lord's will (vs 22-35). For the cursing, Balak took Balaam first to Bamoth-baal (v 41, RSV). There, 7 altars were erected and on each Balak and Balaam offered a bullock and a ram. And Balaam went apart to receive a message from the Lord for Balak (ch 23:1-6). Balaam's first message consisted of a declaration that Israel was different from all other nations and that God had blessed them (vs 7-10). Balak took Balaam next to Mount Pisgah, where the sacrificial procedure was repeated (vs 14-17), but the second message reaffirmed the first. Balak nevertheless made a third attempt, offering the same sacrifices on the top of Mount Peor (vs 27-30), but the results were the same (ch 24:1-9). When ordered to return home, Balaam gave Balak a fourth message that envisioned the Messiah and the establishment of His kingdom (vs 15-19). Subsequently, however, Balaam counseled Balak to seduce the Hebrews into idolatry and immorality, with the result that the curse of the Lord did fall upon Israel (ch 25:1-9; cf. 31:16). A little later Balaam was slain by the Israelites in battle (ch 31:8). His name became a byword for apostasy, particularly for an unholy alliance between God's people and the world (Rev 2:14).

Balac. *See* Balak.

Baladan (băl′å-dăn). [Heb. *Bal'adan,* a transliteration of the Akkadian *Apla-iddin,* meaning "(god) has given a son."] The father of *Merodach-baladan (2 Ki 20:12; Is 39:1). His name has recently been attested in a cuneiform letter written probably by King Sargon to the crown prince Sennacherib, in which a request is made to bring *Apla-iddin* together with other Babylonians. Since this letter comes from the time in which Baladan lived, it is possible that *Apla-iddin* is actually the father

of Merodach-baladan, the king of Babylon (H. W. F. Saggs, *Iraq,* 20 [1958], 183, 184, 207, note 5).

Balah. *See* Baalah, 3.

Balak (bā′lăk), KJV of NT **Balac** (bā′lăk). [Heb. *Balaq,* meaning uncertain; Gr. *Balak.*] A Moabite king in Moses' time who hired Balaam to curse Israel (Num 22:2 to 24:25; Jos 24:9; Jgs 11:25; Mic 6:5; Rev 2:14).

Balances. [Heb. *mo'znayim;* Aramaic *mo'zne';* Ugaritic *mznm;* Gr. (sing.) *zugos.*] Devices used in the ancient world, including Palestine, to weigh produce and money. *See* Weights and Measures. Since fraudulent balances were frequently found, the Bible stresses honest balances (Lev 19:36; etc.). Daniel's statement to Belshazzar, "Thou art weighed in the balances, and art found wanting" (Dan 5:27), was a picturesque and forceful expression of the king's moral deficiency, readily understood by the ancients. The accompanying picture taken from the Egyptian "Book of the Dead" shows the heart of a man weighed on the balances against a symbol that stands for righteousness. Compare Ps 62:9. See fig. 50.

Bald Locust. *See* Locust, 20.

Balm. [Heb. *ṣerî.*] An aromatic resin probably from such trees as the mastic or tere-

50. Balances depicted in the Egyptian "Book of the Dead," showing the weighing of the heart of the deceased (left figure) against a feather, the symbol of righteousness

binth (Gen 43:11; Jer 51:8; Eze 27:17). Gilead was evidently noted for the quality or quantity, or both, of its balm, which it exported (Gen 37:25; Jer 46:11). Jeremiah, mourning over the seemingly incurable sins of his apostate people, inquired whether there was no balm in Gilead to cure their terrible moral disease (Jer 8:22).

Balsam Tree, KJV **Mulberry Tree.** [Heb. *baka'*.] The exact identity of the tree described by the Hebrew term is uncertain. The root, which means "to weep," suggests that it is a shrub or tree exuding sap or gum. In 2 Sa 5:23, 24 and 1 Chr 14:14, 15 David received divine instruction to deploy his forces behind the grove of these trees and wait till he heard "a sound of a going in the tops" of them. From this narrative some have concluded that a species of aspen (*Populus euphratica*), growing 30-45 ft. in height, whose leaves rustle when disturbed by the wind, was meant. But there is little to support this view. The LXX reads *apios,* "a pear tree," in the Chr passage.

Bamah (bä'mä). [Heb. *bamah,* "elevation," "high place."] A term in Eze 20:29 designating either a particular "high place" or, collectively, all "high places," which were centers of idolatry. There is a possible play on the words *ba,* as if from *ba'* (go) and *mah* (what?), as though the prophet asked in contempt, "Where are you going?" *See* High Place.

Bamoth (bā'mŏth). [Heb. *Bamôth,* "high places."] The last camping place of the Israelites before they reached a valley near Pisgah (Num 21:19). The name is probably an abbreviation of *Bamoth-baal; site not identified.

Bamoth-baal (bā'mŏth-bā'ăl). [Heb. *Bamôth Ba'al,* "the high places of Baal."] A place between Dibon and Beth-baal-meon north of the river Arnon in the territory of Reuben (Jos 13:17). It is mentioned on the *Moabite Stone (line 27) as Beth-bamoth. It was apparently from this spot that Balaam was asked to curse Israel encamped in the plains of Moab (Num 22:1, 41, RSV). The place may be identical with *Bamoth (ch 21:19). The site has not yet been identified.

Band. The translation of various Hebrew and Greek words. In many instances it designates a company of persons, such as soldiers (Eze 38:6, RSV "hordes"; etc.). The "band" of Jn 18:12 is a body of soldiers (Gr. *speira,* translated "battalion" in the RSV of Mt 27:27; Mk 15:16).

Speira also denotes the Roman *cohort, and is so translated three times in the RSV of Acts. "Bands" is used to translate words designating bonds used for binding (Jgs 15:14, KJV; etc.). The "bands" of Orion (Job 38:31) are the figurative "chains" or "cords" (Heb. *moshkôth*) that apparently hold the constellation together. For "bands" as the name of a staff *see* Beauty and Bands.

Bani (bā'nī). [Heb. *Bani,* "builder," or if it is a contraction of *Benayah,* "Benaiah," it means "(Yahweh is) the builder." The name occurs in Akkadian as *Bâni, Banini,* and *Bania.*]

1. A Gadite, one of David's "mighty men" (2 Sa 23:36), probably identical with Mibhar (1 Chr 11:38).

2. A Merarite Levite (1 Chr 6:46).

3. A descendant of Judah through Perez (1 Chr 9:4).

4. The founder of a family of which 642 male members returned with Zerubbabel from Babylon (Ezr 2:10). Neh 7:15 calls him Binnui and gives the number who returned as 648. Six men belonging to this family were among those married to foreign wives in the time of Ezra (Ezr 10:29).

5. One of the chief of the people who signed Nehemiah's covenant (Neh 10:14), possibly a representative of the family mentioned under Bani, 4.

6. The father of one of the overseers of the Levites in Nehemiah's time (Neh 11:22).

7. The father of one of the builders of the wall of Jerusalem in Nehemiah's time (Neh 3:17).

8. One of those who explained the Law of God in the time of Ezra (Neh 8:7), probably a Levite (see RSV).

9. A Levite in Ezra's time (Neh 9:4).

10. Founder of a family, of which 27 members were among those married to foreign wives in Ezra's time (Ezr 10:34).

11. A man belonging to the family of Bani, 10, who was married to a foreign wife in Ezra's time (Ezr 10:38).

It is possible that some of the Banis of the time of Ezra and Nehemiah are identical.

Bank. [Gr. *trapeza,* "table," a reference to the table on which the money-changers displayed their coins.] The word as a term to describe a place where money transactions were made occurs only once in the Bible (Lk 19:23). Banks in the modern sense of places where money is kept on deposit were not known in ancient times. Ancient banking consisted of lending money at interest, and of exchanging money from one denomination to another, or from the currencies of one nation to that of another. The Hebrews were forbidden to take interest on loans made to fellow Hebrews (Deut 23:19; cf. Ex 22: 25; Lev 25:37). They were, however, permitted to collect interest on loans made to the Gentiles (Deut 23:20).

For "bank" as a siege mound, *see* Mound.

Banner. A standard, or ensign, such as a military standard, which might be a flag or some other symbol (Song 2:4; 6:4; etc.). Frequently the words thus translated are rendered "standard," or "ensign."

Banquet. *See* Dinner; Meals.

Baptism. [Gr. *baptisma* from *baptizō,* "to dip," "to immerse."] Baptism as a religious rite originated in pre-Christian times. It was practiced by the Jews as a means of receiving proselytes to Judaism, as is attested by various Jewish writings. It is significant that the Jewish leaders did not question John concerning the validity of the rite of baptism, but only his authority to administer it (see Jn 1:19-28). Baptism was also practiced by the Essenes in connection with their religious rites. In *Khirbet Qumrân,* which was probably the center of the Essenes, several tanks with steps leading into them have been discovered (fig. 140). These may have been used for baptismal rites, which apparently involved immersion, as did Jewish proselyte baptism (see Talmud '*Erubin* 4b, Soncino ed., p. 20; *Yebamoth* 47a, 47b, Soncino ed., pp. 311, 312).

Baptism is practiced by almost all Christian communions, although the mode of administering it varies. Some employ total immersion, others sprinkling, still others pouring. That immersion was the mode employed in NT times is clear from the meaning of the Greek term, from Bible descriptions of the performance of the ceremony, and from the spiritual applications made in the Bible respecting the rite. The term *baptizō* was used anciently to describe the immersing of cloth in dye, and of the submerging of a vessel in order to fill it with water. Its most obvious meaning when applied to Christian baptism is "to immerse." Bible references to baptisms show plainly that immersion was the method used. John the Baptist baptized "in Ænon near to Salim, because there was much water there" (Jn 3:23). There would be no reason to require a place where there was "much water" if

sprinkling or pouring were the method used. The description of the baptism of the Ethiopian eunuch states that Philip and the eunuch "went down both into the water," and came "up out of the water" (Acts 8:38, 39), action that most certainly indicates more than sprinkling or pouring. In the spiritual application made by Paul, the figure used by the apostle becomes clear only as baptism by immersion is understood. In discussing the significance of baptism Paul points out that (1) as Christ died for sin, the Christian must die to sins; (2) as Christ, having died, was buried, so the Christian is symbolically "buried" with Him in the watery grave of baptism; and (3) as Christ was raised from the grave, so the Christian is raised to newness of spiritual life (Rom 6:3-5; cf. Col 2:12). Obviously the figure of burial and resurrection is pointless unless total immersion is meant. It is worthy of note that the presence of baptisteries in ancient churches shows that for centuries the Christian church practiced baptism by immersion.

That baptism is required of Christians is clear. Christ instructed His disciples to baptize (Mt 28:18, 19; Mk 16:15, 16), and to teach new converts to observe all things commanded by Him (Mt 28:20). The apostles taught the necessity of baptism (Acts 2:38; 10:48; 22:16), and practiced the rite (chs 8:12; 16:14, 15, 33; 19:5; etc.). Among the prerequisites to baptism noted in the Scriptures are belief in Jesus Christ as the Son of God (ch 8:36, 37; cf. v 12; ch 18:8), and repentance (ch 2:37, 38).

One incident is recorded in which, upon the reception of new and important truths, certain believers at Ephesus who had received "John's baptism" were baptized in the name of the Lord Jesus (Acts 19:1-5). In a difficult passage (1 Cor 15:29) Paul refers to baptism for the dead. A great number of explanations have been suggested, none of which appears to be conclusive (see *SDACom* 6:806, 807).

The term "baptize" is also used figuratively. John the Baptist stated that Christ would baptize with "the Holy Ghost and with fire" (Mt 3:11; Lk 3:16), which may have reference to the outpouring of the Holy Spirit at Pentecost under the symbol of fire (Acts 2:3, 4), or perhaps also to the ultimate destruction of the wicked (see Mt 3:11, 12). Jesus spoke symbolically of His death as a baptism (Mt 20:20-23; Mk 10:37-39; cf Lk 12:50). The experience of Israel in coming out of Egypt is spoken of figuratively as being "baptized unto Moses in the cloud and in the sea" (1 Cor 10: 1, 2).

Bar. [Aramaic *bar,* "son," equivalent to the Heb. *ben,* "son."] A prefix commonly used with personal names to identify a man as the "son" of the person to whose name the prefix is attached. Examples are Bartholomew (Mt 10:3), Bartimaeus (Mk 10: 46), and Barsabas (Acts 1:23).

Barabbas (bá-răb′ăs). [Gr. *Barabbas,* a transliteration of the Aramaic *Bar 'abba',* "father's son."* Jerome's interpretation that the Aramaic was *Bar Rabban,* "son of the rabbi," is now generally rejected.] A Jewish criminal in prison for robbery and murder at the time of Jesus' trial before Pilate. When Pilate offered to release either Jesus or Barabbas the Jews chose Barabbas (Mt 27:16-26; Mk 15:7-11; Jn 18:40).

Barachel (băr′á-kĕl). [Heb. *Barak'el,* "God has blessed." The name occurs in Akkadian as *Barik-ilu.*] The father of Job's friend, Elihu (Job 32:2, 6).

Barachiah (băr′á-kī′á), KJV **Barachias** (băr′á-kī′ăs). [Gr. *Barachias,* Greek form of the Heb. *Berekyah,* "Yahweh has blessed."] Father of the Zechariah who was killed between the Temple and the altar (Mt 23:35).

Barachias. *See* Barachiah.

Barak (băr′ăk). [Heb. *Baraq,* "lightning." The name occurs in inscriptions from Palmyra. Compare the Amorite *jabruq-ilu,* "god has sent lightning"; Gr. *Barak.*] An Israelite from Kedesh in Naphtali whom *Deborah the prophetess called to lead a military campaign against Jabin, king of Canaan. Barak gathered 10,000 men from Naphtali and Zebulun, and defeated Sisera, the commander of Jabin's army (Jgs 4:6-22; 5:1, 12, 15; Heb 11:32).

Barbarian. [Gr. *barbaros,* "foreigner," one who speaks an unintelligible tongue.] A Greek term designating peoples who did not speak Greek, without reference as to whether they were civilized or not (Rom 1:14; Col 3:11; etc.). The word is of onomatopoeic origin, imitating the unintelligible speech of a foreigner.

Barber. [Heb. *gallab.* Professional barbers are mentioned in Phoenician and Babylonian inscriptions by cognate terms.] A term appearing in the Bible only in Eze 5:1. Since the book of Ezekiel was written in Babylonia, it is not certain whether it is a Hebrew or a Babylonian barber that is referred to.

Barhumite. *See* Baharumite.

Bariah (bá-rī′á). [Heb. *Bariach,* "fugitive,"

or, according to the Akkadian, *biriḫu,* "descendant."] A descendant of David (1 Chr 3:22).

Bar-Jesus (bär′jē′zŭs). [Gr. *Bariēsous,* a transliteration of the Aramaic *Bar Yeshua',* "son of Jeshua." "By interpretation" the name is Elymas (ĕl′ĭ-măs) the sorcerer (Acts 13:8). If Elymas is taken to mean "sorcerer," the name is doubtless connected with the Arabic verb *'alima,* "to recognize," "to be clever," from which *'alîm,* "sorcerer," is derived. Others see in the word Elymas a corrupted form of *Hetoimos,* as the Codex Bezae reads, and identify him with the sorcerer of Cyprus mentioned by Josephus (*Ant.* xx. 7. 2).] A false Jewish prophet (Acts 13:6). He was in the retinue of Sergius Paulus, the proconsul of Cyprus, and when he saw that the Roman governor was receptive to the gospel proclaimed by Paul he withstood the apostle. Paul rebuked his action, declaring that as punishment the Lord would strike him with temporary blindness. The sentence was immediately carried out. This miracle made so great an impression on Sergius Paulus that he believed Paul's teachings (vs 5-12).

Bar-Jona (bär′jō′ná). [Gr. *Bariōna,* a transliteration of the Aramaic *Bar Yônah,* "son of Jonah." However, according to the apocryphal Gospel According to the Hebrews it stands for *Bar Yochanan,* "son of John."] A surname of the apostle Peter (Mt 16:17).

Barkos (bär′kŏs). [Heb. *Barqôs,* "son of (the Edomite god) Qaus." The name of this god is attested in an Aramaic ostracon from Ezion-geber which mentions the Edomite name *Qaus'anal* (*BASOR* 71 [1938], 17; 79 [1940], 13).] The head of a family of Nethinim, of which some members returned with Zerubbabel from Babylon (Ezr 2:53; Neh 7:55).

Barley. [Heb. *se'orah;* Gr. *krithē.*] A hardy cereal grain cultivated extensively in Egypt and Palestine (Deut 8:8), providing (1) feed for horses and other livestock (1 Ki 4:28), (2) a coarse flour for bread (2 Ki 4:42; Jn 6:9, 13), and (3) malt for beer (*see* Strong Drink). The common winter and spring varieties are all of the genus *Hordeum.* In general the people of Bible times considered barley meal and the cakes it produces to be an inferior form of food. Only the poorer classes used them for human consumption (see Jgs 7:13, 14; Eze 13:19; Hos 3:2).

The time of the Palestinian barley harvest was the key to the Hebrew calendar, because every year the harvest season must be opened by offering a wave sheaf of new grain during the Feast of *Unleavened Bread, which followed the *Passover in the middle of the 1st month, Abib (Ex 12:2, 6; 13:4-7; Lev 23:6-15). This was barley, which ripens a few weeks before wheat, for *Pentecost, the 50th day from the wave sheaf ceremony, fell in wheat harvest (Ex 34:22; Lev 23:15-17; Deut 16:9). The calendar, therefore, had to be adjusted so that mid-Abib would always come at a time when some of the grain, at least, was ready for harvesting. Barley was the first grain to ripen in Palestine, and was ready for harvest generally about the first week in April. Since each Hebrew *month began with the new *moon, and since 12 such months total 11 days less than the solar, or seasonal, year, the months would have shifted constantly earlier in relation to the seasons, and the proper celebration of the Feast of Unleavened Bread would have been impossible in most of the years unless the Hebrews lengthened their lunar *year periodically to correct this difference. It is assumed that they did this in early times —as they are known to have done later— by adding an extra month every two or three years as the barley harvest required. This simple expedient kept the calendar approximately in step with the solar year, which is the true seasonal year.

Barn. The rendering of: (1) the Heb. *megûrah* (Hag 2:19), which means "grain pit" (*see* Granary); (2) the Heb. *'asam* (Deut 28:8; KJV "storehouse"; Prov 3: 10), which denotes "storeroom" or "storehouse"; (3) the Heb. *goren* (Job 39:12), "threshing floor" (see RSV); and (4) the Gr. *apothēkē* (Mt 6:26; 13:30; Lk 12:18, 24), which also means a storeroom. In ancient times a farmer's storeroom was either a simple shed or a part of his home, where grain and other produce were kept.

Barnabas (bär'nȧ-bǎs). [Gr. *Barnabas*. The exact Hebrew or Aramaic form of which this name is a transliteration is uncertain. Hence it is uncertain how the meanings, "son of consolation," KJV, "Son of encouragement," RSV (Acts 4:36), are derived.] The surname given by the apostles to Joseph (KJV "Joses"), a Cypriote Jew of the tribe of Levi (Acts 4:36), and by which he is thereafter named in the NT. He is described as a "good man, and full of the Holy Ghost and of faith," and as a successful evangelist (ch 11:24). He was a cousin of John Mark (Col 4:10, RSV). An ancient tradition names Barnabas as one of the Seventy sent out by Jesus (Lk 10:1).

Barnabas appears first in the NT account as one of those who sold their property and donated the proceeds for the support of the needy in the Jerusalem church (Acts 4:34, 36, 37). He appears next in connection with the visit Paul made to Jerusalem some three years after his conversion (Gal 1:18). At this time Barnabas helped to dispel the understandable fear and distrust the Christians of that city felt toward Paul, by befriending the converted persecutor, and by urging others to accept him (Acts 9:26, 27).

When news of the spread of the gospel in Antioch of Syria came to the leaders of the Jerusalem church, they dispatched Barnabas to strengthen and expand the work there. He succeeded in adding many new converts to the church (Acts 11: 20-24). Feeling the need of help with the growing work, he made a trip to Tarsus, found Paul, and brought him back to Antioch with him (vs 25, 26). The two labored together in Antioch for one year, during which time the church was further strengthened (v 26). About this time a great famine, which had been predicted by the prophet Agabus, took place (v 28). The Christians of Judea were seemingly especially affected, so the believers at Antioch gathered a contribution and delegated Barnabas and Paul to deliver it to the church leaders at Jerusalem (vs 29, 30).

Their mission accomplished, Barnabas and Paul returned to Antioch (Acts 12: 25). By divine direction they were consecrated as missionaries, and "sent forth by the Holy Ghost" (ch 13:2-4) on what is usually called Paul's 1st Missionary Journey. John Mark, who had returned from Jerusalem with them, began the itinerary with them. The journey took them to the island of Cyprus and onward to the mainland. John Mark, discouraged by the vicissitudes of the journey, left them at Perga, and returned to his home at Jerusalem (vs 5-13). Continuing their trip, Barnabas and Paul preached in some of the important cities of Asia Minor, at Antioch of Pisidia (vs 14, 15), Iconium (ch 14:1-6), Lystra (vs 8-18), and Derbe (vs 20, 21). From Derbe they retraced their way to Perga, thence to the coast, where they took ship to Antioch in Syria (vs 19-26).

After a period of time in Antioch Barnabas was delegated to accompany Paul to Jerusalem, this time to consult the leaders of the church there with respect to the role of various requirements of the Mosaic law in the practices of the new

Christian church (Acts 15:2). The matter being satisfactorily decided (vs 4-21), they again returned to Antioch, accompanied by others from Jerusalem, and bearing letters for the church of Antioch (vs 22, 23). There followed another period of labor in that city (v 35), during which time the dissimulation described in Gal 2:11, 12 evidently took place, in which Barnabas, Peter, and others had a part.

When Paul planned his second tour of the churches of Asia Minor, Barnabas agreed to accompany him (Acts 15:36). Barnabas suggested taking John Mark with them, but Paul, remembering Mark's previous failure, dissented. A severe contention ensued, resulting in the separation of the two missionaries. Barnabas took John Mark with him and embarked for Cyprus. At this point (vs 37-41) the book of Acts terminates the story of Barnabas, but he is mentioned several times in Paul's writings (1 Cor 9:6; Gal 2:1, 9, 13; Col 4:10).

Barracks, KJV **Castle.** As used in Acts 21-23, the strong fortress known in history as the Tower of Antonia, immediately outside the Temple of Jerusalem at its northwestern corner. The first mention of a structure here is by Nehemiah, who speaks of the "palace" (Heb. *bîrah*) "which ap-

51. The Tower of Antonia—lower courses of masonry (left) are remains of the structure of Christ's day

pertained to the house" (Neh 2:8), "house" undoubtedly being the Temple. The fortress seems to have been built between the time of Zerubbabel and that of Nehemiah and was the residence of the governor of the province of Judah. Josephus calls it Baris (*Ant.* xi. 4. 6; etc.), which seems to reflect the Heb. *bîrah,* "palace," the word used by Nehemiah. It was rebuilt in the time of the Maccabees by John Hyrcanus, who there kept the high-priestly vestments which he was entitled to wear (*ibid.* xv. 11. 4; xviii. 4. 3). It was later strongly fortified and embellished by Herod the Great for the purpose of guarding the Temple and also of serving as a special protection for him in the event of an insurrection of the Jews. He called it Antonia in honor of Mark Antony (Jos. *War* i. 21. 1; v. 5. 8).

Josephus gives a detailed description of the fortress of Antonia in the passages referred to above. The fortress contained not only barracks for the soldiers but also rooms and baths for the king. The walls rose to a height of 40 cu. above the rock on which they were founded, the rock itself being about 50 cu. higher than the Temple area. The four corners of the fortress had towers, three of which were 50 cu. high, but one, overlooking the Temple, had a height of 70 cu. Two stairways led down to the Temple area, and a tunnel connected the fortress with a tower at the east gate of the inner Temple. See figs. 51, 189.

A Roman legion was stationed in the fortress during the period of the Roman procurators. The soldiers were ready at any time to rush down into the Temple area and restore order should any violence break out. Sentries always kept watchful eyes on the Temple compound, especially during feasts when great throngs of people were there and public excitement ran high. During important feasts the Roman procurators usually were present at Jerusalem and stayed in the Castle of Antonia to be on hand for any unforeseeable disturbance.

The fortress fell into the hands of the Jews during the Jewish war (A.D. 66-70), but was reconquered by the Roman soldiers under Titus in A.D. 70 in spite of heroic resistance by the rebels. It was then demolished. The site is now occupied partly by the Moslem school of *Kuliat Rawdat el-Ma'arif,* and partly by two convents. Tradition identifies this castle with the Praetorium of Pilate, where Jesus was condemned to the cross. This identification is not certain, although some archeological evidence seems to support it.

It was certainly this castle from which the Roman soldiers rushed down to rescue the apostle Paul when he had been pushed out of the Temple court into the Court of the Gentiles, and was about to be killed by the infuriated people (Acts 21: 30-34). After his rescue Paul addressed his attackers from the stairs leading up to this castle (v 40). He was held inside the fortress until he was sent to Caesarea (chs 22:24, 30; 23:10).

Barrel. In the KJV the rendering of the Heb. *kad* (1 Ki 17:12, 14, 16; 18:33). The *kad* is either a sturdy whole-mouthed jar of cylindrical shape, used to store dry material such as flour, or a large jar with a narrow mouth, used as a water container. Hence the RSV translation "jar" is preferable.

Barsabas. See Barsabbas.

Barsabbas (bär-săb′ăs), KJV **Barsabas** (bär′sá-băs). [Gr. *Barsabbas*, a transliteration of either the Aramaic *Bar Seba'* or *Bar Sa'ba'*, both of uncertain meaning.] The surname of Joseph (*see* Joseph, 12) and of Judas (*see* Judas, 8). In 1945 a family tomb containing several ossuaries (bone receptacles) was discovered outside Jerusalem. The names Simeon, Jesus (fig. 264), Miriam (fig. 333), and Barsabbas (fig. 446) were scratched into the ossuaries together with crosses, perhaps Christian signs. Since the name Barsabbas is not attested outside the NT, this Christian tomb may have belonged to the family of which Joseph Barsabbas and Judas Barsabbas were members (E. L. Sukenik, *AJA* 51 [1947], 351-365, pls. LXXVII, LXXXVIII).

Bartholomew (bär-thŏl′ō-mū). [Gr. *Bartholomaios* from Aramaic *Bar Talmay*, "son of Talmai." Talmai is probably an archaic Hurrian name meaning "great."] One of the twelve apostles (Mt 10:3; Mk 3:18; Lk 6:14; Acts 1:13). Bartholomew was possibly a surname of Nathanael, whom Philip led to Christ (Jn 1:45, 46).

Bartimaeus (bär-tĭ-mē′ŭs). [Gr. *Bartimaios*, from Aramaic *Bar Ţimay*, "son of Timaeus." Timaeus is possibly an abbreviation of Timotheus.] A blind man of Jericho, whom Jesus healed (Mk 10:46).

Baruch (băr′ŭk). [Heb. *Barûk*, "blessed." The name appears also on ostraca from Samaria.]

1. A scribe and close associate of the prophet Jeremiah. Josephus claims he came from an eminent family (*Ant.* x. 9. 1). In Jehoiakim's 4th year Baruch wrote from dictation a series of Jeremiah's denunciatory prophecies, and the following year read them publicly (Jer 36:1-20). The princes informed the king about this, who, when the scroll was read before him, cut it up and burned it piecemeal, ordering also that the prophet and his scribe be seized. They escaped the king's wrath by going into hiding (vs 21-26). There Jeremiah redictated and Baruch rewrote the former prophecies and added many more (vs 27-32). In connection with the writing of the scroll Baruch became so discouraged that the Lord sent a special message of comfort to him (ch 45:1-5).

When Jeremiah bought a field from his uncle in Anathoth during the final siege of Jerusalem, he entrusted the deed to Baruch (Jer 32:6-16, 43, 44). Baruch was with Jeremiah at Mizpah after the fall of Jerusalem, and was later accused of influencing Jeremiah to dissuade the people from going to Egypt after the murder of Gedaliah. The Jews forced him and Jeremiah to accompany them into Egypt (ch 43:1-7), where the story of his life ends. Later, the Jews considered him author of several books.

2. A man who worked on the building of the wall of Jerusalem in Nehemiah's time (Neh 3:20), probably identical with the Baruch who signed the covenant of Nehemiah (ch 10:6).

3. A Judahite (Neh 11:5).

Barzillai (bär-zĭl′á-ī). [Heb. *Barzillay*, "the iron one."]

1. A wealthy man from Gilead and close friend of David. During the rebellion of Absalom, when David fled to Transjordan, Barzillai brought supplies to the fugitive king and his army (2 Sa 17: 27-29). After the victory over Absalom he accompanied David to western Palestine, and was invited to become a member of the royal court. He declined because of his age and requested that his son Chimham take his place (ch 19:31-40).

2. A man from Meholah whose son Adriel married a daughter of Saul (2 Sa 21:8; cf. 1 Sa 18:19). See Merab.

3. The father of a family of priests, some of whom returned with Zerubbabel from Babylon after the Exile (Ezr 2:61; Neh 7:63). The father had taken to wife one of the daughters of Barzillai, 1, and he had adopted the name of his father-in-law.

Basemath (băs′ĕ-măth), KJV **Bashemath** (băsh′ĕ-măth), once **Basmath** (băs′măth). [Heb. *Baśemath*, "perfume."]

1. One of Esau's wives, the daughter of

Elon the Hittite (Gen 26:34), also called Adah (ch 36:2).

2. Another of Esau's wives, the daughter of Ishmael (Gen 36:3, 4, 13, 17), also called Mahalath (ch 28:9).

3. A daughter of Solomon and wife of one of the royal supply officers (1 Ki 4:15).

Bashan (bā'shăn). [Heb. *Bashan,* "a fertile, stoneless plain."] The highland region of northern Transjordan lying north of the central and upper Yarmuk (Map VI, B-5). It was one of the 3 principal parts into which eastern Palestine was divided: "The plain" (*Arabah), Gilead, and Bashan (Deut 3:10; Jos 20:8). However, sometimes some of the territory south of the Yarmuk was also counted as forming part of Bashan (Jos 12:4, 5). Occasionally even the mountainous area lying east of the Sea of Galilee and of Lake Huleh was included in Bashan (Deut 4:43). The country was famous for its pastureland (Jer 50:19; Mic 7:14; Nah 1:4), for its forests (Is 2:13; Eze 27:6), and for its cattle, which Biblical writers set forth as symbols of strength, passion, self-content, and wealth (Deut 32:14; Ps 22:12; Eze 39:18; Amos 4:1). The lions (Deut 33:22) and leopards of Bashan have now become extinct. The territory was thickly populated and under the domination of King Og when the Israelites came into the country (ch 3:3-5). Og was defeated in the battle of Edrei, and his territory was given to the half tribe of Manasseh (Num 21:33-35; Deut 3:1-11, 13; Jos 13:7, 8, 12).

After the secession of the 10 tribes Bashan belonged to the northern kingdom, but was conquered by Hazael of Damascus in the time of King Jehu (2 Ki 10:32, 33); in fact, it had probably been in the possession of Damascus for some time during the reigns of Ahab (1 Ki 22:3), and Joram of Israel (2 Ki 8:28). Jeroboam II reconquered it (ch 14:25), but Tiglath-pileser III (745-727 B.C.) took it after his conquest of Damascus and made it into an Assyrian dependency (ch 15:29). It was in Nabataean hands in the 2d cent. B.C., and later belonged to the kingdom of Herod the Great, then to that of his son Philip, and lastly to that of Agrippa II, its last Jewish ruler. The name Bashan lived on in the Greek-Roman name Batanaea (Map XV, C-5). The country seems to be mentioned in the *Amarna Letters under the name *Ziri-bashani.*

Bashan-havoth-jair (bā'shăn - hā'vŏth - jā'ĭr). [Heb. *Bashan Chawwoth Ya'ir.*] According to the KJV a geographical area (Deut 3:

14). However, the element "Bashan" should obviously be separated from the name and probably be placed earlier in the verse as in the RSV. *See* Havvoth-jair.

Bashemath. *See* Basemath.

Basin and **Bowl.** The distinction between basins (KJV "basons") and bowls is not always clear from the words thus translated. Basins are mentioned in connection with the sacrificial rituals at Sinai (Ex 24:6) and among the vessels of the tabernacle and the Temple (Ex 37:16; 1 Ki 7:50; etc.). A washbasin (Gr. *niptēr*) was used by Jesus when He washed His disciples' feet (Jn 13:5). Bowls, on the other hand, are mentioned as drinking ves-

52. Silver bowl with inscription (see fig. 197) containing the name of "Geshem, King of Kedar"

sels (Jgs 5:25, RSV; etc.), and as the oil reservoirs of lamps in the tabernacle (Ex 25:31; etc.), rendered "cups" in the RSV. The angels seen by John as bringing the last plagues upon the earth carried bowls (Gr. *phialai;* KJV "vials"), from which the plagues were poured out over the doomed earth (Rev 15:7; 16:1; etc.).

Basket. A container made of various flexible materials, such as willow, palm leaf, rush, interwoven to form more or less solid sides and bottom. Basketwork was a major industry in Bible lands, most of the work being done by persons in their own homes. Baskets were used universally—in the home and in the caravan, in the field and in the storehouse. In the OT the word comes from 5 different Hebrew words difficult to distinguish in meaning. The RSV also calls the "ark" of bulrushes into which the infant Moses was laid a "basket." The Hebrew word thus translated (*tebah*) is derived from the Egyptian *db3.t* or *tb.t,* meaning "box." However, the details of its manufacture given in Ex 2:3 show that it was obviously a basket.

Two principal types of basket are mentioned in the NT: (1) *kophinos,* one of the baskets used for the fragments after feeding the 5,000 (Mt 14:20); and (2) *spuris,* one of the baskets used for the fragments after feeding the 4,000 (ch 15:37). The latter word is also used for the "basket" in which Paul was let down from the wall in Damascus (Acts 9:25). Hence *spuri* is thought to be a large hamper, in contrast with *kophinos,* which is probably a small hand basket.

Basmath. *See* Basemath, 3.

Bason. *See* Basin.

Bastard. [Heb. *mamzer;* Gr. *nothos,* both meaning "an illegitimate child."] Post-Biblical Hebrew applies *mamzer* specifically to a child of incest, but it is doubtful that this restricted definition applies to the OT occurrences of this word. According to Deut 23:2 a *mamzer* and his descendants to the 10th generation were excluded from the "congregation of the Lord." This no doubt referred to exclusion from the sanctuary where the congregation worshiped, but not in any sense to exclusion from God's grace. Zechariah uses the term in his denunciation of Philistia, declaring that "a bastard shall dwell in Ashdod" (Zec 9:6). He probably uses *mamzer* figuratively for "mixed population," or "mongrel people" (RSV).

The word appears once in the NT (Heb 12:8, KJV) in the sense of one born outside of wedlock. The Christian who is "without chastisement" is compared· to an illegitimate child who naturally would lack the benefit of a father's discipline.

Bat. [Heb. *'aṭalleph.*] The bat is mentioned in the lists of unclean animals (Lev 11:19; Deut 14:18). Since the animal flies, it is classed with fowls in these lists, but it is actually a mammal whose forelimbs are modified into membranous wings. The ancients regarded it as an animal halfway between birds and beasts (G. R. Driver, *PEQ* 87 [1955], p. 18). Some 15 or 17 kinds are found in Palestine. They swarm everywhere in caves, tombs, or empty

houses. Isaiah mentions the idols being thrown to the moles and bats in the day of the Lord (Is 2:20).

Bath. [Heb. and Aramaic *bath.*] A Hebrew measure of capacity for liquids (1 Ki 7: 26, 38; 2 Chr 2:10; 4:5; Ezr 7:22; Is 5:10). It was 1/10 of a homer, and corresponds to the dry measure ephah in capacity (Eze 45:10, 11, 14). In the excavations of Lachish and *Tell Beit Mirsim* sections of jars were found with inscriptions showing that they had been used as bath measures. Reconstructions of the vessels reveal that the Hebrew *bath* contained about 22 liters 5.81 gals.), a figure that approximates the volume of the bath given by the Jewish rabbis. This equivalent is used in this dictionary as the basis for computing the other measures of capacity: cab, homer or cor, seah, ephah, lethech, log, and hin. See *SDACom* 1:165, 166.

Bathing. The Hebrew word translated "to bathe" (*rachaṣ*) does not distinguish between washing a part of the body or the whole body. Also most of the references to bathing have to do with ceremonial washings, though washing for cleanliness is noted. Public baths were unknown among the Jews until the Greek-Roman period. Among the people of Bible lands it was customary to wash the dust from the feet when one entered a house (Gen 18:4; 19: 2). Pharaoh's daughter was bathing in the Nile when she found the baby Moses (Ex 2:5). It is said that Egyptian priests bathed 4 times each day.

The Hebrew priests were symbolically washed and anointed in preparation for their assumption of the priestly office (Ex 40:12, 13; Lev 8:6), and Aaron and his priestly sons were commanded to bathe their hands and feet each time they entered the tabernacle to offer sacrifice (Ex 30:19-21). The high priest was required to bathe before each official act on the Day of Atonement (Lev 16:4, 24). This ceremonial act was designed to teach the lesson of the virulent and fatal effect of spiritual uncleanness and to give understanding of God's uncompromising rejection of all forms and degrees of sin. It also carried the implication that there *is* provision made to cleanse men from sin. In connection with the slaying of the red heifer (a sacrifice for uncleanness), the priest's ceremonial defilement was counteracted by bathing the body and washing the clothing (Num 19:7). Also in connection with the official priestly pronouncement of cure of a leper, there was a ceremonial bathing (Lev 14:8, 9). Certain of the Levitical laws bearing on ceremonial uncleanness that required bathing as a part of the procedure for restoration to the camp of Israel were obviously based on considerations of health and sanitation (Lev 15:5; 17:15). Elisha instructed Naaman to bathe 7 times in the Jordan, as his token of faith in God's power to heal him (2 Ki 5:10, 14), and for a similar reason Jesus told the blind man to wash in the pool of Siloam (Jn 9:7).

Bath-rabbim (băth'răb'ĭm). [Heb. *Bath-rabbîm*, "daughter of a multitude."] The name of a gate of Heshbon, of which nothing else is known (Song 7:4).

Bathsheba (băth-shē'bà), KJV **Bath-sheba** (băth-shē'bà). [Heb. *Bath-sheba'*, either "daughter of an oath," or "daughter of the seventh (day, that is, the Sabbath)."] Daughter of Eliam, and wife of Uriah, a Hittite soldier in David's army. Attracted by her beauty, David committed adultery with her during her husband's absence, resulting in her pregnancy. When he failed in his attempts to make Uriah visit his home and thus be led later to believe that the child was his, David manipulated events to have his faithful soldier killed during the siege of Rabbah. Following the customary period of mourning, he married Bathsheba. The first child died; the second was the later King Solomon (2 Sa 11:1 to 12:24).

When Adonijah was about to assume the royal throne (1 Ki 1:11-31), Bathsheba, advised by the prophet Nathan, induced the king immediately to crown her son Solomon. She tried later to obtain her son's consent for Adonijah's marriage to Abishag, David's nurse. Her efforts failed, and because of the request Adonijah lost his life (1 Ki 2:13-25). According to 1 Chr 3:5 Bathsheba had three sons besides Solomon: Shimea, Shobab, and Nathan (cf. 2 Sa 5:14; 1 Chr 14:4). Once she is called Bath-shua, the daughter of Ammiel (1 Chr 3:5). The name Bath-shua is a misreading for Bathsheba, probably caused by a partial effacing of the Hebrew letter *b*. The name Ammiel contains the component parts of Eliam in reverse order. Bathsheba is listed in Matthew's genealogy of Christ as "the wife of Uriah" (Mt 1:6, RSV).

Bath-shua (băth'shoo'à). [Heb. *Bath-shua'*, "daughter of Shua."]

1. Wife of Judah (1 Chr 2:3, KJV, "the daughter of Shua").

2. The mother of King Solomon (1 Chr 3:5). *See* Bathsheba.

Battering Ram. A war machine used with great success by the Assyrians to conquer and destroy enemy cities. The Assyrians were probably its inventors. Their reliefs provide us with instructive pictures of these machines (see figs. 201, 210). The battering-ram consisted of a long beam with an iron or bronze war head that was swung by ropes from a tower, sometimes moved on wheels. Behind a protective shield of wickerwork or hides the tower was moved toward the city wall on a wooden platform built by the Assyrian soldiers. The defenders of the attacked cities tried to catch the battering beam by means of chains lowered from the top of their wall, and lift it up, thus making its thrust ineffective. They also shot arrows against the operators of the battering-rams, and hurled fiery torches (see fig. 284) to set them on fire. Hence, the reliefs show Assyrian soldiers standing on top of the towers and shooting arrows into the city to drive the defenders off, and also pouring water on their tower to prevent it from catching afire. A bronze war head of a battering-ram has been found in excavations, and is now in the Baghdad Museum. These war machines are mentioned in Eze 4:2; 21:22; 26:9, RSV.

Battle. Many battles are mentioned in the Bible, but details of tactics, deployment of armies, and detailed descriptions of battles are almost totally absent in the Scriptures. It is known, however, that the armed forces were divided into bands or divisions (*see* Army) in order to confuse the enemy or to conceal the direction of the main attack (Jgs 7:16-18; 1 Sa 11:11; 2 Sa 18:2). To surprise or mislead the enemy, armies employed such methods as ambushments or pretended flights by part of the armed forces (Jos 8:2, 12; Jgs 20:29-34; 1 Sa 15:5), also attacks by night (Jgs 7:16-20; 2 Sa 17:1-3).

53. Temple relief at Karnak depicting a battle of Pharaoh Seti I against Syrians

The battle usually started with the sound of the trumpet (Jgs 7:18), and with a battle cry or alarm (Jer 49:2; Amos 1: 14; etc.), after which the opposing forces charged each other. But how the forces were deployed during the battle is not known (*see* Array). Man fought against man, and their principal weapons were the spear, bow and arrow, and the dagger or sword. From the time of Solomon the Israelites also used chariot forces (1 Ki 1:5; 10:26, 29), but the weapons remained the same, except that the sword and dagger were of no use to the charioteer. In the later period of the kings, cavalry (2 Ki 13: 7; etc.) was introduced after the Assyrian model. In some cases a battle was preceded by a duel between the two foremost champions of the opposing armies. The outcome of such a duel frequently had a decisive effect on the whole battle (1 Sa 17:3-52).

After a battle it was the first duty of the victorious army, which usually occupied the field, to bury its own dead and those of the enemy (1 Ki 11:15; Eze 39:11-13). Lamentations were made over fallen leaders or heroes (2 Sa 3:31). The severed heads of prominent enemies were sometimes carried away as trophies (1 Sa 17:51, 54; 31:8, 9; 2 Sa 20:22). A soldier sometimes cut off a hand (see fig. 209) of the slain enemy (see Jgs 8:6, KJV; RSV is a less literal rendering) or his phallus (1 Sa 18:25, 27), to prove his valor and to claim rewards. Both customs existed among the Egyptians. For reliefs depicting battle scenes see figs. 19, 36, 210, etc. Prisoners were usually treated with great severity, although exceptional cases of leniency are also recorded (1 Ki 20:30-34). Captured kings were usually slain (Jos 10:23, 26), and sometimes also many of the ordinary soldiers (2 Chr 25:12). Captives were frequently sold into slavery (Amos 1:6, 9). The Israelites are recorded as laming the captured horses of their enemies and burning the chariots (Jos 11:6, 9; 2 Sa 8:4) before they themselves used chariots.

The territory of a defeated enemy was often devastated by cutting down trees, stopping springs, and burning cities and villages (Jgs 6:4; 2 Sa 3:19). The spoil obtained was distributed among those who had participated in the battle and those who had guarded the camp (1 Sa 30:24, 25). Precious metal was frequently dedicated to the Temple (2 Sa 8:10, 11), and special trophies were preserved in the sanctuary (1 Sa 21:8, 9; 31:8-10; 2 Ki 11:10). Garrisons were sometimes placed in conquered cities (2 Sa 8:6, 14), and hostages were taken to ensure the fulfillment of agreements (2 Ki 14:14).

Battle Axe. This instrument of war, an important weapon among some ancient nations, such as the Hittites, was of no great importance among the Israelites, and is therefore seldom mentioned. The term "battle axe" is found only in Jer 51:20 (KJV). However, the Hebrew word thus translated (*mappes*) is probably not an ax but the club, or mace, which was a common weapon among the early Egyptians and among Mesopotamian nations. In Prov 25:18 the Heb. *mephis,* in form closely related to *mappes,* is rendered "maul" in the KJV and "war club" in the RSV. The Heb. *sagar* of Ps 35:3 has been

54. Head of a battle-ax found in Palestine

compared with the double ax of the Scythians and Persians, called *sagaris* by Herodotus (i. 215). It is rendered "javelin" in the RSV, but in the KJV as a verb "to stop."

Battlement. A parapet with open spaces that surmounted ancient city walls and fortresses (Song 8:9; Zep 1:16; 3:6; RSV). The KJV has "palace" in the first passage and "tower" in the last two passages. "Battlements" in Jer 5:10, KJV, is an erroneous rendering of the Heb. *netishôth,* which means "branches," "shoots." The "battlement" of Deut 22:8, KJV, is a parapet.

Bavai. *See* Bavvai.

Bavvai (băv′á-ī), KJV **Bavai** (băv′á-ī). [Heb. *Bawwaȳ.*] One of those who helped Nehemiah repair the wall of Jerusalem (Neh 3:18). However, Bavvai is probably a misspelling of Binnui, resulting from the dropping out of the letter *n* in the Hebrew. *See* Binnui, 5.

Bay.

1. An inlet of the sea, generally not as large as a gulf. The Heb. *lashôn,* "tongue," is translated "bay" in Jos 15:2, 5; 18:19 with reference to a southern and a northern bay in the Dead Sea, the exact locations of which are unknown. In the RSV the Gr. *kolpos* (Acts 27:39) is rendered

"bay," referring to the inlet on the coast of Malta where Paul suffered shipwreck. This word is incorrectly rendered "creek" in the KJV.

2. In the KJV of Zec 6:3 the rendering of the Heb. 'amoş, a term of uncertain meaning. The RSV translates the word "gray," but the meaning "strong" is also possible.

Bay Tree. [Heb. 'ezrach, "of one's own land," "native."] A term appearing once (Ps 37:35, KJV). However, the exact meaning of 'ezrach is obscure. "Bay tree," an evergreen (Laurus nobilis) reaching 40 to 60 ft. in height, with leaves like the mountain laurel of North America, is a conjectural translation. The RSV follows the LXX and reads "cedar of Lebanon."

Bazaars. A term appearing in the RSV of 1 Ki 20:34 translating the Heb. chûşôth, meaning literally, "things which are outside." The context and historical background indicates that chûşôth here refers to open market places along the streets, such as are still common in the East.

Bazlith (băz'lĭth), or **Bazluth** (băz'lŭth). [Heb. Başlîth and Başlûth. The variant spelling may be accounted for by the fact that the Hebrew letters y and w, in these names transliterated "i" and "u," are very similar in appearance, and in manuscripts can hardly be distinguished.] The head of a family of Nethinim of which certain members returned with Zerubbabel from Babylon (Ezr 2:52; Neh 7:54).

Bazluth. See Bazlith.

Bdellium. [Heb. bedolach.] A substance found with gold and onyx in the antediluvian land of Havilah (Gen 2:11, 12), to which manna is compared in color (Num 11:7). The substance cannot be definitely identified. To the Greeks bdellium was a transparent and odoriferous resin of a tree native to the Near and Middle East. In Gen 2:12 the LXX reads anthrax, a precious stone of dark-red color.

Bealiah (bē'á-lī'á). [Heb. Be'alyah, "Yahweh is Lord."] One of the "mighty men," a Benjamite, who joined David at Ziklag (1 Chr 12:5).

Bealoth (bē'á-lŏth). [Heb. Be'alôth, "mistresses" or "(female) possessors."]

1. A place in the south of Judah (Jos 15:24); thought by some to be *Baalath-beer.

2. A place near the territory of Asher, according to the RSV (1 Ki 4:16). The KJV translates Be'alôth "in *Aloth."

Beam. Generally, either the thick cylindrical piece of wood in a loom on which the warp is wound, called a weaver's beam (1 Sa 17:7; 2 Sa 21:19; etc.), or a large timber such as one of the main timbers in a building (Song 1:17; Hab 2:11; etc.). In Mt 7:3, 4, 5; Lk 6:41, 42; KJV, Christ uses the term figuratively of the faults of the critic. By contrast, the faults of the one criticized are but as an insignificant speck.

Bean. [Heb. pôl.] A legume, perhaps the broad bean (Vicia faba), or horse bean. Beans were a staple article of diet in Bible lands (see 2 Sa 17:28), and in times of economic stress were even added to flour to produce a coarse bread (see Eze 4:9).

Bear. [Heb. and Aramaic dob; Gr. arktos.] The Biblical animal is the Ursus syriacus, of somewhat lighter fur than the European bear, and is now limited to the forest areas of the Lebanon and the Anti-Lebanon. The bear was widely spread over the whole country of Palestine. For example, it was found near Bethlehem (1 Sa 17: 34) and near Bethel (2 Ki 2:24). Although bears live mainly on fruit and insects, they eat flesh on occasion, and can be dangerous to men if frightened or if robbed of their whelps (2 Sa 17:8; Prov 17:12; Hos 13:8; Amos 5:19).

Beard. [Heb. zakan.] Palestinian Jews generally wore full round beards, as shown by ancient monuments (see figs. 246, 438). They regarded their beards as symbols of manliness and dignity. Thus, when David's envoys to the king of Ammon were mistreated and forced to suffer the indignity of having one side of their beards shaved off, they were bidden to wait at Jericho until their beards were grown (2 Sa 10: 4, 5). The Mosaic law forbade the Israelites to mar the corners or edges of their beards (Lev 19:27; 21:5). It appears from the context that this regulation was designed to secure God's people against identification with a certain heathen custom rather than arbitrarily to refuse the trimming of the beard or even the shaving of it. To allow a beard to become unkempt and untrimmed was a sign of mourning (2 Sa 19:24).

Beast. A mammal of lower order than man, and distinct from fishes, fowls, and creeping things. The word "beast" in the OT comes from several Hebrew words: (1) Behemah, generally domestic cattle and related kinds (Gen 7:2; Ex 22:10; Lev 11:3; Deut 14:4; Joel 1:18; etc.), but occasionally wild beasts (Jer 7:33; 19:7). (2) Be'ir, beasts of burden or cattle (Gen 45:17; Ex 22:5; Num 20:8, 11). (3)

Chayyah, the general term for wild beasts (Gen 1:24; Lev 26:22; Ps 50:10; etc.). The Aramaic form of this word describes the symbolic beasts that Daniel saw (Dan 7:3), beasts that were symbols of world powers in conflict with God's people (v 17), the various characteristics of the animals serving as effective representations of the attitudes and roles of these powers, civil and ecclesiastical. (4) *Nephesh,* generally translated "soul," "life," but meaning "beast" in Lev 24:18. (5) *Ṭebach,* "slaughter animal" (Prov 9:2).

The most common NT word for "beast" is *thērion,* "wild animal." This is the term used for the symbolic animals of the Revelation. For example, Rev 13 presents a beast with lamblike horns that learns to speak like a dragon, a fit symbol of a nation's changing from benignity to intolerance in its attitude. *Ktēnos* represents domesticated animals (Lk 10:34). *Zōon* is, literally, "a living thing," or "a living being," used at times for animals (2 Pe 2:12; Jude 10). In the symbolism of the Revelation it describes the beings John saw near the throne of God (Rev 4:6-9). It is translated "beast" in the KJV but is preferably translated "living being," or "living creature" as in the RSV.

Beaten Oil. *See* Oil.

Beating. Beating, referred to by various terms, is mentioned frequently as a corporal punishment in the OT (Ex 21:20; Deut 22:18; 1 Ki 12:14; Prov 10:13; Jer 20:2; etc.), and seems to have been common among the Israelites as it was also among other Oriental nations of antiquity. Some suggest that the recipient of this punishment was beaten on the soles of his feet (bastinado), and believe that the rule that he had to lie down (Deut 25:2) implies this. This form of punishment was also common among the ancient Egyptians. The humane spirit of the Mosaic legislation prohibited excesses in punishment and limited the number of "stripes" to 40 (v 3). The "scorpion" mentioned as an instrument of beating (1 Ki 12:14; 2 Chr 10:14) was probably a whip consisting of thongs armed with pieces of lead. In the NT beating refers either to the Jewish custom of castigation administered with a whip of three lashes (2 Cor 11:24; cf. Jos. *Ant.* iv. 8. 21) or to the beating the Romans employed to punish slaves and criminals (Jn 19:1; Acts 16:22; 22:25; 2 Cor 11:25). Roman citizens were exempt from this punishment by the Porcian Law (see Acts 16:37; 22:25, 26).

Beatitudes. This term, though not in the Bible, is commonly used to designate the opening portion of Jesus' Sermon on the Mount (Mt 5:3-12; Lk 6:20-23). The English term "beatitudes" is derived from the Latin *beatitudo,* "blessedness." In the Vulgate, Mt 5:3-11 begins with *beati,* "blessed," a word derived from the same root as *beatitudo.* The Greek word for "blessed" is *makarios,* meaning "happy," "fortunate." The Beatitudes as given in Matthew pronounce blessings upon: (1) those who recognize their spiritual poverty; (2) those who mourn; (3) those who are meek; (4) those who desire righteousness as a thirsting, starving man longs for water and food; (5) those who are merciful; (6) those who are "pure in heart," whose thoughts and motives are heavenward; (7) those who seek to promote peace; and (8) those who, for Christ's sake, are persecuted and maligned. Luke lists only the first, fourth, second, and eighth, in that order. In the Beatitudes, Christ announced that the objectives of His ministry and of His kingdom were to bring happiness to humanity. The principles He enumerated cut across the concept that happiness is to be found on the material or carnal level.

Beautiful Gate. A Temple gate in NT times, at which Peter and John healed a lame beggar (Acts 3:1-8). The gate is mentioned nowhere else, either in the Bible or in Jewish literature, and its location is uncertain. The following suggestions have been made: (1) That it is the Shushan Gate, which led from the Kidron Valley into the Court of the Gentiles, the gate now closed with masonry and known as the Golden Gate. (2) That it is the Nicanor Gate, a beautiful bronze gate that led from the Court of the Gentiles into the Court of the Women, and that, according to Josephus, "far exceeded in value those plated with silver and set in gold" (*War* v. 5. 3 [201], Loeb ed., vol. 3, p. 261). (3) That it is the gate that led from the Court of the Women to that of the Men, at the top of a flight of stairs. The most probable identification is the second (see also *SDACom* 6:153).

Beauty and Bands. The symbolic names given two staves (Zec 11:7, 14), the first representing God's gracious covenant with His people, and the second, the brotherly union of Judah and Israel. The breaking of the staves (vs 10, 14) represented the cancellation of the covenant and the dissolution of the union. The RSV renders the expression "Grace" and "Union."

Bebai (bē'bȧ-ī). [Heb. *Bebay,* probably "child." This definition is based on the Akkadian names *Bibi, Bibiya, Bibbi'a,* which have the meaning "child."]

1. The founder of a family of whom 623 males returned with Zerubbabel from Babylon (Ezr 2:11; Neh 7:16 [628]), and another 29 male members with Ezra (Ezr 8:11). Four members of the family of the former group were married to foreign wives in the time of Ezra (ch 10:28).

2. An Israelite who signed the covenant of Nehemiah (Neh 10:15).

Becher (bē'kēr). [Heb. *Beker,* "a young male camel."]

1. A son of Benjamin (Gen 46:21; 1 Chr 7:6-8). He is not mentioned in the genealogical lists of the tribe of Benjamin given in Num 26:38; 1 Chr 8:1-6, probably because of the small number of his descendants in the early history of the tribe.

2. A son of Ephraim and founder of a tribal family (Num 26:35), called Bered in 1 Chr 7:20.

Becherites (bē'kēr-īts), KJV **Bachrites** (băk'-rīts). [Heb. *Bakrî.*] The family name of the descendants of Becher, son of Ephraim (Num 26:35). *See* Becher, 2.

Bechorath. *See* Becorath.

Becorath (bē-kō'răth), KJV **Bechorath** (bē-kō'răth). [Heb. *Bekôrath,* "first-born."] A Benjamite ancestor of King Saul (1 Sa 9:1).

Bed. The word "bed," found frequently in the Bible, does not always designate a piece of furniture, but in many instances simply the place of reclining or lying down (Job 17:13; Ps 63:6; etc.). For the ancients the bed was sometimes no more than a mat on the floor or a blanket spread out in which one would wrap himself (see Jn 5:8, where Jesus commanded the impotent man to take up his bed and walk). However, bedsteads existed from early times. In Israelite and NT times royalty or noblemen had high beds, and the poorer classes low cots. Actual ancient beds have been discovered in Egypt, and the metal cornerpieces of a bed were excavated at *Tell Far'ah* in Palestine.

55. The bed of Queen Hetep-heres, mother of the builder of the Great Pyramid at *Gîzeh.* Footrest at the left and headrest at the right

Ornamented beds or couches (see figs. 55, 213) are mentioned in the Bible as used by kings and wealthy people (Est 1:6; Eze 23:41; Amos 3:12; 6:4). The "bedstead" of King Og of Bashan, which for a long time was kept in Rabbah of the Ammonites (Deut 3:11), was probably his sarcophagus.

Bedad (bē'dăd). [Heb. *Bedad.*] Father of the Edomite king Hadad (Gen 36:35; 1 Chr 1:46).

Bedan (bē'dăn). [Heb. *Bedan,* meaning uncertain.]

1. According to the KJV, an Israelite leader mentioned between Gideon and Jephthah in a list of men who delivered Israel from foreign oppression (1 Sa 12:11; cf. Jgs 6:32). Since he is not mentioned in the book of Judges, many attempts to identify him with a known judge have been made. The LXX and the Syriac Peshitta read Barak instead of Bedan, suggesting thereby that the Hebrew *r* was misread for a *d,* and the *k* for *n* (see RSV). These letters are very similar in the Hebrew. Others suggest that Abdon be read for Bedan, supposing that an initial *'ayin* has dropped out of the Hebrew word.

2. A Manassite (1 Chr 7:17).

Bedchamber. Rear rooms or inner rooms in smaller houses, or rooms on the second floor, were usually reserved for sleeping purposes, and are called bedchambers (2 Sa 4:7; 2 Ki 11:2). These rooms were also the quarters of the women (Jgs 15:1). Of the men, only the head of the house had access to them.

Bedeiah (bē-dē'yȧ). [Heb. *Bedyah,* probably a shortened form of *'Obadyah,* "servant of Yahweh."] An Israelite of Ezra's time who was married to a foreign wife (Ezr 10:35).

Bee. [Heb. *debôrah*]. The honey-producing insect *Apis mellifica.* Beekeeping is not directly mentioned in the OT, but it probably existed in early times. Some scholars (see Koehler, *LVTL,* p. 391) suggest that the Heb. *ya'ar* in 1 Sa 14:26 and possibly also in v 25 should be translated "honeycomb" instead of "wood," or "forest," and that therefore these verses indicate the existence of beekeeping in ancient Palestine. The storage of honey, mentioned in Jer 41:8, presupposes also the existence of beekeeping, as does the characterization of Palestine as a "land flowing with milk and honey" (Ex 3:8; Num 13:27). There is reference to wild bees or their honey in several OT passages (Deut 1:44; 32:13; Jgs 14:8; Ps 118:12; Is 7:18). Beekeeping is mentioned in the Hittite laws (sec. 91, 92 of Tablet I) of the 14th cent. B.C. (*ANET* 193).

Beeliada (bē'ĕ-lī'à-dà). [Heb. *Be'elyada'*, "Baal has known," or, "The lord has known."] A son of David born at Jerusalem (1 Chr 14:7). He is called Eliada, Heb. *'Elyada'*, meaning "God has known," in 2 Sa 5:16 and 1 Chr 3:8, probably to eliminate the reference to Baal.

Beelzebub. *See* Beelzebul.

Beelzebul (bē-ĕl'zĕ-būl), KJV **Beelzebub** (bē-ĕl'zĕ-bŭb). [Gr. *Beelzeboul* and *Beezeboul*, textual evidence being divided between the two. The KJV reading "Beelzebub" is apparently derived from the Vulgate rather than the Greek manuscripts, and is probably based on the belief that Baalzebub, the "Lord of flies" of Ekron, was meant (2 Ki 1:2, 6). However, Canaanite literature of Ugarit shows that a god *Zebul* was known to the ancients, so that the name Beelzebul could mean "Baal is Zebul" or "The lord is Zebul." Another explanation is that Beelzebul means "Lord of dung," since in later Hebrew *zebel* means "dung."] A name given to the chief of the demonic world, Satan (Mt 10:25; 12:24-27; Mk 3:22, 23; Lk 11:15-19).

Beer (bē'ĕr). [Heb. *Be'er*, "well."]

1. A place in Moab where the Israelites encamped. It was called Beer because the leaders of the people there dug a well with their staves (Num 21:16-18). Scholars believe the place was probably in the *Wâdī et-Tamad* in northeastern Moab; the exact site is uncertain.

2. The place to which Gideon's son Jotham fled from his brother Abimelech (Jgs 9:21). It has usually been thought to be in the vicinity of Ophrah, hence identified with *el-Bîreh*, about 8 mi. northwest of Beth-shean. Josephus says only that Jotham fled to the mountains (*Ant.* v. 7. 2), whereas Eusebius locates the place about 7½ mi. north of Eleutheropolis in the neighborhood of Bethshemesh.

Beera (bĕ-ē'rà). [Heb. *Be'era'*, probably "well."] An Asherite (1 Chr 7:37).

Beerah (bĕ-ē'rà). [Heb. *Be'erah*, probably "well."] A chief of the Reubenites who was carried away captive by Tiglathpileser III (1 Chr 5:6).

Beer-elim (bē'ĕr-ē'lĭm). [Heb. *Be'er 'Êlîm*, "well of trees."] A place in Moab (Is 15:8), identified by many scholars with Beer of Num 21:16, which was probably in the *Wâdī et-Tamad*. *See* Beer, 1.

Beeri (bĕ-ē'rī). [Heb. *Be'eri*, "belonging to a well."]

1. A Hittite whose daughter Judith was one of Esau's wives (Gen 26:34).

2. Father of Hosea (Hos 1:1).

Beer-lahai-roi (bē'ĕr-là-hī'roi). [Heb. *Be'er Lachay Ro'i*, usually interpreted to mean "the well of the Living One who sees me," although there is some doubt as to its exact meaning.] A well in the desert between Kadesh and Bered on the way to Shur, where Hagar met an angel of the Lord (Gen 16:7, 14). Isaac lived there for some time after Abraham's death (chs 24:62; 25:11; KJV "the well Lahai-roi"). The place has not been identified.

Beeroth (bĕ-ē'rŏth). [Heb. *Be'erôth*, meaning "wells."]

1. A Canaanite town, whose inhabitants joined the Gibeonites in making a treaty with the Hebrews (Jos 9:17, 18). The town was assigned to the tribe of Benjamin (Jos 18:25; 2 Sa 4:2). It was reoccupied by the Jews after the Exile (Ezr 2:25; Neh 7:29). In NT times it was called Beroea. The place is usually identified with *el-Bîreh*, 11½ mi. southwest of Bethel, but *Râs-et-Tahûneh*, near *el-Bîreh* (Map VI, E-3), is a preferred identification.

2. According to the KJV a place on the border of Edom where the Israelites encamped (Deut 10:6). The RSV calls the place Beeroth Bene-jaakan, that is, "the wells of the Sons of Jaakan" (*see* Jaakan). The KJV translates the last two elements of the longer name as "children of Jaakan." The place is possibly identified with *Birein*, about 7 mi. southeast of the oasis *el-'Aujâ* (Map V, B-6).

Beerothite (bĕ-ē'rŏth-īt), KJV once **Berothite** (bē'rŏth-īt). [Heb. *Be'erothi* and *Berothi*.] A man of Beeroth (2 Sa 4:2, 3, 5, 9; 23:37; 1 Chr 11:39).

Beer-sheba (bē'ĕr-shē'bà). [Heb. *Be'er Sheba'*, "well of seven" (Gen 21:30, 31), or "well of an oath" (ch 26:31-33). Strabo explained it to mean "seven wells" (xvi. 4. 24).] A place in southern Palestine, the temporary residence of the patriarchs Abraham (Gen 21:31-34) and Isaac (ch 26:23-33). From here Jacob went to Haran (ch 28:10), and here on his way to Egypt he stopped to offer sacrifices at the place where his father and grandfather had erected altars and had received divine messages (ch 46:1-5). During the distribution of the country Beer-sheba was assigned to the tribe of Simeon (Jos 19:2). Since it was the southernmost city of the coun-

56. Modern Beer-sheba

try, the expression arose "from Dan even to Beer-sheba" (Jgs 20:1; 1 Sa 3:20), or "from Beer-sheba even to Dan" (1 Chr 21:2; 2 Chr 30:5), to designate the limits of Israel's homeland.

Samuel's sons were judges at Beer-sheba (1 Sa 8:2). Elijah passed through there when he fled to Horeb (1 Ki 19:3). The mother of Jehoash of Judah came from Beer-sheba (2 Ki 12:1). In the days of the prophet Amos the city had a sanctuary that was frequented by people from the northern kingdom (Amos 5:5; 8:14). The postexilic Jews reoccupied Beer-sheba (Neh 11:27, 30). It has been generally identified with the *Tell es-Seba'*, close to modern *Bir es-Seba'*, the successor of the ancient town, now a prosperous city in the state of Israel. Map VI, F-2.

Beeshterah (bē-ĕsh'tē-rå). [Heb. *Be'eshterah,* probably an abbreviation for *Beth 'Ashterah,* "house of Astarte."] A city in Bashan (Jos 21:27), called *Ashtaroth in other texts.

Beetle. *See* Locust, 3.

Beeves. The translation in the KJV in a few instances (Lev 22:19, 21; Num 31:28; etc.) of the frequently occurring Heb. *baqar,* "herd," "cattle."

Beggar. One who for his living depends on the gifts or alms he asks of others. Beggars were common in Bible times. They sat along the dusty roads, or stationed themselves at public disposal heaps or at the city or Temple gates, and called out for gifts from passers-by. "Beggar" occurs twice in the RSV (Mk 10:46; Jn 9:8), in both instances the translation of *prosaitēs,* "beggar." In the KJV the word occurs 3 times (1 Sa 2:8; Lk 16:20, 22), but in each case the word thus translated has the general meaning "poor," "needy." Compassion toward the needy is enjoined in Scripture (Lev 19:10; 25:25; Ps 69:33; etc.).

Behemoth (bē-hē'mŏth). [Heb. *behemôth,* probably an intensive plural of *behemah,* "beast." The word is simply transliterated in Job 40:15. It has been suggested that *behemoth* is derived from Egyptian *p3-îḥ-mw,* "water ox," but this is uncertain.] In the poem of Job 40:15-24 generally believed to describe the hippopotamus. This tremendous animal, weighing up to 6,500 pounds, was found in ancient Egypt, as shown by depictions of it on the monuments of that country. At present it is found only south of the 3d cataract, in the Sudan. The animal feeds on vegetable food, lives mostly in the water, where it swims with great facility, but also feeds on land, especially after sunset. It has a large body (10-12 ft. long), a clumsy head, and short stout legs. Although its size, ugliness, and big mouth give it a terrifying appearance, it is generally harmless, seldom attacking other animals or man.

Beka, KJV **Bekah.** [Heb. *beqa'.*] A Hebrew weight for precious metal equivalent to half a shekel (Ex 38:26). Weights inscribed with the word *bq'* have been found in Palestinian excavations. These weigh from 5.8 to 6.1 grams, but the local weights were not accurate. If the standard

126

shekel was 11.4 grams, a beka was 5.7 grams (.2 oz. avoirdupois). A Hebrew coin of the 5th cent. B.C. that bears the letters *bq'*, "half shekel," has also been discovered (*BASOR* 93 [1944], 26). The Heb. *beqa'* occurs also in Gen 24:22, but there it is translated "half a shekel."

Bekah. *See* Beka.

Bel (bĕl). [Heb. *Bel*; Akkadian *Bêlu,* related to Heb. *ba'al,* "lord," the popular name for Marduk (Heb. *Merodak,* "Merodach"), the chief god of the Babylonians.] Originally Marduk was nothing more than the local god of Babylon, but he rose in importance in the time of Hammurabi, when Babylon became the capital of an empire. From that time on he was considered the chief of all the Babylonian

57. The god Bel, or Marduk, as represented on a piece of lapis lazuli, found at Babylon

gods, excelling even his father, Ea, in importance. He was also the god who bestowed the authority of Babylonian kingship; therefore all Babylonian kings took the hands of Bel, or of Marduk, during the annual New Year festivities, thus receiving confirmation of the kingship for the ensuing year. The great temple *Esagila* in the center of Babylon was dedicated to Bel Marduk. In it was a golden statue of this god, which is referred to in ancient texts of various nations. In Is 46:1 Bel and Nebo are mentioned together. Nebo, or Nabu, was Bel's son. In Jer 50:2 the two names Bel and Marduk (Merodach) appear in parallelism. Bel's end is predicted in ch 51:44.

Bela (bē'lȧ), KJV once **Belah** (bē'lȧ). [Heb. *Bela',* "confusion" or "devoured."]

1. An early king of Edom (Gen 36:32).
2. A Reubenite chief (1 Chr 5:8).
3. A son of Benjamin and founder of a tribal family (Gen 46:21; Num 26:38).
4. One of the 5 cities of the plain attacked by Chedorlaomer, identical with Zoar (Gen 14:2, 8). *See* Zoar.

Belah. *See* Bela, 3.

Belaites (bē'lȧ-īts), [Heb. *Bal'i.*] Members of the family of *Bela.

Belial (bē'lĭ-ȧl). [Heb. *Beliya'al,* "uselessness," "wickedness"; Gr. *Beliar* or *Belial.*] A KJV OT term, usually in such phrases as "children of Belial" (Deut 13:13) or "sons of Belial" (1 Sa 2:12). These phrases are literal translations of Hebrew idiomatic expressions meaning "worthless men," "wicked men." The RSV renders the Hebrew idiom variously as "base fellows," "worthless men," etc. In the NT and in the (non-Biblical) Hebrew Dead Sea scrolls the term is used as a proper name for Satan (2 Cor 6:15).

Bell. Bells are mentioned in the Scripture in only two contexts: (1) As golden objects (Heb. *pa'amonîm*), alternating with golden pomegranates attached to the skirt of the garment of the high priest (Ex 28:33, 34; 39:25, 26). These bells were to be heard when Aaron went "in unto the holy place" (ch 28:35). (2) As objects (Heb. *meṣillôth*), presumably bells hung around the necks of horses (Zec 14:20).

Bellows. [Heb. *mappuach.*] An instrument consisting of a pair of leather bags, which, when expanded, draw in air through a valve and expel it when compressed. Such an instrument was known to the ancients and was used by them for the purpose of blowing air into furnaces to produce sufficient heat so that metals could be melted (Jer 6:29). The Palestinians depicted in a nobleman's tomb at Beni-hasan (19th cent. B.C.) carry two objects that have been interpreted as bellows. If the identification is correct, the depiction is evidence that these Palestinians were wandering smiths (see colored end sheet).

Belshazzar (bĕl-shăz'ēr). [Aramaic *Belsha'ṣṣar;* Babylonian *Bêl-shar-uṣur,* meaning "Bel, protect the king!"] According to Dan 5:2, 30, 31 the last king of the Chaldeans. Belshazzar was long unknown outside of the Bible and Jewish or Christian writings based on Dan 5. All secular sources dealing with the end of the Babylonian Empire listed Nabonidus as the last king. The discoveries of the last hundred years, however, have identified Belshazzar. It is now known from numerous contemporary cuneiform documents that he was the eldest son of Nabonidus, that as early as 560 B.C., 4 years before his father came to the throne, he was already a high officer of the crown, and that Nabonidus in "the third year" (most probably his third regnal year) "entrusted the kingship" to his eldest son (as coregent) and also placed the army at Babylon under his command. The elevation to the kingship took place when Nabonidus was about to conduct a military campaign against Tema in the interior of northern Arabia. After Tema was captured, Nabonidus rebuilt it, made it his residence city, and remained there for 10 years. During these years the official royal duties at Babylon were performed by Belshazzar. Among these was the official mourning for Nabonidus' mother, who died during these years.

Daniel's statement calling Belshazzar "the king" has thus been completely vindicated. Confirmation that Belshazzar was a descendant of Nebuchadnezzar, as Dan 5:2 indicates, has not yet been found, but as a result of the studies of R. P. Dougherty it now seems plausible that Belshazzar's mother was a daughter of the great king, and that Belshazzar was thus the grandson of Nebuchadnezzar. According to Semitic usage "father" stood frequently for "grandfather" or "ancestor."

Dan 5 describes the banquet Belshazzar held the night the Persians captured Babylon. It states that at the time the king drank wine from the sacred vessels of the Jerusalem Temple, his doom was spelled out in a mysterious handwriting on the plastered wall of his banquet hall, also how Daniel interpreted this message, and how it found its fulfillment before dawn came. Xenophon, too, intimates that the king met his death during the capture of Babylon (*Cyropaedia* vii. 5. 30).

Lit.: Raymond P. Dougherty, *Nabonidus and Belshazzar* (New Haven, Conn., 1929); *SDACom* 4:806-808.

Belt. A strip of cloth or leather used to girdle a person's body. The word occurs in RSV as the translation of: (1) The Heb. *meziach* in Job 12:21 (KJV "strength), and the Heb *mezach* in Ps 109:19 (KJV "girdle"). Both terms refer to a leather *girdle or belt worn next to the skin by males who had attained puberty. (2) The Heb. *'ezôr,* "loincloth," "belt," in Eze 23:15 (KJV "girdle"). (3) The Gr. *zōnē,* "belt," "girdle," in Mt 10:9 and Mk 6:8. Money was sometimes carried in these belts, hence the KJV translation "purse."

Belteshazzar (bĕl'tĕ-shăz'ẽr). [Heb. and

Aramaic *Beltesha'ṣṣar* and *Belte'shaṣṣar,* forms of probably the Babylonian *Bêl-balâtsu-uṣur,* meaning "Bel protect his (the king's) life" (see *SDA Com* 4:759).] The name the chief eunuch gave to Daniel when the young captive began his training in the royal palace at Babylon (Dan 1:7; 10:1).

Ben (bĕn). [Heb. *Ben,* "son," probably an abbreviation of a longer name.] A Levite (1 Chr 15:18, KJV).

Ben-abinadab (bĕn'à-bĭn'à-dăb). [Heb. *Ben-'abinadab,* "son of Abinadab."] A son-in-law of King Solomon, and a royal supply officer (1 Ki 4:11, RSV).

Benaiah (bĕ-nā'yà). [Heb. *Benayah* and *Benayahû,* "Yahweh has built." The name occurs also on an ancient Hebrew seal.]

1. A Levite of Kabzeel, in Judah (2 Sa 23:20), whose father, a leader of the priestly house of Aaron, brought 3,700 men to help place David on the throne (1 Chr 12:27). Benaiah, one of David's valiant heroes, had to his credit the slaying of two "lionlike men" (RSV "ariels") of Moab and an Egyptian giant (2 Sa 23:20, 21; 1 Chr 11:22, 23). He was commander of David's bodyguard, the Cherethites and Pelethites (2 Sa 8:18; 20:23), and also commanded the military division for the 3d month (1 Chr 27:5, 6). He and his forces remained faithful to the king during Absalom's rebellion (2 Sa 15:18; 20:23) and during Adonijah's attempt to seize the throne (1 Ki 1:8). He was one of those commissioned to lead Solomon to the coronation ceremony at Gihon (v 38). Under Solomon he became commander in chief of the armed forces (ch 2:35), and carried out the execution of Adonijah (vs 24, 25), Joab (vs 28-34), and Shimei (vs 36-46).

2. A man of Pirathon, one of David's 2d rank "mighty men" (2 Sa 23:30; 1 Chr 11:31), who commanded the military division for the 11th month (1 Chr 27:14).

3. A Levite musician who played the lyre in the company of those who escorted the ark to Jerusalem, and also in the tent David erected for the ark (1 Chr 15:18, 20; 16:5).

4. A priest who blew a trumpet in the company of those who escorted the ark to Jerusalem, and also in the tent erected by David for the ark (1 Chr 15:24; 16:6).

5. A Levite descended from Asaph (2 Chr 20:14).

6. A Simeonite (1 Chr 4:36).

7. A Levite, an overseer in the service of Hezekiah (2 Chr 31:13).

8. Father of Pelatiah, a prince of Judah during the Exile (Eze 11:1, 13).

9, 10, 11, 12. Four Israelites, one of the family of Parosh, one of the family of Pahath-moab, one of the family of Bani, and one of the family of Nebo, each of whom was married to a foreign wife in the time of Ezra (Ezr 10:25, 30, 35, 43).

Ben-ammi (běn'ăm'ī). [Heb. *Ben-'ammî,* "son of my kinsman."] Son of Lot's younger daughter, and founder of the Ammonites (Gen 19:38).

Ben-deker. *See* Dekar.

Beneberak (běn'ĕ-bē'răk). [Heb. *Benê-beraq,* "sons of lightning." The name occurs in Akkadian as *Banai Barqa.*] A place in the territory of Dan (Jos 19:45), modern *Ibn-ibrâq,* 4 mi. east of the city of Jaffa. Map VI, D-2.

Bene-jaakan (běn'ĕ-jā'à-kăn). [Heb. *Benê Ya'aqan,* "sons of Jaakan."] A place belonging to a clan descended from Jaakan, probably identical with the *Jaakan of 1 Chr 1:42. The Israelites camped here near wells belonging to this people (Num 33:31, 32; Deut 10:6). *See* Beeroth, 2.

Benevolence. [Gr. *eunoia,* from *eu,* "well," and *nous,* "mind"; thus, "good will," "favor," "affection."] This word occurs once in the KJV (1 Cor 7:3); however, textual evidence favors its omission, and favors also the reading "obligation" (Gr. *opheilē*) instead of the adjective "due." The passage thus reads literally, "Let the husband give to the wife the obligation, likewise also the wife to the husband." The context plainly reveals that Paul is here speaking of the proper attitude toward sexual relations. The RSV translates *opheilē* "conjugal rights."

Ben-geber. See Geber, 2.

Ben-hadad (běn'hā'dăd). [Heb. *Ben-hadad,* "son of (the god) Hadad."] The name of several rulers of the Aramaean (Syrian) kingdom of Damascus.

1. Ben-hadad I, son of Tabrimmon, grandson of Hezion (1 Ki 15:18), and great-grandson of Rezon (ch 11:23). He reigned from *c.* 912 to *c.* 870 B.C. He was an ally of Baasha, king of Israel, but in the struggle between Judah and Israel he was induced by Asa, king of Judah, to break off his alliance and attack Israel (1 Ki 15:16-21; 2 Chr 16:1-5). He induced Omri to admit Aramaean business firms to Samaria (see 1 Ki 20:34). This Ben-hadad (called Bar-hadad), his father, and his grandfather are mentioned in an Aramaic inscription found at Breidj (see fig. 58), 4½ mi. north of Aleppo (W. F.

Albright, *BASOR* 87 [1942], 23-29).

2. Ben-hadad II (in Assyrian texts *Biridri* or *Adad-idri*), probably son and successor of Ben-hadad I. He ruled over Damascus from *c.* 870 to *c.* 842 B.C. He fought against Ahab of Israel and unsuccessfully besieged Samaria. He was also beaten in the battle of Aphek in a second attempt to subjugate Israel. In this battle he was captured, but Ahab spared his life after the king promised to return to Israel the conquered cities of Galilee, to admit business firms of Israel to Damascus, and to enter into a treaty (1 Ki 20:1-34). Probably this treaty was an alliance against Assyria, for in 853 B.C. both Ahab and Ben-

58. A stele erected by Bar-hadad (Ben-hadad I), king of Damascus, in honor of the god Melkarth

hadad fought as allies in the battle of Qarqar against Shalmaneser III. The battle was not decisive, and the allies were not beaten into submission. Shalmaneser III mentions three further campaigns against Damascus during Ben-hadad's reign (849, 848, 845 B.C.), but they seem to have had no lasting success. The alliance of Damascus and Israel was short-lived. In the same year that the battle of Qarqar was fought Ahab waged war against Ben-hadad and was killed at Ramoth-gilead. Later Ben-hadad invaded Israel again, but lifted the siege on the rumor that the Hittites or Egyptians were approaching to help Israel (2 Ki 6:24 to 7:16). About 842 B.C. he was murdered by Hazael, who became his successor and the founder of a new Aramaic dynasty in Damascus (ch 8:15).

3. Ben-hadad III, son of Hazael (2 Ki 13:3, 24, 25); he reigned as king of Damascus from *c.* 805 - *c.* 750 B.C. He was thrice defeated by Jehoash, king of Israel, and lost to Israel all the cities that Hazael had taken from Jehoahaz (vs 3, 24, 25). He is mentioned in the Aramaic inscription of Zakir, king of Hamath, under the name of Bar-hadad. It is not known how he died.

Ben-hail (bĕn'hā'ĭl). [Heb. *Ben-chayil,* "a brave man."] One of the princes whom King Jehoshaphat sent to teach the law of the Lord in Judah (2 Chr 17:7).

Ben-hanan (bĕn'hā'nắn). [Heb. *Ben-chanan,* "son of grace."] A Judahite (1 Chr 4:20).

Ben-hesed (bĕn-hē'sĕd), KJV **(son of) Hesed** (hē'sĕd). [Heb. *Ben-chesed,* "son of mercy," or "son of grace."] One of King Solomon's supply officers (1 Ki 4:10).

Ben-hinnom. *See* Hinnom, Valley of.

Ben-hur. *See* Hur, 4.

Beninu (bĕ-nī'nū). [Heb. *Beninû,* possibly "our son."] A Levite who set his seal to Nehemiah's covenant (Neh 10:13).

Benjamin (bĕn'jȧ-mĭn). [Heb. *Binyamîn,* meaning "son of my right hand," or "son of the south." The name occurs in the Mari texts of the 18th cent. B.C. as that of a tribe, spelled *Banu-Yamina.* But this tribe has no connection with the Biblical tribe of Benjamin in spite of the assertions of some scholars to the contrary. Gr. *Beniamin.*]

1. The youngest of Jacob's 12 sons, who was born to Rachel on the road from Bethel to Ephrath. His dying mother called him Benoni, "son of my sorrow," but his father gave him the name Benjamin (Gen 35:16-19). It was with great reluctance that Jacob allowed Benjamin to go to Egypt on the second journey of his sons to that country to purchase food during the famine. Joseph also deeply loved Benjamin (chs 43:29 to 44:34). The blessing of Jacob for Benjamin is recorded in ch 49:27. Benjamin had numerous descendants (Gen 46:21; Num 26:38-41; 1 Chr 7:6-12; 8:1-40).

2. A Benjamite (1 Chr 7:10).

3. An Israelite of the family of Harim; he was married to a foreign wife in Ezra's time. (Ezr 10:32); possibly identical with Benjamin, 4.

4. A builder of Jerusalem's wall in Nehemiah's time (Neh 3:23; 12:34), who also signed the covenant (ch 10:28-39); possibly identical with Benjamin, 3.

5. One of the 12 tribes of Israel, the descendants of the youngest son of Jacob and Rachel. When Canaan was divided among the tribes, Benjamin was assigned a territory between Ephraim in the north and Judah in the south (Jos 18:11-20). Its northern boundary ran from Jordan up to Bethel, and as far as nether Beth-horon. From here it ran south until it reached Kiriath-jearim. Its southern boundary began at Kiriath-jearim in the west, went over to Jerusalem's Valley of Hinnom, and from there to the northern end of the Dead Sea. The eastern boundary was formed by the Jordan (Map VI, E-3/4). Although the territory was small and mountainous, it enjoyed great fertility and enclosed within its area many important cities, including Jerusalem, Jericho, Bethel, Gibeon, Mizpah, and others (Jos. *Ant.* v. 1. 22). Ehud, one of the early judges and deliverers (Jgs 3:15), was a Benjamite. The tribe was almost wiped out when it protected the criminal inhabitants of Gibeah (chs 19-21), but it quickly recovered. Saul, Israel's first king, came from Benjamin. Because of this affinity the tribe clung to the house of Saul for some time after the king's death (2 Sa 2:9, 15; 16:5; 20:1-22). However, in the course of time it turned its loyalty to the house of David and cast in its lot with the kingdom of Judah when the remaining tribes seceded after Solomon's death (1 Ki 12:21). After the Exile the members of Benjamin and Judah formed the main contingents of the returned Jews (Ezr 4:1). The apostle Paul (Php 3:5) was one of the tribe's most famous members. Benjamin is listed among the tribes in the prophetic visions of Ezekiel and of John the revelator (Eze 48:23, 24, and Rev 7:8).

6. The name of two gates at Jerusalem: (1) a gate in the northern wall of Jerusalem, not identified (Jer 37:13; 38:7; Zec 14:10); (2) a gate in the north wall of the Temple compound (Jer 20:2). If the northern city wall was at the same time the north wall of the Temple compound, this gate may be identical with (1).

Benjamite (bĕn'jȧ-mīt). [Heb. *Ben-hay-mînî.*] A descendant of *Benjamin.

Beno (bē'nō). [Heb. *Benô,* "his son."] A Merarite priest (1 Chr 24:26, 27).

Ben-oni (běn'ō'nī). [Heb. *Ben-'ônî,* "son of my sorrow."] The name given by Rachel to her second son, at whose birth on the way from Bethel to Ephrath she died. He is better known by the name Benjamin, which was given him by his father (Gen 35:18, 19).

Ben-zoheth (běn'zō'hěth). [Heb. *Ben-zôcheth,* "son of Zoheth."] A Judahite (1 Chr 4:20).

Beon (bē'ŏn). [Heb. *Be'on.*] A contracted form of Beth-meon, or Beth-baal-meon (Num 32:3, 38). *See* Baal-meon.

Beor (bē'ôr), KJV of NT **Bosor** (bō'sôr). [Heb. *Be'ôr,* "burning"; Gr. *Beôr,* textual variant *Bosor.*]
1. Father of the Edomite king Bela (Gen 36:32; 1 Chr 1:43).
2. Father of the renegade prophet Balaam (Num 22:5; etc.). Called Bosor in the KJV of 2 Pe 2:15, but Beor in the RSV on the basis of certain ancient manuscripts.

Bera (bē'rá). [Heb. *Bera',* of uncertain meaning.] The king of Sodom, whom Chedorlaomer and his confederates defeated in battle (Gen 14:2).

Beracah (běr'á-ká), KJV **Berachah** (běr'áká). [Heb. *Berakah,* "blessing."]
1. A Benjamite who joined David at Ziklag (1 Chr 12:3).
2. A valley in Judah near Tekoa. King Jehoshaphat once gathered his army there to bless God for a great victory over the Ammonites, Moabites, and Edomites (2 Chr 20:26), and as a consequence named it *Berakah,* "blessing." The valley has been identified with the depression now called *Wâdî el-'Arrûb,* which runs from the ridge of the mountains of Judea in a southerly direction south of Tekoa.

Berachah. *See* Beracah.

Berachiah. *See* Berechiah, 2.

Beraiah (běr'á-ī'á). [Heb. *Bera'yah,* "Yahweh has created."] A Benjamite (1 Chr 8:21).

Berea. *See* Beroea.

Berechiah (běr'ē-kī'á), KJV once **Berachiah** (běr'á-kī-á). [Heb. *Berekyah* and *Berekyahû,* "Yahweh has blessed."]
1. A Gershonite Levite, father of Asaph (1 Chr 6:39; 15:17).
2. A Levite, a doorkeeper for the ark in David's time (1 Chr 15:23, 24).
3. A chief man of Ephraim in the time of King Pekah of the northern kingdom of Israel (2 Chr 28:12).
4. Son of Zerubbabel (1 Chr 3:20).
5. Son of Asa, a Levite (1 Chr 9:16).

6. The father of one of the leaders who helped repair Jerusalem's city wall in Nehemiah's time (Neh 3:4, 30).
7. Father of the prophet Zechariah (Zec 1:1, 7).

Bered (bē'rĕd). [Heb. *Bered,* "hail."]
1. An Ephraimite (1 Chr 7:20).
2. A place in the Wilderness of Shur (Gen 16:7, 14), to the west of Kadesh. The site has not been identified, but the *Wâdî Umm el-Bâred* in the southern desert seems to have retained the name.

Beri (bē'rī). [Heb. *Berî,* meaning unknown.] An Asherite (1 Chr 7:36).

Beriah (bē-rī'á). [Heb. *Berî'ah,* of uncertain meaning; Akkadian *Barḫu* and *Buraḫu.*]
1. A son of Asher and the founder of a tribal family (Gen 46:17; Num 26:44).
2. A son of Ephraim (1 Chr 7:23).
3. A Benjamite, head of a family of the inhabitants of Aijalon (1 Chr 8:13).
4. A Gershonite Levite (1 Chr 23:10), whose sons, together with those of his brother Jeush, formed one family (v 11).

Beriite (bē-rī'īt). [Heb. *Berî'î.*] A member of the family of Beriah (Num 26:44).

Berites (bē'rīts). [Heb. *Berîm.*] According to the KJV, a people near Beth-maachah (2 Sa 20:14). Scholars think that a scribal error is involved, and that Bichrites (bĭk'rīts), Bachrites, or Barhumites (bär-hū'mīts) should be read (see RSV).

Berith. *See* Baal-berith.

Bernice (bēr-nī'sē). [Gr. *Bernikē.*] The eldest daughter of King Herod Agrippa I. She was married first to a certain Mark, then to her uncle Herod, king of Chalcis. After he died in A.D. 48 she lived in incest for several years with her brother Agrippa II. To quiet this scandal she married Polemon II, king of Olba in Cilicia, some time after A.D. 60. However, she left him about A.D. 65 and returned to her brother. The Roman general Titus (later the emperor) fell in love with her when he was in Judea during the Jewish War, and later lived openly with her in Rome for some time. She appears in the NT accompanying her brother Agrippa II to Caesarea at the time Festus became procurator of Judea. There she and her brother met and heard the apostle Paul (Acts 25:13, 23; 26:30). See fig. 221.

Berodach-baladan. *See* Merodach-baladan.

Beroea (bē-rē'á), KJV **Berea** (bē-rē'á). [Gr. *Beroia.*] A city in Macedonia, about 50 mi. southwest of Thessalonica, and 24 mi. from the sea at the southern edge of the Vardar plain. During the 1st cent. A.D. it was a populous city of Macedonia, al-

59. The place where, according to tradition, Paul is supposed to have preached at Beroea

though other cities, such as Thessalonica and Philippi, exceeded it in commercial and political importance. Its modern name is *Verria*. Paul came to Beroea from Thessalonica during his 2d Missionary Journey, and preached with considerable success. When Jews from Thessalonica came to Beroea and stirred up trouble against the apostle, he withdrew, leaving Timothy and Silas behind (Acts 17:10-14). Nothing further is known of this church. There is probably little doubt that Paul visited the city and church again during his 3d Missionary Journey (ch 20:1-4). Map XX, A-3.

Berothah (bĕ-rō'thà), or **Berothai** (bĕ-rō'thī). [Heb. *Berôthah* and *Berothay*.] According to Eze 47:16 Berothah was a city between Hamath and Damascus, and was probably identical with the Berothai that belonged to the kingdom of Hadadezer of Zobah, from which David obtained much booty in bronze after capturing the city (2 Sa 8:8). Berothah was also called Cun (kŭn) [Heb. *Kûn*] (1 Chr 18:8, "Chun," kŭn, KJV). It has been identified with *Bereitân*, 8 mi. south of Ba'albek.

Berothai. *See* Berothah.

Berothite. *See* Beerothite.

Beryl. [Heb. *tarshîsh;* Gr. *bērullos*.] The Hebrew term is of uncertain identification.

BETHABARA

It has been variously identified as topaz, chrysolite, chalcedony, and carbuncle. It was the first stone in the fourth row of the high priest's breastplate (Ex 28:20; 39:13). It appears in connection with the descriptions of "my beloved" (Song 5:14), Ezekiel's wheels (Eze 1:16; 10:9), "the king of Tyre" (ch 28:13), a heavenly being (Dan 10:6). The Gr. *bērullos* may possibly be identified with the modern beryl. It constitutes the eighth foundation of the New Jerusalem (Rev 21:20). Mineralogists believe that only the green variety was known in John's time.

Besai (bē'sī). [Heb. *Besay*.] The founder of a family of Nethinim. Members of this family returned with Zerubbabel from Babylon (Ezr 2:49; Neh 7:52).

Besodeiah (bĕs'ô-dē'yà). [Heb. *Besôdyah*, "in intimacy with Yahweh."] Father of Meshullam, who aided in the repair of one of Jerusalem's gates (Neh 3:6).

Besom. [Heb. *mat'ate'*, "broom."] A term meaning "broom," found in the KJV of Is 14:23, where the prophet declares that God will sweep Babylon with the besom, or broom, of destruction.

Besor (bē'sôr). [Heb. *Besôr*.] A brook south of Ziklag (1 Sa 30:9, 10, 21), probably the *Wâdī Ghazzeh,* which runs from Beer-sheba in a westerly direction, and enters the Mediterranean south of Gaza.

Bestead. An obsolete word found in the KJV of Is 8:21 translating a Hebrew word meaning "hard-pressed," "oppressed," "distressed" (RSV).

Betah (bē'tà). [Heb. *Betach*, "trust," "security."] A town in Aram-zobah (2 Sa 8:8), called Tibhath in 1 Chr 18:8.

Beten (bē'tĕn). [Heb. *Beten*, "a hollow."] A village in the territory of Asher (Jos 19:25). It has been identified with *Abtûn,* about 12 mi. southeast of Acre (Acco).

Beth. [Heb. *bêth.*] The 2d letter of the Hebrew alphabet, written ב, appearing as the title to the 2d section of Ps 119 in the KJV. *See* Aleph.

Bethabara (bĕth'ăb'à-rà). [Gr. *Bēthabara.*] According to the KJV a place on the Jordan where John baptized (Jn 1:28). However, textual evidence favors the reading *Bēthania,* "Bethany" (see RSV), but Origen, who could find no Bethany at the Jordan, preferred Bethabara on geographical grounds. His preference became the accepted reading for many centuries. But even Origen's Bethabara has not been identified. The Jordan ford '*Abārah,* suggested by some, lies 12 mi. south of the Sea of Galilee, and thus seems to be too

132

60. Bethany

far north. Another conjecture is that Beth-abara is Beth-barah, which Map XVI, D-4 puts, with a question mark, near the confluence of the Jabbok with the Jordan. The location must be considered as still uncertain.

Beth-anath (bĕth'ā'năth). [Heb. *Bêth-'anath,* "house (or temple) of (the Canaanite goddess) Anath."] The name is mentioned in Egyptian topographical lists of Palestine from Ramses II to Shishak as *Bt 'nt.*] A Canaanite city in the territory of Naphtali (Jos 19:32, 38), which remained in the hands of the Canaanites (Jgs 1:33). It has been identified with *el-Ba'neh,* about 11 mi. east of Acre (Acco) (Map VI, C-3).

Beth-anoth (bĕth'ā'nŏth). [Heb. *Bêth-'anôth,* "the house of (the Canaanite goddess) Anath."] A place in Judah (Jos 15:59). Some of the Egyptian references to Beth-anath may actually apply to this town. It has been identified with *Beit 'Ainûn,* 3 mi. northeast of Hebron.

Bethany (bĕth'á-nĭ). [Gr. *Bēthania* from Heb. *Bêth-'ani,* "house of the poor."]
1. A village on the eastern slope of the Mount of Olives, about 1½ mi. east of Jerusalem, on the road from Jerusalem to Jericho. In Bethany was the home of Lazarus, Martha, and Mary, which Jesus visited on several occasions (Mt 21:17; Mk 11:1, 11, 12; Lk 10:38; Jn 11:1); also the home of Simon the leper, where Mary anointed Jesus (Mt 26:6-13; Mk 14:3). The ascension took place not far from the village (Lk 24:50, 51). The place is now called *el-'Azarîyeh* after Lazarus, whose traditional tomb is now exhibited

there. Map XVI, E-3. See figs. 9, 60, 292.
2. A place east of the Jordan, where John baptized (Jn 1:28, RSV); not identified. *See* Bethabara.

Beth-arabah (bĕth'ăr'á-bá). [Heb. *Bêth Ha'arabah,* "house of the wilderness."] A place in the Wilderness of Judah on the border of Benjamin and Judah (Jos 15:6, 61; 18:22), possibly the Arabah of Jos 18:18. It is probably correctly identified with *el-Gharabeh* in the *Wâdî Qelt,* about 3 mi. west of the Jordan River (Map VI, E-3/4).

Beth-aram. *See* Beth-haran.

Beth-arbel (bĕth'är'bĕl). [Heb. *Bêth 'Arbe'l.*] According to Hos 10:14 a town destroyed by Shalman (probably Shalmaneser). Its identification is not certain. Eusebius identified it with an Irbid (Arbela) in Gilead, 16 mi. east of the Jordan (Map VI, C-4), whereas Josephus mentions an Arbela in Galilee (*Ant.* xii. 11. 1), 4 mi. northwest of Tiberias (Map XV, C-3).

Beth-ashbea (bĕth'ăsh'bĕ-á). [Heb. *Bêth 'Ashbea',* "house of plenty."] A place probably in Judah where lived a Judahite family known as workers in fine linen (1 Chr 4:21, RSV); the site has not been identified. The KJV translates the Hebrew term "house of Ashbea," considering Ashbea to have been the head of the family of these weavers.

Beth-aven (bĕth'ā'vĕn). [Heb. *Bêth-'awen,* "house of wickedness."]
1. A place near Ai, east of Bethel and west of Michmash, near a wilderness (Jos 7:2; 18:12; 1 Sa 13:5; 14:23); not identified.
2. A derisive epithet that was used by the

133

prophet Hosea for Bethel after the city became a seat of idolatrous worship (Hos 4:15; 5:8; 10:5).

Beth-azmaveth. See Azmaveth, 5.

Beth-baal-meon. See Baal-meon.

Beth-barah (bĕth′bâr′à). [Heb. *Bêth Barah.*] A place in the Jordan Valley (Jgs 7:24); not identified. Map XVI, D-4, shows a merely conjectural location.

Beth-birei. See Beth-biri.

Beth-biri (bĕth′bĭr′ĭ), KJV **Beth-birei** (bĕth′-bĭr′ē-ĭ). [Heb. *Bêth Bir′i.*] A town in the territory of Simeon (1 Chr 4:31); not identified.

Beth-car (bĕth′kär′). [Heb. *Bêth Kar.*] A place to which the Israelites pursued the Philistines after the 2d battle at Ebenezer (1 Sa 7:11); possibly to be identified with Beth-haccherem.

Beth-dagon (bĕth′dā′gŏn). [Heb. *Bêth-dagôn,* "house (or temple) of (the god) Dagon." The name probably designates early seats of Dagon worship. A topographical list of Palestinian cities of Ramses III mentions a *Bt-dkn,* and cuneiform records mention *Bit-dagarna,* both doubtless referring to one of the two Biblical Bethdagons.]

1. A place in the *Shephelah of Judah (Jos 15:33, 41), possibly *Khirbet Dajûn,* 5 mi. southeast of Jaffa.

2. A place in the territory of Asher toward Zebulun, near Mount Carmel (Jos 19:27); not identified.

Beth-diblathaim. See Almon-diblathaim.

Beth-eden (bĕth′ē′dĕn). [Heb. *Bêth ʻEden,* "house of Eden."] Probably the country called *Bit Adini* in Akkadian inscriptions, which lay on both sides of the Euphrates in northern Mesopotamia (Map XI, B-4) and was inhabited by Aramaeans until the nation was destroyed by Assyria in the 8th cent. B.C. Amos denounced it (ch 1:5, "house of Eden," KJV). Elsewhere it is simply called Eden. Eden is mentioned with Gozan, Haran, Rezeph, and Telassar as conquered by the Assyrians in the time of Hezekiah (2 Ki 19:12; Is 37:12). Ezekiel lists the merchants of Eden with others as those who supplied Tyre when it was in its former heyday (Eze 27:23).

Beth-eked of the Shepherds (bĕth′ēk′ĕd). [Heb. *Bêth-ʻeqed Haroʻim,* meaning uncertain.] A locality on the way from Jezreel to Samaria (2 Ki 10:12, 14, RSV). The KJV has rendered the Hebrew term "shearing house." Some identify it with *Beit Qâd,* near *Jenîn* (ancient En-gannim); others with *Kufr Râʻi;* but both identifications are conjectural.

Bethel (bĕth′′l). [Heb. *Bêth-ʼel,* "house (or temple) of God."]

1. A Canaanite town, originally called Luz. The name Bethel was given to it by Jacob, who there had his dream of the heavenly ladder (Gen 28:16-19). It was west of Ai, south of Shiloh (Gen 12:8; Jgs 21:19), and near Michmash (1 Sa 13:2). Abraham camped twice at Bethel and built an altar there (Gen 12:8; 13:3). When Jacob returned from Laban he followed his grandfather's example and also camped at Bethel (ch 35:1-15). When the Israelites under Joshua invaded the country, the people of Bethel aided the inhabitants of Ai in their resistance (Jos 8:9-17), but both towns fell to the invader (ch 12:9, 16).

In the division of the country Bethel was assigned to Benjamin, but it was on the border of Ephraim (Jos 16:1, 2; 18:11, 13, 21, 22), and the Ephraimites considered it one of their cities (Jgs 1:22-26; 1 Chr 7:20, 28). During the war of the Israelites against Gibeah, Bethel played an important role, for there the Israelites sought God's counsel and offered sacrifices (Jgs 20:1, 18, 26, 27; 21:2-4; RSV). After the Philistines destroyed Shiloh, Bethel was one of the places from which Samuel judged Israel, and where, probably, sacrifices were offered (1 Sa 7:16; 10:3). When the ten tribes seceded from the house of David, Jeroboam I established one of the centers of calf worship at Bethel (1 Ki 12:29-33; 13:1-32; 2 Ki 10:29). King Abijah of Judah temporarily occupied it (2 Chr 13:19).

61. A village street in Bethel

Bethel was repeatedly denounced by the prophets (Jer 48:13; Amos 3:14; 4:4; 5:5, 6), and Hosea called it *Beth-aven, meaning "house of wickedness" (Hos 4:15; 5:8; 10:5). Josiah finally desecrated its sacred place by tearing down its altars and burning there the bones of former idolatrous priests dug up from their graves (1 Ki 13:1-3; 2 Ki 23:4, 15-20).

The descendants of some of Bethel's inhabitants returned from Babylonia with Zerubbabel after the Exile (Ezr 2:28; Neh 7:32), and the city was counted as belonging to Benjamin (Neh 11:31). Bethel played a role in the Maccabean period (1 Macc 9:50), and in the Jewish-Roman war was captured by Vespasian (Jos. *War* iv. 9. 9). It is a small village today, called *Beitin,* about 11 mi. north of Jerusalem (Map VI, E-3). Excavations carried out in 1927 and 1934 by W. F. Albright and J. L. Kelso and again since 1954 by Kelso show that the site was inhabited since the 3d millennium B.C., and that it experienced a severe destruction in the 13th cent. B.C. They give evidence also of the destruction by the Babylonians, and show vestiges of the rebuilding under the Persians and of a period of prosperity in Hellenistic times. See J. L. Kelso, *BA* 19 (1956), 36-43. See figs. 38, 61.

2. A place in the territory of Simeon (1 Sa 30:27). See Bethuel, 2.

Bethelite (bĕth'ĕl-īt). [Heb. *Bêth Ha'elî.*] An inhabitant of *Bethel.

Beth-emek (bĕth'ē'mĕk). [Heb. *Bêth-ha'emeq,* "house of the valley."] A town in the territory of Asher (Jos 19:27); probably *Tell Mîmâs,* about 6 mi. northeast of Acre.

Bether (bē'thĕr). [Heb. *Bether.*] According to the KJV a proper name appearing in the phrase "the mountains of Bether" (Song 2:17). However, it is generally believed that *bether* is not a proper name, but a common noun describing the mountains as rugged (see RSV).

Bethesda. See Beth-zatha.

Beth-ezel (bĕth'ē'zĕl). [Heb. *Bêth-ha'eṣel,* "a place nearby."] A town in the *Shephelah of Judah (Mic 1:11). It has been identified with *Deir el-'Aṣal,* about 2 mi. east of *Tell Beit Mirsim* (probably ancient Debir).

Beth-gader (bĕth'gā'dĕr). [Heb. *Bêth-gader,* "house of a wall."] A town in Judah (1 Chr 2:51), probably the Geder of Jos 12:13. The site is unknown.

Beth-gamul (bĕth'gā'mŭl). [Heb. *Bêth Gamûl,* "house of rewards."] A town in Moab (Jer 48:23), now identified with *Khirbet ej-Jumeil,* 8 mi. east of Dibon.

Beth-gilgal. See Gilgal.

Beth-haccerem. See Beth-haccherem.

Beth-haccherem (bĕth'hă-kē'rĕm), KJV **Beth-haccerem** (bĕth'hăk'sĕ-rĕm). [Heb. *Bêth Hakkerem,* "house of the vineyard."] A place in Judah (Neh 3:14; Jer 6:1), usually identified with *'Ain Kârim,* 4 mi. west of Jerusalem, but recently with *Ramath-Rahel,* 2½ mi. south of Jerusalem, where excavations have uncovered an ancient town (Y. Aharoni, *IEJ* 6 [1956], 102-111, 137-157).

Beth-haggan (bĕth'hăg'ăn). [Heb. *Bêth Haggan,* "house of the garden."] A place to which Ahaziah fled when Jehu killed Joram of Israel (2 Ki 9:27, KJV "garden house"). It is probably the modern *Jenîn,* called *En-gannim (see Map IX, D-3) in Jos 19:21.

Beth-haram. See Beth-haran.

Beth-haran (bĕth'hā'răn). [Heb. *Bêth Haran.*] A place in the Jordan Valley, rebuilt by the people of Gad (Num 32:36), probably identical with Beth-haram (bĕth'-hā'răm; KJV "Beth-aram," bĕth'ā'răm) [Heb. *Bêth Haram*] (Jos 13:27). In NT times it was known as Beth-aramphtha (Jos. *Ant.* xviii. 2. 1; *War* ii. 4. 2), the place where Herod had a palace. Herod Antipas called it Livias in honor of the wife of the emperor Augustus. It has been identified with *Tell Iktanû,* about 7 mi. northeast of the point where the Jordan flows into the Dead Sea (Map XIV, E-4).

Beth-hogla. See Beth-hoglah.

Beth-hoglah (bĕth'hŏg'lä), KJV once **Beth-hogla** (bĕth'hŏg'lä). [Heb. *Bêth Choglah,* "house of the partridge."] A village of Benjamin, on its southern boundary in the Jordan Valley (Jos 15:6; 18:19). It has been identified with *'Ain Hajlah,* 5 mi. southeast of Jericho. Map VI, E-3.

Beth-horon (bĕth'hō'rŏn). [Heb. *Bêth-chorôn,* "house of the (god) Choron"; Egyptian *Bt Hrn.* Records show that this god was worshiped also in Egypt and at Ugarit.] Twin towns in the territory of Ephraim (Jos 16:3, 5), about 2 mi. apart, called Upper and Lower Beth-horon because there is a difference in altitude of *c.* 700 ft. between the two sites.

1. Upper Beth-horon, a border city of Ephraim (Jos 16:5) toward Benjamin, situated on a mountain ridge. It was built by Sheerah, an Ephraimite woman (1 Chr 7:24). It controlled the important entrance from the plain to the central mountain area. This was doubtless the reason Solomon fortified it (2 Chr 8:5). It is identified with the present *Beit 'Ur el-*

Fōqā, 10 mi. northwest of .Jerusalem, about 2,024 ft. above sea level (Map VI, E-3).

2. Lower (or nether) Beth-horon (Jos 16:3; 18:13), on the border of Ephraim at the western exit of the descent from the mountains. It was about 2 mi. west of Upper Beth-horon, and its altitude was about 1,312 ft. above sea level. Lower Beth-horon, a strategically important city, was also fortified by Solomon (1 Ki 9:17; 2 Chr 8:5). It is now *Beit 'Ur et-Taḥtā.* The pass in which the two cities lay was the route by which the Amorites fled before the victorious Israelites under Joshua (Jos 10:10, 11). The Philistines ascended this narrow defile to fight against Saul (1 Sa 13:18). In the Maccabean wars two great battles were fought there (1 Macc 3:15, 16; 7:39, 40), and in this pass the Jews in A.D. 66 almost wiped out the Roman army of Cestius Gallus, legate of Syria (Jos. *War* ii. 19. 8).

Beth-jeshimoth (běth'jěsh'ĭ-mŏth), KJV once **Beth-jesimoth** (běth'jĕs'ĭ-mŏth). [Heb. *Bêth Hayeshimôth,* "house of the wastes."] A place that formed the southern limit of the Israelite camp at Abel-shittim (Num 33:49), probably to be identified with *Tell el-'Azeimeh,* about 10 mi. southeast of Jericho, east of the Jordan (Map VI, E-4). The place is also mentioned in Jos 12:3; 13:20; Eze 25:9.

62. Entrance of the Church of the Nativity at Bethlehem

Beth-jesimoth. *See* Beth-jeshimoth.

Beth-le-aphrah (běth'lě-ăph'rä), KJV (house of) Aphrah (ăf'rä). [Heb. *Bêth Le'aphrah.*] A town in Judah (Mic 1:10). It has been identified with *eṭ-Ṭaiyibeh* between Hebron and *Beit Jibrîn;* but the identification remains uncertain (Abel, *Géographie* II, p. 277).

Beth-lebaoth (běth'lě-bā'ŏth). [Heb. *Bêth-leba'ôth,* "house of lions."] A town in the south of Judah, assigned to the tribe of Simeon (Jos 19:6). The site is unknown.

Bethlehem (běth'lě-hěm). [Heb. *Bêth Lechem,* "house of bread," or "house (i.e., temple) of (the god) Laḥmu."]

1. A town in the hill country of Judah. It seems to have belonged to Jerusalem before the Israelites invaded the country, as a reference to *Bit-Laḥmi* in the *Amarna Letters (ANET* 489) is believed to indicate. It was sometimes called Ephrath (Gen 35:19), and to distinguish it from the Bethlehem in Zebulun was called Bethlehem in Judah (KJV "Beth-lehem-judah") and Bethlehem Ephrathah (Jgs 17:7; Mi 5:2). In the patriarchal period it is first mentioned as the place to which Jacob was traveling when Rachel died (Gen 35:16, 19; 48:7). If the LXX text of Jos 15:59 is reliable it seems to have been assigned to Judah at the division of the country, but the Masoretic text does not include it in the list of Judah's towns. It was the home of several famous Biblical characters: Boaz (Ruth 2:4), Jesse (1 Sa 16:1), the sons of Zeruiah (2 Sa 2:32), and David (1 Sa 17: 12; etc.). According to Micah's prediction (Mi 5:2) the Messiah would come from Bethlehem. Sacrifices seem to have been offered to God in Bethlehem in the time of Samuel (1 Sa 16:2-5; 20:6, 29). In the time of David it was a walled city and for some time was occupied by the Philistines (2 Sa 23:14, 15). Rehoboam refortified it (2 Chr 11:6). After the Babylonian exile the Jews reoccupied it (Ezr 2:1, 21; Neh 7: 26). See figs. 62-64, 241, 330.

Bethlehem is especially well known as the town in which Jesus Christ was born, and where a number of events took place connected with His birth: the announcement of His birth to the shepherds, the visit of the Wise Men from the East, and the murder of the town's infants by Herod the Great (Mt 2:1-18; Lk 2:4-20). Tradition going back to Justin Martyr (*c.* A.D. 148) claims that Jesus was born in a cave. Constantine the Great built a church over that cave, which has attracted

63. The bell tower at Bethlehem, with the bells that are heard over the world in Christmas broadcasts

hosts of pilgrims throughout the centuries. The town, now mostly Christian, lies about 5 mi. south of Jerusalem and is called *Beit Laḥm* (Map VI, E-3).

2. A town in the territory of Zebulun (Jos 19:15), probably the home of Judge Ibzan (Jgs 12:8-11); identified with *Beit Lahm*, 10 mi. north of Megiddo.

Bethlehemite (bĕth′lĕ-ĕm-īt). [Heb. *Bêth-hallachmî.*] An inhabitant of *Bethlehem (1 Sa 16:1; etc.).

Beth-maacah (bĕth′mā′à-kà), KJV **Beth-maachah** (bĕth′mă′à-kà). [Heb. *Bêth Ma'akah.*] A name appearing in the phrase "Abel of Beth-maacah" (2 Sa 20:15). In v 14 the same phrase appears in the RSV, but the KJV reads "Abel, and to Beth-maachah." This is the reading of the Hebrew also, but many scholars believe that Abel of Beth-maacah should be read in v 14 also. Some believe Beth-maachah to be a district in the neighborhood of *Abel-beth-maacah (see Map VIII, B-4).

Beth-maachah. *See* Beth-maacah.

Beth-marcaboth (bĕth′mär′kà-bŏth). [Heb. *Bêth-hammarkabôth,* "house of the chariots."] A town in the territory of the Simeonites, near Ziklag (Jos 19:5; 1 Chr 4:31); not identified.

64. Hillside at Bethlehem with terraced fields and Church of the Nativity in center background

Beth-meon. See Baal-meon.

Beth-millo. See Millo.

Beth-nimrah (bĕth'nĭm'rȧ), or **Nimrah** (nĭm'rȧ). [Heb. *Bêth Nimrah* and *Nimrah,* "(house of) clear water."] A town in Transjordan, assigned to the tribe of Gad and rebuilt by that tribe (Num 32:3, 36; Jos 13:27). Following information given by Eusebius and Jerome, the site has been identified with *Tell el-Bleibil,* which lies 6 mi. east of the Jordan in the *Wâdī Sha'îb* (N. Glueck, *AASOR* 25-28 [1951], 370). Map VI, E-4.

Beth-palet. See Beth-pelet.

Beth-pazzez (bĕth'păz'ĕz). [Heb. *Bêth paṣṣeṣ,* "house of shattering."] A place in the territory of Issachar (Jos 19:21); not identified.

Beth-pelet (bĕth'pē'lĕt), KJV **Beth-phelet** (bĕth'fē'lĕt) and **Beth-palet** (bĕth'pā'lĕt). [Heb. *Bêth Pelet,* "house of escape."] A town in the south of Judah (Jos 15:27; Neh 11:26). It was doubtless near Beersheba, but its exact site has not been ascertained. Petrie identified it with *Tell el-Fâr'ah,* which he excavated, but this tell probably contains the remains of Sharuhen.

Beth-peor (bĕth'pē'ôr). [Heb. *Bêth Pe'ôr,* "house of (the god Baal-)Peor."] A Moabite place near Mount Pisgah, where the Israelites encamped before they crossed the Jordan (Deut 3:29; 4:46). In that vicinity Moses was buried (ch 34:6). It was as-signed to Reuben (Jos 13:20). Abel and Noth identify it with *Khirbet esh-Sheikh Jâyel,* 6 mi. west of Heshbon (Abel, *Géographie* II, 278; Noth, *ZAW* 60 [1944], 19).

Bethphage (bĕth'fȧ-jē). [Gr. *Bēthphagē,* from the Aramaic *Bêth-pagge',* "house of figs."] A small place near Jerusalem mentioned with Bethany (Mk 11:1; Lk 19:29), and lying apparently on the east side of the Mount of Olives (see Lk 19:37). It has been identified as probably the present *Kefr eṭ-Ṭûr* on the summit of the Mount of Olives, somewhat to the northwest of Bethany.

Beth-phelet. See Beth-pelet.

Bethrapha (bĕth'rā'fȧ). [Heb. *Bêth Rapha'.*] The name of a family of Judah or of an unidentified town somewhere in Judah (1 Chr 4:12).

Beth-rehob (bĕth'rē'hŏb). [Heb. *Bêth Rechob,* "house of a wide street."] A city north of Palestine in the valley in which the tribe of Dan settled (Jgs 18:28). In Num 13:21 and 2 Sa 10:8 it is simply called Rehob. According to 2 Sa 10:6 it was a small Aramaean (Syrian) city-state which the Ammonites hired to join them in their war against David but which suffered defeat (v 13). The exact location is unknown. See Aram, 5, a.

Bethsaida (bĕth'sā'ĭ-dȧ). [Gr. *Bēthsaïda,* from the Aramaic *Bêth Ṣayeda',* "house of fishing."] A place on the Sea of Galilee (Mk 6:45), the home town of the apostles

65. Traditional site of Bethsaida, on the Sea of Galilee

BETH-SHAN

Philip, Andrew, and Simon Peter (Jn 1: 44; 12:21), and the place where a blind man was healed (Mk 8:22-26). Jesus denounced the city along with Chorazin and Capernaum for its hardness of heart and unbelief (Mt 11:21-23). The place had been rebuilt and raised to the level of a city (Jn 1:44) by the tetrarch Herod Philip, who named it Bethsaïda Julias in honor of the daughter of the emperor Augustus. Not far from Bethsaida lay the barren area where Jesus fed the 5,000 with 5 loaves of bread and 2 fishes (Mk 6:31-44; Jn 6:1-15). The exact site of Bethsaida has not been identified. The city probably lay near the mouth of the Jordan, either on the northeastern shore of the Sea of Galilee at el-'Araj, or 2 mi. to the north at et-Tell (Map XVI, C-4).

Beth-shan. *See* Beth-shean.

Beth-shean (bĕth'shē'ǎn), or **Beth-shan** (bĕth'-shăn'). [Heb. *Bêth-she'an* and *Bêth-shan*. In the *Amarna Letters the name appears as *Bît-Sâni*, and in Egyptian texts as *Bt-shîr, Bt-shr,* and *Bt-shnrß.*] An ancient Canaanite fortress city in the eastern bottleneck of the Plain of Esdraelon on the river *Jālūd*, near the Jordan. It occupied a strategically important position on the main road to Damascus. Because of this the Egyptians considered it for centuries a key city of their Asiatic empire. Beth-shean was not occupied by the Hebrews in Joshua's time (Jgs 1:27). In the division of the land the city was allotted to Manasseh although it lay in the territory of Issachar and Asher (Jos 17:11). At the time of King Saul's death the Philistines held it, and after the battle at Gilboa hung on its wall the bodies of Saul and his sons (1 Sa 31:10, 12; 2 Sa 21:12). David apparently occupied it, for it belonged to Solomon's kingdom. Solomon placed it under the administration of Baana, whose residence was in Megiddo (1 Ki 4:12).

Pharaoh *Shishak mentions Beth-shean as one of the cities conquered during his Palestinian campaign (cf. 1 Ki 14:25, 26). After a silence of many centuries Beth-shean appears again in history in the 3d cent. B.C., when Antiochus III conquered it (218 B.C.). In 107 B.C. it fell once more into the hands of the Jews and remained briefly under their control (Jos. *Ant.* xiii. 10. 3). Its name in the meantime had been changed to Scythopolis. When Pompey made it a free city in 63 B.C. it joined the cities of the Decapolis. The modern village of *Beisân* has preserved its ancient name. The original

66. The ruin mound of *Tell el-Ḥuṣn*, the site of ancient Beth-shean

site, one of the most conspicuous mounds of Palestine, bears the name *Tell el-Ḥuṣn.* Map VI, C-4.

An expedition of the University of Pennsylvania excavated the ancient site from 1921 to 1933 and uncovered 18 occupation levels. It was found that the city was already under Egyptian influence at the beginning of the 2d millennium B.C. and that it was a strong city-kingdom during the Hyksos period. The excavations revealed also that after Thutmose III's conquest Beth-shean remained in Egyptian possession as a garrison city for three centuries. During that time two temples were built on the foundations of earlier temples, one for Astarte-Anath and another for Mekal-Resheph. About that time also may be dated several monumental Egyptian steles, two of which were erected by Seti I and one by Ramses II, and a statue of Ramses III, discovered by the expedition among the ruins. Many objects shedding light on the pagan cult rites of the Canaanites were also discovered, notably such as were used for the cult of snake worship. For ancient snake monuments see figs. 429, 430.

Lit. (all published in Philadelphia): A. Rowe, *The Topography and History of Beth-Shan* (1930); Rowe, *The Four Canaanite Temples of Beth-Shan, I, The Temples and Cult Objects* (1940); G. M. Fitzgerald, *The Four Canaanite Temples of Beth-Shan, II, The Pottery* (1930).

Beth-shemesh (bĕth'shē'mĕsh). [Heb. *Bêth Shemesh,* "house of the sun." Cities thus named were apparently seats of sun worship.]

1. An old Canaanite city in the *Shephelah, 15 mi. west of Jerusalem in the Valley of Sorek on the highway to Ashdod. The town was assigned to Judah (Jos 15:10) as a city for priests (ch 21: 16). It stood on the boundary between Judah and Dan and was also called

139

67. The mound of ancient Beth-shemesh

Ir-shemesh (Jos 19:41). It was probably not occupied by the Hebrews until several centuries later, but the precise time is not known. They seem to have possessed it by the time of Samuel, for the ark of the Lord, which the Philistines had captured, was returned to Beth-shemesh, where it stayed until it was removed to Kiriath-jearim (1 Sa 6). Beth-shemesh was the scene of battle in which Joash of Israel captured Amaziah of Judah (2 Ki 14:1-14). The Philistines occupied it in the time of Ahaz (2 Chr 28:18). The site is identified with *Tell er-Rumeileh,* near *'Ain Shems,* which still bears the ancient name. Map VI, E-2.

Excavations were carried out by the Palestine Exploration Fund under the direction of Duncan Mackenzie in 1911-1912, and by Elihu Grant for Haverford College from 1928 to 1933. Six levels were discovered. Level VI, the earliest, contained pottery remains of the pre-Hyksos period (2200-1700 B.C.). Level V represents the Hyksos city, which seems to have been destroyed in the 16th cent. during a campaign of Amenhotep I or Thutmose I. The remains found in the next level, IV, show that the Canaanite city experienced its most prosperous period from about 1500 to 1200 B.C., but that it was once destroyed in the middle of this period, perhaps by the Hebrews (*c.* 1350 B.C.). Levels III (1200-1000 B.C.) and II (1000-586 B.C.), which must be ascribed to the Israelite occupation, show that Beth-shemesh was a poor city at that time, without fortifications. The site was not reoccupied after the Exile until the Hellenistic period, when a small settlement established itself there (level I).

Among the more interesting discoveries at Beth-shemesh are: (1) a clay tablet inscribed with Ugaritic cuneiform signs written in reverse order so that they can be deciphered only with the help of a mirror and (2) an ostracon, or potsherd, containing an inscription in proto-Semitic script,

dated about the middle of the 2d millennium B.C.

Lit.: Excavation reports (all published in Haverford): E. Grant, *Beth Shemesh* (1929); E. Grant, *Ain Shems Expedition,* I-III (1931-1934); E. Grant and G. E. Wright, *Ain Shems Expedition,* IV-V (1938-1939).

2. A town in the territory of Naphtali near Beth-anath (Jos 19:38; Jgs 1:33); not yet identified.

3. A city mentioned in or near the eastern end of the Plain of Esdraelon (Jos 19:22). It has been identified with *el-'Abeidiyeh* near Beth-shean.

4. A center of sun worship in Egypt, probably Heliopolis (hē'lĭ-ŏp'ô-lĭs), Biblical *On (Jer 43:13).

Bethshemite (bĕth'shē'mīt). [Heb. *Bêth-hashshimshî.*] An inhabitant of Beth-shemesh (1 Sa 6:13, 14, 18).

Beth-shittah (bĕth'shĭt'à). [Heb. *Bêth Hashshiṭṭah,* "house of acacias."] A town near Zererah in the Jordan Valley, where the Midianites fled from Gideon (Jgs. 7:22).

Beth-tappuah (bĕth'tăp'û-à). [Heb. *Bêth-tappûach,* "house of apples."] A town in the hill country of Judah (Jos 15:53), identified with *Taffûh,* 3 mi. northwest of Hebron.

Beth-togarmah. *See* Togarmah.

Bethuel (bĕ-thū'ĕl). [Heb. *Bethû'el,* probably "man of God."]

1. Son of Nahor and his wife Milcah. He was the nephew of Abraham, and the father of Laban and Rebekah (Gen 22:20, 22, 23; 24:15, 24, 29; 25:20; 28:2, 5).

2. A place in southern Judah belonging to the Simeonites (1 Chr 4:30), called Bethul (bĕth'ŭl) [Heb. *Bethûl*] in Jos 19:4. It was possibly this town to which David sent part of the spoil captured from the Amalekites after they had sacked Ziklag (1 Sa 30:27; the spelling "Bethel" in this text may have been caused by a dropping of the letter *w* from the Hebrew name). It is possible that the Chesil of Jos 15:30 is another name for the same place. The site has not been identified.

Bethul. *See* Bethuel, 2.

Beth-zatha (bĕth'zā'thà), KJV **Bethesda** (bĕ-thĕz'dà). [Gr. *Bēthzatha,* derived from the Aramaic *Bêth Zaytha',* meaning "house of olives," and *Bethesda,* derived from the Aramaic *Bêth Chesda',* "house of grace." Textual evidence is divided between these two readings, but tends to favor the former. Textual evidence may also be cited for the reading *Bēthsaïda,* derived from Aramaic *Bêth Ṣayda',* "house

140

of fishing."] A pool in the vicinity of the Sheep Gate of Jerusalem, with 5 porches or halls (Jn 5:2). In the time of Christ these porches were occupied by many sick people who lay there waiting for a mysterious movement of the water which they believed was caused by an angel and, they thought, healed the first to step into the water. There Jesus healed a man who had been an invalid for 38 years (vs 1-9). The name Beth-zatha points to a location of the pool in the northern quarter of NT Jerusalem, which had the name Bezetha. Also the presence of the Sheep Gate (v 2, RSV) in the vicinity indicates that the pool was north of the Temple, for this gate (Neh 3:1) was at the northeastern corner of the Temple wall.

The present pool was discovered in 1888 to the northwest of the church of Saint Anne, and excavations carried out there since that time show that the whole structure consisted of 5 halls, one of which divided the pool into 2 basins, while the other 4 halls surrounded the pool (L. H. Vincent and F. M. Abel, *Jerusalem* [Paris, 1926], pp. 669-742). See fig. 68, also Map, fig. 259.

Beth-zur (bĕth'zûr'). [Heb. *Bêth Ṣûr,* "house of a rock."] A Canaanite city assigned to Judah (Jos 15:58), and inhabited by Calebites (1 Chr 2:45; cf. v 42). Rehoboam fortified it (2 Chr 11:5, 7), and after the Exile it became the center of a

69. The mound of ancient Beth-zur, from the north

district (Neh 3:16). It played a large role in the Maccabean wars. Judas gained a great victory there over the Syrian general Lysias (1 Macc 4:29; 2 Macc 11:5; 13:19, 22), and afterward fortified the city (1 Macc 4:61; 6:7, 26). It was later lost to Antiochus V Eupator (ch 6:49, 50), and then strengthened by the Syrians under Bacchides (ch 9:52), but was recaptured by the Jews under Simon Maccabeus (chs 11:65, 66; 14:7).

The old name has been retained in *Beit Ṣûr,* 4 mi. north of Hebron, but the actual site of ancient Beth-zur is found at *Khirbet eṭ-Ṭubeiqah,* about 4 mi. northwest of Hebron (Map VI, E-3). In 1931 and 1957, excavations were carried out at Beth-zur that confirmed the history of the city as described by literary records. They also show that it was already a significant town in the 18th cent. B.C. (O. R. Sellers, *The Citadel of Beth-Zur* [Philadelphia, 1933]; R. W. Funk, "The 1957 Campaign at Beth-zur," *BASOR* 150 [Apr., 1958], 8-20).

Betonim (bĕt'ô-nĭm). [Heb. *Beṭonîm,* "pistachio nuts."] A town in Transjordan in the territory of Gad (Jos 13:26), identified with *Khirbet Baṭneh* near *es-Salṭ.*

Betrothal. The Oriental betrothal was a binding contract that was consummated with solemn promises and the payment of money, and which could be broken only by divorce. Certain laws relating to betrothal are stated in Deut 22:23-29. A betrothed man was not required to go into battle (Deut 20:7). God figuratively described the idolatrous northern kingdom of Israel as an adulterous wife, whom He would woo back and betroth unto Himself once more forever (Hos 2:19, 20). In 2 Cor 11:2 Paul likens the middleman who, by ancient custom, arranged a betrothal (KJV "espoused"), to himself as having arranged a betrothal between Christ, the Bridegroom, and the Corinthian church, the bride. Mary the mother of Jesus was betrothed (KJV "espoused")

68. The Pool of Bethesda (Beth-zatha)

to Joseph at the conception of Christ (Mt 1:18; Lk 1:27; 2:5).

Beulah (bū'lȧ). The transliteration of the Heb. *be'ûlah,* meaning "married." The name occurs only in Is 62:4, KJV.

Bewray. An archaic English word translating terms meaning "to reveal," "to disclose," "to call," "to make evident" (Prov 27:16; 29:24; Is 16:3; Mt 26:73).

Beyond the River. *See* Judah, Tribe of, Kingdom of, and Province of, 3.

Bezai (bē'zá-ī). [Heb. *Beṣay.*] Founder of a family of whom 323 male members returned from Babylonia with Zerubbabel (Ezr 2:17; Neh 7:23 [324]). A representative of the family set his seal to Nehemiah's covenant (Neh 10:18).

Bezaleel. *See* Bezalel.

Bezalel (bĕz'á-lĕl), KJV **Bezaleel** (bĕ-zăl'ê-ĕl). [Heb. *Beṣal'el,* "in the shadow of God," with which may be compared the Akkadian *Ina-ṣilli-Nabû,* "in the shadow of Nabu."]

1. A Judahite (of the family of Caleb, (1 Chr 2:20) who was divinely called to be the chief craftsman and artist of the tabernacle and its furniture (Ex 31:1-11; 35:30-35; 2 Chr 1:5).

2. An Israelite of the family of Pahath-moab, who was married to a foreign wife in Ezra's time (Ezr 10:30).

Bezek (bē'zĕk). [Heb. *Bezeq.*]

1. A town ruled by Adonibezek, and captured from him by Judah and Simeon during the invasion of Canaan (Jgs 1:4, 5). The site has not been identified, but *Khirbet Bezqa* near Gezer has been suggested.

2. A place where Saul rallied the Israelites before marching to the relief of Jabesh-gilead (1 Sa 11:8), now *Khirbet Ibzîq,* about 12 mi. northeast of Shechem (Map VI, D-3).

Bezer (bē'zēr). [Heb. *Beṣer,* "fortress."]

1. An Asherite (1 Chr 7:37).

2. A city in Transjordan in the territory of Reuben, assigned to the Levites (Deut 4:43; Jos 21:36), and designated as a city of refuge (Jos 20:2, 8). It was later taken over by Moab, and fortified by King Mesha (*Moabite Stone, line 27). Its site is possibly *Umm el-'Amad,* about 9 mi. northeast of Medeba.

70. The Samaritan high priest holds an ancient Pentateuch scroll at the annual Passover on Mount Gerizim

71. Page from the Codex Vaticanus, of the 4th cent. A.D., containing Luke 7:14-38

Bible. The book containing the collection of sacred writings accepted by Christians as inspired of God and as possessing divine authority. For the Jew the term means the Hebrew Bible, which, as originally arranged, consisted of 24 books, but is now divided into the 39 books designated by Christians as the Old Testament. To it Christians have added a collection of 27 writings which they call the New Testament. In addition to these 66 books of the OT and NT, the Roman Catholic Bible includes 12 other writings which Protestants classify as "Apocrypha." The authoritative text of the Bible for Protestants is the Hebrew OT and the Greek NT; for Roman Catholics, it is the Vulgate, a Latin translation made by Jerome in the 4th cent. A.D.; and for the Greek Orthodox Church, the Septuagint (LXX), together with the Greek NT.

Our English word "Bible" is a transliteration, through the Latin and Old French, of the Gr. *biblia*, literally, "little books." In ancient times the common writing material was papyrus, manufactured from an Egyptian reed or sedge plant of the same name, whence our English word "paper" (*see* Writing Materials). The Greek name for papyrus was *bublos* (later, *biblos*), later given also to manufactured writing material, and finally to a papyrus scroll or *book. The ancient Phoenician city between Sidon and Tripolis known as Byblos (the Gebal of the OT) derived its name from its extensive manufacture and trade in this writing material. *Biblia* is properly the plural of *biblion* (Lk 4:17), the diminutive form of *biblos* (Mt 1:1), and hence means "little books." *Biblos* and *biblion* are used in the LXX in the phrases rendered "the books of the law" (1 Macc 1:56), the "books" of the prophets (Dan 9:2), "the holy books" (1 Macc 12:9), and in the prologue to Sirach for the 3d part of the Hebrew canon of the OT, the Writings.

The usual designation for the sacred writings in the NT is *hai graphai*, "the scriptures," Latin *scriptura* (Mt 21:42;

72. Page from the Codex Sinaiticus, of the 4th cent. A.D., containing Mark 1:1-35

22:29; Lk 24:32; Jn 5:39; Acts 17:2, 11; 18:24; etc.). The singular *hē graphē* is also used to designate the collection of the scriptures as a whole (Jn 7:38; Rom 4:3;

73. Page of the Codex Alexandrinus, of the 5th cent. A.D., containing Luke 18:9-36

etc.), but sometimes it refers to a single specific passage (Lk 4:21; Jn 13:18; etc.). In addition to the simple designation *hai graphai*, "the scriptures," the NT speaks of the *graphai hagiai*, "holy scriptures" (Rom 1:2), the *hiera grammata*, "sacred writings" (2 Ti 3:15, RSV), "the law and the prophets" (Mt 7:12; Lk 16:16), "the law . . . the prophets . . . the psalms" (Lk 24:44), "the law" (Jn 12:34), and "the oracles of God" (Rom 3:2; cf. Acts 7:38).

Liberal critical scholars for nearly a century stressed the diversity in the documents of the Scriptures, but in present-day theological thinking there is a renewed emphasis on the essential unity of the Bible. Its great unifying principle, its central theme, is the redemptive plan, and the working out of that plan in human history. But the unity of the Bible must not be interpreted as uniformity. In the various books of the Scriptures the re-

74. The first page of Genesis from the first printed Bible, the Gutenberg edition produced between 1450 and 1456

these events. God's saving acts find their center in the death, resurrection, and ministry of Christ, and the significance of these acts is made clear in the apostolic witness of the NT.

The Bible, like the person of its Author, Jesus Christ, is the result of a mysterious combination of the divine and the human. As the human mind is incapable of fully explaining the incarnation, so it cannot fully explain the Bible. In writing the various books of the Bible the authors' own personalities had full play, and their own style and vocabulary are reflected in the finished product. Yet the Bible is, nevertheless, "inspired by God" (2 Ti 3:16, 17, RSV). While men did the speaking, they did so as they were moved by the Holy Spirit (2 Pe 1:21). The Bible is therefore in a special sense the Word of God. *See* Inspiration.

For further information regarding the Scriptures, *see* Apocrypha; Apocryphal Books (NT); Canon; New Testament; Old Testament; Pentateuch; Pseudepigrapha; Versions. See figs. 215, 244, 298, 416.

75. Page from Tyndale's New Testament

demptive plan is viewed from various angles, and stress is laid on various aspects, with varying emphasis.

There has also been a shift in emphasis in recent theological thinking from ideas to events as they are portrayed in the Bible. It has even been suggested that we should speak of the Bible as the "Acts of God" rather than the "Word of God." The Bible, it is observed, is the story of redemptive history (*Heilsgeschichte*), the account of what God has done, is doing, and will yet do for the saving of mankind, and of man's responses to these saving acts. While there is much truth in this viewpoint, the Bible is more than this. God's saving acts have also to be interpreted, and these interpretations, too, partake of the nature of divine revelation precisely because they are witness, under the Holy Spirit, to God's unique act of self-revelation in Jesus Christ. Thus the NT contains not only a record of Jesus' saving acts in history but also the authoritative apostolic interpretation of

Bichri (bĭk'rī). [Heb. *Bikrî*, "first-born."] Father of the Sheba who revolted against David (2 Sa 20:1), possibly a member of the family of *Becher.

Bichrites. *See* Berites.

Bidkar (bĭd'kär). [Heb. *Bidqar*, possibly a contracted form of *Ben-deqer*, "the son of Deker."] An army officer under King Jehu of Israel (2 Ki 9:25).

Bier. A litter used to carry human corpses. In the OT this word is a rendering of the Hebrew terms *miṭṭah* (2 Sa 3:31) and *mishkab* (2 Chr 16:14), both words meaning literally "couch." In the NT "bier" is a rendering of the Gr. *soros* (Lk 7:14), literally "coffin."

Bigtha (bĭg'thȧ). [Heb. *Bigtha'*, probably a Persian name, but with uncertain meaning.] A chamberlain of King Ahasuerus (Xerxes) at the time when Vashti was summoned (Est 1:10).

Bigthan (bĭg'thăn), or **Bigthana** (bĭg-thā'nȧ). [Heb. *Bigthan* and *Bigthana'*, probably a Persian name, but with uncertain meaning.] A royal courtier of Xerxes who conspired against the life of the king (Est 2:21; 6:2).

Bigthana. *See* Bigthan.

Bigvai (bĭg'vȧ-ī). [Heb. *Bigway*, a Persian name, attested in Greek as *Bagōas*, and in the Aramaic papyri from Elephantine as *Bgwhy*.]

1. One of the Israelite leaders who returned with Zerubbabel from Babylonia (Ezr 2:2; Neh 7:7).

2. Founder of a family, of which 2,056 male members returned with Zerubbabel from Babylonia after the Exile (Ezr 2: 14; Neh 7:19 [2,067]); later 72 more returned with Ezra (Ezr 8:14). A representative of the family set his seal to Nehemiah's covenant (Neh 10:16).

Bildad (bĭl'dăd). [Heb. *Bildad*, perhaps "Bel loves," unless it is to be compared with the Akkadian *Bil-Adad* (= *apil-Adad*), "the son of (the god) Hadad."] One of Job's friends (Job 2:11; etc.), who is called a Shuhite. He is thought by some to be a descendant of Shuah, son of Abraham (Gen 25:2, 6), but inscriptions now indicate the possibility that Bildad came from *Shûḫu* in the region of the middle Euphrates.

Bileam. *See* Ibleam.

Bilgah (bĭl'gȧ). [Heb. *Bilgah*, "brightness."]

1. A descendant of Aaron, and the ancestral head of the 15th course, or division, of priests (1 Chr 24:1, 6, 14; Neh 12:18).

2. A chief of the priests who returned from Babylon after the Exile (Neh 12:5), possibly a name representing the family mentioned under Bilgah, 1.

Bilgai (bĭl'gȧ-ī). [Heb. *Bilgay*, "brightness." The name occurs on an ancient Hebrew seal.] A chief of the priests who set his seal to Nehemiah's covenant (Neh 10: 8). He may have belonged to the family of Bilgah, 1.

Bilhah (bĭl'hȧ). [Heb. *Bilhah*, meaning uncertain.]

1. Rachel's maidservant, who became Jacob's concubine and the mother of Dan and Naphtali (Gen 30:1-8; 1 Chr 7:13). Reuben committed fornication with her (Gen 35:22).

2. A town in the territory of Simeon (1 Chr 4:29); usually identified with the Baalah of Jos 15:29 and the Balah of ch 19:3; but this identification is uncertain.

Bilhan (bĭl'hăn). [Heb. *Bilhan*.]

1. A Horite of Mount Seir (Gen 36: 27; 1 Chr 1:42).

2. A Benjamite ancestor of several families (1 Chr 7:10).

Bill. A written scroll containing the terms of an agreement or of an action. Two kinds are mentioned in Scripture: (1) Bill of divorce (Deut 24:1, 3; Is 50:1; Jer 3:8), a statement of dismissal the husband was required to give to his wife when he terminated the marriage. Christ said that the arrangement was never approved by God, but was permitted anciently because of the hardness of men's hearts (Mk 10:5). (2) A statement of indebtedness (Lk 16:5-7). The Gr. *gramma*, "a writing," can be any kind of record.

Bilshan (bĭl'shăn). [Heb. *Bilshan*, "their lord," if derived from the Akkadian *Bêlshunu*.] One of the leaders who returned with Zerubbabel from Babylon (Ezr 2:2; Neh 7:7).

Bimhal (bĭm'hăl). [Heb. *Bimhal*.] An Asherite (1 Chr 7:33).

Binea (bĭn'ê-ȧ). [Heb. *Bin'a'*.] A descendant of Saul through his son Jonathan (1 Chr 8:37; 9:43).

Binnui (bĭn'ū-ī). [Heb. *Binnûy*, "built."]

1. Another name for Bani. *See* Bani, 4.

2. An Israelite who was married to a foreign wife in Ezra's time, belonging to the family of Pahath-moab (Ezr 10:30).

3. An Israelite who was married to a foreign wife in Ezra's time, belonging to the family of Bani (Ezr 10:38).

4. A Levite who returned with Zerubbabel from Babylon after the Exile (Neh 12:8).

5. Another Levite, son of Henadad, who built a section of the wall of Jerusa-

lem in Nehemiah's time (Neh 3:24; "Bavvai," v 18, RSV, has been conjectured to be identical with Binnui. The names are the same in vowelless Hebrew except for the dropping of one letter from the term rendered "Bavvai"). He also set his seal to the covenant of Nehemiah (Neh 10:9), and it was probably his son who was one of those who received the money and treasures that Ezra had brought from Babylon (Ezr 8:33).

Birds. Bible writers frequently mention winged creatures, and show by their attention to various details that they were more than casual observers of wildlife. However, positive identification of many of the birds (KJV often "fowl") mentioned in the Bible is impossible. The Mosaic law includes 19 birds in a list of unclean creatures (Lev 11:13-19; Deut 14:11-18) and directs the passer-by or hunter not to take the mother bird from her nest or brood, although he might take the young (Deut 22:6, 7). Doves or young pigeons were recognized as a substitute offering when the transgressor was too poor to bring a lamb for sacrifice (Lev 5:7; 12:8; 14:21, 22, 30). Elijah was fed by ravens during a famine (1 Ki 17:4). The Biblical poetic descriptions of the ostrich (Job 39:13-18), the hawk (v 26), and the eagle (vs 27-30) are unsurpassed in literature. The psalmist compares deliverance of a bird from the fowler with the saints' deliverance from Satan (Ps 91:3). Christ referred to sparrows (Mt 10:29), ravens (Lk 12:24), and chickens (Mt 23:37), and frequently mentioned birds in general. *See* Flora and Fauna; also names of specific birds. See figs. 76, 77.

Birsha (bĭr′shà). [Heb. *Birsha‘*, "ugly."] King of Gomorrah in Abraham's time, one of those defeated by Chedorlaomer and his confederates (Gen 14:2, 8, 10).

Birthday. The day of one's birth, or its anniversary. The Bible mentions two birthday celebrations: (1) Pharaoh's feast when he released the chief butler. from prison and hanged the chief baker (Gen 40:20), and (2) the birthday celebration of Herod Antipas in connection with which he granted Salome's request for the head of John the Baptist (Mt 14:6; Mk 6:21). Herod may have derived the custom of celebrating birthday anniversaries from his Greek and Roman education, for Greeks, Romans, and Persians observed personal birthdays. Antiochus Epiphanes persecuted the Jews by requiring them to partake of special sacrifices on his monthly birthday (2 Macc 6:7). There is no record of the Jews ever celebrating the birthdays of private citizens. *See* Age.

Birthright. Rights or privileges belonging to the first-born son. This, according to Hebrew law, provided for the eldest son to (1) succeed his father as the head of the family, and (2) inherit a double portion of his father's property (Deut 21:17; 2 Chr 21:3). The birthright also carried with it a blessing (Gen 27:1-4, 19, 36).

The first-born inherited a double portion of his father's estate (Deut 21:17). When Reuben, Jacob's eldest son, forfeited his birthright Joseph received the double portion; two tribes were descended from him (1 Chr 5:1, 2).

In the event of a man's having more than one wife, the right was guaranteed to the first-born son in point of time, even if he should be the child of a less-loved wife (Deut 21:15-17).

It is apparent from OT accounts that all these gifts and privileges could be forfeited, as in the case of Esau, who sold his birthright to Jacob (Gen 25:29-34; Heb 12:16), or as in the experience of Reuben, who lost his right through misconduct (1 Chr 5:1, 2).

Birthstool, KJV **Stool.** The rendering of the Heb. *'obnayim*, literally "two stones" (Ex 1:16). Literary and archeological evidence from ancient Egypt shows that Egyptian

76. Birds on an Egyptian 4th-dynasty painting on plaster, from *Meidum*

women gave birth while sitting on 2 bricks or on brick structures in front of which the midwife received the newborn child on her knees. The Israelites evidently used similar methods.

Birzaith (bĭr-zā′ĭth), KJV **Birzavith** (bĭr-zā′vĭth). [Heb. *Birzawith* but to be read *Birzayith* according to Masoretic tradition and certain versions.] Either a son of the Asherite Malchiel (1 Chr 7:31) or, possibly, a town founded by him, identified with *Bir-zeit,* about 4 mi. northwest of Bethel.

Birzavith. *See* Birzaith.

Bishlam (bĭsh′lăm). [Heb. *Bishlam,* "in peace," if the name is Semitic.] A Persian or Samaritan accuser of the Jews in the time of Artaxerxes (Ezr 4:7).

Bishop. [Gr. *episkopos,* "overseer."] As used in the NT this term generally refers to a person serving as an "overseer," "superintendent," or "guardian" over the church. Once (1 Pe 2:25, KJV) it is used of Christ the guardian of souls. The "overseers" or "guardians" (Gr. *episkopoi*) of Acts 20:28 are called "elders" (Gr. *presbuteroi*) in v 17. Such an interchangeableness of the two terms is attested by Chrysostom, who died in 407. He stated that in olden times the elders were called overseers (or bishops) of Christ (*First Homily on Epistle to the Philippians* 1, in Migne, *Patrologia Graeca,* vol. 62, col. 183). Clement of Rome, who lived in the 1st cent., seems to confirm this (*The First Epistle of Clement to the Corinthians,* ch 44).

The character requirements and duties of a bishop are plainly outlined in 1 Ti 3:2-7. An examination of these duties shows that originally he was not at all invested with the authority that some later possessors of that office assumed.

Bishoprick. A term appearing once (Acts 1:20, KJV), the translation of the Gr. *episkopē,* "office" as an overseer. It is used with reference to the position Judas Iscariot held among the Twelve.

Bithiah (bĭ-thī′à). [Heb. *Bithyah.* If a Hebrew name, the consonantal form may mean "daughter (that is, follower) of Yahweh." However, the name may be a transliteration of the Egyptian *bîtyt,* "queen," a term applied in Egyptian texts to the goddesses Hathor, Isis, etc.] An Egyptian princess who became the wife of Mered, a man of the tribe of Judah (1 Chr 4:17, RSV). If her name was Hebrew it may be taken as an indication that she had accepted the religion of her husband. In such a process,

the substitution of a Hebrew name for her Egyptian name would be entirely natural.

Bithron (bĭth′rŏn). [Heb. *Bithrôn,* "gorge."] A district or valley leading from the Jordan to Mahanaim (2 Sa 2:29, KJV); not yet identified with certainty. It is probably the place mentioned in the *Amarna Letters as *Batruna.*

Bithynia (bĭ-thĭn′ĭ-à). [Gr. *Bithunia.*] A coastal area in northern Asia Minor bounded on the east by Pontus, on the south by Galatia and Phrygia, and on the west by Mysia and the Propontis (Map XX, A-4/5). The people of Bithynia were related to the Thracians. In Persian times the country formed a separate satrapy, but in the Hellenistic period it was more or less independent. The last native king, Nicomedes III, in 74 B.C. bequeathed his kingdom to the Romans, who later organized it into a province and added Pontus to it so that the province was called *Bithynia et Pontus.* The capital of Bithynia was Nicomedia. Paul hoped to do missionary work in this area, but was prevented by the Holy Spirit from entering it (Acts 16:7). However, a Christian church was founded there in apostolic times, as the first letter of Peter attests (ch 1:1). The most famous governor of the province was Pliny the Younger, who in the beginning of the 2d cent. A.D. tells us that many Christians were under his jurisdiction. Important church councils were later held in the Bithynian cities of Nicaea and Chalcedon.

Bitter Herbs. [Heb. *merorim.*] One or more edible plants used in the Passover meal. It is generally supposed that such plants as lettuce, chicory, endive, or water cress, or a combination, made up the Passover salad (Ex 12:8; Num 9:11). Most of these are widely distributed throughout Egypt, the Middle East, and western Asia. The dish was to remind the Israelites of their bitter sufferings in Egypt.

Bitter Water. *See* Water of Bitterness.

Bittern. [Heb. *qippod.*] A water bird (*Botaurus stellaris*) belonging to the family of the herons. The Hebrew term is found in three OT texts (Is 14:23; 34:11; Zep 2:14) and is rendered "bittern" in the KJV. The RSV, following the LXX and the Vulgate, renders it "hedgehog" in Is 14:23; Zep 2:14, and "porcupine" in Is 34:11. Some object to the rendering "hedgehog" in Zep 2:14, pointing out that this animal cannot live in capitals of columns as this passage states. Bodenheimer (*Animal Life in Palestine* [1935], pp. 94, 166) and Koehler (*LVTL* 845) declare the *qippod* of the two Isaiah texts to be the hedgehog (*Erinaceus auritus* and *Erinaceus sacer*), but that of Zephaniah to be the short-eared owl (*Asio flammens*). Driver suggests the ruffed bustard as an identification for the *qippod* of all three texts (*PEQ* 87 [1955], 137).

Bitumen, KJV **Slime.** A rendering of the Heb. *chemar* (Gen 11:3; 14:10; Ex 2:3), meaning "asphalt," or "bitumen." This material was common in ancient Mesopotamia and was used in building the tower of Babel (Gen 11:3). It was widely used for public buildings by the ancient Assyrians and Babylonians (see fig. 388). At one time it existed in the Dead Sea region in the vicinity of Sodom and Gomorrah (ch 14:10). Even today considerable quantities of asphalt appear on the surface of the Dead Sea from time to time. This phenomenon was well known to the ancients and is mentioned in several classical sources (Diodorus, ii. 48. 7-9; Strabo, *Geography*, xvi. 2. 42-44; Jos. *War* iv. 8. 4; Tacitus, *Histories* v. 6, 7). It was for this reason that the Dead Sea was frequently referred to as *Mare Asphaltitis*, "Lake of Asphalt." The Dead Sea was the main source of asphalt in the Middle Ages in Europe, and because of its land of origin, was called "Jews' pitch." Moses' mother used it and *pitch (Heb. *zepheth*) to daub the ark into which she placed her son (Ex 2:3). See Pitch.

Biziothiah (bĭz'ĭ-ô-thī'à), KJV **Bizjothjah** (bĭz-jŏth'jà). [Heb. *Bizyôthyah*.] A place in the southern section of Judah (Jos 15:28), if the Masoretic Hebrew text is followed. The LXX reads "and their villages."

Bizjothjah. See Biziothiah.

Biztha (bĭz'thà). [Heb. *Bizzetha'*, probably a Persian name, but with uncertain meaning.] One of the chamberlains of Xerxes (Est 1:10).

Blains. [Heb. *'aba'bu'oth.*] The blisters or sores (RSV) breaking out on the boils of the 6th plague upon Egypt (Ex 9:9). It is impossible with our present knowledge to identify the exact nature of the skin eruption described by the Hebrew term. The most plausible identification is that of skin anthrax (G. Hort, *ZAW* 69 [1957], 101-103).

Blasphemy. A term generally denoting abusive or defamatory language with respect to God. However, the Hebrew and Greek terms thus translated are used also for such language with respect to man. In translating these terms our English versions generally reserve "blaspheme" and "blasphemy" for instances where God's name or character is defamed (Lev 24: 11; Jas 2:7; etc.). The defamation may be direct (Acts 6:11) or implied as in attributing evidences of divine power to the devil (Mt 12:31), or in claiming divinity or divine prerogatives (Mt 9:1-6; 26:65; Jn 10:33, 36).

Blastus (blăs'tŭs). [Gr. *Blastos*, "sprout" or "shoot." The name is Greek and occurs frequently in Greek inscriptions.] The chamberlain of Herod Agrippa I, through whom certain envoys from Tyre and Sidon obtained an audience with the king (Acts 12:20).

Bless, Blessed. ["Bless," generally Heb. *barak;* Gr. *eulogeō;* "blessed," generally Heb. *'ashrê, barûk;* Gr. *makarios, eulogēmenos, eulogētos.*] *Barak* is used to express various shades of meaning. God's blessing of a person means that God bestows good gifts upon him (2 Sa 6:11, 12; Job 42:12), or declares him to be so endowed (Gen 17: 20). In the OT men are frequently mentioned as blessing God, which means that they acknowledge God as the bestower of spiritual and material prosperity (Ps 63: 4; 103:1-5; 145:2; etc.). When one person blesses another he expresses a wish that the other will be endowed with good gifts (Jos 14:13; 1 Sa 2:20). *Eulogeō,* which literally means "to speak well," is used in the NT with essentially the same meanings as *barak.*

Where "blessed" is the translation of *barûk, eulogēmenos,* or *eulogētos* it describes the result of the action of the verbs *barak* and *eulogeō.* *'Ashrê* and *makarios,* however, mean "happy," "fortunate." *'Ashrê* is frequent in the Psalms (1:1; 2:12; 32:1, 2; etc.). *Makarios* is the term introducing the *Beatitudes.

Blessing. [Heb. *berakah;* Gr. *eulogia.*] An advantage or benefit, generally such as conferred by God or Christ (Gen 39:5; Deut 28:8; etc.). Many of God's blessings are conditional upon man's obedience and cooperation (Ex 15:26; Deut 28:1-14; etc.). *Berakah* is used also for a gift bestowed by man as a token of affection or good will (Gen 33:11; 2 Ki 5:15, "present," RSV). This is probably also the meaning of *eulogia* in 2 Cor 9:5 ("bounty," KJV; "gift," RSV). "Blessing" is also used of the act of pronouncing benefits to come upon a person or a people (Jas 3:10).

Blindness. The fact that blindness is mentioned so frequently in the Bible is an indication of its prevalence in Bible times. There was a large variety of eye diseases, all aggravated by the lack of sanitation among the people, the glaring sun, and the abundance of dust. Flies were common, undisturbed carriers of the diseases.

Special mention is made of the care of the blind (Lev 19:14). A blind man was not considered fit for the priesthood (ch 21:18). The opinion prevailed among the Jews that God struck men blind for their sins (Jn 9:1, 2), but Jesus refuted this false belief (v 3). During His brief ministry He healed many sightless (Mt 9:27-30; 12:22; 20:30-34; 21:14). The Bible mentions several instances of men being struck blind temporarily by divine intervention (Gen 19:11; 2 Ki 6:18-22), probably the best-known instance being that of the apostle Paul (Acts 9:8, 9). 2 Ki 25:7 mentions the practice common among the Assyrians and others of conquerors blinding their captives.

Blood. [Heb. *dam;* Gr. *haima.*] The vital fluid circulating through the body, carrying nourishment and oxygen to all parts of the body and carrying off waste products to be excreted (Lev 17:11, 14; Deut 12:23). The ancients were unaware of these detailed functions, but they recognized that the blood was closely connected with life. The Law declared, "For the life of the flesh is in the blood" (Lev 17:11). The ancients were forbidden to eat blood (Gen 9:3, 4; Lev 17:10-14; Acts 15:20, 29). This prohibition doubtless had a hygienic basis, but may have been designed to have instructional value as well. The most significant use of blood in OT times was in the sacrificial services and more largely in the sanctuary services. The shed blood foreshadowed the blood of Christ, the priceless life of the Son of God that was to be sacrificed as the only hope of a fallen and doomed race (1 Cor 10:16; Eph 2:13; Heb 9:14; 10:19; 1 Pe 1:2, 19; Rev 12:11). Salvation through the blood of Christ is the central theme of the gospel (Rom 3:25; 5:9; Eph 1:7; Col 1:20; Heb 9:22; Rev 1:5; etc.).

Blood, Avenger of. *See* Avenger of Blood.

Blood, Issue of. *See* Issue.

Bloodguiltiness. [Heb. *dam,* "blood." When translated "bloodguilt" or "bloodguiltiness" it usually appears in its plural form *damîm.*] The guilt of murder or bloodshed. The term occurs once (Ps 51:14) in a penitential prayer in which David prays to be delivered from guilt, probably his

guilt in the murder of Uriah. However, "bloodguilt," with essentially the same meaning (also the translation of *dam* or *damîm*), is found in the RSV of Ex 22:2, 3; Lev 17:4; 1 Sa 25:26, 33; Hos 12:14.

Bloody Flux. *See* Dysentery.

Blowing of Trumpets. *See* Trumpets, Feast of.

Boanerges (bō'à-nûr'jēz). [Gr. *Boanērges,* the translation of an Aramaic term the exact form of which is uncertain.] The appellation Jesus gave to James and John, the sons of Zebedee, doubtless on account of their impetuous disposition. It is interpreted to mean "sons of thunder" (Mk 3:17).

Boar. [Heb. *chazîr,* translated "boar" only in Ps 80:13; elsewhere (Lev 11:7; Deut 14:8; Prov 11:22; Is 65:4; 66:3, 17) rendered "swine."] Wild boars at least until recently were still found, and may even now not be extinct in some parts of Palestine, as in the Jordan Valley, in the former swamps of Lake Huleh, and on Mount Carmel. The boar fights by ripping up its enemy with its tusks.

Boat. The translation of: (1) The Gr. *ploion,* a general term for vessels, including the rather large seafaring ships (Acts 20:13, 38; etc.) and the small fishing vessels (Mt 4:21; Mk 1:19; etc.). In every instance but one the KJV translates *ploion* "ship," but the RSV uses "ship" only when larger vessels are indicated. (2) The Gr. *ploiarion,* literally, "a little boat," but not always distinguished from *ploion* (Mk 3:9; Lk 5:2; Jn 6:22). (3) The Gr. *skaphē,* a small vessel, probably a rowboat. This is the kind of boat the sailors wanted to let down from the ship at the time of Paul's shipwreck at Malta (Acts 27:30, 32). In 2 Sa 19:18 the KJV mistakenly translates

77. Ancient model of an Egyptian sailing boat, found in a tomb at Thebes

the Heb. *'abarah,* which means "ford," as "ferry boat." Although such is not the meaning of *'abarah,* ferryboats were used by the ancient Egyptians from early times, and may have also been employed at the Jordan. The Mosaic Map at Medeba (see fig. 323) shows two Jordan ferries of the 6th cent. A.D. *See* Ship. See figs. 77, 177.

Boaz (bō'ăz), KJV of NT **Booz** (bō'ŏz). [Heb. *Bo'az,* meaning uncertain. Gr. *Boes.* The name occurs in an inscription found in the Hauran.]

1. A wealthy inhabitant of Bethlehem, a relative of the deceased husband of Ruth. He married Ruth and became an ancestor of David (Ruth 2:3, 4; etc.; Mt 1:5).

2. One of the 2 pillars set up at the entrance to Solomon's Temple (1 Ki 7:15-22; 2 Chr 3:17). The name has not yet satisfactorily been explained in spite of many efforts. For a possible interpretation, *see* Jachin, 3.

Bocheru (bō'kĕ-rōō). [Heb. *Bokerû,* probably "first-born."] A descendant of Saul's son Jonathan (1 Chr 8:38).

Bochim (bō'kĭm). [Heb. *Bokîm,* "weepers."] A place near Gilgal where the Israelites wept for their disobedience (Jgs 2:1-5). It has not yet been identified. Some see in it possibly another name of the place near Bethel called Allon-bacuth.

Body. The body of man was originally molded from the soil (Gen 2:7). God's plan was that the human body should never deteriorate, but that man should live endlessly with all his faculties at maximum perfection (cf. chs 1:26, 31; 2:22-24). But sin brought a change in man's condition. After expulsion from the Garden of Eden, Adam and Eve gradually lost their physical vigor until it was totally expended, and death claimed them. The following centuries brought further degeneration (ch 11:12, 13, 18, 19, 32; cf. Ec 12:1-7), until finally man's age seldom exceeded 70 years (Ps 90:10). At *death the body returns unto the ground (Gen 3:19; Ec 12:7).

At the *resurrection the righteous will receive new, glorified bodies (1 Cor 15:35-50; 2 Cor 5:1-4) resembling Christ's glorified body (Php 3:20, 21). These glorified bodies will be free from all weakness and disability.

Paul likened the church to a body, with Christ as the head (Eph 1:22; 4:15, 16; Col 1:18). As the body has many and varied organs, each designed to do a particular work, none encroaching upon the

functions of others but all performing in perfect harmony, so also should the members of the church, having differing gifts and functions, all work efficiently and harmoniously toward one supreme end (Rom 12:4, 5; 1 Cor 12:12-31).

The bodies of God's servants are declared to be the temple of the Holy Spirit (1 Cor 6:19; cf. 2 Cor 6:16). Paul appealed to believers to dedicate their bodies, that is, every bodily member and faculty, to God (Rom 12:1).

A body was prepared for Christ that He might dwell among men (Heb 10:5). In this body He vicariously bore the sins of men (1 Pe 2:24). Christ referred to His body as bread for the believer, speaking symbolically of His followers' assimilation of His character through an appropriation of the Word of God (Mt 26:26; Mk 14:22; Lk 22:19; cf. Jn 6:35, 48-58). The bread appointed to be eaten at the *Lord's Supper represents the broken body of Christ, and the believer's partaking of this bread represents his appropriation by faith of Christ's sinless life, righteousness, death, and resurrection (cf. Rom 4:24, 25; 8:10; 1 Cor 1:30; 10:17; 11:24; 15:3, 4; Php 3:9; etc.).

Bohan (bō'hăn). [Heb. *Bohan,* "thumb."] Apparently a "son" or "descendant" of Reuben (Jos 15:6; 18:17), not mentioned elsewhere, who gave his name to a landmark on the boundary between Judah and Benjamin, called "the stone of Bohan the son of Reuben." It is possibly to be identified with *Ḥajar el-Aṣbah,* a conspicuous rock about 2 mi. north of *Khirbet Qumrân,* near the Dead Sea.

Boil. *See* Botch.

Bolled. [Heb. *gib'ol.*] A term used in the KJV to describe the condition of the flax when struck by the plague of hail upon Egypt (Ex 9:31). The Hebrew term occurs only here in the OT, and it is impossible to determine whether it means "bud" (RSV), "blossom," or "seed pod."

Bolster. A term appearing in the KJV of the OT translating the Heb. *mera'ashôth,* and *ra'ashôth,* "the place at the head." A pillow or bolster is not necessarily implied, simply a position at the head (1 Sa 19:13, 16; 26:7, 11, 12).

Bolt. The verb "to bolt" is from the Heb. *na'al,* rendered "to bolt" in 2 Sa 13:17, 18 and "to lock" in Jgs 3:23, 24 and Song 4:12 (RSV). The literal meaning of *na'al* is "to bind (with straps)." The bolting of doors was performed by sliding bolts of wood with leather straps, or ropes.

Entrances to ancient houses were not always closed with a door, nor was every door equipped with a lock. The noun translated "lock" (Heb. *man'ûl*) in the KJV really means bolt (see Neh 3:3, 6, 13-15; Song 5:5). Doors equipped with a bolt could be unlocked from the outside by means of a key (Heb. *maphteach*, Jgs 3:25; 1 Chr 9:27). The bolt consisted of a wooden bar that was laid across the door and pushed into a hole in the doorpost. One or more pegs, or wedges, dropped into corresponding notches, or holes in the bar, making it impossible to move the bar unless the pegs or wedges were lifted up. The key also was of wood and had pegs that corresponded to the pegs, or wedges, of the lock. Inserted into a slot or a hole, the key lifted up the pegs so that the bar could be moved and the door opened. Ancient keys were not turned in the hole, but functioned as a lever to lift up the pegs of the lock. The first mention in the Bible of a key by means of which a door could be opened comes from the early period of the judges (Jgs 3:25). Certain ancient keys were apparently so large that they were carried on the shoulder (Is 22:22). Figuratively keys were symbols of authority (Mt 16:19; Rev 1:18; 3:7; 9:1; 20:1).

Bondage. *See* Slave.

Bondmaid. *See* Slave.

Bondman. *See* Slave.

Bonnets. A KJV term translating (1) the Heb. *migba'ôth*, the term used for the headdresses worn by the priests (Ex 28:40; 29:9; 39:28; Lev 8:13, RSV "caps"); (2) the Heb. *pe'erîm*, "headdresses," worn by women (Is 3:20) and by priests (Eze 44:18, RSV "turbans").

Book. [Heb. *sepher* (Ex 17:14; Jer 25:13; etc.), and *siphrah* (Ps 56:8); Aramaic *sephar* (Ezr 4:15; etc.), all of which mean "writing," "roll," or "scroll." The Heb. *dabar*, meaning "word" in spoken or written form, hence, by transfer, a document containing words, is also used (1 Chr 29:29; etc.); Gr. *biblos*, "roll," "scroll," and its diminutives *biblion* and *biblaridion*, "little scroll."]

Books, in the sense of written compositions of some length, were produced in ancient times in various forms and on various materials. In Mesopotamia they were written in cuneiform, and were inscribed on clay tablets or on wooden tablets covered with wax and fastened together like the leaves of a Japanese screen (*Iraq* 17 [1955], 3-20). Egypt developed

the papyrus scroll early in its history, and from there it spread throughout the whole ancient world. A little later, scrolls were made also of leather, and still later of parchment. They consisted of sheets about one foot wide fastened together to make long strips, ordinarily not exceeding 30 ft. in length. It was not until Christian times that the scroll gave way to the codex, a book composed of folded sheets bound into pages like our modern books. The oldest known codex comes from the 2d cent. A.D. There is evidence to indicate that it may have been the Christians who popularized the codex form of books in the Roman world.

Books written by the Hebrews are first mentioned after the Exodus (Ex 17:14), although the art of writing had been known for many centuries. From the time of Moses for about a thousand years a stream of books came from the versatile pens of the Hebrew prophets, historians, and others. Not all Hebrew books found a place in the OT canon, and many titles are mentioned in the OT of books that have been lost (Num 21:14; 1 Chr 29:29; etc.). The canon of inspired writings in Hebrew was closed about 400 B.C. Jewish religious books of the next period are now largely relegated to the realm of apocrypha or pseudepigrapha. The Christian church has accepted as inspired also the NT books, written by Christian writers of the apostolic age over a period of about 50 years. Many other books were written by Christians during that same period and later, which found no place in the NT canon. However, apart from the NT, with the exception of 1 Clement, no book written by a Christian writer up to A.D. 100 is extant today. *See* Apocryphal Books (NT).

Hebrew Scripture manuscripts used in public Jewish and Christian services were produced by trained scribes writing with ink on leather and parchment. The Dead Sea scrolls are the oldest surviving examples of these books (see figs. 244, 298, 416). The common people could not afford such materials, and if they possessed any Bible books they were of papyrus, the type widely circulated in Greek and Roman times and produced by many professional copyists for commercial publishers. The NT writings also were at first circulated on papyrus; in fact, all extant copies of NT books of the first three Christian centuries are either papyrus rolls or papyrus codices (see fig. 215). But when the church became prosperous, by about the 4th cent. A.D.,

expensive Bible copies in parchment codices were produced, of which the Codex Vaticanus and the Codex Sinaiticus are noted examples (see figs. 71, 72).
See Writing; Writing Material.

Book of Life. The concept of a heavenly book containing the names of the righteous seems to have been current from ancient times. Moses evidently had such a record in mind when he asked God to blot his name out of His book (Ex 32:31-33). Daniel spoke of those whose names were found written in a book as being delivered out of a time of trouble when Michael should stand up (Dan 12:1). Jesus told His disciples to rejoice because their names were written in heaven (Lk 10:20). Paul spoke of his fellow laborers' names' being in the book of life, the record of the citizens of heaven (Php 4:3).

In his vision of the judgment, Daniel saw certain books being opened (Dan 7:9, 10). The book of Revelation identifies one of the books used in the final judgment as the book of life (ch 20:11, 12), and states that all whose names are not found therein will be cast into the lake of fire (v 15). The one who steadfastly endures to the end is assured that his name will be retained in the book of life (ch 3:5), but those who practice wickedness will be excluded from the New Jerusalem that comes down from heaven (ch 21:10, 27).

The beast of Revelation 13 will be worshiped by all upon the earth whose names are not written in the book (vs 1, 8). It is this same group that will be amazed at the beast "that was, and is not, and yet is," the beast that "shall ascend out of the bottomless pit, and go into perdition" (ch 17:8).

Boot. The translation, in the RSV of Is 9:5, of the Heb. *se'ôn,* which according to its cognates means "boot," especially the military boot. Assyrian reliefs (see figs. 284, 308) show the Assyrian soldiers with heavy boots that reach almost to the knee.

Booth, KJV often **Tabernacle.** [Heb. *sukkah.*] A temporary shelter, often built of branches of trees and leaves. Farmers used booths in the harvesttime to protect themselves from the heat of the sun while guarding their crops (Job 27:18; Is 1:8). Booths were also used for the accommodation of domestic animals (Gen 33:17). The prophet Jonah built a booth east of the city of Nineveh to provide a comfortable place from which to observe whether his predicted doom of the wicked city would be actually carried out (Jon 4:5).

Booths, Feast of. *See* Tabernacles, Feast of.

Booz. *See* Boaz.

Borashan. *See* Ashan.

Border. A number of Hebrew and Greek terms are rendered "border" in the KJV, most of which mean "boundary," "frontier," or "territory" (Num 22:36; Jos 13:3; etc.). In a few instances "border" is used to refer to the hem or edge of a garment (Num 15:38; Mt 23:5; Mk 6:56; Lk 8:44), or the enclosing edge of a piece of furniture or of some other object (Ex 25:25; 37:12).

Borrow. Borrowing in OT times was generally undertaken to relieve a necessity. Interest was not to be charged a fellow Israelite (Ex 22:25) but could be charged a foreigner (Deut 23:20). In Ex 11:2; 12:35; KJV, the word "borrow" is from the Heb. *sha'al,* "to ask." *Sha'al* implies no intent or promise to return. The Israelites simply asked gifts of the Egyptians as a contribution to assist them in the expenses of the journey.

Boscath. *See* Bozkath.

Bosom. The front, upper portion of the human body (Ex 4:6; Ruth 4:16; etc.). Figuratively the word denotes close association, intimacy, and loving care (Is 40:11; Jn 1:18). *See* Abraham's Bosom.

Bosor. *See* Beor, 2.

Boss. [Heb. *gab.*] A term appearing in the plural in the KJV of Job 15:26. The Hebrew word probably describes the metal pieces attached to ancient shields. These ornaments were often a kind of bronze nail with a wide, flat, round head.

Botch. [Heb. *shechîn,* "boil."] A term appearing twice in the KJV (Deut 28:27, 35). However, elsewhere that version renders *shechîn* "boil" (Ex 9:9, 10, 11; Lev 13:18; etc.). Some suggest that the "botch of Egypt" (Deut 28:27) and the "sore botch" (v 35) may have been smallpox, but this cannot be confirmed.

Bottle. In the KJV a number of Hebrew terms and one Greek term are rendered "bottle," but these are not "bottles" in our modern sense of the word, but either skins or jars. The Heb. *'ôb* (Job 32:19) and *no'd* (Jos 9:4, 13; Jgs 4:19; 1 Sa 16:20; Ps 56:8; 119:83) and the Gr. *askos* (Mt 9:17; Mk 2:22; Lk 5:37, 38) are goatskins (see figs. 78, 474) used for liquids —water, wine, or milk. The Heb. *chemeth* (Gen 21:14, 15, 19) is a small skin, made watertight with date syrup, and is a container for butter, honey, and oil. The Heb. *baqbuq* (Jer 19:1, 10) is a decanter, a narrow-necked clay vessel. The Heb. *nebel*

78. Egyptian boy carrying water in a skin bottle made of goat's hide

(1 Sa 1:24; 10:3; 25:18; 2 Sa 16:1; Job 38:37; Jer 13:12; 48:12) is a large storage jar. The Heb. *chemah* in Hos 7:5 is not a bottle, but means "heat," and the same word in Hab 2:15 should be rendered "wrath."

In the RSV, "bottle" is found only twice— (1) as the translation of *no'd* in Ps 56:8, and (2) as the translation of *ned* in Ps 33:7. The translators considered *ned* as either a variant spelling of *no'd* or a spelling mistake.

Glass bottles as they are known today did not exist in OT times, nor are there any earthenware vessels from that period in the shape of modern bottles. Water was carried and stored in goatskins; and other liquids were either stored in this way or kept in jars of various shapes and sizes. Glass vessels and small glass flasks were known and used in Palestine in the time of Christ and the apostles, but there is no mention of glass vessels of any kind in the NT.

Bottomless Pit. See Abyss.

Bow. A weapon of the hunter and warrior. It was introduced into Canaan in comparatively late times. The Egyptian Sinuhe, who in the 20th cent. B.C. fought with arrow, bow, and dagger, met a Syrian enemy who had simply an ax, dagger, and lances, but no bow (*ANET* 20). Thutmose III (15th cent. B.C.) lists among the spoils taken at the battle of Megiddo 924 chariots but only 502 bows (*ANET* 237). In a nobleman's tomb at Gezer, from the middle of the 2d millennium B.C., only 2 arrowheads were found but 130 spearpoints. The Egyptian bow before the Hyksos period was made of wood strengthened with leather plaiting. The Hyksos, however, introduced the "compound bow," which contained laminations of bone or ivory to increase its elasticity and shooting power. Examples of these bows have been found in Egyptian royal tombs. Some bows had laminations even of metal, probably bronze, for the purpose of increasing their elasticity (2 Sa 22:35; Job 20:24; Ps 18:34; RSV). To handle such a bow, by which almost incredible feats could be accomplished, required long training, as Egyptian records reveal.

In early Israel only the nobility seem to have possessed bows, but in the time of the kings the weapon was in general use among the common soldiers (1 Chr 5:18; 2 Chr 26:11, 12, 14; Ps 78:9). The Aramaeans had bowmen (1 Ki 22:34), as had the enemy Jeremiah predicted would come from the north (Jer 4:29; 6: 23). In the poetical language of the OT the bow stands for might and strength (Gen 49:24; Job 29:20), and to "break the bow" of the enemy means to destroy his forces (Jer 49:35; Hos 1:5). For representations of bows in Assyrian sculptures see figs. 19, 210, 284, 301.

Bowl. See Basin.

Box, I. In 2 Ki 9:1, 3, KJV, the translation of the Heb. *pak*, a container of oil, which should rather be rendered "flask"; in KJV of Mt 26:7; Mk 14:3; Lk 7:37 it appears in the phrase "alabaster box," which is a rendering of the Gr. *alabastros* and *alabastron*, "alabaster jar" and "alabaster flask" (see RSV).

In the RSV, "box" is the translation of (1) the Heb. *'argaz* (1 Sa 6:8, 11, 15), probably a "saddlebag" (KJV "coffer"); (2) the Gr. *glōssokomon* (Jn 12:6; 13:29), "money box" (KJV "bag"). Once the Heb. *battim*, "containers" (literally, "houses"), is translated "boxes" (Is 3: 20).

Box, II. [Gr. *pukteuō*, "to box," "to fight with fists."] Paul apparently has reference to a boxer in his illustration of his determination to win his Christian fight (1 Cor 9:26). In Paul's time boxers were not matched in weight nor confined to a ring. They customarily did not strike the body, but the head only. The boxing "gloves" were made of hard leather, and the Roman type (the *caestus*) had metal weights or spikes inserted.

Bozez (bō'zĕz). [Heb. *Bôṣeṣ*, "shining."] A high rock in the pass of Michmash (1 Sa 14:4).

Bozkath (bŏz'kăth), KJV once **Boscath** (bŏs'-kăth). [Heb. *Boṣqath*.] A place in the south of Judah (Jos 15:39), the home town of Adaiah, the maternal grandfather of King Josiah of Judah (2 Ki 22:1). It was doubtless near Lachish, but has not been identified.

Bozrah (bŏz'rà). [Heb. *Boṣrah*, "fortress."]

1. One of the most important cities of Edom (Gen 36:33; 1 Chr 1:44; Is 34:6;

79. The site (center) of ancient Bozrah in Edom

63:1). It contained palaces whose destruction the prophet Amos predicted (Amos 1:12). Jeremiah prophesied its complete destruction (Jer 49:13, 22). It is identified with the village of *Buṣeirah*, about 30 mi. north of Petra (Map V, B-7), near the highway from Petra to Kerak.

2. A city of Moab which Jeremiah mentions with Kerioth, Beth-meon, Dibon, and other towns (Jer 48:24). It is possibly the Reubenite city of Bezer, for the LXX reads *Bosor* instead of Bozrah.

Bracelet. An ornament made of metal or of strings of beads worn on the wrist or arm by men and women of ancient times. Abraham's servant gave a bracelet to Rebekah as a gift of introduction (Gen 24: 22). The Israelites apparently had Egyptian bracelets in their possession when they left Egypt, which they gave for the vessels of the tabernacle (Num 31:50; cf. Ex 12:35). Saul wore a bracelet (RSV

"armlet") on the battlefield at the time of his death (2 Sa 1:10). A bracelet appears on the arm of King Esarhaddon of Assyria (see fig. 163). Fig 80 shows a golden bracelet consisting of two halves fastened together by pins. It was found in the tomb of the grandson of King *Shishak of Egypt. The hieroglyphic inscription on the inner side identifies it as a gift of Shishak. It may have been made of the gold obtained from his conquest of Jerusalem during Rehoboam's reign.

Bramble. [Heb. *'aṭad, chôach;* Gr. *batos*.] A bush or shrub bearing thorns, probably the buckthorn (*Rhamnus Palestina*). This shrub attains a height of 3 to 6 ft. and has oblong, wedge-shaped evergreen leaves, velvety thorns, and imperfect flowers blooming in March and April. But no certainty exists in identifying the plants re-

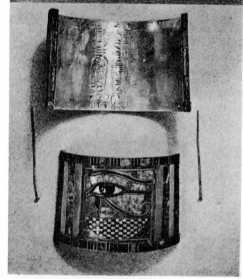

80. Gold bracelet from Tanis, with inscription of Pharaoh Shishak (shown closed and open)

ferred to by the more than 20 different words used in the Bible to describe spiny, brambly plants. The allegory of the trees' choosing a king uses the bramble in contrast to the giants of the forest to symbolize the weak protection offered the Shechemites by Abimelech (Jgs 9:14, 15). Brambles (RSV "thistles") are mentioned as part of the desolation of Edom (Is 34:13) and in an illustration emphasizing the truth that men are known by their words and actions (Lk 6:44).

Branch. A common Biblical word, the translation of various Hebrew and Greek words. In Jer 23:5; 33:15; Zec 3:8; 6:12 it is used as a title of Christ. The Hebrew word in these verses is *ṣemach*, "a sprout," "a shoot." The Messiah is represented as a shoot, or sprout, from the root, or stock, of David.

Brand. The translation of (1) the Heb. *'ûd*, "a stick" or "a log" (Amos 4:11; Zec 3: 2). God compares His people to a brand or stick plucked from the fire, meaning that He had saved them from utter destruction. (2) The Heb. *zîqoth*, "fire-arrows," used only in the plural (see Is 50: 11, RSV). See Firebrand.

Brasen. Literally, "of brass." However, the terms thus translated refer to *bronze or copper and should be thus rendered (Ex 27:4; 1 Ki 4:13; etc.).

Brasen Sea. *See* Sea, Bronze.

Brasen Serpent. *See* Bronze Serpent.

Brass. *See* Bronze.

Bray. A term found in the KJV of Prov 27:22, translating a Hebrew word (*kathash*) meaning "to pound," "to crush."

Brazier. [Heb. *'ach*, probably from Egyptian *'ḥ*, "firepan."] A brazier in a present-day Palestinian house is made of clay or brick placed in a depression in the floor. After the fire is burned out, a wooden frame covered with a rug is placed over it to conserve the heat. Whether the "brazier" (KJV "hearth") in the winter house of King Jehoiakim (Jer 36:22, 23, RSV) was similar, or a portable charcoal-burning firepan, cannot be ascertained.

Breach. A break, a breaking. Breach is the translation of various Hebrew words. In Lev 24:20, KJV, "breach" is from *sheber*, a "break" or "fracture." In 2 Ki 12:5-12; 22:5; KJV, it is the translation of *bedeq*, "fissure," "rent," "leak." In Jgs 21:15 it is from *pereṣ*, "a bursting forth," "gap," "rent," "breach," from *paraṣ*, "to break out," "to burst." In 2 Sa 6:8, where it is said that God "made a breach upon Uzzah," the meaning is that God interfered

with the normal course of human events by exercising supernatural power. In Is 30:13; 58:12 "breach" means a "break" or a "crack."

Bread. Bread was the principal article of food in Palestine. Other items, such as flesh foods, fruits, and vegetables, took a secondary place in the diet. Bread was made of barley (Jgs 7:13; Jn 6:13), or of wheat (Ex 29:2; etc.). The flour was either coarse ground (Lev 2:14, 16), standard ground (Ex 29:2), or fine ground (Gen 18:6). Either a mortar and pestle or revolving stones were used for the grinding (*see* Mill). Kneading bowls are mentioned in Ex 8:3. For the types of ovens used for baking *see* Oven. The form of the loaves differed from ours, being usually thin flat cakes. Both leavened bread (ch 12:34) and unleavened bread (Gen 19:3) were used. The latter played an important part in connection with the feast of the Passover when for 7 days unleavened bread was to be eaten (Ex 13: 6, 7; Lev 23:5, 6). The *showbread was a prominent item in the tabernacle and Temple service (1 Chr 9:32; 2 Chr 13:11; Neh 10:32, 33; etc.). Jesus chose broken bread as a symbol of His broken body in the ordinance that was to memorialize His death (Mt 26:26; etc.). See Bread, Breaking of; Lord's Supper.

Bread, Breaking of. This expression is used in the Bible with reference to the breaking of the bread in connection with the celebration of the Lord's Supper (Mt 26: 26; Mk 14:22; Lk 22:19; 1 Cor 11:24), also for the breaking of bread at ordinary meals (Mt 14:19; 15:36; Mk 8:6, 19; Lk 24:30, 35). In Acts 2:42, 46; 20:7 the term may apply to a communal meal or to the partaking of the Lord's Supper or to both. According to ch 2:46 bread was broken daily, but Christ set no specific time for the observance of the ordinance.

Bread of the Presence. *See* Showbread.

Breastpiece. *See* Ephod.

Breastplate.

1. Part of the sacred dress of the Hebrew priest. *See* Ephod.

2. In 1 Ki 22:34 and 2 Chr 18:33, RSV, the rendering of the Heb. *shiryan*, which is translated "harness" in the KJV. However, there is no archeological evidence that "breastplates" in the sense of armored plates of one piece were worn in the 9th cent. B.C. The meaning of the Heb. *debaqim*, rendered "scale armor" in the RSV of these verses (KJV "joints") is somewhat obscure, but the word probably describes parts of the coat of mail. Lexi-

cographers give its probable meaning as "joints," "appendages," or "scales [of the armor]."

Breath. [Heb. *neshamah*, "breath"; *rûach*, "breath," "wind," "disposition," "spirit"; Gr. *pneuma*, *pnoē*.] The Hebrew words thus translated are close in meaning, though *neshamah* often stresses the physical act of breathing, and *rûach* the life principle, of which breath is one expression. *Rûach* is much the more common word, being used 377 times in the KJV. It is most often translated "spirit" (232 times), "wind" (91 times), and "breath" (28 times). In such passages as Gen 3:8; 8:1; Ex 10:13; 14:21 *rûach* obviously refers to the currents of air in the atmosphere, while in Gen 7:22; Job 4:9; Ps 18:15, for instance, reference is to respiration through the nostrils. Since a living being breathes, the breath is one evidence of the presence of life itself, or of the life principle, which, by extension, *rûach* came also to denote. In addition, it came to denote other characteristics that accompany life, such as mind, intelligence, and the emotions, or disposition. In the latter sense it is usually translated "spirit" (Ps 32:2; Is 54:6; Dan 2:1; etc.).

Breeches [Heb. *miknesîm*, possibly derived from the root *kanas*, "to cover up," "to hide."] An undergarment resembling drawers or trousers. The breeches of the priests were of linen, and reached probably from the waist to a little above the knees. They were to be worn whenever the priests ministered in the tabernacle (Ex 28:42; 39:28; Lev 6:10; 16:4; cf. Eze 44:18).

Brethren of the Lord. Four men—James, Joses, Simon, and Judas—are mentioned as the brothers of Jesus (Mt 13:55; Mk 6:3). There has been much discussion through the centuries as to the exact relationship of these men to Jesus. Three principal views have been advanced: (1) that they were Jesus' actual brothers, that is, half brothers, sons of Joseph and Mary (and therefore younger than Jesus); (2) that they were His stepbrothers, that is, children of Joseph by a previous marriage (and thus all older than He and not His blood relatives at all); (3) that they were the cousins of Jesus on the mother's side, according to some, or on Joseph's side, according to others. Those who hold the first view argue that this is the most natural way to understand the various references to these brethren; also that this is the most obvious intent of Mt 1:25; Lk 2:7. Those who hold the second view

argue that Oriental family ethics would not permit younger brothers to taunt or otherwise meddle with an older brother as Jesus' brothers taunted Him (see Mk 3:31; Jn 7:3, 4). They point out further that the, fact that Jesus left His mother in the care of the apostle John (Jn 19:26, 27) rather than with one of His brothers strongly implies that Mary had no other children. The view that these brethren were the cousins of Jesus on Joseph's side is based on pure conjecture. That they were cousins on Mary's side is based on the uncertain identity of "Mary the wife of Cleophas" with the sister of Mary (Jn 19:25; cf. Mk 15:40), and on the unproved identity of "Clopas" (Jn 19:25, RSV) with Alphaeus (Mk 3:18). See *SDACom* 5:399, 400.

Jesus' brothers are mentioned as accompanying Jesus and His mother to Capernaum after the marriage at Cana (Jn 2:12). Later Mary and these brothers are recorded as seeking an audience with Jesus (Mt 12:46-50; Mk 3:31-35; Lk 8:19-21). Toward the end of Jesus' ministry, His brethren are mentioned as urging Jesus to prove His Messiahship, which they themselves doubted (Jn 7:3-5). That they were later converted is clear, for they are described in Acts as uniting with the disciples and others in "prayer and supplication" prior to Pentecost (ch 1:13, 14). Paul implies that they were all married (1 Cor 9:5). Many commentators hold that the author of the epistle of Jude, who identifies himself as the "brother of James," was one of these brothers (Jude 1). It is also generally believed that the leader of the church at Jerusalem was James, the Lord's brother (see Acts 12:17; 15:13). This seems to be confirmed by Paul's reference to his visit to Jerusalem, in which he states that he saw only Peter, and "James the Lord's brother" (Gal 1:18, 19; cf. 2:9). According to Josephus, James, the Lord's brother, was stoned to death (*Ant.* xx. 9. 1).

Bribery. [Heb. *shochad*, "bribe."] The giving and receiving of a gift or payment with a view to influencing the judgment of someone in a position of trust. The word "bribery" appears but once in the Bible (Job 15:34), but "bribe" occurs several times (1 Sa 8:3; 12:3; etc.) in the KJV, and frequently in the RSV, which reads "bribe" where the KJV has "gift," or "reward," but with the meaning of "bribe." The practice of accepting bribes is repeatedly denounced in Scripture (Ex 23:8; Deut 10:17; Amos 5:12; etc.).

Brick. [Heb. *lebenah*.] Brickmaking was common and highly developed in Egypt (Ex 1:14; 5:7-19) and Mesopotamia (Gen 11:3). The ancient Hebrews were familiar with bricks made of clay, either sun-dried or kiln-baked, although their houses were built mainly of stone. Sun-dried bricks were made with straw and were used for the inner core of walls, and burned brick made without straw was used for the outer coats to make brick structures more durable. Ancient illustrations and inscriptions give us a rather complete picture of the manufacture of bricks paralleling the description of Ex 5:7-19. Many ancient bricks are stamped with the name of the king under whose reign they were made, and this gives us valuable clues as to the age of ancient buildings and ruins. The ordinary dwelling *house was most often built of unbaked bricks, except in areas, like mountainous Palestine, where stone was plentiful. See figs. 81, 82, 388.

Brickkiln. [Heb. *malben*.] A kiln or furnace in which bricks are baked or burned (2 Sa 12:31). In Nah 3:14 *malben* designates the brick mold rather than the brickkiln, and in Jer 43:9 "brick work."

Brier. A prickly or thorny plant. Six different Hebrew words and one Greek word are thus translated, which are generally of

81. A brick from Babylon, inscribed with the name and titles of King Nebuchadnezzar

82. Brickmaking by Semites and Negroes, as depicted in the tomb of Rekh-mi-Re at Thebes

uncertain identification. *See* Bramble; Thorns and Thistles.

Brigandine. *See* Coat of Mail.

Brimstone. [Heb. *gophrîth;* Gr. *theion*.] Sulphur—a yellowish, nonmetallic element which gives off a suffocating odor when burned. It is mentioned frequently with "fire" and in connection of the destruction of the wicked of earth in past ages (as in Gen 19:24), or at the end of time (Rev 20:9, 10).

Broid. An obsolete word meaning "to braid," "to plait," appearing in the phrase "broided hair" (1 Ti 2:9, KJV).

Broidered. An archaic word occurring in Ex 28:4; Eze 16:10, 13, 18; etc., KJV, meaning "embroidered." *See* Checker Work.

Bronze, KJV generally **Brass.** [Heb. *nechosheth, nechûshah, nachûsh;* Aramaic *nechash;* Gr. *chalkos*.] An alloy of copper and tin, used widely in the making of instruments, utensils, and images, as brass is used today. The Hebrew and Greek terms may refer to either bronze or copper, but brass, an alloy of copper and zinc, was not known until perhaps Roman times. Archeological findings reveal that copper ore was smelted at a very early period. At first the product of hillside forges was crude and spongy, but later the artisans learned to remelt the metal to purify it further. Elaborate refineries, with flues to take advantage of the prevailing winds, are known to have existed at Ezion-geber (see fig. 170). Major mines were on Cyprus, in Edom, and in the Sinai Peninsula (see fig 83). Copper, or bronze, was an antediluvian metal (Gen 4:22). It was used widely in the construc-

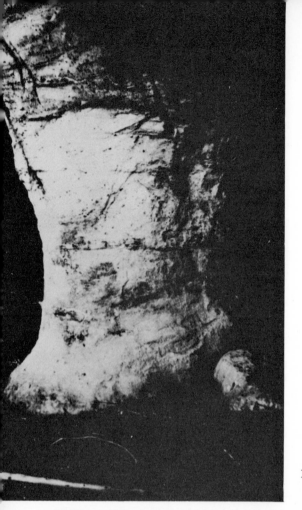

83. Pillar at the entrance of an ancient copper mine at *Umm el-'Amad* in Edom, showing veins and nodules of copper ore

tion of the tabernacle, the Temple, and their equipment (Ex 25:3; etc.), as well as for Moses' serpent (Num 21:9). Doors and gates were overlaid with bronze (see fig. 509). Much of Goliath's armor was bronze (1 Sa 17:5, 6) and the image of Daniel's first vision had belly and thighs of this same metal (Dan 2:32). The word "copper" appears but once in KJV (Ezr 8:27), where probably "bronze" is meant. In the NT Paul describes a coppersmith, Alexander, as an enemy of the gospel (2 Ti 4:14). John speaks of the feet of the Son of God as appearing "like burnished bronze" (Rev 1:15, RSV). The word "bronze" itself is not found in KJV.

Bronze Sea. *See* Sea, Bronze.

Bronze Serpent, KJV Brasen Serpent. The bronze figure of a serpent made and placed by Moses on a pole during a crisis in the wilderness wanderings of Israel.

The Israelites had precipitated the displeasure of God by a fresh outburst of murmuring. As a result God withdrew His protection, and deadly serpents inhabiting the desert regions attacked the people. Many were bitten and died. The bronze serpent was erected as an agency of healing. Those who had been bitten were to look on the figure, after which they would be healed (Num 21:8, 9), provided that faith in God's ability and willingness to be healed were present also. The mere bronze figure had no power to heal, but God had such power and was eager to use it in behalf of His beleaguered children. The gaze was an act of faith on the part of the people. The Israelites were to understand that no symbols, not even the symbols of the sacrificial system, were an end in themselves. The image was preserved, but a later generation made it an object of worship; so Hezekiah destroyed it (called Nehushtan in 2 Ki 18:4). Jesus used the wilderness episode as an illustration of His impending sacrifice (Jn 3:14, 15), and possibly also of His being "lifted up" before the world through the proclamation of the gospel.

"Brasen," which means "of brass," is an erroneous rendering, for brass, an alloy of copper and zinc, was anciently unknown. But bronze, an alloy of copper and tin, was known.

Brooch. In the RSV of Ex 35:22 the rendering of the Heb. *chach* (KJV "bracelet"). *Chach* is a fibula, an ornamental safety pin similar in appearance to a brooch. Fibulas are found in great numbers in the excavations of ancient sites in the Near East. The Israelites had such ornaments when they left Egypt. Later they contributed of them for the building of the tabernacle.

Brook. A small stream, in most instances a rendering of the Heb. *nachal,* designating either the whole valley or ravine or simply the stream bed (Lev 23:40; Deut 2:13; 2 Sa 15:23; etc.). *Nachal* generally desig-

84. A brook in Transjordan

nates a Palestinian stream that flows only in the rainy season or after a rain, drying up in the summer—the equivalent of the Arabic word *wâdī*.

Brook of Egypt. *See* River of Egypt, I.

Broom Tree. [Heb. *rothem*, probably the Arabic *ratam*.] A nearly leafless, branchy bush of the Jordan Valley and Arabian Peninsula (*Retama roetam*), called "juniper" in the KJV, but not to be confused with the modern juniper. Elijah rested under a "broom tree" in his flight from Jezebel (1 Ki 19:4, 5). The root stalk was probably eaten in destitution (Job 30:4, KJV), and was used for making charcoal (see Ps 120:4).

Broth. [Heb. *maraq*, "broth," "soup."] The Hebrew term seems to signify what broth does today, a thin soup, usually a liquid in which a nutritious substance, either a vegetable or animal flesh, has been boiled. The broth of a kid was part of Gideon's presentation at Ophrah, by which he thought to test the identity of the heavenly messenger (Jgs 6:19, 20). Among those provoking God in Isaiah's day were those eating swine's flesh and the "broth of abominable things" (Is 65:4). "Broth" is a conjectural reading in Eze 24:10, RSV, where the Hebrew is obscure. For the clause "spice it well," this version on the basis of evidence from the ancient versions reads "empty out the broth."

Brother. [Heb. *'ach*; Gr. *adelphos*.] This frequently occurring word is used with a variety of meanings. (1) A male person considered with respect to his relationship to any other person having the same parents, for example, Jacob and Esau (Gen 27:6), or having the same father or the same mother (Jgs 8:19). (2) A man more or less closely related by blood. Thus Lot is called Abraham's brother (Gen 13:8; 14:14, 16), though he was a nephew. (3) A person of a kindred race or nation. Moses called the Edomite the "brother" of the Jews (Deut 23:7). Within the Jewish race all men were referred to as brethren (Neh 5:7; Jer 34:9). (4) Any fellow man, as all are descended from the same first ancestor. In this sense the Lord taught the true relationship of brethren (Mt 5:22, 24; 7:3). (5) A fellow believer, as indicated in Mt 23:8; Jn 21:23; Acts 6:3; Gal 1:2. Christ Himself is represented as a brother to those whom He saves (Rom 8:29).

Brown. A color mentioned in the KJV of Gen 30:32, 33, 35, 40, describing certain of Laban's "cattle." However, the Hebrew

word thus translated (*chûm*) is of uncertain meaning. The RSV translates it "black." Some scholars suggest the meaning "in heat."

Bruit. An Old English term appearing in the KJV of Jer 10:22; Nah 3:19, meaning "report," "rumor," "news."

Bucket. A rendering of the Heb. *delî*, which denotes a skin or leather sack used as a bucket to draw water. Its mouth was kept open by crossed sticks. The word occurs in the Bible only in figurative settings (Num 24:7; Is 40:15).

Buckler. The KJV rendering of: (1) the Heb. *magen*, "a small shield" (2 Sa 22:31; 1 Chr 5:18; etc.); (2) the Heb. *ṣinnah*, "a large shield" (Ps 35:2; Eze 23:24; etc.); (3) the Heb. *socherah*, which probably means "bulwark" (Ps 91:4); and (4) the Heb. *romach*, "spear" (1 Chr 12:8). The reason for translating *romach* "buckler" in 1 Chr 12:8 is not clear. Elsewhere the word is generally rendered "spear" (Jgs 5:8; 1 Chr 1:24; etc.).

Bukki (bŭk'ī). [Heb. *Buqqî*, probably a shortened form of *Buqqîyahû*, "Bukkiah."]

1. A Danite prince who helped to allot the land to the 12 tribes (Num 34:22).

2. A descendant of Aaron, and an ancestor of Ezra (1 Chr 6:5, 51; Ezr 7:4).

Bukkiah (bŭ-kī'ȧ). [Heb. *Buqqîyahû*.] A Levite musician, head of the 6th of the 24 companies organized by David for the Temple service (1 Chr 25:4, 13).

Bul. [Heb. *Bûl*; in cuneiform records from Alalakh, *Bale*.] The 8th month of the Hebrew religious year (1 Ki 6:38), called Heshvan or Marheshvan after the Babylonian exile. It began at the new moon of October or November. *See* Year.

Bull. [Heb. and Aramaic generally *par*.] This term occurs frequently in the RSV but rarely in the KJV. The latter version uses the term "bullock" in most instances where the RSV reads "bull" or "young bull." Young bulls were common sacrificial animals (Ex 29:1; Lev 4:3; etc.). The bull was a symbol of strength throughout the ancient world; many gods were represented by or praised as bulls (see fig. 90). This was so of Marduk in Babylon, of Osiris in Egypt, and of El among the Canaanites. In Egypt living bulls were worshiped as reincarnations of the gods Apis and Mnevis. The Israelites followed these heathen practices when they made images of young bulls, one at Mount Sinai (Ex 32) and two which were set up at Bethel and Dan in the time of Jeroboam I (1 Ki 12:28, 29). *See* Calf; Cherub.

Bullock. *See* Bull.

Bulrush. [Heb. *'agmón, gome'.*] Papyrus. Baby Moses' small ark was made from this tall marsh plant (Ex 2:3), as were large craft of the Nile (Is 18:2). The head of the bulrush forms a drooping tassel, illustrative of one who, when fasting or mourning, bows down his head (ch 58:5). The Hebrew terms are sometimes rendered "rush" in the KJV (Job 8:11; Is 9:14; 19:15; 35:7). *See* Writing Material.

Bulwark. A fortification or defense structure. The word is the translation of several Hebrew terms suggesting various types of fortifications (Is 26:1; etc.) and in the RSV the translation also of one Greek term (*hedraiōma,* "foundation," perhaps "mainstay," 1 Ti 3:15). *See* Fortifications.

Bunah (bū′nà). [Heb. *Búnah,* meaning uncertain.] A descendant of Judah (1 Chr 2:25).

Bunch. In the KJV of Is 30:6 this word is used in its now rare sense of "hump" with reference to the humps of camels.

Bunni (bŭn′ī). [Heb. *Bunní,* meaning uncertain.]

1. A Levite belonging to a generation preceding that of Nehemiah (Neh 11:15).

2. A Levite of the time of Ezra and Nehemiah (Neh 9:4).

3. An Israelite who set his seal to Nehemiah's covenant (Neh 10:15).

Burden. The translation of various Hebrew words, chiefly *maśśa',* "burden," "hardship," "heavy load," whether literal (2 Ki 5:17) or figurative (2 Sa 19:35). The prophets commonly use *maśśa'* of a solemn message from God, usually one of judgment (Is 15:1; Eze 12:10; etc.). The RSV translates these occurrences of *maśśa'* as "oracle."

Burial. When death occurred the eyes of the deceased were closed (Gen 46:4), the body washed (Acts 9:37) and wrapped

85. The remains of a burial of the pre-Mosaic period at Jericho (Tomb H 18)

in (linen) cloth (Mt 27:59; Jn 11:44; etc.). Cremation—a European, not a Semitic, custom—was practically unknown among the Hebrews, and is rarely mentioned (1 Sa 31:12; Amos 6:10). Embalming was not practiced by the ancient Hebrews. Jacob and Joseph were embalmed (Gen 50:2, 3, 26) because they died in Egypt, where such a practice was customary (*see* Embalming). However, "spices prepared by the perfumer's art" were sometimes placed on the bier (2 Chr 16:14, RSV), and it seems to have been "the burial custom of the Jews" to treat a body with myrrh and aloes (Jn 19:39, 40, RSV). The deceased was laid in an upper room (1 Ki 17:19; Acts 9:37), and then mourned by relatives, friends, and hired mourning women (Mt 9:23).

Burial took place usually within 24 hours (Acts 5:5, 6, 10). The members of the family, friends, servants, and others accompanied the body as it was carried upon a bier to the burial place (1 Ki 13:29, 30; 2 Ki 23:30; Mt 14:12; Mk 6:29; Lk 7:12). The body was generally buried in a grave without the use of a coffin. In cases where people owned no property the *grave was simply a hole in the ground, into which the body was placed and then covered with earth and stones, so that it would not be disturbed by hyenas or jackals. Such graves were sometimes dug under shade trees (Gen 35:8). Those who were able provided family burial grounds in the form of sepulchers hewn out of the rocks (Is 22:16), or in natural caves (Gen 23). To protect the bodies against wild animals, the openings were covered with large slabs of stone (Mt 27:60). Some tombs of wealthy men were located in gardens (2 Ki 21:18, 26; Mt 27:57, 60; Jn 19:41; see fig. 265). Occasionally, monuments, probably pillars, were erected over such sepulchers (2 Ki 23:17). Tombs were frequently whitewashed on the outside (Mt 23:27), so that the people might recognize them and not become defiled by accidentally touching them.

The Israelites highly valued a proper burial (Ec 6:3), and considered the lack of a burial a divine punishment (Deut 28:26; 2 Ki 9:10; Jer 7:33; etc.). Even enemies were buried (1 Ki 2:31; 2 Ki 9:34), to spare them the additional disgrace of being treated like the carcass of an animal (Jer 22:19; 2 Ki 9:34-36). The Israelites considered it desirable to be buried with their ancestors, that is, in the family burial ground or in the family sepulcher (Gen 47:30; 2 Sa 19:37; cf. Jgs

16:31; 2 Sa 2:32; 17:23; etc.). See fig. 224. To be deprived of a place in the family tomb was considered a divine punishment (1 Ki 13:22), and lying in the family tomb was considered as a sleep with the fathers (1 Ki 2:10; 2 Ki 8:24; etc.).

The *tombs of the kings have never been found in Jerusalem, but well known in other lands are rock-cut or stone-built royal tombs (see figs. 31, 118, 144, 145, 168). Heathen burials of all social strata included articles intended for the use of the dead, from royal treasures (see figs. 102, 103, 422, 501) to common household articles (see fig. 85).

Burnt Offering. *See* Sacrifices and Offerings.

Burnt Sacrifice. *See* Sacrifices and Offerings.

Burying Place. *See* Burial.

Bush. In most of the passages where the term "bush" is used, the reference is to the bush out of which God spoke to Moses (Ex 3:2-4; Deut 33:16; Mk 12:26; etc.). However, the identity of the plant referred to is uncertain. Some suggest the thorny acacia (*Acacia nilotica*), which grows to 12 ft. in height. The identity of the plant in other passages is also uncertain (Job 30:4, 7, KJV). The word translated "bushes" in Is 7:19, KJV, probably

86. Servants carrying cups; relief on south stairway of council hall at Persepolis

means "watering places," or "pastures" (RSV).

Bushel. [Gr. *modios,* from the Latin *modius.*] A Roman dry measure used especially for grain. It contained 16 sextarii, 8.76 liters, or 7.95 U.S. dry qt., approximately a peck. A *modios* measure was used as a domestic utensil (Mt 5:15; Mk 4:21; Lk 11:33).

Business. The translation of various Hebrew and Greek words. In Jos 2:14, 20; 1 Sa 21:8; etc., the term is a translation of the Heb. *dabar,* "word," "report," "matter," "affair." In Gen 39:11; Prov 22:29; Dan 8:27, KJV, the Hebrew word is *mela'kah,* "work," "undertaking," "task." In Lk 2:49 the expression "about my Father's business" (KJV) is literally, "in the things of my Father," which might refer either to matters with which the Father had charged Him or to His "Father's house" (RSV), that is, to the buildings that belonged in a special sense to the Father. The word translated "business" in Rom 12:11, KJV, should be rendered "zeal" (RSV) or "diligence."

Butler. [Heb. *mashqeh,* "one who gives to drink."] Ancient Oriental monarchs lived in constant danger of being poisoned, and therefore employed highly trusted courtiers to be responsible for their drinks. These are called "butlers" or "cupbearers." See fig. 86.

The OT mentions Pharaoh's butler in Joseph's time (Gen 40:1 to 41:13), cupbearers in King Solomon's time (1 Ki 10:5; 2 Chr 9:4), and Nehemiah as cupbearer in the time of Artaxerxes I of Persia (Neh 1:11). The fact that Nehemiah, a Jew, held such an office of trust and responsibility speaks much for his ability and integrity of character.

Butter. [Heb. generally *chem'ah.*] Milk curds, not butter as prepared today. The substance seems to have been made by placing milk in a leather bag or animal-skin bottle and kneading or shaking it until curds formed. Sarah prepared curds for her heavenly guests (Gen 18:8), Jael served them to Sisera (Jgs 5:25), and David and his men received them when they entered Mahanaim (2 Sa 17:29). Along with honey and oil, dairy products were a symbol of abundance (Deut 32:14; Job 20:17; 29:6; Is 7:22). The wise man states that as the pressing of milk makes curds, so the pressing of anger brings strife (Prov 30:33). The RSV consistently renders *chem'ah* "curds," and has butter only once (Ps 55:21), the rendering of *machama'oth* in the idiomatic expression "speech . . . smoother than butter."

Buz (bŭz). [Heb. *Bûz.*]

1. A son of Abraham's brother Nahor (Gen 22:20, 21), and ancestor of an Aramaean tribe that appears to have borne his name. Jeremiah mentions it as a tribe dwelling in Arabia (Jer 25:23). It is mentioned in the inscriptions of Esarhaddon of Assyria as *Bâzu,* and has been located in the hinterland of the island of *Tilmun,* modern Bahrein (W. F. Albright, in *Geschichte und Altes Test.* [Tübingen, 1953], p. 8, note 2).

2. A Gadite, founder of a family (1 Chr 5:14).

Buzi (bū'zī). [Heb. *Bûzî.* The name is attested on an ancient Hebrew seal.] Father of the prophet Ezekiel (Eze 1:3).

Buzite (bū'zīt). [Heb. *Bûzî.*] A member of the tribe of Buz, or a descendant of Buz (Job 32:2, 6).

Buzzard, KJV **Glede.** [Heb. *ra'ah.*] This bird is mentioned only once (Deut 14:13), and there is uncertainty as to its identity.

Instead of *ra'ah* a number of Hebrew manuscripts read *da'ah,* which in Lev 11: 14 is translated "vulture" (KJV), and "kite" (RSV). Some believe that both Hebrew terms refer to the red kite (*Milvus milvus*). The root meaning of *ra'ah* ("to see") suggests a bird of keen sight. The translation "buzzard" was probably selected because this word describes any of various birds of prey.

Byword. A proverbial saying, or a word or phrase, usually expressing scorn or contempt. The term is a rendering of several Hebrew words meaning variously, "byword," "taunt," "proverb." In his misfortune Job became an object of scorn to even the most degraded (Job 30:8-10). Moses predicted that if Israel disobeyed God she would become an object for the taunts of other nations (Deut 28:36, 37). The psalmist complained that Israel had become a proverb to the surrounding nations (Ps 44:14).

C

Cab. *See* Kab.

Cabbon (kăb'ŏn). [Heb. *Kabbôn.*] A town in Judah near Lachish (Jos 15:40), not yet identified, possibly identical with Machbenah (1 Chr 2:49), if the latter is a place name.

Cabul (kā'bŭl). [Heb. *Kabúl,* "circle." The name appears as *Kbr* in a topographical list of Palestinian places by Ramses III.]

1. A town in the territory of Asher (Jos 19:27), now *Kâbûl,* about 8 mi. southeast of Acre (Map VI, C-3).

2. A name Hiram of Tyre as an expression of his dissatisfaction gave to a district of 20 cities in Galilee given to him by Solomon (1 Ki 9:13). It was presumably these cities that Solomon later peopled with Israelites (2 Chr 8:2). In popular etymology it seems to have been interpreted as *kebal,* literally "as nothing," or "good for nothing," though other interpretations have also been suggested.

Caesar (sē'zēr). [Gr. *Kaisar;* Latin *Caesar.*] Originally the surname of Gaius Julius Caesar (100-44 B.C.). When Julius Caesar adopted Gaius Octavius, later the emperor Augustus, he conferred the name Caesar upon him. Thus it became the family name of the early emperors. Later

it remained the general title of every emperor, being practically synonymous with the term "emperor" (Lk 23:2; Jn 19:12, 15). The NT mentions the following Caesars:

1. Caesar Augustus, 27 B.C.-A.D. 14. During his reign Jesus Christ was born (Lk 2:1). *See* Augustus.

2. Tiberius Caesar, A.D. 14-37. The ministry of John the Baptist and of Jesus took place during his reign (Lk 3:1; cf. Mt 22:17, 21; Mk 12:14, 16, 17; Lk 20:22, 24, 25). *See* Tiberius.

3. Claudius Caesar, A.D. 41-54. (Caligula, who reigned from A.D. 37 to 41, between Tiberius and Claudius, is not mentioned in the NT.) Claudius is mentioned in Acts 11:28 as the emperor when a famine raged in Palestine, and as the one who expelled the Jews from Rome (ch 18:2). The reference to "Caesar" in ch 17:7 in the accusation brought against Paul occurred during his reign and would apply specifically to him. *See* Claudius.

4. (Nero), A.D. 54-68. Nero, the successor of Claudius, is not mentioned by name in the NT, but he was the "Caesar" to whom Paul appealed his case and to whose tri-

bunal he was sent (Acts 25 to 28). It was doubtless before him that Paul appeared during his 1st and 2d Roman imprisonments (cf. 2 Ti 4:16, 17). *See* Caesar's Household.

Caesarea (sĕz'ȧ-rē'ȧ). [Gr. *Kaisareia*.] A city on the coast of Palestine, about 23 mi. south of Mount Carmel, originally named Strato's Tower, or Straton's Tower (Map XV, C-2). The city fell into Jewish hands when the Maccabean king Alexander Jannaeus (103-76/75 B.C.) captured it. In 63 B.C. it fell to Rome when Pompey conquered it. Then in 30 B.C. Octavian (who became Augustus) gave it to Herod, who spent 12 years (22-10 B.C.) rebuilding it on a grand scale. The new artificial port was the size of the port of Athens. The sea mole is said to have been 200 ft. wide, standing in 20 fathoms (120 ft.) of water. Herod also built temples, a theater, and an amphitheater. The new city he named *Caesarea* in honor of Augustus Caesar, and called the port *Portus Augusti*. The population consisted mostly of Syrians, but many Jews also lived there. The latter made an unsuccessful claim for Roman citizenship in the time of Nero. There was constant enmity between the pagan and Jewish populations, which culminated in A.D. 66 when the Syrians massacred most of the Jews in the city. This started the Jewish War.

The city was the capital of Palestine and residence of the Roman governor during two periods, first, from A.D. 6, when the ethnarch Archelaus was deposed, until A.D. 41, when Judea and Samaria were given to King Agrippa I; and second, from the time of Agrippa's death, which occurred in Caesarea (Acts 12:20-23) in A.D. 44, until the beginning of the

87. Ancient harbor quay at Caesarea on the Mediterranean coast

Jewish War in A.D. 66. Vespasian then made it a colony and freed it from the payment of tribute. The site is now forsaken, but ruins of its ancient buildings and harbor works are still to be seen. Its present name is *Qeiṣâriyeh*. The state of Israel has announced its intention of rebuilding the city on a grand scale.

The city of Caesarea is frequently mentioned in the book of Acts. The evangelist Philip lived there (chs 8:40; 21:8), also the Roman centurion Cornelius, whose conversion and baptism marked the beginning of mission work among Gentiles (ch 10:1 to 11:18). Other Christians also lived there; during apostolic times the city apparently contained a thriving Christian community (ch 21:16). The apostle Paul passed through the city repeatedly, either when embarking in its harbor for a foreign journey (ch 9:30) or after landing there when returning from missionary journeys (chs 18:22; 21:8-16). He also spent two years in the prison of Caesarea (c. A.D. 58-60), and in that city defended himself before Felix, Festus, and King Agrippa II (ch 23:33 to 27:1). The famous early church writer Origen of Alexandria (c. A.D. 184 - c. 254) made his home at Caesarea, and the church historian Eusebius (c. A.D. 260 - c. 340) was bishop there.

Caesarea Philippi (sĕz'ȧ-rē'ȧ fĭ-lĭp'ī). [Gr. *Kaisareia hē Philippou*.] A city near one of the main springs of the Jordan on the southern slope of Mount Hermon. Some have identified the place with Baal-gad (Jos 11:17), and Baal-hermon (Jgs 3:3), because there is evidence that it was the seat of Canaanite worship, but these identifications are very doubtful. The site appears in historical times first during the Seleucid period by the name of Paneas (or Panias, or Paneion), as the chief place of a district called by one or another form of the same name (Jos. *Ant.* xv. 10. 3; xviii. 2. 1; Pliny *Nat. Hist.* v. 18), because the god Pan was worshiped in a grotto at the site. The tetrarch Philip, son of Herod the Great, embellished the city with many new buildings, and renamed it Caesarea in honor of the emperor (Jos. *Ant.* xviii. 2. 1; *War* ii. 9. 1). To distinguish it from Caesarea on the Palestinian coast it was commonly called Caesarea Philippi (Mt 16:13; Mk 8:27; Jos. *War* iii. 9. 7; *Life* 13). Jesus once visited one of the towns of the region of Caesarea Philippi during His Galilean ministry, and it was on that occasion that Peter made his famous confession declaring

88. The village of *Bâniyâs,* the ancient Caesarea Philippi

Jesus to be the Son of God (Mt 16:16). After Agrippa II became king of the northeastern territories he changed the name of the city again, and called it Neronias in honor of Nero (Jos. *Ant.* xx. 9. 4). Titus conducted games in the city's amphitheater after the destruction of Jerusalem, and made captured Jews fight against one another, and against wild animals (Jos. *War* vii. 2; 3. 1). In the succeeding centuries the city lost its importance, and reverted to its old name Paneas. The ancient name is preserved in *Bâniyâs,* a village now standing on the ancient site. Map XVI, B-4.

Caesar's Household. A term appearing in Php 4:22 designating the place of origin of certain saints or Christians who sent greetings to the brethren in Philippi. The word translated "household" refers to domestic slaves and other retainers; a Christian in the imperial household was not necessarily of the emperor's family; he may have been a government official or clerk, or a servant.

Caiaphas (kā'yȧ-fǎs). [Gr. *Kaiaphas.* The form or meaning of the Aramaic from which it is transliterated is uncertain.] Surname of Joseph, a high priest in Jerusalem, appointed by the Roman procurator Valerius Gratus (Jos. *Ant.* xviii. 2. 2), c. A.D. 18, and deposed by Lucius Vitellius, the legate of Syria (*ibid.* 4. 3),

c. A.D. 36. He was a son-in-law of the former high priest, Annas (Jn 18:13), with whom he is occasionally mentioned (Lk 3:2; Acts 4:6), showing that the former high priest was held in high esteem and allowed to exercise considerable influence. Caiaphas took part in the court procedures against Jesus and was largely responsible for His death (Mt 26:3, 57; Jn 11:49-53; 18:14, 24, 28). He took part also in the procedures against the apostles Peter and John (Acts 4:6).

Cain (kān). [Heb. *Qayin,* commonly "worker in iron," or "spear," but according to Gen 4:1, "one acquired." Gr. *Kain.*]

1. The eldest son of Adam and Eve, brother and murderer of Abel. A farmer by occupation, he offered as a sacrifice the produce of his fields. When God rejected his offering and accepted that of his brother, Cain became jealous and murdered his brother (Gen 4:1-16). The NT indicates an ethical cause for the rejection of Cain. Abel was righteous (Mt 23:35), while the way of Cain (Jude 11) was evil. John says that Cain was of that wicked one and that he slew his brother because his "works were evil, and his brother's righteous" (1 Jn 3:12). The author of Heb 11:4 implies that lack of faith was the reason for the rejection of Cain's offering. As punishment for his crime Cain was forced to live the life of an ex-

164

ile. He was given a mark, the exact nature of which is not known, as a protection or sign of protection against blood revenge (Gen 4:15, 16).

2. A town. See Kain, 1.

Cainan (kā-ī'năn), RSV of OT and KJV once **Kenan** (kē'năn). [Heb. *Qênan;* Gr. *Kaïnam* or *Kaïnan.*]

1. Son of Enosh and father of Mahalalel in the genealogy between Adam and Noah (Gen 5:9-14; Lk 3:37, 38).

2. Son of Arphaxad and father of Shelah (Sala) in the genealogy between Shem and Abraham according to Lk 3:36 and the LXX of Gen 10:24; 11:12, 13. In the Hebrew text of the genealogy in Gen 10 and 11 this second Cainan is absent.

Cake. See Bread.

Calah (kā'lá). [Heb. *Kelach,* spelled *Kalḫu* in cuneiform texts.] An Assyrian city founded by Nimrod (Gen 10:11, 12). It lay at the junction of the Great Zab and Tigris rivers, about 20 mi. south of Nineveh. Ashurnasirpal II (884-859 B.C.) claims that Shalmaneser I (c. 1274-1244

89. General view of *Nimrúd*, the site of Biblical Calah

B.C.) built (or rebuilt) and fortified the city. It afterward fell into decay, but Ashurnasirpal II restored it and made it into a beautiful royal residence, which was used as such by several Assyrian kings. Excavations at the site, now called *Nimrúd,* were carried out first by Henry Layard between 1845 and 1850, then by Hormuzd Rassam from 1852 to 1854, W. H. Loftus from 1854 to 1855, and since 1949 by M. E. L. Mallowan. The excavators have uncovered palaces built by Ashurnasirpal II, Adadnirari III, Tiglath-pileser III, and Esarhaddon, and temples dedicated to Ninurta and Nabu. Many finds have come from Calah (see figs. 249, 347), of which the Black Obelisk of Shalmaneser III is the most important for students of the Bible, since it mentions the name of King Jehu of Israel (see fig. 255). Map XI, B-5.

Calamus. [Heb. *qaneh.*] The Hebrew term is used variously for "reed," "an article in the form of a reed," "measuring rod," "stalk," "shaft," "bone of upper arm," "beam of balances." In a few instances it seems to refer to an aromatic reed, hence the translation "calamus," a reed of aromatic qualities, probably such as ginger grass (*Andropogon calamus aromaticus*), found originally in India and southern Arabia. This grass's roots, stems, and leaves are highly aromatic when bruised, and taste like ginger. A European grass, common sweet sedge (*Acorus calamus*), may be meant in some instances. Calamus or some scented reed was an ingredient of the holy anointing oil for the priests and the tabernacle furniture (Ex 30:23-30; RSV "aromatic cane"). In Song 4:14 calamus appears in a list of various spices. Calamus was bartered in the markets of Tyre (Eze 27:19).

Calcol (kăl'kŏl), KJV once **Chalcol** (kăl'kŏl). [Heb. *Kalkol.*] A descendant of Judah famous for his wisdom, as were also his two brothers, Heman and Darda, or Dara (1 Ki 4:31; 1 Chr 2:6).

Caldron. A cooking vessel, used domestically (Mic 3:3), and in connection with the sanctuary service (1 Sa 2:14; 2 Chr 35:13; etc.). The exact nature of these vessels is a matter of uncertainty. Some of the words thus translated are also rendered "pot." The Heb. *'agmón,* translated "caldron" in Job 41:20, KJV, is more correctly rendered "rushes," as in the RSV.

Caleb (kā'lĕb). [Heb. *Kaleb,* "dog." The name occurs in Nabataean as *Klbw,* in Ugaritic as *Klby,* and in ancient South Arabic as *Klb.*]

1. A son of Hezron and brother of Jerahmeel, of the descendants of Judah (1 Chr 2:18, 42). Among his descendants were Hur, the associate of Aaron in the administration of Israel during Moses' absence on Mount Sinai, and Hur's grandson Bezalel, the master workman who built the tabernacle and its furniture (Ex 31:2; 1 Chr 2:19, 20). In 1 Chr 2:9 Caleb is apparently called Chelubai (kĕ-loo'bī) [Heb. *Kelúbay,* probably a scribal variant]. If Caleb's daughter (or female descendant) Achsah, mentioned in v 49, was the well-known daughter of Caleb, 2, the son of

Jephunneh (Jos 15:16), as some think, then it would follow that the second Caleb was a descendant of the first. Some have wished to identify the two Calebs, but this is impossible since Caleb, 1, the son of Hezron, had a great-grandson, Bezalel, who built the tabernacle at Sinai, whereas Caleb, 2, the son of Jephunneh, was only 40 years old when he went as one of the 12 spies in the year following the building of the tabernacle. Hence Caleb the great-grandfather of Bezalel, and Caleb the spy must be 2 individuals.

2. A son of Jephunneh, a Kenizzite (Num 32:12). He represented the tribe of Judah as one of the 12 Israelite leaders who were sent out from Kadesh-barnea as spies to investigate the land of Canaan, and only he and Joshua returned with encouraging reports; the other spies completely disheartened the people with their pessimistic reports (Num 13; 14). Caleb also took part in the conquest of the land some 40 years later, and was a member of the commission to distribute the land among the 12 tribes (Num 34:19; Jos 14:6-14; 15:13-15). At that time, being 85 years old, he received Hebron and its neighboring territory as an inheritance, and drove out the Anakim from it, while his younger relative Othniel took Debir and thus obtained Caleb's daughter Achsah as wife (Jos 14:13-15; 15:13-17). "The south of Caleb" (1 Sa 30:14) probably refers to the area of Hebron and Debir.

3. A son of Hur, according to the punctuation in the KJV (1 Chr 2:50). However, some believe that a period belongs after "Caleb" so as to make the beginning of v 50 the closing phrase of the preceding section: "These were the sons [or descendants] of Caleb," namely Caleb, 2. Then the following words would begin a new section listing the family of Hur, the son of Ephratah (cf. v 19).

Caleb-ephratah (kā'lĕb-ĕf'rà-tà). [Heb. *Kaleb 'Ephrathah*.] A place where Hezron died, according to the KJV of 1 Chr 2:24. The RSV, following the LXX and Vulgate, reads: "After the death of Hezron, Caleb went in to Ephrathah, the wife of Hezron his father, and she bore him Ashhur."

Calebite (kā'lĕb-īt). [Heb. *Kalibbô* (Q *Kalibbî*). A descendant of *Caleb (1 Sa 25:3).

Calf. [Heb. generally *'egel*; Gr. *moschos*.] Calves in Bible times were used either for food (1 Sa 28:24) or for sacrifices (Lev 9:2; etc.). Idolatrous images of calves representing the God of Israel were set up at Sinai in the time of Moses (Ex 32:4), and at Dan and Bethel in the time of Jeroboam I (1 Ki 12:28, 29). Throughout the ancient world chief gods were represented by bulls or worshiped under this symbol (*see* Bull). In Egypt the bulls of Apis and Mnevis represented gods, and the Hebrews may have become familiar with bull worship there. Hence when the time came that they desired a visible image of their God such as other nations possessed, Aaron made a golden image of a young bull (Ex 32:4; Neh 9:18). The context makes clear that this image was not to represent a foreign god, but Yahweh, the God of the Hebrews (see Ex 32:5). The children of Israel were consequently rebuked and punished, not for replacing their God by another, but for making an idol, thus placing their God side by side with the gods of other nations.

When Jeroboam founded the northern kingdom of Israel, he devised means to draw his people's loyalty away from Jerusalem. One of the measures taken was to erect sanctuaries, one at Bethel and

90. Hittite relief from *Alaça Hüyük* depicting a royal couple worshiping a bullock on a pedestal

another at Dan, each containing a cult image of a young bull (1 Ki 12:28, 29). His choice of bull images may have come from a familiarity with the worship of the bull Apis during his stay in Egypt (ch 11:40), or from an attempt to reinstate the bull worship introduced at Mount Sinai, as his quotation of Ex 32:4 might indicate (1 Ki 12:28). A pictorial relief from *Alaça Hüyük* shows a Hittite royal pair worshiping at an altar behind which a bull stands on a pedestal (see fig. 90). Their worship seems to parallel closely the Biblical calf worship at Sinai and at Dan and Bethel. Many scholars, however, consider that the bull images of Israel were regarded not as images of Yahweh the God of Israel but merely as pedestals for the invisible Yahweh. They base their opinion on the fact that many Hittite, Aramaean, and Assyrian gods are depicted in reliefs as standing upon animals, mostly upon bulls. However, the tenor of the Biblical statements condemning the bull images of Dan and Bethel favors the view that the golden calves were representations of the Deity, and not mere pedestals for His invisible being.

Through His prophets God strongly condemned bull worship at Bethel and Dan. He sent an unnamed prophet to rebuke King Jeroboam immediately after his initiation of this worship in Israel (1 Ki 13:1-9). Later the prophets Hosea and Amos denounced this form of worship in strong terms as a degeneration and corruption of true worship (Hos 8:4-6; Amos 4:4; 5:5, 6; 7:9). Hosea made sport of men who kiss calves (ch 13:2).

One of the Samaria ostraca found by the Harvard excavation in 1910 contained the personal name *'glyw,* meaning either "the calf of Yahweh" or "Yahweh is a calf." This name, which was borne by a citizen of the northern kingdom during the latter part of the 9th cent. B.C., indicates that people actually considered the calf to represent Yahweh. The worship of the bulls ceased, first at Dan and later at Bethel, with the destruction of the northern kingdom under Tiglath-pileser III, Shalmaneser V, and Sargon II. In a text recently excavated at *Nimrûd* (Biblical Calah) Sargon II claims that in the spoils he carried away after the capture of Samaria were "the gods, their trust." Since these gods were objects that could be carried it is quite possible they were the calves of Jeroboam, which might have been removed to Samaria for protection before the siege of the city began.

Call, or Calling. As used in the NT generally an invitation extended by God (2 Ti 1:9), many times seemingly implying that the invitation has been accepted (Eph 4:4; 2 Th 1:11). This is illustrated by Rom 8:30, where it is stated that God justified those whom He called. But justification comes only with acceptance of Jesus (see Acts 13:38, 39; Rom 3:23-25; Gal 2:16; 3:24; etc.). That this term may imply acceptance is further demonstrated in Heb 3:1, where the "holy brethren" are set forth as those who are "partakers of the heavenly calling" (KJV), or those "who share in a heavenly call" (RSV); cf. 1 Cor 1:24, 26; Eph 1:18. Peter admonishes believers continuously to confirm their calling that they might not lose eternal life (2 Pe 1:10).

The word "calling" is also used with the meaning "station in life," "position," "vocation" (1 Cor 7:20-22).

Calneh (kăl'nĕ). [Heb. *Kalneh.*]

1. A city in Babylonia belonging to the kingdom of Nimrod (Gen 10:10). It is either the unidentified *Kulunu,* mentioned in cuneiform records as a city near Babylon, or, according to the Talmud, Nippur (Map III, C-6), which in Sumerian inscriptions is called *Enlil-ki,* "the city of (the god) Enlil." F. Hommel suggests that in Babylonian it may have been called *Ki-Enlil,* pronounced *Ki-Illin,* which may have given rise to the Heb. *Kalneh* (*Grundriss der Geographie* [1904], p. 348; *OLZ* 10 [1907], 382).

Nippur was one of the most sacred cities of Lower Mesopotamia, and was the site of several famous temples. Excavations carried out by American expeditions show that its importance extended from early times until the Persian period. For Calneh the RSV reads "all of them," following a suggestion of W. F. Albright (*JNES* 3 [1944], 254-55), according to which the Hebrew should be read *kullanah* (by supplying different vowels to the consonants), meaning "all of them."

2. A city, presumably in Syria, mentioned with Hamath in Amos 6:2. It has been identified with a Syrian city spelled *Kullani* and *Kulnia* in cuneiform records, perhaps modern *Kullanköy,* 10 mi. southeast of Arpad, and 20 mi. northwest of Aleppo. It is probably identical with the city called Calno (kăl'nō) [Heb. *Kalnô*] in Is 10:9, which the Assyrians mentioned as an example of the futility of offering resistance to them.

Calno. *See* Calneh, 2.

Calvary. *See* Golgotha.

Calves of Our Lips. An expression occurring in Hos 14:2, KJV. It has been suggested that the Hebrew words thus translated should read "fruit of our lips" as in the LXX. In the Hebrew consonantal text the dropping of the final letter *m* from *prym,* "calves," would give *pry,* "fruit." This "fruit" would be the praise that repentant Israel would offer to God in response to forgiveness, acceptance, and blessing.

Camel. [Heb. generally *gamal. Beker* and *bikrah* are used for young male and female camels. These last two words are translated "dromedary" in the KJV. The

91. Camel caravan led by a donkey near Smyrna, in western Asia Minor

word *'achashteranîm* (Est 8:10, 14), translated "camels" in the KJV, is a loan word from the Persian and means "royal" (see *SDACom* 3:485). The Greek term for camel is *kamēlos*.] An animal used widely in the ancient world and in modern times as a beast of burden and for riding (see figs. 8, 19, 91). It is frequently mentioned in the Bible. In Lev 11 and Deut 14 it is listed as an unclean animal.

The camel of the Bible is probably without exception the one-humped camel, or the dromedary, not the two-humped Bactrian camel displayed in Mesopotamian and Persian art. The patriarchs possessed camels (Gen 24:10), and there were camel caravans of Ishmaelites moving between Transjordan and Egypt in their time (ch 37:25). By the time of the judges camels had become so common that the Midianite nomads of the eastern desert overran Palestine with camel forces "without number" (Jgs 6:5). From that time on, camels appear frequently in Bible stories, espe-

cially with reference to desert people and caravans. These animals, generally patient and phlegmatic, can be extremely stubborn and vicious, especially when in heat. It is probably for this reason that the prophet Jeremiah compares idolatrous Israel to "a restive young camel" (Jer 2:23, RSV). The camel is also mentioned in the NT: John the Baptist wore a garment made of camel's hair (Mk 1:6); and Jesus spoke of a camel going through the eye of a needle (Mt 19:24; etc.), and of men straining out a gnat and swallowing a camel (ch 23:24).

Some in recent years have claimed that the camel was not domesticated until the 12th cent. B.C., and that all earlier OT statements mentioning camels as domestic animals are anachronistic. This claim is based mainly on the fact that pictures of camels are not found in early Egyptian reliefs and murals and that the animal is not mentioned in Egyptian and cuneiform texts before the 12th cent. B.C. Although evidence seems to indicate that camels were not widely used before that time, their sporadic domestication and use in small numbers is attested from very early times in Egypt, Palestine, and Mesopotamia. Figurines of burden-carrying camels in early archeological contexts have been discovered, and a pictorial representation of a camel rider appears on an early cylinder seal from Mesopotamia. The evidence for the existence of the domestic camel goes back in some instances to the 3d millennium B.C.

Camel's Hair. [Gr. *triches kamēlou.*] As used in Mt 3:4; Mk 1:6, coarse cloth woven from the hair of the camel. John the Baptist wore a garment of this material. Cf. 2 Ki 1:8.

Camon. *See* Kamon.

Camp. [Heb. *machaneh;* Gr. *parembolē.*] The temporary location of a body of people or soldiers dwelling in tents or booths.

92. The arrangement of the tribes of Israel in camp and their order of march

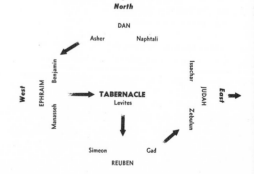

NOTE: Arrows indicate order in line of march. Leading tribes in capitals (Based on Numbers 2)

CAMPHIRE

During the wilderness wanderings the Israelites lived in a camp, in an orderly arrangement of the various tribal units, situated around the portable sanctuary called the tabernacle (Num 1:47 to 2:34; 3:14-39). Strict cleanliness was enjoined in sanitary regulations (Deut 23:9-14).

The arrangement of a military camp in OT times is not known, although the Heb. *ma'gal,* from *'agal,* "to circle," used in two passages (1 Sa 17:20; 26:5, 7; KJV "trench"), indicates that it was circular. The soldiers slept in temporary shelters at night guarded by sentries in 3 shifts (Jgs 7:19). See fig. 20.

Camphire. *See* Henna.

Cana (kā′ná). [Gr. *Kana,* probably a transliteration of the Heb. *Qanah,* "place of reeds."] A town in Galilee, called Cana of Galilee or Cana in Galilee to distinguish it from a Cana in Coelesyria (Jos. *Ant.* xv. 5. 1). It was the scene of Christ's first miracle, the making of water into wine (Jn 2:1-11), and of another miracle, the healing of the nobleman's son (ch 4: 46-54). It was also the home of Nathanael (ch 21:2). Its location is still disputed. Tradition for centuries has identified it with *Kefr Kenna,* a village about 4 mi. northeast of Nazareth, on the road to Tiberias, but many prefer the identification *Khirbet Qânâ,* about 8 mi. north of Nazareth (Map XVI, C-3).

Canaan (kā′năn), KJV of NT twice **Chanaan** (kā′năn). [Heb. *Kena'an.* The name appears repeatedly in cuneiform texts: in the *Amarna Letters in the forms *Kinahna, Kinahni,* and *Kinahhi,* and in the statue inscription of King Idrimi of Alalakh (14th cent. B.C.) as *mât Kinanim.* In Egyptian records of the 2d millennium it is written with the definite article as *p3 Kn'n.* Former commentators explained *Kena'an* to mean "lowland." However, this interpretation lacks linguistic evidence, and has lately been given up. In the Hurrian language the word *kinahhu* means "red purple," and this seems to have been the ancient meaning of the name. This view seems to be supported by the fact that when the Greeks came in contact with the coastal Canaanites they called them "Phoenicians" from *phoinix,* "red purple." Gr. *Chanaan.*]

1. A son of Ham (Gen 9:18).

2. The Biblical name of Palestine west of the Jordan. In the Bible it is usually spoken of as the "land of Canaan." Exceptions are found in a few poetical passages (Is 19:18; Zep 2:5; etc.), and occasionally

93. Relief of the conquest of the "Town of Canaan" by Pharaoh Seti I

elsewhere as in the following expressions: "daughters of Canaan" (Gen 28:1), "inhabitants of Canaan" (Ex 15:15), "wars of Canaan" (Jgs 3:1), "king of Canaan" (ch 4:2), "idols of Canaan" (Ps 106:38).

"The land of Canaan" comprised the whole country west of the Jordan. Its southern border ran from Gaza to the Dead Sea (Gen 10:19), and the eastern border was formed by the river Jordan (see Num 32:32; 33:51; etc.). The northern border is variously designated in different texts: at Sidon (Gen 10:19), at the Lebanon and Euphrates (Deut 11:24), at the Euphrates (Gen 15:18), at Baalgad below Mount Hermon (Jos 11:17), and at Lebo near Hamath (Num 13:21).

The heathen inhabitants of the land of Canaan were called Canaanites. According to Gen 10:6 they were the descendants of Canaan, one of the sons of Ham. Eleven of Canaan's sons are listed in vs 15-18. Of these, 6 are found in the names of Syrian peoples, and 4 in those of Palestinian tribes. Supporting evidence for a Hamitic origin of the Canaanites is provided by the Phoenician tradition that their original ancestor's name was *Chna* or *Chnas.* This name later became that of their country. The Canaanites also claimed that their earliest home was on the Gulf of Erythraea, by which the Persian Gulf is meant. That area was inhabited mainly by Semites, but was also the home of Nimrod, a descendant of Ham (Gen 10:8). Because of their descent from Ham one would expect the Canaanites to speak a Hamitic language; however, in historical times they spoke a Semitic language, which for practical purposes can be identified with Hebrew. *See* Hebrew Language. This seems to contradict the record of their Hamitic origin. This apparent contradiction may be explained by assuming that the Canaanites, by living in a Semitic territory and through close association with Semites, took over a Semitic language. There are other historical cases of one nation adopting another language after migrating to another country.

It is not known when the Canaanites moved into Palestine, but they formed the indigenous population of that country in Abraham's time (Gen 12:6). They were in possession of the largest and strongest cities in the country until dispossessed by the Israelites toward the end of the 2d millennium B.C. Excavations of some of their cities, such as Jerusalem, Megiddo, Beth-shean, Hamath, Gezer, and Byblos, show that Canaanite culture at the time of the Israelite conquest was of a high level. Writing in Babylonian cuneiform script was widely practiced, and several alphabetic systems of *writing had come into use before the Israelites came into the country. Craftsmanship and metallurgy were on a high level, the art of erecting strong fortifications had never been better, music flourished, and a rich literature was produced. In these areas the Israelites, a nomadic desert people who had lived in slavery for generations, were no match for the Canaanites. Because of their inferiority and because of their lack of a firm trust in God, the conquest of the country was much more gradual and incomplete than a superficial reading of the book of Joshua might suggest. Many of the strong Canaanite cities did not come into the possession of the Israelites until the time of David, and one of them, Gezer, was not occupied until Solomon's reign.

After the conquest of the country, remnants of the Canaanites continued as a thriving colony on the Phoenician coast. These took to seafaring and became the merchants and mariners of the then-known world. Founding Canaanite (Phoe-

94. A stone relief from the tomb of Pharaoh Harmhab, depicting Canaanites pleading for admission to Egypt

nician) colonies in various countries bordering on the Mediterranean Sea as far away as Spain and northern Africa (Carthage), they spread Eastern culture and civilization among the primitive nations of the West. In this way they exerted•a great influence on the Greeks at the dawn of their civilization and on other peoples. They taught them, for example, the art of writing, which up to that time had been practically unknown in Europe. They became so famous and successful as merchants that the Heb. *Kena'anî*, *"Canaanite," became a synonym for trader (Job 41:6; Is 23:8; Zec 14:21).

Little was known of the religion of the Canaanites before the discoveries of the rich mythological literature of Ras Shamra. Now, however, the Canaanite gods and goddesses are well known. The chief ones were *El, *Baal, *Anath, *Asherah,* Dagon,* Hadad, some of which are mentioned in the Bible (Jgs 16:23; 2 Ki 10:21; 21:7, RSV). These gods were worshiped in temples, a number of which have recently been excavated, and in open-air sanctuaries (called *"high places" in the Bible, 2 Ki 17:32; etc.). The idolatrous religious rites were connected with gross immorality, and centered around a worship of the fertility of man, flocks and herds, and the land. The sacrificial system was similar to that of the Hebrews, but besides clean animals unclean beasts and sometimes human beings, especially children, were offered on Canaanite *altars. Their nature cults seemed to have a great attraction for the Israelites and were therefore widely adopted by both Israel and Judah. For a time the Canaanite Baal rivaled Yahweh.

Lit.: B. Maisler, *BASOR* 102 (1946), 7-12; W. F. Albright, *Archaeology and the Religion of Israel* (4th ed.: Baltimore, 1956), pp. 68-94.

Canaanite (kā'năn-īt). [Heb. *Kena'anî;* Gr. *Kaninitēs.*

1. A descendant of Canaan, the son of Ham (Gen 10:6, 15-20). Since the Canaanites lived in Palestine, the land bridge between the Semites and the Hamites, they seem to have had close contacts with the Semites in their early history. The fact that the monuments show no traces of a Hamitic language among the Canaanites leads to the conclusion that at an early stage in their history they adopted the Semitic speech. Their language was then taken over by the early migrating Hebrews (cf. Is 19:18), and was spoken by most of the nations of Palestine. It is now called

Hebrew. The Canaanites were doomed by God for their wickedness (Deut 20:17), but the Israelites only partially carried out the commission to exterminate them. Those who were left were made tributary, or were used as slaves (Jgs 1:27-36; 1 Ki 9:20, 21). The remaining Canaanites, to whom the Phoenicians belonged, became known as merchants throughout the ancient world, and the Hebrew word *Kena-'anî*, "Canaanite," came to mean "merchant," and is so translated in several texts of the KJV and RSV (Job 41:6; Prov 31:24; Nah 3:16).

2. For the term in the NT *see* Canaanaean.

Canaanitess (kā'năn-īt'ĕs). [Heb. *Kena'anîth.*] A Canaanite woman (1 Chr 2:3).

Cananaean (kā'nȧ-nē'ăn), KJV **Canaanite** (kā'năn-īt). [Gr. *Kananaïos* from the Aramaic *qane'an*, "a zealous one." The Textus Receptus reads *Kananitēs,* "man from Cana," hence the reading of the KJV.] An epithet of Simon, one of the 12 apostles (Mt 10:4; Mk 3:18). Luke calls him *zēlōtēs,* "the zealot" (Lk 6:15; Acts 1:13), supporting the interpretation given above. He had probably been a member of the extremely nationalistic political party known as the *Zealots.

Candace (kăn'dȧ-sē). [Gr. *Kandakē.*] The title (not name) of the queen of Nubia, or *Ethiopia (Acts 8:27), whose capital was at Meroë, 130 mi. north of Khartum, between the 5th and 6th Nile cataracts. Strabo, Dio Cassius, and Pliny give the titles of several ruling Meroïtic queens as Ka (n)take or Ka (n)dakit (see also Pliny, *Nat. Hist.* vi. 186). Discoveries recently made in the Nubian royal cemeteries at Meroë and Barkal indicate that the queen referred to in Acts 8:27 was Amanitēre, whose title appears as *Kntky,* "Candace," in a cartouche. She reigned from A.D. 25 to 41 (J. A. Wilson, *JNES* 18 [1959], 287). A eunuch from her court, either a born Jew or a proselyte, had come to Jerusalem to attend one of the Jewish feasts, and on his way back was converted to Christianity through the work of Philip the evangelist (vs 26-39).

Candle. *See* Lamp.

Candlestick. *See* Lampstand.

Cane. *See* Calamus; Sweet Cane.

Canker. *See* Gangrene.

Cankerworm. *See* Locust, 6.

Canneh (kăn'ĕ). [Heb. *Kanneh.*] A city in northern Mesopotamia mentioned with Haran and Eden (Eze 27:23). It occurs in cuneiform records as *Kannu'*, but it has not yet been identified. Some commentators consider it a misspelling of *Calneh.

Canon. [A transliteration of the Gr. *kanōn,* "an authoritatively established rule" derived originally from the Semitic name for a straight rod or measuring reed. From this the meaning of standard, norm, or rule was derived.] The collection or list of sacred books composing the Old and New Testaments, which are accepted as inspired by God and therefore as possessing divine authority. *Kanōn* appears several times in the NT: in 2 Cor 10:13, 15, 16 in the sense of limits or sphere of action, in Gal 6:16 to refer to the "rule" of the Christian life, which rule is laid down by divine inspiration, and in Php 3:16, where it is used of a "rule," or standard, of life. In the 2d cent. in the Christian church the term came to signify revealed truth, the rule of faith. The earliest Christian writer to apply the term to the collection of Bible books recognized as the rule of faith and practice was Origen (*c.* 185 - *c.* 254), who said "no one should use for the proof of doctrine books not included among the canonized Scriptures" (*Commentary on Matt.,* section 28). Some years later Athanasius (*c.* 293?-373) designated the whole collection of sacred books the "canon." Thus the term came to mean the catalogue or list of sacred books accepted as inspired, normative, sacred, and authoritative.

The study of the canon involves the question as to when, how, by whom, and why the various books of the Bible were accepted as sacred and authoritative. It seeks to discover who was responsible for collecting and arranging the books of the Bible in their present order. The study of canon is therefore largely a historical investigation. With reference to the canon of the NT there are abundant source materials. With reference to the canon of the OT, however, the investigator is faced with great difficulties because of the lack of external evidence. No historical account of the formation of the OT has been preserved, either in the Scriptures themselves or in other reliable historical documents. In the extra-Biblical Jewish writings 2 accounts (2 Macc 2:13-15; 4 Ezra 14:19-48) bearing on the problem are presented. The first refers to Nehemiah as having gathered books now regarded as canonical, and as having founded a library. The second is usually regarded by modern scholars as purely legendary. It connects the formation, transcription, and promulgation of the canon with Ezra, who is supposed to have rewritten and reissued the sacred books after the Chaldeans had burned them at the fall of Jerusalem.

I. Old Testament Canon. The canon of the OT as accepted by Protestants is the Hebrew Bible, which, as arranged today, consists of 39 books, but which in the time of Jesus was arranged in 24 books (4 Ezra 14:45). It was made up of three divisions: the Law (*Torah*), the Prophets (*Nebī'îm*), and the Writings (*Kethûbîm*). The *Torah* consisted of the Pentateuch, the 5 books of Moses: Gen, Ex, Lev, Num, and Deut. The *Nebī'îm* consisted of 8 books in 2 parts, (1) the 4 books of Former Prophets: Jos, Jgs, Sa, Ki (1, 2 Sa and 1, 2 Ki counted as 2 books); and (2) the 4 of Latter Prophets: Is, Jer, Eze, and the Book of the Twelve (Minor Prophets). The *Kethûbîm,* or Hagiographa, consisted of 11 books including: (1) 3 poetic books: Ps, Prov, Job, (2) the 5 scrolls (*Megilloth*): Song, Ruth, Lam, Ec, Est, (3) Dan, and (4) 2 historical books: Ezr-Neh and Chr. By another calculation, such as in Josephus (*Against Apion* i. 8), the canon was regarded as composed of 22 books. To arrive at this number Ruth was possibly appended to Jgs, and Lam was possibly added to Jer. The LXX and Vulgate take no notice of this tripartite division of the OT, but arrange the books according to the type of literature they contain: historical, poetical, and prophetic. From these versions the arrangement of our English OT is derived.

Various theories have been propounded to explain the threefold division of the Hebrew Bible:

1. The Jewish scholars of the Middle Ages (such as Maimonides) seem to have held that 3 divisions represent 3 degrees of inspiration. In the Torah, Moses spoke directly from God, the Prophets possessed the "Spirit of prophecy," whereas the Writings were inspired by the Holy Spirit. But such a position is untenable. Certainly the NT knows of no degrees of inspiration, and Jesus used the 3 parts of the canon as of equal value (Lk 24:27, 44; 2 Ti 3:16).

2. The division is due to differences in content. There is first of all law, then history and prediction, and finally poetry and wisdom. But these distinctions do not hold. The Torah contains not only law but an extensive amount of history and some prophecy; a large percentage of the Prophets is poetry; and the Writings contain the historical books of Ezra-Nehemiah and Chronicles, and the prophetic

(and partly historical) book of Daniel.

3. The division is due to differences in the official position and status of the Bible writers. This is the view of many modern Protestants. To explain Daniel's position among the Writings, for example, they distinguish between the gift of prophecy (*donum propheticum*) and the office of prophecy (*munus propheticum*). Daniel, they believe, possessed the gift of prophecy but not the office.

4. The divisions represent separate stages in the process of canonization. This is the modern critical position. It contends that the formation of the canon was a gradual process which began with the Torah, and was followed by the Prophets at a considerably later time, and still later by the Writings. While there is much to commend this view, the conservative scholar cannot accept the late dates assigned for the separate divisions of the canon. Also, it seems most likely that the collecting of the Prophets and the Writings was largely carried on synchronously, and that therefore the last 2 divisions represent differences in content and not mere chronology. A conservative study of the evidence, it is believed, will show that all 3 divisions were recognized as Scripture as early as the time of Ezra and Nehemiah, that the Prophets, with the exception of the postexilic, were accepted as Scripture as early as the Exile, and the Law as early as the time of Joshua. These conclusions are, of course, based on the assumption of an early and conservative date for the various OT books.

In tracing the history of the formation of the OT it is helpful to begin with the completed canon as it existed in the 1st cent. and then work backward. The use of such terms as "the scriptures," "the holy scriptures," in the NT makes it evident that there was a definite, fixed, and authoritative collection of sacred writings among the Jews in the 1st cent. of our era (Mt 21:42; 22:29; Lk 24:32; Jn 5:39; Acts 17:2, 11; 18:24; Rom 1:2; 2 Ti 3:15). The words of Jesus also give evidence of the recognition of the tripartite arrangement of the books into the Law, the Prophets, and the Writings (Lk 24:44). Jesus' statement regarding the martyrs as extending from Abel to Zechariah (Mt 23:35; Lk 11:51) is also in harmony with this arrangement. Chronologically, Zechariah was not the last righteous man slain, but his murder is the last recorded in the Hebrew Bible, for it is recorded in Chronicles (2 Chr 24:20, 21), the last book in the Hebrew canon. This evidence regarding the last book of the Writings implies the recognition of the other books in the 3d division of the Hebrew canon.

According to one compilation, the NT contains 433 direct quotations from the OT: 144 from the Pentateuch, 148 from the Prophets, and 141 from the Writings. Thirty of the 39 books of the OT are definitely quoted, the exceptions being 1 Chr, Ezr, Neh, Est, Song, Lam, Nah, Ob, and Zep. However, it is not the mere fact that these books are quoted that is of primary significance, but the manner in which they are quoted. The technical phrase "It is written" is used to introduce OT statements in 73 passages. In about 21 passages taken from 11 OT books the term "scripture" is applied. Quotations from 11 books are attributed to God or to the Holy Spirit. In 46 passages the names of 10 OT books or the authors of these books are mentioned. It may be further added that in no case is any Apocryphal book cited as "Scripture" or attributed to the work of the Holy Spirit.

The evidence from the NT regarding the Hebrew canon is confirmed by 1st-cent. Jewish writings. 4 Ezra (1st cent. A.D.) is the earliest work to give the number of the sacred books as 24 (ch 14:19-48). The writings of the Jewish Alexandrian philosopher, Philo Judaeus (fl. late 1st cent. B.C. and early 1st cent. A.D.), contain quotations from most of the books of the Hebrew canon, but nothing is cited by him from the Apocrypha. The Jewish historian Flavius Josephus (A.D. 37 - c. 100) mentioned 22 books "which contain the records of all the past times" (*Against Apion* i. 8). In this he apparently followed the practice of some Jews in equating the number of books in the canon with the 22 letters in the Hebrew alphabet. Of the books he lists 5 as belonging to Moses and 13 as Prophets (probably Jos, Jgs with Ruth, Sa, Ki, Chr, Ezr with Neh, Est, Job, Dan, Is, Jer with Lam, Eze, and the 12 Minor Prophets). "The remaining four," he declares, "contain hymns to God, and precepts for the conduct of human life" (doubtless meaning Ps, Song, Prov, and Ec). A group of Jewish scholars confirmed this Hebrew canon in the Council of Jamnia toward the close of the 1st cent. While the canonicity of certain books, such as Prov, Ec, Est, and Song had been questioned, they were in the end retained as Scripture. The position was taken that so far as Judaism was concerned the canon was closed; hence the Jewish canon excluded not only the Apocrypha but such Christian books as the Gospels.

In the 1st cent. B.C. there is little evidence regarding the canon. The *Letter of Aristeas,* which some date in the 1st cent., others later, speaks of the Pentateuch as "Scripture" (56), which is the earliest use of this designation. From the 2d cent. B.C. there are several significant statements in the Apocryphal writings. The 1st book of Maccabees (*c.* 100 B.C.) speaks of the encouragement to be derived from "the holy books which are in our hands" (ch 12:9). In ch 1:54 there is a definite allusion to Dan 9:24-27. In 1 Macc 2, where "the deeds of the fathers" are held up before the sons of Mattathias for emulation, the 3 Hebrew worthies and Daniel are listed among such heroes of faith as Abraham, Joseph, Phinehas, Joshua, Caleb, David, and Elijah (1 Macc 2:51-60; cf. Dan 1:7; 3:26; 6:23), indicating that the book of Daniel was regarded as normative and canonical. 1 Macc 7:16, 17 introduces a quotation from Ps 79:2, 3 with the clause "in accordance with the word which was written," indicating that the Psalms were at this time regarded as canonical. 1 Macc also records the efforts of Antiochus Epiphanes to destroy the books of the Law (ch 1:20, 56, 57). The 2d book of Maccabees of about the same date tells how Judas Maccabeus made a collection of the sacred writings (ch 2:14).

Ecclesiasticus, or the Wisdom of Jesus the Son of Sirach (*c.* 180 B.C.), furnishes further important evidence. About 132 B.C. the grandson of this Jewish sage translated the Hebrew text of this work into Greek and wrote the Prologue, in which he refers to "the law and the prophets and the other books of our fathers." This is believed to be the earliest evidence we have of the existence of the threefold division of the Hebrew Bible. Ecclesiasticus either alludes to, quotes, or refers to at least 19 of the 24 books of the Hebrew canon. It clearly refers to the arrangement of the Minor Prophets as a group of "the twelve prophets" (ch 49:10), and the well-known "Hymn to the Fathers" suggests that the 2d division of the canon, the Prophets, was authoritative at that time (chs 44:3, 4; 49:6, 8, 10).

We have no Jewish writings between the 2d cent. B.C. and the time of Ezra and Nehemiah in the 5th cent. However, Josephus (*Ant.* xi. 8. 4, 5) tells the story of Alexander the Great's visit to Jerusalem in the 4th cent., when he was met outside the walls by Jaddua the high priest and persuaded to spare Jerusalem. On this occasion, according to Josephus, Alexander was shown the prophecies of the book of Daniel regarding himself. If the story is true the existence and study of this prophetic work is carried back to the 4th cent.

There can be no doubt that by the 5th cent. B.C. the Pentateuch was regarded as canonical Scripture (cf. Neh 8:1-8). This is shown by the great reverence of the people when the scroll was unrolled. The Pentateuch, in whole or in part, is mentioned as "book of Moses," "law of the Lord" or "book of the law of the Lord" about 24 times in Chr and Ezr-Neh. It is mentioned once in Mal (ch 4:4). Jewish tradition uniformly assigns the collection of the sacred books and the fixing of the Hebrew canon to Ezra and Nehemiah. 2 Macc refers to the "records and memoirs of Nehemiah" and declares that he "founded a library and collected the books about the kings and prophets, and the writings of David . . . " (2 Macc 2:13; cf. 4 Ezra 14:37-48). Josephus also implied the completion of the canon at the time of Ezra and Nehemiah, and definitely asserted that writings since their time were not of the same value "because of the failure of the exact succession of prophets" (*Against Apion* i. 8, Loeb ed.).

But there is evidence that the Law and the Prophets were regarded as Scripture at an earlier date. Zechariah (*c.* 518 B.C.) refers to the pre-exilic Israelites thus: "They made their hearts like adamant lest they should hear the law and the words which the Lord of hosts had sent by his Spirit through the former prophets" (Zec 7:12, RSV). This is a *locus classicus* dealing with the inspiration of the OT prophets. Furthermore, if we follow the conservative dating of the book of Daniel (6th cent. B.C.; *see* Daniel, Book of) we have additional evidence that the writings of Jeremiah were recognized as authoritative, as well as "the law of Moses" (Dan 9:2, 11, 13). If the prophetic canon was made up in the exilic period, it is easy to understand why Daniel was not included in this group. The latest date in Daniel is given as the 3d year of Cyrus (ch 10:1), or 536/35 B.C. The book was probably completed shortly after.

In the 7th cent. there is clear evidence that the Law or some major portion of it was regarded as authoritative and normative. King Josiah and his court accepted it as ancient and as containing the word of God (2 Ki 22:13, 18, 19). This experience is sometimes cited by modern scholars as the beginning of the Hebrew canon, but there is no basis for this. The Law was regarded as normative long before (cf. Ex 24:3, 7). Evidence for this can be cited from the time of Joash (2 Ki 14:6), the charge of David to Solomon (1 Ki 2:2, 3), and back to the time of Joshua (Jos 1:7, 8; 8:31; 23:6).

II. New Testament Canon. The OT was the Bible of the early Christian church. Among Greek-speaking Christians that Bible was in the form of the LXX. But by the side of the OT, Christians from the very first had another equally authoritative source of truth, the sayings of our Lord Himself. The "words of the Lord" and reminiscences of the "Jesus-event" circulated orally. But before many years had passed, written records of Jesus' teachings and saving ministry began to appear. The exact date of the composition of the Gospels is not known. Most scholars today believe that Mark was the earliest and John the latest of the 4 Gospels in our NT. In his writings the apostle Paul makes no reference to any written Gospel, and it is generally believed that most of his letters were produced earlier than the Gospels. Paul's letters constituted a new and distinctive type of religious literature.

The formation of the NT canon was a gradual process from the 2d to the 4th cent. The Gospels, Acts, and most of the epistles of Paul were accepted and used as authoritative early in the 2d cent. There are in existence today important papyrus codices, one containing the 4 Gospels and the book of Acts; another containing 11 epistles of Paul (including Heb) dating from the 1st half of the 3d cent.; a recently discovered manuscript containing 1 Pe, 2 Pe, and Jude from the 3d cent.; and one of John from c. 200. But the inclusion of certain books, such as Jas, 2 Pe, 2 and 3 Jn, Jude, Heb, and the Apocalypse, was disputed for many years. There were some other books that are outside the canon today which at one time were on the fringe of the NT, such as the Epistle of Barnabas, the Shepherd of Hermas, and the Didache. By the 4th cent. the matter was clearly and finally settled and our NT had its present form.

The written Gospels, at least the first 3, were known to the majority of the churches before the end of the 1st cent. This is evident from their use in the writings of the Apostolic Fathers (see Didache VIII. 2; Ignatius, Epistle to the

Philadelphians, 5, 8; Epistle of Mathetes to Diognetus, ch 11). The collection of the 4 Gospels was made early in the 2d cent., for probably in the 2d half of that century Tatian combined the 4 accounts into one continuous narrative known as the Diatessaron.

The collection of Paul's letters may have begun within his lifetime. He himself gave instructions regarding the sharing of at least one of his letters with other churches (Col 4:16), and warned of spurious letters circulating in his name (2 Th 2:2; cf. 3:17). The first certain evidence we have of the existence of a group of his letters is in 2 Pe 3:15, 16. This passage indicates that these letters were not only known among the churches but recognized as on a par with "the other scriptures." It has been suggested that the publication of the book of Acts (c. A.D. 61) promoted the collection and publication of these letters. And certainly Paul's martydom gave them an even greater appeal. For early evidence regarding the knowledge and use of Paul's letters see 1 Clement 47:1; Ignatius, Ephesians, ch 12; Polycarp, and Philippians, ch 3.

The appearance of heretics and heretical books in the church hastened the process of canonization. Marcion (c. A.D. 140) produced the 1st collection of books of the NT, which consisted of Luke (the "Gospel"), 10 epistles of Paul (the *Apostolikon*), plus Marcion's own heretical book (the *Antithesis*). His work forced the church to take a stand with reference to the books of the NT. Hence the idea of a definite NT canon arose at least as early as between the middle and the close of the 2d cent. A.D.

The earliest list of NT books is given in the Muratorian canon of c. 180 A.D. This list omits 4 of our present 27 books: Heb, Jas, 1 Pe, 2 Pe, and possibly also 3 Jn. By the end of the 2d cent. 7 books still lacked general recognition: Heb, Jas, 2 Pe, 2 and 3 Jn, Jude, and Rev. These books gradually made good their claim to inclusion in the canon by the 4th cent. During the persecution of Diocletian (A.D. 303), the burning of all the sacred writings of Christians was decreed. This forced Christians to consider which books they were willing to risk their lives for.

The 4th cent. was marked by authoritative pronouncements by bishops and councils regarding the limits of the canon. Athanasius, bishop of Alexandria, and the leading theologian of the Eastern church, included in his 39th Festal Letter addressed to his bishops a list of the books of the Bible, the first to contain the 27 books of the NT exactly as we have them. This is important, for his influence extended over all Greek-speaking churches in the East, among whom there were doubts concerning the canonicity of Revelation and several epistles. It was several centuries more before a revision of the Syriac Peshitta version included all the general epistles and Revelation. The Latin church soon followed the example of Athanasius. In A.D. 382 a Western council at Rome declared the acceptance of several epistles, including Hebrews, formerly doubted (Revelation was not doubted in the West). Then in North Africa the Council of Hippo (A.D. 393) and finally the 3d Council of Carthage (A.D. 397) ratified this canon and placed all other books outside and banned their use in the churches. By the end of the 4th cent. there was no longer any dispute over the right of any of the 27 books to a place in the canon.

The development of the canon was a gradual process, presided over by the Spirit of God. True, church councils passed upon the canon of Scripture, but the reasons for accepting the present canon lie deeper than the authority of these councils; they are based upon the conviction that the hand of God led in the formation of the canon. The early Christians accepted as reliable only those books written by an apostle or a companion of an apostle. They judged a work on the basis of content, its inner consistency, its harmony with the rest of Scripture, and its general harmony with Christian experience.

Any Christian who desires to convince himself regarding the NT canon can do so by carefully comparing the 27 books accepted by the church with any other early Christian literature of the first 3 centuries. He will without doubt conclude that there is no book in the canon which should be left out, and no book left out that should be included.

Canticles. *See* Song of Solomon.

Cap. [Heb. *migba'ah*.] Headdress worn by the priests (Ex 28:40; 29:9; 39:28; Lev 8: 13), called *bonnet in the KJV.

Capernaum (ka-pûr′na-ŭm). [Gr. *Kapharnaoum*, a transliteration of the Heb. *Kephar Nachûm*, "village of Nahum."] A town on the Sea of Galilee. The fact that it had a customhouse (Mt 9:9) and a Roman garrison suggests that it was probably a border town between the states

95. Ruins of the synagogue at Capernaum, which may be built on the same site as the one in which Jesus taught

of Philip and Herod Antipas. The captain of the garrison was particularly friendly toward the Jews, as indicated by the fact that he built a synagogue for them (Mt 8:5-13; Lk 7:1-10). Capernaum was the home town of Simon Peter and Andrew (Mk 1:29; Lk 4:38), and the place where Matthew (Levi) received his call to the apostleship (Mt 9:9-13; Mk 2:14-17; Lk 5:27-32). Jesus there performed many miracles (Mt 8:5-17; Mk 1:21-28; 2:1-13; Jn 4:46-54; etc.) and preached many sermons (cf. Jn 6:24-71; Mk 9:33-50). In fact it became known as His headquarters and was called His own city (Mt 9:1; cf. Mk 2:1). Yet His ministry made no great impression on the people. They refused to repent, therefore Jesus predicted the complete destruction of the city (Mt 11:23, 24; Lk 10:15).

The identification of the site is still disputed. A late tradition places it at *Khān Minyeh,* 6 mi. north of Tiberias, but the earlier tradition, which is now generally accepted, identifies the site as *Tell Ḥûm,* about 2½ mi. from the mouth of the Jordan on the northwestern shore of the Sea of Galilee (Map XVI, C-4). A Jewish synagogue has been excavated and partly reconstructed at *Tell Ḥûm.* It dates from *c.* A.D. 200, but it is not certain that it stands on the site of the one in which Christ preached (Mk 1:21).

Caph. [Heb. *kaph.*] The 11th letter of the Hebrew alphabet, written כ, appearing as the title to the 11th section of Ps 119 in the KJV. *See* Aleph.

Caphtor (kăf′tôr). [Heb. *Kaphtôr.*] The place from which the Caphtorim (Deut 2:23) and the Philistines originated (Jer 47:4; Amos 9:7). The LXX renders the Caphtor of Deut 2:23 and Amos 9:7 by Cappadocia; hence some scholars identify Caphtor with the southern coast of Asia Minor. Most commentators, however, believe Caphtor to be the island of Crete (Map III, C-2), and identify the name

96. View of central Crete (ancient Caphtor) near Phaestus

with *Kftyw,* the Egyptian name for Crete. The Ugaritic texts mention a country by the name of *Kptr* and the cuneiform records from Mari the gentilic name *Kaptaru,* but these texts provide no clue as to whether the country in question was a mainland site or an island.

Caphthorim. *See* Caphtorim.

Caphtorim (kăf'tŏ-rĭm), KJV once **Caphtorims** (kăf'tŏ-rĭmz), and once **Caphthorim** (kăf'thŏ-rĭm). [Heb. *Kaphtorîm.*] People from *Caphtor, most probably Cretans (Gen 10:14; Deut 2:23; 1 Chr 1:12).

Capital, I. [Heb. *kaphtôr, kothereth, ṣepheth,* and *ro'sh.*] The uppermost part of a pillar or column (1 Ki 7:16, RSV). The ornamentation, style, and shape of capitals varied in different buildings and periods, or times. The earliest stone capitals found in Palestine are those found at Megiddo dating from the time of Solomon. The Megiddo capitals are classified as proto-Ionic because they resemble an early type of capital found on the so-called Ionic columns. Instead of "capital" the KJV generally reads "chapiter" or "knop."

Capital, II. [Heb. *bîrah,* "citadel," "castle," "fortress."] The RSV translates *bîrah* as "capital" in the phrase "Susa the capital" (Neh 1:1; Est 1:2; etc.). The translation is somewhat interpretative. Although Susa was an important capital, *bîrah* is more appropriately rendered "citadel."

Cappadocia (kăp'á-dō'shĭ-á). [Gr. *Kappadokia.*] A mountainous area and Roman province in eastern Asia Minor. The area produced many horses, sheep, and mules. The Romans realized its military importance as a border area, and after the death of the semi-independent king Archelaus in A.D. 17, they annexed it and had it administered by a procurator. Jews from Cappadocia are mentioned as attending the feast of Pentecost in Jerusalem in the year of Christ's death (Acts 2:9), and the early existence of Christian churches in that province is attested by the salutation of Peter's first letter (1 Pe 1:1). Map XIX, D-13.

Captain. A term used in the KJV to designate various officials in the OT, the rendering of 13 Hebrew words and 1 Aramaic word, which are mostly translated by different terms in the RSV, for example: "leader" (Num 2:3), "friend" (Jer 13:21), "sentry" (ch 37:13), "marshal" (ch 51:27), "scribe" (Nah 3:17), "prince" (1 Sa 9:16), "commander" (1 Ki 20:24), "chief" (Jos 10:24), "head" (Deut 29:10), "officer" (Ex 14:7), and others. In harmony with the KJV the RSV uses "captain" as the rendering of the following terms: (1) the Heb. *ro'sh* in Num 14:4, (2) the Heb. *rab* in several texts (2 Ki 25:8; etc.), the Heb. *śar* in numerous texts (Gen 37:36; etc.), and the Aramaic *shallîṭ* (Dan 2:15). The term "captain" is chosen in these passages, apparently because these men were military officers. So far as can be determined, they were in charge of small detachments of soldiers, hence were in rank somewhat equivalent to modern military captains. For higher officers and commanders of armies the RSV prefers the term "commander."

In the NT the picture is similar. Here, however, the terms rendered "captain" in the KJV generally refer to military personnel. There are four such terms, one of which, *stratēgos,* is translated "captain" also in the RSV (Lk 22:4, 52; Acts 4:1; 5:24, 26). It designates a Jewish officer in charge of the Temple guard. The Gr. *chiliarchos,* literally "a ruler over a thousand," is consistently rendered "captain," "high captain," or "chief captain" in the KJV, but "captain" only twice in the RSV, once in Jn 18:12, where the officer in charge of the Temple guard is again referred to, and in Rev 19:18. In the other NT passages the RSV renders *chiliarchos* "officer," "tribune," and "general." The Gr. *archēgos* of Heb 2:10, referring to Christ, is translated "captain" in the KJV, but "pioneer" in the RSV. The Gr. *stratopedarchēs,* rendered "captain" in the KJV of Acts 28:16, occurs in a passage of questioned textual authority, and the term is consequently not translated at all in the RSV.

Captivity. A translation of various Hebrew terms with slightly varying shades of meaning, and designating (1) a state of restriction or confinement, whether literal or figurative; (2) removal to a foreign land. In the OT *shebî* and *shebûth* have a broader range of meaning, including that of exile in a foreign land, while *gôlah* and *galûth* are used exclusively in the latter sense (see RSV), especially with reference to the Assyrian captivity of the northern kingdom, Israel, and that of the southern kingdom, Judah, in Babylonia.

Assyrian captivity of the ten tribes.— Assyria was the first nation of antiquity to practice the wholesale deportation of conquered peoples, or at least of their leading men, to remote regions as a means of preventing revolt in conquered lands (see fig. 37). After a century of intermittent payment of tribute to Assyria, the northern kingdom of Israel crumbled and eventually fell under the successive and increasingly heavy blows of the Assyrian kings Tiglath-pileser III (745-727 B.C.), Shalmaneser V (727-722 B.C.), and Sargon II (722-705 B.C.). It was probably in his campaign of 733/32 that Tiglath-pileser occupied the greater part of Galilee and Gilead and deported the inhabitants of these regions to the east (2 Ki 16:5-9; 15:27-29). At the same time Tiglath-pileser, having possibly arranged for the assassination of the Israelite king, Pekah, set Hoshea (*c.* 732-722 B.C.) on the throne as a vassal king of Assyria, requiring of him a heavy tribute for the privilege. In desperation Hoshea entered into an alliance with Egypt against Assyria, with the result that Shalmaneser, who by that time had succeeded Tiglath-pileser, invaded Israel, laid siege to Samaria, and took the city after three years (ch 18:10), probably during the last year of his reign (723/22 B.C.). Some uncertainty remains as to whether the city of Samaria, capital of the northern kingdom, fell before or after the death of Shalmaneser. *See* Samaria; Sargon; Shalmaneser. A majority of the remaining inhabitants were deported to Mesopotamia and Media (ch 17:5, 6, 18), and colonists from other conquered areas were brought in to take their place. The result of this mixture of the remaining Israelites with these foreigners was the Samaritan race (vs 19-41). To what extent, and for how long, the exiles from the northern kingdom maintained their identity is not certainly known, though later Bible writers occasionally mention 12 tribes (see Ezr 6:17; 8:35; Acts 26:7).

Babylonian captivity of Judah.—Attempts by Sargon II (722-705 B.C.) and Sennacherib (705-681 B.C.) to subjugate Judah proved largely unsuccessful. The former conquered a small coastal area of Judah. On two invasions of Judah, the first in 701 and the second somewhat more than 10 years later, Sennacherib subdued the entire region except for the city of Jerusalem, which was spared by divine intervention (2 Ki 18:13 to 19:37). Greatly reduced in size, Judah remained independent for nearly another century, until the invasion of Nebuchadnezzar in 605 B.C. Recently victorious over the remnants of Assyrian power, Nebuchadnezzar captured Jerusalem in that year, raided the Temple of its treasures, and carried certain members of the royal family and of the nobility captive to Babylon (2 Chr 36:2-7; Dan 1:1-3). Nebuchadnezzar left Jehoiakim on the throne as a vassal king subject to Babylon, but when Jehoiakim rebelled Nebuchadnezzar again sent armed forces into Judah to raid and harass the land (2 Ki 24:1, 2), this time deporting 3,023 Jews to Babylon (Jer 52:28). Late in 598 B.C. the Chaldean army apparently re-entered Jerusalem and bound Jehoiakim for deportation to Babylon, along with additional treasures from the Temple. Jehoiakim died at Jerusalem not long after (2 Chr 36:6, 7; Jer 22:18, 19). He was succeeded on the throne by his son Jehoiachin, who reigned but three months before Nebuchadnezzar returned in person (597 B.C.) and took him to Babylon, along with 7,000 soldiers, all the skilled craftsmen, and the remaining Temple treasure (2 Ki 24:10-16). He left Zedekiah, an uncle of Jehoiachin, on the throne.

Though mildly inclined to follow the course of action prescribed by the prophet Jeremiah, Zedekiah permitted himself to be dominated by the shifting tide of popular opinion, and as a result proved to be a weak and vacillating ruler. This defect of character proved his undoing and made inevitable the utter desolation of Jerusalem. For a time Zedekiah remained in submission to Babylon, and in the 4th year of his reign journeyed to Babylon apparently to renew his pledge of loyalty (Jer 51:59). Some time later he seems to have negotiated an alliance with neighboring nations to throw off the Chaldean yoke (chs 27:1-3, 12-22; 28:1, 2). Anticipating a new invasion of Palestine by Nebuchadnezzar, Zedekiah arranged for the king of Egypt (Psamtik II) to come to his assistance (see ch 37:6-10). Eventually Babylonian forces returned, as expected, laid Jerusalem under siege (approximately Jan. 15, 588 B.C.), and entered it 30 months later (approximately July 19, 586 B.C.; see 2 Ki 25:1, 2; Jer 39:2). The city was systematically looted, its walls were leveled, and a month later it was burned to the ground (Jer 39:8). Zedekiah and most of his subjects were transported to Babylon, leaving only a few of the humblest classes in all of Judah (vs 9, 10). Over this remnant Nebuchadnezzar appointed Gedaliah as governor, but a fanatical royalist named Ishmael killed the governor, his staff, and the Chaldean garrison (ch 41:1-3). Fearful of reprisal, the remnant of Jews fled to Egypt, under the leadership of Johanan, and settled there (ch 43:5-7). Jerusalem and Judea lay desolate and unpopulated for about 50 years, until some 50,000 exiles returned under Zerubbabel. *See* Cyrus; Zerubbabel.

Caravan. A company of travelers, usually merchants, traveling for long distances through the desert, with donkeys or camels as beasts of burden. The word occurs in the RSV (Gen 37:25; Jgs 5:6; 8:11; Job 6:18, 19; Is 21:13) as a rendering of several Hebrew terms variously translated in the KJV as "company," "travelers," "troops," etc.

Carbuncle. [Heb. *'eben 'eqdach, bareqath, bareqeth*.] A precious stone of uncertain identification. "Carbuncle," a red precious stone, is a conjectural translation of the several Hebrew terms thus rendered. Some scholars believe the green beryl is meant. The Akkadian *baraktu*, believed to be related to the Hebrew, designates smaragd. "Carbuncle" is given as the third gem in the top row of the high priest's breastplate (Ex 28:17; 39:10) and as an adornment of Lucifer before his fall (Eze 28:13). The hope of the afflicted is figuratively given as a mansion which has its "gates of carbuncles" (Is 54:12).

Carcas. *See* Carkas.

Carchemish (kär'kĕ-mĭsh), KJV once **Charchemish** (kär'kĕ-mĭsh). [Heb. *Karkemish*.] A city on the Euphrates mentioned in secular records from the beginning of the 2d millennium B.C., as *Karkamis* in Babylonian cuneiform documents, as *Kargamish* and *Gargamish* in Assyrian inscriptions, and as *Krkmsh* in Egyptian records from Thutmose III on. The city came under Hittite influence, and after the fall of the Hittite Empire (*c.* 1200 B.C.) became the most important of the Hittite city-states, the Assyrians even regarding it as the Hittite capital. Carchemish paid tribute to Ashurnasirpal II (884-859 B.C.) and to Shalmaneser III (859-824 B.C.). See fig. 509. It was frequently at war with Assyria during the following century until Sargon II in 717 B.C. thoroughly destroyed

97. **General view of the excavation of the great palace staircase at Carchemish**

it and deported its population. It again played a role from the time Pharaoh-Necho occupied it after the fall and destruction of Nineveh in 612 B.C. (cf. 2 Chr 35:20), until Nebuchadnezzar decisively defeated him in 605 B.C. (Jer 46:2). At that time the city seems to have been destroyed once more. The site is marked by a mound called *Jerablus,* 63 mi. northeast of Aleppo (Map XI, B-4). Excavations were carried out there for the British Museum from 1876 to 1879 and from 1912 to 1914 with great success. These have brought to light many Hittite hieroglyphic inscriptions.

Lit.: D. G. Hogarth, C. L. Woolley, and T. E. Lawrence, *Carchemish,* 3 vols., London, 1914-1921 and 1952.

Careah. *See* Kareah.

Carites (kâr'īts). [Heb. *Kari*.] The RSV rendering of *kari* in 2 Ki 11:4, 19, which the KJV translates "captains." However, the meaning of *kari* is uncertain. It evidently described a body of guards, but whether a proper name was intended is uncertain. If they were Carians, they would have come from Caria (Map XI, B-2), a land in the southwestern part of Asia Minor.

Carkas (kär'kăs), KJV **Carcas** (kär'kăs). [Heb. *Karkas,* probably a Persian name, but not satisfactorily explained.] One of the 7 chamberlains of King Xerxes (Est 1:10).

Carmel (kär'mĕl). [Heb. *Karmel,* "garden" or "orchard."]

1. A 15-mi. range or ridge of mountains and hills (Map II, B-3) between the Mediterranean Sea (Jer 46:18) and the Plain of Esdraelon (cf. 1 Ki 18:42-46). Along its northern limits flows the river Kishon (v 40). The ridge anciently formed the southern boundary of Asher (Jos 19:26). The Carmel range lies between the plains of Acre and Esdraelon to the north and that of Sharon to the south. The highest summit is 1,742 ft. above sea level, but the promontory at the western end rises to

98. The seaward end of the ridge of Mount Carmel, and the city of Haifa

only 556 ft. Many caves in the slopes of the limestone formations have produced skeletons and other remains of very early settlers. The Carmel range is barren and dry during the summer, but covered with gorgeous flowers and a lush green plant growth in the winter, and is much praised by the Bible writers (Song 7:5; Amos 1:2). There are dwarf oaks, wild olive trees, and junipers on the slopes of Mount Carmel, and many cisterns and wine and oil presses show its ancient fertility. A barren and sterile Carmel was therefore the sign of the greatest want and destruction (Is 33:9; Amos 1:2; Nah 1:4).

The Egyptians called Carmel a sacred cape, and the Canaanites seem to have had an open-air sanctuary there, which Elijah chose for the demonstration of the impotence of Baal and of the power of Jehovah (1 Ki 18:17-46). Elisha seems to have lived on Mount Carmel for some time (2 Ki 4:23-25). In the 4th cent. B.C. the Greeks called Carmel the holy mount of Zeus, and a recently discovered base of a statue of the 2d or 3d cent. A.D. carries the inscription: "(Dedicated) to the Heliopolitan Zeus (of Mount) Carmel by G. Julius Eutychas, a colonist of Caesarea." It shows how tenaciously the cult of a pagan god clung to the mountain. The modern name of Carmel is *Jebel Karmel* or *Jebel Mâr Elyâs.* See figs. 98, 152, 281.

2. A town in the mountainous part of Judah (Jos 15:55; 1 Sa 15:12; 25:2). It was the home of Nabal (1 Sa 25:2, 40), the husband of Abigail prior to her marriage to David (chs 25:42; 30:5). It was also the home of Hezro, one of David's "mighty men" (2 Sa 23:35). The site is

CARRION VULTURE

now called *Kermel,* a place about 7 mi. south of Hebron (Map VI, F-3).

Carmelitess (kär'měl-īt'es). [Heb. *Karmelîth.*] A female inhabitant of Carmel (1 Chr 3:1). See Carmel, 2.

Carmi (kär'mī). [Heb. *Karmî,* "vinedresser."]
1. A son of Reuben, and founder of a tribal family called Carmites (kär'mīts; Gen 46:9; Ex 6:14; Num 26:6; 1 Chr 5:3).
2. A descendant of Judah and father of Achan (Jos 7:1; 1 Chr 2:7).
3. The Carmi of 1 Chr 4:1 is usually considered a scribal variant of Caleb. See Caleb, 1.

Carmites. See Carmi, 1.

Carnelian. See Sardius.

Carpenter. [Heb. *charash,* "artisan," the context showing that a worker in wood is meant; *charash 'eṣ,* "one who works in wood (or trees)"; Gr. *tektōn,* "carpenter," "woodworker," "builder."] Although carpentry is implied in earlier books of the Bible (cf. Ex 25:10; Deut 10:1; etc.), the first carpenters mentioned are those sent by Hiram of Tyre to work on a palace for David (2 Sa 5:11; 1 Chr 14:1). They are again mentioned in connection with King Jehoash's repairing of the Temple (2 Ki 12:4, 5, 11). Isaiah describes heathen carpenters making an idol (Is 44:13). Jesus is described as a carpenter's son (Mt 13:55) and as a carpenter (Mk 6:3). See Artisans.

Carpets. A term appearing twice in the RSV (Jgs 5:10; Eze 27:24) translating Hebrew terms of uncertain meaning. "Carpets," like the KJV "judgment" and "chests," is a conjectural translation, but acceptably suits the context.

Carpus (kär'pŭs). [Gr. *Karpos,* "fruit," a name occurring also in Greek inscriptions.] An unknown Christian, probably living in Troas, with whom Paul may have stayed when he was in that city (2 Ti 4:13). Christian legend made him one of the 70 disciples of Jesus.

Carriage. A word used in an obsolete sense in the KJV, to translate words describing the baggage of the army (Jgs 18:21; 1 Sa 17:22; Is 10:28; 46:1) or the luggage of a traveler (Acts 21:15). The RSV uses appropriate modern terms such as "goods" and "baggage" in these texts.

Carrion Vulture, KJV **Gier Eagle.** [Heb. *racham.*] A scavenging bird, probably the *Vultur percnopterus* or the *Neophron percnopterus.* The Hebrew name derived from *racham,* "to love," probably implies that the bird gave tender care to its young or that mated pairs remained together.

The vulture had a wide range and was common in Palestine. It is a creature of unclean and disgusting habits, and is listed among some 20 species of fowl not fit for human consumption (Lev 11:18, RSV simply "vulture"; Deut 14:17). G. R. Driver claims that the Heb. *racham* designates the osprey, a large hawk which lives by feeding on fish (*PEQ* 87 [1955], 16, 17, 20).

Carshena (kär'shĕ-nȧ). [Heb. *Karshena'*, probably a Persian name but not explained.] One of the high courtiers of King Xerxes (Est 1:14).

Cart. [Heb. *'agalah,* a loan word from Egyptian *'g3rt.*] In contrast to the chariot, which was used in war and for the transport of high dignitaries on occasions of state, the cart was a vehicle employed in peaceful occupations and for domestic purposes. It was made of wood (1 Sa 6:14), and in most cases had two wheels, as ancient pictures show. The cow-drawn cart used by the Philistines for the transporting of the ark (vs 7-14) was probably like the Philistine carts depicted on the walls of Ramses III's temple at Medinet Habu. They appear as rude ox-drawn vehicles, consisting of a wooden box fastened to an axle, with two wheels of solid wood. A cart carrying captive Hebrew women is depicted on an Assyrian stone relief illustrating the conquest of Lachish by Sennacherib. This cart has two wheels of 8 spokes each and is drawn by oxen. The cart on which David transported the ark to Jerusalem (2 Sa 6:3; 1 Chr 13:7) was probably like the one on the Lachish relief. Is 28:28 has been understood as indicating that in Judah carts were sometimes drawn by horses and used for threshing in place of the customary threshing sledges. Their use for the hauling of grain is mentioned in Amos 2:13. *See* Wagon.

Carving. The work of impressing, or shaping by means of cutting, in a decorative or artistic manner. In preparation for the building of the tabernacle God gave Bezalel, a Judahite, special skill for carving wood, as well as for other fine work (Ex 31:1-5). The cedar work within the Most Holy Place of the Temple built by Solomon was carved to represent gourds (KJV "knops") and open flowers (1 Ki 6:16, 18). The walls of the Temple had carvings of cherubim, palm trees, and open flowers, as did also the doors of the inner sanctuary (vs 29, 31, 32). The Heb. *chatubôth,* translated "carved works" in Prov 7:16, KJV, refers rather to materials of many colors.

Casement. A term appearing in the KJV of Prov 7:6 translating the Heb. *'eshnab,* meaning "window" or "air hole." Windows of ancient Oriental houses were often covered with a latticework or trelliswork of wood, hence the RSV "lattice."

Casiphia (kȧ-sĭf'ĭ-ȧ). [Heb. *Kasiphya'.*] A place in Babylonia where Levites and Nethinim lived during the Exile (Ezr 8: 15-20); not identified.

Casluhim (kăs'lū-hĭm). [Heb. *Kasluchim.*] A people descended from Mizraim, the ancestor of the Egyptians (Gen 10:14; 1 Chr 1:12; KJV); not identified. Some locate them conjecturally west of Egypt (Map IV, C-3/4).

Cassia. [Heb. *qiddah, qesi'ah.*] Probably *Cinnamomum cassia,* native to India and Ceylon, an aromatic bark, somewhat similar to cinnamon but of not so fine a quality. G. R. Driver believes that *qiddah* is cassia in strips and that *qesi'ah* is powdered cassia (*WO* 2 [1956], 261, 262). Cassia is listed as an ingredient of the holy anointing oil for the priests (Ex 30: 24) and as a perfuming agent (Ps 45:8). It was one of the imports of Tyre (Eze 27:19).

Castanets. In 2 Sa 6:5, RSV, the translation of the Heb. *mena'ane'im,* rendered "cor-

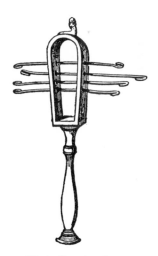

99. An Egyptian sistrum

nets" in the KJV. The Hebrew term designates a sistrum, a rattling instrument used in Egyptian and Mesopotamian temple services (fig. 99). It consisted of a thin oval-shaped metal frame with a handle, and with several metal rods that passed through the frame. The rods were smaller than the holes, and would rattle when the instrument was shaken. The handle of a sistrum was found in the excavations of Bethel.

Castaway. The rendering in 1 Cor 9:27, KJV, of the Gr. *adokimos*, meaning "rejected after testing," "unapproved." The RSV renders the term "disqualified." Paul stated that he disciplined himself strictly, lest, having held God's standard before others, he himself should be unapproved by God.

Castle. A fortified building or group of buildings serving as a residence for a king or prince. However, not all Hebrew and Greek words rendered "castle" in the KJV have this meaning. The RSV uses the term only in Prov 18:19 as the translation of *'armôn*, and in Neh 7:2 as the translation of *bîrah*. The structure built by Nehemiah was probably the forerunner of the later "Castle" of Antonia, built by Herod the Great north of the Temple. The same structure is referred to in Acts (chs 21:34, 37; 22:24; 23:10, 16, 32) by the Gr. *parembolē*, translated "castle" in the KJV, but *"barracks" in the RSV. The other Hebrew terms rendered "castle" in the KJV are variously translated in the RSV as: "encampments" (Gen 25:16; Num 31:10), "settlements" (1 Chr 6:54), "towers" (ch 27:25), "fortresses" (2 Chr 17:12), "forts" (ch 27:4), and "stronghold" (1 Chr 11:5, 7). In the last-mentioned reference the "stronghold" of the Jebusites which David conquered and then used as his own residence could be appropriately termed "castle."

Castor and Pollux. *See* Twin Brothers.

Caterpillar. *See* Locust, 6, 10.

Cattle. As used in the Bible this term describes domesticated animals of several kinds, including horses, camels, sheep, goats, oxen, and asses (Gen 47:16, 17; 1 Chr 5:21). Anciently, a man's cattle frequently indicated his wealth, so much so that the Heb. *miqneh,* literally "possession," is generally translated "cattle" (Gen 4:20; Ex 9:4; Jer 49:32; etc.). Israel's cattle herds furnished the animals for sacrifice in the typical system (Deut 12:6).

Cauda (kô′dȧ), KJV **Clauda** (klô′dȧ). [Gr. *Kauda* and *Klauda;* textual evidence is divided between these two readings.] A small barren island south of Crete without a safe harbor. Paul's ship ran under its lee when it was caught by the storm after leaving Crete (Acts 27:16). The present

population of the island, which is now called Gaudos, is rather small. Map XX, C-3.

Caul. In the KJV the translation of (1) the Heb. *yothereth* (Ex 29:13), "what is left over," here applied to the liver, hence an unidentified appendage to the liver; (2) the Heb. *segôr* (Hos 13:8), "an enclosure," here describing the enclosure of the heart; (3) the Heb. *shabîs* (Is 3:18), probably a headband or hair net worn by Israelite women.

Cave. Mountainous Palestine is a land of many natural caves. These hollowed-out chambers in the earth served as dwelling places in very early times, and in later periods as places of temporary abode (Gen 19:30), or of refuge from invaders or pursuers (Jgs 6:2; 1 Sa 13:6; 22:1; etc.). During all the periods of Palestine's history caves have been used as tombs. The most famous of these is that at Machpelah, which became the family tomb of Abraham (Gen 23; 49:29). Lazarus was buried in a cave (Jn 11:38). Recent discoveries in the Dead Sea area show that many members of a religious order (probably the Essenes) lived in caves in the time of Christ. When the war drove them away from Qumran, their community center, they hid their literary possessions in concealed caves.

100. One of the caves at Qumran where the Dead Sea scrolls were found. The floor level of Cave IV is indicated by the two large openings at the bottom, cut by archeologists after entrance had been made from the small holes above, near the top of the ridge

Cedar. [Heb. *'erez*.] Generally the cedar of Lebanon (*Cedrus libani*). This tree was once widely distributed in the mountains

101. Cedars of Lebanon

of Lebanon, but it now has a limited range. It grows to a height of 80 ft. and assumes a pyramidal shape in early years, later flattening out at the top. Its branches become thick and gnarled. In Bible times the cedar of Lebanon was used in the construction of temples and other buildings (2 Sa 5:11; 1 Ki 5:5, 6; 7:1-12; Ezr 3:7), and served as a symbol of growth, strength, and steadfastness (Ps 92:12; etc.). From it idols (Is 44:14, 15) and masts (Eze 27:5) were made. However, in certain references it is believed that *'erez* refers, not to cedar, but to the fir tree, or, more generally, to any tree from which lumber for building purposes or masts can be obtained. In Egyptian there is a similar use of the word *'sh*, primarily representing "cedar," but also designating any other wood useful for building lumber.

Cedron. *See* Kidron.

Cellar. The translation of the Heb. *'ôṣar* in 1 Chr 27:27, 28, where the meaning seems to be simply "supply." The "cellar" of Lk 11:33, RSV (KJV "secret"), is the translation of the Gr. *kruptē,* "a dark and hidden place," "a cellar."

Cenchreae (sĕn'krĕ-à). [Gr. *Kegchreai,* "millet."] The eastern port of Corinth on the Saronic Gulf, about 7 mi. from the city. It was a town of some size and possessed several temples and baths. Paul embarked at Cenchreae for his voyage to Jerusalem in his 2d Missionary Journey (Acts 18: 18). The book of Romans, written most probably in the winter of A.D. 57-58, mentions a Christian church in the city. It describes Phoebe as the deaconess of "the church which is at Cenchrea" (Rom 16:1). This church was probably founded during Paul's missionary activity at Corinth during his 2d Missionary Journey about A.D. 51-52. Map XX, B-3.

Censer. [Heb. *machtah* and *miqtereth;* Gr. *libanōtos.*] A vessel for the burning of incense. Censers having the form of a hollow hand have been excavated. The censers used in the tabernacle (Lev 16:12; Num 4:14) were of *bronze (Ex 27:3; 38: 29, 30), whereas those of the Temple were of gold (1 Ki 7:50). The Gr. *thumiatērion* of Heb 9:4, rendered "censer" in the KJV, is translated "altar of incense" in the RSV, which is in agreement with the use of this Greek term by Philo and Josephus.

183

Census. A term appearing in the RSV, frequently in the phrase "take a census," instead of which the KJV reads "take the sum" (Num 1:2; etc.). Among the ancient Hebrews only able-bodied males 20 years of age or older were counted, and the registration was made by tribe, family, and house (vs 1-3, 18). The first informal census was taken during the encampment at Mount Sinai, when a tax of half a shekel of silver was levied on each adult male for the construction of the sanctuary. There were 603,550 who paid this tax (Ex 38:25-27), exclusive of 22,000 Levites who were not subject to it (Num 3:39). Some months later a formal census to determine the number of males eligible for military service resulted in the same figure—603,550 (chs 1:1-3, 45-47; 11:21). At the close of the wilderness wanderings some 38 years later a second census revealed a slight decrease in the adult male population, the figure now being 601,730 (ch 26:1-3, 51) and 23,000 Levites (vs 62, 63). A census conducted by David toward the close of his reign counted approximately 1,300,000 adult males available for military service (2 Sa 24:1-9; cf. 1 Chr 21:1-6) and 38,000 Levites (1 Chr 23:1-3). A census of those who returned from Babylon with Zerubbabel at the close of the Captivity tallied 42,360, including priests and Levites (Ezr 2:1, 2, 64).

The "decree from Caesar Augustus, that all the world should be taxed" (Lk 2:1) was, in fact, an order for the taking of a census, as the Greek word *apographō,* "taxed" (literally, "recorded," "registered," "enrolled") shows. The tax levy was based on the census, and normally followed it. About 10 years after the census of Lk 2:1, 2, another Roman enrollment resulted in a revolt led by Judas of Galilee (Acts 5:37).

Centurion. [Gr. *kenturiōn,* a transliteration of the Latin *centurio,* and *hekatontarchēs,* "ruler over a hundred."] The commander of a "century," that is, a hundred men, which formed the 60th part of a Roman legion. He was probably comparable to one of the top-grade noncommissioned officers in our modern military organization.

The NT mentions two centurions by name, Cornelius, one of the first Gentiles baptized by the apostles (Acts 10), and Julius, who conducted Paul from Caesarea to Rome (ch 27:1, 3, 43). Two others are mentioned favorably, the centurion in Capernaum whose servant Jesus healed (Mt 8:5-13), and the one at the cross who declared Jesus to be the "Son of God" (Mt 27:54).

Cephas (sē'făs). [Gr. *Kēphas,* a transliteration of the Aramaic *Kêpha',* "rock" or "stone."] A surname given by Jesus to the apostle Simon, son of Jonas (Jn 1:42; 21:15; 1 Cor 1:12; 3:22; 9:5; 15:5). Peter, a transliteration of the Gr. *Petros,* the equivalent of *Kêpha',* is the better-known form.

Cereal. A term occurring frequently in the RSV, always in the phrase "cereal offering (s)." The phrase is the translation of the Heb. *minchah,* which describes, among other things, the offerings of grain in the form of fine flour, wafers, cakes, crushed and parched new grain, etc. (Lev 2:1, 3, 4, 7, 14-16).

Ceremonial Law. *See* Law.

Chaff. The refuse of grains after they have been threshed. The wicked are likened to chaff blown away by a storm (Job 21:18; Ps 1:4; Is 17:13; etc.). Isaiah describes the day when Israel would thresh the mountains and make the hills like chaff, representing their victory over wicked powers (Is 41:14-16). John the Baptist compared the final destruction of the wicked to chaff being burned (Mt 3:12; Lk 3:17).

Chain. The rendering of various Hebrew, Aramaic, and Greek words. Chains were

102. Golden chains and pectorals from the tomb of Tutankhamen

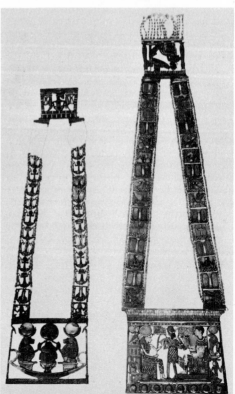

worn, either as ornaments or as symbols of honor and dignity, or were used to restrain prisoners. Examples of men who had chains placed around their necks upon their elevation to high office are Joseph (Gen 41:42) and Daniel (Dan 5:7, 29). Egyptian reliefs and pictures illustrate the granting of such symbols of dignity to high officers of state, and the symbols themselves have been discovered in tombs of kings and noblemen. They usually consist of beads artistically strung together with a golden filigreed pendant hanging at the breast, on which appears the name of the reigning monarch (see fig. 102).

Bronze or iron chains were used to restrain or hold prisoners (Jer 40:1; Nah 3:10; etc.). In NT times it was customary to chain notorious or important prisoners to the soldiers who guarded them, and this custom was most probably followed in the case of Peter and Paul during their imprisonments (Acts 12:7; 21:33; 28:16, 20; 2 Ti 1:16).

Chalcedony. [Gr. *chalkēdōn.*] A gem, named for its source, a town in Asia Minor, but since several gems were mined there it is impossible to identify with certainty the stone named by John as the 3d foundation of the New Jerusalem (Rev 21:19). The RSV rendering is "agate." Stones designated as chalcedony today were apparently anciently known by different names.

Chalcol. *See* Calcol.

Chaldaeans. *See* Chaldeans.

Chaldea (kăl-dē'à). [Heb. *Kaśdîm.*] Originally the area in southern Mesopotamia between the Tigris and the Euphrates where Chaldean tribes (*see* Chaldeans) settled in the late 2d millennium B.C. or the early 1st millennium. After the Chaldeans took over Babylonia and founded the Neo-Babylonian Empire, the name Chaldea was applied to the whole land of Babylonia and is thus used in the OT (Jer 50:10; 51:24; Eze 11:24; etc.). Map XI, C-6.

Chaldeans (kăl-dē'ăns), KJV of OT sometimes **Chaldees** (kăl-dēz'), KJV of NT **Chaldaeans** (kăl-dē'ăns). [Heb. *Kaśdîm;* Aramaic *Kaśda'în;* Gr. *Chaldaioi.* These terms are transliterations of the Akkadian *Kaldu.*]

1. A tribe of Lower Mesopotamia closely related to the Aramaeans. They appear for the first time in Assyrian records of the time of Ashurnasirpal II (884-859 B.C.), which show that they were founders of the tribe known as *Bit-Yakin,* which settled on the western side of the Tigris River at the head of the Persian Gulf, and which constantly threatened Babylon. Chaldeans succeeded several times in gaining control of Babylonia before the founding of the Chaldean Empire. For example, Ukinzer made himself king of Babylon (732/31-729 B.C.), and Marduk-apaliddina, the Merodach-baladan of the Bible, accomplished this feat twice (721-710/09 and 703-702 B.C.). Nabopolassar (626-605 B.C.), the founder of the Neo-Babylonian Empire, was a Chaldean. It is to this Chaldean or Neo-Babylonian Empire that the Bible refers when speaking of the Chaldean nation (Jer 21:4; Eze 1:3; etc.). On "Ur of the Chaldeans" *see* Ur, 1.

2. A designation for scholars, sorcerers, astrologers, and magicians (Dan 2:2, 4, 5; etc.). Since in the Neo-Babylonian Empire the Chaldeans occupied all high offices, including the priesthood, the ethnic name seems to have become a designation for the priestly work and office, which included the arts of divination, etc. The term Chaldeans in this sense is found not only in Daniel but also in the works of Herodotus, Strabo, and Diodorus Siculus, and in Palmyrene inscriptions.

Chaldees. *See* Chaldeans.

Chalkstone. [Heb. *'eben-gir.*] Limestone, common in Palestine. God's people were to crush the stones of the heathenish altars as if they were of chalk (Is 27:9).

Chamberlain. [Heb. *sarîs,* "court official," "eunuch"; Gr. *koitōn* and *oikonomos,* the latter being translated "chamberlain" only in the KJV of Rom 16:23.] Anciently a court official and generally, if not always, a eunuch. Oriental courts employed eunuchs not only for the harem of a king but also as officers in high positions of trust in the royal household and government (*see* Eunuch). Several such officials are mentioned in the Bible: (1) Nathan-melech (2 Ki 23:11). (2) Officials in the Persian court of Ahasuerus, eunuchs, as the Heb. *sarîs* indicates. A number are mentioned by name (Est 1:10, 12, 15; 2:3, 14, 15, 21; 4:4, 5; 6:2, 14; 7:9). (3) Erastus (Rom 16:23, KJV). The word here translated "chamberlain" is *oikonomos,* "steward," "manager." He was probably an *aedile,* or an *aedilis,* commissioner of streets and public buildings, as an inscription found at Corinth indicates (*see* Erastus). (4) Blastus, an official under Herod Agrippa I (Acts 12:20).

Chameleon. [Heb. *koach* and *tinshemeth.* The former term is the one translated "chameleon" in the KJV (Lev 11:30) and the latter the one thus translated in the RSV (Lev 11:30). *Koach* is properly a "lizard," and *tinshemeth,* translated "mole" in the KJV, is another species of lizard, the chameleon.] A small insect-feeding lizard that is able to change the color of its skin according to moods or to the color of the object on which it is sitting.

Chamois. *See* Mountain-sheep.

Champaign. The translation in the KJV of Deut 11:30 of the Heb. *'arabah,* elsewhere translated "desert," "plain," "wilderness." *See* Arabah.

Chanaan. *See* Canaan.

Changer. *See* Money-changer.

Chant. [Heb. *qîn,* "to chant," "to utter a lament."] The RSV rendering in Eze 32:16 of a word uniformly translated "lament" in the KJV, and elsewhere in the RSV. By an Oriental literary figure Ezekiel depicts the desolation of Egypt at the hands of the Chaldeans (v 11).

Chapel. [Heb. *miqdash,* "sacred place," "sanctuary."] A word occurring once (Amos 7:13, KJV), the rendering of a term elsewhere almost always translated "sanctuary." Here, reference is to the national shrine, probably a temple, erected by Jeroboam at Bethel for the worship of the golden calf he set up there.

Chapiter. *See* Capital, I.

Chapman. An archaic English word meaning "merchant" or "trader." It occurs in the KJV of 2 Chr 9:14 as a translation of the Heb. *'enôsh tar.* In 1 Ki 10:15 the plural of the same Hebrew term is translated "merchantmen" in the KJV and "traders" in the RSV, translations supported by the ancient versions.

Chapt. A variable form of "chapped." The word occurs in the KJV of Jer 14:4. However, the Hebrew word (*chathath*) thus translated does not mean "chapt" but "downcast" or "dismayed." In a poetic sense the prophet is ascribing human emotion to the parched fields.

Charashim. *See* Ge-harashim.

Charchemish. *See* Carchemish.

Charger. In the KJV the translation of (1) the Heb. *qe'arah* (Num 7:13, 19; etc.), "plate"; in the context the silver vessels, perhaps platters (RSV "plates"), given by several Israelite princes to the tabernacle at its dedication; (2) the Heb. *'agarṭal* (Ezr 1:9), a vessel of unknown purpose and form (Koehler, *Suppl. ad LVTL,* 134; J. L. Kelso, *BASOR Suppl.,* 5-6 [1948],

33); in the context certain vessels that Nebuchadnezzar had taken to Babylon as war booty but which Cyrus returned; (3) the Gr. *pinax* (Mt 14:8; Mk 6:25; etc.), "a platter"; "a dish," in the context platter on which the head of John the Baptist was presented to Salome.

"Chargers," in the sense of "war horses," appears in the RSV of Nah 2:3, where the KJV reads "fir trees." The Heb. *berôshim* means "Phoenician junipers." However, a change in one letter gives the reading "riding horses," "chargers," which reading is supported by the LXX.

Chariot. A war vehicle which, along with the horse, the Hyksos introduced into Canaan and Egypt. It was a light, 2-wheeled vehicle drawn by 2 horses. In early times the wheels had 4 spokes, later 6, and finally 8. The chariot box was placed on the axle and was made of light material, sometimes covered with metal (cf. Jos 17:16, 18). See fig. 103, also figs. 53, 274, 301. The pictures of Egyptian chariots always show 2 riders, a driver and a warrior, but the Assyrians and Hittites frequently had on the chariot a third man, who carried a shield. The Hebrew chariots also seem to have had 3 riders, as the Heb. *shalîsh,* literally, "the third one (on the chariot)," in 2 Ki 9:25; etc., probably indicates. The first mention of chariots in the OT is in the narrative of Joseph (Gen 41:43). Since Joseph was most probably in Egypt during the Hyksos period, reference to chariots would be completely in harmony with the historical facts. When the Israelites came into Canaan, they found the Canaanites in possession of chariots (Jos 17:16, 18; Jgs 1:19; 4:3). It was not until the time of Solomon that the chariot became part of the standard military equipment of the Hebrews (1 Ki 1:5; 10:26, 29). It became so popular that a century after Solomon, Ahab had more chariots than any of his confederates who took part in the battle of Qarqar against Shalmaneser III. In fact, his 2,000 chariots were more than the total of those supplied by the other kings (*ANET* 278, 279). Besides those of the Israelites, the Bible mentions the chariots of the Egyptians (Is 31:1), Ethiopians (2 Chr 16:8), Syrians (2 Ki 5:9), Hittites (ch 7:6), and Assyrians (Nah 2:3, 4; 3:2). The word translated "chariots" in Rev 18:13 (Gr. *rhedai,* of Gallic or Celtic origin, introduced into the Greek by means of the Latin) describes 4-wheeled vehicles, and should probably be translated "wagons" or "coaches," unless the

103. Chariot of King Tutankhamen in the Cairo Museum

writer had the ancient Babylonian chariots in mind.

Charity. [Gr. *agapē*, "love" in its highest and truest form.] A word appearing repeatedly in the KJV (1 Cor 13, and elsewhere), used in its now obsolete sense of " (selfless) love."

Charran. *See* Haran, II, 2.

Chebar (kē'bär). [Heb. *Kebar*.] A "river" in Babylonia, beside which the prophet Ezekiel had several of his visions (Eze 1:1, 3; 3:15, 23; 10:15, 20, 22; 43:3). Cuneiform tablets found at Nippur from the time of Artaxerxes I mention this river by the name *nâr Kabari*, meaning "great river." It was actually a canal that branched off from the Euphrates near Babylon and rejoined the main river near Uruk, the Biblical Erech, the modern *Warka*. It flowed past Nippur (Map XI, C-6) near which Ezekiel may have lived.

Checker Work. A term used in 1 Ki 7:17 to describe the ornamental embellishment of the capitals of the two bronze pillars that stood on either side of the doorway to Solomon's Temple. This "checker work," or latticework, around each of the capitals probably had the appearance of bronze slats interwoven so as to form a grating. "Checker work" appears in the RSV of Ex 28:4 (KJV "broidered"), where, however, the meaning of the Hebrew word (*tashbeṣ*) is uncertain, and in v 39, where the idea seems to come from the LXX.

Chedorlaomer (kĕd'ŏr-lā-ō'mẽr). [Heb. *Kedorla'omer*.] A king of Elam, the leader (Gen 14:1, 4, 5, 9, 17) of a confederation of Mesopotamian and northern Syrian kings, who invaded Transjordan and subjugated it. After 12 years the subject petty kings of southern Transjordan rebelled against

their overlords, whereupon the 4 kings from the north attacked their rebellious vassals, destroyed their cities, and returned laden with spoil toward their home countries. In the area of Damascus Abraham and his servants overtook them and in a surprise raid defeated the four kings, freed their captives, and recovered the spoil (Gen 14:1-16).

The name "Chedorlaomer" is good Elamite and means "servant of (the goddess) Laqamar." Several names of Elamite kings of Susa and their governors are known with *kuter* or *kudur*, "servant," as the first element; for example: *Kudur-Naḥḥunte, Kudur-Mabug,* and *Kudur-Ellil.* Furthermore, the Elamite goddess Laqamar or Lagamar is repeatedly mentioned, as is a temple built in her honor. One text mentions *Laqamar* and *Naḥḥunte* side by side (F. M. Th. de Liagre Böhl, *Opera Minora* [Leiden, 1953], p. 478, n. 39). But although the two parts of Chedorlaomer's name are well attested as Elamite words, no Elamite king by the name *Kudur-Lagamar* has so far been found in secular sources. W. F. Albright argues for a phonetic identification of Chedorlaomer with *Kudur-Naḥḥunte* (*BASOR* 88 [1942], 34).

Cheese. The translation of several Hebrew words denoting the curd of milk removed from the whey and pressed or molded into form (1 Sa 17:18; 2 Sa 17:29; Job 10:10).

Chelal (kē'lăl). [Heb. *Kelal*, "perfection."] An Israelite of the family of Pahath-moab. He was among those who had married foreign wives in the time of Ezra (Ezr 10:30).

Chelluh. *See* Cheluhi.

Chelub (kē'lŭb). [Heb. *Kelûb*, "basket."]
1. A Judahite (1 Chr 4:11).
2. An Israelite whose son Ezri was an officer of David in charge of the farmers (1 Chr 27:26).

Chelubai. *See* Caleb, 1.

Cheluhi (kē-lōō'hī), KJV **Chelluh** (kĕl'ū). [Heb. *Kelûhi.*] An Israelite of the family of Bani. He was among those who had married foreign wives in the time of Ezra (Ezr 10:35).

Chemarims (kĕm'á-rĭmz). [Heb. *kemarîm,* "priests," but used only for idolatrous priests. The word occurs in ancient Phoenician, Palmyrene, and Nabataean texts and in the *Amarna Letters in the form *kamiru,* and the Jews in Elephantine used the word when speaking of the Egyptian priest of Khnum.] A term occurring in the KJV of Zep 1:4 describing the priests of Baal. However, the Hebrew term should not be rendered as a proper name, but should be translated "priests," or "idolatrous priests," as elsewhere (2 Ki 23:5; Hos 10:5).

Chemosh (kē'mŏsh). [Heb. *Kemôsh;* on the *Moabite Stone *Kmsh.* In cuneiform inscriptions "Chemosh" appears as *Kamûshu.* Examples of ancient theophorous personal names formed from it are *Kmsh-ṣdq, Kmsh-plṭ,* and *Kmsh-ychy* appearing on seals and inscriptions, and *Kammusunadbi* (*ANET* 287) and *Kamashaltu* (*ANET* 298), names of Moabite kings, appearing on cuneiform tablets.] The chief god worshiped by the Moabites (1 Ki 11:7, 33; 2 Ki 23:13; Jer 48:7, 13), who are therefore called the people of Chemosh (Num 21:29; Jer 48:46). His name is mentioned 11 times in the inscription of King Mesha on the *Moabite Stone, and once in combination with that of his consort as Ashtar-Chemosh. This inscription attributes all victories of the Moabites to Chemosh's help, and all defeats to Chemosh's anger. Occasionally human sacrifices were offered to him (2 Ki 3:27). From Solomon's to Josiah's time he was worshiped in Judah (1 Ki 11:7; 2 Ki 23:13). The mention of Chemosh in Jephthah's message (Jgs 11:24) implies that either the Ammonites also worshiped Chemosh or the Moabites had taken part in the illegitimate demands on Israelite territory.

Chenaanah (kē-nā'á-nä). [Heb. *Kena'anah,* meaning uncertain.]

1. A descendant of Benjamin, and head of a tribal family (1 Chr 7:10).

2. Father of the false Samaritan prophet Zedekiah, who lived in the days of Ahab (1 Ki 22:11; 2 Chr 18:10).

Chenani (kē-nā'nī). [Heb. *Kenani,* a shortened form of *Kenanyah,* "Chenaniah," "Yahweh has established."] One of the Levites who led the returned exiles in worship before the people entered into a covenant to serve the Lord (Neh 9:4).

Chenaniah (kĕn'á-nī'á). [Heb. *Kenanyah* and *Kenanyahû,* "Yahweh has established."] A chief of the Levites in David's time. He led the musicians who accompanied David in transporting the ark to Jerusalem (1 Chr 15:22, 27), and also held a judicial office (ch 26:29).

Chephar-ammoni (kē'fär-ăm'ŏ-nī), KJV **Chephar-haammonai** (kē'fär-há-ăm'ŏ-nī). [Heb. *Kephar Ha'ammoni,* "village of the Ammonite."] A place in the territory of Benjamin (Jos 18:24); not identified.

Chephar-haammonai. *See* Chephar-ammoni.

Chephirah (kĕ-fī'rä). [Heb. *Kephîrah,* "village."] One of the cities of the Gibeonites with whom Joshua made the league; assigned to Benjamin (Jos 9:17; 18:26), and reoccupied after the Exile (Ezr 2:25; Neh 7:29). It is identified with *Tell Kefîreh,* 8½ mi. northwest of Jerusalem.

Cheran (kē'răn). [Heb. *Keran.*] A Horite (Gen 36:26; 1 Chr 1:41).

Cherethims. *See* Cherethites.

Cherethites (kĕr'ĕ-thīts), KJV once **Cherethims** (kĕr'ĕ-thĭmz). [Heb. *Kerethî.*] A people closely connected with the Philistines and living in the southern portion of the Philistine coastal area of Palestine (1 Sa 30:14; Eze 25:16; Zep 2:5). Some of them were members of David's bodyguard (2 Sa 8:18; 20:23; cf. chs 23:23; 15:18). They were probably Cretans who had come either with the Philistines at the time of the invasion of the Peoples of the Sea in the 13th cent. B.C., or directly from Crete at a later time, and then found living space among the Philistines, who also had formerly been inhabitants of Crete. Map VIII, F-1. *See* Caphtor.

Cherith (kē'rĭth). [Heb. *Kerîth,* "cut" or "gorge."] A brook in the Jordan Valley where Elijah hid from King Ahab (1 Ki 17:3, 5), probably on the east side of the Jordan, but not identified. N. Glueck believes it to be "one of the easternmost branches of the *Wâdī el-Yâbis* in the highlands of North Gilead" (*AASOR* 25-28 [1951], 219).

Cherub, plural **Cherubim;** KJV, plural **Cherubims.** [Heb. *kerûb, kerûbîm,* and *kerubîm;* Gr. *cheroub.* No Hebrew root word is known from which the term is derived, but there is a possible connection with the Akkadian *karâbu,* "to bless" and "to pray," from which root the terms *karibi* and *karibâti* (see below) were derived.]

1. A class of angels.

Occurrence in the Bible: (1) Cherubim were placed to guard the way to the tree of life to prevent men, expelled from the Garden of Eden, from eating of the fruit of the tree (Gen 3:24). (2) A pair of cherubim made of hammered gold were placed on the ark in the tabernacle. They faced each other and overshadowed the ark (Ex 25:18-20, 22; 37:8, 9), and from between them God is represented as revealing His will (Num 7:89). In Solomon's Temple the two cherubim, made of olivewood and overlaid with gold, were larger, but in appear-

104. A cherub on an altar from Sidon, 5th cent. B.C.

11:22). They had feet resembling those of calves, wings, and human hands, and four different faces each, namely of a cherub ("ox," Eze 1:10), of a human being, of a lion, and of an eagle. The four beings of Rev 4:6-8 probably have some connection with Ezekiel's cherubim. (6) The cherubim are not mentioned in the NT except in Heb 9:5, where the ancient sanctuary, its apartments, and its furniture are discussed.

Oriental parallels. In almost all countries of the ancient Orient, superhuman beings which in form and function resemble those of the Biblical cherubim are depicted or described. (1) Assyria knows the *kāribu* or *karubu* (plural *karibi*), male intercessors, and *kāribatu* (plural *karibāti*), female intercessors, among the gods, although these intercessors were not considered to be gods. In sculpture they appear as huge winged human-headed bulls or lions guarding the gates of palaces, temples, and cities. Some have compared them in name and function with the Biblical cherubim at the gate of the Garden of Eden. See fig. 105. (2) Egyptian representations parallel more closely the cherubim overshadowing the ark. In the tomb of King Seti I, two winged human-shaped beings are represented, who look at each other and spread their wings in such a way as to protect the god or king between them. Similar representations are found carved on temple walls and on shrines. A pair of these beings is also depicted on the two sides of a Phoenician altar found at Sidon, now in the Museum at Istanbul. See fig. 104. (3) Most representations of winged beings appearing on objects found in Palestine or Phoenicia are sphinxlike in appearance, such as those on the ivories from Ahab's palace at Samaria (see fig. 247), the sphinx throne on an ivory from Megiddo, and the sphinx throne of King Ahiram of Byblos carved on his sarcophagus (see fig. 383). (4) In the stone sculptures found in the ruins of the Hittite city-states of northern Syria appear representations of mixed beings with several heads and wings, more like the cherubim of Ezekiel than are those of Mesopotamia.

Interpretation of the evidence. There can be no doubt that the Biblical cherubim designate a class of angels. Nowhere are they represented as objects of worship, and therefore cannot have been divine beings. They appear everywhere in the service of God, and usually in His immediate presence. In poetic, symbolic language they are

ance were probably like those in the tabernacle (1 Ki 6:23-28; 8:6-8; 2 Chr 3:10-13), although their faces looked "inward" (KJV), that is, toward the "nave" (RSV), or holy place of the sanctuary (2 Chr 3:13). (3) Representations of cherubim were used as decorations on the curtains of the tabernacle (Ex 26:1, 31; 36:8, 35) and of the Temple (2 Chr 3:14), and were carved in the wooden paneling of the walls and door leaves of Solomon's Temple (1 Ki 6:29, 32); cherubim were likewise to be carved in Ezekiel's temple (Eze 41:18). (4) In poetic, symbolic language a cherub is referred to as the carrier of God (2 Sa 22:11; Ps 18:10), and God is described as enthroned between cherubim (1 Sa 4:4; 2 Sa 6:2; Ps 99:1) or above them (2 Ki 19:15; 1 Chr 13:6; Is 37:16). (5) In the vision of Ezekiel, complicated forms and groups of cherubim are described (Eze 1:4-25; 9:3; 10:

105. Two Assyrian-type cherubs, guardians of cities, palaces, and temples, in the process of being excavated at Khorsabad, Iraq

represented as carrying God, or as guarding or overshadowing His throne. Their appearance is not uniformly represented and may have varied, as does that of cherubim appearing in pictorial representations of the ancient Orient. The cherubim in the tabernacle and the Temple may have resembled those depicted in Egyptian reliefs. Some scholars think that when the Hebrew poets spoke of God as sitting on the cherubim, or riding on them, they may have had sphinxlike beings in mind similar to those seen on Oriental thrones. The cherubim of Ezekiel's vision, on the other hand, which were mixed creatures, would find their closest parallels in the multi-headed mixed beings of the Syro-Hittite world.

2. A place in Lower Mesopotamia from which Jews who could not prove their Israelite descent returned to Jerusalem in Zerubbabel's time (Ezr 2:59; Neh 7:61); not identified.

Cherubim. See Cherub.

Chesalon (kĕs'á-lŏn). [Heb. *Kesalôn.*] A place on Mount Jearim, in Judah's northern boundary (Jos 15:10), identified with *Keslă,* 10 mi. west of Jerusalem.

Chesed (kĕ'sĕd). [Heb. *Keśed,* a "Chaldean."] A son of Abraham's brother, Nahor, and Milcah (Gen 22:22). Some think that he was the ancestor of the Chaldeans (Koehler, *LVTL* 458).

Chesil (kĕ'sĭl). [Heb. *Kesîl.*] A place in southern Judah (Jos 15:30); not identified. It may possibly be identical with the place called Bethuel in 1 Chr 4:30, and Bethul in Jos 19:4.

Chestnut Tree. See Plane Tree.

Chesulloth (kĕ-sŭl'ŏth). [Heb. *Kesullôth.*] A town on the boundary of Issachar (Jos 19:18), probably identical with Chisloth-tabor (kĭs'lŏth-tā'bĕr) [Heb. *Kisloth Tabor*] (v 12), since it lay in the vicinity of Mount Tabor. It has been identified with *Iksâl,* 2½ mi. southeast of Nazareth (Map VI, C-3).

Cheth. [Heb. *chêth.*] The 8th letter in the Hebrew alphabet, written ח, appearing as the title to the 8th section of Ps 119 in the KJV. See Aleph.

Chezib. See Achzib, 1.

Chidon. See Nacon.

Children of the East. See People of the East.

190

Chileab (kĭl'ē-ăb). [Heb. *Kil'ab*.] A son of David, born at Hebron (2 Sa 3:3); called Daniel in 1 Chr 3:1.

Chilion (kĭl'ĭ-ŏn). [Heb. *Kilyôn*, "wasting."] The younger son of Elimelech and Naomi, and brother-in-law of Ruth (Ruth 1:2, 5; 4:9).

Chilmad (kĭl'măd). [Heb. *Kilmad*.] A place, probably a country, that traded with Tyre, mentioned in connection with Asshur (Eze 27:23, 24); not identified.

Chimham (kĭm'hăm). [Heb. *Kimham*.] The son of David's friend, Barzillai the Gileadite. David invited Barzillai to make his residence at the court in Jerusalem, but he declined and sent his son instead (2 Sa 19:37, 38). Chimham seems to have built a lodging place (Heb. *gerûth*, rendered as a proper name "Geruth," gē'rŭth, in the RSV) at Bethlehem (Jer 41:17).

Chinnereth (kĭn'ē-rĕth) or **Chinneroth** (kĭn'ē-rŏth), KJV once **Cinneroth** (sĭn'ē-rŏth). [Heb. *Kinnereth, Kinnerôth,* and *Kinarôth*, "lyre."]

1. A fortified city in Galilee, mentioned as early as the 15th cent. B.C. as *Knnrt* and *Kn[r]t* by Thutmose III. The city was assigned to Naphtali (Jos 19:35). It is now *Tell el-'Oreimeh*, on the Sea of Galilee, 6 mi. north of Tiberias (Map VI, C-4).

2. The area around the city of Chinnereth (Jos 11:2), usually identified with the Plain of *Gennesaret (Mt 14:34).

3. The lake or "sea" on which Chinnereth is situated (Num 34:11; Jos 12:3; 13:27; 1 Ki 15:20). The lake was known in later times as the Lake of Gennesaret (Lk 5:1), of Tiberias, and of Galilee (Jn 6:1). *See* Galilee, Sea of.

Chinneroth. *See* Chinnereth.

Chios (kī'ŏs). [Gr. *Chios*.] An island off the western coast of Asia Minor, which played a role in the Persian period. Paul's ship passed the island on his voyage to Jerusalem when returning from his 3d Missionary Journey (Acts 20:15). Map XX, B-4.

Chirp. [Heb. *ṣaphaph*, "chirp," "whisper."] The RSV term in Is 8:19, equivalent to "peep" in the KJV. In ch 10:14 *ṣaphaph* is used of the inarticulate chirping of a bird. In ch 8:19 it refers to the strange sounds made by a spirit medium when in a trance.

Chisleu. *See* Chislev.

Chislev (kĭs'lĕv), KJV **Chisleu** (kĭs'lū). [Heb. *Kislew;* Nabataean and Palmyrene *Kslwl;* Aramaic *Kslw;* Akkadian *Kislimu*.] The 9th month of the Jewish religious year (Zec 7:1). It began at the new moon of November or December. *See* Year.

Chislon (kĭs'lŏn). [Heb. *Kislôn,* a personal name attested in Ugaritic as *Ksln*.] A Benjamite whose son Elidad was tribal prince in the time of Moses (Num 34:21).

Chisloth-tabor. *See* Chesulloth.

Chitlish (kĭt'lĭsh), KJV **Kithlish** (kĭth'lĭsh). [Heb. *Kithlîsh*.] A village in Judah, in the Shephelah near Eglon (Jos 15:40); not identified.

Chittim. *See* Kittim.

Chiun. *See* Kaiwan.

Chloe (klō'ē). [Gr. *Chloē*, "verdant." The name occurs in ancient texts as an epithet of the goddess Demeter.] A woman from whose household Paul received information concerning the conditions of the church at Corinth (1 Cor 1:11). She may or may not have been a Christian. Those of her household may have been either her relatives, her employees, or her slaves.

Chor-ashan. *See* Ashan.

Chorazin (kō-rā'zĭn). [Gr. *Chorazin*.] A place in a valley that runs down toward the Sea of Galilee (Map XVI, C-4), identified with *Khirbet Kerâzeh*, about 2 mi. north of *Tell Ḥûm* (Capernaum). It is not mentioned in the OT, but is probably the *Karzayîm* of the Talmud (*Menachoth* 85a). Extensive ruins, including those of an ancient synagogue, mark the site. Christ denounced the city, along with Capernaum and Bethsaida, for having

106. Ruins of the synagogue at Chorazin

witnessed many of His miracles and having heard many of His sermons without responding (Mt 11:21-24; Lk 10:13).

Chosen People. A term designating Israel as God's appointed agent, to be the recipient and custodian of His revealed will, to be an example and witness to the nations of the superiority of the worship of, and service to, the true God, and to be His representatives in effecting the conversion of the world. God first chose Abraham (Neh 9:7), and later his descendants, the Hebrew people (Deut 7:6). The unique status of Israel as the chosen people is stressed throughout the OT (Is 41:8; 43:21; 44:1, 2, 8; Hos 2:23; Amos 3:2, 3; etc.). The relationship between God and Israel under which they became His chosen people is defined in His covenant, first with Abraham and later with Abraham's descendants (Gen 12:1-3; 15:18; 17:7; Ex 19:5-7; Deut 7:12). The prophets often point to the marriage relationship to illustrate the privileges and responsibilities of Israel under the *covenant relationship (Eze 16:6-8; Hos 2:2, 19, 23; etc.). However, the status of chosen people was conditional (Ex 19:5, 6; *see* Prophet, II), and ancient Israel forfeited that status. In the NT the Christian church replaces ancient Israel as the chosen people (Mt 21:43; 1 Pe 2:9, 10), but God's aims and objectives in the new covenant are, in effect, the same as in the old (see Heb. 8:8-11).

Chozeba. See Cozeba.

Christ. (krĭst). [Gr. *Christos,* "anointed," equivalent to the Heb. *Mashiach,* "messiah," "anointed."] The official title of Jesus of Nazareth designating Him as *"the* Messiah" or Promised One of the OT. In OT times the high priest (Ex 30:30), the king (2 Sa 5:3), and sometimes prophets (1 Ki 19:16) were "anointed" upon consecration to holy service. In Messianic prophecy the term came to be applied specifically to *the* Messiah, who, as Prophet (Deut 18:15), Priest (Zec 6:11-14), and King (Is 9:6, 7), was the One ordained to be the Redeemer of the world. In later NT usage the definite article was omitted before the title, and "Christ" became virtually a proper name as in common usage today. Use of the names Christ and Jesus together constitutes a confession of faith that Jesus of Nazareth, Son of Mary, Son of man, is indeed the Christ, the Messiah, Son of God, and thus a profession of belief in the union of the divine and human natures in the one Person. *See* Jesus Christ.

Christian. [Gr. *Christianos,* "a follower of Christ."] A name used first in Antioch of Syria to describe a disciple of Jesus Christ (Acts 11:26). The text does not make clear who originated this term. It has been thought unlikely that it was adopted by the Christians themselves, although there is an ancient tradition that names Evodius, the first bishop of Antioch, as the originator of the term. Nor is it likely that the name was coined by the Jews, for the Gr. *Christos* means "Messiah," and the Jews would hardly call the disciples of Jesus "followers of the Messiah." It appears that the term was first applied to the followers of Jesus by the heathen, doubtless as a nickname to express contempt, but to the Christian it became a name of honor. The word occurs elsewhere in the NT only in Acts 26:28 and in 1 Pe 4:16.

Chronicles, Books of. Two books of the OT that record events during the reign of David and his successors, duplicating in part information that already appears in the books of Samuel and Kings. In Hebrew Bibles the two books of Chronicles appear as one continuous work with the single title *dibrê hayyamîm,* "events of the days," probably an abbreviation for *sepher dibrê hayyamîm,* "book of events of the days," a royal journal of happenings under successive kings. See 2 Ki 14:18, 28; 1 Chr 27:24; Neh 12:23; etc. The English title "Chronicles" comes from the Latin *Chronicon,* the title Jerome used as a fitting translation of the Hebrew title in his Latin translation, the Vulgate. In the Hebrew canon of the OT the book of Chronicles stands as the last book. Its present position following the books of Kings in modern versions, and its division into two books, originated with the Greek translation known as the Septuagint (completed *c.* 150 B.C.), which was followed by the Latin Vulgate.

An examination of the Hebrew text of Chronicles, Ezra, and Nehemiah shows that the three are closely related in language, style, and general point of view. From this it is reasonable to conclude either that all three were the work of one author, or that they were written at about the same time by various men who collaborated with one another. Early Jewish tradition attributes the Chronicles to Ezra, and modern scholarship generally assigns Chronicles, Ezra, and Nehemiah to the same author. Internal evidence suggests a priest of the Persian period as the writer, both of which requirements are met by Ezra (Ezr 7:1-5). The fact that the opening verses of Ezra repeat the closing verses of Chronicles, almost verbatim, also indicates a close relationship between the two. Use by the writer of Chronicles of the Persian monetary system (1 Chr 29:7) points to the Persian period as the time of writing. The fact that the genealogy of the royal line of Judah is carried several generations beyond Zerubbabel, who returned to Judea about 536 B.C., suggests that the date of writing could well have been a century or more after the time of Zerubbabel (ch 3:19-24). This and other evidence are taken as sufficient grounds for assigning Chronicles to about 400 B.C. The author's frequent reference to numerous other works (1 Chr 27:24; 29:29; 2 Chr 9:29; 12:15; 13:22; 20:34; 24:27; 26:22; 32:32; 33:19) suggests that he had access to an excellent source collection and that he made generous use of it, under the guidance of Inspiration.

Essentially, Chronicles is a record of the united kingdom under David and Solomon, and of their successors upon the throne of Judah down to the Babylonian captivity, which is a period of a little more than 4 cent. Considerably more than half of the contents of Chronicles parallels information found in other OT books, especially Samuel and Kings. Nevertheless, in style and emphasis it is clearly an independent work, written from its own distinctive point of view and designed to serve its own particular purpose. With the spiritual lessons of the Captivity vividly in mind, the author sets forth Israel's history as a nation prior to that tragic event in such a way as to show why captivity was inevitable. He stresses the moral and spiritual aspects of the events he records and seeks ever and again to point out that obedience to the revealed will of God brings peace and prosperity, whereas disobedience results in suffering and calamity. He emphasizes the fact that the Lord rewards the righteous and punishes the evildoers (see 1 Chr 10:13; 11:9; 21:7; 2 Chr 13:18; etc.). He assures Israel that she has nothing to fear for the future except as she might forget the lessons taught by her past history.

Chronicles may logically be divided into four parts: (1) Introduction, 1 Chr 1 to 10; (2) Reign of David, chs 11 to 29; (3) Reign of Solomon, 2 Chr 1 to 9; (4) Kingdom of Judah to the Captivity, chs 10 to 36. In the Introduction the historian traces, in a few bold strokes, the history of the world from Creation down to the accession of David. This brief sketch is largely genealogical, with emphasis on the royal tribe of Judah and the priestly tribe of Levi. These genealogical tables are interspersed, here and there, with brief biographical and historical items (1 Chr 4:9, 10, 38-43; 5:9, 10, 16-26; 6:31, 32, 48, 49, 54-81; etc.). With a view to completeness the genealogies are continued on through the time of the united and divided kingdoms, the Captivity, and the Restoration to the time of writing. Nothing is said of Saul's reign except for a brief account of his death in battle, and this only by way of explaining why God rejected him, thus setting the stage for the accession of David.

Nineteen of the 65 chapters in Chronicles—nearly one third—are devoted to the glorious reign of David. David and Solomon together, whose reigns witnessed the golden era of Israelite history, are allotted 28 chapters, or almost half the space. The section covering the reign of David may be further subdivided into 3 parts, the first of which summarizes the outstanding events of the period (1 Chr 11 to 21). Included are the circumstances of his coronation as king over all Israel, his capture of Jerusalem and removal of the capital from Hebron to Jerusalem, the enumeration of his mighty men and army, his transfer of the ark to Jerusalem, the erection of his palace, his wars, and his numbering of the people. The second part of the Davidic section (chs 22:1 to 29:21) deals at length with David's preparations for the erection of the Temple, with his organization of the service of priests and Levites, and his instructions to Solomon regarding the Temple. The third part of this section (chs 23:1; 29:22-30) takes up, briefly, the transfer of authority to Solomon by David, and David's death.

The 3d section, on Solomon (2 Chr 1 to 9), is devoted chiefly to the construction and dedication of the Temple, with brief mention of Solomon's other public works and enterprises, his devotion to wisdom, and the splendor of his reign.

The 4th section (2 Chr 10 to 36) covers the period of the divided kingdom, with emphasis on the kingdom of Judah. The history of this period is arranged under the successive reigns, with each ruler from Rehoboam to Zedekiah being accorded space. The revolt of the 10 tribes is covered rather fully, and thereafter major attention is given to the efforts of the reforming kings Asa, Jehoshaphat, Joash,

Hezekiah, and Josiah to bring the nation back to God. This section closes with the 3d deportation to Babylon and a brief epilogue of Cyrus' edict for the return.

Chronology. [A non-Biblical word derived from the Greek words *chronos,* "time," and *logos,* "word," "speech," "reason."] The study of time relationships between periods and events in the Bible record requires a discussion of methods of reckoning as well as a survey of the different historical periods and the data on which the chronological pattern is based. The subject will be discussed under various heads and summarized in tables of dated or approximately dated events of Bible times.

I. Basis of Ancient Chronology. The ancients did not record dates according to the system we use, nor did the different nations reckon time by one calendar, as practically the whole world does today. Therefore, our success at dating ancient events—that is, at assigning them dates in our own B.C.-A.D. scale of years—depends on our understanding of ancient methods and on the amount of information we have about the events. That is why there is sometimes uncertainty or difference of opinion on Biblical dating.

1. *Various methods of designating years.* Some ancient peoples regularly designated their years by name rather than by number. One early method was to name each year after an important event. Later came the designation of each year by the name of an annual official—in Assyria, that of the *limmu;* in Athens, that of one of the high magistrates, an *archōn;* and in Rome, the names of the two chief magistrates, the *consuls.* However, in Babylonia, Egypt, and other lands of the Near East the common method of dating was by the numbered years of their kings—a method found often in the Bible. A letter, a contract, or the record of an event might be dated in such a formula as: "in the fifth month, on the seventh day of the month, . . . the nineteenth year of king Nebuchadnezzar" (2 Ki 25:8). The year numbering began over for each king.

All these methods required the preservation of lists giving either the sequence of the year names, limmus, archons, or consuls, or the kings and the length of each reign; otherwise there could be no possibility of knowing how many years apart any two events were. Fortunately, there are such lists extant for certain periods of ancient history.

Such cumbersome methods of reckoning are avoided by dating by an era, that is, in a series of years numbered continuously from a single starting point. But the ancients were slow to invent eras, and never employed them for ordinary dating purposes until the reckoning by the Seleucid Era came into use in the late 4th cent. B.C. in the area under the rule of the Seleucid kings (the Eastern kingdom of Alexander's divided empire). The Jews, who for a time were under Seleucid rule, sometimes used this era (beginning, by different reckonings, in the autumn of 312 or the spring of 311 B.C. For example, it is found in the books of the Maccabees in the Apocrypha. For historical purposes, though not for ordinary day-to-day dating, the Greeks reckoned by Olympiads—the 4-year periods between Olympic games—beginning with the supposed date of the origin of the games (776 B.C.); and the Romans counted years A.U.C. (*ab urbe condita,* "from the founding of the city," or, alternately, *anno urbis condita,* "in the year of the founding of the city"), from 753 B.C. But these Greek and Roman eras were artificial, invented long after the true beginning dates had been forgotten, and they were employed only by historians. Moses used what might be termed a Hebrew era when he recorded events of the forty years of wilderness wandering in years numbered from the one in which the Israelites left Egypt (Ex 12:2, 6; 16:1; 40:1, 2, 17; Num 10:11; for a table *see* Wilderness Wandering); and centuries later Ezekiel dated his messages in years from the captivity of Jehoiachin (Eze 1:1, 2; 8:1; 33:21; etc.); but neither Moses' nor Ezekiel's era was used long after as a regular dating system, unless 1 Ki 6:1 is evidence for an otherwise unattested use of the Exodus era.

The era system now employed for designating years in ancient history came into use only in medieval times, yet it covers any ancient date, however remote, by numbering years in reverse from the beginning of the Christian Era. An understanding of this dating system is important because we translate all ancient chronological data into its B.C.-A.D. scale.

The Christian Era, which numbers years from the supposed year of the birth of Christ, was devised so long after that event that its starting point was placed erroneously—approximately 4 years late. It has two disadvantages: (1) It requires a reverse numbering for all the events preceding the time of Christ. (2) Since A.D. 1 is preceded in the scale by 1 B.C., with no zero year between, the computation of any interval between a B.C. and an A.D. date is awkward; for example, the interval from a date in 2 B.C. to that same date in A.D. 2 is not 4 years, as would seem natural, but 3 years. (Astronomers avoid this inconvenience by using negative numbers for the period B.C., substituting 0 for 1 B.C., —1 for 2 B.C., —2 for 3 B.C., etc.)

The reason an error of one year is often made in computing intervals from B.C. to A.D. dates is easily understood when the 2 reckonings are tabulated for comparison:

Chronological Reckoning:	Astronomical Reckoning:
5 B.C.	—4
4 B.C.	—3
3 B.C.	—2
2 B.C.	—1
1 B.C.	0
A.D. 1	1
A.D. 2	2
A.D. 3	3
A.D. 4	4
A.D. 5	5

Except in astronomical works, dates are customarily given by the chronological, or historical, method, in the B.C.-A.D. scale.

2. *Ancient concepts of time.* The people of Bible times, as in many parts of the East today, thought more in terms of round numbers than we do, and did not demand mathematical exactitude. Thus, if a man traveled part of 1 day, all the next day, and part of the 3d day, he was said to have arrived in 3 days; we would say it was 2 days after he left. The siege of Samaria (2 Ki 18:9, 10), extending from the 4th to the 6th year of Hezekiah, or from the 7th to the 9th year of Hoshea, would have lasted 2 years by our method of counting, but the Bible counts it "three years." This method is called inclusive reckoning. Also, at times, a part was counted for the whole; for example, when the Israelites were condemned to wander "forty years," the meaning was that they were to wander the rest of the 40-year period, since they were already in the 2d year of their journeying when the sentence was passed on them (Num 14:33; cf. Deut 2:14).

3. *Certainties and uncertainties.* A few key dates in antiquity, such as the 37th year of the reign of Nebuchadnezzar (568/67 B.C.) and the 7th year of the Persian king Cambyses (523/22 B.C.), can be fixed with certainty. In each of these cases

we have ancient astronomical records, including an eclipse and other data throughout a whole year. By astronomical computation these years can be located exactly in our B.C. system of reckoning. Other regnal years of Babylonian and Persian kings can be determined relatively from these fixed dates by means of king lists covering many centuries.

Certain Biblical events are synchronized with these Babylonian or Persian regnal years; but in dealing with Biblical dates we must take into consideration the fact that the Hebrew calendar was not exactly the same as foreign calendars and that there were 2 different methods of numbering regnal years: (1) the "postdating," or "accession-year," method, by which the "first" year of a reign was the calendar year *beginning* at the next New Year's Day after the king came to the throne; or (2) the "antedating," or "non-accession-year," method, by which the "first" year was the remainder of the year in which he ascended the throne, *ending* with the 1st New Year's Day of the reign. Further, since the Babylonian-Persian regnal year began in the spring, and the Hebrew year had 2 beginnings, in spring and fall (*see* Year), these differences must also be taken into account. Even when we can place an event in a regnal year, such as 568/67 B.C., and know whether the year began in the spring or the fall, we still cannot know whether the event occurred in the latter part of 568 or the earlier part of 567 unless we know the month also. Therefore this dictionary presents most dates qualified by "about" (abbreviated *c.*), or "approximately."

However, in cases where the information is sufficient (as in 2 Ki 25:8), we can be certain as to the year and sometimes approximately to the day. "Approximately" in the case of a date giving month and day means that the possible error is no more than a day or so. But without additional information, such as an exact eclipse date or a double date synchronizing a lunar with a solar calendar date, we cannot by modern computation identify the exact day of the beginning of any specific ancient lunar month, either Hebrew or Babylonian, because of the unknown factors such as the visibility of the moon (*see* Month), etc. There may sometimes be a difference of a month between the Jewish and the Babylonian calendar, if the insertion of the extra month in the lunar *year fell in different years. Since all these variables must be taken into account, it is not surprising that there are sometimes uncertainties and differences of opinion in the interpretation of Bible chronology, even with the relatively abundant source material now available from archeological investigations. However, the possible difference of a day or two, a month, or even a year, in dates thousands of years ago is generally a minor matter.

Older chronologies are built on incomplete, erroneous, or obsolete information and cannot be relied on. Ussher's scheme of dates, as incorporated into the marginal notes of many editions of the Catholic Douay Version and, in modified form, in those of the KJV, was once the best available approximation, but it is 300 years old and now outmoded, as the increasing information coming to us from archeological finds makes possible a much more exact chronology of Biblical events than was possible in Ussher's day.

II. Creation to Exodus. The earliest portion of the Bible, which covers large sections of history with much less detail than some of the later portions, offers the least material for exact chronology, and contains the greatest variations in numbers between the Hebrew, the LXX, and the Samaritan Pentateuch,

1. *Adam to Abraham.* For the earliest period the Bible furnishes no date for any event. It gives only the genealogy of the patriarchs and their life spans. If we follow the Hebrew text, we can arrive at a total from the life spans that puts the Flood in the year 1656 from the Creation (A.M. 1656; A.M. for *anno mundi*, "in the year of the world"), and the Exodus in A.M. 2513. However, it should be remembered that this reckoning represents a minimum, not maximum, possibility; the period becomes longer if we (1) use different interpretations of the figures (such as those given in *The Westminster Dictionary of the Bible* and *The International Standard Bible Encyclopaedia*); or (2) allow the possibility that there were generations not mentioned in the record; or (3) follow the LXX, in which the life spans of the patriarchs total about 1,000 years longer than in the Hebrew. It is possible that the LXX version represents an older Hebrew original, but on the other hand it may be an intentional modification. See table 1 under sec. IX.

Let us examine the alternatives. Laying aside possibility (1) as either conjectural or unacceptable, we find, with regard to possibilities (2) and (3), that in his genealogy of Jesus, Luke mentions one name (Lk 3:36) that is not in the Hebrew OT genealogy (see Gen 11:12), but is included in the LXX list; and that other Bible genealogies sometimes omit names, probably the less important ones: for example, the genealogy of Ezra (Ezr 7:1-5; cf. 1 Chr 6:3-15), and Matthew's genealogy of Christ, which omits four generations—Ahaziah, Joash, Amaziah, and Jehoiakim (Mt 1:8, 11; cf. 1 Chr 3:11, 12, 15). Thus the possibility exists that there were other men in the patriarchal line whose names Inspiration did not see fit to preserve. (On "son" in Biblical usage, meaning "grandson" or "descendant," *see* Son.) Therefore it must be considered that early Bible chronology, at least before Abraham, is not necessarily completely known. For the Bible record, including its chronological data, to be true does not require that the Scriptures contain a *complete* record of everything in the past. The Scriptures nowhere give us the total number of years from Creation to the Flood, from the Flood to the Exodus, or, for that matter, for the series of kings. The totals must be arrived at by the interpretation of the various figures given in the text. That is why this dictionary, although it holds to the accuracy of the account of Creation as given in Genesis, and to the substantial accuracy of whatever chronological data are furnished, does not presume dogmatically to set forth the exact date of the creation of the earth.

2. *Abraham to the Exodus.* The time from Abraham's call to the Exodus is stated definitely to have been 430 years (Gal 3:17; cf. Ex 12:40, LXX); and the story of each generation is told in sufficient detail to make it certain that Jacob and his family entered Egypt 215 years after the call of Abraham; thus the Israelites were in Egypt 215 years. The B.C. dating of Abraham depends on that of the Exodus, which has been placed variously, by differing interpretations of the record, between the latter part of the 17th cent. and the latter part of the 13th cent. B.C. There is insufficient evidence to prove any of these Exodus datings completely. However, since the dates of the end of the kingdoms of Judah and Israel are fixed, the latest dates suggested for the Exodus permit only a very short period to be allotted for the judges, even with a "short chronology" of the kings, whereas the earliest dates for the Exodus require a very long period for the judges and a

"long chronology" of the kings. One theory supposes a two-stage Exodus, with Joshua entering Canaan in the 15th cent. and Moses in the late 13th cent.

Of all the theories for dating the Exodus, the one that involves the least difficulty in regard to either the Biblical records or the historical setting is the one resulting in a mid-15th cent. date, which is based (1) on the acceptance of the 480th year (1 Ki 6:1) as expressing a literal statement of the interval between the Exodus and Solomon's 4th year; (2) on the interpretation that the various periods mentioned in the book of Judges (which total considerably more than 480 years) represent, in some cases, simultaneous judgeships in different areas of Palestine; and (3) on a chronology of the divided kingdom that would place the 4th year of Solomon in the neighborhood of 965 B.C., as is now widely accepted.

This dictionary adopts a tentative system of chronology that dates this 4th year of Solomon in 967/66 B.C., that is, the fall-to-fall civil-calendar year beginning with Tishri, the 7th month (*see* Year), in 967. Consequently, the founding of the Temple in the 2d month, Ziv (Iyyar), of that year (1 Ki 6:1) would be dated in the spring of 966 B.C. Then, if Ziv in the 480th year from the Exodus fell in 966, Ziv in the 1st year of the Exodus would be 479 years earlier, in the spring of 1445 B.C.; and the 1st month, in which the Israelites left Egypt, would be the preceding month, Abib (Nisan) in that year. With the Exodus, then, in 1445 B.C., the call of Abraham exactly 430 years earlier (Gal 3:17; Ex 12:40, 41) would be in 1875 B.C., and Jacob's entry into Egypt, 1660 B.C.

III. Exodus to Kingdom. There is a problem involved in fitting the various periods of the books of Joshua and Judges into the 480 years (1 Ki 6:1) beginning with the Exodus and ending with Solomon's 4th year (*c.* 967/66 B.C.). If the Israelites left Egypt in 1445 B.C., they entered Canaan 40 years later (see tables under Wilderness Wandering), in the spring of 1405, and completed the initial conquest of Canaan and the division of the land about 1400. The series of judges began some considerable time after 1400, for the Israelites "served the Lord all the days of Joshua, and all the days of the elders that outlived Joshua" (Jgs 2:7), before they apostatized and brought the foreign oppressions from which they were saved by the judges. If we allow *x* years for

the interval between the initial conquest and beginning of the oppression under Cushan-rishathaim (Jgs 3:8) and 83 years for the sum of the lengths of Saul's reign (Acts 13:21), David's reign (2 Sa 5:4, 5), and 3 years till the 4th year of Solomon, we have $83+x$ years; then if we subtract this sum from the total years between approximately 1400 B.C. and 967 B.C. we arrive at approximately $350 -x$ years for the period of the judges. However, the various periods of the judgeships and oppressions given in the book of Judges and the unknown period between the conquest and the beginning of the first oppression, add up, not to $350 -x$ years, but to $410 +x$ years. It has become obvious therefore, that these periods cannot all be successive; some must be overlapping. The record does not state that each judge ruled all 12 tribes; rather it draws a picture of disunity and confusion that fits perfectly into a situation in which judges might function in small areas in different parts of Palestine at the same time. In some cases there is an indication in the record that this is so; it could have been true also in other cases. We do not have enough information about this period to construct a detailed chronology, but it is perfectly possible to work out tentatively an approximate scheme of dating in which the total lengths of the judgeships can be harmonized with the statement that the Temple was begun in the 480th year from the Exodus. See table 2 under sec. IX.

IV. The United Hebrew Kingdoms. The OT does not state clearly how long Saul, the first Hebrew king, reigned, but Luke, reporting one of Paul's sermons, gives the length as "forty years" (Acts 13:21). Since neither Luke nor Paul is making a point of exact chronology here, it is entirely possible that this "forty years," like the 450 years in the preceding verse, was meant as a round number. Reasons have been offered for concluding that Saul reigned somewhat less than 40 years. However, the 40 years given for David's reign was obviously not a round number, for 40 is given as the sum of 7 and 33 (1 Chr 29:27). Furthermore, an event occurring shortly before David's death is said to have taken place in the king's 40th year (chs 23:1; 26:31). Solomon reigned 40 years also (1 Ki 11:42), and then the kingdom was divided. From the chronology of the divided kingdom (explained in the next section) we arrive at the following tentative dates for the united kingdom: Saul, *c.* 1050-1011 B.C.; David, *c.* 1011-971; Solomon, *c.* 971-931.

V. The Divided Kingdom—Israel and Judah. The basis for the chronology of the kingdoms of Judah and Israel is a series of time statements giving the accession data and the lengths of the reigns. The following tabulation lists the kings in the order in which they are introduced in the books of Kings. For the tentative B.C. dating of these reigns, see table 3 appearing under sec. IX.

Bible Data for the Reigns of Israel and Judah

Ruler	Kingdom	Accession Synchronism			Years of Reign	
			I KINGS			I KINGS
Rehoboam	Judah		12:1	17		14:21
Jeroboam I	Israel		12:20	22		14:20
Abijam	Judah	18th of Jeroboam	15:1	3		15:2
Asa	Judah	20th of Jeroboam	15:9	41		15:10
Nadab	Israel	2d of Asa	15:25	2		15:25
Baasha	Israel	3d of Asa	15:28	24		15:33
Elah	Israel	26th of Asa	16:8	2		16:8
Zimri	Israel	27th of Asa	16:10	(7 days)		16:15
Tibni	Israel		16:21			
Omri	Israel	31st of Asa	16:23	12		16:23
Ahab	Israel	38th of Asa	16:29	22		16:29
Jehoshaphat	Judah	4th of Ahab	22:41	25		22:42
Ahaziah	Israel	17th of Jehoshaphat	22:51	2		22:51
			II KINGS			II KINGS
Joram ⎱	Israel	⎰2d of Jehoram	1:17			
Joram ⎰	Israel	⎱18th of Jehoshaphat	3:1	12		3:1
Jehoram	Judah	5th of Joram	8:16	8		8:17
Ahaziah	Judah	12th (11th) of Joram	8:25 (9:29)	1		8:26
Jehu	Israel		9:12, 13	28		10:36
Athaliah	Judah		11:1, 3	7		11:3, 4
Joash	Judah	7th of Jehu	12:1	40		12:1
Jehoahaz	Israel	23d of Joash	13:1	17		13:1
Jehoash	Israel	37th of Joash	13:10	16		13:10
Amaziah	Judah	2d of Jehoash	14:1	29		14:2
Jeroboam (II)	Israel	15th of Amaziah	14:23	41		14:23
Azariah (Uzziah)	Judah	27th of Jeroboam	15:1	52		15:2
Zachariah	Israel	38th of Azariah	15:8	(6 mos.)		15:8
Shallum	Israel	39th of Azariah	15:13	(1 mo.)		15:13
Menahem	Israel	39th of Azariah	15:17	10		15:17
Pekahiah	Israel	50th of Azariah	15:23	2		15:23
Pekah	Israel	52d of Azariah	15:27	20		15:27
Hoshea ⎱	Israel	⎰20th of Jotham	15:30			
Hoshea ⎰	Israel	⎱12th of Ahaz	17:1	9		17:1
Jotham	Judah	2d of Pekah	15:32	16 (20)		15:33 (30)
Ahaz	Judah	17th of Pekah	16:1	16		16:2
Hezekiah	Judah	3d of Hoshea	18:1	29		18:2
Manasseh	Judah		21:1	55		21:1
Amon	Judah		21:19	2		21:19
Josiah	Judah		22:1	31		22:1
Jehoahaz	Judah		23:31	(3 mos.)		23:31
Jehoiakim	Judah		23:36	11		23:36
Jehoiachin	Judah		24:8	(3 mos.)		24:8
Zedekiah	Judah		24:17	11		24:18

1. *The problem of the Judah-Israel synchronisms.* Regnal statements such as "In the thirty and eighth year of Asa king of Judah began Ahab the son of Omri to reign over Israel: and Ahab the son of Omri reigned over Israel in Samaria twenty and two years" (1 Ki 16:29) are given for the various kings of Israel and Judah. They furnish two items of information: (1) the length of the reign, and (2) a synchronism between the accession of a particular king and a specific year in the reign of his contemporary in the other kingdom. However, when the figures for the reigns of the kings of the northern kingdom, Israel, are totaled, and those for the reigns of the southern kingdom, Judah, for the same period are totaled, the latter sum is greater than the former by about 20. Because of this apparent discrepancy some have abandoned the Biblical chronological statements as unreliable, and have revised the figures to suit their varying theories. But others have shown that both lines can be reconciled by assuming either overlapping reigns (coregencies) in the longer line or gaps between reigns (interregna) in the shorter line. The method of harmonization used by Ussher and others was to lengthen the shorter line by assuming interregna (the system is therefore called the "long" chronology of the kings); it is no longer accepted generally, because it does not fit the Assyrian chronology as worked out from the *limmu* lists. More recently, however, the opposite method, that of shortening the longer line of kings by assuming coregencies, has come into favor.

2. *Coregencies harmonize synchronisms between reigns.* In some cases the record directly specifies a coregency of one king with his predecessor for a period of years. For example, when Uzziah (Azariah) was smitten with leprosy, his son Jotham ruled for several years before Uzziah's death (2 Ki 15:5); hence Jotham's reign with his father—his coregency—began some time before he succeeded his father as sole ruler. In other cases the record does not tell us what happened, but the chronological data concerning the length of the reigns or the synchronisms between the reigns of Israel and Judah show clearly that a coregency must have occurred. For example, we are told that Jehoram (or Joram) of Judah began to reign in the 5th year of Joram (or Jehoram) of Israel (2 Ki 8:16). This would seem to imply that he came to the throne about 5 years *later* than did Joram of Israel. How-

ever, we are also told that Joram of Israel began to reign in the 18th year of Jehoshaphat (2 Ki 3:1), or the 2d year of Jehoram of Judah (ch 1:17). This would seem to imply that Jehoram of Judah came to the throne a year *before* Joram of Israel. It would seem, further, that this was the beginning of a coregency with his father, since Jehoshaphat reigned more than 18 years. Therefore the supposed contradiction between Jehoram's reign's beginning *a year before* and *5 years after* Joram of Israel is solved. Obviously, Jehoram of Judah began to reign with his father in the year before Joram of Israel came to the throne, and then in the latter's 5th year Jehoshaphat died and his son Jehoram of Judah began his reign as sole ruler. These texts show one thing more: If Jehoshaphat died in the 5th year of Joram of Israel, his last year was not his 25th, but his 22d. Therefore, to count 25 years for his reign (1 Ki 22:42), we must assume that he ruled 22 years after his father Asa, but 25 counting a 3-year coregency with his father. Thus we might say that the synchronisms and the length of Jehoshaphat's reign require us to draw the conclusion that he had a coregency in the beginning with his father Asa and one at the end with his son Jehoram.

There are other examples. Thus a number of supposed inconsistencies in the records of the kings can be reasonably accounted for by coregencies, while many apparent one-year discrepancies may be solved in terms of the difference between the two kingdoms of Israel and Judah in two respects: (1) the two methods of numbering regnal years (see I, 3, above), and (2) the two beginnings of the Hebrew *year. An almost complete chronological pattern has been worked out for these two lines of kings in harmony with both the Bible and the Assyrian and Babylonian chronological data. Consequently, the time statements in the books of Kings and Chronicles are now being increasingly accepted as reliable history by those who were formerly skeptical of them.

3. *Arriving at the* B.C. *dating.* Once a system has been worked out for the reigns of Israel and Judah, we still face the problem of determining the exact dating of the whole interlocked system *in the* B.C. *scale*—a scale of years that did not come into use until many centuries later. Fortunately, the year of Ahab's death can be dated with reasonable certainty in 853/52 B.C. by Assyrian chronology through a record of his participation in

the battle of Qarqar in the 6th year of Shalmaneser III and another record of Jehu's paying tribute in the 18th year of the same king. Then the end of the kingdom of Judah is linked by several synchronisms to the reign of Nebuchadnezzar, whose regnal years are fixed beyond any doubt because his 37th year has been identified by modern astronomical methods as the Babylonian lunar-calendar year beginning with Nisan 1 (April 23), 568 B.C., and ending Adar 30 (April 12), 567. (All month dates, such as April 23, etc., are customarily given in the Julian calendar in B.C. dates and up to A.D. 1582, the time when the Gregorian revision came in.)

With the end of the kingdom of Judah determined (see sec. VI, 1, below), the B.C. dating of earlier events—including the beginning of the Temple in the 4th year of Solomon and the Exodus in the 480th year before that—depends on one's method of working out the chronology of the reigns of the Hebrew kings, on which there is still room for minor difference of opinion. Any arrangement of the reigns that seems to be correct because it "works," when charted on paper, is subject to the possibility that later someone may arrive at a slightly different arrangement that works a little better. Therefore we must adopt the scheme that seems most nearly to fulfill all the requirements, and use that *tentatively*. That is why many dates in this book are given "about" or "approximately." The series of dates used in this dictionary (*see* Chronological Tables under sec. IX) is not based wholly on any one published system of chronology (see lit. cited at end of sec. VIII).

Any future revision is hardly likely to make more than a very few years' difference in this period of the Hebrew kings. The possibility of variation lies, aside from the coregency problem, in the difference between a spring and a fall beginning of the year and in the question of whether the "first year" of a king is the year beginning or the one ending at the first New Year's Day of the reign—either possible difference being that of only one year. And what, from this distance, is a variation of a year in the reign of Uzziah, or even of 10 years as far back as the reign of Solomon? The important facts are that for all practical purposes the chronology of the Hebrew kingdoms is known, and that the Bible gives us a dependable chronology of the period.

VI. Captivity and Restoration. Since the reign of Nebuchadnezzar has been fixed astronomically, and our most exact chronological data belong to the Babylonian and early Persian periods, and since the Bible records of the times of the Captivity and Restoration contain numerous date statements, the chronology of this period is better established than that of any other portion of the Bible.

1. *The seventy years' captivity.* The Babylonian captivity was the result of a threefold deportation of the bulk of the population of the kingdom of Judah:

a. The first stage was in the 3d year of Jehoiakim, when Nebuchadnezzar's captives included Daniel (Dan 1:1-3, 6). This was the year preceding the 4th year of Jehoiakim, which was the 1st year of Nebuchadnezzar, in which Jeremiah first foretold that the Captivity would last 70 years (Jer 25:1-11). We have a Babylonian chronicle covering the summer preceding Nebuchadnezzar's 1st regnal year. It describes his campaign in Palestine, during which he was called home to succeed his father at the latter's death. Josephus mentions this campaign, and says that Jewish captives were taken to Babylonia at this time. The date of this captivity is precisely known. Since Nebuchadnezzar's 37th year was 568/67 B.C. (Nisan to Nisan), then his 1st year was 604/03 B.C.; and the preceding summer, 605 B.C., was the date of his accession to the throne. This agrees perfectly with the Biblical references to the 3d and 4th years of Jehoiakim. Since, however, each nation had its own local calendar, the Jewish writers would be expected to reckon the years by their civil-calendar year beginning with Tishri, in the autumn; and thus to begin the 1st year of Nebuchadnezzar, the 4th of Jehoiakim, in autumn 605, at their own next New Year, or 6 months ahead of the next Babylonian New Year. Since the Captivity began in the Jewish year ending in 605, we should expect the 70-year period to close with the 70th year by Jewish reckoning, which ended in 536, as will be seen in sec. 2.

b. The second stage of the Captivity removed King Jehoiachin and a number of others, including Ezekiel, to Babylon (Eze 1:1-3; 33:21; 40:1), in the 8th year of Nebuchadnezzar (2 Ki 24:8-16). With this agrees the Babylonian record that Nebuchadnezzar took Jerusalem and captured the king on the 2d of Adar (the 12th month), approximately March 16, 597 B.C.. in his 7th year. (Note that this date would be in the 8th year of the reign by the Jewish civil calendar. The reason is that the Jewish civil year, which began in the autumn, and the Babylonian year, which began in the spring, overlapped about 6 months; therefore in half of each year the year number was the same in both calendars, and in the other half there was a difference of one in the number. *See* Year.)

c. The third stage was the final fall of the city and the destruction of the Temple, which is twice dated in the 19th year of Nebuchadnezzar (2 Ki 25:8-12; Jer 52:12-15). This was in 586 B.C., approximately Aug. 15 or 18. (The difference between the 7th and the 10th of the 5th month in these two texts may be the interval from Nebuzar-adan's entry to the burning of the city, or from the beginning to the end of the destruction.)

Some authorities place the fall of Judah in 587 B.C., but they either suppose that the Hebrews numbered Nebuchadnezzar's regnal years a year earlier or assume (from Jer 52:29) that Judah fell in the 18th year instead of the 19th. However, since the same chapter mentions the 19th year (v 12), there is no need to assume an error; vs 12 and 29 do not need to refer to the same event.

Thus we have well-established dates for the end of the kingdom of Judah and the beginning of the Babylonian captivity, dates which are known approximately to the day.

2. *The return from captivity.* Contemporary records tell us that Cyrus conquered Babylon in the 7th month of the 17th year of Nabonidus (the king who in his absence "entrusted the kingship" at home to his eldest son, *Belshazzar). The city of Babylon fell on the 16th of the 7th month, and the victorious Cyrus entered its gates on the 3d of the 8th month. These dates are approximately Oct. 13 and 29, 539 B.C. Babylonian records mention no separate reign for Belshazzar, though they confirm his rule in Babylon as his father's representative during Nabonidus' reign. It seems evident that we are to consider the Biblical "first year of Cyrus" as Cyrus' first regnal year following his conquest of Babylon, as reckoned by the Jewish calendar. There is no reason to suppose that Jewish writers used a reckoning two years later than the official regnal-year numbering of Cyrus, as some older commentators have assumed (*see* Darius, 1).

The 1st year of Cyrus was marked by his decree allowing the Jews to return to Palestine (Ezr 1:1-4). That year in the Babylonian-Persian calendar was 538/37 B.C., beginning Nisan 1, in the spring following the capture of Babylon. In the Jewish civil calendar, however, the accession year would have extended, not to the spring of 538, but to Tishri in the autumn of 538, and the year 1 would have extended from the fall of 538 to the fall of 537.

Thus the decree issued by Cyrus in his "first year" might have been issued as late as the spring of 537 according to the Babylonian-Persian calendar, and by Jewish civil reckoning as late as the summer or autumn of 537. If the decree went out in the latter part of the 1st year, the thousands of returning Jews could hardly have made preparations and set out with all their goods before the next spring, in 536, for spring was the only season that would allow ample time for a 4-month journey (see Ezr 7:8, 9) and leave time to get the settlers under adequate shelter and ready to plant their crops by the time the autumn rains began. We do not know exactly when Cyrus' decree was issued or exactly when the exiles returned; but it is sufficient that there is a reasonable possibility, even a strong probability, in a date that would place the return in 536 B.C.—70 years, inclusive, from the beginning of the Captivity in 605 B.C., in harmony with Jeremiah's prophecy (Jer 29:10).

After the return under Cyrus the work of restoration lagged in the face of difficulties and opposition, but in the 2d year of Darius I (not Darius the Mede; *see* Darius, 1; Darius, 2) the building of the Temple was resumed, led by Haggai and Zechariah (Ezr 5:1, 2). This was in 520/19 (spring to spring in the Persian reckoning, but 520/19 fall to fall in the Jewish civil calendar). The work was authorized by a decree of Darius (whether in or after the 2d year is not specified), and the building was completed on Adar 3, in the 6th year of that reign (ch 6:1-15), which would be approximately March 12, 515 B.C. (by both Jewish and Persian calendars).

3. *Organization under Ezra and Nehemiah.* The next important landmark was the reign of Artaxerxes I, whose regnal years are established by a series of doubledated papyri from Elephantine, Egypt, in which the date lines are given in both the Semitic lunar and the Egyptian solar calendar, thus fixing the B.C. years beyond doubt. Artaxerxes' 1st year was 464/63 B.C.; his 7th, in which Ezra was

sent to Jerusalem, was 458/57; and his 20th, in which Nehemiah was commissioned as governor, was 445/44. In the Jewish civil year, beginning with the 7th month, the 1st month began the second half of the *year, in the spring. This was when Ezra set out (Ezr 7:9), and likewise Nehemiah, in the 20th year, evidently set out about the same month (Neh 2:1). In the Jewish year 458/57, the 1st month fell in 457, and in 445/44, at the same time in 444. The use of the fall-to-fall year is evident from Nehemiah's account that he received bad news from Jerusalem in Chislev (the 9th month) of the 20th year, in consequence of which he asked the king's permission to go there in Nisan (the 1st month) of the same year (Neh 1:1; 2:1). Obviously, the 20th year, in Nehemiah's reckoning, was not the religious year beginning with the 1st month, but the civil year beginning with the 7th month, in which the 9th month would precede the 1st month.

After Nehemiah's governorship there are no chronological data in the OT. The mention, without date, of "the reign of Darius the Persian" (Neh 12:22) refers either to Darius II (424/23-405/04 B.C.) or (extremely unlikely) to Darius III (336/35-331 B.C.), who lost his empire to Alexander the Great.

VII. Between the Testaments. The period between the OT and the NT covers (a) the conquest of the Persian Empire by Alexander the Great (the campaigns lasted from 334 to 323 B.C., with the decisive battle in Mesopotamia in 331); (b) the breakup of Alexander's empire, about 20 years after his death, into four principal parts (301 B.C.), later reduced to three (c. 280), which were eventually absorbed gradually into the Roman Empire (c. 168-30 B.C.; see Greece, II, 3); (c) the brief period of Jewish independence (c. 143-63) growing out of the revolt of the Maccabees (c. 168) against the Seleucid Empire (the dates may vary a year, according to two interpretations of the Seleucid Era—an era widely employed in the Near East at that period; see sec. I, 1), and ending with the subjection of Palestine by Rome in 63; (d) the rule of the Herods, Idumean-Jewish vassal kings under Rome, extending from 40 B.C. into the NT period.

VIII. New Testament Chronology. Chronological data for the Roman period of Palestine are plentiful, that is, for Roman history from the conquest of Syria by Pompey in 63 B.C., on through the early Roman emperors, whose reigns can be dated to the day. Yet, strangely enough, the data for a chronology of the NT are very scanty, and events cannot be dated with as much certainty as in the late OT period. The chief reason for this is that the NT writers, apparently having little interest in chronology as such, mentioned almost no dates. The NT writers set forth the good news of salvation; what Jesus said and did was more important to them than the precise time these events occurred. Further, they expected the return of Jesus soon, an event that they taught would terminate world history.

It may seem strange that there is difference of opinion about the dates in the life of the One by whom we reckon every year of the Christian Era, but it is true that we do not have conclusive answers to certain problems concerning the dates of His birth, His baptism, and His death and resurrection.

1. *The birth of Christ.* The year of Christ's birth was not A.D. 1 (A.D. is *Anno Domini,* "in the year of the Lord"), but about 4 or 5 years earlier. Herod the Great, who was on the throne of Judea when Jesus was born (Mt 2:1), and who lived at least a short time afterward (v 15), died in 4/3 B.C. Some would put Herod's death in the autumn of 4 or later, but it is generally accepted that the eclipse mentioned by Josephus (*Ant.* xvii. 6. 4, 5) in connection with that event was one in the spring of 4 B.C. Then Jesus must have been born as early as late 5 or early 4 B.C., but the exact date cannot be known with the information that we now possess.

The tax enrollment, or census, under Quirinius (KJV "Cyrenius") does not furnish an exact date, because we have no other record of it, and the data that might be regarded as referring to it can be interpreted in more than one way.

The star of Bethlehem (Mt 2:2) cannot be identified as an astronomical event, as some have attempted to do, because it was not an actual star, as is obvious from the description of its motion (v 9).

2. *The baptism of Christ.* The beginning of Christ's ministry is dated by Luke (ch 3:1-3, 21) during the administration of several different officials whose terms of office must be dated somewhere between A.D. 26 and A.D. 34, but the only specific year that Luke mentions is the 15th regnal year of Tiberius. To Luke's original readers this date was clear, but to us it is inconclusive because of the differing ways

of interpreting the regnal-year formula Luke employs. The official Roman method of dating by consulships is known to us; but the dating by regnal years, which was not Roman, but was customarily used in the Eastern provinces, depended on the various local methods of reckoning the year. We do not know exactly what sort of reckoning Luke employed, since there is no source material extant for Jewish regnal dating of a Roman emperor. Therefore there is room for difference of opinion as to the precise year referred to by the 15th year of Tiberius. However, if Luke employed the usual Eastern regnal reckoning of that period, he counted as year 1 the calendar year in which a ruler began his reign. Then the year in which Tiberius succeeded Augustus (who died in August, A.D. 14) would have been, according to the Jewish civil calendar, the year 13/14, autumn to autumn, and Tiberius' 15th year would have been A.D. 27/28, beginning in the autumn. The date for the baptism that fits best the chronological data of the Biblical narrative of the life of Christ, especially on the length of Christ's ministry and on the crucifixion (see secs. 3, 4 following), is the autumn of A.D. 27.

3. *The crucifixion.* Likewise there are alternative interpretations for the date of the crucifixion. To locate the exact year by attempting to discover in what year—during the general period in which Jesus is known to have been crucified—the Passover date could have fallen on Friday, is not the simple problem that many suppose. Astronomers are emphatic in stating that the new-moon and full-moon dates that they furnish for the possible years of the crucifixion are not proof of the ancient *Jewish-calendar* date. The reason is that the 1st of the Jewish month was not the day of the astronomical new moon ("conjunction") but depended on the appearance of the crescent, 1 to 3 days later. Not all the variable astronomical and atmospheric conditions can now be determined for any given *month. Thus a modern reconstruction of an ancient Jewish date, without more detailed information than the mere day of the lunar month, cannot be proved to the exact day. It is true that there are two years that are possible, by different methods of interpretation, for a Friday crucifixion date (A.D. 30 and 31), neither of which can be proved astronomically, but again we may choose the alternative that fits the Biblical and historical specifications.

In consideration of all the Biblical, historical, and calendrical specifications—the birth of Jesus before the death of Herod the Great, His baptism about 30 years later, the 46 years of the building of the Temple, the 15th year of Tiberius, the crucifixion after a 3½-year ministry (see sec. 4 following), the relation of the crucifixion to the Passover and the month date —which cannot be discussed here (see *SDACom* 5:235-266), this dictionary adopts for the 3 key dates in the life of Christ the years 5/4 B.C. for His birth, A.D. 27 for His baptism, and A.D. 31 for His death and resurrection.

4. *The events of Christ's ministry.* Since the Gospels were not written primarily to record the exact timing of the events of the narrative, they do not always follow chronological order. Because of this, and because some events are recorded by only one Gospel and relatively few by all four, it is not possible to be dogmatic about the exact sequence. The length of Christ's ministry has been a matter of difference of opinion; many modern writers contend for a duration of about one year, others for two or more, a few even for seven; but the chronology adopted for this dictionary accepts a duration of 3½ years, which is believed to be indicated by the mention in the Gospel of John of three Passovers (Jn 2:13; 6:4; 12:1) and one unnamed feast (ch 5:1) that seems most reasonably to have been a Passover (*see* Jesus Christ, III).

5. *The chronology of Acts and the epistles.* Since there are no specific statements of dates in the book of Acts or the epistles, any chronology of this portion of the Bible must be considered approximate only. That adopted for this dictionary can be taken as a useful scale for the sequence and approximate dating of the events in accordance with the Biblical narrative and the historical background. The key events that can be dated within a year or so either way are: (1) the rule of Aretas IV in Damascus (probably A.D. 37-40) at the time of Paul's escape; (2) the death of Herod Agrippa I (A.D. 44) shortly after he had imprisoned Peter; (3) the expulsion of the Jews from Rome by Claudius (*c.* A.D. 49), which caused Aquila and Priscilla to go to Corinth; (4) the proconsulship of Gallio in Greece (A.D. 51/52 or 52/53), synchronizing with Paul's 2d Missionary Journey; (5) the accession of Festus (*c.* A.D. 60).

Lit. Introductory articles on chronology and calendars in *SDACom* and the literature listed in their annotated bibliographies. See vol. 1, pp. 174-196; vol. 2, pp. 100-123, 124-164; vol. 3, pp. 85-110; vol. 5, pp. 235-266; vol. 6, pp. 97-107. On general principles and methods: *Cambridge Ancient History*, vol. 1, ch. 4; Siegfried H. Horn and Lynn H. Wood, *The Chronology of Ezra 7* (Washington: Review and Herald, 1953), chs. 1-4. On the period of the Hebrew kingdoms: Siegfried H. Horn (Potomac University, Berrien Springs, Mich.), unpublished tables; Edwin R. Thiele, *The Mysterious Numbers of the Hebrew Kings* (Chicago: University of

Chicago Press, 1951). For the Exile and Restoration: Horn and Wood, *op. cit.*, chs 4, 5. For the Babylonian-Persian chronology and calendar: Richard A. Parker and Waldo H. Dubberstein, *Babylonian Chronology, 626 B.C.-A.D. 45* (Chicago: University of Chicago Press, 1946); this has been published in new form to A.D. 75 (Providence, R.I.: Brown University Press, 1956).

IX. Chronological Tables. The relative dates of various Biblical characters or events, and those of contemporary history are shown in the following tables:

CHRONOLOGICAL TABLES

1. Genealogy of the Patriarchs

Before the Flood (Gen 5):

	Hebrew		Samaritan		LXX		Josephus	
	Age at son's birth	Age at death	Age at son's birth	Age at death	Age at son's birth	Age at death	Age at son's birth	Age at death
Adam	130	930	130	930	230	930	230	930
Seth	105	912	105	912	205	912	205	912
Enos	90	905	90	905	190	905	190	905
Cainan	70	910	70	170	170	910	170	910
Mahalaleel	65	895	65	895	165	895	165	895
Jared	162	962	62	847	162	962	162	962
Enoch	65	365	65	365	165	365	165	365
Methuselah	187	969	67	720	167*	969	187	969
Lamech	182	777	53	653	188	753	182	777
Noah	500	950	500	950	500	950	500	950
Noah's age at Flood	600		600		600		600	

After the Flood (Gen 11):

	Hebrew		Samaritan		LXX		Josephus
	Age at son's birth	Remaining years	Age at son's birth	Remaining years	Age at son's birth	Remaining years	Age at son's birth
Shem (age 2 yrs. after the Flood)	100	500	100	500	100	500	(omits)
Arphaxad	35	403	135	303	135	430†	135
Cainan					130	330	
Salah	30	403	130	303	130	330	130
Eber	34	430	134	270	134	370†	134
Peleg	30	209	130	109	130	209	130
Reu	32	207	132	107	132	207	130
Serug	30	200	130	100	130	200	132
Nahor	29	119	79	69	179†	129†	120
Terah	70	135	70	75	70	135	
Terah (at Abram's birth)	130	75	70	135	130	75	70

* Later editions of the LXX give Methuselah's age at the birth of Lamech as 187 years, in an attempt to avoid the obvious difficulty of having Methuselah live 14 years after the Flood.
† Ancient texts of the LXX disagree on these figures. The figures here given are from the oldest LXX texts known.

2. Tentative B.C. Chronology From Abraham Through the Judges

Abraham's call (430 years before Exodus), probably 1875 B.C.
Exodus (480th year before the building of the Temple), probably 1445 B.C.

ISRAEL UNDER THE JUDGES*		EGYPTIAN KINGS*		HITTITE KINGS*
		Eighteenth Dynasty		
	B.C.		B.C.	
Invasion of Canaan	1405	Amenhotep III	1412-1375	Hattusilis II
Israel under Joshua and the elders	1405-1364	Ikhnaton (Amenhotep IV),		Tudhaliyas III
		Smenkhkare	1387-1366	Arnuwandas II
Othniel's liberation from Cushan-rishathaim's		Tutankhamen, Eye	1366-1353	Suppululiumas
8-year oppression	1356			
Rest of 40 years	1356-1316	Harmhab	1353-1320	
		Nineteenth Dynasty		
				Arnuwandas III
		Ramses I	1320-1319	Mursilis II
		Seti I	1319-1299	
		Seti in Palestine	1319	
Ehud's liberation from 18-year Moabite oppression	1298	Ramses II	1299-1232	Muwatallis
80 years' rest of southern and eastern tribes	1298-1218			
		Battle at Kadesh	1295	
Deborah and Barak's liberation after Jabin's 20 years				Urhi-Teshub Hattusilis III
of oppression in the north	1258			
Rest in the north	1258-1218	Merneptah and other weak		Last weak Hittite kings
Gideon's liberation from 7-year Midianite oppression	1211	kings	1232-1200	End of Hittite kingdom about 1200
		Twentieth Dynasty		
Gideon's rule	1211-1171	Ramses III	1198-1167	
		War against Peoples of		
		the Sea	1194-1191	
Abimelech's kingship over Shechem	1171-1168			
Tola, Jair, Jephthah, Ibzan, Elon, Abdon	1168-1074	Ramses IV-XI	1167-1085	
Beginning of Philistine oppression	1119			
		Twenty-first Dynasty		
Samson's exploits	1101-1081			
Ark taken, Eli's death	1099	(High priests of Amon names		
Battle at Ebenezer, Philistines defeated	1079	on table 3)	1085-950	
Samuel judge	1079-1050			

* It is possible to assign only conjectural dates for the various judgeships and other events of this period; the dates here given set forth a possible solution to the problem of fitting all the periods of the book of Judges into the 480 years of 1 Kings 6:1. The dates of Egyptian kings are approximately correct. No dates for the Hittite kings are given, since their chronology is not yet established. *See* Hittites. For earlier Egyptian dates *see* Egypt, V, 1.

3. Tentative Chronology of the Hebrew Kingdoms* and the Exile

These B.C. dates are not all equally certain; they range from tentatively approximate to astronomically certain.†

EGYPT	HEBREWS	B.C.	ASSYRIA	B.C.
Twenty-first Dynasty, c. 1085 - c. 950			Shamshi-Adad IV	1052-1048
Smendes	Saul	1050-1011	Ashurnasirpal I	1048-1029
Herihor			Shalmaneser II	1029-1017
Psusennes I			Ashur-nirari IV	1017-1011
Pinodjem			Ashur-rabi II	1011-970
Amenophthis	David	1011-971	Ashur-resh-ishi II	970-965
Siamon			Tiglath-pileser II	965-933
Psusennes II	Solomon	971-931		
			Ashur-dan II	933-910
	Judah			
Libyan Dynasties, c. 950 - c. 750	Rehoboam	931-913		
	Abijam	913-911	Adad-nirari II	910-889
Twenty-second Dynasty	Asa	911-869	Tukulti-Ninurta	889-884
Sheshonk I				
Osorkon I				
Takelot I			Ashurnasirpal II	884-859
Osorkon II	Jehoshaphat	872-848*		
	Jehoram	854-841*	Shalmaneser III	859-824
Twenty-third Dynasty	Ahaziah	841		
Pedubast	Athaliah	841-835		
Sheshonk IV	Joash	835-796	Shamshi-Adad V	824-810
Osorkon III	Amaziah	796-767	Adad-nirari III	810-782
Takelot III			Semiramis (regent)	
Amenrud	Azariah	790-739*	Shalmaneser IV	782-772
Osorkon IV	(Uzziah)		Ashur-dan III	772-754
			Ashur-nirari V	754-746
Twenty-fourth Dynasty	Jotham	750-731*	Tiglath-pileser III	745-727
(of Saïs) c. 750-715				
Tefnakht	Ahaz	735-715*		
Bocchoris	Hezekiah	729-686*	Shalmaneser V	727-722
(So)			Sargon II	722-705
			Sennacherib	705-681

Israel

HEBREWS	B.C.
Jeroboam I	931-910
Nadab	910-909
Baasha	909-886
Elah	886-885
Zimri	885
Omri	885-874
(Tibni	885-880)
Ahab	874-853
Ahaziah	853-852
Joram	852-841
Jehu	841-814
Jehoahaz	814-798
Jehoash	798-782
Jeroboam II	793-753*
Zachariah	753-752
Shallum	752
Menahem	752-742
Pekahiah	742-740
Pekah	752-732*
Hoshea	732-722

Twenty-fifth Dynasty (Ethiopian) c. 750-663
Piankhi
Shabaka
Shabataka
Taharka
Tanutamon

Egypt	Judah	Events (B.C.)	Assyria / Babylonia / Persia
			Esarhaddon 681-669
			Ashurbanipal 669-627?
			Ashur-etil-ilani 627?-626?
			Sin-shar-ishkun 626?-612
			Ashur-uballit II 612- ?
	Manasseh 696-641*		
	Amon 641-639		**BABYLONIA**
Twenty-sixth Dynasty 663-525	Josiah 639-608		Nabopolassar 626-605
Psamtik I 663-609			Nebuchadnezzar II 605-562
Necho II 609-594	Jehoahaz 608	608 (*Closing events in last reigns of Judah*)	
	Jehoiakim 608-598	605 1st stage of Babylonian captivity; Daniel taken to Babylon (Nebuchadnezzar's accession yr.)	
	Jehoiachin 598-597	597 Fall of Jerusalem; captivity of Jehoiachin and Ezekiel	
Psamtik II 594-588	Zedekiah 597-586	586 Destruction of Jerusalem (19th yr. of Nebuchadnezzar)	
Apries (Hophra) 588-569			Amel-Marduk 562-560
Amasis 569-526			Nergal-sharusur 560-556
			Labashi-Marduk 556
			Nabonidus 556-539
			Belshazzar co-regent 553?-539
			PERSIA
		539 Fall of Babylon to Cyrus (Oct., Cyrus' accession yr.)	(Darius the Mede 539-537?)
Psamtik III 526-525			Cyrus (Persian) 539-530

---

* The Hebrew reigns thus marked (*) are reckoned as overlapping; that is, the earlier years of one reign coincide with the closing years of the preceding reign, representing coregencies. The one exception is Pekah, whose years seem to have been reckoned from 752 B.C., ten years before he took over actual control of the kingdom by murdering Menahem's son Pekahiah.

† Dates of the *Egyptian* kings of dynasties 22 to 25 are unknown, and the dynasty dates here given are approximate only.

The dates of the *Assyrian* kings from about 900 B.C. and on are generally accepted today as fixed with reasonable certainty within a year (for example, Sargon's reign began at some time between spring 722 and spring 721); a few are more exact than that.

Babylonian dates are well known, for Nebuchadnezzar's B.C. dating is completely certain; an astronomical tablet from his 37th year aligns that year with 568/67 B.C., spring to spring.

The dates assigned to most of the *Hebrew* kings are tentative; the Judah and Israel lines are aligned according to the most reasonably workable interpretation of the Bible data, then the B.C. dates are arrived at on the basis of synchronisms of the last kings of Judah with the known years of Nebuchadnezzar. Since certain B.C. dates of Judah's line are fixed, and there is a synchronization of the years of Ahab and Jehu of Israel with Assyrian data for Shalmaneser III, the chronology of the Hebrew kings may be considered approximately correct. Any difference of interpretation might shift the earlier reigns, but the difference would be a very few years.

These regnal years are not given in exact form (as 931/30, etc., to indicate that the year began in either the spring or fall of 931 and ended in 930, etc.). Hence a plus or minus 1 should be allowed unless exact dates of accession appear in the dictionary articles under names of specific kings.

4. Chronology of Postexilic Period

In this period fall well-established dates, for the Bible gives many regnal dates for Persian kings whose reigns are accurately established.

RESTORATION FROM CAPTIVITY		KINGS OF PERSIA	
B.C.			B.C.
539	Fall of Babylon to Cyrus (October, Cyrus' accession year)	Cyrus	539-530
538/37	Decree for return of Jews (Cyrus' 1st year)		
536	Return of Jews under Zerubbabel (probable; 70 years, inclusive, from 1st phase of captivity in 605)		
		Cambyses	530-522
		Smerdis	522
520/19	Temple building resumed (in 2d year of Darius I)	Darius I (the Great)	522-486
520-518	Ministry of Haggai and Zechariah		
515	Completion of Temple (in spring of 6th year of Darius)		
479/78	Esther made queen (7th year of Xerxes)	Xerxes	486-465
473	Jews delivered from death		
		Artaxerxes I	465-423
457	Return of Ezra to Jerusalem, spring and summer		
444	Return of Nehemiah, spring; building of wall of Jerusalem		
432	End of Nehemiah's first term as governor		
		Darius II	423-405/04
		Artaxerxes II	405/04-359/58
		Artaxerxes III	359/58-338/37
		Arses	338/37-336/35
		Darius III	336/35-331
		Alexander the Great (from his recognition in Babylonia)	331-323

5. Intertestamental Period—Important Dates

Except for difference of one year in a few instances in the Maccabean period (due to two methods of reckoning the Seleucid Era), these dates are undisputed.

B.C.

334-323	Alexander's conquest of Persian Empire (Asia Minor to borders of India)
331	Battle of Arbela (Gaugamela); decisive defeat of Persia
323	Alexander's death at Babylon
301	Division of Alexander's Empire into 4 parts (after battle of Ipsus)
281	Four divisions reduced to 3 (Lysimachus conquered by Seleucus I)
200	Palestine transferred from Ptolemies to Seleucids (after battle of Panium)
168	Rome defeats Macedonia; prevents Antiochus IV Epiphanes from taking Egypt
168	Antiochus Epiphanes persecutes Jews, desecrates Temple
165	Maccabees restore Temple after 3 years' profanation
146	Macedonia a Roman province
143-63	Jews independent under Maccabean rulers
63	Syria (Seleucid kingdom) and Palestine annexed by Rome
40	Herod appointed king of Judea in Rome
37	Herod takes Jerusalem from last Maccabean king
30	Egypt made a Roman province

6. Chronology of the Gospels

Chronological data in the Gospels are scanty; hence A.D. dates for this period are widely disputed among commentators. For the Biblical basis on which these dates are selected see *SDACom* 5:242-266.

B.C.

5-4	Birth of Jesus
4	Death of Herod

A.D.

26-35	Pilate procurator
27	Baptism of Jesus, in autumn
27-31	Ministry of Jesus (*see* Gospels, Harmony of)
31	Crucifixion of Jesus

7. Tentative Chronology of the Acts and the Pauline Epistles

There are virtually no chronological data in this period to synchronize with secular events. Dates here given are interpretative and most are conjectural, though within the range of a few years.

A.D.

31	Christ's ascension; Pentecost
34	Stephen stoned; church persecuted; gospel carried to Samaria
35	Paul converted
35-38	Paul at Damascus and in Arabia
38	Paul's escape from Damascus during reign of Aretas IV; visit to Jerusalem "after three years" (Gal 1:18); departure for Tarsus
44	James the brother of John martyred; Peter imprisoned at Passover time; death of Agrippa I
44-45	Barnabas brings Paul to Antioch; Paul remains there "a whole year" (Acts 11:26)
45	Barnabas and Paul take famine relief to Jerusalem
45-47	Paul's 1st Missionary Journey; on return Paul remains at Antioch "no little time" (Acts 14:28, RSV)
49	Jerusalem Council, "fourteen years after" (Gal 2:1)
49-52	Paul's 2d Missionary Journey; preaches in Phrygia, Galatia, and enters Europe, founding churches in Macedonia and preaching in Athens
51	Paul arrives at Corinth, staying 1½ years
51	Writing of 1 Thessalonians
51 or 52	Writing of 2 Thessalonians
52	End of 2d Missionary Journey; Paul "some time" at Antioch (Acts 18:23)
53-58	Paul's 3d Missionary Journey: through Asia Minor, 3 years at Ephesus, through Macedonia, 3 months at Corinth
57	Writing of 1 and 2 Corinthians
57 or 58	Writing of Galatians
57 or 58	Writing of Romans
58-60	Paul imprisoned at Caesarea "two years" (Acts 24:27); departs in autumn
60-61	Paul's journey to Rome; arrival in spring
61-63	Paul a prisoner in Rome "two whole years" (Acts 28:30)
c. 62	Writing of Ephesians, Colossians, Philemon
63	Writing of Philippians
63	Writing of Hebrews
63-66	Paul's travels in Crete, Asia Minor, Achaia, Macedonia
64	Writing of 1 Timothy
65	Writing of Titus
66	Writing of 2 Timothy
67	Deaths of Peter and Paul

Chrysolite. [Gr. *chrusolithos,* literally, "gold stone."] The 7th foundation of the New Jerusalem (Rev 21:20). The exact meaning of the Greek term is uncertain. Some have suggested that it designates a yellow or perhaps an olive-green form of chrysolite or a topaz.

Chrysoprase. [Gr. *chrusoprasos.*] The 10th foundation of the New Jerusalem (Rev 21:20). The exact meaning of the Greek term is uncertain. Modern chrysoprase is an apple-green transparent variety of chalcedony.

Chub (kŭb). [Heb. *Kûb.*] A people mentioned in the KJV of Eze 30:5 with Ethiopia and other countries as falling by the sword that smites Egypt. Their identity is unknown. The word does not appear in the RSV, which here follows the wording of the LXX, Syriac, and Vulgate to read "Libya."

Chun. *See* Berothah.

Church. [Gr. *ekklēsia,* from *ek,* "out," and *kaleō,* "to call." In secular Greek the term signified a gathering of the people, such as a regularly summoned political body, or an assemblage generally. No clear case can be produced of its use for a religious society. In the LXX *ekklēsia* is the rendering almost exclusively of the Heb. *qahal* (1 Ki 8:14, 22; 1 Chr 13:2; etc.), "gathering," "congregation," "assembly." NT usage of the term seems to be based on the usage of the LXX.]

In NT times this term is most frequently applied to a body of people who believe in Jesus as the Messiah and who accept Him and His teachings, and who are joined to the organization originated by Him (see Mt 16:18; cf. 1 Cor 3:11; Mt 28:19, 20; Mk 16:15, 16; Acts 2:38, 41, 47; 16:31; Rom 12:4, 5; 1 Cor 12:12). In Acts 7:38 the word is used for the congregation of the Israelites. When used of the Christian church it has several shades of meaning: (1) a church meeting (1 Cor 11:18), (2) the total number of Christians living in one place (ch 4:17), (3) the church universal (Mt 16:18).

After Jesus' ascension leadership of the church naturally devolved upon the apostles. As the need arose others were given positions of leadership (Acts 6:2-6). The church centered first in Jerusalem (see Lk 24:47; Acts 1:8; 10:39; 15:2), but later spread to other places (Acts 1:8; 8:1; etc.). The first church members were apparently exclusively Jews (ch 11:19), but later the Gentiles formed the major part of the church. As congregations sprang up in various places, local leaders were chosen (Acts 14:21-23; 20:17; etc. cf. 1 Ti 3:1-13).

The cardinal requirement for entrance into the Christian church was the acceptance of Jesus as the Messiah (Acts 2:38; 4:10-12; 5:30, 31; etc.). In respect to other doctrines, the beliefs of the infant church were much like those of Judaism. The Christians, both Jews and Gentiles, attended the synagogues on the Sabbath, and heard the writings of Moses expounded (chs 13:42-44; 15:13, 14, 21). In time, the need for development and clarification of doctrines became more pressing as various schismatic movements arose in the church (1 Ti 6:20; 2 Pe 2:15-19; 1 Jn 2:18, 19; 4:1-3; 5:10; see Jude 17-19).

The church was intended to take up and fulfill the work that Israel failed to do—that of representing God's character to the world (see Mt 28:19; Rom 2:28, 29; Gal 3:28, 29; Eph 2:8-22; 1 Pe 2:5-10), and of preparing itself for the return of its Lord (1 Cor 1:7, 8; 2 Pe 3:14; Rev 14:5; etc.).

Churches, Robbers of. [Gr. *hierosuloi,* from *hieron,* "temple," and *sulos,* "one who strips," "robber."] An expression occurring only in Acts 19:37, KJV, translated "sacrilegious [persons]" in the RSV. The papyri attest both the literal rendering of the KJV and the figurative sense of the RSV. The KJV translates the related verb *hierosuleō* as "commit sacrilege" (Rom 2:22, RSV "rob temples"). Paul had done nothing in Ephesus that could be interpreted as plundering the temple of Artemis (Diana), but the pagans could regard his preaching of the true God as sacrilege against their gods, especially against Artemis.

Chushan-rishathaim. *See* Cushan-rishathaim.

Chuza (kū′zȧ). [Gr. *Chouzas,* a transliteration of the Aramaic *Kûza'.* The name is of Persian origin and means "jar." It occurs also in Nabataean and Syriac inscriptions.] A steward of Herod (Antipas ?). His wife, Joanna, was one of those who contributed to the support of Jesus (Lk 8:3).

Cilicia (sĭ-lĭsh′ĭ-ȧ). [Gr. *Kilikia.*] An area on the southeastern coast of Asia Minor, bordered on the north by the Taurus Mountains and on the east by Mount Amanus. Its most famous city was Tarsus, the birthplace of the apostle Paul (Acts 21:39; 22:3; 23:34). Cilicia is mentioned in Assyrian and Babylonian inscriptions. Many recognize in the Kue (Heb. *Qeweh*) of 1 Ki 10:28, RSV, and 2 Chr 1:16, RSV, the ancient name of Cilicia. Cilicia is mentioned also in the Phoenician inscriptions of Zakar from Zenjirli, and by Herodotus (iii. 90).

The western part of Cilicia was mountainous, and was consequently called Rugged Cilicia. The eastern part was level, with marshes and swamps. The part of the Mediterranean lying between Cilicia and Cyprus was called the "sea of Cilicia" (Acts 27:5). After having belonged to the Seleucids for some time, Cilicia became a Roman province in 102 B.C., but was subsequently reorganized several times. The population consisted of descendants of the Hittites, Greeks, and Jews (cf. ch 6:9). The Christian church there probably owed its existence to Paul, who spent several years in that area after his conversion (Acts 9:30; 11:25, 26; Gal 1:21). During his 2d Missionary Journey he delivered to the churches there the decrees of the Jerusalem Council (Acts 15:23, 41). Map XIX, D-12/13.

Cinnamon. [Heb. *qinnamôn;* Gr. *kinnamōmon.*] Probably *Cinnamomum zeylanicum* or *Cinnamomum loureirii,* a medium-sized tree of Ceylon, producing an inner bark of aromatic quality and a highly prized oil. It is listed among the merchandise of Babylon the great (Rev 18:13), and its perfuming qualities served both holy and unholy ends (Ex 30:23; Prov 7:17; Song 4:14).

Cinneroth. *See* Chinnereth, 2.

Circle. [Heb. *chûg,* "circle," "vault," "horizon."] A term appearing in Is 40:22, KJV, and in Job 26:10; Prov 8:27; RSV. *Chûg* occurs also in Job 22:14, where the KJV renders it "circuit," and the RSV "vault." *Chûg* describes either the arch of the heavens or the circular horizon of earth or sea, as viewed by an observer from any point on the earth's surface.

Circumcision. [Heb. *mûloth;* Gr. *peritomē.*] A religious rite practiced by the Hebrews and other ancient peoples (see fig. 107), and even today by Jews, Moslems, and others. It consists in the surgical removal of the foreskin of the male, which the Hebrews performed on the 8th day, inclusive, after birth. Among the Hebrews this initiatory rite signified admission to the community of God's chosen people, and was a token of submission to the requirements of the covenant. God required circumcision of Abraham as a token of the covenant that made Abraham and his

descendants representatives of the true God (see Gen 17:1-14). Circumcision was a prerequisite to participation in the Passover ritual (Ex 12:48). The father usually performed the rite of circumcision upon his own children, though any Israelite might do so as proxy for the father. Flint knives were used, apparently even after iron instruments had come into use. During the wilderness wanderings the rite had been discontinued, but was resumed immediately upon entrance into the Promised Land, prior to the celebration of the first Passover observed there (Jos 5:2-9). Non-Jews who chose to unite with the commonwealth of Israel were required to submit to the rite of circumcision (cf. Gen 34:14-17; Ex 12:48). In later times baptism was also required, as well as the offering of sacrifices.

The term "circumcision" was frequently used in a figurative sense. The Philistines are frequently referred to as

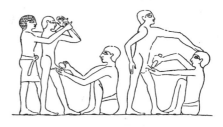

107. Egyptian relief depicting circumcision

"uncircumcised" (Jgs 14:3; etc.). This was, of course, literally true, but the term came to be practically equivalent to the word "heathen" or "gentile." Jeremiah refers to Israel as being "uncircumcised in the heart" (Jer 9:26), and says also of them, "their ear is uncircumcised" (ch 6:10). Moses considered himself as a man "of uncircumcised lips" (Ex 6:12) because he was hesitant in speech. To have uncircumcised ears and hearts was to be unwilling to heed divine instructions.

In NT times Jews commonly spoke of themselves as "the circumcision" (Gal 2:8; Col 4:11; etc.). The Judaizing, or "circumcision," party in the apostolic church maintained that all Gentile converts to Christianity should also accept circumcision and practice various rites and ceremonies of the Jewish faith. At one time this "circumcision" party succeeded in subverting the entire Galatian church (*see* Galatians, Epistle to), and sought to undermine Paul's labors for Gentiles elsewhere as well. Paul took the position that literal circumcision had become meaningless (1 Cor 7:19; Gal 5:6), and that the only kind of circumcision that mattered for the Christian was "that of the heart, in the spirit, and not in the letter" (Rom 2:28, 29).

Cis. *See* Kish.

Cistern. [Heb. *bôr* and *bo'r.*] An artificial, usually subterranean, reservoir for the storing of water. Since Palestine is without rainfall for several months of the year, and the character of the surface of the country is such that water quickly drains off the steep hillsides through numerous ravines, water must be collected and stored by artificial means to keep the country's population alive. Most houses had cisterns into which rain water was collected by means of drains from the roofs. Cisterns for animals were constructed in the open country. Most of them consisted of a narrow shaft that widened into a cylindrical hole cut into the rock, which opening could be covered by a stone or slab. The KJV uses the word "cistern" only rarely (2 Ki 18:31; Prov 5:15; Ec 12:6; Is 36:16; Jer 2:13), at times employing the less correct words "pit" or "well" (Lev 11:36; 2 Sa 3:26; Is 30:14; etc.) where the RSV reads "cistern."

Many ancient cisterns have been discovered and excavated in recent years. They show that the art of making them waterproof by means of a good cement plaster had been mastered at very early historical times. Some cisterns were very large and could hold many thousands of gallons of water. One found at Gezer has been estimated to have held 600,-000 gallons.

Citadel. A fortress commanding a city or palace. The word is found in the RSV as the rendering of the Heb. *'armôn,* (1) where it refers to a fortified section of the king's palace (1 Ki 16:18; 2 Ki 15:25), and (2) with reference to Zion (Ps 48:3, 13).

City. The Biblical record names Cain, Adam's son, as the first builder of a city (Gen 4:17). After the Flood the first city was Babylon, or Babel (ch 11:4, 9), built by men who defied God. The patriarchs did not, for the most part, live in cities, but sometimes pitched their tents near a city (chs 12:6; 13:3; etc.). When the Israelites moved into Canaan, they were content to live in the open country for a time, leaving the cities to the Canaanites (Jgs 7:8; 1 Sa 4:10; cf. Jgs 1:22-36). However, in the course of time the Israelites took over the cities from the indigenous population, and also founded new cities.

Most of the Palestinian city names had a meaning. Sometimes the name had reference to some natural feature in the vicinity, as for example: Ramah, meaning "elevated place"; Beer-sheba, "well of an oath"; En-gannim, "spring of gardens"; Kiriath-jearim, "city of forests"; Beth-haccherem, "house of the vineyard"; and Abel-shittim, "meadow of acacias." Sometimes cities were named after events, as was Bethel, meaning "house of God" (see Gen 28:11-19), or after men, as was Dan (Jgs 18:29).

Most cities were situated either on hilltops, to facilitate defense against attack, or on the slopes of mountains, with their citadels at the highest points. Palestinian cities were usually small; even important cities like Samaria, Megiddo, and Lachish covered only 19, 13, and 21 acres, respectively. The largest ancient city of Palestine known, Hazor, had a size of 182 acres. The city walls were built of stone and had towers at regular or irregular intervals as part of the fortification system. One or more gates gave entrance to the city. Rooms in the gateway were used for judicial trials (Amos 5:12, 15) and meetings of the city's administration (Ruth 4:1, 2, 11). Near the gates wide places were sometimes found which could be utilized for meetings in which the population took part (Neh 8:1). The streets were unpaved, unlighted, narrow, and crooked, a straight street being an exception (Acts 9:11). Some, such as the bakers' street (Jer 37:21), were named after the kind of shops found in them. For a typical city see fig. 282; *see* Fortification; Gate; Mound, 2; Wall.

City of David. *See* David, City of.

City of Destruction. [Heb. *'îr haheres,* literally, "city of the overthrow." However, many manuscripts, the Dead Sea scroll 1QIsᵃ, and some of the versions read, *'îr hacheres,* "city of the sun." The Egyptian city more commonly known by its Greek name Heliopolis, also meaning "city of the sun."] According to the KJV the figurative name of an Egyptian city mentioned in a conditional prophecy envisioning a time when certain cities in that land should be converted to the true God (Is 19:18). However, if the Heb. *'îr hacheres* is adopted (see above) the reference is to the Egyptian city of On, a center of sun worship.

City of Moab. *See* Moab, City of.

City of Palm Trees. *See* Jericho.

City of Refuge. One of 6 cities designated in Canaan, 3 on each side of the Jordan, where one guilty of unintentional manslaughter was accorded the right of asylum (Num 35:9-34). The 6 cities—Bezer, Ramoth-gilead, and Golan east of Jordan (Deut 4:41-43), and Hebron (Kiriath-arba), Shechem, and Kedesh in Naphtali to the west (Jos 20:7)—were selected so as to facilitate the flight of the pursued person in his effort to reach a place of safety. Wherever he might live, no person would have to go more than about 30 mi. in order to reach a city of refuge. Usually the distance would be considerably less. The six were Levitical cities, that is, cities assigned to the Levites, who supervised the administration of justice.

In a comparatively primitive society where the law of an "eye for eye, tooth for tooth, hand for hand, foot for foot, burning for burning, wound for wound, stripe for stripe" (Ex 21:24, 25) prevailed, where the machinery of justice had not been fully developed and made accessible everywhere, men who had unwittingly or accidentally taken human life would be at the mercy of the slain man's relatives who, in the heat of passion, might not distinguish between intentional and unintentional murder. The so-called law of the avenger required the eldest male relative of the slain man to avenge the death. A fugitive claiming the protection of one of the cities of refuge received a fair trial, and if found innocent was to remain there until the death of·the high priest. Apparently, the accession of a new high priest inaugurated a new era that was considered to erase any possible legal claims of the preceding era (Num 35:28, 32)—a wise provision that would prevent family feuds going on from generation to generation.

City of Salt. *See* Salt, City of.

City of Waters. *See* Rabbah.

Clauda. *See* Cauda.

Claudia (klô′dĭ-à). [Gr. *Klaudia,* the transliteration of a common Latin female name.] A Christian woman who sent greetings to Timothy from Rome (2 Ti 4:21).

Claudius (klô′dĭ-ŭs). [Gr. *Klaudios.*] Roman emperor from A.D. 41 to 54, and successor of Caligula. He was a son of Drusus, the stepson of Augustus. Tiberius was his uncle. He was a weak and vacillating, nevertheless conscientious, ruler. Claudius showed his friendship for Agrippa, who had helped him become emperor, by giving him those parts of Palestine not yet under his rule. Early in his reign he generally favored the Jews and restored to those in Alexandria privileges earlier taken away. However, for some unknown reason he later banished all Jews from Rome (Acts 18:2; Suetonius *Claud.* xxv. 4). It was this expulsion that caused Aquila and Priscilla to move from Rome to Corinth. The 5th-cent. historian Orosius (*Hist.* vii. 6. 14) claims that this event took place in the 9th year of Claudius (*c.* A.D. 49), and gives Josephus as his source, but no extant manuscript of Josephus' works mentions the expulsion decree of Claudius. The widespread famine under Claudius (Acts 11:28), during which the impoverished church in Jerusalem suffered greatly, cannot be dated with certainty. Suetonius (*Claud.* xviii. 2) and Tacitus (*Annals* xii. 43) mention a famine in Rome during Claudius' reign. Dio Cassius (lx. 11. 1-3) places it in the emperor's 2d regnal year (A.D. 42/43). Josephus records a famine in Palestine under the procuratorships of Fadus and Alexander (*Ant.* xx. 5. 2), the two procurators following Agrippa I, who died in A.D. 44. Although their terms of office cannot be dated with certainty, various historical evidences make it probable that Alexander's term ended in A.D. 48. Hence the famine must have taken place between 44 and 48. (See *SDACom* 6:98.)

Claudius Lysias (klô′dĭ-ŭs lĭs′ĭ-ăs). [Gr. *Klaudios Lusias.*] The military tribune in charge of the Roman garrison in Jerusalem at the time of Paul's visit to the city at the close of his 3d Missionary Journey. His Greek name Lysias seems to indicate that he was racially a Greek. He claims to have bought his Roman citizenship for a great sum of money (Acts 22:28). It was probably in connection with that event that he adopted the name of the emperor Claudius, whose wife and court carried on a flourishing trade in the sale of Roman citizenships. Luke calls him a *chiliarchos,* literally "a commander of 1,000 men," or "chief captain" (Acts 24:7, KJV). He was stationed with his soldiers in the castle of Antonia. This castle overlooked the Temple court area from the north, and was connected with it by stairs, which gave ready access to the court in case of emergency. Thus, when the Jewish mob attacked Paul, Claudius, with his soldiers, was on hand to rescue him. He first gave orders to examine Paul under torture, but when informed that Paul was a Roman citizen, he unbound him. When he later learned of a further Jewish plot to kill Paul he sent the apostle to the procurator Felix at Caesarea (Acts 21:30 to 23:30).

Clay. [Heb. generally *chomer;* Gr. *pēlos.*] A plastic earthen material used in making bricks and vessels. In Egypt, clay, a Nile alluvium, mixed with sand and straw, was used in the manufacture of brick and served as mortar. The variations in clay as used anciently in different lands depended upon the traces of organic and nonorganic substances mixed with the essential constituent, aluminum silicate. One of clay's basic qualities is its ability to become increasingly miry and workable as water is added, and more fixed as the **mixture dries.**

Clay molds were evidently used for casting the bronze vessels of Solomon's Temple (1 Ki 7:46). The Aramaic word translated "clay" in Dan 2 (*chasaph*) should be thought of as that which is formed from clay, "earthenware." Jesus, by moistening dirt, formed a clay poultice and used it in His healing of the blind man (Jn 9).

Clean. See Unclean Animals; Uncleanness.

Clement (klĕm′ĕnt). [Gr. *Klēmēs,* a transliteration of the Latin *Clemens,* "mild," or "merciful." The Greek form of this name occurs also in inscriptions.] A fellow worker with Paul in the church of Philippi (Php 4:3). It may have been he who was bishop at Rome *c.* A.D. 96 and who was author of the Epistle of Clement (*see* Apochryphal Books [NT]).

Cleopas (klē′ō-păs). [Gr. *Kleopas,* a contraction of *Kleopatros.* Both forms are attested by secular sources.] One of the two disciples who traveled to Emmaus on the resurrection day, who on their journey were joined by the risen Christ (Lk 24: 18). The later Christian tradition identifying Cleopas with Clopas (KJV "Cleophas") of Jn 19:25 cannot be proved or disproved from Scripture.

Cleophas. See Clopas.

Cloak. The translation of several Hebrew (in RSV only) and Greek words. The exact nature of the garment described in each of these cases is not always clear. The *himation* (Mt 5:40; Lk 6:29) was the loose, outer garment usually worn on the street. See Clothing.

Clopas (klō′păs), KJV **Cleophas** (klē′ō-făs). [Gr. *Klōpas,* from Aramaic *Qlwp',* attested in Palmyra.] Husband of one of the Marys who followed Christ to the cross (Jn 19:25).

Closet. In the KJV the translation of: (1) the

Heb. *chuppah,* "(bridal) chamber" (Joel 2:16); (2) the Gr. *tameion,* the innermost, hidden, or secret room of the house, or simply one of the inner rooms (Mt 6:6). In the RSV the word occurs once (Jgs 3:24), the translation of the Heb. *cheder,* in the context a privy.

Clothing. Cloth or other material worn over the body for covering and protection (Job 22:6; Prov 27:26). Adam's first clothing was of skins (Gen 3:21). Later, the art of weaving made available materials of wool (Lev 13:47), linen (ch 16:4; cf. Jos 2:6), and hair (Zec 13:4, RSV). Silk is mentioned 3 times in the KJV OT (Prov 31:22; Eze 16:10, 13). However, the Heb. *shesh,* rendered "silk" in Prov 31: 22, should probably be translated "fine white linen," and the "silk" of Eze 16: 10, 13 is from a word (Heb. *meshî*) of doubtful meaning. The spinning and weaving of cloth of various materials were household tasks, as is indicated by Prov 31:13, 19, 21-24. The Israelites were forbidden to wear garments made of linen mixed with wool (Lev 19:19). The Mosaic law also forbade the wearing of the distinctive clothing of one sex by the other (Deut 22:5).

The almost universal garment of primitive peoples was the loincloth. That it was also used in the ancient Near East is amply attested by the depictions on monuments ranging from Assyria to Egypt. It is found most often on captives of war, who were usually scantily clad. Other pictorial representations show that the loincloth in Bible lands was primarily an undergarment, over which a robe or other attire was usually worn. The word "loincloth" does not appear in the Bible; however, this garment seems to be the one designated at times by the Heb. *'ezôr,* translated "girdle" in the KJV, and generally "waistcloth" in the RSV (Job 12:18; Jer 13:1, 7; etc.).

A long tunic (Heb. *kethoneth* and *kuttoneth;* Gr. *chitōn*), or coat, was the common garment among both sexes in Bible times (Gen 37:3; 2 Sa 13:18, RSV). An outer garment called the *himation* was sometimes worn over the *chitōn.* The distinction between these two items of clothing may be noted in Mt 5:40, where the Lord's words are quoted: "If any man will sue thee at the law, and take away thy coat [*chitōn*], let him have thy cloak [*himation*] also." Jesus is here speaking of a legal act. The claimant was supposed to claim not the outer garment, but the less expensive inner garment. The defendant is advised as a Christian to be willing to let him have even the more costly outer one too. In Lk 6:29 the *himation* is first seized, and the victim is advised to permit his *chitōn* to be taken also, but an act of highway robbery is there under consideration and naturally the outer garment would be the one that would be seized first. *Himation* is also frequently used of clothes in general (see Mt 27:35; Mk 5:28; Lk 8:27). The purple robe placed upon Christ by the Roman soldiers was called *chlamus,* "a man's outer garment," by Matthew (ch 27:28, 31); *esthes,* a general term for clothing, by Luke (ch 23:11); and *himation,* "an outer garment," by John (ch 19:2, 5).

Over the *kethoneth* or *chitōn* a girdle, frequently made of leather (2 Ki 1:8; Mt 3:4), was at times worn, into which the bottom of the long tunic was sometimes tucked when maximum bodily freedom was needed (1 Ki 18:46). Christ's garment (Jn 19:23, 24; Gr. *chitōn*) was seamless; hence the Roman soldiers at the crucifixion decided to cast lots for it rather than tear it apart. The word translated "fisher's coat" in ch 21:7 (Gr. *ependutēs*) simply means "clothes" (see RSV). The terms "vesture" and "vestment" appearing occasionally are a rendering generally of the Heb. *lebûsh,* "clothing" (Gen 49:11; 2 Ki 10:22; etc.), and of the Gr. *himation* (Rev 19:13, 16, KJV), or the related term *himatismos* (Mt 27:35; Jn 19:24; KJV), "clothing," "apparel."

The feet were characteristically protected by sandals (Gr. *hupodēmata*) of varying construction and material, generally of leather (Eze 16:10; KJV "badgers' skin"). John the Baptist declared himself to be unworthy to unloose the thongs of Jesus' sandals (Mk 1:7, RSV). Removal of shoes also served as a mark of humility and reverence in the presence of God (Ex 3:5).

The headdress of Bible times was varied. In NT times the head covering was sometimes a hat of straw or felt, and sometimes a type of head scarf similar to the prayer scarves seen today in synagogues. Women's headdress consisted of a *veil or scarf. See Breeches; Girdle; Mantle; Robe. For the priestly garments see Ephod; Priest. See Dress for references to illustrations.

Cloud. In lands where rain is infrequent, as in Bible lands, rain clouds are watched for eagerly. Bible writers frequently mention clouds (Jgs 5:4; Job 26:8; 37:11; Ps 77:17; Ec 11:3; etc.), notably in figures

of speech (Prov 16:15; Is 18:4; 25:5; Jude 12). For example, the vaporous quality of clouds is used to illustrate life's vicissitudes (Job 30:15; Hos 6:4). For Israel, during the wilderness wandering, the presence of the Lord was marked by a pillar of cloud, which became a pillar of fire by night (Ex 13:21; etc.). Under special circumstances His glory filled the Temple like a cloud (1 Ki 8:10, 11; 2 Chr 5:14; cf. Eze 10:4).

Clouts. An Old English word meaning "cloth patches," or "rags," correctly translating the Heb. *sechabôth* (Jer 38:11, 12). In Jos 9:5, KJV, "clouted," with the meaning "patched," appears as a translation of the Heb. *tala',* "to patch."

Cloven-footed. An expression occurring in Lev 11:3, 7, 26, literally meaning "cleaving the cleft (of the hoof)." In v 26 the expression is distinguished from "divideth the hoof," so obviously is not synonymous with it. "Cloven-footed" seems to indicate a complete separation of the two parts of the hoof, not a partial division only, as perhaps in the case of the camel. According to Levitical law only animals that part the hoof, are cloven-footed, and chew the cud are permissible for food.

Club. The war club, or mace, of Bible times was a pierced pear-shaped stone or ball of metal placed on a stick that served as a handle. It is known to have been used from very early times throughout the ancient Orient as a deadly weapon. The word "club" is not found in the KJV, but in the RSV it is a rendering of the Heb. *mephis* (Prov 25:18; KJV "maul"), and of the Heb. *tôthach* (Job 41:29; KJV "dart"). The Gr. *xulon,* literally "wood" in Mt 26:47, 55; Mk 14:43, 48; Lk 22:52 (KJV "staff"), was probably not a mace but a heavy staff of wood tapering at the end, used as a cudgel or club.

Cnidus (nī′dŭs). [Gr. *Knidos.*] A port city at Cape Krio on the southwestern coast of Asia Minor. Part of the city lay on an island, which was connected with the mainland by a causeway. In NT times the city belonged to the Roman province of Asia. The Rome-bound ship on which Paul was a prisoner passed this city (Acts 27:7). Map XX, B-4.

Coal. As used in the Bible, a burning ember or charcoal, not coal as we know it today. On the Day of Atonement the high priest took "a censer full of burning coals of fire from off the altar" (Lev 16:12). Elijah found cakes baked on "hot stones"

(1 Ki 19:6, RSV) when he awoke from his desert sleep under the broom, or juniper, tree. In Prov 26:21, where the KJV gives "as coals are to burning coals," the RSV has "as charcoal to hot embers." The lifeless ember, known for its blackness, is used to contrast the former and present state of the leaders of Judah—once pure as snow, now with a visage "blacker than soot" (Lam 4:8, RSV). The fire by which Peter warmed himself in the outer court of the high priest's residence and the one over which Jesus cooked a morning meal for His disciples were doubtless charcoal fires (Jn 18:18; 21:9; RSV).

Coast. A word appearing frequently in the KJV in the obsolete sense of "border," "frontier," where no body of water is involved (Num 20:23; Deut 19:8; 2 Chr 11:13; etc.).

Coat. *See* Clothing.

Coat of Mail. [Heb. *siryôn, shiryan,* and *shiryôn,* "shining"; Hurrian *ṣariam* and *sharian.*] Body armor made of pieces of metal sewn on leather, woolen, or linen garments. The coat of mail was a Semitic or Hurrian invention (see fig. 108), as shown by the fact that the Egyptians

108. Fragment of a coat of mail found at Nuzi

adopted the Semitic or Hurrian word to designate this piece of armor, calling it *ṭryn.* The hieroglyphic character following the Egyptian word is the sign for leather, which indicates that the armor consisted of a leather base on which the metal scales were sewn. Armor scales, from 2 to 8 in. long, have been excavated in Palestine and Mesopotamia. The coat of mail was first worn only by eminent warriors or noblemen (1 Sa 17:5, 38; 1 Ki 22:34; 2 Chr 18:33), but later also by common soldiers (2 Chr 26:14). The KJV

reads "coat of mail" only in 1 Sa 17:5, 38, elsewhere reading variously "habergeon," "brigandine," and "double bridle."

Cock. [Gr. *alektōr.*] A male of the domestic fowl *Gallus domesticus.* The word is used in the OT once (Prov 30:31, RSV, where the KJV reads "greyhound"). The meaning of the Hebrew word is obscure, but "cock" is favored by the ancient versions. The earliest representation of a cock in Palestine is found on a seal of Jaazaniah of the period of Jeremiah, discovered at *Tell en-Naṣbeh* (see fig. 250). In the NT the word appears only in the narrative of Peter's denial of Christ, recorded in all four Gospels (Mt 26:34; Mk 14:30; Lk 22:34; Jn 13:38; etc.). The third watch of the night, which immediately preceded dawn, was probably designated as "cockcrowing" (Mk 13:35).

Cockatrice. *See* Serpent.

Cockcrow. The time of the night immediately before dawn.

Cockle. A KJV term translating the Heb. *bo'shah,* a useless, foul-smelling weed. Job declared that if he had been oppressive, let these noisome weeds grow in his fields instead of wheat (Job 31:40, RSV "thorns").

Code. A term used in the RSV of Rom 2:27; 7:6; 2 Cor 3:6 for the Gr. *gramma,* which the KJV renders "letter." In these passages the apostle is describing the literal, legalistic way in which the Jews observed the Mosaic code.

Coffer. [Heb. *'argaz,* perhaps a "saddlebag."] The container in which the Philistines sent offerings when they returned the ark to Israel (1 Sa 6:8, 11, 15, KJV).

Coffin. [Heb. *'arôn,* "chest" or "box."] Coffins were practically unknown among the ancient Hebrews, who were buried wrapped in clothes or sheets. *See* Burial. An exception was the case of Joseph, who died in Egypt (Gen 50:26). His embalmed body was apparently deposited in an Egyptian coffin or mummy case, of which many examples from his time exist.

Cohort. [Gr. *speira;* Latin *cohors.*] A Roman military unit. A legionary cohort in the time of Augustus was one tenth of a *legion and was composed of Roman citizens. In the auxiliary forces, recruited from the provinces, a cohort was of either 500 or 1,000 noncitizens. These were generally infantry, though there was a kind of cohort that had both foot soldiers and cavalry. The auxiliary cohorts not only were numbered but also bore geographical or honorific names. Volunteer troops specially levied were organized into *cohortes voluntariorum* ("cohorts of volunteers"). The geographical names at first indicated the origin of the troops, though later, after the cohorts were replenished with local recruits in the places where they were stationed, the names lost their geographical character. The auxiliary cohorts were commanded by prefects who were ex-centurions. Under the prefect were centurions and decurions. In the NT two specific cohorts are mentioned by name:

a. The Italian Cohort (KJV "Italian band"), apparently a cohort stationed at Caesarea in apostolic times (Acts 10:1). The existence of 32 cohorts by that name is known. The full name of one of these cohorts was *Cohors Italica* I (or II, III, etc.) *civium Romanorum voluntariorum*, but each was usually referred to by the abbreviated form *Cohors Italica*. These Italian cohorts consisted, as their name indicated, of Roman citizens who had volunteered for military service.

b. The Augustan Cohort (KJV "Augustus' band"). This *Speira Sebastē* (Latin *Cohors Augusta*, "imperial cohort") bore a name found frequently among the units of Roman auxiliary forces. There is inscriptional evidence that a cohort named Augusta was stationed in Syria in the 1st cent. A.D. This may have been one of the five cohorts stationed in Caesarea. Some have suggested that it was possibly a cohort of *frumentarii*, "imperial couriers," whose duties might include conducting such a prisoner as Paul to Rome for an appeal to the emperor (Acts 27:1). However, there is no evidence for this title's having been used for a cohort of the latter type.

Coin. A piece of metal issued by authority of the government as a standard currency with guaranteed values to be used as money. The first coined money is supposed to have been issued by the kings of Lydia in the 7th cent. B.C. This coinage was taken over by Cyrus upon the conquest of Sardis in 547 B.C. and subsequently spread through the whole Persian Empire and to other nations. Ancient coins were issued in gold, silver, copper, and bronze, the last mentioned being the most common. The word "coin" does not appear in the KJV, but in the RSV is used in several NT passages as the rendering of the Gr. *dēnarion, drachma, lepton,* and *kerma* (Mt 22:19; Mk 12:15, 42; Lk 15:8, 9; 20:24; 21:2; Jn 2:15). The first 2 terms refer to Greek or Roman silver coins. These coins generally bore the

emperor's bust and titles on the obverse (see fig. 340), and often the image of a genius or a deity on the reverse. The representations upon them caused these coins to be rejected by orthodox Jews as acceptable Temple offerings. Consequently, the Jews in Christ's time used locally minted copper coins, which bore Hebrew inscriptions but no images of living creatures. Hence, money-changers were active in the Temple court on feast days (Mt 21:12; Jn 2:15) exchanging the silver coins that the worshipers brought from other countries into a currency usable in the Temple. *See* Daric; Money.

Colhozeh (kŏl-hō′zĕ). [Heb. *Kol-chozeh,* "he sees all."] A Jew whose son Shallum was a district officer of Mizpah, and a builder of Jerusalem's wall in Nehemiah's time. He was probably also the father of Baruch, an inhabitant of Jerusalem (Neh 3: 15; 11:5).

College. *See* Second Quarter.

Collops. A KJV term appearing in Job 15: 27, where the phrase "collops of fat" describes the thick folds of fat on the flanks of a man. However, the Hebrew term (*pimah*) translated by this phrase may mean simply "fat," with emphasis, probably, on a superabundance of it.

Colony. In NT times a settlement of Roman citizens in subject territories, authorized by the senate of Rome. The settlers retained their Roman citizenship with the privileges connected with it, and usually formed the aristocracy of the area in which they lived. From the time of Augustus colonies were formed by settling veteran soldiers, many of whom were noncitizens, in strategic localities, and giving them special privileges, such as Roman citizenship and a city constitution modeled after that of Rome. The colonies were usually loyal supporters of the Roman cause in distant countries. Philippi in Macedonia was such a colony (Acts 16:12).

Colossae (kŏ-lŏs′ē), KJV **Colosse** (kŏ-lŏs′ē). [Gr. *Kolossai.*] A city of Asia Minor, in southwestern Phrygia, on the Lycus River, not far from where the river joins the Maeander. It lay about 11 mi. from Laodicea and 13 mi. from Hierapolis, and was originally on the great trade route that led from Ephesus, via Magnesia, Colossae, and Tarsus, to Syria. It is mentioned by Herodotus (vii. 30) and Xenophon (*Anab.* i. 2. 6) as a large and wealthy city. It owed its wealth mainly to its wool of violet hue, called *colossinus*. When

109. Site of ancient Colossae

the trade route was changed, Colossae declined. A few ruins of Colossae are visible near the village of *Honaz*. The population of NT times consisted mainly of Phrygians, Greeks, and Jews, with Phrygians predominating. Its Christian church had probably been founded by Epaphras (Col 1:7). Later a certain Archippus was its leader (Col 4:17; Phm 2). In Paul's days the meetings were apparently held in the home of Philemon (Phm 2), the master of Onesimus who was a runaway slave converted by Paul in Rome and later returned to his master (vs 10-12). Paul wrote a letter to the church (*see* Colossians, Epistle to the). Map XX, B-4.

Colosse. *See* Colossae.

Colossians, Epistle to the. One of 4 letters by Paul written, as is generally agreed, from Rome toward the close of his 1st imprisonment there, about the year A.D. 62. The other prison epistles are Ephesians, Philippians, and Philemon. In each of these he speaks of "bonds" or calls himself a "prisoner" (Eph 6:20; Php 1:13, 14; Col 4:3, 10, 18; Phm 1, 9). That at least 3 of these epistles were written at approximately the same time is shown by the fact that the same persons are listed as being with Paul at the time the epistles were written (Eph 6:21; Col 4:7-9; Phm 10-19). During the course of his 3d Missionary Journey Paul had labored at Ephesus for 3 years (see Acts 19:1-41). Although it is not known whether he ever visited Colossae, a little more than 100 mi. to the east, the influence of his ministry during this time extended far beyond the immediate vicinity of Ephesus. Demetrius protested that "almost throughout all [the Roman province of] Asia, this Paul hath persuaded and turned away much people" (v 26). At least one resident of Colossae, Philemon, had found Christ through Paul's ministry (Phm 19), and possibly also Epaphras, who was in charge of the church there (Col 1:7). They may have heard the gospel in Ephesus and carried it back with them to Colossae, since

Paul seems not to have labored there himself (Col 2:1, 5). When Paul wrote to the believers at Colossae, Epaphras had but recently arrived with a report of the love and zeal of believers there (ch 1:7, 8), and it was this report that prompted the writing of the epistle. Tychichus, a companion of the apostle, together with Onesimus, Philemon's slave, was dispatched with the letter (ch 4:7-9). Whatever the case, Paul considered himself as spiritual father and founder of the church at Colossae, and thus responsible for its welfare.

According to the epistle a twofold error was threatening the church at Colossae. The exact nature of this error is not clearly stated, but we can infer its general nature from what Paul writes in warning against it. On the one hand, an effort was apparently being made to persuade Gentile Christians at Colossae to adopt the rites and ceremonies of Judaism (Col 2:11-16) and certain ascetic tendencies (vs 18-23). On the other, there is evidence of a speculative type of philosophy that resembled the later Gnostic heresy (vs 4, 8, 18, 20). Some have traced the Colossian error to the Essenes, or the Qumran sect, who are known to have held and practiced certain of these teachings. What is said of "angels" closely resembles the intermediary beings or "emanations" of Gnosticism (chs 1:16; 2:18). The Greek words for "mystery" (ch 1:26, 27), "fulness" (v 19), and "knowledge" (ch 2:3) appear as technical terms in ancient Jewish and pagan religious and philosophical literature. Here, Paul uses them in a Christian sense.

The apostle meets the errors in the Colossian church by setting forth the pre-eminence of Christ, as infinite God and Creator and sustainer of all things (chs 1:15-17; 2:8, 9), as the author of salvation and the perfecter of Christian character (chs 1:20-27; 2:7; 3:1-3), and as head of the church (ch 2:17, 18). Belief in Christ, therefore, excludes ceremonialism and speculative philosophy. All the mysteries man needs to know have been revealed in Christ, whom the apostle presents as the Christian ideal (ch 3:12-24).

The epistle logically falls into 6 principal sections: (1) The introduction: salutation, commendation, and statement of purpose (Col 1:1-13). (2) The doctrinal section exalting the pre-eminence of Christ to the Christian (chs 1:14 to 2:3). (3) A warning against error (ch 2:8-23). (4) Exhortations to imitate Christ's exemplary life (Col 3:1-17). (5) Duties of social relationships (chs 3:18 to 4:6). (6) The conclusion: salutation and greetings (ch 4:7-18).

Comeliness. In the OT the translation of Hebrew terms signifying "splendor," "excellency," "honor," "beauty" (Eze 16:14; 27:10; Dan 10:8; KJV). In Is 53:2 the Messiah is declared to have no "comeliness," that is, no outward splendor. In the NT, "comeliness" is the translation of a Greek term meaning "presentability" (1 Cor 12:23, KJV).

Comforter. *See* Holy Spirit.

Coming of the Lord. *See* Second Coming of Christ.

Commander. *See* Captain.

Commandments, The Ten. *See* Ten Commandments.

Commentary. [Heb. *midrash,* "exposition," from *darash,* "to inquire," "to search."] A term appearing once (2 Chr 24:27, RSV), where the KJV reads "story." The Hebrew term occurs elsewhere in the OT only in ch 13:22, where, however, both versions render it "story." "Commentary" would be a suitable translation there also. A "commentary" in the sense of a "story" would be a religious narrative whose primary purpose was to teach truth.

Common. The translation of various Hebrew and Greek words meaning "that which belongs to all," "general," "universal," "public," in contrast with what belongs to one person or to a limited group. Thus, "the common faith" is universal in the sense that it belongs to all men everywhere (Tit 1:4). The "common salvation" of Jude 3 is the salvation to which all who believe have access. At times "common" represents that which comes in contact with everybody and everything, and thus means "profane," "impure," "unclean" (see Rom 14:14, where the Gr. *koinos,* generally translated "common," is rendered "unclean").

Commonwealth. In Eph 2:12 a rendering of the Gr. word *politeia,* "state," "commonwealth," used of the economy of Israel from which, by a failure of Israel to fulfill her mission, the Gentiles had been excluded. In Php 2:20, RSV, the word is a translation of the Gr. *politeuma,* with essentially the same meaning. In the KJV *politeuma* is rendered *"conversation," an Old English word meaning one's course of conduct or behavior. Paul reminds the Philippian believers that their commonwealth is in heaven, even though they are at present upon earth.

Conaniah (kŏn'ȧ-nī'ȧ), KJV twice **Cononiah** (kōn-ô-nī'ȧ). [Heb. *Kônanyahû,* "Yahweh has established."]

1. A Levite in charge of the tithes and offerings in Hezekiah's reign (2 Chr 31:12, 13).

2. A Levite in a responsible position in the reign of Josiah (2 Chr 35:9).

Concision. [Gr. *katatomē,* "mutilation," "a cutting in pieces."] A term appearing once (Php 3:2) to refer to circumcision in a derogatory way. Since circumcision had become meaningless, or even harmful, spiritually in that it led the people to trust in an obsolete system, it is referred to as being nothing more than an act of mutilation. The Philippians were told to beware of the Jews who advocated the continuation of the ancient rite. *Katatomē* is used as a play on the word *peritomē,* "circumcision," and seems also to imply that the circumcision party stirred up divisions in the church, that is, it cut it to pieces.

Concubine. An inferior wife in the system of polygamy. Concubines were sometimes taken from among slaves (Gen 16:2, 3), and could be divorced more easily than regular wives (ch 21:10-14). Their sons were also considered inferior to those born to the full-fledged wives (Gen 25:6; Jgs 8:31; 9:18; cf. vs 14, 15).

Conduit. In the Bible this word is used to describe a channel, or aqueduct, generally artificial, which is used to conduct water to a city. The conduit mentioned in 2 Ki 18:17; 20:20 is most probably the rock-hewn tunnel excavated by Hezekiah from the Gihon spring to the Pool of Siloam (see figs. 443, 444), also called Upper Pool. *See* Siloam. The best-known aqueducts of the Greek and Roman period, bringing water into a city over long distances, were closed masonry channels, maintaining a free flow by a slight decline toward the point of delivery. To maintain proper levels they were carried partly in tunnels, on ground level where possible, and over

110. Ancient aqueduct at Smyrna

valleys and streams and into the lower-lying city on arched structures, sometimes many feet above ground. See fig. 110.

Coney. *See* Rock Badger.

Confectionary. In 1 Sa 8:13, KJV, the rendering of the Heb. *raqqach,* "spice mixer," "ointment mixer." When the Israelites demanded a king of the prophet Samuel, he pointed out to them that a king would take their daughters to serve him, among other things, as spice, or ointment, mixers. The same Hebrew term is rendered ***"apothecary" in Neh 3:8; RSV "perfumer."

Confession. Generally an acknowledgment of faith in God and His superiority and authority, or an admission of sin, either of which, according to circumstances, may be made publicly or privately, and either to God or to man. Confession of the power and supremacy of God may be sincere or insincere (1 Ki 8:33, 35; Is 48:1), willing or unwilling (Rom 14:11; Php 2:11), as may also be the confession of sin. In individual confession there must be a specific acknowledgment of the sin or sins involved (Lev 5:5), accompanied by repentance (Mt 3:2, 6, 8; Acts 2:38; cf. Ps 38:18), restitution, if necessary and possible (Lev 6:4; Lk 19:8; cf. Num 5:7, 8), and reformation (1 Ki 8:35; Prov 28:13; Is 55:7; Acts 19:18, 19). The requirements being met, forgiveness is assured (1 Jn 1:9). All sins must be confessed to God, and those where fellow men have been wronged, to them also (Mt 5:23, 24; Lk 17:4; Jas 5:16).

The word "confession" is sometimes used to describe a statement of faith in Christ (Lk 12:8; Rom 10:9; 1 Jn 4:15); an open acknowledgment or profession of one's beliefs (Acts 23:8; Rom 10:10); or a concession to, or affirmation of, a belief or fact (Jn 1:20; Acts 24:14). The word is also found describing Christ's acknowledgment of His own people before the Father (Mt 10:32; Rev 3:5).

There is no Biblical basis for the establishment of an ecclesiastical confessional wherein the absolving of sin becomes a priestly function.

Coniah. *See* Jehoiachin.

Conjugal Rights. *See* Benevolence.

Cononiah. *See* Conaniah, 1.

Conscience. [Gr. *suneidēsis,* "moral consciousness," "conscience."] An inward faculty of consciousness that sits in judgment on the moral rightness of thoughts, words, and actions, independent of the individual's desires or inclinations. The word "con-science" does not appear in the KJV OT, and only once in the RSV OT (1 Sa 25: 31), the translation of the Heb. *leb,* "heart." However, its function and operation are implied in the OT (see Gen 3:8; 1 Sa 24:5; Ps 51:3; etc.). All men are endowed by God with a conscience, but not all consciences are equally enlightened (see Rom 2:14-20).

The Bible describes different kinds of consciences. Paul mentions a "good conscience" (1 Ti 1:5). He himself was always careful to keep his conscience clear before God (Acts 24:16). He taught that a good conscience can remain so only so long as faith and integrity are maintained (see 1 Ti 1:19, 20). Enlightened by the Holy Spirit, Paul's conscience could witness to his truthfulness when he expressed his burden for his fellow Jews (Rom 9:1). He was so confident of his blameless conduct that he could appeal to the consciences of others as witnesses of it (2 Cor 4:2; cf. 2 Ti 1:3; Heb 13:18). Deacons, he instructed, must have a clear conscience in the faith (1 Ti 3:9). In discussing for the Corinthian believers the moral involvements of eating meat offered to idols, he implied that such a practice might not be a sin of itself; however, if one's conscience was disturbed by this practice, or if indulgence became a stumbling block to a brother with a weak conscience, then the practice should be avoided (1 Cor 8; cf. ch 10:19-33; *SDACom* 6:719-723, 746-751). The apostle wrote also of a "conscience seared" (1 Ti 4:2), and a defiled conscience (Tit 1:15), referring perhaps to a conscience which has become insensible to guilt because of protracted sin (cf. Is 5:20; Mi 3:2). The author of Hebrews points out that the various sacrifices of the Mosaic dispensation "could not make him that did the service perfect, as pertaining to the conscience"; only an acceptance of Christ's sacrifice could do that (Heb 9:9-14). Peter admonished the believers in Asia Minor (1 Pe 1:1) to keep their consciences clear by right living, so that evildoers might find nothing by which to accuse them (ch 3:16).

Consecration. The ritual act or ceremony by which a person or place is set aside for the worship and service of God. Aaron and his sons were consecrated to office (Ex 28: 41); David called for the people to consecrate their service to the Lord (1 Chr 29:5, KJV); the Levites consecrated themselves to God in the time of King Hezekiah (2 Chr 29:31). Inanimate objects and also animals were sometimes consecrated to holy use (Ex 19:23, RSV; Lev 8:22; Jos 6:19; 2 Chr 29:33). "Consecrated" (Heb 7:28) is literally "perfected," and in ch 10:20 means "inaugurated," "dedicated." Frequently the RSV reads "consecrate" where the KJV has "sanctify" (Jn 10:36; 17:19; 1 Cor 7:14; etc.).

Constellations. The translation of: (1) The Heb. *kesilim* in Is 13:10, the singular form of which (*kesil*) is rendered "Orion" in Job 9:9; 38:31; Amos 5:8. The plural probably refers to Orion and associated constellations. (2) The Heb. *mazzaloth* in 2 Ki 23:5, RSV, probably meaning the constellations of the zodiac. The KJV translates the term "planets," but this is obviously not its meaning. *See* Orion.

Consumption. The translation of (1) the Heb. *kalah*, "complete destruction" (Is 10:23; 28:22); (2) the Heb. *killayon*, "annihilation" (ch 10:22); (3) the Heb. *shachepheth*, perhaps pulmonary tuberculosis or some other disease causing a wasting away of the body (Lev 26:16; Deut 28:22).

Conversation. Used in the KJV only in the archaic sense of "way of life," "conduct," "manner of living" (Gal 1:13; Eph 4:22; 1 Ti 4:12; etc.), not once with its modern connotation of oral interchange of views, sentiments, etc. Twice it is used in the latter sense in the RSV (Jer 38:27; Lk 24:17).

Conversion. The noun "conversion" occurs once (Acts 15:3), the rendering of the Gr. *epistrophē*, literally, "a turning toward." The verb form "convert" appears a number of times in the KJV in the active sense (Ps 19:7; Jas 5:19, 20), and in the passive sense (Is 60:5; Mt 13:15). The literal meanings of the words thus translated are "to turn," "to turn back," "to turn toward." The RSV prefers these literal renderings, and "convert" as a verb does not appear in that version. However, "convert" as a noun appears in Acts 13:43; Rom 16:5; 1 Cor 16:15; 1 Ti 3:6. Conversion is the turning of the soul from sin to God. The turning from sin is the step of repentance, and the turning to God is the act of faith through which salvation becomes possible (Eph 2:8, 9).

Convocation. [Heb. *miqra'*, "assembly," "convocation."] A term appearing only in the phrase "holy convocation," which phrase is used to describe the sacred assemblies on the Sabbath day (Lev 23:3) and on the festivals (Lev 23). Besides the weekly Sabbaths there were seven special days of "convocation" each year—the first and last days of the Feast of Unleavened Bread (vs 6-8), Pentecost (vs 15-21), the first day of the seventh month (vs 24, 25), the Day of Atonement (vs 26-32), and the first and last days of the Feast of Tabernacles (vs 34-36). No labor was to be performed on any of these days. *See* names of individual feasts.

Coos. *See* Cos.

Coping. An architectural term used in 1 Ki 7:9. However, the Hebrew word thus translated (*tephachoth*) is of uncertain meaning. "Coping" is a conjectural translation.

Copper. *See* Bronze.

Cor. [Heb. and Aramaic *kor;* Phoenician *kr;* Akkadian *kurru.*] A dry and liquid measure. (1 Ki 5:11, RSV; 2 Chr 2:10, RSV; Eze 45:14). It was of Sumerian origin, and came to the Hebrews via the Akkadians. The cor was the equivalent of a "homer" (Eze 45:14) or 10 ephahs as a dry measure (=220 liters, 6.24 bu.), and the equivalent of 10 baths as a liquid measure (=220 liters, 58.12 gal.).

Coral. [Heb. *ra'môth* and *penînîm.*] The calcareous skeletons of certain marine organisms of a low order. The coral of the Mediterranean Sea and of the Red Sea was red (*Corallium nobile*) and was used by the ancients for jewelry and ornaments. It is not certain whether this is the coral mentioned in the Bible. The *ra'môth* of Job 28:18 and Eze 27:16 listed among highly prized articles brought to the markets of Tyre by either Syrian or Edomite traders, is of uncertain meaning. *Penînîm,* translated "rubies" in the KJV, is also of uncertain meaning, but probably in some instances stands for coral (Job 28:18; Prov 8:11; 20:15; 31:10; Lam 4:7). The RSV translates *penînîm* variously as "pearls," "jewels," "costly stones," and "coral."

Corban. [Gr. *korban,* a transliteration of the Heb. *qorban,* "a gift," "an offering," literally, "that which is brought near."] An expression used by a Jew by which he was released from obligation to his parents (Mk 7:11). *Qorban* appears frequently in the OT (Lev 1:3; 2:1; 27:9; Num 7:3, 12, 13, 17; etc.), and signifies an offering. When a Jew pronounced this term under the circumstances described by Jesus, it meant that any benefit that his parents might derive from him was now a gift to the Temple, to which they could henceforth lay no claim. Christ scathingly rebuked the Jews who, in their attempt to defraud their parents, used this pious device, the consequence of which was that a command of God, namely the 5th commandment, was set aside (Mk 7:9-13; cf. Mt 15:3-5). For Jewish traditions concerning vows see Mishnah *Nedarim.*

Cord. A rope (Jos 2:15; Jgs 15:13; Jer 38:6; compare KJV and RSV). The term is frequently used figuratively, for example, of the fetters of Sheol (2 Sa 22:6, RSV), of affliction (Job 36:8), of the plots and devices of the wicked (Ps 129:4; 140:5), and of the love of God that draws men to Him (Hos 11:4). The Heb. *pathîl,* translated "bracelets" in Gen 38:18, 25, KJV, is preferably rendered "cord" (RSV). The expression "signet and . . . cord" in these verses probably refers to Judah's seal and the cord to which it was fastened and by which it was hung around the neck. *See* Seal.

Core. *See* Korah, 4.

Coriander. [Heb. *gad.*] An herb, *Coriandrum sativum,* which grows wild in the Near

East. Its round aromatic fruit, called "coriander seed," is white or yellow-gray and is used for seasoning and medicinal purposes. Moses described manna as being like coriander seed in appearance (Ex 16:31; Num 11:7).

Corinth (kŏr'ĭnth). [Gr. *Korinthos.*] An ancient Greek city lying about 5 mi. southwest of the present canal crossing the Isthmus of Corinth (Map XX, B-3). To the south was a mountain about 1800 ft. high rising steeply from the lowland, on the summit of which, called the *Acrocorinthus,* stood a citadel and a temple of Aphrodite. The location of Corinth on the only land connection between northern Greece and the Peloponnesus, as well as the fact that the city had harbors on two gulfs (the harbor of Cenchreae, about 7 mi. east of Corinth on the Saronic Gulf, and the harbor of Lechaeum, 1½ mi. west on the Corinthian Gulf), was responsible for its importance and wealth. Corinth was connected with Lechaeum by two parallel walls. Since the canal (constructed from 1881 to 1893) through the 5-mile-wide

111. Map of the central area of the ancient city of Corinth

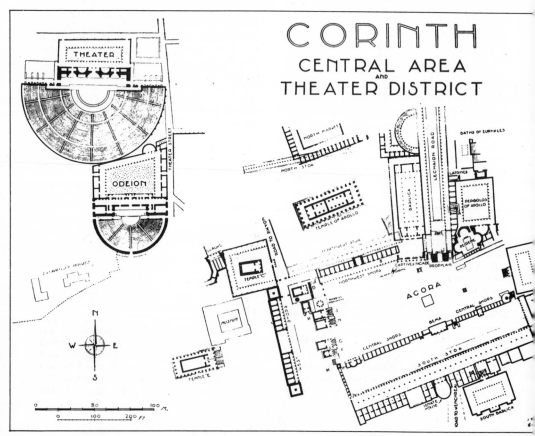

112. Ruins of the temple of Apollo at Corinth

isthmus did not exist in ancient times, small ships were often hauled overland on a track (called the *diolkos*) from the Saronic Gulf to the Corinthian Gulf and vice versa.

The earliest settlers of Corinth were non-Greeks. Later the Phoenicians settled colonists there who were engaged in the manufacture of purple dye from shellfish. They also introduced the manufacture of textiles, pottery, and armor. In the latter part of the 2d millennium people from Attica took Corinth, and later the Dorians conquered it. The city fell into the hands of Philip of Macedon and remained under Macedonian control until declared independent by the Romans in 196 B.C. It rebelled against Rome and was completely destroyed by Mummius in 146 B.C., remaining in ruins for a century. Julius Caesar began to rebuild the city in 44 B.C. It became the capital of the senatorial province of Achaia, with the status of a colony, which was called *Colonia Laus Iulia Corinthiensis.* Its status made it the residence of a proconsul (Acts 18: 12, RSV). This official held his court in the center of the agora, or market place, as excavations reveal. The new city had many temples, basilicas, and a large number of shops.

Many Romans lived in the city, also Greeks and Orientals. There was also a Jewish community large enough to have its own synagogue. A stone lintel with a fragmentary inscription "[Syna]gogue of the Hebr[ews]" has been found there (fig. 468). The script shows that it comes from a building of the 4th cent. A.D., which may, however, have been at the place on which the synagogue of Paul's day had stood (Acts 18:4). The contrast in the social status of the rather mixed population

was great, probably two thirds of the population being made up of slaves. Hence, many were poor, and a small number were exceedingly rich.

The city was universally known for its immorality. The term "Corinthian girl" was synonymous with "prostitute," and "to Corinthianize" meant to lead an immoral life. In later Greek comedies "Corinthian" is occasionally the designation for a drunkard. According to Strabo there were about 1,000 slave girls as temple prostitutes in the sanctuary of Aphrodite located on *Acrocorinthus.* An inscription shows they had their own seats in the theater. These conditions throw light on Paul's references to the immorality of the pagan world in his two letters to the Corinthians (1 Cor 5:1; 6:9-20; 10:8; 2 Cor 7:1), and in his letter to the Romans (Rom 1:18-32), written while he was at Corinth during his 3d Missionary Journey.

American expeditions have carried out intermittent excavations at Corinth since 1896. Practically the whole agora has been excavated, as have sections of the Lechaeum Road, the Odeum, the Theater, the Temple of Asclepius, and some other isolated structures. These excavations have made it possible to gain an amazingly accurate picture of life in ancient Corinth. An inscription containing the name of Erastus (probably the man mentioned in Rom 16:23) has been found, also one from a fish market (cf. the "meat market" of 1 Cor 10:25). See figs. 161, 321. In the agora was found the *Bēma,* the tribunal ("judgment seat," KJV) of the proconsul (Acts 18:12). It was identified by an inscription found in the vicinity. See fig. 113.

113. The agora of Corinth with the *Bēma,* the judgment seat, of Gallio in the left center

Paul came to Corinth on his 2d Missionary Journey and spent 18 months in the city. During that time he founded a church (Acts 18:1-18), which subsequently exerted wide influence. Later Apollos worked in Corinth with considerable success (Acts 18:24, 27, 28; 19:1; 1 Cor 3:4). Paul may have revisited the city during his stay of 3 years at Ephesus (2 Cor 12:14; 13:1). He spent a brief time, probably the largest part of 3 months, there toward the end of the 3d Missionary Journey about the winter of A.D. 57/58 (Acts 20:2, 3). In his letter to Timothy, Paul implies that he made at least one later visit to Corinth after his first Roman imprisonment (2 Ti 4:20). Two of Paul's longest letters now extant were written to the church at Corinth. At least one other letter has been lost (1 Cor 5:9).

Corinthians (kö-rĭn'thĭ-ănz). [Gr. *Korinthioi*.] Inhabitants of the city of *Corinth (Acts 18:8; etc.).

Corinthians, Epistles to the. On the basis of both internal and external evidence the two Corinthian epistles are fully attested as coming from the pen of the apostle Paul. The first was written from Ephesus (1 Cor 16:8) in the spring, probably of the year A.D. 57, and the second from Macedonia (2 Cor 2:13), doubtless in the summer of the same year. The earliest known titles are simply "To the Corinthians 1" and "To the Corinthians 2."

During the course of his 2d Missionary Journey Paul labored at Corinth for a year and a half, about A.D. 51-52, and there founded a flourishing church (Acts 18: 1-11). On his 3d Missionary Journey he devoted 3 years to the city of Ephesus and the Roman province of Asia, about A.D. 54-57. After the apostle's departure from Corinth numerous doctrinal and practical problems had arisen, and word was brought to Paul at Ephesus, perhaps first by Apollos, a learned and eloquent Christian who had labored earnestly to build up that church (Acts 18:24 to 19:1; cf. 1 Cor 16:12). Also, members of Chloe's household, who belonged to the Corinthian church, had come with disconcerting news of the state of affairs there (1 Cor 1:11). Further information came with the arrival of Stephanas, Fortunatus, and Achaicus (ch 16:17, 18), who may also have brought the letter of which Paul speaks in ch 7:1, in which the church asked Paul's judgment on certain matters. Gross practices were corrupting the church and dissipating its life and vitality, and heretical doctrines were being taught.

Paul wrote a letter, now lost, admonishing the Corinthians to amend their scandalous ways and to discipline the guilty persons (1 Cor 5:9, 11). From 2 Cor 2:1; 12:14; 13:1 some have inferred that Paul himself paid a brief, unrecorded visit to Corinth during this period of labor at Ephesus, one that had proved to be a painful and disappointing experience. At least he sent Timothy there (1 Cor 4:17; 16:10), quite likely as the bearer of what we now call his 1st epistle to the Corinthians—actually his 2d letter to them. In this letter he promised to visit Corinth, hoping to leave Ephesus after Pentecost (ch 16:8). However, an unexpected event, the riot led by Demetrius the silversmith, forced him to leave the Asian city sooner than he had intended (Acts 19:21 to 20:3). Paul had also dispatched Titus to Corinth, in a further endeavor to settle affairs at Corinth prior to his own arrival. Titus was to rejoin Paul at Troas (2 Cor 2:13), but his failure to do so led Paul to press on into Macedonia. There Titus met him with the cheering news that the church at Corinth had responded heartily to the admonition he had sent, and was now thoroughly repentant (ch 7:5-7). Thereupon, in joy and commendation, Paul wrote the letter we know as 2 Corinthians.

The 1st Corinthian epistle is objective and practical, carefully organized, and measured in tone. It contains firm reproof for irregularities that had crept into the church, and instruction on the points of faith and practice concerning which the church had sought further information. The author rebukes the factious spirit that had arisen, denounces immorality, especially a certain case of incest, and reproves Christians for resorting to litigation in secular courts. The instruction he gives is concerned with proper marriage relationships, meats sacrificed to idols, propriety in public worship, the proper observance of the Lord's Supper, spiritual gifts—particularly the gift of tongues— and the resurrection. 1 Corinthians may be divided into two parts, the 1st being concerned with problems of church discipline, and the 2d chiefly with doctrinal instruction. Following a brief introduction (ch 1:1-9), Paul deals with the factions that had arisen in the church (chs 1:10 to 4:21). Professing allegiance to Paul or Apollos or Peter or Christ, these factions had already grievously split the young church, and it was in danger of disintegrating. Those who have proclaimed the gospel to them are simply servants of Jesus Christ, and He alone is to be exalted, honored, and followed. In 1 Cor 5 Paul rebukes moral irregularities among Christians, and in particular a shameful case of incest. Chapter 6 admonishes church members to settle their own differences instead of haling one another into court. The church, he says, is fully qualified to administer justice among its members and all should submit to its judgment. The 7th chapter deals with marriage relationships and responsibilities, including problems that arise in a home where husband and wife are not united in the church. In chs 8:1 to 11:1 Paul answers the question of eating meats offered in sacrifice to idols and served at feasts to which Christians had been invited. While denying that idols in any way affect food, he stresses the supreme importance of doing nothing, even when right in itself, that might injure a fellow Christian's conscience and so risk the salvation of his soul. Women are to be veiled in church (ch 11:2-16). The Lord's Supper is not to be an occasion for riotous feasting, but is to be celebrated in discriminating solemnity (vs 17-34). The gifts of the Spirit are to be recognized and honored (ch 12), but even they are of less importance than the spirit of love among brethren (ch 13). The gift of tongues, in particular, must be exercised "decently and in order" (ch 14). The resurrection of the righteous and the bestowal of immortality are vouchsafed by the resurrection of our Lord (ch 15). In the closing chapter Paul takes up his plans for the future—the collection for the poor, his own intention to visit Corinth, his request for the acceptance of Timothy—and Apollos' decision to remain at Ephesus (ch 16:1-12). The letter closes with a series of exhortations and greetings (vs 13-24).

The 2d epistle is largely subjective and personal, and reflects Paul's anxiety for the Corinthian church and his joy at their repentance and reformation. He expresses gratitude and appreciation for their wholehearted reception of his previous epistle, and reviews some of the problems dealt with in it. In the final section, which deals in unwonted severity with a small minority who apparently persisted in opposing his counsel, the apostle sets forth proof of his apostolic authority and vindicates his course in dealing with the church at Corinth.

2 Corinthians logically falls into three main divisions. Following the introduction (2 Cor 1:1-11), Paul reviews his recent relations with the church (chs 1:12 to 7:16). He explains why he could not carry out his original plan to visit them (chs 1:12 to 2:4), counsels restoring a repentant offender to fellowship (ch 2:5-11), and expresses joy at the Corinthians' sincere repentance (vs 12-17). He again vindicates his apostleship, which some at Corinth have challenged, and exalts apostles as the ambassadors of Christ (chs 3:1 to 6:10). He appeals to the Corinthians to lead holy lives, and again expresses his rejoicing at the warmhearted response to his previous admonitions (chs 6:11 to 7:16). In chs 8 and 9, the second main division, Paul makes arrangements for completing the collection for the poor at Jerusalem, appoints Titus to take charge of this work, and appeals to the Corinthians' liberality. In chs 10 to 13, the third main division, it would seem that Paul turns his attention to the unrepentant minority who still refuse to humble themselves and to repent. Again he defends his apostleship (ch 10), and distinguishes between true and false apostles (chs 11:1 to 12:18). In chs 12:19 to 13:10 he makes a final appeal to the unrepentant, and follows this appeal with concluding remarks and greetings (ch 13:11-14).

Cormorant. [Heb. *shalak, qa'ath.*] The identification of both Hebrew terms is uncertain. For *shalak* some suggest *Phalacrocorax carbo,* the common cormorant, well known on Palestine's Mediterranean coast and along inland waterways. It has a ravenous appetite, but does not possess the pouch of the pelican. *Shalak* is listed among the unclean fowl in the Mosaic law (Lev 11:17; Deut 14:17). Similar uncertainty exists concerning the identification of *qa'ath,* a bird mentioned in the prophecies of Isaiah (ch 34:11) and of Zephaniah (ch 2:14). It may have been a species of owl, hawk, or vulture. In any case its presence is symbolic of the desolation of once-inhabited regions. G. R. Driver identifies the *shalak* with the fisher-owl (*PEQ* 87 [1955], 14, 15) and the *qa'ath* with the scops-owl (*ibid,* 16).

Corn. A KJV term for cereal grains, such as barley, rye, oats, or wheat (Gen 27:28; 41:35; 42:1; etc.). Modern versions generally use "grain" where KJV has "corn." The term must not be mistaken for Indian maize, a cereal of American origin, unknown elsewhere until the discovery of the New World. During the famine of Joseph's time the grains harvested in the good years were stored against the 7 lean years (Gen 41-45). A land of "corn and wine" was a land of plenty. When Christ's disciples, plucking grain in the field, were accused of desecrating the Sabbath (Mt 12:1, 2), they were following the custom Mosaic law condoned, that a transient might satisfy his hunger by taking what could be plucked by hand (Deut 23:25).

Cornelius (kôr-nēl′yŭs). [Gr. *Kornēlios,* a transliteration of the Latin *Cornelius,* a frequently occurring Roman name.] A centurion of the Italian Cohort (KJV "Italian band") in Caesarea (Acts 10:1). His devotion and piety were honored by God (1) with a vision directing him to come into contact with Peter, and (2) with the gift of the Holy Spirit as a sign of God's acceptance of the Gentiles. Peter baptized him and his house as apparently the first uncircumcised Gentiles officially received into the Christian church (ch 10).

Corner Gate. [Heb. *sha'ar happinnah.*] One of the gates of Jerusalem, probably located at the northwestern corner of Solomon's city (2 Ki 14:13; 2 Chr 25:23; 26: 9; Jer 31:38; Zec 14:10). It is usually equated with Nehemiah's "old gate" (Neh 3:6). There is uncertainty with regard to its exact location, because the course of the western wall has not been ascertained. Those who include the southwestern hill in Solomon's Jerusalem place this gate at the present Jaffa Gate, whereas those who limit Solomon's city to the two eastern hills believe that the gate was a short distance to the northeast of where the Church of the Holy Sepulchre now stands. Map XVII.

Corners. In Is 11:12 and Eze 7:2 a rendering of the Heb. *kanephôth,* literally, "wings," here meaning "extreme limits," from the idea of the wings of a bird being stretched out. In Rev. 7:1; 20:8, RSV, "corners" is a rendering of the Gr. *gōniai,* "corners," "angles." The phrase "four corners of the earth" may probably refer to the 4 main points of the compass.

Cornerstone. [Heb. *'eben pinnah,* "stone of the corner," or simply *pinnah,* "corner," where the context suggests that a cornerstone is meant. With *ro'sh pinnah,* "chief cornerstone," literally, "head of a corner," may be compared the Akkadian *aban resha;* Gr. *akrogōniaios.*] On the basis of Is 28:16 the cornerstone is usually considered to have been one of the foundation stones, probably the one binding together two connecting walls (cf. Mishnah *Nega'im* 13. 2). In Ps 118:22,

RSV, the psalmist refers to a cornerstone rejected by the builders. In the NT this reference is applied to Christ (Mt 21:42; Mk 12:10; Lk 20:17; Acts 4:11; Eph 2:20; 1 Pe 2:7).

Cornet. See Castanets; Horn, 2.

Corruption, Mount of. [Heb. *Har-hammashchîth,* literally "mount of the destruction."] The place on which Solomon built altars for the pagan gods worshiped by his foreign wives (2 Ki 23:13; cf. 1 Ki 11: 7). It is generally identified with the southern portion of the Mount of Olives, traditionally called Mount of Offense.

Cos (kŏs), KJV **Coos** (kō′ŏs). [Gr. *Koos.*] A long narrow island lying between the promontories of Cnidus and Halicarnassus. After varying fortunes it became a Roman possession, to which in A.D. 53 the emperor Claudius gave autonomy. This was its political standing when Paul passed the island on his voyage to Jerusalem on his 3d Missionary Journey (Acts 21:1). The island was the birthplace of famous men like Hippocrates and King Ptolemy II of Egypt. It possessed a temple dedicated to Asclepius, with which was associated a medical school. The island was known as a rich banking center. It was a favorite resort of Herod the Great. Map XX, B-4.

Cosam (kō′săm). [Gr. *Kōsam,* a transliteration of the Heb. *Qasam,* "oracle."] A descendant of David appearing in Luke's genealogy of Christ (Lk 3:28).

Cote, Sheep. See Sheepcote.

Cottage. A KJV term, a rendering of: (1) the Heb. *melûnah* (Is 24:20; RSV, "hut"), referring to the flimsy structure in a Palestinian field built of sticks and branches, from which the watchman kept a lookout during the night; (2) the Heb. *sukkah,* "covert of foliage" (Is 1:8; RSV, "booth"), a synonym for the shelter described under (1); (3) the Heb. *keroth* (Zep 2:6), the meaning of which is unknown. The RSV rendering "meadows" is conjectural.

Cotton. A soft white cellulose substance produced by a plant of the mallow family *Gossypium herbaceum,* grown first in India. The term appears twice: (1) Est 1:6, RSV, the translation of the Heb. *karpas,* meaning either fine linen or fine cotton. The KJV incorrectly renders *karpas* as "green." (2) Is 19:9, RSV, a conjectural translation of *chôray,* an obscure Hebrew word. It is thus uncertain whether cotton is mentioned in the Hebrew OT.

Couch. It is difficult to distinguish between beds and couches in the Biblical passages that deal with pieces of furniture used for sleeping or resting (Gen 49:4; Song 1:16; Lk 5:19, 24; Acts 5:15). *See* Bed. An Assyrian royal couch is depicted on a famous stone sculpture from Nineveh now in the British Museum. The stone shows King Ashurbanipal resting upon a couch that apparently stands in the palace garden, while the queen sits on a chair and holds him a cup of wine (see fig. 362).

Coulter. A rendering of the Heb. *'eth,* "mattock," an agricultural instrument used for digging and grubbing (1 Sa 13:20, 21, KJV). *'Eth* is translated "mattock" in the RSV.

Council. An assembly convened for consultation, deliberation, advice, consideration, or agreement upon concerted action; in some cases a permanent advisory, legislative, or administrative body. Various kinds of councils are referred to under different terms in the Bible, but nearly all the NT examples refer to a specific body, to which this discussion will be confined: the Great Sanhedrin at Jerusalem, the chief judicial body of the Jews from the Hellenistic period to A.D. 66.

Origin and Name. In the Greek sources (Josephus; 1 and 2 Macc; and NT) it is called *gerousia,* "council of elders," *sumboulion,* "council," and most frequently *sunedrion,* "council." In Jewish writings it was officially called *Bêth dîn haggadôl,* "house of the great judgment," or more frequently as a Greek loan word *Sanhedrin.* It is generally believed that the Sanhedrin originated in the Persian period when the Jews, enjoying a great measure of independence, were allowed to manage their own internal affairs. However, this council cannot be traced back to an earlier time than the Hellenistic period. It is mentioned first in a letter of Antiochus the Great, 223-187 B.C. (Jos. *Ant.* xii. 3. 3), and then in 1 Macc 12:6, as existing in the time of Jonathan, the Maccabean (160-143/42 B.C.).

Membership and Constitution. According to the Mishnah (*Sanhedrin* 1. 6), the Sanhedrin consisted of 71 members, with the high priest as chairman. It was believed to be the continuation of the body of counselors (Num 11:16, 17) who helped Moses in the administration of the people in the wilderness. In the earliest history of the Sanhedrin its members apparently consisted of priests and members of aristocratic families. However, during the reign of Queen Alexandra (76/75-67 B.C.) the Pharisees seem to have succeeded in having members of their own

group, the "scribes" (Gr. *grammateis*), included in the Sanhedrin, so that from that time on it consisted of three classes: (1) elders (*presbuteroi*), that is, representatives of the chief aristocratic families; (2) chief priests (*archiereis*), that is, retired high priests, and members of the four families which provided most high priests (Ananos, Boethos, Phabi, and Kamithos); and (3) the scribes (*grammateis*), mostly belonging to the party of the Pharisees. The three classes are mentioned combined in Mt 27:41; Mk 11:27; 14:43, 53; 15:1; etc. It is not certain how members were appointed to the Sanhedrin. The aristocratic nature of this body seems to exclude the possibility that they, like the senates of Greek communities, were elected to office by popular vote. When death or apostasy reduced its membership, new members were probably appointed for life by the Sanhedrin or the Roman authorities.

History. Under Jonathan and Simon, who were Maccabean leaders and high priests, the Sanhedrin along with its leaders officially represented the Jewish nation, as, for example, when it concluded a military alliance with Sparta. It also took care of building fortresses throughout the country of Judea and strengthened Jerusalem's fortifications (1 Macc 12:6-23; 14:20-23; 12:35, 36). After Pompey conquered Palestine in 63 B.C., Judea was made part of the province of Syria. A few years later, Gabinius, proconsul of Syria (57-55 B.C.), divided Judea into 5 districts and placed each under the administration of a sanhedrin (Jos. *Ant.* xiv. 5. 4; *War* i. 8. 5). A few years later, however, in 47 B.C., Sextus Caesar, governor of Syria, recognized the authority of the Sanhedrin of Jerusalem as a supreme court for the whole country (Jos. *Ant.* xiv. 9. 3, 5; *War* i. 10. 7). When Herod the Great occupied Jerusalem in 37 B.C. he executed many of the members of the Sanhedrin for having supported Antigonus, his rival, and replaced them by men loyal to him (Jos. *Ant.* xiv. 9. 4; xv. 1. 2). This marks the end of any outward semblance of political authority for the Sanhedrin; thereafter it was limited chiefly to religious matters.

When Archelaus fell heir to the provinces of Judea and Samaria after the death of Herod, with the remainder of the kingdom of his father being given to his brothers, the extent of the authority of the Sanhedrin was limited to Archelaus' territory, and it remained thus until the outbreak of the Roman war in A.D. 66. After the fall of Jerusalem in A.D. 70, the Sanhedrin was never reconstituted as an authoritative administrative body, although the Jews organized a sanhedrin at Jabneh (called Jamnia in Greek sources) near Joppa. This latter was merely a religious council with no real judicial authority.

Meeting Place. According to the Mishnah, the hall in which the Great Sanhedrin had its meetings (called *Lishkath haggazîth,* "Hall of hewn stone," in Jewish writings) lay in the Court of Israel,. also called Court of Men (*see* Temple), one of the inner Temple courts (*Middoth* v. 4; *Sanhedrin* xi. 2). A statement by Josephus (*War* v. 4. 2) has been interpreted as locating the meeting place of the Sanhedrin in the southwestern corner of the outer Temple court. However, scholars are divided as to whether the Mishnah or Josephus should be considered more authoritative in this matter. The Jewish literature mentions no meetings of the Sanhedrin in the palace of the high priest, and it must be assumed that the meeting recorded in Mt 26:57 (and parallel texts) was held in the residence of Caiaphas because the Temple precincts were closed at night.

Authority. It was the highest judicial body in the country and had power over life and death (Jos. *Ant.* xiv. 9. 3, 4; Mt 26:3, 4, 59, 66). However, during the administration of the Roman procurators, its death sentences had to be confirmed by the *governor (Jn 18:31), although this seems to have occasionally been circumvented (Acts 7:58). The norm of its action was the *Law of Moses and the oral traditions that were pronouncements of leading Jewish scholars. It is generally agreed that the Roman administration also put in its hands the responsibility of collecting the taxes. This obligation was discharged by selling it to tax purchasers or speculators, known as *publicans in the NT.

Lit.: E. Schürer, *A History of the Jewish People in the Time of Jesus Christ,* § 23, III. New York, n.d.

Counselor. An adviser, often in the general sense, but frequently one who is an official adviser to a king. Royal counselors in David's court are mentioned (1 Chr 27:32-34), among them Ahithophel, who went over to Absalom (2 Sa 15:12). Nebuchadnezzar's counselors are also mentioned (Dan 3:24, 27; 4:36), as are 7 counselors of Artaxerxes (Ezr 7:14, 28;

8:25). It is probably this latter council that is described in Est 1:14 as the 7 princes who "saw the king's face" and "sat the first in the kingdom." This institution of 7 counselors has not yet been attested by inscriptions, but Herodotus says that 7 great Persian families had special privileges exceeding those enjoyed by other families, including the right of unrestricted access to the royal presence (iii. 84). In the NT the KJV calls Joseph of Arimathea a "counsellor," meaning "member of the *council" (Mk 15:43; Lk 23:50; RSV), that is, of the Sanhedrin.

Countenance. Outward appearance or facial expression, considered as expressive of the mental attitudes and emotions (Gen 4:5; Num 6:26; Dan 8:23; etc.).

Couriers, KJV Posts. [Heb. *raṣîm,* "runners."] Messengers, literally "runners," sent with tidings or official proclamations (2 Chr 30:6, 10).

Court. A walled, roofless area, connected with a dwelling (2 Sa 17:18), a palace (1 Ki 7:8), the tabernacle (Ex 40:8), or the Temple (1 Ki 6:36). Some palace courts were so large that they contained a garden (Est 1:5). Since the enclosed area that surrounded the Temple building of Solomon was divided into several sections by walls or buildings, the term "courts" is used (2 Ki 21:5; Ps 65:4; 84: 2). The Temple precinct of Christ's time had four courts: "the court of the Gentiles," accessible to all worshipers regardless of race or religious affiliation; "the court of the women," accessible to all Jews regardless of age or sex; "the court of Israel," into which only male Jews could enter; and "the court of the priests," in which the ecclesiastical personnel functioned. See figs. 238, 408, 486, 517.

Courtyard. The RSV uses this term in Mt 26:58, 69; Mk 14:54, 66, where the KJV reads "palace," and in Lk 22:55, where the KJV reads "hall." The Greek word thus translated in each of these cases is *aulē,* which, although it may mean palace (Mt 26:3), in these scriptures clearly means "courtyard" and refers to the enclosed space connected with Caiaphas' palace. See figs. 238, 517.

Cousin. A word used in Lk 1:36, 58, KJV, translating the Gr. *suggenēs,* "relative," with the degree of relationship unspecified. The term is used of Elizabeth as a relative of Mary. Since the Greek word does not specify the degree of relationship, "kinswoman" (see RSV) would be a preferable translation.

Covenant. [Heb. *berîth,* "covenant," "agreement," "arrangement"; Gr. *diathēkē,* "last will and testament," "decree," "compact," "agreement," "covenant."] A term used in Scripture of agreements between man and man and between man and God. Generally speaking, "covenant" usually appears in the latter sense. Ancient covenants were of 2 kinds, those between equals and those between lord and vassal. In a covenant between equals there was mutual agreement on conditions, privileges, and responsibilities (Gen 21:32; 26:28; etc.). In a covenant between lord and vassal, conqueror and conquered, superior and inferior, the lord or conqueror specified the conditions, privileges, and responsibilities accruing to both parties, and the vassal or subject nation submitted to the conditions imposed upon it (2 Sa 3:21; 5:3; etc.). Such an agreement was proposed to Hezekiah by Sennacherib (Is 36:16, 17). On ancient covenants see G. E. Mendenhall in *BA* 17 (1954), 49-76.

Throughout Scripture, however, the term "covenant" most commonly describes the formal relationship that existed between God on the one hand and Israel as the chosen people on the other. Obviously, this was not a covenant between equals, but between the infinite God and finite man. God Himself determined the provisions of the covenant, made them known to His people, and gave them the choice of accepting or rejecting the covenant. Once ratified, however, it was considered binding upon both God and His people. In brief, the covenant embraced all that was required to make the plan of salvation fully effective. On His part, God promised to bless His people, to give them the land of Canaan for a possession, to make known His will to them, to send them the Messiah, and to make them His chosen instrument for the conversion of the world. On their part, the people were to yield implicit obedience and to cooperate with all of God's requirements.

In a preliminary form this covenant was made with Adam at the Fall (Gen 3:15), and later with Noah (ch 9:12, 15, 16). But it was first with Abraham and his posterity that the covenant became fully effective (chs 12:1-3; 15:18; 17:1-7; etc.). The covenant was ratified in a more formal way at Sinai, when Israel as a nation bound itself to comply with the divine requirements and accepted the promises (Ex 19:5-8; 24:3-8). After centuries of faithlessness to their promise to cooperate with

God, Israel was released from the covenant and permitted to go into captivity as a token that its provisions were no longer operative (see Jer 11:1-16; Eze 16; Heb 8:9; etc.). Returning from captivity, Israel was restored to the covenant relationship, and God promised to "make a new covenant with the house of Israel, and with the house of Judah" (Jer 31:31-34). In rejecting and crucifying Christ the Jewish people renounced the covenant and were rejected as the chosen people (Mt 21:43). At the same time, God transferred the privileges and responsibilities of the covenant relationship to His new chosen people, the Christian church (Mt 21:43; Gal 3:29; Heb 8:8-11; 1 Pe 2:9, 10).

The writer of Hebrews refers to the covenant with ancient Israel as the "first," or "old," covenant, and that with Christian believers as the "second," or "new" (ch 8:7, 13). Essentially, the provisions, conditions, and objectives of the 2 covenants are identical. The chief difference is that the "old" covenant was made with Israel as a nation, whereas the "new" is made with individual believers in Christ. The "new" covenant is also called an "everlasting" covenant (Gen 17:13; Heb 13:20). It became operative in Eden when man sinned, but was not ratified until the blood of Christ was shed on the cross (Heb 13:20). The "old" covenant was ratified at Sinai (Ex 24:3-8). The "old" covenant was, in fact, a temporary arrangement designed to enable those bound by its provisions to enter into the privileges and responsibilities of the "new," or "everlasting," covenant. See *SDACom* 1:1103; 4:632, 633.

Coverlet. A conjectural translation in the RSV of 2 Ki 8:15 of a Hebrew term of uncertain meaning. The translation apparently assumes that some part of the bed clothing was used in the act of assassination there described.

Covert. A protective covering, or booth, or secret place, affording shelter from heat, weather, or protection from enemies (2 Sa 25:20; Job 38:40; Is 16:4; Jer 25:38). The word is sometimes used figuratively to express God's protection of His people (Ps 31:20, RSV; 61:4, KJV).

Covetousness. [Heb. *beṣaʻ,* "gain," "profit"; Gr. generally *pleonexia,* "greediness," "avarice," "covetousness."] An inordinate desire to have more, usually that which belongs to someone else. Covetousness, although in itself not constituting an overt act, is one of the gravest of sins (Eph 5:3), along with idolatry (Col 3:5). In a sense, the 10th commandment summarizes the 2d section of the Decalogue (Ex 20:17), since in one way or another it is covetousness that leads to the other sins against one's fellow men. Covetousness leads men to abandon the faith (1 Ti 6:9, 10) and will eventually exclude them from heaven (1 Cor 6:10).

Cow. [Heb. generally *parah*, the plural of which is usually translated "kine" in the KJV.] A milk-producing animal which has been domesticated since early times. The Palestinian cows are the Arabian kind, which are thin and produce little milk and meat. Cattle breeding was carried out only in the areas where pastureland was available more or less the year round, such as coastal plains. The highland of Bashan was known especially for its fat cattle (Eze 39:18). Except for fattening (Gen 18:7; 1 Ki 4:23; etc.), cattle were generally left to graze in pasture.

Coz. See Koz.

Cozbi (kŏz′bī). [Heb. *Kozbî*, "the luxuriant one." Compare the Akkadian *Kuzâbatum*.] A Midianite princess with whom a Simeonite prince performed idolatrous rites while the Israelites were encamped at Shittim. Phinehas slew both of them, thus staying a plague that had broken out. The father of the princess died later in a war between the Israelites and the Midianites (Num 25:6-8, 14, 15, 18; 31:8).

Cozeba (kŏ-zē′bá), KJV **Chozeba** (kŏ-zē′bá). [Heb. *Kozeba'*, "lying."] A place in Judah (1 Chr 4:22). The name has been preserved in *Khirbet Kuweizîbeh*, 6 mi. northeast of Hebron, but since this place has no remains from earlier than Byzantine times, the ancient site may well have been at neighboring *Khirbet ed-Dilb*, which has remains dating from the 2d millennium B.C. Some commentators identify it with Achzib, 1.

Cracknels. [Heb. *niqqudîm*.] A term appearing once (1 Ki 14:3, KJV) describing a part of the provisions taken by Jeroboam's wife when she went to Ahijah the prophet at Shiloh to seek help for her sick son (v 3). The Hebrew term here may represent some hard, brittle biscuit or a cake sprinkled with some substance. In Jos 9:5, 12 the Hebrew term means "crumbling bread."

Craftsmen, Valley of. See Ge-harashim.

Crane. [Heb. *sûs*, or *sîs*.] The exact meaning of the Hebrew word is obscure. The swallow, swift, and crane have all been suggested. The bird's plaintive call is compared with Hezekiah's cries in his suffering (Is 38:14), and its faithful migratory instinct is contrasted to the delinquency of God's people (Jer 8:7). G. R. Driver identifies the *sîs* with the swift (*PEQ* 87 [1955], 131).

Crawling Things. [Heb. *zochalîm, remeś*.] *Zochalîm* describes creatures that glide away and hide themselves, such as snakes; *remeś*, generally small creatures, creeping things. In Moses' song the Lord is said to give over to the "venom of crawling things" those who forget Him (Deut 32:24, RSV). The nations that defy Jehovah are to lick dust as crawling things (Mic 7:17, RSV). Habakkuk speaks of God making men "like crawling things that have no ruler" (Hab 1:14).

Creation. The word "creation" in its broadest sense implies the formation by the Creator, or God Himself, of the universe, including our world and all living things in it. However, the Creation narrative (Gen 1 and 2) is concerned primarily with the bringing into existence of this earth, the sun, the planets, and the living creatures found on the earth.

The Hebrew word translated "create" (*bara'*) when appearing in Scripture is used exclusively for an act of which God is the subject. Two other Hebrew words are spelled the same, but have different meanings: (1) "to be fat" (1 Sa 2:29); (2) "to cut down" (Jos 17:15, 18; etc.); these words appear in grammatical forms different from the word meaning "to create," so are easily distinguished. Among the various things created (*bara'*) by God noted in the Scriptures are: the heaven and the earth (Gen 1:1; Is 40:28; 42:5; 45:18), man (Gen 1:27), stars (Is 40:26), a clean heart (Ps 51:10), new heavens and a new earth (Is 65:17).

It is sometimes alleged that *bara'* signifies the creation of something out of nothing. This idea is not intrinsic in the word, and if understood in any passage must be deduced from other considerations, such as the context, or related scriptures. A number of instances can be cited of the use of the word for the creation of something new or different from already existing material. The most-noted example is the record of the creation of man, which states that man was formed out of the dust of the earth, but was nevertheless "created" (Gen 1:26, 27).

The record of Creation is exceedingly brief, and is written not in the technical terms of a scientist but in the simple style of the scriptural record. This fact must constantly be borne in mind in any attempt to interpret the passage. Often unwarranted philosophical or scientific deductions are drawn from a simple Hebrew word or phrase, which go far beyond what the original writer had in mind.

The Creation narrative begins with the simple statement, "In the beginning God created the heaven and the earth." The Scriptures make clear that before all else was God, who through Christ brought all things into existence. "All things were made by him; and without him was not any thing made that was made" (Jn 1:3). "For by him were all things created, that are in heaven, and that are in earth, visible and invisible, whether they be thrones, or dominions, or principalities, or powers: all things were created by him, and for him: and he is before all things, and by him all things consist" (Col 1:16, 17). "For in six days the Lord made heaven and earth, the sea, and all that in them is" (Ex 20:11).

According to the narrative of Gen 1, the work of Creation was completed in six days. The most natural way to understand the passage is to regard these days as literal days of 24 hours each. The terms "evening" and "morning" were obviously intended to designate the dark part and the light part of a 24-hour day. On the 7th day God finished His work and rested (Gen 2:2). On this historic fact the Sabbath command is based: "Remember the sabbath day, to keep it holy. . . . For in six days the Lord made heaven and earth, the sea, and all that in them is" (Ex 20:8-11). This command and the reason for it make sense only as the original Creation occupied the same length of time as the interval between two Sabbaths, namely 6 literal days. God's arbitrary use of 7 days for Creation week is, in fact, the origin of the weekly cycle as we have it today. There is no satisfactory theory of origin for this cycle other than the original Creation week.

I. The Biblical Account. As the earth came forth from its Maker's hand it was "without form, and void," shrouded in darkness, which, however, disappeared at the word of God (Gen 1:2, 3). The Creator then "divided the light from the darkness" and thus started the world on its recurring cycle of day and night (vs 4, 5). On the 2d day God created the atmosphere and separated a part of the great water mass from the unfinished earth and evidently diffused it above and around that body as a vaporous envelope

(Gen 1:6-8). On the 3d day the "waters," which hitherto had apparently covered the entire sphere, were gathered together "unto one place," and dry land was made to appear. God immediately clothed the earth with grass and trees and foliage of various kinds (vs 9-12), which were subsequently watered day by day by a "mist" or dew (ch 2:5, 6). This vegetation was given by God to provide food for man, birds, and animals (ch 1:29, 30). Next, the record mentions the creation of 2 great luminaries, the sun and moon. These were set in the heavens to give light upon the earth and to be "for signs, and for seasons, and for days, and for years." God "made the stars also" (vs 14-19). Marine and aerial creatures of every kind, from the largest and most complicated to the smallest and simplest forms, were created on the 5th day (vs 20-23). All other life forms "after his kind, cattle, and creeping thing, and beast of the earth after his kind" appeared upon the earth on the 6th day (vs 24, 25). Man, too, was created on that day (vs 26, 27; ch 2:7). As a home for man, and as a place for him to work, God "planted a garden eastward in Eden" (ch 2:8, 15). In this garden was the tree of life and the "tree of the knowledge of good and evil," the fruit of which man was not to touch or to eat (vs 9, 16, 17). Woman was formed from a rib taken from the side of Adam (vs 21, 22). Creation was climaxed by the sanctifying of the 7th day as a memorial of Creation week and as a day of spiritual and physical rest for man (Gen 2:2, 3; Ex 20:8-11; Is 58:13).

It has been asserted by many commentators that Gen 2:4 to 3:24 constitutes a second and different creation account by a different author, and from a later period, than the account in chs 1:1 to 2:3. Such an assumption is not at all necessary (see *SDACom* 1:201-204). Chapter 2 may logically be considered an amplification of certain details that would not properly have belonged in the summary account of ch 1. Without this additional information our knowledge of the Edenic state would indeed be incomplete (see *SDACom* 1:221, 222).

II. The Creation Story Among Ancient Nations. Among the Sumerians and Babylonians the Creation was connected with a primeval fight between the gods. It is mentioned in several myths, the most important of which is the famous Babylonian myth called *Enûma elish*, "When on high." It tells how the god *Apsû*,

"Chaos," had annoyed the wise god *Ea,* who, as a result, killed *Apsû.* This stirred up the anger of *Apsû's* consort *Ti'âmat,* who gathered followers among the evil gods and made preparations to avenge the death of *Apsû.* The good gods supporting *Ea* then appointed *Marduk* as their champion to fight against *Ti'âmat.* The story deals at great length with the struggle between *Marduk* and *Ti'âmat,* which ultimately ended with the latter's death. *Marduk* then created out of her body the heaven and the earth, put the luminaries in the sky to regulate the seasons, and finally fashioned man out of the blood of *Kingu,* the principal follower of *Ti'âmat.*

Aside from the fact that the Babylonian story is devoid of all ethical values, and presents the gods as extremely anthropomorphic, it lacks the orderly theme of the Biblical narrative in which one act of Creation follows the other in a logical sequence, and which presents the whole work accomplished through the word of the Almighty in 6 days, and crowned on the 7th day by the Sabbath, a day of rest. The few parallels that exist between the Creation story of the Bible and that of the peoples in Mesopotamia simply show that when these myths were originated there was still a vague memory of what had happened at the beginning of this world's history. But it was no more than a vague memory, and it seems quite unnecessary to believe, as many scholars do, that the author of Genesis borrowed his Creation account from the Babylonians.

The Egyptian concept of the creation of the world and of mankind is even farther removed from that of the Biblical Creation story. For example, some mythological texts declare that man was created from the tears of the sun-god Ra. Then there are illustrations that depict the formation of human beings on a potter's wheel by the god Khnum (see fig. 114). The cosmogonies of the Phoenicians, Iranians, and of other ancient peoples also contain references to the creation of the world and of mankind, but they show no parallels to the Biblical Creation story, and in most cases present such absurd concepts about the Creation, that no point is gained in pursuing them.

Lit.: On the Babylonian Creation stories see Alexander Heidel, *The Babylonian Genesis,* 2d ed., Chicago, 1951, and *ANET* 60-72; on the Egyptian myths of origin see *ANET* 3-7; on the cosmogonies of other nations see A. Jeremias, *The Old Testament in the Light of the Ancient East* (New York, 1911), vol. 1, pp. 155-173.

III. Creation Versus Evolution. The evolutionary philosophy assumes that the earth originally was a gaseous, shapeless mass of matter hanging in space for perhaps billions of years. Eventually the matter began to take on a more solid form; the hot gases condensed, and ultimately water was formed. In time the earth cooled until temperatures became low enough for life to exist. By spontaneous generation in some form or another the first living thing came into existence. One textbook suggests the following possibility: "Would it be too much to speculate on the origin of some simple form of life by allowing a flash of lightning to release the pure nitrogen of the air in some form of nitrate which would combine with the life elements found in sea water and the carbon dioxide of the air?" (Hunter, Walter, Hunter, *Biology* [N.Y.: American Book Co., 1937], pp. 407, 408).

Evolutionists assume that the first living thing was a one-celled creature, and that in time it produced offspring with more than one cell. These in turn eventually produced offspring that contained many cells, and in time all the forms of life as we know them today came into being. This is contrary to observed facts today; all life comes only from pre-existing life.

Evolutionists believe that all living things found on earth today have come

114. The Egyptian god Khnum depicted in the temple of Luxor as fashioning King Amenhotep III and his double on the potter's wheel

from ancestors simpler than themselves, by the process of evolution. For proof they point to the processes whereby measurable changes do occur in plants and animals (through mutations, chromosomal aberrations, and geographic isolation) at the present time, whereby new species and varieties do appear on the earth today. However, new species thus formed are always in the same genus, or at least in the same family, as the ancestors, and many times the new species are so similar to the original species that only the expert taxonomists can tell the difference. In all time and under all conditions known yet to science, not one new type of animal or plant has come about by evolution, nor by any other means.

Evolutionists admit that of all the arguments for evolution published in the accounts of the theory, only the evidences from the fossils can be called direct evidence. Yet, when the fossils are examined no evidence for changes from simple to complex can be uncovered. All groups of animals and plants in the fossil beds bear the same relationships to each other as living corresponding examples today! Austin Clark, who for many years was the chief invertebrate paleontologist at the United States National Museum in Washington, D.C., and a world authority on crinoids, a fossil group somewhat related to starfish, makes the following interesting observation: "No animals are known even from the very earliest rocks which cannot be at once assigned to their proper phylum or major group on the basis of the definition of that group as drawn up from a study of living animals alone. A backboned animal is always a backboned animal, a starfish is always a starfish, and an insect is always an insect no matter whether we find it as a fossil or catch it alive at the present day. There can be only one interpretation of this entire lack of any intermediates between the major groups of animals, as for instance between the vertebrates, the echinoderms, the mollusks, and the arthropods. If we are willing to accept the facts at their face value, which would seem to be the only thing to do, we must believe that there never were such intermediates, or in other words that these major groups from the very first bore the same relation to each other that they do at the present day" (*The New Evolution* [1930], pp. 167, 168).

He states further: "The complete absence of any intermediate forms between the major groups of animals, which is one of the most striking and most significant phenomena brought out by the study of zoology, has hitherto been overlooked, or at least ignored" (*ibid.,* p. 168; cf. pp. 128, 129, 167, 168, 189, 190).

There are many who think that Darwin proved evolution beyond any doubt. And elementary discussions of Darwin and his work generally fail to point out the errors and weaknesses in the theories proposed by this great thinker. In his recent book, *A History of Biology,* Charles Singer, a noted British biologist, points out "a series of fallacies and some erroneous assumptions" in Darwin's book *The Origin of Species* (1859). Following are a number of these: " (*a*) All domestic breeds have not been produced by selecting very slight individual differences. On the contrary, some domestic breeds certainly and all domestic breeds possibly have been produced by breeding from individuals which presented very considerable deviations from the normal. . . . (*b*) That a natural variation should confer an advantage is not enough to secure its perpetuation. The advantage must be effective and moreover it must be transmissible. . . . A wing, for instance, so little developed as to confer no power of flight, or at least of gliding, would be no advantage. (*c*) It is assumed that 'advantages' are inherited. On this matter the modern development of the theory of heredity . . . has entirely changed the whole point of view presented by Darwin. . . . (*d*) It is tacitly assumed that species differ from their nearer relatives in having some special advantages that enable them to adapt themselves to slightly different conditions. In fact, however, allied species are found living in identical areas and under identical conditions. This would hardly be the case if one had the advantage over the other, for then one would flourish and the other decline."

"Darwin's view of Natural Selection as an effective agent of Evolution is perhaps at its weakest in dealing with the problem of disuse. Here he assumes the inheritance of acquired characters in a form hardly less crude than that of Lamarck."

" 'Natural Selection means merely that a creature survives.' As to why it survives, or whether its survival be due to one character more than another, and as to how it acquired that character, the theory gives us no information whatever" (pp. 304, 305, 307. Reprinted by permission of the publisher, Abelard-Schuman, Limited, from *A*

History of Biology: Newly Revised Edition, by Charles Singer. Copyright 1959).

Thus it is evident that Darwin did not *prove* evolution; his work was largely theoretical, and is recognized as such by authorities. Nor has science since his day *proved* evolution.

In an attempt to reconcile the scriptural account of Creation with the propositions of the evolutionary philosophy, many Christian scholars have adopted one or the other of two views, or combinations of the elements of these two views:

1. *The Day-Age View.* In this view the days of Creation week are taken to be long periods of time, perhaps even millions of years. The proponents of this idea hold that for millions of years the earth was "without form, and void," then the 2d era brought in the firmament and the dry land. The next era saw the creation of plant life, while the 4th era brought sunshine. The last 2 eras furnished the earth with animal life. A belief in this theory is often linked with the following philosophy.

2. *Creation by Evolution.* Many hold that billions upon billions of years ago God made this earth, and in due time created upon it a simple form of life. During succeeding ages, by the process of evolution, animals and plants evolved to the present-day forms.

But not all Christian scholars have adopted these views. Some competent men of science have taken a new look at the Biblical account and have found nothing in the discoveries of science that disproves the record of the origin of life on this planet given in the Creation narrative, even when the account is taken literally. They note that if one is willing to accept the fact of a miracle-working God, it is then no more difficult to believe that He created life in complex forms than that He created only a single cell from which other life forms developed, and it is no more difficult to believe that these complex forms were brought forth in a moment than to believe that long eras were involved in their development. They consequently find no difficulty in believing that in the course of 6 literal days of creation God created the ancestors of all living plants and animals on this earth. They point out, however, that since Creation there have appeared on earth many new species and varieties not exactly like their ancestors— a development not denied in the Genesis record. These new forms have come about, as science attests, through a combination of factors such as mutations, chromosomal aberrations, geographic isolation, and hybridization. But in every case the new forms are so similar to their ancestors that they can be traced back without great difficulty. See *SDACom* 1:46-63.

Creature. Generally, a living organism, though in the Hebrew the idea of "living" is sometimes conveyed by a separate adjective (Gen 1:21; 9:16; etc.). The idea of being created, though it may be implied, is not inherent in the Hebrew terms translated "creature." It is, however, in the Greek terms thus translated in the KJV.

The RSV uses the term "living creatures" for the beings John saw at God's throne (Rev 4:6-9; etc.). The Greek term thus translated is literally "living things" or "living being." In 1 Ti 4:4 "every creature" (KJV), "everything created" (RSV), probably refers to created things in general, whether animate or inanimate. Figuratively, "creature" is used of the transformed Christian, the whole tenor of whose desires, motives, and actions is directed toward serving God rather than self; he literally thinks and lives as a re-creation of God (2 Cor 5:17, KJV). The RSV translates the term rendered "creature" in the passage "creation."

Creeping Things. [Heb. *remeś, shereś;* Gr. *herpeta.*] In general *remeś* describes small creatures, usually such as creep (Gen 1: 24, 26; 6:7, 20; 7:14; etc.). The expression "creeping things" in the RSV is almost always from *remeś.* In the KJV *shereṣ* is also generally translated "creeping things." *Shereṣ* comes from the root *sharaṣ,* "to swarm," "to team"; hence "swarming things" is a more accurate translation. The term *shereṣ* includes creatures that swarm in the water (Gen 1:20; Lev 11:10), winged insects (Lev 11:20; Deut 14:19), land creatures (Gen 7:21; Lev 11:29; etc.). *Herpeta* refers to reptiles (Acts 10:12; Rom 1:23).

Crescens (krĕs′ĕnz). [Gr. *Krēskēs,* from the Latin *Crescens,* "growing," "increasing."] A Christian, probably a missionary, who had been in Rome during part of Paul's second imprisonment in that city, but had left for Galatia (or possibly Gaul) when Paul wrote the 2d letter to Timothy (2 Ti 4:10). An early tradition makes Crescens a bishop in Galatia. A later tradition, probably reflecting a desire for apostolic origin, names him as a bishop of Gaul.

Crescents. [Heb. *śaharonîm,* "moonlets," "little moons."] A term in the RSV of Jgs 8:21, 26; Is 3:18, variously translated "ornaments" and "round tires like the moon" by the KJV. These were probably crescent-shaped pendants worn on the neck.

Cretans (krē′tăns), KJV **Cretians** (krē′shăns) [Gr. *Krētes.*] Natives or inhabitants of *Crete (Tit 1:12), called Cretes (krēts) in Acts 2:11, KJV.

Crete (krēt). [Gr. *Krētē.*] A large island in the Mediterranean, 160 mi. long and from 7½ to 35 mi. wide, 60 mi. southeast of Greece (Map XX, B-3/4). The island is mountainous, the highest peak being Mount Ida (8,065 ft.) in central Crete, the legendary birthplace of Zeus. According to the Greeks a certain king Minos founded the Cretan civilization. Excavations reveal the existence of a high culture on the island in very early times. The history of this ancient culture is divided into three periods: (1) Early Minoan, contemporary with the Pyramid Age in Egypt; (2) Middle Minoan, contemporary

115. Part of the palace of Minos at Cnossus, Crete

with the Egyptian Middle Kingdom; and (3) Late Minoan, contemporary with the 18th Egyptian dynasty. Several large palaces on the island have been uncovered, notably the one excavated at Cnossus since 1900 by Sir A. J. Evans. This structure contained a maze of chambers, halls, storage rooms, a theater, and a large central court; and was probably the Labyrinth of Greek legend. That the Minoan civilization reached an astonishingly high level is shown by its art: pottery, stone and metal work, tasteful architecture, and fine mural paintings preserved at such places as Cnossus, Phaestus, Hagia Triada, and elsewhere.

The earliest Minoan script was of the hieroglyphic variety; later two forms of linear script were invented. The claim is made that one of them, Linear B, was deciphered by M. Ventris in 1953, revealing, according to him, that the language of the texts written in this script was an early form of Greek. However, some scholars are not convinced of the soundness of the methods used in Ventris' decipherment, and do not accept his results.

The Cretans of the Minoan periods seem to have been a maritime nation having lively trade relations with Egypt, the Syrian coast, and the Aegean area. About 1400 B.C. this Minoan culture was destroyed, and was replaced by that of a far inferior people, probably the Philistines, who in their migration toward the East destroyed the Minoan culture of Crete (*see* Philistines; Caphtor). From that time on Crete lost its outstanding significance in history.

During the Hellenistic and Roman periods many Jews settled on Crete (1 Macc 15:23; Acts 2:11; Tit 1:10-14). The Romans occupied the island in 67 B.C. and made it a senatorial province. Subsequently it was incorporated with Cyrenaica in northern Africa. The Cretans were reputed to be good bowmen, and also great liars, as expressed in the hexameter quoted by Paul in Tit 1:12, which is supposed to have been written by Epimenides. The vessel carrying Paul as a prisoner to Rome entered one of the harbors of Crete (Acts 27:7, 8). This seems to have been Paul's first visit to the island. It was apparently later, during the interval between his 1st and 2d Roman imprisonments, that Paul visited the island, leaving Titus behind to complete the organizing of the church (Tit 1:5).

Cricket, KJV **Beetle**. [Heb. *chargol.*] The Hebrew term describes, presumably, a leaping, winged insect belonging to the family *Orthoptera,* to which belong the grasshopper, locust, and cricket. From the meaning of *chargol* in cognate languages the insect has been identified by some with the locust called *Tettigonia vividissima,* a leaping locust. The *chargol* is considered clean (Lev 11:22).

Crisping Pins. A term appearing in Is 3:22, KJV, translating the Heb. *charîṭîm,* probably "purses" or "handbags."

Crispus (krĭs′pŭs). [Gr. *Krispos,* a transliteration of the Latin name *Crispus,* "curled."] The superintendent of the Jewish synagogue at Corinth, who with his household was converted to Christianity by Paul. He was one of the few converts Paul baptized personally (Acts 18:8; 1 Cor 1:14).

Crocodile, Land. *See* Leviathan; Lizard.

Crocus. [Heb. *chabaṣṣeleth*.] The identity of the Hebrew term is uncertain. Some wildflower is indicated, perhaps a member of the family *Asphodelus*. The Hebrew term appears twice (Song 2:1; Is 35:1) and is translated "rose" in the KJV. The RSV translates the term "rose" in Song 2:1, but has a footnote stating that the Hebrew means "crocus." In Is 35:1 it has "crocus" in the text.

Cross. [Gr. *stauros*, "stake," "pale," "cross."] A stake sunk into the earth in an upright position, often with a crosspiece attached at right angles to its upper part so as to form either a T or a cross. Crucifixion was a characteristic Roman mode of execution. However, Roman citizens were never crucified, this form of punishment being reserved for persons held in utter contempt, such as slaves, the worst criminals, and non-Romans. In submitting to this form of death Christ humbled Himself utterly (Php 2:8). A curse was supposed to rest upon those who were crucified (cf. Deut 21:23; Gal 3:13). This mode of execution is supposed to have been introduced into Palestine by Antiochus Epiphanes about 165 B.C. (see Jos. *Ant.* xii. 5. 4). The lingering death upon a cross was horrible indeed, for victims commonly lived for many hours, sometimes several days. Among the Jews death by stoning was the usual mode of execution, though provision was made for hanging or impaling dead bodies upon a stake or tree to expose them to contempt (Deut 21:22, 23). *See* Hanging.

116. A wall cross with what appears to be a Christian's prayer stool in front of it; discovered in 1939 in a house at Herculaneum that was destroyed in A.D. 79

The Saviour spoke of the cross as a symbol of self-sacrifice (Mt 10:38; 16:24). As proclaimed by the apostles, the gospel centered in the crucifixion and resurrection of our Lord (1 Cor 2:2; etc.), and with Paul the cross stood as a comprehensive term for the message of salvation through Christ (1 Cor 1:18; Gal 6:14; Php 3:18; Col 1:20). "I, if I be lifted up from the earth," said Jesus, "will draw all men unto me" (Jn 12:32).

One of the earliest apparently Christian crosses yet found is that incised in the plaster of a house at Herculaneum, discovered in 1939. Below it is a small wooden cabinet that has been taken to be a prayer stool or an altar (fig. 116). Other early crosses were found scratched on possibly Christian ossuaries (bone receptacles) at Jerusalem. *See* Barsabbas.

Crown. An ornamental headdress worn as a symbol of authority and honor. Various Hebrew and Greek words are used in the Bible without recognizable significant differences in meaning between some of them.

1. *Royal crown.* Neither literary nor archeological evidence tells us anything about the shape of crowns worn by the Hebrew kings. They were presumably made of gold (Ps 21:3), and were probably decorated with precious stones (2 Sa 12:30, RSV; Zec 9:16). We are better informed about the crowns of other nations of antiquity. The Egyptian kings of Upper Egypt in the early days wore a high, round white cap, tapering toward the top; the kings of Lower Egypt wore a flat red cap that rose at the back to a high point, and had a spiraled wire attached to it. When Egypt was united, the two crowns were combined into one that retained the features of both crowns. Sometimes the Egyptian kings wore a simple gold band with the uraeus, or sacred serpent, in front, the symbol of royal power and terror. This simple crown may be termed a diadem (fig. 133). Besides these there were other headdresses worn by Egyptian kings at formal or informal occasions. The Assyrian kings wore crowns that were somewhat similar in shape to the modern fez, except that they were sometimes higher or lower, and topped by a conelike protrusion or a thorn (figs. 163, 420). Persian kings wore crowns made in the form of skull caps encircled by a white and a blue band (fig. 293). The blue band, the "diadem," was the sign of kingship. The Hittite kings seem to have worn skull caps of various shapes as crowns.

2. *The crown of the high priest.* An emblem of the priestly office consisting of a plate of gold and inscribed with the words "Holy to Yahweh." It was worn on the miter, but its actual shape is unknown (Ex 29:6; cf. 28:36, 37; Lev 8:9).

3. *Marriage crown.* Probably a *garland of flowers worn by the bride and bridegroom (Eze 16:12), a custom still observed in some parts of the Orient, as, for example, in Turkey.

4. *Crown of victory.* A wreath of natural leaves, perhaps olive, or of leaves made of metal, given to athletic or military victors (2 Ti 2:5; 4:8; Heb 2:9).

5. In the KJV the word "crown" is sometimes applied to the round edge, or molding, of the ark, of the table of showbread, or of the altar of incense (Ex 25:11, 24; 30:3).

6. In metaphorical language the crown may be the top of the head, as that part of the body on which the crown is ordinarily worn (Job 2:7); also anything that is a reward or a cause for justifiable pride (Prov 12:4; 16:31; 17:6; Is 28:5; Php 4:1; Jas 1:12; Rev 2:10).

Crucify, Crucifixion. The act of fixing a condemned person to a cross, either by tying the hands and feet to it or by fixing them to it by driving nails through them. As with Christ, it was common to scourge victims prior to crucifixion, and then to require them to carry the cross, or one beam of it, to the place of execution (Jn 19:1, 17). See Cross; Hanging.

Cruse. This word appears only in the OT and is the translation of (1) the Heb. *baqbuq* (1 Ki 14:3), "bottle," or "jar" (RSV); (2) the Heb. *selochith* (2 Ki 2:20), "dish," or "bowl" (RSV); (3) the Heb. *sappachath,* a small pot or jug used for oil (1 Ki 17:12, 14, 16).

Crystal. [Heb. *gabish, zekôkîth, qerach;* Gr. *krustallos.*] In general, the Hebrew and Greek terms translated "crystal" in KJV and RSV refer to rock crystal, or to ice, which resembles rock crystal in its scintillating and transparent qualities. According to Job, wisdom cannot be exceeded in value by precious stones or crystal (Job 28:17, RSV "glass"; v 18, RSV). A glittering luminescence of the appearance of scintillating crystal appeared above the heads of the living creatures in Ezekiel's vision (Eze 1:22). The revelator compared various features of the unseen world with crystal: the sea of glass (Rev 4:6); the brilliance of the New Jerusalem (ch 21:11); and the river of life (ch 22:1).

Cubit. [Heb. and Aramaic *'ammah;* Akkadian *ammatu;* Ugarit *'mt;* Gr. *pēchus.* Originally these words meant "elbow"; but the Hebrew, Aramaic, and Greek also meant "forearm." Since the forearm from the elbow to the tips of the fingers was used as a rough linear measure, its name was later adopted as that of the standardized measure of length.] A measure of length used throughout the ancient Orient. Archeological evidence indicates that the Mesopotamian cubit was 19.6 in. long, and the Egyptian cubit, 20.6 in. Since the Hebrews probably used the Egyptian cubit during their long stay in Egypt, it is reasonable to assume that it is this standard they used when building the tabernacle Ex 25:10, 17, 23; etc.). However, the length of the cubit does not seem to have been uniform throughout Israel's history. The Siloam inscription, dating from Hezekiah's time, states that the Siloam tunnel was 1,200 cubits long. Though the exact points between which the 1,200 cubits were computed cannot now be determined with certainty, the length has been measured as 1,749 ft. This would give a cubit of approximately 17.5 in. The mention of an "old standard" (2 Chr 3:3, RSV) implies the existence of a new standard at the time when Chronicles was compiled (probably 5th cent. B.C.). The new measure may have been the "long cubit" (RSV) referred to by Ezekiel (Eze 40:5; 43:13), which consisted of "a cubit and a hand-breadth," hence was about 20 in. long if the ordinary cubit was 17.5 in.

The "cubit" of Jgs 3:16 is the translation of the Heb. *gomed,* a word appearing in the OT only in this text. The exact length of the *gomed* is unknown.

The NT cubit (Jn 21:8; Rev 21:17) is generally considered to have had a length of 17.5 in., because Josephus' writings give the impression that the Hebrew cubit of his day did not differ materially from the Roman-Attic cubit of the 1st cent., which had a length of 17.47 in. An unusual use of the "cubit" is found in Mt 6:27 and Lk 12:25, where it apparently refers to time, a usage unattested in non-Biblical Greek.

Cuckoo. See Sea Gull.

Cuckow. See Sea Gull.

Cucumber. [Heb. *qishshu'ah.*] Fruit of the well-known climbing or trailing vine, *Cucumis chate.* This vegetable had been grown extensively since earliest times, and was a part of the everyday diet of Egypt and Palestine. As a part of the Israelites' accustomed menu, along with fish, melons, leeks, onions, and garlic, cucumbers were greatly missed as the people passed through the desert (Num 11:5). *Miqshah*, a derivative of *qasha'* from which also *qishshu'ah* is derived, is the cucumber field. The desolation of Zion is compared to the vacant booth in the cucumber field, once erected for the watchman (Is 1:8). Heathen idols are compared to scarecrows in a cucumber field (Jer 10:5, RSV).

Cult Prostitute. [Heb. *qadesh, qedeshah;* Ugaritic *qdshm*.] A term appearing in the RSV referring to temple prostitutes, both male and female (Deut 23:17; 1 Ki 14: 24; 15:12; 22:46; 2 Ki 23:7; Hos 4:14). These persons were devotees of various gods and served those who came to worship these gods. Such worship involved the grossest immoralities. *See* Ashtoreth. The KJV translates *qadesh*, "sodomite," and *qedeshah*, "harlot."

Cumi. [Gr. *koum;* in many manuscripts *koumi*, a transliteration of the Aramaic *qûmî*, "rise up" (a feminine imperative).] A term appearing in the phrase "Talitha cumi" (Mk 5:41). The phrase means "Maiden, arise." This is one of the few Aramaic sayings recorded of Jesus (cf. Mt 27:46; Mk 7:34).

Cummin. [Heb. *kammon;* Gr. *kuminon*.] *Cuminum cyminum*, a cultivated plant of the carrot family, bearing seeds used in cooking and medicines. Since ancient times cummin has been grown widely. Its aromatic seeds resemble caraway seeds, but are neither as tasty nor as nutritious. The seeds were separated from the plant by being beaten with a rod (Is 28:27). They were tithed meticulously by some Jews (Mt 23:23).

Cun. *See* Berothah.

Cunning. In the KJV this term is used in its archaic sense of "skillful." Thus Hiram, whom the king of Tyre sent to assist Solomon in the erection of the Temple, was a skillful craftsman (1 Ki 7:14; 2 Chr 2:7, 13). The cherubim were to be skillfully worked into the curtains and veil of the tabernacle (Ex 26:1, 31; etc.). In the RSV "cunning" is used with its present-day meaning of "crafty," "sly," "artful" (Jos 9:4; 1 Sa 23:22; etc.).

Cup. A drinking vessel of earthenware or metal (Gen 44:2; Jer 51:7; Mk 7:4; etc.). The term is frequently used figuratively to indicate something unpleasant and bitter (Is 51:17; Mt 26:39) or joyful and sweet (Ps 23:5; 1 Cor 10:16). Fig. 362 shows a royal cup containing wine being passed to the Assyrian king Ashurbanipal by the queen. *See* Basin; see figs. 86, 362.

Cupbearer. *See* Butler.

Curds. *See* Butter.

Curious. A term appearing in the KJV in its obsolete meaning of "markedly careful," "exhibiting care or nicety." The "curious girdle" in Ex 28:8, 27, 28; 29:5; 39:5, 20, 21; Lev 8:7 was obviously a skillfully woven girdle or belt. The "curious works" of Ex 35:32 were doubtless artistic works. "Curiously wrought" in Ps 139: 15 means "intricately wrought" (see RSV).

Cush (kŭsh). [Heb. *Kûsh*.]

1. A son of Ham and ancestor of 5 principal peoples: Seba, Havilah, Sabtah, Raamah (from whom Sheba and Dedan descended), and Sabteca (Gen 10:6-8; 1 Chr 1:8). These peoples lived for the most part in Nubia, south of Egypt, and in southern and western Arabia.

2. A Benjamite who appears in the title of Ps 7 as an enemy of David.

3. The land of the Cushites, generally called Ethiopia. The Egyptians referred to it as *Kʒsh*, the Assyrians as *Kúsu*, and the Babylonians as *Kûshu*. It is called *Kashi* in the *Amarna Letters. It comprised the land lying south of Egypt, later called Nubia, now the Sudan, which was known to the ancients by the name of Ethiopia, and included also the western area of Arabia and sections of southern Arabia (2 Ki 19:9; Est 1:1; Eze 29: 10; etc.). Map IV, C-5, shows the "Ethiopian" Cush.

Cushan (kū'shăn). [Heb. *Kúshan*, probably a variant name for *Kúsh*, "Cush."] A tribe of Midianites in Arabia (Hab 3:7).

Cushan-rishathaim (kū'shăn-rĭsh'á-thā'ĭm), KJV **Chushan-rishathaim** (kū'shăn-rĭsh'á-thā'ĭm). [Heb. *Kûshan Rish'athayim*.] A king of Mesopotamia who invaded the country of Palestine and oppressed the Israelites for 8 years, at the end of which Othniel, the son-in-law of Caleb, delivered Israel (Jgs 3:5-11). The king has not been identified. Some scholars think the name has been corrupted until unrecognizable. H. Häusler identifies him with Tushratta, a king of Mitanni in the 14th cent. B.C. (*Biblica* 11 [1930], 391-418; 12 [1931], 3-26, 271-296), and A. Malamat with the Syrian Irsu of the end of the 13th cent. B.C., who occupied Egypt for a few years, and who on his way there may have subdued Israel, oppressing them until driven out of Egypt by Setnakht and out of Palestine by Othniel (*JNES* 13 [1954], 231-242). Others suggest identifying him with an Edomite king, a Kassite king, an Aramaean king, or with Aziru of Amurru in northern Syria. However, none of these proposed identifications is conclusive. Malamat's proposal must be rejected for chronological reasons, since Irsu lived at least 150 years too late. So must the suggestion advanced by many scholars that an Edomite king is meant, since this requires a drastic emendation of the text. As to the other suggestions, they represent possibilities, but none can be given preference.

Cushi (kū'shī). [Heb. *Kûshî,* "a Cushite" or "an Ethiopian," attested as a name also in a Phoenician inscription.]

1. One of the ancestors of a servant in Jehoiakim's court, Jehudi. This is the servant who read Jeremiah's prophecies before Jehoiakim (Jer 36:14, 21, 23).

2. The father of the prophet Zephaniah (Zep 1:1).

3. According to the KJV, the name of one of the two messengers who brought David the news about the victory over Absalom (2 Sa 18:21-23, 31, 32). However, in these texts the RSV renders *Kûshî,* "Cushite," a term expressing nationality. If this interpretation is correct, the actual name of this messenger is unknown.

Cushion. The translation in the RSV of the Gr. *proskephalaion* (Mk 4:38), "cushion" or "pillow." Some believe that the definite article in the Greek indicates that Christ's headrest was a regular part of the boat's equipment, possibly the rower's cushion.

Cushite (kŭsh'īt). [Heb. *Kûshî.*] An inhabitant of Cush. The term is used in the RSV of Num 12:1, where the KJV reads "Ethiopian," and of 2 Sa 18:21-23, 31, 32, where the KJV, taking *Kûshî* as a personal name, reads "Cushi."

Custodian. *See* Schoolmaster.

Custom. In Ezr 4:13, 20; 7:24, KJV, a rendering of the Aramaic *halak,* a loan word from the Akkadian *alâku* used to describe feudal fees paid to rulers for certain grants. The RSV translates this term "toll," but translates another Aramaic term appearing in these verses, *belô,* as "custom." *Belô* means tax paid in kind. Two other Aramaic terms appearing in these verses, *mindah* and *middah,* are rendered "toll" in the KJV, and "tribute" in the RSV. *Mindah* and *middah* mean revenues to be paid in money. In a letter to Artaxerxes, enemies of the Jews claimed that if the returned Jews were permitted to rebuild Jerusalem they would refuse to pay tribute, custom, or toll to the Persian Empire (Ezr 4:13). Similar tribute, custom, or toll, had been levied from others by former Hebrew kings ruling in Jerusalem (Ezr 4:20). Artaxerxes decreed that tribute, custom, or toll was not to be required of those who served at the restored Temple (ch 7:24). The "receipt of custom," at which Matthew sat (Mt 9:9; Mk 2:14; Lk 5:27), was a revenue office, or "tax office," as the RSV correctly translates the Gr. *telōnion. See* Publican. The "custom" of Mt 17:25 is a translation of the Gr. *telos,* which means " (indirect) tax," "customs duties." Paul admonished the Roman Christians to pay *telos* to those whose right it was (Rom 13:7).

Cuth (kŭth), or **Cuthah** (kū'thȧ). [Heb. *Kûth* and *Kûthah;* Akkadian *Kutú.*] A city in Babylonia, about 15 mi. northeast of Babylon. The city, containing the temple *E-meslam,* was the center of the worship of the god Nergal. Otherwise Cuth played an insignificant role in the history of ancient Babylonia. People from Cuth are listed as being among those Sargon II (722-705 B.C.) settled in Samaria after its destruction (2 Ki 17:24). These settlers continued to worship their god Nergal in the new country (v 30). Cuth is one of the few Babylonian cities mentioned in the Bible. The later Jews called the Samarians Cuthaeans. The site, now *Tell Ibrāhîm,* was partially excavated by Hormuzd Rassam in 1880. See Cutha on Map XI, C-5.

Cuthah. *See* Cuth.

Cymbals. [Heb. *ṣelṣelîm* and *meṣiltayim;* Gr. (sing.) *kumbalon.*] Percussion instruments. They are mentioned 16 times in the OT (2 Sa 6:5; 1 Chr 13:8; etc.), and once in the NT (1 Cor 13:1). In Ps 150:5 a distinction is made between "loud" and "high sounding" (RSV "sounding" and "loud clashing") cymbals. Ancient pictures show that the cymbals were struck with either a vertical or a horizontal movement of the hand. Two pairs of cymbals have

117. Assyrian with cymbals

been discovered in the excavations of Palestine. Those found at *Tell Abū Hawâm* are of bronze and have a diameter of about 4 in. They have holes in the center through which thongs were probably thrust and knotted on the inside to serve as handles. Another pair of bronze cymbals was found in excavations at Bethshemesh. See *SDACom* 3:30, 31.

Cypress. In the KJV (Is 44:14) the translation of the Heb. *tirzah,* a tree of unknown identification, and translations of the term are only conjectures, as, for example, the RSV translation "holm tree." In the RSV "cypress" is the translation of the Heb. *berôsh,* the exact identity of which is uncertain. Some believe the cypress is meant, others, the Phoenician juniper (1 Ki 5:8, 10; 6:15; etc.).

Cyprus (sī′prŭs). [Gr. *Kupros.*] An island in the northeastern Mediterranean Sea, at a minimum distance of about 45 mi. from the coast of Cilicia and 60 mi. from the Syrian coast. The island is about 150 mi. long and from about 6 to 60 mi. wide. The copper ore in its mountains made it the main copper-producing area for the ancient world. This gave it its name Cyprus, which means "copper."

In the OT its inhabitants are called *Kittim (Gen 10:4), a name that has been recognized in Citium (Gr. *Kition*), the earliest capital of the island. In the 15th cent. B.C. there was a lively contact between Cyprus and Mycenae in Greece. Later the Phoenicians took possession of the island, but the Greek population remained in the majority. The island enjoyed virtual independence until it became an Egyptian possession under the Ptolemies. The Romans occupied it in 58 B.C., and in 27 B.C. made it an imperial province. It was transferred to the Senate in 22 B.C. and was administered by a proconsul as a senatorial province.

When Paul visited the island, Sergius Paulus, who is mentioned in inscriptions, was proconsul of Cyprus. Many Jews lived on Cyprus in NT times, and Barnabas (Acts 4:36) and Mnason, Jewish Christians, came from there (ch 21:16). Christianity was introduced to the island by Christians who fled from Jerusalem during the persecution following the stoning of Stephen (ch 11:19, 20). Barnabas and Paul made Cyprus the first stop of their 1st Missionary Journey, preaching in the large city of Salamis (ch 13:5), near the eastern end of the island (see fig. 412), and in Paphos, the seat of the Roman governor, in the western end (vs 6-13).

Barnabas and John Mark made another missionary journey to Cyprus at a later period (Acts 15:39). Map XX, B/C-5.

Cyrene (sī-rē′nē). [Gr. *Kurēnaios.*] A large Greek city of Libya Cyrenaica in North Africa, about 17 mi. from the sea, on a 2,000 ft. elevation. It was founded in the 7th cent. B.C. by people from Thera, an island belonging to the Greek Sporades. The Cyrenians fought successfully against Egyptians and Libyans, but were subjugated by Cambyses in 524 B.C. and incorporated into the Persian Empire. In 321 B.C. the Cyrenaic Pentapolis, consisting of 5 cities, was organized by Ptolemy I and taken under his protection. In 117 B.C. Cyrene became an independent kingdom, but in 96 B.C. its king, Ptolemy Apion, bequeathed it to Rome. In 67 B.C. Cyrenaica was joined to Crete and made into a Roman province. Map XX, C-3.

During the Hellenistic period many Jews settled in the city (Jos. *Ant.* xiv. 7. 2; *Against Apion* ii. 4). Cyrenian Jews, with the Alexandrian Jews and the Libertines, had a synagogue in Jerusalem (Acts 6:9). Simon, whom the Roman soldiers forced to carry Jesus' cross, was a Jew from Cyrene (Mt 27:32). Some of the early converts to Christianity were from that city, and were active as lay missionaries (Acts 11:20). A leader of the church at Antioch in Syria was Lucius of Cyrene (ch 13:1).

Extensive ruins of the ancient city are still extant. Excavations have been carried out by Italian archeologists. The present name of the city is *Cirene.*

Cyrenius. *See* Quirinius.

Cyrus (sī′rŭs). [Heb. and Aramaic *Kôresh;* Old Persian *Kurush;* Babylonian *Kurash.*] King and founder of the Persian Empire;

118. Cyrus' tomb at Pasargadae

son of Cambyses I. He became king of Anshan in 558 B.C., ruling over Persian tribes as a vassal prince of the Medes. Greek historians name Mandane, the daughter of Astyages, king of Media, as his mother. After *c.* 559 B.C. he united the various Persian tribes into one nation, and between 553 and 550 B.C. defeated his grandfather Astyages and took over the Median Empire with its capital, Ecbatana. A few years later, in 547 B.C., he defeated Croesus, king of Lydia, and conquered Sardis, the "impregnable" Lydian capital. He thus became ruler of all of Asia Minor in addition to Iran (Persia) and the territories lying north of Mesopotamia that he already possessed. Since he was now the most powerful ruler of his time, a clash with the weakened Chaldean empire of Nabonidus was inevitable. In 539 B.C. the forces of Cyrus crossed the "Median wall" erected by Nebuchadnezzar, defeated the Babylonians in the battle of Opis on the Tigris, and shortly afterward captured Sippar and Babylon, the latter city falling without a real battle. Belshazzar, who had ruled in Babylon as coregent, was slain. His father, Nabonidus, fled, but later surrendered to Cyrus and was sent into exile. By bringing to an end the Babylonian Empire and by allowing the exiled Jews to return to their homeland and to rebuild their Temple at Jerusalem (2 Chr 36:22, 23; Ezr 1:1-4; 6:3-5), Cyrus fulfilled the prophecies of Isaiah (Is 44:28 to 45:4).

The Jews were not the only beneficiaries of Cyrus' favors. From the long cuneiform inscription on the famous Cyrus Cylinder (now in the British Museum), we learn that he allowed various other nations exiled by the Babylonians to return to their homelands and to rebuild devastated sanctuaries. He also returned to their former temples cult objects, such as statues of divinities (*ANET* 315, 316), in the same manner as he returned to the Jews the sacred vessels that Nebuchadnezzar had carried to Babylon from the Jerusalem Temple. When he died in a campaign against some tribes in eastern Iran, in 530 B.C., the world lost one of its greatest monarchs. He had been not only a great warrior but also a wise organizer and a tolerant and broad-minded ruler. His empire, reaching from the Aegean Sea in the west to India in the east, and from the Caucasus Mountains in the north to the border of Egypt in the south, was the largest the world had ever seen. His son Cambyses, who followed him on the throne, added Egypt to the empire, which Cyrus himself may have planned. See Map XII.

D

Dabareh. *See* Daberath.

Dabbasheth. *See* Dabbesheth.

Dabbesheth (dăb′ĕ-shĕth), KJV **Dabbasheth** (dăb′á-shĕth). [Heb. *Dabbasheth*.] A town on the boundary of Zebulun, near Jokneam (Jos 19:11); not identified.

Daberath (dăb′ĕ-răth), KJV once **Dabareh** (dăb′á-rĕ). [Heb. *Daberath*.] A city in the territory of Issachar, on the border of Zebulun, assigned to the Gershonite Levites (Jos 19:12 [19:13, RSV]; 21:28; 1 Chr 6:71, 72); now *Debûriyeh,* a village about 4 mi. southeast of Nazareth, on the western slopes of Mount Tabor (Map VI, C-3).

Dagger. A weapon shorter than a sword, used for stabbing. The word occurs only in Jgs 3:16, 21, 22, KJV, and is the rendering of the Heb. *chereb,* which is usually rendered "sword." However, "sword" does not fit the narrative of this passage, for a dagger was most obviously used as the murder weapon. Archeological evidence shows that the dagger was widely used among ancient nations, including Palestine (see figs. 119, 243). Apparently the Heb. *chereb* designated not only the longer sword but also the shorter dagger. It may be that in certain other OT passages *chereb* should be translated "dagger."

119. **Two daggers found in Palestine**

Dagon (dā'gŏn). [Heb. *Dagôn;* Ugaritic *Dgn;* Akkadian *Dagân* and *Dagúna.* The etymology is uncertain. Some derive the name from the Heb. *dag,* "fish," and believe Dagon was a fish-god; others derive the name from the Heb. *dagan,* "grain," and believe he was a grain god. Both of these frequently defended etymologies are questionable, the first despite the fact that the ancient East knew gods half fish and half human, and Greek coins from Aradus and Ashkelon show pictures of fish-gods.] A deity widely worshiped among the western Semites from the time of Sargon of Akkad. Being considered the father of Baal, he was an important god in the Ugaritic pantheon. His temple, adjacent to that of Baal, has been excavated at Ras Shamra. The Canaanites in Palestine also worshiped him, as is evident from the fact that two towns in Joshua's time, one in Judah (Jos 15:41) and another in Asher (ch 19:27), both bore the name Beth-dagon, meaning "house (or temple) of Dagon." It is virtually certain that a Dagon temple was in each of the two places. According to H. Schmökel there are three villages in Palestine that today bear the name *Beit-Deĝan.*

The fact that Dagon appears in the OT as the chief Philistine deity suggests that the Philistines must have adopted this god when they moved into Palestine. Three centers of Dagon worship, all connected with the Philistines, are mentioned in the OT: (1) The temple of Dagon at Gaza, in which Samson met his death (Jgs 16:21-30). (2) The temple of Dagon at Ashdod, to which the ark was taken after the battle of Aphek. It contained a statue of Dagon, probably a human form, since his head, face, and the palms of his hands are mentioned. This statue fell to the ground and was broken when the ark was in its temple (1 Sa 5:1-4). This Dagon temple or its successor existed until the 2d cent. B.C., when it was finally destroyed by Jonathan, the Maccabean (1 Macc 10:83, 84; 11:4). (3) The temple of Dagon at Beth-shan, to which the Philistines took King Saul's head and armor after the battle of Mount Gilboa, in which Saul lost his life (1 Sa 31:9, 10; 1 Chr 10:6-10). Excavations were conducted by the University of Pennsylvania expedition in the ruin mound of ancient Bethshan. It is believed that the south temple found in stratum V from the time of Ramses III was probably the one dedicated to Dagon when the Philistines held the city.

Lit.: H. Schmökel, *RLA* II, 99-101; A. Rowe, *The Four Canaanite Temples of Beth-shan,* I (Philadelphia, 1940), pp. 22-30.

Daily. [Heb. *tamîd,* "continually," "regularly."] *Tamîd* occurs 104 times in the OT both as an adjective (Ex 29:42) and as an adverb (ch 27:20). Six times (Num 4:16; Dan 8:11-13; 11:31; 12:11) it is translated "daily" in the KJV, but usually "continual" or "perpetual" when used adjectively, and "continually," "perpetually," "always," "ever," "evermore" when used adverbially. The rendering "daily" is a modified translation based on the context. The Hebrew expression most often translated "daily" is *yôm beyôm,* literally, "day by day." *Tamîd* is used in connection with the tabernacle and Temple service about 50 times: of the daily morning and evening burnt offering (Ex 29:38, 42), of the candlestick, or lamp (ch 27:20), of the showbread (ch 25:30), of the incense (ch 30:8), of the fire upon the altar (Lev 6:13), of the fire and cloud that hovered over the sanctuary (Num 9:16), of the musical service (1 Chr 16:6, 37), etc. In all instances *tamîd* denotes aspects of the tabernacle or Temple service that were in operation "continually," "regularly," or "daily," in contradistinction to special ritual performed only at specified seasons—such as the Passover, or the Day of Atonement —or for individuals. Thus, the 7 lamps were never extinguished all at once, the fire on the altar of burnt offering was never permitted to go out, the bread of the Presence was always upon its table; a lamb was offered every morning and every evening, and incense burned upon the altar of incense simultaneously. See references above. The "daily" or "continual" service represented God's continuing beneficent provision for man, and pointed forward symbolically to Christ's ministry—Christ, who "ever liveth to make intercession for" us (Heb 7:25).

In Dan the term "daily" occurs 5 times as the translation of *tamîd* (chs 8:11-13; 11:31; 12:11; RSV "continual burnt offering") and is associated with the sanctuary. In ch 8:11-14 the power symbolized by the little horn desolates the sanctuary and halts its regular ritual services, but after a period of 2300 "days" the sanctuary is to be "cleansed" (KJV), or "restored to its rightful state" (RSV). In ch 11:31 the additional information is given that "the abomination that maketh desolate" is substituted for "the daily." Since "the daily" designates the divinely ordained system of worship, the power that removes it stands in opposition to God, and "the abomination that maketh desolate" represents a counterfeit system of worship.

Jews at the time of Christ applied this prophecy of Daniel to the desolation of the Temple by Antiochus Epiphanes, the interruption of its sacred services, and the substitution of heathen ritual for those services, between 168 and 165 B.C. Josephus (writing *c.* A.D. 75-93) specifically so applies the prophecy (*Ant.* x. 11. 7; xii. 5. 3, 4; 7. 6, 7; *War* i. 1. 1, 2). The writer of 1 Macc (*c.* 100 B.C.) seems also so to have understood the prophecy (see 1 Macc 1:20-64; 4:36-60; 6:7; cf. 2 Macc 6:2). Christ applied the expression "abomination of desolation" to the Romans who in A.D. 70 destroyed the Temple and put an end to its services (Mt 24:15; cf. Lk 21:20, 24). Later, the Romans erected a temple to Jupiter Capitolinus on the site of Herod's Temple at Jerusalem. Many Protestant interpreters have applied the year day principle to the 2300 days, thus bringing the termination of this period to near the close of the Christian age. For various interpretations that have been given to the expression "daily" as used in Dan, see *SDACom* 4:842, 843.

Dainties. Delicate and luxurious foods associated anciently with royal tables (Gen 49:20) and the extravagant elements of society (Lam 4:5, RSV). "Dainties" were a part of the departed luxuries of fallen Babylon (Rev 18:14).

Dalaiah. *See* Delaiah.

Dale, King's. *See* King's Valley.

Daleth. [Heb. *daleth.*] The 4th letter of the Hebrew alphabet, written ד, appearing as the heading of the 4th stanza of Ps 119 in the KJV. *See* Aleph.

Dalmanutha (dăl'ma-nū'tha). [Gr. *Dalmanoutha.*] A place probably on the western shore of the Sea of Galilee (Mk 8:10). Its location is unknown. Since the parallel text in Mt 15:39 reads Magdala, or Magadan (RSV, textual evidence favors the latter reading), Dalmanutha has been considered a variant name or a scribal error for *Magadan.

Dalmatia (dăl-mā'shĭ-a). [Gr. *Dalmatia.*] A coastal area of the Balkan Peninsula on the Adriatic Sea. The warlike Dalmatians once belonged to the kingdom of Illyricum. When Greece and Macedonia became Roman possessions the Dalmatians followed a course of semi-independence; sometimes they paid tribute to Rome, but more often they were in revolt. After several military campaigns they were subdued by Octavian in the Illyrian War (35-33 B.C.), and, after another revolt, by Tiberius in A.D. 6-9, before he became emperor. The area was then made into a Roman province. After an unsuccessful rebellion in A.D. 42 it became part of the province of Illyricum, and was probably included in Paul's "Illyricum" in Rom 15:19. Dalmatia is mentioned in the NT only in 2 Ti 4:10, where Paul informs Timothy that Titus had departed for Dalmatia, probably to carry out some missionary activities. Map XX, A-2.

Dalphon (dăl'fŏn). [Heb. *Dalphôn,* probably a Persian or Akkadian name, which, if it is of Semitic origin, as is the Akkadian *Dullupu,* may mean "sleepless."] One of the sons of Haman (Est 9:7).

Damaris (dăm'a-rĭs). [Gr. *Damaris.*] A woman of Athens who became a Christian as the result of Paul's sermon on the Areopagus (Acts 17:34). Her name is unique and is not attested in non-Biblical Greek documents; consequently it has been suggested that it should read Damalis, a frequently occurring Greek female name, meaning "heifer." She must have been a woman of rank, since only such women would attend public meetings such as the one Paul held on the Areopagus. The fact that only she and a high-ranking Athenian official (*see* Dionysius) are named among the converts seems further to support the suggestion that she was a highly respected woman.

Damascene (dăm'a-sēn). [Gr. *Damaskēnos,* "(one) from Damascus."] A citizen of Damascus. The expression occurs only once (2 Cor 11:32, 33, KJV), where, in his narration of his sufferings for the cause of Christ, Paul mentions his escape from "the city of the Damascenes," by being let down through a window by the wall. Thus he escaped from his enemies.

Damascus (da-măs'kŭs). [Heb. *Dammeśeq, Dûmmeśeq,* and *Darmeśeq;* Akkadian *Dimashqa;* Egyptian *Tmśk;* Gr. *Damaskos.*] A city in Syria, east of the Anti-Lebanon Mountains, on a tableland 2,200 ft. above sea level. The region is watered by the river Abana, the modern *Baradā* (see fig. 1), which branches widely just before it reaches the city. There is a tradition that one of these is the Biblical Pharpar (2 Ki 5:12). These waters make the city and its surroundings a large, fertile oasis on the edge of the desert, a circumstance that accounts for its importance, making it to the desert what a good port is to the sea. Important roadways lead from Damascus in every direction. The shortest caravan route from Egypt to Mesopotamia in ancient times went by way of this city. It also lay on the main highway crossing Syria and Transjordan, and connecting Anatolia and northern Mesopotamia with southern Arabia. Its position at the crossroads of the nations made Damascus "the head of Syria" (Is 7:8). Map VI, A-5.

Damascus is one of the oldest continuously inhabited cities of the world. Although, like every ancient city, it has been conquered and repeatedly sacked, it has always risen, phoenixlike, from the ashes of its destruction.

Abraham may have passed through the city on his way from Haran to Canaan; at least he must have been acquainted with it, since Eliezer, one of his chief servants, was a Damascene (Gen 15:2). Damascus appears for the first time in the Egyptian records in Abraham's time. It is again mentioned as a city-state among the conquered kingdoms listed for posterity by Pharaoh Thutmose III (1482-1450 B.C.). During the Amarna period it fell into the hands of the Hittites (c. 1350 B.C.), but regained its independence with the downfall of the Hittite Empire brought about by the invasion of the Sea Peoples, sometime around 1200 B.C.

When David built the Hebrew empire he conquered Damascus (Map VIII, A-5) and garrisoned it with Israelites (2 Sa 8:5, 6; 1 Chr 18:5, 6), but the city was lost in the time of Solomon. In his reign Rezon, who had rebelled against his lord, the king of Zobah, and had organized a band of irregulars at the time of David's defeat of Zobah, became king of Damascus (1 Ki 11:23, 24). Rezon founded an Aramaean kingdom (Map IX, A-5) which lasted for a little more than 200 years. Following is an approximate chronology for this kingdom, established by

120. Bird's-eye view of the city of Damascus, situated in a fertile oasis between the mountains and the desert;

means of Biblical data, and Aramaic and Assyrian inscriptions:

Ruler	References	Date
Rezon	1 Ki 11:23, 24	c. 960-c. 930 B.C.
Hezion	1 Ki 15:18, 19	c. 930-c. 920 B.C.
Tabrimmon	1 Ki 15:18, 19	c. 920-c. 912 B.C.
Ben-hadad I	2 Chr 16:2, 3	c. 912-c. 870 B.C.
Ben-hadad II (Adad-idri)	2 Ki 6:24; 8:7	c. 870-c. 842 B.C.
Hazael	1 Ki 19:15-17; 2 Ki 8:8-15; 9:14, 15	c. 842-c. 805 B.C.
Ben-hadad III (Mari)	2 Ki 13:3-5, 24, 25	c. 805-c. 750 B.C.
Rezin	2 Ki 15:37; 16:5, 6; Is 7:1, 4	c. 750-c. 732 B.C.

These rulers were frequently in conflict with the kings of Israel and Judah, though occasional alliances were formed to meet a common foe. Tabrimmon and Ben-hadad I were allies of Abijam and Asa, kings of Judah, and Ben-hadad I sent armies against Israel to aid Asa (1 Ki 15: 18-22; 2 Chr 16:2-4). Ben-hadad II had several clashes with Ahab, but was defeated; among other things he granted Ahab bazaar rights in Damascus (1 Ki 20:1-34). When King Shalmaneser III of Assyria invaded the West, Ahab of Israel, Ben-hadad of Damascus (called *Adad-idri* in Assyrian records), and several other Syrian and Palestinian kings joined forces and in 853 B.C. met the Assyrians at Qarqar on the Orontes (Map XI, B-4). The Assyrians were forced to retreat, and Syria was safe for the time being. Immediately Israel began once more to attack its former foe, Damascus, but Ahab lost his life in the ensuing battle (ch 22:29-35). The victorious Syrians continued to harass Israel during the reign of Ahab's son Joram (Jehoram). It was probably during the latter king's reign that they besieged Samaria, and caused a famine which brought the city almost to submission (2 Ki 6; 7). Later Hazael, the king's army commander, assassinated Ben-hadad and usurped the throne (ch 8:7-15). Hazael became the great scourge of Israel and Judah, as the prophet Elisha had predicted (vs 11, 12). He occupied

looking southwest toward the Anti-Lebanon Mountains in the background, and Mount Hermon at extreme left

Israelite territory in Transjordan (Amos 1:3, 4), and marched on Jerusalem, sparing that city only because a high tribute was paid by Joash (Jehoash) of Judah (2 Ki 12:17, 18).

Ivory carvings from the royal bed inscribed with King Hazael's name were found in excavations of *Arslan Tash,* in northern Mesopotamia, where the Assyrians had taken it with other loot from Damascus, probably in the time of Hazael's son Ben-hadad III (see fig. 213).

Ben-hadad III, called *Mari* in Assyrian records, had troubles with the Assyrians (*ANET* 281, 282), and was also repeatedly beaten by King Jehoash (Joash) of Israel, who recovered the cities lost to the Aramaeans by his father (2 Ki 13:24, 25). Rezin, the last king of Damascus, recognizing that only a united front of all western states could save them from Assyria, made an alliance with Pekah of Israel, and apparently also attempted to draw Judah into the pact. Probably because Ahaz of Judah refused to join the alliance, Rezin and Pekah invaded Judah (2 Ki 16:5; Is 7:1-8). Ahaz turned to the Assyrian king for help, and Tiglath-pileser III marched against Damascus, captured the city in 732 B.C., abolished the kingship, deported the population, and made the area an Assyrian province.

However, Damascus regained its pros-

121. Looking through the city gate into the "street . . . called Straight" in Damascus

perity, although in the following centuries it passed from one power to another, falling successively to the Babylonians, Persians, and to the Greco-Macedonians. In 64 B.C. it was conquered by the Romans, but subsequently was allowed to join a group of 10 free cities called the Decapolis. In the 1st cent. A.D. it apparently belonged temporarily to Aretas IV, king of the Nabataeans (2 Cor 11:32).

There was a strong community of Jews in Damascus which supported several synagogues (Acts 9:2; Jos. *War* ii. 20. 2), and Christianity took root among them at an early date. It was when Saul of Tarsus went to Damascus to purge the city of the Christians (Acts 9:1, 2) that he was converted by his vision of Christ outside the city (ch 22:6-16).

The traditional "street . . . called Straight," on which Paul is said to have lived in Damascus (Acts 9:11, 19), is about 2 mi. long (fig. 121), crossing the city from northeast to southwest. Its modern name is *Sulṭaniyeh,* and the *Sûq eṭ-Ṭawîleh,* "The Long Bazaar," occupies a considerable portion of the street. Excavations show that this was once a magnificent thoroughfare flanked by colonnades.

The modern city is now called *Esh-Sham,* and its most important building is the Omayyad Mosque. Originally, it is believed, the temple of Rimmon stood on this site (2 Ki 5:18). That temple, however, was replaced in the 4th cent. by a Christian church dedicated to the memory of John the Baptist, which in turn was converted into a Moslem mosque in the 8th cent. The Greek inscription above the south door, which read, "Thy kingdom is an everlasting kingdom, and thy dominion endureth throughout all generations" (Ps 145:13), has never been removed. Until recent years it was visible from the roof of a shop built against the mosque, but now it is plastered over.

Lit.: C. Watzinger and K. Wulzinger, *Damaskus, die antike Stadt* (Berlin, 1921); A. Jepsen, "Israel and Damaskus," *AfO* 14 (1942), 153-172.

Damsel. The KJV translation of various words, chiefly the Heb. *na'arah,* "young woman," as in Ruth 2:5, and of the Gr. *korasion,* "little girl" (Mk 5:41, 42), *paidion,* "little child" (vs 39-41), and *paidiskē,* "maid," "servant girl" (Jn 18:17).

Dan (dăn). [Heb. *Dan,* "judge."]

1. A son of Jacob by Bilhah, Rachel's maidservant (Gen 30:5, 6). He had one son, Hushim (ch 46:23), called Shuham

in Num 26:42. Nothing is recorded of the life of Dan.

2. The tribe of Dan, the descendants of Dan, 1. This tribe was assigned a small area in the northern Shephelah (Map VI, D/E-2/3), to which belonged the cities of Zorah, Aijalon, Ekron, and Eltekeh (Jos 19:40-46; 21:5, 23, 24). The Danites, however, did not occupy all this territory (Jgs 1:34, 35), but sent out spies who found a suitable area in the north of Palestine, to which they migrated. They drove out the inhabitants of Leshem, or Laish, and occupied their territory, calling the city Dan (Jos 19:47; Jgs 18).

Oholiab, one of the craftsmen who made the tabernacle and its furniture in the wilderness (Ex 31:6), and the judge Samson (Jgs 13:2, 24) were Danites. Jacob's prophecy concerning Dan's descendants is found in Gen 49:16, 17. Dan is mentioned among the 12 tribes in Eze 48:1, 2, but not in Rev 7:4-8.

3. A town in a fertile valley near Mount Lebanon at the source of the Leddan, one of the streams forming the Jordan River (Jgs 18:28, 29; Jos. *Ant.* v. 3. 1; viii. 8. 4). It was the northernmost city occupied by the Israelites. The expression "from Dan even to Beer-sheba" or "from Beer-sheba even to Dan" was used to denote the whole extent of the land of Israel from its northernmost limits to its southernmost boundary (Jgs 20:1; 1 Chr 21:2; etc.). The town seems to have belonged to Sidon before Dan conquered it (Jgs 18:7, 27-29). Its original name was Leshem, or *Laish, which was changed to Dan (Map VI, B-4) when the Danites took it and made it an Israelite city (Jos 19:47; Jgs 18:7, 29). The use of this name for the city in earlier times (Gen 14:14; Deut 34:1) is doubtless the work of later scribes who replaced an out-of-date name by a current one. The city of Dan was a seat of idolatry from the beginning of its Israelite history. Its Danite founders brought with them a graven image stolen while on their way to the north (Jgs 18:18-20, 30, 31). Later Jeroboam I of Israel built one of his two calf temples in Dan (1 Ki 12:28-30; 2 Ki 10:29; Amos 8:14).

Dan, with several important neighboring cities, was conquered by Ben-hadad I of Damascus (1 Ki 15:20; 2 Chr 16:4). The whole area was again conquered by Tiglath-pileser III of Assyria in the time of King Pekah of Israel (2 Ki 15:29) and incorporated into an Assyrian province (Map X, B-4). The site has been identified with the *Tell el-Qâdi* which is the equivalent of the old name, for the Arabic *qâdi*, like the Heb. *dan*, means "judge."

Dance. In the Bible dancing is always connected with rejoicing. The nature of this rejoicing may be religious, festive, or

122. Egyptian male and female dancers in the tomb of Mereruka

DANIEL

merely joyous. The Biblical dance bears little resemblance to the society dance (or even to the so-called "square dance") of modern Western civilization. The Biblical version was usually performed by women, but on rare occasions they were joined by men. Even on these occasions there is no evidence of physical contact between the sexes.

Dancing was frequently performed with the accompaniment of musical instruments (Ex 15:20; Jgs 11:34). The dance mentioned in Ps 149:3; 150:4 was of a religious nature. Of such a nature was also the dancing that took place during the bringing of the ark to Jerusalem, when David expressed his sublime joy by leaping and dancing (2 Sa 6:14, 16; 1 Chr 15:29). A certain annual religious festival at Shiloh provided for dancing by groups of women (Jgs 21:21). Frequently, however, dancing had no religious significance, but was simply an expression of special festive joy (Jer 31:4), and as such is often contrasted with mourning (Ps 30:11; Lam 5:15; Lk 7:32).

Daniel (dăn'yĕl). [Heb. and Aramaic *Daniye'l*, and, more correctly, *Dani'el*. The latter form means, "God is my judge." The name occurs in Ugaritic and Nabataean as *Dn'l*, in Palmyrene as *Dny'l*, and in Akkadian as *Dânilu*. Gr. *Daniēl*.]

1. A son born to David by Abigail at Hebron (1 Chr 3:1), called also Chileab (2 Sa 3:3).

2. Jewish statesman and prophet at the court of Nebuchadnezzar during the Babylonian captivity, and author of the book that bears his name. Daniel was of the royal family (Dan 1:3), and thus of the tribe of Judah. He was obviously a young man at the time he was taken captive, for his foreign service, first, for a time, at the court of Babylon, and again briefly under the Persian Empire, spanned a period of at least 67 years (see chs 1:1-4, 7, 21; 10:1; 12:13). Being a prince and a youth of ability and promise (ch 1:3, 4), he was selected, along with others, for a 3-year course of training designed to qualify him for service at court (vs 5, 19). The curriculum consisted among other things of "the learning and the tongue of the Chaldeans [Aramaic]" (v 4). Students taking this course were considered as members of the court and enjoyed certain special privileges (v 5). Apparently from the very first Daniel's gracious personality and integrity of character won him the favor of the court officials in whose charge

123. The peaked dome of the building that is, according to tradition, the tomb of Daniel at Susa

he was placed (Dan 1:8, 9). These qualities soon won for him the opportunity of demonstrating the advantages of a healthful diet (vs 8-16). At the close of the course (3 years, inclusive), Daniel and his 3 companions graduated with highest honors (vs 17-20). Thus even before Daniel formally entered upon his service at court he had earned the respect and confidence of the king and his courtiers, having given evidence of a gracious personality, a healthy physique, and superior intellect —in addition to native talent and integrity of character.

Soon thereafter a situation arose that, in God's providence, launched Daniel on his career as a minister and adviser to the king (Dan 2). Nebuchadnezzar had a dream of a great image, which, most particularly its spectacular climax, was well calculated to arouse the interest of an idolatrous monarch. When he awoke he found that the contents of the dream had been erased from his memory. He summoned his wise men to declare it to him, but they finally admitted that none but "the gods" could answer the king's queries (vs 10, 11). This set the stage for Daniel to prove his own acquaintance with the God of heaven, who not only revealed the dream but so interpreted it as to win Nebuchadnezzar's complete confidence in Daniel as a representative of the true God (vs 46-49). After the passage of an unspecified period of time, Nebuchadnezzar erected a magnificent golden image and required all his officials to bow before it (ch 3). This golden image was probably designed to represent an empire that would never end, in defiance of the pre-

248

diction in the dream of ch 2 that envisioned Babylon giving way to another world power (Dan 2:38, 39). For some reason Daniel was apparently not summoned.

After the passage of another unspecified period of time, and apparently toward the close of Nebuchadnezzar's long reign, the king again dismissed the God of heaven from his mind (Dan 4:4, 30). God accorded him another dream that presaged his humiliation (vs 5-18), and once more Daniel proved to be the only one able to interpret it (vs 19-27). After the humiliating experience foretold by the dream (vs 28-34), the king testified publicly to the greatness of God, to his own submission to God, and implied his own readiness to cooperate with the divine plan for his reign (vs 1-3, 34-37). But Nebuchadnezzar's successors on the throne of Babylon, though they knew all this, refused to follow his course of submission to the will of God (ch 5:22), and actually defied Him (vs 2-4, 23). This persistent and obdurate refusal to comply with the divine plan brought about the downfall of the kingdom only a few years prior to the termination of the 70 years of captivity (Jer 25:12; 29:10; Dan 9:1, 2). Daniel's subsequent installation as a high official in the Persian Empire gave him an opportunity to testify to his faith before the leaders of the nation that was destined of God to bring about the predicted return of the Jews to their homeland and to assist in re-establishing them there. His deliverance from the lions' den resulted in the recognition of Daniel as an ambassador of the court of heaven (Dan 6:22-28), and doubtless opened the way for him to call attention to the prophecies about Cyrus and his role in the restoration of Jerusalem (Is 44:24 to 45:13).

On at least 4 occasions Daniel was the recipient of divine revelation, first the vision of Dan 7 early in Belshazzar's reign, second the vision of ch 8 two years later, third the communication of ch 9 after the conquest of Babylon by the Persians, and fourth the vision of ch 10 and the lengthy explanation that followed it, as recorded in chs 11 and 12 (see SDACom 4:864), in the 3d year of the new empire. (For an analysis of these visions, see Daniel, Book of.) Thus Daniel lived at least till the 3d year of Cyrus, and was at that time almost 90 years of age.

3. A priest of the time of Nehemiah who affixed his signature to a covenant of loyalty to God, probably as head of his father's house (Ezr 8:2; Neh 10:6).

Daniel, Book of. In English translations, as also in the LXX and the Vulgate, the book of Daniel appears with the Major Prophets, following the book of Ezekiel. In the Hebrew canon, however, Daniel is classified with the *Kethûbîm,* or "writings," which included books that appear in English Bibles from 1 Chronicles to Song of Solomon, with Ruth and Lamentations. Various explanations have been given to account for the position of Daniel in the Hebrew canon, of which the more important are: (1) Daniel was not accepted by the Jews as part of the Sacred Canon until after the contents of "the law" (the Pentateuch) and "the prophets" (see Lk 24:44) had become fixed. (2) Daniel, though called a prophet (Mt 24:15; Jos. *Ant.* x. 11. 4, 6), was officially and primarily considered to be a statesman, not a prophet. According to this view he had the prophetic gift but not the prophetic office; that is, he did not address his contemporaries in the name of the Lord and exhort them as did the other prophets. At the same time, he was the recipient of important visions.

The traditional view of both Jews and Christians is that the book of Daniel was written by Daniel, its leading character, during the 6th cent. B.C. Josephus refers to Daniel as a great prophet (*Ant.* x. 11), and to the book as antedating Alexander the Great, who died in 323 B.C. (*Ant.* xi. 8. 5), and even Artaxerxes I, who began to reign in 465 B.C. (*Against Apion* i. 8). Christ similarly spoke of Daniel as a prophet and as the author of the book that bears his name (Mt 24:15). In addition to this external evidence, the writer of the book identifies himself as Daniel, its chief character, and frequently speaks in the first person (Dan 8:1, 2; 9:2; 10:1, 2; etc.). The fact that he also writes in the third person (chs 1; 2; etc.) does not necessarily imply another than Daniel as the author, since this was a common practice with ancient writers.

Since the time of the Neoplatonic philosopher Porphyry (c. A.D. 300), one of the first major critics to attack the historicity of the book of Daniel, its authenticity and inspiration have been challenged. This has been particularly true during the past 2 centuries, and today a majority of Christian scholars attribute it to an anonymous author of the time of the Maccabean revolt during the middle of the 2d cent. B.C. The 3 chief arguments they offer for this conclusion are: (1) That the principal theme of the prophetic portion of Daniel is the great persecuting power depicted in chs 7 and on, and that this refers to Antiochus IV Epiphanes (175-164/63 B.C.). With this is coupled a rejection of the idea that the prophets had the ability accurately to predict the future. Thus, they contend that if what purports to be predictive prophecy appears to have met reasonably accurate fulfillment in history, the prediction must have been written after the occurrence of the event. (2) That the historical sections of the book contain numerous historical inaccuracies, anachronisms, and misconceptions. (3) That the occurrence of Greek and Persian words in the book are evidence of a late date.

With respect to the first of these contentions 3 points may be noted: (a) The fact that some of the prophetic specifications seem to fit Antiochus (and many commentators who accept the book as genuine prediction by Daniel will allow at least some application to Antiochus in ch 8 or 11) does not prove that a later fulfillment might not fit the requirements even better and more completely. (b) The insistence on Antiochus as the persecuting power of ch 7, which is, to say the least, equally subjective with a belief in a later fulfillment, is most necessary to those who assume that the fulfillment is to be sought in or before the time of writing. (c) The inconsistency of this interpretation with historical facts both from Nebuchadnezzar to Cyrus and from Antiochus on, is alleged as proof that the writer was ignorant of those facts and was therefore a pseudo Daniel of the 2d cent. B.C. In other words, in the face of a set of specifications in the prophecy, some of which fit Antiochus and some of which do not, it is illogical to conclude that the specifications that do not fit the facts are an indication that the author was ignorant of his subject; it is more logical to doubt the correctness of the interpretation.

With respect to the 2d of these contentions it may be noted that the author gives repeated evidence of being intimately acquainted with the historical circumstances of which he writes in chs 1-6 concerning the Neo-Babylonian Empire and the first years of the Persian Empire. However, the detailed knowledge of these facts was largely lost during the centuries following. Only with relatively recent archeological finds have these facts once more come to light, thus authenticating the historical narrative of the book at numerous points. Critics who attribute the

book to some person other than its leading character, and who assign it to the Maccabean period (c. 165 B.C.) are at a loss to account for such a late writer's accurate knowledge of historical facts that had been forgotten long before his day and that have but recently again come to light. For instance, Greek writers almost ignore Nebuchadnezzar and make the mistake of attributing his extensive rebuilding of the city of Babylon to Semiramis, who was actually a queen mother of Assyria who had lived 2 centuries earlier. Until recent years, also, there was no known historical evidence regarding Belshazzar as the last king in Babylon, and critics commonly pointed to this silence as evidence that the writer was misinformed. Now, of course, the existence of Belshazzar, his position as joint king ruling in Babylon for his absent father, and his role during the last years before the fall of Babylon, are all amply attested. On the period from Nebuchadnezzar to Cyrus see Babylon; Cyrus; Nebuchadnezzar; Persia. The supposed chronological discrepancy between Dan 1:1 and Jer 25: 1, and between Dan 1:5, 18 and 2:1, with respect to the regnal years of Jehoiakim and Nebuchadnezzar, can be resolved by taking into account the now well-known "accession-year" or "postdating" system of numbering regnal years, and the ancient habit of reckoning inclusively (see Chronology, I, 2, 3).

With respect to the 3d contention, it is now known that Ionian (Greek) and Persian artists were employed at the Babylonian court, who might easily have been responsible for the introduction of foreign terms. Furthermore, the widespread commercial activities of the Phoenicians and Aramaeans, together with the fact that articles of trade commonly retain the names given them in their country of origin, could also have accounted for the use of some of these foreign words. Then, too, some words that were formerly thought to be Persian have been found to be Babylonian.

A characteristic literary feature of the book of Daniel is the fact that it is partly in Hebrew and partly in Aramaic, a language closely akin to Hebrew. The Aramaic portion begins with ch 2:4 and continues to the end of ch 7. Aramaic was a sort of lingua franca used widely throughout western Asia. The Aramaic of Daniel, which is almost identical with that of the Aramaic portions of Ezra, contains a large number of Babylonian and Persian words, as might be expected, and is sometimes improperly called Chaldee. Whether the book of Daniel was originally written in 2 languages, partly Hebrew and partly Aramaic, or whether one part or the other represents a translation, is not known. It has been suggested that the book appeared in 2 editions, one in Hebrew for Palestinian Jews, and one in Aramaic for the Jews of Mesopotamia. According to this theory a portion of the copy at Jerusalem was destroyed during the Maccabean wars of the 2d cent. B.C., and later the lost portion was replaced by the corresponding portion in Aramaic, without translation. More probable is the suggestion that the author began to write in Aramaic at the point where the Chaldeans addressed "the king in Syriack [literally, "Aramaic"]" in ch. 2:4, and that he continued in this language as long as he was writing at the time. When he resumed writing, with ch 8:1, he chose to use Hebrew. It is certain that Daniel knew both languages, having been reared in Jerusalem and having later studied Aramaic at Babylon (ch 1:4). As a statesman he would be expected to be fluent in the official language of the government he served. Thus, when he came in the narrative to a speech made in Aramaic it would be natural for him to report the speech in the language in which it was spoken, and having done so to continue the narrative in that language. Aramaic must have become as familiar to Daniel as his own native Hebrew.

The book of Daniel has 2 parts, the first essentially historical in nature, and the second prophetic. It might appropriately be called a handbook on history and prophecy. The historical section sets forth, by practical example, the principles of the true philosophy of history, and stands as a preface to the prophetic section, in which those principles and that philosophy are projected into the future. A somewhat detailed account of God's dealings with one nation, Babylon, provides a pattern for understanding the rise and fall of other nations that were to follow. As a leading statesman in 2 of the great empires of antiquity, Daniel was well qualified to perceive and understand God's dealings with Babylon and to be the recipient of an inspired delineation of future events. According to the philosophy set forth in the book of Daniel, it is the function of government to protect and upbuild the nation and to

provide its people the opportunity of knowing and attaining to the Creator's purpose for them. A nation is strong in proportion to the fidelity with which it fulfills God's purpose for it; its success depends upon its use of the power entrusted to it; its compliance with the divine principles is the measure of its prosperity; and its destiny is determined by the choices its leaders and people make with respect to these principles.

The historical section of Daniel reveals how, when God's chosen people, the Jews, were at a crisis hour in their history, the king and officials of the Babylonian Empire were confronted with a knowledge of the true God and of His will for them as a nation. King Nebuchadnezzar, genius of the Gentile world, was brought face to face with Daniel, God's man of the hour, that the king's cooperation in the divine plan might be secured. The national apostasy of the Jewish people came to a climax in the Babylonian captivity, and if they were to learn the lesson of loyalty to God that the Captivity was designed to teach, they must be held by a firm hand but without being obliterated as a nation. Daniel's mission at the court of Nebuchadnezzar was to secure the king's submission to the divine will in order that God's purpose might be realized. The first 4 chapters reveal the means by which God secured Nebuchadnezzar's allegiance. Daniel and his 3 companions earned the confidence and respect of the king and his courtiers as men of gracious personality, vigorous health, and superior intellect (Dan 1). By the agency of these 4 worthy men of principle, and in a succession of dramatic interpositions of divine providence, Nebuchadnezzar learned to his satisfaction the knowledge, power, and authority of Daniel's God. The inadequacy of human wisdom, vividly demonstrated in connection with the dream of the golden image of ch 2, led the king to admit to Daniel, "Of a truth it is, that your God is a God of gods, and a Lord of kings, and a revealer of secrets" (ch 2:47). The incident of the golden image and the fiery furnace demonstrated God's power to thwart the king's will when it was exercised in opposition to that of God. "There is no other God that can deliver after this sort," Nebuchadnezzar admitted (ch 3:29). By erecting the golden image Nebuchadnezzar defied God's express declaration in ch 2:38, 39 that his kingdom would fall and be succeeded by other kingdoms. His imperial policy was to found a kingdom that would last forever. The fiery furnace expressed his fixed purpose to silence all opposition to this plan, but the providential deliverance of the 3 worthies from its flames effectively revealed to the king the fact that he had no power to thwart the purposes of the Omnipotent One (Dan 3:28). The experience of ch 4—the 7 years during which his own vaunted wisdom and power were temporarily removed—taught the king not only that the Most High is omniscient (ch 2) and omnipotent (ch 3) but that He rules in the affairs of men (ch 4:17, 25, 32). Nebuchadnezzar was now willing to admit that in wisdom, power, and authority the God of heaven transcends all the prowess of man. But the rulers who succeeded Nebuchadnezzar upon the throne of Babylon deliberately refused to profit from his experience. They openly defied the God of heaven (ch 5:23), in the full knowledge of what they were doing (v 22). Instead of fulfilling the divine purpose in its existence the kingdom of Babylon became proud and cruelly oppressive. It was weighed in the divine balances and found wanting (vs 25-28), and world dominion passed to the Persians (vs 30, 31).

In the deliverance of Daniel from the lions' den God demonstrated His power and authority before the leaders of the Persian Empire (Dan 6:20-23), and led Darius to acknowledge Him as "the living God" (v 26) and to admit that "the law of the Medes and Persians, which altereth not" (v 8) must yield before the decrees of the Most High. Evidently impressed favorably by this, and by the prophecies outlining his role in the restoration of the Jews to their homeland (Is 44:26 to 45:13), Cyrus fufilled his divinely appointed mission and issued the decree for their return. The historical section of the book of Daniel thus demonstrates the principle that divine wisdom, power, and authority operate through the history of nations for the eventual fulfillment of the divine purpose.

The prophetic portions of the book of Daniel contain 4 great lines of prophecy: (1) the great image of ch 2, (2) the 4 beasts and little horn of ch 7, (3) the ram, he-goat, and little horn of chs 8 and 9, and (4) the kings of north and south, of chs 10-12. Each of the 4, in its own particular way and from its own point of view, traces the history of the world from the time of Daniel onward. All 4 converge on the close of earth's history and come to a focus on the eternal kingdom that the God of heaven proposes one day to set up. All 4 are concerned with the struggle between the forces of good and evil on this earth from the time of Daniel to the establishment of that kingdom, and are thus, in general, parallel in scope and nature.

Though the primary purpose of the dream of Dan 2, in its setting in the historical section of the book, was to reveal to Nebuchadnezzar his role as ruler of Babylon, and incidentally to make known to him "what should come to pass hereafter" (vs 29, 30), it is of great value to us today. This prophecy provides a brief outline of world history down through 4 successive world powers, and makes only incidental references to the experiences of God's people. The 2d prophecy—the vision of ch 7—covers the same ground but emphasizes the experiences of God's people, their ultimate victory, and God's judgment upon their adversaries. The 3d and 4th visions came to Daniel after the Babylonian Empire had run its course, or nearly so, and that empire therefore does not figure in either of them. The 3d vision emphasizes Satan's attempts to thwart the plan of salvation as represented by the sanctuary service and the chosen people (ch 8:9-14, 23-26). The restoration from Babylonian captivity is promised (ch 9:24-26), but with this promise comes the warning of a future desolation that will terminate only with the final "consummation" (chs 8:17, 19; 9:26, 27). The 4th vision (chs 10-12) differs from the others in that it is couched in literal, rather than figurative, language. Nevertheless, it covers some of the ground of the ones that precede it, but with added detail and thoroughness at certain points. In particular, it provides a more complete preview of the experiences of God's people prior to the first advent of Christ and also prior to His second advent. The focus of emphasis in the 4th vision is on "what shall befall thy people in the latter days: for yet the vision is for many days" (ch 10:14), and "the time appointed was long" (v 1). The narrative outline of history covered in ch 11:2-39 leads up to "the latter days" (ch 10:14) and the events that were to occur in "the time of the end" (ch 11:40).

The prophecies of Daniel are closely related to those of the book of Revelation. The Revelation covers some of the same ground, but places particular emphasis on the role of the Christian church as God's chosen people. Thus details that may be obscure in the book of Daniel are often clarified by comparison with the Revelation. That portion of the prophecy of Daniel relating to the last days was sealed (Dan 12:4), whereas John was specifically instructed to "seal not the sayings" of his prophecy, since "the time is at hand" (Rev 22:10). Accordingly, certain obscure portions of the book of Daniel are unsealed in the Revelation.

In view of the generally parallel nature of the 4 visions as to scope and content, a composite picture of the information supplied by all 4 on each major point is particularly helpful. All 4 look forward to "the latter days," or "the time of the end," when God will deliver His people from their enemies and when they "shall take the kingdom" (Dan 2:28, 29, 45; 7:1, 2, 18; 8:13, 14, 17, 19, 26; 10:1, 14; 12:1, 6). The first two visions introduce Babylon, one as the golden head of the image (ch 2:32, 37, 38) and the other as a lion with eagle's wings (ch 7:4). The Persian Empire (Map XII) figures in all 4, in the 1st as the breast and arms of silver (ch 2:32, 39), in the 2d as a bear (ch 7:5), in the 3d as a ram with 2 horns (ch 8:3, 4, 20), and in the 4th, in literal language, under several of its kings (chs 10:20; 11:2). "Greece"—that is, the Greco-Macedonian-Oriental Empire of Alexander—and its successors, the Hellenistic kingdoms (Map XIII), appear in the 1st vision as the bronze "belly" and "thighs" of the image (ch 2:32, 39), in the 2d as a leopard with 4 wings (ch 7:6), in the 3d as a male goat with its horns (ch 8:5-8, 21, 22), and in the 4th in literal language, under Alexander and his successors (chs 10:20; 11:2-4). The career of Rome (Map XIX) is depicted in the 1st vision as the iron legs of the image (ch 2:33, 40), in the 2d as an indescribably ferocious beast (ch 7:7, 19, 23), in the 3d as a little horn that became exceedingly powerful (ch 8:9, 10, 23, 24), and in the 4th in literal but somewhat obscure language (commentators disagree as to where Rome is first introduced; some believe as early as ch 11:14; others, later). Rome's opposition to Christ is presented in the 3d and 4th visions (chs 8:11, 12; 11:22, 30). The European nations that succeeded Rome are pictured in the 1st vision as the feet of the image, of iron and clay mixed together (ch 2:33, 42, 43), and in the 2d as the 10 horns of of the indescribably ferocious beast (ch

7:7, 20, 24; possibly also in ch 11:31). The apostasy which developed into the Papacy figures in the 1st vision only incidentally, but comes in for extended comment later. Its opposition to God and Christ is represented in the 2d vision under the symbol of a little horn with a blasphemous mouth (Dan 7:8, 20, 25), in the 3d by the little horn in its later phase (ch 8:9-12, 23-25), and in the 4th—according to one interpretation—as a willful king who exalts himself against God (ch 11:31-38). An alternate interpretation applies vs 36-38 to Turkey and France. Its opposition to God's people and to the truth is similarly depicted (chs 7:21, 22, 25; 8:10-13, 24; 11:30-35; 12:1, 10). Papal policy is delineated in chs 7:8, 20, 25; 8:11-14, 19, 25; and, according to one interpretation, in ch 11:31, 36-39, 44, 45. An alternate interpretation applies the latter to Turkey and France. The ultimate end of earthly kingdoms is spoken of in the 1st vision under the symbol of the shattering of the image by a stone (ch 2:34, 35, 44, 45), in the 2d under the figure of the final judgment (ch 7:9-12, 16), in the 3d by the breaking "without hand" (see chs 8:14, 17, 19, 25; 9:27), and in the 4th by Michael standing up to deliver His people (chs 11:27, 35, 45; 12:1, 2). In the 1st vision the reception by Christ of His kingdom appears under the figure of a stone that fills the earth (ch 2:34, 35, 44, 45), in the 2d it is referred to literally, as the Son of man receiving dominion (ch 7:13, 14), and in the 4th, as Michael standing up (ch 12:1). The 4 visions thus collectively present a composite preview of the process by which God purposed to work out His will through the process of history, how those who love and serve Him would suffer but eventually triumph, and how "the kingdoms of this world" would "become the kingdoms of our Lord, and of his Christ" (Rev 11:15).

Danite (dăn′ĭt). [Heb. *Danî.*] A member of the Israelite tribe of *Dan (Jgs 13:2; etc.).

Dan-jaan (dăn′jā′ăn). [Heb. *Dan Ya'an.*] According to the KJV a place between Gilead and Sidon (2 Sa 24:6); not identified. Some scholars see in it a variant name for Dan. However, the Hebrew text poses difficulties, and various solutions have been suggested. Some render the Hebrew phrase "from Dan to Ijon." The RSV, following the LXX, has Dan twice, rendering the passage in which the phrase occurs: "They came to Dan, and from Dan they went around to Sidon."

Dannah (dăn′à). [Heb. *Dannah*, "fortress."] A place in the hill country of Judah (Jos 15:49); not identified with certainty.

Dappled. *See* Grisled.

Dara. *See* Darda.

Darda (där′dà). [Heb. *Darda'.*] A man of the tribe of Judah, famous for his wisdom (1 Ki 4:31). He is called Dara (dă′rà) [Heb. *Dara'*] in 1 Chr 2:6, the second *d* having been dropped from the Hebrew.

Darics, KJV **Drams.**

1. The translation of the Heb. *darkemonîm* (Phoenician *drkmn;* Gr. *drachmōn*) in Ezr 2:69 and Neh 7:70-72, monetary units used as early as the time of Zerubbabel (6th cent. B.C.). Hebrew silver coins with engravings of the Athenian owl but having Hebrew inscriptions—evidently imitating Greek drachmas (but much smaller)—have come to light in Palestinian excavations (see fig. 124). This is an indication that the Hebrew term actually meant this type of coin which was probably used in this period before darics came into circulation. Hence, the translation "drams" (KJV), an English term denoting drachmas, in these texts is more correct than the "darics" of the RSV. *See* Money.

124. Enlargement of Jewish silver coin of the 4th cent. B.C. from Beth-zur, imitating the Greek drachma (2½ times actual size)

2. The translation of the Heb. *'adarkonîm* (Gr. *darikōn*, sing. *dareikos*), the gold coin introduced by Darius I (522-486 B.C.), which was the equivalent of 20 *sikloi* (shekels), in modern value about $5 (1 Chr 29:7; Ezr 8:27). Actually such gold coins had existed in Lydia before

125. Gold daric of Darius I of Persia (actual size)

Cyrus founded the Persian Empire; he simply took over Lydian coinage after the conquest of Sardis in 547 B.C. However, in the time of Darius the gold coins were named after the king's name, and their minting became the sole right of the crown.

Darius (dá-rī′ŭs). [Heb. and Aramaic *Dareyawesh.* "Darius" is the Latinized spelling of the Greek equivalent of the Old Persian royal name *Dārayavaush*, spelled *Dāriyâwush* in Babylonian texts.] The name of 3 Persian kings, 2 of whom are mentioned in the Bible, and 1 ruler called Darius the Mede, not yet identified conclusively with any ruler known from ancient contemporary documents.

1. Darius the Mede, son of Ahasuerus, unknown by that name except in Daniel. He "took the kingdom" from Belshazzar at about the age of 62 years at the time of Cyrus' conquest of Babylon (539 B.C.), and had at least one regnal year (Dan 5:31; 6:28; 9:1). He appointed various governors, making Daniel one of his three most intimate counselors (ch 6:1-3). Tricked by Daniel's enemies into issuing a decree which the Hebrew statesman could not obey, he was forced to throw his friend Daniel to the lions, and was exceedingly happy when Daniel was miraculously saved (vs 4-27).

Various modern attempts to identify this Darius have resulted in several theories, none of them free from difficulties. One theory equates him with Cambyses, Cyrus' son and successor, who ruled jointly with his father for a time; another equates him with Gobryas, the officer of Cyrus who actually took the city of Babylon, and may have ruled the conquered Babylonian kingdom under Cyrus for a year or so. Another explanation, plausible enough, is that Darius is another name for Cyaxares II, the son of Astyages, who according to the Greek writer Xenophon was Cyrus' uncle and father-in-law, and whom Cyrus might have retained temporarily as a figurehead king to please the Medes. The fact that the Persian account of the fall of Babylon to Cyrus begins Cyrus' reign in Babylon immediately, without any intervening reign of Darius the Mede, does not contradict the Biblical narrative. Darius was evidently recognized as a ruler in Babylon by courtesy of Cyrus, while it was Cyrus who actually held the power (see Is 45:1). It was natural that Daniel, in direct contact with Darius, should speak of him as the "king" and mention his "first year" (Dan 9:1). It seems evident that we are to consider the accession year and 1st year of Darius the Mede as coinciding with the same years of Cyrus. For full discussion of this Darius see *SDACom* 4:814-817. The lack of conclusive evidence as to the identity of Darius the

Mede must not lead one to question the Bible statements concerning this ruler, for future finds may clarify the problem, as archeology has already done for *Belshazzar, who puzzled earlier historians.

2. Darius I Hystaspes, or Darius the Great, king of Persia (522-486 B.C.). Through his father Hystaspes, Darius belonged to the Achaemenid family, as did Cyrus and his son Cambyses, but to a different branch of this family. When Cambyses was in Egypt, during the last year of his reign, a certain Gaumata usurped the throne by pretending to be Smerdis, Cambyses' brother, who had been assassinated secretly before Cambyses started out for his Egyptian campaign in 525 B.C. When Cambyses learned of this usurpation he immediately set out for Persia, but on the way, while in Syria, he died (July, 522 B.C.), as the result of either an accident or suicide, leaving no heir. Darius, a distant cousin of Cambyses, at once set out to gain the throne for himself. With some helpers he slew the false Smerdis in September, 522 B.C., and as-

126. Darius I on his throne; relief on a doorway at Persepolis

sumed the kingship. However, he had to fight against a number of other pretenders and rebels for many months longer before he finally emerged from the struggle the undisputed ruler of the Persian Empire. The story of his successes was engraved in three scripts and languages (Persian, Babylonian, and Elamite), accompanied by a sculptured relief, into a high rock wall of the Behistun mountain, which lies on the main highway between Iran and Iraq. This trilingual Behistun inscription, copied by Henry Rawlinson more than a century ago, became the first key to the decipherment of the cuneiform scripts used in ancient western Asia. See fig. 293; also figs. 6, 31, 138.

Darius proved to be a strong and wise ruler. He was tolerant toward other religions and cultures, promoted learning, agriculture, forestation, and the construction of highways. He also built the great palace cities of Susa and Persepolis. However, he made an extremely unwise choice when he began a war against the mainland Greeks, which ended in the defeat of the Persian army at Marathon (490 B.C.). This battle was the beginning of a series of defeats the Persians suffered under Darius' successors.

When Darius came to the throne the building of the Temple at Jerusalem had been suspended by the false Smerdis because of complaints against the Jews by their jealous neighbors. With the change of government the Jews took heart, and encouraged by the prophets Haggai and Zechariah, resumed their building activity. When the matter was brought to the attention of Darius by the deputy satrap Tatnai, who had visited Jerusalem, the king had the whole case investigated, and after finding that the Jews had legal rights to rebuild their Temple, he issued a decree that favored the Jews even more than the decree of Cyrus had done some 18 years earlier (Ezr 4:24 to 6:15). A number of prophetic utterances and visions of Haggai and Zechariah are dated in terms of regnal years of Darius (Hag 1:1, 15; 2:1, 10; Zec 1:1, 7; 7:1).

3. Darius the Persian (Neh 12:22) is probably Darius II (424/23-405/04 B.C.), the son and successor of Artaxerxes I. The various lists of ecclesiastical officers given in the book of Nehemiah seem to have their terminal point in his reign. Many commentators identify him with Darius III (336-331 B.C.), who was defeated by Alexander the Great, on the basis of identifying Jaddua of Josephus

(*Ant.* xi. 8. 4, 5) with the Jaddua of Neh 12:11 and 22. This identification, however, is very uncertain (see *SDACom* 3: 372, 373).

Darkness. Besides its frequent literal uses "darkness" is used symbolically of spiritual ignorance (Ps 82:5; Is 60:2; Mt 4: 16), wickedness (Prov 4:19; Is 5:20), a spiritual condition that results from spurned or neglected truth (Mt 6:23; Lk 11:35), troubles (2 Sa 22:29), confusion and uncertainty (Job 12:25), the unapproachableness and mystery of God (Ex 20:21, KJV; 1 Ki 8:12).

"Darkness" covered the deep at Creation (Gen 1:2). A plague of "darkness" smote the Egyptians (Ex 10:21, 22). "Darkness" covered the land at the crucifixion of Christ. "Darkness" portends His coming (Mt 24:29; cf. Rev 6:12).

Darkon (där'kŏn). [Heb. *Darqón.*] The founder of a family among Solomon's servants. Some members of this family returned with Zerubbabel from Babylonia after the Exile (Ezr 2:56; Neh 7:58).

Dark Saying or **Dark Speech.** The translation of the Heb. *chîdah*, "an enigmatic statement" or "riddle" (Ps 78:2; Num 12:8). *Chîdah* is frequently rendered "riddle" (Jgs 14:12-19; Eze 17:2), twice "hard question" (1 Ki 10:1; 2 Chr 9:1), and elsewhere variously (Dan 8:23; Hab 2:6).

Darling. The translation of the Heb. *yachîd* (Ps 22:20; 35:17; KJV), meaning "only [one]." *Yachîd* is translated "only" in Gen 22:2, 12, 16; etc.

Dart. A short lance or javelin. In the RSV "dart" is the translation of: (1) the Heb. *massa'* (Job 41:26), a word of uncertain meaning; (2) the Heb. *shebeṭ* (2 Sa 18: 14), literally, "stick," or "staff," here probably a spear shaft; (3) the Gr. *belos,* "an arrow" (Eph 6:16). In two other texts "dart" is used as a verb to indicate quick motion (Eze 1:14; Nah 2:4). Textual evidence attests the omission of "dart" in Heb 12:20. In the KJV "dart" is also from (1) the Heb. *cheṣ* (Prov 7: 23), "arrow"; (2) the Heb. *shelach* (2 Chr 32:5), "missile," "javelin"; (3) the Heb. *tôthach,* "cudgel," "club" (Job 41:29).

Dathan (dā'thăn). [Heb. *Dathan.* The name is attested in Ugaritic inscriptions.] A Reubenite leader, who, with Abiram, his brother, and On, a man of the same tribe, joined the Levite Korah in rebellion against the leadership of Moses and Aaron. He evidently thought that the leadership belonged to his tribe, since Reuben had been Jacob's first-born son. He also accused Moses of having promised to bring the Israelites to a fertile land, while in fact they had been led by him into a barren and forsaken wilderness. With the other rebels, Dathan perished when the ground under them opened, swallowing the group (Num 16:1-34; 26:7-11; Deut 11:6; Ps 106:17).

Daughter. [Heb. *bath;* Gr. *thugatēr.*] A term used variously, with both literal and figurative meanings. Literally, it may refer to any female descendant, whether immediate or remote (Gen 5:7; 2 Ki 8:26; Lk 13:16). *See* Son. Collectively, it may refer to women generally (Gen 34:1; Lk 23:28). It served also as a familiar form of address expressing respect and sometimes compassion (Mk 5:34; Lk 8:48). Commonly in the OT, especially by the prophets, the term was used to personify the inhabitants of towns, cities, or countries (Is 1:8; 47:1; Jer 46:24; Lam 4:21).

David (dā'vĭd). [Heb. *Dawid,* usually interpreted to mean "beloved." However, it has also been suggested that *dwdh* on the Moabite Stone and *dawidum* in the Mari texts mean "chieftain," or "commander," and that this is the true meaning of David's name. This interpretation has not been conclusively proved. Gr. *Dauid.*] The son of Jesse, a Bethlehemite; 2d king of Israel (reigning from *c.* 1011 to 971 B.C.), and an ancestor of Christ.

David's youth. David, the youngest son of Jesse (1 Sa 16:10-13; 17:12-14), is described as a ruddy, handsome boy with beautiful eyes (ch 16:12, RSV). Like many other Palestinian boys, he was early placed in charge of the family's few sheep (ch 17:28). As shepherd boy he showed unusual bravery by killing a bear and a lion singlehanded (vs 34-36). After Saul's rejection as king, God directed Samuel to anoint David king. This ceremony was carried out in secrecy (ch 16:1-13), and its true significance may not have been understood even by the members of David's family. Whatever the case, Saul did not at first hear of it. From the day of his anointing the Spirit of the Lord came mightily upon David (v 13).

As Saul's courtier. Saul, plagued by fits of melancholy after the departure of God's Spirit from him, was counseled to seek relaxation in music. David, a skillful lyre player, was chosen to soothe Saul's troubled mind. Saul liked the boy and made him also an armorbearer and kept him at the court much of the time, though not continuously (1 Sa 16:14-23; 17:15). This must have been of great educational value for the shepherd boy who was destined to become the future king of Israel.

In a war with the Philistines about this time, the eldest three sons of Jesse followed Saul's call to arms and left for the battlefield, about 15 mi. west of Bethlehem. Here a Philistine champion, Goliath, challenged the Hebrews to appoint an opponent, but the challenge remained unanswered and for about 6 weeks the two hostile armies faced each other without being involved in actual fighting (1 Sa 17:1-16). At the end of this period David, who had been at home, was sent to take some provisions to his soldier brothers. Arriving in the Hebrew camp, he heard Goliath utter his challenging call. He was surprised that none of Saul's soldiers dared to fight the Philistine warrior and offered to do so himself (vs 17-27). His eldest brother considered David's offer an unwarranted insolence, but the king assented and allowed the youth to accept the Philistine's challenge. David, laying aside the heavy armor that Saul offered him, went out to meet the Philistine giant with the equipment of a shepherd—a sling and a stick. Skillful in handling the *sling, from a distance David shot a stone that struck Goliath on his unprotected forehead. He fell, stunned, and David ran and struck off the giant's head with Goliath's own sword. Having lost their champion, the Philistines lost heart and fled in panic. The Israelites pursued them as far as Gath and won a great victory (vs 28-53). David kept the giant's armor as a souvenir, and later put his sword in the Lord's tabernacle (v 54; ch 21:9). The fact that Saul asked Abner whose son David was (ch 17:55-58)

does not mean that the king did not know David—though he might have forgotten the name of David's father. He was apparently interested as to whether this boy came from a family of heroes and warriors. When the question was placed before David, the humble youth simply answered that he was the son of Jesse of Bethlehem—he could not point to any spectacular ancestry. David remained humble and made no demand that the king should fulfill his promise of making the victor over Goliath a wealthy man, the king's son-in-law, and tax exempt (1 Sa 17:25). David's behavior, his forthrightness, modesty, bravery, and piety won for him the admiration of Jonathan, the crown prince, and the two became fast friends (ch 18:1, 3). This friendship survived great odds, and never died. Their devotion and loyalty to each other has seldom been duplicated and has probably never been surpassed.

Saul no longer allowed David to leave him (1 Sa 18:2), but his attachment to the young man turned to jealousy and hatred when he saw that David was acclaimed as a greater hero than himself. The king was also plagued by forebodings that David might become king (vs 6-9), and consequently planned his death. While in a fit of anger he attempted to kill the lyre player with his spear (vs 10, 11). Later he sent him away (v 13), and gave his daughter, promised to David, to another man (vs 17-19). Noticing later his younger daughter's love for David, he offered her in marriage, scheming, however, by demanding from him the death of 100 Philistines as a marriage present, to have him slain by the Philistines (vs 20-27). David, however, was victorious in all his skirmishes with the Philistines, and became more and more loved and honored by the people. This only increased Saul's fear and deadly hatred of him (vs 28-30). Eventually Saul demanded that his courtiers, among whom David had enemies (ch 24:9), kill him (ch 19:1). Jonathan's intervention brought a short respite (vs 2-7), but Saul's hatred soon revived, and he made another attempt to kill David with his spear (vs 9, 10). Later he tried to arrest him, but David, with the help of his wife, escaped to Samuel (vs 11-19). After one more attempt to reconcile his father with David, Jonathan became convinced that it was no longer safe for David to remain at the court. The two close friends parted, assuring each other of their devotion (ch 20). They seem to

127. The anointing of David by Samuel, depicted in a wall painting of the 3d cent. synagogue at Dura Europus (Map XIII, C-5)

have met only once more (1 Sa 23:16-18).

As a fugitive. With a few faithful followers David left the capital, and by deception obtained some provisions and the sword of Goliath from the high priest at Nob (1 Sa 21:1-9). As an indirect consequence of his subterfuge all the priests of Nob, except one, were slain (ch 22:6-19). In desperation, David turned for refuge to the national enemy, the Philistines. When he found that his life was in danger in Gath, he escaped by feigning insanity (chs 21:10 to 22:1). Returning to Judah, he stayed in a cave at Adullam in the hill country southwest of Bethlehem, but took his parents to Moab for safety (ch 22:1-4). David gathered around him a band of unfortunate and discontented men, which soon grew to about 400 (v 2), and later to about 600 (ch 23:13). Among them was Abiathar, the only priest to escape Saul's massacre at Nob; hence David's company was not deprived of spiritual guidance (ch 22:20-23).

When the inhabitants of Keilah were troubled by raiding Philistines, David delivered them. Learning where David was, Saul went to attack him, but David fled into the Wilderness of Judah, where Saul chose not to follow. While in the Wilderness of Ziph, David was visited by Jonathan, and was again pursued by Saul and almost captured. However, Saul was recalled from the pursuit by the news of a Philistine invasion (1 Sa 23:1-28).

David then moved into the wild area around En-gedi, near the western shore of the Dead Sea. Saul, returning to the pursuit, unwittingly entered a cave occupied by David, thus giving David an opportunity to revenge himself. However, he spared the king, thus convincing Saul of his innocence. Consequently Saul desisted for a while from molesting the fugitive (1 Sa 23:29 to 24:22).

While in southern Judah David's band protected the people of that area from robbers. In return David hoped the people would supply him and his men with provisions. When they approached Nabal, a wealthy sheep owner, he not only refused to furnish provisions but insulted David. Nabal was saved from David's wrath only by the resourcefulness and wisdom of Abigail, Nabal's wife. When Nabal died soon afterward, Abigail became one of David's wives (1 Sa 25:2-42). Later the Ziphites, who had betrayed David once before (ch 23:19), again informed Saul of David's whereabouts when David

moved into their territory. Forgetting his promise to leave David in peace, Saul began a new campaign against him, and again fell into David's hand. Again David spared him and Saul once more promised peace to his rival (1 Sa 26). David, however, could not trust Saul. Weary of being a fugitive in his own country, he made a second attempt to find refuge among the Philistines. They had become convinced, in the meantime, that David as Saul's enemy was their ally, and therefore allowed him to live in their territory. Achish, king of Gath, gave him Ziklag, a town at the southeastern fringe of Philistine territory (ch 27:1-6). During his stay of a year and 4 months at Ziklag, David made forays against various desert tribes, but told the Philistines that he was fighting against Judah (vs 7-12). When the Philistines gathered for an attack on Saul, at Mount Gilboa, David and his 600 men accompanied them, but were sent back before the battle for fear they might desert to the Israelites. When David and his followers returned to Ziklag, they found the town destroyed by the Amalekites and all their dependents taken prisoners. David quickly pursued and was successful in recovering both prisoners and property (chs 28:1, 2; 29:2 to 30:20). Upon hearing the news of Israel's defeat, and of the death of Saul and Jonathan, he mourned their death in beautiful poetry (2 Sa 1).

As king of Judah. Abner, Saul's commander in chief, immediately placed Saul's son Ish-bosheth on the throne at Mahanaim, east of the Jordan, but the tribe of Judah seceded from Israel and crowned David king at Hebron (2 Sa 2:1-10). This division, with constant wars between the 2 factions, lasted for about 7½ years, until first Abner and then Ish-bosheth were assassinated. At this, the tribes left without a king invited David to assume the kingship over the whole nation (chs 2:11; 3:6 to 5:5). David was now about 37 years of age and had several wives and sons (chs 5:4, 5; 3:2-5).

As king over Israel and Judah. David's first act as king over all 12 tribes was to conquer Jerusalem from the Jebusites. He made that city the capital of the kingdom and called it the "city of David" (2 Sa 5:6-10). Since Jerusalem lay between Judah and the southernmost of the northern tribes, yet had belonged to neither, the choice of this stronghold as the nation's capital aroused no tribal jealousies. In several battles with the Philistines, David succeeded in defeating them so completely that they ceased to be a menace to Israel (2 Sa 5:17-25; 8:1; 21:15-22; 1 Chr 14:8-17; 18:1; 20:4-8). He also waged war against the Moabites, the Aramaeans of Zobah and Damascus, the Ammonites, the Edomites, and the Amalekites (2 Sa 8; 10; 12:26-31). Victorious in every war, he was able to extend his territories into surrounding areas, and thus increased the nation's revenues and his personal fame.

David also assumed leadership in religious matters. He brought the ark from Kiriath-jearim to Jerusalem and placed it in a tent sanctuary (2 Sa 6; 1 Chr 13:1 to 16:6). He laid plans for the permanent Temple, but was prevented by divine command from erecting it. Nevertheless, he made extensive preparations for its construction (2 Sa 7; 1 Chr 17; 22:7-10), and formed an elaborate organization of ecclesiastical personnel—priests, Levites, musicians and singers, Temple police, and other servants (1 Chr 23:2 to 26:28).

However, David encountered not only triumphs but also serious troubles during his reign. His notorious adultery with Bathsheba and his contrivance of her husband's death in battle (2 Sa 11:1 to 12:23) resulted, despite his repentance, in a breakdown of discipline in his own family and a series of lawless acts that finally led to civil war. This occurred when his son Absalom rebelled against him and forced him to flee to Transjordan. In the ensuing battle Absalom was slain and David regained his throne (chs 13-19). A second revolt was instigated by Sheba, and this was also crushed (ch 20). Besides these troubles there was famine (ch 21:1), and a plague occasioned by David's pride which had caused him to take a census of his kingdom (ch 24).

Shortly before his death David had further trouble when his son Adonijah attempted to seize the throne. This time the efforts of Nathan the prophet checked the plot and succeeded in having Solomon proclaimed king (1 Ki 1). Shortly after this David died, having first admonished Solomon with regard to the young king's future course of action. David ruled a total of 40 years after Saul's death, 7 years in Hebron and 33 in Jerusalem (2 Sa 2:11; 5:4, 5; 1 Chr 29:27).

As poet and musician. David must have been a musician of no mean talents to be chosen by Saul as a court musician. Amos (Amos 6:5) attributes to him the invention of musical instruments, and Ezra and Nehemiah also refer to his musical activity (Ezr 3:10; Neh 12:24, 36, 45, 46) in connection with plans for the Temple music. However, the "sweet singer of Israel" (2 Sa 23:1, KJV) made his greatest contribution as poet and composer of numerous religious hymns. He composed elegies over Saul, Jonathan, and Abner (chs 1:17-27; 3:33, 34), and deeply spiritual poems on many occasions during his checkered life: while he was persecuted and living the life of a fugitive (see titles of Ps 34; 56; 57; 59; 63; 142), while in deep repentance over his great sin (Ps 51), at the dedication of the tent sanctuary (Ps 30), when he fled from Absalom (Ps 3), and on days of deliverance and victory (2 Sa 22; cf. Ps 18), etc. Through his psalms, which have been read and sung by Jews and Christians for centuries, he has helped mold the religious concepts of multitudes, and his influence on the Christian church cannot be overestimated.

As a man after God's own heart. This was a designation given him by Samuel (1 Sa 13:14), before he became corrupted by power. Although David did not live a spotless life, and even loaded his soul with heavy guilt (see 1 Ki 15:5), he knew how to repent, and to accept the results of his transgressions without rebellion (2 Sa 12:13; 16:10; Ps 51). He was an illustrious king, the founder of a Hebrew dynasty that lasted for about 425 years, a great religious leader, a true servant of God, and an ancestor of the Messiah, who was at once David's Son and Lord (Mt 22:41-45).

David, City of. [Heb. *'Îr Dawid*.] The ancient citadel of Zion, stronghold of the Jebusites, which was conquered by David, and became the capital of his kingdom (2 Sa 5:6-9; 1 Chr 11:5-7). It later formed the southeastern portion of the expanded Jerusalem (Map XVII, II; fig. 259). The city stood on a ridge that slopes toward the south, now called the southeastern hill, which lies south of, and completely outside of, the present Old City (whose walls date from the 16th cent.). See fig. 259; compare fig. 278 and on fig. 260 note the low ridge extending from the southeast (left) corner of the wall along the Kidron Valley to the extreme left, behind the tower and beyond. The "City of David" measured only 100 by 500 yd. Its particular site was determined by the proximity of the two natural water sources, the Gihon spring to the east and the En-rogel well to the south of the southeastern hill. The other more prominent hills to the north and west lacked both springs and wells. The city was bounded by the Kidron Valley on the east and by the Tyropoeon Valley, now almost obliterated by being filled, on the west. The southern limit was formed by the confluence of the two valleys. The north had no natural boundary. The Jebusites, who held Jerusalem before it was taken by David, had strongly fortified the city, and had created access to the Gihon spring through a subterranean shaft and tunnel, obviating the necessity of leaving the city in times of siege. It was probably through this watercourse that Joab and his men gained access to the city and took it by surprise (1 Chr 11:4-6).

Jerusalem was not enlarged during David's lifetime, but Solomon extended it to the north by adding a palace and Temple area. From that time on the "City of David" is mentioned mainly as the place where the kings of Judah were buried (1 Ki 11:43; 14:31; etc.). Hezekiah added a section in the south and enclosed it with a second wall. He also dug a tunnel from the Gihon spring to this new southern section, channeling the water into a new pool, the Pool of Siloam (2 Chr 32:3, 4, 30; see *SDACom* 2:87). The City of David was still part of Nehemiah's Jerusalem (Neh 3:15; 12:37); in fact, it remained part of the city until medieval times. Today it lies outside of the walls, and thus is, fortunately, accessible to archeological explorations. It is the only section of the Holy City that has actually been excavated. Hence, its archeological history is comparatively well known. Some of its ancient walls have been traced, a gate in its western wall has been excavated, and an impressive piece of the Jebusite eastern bastion, including a tower added to the city by David or Solomon, has been uncovered. The intricate subterranean water systems of the Jebusites and of Hezekiah have been explored, and many caves which originally may have been royal tombs have been found. However, since they were empty when found, having all been robbed in ancient times, they have provided no clues as to their original purpose. *See* Jerusalem; Gihon, 2; Siloam.

Day. A term used variously to mean:

1. The period of daylight in contrast to the night. In postexilic and NT times it was divided into twelve hours (Jn 11:9; cf. Mt 20:1-12), between approximately sunrise and sunset, or dawn and dark.

Thus the sixth hour was at noon. In this system the hours were longer in the summer than in the winter.

2. The period of a day and a night, approximately the time of one rotation of the earth on its axis. The calendar day was reckoned by the Hebrews from evening to evening (Lev 23:27, 32; cf. Gen 1:5, 8, 13; etc.), that is, from sunset to sunset (Lev 22:6, 7; cf. Mk 1:32). The Babylonians began the day likewise with sunset, but the Egyptians with sunrise; and the Romans began it with midnight, whence we derive the custom.

3. A specific time or condition, regardless of duration, as "the day of temptation" (Ps 95:8), "the day of prosperity" (Ec 7:14), "the day of salvation" (2 Cor 6:2), the *"day of the Lord" (Is 2:11). The phrase translated "in the day when" may mean no more than "when," and is sometimes so translated (Lev 13:14; 14:57; Zec 14:3).

Day of Atonement. *See* Atonement, Day of.

Day of Judgment. *See* Judgment.

Day of the Lord. [Heb. *yôm Yahweh;* Gr. *hē hēmera tou Kuriou.*] Consistently in both the Old and New Testaments this and similar expressions denote the time when God intervenes in human affairs to execute judgment upon evildoers or to deliver His people from the hands of their oppressors, or both. The day of divine visitation upon ancient Egypt (Jer 46:10) and Babylon (Is 13:6, 9) is spoken of as "the day of the Lord" upon these nations, but it is also a day when God promises to restore Israel (Is 14:1, 2; Jer 46:27, 28). "The day of the Lord" was also to be a day of judgment upon His own people because of their evil ways (Joel 1:15; 2:1), the Babylonian captivity in particular being thus spoken of (Zep 1:7, 14, 18; 2:2). The expression also came to refer to the great final day when God would subdue the heathen nations of earth and establish His own people in their rightful dominion (Is 2:2, 12; 34:8; Joel 3:14; Ob 15, 17; Zec 14:1; Mal 4:5). As a day of judgment upon evildoers it is called a "day of darkness" (Joel 2:1, 2; Amos 5:18-20), dark because of divine wrath (Eze 7:19).

NT writers likewise picture the day of the Lord as a "day of wrath" (Rom 2:5, 6) and a "day of judgment" (Mt 10:15; 2 Pe 3:7). They refer to it as "the day of the Lord Jesus" (2 Cor 1:14), "the day of Jesus Christ" (Php 1:6), or simply as "the day of Christ" (v 10). In view of the fact that the affairs of earth would all come to a halt at that time—it was to be the last day of this present world—it is variously called "the great day" (Jude 6), "that day" (Mt 7:22; 1 Th 5:4), or simply as "the day" (1 Cor 3:13). "The day of the Lord" is pre-eminently the day when the Lord Jesus Christ appears to summon the righteous from their graves (Jn 6:39), to purge the earth with fire (2 Pe 3:7-12), and to establish His everlasting kingdom of righteousness (Mt 25:31, 34; cf. 2 Pe 3:13, 14).

Day Star. *See* Lucifer.

Day's Journey. [Heb. *derek yôm;* literally "way (journey) of a day"; Gr. *hēmeras hodos.*] An ancient measure describing a distance traveled in one day (Gen 30:36; Ex 5:3; Lk 2:44; etc.). In Talmudic times, according to *The Jewish Encyclopedia,* it was 40 *Sabbath day's journeys, or 80,000 cubits. This, computed from a 17.5-in. cubit, would be about 22 mi. However, in actual practice a day's travel would vary with the circumstances.

Daysman. An archaic English word meaning "arbitrator," or "mediator" (Job 9:33, KJV). The Hebrew term (*môkiach*) is from a word (*yakach*) meaning "to judge between," "to reprove," "to decide." The RSV translates *môkiach* "umpire."

Dayspring. [Heb. *shachar,* "dawn"; Gr. *anatolē,* the "rising" of stars, especially of the sun, and thus "east," or "orient."] The beginning of the day or dawn. The word occurs twice (Job 38:12, RSV; Lk 1:78, KJV). In the latter text the term is used figuratively of Christ, "the light of the world" (Jn 8:12; cf. 1:9; 2 Pe 1:19).

Deacon. [Gr. *diakonos,* "servant," "helper."] An official of the church whose qualifications are described in 1 Ti 3:8-13. It is generally believed that the incident narrated in Acts 6:1-6 is a record of the institution of the office, although the name "deacon" does not there appear. As a result of complaints that the Hellenistic Jewish widows in the church at Jerusalem were not receiving their share of daily relief, "seven men of honest report" were selected to supervise the distribution of food, clothing, etc. (vs 3, 5, 6). These men did not limit themselves to these duties, but labored also in active evangelistic work (v 8; ch 8:5, 26-40). In certain Protestant churches today the deacons are a lower order of the clergy rather than laymen charged chiefly with the temporal affairs of the church, and may officiate as church pastors. The qualifications of a deacon, as described by Paul in 1 Ti 3:8-10, 12, 13, are: he must be "grave," or "serious" (RSV), he must not be "double-tongued" by saying one thing to one person and something else to another, he must not be "given to much wine," not grasping, but must with a clear conscience possess the truth revealed to him. Furthermore, he must be a man who has proved his fitness and who in his family life is exemplary, being the husband of only one wife, and ruling his family well.

Deaconess. A term appearing once (Rom 16:1, RSV), the rendering of the Gr. *diakonos,* here a feminine noun which means literally "servant" or "helper." Phoebe is mentioned as a *diakonos* of the church at Cenchreae. The word and its usage in this text suggest that the office of deaconess may have been established in the church at the time Paul wrote the book of Romans.

Dead Sea. The modern English name of the largest lake of Palestine. In the Bible it is called the "salt sea" (Gen 14:3; Num 34:3, 12; Deut 3:17; Jos 3:16; 12:3; etc.), "sea of the Arabah" (RSV), or "sea of the plain" (Deut 3:17; Jos 3:16; etc.), and the "eastern sea" (RSV), or "east sea" (Eze 47:18; Joel 2:20; etc.).

The Dead Sea is the lowest body of water on earth, its surface level, not computed till 1837, being about 1,300 ft. below sea level. The lake receives a daily average of about 6½ million tons of water from the river Jordan and other streams. However, the evaporation is so great that the level of the lake remains rather constant, rising only about 10-15 ft. above its normal level after the season of heavy rains. The intake of water is nevertheless slightly greater than the evaporation, with the result that its level has slowly risen, so that the lake is now considerably greater than it was 2,000 years ago (see figs. 365, 455).

Since the Dead Sea has no outlet, it retains all incoming minerals and is there-

128. Floating in the Dead Sea

fore so salty that a human being or an animal cannot sink in it (fig. 128); hence the name "the salt sea" (Gen 14:3; etc.). Greek writers called it Lake Asphaltitis because asphalt occasionally comes to the surface at its southern end and is washed to the shore. Greek writers from the 2d cent. A.D. on called it the Dead Sea, an appropriate though not strictly literal name. Practically nothing can live in its briny waters except a few fish near the mouths of streams. The Arabs since the 11th cent. A.D. have called it *Bahr Lût,* "Lake of Lot," in memory of Lot who once lived there. *See* Sodom.

The Dead Sea is approximately 47 mi. long and 6-10 mi. wide, and its surface about 365 sq. mi. Josephus (*War* iv. 8. 4) is therefore incorrect when he states that its size was 580 x 150 furlongs, which would be about 66½ x 11½ mi. Actually it was smaller in Josephus' time than it is now. The greatest measured depth is 1,328 ft. in the northern section. The depth decreases toward the south, measuring 660 ft. just north of *el-Lisân,* "the Tongue," the flat peninsula that juts out from the eastern shore. In the narrows between *el-Lisân* and the western shore the depth is only 16 ft., varying between 3 and 20 ft. south of it.

The Dead Sea contains 28 per cent salt, as compared with the 4 to 6 per cent in ocean water. Natural salt deposits at the southwest shore (see fig. 454), as well as the absence of an outlet, cause this condition. About half of the salt content consists of ordinary table salt (sodium chloride). Other salts in considerable quantities are magnesium chloride, which gives the Dead Sea water its unpleasant taste, and calcium chloride, which makes it feel oily.

The western shore is formed by the steep mountain cliffs of the Wilderness of Judah. The few settlements that existed in that area—such as the Essene community at Qumran, home of the Dead Sea scrolls, or Masada, the last Jewish fortress to fall to Titus in the Jewish-Roman war—were not directly located on the shore, but on elevated plateaus. Similarly the eastern plateau rises steeply out of the Dead Sea, but streams cutting deep canyons through this plateau have formed pockets of habitable land where towns existed in ancient times. Map II, C/D-3. See fig. 368.

Dead Sea Scrolls. *See* Old Testament.

Deal. A term appearing in Ex 29:40; Lev 14: 21; etc.; KJV, in the expression "tenth

deal" (Heb. *'iśśarôn,* "tenth part"). The context apparently implies that 1/10 of an ephah is in each case intended (see RSV; Ephah, II.).

Death. Death entered the world as a consequence of sin (Gen 2:16, 17; 3:19; Rom 5:12), and is labeled an enemy (1 Cor 15:26). All men are appointed to die (1 Cor 15:22; Heb 9:27), but all will be made alive again (Jn 5:28, 29; 1 Cor 15:22).

In the Bible death is frequently called a sleep. David, Solomon, and many other kings of Israel and Judah were after death described as sleeping with their forefathers (1 Ki 2:10; 11:43; 14:20, 31; 15:8; 2 Chr 21:1; 26:23; etc.). Job referred to death as a sleep (Job 7:21; 14: 10-12), as did the psalmist (Ps 13:3), Jeremiah (Jer 51:39, 57), and Daniel (Dan 12:2). In the NT Christ stated that the dead daughter of Jairus was sleeping (Mt 9:24; Mk 5:39). He referred to the deceased Lazarus in the same manner (Jn 11:11-14). Paul and Peter also called death a sleep (1 Cor 15: 51, 52; 1 Th 4:13-17; 2 Pe 3:4). Many saints "which slept" arose from their graves at the resurrection of Christ and appeared to many (Mt 27:52, 53). Luke, the writer of Acts, described the martyrdom of Stephen as a falling asleep (Acts 7:60).

Sleep is a fitting symbol of death, as the following comparisons demonstrate: (1) Sleep is a condition of unconsciousness. "The dead know not any thing" (Ec 9:5, 6). (2) In sleep conscious thought is dormant. "His breath goeth forth . . . ; in that very day his thoughts perish" (Ps 146:4). (3) Sleep brings an end to all the day's activities. "There is no work, nor device, nor knowledge, nor wisdom, in the grave" (Ec 9:10). (4) Sleep dissociates us from those who are awake, and from their activities. "Neither have they any more a portion for ever in any thing that is done under the sun" (v 6). (5) Normal sleep renders the emotions inactive. "Their love, and their hatred, and their envy, is now perished" (v 6). (6) In sleep men do not praise God. "The dead praise not the Lord" (Ps 115:17). (7) Sleep is transitory and presupposes an awakening. "Thou shalt call, and I will answer thee" (Job 14:15). "The hour is coming, in the which all that are in the graves shall hear his voice, and shall come forth" (Jn 5:28, 29). *See* Resurrection.

In the sleep of death the breath ceases (Ps 146:4), the physical body decays and its elements mingle with the earth from whence they came (Ps 146:4; Gen 3:19), and the spirit returns to God, from whence it came (Ec 12:7). However, the spirit thus separated from the body is not a conscious entity (*see* Spirit). It is the character of man, which God preserves until the resurrection (1 Cor 15:51-54; Job 19:25-27), so that every man will have his own character (see *SDACom* 6:1093). At Christ's second coming the righteous will be granted immortality, and will at the same time be clothed with glorified bodies (1 Cor 15:35-49).

Between the time of dying and the resurrection the dead are represented as sleeping in Sheol (Ec 9:10, RSV) or in Hades (Acts 2:27, 31, RSV). They are not in heaven (vs 29, 34), for they are not united with their Lord until the Second Advent (Jn 14:1-3).

The Bible refers to a second death (Rev 20:6). The first death comes to all and is the normal outworking on humanity of the degenerative effects of sin. The second death comes to the finally impenitent at the close of the 1,000 years of Rev 20, when the wicked are eternally annihilated (Mt 10:28). In the conflagration the earth is purified by fire (2 Pe 3:10). With the destruction of Satan and the unrighteous, death itself is destroyed (1 Cor 15:26; Rev 20:14). *See* Second Death.

Figuratively, sinners are described as being "dead in trespasses and sins" (Eph 2:1; cf. Col 2:13). Except as the Holy Spirit touches their hearts, they are insensitive to all spiritual things. In Rom 6:2 Paul, reversing the figure, refers to Christians as now being dead to sin, hence no longer living in it.

Debir (dē′bēr). [Heb. *Debir*.]

1. A king of Eglon, who fought against Israel as an ally of Adoni-zedek, but was defeated, captured, slain, and hung upon a tree (Jos 10:3, 23, 26).

129. Dyeing plant at *Tell Beit Mirsim*, probably ancient Debir

2. An old fortified city of the Canaanites in the Shephelah. It was also called Kiriath-sepher (kĭr′ĭ-ăth-sē′fēr) [Heb. *Qiryath-sepher*, "city of books"], KJV "Kirjath-sepher" (kĭr′jăth-sē′fēr) (Jos 15:15); and Kiriath-sannah (kĭr′ĭ-ăth-săn′ā) [Heb. *Qiryath-sannah*, "city of palm branches"], KJV "Kirjath-sannah" (kĭr′jăth-săn′ā) (v 49). When captured by Joshua it was inhabited by the Anakim (chs 10:38, 39; 11:21; 12:13), who seem to have regained possession of it, for it was later reconquered by Othniel, Caleb's younger brother (Jos 15:15-17; Jgs 1:11, 12). It was assigned to the priests and designated as one of the cities of refuge (Jos 21:13, 15; 1 Chr 6:57, 58). The site has not yet been definitely located, but is probably *Tell Beit Mirsim*, about 12 mi. southwest of Hebron (Map VI, F-2). This tell was excavated by Kyle and Albright in four campaigns (from 1926 to 1932), which revealed 10 successive layers of city remains.

Lit.: M. G. Kyle, *Excavating Kirjath-Sepher's Ten Cities* (Grand Rapids, 1934); W. F. Albright, *The Excavation of Tell Beit Mirsim*, Vols. I, IA, II, III (*AASOR* 12 [1932]; 13 [1933]; 17 [1938]; 21-22 [1943]).

3. A town on the northern boundary of Judah, near the valley of Achor (Jos 15:7), perhaps *Thoghret ed-Debr*, 7½ mi. northeast of Jerusalem, on the road from Jerusalem to Jericho.

4. A place in Transjordan near Mahanaim (Jos 13:26); not identified. The Hebrew term in this text (*lidebir*) is taken by some scholars as meaning "to Debir," while others emend it so as to see in it the name of the town of Lo-debar.

Deborah (dĕb′ô-rà). [Heb. *Debôrah*, "bee."]

1. Rebekah's nurse, who went with her to Canaan. She either later returned to Haran and then followed Jacob back to Canaan or left Isaac's home and joined Jacob's family after their return from Haran, because we find her a member of Jacob's household at Bethel when she died. She must have been exceedingly old at that time. She was buried at the foot of the hill near the town, and the oak over her tomb was called Allon-bacuth, "oak of weeping" (Gen 24:59; 35:8).

2. A prophetess who judged Israel at a place called "the palm of Deborah" (Jgs 4:5, RSV) in the hill country of Ephraim between Ramah and Bethel. After the long oppression by the king of Hazor, Deborah called upon Barak and commissioned him to liberate Israel from the

foreign yoke. She accompanied the army to battle, and later, with Barak, composed a victory hymn (Jgs 4:4-10; 5:1-31).

Debtor. One who owes a debt, financial or otherwise. In the single OT use of the word in the KJV (Eze 18:7), the Hebrew word so translated (*chôb*) is somewhat of a puzzle to commentators, for it properly means "guilt." However, the context of the passage implies that a debt is involved. In the RSV the word "debtor" occurs also in Is 24:2 and Hab 2:7, in both instances referring to financial debtors. In the NT "debtor" is used also of one who owes an obligation other than monetary (Mt 6:12; Rom 8:12; Gal 5:3, KJV). *See* Loan; Sabbatical Year.

Decalogue. *See* Ten Commandments.

Decapolis (dĕ-kăp'ō-lĭs). [Gr. *Dekapolis,* "ten cities."] A league of ten Hellenistic cities, all of which, with one exception, were in Transjordan. The exception is Scythopolis (OT Beth-shean), which lay at the eastern end of the Plain of Esdraelon on an important crossroad west of the Jordan. Since these cities consisted mainly of Hellenistic populations, Pompey in 63 B.C. made them free cities subordinate to the legate of Syria. He probably wanted to further the process of Hellenization of these cities, and prevent their being taken over by the Jews. The cities administered their own affairs and struck their own coins, which they dated by an era of their own. They are listed by Pliny (*Natural History*, v. 18) as: Damascus, Philadelphia (OT Rabbath-ammon), Raphana, Scythopolis (OT Beth-shean), Gadara, Hippos, Dion, Pella, Gerasa, and Kanatha. From time to time some cities were dropped from the league, while others were added to this organization. In the 2d-cent. list of Ptolemy (v. 15, 22) Raphana is missing, but nine other cities are added (Abila, Abila Lysaniae, Capitolias, Saana, Ina, Samulis, Heliopolis,

130. Excavations at *Jerash*, ancient Gerasa, one of the large cities of the Decapolis

Adra, and Gadora), making 18 in all. During the time of Herod the Great, Hippos and Gadara belonged to his kingdom, having been given to him by Augustus. Nero later gave Abila to Agrippa II. The league was finally dissolved in the 3d cent. A.D. and its cities attached to the province of Arabia. The Gospels mention the Decapolis several times. Multitudes from Decapolis followed Jesus (Mt 4:25), the freed demoniac told the story of his deliverance in Decapolis (Mk 5:20), and Christ passed once through this area (ch 7:31). Map XVI, C-4.

Decision, Valley of. [Heb. *'emeq hecharûṣ.*] A term appearing twice in Joel 3:14, a passage dealing with events to take place on "the day of the Lord" in "the valley of Jehoshaphat" (v 12). The occasion is the gathering of all nations into "the valley of Jehoshaphat," where God sits in judgment upon them. "Jehoshaphat" means "the Lord will judge." Since in v 13 the figure is one of cutting grain at harvesttime and of the vintage and pressing of the grapes (cf. Mt 13:39-42; Rev 14:14-20), some prefer to translate *charûṣ* in Joel 3:14 as "threshing," one of the meanings of the Hebrew term (see Is 28:27; Amos 1:3, where *charûṣ* is rendered "threshing instrument," KJV, and "threshing sledge," RSV). Only in the sense that God is rendering a judicial "decision" upon the unrepentant heathen is the translation of *charûṣ* as "decision" in harmony with the meaning of the word and the sense of the context.

Dedan (dē'dăn). [Heb. *Dedan.*]

1. A grandson of Cush, and ancestor of the South Arabic tribe of Dedan, of which nothing more is known (Gen 10:7; 1 Chr 1:9).

2. A grandson of Abraham by Keturah; also his descendants, the tribe of Dedan; or their territory, at the southern border of Edom in northwestern Arabia (Gen 25:3; 1 Chr 1:32), especially in the oasis *el-'Ula* (Map XI, D-4). It was an important tribe controlling caravan routes between southern and northern Arabia, and between Arabia and Egypt or Palestine (Is 21:13; Jer 25:23; 49:8; Eze 25:13; 27:15, 20; 38:13).

Lit.: W. F. Albright, "Dedan," in *Geschichte und Altes Testament* (Tübingen, 1953), pp. 1-12.

Dedanites (dē'dăn-īts), KJV **Dedanim** (dĕd'ȧ-nĭm). Heb. *Dedanîm.*] Inhabitants of *Dedan, in Arabia (Is 21:13).

Dedanim. *See* Dedanites.

Dedication, Feast of. An annual festival, beginning on *Chislev 25 and lasting a week, instituted by Judas Maccabeus (1 Macc 4:59) to celebrate the restoration of the Temple and the dedication of its new altar after its 3-year desecration by Antiochus Epiphanes (168-165 B.C.). It is mentioned once in the Bible (Jn 10:22). It is sometimes referred to as the Feast of Lights. The Jews still observe the feast, calling it Hanukkah. It comes sometimes in December, at other times in January.

Deed. A written and official document bearing the conditions and details of some transfer or contract, asserting the title or right of possession of property involved. "Deed" occurs in this sense in the RSV of Jer 32:10-16 as the translation of the Heb. *sepher*. The KJV translates this term "evidence."

Deep, The. [Heb. *tehôm*, "deep [waters]"; Gr. *abussos*, "abyss," "depth," "underworld"; *bathos* or *buthos*, "depth."] In the OT, a term that refers variously to the primeval ocean (Gen 1:2), the depths of the sea (Ex 15:8), and of subterranean waters (Gen 7:11), and of the place of the dead (Ps 69:15; Eze 26:19, 20; cf. Job 38: 16, 17). In the NT *abussos* refers literally to the depths of the sea (Lk 8:31, RSV "abyss") and figuratively apparently to the abode of the dead (Rom 10:7, RSV "abyss"). *Bathos* is used literally of the depths of the sea (Lk 5:4). *Buthos* is used only of ocean depths (2 Cor 11:25).

Deer, Fallow. See Fallow Deer.

Degrees. See Ascents.

Dehavites (dē-hā'vīts). [Aramaic *dehawe'.*] A term formerly thought to be the name of a people (Ezr 4:9, KJV); but the Aramaic word in question should be vocalized (*dihû'*) so as to mean "that is." The latter part of v 9 would then read, as in the RSV, "the men of Susa, that is, the Elamites."

Deity. See Godhead.

Dekar (dē'kär). [Heb. *Deqer*, "a piercing tool." The name occurs in Akkadian as *Daqirum* and in Ugaritic as *Dqry*.] The father of Solomon's supply officer in the area of Beth-shemesh (1 Ki 4:9). For "son of Dekar" the RSV reads "Bendeker" (bĕn'dē'kĕr).

Delaiah (dē-lā'yá), KJV once **Dalaiah** (dăl'ȧ-ī'á). [Heb. *Delayah* and *Delayahû*, "Yahweh has drawn (me)."]

1. Founder of a priestly family descending from Aaron, which was organized by David into the 23d of the 24 priestly courses (1 Chr 24:18).

2. A prince who urged King Jehoiakim of Judah not to burn the scroll that contained the prophecies of Jeremiah (Jer 36:12, 25).

3. A founder of a family of Nethinim, some members of which returned from Babylon with Zerubbabel after the Exile (Ezr 2:58, 60; Neh 7:62).

4. Father of the Shemaiah who advised Nehemiah to seek refuge in the Temple to save his life (Neh 6:10).

5. A late descendant of David (1 Chr 3:1, 24).

Delilah (dē-lī'lá). [Heb. *Delîlah*, "coquette," or "flirt."] A Philistine woman from the Valley of Sorek who became Samson's mistress and the final cause of his ruin (Jgs 16:4-22).

Demas (dē'măs). [Gr. *Dēmas*, probably a shortened form of *Dēmetrios*.] An associate of Paul during his first Roman imprisonment. He sent greetings to the church in Colossae, and to Philemon (Col 4:14; Phm 24). Later he forsook Paul, probably having given up the faith, and went to Thessalonica (2 Ti 4:10).

Demetrius (dē-mē'trĭ-ŭs). [Gr. *Dēmetrios*, "belonging to Demeter (the goddess of agriculture)."]

1. A silversmith at Ephesus, who made a living by making and selling shrines (probably replicas of the temple) of *Artemis. When his trade suffered as the result of many being converted from paganism to Christianity through the labors of Paul, he stirred up his fellow craftsmen and the whole pagan population of the city against the apostle. A near riot occurred, which the town clerk quelled with difficulty (Acts 19:24-41).

2. A faithful Christian commended by John (3 Jn 12).

Demon. A frequently occurring term in the RSV, the translation of the Gr. *daimonion*, which in the KJV is translated "devil" everywhere except in Acts 17:18, where it is rendered "god" ("divinity," RSV). However, the translation "devil" may be misleading, for when "devil" refers to Satan it is the translation of the Gr. *diabolos*, not *daimonion;* hence "demon" is a preferred translation of *daimonion*. The Greeks applied the term to inferior divinities, nevertheless beings superior to men. In the NT the term is applied to divinities once (v 18), but elsewhere to evil beings superior to men, and able in cases completely to control them. They are described as spirit beings, the terms "spirit" or "unclean spirit"

being paralleled with "demon" (Mt 8:
16; Lk 9:42). They are held to be the
"angels that sinned" (2 Pe 2:4; cf. Jude
6), who fell with Lucifer, termed "his
angels" (Mt 25:41), over whom he is
"prince" (ch 9:34; *see* Beelzebul).

These demons are represented as' possessing superhuman wisdom, for upon
seeing Jesus they immediately declared
Him to be the Son of God (Lk 8:27, 28).
Because they had this knowledge, Jesus
commanded them not to speak (Mk 1:34).

According to the NT picture, these demons, when possessing men, brought disease, such as we generally associate with
mental afflictions. The driving out of
these spirits resulted in recovery. During
His ministry Jesus cast out many demons.
The Gospels mention a number of specific cases of healing, besides noting generally that He cast demons out of many
(Mt 8:16; Mk 1:39). When He sent
out the Twelve He "gave them power
against unclean spirits, to cast them out"
(Mt 10:1). Later He sent out 70 with
the same power, for when they returned
they rejoiced, "saying, Lord, even the devils are subject unto us through thy name"
(Lk 10:17).

Demoniacs manifested various symptoms. One who was brought to Jesus was
dumb, but when the demon was driven
out the dumb man spoke (Mt 9:32, 33).
Another, possessed with a deaf and dumb
spirit, was thrown into terrible convulsions, often falling into fire or water,
foaming at the mouth, and on occasion
crying out (Mk 9:17-29). Still another
was driven by the demon from the haunts
of men and lived unclothed among the
tombs. Attempts to bind him were fruitless, for he broke all chains and fetters
placed upon him. This particular demoniac was possessed of many demons.
These, when rebuked, entered into a herd
of swine, rushing them headlong into a
lake (Lk 8:26-33). *See* Lunatick.

Demoniac. *See* Demon.

Denarius, KJV **Penny.** [Gr. *dēnarion* from
the Latin *denarius*.] A Roman silver coin
about the size of an American dime with
the image of the emperor (or some member of his family) on the obverse, and
usually a genius, or tutelar deity, on the
reverse (see fig. 340). Its normal value was
c. 18 cents, but devaluated to *c*. 8 cents
in the 1st cent. A.D. However, its buying
power in NT times was much greater. It
was the ordinary pay of a laborer for a
day's work (Mt 20:2, 9, 10, 13). The

Samaritan paid 2 denarii to the inn-
keeper to take care of the wounded man,
but promised to pay more later if the expenses exceeded that amount (Lk 10:
35). The disciples of Jesus estimated that
it would cost 200 denarii to feed 5,000
men with bread (Mk 6:37). It is not
known how many women and children
were in the group (Mt 14:21), but it is
immediately apparent that according to
the disciples' estimate 1 denarius, would
buy bread for above 25 people. The denarius was the only legal silver coin used in
the western half of the Roman Empire,
but in the Palestine-Syria area there was
also the Greek *didrachmon* (ch 17:24) and
the *tetradrachmon* (NT *statēr*, (v 27),
the equivalents of 2 and 4 denarii respectively, which were legal tender in the time
of Christ. These two latter coins were
minted in Antioch and Tyre. All other
local mints produced only copper coins.

Deputy. The translation of: (1) The Heb.
niṣṣab, "officer," from *naṣab*, "to take one's
stand, to be appointed" (1 Ki 22:47). (2)
The Heb. *pechah*, "governor" (Est 8:9;
9:3; KJV). The title *pechah* is rather
vague in scope, but has the general meaning "governor," that is, one who rules over
a certain territory, but is subject to a
higher authority. The Hebrew word is
derived from the Akkadian *pâḥatu*,
"governorship." (3) The Heb. *segen*, derived from the Akkadian *shaknu*, "a lesser
official," "a deputy" (Jer 51:28, RSV).
(4) The Gr. *anthupatos*, "a proconsul," a
Roman official, generally an ex-consul,
designated to act in place of a consul in
governing a senatorial province (Acts 13:
7; 18:12). *See* Governor, (2), *a*.

Derbe (dûr'bĕ). [Gr. *Derbē*.] A city in Lycaonia, first mentioned in history in the
1st cent. B.C. It was in a section of the Roman province of Galatia in the days of
Paul. Derbe fell to the Romans in 25 B.C.,
and was added to the province of Galatia
by Claudius in A.D. 41. Paul and Barnabas

131. *Kerti Hüyük,* the site of ancient Derbe

132. Inscribed stone mentioning Derbe, found at *Kerti Hüyük* in 1956

preached there during Paul's 1st Missionary Journey and founded a Christian church in the city (Acts 14:20, 21). Paul again visited Derbe on his 2d Missionary Journey (ch 16:1, 2), and possibly during the 3d (ch 18:23). Gaius, who later joined Paul, was a native of Derbe (ch 20:4).

Several suggestions as to the site of ancient Derbe have been set forth, but the actual site was not discovered until 1956, when M. Ballance found at *Kerti Hüyük* an inscribed limestone block with a Greek inscription mentioning Derbe (fig. 132). *Kerti Hüyük* is a mound of moderate size, lying 52 mi. southeast of Iconium, the modern *Konya*. Map XX, B-5, places Derbe about 45 mi. southeast of Iconium, but this map does not incorporate the newest findings on this site.

Lit.: Anatolian Studies, vol. 7 (1957), pp. 147-151.

Descry. The translation of the Heb. *tûr,* "to seek out," "to spy out," "to detect" (Jgs 1:23, KJV).

Desert. *See* Wilderness.

Destiny. The translation of the Heb. *menî* (Is 65:11, RSV), rendered "number" in the KJV. *Menî* is generally considered to be the name of a Semitic deity to whom apostate Israelites offered libations. This deity has not yet been identified in non-Biblical sources.

Detestable Thing. [Heb. *shiqqûṣ,* "detestable thing," from *shaqaṣ,* "to detest (as unclean)."] An object of heathen worship to be detested because contact with it defiled one (Eze 5:11; 7:20; 11:18, 21; etc.).

Deuel (dū'ĕl). [Heb. *De'û'el,* "knowledge of God."] A Gadite (Num 1:14; 7:42; 10:20), called Reuel, Heb. *Re'û'el,* "friend of God" (ch 2:14), probably as a result of a confusion of the letters *d* and *r,* which in the pre-exilic and postexilic Hebrew scripts are very similar. The Samaritan Pentateuch reads "Deuel" in v 14, but the LXX and the Syriac version read "Reuel."

Deuteronomy, Book of. The 5th of the 5 books of the Pentateuch. In Hebrew Bibles it bears the title *'Elleh haddebarîm,* "these [are] the words," the opening words of the book. The name in our English Bibles, Deuteronomy, comes through the Latin Vulgate, from the title of the book in the Septuagint, *Deuteronomion,* "second law," a title thought to be drawn from ch 17:18, where the expression occurs. Ancient Jewish tradition unanimously attributes the book to Moses. Our Lord and the various NT writers quote from it or allude to it approximately 100 times, often prefixing the citation with such expressions as "Moses wrote unto us" (Mk 12:19). Modern critical scholars deny its Mosaic authorship and attribute the book in its present form to various writers and editors over a period of centuries. For a discussion of these critical theories and a detailed refutation of them see *SDACom* 5:149-175.

As stated in Deut 1:1-5, the 40 years of *wilderness wandering were now in the past, and Israel had encamped to the east of the Jordan River opposite Jericho, in the land of Moab (cf. Num 25:1). The conquest of the region to the east of Jordan had already been completed (Deut 1:4), and now for about 2 months (Deut 1:3; cf. Jos 4:19) preparations were being made for the invasion of Canaan proper, to the west of the river. During this time Balaam essayed to curse Israel, on behalf of Balak, king of Moab (Num 22 to 24); 24,000 of the people died as a result of apostasy (ch 25); Joshua was ordained to succeed Moses (Num 27:18-23; Deut 1:38), and Moses died (Deut 34). Most important of all, Moses delivered 3 memorable addresses summarizing the experiences and lessons of the Exodus, reviewing the laws already revealed and enacted, and writing out these addresses and laws (ch 31:24-26). The generation that had come out of Egypt had died in the wilderness, and a new generation had risen. Before they should enter upon their promised inheritance in the land of Canaan, and upon the arduous conquest of the land, they needed a clear concept of God's purpose in giving them the land and in driving out its former inhabitants. They needed, also, a clear concept of what God expected of them once they had come into possession of the land, and of the laws that were to regulate their conduct. Finally, the people renewed the covenant made at Sinai with their fathers (Deut 5:1-3; 29:1). Whereas in Exodus, Leviticus, and Numbers, God delivers the various laws to Moses at various times, here Moses stands in the role of lawgiver, at God's command (chs 1:1-4; 5:1; 29:1).

The purpose of the book of Deuteronomy is to inspire an intelligent loyalty to God, through a review of His providential guidance in times past and through an exposition of His holy precepts. The lofty spiritual tone of the book is evident from the fact that when Jesus was called upon to summarize the divine requirements, He cited as "the first and great commandment" a passage from Deuteronomy (ch 6:5). The principle set forth in this commandment is repeated again and again in the book (chs 10:12; 30:6). The code of laws recorded in Deuteronomy applies the principles of the Decalogue—love toward God and toward one's fellow men—to the circumstances under which Israel was to live in the land of Canaan. The theme of the book is Israel's unique relationship, as a unique people, to a unique God. In carrying out this theme Moses lays great stress on monotheism, that is, on the fact that there is only one true God (chs 4:35, 39; 6:4; 10:17; 32:39), on God's supreme rulership in heaven and on earth (chs 7:19; 10:14), on His graciousness and faithfulness (chs 7:6-9; 28:58; 32:6), and on His exacting claim to exclusive worship and service (chs 7:4; 29:24-26; 31:16, 17). The great watchword of the Jewish people down through the centuries and millenniums—"Hear, O Israel: The Lord our God is one Lord"—is taken from ch 6:4. Furthermore, God had chosen Israel "to be a special people unto himself, above all people that are upon the face of the earth" (ch 7:6), and graciously invited them to enter into covenant relationship with Him (vs 6-13). Through the covenant they were to become heirs to all the promises formerly made to their forefathers (chs 4:31; 7:12; 8:18; 29:13) and to

be established as God's special representatives to the nations of earth (Deut 4:6-9; 28:1-14). Unprecedented blessings were to be bestowed upon them as a result of compliance and for the purpose of demonstrating the superiority of the worship and service of the true God above all false gods (ch 28:1-14), and corresponding curses for a failure to comply with the requirements of the covenant to which they had voluntarily agreed (chs 27:14-26; 28:15-68). Ever since it was first written, the book of Deuteronomy has been considered by the Jewish people the supreme revelation of the divine will for them as a nation, and was accorded a place of special honor by the sacred ark of the covenant (ch 31:25, 26).

Following a brief historical preface (Deut 1:1-5), Moses delivers the 1st of the 3 addresses, which is recorded in chs 1:6 to 4:49. This address consists primarily of a review of events that had taken place since Israel's departure from Mount Horeb 38 years before, and of instructions of a general nature anticipating the entrance into Canaan. Moses recounts the command to leave Horeb and to set out for the Promised Land (ch 1:6-8), the administrative arrangements for the journey (vs 9-18), and the debacle at Kadesh-barnea that resulted in 38 years of wandering in the wilderness (vs 19-46). Moses next recounts, briefly, events that took place during this period of wandering, through territory that was not to become their possession, until the people arrived at the river Arnon (ch 2:1-23). Then, at greater length, he relates the conquest of the regions to the east of the Jordan belonging to Sihon, king of the Amorites, and Og, king of Bashan (chs 2:24 to 3:11). This land was distributed among the Reubenites, the Gadites, and the half tribe of Manasseh (ch 3:12-17), and provision was made that the tribes thus settled would assist their brethren in the conquest of the land to the west of the Jordan (vs 18-20). Moses tells also of his request to participate in the conquest of Canaan proper and of God's denial of the request (vs 21-29). Appropriately, therefore, he exhorts the people to be faithful to God inasmuch as they are soon to go forward without him (ch 4:1-40). There follows a brief interlude reporting the appointment of 3 cities of refuge in the land already subdued, and a statement of the full possession of the territory to the east of the Jordan (vs 41-49).

The 2d address, delivered on another

occasion a little later than the 1st, occupies Deut 5:1 to 26:19, the major portion of the book. First, Moses relates the awesome circumstances under which God delivered the Decalogue from the heights of Sinai (ch 5:1-5), repeats the Decalogue itself with slight variations in wording from the version recorded in Ex 20: 3-17 (Deut 5:6-21), and stresses the importance of strict obedience based on love for God (vs 22-33). There follows an earnest admonition to observe all the precepts Moses is about to deliver, precepts that had been revealed to Moses and that applied the principles of the Decalogue to the circumstances under which the people were to live in the land of Canaan (ch 6:1-25). Moses then explains Israel's unique relation to God as His chosen people, as epitomized in the covenant relationship, and upon this basis strictly forbids any and all association with the heathen peoples of Canaan that would tend to lure Israel away from their unique privilege as the chosen people and their solemn responsibility to represent the true God (ch 7:1-15). Certain details regarding the conquest and settlement are outlined, and success is assured, subject to loyalty on Israel's part (vs 16-26). Chapter 8 constitutes an exhortation to keep God foremost in the affections and in the daily life (ch 8:1-20). By a narration of repeated occasions of apostasy and backsliding since the departure from Egypt, Moses admonishes the people to humility and loyalty (chs 9:1 to 10:11). Special emphasis is given to the apostasy at Mount Sinai occasioned by the golden calf, as an example of what Israel must, at all costs, avoid in the future. This is followed by another earnest appeal to love God and to obey Him from the heart (chs 10:12 to 11:32). In the next section of the address Moses reviews and comments on the religious precepts and provisions earlier revealed at Mount Sinai (chs 12:1 to 16:17). Israel is to destroy every vestige of heathen worship and to establish a special center for the worship of the true God, and false prophets are to be stoned to death (chs 12; 13). The people are to avoid heathen customs (ch 14:1-21), and to be faithful in supporting the worship of God by their tithes and offerings (vs 22-29). Provision is made for the sabbatic year and for the major religious festivals (chs 15:1 to 16: 17). The final and lengthiest section is a compendium of civil and social legislation (chs 16:18 to 26:19). Judges are

to be appointed (Deut 16:18 to 17:13), and a monarchy, when eventually established, is to be conducted on the basis of the laws now promulgated and on the principles of the covenant (ch 17:14-20). Leadership is to be vested in the Levites and in divinely commissioned prophets (ch 18). Provision is made for the prevention of a miscarriage of justice (ch 19:1-13). Sundry civil and social laws are codified (chs 19:14 to 25:19). As a sort of postscript, Moses again returns to the covenant between God and His people, and to their loyalty to Him (ch 26).

The 3d address focuses attention on the preservation of the covenant relationship and its inviolability (Deut 27:1 to 30:20). Provision is made for the reading of the law and for the erection of a permanent monument on which its provisions are to be inscribed (ch 27:1-13). At a solemn ceremony the people are to renew their vows of obedience to the covenant and its provisions (vs 14-26). The blessings that are to follow obedience (ch 28:1-14) and the curses that are to accompany disobedience (vs 15-68) are outlined in detail. Moses further exhorts to obedience and closes with a tribute to divine graciousness and an appeal to remain loyal to God (chs 29; 30).

In the closing section of the book (Deut 31 to 34) Moses makes arrangements for the preservation of the law and solemnly charges the leaders with the responsibility of teaching its precepts to the people (ch 31); he makes arrangements for Joshua to succeed him (v 23). He praises God for His gracious mercy and guidance (ch 32: 1-43), makes arrangements for his own death (vs 44-52), and pronounces his final blessing upon the tribes of Israel (ch 33). He ascends Mount Nebo, views the Promised Land, dies, and is succeeded by Joshua (ch 34). Concerning the authorship of the closing verses of Deuteronomy see *SDACom* 1:1077.

Devil. [Gr. *diabolos,* "slanderer."] Otherwise called *Satan, wicked one (Mt 13:38), enemy (v 39); presented figuratively as a lion (1 Pe 5:8), a serpent, or dragon (Rev 12:9). He is the leader of all the fallen spirits, or angels (vs 4, 7). Prior to his fall in heaven he was called *Lucifer (Is 14:12-14), and as such occupied the exalted position of covering cherub (Eze 28:14). Pride in the beauty and wisdom with which the Creator had originally endowed him was responsible for his fall (vs 12, 17). He was the author of sin

(1 Jn 3:8) and seduced approximately one third of the angelic host (Rev 12:4), with whom he was cast out of heaven (vs 8, 9). He is characterized as a murderer and a liar (Jn 8:44). He incites men to sin (ch 13:2) and then accuses them before God as worthy of death (Zec 3:1-4; Rev 12:10). He is bent upon their destruction (1 Pe 5:8). Entering Eden under the guise of a serpent he seduced man into sin (Gen 3:1-6), thus bringing sin and death upon the entire human race (Rom 5:12; cf. ch 3:23). His work ever since has been to ensnare, deceive, beguile, and seduce the human family (2 Cor 11:3; 2 Ti 2:26; Rev 12:9; etc.). He snatches away the good seed of truth (Lk 8:12), sows tares (Mt 13:38), and disguises himself as an angel of light (2 Cor 11:14). Christians are admonished to resist him, in the confident assurance that he will flee from them (Eph 4:27; Jas 4:7; cf. Mt 4:10, 11). Sinners are sometimes figuratively called children of the devil in the sense that they resemble him in character as a son does his father (Jn 8:44; 1 Jn 3:8, 10). In this sense Jesus referred to Judas as "a devil" (Jn 6:70, 71). When Peter sought to turn Christ from the cross he was actually collaborating with Satan, and Christ addressed him as if he were Satan in person (Mt 16:23). Christ had come to destroy the works of Satan (1 Jn 3:8). He met him in personal combat in the wilderness of temptation and overcame him (Mt 4:1-11). When He comes again He will destroy the devil himself (Mt 25:41; Rev 20:10). See Demon; Satan.

Devoted Thing. [Heb. *cherem*, "(a thing or person) devoted."] The basic idea of this expression is that something (or someone) has been placed under a ban—the ban involving either seclusion from society or devotion to destruction. The KJV translates *cherem* variously as "cursed thing" (Deut 13:17), "accursed thing" (Jos 6:18), "dedicated thing" (Eze 44:29), "devoted thing" (Lev 27:28); etc. In some instances *cherem* implies that the object is "dedicated," or made sacred, by exclusion from the use of profane society (Lev 27:28, 29; Eze 44:29).

Devotions. The translation of the Gr. *sebasma* (Acts 17:23, KJV), "objects of devotion," "sanctuaries." These were objects of worship Paul observed in the city of Athens which led him to conclude that the Athenians were "too superstitious," or "very religious."

Dew. [Heb. *ṭal*, "dew," "light rain."] Moisture of the air that condenses on cool objects. In Palestine it appears in sufficient quantity to be of agricultural importance during the dry season. Both dew and rain are symbolic of God's blessings (Hos 14:5) and their absence is considered a loss (2 Sa 1:21).

Diadem. The translation of: (1) The Heb. *miṣnepheth* (Eze 21:26, KJV), "turban," from *ṣanaph*, "to wrap around," "to wind up." The turban, an Oriental headdress formed by winding a length of cloth around the head, apparently was used by both men and women. Ezekiel uses the term figuratively of the royal power of Judah. (2) The Heb. *ṣaniph*, "turban," also from *ṣanaph* (Job 29:14; Is 62:3). (3) The Heb. *ṣephirah* (Is 28:5), a word of uncertain meaning, but in a poetic

133. Egyptian royal diadem in the Cairo Museum. The vulture represents Upper Egypt, and the cobra Lower Egypt

couplet it stands as a synonym for "crown."
(4) The Gr. *diadēma* (Rev 12:3; 13:1; 19:12, RSV), "royal crown," "diadem," an Oriental symbol of royalty, in the form of a fillet or headband. *See* Crown; see figs. 133, 293).

Dial. The translation of the Heb. *ma'alôth* in 2 Ki 20:11 and Is 38:8. The Hebrew term has traditionally been rendered "dial" in the phrase *ma'alôth 'Achaz,* "dial of Ahaz." That sundials were known in Palestine in ancient times is attested by an Egyptian dial inscribed with the name of King Merneptah (13th cent. B.C.), discovered in the excavations of Gezer. However, it is not certain that *ma'alôth* designates a dial in the passages referred to. The word may mean "steps" and is frequently thus translated (2 Chr 9:18, 19; etc.). S. Iwry (*BASOR* 147 [1957], 27-33) has recently pointed out that the LXX version of the Isaiah passage, when studied in conjunction with the reading of the 1QIs^a scroll, seems to indicate that the steps of the upper chamber of Ahaz are referred to. A "chamber of Ahaz" is mentioned in 2 Ki 23:12. According to Iwry's view the shadow crept back on the steps of this chamber in the miracle announced by Isaiah, and not on a real dial.

Diamond. [Heb. *yahalom, shamîr.*] Diamond is crystallized carbon—the hardest of all minerals (10 on the Mohs scale). It is highly valued as a gem because of its brilliance and luster, and as a tool or abrasive because of its extreme hardness. However, the Hebrew terms thus translated do not designate the diamond, for that mineral was not known in OT times. The type of stone designated by *yahalom* is unknown, and any translation of the term is only a conjecture. The 3d stone in the 2d row of the high priest's breastplate was a *yahalom* (Ex 28:18; 39:11), as was one of the precious stones decorating the "king of Tyrus" (Eze 28:13). *Shamîr* (Jer 17:1) is probably emery or a related corundum.

Diana. *See* Artemis.

Diaspora. *See* Dispersion.

Diblaim (dĭb-lā'ĭm). [Heb. *Diblayim,* "double fig cakes."] Either the father or mother of Hosea's wife, Gomer (Hos 1:3).

Diblath (dĭb'lăth). [Heb. *Diblah.*] A place mentioned in the KJV of Eze 6:14; not identified. It is generally believed that the Hebrew should read *Riblah,* "Riblah," instead of *Diblah,* "Diblath." The *r* and *d* are so similar in pre-exilic and postexilic Hebrew that they are easily confused. Riblah is a town 50 mi. south of Hamath in Syria and thus on the northernmost limit of the country of Israel, and the expression "from the wilderness to Riblah" (Eze 6:14, RSV) could mean "from the extreme south to the far north."

Dibon (dī'bŏn). [Heb. *Dîbon;* Moabite *Dybn;* Egyptian *Tbn.*]

1. A city of Transjordan. It originally belonged to the Moabites, but was conquered by the Amorites, and later by the Israelites, when they captured the Amorite kingdom of Heshbon (Num 21:26, 30; 32:3-5, 22). It was then rebuilt by members of the tribe of Gad, and consequently was known also as Dibon-gad (dī'bŏn-găd') (chs 32:34; 33:45, 46). It was subsequently given to Reuben (Jos 13:9, 17).

134. Ruins of Dibon

The Moabites reconquered it in later times and held the city for centuries (Moabite Stone, lines 21, 28; Is 15:2; Jer 48: 18, 22). The present village of *Dhîbân*, 3 mi. north of the Arnon River on the highway between Kerak and Medeba, marks the site of ancient Dibon (Map VI, E-4). It was at Dibon that the *Moabite Stone was found in 1868. This discovery was one of the most important ever made in Palestine. Recent excavations have uncovered a thick layer of the Nabataean city under which the Moabite remains are buried.

Lit.: *BASOR* 125 (1952), 7-23; 133 (1954), 6-26.

2. A village in the territory of postexilic Judah (Neh 11:25), probably the same as *Dimonah (Jos 15:22).

Dibon-gad. See Dibon.

Dibri (dĭb′rī). [Heb. *Dibrî*, meaning uncertain.] A Danite, whose descendant was put to death in the wilderness for blaspheming the name of the Lord (Lev 24:11-14).

Didymus (dĭd′ĭ-mŭs). [Gr. *Didumos*, "twin," a translation of the Aramaic *Te 'ōma'* (from which the name Thomas is derived), also meaning "twin."] The Greek form of the apostle Thomas' name (Jn 11:16; 20: 24; 21:2). Instead of the proper name Didymus, the RSV reads "the Twin." See Thomas.

Diklah (dĭk′la). [Heb. *Diqlah*, "date palm."] A southern Arabian tribe descended from the Shemite Joktan (Gen 10:27; 1 Chr 1:21); not identified.

Dilean (dĭl′ē-ăn). [Heb. *Dil'an*.] A town of Judah in the Shephelah near Lachish (Jos 15:38); not identified with certainty.

Dill. [Heb. *qeṣach;* Gr. *anēthon*.] For the identification of *qeṣach see* Fitches. Quite certainly *anēthon* (KJV "anise") represents *Anethum graveolens,* a member of the parsley family growing about 20 in. high and producing small seeds similar to caraway, which are used for flavoring and for medicine. *Anēthon* appears but once (Mt 23:23), where Jesus illustrates the scribes' and Pharisees' legalism with respect to tithing, while they lacked sensitivity to human needs. According to one tradition mentioned in the Mishnah, the plant, seeds, and pods—everything but the root—were subject to tithe (*Maaseroth* 4. 5). Anise, a plant of the same order, is not as generally cultivated in the Orient as is dill, hence probably is incorrectly read in the passage.

Dimnah (dĭm′na). [Heb. *Dimnah.*] A town in Zebulun (Jos 21:35), probably a mistaken transcription of Rimmon. *See* Rimmon, 3.

Dimon (dī′mŏn). [Heb. *Dîmôn.*] According to the KJV, a town in Moab (Is 15:9); not identified. However, many scholars equate it with Dibon and cite textual evidence (including the 1QIsa scroll) for their support. Jerome states that the two names were used interchangeably in his time. The expression "the waters of Dimon" would then probably signify the Arnon, which flows about 3 mi. to the south of Dibon.

Dimonah (dī-mō′na). [Heb. *Dîmônah.*] A town in the southern part of Judah, near Edom (Jos 15:22); not identified with certainty. It is probably the same as Dibon in Neh 11:25.

Dinah (dī′na). [Heb. *Dînah,* probably "judged." The name occurs in cuneiform records as *Dinā,* the name of an Israelite slave at Gozan in Mesopotamia.] A daughter of Jacob by Leah (Gen 30: 21). She was violated by Shechem, the son of King Hamor of the city of Shechem, when Jacob's family lived in the area after their return from Haran. For this shameful act, Simeon and Levi, Dinah's full brothers, killed all the males of Shechem and rescued their sister, who had been taken into Shechem's house to become his wife (ch 34). Jacob did not approve of his sons' crime (v 30), and denounced it on his deathbed (ch 49:5-7). Of Dinah's later life nothing is known.

Dinaites (dī′na-īts). [Aramaic *Dînaye'.*] A name appearing in KJV of Ezr 4:9, formerly understood as that of a nation transplanted to Samaria by Osnappar (Ashurbanipal), and identified with the *Dayeni* of the Assyrian inscriptions. However, the Elephantine papyri have shown that the Aramaic word means "the judges." Hence recent commentators regard the term in that sense in Ezr 4:9 also, vocalizing the Aramaic *dayyanayya'.*

Dinhabah (dĭn′ha-ba). [Heb. *Dinhabah.*] The city of Bela, a king of Edom (Gen 36:32); not identified.

Dinner. The translation of (1) the Heb. *mishteh* (Est 5:4, 5, 8, 14, RSV), "banquet," "feast," and generally thus translated elsewhere; (2) the Heb. *'aruchah* (Prov 15:17), "dish," "portion," "allowance"; (3) the Gr. *ariston,* "breakfast" (thus probably in Lk 14:12, where it is distinguished from *deipnon,* the main meal of the day eaten toward evening), "noon meal," and also any meal generally (Mt 22:4; Lk 11:38). There is no word for "dinner" in the Greek text of 1 Cor 10:27, but the word is implied in the context. The ancients generally ate only 2 full meals a day, the main meal coming at night after the work was done; the early morning snack was hardly a full meal. *See* Meals.

Dionysius (dī'ô-nĭsh'ĭ-ŭs). [Gr. *Dionusios*, "of or pertaining to Dionysus" (a Greek god of fruits and wine, originally worshiped in Thrace and Phrygia and known to the Romans as Bacchus). Dionysius is a common Greek personal name.] A convert of Paul at Athens, and a member of the high council of the Areopagus (Acts 17:34). Since the men of this council were elected from the wealthiest and most influential aristocrats of the city, Dionysius must have belonged to a high-ranking Athenian family. It is doubtless for this reason that Luke mentions him by name as a convert of Athens. The church historian Eusebius (*Eccl. Hist.* iii. 4; iv. 23) quotes Dionysius of Corinth (*c.* A.D. 170) as saying that the Dionysius of the NT was the first bishop of the church at Athens. Later tradition confuses him with the 3d-cent. martyr Dionysius, the St. Denis of France, and also attributes to him mystical theological writings which were actually produced by an anonymous writer now known as Pseudo-Dionysius, who advocated Neoplatonic philosophical ideas.

Diotrephes (dī-ŏt'rĕ-fēz). [Gr. *Diotrephēs*, "fed by Zeus." The name occurs also in Greek literature and on inscriptions.] A Christian leader of authority in an unknown church, who aspired to "preeminence among" the church members. He had not received messengers sent by John, and had expelled from the church those who had received them (3 Jn 9, 10).

Diphath. *See* Riphath.

Disciple. One who, as a student or adherent, follows the teaching of another, especially of a public teacher. In the NT "disciple" is the translation of the Gr. *mathētēs* (Mt 5:1; Mk 2:15; Lk 5:30; Acts 6:1; etc.), which is related to *manthanō*, "to learn," hence means "a learner," "a pupil," "an adherent." The word is used especially of the disciples of Jesus: of the Twelve (Mt 10:1; 11:1; etc.), and of His disciples generally (Lk 6:17; etc.). *See* Apostle.

Disease. A translation of several Hebrew and Greek words denoting any malfunction of the body and its organs, which causes either discomfort, temporary or permanent disability, or death.

Ancient documents, especially from Egypt, and observations made on mummies and skeletons, reveal that most diseases known to modern medical science existed in the ancient world. Such a conclusion is also corroborated by a study of the Bible, although only few diseases are mentioned by name (*leprosy, *blindness, boils, *extreme burning). Most illnesses are mentioned only in vague terms that make it extremely difficult to recognize their true character. The ancient Hebrews generally considered disease, whether organic or mental, a divine punishment for sin, for they had been warned that if unfaithful they would be smitten with diseases (Lev 26:16; Deut 28:22). The book of Job, however, reveals the true author of disease to be Satan. Christ combated the idea that illnesses are always the direct results of personal sins (Jn 9:1-3; cf. ch 11:4). God brings recovery and healing (Ex 15:26; Job 5:18; Ps 6:3; 103:3; Hos 11:3), though He does not always heal (2 Cor 12:7-9).

The place of human help as an aid in recovery from an illness was recognized, and *physicians are mentioned (Is 3:7; Jer 8:22; Mk 5:26). Natural remedies mentioned in the Bible though not necessarily endorsed are: wine and oil (Is 1:6; Lk 10:34; 1 Ti 5:23), balm (Jer 8:22; 46:11; 51:8), a cake of figs (2 Ki 20:7), and ointment (Rev 3:18). *See* Medicine.

Dish. A vessel for serving food (Prov 19:24, RSV; Mt 26:23; etc.), or for ceremonial use (Ex 25:29; 37:16; Num 7:14, 20, 26, RSV; etc.). In the OT the exact vessel specified by the several Hebrew terms translated "dish" is frequently uncertain. Gold dishes (KJV "spoons") for the tabernacle are mentioned (Num 7:14, 20, 26; etc.). God warned that He would make Jerusalem as free of its inhabitants as a dish is wiped clean of its food remnants (2 Ki 21:13). The dish (Gr. *trublion*) used at the Last Supper (Mt 26:23; Mk 14:20) was probably a bowl. Instead of "platter" the RSV reads "dish" in Lk 11:39. See figs 52, 86, 362.

Dishan (dī'shăn). [Heb. *Dîshan.* The Hurrian name *Tai-sheni* has been compared with *Dîshan.*] A Horite chief, but the name probably designates also a Horite clan (Gen 36:21, 28, 30).

Dishon (dī'shŏn). [Heb. *Dîshôn.* Compare the Hurrian name *Tai-sheni.*]

1. A Horite chief, and probably also the name of a Horite clan (Gen 36:21, 30; 1 Chr 1:38).

2. A grandson of Esau, and probably also the name of an Edomite clan (Gen 36:25, 26; cf. 1 Chr 1:41).

Dispensation. The translation in the KJV of the Gr. *oikonomia*, "stewardship," "the office of stewardship" (1 Cor 9:17; Eph 3:2; Col 1:25), or "arrangement," "plan" (Eph 1:10); in the RSV of the Gr. *diakonia*, "service," "ministry," "ministration" (2 Cor 3:7-9). "Dispensation" in these verses should be understood in the sense of a system of principles. The expressions "dispensation of death" and "dispensation of condemnation" refer to the Mosaic system, and the expressions "dispensation of the Spirit" and "dispensation of righteousness" refer to the Christian system. The two systems are contrasted by Paul.

Dispersion. [Gr. *diaspora*.]

Meaning of the term. In the LXX *diaspora* is used euphemistically for several Hebrew expressions, such as *za'awah* "(an object of) terror" (Deut 28:25; Jer 34:17), and *cherpah*, "reproach" (Dan 12:2). On the other hand the LXX never renders the Hebrew technical terms for "exile" (*gôlah* and *galûth*) *diaspora* (see Amos 1:6-9; Jer 52:31; 24:5; 28:4), but *aichmalōsia*, "captivity," *apoichia*, "departure," etc. That version does use the term, however, in Deut 28:25; 30:4; Jer 41:17 (34:17 in other versions) for the dispersion of the Jews. It has been suggested that the Hellenistic Jews preferred the term *diaspora*, for it avoided the connotation that Jews who lived outside of Palestine as the result of earlier deportations were still there because of punishments. To them *diaspora* simply meant the Jews who were found all over the world. The Jews of NT times considered the presence of their kinsmen in many countries of the world as a blessing for the Jewish nation and for the world in general, and they were proud of the *diaspora*.

Extent. Some of the Hebrews may have migrated to other countries before the captivities of the 8th and 6th cent. B.C. There is some evidence, for example, of Jewish colonies in Egypt before the Exile. However, any such movements would not have involved great numbers of people. The first mass deportation came in the 8th cent. B.C. when the Assyrians carried away captive the 10 northern tribes. Most of the deportees were absorbed by the nations among whom they were forced to live, and lost their peculiarities and national consciousness. It was differ-

ent with the 2 tribes of Judah and Benjamin (including the Levites) who were deported by the Babylonians in the 6th cent. B.C. Having great religious leaders such as Ezekiel and Daniel, and the comfort of written prophecies, they retained their ethnic unity. However, when the Persian kings allowed them to return to their homeland, only a minority of the exiles responded to the offer. The many who chose to remain in Babylonia thus became the first great Jewish colony outside of Palestine and until recent times has formed a sizable minority of the population of that country. The many Jews who moved to Egypt before Jerusalem was destroyed in 586 B.C. and after (Jer 43:7 to 44:30), built up strong Jewish colonies there. Of these the one on the Nile island of Elephantine is best known because of the discovery on the island of a large number of Jewish papyri written in Aramaic. After Alexander's conquest facilitated travel to distant countries, Jews moved to many parts of the Hellenistic world. During the Roman Empire period such movements were accelerated. Literary evidence and inscriptions attest the existence of about 150 Jewish colonies outside of Palestine in the 1st cent. A.D. Jews were found throughout Syria, in the various parts of Asia Minor, in the large cities of Greece, Italy, northern Africa, and Egypt, and in the Parthian area, an area outside the Roman Empire. Certain scholars have estimated that the Jews of the Dispersion within the Roman Empire in the 1st cent. A.D. numbered approximately 4½ million out of a total population of about 55 million.

Influence. The Jews of the Dispersion founded synagogues in many cities, and because of the high moral value of their monotheistic religion they attracted thinking Gentiles to their services. Through their association with the outside world they obtained a wider outlook on life than their compatriots in Palestine. Their financial support of the Temple and of their brethren in the homeland was a significant economic factor. They were encouraged to visit the Temple in Jerusalem as frequently as possible during high feasts, and made every effort to do so at least once during their lifetime. This accounts for the great number of foreign Jews present in Jerusalem when the Holy Spirit was poured out on the day of Pentecost (Acts 2:5-11). By acquainting the world with the teachings of the OT and by making their sacred Scriptures available in Greek (the Septuagint), the Jews of the Dispersion prepared the way for the rapid spread of the Christian gospel, which could not have triumphed so quickly if the Jews had not thus spread their religion.

Disposition. A translation of the Gr. *diatagē*, "ordinance," "direction," in Acts 7:53, KJV, where the martyr Stephen refers to the transmission of "the law" by the agency of angels.

Distaff. A small wooden rod used in the spinning process, on which are wound the fibers to be used in making thread. The word as it appears in Prov 31:19, KJV, is a translation of the Heb. *pelek*, "spindle," whereas in the same text "spindle" is a translation of Heb. *kîshôr*, and should perhaps be rendered "distaff," as in the RSV. Some take *kîshôr* to be a synonym of *pelek*, the whorl at the distaff.

Divers. In the KJV a rendering of several Hebrew and Greek words (1 Chr 29:2; Prov 20:10, 23; Mt 4:24; Heb 1:1; etc.), generally meaning either: (1) "several," "many," or (2) "various," "different in kind."

Divination. [Heb. generally *qesem*, from *qasam*, "to practice divination"; Gr. *puthōn*, "python," in Greek mythology, the serpent that guarded the Delphic oracle and was killed by the god Apollo.] A general term for various false systems of seeking supernatural aid, either for information regarding the future or for guidance in present affairs. Those who practiced divination were called diviners (1 Sa 6:2; Is 44:25; etc.). Three types of divination are mentioned in Eze 21:21—divination by arrows, by consulting *teraphim, and by liver. Since in Arabic, a cognate language to the Hebrew, *qaśama* means "to cut" or "to split," it has been suggested that the Hebrew term originally was limited to divination by cutting open an animal and examining its entrails. All types of divination were strictly forbidden by the Mosaic code (Deut 18:10, 11). The expression "Diviners' Oak" (Jgs 9:37, RSV; KJV "plain of Meonenim") was used probably to designate some specific ancient tree, the site of which was connected with soothsaying or necromancy. In Acts 16:16 "a spirit of divination" is literally, "a python-spirit" (see etymology above).

Divorce. [Heb. *kerîthûth*, "dismissal," literally, a "cutting off," from *karath*, "to cut," or "to cut off"; Gr. *apostasion*.] Prior to the promulgation of the law concerning divorce, recorded in Deut 24:1-4, the Is-

raelites, as did the ancient world generally, apparently divorced their wives without any formality by simply ordering them out of the house. This is what Abraham did to Hagar, whom he had married (Gen 16:3; 21:9-14). According to Oriental custom every woman was attached to some man, either her father or her husband, and to be unattached represented disgrace and brought want. Thus when a man dismissed his wife he cast her adrift to fend for herself in a society that had no place for her and that was unsympathetic and hostile toward her. With a view to ameliorating the lot of the divorced woman, God mercifully ordained that a woman thus divorced be given a certificate identifying her as a divorced woman. Thus, she might legally and properly become the wife of another man without any stigma attaching to her. Jesus declared that the provision for divorce in the Mosaic code was introduced because of the hardness of the people's hearts; that originally "it was not so" (Mt 19:3-9; cf. 1 Cor 7:10, 11). Thus the law of Deut 24:1-3 was not intended to sanction free divorce; it simply placed restrictions about a strongly entrenched custom, with a view to protecting a woman from a capricious husband. Jesus reinterpreted the divorce statute, stating that a man who divorced his wife for any reason except marital infidelity committed adultery by remarriage (Mt 5:31, 32; 19:3-9).

Dizahab (dĭ′zȧ-hăb). [Heb. *Dîzahab*, "of gold."] One of the 5 places that define the territory where Israel camped when Moses delivered his final discourses recorded in Deuteronomy (ch 1:1). The site, somewhere in the central Transjordan region, has not yet been identified with certainty.

Doctor. [Gr. *didaskalos*, "teacher," *(nomo)-didaskalos*, "teacher (of the law)."] A term used in Lk 2:46; 5:17; Acts 5:34 (KJV) of Jewish learned men, or in the latter two passages, especially of professional teachers or expositors of Jewish law. They were a professional class who passed through special schooling, and were required to pass certain examinations before being recognized officially. Later their traditions and those of other prominent teachers were codified in the Mishnah and the Talmud.

Doctrine. [Heb. generally *leqach*, "teaching," "instruction"; Gr. *didaskalia*, "act of teaching," "teaching," or "instruction," *didachē,* "teaching," generally, the thing taught.] A common NT term that may denote the act of teaching (1 Ti 4:13; 5:17) but more generally designates the content, or substance, of the information or ideas transmitted (ch 1:10; etc.). *Didaskalia* is used in the active sense of instructing in Rom 15:4, hence translated "instruction" (RSV), and in the passive sense of instruction in Mt 15:9.

Dodai. *See* Dodo, 2.

Dodanim (dō′dá-nĭm). [Heb. *Dodanîm.*] The fourth son of Javan, and his descendants (Gen 10:4). If this spelling is correct, these descendants were doubtless Dardanians, related to the Greeks and living along the northwestern coast of Asia Minor. The LXX, however, reads *Rodioi,* and the Hebrew of the parallel text in 1 Chr 1:7 has *Rodanim,* "Rodanim" (rŏd′á-nĭm), changed in the KJV to Dodanim to agree with the spelling in Gen 10:4. If Rodanim was the original spelling, Greeks on the island of Rhodes are meant (Map IV, B-4). The uncertainty is caused by the confusion of the letters *r* and *d,* which in pre-exilic Hebrew are very similar and in postexilic Hebrew are almost indistinguishable.

Dodavah. *See* Dodavahu.

Dodavahu (dō′dá-vā′hū), KJV **Dodavah** (dō′-dá-vá). [Heb. *Dôdawahû.* The name means "beloved of Yahweh" or "Yahweh is a friend," if *yahû* is read for *wahû.*] A man from Mareshah. His son, the prophet Eliezer, warned Jehoshaphat that for joining the wicked king Ahaziah in a commercial enterprise his fleet of ships would be destroyed (2 Chr 20:37).

Dodo (dō′dō). [Heb. *Dôdô.* The name occurs in Akkadian, *Dudû.*]

1. The grandfather of the judge Tola of the tribe of Issachar (Jgs 10:1).

2. An Ahohite, the father of one of David's 3 most outstanding warriors, Eleazar (2 Sa 23:9; 1 Chr 11:12). He is called Dodai (dō′dī), Heb. *Dôday,* probably a contraction of *Dôdayahû,* in 1 Chr 27:4, where he is presented as commander over the course of the 2d month (v 4).

3. A Bethlehemite, the father of another of David's great warriors, Elhanan (2 Sa 23:24; 1 Chr 11:26).

Doe. [Heb. *ya'alah.*] A female deer, mountain goat, or antelope (Prov 5:19, KJV "roe"). The exact species cannot be ascertained.

Doeg (dō′ĕg). [Heb. *Dô'eg,* "timid."] An Edomite chief of Saul's herdmen (1 Sa 21:7). He was at the tabernacle at Nob for some unknown reason when David arrived requesting and obtaining food and a sword from Ahimelech the priest when fleeing from Saul. Doeg reported this act to Saul, who ordered that Ahimelech and other priests be killed. When the royal bodyguard refused to kill the priests, Doeg became their executioner. He killed not only 85 priests but also their families and livestock (1 Sa 22:7-23). David prophesied his destruction (see the superscription of Ps 52).

Dog. [Heb. *keleb;* Gr. *kuōn,* "dog," and *kunarion,* "little dog," the diminutive of *kuōn.*] The dogs of the Bible were not domesticated to the extent that they are today. There are only two Bible references to domestic dogs: Job 30:1, which mentions the dog of the flock, which probably aided the shepherd, and Mt 15:27; cf. Mk 7:28, which refers to dogs under tables. Other references show that the dogs of the ancient Orient were the same wild street dogs that one finds in the Near East today. They are described as lying lazily around during the daytime (Is 56:10, 11), and

135. Basalt panel from the Mekal temple at Bethshean, with fighting lion and dog

with much noise and barking, seeking food during the night (Ps 59:14, 15). They bark at passers-by (Ex 11:7); eat almost any kind of food (Ex 22:31; Prov 26:11; Mt 7:6), even corpses (1 Ki 14:11; 21:19, 23; Jer 15:3; Ps 68:23), or lick the sores of a helpless sick man on the street (Lk 16:21).

Since the dog was despised by the ancient Semites (Ec 9:4), the word "dog" was a term of insult when applied to human beings (1 Sa 17:43; 2 Sa 3:8; 16:9), or a term used to indicate extreme self-abasement (1 Sa 24:14; 2 Sa 9:8; 2 Ki 8:13). In the NT opponents of the gospel are compared to dogs (Mt 7:6; Php 3:2). Mt 15:26 reflects an attitude of the Jews toward the Gentiles, whom they called dogs. Christ used the term simply to test the faith of His petitioner. In the excavations of Beth-shean a basalt relief was found showing two scenes depicting a lion and a wild dog engaged in deadly combat (fig. 135).

Door Post. The two wooden or stone posts standing on either side of a door (Ex 21:6; Deut 11:20; etc.). The "upper door post" (Ex 12:7, KJV) is the lintel. The word translated "door posts" in Eze 41:16, KJV (Heb. *sippim*), means "threshold."

Doorkeeper. In 1 Chr 15:23, 24, KJV, the rendering of the Heb. *shô'er*, which correctly means "gatekeeper." In Ps 84:10 the Heb. *saphaph*, translated "be a doorkeeper," means "to stand at the threshold," and doorkeeper here should not be understood in the technical sense. In 2 Sa 4:6, RSV, "doorkeeper" is a translation based on the LXX, not the Hebrew. In Ezr 7:24, RSV, the word is the translation of the Aramaic *tara'*. In the NT "doorkeeper" is the rendering of the Gr. *thurōros*, "doorkeeper, porter," from *thura*, "door," and *ouros*, "guardian" (Mk 13:34, RSV).

Dophkah (dŏf'ka). [Heb. *Dophqah*.] A place between the Red Sea and Rephidim where the Israelites encamped on their way to Sinai (Num 33:12, 13). The place has not been identified with certainty, but it must have been either at or near *Serābîṭ el-Khâdim* (Map V, C-5), or in the *Wâdî Magharah* (Map V, D-5).

Dor (dôr). [Heb. *Do'r;* Phoenician *D'r;* Egyptian *Dyr.* A Semitic place name meaning "dwelling."] An old Canaanite city on the Mediterranean coast, some 8 mi. north of Caesarea. The city was founded in the 14th cent. B.C. and occupied about 1200 B.C. by the invading Tjekker, who, like the

Philistines, belonged to the Peoples of the Sea. The city was assigned to Manasseh (Jos 17:11; 1 Chr 7:29), but until the time of David and Solomon it was not occupied (Jgs 1:27) by the Israelites. Solomon placed the whole area of Dor under the administration of Abinadab, his son-in-law (1 Ki 4:11). The Assyrians conquered Dor (called *Du'ru* in their records) in the 8th cent. B.C., and made it a separate province. Later it was given to Sidon, then fell into the hands of the Seleucids, and again belonged to Judea in the time of the Maccabees. In 63 B.C. Pompey made it a free city, responsible to Rome but self-governing. Its present name is *el-Burj*, and the site lies north of *eṭ-Ṭanṭûrah*. J. Garstang carried out some excavations there in 1924. Map VI, C-2.

Dorcas (dôr'kăs). [Gr. *Dorkas,* a translation of the Aramaic *Ṭabyetha',* "gazelle." The name occurs also in Greek literature.] A Christian woman of Joppa who was a great friend and helper of the poor. The apostle Peter raised her from the dead, an event that greatly accelerated the spread of the Christian message (Acts 9:36-42).

136. Mound of ancient Dothan

Dothan (dō'thăn). [Heb. *Dothan* and *Dothayin*.] A Canaanite city near a caravan route between the Plain of Esdraelon and Samaria. It appears first in the Bible in connection with the story of Joseph, who was cast by his brothers into an empty cistern near Dothan (Gen 37:14-28). The city was once besieged by the Syrians, but the prophet Elisha, who was in it, smote the besiegers with blindness, led them to Samaria, and then dismissed them (2 Ki 6:8-23).

The city is mentioned as *Ttyn* in the

list of Palestinian cities captured by Thutmose III in the 15th cent. B.C. The site is now *Tell Dôthā,* about 10 mi. north of Samaria (Map VI, D-3). Excavations carried out since 1953 by Free have shown that it was occupied from the patriarchal period on.

   Lit.: J. P. Free, *BA* 19 (1956), 43-48.

Double Bridle. *See* Coat of Mail.

Dough. The translation of: (1) the Heb. *baṣeq,* used for the unleavened dough the Israelites took with them when they left Egypt (Ex 12:33, 34), and elsewhere for dough generally in 2 Sa 13:8, RSV; Jer 7:18; Hos 7:4; (2) the Gr. *phurama* (1 Cor 5:6, 7), translated "lump" in the KJV; (3) the Heb. *'arîsah* in the KJV of Num 15:20, 21; Neh 10:37; Eze 44:30. *'Arîsah* seems to designate dough in its first stage of mixing. The RSV translates the term "coarse meal."

Dove. [Heb. *yônah;* Gr. *peristera.*] A bird of the family *Columbidae,* characterized by its mournful call (Is 38:14; 59:11; Nah 2:7), gentle disposition (Song 2:14; etc.), and rapid flight. In popular usage "pigeon" is used for the larger *Columbidae* and "dove" for the smaller. Both terms are used to translate *yônah* and *peristera.* The dove was a rabbinical symbol for Israel as a nation, but Christians have come to consider it a symbol of the Holy Spirit, doubtless because the Spirit descended "like a dove" at Jesus' baptism (Mt 3:16). The dove was used in tabernacle (Lev 1:14; etc.) and Temple (Lk 2:24) sacrifices, and was sold in the outer Temple court during NT times (Mt 21:12; etc.). For Turtledove *see* Turtle.

Dove's Dung. An unesthetic substance that became coveted food for the besieged inhabitants of Samaria and for which they paid a high price (2 Ki 6:25). Josephus records that in their extremity people in Jerusalem were reduced to eating dung during its siege (*War* v. 13. 7). Recently an attempt has been made to identify the substance with a cheap, undesirable vegetable produce. This identity cannot be proved.

Dowry. A translation of: (1) The Heb. *zebed,* "endowment," "gift," from *zabad,* "to bestow something on a person" (Gen 30:20). (2) The Heb. *mohar,* "marriage money," "marriage present" (Gen 34:12; Ex 22:17; 1 Sa 18:25; KJV). In accordance with ancient custom, money (or other valuables) was given by the bridegroom to the father of the bride as compensation for his loss of a daughter. The payment gave assurance that the bridegroom was able to support his bride. (3) The Heb. *shilluchîm* (1 Ki 9:16, RSV), a father's parting gift to his daughter who is being married.

Drag. [Heb. *mikmereth,* "fishing net."] A term used in Hab 1:15, 16, KJV, of a large fishing net, or seine, equipped with weights and floats. It is spread out, and then the 2 ends are drawn together, enclosing any fish that may be within the net.

Dragon. [Heb. *tannîn* and *tannîm;* Ugaritic *tnn;* Gr. *drakōn.*] In the modern meaning, a fabulous and monstrous animal with wings, scales, claws, scorpion's tail, and other features of a repelling nature. In the mythology of the ancient world, such monsters appear in primordial conflict with certain gods and represent in a sense the principle of evil. In Babylon dragons were pictured in relief on the Ishtar Gate. These were scaled quadrupeds with horned serpent heads and necks, scorpion tails, lions' forepaws, and hindfeet like an eagle's (see fig. 137). In ancient Persia, Ahriman, the evil principle, was shown on reliefs as a winged bull or lion with a scorpion's tail, and eagle's claws (see fig. 138). For other Mesopotamian representations of dragons see figs. 57, 297.

   In the Bible the figure of the dragon is used strictly as a symbol of enmity against the true God and His chosen people (Ps 74:13; Is 27:1; 51:9; Eze 29:3-5; 32:2-8, RSV). In the book of Revelation it is primarily a symbol of Satan himself, the archenemy of God, and secondarily, of the powers or forces through which he operates in his warfare against the Christian church (Rev 12). In symbolic vision John saw the dragon ultimately consigned to the lake of fire (ch 20:10).

137. A dragon of Babylon decorating the Ishtar Gate; a relief in glazed bricks

138. Darius I fighting against Ahriman, representing the evil principle, depicted as a feathered and winged lion with hind legs like an eagle's legs and a scorpion's tail; relief on a doorway at Persepolis

Dragon's Well. *See* Jackal's Well.

Dram. *See* Daric.

Draught House. *See* Latrine.

Dream. [Heb. *chalôm,* "a dream," from *chalam,* "to dream"; *shenah,* "sleep" (Ps 90:5, RSV). Aramaic, *chelem,* "a dream." Gr. *enupnion,* "a dream," from *en,* "in," and *hupnos,* "sleep"; *onar,* "a dream."] To the ancients a dream often had portentous significance, which, however, was not believed to be obvious except to one gifted or initiated in interpreting dreams (cf. Gen 41:11, 12; Dan 5:12). The Bible records such beliefs as•being held by the Egyptians (Gen 41), the Midianites (Jgs 7:13, 15), and the Babylonians (Dan 2).

God communicated with men through dreams (Num 12:6). Yet the Bible clearly teaches that not all dreams are of divine origin. God gave specific directions as to how certain false dreams might be detected and their dreamers exposed (Deut 13:1-5). In Job 20:8 dreams are used to illustrate that which is fleeting and transitory.

The terms "dream" and "vision" are at times used synonymously. "Dream" stresses something seen while a person is asleep, whereas "vision" stresses "an appearance," "a sight," "something seen." The "vision" may come in a dream at night (Dan 2:19; cf. Acts 12:9), in which case either term would correctly describe the experience (see Is 29:7). In Joel 2:28; Acts 2:17, the 2 terms appear in poetic parallelism and are probably synonymous.

Dress. For garments mentioned in the Bible, *see* Clothing. For national styles of dress, see the following illustrations: Amorite, colored end sheet; Arabian, figs. 19, 20; Assyrian, figs. 117, 163, 201, 210, 212, 255, 362, 502; Babylonian, fig. 328; Canaanite, figs. 93, 94; Egyptian, figs. 50, 94, 122, 177, 211, 510, colored end sheet; Hittite, figs. 90, 232; Israelite, figs. 37, 201, 246, 255, 308; Median, fig. 322; Persian, figs. 6, 322; Philistine, fig. 382; Roman, fig. 42; Syrian, fig. 469.

Drink. Water was the universal beverage of antiquity (Gen 21:14; Ex 23:25; 2 Ki 6:22). Milk was commonly used (Jgs 5:25). For other drinks *see* Strong Drink; Vinegar; Wine. Figuratively, the wicked are described as drinking of God's wrath (Job 21:20; Jer 25:15; Rev 14:10). Jesus referred to the drinking of His blood (Jn 6:53-56), meaning both the partaking of the wine of the Lord's Supper and the reception, by faith, of His life symbolized by it. In Mt 20:22, 23 Jesus spoke figuratively of drinking the cup of His suffering (cf. Mt 26:39; Mk 14:36; etc.).

Drink Offering. *See* Sacrifices and Offerings.

Drink, Strong. *See* Strong Drink.

Dromedary. In the KJV the translation of: (1) the Heb. *beker* (Is 60:6), "a young male camel"; (2) the Heb. *bikrah* (Jer 2:23), "a young female camel"; (3) the Heb. *rekesh* (1 Ki 4:28), "a chariot horse," erroneously translated "dromedary"; (4) the Heb. *rammak* (Est 8:10), "mare," or perhaps "stud." In the RSV "dromedaries" is the translation of the Heb. *kirkarôth* (Is 66:20), "fleet female camels." The KJV translates this Hebrew term "swift beasts." *See* Camel.

Dropsy. [Gr. *hudrōpikos,* derived from *hudōr,* "water."] The Greek term designates a disease most obviously dropsy. The disease is mentioned only once (Lk 14:2).

Drunkenness. The Bible records many cases of individual drunkenness, the first being that of Noah (Gen 9:20, 21). Lot (ch 19: 30-35), Nabal (1 Sa 25:36), Uriah (2 Sa 11:12, 13), Amnon (ch 13:28), King Elah of Israel (1 Ki 16:8-10), and Benhadad of Syria (ch 20:16) are also mentioned as being drunk. Apparently drunkenness was common in the time of the judges, for Eli quickly suspected Hannah of being intoxicated (1 Sa 1:13, 14). The northern kingdom of Israel was reproved for its drunkenness (Is 28:1-3; Amos 4:1, 2); Judah, too, did not escape (Is 5:7, 11, 22; Amos 6:1, 6). Prov 23:29-35 graphically describes the pitiable physical, mental, and moral condition of the drunkard.

Because Jesus ate and drank with sinners He was accused of being a drunkard (Mt 11:19; Lk 7:34). His followers, too, were falsely charged with drunkenness when under the unction of the Holy Spirit on the day of Pentecost (Acts 2:13). Jesus warned His followers against drunkenness, for this would leave them unprepared to meet Him at His second coming (Lk 21:34).

Paul reproached the Corinthian believers, recent converts from heathenism, for drunkenness at the Lord's Supper (1 Cor 11:20, 21). He also admonished the Romans concerning drunkenness (Rom 13:13), and warned the Galatians that indulgence in this vice barred one from the kingdom of God (Gal. 5:21).

Drunkenness is frequently used in a figurative sense. The earth is prophetically described as staggering like a drunkard when God's final judgments are visited upon mankind (Is 24:20). Israel was so stupefied by spiritual indifference and material interests that God's warnings of impending disaster affected the people no more than they would an uncomprehending drunkard (ch 29:9, 10). In Rev 17:2 the inhabitants of the earth are pictured as being drunk with the deceitful doctrines of the religio-political Babylon (cf. vs 4, 5). In v 6 the woman, representing that great system, is described as being drunk with the blood of saints and martyrs. *See* Strong Drink.

Drusilla (droō-sĭl′ȧ). [Gr. *Drousilla*, a transliteration of a feminine form of the Roman name *Drusus*, derived from the Celtic *Drausus*.] Daughter of King Herod Agrippa I, and the wife of the Roman procurator Felix (Acts 24:24). She was born A.D. 38 and was only 6 years old when her father died. At an early age she

became engaged to Epiphanes, the son of King Antiochus of Commagene, but Epiphanes later refused to marry her because this would have required he become a Jew and accept circumcision. She then married King Azizus of Emesa, whom she left shortly afterward to marry Felix. She had a son by Felix, called Agrippa, who lost his life during the eruption of Mount Vesuvius in A.D. 79. When a prisoner, the apostle Paul spoke to Felix and Drusilla about righteousness, temperance, and the coming judgment (Acts 24:24, 25), but the effects on Drusilla are not recorded.

Duke. In the KJV the translation generally of the Heb. *'allûph,* "leader," "leader of a thousand," "chief." The Heb. term occurs some 40 times in Gen 36 with reference to the tribal chieftains of the Edomites. In Jos 13:21, KJV, "duke" is the rendering of the Heb. *nasîk,* "leader," "chieftain."

Dulcimer. *See* Bagpipe.

Dumah (dū′mȧ). [Heb. *Dûmah,* "silence."]
 1. A son of Ishmael, and ancestor of a tribe in Arabia carrying his name (Gen 25:14; 1 Chr 1:30). The region in northwestern Arabia called Doumaitha by Ptolemy and Domata by Pliny is considered to be the homeland of this tribe. Its center is the oasis *Dûmet ej-Jendel* or *ej-Jauf* (Map XI, D-4).
 2. Probably a symbolic name for Edom (Is 21:11).
 3. A town in the hill country of Judah (Jos 15:52), now *ed-Dômeh,* about 10 mi. southwest of Hebron.

Dung. The use of dung for fuel is mentioned only in Eze 4:12, 13, 15, but the prevalence of its use for this purpose today suggests that it must have been widely used anciently. Its use as fertilizer is mentioned in Lk 13:8. *Dove's dung was eaten by the besieged inhabitants of Samaria (2 Ki 6:25). Figuratively dung is used to describe that which is detestable, perishable, and worthless (2 Ki 9:37; Job 20:7; Php 3:8, RSV, "refuse"; etc.).

Dung Gate. A gate in the southern wall of Jerusalem. The gate was given this name because the refuse of the city was taken through it to be burned in the Valley of Hinnom (Neh 2:13; 3:13; 12:31). *See* Jerusalem.

Dungeon. The darkest and worst part of a prison, usually a subterranean vault. It is the rendering of: (1) The Heb. *bôr,* "pit," "cistern" (Gen 40:15; 41:14). (2) The Heb. *bêth habbôr,* "house of a cistern" (Ex 12:29; Jer 37:16). Empty or half-empty cisterns were frequently used to hold prisoners. It can easily be understood that a man could not long survive such inhuman confinement. (3) The Heb. *bêth kele'*, "prison" (Is 42:7, RSV).

Dura (dū′rà). [Aramaic *Dûra'*, according to the Akkadian (*dûru*) meaning "wall."] The name of the plain where Nebuchadnezzar set up the golden image that was to be worshiped by all nations (Dan 3:1). The name survives in that of a tributary of the Euphrates called *Nahr Dûra,* which enters the Euphrates about 5 mi. below Hilla. Some neighboring hills also bear the name of Dura. The local tradition that locates Dura in the area of *Kirkuk* is without historical basis.

Dwarf. [Heb. *daq,* "lean," "small."] In the context of Lev 21:20 the Hebrew term probably describes one who is undersized or emaciated. Only those of the priestly lineage who were physically normal might officiate in the tabernacle.

Dye. The art of dyeing is rarely mentioned in the Bible (see Ex 25:5; 26:14; Eze 23:15, KJV; Jgs 5:30; Job 38:14; RSV), although archeological evidence shows that it was widely known in ancient Palestine. At *Tell Beit Mirsim,* probably ancient Debir, 6 dyeing plants have been excavated (see fig. 139). Several vats and other utensils show that it was used for the dyeing

139. Vats in a dyeing plant at *Tell Beit Mirsim*, probably ancient Debir

of woolen goods. In Gezer a dyeing installation from the Hellenistic period has been discovered.

Lit.: W. F. Albright, *The Archaeology of ·Palestine and the Bible,* 3d ed. (New York, 1935), pp. 119, 120; C. Watzinger, *Denkmäler Palästinas,* Vol. I (Leipzig, 1933), p. 101.

Dysentery, KJV **Bloody Flux.** [Gr. *dusenterion,* "dysentery."] A disease marked by inflammation of the lower intestines, frequently accompanied by fever, and at times by hemorrhage from the bowels. Dysentery is a common and dangerous malady in the Near East even to this day. The father of Publius, chief man of the island of Melita (Malta), was afflicted with this sickness but was miraculously healed by Paul (Acts 28:7, 8).

E

Eagle. [Heb. *nesher;* Aramaic *neshar;* Gr. *aetos.*] A large, majestic bird of prey. The Hebrew term describes both vultures and eagles. Of the latter there are several types that are common in Palestine. The eagle is listed among the unclean creatures (Lev 11:13; Deut 14:12). Noted in the Bible are its characteristics of speed (Deut 28:49; Job 9:26), soaring (Prov 30:19), and nest building (Jer 49:16). One of the faces of the living creatures in Ezekiel's vision of God's throne was likened to that of an eagle (Eze 1:10; etc.); in John's vision one of the living creatures was likened to a flying eagle (Rev 4:7). In the prophetic symbolism of Daniel a lion was equipped with eagle's wings, doubtless to signify its unusual swiftness (Dan 7:4). For Gier Eagle *see* Carrion Vulture.

Ear, Earing. [Heb. *charash,* "to plow," and *charîsh,* "plowing," "plowing time."] Terms used in Gen 45:6; Ex 34:21; 1 Sa 8:12; KJV, with reference to the plowing of the ground. The Old English word "to ear" was derived from the Anglo-Saxon *erian,* which probably came from the Latin *aro,* "to plow."

Early Rain. *See* Palestine, VIII.

Earnest. A rendering of the Gr. *arrabōn* (2 Cor 1:22; 5:5; Eph 1:14; KJV), a loan word from the Heb. *'erabôn,* which is rendered "pledge" in Gen 38:17, 18, 20. *Arrabōn* was used in a legal sense to denote a first installment, deposit, or pledge sealing a contract and making further payments on the part of the contracting party obligatory. Paul states that the Holy Spirit is given to believers as a pledge (RSV "guarantee") of their future inheritance.

Earring. Earrings are mentioned several times, but the word usually thus translated (*nezem*) is a general term for "ring" and may refer to a nose ring (Gen 24:30) as well as to an earring (ch 35:4; Ex 32:2). The context sometimes makes clear what type of ring is intended. The Israelites wore golden earrings, and contributed these for the manufacture of the golden calf (Ex 32:2, 3). In the NT women are counseled against the wearing of gold (1 Ti 2:9; 1 Pe 3:3). The "earrings" of Is 3:20, KJV, were probably amulets. Earrings are listed in the spoil taken from the Midianites (Num 31:50). The Ishmaelites wore earrings of gold (Jgs 8:24-26). See earring on fig. 420.

Earth. The translation of various Hebrew and Greek words. The most common Hebrew term is *'ereṣ,* which occurs about 2,400 times in the OT. It is used of the planet Earth as distinguished from the atmospheric and possibly the stellar heavens above (Gen 1:1; etc.), of a piece of ground (ch 23:15, translated "land"), of the territory occupied by a certain people or nation (Gen 47:13, translated "land" in the phrases "land of Egypt," "land of Canaan"), of the dry land as distinguished from the sea (ch 1:10), of the habitable world (ch 18:18), and figuratively of the inhabitants of the world (Jer 22:29). The Heb. *'adamah,* also frequently translated "earth" (Gen 1:25; 4:11, 14; etc., RSV frequently "ground"), denotes the reddish, arable soil, from the word *'adam,* "to be red." This word is commonly used of the soil from an agricultural point of view, as the source of plant, animal, and human life (ch 2:6, 9, translated "ground"; Deut 7:13, KJV "land," RSV "ground"; etc.). In the NT "earth" is a rendering of the Gr. *gē,* which includes the meanings of both Hebrew words (Mt 5:5; 13:5; Acts 1:8; etc.). The Gr. *oikoumenē* specifies the inhabited earth (Lk 21:26, RSV "world"). Because of the varied meanings of the terms translated "earth," there is uncertainty at times as to whether the whole earth is meant or only a certain portion of it.

Earthquake. [Heb. *ra'ash;* Gr. *seismos.*] A trembling of the earth, caused by volcanic eruption or faulting in the earth's rocky crust—one of the most terrifying of natural disasters. The most memorable earthquake of OT times occurred during Uzziah's reign (Amos 1:1; Zec 14:5). In NT times an earthquake marked Christ's death (Mt 27:54) and resurrection (ch 28:2), as well as God's intervention for Paul and Silas in the Roman prison at Philippi (Acts 16:26). Earthquakes are listed as a sign of the end of time (Mt 24:7; Mk 13:8; Lk 21:11; Rev 6:12). A most sublime description of an earthquake and other natural phenomena is given in Ps 18.

East. The Hebrews had several terms for expressing the direction east: (1) *mizrach,* "the place of sunrising" (Deut 4:47; Jgs 20:43; Is 41:25; etc.); (2) *qadim* and *qedem,* "before," "east." The Hebrews customarily faced east when giving directions. Thus what was before was east (Gen 29:1; Jgs 6:3, 33; 2 Ki 23:13; etc.), what was behind, or on the back side, was west (Jgs 18:12; Eze 41:15; Zec 14:8), what was on the right hand was south (Jos 17:7; 2 Chr 4:10), and what was on the left hand was north (Jos 19:27; Eze 16:46).

For "west" the Hebrews used the term *ma'arab,* "sunset," "west" (Ps 103:12; Is 43:5; 45:6; etc.), and *yam,* "sea," with reference to the Mediterranean Sea, which

140. A water tank at *Qumrân,* with a break in the steps showing the effect of the earthquake of 31 B.C.

was the western boundary of Palestine. For "south" they used a number of expressions, the most common being *negeb,* the desert country to the south of Judah (Gen 28:14; Ex 26:18; etc.). For "north" the most common designation was *ṣaphôn* (Gen 13:14; Jgs 7:1; etc.).

East, Children of the. *See* People of the East.

East Country. The area east of Palestine (Zec 8:7), particularly the Syrian and Arabian deserts (Gen 25:1-7).

East Sea or **Eastern Sea.** *See* Dead Sea.

East Wind. [Heb. *qadîm.*] A wind from the general direction of the east. In the Bible it is usually the wind coming from the Arabian or Syrian deserts (see Hos 13: 15). It is mentioned as drying up the corn of Egypt (Gen 41:23, 27) and scorching the vine and other plants in Palestine (Eze 17:10; 19:12). It is now like the south wind called sirocco in Palestine. In Jon 4:8 the hot desert blast that destroyed Jonah's gourd is called an east wind, probably here simply meaning a hot, dry wind such as in Palestine blew from the east. At Nineveh the hottest winds blew from the south, the southeast, and the southwest. *See* South Wind.

Easter. A mistranslation in Acts 12:4, KJV, of the Gr. *pascha,* a transliteration of the Heb. *pesach,* "the passover." *Pascha* is elsewhere in the NT uniformly translated "passover" (Mt 26:2; etc.). The word "Easter" is never properly used of the Jewish Passover. It is of Anglo-Saxon origin, from the Anglo-Saxon *Eastre,* the goddess of spring, in whose honor a festival was celebrated at the time of the vernal equinox.

Ebal (ē'băl). [Heb. *'Ebal.*]

1. A son of Joktan (1 Chr 1:22), called Obal in Gen 10:28.

2. One of the highest mountains of central Palestine (3,084 ft.; Map II, B-3). It lies north of Mount Gerizim, from which it is separated by a narrow valley. At the eastern exit of this valley lay the important city of Shechem. Mount Ebal (now called *Jebel Eslāmîyeh*) is steep and rocky, and today is almost deprived of vegetation. Moses directed the Israelites to go there after they had crossed the Jordan, and to erect on it an altar and great plastered stones on which they were to write the Law (Deut 27:1-8). Moses ordered that 6 of the Hebrew tribes (Reuben, Gad, Asher, Zebulun, Dan, and Naphtali) were to stand on the slopes of Mount Ebal and pronounce the curses that would overtake the transgressors of

141. Mount Ebal seen from Jacob's Well

the Law (Deut 27:13-26; 28:15-68; etc.). The other 6 tribes were to stand on Mount Gerizim and pronounce the blessings (chs 11:29; 27:11, 12; 28:1-15). Shortly after the Israelites invaded Canaan they carried out these commands (Jos 8:30-35). The Samaritan Pentateuch reads "Gerizim" instead of "Ebal" in Deut 27:4 since Gerizim was the holy mountain of the Samaritans. See figs. 141, 433.

Ebed (ē'bĕd). [Heb. *'Ebed,* "servant." The name occurs also in ancient South Arabic inscriptions.]

1. Father of the rebel Gaal who revolted against Abimelech (Jgs 9:28, 30).

2. The chief of the family of Adin, who returned from Babylonia under Ezra's leadership with 50 men (Ezr 8:6).

Ebed-melech (ē'bĕd-mē'lĕk). [Heb. *'Ebed-melek,* "servant of the king." The name occurs in cuneiform records as *Abdimilki,* and also in Nabataean inscriptions.] An Ethiopian (Cushite) eunuch in the service of King Zedekiah, who obtained the king's permission to rescue Jeremiah from a cistern into which he had been thrown to die. With the help of 3 other men Ebed-melech drew the prophet out of the cistern with cords (Jer 38:7-13). Later he received a message from Jeremiah that he would be preserved in the coming destruction that would be visited upon Jerusalem (ch 39:15-18).

Ebenezer (ĕb'ĕn-ē'zĕr). [Heb. *'Eben Ha'ezer,* "stone of the help."] A stone monument erected by the prophet Samuel between Mizpah and Shen (RSV "Jeshanah"), in the area where the Lord gave Israel, under Samuel's leadership, a great victory over the Philistines (1 Sa 7:10, 12). It was in this same area that the Israelites had been defeated by the Philistines 20 years previously and the ark had been captured (1 Sa 4:1-11). In recording these earlier events the writer used the name Ebenezer, since that was the name by which the place was known at the time of writing.

Eber (ē′bĕr), KJV three times **Heber** (hē′bĕr). [Heb. *'Eber,* "the other side." Gr. *Eber.*]

1. A descendant of Shem through Arpachshad and ancestor of a group of people called "all the children of Eber" (Gen 10:21, 24, 25), which phrase probably means the "Hebrews" in the broadest sense. *See* Hebrews. To his descendants belonged the Joktanite Arabic tribes (vs 25-30) and the Aramaean tribes descending from Nahor and other relatives of Abraham (chs 10:26-29; 11:16-27; 22:20-24), besides Abraham's descendants (ch 11: 16-26), who included—in addition to the Israelites—the Ishmaelite Arabs, the Edomites, and the descendants of Keturah, Abraham's later wife (chs 25:1-16; 36:1, 8, 43). In Num 24:24 the name Eber is probably used collectively for all these peoples. Eber is listed in Luke's genealogy of Jesus Christ (Lk 3:35).

2. A Gadite of Bashan in Transjordan (1 Chr 5:13).

3. A Benjamite, a son of Elpaal (1 Chr 8:12).

4. Another Benjamite, son of Shashak (1 Chr 8:22, 25).

5. The head of a family of priests in the time of the priest Joiakim (Neh 12:20).

Ebez (ē′bĕz), KJV **Abez** (ā′bĕz). [Heb. *'Ebeṣ,* meaning uncertain.] A town in Issachar (Jos 19:20). The site is uncertain.

Ebiasaph. *See* Abiasaph.

Ebony. [Heb. *hobnîm,* a loan word from the Egyptian *hbny.*] A very hard wood, known for its characteristic color—dark brown or black—and appearance, and used as veneer and inlay. Originally the Hebrew term may have designated the heartwood of any of several different tropical African trees. In our day it is either *Diospyros ebenum* of tropical India and Ceylon or *Diospyros dendo* of West Africa. Ebony is given as one of Tyre's imports (Eze 27:15).

Ebron (ē′brŏn), KJV **Hebron** (hē′brŏn). [Heb. *'Ebron.*] A town in Asher (Jos 19: 28). Many scholars believe that Abdon is meant, considering that the almost identical Hebrew *r* and *d* were confused.

Ebronah. *See* Abronah.

Ecbatana (ĕk-băt′à-nà), KJV **Achmetha**

142. General view of Hamadan, Iran; the ancient city of Ecbatana (KJV "Achmetha"), with snow-capped mountains in the background

(ăk′mĕ-thà). [Aramaic *'Achmetha'.*] The capital of the Medes, called *Hagmatâna* in Old Persian. The city is better known by its Greek name, Ecbatana. It lay in the western Iranian mountains, about 6,000 ft. above sea level, and hence enjoyed a pleasant climate. Because of this the Persian kings used it as their summer capital. It was also one of their treasure cities (Herod. i. 98; iii. 64; Xenoph. *Cyrop.* viii. 6. 22). It was apparently in this city that Cyrus issued the decree permitting the Jews to return from their exile, for a copy of the decree was there preserved (Ezr 6:1, 2). Since the modern city of Hamadan (pop. about 100,000) is built on top of the ancient site, no systematic excavations have been carried out, but antiquities are frequently found in clandestine diggings. Map XII, D-8.

Ecclesiastes, Book of. A treatise on moral philosophy traditionally attributed to Solomon. The title "Ecclesiastes" originated with the LXX, which calls the author an *ekklēsiastēs* (ch 1:1), "a presiding officer" or "a speaker" at a public assembly. In Hebrew he is called *Qoheleth,* meaning the "speaker" at a public assembly, or "preacher." This is also the name the book bears in the Hebrew Bible. *Qoheleth* is the title by which the author identifies himself in vs 1, 12. *Qoheleth* is a feminine form, which may imply that Wisdom personified is speaking through "the Preacher." As a man of unusually broad experience (chs 1:1, 16; 2:7, 9), one who has explored every area of human enterprise, both material and intellectual, and who implies that he is now old and feeble in mind and body (ch 12:1-7), *Qoheleth* addresses himself to God's people, particularly to the young (v 1). Figuratively, they are gathered about him, one and all, as he contrasts for them the false philosophy of life with the true. *Qoheleth* introduces himself as "son of David, king in Jerusalem" (ch 1:1). He had "come to great estate" and had acquired "more wisdom" and "great experience of wisdom and knowledge" beyond his predecessors (Ec 1:16), as well as greater wealth (ch 2:7, 9). No "son of David, king in Jerusalem" other than Solomon could honestly have made such claims, though one ancient Jewish tradition attributes the book to Hezekiah. In the Hebrew Bible Ecclesiastes appears 6th from the last, the other 5 being in their order Lamentations, Esther, Daniel, Ezra-Nehemiah, and Chronicles. From a literary point of view it was classified with Song of Solomon, Ruth, Esther, and Lamentations, the 5 miscellaneous "rolls," or books, known collectively as the Megilloth. These 2 considerations are thought to indicate that Ecclesiastes was accepted into the canon toward the close of OT times. Its right to a place in the canon has repeatedly been challenged since ancient times, on the basis of the obvious agnostic quality of some of the sentiments expressed in it. However, close examination each time vindicated its right to be there.

In Ecclesiastes Solomon sets forth his philosophy of life on the basis of his own experience. In succession he had sought ultimate happiness through the pursuit of knowledge, in sensory pleasure and luxury, and by magnificent building projects and vast enterprises (chs 1 and 2). As a powerful young ruler blessed with unique wisdom and wealth, he had lacked no facilities in his quest for happiness, yet when he had secured all that human ingenuity could provide along each path of endeavor he found only "vanity and vexation of spirit" and concluded that in none of them was there any "profit under the sun" (ch 2:11). What distressed him more than anything else, however, was the fact that at the close of a lifetime of labor the wise and diligent man was no better off than the fool, since both were alike in death, and what he had learned and gathered and produced must be left to men who may prove to be fools (vs 14-23). Therefore he despaired of his labors and came to hate life itself (vs 20, 17). Instead of happiness he had found only vexation of heart (v 22). A cynical attitude darkened his outlook on life and, for practical purposes, he became an agnostic. Losing sight of God, his natural tendencies gained the supremacy over reason, and with his reason increasingly subordinated to inclination, his moral sensibilities were blunted, his conscience seared, and his judgment perverted. Toward the close of

life he realized that a lifetime of folly had made him into "an old and foolish king" (Ec 4:13). Conscience awakened and he saw folly in its true light. Spurred on by sincere repentance he sought to retrace his wayward steps, as best he might, and chastened in spirit he finally turned, wearied and thirsting, from earth's broken cisterns to drink once more at the fountain of life.

Having himself learned the great lesson of life the hard way, Solomon sought to counteract his years of evil influence, and to guide others along the pathway to faith in God. Guided by Inspiration, he recorded the history of his wasted years, with their lessons of warning, setting forth a sound philosophy of life and clarifying the purpose of man's existence and stating in simple terms man's duty and destiny. In this life men are to be content with the opportunities and privileges God has afforded them (Ec 2:24; 3:12, 22; 5:18), making the most of them in cooperation with, and obedience to, their Creator. In fact, "the conclusion of the whole matter" is that "the whole duty of man" can be summed up in the one admonition to "fear God, and keep his commandments" (ch 12:13), in view of the fact that when life is over man must be ready to stand in judgment before God (ch 11:9).

In the prologue Solomon dwells upon the futility of life (Ec 1:1-11). Next he relates his own futile experience in quest of happiness (chs 1:12 to 2:26). Nevertheless, he affirms that there is a purpose to life, that there is an appropriate time for everything, and that even the seeming injustices of life are not without purpose (chs 3:1 to 4:8). He then contrasts the value of companionship, wisdom, reverence, and justice (chs 4:9 to 5:9) with the folly of materialism, the incomprehensibility of suffering, and the seeming futility of human effort (chs 5:10 to 6:12). Character, an understanding of God's dealings with men, and a balanced outlook on life are the things worth striving for (ch 7:1-22). The closing chapters of the book summarize the disappointments and conflicts he has encountered in his search for wisdom (chs 7:23 to 8:15). God's ways are often inscrutable, but one may nevertheless be content amid the vicissitudes of life in the certain knowledge that every deed will have its due reward (chs 8:16 to 12:14).

Ed. A word appearing in Jos 22:34, KJV, a transliteration of the Heb. *'ed,* "witness." The Hebrew term, however, does not appear in the Bible text, but is obviously required by the context. The RSV supplies the word "Witness," a translation of *'ed.* The Israelites that settled east of the Jordan erected this altar of "Witness" as a memorial to the fact that they were of the same blood and worshiped the same God as their brethren to the west of the river. The latter at first mistook the altar as evidence of apostasy and prepared for war, but rejoiced when its true purpose was explained to them.

Edar. *See* Eder, 1, 3.

Eden (ē'd'n). [Heb. *'Eden,* "delight."]

1. A Gershonite Levite of the days of King Hezekiah (2 Chr 29:12; 31:15).

2. An antediluvian land in the eastern part of which God planted a garden as the abode of Adam and Eve. Among its trees were two special trees, the "tree of life" and the "tree of the knowledge of good and evil." The fruit of the former would perpetuate man's life as long as he had access to its fruits. The latter tree was placed in the Garden to test man's loyalty to God. By refraining from touching the forbidden fruit of this tree, man would indicate his willingness to obey his Creator. However, since God desired that man should be a free moral being, He gave him the freedom to choose between obedience and disobedience (Gen 2:9, 17). An unnamed river watered the Garden and divided into 4 streams, the names of which are given, as are the names of 3 of the lands through which they flowed (vs 10-14).

Attempts to locate the Garden of Eden by means of the names of these rivers have so far been fruitless, because the surface of the earth after the Flood must have borne little resemblance to its pre-Flood appearance. A catastrophe that elevated lofty mountains and formed oceans and plains left little of the antediluvian world to be recognized after the Flood. True, the names of 2 of these rivers, the Hiddekel (Tigris) and Euphrates (Gen 2:14), are preserved in the names of 2 postdiluvian rivers, but probably the two mighty streams the descendants of Noah found when they moved from Mount Ararat into the Mesopotamian Valley, simply reminded them of 2 of the antediluvian streams, so that they gave to these newly discovered rivers the names of the former rivers. Hence, it is not possible to locate the land of Eden in the Mesopotamian valley on the basis of the names of

its rivers. On the other hand, there is no positive evidence that the Garden was not located there. Likewise, the rivers Pishon and Gihon (Gen 2:11-13) cannot be identified, although for the former the Ganges and Indus rivers in India, some rivers in Armenia, and others have been proposed; the Nile and others have been suggested for the latter.

Cush in postdiluvian times was Ethiopia (now the Sudan), whereas Havilah remains uncertain, but, again, the location of these post-Flood countries has no bearing on the location of Eden in the prediluvian world. References to "Eden," "the garden of the Lord," "the garden of God," or the "garden of Eden," in Gen 13:10; Is 51:3; Eze 28:12; 31:9, 16-18; 36:35; Joel 2:3, are probably to the garden in Eden.

In modern times this garden is sometimes referred to as Paradise, a loan word of Persian origin that has the meaning "park." The corresponding Hebrew term *pardes* is found in Neh 2:8; Ec 2:5; Song 4:13, where it refers to forests or parks. It and the Persian *pairidaēza* seem to have a common origin. It is never used as a designation or name for the garden in Eden. The corresponding Gr. term *paradeisos* is used in the Genesis account for the home of our first parents by the translators of the LXX.

3. A country in northern Mesopotamia. *See* Beth-eden.

Eder (ē'dēr), KJV once **Edar** (ē'där), once **Ader** (ā'dēr). [Heb. *'Eder,* "flock." In Eder 3 and 4, which are personal names, *'Eder* is an Aramaic loan word meaning "help."]

1. A tower between Bethlehem and Hebron, near which Jacob once pitched his tent (Gen 35:21).

2. A place in the south of Judah (Jos 15:21), identified with *el-'Adar,* about 5 mi. south of Gaza on the right bank of the *Wâdī Ghazzeh.*

3. A Benjamite (1 Chr 8:15).

4. A Levite of the family of Merari (1 Chr 23:23; 24:30).

Edom (ē'dŭm). [Heb. *'Edôm,* "red."]

1. Another name for *Esau, called Edom because he sold his birthright for red-colored food (Gen 25:30; 36:1, 8, 19).

2. A collective name for the *Edomites (Num 20:18, 20, 21; Amos 1:6, 11; etc.).

3. The land of the Edomites, called *Udumu* in Akkadian inscriptions, and *'Idwm* in Egyptian hieroglyphic texts, originally named the land of Seir (Gen

143. The valley of Shobak in the land of Edom

32:3; 36:20, 21, 30; Num 24:18). Edom included the depression called the Arabah, extending from the Dead Sea to the Gulf of Aqabah, which is the wilderness of Edom in 2 Ki 3:8, 20. It also included the mountainous territory on both sides of the Arabah. Some of the mountains rise more than 3,500 ft. above the low-lying depression. They consist of sandstone, limestone, and porphyry, with veins of copper and iron in some sections. Parts of Edom could be used for agricultural purposes (Num 20:17-19), but most of the country was barren (Mal 1:3, 4). The capital of Edom was the rock fortress Sela, later called Petra, lying in an impenetrable mountain wilderness. Other important Edomite cities of antiquity were Bozrah and Teman. In Greek times the name Idumea was used for Edom, and applied to the portion west of the Arabah and south of Judah, the area to which the Edomites had been driven by pressure from the Nabataeans (*see* Aretas) from the east. Maps I, D-2; V, B-7; VI-X, G-4; XI, C-4; XIV-XVI, F-2/3. See figs. 79, 83.

Edomites (ē'dŭm-īts). [Heb. *'Adômî.*] The descendants of Edom, or Esau, Jacob's older brother (Gen 36:1, 19). Because of this relationship the Edomites were recognized by the Israelites as a brother nation, and the Mosaic law provided for their admission into the Hebrew nation in the 3d generation, whereas Moabites and Ammonites could not become full-fledged Israelites until the 10th generation (Deut 23:3-8). The Edomites occupied the country south of the Dead Sea after expelling the *Horites (KJV sometimes "Horims"), known from secular sources as Hurrians (Gen 14:6; Deut 2: 12, 22). The Edomites were ruled by tribal chiefs (KJV "dukes") during their early history (Gen 36:15-19, 40-43; 1 Chr 1:51-54), but were later ruled by kings (Gen 36:31-39; 1 Chr 1:43-51).

Toward the end of their wandering in the wilderness, the Israelites requested permission to march peacefully through Edomite territory. This request was refused, and the Israelites were forced to travel around Edom on their way north (Num 20:14-21; Deut 2:8).

Egyptian records of the 13th cent. B.C. mention Edomite Bedouins being given permission to enter Egypt for food during a famine (*ANET* 259). Saul fought against the Edomites (1 Sa 14:47), and David overwhelmingly defeated them (1 Ki 11:15, 16; 1 Chr 18:12; cf. the parallel account in 2 Sa 8:13, where the RSV "Edomites" is probably correct, since an original *'dm*, "Edomites," as indicated by several Hebrew MSS, the LXX, and Syriac versions, could easily have been copied as *'rm*, "Syrians," because the two Hebrew letters *d* and *r* are very similar in the postexilic script). David then put garrisons in Edom (2 Sa 8:14; 1 Chr 18:13), thus fulfilling Balaam's prediction made several centuries earlier (Num 24:18). Archeological explorations have shown that Solomon exploited the rich mines of Edom for their copper and iron, and built the industrial smelter city of Ezion-geber at the Gulf of Aqabah, where the fleet for his Ophir expeditions was based. A revolt against Solomon with unknown results seems to have been instigated by Hadad, an Edomite prince who had escaped to Egypt when the royal family was exterminated by Joab under David (1 Ki 11:14-22). However, Edom seems to have remained in the possession of Judah at least until the reign of Jehoshaphat, during which time it was still ruled by a Hebrew governor who was called "king" (1 Ki 22:47; 2 Ki 3:9). At that time it aided Judah and Israel in their campaign against the Moabite king Mesha (2 Ki 3:6-27). However, the Edomites revolted against Jehoram, Jehoshaphat's son, and re-established their monarchy and independence (2 Ki 8:20-22; 2 Chr 21:8-10). Half a century later Amaziah campaigned against them with much success, smiting 10,000 Edomites in the Valley of Salt, taking their impregnable capital *Sela, and killing another 10,000 of them by pushing them off their rock fortress (2 Ki 14:7; 2 Chr 25:11, 12). Amaziah's son Uzziah rebuilt Elath, a port on the Gulf of Aqabah (2 Ki 14:22). The Edomites retaliated in the time of Ahaz, when Pekah of Israel and Rezin of Damascus attacked Judah, by invading the oppressed kingdom of Ahaz and carrying away captives (2 Chr 28:17). During this period Edom was a vassal state of Assyria and paid tribute successively to Tiglath-pileser III

(*ANET* 282), Sargon II (*ibid.* 287), Sennacherib (*ibid.* 287), Esarhaddon (*ibid.* 291), and Ashurbanipal (*ibid.* 294). When Judah was conquered by Nebuchadnezzar the Edomites rejoiced (Ps 137: 7), and the prophets denounced them for their enmity against their brother-nation (Eze 25:12-14; 35:5, 6; Jer 49:7-22; Lam 4:21, 22; Joel 3:19; Amos 9:12; Ob 10-14). In the period after the fall of Jerusalem in 586 B.C. the Edomites moved into the southern part of Judah. Eventually they occupied its territory at least as far as Hebron, probably at the time they were pushed out of their older area by the Arabian Nabataeans. Hebron and other Jewish towns were reconquered by Judas Maccabeus (1 Macc 5:65; Jos. *Ant.* xii. 8. 6), and about 100 B.C. John Hyrcanus forced the Edomites to adopt the Hebrew religion, including the rite of circumcision (*ibid.* xiii. 9. 1). From these Judaized Edomites, or Idumeans, came the royal house of the Herods of the NT.

Edrei (ĕd′rē-ī). [Heb. *'Edre'i.*]

1. One of the residence cities of King Og of Bashan, whom Moses defeated at the battle of Edrei (Num 21:33-35; Deut 1:4; 3:1, 10; Jos 12:4; 13:12, 31). It is the present large town of *Der'ā*, about 30 mi. east of the confluence of the rivers Yarmuk and Jordan (Map VI, C-5).

2. A fortified city of Naphtali, near Kedesh (Jos 19:37); not identified.

Egg. [Heb. *bêṣah;* once (Job 6:6, KJV) from *challamûth,* a word of uncertain meaning; Gr. *ōon.*] Eggs mentioned in the OT are from various species of wild fowl, and from adders, not from the chicken we know today unless Is 10:14 be such a reference. One of the laws of Moses specified that the fowler who came upon a mother bird on her nest was not to take both mother and eggs or young, but the latter only (Deut 22:6). Ostrich eggs are mentioned in Job 39:14, and egg gathering is employed as a figure of Assyria's might in robbing the "nests" of other nations (Is 10:14). Evil men are like those who hatch adders' eggs (ch 59:5, RSV). Jesus' reference to an egg is probably to a chicken's egg (Lk 11:12), and is evidence that such eggs were eaten in NT times. *See* Hen.

Eglah (ĕg′lä). [Heb. *'Eglah,* "heifer."] One of David's wives and mother of his son Ithream (2 Sa 3:5; 1 Chr 3:3).

Eglaim (ĕg′lä-ĭm). [Heb. *'Eglayim,* "two drops."] A town in Moab (Is 15:8); not identified with certainty.

Eglath-shelishiyah (ĕg′lăth-shĕl′ĭ-shī′yȧ). [Heb. *'Eglath Shelishîyah,* "Eglath of the third part."] A town in Moab (Is 15:5; Jer 48:34; RSV); not identified. The Hebrew term is rendered "an heifer of three years old," in the KJV; however, a town is obviously indicated.

Eglon (ĕg′lŏn). [Heb. *'Eglôn;* compare the Akkadian personal name *Iglânu.*]

1. A king of Moab, who in the period of the early judges captured Jericho, the "city of palm trees," and oppressed Israel for 18 years. He was assassinated by Ehud, who had gained access to the king as an Israelite tribute bearer, and privacy with him on the pretext that he had a secret message for him (Jgs 3:12-30).

2. A Canaanite town belonging to the confederacy that fought against Gibeon and was defeated by Joshua. The city was then assigned to Judah (Jos 10:3-23, 34-37; 12:12). The name has been preserved in *Khirbet 'Ajlân,* a ruin site 16 mi. northeast of Gaza, but the ancient site of Eglon was probably at *Tell el-Ḥesî,* 15 mi. northeast by east from Gaza (Map VI, E-2).

Egypt (ē′jĭpt). [Heb. *Miṣrayim.* The English name is derived from the Gr. *Aiguptos,* which is probably a derivation of the Egyptian name of ancient Memphis, *Ḥ.t-k3-ptḥ,* "house of the (god) Ptah," written *Ḥikuptaḥ* in the Amarna Letters. The ancient Egyptians called their land *Km.t,* "the black (land)," because of the contrast between the dark, rich soil of the fertile Nile valley and the desert land beyond. Usually, however, Egypt was called *T3.wy,* meaning "the two lands," that is, the union of Upper and Lower Egypt. The Amarna Letters show that in the 14th cent. B.C., the Canaanites called Egypt *Miṣri.* The Heb. *Miṣrayim* (*see* Mizraim) has a dual ending, which may point to the two principal parts of the country, Upper and Lower Egypt. The Egyptians today use the Arabic name *Miṣr.*]

I. Country. A country in the northeastern section of Africa. It is part of the great Sahara Desert, but owes its fertility to the Nile, which flows from Central Africa and the highland of Ethiopia, through the whole country from south to north, and forms a narrow valley 1 to 15 mi. wide. To the east, between the valley and the Red Sea, is the Eastern Desert, whose northern portion is sometimes called the Arabian Desert. To the west are the Libyan Desert and the vastness of the Sahara.

About 100 mi. from the Mediterranean Sea the Nile splits into several branches and forms a large delta, which is especially fertile in its southern part. Since there is hardly any rainfall in the Nile valley except in the Delta, Egyptian agriculture depends on the river. Before the Aswan Dam was built, river water was brought to the fields through irrigation canals and by the annual inundation. Beginning in July the river rose from 15 to 20 ft. above its normal level, reaching its peak in September and October. The receding waters, which reached their lowest level from March to June, left rich mud from the Ethiopian highland on the Egyptian fields.

The Nile valley, from the sea to the first cataract of Aswan, anciently the southern border of Egypt, is about 600 mi. long; the average width is only 12 mi. Thus ancient Egypt had only about 13,000 sq. mi. of cultivable land, an area equivalent to little more than that of the combined States of Maryland and Delaware.

There were five oases west of the Nile valley, in the Libyan Desert. There was also the Faiyum, a fertile inland area surrounding Lake Moeris, which was fed by Nile water. Other inhabitable sections were a coastal strip of land lying between the easternmost Nile arm and the *Wâdî el-'Arîsh,* the Biblical "river of Egypt"; and the *Wâdî Ṭumilât* (probably the Biblical Goshen), lying between the Nile and Lake Timsah in the Suez Canal area.

The eastern mountains provided the ancient Egyptians with building material and minerals. Red and black granite came from quarries at Aswan, and limestone and alabaster were found in many quarries throughout the country. The *Wâdî Ḥammâmât,* a dry valley between the Nile and the Red Sea, provided dark-colored hard stone, which the Egyptians preferred for sarcophagi. Copper and turquoise were mined in the Sinai Peninsula and gold came from the mountains of Nubia, an Egyptian dependency during long periods of her ancient history.

Ancient Egypt never had a large variety of plant life. Wheat, barley, flax, and grapevines were the main plants of field and garden. Among the few trees growing in ancient Egypt were the date palm, the fig tree, the acacia, and the sycamore. Since Egypt had no forests it had to import all its lumber, and did so mainly from Lebanon. In the marshes of the Nile grew the papyrus reed, from which was made writing material, the papyrus scroll (see figs. 177, 371, also 417), a principal export of ancient Egypt.

144. The Step Pyramid of King Zoser (3d dynasty) at *Saqqârah*

The domestic animals of the Egyptians were cattle, goats, sheep, a kind of greyhound, and that very common beast of burden, the donkey. The horse did not come into Egypt until the Hyksos period; then it was used mainly for military purposes. The camel was little used in the early periods. Geese and ducks were common, but the chicken was unknown until the middle of the 2d millennium B.C., when Thutmose III introduced it from Syria. The crocodile, hippopotamus, hyena, and jackal were some of the wild animals of ancient Egypt.

II. People. The Egyptians were basically Hamitic (Gen 10:6), belonging to the Mediterranean races. However, early intrusion of Semites (evident from a study of its langauge; see sec. III), and the invasion of Nubians, Hyksos, Greeks, and, in more modern times, of Arabs, has produced a mixed race. The ancient Egyptians were small, with dark complexion and black hair. Most of them were farmers, but there· were also many artisans and craftsmen. Although the average education of the masses must have been low, their intellectual ability was high, as is witnessed by the advanced level of art, literature, architecture, state organization, medicine, and mathematics. For painting see figs. 76, 177, colored end sheet; architecture, figs. 144-148; sculpture, figs. 274, 327; art objects, figs. 102, 133, 422, 501.

III. Language. We are in the fortunate position of being able to trace the Egyptian language to the earliest history of the people and to follow its changes until its latest form, the Coptic, which gave place to the Semitic Arabic. Egyptian belongs to the Hamitic family of languages, but has so many Semitic features that it is called a Hamito-Semitic language. The following 5 linguistic stages can be recognized in the language: (1) OLD EGYPTIAN, spoken during dynasties 1-8, to which the Pyramid Texts are our most extensive witnesses; (2) MIDDLE EGYPTIAN, of dynasties 9-18, considered the classical period of the language; (3) LATE EGYPTIAN, which began in dynasty 18, and was used as a vernacular up to the 24th dynasty, but was employed for inscriptions for a much longer period; (4) DEMOTIC, the vernacular of Egypt from dynasty 24 to the 5th cent. A.D., represented mainly by documents and books written in the demotic script; (5) COPTIC, used from the 3d cent. A.D. onward. It was the language mainly of Christian Egypt, and is still used in church liturgy, although it has not been a living language since the 16th cent. The Bible was translated into the various Coptic dialects in early Christian times.

IV. Scripts. The following 4 scripts were used in Egypt on monuments and in texts: (1) HIEROGLYPHS (a Greek expression, meaning literally "sacred inscription"), a term designating the script used on monuments. This script was originally a pure picture writing and consisted of about 750 signs in the classical period. This number grew in the course of time until in Late Egyptian about 2,500 signs were used. In its early stages every picture represented the actual object depicted; for example, the picture of a house meant "house." These signs are called ideograms, or word signs. As the script developed, pictures of objects were used as phonograms, or sound signs; that is, the pictures were used to represent sounds rather than objects. When a particular sound was desired an object was chosen whose name reproduced that sound, by what is called the rebus principle. For example, in English a picture of a "bee" and a "leaf" (of a plant) placed side by side could, by the rebus principle, be used to represent either the noun *belief* or the verb *believe*. In Egyptian some objects had very short names, and 24 of the signs represented sounds of only one consonant. These have been called alphabetic signs. Besides these there were also determinatives, signs added to words to indicate whether the word written out represented something abstract or concrete, a man or a woman, etc. Vowels were not written; consequently the pronunciation of ancient Egyptian is still uncertain. This hieroglyphic script was used until the Christian Era. See figs. 235, 245, 527. (2) HIERATIC, also meaning "sacred (writing)," a term used by the Greeks to designate the cursive script the ancient Egyptians employed on papyrus, or other material, whenever the writing had no orna-

mental purpose. (3) DEMOTIC, meaning "people's (script)," came into being in the 8th cent. B.C. as a more cursive form of writing than hieratic, and was used mainly on everyday documents. It had a smaller number of characters than either hieroglyphic or hieratic. The appearance of a new script did not eliminate the former; consequently in the Greco-Roman period all 3 scripts were simultaneously in use. (4) COPTIC. When Egypt became a Christian nation in the 4th cent. A.D., the old scripts were discarded and the Greek alphabetic letters were adopted to write the Coptic language. Eight additional characters were borrowed from demotic to express sounds for which the Greek script had no letters.

The knowledge of the Egyptian writing systems, with the exception of that of Coptic, completely died out in the course of centuries; consequently ancient texts, written either on monuments or on papyri, were a mystery. In 1799 the famous Rosetta Stone was found in Egypt. It contains a decree in honor of Ptolemy Epiphanes (erected 196 B.C.) in 3 scripts: hieroglyphic, demotic Egyptian, and Greek (fig. 526). This monument, now in the British Museum, provided the key for the decipherment of ancient Egyptian. The Swedish diplomat Akerblad made a successful beginning at deciphering the demotic portion in 1802. Then Thomas Young took the first successful steps in a decipherment of hieroglyphic signs in 1819. The full decipherment was accomplished by the brilliant young Frenchman, François Champollion, in 1822. This work has been refined and completed by a great host of Egyptologists since Champollion's day, so that Egyptian inscriptions of all kinds and periods can now be read with remarkable ease and certainty.

V. History.

1. *Chronology.* The chief sources of information on this very difficult subject are ancient lists of kings, some astronomical data, and historical data mentioning regnal years of kings, or the length of their reigns. The division into dynasties was made by Manetho, an Egyptian priest who wrote his history on Egypt in Greek in the early 3d cent. B.C. This work has been lost and only portions are available to us in summaries or references to it by Josephus, Africanus, and Eusebius. To arrive at an accurate chronology has been more difficult than any other task undertaken by Egyptologists since ancient

Egyptian records could be read. Scholars have not yet come to unanimous conclusions, and no dates given for the early history are established. Dates given by earlier scholars for the beginning of Egyptian history with the 1st dynasty (Petrie: 4777 B.C.) are now accepted by no one. This event is now dated by Egyptologists between 3100 B.C. and 2800 B.C. It is not until the Middle Kingdom that reliable dates become available, and the first absolute date, arrived at on the basis of astronomical data, is the year 1991 B.C., the beginning of the 12th dynasty. Nevertheless, even in the 2d and 1st millenniums B.C. there are events for which no chronological data are available; for example, for most events that took place during dynasties 13-17. There are also chronological uncertainties during dynasties 21-23. However, dynasties 18-20 are reasonably well established, and the chronology of dynasties 24-30 creates few problems. This varying degree of certainty should be remembered in considering the dates given in the following paragraphs. The dates given in connection with the Egyptian history up to the 12th dynasty are those currently accepted by Egyptologists who are adherents of the lowest chronology, and are not necessarily endorsed as correct.

2. *Prehistory.* Practically nothing is known of Egypt before the art of writing came into existence in the 1st dynasty. Remains of predynastic Egypt consist of some village ruins, pottery, stone vessels, utilitarian objects, weapons, and some crude sculptures and wall paintings. Scholars have divided the prehistoric time into periods to which they have given names based on sites on which characteristic cultural remains were first found —Tasian, Badarian, Amratian, and Gerzean. There is no way of determining the length of these periods.

3. *The Old Kingdom,* dynasties 1-6 (*c.* 2800 - *c.* 2150 B.C.). In the beginning of this period the unification of Egypt took place under a king called Menes by Manetho, although this name is not yet attested in ancient Egyptian records. The kings of dynasties 1 and 2 have left massive tombs at Abydos and *Saqqârah,* built of brick in imitation of the Mesopotamian style of building. Much other evidence points to the valley of the Euphrates and Tigris as the land of origin of Egypt's early culture and achievements. During the 3d dynasty the first monumental stone structures were erected, to which belong the Step Pyramid of King Zoser (fig. 144)

and the numerous structures around it that form a great mortuary compound. Then came the great pyramid builders of the 4th dynasty, Khufu, Khafre, and Menkure, who have left us 3 tremendous pyramids in *Gizeh* (fig. 145). Their mastery of hard stone, as witnessed by sculptures, by monumental structures (such as the pyramids), and by mortuary temples, was never surpassed and seldom equaled in ancient Egypt. The Old Kingdom excelled not only in architecture and sculpture but also in such sciences as mathematics and astronomy, and was regarded in later times as the classical period. During dynasties 5 and 6 royal power declined, as is revealed by the smaller size and poorer quality of the pyramids and other tomb structures. In the 22d cent. the Old Kingdom came to its end and was followed by a period of chaos and anarchy, marked by great poverty among the population and a spiritual re-evaluation of the whole Egyptian outlook on life.

4. *The First Intermediate Period,* dynasties 8-11 (*c.* 2150 - *c.* 2025 B.C.). It must first be noted that no trace of the existence of the so-called Manetho's 7th dynasty has been found in ancient records; consequently it must be assumed that this dynasty never existed, and it must be left out of any historical discussion of Egypt's ancient history. The kings of the First Intermediate Period, mostly local rulers who called themselves kings, were weak successors of those of the Old Kingdom, and attempted unsuccessfully to gain supremacy over the whole country.

During this period there was also an influx of Asiatics—probably Amorites, who appeared at this time in the whole Near East. They ruled over parts of the Delta and used the city of Athribis as their capital. They were usually blamed by their contemporaries for all the troubles and miseries of that time. As the central form of government broke down, much lawlessness was seen on every hand, and a great economic crisis made the country bankrupt. However, when material possessions vanished there was a profound search for true values. This is clearly reflected in the exceptional flourishing of wisdom literature at that time.

5. *The Middle Kingdom,* dynasties 11-12 (*c.* 2025 - *c.* 1780 B.C.). One of the 11th-dynasty kings of Thebes in Upper Egypt was able to end the chaotic conditions of the period and to put the whole country under his rule. The result was the return of a united and strong kingdom with

an orderly administration. This event marked the beginning of the Middle Kingdom. Later a revolution brought a change in dynasties, but the kings of the 12th dynasty continued the powerful rule of their predecessors. They moved the capital to Lisht in central Egypt, and took great care to be responsible rulers of their people. They trained their successors, promoted foreign trade, exploited the mines of Nubia and Sinai, and carried out military expeditions into Palestine and Libya. At the same time they built strong fortifications to protect their borders from the intrusion of foreigners.

6. *The Second Intermediate Period,* dynasties 13-17 (*c.* 1780 - *c.* 1570 B.C.). Once more Egypt experienced a period of chaos and foreign domination. This second breakup of order and centralized government was caused by the intrusion of the Hyksos, a mysterious people whom Josephus called shepherd kings. They seemed to have been part of a great migration of peoples which at that time flooded the Near East, and which was responsible for the destruction of several kingdoms, also the emergence of new ones, such as the Hittite empire in Asia Minor, the Hurrian kingdom of Mitanni on the upper Euphrates, and the kingdom of the Kassites in Lower Mesopotamia.

The Hyksos (their name means "ruler of foreign countries"), who came into

Egypt from Asia, were partly Semites and partly Hurrians. They brought with them a new war vehicle, the horse and chariot, which changed warfare as much as did the invention of the tank in the 20th cent. Whether they entered Egypt in peace and then took over a weak, outmoded administration, or whether they conquered the country by force of arms, is unknown for lack of documentary evidence. The Egyptians later destroyed every trace of evidence that reminded them of their hated foreign oppressors.

The Hyksos had their capital in Avaris (the Greek Tanis; Biblical Zoan) in the eastern Delta. Some of their strong kings probably ruled over the whole Nile valley; others controlled not more than certain restricted areas. Local native rulers continued to be recognized by the Egyptians and Hyksos as administrators over certain territories. About 1600 B.C. the local prince of Thebes began a struggle for the liberation of Egypt from foreign domination. The campaigns of three successive kings—Sekenen-Re, Kamose, and Ahmose—ended with the complete defeat of the Hyksos, the conquest of Avaris, and the expulsion of the oppressors from Egypt. The Hyksos established themselves for a few years in Sharuhen, in southern Palestine, but after a 3-year campaign (or 3 annual campaigns; the record is ambiguous) the Egyptians expelled them from there also, after which they were lost to history. Thus at about 1570 B.C. Egypt was free again, and began the most glorious period of its entire history.

7. *The New Kingdom Before the Amarna Period,* early dynasty 18 (*c.* 1570 - *c.* 1380 B.C.). Ahmose, the liberator king of Thebes, apparently became the father of a new dynasty, although the ancestral line from the 17th-dynasty kings remained unbroken. His successors were mostly strong rulers, but, peculiarly, for several generations only girls were born to the legitimate queens, so that one king after another was a commoner, who held the throne only through his royal wife. This was true of the first three Thutmoses, and was the reason why a woman, the famous Hatshepsut, ruled Egypt for some years as "king."

Under Amenhotep I Nubia again became an integral part of the Nile country, and the Sinai mines were exploited. Thutmose I carried out military campaigns in Palestine and Syria, reaching as far as the Euphrates. Under Hatshepsut

145. The Sphinx and the pyramid of Khufu at *Gîzeh*. Between the paws of the Sphinx stands a stele of Thutmose IV

146. Mortuary temple of Queen Hatshepsut at *Deir el-Bahri* in western Thebes

trading expeditions were sent to Punt (probably Somaliland in eastern Africa) and a great building activity was developed. After Hatshepsut's peaceful but strong rule, Thutmose III, who had already been her coregent for a number of years, began the series of military campaigns into Palestine and Syria that brought Egypt to the height of her glory. He created the most powerful empire that existed in the 2d millennium B.C., one that reached from the Euphrates to the 6th Nile cataract. A strong central government was built up, and for the first time the nation had a powerful army of professionals, with garrisons in all parts of the far-flung empire. The treasures of the world that poured into the Nile valley enabled the Egyptian Pharaohs to engage in building activities of phenomenal proportions. The world had not seen the like of it.

8. *The Amarna Period,* later dynasty 18 (*c.* 1380 - *c.* 1350 B.C.). The Amarna period was only a short interlude in Egypt's history, but a most intriguing and important one. Some developments preceding the Amarna period are noticeable at the end of the 15th cent. and the beginning of the 14th cent. B.C., but nothing tangible is known to the modern historian until Amenhotep IV steps into the

limelight of history as king of Egypt. He appears as a fanatical monotheist worshiping Aton, the sun disk, exclusively. Opposition to his religious revolution was too strong in the old capital, Thebes, where polytheism, especially the Amon cult, was powerfully entrenched; therefore he moved the capital to a new place, Akhetaton (now called Amarna), which lay halfway between Thebes and Memphis. With the old temples closed and their priests dismissed, with the former gods suppressed and their worshipers persecuted, a new sun temple was built in Akhetaton. The king, who had changed his name from Amenhotep to Ikhnaton, devoted himself wholeheartedly to the interpretation and dissemination of the new religion and cult. However, he was not strong enough to change completely the ingrained beliefs of the populace, and toward the end of his reign a less fanatical rejection of the old religion is noticeable. With his death the movement collapsed. A successor, Tutankhaton, a son-in-law, was forced to return to Thebes. By changing his name to Tutankhamen, and by reopening the former temples, he indicated that the original order was restored and that the Amarna revolution was dead. Ikhnaton's revolution was the only attempt to introduce monotheism into Egypt until Christianity appeared and triumphed over paganism some 16 cent. later.

Ikhnaton, more interested in religious reformation than in politics and administrative duties, composed and chanted hymns to Aton instead of lending his ear to the frantic appeals for help coming from his subjects and friends in Asia. Hence, we find that all of Syria and most of Palestine slipped from under Egyptian control in those fateful years, and the kings after him were too weak and too much engaged in work at home to arrest the breakup of the empire.

9. *The New Kingdom After the Amarna Period,* dynasties 18-20 (*c.* 1350-1085 B.C.). After the Amarna revolution collapsed the old religion and former way of life were quickly restored, and soon all traces of the religious upheaval disappeared. Harmhab, the first strong ruler of the restoration period, had his hands too full restoring order and authority within the borders of Egypt to begin the reconquering of lost territories in Asia. This Seti I began to do, subduing several strong cities in the Valley of Esdraelon in Palestine and maintaining control of the coastal area

connecting them with Egypt. Under the circumstances he could do no more.

His successor, Ramses II, ruled for nearly 70 years (1299-1232 B.C.). He fought against the Hittites at Kadesh and then concluded a treaty that left them in possession of Syria. He became better known in history than any other king of Egypt because his long reign enabled him to carry on an extensive building program. He usurped many buildings of former kings, dismantled them, and used the materials for his own buildings, on all of which he placed his own name as the builder.

During the reign of his son and successor, Merneptah, a migration of western barbarians, the so-called Peoples of the Sea, invaded the civilized countries of the East. These newcomers exerted pressure upon the Libyans, who in turn pushed into Egypt, forcing Merneptah to fight against his western neighbors. The Hittite empire vanished under the relentless onslaughts of these Peoples of the Sea, who had overrun Asia Minor. When Ramses III came to the throne, Egypt was in mortal fear of these invaders, but he was able to stem the tide by defeating them and turning them back. Some of their remnants remained, such as the Philistines, who settled on the southwestern coast of Palestine. Ramses III saved Egypt from external danger, and also promoted the internal security of his country. However, a period of decline began in the latter part of his reign, which accelerated under his weak successors, so that Egypt became a second- or third-rate nation. A loss of foreign possessions and overseas trade was the main cause of a serious economic crisis. This in turn resulted in corruption at home, disorder among army personnel, strikes among government workers, the plundering of royal tombs, and a widely felt lack of personal and economic security. At the same time the power of the high priest of Amon increased until the priesthood took over the state.

10. *The Rule of Priest-Kings, Libyans, Ethiopians, and Assyrians,* dynasties 21-25 (1085-663 B.C.). During the 21st dynasty rival kings reigned in Tanis and Thebes, the one in Thebes being the high priest of Amon. Egypt had become so weak by this time that even her envoys received humiliating treatment in foreign countries. Unity was once more achieved by kings of Libyan descent who formed the 22d, or Libyan, dynasty. The first of

these kings, Sheshonk I (Biblical Shishak), made an ambitious attempt to restore the empire. However, his military campaign in Palestine had no lasting success and did not restore the lost territories in the east to Egypt, even though he conquered Jerusalem and many other strongholds of Judah and Israel. Sheshonk's successors were weak rulers, and Egypt continued as only a shadow of its former self. See fig. 438.

After Libyan kings had ruled for 200 years, native Egyptians regained the throne (24th dynasty), but occupied it for only a few years. They were soon replaced by invading Ethiopians from Nubia (*see* Ethiopia), who, as kings of the 25th dynasty, ruled the Egyptians for almost 9 decades. These Ethiopian Pharaohs had to fight against the Assyrians, who by that time had become the most powerful nation on earth. In 670 B.C. Esarhaddon of Assyria conquered Egypt and made it into an Assyrian province, which status it held for several years.

11. *The Saïte Kings,* dynasty 26 (663-525 B.C.). During this dynasty Egypt experienced a period of reasonable prosperity. Its native kings, whose capital was Saïs, in the western Delta, regained for their country some of its long-lost international prestige. Reigning during a time when the Assyrian power declined, the Saïte kings re-established some semblance of a strong rule in Egypt. They dared to dream of rebuilding their old empire in Asia, and challenged the Neo-Babylonian kingdom, which had recently emerged as a new power in Mesopotamia. Necho, king of Egypt, not only campaigned deep into Asia but for several years was in possession of all of Palestine and Syria as far as the Euphrates. However, his defeat at Carchemish, at the hands of the Babylonian crown prince Nebuchadnezzar (605 B.C.), ended all Egyptian aspirations in Asia. From that time the Egyptians were confined to their own country. A broken cuneiform tablet indicates that they probably suffered a Babylonian invasion during the reign of Amasis. However, native Egyptian rulers remained on the throne throughout the period of the Babylonian Empire.

12. *Persian and Last Native Rulers,* dynasties 27-31 (525-333 B.C.). Cambyses, the 2d king of the Persian Empire, conquered Egypt in 525 B.C. and made it a Persian satrapy. However, Egypt was again under native rule from the time of Da-

rius II to the reign of Artaxerxes III, during which time Egyptian kings belonging to 3 dynasties (28-30) occupied the throne of the Pharaohs. The Persians finally came back in 341 B.C. and ended the native rulership. However, this second Persian rule, counted by Manetho as the 31st dynasty, did not last long, ending with Alexander's victorious entry into Egypt in 332 B.C.

13. *Hellenistic and Roman Egypt.* With Alexander's crushing victories over the Persian armies, Hellenistic governors took over the conquered areas, among which was Egypt, which was administered for Alexander by Ptolemy. About 20 years after Alexander's death Ptolemy made himself king of Egypt, and his descendants reigned over Egypt for almost 300 years. Alexandria was founded as a Greek city, and certain sections of the Delta were Hellenized, but the remainder of Egypt continued in its old way, experiencing few changes. With the arrival of the Romans the kingdom of Egypt became a dependency of the pow-

147. The heraldic symbols of Upper and Lower Egypt, the lotus (right) and the papyrus (left), in the temple at Karnak

erful republic on the Tiber. After its conquest by Octavian (Augustus) in 30 B.C., the year following the battle of Actium, it became a Roman province under the direct rule of the emperor. This was its status throughout the age of the apostles.

VI. Religion. Although many temples of the ancient Egyptians have survived, and much is known about their religious rites, the real nature of the Egyptian religion is still extremely obscure. One must distinguish between local deities, mostly identified with animals, such as the cat, the frog, and the crocodile, and national deities, such as Ra and Osiris.

The characteristics of the gods and their spheres of activity changed from time to time. Osiris was first a Nile god, then the god of fertility, and finally the master of the underworld. Ra, the sun-god, was worshiped for many centuries in On (Heliopolis), near Memphis; but when, during the empire period, the ram-headed Amon, the local god of Thebes, became the chief god of Egypt, Amon became identified with Ra and received the name Amon-Ra. The hawk-headed Horus was the god of kingship, and every king called himself Horus. The cow goddess Hathor was the patron of Sinai, of Byblos on the Phoenician coast, and of other places. Thoth, the scribe among the gods, who kept the heavenly records, had the head of an ibis; and Anubis, the guide of the dead, was a jackal-headed god. The Egyptians built great temples to the gods, brought sacrifices for their support, and celebrated feasts in their honor during which the emblems of the gods were carried around in procession. Since all forces of nature, animate or inanimate, were believed to be working under the jurisdiction of one or several gods, the Egyptians felt they had to appease these gods in order to enjoy the blessings of life. It was thought that the good life could be attained only by becoming and remaining a friend of the gods.

The Egyptians believed in a life after death. They held that if they could pass, at death, a rigid examination of their life on earth (see fig. 50), they would continue the earthly life in the underworld. Since the preservation of the body was considered necessary for the welfare of the deceased in this future life, the Egyptians embalmed their dead (see figs. 167, 399). Furthermore, they thought that offerings were needed to be brought on earth for the well-being of the dead; therefore people made provision during life for the continuance of these offerings after their death.

Although Egyptian gods are frequently referred to in the OT, only one of them is mentioned by name, Amon (Amen), of Thebes (Jer 46:25, RSV). However, a number of names of deities appear in theophorous personal names or place names, as in Asenath, Potiphera, Rameses, Pithom, and Pibeseth (Gen 41:45; 46:20; Ex 12:37; 1:11; Eze 30:17).

VII. Egypt and Bible History. Following are the principal Biblical events connected with Egypt, dated in alignment with Egyptian history according to the chronology adopted in this dictionary (*see* Chronology): (1) Abraham found refuge in Egypt during a famine in Palestine in the 19th cent. B.C. during the Middle Kingdom. Hence the Pharaoh with whom Abraham became acquainted,

148. The large Hypostyle Hall in the temple at Karnak; latticed stone window in the upper center

and who treated him with consideration and respect (Gen 12:10-20), must have been one of the 12th dynasty. (2) Joseph was sold into Egyptian slavery in the 17th cent. B.C., when the Hyksos were in power. This explains how he could come to honor and authority as vizier in the Nile country, whereas at any other time it would have been extremely unusual to find a Semite occupying such a position. While he was in office the family of Jacob moved into Egypt because of a famine and settled in the area of Goshen (chs 39:1 to 47:28). (3) Jacob's descendants multiplied in Egypt until they became a formidable group. When the Egyptians liberated their country from the Hyksos, they enslaved the Hebrews, who, with the accompaniment of miracles, were eventually delivered under the leadership of Moses (Ex 1:8-12; 3:10-12; 7 to 12). This took place probably under King Amenhotep II, in 1445 B.C. (4) Merneptah, the son and successor of Ramses II, mentions in a famous inscription on the Israel stele that he defeated Israel, and from the context it appears that this encounter must have taken place in Palestine (see fig. 245). This event, late in the 13th cent. during the period of the judges, is not recorded in the Bible. (5) Solomon married an Egyptian princess, probably a daughter of one of the last kings of the 21st dynasty (1 Ki 3:1). His officer Jeroboam rebelled against him and found refuge at the court of Sheshonk I (Biblical Shishak; ch 11:40). Sheshonk I invaded Judah and Israel shortly after Solomon's death and conquered Jerusalem (I Ki 14:25, 26; 2 Chr 12:2-5; fig. 438). (6) Hezekiah defied the Assyrians by trusting in part in the strength and help of the Ethiopian kings of Egypt (2 Ki 18:19-21). Taharka (Biblical Tirhakah; see fig. 163) is mentioned as actually having made an attempt to rescue Hezekiah (ch 19:9), but nothing is known about the success of this attempt. (7) During the last years of the kingdom of Judah, Egypt played a greater role in the history of the Hebrew nation than it had for a long time. King Josiah, probably bound by an agreement with the Babylonians, attempted to block Pharaoh Necho's march to the north against them, and in the ensuing battle of Megiddo lost his life (2 Ki 23:29, 30; 2 Chr 35:20-24). His son and successor, Jehoahaz, was deposed by Necho after a short reign of 3 months and taken to Egypt as a prisoner (2 Ki 23:31-33; 2 Chr 36:1-3). Jehoiakim was made a vassal king by the Egyptian ruler and continued as such until Nebuchadnezzar ended Egyptian supremacy in Palestine (2 Ki 23:34, 35; 2 Chr 36:4-6). However, a pro-Egyptian party remained among the Jews, and it was trust in Egypt's strength that made Jehoiakim, and later Zedekiah, rebel against the Babylonian king. During the last siege of Jerusalem an unsuccessful attempt was made by Pharaoh Apries (Biblical Hophra) of Egypt to bring relief to the beleaguered city, but it resulted in no more than a short respite for the Jews (Jer 37:5-7). Many Jews who escaped from the destruction of Jerusalem by the Babylonians later went to Egypt (chs 42 to 44) and became the nucleus of the strong Jewish communities in later times. (8) Joseph, following divine instructions, fled to Egypt with his wife Mary and the child Jesus to escape from the wrath of Herod the Great. They remained there until after the death of Herod in the spring of 4 B.C. (Mt 2:13-15).

Egyptian, The. An Egyptian Jew who, shortly after Felix became procurator, claimed to be a prophet and, according to Josephus, deluded 30,000 Jews into following him to the Mount of Olives. There he asserted he would command the walls of Jerusalem to fall, whereupon he would overcome the Roman garrison in the city. His followers were dispersed by the Romans, and many of them killed, but the Egyptian himself escaped (Jos. *Ant.* xx. 8. 6; *War* ii. 13. 5). The chief captain (RSV "tribune") of the *barracks mistook Paul for this Egyptian (Acts 21:37, 38).

Ehi. *See* Ahiram.

Ehud (ē′hŭd). [Heb. *'Ehûd*.]
1. A descendant of Benjamin through Jediael (1 Chr 7:10).
2. A descendant of Benjamin through Gera, described as left-handed. He assassinated Eglon, king of Moab, who had oppressed Israel for 18 years, and became one of the early judges of Israel. He gained access to Eglon as a tribute bearer and succeeded in having all royal attendants removed on the pretext that he had a secret message for the king. He used this opportunity to kill the king, who is described as being "very fat," and then called up Israel to shake off the foreign yoke. In the ensuing war many Moabites lost their lives. After Ehud's deliverance the southern part of Israel had rest for an extended period of time (Jgs 3:15 to 4:1).

Eker (ē'kĕr). [Heb. *'Eqer,* "offspring."] A descendant of Judah of the house of Jerahmeel (1 Chr 2:27).

Ekron (ĕk'rŏn). [Heb. *'Eqrôn,* mentioned in Akkadian texts as *Amqarruna* and in Egyptian inscriptions as *'Ngrn.*] One of the 5 chief cities of the Philistines. It was formerly believed to have lain either at the present site of *Qaṭrā,* 8 mi. northeast of Ashdod, or at *'Āqir,* about 3 mi. farther to the northeast (Map VI, E-2). However, recently evidence has been presented for identifying it with *Khirbet el-Muqanna',* 6 mi. south of *'Āqir* (J. Naveh, *IEJ* 8 [1958], 87-100, 165-170; Y. Aharoni, *PEQ* 90 [1958], 29). The city was in the territory assigned first to Judah (Jos 15:45, 46), but later to Dan (ch 19:43). Although Judah conquered it once, early in the settlement of Canaan (Jgs 1:18), the Israelites probably did not occupy it. In the time of Samuel and Saul, Ekron's surrounding territory was repeatedly conquered by the Israelites, but the city was apparently held by the Philistines (1 Sa 7:14; 17:52) from the time when they settled in Palestine in the 12th cent. B.C. Ekron was one of the cities to which the Philistines took the captured ark (chs 5:10; 6:16). The prophets spoke against it (Jer 25:20; Amos 1:8; Zep 2:4; Zec 9:5, 7). When Hezekiah rebelled against the Assyrians, Padi, king of Ekron, remained loyal to Assyria, but the Ekronites joined the rebellion and handed him over to Hezekiah. As a result Sennacherib came and punished Ekron and re-established Padi on his throne (*ANET* 287, 288). The city was finally given to the Jews by the Seleucid king Alexander Balas in the time of Jonathan the Maccabean (1 Macc 10:89). Its inhabitants worshiped Baal-zebub (2 Ki 1:2).

Ekronites (ĕk'rŏn-īts). [Heb. *'Eqrôni.*] An inhabitant of Ekron (Jos 13:3; etc.).

El (ĕl). [Heb. *'el;* Ugaritic *'il;* Akkadian *ilu;* Phoenician and South Arabic *'l.*] The transliteration of the oldest Semitic designation for god, appearing in the Bible only in compound names. As a generic name in the ancient languages the word appears in both the singular and the plural (*'elim, ilâni*), also in feminine forms (Ugaritic *'ilt;* Akkadian *iltu*) and as a proper name of specific gods.

In Babylonian and Assyrian texts *ilu* usually appears as a generic name, as is evident from a study of personal names such as *Ibashshi-ilum,* "there is a god," *Ibashshi-ilâni,* "there are gods," *Ili-bâni,*

"my god is my creator," *Iluma-ilu,* "my god is god." The god in these cases is Marduk, Nabu, Shamash, Ashur, or some other national god.

The derivation and original meaning of the word is uncertain. It is usually derived from the Semitic root *'wl,* "to be strong," so that the meaning would be "strength," "majesty," and "sublimity." This meaning of *'el* is found in some OT passages where the word does not refer to a god, as for example in Eze 31:11, where *'el* is translated "the mighty one," and in Ps 80:10, where it is translated "mighty" (RSV). Other explanations that have been offered by scholars are less plausible.

Names compounded with "El" are frequent among the Aramaeans, as Aramaic Biblical names show, for example, Kemuel, Bethuel (Gen 22:21, 22), and Tabeel (Is 7:6), and as the inscriptional records of Palmyra, of the Nabataeans, and of other Aramaic-speaking people reveal. Aramaic inscriptions of the 8th cent. B.C. reveal that the Aramaeans worshiped a god named El, and it is safe to conclude that it is he that is referred to in most Aramaic names in which El occurs.

In the Phoenician inscriptions El describes a specific god, but the plural form is used as a generic name. This is also true in Canaanite Ugaritic, which was closely related to the Phoenician language. In Ugaritic inscriptions El is presented as the highest god, and is considered to be the father of practically all gods. He is called "father of years," and must have been considered as the earliest god of the Ugaritic pantheon, the one to whom the whole world belonged, and without whose command nothing could happen. The fact that he was called a "bull" by the Canaanites may have influenced the bull worship of Israel. By the time the Israelites entered Canaan, El's position had already become inferior to that of *Baal.

In the ancient Arabic inscriptions El appears so frequently in personal names that it is quite evident he must have been the earliest and most important god of Arabia. Names meaning "El commanded," "El has heard," "El is lord," "El gives," and others show clearly that the ancient Arabs considered El a good, humane, and sublime deity.

In the OT the name *'El* appears as a generic name for the one and true God (Gen 31:13; Ex 20:5; 34:14; etc.), and in the plural to designate more than one god

(Ex 15:11; Dan 11:36). It appears also as the proper name of the God of Israel (Is 40:18; Ps 10:11, 12; 16:1; 68:20; etc.). It is found in many personal names as in Elijah, "my God is Yahweh" (1 Ki 17:1); Elimelech, "my God is king" (Ruth 1:2); Eliezer, "my God is [my] help" (Gen 15:2); Ishmael, "God has heard" (ch 16:11); and others. Sometimes an attribute is added to the word *'El*, as in *'El-'Elyôn*, "God, the highest" (ch 14:18); *'El-Shaddai*, "God, the Almighty" (ch 17:1); *'El-'Ôlam*, "God, the Ancient one" (ch 21:33); etc. Frequently the word *'El* appears in terms such as "the God of your father" (ch 31:29), "the God of your fathers" (Ex 3:13), "Lord God of . . . Abraham" (Gen 24:12), "the God of . . . Isaac" (ch 46:1). These expressions meant that *'El* was the God who had revealed Himself to their father Abraham or Isaac, who kept a constant connection with His worshipers, and who is not bound to any one place. *See* God; Lord.

Lit.: M. H. Pope, *El in the Ugaritic Texts* (Leiden, 1955); *LVTL* 45-47; W. F. Albright, *Archeology and the Religion of Israel* (4th ed.; Baltimore, 1956).

Ela (ē'lȧ), KJV **Elah** (ē'lȧ). [Heb. *'Ela'*, a name attested in ancient Hebrew inscriptions.] An Israelite whose son Shimei was one of Solomon's supply officers (1 Ki 4:18).

Eladah. *See* Eleadah.

Elah (ē'lȧ). [Heb. *'Elah* and *'Ela'*, a tree not certainly identified, perhaps the terebinth or oak.]

1. A valley in which Saul's army was encamped when the combat between David and Goliath occurred (1 Sa 17:1, 2). It is identified with the *Wâdī es-Sanṭ*, about 19 mi. west of Bethlehem, and a few miles to the west of Socoh (see Map VII, E-2).

2. An Edomite prince (Gen 36:41; 1 Chr 1:52).

3. Son of Caleb the son of Jephunneh (1 Chr 4:15).

4. A Benjamite (1 Chr 9:8).

5. Father of one of Solomon's supply officers (1 Ki 4:18).

6. The 4th king of Israel, the northern kingdom, ruling 886-885 B.C. He was killed by Zimri, a commander of his chariotry (1 Ki 16:6, 8-10), in fulfillment of the prediction of the prophet Jehu to Baasha, Elah's father (vs 1-4).

7. An Israelite whose son Hoshea slew Pekah and took the throne as the last king of Israel (2 Ki 15:30; 17:1; 18:1).

Elam (ē'lăm). [Heb. *'Ēlam*, meaning unknown.]

1. Son of Shem, ancestor of the Elamites (Gen 10:22; 1 Chr 1:17).

2. A Levite of the family of Korah in the time of David (1 Chr 26:3).

3. A Benjamite who lived in Jerusalem (1 Chr 8:24, 28).

4. The ancestral name of a clan of exiles of whom 1,254 returned to Palestine with Zerubbabel (Ezr 2:7; Neh 7:12), and another 71 with Ezra (Ezr 8:7). Some of these people were married to foreign wives in the time of Ezra (ch 10:2, 26). A representative of the family signed Nehemiah's covenant (Neh 10:14).

5. The ancestral name of the clan of exiles called "the other Elam," of whom 1,254 returned to Palestine with Zerubbabel (Ezr 2:31; Neh 7:34).

6. A priest of Nehemiah's time who took part in the dedication of the wall of Jerusalem (Neh 12:42).

7. A country lying in the Zagros Mountains east of Babylonia (Map III, C-6), called Susiana or Elymais by the Greeks (Map XIII, C-6). The Medes were their northern and the Persians their southern neighbors. Their capital was *Susa (KJV Shushan). According to Gen 10:22; 1 Chr 1:17 the Elamites (ē'lăm-īts) [Aramaic *'Elemaye'*; Gr. *Elamitai*] were descendants of Shem, but their language belongs to the Asianic-Armenoid group of languages. The Elamites are mentioned in cuneiform inscriptions as early as the 3d millennium B.C. Their country was defeated by Sargon and Naram-Sin of Akkad. However, in the 20th cent. B.C. they put an end to the 3d dynasty of Ur by an invasion of Mesopotamia. During the following centuries the Elamites were so powerful that they occasionally controlled parts of Mesopotamia. It was during this time that the Biblical Chedorlaomer of Elam with 3 confederate kings

149. Elamite soldiers (upper row) carved on the palace staircase at Persepolis

subjugated certain Palestinian kings for 12 years and raided their country twice (Gen 14). In the time of the Assyrian Empire in the 1st millennium B.C. Elam was one of Assyria's chief opponents. Many times Elam sided with Babylon, which was eventually subjugated by the Assyrians. Sometimes the Elamites were also made vassals, and Elamite soldiers had to serve in the Assyrian army (Is 22:6). Sargon II, Sennacherib, and Ashurbanipal all campaigned against the Elamite capital, Susa. Finally, Ashurbanipal took the city in 639 B.C. Many of its citizens were deported to other parts of the Assyrian Empire, including Samaria (Ezr 4:9). Ezekiel's lament (Eze 32:24) may allude to this event. Elam later became part of the Babylonian Empire, an event to which the prophecy of Jer 49:34-39 may refer. Later it was taken over by Persia. The Persian kings made Susa (KJV "Shushan") one of their residences (Dan 8:2; Est 1:2). The Elamites of Acts 2:9, who attended the feast of Pentecost in Jerusalem, where they came under the influence of the preaching of the gospel by the apostles, were probably Jews living in Elam.

Elamites. *See* Elam, 7.

Elasah (ĕl′à-sà). [Heb. *'El'aśah,* "God has made."]

1. One of King Zedekiah's royal envoys who carried a letter of the prophet Jeremiah to the exiles in Babylon (Jer 29:1-3).

2. An Israelite who was married to a foreign wife in Ezra's time (Ezr 10:22).

Elath (ē′lăth), or **Eloth** (ē′lŏth). [Heb. *'Êlath, 'Êlôth,* probably "a large tree."] An Edomite port city at the northern end of the eastern arm of the Red Sea, called the Gulf of Aqabah or the Aelanitic Gulf, after Elath. Elath and *Ezion-geber were either neighboring cities or the same city with two names. The latter view, defended by Nelson Glueck, the excavator of Ezion-geber (*AASOR* 18, 19 [1939], 1-7), is exemplified in the name of the modern Israeli port of Eilat (sometimes called Elath), west of Ezion-geber (Map XXII, E-2). There is, however, some evidence available to support the view that the two names represented neighboring towns—Ezion-geber being identified with *Tell el-Kheleifeh,* and Elath approximately with the site of the modern Aqabah, a few miles to the east of Ezion-geber (Map V, C-7). The name Elath may have been derived from a sacred tree under which pagans had worshiped. Some com-

150. The Gulf of Aqabah, on whose shore the city of Elath was situated

mentators have seen in the El-paran of Gen 14:6 the first reference to Elath. If this view is correct, it means that the 4 kings of ch 14 swept as far south as the Gulf of Aqabah in their conquest of Palestine. Elath is first clearly mentioned in Deut 2:8 as a station of the Hebrews in their desert wandering. At that time it marked the southernmost border of Edom and an important crossroad for caravans between Arabia and Egypt. The place did not come into the possession of the Israelites until David subjugated the Edomites (see 2 Sa 8:14). After this, *Ezion-geber is mentioned as an industrial center and port city, whereas the name Elath is not mentioned again until the time of Azariah, who is mentioned as recovering it for Judah (2 Ki 14:22), presumably from the Edomites. In Ahaz' time Elath fell into the hands of the Syrians (ch 16:6). However, they seem to have possessed it only briefly, for a few years later, in 732 B.C., the kingdom of Damascus was defeated and uprooted by Tiglath-pileser III (v 9). However, some Syrians seem to have remained at Elath for some time afterward (v 6). Elath is not mentioned again in the Bible, but other sources show that it became a place of some importance during the period of the Roman Empire when the Arabian Nabataeans were in possession of the old Edomite territory. Its name was then Aila.

El-berith. *See* Baal-berith.

El-bethel (ĕl′bĕth′ĕl′). [Heb. *'El Bêth-'el,* "God of Bethel."] The name given to an altar Jacob erected at Bethel after his return from Mesopotamia (Gen 35:7). It commemorated his earlier meeting with God in a dream, when he fled from his brother Esau to Mesopotamia (see ch 28: 10-22).

Eldaah (ĕl-dā′à). [Heb. *'Elda'ah,* "God desires."] Grandson of Abraham through

Midian and ancestor of a Midianite tribe (Gen 25:4; 1 Chr 1:33).

Eldad (ĕl'dăd). [Heb. *'Eldad,* "God is a friend." The name occurs in cuneiform records as *Dâdi-ilu.*] One of the 70 elders chosen to assist Moses in his administrative and judicial duties in the wilderness. He and Medad were absent from the tabernacle when the other elders received God's Spirit in a noticeable manner, yet the Spirit came upon them in the camp where they were. When Joshua, at that time a servant of Moses, heard of this he was displeased, doubtless thinking that such experiences should come only through the intervention of Moses. But Moses told him that he wished the Lord would put His Spirit on all people so that all might be prophets (Num 11:24-29).

Elder. [Heb. *zaqen;* Gr. *presbuteros.*] In the OT the word designates those of a certain official rank and position among their brethren, such as heads of families, households, or tribes (Gen 50:7; Ex 3:16; 2 Sa 5:3). The term does not necessarily mean an old man, but does imply one of maturity and experience. God directed Moses to choose 70 elders to aid him in his great responsibility of governing Israel (Num 11:16, 17). These men were especially prepared by God to do that work (vs 24-26). In cases when the whole nation sinned, the elders were to represent it in making atonement (Lev 4:13-15). Each city had its group of elders, who had certain civil and religious responsibilities (Ex 12:21; Deut 19:11, 12; Ruth 4:2, 4, 9, 11; etc.), and were required to answer for the whole city in certain cases (Deut 21:1-9). The elders of other ancient peoples evidently held responsibilities similar to those of the elders of Israel (Gen 50:7; Num 22:4; Jos 9:3, 4, 11). The elders of Israel held a place of importance even after the nation was ruled by kings (2 Sa 5:3; 1 Ki 8:1; 20:7, 8; 2 Chr 5:2), and continued to do so for some time (Ezr 5:9; Eze 8:1; Joel 1:14; Mt 26:47; 27:1; Mk 8:31; Lk 7:3; Acts 4:8).

The term "elder" is applied first to a member of the Christian church in Acts 11:30, where reference is made to certain church leaders in Judea. A comparison of Acts 20:17 with v 28 (cf. also 1 Ti 3: 2-7; Tit 1:5-9) seems to indicate that the terms *presbuteros* and *episkopos,* literally "overseer," generally translated "bishop," are used synonymously (in Acts 20:28 *episkopos* is rendered "overseer," KJV, and "guardian," RSV). Thus the qualifica-

tions and offices of an elder and bishop would be the same (see 1 Ti 3:2-7; Tit 1:5-9); *see* Bishop. Peter, writing to the churches of Asia Minor (1 Pe 1:1), admonished the elders to have a care for those under their direction, not as if compelled, but willingly. They were not to fulfill their office for personal gain or with a domineering attitude (ch 5:1-3). The sick were advised to request "the elders of the church" to anoint them and to pray for their recovery (Jas 5:14, 15). Elders are mentioned separately from the apostles (Acts 15:2, 4, 6). Apparently there were more than one elder in each church (ch 14:23; Tit 1:5).

Twenty-four elders are presented in the symbols of Revelation. They are represented as seated upon 24 thrones surrounding the throne of God, clothed in white apparel, and wearing golden crowns (Rev 4:4). They join the 4 "living creatures" in praise and adoration to God (vs 8-10, RSV; chs 11:16; 19:4, RSV). On one occasion they are represented as carrying incense bowls and harps, and as singing a new song (ch 5:8, 9). The Biblical information is insufficient for positive identification, especially in the light of the textually attested reading "them" instead of "us" in v 10, and the questioned reading "us" in v 9. See *SDACom* 7:767, 768, 773.

Elead (ĕl'ê-ăd). [Heb. *'El'ad,* "God has witnessed," or "God is a witness."] A son of Ephraim who, when attempting to steal cattle from the city of Gath with one or more of his brothers, was slain by the people of that city. Their father mourned this loss greatly (1 Chr 7:21, 22).

Eleadah (ē'lĕ-ā'dà), KJV **Eladah** (ĕl'à-dà). [Heb. *'El'adah,* "God has adorned."] A descendant of Ephraim (1 Chr 7:20).

Elealeh (ē'lĕ-ā'lĕ). [Heb. *'El'aleh* and *'El'ale'.*] A town which the Israelites took from the Amorite king of Heshbon, and which the Reubenites rebuilt (Num 32:3, 37). Later, when the Moabites extended their territory to the north, they reoccupied it (Is 15:4; 16:9; Jer 48:34). It is now el-'Al, a ruin on top of a hill, 3,082 ft. above sea level, about 2 mi. northeast of Heshbon (Map VI, E-4).

Eleasah (ĕl'ê-ā'sà). [Heb. *'El'aśah,* "God has made."]

1. A descendant of Judah, belonging to the family of Jerahmeel, 1 (1 Chr 2: 33, 39).

2. A descendant of Saul through Jonathan (1 Chr 8:33-37; 9:43).

Eleazar (ĕl'ē-ā'zẽr). [Heb. *'El'azar,* "God has helped." The name occurs also on a Jewish contract among the Dead Sea scrolls; Gr. *Eleazar.*]

1. The third son of Aaron (Ex 6:23; Num 3:2). He served as priest with his father and brothers during the wilderness wanderings (Ex 28:1, 44; Num 3:4; 16:39; 19:3). He outlived his older brothers, whom God slew when they offered strange fire (Lev 10:1-7), and was divinely appointed as high priest when his father died (Num 20:25-28; cf. Deut 10:6). He took part in the division of the Promised Land (Jos 14:1). He was buried near the home of his son Phinehas, who succeeded him as high priest (ch 24:33; Jgs 20:28). Eleazar was the ancestor of the Zadokite priests, who in Solomon's time won precedence over the family of Abiathar, which descended from Ithamar, Eleazar's younger brother (1 Chr 6:4-15; 1 Ki 2:26, 27, 35).

2. A Merarite Levite who died without sons. The inheritance was kept in the family by the marriage of his daughters to relatives within the tribe (1 Chr 23:21, 22), in accordance with the Mosaic regulations of Num 36:6-9.

3. The son of Abinadab. He was given charge of the ark while it was in his father's home after it was returned by the Philistines in Samuel's day (1 Sa 7:1).

4. One of David's "mighty men," the son of Dodo (or Dodai) the Ahohite (2 Sa 23:9; 1 Chr 11:12).

5. A priest who was an official in the Temple treasury in the time of Ezra (Ezr 8:33).

6. A member of the family of Parosh. He was married to a foreign wife in the time of Ezra (Ezr 10:19, 25).

7. A priest who took part in the dedication ceremonies of Jerusalem's wall in the time of Nehemiah (Neh 12:42).

8. A Judahite appearing in Matthew's genealogy of Jesus Christ (Mt 1:15).

Elect, Election. [Heb. *bachîr,* "chosen," "elect"; Gr. *eklektos,* "chosen," "elect," and *eklogē,* "choice," "election," "chosen instrument."] These terms are used in both the OT and NT primarily with reference to ancient Israel as God's chosen instrument for the salvation of the world (Is 45:4; Rom 11:7, 28), and in the NT also with reference to Christian believers (2 Ti 2:10). God chose Abraham and his descendants "to be a special people unto himself, above all people that are upon the face of the earth" (Deut 7:6), to know

Him, to understand His ways, and to be His witnesses to the nations of earth (Is 43:10). The terms "elect" and "election" specifically designate Israel in its Messianic role as God's chosen messengers to convert the heathen (ch 42:1). Neither anywhere connotes an arbitrary choice on God's part with respect to the eternal salvation of individual Israelites. The terms denote Israel's unique status as a nation in the service of God, not the standing of the subjects of that nation individually as subjects of God's grace and mercy. This is evident in Paul's discussion of God's preference for Jacob over Esau as inheritor of the Abrahamic birthright (Rom 9:10-14).

The divine "election" of a chosen people remains valid in NT times (Rom 11:5, 7, 28), but now Gentiles as well as Jews are included (ch 9:24-26). In fact, Christian believers, irrespective of race, are now in a special sense "a chosen generation" and "the people of God" (1 Pe 2:9, 10), having inherited the privileges and responsibilities of the covenant relationship originally entrusted to the Hebrew people (Mt 21:43). Individual Christians are to "give diligence" to making sure that they are numbered among the faithful to whom God will grant entrance into Christ's everlasting kingdom (2 Pe 1:10, 11). In the Gospels Christ uses the term "elect" of the faithful remnant immediately prior to His second coming (Mt 24:22, 24, 31; Mk 13:20, 22, 27; Lk 18:7). They are His chosen ones, rejected and oppressed by their enemies, but soon to be avenged and delivered. In the hour of tribulation immediately preceding their deliverance they bear their final testimony to the world, so bringing to completion the divine purpose that made them His chosen people. See *SDACom* 6:575.

Elect Lady. The rendering in 2 Jn 1 of the Gr. *eklektē kuria,* literally, "chosen lady." The word *kuria* has been taken by some to be a proper name, which would then be transliterated "Kyria," or "Cyria." However, the Greek construction makes this improbable. The second epistle of John is addressed to this "elect lady and her children." Some believe that John was writing to some specific woman and her literal children, others that he was addressing the church as a whole, or some local church body. A combination of these views seems the most plausible: John was addressing a woman who was a prominent religious worker, and her children, that is, those under her spiritual direction.

Elect Sister. *See* Sister.

El-Elohe-Israel (ĕl'ĕ-lō'hĕ-ĭz'rá-ĕl). [Heb. *'El 'Elohê Yiśra'el*, "God is the god of Israel."] The name given by Jacob to an altar erected at Shechem after his return from Mesopotamia (Gen 33:20).

Elements. [Gr. *stoicheia,* the "elemental substances" of which everything in the natural world is made; the "elementary principles" of learning.] A term used in Gal 4:3, 9, KJV, of the system of heathenism from which the Galatian Christians had been delivered, also of the Jewish legal system as being little better, now that the full revelation through Christ had come. In 2 Pe 3:10, 12 *stoicheia* refers to the constituent elements of the physical universe. In Col 2:8, 20 the same Greek word is translated "rudiments," KJV, "elemental spirits," RSV, and refers to the principles of worldly philosophy. In Heb 5:12 it is rendered "first principles," with reference to the elementary steps that lead to salvation.

Eleph. *See* Ha-eleph.

Elephant. *See* Ivory.

Eleven, The. A term referring to the disciples of Jesus after the apostasy and suicide of Judas (Lk 24:9, 33; Acts 2:14). In Jn 20:24; 1 Cor 15:5 they are still called "the twelve" even though the vacancy left by Judas had not been filled at the time referred to.

Elhanan (ĕl-hā'năn). [Heb. *'Elchanan,* "God is gracious." The name occurs on an ancient Hebrew seal, and in Akkadian as *Ilu-ḫananu.*]

1. A warrior who slew Lahmi, the brother of Goliath of Gath (1 Chr 20:5; cf. 2 Sa 21:19).

2. The son of Dodo of Bethlehem, and one of David's 30 "mighty men" of the 2d rank (2 Sa 23:24; 1 Chr 11:26).

Eli, I. *See* Eloi.

Eli, II (ē'lī). [Heb. *'Elî,* probably a short form of *'Eli'el* occurring in Nabataean, meaning "God is exalted," or of *'Elyah,* meaning "Yahweh is exalted."] A high priest, descended from Aaron's youngest son Ithamar (1 Sa 1:9; 1 Ki 2:27; 1 Chr 24:3, 6). He had become high priest of the tabernacle at Shiloh toward the end of the period of the judges, being the first of his line to hold that office, according to Josephus (*Ant.* v. 11. 5; viii. 1. 3). It is not certain which of Eleazar's descendants was his predecessor, or why the office was changed from one family to the

other. Eli also occupied the office of judge for 40 years (1 Sa 4:18). His two sons, Hophni and Phinehas, who also were priests, were extremely wicked (ch 2:12-17). Because Eli failed to deal firmly with their misconduct, an unnamed prophet denounced his house and predicted its downfall (vs 23-36). Later the boy Samuel, who lived at the tabernacle and ministered "to the Lord under Eli," was given a special revelation confirming this message (ch 3:1-18). A partial fulfillment came when Eli's two sons, who carried the ark to the camp of the Israelites as a hoped-for aid in a war against the Philistines, were slain in battle, and the ark was taken. Eli, who was then 98 years of age, upon receiving the news fell from his chair, broke his neck, and died (ch 4:1-18). The final fulfillment came when Solomon removed Abiathar, Eli's descendant, from the high priesthood (1 Ki 2:26, 35). Thereafter, the descendants of Eleazar held the high priesthood.

Eliab (ē-lī'ăb). [Heb. *'Eli'ab,* "my God is a father." The name occurs in Akkadian as *Ili-abi.*]

1. A head of the tribe of Zebulun during the wilderness wanderings (Num 1:9; 2:7; 7:24, 29; 10:16).

2. A Reubenite, the father of Dathan and Abiram (Num 16:1, 12; 26:8, 9).

3. A Levite who was an ancestor of Samuel (1 Chr 6:27), and possibly the Eliel of v 34.

4. David's eldest brother (1 Sa 17:13, 28), who was tall and of impressive appearance (ch 16:6, 7). His daughter Abihail married David's son Jerimoth (2 Chr 11:18).

5. A Gadite hero who joined the fugitive David at Ziklag (1 Chr 12:1, 8, 9).

6. A Levite musician at the sanctuary in David's reign (1 Chr 15:12, 16, 20).

Eliada (ē-lī'á-dá), KJV once **Eliadah** (ē-lī'á-dá). [Heb. *'Elyada',* "God knows." The name occurs in Akkadian as *Ilum-ida.*]

1. A son of David, born at Jerusalem (2 Sa 5:13-16; 1 Chr 3:8), called Beeliada in 1 Chr 14:7.

2. A man whose son Rezon of Zobah became the founder of a dynasty of kings of Damascus (1 Ki 11:23).

3. A Benjamite, a chief captain of King Jehoshaphat (2 Chr 17:17).

Eliadah. *See* Eliada, 2.

Eliah. *See* Elijah, 2 and 4.

Eliahba (ē-lī'á-bá). [Heb. *'Elyachba',* a name that may contain the name of the Hittite deity Chepa as one of its elements, and may therefore be vocalized as *'Eli Chiba'*, "my god is (the Hittite deity) Cheba (or "Chepa")." An alternative explanation links the name with the verb *chaba'*, "to hide," giving it the meaning "God will hide."] One of David's "mighty men" (2 Sa 23:32; 1 Chr 11:33). Since other Hittites are mentioned among David's soldiers (1 Sa 26:6; 2 Sa 11:3, 6), it would not be strange to find Eliahba bearing a Hittite name.

Eliakim (ê-lī′ă-kĭm). [Heb. *'Elyaqîm,* "God establishes." The name occurs also on an ancient Hebrew seal. Gr. *Eliakim.*]

151. Seal impression of Eliakim, steward of King Jehoiachin, found at *Tell Beit Mirsim,* probably ancient Debir (enlarged)

1. A descendant of David named in Luke's genealogy of Jesus Christ (Lk 3:30, 31).

2. The official who was over King Hezekiah's household, and one of the ministers closest to the king. He was one of those who conferred with *Rabshakeh, Sennacherib's envoy (2 Ki 18:18, 26, 37; Is 36:3, 11, 22), and one of those whom King Hezekiah sent to consult Isaiah in the hope of obtaining a message from God in a time of great crisis (2 Ki 19:2; Is 37:2). God's message to him through Isaiah indicates that he must have been an extraordinarily capable and pious man (Is 22:20-25). The name of his father was Hilkiah (2 Ki 18:18).

3. A son of Josiah. *See* Jehoiakim.

4. A priest who took part in the dedication ceremonies of Jerusalem's wall in Nehemiah's time (Neh 12:27, 41).

5. A descendant of Zerubbabel (KJV "Zorobabel") who appears in Matthew's genealogy of Jesus Christ (Mt 1:13).

Eliam (ê-lī′ăm). [Heb. *'Eli'am,* "my God is a kinsman." The name occurs also on an ancient Hebrew seal.]

1. The father of Bathsheba (2 Sa 11:3). He is called Ammiel in 1 Chr 3:5, the two component parts of the same being transposed.

2. Son of Ahithophel and one of David's "mighty men" (2 Sa 23:8, 34), apparently the same as Eliam, 1.

Elias. *See* Elijah, 1.

Eliasaph (ê-lī′ă-săf). [Heb. *'Elyasaph,* "God has added."]

1. A Gadite tribal head during the wilderness wanderings (Num 1:4, 14; 2:14; 7:42).

2. A Levite head of the Gershonite family in the wilderness (Num 3:24).

Eliashib (ê-lī′ă-shĭb). [Heb. *'Elyashîb,* "God restores."]

1. A priest, some of whose descendants formed the 11th of the 24 courses into which David divided the priests (1 Chr 24:1, 12).

2, 3, and 4. Three Jews who had married foreign wives in the time of Ezra. One was a Levite, while the other two belonged to the families of Zattu and Bani, respectively (Ezr 10:24, 27, 36).

5. A high priest in the time of Ezra and Nehemiah. He was the grandson of Jeshua, the high priest under Zerubbabel. He and the priests built the Sheep Gate of Jerusalem under Nehemiah (Neh 12:10; 3:1). He was allied, probably by marriage, to Tobiah, the Ammonite enemy of Nehemiah, and to Sanballat, another foe of Nehemiah, by the marriage of his grandson to the daughter of Sanballat (ch 13:4, 28). During Nehemiah's absence from Jerusalem, Eliashib provided Tobiah with a room within the Temple area (ch 13:5).

6. A descendant of Zerubbabel (1 Chr 3:24).

Eliathah (ê-lī′ă-thá). [Heb. *'Eli'athah,* "my God comes."] A son of Heman and a musician in the time of King David (1 Chr 25:4, 27).

Elidad (ê-lī′dăd). [Heb. *'Elidad,* "my God loves," or "my God is a friend."] A Benjamite tribal head who was on the commission to divide the land of Canaan among the 12 tribes (Num 34:17, 21).

Eliehoenai (ê-lī′ê-hō-ē′nī), KJV once **Elioenai** (ê-lī′ō-ē′nī), once **Elihoenai** (ĕl′ī-hō-ē′nī). [Heb. *'Elyehô'ênay,* "my eyes are toward Yahweh," with which may be compared the Akkadian name *Itti-Nabû-îniya,* "my eyes are with (the god) Nabu."]

1. A Korahite gatekeeper (1 Chr 26:3).

2. A member of the family of Pahathmoab, who, with 200 other male mem-

bers of his family, returned with Ezra from Babylonia (Ezr 8:4).

Eliel (ē'lĭ-ĕl). [Heb. *'Eli'el*, "El is my God," or "my God is god." The name occurs in Akkadian as *Elili*.]

1. A Kohathite Levite, an ancestor of the prophet Samuel (1 Chr 6:34, probably the same as the Eliab of v 27).

2 and 3. Two of David's "mighty men" (1 Chr 11:46, 47).

4. A Gadite warrior who came to David at Ziklag before he had become king (1 Chr 12:1, 8, 11).

5. A Levite of the time of David (1 Chr 15:9, 11).

6 and 7. Two Benjamites of whom nothing but their fathers' names is known (1 Chr 8:20, 22).

8. A family chief of the half tribe of Manasseh in Transjordan (1 Chr 5:24).

9. An officer under King Hezekiah assisting the chief officer in charge of offerings and tithes (2 Chr 31:13).

Elienai (ĕl'ĭ-ē'nī). [Heb. *'Eli'ênay*, probably a contraction of *'Eliyehô'ênay*, "my eyes are toward Yahweh."] A Benjamite, son of Shimei (1 Chr 8:20, 21).

Eliezer (ĕl'ĭ-ē'zẽr). [Heb. *'Eli'ezer*, "my God is a helper." Gr. *Eliezer*.]

1. A servant of Abraham, born in his household, but probably descended from an Aramaean from Damascus (Gen 15:2-4). It was doubtless this Eliezer who was sent to Mesopotamia to obtain a wife for Isaac (ch 24).

2. The younger son of Moses (Ex 18:4; 1 Chr 23:15, 17).

3. A Benjamite (1 Chr 7:8).

4. A captain over the Reubenites under King David (1 Chr 27:16).

5. A priest who blew the ·trumpet before the ark in the reign of David (1 Chr 15:24).

6. A prophet of Mareshah who told King Jehoshaphat that because he had joined with Ahaziah of Israel, the wicked son of Ahab, in building a fleet, his ships would be destroyed (2 Chr 20:37).

7. An Israelite whom Ezra sent out to solicit Levites to return from Babylonia (Ezr 8:15-17).

8. A priest of Ezra's time who had married a foreign wife (Ezr 10:18).

9. A Levite of Ezra's time who had married a foreign wife (Ezr 10:23).

10. An Israelite of Ezra's time who had married a foreign wife. He was of the family of Harim (Ezr 10:31).

11. A Judahite appearing in Luke's genealogy of Christ (Lk 3:29).

Elihoenai. *See* Eliehoenai, 2.

Elihoreph (ĕl'ĭ-hō'rĕf). [Heb. *'Elichoreph*.] One of Solomon's scribes (1 Ki 4:3).

Elihu (ĕ-lī'hū). [Heb. *'Elihû'*, "he is my God."]

1. An ancestor of Samuel, the prophet (1 Sa 1:1).

2. One of the brothers of David (1 Chr 27:18).

3. A Manassite captain who joined David's company when David was on his way to Ziklag (1 Chr 12:20).

4. A gatekeeper of the family of Obed-edom under David (1 Chr 26:1, 4, 7).

5. A man from Buz, one of Job's friends (Job 32:2, 5, 6; 34:1; etc.).

Elijah (ĕ-lī'já), KJV twice **Eliah** (ĕ-lī'á), KJV of NT **Elias** (ĕ-lī'ăs). [Heb. *'Eliyahû* and *'Eliyah*, "Yahweh is my God"; Gr. *Elias*. The name occurs in Akkadian as *Ilu-yâu*.]

1. God's special messenger to the northern kingdom of Israel during the great apostasy under Ahab (c. 874-853 B.C.) and Jezebel, when Baal worship practically supplanted the worship of the true God. He is identified only as "the *Tishbite" (1 Ki 17:1). A man of great faith in God and bold zeal for God, Elijah easily qualifies among the greatest of the prophets. The high esteem in which the Jews of later centuries held Elijah is evident from the popular expectation, based on the prediction of Mal 4:5, 6, that the prophet would return to earth to herald the imminent appearance of the Messiah

152. A place on Mount Carmel pointed out as the traditional site of Elijah's sacrifice

(see Mt 17:10-12). Jesus identified the ministry of John the Baptist with that predicted by Malachi (ch 11:14), having already declared that there was none greater than John (v 11). So far as is known, Elijah was the only person, except Enoch, ever honored by translation to heaven without seeing death (2 Ki 2:11, 12). He was also chosen to accompany Moses, the great lawgiver, at the transfiguration of Christ (Mt 17:3).

When Ahab began his reign, a little more than half a century had passed since the death of Solomon and the division of the kingdom, since which time Israel, the northern kingdom, had rapidly lapsed into apostasy. But Ahab "did evil in the sight of the Lord above all that were before him," in that he married Jezebel, daughter of a Phoenician king, and adopted her religion, thus becoming a worshiper of Baal (1 Ki 16:30, 31). Not only so, but he erected a temple to Baal in Samaria (vs 32, 33) and thus "Ahab did more to provoke the Lord God of Israel to anger than all the kings of Israel that were before him" (v 33). Such were conditions when the Lord commissioned Elijah to visit Ahab at court and announce a severe drought of unspecified duration (ch 17:1) as remedial punishment. The prophet was then instructed to flee for safety to the brook *Cherith, a seasonal tributary of the Jordan River (vs 2, 3), where he was sustained for a time by food miraculously provided (vs 4-6). When the brook dried up, Elijah was instructed to leave Israel altogether and find refuge in Zarephath (see figs. 500, 534), a Sidonian town (NT Sarepta; see Lk 4:26, KJV). There God again made miraculous provision to sustain him (1 Ki 17:7-16) and by him raised to life the son of the widow whose hospitality had given him a temporary home (vs 17-24). After some 3½ years (see Lk 4:25, 26), during which Ahab had spared no effort to find the prophet and bring him to account for the famine (1 Ki 18:10), which had become increasingly severe (vs 2-6), God instructed Elijah to appear once more at Ahab's court (vs 1, 2). The intensity of the famine and the gravity with which Ahab viewed the situation are reflected in the apprehensive reaction of Obadiah, the officer over Ahab's house, to whom Elijah presented himself (vs 7-14). Ahab's initial challenge upon meeting Elijah, "Art thou he that troubleth Israel?" was promptly silenced by the divine indictment that Ahab himself was to blame

for the plight of the nation, and by the order for the king to appear forthwith on Mount Carmel, together with all the prophets of Baal and Asherah (1 Ki 18:17-19). On Carmel the issue of Baal versus the Lord as the true God was put to a dramatic test designed to bring king and people to a decision in the matter (vs 20-40). The prophets of Baal were first given an opportunity to demonstrate their god's power by having him bring fire down from heaven to consume the sacrifice offered to him (vs 22-29), but Baal proved impotent to do so. Elijah then repaired the Lord's altar that had fallen into disrepair, laid a sacrifice upon the altar, drenched it all with water, and then called upon God to vindicate His name. The Lord responded by sending a bolt of fire that consumed the sacrifice, the altar, and the water (vs 30-38). The people acknowledged the Lord as the true God, and at the command of Elijah slew all the prophets of Baal (vs 39, 40). Then, to prove that the drought had been a divine judgment upon the land, and as a sequel to the people's admission that the Lord is the true God, an abundance of rain fell (vs 41-46).

Enraged at the turn of events, Jezebel threatened the prophet's life, with the result that he took refuge in hasty flight southward to the Wilderness of Sinai, where he lodged in a cave; once more he was miraculously sustained (1 Ki 19:1-9). When summoned by the Lord to account for his inglorious flight from the threat to his life by Jezebel, Elijah protested that he alone of all Israel had remained loyal to God, and that now even his life was in jeopardy (vs 10-14). Thereupon God tactfully rebuked His erring prophet and appointed him further tasks—the anointing of Jehu as king of Israel in the place of Ahab, of Hazael as the scourge of Israel because of its apostasy, and of Elisha as Elijah's successor (vs 15-21). After an unspecified length of time, during which Ahab and Jezebel murdered Naboth to secure Naboth's hereditary allotment of land, Elijah went to meet the king, who was on his way to take possession of the land, and announced the fate that awaited Ahab and Jezebel and the entire royal family because of their apostasy and impenitence (ch 21). Upon Ahab's death his son Ahaziah succeeded him briefly upon the throne (ch 22:40). Falling ill, Ahaziah appealed to the Baal of Ekron, but his messengers encountered Elijah on the way, who bade them return to their master with the announcement that he would die (2 Ki 1:1-4). Ahaziah sent for the prophet by 3 companies of soldiers. The first 2 were miraculously consumed by fire, but the last was preserved because of the submission of its leader (vs 5-16). Soon after this event Elijah's ministry came to a close and he was translated to heaven (ch 2:1-11). Elisha, present to witness the event, was endowed with the power and authority that had been Elijah's and was established in the prophetic office (vs 12-15).

2. A son of Jeroham of the tribe of Benjamin, who lived at Jerusalem (1 Chr 8:27, KJV "Eliah").

3. A priest, a son of Harim. He was married to a foreign wife in the time of Ezra (Ezr 10:21).

4. An Israelite, son of Elam. He was among those who had foreign wives in the time of Ezra (Ezr 10:26, KJV "Eliah").

Elika (ê-lī′kà). [Heb. *'Elîqa'*, meaning uncertain.] One of David's "mighty men" (2 Sa 23:25).

Elim (ē′lĭm). [Heb. *'Êlim,* "large trees."] A place between Marah and the desert of Sin where the Israelites made their 2d encampment after they had crossed the Red Sea. At Elim were 12 springs and 70 palm trees (Ex 15:27; 16:1; Num 33:9, 10). It is generally identified with the

153. The oasis in the *Wâdî Gharandel,* on the Sinai Peninsula; generally identified as ancient Elim

Wâdî Gharandel, about 60 mi. southeast of Suez (Map V, C-4), which has a rich vegetation of palm trees, tamarisks, and acacias, and a permanent source of water, which produces 1,260 U.S. gal. per minute.

Elimelech (ê-lĭm′ê-lĕk). [Heb. *'Elimelek,* "my God is king." The name occurs in Ugaritic as *'lmlk,* and in the Amarna Letters as *Ilimilku.*] The husband of Naomi of Bethlehem (Ruth 1:2, 3).

Elioenai (ê-lī′ō-ē′nī). [Heb. *'Elyô'ênay,* "my eyes are toward Yahweh," with which may be compared the Akkadian name *Itti-Nabû-iniya,* "my eyes are with (the god) Nabu."]

1. A descendant of Judah (1 Chr 3:23).

2. A Simeonite (1 Chr 4:24, 36).

3. A Benjamite (1 Chr 7:8).

4. A Jew of the family of Pashhur. He was married to a foreign wife in the time of Ezra (Ezr 10:22).

5. A Jew of the family of Zattu. He was married to a foreign wife in the time of Ezra (Ezr 10:27).

6. For 1 Chr 26:3, KJV, *see* Eliehoenai, 1.

Eliphal (ê-lī′făl). [Heb. *'Eliphal,* "God has judged."] One of David's "mighty men" (1 Chr 11:35).

Eliphalet. *See* Eliphelet, 2.

Eliphaz (ĕl′ĭ-făz). [Heb. *'Eliphaz,* possibly "God is fine gold."]

1. A son of Esau. His mother's name was Adah (Gen 36:4).

2. One of Job's friends, a Temanite (Job 2:11; 4:1; etc.). He was probably a descendant of Eliphaz, 1, who had a son named Teman (Gen 36:11).

Elipheleh. *See* Eliphelehu.

Eliphelehu (ê-lĭf-ê-lē′hū), KJV **Elipheleh** (ê-lĭf′ê-lĕ). [Heb. *'Eliphelehû,* "God distinguishes him."] A Levite singer, musician, and one of the porters who helped bring the ark from the house of Obed-edom (1 Chr 15:14; 15:3, 15-21).

Eliphelet (ê-lĭf′ê-lĕt), KJV twice **Eliphalet** (ê-lĭf′à-lĕt). [Heb. *'Eliphelet,* "my God is deliverance."]

1. A son of David born in Jerusalem (1 Chr 3:6); probably the Elpalet (ĕl-pā′-lĕt) [Heb. *'Elpalet*] (RSV "Elpelet," ĕl-pē′-lĕt) of ch 14:5.

2. Another son of David, also born in Jerusalem, perhaps after the death of Eliphelet, 1 (2 Sa 5:16; 1 Chr 3:8; 14:7).

3. One of David's "mighty men" (2 Sa 23:34).

4. A descendant of Saul through Jonathan (1 Chr 8:33, 39).

5. A member of the family of Adonikam. He returned from Babylonia with Ezra (Ezr 8:13).

6. A Jew of the family of Hashum. He was married to a foreign wife in Ezra's time (Ezr 10:33).

Elisabeth. *See* Elizabeth.

Eliseus. *See* Elisha.

Elisha (ĕ-lī′shȧ), KJV of NT **Eliseus** (ĕl′ĭ-sē′ŭs). [Heb. *'Elîsha'*, probably "God is salvation." The name occurs on an Aramaic ostracon found at *Nimrûd.* Gr. *Elissaios.*] Son of Shaphat, of Abel-meholah; the prophet who succeeded Elijah as God's special envoy to the northern kingdom of Israel. His ministry as pastor-prophet spanned the reigns of Jehoram (Joram), Jehu, Jehoahaz, and Jehoash of the northern kingdom, and thus lasted from at least 852 B.C. to about 798 B.C., a period of more than half a century. On the national scene he completed the eradication of Baal worship begun by Elijah, counseled the king of Israel on national policy, and took an intense personal interest in the problems and needs of the individuals with whom his ministry brought him into contact. He supervised the so-named "schools of the prophets" founded 2 cent. earlier by Samuel, and thus made what was perhaps his greatest single contribution to the spiritual life of the nation. In the presence of need he was ever solicitous and largehearted; in the presence of a limited understanding of the divine will he was tolerant and patient; in the presence of danger he manifested firm unflinching courage; in the presence of evil he was stern and severe without being vindictive. Whereas Elijah tended to be ascetic in dress and diet, in place of abode, and in his limited contacts with people—at least in so far as the record goes

154. "Elisha's spring" at Jericho

—Elisha lived close to the people he served, and loved social life. Unlike the life of Elijah, who appeared on the stage of sacred history for a few striking events, Elisha's life is recorded as a steady ministry during which he constantly ministered to the needs of his fellow men as individuals, as well as to the spiritual life of the nation as a whole. Although for a time there seems to have been an encouraging response on the part of the nation to his leadership as a prophet, the reforms he set in motion were short-lived and did not prevent the complete dissolution of the northern kingdom some 75 years after his death.

The life narrative of the prophet Elisha seems, almost, to be one of an uninterrupted succession of miracles, some consisting essentially of supernatural information, and others of supernatural control over men and the forces of nature. In an era of apostasy and Baal worship, these miracles provided a continuing witness to the Lord as the true God and to Elisha as His messenger. Elisha is distinguished in the annals of sacred history as the greatest miracle-working prophet of all time, next to Jesus Christ.

Abel-meholah, a town of the upper Jordan Valley, was Elisha's home until his call to the prophetic office. At the time of his call he was following the plow (1 Ki 19:19-21). For an unspecified period of time he was a personal attendant of Elijah (2 Ki 3:11). His immediate response to Elijah's call and his persistence in accompanying the prophet to the place of his translation testify to the earnestness with which Elisha took up his appointed work (ch 2:1-12). Returning from Elijah's ascension, Elisha miraculously sweetened the brackish waters of a spring at Jericho (vs 19-22), and on the way from there to Bethel pronounced a curse upon a group of godless youth who ridiculed him as God's messenger (vs 23-25). Later, he miraculously provided water for an expedition by kings Jehoram of Israel and Jehoshaphat of Judah to suppress a revolt in Moab, and assured these kings of success (ch 3:6-27). He provided assistance for the widow of one of the sons of the prophets when she was in financial straits (ch 4:1-7), and at another time foretold the birth of a son to a Shunammite woman who had befriended him, and later raised this son back to life when he died (vs 8-37). During a famine he provided an antidote for poison gourds as a group of the sons of the prophets sat at table (vs 38-41), and miraculously satisfied the hunger of 100 men with 20 barley loaves and a few ears of ripe grain (2 Ki 4: 42:44). He cured Naaman's leprosy (ch 5:1-19) and foretold Gehazi's fate as a leper when the latter dishonored the prophetic office (vs 20-27). He procured the recovery of a valuable axhead that had been lost in the Jordan (ch 6:1-7). He counseled the king of Israel in defending the nation against a Syrian invasion (vs 8-12), and when he was himself surrounded at Dothan, led a group of Syrian soldiers to Samaria, presented them to the king, and then released them to return home (vs 13-23). At another time when Syrian forces had reduced Samaria by siege to the point of famine he foretold an abundance of food on the morrow, implying the lifting of the siege (chs 6:24-31; 7:1-20). He predicted the arrival of a messenger sent to arrest him (ch 6:32, 33). He declared the destruction of the house of Ahab, because of apostasy, and arranged for the anointing of Jehu as king (chs 9:1 to 10:28). His last recorded act was the encouragement of King Jehoash to defend Israel against the Syrians (ch 13:14-19). After Elisha's death another man hastily buried in the same tomb during an emergency was miraculously restored to life when his body touched Elisha's bones (vs 20, 21).

Elishah (ĕ-lī'shà). [Heb. *'Elîshah*.] A son of Javan (Gen 10:4; 1 Chr 1:7). The "isles" or "coasts" (RSV) of Elishah furnished blue and purple cloth for Tyre (Eze 27:7). Since Elishah's father, Javan, was the progenitor of the Greeks, the territory of Elishah must be sought on islands or coasts colonized by Greeks. Because of a similarity of names, Aeolis, Elis, and Hellas have all been identified with Elishah. But if literal "isles" are intended, they may be those of Sardinia and Sicily. (Map IV, B-3, assigns "Elisha" to Sicily and the southern tip of Italy.)

Elishama (ĕ-lĭsh'à-mà). [Heb. *'Elîshama'*, "my God has heard." The name appears on ancient Hebrew seals and in South Arabic inscriptions.]

1. An Ephraimite who was made a tribal chieftain at the beginning of the wilderness wandering (Num 1:10; 2:18). He was the grandfather of Joshua (1 Chr 7:26, 27, RSV).

2. A member of the tribe of Judah (1 Chr 2:41).

3. A son of David, born in Jerusalem (1 Chr 3:6), called Elishua in 2 Sa 5:15 and 1 Chr 14:5.

4. Another son of David, also born in Jerusalem (2 Sa 5:16; 1 Chr 3:8; 14:7).

5. A priest sent by King Jehoshaphat of Judah to teach the Law of God in the cities of Judah (2 Chr 17:7-9).

6. A prince and scribe in the reign of King Jehoiakim of Judah (Jer 36:9, 12, 20, 21).

7. The grandfather of the Ishmael who murdered Gedaliah, the governor of Judah installed by the Babylonians after the destruction of Jerusalem (2 Ki 25:25; Jer 41:1, 2). Probably identical with Elishama, 6.

Elishaphat (ē-lĭsh'à-făt). [Heb. *'Elîshaphaṭ*, "my God has judged."] One of the captains who assisted Jehoiada in the revolt against Queen Athaliah (2 Chr 23:1-15).

Elisheba (ĕ-lĭsh'ĕ-bà). [Heb. *'Elîsheba'*, possibly "my God is fullness," or "my God has sworn."] A daughter of Amminadab of the tribe of Judah. She became Aaron's wife, and the mother of Nadab, Abihu, Eleazar, and Ithamar (Ex 6:23).

Elishua (ĕl'ĭ-shū'à). [Heb. *'Elîshûa'*, "my God is salvation."] A son of David, born in Jerusalem (2 Sa 5:15; 1 Chr 14:5); called Elishama in 1 Chr 3:6.

Eliud (ĕ-lī'ŭd). [Gr. *Elioud*, a transliteration of the Heb. *'Elîhôd*, "my God is majesty."] A Judahite appearing in Matthew's genealogy of Jesus Christ (Mt 1:14, 15).

Elizabeth (ē-lĭz'à-bĕth), KJV **Elisabeth** (ē-lĭz'à-bĕth). [Gr. *Elisabet*, a transliteration of the Heb. *'Elîsheba'*, possibly either "my God is fullness" or "my God has sworn."] The wife of the priest Zacharias, and a descendant of Aaron (Lk 1:5), bearing the name of Aaron's wife Elisheba (Ex 6:23). She became the mother of John the Baptist at an advanced age, as an angel had predicted to her husband (Lk 1:5-25, 57). She was related to Mary, the mother of Jesus (v 36), although the two belonged to different tribes. When Mary visited Elizabeth's home in the hill country of Judea, Elizabeth was inspired by the Holy Spirit to address Mary as the mother of the Lord (vs 39-45).

Elizaphan (ĕl'ĭ-zā'făn). [Heb. *'Elîṣaphan*, "my God conceals" or "my God protects."]

1. A Kohathite Levite who served in the tabernacle and assisted in the removal of the bodies of Nadab and Abihu (Ex 6: 18, 22; Lev 10:4; Num 3:30), called Elzaphan (ĕl-zā'făn) [Heb. *'Elṣaphan*] in Ex 6:22; Lev 10:4. A family was called after him (1 Chr 15:8; 2 Chr 29:13).

2. A prince of the tribe of Zebulun during the Exodus (Num 34:25).

Elizur (ĕ-lī′zēr). [Heb. *'Elîṣûr*, "my God is a rock."] A prince of the tribe of Reuben during the wilderness journey (Num 1:5; 2:10).

Elkanah (ĕl-kā′nȧ). [Heb. *'Elqanah*, "God has redeemed," or "God has created." The name occurs in Akkadian as *Ilu-qanâ*.]

1. A Kohathite Levite and grandson of Korah (Ex 6:24; 1 Chr 6:23).

2. Son of Joel and descendant of Elkanah, 1 (1 Chr 6:25, 36).

3. A descendant of Elkanah, 2 (1 Chr 6: 26, 35).

4. A descendant of Elkanah, 3, and father of Samuel (1 Chr 6:27, 34; cf. v 33). He lived, with his wives Hannah and Peninnah, in Ramathaim-zophim in the hill country of Ephraim and so was called an Ephraimite (1 Sa 1:1; 2:11, 20).

5. One of David's "mighty men" who joined him at Ziklag before he became king (1 Chr 12:6).

6. A gatekeeper for the ark in David's time (1 Chr 15:23).

7. A high official under King Ahaz, slain when Pekah attacked Jerusalem (2 Chr 28:7).

8. A Levite who dwelt in a village of the Netophathites (1 Chr 9:16).

Elkosh. *See* Elkoshite.

Elkoshite (ĕl′kŏsh-īt). [Heb. *'Elqoshî*.] A designation of the prophet Nahum (Nah 1: 1, KJV), probably meaning that he was a native or citizen of Elkosh (ĕl′kŏsh). However, Elkosh cannot definitely be identified. A late tradition identifies it with Alkush in Assyria, and claims that Nahum was born of parents in exile. Another tradition sees in Nahum's point of origin the town of Elcesi in Galilee. The attempt to connect Nahum with Galilee may have had its origin in the fact that Capernaum, which means "village of Nahum," was in Galilee. Another tradition places Nahum's home town near *Beit Jibrîn* in the Shephelah of Judah.

Ellasar (ĕl-lā′sär). [Heb. *'Ellasar*.] The city or country ruled by Arioch, one of the kings who under Chedorlaomer invaded Transjordan in the time of Abraham (Gen 14:1, 9). For a long time Ellasar was identified with the city of Larsa in southern Mesopotamia (Map III, C-6), but this identification poses grave problems, in that it leaves the formative *'el* unexplained, and reverses the sequence of the last two consonants. Recently, scholars have sought Ellasar in northern Mesopotamia. W. F. Albright (*BASOR* 78 [1940], 29, n. 43) and R. de Vaux (*RB* 55 [1948], 333) have suggested identifying it with *Ilanzura*, a city between Carchemish and Haran in northern Mesopotamia. This city is mentioned in a Hittite text and in the Mari Letters.

Elm. [Heb. *'elah*.] A term appearing once (Hos 4:13, KJV), but the type of tree designated by the Hebrew term is uncertain. The terebinth (*Pistacia terebinthus*, var. *palaestina*), a turpentine-producing tree, has been suggested (see RSV). The modern elm is a large spreading tree of the *Ulmacaea* family, but this obviously is not the tree intended.

Elmadam (ĕl-mā′dăm), KJV **Elmodam** (ĕl-mō′dăm). [Gr. *Elmadam*, of unknown Hebrew origin and meaning.] A Judahite appearing in Luke's genealogy of Jesus Christ (Lk 3:28).

Elmodam. *See* Elmadam.

Elnaam (ĕl-nā′ăm). [Heb. *'Elna'am*, "God is graciousness." The name occurs also on an ancient Hebrew seal.] The father either of Jeribai and Joshaviah, two of David's "mighty men," or of some unnamed members of the same corps (1 Chr 11:46).

Elnathan (ĕl-nā′thăn). [Heb. *'Elnathan*, "God has given." The name occurs also on an ancient Hebrew seal, and in ancient Hebrew inscriptions found at Gibeon.]

1. The father of Nehushta, the mother of King Jehoiachin of Judah (2 Ki 24:8); possibly identical with Elnathan, 2.

2. A prince of Judah who lived in Jerusalem (Jer 26:22; 36:12, 25); possibly identical with Elnathan, 1.

3, 4, and 5. Three of the men whom Ezra sent back from Ahava to induce some Levites and Nethinim to join his company of returning exiles (Ezr 8:15, 16).

Eloi (ĕ-lō′ī), or **Eli, I** (ē′lī). [Gr. *Elōi*, a transliteration of the Aramaic *'Elahî*, "my God," and *Ēli*, a transliteration of the Heb. *'Elî*, "my God."] An expression occurring in Mk 15:34; Mt 27:46 in Christ's exclamation on the cross, "Eloi (Eli), Eloi (Eli), lama sabachthani?" meaning "My God, my God, why hast thou forsaken me?" The quotation is from Ps 22:1.

Elon (ē′lŏn). [Heb. *'Êlôn*, "terebinth."]

1. A Hittite whose daughter was married to Esau (Gen 26:34; 36:2).

2. A son of Zebulun and founder of a tribal family, the Elonites (ē′lŏn-īts) [Heb. *'Elonî*] (Gen 46:14; Num 26:26).

3. A Zebulunite who judged Israel 10 years. He was buried in Aijalon in Zebulun (Jgs 12:11, 12).

4. A village in the territory of Dan (Jos 19:43); not identified.

Elon-beth-hanan (ē'lŏn-bĕth-hā'năn). [Heb. *'Êlôn Bêth-Chanan*.] Possibly two geographical names, Elon and Beth-hanan (1 Ki 4:9); possibly the same place as Elon in Dan, which is not now identified. Some identify it with Aijalon, 1.

Elonites. *See* Elon, 2.

Eloth. *See* Elath.

Elpaal (ĕl-pā'ăl). [Heb. *'Elpa'al*, "God has wrought."] An ancestor of a Benjamite family (1 Chr 8:11, 12, 18).

Elpalet. *See* Eliphelet, 1.

El-paran (ĕl-pā'răn). [Heb. *'Êl Pa'ran*, "mighty tree of Paran."] A place in the southern part of Palestine (Gen 14:6), either identical with *Elath at the Gulf of Aqabah or yet unidentified.

Elpelet. *See* Eliphelet, 1.

Elteke (ĕl'tĕ-kē), KJV **Eltekeh** (ĕl'tĕ-kē). [Heb. *'Elteqeh* and *'Elteqe'*. The town is called *Altaqû* in Assyrian records.] A town in the territory of Dan assigned to the Levites (Jos 19:40, 44; 21:20, 23). Sennacherib of Assyria in 701 B.C. defeated the Egyptians in the plain of Eltekeh, and afterward besieged and destroyed the city of Eltekeh (*ANET* 287, 288). The site was identified by W. F. Albright (*AASOR* 2-3 [1923], 5) with *Khirbet el-Muqenna'*, 22 mi. west of Jerusalem (Map VI, E-2). Since the latter site is now believed to be the location of Ekron, a new search has to be made for Eltekeh (see *IEJ* 8 [1958], 170).

Eltekeh. *See* Elteke.

Eltekon (ĕl'tĕ-kŏn). [Heb. *'Elteqon*.] A city in the hill country of Judah (Jos 15:59); not identified with certainty.

Eltolad (ĕl-tō'lăd). [Heb. *'Eltôlad*.] A village in the southern part of Judah—called Tolad (tō'lăd) [Heb. *Tôlad*] in 1 Chr 4:29; assigned to the tribe of Simeon (Jos 15:21, 30; 19:4); not identified.

Elul (ē-lōōl'). [Heb. *'Elûl*; Akkadian *Ulûlu* and *Elûlu*.] The 6th month of the Jewish religious year (Neh 6:15), beginning at the new moon of August or September. *See* Year.

Eluzai (ē-lū'ză-ī). [Heb. *'El'ûzay*, meaning uncertain.] One of David's "mighty men" who joined him at Ziklag (1 Chr 12:5).

Elymas. *See* Bar-Jesus.

Elzabad (ĕl-zā'băd). [Heb. *'Elzabad*, "God has given."]
1. One of the Gadites who joined David in Ziklag (1 Chr 12:12).
2. A Levite doorkeeper of the house of Obed-edom in the time of David (1 Chr 26:7, 8).

Elzaphan. *See* Elizaphan, 1.

Embalming. A method of preserving dead bodies not generally practiced by the Hebrews, but a general custom in Egypt. Jacob and Joseph, both of whom died in Egypt, were embalmed according to Egyptian methods (Gen 50:2, 3, 26). Whether King Asa of Judah was embalmed before his burial is not certain (2 Chr 16:14). It is evident that the friends of Christ planned to preserve His body by some sort of embalming (Lk 23: 56; 24:1; Jn 19:39, 40). Embalming in Egypt was practiced perhaps as early as the 1st dynasty, and this practice continued throughout its history up to the 8th cent. A.D. Information for the later period comes from Herodotus (ii. 86-88) and Diodorus Siculus (i. 91) and, for the earlier period, from ancient records and the study of actual mummies. The methods used were not always the same. During the 2d millennium B.C., when Jacob and Joseph were embalmed, the following procedures were followed: The intestines were removed, but not the heart and kidneys, and the brain was drawn through the nose by means of a metal hook. These organs were then put in a natron solution in four canopic jars, each of which stood under the patronage of one of the four sons of the god Horus. The body was put in a salt solution for some time, and after that the cavities created by the removal of the internal organs were filled with myrrh, cassia, cinnamon, and other spices. The whole body was then rolled in linen bandages from 700 to 1,000 yards long. The mummy was placed in a cartonnage shaped in the form of the deceased, imitating as much as possible his features. This cartonnage coffin was then put in a wooden coffin or in a stone sarcophagus, if the deceased was wealthy enough to pay for one of these. The Egyptian texts frequently mention 70 days as the time of embalming, after which the burial took place, but shorter or longer periods are also mentioned. Jacob's embalming is given as having lasted 40 days, after which a 70-day mourning followed (Gen 50:2, 3).

Emek-keziz (ē'mĕk-kē'zĭz), KJV **Valley of Keziz** (kē'zĭz). [Heb. *'Emeq Qeṣiṣ*.] A valley near Beth-hoglah and Jericho (Jos 18:21); not identified.

Emerald. [Heb. *nophek* from Egyptian *mfk3t*, "turquoise"; Gr. *smaragdos*.] A green-colored and transparent variety of beryl, a double silicate of beryllium and aluminum. However, the exact stone represented by *nophek* is uncertain. If by the term the Hebrews designated the stone the Egyptians called *mfk3t,* then almost certainly turquoise is meant. Some suggest malachite. The gem is mentioned as the 1st stone in the 2d row of the high priest's breastplate (Ex 28:18; 39:11) and as an adornment of the king of Tyre (Eze 28:12, 13). Less doubt exists that the emerald was in John's mind as he described the rainbow above God's throne (Rev 4:3) and the 4th foundation of the New Jerusalem (ch 21:19).

Emerods. The translation in the KJV of: (1) the Heb. *ṭechorîm,* some form of tumors, probably "hemorrhoids" (1 Sa 6:11, 17); (2) the Heb. *'ophalîm,* "tumors," "boils" (Deut 28:27; 1 Sa 5:6, 9, 12; 6:4, 5). The account in 1 Sa 5 and 6 uses both terms to describe the infliction visited upon the Philistines for taking the ark.

Emim (ē'mǐm), KJV **Emims** (ē'mǐmz). [Heb. *'Êmîm,* "terrible men" or "frightening men."] The name the Moabites gave to the * Rephaim, whose country they occupied (Deut 2:10, 11).

Emims. See Emim.

Eminent Place. The translation in the KJV of Eze 16:24, 31, 39, of the Heb. *gab,* protuberance, whether a feature of the body, of the surface of the earth, or in architecture, or otherwise. Ezekiel seems to describe, as reliefs from Asshur seem to indicate, a platform before the altar, set apart for ritual prostitution (O. Eissfeldt, *JPOS* 16 [1936], 289-292). The RSV conjecturally renders *gab* "vaulted chamber."

Emmanuel. See Immanuel.

Emmaus (ĕ-mā'ŭs). [Gr. *Emmaous.*] A village which, according to the best textual evidence, lay 60 stadia (about 7 mi.) from Jerusalem (Lk 24:13). The site has not yet been conclusively identified. Josephus (*War* vii. 6. 6) says that Titus had a colony of soldiers at *'Ammaous,* 30 stadia (about 3½ mi.) from Jerusalem; this is probably *Qalôniyeh,* about 5 mi. to the northwest of Jerusalem. Since the time of the crusaders, *Kubeibeh,* 7 mi. northwest of Jerusalem on the Roman road, has been pointed out as Emmaus; however, some scholars have identified it with the modern *'Amwâs* in the Shephelah (the Emmaus of 1 Macc 3:40, 57; etc.). See Map XVI, E-2. But this is 15 mi. from Jerusalem and too far for Lk 24:13.

Emmor. See Hamor.

Enaim (ĕ-nā'ĭm). [Heb. *'Enayim,* "two springs."] A town or village on the road

155. The village of En-dor

from Adullam to Timnah (Gen 38:14, 21, RSV). The translators of the KJV did not recognize *'Enayim* as the name of a town and rendered it once as "open place" and once as "openly." Enaim is probably identical with Enam.

Enam (ē'năm). [Heb. *'Enam.* Probably a short form of *Enaim,* "two springs."] A place in the Shephelah of Judah (Jos 15:34); probably identical with Enaim.

Enan (ē'năn). [Heb. *'Enan,* meaning uncertain.] A Naphtalite whose son Ahira was a tribal prince (Num 1:15; 2:29; etc.).

Encampment. See Camp.

Enchanter. The translation in the RSV of the Heb. *'ashshaphîm* and the Aramaic *'ashephîn* in Dan 1:20; 2:2; etc. (see Astrologers). In the KJV the term occurs twice, once (Deut 18:10) as the rendering of a word derived from the Heb. *nachash,* "to look for an omen," "to divine," and once (Jer 27:9) as the rendering of a word derived from the Heb. *'anan,* "to appear," or "to cause to appear," hence probably a spirit medium.

Enchantment. Any of various procedures employed in the occult or magic arts whereby supernatural power is invoked to produce desired effects or to gain information (Ex 7:22; Is 47:9; etc.). Sorcery was used to produce magic spells. Soothsaying was the foretelling of future events. In astrology the stars were observed in order to ascertain the will of the gods or to predict the future. Necromancy was the supposed communication with the dead. Divination took various forms, such as examining the entrails of sacrificial animals, the interpretation of dreams, or the observation of various aspects of the natural world. In the Bible the various forms of enchantment are referred to by various names (*see* Divination; Magic).

En-dor (ĕn′dôr). [Heb. *'Ên Dor,* "spring of habitation."] A town in the territory of Manasseh in western Palestine (Jos 17: 11). The psalmist locates Sisera's defeat by Barak in the vicinity of En-dor (Ps 83: 9, 10). It was the home town of the spiritistic medium whom Saul consulted shortly before his last battle against the Philistines (1 Sa 28:8-25). It has been identified with *Endôr,* about 7 mi. southeast of Nazareth (Map VI, C-3). See fig. 155.

En-eglaim (ĕn-ĕg′lȧ-ĭm). [Heb. *'Ên 'Eglayim,* "spring of two calves."] A place near the north end of the Dead Sea (Eze 47:10); now generally identified with *'Ain Feshkha* on the northwestern shore of the Dead Sea (Map XVI, E-3).

En-gannim (ĕn-găn′ĭm). [Heb. *'Ên Gannîm,* "spring of gardens."]

1. A village in the lowland (Shephelah) in Judah (Jos 15:34). It has been identified by some with *Beit Jemâl,* which is not far from Beth-shemesh.

2. A town toward the boundary of Issachar (Jos 19:17, 21), assigned to the Gershonite Levites (ch 21:28, 29). It is the Ginaea of NT times, modern *Jenín,* a large village on the southern edge of the Plain of Esdraelon, about 6 mi. southeast of Taanach (*see* En-gannim, Map VI, D-3; Ginnaia, Map XVI, D-3).

En-gedi (ĕn-gē′dī). [Heb. *'Ên Gedî,* "spring of the kid."] A fertile place on the Dead Sea at about the middle of its western shore (Map VI, F-3). A hot spring, now called *'Ain Jidi,* bursting forth some 400 ft. above the seashore, feeds, in this wilderness area, an oasis that is rich in palm

156. En-gedi, on the Dead Sea

157. The spring of En-gedi

trees, vineyards, and balsam (Song 1:14). The site was formerly called Hazazontamar (hăz′ȧ-zŏn-tā′mẽr), Heb. *Chaṣaṣon Tamar,* "pruning of a palm tree" (Gen 14:7, KJV "Hazezon-tamar," hăz′ê-zŏn-tā′mẽr; 2 Chr 20:2). In the days of Abraham the place was occupied by Amorites, who were smitten by Chedorlaomer (Gen 14:7). David used its wild surrounding area as a hiding place from Saul, and in one of the caves in the vicinity he cut off a piece of Saul's robe (1 Sa 23:29; 24: 1-22). See figs. 156, 157, 365.

Engine. The translation of: (1) The Heb. *chishshabôn,* "device," "invention," hence "a machine." King Uzziah is credited with making "engines, invented by cunning men" to shoot arrows and large stones against an enemy force (2 Chr 26: 15). So far archeology has shed no light on this type of machinery in that period. (2) The Heb. *mechî* (Eze 26:9, KJV), *"battering ram."

Engrafted. The translation in the KJV of Jas 1:21 of the Gr. *emphutos,* meaning "implanted." The "word," that is, the gospel message, is described as implanted in the heart and life of the believer in Christ. James's statement is based on the figure by which truth is represented by a seed sown in the ground. Compare our Lord's parable of the Sower (Mt 13:3-9, 18-23).

En-haddah (ĕn-hăd′ȧ). [Heb. *'Ên Chaddah,* "a swift spring."] A town in the territory of Issachar (Jos 19:21), which has been identified with *el-Hadetheh,* about 6 mi. southwest of the southern tip of the Sea of Galilee.

En-hakkore (ĕn-hăk′ô-rē). [Heb. *'Ên Haqqôre',* "spring of the one who calls" or "spring of the partridge."] A spring in Lehi from which Samson quenched his thirst after the slaying of the Philistines with the jawbone of an ass (Jgs 15:19); not identified.

En-hazor (ĕn-hā′zôr). [Heb. *'Ēn Chaṣôr,* "spring of Hasor."] A fortified city of Naphtali (Jos 19:37), identified with some hesitation with *Ḥazzûr,* about 9 mi. west of Kedesh in Galilee.

En-mishpat (ĕn-mĭsh′păt). [Heb. *'Ēn Mishpat,* "spring of judgment."] A place identical with *Kadesh-barnea (Gen 14:7).

Enoch (ē′nŭk), KJV once **Henoch** (hē′nŭk). [Heb. *Chanôk,* "dedicated one"; Gr. *Enōch.*]

1. The eldest son of Cain. His father built the first city on earth, and called it Enoch after his son (Gen 4:17, 18).

2. The son of Jared and father of Methuselah. For his pious life he was translated at the age of 365 years, and saw no death (Gen 5:18-24; 1 Chr 1:3; Heb 11:5).

3. An antediluvian city, the first built on earth, whose builder was Cain (Gen 4:17).

Enos. *See* Enosh.

Enosh (ē′nŏsh), KJV **Enos** (ē′nŏs), except in 1 Chr 1:1. [Heb. *'Ēnôsh,* "man"; Gr. *Enōs.*] A son of Seth (Gen 4:26; 5:6-11; 1 Chr 1:1; Lk 3:38).

En-rimmon (ĕn-rĭm′ŏn). [Heb. *'Ēn Rimmôn,* "spring of pomegranates."] A postexilic town of Judah (Neh 11:29), identified with *Khirbet Umm er-Ramāmîn,* 8½ mi. north of Beer-sheba.

En-rogel (ĕn-rō′gĕl). [Heb. *'Ēn Rogel,* possibly "spring of the spy."] A well, 125 ft. deep, south of Jerusalem, where the Kid-

158. The well of En-rogel (center foreground) at the confluence of the Kidron and Hinnom valleys at Jerusalem

ron and Hinnom valleys meet. It was on the borderline between Judah and Benjamin (Jos 15:7; 18:16). It is mentioned in the narrative of Absalom's rebellion against David (2 Sa 17:17), and in that of Adonijah's unsuccessful usurpation of the throne (1 Ki 1:9). It is now generally identified with *Bîr 'Ayyûb,* although this water source is a well and not a spring, as a literal interpretation of the Heb. *'ayin* would require. However, *'ayin* is not always used in its strict meaning of "spring" (cf. Gen 16:7 with v 14). See map XVIII; figs. 158, 259.

Enrollment. The translation in the RSV of: (1) a Hebrew term from the verb *yachaś,* "to enroll oneself by genealogy," hence "genealogical register," in 1 Chr 7:7, 9; 2 Chr 31:17; (2) the Gr. *apographē,* "list," "census," "registration," in Lk 2:2; KJV "taxation," "taxing." Reference is to a Roman census registration, which usually preceded a taxation levy.

Ensample. An archaic term meaning "example," "pattern." The Greek terms thus translated mean "model," "pattern," "example" (1 Cor 10:11; Php 3:17; etc.).

En-shemesh (ĕn-shē′mĕsh). [Heb. *'Ēn Shemesh,* "spring of the sun."] A place on the boundary between Judah and Benjamin (Jos 15:1, 7; 18:11, 17), generally identified with *'Ain el-Ḥôd,* about 2 mi. northeast of Bethany on the road from Jerusalem to Jericho.

Ensign. A sign, banner, or standard whose purpose is to identify or to typify certain principles that organizations or peoples stand for (Is 11:10, 12; Eze 27:7, RSV; etc.). *See* Banner.

Ensue. An Old English term in 1 Pe 3:11, KJV, meaning "pursue."

En-tappuah. *See* Tappuah, 3.

Entrance of Hamath (hā′măth). [Heb. *Lebô' Chamath.*] A phrase used to indicate the northern limit of the extension of Israelite power or control (Num 34:8; Jos 13:5; Jgs 3:3; 1 Ki 8:65; 2 Ki 14:25; 1 Chr 13:5; 2 Chr 7:8; Amos 6:14). However, Egyptian and Assyrian texts make clear that in this phrase *Lebô'* does not mean "entrance" but is the name of a place in southern Syria, the modern *Lebweh,* about 20 mi. southwest of *Tell Nebi Mend* (*see* Kadesh, 2), in the Orontes Valley. In Assyrian texts it appears in the form *Lab'u,* and in Egyptian texts as *R₃bîw.* It should be remembered that the Egyptians had no *l*-sound in their language and therefore used the letter *r* to express an *l*-sound in foreign words.

Lit.: M. Noth *ZDPV* 58 (1935), 242-246; *PJB* 33 (1937), 36-51; B. Maisler, *BASOR* 102 (1946), 9; *LVTL* 470.

Epaenetus (ĕ-pē′nĕ-tŭs). [Gr. *Epainetos,* "praiseworthy," a name attested in Greek inscriptions.] The first Christian convert in the province of Asia (KJV "Achaia"). He was living in Rome when Paul wrote his epistle to the Romans and sent greetings to him, calling him "my well-beloved Epaenetus" (Rom. 16:5).

Epaphras (ĕp′à-frăs). [Gr. *Epaphras,* a contraction of *Epaphroditos,* "beloved," a name also attested in Greek inscriptions.] An early Christian from Colossae, and probably the founder of the church in that city (Col 4:12; 1:7). He went to Rome during Paul's first imprisonment there and gave the apostle a good report of his home church. He seems to have shared Paul's imprisonment (Phm 23).

Epaphroditus (ĕ-păf′rŏ-dī′tŭs). [Gr. *Epaphroditos,* "beloved," a frequently occurring Greek name.] A messenger from Philippi by whom the church sent gifts to Paul in Rome during the apostle's first imprisonment there (Php 4:18). He fell seriously ill in Rome, and upon recovery was sent to his home church with the epistle to the Philippians (ch 2:25-30).

Ephah, I (ē′fà). [Heb. *'Êphah,* "darkness."]
1. A grandson of Abraham through Keturah, and a son of Midian (Gen 25:4; 1 Chr 1:32, 33). His descendants, a Midianite tribe in northwestern Arabia, continued to bear the name of their ancestor (Is 60:6), being called *Haiapâ* in Assyrian inscriptions of Tiglath-pileser III, and were known for their wealth in camels.
2. A concubine of Caleb (1 Chr 2:46).
3. A man of Judah (1 Chr 2:47).

Ephah, II. [Heb. *'ephah,* a loan word from Egyptian *ỉpt.*] Originally an Egyptian measure of a capacity yet unknown, taken over by the Hebrews as a measure for grain. The Hebrew ephah (Jgs 6:19; etc.) was equal to the *bath in volume, and equivalent to about 22 liters, or 2.5 pecks U.S. dry measure.

Ephai (ē′fī). [Heb. *'Êphay,* meaning uncertain.] A captain of Judah's dissolved army who came to Gedaliah, the governor of Judah after the fall of Jerusalem, to offer his services (Jer 40:7, 8). He was probably among those slain by Ishmael (ch 41:3).

Epher (ē′fẽr). [Heb. *'Epher,* "gazelle."]
1. A son of Midian and grandson of Abraham through Keturah (Gen 25:4; 1 Chr 1:33).

2. A descendant of Judah (1 Chr 4:1, 17).
3. The head of a family in the half tribe of Manasseh that lived in Transjordan (1 Chr 5:23, 24).

Ephes-dammim (ē′fĕs-dăm′ĭm). [Heb. *'Ephes Dammim,* meaning uncertain.] A place in Judah between Socoh and Azekah, where the Philistines encamped against Saul's forces at the time David fought Goliath (1 Sa 17:1). The place is called Pas-dammim (păs′dăm′ĭm) [Heb. *Pas Dammim*] in 1 Chr 11:13. The site was near the valley of Elah (1 Sa 17:2), but it has not been identified with certainty.

Ephesians, Epistle to the. An epistle of Paul addressed, according to the title appearing on the ancient manuscripts, and according to ch 1:1 in many manuscripts, to Christian believers residing in the city of Ephesus, metropolis of the Roman province of Asia, and possibly intended also for other Christians in the neighboring cities as well. However, since the titles are later additions, and since the words "at Ephesus" in ch 1:1 are lacking in 2 of the most ancient and respected manuscripts, the Vaticanus and the Sinaiticus, and in the Chester Beatty Papyrus (P⁴⁶) as well, and since the epistle records no personal greetings, some have concluded that it was originally addressed to all Christian believers in the province of Asia, but that it was probably sent first to Ephesus, where the oldest and foremost church of that region was situated from which the gospel had spread to the outlying cities of the province (see Acts 19:10, 26). The status of Ephesus as the metropolis of Asia and the position of the Ephesian church as mother of the other churches in the province could account for the attachment of the expression "at Ephesus" in ch 1:1, and subsequently "To the Ephesians" as the title of the epistle. From the earliest times the Christian church has acknowledged the epistle as genuine, and thus as rightfully included in the NT canon. Among those who refer to it are Clement of Rome (*c.* A.D. 90) and Ignatius and Polycarp early in the 2d cent. Paul is mentioned by name as author by a number of Christian writers of the 2d cent. and onward. For a discussion of the critical problem with regard to the authorship of the book of Ephesians see *SDACom* 5:181-183; 6:993, 994.

During the course of his 3d Missionary Journey Paul labored in Ephesus for approximately 3 years (Acts 20:31), and may have personally evangelized some of the other cities of the province as well (Acts 19:10, 26). At the time of writing the epistle he was in prison, a fact to which reference is repeatedly made (Eph 3:1; 4:1; 6:20), apparently at Rome during his first imprisonment there. For this reason Ephesians is commonly grouped with Philippians, Colossians, and Philemon, which were written during this same imprisonment (see Php 1:13, 14; Col 4:18; Phm 1, 9), which continued for 2 years or a little more (Acts 28:30), from A.D. 61-63. In Eph 6:21, 22 Tychicus is mentioned as the bearer of that epistle, and in Col 4:7, 8 as the bearer of that epistle, and when v 9 is taken with Phm 10, 12 it seems evident that Onesimus accompanied Tychicus on the same mission. Apparently the 3 letters were written and dispatched at the same time, perhaps in the year A.D. 62. The numerous and striking parallels between Ephesians and Colossians (Eph 1:1 cf. Col 1:1; 1:13 cf. 1:5; 2:16 cf. 1:4, 9; 2:12 cf. 1:21; 2:15 cf. 2:14; 2:16 cf. 1:22; 6:18 cf. 4:2; 6:21 cf. 4:7) tend to confirm still further the close relationship between the 2 epistles, in subject matter, as well as in point of time. In Col 4:16 Paul mentions a letter addressed to the church at Laodicea, which some have considered identical with the epistle commonly called Ephesians.

The central theme of Ephesians is the pre-eminent position of Christ in the divine provision for man's salvation, and the unity of believers in Him. In a cosmopolitan region such as the coast of Asia Minor bordering on the Aegean, where the Christian church doubtless included Gentiles of several different races in addition to the Jewish believers, there would be an especial need to develop the theme of unity in Christ as a means of binding men of diverse backgrounds together in Christian fellowship. Heresies that later developed in Roman Asia, such as the teachings of the Judaizers (2 Ti 1:15) and Docetism (see 1 Jn 4:1-3), both of which denied Christ His pre-eminent gospel role, may imply that already there were tendencies that Paul sought to check by his emphatic statement on the unique position of Christ in the faith of the believer. The phrase "in Christ," occurring 4 times in the first chapter (Eph 1:3, 10, 12, 20), sets the keynote of the book. In one way or another the Christian's close personal relationship with Christ is mentioned more than 20 times. The epistle

may be considered a treatise on this subject.

After a brief salutation (Eph 1:1, 2) Paul develops the doctrinal theme of the book (chs 1:3 to 3:21) and then proceeds to show how a philosophy of life based on this exalted concept of unity in Christ should affect the believer in meeting the problems of life and church fellowship (chs 4:1 to 6:20). The letter closes with mention of the mission of Tychicus (ch 6:21, 22) and an apostolic benediction (vs 23, 24). In the practical section (chs 4:1 to 6:20) Paul develops an appreciation for the gifts of the Spirit as a means of preserving Christian unity (ch 4:1-16), and then shows how true Christianity will transform the life of the individual believer (chs 4:17 to 5:21). Various home relationships—those of husband and wife, children and parents, servants and masters—are discussed at length, as the basis of unity in the church (chs 5:22 to 6:9). This section closes with a graphic portrayal of the spiritual armor, which alone will give the Christian victory in his contest with the devil (ch 6:10-20).

Ephesus (ĕf′ĕ-sŭs). [Gr. *Ephesos*.] A city in western Asia Minor, near the mouth of the Cayster River (Map XX, B-4). It was situated at the junction of several natural trade routes within the Greek world, and lay on the main road from Rome to the Orient. This strategic position gave it importance, as did its great temple, the center of the cult of *Artemis (Diana); its famous magical books, the *Ephesia grammata* (cf. Acts 19:19); and the economic power of its banking association.

The city was founded by the Ionian Greeks in the 11th cent. B.C., and became the capital of the Ionian confederation consisting of 12 cities. In the 6th cent. B.C. it was taken over by the Lydian king Croesus. After his fall to Cyrus, it was made part of the Persian Empire. Two cent. later it fell to Alexander the Great, and then changed hands several times during the early years of his successors. Eventually it fell to the Seleucids, from whom the Romans took it after defeating Antiochus the Great at Magnesia in 190 B.C. The city was then given to the kingdom of Pergamum. When that kingdom was bequeathed to Rome by Attalus III (133 B.C.), Ephesus became the most important city of the Roman province of Asia.

The city suffered much from an earthquake in A.D. 29, but was rebuilt by scene of the riot against Paul and his teachings recorded in Acts 19:23-41.

The main street connecting the theater with the harbor was called the Arkadiane. Its 1,735 ft. were paved with marble slabs, and it was lined with colonnaded shops. At night the street was lighted, something unusual in an ancient city.

Other excavated ruins of Ephesus are the agora, the library of Celsus, gymnasia, baths, several churches of the Christian period (among which is the large double church in which the council of A.D. 431 was held), and the monumental church that was built in honor of the apostle John, who was believed to have spent the last years of his life in that city.

Nothing remains of the great temple of *Artemis (Diana) but a hole that in the dry season reveals some foundation stones (see fig. 160). This building was four times the size of the Parthenon at Athens, and was counted among the Seven Wonders of the World. Incorporated into the temple structure were 117 columns (Pliny mistakenly says 127), each 66 ft. high, 36 of them sculptured in life-size figures around their lower parts. This temple was the center of great feasts attracting many visitors, especially during the month Artemisios (March-April), the month when the riot against Paul seems to have occurred. It was also the place where the treasures of the great banking association for which Ephesus was famous were kept. Its cult object was an image of the goddess Artemis, made of black olivewood, according to some authorities, or of meteoric iron, according to others (cf. Acts 19:35). Being regarded as a goddess of fertility, her image contained many breasts (see fig. 32). The temple was originally in the center of the city, which was built on alluvial soil on a bank of the Cayster River. However, since the city was frequently flooded by the river, Lysimachus in 286 B.C. moved it beyond the reach of the water. The temple of Artemis was not moved and it then stood outside the city walls. It was destroyed by the Goths about A.D. 260, and was never completely rebuilt. Its columns were used to decorate Christian churches as far away as Constantinople (Istanbul), and the ruined temple remained a quarry for building material until nothing was left.

In Ephesus, as in most large cities, there was a Jewish community, which had a synagogue (Acts 18:19; 19:8, 17). Paul, as usual, began his preaching in the synagogue when he came to Ephesus. He first did this briefly on his way from Corinth to

159. View from the top row of the theater of Ephesus, with the Arcadian way leading to the ancient harbor (now silted up, visible as a dark area at upper part)

Tiberius. It was this new and modern city to which Paul and John came. During the 3d cent. A.D. it suffered from an invasion of the Goths, who destroyed the famous Artemis temple. However, the city recovered, and in A.D. 431 was the seat of the 3d general church council. At this council important pronouncements concerning the nature of Christ were made, and Mary was officially declared the "Mother of God."

Ephesus gradually lost its importance owing to the silting up of the harbor with mud brought down by the Cayster River, and has become a ruined site. Nearby stands an insignificant village.

Excavations were first carried out by a British expedition under J. T. Wood from 1863 to 1874, and in more recent years by Austro-German expeditions. One of the most impressive ruins is the great theater built on the western slope of Mount Pion. Its semicircular auditorium was 495 ft. in diameter, and its orchestra 110 ft. The stage was 22 ft. wide. The theater contained 66 rows of seats accommodating 24,500 people. This was the

160. The site of the great temple of Artemis (Diana) of Ephesus, now merely a hole in the ground with water covering the ancient foundations

Jerusalem during his 2d Missionary Journey, and again for 3 months during his 3d Missionary Journey (Acts 18:18; 19:8). After being expelled from the synagogue Paul held his meetings in a school for more than two years (vs 9, 10) until the riot incited by the silversmith Demetrius made it advisable for him to leave the city (ch 20:1). By that time he had spent 3 years in Ephesus (v 31), and probably had built up a strong center of Christianity from which the message spread into other cities of the province of Asia. This seems evident from the fact that only a few years later Christian churches were found in most of the large cities of that province (Col 4:13-16; Rev 2:1 to 3:22). On his return to Jerusalem about a year after he had left Ephesus, Paul was visited by the church leaders from Ephesus at Miletus (Acts 20:16-38). During his first Roman imprisonment Paul wrote the "Letter to the Ephesians," and he probably paid another visit to Ephesus after his release (1 Ti 1:3).

According to a strong tradition the apostle John spent many years of his life at Ephesus and became the recognized leader of the churches of western Asia Minor. It was to Ephesus that he addressed the first of the 7 letters written during his exile on the island of Patmos (Rev. 2:1-7). See SDACom 7:88-91, 742-745.

Ephlal (ĕf'lăl). [Heb. *'Ephlal*, meaning uncertain.] A Judahite (1 Chr 2:37).

Ephod. [Heb. *'ephod.* A secular garment of an undetermined kind was called *epâdâtum* in Assyrian and *'pd* in Ugaritic (*BASOR* 83 [1941], 40, n. 10).]

1. The sleeveless linen waistcoat worn by priests as the emblem of their sacred office. That worn by common priests was probably plain and unornamented, but that of the high priest was artistically embroidered with gold, blue, purple, and scarlet (Ex 28:3-6). The front and back panels were joined by 2 shoulder pieces,

and there was a woven border of the same materials as the panels (Ex 28:7, 8). Mounted on each of the shoulder straps was an onyx stone with 6 tribal names engraved upon it (vs 9-12), symbolizing the fact that the high priest ministered as the representative of all the people.

Attached to the ephod was the breastpiece (KJV "breastplate") of the same material, bearing the 12 precious stones and the *Urim and Thummim (vs 15-30).

2. A Manassite whose son Hanniel was a member of the commission to divide Canaan among the tribes (Num 34:18, 23).

Ephphatha. A transliteration through the Greek (*ephphatha*) of the Aramaic *'ethpethach* (Mk 7:34), meaning "be opened." This is one of the few Aramaic sayings recorded of Jesus (cf. Mt 27:46; Mk 5:41).

Ephraim (ē'frå-ĭm). [Heb. *'Ephrayim,* "double fruitfulness"; Gr. *Ephraim.*]

1. The second son of Joseph (Gen 41:50-52). Although younger than Manasseh, Ephraim was given pre-eminence over his older brother in the blessing of their dying grandfather Jacob. Jacob declared that these two grandsons should be reckoned as his heirs, along with his own sons, and he indicated the prominent position of Ephraim's descendants (ch 48:5-20). Ephraim suffered a grievous loss when two of his sons were slain by the people of Gath, whose cattle they tried to steal (1 Chr 7:20-22).

2. The descendants of Ephraim, 1, and one of the tribes of Israel (Jos 16:4, 10; Jgs 5:14). Although their ancestor Ephraim was only a grandchild of Jacob, his descendants and those of his brother Manasseh were always treated by the Israelites as two separate tribes equal in rank to those that descended from Jacob's sons. During the desert wandering the tribe of Ephraim was one of the smallest among the Hebrew tribes (Num 1:33; 26:37), but it rapidly increased in importance after the conquest of Canaan, owing probably to the influence of Joshua, who was himself an Ephraimite (Jos 19:50; 24:29, 30). In the distribution of the Promised Land Ephraim received a territory that lay between Benjamin and Manasseh (Map VI, D/E-2/3). Its northern boundary ran from Ataroth near the Jordan to the city of Shechem, which was included in its territory, then to Tappuah, and then along the river Kanah to the Mediterranean Sea. The southern boundary ran from Jericho to Bethel, then to the two Beth-horons, and from

there to the Mediterranean Sea via Gezer (Jos 16:1-8; 21:20, 21). The Ephraimites failed to drive out the Canaanites from Gezer (ch 16:10), but conquered Bethel (Jgs 1:22-26). They also took part in the war against Sisera, and were praised by Deborah for their patriotic aid (ch 5:14). They quarreled with Gideon, a Manassite, for having failed to call them when he warred against the Midianites (ch 8:1-3), and were angry also with Jephthah for not having called them when he fought against the Ammonites. In the ensuing civil war the tribe of Ephraim suffered great losses. They were identified by the enemy because they had a distinctive pronunciation of certain words (ch 12:1-6). *See* Shibboleth. Micah, who set up an idol that eventually became a permanently worshiped cult object at Dan, and Jeroboam, the first king of Israel after the secession of the 10 tribes, were Ephraimites. Jeroboam's tribal affiliation doubtless accounts for his choice of Shechem as his first capital (Jgs 17:1; 18:30, 31; 1 Ki 11:26; 12:25). Ephraim is listed among the 12 tribes (Eze 48:5, 6), but omitted in John's enumeration of the 144,000 (Rev 7:4-8).

3. A designation, sometimes used by the prophets, for the whole northern kingdom of 10 tribes (Is 7:2, 5, 9, 17; 9:9; 17:3; 28:3; Hos 4:17; 5:3; 9:3-17).

4. A town near Baal-hazor, in the vicinity of which Absalom had his sheep range (2 Sa 13:23). Jesus went to Ephraim after having raised Lazarus from the dead (Jn 11:54). In 1 Macc 11:34 it is called Aphairema. It has been identified with Ophrah of Benjamin (*see* Ephron, 3), which is probably the modern village of *eṭ-Ṭaiyibeh*, 4½ mi. northeast of Bethel (Map VI, E-3).

5. The designation of a gate in the wall of Jerusalem. See Ephraim Gate.

6. The designation of a certain forest or wood, which was the scene of the decisive battle between David's forces and those of his rebellious son Absalom (2 Sa 18:6). This forest was certainly in Transjordan, probably not far from Mahanaim, but it has not been located. It may have received its name from a colony of Ephraimites that may have dwelt in this area of Manasseh (cf. Jgs 12:4; Jos 17:14-17).

Ephraim Gate. [Heb. *sha'ar 'Ephrayim*.] A gate in the northern section of the western wall of Jerusalem. It lay at a distance of 400 cubits (=686 ft.) from the Corner Gate (2 Ki 14:13; 2 Chr 25:23). It was

located probably somewhere to the southeast of the site of the modern Church of the Holy Sepulchre, if that church lies outside the ancient wall. However, the exact site of this gate has not yet been ascertained. It had apparently been rebuilt before Nehemiah arrived at Jerusalem, because it is not mentioned in his list of repaired gates and sections of the city wall, although it is mentioned in Neh 12:39 as one of the gates that the procession passed during the dedication of the wall. A square was located in its vicinity (ch 8:16). See Map, fig. 259.

Ephraimites (ē'frá-ĭm-īts). [Heb. *'Ephrayim* and *'Ephrathi*.] Members of the tribe of Ephraim (Jgs 12:4-6).

Ephrain. See Ephron, 3.

Ephratah. See Ephrathah.

Ephrath. See Ephrathah, 1, 3.

Ephrathah (ĕf'rá-thá), KJV **Ephratah** (ĕf'-rá-tá). [Heb. *'Ephrathah*, "fruitfulness."]

1. A wife of Caleb, son of Hezron, and the mother of Hur (1 Chr 2:50; 4:4), called Ephrath (ĕf'răth), Heb. *'Ephrath*, in 1 Chr 2:19.

2. According to the RSV, following the LXX, the widow of Hezron, whom Caleb, son of Hezron, married (1 Chr 2:24).

3. The original name of Bethlehem in Judah, also called Ephrath (ĕf'răth), Heb. *'Ephrath* (Gen 35:19; 48:7; Ruth 4:11), also called Bethlehem Ephrathah (Mic 5:2).

4. A place mentioned in Ps 132:6. Some commentators believe it is identical with Bethlehem (*see* Ephrathah, 3). Others see in it a reference to Kiriath-jearim (1 Chr 2:24, 50), where the ark was for 20 years (1 Sa 7:2). They point out that Ephrathah is paralleled by "the fields of Jaar" (Ps 132:6, RSV), the latter probably representing Kiriath-jearim.

Ephrathite (ĕf'rá-thīt). [Heb. *'Ephrathi*.]

1. An inhabitant of Ephrath, which is Bethlehem in Judah (Ruth 1:2; 1 Sa 17:12; cf. Mic 5:2).

2. In the KJV twice a designation of a member of the tribe of Ephraim (1 Sa 1:1; 1 Ki 11:26).

Ephron (ē'frŏn). [Heb. *'Ephrôn*.]

1. A Hittite of Hebron, and the owner of the field in which was located the cave of Machpelah, which Abraham bought as a burial place (Gen 23:8, 9; 25:9).

2. A mountain between Nephtoah and Kiriath-jearim, on the boundary between Judah and Benjamin (Jos 15:1, 9).

3. A city in the northern kingdom of Israel which Abijah of Judah captured from Jeroboam I (2 Chr 13:19, RSV). It

is commonly identified with Ephraim or Ophrah, which is probably the village of *eṭ-Ṭaiyibeh*, 4½ mi. northeast of Bethel (Map VI, E-3). The KJV, on the basis of Masoretic tradition, here reads "Ephrain" (ē'frā-in). The RSV reading is supported by the LXX.

Epicureans. [Gr. *Epikoureioi.*] The adherents of a school of philosophy originated by Epicurus and his followers. Epicurus, born in 342/41 B.C. of Athenian parents, probably on the island of Samos, showed philosophic interests at the age of 14. After having studied under several philosophers, he began a school of his own, first at Mytilene, later at Lampsacus, and finally at Athens. There for 36 years, until the time of his death in 271/70 B.C., he taught in his own house with its famous garden. He was greatly revered and had a large number of students and followers, among them women. He wrote numerous works (in all, it was said, some 300 rolls), most of which have perished. He did not believe in a creator-god, but considered everything in nature to consist of atoms, which changed, although they were eternal in themselves. There was no afterlife, according to Epicurus, since the body returned to its original atoms. He admitted the existence of gods, but did not believe that they played a role in human affairs or took any interest in them. He aimed to obtain the highest "pleasure," which he understood as freedom from pain, or imperturbability, and to banish fear and superstition. However, by pleasure he did not mean sensual or even sensuous enjoyment, as has been erroneously supposed; he considered ethics and morals of a higher order than knowledge. Members of this philosophical group gave Paul an opportunity to expound his teachings to them, but they rejected his message after listening to him, since his teachings were radically at variance with their own concepts (Acts 17:18-32).

Epileptic. *See* Lunatick.

Epistle. A rendering of the Gr. *epistolē*, "letter," used to designate the epistles of Paul (Rom 16:22; Col 4:16; cf. 2 Pe 3:16), the epistles of Peter (2 Pe 3:1), and other letters (Acts 15:30; 23:33). Today the term "epistles" is used for any of the 21 books from Romans to Jude, inclusive. Most of the epistles were written to a church, or to Christians more generally (1 Cor 1:2; Gal 1:2; 1 Pe 1:1, 2; 2 Pe 1:1; etc.); a few were addressed to individuals (Tit 1:1, 4; 2 Jn 1; etc.). Their writing was occasioned by problems arising in the church, such as moral evils or heresy (1 Cor; Gal), by the desire to clarify or teach certain doctrines (Heb), or to give instructions (1, 2 Ti; Tit). Most of them follow the custom of the period in having a superscription bearing the name of the writer and of the church or individuals to whom the epistle was written. Likewise, most of them close with a salutation.

It appears that Paul's epistles were generally written by an amanuensis, or scribe (see Rom 16:22). However, the apostle apparently preferred to affix his own signature (2 Th 3:17; cf. 1 Cor 16:21). This was probably to prove that the letters were his own, and to discourage forgeries, which appear in one case at least to have been circulating under his name (see 2 Th 2:2). Galatians and Philemon were probably written by him in their entirety (Gal 6:11; Phm 19). Not all of Paul's epistles have been included in the canon (1 Cor 5:9). Three of them—1 and 2 Ti and Tit—are generally referred to as Pastoral Epistles.

Seven epistles—Jas, 1 and 2 Pe, 1, 2, and 3 Jn, Jude—are called Catholic Epistles. Unlike Paul's epistles, these are named not after the churches or individuals to whom they were sent, but after their authors. The notes appearing at the end of certain epistles in the KJV, naming the writer and stating the place of writing, etc., are later additions. *See* names of the various epistles.

Er (ûr). [Heb. *'Er*, "watchful"; Gr. *Ēr.*]
1. A son of Judah by his Canaanite wife Shua. He was married at an early age to the Canaanite Tamar. He was slain by God for his wickedness (Gen 38:1-7; 46:12; 1 Chr 2:3).
2. A descendant of Judah (1 Chr 4:21).
3. A Judahite who appears in Luke's genealogy of Jesus Christ (Lk 3:28).

Eran (ē'răn). [Heb. *'Eran.*] The ancestral head of an Ephraimite tribal family, the Eranites (ē'răn-īts) [Heb. *'Erani*] (Num 26:36).

Eranites. *See* Eran.

Erastus (ē-răs'tŭs). [Gr. *Erastos*, "desirable."] One or more persons closely associated with Paul, mentioned in three NT passages. (1) Acts 19:22 records that Erastus served Paul, and was sent to Macedonia, together with Timothy, to precede the apostle to that province. (2) In Rom 16:23 "Erastus, the city treasurer" (KJV "chamberlain"), is mentioned as sending greetings to Rome. The Greek word trans-

161. The inscription of Erastus the aedile, found near the theater at Corinth

lated "chamberlain," *oikonomos*, can stand for the Latin title *aedilis*, an aedile, or commissioner of streets and public buildings. A paving block found near the large theater of Corinth contains an inscription stating that "Erastus in return for the aedileship laid (the pavement) at his own expense" (ERASTVS PRO AEDILITATE S P STRAVIT). Fig. 161. The liberal Erastus of this inscription may be the convert of Paul mentioned in Rom 16:23. (3) Paul informed Timothy in his last letter, shortly before his death, that Erastus had stayed behind in Corinth (2 Ti 4:20). If the three texts refer to the same individual, and he is identical with the Erastus mentioned in the inscriptions, then Erastus, a commissioner of streets and buildings at Corinth, had become one of Paul's converts and had left his influential office to become Paul's assistant at Ephesus and, later, during his journeys. However, the possibility that Paul refers to more than one Erastus should not be ruled out.

Erech (ē'rĕk). [Heb. *'Erek*; Babylonian *Uruk*.] A city in Mesopotamia that formed part of Nimrod's kingdom in Babylonia (Gen 10:10). The site has been identified with the modern *Warka*, about 50 mi. northwest of Ur. German excavations begun previous to World War I show the city to have been one of the earliest in the Mesopotamian valley. The ancient Babylonians considered it the residence of Gilgamesh, hero of a great Babylonian epic that contains the Flood story. Inhabitants of this city were settled in Samaria by Ashurbanipal, who is called Osnappar in Ezr 4:9, 10 (KJV "Asnapper"). Map III, C-6.

162. The White Temple of Uruk, the Biblical Erech, with its stairway

Eri (ē'rī). [Heb. *'Eri*.] A son of Gad and founder of a tribal family called Erites (ē'rīts) [Heb. *'Eri*] (Gen 46:16; Num 26:16).

Erites. *See* Eri.

Esaias. *See* Isaiah.

Esarhaddon (ĕ'sär-hăd'ŏn). [Heb. *'Esar-Chaddôn*; Assyrian *Ashshur-aḫa-iddin*, "(the god) Asshur has given a brother."] An Assyrian king, the son and successor of Sennacherib; he reigned 681-669 B.C.

163. Stele of Esarhaddon of Assyria depicting the king as holding ropes that lead to the lips of the kings Taharka (Biblical Tirhakah) of Egypt and Ba'lu of Tyre

Upon his accession Esarhaddon began to rebuild Babylon, which his father had destroyed. Since his mother was a Babylonian princess, he was more favorably disposed to the Babylonians than was his father. Esarhaddon is especially known for his conquest of Egypt, which he organized into an Assyrian province. He also waged successful wars against Phoenician and Syrian kings. He had himself depicted on monuments as holding in his right hand ropes attached to rings in the lips of the Egyptian king Taharka (Biblical Tirhakah) and the king of Tyre, one of whom kneels and the other stands shackled before him (fig. 163). In the Bible Esarhaddon is mentioned as the successor of Sennacherib (2 Ki 19:37; Is 37: 38), and as the Assyrian king who settled foreign colonists in Samaria (Ezr 4:2). In his inscriptions he claims that King Manasseh of Judah paid tribute to him. Whether Esarhaddon himself or his son Ashurbanipal was responsible for exiling Manasseh of Israel temporarily to Babylon (2 Chr 33:11-13) is not known (*see* Manasseh).

Esau (ē'sô). [Heb. *'Eśaw*, "hairy"; Gr. *Ēsau*.] The firstborn of the twin sons of Isaac (Gen 25:25). He grew up and became a hunter, endearing himself to his father with his venison, whereas his brother Jacob, as a herdsman, was his mother's favorite. Jacob, not satisfied with being the younger son, schemed to obtain the rights belonging to the first-born, and therefore was glad when an opportunity arose to obtain the coveted birthright in exchange for a meal of red *pottage. Esau, a carefree man, did not realize in a moment of hunger what his rash action involved. For selling his birthright for a dish of red pottage, he received the nickname Edom, the "red one" (Gen 25:27-34; Heb 12:16, 17). His marriage at the age of 40 to two Hittite girls grieved his parents (Gen 26:34, 35; 36:1, 2). In order to please them in this respect he later took as an additional wife one of Ishmael's daughters (chs 28:9; 36:3).

When the time came for Isaac, who was old and almost blind, to confer upon his favored son the blessings due to the first-born, Jacob, induced by his mother, impersonated his older brother and fraudulently obtained the blessings, while Esau was out hunting (Gen 27:1-40). Highly incensed, Esau planned the murder of his brother as soon as his father had passed away, but his parents sent Jacob to Mesopotamia to escape the wrath of Esau (chs 27:41 to 28:5). When Jacob returned after 20 years, he found that Esau had forgiven him, and the two brothers met peacefully near the river Jabbok in Transjordan. Later they were together again at the burial of their father (chs 32:3-8, 13-23; 33:1-16; 35:29). Esau had in the meantime made his abode in the mountainous area of Seir, which lay south of the Dead Sea, and when his descendants increased they dispossessed the inhabitants of Mount Seir and became the powerful nation of the Edomites (Gen 33:16; Deut 2:4, 12, 22). Afterward that area was also called simply the Mount of Esau (Ob 8, 9, 19, 21). Esau's loss of the rights of the first-born is repeatedly discussed in the Bible (Mal 1:2, 3; Rom 9: 12, 13; Heb 12:17).

Eschew. [Heb. *sûr*, "to turn aside," "to depart from," "to withdraw"; Gr. *ekklinō*, "to turn away from," "to shun," "to avoid."] A term appearing in Job 1:1, 8; 2:3; 1 Pe 3:11; KJV, meaning "to abstain from," "to shun." In Old English "eschew" meant "to shy away from."

Esdraelon. *See* Jezreel, 3.

Esek (ē'sĕk). [Heb. *'Eśeq*, "strife."] A well dug by Isaac near Gerar which the Philistine herdsmen claimed (Gen 26:20); not identified.

Eshan (ē'shăn), KJV **Eshean** (ĕsh'ē-ăn). [Heb. *'Esh'an*.] A town in the mountains of Judah in the neighborhood of Dumah and Hebron (Jos 15:52). Its identification is uncertain.

Eshbaal. *See* Ish-bosheth.

Eshban (ĕsh'băn). [Heb. *'Eshban*.] A descendant of Seir the Horite, or Hurrian (Gen 36:26; 1 Chr 1:38, 41).

Eshcol (ĕsh'kŏl). [Heb. *'Eshkol*, "a cluster (of grapes, etc.)."]

1. An Amorite, the brother of Mamre, and one of Abraham's confederates (Gen 14:13, 24).

2. A valley near Hebron, from which the 12 spies, sent out by Moses, brought samples of great clusters of grapes to the Israelites in their wilderness camp (Num 13:22, 23; Deut 1:24, 25). It is generally placed north of Hebron, a valley which to the present day is famous for its luscious grapes. The valley may have received its name from the Amorite Eshcol who lived in this area in the time of Abraham (Gen 14:13, 24).

164. Vineyards in the valley of Eshcol

Eshean. *See* Eshan.

Eshek (ē'shĕk). [Heb. *'Esheq,* "oppression."
The name occurs in South Arabic inscriptions.] A descendant of Saul (1 Chr 8:39).

Eshkalonite (ĕsh'kà-lŏn-īt). [Heb. *'Eshqelônî.*]
An inhabitant of Ashkelon (Jos 13:3).

Eshtaol (ĕsh'tà-ŏl). [Heb. *'Eshta'ol.*] A town
in the Shephelah in the territory of Judah
(Jos 15:33), assigned to the Danites (ch
19:40, 41). It lay in the vicinity of Zorah,
and is frequently mentioned in the Samson stories (Jgs 13:25; 16:31; 18:2, 11).
It is identified with *Eshwa',* about 13 mi.
west of Jerusalem, and about 2 mi. east of
Zorah. Map VI, E-2.

Eshtaolite (ĕsh'tà-ŏ'lĭt), KJV **Eshtaulite**
(ĕsh'tà-ū'lĭt). [Heb. *'Eshta'ulî.*] An inhabitant of Eshtaol (1 Chr 2:53).

Eshtaulite. *See* Eshtaolite.

Eshtemoa (ĕsh'tē-mō'à). [Heb. *'Eshtemôa'*
and *'Eshtemoah,* "place where the oracle
is heard."]

1. A Maachathite, a descendant of Ezra
(1 Chr 4:17, 19), considered by some
commentators to be founder of the town
of Eshtemoa.

2. A town in the hill country of Judah,
assigned to the priests (Jos 21:14; 1 Chr
6:57), called Eshtemoh (ĕsh'tē-mō), Heb.
'Eshtemoah, in Jos 15:50. It received from
David some of the spoil obtained from the
Amalekites who had destroyed Ziklag (1
Sa 30:28). The site has been identified
with *es-Semú',* about 9 mi. south of Hebron. Map VI, F-3.

Eshtemoh. *See* Eshtemoa, 2.

Eshton (ĕsh'tŏn). [Heb. *'Eshtôn.*] A descendant of Chelub and a member of the tribe
of Judah (1 Chr 4:11, 12).

Esli (ĕs'lī). [Gr. *Hesli,* a transliteration possibly of the Heb. *'Aṣalyah,* "Yahweh has
reserved."] A Judahite appearing in Luke's
genealogy of Jesus Christ (Lk 3:25).

Espoused. *See* Betrothal.

Esrom. *See* Hezron, 2.

Esther (ĕs'tēr). [Heb. *'Ester,* thought to come
from a Persian word meaning "star."] The
Jewish queen of King Ahasuerus, or
Xerxes, and heroine of the book of Esther.
(*See* Ahasuerus, 2.) Esther's original Hebrew name was *Hadassah,* "myrtle." She
probably adopted the Persian name Esther upon entering the Persian court.
Esther was the daughter of Abihail, apparently a Benjamite, and the adopted
daughter of her cousin *Mordecai, a courtier of Ahasuerus (Est 2:5, 7, 15). Both
Esther and Mordecai were descendants
of the Hebrew exiles who had been trans-

165. The tomb at Hamadan (ancient Ecbatana),
where, according to tradition, Queen Esther is buried

ported to Babylon by Nebuchadnezzar
more than 100 years earlier, but were
among those who had chosen to remain
in the land of exile when Cyrus granted
permission for the return to Judea. Both
were residents of Susa (Shushan), formerly capital of Elam, but in their time
one of several Persian capitals, situated
about 200 mi. east of Babylon. Map XII,
D-8.

Esther was a remarkably beautiful
young woman whose tact and winsome-
ness brought her into royal favor and
earned for her the title of queen after
the former queen, Vashti, fell into disfavor. Ahasuerus gave her this rank in his
7th year, about the month of January,
478 B.C.; this would have been at some
time soon after the disastrous war in
Greece marked by the battles of Salamis
and Plataea. Four years later, in April,
474 B.C., the royal favorite, Haman, cast
lots and then secured a royal decree authorizing the slaying of all Jews within
the borders of the Persian Empire and the
confiscation of their property (Est 3:7-
15). By this decree he sought revenge
upon Mordecai, who, as he came and
went at the palace gate, had consistently
refused to prostrate himself before Haman (vs 2-6). The decree naturally threw
the Jews into great consternation, and
Mordecai reported the matter to Esther
(ch 4:1-7) with the admonition that God
had providentially overruled that she
should be queen at this hour of crisis
(vs 8-17). In a supreme act of bravery
equaled only by her infinite tact, Esther
appealed to the king on behalf of her
people, apparently for the first time revealing that she herself was Jewish (chs
6 and 7). Upon Haman's execution, the
king elevated Mordecai to Haman's for-

mer position, and in the month of June signed a decree prepared by Mordecai that, in effect, reversed Haman's decree (Est 8). In joyful celebration of their miraculous deliverance the Jews declared a festal period known as *Purim, "Lots," in commemoration of Haman's casting of lots in connection with the decree for slaying the Jews (chs 3:7; 9:17-32). Ever since, the Jews have celebrated this festival in honor of Esther and in commemoration of her spirit of bravery and devotion, which God used as the means of bringing deliverance to His people. See figs. 165, 341.

Esther, Book of. A historical account of the supreme crisis that confronted the Jewish people in 474/73 B.C., when a royal decree of the Persian king Xerxes (*see* Ahasuerus, 2) ordered their extermination, and of the providential means by which God wrought their deliverance. In the Hebrew Bible the book of Esther stands last in a group of 5 books bearing the common title Megilloth, the other 4 being Ruth, Song of Solomon, Ecclesiastes, and Lamentations. Inasmuch as the Hebrew text of Esther begins with the word "and" some have suggested that originally it was attached to some other historical work, possibly Nehemiah—the book it follows in the LXX and in the English translations. Despite the fact that the book nowhere contains the name of God, the Jews gave it a place in the sacred canon. Certain early Christian writers omitted it from their canonical lists, and Martin Luther openly denounced the book.

The identity of the author of the book of Esther is unknown. However, the historical accuracy of the narrative and its many intimate details now confirmed by archeology, together with certain characteristic word forms used in the book, and the fact that the writer had access to the official texts of the various decrees mentioned and quoted, all point to someone as the author who lived in Susa (Shushan) at the time, who was familiar with the palace grounds and buildings, who had access to the royal archives, and who was an educated Jew. Ezra or Mordecai has been suggested as possibly being the writer. The implicit claim of the book that it is a factual account of historical events has been remarkably confirmed by archeological discoveries. Numerous significant details of the royal palace at Shushan mentioned by the writer have

been observed in the ruins that have been unearthed. Copies of royal Persian decrees found in Egypt furnish parallels in form and style that corroborate the authenticity of the decrees cited in the narrative. The true-to-life description of Persian manners and customs corresponds to what is known from other sources. See Est 1:5, 10, 14; 2:9, 21, 23; 3:7, 12, 13; 4:6, 11; 5:4; 8:8, 10, 15; 9:30; 10:1, 2.

The historical setting of the book of Esther is to be found in events closely connected with Xerxes' disastrous Greek campaign that marked the last serious Persian attempt to incorporate the city-states of Greece into the Persian Empire. The 6 months' feast of ch 1, which was attended by officials from all parts of the empire, was apparently the great council of war at which plans were laid for the invasion of Greece, inasmuch as the massive campaign was launched as soon thereafter as preparations could possibly have been completed. Esther was made queen soon after Xerxes' return from Greece, and the crisis occasioned by Haman's decree arose 4 or 5 years later. The precise chronological data provided by the writer (chs 1:3; 2:12, 16; 3:7, 12; 8:9, 12; 9:1, 17-19) for the principal events mentioned in the narrative make possible this close correlation with the known events of secular history. If the writer had located the great feast, the reception of Esther as queen, or the experience with Haman at a time when Xerxes was some 1,500 mi. away in Greece for a period of many months, the implicit claim of the book to be historical would be placed in serious doubt. Conversely, this close correspondence with the facts of history attests its authenticity.

As a literary masterpiece the book of Esther rates high. It consists of a fast-moving sequence of highly dramatic situations of epic quality. Esther is not only beautiful, but a woman of clear judgment, remarkable self-control, infinite tact, firm loyalty, and noble self-sacrifice, who rises to heights of heroic action. Haman is a hateful, clever, unscrupulous, and egotistical villain. The surprising series of providential coincidences that reach a climax in his exposure and death and in deliverance for the Jews, whose extinction as a race he had planned, match in dramatic suspense anything that fiction has to offer. Although God is not mentioned by name, His overruling providence is the great theme of the book from beginning to end. The book highlights, also, the transitory nature of earthly power and prosperity. Doubtless because of these things the medieval Jewish commentator Maimonides exalts the book of Esther above all the books of the Prophets and the rest of the Hagiographa and places it on a par with the Pentateuch. If God can deliver His people from a crisis such as the one that confronted them in the days of Esther, certainly no earthly situation can prove too difficult for Him and no crisis can be so dark as to leave His people without hope.

The narrative logically falls into 5 sections, the 1st of which explains how a Jewish maiden happens to become queen of the Persian Empire (Est 1:1 to 2:20). The narrative develops as Haman is promoted to the office of prime minister and plots to exterminate the Jews (chs 2:21 to 3:15) and Esther sets out to champion the cause of her people (chs 4:1 to 5:8). It reaches its climax with the fall of Haman (chs 5:9 to 7:10) and the triumph of the Jews over their enemies (chs 8:1 to 10:3). The story opens with a description of a high festival of state at which all the princes and nobles of Persia are present, but which becomes the occasion for the deposition of Vashti as queen and the eventual appointment of Esther as her successor to royal favor. Next, the incident by which Mordecai saves Xerxes' life is related, by way of explaining Mordecai's later role in the narrative (ch 2: 21-23). Haman's appointment as prime minister leads indirectly to personal hatred for Mordecai (ch 3:1-6), and to the plot by which he seeks to take revenge by means of a royal decree that sentences all Jews to death (vs 7-15). The Jews are in despair, but Mordecai perceives that Esther's position as queen has placed her in a position to approach the king. He prevails upon her to champion her people's cause at great personal risk (ch 4: 1-17). Esther tactfully approaches the king and makes sure of his favor, step by step, before lodging her accusation against Haman. Her handling of the critical and delicate situation is a demonstration of consummate skill and tact (chs 5:1 to 7:6). During the course of Esther's maneuvers to bring the king and Haman together under circumstances suited to her purpose, Haman is utterly humiliated and disheartened by being required to parade Mordecai about the city in royal splendor at the very time he has purposed to hang his mortal enemy. After the exposure and death of Haman events move rapidly with the promotion of Mordecai to Haman's post as prime minister and the issuance of a decree that effectively checkmates the one promulgated earlier upon the insistence of Haman (Est 8:1 to 9:16). The remainder of ch 9 explains the historical basis for the Feast of Purim, which has been universally observed by the Jews ever since (ch 9:17-32). Chapter 10 constitutes a conclusion that relates briefly the honor that comes to Mordecai as prime minister and notes how he uses this high office not only to the advantage of Persia and its king but also to further the welfare of his own people, the Jews.

Etam (ē′tăm). [Heb. *'Ēṭam.*]

1. A descendant of Judah (1 Chr 4:3). He may have given his name to the town of Etam, 4.

2. A place in the southern portion of the territory of Judah that was assigned to Simeon (1 Chr 4:32). It has not yet been identified with certainty, but must be sought in the neighborhood of En-rimmon (see Map V, A-6).

3. The name of a rock in northern Judah where Samson dwelt for a time after having left Timnah (Jgs 15:8, 11). It has not been identified.

4. A town in the vicinity of Bethlehem, which Rehoboam fortified after the secession of the ten tribes (2 Chr 11:6). Its site is *Khirbet el-Khôkh*, about 2½ mi. southwest of Bethlehem (Map VI, E-3). The neighboring spring of *'Ain 'Aṭān* has preserved the ancient name. The famous so-called pools of Solomon, which formerly provided water for Jerusalem via an aqueduct, are found there. The water from these pools is now channeled to Bethlehem.

Etham (ē′thăm). [Heb. *'Etham.*] The place where the Israelites first encamped after leaving Succoth in Egypt under Moses (Ex 13:20; Num 33:6). Since it lay at the edge of the wilderness, it must be sought somewhere at the eastern end of the *Wâdī Ṭumilât*, near Lake Timsah or near the Great Bitter Lake. (See Map V, B-4, where Etham is shown probably too far north.) The name Etham was applied to that portion of the Wilderness of Shur which lay between the Egyptian border and Marah, and which took three days to traverse (Num 33:8; cf. Ex 15:22).

Ethan (ē′thăn). [Heb. *'Ēthan,* "permanently (flowing with water)."]

1. A Judahite, son of Zerah (1 Chr 2:6).

He was probably the Ezrahite famous for his wisdom, mentioned in 1 Ki 4:31. Some identify him with the "Ethan the Ezrahite" in the superscription of Ps 89, but it is not certain when this Ethan lived.

2. A Gershonite Levite, an ancestor of Asaph (1 Chr 6:42).

3. A Merarite Levite who was one of the Temple singers appointed by David (1 Chr 6:44; 15:17, 19). He may have been identical with Jeduthun in other texts that list the Temple singers (1 Chr 16:41; 25:1, 6; 2 Chr 5:12; 35:15).

Ethanim (ĕth'à-nĭm). [Heb. *'Ethanîm;* Phoenician *'tnm.*] The Jewish (also Canaanite) month (called Tishri after the Babylonian exile) beginning at the new moon of September or October. It was called the 7th month (1 Ki 8:2) because the months were numbered according to the religious year, beginning with Abib (Nisan) in the spring; but Ethanim, or Tishri, began the civil year. Tishri 1 was New Year's Day, the 10th was the Day of Atonement, and the 15th was the 1st day of the Feast of Tabernacles. On the 10th of this month the trumpet sounded to announce the year of *jubilee (Lev 25:9). *See* Year.

Ethbaal (ĕth'bā'ăl). [Heb. *'Ethba'al,* "with Baal." The name, written *'tb'l,* is attested in a Phoenician inscription from Byblos, also in Sennacherib's inscriptions of 701 B.C. as that of a later king of Sidon, written *Tuba'lu* (*ANET* 287).] A king of Sidon (and Tyre), father of Jezebel, and father-in-law of King Ahab of Israel (1 Ki 16:31). He was a priest of Astarte when he killed his brother Phelles, king of Sidon, and usurped the throne *c.* 887 B.C. (Jos. *Ant.* viii. 13. 1, 2; ix. 6. 6; *Against Apion* i. 18).

Ether (ē'thēr). [Heb. *'Ether,* probably "perfume."]

1. A place in Judah (Jos 15:42), identified by some with *Khirbet el-'Ater,* about 13 mi. west-northwest of Bethzur. Others identify it with Ether, 2, or with *Athach.

2. A place assigned to Simeon near En-rimmon (Jos 19:7), identified, on the basis of Eusebius' *Onomasticon,* with *Khirbet 'Attîr,* 15 mi. northeast of Beersheba, but some think Eusebius confuses it with Jattir. Some consider it identical with Ether, 1.

Ethiopia (ē'thĭ-ō'pĭ-à). [Heb. *Kûsh;* Assyrian *Kûsu;* Babylonian *Kûshu.*] In Biblical times the area later called Nubia, lying partly in what is now Egypt and partly in the Sudan. In classical times it was called Nubia. Its northern border was the 1st

Nile cataract at Aswan; the southern border remained undefined. The Heb. name *Kûsh* is derived from the name of Ham's first-born son Cush (Gen 10:6), who became the ancestor of the inhabitants of Ethiopia. The Egyptians called this country *K3sh,* a name in which the Heb. *Kûsh* is easily recognizable (Maps IV, C/D-4/5; XII, F-5). The inhabitants of this country were Hamites, like the Egyptians and Libyans, although the Egyptians referred to the Cushites as Negroes. Their dark color, which is also alluded to in the Bible (Jer 13:23), gave rise to this appellation. See fig. 27 for models of Nubian soldiers.

Ancient Ethiopia included not only Nubia but also part of western Arabia bordering on the Red Sea. This area appears in Assyrian inscriptions by the name of *Kûsu,* and several Bible references to Ethiopia must likewise apply to the Arabian Cush, since they cannot refer to the African Cush. Zerah, the Cushite of 2 Chr 14:9, could not have invaded southern Palestine if he came from African Ethiopia, since Egypt was at that time in firm control of her own country and of Nubia. He must have been an Arabian Cushite. This was doubtless true also of the Cushites of Is 45:14.

Nubia was always coveted by the Egyptians because of the gold mines in its mountains, and its wealth in cattle, ivory, hides, and ebony, and because products of central Africa entered Egypt through Nubian traders. The country was conquered by the strong kings of the 12th Egyptian dynasty, but during the 2d Intermediate Period, which followed, when the Hyksos ruled over part of Egypt, it regained its independence. Afterward the powerful kings of the New Kingdom, who reoccupied Nubia, placed it under an Egyptian governor who was called Prince of Nubia. At this time the Nubians adopted the Egyptian religion and culture, and in the course of time became more conservative in things Egyptian than the Egyptians themselves.

Later Nubia regained its independence, and when Egypt became weak invaded that country (*c.* 750 B.C.). For almost 90 years Egypt was ruled by Ethiopian kings whose capital was at Napata, near the 4th Nile cataract. The Ethiopian dynasty is called the 25th in Egyptian history. The best-known king of that dynasty is Taharka, the Biblical Tirhakah (2 Ki 19:9), who attempted to come to the help of King Hezekiah of Judah during an Assyrian invasion by Sennacherib. Sennacherib's son finally defeated the Ethiopians and drove them back into their own country. From that time on they wielded no more power over foreign countries.

In NT times the land was ruled by a succession of queens whose capital was in Meroe (Map IV, D-5), which lies about 130 mi. northeast of Khartum. Each of these queens carried the title *Candace (Acts 8:27). The Meroitic kingdom existed until c. A.D. 350, and then gave way to the Abyssinian power of Aksum.

The country is frequently mentioned in the Bible, which speaks of its rivers (Is 18:1; Zep 3:10), meaning probably the White and Blue Niles, possibly also the Atbara. Nubia is also mentioned as the land of the origin of certain precious stones (Job 28:19), and as a land noted for trade (Is 45:14). The psalmist predicted that the time would come when Ethiopia would stretch out her hands to God (Ps 68:31). Some of the Hebrew prophets foresaw her doom (Is 20:1-6; Zep 2:12).

Ethiopian (ē'thĭ-ō'pĭ-ăn). [Heb. *Kûsh, Kûshî;* Gr. *Aithiops.*] Inhabitant of *Ethiopia (2 Chr 12:3; Jer 13:23; etc.).

Eth-kazin (ĕth'kā'zĭn), KJV **Ittah-kazin** (ĭt'á-kā'zĭn). [Heb. *'Ithah Qaṣîn.* The name of the place was probably *'Eth qaṣin,* since the ending *ah* in *'Ithah* indicates direction and is not part of the name.] A place on the eastern border of Zebulun (Jos 19:13). Its exact location is unknown.

Ethnan (ĕth'năn). [Heb. *'Ethnan,* "gift."] A descendant of Judah, of the family of Hezron (1 Chr 4:7).

Ethni (ĕth'nī). [Heb. *'Ethnî,* probably a shortened form of *Ethnan,* "gift."] A Gershonite Levite (1 Chr 6:41). Some identify him with the Jeatherai of ch 6:21.

Eubulus (û-bū'lŭs). [Gr. *Euboulos,* "well-advised." The name occurs frequently in Greek inscriptions.] A Roman Christian who sent greetings to Timothy through Paul (2 Ti 4:21).

Eunice (û-nī'sĕ). [Gr. *Eunikē,* "good victory."] The mother of Timothy; a Christian Jewess married to a Greek (2 Ti 1:5; cf. Acts 16:1).

Eunuch. [Heb. *sarîs;* Gr. *eunouchos.*] An emasculated person. Eunuchs were anciently employed in Oriental countries not only as chamberlains but also as courtiers in low and high positions. Since most courtiers in confidential positions in the king's immediate household were emasculated, the term became synonymous with "officer," and may occasionally have been used for men who were in possession of their full virility. On the other hand, there is no proof that a married courtier (Heb. *sarîs*) like Potiphar (Gen 39:1) was not a eunuch. If he were a eunuch the situation would easily account for his wife's approaches to Joseph. *Sarîs* is variously rendered in the English translations, but is found in every one of the OT passages quoted hereafter. Pharaoh's captain of the guard and his chief baker and chief butler were eunuchs (chs 37:36; 40: 2, 7). *Sarîsîm* are also mentioned in the Bible as close servants not only of the kings of Assyria (2 Ki 18:17), Babylonia (2 Ki 20:18; Is 39:7; Jer 39:3, 13; Dan 1:3, 7; etc.), and Persia (Est 1:10, 12, 15; etc.) but also of the kings and queens of Israel and Judah. They are mentioned in the service of King David (1 Chr 28:1), of Ahab, Jezebel, and of their son Jehoram (1 Ki 22:9; 2 Ki 8:6; 9:32), of Jehoiachin (2 Ki 24:15; Jer 29:2) and Zedekiah (2 Ki 25:19). Mosaic law excluded such men from the congregation of the Lord (Deut 23:1), so perhaps many of the eunuchs were foreigners (see Jer 38:7). Isaiah, however, told them that they could have a place and name in the house of the Lord if they were faithful in the performance of their religious duties (Is 56:3-5). Some commentators think that probably Daniel, and certainly Nehemiah, were eunuchs. The only eunuch mentioned in the NT was a treasurer of the queen of Ethiopia, who was accepted into the Christian church by baptism (Acts 8:27-39). The word of Christ in Mt 19:12 uses the term in a context that illustrates the desirability of an unmarried state under certain circumstances.

Euodia (û-ō'dĭ-á), KJV **Euodias** (û-ō'dĭ-ăs). [Gr. *Euodias,* "fragrance," a name frequently occurring in the Greek inscriptions.] A Christian woman in Philippi, whom Paul urged to live harmoniously with Syntyche, a fellow gospel laborer (Php 4:2, 3).

Euodias. See Euodia.

Euphrates (û-frā'tēz). [Heb. *Perath;* in cuneiform texts *Purattu.* The modern name comes from the Gr. *Euphratēs,* derived from Old Persian *Ufrātu.*] One of the great rivers of western Asia, and the main stream of Mesopotamia. It has two sources, one near Erzerum, feeding the western Euphrates, now called *Karasu,* and the other west of Mount Ararat (Map XI, B-5), feeding the eastern branch, the *Muradsu.* After the two

166. Date palms on the bank of the river Euphrates

branches join near *Melid*, the united river flows meanderingly through the Anti-Taurus Mountains, and upon entering Upper Mesopotamia forms the Great Bend of the Euphrates by turning first southward at Apamea and then eastward at Thapsacus (Map XI, B-4). In this Great Bend are located the famous city of Carchemish and the Assyrian city of *Til Barsip* (Map III, B-4). After the eastward turn the river soon turns again and flows in a southeasterly direction, receiving the waters of two important tributaries, the *Balikh*—on which lies Haran (Map XI, B-4)—and the *Khābûr* (Map XI, B-5). In Lower Mesopotamia the Euphrates has changed its course repeatedly since ancient times; consequently the ruins of many large cities that formerly were on its banks—such as Sippar, Babylon, Nippur, Uruk (Biblical Erech), Larsa, Ur, Eridu—are now found at varying distances from it (Map XI, C-5/6). For the river at Babylon see fig. 47. After flowing about 1,780 mi. the Euphrates is now joined by the Tigris, the combined river being called the *Shatt el-'Arab*. In ancient times, however, the Persian Gulf extended farther northwest than now, and the Euphrates and the Tigris entered the gulf separately.

The name Euphrates is first mentioned in the OT in reference to one of the rivers of the Garden of Eden (Gen 2:14), but the identity of the antediluvian Euphrates with the present river must not be assumed. The Euphrates is often referred to simply as the "great river," and is designated as the northern boundary of the Promised Land (Gen 15:18), which it seldom was, except for a short time during the reigns of David and Solomon (2 Sa 8:3; 1 Chr 18:3; 1 Ki 4:21, 24). In Persian times the Euphrates formed the boundary between Mesopotamia and the territory of Syria and Palestine. Consequently the latter territory which was combined administratively as one satrapy, was officially called "Beyond the River" (Ezr 4:10, 11; 5:3; 6:6; Neh 2:7). In the symbolic language of the book of Revelation, angels are mentioned as being "bound at the great river Euphrates" (Rev 9:14, RSV), and the 6th plague is said to be poured out upon the Euphrates (ch 16:12). *See* Armageddon.

Euroclydon (ŭ-rŏk′lĭ-dŏn). [Gr. *eurokludōn*, with variant spellings of *eurukludōn* and *eurakulōn*, a hybrid term from Gr. *euros*, "east wind," and Latin *aquilo*, "northeast wind."] The popular name of a strong eastern or northeastern wind, which brought the ship on which Paul traveled to Rome, first into danger and then to shipwreck (Acts 27:14, KJV).

Eutychus (ū′tĭ-kŭs). [Gr. *Eutuchos*, "fortunate," a name occurring frequently in Greek literature and inscriptions.] A young man of Troas who, while sitting in the window during Paul's last meeting there, fell asleep and dropped from the 3d floor to the ground. He was taken up dead, but was restored to life by the apostle (Acts 20:7-12).

Evangelist. A rendering of the Gr. *euaggelistēs* (Acts 21:8; Eph. 4:11; 2 Ti 4:5), literally, "announcer of glad tidings." The gift of evangelism was one of the several endowments which Christ gave to various members of His church after His ascension (Eph 4:8, 11). This gift, with others, was given that the church might be capable of carrying on every phase of its work, and be perfected in Christ (vs 11-16). Philip, the deacon, was called an evangelist (Acts 21:8; cf. ch 6:5). The youthful Timothy was urged by Paul to do the work of an evangelist (2 Ti 4:5).

Eve (ēv). [Heb. *Chawwah*, the etymology of which is not clear. The word has been interpreted as meaning "ancestress," "mother," "the living one," "the one who gives birth," etc. Gr. *Eua*.] The first woman, Adam's "help meet," and mother of the human race (Gen 2:18-22). Adam first named her *'ishshah*, "woman" (from *'ish*, "man"), and gave her the name Eve after the Fall. Perfect as he was in manly dignity and ability, Adam was an incomplete being, in and of himself. To supply this inherent, divinely ordained deficiency God created Eve "an help meet for him," literally, "as his counterpart," "appropriate to him." Adam was created a social being and it was "not good" that he "should be alone" (v 18). God ordained that Eve should supply what was lacking in him in order that together the two of them should constitute a completeness of being. Eve succumbed to the seduction of the tempter and induced Adam to join her in transgression (Gen 3:1-7). As a penalty Eve was subordinated to Adam (v 16) and told that pain in childbirth would be her lot (v 16). After the reference to her in ch 4:1, 2 as mother of Cain and Abel, she is not mentioned again in the OT, nor even alluded to. In the NT Paul mentions her twice, once with reference to the fact that the serpent beguiled her (2 Cor 11:3) and once with reference to her transgression's being the ground for the subordinate status assigned to women after the Fall (1 Ti 2:13).

Even, Evening, Eventide. These terms cover several meanings: (1) Sunset, at which the Hebrew day began; the equivalence of evening with sunset is clear from Lev 22:6, 7, for example, which states that one who touched any unclean thing was to be "unclean until the evening," and further that he was clean again "when the sun is down" (Lev 22:6, 7, RSV). (2) Twilight, the period between sunset and dark. (3) In several instances "even" and "evening" are the translation of a Hebrew expression meaning literally, "between the two evenings," the time of lighting the lamps of the sanctuary (Ex 30:8; [see (2)]), and of offering the Passover lamb (ch 12:6; see RSV footnote). Originally, this was apparently at "the going down of the sun" (Deut 16:6). However, there have been two interpretations of "between the two evenings": one, that this meant the period between sunset and dark; and the other, that it meant the period between the first visible declining of the sun in the sky and actual sunset. The fact that the slaughter of the Passover lamb was on the 14th of the month, not after sunset that began the 15th, made the Jews, at least of later times, interpret "between the two evenings" as meaning between the declining of the sun (which actually begins as soon as the sun passes noon) and sunset. In the time of Josephus the official custom was to offer the lamb at the 9th hour, or about 3 P.M. (*Ant.* xiv. 4. 3).

Everlasting. [Heb. *'ôlam,* "for a long time," "for all time"; Gr. *aiōnios,* "age-lasting," "for ever," "eternal."] A term Biblically denoting time of long duration, always in a relative sense with respect to the inherent nature of the circumstances or conditions described by the expression. Neither *'ôlam* nor *aiōnios* of itself implies time without beginning or without end,

as does the English term "everlasting." Because the meaning of these words is conditional on the nature of that to which they are applied, the period of time they designate may have neither beginning nor end, or a beginning without an end, or both beginning and end. "Perpetual" would at times be a preferable English translation. *'Ôlam* indicates time of indefinite duration whose limits are either unknown or unspecified. When used of God it means "eternal" in the absolute sense, without beginning or end, because God is eternal (Gen 21:33). When used of the life of the redeemed it specifies time with a beginning but without end, the result of bestowal of immortality (Dan 12:2). The indefinite, durative, but nevertheless finite quality of *'ôlam* is clearly evident from Ex 21:6, where the expression is translated "for ever." Here it is specified that a slave who has already served his master for 6 years but who at the close of this period of indentured service voluntarily elects to bind himself to his master henceforth "in perpetuity," may do so. Obviously, *'ôlam* here has both a beginning and an end, the beginning specified and the term of servitude assumed to end upon the death of the servant. In view of the fact that the NT writers were Hebrews by race and background, they used *aiōnios,* the Greek equivalent of *'ôlam,* in the same sense that they would have used *'ôlam* had they been writing in Hebrew. The noun form from which the adjective *aiōnios* is derived (*aiōn*) means "age" or the "world" considered from the viewpoint of time, as in Mt 12:32; 13:22, 39; etc. The derived adjective *aiōnios* means simply "age-lasting." In every occurrence of the word the nature of the thing or circumstance described as "everlasting," as evident in the context and the analogy of Scripture, must determine the durative and terminal significance of *aiōnios.* The popular concept that "everlasting," as the translation of *'ôlam* or *aiōnios,* always denotes time without end is wholly without scriptural support.

Evi (ē'vī). [Heb. *'Ewî.*] One of the 5 kings of Midian who were vassals of Sihon, king of Heshbon. They were all slain in a war against the Israelites under Moses (Num 31:8; Jos 13:21).

Evil Spirit. *See* Demon.

Evil-merodach (ē'vĭl-mĕ-rō'dăk). [Heb. *'Ewîl Merodak;* Babylonian *Amel-Marduk,* "man of (the god) Marduk."] The son and successor of Nebuchadnezzar on the throne of Babylon. He ruled for 2 years (562-560 B.C.). According to the Babylonian historian Berossus, his reign was "arbitrary and licentious" (Jos. *Against Apion* i. 20, Loeb ed.). The Bible mentions Evil-merodach as showing kindness to King Jehoiachin of Judah, whom he released from prison in the 37th year of his captivity and placed in a more favorable position than that of any other exiled monarch living in Babylon (2 Ki 25:27-30; Jer 52:31-34). The expressions used in both texts are ambiguous as to whether Jehoiachin's release occurred in Amel-Marduk's accession year or in his first regnal year. Amel-Marduk fell victim to a murderous plot of his brother-in-law, Nergal-shar-usur (Neriglissar), who succeeded him on the throne.

Exactor. The translation of a form of the Heb. *nagaś,* "to impose (tribute)," "to drive (to work)," in Is 60:17, KJV, where "tax collectors," "imposers of tribute," or "taskmasters" may be meant; and in Dan 11:20, RSV, where an "exactor of tribute" is apparently referred to.

Executioner. A word appearing once in the KJV (Mk 6:27) and once in the RSV (Eze 9:1). In the KJV "executioner" is the translation of the Gr. *spekoulatōr,* "spy," "scout," "courier," but also "executioner." The word is used of the man who was dispatched to behead John the Baptist. In the RSV "executioners" appears as the translation of the Heb. *pequddôth,* which may be rendered "executioners" but may also simply mean "punishments," "visitations." If these latter meanings are adopted the passage would read, "the punishments [or "visitations"] of the city are near."

Exercise. In the NT "exercise" is usually the translation of *gumnazō,* "to exercise," "to train." It is in the latter sense that it is used in 1 Ti 4:7; Heb 5:14; 12:11; 2 Pe 2:14. Otherwise, in both the Old and New Testaments "exercise" carries the usual meaning associated with the term in English.

Exile. *See* Captivity.

Exodus. The departure, or journey, of the Israelites from Egypt after they had lived in that country for more than 2 centuries and had been held in slavery for some time. This migration, accomplished under the leadership of Moses, was accompanied by many miracles.

Historicity. The Egyptian records mention neither the stay of the Israelites in Egypt nor their departure. This complete lack of contemporary evidence has sometimes been employed as an argument against the historicity of the Exodus. However, the deliverance from bondage is so often referred to in Jewish poetical and historical records, that scholars now generally admit that the Exodus must be considered a historical event.

However, scholarly opinions differ widely as to the time of the Exodus, and as to whether the whole nation was involved in this great event or only some of the tribes of Israel. Many modern scholars place the Exodus in the 13th cent. B.C., believing that the mention of the city of Raamses or Rameses (Ex 1:11; 12:37; Num 33:3, 5) and "the land of Rameses" (Gen 47:11) indicates that the Exodus could not have taken place before the reign of Ramses II (*c.* 1299 - *c.* 1232 B.C.); others place the Exodus in the Hyksos period (*c.* 1730 - *c.* 1570 B.C.); others advocate 2 migrations, the 1st, led by Joshua, in the 15th cent. B.C.—perhaps related to the Habiru invasion of Canaan mentioned in the *Amarna Letters —and the 2d, led by Moses, in the 13th cent. B.C. Still others place it in the 15th cent. B.C. Each of these theories with respect to the time of the Exodus encounters certain historical and archeological difficulties, but the 15th cent. B.C. Exodus, which harmonizes with the scheme of chronology based on the 4th year of Solomon as the 480th year from the Exodus (*see* Chronology, II, 2), agrees more fully with Biblical data than any other theory, and is the one adopted in this dictionary.

The Biblical Story. The story of the departure from Egypt is related primarily in the book of Exodus, chs 1 to 14, with the preceding events narrated in the last chapters of Genesis. The family of Jacob had migrated to Egypt during a severe famine at a time when Joseph was the food administrator of Egypt. Some time after Joseph's death there "arose up a new king over Egypt, which knew not Joseph" (Ex 1:8). Fearing that the rapidly increasing Israelites might join possible enemies, the king of Egypt enslaved them in an attempt to weaken them. During that time Moses, the future leader of Israel, was born. Hidden in a floating basket on the Nile, the infant Moses was found by a princess of Egypt, who adopted him and brought him to the royal court. At the age of 40 he fled from Egypt into the Wilderness of Sinai, fearing punish-

167. The mummy of Amenhotep II, the possible Pharaoh of the Exodus

ment for having slain an Egyptian who mistreated a Hebrew. There he became a shepherd. Forty years later God commissioned him to go back to Egypt to lead His people out of their humiliation. After showing some reluctance at the first, Moses accepted the divine call and became his nation's greatest leader.

Arriving in Egypt, Moses requested that Pharaoh release the Israelites. His request met only with refusal and ridicule, as did subsequent requests. As a result 10 plagues in all were brought upon Egypt, some of them real catastrophes. Only after the Egyptians had lost heavily of their crops and domestic animals, had been smitten with diseases, and had lost their first-born children, did Pharaoh give in and allow the Israelites to leave Egypt. The departure took place on the 15th day of the month *Abib, the morning after the *Passover supper, which was initiated at that time by divine order, to be celebrated by the Israelites henceforth as a feast in memory of their liberation from slavery.

Leaving Goshen, the area of their habitation, they were led in a southerly direction until they reached the northwestern shore of the Red Sea. They were prevented from taking the shortest route to Canaan, because they were unprepared to meet the opposition of the nations they would face on that route. At the Red Sea, Pharaoh, who in the meantime had recovered from his initial shock of losing the crown prince, and who now regretted having allowed the Israelites to depart, overtook the Israelites, hoping to force them to return to Egypt. It was then that God divided the waters of the Red Sea and enabled His people to pass through to the eastern shore. The pursuing Egyptians, on the other hand, were swallowed up by the returning waters. The crossing of the Red Sea marked the accomplishment of the departure or exodus from Egypt proper and the beginning of the *Wilderness Wandering. The term "Exo-

dus" is here used in this restricted sense though it is recognized that it is often used to include the entire 40-year wilderness journey.

The Historical Background. The chronological statement of 1 Ki 6:1 places the beginning of the building of Solomon's Temple at Jerusalem in the 480th year after the Exodus. The date for the beginning of the building in Solomon's 4th regnal year is established with reasonable certainty (authorities differ by a few years). According to the chronological system of the Hebrew reigns that follows most closely the Biblical data for the period, the 4th year of Solomon was 967/66 B.C., and the Temple was begun in the spring of 966. This leads to c. 1445 B.C. as the date of the Exodus (*see* Chronology, II, 2), the time when Egypt was ruled by the powerful kings of the 18th dynasty.

Joseph had probably served one of the Semitic Hyksos kings of the 15th dynasty. His high position as a foreigner can best be understood as having been held during the period when the Hyksos, who were also aliens, were in power. The conversion of privately owned land in Egypt into crown property, described in Gen 47:13-26, probably made Joseph extremely unpopular, especially after the emergency had passed, since all Egyptians then found themselves serfs of an alien king. Finally, Sekenen-Re, a local prince of Thebes, undertook to fight the Hyksos. His sons, 1st Kamose, then Ahmose, continued the struggle until, after a long war, the Hyksos were expelled from Egyptian soil. Ahmose became the founder of a new dynasty, one which was exceedingly nationalistic in spirit, and which became extremely powerful at home and abroad. Its kings built an empire eventually reaching from southern Nubia in Africa to the river Euphrates in Asia. According to the chronology of the Exodus adopted in this dictionary, it was one of the early kings of the new dynasty who, after expelling the Hyksos, took measures to reduce the Semitic Israelites to servitude, and to arrest the rapid increase of their population by devising means of killing their newborn infants. It would be this new (18th) dynasty (for the 16th and 17th dynasties *see* Egypt, V, 6) that is designated by the expression "there arose up a new king over Egypt, which knew not Joseph" (Ex 1:8).

According to this chronology it would be during this time of oppression, probably under Thutmose I (c. 1525 - c. 1508

B.C.), that Moses was born (1525 B.C.), and a few years later entered the Egyptian court. Thutmose I, a commoner, had come to the throne because his wife, the daughter of Ahmose, was a royal princess. Having no legitimate son, he gave his daughter Hatshepsut as wife to her half brother, a son from a commoner wife. This half brother took the throne as Thutmose II after his father's death and occupied it for 4 years (c. 1508 - c. 1504 B.C.). He also had only daughters, and so upon Thutmose II's death Hatshepsut assumed the rule of the kingdom. She ruled successfully until a temple revolution several years later forced her to accept as coruler an illegitimate son of her late half brother and husband, who took the name of Thutmose III. About 1482 B.C. Hatshepsut disappeared, perhaps died, and her coregent took over as sole ruler. Because of his deep hatred for his aunt and stepmother, he mutilated her inscriptions after her death, by erasing her name from the monuments, and by smashing her statues. Thutmose III ruled over Egypt for some 32 years (c. 1482 - c. 1450 B.C.). He became a great war lord and built the greatest empire Egypt had ever seen. He was probably the king from whom Moses fled in 1485 B.C., in which case the flight probably preceded the death of Hatshepsut, for she seems the most likely person to have been his adoptive mother. Since Moses grew up in a royal household in which for several generations no legitimate male heirs were born, it is logical to surmise that Hatshepsut might have planned to have Moses marry one of her daughters and to put him on the throne if circumstances should allow. However, any such plans would have been foiled by the revolution forcing her to accept Thutmose as coruler. Such plans would account for Thutmose III's hatred for Hatshepsut, and would explain why Moses, with no future for him at the royal court, and hated by the future king, would make the decision to assume leadership of his subjugated people, fully expecting that they would welcome such a move. It would also explain why his clumsy attempt to aid them by killing an Egyptian, whom he saw mistreating a Hebrew, was considered a crime so grave that Moses' life was no longer safe in Egypt.

Forty years later, after the death of the king who had sought the life of Israel's would-be deliverer (Ex 2:23), God called Moses to become Israel's leader. By that time Thutmose III had been followed by Amenhotep II, a cruel and ruthless son. It was probably Amenhotep II to whom Moses was sent, under whom all the plagues occurred, and who lost his son in the 10th plague and his army in the Red Sea. According to accepted Egyptian chronology of this period (considered to be exact within a margin of perhaps 10 years) he reigned from c. 1450 to c. 1425 B.C. If this is correct, then his death did not come until some 20 years after 1445 B.C., the suggested date for the Exodus. Since the Bible seems to indicate that the Pharaoh of the Exodus was with his forces that perished in the Red Sea, the placement of the end of his reign in 1425 B.C. poses a chronological problem, which has not yet been solved. However, there is nothing in the historical records that would bar the possibility of his having drowned with his army in the Red Sea. The fact that his mummy, like many others, has been preserved (see fig. 167) proves merely that if he was drowned his body was recovered. His son and successor on the throne, Thutmose IV (1425-1412 B.C.), left to posterity a monument that mentions his unexpected elevation to the throne (see fig. 145), thus indicating that he had not originally been the crown prince—a situation that would be true if it was his older brother that had perished in the 10th plague, in which all the firstborn were slain.

With the exception of the chronological problem connected with Amenhotep II's reign, the Biblical story of the Exodus fits remarkably well into the historical background of the 15th cent. B.C., better, in fact, than into any other known historical period of Egypt.

The Route of the Exodus. The exact route taken by the Israelites until they reached the Red Sea is difficult to ascertain, because only 2 of the 6 places mentioned by name can be identified with reasonable certainty. The point of departure was *Rameses (Ex 12:37), in the northeastern Delta (Map V, B-3, gives 2 alternative locations). From there they went to *Succoth, probably the first rallying place, since it lay in the land of Goshen, the home of the Israelites for over 200 years. Succoth has been plausibly identified with *Tell el-Maskhûṭah*, the *Theku* of the Egyptian texts. It lies in the eastern part of the *Wâdî Tumilât*, the "land of Goshen."

The shortest and most natural route to Canaan would have been the coastal desert road via Raphia to Gaza, called

168. The burial chamber of Amenhotep II, the possible Pharaoh of the Exodus, in the Valley of the Kings at western Thebes (for his mummy see fig. 167)

in Ex 13:17 "the way of the land of the Philistines." The people, however, were not allowed to use this route, not being ready to fight their way through a well-fortified area. They were led, instead, in a southeasterly direction, by "the way of the wilderness of the Red sea" (v 18). *Etham, at "the edge of the wilderness" (v 20), was their 1st camping place after leaving Succoth. It has not yet been identified. At Etham they changed direction and made their next stop in front of *Pi-ha-hiroth (ch 14:2), which also remains unidentified, as do the next 2 sites mentioned, *Migdol, probably one of the fortresses of the eastern fortification system, and *Baal-zephon (vs 2, 9).

The Israelites reached the sea near Pi-ha-hiroth. The identification of this sea has been frequently debated. The Hebrew term applied to it in Ex 13:18 is *yam-sûph,* which means literally "sea of reeds." Since the Red Sea contains no reeds, some have suggested that one of the eastern lakes—Lake Timsah or one of the Bitter Lakes—is actually meant. However, in 1 Ki 9:26 *yam-sûph* is identified with the eastern arm of the Red Sea, the Gulf of Aqabah, and it would seem logical to apply *yam-sûph* to the Red Sea in other texts also. However, whatever identification is accepted, the exact site where the crossing took place is unknown. One likely place is in the northern part of the Gulf of Suez south of the city of Suez, but north of the mountains of the Egyptian desert that reach to the seashore a short distance below, making passage there impossible. If the crossing occurred here the Israelites' fear at the approach of Pharaoh's armies can be easily understood, for the way to the south was blocked by mountains and the sea formed an impassable barrier to the east. It was then that the miracle of the dividing of the sea saved them from what appeared a hopeless predicament. The crossing at this point is not shown on Map V, which shows routes according to several other theories. The route based on the "sea" being the Red Sea is the red line. However, it makes the crossing take place north rather than south of the city of Suez.

When the Israelites left the Red Sea, they began the long journey through the wilderness which ended 40 years later. *See* Wilderness Wandering.

Exodus, Book of. The 2d book of the Pentateuch, in Hebrew Bibles bearing the title *we'elleh shemôth,* "and these are the names," the opening words of the Hebrew text. The English title originated with the title given the book by the translators of the Septuagint, who called it *Exodos,* an appropriate characterization based on the book's central theme, the departure of the Hebrew people from Egypt. The Hebrew word "and" with which the narrative of Exodus begins indicates that the writer considered it to be a continuation of the account in the book of Genesis. From the most ancient times Jewish scholars have attributed the Pentateuch, in which the book of Exodus is found, to Moses. Internal evidence clearly points to him as the author. The use of many Egyptian terms, the minute description of certain Egyptian customs, the intimate knowledge of the land of Egypt itself and of the route of the Exodus, all clearly point to an educated Jew who at one time lived in Egypt (see Acts 7:22) and who was familiar with parts of the Sinai Peninsula as well. The vivid description of incidents connected with the departure from Egypt and the journey to Mount Sinai, as well as of the events that took place there, is such as none but an eyewitness could be expected to give. This internal evidence, together with the fact that our Lord quotes from the book of Exodus and specifically calls it "the book of Moses" (Mk 12:26), is sufficient to establish him as the writer for all who accept the divine origin of Scripture and the deity of the Son of God.

At the time of the Exodus (*c.* 1445 B.C.) Israel had been in Egypt about 215 years (*see* Chronology II, 2). The friendly kings of the Hyksos period, during whose dynasty Joseph and later Jacob settled in Egypt, had given way to the native Egyptian kings of the 18th dynasty about 135 years before the Exodus (see Ex 1:8). It was between this event and the birth of Moses, 80 years before the Exodus (ch 7: 7), that the oppression of ch 1:9-22 began. The book of Exodus traces briefly the personal experiences of Moses during this preparatory period of his life, and then deals at length and in great detail with events of the 6 months or so preceding the departure from Egypt and the first 2 years thereafter—a period of approximately 2½ years altogether. During this comparatively brief period the Hebrew people were transformed from a race of slaves into an independent nation, and the book of Exodus explains how this came about.

The book may be divided into 5 major sections: (1) the early life and training of Moses, Ex 1:1 to 4:31; (2) the 10 plagues upon the land of Egypt, chs 5:1 to 12:30; (3) the Exodus and the journey to Sinai, chs 12:31 to 19:2; (4) Israel constituted a nation at Sinai, chs 19:3 to 24: 18; (5) construction of the tabernacle and arrangements for the ritual service, chs 25:1 to 40:38. In ch 1 a brief account is given of the enslavement of the Hebrew people by the Egyptians, whereas ch 2 traces the life of Moses down to the close of his sojourn in the land of Midian. Moses' call to liberate the Hebrew people and his return to Egypt are related in chs 3 and 4. Chapters 5 and 6 deal with preliminary moves to secure the release of the Hebrews. In chs 7 to 10 the first 9 plagues are described. In chs 11:1 to 13: 16 we find a record of the 10th plague and of the institution of the Passover, which took place simultaneously. Outstanding events on the way to Mount Sinai—the crossing of the Red Sea, the miraculous provision of water and food, the repeated murmuring of the people, the victory over Amalek—occupy chs 13: 17 to 19:2. While Israel was encamped at Mount Sinai God revealed to them His moral law (chs 19:3 to 20:21), and a civil code, applying the principles of the moral law to the polity of Israel as a nation (chs 20:22 to 23:33). He revealed also His covenant that constituted Israel a theocracy (ch 24), and gave detailed instructions for the erection of the tabernacle and for the preparation of facilities to be used in connection with it (chs 25:1 to 31:18). A brief interlude relates Israel's apostasy and restoration to divine favor (chs 32:1 to 34:35). In chs 35:1 to 40:38 we find a detailed record of the actual construction of the tabernacle and the fabrication of such items as anointing oil, incense, and the priestly vestures to be used in connection with it, and finally the account of Moses' inspection and approval of the workmanship, and the erection of the structure, ready for use. The departure from Mount Sinai took place less than 2 months after the events of the book of Exodus came to a close (Ex 40:17; Num 10:11, 12).

Exorcist. The translation of the Gr. *exorkistēs,* one who, by the use of magical formulas, professes to cast out demons and remove their influence (Acts 19:13).

Expiate, Expiation. Terms used in the RSV for the Heb. *chatta'th* (Num 8:7) and *kaphar* (Num 35:33; Deut 32:43; 1 Sa 3:14; 2 Sa 21:3; Is 27:9; 47:11), and for the Gr. *hilastērion* (Rom 3:25), *hilaskomai* (Heb 2:17), and *hilasmos* (1 Jn 2:2; 4:10). Since these terms may imply appeasement they can give a wrong concept, especially when applied to the work of Christ. *See* Atonement.

Extortion. The practice of wresting property or money from another by force or subterfuge, sometimes by employing intimidation (Ps 109:11; Is 16:4; KJV; Eze 22:12; Lk 18:11; etc.). God warned that trust is not to be put in money gained by extortion (Ps 62:10; KJV "oppression"), and condemned the Jews for practicing this evil (Eze 22:7, 29, RSV; etc.). Christ scathingly rebuked the scribes and Pharisees for their extortion hidden under a cloak of sanctimoniousness (Mt 23:25). Paul exhorted the Corinthian believers not to associate with extortioners, stating that such men cannot enter heaven (1 Cor 5:10, 11; 6:10; RSV "robbers," a translation of the same Greek word translated "extortioners" in Lk 18:11).

Extreme Burning. A rendering of the Heb. *charchur* (Deut 28:22), translated "fiery heat" in the RSV. The specific malady referred to is uncertain.

Eye. Literally, the organ of physical sight perception, and figuratively, the faculty of mental and spiritual perception. The Law of Moses provided that deliberate injury to the eye should be punished by the infliction of a similar injury to the eye of the guilty person—"eye for eye" (Ex 21:24; Deut 19:21). In a sense this was merciful, in that the infliction of a greater injury was prohibited for a lesser one. To "lift up" one's eyes (Gen 13:10; 18:2; 22:13; 24:63; etc.) is to observe carefully. Figuratively, the psalmist prayed that God would open his eyes to understand His revealed will (Ps 119:18). The "eye" also stands for the disposition or character, as in Ps 18:27; 131:1; Prov 22:9; 2 Pe 2:14. The many eyes of the living creatures of Ezekiel (Eze 1:18; 10:12; Rev 4:6) probably stand figuratively for the omniscience of God.

Eyesalve. [Gr. *kollourion*.] A reference probably to a famous powder produced in Phrygia and used in the school of medicine at Laodicea. The term is used figuratively of Heaven's cure for spiritual blindness (Rev 3:18).

Ezar. *See* Ezer, I.

Ezbai (ĕz'bȧ-ī). [Heb. *'Ezbay*, meaning uncertain.] The father of one of David's "mighty men," Naarai, or Paarai (2 Sa 23:35; 1 Chr 11:37).

Ezbon (ĕz'bŏn). [Heb. *'Eṣbôn*.]
1. A son of Gad and founder of a tribal family (Gen 46:16). It is apparently he who is called Ozni in Num 26:16.
2. The head of a tribal family of Benjamin (1 Chr 7:7).

Ezekias. *See* Hezekiah.

Ezekiel (ê-zē'kĭ-ĕl). [Heb. *Yechezqe'l*, "God will strengthen."] A priest, the son of Buzi, born in Judah but transported to Babylonia with the group that went into captivity with Jehoiachin in 597 B.C. (Eze 1:1-3). He was then about 25 years of age if "the thirtieth year" (ch 1:1) is a reference to his age (cf. v 2). He was with a group of Jews settled at Tel-abib (chs 1:1, 3; 3:15) by "the river Chebar" (ch 1:1), an irrigation canal known from cuneiform records as *Nār Kabari*, which passed the city of Nippur. Archeological evidence testifies to a large Jewish settlement in this vicinity during the time of the Babylonian captivity. Ezekiel was happily married, but his wife died about 9 years after their captivity began (ch 24:1, 16). He seems to have had a house of his own (Eze 3:24; 8:1; cf. Jer 29:5). In the 5th year of his captivity he was called to the prophetic office (Eze 1:2, 3; 2; 3), and served in this capacity for some 22 years (ch 29:17), from about 593 to 571 B.C. At a time when the Temple lay in ruins and the people were in exile it was particularly appropriate that the offices of priest and prophet should be united in one person. Jeremiah, whose ministry was, in part, contemporary with that of Ezekiel, was likewise a priest-prophet (Jer 1:1), as was Zechariah, and also doubtless others (Zec 1:1; cf. Ezr 5:1; 6:14; Neh 12:4, 16). In a special sense Ezekiel was God's messenger to the Jews in captivity, as Jeremiah was to the Jews who remained in Judah and Jerusalem, and as Daniel was to Nebuchadnezzar and the court at Babylon. All 3 were divinely commissioned with the purpose of securing the divine objectives in the Captivity. Apparently Ezekiel was well liked by the people to whom he bore his inspired messages, but his mission seems to have met with limited success (Eze 20:49; 33:32).

Ezekiel, Book of. The book containing the messages of Ezekiel the prophet to the Jews of the Babylonian exile from 593/92 to 571/70 B.C. In the English Bible Ezekiel follows the writings of Jeremiah and precedes those of Daniel. In Hebrew Bibles

Ezekiel is preceded by Jeremiah and followed by Hosea, the book of Daniel being classified in the section known as the Hagiographa, or Writings. The book of Ezekiel seems to have been accepted into the prophetic canon at an early date, and its right to a place there has never been challenged. Unlike many other books of the OT, Ezekiel is usually recognized as genuine even by critical scholars, although some attacks have been made upon it.

By the time of the Babylonian captivity more than 8 centuries had passed since the formal covenant at Mount Sinai by which Israel as a nation had accepted God's invitation to become His chosen people and had pledged itself to Him as theocratic ruler. In the divine purpose the Jewish people, by strict obedience to God's wise and just requirements, were to reflect God's character and to become the recipients of spiritual and material blessings that would testify to the nations of the earth of the superiority of the worship and service of the true God above all false gods. But continued and increasing apostasy finally made it clear that only by the most severe measures could the Jewish nation ever be expected to realize its high mission. The people had forgotten that it was only by virtue of their covenant agreement with God that they occupied the Land of Promise, and that apostasy meant the forfeit of that right. Accordingly, God sent them into exile to learn under adverse circumstances the lesson they had failed to learn in times of prosperity, namely, that they must accept the responsibilities of the covenant relationship if they would enjoy its privileges. God purposed that the leaders of Israel, who were chiefly at fault, should be sent into exile (Is 3:12; 9:16; Eze 34:2-19; Dan 1:3, 4), but that the vast majority of the people were to remain in their homeland, awaiting there the return of a chastened leadership. In order that the people might understand and cooperate with the divine purpose in the Captivity, God sent the prophet Jeremiah to instruct those who remained behind, and commissioned Ezekiel to be His spokesman to the exiles in Babylon. Simultaneously God sent Daniel as His ambassador to the court of Babylon, to secure Nebuchadnezzar's submission to, and cooperation with, His purpose.

As Ezekiel himself relates, he "was among the captives by the river of Chebar" (Eze 1:1), probably at Tel-abib (ch 3:15), having been transported there with the 2d contingent of exiles, at the time of Jehoiachin's captivity in 597 B.C., from which event the numerous chronological notices in the book are computed (Eze 1: 2). Apparently the exiles at Tel-abib were permitted to administer their own local affairs through a group of "elders" (see chs 8:1; 14:1; 20:1, 3), and were permitted to communicate with the leaders who remained in Jerusalem (Jer 29:1, 24-29). As a whole, the exiles doubtless led a reasonably normal social and economic life (see ch 29:5-10, 28).

Ezekiel was called to the prophetic office in midsummer, in 593/92 B.C. (Eze 1:2). Whereas former prophets had largely been content simply to date their messages by noting the reign of the king under which the messages were given, Ezekiel and Jeremiah often provide practically complete chronological information, giving the month and day as well as the year, so that it is possible to correlate the messages with specific historical developments. This greatly helps in understanding the import of the successive messages, since each is thus dated. Ezekiel's ministry, at least in so far as his recorded messages are concerned, seems to have been concentrated largely within the 7 years immediately preceding the destruction of Jerusalem and the Temple in 586 B.C. and in the next few months thereafter. His ministry extended at least some 15 years later, to 571/70 B.C.

If a title were to be given the book appropriate to its contents, perhaps none would serve better than "Captivity and Restoration," since these subjects are the 2 foci around which the messages cluster. Chapters 1-33 are concerned with the former; chs 34-48 deal with the latter, the arrival of news concerning the fall of Jerusalem (ch 33:21) logically dividing the book into 2 parts. The constantly recurring theme that binds the 2 sections together is "Ye shall know that I am the Lord" (chs 6:7; 7:4; etc.). This expression or its equivalent occurs more than 60 times and emphasizes the fundamental cause of Israel's failure hitherto— they did not understand or appreciate God's righteous character or the exalted purpose and destiny that the covenant relationship vouchsafed to them as a nation. The Captivity was ordained to teach them this all-important lesson. Messages borne by Ezekiel prior to the arrival of word that Jerusalem had fallen were designed to secure the cooperation of the exiles with God's plan for the Captivity.

The exiles were to submit to Nebuchadnezzar (for a period of 70 years; Jer 25: 12; 29:10).

About the time Ezekiel received his call to the prophetic office in Babylonia, King Zedekiah at Jerusalem was entertaining envoys from neighboring nations seeking an alliance to rise in revolt and throw off the Babylonian yoke (Jer 27:2, 3). Jeremiah warned that the yokes of wood they proposed to break would be replaced with yokes of iron (see ch 28:10, 12). Among the false prophets at Jerusalem were some who predicted the end of the Captivity and the return of the captives "within two full years" (vs 3, 4, 11). The Jews in Babylonia apparently shared the expectation of a brief captivity (see ch 29:28). It was these circumstances that led Jeremiah to counsel submission to God's plan for an extended captivity (chs 27:4-17; 29:5-13, 28) and that formed the background for Ezekiel's messages recorded in Eze 1-23. Jeremiah 24-33, on the other hand, deals more particularly with the siege of Jerusalem and its fall in 586. With a spirit of unwarranted optimism the Jews blindly believed that God would not allow this calamity to come (Jer 7:4; 17:15; 26:8, 9; Eze 11:3, 15; etc.), but both Jeremiah (Jer 26:6) and Ezekiel (Eze 11:5-11) sought to dispel this vain hope. When the destruction of the city and the Temple eventually dashed this vain hope to the ground the Jewish people gave themselves up to despair, apparently fearing that the Captivity would be permanent and that their nation would never be restored. Their national pride thus fully humbled, the people stood in need of encouragement, lest their loss of hope should incapacitate them for learning the great lesson of the Captivity and for responding to the eventual summons to return and rebuild Jerusalem. Such encouragement God sent through the prophet Jeremiah (Jer 31:27 to 33:26) to the Jews who remained in Jerusalem, and through Ezekiel to the exiles in Babylonia (Eze 34-48).

The mysterious vision of God's throne and the "wheel in the middle of a wheel" (Eze 1:26, 16) that accompanied Ezekiel's commission to the prophetic office was designed to impress upon the prophet the greatness and majesty of God (cf. Is 6: 1-8). Boldly he was to proclaim the words that God gave him to speak (Eze 2:3-8), not quailing at the people's dullness of perception and their hardness of heart (ch 3:1-11). He became not only God's spokesman (Eze 2:8; 3:1) but His watchman over the house of Israel (ch 3:15-21). As a reminder of Ezekiel's role as spokesman and watchman, God inflicted dumbness upon him (v 26) and gave him the faculty of speech only when bearing the messages God should bid him speak (v 27). This experience served also as a testimony to the people that God was indeed speaking through the prophet. With the arrival of news that Jerusalem had fallen, his tongue was loosed (ch 33: 21, 22).

Ezekiel's first message (Eze 4-7) announces the inevitability of the fall of Jerusalem. He is to act out the siege in pantomime in order to impress the exiles (ch 4:1-8) and to depict the sufferings of the people during that time (chs 4:9 to 6:7). A remnant will escape, however (ch 6:8-14). But an "end is come" (ch 7), and the centuries of warning are to be fulfilled without further delay. The 2d message (chs 8-19) delineates in bold strokes the reason for the Captivity, particularly for the impending blow of 586 B.C. that was to lay Jerusalem waste—Israel's now absolute apostasy. Chapter 8 etches a vivid picture of how the sacred precincts of the Temple were at that very time being prostituted to various forms of heathen worship, and the vision of the man with a writer's inkhorn in ch 9 announces the close of the city's period of probation. The coals of fire scattered over the city (ch 10:2) depict the same idea, which is confirmed by a repetition of the vision of ch 1, thus stressing the fact that what is to take place is the divine will (ch 10:3-22). In ch 11 Ezekiel is shown the stubborn opposition of the people in Jerusalem to the idea that the city will fall. By the graphic device of moving his own household effects (ch 12:1-7) he reinforces the divine proclamation concerning the city's fate (vs 8-20) and declares that God will no longer delay the fulfillment of His word (vs 21-28). Ezekiel then warns against the messages of the false prophets (ch 13), and when the elders come to restrain him, he boldly declares their sins and repeats the warning of judgment (chs 14; 15). By an allegory he sets forth God's persistent efforts to exalt Israel, and their persistent apostasy (ch 16). It is the failure of the contemporary leaders that has made the fall of Jerusalem inevitable (ch 17), and they cannot escape responsibility by blaming their woes on the sins of their fathers (chs 18; 19). The 3d message (chs 20-23) covers generally the same ground as the 2d and closes with another lengthy allegory depicting Israel's apostasy. The 4th message (Eze 24; possibly also ch 25) announces the beginning of the siege, and the destruction of the Temple is graphically portrayed by the death of the prophet's own wife—the "desire" of his eyes, as the Temple was the "desire" of every Jew. In ch 25 Ezekiel inveighs against the neighbor nations for taking advantage of the Jews in their hour of extremity. The next section (chs 26-32) consists of a series of messages given at different times, in which God declares His purpose to judge the neighboring nations as well as Israel, with particular attention given to the Phoenician capital of Tyre and to Egypt. Chapter 33 consists mostly of messages addressed to the prophet himself, reiterating his status as a watchman over Israel, though vs 21, 22 relate the incident (dated 2 mos. earlier than ch 32) of the arrival of news of the fall of Jerusalem.

The 2d part of the book of Ezekiel (chs 34 to 48) consists of a series of messages dealing with various aspects of the restoration from captivity. God will restore His people to their land and enter into a new covenant with them (ch 34). The triumph of Israel will be accompanied by the desolation of their foes (ch 35). God will give His people a new heart, to obey Him, and will do better by them than ever before (ch 36). The nation will be revived, and the 2 kingdoms, Judah and Joseph (the 10 tribes), will be reunited under the house of David (ch 37). All of their enemies will be destroyed (chs 38; 39). The Temple will be rebuilt, more ample and glorious than ever (chs 40-42), God will again take up residence among His people, and the priestly service will be reinaugurated (chs 43; 44). The land will be reapportioned (ch 45), and "the prince" (Messiah) will come and go among them (ch 46). From the Temple there will flow forth a healing stream that restores the

169. The site of ancient Ezion-geber at the head of the Gulf of Aqabah

entire earth to Edenic beauty, thus depicting the extension of God's sovereignty over the whole earth (Eze 47). The city itself is described (see fig. 464), and its name given as "The Lord is there" (ch 48).

It should be remembered that Ezekiel was describing for the exiles in Babylon God's plans for their return and for the restored state of 12 tribes, plans centering on the city and Temple to which the Messianic Prince would come. However, because of unfaithfulness the returned Jews failed to realize what was envisioned by Ezekiel. For a discussion of prophecies of this type *see* Prophet, II.

Ezel (ē′zĕl). [Heb. *Ha'azel,* of which the *ha* is the article.] According to the KJV, a stone where David hid until Jonathan could inform him of King Saul's attitude (1 Sa 20:19). Its location is unknown. The RSV follows the LXX in this passage, reading "stone heap" instead of "stone Ezel."

Ezem (ē′zĕm), KJV twice **Azem** (ā′zĕm). [Heb. *'Eṣem,* "mighty."] A town in southern Judah later assigned to Simeon (Jos 15:29; 19:3; 1 Chr 4:29). It has been identified with *Umm el-'Aẓam,* about 12 mi. southeast of Beer-sheba.

Ezer, I (ē′zĕr), KJV once **Ezar** (ē′zĕr). [Heb. *'Eser.*] A son of Seir the Horite (Gen 36: 21, 30; 1 Chr 1:38).

Ezer, II. [Heb. *'Ezer,* "helper," a name occurring also on ancient Hebrew seals.]

1. A son of Ephraim. While he and his brother Elead were stealing cattle from Gath they were slain by the inhabitants of the town (1 Chr 7:21, 22).

2. A descendant of Judah (1 Chr 4:4).

3. A Gadite warrior who joined David at Ziklag (1 Chr 12:9).

4. A ruler of Mizpah who in Nehemiah's time repaired part of the wall of Jerusalem (Neh 3:19).

5. A priest who took part in the dedication ceremony of the rebuilt wall of Jerusalem (Neh 12:42).

Ezion-gaber. *See* Ezion-geber.

Ezion-geber (ē′zĭ-ŏn-gē′bĕr), KJV 4 times **Ezion-gaber** (ē′zĭ-ŏn-gā′bĕr). [Heb. *'Esyón Geber.*] A town at the northern end of the Gulf of Aqabah, the eastern arm of the Red Sea. It is first mentioned in the Bible as one of the stations where the Israelites camped during their desert wanderings (Num 33:35, 36; Deut 2:8). See fig. 169. It came into prominence as a port during the period of the united Hebrew monarchy; Solomon made it the port city from which his expeditions to Ophir originated (1 Ki 9:26; 2 Chr 8:17). Jehoshaphat attempted to revive these expeditions, but his fleet was destroyed in a storm at Ezion-geber (1 Ki 22:48). Because of this disaster he gave up all further attempts

170. A wall of King Solomon's smelters at Ezion-geber, showing two rows of flue holes

to rebuild the fleet, although Ahaziah, the son of Ahab, offered to help him (1 Ki 22:49; 2 Chr 20:36, 37). When in its revolt against Joram, Jehoshaphat's son, Edom gained its independence, Judah's rule over Ezion-geber must also have ended temporarily. But Amaziah defeated the Edomites, and again gained control over that area. His son Uzziah built *Elath, apparently the twin city of Ezion-geber, lying probably east of it (2 Ki 14:7, 22; 2 Chr 25:11, 12; 26:1, 2). From that time Ezion-geber is not mentioned again in historical records. It probably passed from the hands of the Israelites back into those of the Edomites. When the Edomites were replaced by the Arabian Nabataeans, the city of Ezion-geber became a Nabataean possession.

After a period of unsuccessful searching, the site (Map V, C-6) was discovered by F. Frank (*ZDPV* 57 [1934], 243, 244) to be *Tell el-Kheleifeh*, which was then excavated in three seasons under the direction of Nelson Glueck from 1938 to 1940. It was found that the strongly fortified city had been a great metal-producing center. It had a whole row of smelters in which the copper and iron ore extracted from the mines of Edom (cf. Deut 8:9) were refined and made into ingots and finished products. The town lay between the mountains of Palestine and Edom at the end of the troughlike *Wâdî 'Arabah*,

through which a constant wind blew in a southerly direction, thus automatically furnishing the necessary draft for the refinery smelters. Because of this, all furnaces were located in a row at the northwestern end of the town, with flue openings toward the north (see fig. 170). The wind reached the furnaces by means of air channels.

Lit.: Nelson Glueck, *BA* 1 (1938), 13-16; 2 (1939), 37-41; 4 (1940), 51-55; *BASOR* 71 (1938), 3-17; 75 (1939), 8-22; 79 (1940), 2-18.

Eznite. *See* Adino.

Ezra (ĕz'rá). [Heb. and Aramaic *'Ezra'*, thought to be either a late form of *'ezrah*, "help," "assistance," or an abbreviation of *'Azaryahû*, "Azariah," "Yahweh has helped," or "Yahweh gives assistance."]

1. For 1 Chr 4:17, KJV, *see* Ezrah.

2. A leading priest who accompanied Zerubbabel upon the return from Babylonian captivity (Neh 12:1, 7), probably founder of the postexilic house of Ezra (vs 12, 13).

3. A priestly descendant of Zadok, of the house of Phinehas (Ezr 7:1-6), probable author of the canonical book of Ezra. He was commissioned by a decree of the Persian king Artaxerxes issued in his 7th year, to journey to Jerusalem, to set up civil and religious administration, and to take whatever measures might be found necessary for the welfare of Jerusalem and its inhabitants (vs 6-26). He was "a ready scribe in the law of Moses" (v 6), and thus a well-educated Jew of the priestly class. Jewish tradition identifies him as the first of the order of "scribes," who, in the days of Christ, were the official interpreters of the Jewish law. With the royal decree in his hand and accompanied by a 2d band of Jewish exiles numbering more than 1,700 men, Ezra arrived in Jerusalem in the 5th month (v 8), approximately in August. (This would be August, 457 B.C., if the 7th year of the reign is to be reckoned according to the Jewish fall-to-fall civil year beginning half a year later than the Persian year, which ran from spring to spring.) Finding the Jews of Palestine lax in observing the requirements of the Law, he instituted a thoroughgoing series of reforms. Many of the priests and others who had married heathen wives were persuaded to divorce them (chs 9; 10). Under the governorship of Nehemiah some 13 years later, Ezra led in the public reading and exposition of the Law (Neh 8), and had a leading role

in the dedication of the new city wall (Neh 12:36) after its rebuilding under the leadership of Nehemiah.

171. Ezra reading the Law, as depicted in a mural in the 3d cent. synagogue at Dura Europus (Map XIII, C-5)

Ezra, Book of. A canonical work that records the return of the Jewish exiles from captivity in Babylonia and their re-establishment in Jerusalem, together with relevant genealogical lists and copies of the royal documents that authorized the restoration in its successive stages. Prior to A.D. 1448 Ezra and Nehemiah stood as one book in all Hebrew Bibles and were counted as one. In the LXX the book Ezra-Nehemiah appears as one book with the title 2 Esdras, with an Apocryphal book bearing the title Esdras preceding it as 1 Esdras. About A.D. 400 Jerome, translator of the Latin Vulgate, separated Ezra-Nehemiah into 2 books, as they appear in all English translations, but called them 1 Esdras and 2 Esdras. He also transposed the LXX Apocryphal work 1 Esdras and gave it the title 3 Esdras, and

to these 3 added a spurious apocalypse bearing the name of Ezra and called it 4 Esdras. In Hebrew Bibles Ezra-Nehemiah appears near the close of the 3d and last section of the OT, the Hagiographa, or Writings, with only Chronicles following. This position in the canon suggests that Ezra-Nehemiah and Chronicles were either the last of the OT books to be written or the last to be accepted into the canon, or both. The translators of the LXX transposed this group of historical works to the position they now occupy in English translations, next to Kings, near the close of the historical section of the OT. The LXX also transposed Chronicles, which it divided into 2 books, so as to precede Ezra and Nehemiah, probably on the basis that when read in this order the 4 books provide a chronological historical narrative from David to near the close of OT times, with genealogical records from the Creation to David. In view of the fact that the Hebrew text of Ezra begins with the word "and," together with the additional fact that the last 2 verses of 2 Chr 36 are repeated verbatim in Ezra 1:1-3, it is thought likely that at one time Ezra may have followed Chronicles in the Hebrew canon, or at least in some Hebrew manuscripts.

Jewish tradition (Talmud, *Baba Bathra* 15a) identifies Ezra as the principal writer of Ezra-Nehemiah. Certain passages are written in the first person (Ezr 7:28 to 9:1-15), but without identifying the writer by name. Ezra is mentioned by name 7 times in ch 7 (vs 1, 6, 10-12, 21, 25) and 6 times in ch 10 (vs 1, 2, 5, 6, 10, 16), but nowhere else in the book. Narrative sections in the 3d person are chs 7 1-26; 8:35, 36; 10:1-44. The book thus leaves the matter of authorship undetermined. However, certain considerations clearly point to a Jew of the time of Ezra, or soon thereafter, as responsible for the composition of the book. In view of the fact that Ezra-Nehemiah originally constituted one work, and that the genealogical lists of Neh 12 terminate about 400 B.C., it is reasonable to suppose that the combined work was completed by that time. The precise details enumerated in connection with the return from Babylon, together with the royal Persian decrees quoted at length, possibly in full, point to the writer as a person familiar with these events and one who had access to the documents themselves. Two sections (Ezr 4: 8 to 6:18; 7:12-26) are in Aramaic, and the remainder in Hebrew, a bilingual characteristic found also in the book of Daniel. Since Aramaic was the official language of the Persian Empire and a sort of lingua franca spoken widely even where it was not the native tongue, the bilingual nature of the book points to an educated Jew, possibly one in the service of the government, as the writer (see Ezr 7:6). The great linguistic similarities between the Aramaic portions of Ezra on the one hand, and a group of recently recovered *Aramaic Jewish documents dating from the same period, on the other, provide further testimony concerning a 5th-century date for the book. Similarly, the Hebrew portions of Ezra are strikingly similar in language and literary style, not only to Nehemiah, as might be expected, but also to Chronicles, and to a remarkable extent to Daniel and Haggai as well. Some have suggested that one writer was responsible for both Chronicles and Ezra-Nehemiah. Ezra, "a ready scribe," qualifies in every way as the writer, and there is no valid reason to deny his authorship.

Ezra, Nehemiah, and Esther are the only historical books dealing with the postexilic period, and are most important as source material for events of that time, concerning which the Sacred Canon is otherwise silent, with the exception of slight information provided by the prophetic books of Haggai, Zechariah, and Malachi. The close of the 70-year period foretold by Jeremiah (Jer 25:11; cf. 29:10) witnessed the decree by Cyrus for the return of the Jews and the rebuilding of Jerusalem with its Temple. Apparently but a small fraction of the Jewish exiles returned to their homeland, leaving by far the larger number behind. Beset by enemies without (Ezr 4) and lethargy within (Hag 1:1-5), work on the Temple came to a halt. Some 15 years after the return under Zerubbabel, God raised up the prophets Haggai and Zechariah to encourage the people to a renewed effort, which, strengthened by a new decree issued by Darius, led to the completion of the Temple in 515 B.C. (see Ezr 5:1 to 6:15; Hag 1:12, 13; 2:10-19). In half a century more, however, the moral and religious tone of Jerusalem had deteriorated, and it was under these circumstances that God inspired Ezra, the priest-scribe, to return from Babylonia to Jerusalem, where he instructed leaders and people in the law and led the way to a thoroughgoing reform (Ezr 9; 10). Some years afterward, however, temporal matters were still in a lamentable state (Neh 1:3), and Nehe-

miah sought, and obtained, a royal commission to administer the affairs of Jerusalem and Judah (Neh 2:1-8). The united efforts of Ezra and Nehemiah, with the assistance of the Persian government and under God's blessing, completed the work of restoration—material, civil, economic, moral, and religious.

The books of Ezra and Nehemiah constitute our chief historical source for information concerning the restoration period of Judaism. They provide a record, as well, of the fulfillment in part of the prophecies of Isaiah and Jeremiah and Ezekiel regarding the return from captivity. They provide the historical background for understanding the prophetic messages of Haggai, Zechariah, and Malachi. Ezra opens with an account of Cyrus' decree for the return of the Jews and their response to the call (Ezr 1:1-11). Chapter 2 lists and enumerates the returning exiles by families, the pedigrees of priest and Levite being of special importance. The restoration of the altar and the resumption of the daily sacrifices and the earlier stages of reconstruction occupy ch 3. Chapter 4 tells of the success of Samaritan efforts to halt the process of rebuilding, and chs 5 and 6 relate the means by which God opened the way for work to be again set forward, together with the completion of the new Temple and its dedication and the celebration of the Passover. In ch 7 Ezra relates the circumstances of his journey to Jerusalem and quotes the decree of Artaxerxes authorizing him to complete the work of restoration, whereas in ch 8 he tells of the actual preparations for return, of the Jews who accompanied him, and of the arrival at Jerusalem. The lax moral conditions, particularly among the priests and the Levites, which Ezra found are recounted in ch 9, and in ch 10 the measures taken to effect a reform, together with a long list of the offenders.

Ezrah (ĕz′rȧ), KJV **Ezra** (ĕz′rȧ). [Heb. *'Ezrah,* "help."] An otherwise unidentified descendant of Judah (1 Chr 4:17).

Ezrahite (ĕz′rȧ-hīt). [Heb. *'Ezrachi.*] Probably an alternate form of Zerahite. Ethan is called an Ezrahite in 1 Ki 4:31 and in the title of Ps 89, and Heman in the title of Ps 88. Both Ethan and Heman were sons of Zerah (1 Chr 2:6). *See* Zerahite.

Ezri (ĕz′rī). [Heb. *'Ezri,* "my help."] A superintendent of David's farms (1 Chr 27:26).

F

Fable. [Gr. *muthos*, "tale," "legend," "myth," "fable."· Compare the English word "myth," which is derived from *muthos*.] A story, historically untrue, designed to teach some spiritual or moral lesson, or to convey a supernatural message. Some believe that the various occurrences of this word in the Bible (1 Ti 1:4; 4:7; 2 Ti 4:4; Tit 1:14; 2 Pe 1:16) refer to certain legendary accounts preserved by the Jews, later recorded in such works as the Mishnah (cf. the "Jewish fables" mentioned in Tit 1:14); others believe that the "fables" mentioned in the NT refer to certain legends of the Gnostics. Perhaps both types. of legends were in the author's mind in certain passages. The RSV translates *muthos* as "myth."

Fair Havens (fâr hã′vĕnz). [Gr. *Kaloi Limenes,* a name perpetuated in the modern *Limenes Kali.*] A harbor on the southern coast of Crete, near Lasea (Map XX, C-3). Its bay is open to the east, but there are two small islands that provide shelter on the southwest. The sailors of the vessel in which Paul traveled as a prisoner did not consider it safe to keep the ship there all winter, and left against Paul's advice, attempting to reach Phoenix, a good port on the southwestern coast of Crete (Acts 27:8-12).

Fairs. [Heb. *'izbônîm,* "things left by ships and caravans," "goods," "wares."] An Old English word, meaning "wares," occurring in Eze 27:12-27, KJV, describing the goods that made up Tyre's extensive trade with other countries.

Faith. [Heb. *'emûn; 'emûnah;* Gr. *pistis.*]
  1. A confidence of heart and mind in God and His ways that leads one to act in accordance with His sovereign will (2 Cor 5:7; Heb 11:8). This faith is not based upon a blind, unintelligent acquiescence, but upon a supreme trust in the ability and integrity of God (Deut 7:9; 1 Ki 8:56; 1 Cor 1:9; Heb 10:23; 2 Ti 1:12; etc.). Such a faith is a prerequisite for any approach to Deity (Heb 11:6). It is by means of faith in Christ that one is justified (Rom 3:28; 5:1; Gal 2:16; 3:8, 25; etc.). Christ's righteousness becomes ours through faith in Him (Php 3:9). The believer's faith in God enables the Lord to do miraculous things for him

and through him (Mt 9:21, 22; Jas 5:14, 15; etc.). True faith cannot be passive, but manifests itself in works of righteousness (Gal 5:6; Jas 2:17, 18, 20, 21, 26; etc.). Paul emphatically denied that faith abolished the law (Rom 3:31) or one's obligations to the law (ch 6:1); rather it placed one in a position where, through Christ, the righteousness of the law might be fulfilled in him (ch 8:1-4).
  2. That which is believed; the system of Christian doctrines. Because of the power and conviction that accompanied the preaching of the gospel by the apostles "a great company of the priests were obedient to the faith" (Acts 6:7). The sorcerer Elymas endeavored to prejudice Sergius Paulus, the deputy of Cyprus, against "the faith" (ch 13:6, 7). Paul exhorted his converts "to continue in the faith" (ch 14:22). See also Php 1:27; Jas 2:1; Jude 3.
  3. Faithfulness, fidelity. This is the meaning particularly of the Heb. *'emûnah,* rendered "faith" in Hab 2:4. Where Paul quotes this text in Rom 1:17 he may be giving to faith the more extended meaning of NT faith. *Pistis* does, however, have the meaning "faithfulness" in Rom 3:3; Tit 2:10; Gal 5:22 and doubtless in other texts to a greater or lesser degree.

Falcon. [Heb. *'ayyah,* a name imitating the cry of the bird.] A bird of prey related to kites, eagles, and hawks (Lev 11:14; Job 28:7; RSV). The RSV translates *'ayyah,* "kite," in Deut 14:13, as does the KJV, which has "kite" also in Lev 11:14, but "vulture" in Job 28:7. The bird was unclean for food. Job declares that there are some paths of the wild that are not seen even by the keen eye of this bird (ch 28: 7). G. R. Driver identifies the *'ayyah* with the common buzzard (*PEQ* 87 [1955], 20).

Fall, The. A term commonly applied to the experience by which Adam and Eve lost their original innocence and sinlessness and abased themselves and their progeny, as recorded in Gen 3. How long after the creation of our first parents this event took place is not known, though the silence of Scripture may be taken to imply that no great time had elapsed. At most it would be less than 130 yrs. (Gen 5:3). In the Garden of Eden God set the tree of the knowledge of good and evil as a test of man's love, loyalty, and obedience, and gaγe Adam and Eve explicit instructions not to eat of the fruit of that tree, on pain of death (Gen 2:17). It was the deliberate violation of that express command that occasioned the Fall. In the guise of a serpent seemingly possessed of the power of speech, Satan engaged Eve, standing alone in curiosity before the tree, in conversation. Echoing her unspoken question as to why God had forbidden them the fruit of that tree, he declared that, in reality, the prohibition was a sinister device by which God purposed to prevent her and her companion from attaining to the high destiny of which they were capable (ch 3:1-5). He challenged the validity of the divine warning that death would be the penalty for eating of the fruit, and declared that instead of suffering this penalty they would attain to a higher state of existence. Satan convinced Eve that the tree so "pleasant to the eyes," was "good for food" (v 6) and "to be desired to make one wise" (v 6). This appeal was a subtle mixture of truth with error, for the fruit was attractive in appearance, it was, as claimed, good for food, and by eating it Eve and her companion would, indeed, attain to a certain, if questionable, state of wisdom. The falsity of Satan's claims for the fruit centered in his declaration that it was to be *desired* as a means to a higher state of wisdom, in view of God's specific prohibition. Eve was deceived and became the agent of the tempter to bring about her husband's fall (1 Ti 2:14). With Adam it was deliberate sin, prompted by his love for Eve. As the result of their transgression our first par-

172. Babylonian cylinder-seal impression interpreted by some as depicting possibly the story of the Fall. Two people sit at a tree and stretch out their hands to its fruits. Behind the person on the left is a serpent

ents forfeited their original innocence of character and their right of access to the tree of life, incurred a natural bent to evil, and were driven from their Eden

home. They went forth under sentence of death, and became the parents of a degenerate race.

After the account in Gen 3 the Fall is not mentioned again in the OT, and is mentioned but briefly in the NT (Jn 8:44; Rom 5:12-19; 1 Cor 15:22; 2 Cor 11:

173. Babylonian cylinder-seal impression interpreted by some as possibly depicting a Babylonian version of the expulsion from Paradise. A god (in the center) rebukes with raised arm the person at the right. Between the god and the nude woman stands a serpent

3; 1 Ti 2:14). Nevertheless, this tragic event is fundamental to the Scriptures from beginning to end, for if there had been no fall, how could there be need of salvation and restoration? The sum total of human experience testifies to the depravity of human nature, to man's own innate inability to change that nature, and to the need of a transformation of character by faith in Jesus Christ (Jer 13:23; 17:9; Acts 4:12). The idea of a fall from an original state of innocence and the concept that the history of the human race has been a process of evolution upward are mutually exclusive.

Fallow Deer. The KJV translation in Deut 14:5; 1 Ki 4:23, of the Heb. *yachmûr,* meaning *"roebuck," as the Arabic cognate indicates.

Familiar Spirit. An expression appearing in the KJV in phrases such as "them that have familiar spirits," "one that hath a familiar spirit." The phrases are the translation of the Heb. *'ôb,* "spirit medium," "necromancer," pl. *'ôbôth.* The LXX usually renders *'ôbôth* as *eggastrimuthoi,* "ventriloquists," literally, "bellyspeakers." The word *'ôb* is also used for "wineskin," and possibly came to be applied to spirit mediums because of the unnatural, indistinct, and sonorous quality of the voice when presumably possessed by the "familiar spirit," a voice such as might be produced by speaking into a wineskin, or bottle. Ventriloquism was a common device used by ancient practitioners of the occult arts, and perhaps by the spirit mediums of Bible times (see Is 29:4). The "familiar spirit" impersonated the dead and presumed to place the living in communication with the spirits of the departed dead. The Mosaic law provided the death penalty for anyone who claimed to have the power to consult with a "familiar spirit" (Lev 19:31; 20:6, 27; Deut 18:11). The most notable incident of consultation with a spirit medium in Bible times is Saul's interview with the witch of En-dor (1 Sa 28:3-25).

Famine. Famines were of frequent occurrence in Palestine, and were caused by drought (1 Ki 17:1; 18:2), enemy inroads (Deut 28:49-51), blight and mildew (Amos 4:9), and wartime besiegement (2 Ki 6:24 to 7:20; 25:1-3; Jer 32:4, 5). They were sometimes the results of God's judgments (Jer 29:17; Eze 5:5, 7, 8, 12; etc.). Abraham was forced by famine to leave Canaan (Gen 12:10), and his descendants more than once had to do likewise (chs 26:1; 41:56 to 42:5). Famine was known in the days of Job (Job 5:22; 30:3). In the days of the judges it was famine that drove Elimelech and his family to Moab (Ruth 1:1). The 3-year famine in David's time (2 Sa 21:1) was declared to be the result of Saul's disobedience in the matter of the Gibeonites, and the 3 years without rain invoked by Elijah indicated God's displeasure with Ahab's wicked leadership (1 Ki 17; 18). Acts 11:28 mentions a famine (KJV "dearth") that occurred (c. A.D. 44) during the reign of Claudius. The parable of the Prodigal Son mentions a famine (Lk 15:14), and Paul mentions famine, among other things, as being unable to separate us from Christ's love (Rom 8:35). Famines are mentioned as a sign of the last days (Mt 24:7; Mk 13:8; Lk 21:11).

Fan. In the KJV a rendering of: (1) The Heb. *mizreh* (Is 30:24; Jer 15:7), a six-pronged fork with which the Palestinian farmers threw up the grain after it had been threshed, so that the wind would blow off the chaff (the RSV translates *mizreh* "fork" and "winnowing fork," respectively). (2) The Gr. *ptuon* (Mt 3:12; Lk 3:17), "a winnowing shovel," a forklike shovel similar to the above (RSV "winnowing fork").

Farewell, Fare Ye Well. An exclamation used by friends when parting (Acts 18:21), or by a writer at the conclusion of a letter (2 Cor 13:11; cf. Acts 15:29). The expression occurs in the RSV of Gen 31:28 as

the translation of the Heb. *nashaq*, which literally means "to kiss." In the NT it appears as the translation of several Greek words: (1) *rhōnnumi*, literally, "to be strong" (Acts 15:29; 23:30); (2) *chairō*, literally, "to rejoice" (2 Cor 13:11); (3) *apotassomai*, "to say farewell [to]," "to take leave of" (Lk 9:61; Acts 18:21).

Farthing. *See* Penny.

Fashion. A term appearing frequently in the KJV with the Old English meaning, "shape," "appearance," etc., the translation of the Heb.: (1) *demûth*, "likeness," "shape," "pattern" (2 Ki 16:10); (2) *mishpat*, literally, "judgment" (rarely, "plan," "sketch," as in Ex 26:30; 1 Ki 6:38; Eze 42:11); (3) *tekûnah*, "arrangement" (Eze 43:11); and of the Gr.: (1) *eidos*, "appearance" (Lk 9:29); (2) *prosōpon*, literally, "face" (Jas 1:11); (3) *schēma*, "outward appearance," "form," "shape" (1 Cor 7:31; Php 2:8); (4) *tupos*, "type," "pattern," "model," "image" (Acts 7:44).

Fast, Fasting. [Heb. *ṣûm*, "to fast," *ṣôm*, "fast"; Gr. *nēsteuō*, "to fast," *nēsteia*, "fast."] The abstinence from food, whether for religious purposes or because of a lack of food; or the period of such abstinence. The OT records no divine command requiring abstinence from food as a matter of religious duty; however, there are numerous instances of voluntary fasting prompted by religious motives. Under such instances fasting presumably reflected a spirit of willing self-denial and of humility before God, sometimes of penitence for sin. Often when accompanying intercession with God for certain specific requests it expressed sincerity and selflessness. The Israelites fasted after their slaughter of the Benjamites (Jgs 20:26). They did so again as a mark of repentance from idolatry when interceding with God for deliverance from the Philistines (1 Sa 7:6). The men of Jabesh-gilead fasted after burying Saul and his sons, apparently in contrition or sorrow for Israel's defeat (ch 31:13). David and his retainers did likewise upon receipt of the news of Saul's death (2 Sa 1:12). Later, David fasted while interceding with the Lord for the life of the son born to him by Bathsheba (ch 12:21-23). Daniel fasted when interceding with God for the close of the Captivity (Dan 9:3). Ezra and his group of returning exiles fasted as they prayed for divine protection on their journey back to Jerusalem from Babylonia (Ezr 8:23). Nehemiah abstained from food upon hearing of the "great affliction and reproach" suffered by the returned exiles at Jerusalem (Neh 1:4). Esther did the same prior to interceding with Ahasuerus for her people (Est 4:16), and invited the Jews to do likewise. Only rarely in the OT is the divine attitude concerning the practice of fasting expressed. In Is 58:3-7 God rejects the fasting of His people in a time of national apostasy, declaring that the "fast" He has "chosen" consists of justice and mercy exercised toward others. In Jer 14:12 He refuses to accept fasting unaccompanied by a reformation of the life. During the Babylonian captivity the Jews became accustomed to fast on certain anniversaries connected with the fall of Jerusalem and the destruction of the Temple, and perhaps with the murder of Gedaliah (Zec 7:5; cf. 2 Ki 25:1-4, 8, 9, 25; Jer 52:6, 7), but God was not interested in these outward, presumed tokens of humility and repentance (Zec 7:5). Only once (Joel 2:12) is God spoken of as summoning the people to fast, as evidence of repentance.

Moses (Ex 34:28) and Jesus (Mt 4:2) each fasted for 40 days, but under circumstances in which food was not readily available. Pious Jews fasted twice each week (Lk 18:12), on Mondays and Thursdays, a practice which Jesus neither approved nor disapproved, although He and His disciples did not observe these ritual fasts (Mt 9:14, 15; Mk 2:18-20; Lk 5:33-35). His only instruction relative to fasting was that it should not be ostentatious (Mt 6:16-18), but sincere. The leaders at Antioch fasted prior to ordaining Paul to the gospel ministry (Acts 13:2, 3). The apostle later followed the same practice when ordaining elders in the local churches he established (ch 14:23). There is strong textual evidence for omitting the word "fasting" altogether in Mt 17:21; Mk 9:29; Acts 10:30; 1 Cor 7:5. If this evidence be accepted, the NT stands without any specific divine requirement for fasting or expressed approval of the practice. To afflict the body for the sin of the soul is to dodge the issue and to miss the true nature of repentance, since sin is a disease of the soul and not of the body. The chief benefit to be obtained from fasting is a clarity of mind that comes with complete or partial abstinence from food and that enables a person to perceive God's will more distinctly. On the other hand, there is often such a concentration upon the seeking of divine help in a time of crisis that physical need and

desire for food are sometimes by-passed.

Fat. The Israelites were forbidden to eat fat (Lev 3:17; 7:23, 24; etc.), because "all the fat is the Lord's" (ch 3:16). It was to be burned on the altar (Ex 29:13; Lev 3: 3-5; etc.), as "a sweet savour unto the Lord" (Lev 17:6). The term is often used figuratively in passages dealing with material prosperity and personal blessings (Gen 45:18; cf. 1 Chr 4:40; Ps 92:14; Prov 11:25; Is 30:23; KJV; etc.).

Father. This term denotes primarily the immediate male parent (Gen 22:7; 27:22, 38; Mt 4:21; Lk 1:59), but may also denote the grandfather (Gen 28:10, 13), or any male ancestor no matter how remote (2 Ki 15:38; Jn 8:53). "Father" may also mean the founder of a particular social or occupational group (Gen 4:21); thus Jabal "was the father of such as dwell in tents" (v 20), and Joseph and Levi are spoken of as the fathers of their houses or tribes (Jos 17:16; Num 3:6). In 1 Chr 2:51, 52, the founders of the cities of Bethlehem, Beth-gader, and Kiriath-jearim, are called "fathers" of these cities, and in 1 Chr 4:14, RSV, one, Joab, is called the "father" of Ge-harashim, meaning "valley of craftsmen" (see RSV footnote and KJV text). One acting with paternal kindness, or as a guide or teacher, is sometimes called a father (Jgs 17:10; 2 Ki 2:12). In a special sense God, as Creator, is represented as Father (Mal 2:10), a relationship made explicit by the life of Christ (Mt 11:26; Mk 14:36; Lk 22:42; Jn 14:9). Paul likens spiritual regeneration to an adoption by which God becomes our spiritual Father (Rom 8:15; Gal 4:5, 6).

Fathom. [Gr. *orguia*.] A linear Greek measure used for reckoning the depth of bodies of water (Acts 27:28), as well as land measures. Its length was derived from the measurement of a man's horizontally outstretched arms, and is given by Herodotus (ii. 149) as 4 cubits, or 24 palms. Thus it was roughly equivalent to the modern fathom of 6 English ft. (1.78 m., or 5.84 ft., as based on a *cubit of 17.5 in.).

Fatlings. Cattle, sheep, etc., fattened for feast or sacrifice (Ps 66:15; Eze 39:18; etc.).

Fauna. *See* Flora and Fauna.

Favor, Favour. The translation of a number of different Hebrew and Greek words, most of which center around the concepts of "grace," "kindness," "delight," etc. For example, in the KJV, "favour" appears 26 times in the OT as a translation of the Heb. *chen,* which is also often translated "grace." Similarly, in the NT, "favour" is found 6 times as a translation of the Gr. *charis,* which is usually rendered "grace." In the expression "well favoured" (as in Gen 29:17; 39:6; Dan 1:4; etc.), the word occurs in an Old English phrase that refers to physical attractiveness. The corresponding expressions in the RSV are "lovely," "good-looking," etc. *See* Grace.

Fear. The translation of various Hebrew and Greek words, which originally must have emphasized different types and varying degrees of fear. However, most of the occurrences of the word are translations of the following: (1) the Heb. *yara',* "to fear" (with the related noun, *yir'ah,* "fear," and the verbal adjective, *yare',* "fearful"); (2) the Heb. *pachad,* "to tremble," "to dread" (with the related noun, *pachad,* "trembling," "dread"); (3) the Gr. *phobeomai,* "to fear" (with the related noun *phobos,* "fear").

The concept of fear as expressed in the Bible covers a wide range of emotions. Its force ranges from deep concern (as in 2 Cor 11:3; 12:20; Jude 23) to abject terror (as in Mt 14:26). Occasionally, fear merely involves a sense of respect for one's superiors (as in Rom 13:7; 1 Pe 2:18; cf. Job 32:6, where the Heb. *yara',* "to fear," is translated "was afraid") or for one's parents (as in Lev 19:3, RSV "revere"). Sometimes it describes a feeling of awe (Is 60:5; Lk 5:26, RSV "awe"; 7:16). The exact shade of thought or degree of fear generally needs to be determined from the context; but in most cases the Biblical usage of "fear" reasonably approximates our modern English usage of the term.

A number of occurrences of the word "fear" involve the reverential awe that man should feel for the majesty, power, and position of his divine Maker. In this sense the term would include any of the varying degrees of emotional response comprehended in our words "reverence," "respect," "awe," and "fear"; and it may occasionally signify even the more extreme reaction of awe mingled with terror that a mortal man would naturally feel when in the immediate presence of God (Heb 12:21; Jgs 6:22, 23) or of angels (Lk 1:12, 13). This type of fear is, of course, not to be included in the harmful emotion that is disparaged in 1 Jn 4:18, but is rather commended in the Scriptures (Rev 14:7; Job 28:28; Ps 2:11; 111:10; etc.).

Feasts. *See* Festivals; names of individual feasts.

Felix (fē′lĭks). [Gr. *Phēlix,* from the Latin, *felix,* "happy."] A Roman procurator of Judea and Samaria (*c.* A.D. 52 - *c.* 60), whose full name was Marcus Antonius Felix. He was a freedman serving the emperor Claudius, and a brother of Pallas, who was a minister of Claudius. Felix was married 3 times; his 1st wife was Drusilla, a granddaughter of the triumvir Antony and of Cleopatra; his 2d wife, also named Drusilla, was the youngest daughter of Herod Agrippa I. The name of his 3d wife is unknown. He was ill qualified for the high office he held in Palestine, and the Roman historian Tacitus said of him that he practiced every kind of cruelty and lust, "wielding the power of king with all the instincts of a slave" (*Hist.* v. 9). He is said to have encouraged the murder of the Jewish high priest Jonathan. He suppressed several rebellions of the Jews against his despotic rule. The apostle Paul appeared before him and his Jewish wife Drusilla, and talked to them about righteousness, temperance, and the coming judgment. This made Felix tremble, but left no lasting impressions upon him. Felix was convinced of Paul's innocence, and would have released him if Paul had paid a ransom, but when no such offer was made, he left Paul in prison in the hope of gaining favor with the Jews (Acts 24:24-26). On his return to Rome, after his term of office expired, certain accusations were brought against him by the Jews, but he was acquitted.

Felloe. [Heb. *chishshuq,* "spoke of a wheel."] An archaic English word meaning "rim of a wheel" (1 Ki 7:33, KJV). However, the Hebrew term signifies a spoke, not a rim.

Fellow. The translation of a number of Hebrew and Greek words. Most of the occurrences of this term reflect words in the original tongues that may be classified as follows: (1) various more or less synonymous expressions for "friend," "companion," "neighbor," etc. (especially Heb. *rea',* as in Jgs 7:13; 1 Sa 14:20; Zec 3:8; and *chaber,* as in Ps 45:7); (2) compound words or expressions that refer to a close associate in some activity or state, for example, "fellowcitizen" (Eph 2:19), "fellowservant" (Rev 19:10), "fellowworker" (Col 4:11), "fellow townsmen" (Ruth 3:11, RSV), etc.; (3) expressions in their context of contempt, for example, Gen 19:9; 1 Sa 21:15; 25:21; 1 Ki 22:27; Mt 26:61; Acts 22:22; 24:5.

Fellowship. [Gr. generally *koinōnia,* "association," "communion," "participation," "sharing (in something)."] A mutual sharing in some blessing or experience. In the NT the term is used to express the concept of joint participation in such experiences as sharing together in the blessings of the gospel (Php 1:5, RSV "partnership"). The word is particularly found in passages that refer to the close relationship that Christians experience with God (1 Jn 1:3), with Christ (1 Jn 1:3; 1 Cor 1:9), with the Holy Spirit (2 Cor 13:14, RSV), and with fellow believers (1 Jn 1: 3, 7). The closeness of this relationship finds unique expression in connection with the Lord's Supper, in which the Christian symbolically partakes of the flesh and blood of Christ. In 1 Cor 10:16, Paul describes the cup and the bread of the Lord's Supper as "the communion [Gr. *koinōnia,* "fellowship"] of the blood of Christ" and "the communion [Gr. *koinōnia,* "fellowship"] of the body of Christ." In contrast, the believer is urged to have no fellowship with "devils" (v 20), nor with the "works of darkness" (Eph 5:11; cf. 2 Cor 6:14, RSV).

In addition to its usual meaning, *koinōnia* was used by the early church to describe the act of sharing one's temporal blessings with fellow believers (2 Cor 8:4); as such, it may appropriately be translated "contribution" (Rom 15:26; 2 Cor 9:13, RSV).

Fen. A rendering of the Heb. *biṣṣah* (Job 40:21, KJV), meaning "marsh." Elsewhere the KJV renders *biṣṣah* "mire" (ch 8:11) and "miry place" (Eze 47:11).

Fenced Cities. *See* Fortifications.

Ferret. *See* Lizard.

Ferry Boat. [Heb. *'abarah,* "ford," "crossing."] A term found only in 2 Sa 19:18, KJV, the translation of a Hebrew word the exact meaning of which is somewhat obscure. The passage in which it appears reads literally, "And the crossing crossed over to bring over the household of the king." The translators of the KJV apparently assumed that *'abarah* denoted some means of conveyance by which to cross a river, hence the rendering "ferry boat." Other translators and scholars assume a scribal error, and by changing one letter in the verb of the sentence arrive at the translation, "And they crossed the ford . . . " (see RSV).

Festivals. Celebrations or observances recurring yearly, mostly connected with the ceremonial law. Three times in the year all Hebrew men were required to gather at Jerusalem (Ex 23:14-17; Deut 16:16) to celebrate the three harvest festivals— (1) the Feast of *Unleavened Bread (which immediately followed the Passover supper held the preceding night) in the middle of the 1st month, at the beginning of the *barley harvest (Lev 23:5-14); (2) the Feast of Weeks (*Pentecost), fifty days later, celebrating the season of the wheat harvest (Lev 23:15-21; Ex 34:22); and (3) the Feast of Ingathering, or the Feast of Booths or Tabernacles (*see* Tabernacles, Feast of), in the middle of the 7th month, at the close of the olive and fruit harvest (Lev 23:34-44; Deut 16:13). There were several other annual observances included in the Levitical law: the Blowing of *Trumpets on the 1st of the 7th month (Lev 23:24, 25), which was the civil New Year's Day, and is still observed as such; and the Day of *Atonement, on the 10th of the month (ch 23:27-32), on which the Israelites were to "afflict" their souls (ch 23:27-29), even though they were not all required to assemble at Jerusalem. These festivals included 7 festival sabbaths in addition to and separate from the weekly Sabbath of the 4th commandment (Lev 23: 38; Ex 20:8-11). These were on fixed days of the month and hence fell on various days of the week in different years. (For these sabbaths, *see* tabulation under Year.) The "new moons" might also be considered monthly festivals (2 Ki 4:23; Is 1:13, 14; etc.).

To these festivals others were later added. The deliverance of the Jews from destruction by Esther was commemorated by the feast of *Purim in Adar (Est 9:21, 22, 26). Then the restoration and rededication of the Temple after its desecration by Antiochus Epiphanes was celebrated by the Feast of the *Dedication in Kislev (Jn 10:22). *See* names of specific feasts, also tabulation under Year.

The Jews observe these festivals to the present day, without, of course, the sacrificial rites. One change has taken place since the scattering of the Jews from Jerusalem: the sacred days are observed on two successive days instead of one. This practice was adopted by the Jews of the Diaspora, or *Dispersion, so as to be sure of not missing the correct day. Originally the Jews of Syria and Babylonia were notified by fire signals from hilltop to hilltop from Jerusalem as to the time of the new moons preceding the important feasts, so that all could be sure of celebrating the same days. After enemies caused confusion by sending false fire signals, messengers were substituted, but the time came when Jerusalem could no longer be the headquarters for all the scattered Jews. It was then that the custom of a two-day observance became established, a custom that is still retained even though it is unnecessary, for the Jewish calendar, long ago standardized, is no longer dependent on the observation of the moon at Jerusalem.

Festus (fĕs'tŭs). [Gr. *Phēstos*, from the Latin *festus*, "festal."] A procurator of Judea (*c.* A.D. 60 - *c.* 62), whose full name was Porcius (pôr'shĭ-ŭs) Festus. He possessed greater integrity than his predecessor, but in the short time of his rule was unable to undo the evil done by Felix. He fought against Jewish assassins (the Sicarii) and against the followers of a pseudoprophet. He was also involved in a controversy between the Jews and Agrippa II. In taking office he found the apostle Paul in prison where Felix had left him. Festus became convinced of Paul's innocence, but desiring to satisfy the Jews, proposed that the trial should take place in Jerusalem. Paul, knowing that his life would not be safe in Jerusalem, was thus forced to use a right which he possessed as a Roman citizen, namely to appeal to the emperor, whereupon he was sent to Rome (Acts 25:26). Festus died in office, and was succeeded by Albinus, a man of extremely mean principles.

Fetter. A means used for confining or binding persons, probably usually a *chain. Such fetters were made of iron (Ps 149:8) or bronze (2 Chr 33:11, RSV). In 2 Sa 3:34; Ps 105:18 fetters are mentioned as being placed on the feet. The "fetters" of Mk 5:4; Lk 8:29 are a rendering of the Gr. *pedē*, meaning literally, "fetters for the feet."

Fever. The translation in the OT of the Heb. *qaddachath,* "fever," or "burning heat." "Fever" was one of the curses that were to fall upon Israel if they rejected God's plan for their lives (Lev 26:16;

KJV "burning ague"; Deut 28:22). In the NT "fever" is the translation of Greek words having the root meaning "fire." Several of Christ's healing miracles involved the cure of fevers (Mt 8:15; Mk 1:31; Lk 4:38; Jn 4:52; Acts 28:8). Galen and the Greek physicians classified fevers as "greater" and "lesser," which classification may be indicated by Luke's mention of a "great fever" (Lk 4:38).

Fiery Serpent. *See* Serpent.

Fig. [Heb. *pag,* "unripe fig," *te'enah,* "fig tree (or fruit)," *bikkûrah,* "early fig," *debelah,* "cake of pressed figs"; Gr. *olunthos,* "unripe fig," *sukon,* "fig," *sukē,* "fig tree."] The fleshy fruit of a tree, *Ficus carica,* and the tree itself. The tree was common in Bible lands from early times (Deut 8:8), and is thought to have been originally native to southwestern Asia. It may grow somewhat as a vine in rough, stony ground, or assume the expected shape of a tree in good soil, attaining a height of 20 to 30 ft. It is now widely distributed in Palestine and is one of few plants found wild throughout the land. The near-spherical or conical fruit hangs from the branch by its small end. Figs are the first plants mentioned by name in the Bible (Gen 3:7) and among the last (Rev 6:13). The trees bear twice a year, in June and in August or September. The June figs, or "firstripe" (Hos 9:10; Mic 7:1, RSV), grow on the old wood and are considered a delicacy. The August crop grows on the new wood, and when harvested is often dried and pressed into cakes or strung on cords for winter use. Figs were believed to have medicinal value and the cakes were used as poultices for boils and similar skin eruptions (2 Ki 20:7). To sit under one's vine and one's own fig tree symbolized prosperity to the Hebrew (1 Ki 4:25; Mic 4:4; Zec 3:10). In the spring the fruit appears before the leaves. One of Jesus' most striking parables concerned the deceptive fig tree which gave

174. A typical fig tree in Palestine as it appeared in normal condition, in full leaf

175. The same fig tree, after locusts had eaten up all its leaves. This denudation took only fifteen minutes

evidence of having borne fruit but had none (Mk 11:12-14, 20). Because the fig and the grape were so important in Jewish agriculture, the prophets, when upbraiding the people for their sins, warned that the vines and fig trees would be destroyed. When the prophets offered the people prosperity through obedience, they pictured an abundance of these 2 crops (Is 36:16; Joel 1:7; Amos 4:9).

Figure. The translation of a number of Hebrew and Greek words. These may be generally subdivided into (1) various terms for "likeness," "image," "replica," etc., and (2) terms representing figures of speech. Most of these words are generally given other renderings. For example, *tabnith,* "plan," "image," occurs only in Is 44:13 as "figure"; elsewhere it has been translated by such synonyms as "pattern" (Ex 25:9), "likeness" (Deut 4:16), etc. Other words that have been rendered "figure" include: *antitupon,* "copy," "antitype," "representation" (Heb 9:24; 1 Pe 3:21); *parabolē* (Heb 9:9; 11:19), which is generally translated "parable"; *tupos,* "type," "copy," "pattern" (Rom 5:14), "image" (Acts 7:43); *paroimia,* "proverb," "figure of speech" (Jn 10:6; 16:29; RSV).

File. The conjectural rendering in the KJV of the Heb. *happeṣîrah phîm* (1 Sa 13:21). Since the discovery of stone weights in Palestinian excavations on which the Hebrew characters *pym* are inscribed, there can be little doubt that the *happeṣîrah phîm* should be translated "the charge was a pim," as in the RSV. A pim was equivalent to ⅔ of a shekel, and had a monetary value of about 27 cents. *See* Pim.

Filigree. A delicate, open ornamental work, usually in fine wire, done in rarer metals. The word appears in the RSV of Ex 28:11, 13, 20, 25; 39:6, 13, 16, 18, where precious stones are described as being enclosed in settings of gold filigree.

Fillet. A rendering of: (1) The Heb. *chashûq* (Ex 27:10, 11; 36:38; etc.), from a root meaning "to join." The term probably refers to rods that extended between the pillars of the tabernacle, upon which the curtains were hung. (2) The Heb. *chût* (Jer 52:21, KJV), "thread," and thus rendered in Gen 14:23; Jgs 16:12; etc. A cord of some kind, perhaps one to measure the circumference of the pillar, may be referred to in Jer 52:21, hence probably the RSV translation "circumference."

Fine Flour. *See* Flour.

Fine Linen. Generally a rendering of the Heb. *shesh* and *bûṣ* and the Gr. *bussos* and *bussinos.* All 4 of these words were used anciently to designate a fine quality of linen cloth, and should be distinguished from the Heb. *bad,* which signifies linen (or cloth) in a general sense. Several other words have also been rendered "fine linen," but these are quite rare. Linen was highly prized by the ancient peoples. Egypt was renowned for its fine linen (cf. Gen 41:42; Is 19:8, 9), and Solomon referred to it as an item of luxury (Prov 7:16). Ezekiel likened Tyre to a ship with fine Egyptian linen for its sails (Eze 27:7). The curtains of the tabernacle (Ex 26:1; 36:8), as well as the hangings of the court (ch 27:9), were of fine linen. The priests' garments were also made of this material (ch 39:1-5, 8, 27-29; etc.). Joseph of Arimathea wrapped the body of Jesus in "fine linen," Gr. *sindōn* (Mk 15:46, KJV; RSV "linen shroud"). The mystic Babylon the great of Rev 18 is described as dealing in, and as being clothed with, fine linen (vs 12, 16). Rev 19:7, 8 states that the bride of the Lamb is clothed in fine linen, which symbolizes the righteousness (RSV "righteous deeds") of the saints.

Finer. A term occurring in the KJV of Prov 25:4, meaning "one who refines metals."

Finger. [Heb. *'eṣba'.*] As a linear measure (Jer 52:21), derived from the thickness of the finger, 1/24 of a cubit, either 2.18 cm. (.86 in.) or 1.85 cm. (.73 in.), depending on which of the 2 kinds of *cubit discussed in this dictionary is used.

Fining pot. [Heb. *maṣreph,* "a crucible," from *ṣaraph,* "to smelt (metal)," "to refine," "to test."] A crucible used for refining precious metals. The fining pots mentioned in the Bible were for silver (Prov 17:3; 27:21).

Fir. [Heb. *berôsh.*] There is uncertainty as to the exact identity of the tree designated by *berôsh.* Many commentators suggest the cypress (*Cypressus sempervirens*), as does the RSV in the majority of occurrences of *berôsh.* According to Moldenke, the Aleppo pine (*Pinus halepensis*) is also a possibility.

The cypress, said to have the middle mountain zones as its habitat, grows to 50 or 60 ft. in height in Palestine, and produces a hard and durable wood especially valued by ancients for carving idols and for cabinetwork.

Along with the cedar, the *berôsh* was brought from Lebanon and used for the woodwork of Solomon's Temple (1 Ki 5:8, 10; 6:15, 34). The wood was also used for musical instruments (2 Sa 6:5) and for planking on ships (Eze 27:5).

Fire. An important element to the ancients, mentioned frequently in the Scriptures. Fire is often associated with the presence of God (Gen 15:17; Ex 3:2; 13:21, 22; 19:18; etc.). God is likened to a devouring or consuming fire (Deut 4:24; Heb 12:29; cf. Ex 24:17; Is 33:14), and a refiner's fire (Mal 3:2). Fire plays an important role in symbolic visions of Deity (Eze 1:27; Dan 7:9, 10; Rev 1:14; 2:18). God's word is likened to fire (Jer 23:29; cf. chs 5:14; 20:9). God punished sinners with fire (Lev 10:2; Num 11:1; 16:35; 2 Ki 1:10, 12; Jude 7), and with fire He will eventually annihilate them (Rev 20:9). Fire from heaven expressed His acceptance of an offering made to Him (Lev 9:24; Jgs 6:21; 2 Chr 7:1). Angels are described as "ministers" made "a flaming fire" (Ps 104:4, KJV).

Because of the difficulty of starting fires in ancient times, lamps were kept burning continually (*see* Lamp) as a ready source of fire. When traveling to Mount Moriah to sacrifice Isaac, Abraham carried fire with him with which to ignite his sacrifice (Gen 22:6, 7). Fire was used for cooking, lighting, heating, and refining metals.

Fire Pan. [Heb. *machtah.*] A flat metal vessel of bronze, silver, or gold used in the tabernacle and Temple service for the carrying of fire (Ex 27:3; 38:3; 1 Ki 7:50; 2 Ki 25:15). The KJV generally translates *machtah* as *censer.

Firebrand. The translation of: (1) The Heb. *'ûd,* "log." The context reveals it to be a burning log, hence "firebrand" (Amos 4:11; RSV "brand"). In Is 7:4 God declared Rezin, king of Syria, and Pekah, king of Israel, to be no more dangerous than two pieces of smoldering logs. *'Ûd* is translated "brand" in Zec 3:2. (2) The Heb. *lappîd,* "torch," "lamp." Such were the firebrands Samson used to destroy the grain of the Philistines (Jgs 15:4, 5; RSV "torch"). (3) The Heb. *ziqqîm,* "fire arrows." In Prov 26:18 (RSV), a deceiver who makes the excuse that he is only joking is compared to one who throws "firebrands, arrows, and death." Firebrands were thrown as weapons during a siege (see fig. 284).

Firkin. The translation in Jn 2:6, KJV, of the Gr. *metrētēs,* a liquid measure originating in Attica. It held about 10 gal. U.S. (39.39 liters, according to Hultsch; 38.88, according to Walter-Hirt). Some authorities, taking *metrētēs* as the equiv-

alent of the Heb. *bath* (see 2 Chr 4:5, LXX), assign to *metrētēs* the measure of the bath, which has been calculated at 5.81 gal. U.S. (*see* Bath).

Firmament. [Heb. *raqîa',* "beaten-out (iron) plate," "solid vault (of heaven)," "firmament."] The usual OT term for the vault of the sky as it appears from any point on earth, bounded on all sides by the horizon. The firmament was made on the 2d day of Creation week (Gen 1:6-8), and to it God assigned the designation "heaven." Reference here is to the atmospheric heavens which give rise to the appearance of a canopy or dome overhead. In these heavens the clouds move from place to place and the birds fly. The sun, moon, and stars appear to move across the vault of heaven each day (see vs 14, 17). The psalmist (Ps 19:1) speaks of the firmament as evidence of the creative power of God. In his vision of the throne of God Ezekiel saw a "firmament" supporting the throne and the Divine Being seated thereon (Eze 1:22-26).

First Begotten. A term appearing only in Heb. 1:6; Rev 1:5; KJV, as a variant translation of the Gr. *prōtotokos,* elsewhere rendered *"firstborn."

First Day of the Week. This term appears 8 times in the NT (Mt 28:1; Mk 16:2, 9; Lk 24:1; Jn 20:1, 19; Acts 20:7; 1 Cor 16:2). The term is generally a rendering of the Gr. *mia sabbatōn* or *mia tōn sabbatōn.* Since *sabbatōn* may mean "Sabbath," as well as "week," some have translated it "Sabbath" and have rendered the Greek phrase as it appears in Mt 28:1 "first of the sabbaths," a translation ruled out by both Greek syntax and the context (see *SDACom* 5:554, 555). The Gospel passages where the phrase occurs establish the resurrection as having taken place on the first day of the week, the day now called Sunday.

In Acts 20:7 reference is made to a religious meeting held by Paul on the first day of the week. Commentators have not been agreed as to whether in this passage Luke used Roman time reckoning, which began the day at midnight, or Jewish time reckoning, which began the day at sunset. If Roman reckoning was used, the meeting in question was held Sunday evening, going over into Monday morning, for Paul "continued his speech until midnight." If Jewish reckoning was used, the meeting was held Saturday evening, going over into Sunday morning, that is, provided the meeting began after sunset, otherwise it would have been a Sunday afternoon meeting. The occasion was a farewell meeting, for Paul was "ready to depart on the morrow." The passage offers no proof that the early church observed the first day of the week, as is sometimes alleged. See *SDACom* 6:387.

Paul's instruction to the Corinthian church to lay aside a certain portion as a contribution to the Jerusalem church upon "the first day of the week" (1 Cor 16:2, 3) has also been used as proof that the apostolic church met for worship on Sunday. However, the Gr. *par heautō*, rendered "by him" in this text, means literally "by himself," and is the equivalent of the English "at home." Thus reference is made not to an offering given at a Christian assembly, but rather to a portion set aside privately at home.

First Fruits. [Heb. *bikkûrim,* "first (or earliest) fruit"; *re'shîth,* "beginning (fruit)," "choicest (fruit)"; once *bikkûrah,* "first ripe fruit" (Hos 9:10, RSV); Gr. *aparchē,* "the beginning of a sacrifice," "first fruits."] Offerings presented to God as a sign of allegiance on the part of the worshiper. Upon being presented, these offerings ordinarily became the property of the priest (Num 18:11; Deut 18:4), although on occasions it seems to have been permissible to present them to a prophet (2 Ki 4:42). The nature of the offering of the first fruits is emphasized by the 2 Hebrew words used for it: (1) it consisted of the earliest ripened portion of the crops, *bikkûrim;* and (2) it was the choicest part of the early crops, *re'shîth.*

Special offerings of first fruits were made at each of the 3 great annual feasts of Israel—Unleavened Bread, Pentecost, and Tabernacles. On the 16th of Nisan, the day after the yearly Passover sabbath, a sheaf of freshly ripened grain (barley) was waved before the altar (Lev 2:12; 23:10, 11). On the day of Pentecost 2 loaves of bread, baked with leaven and wheat flour from the new crop, were presented to the Lord (Lev 23:17; cf. Ex 34:22). The Feast of Ingathering (or Tabernacles) in the 7th month was in itself an act of thanksgiving to God for all the harvested crops, and apparently first or choice fruits were offered in connection with it also (cf. Ex 23:16, 19; Lev 23:39). Besides these national presentations of first fruits, individuals might present their personal freewill offerings (Num 15:20, 21; Deut 26:2, 10).

In Rom 16:5, KJV, Epaenetus is called "the firstfruits . . . unto Christ," meaning that he was the first convert, or one of the first converts. In 1 Cor 15:20 Christ is declared to be "the firstfruits of them that slept." He was the pledge of the great harvest that will follow when the righteous dead are raised at the second advent of Christ (v 23). The 144,000 are also called "firstfruits" (Rev 14:4), either as being the pledge of the great harvest of the redeemed, or as being a special gift or offering to God.

First Fruits, Feast of. *See* Pentecost, Feast of.

First-born. [Heb. *bekor, bekîrah;* Gr. *prōtotokos,* "first-born."] The first offspring of either man or beast. As a figurative expression the term may also indicate superiority in size, rank, strength, etc., or preeminence in character or position.

Among the ancient Hebrews the first-born son held a position of special importance, in accordance with well-defined customs and God-given laws (cf. Gen 48:13, 14, 17, 18; Deut 21:15-17; 2 Chr 21:3). This position was closely linked with the *birthright and its special privileges, which included not only a favored portion of the *inheritance but also certain spiritual blessings and responsibilities in the family. After the experience of the Passover and the slaying of the first-born of the Egyptians, the Lord emphasized the special position of the eldest son by commanding that all the first-born of man or beast were to be especially devoted to Him (Ex 13:2, 12; Num 3:13). The first-born son was to be redeemed by a ransom payment (Ex 13:13, 15; Num 18:15, 16). Apparently, the devoting of the first-born son to God was intended to be a special dedication to the service of God, but this aspect was later modified by dedicating the tribe of Levi to religious service in place of the first-born (Num 3:12, 45). In all of this the Israelites were to be reminded of the deliverance of the first-born of God's people during the Passover night in Egypt (Ex 12:22, 23, 29), and to be pointed to Christ, the antitypical First-born.

The term was also used in a figurative sense, in such phrases as "the firstborn of death" (Job 18:13), probably denoting a disease so virulent that it was considered the chief among all fatal maladies, and "the firstborn of the poor" (Is 14:30), signifying "the poorest of the poor." This usage would explain how David could become the "firstborn" (Ps 89:27), even though he was actually the youngest son of Jesse (1 Sa 17:14). What was apparently meant was that David would have a place of special distinction and excellence. Similarly, when the Lord designated Israel, as a nation, as "my first-born" (Ex 4:22, RSV), He had reference to Israel's pre-eminence among the nations in God's sight, even as a first-born son held a position of pre-eminence among his brothers. Likewise the expression "assembly and church [RSV "assembly"] of the firstborn [ones]" emphasizes the exalted condition of the saints (Heb 12:23). When Christ is called "the firstborn of every creature" (Col 1:15, KJV), His superiority over all created beings is emphasized. Paul speaks of Him also as "the firstborn from the dead" (v 18), after which he adds this significant explanation: "That in all things he might have the preeminence"; see also Rom 8:29, KJV, where Christ is spoken of as "the firstborn among many brethren." In Heb 1:6; Rev 1:5; RSV, the expression "first-born" (KJV "firstbegotten") is probably used in this same figurative sense of pre-eminence. In addition to its figurative usage, as an epithet of Christ, the term is used in a literal sense when it refers to Jesus as the "firstborn son" of Mary (Mt 1:25; Lk 2:7; KJV).

Firstling. *See* Firstborn.

Fish Gate. [Heb. *sha'ar haddagîm.*] A gate which lay approximately in the middle of the northern wall of Jerusalem (2 Chr 33:14; Neh 3:3; 12:39; Zep 1:10), somewhere near the northwestern corner of the present *Ḥaram esh-Sherif* (fig. 259).

Fisher's Coat. The translation in the KJV of Jn 21:7 of the Gr. *ependutēs,* "an outer garment." The term is general and does not describe a coat peculiar to fishermen. The RSV translates the term "clothes."

Fishing. Since Israel was an inland nation, the coast being nearly always held by non-Israelite peoples, deep-sea fishing is not mentioned in the Bible. Apparently fishing was confined to the Sea of Galilee and the few rivers of Palestine. River fishing by means of nets, hooks, or fish spears (*see* Hook) is depicted on Egyp-

176. Fishing nets spread out for drying at ancient Sidon

tian murals and reliefs (see fig. 177). The Israelites may have had their first experience in fishing in Egypt (Is 19:8), where they ate fish freely (Num 11:5). In Palestine they bought fish from the Phoenicians, who controlled the sea and hence deep-sea fishing (Neh 13:16). The fact that one of Jerusalem's gates was called the Fish Gate (2 Chr 33:14; etc.) is generally taken as an indication that there was a fish market in that city, for marketing was usually conducted at the gates (*see* Market Place). Fishing by means of nets was carried on in the Sea of Galilee (Lk 5:1-6; *see* Galilee, Sea of). There the dragnet (Heb. *mikmereth;* Gr. *sagēnē*) was used (Hab 1:15; Mt 13:47), as well as the round throwing net (Heb. *cherem;* Gr. *amphiblēstron;* Eze 26:5; Mk 1:16). The Gr. *diktuon* is a general term for "net," without indication of its specific use or shape (Mt 4:20, 21; etc.). Several of Jesus' disciples were fishermen.

Recent studies of the behavior and movements of fish in the Sea of Galilee throw valuable light on the narrative of the miraculous draught of fish recorded in Lk 5:4-8. The narrative relates that after Peter and his companions had spent a night in fruitless efforts to catch fish, Christ asked Peter to go out into the open sea and throw out the nets. Peter and his companions obeyed, although their experience as fishermen told them it would be a waste of time and effort. When, against all expectations, a tremendous catch of fish resulted, they were amazed, and recognized that this draught was the result of a miracle performed by their Master. Why in the Sea of Galilee fishermen can expect to catch fish with deep-sea nets and with dragnets only at night, and not after daybreak, has recently been explained by a careful study of the behavior of fish in that lake. It has been discovered that at night the fish stay below the steep eastern shore, or in those deep parts of the lake where the mineral springs bubble forth. Toward morning the fish move to shallower places, either at the mouth of the Jordan, where they find much food in the water entering the lake, or to the Seven-Springs near Capernaum, whose radium-containing water attracts them. Because of these factors, fishermen find it useless to sail out after daybreak to catch fish by means of deep-sea nets or dragnets. Therefore they fish during the day near the shore at Bethsaida or at the Seven-Springs, with throwing nets. These discoveries explain

177. Fishing and hunting in the marshes, as depicted on a mural painting of ancient Egypt

what Peter knew by experience, that it was useless to launch out into the deep for a draught in daylight hours, and prove that the great catch made that day was indeed miraculous.

Lit.: J. Jeremias, *ZDPV* 70 (1954), 88.

Fitches. A translation of: (1) The Heb. *qeṣach* (Is 28:25, 27, KJV), identified by some with black cummin, or fennelflower (*Nigella sativa*), of the crowfoot family, by others with *dill (see RSV). Black cummin grows to a height of about 1½ ft. and has yellow and sometimes blue blossoms. Its numerous black, acrid, and aromatic seeds are used in the Orient as a seasoning and as medicine. (2) The Heb. *kussemîm. See* Spelt.

Flag. The translation of: (1) the Heb. *'achû,* "marsh plant," "reed" (Job 8:11, KJV), a loan word from the Egyptian *îḥy* and *îyḥ,* "marsh plant." (2) The Heb. *sûph,* "reeds," "rushes," "water plants." It was among such aquatic plants that Moses' mother placed the ark in which she hid him (Ex 2:3, 5). In divine judgments upon Egypt that would dry up its rivers its *sûph* would wither (Is 19:6). *See* Bulrush; Reed.

Flagon. The translation of: (1) the Heb. *nebel* (Is 22:24), a storage jar for wine, oil, and grain. (2) In the KJV the rendering of the Heb. *'ashîshah* (2 Sa 6:19; 1 Chr 16:3; Song 2:5; Hos 3:1), "a cake of raisins."

Flask. The rendering in the RSV of several Hebrew and Greek words, all of which, with the exception of one (*alabastron,*

"an alabaster flask," mentioned in Lk 7:37), designate earthenware vessels used to carry oil or other liquids (2 Ki 9:1, 3; Jer 19:1, 10; Mt 25:4). The word does not occur in the KJV.

Flax. [Heb. *pishtah;* Gr. *linon.*] A slender, wiry plant (*Linum usitatissimum*) from 1 to 4 ft. tall, bearing pale-blue flowers. The fibers of its bark are woven to make linen, and its seeds yield the familiar linseed oil. As one of the earliest textile fibers, it was employed by Egyptians and Palestinians for clothing, towels, measuring lines, nets, sails, flags, and wicks. Flax was one of the crops ruined by the plague of hail in Egypt (Ex 9:31), and the spies sent by Joshua to Jericho were hid by Rahab among bundles of flax stalks put on her roof to dry (Jos 2:6). Homemakers worked with flax (Prov 31:13), as did textile craftsmen (Is 19:9). Literary figures employing flax occur in Jgs 15:14 and Is 42:3 (cf. Mt 12:20).

Flay. [Heb. *pashat,* "to strip off," "to skin."] An Old English word meaning "to strip off the skin," "to skin." It occurs in this sense in the following texts which refer to the preparation of animals for sacrifice: Lev 1:6; 2 Chr 29:34; 35:11-13. Flaying is used figuratively in Mic 3:3 to describe the greed and rapaciousness of the leaders of Israel toward their people. The Hebrew word involved is somewhat more flexible in its meaning than the English word and appears a number of times elsewhere in passages that refer to the stripping off of clothing, armor, etc. (1 Sa 19:24; 31:9; 1 Chr 10:8; Job 19:9; etc.).

Flea. The translation of the Heb. *par'osh,* the *pulex irritans,* an insect that is a universal pest in Palestine. In self-abasement David called himself a flea (1 Sa 24:14; 26:20, RSV "life," on the basis of the LXX).

Fleece. [Heb. *gez* and *gizzah,* "a shearing (of wool)," "that which is shorn."] The wool of sheep. The term occurs only in Deut 18:4, Job 31:20, and Jgs 6:37-40. Although the English word "fleece" may refer to either sheared or unsheared wool, the Biblical word appears to be restricted in its meaning to sheared wool, as is evident from the meaning of the cognate Hebrew verb *gazaz,* which signifies "to shear (sheep)" or "to cut (hair)." Instead of "fleece of wool" in Jgs 6:37, the significance of the Hebrew might be clearer if translated "a shearing of wool" or "wool that has been shorn."

Flesh. This term is generally a rendering of the Heb. *baśar* (Gen 2:21; Num 27:16; etc.) and the Gr. *sarx* (Mt 16:17; Rom 1:3; etc.). It is used: (1) nontechnically to describe the physical parts of man and animals other than the bones (Gen 9:4; 29:14; Lk 24:39; 1 Cor 15:39); (2) as referring to living things in general (Gen 6:13; 1 Pe 1:24); (3) as meaning material things as contrasted with spiritual things (Jer 17:5; Zec 2:13; Mt 16:17; Mk 14:38; Lk 24:39); (4) figuratively, to describe the carnal, lower nature of man which is opposed to spiritual things (Rom 7:18; 8:3; Gal 5:16-21; etc.).

Fleshhook. [Heb. *mizlag* and *mazleg,* "fork."] A forklike instrument used by the priests in the ancient sacrificial services, more exactly translated "fork" in the RSV. The exact size and shape of the implement remain somewhat uncertain, but its general nature seems clear. The fleshhooks for the tabernacle were made of "brass," RSV "bronze" (Ex 27:3; 38:3), whereas those for the Temple built by Solomon were of gold (1 Chr 28:17). The fork referred to in 1 Sa 2:13, 14 as having 3 tines, or "teeth," probably involved a style or size slightly different from that mentioned in other references.

Flint. [Heb. *challamîsh, ṣor.*] A very compact form of silica, gray or black in color, which characteristically fractures to form sharp edges suitable for primitive cutting tools (Ex 4:25; Jos 5:2, RSV), such as knives (fig. 178). Flint was used symbolically of extreme hardness (Is 5:28;

178. A flint knife from ancient Egypt

Eze 3:9), and figuratively of determination (Is 50:7).

Flood, I. Frequently, as used in the KJV, the translation of the Heb. *nahar,* "river" (Jos 24:2, 3, 14, 15; Job 14:11; etc.).

Flood, II. [Heb. *mabbûl;* Gr. *kataklusmos.*] The Deluge of the time of Noah, visited as a judgment upon the wicked inhabitants of the earth (Gen 6 to 9).

I. The Biblical Account. Early in Biblical history intermarriage of those who had hitherto been loyal to God with those who were wicked brought the human family to such a level of moral corruption and anarchy that every thought of the heart "was only evil continually." Men were so incorrigibly evil that, although "it grieved him at his heart," God concluded that they, with other living things, must be destroyed. Only Noah and his immediate family were to be saved of the entire race of men. This was because Noah was "a just man"; therefore he "found grace in the eyes of the Lord" (Gen 6:8-10).

God instructed Noah to build an ark (*see* Ark, II, 1) for the preservation of the lives of himself and his family, and also the lives of representative groups of living creatures (Gen 6:13-21). There was a period of 120 years from the time God warned Noah that a flood was impending until the Flood itself (see v 3). During this time Noah built the ark and warned the antediluvians of the coming cataclysm (Gen 6:22; 1 Pe 3:20; 2 Pe 2:5). Seven days before the Flood, Noah and his wife, his 3 sons and their wives, and the living creatures that were to be saved, entered the ark, and were shut in by the Lord (Gen 7:1-9, 13-16). Seven days after the entrance into the ark, the Flood began (v 10). The combination of torrential rains, which lasted for 40 days, and immense volumes of water which poured forth from the earth itself soon completely inundated everything until "all the high hills, that were under the whole heaven, were covered," and the highest mountain peak was submerged. The ark floated safely upon the water (vs 11, 12, 17-20). As a result of this inundation man and every living thing on the earth were destroyed (vs 21-23). Although the Genesis story clearly mentions a distinct period of 40 days and nights during which the rain fell, it would appear that the rains continued to fall, and the waters continued to issue from the earth, though doubtless with decreased intensity, or perhaps now intermittently, for 150 days (see Gen 7:11, 12, 24; 8:2). At the end of the 150 days God sent a wind to blow upon the earth (ch 8:1). Apparently about the same time the rain was restrained, water no longer issued from the earth, and the water level began to recede. The ark eventually came to rest "upon the mountains of *Ararat" (vs 3, 4). Finally, about 2½ months after the ark had come to rest, and some 7½ months after the Flood began, the tops of the mountains were seen (cf. chs 7:11; 8:4, 5). Forty days later Noah, anxious to discover to what extent the land had dried up, opened the "window" of the ark and released a raven. This bird evidently flew to and from the ark until the adjacent land was dry (ch 8: 6, 7). Noah also released a dove, which came back to the ark because it could find no place to rest (vs 8, 9). One week later he released the dove again, which returned in the evening with an olive leaf, an indication that the earth was drying up (vs 10, 11). When he sent the same bird out another week later the ground was sufficiently dry that it did not return (v 12). After another period of waiting Noah removed what was evidently a portion of the roof of the ark and observed that the "face of the ground" was dry. Apparently the position of the "window" was such that the ground could not be seen. However, it was about 8 weeks after this before the earth was sufficiently dry for the people and animals that were in the ark to leave (vs 13-19), a year and

10 days after the Flood had begun (cf. Gen 7:11; 8:14-18).

The Flood is attested by both OT and NT writers. Through the prophet Isaiah God reminded His people of His promise no more to destroy the earth with a flood (Is 54:9). Jesus plainly testified concerning the Flood, mentioning the condition of the antediluvians, the entrance of Noah into the ark, the coming of the waters, and the destruction of all the wicked (Mt 24:37-39; Lk 17:26, 27). Peter, too, attested the historicity of the Flood (1 Pe 3:20; 2 Pe 2:5), as did also the writer of Hebrews (Heb 11:7).

II. Flood Stories Among Ancient Nations. Stories about the destruction of the world by a great flood, from which only a few people were saved, have been found among many peoples on every continent and even on islands of the Pacific. See fig. 180. R. Andree, *Die Flutsagen ethnographiṣh betrachtet* (1891), lists 88 Flood stories found all over the world, and B. C. Nelson, *The Deluge Story in Stone* (1949), reports on 41 Flood stories. Nelson points out that most stories have certain features in common, namely, that the destruction occurred by water, that an ark was provided, and that human seed was saved. Many stories stress the universality of the Flood, but other details vary, such as the question as to the cause of the Flood, the saving of animals, the place of the landing of the ship, and the sending out of birds. Although it is possible that some of these stories originated in a disastrous local catastrophe, the worldwide distribution of the Flood stories cannot be accidental and must be accepted as evidence for the historicity of the Biblical Flood narrative.

179. The duration of the Flood. The total was 1 calendar year and 10 days, but the exact number of days cannot be calculated since it is not known what form of calendar Noah used. The broken lines and the numbers in parentheses indicate uncertain periods that are reckoned conjecturally on the basis of a 360-day year (consisting of twelve 30-day months)—a theoretical year not employed in any known calendar

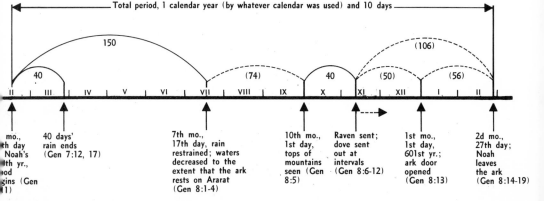

Of all the extant non-Biblical Flood stories, the oldest transmitted to us in written form is that of the Sumerians and Babylonians. None provides so many close parallels to the Biblical Flood record as this account, several copies of which have been discovered. It is found in its fullest form on the 11th tablet of the Babylonian Gilgamesh Epic. According to the story Gilgamesh, a king of Erech, in search for immortal life, traversed the nether world, and there met Utnapishtim (called Ziusudra in the Sumerian version), the hero of the Flood, from whom he learned the story of that great catastrophe: The gods had been angry with the world and decided to destroy it by a flood, but Utnapishtim, the king of Shuruppak, was warned by the god Ea of the coming event, and was advised to forsake all his possessions, build a ship, and thus save his life. He was counseled to satisfy the curiosity of his citizens who would wonder about his ship-building activity by telling them that the gods were angry with him and had decreed to banish him to a distant land. After he had completed the ship according to the instructions and measures given to him, he and his family, also a pilot, foodstuff, and many animals, went into the ship. Thereupon a tempest began,

which in the course of days destroyed the earth and everything on it, turning all mankind to clay. The storm was of such a terrifying nature that even the gods became frightened and cowered like dogs in Anu's heaven. After several days the tempest calmed down and the ship landed on Mount Nisir, one of the peaks of the Zagros Mountains east of Mesopotamia. After waiting a few days Utnapishtim at intervals sent forth birds, first a dove, then a swallow, and finally a raven. The first 2 came back, since they found no place to alight, except the ship. However, the last one did not return, thus indicating to the hero of the Flood that the land had sufficiently dried up so that he could leave his ship. Like the Biblical Noah, he offered a sacrifice upon leaving the ship, which the gods accepted by hovering around it like flies. Later Utnapishtim and his wife received the gift of immortality and then lived among the gods. For a full translation of the Babylonian Flood story see *ANET* 93-95, and for a translation of the Sumerian story, *ANET* 42-44.

Ever since the discovery of the 1st tablet of this cuneiform Flood story in 1872, to which others have been added by new discoveries from time to time, scholars have

180. The worldwide distribution of Flood stories; each dot represents a local version

FLOOD

claimed that the Biblical story borrowed its theme from the Babylonians or Sumerians. The reverse, that the Sumero-Babylonian story is based on the written Biblical narrative, is, of course, impossible, because cuneiform tablets containing the Flood story have been found written before Moses composed the book of Genesis. Yet, it is not necessary to accept the theory that the author of Genesis borrowed his story from the Babylonians. Both accounts doubtless go back to a common source. The Sumerians, probably early descendants of Noah, lived in the country in which the early postdiluvians settled soon after the Flood (Gen 11:2), and therefore retained a more vivid memory of the Flood than people who moved away from that area and did not write down an account of the Flood as early as the Sumerians. These considerations account for the many parallel details contained in the Sumero-Babylonian Flood story. Being idolaters and polytheists they corrupted the story and robbed it of the ethical features found in the Biblical story, and even depicted the gods who decreed the Flood as miserable characters.

III. Archeology and the Flood. In several ancient Mesopotamian sites, notably Ur, Erech, Kish, Lagash, Shuruppak, and Nineveh, thick levels of sediment have been uncovered that show that at various times in the distant past there had been great inundations, probably caused by a disastrous flooding of the rivers Euphrates and Tigris. The archeological contexts indicate that the various destructions were local in character. Some archeologists, believing that the Babylonian story of the Flood (see sec. II) and also the Biblical Flood record in reality refer to no more than a local disaster, take the sediment levels from Ur and other Mesopotamian sites as evidence for the great Flood described in the ancient records of Babylonia and the Bible (see Sir Charles Leonard Woolley, *Excavations at Ur* [London, 1955], pp. 19-36). Since it is rather obvious and generally recognized that these Flood levels are indications of local disasters, students of the Bible who believe in the universality of the Flood should not use the archeological evidence of Ur and other Mesopotamian sites as proof for the historicity of the Flood.

IV. Fossils and the Flood. Evolutionists call attention to the somewhat constant sequence of fossil forms characteristically

181. A cuneiform tablet containing the Babylonian story of the Flood

found in the layers of sedimentary rock, and have fitted the evidence to their unproved theory (*see* Creation), which they accept as fact. Hence, following the uniformitarian idea popularized by Sir Charles Lyell in the early decades of the 19th cent., they assume that long ages of gradual deposition, together with the rise and death of increasingly complex kinds of life, provide the explanation of the fossil sequence. This, of course, denies both the Genesis record of Creation and the inspired record of the Flood. Actually, the fossil evidence can be explained adequately from a creationist viewpoint.

At the beginning of the Flood sediment was doubtless carried down the streams and deposited in the oceans, burying animals and plants. As the rains continued, more and more sediment was deposited in the seas, until finally they became filled. As the waters increased, sediments were deposited everywhere. When the water reached its greatest depth (at the end of the first 150 days) all life was dead upon the earth. Bodies of dead creatures were soon buried under quantities of sediment. Water movements would cause disturbances of the fresh sediments, accounting for deposits of great thickness in some places and the lack of any deposits in other regions. It would account also for alternating layers of sand and coal, and the layering of sandstone on a large scale in many regions.

The animals and plants living at the bottom of the preflood seas would be

357

182. Skeleton of an extinct animal, the *Stegosaurus stenops*, one of the ancient dinosaurs that once roamed in what is now the northwestern United States

buried down deeply—at the bottom of the sea. Trilobites and brachiopods were common forms found at the bottom of the seas, and we find them in the deepest fossil beds today. Clams, snails, starfish, crinoids and many other marine animals are also found deep in the sediment of the pre-Flood seas. Great quantities of fishes, and especially plankton (microscopic animals and plants of the ocean), form deposits so large as to produce our major oil fields.

Land animals in general are found in higher layers of fossils, since they lived on dry land before the Flood, and often at higher elevations. Also, they were the more mobile, and therefore would logically be the last of the life forms to drown and be carried away and buried in the deposited mud. Thus, today we usually find the land animals in fossil layers nearer the surface. There are a few places where this order is exactly reversed, but a geological process known as overthrusting or thrust-faulting accounts for this. It is a case where sedimentary layers are folded so violently that they are actually pushed over on top of themselves and form an order of layers reversing the position they had formerly assumed. Of course, it is conceivable that one of the higher forms of animal would occasionally have been overwhelmed early in the Flood and would be found buried in the lower layers of rock.

Flora and Fauna. The following tables furnish a convenient comparative list of the various plants and animals of the Bible as they appear in the KJV and RSV. The KJV is used as the basis; its terms appear in the 1st column, the corresponding RSV terms in the 2d, and the Hebrew, Aramaic, and/or Greek expressions of which these KJV and RSV terms are translations in the 3d and 4th columns.

The KJV terms in the 1st column of each table provide a ready reference and an alphabetical listing of the animals and plants. There are a few exceptions to the alphabetical arrangement. Occasionally a word appears that does not belong in the tabulation; it is included because the RSV equivalent (sometimes the result of an emendation) properly belongs in the table. Such terms are put in parentheses and appear indented in the space corresponding to the RSV rendering, not in alphabetical order. For example, " (vessel)" appears indented under "ram" because its RSV equivalent is "ram."

The 2d column provides an equally complete, though not alphabetical, list of the RSV renderings, arranged in the order of the corresponding KJV entries. Because the Hebrew, Aramaic, and/or Greek words are often variously rendered, RSV terms are at times repeated. For example, the RSV "vulture" is found opposite the KJV "eagle," "ossifrage," and "pelican."

The following examples show how the tables are to be interpreted. In the table of mammals appears the entry "beef" in column 1, "ox" in column 2, and *baqar* in column 3. This means simply that where the KJV has "beef" and the Hebrew, *baqar*, the RSV has "ox." However, this must not be construed to mean that where the RSV has "ox" the KJV will always have "beef" (as a glance at the entry "ox" reveals), or that *baqar* is rendered only "ox" in the RSV and "beef" in the KJV (as a glance at the entries "bull" and "kine" reveals). The table is broken down so that for every item appearing, not only in the KJV column but in the RSV column as well, the corresponding Hebrew, Aramaic, and/or Greek words may be known.

In a few cases the RSV offers variant translations based either upon the LXX or other ancient versions, or upon textual emendations. Such translations are indicated by †. An asterisk (*) before a term indicates, as elsewhere in the book, that a discussion of that item may be found by looking under that particular entry. It is suggested that these tables be studied in connection with the individual discussions of the various plants and animals.

KJV	RSV	Hebrew	Greek
algum (see almug)	algum	'algûmmîm	
*almond	almond	shaqed	
*almug	almug	'almuggîm	
*aloe	aloe	'ahalîm (pl.), 'ahalôth (pl.),	aloē
aloe, lign	"	'ahalîm (pl.)	
*apple	apple	tappûach	
*ash	cedar	'oren	
*bay tree	cedar †	'ezrach	
box	*pine	te'ashshûr	
camphire	*henna	kopher	
*cassia	cassia	qeṣi'ah, qiddah	
*cedar	cedar	'erez	
chestnut	*plane	'ermôn	
*cinnamon	cinnamon	qinnamôn	kinnamōmon
*cypress	holm	tirzah	
*ebony	ebony	hobnîm (pl.)	
*elm	terebinth	'elah	
*fig	fig	te'enah	sukē
fig, green	"	pag	
*fig, untimely	winter fruit		olunthos
*fir	cypress, fir	berôsh	
"	*pine	berôth	
*frankincense	frankincense	lebonah	libanos
*gopher	gopher	gopher	
(grove)	*tamarisk	'eshel	
hazel	*almond	lûz	
*heath	(wild ass)	'arô'er	
"	shrub	'ar'ar	
juniper	*broom tree	rothem	
mulberry	*balsam	baka'	
*myrtle	myrtle	hadas	
*nut	nut	'egôz	
"	pistachio nut	boṭnah	
*oak	oak	'allah, 'allôn, 'ayil, 'elah	
(Allon)	"	'elôn	
(hind)	oak†	'ayyalah	
(idol)	"	'elah	
(plain)	"	'elôn	
*oil tree	olive	'eṣ shemen	
*olive	"	zayith	elaia
olive tree	olivewood	'eṣ shemen	
olive tree, good	cultivated olive tree		kallielaios
olive, wild	wild olive		agrielaios
*palm	palm	tamar, timmorah	phoinix
"	palm, (idol)†	tomer	
pine	*plane	tidhar	
"	wild olive	'eṣ shemen	
*pomegranate	pomegranate	rimmôn	
*poplar	poplar	libneh	
shady tree	*lotus, plant or tree	ṣe'elîm (pl.)	
*shittah	acacia	shiṭṭah	
shittim (see shittah, above)	acacia	shiṭṭîm (pl.)	
*sycamine	sycamine		sukaminos
*sycomore	sycamore	shiqmah	sukomorea
*teil	*terebinth	'elah	
*thyine	(scented)		thuïnos
tree	tamarisk	'eshel	
*willow	willow	'arabah, ṣaphṣaphah	

† Emendation or ancient versions

KJV	RSV	Hebrew or Aramaic	Greek
anise	*dill		anēthon
*barley	barley	še'orah	krithē
*bean	bean	pól	
*bramble	bramble	'aṭad	batos
"	thistle	chóach	
*brier	brier	barqonîm (pl.), chedeq, sarab, shamîr, sillón, sirpad	
"	thistle		tribolos
*bulrush	bulrush, papyrus (see Writing Material)	gome'	
"	rush	'agmón	
*calamus	calamus, cane	qaneh	
cane (see Calamus)	cane	qaneh	
*chaff	dry grass	chashash	
"	chaff	moṣ, 'ûr‡	achuron
"	straw	teben	
*cockle	foul weed	bo'shah	
*coriander	coriander	gad	
*corn	fodder	balîl	
"	grain	bar, gereś, karmel, qalî, sheber, shibboleth	kokkos, sitos, sporima, stachus
"	grain, *bread	dagan	
"	grain, standing grain	qamah	
"	(threshing floor)	goren	
corn, standing	stacked grain, standing grain	qamah	
*cucumber	cucumber	miqshah, qishshu'ah	
*cummin	cummin	kammon	kuminon
*fitch	dill	qeṣach	
"	*spelt	kussemeth	
*flag	reed	'achû	
"	reed, rush	sûph	
*flax	flax, (wick)	pishtah	
"	(wick)		linon
*galbanum	galbanum	chelbenah	
*gall	gall, poison, (bitterness)	mererah, merorah, ro'sh, rósh	
"	gall		cholē
garlick	*garlic	shûmim (pl.)	
*gourd	plant	qîqayón	
gourd, wild	wild gourd	paqquʻoth (pl.)	
(knop)	gourd	peqa'îm (pl.)	
(oxen)	gourd†	baqar	
grape (see vine below)	grape	'enab, pereṭ	staphulē
grape, sour	grape, sour grape	boser	
grape, tender	blossom, grape blossom	semadar	
grape, unripe	unripe grape	beser	
grape, wild	wild grape	be'ushîm (pl.)	
*grass	grass	'aśab, chaṣîr, deshe'‡, yereq	chortos
"	grass, vegetation	deshe'	
"	grass, herbage, vegetation	'eśeb	
grass, mown	mown grass	gez	
(meadow)	reed grass	'achû	
*hemlock	wormwood	la'anah	
"	poisonous weed	ro'sh	

† Emendation or ancient versions
‡ Aramaic

KJV	RSV	Hebrew or Aramaic	Greek
*herb	herb, (light)	'órah	
"	(sunshine)	'ór	
"	plants	chaṣir	
"	herb, *vegetable	yaraq	
"	grass, herb, plant, vegetable	'eśeb	
"	vegetation		botanē
"	herb, shrub, *vegetable		lachanon
*herb, bitter	bitter herb	merorím (pl.)	
herb, tender	grass, herb, tender grass	deshe'	
*hyssop	hyssop	'ezób	hussōpos
*leek	leek	chaṣir	
*lentil	lentil	'adashím (pl.)	
*lily	lily	shóshan, shóshannah, shúshan	krinon
*mallow	mallow	mallúach	
(all)	mallow†	kol	
*mandrake	mandrake	dúda'ím (pl.)	
*melon	melon	'abaṭṭichím (pl.)	
*millet	millet	dochan	
*mint	mint		hēduosmon
*mustard	mustard		sinapi
*nettle	nettle	charúl, qimmóś	
*onion	onion	baṣal	
*pannag	(early fig)	pannag	
paper reed	(bare place)	'arah	
*reed	reed, rod	qaneh	kalamos
"	(bulwark)	'agam	
rie	*spelt	kussemeth	
*rose	*crocus, rose	chabaṣṣeleth	
*rue	rue		pēganon
rush (see Bulrush)	*papyrus	gome'	
"	reed	'agmón	
*saffron	saffron	karkóm	
*spikenard	nard	nerd	nardos pistikē
*tare	weed		zizanion
thistle (see Thorns and Thistles)	thistle	dardar	tribolos
thistle	thistle, thorn	chóach	
thorn (see Thorns and Thistles)	thorn	'aṭad, chedeq, qimma-shón, qóṣ, ṣen, seniním (pl.), shayith, sillón, sír	akantha, akan-thinos, skolops
thorn	*bramble, hook	chóach	
"	thornbush	na'aṣúṣ	
*vine	vine	gephen, nazír, śoreq, śoreqah	
"	grapevine, vine, vintage		ampelos
"	(vineyard)	kerem	
*vine of Sodom	vine of Sodom	gephen Sedom	
weed	weed	súph	
*wheat	wheat	chinṭah‡, chiṭṭah	sitos
"	grain, wheat	bar	
"	grain	dagan	
"	crushed grain	ríphóth (pl.)	
*wormwood	bitter fruit, wormwood	la'anah	
"	wormwood		apsinthos

† Emendation or ancient versions
‡ Aramaic

MAMMALS

KJV	RSV	Hebrew or Aramaic	Greek
*ape	ape	qôph	
*ass	ass, she-ass	'athôn	
"	ass	chamor, chamôr	hupozugion, onos
ass colt	ass, ass colt	'ayir	
ass, wild	*wild ass	'arad‡, 'arôd, pere'	
ass, young	ass	'ayir	onarion
*badger	goat, sheep, (leather)	tachash	
*bat	bat	'aṭalleph	
*bear	bear	dob‡, dób	arktos
*beef (see Beeves)	ox	baqar	
*behemoth	Behemoth	behemôth	
*boar	boar	chazîr	
*bull	bull, *stallion	'abbîr	
"	bull	baqar, par, shôr	tauros
bull, wild	*antelope	te'ô	
bullock	*bull	par, tôr‡	
"	bull, *ox	ben baqar, shôr	
"	*calf	'egel	
*calf	"	ben baqar, 'egel, 'eglah	
"	calf, ox		moschos
*camel	camel	gamal	kamēlos
"	(used in the royal service)	'achashteranîm (pl.)	
*cattle, lesser or small	*sheep	śeh	
chamois	*mountain-sheep	zemer	
coney	badger, *rock badger	shaphan	
*cow	cow	parah, shôr	
cow, young	cow, young	'eglath baqar	
deer, *fallow	*roebuck	yachmûr	
*dog	dog	keleb	kunarion, kuōn
(dragon)	*jackal, (dragon)	tan	
*dromedary	swift steed	rekesh	
"	royal stud	rammak	
"	young camel	beker	
dromedary, swift	" "	bikrah	
ewe	ewe	kabśah, kibśah, rachel, śeh, 'ûl	
*fatling	fatling	meach, merî', mishneh	
"	fatted calf		sitistos
ferret (see Lizard)	(gecko)	'anaqah	
foal	foal, he-ass	'ayir	
*fox	fox	shú'al	alōpēx
"	*jackal	shú'al	
*goat	goat	'ez	eriphion, eriphos, tragos
"	he-goat	'ez	
"	he-goat, male goat	'attûd	
goat, he	he-goat	śa'îr, śephîr‡, tayish	
goat, (he)	goat, he-goat	śaphîr	
" "	he-goat, male goat	attûd	
goat, she	female goat, she-goat	'ez	
*goat, wild	wild goat	'aqqô	
" "	mountain goat, wild goat	ya'el	
greyhound	(strutting *cock)†	zarzîr mothnayim	
*hare	hare	'arnebeth	
*hart	hart, stag	'ayyal	
heifer	heifer	'eglah, parah	damalis
heifer of 3 yrs	(Eglath-shelishiyah)	'eglath shelishîyah	

† Emendation or ancient versions
‡ Aramaic

MAMMALS (Continued)

KJV	RSV	Hebrew or Aramaic	Greek
*hind	hind, (oak)	'ayyalah	
"	hind	'ayyeleth	
*horse	horse	sûs	hippos
"	stallion	sûs	
*kid	goat, he-goat, male goat	śa'îr	
"	kid	ben-'ez, gedî, gedîyah	eriphos
"	goat, kid	'ez	
"	goat	śe'îrah	
kine	*cow	parah	
"	cattle	'eleph	
"	herd	baqar	
*lamb	lamb	ben ṣo'n, kabśah, kar, kebeś, keśeb, kibśah, kiśbah, ṣo'n, ṭaleh, ṭelî	amnos, arnion
"	lamb, sheep	'immar‡, śeh	
*leopard	leopard	namer, nemar‡	pardalis
*lion	lion	'arî, 'aryeh, kephîr, laba', labî', layish, shachal	leōn
lion, great	lion	labî'	
lion, old	"	labî'	
" "	lion, strong lion	layish	
lion, stout	"	labî'	
lion, young	young lion	'arî, kephîr	
" "	lioness	labî'	
lioness	"	leba'ah, lebîya'	
lion's whelp	(proud beast)	shachaṣ	
mole	* (chameleon)	tinshemeth	
*mole	mole	chapharpar, chaphar-parah	
*mouse	mouse	'akbar	
*mule	mule	pered, pirdah	
"	horse	rekesh	
"	(hot spring)	yemim (pl.)	
*ox	cow	shôr	
"	ox	'eleph, tôr‡	bous, tauros
"	bull, ox	baqar	
"	cattle	'alûph	
"	bull	par	
ox, wild	*antelope	te'ô	
(passover)	Passover lamb, paschal lamb	pesach	pascha
pygarg	*ibex	dîshôn	
ram (see Ram, I)	ram	'ayil, dekar‡	
"	goat, he-goat	'attûd	
(vessel)	ram†	kelî	
*roe	gazelle	ṣebî, ṣebîyah, ya'alah	
*roebuck	"	ṣebî	
*sheep	sheep	kebeś, śeh, ṣona', ṣoneh	probaton
"	lamb, sheep	keśeb	
"	flock, sheep	ṣo'n	
"	ewe, sheep	rachel	
(strong [one])	stallion	'abbîr	
swift beast	*dromedary	kirkarôth (pl.)	
" "	steed	rekesh	
*swine	swine	chazîr	choiros
*unicorn	wild ox	re'em	
*weasel	weasel	choled	

† Emendation or ancient versions
‡ Aramaic

KJV	RSV	Hebrew or Aramaic	Greek
*whale	sea monster	*tannín*	
"	dragon	*tanním*	
"	whale		*kētos*
wild beast	(all that moves)	*zíz*	
wild beast of the desert	wild beast	*ṣí*	
wild *beast of the islands	*hyena, *jackal	*'í*	
*wolf	wolf	*ze'eb*	*lukos*

BIRDS

KJV	RSV	Hebrew or Aramaic	Greek
bird, *speckled	speckled bird	*'ayiṭ ṣabûa'*	
*bittern	(hedgehog), (porcupine)	*qippod*	
*cock	cock		*alektōr*
*cormorant	cormorant	*qa'ath, shalak*	
"	*hawk	*qa'ath*	
*crane	swallow	*sís, sûs*	
cuckow	*sea gull	*shachaph*	
*dove	dove	*yónah*	*peristera*
"	pigeon		*peristera*
*eagle	eagle	*neshar‡, nesher*	*aetos*
"	*vulture	*nesher*	
gier eagle	*carrion vulture	*racham*	
"	vulture	*rachamah*	
glede	*buzzard	*ra'ah*	
(greyhound)	strutting *cock	*zarzír mothnayim*	
*hawk	hawk	*neṣ*	
*hen	hen		*ornis*
*heron	heron	*'anaphah*	
*kite	kite, *falcon	*'ayyah*	
lapwing	*hoopoe	*dûkíphath*	
*night hawk	nighthawk	*tachmas*	
ospray	*osprey	*'oznîyah*	
*ossifrage	ossifrage, *vulture	*peres*	
*ostrich	ostrich	*chasîdah, ya'anah*	
*owl	owl	*kôs, yanshûph*	
"	*ostrich	*bath ya'anah*	
owl, great	great owl, *ibis	*yanshûph*	
" "	*owl	*qippóz*	
owl, little	little owl, owl	*kôs*	
owl, screech	*night hag	*lílíth*	
*partridge	partridge	*qore'*	
*peacock	peacock	*tukkíyím* (pl.)	
"	*ostrich	*renaním* (pl.)	
*pelican	pelican, *vulture	*qa'ath*	
pigeon (*see* Dove)	pigeon	*yónah*	*peristera*
pigeon, young	pigeon, young	*gózal*	
*quail	quail	*śelaw*	
*raven	raven	*'oreb*	*korax*
(desolation)	raven†	*choreb*	
*sparrow	sparrow	*ṣippór*	*strouthion*
"	lonely bird	*ṣippór*	
*stork	stork	*chasîdah*	
*swallow	swallow	*derór*	
"	*crane	*'agûr*	
*swan	water hen	*tinshemeth*	
turtle	*turtledove	*tôr*	
*turtledove	"	*tôr*	*trugōn*
"	dove	*tôr*	
*vulture	kite	*da'ah, dayyah*	
"	falcon	*'ayyah*	

† Emendation or ancient versions
‡ Aramaic

KJV	RSV	Hebrew	Greek
adder (see Serpent)	adder	pethen, ṣiph'oni	
"	*viper	'akshûb, shephiphon	
asp (see Serpent)	asp	pethen	aspis
*chameleon	land crocodile	koach	
cockatrice (see Serpent)	adder	ṣepha', ṣiph'oni	
*dragon	dragon		drakōn
dragon (see list of Mammals)	serpent, (monster, sea monster)	tannin	
(ferret)	gecko (see Lizard)	'anaqah	
*frog	frog	sephardea'	batrachos
*leviathan	Leviathan	liwyathan	
*lizard	lizard	leṭa'ah	
(mole)	*chameleon	tinshemeth	
*serpent	serpent	nachash, śaraph, tannin	ophis
"	crawling thing	zachal	
"	*reptile		herpeton
tortoise (see Lizard)	great lizard	ṣab	
*viper	viper	'eph'eh	echidna

INSECTS AND OTHER INVERTEBRATES

*ant	ant	nemalah	
*bee	bee	debôrah	
beetle (see Locust, 3)	cricket	chargol	
cankerworm (see Locust, 6)	hopper, hopping locust, locust	yeleq	
caterpiller (see Locust, 10)	caterpillar, destroyer, destroying locust	chasil	
caterpiller	locust, young locust	yeleq	
*flea	flea	par'osh	
*fly	fly	'arob, zebûb	
*gnat	gnat		kōnōps
grasshopper (see Locust, 1, 4)	locust	'arbeh, chagab	
grasshopper (see Locust, 7)	grasshopper	gôbay	
*hornet	hornet	ṣir'ah	
horseleach	*leech	'alûqah	
*lice	gnat	ken, kinnam	
(in like manner)	gnat†	(kemô) ken	
*locust	grasshopper, locust, swarming locust	'arbeh	
"	locust	chagab, geb, ṣelaṣal	akris
locust, bald	bald locust	sal'am	
*moth	moth	'ash	sēs
"	(spider's web)†	'ash	
palmerworm (see Locust, 5)	cutter, cutting locust, locust	gazam	
*scorpion	scorpion	'aqrab	skorpios
*snail	sand lizard	chomeṭ	
"	snail	shabbelûl	
*spider	spider	'akkabish	
"	*lizard	śemamith	
*worm	worm	rimmah, sas, tola', tôla'ath, tôle'ah	skôlēx
"	crawling thing	zachal	

† Emendation or ancient versions

Flotes. A rendering of the Heb. *raphsodôth* (2 Chr 2:16, KJV), meaning "rafts" (RSV).

Flour. Two types of flour were used by the ancient Hebrews: (1) *Soleth,* "fine flour." It was this type of flour that was offered in the ancient tabernacle and Temple offerings (Ex 29:2, 40; Lev 2:2; Num 15: 4; 28:5, 9, 12). It was, of course, also used domestically (1 Ki 4:22). (2) *Qemach,* "ordinary flour," of varying grades of coarseness (Gen 18:6; Jgs 6:19; 1 Sa 1: 24; 28:24; etc.). Wheat and barley were the principal grains from which flour was made, the poorer classes using chiefly barley (Jgs 7:13; Jn 6:13). The word "flour" appears in the NT only in Rev 18:13, where it is named among the luxuries of mystic Babylon. It is a translation of the Gr. *semidalis,* which indicates the finest grade of flour. *See* Bread; Mill.

Flower.

1. Palestine has a great number of spring flowers, which lend a colorful but brief beauty to a land that is otherwise bare and sun baked for much of the year (see fig. 183). However, the Bible speaks but rarely of these flowers and names only a few of the many varieties flourishing in ancient Bible lands (*see* names of individual flowers; *see also* Flora and Fauna). Ornamental flowers embellished the candlestick of the tabernacle (Ex 25:31, 34; etc.), decorated the "molten sea" of Solomon's Temple, and were carved in the interior cedar boards (1 Ki 6:16, 18; 7:26; 2 Chr 4:5; etc.). The life of man is frequently likened to a flower that blossoms briefly, then withers and perishes (Job 14:1, 2; Ps 103:15; Is 28:1; 40:6-8; Jas 1:10, 11; 1 Pe 1:24; etc.).

2. The menses or menstrual discharge (Lev 15:24, 33; RSV "impurity").

Flute. One of the earliest musical instruments, often found depicted on the Egyptian monuments. It was a simple hollow reed with a mouthpiece at one end, and, toward the other end, holes that were covered by the fingers of the one playing, to vary the pitch. The word "flute" occurs in the KJV only in Dan 3:5, 7, 10, 15 as an instrument in Nebuchadnezzar's band, but the word thus translated describes instead a whistle or pipe. The true

183. Spring flowers on the shore of the Sea of Galilee, with Mount Hermon in the distance

flute is probably the Heb. *'ûgab,* translated "organ" in the KJV and "pipe" in the RSV (Job 21:12; 30:31; Ps 150:4). It is mentioned in Gen 4:21 as an instru-

184. Egyptian playing a flute

ment invented very early in this world's history. In the NT the flute, Gr. *aulos,* occurs in 1 Cor 14:7 (KJV "pipe"), and the flute players, Gr. *aulētēs,* are mentioned as playing on occasions of both mourning (Mt 9:23, RSV) and joy (Rev 18:22, RSV). The Heb. *chalil,* translated "flute" (RSV generally), "pipe" (KJV), is probably the double flute or oboe (see fig. 387).

Flux. *See* Dysentery.

Fly. The translation of: (1) The Heb. *zebûb,* an insect mentioned only twice in the Bible, although it is a real pest in Palestine, incessantly attacking man and beast. The fly belongs to the order *Diptera,* and the common housefly (*Musca domestica*) can be found everywhere in Bible lands. Is 7:18 mentions the fly as a figure of the Egyptian forces, and Ec 10:1 reminds the reader that a dead fly, falling into the ointment bottle, spoils the entire contents. The Philistines at Ekron had a special god of the flies, *Baal-zebub, who would supposedly be appeased by sacrifices and thus deliver from the plague those who consulted him (2 Ki 1:2). In

185. Golden replicas (actual size) of flies found at *Tell el-'Ajjúl,* a Philistine site. These were probably objects offered to appease the Philistine god of flies

the excavations of Philistine sites numerous golden images of flies were found (see fig. 185), which had probably been dedicated to this god. (2) The Heb. *'arob,* the swarms of flies that brought the 4th plague upon Egypt (Ex 8:21-31; Ps 78:45; 105:31). Following the ancient

versions commentators have seen in this noxious insect the dogfly, also called gadfly, which sucks the blood and can be very annoying to horses and other domestic animals, as well as to human beings.

Fold. *See* Sheepfold.

Folly. The thoughts and acts of a *fool.

Food. The original food of man, appointed him by his Creator, was grains, nuts, and fruits (Gen 1:29; 2:16). Immediately after the *Flood, which had destroyed these foods, God permitted man to eat the flesh of animals (ch 9:3), although He specified that blood was not to be eaten (v 4). The prohibition concerning blood was later repeated to the Israelites (Lev 3:17; 7:26; 17:10; etc.). God also designated that only certain animals, birds, and fish were fit for food (Lev 11; Deut 14). However, meat never played a large part in the diet of the Hebrews, nor in that of Orientals generally. Their principal food was grains, such as wheat, barley, millet, and spelt (Ruth 2:23; 2 Sa 17:28; Eze 4:9). Among the legumes, beans and lentils are mentioned (2 Sa 17:28; Eze 4:9). Fruits included grapes, figs, apples, pomegranates, and olives (Num 13:20; 20:5; Deut 8:8; Joel 1:12). While in the wilderness the Israelites longed for the cucumbers, melons, leeks, onions, and garlic they had had in Egypt (Num 11:5), and these were doubtless a part of their diet when they settled in Canaan. Honey was regarded as a delicacy (Ps 19:10; Song 5:1); and thus "a land flowing with milk and honey" signified a land of great productivity (Ex 3:8; Lev 20:24; Deut 11:9; etc.). Of the dairy products, milk curds (KJV "butter") and cheese are mentioned (Gen 18:8; Deut 32:14; 2 Sa 17:29). Lk 11:12 implies that eggs were eaten (cf. Is 59:5). *See* names of individual foods.

Fool. In the OT the translation generally of the Heb. *'ewil* and *kesil.* Both words occur frequently in Proverbs and Ecclesiastes, but rarely in other books. The wise man contrasts the fool with the man who pursues wisdom. The wise man is one who fears God, whereas the fool has no fear of God in his heart. He either neglects God because of a love of ease and pleasure, or willfully defies Him. Foolishness and wickedness are thus almost synonymous expressions. The words translated "fool" in the NT generally designate one who is "foolish," "stupid," "ignorant," or "senseless" (Mt 5:22; 23:17, 19; Lk 12:20; 2 Cor 11:16, 23; etc.).

Foot. Anciently, as today, in Oriental lands, reverence was shown by baring the feet (Ex 3:5; Jos 5:15). The Hebrews also bared their feet in times of great misfortune and mourning (2 Sa 15:30). Respect for another was shown by falling at his feet (2 Ki 4:37; Est 8:3; Mk 5:22; Rev 19:10). Victors placed their feet upon the necks of the conquered as a sign of conquest (Jos 10:24). The psalmist declared that because he faithfully served God his feet stood "in an even place" (Ps 26:12). Being overtaken by the results of sin or falling into sin was figuratively represented as the feet stumbling or slipping (Deut 32:35; Ps 73:2, 3). The expression "to sit at the feet of a teacher" was anciently literally true (cf. Acts 22:3). The prophet called for his people to turn away their feet from the Sabbath (Is 58:13), meaning that they were to stop desecrating that day. At the Last Supper Jesus washed the disciples' feet, taking the part of the servant who commonly washed the soiled feet of arriving guests (Jn 13:4-14; cf. Lk 7:44).

Footmen. Soldiers who fought on foot in contrast to horsemen and charioteers (Num 11:21; Jgs 20:2; 1 Sa 4:10; etc.), RSV variously, "on foot," "men on foot," "foot soldiers." The word translated "footmen" in 1 Sa 22:17, KJV, literally means "runners," and is a term sometimes applied to guards (1 Ki 14:27; etc.). Here, members of the royal bodyguard and not footmen are meant.

Footstool. [Heb. *kebesh* and *hadom raglayim;* Gr. *hupopodion tōn podōn.*] A low, box-like stool to support the feet of one sitting on a high chair, especially used in connection with thrones. In the Bible the term is generally used in poetical passages where, symbolically, the earth or Jerusalem are spoken of as being God's footstool (Is 66:1; Lam 2:1; Acts 7:49; etc.). In several texts (Ps 110:1; Lk 20:43; Heb 1:13; etc.) God's enemies are said to be made His footstool. This metaphorical expression was well understood in the ancient world, for pictures of bound enemies were painted on, or carved in, the footstools of kings, for example, Tutankhamen's footstool (fig. 501).

Ford. [Heb. *ma'abar, ma'barah,* and *'abarah.*] Since bridges were uncommon in the ancient world, rivers were usually crossed at fords, where the water was ordinarily shallow. The OT mentions fords of the rivers Jabbok (Gen 32:22), Arnon (Is 16:2), Jordan (Jos 2:7; Jgs 3:28; etc.),

and the river of Babylon, presumably the Euphrates (Jer 51:32, RSV).

Forecast. [Heb. *chashab,* "to devise," or "to plot."] A term used only in Dan 11:24, 25, KJV, with the archaic English meaning "to contrive beforehand," "to scheme beforehand." Elsewhere *chashab* is rendered: "devise" (Ex 31:4; 35:32); "imagine" (Zec 7:10; 8:17; KJV); "purpose" (Jer 26:3, KJV; 49:20); etc.

Foreigner. One who is an alien or a stranger. In the OT several types of aliens are delineated: (1) *Nokrî,* "strange," "foreign," "foreigner." This Hebrew term is translated "foreigner" in the KJV only in Deut 15:3 and Ob 11, though this rendering is frequent in the RSV (Deut 15:3; 23:20; 1 Ki 8:41; Prov 20:16; Ob 11; etc.). *Nokrî* does not necessarily denote a non-Jew, but simply designates a person or an object that is distinctly alien to the locality. When used by the Hebrews, however, the expression usually refers primarily to non-Hebrews, either those who remained in Canaan after the Israelite conquest, or those who subsequently settled there. Ruth the Moabitess refers to herself by this term (Ruth 2:10, KJV "stranger"; RSV "foreigner"). Ittai the Gittite, a Philistine, is referred to in 2 Sa 15:19 by this expression; and Solomon's foreign wives are similarly described in 1 Ki 11:1, RSV (KJV "strange"). (2) *Ben nekar,* literally, "son of a foreign country." This term appears frequently in the OT as a synonym of *nokrî,* and in the RSV is usually rendered "foreigner" (Gen 17:12; Ex 12:43; Is 56:3, 6; etc.); but in the KJV usually "stranger" or "son of the stranger." (3) *Zar,* "strange," "illicit," "foreign" (Eze 7:21; 11:9; 28:10; etc.; RSV; KJV usually "stranger"). This word often appears as a synonym of *nokrî,* but contains the added implication that the person so designated is an "outsider" (Lev 22:10) who must not expect to participate in the privileges of the community or class. (4) *Tôshab,* "sojourner," "inhabitant." Translated "foreigner" only in Ex 12:45 (RSV "sojourner"). Although the word refers to the more or less settled state of the individual involved, it implies that the original home of the person was elsewhere. In other texts the KJV usually translates it "sojourner" (Gen 23:4; Lev 25:35, 40, 47; etc.).

In the NT the expression "foreigner" occurs once in the KJV and 5 times in the RSV, a rendering of the following words: (1) *Paroikos,* Eph 2:19, KJV "stranger," "alien." The term not only refers to one who is an alien within a given community but also implies (like *tôshab* above) that the person maintains a more or less permanent residence in that place. Such an individual, as a citizen of some remote land, could not expect all the rights and privileges naturally belonging to the local citizens; but he could live there and conduct business at the option of the local populace. *Paroikos* appears also in 1 Pe 2:11, where the plural form is rendered "strangers" in the KJV and "aliens" in the RSV. Compare its use in Acts 7:6, 29. (2) *Allogenēs*, "foreigner" (Lk 17:18, RSV; KJV "stranger"). (3) *Barbaros*, "non-Greek," "foreigner," "one who speaks a foreign language" (1 Cor 14:11, RSV; KJV *"barbarian"). (4) *Heteros*, "other," "different," "strange (one)," hence "foreigner" (1 Cor 14:21, RSV; KJV "other"). (5) *Xenos*, "stranger," "alien" (Acts 17:21, RSV "foreigner"; KJV "stranger").

It should be noted that a distinction seems to have been made between these Hebrew and Greek words rendered "foreigner," which designate one of any race who was living as an alien at a distance from his native land, and those rendered "Gentile," which designate a member of any race other than Jewish, without reference to place. *See* Gentiles; Stranger.

Foreknowledge. [Gr. *prognōsis*, "a knowing beforehand," "foreknowledge."] That aspect of God's omniscience by which future events are known to Him before, and apart from, any objective indication that they are to take place. The term appears only in Acts 2:23 and in 1 Pe 1:2, KJV. The related verb form, "to foreknow" (*proginōskō*), is used in Rom 8:29; 11:2; etc. The Scriptures in no way circumscribe the foreknowledge of God; in fact, they point to this ability to discern the future as a primary evidence that He is God (Is 42:9; 45:21; 46:10; 48:3-8).

It is important to distinguish between foreknowledge and predestination. "To know" does not mean "to determine," and "to foreknow" must not be construed to mean "to predetermine." In Acts 2:23 God's foreknowledge concerning Christ's vicarious death is connected with His infinite purpose, or "plan," that Christ should die for sinners. God foresaw, as well, that some would accept the salvation thus provided, and to such He purposed to give the privilege of becoming the sons of God (Jn 1:12). He foreordained, or predestined, all who would voluntarily accept the gift of salvation "to be conformed to the image of his

Son" (Rom 8:29). Thus, in the case of human beings as free moral agents, predestination is based on foreknowledge. According to v 30, those thus predestined to conformation to the image of Christ are said to be "called," "justified," and "glorified." Similarly in 1 Pe 1:2 the divine election must be considered as based on "the foreknowledge of God" with respect to those who accept His gift of salvation. *See* Predestination.

Forerunner. A rendering of the Gr. *prodromos* (Heb 6:20), "one who runs before." Jesus is described as having gone before into the presence of the Father; His followers will arrive there later (cf. Jn 14:1-3).

Foresail. [Gr. *artemōn*, "sail," "foresail."] In NT times a small sail hoisted above the bow (KJV "foreship," "forepart"; cf. Acts 27:30, 41) of sailing ships (v 40, RSV). It was not the mainsail (as the KJV mistakenly renders *artemōn*), but was placed ahead of the mainsail on a small mast that usually slanted forward above the bow.

Foreship. *See* Foresail.

Foreskin. *See* Circumcision.

Forest. The translation of: (1) the Heb. *choresh*, "wooded place" (2 Chr 27:4, KJV); (2) the Heb. *ya'ar*, "thicket," "wood" (Is 21:13; Mi 3:12; etc.); (3) the Heb. *pardes*, "park," "forest" (Neh 2:8). Palestine was a thickly wooded land in the 3d millennium B.C. and still had extensive forests in the 2d millennium B.C., according to occasional Egyptian records. The present country, denuded of wooded areas with the exception of Gilead, which still has some remnants of forests (see fig. 205), gives a wrong impression of the appearance of Palestine as it was some four thousand years ago. In these ancient forests, oak and cypress, terebinth and mastic tree, wild locust tree and wild olive tree, the strawberry tree and the willow, were frequently found. Forests mentioned in the OT are those of the hill country of Ephraim (Jos 17:15, 18), of Judah (1 Sa 22:5), and the "forest [KJV "wood"] of Ephraim," near Mahanaim in Transjordan (2 Sa 18:6), besides the forests of the Lebanon (1 Ki 7:2). The "forest in Arabia" (RSV "thickets in Arabia"; Heb. *ya'ar ba'erab*) of Is 21:13, described as a lodging place for the merchants of the tribe of Dedan, has not been identified. Some translators suggest that the vowel points of the second word in the Hebrew phrase should be changed so that this word would read "in the evening."

Forest in Arabia. *See* Forest.

Forest of Hareth. *See* Hereth.

Forest of Lebanon. *See* Lebanon.

Forgive, Forgiveness. The translation of various Hebrew and Greek words which have in common the idea of releasing an offender from guilt and of restoring the personal relationship that existed prior to the offense. The 2 most common Hebrew words so translated are *naśa'*, "to take away [guilt]," literally, "to lift up," and *salach,* "to pardon," "to forgive." The more common Greek terms are *charizomai*, "to remit," "to forgive," "to pardon," literally, "to give graciously [as a favor]," and *aphiēmi*, "to cancel," "to remit," "to pardon," literally, "to let go," "to send away." Forgiveness always implies an offense committed against the person extending forgiveness, and should be preceded by the offender's repentance.

All men have sinned against God (Rom 3:23) and stand before Him condemned to death (ch 6:23) unless they repent of their sins (Lk 13:3, 5; Acts 3: 19) and thereby obtain forgiveness (1 Jn 1:9), so being restored to a right relationship with Him (Rom 5:1). God is not obliged to forgive the guilty sinner, but His gracious character impels Him to do so whenever forgiveness is desired and requested (Ex 34:6, 7; Lam 3:22). The request, however, must be made in all sincerity and with the intent not to take advantage of the grace thus freely bestowed. When God forgives He does so completely and without reserve, restoring the sinner to the same state of favor he formerly enjoyed and removing all estrangement and alienation. In Scripture various expressions are used in the endeavor to convey to human minds the completeness with which God forgives. He casts men's sins, as it were, into the depths of the sea (Mic 7:19); He removes them as far from them and Him as "the east is from the west" (Ps 103:12); He casts them behind His back (Is 38:17); He promises to blot them out and forget them (Is 43:25; Jer 31:34). God's forgiveness is perfect, even as God Himself is perfect.

In so far as his finite limitations permit, the Christian will emulate the perfect and complete manner of God's forgiveness whenever someone offends him. The spirit of forgiveness accompanies the external act of forgiveness. Furthermore, the fact that the Christian has been the recipient of a full measure of divine forgiveness places him under the most strict obligation to forgive his fellow men when occasion arises to do so—to the same extent that he has been forgiven. In fact, the Christian who declines to forgive others thereby forfeits the forgiveness of God for himself (Mt 6:12-15), and an unforgiving spirit is a most heinous sin before God. The utter abhorrence with which God looks upon an unforgiving spirit Jesus illustrated by the parable of the Unforgiving Servant (ch 18:23-35). He who refuses to forgive cannot, by the very nature of things, be forgiven so long as he harbors an unforgiving spirit. As Christ explained to Peter, there are no limits on the extent to which, or the number of times, the Christian is obliged to forgive one who comes to him for forgiveness (vs 21, 22). The Christian must ever entertain the *spirit* of forgiveness, even before he is given the opportunity to forgive. Not only so, but he will take the initiative in making every reasonable effort to win the wrongdoer and to make it easy for him to ask forgiveness (vs 15-17).

Fork. The rendering in the KJV of the Heb. *shelosh qilleshôn* in 1 Sa 13:21. The first word of the Hebrew phrase means "three," but the meaning of the second word is unknown. Hence the translators of the KJV conjectured that a "three-pronged fork" or "trident" was meant. The translators of the RSV assumed that the letters of the second word had become transposed and rearranged them to make the phrase read "a third of a shekel."

Fornication. The terms thus translated denote every kind of unlawful sexual intercourse. The prohibition of the 7th commandment (Ex 20:14) must be understood to include fornication (*see* Adultery). Fornication was part of the religious ritual of the native Canaanite cults (*see* Cult Prostitute), in which the Israelites sometimes became involved (2 Chr 21:11). Jesus stated that a man could not divorce his wife except "for the cause of fornication" (Mt 5:32; "on the ground of unchastity," RSV). The Gentile element in the early Christian church was cautioned against this impurity (Acts 15: 20, 29), and Paul had to write plainly to the Corinthian church because of fornication in its midst of a type not practiced even by the notoriously profligate pagans of that area (1 Cor 5:1). He warned the members of the church not to maintain social contact with a fornicator even if he claimed to be a believer (1 Cor 6:9, 11). He further warned that fornicators ("the immoral," RSV) could have no part in Christ's kingdom (v 9). The book of Revelation uses the term figuratively to mean spiritual apostasy (Rev 17:2; 19:2).

Forswear. A word meaning "to commit perjury," "to swear falsely," appearing in Mt 5:33, KJV, as a rendering of the Gr. *epiorkeō*, "to swear falsely," "to break one's oath" (RSV "swear falsely"). *Epiorkeō* is somewhat ambiguous and may refer either to making a false oath or to breaking an oath after it has been made.

Fortifications. From very early times until comparatively recently, inhabitants of cities protected themselves by surrounding their cities with strong walls. In times of war those who lived in the open country or in villages sought protection inside the nearby "fenced," or fortified, city. There were various types of fortifications in different periods. *See* Wall.

Before 1800 B.C. The excavations of Jericho show that this city had a succession of walls in very early times. On the other hand, places such as the settlements of *Teleilât el-Ghassûl*, which flourished before the end of the 3d millennium, show no city walls at all. The northern city of *Tell el-Fâr'ah* (probably Tirzah) possessed a circular wall 27 to 30 ft. thick, consisting of an inner and an outer face built of medium-sized stones, with the space between filled with earth and gravel. This wall was strengthened by buttresses inside the city. In addition, a smaller wall was placed outside the main wall as extra protection.

The Middle Bronze Age, 1800-1600 B.C. The strongest fortifications built at any time were constructed in the Middle Bronze period. Strong walls, thicker at the bottom, with a sloping outer face, were set in shallow trenches to make the work of undermining more difficult. The lower part was built of stone, the upper, of bricks. At this period the wall of Jericho consisted of a stone revetment, or retaining wall, about 12 ft. high, surmounted by plastered masonry rising to another 37 ft. at an angle of 35°, making it extremely difficult, if not impossible, to scale. It culminated in a brick wall of unknown height. The result was a most imposing defense system, which was much like that of a great medieval castle.

The Hyksos, who appeared in the Fertile Crescent in this period and introduced horse and chariot, built large for-

tified camps for their chariot forces. That of Hazor in Galilee measured more than 1,000 by 400 yards. These Hyksos camps were protected by sloping ramparts of packed earth overlaid with stone. Surrounding the wall in *Tell el-'Ajjûl*, near Gaza, was a moat 20 ft. deep with its inner side sloping up to the city at an angle of 35°. Never again in ancient Palestine were walls built that equaled the fortifications of this period in impressiveness and strength.

The Late Bronze Age, 1600-1200 B.C. This was the latest Canaanite period, before the cities were gradually taken over by the Hebrews in the period of the judges. The techniques of the preceding period were continued, but larger stones were used; and to the walls were now added projecting towers which enabled the defenders to cover attacking forces with cross fire. Likewise, the gates were provided with two or three pairs of towers which reduced the thoroughfare by half, thus facilitating its barricading in times of attack.

To this period belonged the cities described in the Bible as "fenced with high walls, gates, and bars" (Deut 3:5; cf. Num 13:28; Jos 14:12). Subterranean tunnels were often dug to provide protected access to springs. In most cases these sources of water lay outside the city walls at the foot of the hills on which the cities were built. Such waterworks have been found at Jerusalem, Gezer, Megiddo, Gibeon, and other sites.

The Iron Age, during which the Israelites were mainly in control of Palestine, 1200-600 B.C. The Israelites, awed by the sight of the strong Canaanite cities (Num 13:28), attempted, after their conquest of Canaan, to imitate the Canaanites in the building of fortifications. However, excavations show that walls built by the Israelites were of crude masonry construction and were much thinner and much less substantial than those of their predecessors. The small fortified castle of *Saul at *Gibeah is an example. It was not until the time of the great city builder, Solomon (1 Ki 9:17-19), that the Israelite city walls show the same strength and excellence of construction as those of the Canaanites (see fig. 482). The walls of Megiddo, Ezion-geber, and Gezer reveal that the Israelites, perhaps with Phoenician help (chs 5:18; 7:13, 14), mastered the art of constructing strong and well-built stone walls in the 10th cent. B.C.

It is expressly recorded that Rehoboam,

Solomon's son and successor, fortified many cities (2 Chr 11:5-12). Asa and Jotham also built fortified cities (chs 14: 2, 6, 7; 27:1, 4). Jotham and Hezekiah were especially active in strengthening Jerusalem's walls (chs 27:3; 32:2, 5). Such activity is also recorded of the kings of Israel. Jeroboam I built Shechem and Penuel (1 Ki 12:25); Baasha made an unsuccessful attempt to fortify Ramah (ch 15:17, 21); and Omri founded and built the strong fortress-capital of Samaria (ch 16:24).

One of the best preserved city walls from the period of the Hebrew kings is that of *Tell en-Naṣbeh,* probably ancient Mizpah. The fortifications, built about 900 B.C., were some 13 ft. thick, but the thickness was greatly increased by retaining, or supporting, walls at the bottom. Eleven rectangular towers at intervals gave additional strength to the wall. The city's only gate did not open directly through the wall, but was built between (and at right angles to) two parallel sections of the wall where its two ends overlapped and ran parallel to each other for a short distance (see fig. 193; cf. fig. 336). The purpose was to force the attacking soldiers to approach the gate along the wall with their right sides, usually not protected by a shield, exposed to the defenders. The gates of Megiddo and Lachish were similar in principle, although different in detail. Assyrian reliefs of Palestinian cities of the 8th and 7th cent. also enable us to gain some impression of the fortifications built by the Hebrews during the period of the divided kingdoms. See figs. 201, 284.

In Later Periods. No remains of city walls from the Persian period have been found, although we have a detailed account of the restoration of the wall of Jerusalem by Nehemiah, who lived during that period (Neh 3:4, 6). From the Hellenistic period comes a round tower excavated at Samaria, the fortifications of Beth-zur, and the castle of the Tobiads in western Transjordan. Monumental remains of fortifications built during the Roman period are found at several places. There is the so-called "David's Tower," erected by Herod the Great, incorporated into the present Citadel (see fig. 263), as well as the lower courses of masonry of the Castle Antonia (*see* Barracks); with several courses of stone blocks at the famous Wailing Wall, which formed part of the outer Temple wall of Christ's time; and various structural remains at Hebron, Samaria, Masada, and other sites. This period is distinguished by the extraordinary size of the individual stone blocks (up to 23 ft. in length), which gave to the walls the impression of invulnerability.

Lit.: A. G. Barrois, *Manuel d'archéologie biblique* (Paris, 1939), vol. 1, pp. 127-212; Millar Burrows, *What Mean These Stones?* (New Haven, 1941), pp. 136-156.

Fortified Cities. *See* Fortifications.

Fortress. *See* Fortifications.

Fortunatus (fôr-tu̇-nā'tu̇s). [Gr. *Phortounatos,* the equivalent of a common Latin name meaning "fortunate."] A member of the church at Corinth who, with Stephanas and Achaicus, came to Paul at Ephesus (1 Cor 16:17), probably bringing a letter of inquiry from the Corinthian believers and possibly being also the bearers of Paul's letter known as First Corinthians to the church at Corinth.

Fortune. The rendering in the RSV of the Heb. *gad* in Is 65:11 ("that troop," KJV). This is a reference to the god Fortune, who is attested in inscriptions of southern Arabia and Palmyra. The passage indicates that this god was at one time worshiped by the Israelites. Such place names as Baal-gad (Jos 11:17; 12:7; 13:5) and Migdal-gad (ch 15:37) suggest that at one time sanctuaries were dedicated to this god in these places.

Forum of Appius (fō'rŭm ŭv ăp'pĭ-ŭs), KJV **Appii Forum** (ăp'ĭ-ī fō'rŭm). [Gr. *Appiou phoron,* a transliteration of Latin *Apii Forum,* "market of Appius."] A town at the northern end of the Pontine Marshes,

186. The Appian Way, looking south

about 40 mi. southeast of Rome. It was founded about 312 B.C. by the censor Appius Claudius Caecus. The market as well as the road on which it lay, *Via Appia* (Appian Way), perpetuated the builder's name. In the course of time it developed into a large trading center. Paul was met at the Forum, or Market, of Appius by Roman Christians who had come to accompany him to Rome (Acts 28:15). Map XX, A-1.

Forward, Forwardness. These terms appear in such texts as 2 Cor 8:8, 17; Gal 2:10; KJV, as translations of Greek words meaning eagerness to carry out some action. In 2 Cor 8:10, KJV, "to be forward" is the translation of a Greek term signifying a simple desire to act. In ch 9:2, KJV, "forwardness" is translated from a word literally meaning "willingness" or "readiness" (see RSV).

Foul Spirit. *See* Unclean Spirit.

Founder. A rendering of a form of the Heb. *ṣaraph* (Jgs 17:4; Jer 6:29; 10:9, 14; 51:17; KJV), "to smelt," designating variously "silversmith," "goldsmith," depending on the context. In Jer 6:29, KJV, "founder" is an inexact translation from a verb form of *ṣaraph* (see RSV).

Fountain. *See* Spring.

Fountain Gate. [Heb. *sha'ar ha'ayin.*] One of the gates of ancient Jerusalem (Neh 2:14; 3:15; 12:37). Since it was close to the Pool of Siloam (Neh 3:15; cf. Jn 9:7, 8), it must have been in the southernmost portion of the City of David. It was probably the one in the southeastern corner of the city leading to En-rogel, the well or spring at the confluence of the valleys of Kidron and Hinnom (Map XVII; see figs. 158, 259). Some commentators have identified it with "the gate between the two walls" (2 Ki 25:4; Jer 39:4; 52:7).

Fowl. A word occurring frequently in the KJV (only twice in the RSV, Lev 7:26; 1 Ki 4:23), translating Hebrew and Greek terms denoting *birds in general.

Fowler. One who hunts fowls by any of several means, but generally by use of a snare or a trap device (Ps 91:3; 124:7; Prov 6:5; Jer 5:26; Hos 9:8).

Fox. [Heb. *shû'al;* Gr. *alōpēx.*] The Hebrew term seems clearly to refer in some instances, at least, to the *jackal as, for example, in Jgs 15:4, where it may be implied that the animals Samson caught ran in packs. Jackals, unlike foxes, often run in packs, and Samson could have captured 300 jackals more easily than 300

foxes. Also Ps 63:10 most probably refers to jackals, since foxes do not feed on corpses. The description of the animal as roaming in the desert or ruins, and destroying vineyards (Lam 5:18; Eze 13:4; Song 2:15), may apply to foxes as well as jackals. Palestine has two kinds of foxes, the *Vulpes nilotica* in southern Palestine, and the larger kind, the *Vulpes flavescens* in northern Palestine. Jesus mentions the holes of the foxes (Mt 8:20; Lk 9:58), and compares Herod Antipas to a clever fox (Lk 13:32).

Frankincense. [Heb. *lebonah,* from *laban,* "white"; Phoenician and South Arabic *lbnt;* Aramaic *lbwnt'* and *lbnt';* Gr. *libanos.*] A white resin, as its Hebrew name implies, obtained from the frankincense tree, which belongs to the genus *Boswellia.* Of its 5 species the following 2 produce frankincense of commercial value: *B. Carteri* and *B. Frereana.* These trees grow only in the *Dhofâr,* a part of the Hadhramaut in South Arabia, and in the northern part of British Somaliland. The dry gum resin, called frankincense, has a pleasing, balsamlike odor, especially so when it is burned.

Frankincense was one of several ingredients composing the holy incense used in the tabernacle (Ex 30:34). It was also an ingredient of the cereal offerings (Lev 2:1, 2, 15, 16; 6:15), and was put on the loaves of showbread (ch 24:7). However, its use was prohibited in connection with the sin offerings (ch 5:11) and the offerings of jealousy (Num 5:15). Frankincense was brought to Palestine from Arabia by caravans of Midian, Ephah, and Sheba (Is 60:6; Jer 6:20, RSV), and was stored, along with other ingredients needed for the offerings, in a special room within the Temple precinct (Neh 13:5). Commentators are generally uncertain about the meaning of the "hill of frankincense" mentioned in Song 4:6. Some think that it was the name of a real hill in the palace garden of Jerusalem, whereas others consider it and the "mountain of myrrh" of the same verse to be poetical terms for the breasts of the author's beloved. The gifts of the Wise Men included frankincense (Mt 2:11).

Lit.: G. W. Van Beek, *JAOS* 78 (1958), 141-152.

Fray. An archaic English term meaning "to frighten." It appears only in Deut 28:26; Jer 7:33; Zec 1:21; KJV, as the translation of a form of the Heb. *charad,* "to frighten," "to cause to tremble."

Freckled Spot. *See* Tetter.

187. Greek inscription of Theodotus, who had built the synagogue at Jerusalem for Jews from the Dispersion

Freedmen, KJV **Libertines.** [Gr. *Libertinoi.*] The name of a group of Jews who, with certain Alexandrians and Cyrenians, had a synagogue in Jerusalem (Acts 6:9). These freedmen may have been descendants of Jews taken captive by Pompey in 63 B.C. but who had regained their liberty. Since they had grown up in foreign countries, they belonged to Hellenistic Jewry, and had therefore joined the Alexandrian and Cyrenian Jews in Jerusalem. On the other hand, Acts 6:9 may be understood as meaning that the Alexandrians and Cyrenians were themselves the freedmen referred to.

During excavations at Jerusalem in 1914 R. Weill discovered an inscription that may have come from this synagogue, mentioning that the place was built for the use of Jews from the Dispersion (see fig. 187). The inscription, still almost completely legible, reads:

"Theodotus the son of Vettenus, priest and ruler of the synagogue, son of a ruler of the synagogue, son's son of a ruler of the synagogue, built the synagogue for reading of the law and for teaching of the commandments, also the strangers' lodging and the chambers and the conveniences of waters for an inn for them that need it from abroad, of which (synagogue) his fathers and the elders and Simonides did lay the foundation" (Adolph Deissmann, *Light From the Ancient East* [New York, 1927], 440).

Freshets. [Heb. *'aphiqim,* "stream beds," "channels of a stream."] A term appearing once in the RSV (Job 6:15), where the context suggests that streams full of water are meant. Job compares his brethren to well-filled streams that in time of heat dry up and disappear (vs 16, 17).

Fried. An expression appearing twice in the KJV (Lev 7:12; 1 Chr 23:29), the translation of a Hebrew word (*rabak*) not meaning "fried," but "mixed." *Rabak* is closely related to the Arabic *rabaka,* "to mix (dough)," "to stir (dough)."

Friend. No less than 16 different Greek and Hebrew words and expressions have been translated "friend" in the KJV. Most of these are practically synonymous or at least interchangeable, but others draw fine distinctions in social relationships. Some of the more important Biblical terms for "friend" include: (1) A form of the Heb. *'ahab,* "to love," hence, "one who loves," "a fond friend." The term emphasizes an affectionate attachment. Examples of the use of this word are: 2 Sa 19:6; 2 Chr 20:7; Est 5:10; Prov 18:24; etc. (2) The Heb. *rea',* "neighbor," "companion," "friend." Although this term may at times refer to affectionate attachments (as in Prov 17:17), the primary emphasis is upon proximity and acquaintance. Like its English equivalent, the Hebrew expression usually describes a person with whom one enjoys amicable, sociable relationships (Ex 33:11; 1 Sa 30:26; Job 2:11; 6:14; 17:5; etc.); but, as in English, the term may sometimes include those whose friendship is somewhat shallow or even selfish, as in Job 16:20; Ps 38:11; Prov 19:4, 6; Lam 1:2. (3) The Gr. *hetairos,* designating simply a person in one's immediate presence. It may denote one whose name is unknown; and, occasionally, its use may convey mild reproach. In the NT it is found only in Mt 11:16 (KJV "fellows"; RSV "playmates"); 20:13; 22:12; 26:50. (4) The Gr. *philos,* the general word for "friend." But like the form of the Heb. *'ahab* above, the term usually includes more than the Eng-

374

lish "friend"; it primarily indicates one who is dear, beloved, or close in friendship (Lk 15:6, 29; Jn 3:29; 11:11; 15:14, 15). Quite often, however, the expression closely approximates the English "friend" in a general sense, as in Lk 11:5; 23:12; Jn 19:12.

"Friendship" is found twice in the KJV and 5 times in the RSV. In 1 Chr 12:17, RSV, it appears as the translation of the Heb. *shalôm*, "peace," "friendship"; in Job 29:4; Ps 25:14; RSV, of the Heb. *sôd*, a word that depicts confidential information or conversation, hence the translation "secret" (KJV). Elsewhere the RSV frequently renders *sôd* "secret," for example, Prov 11:13; 20:19; Amos 3:7; etc. In Prov 22:24 the Heb. *ra'ah*, meaning "to make friends with," "to have as a companion," is rendered "make friendship" in both the KJV and RSV. In Jas 4:4 "friendship" appears as a translation of the Gr. *philia*, a translation that favorably approximates the idea of the Greek word.

Friend of the King. *See* King's Friend.

Fringe. In the OT (KJV only) the translation of two Hebrew words, each of which means "tassel." The Israelites were bidden to wear tassels on the corners of their garments. These tassels had religious significance, serving as reminders of the law (Num 15:38-40; cf. Deut 22:12). "Fringe" appears in the RSV of the NT as the translation of the Gr. *kraspedon*, "edge," "border," "hem," "tassel." The last meaning probably applies in Mt 23:5. Some think this meaning applies also in Mt 9:20; 14:36; Mk 6:56; Lk 8:44, but it is not known how strictly Jesus followed the Mosaic law in the matter of the wearing of tassels.

Frog. [Heb. *sephardea'*; Gr. *batrachos*.] An amphibious animal, several kinds of which occur in the Near East. The OT references are all to the 2d plague that Moses brought upon Egypt (Ex 8:1-15; Ps 78:45; 105:30). In the NT frogs are a symbol of impurity (Rev 16:13). In ancient Egypt the frog was a symbol of life and origin, and was an emblem of the goddess Heqet, the patroness of birth and the consort of Khnum, the god who is represented as a potter forming a man on a potter's wheel (see fig. 114). Heqet, a female deity with a frog's head, is depicted as giving life to the newborn. The 2d plague, an infliction of creatures that were symbols of a deity the Egyptians considered as beneficent, was, like the others, directed against the gods of Egypt and was intended to discredit them and to demonstrate the power of the God of the Hebrews.

Frontier. *See* Coast.

Frontlets. [Heb. *tôtaphoth*.] God commanded Israel to "bind" His revealed instructions "for a sign upon thy hand, and . . . as frontlets between thine eyes" (Deut 6:8; 11:18). From Ex 13:16 it would appear that God meant this in a figurative sense. Events connected with the departure from Egypt were to be kept as clearly in mind as if the record were written upon the forehead. Similarly, the people were to remember His revealed commands. The Jews, however, took the command literally and wore portions of the law upon their foreheads and their arms, as *phylacteries.

Froward. A rendering in the KJV of several more or less synonymous Hebrew and Greek words signifying "contrary," "perverse," etc. Two of these, the Heb. *haphakpak* (Prov 21:8; RSV "guilty") and *tahpukoth* (Deut 32:20; Prov 2:12; 8:13; 10:31; etc.; "perverse," "perverted," RSV), are derived from *haphak*, "to turn," "to turn around," and emphasize a perversity that turns from what is right and good. The Heb. *'iqqesh* (2 Sa 22:27; Ps 101:4; Prov 11:20; etc.; RSV "perverse" or "perverseness") and its derivative, *'iqqeshûth* (Prov 4:24; 6:12; RSV "crooked"), describe the perversity of an evil person or an evil deed as something "crooked" and "bent" out of shape; not aligned with God's ways. Other terms translated "froward" in the KJV stress similar aspects of the stubborn perversity of the unregenerate heart.

Fruit. [Heb. generally *perî*, "fruit"; *tabû'ah*, "yield," "product (of soil or toil)"; Gr. generally *karpos*.] Basically, the product of trees and vines, but frequently, in figures of speech, the end result of any work or activity. Thus, the produce of the land is designated "fruit" (Gen 4:3; Lev 25:19; etc.), as is the offspring of man and beast (Gen 30:2; Deut 28:4; Mic 6:7; etc.). Speech is poetically designated "the fruit of his mouth" (Prov 18:20); work, "the fruit of her hands" (ch 31:16); and the rewards of evil deeds as the fruit of one's deeds (Is 3:10, RSV); etc. In the NT, in addition to its usual meaning, "fruit" is frequently used as a figure of speech for the outward actions of one's life, particularly those indicating whether the heart is righteous or evil (Mt 3:8; 7:16, 17; Lk 6:43, 44; Php 1:11). Similarly, in Gal 5:22, 23, the Christian graces are called "the fruit of the Spirit."

Fryingpan. The translation of the Heb. *marchesheth* (Lev 2:7; 7:9; KJV), an earthenware or metal cooking pot probably wide-mouthed and lidded. The RSV translates the term "pan."

Fugitive. An escapee; one who runs from pursuit or danger; an OT term, the translation of several closely synonymous Hebrew words, usually designating one who has fled from danger. Twice the thought of homelessness is emphasized (Gen 4:12, 14). Other contexts involve desertions (2 Ki 25:11; RSV "deserters") or escapees from battle (Ob 14, ·RSV).

Fuller. One who cleansed and bleached soiled clothes (Mk 9:3), which were usually made of wool, except in Egypt, where garments were commonly of linen. Little is known from the Bible of the procedures followed by the Palestinian fullers. The Heb. *kabas,* from which the word rendered "fuller" is derived, means literally to tread, knead, or beat. This shows that the process of cleaning was performed by treading or beating the cloth in water and "soap" (Mal 3:2), not true *soap, but some alkali. The "fuller's field," that is, a place where the fullers plied their trade, lay outside Jerusalem, probably near the Gihon fountain in the Kidron Valley (2 Ki 18:17; Is 7:3; 36:2). The fullers needed large quantities of water for their work, and this could not easily be obtained inside Jerusalem, which lay mostly on hills much higher than the water supply; then, too, it would be desirable to have such establishments some distance from the city because of their offensive odor. The ancients used a method by which the garments were trodden in a solution of some alkali, usually urine, and were afterward purified with sulphur. This process of cleaning woolen garments is well attested among the Greeks and Romans, and probably was used by the Hebrews, although there is no literary evidence to this effect.

Fuller's Field, The. *See* Fuller.

Furlong. *See* Stadia.

Furnace. The following types may be noted:

1. A *smelter* or furnace to smelt and refine metals (Gen 19:28 [Heb. *kibshan*]; Deut 4:20; 1 Ki 8:51; etc. [Heb. *kûr;* Akkadian *kûru*]). The Heb. *'alîl,* rendered "furnace" in Ps 12:6, is of somewhat uncertain meaning. In the NT the smelting furnace appears as the *kaminos* of Rev 1:15. Simple furnaces for the "roasting" of iron and copper ore have been discovered in Edom. They were built of field stones and were heated with charcoal in the most primitive manner. At Eziongeber, however, were found a row of smelters with an intricate system of flues and crucibles made of hard-baked clay, in which the iron and copper were refined and converted into ingots (see fig. 170). Another metal smelter was uncovered at *Tell Qasîleh* near Tel Aviv in Israel (fig. 188).

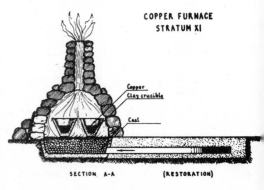

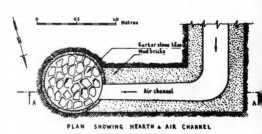

188. Archeologist's reconstruction and cross section of copper furnace (11th cent. B.C:) found at *Tell Qasîleh*

2. *Baking ovens* (Heb. *tannûr;* Akkadian *tinûru;* Aramaic *tannûra'*) are repeatedly mentioned in the OT (Neh 3:11, RSV "ovens"; Is 31:9; etc.). A well-preserved ancient *tannûr* that was excavated at Megiddo varied but little from the modern Arabic ovens. Such an oven consisted of a pit in the ground in which the fire was made, over which was a wide conical clay pipe, or pan, with an open top through which the smoke escaped. The flat pancakelike bread was stuck on the outside walls of this cone and thus baked.

3. A *brickkiln* or furnace (Aramaic *'attûn;* Akkadian *atûnu*) is mentioned in Dan 3 in connection with the attempted burning of Daniel's three friends for their refusing to worship Nebuchadnezzar's

golden image. This type of kiln was a cone-shaped brick structure, with an opening in one side of the wall. The unbaked bricks were stacked around the inner wall, after which the fire was set. The material for the fire was probably the same as is used in Mesopotamia today: chaff mixed with crude oil obtained from the open oil wells. In other countries charcoal and other fuels were used. The *kaminos* of Rev 9:2 probably refers to a brick-kiln.

Furniture. Household equipment and movable furnishings. In 7 of its 8 occurrences in the KJV, the term is a rendering of the Heb. *kelî,* "vessel," "utensil," "implement," "furniture," the exact meaning being determined by the context (Ex 31:7-9; 35:14; 39:33; Nah 2:9; RSV generally "utensil"). In Gen 31:34 the Hebrew term is *kar,* a word that denotes a canopied saddle, often curtained and cushioned, and used especially by women when riding upon camels. In the RSV "furniture" occurs in Ex 25:9; 40:9; 1 Chr 9:29; Neh 13:8, in each case the translation of *kelî.*

G

Gaal (gā′ăl). [Heb. *Ga‘al,* "scarab." The name occurs also in ancient South Arabic inscriptions.] A son of Ebed, and organizer of a revolt of the Shechemites against Abimelech. He was defeated in the ensuing battle (Jgs 9:26-41). It is uncertain whether he was an Israelite or a Canaanite, a patriot, or an adventurer who aspired to leadership.

Gaash (gā′ăsh). [Heb. *Ga‘ash.*] A hill in the vicinity of Timnath-serah in the hill country of Ephraim. Joshua was buried north of this hill (Jos 24:30; Jgs 2:9; 2 Sa 23:30; 1 Chr 11:32). Map VI, E-3.

Gaba. *See* Geba.

Gabbai (găb′ȧ-ī). [Heb. *Gabbay.*] A Benjamite inhabitant of Jerusalem in Nehemiah's time (Neh 11:8).

Gabbatha (găb′ȧ-thȧ), or **The Pavement** (pāv′měnt). [Gr. *Gabbatha,* the transliteration of an uncertain Aramaic word, perhaps *gabbetha′,* "height," *gabbachta′,* "a free place," *gubabta′,* "ridge," or *gaphtha′,* "hill"; and *Lithostrōton,* "pavement."] A stone pavement on which the judgment seat of Pilate stood (Jn 19:13). Its exact site is unknown. L. H. Vincent identifies it with the pavement that lay originally in the inner court of the Castle Antonia. That area is now partly in the monastery of Notre Dame de Sion and partly in the adjoining Franciscan monastery. A Roman game scratched in the stones of the pavement shows that Roman soldiers whiled away their time at this spot (see fig. 189). However, there is no positive proof that the Castle Antonia was the place where Pilate stayed when in Jerusalem, or that this castle was the judgment hall referred to in the Gospels. Some scholars seek Gabbatha in or in front of the palace of Herod at the site of the present Citadel in the western part of the old city of Jerusalem. See fig. 263.

189. **Roman game board cut in the pavement (possibly the NT Gabbatha) of the Castle Antonia**

Gabriel (gā′brĭ-ĕl). [Heb. *Gabrî′el,* "man of God," or "God has shown Himself strong"; Gr. *Gabriēl.*] An angel who stands in the presence of God (Lk 1:19). He appeared to the prophet Daniel and explained to him the prophecy of the ram and the goat (Dan 8:16-26), and the 70-week prophetic period (ch 9:21-27). He announced the birth of John the Baptist to Zacharias (Lk 1:11-20), and informed Mary of the birth of Jesus (vs 26-38).

Since he stands in the presence of God (Lk 1:19), post-Biblical tradition describes him as an archangel, but he is not thus designated in the Bible. He is also mentioned in Jewish apocryphal literature (Apocalypse of Moses 40:1; First Book of Enoch 9:1; 10:9; 20:7; 40:9; 54:6; etc.).

Gad (găd). [Heb. *Gad,* "good fortune"; Gr. *Gad.*]

1. A son of Jacob by Zilpah, Leah's maidservant (Gen 30:10, 11). Jacob predicted that Gad's descendants would be hard pressed by hostile forces, but would stand against them (ch 49:19). Of Gad's 7 sons (ch 46:16), at least 6 were heads of tribal families (Num 26:15-18).

2. The tribe of Gad, the descendants of Gad, 1. Moses compared this valiant tribe to a lion (Deut 33:20, 21). The first census recorded 45,650 Gadites ready for war (Num 1:24, 25); a later census gave 40,-500 (ch 26:15-18). The Gadites were assigned part of the territory east of Jordan taken from the Amorite kings of Heshbon and of Bashan. They were permitted to occupy it only after they had helped the other tribes to conquer their territories west of the Jordan (ch 32:20-32). The boundaries of their territory were somewhat fluid and are difficult to define. They seemed to overlap those of Reuben to the south and Manasseh to the north. Generally speaking, Gad's territory lay between the river Jabbok and the city of Heshbon, and included the southern part of Gilead, extending along the Jordan Valley to the Sea of Galilee (Jos 13: 24-28; Deut 3:12, 16, 17). The *Moabite Stone mentions the "men of Gad" as the immediate northern neighbors of the Moabites (lines 10, 11). Some valiant Gadites joined David at Ziklag before he became king of Judah (1 Chr 12:8). Ezekiel included Gad among the other tribes in his prophecy of Israel's restoration (Eze 48). Gad is mentioned as one of the 12 tribes sealed in Rev 7 (v 5).

3. A prophet, usually called the "seer," who was counselor to David when David was persecuted by Saul (1 Sa 22:1, 5). He was sent by God to rebuke David after the king's census of Israel, and to give him a choice of three punishments (2 Sa 24: 11-14; 1 Chr 21:9-13). He and the prophet Nathan helped David organize the services of the sanctuary (2 Chr 29:25). He later wrote a biography of David (1 Chr 29:29).

Gad, River of. [Heb. *hannachal haggad.*] According to the KJV, apparently the river

on which Aroer is situated, namely, the Arnon (2 Sa 24:5). The RSV translates the Hebrew phrase "the valley, toward Gad." This translation is supported by the fact that the two Hebrew words involved both have the definite article, showing that "river of Gad" is an incorrect translation.

Gadarenes (găd'*à*-rēnz'). [Gr. *Gadarēnoi.*] Inhabitants of Gadara, a Greek city belonging to the Decapolis, according to Josephus (*Ant.* xvii. 11. 4). Eusebius tells us that it lay about 6 mi. southeast of the Sea of Galilee. It has therefore been identified with *Muqeis* (Map XVI, C-4), which lies south of the river Yarmuk. Its territory must have extended to the Sea of Galilee, as is indicated by the record of Jesus' deliverance of a demon-possessed man (Mt 8:28-32, RSV; Mk 5:1-17; Lk 8:26-37). This Gadara is not to be confused with the city of Gadara, or Gador (Map XVI, D-4), which was the capital of Perea in the 1st cent. B.C. (not mentioned in the NT). *See* Gergesenes; Gerasenes.

Gaddi (găd'ĭ). [Heb. *Gaddi,* probably "my fortune."] The representative of the tribe of Manasseh among the 12 spies sent out to explore Canaan (Num 13:11).

Gaddiel (găd'ĭ-ĕl). [Heb. *Gaddi-'el,* "God is my fortune." The name occurs in Akkadian as *Gadi-ilu.*] The representative of the tribe of Zebulun among the 12 spies sent out to explore Canaan (Num 13:10).

Gadfly. The translation in the RSV of the Heb. *qeres,* apparently an annoying, biting insect (Jer 46:20), but the exact identity is a matter of conjecture. Some think the mosquito is meant.

Gadi (gā'dĭ). [Heb. *Gadi,* "a Gadite."] Father of King Menahem of Israel (2 Ki 15:14, 17).

Gadite (gad'ĭt). [Heb. *Gadi.*] A member of the tribe of Gad (Deut 3:12; etc.).

Gaham (gā'hăm). [Heb. *Gacham,* "burning brightly."] A son of Abraham's brother, Nahor. His mother was Nahor's concubine, Reumah (Gen 22:24).

Gahar (gā'här). [Heb. *Gachar,* "born in (a year of) little rain."] The head of a family of Nethinim. Some members of this family returned from Babylon with Zerubbabel (Ezr 2:47; Neh 7:49).

Gaius (gā'yŭs). [Gr. *Gaïos,* a transliteration of the Roman personal name Gaius or Caius. This name occurs frequently in Greek inscriptions and texts.]

1. A Macedonian Christian whom the Ephesian mob dragged into the theater during the riot against Paul (Acts 19:29).

2. A Christian of Derbe who, when Paul returned from his 3d Missionary Journey, accompanied him (Acts 20:4).

3. A Christian of Corinth who had been baptized by Paul (1 Cor 1:14), and probably the same as the Gaius of Rom 16:23.

4. A Christian to whom John addressed his 3d epistle (3 Jn 1). He is otherwise unknown.

Galal (gā′lăl). [Heb. *Galal*, "rolling." The name occurs in Akkadian as *Galalânu*.]

1. A postexilic Levite (1 Chr 9:15).

2. A postexilic Levite, the son of Jeduthun (1 Chr 9:16; Neh 11:17).

Galatia (gȧ-lā′shĭ-ȧ). [Gr. *Galatia*.] An area and Roman province in the central part of Asia Minor. The inhabitants, the Galatians, were Celts or Gauls, whose former homes had been in Gaul (Latin *Gallia*). They began a migration toward the southeast in the early part of the 4th cent. B.C., invaded Italy about 360 B.C., and nearly a century later invaded Macedonia and Greece. They migrated into Asia Minor, especially after Nicomedes I (278-250 B.C.) of Bithynia took them into his service. The area inside the curve of the river Halys was assigned them for settlement. Gradually they enlarged their territory by seizing areas from Phrygia, Cappadocia, and Pontus. In their efforts to expand they clashed with the Seleucid king Antiochus I (281-261 B.C.), later with Attalus I of Pergamum (241-197 B.C.), and were defeated by both. Afterward they joined Antiochus IV (175-163 B.C.) against the Romans, but a century later they joined the Romans against Mithridates of Pontus (73-64 B.C.). Pompey rewarded them for this help by enlarging their territory and granting to their leader Deiotarus the title king of Galatia. When Deiotarus died in 40 B.C. his successor, Amyntas, received from Antony further territories, namely, parts of Pamphylia, Lycaonia, and Cilicia, in the eastern area of· Phrygia and Isauria. After the death of Amyntas (25 B.C.) his whole kingdom was made into the province of Galatia under the administration of a *propraetor* whose residence was at Ancyra (now the Turkish capital, Ankara). The population was mixed and consisted in its central part of Galatians (Gauls), in the other areas, of Anatolians or Greeks. Some of the cities had flourishing Jewish communities. The Galatians retained their language and customs, and their native religious rites, but to these they added Phrygian mystery-cult elements.

Since the term Galatia can refer to the Roman province or any part of it, and also to the central section in which the ethnic Galatians (Gauls) lived, its use in various NT passages is open to differences of opinion. Some commentators hold that the Galatia of Acts 16:6 refers to the Roman province, and therefore to churches founded by Paul during his 1st Missionary Journey. Others think that it refers to the country of the Galatian people, in the northern and central section of the province. The same difference of opinion is found with regard to the interpretation of Acts 18:23 and the identification of the recipients of the letter to the Galatians. If "Galatia" in Gal 1:2 means the Roman province, the letter could have been addressed to the members of Derbe, Lystra, Iconium, and Antioch in Pisidia (Acts 13; 14). If it refers to the land of the ethnic Galatians, it has to be assumed that Paul addressed the letter to churches organized during his 2d and 3d Missionary Journeys (ch 16:6; 18:23). This dictionary favors the latter view. The churches in Galatia are also mentioned in 1 Cor 16:1, and 2 Ti 4:10 states that Crescens had gone to Galatia, although in this latter passage there is a possibility that Paul speaks there of Gaul in western Europe (now France). In 1 Pe 1:1 "Galatia" refers certainly to the province. Map XX, B-5.

Galatians (gȧ-lā′shȧnz). [Gr. *Galatai*.] Inhabitants of *Galatia (Gal 3:1).

Galatians, Epistle to the. A letter written by the apostle Paul to Christian believers of churches he had established in the Galatian region of central Asia Minor. There are differences of opinion as to the exact region here spoken of as Galatia— whether it is the Roman province by that name or the older region to the north settled by a body of migrating Gauls—and, as a result, differing views as to the point in Paul's ministry when the circumstances that occasioned the epistle arose. The expression "so soon" of Gal 1:6 has been understood as indicating either soon after the founding of the Galatian churches or relatively soon after a later visit to them. According to one theory (South Galatian), the cities of Antioch, Iconium, Lystra, and Derbe, which Paul visited on his 1st journey (Acts 13:14 to 14:23) and revisited on his 2d journey (chs 15:35 to 16:6), were in the Galatia of Gal 1:2. According to this theory the epistle was written in the course of Paul's 2d journey. According to another theory

(North Galatian), the region referred to as Galatia lay to the north, and the time of the writing of the epistle was during the course of his 3d journey, so as to allow for the 2 prior visits (cf. Gal 4:13). The great similarity to Romans in subject matter may be understood to indicate that the 2 epistles were prompted by the same problem—the Jewish heresy—and that they were written at about the same time. If so, the date of writing would be the winter of A.D. 57-58, and the place of writing doubtless Corinth. Furthermore, facts mentioned in connection with the visit alluded to in Gal 4:13-15—Paul's illness, his cordial reception by the Galatians, and the implication that they were indebted to him alone—do not comport with the known circumstances of the 1st journey described in detail in Acts 13:14 to 14:23. This dictionary adopts a modified form of the North Galatian theory (see *SDACom* 6:337, 338). The authenticity of the Galatian epistle and its right to a place in the canon have never been seriously questioned. The historical situation reflected in it is fully in accord with known facts and the style is distinctly that of the apostle Paul.

The book of Galatians deals with the greatest single doctrinal problem of the apostolic era—the relationship between Christianity and Judaism. To Christian believers of that time, and to Jewish Christians in particular, this was a perplexing problem. To begin with, Christianity was strictly Jewish. Our Lord, Himself a Jew (Rom 1:3), had declared salvation to be "of the Jews" (Jn 4:22). At His ascension He commanded that the gospel should first be preached to the Jews (Acts 1:8; cf. ch 13:46), and for some years thereafter most Christians were Jews and as such continued to practice the Mosaic rites and ceremonies. As devout Jews they naturally expected Gentile converts to conform to Jewish ritual requirements. But evidence that God accepted Gentile believers apart from Judaism (chs 10:44-48; 11:1-18; 15:1-20) posed the question as to whether the ancient rites and ceremonies were still essential to salvation. About A.D. 49 the Jerusalem Council (ch 15) officially resolved the issue, declaring Gentile Christians to be free from the requirements of Jewish law (vs 19, 20), but in actual practice a great many Jewish Christians seem never to have fully understood or accepted the decision. It was difficult for them to grasp that the ritual system divinely ordained 15 cent. before had now be-

come obsolete and unnecessary. A Judaizing party arose that advocated that all Gentile converts should become practicing Jews, and sought to force their point of view upon Paul's Gentile converts. Such were the circumstances that called forth the Galatian epistle, which deals with the problem in terms of a particular situation that had arisen.

Against the Judaizing argument that Gentile believers must accept circumcision, the sign of the covenant and of admission to the commonwealth of Israel, Paul maintained that justification comes by faith in Christ alone (Gal 6:13; 5:1-4). Whereas the Judaizers held that salvation depends upon compliance with the legal requirements of the law of Moses, that is, upon "the works of the law" (ch 2:16), the book of Galatians declares this concept to be altogether incompatible with the principle of justification by faith (chs 2:21; 5:1-4; 6:15). Salvation cannot be earned, but must be accepted as a free gift. After a short introduction (ch 1:1-5) Paul briefly outlines the problem in Galatia (vs 6, 7). He then affirms the divine origin of his version of the gospel and cites evidence to prove that the apostles in Jerusalem acknowledged its validity and his right to build up the Gentile church on that basis (chs 1:8 to 2:14). In the doctrinal argument that follows—the heart of the epistle—he essays, by setting forth evidence from the OT Scriptures, to prove that "a man is not justified by the works of the law, but by the faith of Jesus Christ" (chs 2:16 to 5:12). In chs 5:13 to 6:10 he makes a practical application of the principle of justification by faith by showing the fruit it will produce in the life of the believer.

The line of argument in the doctrinal section (Gal 2:16 to 5:12) proceeds thus: Salvation cannot be earned by compliance with the "works" prescribed by the Jewish law, but only by faith in Christ's death for sins and in His living out His life within the believer (ch 2:16-21). This the Galatians knew to be true because they had received the Holy Spirit by faith, altogether apart from works of law (ch 3:1-5). Abraham himself was justified by faith, and is therefore the spiritual father of believing Gentiles, who thereby become eligible to the blessings promised to him (vs 6-9). No one has ever complied perfectly with the requirements of the law, and all are accordingly under the curse of the law and can be redeemed only by faith in Christ (vs 10-14). The law was added 430 years after the covenant was vouchsafed to Abraham, as a "schoolmaster" until the coming of Christ, the covenant "seed," in order that men might the more readily enter into the covenant experience of salvation by faith. The law did not annul the covenant promise of salvation by faith in Christ, nor did it provide another way of salvation (Gal 3:15-29). Prior to the coming of Christ the Jews were like an heir during his nonage, with "the law" as their appointed guardian. But since Christ came men are no longer under the tutelage, or jurisdiction, of the legal system with its rites and ceremonies (ch 4:1-12). In a brief interlude Paul next reminds the Galatians of their joy upon accepting the gospel as he preached it (vs 13-20). Then, by the allegory of Abraham's 2 sons (vs 21-31), he stresses the point that believing Christians are, like Isaac, children of the covenant promise and thus not under bondage to the law as the children of a bondwoman would be. The line of argument is brought to a conclusion in ch 5: 1-12, where Paul declares categorically what he has already proved, that circumcision and the other requirements of the legal system avail nothing for the Christian, and that anyone who seeks justification by the works of the law has fallen from grace.

The epistle to the Galatians was written to meet a specific situation in the apostolic church, but the principle therein set forth—that men are saved, not by supposed works of merit, but by faith alone—is as true today as it was then. Legalism of any kind—the seeking of merit with God by the performance of certain acts—is worthless, since "man is not justified by the works of the law, but by the faith of Jesus Christ (Gal 2:16).

Galbanum. [Heb. *chelbenah,* "fatty."] An odorous gum used in making incense and perfume. It may have been derived from *Ferula galbaniflua,* a plant allied to the fennel in the carrot family, but definite identity of the Biblical substance has not yet been established. The gum from this plant is obtained by cutting into the stem a few inches above the ground. The milky juice that exudes soon hardens into a mass of pungent, yellowish-brown resin containing a chemical substance, umbelliferone. Today this gum is a constituent of varnish and of a medicine. Galbanum was an ingredient of the tabernacle incense (Ex 30:34, 35).

Galeed (găl′ĕ-ĕd). [Heb. *Gal′ed,* "heap of witness."] A stone heap that Jacob erected in the mountains of Gilead as a memorial of the covenant concluded there between himself and Laban (Gen 31:45-54). It was also called Mizpah, "watchtower," signifying that God was a watcher between the covenanting parties (vs 48, 49). The site has not been identified, unless it is the town Mizpah in Gilead. *See* Mizpah, 1.

Galilaean. *See* Galilean.

Galilean (găl′ĭ-lē′ăn), KJV **Galilaean** (găl′ĭ-lē′ăn). [Gr. *Galilaios.*] A native or inhabitant of Galilee (Mt 26:69; Lk 13:1, 2; 22:59; 23:6; Jn 4:45; 7:52; Acts 1:11; 2:7; 5:37). A Galilean could be recognized by his accent, or perhaps dialect (Mk 14:70).

Galilee (găl′ĭ-lē). [Gr. *Galilaia,* from Heb. *galil,* "circle," "region."] Originally the name applied to only part of the territory of Naphtali (2 Ki 15:29; 1 Chr 6:76); gradually it came to mean the northern part of Palestine, bounded on the south by the Plain of Esdraelon and on the north by the southern slopes of the Lebanon and Mount Hermon, an area about 40 mi. long and 25 to 30 mi. wide. Most of the country is mountainous, with fertile valleys. The mountains of the northern portion reach as high as 4,000 ft. above sea level, and consequently that part of Galilee has always been sparsely populated. The less mountainous southern portion (with mountains not exceeding 1,850 ft. above sea level) is a grain-producing region.

The Canaanites remained in possession of Galilee for a long time after the invasion of the Israelites (Jgs 1:30-33), and when the Israelites finally possessed that area the Canaanites merged with them. Because Galilee contained a mixed population, Solomon felt that he could give 20 of its cities to Tyre without great loss to his nation (1 Ki 9:11). After Tiglath-pileser III conquered Galilee (2 Ki 15: 29) *c.* 732 B.C. and made it part of the Assyrian province of Megiddo, it became a predominantly Gentile country. Consequently it could fittingly be called "Galilee of the nations" (Is 9:1; cf. Mt 4:15). Only a few Jews settled there after the Babylonian exile, and even these were later removed to Judea by Judas Maccabeus (1 Macc 5:23) in 164 B.C. After being joined to the kingdom of Judea in Herod's time, Galilee attracted so many Jews that it soon became thoroughly Jewish. According to Josephus it was so

densely populated that it could furnish an army of 100,000 men to fight against the Romans (Jos. *War* ii. 20. 6). The same author claims that there were 240 cities and villages in Galilee (*Life* 45). However, what he says about the size of the villages of Galilee seems to be exaggerated (*War* iii. 3. 2).

After Herod the Great died, Galilee became part of the tetrarchy of Herod Antipas (4 B.C. - A.D. 39), who was ruler during the time of Christ's ministry. After Antipas was deposed it was part of the kingdom of Agrippa I from A.D. 39 to 44, but was joined to the province of Judea after Agrippa's death. Agrippa II received part of Galilee *c.* A.D. 54 and administered it until the outbreak of the Jewish war in A.D. 66. The population of Galilee had a distinct accent, perhaps even a different dialect (Mk 14:70; Lk 22:59). The region was the main scene of Christ's activity. Not only was He reared in Galilee, but most of His apostles came from there. Galilean cities mentioned in the NT are Chorazin, Capernaum, Nain, Cana, Nazareth, Tiberias, and Bethsaida. Map XVI, C-3.

Galilee (găl'ĭ-lē), **Sea of.** A fresh-water lake, fed and drained by the Jordan River. It is 12¾ mi. long, and 7½ mi. wide at its greatest breadth, at the latitude of Magdala. It lies about 685 ft. below the level of the Mediterranean Sea, and is 130 to 148 ft. deep. The low altitude of this lake is responsible for its semitropical climate. It is surrounded by high hills, except where the Jordan enters and leaves, and is subject to sudden and extremely violent storms (Mt 8:23-27; 14:24-33; Mk 4:35-41). The abundance of its fish made fishing a lucrative trade in the time of Jesus. Tristram lists 22 species of fish found in the lake. It was originally called Sea of Chinnereth (Num 34:11), and in NT times Lake of Gennesaret (Lk 5:1; Jos. *Ant.* xviii. 2. 1), and Sea of Tiberias (Jn 6:1; 21:1), as well as Sea of Galilee. The name Sea of Tiberias is preserved in Arabic as *Bahr Ṭabarîyeh.* Map XVI, C-4.

Gall. The translation of: (1) The Heb. *ro'sh* or *rôsh* (Ps 69:21; Amos 6:12; etc.), a bitter and poisonous plant, also poison in general. The plant may have been the hemlock, the colocynth, the poppy, or the

nightshade. (2) The Heb. *mererah,* "gall," or "gall bladder" (Job 16:13), and *merorah,* "gall," "poison" (ch 20: 14, 25). (3) The Gr. *cholē,* a substance with an unpleasant taste (Mt 27:34). According to Mk 15:23 the gall given to Jesus was myrrh.

Gallant Ship. [Heb. *ṣi 'addîr,* "a mighty ship," "a magnificent ship."] A stately ship, magnificent in its appearance or mighty in its performance. The expression occurs only in the KJV of Is 33:21 (RSV "stately ship"). The particular type of ship involved is somewhat uncertain. Since the Heb. *ṣi* is a loan word from the Egyptian *d3y,* "a river boat," it must be assumed that a large vessel of an Egyptian type is meant.

Gallery. A corridor or a narrow room, often elevated or projecting above other rooms. The term occurs in Eze 41:15, 16; 42:3, 5; KJV, as the translation of *'attiq,* a Hebrew architectural term of unknown significance. *'Attiq* is a loan word from the Akkadian *etēqu,* "to pass," and may therefore mean "passage." In Song 7:5 the term appears in the KJV as the translation of the Heb. *rahat,* a term equally obscure. Here, the RSV has "tresses," as a conjectural translation.

Galley. The translation in Is 33:21 of the Heb. *'onî,* "ship(s)," "fleet." The term is general and does not necessarily refer to the classical "galley" propelled chiefly by rowers.

Gallim (găl'ĭm). [Heb. *Gallîm,* "heaps."] A place near Saul's fortress of Gibeah and Anathoth (Is 10:29, 30). From a comparison of 1 Sa 25:44 and 2 Sa 3:13-16 Gallim would seem to have been near Bahurim, which lies immediately east of Mount Scopus, the northern extension of the Mount of Olives. Gallim has therefore been identified with *Khirbet Ka'kûl,* ¾ mi. west of Anathoth.

Gallio (găl'ĭ-ō). [Gr. *Galliōn.*] A Roman proconsul of *Achaia (Greece) at the time the apostle Paul first visited Corinth. He was born Marcus Annaeus Novatus, about 3 B.C. at Cordoba in Spain, but upon his adoption by the rhetor Lucius Junius Gallio, his name was changed to Junius Annaeus Gallio. His two brothers were Seneca, the philosopher and tutor of Nero, and Marcus Annaeus Mela, the geographer and father of the poet Lucan. All three brothers were forced by Nero to commit suicide *c.* A.D. 66. Gallio was a statesman, who was senator of Rome and also held the consulship once. That he was proconsul of Achaia is known from

←

Acts 18:12-17 and from a letter of Seneca, but the time of his governorship was not known until a fragmentary inscription found at Delphi in Greece was made known in 1905 by E. Bourguet. In this in-

191. The Gallio inscription from Delphi

scription Gallio is called by the emperor Claudius his "friend and proconsul of Achaia." A time statement in this inscription, together with other known data, indicates that Gallio was governor either A.D. 51/52 or 52/53. Gallio proved himself an impartial judge when Paul was taken before him by his Jewish opponents, and acted the part of a worthy Roman official by refusing to take sides in a dispute about Jewish religion. Probably because he despised the Jews, as most Romans did, he did not even interfere when Sosthenes, the superintendent of the synagogue, was cruelly beaten in the governor's presence. Thus Gallio unconsciously aided Paul and his work. See fig. 113.

Lit.: A. Deissmann, *St. Paul* (London, 1912), pp. 235-260.

Gallon. A term appearing in Jn 2:6, RSV, in the phrase "twenty or thirty gallons," which is not a direct translation, but a computation, from the expression "two or three *metrētes,*" rendered "two or three firkins" in the KJV. *See* Firkin.

Gallows. [Heb. *'eṣ,* "tree."] A word occurring only in the book of Esther. Haman the Agagite had a "gallows" made, 50 cubits high, on which he hoped to hang Mordecai but on which he met his own end (Est 5:14; 7:9, 10). Since the Persians did not practice hanging involving strangulation, but impaled their criminals, there can be little doubt that the "gallows" was a pole or stake on which Haman planned to impale Mordecai.

Gamad (gā'măd), **Men of,** KJV **Gammadims** (găm'á-dǐmz). [Heb. *Gammadîm.*] A people mentioned only in Eze 27:11. They were probably the inhabitants of *Kumidi,* an unidentified city of northern Phoenicia mentioned in the *Amarna Letters. The city was near Arvad.

Gamaliel (gȧ-mā'lǐ-ĕl). [Heb. *Gamlī'el,* "God has rewarded"; Gr. *Gamaliēl.*]

1. A prince of Manasseh during the Exodus, who assisted in taking the census in the wilderness, and who brought gifts for the tabernacle (Num 1:10; 2:20; 7: 54, 59; 10:23).

2. A member of the Sanhedrin in the apostolic age (died *c.* A.D. 50), a grandson of the great rabbi Hillel, and a famous Hebrew scholar whose most illustrious pupil was Saul of Tarsus (Acts 22: 3). He was a student of Greek literature, and a leader of the liberal school of thought among the Jews. To distinguish him from a later namesake, he is usually referred to as Gamaliel I. Gamaliel prudently advised the Sanhedrin to leave John and Peter alone, when the two apostles were on trial, stating that their work would come to nought if it were merely human, and could not be stopped if it were of divine origin (ch 5:34-39).

Game. [Heb. *ṣayid,* "game," "wild animal(s) hunted for food."] A wild animal or bird, hunted for its flesh. The expression occurs only in the narrative of Esau (Gen 25:28; 27:3, 5, 7, 19, 25, 31, 33; RSV), whose wild game was much prized by his father, Isaac (ch 25:28). In each of these passages the KJV renders *ṣayid* "venison," but this translation is too restricted.

Games. *See* Play.

Gammadims. *See* Gamad, Men of.

Gamul (gā'mŭl). [Heb. *Gamûl.*] A descendant of Aaron, and head of the family that was made the 22d of the 24 courses of the priests (1 Chr 24:17).

Gangrene. [Gr. *gaggraina,* "cancer," "gangrene," "an ulcerative and spreading sore."] A term appearing once (2 Ti 2:17, RSV), the translation of an ancient medical term that could refer to any spreading and ulcerative sore of a gangrenous or cancerous type, usually fatal. The KJV translates *gaggraina* "canker."

Garden. [Heb. *gan, gannah, ginnah;* Gr. *kēpos.*] The first garden mentioned in the Bible is the garden in Eden (Gen 2:8, 15; etc.), designed and planted by God for man, but lost by him because of sin. Gardens in the OT are mostly fruit gardens (Jer 29:5, 28; Amos 9:14). Some of them had a well (Song 4:15), and some were enclosed with a hedge or wall (Song 4: 12; Is 5:2, 5). Some even had a booth for a watchman (Is 1:8). Gardens were connected with palaces (2 Ki 25:4; Est 1:5; Jer 39:4), and some kings were buried in their palace garden (2 Ki 21:18, 26). The NT mentions the Garden of Gethsemane, which seems to have been an olive grove. Thither Jesus customarily retreated for meditation and prayer, and there He was arrested (Jn 18:1, 26). He was buried in a garden (ch 19:41; cf. 20:15).

Gareb (gā'rĕb). [Heb. *Gareb*. The name occurs in Akkadian as *Gurrubu*, in Palmyrene as *Grb'*, and in ancient South Arabic with the same spelling as the Hebrew.]

1. An Ithrite listed among David's "mighty men" (2 Sa 23:38; 1 Chr 11:40).

2. A hill probably on the western or southwestern side of Jerusalem (Jer 31:39); not identified.

Garland. The rendering of: (1) The Heb. *liwyah* (Prov 1:9; 4:9; RSV), "wreath." The instruction of the father, the law of the mother, and wisdom, are likened to a garland (KJV "ornament") upon the head. In ch 14:24 the translators of the RSV emended the Heb. *'iwweleth*, "foolishness," to *liwyath*, making the expression read "garland of fools" instead of "foolishness of fools." The emendation preserves the poetic balance of the passage. (2) The Heb. *pe'er* (Is 61:3, 10, RSV), "headdress." The Messiah would give the mourner a "garland" (KJV "beauty") in place of ashes of mourning; he would be clothed with the robe of righteousness as an Oriental bridegroom is arrayed with garlands (KJV "ornaments"). (3) The Gr. *stemma* (Acts 14:13), "garland," "wreath (of flowers)." Wreaths of flowers or leaves were placed by heathen priests upon sacrificial animals and upon idols in preparing for a sacrifice. In Acts 14:13 the priest of the heathen temple at Lystra is described as preparing to offer sacrifices to Paul and Barnabas by bringing oxen and garlands. The garlands in this case may have been intended either for the sacrificial victims or as honorary wreaths for the apostles themselves, whom the men of Lystra supposed to be deities.

Garlic, KJV **Garlick.** [Heb. *shûmîm*.] A bulbous perennial plant (*Allium sativum*) resembling the onion. As an article of diet, it has been and is very popular with the peoples of the Mediterranean basin. It has a more pungent flavor than the onion, yet is eaten raw with bread and is used frequently in cooking. The Hebrews ate garlic while in Egypt and longed for it while living almost wholly on honey-flavored manna (Num 11:5).

Garmite (gär'mīt). [Heb. *Garmi*.] A gentilic

name applied to one Keilah, a Judahite (1 Chr 4:19). Its meaning is unknown.

Garner. A granary or storehouse (Ps 144:13; Joel 1:17, RSV "storehouse"; Mt 3:12, RSV "granary").

Garrison. In the OT the translation of two Hebrew words both derived from the root *naṣab:* (1) The Heb. *maṣṣab* or *maṣṣabah*, "post," "outpost," "guard," that is, a military force in a fort or a fortified town, or in an occupied country or city (1 Sa 13:23; 14:1, 4, 6, 11, 12, 15; 2 Sa 23:14). (2) The Heb. *neṣib* (1 Sa 10:5; 13:3, 4; 2 Sa 8:6, 14; 1 Chr 11:16; 2 Chr 17:2). Whether the *neṣib* in all of these texts is correctly rendered "garrison" is disputed among scholars. Some think that in certain verses a "governor" is meant. *Neṣib* is translated "officer" in 1 Ki 4:19. In the NT "garrison" occurs once in the translation of the Gr. *phroureō*, "to guard" (2 Cor 11:32, KJV). The idea of "garrison" is not in the Greek term and was apparently assumed by the translators of the KJV from the context. The guard in this case was probably a detachment of soldiers guarding the city gates from within.

Gashmu. *See* Geshem.

Gatam (gā'tăm). [Heb. *Ga'tam*.] A chieftain of Edom (Gen 36:11, 16; 1 Chr 1:36).

Gate. An entrance, generally protected, to a city, palace, or temple. The gate of a city served as a watchtower (2 Sa 18:24; 2 Ki 9:17), and as a place where business was conducted (2 Ki 7:1), public hearings were held (1 Ki 22:10), legal transactions were carried on (Gen 23:10, 18; Ruth 4:1-11), and cases were tried and judgment pronounced (Deut 21:19-21; 22:13-21; Amos 5:15). Open places near city gates were public meeting places and centers of community life (Neh 8:1, 3).

The excavations of Palestinian sites have brought to light a number of different gate structures. The earliest city gates were simple, not much more than an opening in the wall closed with a door (see fig. 192). With the turn of the 2d millennium B.C. the gate became an elaborate roofed-over structure. From 1 to 4 pairs of towers might be built in the gate opening to make its capture as difficult as possible. During the 2d millennium most cities had only 1 gate, or at the most 2, since such breaks in the wall were always weak spots in the defense system. When the gate structures became stronger and more elaborate, the number of gates increased. For example, Jerusalem had 7 gates in the time of the kings of Judah.

GATE

The wooden doors, no doubt covered or reinforced with bronze (see fig. 509), were probably in pairs fastened to upright beams; the lower end of such a beam turned in a stone door socket, while the upper end turned in a metal socket. To secure the gates, bars were laid across the closed doors and anchored in recesses in the walls of the towers, between which the doors stood (see Deut 3:5; 1 Ki 4:13; 2 Chr 8:5; 14:7). At Gezer, Megiddo, and Hazor, almost identical city gates from Solomon's time have been excavated (see figs. 482, 483). They are also similar in lay-out and size to the temple gates of Ezekiel's vision (Eze 40:6-19). See figs. 482, 483.

Fig. 193 is a picture of a model of the city gate of *Tell en-Naṣbeh* of the period of the Hebrew kings as this gate appeared when excavated by Dr. W. F. Badè in 1932. The foreground shows the entrance court lined along the sides with stone benches. Between the two towers on either side of the passageway were rooms that had stone seats facing each other. The gateway was about 14 ft. wide. The door wings turned on pivots in stone sockets. A stone in the middle of the gate-way served as doorstop. In the eastern bastion tower (left in the picture) was a slot for the bar that was drawn across the doors after they were closed.

193. Model of the foundations of the city gate of *Tell en-Naṣbeh*, probably ancient Mizpah, from the period of the Hebrew kings. Tower (left) in outer wall has slot for gate bar; note seats in gatehouse and outside

Gate Miphkad. *See* Muster Gate.

Gate, Upper. *See* Upper Gate.

Gath (găth). [Heb. *Gath,* "wine press." The city is mentioned in the *Amarna Letters of the 14th cent. B.C. as *Gimti* and *Ginti;* and in Sargon's records as *Gimtu.*] A city in Philistia, whose Semitic name seems to indicate that it was founded by Semites. At the time of Joshua it was inhabited by remnants of the Anakim, men of great stature (Jos 11:22). The giant Go-liath, who came from Gath (1 Sa 17:4, 23), was probably one of them (cf. Num 13:33; Jos 11:22). Gath became the capital of the Philistine confederation of 5 chief cities (Jos 13:3; 1 Sa 5:7-10; 6:17). To Gath belonged the subordinate cities of Ziklag (1 Sa 27:6), Jabneh (2 Chr 26:6), and Moresheth-gath—literally, "posses-sion of Gath"—(Mic 1:14). During the reign of Saul, Gath was ruled by a king named Achish (1 Sa 27:2-11), with whom David found refuge. After David came to the throne he conquered Gath (1 Chr 18:1), and his grandson Rehoboam fortified it (2 Chr 11:8). Hazael of Damascus took it later from Judah (2 Ki 12:17), but Uz-ziah of Judah reconquered it and broke down its wall (2 Chr 26:3, 6). From that time on it is not mentioned among the Philistine cities. Later, however, Sargon II tells us that he took the city (*Gimtu*) dur-ing his campaign against Ashdod in 711 B.C. (*ANET* 286, 287).

Although the city must have been an important metropolis, it has not been identified. Most scholars consider the tell of *'Arâq el-Menshîyeh,* which lies about 6½ mi. west of *Beit Jibrîn* (Eleuthero-polis), to be the site of Gath (Map VI, E-2). But *Tell eṣ-Ṣâfi,* usually considered to have been Libnah, and *Beit Jibrîn*

192. An ancient gate in the city wall of Ugarit (*Ras Shamra*)

have also been suggested. The latest suggestion, one which has much support from Israeli scholars, is *Tell Sheikh el-'Areini*, 9 mi. west of *Beit Jibrin*. This tell is a large mound rising 100 ft. above its surroundings. Excavations were started there in 1956 by the Department of Antiquities of the state of Israel, and remains from the earliest historical times until the Persian period have been discovered (*IEJ* 6 [1956], 258, 259).

Gath-hepher (găth'hē'fẽr), KJV once **Gittah-hepher** (gĭt'à-hē'fẽr). [Heb. *Gath Hachepher*, "the wine press of Hepher."] A town on the boundary of Zebulun (Jos 19:13), the home of the prophet Jonah (2 Ki 14:25). It is the modern *Khirbet ez-Zurrâ'*, about 3 mi. northeast of Nazareth, near which is an alleged tomb of Jonah. Map IX, C-3.

Gath-rimmon (găth'rĭm'ŭn). [Heb. *Gathrimmôn*, "press of pomegranates."]

1. A town in the territory of Dan, assigned to the Kohathite Levites (Jos 19:45; 21:24; 1 Chr 6:69), possibly to be identified with *Tell ej-Jerîsheh*, about 5 mi. northeast of Jaffa.

2. A town west of the Jordan in the territory of the tribe of Manasseh, assigned to the Kohathite Levites (Jos 21:25). It has been located at *Rummâneh*, about 1 mi. northwest of Taanach, but some scholars consider the Gath-rimmon of v 25 a copyist's error and that *Ibleam or Bileam should be read in its place.

Gaza (gā'zà), KJV three times **Azzah** (ăz'à). [Heb. *'Azzah;* Gr. *Gaza.*]

1. The most important of the 5 Philistine cities of Palestine. It was an old Canaanite city (Gen 10:19) and is mentioned in the *Amarna Letters as *Ḥazati*, in Egyptian records as *Qȝḏȝtî*, and in Assyrian inscription as *Ḥazzatu* and *Ḥazzutu*. From the time of Thutmose III Gaza was the point of departure in Palestine for Egyptian military campaigns, and became the center of the Egyptian administration of Palestine during the 18th dynasty when Egypt controlled most of that country. Seti I fortified the city, but in the 12th cent. it was taken over by the Philistines, who had come into the country with the Peoples of the Sea. Gaza was assigned to Judah in the time of Joshua (Jos 15:47), and was also captured by that tribe (Jgs 1:18). They probably did not hold it for long, for it was in the hands of the Philistines in the time of the judges (chs 16:1-3, 21-31). Solomon's kingdom reached to Gaza but probably did not include the city (1 Ki 4:21, 24, KJV "Azzah"). Tiglath-pileser III subjugated its king, Hanno, in 734 B.C. (*ANET* 283), Sargon II took the city in 720 B.C. (*ANET* 285), and Sennacherib in 701 B.C. (*ANET* 288). Hezekiah fought against it (2 Ki 18:1, 8), and a century later it was taken by Pharaoh Necho (Jer 47:1). The prophets denounced the wicked city repeatedly (chs 25:20; 47:1, 5; Amos 1:6; Zep 2:4; Zec 9:5). Gaza refused to surrender to Alexander the Great, but was captured after a siege of several months. Its inhabitants were then massacred. The Maccabees fought against the city repeatedly and took it twice (1 Macc 13:43-48; Jos. *Ant.* xiii. 5. 5). When Pompey took Palestine, he made Gaza part of the province of Syria. In Acts 8:26 the road to Gaza is mentioned. Gaza remained an important city throughout the succeeding centuries, and still plays its role in history under its present name, *Ghazzeh*. However, *Ghazzeh* is probably not on the same location as the ancient city, the exact site of which has not yet been identified. Map VI, E-1.

2. According to the KJV, an Ephraimite town. *See* Ayyah.

Gazathite (gā'zăth-īt). [Heb. *'Azzathi.*] An inhabitant of Gaza (Jos 13:3, KJV).

Gazelle. The translation in the RSV of the Heb. *ṣebî* and *ṣebîyah* and the Gr. *dorkas.* The gazelle (*Gazella dorcas*) was found all over Palestine and still occurs there today. It is a small animal (3 ft. 6 in. long by 1 ft. 9 in. high), and very beautiful and graceful. Both males and females have horns, but those of the males are larger. The gazelle was counted among the clean animals and hence was permitted to be eaten (Deut 14:5, RSV). It was hunted for Solomon's table (1 Ki 4:23). It was admired by Bible writers for its swiftness (2 Sa 2:18; 1 Chr 12:8; Song 2:17) and grace (Song 2:7; 4:5); its name occurs as that of Hebrew men and women ("Zibia," 1 Chr 8:9; "Zibiah," 2 Ki 12:1; and "Dorcas," Acts 9:36).

Gazer. *See* Gezer.

Gazez (gā'zĕz). [Heb. *Gazez*, "shearer."]

1. A son of Caleb's concubine Ephah (1 Chr 2:46a).

2. A son of Haran, another son of Caleb's concubine Ephah (1 Chr 2:46b).

Gazite (gā'zīt). [Heb. *'Azzathi.*] An inhabitant of Gaza (Jgs 16:1, 2).

Gazzam (găz'ăm). [Heb. *Gazzam*, "cutter."] Founder of a family of Temple servants, or Nethinim (Ezr 2:48; Neh 7:51).

Gear. [Gr. *skeuos,* "a thing," "an object," the specific type being determined by the context or by an added statement.] A word occurring once (Acts 27:17, RSV), in a context that shows that it applies to the sails and such other equipment as might be removed from the masts to help the ship ride out the storm.

Geba (gē′bȧ), KJV three times **Gaba** (gā′bȧ). [Heb. *Geba',* "hill."] A city in the territory of Benjamin (Jos 18:24; 1 Chr 8:6), which was assigned to the priests (Jos 21:17). It should not be confused with the neighboring Gibeah, the fortress-capital of Saul. In Is 10:29 the two cities are mentioned together. Geba was the northernmost city of the kingdom of Judah (2 Ki 23:8; Zec 14:10). It is mentioned in the records of Thutmose III and Ramses II. The site has been identified with the modern *Jeba',* 2 mi. southwest of Michmash and about 7 mi. north-northeast of Jerusalem. Map VI, E-3.

Gebal (gē′băl). [Heb. *Gebal;* Phoenician and Ugaritic *Gbl;* Egyptian *Kbn;* Akkadian *Gubla.*]

194. The temple of obelisks at Byblos, Biblical Gebal

1. A famous Phoenician seaport city (Jos 13:5; Eze 27:9), better known by its Greek name Byblos. It is the earliest Asiatic city mentioned in Egyptian records of the Old Kingdom, and was under the strong cultural influence of Egypt for centuries. It was the most important Phoenician city long before Tyre and Sidon came on the scene of action, and was for many centuries a great exporter of cedarwood. Among the *Amarna Letters are many written by Rib-Addi, king of Gebal. After the 2d millennium B.C. the city declined and lost its prominence. It is some 20 mi. north of Beirut and presently bears the name *Jebeil.* Excavations carried out since 1921 by French expeditions have uncovered temples, royal tombs, inscriptions, and a wealth of other structures and objects. In 1 Ki 5:18 the word translated "stonesquarers" (KJV) is more properly rendered "men of Gebal," as in the RSV. Map III, C-4. See fig. 383.

Lit.: P. Montet, *Byblos et l'Égypte* (Paris, 1928), 2 vols.; M. Dunand, *Fouilles de Byblos* (Paris, 1939-54), 4 vols.

2. A place mentioned in Ps 83:7; probably an Edomite territory north of Petra, now known as *Jibâl.*

Gebalites (gē′băl-īts), KJV **Giblites** (gĭb′lĭts). [Heb. *Giblî.*] The inhabitants of Gebal (Jos 13:5), that is, Byblos. The "men of Gebal" are mentioned in 1 Ki 5:18, RSV.

Geber (gē′bēr). [Heb. *Geber,* "man."]

1. Solomon's supply officer in Gilead (1 Ki 4:19).

2. A man whose son (called Ben-geber in the RSV) was Solomon's supply officer in Ramoth-gilead (1 Ki 4:13); possibly identical with Geber, 1.

Gebim (gē′bĭm). [Heb. *Gebîm,* "cisterns."] A place in Benjamin between Madmenah and Nob, north of Jerusalem (Is 10:31, 32); not identified.

Gecko. *See* Lizard.

Gedaliah (gĕd′ȧ-lī′ȧ). [Heb. *Gedalyah* and *Gedalyahû,* "Yahweh is great." The name appears on a Hebrew seal as *Gdlyh.*]

1. The son of Jeduthun, and an inspired lyre player in the time of David (1 Chr 25:3). He became the head of the 2d of the 24 companies of 12 musicians each, whom David appointed for service in Solomon's Temple (v 9).

2. The grandfather of the prophet Zephaniah (Zep 1:1).

3. The son of Pashhur and an opponent of the prophet Jeremiah (Jer 38:1).

4. The son of Ahikam, a citizen of Judah of high birth. He must have been

known for his pro-Babylonian sympathies, since Nebuchadnezzar made him governor over the province of Judah after Jerusalem's capture and the abolition of the kingship of Judah in 586 B.C. Gedaliah chose Mizpah as his capital and residence, and began at once to rally around him the remnants of the nation which had not been taken captive to Babylonia (2 Ki 25: 22-24; Jer 40:7-13). His efforts were cut short when he was treacherously assassinated by the former army general, Ishmael, a relative of the royal family, who was either a personal enemy of Gedaliah or considered him a usurper (2 Ki 25:25; Jer 40:13 to 41:3). In the excavations at Lachish was found a seal impression on clay that had once been attached to a papyrus scroll, bearing the inscrip-

195. Left: Seal impression of "Gedaliah who is over the house" (actual size)

Right: Back of the Gedaliah seal showing the fiber of the papyrus to which it had been attached

tion: "(Belonging) to Gedaliah [w]ho is over the hou[se]" (see fig. 195). The title "over the house" means "administrator of the palace," and indicates that the owner of the seal was a high government official. It is generally assumed that the Gedaliah of the Lachish seal became the governor of the province of Judah, after Jerusalem's capture.

5. A priest who had married a foreign wife in the time of Ezra (Ezr 10:18).

Gedeon. *See* Gideon.

Geder (gē'dēr). [Heb. *Geder*, "wall" or "fence."] A city in Judah (Jos 12:13); not identified. It is probably the *Beth-gader of 1 Chr 2:51, and is possibly identical with *Gedor, 3.

Gederah (gĕ-dē'rá). [Heb. *Gederah*, "a walled place," or "sheepfold."]
1. A place in the Shephelah in the territory of Judah (Jos 15:36), identified with *Jedireh*, 3 mi. southeast of Gezer.
2. A village in the territory of Benjamin and the home of Josabad, the Gederathite (1 Chr 12:4, KJV). It has been identified with *Jedireh* near Gibeon, about 6 mi. northwest of Jerusalem.

Gederathite (gĕ-dē'rá-thīt). [Heb. *Gederathi*.] An inhabitant of *Gederah, 2.

Gederite (gĕ-dēr'īt). [Heb. *Gederi*.] An inhabitant either of Geder or of Gederah (1 Chr 27:28).

Gederoth (gĕ-dē'rŏth). [Heb. *Gederôth*, "enclosures" or "sheepfolds."] A place in the Shephelah in the territory of Judah (Jos 15:41), which has not been identified with certainty. It was captured by the Philistines during the reign of King Ahaz (2 Chr 28:18).

Gederothaim (gĕd'ē-rŏ-thā'ĭm). [Heb. *Gederothayim*, "two enclosures" or "two sheepfolds."] A city in the territory of Judah (Jos 15:36). However, the LXX has not taken it as a place name, but renders the term "its cattle shelters." This may be correct since vs 33-36 lists 15 cities including Gederothaim, whereas there should be only 14 according to v 36.

Gedor (gē'dôr). [Heb. *Gedôr*, "pockmarked."]
1. A brother of King Saul's grandfather, Ner (1 Chr 8:30, 31; 9:35-39).
2. A city in the hill country of Judah (Jos 15:58), probably identical with the Gedor of 1 Chr 4:4, 18. It is identified with *Khirbet Jedûr*, about 8 mi. north of Hebron.
3. A town in southern Simeon (1 Chr 4:39); not identified. It is possibly the Geder of Jos 12:13 and the Beth-gader of 1 Chr 2:51.
4. A place in the territory of Benjamin (1 Chr 12:7); site uncertain.

Ge-harashim (gē'há-rā'shĭm), KJV **Valley of Charashim** (kăr'á-shĭm). [Heb. *Ge' Charashim*, "valley of craftsmen."] A valley in Judah (1 Chr 4:14), inhabited by Benjamites after the Exile (Neh 11:35, KJV "valley of craftsmen"). Most commentators place it in the region of Ono and Lod. It is therefore identified with the *Wâdī esh-Shellâl*, which runs into the *Wâdī el-Kebîr*, a tributary of the Auja (*Me-jarkon*) River, then into the Mediterranean Sea.

Gehazi (gĕ-hā'zī). [Heb. *Gêchazi*, meaning uncertain.] Elisha's servant. He appears first in favorable light when he showed sympathy with a childless Shunammite woman (2 Ki 4:14), and when he showed zeal for the honor of the prophet, who he thought was not being shown the proper respect (v 27). Later he is pictured as covetous and lying. To Naaman, the Syrian commander whom Elisha had healed of leprosy, he made it appear that the prophet had broken his word. As punishment the leprosy of Naaman fell on him (ch 5:20-27). His meeting with the king of Israel after a seven-year famine (ch 8:4-6) seems to have occurred before he was punished with perpetual leprosy.

Geliloth (gḗ-lī′lŏth). [Heb. *Gelilôth,* "circles" or "regions."] A place on the boundary between Judah and Benjamin (Jos 18:17); not identified. It is probably identical with Gilgal in ch 15:7.

Gemalli (gḗ-măl′ī). [Heb. *Gemalli,* meaning uncertain.] Father of the spy who represented the tribe of Dan (Num 13:12).

Gemariah (gĕm′à-rī′à). [Heb. *Gemaryah* and *Gemaryahû.* The name occurs also in the Lachish Letters.]

1. One of the 2 envoys sent to Nebuchadnezzar by King Zedekiah to deliver either the annual tribute or a royal message. These messengers carried with them a letter from Jeremiah to the exiles in Babylon (Jer 29:3).

2. A prince of Judah who was evidently favorably disposed toward Jeremiah. He urged King Jehoiakim not to burn the scroll containing Jeremiah's prophecy. His high position is indicated by the fact that he occupied a room in the Temple (Jer 36:10-12, 25).

Genealogy. [Heb. generally *yachaś,* as a noun, "genealogy," and as a verb, "to reckon genealogically"; Gr. *genealogia,* "genealogy."] An ancestral record giving one's line of descent. The "book of the generations" (Gen 5:1) and the "book of the generation" (Mt 1:1, KJV) were genealogical lists or family registers. The tribal organization of Hebrew society, with its strong emphasis on family relationships, demanded accurate genealogical lists (Num 1:2, 18). Status in the community and before the law depended on one's personal identity as belonging to a certain family and tribe. The Hebrew economy was essentially pastoral-agricultural, and each tribe and family had its own allotment of land (Jos 13 to 19). The legal right of inheritance was based on kinship, and land was not to pass from one tribe to another (Num 36:7, 9), nor, except in walled cities, was it to be permanently transferred from one family to another (Lev 25:23, 28-31; Num 27:8-11). Headship in the tribe, the tribal family, and the father's house, was likewise a matter of lineage. The high priesthood, the priesthood, the Levitical service, and the royal succession were all hereditary. At one time inability to prove Aaronic descent automatically excluded certain persons from the priesthood (Ezr 2:62; Neh 7:64). The fact that Messiah was to be of the house of David (Is 9:6, 7; 11:1; cf. Rom 1:3) gave members of that family an additional incentive for preserving an accurate record of their family pedigree. A valid genealogy was thus essential to the stability of the throne, to the purity of the priesthood, and to family and tribal status, and for every Hebrew male there were compelling ethnic, social, economic, political, and religious reasons for the preservation of precise and accurate family records.

Certain Jewish customs and modes of expression must be kept in mind in any study of the genealogical lists of the Bible. For instance, the term "son" is also used to mean "grandson" or an even more remote descendant (1 Ki 19:16; cf. 2 Ki 9:2, 14, 20; Mt 1:1, 8; cf. 1 Chr 3:11, 12; *see* Son). Thus there are skeleton genealogical lists in which only the more important ancestors are mentioned, with the gaps bridged by the word "son" as if each person in the list were the immediate descendant of the one previously named (see Ezr 7:1-5; 1 Chr 6:7-9; Mt 1:8, 11; cf. 1 Chr 3:10-12, 15, 16). Furthermore, by the levirate ("husband's brother") marriage law, the next of kin was required to marry the widow of a deceased person and provide him with a successor and heir (Deut 25:5-10; cf. Ruth 2:20; 4:5, 10, 13, 14; Mt 22:23-28). Thus a person could be the actual son of one man and yet be referred to as the son of another. Obviously, great care must be taken in the interpretation of the genealogical data of the Bible.

For Christians the most important genealogy of Scripture is that of Jesus Christ. The 2 versions of this genealogy given by Matthew (ch 1:1-16) and Luke (ch 3:23-38) differ in certain important respects, and each has problems of its own. Internal evidence leads to the conclusion that Matthew composed his account of the life of Jesus primarily for readers of Jewish birth. In his Gospel, Matthew stresses the fact that Jesus of Nazareth was, indeed, the One to whom Moses and the prophets bore witness, and begins his account in typical Jewish style by giving Jesus' family pedigree. Since Messiah was to be of the seed of Abraham (Gen 22:18; Gal 3:16), the father of the Jewish nation, and of David, the founder of its royal line (Is 9:6, 7; 11:1), Matthew presents evidence that proves Jesus to be the legal descendant of these two illustrious men. Lacking such proof, the Jews would declare His claim to Messiahship invalid and summarily dismiss other evidence without examination. On the other hand, Luke, writing for Gentile readers, carries his ancestral list back to Adam, the progenitor of both Jews and Gentiles, in order to prove Christ to be the Saviour of both. Matthew gives the direct descent, from Abraham to Jesus, whereas Luke presents it in reverse order, from Jesus back to Adam. One noteworthy characteristic of Matthew's genealogy is the division of Christ's ancestors into 3 groups of 14 generations each—from Abraham to David, from David to the Captivity, and from the Captivity to Christ (Mt 1:17). His omission of Ahaziah, Joash, and Amaziah in v 8 (cf. 1 Chr 3:11, 12) and Jehoiakim in v 11 (cf 1 Chr 3:15, 16), marks his as an intentionally abbreviated list like that of Ezr 7:1-5; cf. 1 Chr 6:7-9, perhaps as an aid to memory. Furthermore, there are only 41 names in the 3 sections, instead of 42, which makes it necessary to count either David or Jechoniah twice— as the last member of one group of 14 and as the 1st member of the next group.

Chief points of difference between the genealogies of Matthew and Luke are: (1) Luke names 41 descendants of David as ancestors of Jesus, whereas Matthew gives only 26. (2) Except for Salathiel, Zerubbabel, and Joseph, the 2 lists are altogether different between David and Jesus. (3) The 2 genealogies converge briefly, with Salathiel and Zerubbabel, but Matthew identifies Salathiel as the son of Jechoniah (Mt 1:12) and Luke lists him as the son of Neri (Lk 3:27). (4) Matthew identifies Joseph as the son of Jacob (ch 1:16), and Luke, as the son of Heli (ch 3:23). The complete absence of information on nearly all of the 64 persons between David and Jesus named in the 2 lists makes a positive reconciliation of the differences between the lists practically impossible. However, enough is known of ancient Jewish customs and modes of thought and expression to offer an entirely plausible explanation of the points of difference to justify both lists as inherently correct. These seeming discrepancies may be explained as follows. (1) Luke's 41 generations, spanning more than 900 years from David's death to the birth of Christ about 5 B.C., average about 24 years each, as compared with Matthew's 26 generations averaging 37 years each. The intentional omission of at least 4 names by Matthew suggests the possibility that he may have omitted still others in the relatively obscure period between the Testaments. An average span of 24 years between a man's own birth and that of his successor is far more probable than 37 years. (2) From David to the Captivity, Matthew traces Jesus' ancestry through the royal line, and doubtless does so with potential heirs to the throne following the

Captivity, whereas Luke follows a nonruling branch of the royal family back to Nathan, another son of David by Bathsheba (Lk 3:31; cf. 1 Chr 3:5). Intermarriage within the limits of the royal family could easily account for Christ's ancestry being traced back to David through 2 almost entirely distinct family lines. (3) Salathiel may have been both the literal son of Neri as Luke states (ch 3:27) and the adopted son of Jeconiah, or the legal successor to Jeconiah by the extinction of Jeconiah's family (Mt 1:12). (4) The absence of literal blood relationship between Joseph and Jesus, the fact that the Jews never introduce women as direct genealogical links, and the loose way in which Bible writers use the terms "son" and "father" are probably responsible for the seeming discrepancy by which Matthew lists Jacob as Joseph's father, and Luke gives Heli. Either Luke or, more probably, Matthew uses the expression "son of" (in Lk 3:23) or "begat" (in Mt 1:16) in a strictly legal and genealogical sense rather than in a strictly literal sense, since Joseph the husband of Mary could not be the literal son of both Heli and Jacob. This seeming discrepancy has been explained on the basis that Luke presents Jesus as the actual blood descendant of David through Mary (cf. Rom 1:3, 4), but without listing Mary as a link in the chain of progenitors, whereas Matthew gives the royal and legal line of descent through Joseph, who was Jesus' father by Jewish law. Joseph could have been the literal son of either Jacob or Heli and the adopted son of the other, perhaps through a levirate marriage by either.

General. A rendering of: (1) The Heb. *śar*, "chieftain," "leader," "prince" (Jgs 4:7, RSV; 1 Chr 27:34, KJV). *Śar* is very common in the OT, occurring 419 times, but only in these two passages is it rendered "general," apparently because the commander in chief of the entire army may have been involved. (2) The Gr. *chiliarchos*, literally "commander of a thousand" (Rev 6:15, RSV), with a rank roughly comparable to that of a modern colonel.

Generation. [Heb. *dôr*, "period," "age," "generation"; *tôledôth* (always in the plural), "descendants," "genealogy," "life record," literally, "begettings"; Gr. generally *genea*, "descendant," "race," "age," "generation," "contemporaries."] The translation of various Hebrew and Greek terms signifying either a person or persons in relation to their ancestors or the human race as a whole, or the period of time during which they live. The Heb. *dôr* usually stresses the time element, as in Gen 7:1; 15:16; Deut 23:2, and *tôledôth,* the personal element, as in Gen 5:1; 10:1, 32; 1 Chr 26:31, or the idea of birth or origin, as in Gen 2:4; Ex 28:10 ("birth"). *Genea* combines both ideas in one word (Mt 1:17; 11:16; 17:17).

The expression "this generation" of Mt 24:34; Mk 13:30; Lk 21:32 must be understood in the context of the subject under discussion and the context of Christ's use of the word "generation" elsewhere in the Gospels. In all other instances (Mt 11:16; 12:39, 41, 42, 45; 16:4; 17:17; 23:36, and in the parallel passages in Mk and Lk) He refers to His contemporaries, the people then living, particularly the Jews of His time. The discourse of Mt 24 envisions, and to a certain extent blends, the fall of Jerusalem in A.D. 70 and events associated with His return and the end of the world. As applied to the fall of Jerusalem "this generation" denoted Jews then living. As applied to the end of the world it refers to the people who witness the signs presaging that event. To make "this generation" the basis for reckoning a period of time supposedly terminating with Christ's return violates both the letter and the spirit of His instructions (see vs 36, 42).

Genesis, Book of. First book of the Pentateuch, giving the record of sacred history from the 1st day of Creation week to the death of Joseph in Egypt. The title of the book in Hebrew Bibles is *Bere'shîth,* the word with which the book opens, translated "in the beginning." The title "Genesis," meaning "birth," or "origin," was assigned the book by the translators of the LXX, as being appropriate to its contents. From ancient times Jewish and Christian scholars consistently attributed the book to Moses, but about the middle of the 18th cent. critical scholarship began its attack on the authenticity of the Scriptures as a divine revelation and as a reliable history of antiquity, and set forth the view that Genesis is a composite work consisting of documents written at various times by different authors, and later combined into its present form by one or more editors. The basis of this supposition was the conjecture that the use of different names for God in different sections—*'Elohîm,* "God," and *Yahweh,* "Lord"—was an indication of different authors, and that the authorship of a given passage may be determined by the name used. However, a careful study of ancient versions, such as the LXX, and more recently of the Dead Sea scrolls, has proved conclusively that ancient Hebrew scholars used these terms interchangeably, and thus that the imaginary distinction contrived by modern critics is invalid. Historically, the critics labeled the book as myth and legend. But a remarkable series of archeological discoveries spanning the past century has conclusively proved the historicity of passage after passage that had formerly been challenged. Among the passages thus attested are those that refer to the Hittites and the Philistines, and to the use of iron and camels in the patriarchal age. The section of the book that deals with Egypt shows a remarkable familiarity with that country, its language, and customs. The successive narratives are true in every respect to what is known of the patriarchal age as a result of archeological discoveries.

The book was written with the object of enlightening the Hebrew people with respect to their high destiny, and to preserve for all future generations a reliable record of sacred history prior to that time, particularly concerning God's dealings with those who were faithful to Him. It contains the world's only authentic written record of Creation and of the history of the antediluvian world, and the only reliable account of the Deluge. It tells of the origin of man, the entrance of sin, the promise of salvation, and relates the early stages of history that prepared the way for the later fulfillment of that promise.

The book logically divides itself into 4 major sections: (1) from Creation to the Flood, and the peopling of the world following the Flood (Gen 1:1 to 11:26); (2) the patriarchs Abraham and Isaac (chs 11:27 to 26:35); (3) the patriarch Jacob (chs 27 to 36); (4) Joseph (chs 37 to 50). Chs 1 and 2 describe the creation of this planet and its change from a state described as "without form, and void" (ch 1:2) to one perfectly adapted to be the home of human beings. Particular attention is given to the establishment of the 1st home and the observance of the 1st Sabbath day. Ch 3 delineates the fall of man, marks its results, and contains the 1st promise of salvation. Chs 4 and 5 relate the murder of Abel and trace the history of Adam's descendants during antediluvian times. In chs 6 to 9 an account is given of the destruction of the antediluvian world by a flood and of the means by which human and animal life was preserved, together with a brief report of the experiences of Noah and his sons after the Flood. Chapters 10 and 11 record the peopling of the earth by Noah's descendants, down to the time of Abraham.

In the 2d major division Abraham is the chief character. God called Abraham and his descendants to be His chosen representatives on earth, and guided him to the land of Canaan (Gen 11:27 to 12:9). After many years of sojourning, with its vicissitudes, Abraham received a son of promise, Isaac, who became heir to the covenant promises (chs 12:10 to 25:18). Isaac was passed over in comparative silence, a far less forceful character than his illustrious father (chs 25:19 to 26:35). His chief function seems to be to provide a link between Abraham and Jacob.

The 3d major section relates how Jacob received the birthright by deceit and was compelled to flee to Haran, where he reared a large family and accumulated considerable wealth (Gen 27 to 30). He returned finally to Canaan, migrating from place to place as circumstances required (chs 31 to 35). Chapter 36 enumerates Esau's descendants. In ch 37 an account is given that explains how Joseph was exiled to Egypt, and chs 39 and 40 tell of his early experiences in that land. Chapters 41 to 47 tell of the famine and of the circumstances under which Jacob and his sons migrated to Egypt and settled there. Chapters 48 and 49 record the blessings pronounced by the patriarch Jacob upon his sons, and ch 50 tells of his death and of that of Joseph.

Gennesaret (gĕ-nĕs'á-rĕt). [Gr. *Gennēsaret*, derivation and meaning uncertain.]

1. The land of Gennesaret (Mt 14:34; Mk 6:53), a fertile plain on the northwestern shore of the Lake of Gennesaret, or Galilee. Josephus describes it as being about 3½ mi. long and 2¼ mi. wide (30 by 20 stades), rich in walnuts, palms, fig trees, olives, and grapes (*War* iii. 10. 8). This plain, which lay around Capernaum, later became known by the Arabic name of *el-Ghuweir*.

2. The Lake of Gennesaret (Lk 5:1), another name for Sea of *Galilee.

Gentiles. [Heb. generally *góyim;* Gr. generally *ethnoi*, both of which signify "nations," "heathen," "gentiles."] Generally those who are non-Jewish in faith or in race. The terms thus translated are actually less restricted in their basic meaning than the translation itself, and denote simply "nations" and were used in referring to any ethnic group, even Jews. However, Jewish writers usually applied these terms to those races or nations not descended from Abraham, and thus these terms came to emphasize the spiritual and racial distinction between Israelites and the various pagan nations surrounding them. When the scriptural words involved seem to have been used especially in the sense of designating a person or a nation as non-Jewish, the KJV (and frequently the RSV) renders these words as "Gentiles" (Jer 16:19; Mt 10:5; Acts 13:46; etc.) or "heathen" (Lev 26:33; 1 Cor 12:2, RSV; etc.). When these same terms, however, seem to have been used in a broader sense, or may have referred to Israel directly, or to other nations, in a purely ethnic sense, both versions use more general terms, such as "people" or "nation" (Jos 3:17; 4:1; Jgs 2:20; Acts 10:22; etc.).

Although a distinction was made in OT times between Jews and other nations (cf. Lev 20:24, 26, where the Lord said that He had separated Israel from the *góyim*, "peoples," RSV), this demarcation was not intended to preclude the Gentiles from the blessings of salvation (cf. Ps 22:27; Is 56:6-8; Gal 3:8; etc.). And in the NT era the breaking down of "the middle wall of partition" (Eph 2:14) by the death of Christ clearly showed that there was to be no longer a distinction between Jews and other races in spiritual privileges (Rom 10:12; Gal 3:28; Col 3:11); both Jews and Gentiles were to share alike in the blessings of the gospel (cf. Acts 10:34, 35, 45).

Genubath (gĕ-nū'băth). [Heb. *Genubath*, "theft."] The son of the Edomite prince Hadad. His mother was the sister of Queen Tahpenes of Egypt. He grew up with the royal children of Egypt (1 Ki 11:20).

Gera (gē'rá). [Heb. *Gera'*, meaning uncertain.]

1. A son of Benjamin (Gen 46:21).

2 and 3. Two sons of Bela (son of Benjamin; 1 Chr 8:3, 5).

4. A son of Ehud (1 Chr 8:6, 7).

5. A Benjamite, the father or ancestor of the judge Ehud (Jgs 3:15).

6. A Benjamite whose son Shimei cursed David and was later executed by Solomon (2 Sa 16:5; 19:16-23; 1 Ki 2:36-46).

It is possible that some of these men are identical.

Gerah. [Heb. *gerah*, "bean" or "grain," a loan word from the Akkadian *girû*, a weight which is 1/24 of a shekel, probably originally based on that of a carob seed.] The smallest Hebrew weight, equivalent to 1/20 of a shekel (Ex 30:13; Num 3:47; 18:16; Eze 45:12). Hence a gerah's weight was .57 gram, or .02 ounce avoirdupois.

Gerar (gē′rär). [Heb. *Gerar*.] An ancient city at the southwestern border of Canaan near Gaza (Gen 10:19; 2 Chr 14:13). It was inhabited by Philistines in the patriarchal age, when Abraham and Isaac had dealings with its king (Gen 20:1, 2; 26:1, 6). Sir Flinders Petrie identified it with a place about 9 mi. south of Gaza, called *Tell ej-Jemmeh*, which he excavated in 1926 and 1927. Map VI, F-2; XXI, E-2. He uncovered many grain bins of the Persian period, showing that the city had served as a storage place. Other scholars have identified it with *Tell esh-Sherī'ah*, 16 mi. east-southeast of Gaza, but the evidence seems to point to *Tell Abū Hureirah*, 11 mi. southeast of Gaza, as the most likely site of ancient Gerar.

Gerasenes (gĕr′à-sēnz). [Gr. *Gerasēnos*.] Inhabitants of Gerasa. Certain NT manuscripts have this reading, in Mt 8:28; Mk 5:1; Lk 8:26, 37 (the RSV has adopted this reading in the Mk and Lk passages), where other manuscripts have *Gadarenes and still others *Gergesenes. The Decapolis city of Gerasa, now *Jerash* (Map XVI, D-4; fig. 130) lies about 35 mi. southeast of the Sea of Galilee, hence cannot be the one to which the above passages refer, for they locate the event near the shore of the Sea of Galilee. It has therefore been suggested that another Gerasa, otherwise unknown, may have lain near the shore.

Gergesenes (gûr′gĕ-sēnz′). [Gr. *Gergesēnoi*.] Inhabitants of Gergesa (Mt 8:28, KJV; and given as variant reading of Mk 5:1; Lk 8:26, 37 in the RSV). It is said that Origen felt that Gadara was too far from the Sea of Galilee to have been the city mentioned in the story of Christ's healing a demon-possessed man, and that since he had been told that there was a place by the name of Gergesa near the shore of the Sea of Galilee, he therefore introduced the reading Gergesenes instead of *Gadarenes into the text. The ruined site of *Kursī*, lying at the latitude of Magdala on the eastern shore of the Sea of Galilee, is usually identified with the Gergesa of Origen.

Gerizim (gĕr′ĭ-zĭm). [Heb. *Gerizzim*.] One of the highest mountains of central Pales-

196. The village of *Askar* (possibly ancient Sychar) and Mount Gerizim

tine, with an elevation of 2,891 ft. It lies south of Mount Ebal, from which it is separated by a narrow valley. In the eastern exit of this valley lay the important city of Shechem. Mount Gerizim is now called *Jebel eṭ-Ṭôr* (Map II, B-3), and is a rocky, barren mountain, almost wholly deprived of vegetation. Older textbooks generally represent Mount Gerizim, the mount of blessings, as covered with vegetation, and Mount Ebal, the mount of curses, as barren. This is certainly not true today, and such a contrast probably never existed. Moses directed that after the Israelites crossed the Jordan they go to Ebal and Gerizim and that six of their tribes (Simeon, Levi, Judah, Issachar, Joseph, and Benjamin) stand on the slopes of Mount Gerizim and pronounce the blessings on those who keep God's Law (Deut 11:29; 27:12, 13). Shortly after the Israelites invaded Canaan they carried out this command (Jos 8:33-35).

The mountain is known as the holy mount of the Samaritans, who erected a temple there after the return of the Jews from exile. Josephus claims that this temple was built in the time of Alexander the Great by Sanballat for his son-in-law Manasseh, who had been expelled from the priesthood by his brother Jaddua, high priest in Jerusalem (*Ant.* xi. 8. 2. 7). Either Josephus confuses the time by making two men named as living in the days of Nehemiah (Neh 4:7; 12:22), contemporary with Alexander the Great, who lived a hundred years later, or we must assume a coincidence of names and offices.

John Hyrcanus destroyed this Gerizim temple in 128 B.C., but the Samaritans continued to use the mountain as their place of sacrifice and worship and still use it today. This worship was mentioned by the Samaritan woman in her conversation with Jesus at Jacob's Well (Jn 4:20, 21). See figs. 415, 433.

Gershom (gûr'shŏm). [Heb. *Gershom*, by popular etymology "sojourner," or "banishment," from the verb *garash*, "to drive out." The name is attested in ancient South Arabic.]

1. A son of Levi (1 Chr 6:16, 17, 20, 43, 62, 71). In the Pentateuch (Gen 46: 11; Ex 6:16; Num 3:17) he is called Gershon (gûr'shŏn) [Heb. *Gershôn*], a name having the same meaning as Gershom. The tribal family of the Levitic *Gershonites descended from him.

2. The elder son of Moses and Zipporah, born in Midian (Ex 2:22; 18:3). His descendants formed a Levitic family but were not priests (1 Chr 23:14-16). This son of Moses was the father or ancestor of Jonathan, the priest of the sanctuary at Dan (*see* Jonathan, 1).

3. A descendant of Phinehas, and the head of a priestly family (Ezr 8:2).

Gershomites. *See* Gershonites.

Gershon. *See* Gershom, 1.

Gershonites (gûr'shŏn-īts). [Heb. *Gershunnî*.] The descendants of Gershon, or Gershom, 1, and one of the 3 main divisions of the Levites, called Gershomites (gûr'shŏm-īts) [Heb. *Benê Gershôm*] in 1 Chr 6:62, 71, RSV. Moses placed them in charge of the tabernacle and the curtains of the court,

for whose transport they had the use of 2 wagons and 4 oxen (Num 7:7). In the wilderness they camped to the west of the tabernacle (chs 3:23-26; 4:21-28). The Gershonites were subdivided into two families, those of Libni and those of Shimei, the two sons of Gershon (Ex 6:17; Num 3:18; 1 Chr 6:17). At the time of the first census these families numbered 7,500 (Num 3:21, 22). Eleven cities in western Canaan, 4 in Issachar, 4 in Asher, and 3 in Naphtali (Jos 21:28-33), and 2 cities in Transjordan (v 27) were assigned to them.

Geruth Chimham. *See* Chimham.

Gesham. *See* Geshan.

Geshan (gē'shăn), KJV **Gesham** (gē'shăm). [Heb. *Gêshan*.] A Judahite (1 Chr 2:47).

Geshem (gē'shĕm), KJV once **Gashmu** (găsh'mū). [Heb. *Geshem* and *Gashmû*, "(born in) the rainy season."] An Arabian opponent of Nehemiah. He tried in every way to prevent the Jews from fortifying Jerusalem. First he asserted that such a course would be equal to rebellion against Persian rule (Neh 2:19). Then when this did not deter the Jews he, with Sanballat, the governor of Samaria, and Tobiah, an Ammonite official, plotted violence, apparently planning even to assassinate Nehemiah (ch 6:1, 2). So that he might discredit Nehemiah in the eyes of the Persian officials Geshem also circulated the rumor that Nehemiah was planning to rebel against Persia and would soon proclaim himself king (vs 6, 7). The name Geshem has been recognized in a Lihyanite inscription found at Dedan, now el-'Ulā, in northwestern Arabia, and in an Aramaic inscription ón a recently found silver vessel, now in the Brooklyn Museum (see fig. 52). This inscription mentions a certain Qainû, son of Geshem, king of Kedar (see fig. 197). Kedar is the

197. The rim of the bowl depicted in fig. 52, showing the inscription that mentions "Geshem, King of Kedar"

198. The Garden of Gethsemane, on the western slope of the Mount of Olives, beyond the road, with the Kidron Valley in the foreground, seen from the eastern edge of Jerusalem. Fig. 260 was photographed from the tower at upper left

name of an Arab tribe frequently mentioned in the Bible (Is 21:16; etc.). Since the Aramaic inscription can be dated in the late 5th cent. B.C., which was probably in the lifetime of Nehemiah, there can be little doubt that the Geshem of the Kedar Arabs is the opponent of Nehemiah. His high position makes clear why his opposition was so dangerous for Nehemiah (I. Rabinowitz, *JNES* 15 [1956], 1-9).

Geshur. *See* Aram, 5, c.

Geshuri. *See* Geshurites.

Geshurites (gĕsh′ū-rīts), KJV twice **Geshuri** (gĕ-shoo′rī). [Heb. *Geshuri*.]

1. The inhabitants of Geshur (Deut 3: 14; Jos 12:5; 13:11, 13). *See* Aram, 5, c.

2. A tribe living in the desert area between the Philistine coastland and Egypt (Jos 13:2; 1 Sa 27:8); not identified.

Gether (gē′thĕr). [Heb. *Gether*.] A son of Aram (Gen 10:23; 1 Chr 1:17), and founder of an Aramaic tribe of which nothing else is known.

Gethsemane (gĕth-sĕm′ȧ-nĕ). [Gr. *Geth-sēmani*, a transliteration of the Aramaic *Gath Shemani*, "oil press."] A place on the western slope of the Mount of Olives, where Jesus prayed in agony shortly before He was arrested there (Mt 26:36; Mk 14:26, 32; Lk 22:39). It probably re-

ceived its name from an olive press in the area. It is called a garden in Jn 18:1. It may have belonged to a disciple of Christ, since He used it frequently as a favorite retreat (Lk 22:39; Jn 18:1, 2). The traditional site lies at the lower section of the slope of the Mount of Olives immediately east of the bridge by which the road from St. Stephen's Gate of Jerusalem crosses the Kidron Valley. It is now divided into several sections, held by Roman Catholics, Orthodox, and Armenian church groups. The olive trees found there are extremely old, but they do not go back to the time of Jesus' ministry, for Titus had all the trees around Jerusalem cut down during the siege of that city in A.D. 70 (Jos. *War* v. 12. 4), and Christian pilgrims of the early centuries lamented that no olive

199. Olive trees in the Garden of Gethsemane

trees were found at the site of Gethsemane. The present Franciscan church (fig. 198, center) is on the site of a church that was erected in the 4th cent. A.D. Although it is not certain that the traditional Gethsemane is the actual site of Jesus' agony, the place must, in any case, have been nearby.

Geuel (gē̆-ū'ĕl). [Heb. *Ge'û'el*, "majesty of God."] The spy representing the tribe of Gad (Num 13:15).

Gezer (gē'zẽr), KJV twice **Gazer** (gā'zẽr). [Heb. *Gezer;* in the *Amarna Letters, Gazri,* but *Gazru* in Assyrian inscriptions; *Qḏr* in Egyptian records.] A place about 18 mi. northwest of Jerusalem and about 5 mi. east of Ekron; now called *Tell Jezer.* Gezer was an important city because of its geographical position on one of the two main routes from Joppa to Jerusalem. Gezer's importance is also indicated by its unusual size of 27 acres, twice that of Megiddo. Although the inhabitants of Gezer were defeated in Joshua's time

200. High place with standing stones at Gezer

(Jos 12:12), and were put under forced labor for a time by the Ephraimites (ch 16:10), the city remained in Canaanite hands (Jgs 1:29) for centuries. Consequently it could not be used by the Levites, to whom it had been assigned (Jos 21:21; 1 Chr 6:67), until the reign of Solomon. At that time one of the last Pharaohs of the 21st dynasty captured the city and gave its ruins to Solomon as a dowry when his daughter was married

201. The conquest of Gezer, as depicted on an Assyrian relief

to the Hebrew king. The city was at once rebuilt (1 Ki 9:15, 16). When Solomon's kingdom split up into two states after his death, Gezer became part of the northern kingdom. Tiglath-pileser III conquered the city, as an inscribed relief from Calah shows (see fig. 201), and probably incorporated it in the Assyrian province of Megiddo. It played an important role as a strong fortress city in the wars of the Maccabees.

Ch. Clermont-Ganneau was the first correctly to identify *Tell Jezer* with ancient Gezer (Map VI, E-2). This identification was afterward confirmed by the discovery of 6 inscribed ancient boundary stones. Excavations were conducted by the Palestine Exploration Fund, directed by R. A. S. Macalister from 1902 to 1905 and 1907 to 1909 and by A. Rowe in 1934. Macalister made extremely important discoveries which were published in a superb manner. Of these may be mentioned a tunnel dug early in the 2d millennium B.C. which ran to a strong spring lying 94 ft. below the rock surface. A reservoir large enough to hold 600,000 gal. was also uncovered. An interesting open-air sanctuary was discovered which has been plausibly explained as a high place (fig. 200). See High Place. It contained a whole row of pillars, several altars, many caves, and cup holes used for libation offerings. Among the important literary finds, the so-called Gezer Calendar of the 10th cent. B.C. deserves special mention as one of the oldest Hebrew inscriptions ever found in Palestine. In 1929 an ostracon (*see* Potsherd) was found which contains a few signs in proto-Semitic script (*see* Writing).

Lit.: Excavation reports: R. A. S. Macalister, *The Excavation of Gezer* (London, 1912), 3 vols.; A. Rowe *PEFQS* 67 (1935), 19-33. On the Gezer Calendar: W. F. Albright, *BASOR* 92 (1943), 16-26.

Gezrites. *See* Girzites.

Ghost. A frequently occurring term in the KJV used in the more or less archaic sense of "spirit," "breath," "life." It frequently appears in the expression Holy Ghost, in which it is the translation of the Gr. *pneuma* (Mt 1:18; 3:11; Mk 12:36; etc.). Elsewhere in the KJV, "ghost" is used in various euphemistic expressions connected with dying, such as in the expression "give up the ghost." This phrase is the translation of: (1) the Heb. *gawa'* (Gen 25:8; etc.), "to expire"; (2) the Gr. *ekpneō* (Mk 15:37; etc.), "to breathe out," "to expire"; (3) the Gr. *ekpsuchō* (Acts 5:5, 10; etc.), "to expire." In the RSV the term is found only 3 times: in Is 29:4, as the translation of the Heb. *'ôb,* "familiar spirit" (an underworld demon that communicates messages through a medium or an enchantress, etc.); and in Mt 14:26 and Mk 6:49 of the Gr. *phantasma,* "specter," "apparition," "phantom." *See* Spirit.

Ghost, Holy. *See* Holy Spirit.

Giah (gī′à). [Heb. *Gîach,* "bubbling spring."] A place near Gibeon in the territory of the tribe of Benjamin (2 Sa 2:24); not identified.

Giant. Persons of great stature are mentioned several times in the Bible. The *Rephaim are mentioned as "a people great . . . and tall as the *Anakim" (Deut 2:10, 11, 21, RSV). The *Nephilim (Gen 6:4; KJV "giants") were so tall that the 12 Hebrew spies felt like grasshoppers in comparison with them, and were so regarded by that people (Num 13:33). Individual giants are mentioned, such as Og, king of Bashan, whose bed (or sarcophagus) was 9 cu. long and 4 cu. wide (Deut 3:11), Goliath of Gath, whose height was 6 cu. and a span (1 Sa 17:4), and Ishbi-benob (2 Sa 21:16).

Giants, Valley of. *See* Rephaim, Valley of.

Gibbar (gīb′är). [Heb. *Gibbar.*] A town to which 95 descendants of its former inhabitants returned from Babylonia (Ezr 2:20). The name may be either a variant form of Gibeon, or a scribal error for the same name, as the parallel passage in Neh 7:25 reads.

Gibbethon (gīb′ê-thŏn). [Heb. *Gibbethôn,* "mound" or "height."] A town in the southern territory of Dan (Jos 19:44). It was assigned to the Kohathite Levites (ch 21:20-23), but was later taken by the Philistines. Nadab, king of Israel, made an attempt to reconquer it but was assassinated by Baasha during the siege of the city (1 Ki 15:27). Some 24 years later another Israelite army besieged the city in an attempt to reconquer it from the Philistines. When the army heard that the Israelite king Elah had been murdered by Zimri, it made their commander, Omri, king of Israel (ch 16:15-17). Gibbethon is identified with *Tell el-Melât,* about 6 mi. south of Lydda (Map VI, E-2).

Gibea (gīb′ê-à). [Heb. *Gib'a',* "hill."] A grandson of Caleb the son of Hezron (1 Chr 2:49); he may have given his name to a place called Gibeah. *See* Gibeah, 1.

Gibeah (gīb′ê-à), KJV once **Gibeath** (gīb′ê-ăth). [Heb. *Gib'ah,* "hill."]

1. A city in the hill country of Judah apparently somewhere southeast of Hebron (Jos 15:57); not identified. *See* Gibea.

2. A city in the territory of Benjamin. Its name was "Gibeah of Benjamin" (Jgs 20:10 [Hebrew here is *Geba',* the final *h* having been dropped]; 1 Sa 13:15; etc.), "Gibeah of the children of Benjamin" (2 Sa 23:29), and "Gibeah of Saul" (1 Sa 11:4; 15:34; etc.). The inhabitants of the city are described as having been extremely wicked during the period of the judges. As a result they brought upon themselves and upon the whole tribe a fratricidal war in which they were almost exterminated (Jgs 19; 20). Gibeah became important as the home town of Saul, Israel's first king, whose city of residence it remained during his reign (1 Sa 10:26; 15:34; 22:6; 23:19). It is mentioned by

202. The mound of *Tell el-Fûl,* Saul's ancient capital, Gibeah

the prophets Isaiah and Hosea, in whose time it was still an inhabited city (Is 10:29; Hos 9:9; 10:9).

Gibeah was located on the highway from Jerusalem to Ramah (Jgs 19:13; Jos. *Ant.* v. 2. 8), and has been identified with *Tell el-Fûl* (fig. 202), a prominent hill about 4 mi. north of Jerusalem (Map VI, E-3). W. F. Albright, excavating for the American Schools of Oriental Research in 1922 and 1933, uncovered parts of Saul's small castle, which was a two-story citadel estimated to be 170 x 114 ft. in size. The outer walls, built in case-mate style, were 6 to 7 ft. thick. Protruding towers at the four corners gave strength to the structure, which served as a model for other Israelite fortresses of that period (see fig. 421). The largest hall of this building, measuring 7 x 25 ft., was probably the audience chamber of Saul, where David played his lyre for the king.

Lit.: W. F. Albright, *AASOR* 4 (1924), 1-89; *BASOR* 52 (1933), 6-12.

3. A hill or village in the territory of Ephraim, belonging to Phinehas. It became the burial place of the high priest Eleazar, Aaron's son (Jos 24:33, KJV "hill"; Jos. *Ant.* v. 1. 29).

Gibeath (gĭb'ē-ăth). [Heb. *Gibe'ath*, "hill."] A town in the territory of Benjamin (Jos 18:28, KJV), usually identified with Gibeah of Saul. *See* Gibeah, 2.

Gibeathelohim. [Heb. *Gibe'ath 'Elohim*, "hill of God."] Either a variant name of Saul's home town Gibeah (*see* Gibeah, 2), or a hill near the town (1 Sa 10:5). The KJV renders the name "hill of God."

Gibeath-haaraloth (gĭb'ē-ăth-hȧ-ā'rȧ-lŏth). [Heb. *Gib'ath Ha'aralôth*, "hill of the fore-skins."] According to the RSV, a place west of the Jordan that received its name from the fact that the Israelites were circumcised there immediately after they crossed the Jordan and entered the Promised Land. They had not during their wilderness wandering performed this rite, which was a sign of the covenant with God (Jos 5:3). The place is called "hill of the foreskins" in the KJV. It has not been identified.

Gibeathite (gĭb'ē-ăth-īt). [Heb. *Gib'athi.*] An inhabitant of Gibeah (1 Chr 12:3, KJV). The RSV reads simply "of Gibeah."

Gibeon (gĭb'ē-ŭn). [Heb. *Gib'ôn*. The name occurs on 27 ancient Heb. inscriptions found at Gibeon.] An old Canaanite city, the chief city of a confederation to which Chephirah, Beeroth, and Kiriath-jearim belonged (Jos 9:17). The early inhabitants

203. The great well shaft at *ej-Jib*, ancient Gibeon

of Gibeon were *Hivites (ch 11:19), "of the remnant of the *Amorites" (2 Sa 21:2). Using false pretenses they succeeded in concluding a treaty of friendship with Joshua and the children of Israel. When the Israelites discovered the deceit, they made slaves of the Gibeonites; nevertheless, they honored the treaty and rendered military aid when the Gibeonites were attacked by other Canaanite cities (Jos 9:1 to 10:11). The city of Gibeon lay in the territory of Benjamin (ch 18:25), but was assigned to the family of Aaron (ch 21:17). This was probably the reason why the tabernacle was located there during the reign of David and Solomon, before the Temple was built (1 Chr 16:39, 40; 21:29; 2 Chr 1:3, 6, 13). Although his ancestors had lived at Gibeon for some time (1 Chr 8:29; 9:35), Saul unjustifiably massacred some of its inhabitants; consequently 7 of his sons were executed in David's time to satisfy the Gibeonites (2 Sa 21:1-9). At Gibeon David fought a battle against Ishbosheth (ch 2:8-17, 24; 3:30), and defeated the Philistines (1 Chr 14:16); near there Joab murdered Amasa (2 Sa 20:8-10). In the sanctuary at Gibeon Solomon received a divine vision (1 Ki 3:4-15). The city seems to have declined in importance later. It is not mentioned again until after the Exile (Neh 7:25). Its inhabitants helped Nehemiah to erect the city wall of Jerusalem (ch 3:7).

The site is now conclusively identified with the present village of *ej-Jib*, 6 mi. northwest of Jerusalem (Map VI, E-3). It is a steep hill, consisting of well-stratified layers of limestone rock formations, and lies in a broad valley. The village of *ej-Jib* is found on the summit and slopes of the hill. Excavations have been carried out since 1956 by J. B. Pritchard. He has cleared out a great well shaft, 38 ft. in diameter and 82 ft. deep, with a remarkable staircase of 79 steps leading to the bottom (fig. 203). The debris removed from the shaft brought to light numerous jar handles inscribed with the name of Gibeon. The bottom of the shaft gave access to a spring. Access to a second spring at the slope of the hill was obtained by means of a rock-hewn tunnel, 168 ft. in length, which Pritchard cleared out during the first season of the excavations.

Lit.: J. B. Pritchard, BA 19 (1956), 65-75; University Museum Bulletin 21 (1957), 2-26; 22 (1958), 12-24.

The high place of Gibeon may have been the neighboring hill of Nebī-Samwîl, although this is by no means a certain identification. The "pool of Gibeon" (2 Sa 2:13), or "the great waters that are in Gibeon" (Jer 41:12), may be identified with the tank called el-Birkeh, 11 x 7 ft. in size, cut in the solid rock, lying to the west of the hill. Others have identified it with a lake of 6 to 8 acres, which is formed in the shallow part of the valley every year by the winter rains. The wilderness of Gibeon (2 Sa 2:24) was either the somewhat barren plateau between Gibeon and Ramah or the desert toward the Jordan Valley farther away.

Gibeonites (gĭb'ĕ-ŭn-īts). [Heb. Gib'onîm.] The inhabitants of Gibeon. However, the term may also have included the people of Chephirah, Beeroth, and Kiriath-jearim (2 Sa 21:1-4; cf. Jos 9:3, 7, 17), the other cities of the *Hivite confederacy.

Giblites. See Gebalites.

Giddalti (gĭ-dăl'tī). [Heb. Giddaltî, "I have magnified (God)."] A Levite singer, son of Heman, and the head of the 22d of the 24 companies of singers into which David organized the choir for Solomon's Temple (1 Chr 25:4, 29).

Giddel (gĭd'ĕl). [Heb. Giddel, "he (God) has made great."]

1. Head of a family of Nethinim, some of whom returned with Zerubbabel from Babylonia (Ezr 2:47; Neh 7:49).

2. Head of a family of Solomon's servants, some of whom returned with Zerubbabel from Babylonia (Ezr 2:56; Neh 7:58).

Gideon (gĭd'ĕ-ŭn), KJV of NT **Gedeon** (gĕd'ĕ-ŭn). [Heb. Gid'ôn, "hewer" or "feller"; Gr. Gedeon.] A judge and deliverer of the Hebrews, son of Joash of the family of Abiezer, living at Ophrah in western Manasseh (Jgs 6:11). During an oppression by the Midianites, Gideon, while threshing wheat in the wine press at Ophrah to hide his harvest from the Midianites, was called by an angel of the Lord to deliver Israel. He responded with a sacrifice, and the following night threw down the local altar of Baal and built one dedicated to Yahweh (Jgs 6:12-27). The enraged local inhabitants protested violently and demanded Gideon's death, but his father defended him by insisting that Baal should be able to defend himself. It was this event that won for Gideon the name Jerubbaal (jĕr'ŭb-bā'ăl) [Heb. Yerubba'al, "let Baal contend against him"] (vs 28-32, RSV); later, when the word "Baal" was abhorred, this name was changed to Jerubbesheth (jĕr'ŭb-bē'shĕth) [Heb. Yerubbesheth, "let the shameful thing contend"] (2 Sa 11:21).

After having received his divine appointment Gideon summoned the men of Manasseh, Asher, Zebulun, and Naphtali for an attack against the Midianites (Jgs 6:33-35). Then, becoming fearful, he requested a confirmation of his divine call, which was granted him (vs 36-40). So that the people might recognize that the victory would not be the result of human resourcefulness or strength, God directed that the fighting forces be reduced, with the result that all but 300 men were eliminated. With the 300 men, blowing their horns, shouting, and breaking the jars in which they had concealed torches, Gideon attacked at night. Caught by surprise, the Midianites fell into confusion, every soldier fighting his fellow soldier, and then the army fled. The Ephraimites, instructed by Gideon to block the escape routes at the Jordan, caught two of the Midianite princes and sent their heads to Gideon. Gideon continued the pursuit across the Jordan, capturing and killing two more Midianite princes (chs 7:1 to 8:21). This notable victory later became known as the "day of Midian" (Is 9:4; cf. 10:26; Ps 83:11).

Gideon refused the people's offer to make him king, recognizing that God was their only king (Jgs 8:22, 23). He acted foolishly, however, by making an ephod of the jewelry of the Israelites, and displaying it in his home town of Ophrah. This ephod became an object of worship and a means of seduction to idolatry (vs 24-27). He had a large harem and seems to have lived on a grand scale. After a judgeship of 40 years, he died at an advanced age and was buried at Ophrah (vs 28, 32). After Gideon's death Abimelech, his son by a concubine, slew all but one of the sons of Gideon and made himself king (vs 30, 31; ch 9:1-6).

Gideoni (gĭd'ĕ-ō'nī). [Heb. Gid'oni.] Father of a prince of the tribe of Benjamin during the wilderness wandering (Num 1: 11; 2:22; 7:60, 65; 10:24).

Gidom (gī'dŏm). [Heb. *Gid'om*.] A place in Benjamin between Gibeah and the rock of Rimmon (Jgs 20:43-45); not identified.

Gier Eagle. *See* Carrion Vulture.

Gifts. Concrete objects or special favors given to a person without his having earned it. Various terms are translated "gift" in the Bible with probably originally fine shades of distinction in meaning between some of them of which we no longer have accurate knowledge apart from observation of the context in which the words are used. Gifts were given by a father to a son (Gen 25:6), as were dowries to daughters (1 Ki 9:16, RSV), and a marriage present by the bridegroom to the bride's father (Gen 34:12; Ex 22:17; etc.). Tribute given by the defeated to their conqueror was sometimes referred to as a gift (2 Sa 8:6, KJV). Giving was a method of expressing joy and good will (Est 9:22), and gifts were brought to the Temple altar in worship (Mt 5:23, 24; Lk 21:1). In the KJV "gift" often stands for "bribes" (Ex 23:8; Deut 16:19; etc.). God's supreme gift to men is His Son. Through Him men are saved and sanctified (Jn 3:16; 1 Cor 1:30). The Holy Spirit is also one of God's choicest gifts (Jn 14:16, 26; 16:7-11; Acts 2:38); and through the Spirit come "spiritual gifts," such as healing, miracles, prophecy, tongues, teaching ability, and—best of all—love (1 Cor 12 to 14; cf. Rom 5:5). Through the Spirit come also faith, joy, peace, long-suffering, gentleness, goodness, meekness, temperance (Gal 5:22; Eph 2:8). God's gifts to us, whether temporal or spiritual, are fitly summed up in the apostle's words, "Every good gift and every perfect gift is from above" (Jas 1:17).

Gihon (gī'hŏn). [Heb. *Gîchôn*, "gusher."]

1. One of the four rivers of Eden (Gen 2:13). Identification of this river is impossible in spite of the observation that it flowed around the land of Ethiopia, or Cush. The appearance of the face of the earth was radically changed at the time of the Flood, making identification of prediluvian rivers with known rivers impossible.

2. A subterranean spring in the Kidron Valley, now called *'Ain Sittī Maryam,* usually translated freely "Virgin's Spring." It is a dependable spring, with continuous but periodically varying flow. The pre-Israelite Jebusites obtained access to the spring from within the city by dig-

204. The entrance to the Virgin's Fount, the Biblical spring Gihon

ging a horizontal tunnel westward from the spring 50 ft. into the rock, where they opened a 40-foot shaft through which the water could be drawn up. At the upper end of the shaft was a platform connected with the surface of the city by a sloping passage 125 ft. long. It was probably through this tunnel and shaft that Joab gained access to the city, conquering it for David (2 Sa 5:8; 1 Chr 11: 6). The Gihon spring was the scene of Solomon's coronation (1 Ki 1:33 ff.). King Hezekiah dug a tunnel (see fig. 444) from the spring to a pool in the lower part of the city (*see* Siloam) and thus created a lower spring in addition to the original spring. The cave containing the upper spring was then closed and its location concealed (2 Chr 32:30; 2 Ki 18: 17). Maps XVII, XVIII; fig. 204.

Gilalai (gĭl'ȧ-lī). [Heb. *Gilalay,* meaning uncertain.] A Levite musician who took part in the dedication of the wall of Jerusalem in Nehemiah's time (Neh 12:36).

Gilboa (gĭl-bō'ȧ). [Heb. *Gilboa'.*] A mountain ridge about 8 mi. long running from Jezreel first southeast, and then south. It now bears the name *Jebel Fuqû'ah.* It is between 3 and 5 mi. wide, and the highest point is about 1,700 ft. above sea level. Its northern and eastern slopes are precipitous and rugged, but the western surface is gently sloping and fertile. On the gentle western slopes barley, wheat, figs, and olives grow. The ridge forms the watershed between the Plain of Esdraelon and the smaller plain of Beth-shean. The ancient name Gilboa is preserved in the village of *Jelbōn,* which lies on the slopes of one of the ridges. Gilboa is famous as the battlefield on which the Israelites pitched their camp during the battle against the Philistines, in which King Saul lost his life (1 Sa 28:4; 31:1, 8; 2 Sa 1:6, 21; 21:12; 1 Chr 10:1, 8). Map XVI, D-3.

Gilead (gĭl′ê-ăd). [Heb. *Gil'ad,* "hard" or "rough."]

1. A son of Machir, grandson of Manasseh, and founder of a tribal family (Num 26:29, 30; Jos 17:1).

2. The father of Jephthah (Jgs 11:1).

3. A Gadite (1 Chr 5:14).

4. The mountainous region between the tableland of Moab and the river Yarmuk, an area about 70 mi. long and approximately 20 to 25 mi. wide. The name was probably derived from that of a mountain south of the Jabbok, which still bears the name *Jebel Jele'ād.* The territory was divided into two parts by the river Jabbok (Jos 12:2). The southern section was occupied by the tribe of Gad and the northern by the half tribe of Manasseh that resided in Transjordan (Deut 3:12, 13; Jos 13:24-31). Since Gilead was the most important region of Transjordan, the whole of Transjordan was sometimes designated by this name (Deut 34:1; Jos 22:9; Jgs 20:1; 2 Sa 2:9). The country was well suited to cattle (Num 32:1; 1 Chr 5:9), was thickly forested in parts (see 2 Sa 18:6, 8, 9), and was famous for its balm (Gen 37:25; Jer 8:22). Map VI, D-4.

5. A mountain on the edge of the Valley of Jezreel (Jgs 7:3; cf. chs 7:1; 6:33). Some think that Gilead is a misreading of Gilboa, because the region of Gilead was on the east side of the Jordan and there was a mountain ridge west of the Jordan by the name of Gilboa. However, there may have been a mountain by the name of Gilead adjacent to the Valley of Jezreel, as suggested by the name of a stream now known as *Nahr Jālūd,* which

205. In a forest of Gilead

flows along the northern foot of Mount Gilboa and passes Beth-shean.

6. A city in the region of Gilead (Hos 6:8; 12:11); not identified.

Gilead, Balm of. *See* Balm.

Gileadite (gĭl′ê-ăd-īt). [Heb. *Gil'adî.*] A descendant of *Gilead.

Gilgal (gĭl′găl). [Heb. *Haggilgal,* "the (stone) circle."] The name of several places in western Palestine, but scholars do not agree as to the number of Gilgals involved in the various texts mentioning that name. At least three Gilgals are to be distinguished:

1. The site of Israel's first encampment after the crossing of the Jordan, and the place of departure for their various military campaigns under Joshua (Jos 4:19-24; 5:10; 10:6, 7, 15, 43). A town seems to have been built on that site, which lay on the northern boundary of Judah (ch 15:7). Samuel included it in his annual circuits and offered sacrifices there (1 Sa 7:16), and Saul used it as a rallying place for the Israelites in a battle against the Philistines. It was here that in rash haste Saul offered sacrifices, and was told by Samuel that he could · not become the founder of a dynasty (1 Sa 13:4-14). It was here also that, after the battle against the Amalekites, Saul met Samuel, who told him that he had lost his right to the throne for his failure to carry out completely God's directions (chs 15:20-23; 16:14). When David returned from Transjordan after the breakdown of the rebellion of Absalom, representatives of the tribe of Judah came to Gilgal to conduct the king across the Jordan and to welcome him home (2 Sa 19:15, 40).

Later Gilgal became a place of idolatry for which it was denounced (Hos 4:15; 9:15; 12:11; Amos 4:4; 5:5). The last mention of the site is in Neh 12:29 (called "Beth-gilgal" (bĕth'gĭl′gal), RSV; "house of Gilgal," KJV), from which we learn that it had been resettled after the Babylonian exile. The site has not yet been definitely identified. The name of *Jiljûlieh* (in which the name "Gilgal" is preserved) has sometimes been given by modern Arabs to *en-Nitleh,* 2⅓ mi. southeast of ancient Jericho, but this site shows no archeological remains going back to the Exodus period. However, such remains have been found at *Khirbet el-Mefjer,* 2 mi. northeast of ancient Jericho, and several scholars are inclined to identify it with Gilgal. (J. Muilenburg, *BASOR* 140 [1955], 11-27). Map VI, E-4.

2. The place from which Elijah and Elisha departed on their last journey together before Elijah's translation. Since they went from Gilgal *down* to Bethel, the Gilgal in the Jordan Valley cannot be meant (2 Ki 2:1, 2). The place has been identified with *Jiljilia*, 7 mi. northwest of Bethel. Whether the Gilgal of ch 4:38 is 1 or 2 is uncertain.

3. A Canaanite city, mentioned after Dor in Jos 12:23 (KJV). It was in the Plain of Sharon according to the context. It has been identified with *Jiljûlieh*, 14 mi. northeast of Jaffa. For "Gilgal" the RSV, following the Septuagint, here reads "Galilee." Map VI, D-2.

Gilo. *See* Giloh.

Giloh (gī′lō). [Heb. *Giloh*.] A town in the hill country of Judah (Jos 15:51), now probably *Khirbet Jâlâ*, only a short distance northwest of Hebron. It was the home of Ahithophel (2 Sa 15:12). It is called Gilo (gī′lō) in ch 23:34, RSV.

Gilonite (gī′lō-nīt). [Heb. *Gîlonî*.] An inhabitant of Giloh. Ahithophel, David's counselor, was a Gilonite (2 Sa 15:12; 23:34).

Gimel. [Heb. *gimel*, "camel."] The 3d letter of the Hebrew alphabet, written ג, corresponding in pronunciation to the English letter *g* (as in "game"). It appears in Ps 119, KJV, as the heading of the 3d stanza, in which in Hebrew each line begins with a word having ג as its initial letter. *See* Aleph.

Gimzo (gĭm′zō). [Heb. *Gimzô*.] A town in Judah, conquered by the Philistines during the reign of King Ahaz (2 Chr 28:18), now *Jimzū*, about 3 mi. southeast of Lydda.

Gin. The translation of: (1) the Heb. *môqesh*, "bait (of fowler)," "bird trap," or "snare" (Ps 140:5; 141:9; Amos 3:5, KJV); (2) the Heb. *pach*, "bird trap" or "snare" (Job 18:9; Is 8:14, KJV). Ancient monuments depict several types of snares or traps for catching birds.

Ginath (gī′năth). [Heb. *Gînath*.] A man whose son Tibni was the rival of King Omri of Israel (1 Ki 16:22).

Ginnetho. *See* Ginnethoi.

Ginnethoi (gĭn′ĕ-thō′ī), KJV **Ginnetho** (gĭn′ĕ-thō). [Heb. *Ginnethôy*.] A chief priest who returned with Zerubbabel from the Babylonian exile (Neh 12:4). Later a family of priests is mentioned by the name of Ginnethon (v 16). Since the difference in spelling between the two names in Hebrew is only the final *yod* or *nun,* two Hebrew letters very similar in postexilic script, it

is usually thought that Ginnethon is identical with Ginnethoi.

Ginnethon (gĭn′ĕ-thŏn). [Heb. *Ginnethôn.*]
1. A priestly family in the days of the high priest Joiakim (Neh 12:16), probably identical with the *Ginnethoi of Neh 12:4.
2. A priest who set his seal to Nehemiah's covenant (Neh 10:6).

Girdle. The translation of several Hebrew and Greek words meaning variously, "sash," "loincloth," "girdle," "belt," or "band." Part of the high priest's garments was a girdle made of fine linen and of blue, purple, and scarlet materials (Ex 39:29). The prophet Elijah wore a leather girdle (2 Ki 1:8). In vision John the revelator saw Christ wearing a golden girdle (Rev 1:13). *See* Belt; Clothing.

Girgashites (gûr′gȧ-shīts), KJV once **Girgasite** (gûr′gȧ-sīt). [Heb. *Girgashî*.] One of the tribes of western Palestine who were descendants of Canaan (Gen 10:15, 16; 15:21; Deut 7:1; Jos 3:10; 24:11; Neh 9:8). Nothing is known of these people from extra-Biblical sources, but the frequent occurrence of the personal names *Grgshy, Grgsh,* and *Grgshm* in the vowelless Punic texts from Carthage, and of the name *Grgsh* in the vowelless texts of Ugarit, seems to indicate that the Girgashites were closely related to the Phoenicians. Such a deduction would be in perfect agreement with Gen 10:15, 16, where Sidon is mentioned in the genealogy as a son of Canaan.

Girgasite. *See* Girgashites.

Girzites (gûr′zīts), KJV **Gezrites** (gĕz′rīts). [Heb. *Gizrî*. The *r* and the *z* are transposed in pre-Masoretic Hebrew.] An unidentified non-Israelite tribe which lived in the south of Palestine, mentioned with the Amalekites and Geshurites (1 Sa 27:8); not identified.

Gishpa (gĭsh′pȧ), KJV **Gispa** (gĭs′pȧ). [Heb. *Gishpa'*.] An overseer of the Nethinim, or Temple servants, in Nehemiah's time (Neh 11:21).

Gispa. *See* Gishpa.

Gittah-hepher. *See* Gath-hepher.

Gittaim (gĭt′ȧ-īm). [Heb. *Gittayim*, "two wine presses."] A town in Benjamin, to which the inhabitants of Beeroth fled (2 Sa 4:3), probably in Saul's time, and possibly after he massacred the Gibeonites (ch 21:1), among whom were the people of Beeroth (see Jos 9:17). The town was inhabited after the Exile (Neh 11:33). It has not been identified with certainty.

Gittite (gĭt′ĭt). [Heb. *Gittî.*] An inhabitant of Gath (Jos 13:3; 2 Sa 6:10, 11; etc.).

Gittith (gĭt′ĭth). [Heb. *Gittîth.*] A term appearing in the titles of three psalms (Ps 8; 81; 84). For a long time it was considered to be the name of a musical instrument not identified. However, most scholars now agree that the term does not designate a musical instrument, but a melody or a style of singing.

Gizonite (gĭ′zŏ-nīt). [Heb. *Gizônî.*] A designation borne by Hashem, one of David's "mighty men" (1 Chr 11:34), not explained. No name of a place or country by the name of Gizon or Gizoh is known.

Glass. The rendering of: (1) The Heb. *zekôkîth* (Job 28:17, RSV), translated "crystal" in the KJV. The Hebrew term most probably means *glass,* as the cognate languages indicate. The manufacture of glass was understood in Egypt from the time before the Exodus, but glass was little used by the Hebrews of OT times, as archeological evidence shows. (2) The Gr. *hualos* (Rev 4:6; 15:2; 21:18, 21), "glass." In the Roman Empire period very beautiful objects of glass were in circulation and widely used.

"Glass" appears in other passages in the KJV but with the meaning *"mirror."

Gleaning. The act of picking or picking up that part of a given crop that may have been passed by or dropped in the process of harvesting. Hebrew vineyard owners and grain growers were instructed to leave gleanings for the poor (Lev 19:9, 10; 23:22; Ruth 2; cf. Jgs 8:2; Is 24:13; Jer 49:9; Mic 7:1).

Glede. *See* Buzzard.

Glory. In Biblical literature a term that expresses 2 general concepts: (1) "honor," "praise," "esteem," and those distinctive qualities that bring honor or excite admiration; (2) "brilliance" that emanates from or surrounds a radiant being or object, or "splendor." In the KJV the term appears as the translation of numerous Hebrew and Greek words, though most of these occur rather infrequently. Although these various Biblical words occasionally include certain shades of distinction not precisely delineated by the English word "glory," usually the original meaning is reasonably close to the English term and the context sufficiently clear to guide one to the intended thought.

In the OT, "glory" is the rendering most frequently of the Heb. *kabôd,* a noun that is quite close in meaning to the English word "glory." In its primary usage the Hebrew term denotes "esteem," "honor," "admiration," a meaning that is reflected in 29 passages where the word is simply translated "honour" in the KJV (Num 24:11; 1 Ki 3:13; etc.). With this significance "glory" appears in some contexts that speak of the honor and majesty that are linked with high position or royalty (Gen 45:13; Est 1:4, RSV; Is 8:7; etc.), or the honor that results from wealth (Est 5:11). In passages involving praise offered to the Lord, the term "glory" may refer to the honor and esteem that His worshipers ascribe to Him (1 Chr 16:28, 29; Ps 29:1, 2; etc.). Like its English counterpart, *kabôd* occasionally designates those attributes or characteristics that produce esteem or admiration. For example, when Moses asked to see the glory of God (Ex 33:18), the response of the Lord indicated that He regarded the virtues and graces of His character as His special "glory" (chs 33:19; 34:6, 7). The term is also used in referring to personal wealth and property (Gen 31:1; RSV "wealth") as well as to the honor or glory that results from such wealth. In addition to these uses, the Heb. *kabôd* also appears in contexts referring to the dazzling brilliance and light that accompanies the presence of God (Ex 24:16, 17; Eze 10:4; etc.).

A number of other Hebrew words have also been rendered sporadically as "glory." Among these the following are the most frequent: (1) *Hadar,* a close synonym of *kabôd.* The main emphasis of this term is upon "honor" and "esteem." In the KJV it is translated "glory" 7 times (Ps 90:16; Is 2:10, 19, 21; etc.), "honour" 5 times (Ps 8:5; 145:5; etc.), "majesty" 7 times (Ps 29:4; 45:3, 4; etc.), and occasionally "beauty" (Job 40:10; RSV "splendor"; Prov 20:29), "excellency" (Is 35:2; RSV "majesty"), "comeliness" (ch 53:2), etc. (2) *Hôd,* another synonym of Heb. *kabôd,* generally denoting "splendor," "majesty." In the KJV it is translated "glory" 9 times (1 Chr 16:27; RSV "honor"; Job 39:20; Ps 45:3; Zec 6:13; RSV "royal honor; etc.), "honour" 6 times (Ps 21:5; 104:1; Dan 11:21; etc.), "comeliness" once (Dan 10:8); "beauty" once (Hos 14:6); etc. (3) *Ṣebî,* a term generally emphasizing a glory and honor that excites admiration or pride (Is 13:19; Eze 20:6, 15; 25:9; etc.). (4) *Tiph'ereth,* "honor" that often emphasizes that which is beautiful; however, the term frequently refers merely to that which is especially prized. It is rendered "glory" 22 times in the KJV (1 Chr 22:5; Prov 16:31; 17:6; 19:11; 20:29; Is 60:7; etc.),

16 times "beauty" or "beautiful" (Ex 28: 2, 40; Is 52:1; 64:11; etc.), and occasionally "fair," "excellent," and "comely."

In the NT the usual Greek word for "glory" is *doxa*. In many of its occurrences *doxa* parallels the Heb. *kabôd* in meaning; but whereas the OT term usually emphasizes "honor" and related ideas, the NT *doxa* is often linked with "brilliance," such as the brightness or radiance that emanates from a brilliant light (1 Cor 15:41), the splendor that radiates from the presence of a heavenly being (Lk 9:32; Acts 22:11; RSV "brightness"; Rev 21:23; etc.), or the radiance that surrounds one who has been in the presence of God (Lk 9:31; 2 Cor 3:7; etc.). It is similarly used of the splendor of our future life and heavenly home (Rom 8:18; 2 Cor 4:17; 2 Ti 2:10; etc.) as well as of the glory of our resurrected bodies (1 Cor 15:43). In many contexts, however, the thought of the word is abstract and involves such concepts as "fame," "renown," and "honor" (Jn 7: 18; 8:50; etc.; cf. Jn 5:41, 44; 2 Cor 6:8, where the KJV translates *doxa* "honour"). Because of this significance *doxa* frequently occurs in various expressions of praise to God, in which men and angels ascribe honor and adoration to the Lord (Lk 2:14; Rom 11:36; etc.; cf. the command in Rev 14:7 to "give glory" to God). In still another sense, though obviously related, the word is found in other contexts with the meaning of "magnificence" or "grandeur" (Mt 4:8; Lk 12:27; etc.).

Gnat. The Greek word thus translated (*kōnōps*) is generally believed to designate a "gnat" or "mosquito," although Aristotle uses *kōnōps* of a certain worm found in wine (*Hist. An.* 5. 19). The word appears in a proverb in which the Pharisees are said to strain out a gnat, one of the smallest creatures, and swallow a camel, the biggest animal common in the Near East; meaning that these religionists were extremely careful to observe the smallest detail of every religious rule, while they were unconcerned about the essential matters (Mt 23:24).

In the RSV "gnat" appears also as a rendering of the Heb. *ken* and *kinnam*, the insect that plagued the Egyptians (Ex 8:16-18; Ps 105:31), and to which the inhabitants of the earth are likened (Is 51:6).

Go To. An archaic English interjection that usually introduces an invitation to participate in some activity. The phrase occurs 11 times in the KJV, but is not found in the RSV. In Gen 11:3, 4, 7 and 38:16,

the expression is used to translate a Hebrew interjection that is approximately equivalent to "arise" or "come on" (as it is rendered in Ex 1:10; RSV "come"). In 2 Ki 5:5 the Hebrew actually contains 2 synonymous commands each signifying "go" or "depart" (RSV "go now"). The expression occurs elsewhere in Jgs 7:3; Jas 4:13; 5:1.

Goad. A long stick with a sharpened or metal-tipped point, used to urge cattle forward. Shamgar, probably using an ox-goad (Heb. *malmad*) as a spear, slew with it 600 Philistines (Jgs 3:31). The "goad" of 1 Sa 13:21 (Heb. *darban*) is most probably the metal point of the goad. The "pricks" of Acts 26:14 (Gr. *kentra*) were "goads."

Lit.: W. F. Albright, *AASOR* 21-22 (1943), 33, pl. 62:2.

Goah (gō'ȧ), KJV **Goath** (gō'ăth). [Heb. *Goʻah.*] A place near Jerusalem (Jer 31: 39); not identified.

Goat. [Heb. *ʻez, ʻattûd, ṣaphîr, śaʻîr, tayish;* Aramaic *ʻez, ṣephîr;* Gr. *eriphos, eriphion, tragos.*] The Biblical goat is, as far as it is known, in all cases the *Capra mambrica,* which is somewhat larger than the European goat. Its hair is generally black, so that a goat's hair could be confused with human hair (1 Sa 19:13). The Palestinian goat has ears that hang down and horns that are generally curved back. Goats with more than one color were an exception (Gen 30:32). The meat of young he-goats was popular; both Gideon and Manoah prepared a young goat for the angel of the Lord (Jgs 6:19; 13:15-23). The milk of goats was used as a drink (Prov 27:27), the skins were used as containers for water and wine (*see* Bottle), and the hair was woven into tent cloth (Ex 35:26). The he-goat was also used for sacrifices (Num 7:16; etc.). In the symbolic vision of Daniel a he-goat was used to represent the Hellenistic empire of Alexander (Dan 8:5, 21), and in Mt 25: 32 goats symbolize evil men. *See* Goat, Wild.

Goat, Wild. [Heb. *yaʻel.*] An animal found in the high hills (Ps 104:18) and rocks (Job 39:1), hence in the rocky wilderness near En-gedi (1 Sa 24:1, 2). It has been identified with the mountain goat, the *Capra walu* or *Capra nubiana* (F. S. Bodenheimer, *Animal Life in Palestine* [1935], p. 93). The animal is similar to the European ibex, but somewhat lighter of color, and its horns are more slender, are curved, and even wrinkled. The Heb. *ʼaqqô* of

Deut 14:5 is also rendered "wild goat" in the modern translations, but some define *'aqqô* simply as "young goat," seeing in the Akkadian *unîqu*, "young goat," a cognate word.

Goath. *See* Goah.

Goat's Hair. A material used for weaving coarse cloth. Curtains of goat's hair were used as protective coverings for the tabernacle (Ex 26:7; 36:14). Certain items used by warriors were made of goat's hair (Num 31:20), probably tents or some article of clothing. Pillows were also made of that material (1 Sa 19:13, 16). Near Eastern Bedouins still weave tent cloth of goat's hair. The tent shown in fig. 492 is made of this material.

Goatskin. In the RSV OT a rendering of the Heb. *'ôr tachash* (Ex 25:5; 26:14; Num 4:6-14; etc.), translated "badgers' skin" in the KJV (*see* Badger). The hairy skin of a goat was used as a garment in cases of extreme poverty (Heb 11:37). Goatskins were also used for leather bottles. *See* Bottle.

Gob (gŏb). [Heb. *Gôb*.] A town of the Philistines, where David had 2 encounters with the Philistines (2 Sa 21:18, 19); not identified. It is mentioned in the *Amarna Letters as *Gubbu*. For "Gob" the parallel text in 1 Chr 20:4 reads "Gezer." Gob may have been near the better-known Gezer, the name by which the battles later became known.

Goblet. A rendering of: (1) The Heb. *'aggan* (a loan word from the Egyptian *ikn*), "bowl" (Song 7:2, KJV). The context suggests a large deep bowl or basin. (2) The Heb. *keli*, "utensil," "vessel," "receptacle" (Est 1:7, RSV), in the context, cups in which wine was served.

God. [Heb. *'El, 'Elohim, 'Elôah, YHWH;* Aramaic *'Elah;* Gr. *Theos.* See *SDACom* 1:170-173.]

Philosophy and religion have met their greatest challenge in their endeavors to define God. Philosophy, for the most part, has equated God with "first cause," "natural law," "cosmic force," or at best has accepted God as "ultimate reality." The Bible attributes personality to God, and describes Him as creator, sustainer, lawgiver, judge, ruler, and father (Gen 18:25; Deut 33:2; Ps 103:13; 104:27-29; Is 40:28; Dan 4:17; Acts 17:25-28; Rom 8:15). Religious philosophy describes God by such terms as "omnipotent," "omniscient," and "omnipresent." These terms teach certain important truths about God.

The existence of God is universally attested by His creation, and is witnessed to by the nature of man (Rom 1:19, 20; 2:14, 15), but this witness, apart from the revelation that God has given of Himself in the Scriptures, provides but a limited and often erroneous concept, and in the Bible itself God has revealed only as much of Himself as we need to know. But to this we must go for our definition of God. Speculation beyond revelation is useless and even dangerous.

The Bible portrays God as a being who is able to create, to communicate, to love. God's relationship to Abraham illustrates this warm, personal relationship. God had a plan for Abraham as expressed in the "covenant" He made with him. Six times this covenant is repeated: 1st, when God called Abraham to leave his family home (Gen 12:1-3); 2d, when Abraham arrived in the land to which God had called him (vs 6, 7); 3d, when Abraham had experienced the disappointment of Lot's selfish choice (ch 13:14-17); 4th, when Abraham needed his confidence restored after the battle of the kings (ch 15:1, 5, 6); 5th, when Abraham had sinned and needed forgiveness (ch 17:1-8); and 6th, when Abraham had proved his faithfulness in a severe crisis (ch 22:15-18). Others experienced this same kind of friendship (Ex 33:11; Num 14:13, 14; Ps 139:7-10; Is 40:28, 29; etc.).

The God of the Bible is portrayed as a God of love (Jn 3:16; 1 Jn 4:7, 8; etc.). He is described as "merciful and gracious, longsuffering, and abundant in goodness and truth, keeping mercy for thousands, forgiving iniquity and transgression and sin" (Ex 34:6, 7), yet also as a God of justice who will "by no means clear the guilty" (v 7). These same 2 aspects are set forth in the NT statement: "Behold therefore the goodness and severity of God" (Rom 11:22).

The OT witness regarding God is significant and revealing. In an age when the gods of the nations were represented as being earthy and sensual, the OT writers set forth the ethical nature of God (Ps 24:4; Hab 1:13). They also saw God as universal rather than tribal, and as one God rather than a proliferation of competing deities (Gen 14:22; Deut 6:5; Is 45:25; 66:1; Dan 4:17). Man's conception of God could not be complete until He revealed Himself in the person of Jesus. "No man hath seen God at any time; the only begotten Son, which is in the bosom of the Father, he hath declared him" (Jn 1:18). Thus the most complete information man may find about God is not to be found in nature, or in personal experience, or even in the scrolls of the prophets of old, but in the Gospel narratives, and in the teachings of the apostles. These revelations are the norm by which all other revelations of God must be measured.

This revelation is described in Jesus' instruction to His disciples (Jn 14:1-10), in the prayer of Jesus for His disciples (ch 17), and in Heb 1:1-5. To a world that misunderstood God, Jesus portrayed His Father's character (Mt 5:44, 45; Lk 1:78, 79; 6:35). In the sacrifice of Christ was seen the infinite wisdom, love, justice, and mercy of God. An understanding and appreciation of this will not only inform but transform (2 Cor 3:18; Eph 3:14-19; Col 1:9-11).

God is portrayed as One who demands much but who gives freely (Mt 16:24; Rom 8:32). He expects obedience, but pays an infinite price to make obedience possible (Ex 23:21; Deut 11:27-28; Is 5:4; Hos 14:4; Jn 3:16). He has an immutable law, but He supplies inexhaustible grace (Mt 5:17-19; Rom 5:20; Php 4:13). He hates sin with bitter hatred, but loves the sinner with wonderful love (Ps 101:3; Is 63:9; Jer 31:3; Rom 2:8, 9; 9:25). He is the Creator and sustainer of the limitless universe, yet He is the anxious father waiting at the gate for the prodigal's return (Ps 33:6, 13, 14; 104:27, 28; Is 44:22; Lk 15:20). He challenges the intellect of the most brilliant men the world has known, yet He accepts the devotion of a little child (Job 36 to 41; Is 45:20, 21; Jer 9:12; Ps 103:13; Mt 7:11). Jesus referred to Him as merciful (Lk 6:36), concerned about human needs (Mt 6:32), generous (ch 7:11), loving (Jn 3:16), spiritual (ch 4:24).

Occasionally the Bible writers break forth in rhapsodies of praise to God. What the prose of intellect fails to express the poetry of praise is able to portray. After describing God's plan for saving men, Paul declared, "O the depth of the riches both of the wisdom and knowledge of God! how unsearchable are his judgments, and his ways past finding out! For who hath known the mind of the Lord? or who hath been his counsellor? or who hath first given to him, and it shall be recompensed unto him again? For of him, and through him, and to him, are all things: to whom be glory for ever. Amen" (Rom 11:33-36).

God Forbid. An archaic English interjection indicating shocked disapproval. Grammatically, the phrase implies an abbreviated but pious prayer or wish that God might intervene and prevent the occurrence of an action just mentioned. However, one might well question the appropriateness of the expression as an exclamation, since its casual use would be forbidden by the 3d commandment.

In the OT the exclamation occurs in a number of passages in the KJV as the translation of the Heb. *chalilah,* literally, a "profane" or "unthinkable" thing (Gen 44:7; Jos 22:29; 1 Sa 12:23; 14:45; 20:2; etc.). Usually, the RSV translates this Hebrew term with more appropriate renderings, such as "Far be it from . . . ," "Far from it!" etc. (compare similar translations in the KJV in Gen 18:25; 1 Sa 2:30; etc.). In a few places the KJV translates *chalilah* "the Lord forbid" (1 Sa 24:6; 26: 11; 1 Ki 21:3).

In the NT the expression is used by the KJV to translate the Gr. *mē genoito,* an exclamation meaning "may it not happen" or "may it not be." In the RSV the same exclamation is usually translated by such expressions as "By no means!" "Never!" or "Certainly not!" The phrase is found almost exclusively in the writings of Paul (Rom 3:4, 6, 31; 1 Cor 6:15; Gal 2:17; 3:21; etc.); outside of Paul's epistles it appears only in Lk 20:16.

God, Son of. *See* Jesus Christ.

Godhead. A KJV term, a rendering of: (1) the Gr. *theion* (Acts 17:29), "divinity," "the Deity"; (2) the Gr. *theiotēs* (Rom 1: 20), "divine nature," "divinity"; (3) the Gr. *theotēs* (Col 2:9), "deity," "divinity." The English term "Godhead" means "godhood," that is, "godship," "divine nature," "divine essence."

Godless. Acknowledging no god, irreligious. The expression occurs only in the RSV, appearing as the translation of several Hebrew and Greek terms: (1) Heb. *beliya'al* (only in 2 Sa 23:6), literally, "uselessness" (*see* Belial); (2) Heb. *chaneph,* "alienated (from God)," usually rendered "godless" or "godless man" (Job 8:13; Prov 11:9; etc.) and "hypocrite" by the KJV; (3) Heb. *zed,* "insolent," "presumptuous" (Ps 119:51, 69; etc.), usually translated "proud" in the KJV. The same term also appears occasionally in the RSV in such renderings as "arrogant" (Is 13: 11), "insolent men" (Jer 43:2), etc.; (4) Gr. *bebēlos,* "profane," "irreligious"; rendered "godless" 3 times by the RSV (1 Ti 4:7; 6:20; 2 Ti 2:16) and once "profane" (1 Ti 1:9). The KJV consistently renders *bebēlos* "profane."

Godliness. [Gr. generally *eusebeia*, "piety," "godliness," "religion."] *Eusebeia* emphasizes the thought of piety and reverence for God. The basic force of the Greek term, however, is quite close to the English expression "godliness," and it is so rendered in most of its occurrences (1 Ti 4:7, 8; 6:3; 2 Pe 1:3, 6, 7; etc.). At times *eusebeia* seems to assume an additional significance so as to denote "religion," and in the NT, especially the Christian religion (1 Ti 3:16; 2 Ti 3:5; RSV).

Gog (gŏg). [Heb. *Gôg;* Gr. *Gōg.*]
1. A son of Joel of the tribe of Reuben (1 Chr 5:4).
2. The leader of the pagan host that Ezekiel predicted would attack the restored Jewish state (Eze 38:2, 3, 14, 16, 18; 39:1, 11, 15). All attempts to identify him with a historical figure of Ezekiel's time or of a later period have been unsuccessful and unconvincing (see *SDACom* 4:704). Gog seems, therefore, to be simply an ideal name for the leader of heathen hordes that would combine to attack Israel. On prophecies about Israel restored *see* Prophet, II; *SDACom* 4:25-38.
3. Either a person similar to the heathen leader mentioned in Eze 38 and 39 (*see* Gog, 2) or a nation hostile to God symbolizing those nations of the wicked whom Satan assembles after the millennium to attack Christ and to seize the New Jerusalem (Rev 20:8).

Goiim (goi'ĭm). [Heb. *Gôyim,* "nations."] A name appearing in the RSV of Gen 14:1, 9 and Jos 12:23. In these verses *Gôyim* is probably not a common noun meaning "nations" or "peoples," but the name of a country or nation. An inscription of Shalmaneser III (859-824 B.C.) mentions the people of *Guâ,* probably *Que,* apparently living in Cilicia (southeastern Asia Minor), and Tidal may have been king over that country (Gen 14:1, 9). A Genesis Apocryphon among the Dead Sea scrolls of Cave I says that Tidal was "King of Goiim which is between the Rivers" (col. xxi, 23, 24), identifying the area with northern Mesopotamia. However, the same country cannot be meant in Jos 12:23, which speaks of a "king of Goiim in Galilee." The "Goiim" in this text remains unidentified.

Golan (gō'lăn). [Heb. *Gôlan,* "circuit."] A city in Bashan in the territory of the half tribe of Manasseh of Transjordan. It was assigned to the Gershonite Levites, and designated as one of the cities of refuge (Deut 4:43; Jos 20:8; 21:27; 1 Chr 6:71). The ancient site has tentatively been identified with the present *Sahem el-Jôlân,* about 17 mi. east of the Sea of Galilee at the latitude of Tiberias near the *Nahr el-'Allân,* a northern tributary of the Yarmuk (Map VI, C-4). It later gave its name to the small country of Gaulanitis, mentioned repeatedly in the writings of Josephus (*Ant.* viii. 2. 3; etc.), which lay between Mount Hermon and the Yarmuk River (Map XVI, B/C-4). This area is today called *Jôlân.*

Gold. [Heb. generally *zahab;* Aramaic *dehab;* Gr. *chrusos.*] A widely distributed metal, valued for its ornamental uses. It was one of the oldest known metals in Egypt, and was used even to make royal coffins. Before the Flood it was plentiful in Havilah (Gen 2:11, 12), and soon after the Flood the metal became popular for ornamentation and jewelry (Gen 24:53; Ex 3:22; 1 Chr 21:3; etc.). Mining centers were Sheba (Ps 72:15; cf. 1 Ki 10:2), Ophir (1 Ki 10:11; 1 Chr 29:4; Job 28:16; Is 13:12), and apparently Arabia (2 Chr 9: 14). Both in the tabernacle and in the Temple gold was used extensively to overlay woodwork and furniture and to form utensils (Ex 25:10, 11, 31, 38; 1 Ki 6). See fig. 501. This precious metal symbolized great worth and value (Prov 25:12; Lam 4:2; Rev 3:18). G. Ryckmans has pointed out that the ancient Arabic word *dhb,* a cognate of the Heb. *zahab,* means not only "gold" but also "perfume," and it is possible that in some texts, especially those which mention *zahab* from Ophir, Havilah, and Sheba, the term may refer to perfumes rather than gold (*RB* 58 [1951], 372-376; *JEOL* 14 [1955-56], 81).

Golden City. [Heb. *madhebah,* an obscure word.] A term in Is 14:4, KJV, describing Babylon, and poetically parallel to "oppressor." It is thought that an ancient scribe mistook the Hebrew letter *r* for *d,* which is almost identical with it. The ancient versions—the LXX, the Syriac, the Targums, and the Vulgate—together with the Dead Sea scroll 1QIs[a], attest the reading *marhebah,* which the RSV appropriately translates "insolent fury."

Goldsmith. An artisan who made utilitarian and ornamental objects from gold. That goldsmiths were found in early times is indicated by the record of Gen 24:22, where Abraham's servant is described as

presenting gold ornaments to Rebekah.
These artisans refined gold (Job 28:1),
they formed objects by melting it (Ex 32:
4), they beat it into thin "gold leaf" (ch
39:3, RSV), and they apparently made
threads of the metal which were woven
into cloth (ch 28:6). The prophets denounced heathen goldsmiths who fashioned idols (Is 40:19, 20;. Jer 10:8, 9, 14).

Golgotha (gŏl′gô-thà). [Gr. *Golgotha*, a transliteration of the Heb. *gulgoleth* or Aramaic *gulgulta'* or *golgolta'*, simplified to
gulgotha', meaning "skull."] The place
of Christ's crucifixion, the name of which
is interpreted by Luke to mean "skull"
(Mt 27:33; Mk 15:22; Jn 19:17). In Luke
23:33 "Calvary" (Gr. *kranion*) is literally
"skull," being derived from the Latin
calvaria, "skull." It is now generally believed that the name was given to the
place because of its appearance resembling a skull, but the early Church Fathers claim that the name came from either Adam's skull being buried there
(Origen), or from the many skulls of
executed criminals lying around (Jerome). From the Gospel records it is
clear that it was a conspicuous place (Mk
15:40; Lk 23:49), outside the city wall
(Jn 19:20; Heb 13:11-13), near a garden
(Jn 19:41).

The location of the actual site has not
been ascertained with certainty, although
numerous attempts have been made to
do so. Many spots around the city, and
some inside of it, have been at one time
or another identified with Golgotha. Eusebius (*c.* A.D. 264 - *c.* 339), the first Christian historian who provides any information on the subject, claims that wicked
men covered the sacred spot with earth
and built on it the temple of Venus,
which lay in the Forum constructed by the
emperor Hadrian in the 2d cent. A.D.
Constantine removed this pagan structure and erected a church at that spot,
which is now occupied by the Church of
the Holy Sepulchre (fig. 266). Although
it is reasonable to believe that the Palestinian Christians did not soon forget the
place of their Saviour's sufferings, this
identity has not been established. The site
lies well within the present walled city of
Jerusalem, and it is unknown whether
the wall in the time of Christ included
this site. Only extensive excavations,
which have not been carried out there,
could provide the answer to this unsolved problem.

The rocky hill known as Gordon's Calvary, about 250 yards northeast of the

Damascus Gate (fig. 206), has in its favor
that it has the appearance of a skull, and
that a Roman tomb, the so-called Garden
Tomb, is in its vicinity (fig. 265). This
identification was made for the first time
as late as 1849 by Otto Thenius, and was

206. The hill called Gordon's Calvary, north of the
Damascus Gate at Jerusalem

given weight by its acceptance by Gen.
Charles G. Gordon of China and Khartum fame. The opponents of this site
claim that the Turks quarried at the hill
until comparatively recent times, so that
the present skull-like shape is of recent
origin. The true site of the crucifixion is
therefore a matter of uncertainty.

Goliath (gô-lī′ăth). [Heb. *Golyath,* meaning
uncertain.] A giant from the city of Gath,
a member of the Philistine army. He was
6½ cubits (about 9½ ft.) tall. His challenge to a combat was accepted by David,
who defeated and slew him (1 Sa 17; 21:
9, 10). Another giant of Gath (called
Goliath in 2 Sa 21:19) was killed by
Elhanan of Bethlehem, one of David's
"mighty men." Since 1 Chr 20:5 says that
Elhanan slew the brother of Goliath, it
must be assumed that the word "brother"
was somehow lost from the text of 2 Sa
21:19.

Gomer (gō′mēr). [Heb. *Gomer,* "perfection."]
1. The eldest son of Japheth (Gen 10:
2; 1 Chr 1:5, 6), and ancestor of a group
of nations. *See* Gomer, 2.

2. A people descended from Gomer, 1,
mentioned by Ezekiel (ch 38:6). They are
known from Assyrian inscriptions as *Ga-
mir* or *Gimirri,* and from Greek literature as the Cimmerians. They were Indo-
Europeans who came to the Near East
from northern Europe via the Caucasus

in the 8th cent. B.C. The Assyrians pushed them westward, where they overthrew the Phrygian and Lydian kingdoms, but were gradually absorbed by the Anatolian peoples.

3. Daughter of Diblaim, and wife of Hosea, the prophet (Hos 1:3).

Gomorrah (gŏ-mŏr′å), KJV of NT **Gomorrha** (gŏ-mŏr′å). [Heb. ′*Amorah;* Gr. *Gomorra.*] A city in the Jordan plain (Gen 10:19; 13:10), a sister city of Sodom and one of the 5 cities conquered by Chedorlaomer and his confederates in the time of Abraham (ch 14:8-11). Shortly after this event it was destroyed by fire from heaven because of its wickedness (Gen 18:20; 19:24-28; Deut 29:23; Is 1:9; Jer 23:14; 49:18; Amos 4:11; Zep 2:9; Mt 10:15). Its location is still uncertain, but the site is now generally sought underneath the waters of the southern part of the Dead Sea. The portion below the present eastern peninsula is very shallow, the land having been covered by a rising of the water level. *See* Sodom.

Gomorrha. *See* Gomorrah.

Goodman. An archaic English word designating the master of the house or the head of a family. It occurs occasionally in the KJV, and is a rendering of: (1) the Heb. ′*ish,* "man" (Prov 7:19), in the context "husband"; (2) the Gr. *oikodespotēs,* "master of the house" (Lk 22:11). In Mt 20:11; 24:43; Mk 14:14; Lk 12:39, the KJV renders *oikodespotēs* "goodman of the house." Elsewhere the KJV renders the term "householder" (Mt 13:52; 20:1; etc.), as the RSV does consistently, and "master of the house" (Mt 10:25; Lk 13:25; 14:21).

Goodness. Moral or religious excellence, virtue, the quality of being good. It is the rendering of a number of Hebrew and Greek words usually emphasizing that which is kind, benign, or good. In the OT the expression is most frequently a rendering of the Heb. *ṭûb* or *ṭôb,* 2 words closely related in derivation and significance, which refer to that which possesses desirable qualities or excellency of character. Typical examples of *ṭûb* are Neh 9:25, 35; Ps 27:13. In Ex 33:19 it seems to comprehend all the graces and virtues and benignity of God. The related word, *ṭôb,* is normally used as an adjective but may occasionally be used in a sense almost identical to *ṭûb,* as in Num 10:32; Jgs 8:35; Ps 23:6. Occasionally "goodness" is given in the KJV as the translation of the Heb. *chesed,* a word that emphasizes *kindness (as it is frequently also rendered in the

KJV) and mercy (Ex 34:6; 2 Chr 32:32; etc.). In the NT the expression is used to translate the Greek words *agathōsunē* (Rom 15:14; Gal 5:22), *chrēstotēs* (Rom 2:4; 11:22; RSV "kindness"), and *chrēstos* (Rom 2:4; RSV "kindness"). These Greek terms are close to the English word "goodness" in their general meaning, though *chrēstotēs* and *chrēstos* lean more to the concept of "kindness."

Gopher Wood. [Heb. ′*aṣê-gopher;* Sumerian *gipar,* an unidentified wood.] The wood used by Noah to construct the ark (Gen 6:14), identified by some with the cypress. Translators, not knowing the identity of the tree referred to by *gopher,* simply transliterated the term.

Goshen (gō′shĕn). [Heb. *Goshen.*]

1. A fertile pastureland within the borders of Egypt, given to the family of Jacob upon their migration into the Nile valley (Gen 45:10; 46:28, 29; 47:1, 4, 6, 27; 50:8; Ex 8:22; 9:26). Since the name has not yet been found in ancient Egyptian texts, the exact location of the region is unknown. Some scholars have sought it in the coastal region of the eastern Delta, but the majority of commentators have identified it with the fertile *Wâdī Ṭumilât,* which lies between the easternmost branch of the Nile and Lake Timsah in the Suez Canal region (Map V, B-3).

2. A city in the hill country of Judah, lying near Anim (Jos 15:50); not identified. It has been suggested that it was the city that gave its name to the area of Goshen, 3, but this interpretation is rejected by many scholars, since the city seems to have been in the hill country, whereas Goshen, 3, was in the southern section of Judah. Martin Noth has suggested the identification of the town of Goshen with *Tell Beit Mirsim,* identified by W. F. Albright with Debir. (M. Noth, *Das Buch Josua* [Tübingen, 1938], 69, 70.)

3. A region in the south of Palestine (Jos 10:41; 11:16), of unknown location. See Map VI, F-2.

Gospel. [Gr. *euaggelion,* "good news."] The message of Christianity, the message of salvation through Jesus Christ. This "good news" was revealed in embryo from the beginning (Gen 3:15; 12:3), but was disclosed more fully by later Bible writers, especially by Isaiah, who is sometimes called the gospel prophet (see Is 49; 60 to 62; *SDACom* 4:25-36, 278, 279). Jesus announced His ministry to the people of His own village of Nazareth in the words of Is 61:1, 2 (Lk 4:18, 19). The "good news" is described as "the gospel of Christ" (Rom 15:19; 2 Cor 4:4; etc.), "the gospel of God" (Rom 1:1), and the "gospel of the grace of God" (Acts 20:24). It is called a *"mystery" (Eph 6:19). The phrase "the gospel of the kingdom" (Mt 9:35; Mk 1:14; etc.) has reference primarily to the gospel of the "kingdom of heaven," or "kingdom of God" (Mt 12:28; 13:24; Mk 1:15; Lk 17:20, 21). Christ commanded His followers to preach the gospel to "every creature" (Mk 16:15, 16; cf. Mt 28:19; Acts 1:8). The preaching of the "gospel of the kingdom" to all the world is given as a sign of Christ's coming (Mt 24:14). In vision John saw an angel with the "everlasting gospel" to preach to every "nation and tribe and tongue and people" (Rev 14:6, RSV).

The use of the term "Gospel" to refer to any of the first 4 books of the NT is extra-Biblical. Some see a suggestion of such a use in Mk 1:1.

Gospels, Harmony of. The authors of the Gospels give independent accounts of the life of Jesus. Some record incidents that others omit, and many events are related without a statement of their exact time relationship with other incidents. The time order cannot always be deduced from the sequence of the narratives, for the 4 Gospels show variations in the order in which the events are narrated. There are many problems involved in arranging the various incidents in one time sequence, and many solutions have been proposed. The sequence here followed is that presented in the *SDACom*, vol. 5, pp. 196-203; the

reasons for adopting this are found in the comments on the Scripture passages involved.

How to use the Harmony of the Gospels: The following tables present in a continuous chronological sequence the events in the life of Jesus recorded in all 4 Gospels, subdividing the whole series into 8 periods. After each of the 179 incidents listed, in the last 4 columns appear the Scripture passages in the respective Gospels narrating the incident. It will be noticed that certain events are found in only 1 of the Gospels, others in 2 or 3, and still others in all 4.

The tables provide a convenient means of locating any incident chronologically, as well as of comparing the accounts of that event by the various Gospel writers. For example, the incident of Jesus' walking on the water appears as No. 67. The fact that this item appears in section IV, "Ministry in Galilee," dates the incident during Jesus' stay in Galilee from the spring of A.D. 29 to the spring of A.D. 30, between the feeding of the five thousand (No. 66) and the sermon on the bread of life (No. 68). The 3 Scripture references following (Mt 14:22-36; Mk 6:45-56; Jn 6:15-24) show the places in the Gospels where the story of Jesus' walking on the sea is narrated.

Any specific incident may be found either by scanning the list or, if a Scripture reference for the story is known, by consulting the Index to the Harmony of the Gospels which follows the Harmony table.

A HARMONY OF THE GOSPELS

No.	Incident	Matthew	Mark	Luke	John
	I. Infancy to Manhood (Autumn, 5 B.C.-Autumn, A.D. 27)				
1	Prologue to John's Gospel	- -	- -	- -	1:1-18
2	Prologue to Luke's Gospel	- -	- -	1:1-4	
3	The Human Ancestry of Jesus	1:1-17	- -	3:23b-38	
4	The Announcement to Zacharias	- -	- -	1:5-25	
5	The Annunciation	- -	- -	1:26-38	
6	Mary's Visit to Elizabeth	- -	- -	1:39-56	
7	Birth of John the Baptist	- -	- -	1:57-80	
8	The Announcement to Joseph; His Marriage	1:18-25			
9	Birth of Jesus	- -	- -	2:1-7	
10	The Announcement to the Shepherds	- -	- -	2:8-20	
11	The Circumcision	- -	- -	2:21	
12	Presentation at the Temple	- -	- -	2:22-38	

No.	Incident	Matthew	Mark	Luke	John
13	Visit of the Magi	2:1-12			
14	Flight to Egypt	2:13-18			
15	Return to Nazareth	2:19-23	- -	2:39, 40	
16	First Passover Visit	- -	- -	2:41-50	
17	Youth and Young Manhood	- -	- -	2:51, 52	

II. Early Ministry (Autumn, A.D. 27-Spring, A.D. 28)

No.	Incident	Matthew	Mark	Luke	John
18	Ministry of John the Baptist	3:1-12	1:1-8	3:1-18	
19	The Baptism	3:13-17	1:9-11	3:21-23a	
20	The Temptation	4:1-11	1:12, 13	4:1-13	
21	Jesus Declared "the Lamb of God"	- -	- -	- -	1:19-34
22	The First Disciples	- -	- -	- -	1:35-51
23	The Wedding Feast at Cana	- -	- -	- -	2:1-12

III. Ministry in Judea (First Passover, A.D. 28-Second Passover, A.D. 29)

No.	Incident	Matthew	Mark	Luke	John
24	*First Passover:*				
	First Cleansing of the Temple	- -	- -	- -	2:13-25
25	Discussion With Nicodemus	- -	- -	- -	3:1-21
26	Ministry in Judea	- -	- -	- -	3:22-36
27	The Samaritan Woman	- -	- -	- -	4:1-42
28	The Nobleman's Son	- -	- -	- -	4:43-54
29	John Imprisoned	14:3-5	- -	3:19, 20	
30	*Second Passover:*				
	The Invalid at Bethesda	- -	- -	- -	5:1-15
31	Rejection by the Sanhedrin: Close of the Judean Ministry	- -	- -	- -	5:16-47

IV. Ministry in Galilee (Second Passover, A.D. 29-Third Passover, A.D. 30)

No.	Incident	Matthew	Mark	Luke	John
32	Opening of the Galilean Ministry	4:12	1:14, 15	4:14, 15	
33	First Rejection at Nazareth	- -	- -	4:16-30	
34	Removal to Capernaum	4:13-17	- -	4:31a	
35	The Call by the Sea	4:18-22	1:16-20	5:1-11	
36	The Demoniac in the Synagogue	- -	1:21-28	4:31b-37	
37	Peter's Mother-in-law; The Sick Healed at Even	8:14-17	1:29-34	4:38-41	
38	*First Galilean Tour:*	4:23-25	1:35-39	4:42-44	
39	The First Leper	8:2-4	1:40-45	5:12-16	
40	The Paralytic Lowered Through the Roof	9:2-8	2:1-12	5:17-26	
41	Call of Levi Matthew	9:9	2:13, 14	5:27, 28	
42	Plucking Grain on the Sabbath	12:1-8	2:23-28	6:1-5	
43	The Man With a Withered Hand	12:9-14	3:1-6	6:6-11	
44	Jesus' Popularity	12:15-21	3:7-12		
45	Appointment of the Twelve	- -	3:13-19	6:12-16	
46	Sermon on the Mount	5:1-8:1	- -	6:17-49	
47	The Centurion's Servant	8:5-13	- -	7:1-10	
48	Two Blind Men	9:27-31			
49	A Dumb Demoniac	9:32-34			
50	*Second Galilean Tour:*	9:35	- -	8:1-3	
51	The Widow's Son at Nain	- -	- -	7:11-17	
52	A Blind and Dumb Demoniac; The Unpardonable Sin	12:22-45	3:20-30	11:14-32	
53	Visit of Jesus' Mother and Brothers	12:46-50	3:31-35	8:19-21	

No.	Incident	Matthew	Mark	Luke	John
54	Sermon by the Sea:	13:1-53	4:1-34	8:4-18	
	The Pearl of Great Price			[13:18-21]	
	The Mustard Seed				
	The Tares				
	The Sower, the Seed, the Soils				
	Hidden Treasure				
	The Growing Seed				
	The Leaven				
	Treasures Old and New				
	The Dragnet				
55	The Privations of Discipleship	8:19-22			
56	The Storm on the Lake	8:18, 23-27	4:35-41	8:22-25	
57	The Demoniacs of Gadara	8:28-9:1	5:1-20	8:26-39	
58	Matthew's Feast	9:10-13	2:15-17	5:29-32	
59	The Question About Fasting	9:14-17	2:18-22	5:33-39	
60	The Invalid Woman; Jairus' Daughter	9:18-26	5:21-43	8:40-56	
61	The Inquiry by John's Disciples	11:2-6	- -	7:18-23	
62	Jesus' Eulogy of John	11:7-30	- -	7:24-35	
63	*Third Galilean Tour:*				
	Mission of the Twelve	9:36-11:1	6:7-13	9:1-6	
64	Second Rejection at Nazareth	13:54-58	6:1-6		
65	Martyrdom of John the Baptist	14:1, 2, 6-12	6:14-29	9:7-9	
66	*Third Passover:*				
	Feeding the Five Thousand	14:13-21	6:30-44	9:10-17	6:1-14
67	Jesus Walks on the Sea	14:22-36	6:45-56	- -	6:15-24
68	Sermon on the Bread of Life; Rejection in Galilee	- -	- -	- -	6:25-7:1
69	Contention About Tradition and Ceremonial Defilement	15:1-20	7:1-23		

V. Retirement From Public Ministry (Third Passover, A.D. 30-Autumn, A.D. 30)

No.	Incident	Matthew	Mark	Luke	John
70	Withdrawal to Phoenicia	15:21-28	7:24-30		
71	A Deaf-mute Healed; Other Miracles in Decapolis	15:29-31	7:31-37		
72	Feeding the Four Thousand	15:32-39	8:1-10		
73	The Demand for a Sign	16:1-12	8:11-21		
74	The Blind Man Near Bethsaida	- -	8:22-26		
75	Withdrawal to Caesarea Philippi; The Great Confession	16:13-28	8:27-9:1	9:18-27	
76	A Secret Journey Through Galilee	17:22, 23	9:30-32	9:43b-45	
77	Humility, Reconciliation, and Forgiveness	18:1-35	9:33-50	9:46-50	
78	The Transfiguration	17:1-13	9:2-13	9:28-36	
79	The Demon-possessed Boy	17:14-21	9:14-29	9:37-43a	
80	The Temple Half Shekel	17:24-27			

VI. Ministry in Samaria and Perea (Autumn, A.D. 30-Passover, A.D. 31)

No.	Incident	Matthew	Mark	Luke	John
81	Secret Journey to the Feast of Tabernacles	- -	- -	- -	7:2-13
82	Teaching in the Temple	- -	- -	- -	7:14-52
83	The Adulteress	- -	- -	- -	7:53-8:11
84	The Light of the World	- -	- -	- -	8:12-30
85	The Argument About Descent From Abraham	- -	- -	- -	8:31-59
86	The Man Born Blind	- -	- -	- -	9:1-41
87	The Good Shepherd	- -	- -	- -	10:1-21

No.	Incident	Matthew	Mark	Luke	John
88	Final Departure From Galilee; Opening of the Samaritan-Perean Ministry	19:1, 2	10:1	9:51-56	
89	Tests of Discipleship	- -	- -	9:57-62	
90	Mission of the Seventy	- -	- -	10:1-24	
91	The Good Samaritan	- -	- -	10:25-37	
92	Visit to the Home of Mary and Martha	- -	- -	10:38-42	
93	At the Feast of Dedication	- -	- -	- -	10:22-42
94	Return to Perea: Instruction on Prayer	- -	- -	11:1-13	
95	The Inner Light	- -	- -	11:33-36	
96	Dining With a Pharisee	- -	- -	11:37-54	
97	A Warning Against the Pharisees	- -	- -	12:1-12	
98	The Folly of Riches	- -	- -	12:13-34	
99	Awaiting the Master's Return	- -	- -	12:35-59	
100	Divine Justice and Mercy	- -	- -	13:1-9	
101	The Crippled Woman	- -	- -	13:10-17	
102	Growth of the Kingdom of Heaven	- -	- -	13:18-30	
103	A Warning of Divine Judgment	- -	- -	13:31-35	
104	Dining With a Chief Pharisee	- -	- -	14:1-15	
105	The Great Banquet	- -	- -	14:16-24	
106	The Cost of Discipleship	- -	- -	14:25-35	
107	The Lost Sheep	[18:12-14]	- -	15:1-7	
108	The Lost Coin	- -	- -	15:8-10	
109	The Prodigal Son	- -	- -	15:11-32	
110	The Dishonest Steward	- -	- -	16:1-18	
111	The Rich Man and Lazarus	- -	- -	16:19-31	
112	Forgiveness, Faith, and Service	- -	- -	17:1-10	
113	The Raising of Lazarus	- -	- -	- -	11:1-45
114	Withdrawal to Ephraim	- -	- -	- -	11:46-57
115	The Ten Lepers	- -	- -	17:11-19	
116	When and How the Kingdom Comes	- -	- -	17:20-37	
117	The Unjust Judge	- -	- -	18:1-8	
118	The Pharisee and the Publican	- -	- -	18:9-14	
119	Marriage and Divorce	19:3-12	10:2-12		
120	Blessing the Children	19:13-15	10:13-16	18:15-17	
121	The Rich Young Ruler	19:16-30	10:17-31	18:18-30	
122	Laborers in the Vineyard	20:1-16			
123	Jesus Foretells His Death	20:17-19	10:32-34	18:31-34	
124	The Ambition of James and John	20:20-28	10:35-45		
125	Blind Bartimaeus	20:29-34	10:46-52	18:35-43	
126	Zacchaeus	- -	- -	19:1-10	
127	The Nobleman and the Pounds	- -	- -	19:11-28	
128	Simon's Feast	26:6-13	14:3-9	7:36-50	12:1-9
129	The Betrayal Plot	26:1-5, 14-16	14:1, 2, 10, 11	22:1-6	12:10, 11

VII. Passion Week (Fourth Passover, A.D. 31)

No.	Incident	Matthew	Mark	Luke	John
130	*Fourth Passover:* The Triumphal Entry	21:1-11	11:1-11	19:29-44	12:12-19
131	The Fruitless Fig Tree	21:18-22	11:12-14, 20-26		
132	The Second Cleansing of the Temple	21:12-17	11:15-19	19:45-48	

No.	Incident	Matthew	Mark	Luke	John
133	The Leaders Challenge Jesus' Authority	21:23-27	11:27-33	20:1-8	
134	The Two Sons	21:28-32			
135	The Wicked Husbandmen	21:33-46	12:1-12	20:9-19	
136	The Man Without a Wedding Garment	22:1-14			
137	Paying Tribute to Caesar	22:15-22	12:13-17	20:20-26	
138	Marriage and the Resurrection	22:23-33	12:18-27	20:27-38	
139	The Great Commandment	22:34-40	12:28-34	20:39, 40	
140	Jesus Silences His Critics	22:41-46	12:35-37	20:41-44	
141	Woes Upon Scribe and Pharisee	23:1-39	12:38-40	20:45-47	
142	The Widow's Mite	- -	12:41-44	21:1-4	
143	Interview With Certain Greeks	- -	- -	- -	12:20-36a
144	Final Rejection by the Jewish Leaders	- -	- -	- -	12:36b-50
145	Retirement to the Mount of Olives; Signs of Christ's Return	24:1-51	13:1-37	21:5-38	
146	The Ten Virgins	25:1-13			
147	The Talents	25:14-30			
148	The Sheep and the Goats	25:31-46			
149	Preparation for the Passover	26:17-19	14:12-16	22:7-13	
150	Celebration of the Passover	26:20	14:17, 18a	22:14-16	
151	Washing the Disciples' Feet	- -	- -	22:24-30	13:1-20
152	The Lord's Supper	26:26-29	14:22-25	22:17-20	
153	The Betrayer Revealed	26:21-25	14:18b-21	22:21-23	13:21-30
154	Parting Counsel	- -	- -	- -	13:31-14:31
155	Retirement to Gethsemane	26:30	14:26	22:39	
156	A Warning to Peter and the Ten	26:31-35	14:27-31	22:31-38	[13:36-38]
157	The True Vine	- -	- -	- -	15:1-17
158	A Warning of Persecution	- -	- -	- -	15:18-16:4
159	The Coming of the Comforter	- -	- -	- -	16:5-33
160	Jesus' Intercessory Prayer	- -	- -	- -	17:1-26
161	Gethsemane	26:36-56	14:32-52	22:40-53	18:1-12
162	Hearing Before Annas	- -	- -	- -	18:13-24
163	Night Trial Before the Sanhedrin	26:57-75	14:53-72	22:54-65	18:25-27
164	Day Trial Before the Sanhedrin	27:1	15:1	22:66-71	
165	Judas' Confession and Suicide	27:3-10			
166	First Trial Before Pilate	27:2, 11-14	15:2-5	23:1-5	18:28-38
167	Hearing Before Herod Antipas	- -	- -	23:6-12	
168	Second Trial Before Pilate	27:15-31a	15:6-19	23:13-25	18:39-19:16
169	The Crucifixion	27:31b-56	15:20-41	23:26-49	19:17-37
170	The Burial	27:57-61	15:42-47	23:50-56	19:38-42
171	The Guard at the Tomb	27:62-66			

VIII. Resurrection to Ascension (Spring, A.D. 31)

No.	Incident	Matthew	Mark	Luke	John
172	The Resurrection	28:1-15	16:1-11	24:1-12	20:1-18
173	The Walk to Emmaus	- -	16:12	24:13-32	
174	First Appearance in the Upper Room	- -	16:13	24:33-49	20:19-23
175	Second Appearance in the Upper Room	- -	16:14	- -	20:24-29
176	Appearance by the Sea of Galilee	- -	- -	- -	21:1-23
177	Appearance on a Mountain in Galilee	28:16-20	16:15-18		
178	The Ascension	- -	16:19, 20	24:50-53	
179	Epilogue to John's Gospel	- -	- -	- -	20:30, 31; 21:24, 25

How to use the Index to the Harmony of the Gospels: The following Index lists in chapter-and-verse order the Bible passages narrating the incidents listed in the preceding Harmony, and gives for each reference the number under which it is found in those tables. If a Bible reference for an event is known, such as Lk 7:36-50 for the feast given for Jesus by Simon, the entry in the Harmony can be found in the Index under Lk 7; after vs 36-50 appears the number 128. The Harmony entry No. 128, "Simon's Feast," gives the Luke reference and parallel passages in the other Gospels, Mt 26:6-13; Mk 14:3-9; and Jn 12:1-9.

INDEX TO THE HARMONY OF THE GOSPELS

Matthew

Chapter and Verse	Harmony Entry	Chapter and Verse	Harmony Entry	Chapter and Verse	Harmony Entry	Chapter and Verse	Harmony Entry
1: 1-17	3	27-31	48	14-21	79	24: 1-51	145
18-25	8	32-34	49	22,23	76	25: 1-13	146
2: 1-12	13	35	50	24-27	80	14-30	147
13-18	14	36-11:1	63	18: 1-35	77	31-46	148
19-23	15	11: 2-6	61	19: 1,2	88	26: 1-5,14-16	129
3: 1-12	18	7-30	62	3-12	119	6-13	128
13-17	19·	12: 1-8	42	13-15	120	17-19	149
4: 1-11	20	9-14	43	16-30	121	20	150
12	32	15-21	44	20: 1-16	122	21-25	153
13-17	34	22-45	52	17-19	123	26-29	152
18-22	35	46-50	53	20-28	124	30	155
23-25	38	13: 1-53	54	29-34	125	31-35	156
5: 1-8:1	46	54-58	64	21: 1-11	130	36-56	161
8: 2-4	39	14: 1,2,6-12	65	12-17	132	57-75	163
5-13	47	3-5	29	18-22	131	27: 1	164
14-17	37	13-21	66	23-27	133	2,11-14	166
18,23-27	56	22-36	67	28-32	134	3-10	165
19-22	55	15: 1-20	69	33-46	135	15-31ª	168
28-9:1	57	21-28	70	22: 1-14	136	31ᵇ-56	169
9: 2-8	40	29-31	71	15-22	137	57-61	170
9	41	32-39	72	23-33	138	62-66	171
10-13	58	16: 1-12	73	34-40	139	28: 1-15	172
14-17	59	13-28	75	41-46	140	16-20	177
18-26	60	17: 1-13	78	23: 1-39	141		

Mark

Chapter and Verse	Harmony Entry	Chapter and Verse	Harmony Entry	Chapter and Verse	Harmony Entry	Chapter and Verse	Harmony Entry
1: 1-8	18	35-41	56	2-12	119	12-16	149
9-11	19	5: 1-20	57	13-16	120	17,18ª	150
12,13	20	21-43	60	17-31	121	18ᵇ-21	153
14,15	32	6: 1-6	64	32-34	123	22-25	152
16-20	35	7-13	63	35-45	124	26	155
21-28	36	14-29	65	46-52	125	27-31	156
29-34	37	30-44	66	11: 1-11	130	32-52	161
35-39	38	45-56	67	12-14,20-26	131	53-72	163
40-45	39	7: 1-23	69	15-19	132	15: 1	164
2: 1-12	40	24-30	70	27-33	133	2-5	166
13,14	41	31-37	71	12: 1-12	135	6-19	168
15-17	58	8: 1-10	72	13-17	137	20-41	169
18-22	59	11-21	73	18-27	138	42-47	170
23-28	42	22-26	74	28-34	139	16: 1-11	172
3: 1-6	43	27-9:1	75	35-37	140	12	173
7-12	44	9: 2-13	78	38-40	141	13	174
13-19	45	14-29	79	41-44	142	14	175
20-30	52	30-32	76	13: 1-37	145	15-18	177
31-35	53	33-50	77	14:1,2,10,11	129	19,20	178
4: 1-34	54	10: 1	88	3-9	128		

Luke

Chapter and Verse	Harmony Entry	Chapter and Verse	Harmony Entry	Chapter and Verse	Harmony Entry	Chapter and Verse	Harmony Entry
1: 1-4	2	6-11	43	37-54	96	20: 1-8	133
5-25	4	12-16	45	12: 1-12	97	9-19	135
26-38	5	17-49	46	13-34	98	20-26	137
39-56	6	7: 1-10	47	35-59	99	27-38	138
57-80	7	11-17	51	13: 1-9	100	39,40	139
2: 1-7	9	18-23	61	10-17	101	41-44	140
8-20	10	24-35	62	18-30	102	45-47	141
21	11	36-50	128	31-35	103	21: 1-4	142
22-38	12	8: 1-3	50	14: 1-15	104	5-38	145
39,40	15	4-18	54	16-24	105	22: 1-6	129
41-50	16	19-21	53	25-35	106	7-13	149
51,52	17	22-25	56	15: 1-7	107	14-16	150
3: 1-18	18	26 39	57	8-10	108	17-20	152
19, 20	29	40-56	60	11-32	109	21-23	153
21-23ᵃ	19	9: 1-6	63	16: 1-18	110	24-30	151
23ᵇ-38	3	7-9	65	19-31	111	31-38	156
4: 1-13	20	10-17	66	17: 1-10	112	39	155
14,15	32	18-27	75	11-19	115	40-53	161
16-30	33	28-36	78	20-37	116	54-65	163
31ᵃ	34	37-43ᵃ	79	18: 1-8	117	66-71	164
31ᵇ-37	36	43ᵇ-45	76	9-14	118	23: 1-5	166
38-41	37	46-50	77	15-17	120	6-12	167
42-44	38	51-56	88	18-30	121	13-25	168
5: 1-11	35	57-62	89	31-34	123	26-49	169
12-16	39	10: 1-24	90	35-43	125	50-56	170
17-26	40	25-37	91	19: 1-10	126	24: 1-12	172
27,28	41	38-42	92	11-28	127	13-32	173
29-32	58	11: 1-13	94	29-44	130	33-49	174
33-39	59	14-32	52	45-48	132	50-53	178
6: 1-5	42	33-36	95				

John

Chapter and Verse	Harmony Entry	Chapter and Verse	Harmony Entry	Chapter and Verse	Harmony Entry	Chapter and Verse	Harmony Entry
1: 1-18	1	25-7:1	68	12-19	130	28-38	166
19-34	21	7: 2-13	81	20-36ᵃ	143	39-19:16	168
35-51	22	14-52	82	36ᵇ-50	144	19: 17-37	169
2: 1-12	23	53-8:11	83	13: 1-20	151	38-42	170
13-25	24	8: 12-30	84	21-30	153	20: 1-18	172
3: 1-21	25	31-59	85	31-14:31	154	19-23	174
22-36	26	9: 1-41	86	15: 1-17	157	24-29	175
4: 1-42	27	10: 1-21	87	18-16:4	158	30,31	179
43-54	28	22-42	93	16: 5-33	159	21: 1-23	176
5: 1-15	30	11: 1-45	113	17: 1-26	160	24,25	179
16-47	31	46-57	114	18: 1-12	161		
6: 1-14	66	12: 1-9	128	13-24	162		
15-24	67	10,11	129	25-27	163		

Gourd. A translation of: (1) The Heb. *paqqu'oth* (plural), the fruit gathered by one of the sons of the prophets at Gilgal, perhaps a kind of wild cucumber known in Palestine for its bitter taste and painful effects when eaten (2 Ki 4:39). Some commentators follow the LXX and the Vulgate in suggesting the colocynth (*Citrullus colocynthis*), a creeping plant with tendrilled vines, small light-green leaves, and melonlike fruit, which can have fatal effects if eaten. A related Hebrew form, *peqa'im,* of apparently the same meaning is translated "gourd" in 1 Ki 6:18; 7:24; RSV. In 2 Chr 4:3, RSV, where "gourd" appears, the Heb. *beqarim* is corrected to *peqa'im* in harmony with 1 Ki 7:24. (2) The Heb. *qiqayôn* (Jon

4:6-10, KJV), a plant of unknown identification. Since it appeared miraculously some suggest it needs no more to be identified with a known plant than the "great fish" of Jon 1 requires specific identification. Some writers have suggested the pumpkin or the castor oil plant. The RSV simply translates the Hebrew term "plant."

Government. The translation of: (1) The Heb. *memshalah,* "dominion" or "rule," translated "government" only in the KJV of Is 22:21, where the RSV gives "authority." Elsewhere the KJV usually renders *memshalah* "dominion" (1 Ki 9:19; 2 Ki 20:13; etc.). (2) The Heb. *miśrah,* "dominion," "empire," a close synonym of *memshalah* (Is 9:6, 7). (3) The Gr. *kubernēsis,* "administration," from a Gr. word meaning "to act as helmsman." It occurs only in 1 Cor 12:28, where its plural form refers to various types of administration or management that God has placed in the church. (4) *Kuriotēs,* "lordship," "dominion," rendered "government" only in 2 Pe 2:10, KJV, where the exact force of the Greek term is somewhat uncertain. Since it is derived from the Gr. *kurios,* a word that signifies a "lord" or "master" in general, as well as the divine "Lord," it is not clear whether *kuriotēs* here denotes earthly "lordship" or the "lordship" that Christ, the Lord, exercises. Elsewhere the KJV renders the term "dominion."

Governor. A number of terms are rendered "governor," which, although they denote leadership or authority, do not have the technical significance of a governor. The following terms are correctly rendered governor:

(1) The Heb. *pechah* (Akkadian *pâhatu*), in the Persian period either the satrap, who administers a satrapy—one of the many main divisions of the Persian Empire (Est 3:12; 8:9; 9:3)—or a deputy satrap such as Tatnai (Ezr 5:3), who was the deputy of Ushtani, the satrap of the satrapy "Beyond the River," embracing all the area between the Euphrates and Egypt. *Pechah* was also used as the title of the governor of the province of Judea during the Persian period. The following Jews as chief administrators of Judah under Persian suzerainty received this title: Sheshbazzar (ch 5:14), Zerubbabel (Hag 1:1, 14; 2:2, 21), and Nehemiah (Neh 12:26). The word "Tirshatha," a transliteration of the Heb. *tirshatha'* (Ezr 2:63; Neh 7:65, 70; 8:9; 10:1, "governor," RSV), is from the Persian *tarshta,* an honorific title

for the governor of a province, with the literal meaning "the feared one," equivalent to "His Excellency."

(2) The Gr. *hēgemōn* and *anthupatos,* terms designating the three classes of high Roman officials who acted as governors in provinces:

a. The proconsul (Gr. *anthupatos,* a translation of the Latin *proconsul*) was, during the later period of the Roman republic, the governor of a province, generally an ex-consul (or ex-praetor) who acted in his province for (*pro*) the consuls. Under the empire "proconsul" was usually the title given to the governor of a senatorial province (one under the jurisdiction of the senate), as distinguished from the imperial provinces (see *b* below). The holders of this office were ordinarily appointed for 1 year, and exercised all administrative, judicial, and military power in their territories. They were usually career officials of the senatorial class, coming from Rome's nobility, who had a name and family tradition to defend, making them, in general, better administrators than the governors of imperial provinces (*b*) and the procurators (*c*), who were creatures of the emperor alone. The proconsul was attended by quaestors who served as tax collectors. In the NT 2 proconsuls are mentioned by name, Sergius Paulus, proconsul of Cyprus (Acts 13:7, 8, 12), and Gallio, proconsul of Achaia, or Greece (ch 18:12). Acts 19:38 simply refers to the proconsular administration of the province of Asia.

b. The legatus Augusti pro praetore, whose term of office was undefined, was the administrator of an imperial province, that is, a province that was (in contrast to a senatorial province) under the control of the emperor, through his legatus, or envoy. The imperial provinces were those requiring the presence of a Roman military force, and the legatus, answerable only to the emperor, had an indefinite term of office. Only one such legate is mentioned in the NT, Cyrenius of Syria, who had his seat at Antioch on the Orontes (Lk 2:2). The Greek term used for his office is *hēgemoneuō,* "to function as *hēgemōn* ["leader," "governor"]."

c. The procurator (Gr. *hēgemōn,* "leader," "chief," "governor," used for the Latin *procurator*) was usually a financial representative of the emperor assigned to a province for an indefinite term, of lower rank than the governor, yet independently responsible to the emperor. A few of the smaller provinces or those not fully organized were placed under procurators, who in addition to their financial responsibilities became the civil administrators and general commanders of the small military forces of their respective territories. When Herod's son Archelaus, ethnarch of Judea, was deposed by Augustus (in A.D. 6) his territory, consisting of Samaria, Judea, and Idumea, was made an imperial province in the charge of a procurator ("governor," Mt 27:15, 21, 27; etc.). The procurator of this province was subject in part to the legate of Syria; however, he was also directly responsible to the emperor who appointed him, and in his own province had the power of life and death (Jos. *War* ii. 8. 1). Most of these procurators were of the equestrian class (a class lower than the senatorial aristocracy), though one at least, Felix, was a freedman. They resided in Caesarea in Herod's magnificent palace, but were usually in Jerusalem during the religious feasts of the Jews, so that they might be on hand in the case of a riot (Jos. *Ant.* xviii. 2. 2). When they were in Jerusalem they stayed either in Herod's palace or in the Tower of Antonia, a palatial fortress built by Herod. *See* Barracks.

Judea was twice placed under the rule of procurators, first from A.D. 6 to 41 and again from A.D. 44 to 66. In the interval (A.D. 41-44) it was part of the kingdom of Agrippa I. Following is a list of the 14 procurators who ruled Judea, 7 in the 1st period and 7 in the 2d. Little is known concerning some of them, and the dates given for their administration are in most cases only approximate.

A. The first 7 procurators, A.D. 6-41:
1. Coponius, A.D. 6 - *c.* 9 (Jos. *Ant.* xviii. 1. 1; *War* ii. 8. 1).
2. Marcus Ambibulus or Ambivius, A.D. *c.* 9 - *c* 12.
3. Annius Rufus, A.D. *c.* 12 - *c.* 15.
4. Valerius Gratus, A.D. *c.* 15 - *c.* 26; governor for 11 years (Jos. *Ant.* xviii. 2. 2).
5. Pontius Pilate, A.D. *c.* 26-36; appointed by Tiberius, and deposed after 10 years. He arrived in Rome shortly after Tiberius' death, which occurred in March A.D. 37 (Jos. *Ant.* xviii. 2. 2; 4. 2; 6. 5; *War* ii. 9. 2; Tacitus *Ann.* xv. 44). It was he who sentenced Jesus Christ to die on the cross (Mt 27:24-26; etc.). *See* Pilate.
6. Marcellus, A.D. 36 - *c.* 37.
7. Marullus, A.D. *c.* 37-41 (Jos. *Ant.* xviii. 6. 10). In A.D. 41 Claudius handed over Judea and Samaria to Agrippa, who held them until his death in A.D. 44.

B. The later 7 procurators, A.D. 44-66:
1. Cuspius Fadus, A.D. 44-?; appointed by the emperor Claudius (Jos. *Ant.* xix. 9. 2).
2. Tiberius Alexander, A.D. ? - *c.* 48; of Jewish descent (Jos. *Ant.* xx. 5. 2; *War* ii. 11. 6).
3. Ventidius Cumanus, A.D. *c.* 48 - *c.* 52; appointed by Claudius after the death of Herod of Chalcis (Jos. *Ant.* xx. 5. 2; 6. 2 and 3; *War* ii. 12. 1).
4. Antonius Felix, A.D. *c.* 52 - *c.* 60; a freedman, married to Drusilla, sister of King Agrippa II. Under him Paul was held prisoner in Caesarea for 2 years (Acts 23:24 to 24:27; see Jos. *Ant.* xx. 7. 1; *War* ii. 12. 8; Tacitus *Hist.* v. 9). *See* Felix.
5. Porcius Festus, A.D. *c.* 60 - *c.* 62; one of the best procurators; appointed by Nero, but died after 2 years in office. He sent Paul to Rome (Acts 25:1 to 26:32; see Jos. *Ant.* xx. 8. 9; *War* ii. 14. 1). *See* Festus.
6. Albinus, A.D. *c.* 62 - *c.* 64; an extremely mean character (Jos. *Ant.* xx. 9. 1; *War* ii. 14. 1).
7. Gessius Florus, A.D. *c.* 64-66; the worst of all procurators. He was directly responsible for the outbreak of the 1st Jewish war (Jos. *Ant.* xx. 11. 1; *War* ii. 14. 2 ff.; Tacitus *Hist.* v. 10).

Gozan (gō'zăn). [Heb. *Gôzan.*] A district and city on the river Habor (*Khābûr*) in Mesopotamia, in which some of the exiled citizens of Samaria were settled by the Assyrian king Sargon II after the fall of their capital in 723/22 B.C. (2 Ki 17:6; 18:11; 19:12; Is 37:12). Cuneiform inscriptions mention the city by the name *Guzana,* the present *Tell Ḥalâf* (Map XI, B-5), which has been excavated by expeditions led by Baron Max von Oppenheim. These excavations have brought to light a previously unknown culture. The archeological evidence shows that it had been founded in an early phase of Mesopotamian history. Assyrian cuneiform texts from *Guzana* mention certain Israelites, probably exiles. "The river Gozan" (1 Chr 5:26) probably refers to the *Khābûr,* which in this text borrows the name of its main city, hence should probably more properly read, "the river *of* Gozan."

Grace. Generally the translation of the Heb. *chen* and the Gr. *charis,* meaning "favor," or "kindness," especially when unearned or undeserved. The Hebrew term is found frequently in the OT in phrases such as those translated, "If I have found favour [or "grace"] in thine eyes" (Gen 30:27; Ex 33:13). Such phrases are used repeatedly as a formula of courteous address, either to God or to a person.

In most OT usages of the word the meaning is simply "favor" without any special philosophical or theological implication. However, the NT concept of grace as God's saving love toward sinners is not absent from the OT, but this idea was expressed more nearly by the Heb. *chesed*, frequently translated "lovingkindness" in the KJV and "steadfast love" in the RSV (Ps 17:7; 40:11; Is 63:7; Jer 16:5; etc.), and was illustrated in the experience of OT saints. Adam and Eve received a promise of salvation despite their disobedience (Gen 3:15), and were provided with physical protection (v 21); Noah was saved from the general destruction of the Flood (chs 6:8; 7:1); Abraham was selected, despite his imperfections, to keep alive the knowledge of God (ch 12:1); Moses was prepared for leadership by specific, divine guidance (Ex 3:10); Israel was chosen of God and patiently nurtured through centuries of waywardness as God's chosen people (Ps 135:4; etc.). The prophets continually portrayed the steadfast love of God in His dealings with rebellious children (Ps 92:2; Is 54:10; Jer 9:24; Hos 2:19; Jon 4:2; etc.). The OT reveals not only God's displeasure with sin but also His patience and love for sinners, and the grace provided for their salvation.

It remains, however, for the NT to proclaim the fullness of divine grace, "For the law was given by Moses, but grace and truth came by Jesus Christ" (Jn 1:17).

The principal exponent of the doctrine of salvation by grace is Paul. His thesis is that salvation is the result not of law or of books or of nationality but of divine favor freely bestowed, and human faith. "For by grace are ye saved through faith" (Eph 2:8). Paul pictures one of the blessings of the gospel as "access by faith into this grace wherein we stand" (Rom 5:2). Grace is the hand of God reaching earthward. Faith is the hand of man reaching up to take hold of God's hand. The saving dynamic is the grace of God. God has decreed that His grace shall be available to all men of all nationalities and conditions of life in all time, provided they practice faith (Eph 4:7; Tit 2:11).

Paul knew the grace of God to be the dynamic force in his own life: "But by the grace of God I am what I am: and his grace which was bestowed upon me was not in vain; but I laboured more abundantly than they all: yet not I, but the grace of God which was with me" (1 Cor 15:10). His appreciation of divine grace is revealed by the fact that he refers to it in the salutation and conclusion of all of his epistles (Rom 1:7; 16:20; 1 Cor 1:3; 16:23; 2 Cor 1:2; 13:14; Gal 1:3; 6:18; Eph 1:2; 6:24; Php 1:2; 4:23; Col 1:2; 4:18; 1 Th 1:1; 5:28; 2 Th 1:2; 3:18; 1 Ti 1:2; 6:21; 2 Ti 1:2; 4:22; Tit 1:4; 3:15; Phm 3, 25). Peter and John follow a similar pattern (1 Pe 1:2; 2 Pe 1:2; 3:18; 2 Jn 3; Rev 1:4; 22:21).

It is through grace that God calls men to His service (Gal 1:15, 16), and it is the operation of divine grace that influences men to respond to God's call (Acts 20:32). God's grace leads men to repent (2 Ti 2:25) and imparts faith (Rom 12:3; Heb 12:2). The grace of God was mediated to man through Jesus Christ (Rom 5:15) and imparts consolation and hope (2 Th 2:16). God's throne is not only a symbol of judgment and power but of grace (Heb 4:16).

Gracious. The translation of several Hebrew and Greek words with variant shades of meaning. It appears frequently in verb phrases that translate the Heb. *chanan*, "to favor," "to be gracious," often in contexts referring to God (Ex 33:19; Num 6:25; etc.), and often in the RSV in the phrase "be gracious to me" (Ps 4:1; 6:2; 9:13; etc.; KJV "have mercy upon me"). Occasionally *chanan* is rendered by such expressions as "grant . . . graciously" (Jgs 21:22; KJV "be favourable"; Ps 119:29; RSV "graciously teach"), "graciously given" (Gen 33:5), etc. Related to *chanan* is *chanûn*, an adjective closely linked in meaning to *chanan*. In the 13 occurrences of this term it always refers to God (Ex 22:27; 34:6; 2 Chr 30:9; Ps 86:15; etc.). The related noun *chen*, "grace," "favor," is rendered "gracious" in Prov 11:16; Ec 10:12; KJV. The Heb. *na'îm*, "pleasant," "delightful," is translated "gracious" in the RSV of Ps 135:3 and 147:1; KJV "pleasant," and the Heb. *nasa' ro'sh*, literally, "he lifted up the head," is rendered " (he) graciously freed" in 2 Ki 25:27, RSV. The Heb. *tôb*, "good," translated "graciously" in Hos 14:2, KJV, is better rendered "that which is good" (see RSV), or "good" in Zec 1:13, RSV, where it is translated "gracious." In the NT "gracious" appears generally in expressions translating phrases built around: (1) The Gr. *charis,* "grace." The expression "gracious words" (Lk 4:22) is literally, "words of grace" (compare the RSV and KJV of Col 4:6). In 2 Cor 8:6, 7, 19, the RSV renders *charis* as "gracious work," referring to the grace of liberality. (2) The Gr. *eudokia,* "good will," "favor," "good pleasure" (Mt 11:26; Lk 10:21; RSV). (3) The Gr. *euphēma,* "well-sounding," "attractive" (Php 4:8, RSV). The adjective *chrēstos,* "kind," "loving," is rendered "gracious" in 1 Pe 2:3, KJV.

Graff. *See* Graft.

Graft, KJV **Graff.** [Gr. *egkentrizō,* "to engraft."] The word occurs 6 times in Rom 11. The art of grafting olives was doubtless well known to Paul's readers. Improved olive twigs could be grafted into a wild olive stem, to combine the background reservoir of solidarity and establishment built into the root stock with the youthful vigor and potential for greater yield and better fruit that was found in the bud stock. However, in Paul's figure this process was reversed: wild olive shoots were grafted into a cultivated tree. Such shoots could not, according to nature, bear anything except wild berries, and we must not assume that Paul believed otherwise. His figure must not be pressed too far. It was adequate for the purposes for which it was intended. The Gentiles could become part of Israel and with them partake of the blessings of the original covenant (Rom 11:17, 19, 23, 24).

Some light may be thrown on Paul's figure by the observations of Sven Linder, who claims that in Greece the grafting of wild olive branches into cultivated trees is often a stage in the process of developing a healthy, productive olive tree. According to the practice, a wild branch is grafted into the root of an old olive tree, because wild shoots grow faster than those of cultivated trees. When the shoot has grown to a strong trunk, its branches are trimmed and shoots of cultivated trees are grafted into the wild trunk. As soon as they have established themselves the old tree is cut off. (*PJB* 26 [1930], 41-43.)

Granary. An RSV term, the rendering of: (1) the Heb. *ma'abûs* (Jer 50:26, KJV "storehouse"); (2) the Heb. *mammegurah,* "pond," "water pit," corrected to *megûrah,* "grain pit" (Joel 1:17, KJV "barn"); (3) the Gr. *apothēkē,* "storehouse," "barn" (Mt 3:12; Lk 3:17; KJV "garner"). The style and construction of ancient Egyptian granaries are well

known through pictures, models found in tombs, and excavated ruins. They were built of bricks, and were cylindrical in the lower part and conical in the upper part. The grain was poured into them through a hole in the top, which was reached by a ramp. Remains of granaries have been excavated also in several Palestinian sites, especially of bins dug into the ground and plastered. In *Tell Jemmeh* a large number of gigantic granaries of the Persian period were discovered, which had diameters of from 20 to 33 ft. and tapered toward the top.

Grape. *See* Vine.

Grass. A general term covering a vast number of herbaceous plants, cereals, rushes, sedges, and true grasses. Since many of its appearances are in a figurative setting where a quick withering in drought is implied, we may justifiably include tender herbaceous plants in general, for some true grasses are tough and drought resistant. Grasses provide forage for animals (Num 22:4; 1 Ki 18:5; Ps 104:14). Figuratively grass symbolizes temporality in general or the brevity of man's life in particular (Ps 90:5, 6; 103:15; Is 40:6-8).

Grasshopper. *See* Locust.

Grave. The translation of a number of Hebrew and Greek words. Some of these words refer to the grave simply as a physical place of interment; others depict it in highly poetic imagery or in figures of speech.

In the OT the grave is especially represented by the following terms: (1) The Heb. *qeber,* the basic word for "grave," and in the KJV so rendered 34 times (Ps 88:11; Is 53:9; etc.), also frequently "sepulchre" (Gen 23:6; Neh 2:3, 5; etc.). The RSV usually renders the term "tomb" (Jgs 8:32; etc.) or "grave" (Ps 88:5; etc.), and occasionally "sepulchre" (Gen 23:6), etc. (2) The Heb. *she'ôl,* a poetic expression for the grave, difficult to translate. The derivation of *she'ôl* is uncertain. Kohler derives it from the Heb. *sha'ah,* "to be desolate," "to be waste," to which an *l* was added (*LVTL* 935). Other authorities seek to find its linguistic basis in either Akkadian, Sumerian, or Egyptian terms. In poetic sections of the Bible it frequently appears in parallel constructions with "death" (Ps 6:5; Is 38:18; RSV) and "pit," a poetic word for the grave (Ps 30:3; Prov 1:12; RSV). In the KJV, *she'ôl* is rendered "grave" 31 times, and "hell" 31 times, but, because of the theological implications of "hell" (not inherent in the Hebrew word), this rendering is less desirable than "grave." The RSV consistently transliterates the term as "Sheol," except in 1 Ki 2:9; Song 8:6, where it renders it "grave." (3) The Heb. *shachath* (Job 33:22, KJV), literally, "pit," usually so rendered in the KJV and always in the RSV. It is a poetic term for the tomb. (4) The Heb. *qebûrah,* "grave," is so translated only in Gen 35:20; Eze 32:23, 24. Elsewhere it is rendered "burial," "sepulchre," etc.

In the NT the term appears as the translation of: (1) The Gr. *mnēmeion* (Lk 11:44; etc.), "grave," "tomb," usually translated "sepulchre" (KJV) and "tomb" (RSV). (2) The Gr. *mnēma,* a closely related word, translated "grave" (Rev 11:9; RSV "tomb"). (3) The Gr. *hadēs,* the poetic expression for "grave" and the state of man in death, a term signifying (on the basis of its derivation) the "unseen place." It is usually translated "hell" in the KJV, an unsatisfactory rendering, as in the case of *she'ôl.* The RSV usually transliterates the term as "Hades." The revelator saw both death and Hades (KJV "hell") thrown into "the lake of fire," described as "the second death" (Rev 20:14).

Graven Image. [Heb. *pesel,* "idol," "image," "carving," from *pasal,* "to cut," "to hew," "to carve."] An image made by cutting stone, shaping clay (see fig. 493), carving wood, casting metal, or carving metal. The Israelites were forbidden to make, possess, or worship such objects representing Deity (Ex 20:4). Because "graven images" were universally identified with heathen worship, as in Canaan (Deut 7:1, 5), Assyria (Nah 1:14; cf. v 1), and Babylon (Jer 50:38; cf. v 34), the Hebrew people were commanded to erect altars of uncut stone (Ex 20:25), lest religious symbols carved into the stone become objects of worship.

Graving. The art, also the product, of that class of artisans who carved, chiseled, or engraved images, statues, plaques in bas-relief, and engravings. Aaron fashioned the golden calf for the idolatrous Israelites with a "graving tool" (Ex 32:4). The golden plates on the high priest's miter were engraved with the words "Holiness to the Lord" (ch 28:36, KJV), and on two onyx stones were engraved the names of the sons of Israel (v 9). Huram king of Tyre sent an engraver for the intricate work in Solomon's Temple (2 Chr 2:13, 14). In addition to all the cast figures, the Temple contained many excellent examples of the graver's art—cherubim, lions, palms, oxen (1 Ki 7:25, 29, 31, 36; 2 Chr 3:7). Anciently, significant

messages were sometimes graven in rock (Job 19:24). *See* Graven Image.

Great Owl. *See* Owl.

Great Sea. The sea now known as the Mediterranean Sea (Num 34:6; Jos 1:4; 15:12), also called "hinder sea" or "western sea" (Deut 11:24; Joel 2:20; Zec 14:8), or simply "sea" (Num 13:29; Acts 10:6), since it was the chief sea known to the Hebrews. It lies between Europe, western Asia, and northern Africa, and is about 2300 mi. long and from 100 to 600 mi. wide (Map VI, A-1, etc.; XIX, D-5, etc.). In much of OT times this sea was the highway chiefly of the Phoenicians, who had connections with all parts of the Mediterranean world. The Hebrews, who lived in a country void of natural harbors, were not a seafaring people. They obtained their overseas products through the Phoenicians, as did many other nations at that time. In the time of Jesus, however, Palestine was in direct communication with the overseas world. It now had artificial harbor installations at Caesarea and Ptolemais, and the Mediterranean Sea had become virtually a Roman lake, which served the double purpose of connecting all parts of the far-flung empire and of providing the capital with essential food and other products of the provinces. Because of fierce gales from the northeast that often sweep down on the Mediterranean Sea during the winter, and the ancient sailors' great fear of the shallows off the shores of Africa (*see* Syrtis), as well as the straits of Messina between Sicily and Italy, and Cape Malia on the southern tip of Greece, sea traffic came to a practical standstill during the winter months.

Greaves. Thin plates of metal worn by soldiers to protect their legs below the knees. Greaves are mentioned once as part of the armor of the Philistine Goliath (1 Sa 17:6). They were unknown among ancient Oriental soldiers, including the Egyptians, but were used by Greek warriors. The Philistines, coming from Crete, may have adopted this piece of armor from their Greek neighbors. In Near Eastern excavations greaves have been found only at Enkomi on Cyprus and at Carchemish.

Grecia. *See* Greece.

Grecians. *See* Greek(s); Hellenist.

Greece (grēs). [Heb. *Yawan;* Gr. *Hellas.* The names Greek and Greece have come to us from Latin *Graecus* and *Graecia;* the Romans became acquainted with the name

Graikoi in southern Italy, where it was the name of a Greek tribe that had settled there.] The name given to the southern section of the Balkan Peninsula (see Hellas on Map XIII, B-1; Achaia on Map XIX, D-10). Ancient Greece was bounded on the north by Macedonia, on the east by the Aegean Sea, and on the west by the Ionian Sea. From its mountains in the north, where Mount Olympus' highest peak reaches up 9,793 ft., to its southernmost point, Cape Matapan, is 250 mi. Continental Greece is mountainous, so land connections are difficult, but its coast is so indented that most of the country can easily be reached from the sea. Thus the sea is not considered a hindrance to traffic, but rather a bridge. Many islands in the Ionian and Aegean seas belonged to Greece. The ancient Greeks also settled in colonies in Asia Minor, the Black Sea region, southern Italy, Sardinia and Sicily, northern Africa, and southern France.

I. Historic Greece. 1. *Origins.* The ancient Greeks traced their origin to legendary Hellen, from whom came the name "Hellenes," which they applied to themselves in ancient times, and the name "Hellas" for Greece, which they use to this day. Four main groups appear among the early Greeks, who spoke different dialects of a common language and had the same ethnic features. They were the Achaeans, Aeolians, Ionians, and Dorians. The Achaeans played the greatest role in the earliest period, and Homer sometimes refers to all Greeks as Achaeans. The Ionians and Dorians were the most important ethnic groups of later times, being the founders, respectively, of Athens and Sparta, the two most important cities on mainland Greece. The Ionians also founded many of the important coastland cities of western Asia Minor. The OT calls Greece and the Greeks by the Heb. *Yawan,* "Ionia," probably since the Ionians were the most important and the most representative of all Greek tribes. *See* Javan.

2. *Classical Greece.* Because of the lack of earlier written documents Greek history begins only about the 8th cent. B.C. The earliest periods are shrouded in mystery. Some legends and epics deal with the earlier heroic age, to which can now be added the results of excavations at prehistoric sites like Mycenae and Troy, which throw light on some of the epics. At the time when Greece enters into the light of history we find it divided into many city-states, each fostering its own interests, although they were all bound together by a common culture and language. Wars between the states took place occasionally, but the Olympic games, held every four years, served as a kind of unifying bond. Greece appeared on the horizon of the Hebrew people as a faraway country (Is 66:19; Eze 27:13, 19; Dan 8:21; 10:20; 11:2; Joel 3:6; Zec 9:13) during the two cent. (from 700 to 500 B.C.) that preceded the Greco-Persian War, when the foundation of Greek literature, architecture, art, and philosophy was being laid. It was this culture that became the ancestor of all Western culture and was its model for many centuries.

The first prominent role of Greece in world history resulted from the Greco-Persian Wars. These began in the time of Darius I, long after Cyrus had incorporated into his realm Ionian Greek cities of Asia Minor that had belonged to Lydia. But when the Persians entered the homeland of the Greeks, that small people revealed its finest qualities. The hitherto invincible Persians, who had overpowered the forces of empires and kingdoms such as those of Media, Lydia, Babylonia, and Egypt, were amazed to meet one humiliating defeat after another from the small armies of Greeks. That the Persians could be defeated was first demonstrated at Marathon in 490 B.C. and was proved again at Salamis, Plataea, Mycale, the Eurymedon, and in other battles in subsequent years. As a result of these wars the Greek city-states united under the leadership of one city, Athens, for a time; however, as soon as the danger passed they again fell apart. From about 479 to 431 B.C., Athens was the center of the Greek states and experienced its golden age, particularly under Pericles. Then came the Peloponnesian War (431-404 B.C.), which began with a quarrel between Athens and her colonies, but eventually involved all the Greek states and their navies, and ended with the downfall of Athens and the temporary supremacy of Sparta (404-371 B.C.). Sparta's supremacy was replaced in turn by a short-lived supremacy of Thebes (371-362 B.C.). A few years later (338 B.C.) practically all of Greece fell under the power of Philip of Macedon and soon after that became part of the Macedonian Empire of his son Alexander the Great.

II. Alexander's Greco-Macedonian Empire—Hellenistic Period. It was in this new role that the Hellenes, or Greeks, now united with the kindred Macedonians, played a role in the Macedonian world power.

It should be noted that the "Greece" (KJV "Grecia," grē'shĭ-à) that overthrew Persia (Dan 8:20, 21) was not the classical Greece of history, composed of a number of city-states, of which Athens represented the peak of Greek civilization; it was rather this Greco-Macedonian Empire of Alexander, which followed the classical period, after Greece proper had been absorbed by Macedonia.

1. *Alexander's conquests in the East.* Alexander the Great, being a Macedonian with a Greek education, promoted the spread of Greek language and culture in all conquered countries by forceful and by peaceful means. In a few years (334-323 B.C.) he crushed the Persian armies of Darius III, Persia's last king, and led his Macedonian and Greek soldiers victoriously through Asia Minor, Syria, and Palestine to the ancient land of the Nile, which easily fell to him. He then took Mesopotamia and the Persian homeland, pressing on until he reached the Indus Valley; finally, his soldiers refused to continue farther the conquest of unknown lands and kingdoms. He then set about to consolidate his empire and establish a union between the Orient and the Occident, choosing the ancient city of Babylon as his capital and residence, but his death ended his plans of a united Greco-Macedonian-Oriental empire (Map XIII). Yet one result of his conquest remained. Although his successors fought for decades against one another, and split up the inheritance of Alexander into sections of varying sizes and strength, they continued to promote the spread of Greek language and culture over the eastern Mediterranean world.

2. *Hellenistic civilization.* This culture —which we call Hellenistic in distinction from that of the Hellenic, or classical Greek, period that preceded it—survived the political power of the Macedonian kingdoms by centuries and molded Roman civilization. It is called Hellenistic (Grecized) because the Greek language, culture, and customs as spread over the Near East by Alexander's conquests was not purely Greek, but modified by the Macedonian customs of the rulers and the Oriental civilization of the subject peoples. But in the eastern Mediterranean area, Greek was almost universally spoken, Greek settlers were scattered everywhere, and Greek ways were taken up by the earlier inhabitants. (That is why the Jews, who resisted the process of Hellenization, did not distinguish between Greeks and Hellenized Easterners, but spoke of all their non-Jewish contemporaries as "Greeks.")

3. *The divided empire.* This Hellenistic world, composed of Greece, Macedonia, and the Hellenized East, remained a single Greco-Macedonian-Oriental civilization, more or less unified by its Greek elements, long after it lost political unity (Map XIII). After the death of Alexander his Macedonian leaders put on the throne his half brother Philip, a mental defective, and Alexander's posthumous son, Alexander. The successive regents for these puppet kings tried to hold the empire together, but others, who governed various territories as satraps of the empire, strove to divide it among themselves. Scarcely more than 20 years after Alexander's death the last strong claimant to the central power was defeated, at the battle of Ipsus (301 B.C.), by a coalition of 4 (Ptolemy, Cassander, Lysimachus, and Seleucus) who split the empire into 4 kingdoms. In 20 years more these 4 were reduced to 3 when Seleucus I, ruler of the eastern division, conquered the northern division. From then on the territory of Alexander's empire comprised three principal Hellenistic kingdoms plus numerous small, unstable, or short-lived states. These three kingdoms, ruled by the descendants of Alexander's Macedonian leaders, were Macedonia (generally including Greece), Egypt, and the Seleucid Empire (later called Syria, after it had lost its easternmost lands); and they continued until the Hellenistic world was taken over, piece by piece, by the rising power of Rome. Though they were annexed as the Roman provinces of Macedonia (146 B.C.), Syria (64/63 B.C.), and Egypt (30 B.C.), they retained the influence of Greek thought. Greek continued to be the language of the eastern half of the Roman Empire.

III. The Greek Peninsula Under Macedonian and Roman Rule. During the Hellenistic period the Greek homeland had passed through the hands of successive Macedonian overlords, who with incomplete success attempted to keep it under control. Athens continued to be recognized as the intellectual leader of the Greek world but lost its commercial importance, whereas Sparta attempted, without much success, to become the political leader of Greece. The rest of Greece was for the most part incorporated into two sectional confederacies—called the Aetolian League, comprising most of central Greece, and the Achaean League, to which belonged a large part of the Peloponnesus. In the 2d cent. B.C. it fell to the Romans, who interfered repeatedly in Greek affairs. When Mummius broke up the Achaean League and destroyed Corinth in 146 B.C., Greece was put under the governor of *Macedonia, which was annexed at that time as a Roman province. In 27 B.C. Greece was organized as a separate province under the name of *Achaia, by which name it appears in the NT except in Acts 20:2, where the name Greece occurs.

Greek(s) (grēk). [Heb. *Benê Hayyewanim*, "sons of the Ionians" (*see* Javan); Gr. *Hellēn*, "a Hellene."]

1. A native of *Greece or one of Greek descent. Joel 3:6 mentions the Greeks (KJV "Grecians," grē′shănz) as a distant nation. In the NT a *Hellēn* (Acts 17:4; 18:4; etc.) is distinguished from a *Hellēnistēs*, a *"Hellenist" (KJV "Grecian"), a Jew who spoke only Greek or had adopted Greek customs but was not of Greek descent.

2. In Jewish usage, a Gentile. In the NT the term "Greeks" (*Hellēnes*) is often used to designate foreigners in general in contrast to Jews (Rom 1:14, 16; 10:12; etc.). It is not certain whether the "Greeks" of Jn 12:20 were Greek proselytes to Judaism or merely Greek-speaking Gentiles, in which sense Paul often uses this term (Rom 1:14; etc.), though he uses it also of actual Greeks (Acts 18:4; etc.). Once he subdivides Gentiles into "Greeks" and "barbarians" (Rom 1:14, KJV), but this was the Greek, not the Jewish concept. To a Greek all the world was divided between Greeks and *barbarians—the latter being merely "foreigners," or those speaking a foreign language (as in 1 Cor 14:11, RSV). However, after Alexander the Great, with his Macedonian and Greek army, conquered the Near East and set up his Macedonian Empire, he introduced Greek language and culture among these "barbarians." Alexander and the Macedonian rulers who succeeded to his empire founded many "Greek cities," including a number in Palestine (*see* Decapolis), in which Macedonian and Greek settlers were the ruling class and the natives adopted Greek customs, Greek ideas, and the Greek language. Even outside these cities—the eastern Mediterranean area—Greek was the universal language. This transplanted and modified Greek civilization in the period after Alexander is called Hellenistic

(Grecizing) rather than Hellenic (Greek). Consequently, strictly speaking, non-Greeks who adopted Greek ways should be called Hellenists. But to the Jews in Palestine, their Hellenized neighbors were all "Greeks"; and the term "Hellenists" (KJV "Grecians") was applied to Jews who adopted Greek ways, or to Greek-speaking Jews of the Dispersion, born in countries outside Palestine. That is why "Jews and Greeks" came to mean merely "Jews and foreigners," or "Jews and heathen."

Greek (language). The language of the ancient Greeks, belonging to the Indo-European family of languages. Discoveries made during the last 60 years have shown that a distinction must be made between classical Greek, used by writers such as Herodotus, and the later Greek, called *Koinē*, spoken throughout the countries surrounding the eastern part of the Mediterranean Sea after the conquests of Alexander spread the language eastward. It was into this kind of Greek that the OT was translated in Alexandria during the 3d and 2d cent. B.C., producing the version commonly called the Septuagint (LXX), the Greek Scriptures used in the time of Jesus and the apostles by Jews who spoke Greek. Also the NT books were written in *Koinē*. By using the colloquial tongue the Bible became a people's book, and not a literary work in which only a few highly educated men of that time would have been interested. See fig. 215; *see* Writing.

Greetings. Many forms of greetings are recorded in the Bible, such as, "God be gracious unto thee" (Gen 43:29); "The Lord be with you" (Ruth 2:4); "Peace be to this house" (Lk 10:5). Greetings frequently took the form of, or were accompanied by, kisses (Gen 48:10; Ex 18:7; etc.). Customarily the cheek, forehead, beard, hands, or feet were kissed. In the NT the term "holy kiss" is sometimes found, indicating a token of Christian affection among believers (Rom 16:16; 1 Cor 16:20; 1 Th 5:26). Judas used a kiss to betray the Saviour (Mt 26:49; cf. Prov 27:6). Paul's letters abound with greetings from himself and those with him to friends and fellow laborers in the churches addressed (Rom 16:3-16; 1 Cor 16:20; 2 Cor 13:12; Php 4:21; 1 Pe 5:14; 3 Jn 14; etc.). The scribes and Pharisees fell under condemnation for their egocentric love of "greetings in the markets," which were doubtless involved and time consuming, as Oriental salutations sometimes are (Mt 23:7; Lk 11:43). It was probably because of the time involved in ancient greetings that Elisha, sending his servant Gehazi to lay a staff upon the dead son of the Shunammite woman, directed him to salute no one (2 Ki 4:29). Similarly, when Christ sent out the Seventy He told them to "salute no man by the way" (Lk 10:4), probably to impress upon them a sense of urgency in their preaching of the gospel. Elsewhere Christ admonished His followers not to be exclusive in their greetings, but that all, Jew and Gentile, friend and enemy, were to be regarded as brethren (Mt 5:43-47).

Greyhound. A rendering of the Heb. *zarzîr mothnayim* (Prov 30:31, KJV). The meaning of the Heb. *zarzîr* is unknown, but the LXX, the Syriac version, and the Targums render it "cock," a term taken over into the RSV. Others render it "starling" or "war horse." Since all of these animals, the greyhound, cock, starling, and horse, were known to the Hebrews of the 1st millennium B.C., none is ruled out as a possible definition of *zarzîr*, but it is impossible on the basis of present knowledge to make a positive identification.

Griddle. A rendering of the Heb. *machabath* (Lev 2:5; 6:21; 7:9; RSV), describing, apparently, some flat pan. It was used for baking cereal offerings.

Grind, Grinding. *See* Mill.

Grinders. A rendering of the Heb. *ṭochanôth* (Ec 12:3), "molars," literally, "grinding ones" or "grinding (teeth)," from *ṭachan*, "to grind." The form of the Hebrew word indicates that "teeth" should be supplied. Forms similar to *ṭochanôth*, derived from the same root, are found in both Arabic and Syriac, as metaphors for the molar teeth.

Grisled. The translation of the Heb. *barod*, "speckled" (Gen 31:10, 12; Zec 6:3, 6; KJV). It is related to the cognate Arabic word *'arbad*, "speckled." *Barod* is translated "dappled" in Zec 6:3, 6, RSV.

Gross. A term appearing in phrases translating: (1) The Heb. *ṭaphash* (Ps 119:70, RSV), literally, "to be fat," and figuratively, "to be stupid" or "to be dull." (2) The Heb. *'araphel* (Is 60:2; Jer 13:16; KJV), "darkness" or "gloom." The RSV translates *'araphel* "thick darkness" and "deep darkness," respectively. (3) The Gr. *pachunō* (Mt 13:15; Acts 28:27; KJV), "to make fat," figuratively, "to make impervious or dull."

Grove. The translation in the KJV of: (1) The Heb. *'eshel* (Gen 21:33), "a *tamarisk tree," not a group of trees as the word "grove" indicates. In 1 Sa 22:6 and

31:13 *'eshel* is rendered "tree" ("tamarisk tree," RSV). (2) The Heb. *'Asherah, *"Asherah," incorrectly rendered "grove" in Ex 34:13 and many other texts.

Grudge. A word used once with its obsolete meaning of "grumble" (Jas 5:9, KJV), a rendering of the Gr. *stenazō*, "to groan," "to complain."

Guarantee. *See* Earnest.

Guard. Oriental monarchs were protected by a bodyguard, a group of picked men who could be depended upon to guard the life of the king and to fulfill his commands. The captain of this guard held a most responsible position. Several of these captains are mentioned in the Bible: Potiphar, captain of the Egyptian guard (Gen 37:36), and Nebuzaradan and Arioch, captains of the Babylonian guard (Jer 39:9; Dan 2:14, 15). David seems to have had a bodyguard of Cherethites and Pelethites, that is, Cretans and Philistines (2 Sa 15:18; 1 Ki 1:38, 44). These foreign mercenaries, with 600 soldiers from Gath, were practically the only soldiers who remained faithful to David at the time of Absalom's rebellion. These foreign elements were less likely to sympathize with any popular uprising among the people. Ramses III also followed the custom of hiring Philistines, Sardinians, and other Peoples of the Sea in his army.

Guardians. The translation in the RSV of: (1) The Heb. *'omenim*, "caretakers of children," "guardians." Ahab's 70 sons were in the care of guardians (2 Ki 10:1, 5). (2) The Gr. *epitropoi*, persons who by law are charged with the care and supervision of minors. It is well known that guardians, according to ancient laws, were placed in charge of orphaned minors until such came of age legally, but it is not clear what legal system Paul had in mind when he stated that the father determined the date at which the responsibility of the guardians ceased (Gal 4:2). *Epitropoi* is translated "tutors" in v 2, KJV.

Gudgodah. *See* Hor-haggidgad.

Guest. Hospitality, even for total strangers, was expected of the Eastern household. The guest could share this hospitality without the least obligation of payment. In his defense Job contends that he had ever been attentive to the needs of travelers (Job 31:31, 32). Abraham was hospitable to strangers, who he later discovered were heavenly beings (Gen 18). Lot entertained two of these beings, not knowing at first that they were heavenly visitants (ch 19:1-3). So seriously did he consider his obligation toward his guests that for their protection he was willing to sacrifice his daughters' purity (Gen 19:4-8). Paul may have had these experiences in mind when he counseled Christians to exercise hospitality, stating that thereby some had entertained angels unawares (Heb 13:2). The Israelites were commanded to protect, and be hospitable to, strangers in their midst (Lev 19:33, 34). Simon failed to honor Christ with the courtesies a guest might ordinarily expect (Lk 7:44-46). Guestchambers are mentioned in the Bible (Mk 14:14; Lk 22:11). Elisha was frequently the guest of a Shunammite woman, who finally had a special guestchamber built for him (2 Ki 4:8-10).

Guest Room. Smaller houses (*see* House) of the ancient Orient had no special accommodation for guests, and visitors had to sleep and live in the rooms occupied by the members of the family. Larger houses of wealthy people, however, contained special guest rooms, usually in the upper story (Mk 14:14; Lk 22:11; KJV "guestchamber"; cf. 2 Ki 4:10).

Guilt Offering. See Sacrifices and Offerings.

Gulf. [Gr. *chasma*, "a gaping opening," literally, "a yawning."] A term appearing once (Lk 16:26), in the parable of the Rich Man and Lazarus, where it describes the unbridgeable space between Abraham and the rich man. Figuratively the chasm has been thought of as representing the fundamental difference in character between the righteous and the wicked.

Gum. A rendering of the Heb. *neko'th* (Gen 37:25; 43:11), translated "spicery" and "spices," respectively, in the KJV. The Hebrew term refers apparently to the resin of some tree, probably of the genus *Cistus*.

Guni (gū'nī). [Heb. *Gûnî,* "spotted sand grouse."]
1. A son of Naphtali and founder of the tribal family of the Gunites (gū'nīts) [Heb. *Gûnî*] (Gen 46:24; Num 26:48; 1 Chr 7:13).
2. A Gadite (1 Chr 5:15).

Gunites. See Guni.

Gur (gûr). [Heb. *Gûr,* "lion's whelp."] The name of an ascent near Ibleam, where Ahaziah, king of Judah, was mortally wounded (2 Ki 9:27). The site is unknown, although it is also mentioned as *Gurra* in the cuneiform tablets found at neighboring Taanach.

Gurbaal (gûr-bā'ăl). [Heb. *Gûr-ba'al.* The LXX and the Vulgate suggest the reading *ṭur Ba'al,* "the rock of Baal."] A place, probably in Edom, where Arabs lived in the time of King Uzziah (2 Chr 26:7); not identified.

Gutter. The translation in the KJV of: (1) The Heb. *rahaṭ* (Gen 30:38, 41), better rendered "trough" as in Ex 2:16. (2) The Heb. *ṣinnôr* (2 Sa 5:8), in the context probably the subterranean water course, consisting of a tunnel and a shaft, installed by the Jebusites, by which they could reach the spring of *Gihon in the Kidron Valley without leaving their city. Joab and his men, probably knowing of this waterwork, may have used it in a surprise attack to obtain access to the city. The RSV renders *ṣinnôr* "water shaft." The Jebusite waterworks in Jerusalem were discovered by Charles Warren in 1867, hence the shaft now bears the name "Warren's Shaft." It was more scientifically explored by L.-H. Vincent from 1909 to 1911 in connection with the work of the Parker Mission.

H

Haahashtari (hā'ȧ-hăsh'tȧ-rī). [Heb. *Ha-'achashtarî,* "the Ahashtarite."] A descendant of Judah through Hezron and Ashhur (1 Chr 4:6; cf. 4:5 and 2:24).

Habaiah (hȧ-bā'yȧ), RSV once **Hobaiah** (hȯ-bā'yȧ). [Heb. *Chabayyah* and *Chobayah,* "Yahweh has hidden."] The ancestor of a priestly family. Members of this family could not establish their genealogy (Ezr 2:61; Neh 7:63).

Habakkuk (hȧ-băk'ŭk). [Heb. *Chabaqqûq,* possibly from Akkadian *habbaququ,* an undefined fruit tree, or plant, or from Arabic *habaq,* the "water mint" (*Mentha aquatica*), an aromatic garden plant, or from the Arabic *habaqiyaq,* the "basil" (*Ocimum basilicum*). Some connect the name with the Heb. *chabaq,* "to embrace."] A prophet of Judah who lived a few years prior to the Babylonian captivity, and author of the 8th book of the Minor Prophets. The prayer-psalm of Hab 3, with its instructions to the "chief singer" of the Temple (v 19), has led some to suggest that Habakkuk may have been a Temple singer.

Habakkuk, Book of. The 8th of the so-called Minor Prophets, written by the prophet whose name is its title. No serious challenge has been raised as to the authenticity of the book or its right to a place in the Sacred Canon. An ancient Hebrew commentary on the book of Habakkuk found among the Dead Sea scrolls at *Khirbet Qumrân* in 1947 contains the Hebrew text of the 1st 2 chapters of the book, with many gaps, divided into short passages, each with accompanying comment Though written approximately 1,000 years earlier than the oldest Hebrew text previously available, the 2 texts are practically identical, thus providing additional evidence of the reliability of the transmitted text of the OT. Interesting, but minor, variant readings occur in chs 1:12, 14, 17; 2:1, 5, 16. *See* Scrolls, Dead Sea.

After the great work of reform under good King Hezekiah a century or so before Habakkuk's time, the kingdom of Judah lapsed once more into a state of apostasy that continued through the reigns of Manasseh and Amon and the 1st part of Josiah's reign. Apostasy consisted of

207. A column of the Habakkuk Commentary, one of the Dead Sea scrolls. The name of God, *YHWH*, is twice written in the archaic pre-exilic Hebrew (lines 7 and 14), distinguishable from the other lettering

idolatry, with its attendant evils, which was reflected in demoralized social and political conditions. Then Josiah in his 12th year (2 Chr 34:3) "began to purge Judah and Jerusalem" from idolatry, and in his 18th year, prompted by the discovery of the book of the Law (2 Ki 22:8-12), and under the influence of the prophetess Huldah (v 14), the prophet Jeremiah (Jer 1:2) and possibly Nahum, Habakkuk, and Zephaniah, Josiah instituted a series of reforms (2 Ki 23:1-25). Presumably, Habakkuk bore his recorded message prior to the time these reforms became effective, possibly during the latter part of the reign of Manasseh (ending in 641 B.C.), the short reign of Amon (641-639), or the early years of Josiah's reign (639-608). With a reasonable degree of accuracy the book may be dated about 630 B.C., a few years before the fall of Assyria and the resurgence of Babylon under Nabopolasser and Nebuchadnezzar, and some 25 years before the 1st Babylonian captivity, in 605 B.C.

The great theme of the book of Habakkuk is that God is still in control of the affairs of earth, even though sin and violence make the opposite appear to be true, and that ultimately righteousness and justice will prevail. The brief prophecy answers the troublesome question as to why God permits sinners to flourish, in somewhat the same vein that Job explains why God sometimes permits saints to suffer. Habakkuk sincerely loved the Lord and longed earnestly for the triumph of righteousness and justice, but he could not understand why God let apostasy and oppression go unchecked and unpunished among His chosen people (Hab 1:1-4). God answers the prophet's plaintive plea by assuring him that He is about to visit Judah for its sins and that the Chaldeans, "that bitter and hasty nation," are about to "march through the breadth of the land" as instruments of remedial justice (vs 5-11). Staggering at the thought, Habakkuk asks in reply, "O Lord, thou hast ordained *them* for judgment"? How could a just God permit "the wicked" to devour "the man that is more righteous than he?" (vs 12-17). In all earnestness and innocence Habakkuk demands an answer to what seems to him an unanswerable question (ch 2:1). In reply, God patiently assures the rash prophet of the certainty of the Babylonian invasion, and then quietly rebukes him for his temerity (vs 2-4). God outlines at length the sins of the Babylonians, by way of informing Habakkuk that He knows full well their evil ways (Hab 2:5-19). Nevertheless, God is still in charge of human affairs, and it is appropriate that all the earth—including the prophet Habakkuk—"keep silence before him." None may question His wisdom and justice (v 20). Meek and repentant, Habakkuk acknowledges God's wisdom and justice, yet in earnest devotion to Judah as the chosen instrument of God's plan on earth, he enters a humble plea that "in wrath" God will "remember mercy" (ch 3:1, 2). The prayer-song of ch 3 consists of an ecstatic vision in which the prophet foresees the coming of the Lord in judgment upon the nations and for the salvation of His chosen people. At this righteous prospect the prophet rejoices and ascribes praise to God (vs 3-19).

Habaziniah. *See* Habazziniah.

Habazziniah (hăb′á-zĭ-nī′á), KJV **Habaziniah** (hăb′á-zĭ-nī′á). [Heb. *Chabaṣṣinyah,* "Yahweh is exuberant."] The ancestor of a Rechabite of the time of Jeremiah (Jer 35:3).

Habergeon. A short jacket of mail worn by soldiers to protect their chest and arms. The word appears only in the KJV and is the translation of: (1) the Heb. *shiryôn,* *"coat of mail" (2 Chr 26:14; Neh 4:16); (2) the Heb. *shiryah,* "arrowhead" (Job 41:26, "javelin," RSV); (3) the Heb. *tachara′* (Ex 28:32; 39:23), a word of uncertain meaning. It may be a loan word from the Egyptian *dhr,* "shield," or "thong of leather," in which case it would probably designate a "leather cuirass."

Habor (hā′bôr). [Heb. *Chabôr;* Akkadian *Ḫabûru.*] A river of Mesopotamia, one of the two main tributaries of the upper Euphrates, which it joins after an independent flow of 190 mi. Captives from Israel were taken to the area by Tiglath-pileser III (1 Chr 5:26), and later by Sargon II after the capture of Samaria in 723/22 B.C. (2 Ki 17:6; 18:11). The river is now called *Khābûr* (see Map III, B-5).

Hacaliah (hăk′á-lī′á), KJV **Hachaliah** (hăk′á-lī′á). [Heb. *Chakalyah,* meaning uncertain.] The father of Nehemiah (Neh 1:1).

Hachaliah. *See* Hacaliah.

Hachilah (há-kī′lá). [Heb. *Chakîlah.*] A hill between Maon (1 Sa 23:19, 24-26) and the Wilderness of Ziph (ch 26:1-3) southeast of Hebron. The site has not been identified, although the sites of Ziph and Maon are known (Map VI, F-3). Hachilah was one of the places where David hid from Saul.

Hachmoni (hăk′mô-nī). [Heb. *Chakmônî,*

"a wise one."] The father of Jehiel (1 Chr 27:32).

Hachmonite (hăk′mô-nīt). [Heb. *Chakmônî.*] The family name of Jashobeam, one of David's "mighty men" (1 Chr 11:11). The family name is given as Tachmonite (RSV "Tahchemonite") in 2 Sa 23:8, a possible scribal error.

Hadad, I (hā′dăd). [Heb. *Hadad;* Akkadian *Adad, Addu,* or *Ḫaddu;* alphabetic Ugaritic *Hd.* The name of an ancient Semitic storm god identified by the Assyrians with their god of wind and storm, Ramman, who was called Rimmon in Damascus. *See* Ben-hadad; Hadadezer.]

1. An early king of Edom, from the city of Avith, who smote Midian in the country of Moab (Gen 36:35, 36; 1 Chr 1:46, 47).

2. The last in the list of kings of Edom, whose city was Pau or Pai (1 Chr 1:50). In Gen 36:39 he is called Hadar (hā′där) [Heb. *Hadar*], evidently through a confusion in the Hebrew of the letters *r* and *d,* which are very similar.

3. An Edomite prince (possibly the son of Hadad, I, 2), who, as a little child, escaped with his guardians to Egypt at the time Joab subjugated Edom and slew all members of the royal house. He was well received by the Pharaoh, and was later given the Egyptian queen's sister as wife. He returned to Edom after the death of David and Joab and became an adversary against Solomon (1 Ki 11:14-22).

Hadad, II (hā′dăd). [Heb. *Chadad,* "sharp," "pointed."] A son of Ishmael and founder of the tribe of the same name (1 Chr 1:30), called Hadar in Gen 25:15, KJV. The existence of this tribe is attested in cuneiform records that call the tribe *Ḫudadu.*

Hadadezer (hăd′ăd-ē′zēr), KJV frequently **Hadarezer** (hăd′á-rē′zēr). [Heb. *Hadad′ezer* and *Hadar′ezer,* "(The god) Hadad is a help." In the form *Hadar′ezer* the first *r* is a scribal substitution for *d,* a mistake easily made in Hebrew, since these two characters show great similarity in both pre- and postexilic Hebrew script.] King of the Aramaean state of Zobah in Syria, whom David twice defeated, first when setting out to restore Israelite power at the Euphrates (2 Sa 8:3-13; 1 Chr 18:3-10) and later when Hadadezer came to the aid of the Ammonites (2 Sa 10:6-19; 19:6-19).

Hadadrimmon (hā′dăd-rĭm′ŏn). [Heb. *Hadadrimmôn,* a compound name made up of the two names of a Semitic god of thunder, lightning, and rain—Hadad and Rimmon.] A name mentioned in Zec 12:11 which some regard as that of a locality near Megiddo, where Josiah's death was lamented, and which they identify with the present site of *Rummâneh,* lying about 1½ mi. northwest by west of Taanach. It is, however, more likely that "the mourning for Hadadrimmon" (RSV) refers to a pagan rite connected with the worship of the Syrian God Hadad-Rimmon. *See* Rimmon, 5.

Hadar. *See* Hadad, I, 2; Hadad, II.

Hadarezer. *See* Hadadezer.

Hadashah (há-dăsh′á). [Heb. *Chadashah,* "the new (city)."] A town in the Shephelah of Judah, near Lachish (Jos 15:37); not identified.

Hadassah (há-dăs′á). [Heb. *Hadassah,* "myrtle."] The transliteration of the Hebrew name originally borne by Queen Esther (Est 2:7).

Hadattah (há-dăt′á). [Heb. *Chadattah,* "new."] A town in the southern part of Judah (Jos 15:25). In the RSV the name is joined to the preceding word Hazor, to form the compound name Hazor-hadattah. *See* Hazor, 4; Hazor-hadattah.

Hades. *See* Hell.

Hadid (hā′dĭd). [Heb. *Chadîd.*] A town in Benjamin, mentioned first in Egyptian records as *Hdyt,* but in the Bible only in postexilic literature and in connection with Lod (in NT times, Lydda) and Ono (Ezr 2:33; Neh 7:37; 11:34, 35). It is identified with *el-Haditheh,* 3½ mi. east-northeast of Lydda.

Hadlai (hăd′lī). [Heb. *Chadlay,* "a stout one."] An Ephraimite (2 Chr 28:12).

Hadoram (há-dō′răm). [Heb. *Hadôram.*]
1. A son of Joktan (Gen 10:27; 1 Chr 1:21), and ancestor of the South Arabic tribe of the Adramites.
2. A son whom the king of Hamath sent to David with a congratulatory message after David's defeat of Hadadezer (1 Chr 18:10). In 2 Sa 8:9, 10 he is called Joram.
3. An officer over Rehoboam's levy (2 Chr 10:18), also called *Adoniram (1 Ki 4:6) and Adoram (ch 12:18).

Hadrach (hā′drăk). [Heb. *Chadrak,* spelled *Chzrk* in the Aramaic inscription of Zakar, and *Hatarikka* in cuneiform inscriptions.] An area and city in Syria mentioned in Zec 9:1 in connection with Damascus and Hamath. The city may be identified with the present *Tell el-ʿAfis* in the plain of Aleppo. For Aleppo see Map XI, B-4.

Ha-eleph (há-ē′lĕf), KJV **Eleph** (ē′lĕf). [Heb. *ʾEleph,* "ox."] A village near Jerusalem assigned to Benjamin (Jos 18:28); site not identified.

Hagab (hā′găb). [Heb. *Chagab,* "locust." The name occurs in Ugaritic as *Hgb,* and is also found on the Lachish ostraca from Jeremiah's time.] The ancestor and founder of a family of Nethinim, or Temple servants, some members of which returned from Babylon with Zerubbabel (Ezr 2:46).

Hagaba. *See* Hagabah.

Hagabah (hăg′á-bà), or **Hagaba** (hăg′á-bà). [Heb. *Chagabah,* variant *Chagaba′,* "locust." The name occurs in Ugaritic as *Hgbt.*] An ancestor and founder of a family of Nethinim, or Temple servants (distinct from the Hagab of Ezr 2:46), some members of which returned from Babylon with Zerubbabel (Ezr 2:45; Neh 7:48).

Hagar (hā′gär), KJV of NT **Agar** (ā′gär). [Heb. *Hagar,* "flight." The name appears in the same form in ancient South Arabic, Nabataean, and Palmyrene inscriptions, and on a seal found at Jericho. Gr. *Hagar.*] An Egyptian maidservant of Abraham, probably acquired during his Egyptian sojourn (Gen 16:1; cf. ch 12:10, 16). At Sarah's insistence, Hagar was taken by Abraham as his secondary wife, according to the custom of the times (see *SDACom* 1:317, 318), after he had been in Canaan for 10 years. He was then 85 years old and sonless, and by this action hoped that he would have an heir. When Hagar knew she was to have a child she became overbearing toward her mistress. This led Sarah to deal harshly with her, with the result that Hagar fled into the wilderness. As she wandered between Kadesh and Bered on the desert road to Egypt an angel of the Lord found her at a well and sent her back to her mistress, promising that her child would become the ancestor of a great nation. This experience led her to call the well Beer-la-hai-roi, "the well of the living one who sees me." She obeyed the angel, returned to Abraham's household, and subsequently gave birth to a son whom Abraham named Ishmael (ch 16:1-16).

Some years later Ishmael is described as mocking the child Isaac, who in the meantime had been born to Sarah (Gen 21:9). The "mocking" is described in Gal 4:29 as an act of persecution. Sarah then demanded that Hagar and Ishmael be expelled from the household. Abraham was displeased by this demand, but received divine directions to comply. Hagar with her son was therefore sent away. They lost their way in the wilderness of Beer-sheba and seemed about to perish of thirst when the angel of the Lord appeared again, directed them to a well of water, and reminded Hagar of the previous promise made to her concerning Ishmael (Gen 21:9-19). The last mention of Hagar in the OT is a reference to her choice of a native Egyptian woman as a wife for her son (v 21). In the NT she is referred to as a symbol of the old covenant (Gal 4:22-26).

Hagarenes. *See* Hagrite.

Hagarite. *See* Hagrite.

Hagerite. *See* Hagrite.

Haggai (hăg'á-ī). [Heb. and Aramaic *Chaggay,* "one born on a feast day." The name occurs also on an ancient Hebrew seal, and on an inscribed jar handle.] A prophet of the Restoration period used by God to inspire the returned exiles to complete the rebuilding of the Temple, and author of the book that bears his name. It has been inferred from Hag 2:3 that Haggai was now an old man who had seen the 1st Temple prior to its destruction in 586 B.C., and from vs 10-19 that he was a priest. Aside from the book that bears his name he is mentioned only in Ezr 5:1; 6:14. He was a contemporary of the prophet Zechariah (Ezr 5:1; cf. Zec 1:1).

Haggai, Book of. The 10th of the so-called Minor Prophets, addressed to the returned exiles at Jerusalem, who had become disheartened in their efforts to rebuild the Temple. The book consists of 5 messages that inspired the people to arise and complete the task. Four messages (the 1st, 3d, 4th, and 5th) are precisely dated, to the year, month, and day in the 2d year of Darius I, and cover a period of about 3½ months toward the close of the year 520 B.C. (chs 1:1; 2:1, 10, 20). A 5th (the 2d) is approximately dated (ch 1:13-15). With the return of nearly 50,000 Jews under Zerubbabel in 536 B.C., by the decree of Cyrus, the work of rebuilding the Temple was begun (Ezr 3), but the immensity of the task and the interference of enemies had brought the work to a halt (ch 4). As a result of the encouragement of Haggai and Zechariah work was recommenced in 520/19 B.C. and completed 4 or 5 years later, c. 515 B.C. (ch 6:15).

The theme of the book is active co-operation in the work of the Lord and the assurance that faithful service will be richly rewarded. The hearty response of leaders and people to the 1st message, dated approximately Aug. 29, 520 B.C., a call to arise and build the house of the Lord that still lay in ruins, constitutes one of the brightest episodes of sacred history (Hag 1:1-12). The eager obedience of the people elicited a 2d message giving the assurance that God would be with them in the task (vs 13-15). As the work progressed it became evident that the new structure would fall far short of Solomon's Temple in size and beauty, but in his 3d message, some 7 weeks after the 1st, Haggai assured the builders that "the desire of all nations" would come and "fill this house with glory" (ch 2:1-9). When, at the end of about 3½ months, the work of preparation had progressed to the point where the foundation was laid, a 4th message came proclaiming that henceforth God would richly bless His people for their zeal and faithfulness (vs 10-19). A 2d message on the same day envisioned the overthrow of the heathen nations and confirmed Zerubbabel as a "signet" (vs 20-23).

Haggedolim (hăg'ē-dō'lĭm). [Heb. *Haggedôlim,* "the great ones."] According to the RSV the father of an overseer of the priests in Nehemiah's time (Neh 11:14, RSV). The KJV translators did not consider *Haggedôlim* a personal name, and rendered the term "the great men."

Haggeri. *See* Hagri.

Haggi (hăg'ī). [Heb. *Chaggî,* "my feast." The name occurs in a Phoenician text and is found repeatedly in ancient Hebrew inscriptions.] A son of Gad, and founder of the tribal family, the Haggites (hăg'īts) [Heb. *Chaggî*] (Gen 46:16; Num 26:15).

Haggiah (hă-gī'á). [Heb. *Chaggîyah,* "feast of Yahweh."] A Merarite Levite (1 Chr 6:30).

Haggith (hăg'ĭth). [Heb. *Chaggîth,* "festal."] A wife of David and mother of Adonijah (2 Sa 3:4; 1 Ki 1:5, 11; 2:13; 1 Chr 3:2).

Haggites. *See* Haggi.

Hagri (hăg'rī), KJV **Haggeri** (hăg'ĕ-rī). [Heb. *Hagrî.*] The father of one of David's "mighty men," Mibhar (1 Chr 11:38).

Hagrite (hăg'rīt), KJV **Hagarite** (hā'gär-īt), **Hagerite** (hā'gĕr-īt), and **Hagarenes** (hăg'á-rēnz). [Heb. *Hagrî.*] A nomadic people who dwelt throughout Transjordan, and were apparently rich in sheep, asses, and camels. The Reubenites and others waged a war with them (1 Chr 5:18-20), and Saul destroyed them (v 10). They are mentioned in Ps 83:6, and one of them had charge of David's flocks (1 Chr 27:31). They are called *Hagaranu* in inscriptions of Tiglath-pileser III and of Sennacherib and *Agraioi* by Strabo.

Hahiroth. *See* Pi-hahiroth.

Hai. *See* Ai.

Hail. [Heb. *barad;* Gr. *chalaza.*] Ice particles or stones that form in thunderheads and that occasionally grow to a sufficient size to fall to the ground before melting. Isaiah compared the judgments of God to a storm of hail (Is 28:2). A severe hailstorm constituted the 7th plague on Egypt (Ex 9:23, 24; Ps 78:47, 48), and huge hailstones are described as descending upon men in the last of the 7 last plagues at the end of time (Rev 16:21). Following Joshua's defeat of Adoni-zedek and his allies at Gibeon, the Lord rained down hailstones and slew more than the armies of Israel had slain (Jos 10:11). At the present time hail is rare in Egypt, more frequent in Palestine.

Hair. The ancients often manifested extreme sorrow by cutting the hair (Job 1:20; cf. Is 15:2; Jer 16:6; etc.). In sorrowful astonishment or anger, or as an insult, the hair was sometimes torn or plucked (Ezr 9:3; Neh 13:25; Is 50:6). In OT times the Hebrews apparently wore their hair comparatively long (see fig. 246), as did the Assyrians. By contrast the Egyptians customarily shaved their heads. The Hebrews under the *Nazirite vow did not cut their hair at all (Num 6:2, 5; Jgs 13: 5; 16:17). Samson's long hair was a token of his Nazirite vow. When his hair was cut the Lord left him and his strength departed (Jgs 16:17-20). Absalom apparently had unusually luxuriant hair (2 Sa 14:25, 26). According to Josephus (*Ant.* viii. 7. 3) Solomon's charioteers wore very long hair which was sprinkled each day with gold dust. Christ illustrated God's intimate care of us by stating that the hairs of our heads are numbered (Mt 10:30). Paul stated that it is a shame for a man to have long hair, but that a woman's hair is "a glory to her," given to her "for a covering" (1 Cor 11: 14, 15). Women, he warned, were not to adorn themselves with "broided hair" and artificialities, but rather with good character and good works (1 Ti 2:9, 10; cf. 1 Pe 3:3, 4). *See* Goat's Hair.

Hakkatan (hăk'à-tăn). [Heb. *Haqqaṭan,* "the little one." The name occurs in Akkadian as *Qiṭinu* and *Kuttunu.*] A Jew whose son Johanan led 110 male members of his family from Babylonia with Ezra (Ezr 8:12).

Hakkoz (hăk'ŏz), KJV generally **Koz** (kŏz). [Heb. *Haqqôṣ,* possibly "the thorn."] A descendant from Aaron whose family was organized by David into the 7th of the 24 priestly courses (1 Chr 24:1, 10). The

genealogical records of members of the family seem to have been lost during the Exile, so that after the return to Palestine these members could not prove their claims to the priesthood. Consequently they were not immediately admitted to their offices (Ezr 2:61, 62; Neh 7:63, 64). However, later they must have succeeded in proving their rights, for a descendant of Hakkoz is found in office in the time of Ezra and Nehemiah (cf. Ezr 8:33 with Neh 3:21).

Hakupha (hà-kū'fà). [Heb. *Chaqûpha',* meaning uncertain.] The ancestor and founder of a family of Nethinim. Some members of his family returned from Babylonia with Zerubbabel (Ezr 2:51; Neh 7:53).

Halah (hā'là). [Heb. *Chalach.*] An area to which the captured inhabitants of Samaria were transported by the Assyrian king after the fall of their capital city (2 Ki 17:6; 18:11; 1 Chr 5:26). It is probably "the land of *Ḥalaḥḥu*" mentioned in Assyrian inscriptions, which seems to have lain northeast of Nineveh (Map XI, B-5). One of Nineveh's gates was called "Gate of the land *Ḥalaḥḥu.*" On the basis of a textual emendation Halah occurs in the RSV of Ob 20, where the KJV reads "this host."

Halak (hā'lăk). [Heb. *Chalaq,* "smooth" or "bare."] A mountain in the south of Palestine toward Mount Seir (Jos 11:17; 12:7). It has been identified with the mountain ridge *Jebel Halâq* or Mount Halak, about 30 mi. southwest of the Dead Sea (Map II, D-2).

Half Shekel. *See* Shekel.

Halhul (hăl'hŭl). [Heb. *Chalchûl.*] A city in the hill country of Judah (Jos 15:58), identified with the present village of *Ḥalḥûl,* about 3 mi. north of Hebron (Map VI, E-3).

Hali (hā'lī). [Heb. *Chali,* "ornament."] A place on the boundary of Asher (Jos 19: 25); not yet identified with certainty.

Hall. The translation in the KJV of: (1) The Gr. *aulē,* meaning "palace" in Mk 15:16 and "courtyard" in Lk 22:55. (2) The Gr. *praitōrion* (Mt 27:27), transliterated "praetorium" in the RSV, but translated "common hall" in the KJV. The reference in this passage is to Pilate's official residence in Jerusalem, but there is uncertainty as to whether this was in the palace of Herod or in the Tower of Antonia (*see* Barracks). In the RSV "hall" is a rendering of several Hebrew and Greek terms probably less accurately rendered in the KJV by such words as "parlour" (1 Sa 9:22), "porch" (1 Ki 7:6-8), and "house" (Est 5:1; Dan 5:10). "Wedding hall" (Mt 22:10, RSV) is a rendering of the Gr. *numphōn*. However, the Greek text followed by the KJV reads *gamos*, "wedding." Important textual evidence may be cited for either reading. The RSV translation "audience hall" for the Gr. *akroatērion* of Acts 25:23 is preferable to the KJV term "place of hearing." However, the Gr. *scholē* of Acts 19:9, rendered "hall" by the RSV, is more correctly translated "school" as in the KJV.

Hallelujah, KJV **Alleluia.** [Gr. *allēlouia*, a transliteration of the Heb. *halelú-yah*, "praise ye Jah."] A pious interjection meaning "praise Jah" or "praise the Lord" (Rev 19:1, 3, 4, 6). The term is a transliteration of an imperative form of the Heb. *halal*, "to praise," to which is added a shortened form of the Heb. *Yahweh*, the personal name of God. The Hebrew phrase is found a number of times in the Hebrew OT, chiefly in the "hallel," that is, "praise" psalms, but it is always translated "Praise the Lord" or "Praise ye the Lord." In many of these psalms the exclamation appears at both the beginning and the end (Ps 106; 113; 146-150), in others only at the beginning (Ps 111; 112), and in others at the close (Ps 104; 105). These expressions of praise in such psalms may have served certain liturgical purposes in ancient times, or they may have been simply used as expressions of profound praise and gratitude to God. Since the interjection contains a reference to the name of God, its casual or irreverent use would be prohibited by the 3d commandment.

Hallohesh (hă-lō′hĕsh), KJV once **Halohesh** (há-lō′hĕsh). [Heb. *Hallôchesh*, "the enchanter." The name occurs in Babylonian as *Laḥishu*.] The father of the Shallum who, with his daughters, helped to repair the wall of Jerusalem (Neh 3:12). He also set his seal to Nehemiah's covenant (ch 10:1, 24).

Hallow. [Heb. generally *qadash*, "to be holy," "to make holy," "to consecrate," "to sanctify"; Gr. *hagiazō*, "to sanctify," "to reverence."] To sanctify or make holy, to set apart for a holy use, in the Biblical sense. The consecrating of some thing or person to a sacred purpose, with the implication that the object or person thus dedicated is separated from common usage. Thus the seventh day was sanctified, or hallowed, by the Lord at the end of the Creation week (Gen 2:3; Ex 20:11), dedi-

cating it to a holy purpose. The priests were consecrated to their sacred responsibilities (Ex 29:1), the tabernacle and all the sanctuary equipment were hallowed for holy uses (ch 40:9). The first-born sons were set apart and devoted to the Lord (Num 3:13). The same concept, translating the same Hebrew and Greek expressions, occurs frequently in several other renderings, such as "consecrate," "dedicate," and "sanctify."

Halohesh. See Hallohesh.

Halt. In the KJV the translation of: (1) The Heb. *pasach*, "to be lame," "to limp" (1 Ki 18:21). (2) The Heb. *ṣela'*, "limping," "stumbling." Jacob is described as "limping" (RSV) because of his lame thigh (Gen 32:31). The psalmist was ready to stumble (RSV "fall") because of his discouragement and sense of guilt (Ps 38:17). (3) The Gr. *chōlos*, "lame," "crippled" (Mt 18:8; Mk 9:45; Lk 14:21; Jn 5:3). Christ stated that it was better to gain eternal life in a crippled condition than to suffer the final judgments of God (Mt 18:8). The RSV uses "halt" only in the sense of coming to a stop (2 Sa 15:17; 2 Ki 5:9; etc.).

Ham, I (hăm). [Heb. *Cham*, probably "hot."] 1. The youngest son of Noah, born after his father was 500 years old (Gen 5:32; 9:24). During his father's drunkenness Ham acted shamefully and thus incurred the displeasure of Noah and brought a curse upon Canaan, Ham's son, who seems to have been involved in his father's sin (ch 9:22-27). To Ham's descendants belong the African and Arabian Cushites (Ethiopians; see Ethiopia), the Egyptians, and the Canaanites.

2. A name used for Egypt in poetical passages of the OT (Ps 78:51; 105:23, 27; 106:22).

Ham, II (hăm). [Heb. *Ham*.] A place in Transjordan, probably between Moab and Ashteroth-karnaim in Bashan (cf. Gen 14:5; Deut 2:9-11). Here Chedorlaomer and his confederates defeated the Zuzim in Abraham's time (Gen 14:5). It has been identified with the *Hm* of the Egyptian Palestine lists of Thutmose III and Shishak I, which is the present *Hâm*, about 5 mi. south-southwest of Irbid.

Haman (hā′măn). [Heb. *Haman*, a name of doubtful etymology, possibly connected with the Elamite divinity *Humman* or *Humban*.] The son of Hammedatha (a Persian name), an Agagite (Est 3:1; 9:24), and a high-ranking official at the court of Ahasuerus (Xerxes). Josephus claims that he was related to the Amalekite royal house (*Ant.* xi. 6. 5). Two Amalekite kings named Agag are known (Num 24:7; 1 Sa 15:8). This relationship would explain Haman's deep-seated hatred for the Jews and his desire to destroy not only his personal enemy Mordecai but the whole nation that had been the archenemy of his people. Having become a favorite of Xerxes, Haman was offended and chagrined when Mordecai refused to pay him the honors to which he felt he was entitled. He therefore planned the destruction of Mordecai and of all the Jews (Est 3; 5:14). His plan was foiled by Queen Esther's interference, and instead of the Jews' being destroyed, he and his sons perished miserably (chs 7:10; 9:7-10).

Hamath (hā'măth), KJV once **Hemath** (hē'măth). [Heb. *Chamath,* "fortress"; in cuneiform texts *Amatû* and *Hammâtu;* and in Egyptian inscriptions *Ḥmt.*] An ancient and important city on the Orontes in central Syria about halfway between Damascus and Aleppo, today called *Ḥamā* (Map XI, B-4). Its early inhabitants are reckoned among the Canaanites in Gen 10:15-18. In the last centuries of the 2d millennium B.C. the Hittites took over the city, as is shown by the many Hittite inscriptions found at *Ḥamā.* Later the city was taken over by the Aramaeans, who held it until it fell into the hands of the Assyrians.

David lived in friendly relationships with Hamath (2 Sa 8:9, 10; 1 Chr 18:3, 9, 10), but Solomon seems to have occupied parts of its territory, for he built cities there (2 Chr 8:4). However, it must have regained its independence with the breakup of Solomon's kingdom, for in Ahab's time it joined other Syrian and Palestinian states in their fight against Assyria. Hamath took part in the battle against Shalmaneser III at Qarqar in 853 B.C. with 700 chariots, 700 cavalrymen, and 10,000 foot soldiers (*ANET* 279).

208. The modern city of *Ḥamā* in Syria with the ruin hill of ancient Hamath in the background

Some years later it was still influential, for Amos called it "Hamath the great" (Amos 6:2). Hamath was again temporarily incorporated into the kingdom of Israel when Jeroboam II recovered the city (2 Ki 14:28). However, it soon became independent again, but later fell to the Assyrians (chs 18:34; 19:13), who deported some of its population to Samaria, whereas Sargon II settled some from vanquished Samaria at Hamath (2 Ki 17: 24, 30; Is 11:11). It may have become part of the Assyrian province of Damascus, since Jeremiah mentions it in connection with that city (Jer 49:23). Ezekiel's vision of the restored country of Israel placed its northern border at Hamath (Eze 47:16, 17, 20; 48:1).

Excavations carried out from 1931 to 1938 at the tremendous tell of ancient Hamath by a Danish expedition under H. Ingholt showed that the city had been in existence from the earliest historical times.

Lit.: H. Ingholt, *Rapport préliminaire sur la première campagne des fouilles de Hama* (Copenhagen, 1934); *Rapport préliminaire sur sept campagnes de fouilles à Hama en Syrie* (Copenhagen, 1940).

Hamath, Entrance of. See Entrance of Hamath.

Hamathites (hā'măth-īts). [Heb. *Chamathi.*] The people of Hamath (Gen 10:18; 1 Chr 1:16).

Hamath-zobah (hā'măth-zō'bà). [Heb. *Chamath Ṣôbah,* "fortress of Zobah."] A city in Syria conquered by King Solomon (2 Chr 8:3). It seems to have been located somewhere near Tadmor and Hamath. It is of interest to note that 3 bricks found in the excavations of Hamath are inscribed with the name *Ṣbh* (= *Ṣobah*).

Hammath (hăm'ăth), KJV once **Hemath** (hē'măth). [Heb. *Chammath,* "hot spring."]

1. The ancestral head of the Rechabite family (1 Chr 2:55).

2. A fortified town in the territory of Naphtali (Jos 19:35). Because of its name it has been identified with *Ḥammâm Ṭabarîyeh,* a village with warm baths, a short distance south of Tiberias. It is generally thought that the Hammoth-dor of Jos 21:32 and the Hammon of 1 Chr 6:76 are identical with Hammath.

Hammedatha (hăm'ē-dā'thà). [Heb. *Hammedatha',* a Persian name, probably "given by (the sacred drink) *Hâma.*"] The father of Haman (Est 3:1, 10; 8:5; 9:10, 24).

Hammelech (hăm'ē-lĕk). [Heb. *Hammelek,*

"the king."] According to the KJV the name of the father of Jerahmeel and Malchiah, two high officials at the court of King Jehoiakim (Jer 36:26; 38:6). However, it is more likely that "Hammelech" should be rendered literally as "the king," thus making Jerahmeel and Malchiah sons of the king, or royal princes.

Hammer. The translation of: (1) the Heb. *maqqebeth* (1 Ki 6:7; Is 44:12; Jer 10:4), the hammer of the carpenter, smith, or stonemason, as well as the mallet used to drive tent pins into the ground (Jgs 4:21); (2) the Heb. *halmûth* (ch 5:26, KJV), "hammer" or "mallet" (RSV); (3) the Heb. *pattish* (Is 41:7), the forging hammer of the smith, used figuratively of the Chaldeans under Nebuchadnezzar (Jer 50:23); (4) the Heb. *kêlappôth* (Ps 74:6), a loan word from Akkadian *kalapâti*, which denotes a crowbar rather than a hammer; (5) the Heb. *mappeṣ*, probably a "club" or "mace" (*see* Battle Axe).

Hammolecheth (hă-mŏl′ĕ-kĕth), KJV **Hammoleketh** (hă-mŏl′ĕ-kĕth). [Heb. *Hammoleketh*, "the queen."] A sister of Gilead, and ancestress of several Gileadite clans (1 Chr 7:18).

Hammoleketh. *See* Hammolecheth.

Hammon (hăm′ŏn). [Heb. *Chammôn*, "hot spring."]

1. A border town in the territory of Asher (Jos 19:28). Two Phoenician inscriptions mentioning the worship of a Baal Hammon have been found at *Umm el-ʿAwâmîd*, 10 mi. south of Tyre. This would suggest that the Israelite town be sought there, but the identification is uncertain.

2. A Levitical town of Naphtali (1 Chr 6:76), probably Hammath. *See* Hammath, 2.

Hammoth-dor (hăm′ŏth-dôr′). [Heb. *Chammoth Do'r*.] A Levitical city in Naphtali, probably Hammath (Jos 21:32). *See* Hammath, 2.

Hammuel (hăm′û-ĕl), KJV *Hamuel* (hăm′-û-ĕl). [Heb. *Chammû'el*, meaning uncertain. The name occurs also in South Arabic inscriptions.] A son of Mishma, a Simeonite (1 Chr 4:26).

Hamonah (há-mō′ná). [Heb. *Hamônah*, "multitude."] A symbolic name for a city where the armies of Gog were to be buried (Eze 39:16).

Hamon-gog (hā′mŏn-gŏg′). [Heb. *Hamôn Gôg*, "multitude of Gog."] A symbolic valley where the dead bodies of Gog's host were to be buried (Eze 39:11, 15).

Hamor (hā′môr), KJV of NT **Emmor** (ĕm′ŏr).

[Heb. *Chamôr*, "ass"; Gr. *Emmôr*.] A *Hivite prince of the city of Shechem, from whose sons Jacob bought a piece of land, where later the bones of Joseph were buried (Jos 24:32; Acts 7:16). Hamor and Shechem, his son, were slain by Simeon and Levi, Jacob's sons, for Shechem's rape of Dinah, Jacob's daughter (Gen 34:1-31; Jgs 9:28).

Hamran. *See* Hemdan.

Hamstring, KJV generally **Hough.** The act of laming or disabling an animal by cutting the large tendons of its legs. Joshua and David thus crippled the horses of enemy war chariots (Jos 11:6, 9; 2 Sa 8:4; 1 Chr 18:4), because they had no use for them. After the Israelites employed horses in their army, they no longer followed this practice.

Hamuel. *See* Hammuel.

Hamul (hā′mŭl). [Heb. *Chamûl*, "pitied."] The younger son of Perez, and founder of one of the clans of Judah (Gen 46:12; Num 26:21; 1 Chr 2:5).

Hamulites (hā′mŭl-īts). [Heb. *Chamûli*.] Descendants of *Hamul (Num 26:21).

Hamutal (há-mū′tăl). [Heb. *Chamûṭal*, "my husband's father is the dew."] A daughter of Jeremiah of Libnah, and wife of King Josiah, and mother of Kings Jehoahaz and Zedekiah (2 Ki 23:31; 24:18; Jer 52:1).

Hanameel. *See* Hanamel.

Hanamel (hăn′á-mĕl), KJV **Hanameel** (há-năm′ĕ-ĕl). [Heb. *Chanam'el*, probably "God is kind."] A cousin of Jeremiah, from whom the prophet bought an ancestral field during the siege of Jerusalem. This purchase demonstrated Jeremiah's faith that the country would again be inhabited (Jer 32:7-15).

Hanan (hā′năn). [Heb. *Chanan*, "gracious." The name occurs in ancient Hebrew, South Arabic, and Aramaic inscriptions.]

1. One of David's "mighty men" (1 Chr 11:43).

2. A Benjamite (1 Chr 8:23).

3. A Benjamite, a descendant of Saul through Jonathan (1 Chr 8:38; 9:44).

4. A man of God whose sons had a chamber in the Temple (Jer 35:4).

5. The ancestral head of a family of Nethinim, some of whom returned from Babylonia with Zerubbabel (Ezr 2:46; Neh 7:49).

6. A man of Nehemiah's time who, with Ezra and others, explained the Law of God to the people (Neh 8:7). He was probably one of those who sealed Nehemiah's covenant (ch 10:10).

7 and 8. Two principal men of the Jews who sealed Nehemiah's covenant (Neh 10:22, 26).

9. One of the treasurers appointed by Nehemiah during his 2d term in office as governor of Judea (Neh 13:13).

Hananeel. *See* Hananel.

Hananel (hăn′á-něl), KJV **Hananeel** (hăn′á-nē-ĕl). [Heb. *Chanan'el*, "God is gracious." The term is attested as a personal name in ancient Hebrew and Aramaic inscriptions.] The name of one of Jerusalem's towers (Neh 3:1; 12:39; Jer 31:38; Zec 14:10). It is mentioned as being near the Sheep Gate and the Tower of Meah; hence it must be sought in the eastern portion of the northern wall of the Temple and city. It was probably part of the Temple fortress. Map XVII; fig. 259.

Hanani (há-nā′nī). [Heb. *Chanani*, "gracious." The name occurs also in South Arabic inscriptions.]

1. A son of Heman. He was placed in charge of the 18th of the 24 courses of musicians appointed by David to serve in Solomon's Temple (1 Chr 25:4, 25).

2. A seer, and father of the prophet Jehu (1 Ki 16:1). He was imprisoned when he rebuked King Asa for relying on Syria (2 Chr 16:7-10).

3. A priest in the time of Ezra who was married to a foreign wife (Ezr 10:20).

4. Brother of Nehemiah, and bearer of information about the conditions in Jerusalem (Neh 1:2). He and the governor of the castle were later given charge of the city police in Jerusalem (ch 7:2).

5. A Levite musician who took part in the dedication of the wall in Nehemiah's time (Neh 12:36).

Hananiah (hăn′á-nī′á). [Heb. *Chananyah* and *Chananyahû*, "Yahweh is gracious." The name occurs also in ancient Hebrew and Aramaic inscriptions.]

1. A Benjamite (1 Chr 8:24).

2. A son of Heman, and leader of the 16th of the 24 courses of musicians appointed by David to serve in Solomon's Temple (1 Chr 25:4, 23).

3. A military officer of King Uzziah (2 Chr 26:11).

4. The father of a prince in Jeremiah's time, Zedekiah (Jer 36:12).

5. A false prophet from Gibeon who in the 4th year of Zedekiah's reign prophesied that the captives of Judah would return from Babylon after 2 years. Jeremiah predicted that he would die for his false prophesying. The prediction was fulfilled 2 months later (Jer 28:1-17).

6. A man whose descendant Irijah, an officer, arrested Jeremiah (Jer 37:13-15).

7. One of Daniel's 3 Hebrew friends. The Chaldeans named him Shadrach (Dan 1:6, 7, 11, 19).

8. A son or grandson of Zerubbabel (1 Chr 3:19, 21); possibly the Joanna (RSV "Joanan") of Lk 3:27 in the genealogy of Jesus, the two component parts of the name being transposed.

9. A member of the family of Bebai. He was among those who had foreign wives in the time of Ezra (Ezr 10:28).

10. A perfumer who helped to rebuild the wall of Jerusalem in Nehemiah's time (Neh 3:8).

11. A priest who took part in the dedication of the wall in Nehemiah's time (Neh 12:41).

12. A Judahite chief who set his seal to Nehemiah's covenant (Neh 10:23).

13. The governor of the castle of Jerusalem who, with Nehemiah's brother Hanani, was placed in charge of the police in Jerusalem (Neh 7:2).

14. A postexilic priest, and head of a house (Neh 12:12).

Hand. [Heb. generally *yad*; Gr. *cheir*.] A term used with a variety of meanings. In Deut 32:36; Jos 8:20 *yad* is used as a synonym for "power," and is thus translated. *Yad* may also mean "side" (1 Sa 4:18), "place" or "position" (Num 2:17; Deut 23:12), "bank" of a river (Deut 2:37, RSV), "monument" (1 Sa 15:12, RSV), "authority" (Gen 41:35, RSV), etc. The hand of the Lord is spoken of as being "heavy" to punish (1 Sa 5:6), "strong" to deliver (Ex 13:3, 14, 16), not "shortened" (Num 11:23), "stretched out" to smite sinners (Is 5:25).

The expression "thou shalt consecrate Aaron and his sons" (Ex 29:9) is literally, "thou shalt fill the hand of Aaron and the hand of his sons." To wash one's hands was to declare one's innocency (Deut 21:6-8; Mt 27:24). To pour water on the hands of someone meant to serve him (2 Ki 3:11). Hands were lifted up in prayer (Ps 28:2), clapped in joy (Ps 47:1), became defiled with blood (Is 59:3), and were laid upon a man to ordain him for the Lord's service (1 Ti 4:14). Christ was delivered into "the hands of sinful men" (Lk 24:7), but He committed His life into the hands of His Father (ch 23:46).

Egyptian reliefs depicting battle scenes show that it was customary for soldiers to cut off a hand from each of the enemy

209. Hands of enemies killed in battle are counted before Ramses III; scene is from the temple wall at *Medinet Habu*

soldiers they had slain to prove their valor and receive the rewards promised for acts of bravery (see fig. 209, which shows the recording of the hands of slain enemies after a battle). There seems to be a reference to such a custom in a question the people of Succoth asked Gideon, "Are the hands of Zebah and Zalmunna [the 2 kings of the Midianites, whom Gideon pursued] now in thine hand?" (Jgs 8:6).

Handbreadth. [Heb. *ṭephach* and *ṭophach*.] A linear measure derived from the breadth of the hand, or·palm (Ex 25:25; 1 Ki 7:26; 2 Chr 4:5; Ps 39:5; Eze 40:5, 43; 43:13), 1/6 of a *cubit. It was either 8.72 cm. (3.43 in.) if the Egyptian cubit is followed, or 7.41 cm. (2.92 in.) if the Hebrew cubit of the 8th cent. B.C. is followed. In Ps 39:5 a handbreadth is used figuratively for the shortness of life.

Handkerchief. A rendering of the Gr. *soudarion* (Acts 19:12), a loan word from the Latin, meaning "cloth for wiping perspiration." It is rendered "napkin" in Lk 19:20; Jn 20:7. Handkerchiefs touched by Paul were brought to the sick, who were then healed.

Handmaid. [Heb. *'amah, shiphchah*; Gr. *doulē*.] A female slave, servant, or attendant. The keeping of female slaves or servants was followed from earliest times (Gen 16:1; 29:24; etc.). God gave the Hebrews definite instructions concerning the rights of slaves (Ex 20:10; 21:7-9, 27, 32; etc.). The term was sometimes used as an expression of humility (1 Sa 25:24; 2 Sa 14:12; Lk 1:38).

Handpike, KJV **Handstaff.** [Heb. *maqqel yad*, "handstaff."] A weapon used by the forces of Gog (Eze 39:9). *Maqqel* generally means simply "rod" or "staff," items not usually used in warfare, but since in Eze 39:9 it is listed as a weapon, commentators suggest that it refers to a mace with a long handle, and that the handle, being a characteristic part of the weapon, gave it its name.

Handstaff. *See* Handpike.

Handwriting. The literal rendering of the Gr. *cheirographon* (Col 2:14, KJV). The word is attested in many Greek papyri and may designate any handwritten document, but in the papyri is used especially of a certificate of indebtedness, or a bond, hence the translation "bond" in the RSV. According to some commentators, Paul uses "handwriting" of the Mosaic law, the validity of which ended at the cross; according to others, of the condemnation of the law.

Hanes (hā′nēz). [Heb. *Chanes*.] An Egyptian city (Is 30:4), probably the one called *Ḥt-nn-nśwt* in Egyptian, *Hnēs* in Coptic, and Heracleopolis Magna by the Greeks, and now called *Ahnâs el Medîneh*. It lies about 30 mi. southeast of Lake Moeris in the Faiyum (Map V, C-2). However, some scholars have sought Hanes in the eastern delta, where a Heracleopolis once stood, but on a site yet unidentified.

Hanging. Death by hanging, as capital punishment, is not attested in pre-Hellenistic times. However, the bodies of those who had been put to death by other means were sometimes hung on poles. This ex-

437

210. Relief from *Nimrûd* showing captured men impaled by soldiers of Tiglath-pileser III

posure was designed to increase the disgrace suffered by the criminal (Gen 40: 19, 22; Deut 21:22; Jos 10:26; 2 Sa 4: 12). In some Biblical passages where a Persian practice is mentioned, the "hanging" refers to impaling (*see* Gallows), a form of capital punishment depicted on many Assyrian reliefs of war scenes. A pointed pole was fastened upright in the ground, and the victim was impaled in one of two ways: the point was either run into his body from his buttocks upward, or was thrust beneath the ribs upward (see fig. 210). Darius threatened to punish all transgressors of his decree with impaling (Ezr 6:11), and Haman planned this form of death for Mordecai, but suffered it himself (Est 5:14; 7:10). However, there are records of suicide by hanging in early times before it became an official manner of execution (2 Sa 17:23). In the time of Christ, death by hanging was common (see Mt 27:5).

Hangings. *See* Screen.

Haniel. *See* Hanniel.

Hannah (hăn'à). [Heb. *Channah*, "graciousness."] One of the 2 wives of the Levite Elkanah, and mother of Samuel, who was born to her in answer to special prayer and whom she dedicated to God. She later became the mother of 5 more children (1 Sa 1:1 to 2:21).

Hannathon (hăn'à-thŏn). [Heb. *Channathôn*, spelled *Ḥinnatuni* in the Amarna Letters.] A town on the border of Zebulun (Jos 19:14). It has tentatively been identified with *Tell el-Bedeiwîyeh*, 16 mi. west of Tiberias (Map VI, C-3).

Hanniel (hăn'ĭ-ĕl), KJV once **Haniel** (hăn'-ĭ-ĕl). [Heb. *Channî'el*, "God is grace," or "God is kind to me." The name occurs in cuneiform records as *Ḥinni-el*.]

1. The prince representing the tribe of Manasseh serving on the committee to divide the land (Num 34:23).

2. An Asherite (1 Chr 7:39).

Hanoch (hā'nŏk), KJV once **Henoch** (hē'-nŏk). [Heb. *Chanôk*, "dedicated." This same Hebrew term is also rendered "Enoch."]

1. A descendant of Abraham through Midian, and head of a tribal clan (Gen 25:4; 1 Chr 1:33).

2. A son of Reuben and founder of the Hanochites (hā'nŏk-īts) [Heb. *Chanoki*], a tribal family (Gen 46:9; Ex 6:14; Num 26:5; 1 Chr 5:3).

Hanochites. *See* Hanoch, 2.

Hanun (hā'nŭn). [Heb. *Chanûn*, "pitied." The name is attested in Phoenician and Aramaic inscriptions, and in cuneiform texts, as the name of the king of Gaza, spelled *Ḥanûnu* (*ANET* 282).]

1. Son of Nahash and king of Ammon. His disgraceful treatment of David's envoys, who had been sent to congratulate him on his accession to the throne, resulted in a war in which his kingdom lost its independence (2 Sa 10:1 to 11:1; 1 Chr 19:1 to 20:3).

2 and 3. Two Jews who helped Nehemiah rebuild the wall of Jerusalem (Neh 3:13, 30).

Hap. A chance occurrence (Ruth 2:3, KJV). The Hebrew term thus translated (*miqreh*) means "what happens of itself."

Hapharaim (hăf-à-rā'ĭm), KJV **Haphraim** (hăf-rā'ĭm). [Heb. *Chapharayim*, "two pits."] A border town of Issachar (Jos 19: 19). It has been identified with *eṭ-Ṭaiyibeh*, 7 mi. northeast of Jezreel.

Haphraim. *See* Hapharaim.

Happizzez (hăp'ĭ-zĕz), KJV **Aphses** (ăf'sēz). [Heb. *Happiṣṣeṣ*.] An Aaronic priest, head of the 18th of the 24 courses into which David divided the priesthood (1 Chr 24:15).

Hara (hā'rá). [Heb. *Hara'*.] A place to which captives from the kingdom of Israel were deported by Tiglath-pileser III (1 Chr 5:26); not identified.

Haradah (há-rā'dá). [Heb. *Charadah*.] A place in the wilderness between Sinai and Kadesh where the Israelites camped (Num 33:24).

Haran, I (hā'răn). [Heb. *Haran*, "sanctuary."]

1. A son of Terah, and brother of Abraham and Nahor. He died in his native city of Ur of the Chaldees, leaving a son, Lot, and two daughters, Milcah and Iscah (Gen 11:26-31). It is uncertain whether the city of Haran (Heb. *Charan*) is named after him, since the Hebrew spelling of the names is different.

2. A Gershonite Levite (1 Chr 23:9).

Haran, II (hā'răn), KJV of NT **Charran** (kăr'ăn). [Heb. *Charan.* The name occurs also in ancient South Arabic. Gr. *Charran.*]

1. A son of the Caleb who was of the family of Hezron (1 Chr 2:18, 46).

2. An old city in Upper Mesopotamia (2 Ki 19:12). It lay on the Balikh, one of two important tributaries of the Euphrates. Its name in cuneiform texts (*Harrânu*) means "street" in Akkadian. It may have received this name because of its location on important ancient crossroads between Babylonia and Syria, Egypt and Asia Minor. It was, like Ur, the seat of a Moon cult, and King Nabonidus' mother was high priestess in its temple. Terah, Abraham's father, settled in this area with his family on his way from Ur to Canaan (Gen 11:31, 32; 12:4, 5), and the descendants of Terah's son Nahor remained there when Abraham and Lot were called away (chs 28:10; 29:4, 5). If this city was named after Terah's son, Haran (*see* Haran, I, 1), it was not because he founded it, because he had died before the family left Ur (ch 11:28). The conquest of the city by the Assyrians is mentioned in 2 Ki 19:12. The ruined site of *Harrân* has been identified with ancient Haran. Its modern population is very small. The ruins of the great mosque are probably located at the site of the famous Moon temple, as indicated by the discovery of 3 inscribed steles of Nabonidus in this structure by D. S. Rice in 1956. See Map III, B-4.

Hararite (hā'rá-rīt). [Heb. *Harari,* either "the man from Harar" or "a mountain-

eer."] An appellative of several of David's "mighty men" (2 Sa 23:11, 33; 1 Chr 11: 34, 35). A place by the name of Harar is unknown, hence Hararite should probably be understood as signifying a mountaineer, or a man of the mountains.

Harbona (här-bō'ná), KJV once **Harbonah** (här-bō'ná). [Heb. *Charbôna'* and *Charbônah,* an ancient Persian name with uncertain meaning.] One of the 7 chamberlains of Ahasuerus (Est 1:10; 7:9).

Harbonah. *See* Harbona.

Harden (the Heart). The translation of various Hebrew and Greek words denoting in their contexts obdurate and persistent refusal to submit to God's revealed will. The most common Hebrew word thus translated is *qashah,* which means "to make hard," "to be severe," "to become stubborn" (Ex 7:3; Ps 95:8). Similarly used are *kabed,* "to be heavy," "to be insensible," "to be dull," "to be unresponsive" (Ex 8:15, 32; 9:34; 10:1), and *chazaq,* "to make firm," "to become strong" (ch 4:21; etc.). The corresponding Greek words are *pōroō,* "to harden," "to petrify," "to make dull" (Mk 8:17; Jn 12:40), and *sklērunō,* "to harden," "to make stiff" (Rom 9:18; Heb 3:8, 15; 4:7). Bible writers attribute the act of hardening both to God (Ex 4:21; Rom 9:18) and to man (Ex 8:15; Heb 3:8). Nearly half of the Bible passages that refer to the hardening of the heart relate to the refusal of Pharaoh and the Egyptians to release God's chosen people from bondage. *Qashah, kabed,* and *chazaq* are used interchangeably, both of the Lord's hardening Pharaoh's heart (Ex 4:21; 7:3; 9: 12; 10:1, 20, 27; 11:10; 14:4, 8) and of the act of hardening as Pharaoh's own (chs 8:15, 32; 9:34; 13:15). Each successive manifestation of divine power left the haughty monarch more determined to do as he pleased. He despised and rejected the light of duty until he became insensitive to it, and the light was finally withdrawn. It was his resistance to the light that hardened his heart. God was responsible for the hardening process only in the sense that He had provided the light and that He eventually withdrew it, thus confirming the king in his evil course. The Bible often represents God as doing that which He does not prevent. Even the heathen recognized that Pharaoh and the Egyptians were responsible for the hardening of their hearts (1 Sa 6:6).

God takes no pleasure in the suffering and death of the wicked, but desires that all shall repent and be saved (Eze 33:11; 1 Ti 2:4; 2 Pe 3:9). He leaves nothing undone that can be done to encourage men in the way of salvation (Is 5:4), and does nothing to discourage or quench the least flickering of desire for divine grace (ch 42:3). The same manifestation of divine mercy that leads some men to find salvation in Christ results in condemnation and death to those who resist and reject that mercy. Rom 9:18 is sometimes construed to mean that God extends salvation to some and deliberately withholds it from others. The context, however, makes evident that Paul here refers, not to the grace that brings salvation, as such, but to cooperation with God in the advancement of His will on earth. The eventual result of refusing to cooperate with God's will in history is a withdrawal of the opportunity to do so, and this withdrawal may also be considered as a further hardening of the heart.

Hare. [Heb. *'arnebeth*.] An animal mentioned in the Bible in the lists of unclean animals (Lev 11:6; Deut 14:7). Palestine has several kinds of hares. The most common are the Syrian and Egyptian hares (*Lepus syriacus* and *Lepus aegyptiacus*). The hare is not a ruminant, although it moves its jaws as if it were chewing the cud. As in the case of the *rock badger (Lev 11:5, RSV), the Biblical statement that the hare chews the cud (Lev 11:6; Deut 14:7) should doubtless be understood as referring to this movement of the jaws.

Hareph (hā'rĕf). [Heb. *Chareph*, "harvested." The name is attested on an ancient Hebrew seal inscription.] One of the sons of Caleb, and ancestor of the inhabitants of Beth-gader (1 Chr 2:51).

Hareth. *See* Hereth.

Harhaiah (här-hā'yȧ). [Heb. *Charchayah* and *Charhayah*.] A Jew whose son Uzziel, a goldsmith, helped Nehemiah rebuild the wall at Jerusalem (Neh 3:8).

Harhas (här'hăs). [Heb. *Charchas*.] The grandfather of the Shallum who was the husband of the prophetess Huldah (2 Ki 22:14). In 2 Chr 34:22 he is called Hasrah (hăz'rȧ) [Heb. *Chasrah*]. The transposition of letters is probably a scribal error. Similarly, the letters *ch* and *h*, because of their similarity in postexilic Hebrew, are easily confused.

Har-heres. *See* Heres, 1.

Harhur (här'hûr). [Heb. *Charchûr*, probably " (born during) a fever (of the mother)."] The ancestral head of a family of Nethinim. Some members of this family re-

turned from Babylonia with Zerubbabel (Ezr 2:51; Neh 7:53).

Harim (hā'rĭm). [Heb. *Charim*, "dedicated."]
1. The ancestral head of a large priestly family which bore his name. In the time of David this family formed the 3d of the 24 courses into which the priests had been organized (1 Chr 24:8). Some members returned with Zerubbabel from Babylonia (Ezr 2:39; Neh 7:42), and certain ones are listed as being married to foreign wives in Ezra's time (Ezr 10:21). The Harim who set his seal to Nehemiah's covenant (Neh 10:5) and the priest Adna of ch 12:15 seem to have belonged to this family.
2. The ancestral head of a large family which bore his name. A group of 320 male members of this family returned with Zerubbabel from Babylonia (Ezr 2:32; Neh 7:35). Ezra lists 8 members of the family among those married to foreign wives (Ezr 10:31). One member of this family is mentioned as assisting Nehemiah in rebuilding Jerusalem's wall (Neh 3:11).

Hariph (hā'rĭf). [Heb. *Chariph*, "harvest."]
1. The ancestral head of a family of whom 112 male members returned with Zerubbabel from Babylonia (Neh 7:24); apparently called Jorah (jō'rȧ) [Heb. *Yorah*, "early rain"] in Ezr 2:18.
2. A Jew who set his seal to Nehemiah's covenant (Neh 10:19).

Harlot. A prostitute, one whose body is yielded in illicit sexual relations for the sake of monetary gain, often called "whore" in the KJV. Israel's connections with other nations, which indicated apostasy from God, is called harlotry (Eze 16:15-29). There were 2 classes of harlots—those who pursued harlotry for personal gain, and those who served worshipers in idol sanctuaries (*see* Cult Prostitutes). Harlotry is consistently condemned in the Scriptures (Deut 22:21; 23:18; etc.) and young men are warned against being ensnared by the wiles of the harlot (Prov 6:24-28; 7). By forsaking their sin harlots may gain an entrance into the kingdom of heaven, and there is more hope for them than for the self-righteous religionist (Mt 21:31). Figuratively, Israel's apostasy is described as harlotry (Eze 16). Apocalyptic Babylon is called mother of harlots" (Rev 17:5).

Harmon (här'mŭn). [Heb. *Harmôn*.] A place of unknown locality (Amos 4:3, RSV). The KJV, with insufficient linguistic justification, renders *Harmôn* as "palace."

Harnepher (här'nĕ-fẽr). [Heb. *Charnepher*,

211. Wall picture of Egyptian dancing girls playing the harp, lute, double flute, and lyre

a transliteration of the Egyptian name *Ḥr nfr,* meaning "(the god) Horus is good."] An Asherite (1 Chr 7:36).

Harness. *See* Breastplate, 2.

Harod (hā'rŏd). [Heb. *Charod,* probably "intermittently flowing spring," or "spring of terror."]

1. A spring by which Gideon encamped with his army while the camp of the Midianites was at the hill of Moreh, down in the valley (Jgs 7:1). It is identified with *'Ain Jâlûd,* 8 mi. west-northwest of Beth-shean on the northwest slope of Mount Gilboa. Map VI, C-3.

2. According to the RSV apparently a place from which two of David's "mighty men," Shammah and Elika, came (2 Sa 23:25). It has not been identified with certainty. *See* Harodite.

Harodite (hā'rŏd-īt). [Heb. *Charodi.*] An inhabitant apparently of a town called Harod (2 Sa 23:25, RSV "of Harod"), which has not yet been identified with certainty. The appellation appears as Harorite (hā'rō-rīt) [Heb. *Harôri*] in 1 Chr 11:27 (RSV "of Harod"), probably a confusion of the letters *ch* and *h* on the one hand, and of *d* and *r* on the other, letters very similar in postexilic Hebrew. *See* Harod, 2.

Haroeh. *See* Reaiah, 1.

Harorite. *See* Harodite.

Harosheth of the Gentiles. *See* Haroshethha-goiim.

Harosheth-ha-goiim (hȧ-rō'shĕth-hȧ-goi'ĭm), KJV **Harosheth of the Gentiles** (hȧ-rō'shĕth). [Heb. *Charosheth Haggôyim,* "Harosheth of the heathen."] The city of Jabin's general, Sisera (Jgs 4:2, 13, 16). It has been identified with *Tell 'Amr,* on the bank of the Kishon, opposite the village of *el-Hârithîyeh,* 10½ mi. west of Nazareth, at the southeastern edge of the plain of Acre. Map VI, C-3.

Harp. The translation in the KJV of the Heb. *kinnôr* and of the Aramaic *qîthros,* which, however, designate the *lyre. The true harp is the Heb. *nebel,* which the KJV generally translates "psaltery" (1 Sa 10:5; 2 Sa 6:5; etc.), but several times "viol" (Is 5:12; 14:11; Amos 5:23; 6:5). The Gr. *kithara* is rendered "harp" in both versions (1 Cor 14:7; Rev 5:8; etc.). Harps were common from very early times in Egypt and Mesopotamia. The earliest extant pictorial representation of a harp is of an 11-stringed instrument. It appears on a stone relief from Lagash in Lower Mesopotamia and was made 2000 B.C. Egyptian harps generally had

their sounding boxes at the bottom and were usually so large that they were set on the floor when played. Mesopotamian harps had sounding boxes either at the top or at the bottom.

The harps mentioned in the Bible were used almost exclusively for religious purposes (1 Chr 15:16, 20, 28; etc.).

The Aramaic *pesanṭerîn* and *pesanterîn* in Dan 3:5, 7, 10, 15, translated "harp" (RSV) and "psaltery" (KJV), is a loan word from the Gr. *psaltērion,* "psaltery," which designates a triangular stringed instrument with the sounding board above the strings. Cuneiform documents of Nebuchadnezzar's time prove that among the

212. Assyrian harpist

many foreigners employed on royal building projects in Babylon were Greek-speaking Ionians and Lydians. These artisans may have introduced into Babylonia certain musical instruments formerly unknown there. It would be only natural that, with the acceptance of these instruments by the Babylonians, their Greek names would be taken over. This would explain the use of a Greek name for a certain musical instrument in 6th-cent. B.C. Babylon. See Ten-stringed Harp.

Harrow. It is unknown whether the ancients had a harrow in the modern sense of the word. That the Israelites broke the clods in their fields in some manner may be concluded from texts like Job 39:10, Is 28:24, and Hos 10:11, although the Heb. *śadad,* rendered "to harrow" or "to break the clods," is of somewhat questionable meaning. The instrument mentioned in 2 Sa 12:31 and 1 Chr 20:3, Heb. *charîṣ,* rendered "harrow" in the KJV and "pick" in the RSV, is of an unknown nature. Hence it is impossible to describe the ancient agricultural instrument that performed the work of a modern harrow.

Harsha (här'shá). [Heb. *Charsha',* "the silent one," or "the deaf one."] The ancestral head of a family of Nethinim. Some members of this family returned from exile with Zerubbabel (Ezr 2:52; Neh 7:54).

Hart. [Heb. *'ayyal.*] The stag, deer, or hart, an animal belonging to the family *Cervidae.* Since there are few wooded areas left in Palestine, the deer is no longer found there. During the 19th cent. two kinds of deer still existed in Palestine, the *Cervus capreolus,* "roebuck," and the *Cervus dama,* "fallow deer." However, the bones of the red deer (*Cervus elaphus*), the reindeer (*Cervus tarandus*), and the elk (*Cervus alces*) have been found in caves of the Lebanon, which show that a great variety of deer existed there in ancient times. The Heb. *'ayyal,* "hart," may stand for the red deer or the fallow deer. It was a clean animal eaten by the Hebrews (Deut 12:15; 14:5), and was popular meat on Solomon's table (1 Ki 4:23). See Hind; Roebuck.

Harum (hä'rŭm). [Heb. *Harûm* and *Harum.* The name occurs in both spellings, also in ancient South Arabic inscriptions.] A Judahite (1 Chr 4:8).

Harumaph (há-roo'măf). [Heb. *Charûmaph,* "having a slit nose."] A Jew whose son Jedaiah assisted Nehemiah in the rebuilding of the wall of Jerusalem (Neh 3:10).

Haruphite (há-roo'fît). [Heb. *Charûphî,* in pre-Masoretic spelling *Charîphî.*] The appellative of Shephatiah, a Benjamite (1 Chr 12:5), who came to David at Ziklag. No town by the name Haruph is known from which the appellative may have been derived. Perhaps Shephatiah belonged to the family of *Hariph.

Haruz (hä'rŭz). [Heb. *Charûṣ,* probably "gold" or "diligent." The name occurs in

Assyrian as *Ḥarruṣu.*] Father of King Manasseh's wife, Meshullemeth (2 Ki 21:19).

Harvest. The 1st Palestinian grain to be harvested was barley, which in general was ripe for harvest in the early part of April. The harvesting of this crop was preceded by the offering of the wave sheaf (Lev 23:10, 11) on the 16th of Nisan (see 2 Sa 21:9). The barley harvest was closely followed by the wheat harvest (Ruth 2:23), which was spread over several weeks, beginning early in the lowlands but ending about June or July in the uplands. The wheat harvest was celebrated by the presentation of loaves in the Temple on the 50th day from Nisan 16 (Lev 23:15-21; Deut 16:9-12). In the autumn came the fruit harvest. When all the harvests were completed the Feast of Ingathering (Ex 23:16), or Tabernacles (Lev 23:34-43), was celebrated. This was a time of great rejoicing and thanksgiving to the Lord for the blessings of field and forest (Neh 8:14-18; cf. Is 9:3). Ps 65 and, possibly, Ps 67 are harvest hymns of rejoicing.

Jesus referred to the world as a field ripe for the gospel harvest, but with few laborers to do the work (Mt 9:37, 38; Lk 10:2; Jn 4:35). The harvest is also used to represent a time of judgment (Hos 6:11; Joel 3:13). Christ likened the judgments of the last days to a harvest (Mt 13:24-30; cf. Rev 14:15). Jeremiah likens the end of the harvest to the close of human probation (Jer 8:20; cf. Rev 22:11).

Hasadiah (hăs-á-dî'á). [Heb. *Chasadyah,* "Yahweh is gracious."] A son of Zerubbabel (1 Chr 3:20).

Hasenuah. See Hassenuah.

Hashabiah (hăsh'á-bî'á). [Heb. *Chashabyah* and *Cheshabyahû,* "Yahweh has taken account."]

1. A Merarite Levite (1 Chr 6:44, 45).

2. A Merarite Levite who was in charge of the 12th of the 24 courses of musicians appointed by David for the sanctuary (1 Chr 25:3, 19).

3. A Levite of Hebron who was an overseer in secular and religious matters of Israel west of the Jordan in David's time (1 Chr 26:30).

4. A prince of the tribe of Levi in David's time (1 Chr 27:17).

5. A chief of the Levites in the reign of King Josiah (2 Chr 35:9).

6. A Levite, ancestor of Shemaiah (Neh 11:15; 1 Chr 9:14).

7. A Levite, descendant of Asaph (Neh 11:22).

8. The head of a family of priests in

the time of the high priest Joiakim (Neh 12:12, 21).

9. A Merarite Levite priest, who returned from Babylonia with Ezra (Ezr 8:19) and was one of those to whom the treasures were entrusted for transport to Jerusalem (v 24). He was probably also one who set his seal to Nehemiah's covenant (Neh 10:11), and who belonged to the Temple musicians (ch 12:24).

10. The ruler of half of Keilah, who helped Nehemiah in the rebuilding of the wall of Jerusalem (Neh 3:17).

11. For Ezra 10:25, RSV, *see* Malchijah 4 and 5.

Hashabnah (ha-shăb′na). [Heb. *Chashabnah.*] A prominent Jew who set his seal to Nehemiah's covenant (Neh 10:25).

Hashabneiah (hăsh′ăb-nê-ī′a), KJV **Hashabniah** (hăsh′ăb-nī′a). [Heb. *Chashabneyah,* "Yahweh has thought of me."]

1. A Jew whose son Hattush assisted Nehemiah in the rebuilding of the wall of Jerusalem (Neh 3:10).

2. A Levite who assisted Ezra in teaching the people (Neh 9:5).

Hashabniah. *See* Hashabneiah.

Hashbadana. *See* Hashbaddanah.

Hashbaddanah (hăsh-băd′a-na), KJV **Hashbadana** (hăsh-băd′a-na). [Heb. *Chashbaddanah.*] One of the leaders who assisted Ezra in teaching the Law (Neh 8:4).

Hashem (hā′shĕm). [Heb. *Hashem.*] One of the "mighty men" of David (1 Chr 11:34); called Jashen (jā′shĕn) [Heb. *Yashen*] in 2 Sa 23:32.

Hashmonah (hăsh-mō′na). [Heb. *Chashmonah.*] An encampment of the Israelites in the wilderness (Num 33:29, 30); not identified.

Hashub. *See* Hasshub.

Hashubah (ha-shoo′ba). [Heb. *Chashubah,* "esteemed."] A son of Zerubbabel (1 Chr 3:20).

Hashum (hā′shŭm). [Heb. *Chashum,* meaning uncertain.]

1. The ancestral head of a family of which 223 male members (Ezr 2:19), or 328 (Neh 7:22), returned from Babylonia with Zerubbabel. In the time of Ezra several members of this family were married to foreign wives (Ezr 10:33). Either one member signed Nehemiah's covenant in the family name or he himself bore the name Hashum (Neh 10:18).

2. One of the leaders of Judah who assisted Ezra in teaching the people (Neh 8:4). He is possibly identical with the Hashum who signed Nehemiah's covenant (ch 10:18). *See* Hashum, 1.

Hashupha. *See* Hasupha.

Hasrah. *See* Harhas.

Hassenaah (hăs′ê-nā′a), or **Senaah** (sê-nā′a). [Heb. *Hassena'ah* and *Sena'ah.* The two forms are identical except that the former has the definite article. The meaning of the name is uncertain.] It is uncertain whether this name refers to a town (which is the least probable solution; no site by this name has been identified), or to an ancestor, or whether "children of Senaah" describes a large but otherwise undefinable group of exiles. Of the "children of Senaah" 3,630 male members returned from Babylon with Zerubbabel (Ezr 2:35; Neh 7:38 [3,930]). The "sons of Hassenaah" built the Fish Gate of Jerusalem in the time of Nehemiah (Neh 3:3).

Hassenuah (hăs′ê-nū′a), KJV once **Hasenuah** (hăs′ê-nū′a) and once **Senuah** (sê-nū′a). [Heb. *Hassenú'ah,* probably "the hated one." The form "Senuah" ignores the presence of the definite article in the Hebrew.]

1. A Benjamite (1 Chr 9:7).

2. A Jew whose son Judah was the vice-mayor of Jerusalem in Nehemiah's time (Neh 11:9).

Hasshub (hăs′shŭb), KJV generally **Hashub** (hā′shŭb). [Heb. *Chashshúb,* "thought of (that is, by God)." The name occurs in an ancient Hebrew inscription.]

1. A Jew who assisted Nehemiah in rebuilding the wall of Jerusalem (Neh 3:11), a member of the family of Pahath-moab.

2. Another Jew who repaired the wall of Jerusalem in Nehemiah's time (Neh 3:23). Either he or Hasshub, 1, set his seal to Nehemiah's covenant (ch 10:23).

3. A Merarite Levite in the time of Nehemiah (1 Chr 9:14; Neh 11:15).

Hassophereth. *See* Sophereth.

Hasty Fruit. [Heb. *bikkúrah,* "first fruit," especially "early ripened figs."] An archaic English expression meaning "early fruit" (Is 28:4, KJV). The Hebrew suggests the first or early crop of figs, which ordinarily ripens in June.

Hasupha (ha-sū′fa), KJV once **Hashupha** (ha-shoo′fa). [Heb. *Chasúpha',* meaning uncertain.] Ancestral head of a family of Nethinim, some of whom returned from Babylonia with Zerubbabel (Ezr 2:43; Neh 7:46).

Hat. A term found only in Dan 3:21, a rendering of the Aramaic *karbelah,* "cap," a loan word from the Babylonian *karballatu.* The headdress referred to was probably a high, pointed cap of a type occasionally worn by the Babylonians and Assyrians.

Hatach. *See* Hathach.

Hatchet. A short-handled ax with a hammer head. "Hatchet" appears in the RSV of Ps 74:6 as the rendering of the Heb. *kashshîl,* translated "ax" in the KJV. Hatchets of iron and bronze have been found in Palestinian excavations.

Hathach (hā'thăk), KJV **Hatach** (hā'tăk). [Heb. *Hathak,* a Persian name of uncertain etymology.] A eunuch at Ahasuerus' court, who was appointed to attend Esther (Est 4:5, 10).

Hathath (hā'thăth). [Heb. *Chathath,* possibly "terror."] The son of the judge Othniel (1 Chr 4:13).

Hatipha (hȧ-tī'fȧ). [Heb. *Chaṭipha',* "carried away," "seized."] The ancestral head of a family of Nethinim. Some members of this family returned from Babylonia with Zerubbabel (Ezr 2:54; Neh 7:56).

Hatita (hȧ-tī'tȧ). [Heb. *Chaṭîṭa',* "smooth."] The ancestral head of a family of porters. Some members of this family returned from Babylonia with Zerubbabel (Ezr 2:42; Neh 7:45).

Hattil (hăt'ĭl). [Heb. *Chaṭṭîl,* possibly "long-eared."] The ancestral head of a family of Solomon's servants, some members of which returned from Babylonia with Zerubbabel (Ezr 2:55, 57; Neh 7:57-59).

Hattush (hăt'ŭsh). [Heb. *Chaṭṭûsh.*]
1. A man of Judah and descendant of David (1 Chr 3:22).
2. A chief of the priests who returned from Babylonia with Zerubbabel (Neh 12:1, 2, 7).
3. Head of a house, who returned with Ezra from Babylonia (Ezr 8:2).
4. A Jew who assisted Nehemiah in rebuilding the wall of Jerusalem (Neh 3:10).
5. A priest who signed Nehemiah's covenant (Neh 10:4).

Hauran (hou-rän'). [Heb. *Chawran.* The name occurs in cuneiform as *Ḥaurânu.*] An area in Transjordan marking the northeastern border of Canaan as seen in Ezekiel's vision of restored Israel (Eze 47:16, 18). It has been identified with the fertile basin, which lies south of the *Leja.* In its eastern section is found the *Jebel Haurân,* also known as *Jebel ed-Druz* (Map X, C-6). During the Roman period the area was called Auranitis, and was given to Herod the Great (Map XV, C-5). After his death it was one of the four provinces which made up the te-

trarchy of Philip, Herod's son (Jos. *Ant.* xvii. 11. 4).

Haven. Generally, a harbor or port providing a refuge or retreat for ships. The term is a rendering of: (1) The Heb. *chôph* (Gen 49:13), a coast or shore of a sea. See Deut 1:7, KJV, where *chôph* is rendered "side" (RSV "coast"), and Jos 9:1, KJV, where it is rendered "coasts" (RSV "coast"). (2) The Heb. *machôz* (Ps 107:30), a rare word of uncertain meaning, which on the basis of context may denote a "harbor" or even a "dock"; but the cognate word in several of the sister languages of Hebrew signifies a "city," and this may be its actual significance in Hebrew also. (3) The Gr. *limēn* (Acts 27:12), "harbor." "Haven" occurs also in Is 23:1, RSV, but the meaning of the corresponding Hebrew term is uncertain.

Havens, Fair. *See* Fair Havens.

Havilah (hăv'ĭ-lȧ). [Heb. *Chawilah,* "stretch of sand."]
1. A son of Cush (Gen 10:7; 1 Chr 1:9), whose descendants probably lived in northwestern Arabia. *See* Havilah, 4.
2. A son of Joktan (Gen 10:29; 1 Chr 1:23), whose descendants, with other Joktan Arabs, doubtless lived in southern Arabia.
3. An antediluvian country around which the unidentified river Pishon flowed (Gen 2:11). Since it is called a land in which gold, bdellium, and onyx stones were found, it has been identified with India, Arabia, Africa, and other parts of the ancient world. However, the Flood must have changed the surface of the earth to such an extent that the original features were lost; hence any identification is of doubtful value.
4. An area probably in northwestern Arabia (Gen 25:18; 1 Sa 15:7), which most likely received its name from the Cushite people of Havilah, 1. Map IV, C-6.

Havoth-jair. *See* Havvoth-jair.

Havvoth-jair (hăv'ŏth-jā'ĭr), KJV **Havoth-jair** (hā'vŏth-jā'ĭr). [Heb. *Chawwoth Ya'ir,* "tent villages of Jair."] The collective name given to certain small settlements in northern Gilead (see Map VI, C-4), which the clan of the descendants of Jair, a son of Manasseh (Deut 3:14), conquered and occupied (Num 32:41). In Deut 3:14 they are mentioned as lying in Bashan. The somewhat undefined and overlapping borders of Gilead and Bashan permit the same district to be described as lying in both Bashan and

Gilead. The number of the "towns of Jair" varied from 60 (Jos 13:30; 1 Chr 2:23) to 30 (Jgs 10:4). In the late period of the judges these places, now called cities, were administered by 30 sons of the Gileadite judge Jair, who was probably a prominent native of that region and a descendant of the ancient Jair (Num 32:41). The group of settlements is last mentioned in Solomon's time, when these villages were administered by a royal officer from Ramoth-gilead (1 Ki 4:13).

Hawk. The translation of: (1) The Heb. *neṣ,* a bird of prey, generally of the family Falconidae, but no specific identification is possible. Both the sparrow hawk and the kestrel are abundant in Palestine, and may possibly be intended. It was prohibited as food (Lev 11:16; Deut 14:15). Job presents its soaring ability as an illustration of the creative wisdom of God (Job 39:26). (2) The Heb. *qa'ath* (Is 34:11, RSV), a bird of unknown species, conjecturally translated "cormorant" in the KJV. The RSV translates *qa'ath* "pelican" in Lev 11:18; Deut 14:17. Driver suggests the scops-owl (*PEQ* 87 [1955], 20). *See also* Nighthawk.

Hay. [Heb. *chaṣîr,* "grass"; Gr. *chortos,* "grass," "hay."] Cut or mown grass intended for fodder. In both OT texts where *chaṣîr* is rendered "hay" in the KJV (Prov 27:25; Is 15:6), the meaning is probably "grass." In the NT Paul uses "hay" figuratively of the worthless "materials" certain persons were employing in building up the work in Corinth (1 Cor 3:12).

Hazael (hăz'à-ĕl). [Heb. *Chaza'el* and *Chazah'el,* "God has seen." The name occurs also in Aramaic inscriptions and as *Ḥazâ-'ilu* in Assyrian records.] A king of Damascus, and before assuming that office a high royal officer of Ben-hadad II, whom he succeeded on the throne. He was sent to Elisha, who was then in Damascus, to inquire whether the king would recover from an illness. He was told that his master would die, that he would become king of Damascus, and that he would commit great atrocities against the people of Israel. In delivering this message Elisha carried out a divine commission given some time earlier to his master Elijah (2 Ki 8:7-13; 1 Ki 19:15). Upon hearing the prophet's words Hazael returned to the palace, assassinated the king, and ascended the throne (2 Ki 8:14, 15). His reign lasted from *c.* 842 to *c.* 805 B.C.

In his wars against Israel, Hazael smote King Joram at Ramoth-gilead (2 Ki 8:

28, 29; 9:14, 15), took from Jehu all his Transjordan territories (ch 10:32, 33), and fought Jehoahaz (ch 13:3, 22). It was not until after the death of Hazael that Israel freed itself from the heavy yoke of the Aramaeans (vs 24, 25). Judah was also the object of Hazael's military conquests, and Joash of Judah was able to save Jerusalem from siege and possible capture only by paying a huge tribute when the Aramaeans campaigned against Gath (ch 12:17, 18). The prophet Amos calls Damascus the "house of Hazael" (Amos 1:4).

Hazael fought twice against King Shalmaneser III of Assyria, first in 841 B.C. and again in 838 B.C. Shalmaneser claimed to have inflicted a severe punishment on Damascus (*ANET* 280). When Damascus was attacked by Adad-nirari III of Assyria, a few years later, Hazael (for some strange reason referred to as *Mari* in the Assyrian records) paid a heavy tribute to avert full destruction. Among the tribute a "bed (inlaid) with ivory" is mentioned in the Assyrian records (*ANET* 281, 282). The ivory inlays of that bed,

213. Piece of ivory inlay from the couch of King Hazael of Damascus. Inscription bears his name

inscribed with Hazael's name, were found during the excavations of *Arslan Tash* in northern Syria. See fig. 213.

Hazaiah (hà-zā'yà). [Heb. *Chazayah,* "Yahweh has seen."] A Judahite whose descendant lived in Jerusalem in Nehemiah's time (Neh 11:5).

Hazar-addar (hā'zär-ăd'är). [Heb. *Chaṣar-'addar,* "strong enclosure."] A town in the south of Judah (Num 34:4), called Addar in Jos 15:3. It has been identified with *Khirbet el-Qudeirât* in the *Wâdī Qudeirât* near *Qeṣeimeh* at the Egyptian-Israeli border.

Hazar-enan (hā'zär-ē'năn), or **Hazar-enon** (hā'zär-ē'nŏn). [Heb. *Chaṣar 'ênan* and *Chaṣar 'ênôn,* "enclosure of fountains."] A place on the northeastern boundary of the land of Israel as originally planned (Num 34:9), and as set forth in the visions of Ezekiel (Eze 47:17; 48:1). This boundary was not attained in the conquest of Canaan. The place has been tentatively identified with *Qaryatein,* about 75 mi. northeast of Damascus on the road to Palmyra.

Hazar-enon. *See* Hazar-enan.

Hazar-gaddah (hā'zär-găd'ȧ). [Heb. *Chaṣar gaddah,* "enclosure of good fortune."] A place in the south of Palestine, near Beer-sheba (Jos 15:27); not identified.

Hazar-hatticon. *See* Hazer-hatticon.

Hazarmaveth (hā'zär-mā'vĕth). [Heb. *Chaṣarmaweth,* "village of death." The name occurs in ancient South Arabic inscriptions as *Chṣrmwth,* identical with the OT form, also with the spelling *Chṣrmth.*] A son of Joktan, and ancestor of a South Arabic tribe (Gen 10:26; 1 Chr 1:20) that gave its name to the area now called *Hadramaut.* Map IV, D-6/7.

Hazar-shual (hā'zär-shoō'ăl). [Heb. *Chaṣar shú'al,* "village of the fox."] A town in the south of Judah, near Beer-sheba, assigned to the tribe of Simeon (Jos 15:28; 19:3; 1 Chr 4:28). It was reoccupied after the Exile (Neh 11:27). The site has not been identified.

Hazar-susah (hā'zär-sū'sȧ), or **Hazar-susim** (hā'zär-sū'sĭm). [Heb. *Chaṣar Súsah,* "horse village," and *Chaṣar Súsim,* "horses' village."] A town in southwestern Judah, assigned to the tribe of Simeon (Jos 19:5; 1 Chr 4:31). It has been identified with *Sbalat Abū Súsein,* 20 mi. west of Beer-sheba.

Hazar-susim. *See* Hazar-susah.

Hazazon-tamar. *See* En-gedi.

Hazel. *See* Almond.

Hazelelponi. *See* Hazzelelponi.

Hazer-hatticon (hā'zēr-hăt'ĭ-kŏn), KJV **Hazar-hatticon** (hā'zär-hăt'ĭ-kŏn). [Heb. *Chaṣer hattîkôn,* "the middle village."] A place in the Hauran on the northeastern border of Ezekiel's Canaan (Eze 47:16); not identified.

Hazerim (hȧ-zē'rĭm). [Heb. *chaṣerîm,* "villages."] According to the KJV, the place where dwelt the Avvim, the aboriginal inhabitants of the southern coast of Palestine who were replaced by invaders from Crete (Deut 2:23). The RSV correctly renders *chaṣerîm* "villages."

Hazeroth (hȧ-zē'rŏth). [Heb. *Chaṣerôth,* "enclosures."] One of the wilderness camping places of the Israelites between Sinai and Kadesh. It was here that Miriam and Aaron murmured against Moses (Num 11:35; 12:16; 33:17; Deut 1:1). The site is possibly to be identified with the *'Ain Khaḍrā,* some 37 mi. northeast of Mount Sinai (Map V, D-6).

Hazezon-tamar. *See* En-gedi.

Haziel (hā'zĭ-ĕl). [Heb. *Chazî'el,* "God sees."] A Gershonite Levite (1 Chr 23:9).

Hazo (hā'zō). [Heb. *Chazô.*] A son of Nahor (Abraham's brother) and Milcah (Gen 22:22). He was the ancestor of an Aramaean tribe, which gave its name (*Hazû*) to a mountainous area in the Syrian Desert (see Luckenbill, *AR* II, 214).

Hazor (hā'zôr). [Heb. *Chaṣôr,* "enclosure."] 1. A large fortified city in northern Canaan. It appears in Egyptian records from Thutmose III to Ramses III as *Ḥḍr.* In the *Amarna Letters it appears as *Hazura,* and in the archives of Mari on the Euphrates as *Haṣura.* Its importance in the early periods can be seen from the fact that in the Mari records, which date from the patriarchal period, it is the only city of Palestine mentioned. The city was taken by Joshua and burned (Jos 11:1-13; 12:19), and was subsequently assigned to the tribe of Naphtali (ch 19:36). However, it seems that the Hebrews were unable to hold it for long, for it is later found to be the seat of a strong Canaanite king who for 20 years oppressed the northern tribes of Israel in the period of the judges (Jgs 4:2, 3). Barak, a judge, and Deborah, a prophetess, led the Israelites in a successful war against Jabin, king of Hazor, and his commander Sisera (Jgs 4:4-24). It was most probably this Hazor that was fortified by Solomon (1 Ki 9:15), and whose population was carried to Assyria by Tiglath-pileser III about 732 B.C. (2 Ki 15:29).

The site was identified by J. Garstang in 1928 with the large hill *Tell el-Qedah,* or *Tell Waqqâṣ,* in the Huleh plain (Map VI, B-4). From 1955 to 1958, systematic and highly successful excavations were carried out there under the direction of Yigael Yadin. The preliminary reports reveal that the city had a complicated history before it was finally abandoned in the 2d cent. B.C. One destruction

214. Israelite private houses of the 8th cent. B.C., excavated at Hazor

of the city is dated by the excavators in the time of Thutmose III or Amenhotep II in the 15th cent. B.C. If the Exodus took place in the middle of the 15th cent. B.C. and the invasion of Canaan toward the end of that same century, according to the chronology adopted in this dictionary, the destruction attributed by Yadin to Thutmose III or Amenhotep II may have been carried out by Joshua. A later destruction, revealed to have taken place in the 13th cent., is believed by the excavators to have been the work of Joshua, but it seems equally reasonable to assume that it was done by the Israelites under Barak and Deborah. It is quite possible that Barak took Hazor after he routed the entire army of Jabin's general, Sisera. The excavations also show that Hazor was rebuilt in Solomon's time as a fortified city, and that additional building operations were carried out by Ahab and his successors. This city was totally destroyed in 732 B.C. by Tiglath-pileser III, but was rebuilt once more and was inhabited during the Assyrian, Persian, and Hellenistic periods.

The excavations have uncovered two Canaanite temples and yielded many objects of unusual interest, among them cult steles, sculptures, a silver-plated bronze standard, and some inscriptional material. See figs. 12, 214, 482.

Lit.: Y. Yadin, *BA* 19 (1956), 1-12; 20 (1957), 34-47; 21 (1958), 30-47; 22 (1959), 1-20; *IEJ* 6 (1956), 120-125; 7 (1957), 118-23.

2. A place in the extreme south of Judah, near Kadesh-barnea (Jos 15:23), which has been identified with *el-Jebariyeh* in the *Wâdî Umm Ethnân*, about 16 mi. northeast of the *'Ain Qudeirât* in which some see the site of *Kadesh-barnea.

3. A place in southern Judah, also known as Kerioth-hezron (Jos 15:25b, RSV); not identified.

4. A village in Benjamin (Neh 11:33), tentatively identified with *Khirbet Hazzûr,* 4 mi. north-northwest of Jerusalem.

5. A locality in the Arabian Desert mentioned in connection with Kedar (Jer 49: 28-33); not identified.

Hazor-hadattah (hā'zôr-hȧ-dăt'ȧ). [Heb. *Chaṣôr-chadattah,* probably "new Hazor."] According to the RSV, a city in the south of Judah (Jos 15:25); not identified. The KJV makes this not one city, but two separate place names. See Hazor, 4; Hadattah.

Hazzelelponi (hăz'ĕ-lĕl-pō'nī), KJV **Hazelel-poni** (hăz'ĕ-lĕl-pō'nī). [Heb. *Haṣlelpôni,*

"give shade thou who turnest toward me."] A Judahite woman (1 Chr 4:3).

He. [Heb. *he'.*] The 5th letter of the Hebrew alphabet, written ה, corresponding in pronunciation to the English letter *h.* It appears as the heading of the 5th stanza of Ps 119 in the KJV. See Aleph.

Headbands. *See* Sashes.

Healing, Gifts of. *See* Spiritual Gifts.

Heart. This term, very frequent in the Scriptures, is used only rarely of the literal body organ (1 Sa 25:37; 2 Ki 9:24; etc.). It generally denotes the seat of various attitudes, emotions, and of intelligence. King Abimelech's "integrity of . . . heart" expressed honesty of intention (Gen 20:5). The hardening of Pharaoh's heart (Ex 8:32) indicated an attitude of rebellion against God (cf. Heb 3:7-10). The hearts of the citizens of Jericho "melted" when they heard of how God was working for Israel; that is, fear and consternation seized them (Jos 2:11). A "stony heart" describes a state of spiritual insensitivity and moral indifference (Eze 11:19). Although men may be "hypocrites in heart" (Job 36:13, KJV); may have perverted hearts (Prov 6:16, RSV); proud hearts (ch 21:4); fearful hearts (Is 35:4); evil, unbelieving hearts (Heb 3:12); stubborn, rebellious hearts (Jer 5:23); and may have "idols" in their hearts (Eze 14:3), yet God is able to give each an "heart of flesh," a "new heart" (chs 11:19; 18:31), indicating a complete change of attitudes, desires, and ambitions (2 Cor 5:17). Jesus Christ dwells in the heart through faith (Eph 3:17). Such expressions as "the wise in heart" (Prov 10:8) and "reasoning in their hearts" (Mk 2:6, KJV) show that the heart was thought of also as the seat of intelligence (cf. Ex 31:6; Deut 29:4; 1 Ki 3:9). In Mt 12:40 is a reference to "the heart of the earth," meaning the grave.

Hearth. *See* Brazier.

Heath. A rendering of: (1) The Heb. *'ar'ar* (Jer 17:6, KJV), probably a juniper such as *Juniperus oxycedrus,* rather than the true heath, most varieties of which are not seen in Palestine. The *J. oxycedrus,* or brown-berried cedar, is a low-growing shrub seldom attaining a height of more than 20 ft. even in the most ideal habitat. Usually it is found in barren and rocky parts of the desert or on inaccessible mountain crags. The shrub's appearance and habitat serve as a forceful illustration of the desolation experienced by the one who puts his trust in man. (2) The Heb.

'arô'er (Jer 48:6, KJV), "Aroer," or "juniper" (see above). However, the LXX reads "wild ass," as though from the Heb. 'arôd, a reading more suited to the context, and adopted by the RSV.

Heathen. [Heb. *gôyim* and Gr. *ethnoi*, "nations," "heathen," "Gentiles."] Idolaters, gentiles, those who do not acknowledge the true God. In the Bible the term "heathen" is used as a translation of words not as restricted in their general meaning as the English translation suggests. Basically, the Biblical words simply denote "nation(s)" and are frequently (437 times in the KJV) thus translated. But since the nations referred to were often idolaters, the Hebrew and Greek words seem many times to have been equivalent in their resultant meaning to the English word "heathen," and are often given this rendering (2 Ki 16:3; 2 Chr 33:2; Ezr 6:21; etc.). The RSV usually prefers the more neutral translation "nation(s)" (Lev 26:33; 2 Sa 22:44; Ps 2:1; etc.). *See* Gentiles.

Heave Offering. *See* Sacrifices and Offerings.

Heaven. [Heb. *shamayim;* Gr. *ouranos.*] This term describes (1) the atmospheric heavens, (2) the astronomic, or starry heavens, and (3) the dwelling place of God. The atmospheric heavens are the space in which the birds fly (Gen 1:20), from which the rains descend (Gen 7:11; Deut 11:11), and where the winds move (Dan 8:8.) In the day of judgment the atmospheric heavens, along with the earth, will be dissolved in fire (2 Pe 3:10; cf. Is 51:6), following which God will create new heavens and a new earth (2 Pe 3:13; Rev 21:1).

The astronomic, or starry, heavens are the space in which the sun, moon, and stars have their orbits (Gen 1:14, 16, 17; Is 13:10; Joel 2:30, 31; Mt 24:29).

The dwelling place of God is repeatedly represented as heaven (1 Ki 8:30, 39; Ps 11:4; 53:2; 80:14; 102:19; 139:8; etc.). Jesus frequently referred to the Father as being in heaven (Mt 5:16, 45, 48; 6:9; etc.). Christ came down from heaven at His incarnation (Jn 3:13, 31; 6:38) and ascended into heaven after His resurrection (Heb 9:24). He will descend from heaven at His second coming, and will take the redeemed back with Him (Jn 14:1-3; 1 Th 4:13-18; 1 Pe 1:4). Heaven will be the abode of the blessed until the saints inherit the new earth at the close of the millennium (Rev 21:1-7).

The term "heaven" is sometimes used as a substitute for the divine name (Mk 11:30; Lk 15:18, 21), reflecting the Jews' reluctance to pronounce God's name.

Heber (hē'bēr). [Heb. *Cheber,* "companion."]
1. Descendant of Asher and founder of a tribal family (Gen 46:17; Num 26:45).
2. A Kenite, descendant of Moses' brother-in-law Hobab. His wife Jael slew Sisera (Jgs 4:11-22).
3. A Judahite (1 Chr 4:18).
4. A Benjamite (1 Chr 8:17).
5. For 1 Chr 5:13, KJV, *see* Eber, 2.
6. For 1 Chr 8:22, KJV, *see* Eber, 4.
7. For Lk 3:35, KJV, *see* Eber, 1.

Heberites (hē'bēr-īts). [Heb. *Chebri.*] Descendants of *Heber, 1 (Num 26:45).

Hebrew (hē'broō). [Heb. *'Ibri;* Gr. *Hebraios.*] It is uncertain whether the Hebrew term means "one from the other side" or "pertaining to *'Eber.*" Both interpretations have been defended by commentators. The fact that Abraham, the ancestor of the Hebrews, came from the other side of the Euphrates (Gen 11:28-32; 12:4, 5; Jos 24:2, 3, 15), and was the first to be called a "Hebrew" in the Bible (Gen 14:13), has been set forth to support the first meaning. However, ch 10:21 refers to Shem as "the father of all the children of Eber," as if these children were, in the opinion of the author of Genesis, more important than his other descendants. According to ch 10:25 Eber had two sons, one Joktan, from whom all the Joktan Arabs descended (vs 26-29), and the other his elder brother Peleg, through whom the chosen people came (ch 11:16-26). It seems more reasonable therefore to regard the term *'Ibri* as meaning "descendant of *'Eber,*" and to consider the definition "one from the other side" as merely coincidental.

The term "Hebrew" appears relatively infrequently in the OT, and in most cases was employed by foreigners speaking about Israelites (Gen 39:14, 17; 1 Sa 4:6; 13:19; etc.), or by the Israelites speaking about themselves or their country to foreigners (Gen 40:15; Ex 3:18; 7:16; etc.). It is never used in the prophetic exhortations or in the poetical literature of the OT, in both of which the name Israel appears hundreds of times, and names like Judah, Ephraim, or Samaria are often employed.

Since the discovery of the *Amarna Letters a controversy has raged among scholars as to whether the *Ḥabiru* have any connection with the Hebrews. This term has been found in Old Babylonian, Hurrian, and Assyrian texts of Mesopotamia, in Hittite records of Asia Minor, in texts from Ugarit and Alalakh in northern Syria, in Egyptian documents found in Egypt and Palestine, and in the *Amarna Letters found in Egypt but originating in Palestine and Syria. In Ugaritic and Egyptian texts the name is spelled with a *p* (*'Apiru*) instead of a *b* (*Ḫabiru*) as in Hebrew or Akkadian texts. Since *b* and *p* were sometimes used interchangeably, the linguistic problems of equating the Hebrews with the *Ḫabiru* or *'Apiru* are minor.

The question still remains, Who were these people of the ancient world who appear in so many countries from the end of the 3d millennium down to the 11th cent. B.C.? Some texts represent the *Ḫabiru* as slaves, others as mercenaries. In Babylonian and Hurrian texts especially, the word seems to be an appellative rather than an ethnic term. However, there can be little doubt that in some texts a specific people is meant. King Idri-Mi of Alalakh says that he spent 7 years as a refugee among the *'Apiru,* and King Amenhotep II of Egypt claims to have taken 3,600 *'Apiru* captives in a Palestinian campaign. He mentions them in a list of captives with Hurrians and other ethnic groups (*ANET* 247). In the Amarna Letters they are frequently mentioned by the hard-pressed local princes of Palestine as invaders of Palestine and Syria. If the Exodus took place in the 15th cent. B.C., which is the view accepted for the *chronology of this dictionary, there can be little doubt that the *Ḫabiru* mentioned in the Amarna Letters from Palestine were the Biblical Hebrews. However, this does not equate all *Ḫabiru* or *'Apiru* of ancient records with the Hebrews. Although it can be said that all Biblical Hebrews belonged to the group called *Ḫabiru* or *'Apiru,* not all *Ḫabiru* or *'Apiru* were Biblical Hebrews. If we take the term "Hebrew" in the broad sense as meaning all the descendants of Eber, it would include the descendants of Joktan, Peleg, Reu, Serug, Nahor, Terah, and of Abraham's brothers (Gen 10:25-29; 11:17-26). It would also include Abraham's children through his second wife, Keturah (ch 25:1-5). All of these could in that sense be "Hebrews," or *Ḫabiru* or *'Apiru,* without falling into the narrower classification of Jacob's descendants, to whom the Biblical term "Hebrews" was ultimately restricted.

By the time the NT was written the term "Hebrews" was applied to the Jews of Palestine whose mother tongue was Hebrew, or rather Aramaic, in distinction to the "Hellenists" (KJV "Grecians"), who were Greek-speaking Jews (Acts 6: 1). A "Hebrew of the Hebrews" was a full-blooded Israelite, whose parents, like those of the apostle Paul, were both Hebrews (Php 3:5; cf. 2 Cor 11:22).

Hebrew Language. In the OT this language is called the "language of Canaan" (Is 19:18) or the "Jews' language" (2 Ki 18: 26, 28; 2 Chr 32:18; Neh 13:24; Is 36:13). It was the language spoken from at least the time of Moses to that of Nehemiah. With the exception of portions of the books Ezra and Daniel, and a few phrases in other books, which were written in Aramaic, the whole OT was originally written in Hebrew. It has long been known that Hebrew belonged to the group of Semitic languages, to which, for example, ancient Babylonian and Assyrian, and ancient and modern Arabic belong. However, the discoveries of the *Amarna Letters, the *Moabite Stone, and inscriptions from Phoenicia, Edom, and Ammon have shown that Hebrew was only a branch of the Canaanite family of Semitic languages, being distinguished only by peculiarities of dialect from those spoken by the Phoenicians, Moabites, Ammonites, or Edomites. The experience recorded in Jgs 12:5, 6 shows that such dialectal differences existed even between certain Israelite tribes.

The Hebrew pronunciation determined by the vowel signs appearing in modern Hebrew Bibles is that of the Jews of Palestine in the 9th and 10th cent. A.D. Up to that time the Hebrew script had been written without vowels. But the scholars of that time, called Masoretes, invented a system of vowel signs that showed how Hebrew was pronounced in their own time. However, the Hebrew language had undergone changes in the interval of almost 2400 years between Moses and the Masoretes, as does every living language in the course of time. The Amarna Letters, which contain Canaanite words and phrases written in the syllabic Babylonian script, which contains vowels, have revealed the approximate Hebrew pronunciation of these words as used in the 14th cent. B.C. Later texts, such as the Dead Sea scrolls of the time of Christ, show certain pronunciations at a later stage in the history of the Hebrew language.

For the Hebrew script *see* Writing.

Up to the Babylonian exile the Israelites spoke pure Hebrew. During the Exile Aramaic began to exert an influence on Hebrew, and after the Exile, when Aramaic became the official language of the Persian Empire, the influence was even greater. Finally Aramaic superseded the spoken Hebrew. It seems to have been the colloquial tongue in Christ's time, as shown by the fact that Jesus' sayings given in the vernacular by the Gospel writers are in Aramaic (Mk 5:41; 7:34; 15:34). However, Hebrew was still used for literary purposes, as is evident from the non-Biblical Dead Sea scrolls produced in Hebrew during the last 2 centuries of the pre-Christian era and in the 1st cent. A.D., as well as by the Mishnah, written in Hebrew (called Mishnaic Hebrew), about A.D. 200. In the time of the Masoretes, Hebrew was evidently no longer a living language, which accounts for their invention of vowel points to preserve the pronunciation. Hebrew was henceforth a dead language, used only by scholars and rabbis until it was revived as a living language by modern Zionists, who have made it the official language of the State of Israel. Modern Hebrew uses the classical forms and grammar of Jeremiah's time, but employs a large number of new words necessitated by technology and 20th-cent. living, and uses a modern European pronunciation avoiding the Semitic laryngeals; consequently a knowledge of Biblical Hebrew is not sufficient to understand the modern Hebrew of Israel.

The NT expressions "Hebrew tongue" (Jn 5:2; Acts 21:40; 22:2; 26:14; Rev 9: 11; 16:16), "the Hebrew" (Jn 19:13, 17), and "Hebrew" (Lk 23:38; Jn 19:20) all refer to the colloquial language of Palestine in the 1st cent. A.D., which was evidently Aramaic, and not Hebrew in the sense in which we understand the term now.

Hebrews, Epistle to the. An anonymous epistle of the NT. The oldest Greek manuscripts have the simple title *Pros Hebraious,* "To the Hebrews." The epistle assumes that its intended readers are well informed concerning Jewish history and the Jewish religion, and that they hold Abraham, Moses, Aaron, the covenants, the priesthood, and the Temple service in highest esteem—in other words, that they are Jews. They also believe in Christ as Messiah, though not to the point of forsaking Jewish ritual practices. It is thus evident that the epistle is addressed to Jewish Christians (see Heb 2:1; 3:12; 4:1,

11; 5:12; 6:6, 10; 7:14; 10:23-25, 29, 34-39), and the epistle constitutes an appeal to them to turn from reliance on the rites and ceremonies of Judaism to faith in Jesus Christ as an all-sufficient Saviour. Internal evidence attests that the epistle was originally written in Greek. This, together with the fact that the majority of quotations from the OT are verbatim from the LXX, the Greek translation in common use among non-Palestinian Jews, suggests that the writer had Jewish Christians of the Dispersion particularly in mind as he wrote.

The epistle itself affords no direct clue by which to identify its author. His familiarity with Hebrew history and insight into its significance (Heb 3; 4; 7:1-4; 11), his own profound respect for heroes of the faith such as Abraham (ch 11:8-19), Moses (chs 3:1-5; 11:23-29), and Aaron (chs 5:4; 7:11; 9:4), and his intimate knowledge concerning the covenants, the priesthood, and the ritual system (chs 7 to 10), point to him as a devout, educated Jew. On the other hand, as the literary features of the epistle reveal, he was also a man of culture and had a masterly command of the Greek language. Repeated reference to the Temple service as currently in operation (chs 8:4, 5; 9:22; 10: 3, 11) implies that the epistle was written prior to the fall of Jerusalem and the destruction of the Temple in A.D. 70. The author fully appreciates the divine origin of the Jewish religious system (chs 5:4; 8: 3, 5; 9:9; 10:1), but insists that it is now obsolete and inefficacious for salvation (chs 4:9-11; 7:11, 18, 19; 8:6; 9:8-15; 10: 1-10). Throughout the epistle he exalts Christ and assumes that his readers likewise honor Him as Lord and Master (chs 1:1-9; 3:1, 6; 6:18-20; 7:25-28; 8:1, 2; 9:11, 12, 15; 10:12, 19-22; 12:2, 4). Accordingly, it would seem that the author was a devout, Jerusalem-educated Jew of the Diaspora with a Greek cultural background, who had been converted to Christianity and had subsequently renounced Judaism as an effective means to salvation. Till about the close of the 4th cent. great difference of opinion existed as to the identity of this remarkable person. Some held that it was Paul, but many favored Barnabas, Apollos, Luke, or Clement of Rome. Origen, one of the early Church Fathers (c. A.D. 184 - c. 254), declared that God alone knew the identity of the author (quoted by Eusebius *Ecclesiastical History* vi. 25. 14; Loeb ed., vol. 2, p. 79). Since proved apostolic authorship was considered by early Christians an essential prerequisite for the admission of a document into the NT canon, and since uncertainty as to who was the author of Hebrews prevailed, centuries passed before the epistle was universally accepted into the canon. The church in the West in particular long remained dubious. By the time that Hebrews had been deemed worthy of a place in the canon Paul had come to be rather generally accepted as its author, not so much on the basis of objective evidence as apparently upon a general impression that he alone could have written it. With the reasonably full identification of the leaders of the apostolic church provided by the various NT writers, a cultured and scholarly Jewish Christian with the profound spiritual insight that evidently characterized the writer of Hebrews could hardly have remained in obscurity at a time when Christian leaders—especially those with Paul's enlightened point of view—were few. Paul alone seemed to qualify as author of the epistle.

Modern critics reject Pauline authorship chiefly on the basis of certain literary differences between Hebrews and the epistles that are known certainly to have come from his pen. Though a writer's vocabulary and style may vary as he turns from one subject to another, such variations are usually to be found in words and expressions relating to those particular subjects. But in Hebrews the words and expressions common to all discourse —prepositions, conjunctions, and adverbs —differ consistently from the language of the known Pauline epistles. Furthermore, the numerous and often extended OT quotations in Hebrews are virtually always verbatim from the Greek LXX, whereas in his certified epistles Paul often quotes directly from the Hebrew as well as from the LXX, and at times apparently gives his own free translation. The characteristic phraseology with which the writer of Hebrews introduces these quotations also differs from that commonly employed by Paul. Finally, the polished rhetoric of Hebrews and the clear, systematic organization of the argument presented differ markedly from Paul's usual style, with its lengthy digressions of thought and its involved reasoning. To sum up the matter of authorship, the point of view expressed in the epistle is characteristically and uniquely that of the apostle Paul as expressed in Romans, Galatians, and elsewhere, but the style of

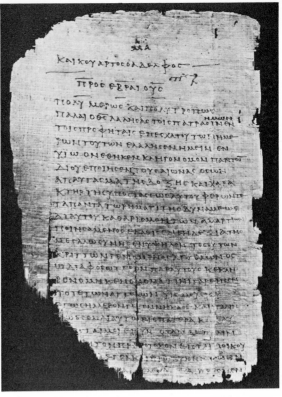

215. A leaf from the Chester Beatty Papyri, containing the end of the book of Romans and the beginning of Hebrews

writing is not his. This suggests the possibility that the content of the epistle may have come from the great apostle himself, guided by the Holy Spirit, but that the actual writing or editing was done by a trusted assistant under his direct supervision, such as Timothy or Luke. To a conservative Bible scholar the mechanical differences in style are far less impressive than the identity of the theme with Paul's point of view. Conclusive evidence of Pauline authorship may thus be lacking, but the presumptive evidence is strongly in his favor.

Among the issues that arose in the apostolic church none brought more perplexity than the problem of the place of Jewish ritual requirements in the life of the Christian. To Jewish Christians it seemed incredible that the Jewish religious system, ordained by God Himself, could have become obsolete and that its ritual requirements were no longer binding. With the veil of Jewish nationalism before their eyes they failed to see that the ceremonial system, in whole and in part, simply foreshadowed the coming Messiah and His ministry for sinners, and that in Him the system reached its climax and end (see

Rom 10:4; 1 Cor 5:7; Col 2:14-17; Heb 7:19-25; 8; 9:11-15). The Jerusalem Council had already released Gentile converts to the Christian faith from the ritual requirements of Judaism, but its silence with respect to the duty of Jewish Christians in this matter implied that the latter were still obliged to comply with them. Nevertheless, a large and influential body of Jewish Christians never assented to the release of Gentile believers from the requirements of the Jewish legal system, and actively sought to impose their point of view on Paul's converts (Gal 1:7-9; 2:4, 5, 11-14; 3:1-3; 5:7-9; 2 Ti 1:15; etc.). But to Paul and those who shared his point of view, reliance on Jewish ritual requirements as a means to favor with God incapacitated even Jewish Christians from entering fully into the blessings of salvation by faith in Christ, and for Gentile Christians it involved falling from grace altogether (Gal 5:1-4). Though the intended readers of Hebrews knew it not, the Temple services were soon to cease forever, with the result that continued faith in these outward forms as essential to salvation would bewilder and perplex those who relied on them. In view of momentous events soon to take place, these Jewish Christians needed to turn their eyes, and transfer their loyalty, to Christ as their high priest in heaven above, and to rely completely on His ministry as efficacious for salvation instead of on an earthly priesthood. The inspired writer of Hebrews therefore sets forth the true relation of the ancient sacrificial system to the plan of salvation and explains how and why it terminated with the great sacrifice of Christ on the cross and His inauguration as high priest. "He is able also to save them to the uttermost that come unto God by him, seeing he ever liveth to make intercession for them" (Heb 7:25). The epistle constitutes an enlightened and enlightening appeal not only to Christian Jews of the 1st cent. but to all men of all time to turn their eyes heavenward and to enter fully into the gracious provisions made for them in the perfect and perpetual ministry of their Lord (chs 1:1-4; 2:14-17; 3:1; 4:14, 15; 6:20; 7:26, 27; 8:1, 2; 9:11-14, 24-28; 10:19-22).

Christ's ministry since His ascension is the central theme of the epistle to the Hebrews (chs 2:17, 18; 3:1; 4:14-16; 6:18-20; 7:25-28; 8:1, 2; 9:11, 12, 15; 10:12, 19-22; 12:2, 4). Believers are to follow Him by faith into the courts of heaven above, where, in His presence, they find rest of soul (Heb 4:16; 6:19, 20). Christ is set forth as God's spokesman to the church (ch 1:1, 2). He is superior to the angels (v 4), to Abraham (ch 7:2, 4, 17), and to Moses (ch 3:3). As a priest forever after the order of Melchizedek He is superior to the Aaronic priests (ch 7:11) and to Levi (vs 9, 10). The new covenant is superior to the old covenant (ch 8:6), the heavenly sanctuary to that on earth (chs 8:1, 6; 9:8, 9), and Christ's ministry in heaven above to that of Aaron and his sons on earth (chs 7:11; 9:11). The Saviour's blood is infinitely superior to that of bulls and goats (ch 9:12-15). In fact, in and of itself the ritual system availed nothing at all (chs 7:19; 9:9; 10:1), and even in past ages Jews who found salvation had done so by faith in the promised Messiah yet to come and in His ministry (ch 11).

Developing his theme, the writer shows Christ to be equal with the Father (Heb 1) and sets forth the purpose of His mission to earth (ch 2). In chs 3 and 4 he surveys Hebrew history to show that, despite God's gracious promises and guidance, the Jewish people did not enter into the rest of soul God intended them to have, and that since the Jews as a nation had never entered truly into that rest, the truehearted may now do so by coming boldly to the throne of grace. Chapters 5 through 8 develop the theme of the transcendence of Christ's ministry over that of Aaron, so much so, in fact, as to render the ancient ministry obsolete and superfluous. In chs 9:1 to 10:22 the writer turns to the nature of Christ's ministry, explaining it in terms of the services of the earthly sanctuary, which foreshadowed it. He closes this section by stressing the efficacy and permanence of Christ's sacrifice, and appeals to his readers to accept Christ's priestly ministry on their behalf. This is followed by a practical application of the principles already set forth, to the Christian faith and practice. Christians are to be faithful even as the great spiritual heroes of preceding ages had been faithful in their day (chs 11:1 to 12:2). Despite trial, persecution, temptation, and the vicissitudes of daily life, believers are to live worthy of their high calling in Christ Jesus (chs 12:3 to 13:17). The epistle closes with a benediction and personal salutation (ch 13:18-25).

Hebron (hē'brŏn). [Heb. *Chebrôn.*]

1. A Levite, son of Kohath and founder of a family (Ex 6:18; 1 Chr 6:2) whose

HEBRON

members are called Hebronites (Num 3: 27; 1 Chr 15:9; 26:30, 31).

2. An important city in the southern hill country of Judah (Jos 15:48, 54), which had been built 7 years before *Zoan (i.e. Tanis) in Egypt (Num 13: 22). Its original name was Kiriath-arba (Gen 23:2; Jos 20:7; etc.). The town existed as early as the time of Abraham, who for a time lived in its vicinity, and purchased a burial site (the Cave of Machpelah; see figs. 3, 311; Gen 13:18; 23:2-20). Isaac and Jacob also resided at Hebron for some time (chs 35:27; 37:13, 14). Its original inhabitants were the gigantic Anakim (Num 13:22; Jos 11:21; etc.), but Hittites are also mentioned as early dwellers there (Gen 23:3-16, see especially v 10). Hoham, the king of Hebron in the time of the Israelite invasion, is called an Amorite (Jos 10:3, 5).

Hebron was one of the Canaanite cities that terrified the Israelite spies in Moses' time (Num 13:22, 28, 29, 32, 33). Its king, Hoham, fought against Joshua, but was defeated and killed and his city captured (Jos 10:1-27, 36, 37). Yet remnants of its population seem to have returned, for it had to be recaptured by Caleb, to whom the city had been assigned when the country was divided among the tribes (Jos 14:12-15; 15:13; Jgs 1:20). The city was also assigned to the priests and designated as a city of refuge (Jos 20:7; 21:8-13; 1 Chr 6:54-57). After Saul's death David made friends with the people of Hebron by sending them part of the spoil taken from the Amalekites who had destroyed Ziklag (1 Sa 30:26, 31). When he was crowned king over Judah, he reigned in Hebron for 7½ years, after which he captured Jerusalem and made that city the capital of the united kingdom (2 Sa 2:1-3, 11, 32; 5:1-5; 1 Ki 2:11; 1 Chr 29:27). Hebron was the seat of Absalom's rebellion against David (2 Sa 15: 7-10). Hebron is mentioned once more in the Bible, as one of the cities which Rehoboam fortified (2 Chr 11:5, 10). Later Hebron fell into the hands of the Edomites, and is not mentioned as one of the cities of Judah reoccupied after the Exile. Judas Maccabeus recaptured the city, which was strongly fortified, from the Edomites (1 Macc 5:65). The city is now called el-Khalîl, meaning "the friend (of God)," a reference to Abraham. It lies partly in a valley and partly upon the adjoining hill at an elevation of 3,040 ft. above sea level, about 19 mi. south-southwest of Jerusalem on the main road from Jeru-

216. A view of Hebron. Center: the *Ḥaram*, a sacred Moslem enclosure under which lies the Cave of Machpelah

salem to Beer-sheba. Its population is 26,390. Its main attraction is the sacred Moslem enclosure, the Haram, which includes a mosque built over the Cave of Machpelah, said to contain the tombs of several patriarchs and their wives.

Hebronites (hē′brŏn-īts). [Heb. *Chebronî*.] The descendants of Hebron, a Kohathite Levite (Num 3:27; 26:58; 1 Chr 26:23, 30, 31).

Hedge. [Heb. *gader*, "a wall (of stones)"; *gederah*, "pen," "(sheep)fold"; *meśûkkah*, "a hedge," from *śakak*, "to cover," "to fence," "to screen"; *meśukah*, "a hedge," from *śûk*, "to hedge," "to fence about"; and *meśûkah*, "a hedge," from *sûk*, "to cause to bristle," "to stimulate." Gr. *phragmos*, "a fencing in"; "a fence."] Rather than being a "hedge," a *gader* was simply a division wall of stones roughly heaped together, without the mortar usually used in making walls (Ps 80:12; Ec 10:8; Eze 13:5; 22:30). *Gederah* is the feminine form of *gader* and describes a fold for sheep or goats. The words *meśûkkah* (Is 5:5), *meśukah* (Prov 15:19), and *meśûkah* (Mic 7:4) are closely related, possibly merely variant spellings of the same word. They all refer to a hedge composed of sharp thorns, strictly for utilitarian rather than ornamental purposes. It is probable that the ancient stone "hedges" were topped with thorns (a custom still followed in some regions of Palestine), though the highly perishable nature of thorns makes it impossible either to prove or disprove this supposition.

Hedgehog. See Bittern.

Hegai (hĕg′á-ī), KJV once **Hege** (hē′gē). [Heb. *Hegay* and *Hege′*, probably a Persian name, but the meaning is uncertain.] A eunuch in charge of the royal harem of King Ahasuerus (Est 2:3, 8, 15).

Hege. See Hegai.

He-goat. See Goat.

Heir. See Inheritance.

Helah (hē'lȧ). [Heb. *Chel'ah,* probably "rust."] One of the two wives of Ashhur, a Judahite, the ancestor of the people of Tekoa (1 Chr 4:5, 7).

Helam (hē'lăm). [Heb. *Chêlam.*] A place in northeastern Transjordan, where David defeated Hadadezer, king of Syria (2 Sa 10:16-19). The city appears in early Egyptian records as *H3im,* and can probably be identified with the Alama of 1 Macc 5:26, which is either the present *'Alma* in the Hauran, or *Elamûn* on the Jabbok, according to Abel (*Géographie* II, 347).

Helbah (hĕl'bȧ). [Heb. *Chelbah.*] An old Phoenician town assigned to Asher, which at first was not conquered (Jgs 1:31). The site has not been identified with certainty. Some commentators think that Helbah is a twin city of Ahlab mentioned in the same text, others that it is a scribal variant of Ahlab, which came into the text by mistake. *See* Mahalab.

Helbon (hĕl'bŏn). [Heb. *Chelbôn,* "fat," or "fertile."] A city in Syria famous for its wines (Eze 27:18). It is mentioned in cuneiform records in connection with the same product under the name *Ḥilbûnu.* It is the modern *Ḥalbûn,* a village 13 mi. north-northwest of Damascus, lying in a steep valley, in which a successful vine culture has been carried on to the present day. Map XVI, A-5.

Heldai (hĕl'dȧ-ī). [Heb. *Chelday,* "enduring."]

1. A Netophathite, a descendant of the judge Othniel; one of David's "mighty men," captain for the 12th month (1 Chr 27:15). He is probably identical with Heleb (2 Sa 23:29) and Heled (1 Chr 11:30).

2. One of a small band who came, probably with gifts for the Temple, from Babylon to the exiles who had returned under Zerubbabel (Zec 6:10); called also Helem (v 14, KJV).

Heleb (hē'lĕb). [Heb. *Cheleb,* "fat."] One of David's "mighty men" (2 Sa 23:29), probably identical with Heldai (1 Chr 27:15) and Heled (ch 11:30).

Helech (hē'lĕk). [Heb. *Chêlek.*] According to the RSV a city or land mentioned together with the Phoenician port city of Arvad (Eze 27:11, RSV). It is probably *Cilicia in southeastern Asia Minor, mentioned in cuneiform sources as *Ḥilaku* and *Ḥiliku* (see Khilaku, Map XI, B-3), and the people from there in Aramaic documents from Egypt as *Ch(y)lky.* The KJV renders the Hebrew term "thine army."

Heled (hē'lĕd). [Heb. *Cheled,* "duration." The name occurs also in South Arabic inscriptions.] One of David's "mighty men" (1 Chr 11:30), probably identical with Heldai (ch 27:15) and Heleb (2 Sa 23:29).

Helek (hē'lĕk). [Heb. *Cheleq,* "portion."] A son of Gilead, and founder of a tribal family of Manasseh (Num 26:30; Jos 17:2).

Helekites (hē'lĕk-īts). [Heb. *Chelqi.*] Descendants of *Helek (Num 26:30).

Helem, I (hē'lĕm). [Heb. *Helem,* meaning uncertain.] An Asherite and founder of a tribal family (1 Chr 7:35), probably identical with Hotham (v 32).

Helem, II (hē'lĕm). [Heb. *Chelem,* "strength."] An exile returned from Babylonia (Zec 6:14), called Heldai (v 10).

Heleph (hē'lĕf). [Heb. *Cheleph,* "change."] A town on the border of Naphtali (Jos 19:33); not identified. The context indicates that it was probably near Mount Tabor.

Helez (hē'lĕz). [Heb. *Cheleṣ,* meaning uncertain.]

1. A Judahite (1 Chr 2:39).

2. A Paltite, one of David's "mighty men" (2 Sa 23:26), possibly identical with Helez, 3.

3. A Pelonite, one of David's "mighty men" (1 Chr 11:27), who was also the captain of David's forces for the 7th month (ch 27:10); possibly identical with Helez, 2.

Heli (hē'lī). [Gr. *Hēli,* a transliteration of the Heb. *'Ēlî.*] Probably the father of Joseph, appearing in Luke's genealogy of Christ (Lk 3:23). Some prefer to read vs 23, 24 as follows: "And Jesus began at the age of about 30 years, being the son (it was thought, of Joseph) of Heli, the son of Matthat. . . ." They assume that the genealogy in ch 3 is that of Mary, and consider Heli to be the father of Mary and thus the actual, not merely the legal, grandfather of Jesus. *See* Genealogy.

Heliopolis. *See* Beth-shemesh, 4.

Helkai (hĕl'kȧ-ī). [Heb. *Chelqay,* probably a contraction of *Chilqîyah,* "Hilkiah," "Yahweh is my portion."] The head of a priestly family (Neh 12:15).

Helkath (hĕl'kăth). [Heb. *Chelqath,* "field," or "portion of land."] A town of Asher (Jos 19:25), assigned to the Gershonite Levites (ch 21:31). It is called Hukok (hū'kŏk) [Heb. *Chúqoq*] in 1 Chr 6:75, and is mentioned as *Ḥrqt* in a list of Palestinian cities conquered by Thutmose III. It is tentatively identified with *Tell el-Har-*

baj, 11½ mi. south of Acre (Map VI, C-3).

Helkath-hazzurim (hĕl'kăth-hăz'ú-rĭm). [Heb. *Chelqath haṣṣûrim*, "the field of flints."] The name given to the scene of a combat at the pool of Gibeon between 12 men of King Ish-bosheth and 12 men of David (2 Sa 2:16).

Hell. [Heb. *she'ôl;* Gr. *hadēs* and *geenna;* the Greek verb *tartaroō*, "to cast (down) to hell," occurs once (2 Pe 2:4).] The Heb. *she'ôl* and the Gr. *hadēs* refer to the unseen world, the world of the dead, as does the English word "hell" in one of its meanings. However, since the English term "hell" connotes also a place of punishment for the impenitent, such a translation often creates confusion. Consequently, the RSV and other modern translations prefer to transliterate the Heb. *she'ôl* as Sheol and the Gr. *hadēs* as Hades. This trend in translation is a recognition of the difference in meaning between the English "hell" as often understood today and the Hebrew and Greek terms.

The close connection between Sheol and death may be illustrated from Hebrew parallelisms. For example, in the song of David recorded in 2 Sa 22:2-51 the following appears: "When the waves of death compassed me, the floods of ungodly men made me afraid; the sorrows of hell compassed me about; the snares of death prevented me" (vs 5, 6). In Isaiah appears this parallelism: "We have made a covenant with death, and with hell we are at agreement" (Isa 28:15; cf. v 18).

Hadēs, the Greek equivalent of *she'ôl,* occurs 10 times in the NT and is generally transliterated in the RSV as "Hades." The following are instances of its use: Capernaum shall be "brought down to hell" (Mt 11:23; Lk 10:15). "The gates of hell" shall not prevail against the church (Mt 16:18). The Messiah's "soul was not left in hell" (Acts 2:27, 31). Jesus holds "the keys of hell and of death" (Rev 1:18). "Hell" followed with the pale horse (ch 6:8). "Death and hell" delivered up their dead (ch 20:13), and "death and hell were cast into the lake of fire" (v 14). The Revelation passages particularly reveal the close connection between "death" and "hell." In only one Bible reference is punishment in Hades indicated (Lk 16:23, RSV), but this is in a parable which by itself must not be regarded as doctrinally definitive.

The Greek term denoting a place of punishment is *geenna,* used 12 times in the NT. *Geenna* is the Grecized form of *Gê Hinnom,* "Valley of Hinnom," a gorge near Jerusalem repeatedly mentioned in the OT (Jos 15:8; 2 Ki 23:10; 2 Chr 33:6; Jer 7:31). Here the barbaric heathen rite of burning children to Molech was conducted (2 Chr 28:3; 33:1, 6), an abomination that King Josiah abolished, desecrating the high places where this form of worship had been practiced. Jeremiah predicted that because of this sin the Lord would make the valley of the son of Hinnom a "valley of slaughter" where the corpses of the Israelites would be buried till there was no more place for them, and the remaining dead bodies would be food for the fowls of the heavens (Jer 7:32, 33). This doubtless led to the valley's being regarded as a place of judgment of the wicked. *See* Valley of Hinnom. Later rabbinical tradition claims that the Valley of Hinnom was also a place outside the city for burning carcasses and rubbish.

The expression *geenna* occurs 3 times in the Sermon on the Mount (Mt 5:22, 29, 30). In ch 10:28 Jesus spoke of Him who "is able to destroy both soul and body in hell," and in ch 18:9 of "hell fire." He warned the Pharisees of "the damnation of hell" (ch 23:33). He stated that it is better to be maimed and yet gain eternal life than to be cast into hell-fire (Mk 9:43, 45, 47). His reference to hell in Lk 12:5 makes clear that hell is an experience beyond death.

These references to a final punishment of sinners by the fire of hell are further clarified in such texts as Mt 3:12, where sinners are likened to chaff that is burned with unquenchable fire (cf. Mk 9:43-48; Lk 3:9). In Mt 25:41 the wicked are represented as being consigned to "everlasting (*aiōnios*) fire," which is defined as "everlasting (*aiōnios*) punishment" (v 46). This fire, which will purge the earth (2 Pe 3:10-12; cf. Mt 3:12; Lk 3:17), will be kindled at the close of the *millennium, when both soul and body of the finally impenitent will be annihilated by fire (Mt 10:28; Rev 20:9).

A study of the usage and meaning of the Greek term *aiōnios,* as used in connection with the fire of the last days, shows that the emphasis is on its destructiveness rather than on its duration. For example, Sodom and Gomorrah met with the punishment of eternal (*aiōnios*) fire (Jude 7). The fire completely destroyed these cities, but became extinct long centuries ago. Jude set forth the destruction of these cities as an "example" of the fate that awaited the licentious apostates of his day. The term "unquenchable" may be similarly understood. Jeremiah predicted that God would kindle a fire in the gates of Jerusalem that would "not be quenched" (Jer 17:27). This prediction was fulfilled when the city was destroyed by Nebuchadnezzar (Jer 52:12, 13; cf. Neh 1:3). Obviously that fire is not burning today. Clearly the meaning is that it would not be quenched but would thoroughly destroy.

Although *aiōnios* fire denotes fire that is effectively destructive, the expression also implies that the fire will endure for a time (*see* Everlasting). This is consonant with the teaching that hell will be a place of punishment (Mt 25:41, 46; 2 Pe 2:9), and that there will be degrees of punishment. Christ comes "to give every man according as his work shall be" (Rev 22:12). The servant who "knew his lord's will, and prepared not himself . . . shall be beaten with many stripes," whereas the servant who did not know his lord's will, and committed things worthy of stripes, "shall be beaten with few stripes" (Lk 12:47, 48). The punishment is described as much more severe than the death penalty anciently inflicted in the Jewish economy (Heb 10:28, 29, 31). So, although hell's fires will eventually annihilate the wicked (Mt 10:28), it is obvious that the destruction is not instantaneous. *See* Death.

Tartaroō, "to cast into Tartarus," is used only once (2 Pe 2:4). According to the Greeks and to Jewish apocalyptic literature Tartarus was a place lower than Hades where divine punishment was meted out. Peter uses the term to describe the place where the rebellious angels were cast (cf. Jude 6).

Hellenist. (hĕl′ĕn-ĭst). [Gr. *Hellēnistēs*.] According to the generally accepted view, a non-Greek who adopts the Greek language or ways (Acts 6:1; 9:29; KJV "Grecian"); Biblically, a Jew usually living outside of Palestine who spoke Greek. Such Jews were called "Hellenists," in contrast with the Palestinian Jews, who spoke Aramaic and were called "Hebrews." In ch 11:20 textual evidence is divided between the reading *Hellēnistai*, "Hellenists," and *Hellēnes*, "Greeks." The presence of Hellenists in Jerusalem was verified in 1914 by the discovery on the hill of Ophel of the Greek inscription of the Theodotus synagogue (see fig. 187).

217. The gold helmet of Prince Meskalamdug of Ur

Helmet. Earliest helmets were made of leather, and had the form of skullcaps or pointed caps, occasionally with earflaps. In later periods helmets were made of metal. Egyptian reliefs of battle scenes show a great variety of helmets among various nations, especially among the Peoples of the Sea in the time of Ramses III. The Philistines are shown with a headgear of feathers (see fig. 382). It is uncertain what kind of helmet Goliath wore (1 Sa 17:5). The Bible mentions a helmet belonging to King Saul (v 38) and the helmets of Uzziah's soldiers (2 Chr 26: 14). The Hebrew defenders of Lachish are depicted on an Assyrian relief as wearing pointed helmets with earflaps. The metal crest mount of an Assyrian helmet, the base into which the plumes were fastened, was found in the excavations of Lachish (see fig. 218). Paul likens "salvation" and the "hope of salvation" to helmets (Eph 6:17; 1 Th 5:8).

218. Crest mount from an Assyrian helmet, found at Lachish: left and center, as found; right, a reconstructed replica

Helon (hē'lŏn). [Heb. *Chelon,* meaning uncertain. The name is attested in South Arabic inscriptions.] A Zebulunite whose son Eliab was the tribal prince (Num 1: 9; 2:7; 7:29; 10:16).

Helps. A rendering of: (1) The Gr. *boētheiai,* literally, "helps" (Acts 27:17, KJV), in a context that indicates that some sort of ropes or undergirding supports were intended. The RSV cautiously renders the term as "measures," with a marginal note defining *boētheiai* as "helps." (2) The Gr. *antilēmpseis* (1 Cor 12:28, KJV), "helps" or "helpful deeds" (RSV "helpers"), in a passage describing special gifts that God has placed in the church. *Antilēmpseis* is not found elsewhere in the NT; but in the LXX and other Hellenistic Greek writings it occurs frequently and is used to refer to acts of assistance.

Hem. In the KJV OT the translation of the Heb. *shûl,* meaning the skirt, or the lowest part of a garment, as applied to the garments of the high priest (Ex 28:33, 34; 39:24-26). In the KJV NT the word is used of the edge or border of Christ's garment, which was touched in faith by the sick, with the result that they were healed (Mt 9:20; 14:36).

Hemam (hē'măm). [Heb. *Hêmam,* "confusion."] Son of Lotan and grandson of Seir (Gen 36:22), called Homam (hō'măm) [Heb. *Hômam*] in 1 Chr 1:39, doubtless because of a confusion in the Hebrew *y* and *w,* two similar characters. For some unexplained reason the RSV reads "Heman" in Gen 36:22, perhaps on the basis of the LXX.

Heman (hē'măn). [Heb. *Hêman,* probably "faithful."]

1. One of the four wise men with whom Solomon is compared (1 Ki 4:31). He belonged to the tribe of Judah (1 Chr 2:6). Some think that it is this Heman whose name appears in the superscription of Ps 88.

2. A son of Joel and grandson of the prophet Samuel (1 Chr 6:33). He was of the Levite family of Korah and was one of David's prominent singers and cymbalists (1 Chr 6:33; 15:17, 19; 16:41, 42).

3. According to the RSV a descendant of Seir (Gen 36:20-22, KJV "Hemam"). He is called Homam in 1 Chr 1:39.

Hemath. *See* Hammath.

Hemdan (hĕm'dăn). [Heb. *Chemdan,* "pleasant" or "desirable."] A descendant of Seir, a *Horite (Gen 36:26) or Hurrian. In the parallel text in 1 Chr 1:41 the RSV has Hamran (hăm'răn) [Heb. *Chamran*].

In the KJV *Chamran* is transliterated Amram. In the vowelless postexilic Hebrew the only difference between *Chemdan* and *Chamran* is in the almost identically appearing Hebrew letters *d* and *r,* which are easily confused.

Hemlock. A translation of: (1) the Heb. *la'anah* (Amos 6:12, KJV), "wormwood," a plant of the genus *Artemisia;* (2) the Heb. *ro'sh* (Hos 10:4, KJV), an unspecified poisonous herb. Israel's perversion of righteousness and judgment was likened to bitter and poisonous herbs.

Hen, I (hĕn). [Heb. *Chen,* "grace."] A personal name, according to the KJV of Zec 6:14. The LXX translates the Hebrew term, rendering the phrase in which it appears "and for the favour of the son of Sophonias [Zephaniah]." The translators of the RSV consider *Chen* an error for *Yo'shîyah,* "Josiah" (cf. v 10), and emend the text in this way.

Hen, II. [Gr. *ornis,* "bird."] The common domestic fowl. It is directly mentioned only twice in the Bible (Mt 23:37; Lk 13:34). The chicken was known in Syria in the 15th cent. B.C., and a rooster is depicted on a Hebrew seal dated about 600 B.C. (fig. 250).

Hena (hē'nä). [Heb. *Hena'.*] A city which, along with others, is mentioned as having been captured by the Assyrians (2 Ki 18: 34; 19:13; Is 37:13); identified with the ancient *Hana,* also written *Hanat,* now called *Anat,* on the middle Euphrates (Map XI, C-5).

Henadad (hĕn'à-dăd). [Heb. *Chenadad,* probably "favor of Hadad."] Founder of a family of Levites whose members assisted Zerubbabel in laying the foundation for the new Temple (Ezr 3:9), and later assisted Nehemiah in the rebuilding of the wall of Jerusalem (Neh 3:18, 24). A member of the family set his seal to Nehemiah's covenant (ch 10:9).

Henna, KJV **Camphire.** [Heb. *kopher.*] An Old World tropical shrub bearing odoriferous flowers (Song 1:14; 4:13). The Hebrew term is believed to describe the "henna." This henna-flowering shrub (*Lawsonia alba,* or *intermis*), said to have been a native of northern India, has become common throughout the Orient, having escaped cultivation. It is from 4 to 12 ft. tall and bears yellow and white flowers of great fragrance. The plant and twigs were sometimes ground into a powder from which Oriental women made a reddish-orange dye to stain the palms of their hands, the soles of their feet, and their fingernails and toenails. Israel's ordinances dealing with taking a captive heathen woman to wife may have been given with reference to these uses of henna dye (Deut 21:11, 12). A nosegay of henna flowers is regarded by Eastern young women as a most generous token of love.

Henoch. See Enoch; Hanoch.

Hepher (hē'fĕr). [Heb. *Chepher*, "pit."]
1. A son of Gilead and founder of a tribal family in Manasseh (Num 26:32; 27:1; Jos 17:2).
2. A man of Judah whose father, Ashhur, was the ancestor of the inhabitants of Tekoa (1 Chr 4:6).
3. One of David's "mighty men," called a Mecherathite (1 Chr 11:36).
4. A Canaanite city in western Palestine (Jos 12:17); not identified.
5. A district of Judah in the neighborhood of Socoh (1 Ki 4:10); not identified.

Hepherites (hē'fĕr-īts). [Heb. *Chephrî.*] Descendants of Hepher, 1 (Num 26:32).

Hephzibah (hĕf'zĭ-bá). [Heb. *Chephsî-bah,* "my delight is in her."]
1. The mother of King Manasseh of Judah (2 Ki 21:1).
2. In the KJV a symbolical name to be given to the Zion of prophecy (Is 62:4). The RSV gives the literal rendering "My delight is in her."

Herald. Messenger, public crier. In Dan 3:4, the term thus translated (*karôz*, an Aramaic loan word from the Old Persian *xrausa*) denotes a "herald," or "public crier." In Is 40:9; 41:27; RSV, "herald" is a rendering of the Heb. *mebasser* and *mebassereth,* "messenger," and in 2 Pe 2:5, RSV, of the Gr. *kērux,* "public crier," "preacher."

Herb. Any of the large number of plants of varying complexity that do not develop woody persistent tissue as do shrubs and trees. Instead of "herbs," the RSV often reads "plants." Herbs were created on the 3d day of the Creation week and were to serve both man and animal for food (Gen 1:11, 12, 29, 30). In the plagues of Egypt herbs were destroyed by both the hail and the locusts (Ex 9:25; 10:15). The psalmist and the prophets spoke of herbs and grasses figuratively and in illustrations, as did Christ in the parable of the Mustard Seed (Mt 13:32). See Bitter Herbs; Grass.

Herdsman. See Shepherd.

Heres (hē'rēz). [Heb. *Cheres,* "sun."]
1. The name of a mountain in the territory of Dan (Jgs 1:35), probably identical with Ir-shemesh (Jos 19:41), which

is *Beth-shemesh. The site is called Harheres (här-hē'rēz) in the RSV.
2. The "ascent of Heres" (Jgs 8:13, KJV "before the sun was up") is an ascent east of the Jordan on which Gideon traveled after the defeat of Zebah and Zalmunna.

Heresh (hē'rĕsh). [Heb. *Cheresh,* "dumb," "silent," or "skillful."] A Levite (1 Chr 9:15).

Heresy. A rendering of the Gr. *hairesis,* which properly means "sect" in Acts 24: 14; "dissension" or "faction" in 1 Cor 11:19 and Gal 5:20; and "opinion," "dogma," "way of thinking" in 2 Pe 2:1.

Hereth (hē'rĕth), KJV **Hareth** (hā'rĕth). [Heb. *Chareth.*] A forest in Judah near Keilah, in which David hid from Saul (1 Sa 22:5); not identified.

Hermas (hûr'măs). [Gr. *Hermas.* The name is attested by Greek inscriptions.] A Christian at Rome to whom Paul sent greetings (Rom 16:14). The tradition current since Origen, that he was the author of *The Shepherd of Hermas,* is without foundation, since this apocryphal Christian work was written probably about a century after Paul's letter to the Romans.

Hermes (hûr'mēz), KJV **Mercurius** (mûr-ku'rĭ-ŭs). [Gr. *Hermēs.* Mercurius is the Latin name (Anglicized as Mercury) of the god.]
1. A Greek god, spokesman and messenger of the gods. He is usually depicted with winged sandals and a winged hat, and as carrying the caduceus—a winged standard decorated with a pair of entwined serpents. When Paul and Barnabas healed a cripple at Lystra, the people took the apostles to be two visiting deities, and acclaimed Barnabas as Zeus, or Jupiter, and Paul, the speaker, as Hermes or Mercury (Acts 14:11, 12).
2. A Christian at Rome, to whom Paul sent greetings (Rom 16:14).

Hermogenes (hûr-mŏj'ĕ-nēz). [Gr. *Hermogenēs,* "sprung from Hermes," a Greek personal name attested by inscriptions.] A one-time Christian in Asia Minor who turned away from Paul (2 Ti 1:15). That he and Phygelus are the only ones mentioned by name of "all they which are in Asia" who had apostatized seems to indicate that the two were leaders in the apostate movement referred to by the apostle. Apocryphal stories concerning him are found in the *Acts of Paul and Thecla.*

Hermon (hûr'mŏn). [Heb. *Chermôn,* meaning unknown.] The southern portion of the Anti-Lebanon Mountains, which form the eastern of the two mountain ranges of

219. Snow-capped Mount Hermon

Syria. The Amorites called it Shenir (shĕ'-nẽr) or Senir (sē'nĭr) [Heb. *Senir*] (Deut 3:9), attested in Akkadian as *Saniru;* the Phoenicians called it Sirion (sĭr'ĭ-ŏn) [Heb. *Siryon*] (Deut 3:9; Jer 18:14, RSV), attested in Ugaritic as *Shryn.* It appears in Hittite as *Shariyana.* One of its summits was apparently called Sion [Heb. *Si'on*] (Deut 4:48). This majestic mountain ridge, which is about 15 mi. long and rises over 9,000 ft. above sea level, is snow capped most of the year and can be seen from many parts of northern Palestine. Its summit affords a marvelous view of the Lebanon, Galilee, the Jordan Valley with its two northern lakes, the Hauran, and the area around Damascus. See figs. 120, 183. It was the northeastern limit of the Israelite conquest of Canaan under Moses and Joshua (Deut 3:8, 9; Jos 11:3, 17; 12:1; 13:5, 11; 1 Chr 5:23). Hebrew poets mention it together with Mount Tabor (Ps 89:12), with Mount Zion (Ps 133:3), and with the Lebanon (Song 4:8). In Ps 42:6 the Hebrew plural form *Chermónîm,* literally "Hermons," is found, a reference probably to the three principal peaks of Mount Hermon rather than to "Hermonites" (hŭr'mŏn-īts, KJV), dwellers of Mount Hermon. On the slopes of Mount Hermon lie the sources of the various streams that form the river Jordan. Map II, A-3.

Hermonites. *See* Hermon.

Herod (hĕr'ŭd). [Gr. *Hērōdēs*, "offspring of a hero" or "like a hero." The name was very common among Greeks and is attested in inscriptions and literature from the 5th cent. B.C.] The name of a family of rulers of Palestine, of whom only 3 (Nos. 1, 3, and 6 below) are mentioned by the name Herod in the NT.

1. HEROD THE GREAT. *King of Judea and all Palestine at the time of Jesus' birth.* He was the 2d son of the Idumean Antipater, and thus a descendant of the ancient Edomites, but he was a Jew by citizenship and religious profession. The Idumeans had been conquered by John Hyrcanus I in 125 B.C. and had been forced to accept the Jewish religion, including circumcision; hence they had nominally become Jews. Antipater was made procurator of Judea by Caesar in 47 B.C. His son Herod (born *c.* 73 B.C.) was brought up at the court of the high priest and ruler, Hyrcanus II (63-40 B.C.), to whom his father was political adviser. When Antipater became procurator he induced Caesar to make his son Herod strategus (chief magistrate) of Galilee, and Phasael, another son, strategus of Judea. Shortly afterward Sextus Caesar, the legate of Syria, made Herod strategus of Coelesyria also. Herod made a shift in political affiliation after Caesar's death (44 B.C.), and gave his support to the party of Caesar's murderers. This resulted in Herod's confirmation in his office by G. Cassius, proconsul of Syria. When Antony and Octavian defeated Cassius, Herod succeeded in gaining the favor of Antony. He and his brother Phasael were then appointed tetrarchs of their territories in Palestine, offices they held until the Parthians conquered all of Syria and Palestine (40 B.C.). Hyrcanus II and Phasael went into the Parthian camp to negotiate a peace but were treacherously imprisoned. Phasael, unable to bear the shame, committed suicide. Herod fled to Rome and was there appointed king over Judea, in opposition to Antigonus, a Maccabean, who had been made king in Judea with the support of the Parthians. Herod returned to Palestine and, with the help of Roman forces, defeated Antigonus and conquered Jerusalem the following year (37 B.C.). Herod revealed at once that he would show no mercy to anyone who had withstood him. He massacred a large number of noblemen, among them 45 leaders who had supported Antigonus, and also put to death all members of the Sanhedrin but one, for having withstood his ambitions on an earlier occasion. The Sanhedrin under Herod was reduced to such impotency that some scholars question its existence during his reign.

The kingdom of Herod initially comprised Judea (including Samaria and Idumea); however, Antony took Jericho and its territory and gave it to Cleopatra of Egypt. After the battle at Actium in 31 B.C., from which Octavian emerged victor over Antony, Herod made another switch in affiliation, went to Rhodes where Octavian was, and succeeded in gaining his favor. The victorious Octavian, who became better known as Augustus, added Jericho, Gadara, and Gaza to Herod's territory after Cleopatra's death, and later (23 B.C.) the northeastern territories of Batanaea, Trachonitis, and Auranitis also. Herod ruled his kingdom without any serious threats from the outside, so that his reign can be called a period of prosperity.

Herod's family life was full of tragedies, and was soiled with the blood of his closest relatives, including three of his own sons and one of his ten wives. Only the most important of his many children will be mentioned here. His eldest son, Antipater, was borne by his Idumean wife Doris. His second wife was Mariamne, a granddaughter of the ruler-priest Hyrcanus II; by this marriage Herod connected his own house with that of the Hasmonaeans (Maccabeans), and thus attempted to legalize his kingship in the eyes of the Jews. He seems to have loved Mariamne with all his heart, although she hated him. Mariamne bore him Aristobulus and Alexander. By Malthace, a Samaritan wife, he had Archelaus and Herod Antipas; by Cleopatra, a wife from Jerusalem, was born Herod Philip (who became a tetrarch); and by another Mariamne (the daughter of Simon of Jerusalem, whom Herod made high priest) he had a son also known as Herod Philip, or Philip of Rome. Since Herod did not trust his Hasmonaean relatives, he killed many of them. In 35 B.C. Aristobulus III, brother of Herod's second wife, was murdered, being drowned in Herod's palace pool at Jericho, although he had been made high priest by Herod only a few months earlier. In 30 B.C. he had the aged Hyrcanus II, the grandfather of his wife Mariamne, killed, and then, a year later, put Mariamne herself to death because he suspected her of plotting against his life. From that time on his suspicions gave him no rest. At first he seems to have designated as his heirs Mariamne's sons Aristobulus and Alexander. However, when their older half brother Antipater, the son of Doris, accused them of treason Herod imprisoned and killed them (7 B.C.). He then named Antipater as his successor, with Herod Philip, the son of Mariamne II, as second in line of succession. Antipater, having been successful in eliminating two of his competitors for the throne, accused his half brothers Archelaus, son of Malthace, and Philip, son of Cleopatra, as well as his aunt Salome, Herod's sister, of plotting against the life of the king. However, Herod, discovering

that the accusation was false, appointed Antipas as his successor, and had Antipater put to death only a few days before he himself passed away. After Antipater's death, and shortly before his own, Herod again changed his will and now designated Archelaus, Antipas, and Philip as his heirs on the throne. This last will of Herod was honored by Augustus. Archelaus (*see* Herod, 2) was given Judea (Mt 2:22), Samaria, and Idumea, with the title ethnarch; Antipas (*see* Herod, 3) was made tetrarch over Galilee (Lk 3:1, 19) and Perea; and Philip (*see* Herod, 4) became tetrarch over the northeastern territories (v 1). Herod Philip, son of Mariamne II, remained a private citizen (*see* Herod, 5). Because of this his wife *Herodias (who was also his niece, being daughter of his brother Aristobulus) left him and lived with Antipas.

Herod was a great builder and the founder of several magnificent cities, which were built in Hellenistic style and splendor. These included two cities named in honor of the emperor Augustus: Samaria, which he called Sebaste (Greek for "Augusta"), and the old Strato's Tower, on the coast, which he named Caesarea, and which later became Herod's capital; two that he named for members of his family: *Antipatris (formerly Aphek), northeast of Joppa and Phasaelis, in the Jordan Valley; and two cities which bore the name Herodium (Gr. *Hērōdeion*), one in Transjordan and the other southeast of Bethlehem (for the latter see Map XV, E-3). Other cities or fortresses built by him were Machaerus, east of the Dead Sea (Map XV, E-4), Masada, near the western shore of the Dead Sea (Map XV, F-3), Gaba in Galilee (Map XV, C-3), and Esbon (formerly Heshbon) in Perea (Map XV, E-4).

The city of Jerusalem also received his attention. Beginning *c.* 20 B.C. he rebuilt Zerubbabel's Temple, which was in a dilapidated condition, and began to erect magnificent buildings in and around the Temple (*see* Temple, IV), including the *"barracks" of Antonia. These structures were not completed until shortly before the outbreak of the Jewish-Roman war in A.D. 66 (cf. Jn 2:20). He also built a royal palace in Jerusalem, one tower of which is still partly visible in the lower section of the so-called "Tower of *David" in the citadel. Herod also erected a theater and an amphitheater. These structures, because they were the scene of plays and games such as were held in Hellenistic cities, were highly offensive to the orthodox Jews.

Although Herod was a *Hellenist in heart and practice, and surrounded himself by Hellenistic counselors, he was prudent enough to refrain from suppressing or openly defying the Jewish religion as Antiochus IV had done in the preceding century. However, the Jews hated him because he was an Idumean and a friend of the Romans, and because of his scandalous private life. They resented his extreme cruelty and the imposition upon them of a heavy tax burden necessitated

220. Reverse of a coin of Herod the Great, king of Judea (actual size). The objects shown are a cult vessel and 2 palm branches

by his extensive building program. The absence of open rebellion during his long reign was due to his unwavering loyalty to the Romans, to his ruthlessness in suppressing every opposition, and to the fact that there was external peace in his day.

Herod the Great appears in the NT in the date formula of Lk 1:5, and in the narrative of the "wise men from the east" as told in Mt 2:1-18. Upon hearing that a descendant of David was born in Bethlehem according to an ancient prophecy, the king gave orders to kill all infants in that city. This cruel act is not recorded in secular history. It is in full harmony with his other known acts of atrocity and cruelty. The last atrocity planned by Herod was fortunately never carried out. Knowing that there would be great rejoicing in the kingdom when the people would learn of his death, he had the principal Jews shut up in the stadium in Jericho, and gave orders to have them killed as soon as he died, in order to provide some mourning over his death. However, his sister Salome and her husband Alexas, who were charged with carrying out this order, foiled his plan by releasing the unfortunate noblemen after his death, thus bringing great joy to many Jewish homes. Herod passed away in his 34th regnal year at the age of 69, in 4/3 B.C., most probably in the spring of 4 B.C.

2. (HEROD) ARCHELAUS (är'kė-lā'ŭs). [Gr. Archelaos, "people's ruler," or "people's prince."] Ruler of Judea and Samaria during Jesus' childhood. Archelaus was a son of Herod the Great and Mal-

thace. He, his full brother Antipas, and their half brother Philip the tetrarch (the son of Cleopatra of Jerusalem) were all educated in Rome. They were named as their father's successors in his final will, which was honored by Augustus. The emperor gave Archelaus Judea, Samaria, and Idumea, and granted him the title ethnarch, meaning "people's prince." He ruled in this capacity from 4 B.C. to A.D. 6. Like his father he loved luxury and power, and on several occasions demonstrated his cruel nature. In suppressing a riot during the 1st year of his reign his troops killed 3,000 people. It is easy to understand why Joseph was afraid to live in Judea under Archelaus when he brought Mary and the child Jesus back from Egypt (Mt 2:22).

Archelaus' choice of high priests, his private life, and his cruelties annoyed the Jews, who, joined by the Samaritans, sent deputations to Rome, and finally persuaded Augustus to recall Archelaus. The deposed ethnarch was banished to Vienne, on the Rhone, in what is now southern France, and his territory was placed under a Roman procurator, who served as a direct representative of the Roman provincial administration (see Governor, 3).

3. HEROD (ANTIPAS) (ăn'tĭ-păs). Ruler of Galilee and Perea during Jesus' ministry, called "Herod the Tetrarch" in the NT, but usually referred to in history as "Herod Antipas." He was the son of Herod the Great and his Samaritan wife Malthace, and was educated in Rome with his brother Archelaus and his half brother Philip. Antipas was designated successor to the throne in his father's 2d will, yet in Herod's final will he was given only Galilee and Perea, with the title of tetrarch. Mark refers to him by his popular title, king (ch 6:14). Since he is simply called Herod in the Gospels, a name found also on his coins, readers of the Bible have frequently confused him with his father. He was married to the daughter of Aretas, king of the Nabataeans, whose capital was Petra, south of the Dead Sea (Map XIX, E-13). This marriage may have been contracted with the purpose of making the eastern and southern borders of Perea safe from Nabataean attacks.

During a visit to Rome, Herod Antipas fell in love with Herodias, his niece, who was the wife of his half brother, Herod Philip. Herodias thereupon left her husband and lived with Antipas. His discarded wife's father was deeply offended and consequently waged war against Antipas, in which he succeeded in occupying parts of Antipas' Transjordan territories. John the Baptist severely rebuked Antipas (perhaps publicly) for his adultery and as a result was incarcerated, probably in Machaerus, a fortress east of the Dead Sea. Herodias deeply hated John for his interference in her private life and could not rest until she brought about his death (Mt 14:1-12). Antipas was known for his cunning (Jesus called him "that fox," Lk 13:32), his ambitions, and his love of luxuries, yet he lived as an orthodox Jew, and went to Jerusalem on feast days (ch 23:7). For years he was an enemy of Pilate (v 12), because he could not condone the procurator's anti-Jewish acts. In harmony with the Jewish aversion to images he refrained from having his portrait put on his coins. He rebuilt Sepphoris in Galilee, added to its fortifications, and made it his capital. He also built Tiberias and other cities and strengthened the borders of his possessions.

Herod Antipas is mentioned in the NT in connection with the imprisonment and execution of John the Baptist (Mt 14:3-12). He may have planned to arrest and kill Jesus of Nazareth, as the Pharisees claimed (Lk 13:31), but this is not certain. He considered Jesus to be the risen Baptist (Mk 6:14-16). When he finally met Jesus in Jerusalem, he showed interest in Him, but his interest turned to ridicule when Jesus refused to answer him (Lk 23:8-12). Pilate's act of sending Jesus to him, in recognition of Herod's authority over Galileans even in Jerusalem, resulted in a friendship between the two former antagonists. In A.D. 37 Agrippa, Herodias' brother, was made king over the northeastern territories of Palestine that Philip (see Herod, 4) had held. Herodias, dissatisfied that her husband had the title only of tetrarch, induced him to go with her to Rome and to seek a royal crown from Caligula. Agrippa, however, sent letters to Rome accusing his uncle Antipas of treasonable activities. As a result, instead of being made a king, Herod was banished in A.D. 39, to either Gaul or Spain, where Herodias followed him into exile. His territory was added to that of his accuser, Agrippa.

4. (HEROD) PHILIP (fĭl′ĭp). [Gr. Philippos, "a friend of horses."] Tetrarch of the territories northeast of the Sea of Galilee, the son of Herod the Great and of Cleopatra of Jerusalem. Educated in Rome with his half brothers Archelaus and Antipas, he was given part of his father's realm upon Herod's death. Receiving the title tetrarch, he was placed over the northeastern territories of Palestine— including Ituraea, Trachonitis (Lk 3:1), Batanaea, and Auranitis and ruled from 4 B.C. to A.D. 33/34. He was the best of all the Herodian rulers, and the historians of his time report nothing evil of him. His building activities were many. He enlarged the city of Paneas, situated at the source of the Jordan, and called it Caesarea. Later it was generally referred to as Caesarea Philippi (Mt 16:13) to distinguish it from the Caesarea of western Palestine. Philip also made the village of Bethsaida into a city and called it Bethsaida Julias in honor of Augustus' daughter, who was the wife of Tiberius. Toward the end of his life he married his niece, Herodias' daughter (ch 14:11) Salome, who was about 30 years his junior. When he died without leaving any children, his tetrarchy was annexed to Syria, but about 3 years later it was given to Agrippa I as a kingdom.

5. (HEROD) PHILIP. Brother of Antipas and first husband of Herodias. He was a son of Herod the Great and of Mariamne II, daughter of the high priest Simon. Philip was not a ruler, but a private citizen. He was married to his niece, Herodias, who after a time fell in love with her uncle Antipas (see Herod, 3), a half brother of her husband, and went to live with him, taking her daughter Salome with her. Salome later married her great-uncle, Philip the tetrarch, and after her husband's death married one of her cousins, Aristobulus.

Herod Philip is called simply Philip in the Gospels (Mt 14:3; Lk 3:19), but is called Herod by Josephus (Ant. xviii. 5. 4). The NT agrees with Josephus in making him a (half) brother of Herod Antipas.

6. HEROD (AGRIPPA I) (ȧ-grĭp′ȧ). [Gr. Agrippas.] King of Judea and all Palestine who persecuted the apostles (Acts 12:1). His official Roman name was Marcus Julius Agrippa Herodes, but he is called simply "Herod the king" in the NT. He was born in 10/9 B.C. as a son of Aristobulus and Bernice and grandson of Herod the Great. He married Cypros, and had four children, Bernice, Mariamne, Drusilla, and Agrippa (II). Of these the 1st, 3d, and 4th are mentioned in the Bible (chs 24:24; 25:13). He received part of his education in Rome, later became superintendent of markets at Tiberias, and

also lived for a while in Damascus. Upon his return to Rome in A.D. 37 he was imprisoned by Tiberius for having sided with Germanicus' son, Gaius, or Caligula, who became emperor only 6 months later. Caligula immediately made his friend Agrippa king of the tetrarchy over which Agrippa's late uncle Philip (*see* Herod, 4) had ruled, and over the tetrarchy of Lysanias. In A.D. 39 he was made ruler over Galilee and Perea, the tetrarchy of his uncle Antipas, whom he had ousted and whose banishment he precipitated by accusing him to Rome of conspiring against the empire. Two years later the emperor Claudius, with whom Agrippa had also ingratiated himself, added to Agrippa's kingdom the territory of Judea and Samaria, which since A.D. 6 had been governed by Roman procurators. Agrippa thus became king over an area equal to that held by his grandfather Herod the Great. Anxious to obtain the good will of his people, he strictly observed the religious rules of the Jews. His execution of James, the brother of John, and the imprisonment of Peter (Acts 12:1-7) were ordered with this purpose in mind. Attempting to strengthen Jerusalem's fortifications, he began to build a new wall to the north of Jerusalem, but gave up the project on the demand of Claudius. Although he tried to show himself an orthodox Jew, he was also a great lover and promoter of Greek athletic games and of the theater. He died in A.D. 44 in his capital, Caesarea, after a brief but violent intestinal illness, which suddenly overtook him when he accepted divine honors after an oration at a public appearance (Acts 12:20-23; Jos. *Ant.* xix. 8. 2).

7. (HEROD) AGRIPPA (II). *Ruler of the northeast; the Agrippa who heard Paul.* His official Roman name was Marcus Julius Agrippa Herodes II. He was the son of Agrippa I and was born and educated in Rome. Since he was only 17 years old when his father died in A.D. 44 he was considered by the emperor Claudius to be too young to take over the kingship. However, in A.D. 50 he was made king of Chalcis (Chalkis on Map XVI, A-4), a small area in the Lebanon region, which had been ruled by his uncle Herod from A.D. 41 to 48. In A.D. 53 he was given the former tetrarchies of Philip and Lysanias in northeastern Palestine in exchange for the kingdom of Chalcis. Nero added large areas of Galilee and Perea to his territory. He was also assigned the supervi-

sion of the Temple of Jerusalem and the right to appoint the high priest. It was during his reign that the Temple begun under his great-grandfather, Herod the Great, was completed (A.D. 62 or 64). Like his father he attempted to live the life of an orthodox Jew, and whenever he had an opportunity he pointed out to his noble pagan acquaintances the high moral advantages of Jewish monotheism over their religions. However, he lived in incest with his sister Bernice, so that his own private life was scandalous.

Agrippa II enlarged and beautified Caesarea Philippi, built an addition to Herod's palace in Jerusalem, and sponsored theatrical performances in Berytus (Beirut). A monumental stone inscription mentioning him and his sister Bernice was recently found in the excavations of Beirut and is now in the Beirut Museum (see fig. 221). Agrippa is men-

221. An inscription of King Herod Agrippa II and his sister Bernice

tioned in the NT in connection with Paul's appeal to the emperor. After the procurator Festus took over his governorship, Agrippa and Bernice paid a courtesy visit to Caesarea. Festus used this opportunity to bring Paul before Agrippa, whom he considered an expert in Jewish affairs, to obtain legal counsel as to what report he should send to Rome. Agrippa became convinced of Paul's innocence, but could not release him since the case had already been appealed to the emperor (Acts 25:13-27; 26:32).

When the Jewish war broke out in A.D. 66, Agrippa II failed in his efforts to persuade the Jews to refrain from rebelling against the Romans. Thereupon he placed himself without reservation on the side of the Romans, and was richly honored for his loyal stand. Little is known about his later private life in Rome, where he died either *c.* A.D. 93 or *c.* A.D. 100.

For women of the Herod family mentioned in the Bible, *see* Bernice; Drusilla; Herodias.

Herodians (hĕ-rō′dĭ-ănz). [Gr. *Hērōdianoi*.] The name of a group mentioned in the NT, which on two occasions joined the

Pharisees in an attempt to trap Jesus (Mt 22:16; Mk 3:6; 12:13). No political party by that name is known, so it is usually thought they were people who supported Herod Antipas, who did much to please the Jews by living an orthodox Jewish life and must therefore have had Jewish sympathizers. It is possible they were in favor of the Hellenization movement supported by the Herods. They may also have been wealthy people to whom the stable government of the Herods meant continued prosperity and security. Jerome thought that the Herodians were Herod's soldiers, whereas other commentators have seen in them court officials of Herod.

Herodias (hē-rō'dĭ-ăs). [Gr. *Hērōdias.*] Daughter of Aristobulus, and granddaughter of Herod the Great. She was married to her uncle Herod Philip (called simply Philip in Mt 14:3; Lk 3:19), who was a private citizen (*see* Herod, 5). Later she fell in love with her husband's half brother Antipas, and lived with him after he had divorced his first wife, the daughter of the Nabataean king Aretas. John the Baptist rebuked (perhaps publicly) the adulterous pair, and was therefore imprisoned. Herodias, who hated him more than her husband did, succeeded in having the Baptist executed (Mt 14:3-12; Mk 6:17-29; Lk 3:19, 20). After Caligula made her brother Agrippa king she became dissatisfied with her husband's status, which was merely that of tetrarch. She therefore induced Antipas to go with her to Rome to request the kingship for himself. Accused by Agrippa of treasonable activities, Antipas was banished either to Gaul or Spain. Herodias followed him there, although she had been pardoned by the emperor.

Herodion (hē-rō'dĭ-ŏn). [Gr. *Hērōdiōn.*] A Jewish Christian in Rome, to whom Paul sent greetings (Rom 16:11). Paul calls him a "kinsman," but this may simply indicate that Herodion was a fellow Jew. He may have been a freedman of Herod.

Heron. [Heb. *'anaphah.*] A bird of the family Ardeidae, wading birds with long neck and legs, a tapering bill, and soft plumage. They feed on fish and reptiles found along the shores and in shallow ponds. The larger members attain to a length of about 50 in. Some Ardeidae are abundant in the Jordan Valley and on the seacoast of Palestine. However, the exact species of bird represented by *'anaphah* is uncertain, "heron" being merely a conjectural translation. Driver suggests the

cormorant (*PEQ* 87 [1955], 20). The bird is mentioned only in the 2 parallel lists of unclean creatures in the Pentateuch (Lev 11:19; Deut 14:18).

Hesed. *See* Ben-hesed.

222. The mound of ancient Heshbon

Heshbon (hĕsh'bŏn). [Heb. *Cheshbôn,* "device."] A city of Transjordan strategically located on two hills of a plateau which give an extensive view over the lower Jordan Valley. The Israelites captured it from Sihon, an Amorite king, who had taken it from the Moabites and made it his capital (Num 21:25-30). The city was given to the Reubenites and rebuilt by them (Num 21:34; 32:37; Jos 13:17). However, since it lay on the border between Reuben and Gad, the latter tribe seems eventually to have occupied it (Jos 13:26). It was later assigned, as a town of Gad, to the Levites (Jos 21:39; 1 Chr 6:81). The Moabites reconquered the city in the period of the divided kingdom and occupied it in the time of Isaiah and Jeremiah (Is 15:4; 16:8, 9; Jer 48:2, 33, 34). It was in the possession of Alexander Jannaeus in the time of the Maccabees, and was later ruled by Herod the Great (Jos. *Ant.* xiii. 15. 4; xv. 8. 5). The site is now called *Ḥesbân,* about 6 mi. north of *Madeba* (Map VI, E-4). Extensive ruins indicate that it was an important city in Roman times. A large reservoir east of the ruins has been identified with one of the pools mentioned in Song 7:4.

Heshmon (hĕsh'mŏn). [Heb. *Cheshmôn.*] A town in the south of Judah, near Beersheba (Jos 15:27); not identified.

Heth. *See* Hittites.

Hethlon (hĕth'lŏn). [Heb. *Chethlon.*] A place mentioned in Ezekiel's vision as being on the northern boundary of restored Israel (Eze 47:15; 48:1); not identified with certainty. Some have identified it with *Ḥeitela,* northeast of Tripoli on the Lebanon coast; others with *'Adlûn,* on the Lebanon coast, halfway between the mouth of the Litani River and Sarepta.

Hezeki. *See* Hizki.

Hezekiah (hĕz'ē-kī'ȧ), KJV of OT once **Hizkijah** (hĭz-kī'jȧ), KJV of NT twice **Ezekias** (ĕz'ē-kī'ăs). [Heb. *Chizqîyah* and *Chizqîyahû,* "Yahweh has strengthened"; in Assyrian cuneiform records the name of the king of Judah is spelled *Ḥazaqi(i)aú;* Gr. *Hezekias.*]

1. The son of Ahaz and the 13th king of Judah. His reign of 29 years (as recorded in 2 Ki 18:2; 2 Chr 29:1) is probably reckoned from his father's death (*c.* 715 B.C.). During 10 years of the 29 his son Manasseh was probably coregent with him. But apparently Hezekiah had ruled jointly with his father for 14 years before that, thus being on the throne a total of 43 years (*c.* 729 - *c.* 686 B.C., according to the synchronisms of the Bible and the Assyrian chronology). Hezekiah was a good ruler and broke with his father's evil practices as soon as he was free to do so. He repaired and cleansed the Temple, reorganized the religious services, and celebrated a great Passover to which he invited the ten tribes of the north. He removed the high places, destroyed the idols, and even the bronze serpent dating from Moses' time, since it was being used for idolatrous purposes (2 Ki 18:3-6; 2 Chr 29:1 to 31:21). He also had unpublished proverbs of Solomon collected and recorded (Prov 25:1).

His reign was marked by remarkable prosperity. He gained control over the Philistine Plain (2 Ki 18:8), built store cities and sheepfolds (2 Chr 32:27-29), and fortified the wall of Jerusalem (Is 22:10). But his greatest technical accomplishment was bringing water inside Jerusalem. His rock-cut Siloam tunnel, 1,749 ft. long, connected an old tunnel from the spring of Gihon, in the Kidron Valley, with a new, lower pool inside the city (2 Ki 20:20; 2 Chr 32:4, 30; cf. Ecclus 48:17. *See* Siloam).

Hezekiah is best known for his brave fight against the powerful Assyrian Empire, and for his faith in God during one of Sennacherib's invasions, a faith that was rewarded by a miraculous destruction of a large Assyrian army. In the 6th year of Hezekiah (evidently of his coregency with his father) he witnessed the destruction of Samaria and the end of the northern kingdom (2 Ki 18:10). His father Ahaz had made himself an Assyrian vassal (ch 16:7-18). Detesting this situation, Hezekiah determined to shake off the Assyrian yoke. He seems to have made an alliance with Egypt despite the prophet Isaiah's opposition to such an unwise action (Is 30:1-5; 31:1-3). Whether he had already severed his connections with Assyria in Sargon's time is not certain. A broken cuneiform inscription mentions an Assyrian campaign conducted by Sargon's army commander against the Philistine city of Ashdod in 711 B.C., recorded also in Is 20:1. The inscription says that attempts had been made to incite Judah, Edom, and Moab to rebel against Assyria (*ANET* 287). However, the text is broken and the reference to Judah is somewhat vague. It is possible that Hezekiah had already clashed with Sargon, since in a Nimrud inscription the Assyrian king calls himself "the subduer of the country Judah which is far away" (*ANET* 287). A test came in 701 B.C. when Sennacherib, who had followed Sargon II in 705 B.C. on the throne of Assyria, carried out a successful campaign against Palestine in general, and against Hezekiah in particular. Of this invasion both Biblical and cuneiform records are available. The Biblical records (2 Ki 18:13 to 19:36; 2 Chr 32:1-21; Is 36 and 37) combine two invasions of Sennacherib in such a way that it is difficult to know where the account of the campaign of 701 B.C. ends and that of the later one (which took place after 690 B.C.) begins. Sennacherib's records of his 1st invasion, inscribed on clay prisms, are well preserved (see fig. 223; see *ANET* 287, 288). The campaign was also pictured on stone reliefs in Sennacherib's palace at Nineveh (see fig. 284). Hezekiah had weak allies. Isaiah had warned the nation not to put any hope in Egypt and Ethiopia, whose conquest by Assyria the prophet predicted (Is 20:2-6). Egypt, ruled at that time by Nubian kings, was so impotent that Sennacherib's general was fully justified in describing the nation as a "bruised reed, . . . on which if a man lean, it will go into his hand, and pierce it" (2 Ki 18:21). Another impotent supporter of Hezekiah was Merodach-baladan (*Marduk-apal-iddin*), a Chaldean who twice was king of Babylon, first from 722/21 to 710/09 B.C., and again for several months in 703/02 B.C. Each time he was driven from his throne and kingdom by the Assyrian army. It was apparently about the time of Sennacherib's first invasion of

Judah that Hezekiah's miraculous recuperation from a mortal disease caused Merodach-baladan to send envoys to him (2 Ki 20:12, 13). Yet the Chaldean leader at that time would have been in no position to help Hezekiah in his struggle for freedom from the Assyrian yoke. The Biblical record says that Sennacherib took all the fortified cities of Judah, and then threatened Jerusalem with a great army commanded by some of his highest officers. In the meantime the king besieged and took the strong fortress of Lachish, and later, Libnah. Hezekiah paid a large tribute to Sennacherib, consisting of 300 talents of silver and 30 talents of gold (2 Ki 18:13 to 19:8; Is 36:1 to 37:8). An

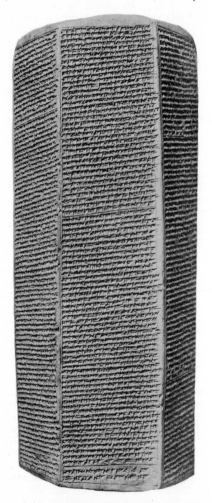

223. Clay prism of King Sennacherib with inscription containing the story of the Assyrian campaign against Hezekiah of Judah

examination shows that the Assyrian records (*ANET* 287, 288) agree in all major points with the Biblical narrative, although there are some differences in details. Sennacherib claims that he met no opposition in Syria or Phoenicia, and that many kings, including Judah's neighbors, such as the kings of Ammon, Moab, and Edom, paid tribute and bowed to his yoke. The only opponents seem to have been Sidqia of Ashkelon, the population of Ekron, and Hezekiah. Sennacherib first captured Ashkelon and deported Sidqia and his family to Assyria; then he fought a battle at Eltekeh against the army of Ekron, punishing Ekron's nobility in a cruel manner. Next he attacked Judah, besieging and taking 46 fortified cities and countless small villages, and capturing in all 200,150 citizens of Judah. He claims that he made Hezekiah "a prisoner in Jerusalem, his royal residence, like a bird in a cage," but he does not say that he conquered his city. His words concerning the siege of Jerusalem probably refer to the unsuccessful attempt of Rabshakeh to take the capital by persuasion. Sennacherib also mentions the tribute paid by Hezekiah, although there are discrepancies in the figures, Sennacherib's being the higher. These can be explained by assuming that Sennacherib either gave an exaggerated figure with regard to the amount of silver paid by Hezekiah or included a later payment made by Hezekiah, one that is not mentioned in the Bible.

At a later time, after Tirhakah (Taharka), the Nubian king, had ascended the throne of Egypt, *c.* 689 B.C., Sennacherib must have made another attempt to subjugate Hezekiah. Hezekiah received a blasphemous letter from Sennacherib demanding the surrender of the city, but Judah's king, trusting in Isaiah's words that God would save Jerusalem, refused to surrender it. His trust was rewarded when by divine intervention the Assyrian army was smitten at night (2 Ki 19:9-36; 2 Chr 32:21; Is 37:9-37). The chroniclers of Sennacherib did not record this disaster. Defeats or catastrophes were seldom if ever recorded by the Assyrian historians. Among other nations, however, the Assyrian disaster was not so quickly forgotten. According to Herodotus, the army of "Sennacherib, king of the Arabians and Assyrians," suffered greatly during a campaign against Egypt. He attributes the catastrophe to an attack by field mice, resulting in a grave defeat (ii. 141). Scholars have thought that Herodotus' story refers to an epidemic of bubonic plague which broke out in the Assyrian army.

Besides Isaiah, the prophets Hosea and Micah were active in Hezekiah's time (Hos 1:1; Mic 1:1). When Hezekiah died, c. 686 B.C., his son Manasseh, who seems to have been associated with him for some years on the throne, became sole ruler.

2. An ancestor of the prophet Zephaniah. Since the Hezekiah to whom Zephaniah traces his genealogy would be some illustrious person, this was probably Hezekiah, 1 (Zep 1:1; KJV "Hizkiah").

3. For 1 Chr 3:23, KJV, see Hizkiah, 1.

4. An ancestor of a group of exiles who returned with Zerubbabel (Ezr 2:16; Neh 7:21).

5. An influential man of Judah who set his seal to the covenant under Nehemiah (Neh 10:17; KJV "Hizkijah").

Hezion (hē'zĭ-ŏn). [Heb. *Chezyôn,* if Semitic, "vision." The name, probably non-Semitic, is attested in Ugaritic as *Hdyn,* and in Akkadian as *Haziânu* and *Hazânu,* occurring as a rather common term for the mayor of a city.] One of the first kings of Damascus and grandfather of Ben-hadad I (1 Ki 15:18). This king is possibly mentioned by name on the Ben-hadad Stele (*BASOR* 87 [1942], 25).

Hezir (hē'zēr). [Heb. *Chezîr,* "wild pig." The name occurs in Ugaritic as *Hzrn,* and in the Amarna Letters as *Hiziri.*]

1. A descendant of Aaron, and ancestral head of a family of priests who in David's time became the 17th of the 24 courses into which the priests were organized (1 Chr 24:15). A tomb of this priestly family which was found in the

224. The tomb of the priestly family of Hezir in the Kidron Valley at Jerusalem

Kidron Valley contains the following Hebrew inscription from the 1st cent. A.D. which certifies its identification:

"This is the tomb and the *nephesh* (=memorial?) of Eleazar, Haniah, Jo'ezer, Jehudah, Sime'on, Johannan, sons of Joseph, the son of 'Oreb; (also of) Joseph and Eleazar, sons of Haniah, priests (of the family) of the sons of Hezir." (See L.-Hugues Vincent and A.-M. Steve, *Jérusalem de l'Ancien Testament,* vol. 1 [Paris, 1954], 335-37.)

2. A prominent Jew who set his seal to Nehemiah's covenant (Neh 10:20).

Hezrai. *See* Hezro.

Hezro (hěz'rō), KJV once **Hezrai** (hēz'rå-ī). [Heb. *Chesray* and *Chesrô.*] One of David's "mighty men," who came from Carmel, in the mountainous part of Judah (2 Sa 23:35; 1 Chr 11:37).

Hezron (hěz'rŏn), KJV of NT **Esrom** (ěs'rŏm). [Heb. *Chesrôn,* meaning uncertain; Gr. *Esrôm.*]

1. A son of Reuben and founder of a tribal family (Gen 46:9; Ex 6:14; Num 26:6; 1 Chr 5:3).

2. Grandson of Judah through Perez, and founder of a tribal family (Gen 46:12; Num 26:21; Ruth 4:18; 1 Chr 2:5). He was an ancestor of David and thus is listed in both genealogies of Christ (Ruth 4:18; Mt 1:3; Lk 3:33).

3. A place in Judah (Jos 15:3), called *Hazar-addar in Num 34:4.

4. A town in Judah (Jos 15:25), also called Hazor. *See* Kerioth-hezron.

Hezronites (hěz'rŏn-īts). [Heb. *Chesrôni.*] Descendants of Hezron, 1 and 2.

Hiddai (hĭd'å-ī). [Heb. *Hidday,* meaning uncertain.] One of David's "mighty men" who came from near Mount Gaash (2 Sa 23:30). He is called Hurai (hū'rå-ī) [Heb. *Chûray*] in 1 Chr 11:32. The two forms are probably the result of a confusion in the Hebrew of *r* and *d,* and of *h* and *ch,* letters very similar in postexilic Hebrew.

Hiddekel (hĭd'ĕ-kĕl). [Heb. *Chiddeqel,* the Hebrew name of the Tigris River, called *Idigna* in Sumerian, *Idiqlat* in Assyrian texts, and *Tigrâ* in Old Persian, from which the Greeks derived the names *Tigrēs* and *Tigris.*]

1. A river of Eden (Gen 2:14).

2. The Tigris (tī'grĭs), one of the two rivers of the Mesopotamian valley, the scene of one of Daniel's visions (Dan 10:4). Two of the 3 sources of the Tigris lie south of Lake Van in Armenia. The streams from these two sources are called *Bitlis Chai* and *Bohtan Chai,* and each

225. The Tigris River (the Biblical Hiddekel) at Baghdad. Bricks are unloaded from *ghuffas*, round basketlike boats of wickerwork coated with pitch

flows about 100 mi. before joining the main river, which comes from the western source originating on the southern slopes of the Anti-Taurus, about 150 mi. west of the junction. The river then flows in a southeasterly direction through Mesopotamia (Map III, B-5), receiving the water of several tributaries along the way, the most important of which come from the Zagros Mountains in the east, namely the Great Zab, the Little Zab, and the Diyala (Map XI, C-5/6). The city of Nineveh was situated about 26 mi. north of the Great Zab on the left bank of the Tigris. The modern city of Mosul lies opposite the ruins of Nineveh on the right (western) bank of the river. Near the junction of the Great Zab and the Tigris, on the left bank, lay the important city of Calah (now *Nimrûd*). The old capital city of Asshur lay near the junction of the Little Zab, but on the right bank. At the junction of the Diyala lies Baghdad, the present capital city of Iraq, and some 20 mi. south, on the east bank, are found the ruins of Ctesiphon, the Parthian capital. On the western bank, just south of Ctesiphon, can be seen the ruins of Seleucia, the famous capital of the Seleucids (Map XIII, C-5). The Tigris joins the Euphrates after an independent flow of 1,146 mi., which is about 3/5 the length of the Euphrates. In ancient times each of the two rivers entered the Persian Gulf separately, because the gulf then extended north above the present junction of the two rivers.

Hiel (hī'ĕl). [Heb. *Chî'el*, "God lives." The name occurs in a Nabataean inscription.] A Bethelite who rebuilt Jericho in Ahab's time and brought upon himself the curse Joshua pronounced over that city (Jos 6:26; 1 Ki 16:34). He lost two of his sons in the venture. Some have suggested that they may have been sacrificed by Hiel in order to appease God. The fact that pagan practices, idolatry, and polytheism were widespread in Israel at that time is presented as giving plausibility to this suggestion.

Hierapolis (hī'ĕr-ăp'ô-lĭs). [Gr. *Hierapolis*.] A city in southwestern Phrygia, at the edge of the valley of the Lycus River, not far from its confluence with the Maeander. It lay on the slope of a mountain close to Laodicea and was about 10 mi.

226. Ruins of the warm baths of Hierapolis

from Colossae. It was founded probably by Eumenes II (197 - c. 160 B.C.), king of Pergamum, and became part of the Roman province of Asia after 133 B.C. Hierapolis owed its name, meaning "holy city," to its mineral-containing warm-water baths considered to have healing effects. Its chief goddess was the Syrian Atargatis. According to Col 4:13, a church was founded in the city early in the Christian Era. Impressive ruins at the site of the ancient city witness to its former importance. Map XX, B-4.

Higgaion. A transliteration of the Heb. *higgayón* (Ps 9:16), a word of uncertain meaning. It is usually thought to be used here as a technical musical term, possibly indicating a quieter rendering of the passage involved.

High Place. [Heb. *bamah*.] In many cases the Hebrew term means simply "height" or "elevation" (Deut 32:13; 2 Sa 1:19, 25; Mic 1:3). Frequently, however, it designates an open-air place of worship, or a sanctuary situated on an elevated area, not necessarily a place of pagan worship (1 Sa 9:12, 13). Some high places were on a hill or mountain in the open country (Num 22:41), others near or within a town (1 Ki 11:7; 2 Ki 17:9), and still others in a valley (Jer 7:31). But almost without exception, such local sanctuaries were established on elevated places, where the worshipers felt nearer to their deities.

Pagan high places have been discovered in excavations, such as the high place at Gezer, and a well-preserved Nabataean high place on top of one of the mountains of Petra (see fig. 227). Furthermore, an ancient bronze model (now in the Louvre) of a high place provides a true picture of one of these open-air sanctuaries (see fig. 228). The high place of Gezer contained a row of pillars, which were symbols of deities and objects of worship (see fig. 200). There were also altars for bloody sacrifices, and cup-holes in the rock surface for libations, probably of oil or wine.

The great high place at Petra, which is cut out of solid rock, contains two standing pillars, a water tank, probably for ablutions, and a large court with a raised platform on which the victim was killed. At one side was a long bench on which the sacrifice was prepared for the burnt offering. The altar on which the sacrifi-

227. The high place on one of the mountaintops at Petra. The man is standing beside the altar of sacrifice, on his right. The round altar for drink offerings appears at the left of the picture

cial beast was burned was approached by several steps. Near the cubical altar of burnt offerings was a round altar for drink offerings. A channel cut in the rock led to

a tank that caught the liquid (see fig. 227). Missing now, of course, are the wooden Asherahs (tree stumps) that were objects of Canaanite worship.

Before the Israelites came to Canaan they were commanded to destroy the high places with all their cult objects (Num 33:52; Deut 7:5; 33:29), since these were places of idolatry and licentiousness (Hos 4:11-14; Jer 3:2). God planned that Israel should look to one central place of worship; first to the tabernacle during the period of Israel's early history, and later to the Temple, after it had been built on the site God would choose for it (Deut 12). However, after the destruction of Shiloh, where the tabernacle had been for 300 years, and before the Temple had been erected, the worship of God was permitted at other altars (1 Sa 9:11-14; 1 Ki 3:2-4; Ps 78:60, 61, 67-69). It was also permitted elsewhere at times when the people of God were prevented from worshiping at the Temple site, such as when Jeroboam I of Israel made it impossible for his citizens to visit Jerusalem for the fulfillment of their religious duties (1 Ki 12:26-33). However, the divinely given regulations were frequently transgressed. Solomon built high places on the Mount of *Corruption near Jerusalem for *Ashtoreth, *Chemosh, and *Milcom, pagan gods of surrounding nations (2 Ki 23:13). Jeroboam I "made houses on high places" (RSV) at Bethel, one of the chief centers of worship in his kingdom after the ten tribes broke away from the house of David (1 Ki 12:31, 32; 13:2). In the course of time high places were also dedicated on other sites in the northern kingdom (1 Ki 13:32; 2 Ki 17:9). Nor was Judah entirely free of these sanctuaries (2 Ki 18:22; cf. 1 Ki 15:14; 22:43). Although the true God was worshiped on some of them, the prophets denounced these cult places and spoke openly against them (Is 1:29, 30; 57:7; 65:7; Jer 2:20; Eze 6:13; 16:16; Hos 4:13). Some of the kings of Judah, for example, Jehoram and Ahaz, built new high places (2 Chr 21:11; 28:25). Hezekiah, the son of Ahaz,

228. An ancient model of a high place of the Elamites

broke them down (2 Ki 18:4, 22), but his son Manasseh re-erected them (2 Ki 21: 3; 2 Chr 33:3). Josiah, however, destroyed them thoroughly (2 Ki 23:5, 8, 13). However, according to Eze 6:3 some such cult places seem to have been in existence in Judah in Ezekiel's time. The Babylonian exile finally ended Israelite worship at high places. There is no record of any being rebuilt after the restoration of the nation. No remains of such places from postexilic times have so far been found in excavations.

High Priest. *See* Priest.

Higher Gate. *See* Upper Gate.

Highway and **Road.** In the OT "highway" is generally a translation of the Heb. *mesillah,* "that which is thrown up," evidently referring to a road produced by throwing up an embankment or dike. In ancient times such roads consisted of loose gravel and earth; consequently heavy traffic tended to lower the center of the roadbed, which made necessary a regular "throwing up" of the gravel and dirt from the edges toward the middle of the road. This method of building new highways and of repairing worn-out ones can still be observed in some parts of the Near East today. "Road" is generally the translation of the Heb. *derek,* for which the KJV usually reads "way."

The road system of Palestine and Syria followed the natural features of the country. A map of the ancient roads (see fig. 229) shows that the main arteries ran in a north-south direction. One such highway came from Mesopotamia via Aleppo toward Kadesh on the Orontes, from where it ran to the coast, and followed it as far as Accho (Ptolemais, Acre). It then crossed the Carmel ridge and followed the foothills of the mountains of Samaria and Judah through the Plain of Sharon and the Philistine Plain, from where it continued through the desert to Egypt. This was the so-called "way of the land of the Philistines" (Ex 13:17). A second road led from Kadesh in the north toward Damascus, skirting the Anti-Lebanon Mountains on the east. From Damascus one road led to western Palestine, crossing the Jordan south of the Sea of Galilee, and passing such important cities as Beth-

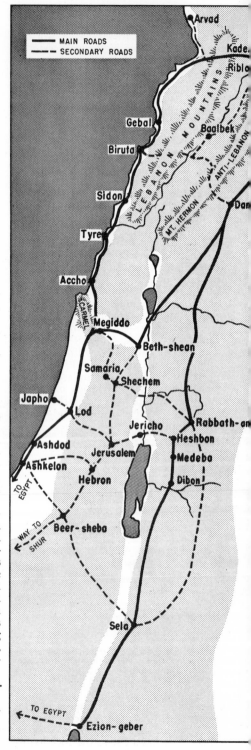

229. Road map of ancient Palestine

shean and Megiddo before joining the coastal road south of the Carmel ridge. This is the *via maris* of the Middle Ages, called "the way of the sea" (*derek hay-yam*) by Isaiah (Is 9:1). The all-important road of Transjordan was the "king's high way" (*derek hammelek*) from Damascus to the Gulf of Aqabah via Rabbath-ammon, Heshbon, and Dibon, and past Petra. The Edomites and Sihon of Heshbon forbade the Israelites the use of this road (Num 20:17-21; 21:21-23). The name "king's high way" was probably not given to this road because of its good quality; it was more likely an official name given to it as a result of some important event in history, such as a king's construction or special use of it. Its entire length can be traced by ruins of cities dating from the 4th millennium B.C. This highway was probably the invasion route of Chedorlaomer and his confederates in the time of Abraham (Gen 14). In the 2d cent. A.D. the emperor Trajan made it a paved Roman road. It is now a hardtopped modern motor road.

The most important of the secondary roads of Palestine was the mountain road from Hebron to Shechem and Samaria via Jerusalem, which followed the ridge of the mountains. Then there were a number of heavily traveled roads that crossed the country from west to east, such as the one that connected the Palestinian coast with Transjordan via Jerusalem and Jericho, and farther north, one that ran from the port city of Biruta (*Beirût*) to Damascus over the Lebanon and Anti-Lebanon Mountains. The roads from Petra to Gaza and from Ezion-geber to the west formed the main connections between Arabia and Egypt. One more road deserves mention, namely the "way to Shur" (*derek Shûr*), which led from Beer-sheba through the desert toward Egypt (Gen 16:7). For an understanding of Israel's history it is important to realize that although Palestine was situated between Egypt and the kingdoms of Mesopotamia, yet only one international road actually cut through the northern kingdom of Israel. The kingdom of Judah lay off all international highways, and was thus spared from conquest when the northern kingdom was constantly engaged in wars with the great powers of its time. Besides the main roads of international and national importance (fig. 229), there were many minor roads connecting small towns and villages with the more important trunk roads.

Hilen. *See* Holon.

Hilkiah (hĭl-kī'à). [Heb. *Chilqîyah* and *Chilqîyahû*, "my portion is Yahweh." The name occurs also on an ancient Hebrew seal.]

1. A Merarite Levite, son of Amzi (1 Chr 6:45, 46).

2. Another Merarite Levite, son of Hosah (1 Chr 26:11).

3. A man whose son Eliakim was over the royal household in Hezekiah's time (2 Ki 18:18, 26; Is 22:20; 36:3).

4. A priest of Anathoth and father of the prophet Jeremiah (Jer 1:1).

5. A man whose son Gemariah was a contemporary of Jeremiah (Jer 29:3).

6. The high priest in the reign of Josiah, who assisted the king in the religious reformation. He found the book of the Law in the Temple while that building was being repaired (2 Ki 22:4-14; 23:4; 1 Chr 6:13; 2 Chr 34:9-22).

7. A chief of the priests who returned from Babylonia with Zerubbabel (Neh 12:7). He was probably also the founder of a priestly family (v 21).

8. An assistant to Ezra when the Law was read to the people (Neh 8:4).

Some commentators think that Hilkiah, 4 and 5, were identical, or Hilkiah, 5 and 6, or even Hilkiah, 4, 5, and 6.

Hill. Generally speaking, the distinction between a hill and a mountain in the Bible is in their height, the hill being the lesser eminence. Sometimes, however, the designations hill and mountain are used for the same locality (Is 31:4). Hill is usually the rendering of the Heb. *gib'ah* (Ex 17:9; Jos 24:33; Jgs 7:1; etc.) and *har* (Num 14:45; Deut 1:41; Jos 9:1; etc.); the latter word is generally rendered "mount" or "mountain" (Ex 19:18; Num 20:27; Deut 1:2; etc.); the Gr. *bounos* appears twice in the NT and is translated "hill" in both cases (Lk 3:5; 23:30). The Gr. *oros* is translated variously "hill" (Mt 5:14; etc.), "mount" (ch 21:1; etc.), and "mountain" (ch 5:1; etc.).

Hill Country. This term appears only once in the KJV OT (Jos 13:6), and is a translation of the Heb. *har*, "mountain," "hill," in the context designating the mountainous coastal area from Lebanon to Misrephoth-maim, some 12 mi. north of Accho (Ptolemais, Acre). In the KJV NT the expression is found twice (Lk 1:39, 65) and refers to the mountainous country of Judah, which extended approximately from Hebron in the south to Jerusalem in the north. The home of Zacharias and

Elizabeth was located in this area, either in the priestly city of Hebron or in Holon (Hilen). The "hill country" appears frequently in the RSV and is used to refer to areas in such places as Naphtali (Jos 20:7), Ephraim (chs 17:15; 20:7), and Judah (ch 21:11). The hill country of Naphtali refers to upper Galilee, that of Ephraim to the mountainous area between Bethel and Shechem.

Hillel (hĭl'ĕl). [Heb. *Hillel*, "he has praised."] Father of the judge Abdon (Jgs 12:13, 15).

Hin. [Heb. *hîn;* Egyptian *hnw.*] A liquid measure, taken over from Egypt where it had been in use since the Middle Kingdom. According to Jewish tradition the Hebrew hin, used mainly for wine and oil, was equal to 1/6 of a bath, or 3.67 liters, which is 3.87 qt. (Ex 29:40; 30:24; Num 15:4, 5, 9; etc.).

Hind. [Heb. *'ayyalah* and *'ayyeleth*.] The female hart (Gen 49:21; 2 Sa 22:34; Job 39:1; Ps 18:33; Prov 5:19; Song 2:7; Jer 14:5; etc.). *See* Hart.

Hinder Sea. *See* Great Sea.

Hinge. In ancient times a pivot arrangement on which doors were suspended, and by which they were opened and closed. The bottom part consisted of a pivot which projected downward from the lower inside corner of the door and turned in a stone socket (Prov 26:14). The upper pivot turned in a metal loop fastened to the doorpost, or the wall, or in a hole in the lower side of a stone slab at the top. It is uncertain what is meant by the golden "hinges" (RSV "sockets") of the Temple mentioned in 1 Ki 7:50. They were probably either gold-plated door sockets, or gold-plated metal hinges in which the upper door pivots turned. Pure gold would be too soft for such a use.

Hinnom (hĭn'ŏm), **Valley of**. [Heb. *Gê Hinnom*.] A valley running south of Jerusalem, mentioned as the boundary between Judah and Benjamin in the period of the judges (Jos 15:8; 18:16), leaving that city completely in the territory of Benjamin (cf. Jer 6:1). The valley is also called "valley of the son of Hinnom" (Jos 18:16) or "valley of the children of Hinnom" (2 Ki 23:10). The place has been identified with the *Wâdī er-Rabâbeh*, the broad valley that encloses Jerusalem on the west and south. Map XVII; figs. 259,

230. The Valley of Hinnom at Jerusalem, looking toward the southeast. The valley runs south, from the left to the center of the picture, then turns east (cf. fig. 259)

230. In this valley the Israelites sacrificed their children to Molech in the days of Ahaz and Manasseh (2 Ki 16:3; 21:6; 2 Chr 28:3; 33:6). Jeremiah predicted that this great wickedness would bring a sore punishment upon the people, and that the valley would become known as the valley of slaughter (Jer 7:31-34; 19:2, 6; 32:35). In connection with his religious reformation King Josiah defiled the site probably by burning bones on the pagan altar, as he had done at Bethel (2 Ki 23: 10, 16). Hence the valley became for the inhabitants of Jerusalem a place of abhorrence and punishment and shame. *See* Hell. The identity of the original Hinnom, after whom the valley was named, is not known. If the valley already bore this name at the time of the invasion under Joshua, he was probably a Canaanite.

Hippopotamus. *See* Behemoth.

Hirah (hī′rả). [Heb. *Chîrah,* meaning uncertain.] A Canaanite friend of Judah from the city of Adullam (Gen 38:1, 12).

Hiram (hī′răm), or **Huram** (hū′răm). [Heb. *Chîram, Chîrôm,* and *Chûram.* The name occurs in Phoenician texts as *Chrm* and *'chrm,* and in cuneiform texts as *Hirummu.*]

1. A Phoenician king of Tyre, who had cordial relations with David and Solomon and whose reign overlapped their reigns (1 Ki 5:1; 2 Chr 2:3). Josephus states that he was the son of Abibaal, that he reigned for 34 years, and that he died at the age of 53. He also claims that the Temple of Solomon was begun in the 11th or 12th year of Hiram (*Ant.* viii. 5. 3; 3. 1; *Against Apion* 1. 17, 18). His chronological statements are difficult to reconcile with the Biblical evidence, and all attempts at solution are unconvincing; hence it must be assumed that Josephus' statements are in part erroneous. After the capture of Jerusalem, Hiram furnished David with cedarwood and with masons and carpenters to assist in the building of David's palace (2 Sa 5:7, 11). When Solomon came to the throne Hiram sent congratulations to the young king (1 Ki 5:1), and later furnished him with cedarwood and skilled workmen to build new palaces and the Temple (1 Ki 5:1-12; 9:10, 11; 2 Chr 2:3-16). Solomon also received a gift of 120 talents of gold from him (1 Ki 9:14). For the services rendered, Solomon paid Hiram in wheat, barley, oil, and wines—products of Palestine (1 Ki 5:11; 2 Chr 2:15). Hiram found unacceptable 20 towns of Galilee that Solomon offered him

231. A monumental ancient tomb near Tyre, popularly known as "King Hiram's Tomb"

as partial reimbursement for his help (1 Ki 9:10-12; 2 Chr 8:1, 2). Hiram joined forces with Solomon in organizing trading expeditions to Ophir for precious metal and exotic tropical products (1 Ki 9:26-28; 2 Chr 9:21).

2. An artificer whom the king of Tyre sent to Solomon to assist in the construction and decoration of the Temple and its furniture (1 Ki 7:13-46; 2 Chr 2:13, 14; 4:11, 16). Hiram's mother was apparently a Danite (2 Chr 2:14), who had at first been married to a Naphtalite, but who, upon his death, married a Tyrian who became the father of Hiram (1 Ki 7:13, 14). Thus Hiram was half Hebrew. In 2 Chr 2:13 and 4:16, KJV, the term "father" (Heb. *'abî*) is added to his name. This has been taken by some commentators to be an honorable title, meaning perhaps "master workman" or "counselor." Others think that his full name was Huram-abi (hū′răm-ā′bī; see RSV), of which Hiram, or Huram, was only an abbreviation.

See also Huram.

Hireling. [Heb. *śakîr,* "hired," "hireling," "hired worker." Gr. *misthōtos,* "a hired servant," from *misthoō,* "to let out for hire," which in turn is related to *misthos,* "wages," "hire," "reward."] *Śakîr* simply means someone or something "hired for recompense." This may be an animal (Ex 22:14), or an inanimate object (Is 7:20). The term may be applied also to mercenary soldiers or troops (Jer 46:21). But the most common usage of the term is in reference to ordinary laborers hired to perform some task (frequently menial) for their employer (Job 7:2; Is 16:14; etc.). This last usage is also properly the meaning of the Gr. *misthōtos.*

History, Biblical. Limitations of space permit only a brief sketch of the early history of the world and of God's people as presented in the Bible. Since Biblical authors recorded history from the point of view of

God's dealings with His people, their records provide only a limited picture of the ancient world. Some periods are described in great detail, whereas others are treated in cursory fashion. Since this article follows the main theme of Biblical history, the reader is referred to other articles in this dictionary for the history of nations not discussed here. For example, *see* Assyria; Babylonia; Egypt; Greece; Hittites; Phoenicia; Rome; etc. See also *SDA-Com* 1:133-148; 2:17-99; 3:43-84; 5:17-43; 6:17-96.

I. The Protohistoric Period: From the Creation to Abraham. The earliest history of this world, comprising many centuries, is compressed into the first 11 chapters of the OT. It begins with the story of the creation in 6 days of this planet, and of life upon it (Gen 1; 2:7). On the 7th day God rested from His work, and instituted the Sabbath as a weekly day of rest and worship (ch 2:2, 3). The first human couple was placed in an ideal environment, the garden in Eden, and charged with the administration of God's created world. They were commanded to increase and thus fill the earth with their numerous descendants (chs 2:15, 21-25; 1:27, 28).

However, through the medium of a serpent Satan led the woman to disobey God's command not to eat of a certain tree. She also persuaded her husband to eat of the forbidden fruit, with the result that both were expelled from the Garden and deprived of eternal life (Gen 3; 1 Ti 2:14). From that time they were compelled to live under changed conditions, in a world marred by sin (Gen 3:16-19). However, God revealed to them the plan of redemption (v 15), presenting to them the hope of regaining the sinless state they had lost. Some of Adam's descendants became nomadic shepherds, others became agriculturists, and still others city dwellers (ch 4:12, 16, 17, 20). Metalworking was introduced, and musical instruments were invented (vs 21, 22). Some descendants of Adam worshiped God, but the majority turned from Him, with the result that within 10 generations humanity became so wicked that God decided to destroy the world by means of a flood, preserving only the righteous. Eventually only 8 persons were saved, all of them members of Noah's family (ch 6:5 to 8:22).

After the Flood had swept away the works of man, changed the face of the earth, and destroyed every living being upon it except those saved in Noah's ark, a new chapter in human history began—the postdiluvian world. From Noah's 3 sons—Shem, Ham, and Japheth—came the Semites, Hamites, and Japhethites (Gen 10:1, 32), from whom are descended all races on earth (Map IV). The ark landed in the mountains of Ararat (Armenia; Gen 8:4; cf. 2 Ki 19:37), and the descendants of Noah moved first into the Euphrates and Tigris valleys. Archeologists agree that the cradle of civilization is found in the Mesopotamian valley.

Again, as in the antediluvian world, wickedness, polytheism, and idolatry became widespread. Noah's descendants founded the city of Babel, in which, in order to defy God and glorify themselves, they planned a tower that would reach to heaven. But God confounded their speech and thus forced them to spread into different countries according to their language groups (Gen 11:1-9). This may have happened in the time of Peleg, the 5th generation after Noah (ch 10:25). By the time Abraham was born (*c.* 1950 B.C.) the human race had increased to the extent that many nations existed (see chs 12:6, 10; 13:7; 14:1, 2; etc.). These nations had developed their own forms of civilization and government, had built cities, and had erected monuments, such as the pyramids. They worshiped various gods in numerous temples and open-air sanctuaries. They had become skilled in many arts and crafts, such as pottery making, weaving, sculpturing, and metallurgy, and had the art of writing—perhaps the most remarkable invention of all. With the appearance of Abraham the Biblical historians leave the treatment of other nations, except for more or less incidental references, and deal chiefly with Abraham and his descendants.

See Abel; Adam; Babel; Cain; Creation; Eden; Enoch; Flood; Noah; Satan; Sin.

II. The Patriarchal Period: From Abraham to the Exodus. The 430 years (*c.* 1875-*c.* 1445 B.C.; see Ex 12:40; Gal 3:17) from Abraham's call out of Haran to the Exodus are described in the last 39 chapters of Gen and the early chapters of Ex. With Abraham's call the center of Biblical historical interest shifts from Mesopotamia, where his patriarchal family originated, to Palestine, the country assigned to him by God. Abraham, the youngest son of Terah, was divinely chosen to become the ancestor of God's people (Gen 12:1-3). His wanderings through Palestine, his trials and temptations, his moral victories and defeats, are recorded in some detail, as well as the experiences in which he demonstrated his superb faith in the Almighty that merited him the title "the Friend of God" (Jas 2:23; cf. 2 Chr 20:7; Is 41:8). Little is said about the life of Isaac, Abraham's son (Gen 21:3), who played a less important role in the patriarchal period than his father. Isaac's twin sons, Esau and Jacob (ch 25:21-26), who were entirely different in character (v 27), became the ancestors of the Edomites (ch 36:1-9) and the Israelites, respectively (cf. Gen 32:28; Ex 1:1-7). The colorful life story of Jacob is told in detail. We learn of how he cheated his brother out of his blessing, fled to Haran, married two sisters (Gen 25:29 to 35:21), and founded a large family, begetting 12 sons, who became the ancestors of the 12 tribes of Israel (ch 35:22-26).

After Jacob's return to Palestine, the story centers around Joseph, the eleventh of Jacob's sons. Sold as a slave by his jealous brothers, Joseph passed through humiliating experiences in Egypt without, however, losing his courage or his clear vision of his duty toward God and man, and finally became prime minister of the Nile country (Gen 37:3-36; 39:1 to 41:57). This was evidently during the time that the Semitic Hyksos were ruling Egypt (see Exodus). During a period of famine the whole family of Jacob was invited by Pharaoh to move to Egypt, which invitation they accepted, settling in the fertile valley of Goshen in the eastern Delta (chs 45:17-21; 46:28). Favorable circumstances permitted them to become a strong and rich people within a relatively short time (Ex 1:7).

After a time the native Egyptians rose up against their foreign rulers and expelled the hated Hyksos from their country (c. 1570 B.C.). The new Egyptian rulers were no longer favorable to Semitic foreigners. A Pharaoh who "knew not Joseph" (Ex 1:8) began to oppress the Hebrews. The Egyptians probably associated them with the Hyksos and feared that the Hebrews might turn against them in the event of another invasion by Asiatics. Hence they reduced them to slavery and attempted to decrease their number by killing their male infants (vs 9-16). Under these cruel circumstances Moses, the future leader of the nation, was born (ch 2:1, 2). Rescued from the Nile by a royal princess, he was taken after some years to the palace and reared as an Egyptian prince (vs 3-10). At the age of 40 (Acts 7:23), Moses decided to join his oppressed people and to become their leader. However, unwisely he used force, murdered one of the oppressors, and was forced to flee from Egypt (Ex 2:11-15). During the next 40 years he lived the life of a shepherd in Midian, on the Sinai Peninsula, until God finally called him to the leadership of His people and commanded him to return and to lead them out of the land of Egypt (Ex 3:1 to 4:17; Acts 7:30-34).

See Abraham; Isaac; Jacob; Joseph; Moses.

III. The Theocratic Period: From the Exodus to Samuel. This period of almost 400 years (c. 1445 - c. 1050 B.C.) is described in the following books: Ex, Lev, Num, Deut, Jos, Jgs, and 1 Sa, portions in only cursory form. The *Exodus was one of the most momentous events in Hebrew history; it was the birth of Israel as a nation. It was accomplished by a revelation of God's supreme power over the Egyptian gods and people through great plagues that forced the humiliated Egyptians to permit the Hebrews to leave their land (see Ex 5 to 13). After experiencing another miraculous proof of God's power at the crossing of the Red Sea (ch 14), the Hebrews were led to Mount Sinai, where, amidst supernatural manifestations, God audibly revealed Himself to them and gave them the Decalogue (chs 19; 20). The Israelites covenanted with God that from that time He would be their supreme leader, king, judge, and object of worship. He was to be represented (1) in religious matters by the hereditary high priest and assisting priests who served in the tabernacle, the place of worship for all; and (2) in administrative and judicial matters by a divinely appointed leader under whom 70 men served in a subordinate capacity (Num 11:16, 24). The first high priest was Aaron (Ex 28:1; 29:28) and the first administrative leader was Moses (see Num 12:7, 8). This latter office was not hereditary, but was transmitted by divine appointment. The people of Israel solemnly entered into the covenant (Ex 24:7; cf. chs 20-23), but almost immediately broke it (ch 32:1-35) by worshiping the golden calf. They repeatedly provoked God to anger by their complaints about His leadership. They rebelled against His appointed representatives, and failed to follow His bidding (see Num 11:1 to 14:45; 16:1 to 17:13; etc.). The result was that their wanderings in the wilderness were prolonged, lasting 40 years, during which time almost the whole generation that had left Egypt perished in the desert (Num 14:34, 35). Map V.

Skirting Edom and Moab (Num 20:20, 21; 21:11, 12), and conquering the countries of two Amorite rulers in Transjordan (ch 21:21-35), the Israelites finally reached the Jordan Valley and were ready to invade Canaan, or western Palestine, when Moses, their leader of 4 decades, died (Deut 29:5; 32:48-52; 34:6). Joshua, Moses' divinely appointed successor, then led the Israelites over the Jordan into Canaan (Deut 31:3; 34:9; Jos 3:7-17). Jericho, the first fortress that blocked their way, fell through divine intervention (Jos 6). Subsequent military campaigns brought Israel's army into the central, southern, and northern parts of the country (see Jos 7; 8; Num 21:1-3; Jos 11:1-13; etc.). However, the Israelites did not dislodge the Canaanites from all of their cities, and by entering into pacts of friendship with some of the Palestinian tribes disregarded God's command not to make any treaties with the Canaanites (Ex 23:32; 34:12; cf. Jgs 1). The country, including unoccupied sections, was then divided by lot among the 12 tribes of Israel (Jos 13 to 21). Map VI.

The indigenous populations of Canaan left in the land influenced the Israelites to adopt many pagan religious practices. The Hebrews took over many open-air sanctuaries, called *high places, and also worshiped many of the local gods besides the true God (1 Ki 3:2; 2 Ki 23:15; 2 Chr 11:15; Hos 4:11-14; etc.). As punishment for their apostasy God permitted neighboring nations to oppress them (Lev 26:15, 25-33; Jgs 10:7, 9; etc.). When the people repented, a deliverer was usually raised up by God (Jgs 2:16). These men were called *shophetim,* rendered *"judges,"* but signifying leaders who united in their hands all administrative, military, and judicial power. Their office was not hereditary, and each judge was appointed by God. Most of these were men of integrity and high moral character. But the people lapsed repeatedly into idolatry and immorality, which resulted in foreign oppression and, consequently, in breaks in the office of judgeship (chs 3:12-31; 6:1; 8:22; etc.). The outcome was chaotic social and political conditions, of which the book of Judges presents several examples (see ch 21:25). The last judge, Samuel, was also a priest and prophet (1 Sa 3:19, 20; 12:18; 16:2,

5). During his lifetime, upon popular demand and with the permission of God, a monarchy was instituted, and the theocratic form of government came to an end (1 Sa 8:4-22; 10:20-24).

See Exodus; Joshua; Judges; Moses; Samuel; and names of the other judges.

IV. The Monarchy. Foreseeing the monarchy, God through Moses had given regulations regarding the rule of any future king (Deut 17:14-20). Toward the end of Samuel's judgeship the nation felt that a hereditary kingship with its continuity was preferable to a sporadic theocratic leadership as Israel had known it during the period of the judges. Hence they demanded a king, and God granted their wish. The sources for the period of the monarchy are the historical books 1 and 2 Sa, 1 and 2 Ki, 1 and 2 Chr, with additional information in some of the psalms and in prophetic books such as Isaiah and Jeremiah.

1. *The United Kingdom* (c. 1050 - c. 931 B.C.). With the exception of a short interruption after Saul's death, Israel's 12 tribes were ruled as a united monarchy for about 120 years. Saul, the first king, was a Benjamite (1 Sa 9:1, 2). *Gibeah, his capital, was a little town, and his palace a strong but unpretentious fortress (1 Sa 11:4; 2 Sa 21:6). He did not hold much more than the mountainous regions and the Jordan Valley (Map VII), and had neither a luxurious court nor a large retinue; he was actually not much more than a chieftain. Under the tutelage of Samuel he began as a good king, and his military victories over Israel's enemies brought courage and hope to his people, who had experienced many humiliations from neighboring nations (1 Sa 10:1-13; 11:6-15). However, he had a stubborn character, and his refusal to submit completely to God's will and carry out divinely given instructions brought about his downfall and God's rejection of his kingship (chs 13:1-14; 15). During the last years of his reign, the king, then a melancholiac, was haunted by a senseless urge to destroy David, in whom he saw his rival (chs 16:14, 15, 23; 18:6-12; 16:12, 13).

David, the second king, was a better man than Saul. He was deeply spiritual and had a childlike faith in God (see Ps 48; 51; 57; 60; etc.). He was also a brave warrior, a great general, a prudent administrator, and a clever politician (1 Sa 17:39-54; 18:7, 14, 30; 1 Chr 27; etc.). He conquered Jerusalem and made it his capital (2 Sa 5:6-9), and extended his power over areas adjoining his nation's territory until his kingdom reached the boundaries which God had originally planned to give His people (see 2 Sa 8:3; 1 Ki 8:65). When David died after a reign of 40 years, he left his son a kingdom respected and feared by its neighbors, free from internal enemies, and economically sound (Map VIII). On the whole, David seems to have had a wholesome influence on the spiritual life of his people. He prepared for the building of the Temple, reorganized the sanctuary service, and composed numerous psalms.

Solomon, David's son and successor (1 Ki 1:32-40), reaped the fruit of his father's military successes. He enjoyed a long, peaceful reign (see chs 3:11-14; 4:20, 25), being thus enabled to use the nation's great resources for unparalleled building activity; and for the organization of a large and strong army (1 Ki 10:26; 2 Chr 1:14). He built palaces (1 Ki 7:1, 2) and the magnificent Temple at Jerusalem (ch 6), fortified strategically located cities and converted them into garrison cities (2 Chr 8:1-6), exploited the copper and iron mines of Edom, and built a metal refining and manufacturing center at Ezion-geber on the shore of the Gulf of Aqabah (1 Ki 9:26-28; 2 Chr 8:17, 18). Yet his idolatry had a deleterious effect on himself and the whole nation, and his ruthless methods of exploiting the nation's manpower through forced labor made him extremely unpopular, and caused the kingdom to break up after his death (1 Ki 11:1-11; 5:13-15; 9:15, 20, 21; 12:1-20). Map IX.

2. *The Northern Kingdom of Israel* (c. 931 - 723/22 B.C.). The kingdom of Israel, consisting of the 10 northern tribes, experienced much bloodshed and misery during the 2 centuries of its existence. Twenty kings belonging to 10 different dynasties ascended the throne, many of whom died violently. The city of Samaria eventually became the capital of the nation (1 Ki 16:23, 24, 29; 22:51; etc.). The 10 tribes gave themselves over to idolatry. They set up bull-idols in 2 sanctuaries at Dan and Bethel and later adopted *Baal and *Asherah worship (chs 12:26-30; 16:31, 32; 18:19). Thus the religious life of the nation at times differed little from that of the surrounding pagan peoples. If God had not raised up a few courageous reformers such as Elijah and Elisha (1 Ki 17; 18; 2 Ki 2:9-15; etc.), the kingdom would probably not have

lasted as long as it did. Not only was the nation internally weak through its religious instability, but it constantly had to fight a host of enemies, among whom the Syrians of Damascus and the powerful Assyrians were the most dangerous (1 Ki 20:1; 2 Ki 15:19, 29; 17:3; etc.). Assyria eventually overran Israel, bringing the nation to an end in 723/22 B.C. (2 Ki 17:5, 6). Most of its citizens went into captivity and were absorbed by the nations among whom they were settled.

3. *The Southern Kingdom of Judah* (c. 931-586 B.C.). After the secession of the northern tribes, Solomon's son Rehoboam retained only Judah and Benjamin (1 Ki 12:21) with about one fourth of the territory his father had possessed. However, the dynasty of David was stable, and continued 136 years longer than the northern kingdom. During the 3½ centuries of its existence 20 rulers (including Queen Athaliah) sat on the throne. Some of them, such as Hezekiah (2 Ki 18:1-3) and Josiah (ch 22:1, 2), were good kings, whereas others, such as Manasseh (ch 21:1, 2) and Amon (2 Chr 33:21, 22), were as wicked as the worst kings of Israel. However, on the whole the southern nation did not reach the depths of immorality and idolatry that the northern kingdom did. The presence of the Temple at Jerusalem, dedicated to the worship of the true God, and the ministry of great prophets, such as Isaiah (2 Ki 19:2), Jeremiah (Jer 37:1, 2), and others, were doubtless responsible in part for the fact that Judah did not separate itself from its God to the extent that Israel did. The southern kingdom, being less exposed than its northern sister nation, had fewer wars during the time of their coexistence, although it had its share of warfare. However, after the downfall of Samaria (Map X) Judah experienced at least two invasions of the Assyrian armies, and consequently became a vassal nation (Map XI, C-4) to the Assyrians (2 Chr 28:19-21; 33:11). The long reign of a wicked king, Manasseh (ch 33:1), brought the nation to the brink of political destruction, and disaster was postponed only through the noble reform of the young king Josiah (chs 34; 35). After his untimely death the nation reversed its course once more and forsook God (ch 36:5, 9, 11-16). Finally, Judah became a vassalage of Babylon but rebelled (2 Ki 24:10-20). The results were several invasions by the Chaldean armies, the destruction of their country and of Jeru-

salem, the cessation of the kingship, and the deportation of a major portion of the population to Babylonia (2 Ki 25; 2 Chr 36:17-21; Jer 39:1-10).

See Assyria; Babylonia; Damascus; David; Egypt; Isaiah; Jeremiah; Nebuchadnezzar; Saul; Solomon; and the names of the various Hebrew kings.

V. Exile and Restoration. The last section of the OT history, which deals with the exile of Judah in Babylonia and the restoration of the nation under the Persian kings, covers a period of approximately 150 years. No historical books deal directly with the Exile, but the narratives of the book of Daniel shed some light on the period (chs 1 to 6), and certain phases of the restoration period are described in detail in Ezr, Neh, and Est. The exiles of Judah and Benjamin had a strong spiritual leader in the land of their captivity, in Ezekiel (Eze 1:1-3), who by precept and example encouraged his discouraged and humiliated compatriots to seek a religious revival, with the result that most of the Jews returning from exile were in some respects, at least, better men and women than their ancestors who went into exile had been. They abhorred idolatry, and rallied around the Scriptures and the law of God, and it was probably they who initiated a kind of synagogue service, which in later centuries proved to be a great unifying factor among the Jews of the Dispersion (see Ezr 6; 10; Neh 9 to 13).

When Cyrus of Persia conquered Babylon in 539 B.C. he applied his attitude of religious tolerance toward subject nations. He issued a decree allowing any and all who worshiped God—which would include exiles from Israel—to return to their homeland and rebuild their Temple and their destroyed homes (2 Chr 36:22, 23; Ezr 1:1-4). Under the leadership of Zerubbabel, a royal prince of Judah (Ezr 2:1, 2; cf. ch 3:2; 1 Chr 3:17-19), about 50,000 exiles returned to Palestine (Ezr 2:64, 65), probably in 536 B.C. Judah became a province of the Persian Empire, part of the larger satrapy of "beyond the River" (see *Abar Nahara* on Map XII, C/D-5/6). The resettling in the old homeland was made difficult by the animosity of the Samaritans and other peoples in Palestine, and the rebuilding of the Temple was carried out under great difficulties (Ezr 4; Neh 4 to 6). It was finally completed during the reign of Darius I in 515 B.C. (Ezr 6:15). During the reign of Ahasuerus (Xerxes) a con-

certed effort was made to destroy the Jews, but they emerged from this crisis stronger than before because God had made provision for this emergency by allowing the Jewess Esther to be placed in the king's palace as the queen.

Xerxes' successor, Artaxerxes I, sent Ezra, a teacher of the Law of God, to Palestine with authority over the whole administrative and judicial system of Judah (Ezr 7:12-26). In 457 B.C. Ezra carried out the royal commission to reorganize the civil administration in harmony with the Law of Moses. About another 5,000 to 6,000 Jews returned with him from Babylonia to the homeland of their ancestors. Some 13 years later Nehemiah, a royal cupbearer, was appointed as governor over Judah (Neh 2:5-8). He completed the work of rebuilding Jerusalem's fortifications, and also strengthened the religious life of the nation by his strong personality and deep spiritual fervor. Nehemiah's activities are described in the last historical records that the OT contains.

It is noteworthy that the postexilic Jews did not, as a people, lapse into the sins of their pre-exilic ancestors. Idolatry and polytheism were never practiced again. After the Exile their religion was purely monotheistic, and the Jews made serious efforts to live according to the Law of God. However, they fell into the sins of legalism and self-righteousness, which, in succeeding centuries, were most fully represented by the sect of the Pharisees (see Mt 23).

See Ahasuerus; Cyrus; Ezra; Nehemiah.

VI. The Intertestamental Period. There are apocryphal writings dealing with the 4 centuries between the time of Nehemiah and Malachi and the birth of Jesus Christ, but one cannot speak of *Biblical* history with regard to this period. However, to omit this part of Jewish history would break the historical continuity. Therefore a brief résumé is here included, which, however, is entirely inadequate to do justice to the rich history of that period. The apocryphal book 1 Maccabees and the writings of Josephus contain detailed information concerning the latter part of the intertestamental period, but hardly anything is known about the history of the Jews under the Persians between Nehemiah's administration and the coming of Alexander the Great about a century later. During the next 150 years and more the Jews lived under Macedonian rulers, the Ptolemies and Seleucids, who fell heir to Alexander's divided empire (Map XIII). During this period the Jews were governed by their own high priests, with little contact with their overlords except the payment of tribute by the priest-ruler, until Antiochus IV Epiphanes made an intensive effort to enforce the Hellenization of the Jewish nation. He forbade the practice of the Jewish religion and defiled the Temple with pagan sacrifices. The result was the rebellion of Mattathias, and the Maccabean wars, which ended with the liberation of the country and an independent kingdom under the Hasmonaean (Maccabean) priest-kings (Map XIV). In 63 B.C. the Romans under Pompey conquered Judea, though they left the Hasmonaean rulers as vassal kings. In 40 B.C. the Romans appointed Herod as king of the Jews. During the reign of Herod the Great (Map XV), Jesus Christ was born and NT history began.

VII. Christ and His Church. The 4 Gospels are our main source for a history of the life and ministry of Jesus Christ, and the book of Acts is our principal source for the history of the early church and the spread of the gospel message through the world. Some additional information can be gleaned from other books of the NT. This whole period comprises about 100 years, from *c.* 5/4 B.C., the approximate year in which Jesus was born, until *c.* A.D. 95, when the last of the NT books was written.

Jesus Christ was born in Bethlehem, but reared in the little Galilean town of Nazareth (Lk 2:1-7; Mt 2:19-23). Little is known of His life until about the age of 30 years, when He was baptized by John in the Jordan (Mt 3:13-17; Mk 1:9-11; Lk 3:21-23). This event marked the beginning of His ministry, the greater part of which was performed in Galilee, although He made a number of journeys to Jerusalem, and also visited Phoenicia, the northeastern territory of the tetrarch Philip, and the Decapolis (see Mt 2:22; 4:23, 25; 16:13; etc.). His work consisted mainly of teaching, preaching, and the performing of miracles (Mt 5:2; Lk 3:18; 4:40; etc.). He gathered around Him a group of followers, of whom He chose 12, and trained them thoroughly in order that they might be able to continue His work after His departure (Lk 6:13-16). He was arrested during the Passover feast in A.D. 31 (*see* Chronology, VIII, 3; Gospels, Harmony of; Jesus Christ) after He had worked for about 3½ years and, after being accused of blasphemy in a mock trial, was sentenced to death by the Sanhedrin (Mt 26:47-66; Mk 14:43-64; Lk 22:47-71; Jn 18:1-24). The Jewish leaders succeeded in having their sentence confirmed by Pilate, the Roman procurator, who, although convinced of Jesus' innocence, had Him crucified (Mt 27; Mk 15; Lk 23; Jn 18:28 to 19:42). He arose on the 3d day (Mt 28:1-6; Mk 16:1-6; Lk 24:1-7; Jn 20: 1-9), and met with His disciples on several occasions, teaching them further concerning their future tasks as His representatives (Mt 28:16-20; Mk 16:14-18; Lk 24:36-48; Jn 20:19-30). After promising to send the Holy Spirit, He finally departed to heaven from the summit of the Mount of Olives (Lk 24:49-51; Acts 1: 8, 9).

The promised Holy Spirit was poured out upon the apostles a few days later, on the Feast of Pentecost (Acts 2:1-12). As a consequence their preaching became so powerful that thousands were converted in one day (vs 41, 47). For some time the gospel was preached mainly to the Jews, and only in exceptional cases to Gentiles (see Acts 3:12; 5:21, 42; 8:26-39; chs 10; 11). Persecution, however, drove Christ's followers from Jerusalem, with the result that the message of salvation spread into foreign countries and cities, among which Antioch in Syria became an important center (chs 8:1, 4; 11:19-25). It was there that the followers of Christ received the name *"Christians"* (v 26).

During the period of persecution that followed the martyrdom of Stephen, Paul the Pharisee was miraculously converted when the Lord Jesus appeared to him near Damascus (Acts 9:1-19). Subsequently, Paul became one of the most ardent followers of his new Master and the most successful Christian missionary of all times. He worked for several years in his native Tarsus in Cilicia (Acts 9:30; Gal 1:21). Later he labored with Barnabas in Antioch and then in Cyprus and southern Asia Minor, where several churches were established (Acts 11:25, 26; chs 13; 14). After this they returned to Antioch, where a question arose as to whether the Gentile Christians needed to keep the Jewish ceremonial law (chs 14:25-28; 15: 1). To solve this question a church council was held at Jerusalem (ch 15:2, 6). It declared the Gentile church free from the obligation to keep the ceremonial laws and rites of the OT (vs 4-29). Fortified with this decision, Paul and Barnabas set out on new but separate missionary expeditions (vs 36-41). On this 2d Journey

Paul took Christianity to Europe and founded strong churches in several major cities of Macedonia and Greece (Acts 15: 40 to 18:22). Later he worked for several years in western Asia Minor, making the metropolis of Ephesus his headquarters (chs 18:23 to 20:38). On returning to Jerusalem Paul was arrested as the result of the intrigues and enmity of foreign Jews (chs 21:27 to 22:29). He then spent 4 years as a Roman prisoner; the first 2 at Caesarea (ch 24:27) and the last 2 in Rome (ch 28:16, 30). With the record of this imprisonment the historical narrative of Luke closes, but from some of Paul's letters we learn that he regained his liberty and was able to carry on his missionary activities for a few more years, after which he was once more imprisoned (see 2 Ti 1:15; 4:10, 11, 16). That he then died as a martyr in Rome, Christian tradition uniformly attests.

Little is known of the life and work of the other disciples. James, the brother of John, was beheaded by King Herod Agrippa I (Acts 12:1, 2). There are traditions that Peter worked successfully as a Christian missionary in different countries before he was crucified by Nero in Rome, and that John, the beloved disciple, moved to Ephesus, and in the persecution of the Christians under the emperor Domitian was banished to the island of Patmos. On that island he wrote the book of Revelation, giving in prophetic outline the history of the Christian church and of the world (Rev 1:9) to the end of time.

See Acts; Barnabas; Gospels; Governor; Herod; Holy Spirit; James; Jesus Christ; John the Baptist; John; Paul; Pentecost; Peter; Pilate; Stephen.

Hittites (hĭt'īts). [Heb. *Chitti;* Akkadian *Ḫatti;* Ugaritic *Ḫty;* Egyptian *Ḫt3.*] The Hittites are mentioned frequently in the OT, but nothing was known of them from secular records until the late 19th cent. The resurrection of their history, culture, religion, and language is one of the sagas of modern archeology. Nineteenth-cent. scholars began to notice that newly deciphered ancient records mentioned an important but hitherto unknown country and nation which was called *Kheta* in Egyptian inscriptions and *Ḫatti* (sometimes transliterated as *Khatti;* see Khatti on Map III, B-3) in Assyrian texts. In 1884 two scholars, A. H. Sayce and W. Wright, published their views that certain undeciphered hieroglyphics in rock sculptures and inscriptions in many parts

of Asia Minor and northern Syria belonged to these people, and that they were the Biblical Hittites, the descendants of Heth (hĕth) [Heb. *Cheth*]. Later discoveries proved their theory to be correct. Hugo Winckler, the Berlin Assyriologist, conducting excavations at *Boghazköy* in central Asia Minor (in 1906-07 and in 1911-12), found that the ancient capital of the Hittites, called Khattushash (Map III, B-3), had been situated there. He also discovered the royal archives of the Hittite kings, consisting of more than 10,000 clay tablets written in Babylonian cuneiform. Some of these texts were written in Akkadian and could be read immediately, whereas others were in an unknown language. When this latter language was deciphered by B. Hrozny in 1915 it was found to be Hittite and to belong to the Indo-European family of languages. Later excavations at *Boghazköy,* carried out intermittently to the present day, have added to our knowledge of the Hittites. Further light was shed on these people by explorations in other Hittite cities, especially Carchemish, which in later Assyrian texts is called the capital of the Hittites. Texts in several ancient languages of Anatolia have been found and deciphered, and recently the hieroglyphic Hittite inscriptions, referred to above as appearing in various rock sculptures and in inscriptions in Asia Minor which for a long time could not be read, have begun to reveal their secrets. This decipherment has been made possible by H. Th. Bossert's discovery in 1947 of bilingual inscriptions at Karatepe, in eastern Anatolia (Map III, B-4), containing parallel texts written in Phoenician script and in hieroglyphic Hittite.

The Ethnic Affiliation of the Hittites. The racial origin of the Hittites is still an unsolved problem. Ancient reliefs show them as a small people with large noses, retreating foreheads, and thick lips. They are customarily depicted on monuments as wearing thick clothes, and shoes with upturned toes. Since the decipherment of their language has shown that they spoke an Indo-European language, some scholars have concluded that they must have belonged to the same race as the Greeks, Medes, and other peoples who spoke Indo-European languages, and who are listed in the Bible as descendants of Japhath. However, Gen 10:15 lists Heth, the ancestor of the Hittites, among the descendants of Ham through Canaan. The so-called Hittites who have left us records called themselves *Neshumli,* and used the term *Ḥattili* to designate the people they replaced when they came into Anatolia sometime in the early 2d millennium. These replaced people are now usually called Proto-Hittite, and it is these that may have been the real descendants of Heth, who was a son of Canaan. These Proto-Hittites were absorbed by, and gave up their language for that of Indo-European *Neshumli,* or Japhethite Hittites, who took their territory, and who themselves became known as Hittites by the surrounding nations. Little is known of the earlier Hittites. A few religious texts in their language, with later Hittite translations, have survived.

The History of the Hittites. The earliest written records from the territory of the Hittites come from Assyrian colonists in the 19th cent. B.C. who lived in various Anatolian cities as merchants with their headquarters in `Kanesh, near the modern *Kültepe,* immediately south of the Halys River (Map III, B-4). For some unknown reason these colonies ceased to exist after having continued for about a century. There followed an Anatolian kingdom ruled by a certain Anittas, but whether he was a Hittite or not is uncertain. The first Hittite king of whom we have any certain knowledge is Labarnas, whom later Hittite kings considered as their revered ancestor, and whose name they used as a title. Labarnas' reign occurred in the end of the 17th cent. B.C. according to the lowest chronology. The Hittites were by that time securely settled in central Asia Minor, with the mountain city of Khattushash, now *Boghazköy,* within the great Halys bend, as capital. Labarnas' great-grandson, Mursilis I, was the first Hittite king to raid Mesopotamia, thereby making a name for himself in history. He conquered Babylon (*c.* 1550 B.C.), put an end to the 1st dynasty of Babylon, and carried away the golden statue of Marduk. During the following century the Hittites struggled to preserve their position in Anatolia against various hostile tribes. At the same time a fierce internal struggle was going on within the royal family, which resulted in the violent death of several Hittite kings. The first great king after Mursilis I, and the first Hittite empire builder, was Suppiluliumas, who lived in the 1st half of the 14th cent. and was a contemporary of Amenhotep III and IV of Egypt. During his reign all of eastern Asia Minor became a Hittite territory, and Hittite power was

232. Hittite soldiers on a sculptured slab from Carchemish

extended eastward into Upper Mesopotamia and southward into Syria as far as Kadesh on the Orontes and Lebanon (Map III, B/C-3/4). Two of Suppiluliuma's sons were made kings, one over Carchemish and the other over Aleppo. During this period the Hittite empire reached the height of its power, and became a strong rival of Egypt. The magnitude of Hittite power is illustrated by the fact that an Egyptian queen—King Tutankhamen's widow—asked Suppiluliuma to send her one of his sons to become her husband and Egypt's king. Although this Hittite prince never occupied the throne of Egypt, having been murdered on his way to Egypt, the attempt to make him king was significant. The Hittites remained strong for some time after Suppiluliuma's death, and it became obvious that a clash between the two world powers, the Hittite empire and Egypt, was imminent. This clash finally came in the reign of Muwatallis, who fought the famous battle at Kadesh on the Orontes (Map III, C-4) against Ramses II of Egypt, in 1295 B.C. The battle apparently ended in a draw, and the Hittites kept all of Syria, and in fact made some territorial gains. A few years later Ramses II concluded a treaty of friendship with the Hittites under Hattusilis III (1278 B.C.), and married a Hittite princess. From that

17

time on, the Hittites and Egypt lived in peace with each other.

However, the Hittites soon had to contend with a new power that invaded Anatolia from the west, the Peoples of the Sea, among whom were the Philistines. Under their onslaught Khattushash and many other Hittite cities were destroyed and the empire disintegrated rapidly and vanished about 1200 B.C. However, Hittite remnants held out in Upper Mesopotamia and northern Syria for more than 300 years in the form of city-states. The best known of these is Carchemish on the Euphrates, where many Hittite monuments of the later period have been found. Other Hittite city-states were Karatepe on the Ceyhan River and Hamath on the Orontes (Map III, B-4). These states finally became involved in a life-and-death struggle with the Assyrians and were gradually annihilated by the cruel Assyrian war machine in the 9th and 8th cent. B.C. By the end of the 8th cent. B.C. the last Hittite power had ceased to exist. Even their memory was forgotten, as shown by the fact that they are never mentioned in classical literature. Only the Bible perpetuated records of this nation lost to secular history.

The Culture and Religion of the Hittites. The Hittites were a hardy mountain people, who possessed higher ethical values than most other ancient nations. This is especially noticeable in the Hittite laws and their penal code, which is the most humane of any known from that period of antiquity.

The Hittites were not artistic, and their productions in the field of art compare most unfavorably with those of their contemporaries in Egypt and Mesopotamia. Their craftsmanship was mediocre, yet they had the advantage over their neighbors of possessing iron mines, which for a time gave them a virtual monopoly in the production of iron, and of iron weapons and tools.

The religion of the Hittites is still somewhat obscure. A whole pantheon of gods was worshiped, most of them having been adopted from local cults or from foreign nations. The Hurrian weather god Teshub was the chief god of the Hittites; the Hurrian form of the Babylonian Ishtar was worshiped and also the sun-god, besides many other deities which, according to the concepts of the ancients, controlled the various forces of nature. Some of the later Anatolian divinities encountered in NT times had their origin in the

Hittite religion. For example, Cybele, the Magna Mater, or mother goddess, had a Hittite prototype by the name of *Kubaba,* who played a great role in the popular religion of Asia Minor for many centuries. Worship consisted mainly in rituals, in some cases in orgiastic rites, and in the offering of sacrifices. The will of the gods was searched out through oracles, and the decisions were guided into desired directions and channels by magic. The dead were cremated, and the remaining bones gathered and put in a separate building, where appointed personnel performed rites for the well-being of the deceased.

The Hittites in the Bible. The word "Hittite(s)" occurs frequently in the OT. The Heth of Gen 10:15, who was a son of Canaan and a grandson of Ham (cf. v 6), must have been the ancestor of the Proto-Hittites who had settled in Asia Minor, and who were absorbed by the Indo-European Hittites when these people moved into Anatolia from the northeast. Some of these Proto-Hittites must have lived in Palestine in the time of Abraham (chs 15:18-20; 23:3-20). Probably these were also the people to whom two of Esau's wives belonged (ch 26:34), and were the "Hittites" in the lists of nations who inhabited Canaan when the Israelites came into the country (Ex 3:8; Deut 7:1; 20:17; Jos 3:10; 11:3; 24:11), though it is possible that by the time of the Israelite invasion there were settlers in Canaan from the Indo-European Hittites. Remnants of the Proto-Hittites may also have been among those with whom the Israelites intermarried in the time of the judges (Jgs 3:5, 6). Addressing the inhabitants of Jerusalem, Ezekiel tauntingly said, with reference to the pre-Israelite population of Jerusalem, "Thy father was an Amorite, and thy mother an Hittite" (Eze 16:3, 45). Amorite names of kings of Jerusalem are known from 19th-cent. B.C. Egyptian execration texts, but Jerusalem's king who wrote letters to the Pharaoh of Egypt in the *Amarna period had a Hittite name, Abdu-Khepa, "servant of (the Hittite goddess) Khepa," which seems to indicate that he was a Hittite. Hittites still formed part of the population of Palestine in the time of David and Solomon as is evident from the Biblical records. David had valiant Hittite soldiers in his army, such as Ahimelech (1 Sa 26:6), and Uriah, the husband of Bathsheba (2 Sa 11:3 to 12:10). The Hittites whom Solomon incorporated into his forced labor corps (1 Ki 9:20-22; 2 Chr 8:7-9) were probably also descendants of the early Hittites of the empire period. Solomon's Hittite wives, however (1 Ki 11:1), were most probably princesses from the north Syrian Hittite city-states which flourished in his time, and among whose rulers were evidently the "kings of the Hittites" with whom Solomon had lively trade dealings (1 Ki 10:29; 2 Chr 1: 17). Kings of the Hittite city-states are also referred to in 2 Ki 7:6, where the Biblical record tells us that an army· of Syrians besieging Samaria lifted the siege and fled in disorder when they fancied they heard a Hittite army approaching to relieve the Israelites.

Hivites (hī'vīts). [Heb. *Chiwwî*.] One of the tribes descended from Canaan (Gen 10:17). A Hivite is mentioned as living in the area of Shechem in the patriarchal period (ch 34:2), and another is listed as a grandfather-in-law of Esau (ch 36:2). In the time of the Israelite conquest of Canaan the Hivite inhabitants of Gibeon (Jos 9:1-7) were able by deceit to make a treaty of friendship with the Hebrews. Hivites also lived at the foot of the Lebanon Mountain range at that time, especially at Mount Hermon (Jos 11:3; cf. Jgs 3:3) and were still found in the Phoenician area in the time of David (2 Sa 24:7). Solomon pressed their remnants into forced labor for his extensive building operations (1 Ki 9:20-22; 2 Chr 8:7, 8).

It is not certain, however, whether the Hivites really were a separate tribe, or whether they are to be identified with the *Horites. The Horites who, according to Biblical and extra-Biblical records, lived in Palestine before and at the time of the conquest, never occur in the lists of tribes the Israelites were asked to replace, nor in the genealogy of Gen 10. But those lists do mention the Hivites, who, on the other hand, are not mentioned in secular sources. Many commentators have therefore thought that the Hivites were the Horites, and that the confusion of names was caused by a scribal error. In the vowelless Hebrew texts the only difference between the word Hivites, transliterated *Chwy*, and Horites, transliterated *Chry*, is in the Hebrew letters *w* and *r*. In postexilic Hebrew these two letters are so similar that a scribe might easily mistake an *r* for a *w* or vice versa. It is noteworthy that the LXX reads Horites in Jos 9:7 and Gen 34:2, where the Hebrew texts contain the word Hivites. Also Gen 36 seems to show a confusion between Ho-

rites and Hivites. There Zibeon the Hivite of Gen 36:2 is probably identical with the Zibeon of vs 20 and 29, who, however, is called a Horite.

Hizki (hĭz'kī), KJV **Hezeki** (hĕz'ĕ-kī). [Heb. *Chizqî*, "my strength." Possibly a contraction of *Chizqîyah*, "Hezekiah."] A Benjamite (1 Chr 8:17).

Hizkiah (hĭz-kī'á), KJV **Hezekiah** (hĕz'ĕ-kī'á). [Heb. *Chizqîyah*, "Yahweh has strengthened."]

1. Son of Neariah and postexilic descendant of Judah's kings (1 Chr 3:23).

2. For Zep 1:1, KJV, *see* Hezekiah, 2.

Hizkijah. *See* Hezekiah, 5.

Hobab (hō'băb). [Heb. *Chobab*, probably "beloved." The name is attested in ancient South Arabic as *Chbb*, in Ugaritic as *Ḥbb*, and in Assyrian as *Ḥababa*.] The son of *Reuel, 2, and brother-in-law of Moses (Num 10:29). Owing to an error in vowel pointing he is called Moses' "father in law" in Jgs 4:11. Masoretes who added the vowel points to the original vowelless Hebrew made *chtn* read *choten*, "father-in-law." The reading should be *chatan*, "brother-in-law." Hobab was the son of Reuel, Moses' father-in-law (Ex 2: 16-21), hence Moses' brother-in-law. When the Israelites left Sinai for Canaan, Moses asked Hobab to serve as their guide in the desert (Num 10:29-32). After some hesitation he consented, and from that time members of his family, referred to as Kenites, lived with the tribe of Judah, and after the conquest of Canaan settled in the southern part of the country (Jgs 1:16; cf. 1 Sa 15:6; 27:10; 30:29). One family of Kenites separated from the group and moved north to Kedesh in Naphtali (Jgs 4:11; cf. v 6).

Hobah (hō'bá). [Heb. *Chôbah*, "reed country."] A place near Damascus, described as the limit of Abraham's pursuit of Chedorlaomer and his confederates (Gen. 14: 15). It is identified with the land of *Upe* of the *Amarna Letters, with the *Apum* of the Mari archive, and with *'Ipwm* of the Egyptian execration texts. These names refer to the area in which Damascus lay, probably also to the name of a town in the same area (*BASOR* 83 [1941], 34, 35).

Hobaiah. *See* Habaiah.

Hock. *See* Hamstring.

Hod (hŏd). [Heb. *Hôd*, "majesty."] An Asherite (1 Chr 7:37).

Hodaiah. *See* Hodaviah.

Hodaviah (hō'dá-vī'á), KJV once **Hodaiah** (hō-dā'yá). [Heb. *Hôdawyah* and *Hôdaw-*

yahû, "praise Yahweh." The name occurs in the Aramaic texts from Elephantine.]

1. The head of a tribal family of Manasseh in Transjordan (1 Chr 5:24).

2. A son of Elioenai and descendant of David (1 Chr 3:24).

3. A Benjamite (1 Chr 9:7).

4. For Ezr 2:40, *see* Hodevah.

Hodesh (hō′dĕsh). [Heb. *Chodesh,* "(born on the day of the) new moon."] A wife of the Benjamite Shaharaim (1 Chr 8:9).

Hodevah (hŏ-dē′vá). [Heb. *Hôdewah,* "praise Yahweh."] The founder of a Levite family, some members of which returned from Babylonia with Zerubbabel (Neh 7:43). He is called Judah in Ezr 3:9, and Hodaviah in ch 2:40.

Hodiah (hŏ-dī′á), KJV generally **Hodijah** (hŏ-dī′já). [Heb. *Hôdîyah,* "Yahweh is my glory." The name occurs also on an ancient Hebrew seal.]

1. A man of the tribe of Judah (1 Chr 4:19). The word order and punctuation of the KJV give the incorrect impression that Hodiah was a woman.

2. A Levite who assisted Ezra in explaining the Law of God to the people (Neh 8:7; 9:5). He was probably one of three men by this name who signed Nehemiah's covenant (ch 10:10, 13, 18).

3 and 4. Two other men, apparently besides Hodiah, 2, who signed Nehemiah's covenant (Neh 10:10, 13, 18).

Hoglah (hŏg′lá). [Heb. *Choglah,* "partridge." The name appears in the Samaria ostraca as the name of a place.] One of the daughters of the Manassite Zelophehad (Num 26:33; 27:1; 36:11; Jos 17:3).

Hoham (hō′hăm). [Heb. *Hôham.*] The Canaanite king of Hebron, a member of the Canaanite confederacy against the Israelites. After its defeat, Joshua slew and hanged its 5 kings, among whom was Hoham (Jos 10:3-27).

Hold. This word appears occasionally in the KJV in the obsolete sense of "secret retreat," "fortification," "cellar," "prison," and is variously a translation of: (1) The Heb. *meṣad, meṣûdah,* or *meṣodah,* the root meaning of which is "to hunt." The term is usually rendered "stronghold" in the RSV. The fugitive David hid from King Saul in a "hold" in Moab (1 Sa 22:4, 5), probably one of the fortresses in the Moabite hills. Some time later David and his men again sought the protection of "the hold" (ch 24:22). In Jer 51:30 the soldiers of Babylon are pictured as remaining inside their "holds," or fortifications, too fearful to battle the Medes.

Jehoiachin, king of Judah, was taken captive, and placed in "holds," "custody" (RSV), by the king of Babylon (Eze 19:9). (2) The Heb. *ṣarîach,* "dugout," "hollow" (Jgs 9:46, 49). In this instance the word seems to describe a stronghold in the form of a cellar connected with the temple of the god Berith. (3) The Gr. *tērēsis,* "prison." Peter and John were placed in "hold" (Acts 4:3). (4) The Gr. *phulakē,* "a place of guarding." In Rev 18:2 mystic Babylon is described as being the "hold," perhaps meaning "haunt," of every foul spirit.

Holiday. A term appearing twice in the RSV translating the Heb. *yôm ṭôb,* literally "good day." It refers to the period of rejoicing that the Jews celebrated after being saved from the plot of Haman the Agagite (Est 8:17; 9:22). This event was subsequently remembered annually in the Feast of *Purim (ch 9:26).

Holiness. *See* Sanctification.

Holm Tree. *See* Cypress.

Holon (hō′lŏn). [Heb. *Cholôn,* meaning uncertain.]

1. A town in the hill country of Judah (Jos 15:51), assigned to the priests (ch 21:15). In 1 Chr 6:58 it is called Hilen (hī′lĕn) [Heb. *Chîlen*]. It has been identified with *Khirbet 'Alin,* a ruin close to Beth-zur.

2. A town in Moab, sought in the area between Medeba and Dibon (Jer 48:21), but not identified with certainty.

Holy. The rendering of several closely synonymous Greek and Hebrew words which refer in general to that which is sacred or set apart from the common. Besides connoting a separation from all that defiles, the terms also usually include, when referring to people of God, the concept of moral perfection, and there is often a strong emphasis upon dedication to religious or sacred use (cf. Ex 19:6; 30:31, 32; Lev 21:6; Heb 3:1; etc.). The term appears in: (1) references to the absolute holiness of God (1 Sa 2:2; Ps 99:9; Is 6:3; Rev 15:4; etc.); (2) the expression "Holy One of Israel," a title of the Lord (Is 47:4; Eze 39:7; etc.); (3) the names of the compartments of the sanctuary and Temple (Ex 26:33; 2 Chr 4:22; Heb 9:12; etc.); (4) references to the holy character expected of the people of God (1 Pe 1:15, 16); etc.

Holy Ghost. *See* Holy Spirit.

Holy of Holies. *See* Tabernacle; Temple.

Holy One of Israel. [Heb. *Qedôsh Yiśra'el,* "Holy One of Israel."] A title of God ascribing to Him absolute perfection of character and implying that His people Israel should aspire to the same standard of character. The heathen did not ascribe perfection of character to their deities, and considered them "holy" only in the sense of being held sacred and inviolable. The term "Holy One of Israel" is characteristic of Isaiah, who uses it 25 times compared with only 7 occurrences elsewhere. His vision of the character of God (Is 6) effected a reformation in his own life and led him to stress the divine perfection in the endeavor to inspire Israel to strive perseveringly for holiness of character.

Holy Place. *See* Tabernacle; Temple.

Holy Spirit. [Heb. *Rûach Qodesh;* Gr. *Hagion Pneuma,* usually translated in the KJV by the Old English term, "Holy Ghost," but in a few instances, "Holy Spirit" (Lk 11:13; Eph 1:13; 4:30; 1 Th 4:8). Often the word *pneuma* is used without the qualifying *hagion,* but the context frequently indicates that the Holy Spirit is meant (Rom 8:26; 1 Cor 2:10; 12:4).] The 3d person of the Godhead, or Deity (Mt 28:19). The operations of God's Spirit are evident throughout Scripture history. When man became insufferably wicked, God said, "My spirit shall not always strive with man" (Gen 6:3). Concerning various men it is reported, "The Spirit of the Lord came upon him" (1 Sa 11:6; 19:23; 2 Chr 15:1; 20:14; etc.). The psalmist recognized the importance of God's Spirit in spiritual experience (Ps 51:11); he also declared His omnipresence (Ps 139:7-12). Joel prophesied that God's Spirit would be poured upon all flesh (Joel 2:28, 29), a promise that was quoted by Peter when the Holy Spirit was poured out on the day of Pentecost (Acts 2:17-21). By and large the OT writers understood the Spirit of God as a vitalizing, sustaining, stimulating, enabling force identified with God.

It was not until NT times, however, that a clearer picture of the work and personality of the Holy Spirit was seen. Christ taught His disciples that the Holy Spirit would teach them and help them to remember things formerly learned (Jn 14:26), would testify of, and glorify Him (chs 15:26; 16:14), would convict men of sin and of their need of righteousness (ch 16:8), and would guide into all truth (v 13). Paul revealed that the Spirit intercedes for us (Rom 8:26), dwells in us (v 9), endows us with various spiritual gifts (1 Cor 12:4, 8-11, 28; Eph 4:11), and brings forth fruit in the life of the Christian (Gal 5:22, 23). He spoke of the body as the temple of the Holy Spirit (1 Cor 6:19), and warned against grieving the Holy Spirit whereby the Christian is sealed unto the day of redemption (Eph 4:30).

There has been much speculation regarding the nature of the Holy Spirit, but revelation has been largely silent on this subject. His personality is implied, for He is presented as performing the acts of a person. He searches, knows, intercedes, helps, guides, convicts. He can be grieved, lied to, resisted. He is listed with other persons—God the Father and Jesus Christ the Son—in such a way as to imply that He, too, is a person. But regarding His essential nature, silence is golden.

The Holy Spirit had a part, mysterious to us, in the conception of Jesus (Mt 1:18, 20). Elizabeth (Lk 1:41), Zacharias (v 67), and Simeon (ch 2:25, 26) acted under the influence of the Holy Spirit. The Spirit descended in the form of a dove on the occasion of Jesus' baptism (Mk 1:10), and the same Spirit led Him into the wilderness of temptation (v 12). Jesus was spoken of as being "full of the Holy Ghost" (Lk 4:1), and John the Baptist predicted that He would baptize with the Holy Ghost (Mt 3:11). Jesus warned the Jewish leaders of the danger of blaspheming the Holy Ghost (Mt 12:32; Mk 3:29; Lk 12:10).

On His last night with His disciples Jesus promised "another Comforter" who would abide with His followers forever (Jn 14:16). The term *paraklētos,* translated "Comforter" (KJV), "Counselor" (RSV), means, literally, "one called alongside." The promised Holy Spirit was to carry on the functions of Jesus in all the world throughout all ages.

The fulfillment of Jesus' promise of the Holy Spirit began shortly after His ascension, as the book of Acts reveals. The book opens with Jesus' instructions to His disciples to witness for Him throughout all the world after the Holy Spirit would come upon them (Acts 1:8). The Holy Ghost descended at Pentecost and many conversions followed (ch 2). Seven deacons "full of the Holy Ghost" (ch 6:3) were chosen to care for certain interests in the infant church. One of their number, Stephen, was used of the Spirit to do a mighty work (v 8). Barnabas was filled with the Holy Spirit (ch 11:24).

Homam. *See* Hemam.

Home. The rendering of various Hebrew and Greek expressions, especially the Heb. *bayith,* "house," and the Gr. *oikos,* "house," which usually refer particularly to the building in which a family lives (Gen 43:26; 1 Sa 2:20; etc.). There is no special word in Biblical Hebrew or Greek to convey the unique meaning of our English word "home." *See* House.

Homer. [Heb. *chomer;* attested as *hmr* in Ugaritic and as *imêru* in Akkadian.] A dry measure, containing 10 baths (Eze 45:14), equivalent to 220 liters, or 6.24 bushels.

Homosexuals. [Gr. *arsenokoitai.*] A term appearing once in the RSV (1 Cor 6:9), where the KJV reads "abusers of themselves with mankind." The Greek term denotes male homosexuals, pederasts, or sodomites.

Honest. A term that usually means "truthful," "free from duplicity," "upright," etc. The RSV uses the term to render several Hebrew and Greek more or less synonymous expressions. In the KJV the term appears in the archaic sense of "honorable," "respectable," and "worthy of esteem." Thus the Gr. *kalos* ("good," "blameless," "excellent") is rendered "honest" in Rom 12:17; 2 Cor 8:21; and 1 Pe 2:12 (RSV "noble," "honorable," "good," respectively).

Honey. [Heb. generally *debash;* Gr. *meli.*] A viscid concentrate of a natural sweet, produced by bees from the nectar of flowers, or made artificially from fruit juices. The gift that Jacob sent to the prime minister of Egypt at the time of the great famine was probably grape honey or syrup, for bee's honey was apparently abundant in Egypt (Gen 43:11). Repeatedly Canaan was called "a land flowing with milk and honey," a metonym for the fertility and natural loveliness of the land (Ex 3:8; etc.). The wise man pointed out that as it is not good to eat too much honey, so too, an overabundance of flattering words is unwise (Prov 25:27, RSV). In the NT honey is mentioned as a part of the Baptist's diet (Mt 3:4; Mk 1:6), and as symbolic of the good taste of the little book of Rev 10, which later turned to bitterness (vs 9, 10).

Hood. A term appearing once (Is 3:23, KJV), the translation of the Heb. *ṣeniphah,* "turban," in the context a woman's headdress.

Hook. The rendering of: (1) The Heb. *waw* of Ex 26:32; 38:28; etc., a "hook" or "peg," such as was attached to the posts of the tabernacle to facilitate the hanging of the curtains. (2) The Heb. *chach* (2 Ki 19:28; Is 37:29; Eze 29:4; 38:4), a "hook" drawn through the nose or lips of a captive. Captives thus treated are depicted on Assyrian stone reliefs (see fig. 163). (3) The Heb. *chakkah* and Gr. *agkistron* (Hab 1:15; Mt 17:27), a "fishhook" resembling a horn. (4) The Heb. *chôach* (Job 41:2, RSV; KJV "thorn"), in this passage a "hook," probably a thorn, put through the jaw of a large fish. This was fastened to a cord, and the fish could thus be kept alive in the water though he was unable to escape. (5) The Heb. *ṣinnôth* (plural, Amos 4:2), the barb or hook of a fishing spear popular in Egypt, as ancient pictures show (see fig. 177). (6) The Heb. *shephattayim* (Eze 40:43), a word of uncertain meaning, probably referring to hooks on which the carcasses of animals were hung, or stone ledges on which articles could be placed. (7) The Heb. *'agmôn* (Job 41:2; RSV "rope").

Hoopoe, KJV **Lapwing.** [Heb. *dûkiphath.*] The Hebrew term probably represents not the "lapwing" (*Vanellus cristatus*), one of the true plovers, but the "hoopoe" (*Upupa epops*), a type of a large family of Old World birds with deeply cleft, slender, curved bills and a large crest. The bird and its kind are excluded from the diet as unclean (Lev 11:19; Deut 14:18).

Hope. The translation of terms meaning variously "confidence," "expectation," "trust," "security," "hope," "expectant desire," and "confidence." In the Bible these attitudes are frequently expressed as directed toward, or settled upon, Deity or heavenly things. The psalmist, meditating upon the uncertainty and vanity of life, turned to God as the solid ground for his hope (Ps 39:7; cf. Ps. 71:5; 146:5), and focused his hope of salvation upon God (Ps 119:116).

The coming of Jesus into this world gave new substance and form to hope. The Christian is saved by "hope" (Rom 8:24), which hope comes by grace (2 Th 2:16). Apart from Christ there is no hope (Eph 2:12, 13), but Christ is to be the believer the "hope of glory" (Col 1:27). Justification by faith brings in its train peace and rejoicing "in hope of the glory of God" (Rom 5:1, 2). Through the Spirit the Christian waits "for the hope of righteousness by faith" (Gal 5:5). The second coming of Christ is to him the blessed hope (Tit 2:13).

Hope is spoken of as "an anchor of the soul" (Heb 6:19). Based on the sound foundation of Christian faith, it imparts courage, enthusiasm, optimism, and joy. It is an antidote for despair and discouragement. It encourages purposeful activity, particularly in the advancement of the kingdom of God.

Hophni (hŏf'nī). [Heb. *Chophnî,* from the Egyptian *ḥfn(r),* "tadpole."] One of Eli's two sons. He and his brother Phinehas were priests of the tabernacle at Shiloh. Their wickedness, and Eli's failure to punish them or remove them from office, although he was twice rebuked by prophetic utterances (1 Sa 2:27-36; 3:11), brought a curse upon the family. The two sons lost their lives in the battle at Aphek, and the ark of the covenant, which they had carried into battle, fell into the hands of the Philistines (ch 4: 4-18).

Hophra (hŏf'rà). [Heb. *Chophra';* Egyptian *Ḥ'-ib-R',* "the heart of Ra rejoices."] The 4th king of the 26th dynasty of Egypt (588-569 B.C.), better known by the Greek form of his name, Apries. Hophra continued the anti-Babylonian policy of his predecessors and attempted to bring relief to Jerusalem when that city was besieged by Nebuchadnezzar sometime between 588 and 586 B.C. (Jer 37:5-11). The effort failed and the Egyptian army was forced to retreat. After the destruction of Jerusalem many Jews fled to Egypt, especially after the assassination of the governor Gedaliah and the slaughter of the Chaldean garrison of Mizpah. Among those who went to Egypt against their will was the prophet Jeremiah and his secretary Baruch (chs 41 to 43). Jeremiah predicted that Hophra would die by the hand of his enemies (ch 44:30), a prediction that was later fulfilled. In a military revolt Hophra was forced to recognize the army commander Ahmose (Amasis) as coregent. Two years later a quarrel broke out between the two rulers, which resulted in bloody battle between their respective supporters and in the death of Hophra. Greatheartedly, Ahmose gave him a royal burial.

Hopper. A rendering of the Heb. *yeleq* in Joel 2:25, RSV, identified by some with the locust in an immature stage, when it can jump but not yet crawl. *See* Locust.

Lit.: O. R. Sellers, *JAOS* 53 (1933), 405.

Hor (hôr). [Heb. *Hor,* "mountain."]

1. A mountain on the border of Edom, where Aaron died and was buried (Num 20:22-29; 33:37-39; Deut 32:50). A tradition going back at least to the 1st cent.

233. A mountain near Petra, traditionally called Mount Hor

A.D. (Jos. *Ant.* iv. 4. 7) places this mountain near Petra, at what is now known as the *Jebel Harûn,* "Aaron's mountain," a two-topped sandstone mountain, almost 5,000 ft. high, southwest of Petra (Map V, B-7). The tomb structure now on its summit is a Moslem mosque. Since this traditional Mount Hor lies in the heart of the Edomite country, the identification is seriously doubted. H. C. Trumbull (*Kadesh-Barnea,* pp. 128 ff.) has suggested *Jebel Maderah,* a mountain 15 mi. northeast of Kadesh, as the correct Mount Hor, but this identification is also uncertain.

2. A mountain on the northern boundary of Palestine (Num 34:7, 8); not identified. It may describe a prominent peak of Lebanon.

Horam (hō'răm). [Heb. *Horam.*] A Canaanite king of Gezer, who came to the aid of Lachish when that city was besieged by the Israelites, but who was defeated by Joshua (Jos 10:33).

Horeb. *See* Sinai.

Horem (hō'rĕm). [Heb. *Chorem,* "sacred."] A fortified city in Naphtali in upper Galilee (Jos 19:38); not identified.

Horesh (hō'rĕsh). [Heb. *Choreshah,* "wood," which is the KJV rendering of this word.] A locality in which David hid from Saul (1 Sa 23:15-19, RSV). It has been identified with *Khirbet Khoreisa,* 2 mi. south of *Tell Zif,* the site of the ancient city of Ziph.

Hor-haggidgad (hôr'hȧ-gĭd'găd), KJV **Horhagidgad** (hôr'hȧ-gĭd'găd). [Heb. *Chor Haggidgad,* "cave of Gidgad."] A station in the wilderness where the Israelites camped (Num 33:32), not identified with certainty. It is called Gudgodah (gŭd-gō'dȧ) [Heb. *Gudgodah*] in Deut 10:7. Its name seems to have been preserved in the *Wâdī Jadejed,* a tributary of the *Wâdī Jerâfi,* north of *Kuntilet el-Jerāfi,* to the northwest of the Gulf of Aqabah.

Lit.: Ant. Jaussen, *RB* 15, N.S. 3 (1906), 459 and map.

Hori (hō′rī). [Heb. *Chori.*]

1. A grandson of Seir and son of Lotan (Gen 36:22; 1 Chr 1:39).

2. A Simeonite whose son Shaphat was the tribal representative on the deputation that spied out the land of Canaan (Num 13:5).

Horims. *See* Horites.

Horites (hō′rīts), KJV twice **Horims** (hō′-rīmz). [Heb. *Chorim.* In the KJV of Deut 2:12, 22 the English plural *s* is added unnecessarily to a transliteration of the Hebrew plural; Egyptian *Ḥꜣrw;* Akkadian *Ḥurru;* Ugaritic *Ḥry.*] The Horites appear in the OT as the original inhabitants of Mount Seir (Gen 36:20, 21, 29, 30), who were defeated by 5 kings in the time of Abraham (ch 14:6), and who were eventually replaced by the Edomites, the descendants of Esau (Deut 2:12, 22). For a long time it was thought that the name Horites was derived from *chor,* "cave," and that the Horites were therefore cave dwellers or troglodytes. Recently discovered historical and archeological evidence has made this view untenable. It is now recognized that they are to be identified with the Hurrians, an ethnic group of people known from Egyptian hieroglyphic inscriptions and also from cuneiform texts of Mesopotamia. This source material reveals that the Hurrians lived in the mountains north of Mesopotamia in the 3d millennium B.C., but poured into the Mesopotamian valley in the early 2d millennium B.C., and some of them subsequently pushed their way into Syria and Palestine. One Hurrian center existed east of Assyria in the patriarchal age. Many Hurrian texts have been found at Nuzi, near modern Kirkuk in Iraq (Map III, B-5), which throw an unusually interesting light on patriarchal conditions.

The pressure of the Hurrians on Syria and Palestine seems to have been responsible for the Hyksos invasion of Egypt in the 18th cent. B.C. The first waves of these invaders were Semites, who had been pushed out of their countries; the later waves were Hurrians. This conclusion is reached by a study of the names of the Hyksos kings. Even after the expulsion of the Hyksos from Egypt, a strong Hurrian element remained in Palestine, and the Egyptians sometimes called the whole country of Palestine "Kharu." Amenhotep II (1450-1425 B.C.) claims to have brought back 36,300 Kharu as captives from a military campaign in Palestine (*ANET* 247).

The Hurrians also founded the kingdom of Mitanni (Map III, B-4/5), which comprised all of Upper Mesopotamia, and which became a formidable opponent of the Egyptian kings of the 18th dynasty, who fought against it repeatedly. The Hurrians were later defeated by the Hittites and Assyrians, and absorbed by these new powers.

That a Hurrian language existed, first became known through one *Amarna Letter (No. 24). Since then texts in this language have come to light in various places, including the Hittite capital, Khattushash, and Ugarit. The language is not yet fully understood. The Hittites adopted many of their religious practices from the Hurrians, as well as the chief Hurrian god, Teshub, the famous god of thunder and storm.

Hormah (hôr′mȧ). [Heb. *Chormah,* "devoted."] An old Canaanite city whose original name was Zephath (Heb. *Ṣephath*). The Israelites changed this name to Hormah after they destroyed the city (Jgs 1:17). Hormah was in the southernmost part of Judah, toward the border of Edom. It is mentioned (Num 14:45; Deut 1:44) as the place to which the Amalekites and the Canaanites drove the Israelites in an attack in the 2d year of the Exodus. When the king of Arad attacked the Israelites some 38 years later and took some of them captive they vowed the destruction of the whole area (Num 21:1-3), which vow they later fulfilled (Jgs 1:17). During the distribution of the country the city was first allotted to Judah, but later transferred to the tribe of Simeon (Jos 15:30; 19:4). The city was apparently reoccupied by the Canaanites, but after Joshua's death the Simeonites, aided by Judah, recaptured it, and for a time retained it, calling it Hormah (Jgs 1:1, 17; 1 Chr 4:24, 30). When David was a fugitive he lived on friendly terms with the people of Hormah, and after he had revenged Ziklag, he sent them spoil captured from the Amalekites (1 Sa 30:30). The site has not been identified with certainty, but may be either *Tell el-Mshāsh,* 3 mi. east of Beer-sheba, or *Tell es-Ṣebaʿ,* which lies slightly to the northeast of *Tell el-Mshāsh.* (The site shown on Map VI, F-2 is *Tell el-Mshāsh*).

Horn. Since Palestine was a country of flocks, the Israelites from their early history used the horns of their animals in various ways.

1. Signaling instruments (Jos 6:5). The Hebrew term is generally *shôphar,* "ram's horn," usually translated *"trumpet"; but in 4 passages (1 Chr 15:28; 2 Chr 15:14;

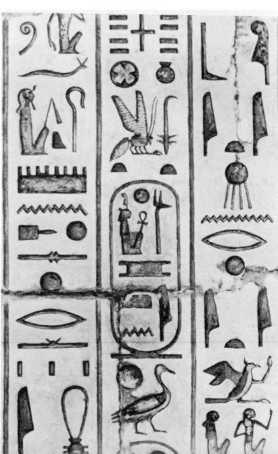

234. Top: A Jewish horn of the 12th cent. A.D. Bottom: An inscribed horn belonging to the Great Synagogue of London

Ps 98:6; Hos 5:8) it is translated "cornet" in the KJV and "horn" in the RSV, because in each of these 4 passages metal trumpets are also mentioned from which it was necessary to distinguish the signaling instruments made of ram's horns. In Dan 3:5, 7, 10, 15 the Aramaic *qeren,* "horn (of a goat or ram)," is translated "cornet" (KJV) and "horn" (RSV).

2. Containers for oil used for anointing (1 Sa 16:1, 13; 1 Ki 1:39).

3. Corner projections on altars, sometimes in the shape of horns (Ex 30:10; 1 Ki 1:50, 51; etc.).

Figuratively the horn was the symbol of arrogance and insolence (Ps 75:4, 5), of strength or political power—from the fact that the horns of an animal were symbols of its strength (Ps 132:17; Jer 48:25). In prophetic symbolism horns stand for kings, kingdoms, or other powers (Dan 7:8, 20, 21, 24; Rev 17:12, 16).

Hornet. The hornet, or wasp, an insect (*Vespa crabro*) with a painful sting. In harmony with the ancient versions the Heb. *ṣir'ah* is translated "hornet" in Ex 23:28; Deut 7:20; and Jos 24:12, where it is stated that the Lord would drive out the enemies of the Hebrews by the *ṣir'ah.* It has been suggested that if "hornet" is the correct rendering in these texts the insect must be a symbol of some nation. The suggestion has been made that it means the Egyptians, since one of the titles of the Pharaoh in hieroglyphs is written with the sign of a bee (*bît*), sometimes interpreted as "wasp" (see fig. 235). Some think, therefore, that the Lord used the Egyptians to weaken the Canaanites before the Israelites arrived to facilitate the conquest of the country. Other scholars reject

the rendering "hornet" and see in *ṣir'ah* a noun meaning "discouragement." The verb *ṣara'* means "to be struck with a disease." They believe that the Lord promised to weaken the nations of Canaan by discouragement even before the arrival of the Israelites.

Horonaim (hôr'ō-nā'ĭm). [Heb. *Choronayim,* "two caverns," spelled *Chwrnn* on the Moabite Stone (lines 30, 31).]

1. A Moabite city near Zoar (Is 15:5; Jer 48:3, 5, 34). In Jer 48:5, RSV, the "descent of Horonaim" is mentioned, and the *Moabite Stone speaks of the city as one to which one descends, but its location, most probably south of the river Arnon, has not been ascertained.

2. According to the RSV, the designation of a certain road (2 Sa 13:34). The RSV reading is based not on the Hebrew, which reads "behind him," but on the LXX. Horonaim is here considered to refer to the two towns called Upper *Beth-horon and Lower Beth-horon.

Horonite (hôr'ō-nīt). [Heb. *Choroni.*] A native either of Beth-horon, or more prob-

235. Egyptian hieroglyphs, including the sign of a bee or wasp (upper center), forming part of the Pharaoh's titles

ably of Horonaim in Moab. If the latter is correct, its application by Nehemiah to Sanballat, the bitter enemy of the Jews (Neh 2:10, 19; 13:28), may have been an expression of Nehemiah's contempt for Sanballat as a Moabite. It has also been suggested that Horonite means "a man of the Hauran."

Horse. [Heb. *sûs*; Gr. *hippos*.] An animal that was originally not native to the ancient Near East. It was probably domesticated by Indo-European people north of the Caucasus, and introduced into the area of the Fertile Crescent in the 18th cent. B.C. It seems to have come into Egypt at the time the Hyksos ruled that country. The horse is therefore not mentioned until the time that Joseph came to Egypt, probably in the 17th cent. B.C. (see Gen 47:17; 49:17; etc.). Joseph rode in a chariot drawn by horses, and Pharaoh pursued the children of Israel with horses and chariots (Ex 14:9; 15:1; cf. Gen 41:42, 43). Horseback riding was practically unknown among the Egyptians at that period, and the "horsemen" of Ex 14:9 and the "riders" of ch 15:1 and of similar texts of an early period should rather be translated "charioteers," that is, men who rode in chariots, either as drivers or as soldiers. Since the Israelites did not have horses and chariots during the early periods of their history, whereas the Canaanites, Philistines, and Syrians did, the Israelites without divine aid were at a disadvantage in meeting their enemies (Jos 17:16; Jgs 4:3; 1 Sa 13:5; 2 Sa 8:4). Yet, for a long time Israel refrained from introducing horse and chariot into their armed forces (cf. Deut 17:16). In their fight with the Canaanites of the plain they hamstrung (KJV "houghed") the captured war horses by cutting the tendons of the horses' hind legs (Jos 11:9). This practice seems

236. Ruins of Israelite stables at Megiddo; note stone mangers between posts at center

to have prevailed until the time of David, who hamstrung the horses captured from Zobah but reserved for himself enough horses for 100 chariots (2 Sa 8:4). His sons also possessed horses and chariots (2 Sa 15:1; 1 Ki 1:5). Solomon was the first to introduce chariotry into Israel on a grand scale, and perhaps also cavalry. He imported horses from Kue (Cilicia) and chariots from Egypt (1 Ki 4:26; 10: 26, 29; see *SDACom* 2:782). The University of Chicago excavators of Megiddo uncovered several large horse stables, with room for about 480 horses, and spacious grounds for 160 chariots, showing that Megiddo was a chariot city in the period of the kings (1 Ki 9:15, 19; 10:26). See figs. 236, 316, 460. From Solomon's time on, horsemen and chariots were part of Israel's war machine (1 Ki 16:9; 22:4; 2 Ki 13:7), although the prophets denounced Israel's reliance on horses and horsemen (Is 2:7; 31:1; Hos 14:3). In Ahab's time the northern kingdom of Israel mustered 2,000 chariots against the Assyrians, and furnished more than 50 per cent of all the chariots that the kings of the anti-Assyrian alliance employed to fight against Shalmaneser III at Qarqar in 853 B.C. In contrast with the many texts that speak of the use of the horse in war there is only one that mentions the horse in connection with agriculture (Is 28:28). Saddles, stirrups, and horseshoes seem to have been unknown in ancient times, and horses with hard hoofs were highly valued (cf. ch 5:28).

In Biblical poetry the strength, courage, and speed of the horse are praised (Job 39:19-25; Jer 4:13; Hab 1:8), and rebuke is uttered against men who, like the horse, needed bridle, whip, and bit (Ps 32:9; Prov 26:3; Jas 3:3). Symbolic horses of different colors are mentioned by Zechariah (Zec 1:8; 6:2, 3) and in Revelation (Rev 6:2-8). Christ is symbolized as riding a white horse, and leading armies on white horses at His second coming (ch 19:11, 14).

Horse Gate. [Heb. *sha'ar hassûsim*.] One of the gates of Jerusalem. A comparison of 2 Ki 11:6 with 2 Chr 23:14, 15 seems to indicate that this gate was not far from the Temple and the royal palace. Neh 3:27, 28 indicates that it stood in the neighborhood of the wall of Ophel, and might appropriately be regarded as belonging to it. Thus it was probably located at the southeastern corner of the Temple area, on the slopes of Mount Moriah.

Horseleach. *See* Leech.

Horsemen. Soldiers who rode on horses, in contrast to foot soldiers, who traveled and fought on foot. Up to the Assyrian period horsemen did not ride on horseback, but were instead charioteers—either the drivers of the chariots or men who fought from chariots (Gen 50:9; Ex 14:17, 18; etc.). During the Assyrian period cavalry as we know it was introduced (Jer 4:29; 6:23; 46:4; etc.). This is attested by the many Assyrian battle scenes on stone that portray Assyrian soldiers on horses.

Hosah (hō'sà). [Heb. *Chosah*, "refugee."]
1. A gatekeeper in the time of David (1 Chr 16:38; 26:10, 11, 16).
2. A place on the boundary of Asher, apparently south of Tyre (Jos 19:29). The proposed identification with *Ushu* of the Assyrian inscriptions, the *Palaituros* of Greek writers, namely, mainland Tyre, is very uncertain and questionable.

Hosanna. A transliteration through the Gr. *hōsanna* of the Aramaic *hôsha' na'* of which the Hebrew equivalent is *hôshî'ah nnâ'* (Ps 118:25). The expression means "save, I pray," or "help, I pray." The multitude at Jesus' Triumphal Entry cried, "Hosanna," probably as a prayer that salvation would come to Israel through the Messiah (Mt 21:9, 15; Mk 11:9, 10; Jn 12:13).

Hosea (hō-zē'à), KJV of NT **Osee** (ō'zē). [Heb. *Hôshea'*, probably an apocopated form of *Hôsha'ayah*, "Yahweh saves"; Gr. *Ōsēe*. The name occurs on ancient Hebrew seals.] The last prophet whose ministry was devoted exclusively to the northern kingdom of Israel; first of the so-called Minor Prophets. His father, Beeri, "my well," was presumably a member of one of the families of an unspecified northern tribe. Hosea bore his message during the reigns of Uzziah, Jotham, Ahaz, and Hezekiah, kings of Judah, and Jeroboam II, the last strong king of the northern kingdom (Hos 1:1), beginning some years prior to 753 B.C. and continuing until some time after 729 B.C. During these years he witnessed the moral and political collapse of the northern kingdom and sought unsuccessfully to stay the course of apostasy and national disintegration. The fact that only 1 king of Israel (Jeroboam II) is mentioned, but several kings of Judah who lived after Jeroboam, may suggest a later ministry in the southern kingdom of Judah.

Hosea, Book of. The title of the book gives the name of its author. Hosea stands first among the Minor Prophets, which are thus designated only because of their comparative brevity and without any implication that the ministry of the men who wrote them was either of brief duration or minor consequence, or that their writings are of less importance or of lesser inspiration. The chronological statement with which the book opens indicates that Hosea's ministry extended over a period of at least 24 years, that is, assuming that he began his ministry in 753 B.C., the closing year of the reign of Jeroboam II, and ended it in 729 B.C., the 1st of Hezekiah, but his ministry doubtless extended some years before 753 B.C. and perhaps a short time after 729 B.C. Inasmuch as Hosea makes no reference to the fall of Samaria in 723/22 B.C., it may be assumed that his service ended prior to that tragic event. For a number of years his ministry was contemporary with that of Amos (ch 1:1), Micah (ch 1:1), and Isaiah (ch 1:1). Although a specific statement linking Hosea's ministry to the northern kingdom, Israel, is lacking, the familiarity with which the prophet speaks of various localities in that part of the divided kingdom strongly implies that his prophetic ministry was largely conducted there (Hos 4:15; 5:1; 6:8, 9; 9:15; 10:5, 8, 15; 12:11; 14:5-8). The course of apostasy in Judah was less advanced than in Israel (chs 11:12; 12:2), and references to the former are more general in tone and somewhat incidental (chs 5:14; 6:4, 11; 8:14; 10:11; 11:12).

Hosea's ministry spans the closing decades of the history of the northern kingdom, and his message constituted God's final appeal to the 10 tribes prior to the disintegration of the kingdom and the permanent captivity of a majority of its people at the hands of the Assyrians. Hosea began his ministry sometime during Jeroboam II's long and successful reign, at a time when the nation was basking in the temporary light of an imposing but deceptive political and material prosperity. Jeroboam's success at pushing back the northern borders of the country practically to the limits attained in the days of David and Solomon had introduced an era of unprecedented luxury, but this served only to hasten the moral and spiritual decline that began nearly 2 cent. earlier in the nation with Jeroboam I, its 1st king. Apostasy, often referred to as "whoredom" or "adultery" (chs 1:2; 6:10; 9:1), had taken the form of *Baal worship (chs 2:8, 13, 17; 9:10; 11:2; 13:1). Adultery had become a national custom (ch 7:4). Increasing prosperity had brought with it increased sin and corruption (Hos. 4:7; 9:9), and the people pursued their iniquitous course with a greedy appetite (ch 4:8). Apostasy, based on a deliberate rejection of the revealed will of God (v 6), was practically universal (vs 16, 17; cf. chs 6:7; 7:7, 13-16; 8:1, 14; 11:7), and the nation had refused God's repeated invitations to return to Him (chs 5:4; 7:10). The degrading effects of idolatry were inevitably reflected in the moral tone of society until there was "no faithfulness or kindness, and no knowledge of God in the land," but only "swearing, lying, killing, stealing, and committing adultery" (ch 4:1, 2, RSV). Lamented the prophet, "They break all bounds and murder follows murder (vs 1, 2, RSV). The religious leaders engaged in the grossest crimes (ch 6:9), and the monarchy had fallen on evil days. Four of its last 5 kings assassinated their predecessors in order to become king (cf. ch 7:7). As a nation the people of Israel had plowed wickedness and were reaping a harvest of iniquity (ch 10:13). The nation was ripe for dissolution, but in mercy God prolonged her day of grace for a few brief years before the Assyrians ended her national existence.

The dominant theme of the book is the infinite love and patient long-suffering of God. God's care for His people is presented in terms of a faithful husband's solicitous affection for an erring wife, as acted out in the tragic personal narrative of Hos 1 to 3. The prophet was instructed to "take . . . a wife of whoredoms and children of whoredoms" (ch 1:2). Hosea's wife, Gomer, soon proved unfaithful (ch 2:2-5) and bore a succession of illegitimate children (chs 1:6, 9; 2:4, 5). His love for the erring wife was unabated, and he sought by every means possible to retrieve her affections (ch 2:2-9, 14, 15), but to no avail. Eventually he found her in a slave market and bought her back (ch 3). Opinion is divided as to whether this narrative relates an actual experience, or whether it is to be considered an allegory or a dream. Those who deny it as an actual experience base their argument on the contention that God would not authorize a prophet to marry an adulteress, while those who consider it an account of Hosea's own experience hold that Gomer was not an adulteress at the time Hosea married her (ch 1:2). Either way, the national apostasy is accurately reflected in Hosea's attitude toward her (chs 1:10, 11; 2:16-23). The

state of national affairs is a projection of the situation in Hosea's home.

The broken heart of Hosea for his wayward wife finds its counterpart in the broken literary pattern of God's message to Israel in Hos 4 to 14. There is no logical development of the theme, but a passionate alternation between passages mourning the waywardness of Israel and others appealing to her to return to her Lord and Master. Hosea's passionate appeals to Gomer are matched by God's appeals to Israel, and the sentences follow one another abruptly and sometimes almost incoherently, like the sobs of a broken heart. Like Jeremiah a century later, Hosea mourns for his people, unreconciled to the evil course they have chosen to follow and the evil fate that awaits them. The book is replete with vivid illustrations drawn from nature and from everyday life: a backsliding heifer (ch 4:16), the early and latter rains (ch 6:3), an overheated oven (ch 7:4-7), a cake unturned, perhaps burned to a cinder on one side and doughy on the other (v 8), an old man who still lives the life of a playboy (v 9), a wild ass in heat (ch 8:9), an empty vine (ch 10:1), and many others.

Though the book of Hosea does not readily lend itself to a logical analysis, the following general approximate line of thought development is evident: In the first 3 chapters, as already noted, Hosea recounts his personal experiences with Gomer, while in chs 4 to 14 he addresses Israel as if she were an unfaithful spouse to God. In ch 4 the Lord has "a controversy with the inhabitants of the land" (v 1), and in ch 5 he addresses the religious leaders, warning them of impending judgment (vs 1, 15). In chs 6, 7 the prophet extends to Israel an invitation to return to the Lord, but then goes on to show how earlier invitations to return have only met with treachery on Israel's part, and, at best, halfhearted reform (chs 6:4, 7; 7:8, 11, 16). Chapters 8 and 9 announce impending captivity as the punishment for apostasy (chs 8:1, 7, 8; 9:3, 7, 15, 17). Reasons for the fearful fate soon to overtake the nation are outlined in chs 10 to 13, where God recounts what He has done for His people and charges them with being "an empty vine" (ch 10:1). Interspersed with the charges are tender appeals to return (chs 10:12; 11:8, 9; 12:6; 13:9, 10). Chapter 14 constitutes God's final invitation to return to Him, and He promises to "love them freely" and to "heal their backsliding" (v 4).

Hosen. An archaic English word for "trousers." The term occurs only in Dan 3:21 (RSV "tunics"), and is a rendering of the Aramaic *paṭṭîsh,* a word of uncertain significance, denoting some article of clothing. Cognate words in Syriac designate "turbans," "trousers," and even "shoes." Some consider the Aramaic word a loan word from the Persian *patyushe,* "dress."

Hoshaiah (hǒ-shā′yà). [Heb. *Hôshaʻayah,* "Yahweh saves." The name occurs also on an ancient Hebrew seal inscription.]
1. Father of Jezaniah and Azariah (Jer 42:1; 43:2).
2. A prominent Jew who assisted in the dedication of the wall of Jerusalem in Nehemiah's time (Neh 12:32).

Hoshama (hǒsh′à-mà). [Heb. *Hôshamaʻ,* a shortened form of *Yehôshamaʻ,* "Jehoshama," "Yahweh has heard."] A son of King Jehoiachin (Jeconiah) of Judah (1 Chr 3:18).

Hoshea (hǒ-shē′à), KJV twice **Oshea** (ô-shē′à). [Heb. *Hôsheʻa,* probably an apocopated form of *Hôshaʻayah,* "Yahweh saves." The name occurs on ancient Hebrew seals.]
1. The original name of the son of Nun that was changed by Moses to *Joshua (Num 13:8, 16; Deut 32:44).
2. A prince of Ephraim in the time of David (1 Chr 27:20).
3. The 20th (if Tibni is included) and last king of Israel (732-722 B.C.). With the probable connivance of Tiglath-pileser III, king of Assyria, Hoshea slew Pekah and usurped the throne. When Shalmaneser V, Tiglath-pileser's successor, appeared in Palestine, Hoshea paid tribute to Assyria and was confirmed in his office. Later, however, he made an alliance with Egypt and broke away from Assyria, with the result that Shalmaneser marched against Israel and besieged Samaria, taking the city after three years. This probably took place in the last year of Shalmaneser's life, although Sargon II, his successor, claimed to have captured the city. Hoshea was taken captive and incarcerated (2 Ki 15:30; 17:1-6).
4. One of the men who set his seal to Nehemiah's covenant (Neh 10:23).

Host. *See* Sabaoth.

Host of Heaven. [Heb. *ṣebaʼ hashshamayim,* "army of heaven."] A figurative expression depicting the various celestial bodies as an army. These were often worshiped by the nations surrounding Israel; hence the Lord early warned His people against this practice (Deut 4:19; 17:3). However, later such worship came to have a prominent place in the degraded religious life of the kingdoms of Judah and Israel (2 Ki 17:16; 21:3, 5; Jer 8:2; 19:13; Zep 1:5; Acts 7:42); and it formed an important target for the efforts of such spiritual reformers as King Josiah (2 Ki 23:4, 5). The expression occurs in prophetic symbolism in 1 Ki 22:19; Dan 8:10.

Hosts, Lord of. *See* Sabaoth.

Hotham (hō′thăm), KJV once **Hothan** (hō′thăn). [Heb. *Chôtham,* "seal."]
1. An Asherite and founder of a tribal family (1 Chr 7:32), probably identical with Helem (v 35, RSV "Heler").
2. A man from Aroer, two of whose sons belonged to the "mighty men" of David (1 Chr 11:44).

Hothan. *See* Hotham, 2.

Hothir (hō′thēr). [Heb. *Hôthîr,* meaning uncertain.] A musician, one of the sons of Heman (1 Chr 25:4, 28).

Hough. *See* Hamstring.

Hour. In ancient times, the 12th part of the period of daylight (Jn 11:9; cf. Mt 20:1-12); thus the length of the hour varied somewhat according to the seasons. Probably the time of day was loosely approximated by looking at the sun; certainly for ordinary purposes time was not measured exactly. But at least as early as the time of Isaiah the Hebrews evidently had some method of telling time by the sun's shadow, for the miraculous sign granted to Hezekiah was the backward movement of the shadow on the *"dial" of Ahaz (2 Ki 20:11). Timepieces existed in Egypt in the form of water clocks, which indicated the hour of the day by the amount of water that had been lost through a carefully measured opening. Scales differing according to the months of the year made allowance for the different length of the hours (see fig. 237).

237. An Egyptian water clock of Amenhotep III, in the Cairo Museum

HOUSE

House. [Heb. generally *bayith;* Gr. generally *oikia* and *oikos.*]

1. **Dwelling.** Anciently farmers and townspeople lived in houses, while nomads lived in tents. Throughout the ancient Near East houses were generally built of bricks, but in some countries, such as Palestine, where stone was plentiful and soft, they were constructed also of stone. Bricks used for the walls were mostly of sun-dried mud. Foundations were either of stone or of burned brick. The roofs were mostly flat, although there is evidence of some gabled ones. The beams of the roof consisted of undressed trees, upon which branches and a thick layer of earth were laid. This was covered with a plaster to make it somewhat waterproof. The roof was smoothed with a stone roller and needed frequent repairs to keep it from leaking. Houses of many common people consisted of only one

239. Model of a Palestinian house at *Tell en-Naṣbeh,* probably ancient Mizpah, 4, in the time of the kings

room, which, however, had 2 different floor levels, a lower for the domestic animals, and one a few feet higher, for the family. The door from the outside led into the lower section. The Mosaic law required that flat roofs be surrounded by battlements to prevent accidents (Deut 22:8). These roofs were used for recreation (Dan 4:29, RSV), a place to sleep (1 Sa 9:25, RSV), ostentatious lamentations (Is 15:3; Jer 48:38), prayers and meditation (Acts 10:9), or for idolatrous worship (2 Ki 23:12, RSV). Usually access to the roof was gained by an outside stairway (Mt 24:17).

The houses of better-class people consisted of a series of rooms arranged around a central court, which in some cases contained a well (2 Sa 17:18). Two-story houses had the bedrooms on the 2d floor (Jgs 3:20, RSV), and also guest rooms (1 Ki 17:19; 2 Ki 4:10, RSV). They could be reached by means of a stairway from the court. The inside walls were whitewashed or brightly painted, sometimes covered with wooden paneling or ivory plaques (1 Ki 22:39; Jer 22:14; Hag 1:4). The ordinary floor usually consisted of a layer of clay or plaster upon which straw mats were spread; the floor in the better houses was laid with boards or flagstones, as excavations have shown (see fig. 214). Windows were small, in most cases being nothing more than slits in the wall. Larger windows had lattices to keep intruders out. Glass windows did not exist until late Roman times. Doors were usually of wood, and had wooden or bronze pivots, the lower of which turned in a stone socket or in a hole in the threshold, and the upper turned either in a hole in the stone lintel or in a metal ring attached to one of the doorposts. The doors could be locked from the outside by bars moved into place by keys

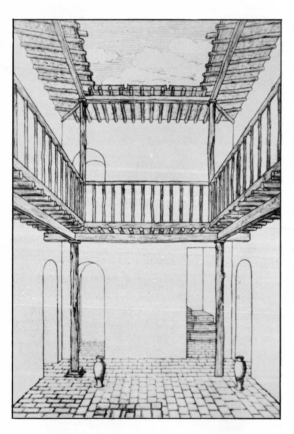

238. The inner court of a private house in Ur from the time of Abraham; drawing based on actual remains (cf. fig. 517)

HOUSE

(Jgs 3:25; Is 22:22; see Bolt) or from the inside by placing the bars in position.

By NT times shop-houses and multiple-apartment buildings were common in the cities of the Roman world. In Rome only a wealthy family could afford a separate house built around a court or courts (see fig. 408); the bulk of the population, including, presumably, most of the early Christians, lived in rented apartments above the shops in many-storied buildings (see fig. 410). The "hired house" in which Paul lived for 2 years, while awaiting trial in Rome, must have been such an apartment.

2. Household. The family establishment (Gen 39:4) and its people (Jos 24:15; Neh 1:6; Acts 10:2; 11:14). The household included not only the family but all inmates of the house—servants, slaves, and retainers (Gen 14:14; 17:27). The meaning of house was sometimes extended to cover ancestral line, as in "the house and lineage of David" (Lk 2:4); tribe, as in "the house of Ephraim" (Jgs 10:9); and even nation, as in "the house of Israel" (1 Sa 7:3; Mt 15:24).

241. House in Bethlehem with stable on the 1st floor and living quarters upstairs

240. The house at Joppa shown as the traditional home of "Simon, a tanner"

Hukkok (hŭk'ŏk). [Heb. *Chuqqoq,* meaning uncertain.] A town on the boundary of Naphtali (Jos 19:34); identified with *Yāqûq,* 2½ mi. west of Chinnereth.

Hukok. *See* Helkath.

Hul (hŭl). [Heb. *Chûl,* meaning uncertain.] The 2d son of Aram (Gen 10:23; 1 Chr 1:17). He was probably, like his brothers, also the ancestral head of an Aramaean tribe of which nothing, however, is now known.

Huldah (hŭl'dá). [Heb. *Chuldah,* "mole."] A prophetess of renown who lived in the 2d section of Jerusalem during the reign of Josiah. She was the wife of Shallum, keeper of the priestly or the royal wardrobe. Her advice was sought by King Josiah after the Book of the Law was found in the Temple. She told the king that Jerusalem would be destroyed, but that because of his pious life this would not occur during his lifetime (2 Ki 22:14-20; 2 Chr 34:22-28).

Humtah (hŭm'tá). [Heb. *Chumṭah,* "reptile."] A place in the hill country of Judah near Hebron (Jos 15:54); not identified.

Hundredweight. *See* Talent.

Hupham. *See* Huppim.

Huphamites. *See* Huppim.

Huppah (hŭp'ȧ). [Heb. *Chuppah,* meaning uncertain.] A descendant of Aaron, and the ancestral head of the 13th of the 24 courses into which David organized the priests (1 Chr 24:13).

Huppim (hŭp'ĭm). [Heb. *Chuppim.*] A son of Benjamin, and head of a tribal family (Gen 46:21; 1 Chr 7:12, 15). He is called Hupham (hū'făm) [Heb. *Chûpham*] in Num 26:39, and from him the Huphamites (hū'făm-īts) [Heb. *Chûphamî*] descended.

Hur (hûr). [Heb. *Chûr,* "whiteness," but for Hur, 1, and Hur, 2, the meaning is possibly "(the Egyptian god) Horus." The name occurs also on an ancient Hebrew seal, and is found in Akkadian as *Ḫûru,* "child."]

1. One of Moses' trusted companions who, with Aaron, held up Moses' arms during the battle with the Amalekites (Ex 17:10-13). He was associated with Aaron in the administration of the people at Mount Sinai (ch 24:14). Jewish tradition makes him the husband of Miriam and brother-in-law of Moses (Jos. *Ant.* iii. 2. 4). He is possibly to be identified with Hur, 2.

2. Grandfather of the artist Bezalel of the tribe of Judah (Ex 31:1, 2; 35:30-33; 38:22; 1 Chr 2:20; 2 Chr 1:5). He is possibly identical with Hur, 1.

3. A king of Midian, slain by Moses (Num 31:8; Jos 13:21).

4. Father of Solomon's supply officer in Mount Ephraim (1 Ki 4:8). The son is called Ben-hur (bĕn-hûr) in the RSV.

5. A Jew whose son, Rephaiah, was ruler of half of Jerusalem and one of the builders of the wall in Nehemiah's time (Neh 3:9).

Hurai. *See* Hiddai.

Huram (hū'răm). [Heb. *Chûram,* a variant spelling of *Chîram. See* Hiram.]

1. A king of Tyre (2 Chr 2:3; etc.). *See* Hiram, 1.

2. A Tyrian artificer of the time of Solomon (2 Chr 4:11, 16; etc.). *See* Hiram, 2.

3. A Benjamite (1 Chr 8:5).

Huramabi. *See* Hiram, 2.

Huri (hū'rī). [Heb. *Chûri,* meaning uncertain.] A descendant of Gad (1 Chr 5:14).

Husband. The rendering of various Hebrew and Greek words, none of which are exactly equivalent to the English word "husband." Occasionally the thought of the Biblical word is "master" or "owner," thus picturing a husband as one who possesses a wife (Ex 21:22; Est 1:17, 20; etc.); but usually the English term is a translation of various Biblical words that mean simply "man" (Gen 3:6; Ruth 1:12; Mt 1:19; 1 Cor 7:2; etc.).

Husbandman. [Heb. generally *'ikkar,* a loan word from the Akkadian *ikkaru,* which in turn was borrowed from the Sumerian *engar,* "farmer"; Gr. generally *geōrgos,* "farmer," "tenant farmer."] The KJV word for "farmer." The RSV usually translates the Biblical expressions as "tiller(s) of the soil" (Gen 9:20; Joel 1:11; Zec 13:5) or "farmer(s)" (2 Chr 26:10; Jer 31:24; 2 Ti 2:6). In Christ's parable of the Lord's Vineyard (Mt 21:33-41; Mk 12:1-9; Lk 20:9-16), in which the farmers did not own the property involved, the RSV renders the Biblical term "tenants."

Hushah (hū'shȧ). [Heb. *Chûshah,* "haste."] A descendant of Judah (1 Chr 4:4), and ancestral head of a family whose members are called Hushathites (hū'shăth-īts) [Heb. *Chushathî*] (ch 27:11). Some commentators take Hushah to be the name of a town.

Hushai (hū'shī). [Heb. *Chûshay,* "hasty."] An Archite, who was a friend and leading counselor of David. His success in defeating Ahithophel's wicked counsel saved David during Absalom's rebellion (2 Sa 15:32-37; 16:16-18; 17:5-16; 1 Chr 27:33). Baana, one of Solomon's supply officers, may have been his son (1 Ki 4:16).

Husham (hū'shăm). [Heb. *Chusham,* meaning uncertain.] A king of Edom from Teman (Gen 36:34, 35; 1 Chr 1:45, 46).

Hushathite. *See* Hushah.

Hushim (hū'shĭm). [Heb. *Chûshîm.*]

1. A son of Dan and ancestral head of a tribal family (Gen 46:23), called *Shuham in Num 26:42.

2. A Benjamite (1 Chr 7:12).

3. One of the 3 wives of the Benjamite Shaharaim (1 Chr 8:8, 11).

Husk. The rendering of: (1) the Heb. *zag* (Num 6:4), "skin (of grape)"; (2) the Heb. *şiqqalôn* (2 Ki 4:42), a word not understood until discovered in Ugaritic with the meaning "green ear of grain" (W. F. Albright, *JBL* 71 [1952], 250); (3) the Gr. *keration* (Lk 15:16), literally, "little horn," in the context probably designating the carob pod.

Huz. *See* Uz, 2.

Huzzab (hŭz'ăb). [Heb. *Huşşab,* of uncertain derivation.] According to the KJV either an Assyrian queen or a name personifying Nineveh (Nah 2:7). However, the meaning of the Hebrew word is uncertain. The RSV conjecturally translates *huşşab,* "mistress."

Hyena. The translation in two instances (Is 13:22; 34:14; RSV) of the Heb. *'î*, generally meaning "isle" or "coastland," but obviously not in these verses, where some animal, or creature, seems clearly to be indicated by the context. The KJV conjecturally translates the plural form "wild beasts of the island(s)," but the RSV "hyenas." Some scholars think that ghostlike island creatures or demons are meant. The hyena (*Hyaena striata*) is a wild animal found in all parts of Palestine today, and must have been as common in ancient times. It lives in tombs and caves, and emerges after dark to plunder graves and to hunt for prey. In the apocryphal book of Ecclesiasticus (ch 13:18) "hyena" is the translation of the Heb. *sabúa'*. This definition would make the "valley of Zeboim" (1 Sa 13:18) mean "valley of hyenas."

Hymenaeus (hī'mĕ-nē'ŭs). [Gr. *Humenaios*, "pertaining to Hymen (the god of marriage)."] A Christian who apostatized, being guilty of blasphemy and of disseminating the false teaching that the resurrection was an event of the past (1 Ti 1:19, 20; 2 Ti 2:17, 18). For their blasphemy he and his associate, Alexander, were delivered "unto Satan," an action that doubtless included disfellowshiping from the church. If Paul had hoped that this act would have a salutary effect on the offenders, he was disappointed, at least with regard to Hymenaeus, for when Paul wrote the second letter to Timothy, Hymenaeus was still active in apostasy.

Hymn. [Gr. *humnos, psalmos*.] Matthew and Mark record that Jesus and His disciples sang a hymn after the Passover meal (Mt 26:30; Mk 14:26). They doubtless sang a part of the Passover Hallel (Ps 113 to 118), which the Jews were accustomed to sing in connection with the Passover feast. Paul and Silas sang hymns while imprisoned at Philippi (Acts 16:25). Paul admonished Christians to communicate with one another in "psalms and hymns and spiritual songs," perhaps in the form of antiphonal singing (Eph 5:19; Col 3:16). The exact difference between these 3 terms is not certain. It has been suggested that the "hymns" and "spiritual songs" may have been songs or odes distinctively Christian rather than Jewish in character, such as the OT psalms were. The "hymn" (Gr. *psalmos*) mentioned in 1 Cor 14:26, RSV, rendered "psalm" in the KJV, was probably one of the psalms of the book of Psalms.

Hypocrisy. *See* Hypocrite.

Hypocrite. One who pretends to be someone, or something, other and often better than he really is. In the OT, "hypocrite" is used in the KJV to render the Heb. *chaneph*, "godless," one who has turned away and alienated himself from God rather than one who has acted a deceptive part. The RSV usually renders *chaneph* as "godless" and "godless man" (Job 8:13; Prov 11:9; Is 33:14). The related noun *choneph*, which appears in the KJV of Is 32:6 as "hypocrisy," is properly rendered "ungodliness" by the RSV. In the NT both the RSV and the KJV correctly use "hypocrite" to render the Gr. *hupokritēs* (from which the English word is derived), a term that was often used by the ancient Greeks in the sense of "actor," that is, one who acted a part in one of the dramas of which the Greeks were fond. Related to this word is the Greek noun *hupokrisis*, usually rendered "hypocrisy" in the KJV (Mt 23:28; Mk 12:15; etc.), but also "insincerity" (1 Pe 2:1) and "pretension" (1 Ti 4:2) in the RSV.

Hyssop. [Heb. *'ezôb;* Akkadian *zûpu;* Gr. *hussōpos*.] The Hebrew and Greek terms thus translated most probably refer to the gray-green marjoram (*Origanum maru*). The plant is small and has hairy stems ending in a mass of tiny white flowers. It has a pungent, fragrant smell, and its taste is not unlike peppermint. Its leaves and stems are succulent, and in modern times the plant has been used as a spice or condiment, even medicinally. It is found everywhere in Palestine, springing up among rocks, in terraces, and from walls (1 Ki 4:33). In addition to its use in the original Passover ritual (Ex 12:22), hyssop was employed on the day of the cleansing of a leper or a house (Lev 14:6, 7, 49), in connection with the offering of the red heifer, and with the purification of men and items unclean through contact with the dead (Num 19:6, 17, 18). According to Heb 9:19, 20 Moses used hyssop at the ratification of the covenant. To the psalmist hyssop was symbolic of cleansing (Ps 51:7).

There has been much discussion over the reading "hyssop" in Jn 19:29, for a plant with a long stem seems to be indicated. Some conjecture that the original reading was *hussos*, "javelin," instead of *hussōpos*, "hyssop," and an 11th-cent. manuscript actually reads *hussos*. Others conjecture that there is some connection with the hyssop of the original Passover (Ex 12:22).

I

Ibex, KJV **Pygarg.** [Heb. *dîshôn.*] An animal classified in Deut 14:5 as clean and hence fit for food. The exact identity of *dishôn* is uncertain. Both "ibex" and "pygarg" are conjectural translations. The ibex is a species of wild goat, the male of which has large recurved horns. The pygarg (*Antilope addax*) belongs to the family of antelopes, and is a native of northeastern Africa. It is about the size of an ass, and has twisted and ringed horns.

Ibhar (ĭb′här). [Heb. *Yibchar,* "he chooses."] A son of David born at Jerusalem (2 Sa 5:15; 1 Chr 14:5).

Ibis. [Heb. *yanshûph,* from *nashaph,* "to blow."] A term appearing once (Lev 11:17, RSV); however, in Deut 14:16 the RSV renders the same Hebrew word "great owl," and in Is 34:11, "owl." The exact species of unclean bird designated by *yanshûph* is uncertain. Some suggest the Egyptian eagle owl, others the long-eared owl. Driver suggests the screech owl (*PEQ* 87 [1955], 20). The ibis is a wading bird of the family *Threskiornithidae,* related to the *herons. The sacred ibis was venerated by the ancient Egyptians.

Ibleam (ĭb′lĕ-ăm). [Heb. *Yible'am,* "people's canal."] The city is mentioned in the list of Palestinian cities of Thutmose III as *Ybr'm.*] A Canaanite city south of Jezreel, in the territory of Manasseh, which was not captured from the Canaanites at the time of the conquest (Jos 17:11; Jgs 1:27). In its vicinity King Ahaziah of Judah was fatally wounded (2 Ki 9:27), and, according to the LXX version of ch 15:10, which is followed by the RSV, King Zechariah of Israel was slain there. Ibleam was assigned to the Levites according to 1 Chr 6:70 (there called Bileam, bĭl′ĕ-ăm, Heb. *Bil'am*). It has been identified with *Tell Bel'ameh,* about 5 mi. northeast of Dothan (Map VI, D-3).

Ibneiah (ĭb[nē′yá). [Heb. *Yibneyah,* "Yahweh builds."] A Benjamite and head of a tribal family (1 Chr 9:8).

Ibnijah (ĭb-nī′já). [Heb. *Yibniyah,* "Yahweh builds."] A Benjamite and ancestor of Ibneiah (1 Chr 9:8).

Ibri (ĭb′rī). [Heb. *'Ibri,* "Hebrew."] A Merarite Levite (1 Chr 24:27).

Ibsam (ĭb′săm), KJV **Jibsam** (jĭb′săm). [Heb. *Yibsam,* "perfume."] The ancestral head

of a tribal family of Issachar (1 Chr 7:2).

Ibzan (ĭb′zăn). [Heb. *'Ibsan,* meaning uncertain.] A judge who ruled Israel for 7 years. He was a native of Bethlehem in Zebulun, a city about 7 mi. west-northwest of Nazareth (Map VI, C-3). He had 30 sons and 30 daughters (Jgs 12:8-10). Nothing more is known of him.

Ice. [Heb. *qerach.*] Scriptural writers recognized ice as one of nature's phenomena and saw in this substance a reflection of the glory of the Creator (Job 38:29; Ps 147:17). *Qerach,* depending on the context, may also mean "frost" (Jer 36:30), or "crystal" (Eze 1:22). *See* Crystal; Snow.

Ichabod (ĭk′á-bŏd). [Heb. *'Ikabod,* "the glory is departed," according to the interpretation given in 1 Sa 4:21. The name is probably an abbreviation of *'achi-kabôd,* "woe (that is, gone is) the glory," or stands for *'i-kabôd,* "where is the glory?"] A son of the priest Phinehas, and grandson of the high priest Eli. He was born immediately following his mother's receiving the tragic news of the death of her husband and father-in-law, and of the capture of the ark by the Philistines. She died shortly afterward but before her death named her son Ichabod to commemorate Israel's shameful defeat (1 Sa 4:19-22; 14:3).

Iconium (ī-cō′nĭ-ŭm). [Gr. *Ikonion.*] An important city of inland Asia Minor, lying as an oasis in the high, waterless plain of Lycaonia. Xenophon called it a border town of Phrygia, but otherwise it was considered the capital of Lycaonia, until it was incorporated into the Roman province of Galatia in 25 B.C. The city has been continuously inhabited and is now called *Konya.* Paul and Barnabas preached in Iconium during their 1st Missionary Journey and founded a Christian church there, but had to flee when persecution broke out (Acts 13:51; 14:1-6). Jews from that city stirred up hatred against them in Lystra (ch 14:19). However, later on the same journey Paul returned to Iconium (v 21), and again visited there on his 2d Missionary Journey (ch 16:2), possibly also on his 3d Journey (ch 18:23). Map XX, B-5.

Idalah (ĭd′á-lá). [Heb. *Yid'alah.*] A border town of Zebulun (Jos 19:15), identified with *Khirbet el-Ḥawârah*, ⅔ mi. south of Bethlehem in Galilee.

Idbash (ĭd′băsh). [Heb. *Yidbash*, "honey."] A Judahite (1 Chr 4:3).

Iddo, I (ĭd′ō). [Heb. *'Iddô*, a name occurring in cuneiform records as *Iddûa*.] The head of a community of Levites and Nethinim at Casiphia in Babylonia whom Ezra asked to send certain members of that community to accompany him to Jerusalem (Ezr 8:17-20).

Iddo, II (ĭd′ō). [Heb. *Yiddô*, meaning uncertain.] A chief of Manasseh in Gilead under David (1 Chr 27:21).

Iddo, III (ĭd′ō). [Heb. *'Iddo'*.] A man whose son Ahinadab was one of Solomon's supply officers (1 Ki 4:14).

Iddo, IV (ĭd′ō). [Heb. *'Iddô*, once (2 Chr 9:29) *Ye'di* (Q *Ye'dô*).]

1. A seer, or prophet, who wrote accounts of the reigns of Solomon, Jeroboam, Rehoboam, and Abijah (2 Chr 9:29; 12:15; 13:22).

2. A Gershonite Levite (1 Chr 6:21).

Iddo, V (ĭd′ō). [Heb. *'Iddô'*, once (Zec 1:1) *'Iddô*; Aramaic *'Iddô'*.]

1. The head of a priestly family who returned with Zerubbabel from Babylonia (Neh 12:4, 16).

2. The (grand)father of the prophet Zechariah (Zec 1:1, 7; Ezr 5:1; 6:14). He may be identical with Iddo, V, 1.

Idol, Image. A figure, statue, likeness, etc., venerated as a representation of a deity. An idol, in a broad sense, may refer to any tangible object that is worshiped as a god or as the symbol of a god. "Image," being somewhat more restricted in meaning, usually designates a manufactured likeness that supposedly pictures the deity involved. In the Bible these terms are used as a translation of many Hebrew and Greek terms, few of which correspond exactly to the English renderings. A number of the Biblical words are technical terms that refer to the form or nature of the idol or to the manner in which it was made; others represent various expressions of contempt for the absurdities and degradation of idolatry. Important Biblical words include: (1) the Heb. *'elîl*, "no god," "nothing" (Ps 96:5; Is 2:8); (2) the Heb. *gillûlîm*, "dung pellets," a contemptuous term for false gods (1 Ki 21:26; Eze 14:3-7); (3) the Heb. *pesel*, an idol that is carved, but, in later writings, also a molten or cast image; in the KJV, usually translated "graven image" (Ex 20:4; Is 40:19, 20; 44:9, 10); (4) the Heb. *ṣelem*, "image," "likeness," generally close

to the English "image" in its force (Eze 23:14; Amos 5:26); (5) the Gr. *eidôlon* (from which English "idol" is derived), "idol" (Acts 7:41; 1 Cor 12:2; 1 Jn 5:21); (6) the Gr. *eikōn*, "image," "likeness" (Rom 1:23; cf. its basic meaning of "likeness" in Mt 22:20; 2 Cor 4:4; etc.). See figs. 32, 493.

Idolatry. [Heb. *teraphîm, gillûlîm*; Gr. *eidôlolatria*.] According to Bible usage idolatry includes both the worship of false gods in various forms and the worship of images as symbols of Jehovah. The NT broadens the concept of idolatry to include such practices as gluttony (Php 3:19) and such attitudes as covetousness (Eph 5:5). This is in harmony with the spiritualizing emphasis of the NT.

Idolatry has been practiced from early times. The immediate ancestors of Abraham "served other gods" (Jos 24:2). The patriarchs were committed to a monotheistic worship of Jehovah, but members of their households were sometimes influenced by idolatry (Gen 31:30, 32-35; 35:1-4). Idolatry was a frequent sin of Israel (Deut 32:16; 2 Ki 17:12; Ps 106:38), and was of more than passing concern to the early Christian church (1 Cor 12:2). Canaanitish heathenism was popular because of its low ethical standards in contrast to the high standards of right and wrong of the Hebrews' religion, and the more demanding religion was often denied for the easier worship of Baal.

The problem of idolatry was so acute that the 1st 2 commandments of the Decalogue dealt in a very definite way with this phase of religious life (Ex 20:3-6). During the Exodus period there were 2 noteworthy violations of these commandments. The 1st was the worship of the golden calf (ch 32), and the 2d the apostasy at Shittim, during which Israel became involved in the licentious practices of Moabitish idolatry (Num 25:1, 2).

From the time of the conquest of Canaan to the Babylonian captivity idolatry was a persistent, undermining influence in the experience of Israel. In the earlier period there was a series of cycles: Israel would lapse into idolatry and would fall victim of aggression. In time a judge would arise who would free the people from oppression and restore the worship of Jehovah. This pattern was repeated over and over (see Ps 106). This fluctuating between the worship of Israel's God and idolatry continued during the time of the kings, and idolatry was frequently strengthened by intermarriage and political alliances (1 Ki 11:1-13; etc.). The battle against idolatry in these times was spearheaded by the prophets. Elijah defied idolatrous Ahab (ch 21:17-27); Amos warned of the captivity that would be the result of idol worship (Amos 5:1, 26, 27). Hosea denounced "the calf of Samaria" (Hos 8:4-6); Isaiah ridiculed the folly of worshiping the works of one's own hands (Is 44:9-20); Jeremiah foretold divine fury as a result of idol worship (Jer 7:16-20, 29-34); Ezekiel predicted desolation because of idolatry (Eze 6). Repetition of these warnings is extremely frequent, indicating the seriousness of the problem in OT times.

During the Captivity the Israelites learned their lesson regarding idolatry. Their revulsion against images became so strong and was so lasting that centuries later the Jews considered even the ensigns of the Roman army as polluting (Jos. *War* ii. 9. 2, 3); they went so far as to destroy the golden eagle on Herod's Temple (Jos. *Ant.* xvii. 6. 2, 3), and every effort was made to isolate themselves from every influence that might lead toward idolatry. The new synagogue worship, which was common in NT times, was an effective protection against foreign influence. The former tendency to fraternize with surrounding nations gave place to a fanatical isolationism (Jn 4:9; Acts 10:28) that had its unwholesome aspects.

Converts from heathenism in NT times were in constant danger of lapsing back into idolatry, hence the frequent warnings of the NT (1 Cor 5:10, 11; 6:9; 10: 7; Eph 5:5; Rev 21:8; 22:15; etc.). One of the perplexing problems that arose was the propriety of eating foods sacrificed to idols. Some converts from heathenism could not with a clear conscience eat foods that had thus been dedicated. Paul urged that these Christians be treated with consideration, and their consciences not be violated by the more enlightened Christian to whom an idol was nothing and food sacrificed to idols not different from ordinary food (1 Cor 8; cf. Rom 14).

The genius of Judaism and Christianity has been ethical monotheism. The beliefs that "God is one" and that "God is concerned about what people do" stand in contrast with the degraded polytheism of the centuries.

Idumea (ĭd′ū-mē′ȧ). [Heb. *'Edôm;* Gr. *Idoumaia.*] The name used by the Greeks and Romans for Edom (Mk 3:8). In the KJV OT the term occurs several times for Edom, the land area between the Dead Sea and the Gulf of Aqabah. In the intertestamental and NT periods the name Idumea designated an area to the west and northwest of old Edom in southern Judah (Map I, C-1/2). This area received the name Idumea from the Edomites because they had moved into the south of Judah after the fall of Jerusalem in 586 B.C., and again after being driven out from their former homeland by the Arabic Nabataeans in the 4th cent. B.C. In Maccabean times the Edomites held such important Hebrew cities as Beth-zur and Hebron (1 Macc 4:29; 5:65). The Maccabean ruler John Hyrcanus finally subjugated them and forced them to accept the Jewish religion (Jos. *Ant.* xiii. 9. 1). As Jewish proselytes they thus technically became Jews and were regarded as part of the Jewish nation. The Herods were of Idumean descent.

Iezer. See Abiezer, 1.

Iezerite. See Abiezerite.

Igal (ī′găl), KJV once **Igeal** (ī′gē-ăl). [Heb. *Yig'al,* "he redeems."]
1. The spy representing the tribe of Issachar (Num 13:7).
2. A son of Nathan of Zobah; one of the "mighty men" of David (2 Sa 23:36), considered by some to be either identical with the Joel of 1 Chr 11:38, or his relative.
3. A son of Shemaiah, and descendant of Jehoiachin (Jeconiah, 1 Chr 3:22).

Igdaliah (ĭg′dȧ-lī′ȧ). [Heb. *Yigdalyahû,* "Yahweh is great."] The father of Hanan (Jer 35:4).

Igeal. See Igal.

Iim (ī′ĭm), RSV once **Iyim** (ī′yim). [Heb. *'Îyîm,* "ruins."]
1. An abbreviated form of *Iye-abarim (Num 33:45; cf. v 44).
2. A town in the extreme south of Judah near Edom (Jos 15:29); not yet identified with certainty.

Ije-abarim. See Iye-abarim.

Ijon (ī′jŏn). [Heb. *'Îyôn,* "ruin."] A city in the extreme north of Israel, near Dan. It was captured by Ben-hadad of Damascus at the request of Asa of Judah (1 Ki 15:20; 2 Chr 16:4), and was later taken and depopulated by Tiglath-pileser III of Assyria (2 Ki 15:29). It is mentioned in Egyptian records of the Middle Kingdom as *'ynw.* The ancient name has survived in that of the plain of *Merj 'Ayyûn.* The site has been tentatively identified with *Tell ed-Dibbin,* about 11 mi. northwest of Banias (Map IX, B-4).

Ikkesh (ĭk'ĕsh). [Heb. *'Iqqesh,* "crooked."] A man whose son Ira was one of David's "mighty men" (2 Sa 23:26; 1 Chr 11:28; 27:9).

Ilai (ī'lȧ-ī). [Heb. *'Ilay.*] One of David's "mighty men" (1 Chr 11:29), apparently called Zalmon in 2 Sa 23:28.

Illyricum (ĭ-lĭr'ĭ-kŭm). [Gr. *Illurikon.*] A coastal area on the Adriatic Sea north of Macedonia. It is a mountainous territory and was inhabited in early times by a wild, warlike, and independent people. It was not until the 3d cent. b.c. that the first kingdom was formed, uniting under one head the various tribes of the area. The Romans fought against this kingdom at different times with varying success. In 229 and 219 b.c. they partially subdued the Illyrians; in 168 they annexed the country, but for many years the Illyrians in Dalmatia resisted with considerable success, until Octavian defeated them in 33 b.c. A few years later rebellion broke out again, and still later they joined the Pannonians in the great revolt of a.d. 6-9. This rebellion was put down by Tiberius, and Dalmatia, Iapydia, and Liburnia were united as the province of Illyricum. This was the political status of the area during Paul's ministry in Macedonia and Achaia. In Paul's reference to Illyricum in Rom 15:19 the Roman province consisting of Illyricum and Dalmatia is probably meant. However, it is not clear whether the apostle had included that province in his missionary itinerary or whether it merely marked the limit of the territory of his labors. Map XX, A-3.

Image. *See* Idol.

Image of Jealousy. [Heb. *semel haqqin'ah.*] An image Ezekiel saw in vision at the gate of the inner court of the Temple at Jerusalem (Eze 8:3). No image by this name is mentioned elsewhere in the Bible or in extant ancient literature. Some have suggested that it represented Baal, Molech, or Astarte. The image may have represented some specific idol that provoked God to jealousy, or idolatry in general carried out in the Temple precincts.

Imlah (ĭm'lȧ), KJV twice **Imla** (ĭm'lȧ). [Heb. *Yimlah* and *Yimla'*, "he fills."] An Israelite whose son Micaiah was a prophet in the time of King Ahab (1 Ki 22:8, 9; 2 Chr 18:7, 8).

Immanuel (ĭ-măn'ū-ĕl), or **Emmanuel** (ĕ-măn'ū-ĕl). [Heb. *'Immanû 'El*, "God is with us"; Gr. *Emmanouēl.*] The sign-child foretold by the prophet Isaiah in conversation with Ahaz, king of Judah (Is 7:14), applied by Matthew to Jesus of Nazareth (Mt 1:23). Alarmed at an alliance between Pekah, king of Israel, and Rezin, king of Syria, against Judah (Is 7:2, 5, 6), Ahaz turned to Tiglath-pileser III, king of Assyria, for help (2 Ki 16:6-9; 2 Chr 28:16; Is 8:9-12). Anticipating imminent attack, Ahaz went out to inspect the water supply of the city. Isaiah met him on the way with the message not to fear Pekah and Rezin but to trust in the Lord (Is 7:4-7; 8:13, 14). In token of the promised deliverance, Isaiah, whose name means "Yahweh saves," foretold the birth of a son to be named Immanuel, meaning "God is with us," as a token and reminder of God's abiding presence. Before this sign-child should reach the age of accountability Pekah and Rezin would both fall before the Assyrians (ch 8:7, 8, 16). This prediction, made about 734 b.c., was literally fulfilled. Tiglath-pileser captured Damascus and killed Rezin 2 years later (2 Ki 16:9, 10), then devastated Gilead and Galilee, took a vast number of captives, and arranged for the assassination of Pekah (2 Ki 15:29, 30; 1 Chr 5:26; Is 8:4). The kingdom of Israel disappeared altogether 12 years later, with the fall of Samaria to the Assyrians in 723/22 b.c. (cf. Is 7:8). Repeated Assyrian invasions during the next few years also devastated all the land of Judah, except for Jerusalem itself (2 Ki 18:13 to 19:34; 2 Chr 32:1-20; Is 36:1 to 37:20). Nevertheless, God was with His people to spare the remnant in Jerusalem in a miraculous way (2 Ki 19:35-37; 2 Chr 32:21, 22; Is 37:21-38). Had Ahaz trusted the Lord, Judah would have been spared this fearful experience altogether, as implied in the name of the sign-child—"God is with us" (Is 7:14). But Ahaz' persistent refusal to rely on the Lord instead of on the Assyrian alliance resulted in great suffering for Judah (ch 8:7, 8, 21, 22). In irony the prophet speaks of Judah as Immanuel's land—"God is with us"—comparing what actually took place with what might have been (vs 8, 10).

Matthew (Mt 1:23; cf. Is 7:14) quotes Is 7:14 and applies it to Christ. The name Immanuel thus originated in an actual historical situation as a promise that God would be with His people to deliver them from their immediate enemies. But Isaiah also looked forward by inspiration to the time when God would send His own Son, the true Immanuel, who would deliver His people from all their enemies.

By inspiration Matthew thus picked up the prophecy of Isaiah and declared that it was to meet its fulfillment in the person of Jesus Christ, who was born of a virgin, and who was in the supreme sense "God with us."

Immer (ĭm′ẽr). [Heb. *'Immer,* "lamb."]

1. The ancestral head of the 16th of the 24 courses into which David organized the priests (1 Chr 9:12; 24:14). Members from this priestly family returned from Babylonia with Zerubbabel (Ezr 2:37; Neh 7:40), two of whom were married to foreign wives (Ezr 10:20). One member of this family, Amashai, was apparently occupying a prominent position in the time of Nehemiah (Neh 11:13). Those listed under Immer, 2 and 3, may be identical with Immer, 1.

2. A priest, the father or ancestor of Pashhur (Jer 20:1). He may be identical with Immer, 1.

3. A Jew whose son or descendant, Zadok, assisted Nehemiah in rebuilding the wall of Jerusalem (Neh 3:29).

4. A place in Babylonia from which some of the Jews returned to Jerusalem with Zerubbabel after the Exile (Ezr 2:59; Neh 7:61); not identified.

Immortality. [Gr. *athanasia,* "deathlessness"; *aphtharsia,* "incorruptibility."] The term "immortality" occurs only 5 times in the Bible. "Immortal" (Gr. *aphthartos*) occurs twice (once in KJV). God is described as being immortal (1 Ti 1:17; Rom 1:23, RSV), and as alone possessing immortality (1 Ti 6:16). The Christian is described as seeking for immortality (Rom 2:7), which Christ brought to light through the gospel (2 Ti 1:10), and which the overcomer receives "at the last trump" (1 Cor 15:53, 54). It is obvious that not one of these texts gives the least support to the widely held view that immortality is inherent in man.

According to Gen 2:7 at Creation "man became a living soul" as the result of the reception of the breath of life from God. Thus is established the principle that life is derived from God. The corollary of this principle is that the continuation of human life is in the hands of God. This is the philosophical basis of the Bible doctrine of the resurrection (Dan 12:2; 1 Cor 15:51-54; 1 Th 4:16, 17).

The fate of the unredeemed is not immortality in hell, but the denial to them of immortality. The Scriptures declare concerning the wicked, "Fire came down from God out of heaven and devoured them"

(Rev 20:9). By contrast those who believe on Christ will not "perish but have eternal life" (Jn 3:16, RSV; cf. v 36). At the "last trump" they "put on immortality" (1 Cor 15:51-53; cf. 2 Cor 5:4). Contrary to Bible teaching, many devout theologians through the centuries have held the belief that man is inherently immortal. Others have upheld the doctrine of conditional immortality, among them William Temple, late Archbishop of Canterbury, who writes: "Man is not immortal by nature or of right; but he is capable of immortality and there is offered to him resurrection from the dead and life eternal if he will receive it from God and on God's terms" (*Nature, Man, and God* [New York: Macmillan & Company, Ltd., St. Martin's Press, 1949], p. 472).

Emil Brunner, of the University of Zurich, declares: "The opinion that we men are immortal because our soul is of an indestructible, because divine, essence is, once for all, irreconcilable with the Biblical view of God and man" (from *Eternal Hope,* by Emil Brunner [tr. by Harold Knight, published 1954, Westminster Press, Philadelphia], pp. 105, 106).

The NT teaches that man, through his acceptance of Christ, may enjoy a foretaste of immortality in his spiritual experience in the present life. "And this is life eternal, that they might know thee the only true God, and Jesus Christ, whom thou hast sent" (Jn 17:3; cf. Rom 6:8; 8:11). Eternal life, or immortality, is a gift of God's grace to those who have faith.

Imna (ĭm′nȧ). [Heb. *Yimna',* "he withholds."] An Asherite (1 Chr 7:35).

Imnah (ĭm′nȧ), KJV once **Jimna** (jĭm′nȧ) and once **Jimnah** (jĭm′nȧ). [Heb. *Yimnah,* "he counts."]

1. Son of Asher and founder of a tribal family called the Jimnites (jĭm′nīts) or Imnites (ĭm′nīts) [Heb. *Yimnah*] (Gen 46:17; Num 26:44; 1 Chr 7:30).

2. A Levite whose son Kore served in King Hezekiah's time (2 Chr 31:14).

Imnites. *See* Imnah, 1.

Imrah (ĭm′rȧ). [Heb. *Yimrah,* "he resists."] An Asherite (1 Chr 7:36).

Imri (ĭm′rī). [Heb. *'Imri,* a contracted form of Amariah, "Yahweh speaks."]

1. A Judahite (1 Chr 9:4).

2. An Israelite whose son Zaccur assisted Nehemiah in rebuilding the wall of Jerusalem (Neh 3:2).

Incense. [Heb. *qeṭoreth;* Phoenician *qṭr;* Ugaritic *qṭr;* Akkadian *qutrênu;* all are loan words from the Egyptian *qdrt;* Gr.

thumiama.] A mixture of fragrant substances, such as gum resins and spices, used in connection with religious worship. The incense prescribed for use in the tabernacle consisted of equal parts of *stacte (possibly opobalsamum), *onycha, galbanum, and frankincense, and was seasoned with salt. It was forbidden to use a mixture made according to this recipe for other purposes (Ex 30:34-38). In the Mosaic system incense was burned morning and evening upon a special *altar that stood in the holy place of the sanctuary (see fig. 471) in front of the curtain that separated this apartment from the Most Holy Place (Ex 30:1-9; Lk 1:8-10). At the annual Day of Atonement the high priest entered the Most Holy Place and burned incense in a censer, the smoke of which enveloped the ark (Lev 16:12, 13). Burning of incense was also connected with the religious rites of the pagans (2 Chr 34:25; Jer 48:35).

Incense Altar. Most of the small altars in homes throughout the ancient world were probably used as incense altars. Many have been found in the excavations of ancient sites (*see* Altar). One discovered at Lachish carries an inscription in Aramaic that indicates that it was used for offering incense (W. F. Albright, *BASOR* 132 [1953], 46, 47). Incense altars devoted to pagan deities are frequently mentioned in the Bible (2 Chr 14:5; 34:4, 7; Is 17:8; RSV; etc.). For the incense altar in the tabernacle *see* Altar; fig. 471.

India (ĭn'dĭ-à). [Heb. *Hoddû,* from the Old Persian *Hidauw* and *Hinduish.*] India is mentioned in the Bible only in Est 1:1 and 8:9 and there as part of the Persian Empire in the time of Ahasuerus, or Xerxes. Darius I, Xerxes' father, had conquered an area on the lower Indus (the present Sind; Map XII, E-12/13), and incorporated this into his empire (Herod. iii. 94; iv. 44). Consequently it is found in several lists of Darius and Xerxes as one of the countries of the Persian Empire (R. G. Kent, *Old Persian* [New Haven, Conn., 1953], p. 214; under "Hindu" all references are given).

Indite. A term found only in the KJV of Ps 45:1, as the rendering of the Heb. *rachash,* which means "to be excited," or "to be stirred."

Infidel. A term appearing twice (2 Cor 6:15; 1 Ti 5:8; KJV), a rendering of the Gr. *apistos,* "lacking in faith," "unbelieving." *Apistos* is translated "unbeliever" in 2 Cor 6:14.

Infirmity. The rendering of various Hebrew and Greek synonyms that refer to sickness in general or to feebleness and weakness of any kind. In the NT "infirmity" is most frequently the translation of the Gr. *astheneia,* "weakness" or "sickness" (Lk 5:15; 13:11; Rom 8:26; Heb 4:15; KJV; etc.).

Inflammation. The rendering in Deut 28:22 of the Heb. *dalleqeth,* "burning fever," a term regarded by Jewish writers as referring to ague. In Lev 13:28, KJV, "inflammation" appears as the rendering of Heb. *ṣarebeth,* a word that means "scar (from a burn)" (see RSV).

Ingathering, Feast of. *See* Tabernacles, Feast of.

Inheritance. [Heb. generally *nachalah;* Gr. *klēronomia,* both denoting "hereditary property," "family estate."] In the Biblical sense, especially the property allocated to the various Israelite tribes and families when they settled in Canaan. The allotment of land (designated by the Heb. *cheleq,* "share" [RSV "portion"], as in Jos 15:13, or *nachalah,* "family estate," "inheritance," as in Num 26:54) was to remain in the permanent possession of the original family, as a trust from the Lord. It was not to be sold (Lev 25:23) except in case of financial distress; and even then the sale was to be only temporary, with the right of redemption (vs 25-27) at any time and with compulsory return to the first family in the year of jubilee (vs 10, 28). Guiding principles for the transmission of the ancestral property included: (1) The principal heir to the family estate was ordinarily the first-born son who, because of the birthright, received a double portion of all his father's wealth (*see* Birthright). (2) When there was no son, the inheritance passed to the daughters, who kept the property title if they married within their own tribe (Num 27:8; 36:6-9). (3) If there was no son or daughter to be the heir, a near relative could assume the inheritance (ch 27:9-11), with the right to redeem any land that had been temporarily sold (Lev 25:25; cf. Ruth 4:3-9). Such a relative was required by the "levirate marriage" law (Deut 25:5-10) to marry the surviving widow and to name their first-born son as the legal heir and successor of the deceased (cf. Ruth 4:10).

"Inheritance" is also used in figurative expressions and for symbolic concepts. For example, the people of God were anciently described as the "portion" or "lot of his [God's] inheritance" (Deut 32:9),

or simply "his inheritance" (Ps 78:71).
And in the NT Jesus represented Himself as the "heir" who came to the family
property which was in the hands of tenant
farmers (Mt 21:33-38). "Inheritance" is
also used to describe the future home of
the saved (Col 3:24; 1 Pe 1:4; etc.), and
the followers of Christ are spoken of as
"heirs" (Gal 3:29; Tit 3:7; etc.) and
"joint-heirs with Christ" (Rom 8:17).

Iniquity. *See* Sin, 1.

Ink. [Heb. *deyô;* Gr. *melan.*] A writing fluid
of red or black color used on papyrus,
leather, parchment, or on potsherds. Red
ink was made of ocher and a gum solution. The earliest black ink was made of
soot or powdered charcoal which was

242. Three inkpots from the 1st cent. A.D. found at
Khirbet Qumrán. The one in the center is of bronze,
the others of burned clay

mixed with a gum solution, but metallic
ink was used in the ancient East long before the Roman period. This was demonstrated by a scientific analysis of the ink
used in the Lachish Letters from the time
of Jeremiah. The analysis showed that it
contained iron, probably derived from
oak galls (A. Lewis, in *Lachish I* [London, 1938], pp. 188-193). Examinations
thus far have revealed that the ink used
in writing the Dead Sea scrolls is of pure
carbon. Egyptian scribes usually carried
dry ink in the form of little cakes which
they mixed with a fluid on a palette before use. Ink is mentioned in the following Biblical passages: Jer 36:18; 2 Cor
3:3; 2 Jn 12; 3 Jn 13.

Inkhorn. *See* Writing Case.

Inlaid. A term occurring once (Eze 27:6,
RSV), where the word has been supplied

by the translators. The exact meaning
of the Hebrew passage is not clear.

Inn. [Gr. *kataluma,* "lodging," literally, a
place of loosening burdens for a rest;
pandocheion, "inn," from *pas* and *dechomai,* "to receive every one."] The ancient world knew of no hotels in the
modern sense, and guesthouses differed
considerably from those of our time. Caravansaries were mere shelters for beasts and
men (see fig. 17) around a courtyard that
had a well or spring. Any rooms provided
were unfurnished; travelers slept on their
own mats or garments, and brought their
own food. For the OT word rendered
"inn" in the KJV, *see* Lodging. The
"inn" (*kataluma*) of Lk 2:7 is held by
some to be a guest room or rather a guestchamber, because *kataluma* is rendered
thus in the other two NT passages where
it occurs (Mk 14:14; Lk 22:11). The
"inn" (*pandocheion*) of Lk 10:34, however, may have been a real guesthouse. In
the story of the good Samaritan the term
"inn" is a justified rendering.

Inquisition. An inquiry or an investigation.
The word occurs 3 times (Deut 19:18; Est
2:23; Ps 9:12; KJV), always in the phrase
"to make inquisition." The phrase is the
rendering of several Hebrew verbs meaning "to inquire" or "to search (into)."

Insects. [Heb. *sheres.*] A term occurring 4
times (Lev 11:20, 21, 23; Deut 14:19;
RSV), always in the phrase "winged insects." *Sheres* describes swarming things
in general, and the adjective "winged"
suggests that insects are meant in the passages cited above. *See* Creeping Things.

Inspiration. God's method of influencing and
directing the minds of men in the process
of making them channels of divine revelation. This word does not appear in the
RSV, although the term "inspire" is occasionally used (Mt 22:43; 2 Ti 3:16;
etc.). "Inspiration" is found twice in the
KJV: (1) Job 32:8, where "inspiration" is
literally "breath," and (2) 2 Ti 3:16, where
the phrase, "all scripture is given by inspiration of God," is literally, "all scripture is
God-breathed." "The prophecy came not
in old time by the will of man: but holy
men of God spake as they were moved by
the Holy Ghost" (2 Pe 1:20, 21; cf. Mt 22:
43; Mk 12:36; 1 Cor 2:13; Heb 3:7;
etc.). Many of the OT authors asserted
the inspiration of their message by prefacing or closing their statements with
such words as, "saith the Lord" (Is 1:
24; Jer 17:24; Amos 2:1; Zep 1:3; Zec 1:
4; Mal 1:2; etc.), "the Lord spake thus"

(Is 8:11), "the word of the Lord came unto me" (Eze 6:1; 7:1; 14:2; cf. Jon 1:1; etc.), "the Lord said" (Hos 1:2), "the Lord hath spoken it" (Ob 18), etc. The NT writers, and Christ Himself, attested the inspiration of the OT by making reference to it as the word and record of God (Mt 1:22, 23; 3:2, 3; 5:18; 21:42; Mk 1:2, 3; Lk 20:17, 18; Jn 2:15-17; Acts 13:33-37; Rom 15:3; etc.), and Jesus affirmed its authority by stating that "the scripture cannot be broken" (Jn 10:34, 35). Of the NT writers Paul claimed that what he taught was not "by human wisdom but . . . by the Spirit" (1 Cor 2:13, RSV; cf. ch 7:40; 1 Th 2:13; 4:2), and Peter acknowledged Paul's writings as on a par with "other scriptures" (2 Pe 3:15, 16). The revelator claims that his message had its source in God and came to him through an angel (Rev 1:1).

God seems to have employed a variety of means in inspiring the writers of the Bible and others of His servants. To some He gave visions and dreams. To others He gave a spirit of understanding—an insight into the mysteries of God. Others were guided in their recording of events and historical incidents. The human personality was not blotted out or short-circuited, but was enhanced and stimulated.

One of the greatest attestations of the divine inspiration of Scripture is predictive prophecy. God repeatedly referred to His ability to foretell future events as a proof of His own divinity (Is 41:4, 26; 42:9; 43:9; 44:7; 45:11, 21; 46:9, 10; 48:3-7), and challenged the worshipers of idols to prove the genuineness of their gods by having them foretell the future (ch 41:21-23). The Scriptures record many predictions, some of them in remarkable detail, and the fulfillment of them inspires confidence in the authenticity and divine origin of the Bible (Jn 14:29).

See *SDACom* 7:944-946.

Instant. Besides its usual connotation of a brief moment of time, the expression appears occasionally in the KJV as an adjective meaning "pressing" or "urgent," in verb phrases translating: (1) the Gr. *epikeimai*, "to be urgent" (Lk 23:23); (2) the Gr. *proskartereō*, "to persist in" (Rom 12:12); (3) the Gr. *ephistēmi*, "to be ready," "to be on hand" (2 Ti 4:2).

Instrument. In the OT generally a rendering of the Heb. *keli*, a term that broadly designates all sorts of pottery and vessels as well as various tools to aid man in his work. *Keli* is ordinarily rendered "vessel" in the KJV; but it appears as "instru-

ment" when referring to implements of war (1 Sa 8:12; etc.), musical instruments (1 Chr 15:16; Amos 6:5), sacrificial implements (Eze 40:42), and similar but undefined tools, furnishings, utensils, etc. (Num 3:8; 1 Chr 28:14). The Heb. *mórag*, "threshing sledge" is translated "threshing instrument" in 2 Sa 24:22; Is 41:15; KJV. In Rom 6:13 "instruments" is a rendering of the Gr. *hopla*, "weapons."

Intercession. An entreaty or prayer for others; a mediation. The expression appears infrequently in the Bible, though a number of examples of intercessory prayer may be found. In the OT the term occurs in the phrase "to make intercession," as the rendering of the Heb. *paga'*, "to meet," and, in a derived sense, to approach someone in order to plead with him, hence, "to entreat" or "to intercede" (Jer 7:16; 27:18; 36:25; Is 53:12). In the NT this same concept is expressed by several Greek verbs, especially *entugchanō*, that closely parallel *paga'* in their meaning (Rom 8:26, 27, 34; 11:2; Heb 7:25). In 1 Ti 2:1 "intercessions" is the appropriate rendering of the Greek noun *enteuxeis*.

Interdict. A prohibition, an official decree that forbids something. The expression is found only in Dan 6:7-9, 12, 13, 15, RSV, as the rendering of the Aramaic *'esar*, "prohibition" (KJV "decree").

Interest. *See* Loan.

Iob. *See* Jashub.

Iota, KJV **Jot.** [Gr. *iōta*.] The 9th letter of the Greek alphabet transliterated *i*. Jesus declared that not one iota was to pass from the law until all be fulfilled (Mt 5:18, RSV). He was most probably preaching in Aramaic when this saying was uttered, in which case the iota would stand for the Aramaic *yôd*, transliterated *y*, the smallest letter in the Aramaic alphabet.

Iphdeiah (ĭf-dē'yà), KJV **Iphedeiah** (ĭf'ĕ-dē'yà). [Heb. *Yiphdeyah*, "Yahweh redeems."] A descendant of Benjamin (1 Chr 8:25).

Iphedeiah. *See* Iphdeiah.

Iphtah (ĭf'tà), KJV **Jiphtah** (jĭf'tà). [Heb. *Yiphtach*, "he opens."] A town in Judah near Libnah (Jos 15:43); not identified.

Iphtahel (ĭf'tà-ĕl), KJV **Jiphthah-el** (jĭf'-thà-ĕl). [Heb. *Yiphtach-'el*, "God opens."] A valley on the boundary between Zebulun and Asher (Jos 19:14, 27). It has been identified with the *Wâdī el-Melek*, which runs in a northwesterly direction north of Bethlehem in Galilee.

Ir (ĭr). [Heb. *'Ir,* meaning uncertain.] A Benjamite (1 Chr 7:12), considered by some to be identical with Iri (v 7).

Ira (ī'rȧ). [Heb. *'Ira',* meaning uncertain.]
1. A Jairite, David's priest or chief minister (2 Sa 20:26).
2. An Ithrite, one of David's "mighty men" (2 Sa 23:38; 1 Chr 11:40).
3. A Tekoite, also one of David's "mighty men" (2 Sa 23:26; 1 Chr 11:28).

Irad (ī'răd). [Heb. *'Irad,* meaning uncertain.] A descendant of Cain (Gen 4:18).

Iram (ī'răm). [Heb. *'Iram,* meaning uncertain.] A chieftain (KJV "duke") of Edom (Gen 36:43; 1 Chr 1:54).

Iri (ī'rī). [Heb. *'Iri,* meaning uncertain.] A Benjamite (1 Chr 7:7), considered by some to be identical with Ir (v 12).

Irijah (ī-rī'jȧ). [Heb. *Yir'iyayh,* "Yahweh sees."] A guard captain who arrested Jeremiah and accused him of attempting to desert to the enemy when the prophet was leaving Jerusalem to go to the land of Benjamin (Jer 37:13).

Irnahash (ĭr'nȧ'hăsh). [Heb. *'Ir-nachash,* "city of the serpent."] A descendant of Judah (1 Chr 4:12), but generally considered to be the name of a place, because of the meaning of the name. However, no town by such a name has been identified. Nelson Glueck identifies it with the *Khirbet Naḥâs* in the *Wâdī el-'Arabah,* where he found great copper slag heaps and the ruins of smelting furnaces (*PEQ* 72 [1940], 24; *AASOR* 15 [1935], 26-30).

Iron, I. [Heb. *barzel;* Aramaic *parzel;* Gr. *sidēreos.*] In Deut 8:9 the Promised Land is described as "a land whose stones are iron, and out of whose hills thou mayest dig brass." Modern explorations have found ancient iron mines in western Edom, in Midian east of the Gulf of Aqabah, and in the Lebanon Mountains. Since the smelting of iron requires high temperatures, the craft of ironworking took a long time to develop. It was not until the 13th cent. B.C. that iron became common in the ancient world; however, it is wrong to conclude that the metal was unknown in the early centuries of the 2d millennium B.C. or even in the 3d millennium B.C. The earliest iron objects found are usually pieces of jewelry discovered in tombs from periods for which no written records exist. They are of meteoric iron fashioned by beating. That it is meteoric iron is proved by its nickel content, an element not found in terrestrial iron. In Egypt as well as in Sumeria the name for iron was "heavenly metal,"

which indicates a meteoric origin. However, iron in small quantities was produced from terrestrial ores in the 3d millennium B.C. This is shown by tools found embedded in two 4th-dynasty pyramids, as well as by iron implements discovered in Mesopotamia in the early levels of Tell Asmar, Tell Chagar Bazar, and Mari. Furthermore, texts of the time of Hammurabi (18th cent. B.C.) and the *Amarna Letters (14th cent. B.C.) furnish evidence that iron was used in Mesopotamia and Egypt in patriarchal and Mosaic times.

This brief review of non-Biblical evidence for the early use of iron is in harmony with the Biblical record which mentions iron from earliest times. Tubalcain, of the race of Cain, worked in iron (Gen 4:22). Iron objects were used in the Mosaic age (Num 35:16; Deut 3:11; Jos 6:19, 24). The Canaanites' "chariots of iron" (Jos 17:16; Jgs 1:19; 4:3, 13) were not war vehicles made completely of iron but vehicles on which some fittings or trimmings were of iron. This may be illustrated by Thutmose III's reference to Canaanite chariots which he mentions in one place as having gold decorations, but in another as "chariots of gold."

In the time of Saul iron was still extremely scarce among the Hebrews, and the Philistines, who seem to have obtained it either from Anatolia or Cyprus, monopolized it (cf. 1 Sa 17:7; 13:19-22). However, from the time of David onward it became more plentiful, and was used for many things, such as harrows and axes (1 Chr 20:3), builders' tools and nails (1 Ki 6:7; 1 Chr 22:3), tools of engraving (Jer 17:1), bars, fetters, and sheets to cover city gates (Ps 105:18; 107:10, 16; 149:8; Is 45:2; Acts 12:10) and idols (Dan 5:4). In Jer 15:12 the expression

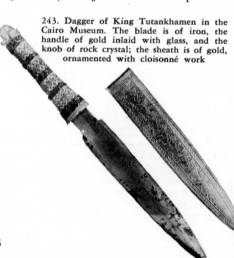

243. **Dagger of King Tutankhamen in the Cairo Museum.** The blade is of iron, the handle of gold inlaid with glass, and the knob of rock crystal; the sheath is of gold, ornamented with cloisonné work

"northern iron" is used. The term "northern" probably suggests that the Hebrews got their iron from the Phoenicians to the north, who themselves probably brought it from Anatolia (Eze 27:12, 19).

Iron, II. *See* Yiron.

Irpeel (ĭr′pē-ĕl). [Heb. *Yirpe'el,* "God heals."] A city in the territory of Benjamin (Jos 18:27); not identified.

Ir-shemesh (ĭr′shē′mĕsh). [Heb. *'Ir Shemesh,* "city of the sun."] A city in Dan (Jos 19: 41), usually called Beth-shemesh. *See* Beth-shemesh, 1.

Iru (ī′rōō). [Heb. *'Irû,* meaning uncertain.] A son of Caleb, son of Jephunneh (1 Chr 4:15).

Isaac (ī′zăk). [Heb. *Yiṣchaq,* "he laughs"; Gr. *Isaak.*] The son of Abraham, according to the promise (Gen 21:1-3; Gal 4:28). The name Isaac, "he laughs," reflects his parents' joy at the time of his birth (Gen 21:6, 7). Both Abraham and Sarah had laughed questioningly and somewhat incredulously at the promise that Sarah should have a son (chs 17:17-19; 18:9-15), but with joy when the promise was fulfilled (ch 21:3, 6). From Abraham's entrance into Palestine 25 years prior to Isaac's birth, God had repeatedly promised him a son and heir (chs 12:2, 4; 13:15, 16; 15:4, 5, 13, 18; 17:2-7; 18:10), finally even specifying his name and the time when he would be born (ch 17:16-21). Remaining childless at an advanced age, and not fully understanding the divine purpose, Abraham had at one time proposed adopting Eliezer, his servant, as son and heir, but God told him that the heir was to be his own son (ch 15:1-6). Soon thereafter Abraham married Hagar, Sarah's maid, who bore him Ishmael when he had been in Canaan 11 years (ch 16:1-5, 15, 16). When, 13 years later, God announced the imminent birth of Isaac (ch 17:1-8, 15-17), Abraham interceded on behalf of Ishmael, whom he dearly loved and to whom he had looked as his son and heir (vs 18, 19). A year later Isaac was born, Abraham being 100 and Sarah 90 years of age (ch 17:17; cf. v 1; ch 21:5). Isaac was circumcised on the 8th day (ch 21:4), in recognition of the covenant promise (ch 17: 2-17). Because of jealousies and frictions Hagar and Ishmael were expelled from the household when Isaac was weaned (ch 21:9-14). When Isaac was a young man God put Abraham to the supreme test of faith with the command to offer his son Isaac as a burnt offering (ch 22: 1-14). Abraham obeyed in faith that God

would raise Isaac from the dead (Heb 11:17-19), but at the last moment his hand was stayed by a voice from heaven. This test demonstrated his complete submission to God and reliance upon Him. Three years after Sarah's death (Gen 23:1; cf. ch 17:17), when Isaac became 40 years of age (chs 24:1-20; 25:20), Abraham arranged for a wife for him—Rebekah—from among relatives in the vicinity of Haran. The old patriarch feared that intermarriage with the idolatrous Canaanites would pervert Isaac's faith and defeat the divine purpose (ch 24). Isaac, who continued to dwell in the southland where he had been born (ch 24:62; cf. ch 20:1), appears to have been of a retiring and contemplative disposition, affectionate and indulgent (chs 24:63, 67; 25:28; 27:1-5, 30-40). With the coming of drought and famine, Isaac moved his encampment some 50 mi. north to Gerar in the fertile plain south of Gaza (ch 26:1, 6). There God appeared to him and renewed the covenant formerly made with Abraham (vs 2-5). While sojourning at Gerar Isaac incurred the displeasure of Abimelech, a Philistine chieftain, through claiming that Rebekah was his sister, not his wife (vs 6-16). Prosperous, and the head of a large household, Isaac kept extensive flocks and herds (ch 26:13-16; cf. ch 23:6). As a result of competition for the limited water supply of the region, Isaac dug 2 wells only to surrender them without an argument when his right to them was challenged (ch 26: 17-23). He later found an adequate water supply at Beer-sheba, "the well of the oath." Here he and the Philistine Abimelech entered into a peace pact (ch 26:23, 26-33; cf. ch 28:10), and here God again renewed the covenant promise (ch 26: 24, 25).

Twenty years after their marriage, Rebekah gave birth to twins, whom they named Esau and Jacob (Gen 25:25, 26; cf. v 20). God revealed that the pre-eminence should go to Jacob (v 23), but Isaac favored Esau (v 28) and, in his old age, prepared to confer the birthright on him (ch 27:1-5). Taking advantage of Isaac's advanced age and dull senses, Rebekah contrived with Jacob to trick her husband into awarding the birthright to Jacob instead (vs 6-29). The plot was successful, but Jacob, to avoid Esau's revenge, was forced to flee to Haran, where he sojourned for about 20 years (chs 27:46 to 28:5). Isaac died at the great age of 180 years and his sons, Jacob and Esau, buried him at Mamre, near Hebron, in the family

burial place (Gen 35:27-29; 49:30, 31).
Isaiah (ī-zā'yȧ), KJV of NT **Esaias** (ĕ-zā'yȧs).
[Heb. *Yesha'yahû*, "Yahweh saves." The name occurs on an ancient Hebrew seal. The Hebrew names *Yesha'yahû* and its shortened form *Yesha'yah* were borne by several men mentioned in the Bible, but their names are transliterated *Jeshaiah (also Jesaiah); Gr. *Ēsaïas*.] Greatest of the Hebrew prophets and author of the book that bears his name. He was a son of Amoz (Is 1:1; not Amos) and came to the prophetic office toward the close of the reign of Uzziah (Azariah), *c.* 790 - *c.* 739 B.C. and served also under Jotham, Ahaz, and Hezekiah (d. *c.* 686). Tradition makes him cousin of Uzziah. The chronology of Sennacherib's campaigns into Judah (chs 36 and 37) shows that Isaiah remained active in the prophetic office approximately to the close of Hezekiah's reign, and that his ministry therefore spanned more than half a cent. Called to be a prophet in his youth, Isaiah fully dedicated himself to God's service at the time of his only recorded vision, in which a realization of God's infinite holiness of character effected a more thorough conversion and response on his part than had earlier been experienced (ch 6). His contemporaries in the prophetic office were Hosea in the northern kingdom of Israel (Hos 1:1) and Micah in the southern kingdom of Judah (Mic 1:1). Isaiah, an eloquent, educated, and cultured man, lived in Jerusalem and served as the political and religious counselor of the nation. He attempted to hold Judah steady and loyal to God during the turbulent and uncertain years that witnessed the dissolution of the northern kingdom of Israel and its fall in 723/22 B.C., and through the repeated Assyrian invasions of Judah in the years that followed. Fearlessly he rebuked the sins of the people, counseled the rulers to rely on the Lord instead of depending on entangling foreign alliances, foresaw the Babylonian captivity, and wrote at length concerning the glorious restoration that would culminate in the coming of Messiah and the establishment of His eternal kingdom—should God's people cooperate with Him. Isaiah's influence was largely responsible for the reformation effected by Hezekiah, whom he encouraged and guided throughout his reign. His counsel and admonition were chiefly responsible for persuading king and people to stand firm when *Sennacherib threatened to take Jerusalem. According to tradition Isaiah fell a martyr to Heze-

kiah's son, Manasseh, who abolished the reforms instituted by his father and, presumably, had the prophet sawn asunder (cf. Heb 11:37).

Isaiah, Book of. First of the so-called Major Prophets, the work of the greatest of the OT prophets. In the Hebrew Bible Isaiah stands in the section known as The Prophets, preceded by the combined book of Kings, and followed by Jeremiah, Ezekiel, and The Twelve (the so-called Minor Prophets). Isaiah's unsurpassed beauty of style and expression make his book the literary masterpiece of all Hebrew literature. Isaiah was a gifted orator and poet as well as the prince of prophets, and in proclaiming his inspired messages he employed a richer vocabulary than that found in any other OT book. A glossary of Isaiah would list more than 2,000 individual words. His exalted concept of the majesty, power, and character of God surpasses that reflected in the writings of the other prophets. Isaiah's understanding of the Messianic role of Israel, of the coming Messiah, and of the Messianic kingdom has earned him the honored title of Messianic prophet and gospel prophet.

From earliest times Jewish and Christian tradition unanimously assented to the entire book of Isaiah as coming from the pen of the man whose name appears as its title. A century and a half ago, however, critical Biblical scholars in Germany set forth the conjecture that the book is, in reality, a composite work written by several writers at widely separated times. As the years passed a great variety of conflicting theories were proposed to distinguish between portions written by Isaiah and those supposedly written by others. Critical scholars now generally assign chs 1 to 39 to the prophet Isaiah who lived during the last half of the 8th cent. B.C., and chs 40 to 66 to a so-called Deutero-Isaiah, or Second-Isaiah, supposed to have lived among the Jewish exiles in Babylonia toward the close of the 70 years of captivity 2 cent. later. Some have proposed a further subdivision that would assign chs 56 to 66 to a Trito-Isaiah, or Third-Isaiah, of the restoration period, about the middle of the 5th cent. B.C. Some of the more radical critics have assigned certain chapters and shorter passages throughout the book to the Maccabean period, about the middle of the 2d cent. As the prophet Isaiah was sawn asunder by his ancient critics, according to tradition, so his prophecy has been dismembered by his critics in more recent years. The basic assumption of the critical approach to a study of the prophets is that each prophetic message grew out of a definite historical situation and was designed to meet the particular needs of Israel at the time. Corollary to this is the idea that a careful examination of each passage can afford clues by which to determine, at least approximately, when the message was given. Conservative scholars will agree that, within limits, such an analysis, which places the messages of the prophets in the setting of the historical circumstances that called them forth, is of great value in determining their true meaning and their import for modern readers. But critical scholars reject the validity of predictive prophecy and arbitrarily assign the writing of passages containing prophecies that have met strik-·ing historical fulfillment to a time *after* the predicted events described took place. Inasmuch as chs 40-66 of Isaiah deal largely with the deliverance of God's people from the Babylonian captivity, an event yet future at the time of writing, and present a glorious picture of Israel's destiny as a nation after the restoration of Jerusalem in the 5th cent., culminating in the Messianic age, the critics assert that this part of the book could not possibly have been composed in the 8th cent., long before the rise of the Neo-Babylonian Empire and the later coming of Cyrus to free the Jewish exiles. The critics further deny that Isaiah wrote the many Messianic passages in the book, inasmuch as these critics arbitrarily relegate the Messianic hope to a later age.

The fundamental fallacy and weakness of the critical position on Isaiah is the complete lack of objective proof. The arguments submitted are wholly subjective, and are based on the a priori suppositions of the critics. Conservative scholars cite both internal and external evidence in favor of their contention that the book is a literary unit and not a composite work. Among other things they point to the similarity in point of view that pervades the entire book and to certain characteristic words and expressions that occur indiscriminately in the various sections, reflecting the thought and style of one person instead of two or more writers. Particularly noteworthy is Isaiah's unusual title for God, "Holy One of Israel [or, Jacob]," which occurs 13 times each in chs 1-39 (chs 1:4; 5:19, 24; 10:20; 12:6; 17:7; 29:19, 23; 30:11, 12, 15; 31:1;

37:23) and Is 40-66 (chs 41:14, 16, 20; 43:3, 14, 16; 45:11; 47:4; 49:7; 54:5; 55:5; 60:9, 14), and twice in the section assigned by some critics to a so-called Trito-Isaiah. This title, which appears only 6 times elsewhere in all the OT, clearly marks the book of Isaiah as the work of one author. The same is true of Isaiah's use of the words "highway" (see chs 11: 16; 35:8; 40:3; 49:11; 62:10) and "remnant" (chs 10:20; 37:32; 46:3; etc.). Other characteristic words and expressions might be cited. Two characteristic literary devices are the frequent emphatic reduplication of thoughts and ideas, as in chs 2:7, 8; 8:9; 24:16, 23; 40:1; 43:11, 25; 48:15; 51:12; 62:10, and the statement of an idea in both positive and negative forms, as in chs 1:19, 20; 42:1-4, 16; 46:9; 48:21; 49:10; 55:7, 8, 9; 65:13, 14, 17, 19, 21, 22, 25. Lengthy passages in poetic form (see chs 1 to 6; 9 to 19; 21; 23 to 35; 40 to 66), the same graphic metaphors and other skillfully turned figures of speech, and a comparable quality of literary elegance are found throughout. The great similarities in outlook, language, and literary style are far more impressive than the supposed dissimilarities. No one will deny that chs 40 to 66, with their exalted concept of the divine purpose and their superb beauty of expression, surpass the earlier portions of the book, but this can easily be attributed to a maturity of outlook and experience that characterized Isaiah's later years. The basic theme—of deliverance from foes without and foes within—and the point of view that runs through the book from beginning to end, are even more important than the strictly mechanical similarities between the various sections. Isaiah's name, meaning "Yahweh saves," aptly summarizes the teaching of all the different sections.

External evidence of the unity of the book comes chiefly from 2 sources. In the apocryphal work called Ecclesiasticus (ch 48:23-28), written about 180 b.c., the author, Jesus ben Sirach, attributes the several sections of the book to 1 writer. Even more important in this respect is evidence recently provided by 2 copies of Isaiah which were found in Cave 1 at *Khirbet Qumrân*. One (designated 1QIsa) is from the 2d cent. b.c., and the other (designated 1QIsb) is from the 1st cent. b.c. In both of these ancient manuscripts Isaiah appears as a unit, without any indication that the book ever existed as a group of independent documents. For the conservative Christian, however, the highest evidence of unity of authorship is the fact that Jesus and the NT writers, who cite Isaiah more often than any other OT book except Psalms—and more often than Psalms when the proportionate lengths of the 2 books are taken into consideration—uniformly attribute all portions of the book to Isaiah (Is 6:9, 10; cf. Mt 13:14, 15; Jn 12:40, 41; Acts 28:25-27; Is 40:3; cf. Mt 3:3; Mk 1:3; Jn 1:23; Is 53:1; cf. Jn 12:38; Rom 10:16; Is 61:1, 2; cf. Lk 4:18, 19; etc.). Christ and the apostles obviously accepted Isaiah as the author of the entire book that bears his name.

The 2 Dead Sea scrolls of Isaiah, already mentioned, have proved to be of major importance in confirming the Masoretic text of the OT. They provide conclusive evidence of the reliability of the OT text as it has come down to us, and show that, for all practical purposes, it is identical with the text as it existed in Christ's day. 1QIsa is complete but contains a number of scribal errors and is not as well written as other scrolls from the collection. Some of the more interesting textual variations are noted in the SDA-Com (see comment on chs 1:15; 3:24; 4:4; 5:24, 27; 9:17; 34:4; 36:5; 37:28; 38: 6, 13; 45:8, 9; 49:5, 12; 51:3; 52:8, 12; 53: 11; 63:11; 65:3, 15; 66:16). 1QIsb is far less complete than 1QIsa, but superior in

quality. Chapters 37 to 41 and 43 to 66 are fairly well preserved. It contains remarkably few scribal errors, and is practically identical with the Masoretic text. Of the relatively few variant readings the more important ones occur in chs 38: 13; 41:11; 43:6; 53:11; 60:19, 21; 63:5; 66:17 (see comment on these passages in the SDACom). Another, and even more fragmentary, text of Isaiah found in Cave 4 at Khirbet Qumrân resembles the text of the LXX more closely than it does the Masoretic text. See Scrolls, Dead Sea.

The earliest date given in the book of Isaiah is "the year that king Uzziah died" (Is 6:1), or 739 B.C., and the last events mentioned are Sennacherib's invasions of Judah in 701 B.C. and some years later (chs 36; 37; see Hezekiah; Sennacherib; Tirhakah). Isaiah gives as the period of his prophetic ministry the reigns of Uzziah, Jotham, Ahaz, and Hezekiah (ch 1:1). He began his work during the closing years of King Uzziah (Azariah), and was still active during Sennacherib's 2d invasion toward the close of Hezekiah's reign, possibly about 690 B.C. or even later. According to an ancient Jewish tradition quoted in the Babylonian Talmud, Isaiah was slain by Manasseh, doubtless soon after Manasseh began to reign, approximately in 686 B.C. It is thus evident that Isaiah's ministry spanned somewhat more than half a century. This period of time

244. The complete book of Isaiah, one of the Dead Sea scrolls, opened to chs 38-40

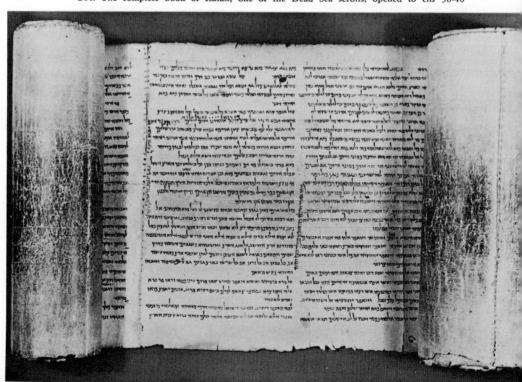

witnessed the peak of Assyria, under Tiglath-pileser III (745-727), Shalmaneser V (727-722), Sargon II (722-705), Sennacherib (705-681), and Esarhaddon (681-669), its most powerful rulers. From 743 onward Assyrian armies repeatedly invaded Palestine and progressively absorbed the northern kingdom into their expanding empire. Shalmaneser V besieged Samaria for 3 years, and it fell in 723/22 B.C., thus bringing the northern kingdom to its end. In 701 Sennacherib embarked on a major campaign that brought Assyria practically all of Mediterranean Asia, including all of Judah except Jerusalem. A few years later another Assyrian army was destroyed by the angel of the Lord at the gates of Jerusalem (Is 37:36, 37).

The period of Isaiah's prophetic ministry was thus a time of turmoil and uncertainty, during which the 10 tribes went into permanent captivity, and when, to all appearances, it was only a matter of time until the same fate would overtake Jerusalem itself. Judah had been blessed from time to time with devout leaders who checked the tide of evil and carried out reforms, with varying success. Uzziah and Jotham were, for the most part, themselves loyal to God, but proved to be only halfhearted in encouraging the people to follow their example. King Ahaz was an apostate and desecrated the Temple (2 Ki 16:3, 4, 10-18; 2 Chr 28:1-5, 22-25; cf. 29:1-7). With the encouragement of Isaiah and others, Hezekiah instituted a series of thoroughgoing reforms that brought about a great spiritual revival (2 Chr 29:1 to 30:13). The northern kingdom had filled its cup of iniquity, and its apostasy was complete and without remedy, but the contemporary prophet Hosea declared, "Judah yet ruleth with God, and is faithful" (Hos 11:12). Isaiah's mission as a prophet was to call the people of Judah back to the true God and to encourage them to trust Him in spite of the evil fate that appeared about to overtake them.

Isaiah's name, meaning "Yahweh saves," is especially appropriate to the theme of his book—deliverance. In Is 1 to 39 first Syria and then Assyria pose a threat to Judah, but the prophet repeatedly assures king and people that God will deliver them (chs 7:1-9; 10:12-27; 11:10-16; 19:23-25; 37:21-36; 38:6). Chs 40 to 66, looking ahead to the time when God's people languish in Babylonian captivity, constitute a great epic of deliverance from that foreign power (see especially Is 40:2; 41:10; 43:1, 2; 44:26 to 45:13; 47; 48:20-22). But, says Isaiah, in effect, deliverance from outward enemies is of secondary importance to deliverance from the oppressive power of sin within, and is contingent upon it (see especially chs 1:16-20; 4:3, 4; 6:5-7; 8:19, 20; 12:3; 53:4-6; 55:6, 7; 58; 61:10; 66:1, 2; etc.). Deliverance reaches its climax with the coming of Messiah, the Great Deliverer who will one day rule in righteousness upon the throne of David (chs 9:6, 7; 11:1-5, 10-12; 25:8, 9; 40:1-5; 52:7 to 53:12; 61:1-3; 63:1-6). He will vanquish His enemies (chs 2:10-21; 10:12; 11:4; 13:1 to 14:27; 24:21, 22; 26:20, 21; 28:21; 33:1-3; 47; 63:1-6; 64:1-3; 65:15; 66:1, 15, 16) and establish His people in never-ending peace and security (chs 4:2-6; 11:5-9; 25:6-8; 35; 51:11; 65:17-25; 66:22-24). He will greatly honor, exalt, and bless them. He will make them a light to the Gentiles, and from all nations of earth a great host will be gathered in to serve the Lord at Jerusalem (chs 2:1-4; 11:10-16; 49:6-8; 54:1-5; 55:5; 56:6-8; 60; 62:1-7). The prophetic insight into the glorious destiny that awaited Israel, as set forth in chs 40 to 66, is without equal elsewhere in Scripture. Isaiah has appropriately been called the Messianic prophet because of the many sublime passages that foretell the coming of Messiah and the establishment of His reign of righteousness.

The prophecy of Isaiah logically falls into 2 sections, the 1st of which (chs 1 to 39), for the most part, deals with the problems then facing God's people. Foremost is the problem of sin, and 2d, the succession of crises that arose from the current historical situation. There are also occasional glimpses of the future. The 2d section (chs 40 to 66) turns to the future, glorious destiny that awaits Israel, and to the coming of the Messiah and the establishment of His eternal kingdom. Chapters 1 to 6 record Isaiah's call to the prophetic ministry and his early prophetic messages. The immediate historical circumstances, which found Judah in mortal danger from Syria, together with a prediction of the impending Assyrian invasions and a promise of deliverance for Judah from both Syria and Assyria, constitute the theme of chs 7 to 12. This section reaches a glorious climax as it predicts the coming of Messiah to champion the cause of His beleaguered people (Is 11:1-9), and the ingathering of the Gentiles and Jewish exiles (ch 11:10-16), and ends with a ringing song of triumph (Is 12). Chapters 13 to 23 constitute an epic of deliverance from Babylon and all the other nations round about that had, at one time or another, oppressed Israel. In chs 24 through 29 the prophet presents a graphic narrative of the desolation of the earth when the Lord would come in judgment upon the nations (ch 24), of the rejoicing of Israel at their deliverance (chs 25 to 27), and of a solemn warning to them to turn to the Lord and to trust in Him (chs 28; 29). The folly of reliance on Egypt and Assyria, with whom the kings of Judah have entered into alliances, is then set forth in stark contrast with the happy fortune of those who put their trust in God (chs 30; 31). This section appropriately closes with another graphic picture of the Messianic kingdom, Messiah reigning in righteousness and His people dwelling in peace and security (chs 32 to 35). This is followed by a brief historical interlude that recites in detail Sennacherib's invasions of Judah and the miraculous deliverance of Jerusalem from the Assyrian armies (chs 36; 37), the sickness and recovery of Hezekiah (ch 38), and the visit of envoys from Babylon (ch 39).

Part 2 (Is 40 to 66) may be divided into 3 major sections: Future deliverance and restoration (chs 40 to 53), Israel a light to the nations, and the ingathering of the Gentiles (chs 54 to 62), and the establishment of the Messianic kingdom (chs 63 to 66). In chs 40 to 47 the prophet encourages his people to look forward to deliverance from the Babylonian captivity. They are to have confidence in God (chs 40 and 41). Deliverance will come through Messiah, God's "servant" (ch 42), and Israel will then become God's "servant" to represent Him before the nations of earth (chs 43 and 44). Cyrus is also God's "servant," the human agent chosen to deliver the people of God from Babylon (chs 44 to 46), whose fall is vividly portrayed in ch 47. In chs 48:1 to 52:12 God challenges His people to learn the lesson of the Babylonian captivity—of loyalty to Him—(ch 48), to accept their role as His messenger of truth to the Gentiles (ch 49), to turn from earthly goals and objectives (ch 50), and to respond courageously to His gracious invitation (chs 51:1 to 52:12). Then, Messiah will come as the suffering "servant," to redeem them from their sins (chs 52: 13 to 53:12). In chs 54 to 56 Israel's role in the divine plan for evangelizing the

world is vividly set forth. In view of this destiny, God summons His people to a revival of true religion (Is 57 to 59). This reformation will usher in Israel's glorious hour of destiny, when she is to arise and let her light shine forth to all men (chs 60 to 62). When the evangelization of the world has been completed the great day of God will come, the day of vengeance upon those who have rejected His gracious call of mercy. The prophet then makes a final appeal to His people to enter wholeheartedly into the work of reformation that must precede the glorious events already foretold (chs 63:1 to 65:16). The earth is restored (ch 65:17-25), men are rewarded according to their deeds (ch 66:1-21), and God's people worship Him in peace and righteousness forever (vs 22-24). The return from Babylon was realized, but the glorious destiny of world mission and leadership that was to follow was forfeited by Israel and now belongs to the spiritual children of Abraham. *See* Prophet, II.

Iscah (ĭs′kȧ). [Heb. *Yiskah.*] A daughter of Haran, Abraham's oldest brother, and a sister of Milcah and Lot (Gen 11:29), hence a niece of Abraham. According to Jewish tradition Iscah was another name for Sarai (Jos. *Ant.* i. 6. 5), but there is no evidence that this tradition is correct.

Iscariot (ĭs-kăr′ĭ-ŏt). [Gr. *Iskariōth* and *Iskariōtēs*, usually considered to be derived from the Heb. *'ish Qerîyôth*, "man of Kerioth," but this derivation is uncertain.] A name given to Judas, the betrayer of Jesus (Mt 10:4; Lk 6:16), which he apparently shared with his father, Simon (Jn 6:71; 13:26, RSV). The appellation distinguishes him from the other disciple called Judas (Lk 6:16; Acts 1:13, 16). If the interpretation "man of Kerioth" is correct, Judas came from Judah, since Kerioth was in the south of Judah, near Hebron. All the other disciples seem to have been natives of Galilee.

Ishbah (ĭsh′bȧ). [Heb. *Yishbach*, "he praises," or "he soothes."] A descendant of Judah, and apparently the ancestor of the people of Eshtemoa (1 Chr 4:17).

Ishbak (ĭsh′băk). [Heb. *Yishbaq*, meaning uncertain.] An Arab tribe descended from Abraham through Keturah (Gen 25:2). It is undoubtedly the tribe in northern Syria mentioned in Assyrian documents (858 B.C.) as *Iasbuq* (*ANET* 277, 278).

Ishbi-benob (ĭsh′bĭ-bē′nŏb). [Heb. *Yishbi Benob,* according to the emendation and vocalization of the Masoretes. The unpointed Hebrew text can also be read, "And there dwelt in Nob one."] A Philistine giant who attempted to kill David, but was slain by Abishai (2 Sa 21:16, 17). However, the Hebrew text has some difficulties, and if the variant reading suggested above is adopted the name disappears.

Ish-bosheth (ĭsh'bō'shĕth). [Heb. *'Ish-bosheth,* "man of shame."] One of Saul's younger sons (2 Sa 2:8), originally called Eshbaal (ĕsh'bā͏ăl) [Heb. *'Eshba'al*], "man of Baal (or the lord)" (1 Chr 8:33). The name Ish-bosheth may have been applied to him after his death, which ended the dynasty of Saul. If the change of name occurred during his lifetime, it must have come after the decline of his power. After the battle of Gilboa, in which Saul and 3 of his sons lost their lives, Abner, Saul's general, made Ish-bosheth king over the northern tribes, who did not join Judah in accepting David as their king. He was about 40 years of age when he began to reign and reigned two years (2 Sa 2:10). He made his headquarters at Mahanaim in Transjordan doubtless because of the hostility of the Philistines (vs 8, 9). His efforts to reunite the country by force were unsuccessful (vs 12-17; ch 3:1). Soon, too, he lost his strongest supporter, Abner (ch 3:6-11), whom he accused of serious misdemeanor. Abner thereupon negotiated to transfer the whole northern kingdom to David (vs 12-21). During the negotiations Abner was assassinated by Joab (v 27), and Ish-bosheth gave up hope of retaining his power. Shortly afterward Ish-bosheth was murdered by 2 of his own army officers, who took his head to David in expectation of a reward. David ordered them to be executed instead, and buried Ish-bosheth's head in Abner's grave at Hebron (ch 4:1-12).

Ishhod (ĭsh'hŏd'), KJV once **Ishod** (ĭ'shŏd). [Heb. *'Ishhod,* "man of majesty."] The ancestral head of a tribal family in Manasseh (1 Chr 7:18).

Ishi, I (ĭsh'ī). [Heb. *'Ishi,* "my husband."] According to the KJV of Hos 2:16, the name that Israel would apply to God after returning to Him. The RSV renders the name literally as "My husband." *See* Baali.

Ishi, II (ĭsh'ī). [Heb. *Yish'i,* "my help." The name occurs also on an ancient Hebrew seal.]

1. A man of Judah of the house of Jerahmeel (1 Chr 2:31).

2. A Judahite (1 Chr 4:20).

3. A descendant of Simeon. His sons were leaders in a raid upon the Amalekites of Mount Seir (1 Chr 4:42).

4. The head of a tribal family of Manasseh in Transjordan (1 Chr 5:23, 24).

Ishiah. *See* Isshiah.

Ishijah. *See* Isshijah.

Ishma (ĭsh'má). [Heb. *Yishma',* meaning uncertain.] A descendant of Judah (1 Chr 4:3).

Ishmael (ĭsh'má-ĕl). [Heb. *Yishma'e'l,* "God hears." The name occurs also on an ancient Hebrew seal. In Akkadian it appears in various forms: *Ishme-ilum, Yashmah-ilu,* and possibly *Sumu'-ilu.*]

1. The son borne to Abram by his Egyptian slave Hagar, as the result of Sarai's plan to obtain a child through giving her maidservant to her husband (Gen 16:1-3). This method was in harmony with Mesopotamian custom in the patriarchal age. However, it showed a lack of faith on the part of Sarai and Abram, to whom God had promised an heir (ch 15:4), and was productive of much trouble in the household (ch 16:4-9). Abram was 86 years of age when Ishmael was born, and 11 years had passed since he had come to Canaan (chs 12:4; 16:16). When Ishmael was 13 years old, the institution of circumcision was given to Abraham, and all male members of his household, including Ishmael, were circumcised (ch 17:23-27). A year later Isaac was born (cf. chs 17:24; 21:5). Later, because of jealousy toward Isaac, Ishmael and his mother were expelled from Abraham's household (ch 21:10-14). Wandering aimlessly in the southern wilderness, they almost perished of thirst, but were saved when an angel showed them a well of water (vs 15-19). Ishmael later settled in the Wilderness of Paran, which lies to the south of Palestine. He lived by his bow, and in the course of time married a girl from his mother's homeland (vs 20, 21). God repeatedly promised to make Ishmael the progenitor of a great nation (chs 16:10-12; 17:20; 21:13, 18), which promise was later fulfilled (ch 25:12-16). *See* Ishmaelite. Although expelled from Abraham's household, Ishmael seems to have maintained good relations with his relatives in Palestine, as shown by the fact that one of his daughters was later married to Esau (ch 28:9), and that he took part in the funeral rites for his father (ch 25:9). He died at the age of 137 (v 17).

2. A descendant of King Saul through Jonathan (1 Chr 8:38; 9:44).

3. A man whose son Zebadiah was a

high court official under King Jehoshaphat of Judah (2 Chr 19:11).

4. An officer who assisted the high priest Jehoiada in deposing Queen Athaliah (2 Chr 23:1).

5. Son of Nethaniah (2 Ki 25:23-25). He was an army officer of royal blood under King Zedekiah of Judah (v 25; cf. v 2). Ishmael was not taken captive when Nebuchadnezzar dissolved the kingdom of Judah and captured Jerusalem (v 23). After Gedaliah was established as governor of the newly formed Babylonian province of Judah, with the capital at Mizpah, Ishmael, being in the pay of the king of the Ammonites, made his way to Mizpah to kill Gedaliah. Gedaliah was warned of Ishmael's murderous intent, but disbelieved his informer, and did nothing to protect himself (Jer 40:7, 14-16). When Ishmael arrived he assassinated Gedaliah and massacred many others, including the Chaldean garrison (2 Ki 25:25; Jer 41:1-3). After some further murders (Jer 41:4-8) he took the rest of the people, including the daughters of the king and presumably Jeremiah, and set out to go over to the Ammonites (vs 10-12). However, Johanan, son of Kareah, and his followers met Ishmael at Gibeon. They retrieved the captives, but Ishmael and 8 of his followers succeeded in escaping from Johanan and went to the Ammonites (vs 13-15).

6. A priest of the family of Pashhur; he had married a foreign wife in the time of Ezra (Ezr 10:22).

Ishmaelite (ĭsh'mȧ-ĕl-īt), KJV frequently **Ishmeelite** (ĭsh'mĕ-ĕl-īt). [Heb. *Yishme'e'lî.*] A descendant of Ishmael, and thus partly Egyptian and partly Semitic (see Gen 16: 1, 2, 15). From Ishmael sprang twelve princes who became tribal ancestors (chs 17:20; 25:12-16). The tribes generally lived a nomadic life, as untamed as the "wild ass" of the wilderness (ch 16:12, RSV). Their home was the desert of northern Arabia and eastern Syria. However, some of the Arabian tribes, such as the Nabataeans (Map XIII, C-4), came to fame and power. Like their ancestor Ishmael (ch 21:20), the Ishmaelites were skilled bowmen (Is 21:17). They were also caravan leaders who brought the products of Arabia to Egypt and Mesopotamia (Gen 37:25). Eventually their name became almost synonymous with desert people, perhaps because they mixed with other tribes, or perhaps because the Ishmaelites were the most important or the most outstanding of the desert peoples. In Jgs 8:5, 21-24 their name is applied to Midianites. Furthermore, it has been usual for Arabs, even down into modern times, to look to Ishmael as an ancestor.

Ishmaiah (ĭsh-mā'yȧ), KJV once **Ismaiah** (ĭs-mā'yȧ). [Heb. *Yishma'yahú* and *Yishma'yah,* "Yahweh hears."]

1. A Gibeonite who joined David at Ziklag (1 Chr 12:4).

2. The head of the tribe of Zebulun in David's reign (1 Chr 27:19).

Ishmeelite. See Ishmaelite.

Ishmerai (ĭsh'mĕ-rī). [Heb. *Yishmeray,* "Yahweh watches."] A descendant of Benjamin (1 Chr 8:18).

Ishod. See Ishhod.

Ishpah (ĭsh'pȧ), KJV **Ispah** (ĭs'pȧ). [Heb. *Yishpah,* meaning uncertain.] A man of the tribe of Benjamin, of the house of Beriah (1 Chr 8:16).

Ishpan (ĭsh'păn). [Heb. *Yishpan.*] A descendant of Benjamin (1 Chr 8:22).

Ish-tob (ĭsh'tŏb). [Heb. *'Ish-ṭôb,* "man of Tob."] According to the KJV a proper name (2 Sa 10:6-8), but the Hebrew term should probably be translated, "men of Tob," as in the RSV, which considers *'îsh,* "man," as a collective for "men."

Ishuah. See Ishvah.

Ishuai. See Ishvi.

Ishui. See Ishvi.

Ishvah (ĭsh'vȧ), KJV once **Ishuah** (ĭsh'ū-ȧ), once **Isuah** (ĭs'ū-ȧ). [Heb. *Yishwah,* meaning uncertain.] The 2d son of Asher (Gen 46:17; 1 Chr 7:30). The fact that his name does not appear in the later lists of the tribal families of Asher suggests that he left no male heirs.

Ishvi (ĭsh'vī), KJV once **Ishuai** (ĭsh'ū-ī), once **Ishui** (ĭsh'ū-ī), once **Isui** (ĭs'ū-ī), and once **Jesui** (jĕs'ū-ī). [Heb. *Yishwî,* meaning uncertain.]

1. The 3d son of Asher, and founder of a tribal family called Jesuites (jĕz'ū-īts) or Ishvites (ĭsh'vīts) [Heb. *Yishwî*] (Gen 46:17; Num 26:44; 1 Chr 7:30).

2. A son of King Saul (1 Sa 14:49).

Ishvites. See Ishvi, 1.

Isle, Island. [Heb. *'î* (plural *'iyîm*); Gr. *nēsos.*] These terms occur frequently in the KJV, but the Hebrew word (*'î*) thus translated does not always mean "isle" or "island." The following are the meanings of *'î* in the OT: (1) a tract of land surrounded by water (Is 40:15); (2) a coastland like that of Phoenicia or Philistia (chs 20:6; 23:2, 6; etc. See RSV); (3) habitable land in contrast to water (ch

42:15); (4) remote regions of the earth (Is 41:5; Zep 2:11); (5) some animal or, according to certain scholars, a ghost-like creature believed to inhabit certain islands (Is 13:22; 34:14; Jer 50:39). *See* Hyena.

Ismachiah (ĭs'mȧ-kī'ȧ). [Heb. *Yismakyahŭ,* "Yahweh supports."] A Temple overseer in the time of King Hezekiah (2 Chr 31:13).

Ismaiah. *See* Ishmaiah.

Ispah. *See* Ishpah.

Israel (ĭz'rȧ-ĕl). [Heb. and Aramaic *Yiśra'el,* "God contends." The name occurs on the *Moabite Stone as *Yśr'l,* and in Ugarit as *Yśr'il,* as that of a craftsman. The name as that of the people of Israel is found as *Isr'r* on the Israel stele of Merneptah, the 2d *r* representing the Heb. *l,* for which Egyptian scripts have no character. Gr. *Israēl.*]

1. The covenant name of Jacob, which was given to him at daybreak after a night wrestling with an unrecognized Antagonist at the brook Jabbok, on his way home to Canaan after 20 years as an exile in Haran (Gen 32:22-32). Subsequent to this occasion, the name is used interchangeably with Jacob (ch 46:5), particularly when Jacob is considered in his role as progenitor of the chosen race (see ch 48:1-3).

2. The descendants of Jacob, whether all of those living at one time (Ex 1:9), or the successive generations taken collectively (Gen 32:32). With these connotations the term commonly occurs in such expressions as "congregation of Israel" (Ex 12:3) and "children (or "people") of Israel" (Hos 3:5). As referring to Jacob's descendants, "Israel" is used interchangeably with the name Jacob (Is 44:1). Applied to the Hebrew people, "Israel" stresses their role as the *chosen people in terms of the covenant between God and Abraham, their forefather (Gen 15:18; cf. Ps 105:9, 10).

3. The 10 northern tribes that seceded from the united monarchy *c.* 931 B.C., in contradistinction to the southern kingdom of Judah (1 Ki 12:1, 16, 19). The dominant position of Judah among the 12 tribes predisposed the others against the reigning house of David and Solomon. The oppressive taxes levied by Solomon to support his luxurious court and for the erection of his magnificent buildings and extensive public works, together with the worldly influence of his personal example, loosened still further the tenuous ties that bound the united kingdom to-

245. The "Israel Stele" of Merneptah, the only Egyptian monument mentioning the name of Israel (in white box) in hieroglyphs

gether. The harsh policy of Rehoboam, son and successor of Solomon, led the 10 northern tribes *c.* 931 B.C. to secede and make Jeroboam king (1 Ki 12:1-24). To consolidate his rule, Jeroboam established a new religion in which he blended the worship of Jehovah with the calf worship of Egypt, with the avowed purpose of diverting the affections of his people from Jerusalem, from the Temple, and from the house of David (vs 25-33). Like a virus, the influence of this apostate religion infected the new kingdom and turned its people away from the true God. Later, under *Ahab, Baal worship was also promoted (ch 16:30-32). Despite the earnest labors of prophets such as Elijah, Elisha, Jonah, Amos, and Hosea, the northern kingdom never experienced a genuine reformation such as the revivals that came to Judah under Jehoshaphat in the 9th cent. B.C., Hezekiah in the 8th cent. B.C., and Josiah in the 7th cent. B.C. The entire course of the Israelite history down to its disruption in 723/22 B.C. was one of ever-deepening apostasy and corruption. In contrast with the single dynasty and 20 rulers of Judah—reflective of the comparative stability that characterized the southern kingdom—the deteriorating social, political, and religious conditions that prevailed in Israel brought several dynasties and 20 kings to the throne in a period of time less than two-thirds as long. (The dates here given are approximate; see table, pp. 205, 206.)

During his reign of 22 years Jeroboam I (931-910 B.C.) was involved in a succession of wars with Rehoboam of Judah and suffered a damaging Egyptian invasion. His dynasty came to an end with the murder of his son Nadab (910-909 B.C.) by Baasha (909-886 B.C.), whose wicked reign was marked by wars with Judah and Syria. With the murder of Baasha's son Elah (886-885 B.C.) by one of his generals, Zimri (who reigned for 7 days in 885 B.C.), the 2d Israelite dynasty came to an end. A military coup led by Omri (885-874 B.C.), who was currently on a campaign in Philistia, in turn terminated Zimri's brief tenure as king. Tibni, a rival contender with Omri for the throne, was soon eliminated, and Omri founded a dynasty that survived 44 years. Omri's selection of the easily fortified hill of Samaria gave Israel an impregnable capital, so that when it was besieged in later years it capitulated only when its food and water were exhausted. Omri entered into cordial commercial and political relations with Phoenicia, and arranged for the marriage of his son Ahab to Jezebel, daughter of the king of Tyre. As the *Moabite Stone erected by King Mesha of Moab states, Omri subdued Moab and placed it under tribute.

With the accession of Ahab (874-853 B.C.) to the throne, Israel took a significant step into deeper apostasy, largely because of his weakness of character and the aggressive policy of his Phoenician wife, Jezebel. She embarked on a determined program to eradicate the worship of Jehovah and to make Baal worship the national religion of Israel. In this spiritual crisis the prophets Elijah and Elisha boldly championed the faith of their fathers. Ahab's reign saw a degree of material prosperity and military success. In coalition with Ben-hadad of Damascus

and other kings, he temporarily checked the westward advance of the Assyrians at the famous battle of Qarqar in 853, but lost his life shortly thereafter in a futile attempt to retake Ramoth-gilead (1 Ki 22). Ahab's son Ahaziah (853-852 B.C.) succeeded briefly to the throne, and was followed by his brother Jehoram (852-841 B.C.). The latter made a futile attempt to perpetuate Israelite hegemony over the land of Moab (2 Ki 3:4-27), and occupied himself with a series of unsuccessful military engagements against the Syrians (chs 6 and 7). While recuperating from battle wounds at Jezreel, Jehoram was assassinated by his army commander Jehu, who obliterated the house of Omri, including Jezebel, and made himself king (chs 8:28, 29; 9:24 to 10:17).

246. Five Israelite tribute bearers, a panel from the Black Obelisk of Shalmaneser III in the British Museum

The dynasty founded by Jehu (841-814 B.C.) lasted for 90 years, or nearly half of the entire period of Israel's history as a separate kingdom. Jehu eradicated Baal worship, but his reforms left the calf worship established by Jeroboam untouched. Jehu voluntarily made himself a vassal of Assyria, paying tribute to Shalmaneser III (see figs. 246, 255), probably in return for assistance against Hazael of Syria. Throughout the reign of Jehoahaz (814-798 B.C.), son and successor of Jehu, there was almost continuous war between Israel and Syria, and Israel was reduced to a state of impotence. Succeeding his father Jehoahaz to the throne, Jehoash (798-782 B.C.) recovered all the area his father had lost to the Syrians. Jehoash was also forced into a war with

Judah, during the course of which he captured its king, entered Jerusalem, and carried a quantity of treasure and exiles back with him to Samaria (2 Ki 14:8-14). Apparently to provide for the continuity of the dynasty, Jehoash seems to have associated his son, Jeroboam II, with him on the throne for about 12 years (c. 793-c. 782 B.C.). After the death of Jehoash, Jeroboam II enjoyed a long and prosperous sole reign of nearly 30 years (782-753 B.C.), during which he regained, with the exception of the territory of Judah, practically all of the territory that Israel had lost since the golden era of David and Solomon (vs 23-27). A period of political weakness on the part of Israel's neighbor nations, particularly Assyria, prevented them from taking effective counter action. As the book of Hosea makes evident, the deceptive material and political prosperity that marked the reign of Jeroboam II was accompanied by the grossest moral and social corruption. His son, Zachariah, reigned for only 6 months (c. 753-752 B.C.) before being assassinated by Shallum (ch 15:8-12).

Thirty years of political anarchy and national chaos followed the death of Zachariah. After the fall of the dynasty founded by Jehu, 5 kings followed one another in quick succession. Shallum (752 B.C.), the assassin of Zachariah, in turn was murdered by Menahem after a brief reign of only 1 month. Menahem (752-742 B.C.) cruelly suppressed all opposition to his rule, and levied a burdensome tax upon his people in order to buy off Tiglath-pileser III of Assyria (2 Ki 15:19, 20). By the close of Menahem's reign, Israel had once more lost the territory that had been reclaimed under Jeroboam II. Menahem's son Pekahiah held the throne for 2 years (742-740 B.C.), only to be assassinated by Pekah (740-732 B.C.). Pekah concluded an alliance with Syria for an unsuccessful joint campaign against Jerusalem, probably seeking to compel Ahaz to join them against Assyria (chs 15:37; 16:5-9). Instead, Ahaz sought and secured the help of Tiglath-pileser. Pekah lost to Assyria his northern and eastern territories (ch 15:29; see fig. 37). His inglorious reign ended with his assassination by Hoshea (732-722 B.C.), who succeeded him as Israel's 20th and last king. A hopeless alliance with So, an Egyptian king, failed to halt the dissolution of his kingdom and the capture of his capital, Samaria, by Shalmaneser V or Sargon II (723/22 B.C.). The northern kingdom of

Israel thus came to a tragic end, an unwilling witness to the fate of a nation that refuses to walk in the ways of the Lord.

4. The term Israel is sometimes applied equally to the kingdoms of Israel and Judah during the time of the divided kingdom (Is 8:14), probably in the covenant sense. Following the dissolution of the northern kingdom the name is commonly used as referring to the people of the kingdom of Judah, even during the period of the Babylonian captivity (Is 1:3; cf. v 1; Eze 3:1, 7; etc.).

In the NT Israel is applied in a spiritual sense to Christians (Gal 6:16; etc.).

Israelite (ĭz'rĭ-ĕl-īt). [Heb. *Yisre'elî*. The name, spelled *Sir'ilaia*, occurs in cuneiform records as an appellative of King Ahab. Gr. *Israēlitēs*.] A descendant of Israel, that is, of Jacob (Jos 3:17). The term implies participation in the covenant relationship, and thus heirship to the promises made to Abraham, Isaac, and Jacob (Gen 15:18; 26:4; 28:13, 14; Rom 9:4-13).

Issachar (ĭs'á-kär). [Heb. *Yiśśakar*. The name is interpreted to mean "there is hire" in Gen 30:18, which presumes a Hebrew form as *yesh śakar*; Gr. *Issachar*.]

1. The 9th son of Jacob, and the 5th of Leah (Gen 29:32 to 30:18; 35:23). Issachar had 4 sons born to him before he went to Egypt with his father's family (Gen 46:13; Ex 1:1, 3; 1 Chr 7:1). When Jacob pronounced blessings upon his own sons shortly before his death, he prophetically likened Issachar and his children to a strong ass crouching down and submitting to foreign yokes as long as he was permitted to remain in his pleasant land (Gen 49:14, 15).

2. The tribe that descended from Jacob's 9th son. It consisted of 4 tribal families comprising the descendants of Issachar's 4 sons (Num 26:23, 24). Nethanel, son of Zuar, was the first leader of the tribe during the wilderness wandering (chs 1:8; 2:5; 7:18; 10:15), and later Paltiel, son of Azzan, held the office (ch 34:26). In the 1st census 54,400 members of the tribe, ready for war, were counted (ch 1:28, 29), at a later census 64,300 (ch 26:25), and in David's time 87,000 (1 Chr 7:5). When the country was divided among the tribes of Israel, Issachar, to whom the 4th lot fell, received an area (Map VI, C-3/4) to the south and east of Zebulun and Naphtali, east and north of Manasseh, and west of the Jordan (Jos 19:17-23). Its most important cities were Shunem and Jezreel (v 18). Some towns

within its territory were held by Manasseh (Jos 17:10, 11), and some were assigned to the Gershonite Levites (Jos 21:6, 28, 29; 1 Chr 6:62-72). The tribe distinguished itself in the war against Jabin of Hazor and Sisera, and was commended for its bravery by Deborah (Jgs 5:15). It provided one of Israel's judges, Tola (ch 10:1). Many of that tribe "had understanding of the times" and joined David's forces at Hebron (1 Chr 12:32). Omri, son of Michael, was head of the tribe under David (ch 27:18). Under Solomon, Jehoshaphat, the son of Paruah, was the king's supply officer for the territory of Issachar as one of the divisions of the state (1 Ki 4:17). Baasha, the assassin of King Nadab, and usurper of the throne of Israel, was from Issachar (ch 15:27, 28), and possibly also King Omri, since his descendants held property in Jezreel (chs 16:28; 21:1). Although the tribe occupied territory in northern Israel, many of its people attended Hezekiah's Passover at Jerusalem (2 Chr 30:18). In Ezekiel's vision of restored Israel, Issachar received a section of the land between the territories of Simeon and Zebulun (Eze 48:33). Issachar is in the list of tribes mentioned as sealed by the angel of Rev 7 (v 7).

3. A Levite doorkeeper in David's reign (1 Chr 26:5).

Isshiah (ĭs′shī′à), KJV once **Ishiah** (ĭ-shī′à), twice **Jesiah** (jĕ-sī′à). [Heb. *Yishshiyah* and *Yishshiyahu*, meaning uncertain.]

1. The head of a tribal family of Issachar (1 Chr 7:3).

2. An Israelite who joined David's band at Ziklag (1 Chr 12:6).

3. The head of a Levite family descended from Moses (1 Chr 24:21).

4. A Kohathite Levite (1 Chr 23:20; 24:25).

Isshijah (ĭs-shī′jà), KJV **Ishijah** (ĭ-shī′jà). [Heb. *Yishshiyah,* meaning uncertain.] A man who had married a foreign wife in Ezra's time (Ezr 10:31).

Issue. A term used with various meanings: (1) A body discharge due either to normal or to diseased conditions. The Mosaic health laws declared that such discharges made the Israelites unclean for varying periods and required cleansing of various kinds, depending upon the nature of the issue, RSV "discharge" (Lev 15). A woman healed by Christ had an "issue of blood" for 12 years (Mt 9:20; Mk 5:25; Lk 8:43, 44). (2) As a verb, a proceeding forth. A fiery stream "issued" from the presence of the "Ancient of days"

(Dan 7:9, 10). In vision the revelator saw flashes of lightning issue from the throne of Deity (Rev 4:5, KJV "proceed"), and a sharp sword issue (KJV "go out") from the mouth of Christ (ch 1:16), and from the mouth of One upon a white horse (ch 19:11, 15, KJV "goeth"). The noun idea of a proceeding forth is probably intended in Deut 21:17; Ps 78:51; 105:36; RSV, where "first issue" translates a Hebrew term meaning "first." (3) Children, or offspring, for example, of Joseph (Gen 48:5, 6, RSV "offspring"). The man who had 7 wives left no "issue" (Mt 22:25, RSV "children"). (4) Source. Prov 4:23 refers to the heart as the source from which come the "issues" (RSV "springs") of life, meaning poetically that the heart is the source of our thoughts and motives which flow forth into actions. (5) Outcome, or result (Dan 12:8, RSV).

Isuah. *See* Ishvah.

Isui. *See* Ishvi.

Italian Band. *See* Cohort, *a.*

Italian Cohort. *See* Cohort, *a.*

Italy (ĭt′à-li). [Gr. *Italia.*] The homeland of the Romans, with Rome as its capital city and also the capital of the empire. In pre-Christian times "Italy" was used for a small district in the south of the peninsula that is now called Italy, but by NT times the name was applied as it is today to the whole peninsula. (Map XIX, C-8.)

Italy was inhabited by various peoples, such as the Gauls who lived in the north, the Greeks who lived in the south, and the Latins, Sabines, Etruscans, and others who lived in the central part. Not long after 300 B.C. the city-state of Rome had extended its control over most of Italy, and by NT times had given the Italian peoples Roman citizenship. Italy is mentioned 4 times in the NT: (1) as the country from which Aquila and Priscilla, who later became Paul's helpers, migrated when the Jews were expelled from Rome by Claudius (Acts 18:2); (2) as the country to which Paul was sent as a prisoner (ch 27:1); (3) as the destination of an Alexandrian ship which Paul and the others boarded at Myra in Lycia on the southern coast of Asia Minor (vs 5, 6); (4) as the country where Christians who sent greetings to the recipients of the letter to the Hebrews either were living or had lived (Heb 13:24).

Itch. In the RSV a rendering generally of the Heb. *netheq* (KJV "scall"), a skin disease, the symptoms of which simulated those of the early stages of leprosy. Hence one afflicted with *netheq* was isolated, and the diseased portion of the skin closely watched (Lev 13:30-37). As a consequence of disobedience, the Lord threatened to send upon the Israelites, among other diseases, the itch (Heb. *cheres,* probably "scabies," Deut 28:27). Once, "itching" is used in a figurative sense where certain Christians are described as having "itching ears," that is, ears searching for interesting and spicy bits of information. This "itching" was satisfied by the strange doctrines of the new teachers (2 Ti 4:3).

Ithai. *See* Ittai, 1.

Ithamar (ĭth′a̍-mär). [Heb. *'Ithamar,* meaning uncertain.] The youngest of Aaron's four sons (Ex 6:23; 1 Chr 6:3; 24:1). He was consecrated to the priesthood along with his father and three brothers (Ex 28:1; 1 Chr 24:2). He was charged with the responsibility of keeping the records of the building material gathered for the construction of the tabernacle and its furniture (Ex 38:21), and was made supervisor of the Gershonite and Merarite Levites (Num 4:21-33). Although the office of high priesthood was generally held by the descendants of Eleazar, it was occupied for a few generations by the descendants of Ithamar, namely from Eli to Abiathar in the time from Samuel to Solomon. Eight of the 24 courses into which David organized the priests belonged to the line of Ithamar (1 Chr 24:4-18). Ithamar's descendants are mentioned among the postexilic priests (Ezr 8:2).

Ithiel (ĭth′ĭ-ĕl). [Heb. *'Ithi'el,* probably "God is with me."]

1. One of the 2 to whom Agur addressed the message of Prov 30 (v 1).

2. A Benjamite whose descendant lived in Jerusalem in Nehemiah's time (Neh 11:7).

Ithlah (ĭth′la̍), KJV **Jethlah** (jĕth′la̍). [Heb. *Yithlah,* meaning uncertain.] A town in the territory of Dan (Jos 19:42); not identified with certainty, but the context indicates that it was in the vicinity of Aijalon.

Ithmah (ĭth′ma̍). [Heb. *Yithmah,* meaning uncertain. The name occurs in Assyrian records as *Yatamâ.*] A Moabite, who was one of the "mighty men" of David (1 Chr 11:46).

Ithnan (ĭth′năn). [Heb. *Yithnan,* meaning uncertain.] A town in the extreme south of Judah (Jos 15:23). It is identified with *el-Jebariyeh,* about 16 mi. northeast of Kadesh-barnea, in the *Wâdī Umm Ethnân,* which preserves the ancient name.

Ithra. *See* Jether.

Ithran (ĭth′răn). [Heb. *Yithran,* "superabundance." The name occurs in Assyrian as *Itranu.*]

1. A Horite, son of Dishon (Gen 36:26; 1 Chr 1:41).

2. A descendant of Asher (1 Chr 7:37), probably identical with the Jether (Heb. *Yether*) mentioned in v 38. *See* Jether, 3.

Ithream (ĭth′rē-ăm). [Heb. *Yithre'am,* "the kinsman has been abundant."] The 6th son born to David at Hebron. His mother was Eglah (2 Sa 3:5; 1 Chr 3:3).

Ithrite (ĭth′rīt). [Heb. *Yithri.*]

1. The name of a family of Kiriath-jearim (1 Chr 2:53).

2. An appellation of Ira and Gareb, two of David's "mighty men" (2 Sa 23:38; 1 Chr 11:40). They were probably descendants of a certain Jether, or natives of the town of Jattir in Judah.

Ittah-kazin. *See* Eth-kazin.

Ittai (ĭt′a̍-ī). [Heb. *'Ittay,* probably a shortened form of *'Ittiyahû* (Ittiah), "with me is Yahweh," or *'Itti'el* (Ittiel), "with me is God."]

1. A Benjamite from Gibeah who belonged to David's "mighty men" (2 Sa 23:29); called Ithai (ĭth′a̍-ī) [Heb. *'Ithay*] in 1 Chr 11:31.

2. A man from the Philistine city of Gath, who with 600 of his followers joined David and became a commander in David's army. He remained faithful to King David and led a 3d part of the army that crushed Absalom's rebellion (2 Sa 15:18-22; 18:2, 5).

Ituraea (ĭt′û-rē′a̍). [Gr. *Itouraios.*] An area northeast of Palestine (Lk 3:1), including part of the Anti-Lebanon Mountains. Its capital was Chalcis at certain periods (Map XV, A-4). It probably received its name from the Arabic tribe of Jetur, a tribe descended from Ishmael (Gen 25:15; 1 Chr 1:31). When the Transjordan tribes of Israel extended their territories they overthrew Jetur (1 Chr 5:19), who then seems to have settled between the Lebanon and Anti-Lebanon Mountains. Nothing further is known of the history of this tribe until it was subjugated by the Maccabean king Aristobulus, who forced the Ituraeans to accept the Jewish religion, including the rite of circumcision, *c.* 104 B.C. (Jos. *Ant.* xiii. 11. 3). Later, the area was ruled by Ptolemy, son of Mennaeus (*ibid.* 16. 3; xiv. 3. 2). He warred with Damascus, but submitted to Pompey of Rome in 65 or 64 B.C. Having paid an indemnity of 1,000 talents to the

Romans, Ptolemy continued to reign until 40 B.C., when he was succeeded by his son Lysanias (I), who was executed by Antony in 34 B.C. (*ibid.* xv. 4. 1). The territory was then left in the hands of Lysanias' son Zenodorus (*ibid.* xv. 10. 1). However, part of it was handed over to Herod the Great in 24 B.C., and the rest in 20 B.C. After Herod's death in 4 B.C., the territory passed to his son Philip (Lk 3:1), who ruled over it until he died in A.D. 33/34. It later became part of the kingdom of Agrippa I, and after his death was governed by procurators for several years. It was finally given to Agrippa II in A.D. 52, who ruled it as the last of the Herodian kings.

Lit.: E. Schürer, *A History of the Jewish People in the Time of Jesus Christ* (New York, n.d.), Appendix I.

Ivah. *See* Ivvah.

Ivory. [Heb. *shen*, "tooth," and *shenhabbîm*. The *habbîm* is usually thought to mean "elephant," although this is not yet attested. Gr. *elephantinos*.] The tusks of ele-

247. An ivory panel from Samaria, probably a decorative piece from Ahab's "ivory house"

phants was a material in great demand in the ancient world for making luxury articles. The elephant is not mentioned in the Bible but is referred to in the books of Maccabees. It is there described as being used by the Syrian kings as a war animal. In such a service the animals were led by Indian drivers and had on their backs wooden towers in which were archers (1 Macc 1:17; 6:30-46; 8:6; 11:56; 2 Macc 13:2-15). In ancient times elephants were found in northern Syria and northern Mesopotamia. Thutmose III (c. 1482 - c. 1450 B.C.) claims to have hunted 120 ele-

248. An ivory panel of Egyptian design from Samaria, showing the infant Horus, probably a decorative piece from Ahab's "ivory house"

phants at Ni, southeast of Aleppo (*ANET* 240), and the Assyrian kings Tiglath-pileser I (1113-1074 B.C.) and Adad-nirari II (910-889 B.C.) tell us that they hunted elephants in the region of Haran and on the river Khabur (Luckenbill, *AR* I, pars. 247, 375, 392). An elephant received as tribute by Thutmose III of Egypt is depicted in the tomb of his vizier Rekh-mi-Re, and another received as tribute by Shalmaneser III of Assyria (859-824 B.C.) is shown on the Black Obelisk. These elephants were the Indian and not the African species. The numerous ivory objects excavated throughout the Near East prove that elephants must have been common in those regions in ancient times.

The Egyptians imported ivory from Punt (Somaliland) via the Red Sea, or traded for it at Elephantine on the south Egyptian border. Solomon obtained his ivory from abroad (1 Ki 10:22; 2 Chr 9:21) through the Red Sea port of Eziongeber, and may have received it from the same sources as the Egyptians. The ivory

249. An ivory panel from *Nimrûd*, Biblical Calah, showing a woman looking through a window

traded by the Phoenicians and that used in Mesopotamia may have come from the Syrian elephant, or may have been obtained from caravans from Africa. The OT mentions ivory in connection with Solomon's throne (1 Ki 10:18), couches (Amos 6:4), a palace (1 Ki 22:39; Ps 45: 8; Amos 3:15), and a tower (Song 7:4). It is obvious that in these cases the ivory was not the building material, but was prominent in its decorations. The author of Song of Solomon compares the body of the bridegroom (ch 5:14) and the neck of the bride (ch 7:4) to white ivory.

The excavations of many Near Eastern sites, including those of Palestine, have brought to light various ivory objects. Figurines representing gods and animals, amulets, plaques, reliefs, combs, balances, game pieces, tools for anointing, and strips with which wooden boxes (now decayed) had been inlaid, have been uncovered. The finest pieces of Palestinian ivory work were found at the southern *Tell el-Fâr'ah*, at Megiddo, and at Samaria. Those from Samaria came doubtlessly from Ahab's "ivory house." Similar objects have been found at *Arslan Tash* in northern Mesopotamia, among which were the inscribed pieces of a bed of King Hazael of Damascus. At *Nimrûd* (Biblical Calah), ivory objects were found, some of which show such a great similarity to the Samaria ivories that it may be assumed that they either came from Ahab's palace, or were made by the same craftsmen in Assyria. In Rev 18:12 vessels of ivory are listed among the many treasures possessed by the mystic Babylon. See figs. 213, 247, 248, 249.

Lit.: J. W. and G. M. Crowfoot, *Early Ivories From Samaria* (London, 1938); R. D. Barnett, *PEQ* 71 (1939), 4-19; G. Loud, *The Megiddo Ivories* (Chicago, 1939); Barnett, *The Nimrud Ivories* (London, 1957).

Ivvah (ĭv′à), KJV **Ivah** (ī′và). [Heb. *'Iwwah.*] A city conquered by the Assyrians under either Sargon II or Sennacherib (2 Ki 18:34; 19:13; Is 37:13). It is probably the same as Ava, Heb. *'Awwa'* (2 Ki 17: 24), from which colonists were brought to people the former Israelite cities in Samaria. The site has not been identified with certainty. See Avva.

Iye-abarim (ī′yĕ-ăb′à-rĭm), KJV **Ije-abarim** (ī′jĕ-ăb′à-rĭm). [Heb. *'Iyê ha'abarîm,* "Iyim of the further regions."] An encampment of the Israelites in the highland of Moab near the Zered (Num 21:11; 33:45), abbreviated to Iyim (KJV "Iim") in ch 33: 45. Map V, A-7.

Iyim. See Iim and Iye-abarim.

Izehar. See Izhar, I.

Izhar, I (ĭz′här), KJV once **Izehar** (ĭz′ĕ-här). [Heb. *Yishar,* probably "He (God) shines."] A son of Kohath, and founder of a tribal family (Ex 6:18, 21; Num 3:19, 27); called Amminadab in 1 Chr 6:22.

Izharites (ĭz′här-īts), KJV once **Izeharites** (ĭz′ĕ-här-īts). [Heb. *Yishari.*] Descendants of *Izhar, I (Num 3:27).

Izhar, II (ĭz′här), KJV **Jezoar** (jĕ-zō′ĕr). [Heb. *Yischar,* "he is yellowish-red."] A descendant of Judah, of the family of Hezron (1 Chr 4:7).

Izliah (ĭz-lī′à), KJV **Jezliah** (jĕz-lī′à). [Heb. *Yizli'ah,* meaning uncertain.] A son of Elpaal, and a Benjamite chief (1 Chr 8:18).

Izrahiah (ĭz′rà-hī′à). [Heb. *Yizrachyah,* "Yahweh shines."] A descendant of Issachar through Tola (1 Chr 7:3).

Izrahite (ĭz′rà-hīt). [Heb. *Yizrach,* "He (God) shines."] Either a member of a family of Izrah or a native of a town of the same name (1 Chr 27:8), neither of which has been identified. Some think that Izrahite is a mistake for Zerahite, mentioned in 1 Chr 27:11.

Izri. See Zeri.

Izziah (ĭz-ī′à), KJV **Jeziah** (jĕ-zī′à). [Heb. *Yizziyah,* meaning uncertain.] An Israelite who had married a foreign wife in Ezra's time (Ezr 10:25).

J

Jaakan (jā′à-kăn), KJV **Jakan** (jā′kăn), or **Akan** (ā′kăn). [Heb. *Ya'aqan* and *'Aqan.*] A descendant of the Horites, or Hurrians, and possibly the ancestor of a clan that apparently merged with the Edomites without completely losing its identity (Gen 36:27; 1 Chr 1:42). It has been suggested that the spelling "Jaakan" (KJV "Jakan") in Chronicles is the result of reading the Hebrew term translated "and Akan" in Genesis as *Ya'aqan,* "Jaakan." However, this is not certain. If the man was actually known as Jaakan, the *Bene-jaakan (sons of Jaakan) may have been his descendants (see Deut 10:6).

Jaakobah (jā'á-kō'bá). [Heb. *Ya'aqobah*, probably "deception."] The head of a family of Simeonites (1 Chr 4:36).

Jaala. *See* Jaalah.

Jaalah (jā'á-lá), or **Jaala** (jā'á-lá). [Heb. *Ya'alah* and *Ya'ala'*, "mountain goat."] The ancestral head of a family of Solomon's servants, some members of which returned from Babylonia with Zerubbabel (Ezr 2: 56; Neh 7:58).

Jaalam. *See* Jalam.

Jaanai. *See* Janai.

Jaar (jā'är). [Heb. *Ya'ar*, "wood."] A name appearing in the RSV of Ps 132:6, probably a shortened form of *Kiriath-jearim (Jos 9:17). The KJV translators considered the Heb. *Ya'ar* a common noun and translated it "wood," but it is more probably a proper name.

Jaareoregim. *See* Jair, II.

Jaareshiah (jā'á-rĕ-shī'á), KJV **Jaresiah** (jār'-ĕ-sī'á). [Heb. *Ya'areshyah*, probably "Yahweh plants."] A descendant of Benjamin (1 Chr 8:27).

Jaasau. *See* Jaasu.

Jaasiel (já-ā'sĭ-ĕl), KJV once **Jasiel** (jā'sĭ-ĕl). [Heb. *Ya'aśî'el*, "God makes."]

1. One of David's "mighty men," called a Mezobaite (1 Chr 11:47). It is not certain whether Mezobaite means that he descended from a family by that name, not identified, or whether he was a native of a place called Mezoba, or Zobah, not identified.

2. A Benjamite (1 Chr 27:21).

Jaasu (jā'á-sū), KJV **Jaasau** (jā'á-sô). [Heb. *Ya'aśaw* (Q *Ya'aśay*), "he makes."] An Israelite of the family of Bani. He was married to a foreign wife in the time of Ezra (Ezr 10:37).

Jaazaniah (já-ăz'á-nī'á). [Heb. *Ya'azanyah* and *Ya'azanyahû*, "Yahweh hears." The

250. The agate seal (left) and seal impression (right) of "Jaazaniah, servant of the king," with one of the earliest representations of the rooster found in Palestine. From *Tell en-Naṣbeh* (actual size)

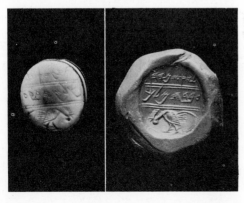

name occurs also on an ancient Hebrew seal, and on the Lachish ostraca.]

1. A Maacathite, who was an army officer in the reign of Zedekiah (2 Ki 25: 23), called Jezaniah (jĕz'á-nī'á) [Heb. *Yezanyahû*], a shortened form, in Jer 40: 8; 42:1, KJV. He escaped from the fighting that culminated in the fall of Jerusalem and the captivity of the nation, and when Gedaliah was appointed governor over Judea he came to Mizpah, the seat of the provincial government, and gave allegiance to the new governor. After Gedaliah's murder he with other leaders approached Jeremiah the prophet to seek divine advice with regard to their plans to migrate to Egypt (ch 42:1-3).

2. A Rechabite leader, son of a certain Jeremiah. The prophet Jeremiah offered him and other members of his family wine so as to make their refusal to touch it an example of obedience to the rebellious house of Judah (Jer 35:3-10).

3. One of 70 elders in Jerusalem whom Ezekiel in vision saw offering incense to idols (Eze 8:11).

4. A prince of the people in Judah, who was shown to Ezekiel in vision as devising wickedness (Eze 11:1, 2).

Jaazer. *See* Jazer.

Jaaziah (jā'á-zī'á). [Heb. *Ya'azîyahû*, "Yahweh strengthens."] A Merarite Levite (1 Chr 24:26, 27). On the textual difficulties of v 26 see *SDACom* 3:193.

Jaaziel (já-ā'zĭ-ĕl). [Heb. *Ya'azî'el*, "God strengthens."] A Levite musician of the 2d degree in the time of David (1 Chr 15:18). Some commentators identify him with the "Aziel" of v 20, and with the "Jeiel" of ch 16:5.

Jabal (jā'băl). [Heb. *Yabal*, possibly "sprout," "leader," or "stream."] Son of Lamech of the line of Cain. He was "the father" of nomadism and of cattle breeding (Gen 4:20).

Jabbok (jăb'ŏk). [Heb. *Yabboq*.] A river in Transjordan which in the time of Moses formed the northern border of the Amorite kingdom of Sihon (Num 21:23, 24; Jos 12:2; Jgs 11:22), as well as the northern boundary line of the Ammonite territory (Deut 2:37; 3:16). The sources of this river are near Rabbath-ammon. From these it flows first in a generally northerly direction but after about 20 mi. it turns west and enters the Jordan about 23 mi. north of the Dead Sea. Its modern name is *Nahr ez-Zerqā*, the "blue river." Jacob's struggle with the angel occurred at a ford of the Jabbok (Gen 32:22-32). When

After Saul's death in battle the inhabitants of Jabesh-gilead demonstrated their loyalty and gratitude to Saul by rescuing his body, and the bodies of his sons, from the wall of Beth-shean, where the Philistines had fastened them, burying them near their own town (1 Sa 31:11-13; 1 Chr 10:11, 12). Later the remains were transferred to Saul's family sepulcher in western Palestine (2 Sa 21:12-14). David sent the people of Jabesh-gilead a special message of thanks for their kindhearted act (ch 2:4-7). Eusebius claims that the town lay 6 Roman mi. from Pella. The *Wâdī Yâbis* has retained the ancient name. The site has been identified by Glueck with the large joint site of *Tell el-Meqbereh* and *Tell Abū Kharaz* (*BASOR* 89 [1943], 2-6; 91 [1943], 8-9). Others have identified it with *Tell el-Maqlûb* (see Map VI, D-4).

Jabez (jā'bĕz). [Heb. *Ya'beṣ,* meaning uncertain. However, in 1 Chr 4:9 his name is connected with "sorrow" (Heb. *'oṣeb,* "pain"), so that the idea of "pain" may somehow be connected with it.]

1. A man of Judah whose mother gave him this name because she had borne him in pain (1 Chr 4:9). Because of his personal piety God blessed him and increased his possessions (v 10).

2. A town in which certain families of scribes lived (1 Chr 2:55). It was probably in Judah.

Jabin (jā'bĭn). [Heb. *Yabin,* "he understands."]

1. The Canaanite king of the city of Hazor in the time of Joshua. He stood at the head of a confederation of city-states in northern Canaan, which the Israelites defeated. After the battle Jabin was slain and Hazor burned (Jos 11:1-14).

2. A king of Hazor who oppressed Israel during the period of the judges for 20 years. He was probably a descendant of Jabin, 1. His army, led by Sisera, was defeated by Barak and Deborah of Israel. He continued his opposition for a time, but was eventually destroyed (Jgs 4:2-24).

Jabneel (jăb'nē-ĕl). [Heb. *Yabne'el,* "God causes to be built."]

1. The westernmost town of Judah on its northern boundary (Jos 15:11). If, as generally held, Jabneel is identical with Jabneh (jăb'nĕ) [Heb. *Yabneh*] (2 Chr 26:6), then it was Jabneel that King Uzziah of Judah captured from the Philistines. Later, Jabneh was known as Jamnia (1 Macc 4:15; 5:58; 2 Macc 12:8, 9). It

251. The river Jabbok near the traditional site of Jacob's struggle

Transjordan was taken over by the Israelites, the Jabbok, which divided Gilead into two parts, formed the northern boundary of the tribe of Gad and the southern boundary of Manasseh. Map VI, D-4. See figs. 251, 272.

Jabesh (jā'bĕsh). [Heb. *Yabesh,* "dry."]

1. An Israelite whose son, Shallum, usurped the throne of Israel but reigned only 1 month (2 Ki 15:10).

2. A shortened form of the name *Jabesh-gilead.

Jabesh-gilead (jā'bĕsh-gĭl'ē-ăd). [Heb. *Yabesh Gil'ad.*] A city in Gilead whose Israelite inhabitants were destroyed by other Israelites in the period of the judges. This wholesale slaughter was in punishment for the inhabitants' refusal to take part in the war waged by the various tribes against the Benjamites. Only 400 unmarried girls were spared and given to 400 surviving men of Benjamin as wives (Jgs 21:8-15). However, the city seems to have been quickly repopulated. King Saul rescued it early in his reign when the Ammonites besieged it (1 Sa 11:1-11).

gained fame after the destruction of Jerusalem in A.D. 70, when it became the seat of the reorganized Jewish council and a center of rabbinical learning. A Jewish council, held at Jamnia toward the end of the 1st cent. A.D., confirmed the canon of the OT. It is now the village of *Yebnā*, about 12 mi. south of Jaffa near the left bank of the *Nahr Rûbin*, on the Gaza-Jaffa road. See Jabneh on Map VI, E-2.

2. A place on the boundary of Naphtali (Jos 19:33), called *Kaphar Yama* in later Jewish writings. It may be the site of *Yemmā* between Mount Tabor and the Sea of Galilee.

Jabneh. *See* Jabneel, 1.

Jacan (jā′kăn), KJV **Jachan** (jā′kăn). [Heb. *Ya'kan*.] A Gadite (1 Chr 5:13).

Jachan. *See* Jacan.

Jachin (jā′kĭn). [Heb. *Yakin*, "he establishes." The name occurs also in Phoenician, and in Assyrian it is spelled *Yakini*.]

1. Son of Simeon, and founder of a tribal family, the Jachinites (jā′kĭn-īts) [Heb. *Yakîni*] (Gen 46:10; Ex 6:15; Num 26:12). He is apparently called Jarib in 1 Chr 4:24.

2. A descendant of Aaron. His family formed the 21st of the 24 courses into which David organized the priests (1 Chr 24:17). Representatives of this family are also mentioned in ch 9:10 and in Neh 11:10.

3. The name of the right-hand pillar set up in the porch of Solomon's Temple (1 Ki 7:15-22; 2 Chr 3:17). It has not definitely been explained why the pillar was named Jachin, but there is a probability that the name was an abbreviation of an inscription engraved on it. An analogy may be seen in a pillar discovered in the temple of *Ṣirwâh* in Arabia on which the word *knt*, "strength," was engraved.

Jachinites. *See* Jachin, 1.

Jacinth. [Heb. *leshem;* Gr. *huakinthos.*] The precious stone referred to by the Hebrew and Greek terms rendered "jacinth" (Ex 28:19; 39:12; RSV; Rev 9:17, KJV; 21:20) cannot be identified. *Leshem*, translated "ligure" (KJV) and "jacinth" (RSV), was one of the precious stones on the third row of gems on the high priest's breastplate (Ex 28:19; 39:12). In Rev 9:17 the adjectival form *huakinthinos* describes some characteristic, perhaps a color, of the breastplates of the horsemen under the 6th trumpet. *Huakinthos* is the 11th foundation of the New Jerusalem (ch 21:20).

Jackal. The term "jackal" does not occur in the KJV, but appears in the RSV as a rendering of the Heb. *tan, 'i,* and *shû'al.* In the KJV *tan* is translated "dragon," "sea monsters," etc., *'i* "wild beast of the islands," and *shû'al* "fox." The jackal (*Canis aureus*) belongs to the family of dogs, but has a longer and more pointed muzzle. It differs also in its fur, which is of a brownish yellow color, mottled with black, gray, and brown hair. It roams the desert and ruined places (Is 13:22; 34:13; 43:20; Jer 9:11; 10:22; 49:33; 50:39; 51:37), alone and in packs, and lives largely on corpses and carcasses. Its nightly howlings (Job 30:29; Mic 1:8) are extremely unnerving. Jackals are still found all over Palestine and in other countries of the Near East.

Jackal's Well, KJV **Dragon Well.** [Heb. *'Ēn Hattannin*, "spring of the water monster."] A spring outside of Jerusalem between the Valley Gate and the Dung Gate (Neh 2:13), frequently identified with En-rogel, now *Bir Ayyûb*. However, it is more likely a spring or well now dry in the Tyropoeon Valley, between the southeastern and southwestern hills of Jerusalem.

Jacob (jā′kŭb). [Heb. *Ya'aqob*, "he takes by the heel," "he supplants." The name occurs repeatedly in cuneiform records, usually spelled *Yaqub-El*, "Jacob of (the god) El," and in Egyptian texts as *Y'qbir*. Gr. *Iakōb*.]

1. Isaac's 2d son, twin of Esau, father of the 12 patriarchs, and a progenitor of the Hebrew people. Rebekah, Isaac's wife, bore Esau and Jacob 20 years after her marriage to Isaac. She had been childless, and Isaac had interceded with the Lord on her behalf when he was about 60 years old (Gen 25:21, 22). Prior to the birth of the twins the Lord told Rebekah that the elder should serve the younger, thus indicating that Jacob was to become inheritor of the birthright (v 23). The name Jacob commemorates the fact that Jacob was born grasping Esau's heel, an incident the parents noted and later seem to have taken as an omen of the destined relationship between the 2 brothers (Gen 25:26; 27:36; Hos 12:3). While Esau took to the adventuresome life of the hunter, at which he excelled, Jacob grew up to be a "quiet man" who preferred the domestic, pastoral routine of the encampment (Gen 25:27, RSV). Rivalry developed between the 2 brothers because Isaac favored Esau, his first-born, while Rebekah was partial to Jacob. Isaac seems never to have been wholly reconciled to the idea that Jacob

should become his heir, as implied by the prenatal communication from the Lord to Rebekah (Gen 25:23), but apparently preferred Esau because he admired his bold, adventuresome, masculine traits. Rebekah, on the other hand, remained loyal to the prenatal admonition, doubtless also appreciating Jacob's practical, industrious disposition (v 28).

The incident recorded in Gen 25:29-34 graphically portrays the dominant character traits of Jacob and Esau, and provides a clue that explains why God rejected Esau as custodian of the covenant trust (cf. Rom 9:10-13). Jacob was preparing a meal of red lentil pottage when Esau, faint and discouraged after a fruitless hunting expedition, approached and asked for a portion. Grasping what he saw as an opportunity to obtain the birthright, Jacob covetously demanded that Esau sell him his birthright before he could have any food. Esau, manifesting his lack of a sense of relative values and of emotional stability, renounced the birthright for a dish of lentils (see Heb. 12:16).

At the age of about 137 Isaac proposed to Esau that the time had come for the formal transfer of the patriarchal blessing to him as the first-born (Gen 27:1-4). The rite was to take place over a meal of venison which Esau was to bring in fresh from the field (vs 3, 4). However, on Rebekah's initiative, Jacob conspired to impersonate Esau before the nearly blind Isaac in order to secure the blessing by subterfuge, in the mistaken belief that the prenatal promise of primacy would otherwise be lost (vs 5-29). Dressed in Esau's clothes and wearing hairy skins to make him as much as possible like Esau, who was hairy, Jacob presented his father with food hastily prepared by Rebekah, and received the blessing. This thinly disguised intrigue at first shocked Esau into utter despair (vs 30-38), which, however, soon turned into hatred and a desire for revenge (v 41). Learning of Esau's furtive plot to slay his brother, Rebekah, under the guise of finding a suitable wife for Jacob, arranged that Jacob should temporarily leave Canaan for the safety of her childhood home in Haran (vs 42-46).

On his way into 20 years of exile, during which Rebekah died, the 77-year-old Jacob, for the first time as heir to the privileges and responsibilities of the covenant, experienced a personal encounter with God and vowed to fulfill his part

should he be able to return home (Gen 28:10-22). Upon arriving in the vicinity of Haran, Jacob met Rachel, his mother's niece, under circumstances reminiscent of those in which Abraham's trusty steward had found a wife for his father in the same vicinity nearly a century before (ch 29:1-12; cf. ch 24:10-28). Now, perhaps, Jacob sensed the blessing of God on his own mission. About a month after his arrival, Jacob arranged to marry Rachel by serving her father, Laban, for 7 years (ch 29:14-20). At the end of the period Jacob, the artful deceiver, was deceived into marrying Rachel's older sister Leah, and was then required to serve an additional 7 years for Rachel (vs 21-30). During the second 7 years 11 sons and 1 daughter were born to Jacob—Reuben, Simeon, Levi, Judah, Issachar, Zebulun, and Dinah by Leah; Gad and Asher by Leah's maid, Zilpah; Joseph by Rachel; and Dan and Naphtali by Rachel's maid, Bilhah (chs 29:32 to 30:24). After 6 additional years of service, during which Jacob developed his own flocks of cattle and herds of sheep, thereby arousing the jealousy of Laban and his sons (ch 31:1, 43), Jacob suspected a plot to deprive him of his property, and departed surreptitiously for his home in Canaan (chs 30:25 to 31:18-21, 31). Learning of Jacob's flight, Laban and his sons pursued Jacob and overtook him 7 days later (ch 31:19-25). Warned on the way by God, Laban confined himself to expostulating with Jacob (vs 24-35), and the 2 men entered into a mutual nonaggression pact before parting (vs 36-55).

Tokens of divine presence and blessing marked Jacob's return journey to Canaan, 1st a vision of angels at Mahanaim (Gen 32:1, 2), and then the encounter with the Angel of the Lord in person at the *Jabbok (Gen 32:24-30; cf. Hos 12:4). Prior to the 2d token Jacob had sent a peace mission to placate Esau's anger, but Esau had responded by setting out with 400 men, ostensibly to attack Jacob (Gen 32:3-8). This confronted Jacob with the crisis of his life, later called "the time of Jacob's trouble" (Jer 30:7). In this, his 2d recorded personal encounter with the Lord, Jacob experienced a thorough conversion and change of heart (Gen 32:9-30). He was also given a new name— Israel, "God contends" or "God rules"—in token of his submission to God under the covenant relationship (v 28). The next day Jacob met Esau, and a spirit of brotherhood was re-established between them (Gen 33:1-15). Jacob remained for a time at Succoth, east of the Jordan, and later moved to the vicinity of Shechem, where he bought a piece of land (vs 17-20). Here his sons dealt treacherously with the men of Shechem in the matter of their sister Dinah, and greatly embarrassed and perplexed Jacob (ch 34), so that he removed to Bethel (ch 35:1-8), where God again confirmed His covenant with him (vs 9-15). As Jacob journeyed from Bethel to meet his father at Mamre, near Hebron (v 27), Rachel died in giving birth to Benjamin, and Jacob buried her near Ephrath (vs 16-20). A little later Isaac died, and his 2 sons laid him to rest in the family burial ground at Hebron (vs 28, 29; cf. ch 49:31). For several years Jacob remained in the southland, where Abraham and Isaac had spent so many years, doubtless moving from place to place to find pasture for his flocks and herds (ch 37:1).

During this time Jacob manifested the same unwise partiality for his favorite son, Joseph (Gen 37:3, 4), that his father Isaac had shown toward Esau (ch 25:28), with similarly disastrous results. The crisis came about 12 years before the death of Isaac (cf. chs 25:26; 37:2; 41:46, 47, 54; 45:6; 47:9) when Joseph was sold as a slave into Egypt by his older brothers (ch 37:23-36). Bereft of Joseph (vs 32-35), whom for about 22 years he had thought to be dead, Jacob at first reacted with incredulity upon hearing that Joseph not only was alive but was a prince in the land of Egypt (ch 45:25, 26). But upon Joseph's invitation, and because of the severe drought then prevailing in Palestine (vs 9-15), Jacob migrated to Egypt (chs 45:27, 28; 46:1) at the age of 130 (ch 47:9), and spent the 17 remaining years of his life there. At the age of 147 he summoned his 12 sons, pronounced a blessing upon each, and then died (chs 48; 49). Joseph had his father embalmed, and buried him in the Cave of *Machpelah near Hebron, the ancestral burial ground (ch 50:1-13; cf. chs 23:3-20; 49:29-33).

2. The descendants of Jacob, collectively, in all generations (Num 23:21; Is 2:5; etc.).

3. The father of Joseph, husband of Mary according to Matthew's *genealogy of Christ (Mt 1:15, 16).

Jacob's Well. A deep well about ½ mi. south of 'Askar (a possible site of NT Sychar) and about 2 mi. east of Nablus, at the

eastern slope of Mount Gerizim. It is near a fork of a road coming from Jerusalem, one branch of which leads to Samaria, and the other to Tirzah and Beth-shean. The well was dug by Jacob when he encamped in the vicinity of Shechem, probably to obtain water for his family without getting into conflict with the people of Shechem (Jn 4:12; Gen 33:18-20; 37:12). It was here that the memorable conversation between Jesus and the Samaritan woman as recorded in Jn 4:5-26 took

252. Jacob's Well, with the ancient well top before modern repair work changed it

place. The present well (see fig. 252), which is doubtless authentic, was originally much deeper than its present 75 ft., since the lower part has been filled with rubbish. Its diameter is 7½ ft.; its upper part is built of masonry, whereas its lower part is cut through limestone rock. The quality of water is much better than that of other springs in the valley. The well now lies in a crypt of an ancient Greek church. The church has been in the process of rebuilding for many years.

Jada (jā'dá). [Heb. *Yada'*, "he knows." The name occurs also in ancient South Arabic.] A Judahite of the family of Hezron (1 Chr 2:28, 32).

Jadau. *See* Jaddai.

Jaddai (jăd'ī), KJV **Jadau** (jā'dô). [Heb. *Yaddaw* (Q *Yadday*]. A Jew who was married to a foreign wife in Ezra's time (Ezr 10:43).

Jaddua (jă-dū'á). [Heb. *Yaddúa'*, "known." The name occurs also in ancient South Arabic inscriptions and in the Lachish Letters.]
1. A leading Jew who set his seal to Nehemiah's covenant (Neh 10:21).
2. A high priest, son of Jonathan, and the 5th in descent from Jeshua, the first postexilic high priest (Neh 12:11, 22). Whether he is to be identified with the Jaddua of the time of Alexander the Great mentioned by Josephus (*Ant.* xi. 7. 2; 8. 4-7) is uncertain, in view of the unreliability of Josephus with regard to the history of that period. If Jaddua was the name of the high priest who met Alexander, he may have been the grandson of the Jaddua mentioned in the book of Nehemiah (see *SDACom* 3:372, 373).

Jadon (jā'dŏn). [Heb. *Yadón*, "he judges."] A man from Meronoth, a place not identified. He assisted Nehemiah in rebuilding Jerusalem's wall (Neh 3:7).

Jael (jā'ĕl). [Heb. *Ya'el*, "mountain goat."] The wife of Heber, the Kenite (Jgs 4:17). Sisera, the general of Jabin, king of Hazor, fleeing from the forces of Barak, found shelter in her home. At this time there had been peace between Heber's clan and the kingdom of Hazor. Utterly exhausted, Sisera fell asleep, whereupon Jael killed him by driving a tent pin through his temple with a hammer. For this she was praised by Deborah and Barak in their song of victory (vs 11-22; ch 5:6, 24-27).

Jagur (jā'gẽr). [Heb. *Yagûr*.] A town in the extreme south of Judah, near Edom (Jos 15:21); not identified.

Jah (jä). A transliteration of the Heb. *Yah* (Ps 68:4, KJV), an abbreviated form of the divine name *YHWH*. The Hebrew term occurs repeatedly, but is elsewhere translated "Lord" (Ex 15:2; Is 12:2; etc.). *See* Yahweh.

Jahath (jā'hăth). [Heb. *Yachath*, meaning uncertain.]
1. A Judahite belonging to the family of Hezron (1 Chr 4:2; cf. ch 2:52-54).
2. A Gershonite Levite, the son of Libni (1 Chr 6:20, 43).

3. The head of a subdivision of Gershonite Levites (1 Chr 23:10, 11).
4. A Kohathite Levite (1 Chr 24:22).
5. A Merarite Levite in charge of the workmen who repaired the Temple in the reign of Josiah (2 Chr 34:12).

Jahaz (jā'hăz), or **Jahzah** (jä'zá), KJV once **Jahaza** (já-hā'zá), twice **Jahazah** (já-hā'zá). [Heb. *Yahas* and *Yahsah*.] A city in Transjordan, where Israel slew the Amorite king Sihon of Heshbon (Num 21:23; Deut 2:32, 33; Jgs 11:20, 21). After the division of the land the city lay in the territory of Reuben (Jos 13:15, 18), but was assigned to the Merarite Levites as a residence city (Jos 21:36; 1 Chr 6:77, 78). Mesha, king of Moab, took it from the Israelites (Moabite Stone, lines 18-20). Subsequently it remained in the hands of the Moabites (Is 15:4; Jer 48:20, 21, 34). The site has not been identified with certainty. It may be either *Jālûl*, 2 mi. southeast of Medeba, or *Khirbet et-Teim*, 3½ mi. east of Medeba.

Jahaza. *See* Jahaz.

Jahazah. *See* Jahaz.

Jahaziah. *See* Jahzeiah.

Jahaziel (já-hā'zī-ĕl). [Heb. *Yachazi'el*, "God sees."]
1. A Kohathite Levite of the house of Hebron (1 Chr 23:19; 24:23).
2. A Benjamite who joined David at Ziklag (1 Chr 12:4).
3. A priest employed by David as a trumpeter before the ark (1 Chr 16:6).
4. An Asaphite Levite who prophesied in the time of King Jehoshaphat and encouraged him against Moab (2 Chr 20:14, 15).
5. A Jew in Babylon whose son returned with Ezra from Babylonia (Ezr 8:5).

Jahdai (jā'dâ-ī). [Heb. *Yahday*, meaning uncertain.] A Judahite of the family of Caleb (1 Chr 2:47).

Jahdiel (jā'dī-ĕl). [Heb. *Yachdi'el*, "God gives joy."] A chieftain of the half tribe of Manasseh (1 Chr 5:24).

Jahdo (jā'dō). [Heb. *Yachdô.*] A Gadite (1 Chr 5:14).

Jahleel (jä'lĕ-ĕl). [Heb. *Yachle'el*, meaning uncertain.] A son of Zebulun and founder of the tribal family, the Jahleelites (jä'lĕ-ĕl-īts) [Heb. *Yachle'eli*] (Gen 46:14; Num 26:26).

Jahleelites. *See* Jahleel.

Jahmai (jä'mâ-ī). [Heb. *Yachmay*, "he protects."] A prince of Issachar (1 Chr 7:2).

Jahzah. *See* Jahaz.

Jahzeel (jä′zĕ-ĕl), or **Jahziel** (jä′zĭ-ĕl). [Heb. *Yachṣe'el* and *Yachṣî'el*, "God distributes."] A son of Naphtali, and ancestor of the Jahzeelites (jä′zĕ-ĕl-īts) [Heb. *Yachṣe'elî*] (Gen 46:24; Num 26:48; 1 Chr 7:13).

Jahzeelites. *See* Jahzeel.

Jahzeiah (jä-zē′yȧ), KJV **Jahaziah** (jä′hȧ-zī′ȧ). [Heb. *Yachzeyah*, "Yahweh sees."] One of the 4 men who opposed Ezra's plan for putting away foreign wives (Ezr 10:15).

Jahzerah (jä′zĕ-rȧ). [Heb. *Yachzerah,* meaning uncertain.] A priest descended from Immer (1 Chr 9:12). He was probably the *Ahzai (KJV "Ahasai") of Neh 11:13.

Jahziel. *See* Jahzeel.

Jair, I (jä′ẽr). [Heb. *Ya'îr,* "he enlightens." The name occurs in Akkadian as *Ya'iru.*]
1. A descendant of Judah (1 Chr 2:3, 21, 22), who seems to have been reckoned to Manasseh (Num 32:40, 41; Deut 3: 14), probably because his grandfather Hezron married a woman of the tribe of Manasseh. At the time of the conquest of Transjordan under Moses, Jair took villages on the border of Bashan and Gilead, which were in Manassite territory (1 Chr 5:23), and called them Havvoth-jair, "tent villages of Jair" (Num 32:41; Deut 3:14).
2. A Gileadite who judged Israel for 22 years. He had 30 sons whom he installed as administrators over the 30 villages of Jair. He may have been a direct descendant of Jair, 1, and thus may have had some rights to these communities (Jgs 10: 3-5).
3. A Benjamite, the father or ancestor of Mordecai (Est 2:5).

Jair, II (jä′ẽr). [Heb. *Ya'îr,* "he arouses." The name occurs also in ancient South Arabic.] A man whose son Elhanan slew Lahmi, the brother of Goliath the Gittite (1 Chr 20:5). He is called Jaareoregim (jä′ȧ-rĕ-ôr′ĕ-jĭm) [Heb. *Ya'rê 'oregîm*] in 2 Sa 21:19, where a scribe may have inserted the word *'oregîm,* "weavers," from the next line of the same verse.

Jair, Villages of. *See* Havvoth-jair.

Jairite (jä′ẽr-īt). [Heb. *Ya'iri.*] A descendant of a certain Jair (2 Sa 20:26).

Jairus (jä′ĭ-rŭs). [Gr. *Iaïros,* from Heb. *Ya'îr.*] A ruler of a synagogue, probably at Capernaum, who requested Jesus to heal his dying daughter. While the two were on the way to his home, word came that the girl had died. Encouraging the father not to fear, Jesus proceeded to the home. Taking only her parents and the disciples Peter, James, and John, He entered the room in which the child lay, took the girl by the hand, and said in Aramaic, *telitha' qûmî,* "girl, arise," and she immediately obeyed Him. In spite of Jesus' request that the matter be kept secret, news concerning the miracle spread rapidly (Mt 9:18, 19, 23-26; Mk 5:22-24, 35-43; Lk 8:41, 42, 49-56).

Jakan. *See* Jaakan.

Jakeh (jä′kĕ). [Heb. *Yaqeh,* meaning uncertain.] A man whose son, Agur, is presented as the author of the confessions and instructions recorded in Prov 30 (v 1).

Jakim (jä′kĭm). [Heb. *Yaqîm,* "he raises."]
1. A descendant of Aaron, and ancestral head of the 12th of the 24 courses into which David organized the priests (1 Chr 24:12).
2. A Benjamite (1 Chr 8:19).

Jalam (jä′lăm), KJV **Jaalam** (jä′ȧ-lăm). [Heb. *Ya'lam.*] A son of Esau by his wife Oholibamah (KJV "Aholibamah"). He was one of the chieftains of Edom (Gen 36:5, 14, 18; 1 Chr 1:35).

Jalon (jä′lŏn). [Heb. *Yalôn.*] A Judahite, the son of Ezrah (1 Chr 4:17).

Jambres (jăm′brēz). [Gr. *Iambrēs.*] One of 2 Egyptians, presumably magicians, who opposed Moses (2 Ti 3:8). *See* Jannes.

James (jāmz). [Gr. *Iakōbos,* from the Heb. *Ya'aqob,* Jacob.] At least 4 persons mentioned in the NT bore this name—2 of the Twelve (a son of Zebedee and a son of Alphaeus), a brother of Jesus, and the father of Judas, one of the Twelve. One of the early leaders of the church at Jerusalem was named James, as was also the author of an epistle, though these have generally been identified with either the son of Alphaeus or with the brother of Jesus. Possibly "James the less" (Mk 15:40) may be similarly identified.
1. A son of Zebedee and a brother of John (Mt 4:21). The 2 brothers were formally called to discipleship at the time Peter and Andrew were called (Mt 4:18-22; Lk 5:10). Nothing is known of James's life or background prior to the call by the sea at the opening of Jesus' Galilean ministry. He was doubtless a Galilean by birth. That Zebedee had hired servant assistants (Mk 1:20) implies that the family possessed a superior economic status, and the fact that his brother John was known to the high priest and secured ready access to his house on the night of the betrayal (Jn 18:16) similarly implies some degree of social standing. With Peter and John, James made up the inner circle who enjoyed a more intimate association with Jesus upon numerous occasions than

their fellow disciples, apparently because they understood better and entered more fully into the spirit of His mission to earth (Mk 3:17; 9:2; 13:3; 14:33). Because James is usually named first when he and his brother John are mentioned together (ch 1:19; etc.), it has been inferred that James was the elder of the 2. The occasional mention of John first (Lk 9:28) is doubtless attributable to John's greater prominence as a disciple and later as an apostle. The epithet Boanerges, interpreted as "sons of thunder," applied to both James and John by Jesus (Mk 3:17), evidently characterizes them as of a naturally impetuous disposition, quick to take offense (Lk 9:54, 55) and to offend (Mk 10:41). James was present at the healing of Peter's mother-in-law, soon after the call by the sea (ch 1:29-31), and a few weeks or months afterward he was ordained one of the Twelve (ch 3:17). Later, in the Galilean ministry, he witnessed the raising of Jairus' daughter to life (ch 5:37), and was with Jesus on the mount of Transfiguration during Jesus' period of retirement from public ministry (ch 9:2-8). On the last journey from Galilee, James and John, offended by the open hostility of a certain Samaritan village that refused hospitality to Jesus and His disciples, proposed the destruction of the village by fire and were rebuked by Jesus (Lk 9:51-56). On the way to Jerusalem, James and John incurred the displeasure of their fellow disciples by seeking positions of honor in the kingdom they supposed Jesus was soon to establish, and again suffered rebuke by Jesus (Mk 10:32, 35-45). With Peter, John, and Andrew, James was present on the Mount of Olives for the Saviour's discourse on the signs of His coming (ch 13:3, 4), and was with Jesus in the Garden of Gethsemane on the night of the betrayal (ch 14:33). In addition to these instances where James is mentioned by name, he is assumed to have been present upon other occasions when the Twelve as a group are mentioned. James was the 1st of the Twelve to suffer martyrdom, being slain by Herod Agrippa I, about A.D. 44, not long before Herod's own death (Acts 12: 1, 2). James thus figuratively drank the cup he and John once rashly declared themselves able to drink (Mk 10:39).

2. The son of Alphaeus, clearly identified 4 times, always as one of the Twelve (Mt 10:3; Mk 3:18; Lk 6:15; Acts 1:13). Otherwise nothing certain is known concerning him. Inasmuch as Levi Matthew

was also the son of a man named Alphaeus (Mt 9:9), it is not impossible that he and this James were brothers. Matthew (Mt 10:3) and Mark (Mk 3:18) pair this James with Lebbaeus Thaddaeus, whereas Luke (Lk 6:15; Acts 1: 13), whose lists do not include a disciple by that name, pairs him with Simon the Zealot.

3. The Lord's brother, named first and thus presumably the eldest of Jesus' brothers (Mt 13:55; Mk 6:3), the others being Joses (RSV "Joseph," Mt 13:55), Simon, and Judas (see Brethren of the Lord). Like "James the less" he had a brother named Joses (Mt 27:56; see James, 5). In Gal 1:19 Paul refers to "James the Lord's brother" as one of the "apostles" he saw in Jerusalem upon his first visit to the city 3 years after his conversion. Aside from these references, this James is not certainly mentioned elsewhere. However, it is commonly believed that he is to be identified with the prominent leader of the church at Jerusalem mentioned several times in Acts and Galatians (see James, 4). This James is doubtless included elsewhere with the "brethren of the Lord," as in Jn 7:5 and Acts 1:14. The "brethren" of the Lord appear not to have believed in Jesus as the Messiah during His earthly life and ministry (Mt 12:46, 47; Jn 7:5), but are mentioned among the believers at Pentecost 10 days after the ascension (Acts 1: 14). In view of the fact that the "brethren" of the Lord are mentioned as accompanying Mary, the mother of Jesus (Mt 12:46, 47; Lk 8:19; Jn 2:12), and because they assumed the right to direct His ministry at various times (Mt 12:46, 47; Jn 7:3), it may be assumed that they were his older stepbrothers, the sons of Joseph by a previous marriage.

4. A church leader at Jerusalem. In the book of Acts (chs 12:17; 15:13; 21:18) and in 2 of Paul's epistles (1 Cor 15:7; Gal 2:9, 12) mention is made of a certain James who was a prominent leader in the church at Jerusalem, apparently head of the board of elders. He is mentioned first in this office soon after the death of James, the brother of John, c. A.D. 44 (Acts 12: 2, 17). This James is next mentioned as moderator of the Jerusalem Council, c. A.D. 49, at which he summed up the arguments presented and announced the decision (ch 15:13). About A.D. 58 this James still held his pre-eminent position at Jerusalem, when Paul presented a report of his ministry among the Gentiles and de-

livered the Gentile gift for poor Christians at Jerusalem (Acts 21:17-20). This leader of the church is always mentioned in such a way as to make evident that both Luke and Paul considered him sufficiently well known to require no further introduction to readers. In Gal 1:19 Paul speaks of seeing "James the Lord's brother" upon the occasion of his first postconversion visit to Jerusalem, and a few verses later (ch 2:9, 12) refers to a James as one of 3 "pillars" of the church there, without further identification, thus implying identity. James the leader at Jerusalem seems to have been a conservative Christian Jew who adhered closely to the rites of Judaism himself and who firmly believed that Jewish believers should do likewise (Acts 21:20; Gal 2:12), but who took a liberal view on such matters in so far as Gentile converts were concerned (Acts 15:13, 19). From early times it has been generally believed that James, the leader of the Jerusalem church, was James, the brother of our Lord.

5. Author of the epistle of James, who identifies himself simply as "a servant of God and of the Lord Jesus Christ" (ch 1:1). Many believe that he was James the Lord's brother, but there is no certain Biblical evidence either to prove or to disprove this. That the author considered it unnecessary to identify himself otherwise implies that he was well known to his intended readers, "the twelve tribes which are scattered abroad" (ch 1:1). Of other NT persons named James, only the son of Alphaeus and the Lord's brother seem to qualify. The weight of evidence may be construed as tending to favor the latter over the former.

6. The son of a certain Mary (see Mary, 5). He is described as "the less" (in years or in stature) and had a brother named Joses. He is referred to only in Mt 27:56; Mk 15:40; Lk 24:10, and there as the son of one of the Marys who attended Jesus at the cross and visited the tomb. James the brother of our Lord also had a brother named Joses (Mt 13:55), but it would seem strange for Mary the mother of Jesus to be identified at the cross as the mother of others than the Saviour Himself (cf. Jn 19:25-27). Some have identified James "the less" with James the son of Alphaeus, but this identification remains also in the realm of doubt.

7. The father (not the "brother" as in the KJV) of Judas (not Iscariot), one of the Twelve (Lk 6:16). Unless he was the brother of Jude, author of the epistle by

that name (Jude 1), he is otherwise unknown.

James, Epistle of. A general, or catholic, epistle addressed to "the twelve tribes which are scattered abroad" (Jas 1:1), that is, one not written to a particular individual or church. In the earliest manuscripts it either bore no title, or had the simple title "Epistle of James." In the Codex Sinaiticus "Epistle of James" appears as a subscript at the close. In the early extant NT manuscripts the 7 epistles from James to Jude immediately follow Acts and precede the epistles of Paul. The right of James to a place in the canon has never been seriously challenged.

The identity of the author is uncertain, inasmuch as the writer identifies himself as simply James, "a servant of God and of the Lord Jesus Christ" (Jas 1:1), and several persons by the name of James are mentioned in the NT. This simple introduction would indicate that at the time of writing apparently only one James was well-known to the church "scattered abroad" as a prominent, acknowledged leader. This would seem to date the epistle at least after the death of James the brother of John, c. A.D. 44, and thus leave only James the son of Alphaeus and James the brother of our Lord—commonly identified with James, a prominent leader in the church at Jerusalem—as possible authors. See James, 2, 5. The writer evidently expects that his readers will not question his authority. Accordingly, of known NT leaders, James the elder at Jerusalem seems best to qualify.

Whether the "twelve tribes . . . scattered abroad" (Jas 1:1) were literal Jews of the Diaspora or Christian believers generally, including Gentiles, cannot be determined with certainty. However, the instruction contained in the epistle seems most appropriate to literal Jews (see, for example, ch 2:21) who had already accepted Jesus Christ as "Lord" (chs 1:1, 7, 12; 2:1; 5:7, 11).

The epistle deals in a concrete way with practical problems within the church rather than with doctrinal problems, as such, and stresses the effect of faith upon the life. The works that result from faith mark off the true Christian from the one who has not experienced genuine conversion (Jas 2). By "works" James denotes the deeds that result from a living faith, not the "works" of the law by which Jews generally thought to attain to righteousness. Misunderstanding of this point has led some erroneously to consider James at variance with the teachings of Paul in Romans and Galatians. Although the epistle does not present a single, tightly knit argument, its component parts are nevertheless closely related, being aspects of practical Christianity. The epistle is written in plain but excellent Greek, and its effective imagery drawn from nature is reminiscent of such OT prophets as Hosea and Amos. The author's literary skill is evident in the graphic language with which he presses simple but vital truths home to his readers (Jas 1:6, 11; 2:1-4, 15, 16; 3:1-12, 17; 4:13-16; 5:1-6; etc.). There are a number of statements that appear to be allusions to the Sermon on the Mount.

After the briefest of introductions (Jas 1:1) the author plunges immediately into his subject, first taking up the need of patient endurance in the face of affliction and temptation (vs 2-18). Next he stresses the importance of applying the principles of religion to the life, contrasting this with the vain, deceptive attitude that insulates theoretical religion from conduct (vs 19-27). In ch 2:1-13 he lays emphasis on the principle of love as enunciated in the 2d table of the Decalogue, and in vs 14-26 upon the worthlessness of a profession unattested by corresponding "works." In ch 3 he stresses the supreme importance of pure, gracious speech. In ch 4 he sets forth the principles by which Christians are to maintain peace and good will among themselves and, conversely, to avoid strife and contention. The closing chapter deals briefly but emphatically with the fact that laborers deserve a just wage (ch 5:1-6). In closing, James admonishes his readers to be patient and circumspect, in anticipation of the coming of the Lord (vs 7-13). He gives special instruction with respect to prayer for the sick (vs 14-18), and appeals to Christians to take a sincere interest in the spiritual welfare of their fellow believers (vs 19, 20).

Jamin (jā'mĭn). [Heb. *Yamin*, "the right side," "south," or "fortune."]

1. A son of Simeon, and founder of the tribal family of the Jaminites (jā'mĭn-īts) [Heb. *Yamini*] (Gen 46:10; Ex 6:15; Num 26:12; 1 Chr 4:24).

2. A man of Judah of the family of Jerahmeel (1 Chr 2:27).

3. A Levite who assisted Ezra in reading the Law and teaching the people (Neh 8:7, 8).

Jaminites. *See* Jamin, 1.

Jamlech (jăm'lĕk). [Heb. *Yamlek*, "he grants dominion." A similar name, *Yamlik-ilu*, occurs in Old Babylonian.] A Simeonite prince (1 Chr 4:34).

Janai (jā'nȧ-ī), KJV **Jaanai** (jā'ȧ-nī). [Heb. *Ya'nay*, meaning uncertain.] A chief of the tribe of Gad (1 Chr 5:12).

Janim (jā'nĭm), KJV **Janum** (jā'nŭm). [Heb. *Yanim* (Q *Yanûm*).] A town near Hebron (Jos 15:53); not identified.

Janna. *See* Jannai.

Jannai (jăn'ȧ-ī), KJV **Janna** (jăn'ȧ). [Gr. *Iannai*.] A Judahite appearing in Luke's genealogy of Christ (Lk 3:24).

Jannes (jăn'ēz). [Gr. *Iannēs*.] One of 2 Egyptians, presumably magicians, who opposed Moses, the other being Jambres (2 Ti 3:8). The events referred to are probably those described in Ex 7:11, 12, 22; 8:7, 18, 19; 9:11, where, however, neither the number nor the names of the magicians are given. Origen and other early church writers mention a now-lost Jewish apocryphal work by the title of *Jannes and Jambres.* Later Jewish literature has also preserved the 2 names in various spellings. The names are probably of Egyptian etymology, but they have not yet been satisfactorily explained.

Janoah (jȧ-nō'ȧ), KJV once **Janohah** (jȧ-nō'hȧ). [Heb. *Yanoach*, "he rests."]

1. A town on the boundary of Ephraim (Jos 16:5, 6, 7), identified with *Khirbet Yānûn,* 7 mi. southeast of Shechem (Map VI, D-3).

2. A town in the northern part of Israel captured by Tiglath-pileser III (2 Ki 15:29); not identified with certainty. This is probably the Janoam captured by Seti I in his Palestine campaign (see fig. 253).

Janohah. *See* Janoah.

253. An attack on the town of Janoam (perhaps Janoah, 2) in Palestine by Seti I

Janum. *See* Janim.

Japheth (jā′fĕth). [Heb. *Yepheth,* "beauty," or "let him make wide."] Noah's eldest son (Gen 10:21; see *SDACom* 1:247, 248), born in the 500th year of Noah (chs 5:32; 6:10). He was married at the time of the Flood (ch 7:7) but apparently had no children at that time (see 1 Pe 3:20). The only recorded incident concerning him tells of his and his brother Shem's effort to save the honor of their father, whom Ham treated with disrespect. For this the two received special blessings. It was predicted of Japheth that his descendants would occupy wide territories, and that they would "dwell in the tents of Shem" (Gen 9:20-27). Japheth became the progenitor of the Japhethite races, among whom were the Medes, Ionians, and several nations who in OT times lived in what is now Asia Minor and southern Russia (ch 10:2-5).

Japhia (jȧ-fī′ȧ). [Heb. *Yaphia‘,* "he shines," or "shining."]

1. A Canaanite king of Lachish who in the time of Joshua joined a confederation against the Israelites but was defeated, captured, and killed (Jos 10:3-27).

2. A son of David, born at Jerusalem (2 Sa 5:15; 1 Chr 3:7; 14:6).

3. A town in Galilee on the boundary of Zebulun (Jos 19:10, 12); identified with *Yâfȧ,* about 1½ mi. southwest of Nazareth (Map VI, C-3).

Japhlet (jăf′lĕt). [Heb. *Yaphleṭ,* "he will deliver."] An Asherite (1 Chr 7:32).

Japhleti. *See* Japhletite.

Japhletite (jăf′lĕ-tīt), KJV **Japhleti** (jăf′lĕ-tī). [Heb. *Yaphleṭi.*] A people who were either descendants of a certain Japhlet, or inhabitants of a town by the name of Japhlet, near Lower Beth-horon (Jos 16: 3). It has been suggested that the Japhletites could possibly have been an Asherite group living in Ephraimite territory.

Japho. *See* Joppa.

Jar. A frequently occurring word in the RSV where the KJV has variously "pitcher," "pot," "cruse," "bottle," etc. Many varieties of jar were used in the Orient. In the OT the word is the translation of: (1) The Heb. *'asûk* (2 Ki 4:2), a special kind of oil jar standing a foot high, with three handles and a widely flared but shallow vertical spout, pierced by a small hole. (2) The Heb. *kad* (Gen 24:45; etc.), primarily a large jar used for carrying water. It was a *kad* that Rebekah used at the well (vs 14-20). This vessel was smaller in volume than the large storage jar, but was closely related to it in form. It had an egg-shaped bottom, and usually two handles. This jar was also used for the storage of flour (1 Ki 17:12-16). (3) The Heb. *nebel* (Jer 13:12; etc.), a storage jar used especially for wine, oil, and grain. The largest ones held a bath and measured about 25 in. in height and about 16 in. in diameter. The larger ones had 4 handles, whereas the smaller ones had two. (4) The Heb. *ṣappachath* (1 Ki 17:12-16; etc.), a small oil jar.

Lit.: James L. Kelso, *BASOR, Suppl. Studies,* 5-6 (1948), 16, 17, 19, 25, 26, 31.

In the NT "jar" is the rendering of the Gr. *keramion* (Mk 14:13; Lk 22:10; KJV "pitcher") and *hudria* (Jn 2:6, 7; 4:28; KJV "waterpot"). The 2 Greek words are general terms and provide no information about the shape and size of the vessels involved. The former simply means "earthenware vessel" and the latter "water vessel." The jars of Jn 2:6, 7 were rather large stone vessels as the texts make clear. Those of Mk 14:13; Lk 22:10 were probably water jars of the type ordinarily used in Palestine to fetch water from a well. For the alabaster jar of Mt 26:7 and Mk 14:3, *see* Alabaster.

Jarah (jā′rȧ). [Heb. *Ya‘rah,* "honeycomb."] A descendant of King Saul through Jonathan (1 Chr 9:42); called Jehoaddah in ch 8:36, through a confusion of the Heb. *d* and *r,* 2 letters very similar.

Jareb (jā′rĕb). [Heb. *Yareb.*] According to the KJV, a king of Assyria (Hos 5:13; 10: 6). Since no Assyrian king by this name is known, expositors have sought an explanation of the passage in the meaning of the Hebrew expression translated "king Jareb." Taking it as a descriptive term they read *melek yareb* and render it "the warlike king." However, a comparison with the Assyrian title *sharru rabû* (Ugaritic *mlk rb*), "the great king," suggests that the reading should be *melek rab,* "the great king."

Jared (jā′rĕd), KJV once **Jered** (jē′rĕd). [Heb. *Yered,* probably "servant," like the Akkadian *wardu;* Gr. *Iaret.*] Son of Mahalalel and father of Enoch (Gen 5:15-20; 1 Chr 1:2; Lk 3:37).

Jaresiah. *See* Jaareshiah.

Jarha (jär′hȧ). [Heb. *Yarcha‘.*] An Egyptian slave of Sheshan (1 Chr 2:34). He married into the family of his master and had many descendants (vs 35-41).

Jarib (jā′rĭb). [Heb. *Yarîb,* "he strives."]

1. A son of Simeon (1 Chr 4:24). *See* Jachin, 1.

2. One of the chief men of the Jews who was in Ezra's company at Ahava (Ezr 8:15, 16).

3. A priest who was married to a foreign wife in the time of Ezra (Ezr 10:18).

Jarmuth (jär'mŭth). [Heb. *Yarmûth,* meaning uncertain.]

1. A Canaanite city, whose king Joshua defeated, captured, and slew (Jos 10:3-27; 12:11). The city was assigned to Judah (ch 15:35). It was again inhabited after the Exile (Neh 11:29). It is identified with *Khirbet Yarmûk,* 14 mi. west of Bethlehem (Map VI, E-2).

2. A town in the territory of Issachar, assigned to the Levites (Jos 21:28, 29), called Ramoth in 1 Chr 6:73, and Remeth (Map VI, C-4) in Jos 19:21, names which in the Hebrew have the same consonants as *Yarmûth* except that they do not have the initial letter *y,* which was probably lost in transcription.

Jaroah (já-rō'á). [Heb. *Yarôach,* meaning uncertain.] A Gadite (1 Chr 5:14).

Jashar (jä'shēr), KJV **Jasher** (jä'shēr), **Book of.** [Heb. *Sepher Hayyashar,* "book of the upright."] The title of an ancient Hebrew songbook mentioned in Jos 10:13 and 2 Sa 1:18. The Syriac translation of Jos 10:13 calls it "Book of Praises," or "Book of Hymns." According to Jos 10:13 it contained a ballad of victory celebrating Joshua's triumph over an alliance of 5 Canaanite kings at Gibeon. In 2 Sa 1:18 the book of Jashar is cited as the source of David's ode on the death of Saul and Jonathan, which seems to be quoted in vs 19-27. The vivid account of the slaying of Saul and Jonathan suggests that this ode was composed soon after the event it memorializes. From these 2 references to the book by canonical writers it has been concluded that it was a collection of songs celebrating memorable men and events in the early history of Israel. These heroes are apparently the "upright" men alluded to in the title. The book has been lost, and the one circulating under that name since 1751 is a modern forgery.

Jashen. *See* Hashem.

Jasher, Book of. *See* Jashar, Book of.

Jashobeam (já-shō'bē-ăm). [Heb. *Yashob'am,* "may the people return."]

1. A man of the family of Hachmoni, and chief of David's "mighty men" (1 Chr 11:11). In ch 27:2, 3, RSV, he is said to be a descendant of Perez, hence was of the line of Judah (ch 4:1). He was made captain over the forces of the 1st month. In 2 Sa 23:8, RSV, he is called

Josheb-basshebeth (jō'shĕb-băs-shē'bĕth) [Heb. *Yosheb bashshebeth*], which the KJV translates "that sat in the seat." This name seems to be the result of a textual corruption.

2. A Benjamite who joined David at Ziklag (1 Chr 12:6). Since he is called a "Korahite," he may also have been related to the Korahite Levites.

Jashub (jä'shŭb). [Heb. *Yashûb,* "he returns."]

1. A son of Issachar, and founder of a tribal family (Num 26:24; 1 Chr 7:1). He is called Iob (yōb) [Heb. *Yôb*] (KJV "Job") in Gen 46:13, probably through the dropping of the letter *sh* from the Hebrew name.

2. A Jew of the family of Bani; he had married a foreign wife in Ezra's time (Ezr 10:29).

Jashubi-lehem (já-shoo'bī-lē'hĕm). [Heb. *Yashubî lechem,* "bread shall return."] According to the KJV a man of the tribe of Judah, of the family of Shelah (1 Chr 4:22). The RSV takes "Lehem" to be the name of a locality and translates the Hebrew phrase "returned to Lehem."

Jashubites (já'shŭb-īts). [Heb. *Yashubî.*] The family of Jashub, 1 (Num 26:24).

Jasiel. *See* Jaasiel.

Jason (jä'sŭn). [Gr. *Iasōn.* A common Greek name used by Hellenistic Jews, often as an equivalent for Joshua, or Jesus.] A man of Thessalonica, in whose home Paul stayed during his visit to that city, and who apparently became a Christian. In an uprising against Paul and Silas the Jews dragged Jason before the city authorities for having lodged the missionaries. He was released on bail (Acts 17:5-9). It is generally thought that he is the Jason to whom Paul sent greetings (Rom 16:21; called Paul's kinsman, but the word thus translated probably means "fellow countryman").

Jasper. [Heb. *yashepheh;* Akkadian *yashpú* and *ashpú;* Gr. *iaspis.*] A gem known to ancients, but quite evidently not the gem we call jasper today. Suggested identifications include a kind of chalcedony, agate, opal, jade, and nephrite. It was the last gem in the high priest's breastplate (Ex 28:20; 39:13) and was an adornment of the king of Tyrus (Eze 28:13). The King of the universe, as seen in vision, appeared to John "like a jasper" (Rev 4:3), and he chooses the same word to describe the Holy City's glory (ch 21:11) as well as her wall and 1st foundation (vs 18, 19).

Jathniel (jăth'nĭ-ĕl). [Heb. *Yathni'el*, "God gives."] A Korahite gatekeeper (1 Chr 26:2).

Jattir (jăt'ẽr). [Heb. *Yattîr*, "pre-eminence," or "abundance."] A town in the hill country of Judah, assigned to the priests (Jos 15:48; 21:14; 1 Sa 30:27; 1 Chr 6:57); identified with *Khirbet 'Attîr*, about 12 mi. northeast of Beer-sheba (Map VI, F-3).

Javan (jā'văn). [Heb. *Yawan;* Akkadian *Yâmanu* and *Yâuanu;* Old Persian *Yaunā:* the oldest name for Greece.]

1. One of the sons of Japheth (Gen 10: 2; 1 Chr 1:7); he became the ancestor of the Ionians, one of the principal tribes of the Greeks. The name Javan was used by the Hebrews to describe all the Greek tribes. In Dan 8:21; 10:20; 11:2; Zec 9: 13, the term "Grecia," or *"Greece," is translated from the Heb. *Yawan*. Since Greece was little known by the OT writers, they mention it only incidentally, as a distant country where God's name had not been heard (Is 66:19), and as a country with which the Phoenicians had commercial relations (Eze 27:13; Joel 3: 6). Map IV, B-4.

2. Possibly an unidentified tribe, a Greek colony in Arabia (Eze 27:19, KJV). However, the Hebrew word rendered "Javan" should probably be read *yayin*, "wine." The RSV, following the LXX, so renders the term.

Javelin. In the RSV a translation generally of the Heb. *kîdón*, usually meaning a small throw weapon, consisting of a shaft shorter than that of a spear, and a head slightly thicker than that of an arrow (Jos 8:18, 26; 1 Sa 17:6, 45; Job 39:23; 41:29). Elsewhere (Jer 6:23; 50:42) the RSV renders *kîdón* "spear." A difficult passage in the "War" document of the Dead Sea scrolls states that the *kîdón* was 1½ cu. long and 4 fingers wide. This description fits a dagger better than a javelin (Molin, *JSS* 1 [1956], 334-337). In Job 41:26 "javelin" is a translation of the Heb. *shiryah*, probably an arrowhead. In the KJV "javelin" is the translation of (1) the Heb. *chanith*, "spear" (1 Sa 18:10; etc.), and (2) the Heb. *romach*, "lance" (Num 25:7).

Jazer (jā'zẽr), KJV twice **Jaazer** (jā'á-zẽr). [Heb. *Ya'zer*, and *Ya'zêr*.] An Amorite town that the Israelites conquered under Moses' leadership (Num 32:1, 3). It was given to the tribe of Gad, and rebuilt by it (Jos 13:25; Num 32:34, 35; 2 Sa 24: 5). The place was later assigned to the Merarite Levites as a residence city (Jos

21:39; 1 Chr 6:81). Its surrounding territory was well suited for grazing (Num 32:1, 3) and for wine production (Is 16: 8, 9; Jer 48:32). In the period of the divided kingdoms it passed into the hands of the Moabites (Is 16:8, 9, 11). It must have changed hands once more, for Judas Maccabeus took it from the Ammonites in the 2d cent. B.C. (1 Macc 5:8). Eusebius claims that Jazer was situated 10 Roman mi. to the west of Rabbath Ammon and 15 mi. from Heshbon (Map VI, E-4). However, no known site in that area fits the distances or has a name similar to Jazer. None of the various identifications so far proposed are certain.

Jaziz (jā'zĭz). [Heb. *Yazîz.*] A Hagrite, David's chief shepherd (1 Chr 27:31, KJV).

Jealousy. Human jealousy is an attitude toward another or others caused by fear, mistrust of loyalty, resentment of his or their advantage (Prov 6:34; Song 8:6; Rom 13:13, RSV; 1 Cor 3:3, RSV). Divine jealousy, frequently mentioned in the Bible, must not be confused with the human emotion; God's jealousy is a zeal He possesses for the welfare of His people because of a determination that nothing shall come between Him and them that could deceive, undermine, and destroy them (Ex 20:5; Deut 5:9; Jos 24:19). Since He is the only true God, salvation resides only with Him. For the people to follow any other god is deception to them, leading to death and destruction. Divine jealousy or indignation often manifested itself in forms that appeared severe but which could later be seen as necessary discipline for the ultimate benefit of a stiff-necked people. Thus God is mentioned as being jealous of His right to human worship (Ex 20:4-6; 34:14; Deut 4:23, 24; etc.), which jealousy was often stirred by the Israelites (see Deut 32:21; 1 Ki 14:22, 23; Ps 78:58; etc.). He is jealous because of the indignity and suffering occasioned His people (Eze 36:6, 7), and for the honor of His name, which had been dishonored by His chosen people's going into captivity (ch 39:25-28). God hoped that the giving of the gospel to the Gentiles would arouse the Jews to jealousy, and thus bring them back to Him (Rom 10:19; 11:11). Paul expressed a "godly jealousy" over the Corinthian church, which he had "espoused" to Christ, fearing that it would be wooed from its divine Suitor (2 Cor 11:2, 3).

Jearim (jē'á-rĭm). [Heb. *Ye'arim*, "forests."] A mountain about 10 mi. west of Jeru-

salem on the boundary line of Judah, on
which Chesalon was situated (Jos 15:10);
not identified.

Jeaterai. See Jeatherai.

Jeatherai (jē-ăth′ē-rī), KJV **Jeaterai** (jē-ăt′-
ē-rī). [Heb. *Ye'othray.*] A Gershonite Levite (1 Chr 6:21). He may be identical
with the Ethni of v 41.

Jeberechiah (jē-bĕr′ē-kī′ȧ). [Heb. *Yeberek-
yahû,* "Yahweh blesses."] A man whose
son Zechariah was a contemporary of
Isaiah (Is 8:2).

Jebus (jē′bŭs). [Heb. *Yebûs.*] An early name
for Jerusalem, used of the time the city
was inhabited by Jebusites (Jgs 19:10,
11; 1 Chr 11:4, 5). The name has not yet
been attested from extra-Biblical sources.
On the basis of the LXX, the Syriac, and
the Vulgate, the RSV reads "Jebus" in Jos
18:28 where the Hebrew is *Yebûsi,* transliterated Jebusi (jĕb′û-sī) in the KJV. This
term is generally translated "Jebusites."

Jebusi. See Jebus.

Jebusites (jĕb′û-zīts). [Heb. *Yebûsî.*] One of
the tribes of western Palestine descended
from Canaan (Gen 10:15, 16; 15:21).
They were the inhabitants of Jerusalem
when David conquered that city (Jos
15:8; Jgs 19:11); hence Jerusalem is occasionally called *Jebus (Jos 18:28, RSV;
Jgs 19:10, 11; 1 Chr 11:4). A part of the
Jebusite wall still stands (see fig. 254). The
Jebusites continued to live in Jerusalem or outside of it. Araunah (or Ornan), the owner of the threshing floor
that David bought and later chose as the
site for the Temple, is called a Jebusite
(2 Sa 24:16, 18; 2 Chr 3:1). His name is
of Hurrian origin. However, this fact
throws little light on the problem of the
Jebusites, unless it is an indication that
they might have been a subtribe of the
Hurrians. Solomon incorporated the remnants of the Jebusites into his forced
labor corps (1 Ki 9:20).

Jecamiah. See Jekamiah.

Jecholiah. See Jecoliah.

Jechoniah. See Jehoiachin.

Jechonias. See Jehoiachin.

Jecoliah (jĕk′ō-lī′ȧ), KJV once **Jecholiah**
jĕk′ō-lī′ȧ). [Heb. *Yekolyahû* (once in K
Yekîlyah), "Yahweh has prevailed." The
mother of King Uzziah (2 Ki 15:2; 2 Chr
26:3).

Jeconiah. See Jehoiachin.

Jedaiah, I (jē-dā′yȧ). [Heb. *Yedayah,* "Yahweh praises."]
  1. A Simeonite chieftain (1 Chr 4:37).
  2. An inhabitant of Jerusalem in Ne-

hemiah's time who repaired the part of
the wall of the city that was opposite his
own house (Neh 3:10).

Jedaiah, II (jē-dā′yȧ). [Heb. *Yeda'yah,* "Yahweh knows." The name occurs also on
ancient Hebrew seals.]
  1. A descendant of Aaron and possibly
related to Jedaiah, II, 2 and 3. He was
ancestral head of a family whose members formed the 2d of the 24 courses into
which David organized the priests (1 Chr
24:1, 7). Members of this family returned
from Babylonia with Zerubbabel (Ezr 2:
36; Neh 7:39).
  2 and 3. Two chief priests who returned
from Babylonia with Zerubbabel (Neh
12:6, 7), possibly related to Jedaiah, II,
1. Their names were used as family
names in the next generation (vs 19, 21).
  4. An exile who came from Babylonia
and brought gifts for the Temple when
Joshua was high priest (Zec 6:10, 14).

Jediael (jē-dī′ȧ-ĕl). [Heb. *Yedî'a'el,* "known
of God." The name occurs in Amorite as
Yadi-ilu, in Old Babylonian as *Yadih-ilu,*
and in late Babylonian as *Yâdih-el.*]
  1. A son of Benjamin and founder of a
tribal family (1 Chr 7:6, 10, 11).
  2. A warrior from Manasseh who
joined David at Ziklag (1 Chr 12:20).
  3. One of David's "mighty men" (1
Chr 11:45).
  4. A Korahite gatekeeper in the reign
of David (1 Chr 26:1, 2).

Jedidah (jē-dī′dȧ). [Heb. *Yedîdah,* "beloved."] Wife of Amon, king of Judah,
and mother of Josiah (2 Ki 22:1).

Jedidiah (jĕd′ĭ-dī′ȧ). [Heb. *Yedîdyah,* "beloved of Yahweh."] A name that was given

254. Jebusite bastion at Jerusalem (right) with a
tower from the time of David or Solomon built into
it (left)

to Solomon at his birth. Whether it was given by David or Nathan is not certain (2 Sa 12:25). Some think that Jedidiah was Solomon's personal name and Solomon his royal or throne name.

Jeduthun (jě-dū'thŭn). [Heb. *Yedûthûn* and *Yedîthûn*, "praise."]

1. A Levite, one of the 3 chief singers or musicians in the time of David, and founder of a family of musicians (1 Chr 16:41; 25:1, 6; 2 Chr 5:12; 35:15; Neh 11:17; Ps 39, 62, and 77, titles). His earlier name seems to have been Ethan. *See* Ethan, 3.

2. A Kohathite Levite, father of the gatekeeper Obed-edom (1 Chr 16:38).

Jeezer. *See* Abiezer.

Jeezerite. *See* Abiezrite.

Jegar-sahadutha (jē'gär-sā'ha-dū'tha). [Aramaic *Yegar śahadûtha'*, "heap of witness," the Hebrew equivalent of which is *Gal'ed*.] A name given to the heap of stones erected by Laban and Jacob as a memorial of the treaty of friendship concluded there (Gen 31:47). *See* Galeed; Mizpah, 1.

Jehaleleel. *See* Jehallelel.

Jehalelel. *See* Jehallelel.

Jehallelel (jē-hăl'ĕ-lĕl), KJV **Jehaleleel** (jē'-ha-lē'lĕ-ĕl) and **Jehalelel** (jē-hăl'ĕ-lĕl). [Heb. *Yehallel'el*, "God praises."]

1. A Judahite (1 Chr 4:16).

2. A Merarite Levite (2 Chr 29:12).

Jehdeiah (jě-dē'ya). [Heb. *Yechdeyahû*, "Yahweh is glad."]

1. A Kohathite Levite of the house of Amram (1 Chr 24:20).

2. A Meronothite who was in charge of David's asses (1 Chr 27:30).

Jehezekel. *See* Jehezkel.

Jehezkel (jě-hĕz'kĕl), KJV **Jehezekel** (jě-hĕz'ĕ-kĕl). [Heb. *Yechezqe'l*, "God strengthens."] A descendant of Aaron, and ancestral head of the 20th of the 24 courses into which David organized the priests (1 Chr 24:16).

Jehiah (jě-hī'a). [Heb. *Yechîyah*, "Yahweh lives."] A Levite doorkeeper for the ark in David's reign (1 Chr 15:24).

Jehiel (jě-hī'ĕl). [Heb. *Yechî'el*, "God lives."]

1. A Levite of the 2d order, who played a *harp when the ark was brought to Jerusalem, and who afterward became a regular musician in the tent sanctuary at Jerusalem (1 Chr 15:18, 20; 16:5).

2. A Gershonite Levite and chief of a family in David's time (1 Chr 23:8; 29:8). Members of that family were called *Jehieli (ch 26:21, 22), but the Hebrew is obscure.

3. A member of David's court (1 Chr 27:32).

4. A son of King Jehoshaphat of Judah (2 Chr 21:2). He was placed in charge of one of the fortified cities of Judah, but he and his brothers were slain by Jehoram, Jehoshaphat's successor (vs 3, 4).

5. A Levite of the house of the singer Heman (2 Chr 29:14). *See* Jehuel.

6. One of the assistants in charge of the Temple revenue in Hezekiah's time (2 Chr 31:13).

7. A high official in the Temple at the time of Josiah's religious reforms (2 Chr 35:8).

8. A man whose son Obadiah returned with Ezra from Babylonia (Ezr 8:9).

9. A member of the family of Elam. His son, Shecaniah, encouraged Ezra to proceed with reforms concerning the foreign wives (Ezr 10:2), although Jehiel himself had a foreign wife (v 26).

10. A priest of the family of Harim who was married to a foreign wife in the time of Ezra (Ezr 10:21).

For others whose names are spelled Jehiel, in the KJV, *see* Jeiel, 2, 3.

Jehieli (jě-hī'ĕ-lī). [Heb. *Yechî'eli*.] According to the RSV the father of 2 men who were Temple treasurers in David's time; according to the KJV, a Gershonite family (1 Chr 26:21, 22).

Jehizkiah (jě'hĭz-kī'a). [Heb. *Yechizqîyahû*, "Yahweh strengthens."] A chief of the tribe of Ephraim under King Pekah of Israel. He, with others, succeeded in bringing about the release of captives from Judah (2 Chr 28:12-15).

Jehoadah. *See* Jehoaddah.

Jehoaddah (jē'hō-ăd'a), KJV **Jehoadah** (jē-hō'a-da). [Heb. *Yehô'addah*, probably "Yahweh has decorated."] A descendant of King Saul through Jonathan (1 Chr 8:36), called *Jarah in ch 9:42.

Jehoaddan (jē'hō-ăd'ăn), RSV once **Jehoaddin** (jē'hō-ăd'ĭn). [Heb. *Yehô'addân* and *Yehô'addîn*, probably "Yahweh makes glad."] A woman from Jerusalem who became the mother of King Amaziah of Judah (2 Ki 14:2; 2 Chr 25:1).

Jehoaddin. *See* Jehoaddan.

Jehoahaz (jě-hō'a-hăz). [Heb. *Yehô'achaz*, "Yahweh has grasped (my hand)." The name occurs in cuneiform records as *Yauhazi*.]

1. A variant form of Ahaziah in which the 2 component parts of the name are given in reverse order (2 Chr 22:1; cf. ch 21:17). *See* Ahaziah, 2.

2. The 12th king of Israel (if Tibni is

included in the count), son and successor of Jehu. He ruled 17 years (c. 814 - c. 798 B.C.). The weakened kingdom which he inherited from his father suffered numerous disasters as penalty for his own apostasy (2 Ki 13:1-3). Two kings of Damascus, first Hazael and later Ben-hadad III, oppressed Israel, reducing its defenses to 50 horsemen, 10 chariots, and 10,000 foot soldiers (vs 3, 7). If we remember that Ahab was able to muster 2,000 chariots less than 50 years earlier, the extent of the military decline of the kingdom is clearly evident. In desperation Jehoahaz turned to the Lord, and as a result of a partial conversion received some unexpected relief through a "saviour" (vs 4, 5), by which the Assyrian king Adad-nirari III (c. 810-782 B.C.) is probably indicated. Adad-nirari invaded Syria in 806 and forced the king of Damascus to pay tribute, impoverishing the kingdom to such an extent that for some time the kings of Damascus were unable to molest Israel. Some see evidence of this identification of the "saviour" in the fact that the second part of the name of Adad-nirari, which is derived from the Akkadian verb *narâru*, "to help," means "helper," a word closely related to "saviour." Jehoahaz was buried in Samaria and was succeeded on the throne by his son Jehoash, or Joash (v 9).

3. The 17th king of Judah (2 Ki 23: 31), who reigned only 3 months (609/08 B.C.). His original name was Shallum (1 Chr 3:15; Jer 22:11, 12; cf. 2 Ki 23:31). He probably took the name Jehoahaz as his throne name. After his father was killed in the battle of Megiddo, fighting against Pharaoh Necho, Jehoahaz was put on the throne by popular demand, although he was not the eldest prince. Belonging probably to the anti-Egyptian party, Jehoahaz continued his father's policies, and after a reign of 3 months was summoned to Riblah in Syria by Necho, who replaced him by his older brother Jehoiakim. He was then deported to Egypt, where he died (2 Ki 23:31-34; 2 Chr 36:1,4).

Jehoash (jĕ-hō′ăsh), or **Joash** (jō′ăsh). [Heb. *Yehô′ash* and *Yô′ash*, "Yahweh has given." The name occurs in the Hebrew Lachish Letters as *Y'wsh*.]

1. The 8th ruler of the southern kingdom of Judah, more often called Joash. He reigned 40 years (c. 835 - c. 796 B.C.). In 841 B.C., when he was but an infant, his father, Ahaziah, was slain by King Jehu of Israel. Thereupon Athaliah, Ahaziah's mother, took the throne after slaying all of Ahaziah's children but one infant son. This child was saved only because his father's sister Jehosheba, wife of the high priest Jehoiada, spirited him away and kept him in hiding (2 Ki 11:1-3; 2 Chr 22:10-12). In the 7th year of Athaliah's reign Jehoiada presented the young prince to the army officers and gained their support in his plan to overthrow Athaliah and make Joash king. Under the protection of the army the plan was put into effect and the boy was proclaimed king in the Temple. Athaliah, attracted by the acclamations, made her way to the Temple but was slain en route (2 Ki 11:4-16; 2 Chr 23:1-15). Jehoiada at once set out to restore the worship of God and to destroy the Baal temple. When the young king grew to manhood, he repaired the Temple, which was now nearly 150 years old, but he allowed the high places to continue and to be used as places of worship (2 Ki 11:17 to 12:16; 2 Chr 23:16 to 24:16). However, after Jehoiada's death, the king changed considerably and became a worshiper of Asherah and other idols. When rebuked for this by his benefactor's son, Zechariah, he ordered him stoned (2 Chr 24:17-22; cf. Lk 11:51). He also suffered a serious military defeat when Hazael of Damascus invaded Judah after taking the Philistine city of Gath. He could buy himself and Jerusalem off only by handing over to the Aramaeans all the treasures of the palace and of the Temple (2 Ki 12:17, 18; 2 Chr 24:23, 24). Soon after this defeat he was assassinated in bed by 2 of his own courtiers (2 Ki 12:20, 21; 2 Chr 24:25, 26). He was buried in the City of David, but not in the royal tombs. His son Amaziah followed him on the throne.

2. The 13th king of the northern kingdom of Israel (if Tibni is included in the count). Jehoash (frequently called Joash) succeeded his father, Jehoahaz, as the 3d king of the dynasty of Jehu, and ruled 16 years (c. 798 - c. 782 B.C.). He retained the national worship of Jeroboam's calves, but was an admirer of Elisha, from whom he received the promise that he would defeat the Aramaeans (2 Ki 13:10-19). He was a successful warrior, and in 3 campaigns against Ben-hadad III recovered the Israelite territories in Transjordan which his father Jehoahaz had lost to Hazael (v 25). His relations with Judah seem to have been cordial in his early years, for when

Amaziah of Judah prepared a campaign against the Edomites he allowed a large armed force of Israelites to enter the service of the king of Judah. Amaziah, however, discharged them on the advice of a prophet before the campaign started. This offended the Israelite soldiers, who, in retaliation, on their way home ravaged the northwestern section of the kingdom of Judah (2 Chr 25:5-10, 13). After Amaziah returned victoriously from the Edomite campaign, he declared war on Jehoash of Israel, presumably in an attempt to avenge himself for the damage done by the Israelite soldiers. The Israelite king was very unhappy about the affair and went to battle against the southern state with great reluctance, contemptuously describing the situation by a parable of the cedar and the thistle (2 Ki 14:8-10; 2 Chr 25:17-19). In the ensuing battle of Beth-shemesh Amaziah was defeated, and the victorious Jehoash looted Jerusalem and broke down 400 cubits of the city's wall before retreating with his spoil and hostages (2 Ki 14:11-14; 2 Chr 25:20-24). There is evidence that his able son Jeroboam II was associated with him on the throne for about 11 years (*see* Chronology V, 2). Jehoash was buried in the royal tombs of Samaria (2 Ki 14:16).

Jehohanan (jē'hō-hā'năn). [Heb. *Yehô-chanan*, "Yahweh is gracious." The name occurs also in the Aramaic documents from Elephantine.]

1. A Korahite Levite, who was in charge of the 6th division of Temple gatekeepers appointed by David (1 Chr 26:3).

2. Commander of 280,000 men of King Jehoshaphat's army (2 Chr 17:15); possibly the same as Jehohanan, 3.

3. A man whose son Ishmael, an army officer, supported Jehoiada in the revolt against Queen Athaliah (2 Chr 23:1); possibly the same as Jehohanan, 2.

4. A priest and one of the heads of fathers' houses in the time of the high priest Joiakim (Neh 12:13).

5. A son of Eliashib (Ezr 10:6; KJV "Johanan"); possibly identical with Johanan, 10.

6. A man who was married to a foreign wife in Ezra's time, of the family of Bebai (Ezr 10:28).

7. A son of Tobiah the Ammonite (Neh 6:18; KJV "Johanan").

8. One of those who assisted Nehemiah in the dedication of the wall of Jerusalem (Neh 12:42).

Jehoiachin (jĕ-hoi'ȧ-kĭn), or **Jeconiah** (jĕk'ō-nī'ȧ), or **Coniah** (kō-nī'ȧ); RSV of NT **Jechoniah** (jĕk'ō-nī'ȧ), KJV of NT **Jechonias** (jĕk'ō-nī'ăs). [Heb. *Yehôyakin, Yekonyah, Yekonyahû,* and *Konyahû,* all meaning "Yahweh establishes"; although different roots which, however, are cognate are used in the verbal part of the names, and the two component parts are reversed. In Babylonian cuneiform records the name is written *Ya'ûkinu.* The name occurs on Hebrew seals as *Ywkn.* Gr. *Iechonias.*] The 19th ruler of the southern kingdom of Judah, who reigned only 3 months and 10 days (598-597 B.C.). He was the son and successor of Jehoiakim, and came to the throne at the age of 18 years (2 Ki 24:8). In 2 Chr 36:9 his age is given as 8 years, with the Syriac and LXX versions, however, reading "18." That 18 is correct is shown by the fact that he was old enough to have "wives" (2 Ki 24:15) when he was taken captive to Babylon at the close of his brief reign. According to cuneiform tablets in Babylonia he was the father of 5 sons only 5 years later. Thus he must have been 18, not 8, years old when he became king.

The recently discovered Babylonian Chronicle dealing with the 7th Babylonian year of Nebuchadnezzar's reign (598/97 B.C.) describes the capture of Jerusalem in 597 B.C. and Jehoiachin's captivity as well as his uncle's accession to the throne in the following brief sentences: Nebuchadnezzar "encamped against the city of Judah and on the 2d day of the month of Adar he seized the city and captured the king. He appointed there a king of his own choice (lit. "heart"), received its heavy tribute and sent (them) to Babylon." This text gives an exact date for the beginning of Jehoiachin's captivity, which, in terms of our calendar, was approximately March 16, 597 B.C. The young king surrendered to Nebuchadnezzar and was subsequently carried away captive to Babylon, along with his mother, his wives, his courtiers, and some 10,000 other captives, among whom was the prophet Ezekiel (2 Ki 24:10-16; 2 Chr 36:9, 10; Eze 1:1-3; 33:21). Jehoiachin's uncle, Zedekiah (2 Ki 24:17), was placed on the throne in his stead.

Not only the discovery of the Babylonian Chronicle but also several other discoveries in Palestine and Babylon have shed light on Jehoiachin's reign. Three clay impressions of a stamp seal were found at *Tell Beit Mirsim* and Beth-shemesh in Palestine. They bear the inscription: "Belonging to Eliakim, steward of Yaukin" (see fig. 151). "Yaukin" is a short form of "Jehoiachin." W. F. Albright is probably right in regarding them as evidence that Jehoiachin's deposition was intended to be only temporary, and that he was held in reserve to reoccupy the throne if Nebuchadnezzar should find such a move advantageous. Thus, according to this view, Jehoiachin's property in Palestine had not been confiscated by Zedekiah but was still administered in Jehoiachin's name by his chief steward. Several cuneiform tablets from Babylon support this view. They belong to 300 tablets giving a record of the issuance of government rations to palace dependents during the years 595-570 B.C. On some of the tablets from 592 B.C. "King *Ya'úkinu* of Judah" with 5 of his sons and their tutor Kenaiah are mentioned as recipients of royal rations. It seems that at that time Jehoiachin was still regarded as a king, was still at liberty, and could freely move about the city of Babylon. His imprisonment must have come later, at a time when the political situation in Judah and the unrest among the exiles (see Jer 29) made it advisable to put him in prison. It was not until the 37th year of his captivity that Evil-Merodach (Amel-Marduk), Nebuchadnezzar's son and successor, released him from prison and exonerated him (2 Ki 25:27-30; Jer 52:31-34).

Lit.: W. F. Albright, *JBL* 51 (1932), 77-106; *BA* 5 (1942), 49-55; D. J. Wiseman, ed., *Chronicles of the Chaldaean Kings (626-556 B.C.) in the British Museum* (London, 1956), pp. 32-34, 73.

Jehoiada (jē-hoi′á-dá). [Heb. *Yehóyada'*, "Yahweh knows."]

1. A man whose son Benaiah was one of David's "mighty men" and a high military officer in David's and Solomon's army (2 Sa 8:18; 23:22; 1 Ki 1:8; 4:4; 1 Chr 11:22; etc.). Jehoiada lived presumably in Kabzeel (2 Sa 23:20), and was a priest (1 Chr 27:5, RSV), not "chief priest" as in the KJV.

2. Leader of 3,700 Aaronites who came to Hebron to turn the kingdom over to David (1 Chr 12:27); possibly identical with Jehoiada, 1.

3. A son of Benaiah and successor of Ahithophel, David's counselor (1 Chr 27:34). Instead of "Jehoiada the son of Benaiah" 2 Hebrew manuscripts read "Benaiah the son of Jehoiada," thus making this Jehoiada identical with Jehoiada, 1. However, Jehoiada, 2, may have

been the grandson of Jehoiada, 1. There is insufficient reason to doubt the reading of the Masoretic text.

4. The high priest during the reigns of Queen Athaliah and King Joash of Judah. He was married to Jehosheba, or Jehoshabeath, the daughter of King Jehoram and sister of King Ahaziah (2 Ki 11:2; 2 Chr 22:11). When Athaliah usurped the throne after her son's death, she slew all the royal children except the infant prince Joash whom Jehoiada's wife rescued and concealed in the Temple for 6 years. At the end of this period Jehoiada proclaimed Joash, his nephew, king and slew Athaliah (2 Ki 11:1-16; 2 Chr 22:10 to 23:15). He then led the people to make a covenant with God and with the king (2 Ki 11:17), and was instrumental in causing the destruction of the Baal temple (v 18). For many years he exercised a good influence on the young king, so that Joash followed God as long as his uncle lived (2 Chr 24:2). Jehoiada died at the age of 130, and in recognition of his service to the nation he was buried among the kings of Judah in the City of David (vs 15, 16). Joash revealed shocking ingratitude after Jehoiada's death not only by allowing the people to relapse into idolatry but also by stoning his benefactor's son, Zechariah, who cried out against the people's return to idolatry (vs 17-22).

5. A priest in the time of Jeremiah (Jer 29:26).

6. For Neh 3:6, KJV, *see* Joiada, 1.

Jehoiakim (jē-hoi′á-kĭm). [Heb. *Yehóyaqîm*, "Yahweh raises up."] The 18th ruler of the southern kingdom of Judah, who reigned for 11 years (609/08-598 B.C.). He was the second son of Josiah (1 Chr 3:15), and followed his younger brother, Jehoahaz, on the throne, when Jehoahaz was deposed by Pharaoh Necho and carried captive to Egypt. Jehoiakim's original name was Eliakim, "God raises up," but Necho changed it to Jehoiakim, which became his throne name (2 Ki 23:34; 2 Chr 36:4). Jehoiakim seems to have belonged to the pro-Egyptian party, as indicated by the fact that Necho considered him a trustworthy candidate for the kingship in Judah. In order to pay the heavy tribute laid upon him by Necho, Jehoiakim taxed the whole population (2 Ki 23:35). He is described as a wicked king (2 Ki 23:37; 2 Chr 36:5), who quickly undid everything his pious father Josiah had achieved in religious reforms. During his reign Jeremiah bade Baruch, his servant, put in writing and read publicly a prophecy predicting Judah's inevitable doom. When Jehoiakim learned about it he requested that the scroll be read before him. Annoyed at its contents, he destroyed it, and ordered the arrest of Jeremiah and Baruch (Jer 36). Another prophet, Uriah, who proclaimed the same message of doom, was executed (ch 26:20-23). *See* Uriah, 3.

During the first 3 years of his reign Jehoiakim was apparently a vassal of the Egyptian king. However, in 605 B.C. Nebuchadnezzar decisively defeated the Egyptian army at Carchemish and entered Palestine. Jehoiakim surrendered, and Nebuchadnezzar carried away some of the Temple vessels and a group of hostages, among whom were Daniel and his three friends (Dan 1:1-6). This event must have taken place shortly before the death of Nabopolassar, Nebuchadnezzar's father, for the news of Nabopolassar's death reached Nebuchadnezzar while he was on his way to Egypt. Jehoiakim became Nebuchadnezzar's vassal for 3 years, but rebelled (2 Ki 24:1), apparently at a time of resurgence of Egyptian power, for in 601 B.C. Egypt succeeded in inflicting heavy losses on Nebuchadnezzar's army, as the Babylonian Chronicle reveals. Nebuchadnezzar then allowed Judah's neighboring nations and his own garrison stationed near Judah to invade Jehoiakim's kingdom. The Babylonians captured Jehoiakim, but he seems to have died before he could be transported to Babylon, possibly by accident or possibly as the result of rough treatment from the Babylonian soldiers (2 Ki 24:2; 2 Chr 36:6). His death must have occurred in early Dec., 598 B.C., because the date of his son Jehoiachin's captivity, which occurred after a reign of only 3 months and 10 days (2 Chr 36:9) is, on evidence found in the Babylonian Chronicle, placed at March 16, 597 B.C. The king's death was not lamented. His body was cast outside the gate of Jerusalem and was finally unceremoniously buried (Jer 22:18, 19; 36:30). His son Jehoiachin followed him on the throne (2 Chr 36:8).

Jehoiarib (jĕ-hoi'á-rīb). [Heb. *Yehôyarib,* "Yahweh pleads," or "Yahweh contends."] A descendant of Aaron and ancestral head of the 1st of the 24 courses into which David organized the priests (1 Chr 9:10; 24:1, 6, 7). His family may be that of Joiarib. *See* Joiarib, 1.

Jehonadab (jĕ-hŏn'á-dăb), or **Jonadab** (jŏn'-á-dăb). [Heb. *Yehônadab,* and *Yônadab,* "Yahweh is bounteous."] A son of Rechab, a Kenite (Jer 35:6; 1 Chr 2:55). Jonadab, a chief of the Rechabites, made the rule for the tribe that they should dwell in tents, lead a nomadic life without engaging in agriculture, and abstain from wine (Jer 35:6, 7). When Jehu became king of Israel and was about to destroy the worship of Baal in his kingdom, he took Jehonadab with him to Samaria, knowing that he sympathized with his zeal against the foreign cult (2 Ki 10:15-28).

Jehonathan (jĕ-hŏn'á-thăn). [Heb. *Yehônathan,* "Yahweh has given." The name occurs in cuneiform records as *Yâhû-natunnu.* Its shorter form is *Jonathan.*]

1. One of the Levites whom King Jehoshaphat of Judah sent to teach the people (2 Chr 17:8).

2. The head of a family of priests in the days of the high priest Joiakim (Neh 12:18). Some identify him with Jonathan, 13.

3. A treasurer of David (1 Chr 27:25, KJV). *See* Jonathan, 7.

Jehoram (jĕ-hō'răm). [Heb. *Yehôram,* "Yahweh is exalted"; Gr. *Iôram.*]

1. The 10th king of the northern kingdom of Israel (if Tibni is included in the count), frequently called Joram (2 Ki 8:16, 25; etc.). Jehoram was the son of Ahab and Jezebel (chs 8:28; 9:22), and followed his elder brother Ahaziah (1 Ki 22:40; 2 Ki 1:17) as the last king of the dynasty of Omri. He reigned for 12 years (2 Ki 3:1; *c.* 852-841 B.C.). He was somewhat less idolatrous than his father and removed the pillar of Baal (v 2), though Baal worship seems to have continued until the time of Jehu though in a less official form (ch 10:18-28). When the Moabite king Mesha rebelled against Israel after Ahab's death, Jehoram attempted to bring him back into subjection. For this enterprise he enlisted the assistance of Jehoshaphat of Judah and of the king of Edom. The armies of the 3 kings marched toward Moab via Edom, intending to attack Moab from the south. They almost perished of thirst in the southern desert, but water was miraculously produced through the instrumentality of Elisha. The campaign was successful in its initial stages, and Mesha's capital, Kir-hareseth, was besieged. When a sortie of the beleaguered Moabites brought no relief, the desperate Moabite king sacrificed his first-born son on the

city's wall. Shortly afterward for some unknown reason the allied armies lifted the siege and returned (2 Ki 3:1-27). The *Moabite Stone of King Mesha treats this same period and contains much additional information.

Jehoram was probably the king to whom Ben-hadad II of Damascus sent his commander Naaman to be cured from leprosy (2 Ki 5:1-7), and the unidentified king to whom Elisha revealed the movements of the Syrian army, and who fed the enemy soldiers and sent them back disarmed to Syria after they had been smitten with blindness at Dothan (ch 6:8-23). He was probably also the king who, during a siege of Samaria, blamed Elisha for the sufferings of the people (vs 24-33). The city experienced an unexpected deliverance as the prophet had predicted (ch 7:1-20). Jehoram's eventful life came to a tragic end. He was wounded at Ramoth-gilead in a war against the Syrians, and while recuperating at Jezreel he was assassinated by Jehu, his army commander, who usurped the throne of Israel for himself (ch 9:14-28). With Jehoram at the time was Ahaziah of Judah, whom Jehu mortally wounded.

2. One of the two priests who were sent out by King Jehoshaphat to instruct the people in the Law of God (2 Chr 17:8).

3. The 5th king of Judah, frequently called Joram. Biblical chronological data (1 Ki 22:42; 2 Ki 1:17; 3:1) indicate that Jehoram was associated with his father Jehoshaphat on the throne for about 5 or 6 years (c. 854 - c. 848 b.c.), before he became sole ruler (see Chronology, V, 2). He ruled for less than 8 years (2 Chr 21:5), c. 848-841 b.c. He was married to Athaliah, a daughter of Ahab, and followed his wife in Baal worship, as· his father-in-law had followed Jezebel (2 Ki 8:18, 26; 2 Chr 21:6, 11). After his father's death, Jehoram murdered all his brothers and other princes of Judah (2 Chr 21:1-4). His wickedness did not go unpunished, for one calamity after another befell him, as Elijah in a letter to him had predicted (vs 12-15). First the Edomites revolted, and though Jehoram was able to defeat them, they remained independent (2 Ki 8:20-22; 2 Chr 21:8-10). Thus Judah lost the copper mines of Edom and the city of Ezion-geber with its production center, along with the city's port facilities. Then Libnah revolted (2 Ki 8:22; 2 Chr 21:10); and during an invasion of the Philistines and

tribesmen from northwestern Arabia Jerusalem was looted, the palace ransacked, and the king's harem and all his sons, except the youngest, carried into captivity (2 Chr 21:16, 17; 22:1). Finally an incurable intestinal disease tormented the king during the last two years of his life (ch 21:18, 19). He died unmourned and was buried in Jerusalem but not in the royal tombs (v 20).

Jehoshabeath. *See* Jehosheba.

Jehoshaphat (jē-hŏsh′á-făt), KJV of NT **Josaphat** (jŏs′á-făt). [Heb. *Yehôshaphat,* "Yahweh has judged"; Gr. *Iōsaphat.*]

1. Son of Ahilud and a high court official under David and Solomon (2 Sa 8:16; 20:24; 1 Ki 4:3).

2. A priest (1 Chr 15:24). *See* Joshaphat, 2.

3. Son of Paruah and a supply officer of Solomon's in Issachar (1 Ki 4:17).

4. The 4th king of the southern kingdom of Judah, who reigned 25 years (c. 872 - c. 848 b.c.). There is reason to believe that he was associated with his father Asa on the throne during Asa's last regnal years when the elder monarch was plagued by a foot disease. Jehoshaphat's son, Jehoram (see Chronology, V, 2) was coregent with his father toward the end of Jehoshaphat's reign (2 Ki 8:16; cf. ch 1:17; 2 Chr 20:31). Jehoshaphat's sole rule lasted only about 17 years. He is described as a good king who did not serve foreign gods, although many of his subjects still worshiped at high places that had not been removed (1 Ki 22:43; 2 Chr 17:3). In his 3d year he sent princes, Levites, and priests through the country of Judah to teach the people the principles of the Law of God (2 Chr 17:7-9). God blessed him because of these things. He was able to make peace with Israel and also to gain the respect and favor of the surrounding nations, some of whom sent him gifts (1 Ki 22:44; 2 Chr 17:11). It was regrettable that he connected his house with that of Omri of Israel, by taking Athaliah, the idolatrous daughter of Ahab, as wife for his son (2 Ki 8:18).

While visiting Ahab after the battle of Qarqar in 853 b.c. Jehoshaphat was induced by the Israelite king to accompany him on a campaign to regain Ramoth-gilead from the Syrians. The campaign was unsuccessful and in the ensuing battle Ahab was mortally wounded, but Jehoshaphat escaped (1 Ki 22:1-38; 2 Chr 18:1-34). Jehoshaphat's fraternization with the wicked king of Israel was severely rebuked by the prophet Jehu, son of Hanani (2 Chr 19:1, 2). Returning from the north, Jehoshaphat continued the religious and judicial reforms started by his father (1 Ki 22:46; 2 Chr 17:6). He also instituted a judicial body in Jerusalem to act as the highest court in the country (2 Chr 19:4-11). He is called Josaphat in Mt 1:18, KJV.

Later in his reign the Ammonites, Moabites, and Edomites joined forces and invaded Judah from the south. Jehoshaphat sought the Lord for deliverance, and the Lord honored his request. The enemy allies began quarreling among themselves and in a bloody battle destroyed one another (2 Chr 20:1-30). It was probably this disaster that gave Jehoshaphat access to the Edomite fort of Ezion-geber, seemingly not occupied by Judah since the time of Solomon. Ahaziah of Israel joined him in an enterprise to build a fleet of ships to be used for trading expeditions. But the ships were wrecked, presumably in a gale. Ahaziah seems to have suggested a second attempt, but Jehoshaphat refused, for he had been rebuked by the prophet Eliezer for uniting himself with the wicked king of Israel (1 Ki 22:48, 49; 2 Chr 20:35-37). Later, Jehoshaphat joined Jehoram (*see* Jehoram, 1), another son of Ahab, in a campaign against Moab which met with a measure of success (2 Ki 3:4-27). Jehoshaphat was buried in the royal tombs of Jerusalem (2 Chr 21:1).

5. Son of Nimshi and father of Jehu, king of Israel (2 Ki 9:2, 14).

Jehoshaphat (jĕ-hŏsh′à-făt), **Valley of.** [Heb. *'emeq Yehôshaphat*.] A valley mentioned in Joel 3:2, 12 as the place where God would gather the heathen for judgment. In the time of Eusebius (4th cent. A.D.) the term was applied to the Kidron Valley, which lies between Jerusalem and the Mount of Olives. However, there is no evidence that this valley was ever called "valley of Jehoshaphat" in ancient times. It is more likely that since Jehoshaphat means "Yahweh judges" or "Yahweh has judged," Joel used the term as descriptive of God's dealings with the enemies of ancient Israel. These texts have also been applied to God's final judgment of the wicked.

Jehosheba (jĕ-hŏsh′ĕ-bà), or **Jehoshabeath** (jĕ′hŏ-shăb′ĕ-ăth). [Heb. *Yehôsheba'* and *Yehôshab'ath*, "Yahweh is an oath."] A daughter of King Jehoram of Judah, sister of King Ahaziah, and wife of Je-

hoiada, the high priest. When Athaliah attempted to assassinate all the royal children at the death of her son, King Ahaziah, so that there might be no rival to the throne she planned to usurp, Jehosheba rescued the young prince Joash, and for 6 years concealed him in the Temple until her husband could safely proclaim him king of Judah (2 Ki 11:2; 2 Chr 22:11).

Jehoshua. *See* Joshua.

Jehoshuah. *See* Joshua, 1.

Jehovah. *See* Yahweh.

Jehovah-jireh (jĕ-hō′và-jī′rĕ). [Heb. *YHWH yir'eh*, "Yahweh sees," or "Yahweh provides."] According to the KJV, the name given by Abraham to the place where God provided a ram to be offered instead of Isaac. The RSV translates the name "The Lord will provide" (Gen 22:14). The Temple at Jerusalem was later built on this site. *See* Moriah.

Jehovah-nissi (jĕ-hō′và-nĭs′ī). [Heb. *YHWH nissî*, "Yahweh is my banner."] According to the KJV, the name Moses gave to the altar he erected at Rephidim as a memorial of the victory of Israel over the Amalekites (Ex 17:15, 16). It is translated "The Lord is my banner" in the RSV (v 15).

Jehovah-shalom (jĕ-hō′và-shā′lŏm). [Heb. *YHWH shalôm*, "Yahweh is peace."] According to the KJV, the name Gideon gave to the altar he built at Ophrah. The RSV translates the term "The Lord is peace." Having seen an angel, and fearing for his life, Gideon was given assurance by the words, "Peace be unto thee." This benediction of peace became the motif expressed in the name of the altar erected in God's honor, and in memory of the event (Jgs 6:23, 24).

Jehozabad (jĕ-hŏz′à-băd). [Heb. *Yehôzabad*, "Yahweh gives."]

1. A Korahite porter whose father was Obed-edom (1 Chr 26:1, 4).

2. A son of a Moabitess. He became a servant of King Joash of Judah, whom he and other conspirators assassinated (2 Ki 12:21; 2 Chr 24:26). For this act King Amaziah, Joash's successor, executed him, but permitted his family to go unpunished in harmony with a Mosaic injunction (2 Ki 14:6; 2 Chr 25:3, 4; cf. Deut 24:16).

3. A Benjamite military officer under King Jehoshaphat of Judah (2 Chr 17:18).

Jehozadak (jĕ-hŏz′à-dăk), or **Jozadak** (jŏz′à-dăk), KJV 6 times **Josedech** (jŏs′ĕ-dĕk).

[Heb. *Yehôṣadaq* and *Yôṣadaq*, "Yahweh is just."] Father of Jeshua, the high priest (Ezr 3:2, 8; etc.; Neh 12:26; Hag 1:1; etc.; Zec 6:11; *see* Jeshua, 4). Jehozadak was carried captive to Babylonia by Nebuchadnezzar (1 Chr 6:14, 15).

Jehu (jē'hū). [Heb. *Yehû'*, probably "Yahweh is He (namely, the God)"; spelled *Yaua* in cuneiform records.]

1. A man from Anathoth who joined David at Ziklag and became one of his officers (1 Chr 12:3).

2. A prophet who denounced King Baasha of Israel for continuing in the sins of Jeroboam (1 Ki 16:1-4, 7), and who rebuked King Jehoshaphat of Judah for joining Ahab (2 Chr 19:2). He wrote a biography of King Jehoshaphat (ch 20:34). His father's name was Hanani (1 Ki 16:1).

3. The 11th king of Israel (if Tibni is included in the count), who reigned for 28 years (*c.* 841 - *c.* 814 B.C.), and became the founder of the strongest and longest-reigning dynasty of the northern kingdom. He was the son of Jehoshaphat (not the king of Judah) and grandson of Nimshi. However, he sometimes is called simply the son of Nimshi (1 Ki 19:16; 2 Ki 9:2). Jehu was an army officer under Ahab and Jehoram (Joram), and was noted for his furious chariot driving (2 Ki 9:20). While engaged in besieging Ramoth-gilead he was anointed king to succeed Ahab by one of Elisha's young helpers (1 Ki 19:16; 2 Ki 9:1-10). Supported by his fellow officers he immediately

drove to Jezreel, where King Jehoram (Joram) was recovering from wounds received at Ramoth-gilead. Arriving there he slew the king (2 Ki 9:11-26) and mortally wounded Ahaziah, king of Judah, who was visiting Jehoram (v 27). He also slew Jezebel, the queen mother of Israel (vs 30-37), 70 princes of the house of Ahab (ch 10:1-11), and 42 close relatives of Ahaziah of Judah (2 Ki 10:12-14; 2 Chr 22:8; cf. Hos 1:4). After Jehu had thus exterminated the house of Ahab, which had originated Baal worship in Israel, he turned against the Baal worshipers in general. He cleverly proclaimed himself an ardent follower of Baal and invited all like-minded men to the Baal temple. When they were all assembled and worshiping, he ordered his soldiers to slay everyone in the Baal temple. The building was then desecrated and made into a latrine (2 Ki 10:18-28). Because Jehu had been zealous in uprooting Baal worship, the Lord promised that his dynasty would continue for 4 more generations (v 30). However, Jehu did not break with the bull worship of Jeroboam, and was thus responsible for the continuation of Israel's idolatry (vs 29, 31).

During the year that Jehu came to the throne (841/40 B.C.) King Shalmaneser III of Assyria invaded Syria, and Jehu considered it prudent to meet him as a vassal with tribute rather than as an enemy. This submission of Jehu is recorded on the famous Black Obelisk, which was found by Layard in the ruins

255. A panel of the Black Obelisk of Shalmaneser III, showing King Jehu of Israel kneeling before the Assyrian king

of Nimrud (Biblical Calah) and which is now in the British Museum (see fig. 255). This obelisk has on it a pictorial representation of Jehu, the only contemporary pictorial representation of any Hebrew king. Shalmaneser III was followed by weak kings, a circumstance that gave Hazael of Damascus a free hand to turn against Israel. Because Jehu was not strong enough to stand up against the Aramaeans, they took from him all Israelite territories east of the Jordan (2 Ki 10:32, 33; cf. Amos 1:3).

4. A Judahite of the family of Jerahmeel (1 Chr 2:38; cf. v 33).

5. A Simeonite (1 Chr 4:35).

Jehubbah (jĕ-hŭb′á). [Heb. *Yachbah* (Q *Chubbah*), probably "he hides."] An Asherite (1 Chr 7:34).

Jehucal (jĕ-hū′kăl), or **Jucal** (jōō′kăl). [Heb. *Yehûkal* and *Yûkal*, "Yahweh is able." The name occurs on an ancient Hebrew seal impression.] A prince of Judah in the time of King Zedekiah. The king sent him to Jeremiah to request prayer for Jerusalem (Jer 37:3). Later, believing that Jeremiah's message discouraged the people, Jehucal became an enemy of the prophet and sought his death (ch 38:1-6).

Jehud (jē′hŭd). [Heb. *Yehud.*] A town in the territory of Dan (Jos 19:45). The LXX reads *Azōr,* and on this basis it has been identified with the present *Yazûr,* 3½ mi. southeast of Joppa (Map VI, D-2).

Jehudi (jĕ-hū′dī). [Heb. *Yehûdî,* "a Jew."] An official in the service of King Jehoiakim, who was sent to Baruch, Jeremiah's secretary, to get a scroll containing Jeremiah's prophecies. When Jehudi read the scroll to Jehoiakim, the king became so enraged at its contents that he burned it (Jer 36:14, 21, 23).

Jehudijah (jē′hŭ-dī′já). [Heb. *Yehudîyah,* "the Jewess."] According to the KJV the name of one of the two wives of Mered, the other being Bithiah, an Egyptian princess (1 Chr 4:18). However, the complete Hebrew expression *'ishtô hay-yehudîyah* means "his Jewish wife" (RSV), as is evident from the presence of the article in the Hebrew. Hence her name is not given; she is simply distinguished from Mered's Egyptian wife by being called his Jewish wife.

Jehuel (jĕ-hū′ĕl), KJV **Jehiel** (jĕ-hī′ĕl). [Heb. *Yechû'el* (Q *Yechî'el*), "God lives." The name occurs in cuneiform records as *Yaḫi-ilu.*] A Levite of the house of Heman the singer (2 Chr 29:14).

Jehush. *See* Jeush, 4.

Jeiel (jĕ-ī′ĕl), KJV 4 times **Jehiel** (jĕ-hī′ĕl). [Heb. *Ye'î'el,* meaning uncertain.]

1. A Reubenite chief (1 Chr 5:7).

2. Ancestor of the Hebrew inhabitants of Gibeon and also of King Saul (1 Chr 8:29, RSV; 9:35; cf. vs 36, 39).

3. One of-David's "mighty men" (1 Chr 11:44); possibly identical with Jeiel, 1.

4. A Levite musician in David's time (1 Chr 16:5, third name); identified by many commentators with Aziel of ch 15:20 and Jaaziel of v 18.

5. A Levite musician in David's time (1 Chr 15:18, 21; 16:5, tenth name).

6. A Levite of the sons of Asaph (2 Chr 20:14).

7. A recording scribe in Uzziah's army (2 Chr 26:11).

8. A Levite who gave offerings for Josiah's Passover (2 Chr 35:9).

9. An Israelite who was married to a foreign wife in Ezra's time (Ezr 10:43).

For other names spelled Jeiel in the KJV, *see* Jeuel, 2, 3.

Jekabzeel. *See* Kabzeel.

Jekameam (jĕk′á-mē′ăm). [Heb. *Yeqam'am,* "may the kinsman establish."] A Kohathite Levite of the house of Hebron (1 Chr 23:19; 24:23).

Jekamiah (jĕk′á-mī′á), KJV once **Jecamiah** (jĕk′á-mī′á). [Heb. *Yeqamyah,* "Yahweh establishes." The name occurs also in an ancient Hebrew seal inscription.]

1. A Judahite (1 Chr 2:41).

2. A son or descendant of King Jehoiachin of Judah (1 Chr 3:18).

Jekuthiel (jĕ-kū′thĭ-ĕl). [Heb. *Yeqûthî'el,* possibly "God is perfection."] A descendant of Caleb, and ancestor of the inhabitants of Zanoah (1 Chr 4:15, 18).

Jemima. *See* Jemimah.

Jemimah (jĕ-mī′má), KJV **Jemima** (jĕ-mī′má). [Heb. *Yemimah,* "dove."] The eldest of Job's 3 daughters born to him after his great affliction (Job 42:14).

Jemuel (jĕ-mū′ĕl). [Heb. *Yemû'el.*] A son of Simeon, and ancestral head of a tribal family (Gen 46:10; Ex 6:15). He is called Nemuel (Heb. *Nemû'el*) in Num 26:12 and 1 Chr 4:24. The letters *y* and *n* are very similar in postexilic Hebrew.

Jephthae. See Jephthah.

Jephthah (jĕf′thá), KJV of NT **Jephthae** (jĕf′-thē). [Heb. *Yiphtach,* "he opens"; Gr. *Iephthae.*] One of the major judges of Israel (Jgs 11:1 to 12:7). He was a Gileadite in a double sense: (1) he was a native of Gilead, and (2) his father's name was Gilead. Because he was an illegitimate child his brothers, who seem to have belonged to the elders of Gilead, expelled him from his home and forced him to flee into the country of *Tob, possibly somewhere in the northeast, where he lived as chief of a band of other outcasts (Jgs 11:1-3). He probably raided caravans or extracted tolls from caravans as protection money for safe passage through the territory controlled by his band. The fact that he was later called to become a military leader of the Transjordan tribes shows that he had gained fame in matters of warfare.

During Jephthah's exile the Ammonites moved into Israelite territory, occupied it, and oppressed the Israelites for many years. Finally the eastern Israelites recalled Jephthah and placed him as judge and general over them to free them from the Ammonites (Jgs 11:4-11). He invited the Ephraimites to help but seems to have received no response (ch 12:2). He attempted to negotiate with the Ammonites to induce them to end their unlawful occupation of Israelite territories. But these efforts failed; so he began military action that resulted in the defeat of the Ammonites and the restoration of the occupied territories to Israel (ch 11:12-27). Before the battle he rashly vowed that if given victory he would offer as a burnt offering to the Lord the first member of his household to meet him on his return (vs 30, 31). Returning victoriously, he was greatly dismayed to be met by his only child, a daughter. According to the narrative he "did with her according to his vow" (vs 34-40), although some commentators attempt to explain that he simply devoted her to perpetual virginity.

Jephthah had trouble with the Ephraimites, who complained that they had been slighted when he made his preparations for the Ammonite campaign. He denied this, but civil war broke out between Ephraim and the Transjordan tribes. Jephthah again emerged as victor (Jgs 12:1-6). He judged Israel for 6 years (v 7). He is referred to by Samuel as proof of the faithfulness of the Lord in sending Israel deliverers at the right time (1 Sa 12:11). In Heb 11:32 Jephthah is praised as a man of faith.

Jephunneh (jĕ-fŭn′ĕ). [Heb. *Yephunneh,* "he turns."]

1. A man whose son Caleb was the spy representing the tribe of Judah (Num 13:6; 14:6, 30, 38; etc.).

2. An Asherite (1 Chr 7:38).

Jerah (jē′rá). [Heb. *Yerach,* "moon."] A son

of Joktan, and ancestral head of an Arabic tribe not identified (Gen 10:26; 1 Chr 1:20).

Jerahmeel (jĕ-rä′mĕ-ĕl). [Heb. *Yerachme'el,* "may God have mercy." The name is attested among the Amorites as *Yarham-ilu.*]

1. A descendant of Judah through Perez and Hezron. He had two wives, and his numerous descendants, who lived in the south of Judah, are called Jerahmeelites (jĕ-rä′mĕ-ĕl-īts) [Heb. *Yerachme'lî*] (1 Sa 27:10; 30:29; 1 Chr 2:9, 25-41).

2. A son of the Levite Kish (1 Chr 24:29), not related to Saul.

3. One of the officers King Jehoiakim of Judah sent to arrest Jeremiah and his secretary Baruch. He was apparently a royal prince (Jer 36:26, RSV). *See* Hammelech.

Jerahmeelites. *See* Jerahmeel, 1.

Jered (jē′rĕd). [Heb. *Yered,* related to the Akkadian *(w)ardu,* "servant."]

1. For 1 Chr 1:2, KJV, *see* Jared.

2. A man of Judah and father of Gedor. By Gedor probably the inhabitants of the town of Gedor are meant (1 Chr 4:18).

Jeremai (jĕr′ĕ-mī). [Heb. *Yeremay,* probably a shortened form of Jeremiah, "Yahweh establishes."] A member of the family of Hashum. He was married to a foreign wife in the time of Ezra (Ezr 10:33).

Jeremiah (jĕr′ĕ-mī′á), KJV of NT **Jeremy** (jĕr′ĕ-mī) and **Jeremias** (jĕr′-ĕ-mī′ás). [Heb. *Yirmeyah* and *Yirmeyahu,* "Yahweh is exalted," or possibly "Yahweh strikes." The name occurs on an ancient Hebrew jar handle, and in the Lachish Letters. Gr. *Ieremias.*]

1. The head of a family in the tribe of Manasseh (1 Chr 5:24).

2, 3, and 4. The name of 3 men who joined David's band at Ziklag (1 Chr 12:4, 10, 13).

5. A native of Libnah whose daughter Hamutal became the wife of Josiah and mother of Jehoahaz (2 Ki 23:30, 31).

6. A son of Habaziniah and father of Jaazaniah, of the Rechabites (Jer 35:3).

7. A prophet who encouraged the work of reform under King Josiah. He counseled the Jews in Jerusalem prior to and during the Babylonian captivity and wrote the book that bears his name. Jeremiah is perhaps the most colorful of all the OT prophets. Interspersed with his prophetic messages are frequent glimpses into his own soul that give a vivid picture of the feelings and experience of a prophet who was called to bear unpopular messages in a time of na-

tional crisis. Jeremiah's prophetic ministry continued for more than 40 years, beginning about 626 B.C. (Jer 1:2) and extending beyond the Captivity in 586 B.C. (ch 39:1, 2)—perhaps the most critical period of Israelite history in all OT times.

The history of the southern kingdom of Judah since the captivity of the 10 tribes a century earlier was one of deepening national apostasy. By Jeremiah's time it had become apparent that drastic measures must be taken if God's purpose for Israel was ever to be fulfilled. Canaan was theirs only by virtue of their covenant relationship with God, and by their persistent violation of the covenant provisions they forfeited their right to the land. Captivity was inevitable, not as retributive punishment but as remedial discipline, and it fell to Jeremiah to explain the reasons for the Captivity and to encourage cooperation with God's plan in that experience. Again and again, through Jeremiah, God appealed to His people to submit to the king of Babylon and to be willing to learn the lesson this bitter experience was ordained to teach. The 1st captivity came in 605 B.C., but their refusal to cooperate led to a 2d in 597 B.C., and a 3d in 586 B.C. that was accompanied by the utter desolation of the city and the Temple. Ezekiel was called to a similar role for the exiles in Babylonia, and about the same time God appointed Daniel to the court of Nebuchadnezzar for the purpose of mitigating the natural harshness and severity of the Babylonians toward the Jews. The messages of Jeremiah, Ezekiel, and Daniel were designed to make clear the nature and purpose of the Captivity and to hasten the return of the exiles to their homeland.

Jeremiah was the son of Hilkiah, a priest of *Anathoth (Jer 1:1). He was called to the prophetic office while still a young man (vs 6, 7). At first he was reluctant to accept the call, but God assured him that although he would encounter violent opposition he could also expect divine help in the accomplishment of his mission (vs 8, 17-19). By nature Jeremiah was gentle and tenderhearted, and the conflict between his personal feelings and the stern messages of rebuke and warning he was commissioned to bear caused him great personal distress. As he foresaw the sad fate that awaited his beloved people he exclaimed, "I am pained at my very heart" (ch 4:19). Captivity was inevitable (v 28), but God comforted Jeremiah with the promise that it would

not mark the "full end" of the nation as God's chosen people (Jer 4:27; 5:10). To impress upon him their hopeless moral and spiritual degeneracy, God sent him on an expedition through the streets of Jerusalem in quest of a man who sincerely sought to know and do God's will (ch 5:1). Unsuccessful, Jeremiah turned hopefully to the leaders, but found not even one to lead the nation in ways of righteousness (vs 3-5). Now realizing more fully the backslidden condition of his people, Jeremiah was instructed to "stand in the gate of the Lord's house" and warn them of the fate that awaited them unless they should repent. This sermon, commonly called "the Temple discourse," is recorded in chs 7-10. The gravity of the message is evident from God's warning to Jeremiah, "Pray not thou for this people . . . : for I will not hear thee" (ch 7:16). Mourning over its solemn import, he exclaimed, "Oh that my head were waters, and mine eyes a fountain of tears, that I might weep day and night for . . . my people!" (ch 9:1, 2). "Woe is me for my hurt! my wound is grievous," he protested to the Lord, but reconciled himself with the thought, "Truly this is a grief, and I must bear it" (ch 10:19). Acknowledging divine justice in the judgments foretold, the prophet nevertheless appealed for mercy (vs 23-25). The Lord next sent Jeremiah out into the cities of Judah and the streets of Jerusalem with the message, "Hear ye the words of this covenant, and do them," but despite his earnestness the people paid no attention (ch 11:6-8). In fact, his own relatives, the priests of Anathoth, plotted to silence him by taking his life. When the Lord told Jeremiah of the plot the prophet appealed to the Lord for justice and vengeance, for had he done more than speak the words God gave him? See vs 9-23. Seeing in the conspiracy to take his life a reflection of the nature of Judah's conspiracy against the Lord, the prophet inquired of the Lord, "Wherefore doth the way of the wicked prosper?" (ch 12:1). The Lord replied by asking Jeremiah what he would do in the future when the whole nation turned against him if this first taste of opposition wearied him (v 5; cf. ch 1:19). As the affections of Jeremiah's own blood relatives were alienated from him to the point that they were ready to take his life, so the affections of Israel were alienated from God (ch 12:6-11). A 2d time he exclaimed, "My soul shall weep . . . ; and mine eye shall weep sore, and run down with tears, because the Lord's flock is carried away captive" (Jer 13:17). A 3d time (cf. chs 7:16; 11:14) God said to Jeremiah, "Pray not for this people for their good" (ch 14:11), and the prophet lamented, "Let mine eyes run down with tears night and day, and let them not cease" (v 17). Jeremiah concluded that perhaps God had "utterly rejected Judah" (v 19), and like Moses of old (see Ex 32: 31, 32) confessed the sin of his people and pleaded with God not to break His covenant with them (Jer 14:20-22). But God replied that it would be useless even for Moses to pray for them—captivity was inevitable (ch 15:1). He would "destroy" His people, "since they return not from their ways" (v 7). Lamenting the abuse he had suffered, Jeremiah complained again to the Lord, "Revenge me of my persecutors; . . . for thy sake I have suffered rebuke. . . . Why is my pain perpetual, and my wound incurable?" (vs 15-18). Once more God assured the prophet of divine protection and deliverance (vs 20, 21). Jeremiah was not to take a wife (ch 16:2) or to rear a family because, in view of the Captivity, they would "die of grievous deaths" (vs 3, 4). The prophet was next commissioned to bear a solemn message of warning at the gate of Jerusalem, based on a symbolic visit to the potter's house. As he did so, the plot against his life deepened, and he pleaded once more (cf. ch 17:18) with the Lord because of his enemies (ch 18:18-23). About this time Pashhur, governor of the Temple, put Jeremiah in the stocks at the gate of Benjamin, hard by the Temple, and left him there overnight (ch 20: 1-3). The prophet complained to the Lord, "I am in derision daily, every one mocketh me," and decided to resign his prophetic commission (vs 7-9). But the Lord would not release him (v 9). In consequence the prophet cursed the day of his birth and lamented the role God had assigned him (vs 14-18).

Shouldering the prophetic yoke once more, Jeremiah did so reflecting greater maturity. No longer did he weep or complain about his lot but bore a forthright and fearless message, without hesitancy or regret. Sent first to "the court of the Lord's house," he announced the 70 years' captivity and the utter desolation of the city of Jerusalem and the Temple (Jer 26:2). Immediately following this discourse the priests and prophets arrested Jeremiah and threatened to kill him (v 8),

and would doubtless have done so had not the princes of Judah come to his rescue (vs 10-16). Jeremiah's maturity of spirit at this time is evident from his calm response to those who proposed to take his life: "As for me, behold, I am in your hand: do with me as seemeth good . . . unto you" (v 14). Forbidden henceforth to teach in the Temple courts, Jeremiah had his assistant, Baruch, write his messages on a scroll and read them in the Temple on a certain fast day (ch 36:1-6). Word of what was going on came to the princes, who requisitioned the scroll and took it to King Jehoiakim, who in turn burned it in the fire (vs 11-26). Thereupon the prophet had the scroll rewritten with additional material warning that the throne of Judah would become extinct and that Jehoiakim would die a violent death (vs 27-32). Jeremiah later appeared before King Jehoiachin with a stern message warning of captivity by Nebuchadnezzar and death in the land of exile (ch 22:20-30).

Early in the reign of Zedekiah, Jeremiah counseled the king to "serve the king of Babylon, and live" lest "this city be laid waste" (Jer 27:12, 17). This policy was opposed by a group of false prophets, but the death of their leader, Hananiah, within the period of time predicted by Jeremiah attested the mission and message of Jeremiah (ch 28:9, 16, 17). About this time Jeremiah also wrote to the exiles in Babylon to settle down for a long captivity (ch 29). The Jewish leaders in Babylon wrote back to Jerusalem demanding that Jeremiah be imprisoned as a false prophet (vs 24-27). Soon after this, Nebuchadnezzar again invaded Judah and laid siege to Jerusalem. Jeremiah was "shut up in the court of the prison" (ch 32:1-3), but apparently was released when the siege was lifted briefly while Nebuchadnezzar left temporarily to do battle with an Egyptian army that had come to assist Zedekiah (ch 37:11). The prophet set out for his home in Benjamin to inspect a piece of property he had recently bought, but was apprehended as he left Jerusalem and was charged with defecting to the Chaldeans and was again imprisoned (vs 11-15). At this time Zedekiah secretly inquired of him what course to take (vs 16-21), and the prophet advised surrender to the Chaldeans. But the princes and army commanders demanded his death (ch 38:1-4), and Jeremiah was remanded to an empty cistern, the floor of which was covered with soft mud into which he sank (vs 5, 6). His life was spared when an Ethiopian eunuch by the name of Ebed-melech appealed to Zedekiah and received permission to draw him up out of the dungeon and place him in the courtyard of the prison (Jer 38:7-13). Here the prophet stayed until Jerusalem fell (v 28).

Upon the surrender of the city, Jeremiah enjoyed the personal protection of King Nebuchadnezzar, apparently because the prophet's policy of urging the Jews to surrender and to cooperate with the Chaldeans had become known (Jer 39; 40). Permitted to choose whether he would go to Babylon or remain in Judah, Jeremiah attached himself to Gedaliah, whom Nebuchadnezzar had appointed governor of Judah (ch 40:4-16). When a group of fanatics assassinated Gedaliah, the people who remained, fearing the Chaldeans, fled to Egypt, forcing Jeremiah to accompany them (chs 41: 17 to 43:13). In Egypt, Jeremiah continued his efforts to turn the people's hearts back to God, but without success (ch 44). How long his ministry in Egypt continued is not known. According to tradition, Jeremiah was stoned to death by his own countrymen at Daphnae.

Jeremiah, Book of. The book by the prophet of that name, containing messages he bore prior to and during the early years of the Babylonian captivity, from about 626 to sometime after 586 B.C., and a record of his personal experiences. No serious question has been raised as to the authenticity of the book or its right to a place in the sacred canon. The actual writing was done by Jeremiah's trusted amanuensis, Baruch (see ch 36:4, 6, 28, 32). The closing words of ch 51, "thus far are the words of Jeremiah" (v 64), imply that the final chapter of the book (ch 52) was appended by another writer, possibly Baruch.

When called to the prophetic ministry in 627/26 B.C. Jeremiah faithfully supported the work of reformation already begun by King Josiah (2 Ki 22:1 to 23: 25). Their efforts met with little success, however, and on Josiah's death in 609/08 B.C. the program came to a halt. Josiah's son Jehoahaz reigned 3 months, when he was taken captive into Egypt (2 Ki 23: 29-33). Another son of Josiah, Jehoiakim, who came to the throne as a vassal of Egypt, opposed Jeremiah's attempts to turn the nation back to God (vs 34-37). Three years later (605 B.C.) Nebuchadnezzar invaded Judea and took a select group of captives, including Daniel, with

him back to Babylon (Dan 1:1-3). Jehoiakim was left on the throne as a Chaldean vassal, but later rebelled, and in Dec. 598 met a violent death. His son Jehoiachin succeeded him on the throne and reigned for 3 months (2 Ki 24:6-9), but Nebuchadnezzar took him captive in March, 597 B.C., carried him to Babylon, and placed Zedekiah on the throne (vs 9-19). When, a few years later, Zedekiah rebelled, Nebuchadnezzar invaded Judah a 3d time, laid siege to Jerusalem, and took it in 586 B.C., after a 30 months' siege (ch 25:1-10). The city was looted and burned, the Temple was destroyed, the monarchy abolished, most of the people were taken captive to Babylon, and Gedaliah, a Jew, was made governor over the few who remained (vs 4-22). It was not long, however, till a group of fanatical Jews slew Gedaliah, and then fearing reprisal by the Chaldeans, they fled to Egypt (vs 23-26). Such were the turbulent times during which Jeremiah bore the messages recorded in his book.

As the chronological data given by Jeremiah indicate, the messages and historical notes as they appear in the book are not arranged in chronological order.

The messages were given at intervals during the last 18 years of Josiah's reign, the 3 months of Jehoahaz' rule, the 11 years of Jehoiakim's reign, the 3 months of Jehoiachin's reign, and the 11 years and 5 months of Zedekiah's reign, and during the Exile, first in Palestine, and later in Egypt. The following arrangement of the book in chronological order is based on the chronological data stated and implied in the book itself:

Josiah (c. 639-609/08 B.C.): chs 1-6; 14-16.

Jehoiakim (608-597 B.C.): chs 7-11; 17; 26; 35; 22:1-19; 25; 18-20; 36:1-4; 45; 36: 5-32; 12.

Jehoiachin (597 B.C.): chs 22:20-30; 13; 23.

Zedekiah (597-586 B.C.): chs 24; 29-31; 46-51 (?); 27; 28; 21; 34; 32; 33; 37-39.

During the Exile: chs 40; 42-44.

Jeremiah is known as the weeping prophet. His message consisted of stern rebuke for the sins of Israel and of warning that divine judgment could not be averted. Through him God sought first to turn the hearts of the people back to Him, and failing that, to secure their cooperation with His purpose in the Captivity, which came not as retributive punishment but as remedial discipline. At this crucial period of history Jeremiah's call for submission to the Babylonians earned for him the implacable hatred of rulers and people alike, and he suffered much at their hands. Repeatedly he wept over the sins of Israel, over the doom that threatened his beloved nation, and over the harsh treatment he suffered at the hands of the leaders. Jeremiah had cause for weeping if any prophet ever had, but he bore his message faithfully.

Besides his messages to Judah and Jerusalem, Jeremiah also uttered prophecies concerning foreign nations (Jer 46:1 to 51:64). *See* Jeremiah.

There are certain significant differences between the Hebrew text of Jeremiah and that of the LXX. The LXX is approximately 1/8, or about 2,700 words, shorter than the Hebrew, although a few sections are longer in the LXX, these additions amounting to about 100 words. Furthermore, the arrangement of materials differs in the 2 texts, although neither follows a strict chronological order. A fragmentary Hebrew manuscript of Jeremiah found in Cave 4 at *Qumrân* shows in its preserved portions a faithful agreement with the LXX, both in length and in sequence of materials. This indicates that the Greek translator cannot be held responsible for the differences that exist between the LXX and the Masoretic text, for he most probably followed closely a Hebrew recension, such as the one found in this cave, shorter than the Masoretic and differing from it in the arrangement of materials. The fact that there were these 2 differing Hebrew recensions in circulation leads to the conclusion that Jeremiah's prophecies at first circulated separately and that their collection was accomplished at a later time. It seems that at least 2 such collections were made and that one of the collectors had more of Jeremiah's works available than the other, which accounts for the difference in the lengths of the 2 recensions and also for the different arrangements of the text material. That this collection of Jeremiah's prophecies was not made until after the Exile seems evident from Dan 9:1, 2, according to which Daniel's information concerning the length of the Exile came from "books" containing the word of the Lord to Jeremiah the prophet. Such a prophecy from Jeremiah is found in 2 places, Jer 25:12 and ch 29:10 in the Masoretic text, and chs 25:12 and 36:10 in the LXX. In Daniel's time these 2 statements were evidently found in 2 different books (*sepharîm*, "scrolls"), and when incorporated into the collections of Jeremiah's proph-

ecies, found different places in the 2 recensions, which are now represented by the Masoretic text and the LXX.

Jeremias. *See* Jeremiah, 7.

Jeremoth (jĕr′ĕ-mŏth), KJV twice **Jerimoth** (jĕr′ĭ-mŏth). [Heb. *Yeremôth* and *Yerîmôth,* meaning uncertain.]

1. A Benjamite, son of Becher (1 Chr 7:8).

2. A Benjamite, descended through Elpaal (1 Chr 8:14).

3. A Merarite Levite, son of Mushi (1 Chr 23:23), called "Jerimoth" in ch 24:30.

4. A descendant of Heman, and head of the 15th course of musicians under David (1 Chr 25:22), called "Jerimoth" in v 4.

5. A prince and head of the tribe of Naphtali in David's reign (1 Chr 27:19).

6 and 7. Two men of the time of Ezra (of the family of Elam and Zattu, respectively) who were married to foreign wives (Ezr 10:26, 27).

8. A member of the family of Bani, and one who was married to a foreign wife in the time of Ezra (Ezr 10:29, RSV; the KJV reads "Ramoth," probably the earlier reading).

Jeremy. *See* Jeremiah.

Jeriah (jē-rī′à), or **Jerijah** (jē-rī′jà). [Heb. *Yerîyah* and *Yerîyahû,* "Yahweh sees."] A Kohathite Levite of the house of Hebron (1 Chr 23:19; 24:23; 26:31).

Jeribai (jĕr′ĭ-bī). [Heb. *Yerîbay,* meaning uncertain.] One of David's "mighty men" (1 Chr 11:46).

Jericho (jĕr′ĭ-kō). [Heb. *Yerichô,* either "city of the moon (god)" or "place of fragrance"; Gr. *Ierichô.*] An important city in the Jordan Valley, sometimes called "the city of palm trees" (Deut 34:3; Jgs

256. The mound of OT Jericho from the west, showing excavators' trenches

1:16; 3:13; 2 Chr 28:15). It is situated about 5 mi. west of the river, about 8 mi. north of the Dead Sea, and 15 mi. northeast of Jerusalem in a straight line (Map VI, E-3; fig. 523), at the foot of the Judean mountains, on the higher ledge of the Jordan Valley. It is 820 ft. below sea level, but 460 ft. above the river bed. It has an almost tropical climate, so that palms, and, in modern times, banana trees grow there. See fig. 365.

Although excavations show that Jericho is one of the oldest cities in the world, it is nowhere mentioned in ancient records outside of the Bible. When the Israelites invaded Canaan, Jericho, lying on the main east-west highway, was the first obstacle to their invasion of western Palestine. Since it was the first city to be conquered in the Promised Land, Joshua directed that it be devoted to God as an offering (Jos 6:17-19). The story of Jericho's fall is well known. Men were sent out from the camp east of the Jordan to spy out the city. They were shown hospitality in the home of Rahab, who also protected them and aided their escape when they were hunted by the inhabitants of Jericho. As a reward for her help and for her faith in the God of the Israelites, the spies promised to save her life and property, a promise that was faithfully kept (chs 2:1-22; 6:22, 23, 25). After the Israelites crossed the Jordan, they camped at Gilgal, near Jericho (ch 5:10), and marched around the city once a day for 6 days. On the 7th day they marched around it 7 times, and then, at the signal of trumpets, made a great shout. At that the walls of the strong fortress collapsed (ch 6:8-21). The Israelites entered the city, destroyed its inhabitants, except Rahab and her family, and burned everything, saving only certain precious objects for use in the sanctuary (vs 1-21, 24). Joshua then pronounced a curse over anyone who should build Jericho in the future (v 26).

Although the city as such was not rebuilt until the time of Ahab, people must have lived in its vicinity, for the name Jericho continued to be used (see 2 Sa 10:5). In the division of the country, Jericho was on the boundary between Ephraim and Benjamin and was assigned to Benjamin (Jos 16:1, 7; 18:12, 21). When Eglon, the king of Moab, oppressed the Israelites in the early judges period, he took Jericho from them (Jgs 3:13). David's envoys, returning from the Am-

monite king, who had insulted them by shaving off half their beards, stayed at Jericho until their beards were grown (2 Sa 10:5; 1 Chr 19:5). In Elijah's time Hiel rebuilt the city, thus incurring the curse pronounced by Joshua, the loss of 2 sons (1 Ki 16:34). In the prophet Elijah's time a community of prophets lived there (2 Ki 2:4, 5, 15, 18), and later Elisha healed its spring (vs 19-22). See fig. 154 for "Elisha's spring." A century later Jericho was the scene of the liberation of captives of Judah taken by the army of King Pekah of Israel (2 Chr 28:15). In the last days of the kingdom of Judah, the Babylonian army captured Zedekiah in its vicinity (2 Ki 25:5; Jer 39:5; 52:8). The population of Jericho must also have been taken captive, because 345 descendants of former inhabitants returned from the Babylonian exile with Zerubbabel (Ezr 2:34; Neh 7: 36). Some people of Jericho helped Nehemiah rebuild the wall of Jerusalem (Neh 3:2).

Jericho is again mentioned in the period of the Maccabees, when Bacchides, the Syrian general, repaired its fortifications (1 Macc 9:49, 50). Antony gave the city to Cleopatra as a winter resort. When Herod the Great later received it as a gift from Augustus, he beautified it, built a palace, and erected a fortress behind the city called Cypros (Jos. Ant. xvi. 5. 2; War i. 2. 4, 9). Herod the Great died at Jericho.

Jesus passed through the NT Jericho (Lk 19:1), which lay to the south and east of the OT city, at the entrance to the Wâdī Qelt, through which the road led up to Jerusalem. Jericho was the home of the tax collector Zacchaeus, whose hospitality Christ enjoyed, and whose conversion is recorded in vs 1-10. It was in the vicinity of the NT Jericho that Jesus healed blind Bartimaeus and his companion (Mt 20:29-34; Mk 10:46-52; Lk 18:35-43). The modern city of Jericho, called Erîkhâ, was founded in the time of the Crusaders and lies to the east of NT Jericho and southeast of OT Jericho.

Because of its great Biblical and historical importance Jericho has received the attention of several archeological expeditions. The OT site has been identified with Tell es-Sulṭân, at the northern edge of modern Jericho (see figs. 256, 257). In 1868 Charles Warren made preliminary explorations that did not materially increase our knowledge of the city's ancient history. From 1907 to 1909 Ernst Sellin and Carl Watzinger excavated parts of the mound, but found its ruins confusing and disturbed by later building activities and by erosion. Since Palestinian archeology was still in its infancy, the conclusions of these scholars were unsatisfactory and later had to be revised when explorations carried out on other sites showed that their interpretations of certain evidence could not be maintained. John Garstang, who carried out diggings at Jericho for 6 seasons, from 1930 to 1936, discovered a Late Bronze Age cemetery, the burial place of the inhabitants of Jericho until about 1350 B.C., as indicated by inscribed Egyptian seals. The remains of the city's fortifications were so confused, however, that some walls were erroneously identified, as later excavations have shown.

Garstang's interpretation of the city's archeological history is now out of date and need not be repeated here. From 1952 to 1957 Kathleen M. Kenyon dug at Jericho, using the latest scientific methods. She discovered another cemetery, Middle Bronze Age tombs, including funerary equipment such as wooden tables, stools, and dishes, foodstuff in vessels, cloth, baskets, etc. (see fig. 85), all amazingly preserved owing to the infiltration of deadly gases that killed the germs and thus prevented the disintegration of ancient material otherwise never preserved in Palestine. The excavations of the mound itself have brought to light levels that were occupied in very early times. They have shown that Jericho was a city long before there was any pottery. In fact, it now seems that the city's walls and towers are the oldest ever discovered in the Near East. The city was destroyed several times, and the remains of at least 7 successive walls of the Early Bronze period (3d millennium B.C.) have been uncovered. The latest of these was destroyed by an earthquake. At that time the "city" was about 750 ft. long and not more than 250 ft. wide. In the Middle Bronze Age, the Hyksos period, it had been enlarged to a length of about 850 ft. and a width of about 425 ft., and was surrounded by a tremendous stone wall with a glacis, or gently sloping bank. This city was destroyed by one of the Egyptian kings of the 18th dynasty in the 15th cent. B.C. Nothing was found of the walls of the Late Bronze Age, which would be those destroyed in Joshua's time. Unfortunately, the forces of man and nature seem to have denuded the upper levels of the mound

257. Outskirts of modern Jericho, the city of palm trees, as seen from the mound of OT Jericho

to such an extent that practically nothing remains of them. The excavation by Kenyon unearthed only a small spot, a portion of a floor level, which dated from Joshua's Jericho. At the foot of the slope some of the latest structures of Jericho, built in the Iron Age (after 1200 B.C.), came to light.

Although the results of the excavations have been very interesting for the archeologist, and have shed light on the early history of this important city, they have unfortunately contributed little that is of direct interest to the Bible student. However, the cemeteries of Jericho have shown that as burial places they ceased to be used in the 14th cent., which may be considered evidence that the city could not have been destroyed much later than that period. See fig. 256.

A portion of NT Jericho, namely *Tulûl Abû el-'Alâyiq,* was excavated in 1951 and 1952 by the American School of Oriental Research in Jerusalem under the direction of J. L. Kelso and J. B. Pritchard. The excavation uncovered part of Herod's winter palace with a façade 330 ft. long and a pool, probably the one in which Herod had his brother-in-law, the high priest Aristobulus III, drowned.

Lit.: John Garstang and J. B. E. Garstang, *The Story of Jericho,* 2d ed. (London, 1948); S. H. Horn, *The Ministry,* Feb., 1954, pp. 29-31 (has exhaustive literature references); Kathleen M. Kenyon, *Digging Up Jericho* (New York, 1957). On the excavations of NT Jericho see J. L. Kelso, *et al., AASOR* 29-30 (1955); J. B. Pritchard, *AASOR* 32-33 (1958).

Jeriel (jē'rĭ-ĕl). [Heb. *Yerî'el,* "God sees."] A descendant of Issachar through Tola (1 Chr 7:2).

Jerijah. *See* Jeriah.

Jerimoth (jĕr'ĭ-mŏth). [Heb. *Yerîmôth,* meaning uncertain.]

1. A Benjamite, son of Bela (1 Chr 7:7).

2. A Benjamite warrior who joined David at Ziklag (1 Chr 12:5).

3. A son of David, who was also the father of Mahalath, a wife of King Rehoboam (2 Chr 11:18).

4. A Levitical Temple overseer in Hezekiah's time (2 Chr 31:13).

5. For the Jerimoth of 1 Chr 24:30 see Jeremoth, 3.

6. For the Jerimoth of 1 Chr 25:4 see Jeremoth, 4.

Jerioth (jĕr'ĭ-ŏth). [Heb. *Yerī'ôth*, "tent curtains."] One of Caleb's wives (1 Chr 2:18).

Jeroboam (jĕr'ô-bō'ăm). [Heb. *Yarob'am*, "may the people multiply." The name occurs on an ancient Hebrew seal.]

1. The first king of the northern kingdom of Israel, usually referred to as Jeroboam I (*c*. 931 - *c*. 910 B.C.). He was an Ephraimite from Zeredah, the son of Nebat and of Zeruah (1 Ki 11:26). While foreman over a company of builders during the construction of the *Millo at Jerusalem, Jeroboam was told by the prophet Ahijah of Shiloh that he would become king over 10 of Israel's tribes (vs 27-39). Jeroboam was not a man to wait patiently for God to work out His plans and to give him the promised kingdom, as David had done under similar circumstances. Instead he seems to have begun at once to plot against Solomon (v 27). When this was discovered, Solomon attempted to kill him, but Jeroboam fled to Egypt (v 40). There he found refuge with Pharaoh Shishak, the founder of the 22d dynasty, who seems to have discontinued his predecessor's friendly policy toward Solomon. When news of Solomon's death and news that the new king of Israel was to be crowned at Shechem reached Jeroboam in Egypt, he returned to Palestine (ch 12:1-3). At once he became spokesman for the people and demanded a promise from Rehoboam, Solomon's son, that the public burden be alleviated (vs 3-5). Rehoboam, misled by the foolish advice of inexperienced counselors, refused to meet the justified grievances of the people. As a result the 10 northern tribes declared their independence from the house of David and proclaimed Jeroboam their king (vs 6-20).

Jeroboam immediately took drastic measures to prevent the two kingdoms from reuniting. He founded 2 new temples, one at Dan on the northern border

of the country and the other at Bethel on the southern border not far from the main highway to Jerusalem. In both places bull images were set up as visible cult symbols for the worship of Yahweh (1 Ki 12:26-30). In his proclamation calling upon the people to worship at these places, Jeroboam echoed the words that Aaron had pronounced at Mount Sinai to gather the people for the worship of the golden calf (cf. 1 Ki 12:28 with Ex 32:4). This bull worship, which was probably an imitation of the Canaanite worship of Él under the image of a bull, became the "sin of Jeroboam," which was followed by practically every ruler of the northern kingdom (1 Ki 15:26, 34; 16:19, 31; 22:52; etc.). Jeroboam also appointed as priests men who were not of the tribe of Levi, and ordered that the chief feasts should be celebrated during the 8th month, not in the 7th, as was done in Judah (ch 12:31, 32). He also seems to have put the New Year's Day, celebrated in the autumn in Judah, in the spring, and to have adopted the Egyptian way of reckoning the regnal year of the king by the "non-accession-year" system, in order to be different from the kings of Judah, who appear to have counted their years according to the "accession-year" system (*see* Chronology, I, 3). By these measures he hoped to alienate the 10 tribes from the south and to make the break between the 2 nations permanent and irreparable. In this he succeeded, although he brought the curse of God upon himself and his people. An anonymous "man of God" from Judah rebuked him severely for his acts (ch 13:1-6), as did also Ahijah, who had predicted his kingship (ch 14:6-18).

Jeroboam seems to have chosen Shechem, which he fortified, as his first capital. Later he moved to Penuel in Transjordan (1 Ki 12:25), perhaps at the time of Shishak's invasion (see below), and carried out building activities there. Finally, he chose Tirzah, a city northeast of Shechem, as his capital and royal residence (ch 14:17). This city remained Israel's capital until the time of King Omri (ch 16:23).

Divine intervention prevented an immediate outbreak of warfare between the seceding northern kingdom and Judah (1 Ki 12:21-24; 2 Chr 11:1-4); however, repeated military campaigns against each other's territory must have taken place, since "there was war between Rehoboam and Jeroboam continually" (1 Ki 14:30, RSV; cf. 15:6), and also "between Abijam and Jeroboam" (1 Ki 15:7; 2 Chr 13:3-20). In these wars Jeroboam temporarily lost to Judah the southern cities Jeshanah, Ephron (KJV "Ephrain"), and even the new temple city of Bethel (2 Chr 13:19).

Israel also suffered from the invasion of Pharaoh Shishak in the 5th year after the separation from Judah. The Bible is silent about the invasion of the northern kingdom (see 1 Ki 14:25, 26; 2 Chr 12:2-4), but Shishak's victory inscription on the temple wall at Karnak mentions well-known cities of Jeroboam's realm among the conquered places: Taanach, Shunem, Rehob, Mahanaim, Megiddo (see fig. 438). This was no hollow boast, for a fragment of a victory monument with Shishak's name on it was discovered during excavations of Megiddo. Shishak may have thought that the political weakness of Palestine, created by the civil war between the north and the south, would make it easy for him to rebuild the Egyptian Empire in Asia, lost since the *Amarna age.

One of Jeroboam's sons died in infancy (1 Ki 14:1, 17); another, Nadab, followed his father on the throne of Israel (v 20).

2. The 14th king of Israel (if Tibni is included in the count), son of Joash (or Jehoash), sometimes called Jeroboam II to distinguish him from Jeroboam, 1. His reign lasted 41 years (c. 793 - c. 753 B.C., including an 11-year coregency with his father c. 793 - c. 782 B.C., as seems to be indicated from chronological synchronisms; see Chronology, V, 2). Either prior to the reign of Jeroboam or during the early years of his rule, the prophet *Jonah predicted that the new king would recover the territories in the north and east that in former times had belonged to Israel (2 Ki 14:25). Jeroboam fulfilled this prophecy. He became the strongest king of the dynasty of Jehu, if not of all the kings who occupied the throne of the northern kingdom. The Biblical record about his reign is extremely brief, consisting of only 7 verses (vs 23-29), yet the brief account of his military successes shows clearly that no ruler of the northern kingdom either before or after him could point to greater achievements than Jeroboam II. He conquered Damascus and Hamath on the Orontes, and recovered most of the territory of Syria and Transjordan down to the Dead Sea, so that his territory included all that David and Solomon had held, with the exception of Judah. It was fortunate for him that Assyria was experiencing a period of weakness during

his reign, and could therefore not interfere with his expansionist activities.

While the kingdom of Israel enjoyed political prestige and economic prosperity, the moral and religious state was extremely low. The gloomy picture painted by the prophets Amos and Hosea of the conditions prevailing under Jeroboam show that in spite of extravagant sacrifices and the celebration of religious feasts, the country was morally corrupt (Amos 5:21, 22; 2:6-8; Hos 6:6-10). Only 6 months after Jeroboam's death his dynasty met its end by the assassination of his son Zechariah (2 Ki 15:8-11). It is amazing that in spite of the gross wickedness prevailing, a certain measure of religious tolerance was exercised. When Amos, a citizen of the southern kingdom, uttered his prophecies of woe against the house of Jeroboam in the sanctuary city of Bethel, the priest of Bethel reported the matter to the king, yet nothing was done to Amos except that he was bidden to leave the territory of the northern kingdom (Amos 7:10-17).

258. Seal impression of "Shema, the minister of Jeroboam," found at Megiddo (approximate size)

During the excavations of Megiddo in 1904 a beautiful stamp seal of jasper was found with a picture of a roaring lion and the following Hebrew inscription: lshm' 'bd yrb'm, "Belonging to Shema, the servant (that is, the minister) of Jeroboam." It is generally believed that this seal, which is now in Istanbul, belonged to one of Jeroboam's high officers (see fig. 258).

Jeroham (jě-rō'hăm). [Heb. Yerocham, "may he have compassion."]

1. A Levite, an ancestor of the prophet Samuel (1 Sa 1:1; 1 Chr 6:27, 34).

2. A Benjamite, whose sons were influential citizens of Jerusalem (1 Chr 8:27); perhaps identical with Jeroham, 3.

3. A Benjamite whose son lived in Jerusalem (1 Chr 9:8); perhaps identical with Jeroham, 2.

4. A Benjamite of Gedor, whose warrior sons, Joelah and Zebadiah, joined David at Ziklag (1 Chr 12:7).

5. Father of the chieftain of the tribe of

Dan in the reign of David (1 Chr 27:22).

6. Father of one of the captains who supported the high priest Jehoiada in making Joash king (2 Chr 23:1).

7. A priest (1 Chr 9:12; Neh 11:12).

Jerubbaal. *See* Gideon.

Jerubbesheth. *See* Gideon.

Jeruel (jĕ-rōō′ĕl). [Heb. *Yerŭ′el*, meaning uncertain.] A portion of the Wilderness of Judah in the vicinity of En-gedi (2 Chr 20:16; cf. vs 2, 20); not identified.

Jerusalem (jĕ-rōō′sȧ-lĕm). [Heb. *Yerŭshalayim*. Since this name is attested, in differing forms, at least from the 19th cent. B.C., long before the Hebrews invaded the country, it is of Canaanite or Amorite origin, meaning probably "city of (the god) Shalim," but in Hebrew probably "city of peace." In Egyptian execration texts of the 19th and 18th cent. B.C. the name is spelled *ꝫwshꝫmm*, pronounced probably *Urusalimum*. In the *Amarna Letters of the 14th cent. B.C. it occurs as *Urusalim*. The Assyrian inscriptions of Sennacherib call it *Urusalimmu*. Aramaic *Yerŭshelem*. Gr. *Ierosoluma* and *Ierousalēm*.] One of the most important cities of the world, the Holy City of 3 great religious faiths: Judaism, Christianity, and Islam. To the Jews it was the site of the Temple and the capital of the nation; to the Christians it is the scene of the suffering, death, resurrection, and ascension of Jesus Christ; and to the Moslem it is the traditional place of Mohammed's ascension to heaven. It is located about a third of the distance from the north end of the Dead Sea to the Mediterranean, in the Judean mountains (Map VIII, E-3; see also fig. 365). After the Arab-Israeli armistice of 1949 Jerusalem became the name of 2 cities; the Arab-held Old City within the walls became the major part of Jerusalem, Jordan, while the New City west of the walls became Jerusalem, Israel. (Map XXII, E-3, shows the border situation of Jerusalem.)

The name *Salem (Heb. *Shalem*), which occurs twice in the OT (Gen 14:18; Ps 76:2), is probably an abbreviated form of the full name. The city was known under the name of *Jebus in the period of the judges (Jgs 19:10, 11) and when David took the city (1 Chr 11:4, 5). This was because the inhabitants of that time were Jebusites. This name is not attested outside of the Bible. Its modern Arabic name is *el-Quds*, "the holy one," but to all non-Arabs—Jews, Christians, and others—it is still known as Jerusalem.

I. The Site. The walled city of Jerusalem lies between 2 main valleys: the *Kidron on its eastern side and the *Hinnom on the western and southern sides. The uneven plateau between these valleys, upon which the city is built, is connected with the tableland of Judea on the north. This plateau is roughly divided into 2 ridges by a central valley which is not named in the Bible, but which is called the Tyropoeon Valley, or "Valley of the Cheesemakers," by Josephus (*War* v. 4. 1). This valley was narrow and deep, but in the time of the Maccabees was filled with the debris of the Acra, the fortress of the Syrians, which Judas Maccabeus demolished. Today it begins at the present Damascus Gate and is visible only as a shallow depression. Excavations have shown that the debris fills it up to a depth of about 100 ft. The eastern ridge rises to an altitude of about 2,440 ft. above sea level at the point where the "castle" (KJV) or *"barracks" (RSV) of Antonia once stood, just north of the Temple. This northern hill of the eastern ridge is called the Temple hill, or the northeastern hill. It is called *Moriah in the OT (Gen 22:2; 2 Chr 3:1). The eastern ridge was divided into a northern and southern section by a shallow depression, now filled up with debris. The southern section, the spur that slopes toward the junction of the Hinnom and Kidron valleys, was the site of the original City of David, which has been variously known as Jebus, Salem, and *Zion. Its highest part had an elevation of about 2,280 ft. above sea level. This area—the original Jerusalem —is left completely outside the present city wall, which passes immediately south of the Temple area. *See* David, City of; Ophel; figs. 259, 260, 278; Maps XVII, XVIII.

The western ridge is higher than the eastern one, rising to an altitude of about 2,550 ft. above sea level, which is about 100 ft. higher than the Temple hill. There are no ancient names known for the different eminences of the western ridge, but the southwestern hill has for many centuries been erroneously identified with "Zion" and carries this name today, although it was probably not even included in the ancient city until Hellenistic times. A good portion of the northwestern hill now lies in the northwestern part of Jerusalem's present Old City and includes as its most famous structure the Church of the Holy Sepulchre. See fig. 259.

The *Kidron Valley, often mentioned in the Bible (2 Sa 15:23; Jn 18:1; etc.), and presently called *Wâdī en-Nâr,* separates the city from the Mount of *Olives, whose highest summit rises to 2,737 ft. above sea level (see fig. 365). The Kidron is a deep and narrow gorge that aided the eastern defenses of the city. In it are found the only water sources of Jerusalem: the *Gihon spring, on the western slopes of the valley, and *En-rogel, a well near the confluence of the Hinnom and Kidron valleys. The *Hinnom Valley, now called *Wâdī er-Rabâbeh,* is also frequently mentioned in the OT (Jos 15:8; 18:16; etc.). It is much wider than either the Kidron or the Tyropoeon, and its slopes are gentler. This valley separates the higher hills to the west and south of it from the southwestern ridge of the Jerusalem plateau. See figs. 230, 259, 260, 277, 278.

II. History. It is not known at what time Jerusalem was founded, but excavations have uncovered evidence proving its existence during the 12th Egyptian dynasty (19th and 18th cent. B.C.), from which time the Egyptian execration texts mention the city and its Amorite rulers, *Yaqar-'Ammu* and *Sasa'-'Anu* (spelled *iyk3'mw* and *st'nw* in the Egyptian hieratic texts) as real or potential enemies of Egypt. During this period the OT mentions the city for the first time under the name of Salem, whose ruler, Melchizedek, was at the time a priest of the most high God, and therefore entitled to bless Abraham and to receive a tithe from the spoil that the patriarch had taken from Chedorlaomer and his confederates (Gen 14:18-20). *See* Melchizedek; Salem.

Jerusalem is mentioned in the book of Joshua as the leading city in a coalition of Canaanite city-states that fought against the invading Israelites. Its king at that time was Adoni-zedek, who, with his allies, was defeated at the battle at Azekah, then captured and executed by Joshua (Jos 10:1-27). Shortly afterward, in the time of King Ikhnaton of Egypt, a king by the name of 'Abdu-Heba sat on the throne of Jerusalem. His name means "Servant of (the Hittite goddess) Heba," and it is possible that he was of Hittite descent. If so, he and the 2 Amorite kings already mentioned are evidence that the early population of Jerusalem included Hittites and Amorites. This is also reflected in the words of Ezekiel, who said of Jerusalem, "Thy father was an Amorite, and thy mother an Hittite" (Eze 16:

3; cf. v 45). Among the *Amarna Letters are several written by 'Abdu-Heba to Ikhnaton, in which he bitterly complained of the invasion of the 'Apiru, or Habiru (probably the Hebrews), and of the inactivity of Egypt, which resulted in one section of the country after another being lost to the invaders (*ANET* 487-489). A capture and destruction of Jerusalem by Judah after Joshua's death is recorded in Jgs 1:8, but this victory was not followed up by an occupation by the Israelites; it remained in the hands of the Canaanites or Jebusites until the time of David's conquest of it (Jos 15:63; cf. Jgs 19:11, 12).

After David was made king over all the tribes of Israel, he decided to move his capital from the important Judahite city of Hebron to a neutral site. He therefore chose Jerusalem, which lay on the border of Judah and Benjamin, but belonged to neither tribe. The Jebusites mocked him when he began the siege, for they were convinced that they could easily hold the well-fortified mountain city. However, Joab and his men found access to the city by climbing up the *ṣinnôr,* by which is meant probably the water shaft that connected the *Gihon spring with the interior of the city (2 Sa 5:6-8; 1 Chr 11:4-6). In David's time it became known as "the city of David" (1 Chr 11:7; 2 Sa 5:7). He built a palace (2 Sa 5:11) and also some fortifications (see fig. 254; see also Song 4:4, which mentions the tower of David; cf. 1 Chr 11:8). This tower is not the one of the same name in the present Citadel of Jerusalem, since the latter is actually one of the towers of the palace built by Herod the Great. David also built a place, or structure, called the "Millo" (2 Sa 5:9; 1 Chr 11:8). From other texts (1 Ki 9:15, 24; 11:27; 2 Chr 32:5) it seems probable that the Millo lay in the city and that it was periodically enlarged or strengthened. It was apparently part of the fortification system of the city at its weakest spot, which would have been the northern end of the southeastern hill (see fig. 259). The LXX identifies it with the Acra, a citadel south of the Temple, which stood there until the time of Judas Maccabeus. The Hebrew name *millô',* meaning "filling," has been variously explained. It may have been a double wall filled with earth, such as was discovered in excavations of a wall at Gezer.

When David moved the ark into Jerusalem, he housed it in a temporary tent.

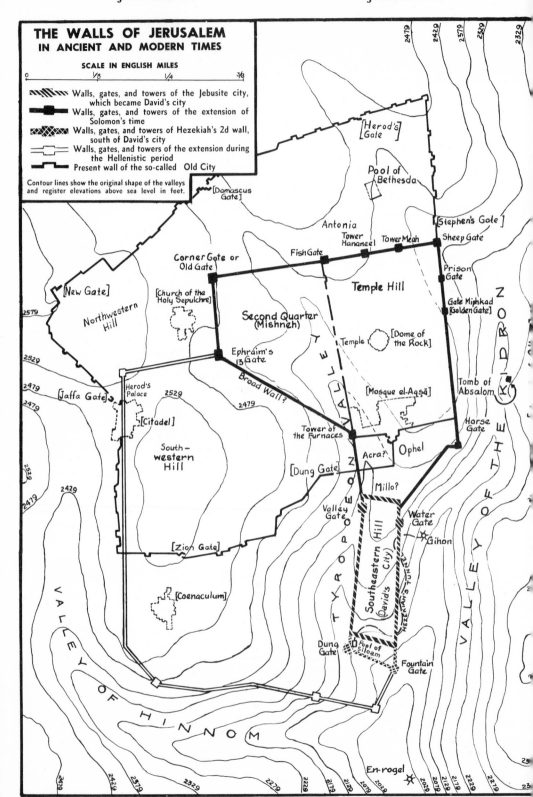

THE WALLS OF JERUSALEM
IN ANCIENT AND MODERN TIMES

SCALE IN ENGLISH MILES

0   1/8   1/4   3/8

⫸⫸⫸ Walls, gates, and towers of the Jebusite city,
   which became David's city
� Walls, gates, and towers of the extension of
   Solomon's time
⫷⫸⫷ Walls, gates, and towers of Hezekiah's 2d wall,
   south of David's city
⫸ Walls, gates, and towers of the extension during
   the Hellenistic period
▬ Present wall of the so-called Old City

Contour lines show the original shape of the valleys
and register elevations above sea level in feet.

[Damascus Gate]

[Herod's Gate]

Pool of Bethesda

Antonia
Tower Hananeel   Tower Meah

[Stephen's Gate]

Sheep Gate

Corner Gate or Old Gate

Fish Gate

Prison Gate

Temple Hill

Gate Miphkad
[Golden Gate]

[New Gate]

Northwestern Hill

[Church of the Holy Sepulchre]

Second Quarter (Mishneh)

Temple   [Dome of the Rock]

Ephraim's Gate

Broad Wall?

[Mosque el-Aqsa]

2579

2529

2479

[Jaffa Gate]

Herod's Palace

[Citadel]

2529

2479

South-western Hill

Tower of the Furnaces

Tomb of Absalom

Horse Gate

Ophel

Acra?

[Dung Gate]

Millo?

Valley Gate

Water Gate

Gihon

2429

[Zion Gate]

Southeastern (Hill City) (David's City)

[Coenaculum]

Dung Gate

Pool of Siloam

Fountain Gate

VALLEY OF HINNOM

VALLEY OF THE KIDRON

TYROPOEON VALLEY

HEZEKIAH'S TUNNEL

En-rogel

259. Map of Jerusalem

God did not permit him to build a Temple. However, he made preparations for its construction, and the threshing floor of Araunah, which he had bought, was used as the site for the Temple built by Solomon (2 Sa 6:17; 24:24; 1 Chr 28:2, 3, 19-21; 2 Chr 3:1). When King David died he was "buried in the city of David" (1 Ki 2:10). All the kings of Judah down to Ahaz were buried in the royal sepulcher, the site of which is still unknown except that a comparison of Neh 3:16 with vs 15 and 26 seems to show that it lay between the Pool of Siloam and the Water Gate. It has been suggested that the winding course of the Siloam tunnel was the result of attempting to avoid the royal tombs. See fig. 259.

With Solomon, who was a great .builder, a new era dawned for Jerusalem. The city was extended toward the north, and possibly toward the northwest. The Temple, which was surrounded by a court, was erected on the northern hill, just west of the present Dome of the Rock (see figs. 259, 262), which covers the rock that is believed to be that on which the altar of burnt offering had stood (1 Ki 6:1-38; 2 Chr 3:1). It was probably between the Temple and the City of David that Solomon erected a palace for himself (1 Ki 7:1), called the "king's house" (ch 9:1). This may have been a complex of structures including: (1) a "house for Pharaoh's daughter," which was probably part of the harem (chs 7:8; 9:24) and with the palace may have formed a unit. This was surrounded by "another court," probably the same as the "middle court" and the "court of the guard" (1 Ki 7:8; 2 Ki 20:4; Jer 32:2; etc.); (2) a porch, or hall (RSV), of judgment (1 Ki 7:7), in which his throne stood; (3) a porch of pillars, perhaps an audience hall (v 6), which was possibly an entrance to the main hall if not a separate building; (4) the "house of the forest of Lebanon," probably so named because its 45 pillars, built in 3 rows (vs 2-5), were made of the cedars from Lebanon. Solomon thus added a whole new quarter to the city, and there can be little doubt that the expansion of his administration brought to Jerusalem many new people for whom residences had to be provided. These new quarters were then surrounded by a wall that enclosed "Jerusalem round about" (ch 3:1; cf. ch 9:15). That the public buildings were erected on the northeastern hill is certain, but how much more area was included in his city is disputed.

Some scholars think that the whole western ridge was included; others limit the expansion to the northern portion of the western ridge. In fact, it seems unlikely that the southwestern hill was included in the city at that early time, because no pre-Hellenistic remains have been found in that area by archeologists. Some scholars question whether even the northwestern hill was included in Solomon's city.

When the kingdom broke up after Solomon's death, more than three fourths of its domain was taken from Judah, and Jerusalem lost much of its importance. Consequently no new expansions of the city were required for several centuries, though some repair work became necessary from time to time, especially after wars. In the time of Rehoboam, Solomon's son, Shishak of Egypt conquered Jerusalem and carried away much loot (1 Ki 14:25-28; 2 Chr 12:2-11). It is not known whether at that time the city fell after a siege, whether it suffered any damage, or whether Rehoboam surrendered it without a fight. It was also taken in the time of King Amaziah by Jehoash of Israel, who broke down 400 cu. of its western wall from the Ephraim Gate to the Corner Gate (2 Ki 14:13). This damage to Jerusalem's fortifications must have been repaired, although this is not recorded. In fact, no building activities are recorded from Solomon to Uzziah, with the exception of some repair work on the Temple carried out by Joash (Jehoash) of Judah (2 Ki 12:4-15; 2 Chr 24:4-14).

King Uzziah seems to have been the 1st king in 200 years who did any appreciable building in Jerusalem. He constructed an undisclosed number of towers at the Corner Gate, the Valley Gate, and the Angle, or turning, of the wall (2 Chr 26:9). His son Jotham continued his work by building the Upper Gate of the Temple and by doing some work on the wall of Ophel (ch 27:3). Great building activity is recorded from the time of Hezekiah, who made feverish preparations to strengthen Jerusalem's fortifications so that the city would be able to withstand a siege by the Assyrians. He constructed the long tunnel from the Gihon to the Pool of *Siloam (2 Ki 20:20; 2 Chr 32:4, 30) and thus brought spring water into the city. At the same time he built a 2d wall in the south, by which he enclosed the newly built pool within the city's fortifications, and repaired the Millo in the ancient City of David (2 Chr 32:5; Is 22:

10, 11). For Siloam see figs. 259, 204, 443.

Although most other fortified cities of Judah were destroyed in Hezekiah's time by Sennacherib's invasion forces (2 Ki 18:13), Jerusalem was spared this ordeal, and emerged from this difficult period unscathed (ch 19:32-36). Manasseh, Hezekiah's son, built a 2d wall in the northeast near the Fish Gate (2 Chr 33:14). It is unknown whether Jerusalem suffered during Manasseh's reign, although it is recorded that he was taken captive by the Assyrians and that he spent some time in a Babylonian prison (v 11). He may have surrendered to the Assyrians without a fight, although it is possible that the city at that time experienced a siege and a capture. Shortly afterward, in the reign of Josiah, mention is made for the first time of the "Second Quarter" (Heb. *mishneh*, KJV "college"), in which Huldah the prophetess lived (2 Ki 22:14; 2 Chr 34:22; cf. Zep 1:10). It is not certain whether this refers to a new city quarter added to Jerusalem by Manasseh or to the northwestern quarter already enclosed in the time of Solomon. See fig. 259.

The good king Josiah did additional repair work on the Temple (2 Ki 22:3-7; 2 Chr 34:8-13), and during his reign Je-

rusalem experienced a great religious reform. However, his sudden death ended this last spiritual revival, and his successors lapsed into wickedness and idolatry, with the result that Jerusalem was captured 3 times within 20 years: 1st in 605 B.C., during the reign of Jehoiakim (Dan 1:1, 2); then in 597 B.C., when Jehoiachin was carried away captive (2 Ki 24:10-16); and finally in 586 B.C., in the 11th year of Zedekiah, when Jerusalem was destroyed after a long siege and Zedekiah was carried captive to Babylon with most of Judah's population (ch 25:1-21).

After Jerusalem had lain in ruins for about 50 years, the 1st large group of exiles returned from Babylon, led by Zerubbabel. This was probably in 536 B.C., which was 70 years, inclusive, from the 1st deportation in 605 (see Jer 25:11, 12; 29:10). Immediately they set out to rebuild the Temple, but experienced so much opposition from the Samaritans, and other difficulties, that this work did not really get into full swing until the 2d year of Darius I, 520/19 B.C.; the Temple was finally completed and dedicated in 515 B.C., in the 6th year of Darius I (Ezr 1:1-4; 3:1-13; 4:1-5, 24; 5:1 to 6:16). In the 7th year of Artaxerxes I, Ezra was

260. View of Jerusalem, looking west from the Mount of Olives. Between the buildings in the foreground and the east wall of the city lies the deep Kidron Valley. The large open area inside the wall is the sacred Moslem *Ḥaram esh-Sherif*—the ancient Temple area. The domed building (center) covers the rock believed to be the

authorized to take a 2d group of exiles to Jerusalem (Ezr 7:6 to 8:32). He reorganized the province and set up an administration, based on Jewish law, in 457 B.C. It was probably during the next years that the Jews of Jerusalem began again to rebuild their city's wall. However, once again they were hindered by their enemies (Neh 1:3), until Nehemiah succeeded in having himself appointed as governor by Artaxerxes I. He went to Jerusalem in 444 B.C. and completed the rebuilding and repair work in a few weeks in spite of many hindrances (chs 2:1 to 4:23; 6:15).

Nehemiah's wall, about which detailed information is available (Neh 2:12-15; 3: 1-32; 12:27-40), seems to have followed the Old City wall as it had stood at the time Jerusalem was destroyed by Nebuchadnezzar. In his description he mentions most of the city gates, as well as other topographical features, although not all can definitely be identified. The locations of the various city gates, towers, and other structures named by Nehemiah are discussed under their respective names in separate articles. See fig. 259.

Little is known of Jerusalem's history during the 250 years following Nehemi-

ah's time. Josephus reports a quarrel concerning the high priesthood during which Johanan killed his brother in the Temple, with the result that the Persian governor placed a heavy penalty on the nation. *See* Johanan, 10. Josephus also tells of a visit of Alexander the Great to Jerusalem, at which time a prophecy of Daniel (apparently ch 8) was explained to him. According to Josephus this made such an impression on him that he became a friend of the Jews (*Ant.* xi. 8. 5, 6). Under Alexander's successors Jerusalem was the capital of a "Temple state" administered by the high priests, sometimes under the overlordship of the Ptolemies of Egypt and sometimes under that of the Seleucids of Syria.

During this period Jerusalem was considerably influenced by Hellenism. Greek language, thought, dress, and customs became fashionable, especially among the ruling classes, who were in direct contact with the foreigners. A faction known as the Hellenizers wanted to make Jerusalem a Greek city like so many others founded or rebuilt by the Hellenistic rulers in neighboring areas, and introduced a Greek gymnasium and athletic games. But the mass of Jewish people rose in

site of the altar of burnt offering. In the city wall, a little to the right of the "Dome of the Rock," is the "Golden Gate," a double-arched gate now walled up. The "City of David" (early Jerusalem) lay to the south of the Temple area and outside the present wall (extending behind the tower in the extreme left foreground)

desperate resistance when one of the Seleucid rulers, Antiochus IV Epiphanes, made a determined attempt to Hellenize the Jews by force, and desecrated the Temple by the sacrifice of unclean beasts to heathen deities. This caused the Maccabean revolt and the wars between the Syrians and the Jews, from which the Maccabeans emerged as victors. When they made Jerusalem the capital of their independent nation, it underwent a tremendous growth, both physically and in importance. The first change came when Judas Maccabeus took Jerusalem in 165 B.C. and rededicated the Temple. Some years later his brother Simon captured the Citadel, the Acra, which seems to have been located just south of the Temple; he destroyed it completely and cut off the crest on which it stood, using the debris to fill the central Tyropoeon Valley, which lies between the western and eastern ridges of the city. The Maccabean rulers of Judea built a palace on the western hill, which by that time was completely included in the city's defense system. They also built a citadel north of the Temple, later called the Castle, or Tower, of Antonia (fig. 259). *See* Barracks.

Pompey and his Roman army captured Jerusalem in 63 B.C. and broke down part of its wall. Crassus plundered the Temple in 54 B.C., and the Parthians looted the city in 40 B.C. Three years later Jerusalem was captured by Herod the Great. He repaired its walls and adorned the city with many new structures, such as a palace with 3 strong towers called Hippicus, Phasaelus, and Mariamne (where the "Citadel" now stands; see fig. 263), also a gymnasium, a hippodrome, and a theater. He also rebuilt the stronghold known as the Tower, or "castle" (KJV), "barracks" (RSV), of Antonia (Acts 21:34, 37; 22:24; etc.). At that time the Temple was 5 cent. old, and badly in need of repairs. Herod wanted to do more than repair it; he planned a complete rebuilding that involved extensive alterations in the walls and fortifications of the Temple hill. This, his most ambitious work, was begun in 20/19 B.C. The central Temple building was completely rebuilt in 18 months, but the other buildings of the large Temple area were not completed until about A.D. 64, only 2 years before the outbreak of the Jewish revolt against the Romans.

No major building activity by Archelaus, Herod's successor, is recorded, but Agrippa I built what has been called the 3d wall. Some think that it followed the course of the northern and western wall of the present Old City as far as the Jaffa Gate. Others, however, believe that the 3d wall ran about 1,500 ft. north of the present Old City, to where remains of an ancient wall have been excavated at several places, so that it can be followed for large sections. Others hold that the 3d wall was a structure hastily erected in the 2d cent. A.D. at the time of the Bar Cocheba revolt.

During the time of Herod the Great (37-4 B.C.) and during the reign of his son Archelaus (4 B.C.-A.D. 6), and of Agrippa I (A.D. 41-44), Jerusalem was the capital of the country, but not during the 2 periods when Roman procurators ruled over Judea (A.D. 6-41 and 44-66). They made Caesarea their capital city and were in Jerusalem only during important feasts in order to be on hand if trouble developed. Ordinarily, only a Roman garrison was stationed in the Castle of Antonia to guarantee law and order in the city.

When the revolt against Rome broke out in the spring of A.D. 66, Jerusalem saw much bloodshed. Under Gessius Florus, the last procurator of Judea, Jews began to massacre Gentiles, and Gentiles Jews, until all semblance of order and government was gone. Cestius Gallus, the legate of Syria, took command of Judea and in the autumn of A.D. 66 marched against Jerusalem. Although at one point he penetrated as far as the northern wall of the Temple he was repelled and for some unknown reason retreated, losing many of his soldiers on the march. The Christians, heeding the warning of Jesus (Mt 24:15-20), took this opportunity to leave Jerusalem and found refuge at Pella in Perea. From late A.D. 66 until the spring of A.D. 70 Jerusalem did not suffer any direct attacks of the Romans. Vespasian, upon his arrival in the country in A.D. 67, followed the plan of reducing the country to submission, allowing the various political factions in Jerusalem to fight against, and weaken, one another. In A.D. 69, when Vespasian was proclaimed emperor, most of Palestine was in Roman hands, but had been converted into a wilderness. Titus, Vespasian's son, took over the command of the army, and immediately made preparations to capture Jerusalem, the strong capital city of Judea.

During the 3 years of war with Rome there had been a tremendous influx of people into Jerusalem. Refugees had poured into the city without cessation, among them being bands of soldiers belonging to different factions and commanded by opposing leaders. John of Gischala from Galilee was the leader of the Zealots, and they established themselves in the lower Temple court. Simon bar Giora, a leader of marauders, held the upper city; and Eleazer, son of Simon, also an insurgent leader, was in command of the upper part of the Temple compound. When Titus began his siege of Jerusalem with 80,000 Roman soldiers in April A.D. 70, the 3 leaders and their followers were engaged in bloody battles against one another. Fighting was bitter during the 5 months of the siege, while one section after another was captured, and starvation was rife. More than 100,000 Jews died in the city between early May and late July. At that time the Castle of Antonia was taken, and the sacrifices in the Temple ceased. In August, according to Josephus' account, the Temple was conquered and against the command of Titus burned to the ground. The southwestern hill of Jerusalem, called the upper city, fell to the Romans in September. Josephus claims that more than 1 million Jews lost their lives during the siege of Jerusalem, and that 97,000 were made prisoners, among them John of Gischala and Simon bar Giora. The city and the Temple were razed in order to show the world that even the strongest fortifications were no match for the Roman army. Only the 3 towers of Herod's palace and part of the western wall were left standing as monuments of Jerusalem's former glory and to furnish a military post for the Roman garrison.

Jerusalem slowly recovered from this catastrophe, but when the emperor Hadrian refortified it and started to rebuild it as a Gentile city, the Jews rose up in a new revolt under Bar Cocheba in A.D. 132. After this had been crushed in A.D. 135, the rebuilding of the city was resumed and completed, and all Jews were banned from it. Its new name was Colonia Aelia Capitolina, indicating that it was a Roman colony, named in honor of Hadrian, whose full name was Publius Aelius Hadrianus, and that it was dedicated to Jupiter Capitolinus. A temple to this Roman god was built on the old Temple site. Christians also settled in Jerusalem, and in the 4th cent. it became practically a Christian city. Helena, mother of Constantine, built a church on the Mount of Olives in A.D. 326, and in A.D. 333 Constantine built the Church of the Holy

261. The Via Dolorosa in Jerusalem

Sepulchre on the supposed site of the resurrection of Jesus. The ban against Jews was also lifted at that time.

In A.D. 614 the Persians under Chosroes II captured Jerusalem, destroyed the Church of the Holy Sepulchre, massacred thousands of inhabitants, and carried thousands of others into captivity. The city was recaptured by the Roman emperor Heraclius 14 years later, and surrendered to the Arabs under Omar in A.D. 638. From that time on it has been under Moslem rule most of the time. The Temple site became a sacred Moslem enclosure called *Ḥaram esh-Sherîf*, within which is the 2d most sacred Moslem shrine, the Dome of the Rock (erroneously called Mosque of Omar), on the spot where Solomon's bronze altar is believed to have stood. At the southern end of the enclosure is the Mosque *el-Aqsa*, possibly on the site of a Christian church. Although there were periods when Christians suffered humiliation in Jerusalem, on the whole they did not fare too badly and were usually tolerated. The situation changed when the barbaric Seljuk Turks took over Jerusalem in A.D. 1077. All of

262. The Dome of the Rock, believed to be built over the spot on which Solomon's altar of burnt offering stood

Europe rose up in indignation over the humiliations suffered by Christians in the Holy City. The Crusades were the result. In A.D. 1099 Jerusalem was conquered and a Christian kingdom established which lasted for 88 years. In 1187 Saladin, sultan of Egypt and Syria, took the city, and began to rebuild its fortifications. For 2 more short periods Jerusalem was restored to the Christians, first in A.D. 1229 when the Emperor Frederick II of Germany obtained it by treaty and Christians held it for 10 years, and again in A.D. 1243 when it was given to the Christians unconditionally. But only 1 year later it was taken by the Khwarazm Turks, then fell to the Egyptians and, in 1517, to the Ottoman Turks, who held it until 1917 when Jerusalem surrendered to the British under General Allenby. The present wall surrounding the so-called Old City was built by the Turkish sultan Suleiman the Magnificent in 1542. During the time that Palestine was a mandated territory under a British government (1923-1948) Jerusalem served as capital. During the Jewish-Arab war heavy fighting raged at Jerusalem and the Jewish quarter of the walled Old City was completely destroyed. Since the armistice the main part of the modern city outside the walls, lying mostly to the west of the Old City, has been in Israeli hands, and has become the capital of the State of Israel. Its population in 1959 was about 200,000. The Old City, inside the walls, is in Arab hands and forms part of the Hashemite Kingdom of Jordan. A new Arab city has sprung up to the north of the Old City. Arab-held Jerusalem has a population of nearly 50,000.

III. History of Archeological Research at Jerusalem. Archeological work of a scholarly nature has been carried on in Jerusalem for about 100 years; on the one hand by resident scholars, ministers, and others, and on the other by organized excavations. To the first group belong

Charles Clermont-Ganneau (1846-1923), who went to Jerusalem in 1867 and lived in the Orient for many years. His discoveries, topographical studies, and publications laid a sound foundation upon which other scholars have built. Among his most important discoveries were the Greek Warning Inscriptions from Herod's Temple (fig. 487), and 2 tomb inscriptions of the time of Hezekiah, found at Silwan. Another resident of Jerusalem for many years, an architect, Dr. Conrad Schick (1822-1901), was untiring in his researches to reconstruct the ancient history of the Holy City. Gustaf Dalman (1855-1941), the director of the German Archeological Institute in Jerusalem from 1902 to 1914, L.-H. Vincent of the French École Biblique for half a century, and W. F. Albright, for 10 years director of the American School of Oriental Research in Jerusalem, take first place among those who have clarified the extremely difficult topographical and archeological history of ancient Jerusalem.

Systematic excavations began in 1867 when Charles Warren worked at Ophel for the newly founded Palestine Exploration Fund. By means of deep shafts and tunnels (up to 80 ft.) he located some of the earliest wall remains. To his discoveries belongs "Warren's Ophel Wall," south of the southeastern corner of the *Ḥaram esh-Sherif,* dating from the time of ancient Israel. He also found the shaft which the Jebusites had dug to provide an access from the city to the Gihon spring, and he made diggings at the Gate of the Chain at the *Ḥaram esh-Sherif* which proved that the present street to that gate leads over "Wilson's Arch," an ancient viaduct which crossed the Tyropoeon Valley. From 1880 to 1881 Hermann Guthe, assisted by Conrad Schick, carried out some excavations around the outlet of the Siloam Tunnel, on the southern slopes of the southeastern hill, and uncovered a few portions of the ancient city wall on the east side of the southeastern hill. From 1894 to 1897 F. J. Bliss and A. C. Dickie explored the southern fortifications of the ancient city on behalf of the Palestine Exploration Fund. They discovered an ancient buttressed wall to the southeast of the Pool of Siloam, uncovered some sections of the later wall crossing the Tyropoeon Valley, which continued on the southern slopes of the southwestern hill. During the clandestine excavations carried out from 1909 to 1911 by Capt. M. Parker in search of the hidden Temple treasures, the Siloam Tunnel was cleared, and L.-H. Vincent was able to map this tunnel and also other parts of the ancient waterworks connected with the Gihon spring. In 1913 Raymond Weill began an ambitious excavation on behalf of Baron E. de Rothschild, planning systematically to uncover the whole southern part of the southeastern hill. The outbreak of World War I soon ended his work. But he discovered in the southern part of the southeastern hill a great round tower, probably of Hebrew origin, and found a Greek inscription of the synagogue of Theodotus (see fig. 187). He continued his excavations for one more season (1923 to 1924), during which he discovered the great tower at the southern end of the Jebusite fortress and a portion of the southern wall, and also uncovered a tomb which may have belonged to the royal necropolis of the kings of Judah; since the tombs of this area were all destroyed long ago, and lacked stratigraphically undisturbed material, their nature remained uncertain. R. A. S. Macalister and J. G. Duncan dug on the eastern side of Ophel from 1923 to 1925 for the Palestine Exploration Fund. Their main discovery was part of the Jebusite bastion of the oldest city and an abutting tower of the time of David or Solomon. These structures (see fig. 254) have been preserved as a national monument by the Antiquities Department. Another important excavation campaign for the British School of Archeology in Palestine and the Palestine Exploration Fund was carried out by J. W. Crowfoot and G. M. FitzGerald at the western side of the southeastern hill in 1927. They discovered a city gate, perhaps the "valley gate" of the OT, with a stepped street leading up to it from the Tyropoeon Valley.

In the north 3 important archeological enterprises have been carried out. From 1925 to 1927 E. L. Sukenik and L. A. Mayer of the Hebrew University at Jerusalem uncovered long portions of the northernmost city wall, labeled by them "the Third Wall." C. N. Johns of the Department of Antiquities of the British Mandate excavated inside the Citadel from 1934 to 1940, showing that the towers of Herod's palace rested on foundations which go back to Hellenistic times. From 1937 to 1938 R. W. Hamilton, also of the Antiquities Department, carried out a number of soundings outside the northern wall of the present Old City and at the Damascus Gate, the results of which are somewhat ambiguous.

Excavations have also been carried out inside the city, mainly at sites of convents or churches. They have shed some light on questions concerning the extent of the Tower of Antonia, the location of the Pool of Bethesda, the city of Constantine's time, and structures erected in his day, but have made no real contribution to the solution of some important questions such as that of the course of the 2d wall, which determines whether the site of the Holy Sepulchre was outside or inside the city in the days of Christ.

IV. The Results of a Century of Archeological Research in Jerusalem. Although many historical and topographical problems have not yet been solved, a few positive results can be listed. The location and size of the Jebusite Jerusalem and of David's city have definitely been ascertained. Also the course of the walls of that oldest city and the location of some of its gates are now established. The waterworks of the Jebusites and of Hezekiah have been explored. Also the approximate extent of the Temple area and the location of the Temple within this area are known. Equally known is the location and extent of the Tower of Antonia, also of Herod's palace, the Pool of Bethesda, the Pool of Siloam, the Gihon spring, the well En-rogel, and the valleys of Kidron and Hinnom. To the unsolved problems belong the following: the extent of Solomon's city in the north and west; the time of the inclusion of the southwestern hill in the city; the course of the 2d northern wall with its bearings on the problem of the location of Golgotha; and the course of the 3d northern wall.

Lit.: Much has been written on the history and archeology of Jerusalem. Following is a partial listing of the more im-

263. The Citadel at Jerusalem with the so-called Tower of David (right), the lower part of which was built by Herod the Great

portant works: L.-H. Vincent, *Jérusalem antique*, Paris, 1912; L.-H. Vincent and F. M. Abel, *Jérusalem nouvelle*, Paris, 1914-1926; L.-H. Vincent and A.-M. Steve, *Jérusalem de l'Ancien Testament*, vols. i-iii, Paris, 1954-1956; J. Simons, *Jerusalem in the Old Testament*, Leiden, 1952; E. L. Sukenik and L. A. Mayer, *The Third Wall of Jerusalem*, London, 1930.

Jerusha (jĕ-rōō'shä), or **Jerushah** (jĕ-rōō'shä). [Heb. *Yerûsha'* and *Yerûshah*, "possessed."] Wife of King Uzziah of Judah, and mother of Jotham, Uzziah's son and successor (2 Ki 15:33; 2 Chr 27:1).

Jerushah. See Jerusha.

Jeshaiah (jĕ-shā'yä), KJV twice **Jesaiah** (jĕ-sā'yä). [Heb. *Yesha'yahû* and *Yesha'yah*, "Yahweh saves." The name occurs also in an ancient Hebrew seal inscription.]
1. A son of Jeduthun, and ancestral head of the 8th of the 24 courses into which David organized the musicians (1 Chr 25:3, 15).
2. A Levite who was a treasury official in David's reign (1 Chr 26:25).
3. A leader of the family of Elam. He with 70 male members of his family returned from Babylonia under Ezra's leadership (Ezr 8:7).
4. A Merarite Levite who returned with Ezra from Babylonia (Ezr 8:19).
5. A descendant of Zerubbabel (1 Chr 3:21).
6. A member of the tribe of Benjamin (Neh 11:7).

Jeshanah (jĕsh'ä-nä). [Heb. *Yeshanah*, "old." The name is mentioned in Egyptian records of Ramses III as *Yśnt*.] A town in the hill country of Ephraim, near Bethel, captured by Abijah, king of Judah (2 Chr 13:19). It has been identified with *Burj el-Isâneh*, about 6 mi. north of Bethel. The RSV, on the basis of the LXX and the Peshitta, reads Jeshanah in 1 Sa 7:12 also, where the Hebrew reads *hashshen*, "Shen" (see KJV).

Jesharelah (jĕsh'ä-rē'lä). [Heb. *Yeśar'elah*, meaning uncertain.] The ancestral head of the 7th of the 24 courses into which David organized the musicians (1 Chr 25:14). He is called Asharelah (KJV "Asarelah"; Heb. *'Aśar'elah*) in v 2.

Jeshebeab (jĕ-shĕb'ĕ-ăb). [Heb. *Yesheb'ab*, meaning uncertain.] A descendant of Aaron, and ancestral head of the 14th of the 24 courses into which David organized the priests (1 Chr 24:13).

Jesher (jē'shĕr). [Heb. *Yesher*, "uprightness."] A son of Caleb the son of Hezron (1 Chr 2:18).

Jeshimon (jĕ-shī'mŏn). [Heb. *Yeshîmôn*, "barren desert."]
1. A wilderness at the northeastern end of the Dead Sea. According to Num 21:20 Pisgah looks down upon Jeshimon, and according to ch 23:28 Peor looks toward Jeshimon. In both these passages the RSV renders *Yeshîmôn*, "the desert."
2. A wilderness near Ziph and Maon, in which David hid from Saul (1 Sa 23:19, 24; 26:1, 3). It lay to the southeast of Hebron toward the Dead Sea.
Some scholars think that Jeshimon is simply another name for the Wilderness of Judah.

Jeshishai (jĕ-shīsh'ä-ī). [Heb. *Yeshishay*, probably "old."] A Gadite, descendant of Buz (1 Chr 5:14).

Jeshohaiah (jĕsh'ō-hā'yä). [Heb. *Yeshôchayah*.] A Simeonite prince (1 Chr 4:36).

Jeshua (jĕsh'ū-ä), KJV once **Jeshuah** (jĕsh'ū-ä). [Heb. and Aramaic *Yeshûa'*, a late form of *Yehôshûa'*, "Yahweh is salvation." The name occurs also on ancient Hebrew seals, and in secular documents found among the Dead Sea scrolls.]
1. The successor of Moses, and leader of the Israelite tribes during the invasion of Canaan (Neh 8:17). See Joshua, 1.
2. Ancestral head of the 9th of the 24 courses into which David organized the priests (1 Chr 24:4-6, 11).
3. A man in Hezekiah's reign who helped to distribute the offerings in the cities of the priests (2 Chr 31:14, 15).
4. The high priest who returned with Zerubbabel from Babylonia; the son of Jozadak (Ezr 2:2; 3:2; Neh 7:7). He officiated as high priest in Jerusalem for the first 20 years of the restoration period, and with Zerubbabel rebuilt the altar on the old Temple site and took the lead in the preparations for the rebuilding of the Temple (Ezr 3:2, 8, 9). When, after a period of inactivity, the rebuilding of the Temple was resumed in the 2d year of Darius I, Jeshua was still spiritual head of the community, and engaged actively in the work (ch 5:2). In Haggai and Zechariah he is called Joshua (Hag 1:1, 12, 14; 2:2, 4; Zec 3:1, 3, 6, 8, 9). In vision Zechariah saw him clothed in filthy rags, symbolic of sin. These garments were replaced by a clean garb representing spiritual cleansing (Zec 3:1-10).
5. A leading Jew of the family of Pahath-moab who returned from Babylonia under Zerubbabel (Ezr 2:2, 6; Neh 7:7, 11).
6. The head of a family of Levites, sons

of Hodaviah, who returned with Zerubbabel from Babylonia (Ezr 2:40; Neh 7:43; 12:8). He aided Jeshua, the high priest, in rebuilding the Temple (Ezr 3:9). Jeshua, 8, may have belonged to this family.

7. A man whose son Ezer assisted Nehemiah in the building of the wall of Jerusalem (Neh 3:19).

8. A Levite whose father was Azaniah (Neh 10:9). He assisted Ezra in reading and expounding the Law to the people (ch 8:7), and helped to lead the people in worship on a fast day (ch 9:4, 5). He also set his seal to Nehemiah's covenant (ch 10:9). He is probably the chief of the Levites mentioned in ch 12:24. In that text the Hebrew word *ben* following his name, rendered "the son of," should probably be read *Bani* as in ch 9:4, 5; hence, instead of reading "Jeshua the son of Kadmiel," it would read "Jeshua, Bani, Kadmiel." This Jeshua may have belonged to the family of Jeshua, 6.

9. A postexilic town in the south of Judah (Neh 11:26), which is probably the present *Tell es-Sa'wi*, 8½ mi. east-northeast of Beer-sheba. This Jeshua is identified by some with the town of Shema mentioned in Jos 15:26.

Jeshuah. *See* Jeshua, 2.

Jeshurun (jĕsh'ŭ-rŭn), KJV once **Jesurun** (jĕs'ŭ-rŭn). [Heb. *Yeshurûn,* "the upright one."] A poetical name designating the ideal character of Israel (Deut 32:15; 33:5, 26; Is 44:2).

Jesiah. *See* Isshiah, 2, 4.

Jesimiel (jĕ-sĭm'ĭ-ĕl). [Heb. *Yeśîmi'el,* "God places."] A prince of Simeon (1 Chr 4:36).

Jesse (jĕs'ĕ). [Heb. *Yishay,* meaning uncertain. The name occurs in an Aramaic document from Egypt, and in a cuneiform text, written *Ishya,* as the name of a Babylonian Jew in the 5th cent. B.C. Gr. *Iessai.*] A descendant of Judah, and grandson of Boaz and Ruth (Ruth 4:18-22; Mt 1:2-5; Lk 3:32). Jesse had 8 sons, of whom David was the youngest (1 Sa 17:12-14). The list in 1 Chr 2:13-15 names only 7, but the 8th seems to have been Elihu, who may have died without leaving any progeny (ch 27:18). Jesse also had 2 daughters, or possibly stepdaughters (1 Chr 2:16; cf. 2 Sa 17:25). Jesse and his family lived at Bethlehem when Samuel, by divine command, came to anoint David as future king of Israel (1 Sa 16:1-13). Later, when fleeing from Saul, David, fearing for the safety of his relatives, took his parents to Moab and

placed them under the protection of the king of that country (1 Sa 22:3, 4). The Scriptures do not mention Jesse's death.

Jesui. *See* Ishvi, 1.

Jesuites. *See* Ishvi, 1.

Jesurun. *See* Jeshurun.

Jesus (jē'zŭs). [Gr. *Iēsous,* from the Heb. *Yeshûa',* the late form of *Yehôshua',* "Joshua," meaning "Yahweh is salvation." The English form "Jesus" comes from the Latin. The name occurs on ossuaries (bone receptacles) discovered in Palestine, dating from, or soon after, the time of Christ (see fig. 264).]

264. Greek inscription on a Jewish ossuary (bone receptacle) reading *"Iēsous Alōth"*

1. According to the KJV NT the name of Joshua, the successor of Moses, and leader of the Israelite tribes during the invasion of Canaan (Acts 7:45; Heb 4:8). The RSV renders the name in both passages by the OT form, "Joshua."

2. According to the RSV, a Judahite whose name appears in Luke's genealogy of Jesus Christ (Lk 3:29, RSV). The KJV, following a different Greek text, reads "Jose" (jō'sĕ).

3. A Jewish Christian, also called Justus, who was an associate of Paul during his 1st imprisonment in Rome, and who sent greetings to the church at Colossae (Col 4:11).

4. The Saviour, *Jesus Christ, born of the virgin Mary.

Jesus Christ (jē'zŭs krīst). [Gr. *Iēsous* (a transliteration of the Aramaic *Yeshûa'* from the Heb. *Yehôshûa',* "Joshua," meaning "Yahweh is salvation"), *Christos* (a translation of the Heb. *Mashiach,* "Messiah," meaning "anointed," or "anointed one").] The Saviour of the world, the Messiah. In NT times *Yeshûa',* "Jesus," was a common given name for Jewish boys. It expressed the parents' faith in God and in His promise of One who would bring salvation to Israel. The angel Gabriel instructed Joseph to call Mary's first-born by this name, the reason given being, "He shall save his people from their sins" (Mt 1:21). "Christ" was not a personal name by which people knew Him while on earth, but a title used to identify Him as the One in whom the Messianic promises and prophecies of the OT met their fulfillment. To those who believed in Him as sent of God He was *the* Christ, that is, the Messiah, the One "anointed" by God to be the Saviour of the world. When used together, as in Mt 1:18; 16:20; Mk 1:1, the 2 names Jesus and Christ constitute a confession of faith that Jesus of Nazareth, the Son of Mary, is indeed the Christ, the Messiah (Mt 1:1; Acts 2:38). He was also to be known by the title Emmanuel, "God with us," in recognition of His deity and virgin birth (Mt 1:23; cf. Is 7:14; 9:6, 7). Christ's usual designation for Himself was "the Son of man" (Mk 2:10; etc.), an expression never used by others when speaking of or to Him. By this title, which seems to have Messianic implications, Jesus emphasized His humanity, doubtless thinking of Himself as the promised Seed of Gen 3:15; 22:18; cf. Gal 3:16. Jesus seldom used the title "Son of God," which stresses deity, of Himself (Jn 9:35-37, KJV; 10:36), though He often referred to God as His Father (Mt 16:17; etc.). However, the Father called Him His son (Lk 3:22; 9:35), and John the Baptist (Jn 1:34) and the Twelve (Mt 14:33; 16:16), "Son of God." It was Jesus' claim that God was His Father in a special sense, and later His admission that He was the Son of God, that the Jews seized upon as warranting His condemnation and death (Lk 22:70, 71). Gabriel explained that Jesus was to be called the Son of God by virtue of His birth to Mary by the power of the Holy Ghost (Lk 1:35; cf. Heb 1:5), and Paul declared that Jesus' resurrection from the dead designated Him "Son of God" in power (Rom 1:4, RSV). His disciples frequently addressed Him as "Master" (Mk 4:38; 9:38; etc.), and eventually, in recognition of His deity, as "Lord" (Jn 14:5, 8; 20:28). The term "son of David" was a popular Messianic designation used by rulers and people alike (Mt 12:23; 22:42; Mk 12:35; etc.) as an expression of hope for deliverance from political oppression.

I. Historical Background. More than anything else it was faith in the promised Messiah that bound the Jews as a race together down through the centuries and gave point to their existence as a nation. The Messianic hope is the central theme of the OT, from the announcement of a Redeemer in Gen 3:15 to the promise of one who would come before Him to prepare His way in Is 40:3-5; Mal 4:5. Correctly understood, the OT Scriptures all anticipate His coming and bear witness to Him (Lk 24:25-27; Jn 5:39, 47). The Gospel writers frequently refer to OT prophecies as meeting their fulfillment in Jesus of Nazareth (Mt 1:23; 2:6, 15, 18; 3:3; etc.), and Christ Himself repeatedly cited the OT Scriptures as evidence that He was the Messiah (Lk 4:18-21; 24:25-27; Jn 5:39, 47; etc.).

For some 375 years after the restoration from Babylonian captivity in 536 B.C., Judea was, successively, tributary to the Persians, to Alexander the Great, and to his successors, the Ptolemies of Egypt and Seleucids of Syria. Then for approximately a century the Jews enjoyed a measure of independence from foreign rule, under a series of rulers known as the Maccabees, or Hasmonaeans. From 63 B.C. onward Palestine was tributary to the Romans—though largely autonomous in the administration of its internal civil and religious life—until A.D. 70, when the nation became extinct. About 15 years after Pompey's subjugation of Palestine, Herod, later known as "the Great," was appointed chief magistrate of Galilee. At the time of the Parthian invasion, when 2 Hasmonaean rulers fought for the throne, Herod was appointed king of Judea by the Romans (40 B.C.), and with the aid of the Romans, took Jerusalem in 37 B.C. This terminated the long series of sanguinary wars that had marked the years 63-37 B.C., during which, it is said, more than 100,000 Jews were slain. Over the next 70 years, to A.D. 34, another 100,000 Jews are said to have lost their lives in abortive attempts to cast off the Roman-Herodian yoke. Herod murdered various members of the Hasmonaean family, to which members one after another the Jews had rallied in a futile attempt to regain their freedom. He also murdered scores of the Jewish nobles on various occasions, either out of dislike or fear or in order to confiscate their property. He further incurred the hatred of his subjects by oppressive taxes, one of the means by which he raised the necessary funds for his grandiose building projects. It is said that whereas he found the nation reasonably prosperous, he left it at his death in abject poverty. The Jews also hated Herod for his paganizing activities and his untrammeled, unbounded cruelties. They called him "that Edomite slave" and looked upon him as Satan incarnate. Despicable though he was, he had an insatiable desire to be liked and honored, but realizing that the Jews would never accord him either, he bestowed rich favors and grand buildings upon the inhabitants of Gentile cities, near and far. A disastrous earthquake in 31 B.C. and a severe famine 6 years later added to the suffering of the Jewish people during his reign of about 33 years. One of his last acts prior to his death, probably in 4 B.C., was the slaughter of the infants of Bethlehem (Mt 2). As his successors he appointed his son Archelaus over Judea and Samaria, another son, Herod Antipas, over Galilee and Perea, and a 3d son, Philip, over the region to the north and east of the Sea of Galilee. Philip, whose subjects were mostly Gentiles, is said to have made his leadership a blessing. Upon occasion Jesus retired briefly to areas under Philip's jurisdiction, where He enjoyed momentary freedom from the harassment of the scribes and Pharisees. Much of Jesus' ministry was devoted to Galilee and Perea, which were under the jurisdiction of Herod Antipas.

Archelaus inherited his father's fiendish character, but lacked his father's capabilities. He was barbaric and tyrannical in the worst sense of the words. He inaugurated his reign over Judea by the senseless slaughter of 3,000 persons in the Temple courts. This massacre aroused public sentiment and provoked a series of unprecedented riots. Hatred for Herodian-Roman rule reached such a pitch that complete anarchy prevailed for a time. Finally, in A.D. 6, Augustus banished Archelaus to Gaul and annexed Judea and Samaria to the Roman province of Syria, thus placing the Jews directly under Roman rule for the first time. As could be expected, the Jews bitterly resented the presence of Roman administrators and soldiers, but with occasional exceptions the affairs of Palestine were relatively quiet for many years. When Coponius, first of the procurators, attempted to levy a direct Roman tax, many Galilean Jews rose in revolt under Judas (Acts 5:37). Abandoning the attempt, the Romans farmed out the collection of taxes to Jews, who are known in the NT as "publicans." These were hated both because they were representatives of a detested foreign government and because they systematically fleeced their own countrymen. The emperor Tiberius himself, according to Josephus (*Ant.* xviii. 6. 5), observed that the Roman procurators, financial officials (*see* Governor, *c*), were like flies on a wound, since those al-

ready sated with blood did not suck as hard as the newcomers. Most of the procurators proved to be unscrupulous, incompetent men who provoked the Jews to ever greater hatred of Rome. They sat, so to speak, on a volcano, which eventually erupted in the great revolt of A.D. 66-73. Under the procurators the Jews still enjoyed a large measure of local autonomy in the administration of their local civil and religious affairs. The great Sanhedrin at Jerusalem (*see* Council) had a measure of civil, as well as religious, jurisdiction. The high priest was its presiding officer, and it had a police force to enforce its authority. In addition, there were 11 regional Sanhedrins in Judea. As the heartland of Judaism the Judea of Jesus' day was ultraconservative. Galilee, on the other hand—called "Galilee of the Gentiles"—was more cosmopolitan, with a larger admixture of non-Jews in its population. Greek influence prevailed there to a much greater extent than in Judea. There were few large cities, and the region was almost wholly under cultivation.

II. Jewish Religious Life. Jewish religious life revolved, to a great degree, around the local *synagogues. However, at the great annual feasts—Passover or Unleavened Bread, Pentecost, and Tabernacles—Jewish pilgrims and Gentile proselytes from all parts of the civilized world flocked by the thousands to the Temple in Jerusalem. Upon these occasions the sacred vestments of the high priest, which the Romans ordinarily kept in the Tower of Antonia adjoining the Temple, were released for use.

The two major religious parties were the *Pharisees and the *Sadducees. The Pharisees, who originated as a political sect in the 2d cent. B.C., represented the popular, orthodox middle class of the towns and villages. They believed that personal salvation and the welfare of the Jewish nation depended upon strict adherence to the laws of Moses. They were the party of the scribes and theologians, and were usually the ones who challenged Christ in argument. Seeking to keep religion separate from the state, they avoided civic duties themselves and promoted a passive resistance to the Herodian-Roman government. On the other hand, the Sadducees, the practical political party of the day, were made up for the most part of the wealthy, cultured, liberal, progressive, Hellenizing segment of the Jewish nation. They were not antireligious, but saw no point in letting religion dominate other aspects of life. Whereas the Pharisees stressed dependence upon God, the Sadducees depended upon themselves, believing each man to be the arbiter of his own destiny. They took a strong interest in the secular concerns of the nation and cooperated—actively but reluctantly—with the Roman authorities. By mutual consent with the Pharisees, the high priest, who was a political appointee in NT times, was always a Sadducee, but on condition that he conduct the duties of his office in harmony with Pharisee tradition.

A 3d religious group, the Essenes, extreme conservatives, possibly numbered no more than 3,000. Their beliefs were similar to those of the Pharisees, but unlike the Pharisees they lived apart from society in monastic communities and shunned the Temple and its sacrifices. They advocated purity of life, the strict observance of the Torah, and high ethical standards. The community at *Khirbet Qumrân* on the shores of the Dead Sea is thought to have been an Essene community. The now famous Dead Sea scrolls were once a part of the *Khirbet Qumrân* library. At several points the beliefs and teachings of the Qumran community closely resemble those of John the Baptist and Christ. They claimed to be the "voice . . . in the wilderness" of Is 40:3-5, and stressed the coming of the Messiah. Their founder was a "teacher of righteousness" who organized his followers under a "new covenant" or "new testament," in anticipation of the Messianic kingdom they believed would soon be established. They practiced ceremonial washings, but taught that these rites were without value unless accompanied by the spiritual cleansing of a holy spirit.

The Zealots, constituting a 4th Jewish party, agreed mainly with the Pharisees, though politics was their chief concern. Josephus (*Ant.* xviii. 1. 1, 6; *War* ii. 8. 1) attributes their origin to Judas of Galilee, who led the revolt against direct Roman taxation in A.D. 6 or 7 (Acts 5:37). They seem to be identified with the Sicarii, or "daggermen," of the first Jewish revolt, A.D. 66-70. They were hotheaded enthusiasts, the fanatical extremists of Judaism. One of Christ's disciples, Simon the Zealot, is thought to have been a member.

The Herodians, or "partisans of Herod" (Jos. *Ant.* xiv. 15. 10), made up a 5th group, with interests solely political.

The scribes, or "lawyers" (Mt 7:29;

Lk 7:30), did not constitute a separate group, though most of them were Pharisees. They were the professional interpreters of the civil and religious laws of Moses and made it their business to apply these laws to the affairs of daily life. Their collective interpretation of the Mosaic law, later codified in the Mishnah and the Talmud, constituted the "tradition" against which Christ spoke so positively. It should be remembered, however, that only a small fraction of the population of Palestine belonged to these religious and political sects and that the great masses of the people were uneducated and despised by the leaders on account of their ignorance and lax observance of ritual. It was among these simple folk that Jesus did most of His work and with whom He was classed by the so-called elite of His time. It was the common people, many of whom were God-fearing and took religion seriously, who heard Him gladly (Mk 12:37).

In the days of Christ there were many who earnestly looked for the Messiah (see Mk 15:43; Lk 2:25, 38). Non-Biblical Jewish literature both before and after Christ reflects a great interest in the coming of Messiah and the establishment of His kingdom. The interminable and bloody wars of the Roman-Herodian period, the great earthquake of 31 B.C., in which many thousands were killed, and the disastrous famine of 25-24 B.C. were looked upon by many as signs of the nearness of Messiah's coming. There was also throughout the Gentile world a great expectation of a savior. When Augustus became emperor in 27 B.C. and centuries of strife gave way to almost universal peace, popular sentiment applied messianic legends and prophecies to him.

In the minds of many his long and tranquil reign seemed to justify this opinion. Of general messianic expectation the Roman historian Seutonius wrote: "There had spread over all the Orient an old and established belief, that it was fated at that time for men coming from Judaea to rule the world. This prediction, referring to the emperor of Rome, as afterward appeared from the event, the people of Judaea took to themselves" (*The Lives of the Caesars* viii. 4; Loeb ed., vol. 2, p. 289). Another Roman historian, Tacitus, attributed the Jewish revolt that ended in the destruction of Jerusalem in A.D. 70 to this Messianic hope of the Jews, the belief that one of their race was destined to rule the world.

III. Chronology of the Life of Christ.

The exact dates of Christ's birth, ministry, and death are not precisely known but can be determined with reasonable accuracy. *See* Chronology, VIII. By an error of 4 or 5 years in determining the year of Christ's birth, Dionysius Exiguus, a 6th-cent. Roman abbot, misnumbered the years of his new Christian Era. He placed the birth of Christ at least 4 or 5 years too late. That is why the birth date can be 4 or 5 B.C. With reasonable certainty Herod's death can be assigned to the early spring of 4 B.C., and by that time Christ must already have been several weeks or months old (see Mt 2). Accordingly, His birth may doubtless be assigned to the late fall of 5 B.C. or winter of 5/4 B.C. John the Baptist began to preach in "the fifteenth year of the reign of Tiberius" (Lk 3:1), a short time—perhaps about 6 months (cf. ch 1:24, 26-31)—before Jesus' baptism, from which time Jesus' public ministry is reckoned. Jesus was then approximately "thirty years of age" (ch 3:23) and soon thereafter it was said that the Temple had been "forty and six years . . . in building" (Jn 2:20). Since gaps in our present knowledge make the precise coordination of these chronological data with one another and the Christian Era difficult if not impossible, only an approximate date can be suggested for the opening of Christ's public ministry. All things considered, the autumn of A.D. 27 seems to harmonize most closely with the known data.

On the basis of the record of the Synoptic Gospels alone (Mt, Mk, and Lk) it might be concluded that Jesus' ministry continued for only a little more than one year, since events at only 2 Passovers are reported. John, however, mentions 3 Passovers (Jn 2:13, 23; 6:4; 13:1) and an unspecified "feast of the Jews" (ch 5:1). The imprisonment and death of John the Baptist, taken in connection with related events in Christ's ministry, help to determine that this unnamed feast was most likely a Passover also. Four Passovers would make the duration of Christ's ministry about 3½ years.

The data for these events (*see* Gospels, Harmony of) can be interpreted thus: According to Mt 4:12 and Mk 1:14, it was the imprisonment of John that led Jesus to transfer His labors from Judea to Galilee, and according to Mt 14:10-21 (cf. Jn 6:4-15), John was beheaded at Passover time one year prior to Jesus' death on the cross (cf. Jn 11:55). Furthermore, the public Galilean ministry closed at Passover time one year before the crucifixion (cf. Jn 5:1; 6:66). The Galilean ministry thus coincides with the period of John's imprisonment. Now, Jesus' Judean ministry began immediately after the Passover in the spring following His baptism, that is, the spring of A.D. 28, and continued for an unspecified but somewhat extended period of time (chs 2:13, 23; 3:22, 26, 30; 4:1). But "John was not yet cast into prison" during the course of Jesus' Judean ministry (ch 3:22, 24). To avoid controversy between His disciples and those of John (see chs 3:25 to 4:3), Jesus temporarily interrupted His ministry in Judea and went to Galilee, going through Samaria on the way (ch 4:3, 4). Therefore the incidents of John 4, in Samaria and Cana of Galilee, took place while John was still at liberty and thus before the formal opening of Jesus' Galilean ministry. Inasmuch as there was probably not sufficient time between the Passover of ch 2:13, 23 and the Feast of Pentecost, 7 weeks later, for the events of chs 3 and 4, the "feast" of ch 5:1 could not be earlier than the Feast of Tabernacles, 6 months after that Passover. But if the feast of ch 5:1 is to be considered the Feast of Tabernacles that year, it is necessary to conclude, on the basis of facts already noted, that all the events and developments recorded in connection with Jesus' Galilean ministry took place within a period of less than 6 months, from this "feast" to the Passover of ch 6:4. But a careful study of all that is told of the Galilean ministry leads to the conclusion that it would be impossible to compress the Galilean ministry into a period of 6 months. It is, therefore, reasonable to conclude that the "feast" of Jn 5 was the 2d Passover of Jesus' ministry (cf. ch 2:13-15), one year after the Passover of ch 2:13, 23, and a year before the Passover of ch 6:4, and that Jesus' ministry extended over a period of 3½ years. With the autumn of A.D. 27 as the time of Jesus' baptism, His ministry would extend to the spring of A.D. 31. On the basis of this chronological pattern about 6 months elapsed between His baptism in the autumn of A.D. 27 and the 1st Passover in the spring of A.D. 28. During this time Jesus labored quietly in Judea and Galilee without attracting public attention. Between the 1st and 2d Passovers, of A.D. 28 and A.D. 29, His efforts were devoted chiefly to Judea. The Galilean ministry occupied the next year, to Passover time in A.D. 30. From the Passover of A.D. 30, His 3d, to the Feast of Tabernacles the next autumn, Jesus discontinued His public ministry in Galilee and spent considerable time in the Gentile regions to the north and east, and in private conversations with His disciples. From the Feast of Tabernacles to the 4th Passover in the spring of A.D. 31 Jesus labored principally in Samaria and Perea. Only John (chs 2 to 5) reports the 1½ years of Jesus' ministry from the autumn of A.D. 27 to the Passover of A.D. 29. The Synoptic writers cover the year of Galilean ministry and 6 months in retirement (Passover A.D. 29 to Feast of Tabernacles, A.D. 30), in detail. John relates only 2 or 3 events of this period (ch 6). Luke (chs 9 to 19) is our primary source for what Jesus did during the final 6 months in Samaria and Perea, to Passover A.D. 31. The formal appointment of the Twelve as apostles did not take place till the summer of A.D. 29, about midway of the 3½ years of ministry. The last year of this ministry is clearly marked off by the Passovers mentioned in Jn 6:4 and 11:55, probably the Passovers of A.D. 30 and 31 respectively.

IV. Life and Public Ministry. The outline of events in this section follows the pattern adopted in the Harmony of the Gospels appearing in this dictionary (*see* Gospels, Harmony of). For a discussion of the reasons for the positions taken in this harmony, see *SDACom* on Scripture passages involved.

1. *Infancy to Manhood.*—Jesus was born in Bethlehem, David's city, in order that He might be identified the more readily as the Son of David, and thus the Messiah of OT prophecy (Lk 2:1-7; cf. Mic 5:2). On the 8th day He was circumcised (Lk 2:21), circumcision being the sign of the covenant and a pledge of obedience to its requirements. Jesus was born "under the law" of Moses and submitted to its jurisdiction (Gal 4:4). Later Joseph and Mary took Him to the Temple for the ceremony of the dedication of the first-born (Lk 2:22-38, 39; cf. Lev 12:1-4). From early times this rite had been followed by the Hebrews in acknowledgment of God's promise to give His first-born to save the lost. In the case of Jesus it was an acknowledgment of God's act in giving His Son to the world, and of the Son's dedication to the work He had come to do. After the visit of the Magi (Mt 2:1-12), by means of which God called the attention of the leaders of the Jewish nation to the birth of His Son, Joseph and Mary briefly took refuge in Egypt from Herod's fury (Mt 2:13-18). Returning to Palestine, they were divinely instructed to settle in Galilee rather than in Judea, doubtless in order to avoid the state of anarchy that prevailed in Judea during the turbulent reign of Archelaus (Mt 2:19-23; Lk 2:39, 40). At the age of 12 a Jewish boy was considered as crossing the threshold from childhood to youth. As a "son of the law" he became personally responsible for fulfilling the requirements of the Jewish religion, and was expected to participate in its sacred services and festivals. Accordingly, at the age of 12 Jesus attended His first Passover, where for the first time He gave evidence of an understanding of His own special relation to the Father and His life mission (Lk 2:41-50).

2. *Early Public Ministry.*—Jesus' baptism and anointing by the Holy Spirit, possibly about the time of the Feast of Tabernacles in the autumn of A.D. 27, was for Him an act of consecration to His lifework that set Him apart for His ministry (Mt 3:13-17; cf. Acts 10:38). The Father publicly declared Jesus to be His own Son (Mt 3:17), and John the Baptist recognized the sign given him by which to identify the Lamb of God (Jn 1:31-34). After His baptism Jesus retired into the wilderness that He might contemplate His mission. There the tempter pressed upon Him temptations designed to appeal to the senses, to pride, and to His own sense of mission. Before He could go forth to men He Himself must gain victory over the tempter (Mt 4:1-11; cf. Heb 2:18). Later Jesus returned to the Jordan where John was preaching (Jn 1:28-34), and shortly afterward gathered about Him a small group of followers —John, Andrew, Simon, Philip, and Nathanael (vs 35-51). His first miracle, at Cana of Galilee (ch 2:1-11), strengthened their faith in Him as the Messiah and gave them an opportunity to testify of their new-found faith to others.

3. *Judean Ministry.*—By the cleansing of the Temple at Passover time the following spring, some 6 months after His baptism, Jesus publicly announced His mission to cleanse men's hearts from the defilement of sin (Jn 2:13-17). Challenged by the Temple authorities for this act, He pointed forward cryptically to His death on the cross as the means by which He proposed to cleanse the soul temple (vs 18-22). The nocturnal visit of Nicodemus, a chief counselor, gave Jesus an opportunity, at the very beginning of

His ministry, to explain the purpose of His mission to a member of the Sanhedrin (Jn 3:1-21) whose mind was receptive. Later Nicodemus temporarily thwarted the schemes of the priests to destroy Jesus (cf. ch 7:50-53). Leaving Jerusalem, Jesus ministered for a protracted period in Judea (ch 3:22). The people thronged to hear Him, and the tide of popularity gradually turned from John to Jesus (ch 4:1). When dissatisfaction arose among John's disciples because of this (ch 3:25-36), Jesus, wishing to avoid all occasion for misunderstanding and dissension, quietly ceased His labors and withdrew, for a time, to Galilee (ch 4:1-3). He took advantage of this interruption in His Judean ministry to prepare the way for His later successful ministry in Samaria and in Galilee. Returning to Jerusalem for the Passover of A.D. 29, Jesus healed a paralytic at the Pool of Bethesda on the Sabbath day, probably the worst, and best-known, case there (ch 5: 1-15). The Jewish leaders had had a full year to observe Jesus and to evaluate His message, and Jesus doubtlessly designed by this miracle to force them to an open decision. Accused by the Jews of Sabbath-breaking, Jesus defended Himself by stating: "My Father worketh hitherto, and I work" (vs 16-18). They had before them various evidences of His Messiahship: (1) They had heard, and professed to accept, the message of John the Baptist—and John had declared Jesus to be the Son of God (vs 32-35; cf. ch 1:31, 34). (2) The many miracles Jesus had performed during His Judean ministry (see ch 2:23), and particularly the healing of the paralyzed man that very Sabbath day, attested His claim (ch 5:36). The very fact that He was doing the works of His Father (v 36; cf. v 17) testified that He had come from the Father. (3) The Father Himself had declared Jesus to be His Son (vs 37, 38). (4) The supreme evidence of Jesus' Messiahship was to be found in the writings of Moses, whom they professed to accept and who would be their judge if they rejected Him (vs 39-47).

The priests and rulers would doubtless have slain Jesus on the spot had they dared to do so, but popular sentiment was too strong in His favor (cf. Lk 5:16, 18). They did, however, reject His claims and they determined to take His life at some future time (v 18). Henceforth the Gospel writers frequently mention spies sent to watch and report what Jesus said and did, showing that these priests and rulers

were attempting to build up a case against Him (cf. Lk 11:54; 20:20; etc.). Also, about this time, Herod Antipas imprisoned John the Baptist (Lk 3:19, 20). These 2 events—the rejection by the Sanhedrin and the imprisonment of John the Baptist—mark the close of Jesus' Judean ministry (Mt 4:12; cf. Jn 7:1). To avoid useless conflict with the teachers of Jerusalem, Jesus henceforth restricted His labors chiefly to Galilee and, in fact, did not revisit Jerusalem until the Feast of Tabernacles about a year and a half later.

4. *Galilean Ministry.*—The Galileans were less sophisticated and less dominated by their leaders than the Jews of Judea, and their minds were thus more open to receive truth. During the Galilean ministry enthusiasm ran so high that Jesus was, at times, obliged to hide Himself lest the Roman authorities be given occasion to fear insurrection. For a time it seemed that the Galileans would receive Jesus as the Messiah. Jesus opened His work in Galilee at Nazareth, whose people knew Him best and who should have been best prepared to welcome Him as the Messiah (Lk 4:16-30). In the synagogue on the Sabbath day Jesus explained to them the nature and purpose of His mission, but they refused to accept Him and set about to take His life.

Turning from Nazareth, Jesus made Capernaum the center of His Galilean labors (Mt 4:13-17). By the sea one morning Jesus summoned Peter and Andrew, James and John, to unite themselves fully as colaborers with Him and to follow Him henceforth as full-time disciples (Lk 5:1-11; cf. Mt 4:18-22). Sentiment soon rose to such a pitch that Jesus felt compelled to leave Capernaum for a time and labor elsewhere (Mk 1:28, 33, 37, 38). Thus Jesus set out on His 1st journey through the towns and villages of Galilee, proclaiming "the kingdom of God" to be "at hand" (Mk 1:14, 15; Lk 4:31, 43). Returning to Capernaum, He healed the paralytic let down through the roof (Mk 2:1-12). Present to witness the miracle were a delegation of "Pharisees and doctors of the law" from all parts of Judea and Galilee and also representatives of the authorities at Jerusalem (Lk 5:17) who had doubtless come to investigate and interfere with His successful labors in Galilee. By forgiving and healing the paralytic Jesus gave them undeniable evidence that divine power was at work, and that His authority was divine (vs 18-24).

265. The "Garden Tomb" north of the Damascus Gate at Jerusalem, which some have identified with the tomb of Jesus Christ

The failure of attempts to discredit Jesus is evidenced by the increasing popularity that marked His work (cf. Mk 3:7, 8).

During the interval between the 1st and 2d Galilean tours, Jesus ordained 12 of His followers to be apostles (Mk 3:13-19). The same day (see Lk 6:13-20) He delivered the Sermon on the Mount, which was meant chiefly for His disciples, but given in the hearing of a great throng (Mt 5 to 7). In this sermon, which may be thought of as His inaugural address as King of the kingdom of divine grace and as the charter of His kingdom, Jesus set forth its fundamental principles. Soon thereafter He departed on His 2d Galilean tour (Lk 8:1-3), which is more fully reported than either of the others. During its course Jesus demonstrated the power of His kingdom and its value to men. It opened (ch 7:11-17) and closed (Mk 5:21-43) with demonstrations of power over death. Jesus also demonstrated His power over nature (Mt 8:23-27) and over demons (Mt 12:22-45; Mk 5:1-20). As King of the kingdom of divine grace, Jesus could set men free from the fear of death, the fear of the elements of nature, and the fear of demons—which well summarize the popular fears of that day.

During the course of this tour Jesus gave His sermon by the Sea (Mt 13:1-53), in a series of parables setting forth the same principles He had taught in a more formal way in the Sermon on the Mount. On the 3d Galilean tour Jesus sent out the Twelve, two by two, to gain experience in personal evangelism (chs 9:36 to 11:1). In their absence, in company with other disciples, He revisited Nazareth, where His townsmen rejected Him a second time (Mk 6:1-6). This tour ended about Passover time the spring of A.D. 30. The evidence of divine power in the miracle of the loaves and fishes (vs 30-44) was taken by the 5,000 men present as crowning evidence that the long-looked-for Deliverer was among them. Here was a man who could supply whole armies with food, who could heal wounded soldiers and raise the dead, and who could conquer the nations, restore the dominion to Israel, and turn Judea into the earthly Paradise foretold by the prophets of old. They endeavored to crown Him king, but Jesus refused (Jn 6:14, 15). This was the turning point in His ministry. After a stormy night on the sea (Mt 14:22-36) Jesus returned to Capernaum, where He gave the sermon on the Bread of Life (Jn 6:25 to 7:1). The people who had thought of Jesus as ruler of an earthly kingdom now realized that His was a spiritual kingdom, and most of them "went back and walked no more with him" (ch 6:66). The current of popular sentiment turned against Jesus in Galilee as it had in Judea the year before.

5. *In Retirement.*—Jesus now discontinued His public labors for the people of Galilee. Rejected by leaders and people alike, He realized that His work was rapidly drawing to a close. Before Him loomed in vivid outline the scenes of His suffering and death, but this even His disciples did not yet realize. Like the people generally, they still conceived of His kingdom as an earthly dominion. Upon repeated occasions Jesus now discussed His Messiahship and mission with them in an endeavor to prepare them for the great disappointment they were to experience. At Caesarea Philippi (Mt 16:13-28), on the mount of Transfiguration (ch 17:1-13), and as they journeyed by the way (vs 22, 23), He explained to them that as the Messiah He must suffer and die. Also, during this period, Jesus retired to the non-Jewish regions of Phoenicia (ch 15:21-28), Caesarea Philippi (ch 16:13-28), and Decapolis (Mk 7:31 to 8:10), purposing to awaken in His disciples a sense of responsibility for the heathen. The confession of faith at Caesarea Philippi (Mt 16:13-20) marked an important turning point in the relationship of the disciples to Jesus. Their understanding of His mission had been growing during the time of their association with Him. Now for the first time they gave evidence of a more mature understanding and appreciation of that mission.

6. *Samarian-Perean Ministry.*—In the autumn of the year Jesus, with His disciples, attended the Feast of Tabernacles (Jn 7:2-13). This was His 1st visit to Jerusalem since the healing of the paralytic at the Pool of Bethesda and His re-

jection by the Sanhedrin 18 months earlier. The issue of Christ's Messiahship was now uppermost in people's minds, and they knew also of the plot against His life (Jn 7:25-31). There was a sharp division of opinion as to whether Jesus should be accepted as the Messiah or put to death (vs 40-44). When an abortive attempt was made to arrest Jesus, Nicodemus silenced the plotters (vs 45-53). A further attempt was made to ensnare Him (ch 8:3-11). As Jesus was teaching in the Temple the Jewish authorities again challenged Him, and He in turn openly claimed God as His Father and declared Himself to be the Sent of God—with the result that they proceeded to stone Him on the spot (vs 12-59). However, He escaped (v 59) and apparently returned briefly to Galilee before departing thence on His last journey to Jerusalem (cf. Lk 9:51-56).

The next few months Jesus spent laboring in Samaria and Perea, and during this time sent the Seventy forth on their mission (Lk 10:1-24). Little is known of the exact route Jesus took, but Luke records at length the parables spoken and the experiences encountered during this period (chs 9:51 to 18:34). He now went about in the most public manner and sent messengers ahead to announce His coming (chs 9:52; 10:1). He was going forward to the scene of His great sacrifice, and the attention of the people must be directed toward Him. During His ministry in Perea the multitude again thronged His steps as during the early days of His ministry in Galilee (see ch 12:1). Some 3 months before the Passover He went up to Jerusalem to attend the Feast of Dedication (Jn 10:22). The authorities again accosted Him in the Temple, demanding, "If thou be the Christ, tell us plainly" (v 24). After a brief discussion the Jews again took up stones to stone Him for making Himself out to be God (vs 25-33). A little later they sought to arrest Him, but again He escaped out of their hands and returned to Perea (vs 39, 40). The death of Lazarus a few weeks before the crucifixion later brought Jesus back briefly to the immediate vicinity of Jerusalem for His supreme miracle, which was performed in the presence of a number of the Jewish leaders and which provided evidence the priests could not misinterpret or deny (see ch 11:1-44). This miracle affixed the seal of God to Jesus' work as the Messiah, but when it was reported to the leaders in Jerusalem (vs 45, 46), they determined to put Jesus

out of the way at the earliest possible opportunity (Jn 11:47-53). This evidence of power over death was the crowning evidence that in the person of Jesus God had, indeed, sent forth His Son into the world for the salvation of men from sin and its penalty, death. The Sadducees, who denied a life after death, were now undoubtedly thoroughly alarmed, and united with the Pharisees in a fixed determination to silence Jesus (cf. v 47). Not desiring to hasten the crisis before its appointed time, Jesus again retired from Jerusalem for a season (v 54).

7. *Closing Ministry at Jerusalem.*—A few weeks after the raising of Lazarus, Jesus once more turned His steps toward Jerusalem. Resting at Bethany over the Sabbath (see Jn 12:1), He was entertained in the home of Simon (Mt 26:6-13; cf. Lk 7:36-50). About that time Judas went to the palace of the high priest with an offer to betray Jesus into their hands (Mt 26:14, 15). On Sunday Jesus rode triumphantly into Jerusalem, publicly manifesting Himself to be Messiah-King (ch 21:1-11). The excitement of the people who had come to Jerusalem to attend the Passover was aroused to the highest pitch and they hailed Him as king. Jesus' disciples doubtless took His ac-

266. The Church of the Holy Sepulchre, covering the cave which since the 4th cent. has traditionally been identified with the tomb of Jesus Christ

ceptance of this homage as proof that their glad hopes were about to be fulfilled, and the multitude believed that the hour of their emancipation from the Romans was at hand. Jesus realized that this course of action would bring Him to the cross, but it was His purpose thus publicly to call the attention of all to the sacrifice He was about to make. On Monday He cleansed the Temple a 2d time (Mt 21:12-16), thus repeating at the close of His ministry the same act by which He had opened His work 3 years before. This was a direct challenge to the authority of the priests and rulers. When they contested His right to act as He did—"By what authority doest thou these things?" (v 23)—Jesus replied in such a way as to reveal their incompetence to weigh His credentials as Messiah (vs 24-27). By a series of parables (chs 21:28 to 22:14) He pictured the course that the Jewish leaders were then taking in rejecting Him as the Messiah, and in His answers to a series of questions put to Him (ch 22:15-46) confuted His critics to the extent that none of them dared to question Him further (v 46).

After publicly exposing the corrupt character of the scribes and Pharisees, Jesus departed from the Temple forever (Mt 23), declaring, "Behold, *your* house is left unto you desolate" (v 38), whereas only the day before He had referred to the Temple as "my house" (ch 21:13). By this declaration Jesus disinherited the Jewish nation from the covenant relationship. He took "the kingdom of God" away from the Jews in order that He might give it "to a nation bringing forth the fruits thereof" (v 43). That night Jesus retired with 4 of His disciples (Mk 13:3) to the Mount of Olives, where He outlined what must yet take place before the establishment of His visible kingdom upon earth (Mt 24; 25). Wednesday of Passion Week Jesus spent in retirement with His disciples. On Thursday night He celebrated the Passover with them, at the same time instituting the ordinance of the Lord's Supper (Lk 22:14-30; Mt 26:26-29; Jn 13:1-20). After the supper He counseled them at length concerning the future and His eventual return (Jn 14 to 16). As He entered the Garden of Gethsemane the weight of the sins of the world fell upon Him (Mt 26:37) and He seemed shut out from the light of His Father's presence, experiencing the sinner's fate of eternal separation from God. Tortured by the fear that He was to be shut out forever from the Father's love, that in His humanity He could not endure the suffering that lay ahead, and that He was to be rejected by the very ones He had come to save, He was tempted to turn from His mission and let the human race bear the consequences (cf. Mt 26:39, 42). But He drank the cup of suffering to the dregs. As He fell dying to the ground, having tasted the sufferings of death for every man, an angel from heaven strengthened Him to endure the hours of torture ahead (Mt 26:30-56; Lk 22:43).

That night Jesus was arrested, and the following morning He appeared 1st before the Jewish authorities (Jn 18:13-24; Mt 26:57-75; Lk 22:66-71), and later before Pilate (Jn 18:28 to 19:16) and before Herod (Lk 23:6-12). Jesus was condemned to death by the Jews, and the sentence received the reluctant ratification of the Roman procurator. That same day Jesus was led forth to be crucified (Jn 19:17-37). By His death on the cross Jesus paid the penalty for sin and vindicated the justice and mercy of God. At the foot of the cross the selfishness and hatred of a created being who aspired to be equal with God but cared so little about God that he was willing to slay God's Son, came face to face with the selfless love of the Creator, who cared so much for the beings He had created that He was willing to take the nature of a slave and to die the death of a criminal in order to save them from their own evil ways (see ch 3: 16). The cross demonstrated that God could be both merciful and just when He forgave men their sins (cf. Rom 3:21-26). Jesus died on the cross at about the time of the evening sacrifice on Friday afternoon, and rose from the dead the following Sunday morning (Mt 27:45-56; 28:1-15). After His resurrection Jesus tarried on earth for a season in order that His disciples might become familiar with Him as a risen, glorified Being, His repeated appearances (Lk 24:13-45; Jn 20: 19-21, 25; etc.) authenticating the resurrection. Forty days later He ascended to the Father, thus bringing His earthly ministry to a close (Lk 24:50-53). "I ascend unto my Father, and your Father," He said (Jn 20:17). His parting instruction to His followers was that they were to proclaim the good news of the gospel to all the world (Mt 28:19, 20). Confidence that Jesus had truly come forth from the tomb and had ascended to the Father (Lk 24:50-53) gave dynamic power to the gospel as the apostles went forth to proclaim it to all the known world in their generation (see Acts 4:10; 2 Pe 1:16-18; 1 Jn 1:1-3).

For the ministry of Christ in heaven as man's great high priest *see* Hebrews, Epistle to; Priest.

Jether (jē′thẽr). [Heb. *Yether*, "abundance."]

1. A descendant of Judah through Jerahmeel (1 Chr 2:32).

2. A descendant of Judah through Ezrah (1 Chr 4:17).

3. A descendant of Asher (1 Chr 7:38); probably the same as Ithran (Heb. *Yithran*) of v 37.

4. The eldest son of Gideon. His father commanded him to slay 2 captured Midianite kings, but because of his youth he declined. Probably fearing to be mutilated by the youth, the kings requested that Gideon slay them (Jgs 8:20, 21).

5. An Ishmaelite, whose son, Amasa, was Absalom's commander in chief (1 Ki 2:5, 32; 1 Chr 2:17). In 2 Sa 17:25, RSV, he is called Ithra (ĭth′rà) the Ishmaelite (Heb. *Yithra*'), and in the KJV, an Israelite. The RSV apparently assumes this to be a textual error for "Ishmaelite," as he is called in 1 Chr 2:17. It is possible, on the other hand, that Jether had become an Israelite, in which case both "Ishmaelite" and "Israelite" would be correct.

Jetheth (jē′thĕth). [Heb. *Yetheth*.] A chieftain of Edom (Gen 36:40; 1 Chr 1:51).

Jethlah. *See* Ithlah.

Jethro (jĕth′rō). [Heb. *Yithrô*, "excellence."] A priest in Midian and father-in-law of Moses (Ex 3:1), also called Reuel, "friend of God" (ch 2:18). On the basis of the meaning of the two names it has been thought that Reuel may have been his personal name received at birth, and Jethro an honorary title given to him as a tribal priest. He had 7 daughters, who tended his flocks. When Moses fled from Egypt and arrived in the area of Midian, where Jethro lived, he helped Jethro's daughters water the animals and was subsequently introduced to their father. Jethro later gave Moses one of the daughters, Zipporah, as his wife (vs 15-21). Moses worked for Jethro as his shepherd for about 40 years (Ex 3:1; Acts 7:30). After his divine call to return to Egypt to lead his people out, Moses began the journey with his wife and their two sons (Ex 4:20), but doubtless later sent them back to her father. After the Exodus, Jethro brought Zipporah and her sons to Moses in the wilderness. Jethro observed that Moses was constantly engaged in straightening out trivial matters and that for this he had no administrative or judicial help, so he advised him to choose helpers (Ex 18:1-27).

In Jgs 4:11 Hobab is called Moses' "father in law." However, this should rather read "brother-in-law" in harmony with other texts. *See* Hobab.

Jetur (jē′tẽr). [Heb. *Yeṭûr*.] A son of Ishmael (Gen 25:15; 1 Chr 1:31), and ancestor of an Ishmaelite tribe (1 Chr 5:19), later known as the Ituraeans. *See* Ituraea.

Jeuel (jē-ū′ĕl), KJV twice **Jeiel** (jē-ī′ĕl). [Heb. *Ye‘û'el* (Q *Ye‘î'el*), meaning uncertain.]

1. A Judahite who belonged to the family of Zerah. He lived in Jerusalem with 690 members of his family (1 Chr 9:6).

2. A Levite who assisted Hezekiah in religious reform (2 Chr 29:13).

3. A Jew who, with 62 males, returned with Ezra from Babylonia; a leader of the family of Adonikam (Ezr 8:13).

Jeush (jē′ŭsh), KJV once **Jehush** (jē′hŭsh). [Heb. *Ye‘ûsh*, "helper." The name occurs also on the Samaria ostraca.]

1. A son of Esau by his wife Oholibamah; he became a chieftain in Edom (Gen 36:5, 14, 18; 1 Chr 1:35).

2. A Benjamite (1 Chr 7:10).

3. A Gershonite Levite (1 Chr 23:10, 11).

4. A descendant of Saul through Jonathan (1 Chr 8:39).

5. A son of King Rehoboam of Judah (2 Chr 11:19).

Jeuz (jē′ŭz). [Heb. *Ye‘ûṣ*, "he counsels."] A Benjamite (1 Chr 8:10).

Jew (jōō). [Heb. *Yehûdi*; Aramaic *Yehûday*; Gr. *Ioudaios*; Akkadian *Yaûdai*.] A term occuring first in the time of Jeremiah designating a citizen or subject of the kingdom of Judah (2 Ki 25:25; Jer 32:12; 34:9; etc.). But the derived Hebrew term *Yehûdith* occurs much earlier, in the days of King Hezekiah, to designate the Hebrew language (2 Ki 18:26; Is 36:11). Most of the returning exiles belonged to the tribe of Judah, since this restored community was established by those who had been carried captive from the kingdom of Judah nearly 70 years before. However, Cyrus' decree was applicable to members of all the tribes, since it included all the worshipers of God, "who is there among you of all his people" (Ezr 1:3). Hence the term "Jew" came to be applied to all the returned exiles in general (Ezr 4:12, 23; Neh 1:2; etc.), and obviously includes others besides Judahites. It is clear also that Judah included inhabitants from other tribes (1 Chr 9:

3). Indeed, since the time of the division, many from the seceded northern kingdom had gone over to Judah in order to worship the true God (2 Chr 11:13-16; 15:9). Both "Judah" and "Israel" were included in postexilic Judah (Zec 8:3-5, 13), and the "Jews" who rebuilt the Temple probably included "all Israel," at least they sacrificed 12 goats for the twelve tribes (Ezr 6:14-17). Later, the term "Jew" came to include all persons of the Hebrew race in whatever country they lived (Acts 2:10; etc.). These were distinguished from Gentiles (Mk 7:3; Jn 2:6; etc.), and from Samaritans (Jn 4:9).

Jewels, Jewelry. In general the words thus translated in the OT do not refer primarily to precious stones as such, but simply to some type of personal adornment fashioned from a precious metal, such as gold or silver (Ex 3:22; 11:2; etc.). In the NT these terms occur only in the RSV and are the rendering generally of the Gr. *lithos timios*, literally, "precious stone" (Rev 17:4; 18:12, 16). The monuments depict numerous varieties of jewelry for personal adornment. In spite of the work of grave robbers through the centuries, archeological excavations have uncovered a wealth of jewelry, much of which exhibits a careful and intricate workmanship of the precious metals (see figs. 80, 102, 404). *See* names of individual jewels or pieces of jewelry; *see also* Precious Stones.

Jewess (jŏ̄o'ĕs). [Gr. *Ioudaia*.] A woman who is Hebrew by blood or religion (Acts 24:24). The term appears also in the KJV of

Acts 16:1, where, however, *Ioudaia* should be translated "Jewish."

Jewry (jŏ̄o'rĭ). [Gr. *Ioudaia*, "Judea."] A term appearing twice (Lk 23:5; Jn 7:1; KJV). The Greek term thus translated appears 44 times but in only these 2 instances is it translated "Jewry," elsewhere always "Judea." Properly, *Ioudaia* designates the southern part of Palestine in contrast to Samaria, Galilee, Perea, and Idumea; however, it is thought that at times *Ioudaia* is used in a wider sense for the region occupied by the Jewish nation. This latter could be its meaning in Lk 23: 5, but not in Jn 7:1.

Jezaniah. *See* Jaazaniah, 1.

Jezebel (jĕz'ē-bĕl). [Heb. *'Îzebel,* meaning uncertain. The name occurs in Phoenician with the name of Baal prefixed as *B'l'zbl.* Gr. *'Iezabel.*] The infamous wife of King Ahab of Israel and daughter of Ethbaal, who was king of Tyre and Sidon (1 Ki 16:31; Jos. *Ant.* viii. 13. 1) and the priest of Astarte (Jos. *Apion* i. 18). As a pagan of strong will she made a determined and successful attempt to introduce her religion into Israel. She killed worshipers of Yahweh, persecuted the prophets, and supported hundreds of prophets of Baal for whom Ahab built a temple in Samaria (1 Ki 16:32; 18:4, 13, 19). The prophet Elijah, who had incurred her wrath by his vocal and active opposition to Baal worship, by slaying all the prophets of Baal at Mount Carmel (ch 18:40) excited her wrath even more (ch 19:1-3). Jezebel was responsible for the murder of Naboth, the owner of a

Esdraelon, the Biblical Valley of Jezreel

vineyard that her husband Ahab desired to possess (1 Ki 21:1-16). Elijah predicted a speedy and gruesome punishment for this crime (vs 17-24), a prophecy that was fulfilled 11 years after Ahab's death, when Jehu usurped the throne. Arriving at Jezreel after slaying Joram, Jehu saw Jezebel looking out of the window of her palace. He challenged her eunuchs to throw her down, which they did, pushing her through the window. She fell in front of Jehu's chariot, and he drove over her body. A little later he gave orders to bury her, since she was of royal blood, but only her skull, feet, and hands were found; the rest of her body had already been eaten by dogs, the scavengers of the East (2 Ki 9:7, 30-37). Because of Jezebel's seduction of the Israelites to idolatry, her name is used in Rev 2:20 as a symbol of that form of seduction in later periods.

Jezer (jē′zēr). [Heb. *Yeṣer,* "form" or "purpose."] A son of Naphtali (Gen 46:24; 1 Chr 7:13), and head of the tribal family of Jezerites (jē′zēr-īts) [Heb. *Yiṣrî*] (Num 26:49).

Jezerites. See Jezer.

Jeziah. See Izziah.

Jeziel (jē′zǐ-ĕl). [Heb. *Yezî′el,* meaning uncertain.] A Benjamite warrior who joined David at Ziklag (1 Chr 12:1, 3).

Jezliah. See Izliah.

Jezoar. See Izhar, II.

Jezrahiah (jĕz′ra-hī′a). [Heb. *Yizrachyah,* "Yahweh will arise" or "Yahweh will shine."] A leader of the singers at the dedication of Nehemiah's wall (Neh 12:42).

Jezreel (jĕz′rĕ-ĕl). [Heb. *Yizre′e′l,* "God sows."]

1. A descendant of Judah (1 Chr 4:3).

2. The first-born son of the prophet Hosea. His name stood for a sign that God would avenge the blood spilled by King Jehu at Jezreel (Hos 1:4, 5).

3. A city in the territory of Issachar (Jos 19:17, 18). In a war with the Philistines the Israelites encamped at the fountain of Jezreel (1 Sa 29:1, 11). The city is specifically named as belonging to the realm of Ishbosheth, Saul's son (2 Sa 2:8, 9). Ahab chose the city as the place for a palace and for his residence. It was there that Naboth was murdered for refusing to sell his vineyard to the covetous king (1 Ki 21:1-6). Jezebel lost her life there, as did also 70 sons of Ahab, whose heads were afterward piled up in heaps at the gate of Jezreel by order of Jehu (2 Ki 9:30 to 10:11). Hosea prophesied that this blood guilt at Jezreel would be avenged on the house of Jehu (Hos 1:4).

The Hellenistic name of the city, and of the plain in which the city stood, was Esdraelon. The present name of the site is *Zer′in,* a place 8 mi. southeast of Megiddo (Map VI, C-3). Though lying in a plain *Zer′in* is prominently and strategically situated so that it commands a splendid view of the surrounding country, to the east as far as the Jordan.

4. The name of a valley. In OT times the name applied only to the eastern section of the great plain that lies north of the Carmel ridge and south of the Galilean mountains. This valley was the scene

of Gideon's attack on the encamped Midianites and Amalekites (Jgs 6:33). Later, however, the term Valley of Jezreel was extended to include the whole plain north of the Carmel ridge. In Hellenistic times this area was called the Plain of Esdraelon (a Greek modification of the name Jezreel). Map I, B-2.

5. A town in the hill country of Judah (Jos 15:56); not identified. David's wife Ahinoam came from there (1 Sa 25:43; 27:3).

Jezreelite (jĕz′rĕ-ĕl-īt), **Jezreelitess** (jĕz′rĕ-ĕl-ĭt′ĕs). [Heb. *Yizre'e'li* and *Yizre'e'lith*.] Inhabitants of *Jezreel (1 Ki 21:1; 1 Sa 27:3, KJV; etc.).

Jibsam. *See* Ibsam.

Jidlaph (jĭd′lăf). [Heb. *Yidlaph*, "he is sleepless."] A son of Abraham's brother Nahor by his wife Milcah (Gen 22:22).

Jimna. *See* Imnah, 1.

Jimnah. *See* Imnah, 1.

Jimnites. *See* Imnah, 1.

Jiphtah. *See* Iphtah.

Jiphthah-el. *See* Iphtahel.

Joab (jō′ăb). [Heb. *Yô'ab*, "Yahweh is father."]

1. A Judahite, head of a family of craftsmen (1 Chr 4:13, 14).

2. A son of David's sister Zeruiah, and commander in chief of David's armies (2 Sa 20:23; 1 Chr 2:16). He appears first in the battle between David's forces and those of Saul's son Ishbosheth, at Gibeon, in which he led David's army to victory. In the battle, Abner, Ishbosheth's commander in chief, killed Joab's younger brother Asahe (2 Sa 2:12-32). Later Abner, after quarreling with Ishbosheth and negotiating with David to turn the kingdom over to him, was assassinated by Joab and Joab's brother, Abishai (ch 3:12, 20-30). This was done ostensibly in revenge for the slaying of Asahel, but probably also because Joab feared that Abner might be given his place. David apparently did not feel strong enough to bring the two brothers to justice; however, he did not condone their crime (vs 31-39).

The capture of Jerusalem was due mainly to Joab's bravery. As a reward David made him chief of the army of the united kingdom (1 Chr 11:6). As such, Joab became an extremely powerful man in the realm, not only fighting David's wars but also performing peaceful works, such as repairing the city of Jerusalem (v 8). For 6 months he campaigned in Edom, slaughtering all males (1 Ki 11:

16). He also successfully operated against the Syrians and Ammonites (2 Sa 10:6-14; 1 Chr 19:6-15). A year later he besieged the Ammonite capital Rabbah (or Rabbath-ammon). In the final stages of the siege he sent for David so that the king might lead the army in the final assault on the citadel and so receive the honor of the victory (2 Sa 11:1; 12:26-29; 1 Chr 20:1-3). It was during the siege of Rabbah that Joab, at David's instructions, placed Uriah in an exposed position with the result that Uriah was killed, leaving David free to take Uriah's wife (2 Sa 11: 6-27). Joab sympathized with Absalom during the prince's banishment, and influenced the king to recall his son (ch 14: 1-24), but turned against Absalom when that young prince began an open rebellion against his father. He not only personally conducted the battle against Absalom's forces, but in defiance of David's expressed wishes killed Absalom, thus bringing the revolt to an end (ch 18:1, 2, 11-17). His rebuke of David's excessive sorrow for his fallen son was justified (ch 19:1-8). After the incident, David, impatient of Joab's independent and sometimes insubordinate actions, appointed Amasa as commander in chief over the army (v 13). Later, when the Benjamite Sheba revolted, Amasa was charged with subduing the revolt (ch 20: 1-4). Joab, however, driven by jealousy, assassinated Amasa, took matters in his own hand and, with his brother Abishai, crushed the revolt (vs 5-22). Apparently he was later reinstated as chief general of David's army (v 23).

When commissioned by David to take a census of the kingdom, Joab opposed the action, and carried it out only halfheartedly and incompletely (2 Sa 24:1-9; 1 Chr 21:1-6). He also opposed David's desire to set Solomon on the throne. Joab favored Adonijah, and even took part in the abortive preparations to make him the new king (1 Ki 1:7, 18, 19). However, when Solomon was proclaimed king, Joab forsook Adonijah's cause (v 49). On his deathbed, David, who had never felt strong enough to handle Joab himself, asked Solomon to bring the general to justice for his past crimes (ch 2:5, 6). This Solomon did, ordering Benaiah, the commander of the royal bodyguard, to execute Joab, who had fled to the tabernacle for refuge (vs 28-34). Joab was buried in his own house in the wilderness, and Benaiah was appointed to his office (vs 34, 35).

3. A leading Jew of the family of

Pahath-moab, from which family 2,812 or 2,818 male members returned from Babylonia in the time of Zerubbabel (Ezr 2:6; Neh 7:11). Some of his descendants remained behind at that time, for 218 more males of his family returned with Ezra some 80 years later (Ezr 8:9).

4. Part of a place name (1 Chr 2:54). *See* Ataroth, 4; Atroth-beth-joab.

Joah (jō′ā). [Heb. *Yô'ach,* "Yahweh is a brother."]

1. A gatekeeper, son of Obed-edom (1 Chr 26:4).

2. A Gershonite Levite (1 Chr 6:21).

3. One of the Levites who assisted King Hezekiah in his religious reformation (2 Chr 29:12).

4. A recording officer under King Hezekiah (2 Ki 18:18, 26; Is 36:3, 11, 22).

5. A recording officer under King Josiah (2 Chr 34:8).

Joahaz (jō′ā-hăz). [Heb. *Yô'achaz,* "Yahweh strengthens."] A man whose son Joah was a recording officer under King Josiah (2 Chr 34:8).

Joanan (jō-ā′năn), KJV **Joanna** (jō-ăn′ā). [Gr. *Iōanan* from the Heb. *Yôchanan,* "Yahweh has been gracious." The KJV spelling is based on the Textus Receptus, which reads *Iōannas.*] A Judahite appearing in Luke's genealogy of Christ (Lk 3:27).

Joanna, I (jō-ăn′ā). [Gr. *Iōanna,* from the Heb. *Yôchanan,* "Yahweh has been gracious."] The wife of a steward of Herod Antipas, tetrarch of Galilee and Perea. She was a faithful disciple of Jesus and helped to support Him financially (Lk 8:3). She was with the group of women who went to the tomb with the purpose of embalming the body of Jesus, only to learn that He had risen (Lk 23:55 to 24:10).

Joanna, II. *See* Joanan.

Joash, I (jō′ăsh). [Heb. *Yô'ash,* probably "Yahweh has given."]

1. A Judahite of the family of Shelah (1 Chr 4:22).

2. The father of Gideon (Jgs 6:11). Although his name implies Yahweh worship, he was the owner of a Baal altar and of an Asherah cult object, indicating that he was a worshiper of these deities (ch 6:25). When his son Gideon destroyed the pagan shrine the local idolaters threatened to take Gideon's life, but Joash defended his son, telling them that their god Baal should plead for himself (vs 27-32).

3. A Benjamite of Gibeah, who joined David at Ziklag (1 Chr 12:3).

4. A son of King Ahab of Israel (1 Ki 22:26; 2 Chr 18:25).

5. A king of Judah. *See* Jehoash, 1.

6. A king of Israel. *See* Jehoash, 2.

Joash, II (jō′ăsh). [Heb. *Yô'ash,* probably "Yahweh has helped." The name occurs also on the Samaria ostraca.]

1. A Benjamite of the family of Becher (1 Chr 7:8).

2. A keeper of David's oil stores (1 Chr 27:28).

Joatham. *See* Jotham, 3.

Job (jōb). [Heb. *'Iyyôb,* "where is (my) father?" The name occurs in the *Amarna Letters as *Ayyâb,* and in the Mari texts as *'Ayyâbum.* Gr. *Iōb.*]

1. A pious believer in the true God who lived in the land of Uz; principal character in the book of Job (Job 1:9). Ezekiel (Eze 14:14, 16, 20) and James (Jas 5:11) refer to him as an ideal example of patience and righteousness. Job doubtless lived in patriarchal times, as the social, historical, and cultural setting of the book suggests. The land of Uz has not been identified with any particular locality, but references in the book of Job and data provided by Josephus (*Ant.* i. 6. 4) and Ptolemy locate Uz east of Palestine proper on the borders of the Arabian Desert, certainly south of Damascus and probably in the vicinity of Edom (see Lam 4:21). The land of Uz may have taken its name from a son of Shem (1 Chr 1:17) who settled there in early times. A son of Nahor, the brother of Abraham, bore the same name (Gen 22:21, RSV); the Hebrew word translated "Huz" is identical with that translated "Uz." The Chaldeans (Job 1:17) are known to have crossed the Arabian Desert and raided the region of Edom. The Sabeans were the people of Sheba (ch 1:15), far to the south of Edom (cf. Is 45:14). Teman (Job 2:11) was in the land of Edom. The land of Shuah (ch 2:11) was probably to the north of Edom and southwest of the Euphrates. Job was apparently a wealthy herdsman (see chs 1:3, 4; 42:12), a leader honored and respected by his fellow townsmen for his wisdom and good counsel and who took a practical interest in the welfare of all who needed his help (ch 29:7-17). He lived in a "city" and was apparently one of its elders (v 7). From a human point of view there was no reasonable explanation of why an upright man like Job should suffer the terrible calamities that came upon him (ch 1:13-21). He did not understand why tragedy had

come, but nevertheless maintained his confidence in God (Job 23). Despite the mistaken admonition of his wife and his friends Eliphaz, Bildad, Zophar, and Elihu (chs 2:9, 11; 32:2), he maintained his "integrity." In the end God sternly rebuked the misguided philosophy of Job's friends, that Job's calamities were a divine retribution for his misdeeds (ch 42: 7). The turning point in Job's experience came when he prayed for his friends, and the Lord gave him "twice as much as he had before" (v 10).

2. For Gen 46:13, KJV, *see* Jashub.

Job, Book of. A dramatic poem of human experience, in which Job's patience and integrity in the face of overwhelming tragedy vindicate the righteousness of God in His dealings with men and confute the theory that suffering is a divine retribution for human misdeeds. In the Hebrew printed Bibles the book of Job stands in the 3d section, the Hagiographa, or Writings (*see* Old Testament), and stands between Psalms and Proverbs. In the Septuagint, the Vulgate, and modern translations, it appears as the first of the poetical books. From ancient times the book has been held in highest esteem, inasmuch as unaccountable suffering and disappointment have ever been man's lot, and men have drawn solace, courage, and hope from the example of Job. The dramatic conversational form and the graphic imagery of the book make it fascinating to read, even in translation. As literature it easily deserves a place among the great classics of all time. Early Jewish tradition, though not unanimous, attributed the book to Moses, whereas modern scholars have suggested Elihu, Solomon, and Ezra as possible candidates for authorship. The following reasons have been deduced for ascribing the book to Moses. Moses sojourned in Midian (Ex 2:15), which was possibly in the vicinity of the land of Uz itself. The land of Uz appears to have been in or near the land of Edom (see Lam 4:21). Thus during his sojourn in Midian, Moses could easily have been acquainted with Job or with his descendants or some who had known him personally. Being "learned in all the wisdom of the Egyptians" and "mighty in words and in deeds" (Acts 7:22), Moses unquestionably possessed the literary background for writing this poetic masterpiece. In recent years texts in alphabetical Semitic script dating from the same period have come to light in the region of Moses' sojourn (*see*

Writing), disproving the former critical position that writing was not known at the time of Moses. The strong Arabic flavor that permeates the narrative of Job, coupled with allusions to Egyptian life and customs that occur in the book, points to a writer who was personally acquainted with both cultures. Furthermore, the concept of God as Creator, reflected in Job 38 to 41, harmonizes with the Creation narrative in the book of Genesis, which Moses wrote. Also, certain words found in the book of Job appear also in the Pentateuch, but rarely elsewhere in the OT. One noteworthy illustration of this is *Shaddai*, "the Almighty," which occurs 31 times in Job and 6 times in Genesis, and only eight times elsewhere. Words occurring in the Pentateuch and in Job but nowhere else are: *'achû*, "meadow"; *tenû'ah*, "opposition," "amazement"; *neṣ*, an unclean bird; *palil*, "judge"; *yaraṭ*, "to throw."

Arguments that have been advanced against Mosaic authorship on the grounds of a dissimilarity of style as compared with other books attributed to him cannot be taken seriously in view of the vast difference in content. The argument that Job resembles the so-called "wisdom literature" of a later period in no way precludes the existence of this literary style at a much earlier time. The historical data in the book, scanty though they are, clearly imply that Job was an actual person, to whose experience an inspired account of the supernatural background of the tragedy that befell him is added. Following this simple, historical record of what befell Job, the solution to his problem of suffering is presented in a series of dialogues between Job and his friends, and later between Job and God. To this is appended a brief historical epilogue that reports the sequel to Job's experience.

The problem to which the book of Job seeks a solution is, "Why do the righteous suffer?" The answer is that Satan is the author of suffering, as he is of the theory that makes suffering out to be divine punishment for sin. Suffering is the result of an evil genius at work in the universe, and not necessarily of particular acts of wrongdoing on the sufferer's part. God's role in human suffering is permissive. This is not to deny the law of reward and punishment (see Gal 6:7-9). It is true that persistent refusal to comply with the divine will brings misfortune (Ex 23:20-33; Deut 28; Ps 1; Jer 31:29, 30; Eze 18), but the fact that suffering is a natural result of sin at work in the universe does not necessarily imply that suffering can be traced to some particular antecedent sin. In a world where sin prevails, the righteous often suffer along with the guilty, while the wicked sometimes appear, for a time, to prosper (cf. Ps 37:7; Jer 12:1).

The narrative of the book of Job opens with Job at the summit of prosperity, a man "perfect and upright, and one that feared God, and eschewed evil" (Job 1:1). But suddenly and without apparent cause he is reduced to a state in which death appears more desirable than life (chs 1:13-21; 2:9; 3:1-3, 20, 21), yet "in all this Job sinned not, nor charged God foolishly" (ch 1:22). On the basis of the tradition that suffering is punishment for sin, Job's wife gives the situation up as hopeless (ch 2:9), and his best friends, who presumably come to comfort him (v 11), succeed only in deepening his misery (ch 16:2). It seems to Job that even God no longer understands or cares (ch 23). Apparently forsaken thus alike by God and man, and prostrate in a deep, dark pit of discouragement, Job nevertheless maintains a degree of spiritual poise. He does not claim to be without sin, but protests that he knows of no rational explanation for his suffering, on the premise that punishment is retribution for a supposed crime. In a supreme act of faith he commits his way to the Lord, even in death, confident that in time God will "have a desire" to the work of His hand (ch 14:12-15). His faith that God is good leads him to triumph over the most forbidding circumstances. Slowly but surely this faith lifts him from the pit into which Satan has plunged him, until finally God sharpens his vision to see circumstances in their true perspective from the standpoint of the divine philosophy.

The poem proper is composed of 3 parts, in the 1st of which Job debates the problem with his friends, Eliphaz, Bildad, and Zophar (chs 3-31). In the 2d part he debates the problem with Elihu (chs 32:1 to 37:24), and in the 3d God intervenes and explains the problem to Job (chs 38 to 42). Job's debate with Eliphaz, Bildad, and Zophar is in 3 cycles, each of which contains 3 speeches by Job and one by each of his 3 friends in response, except that the 3d cycle contains no speech by Zophar. The speeches of the 3 friends have been compared to a number of wheels rotating on the same axle, in that

all attempt to prove misfortune to be divine punishment for sin.

After the prose prologue (Job 1:1 to 2:13), which sets the stage with Job prostrate upon a heap of ashes and surrounded by his 3 well-meaning but mistaken friends, the 1st cycle of the argument between Job and his friends begins (chs 3:1 to 11:20). Job makes 3 speeches and is answered, in turn, by Eliphaz, Bildad, and Zophar. Job tells of his affliction and expresses his inability to understand why God permitted all this to happen to him. His friends assert that he must have committed some heinous sin, to have deserved a punishment such as this, and appeal to him to repent. In the 2d cycle (chs 12:1 to 20:29) Job maintains his integrity—he has not been guilty of such a sin. He then laments the unjust and unmerciful accusations of his would-be "comforters," and affirms his belief that someday God will vindicate his cause. Again replying in turn, Job's friends reprove him for maintaining his integrity, which, because of their mistaken concept of suffering as the penalty for particular sins, is gross impiety. The 3d cycle (chs 21:1 to 31:40) once more presents Job giving 3 speeches in which he observes that the wicked sometimes prosper even as the righteous sometimes suffer. He appeals to God to hear his case, reviews his experience, and maintains his innocence. Eliphaz replies to Job's 1st speech, Bildad to the 2d. They appeal to him to repent, and seek to prove that Job is foolish to expect God to justify him. Silenced at last, Eliphaz, Bildad, and Zophar retire from the stage. Then Elihu, a young man who has been standing by, offers another philosophical approach to the subject (chs 32 to 37), reasoning that suffering is not so much divine punishment as it is corrective discipline. After Elihu has spoken for some time God interrupts (chs 38 to 41), and in 3 addresses emphasizes His concern for man's well-being. He directs Job's attention to countless aspects of the natural world that reveal God as the Creator and Sustainer of all things. If God takes an interest in all of these, can He be unconcerned for Job in his abject misery? The climax comes in a declaration of God's omniscience and omnipotence (ch 41:34). Job can therefore have implicit confidence in Him. In the prose postlude (ch 42) Job acknowledges God's great power and wisdom. Through this experience he has attained to a richer and deeper appreciation of God and of God's ways of dealing with man. God then denounces the false philosophy of Eliphaz and his companions and summons Job to pray for them (Job 42:7), but does not include Elihu in His censure. Then "the Lord turned the captivity of Job" and gave him "twice as much as he had before" (v 10). A rich reward awaits those who endure the vicissitudes of life with patience and courage, a reward that will compensate them fully for all they have endured because of sin—"an hundredfold now in this time, . . . and in the world to come eternal life" (Mk 10:30).

Jobab (jō′băb). [Heb. *Yôbab*. The name occurs in ancient South Arabic as *Yhwbb* and in Akkadian as *Yâbibi*.]

1. A son of Joktan (Gen 10:29; 1 Chr 1:23).

2. A king of Edom originally from Bozrah (Gen 36:33; 1 Chr 1:44).

3. A king of the city of Madon who as a member of a northern coalition fought against Joshua but was defeated at the waters of Merom (Jos 11:1-8; 12:19).

4 and 5. Two men of the tribe of Benjamin (1 Chr 8:9, 18).

Jochebed (jŏk′ė-bĕd). [Heb. *Yôkebed*, "Yahweh is glory."] Wife of Amram and mother of Miriam, Aaron, and Moses (Ex 2:1-4; 6:20; Num 26:59).

Jod. [Heb. *yôd*.] The 10th letter of the Hebrew alphabet, written ', appearing as the title to the 10th section of Ps 119, KJV. See Aleph.

Joda (jō′dȧ), KJV **Juda** (jōō′dȧ). [Gr. *Iōda*, probably from a variant rendering of the Heb. *Yehûdah*, "Judah." "Juda" comes from *Iouda*, the reading of the Textus Receptus.] A Judahite appearing in Luke's genealogy of Christ (Lk 3:26).

Joed (jō′ĕd). [Heb. *Yô′ed*, "Yahweh is a witness."] A Benjamite (Neh 11:7).

Joel (jō′ĕl). [Heb. *Yô′el*, "Yahweh is God"; Gr. *Iōēl*.]

1. A Kohathite Levite, and ancestor of Samuel (1 Chr 6:36), considered by some to be identical with the Shaul of v 24. See Shaul, 3.

2. The eldest son of Samuel (1 Sa 8:2), and father of Heman the singer under David (1 Chr 6:33; 15:17). Samuel's first-born is called Vashni (văsh′nī) [Heb. *Washni*] in ch 6:28, KJV. *Washni* means "and the second." The name Joel was probably inadvertently omitted by some scribe. With the help of the Greek version of Lucian and the Syriac version the text may be reconstructed as follows: "And the

sons of Samuel; the first-born Joel and the second Abiah," or "Abijah."

3. A Gershonite Levite who with 130 fellow Levites assisted David in bringing the ark from Obed-edom's house to Jerusalem (1 Chr 15:7, 11, 12).

4. A Gershonite Levite who with his brother was placed in charge of the treasures dedicated to God in David's time (1 Chr 23:8; 26:21, 22).

5. A chief of the tribe of Issachar (1 Chr 7:3).

6. One of David's "mighty men," a brother of Nathan (1 Chr 11:38), considered by some to be identical with Igal, or related to him (2 Sa 23:36).

7. A chief of the western half tribe of Manasseh in the time of David (1 Chr 27:20).

8. A Gadite chieftain in Bashan (1 Chr 5:12).

9. A Reubenite (1 Chr 5:4, 8).

10. A Kohathite Levite who helped cleanse the Temple in the time of Hezekiah (2 Chr 29:12).

11. One of the Simeonite princes who seized rich pastureland at Gedor (1 Chr 4:35-41).

12. One of the so-called Minor Prophets, the author of the book that bears his name (Joel 1:1). Nothing is known about his history. See Joel, Book of.

13. A man of the family of Nebo; he had married a foreign wife in Ezra's time (Ezr 10:43).

14. A Benjamite overseer who lived in Jerusalem (Neh 11:9).

Joel, Book of. Second of the so-called Minor Prophets. The author's name gives it its title. In the Hebrew printed Bibles Joel stands, as it does in English, between Hosea and Amos, though in the Septuagint it appears 4th in the so-called Minor Prophets, and follows Micah, Hosea and Amos being the first two. Nothing is known of the author other than that he was the son of Pethuel (Joel 1:1). The date of the book has been variously assigned by conservative Bible students to the 9th cent. B.C. and the 7th cent. The book contains no historical or chronological data of assistance in determining its date. Those who advocate the 9th cent. point to the fact that Assyria and Babylonia are not mentioned as enemies of Judah (cf. ch 3:4-6, 19), a mention which we would expect if the book had been written in the 8th cent., or later. The fact that Joel mentions no king as reigning at the time he prophesied is cited as evidence that the book was written during the regency of

Jehoiada while Joash was yet a child (2 Ki 11:17 to 12:2), about 825 B.C. Attention is also called to the fact that there is no stern denunciation for sin that is characteristic of the later prophets. In fact, no national sin, as such, is mentioned. Advocates of the 7th-cent. view assign Joel's ministry to the early years of Josiah's reign, approximately 635 B.C., when Assyrian power was waning and Babylonia had not yet come into prominence. Because Josiah came to the throne as a child, it is conjectured that he must have lived under a regent. The fact that Tyre and Sidon (Joel 3:4-6) do not appear in history as enemies of Judah until the closing decades of its history is cited as favoring this view. Presumably also, the Jews had little contact with the Greeks (v 6) in the 9th cent.

The book of Joel is a masterpiece of Hebrew poetic form marked by systematic organization, a skillful use of language, well-balanced syntax, and vivid figures of speech. It is a classic of Hebrew prophetic literature unexcelled in vividness of description and picturesque diction. In sublimity of style it ranks with Isaiah and Habakkuk.

The prophet's message appears in the form of a sermon or a series of sermons addressed to all Israel (e.g. chs 2:19-21; 3:4, 9, 11, 13). The theme is reformation. The message opens with a stark picture of gloom, but closes with a brief glimpse of glory. The prophet explains why a reformation is needed, calls attention to the calamities God has sent to remind His people of their need, stresses the urgency of reformation, and points out what a genuine reformation will involve. He then turns to the results of such a reformation. The book may be divided into 2 main sections: (1) Adversity and the call to repentance (chs 1:1 to 2:17). (2) The promise of deliverance and restoration (chs 2:18 to 3:21). First, Joel gives a vivid description of the distress occasioned by a severe plague of locusts, which he describes under the symbol of an invading army (ch 1:4-6). The plague is more severe than any in 5 generations (vs 2, 3), with the result that a countryside has already been denuded of verdure (vs 6, 7). Crop after crop has been ruined (vs 11, 12), and there remains not enough even for the offerings of the Lord's house (vs 9, 10). In view of the crisis that confronts the nation Joel calls for a period of fasting and summons the inhabitants of the land to the Temple for a solemn assembly (Joel 1:14). Accompanying the plague of locusts is a severe drought (vs 15-20), so severe that the nation faces extinction, and thus "the *day of the Lord" (chs 1:14, 15; 2:1). The present calamities presage that time of divine retribution. In ch 2:2 the prophet repeats what he has already said in ch 1:2, 3 concerning the severity of the plague and the unprecedented suffering that it has brought about. Even now the land appears as if it had been swept by fire (ch 2:3). In vs 4-11 the locusts are declared to be the "army" of the Lord, whose coming none can abide—unless God intervenes (v 11). Here Joel compares the locusts to a horde of mounted invaders who cover the countryside like a tidal wave. In vs 12-17 the prophet directs attention to what the people of God should do in view of the crisis now confronting the nation. Nothing less than wholehearted repentance, in fact as well as form, will suffice to avert complete annihilation, and the people are admonished to rend their hearts and not their garments (v 13) as they gather together before the Lord. To stress the urgency of reformation the prophet summons the aged, little children, and infants to accompany the men and women of Israel as the nation gathers in solemn assembly; even marriage festivities are to be postponed (v 16).

Beginning with ch 2:18 it is assumed that the people have responded to the prophet's summons. They have gathered together before the Lord, they have repented with all of their hearts, and now they await His gracious reply. The first effect of their repentance is the removal of the plague of locusts. God promises corn, wine, and oil sufficient to satisfy the needs of all, but has even greater blessings in store for His people (v 21). Not only will He send the usual early and latter rains, in the fall and the spring of the year, but the soil will prove to be so productive as to make up for the losses occasioned by the plague of locusts. The people will "eat in plenty, and be satisfied" (vs 23-26). God's blessing will not be limited to supplying their material needs, however. As He pours out the former and latter rain upon the ground, so He will pour out His Spirit upon the hearts of the people (vs 28, 29). Then extraordinary omens in the natural world will herald the coming of "the great and the terrible day of the Lord" (vs 30, 31), but God's people need not fear, since all who "call on the name of the Lord shall be delivered" (Joel 2:32). Instead of being a day of judgment upon Israel (cf. chs 1: 15; 2:1), the day of the Lord will prove to be a time of judgment upon the heathen nations that have oppressed God's people (ch 3:1-17). As repeatedly elsewhere in the OT prophets (Eze 38:8, 23; Zeph 3:8, 9; Zech 12:2-10; 14:2-13; etc.) God is pictured as gathering the heathen nations to the vicinity of Jerusalem, where He will execute judgment upon them. The Phoenicians (Joel 3:4) and Greeks (v 6) who assemble in the "valley of Jehoshaphat" purposing to take the city of Jerusalem (v 2) here stand for all of Israel's oppressors. Once the heathen have assembled and are on the point of capturing the city, God causes His "mighty ones to come down" (v 11). He delivers His people (v 1) and annihilates their enemies (vs 1, 16). Never again will the nations oppress Israel, and the land of Judah will stand forth in perpetual fertility and beauty. From generation to generation the Lord will dwell in the midst of His people (vs 20, 21). For a discussion of prophecies of this type *see* Prophet, II.

Joelah (jô-ē'là). [Heb. *Yô'e'lah,* meaning uncertain.] A warrior of Gedor who joined David at Ziklag (1 Chr 12:7).

Joezer (jô-ē'zẽr). [Heb. *Yô'ezer,* "Yahweh is a help." The name occurs on an ancient Hebrew seal inscription in the form of *Yhw'zr.*] A Korahite who joined David at Ziklag (1 Chr 12:6).

Jogbehah (jŏg'bĕ-hà). [Heb. *Yogbohah,* probably "elevation."] A fortified town of Gad (Num 32:35; Jgs 8:11), now the modern village of *Jubeihât,* 6 mi. northwest of Amman (Map VI, E-4).

Jogli (jŏg'lī). [Heb. *Yoglî,* probably "exiled."] A Danite (Num 34:22).

Joha (jō'hà). [Heb. *Yôcha'.*]
1. A Benjamite (1 Chr 8:16).
2. A Tizite, one of David's "mighty men" (1 Chr 11:45).

Johanan (jô-hā'năn). [Heb. *Yôchanan* and *Yehôchanan,* "Yahweh is gracious." The name occurs in the Aramaic Elephantine papyri (*see* Papyrus) in the longer form as the name of Johanan, 10.]
1. A Benjamite who joined David in Ziklag (1 Chr 12:4).
2. A Gadite who joined David in Ziklag and was later made an officer in David's army (1 Chr 12:12; cf. v 14).
3. A member of the Zadokite high-priestly line (1 Chr 6:9, 10).
4. An Ephraimite (2 Chr 28:12).
5. The eldest son of King Josiah of Judah. He may have died young (1 Chr 3:15), since he did not succeed to the throne and is not mentioned elsewhere.
6. Son of Kareah and a captain of Zedekiah's army who escaped capture at the time of Jerusalem's destruction. Later he made his way to Mizpah, to Gedaliah, who had been appointed governor over Judea by Nebuchadnezzar, and submitted to him. When he learned of Ishmael's plot to murder Gedaliah he warned Gedaliah, but could not convince him, of Ishmael's intent. When the plot materialized and Gedaliah was assassinated, Johanan led the force that opposed Ishmael, and retrieved Ishmael's captives. He sought Jeremiah's counsel with regard to newly proposed plans to migrate to Egypt, but Jeremiah counseled against the move. Nevertheless Johanan carried out his plan (2 Ki 25:22, 23; Jer 40:8, 9, 13-16; 41:11-16; 42:1 to 43:7).
7. A descendant of David (1 Chr 3:24).
8. A man of the family of Azgad; he accompanied Ezra from Babylonia with 110 men (Ezr 8:12).
9. For Neh 6:18, KJV, *see* Jehohanan, 7.
10. A high priest in the days of Ezra. He is called the son of Eliashib in Neh 12:23, but in v 22 he is named as the successor of Joiada, who succeeded Eliashib. Thus the term *son is here doubtless used in the sense of grandson as attested by Josephus (*Ant.* xi. 7. 1). He is called Jonathan in Neh 12:11, probably by a copyist's error, or perhaps Jonathan was an alternate name for Johanan. He may have been the Johanan (RSV "Jehohanan"), to whose room, presumably in the Temple compound, Ezra withdrew and fasted when he learned that many returned Jews had married foreign wives (Ezr 10:6). Johanan is confirmed by the Elephantine papyri as high priest in 410 B.C., probably also in 407, when the papyri, containing his name in the form *Yehôchanan,* were written (see fig. 417). The Jews in Elephantine requested his permission to rebuild their temple, which the Egyptians had destroyed. Josephus, who speaks of him as Joannes (John), says that he murdered his own brother, Jesus (Jeshua, or Joshua), in the Temple, when Jeshua attempted to wrest the high priesthood from him through the influence of the Persians. This in turn gave Bagoas, the general of Artaxerxes II (Mnemon), an opportunity to take severe measures against the Jews (*Ant.* xi. 7. 1). This information may be correct,

268. The Jordan River at the place where, according to tradition, John the Baptist baptized his converts

for the Elephantine papyri give the name of the Persian governor in Johanan's time as Bigvai, the Persian equivalent of the Gr. *Bagoas,* or *Bagoses.*

John (jŏn), KJV 3 times **Jonas** (jō'năs), once **Jona** (jō'nà). [Gr. *Iōannēs,* probably from the Heb. *Yôchanan,* or *Yehôchanan,* "Yahweh is gracious"; variant reading *Iōnas,* "Jonah," on which the KJV renderings "Jonas" and "Jona" are based.]

1. John the Baptist, the forerunner of Jesus Christ and son of Zechariah (KJV "Zacharias"), a priest of the course of "Abia," and Elizabeth (Lk 1:5). It was while Zacharias was performing his priestly function of burning incense in the Temple that Gabriel informed him of the birth of the child and instructed him to call his name John and to bring him up as a Nazirite. The angel predicted that the child would be filled with the Holy Spirit from his mother's womb, and would go forth in the spirit and power of Elijah to "make ready a people prepared for the Lord" (vs 8-17). Remembering his own and his wife's advanced age, Zacharias expressed doubt at the word of the angel, and because of his unbelief was struck dumb (vs 18-22). In due course the child was born, and 8 days later was circumcised. The neighbors and relatives assumed that the child would be called Zacharias. However, Elizabeth, following the directions of the angel (v 13), insisted upon the name John. When Zacharias was consulted by means of signs, he wrote upon a tablet . that the name should be John. At that very moment his speech was restored. These strange happenings astonished the people of the area, so that all wondered what kind of child John would be (vs 57-66). John's father, filled with the Holy Spirit, prophesied that his son would be called "the prophet of the Highest" for he would "go before the face of the Lord to prepare his ways" (vs 67-79).

John grew up in the wilderness, where he remained until his ministry began (Lk 1:80). This wilderness was probably the "wilderness of Judaea" mentioned in Mt 3:1, a region of barren hills between the Dead Sea and the highest parts of the central mountain range of Palestine (see fig. 523). The Bible offers no information concerning the early life and training of John beyond stating that "the child grew, and waxed strong in spirit, and was in the deserts till the day of his shewing unto Israel" (Lk 1:80).

John was a cousin of Jesus, and was about 6 months older than He (Lk 1:36), hence probably began his ministry 6 months before Jesus, also about the age of 30. This was the age at which Jews regarded a man as having reached his full maturity and as being therefore eligible for the responsibilities of public life (cf. ch 3:23).

John was apparently a rugged man in both character and appearance. He did not hesitate to speak cutting truth when it was necessary (Mt 3:7-11; Lk 3:7-9). He was a man of austere, indeed almost might even appear to be almost unsocial, habits (Mt 11:19; Lk 7:33), who ate the simplest foods, *locusts and "wild honey" (Mt 3:4; Mk 1:6). His clothing was a garment woven of camel's hair, and a leather girdle about his waist (Mt 3:4; Mk 1:6; cf. Mt 11:8).

All of John's preaching, it would seem, was done in the "wilderness of Judaea" (Mt 3:1). Luke states that he labored in the country about Jordan, and that his preaching in desert areas was in fulfillment of the prophecy of Isaiah that he would preach in the wilderness (Lk 3:3, 4). One reason for his preaching near the Jordan was doubtless the suitability of the river for baptisms (cf. Jn 3:23). The power of his message is attested by the fact that crowds streamed out of the cities and from the countryside around to hear him and to be baptized of him (Mt 3:5, 6; Mk 1:4, 5; Lk 3:7). Not only did his preaching bear fruit among the Jews of Judea (see Jos. *Ant.* xviii. 5. 2), but the effects of his message spread to areas outside Palestine (Acts 18:25; 19:3).

The peak, and the beginning of the decline, of John's ministry was reached on the day he baptized Jesus (Jn 1:33). When Jesus came to the Baptist requesting immersion, John demurred, stating that he himself needed to be baptized by Jesus, but Jesus requested him to perform the ceremony, "for thus it becometh us to fulfil all righteousness" (Mt 3:13-

15). After the baptism John saw the Holy Spirit in the form of a dove descending upon Jesus, and heard a voice from heaven attesting that Jesus was the Son of God (Mt 3:16, 17; Mk 1:9-11; Lk 3:21, 22; Jn 1:30-34). "The next day" John pointed out Christ to those around him as the Lamb of God (Jn 1:29). Later, when he repeated his statement 2 of his disciples who heard his words began to follow Jesus (vs 36-42), symbols of the shift of the multitudes away from John to the new and greater Teacher (ch 3:26).

At no time was John's greatness more apparent than when some of his disciples came to him with the message that all men were going after Jesus. His answer was one of complete self-abnegation, and self-surrender to the will of God: "A man can receive nothing, except it be given him from heaven. . . . He must increase, but I must decrease" (Jn 3:25-36).

Some months, perhaps a year or more, after the baptism of Jesus, John was imprisoned by Herod Antipas (*see* Herod, 3), whom he had fearlessly reproved for abandoning his wife in order to marry his niece Herodias, who was already the wife of his half brother, Herod Philip (Mt 14: 3, 4; Lk 3:19, 20).

Some time after his incarceration John sent 2 of his disciples to Jesus to inquire whether or not He was the Messiah. Jesus told the disciples to tell John of the things they had seen and heard; how the sick were healed, the dead were raised to life, and the gospel was preached to the poor (Mt 11:2-6; Lk 7:18-23). After their departure Jesus delivered a wonderful eulogy concerning John; John was not wavering and irresolute, as a reed bent in whatever direction the wind blows; he was not a man of courtly dress and manners, but he was a prophet, and much more than a prophet, to whom had been given the great task of heralding the Messiah (Mt 11:7-18; Lk 7:24-35).

Perhaps some 6 months after this event John was beheaded. His death was brought about through the scheming of Herodias, who hated John for his reproval of Herod's actions concerning her (Mk 6:19). On the occasion of one of Herod's birthdays, when he was entertaining some important guests, Salome, the daughter of Herodias by Herod Philip, danced before them. Her performance so pleased Herod that he offered to give her whatever she asked, even to half of his kingdom. Salome consulted her mother, who directed her to request the head of John. This greatly upset Herod, for he had respect for, and fear of, John. However, he felt he could not withdraw his promise; so he gave orders that the prophet be beheaded. This command was performed, and the Baptist's head was delivered to Herodias' daughter on a platter (Mt 14:3, 6-11; Mk 6:19-28). John's body was buried by his disciples (Mt 14: 12; Mk 6:29). When later Herod heard of Jesus and His marvelous works, he thought that Jesus was John, risen from the dead (Mt 14:1, 2; Mk 6:14, 16; Lk 9: 7). According to Josephus, John's imprisonment and death occurred in the fortress of Machaerus in Perea, east of the Dead Sea (Jos. *Ant.* xviii. 5. 2).

The Dead Sea scrolls, discovered since 1947, and the excavations at Qumran reveal several close parallels between the Qumran sect and John the Baptist with regard to customs and teachings. Like John, the members of the Qumran community, probably Essenes, lived in the desert of Judah and denied themselves most of the comforts of life. They believed in a separation from the world and in a life of self-denial in order to "clear the way of the Lord" quoting, as did John, Is 40:3 (1 QS viii. 13-16; cf. Mt 3:3). They practiced ritual washings in tanks, in rivers, and in the sea, and novices seem to have had to submit to a kind of baptism. Their beliefs, as contained in their books, with regard to their expectation of the Messiah and other teachings also show parallels to those of John. These parallels have led some to suggest that before his public ministry John may have been a member of the Qumran community, and as such had shared many of their convictions and ideals, but that he had broken with them and their world-removed life when God called him to a public work that would prepare the way for Jesus' ministry (see W. H. Brownlee, in *The Scrolls and the New Testament* [New York, Harper, 1957], pp. 33-35).

2. The father of Simon Peter (Jn 1:42; 21:15-17; RSV; KJV "Jona" and "Jonas").

3. John, a son of Zebedee, and apparently *Salome, and brother of James (Mt 4:21; 27:56; cf. Mk 15:40; 16:1; Jn 19:25; Acts 12:1, 2). The fact that James is usually mentioned first when the names of the 2 disciples appear together implies that John was the younger of the two. Zebedee and his 2 sons were fishermen by trade, and apparently reasonably prosperous (Mk 1:19, 20). John apparently enters the Gos-

pel narrative in Jn 1:35-40, as an unnamed disciple, among the throng listening to John the Baptist by the river Jordan. In that case he and Andrew, Simon Peter's brother, were the first of John the Baptist's disciples to follow Jesus. John apparently returned with Jesus to Galilee a few days later and attended the wedding festivities at Cana (ch 2:1-11). John was with Jesus intermittently during the next year, the period of His Judean ministry, but also evidently devoted part of his time to the fishing business; but as Jesus began His Galilean ministry, He invited John and his brother, and Peter and Andrew as well, to become permanent disciples (Lk 5:1-11). Some months later John was among the 12 chosen to be apostles (Mt 10:2). Henceforth John was intimately associated with Jesus in His labors. With Peter and James, John was a member of Jesus' inner circle of associates. He witnessed the raising of Jairus' daughter (Mk 5:37), and was present at the Transfiguration (ch 9:2) and again at Gethsemane (ch 14:33). John gave evidence of an impetuous disposition upon various occasions, as when he rebuked someone who labored in Christ's name but had not formally become a disciple (Lk 9:49), and when he proposed to call fire down from heaven on the inhabitants of a Samaritan village who had refused Christ the privilege of sleeping in their village (vs 52-56). He revealed selfishness upon the occasion when he with his brother sought places of honor beside Jesus in His future kingdom, but also demonstrated zeal and loyalty by declaring himself ready to face death with his Master (Mt 20:20-24; Mk 10:35-41).

During his association with Jesus, John seems to have yielded himself fully to the softening, subduing influence of the Saviour, with the result that his character was transformed. Apparently he entered into a fellowship with Jesus deeper and richer than that of the other apostles (see Jn 21:20). At the Last Supper he occupied the place next to Jesus (ch 13:23). When Jesus was arrested in Gethsemane, John followed Him into the palace of the high priest, where he seems to have been known, and later to Calvary (chs 18:15; 19:26). At the cross Jesus entrusted His mother Mary to the loving care of John (ch 19:27). Early Sunday morning, upon hearing the report that Jesus' tomb was empty, John and Peter ran together to the sepulcher to investigate, and became witnesses of the fact that Jesus had indeed risen (ch 20:1-10). John was present the evening of the day of the resurrection, when Jesus appeared to the disciples in the upper room, and also a week later (Lk 24:33-43; Jn 20:19-30; 1 Cor 15:5). He was one of a group of disciples who had gone fishing, to whom Jesus appeared on the shores of Galilee (Jn 21:1-7).

After the ascension John remained with the other 10 apostles in the upper room at Jerusalem (Acts 1:13), and subsequently joined with Peter in missionary labor in the city of Jerusalem (ch 3:1). Despite imprisonment, both apostles witnessed boldly to their faith in Jesus (ch 4:19). Later, Peter and John went to Samaria to assist Philip (ch 8:14). John was possibly among the "apostles and elders which were at Jerusalem" for a number of years (see Acts 16:4; Gal 2:9). Tradition, supported by the implication in Rev 1:11, suggests that during the later years of his life John was in charge of the churches in the Roman province of Asia Minor, with headquarters at Ephesus. From there he was banished by Domitian to the island of Patmos (v 9) but is thought to have been released when Nerva became emperor in A.D. 96 (see figs. 372, 373, for views of Patmos). According to tradition, Polycarp, Papias, and Ignatius were pupils of John. Following his release, according to tradition, John resided at Ephesus, and died during the reign of Trajan, A.D. 98-117. Toward the close of his life John wrote the book of Revelation and also the Gospel and the 3 epistles that bear his name.

4. **John Mark** (märk), author of the 2d Gospel, according to the consistent and unanimous witness of early Christian tradition. He is called Marcus (mär'kŭs) 3 times in the KJV (Col 4:10; Phm 24; 1 Pe 5:13). John Mark was apparently a citizen of Jerusalem, for his mother, Mary (see Mary, 7), had her home in that city, which home was evidently used as a gathering place for the Christians (Acts 12:12). It has been conjectured that the "upper room" where Jesus held the Passover with His disciples, and where the believers later met to await the Holy Spirit, was in John Mark's home (Mt 26:18; Mk 14:15; Lk 22:12; Acts 1:13). Because no mention is made of his father, it is assumed that he was dead. John Mark was a cousin of Barnabas (Col 4:10, RSV). It has been conjectured that the young man "having a linen cloth cast about his naked body" during the arrest of Jesus was John Mark (Mk 14:51). However, this cannot be proved. Because Peter calls him his

"son" in 1 Pe 5:13, some suggest that Mark was a convert of that apostle.

John Mark accompanied Paul and Barnabas to Antioch upon their return from Jerusalem, where they had delivered a contribution to the needy church (Acts 11:28-30; 12:25). He subsequently accompanied them as their "minister," on their 1st Missionary Journey (ch 13:5). This journey took them to the island of Cyprus, where they preached the gospel in the Jewish synagogues. Following their experience at Paphos with the sorcerer, Bar-Jesus, and Sergius Paulus, the Roman proconsul (vs 6-12), the 3 set sail for Perga, a city on the mainland of Asia Minor, in a northwesterly direction from Paphos. At that city John Mark, overcome by the difficulties and hardships already encountered, and anticipating still greater ones, left the other men and returned to his home in Jerusalem (v 13). When Paul and Barnabas planned a 2d Missionary Journey, Barnabas insisted that John Mark accompany them, but Paul would not agree, feeling that, because Mark had forsaken them previously, he could not be depended upon (ch 15:36-38). The result of this difference of opinion was that Paul and Barnabas separated. Barnabas took John Mark and went to the island of Cyprus (v 39).

John Mark does not appear again in the Biblical narrative until he is mentioned by Paul in his letter to the church at Colossae and his letter to Philemon, written during his 1st imprisonment at Rome. In these he calls Mark his "fellow-prisoner" and "fellowlabourer" (Col 4:10; Phm 24). During his 2d imprisonment Paul again mentions Mark. Writing to Timothy, the apostle says: "Take Mark, and bring him with thee: for he is profitable to me for the ministry" (2 Ti 4:11). These words show that Mark had vindicated himself before Paul, and had proved himself to be a worthy minister of the gospel.

According to tradition John Mark later went to Egypt and founded the church at Alexandria, becoming its presiding elder, and was martyred in that country during the Neronian persecutions. Tradition also indicates that, in his Gospel, he served as an interpreter for Peter. Papias of Hierapolis, writing c. A.D. 140, recorded a tradition of John the presbyter that "'Mark became Peter's interpreter and wrote accurately all that he remembered, not, indeed, in order, of the things said or done by the Lord. For he had not heard the Lord, nor had he followed him, but later on, as I said, followed Peter, who used to give teaching as necessity demanded but not making, as it were, an arrangement of the Lord's oracles, so that Mark did nothing wrong in thus writing down single points as he remembered them. For to one thing he gave attention, to leave out nothing of what he had heard and to make no false statements in them'" (Eusebius *Hist. Eccl.* iii. 39. 15).

5. A Jewish leader who participated in the prosecution of Peter and John after their healing of the lame man at the Beautiful Gate of the Temple (Acts 4:6).

John, Epistles of. Three epistles traditionally attributed to the apostle John, belonging to the 7 "general" or "catholic" epistles. 1 Jn is properly called a "general" epistle in view of the fact that it is not addressed to a specific church or individual. Strictly speaking, 2 Jn and 3 Jn are not "general" epistles, but private letters to individual members of the churches which John had served as pastor. In the earliest extant Greek manuscripts the titles of the 3 epistles are simply *Iōannou A,* "of John 1," *Iōannou B,* "of John 2," and *Iōannou Γ,* "of John 3." The author does not identify himself in any of these epistles, but Johannine authorship is attested from earliest times, and the epistles are quoted by many of the Church Fathers. Polycarp, reputed to have been an associate of John the apostle, seems to quote from 1 Jn 4:3 in ch 7 of his epistle to the Philippians, which was written c. A.D. 115. According to the church historian Eusebius, Papias (d. c. A.D. 163) "used testimonies from the first [former] epistle of John" (*Hist. Eccl.* iii. 24). Writing between A.D. 182 and A.D. 188, Irenaeus quoted various passages from the first 2 epistles (*Against Heresies* iii. 16. 5, 8). The Muratorian Fragment (written c. A.D. 170) attributes both 1 Jn and 2 Jn to the apostle John. Thus from earliest times the authenticity and right of these epistles to a place in the canon is firmly fixed. The ancient tradition of Johannine authorship is still further strengthened by the resemblance between 1 Jn and the Gospel of Jn in style, vocabulary, word order, grammatical construction, and the pairing of opposite ideas. For instance, both begin with John's unique designation of Christ as the "Word" that came forth from the Father (1 Jn 1:1-3; cf. Jn 1:1-3, 14). Both express the wish that the recipients' "joy may be full" (1 Jn 1:4; cf. Jn 16:24). Both speak of "a new commandment" (1 Jn 2:8; cf. Jn 13:34) and refer to Jesus Christ as "the true light" (1 Jn 2:8; cf. Jn 1:9). Both encourage believers to "love one another" (1 Jn 3:11; cf. Jn 15:12). Both speak of the Christian as passing "from death unto life" (1 Jn 3:14; cf. Jn 5:24). Both refer to the Holy Spirit as the "Spirit of truth" (1 Jn 4:6; cf. Jn 14:17). Both speak of God as sending "his only begotten Son" into the world (1 Jn 4:9; cf. Jn 3:16), and declare that "life" is to be found in Him (1 Jn 5:11; cf. Jn 1:4). For other close verbal similarities between the Epistles and the Gospel compare 1 Jn 2:1 with Jn 14:16; 1 Jn 2:3 with Jn 14:15; 1 Jn 2:11 with Jn 12:35; 1 Jn 2:17 with Jn 8:35; 1 Jn 2:23 with Jn 15:23; 1 Jn 2:27 with Jn 14:26; 1 Jn 3:22 with Jn 8:29. For a characteristic pairing of opposite ideas compare 1 Jn 3:14 with Jn 1:5; 1 Jn 2:9, 10 with Jn 12:25; 1 Jn 2:8 with Jn 5:24. The few differences that exist between the Gospel and the Epistles can easily be attributed to difference in subject matter and degree of organization. The similarities far outweigh the dissimilarities, a fact that bears silent but impressive witness to identity of authorship between the Epistles and the Gospel. The author identifies himself as one of the apostles who personally saw and heard Christ during His earthly ministry (1 Jn 1:1; 2; 4:14; cf. Jn 1:14), and affectionately addresses his converts as "little children" (1 Jn 2:1, 12, 18, 28; 3:7, 18; 4:4; 5:21), implying that he was advanced in age at the time of writing. For a discussion of John as the author of the Gospel that bears his name *see* John, Gospel of. The Gospel and the Epistles give evidence of having been written at approximately the same time. Whereas some 19th-cent. critics formerly assigned both to the latter part of the 2d cent., it is now generally agreed that manuscript evidence points conclusively to the close of the 1st cent. as the time of writing. *See* John, Gospel of.

I. The First Epistle of John. Despite the fact that 1 Jn makes no specific identification of its author, its intended readers, the place of writing, its destination, or the time of writing—and thus lacks the usual characteristics of a Greek letter—it is obviously an epistle. Apparently it was addressed to believers with whom the writer had been closely associated (see chs 2:1, 12, 18, 28; 3:7, 18; 4:4; 5:21). The apostle John is known to have spent the closing years of his min-

istry at Ephesus, as pastor of the Christian churches in the Roman province of Asia. Presumably, this epistle was addressed to these believers.

The author writes, as a pastor, to his spiritual children, assuming that they are already familiar with the principles of salvation, and admonishes them to put these principles into practice. He stresses love—solicitous concern for the well-being and happiness of others—as the primary Christian virtue. Such love is the basic attribute of God (1 Jn 4:8), and comes from God (v 7). God sent His Son to reveal this love (v 10), and believers ought to love one another (v 11). In so doing they testify to the world that they know God (v 8) and are truly converted (vs 16, 20). The love of the world and the love of the Father are mutually exclusive (ch 2:15-17). John bases his urgent appeal to make the principle of love effective on his earnest conviction that Christ's return is imminent (v 18). It is already "the last time" as evidenced by the appearance of many antichrists (v 18), who were once Christians (v 19). But now they deny that Jesus of Nazareth is "the Christ," that is, the Messiah foretold by the prophets of old. They deny that Jesus is the Son of God (v 22), and that true divinity and true humanity were united in the one Person, Jesus Christ (1 Jn 4:3; 5:5; cf. Jn 3:16). These heretical teachings are identical with those of the Docetists, who taught that Christ was merely a phantom, without a real body, and with those of the followers of Cerinthus, a Judaizing proto-Gnostic, who taught that Jesus was the natural-born son of Joseph and Mary, and that the spirit of the Christ entered His body at baptism and withdrew prior to His death on the cross. The Docetic heresy thus denied the true humanity of Christ, where that of Cerinthus denied His true divinity. It is generally accepted that John wrote his 1st epistle particularly with the Docetic heresy in mind.

Following the introduction (1 Jn 1:1-4) in which John affirms Christ's true divinity and humanity as the central truth of the gospel, he goes on (chs 1:5 to 2:6) to the supreme importance of walking in the light, by which he means making a practical application of the truths of the gospel to the daily life. When the Christian obeys Christ's commands he can know that he is "in him." In ch 2:7-14 John sets forth as evidence of obedience to Christ a selfless love for the brethren.

Next (1 Jn 2:15-28), John warns against false teachers. A Christian's only safety is to hold fast the gospel as he has received it, in order to have confidence when Christ appears (v 28). Those who aspire to be sons of God will aim to be like Christ in word and deed, thus purifying their lives, even as Christ is pure (ch 2:28 to 3:24). Duty toward God, John says, is summed up in believing on Jesus Christ as the Son of God and in loving one another as He commanded (ch 3:23). In chs 4:1 to 5:12 John explains the principles by which Christian believers may tell the difference between teachers of truth and error. The first test to be applied is whether they acknowledge or deny that "Jesus Christ is come in the flesh." The 2d test is whether they adhere to the gospel as it was originally proclaimed by the apostles (ch 4:6). The 3d test is whether they genuinely love the members of the household of God (vs 7, 8, 13, 20). The eternal life God has promised is in His Son, and unless men accept Jesus Christ as His Son they do not have access to this priceless gift (ch 5:11, 12). In his conclusion (vs 13-21) John reaffirms the importance of believing in Jesus as the Son of God who came to this world to impart eternal life to all who believe in Him.

II. The Second Epistle of John. This epistle is in the form of a private letter addressed to "the *elect lady" and her "children" (2 Jn 1). Similarity of language and expression makes evident that 2 Jn was written by the same author as 1 Jn. Note, for instance, the expressions: "antichrist" in v 7 (cf. 1 Jn 2:18, 22; 4:3); "walking in truth" (2 Jn 4; cf. 1 Jn 1:7); "a new commandment" (2 Jn 5; cf. 1 Jn 2:8); "love one another" (2 Jn 5; cf. 1 Jn 3:11); and "he hath both the Father and the Son" (2 Jn 9; cf. 1 Jn 5:12). 2 Jn 5-7, 9, 12 may be based on 1 Jn 1:4; 2:4, 5, 7, 18; 5:10-12, and if so would indicate the order in which the epistles were written. The writer identifies himself simply as "the elder," an appropriate title for the aged apostle John. As to length, the 2d epistle is of the usual length for one sheet of papyrus then in common use. In this epistle John speaks of the fellowship that binds Christian believers together (2 Jn 2), praises the recipients of the letter for their faithfulness, and exhorts them to continue in the love of Christ (vs 4-6). He warns against false teachers and suggests how to deal with these heretics (vs 7-11). The letter closes with the

hope that writer and recipients may soon meet again (2 Jn 12, 13).

III. The Third Epistle of John. A comparison of this epistle with the 2d indicates a common authorship. This epistle is a personal letter addressed to a certain *Gaius, otherwise unknown, a faithful believer whom John commends for his hospitality toward the apostles and other traveling teachers. The letter deals with the Christian's duty to extend hospitality to true teachers, and to beware of false teachers. As one who has distinguished himself by extending hospitality to itinerant preachers, Gaius will appreciate the counsel John gives. The schismatic tendencies of Diotrephes are to be firmly rejected. He seems to have been an elder in the church or to have held some other prominent position in it that afforded him an opportunity to speak against John (vs 9, 10). Furthermore, he had refused to entertain visiting preachers and had forbidden those under his charge to do so, and even had gone so far as to deprive them of membership in the church (v 10). Other instruction John has in mind must wait; he expects soon to visit the church of which Gaius is a member (vs 13, 14).

John, Gospel of. Since earliest times Christian tradition has unanimously attributed the Fourth Gospel to John the apostle. Like the other Gospel writers, the author of this Gospel does not identify himself directly. It is believed that "that disciple" of Jn 21:23, who is identified in v 20 as "the disciple whom Jesus loved" and in v 24 as "the disciple which testifieth of these things, and wrote these things," refers to John the apostle. On the basis that certain characteristic Gnostic terms, such as *logos,* "Word" (ch 1:1), and *plērōma,* "fulness" (v 16), occur in the Gospel of John, some 19th-cent. critical scholars asserted that the Fourth Gospel could not have been written until the latter half of the 2d cent. A.D., in view of the theory that Gnosticism did not flourish until that time. Accordingly, the critics concluded that the apostle John, who died toward the close of the 1st cent., could not possibly have been its author. Furthermore, some critics formerly held that John reflects a state of development in Christian thought, so they conjectured, that was not reached until the middle of the 2d cent. or later. Beginning in 1935, however, a series of remarkable discoveries has compelled critical scholars to abandon their theory of a late date for the Gospel of John. In that year a small scrap of papyrus smaller than the palm of one's hand, and containing portions of John 18 (vs 31-33, 37, 38)—known as the John Rylands Papyrus 457 (see fig. 269) and commonly designated P⁵²—was published. Leading authorities in papyrology agreed that this fragment must have been written about A.D. 125, making it the oldest known portion of any known NT manuscript. The same year there came to light in Egypt fragments of a previously unknown gospel narrative known as Egerton Papyrus II. The gospel narrative preserved in these fragments so closely resembles that of the canonical Gospels as to make it obvious that the writer borrowed from all of them in compiling his composite account. There are several close parallels to rather widely separated passages in the Fourth Gospel, as, for instance, its version of Jn 5:39: "Ye search the scriptures; in which ye think to have life, they are those that witness concerning me." Scholars agree that these fragments of an unknown Gospel must have been written in Egypt before the middle of the 2d cent., and that notable parallels to the canonical Gospels indicate that all 4 Gospels were in circulation in Egypt during the 1st half of the 2d cent. A.D. Furthermore, at Nag Hammadi (Chenoboskion) in Upper Egypt a large Gnostic library, of 40 different works contained in 13 volumes, was found in 1945. These manuscripts demonstrate conclusively that certain previously held opinions about the Gnostics are invalid, and that supposedly Gnostic terms in the Gospel of John were actually in common use in apostolic times. With these discoveries the entire argument for a late date for the Gospel has vanished, and critical scholars themselves admit that it must have been written toward the close of the 1st cent., which would be within the lifetime of the apostle whose name it bears. Some are still reluctant to acknowledge John the apostle as its author, and prefer to attribute it to the presbyter John or to some other person by that name. But the fact remains that the arguments formerly held to prove that John the apostle could not have written it have now been discredited. The publication since 1956 of Papyrus Bodmer II (designated P⁶⁶), containing almost the entire Fourth Gospel and assigned by scholars to the closing years of the 2d cent. —and thus only about 100 years after the writing of the Gospel—reveals a text almost identical with the one that has come down to us, further evidence of the care-

269. Both sides of the John Rylands Papyrus fragment of the Gospel of John (from the 1st half of the 2d cent.)

fulness with which the Scriptures have been copied.

When John wrote his Gospel, toward the close of the 1st cent., 3 great dangers threatened the life and purity of the church. One of these dangers was waning piety (Rev 2:4), a second was persecution, and the third was heretical teaching about the nature of Christ (see 1 Jn 2:19, 26). A certain Judeo-Gnostic, Cerinthus of Alexandria, taught that Jesus was the natural-born son of Joseph and Mary, and that the divine spirit entered His body at baptism and withdrew prior to His death on the cross. Another group of heretical teachers held Christ to have been only a phantom, and not a true human being at all. This latter teaching is known as the Docetic heresy. Both groups thus denied that Jesus of Nazareth was the Son of God, and that true divinity and true humanity were united in His one Person. In his 1st epistle, written, as generally held, about the same time as his Gospel, John refers to these false teachers as "antichrist" (chs 2: 18, 19, 22-24; 4:3-5). John repeatedly stresses the true humanity and true deity of Jesus Christ, and affirms that in Jesus Christ the two natures were united in the one Person (see chs 1:1-3; 2:22-24; 4:2, 3, 14; 5:20). John obviously wrote his Gospel to prove that Jesus Christ is indeed the divine Son of God (see Jn 1:1-3, 14; 3:13-17; 4:29; 5:17-39; 17:3-5; 19:7; etc.), presumably to confute the heretical teachings concerning the nature of Christ that gained acceptance during the closing decades of the 1st cent. The Fourth Gospel differs from the first 3 Gospels, commonly known as the Synoptics, in its manner of dealing with the gospel narrative. In scope and content it is almost altogether different from the Synoptic Gospels, being more theological than historical in its approach. John records only a little more than one fourth of the incidents of Christ's ministry that are recorded in the 4 Gospels, and of those reported nearly one third are not mentioned by the Synoptic writers. Thus, for information on the first year and a half of Jesus' ministry we are forced to depend almost exclusively on the Fourth Gospel. The successive mention of specific Passovers and other Jewish feasts strongly implies that John, alone among the Gospel writers, follows a strictly chronological sequence from beginning to end, by which it is possible to determine with reasonable exactness the length of Jesus' ministry and the general sequence of events.

Generally speaking, the incidents of Christ's life that John selected mark turning points and crises in the development of His mission, but in each instance John shows a greater interest in the significance of the event than he does in the event itself. This is evident from the fact that, in reporting an incident, he devotes most of his comment to its significance as explained in the discourses of the Saviour. He reports several such discourses at considerable length (for example, Jn 6 to 8; 14 to 17). These discourses are concerned almost exclusively with Jesus' identity as the incarnate Son of God and with the purpose of His earthly mission. Upon the solid historical framework of the life and ministry of Jesus, from which he selects incidents appropriate to his purpose, John builds an unanswerable argument designed to prove that Jesus of Nazareth is in reality the divine Son of God, the Messiah of the OT prophets. For a discussion of the value of the Fourth Gospel in arranging a chronology of the life of Christ, *see* Jesus Christ, III. John frankly declares that he wrote this account that his readers "might believe that Jesus is the Christ, the Son of God; and that believing" they "might have life through his name" (ch 20:31). He could have told much more (v 30) had he deemed it desirable to do so.

In his prologue John sets Jesus Christ forth as the Word of God incarnate (Jn 1:1-18). He next deals with Jesus' early public ministry, from His baptism to the 1st Passover (chs 1:19 to 2:12). John deals more fully with events during this period of Jesus' ministry, from His 1st to His 2d Passover (Jn 2:13 to 5:47), than he does with events during the Galilean ministry, between the 2d and 3d Passovers (ch 6). He discusses at some length incidents at the 1st Passover (chs 2:13 to 3:21) and the 2d Passover (ch 5). He passes over in silence the entire Galilean ministry, which is covered so fully by the Synoptic writers, relating only the incident that marked its close, the miracle of the loaves and the fishes, and Jesus' subsequent discussion of His mission to earth (ch 6). John is again silent on the period of Jesus' retirement from public ministry covering the 6 months following His 3d Passover at the close of the Galilean ministry, but takes up in great detail certain incidents that occurred during the Samarian-Perean ministry (chs 7 to 11), though he says nothing whatever of the ministry in Samaria and Perea. The incidents he does select all take place in Jerusalem or its vicinity, and all depict Jesus in conflict with the Jewish leaders— at the Feast of Tabernacles (chs 7:2 to 10:21), the Feast of Dedication (ch 10:22-42), and the raising of Lazarus (ch 11). John's obvious purpose is to trace in considerable detail the steps by which the Jewish leaders came to condemn Jesus and to reject Him as the Messiah. John devotes nearly half of his Gospel to the crucifixion week (chs 12:1 to 19:42) and the postresurrection period. The resurrection is discussed in ch 20:1-18, and certain postresurrection appearances in considerable detail in chs 20:19 to 21:23. A brief epilogue states his purpose in writing.

John, The Revelation of. *See* Revelation, Book of.

Joiada (joi′á-dá), KJV once **Jehoiada** (jĕ-hoi′á-dá). [Heb. *Yôyada‘*, "Yahweh knows."]

1. A Jew who repaired one of Jerusalem's gates in the time of Nehemiah (Neh 3:6).

2. A high priest who was great-grandson of Jeshua and son of Eliashib (Neh 12:10, 11, 22). When Nehemiah returned to Jerusalem for his second term as governor of Judea, he found that a son of Joiada had married a daughter of Sanballat of Samaria. Nehemiah therefore expelled him, probably from Jerusalem (ch 13:28).

Joiakim (joi′á-kĭm). [Heb. *Yôyaqîm*, "Yahweh establishes."] A high priest in postexilic Jerusalem, son of Jeshua and father of Eliashib (Neh 12:10, 12, 26).

Joiarib (joi′á-rĭb). [Heb. *Yôyarîb*, a short-

ened form of *Yehôyarîb*, Jehoiarib, "Yahweh pleads" or "Yahweh contends."]

1. The head of a priestly family, who
returned from Babylonia with Zerubbabel
(Neh 12:6). The family of Joiarib is also
mentioned in the next generation (v 19),
and in the time of Nehemiah (ch 11:10).
The Hasmonaeans, the famous king-
priests of the 2d and 1st cent. B.C., are said
to be descended from a certain Joarib (1
Macc 2:1). The priestly family of Joiarib
may be that of Jehoiarib. *See* Jehoiarib.

2. A "man of understanding" who returned from Babylonia with Ezra. Ezra
sent him with some other men from the
camp on the river Ahava to solicit Levites
and Nethinim (Temple servants) for the
service of the Temple (Ezr 8:16, 17).

3. A Judahite whose father's name was
Zechariah (Neh 11:5).

Jokdeam (jŏk'dē-ăm). [Heb. *Yoqde'am*.] A
town in the hill country of Judah (Jos
15:56), which is probably *Khirbet Raqa'*,
about 4 mi. south of Hebron.

Jokim (jō'kĭm). [Heb. *Yôqîm*, "Yahweh establishes."] A Judahite (1 Chr 4:22).

Jokmeam (jŏk'mē-ăm), KJV once **Jokneam**
(jŏk'nē-ăm). [Heb. *Yoqme'am*, "let the
people arise."]

1. A city in the territory of Ephraim
assigned to the Levites (1 Chr 6:68). It
may be the city called Kibzaim (kĭb-zā'ĭm)
[Heb. *Qibṣayim*] in Jos 21:22.

2. A town in the neighborhood of
Abel-meholah (1 Ki 4:12). Some identify
this town with Jokmeam, 1, but such an
identification is uncertain.

Jokneam (jŏk'nē-ăm). [Heb. *Yoqne'am*; mentioned in Egyptian texts of Thutmose III
as *'n-qn'm*.]

1. One of the royal Canaanite cities,
located in the area of Mount Carmel (Jos
12:22). It was a border town of Zebulun
(ch 19:11), and was assigned to the Merarite Levites (ch 21:34). It has been identified with *Tell Qeimûn*, 7 mi. northwest
of Megiddo.

2. For 1 Ki 4:12, KJV, *see* Jokmeam, 2.

Jokshan (jŏk'shăn). [Heb. *Yoqshan*.] A son
of Abraham and Keturah (Gen 25:1-3;
1 Chr 1:32). He became the ancestor of
the Dedan and Sheba tribes of Arabia.

Joktan (jŏk'tăn). [Heb. *Yoqtan*, probably
"the small one," that is, "the younger
(brother)."] A descendant of Shem through
Eber, and ancestor of 13 tribes of Arabia
(Gen 10:25-29; 1 Chr 1:19-23). Map IV,
C-6.

Joktheel (jŏk'thē-ĕl). [Heb. *Yoqthe'el*, a
shortened form of *Yeqûthî'el* (Jekuthiel),

meaning, possibly, "God is perfection."]

1. A town in Judah near Lachish
(Jos 15:33, 38); not identified.

2. A name given by Amaziah, king of
Judah, to Sela (later called Petra, Map V,
B-7), the capital of the Edomites (2 Ki
14:7).

Jona. *See* John, 2.

Jonadab (jŏn'à-dăb). [Heb. *Yônadab* and
Yehônadab, "Yahweh is bounteous."]

1. David's nephew who planned his
cousin Amnon's rape of Tamar (2 Sa 13:
3-6).

2. For the Rechabite *see* Jehonadab.

Jonah (jō'nà), KJV of NT **Jonas** (jō'nàs).
[Heb. *Yônah*, "dove"; Gr. *Iōnas*.] A
prophet of the northern kingdom of Israel whose ministry came probably before
or during the early part of the reign of
Jeroboam II (*c.* 793 - *c.* 753 B.C.), nearly 1½
cent. after the death of Solomon and
the division of the kingdom *c.* 931 B.C.
He was the son of Amittai (Jon 1:1), and
his home was Gath-hepher in Galilee (2
Ki 14:25). Aside from the information
given in the book of Jonah, the only fact
known about him is that at some time
during the reign of Jeroboam, or earlier,
he predicted the restoration of the northern border of Israel (v 25). Somewhat in
the manner of Elijah the Tishbite, Jonah
appears suddenly on the scene when
God sends him to Nineveh (Jon 1:2).
Having no desire to go as a prophet to a
foreign city such as Nineveh, and being
unconcerned about the conversion of its
inhabitants, Jonah sets out in the opposite direction, for Tarshish, probably the
classical Tartessus on the southern coast
of Spain (v 3). As the ship sails most
probably northward within sight of the
coast, it encounters a violent storm, which
its master attributes to the anger of the
gods against someone on board. By the
casting of lots Jonah is revealed as the

270. The mound of *Nebi Yûnus*, inside the city of
ancient Nineveh. The mosque in the right center is
believed by the local population to be the burial place
of the prophet Jonah

guilty person (Jon 1:7-11). With remarkable physical courage he proposes that he be cast overboard, in order that the storm may abate and the ship be saved (v 12). This demonstration of physical courage stands in sharp contrast with Jonah's moral cowardice in attempting to run away from God. Although Jonah is cast overboard, his life is spared by "a great fish" (v 17), in whose belly he spends the next "three days and three nights"—one 24-hour period, together with unspecified portions of the day preceding and the day following. Jonah's prayer of repentance is honored, and the fish deposits him "upon the dry land" (ch 2:1, 10). He may now have found himself opposite the island of Cyprus, as much as 150 mi. nearer to Nineveh than when he had boarded the ship. God once more commissions him to go to Nineveh, and he responds without further question (ch 3:1-3). The Ninevites repent and God spares the city (vs 5-10). Despite the mercy shown him, Jonah resents God's mercy extended to the people of Nineveh (ch 4:1, 2), and is "very angry." But by an object lesson God shows Jonah the folly of his attitude and justifies the decision to spare the people of Nineveh (vs 4-11).

Jonah, Book of. Fifth of the so-called Minor Prophets. Ancient Jewish tradition attributed the book to Jonah, a position uniformly rejected by modern critical scholarship. The book nowhere claims the prophet Jonah as its author, but reasoning by analogy from the fact that other prophetic works of the OT bear the writer's name as the title, there is no valid reason for assuming the book of Jonah to be an exception to what is otherwise the general rule. Of course, the title of the book might be considered simply as the name of its principal character, which would not challenge its authenticity. On the basis of certain Aramaic words and expressions, many modern scholars have suggested a postexilic authorship, though without necessarily denying its historical basis. However, recent discoveries have proved that the supposedly late Aramaic words and expressions were actually in use centuries before the time of Jonah. There is no objective evidence to indicate that the book of Jonah could not have been written at the time the prophet himself lived. Jonah's use of the 3d person personal pronoun is in keeping with the style of other prophets, such as Isaiah (see Is 8:3), Jeremiah (Jer 20:1-3), Dan-

iel (Dan 1:6-12), etc., and by numerous other ancient writers, such as Xenophon and Caesar. According to 2 Ki 14:25, Jonah prophesied the restoration of Israel's northern boundary in the reign of Jeroboam II. Accordingly, his ministry may be dated in the early part of the 8th cent., probably during the early part of the reign of Jeroboam II (c. 793 - c. 753 B.C.). The record in v 25 also makes clear that Jonah bore a message to his own people as well as to the Assyrians in Nineveh. For a century and a half the northern kingdom had been separated from Judah, and the course of its history was characterized by ever-deepening apostasy and national corruption. The long reign of Jeroboam II witnessed a revival of prosperity and an extension of the boundaries of Israel to include all except Judah that had belonged to the Hebrew kingdom during the golden age of David and Solomon. Jonah had pictured this state of affairs, it apparently being God's intention to grant the nation a period of favor as an inducement to return to the true God. Nevertheless, Jeroboam "did that which was evil in the sight of the Lord" (v 24), as did his successors, and some 30 years later the kingdom came to an inglorious end.

The book of Jonah differs from the books of all the other OT prophets in that its only message was addressed to the people of a foreign nation. Furthermore, the book is strictly narrative in form, and contains no direct message from the Lord except His command to the Ninevites to repent. The question naturally arises as to why the book of Jonah was accorded a place in the sacred canon. The answer doubtless lies in the fact that the narrative contained a lesson of value to Israel. In the first place, it condemns the intolerant prejudice of the Hebrew patriot, who refused to admit that non-Israelites could be considered eligible to salvation. It is certainly not likely that Jonah would have related a story that places him in so unfavorable a light unless, later, he came to realize his error and to sense that a report of the experience would help his fellow Israelites. In addition, the book lays stress on God's great mercy, demonstrated in sparing the lives of the heathen seamen (Jon 1:15), in sparing Jonah's life despite his disobedience (chs 1:17 to 2:10), in giving the Ninevites an opportunity to repent and in averting punishment when they did so (ch 3:2, 10), and in His patient dealings with Jonah

(Jon 4:1-11). The narrative also reveals the simple means God often employs to accomplish His will (see chs 1:4, 17; 2:10; 4:6-8).

The book of Jonah has doubtless attracted sharper criticisms than any other portion of Scripture. From a human point of view the account is incredible, despite recent documented instances of similar character, since in the natural course of events Jonah could never have come through his experience alive. However, the question is not whether Jonah's experience can be demonstrated on a scientific basis, but whether God ever acts in supernatural ways to accomplish His purposes. For those who accept Jesus Christ as the Son of God, our Lord's simple declaration that the prophet "was three days and three nights in the whale's belly" (Mt 12:39, 40) is sufficient documentation of the miracle.

Summoned to announce the doom of Nineveh—obviously with an invitation to repent (cf. Jon 3:5-10)—Jonah sets out in the opposite direction, intending to flee "from the presence of the Lord" (ch 1:2, 3). The seeming hopelessness of the mission to Nineveh and of the prospect that its non-Israelite population might repent, led Jonah to shrink from the commission. His escape is thwarted, however, by a great storm, and as he is thrown overboard his life is spared by "a great fish" (vs 4-17). Now repentant, the prophet prays for deliverance, and is returned to land (ch 2). Bidden again to go preach in Nineveh, Jonah complies (ch 3:1-3), and the people repent (vs 4-10). Strangely enough, however, Jonah himself remains perversely impenitent, and is, in fact, so angry because the Ninevites heeded his warning that he implores the Lord to let him die (ch 4:1-3). His distorted sense of values is evident from his utter indifference toward the Ninevites and his great concern over the gourd that has withered. To God's question, "Doest thou well to be angry for the gourd?" he petulantly replies, "I do well to be angry, even unto death" (v 9). The story closes abruptly with God's affirmation that the lives of the people of Nineveh are of infinitely greater value than the gourd (vs 10, 11).

Jonam (jō′năm), KJV **Jonan** (jō′năn). [Gr. *Iōnam*, possibly from Heb. *Yôchanan*, "Yahweh is gracious."] A Judahite appearing in Luke's genealogy of Jesus Christ (Lk 3:30).

Jonan. *See* Jonam.

Jonas. *See* John, 2.

Jonathan (jŏn′á-thăn). [Heb. *Yônathan* and *Yehônathan*, "Yahweh has given."]

1. A Gershonite Levite and descendant of Moses (Jgs 18:30, RSV). The KJV, following Masoretic tradition, makes him a grandson of Manasseh. The Jews of the Masoretic age, thinking it a disgrace for Moses that one of his descendants had become an idol priest, inserted an *n* above the line in the name of Moses of Jgs 18:30 so that in the Hebrew consonantal spelling it would be read Manasseh (*Mnshh*) instead of Moses (*Mshh*). Since the inserted letter was not incorporated into the text, but was suspended above the line, it is easily recognized as not being part of the original text.

Jonathan was an inhabitant of Bethlehem. While traveling through Ephraim in search of work he met Micah, an Ephraimite, who hired him to officiate as the priest of an idol that he had set up in his house (Jgs 17:1-13). When, shortly afterward, the Danites passed through Ephraim on their way north in search of new territory, they stole Micah's idol and persuaded Jonathan to go with them and to continue to be the officiating priest for this idol, but now on behalf of the tribe of Dan. They set up the idol in a shrine at Dan, and the descendants of Jonathan long remained priests of this idolatrous shrine (ch 18:2-6, 14-30).

2. The eldest son of King Saul (1 Sa 14:49), and commander of an army corps (ch 13:2). He smote a Philistine garrison stationed at Geba, and as a result, precipitated war between Israel and the Philistines. He then made a surprise attack on the Philistines at Michmash, which created such confusion in their camp that Saul won an easy victory. In the ensuing pursuit Jonathan ate some wild honey, and thus unknowingly broke a prohibition of his father that no one, under penalty of death, should eat anything during the pursuit of the enemy. This nearly cost Jonathan's life, but the people intervened and prevented Saul from killing his son (chs 13:3-7; 14:1-46). When David slew Goliath, Jonathan became a friend of the valiant shepherd boy from Bethlehem (ch 18:1-4). Their friendship grew deeper as the years went by, in spite of the enmity of Saul against David. This unselfish friendship almost cost Jonathan his life when Saul in a fit of anger threw a javelin at him for defending David, who he knew would be-

come the future king of Israel (1 Sa 19: 1-7; 20:1-42). Later, when David lived in southern Judah as a fugitive from Saul's wrath, the two friends had their last recorded meeting (ch 23:16-18). Jonathan perished with his father and two brothers in the battle of Gilboa, in which the Israelites were defeated by the Philistines (1 Sa 31:1, 2; 1 Chr 10:1, 2). His body, with those of other members of the royal family, was fastened to the wall of Beth-shean. But the men of Jabesh-gilead, in gratitude for having been saved by Saul on an earlier occasion, crossed the Jordan, rescued the bodies, and gave them an honorable burial (1 Sa 31:10-13; 1 Chr 10:8-12). David was deeply moved by Jonathan's death and mourned for him, composing the beautiful elegy recorded in 2 Sa 1:17-27. Jonathan left one lame son, Mephibosheth (or Merib-baal), to whom David showed kindness for Jonathan's sake (chs 4:4; 9:1-13; 19:24-30). Jonathan's descendants of several generations are listed in the Bible (1 Chr 8:34-40; 9: 40-44).

3. An uncle of King David, who was a wise counselor and a scribe (1 Chr 27: 32). Some commentators think that the word "uncle" here has the meaning of "relative" and that this Jonathan is identical with Jonathan, 4, a nephew of David.

4. A son of David's brother Shimei. He distinguished himself by slaying a giant from Gath (2 Sa 21:21, 22; some think he is identical with Jonathan, 3).

5. A son of the high priest Abiathar; he served, during Absalom's rebellion, as a messenger between David and the loyal courtiers in Jerusalem. With Ahimaaz, Zadok's son, he hid in a well at Bahurim, northeast of Jerusalem, and passed on to David the information that came to him (2 Sa 15:27, 36; 17:15-22). He was also the first to bring the news of Solomon's coronation to Adonijah and his fellow conspirators, who had gathered to proclaim Adonijah king (1 Ki 1:41-49).

6. One of David's "mighty men" (2 Sa 23:32; 1 Chr 11:34).

7. Son of Uzziah; one of David's treasurers (1 Chr 27:25, RSV).

8. A secretary, or scribe, in whose house the prophet Jeremiah was imprisoned (Jer 37:15). He is possibly identical with *Jonathan, 9.

9. According to the KJV, an officer of Zedekiah's army who had not been captured by Nebuchadnezzar's army and who went to Mizpah in submission to Geda-

liah's new regime (Jer 40:8). If his name belongs to the text he may be identical with Jonathan, 8. (The RSV omits this name on evidence from certain versions and manuscripts.)

10. A Judahite (1 Chr 2:32, 33).

11. The father of the leader of 50 men of the family of Adin who were among those returning from Babylonia with Ezra (Ezr 8:6).

12. A man in Jerusalem in Ezra's time who opposed the method adopted for the putting away of the foreign wives certain Jews had married (Ezr 10:15).

13. A priest, head of a family in Nehemiah's day (Neh 12:35). Some make him identical with *Jehonathan, 2.

14. A priest in the days when Joiakim was high priest (Neh 12:14).

15. A high priest, son of Joiada (Neh 12:11), apparently the priest otherwise known as Johanan. See Johanan, 10.

Jonath-elem-rechokim (jō'năth-ē'lĕm-rē-ko'-kĭm). [Heb. *yônath 'elem rechoqîm*.] An expression appearing in the superscription of Ps 56, KJV. The Hebrew phrase may be translated "The Dove of the Far-off Oaks," or "The Dove on Far-off Terebinths" (RSV). The expression may reflect the feelings of the psalmist, who, as a fugitive in a foreign land, felt like a dove driven from its nesting place. More probably it is the title of a song according to the melody of which Ps 56 was to be intoned.

Joppa (jŏp'à), KJV once **Japho** (jā'fō). [Heb. *Yaphô'.* "beauty"; mentioned by Thutmose III in the 15th cent. B.C. as *Ypw*, in the *Amarna Letters, a century later, as *Yapu*, and in Phoenician inscriptions as *Ypy*; Gr. *Ioppē.*] An ancient Canaanite city on the coast of Palestine, mentioned as a city on the border of the tribe of Dan (Jos 19:46), but apparently never occupied by the Israelites in OT times. Being the only seaport between Egypt and the Carmel ridge, unless Dor is counted, it was of great importance for inland Palestine. It was about 34 mi. northwest of Jerusalem (*see* Japho on Map VI, D-2). The cedars from Lebanon used in the building of the Temple of Solomon and that of Zerubbabel entered Palestine through this port (2 Chr 2:16; Ezr 3:7). It was there that the prophet Jonah, fleeing from God's command, embarked on a ship bound for *Tarshish, probably in Spain (Jon 1:3). Joppa was brought under Jewish control, probably for the first time, by the Maccabees, who settled Jews in the city, enlarged the harbor and strength-

271. The old city of Joppa, on the Mediterranean Sea

ened its fortifications (1 Macc 10:74, 75; 12:33, 34; 14:5, 34). Pompey made it a semi-free city in 63 B.C., but Caesar restored it to the Jews. In the time of the Herods it became a stronghold of orthodox Jewry. When the Jewish rebellion broke out in A.D. 66 the Jews of Joppa showed such a fanatical opposition against the Romans that Cestius Gallus massacred more than 8,000 of them. Although the city recovered from this catastrophe, it was completely destroyed by Vespasian a little later.

Christianity found an early entrance into Joppa. The city was the home town of Tabitha, or Dorcas, a great benefactor of the poor. When she died, Peter raised her from the dead, with the result that "many believed" in the message of the apostle (Acts 9:36-42). Peter remained in the city for some time with Simon the tanner (see fig. 240) and had a vision that showed him that the gospel had to go to the Gentiles, and that no distinction was to be made between Jews and Gentiles (ch 10:5-48). Joppa, now called Jaffa, is at the present time a section of the twin cities Jaffa-Tel Aviv with a combined population of 365,000, being thus the largest city of the State of Israel.

Joppa, Sea of. An expression found in Ezr 3:7, KJV, where a preferable translation would be "to the sea, to Joppa" as the RSV has it.

Jorah. *See* Hariph, 1.

Jorai (jō′rā-ī). [Heb. *Yôray.*] A Gadite (1 Chr 5:13).

Joram (jō′răm). [Heb. *Yôram,* "Yahweh is exalted." The name is a shortened form of *Yehôram,* Jehoram; Gr. *Iôram.*]
1. A son of King Toi of Hamath on the Orontes in Syria. His father sent him to congratulate David, who had gained a noted victory over Hadadezer (2 Sa 8:10). He is called Hadoram in 1 Chr 18:10, meaning probably "Hadad is exalted."
2. A Levite descended from Eliezer, a

JORDAN

son of Moses (1 Chr 26:25; cf. ch 23:15-17).
3. A king of Israel. *See* Jehoram, 1.
4. A king of Judah. *See* Jehoram, 3.

Jordan (jôr′d'n). [Heb. *Yarden,* "descender"; Gr. *Iordanēs.*] The most important river of Palestine, which divides the country into 2 parts: western Palestine (the land of Canaan), the more important and richer part, and Transjordan. Map II, B-3. The sources of the Jordan are located on the western side of Mount Hermon, the southernmost ridge of the Anti-Lebanon Mountains. Four streams eventually combine to form the river Jordan.

The easternmost of these 4 rivers is the 5-mi.-long *Nahr Bâniyâs,* the Paneas River. Its source lies 1,085 ft. above sea level at the famous grotto of Paneas, named in Hellenistic times after the Greek god Pan. The next, the *Nahr el-Leddan,* is a much shorter river, emanating from a copious spring near the ancient city of Dan, now *Tell el-Qâdî,* 476 ft. above sea level. The next, the *Nahr el-Ḥasbânî,* is the longest of the 4 feeder rivers. From its source, which lies at an altitude of 1,730 ft., it flows for about 24 mi. along the western slope of Mount Hermon. The westernmost river is the *Nahr Bereighith,* originating near the ancient city of Ijon, now *Tell ed-Dibbin,* also 1,800 ft. above sea level.

The 4 rivers join south of Hermon and then form 1 stream, the Jordan, called *esh-Sheri'ah el-Kebireh* by the Arabs. From the last junction, 142 ft. above sea level, the river flows for 7 mi. through a fertile plain with subtropical vegetation. Part of it is marshland, with a profuse growth of papyrus plants that until recently were made into mats by the Arabs. The government of Israel has been draining the marshes in order to reclaim the land for useful purposes.

The first of the 3 lakes formed by the Jordan is Lake Huleh (*Bahret el-Hûleh*), called Lake Semechonitis by Josephus. Many modern writers have mistakenly identified this lake with the "waters of Merom" (Jos 11:5), which are some 10 mi. southwest of Lake Huleh (*see* Merom). This little lake was formerly 7 ft. above sea level, 3 mi. long and 2 mi. wide in its northern part, and its depth varied from 9 to 16 ft.; but it has now been drained by the Israelis and converted into fields through which the Jordan flows.

After leaving Lake Huleh the river flows for about 2 mi. at a steady rate until it reaches the "Bridge of the Daughters of Jacob" (*Jisr Banat Ya'qub*), over

597

272. Air view of the tortuous course of the Jordan at the junction of the Jabbok

which runs the main highway from Galilee to Damascus. Then the river runs through a narrow, steep basalt gorge, which forms many cataracts, and descends about 600 ft. in the next 7 mi. Emerging from this gorge it enters a small plain, and for the last mile before entering the Sea of Galilee flows rather quietly. In the distance of about 10 mi. between the 2 lakes, the level of the river has dropped from 7 ft. above sea level to about 685 ft. below sea level, a drop of nearly 700 ft.

The Sea of Galilee, well known to every Christian from the stories of Christ's life, is called the Sea of Chinneroth, or Chinnereth, in the OT (Jos 12:3; 13:27), from a city named *Chinnereth, near its northwestern shore. The lake is about 13 mi. long and has a maximum width of about 8 mi. near the center. Its maximum depth is 150 ft. The lake is fed not only by the Jordan but also by a number of lesser streams that enter it at the northeastern shore and at the western bulge, and by many hot and cold underwater springs. The lake has always contained an abundance of fish.

The Jordan leaves the Sea of Galilee at its southwestern corner and then becomes the most crooked river in the world, meandering toward the south in innumerable curves. Because of the many twists and turns the river travels 200 mi. to cover the straight-line distance of less than 65 mi. between the Sea of Galilee and the Dead Sea (see fig. 272). A number of tributaries swell the volume of water in the river. The tributaries from the west are insignificant, but the Yarmuk and Jabbok of Transjordan are important rivers; the former carries, at its junction with the Jordan, almost as much water as the Jordan itself.

In its course from the Sea of Galilee the Jordan descends another 600 ft. until it reaches the level of the Dead Sea, 1,286 ft. below sea level, the lowest area on earth (see Dead Sea). The average fall of the river is therefore about 9 ft. for every mile in a straight line, or 3 ft. for every mile of its winding river bed. Its flow is swift, causing many whirlpools and rapids that make navigation perilous, although it has been navigated a few times, notably in small steel boats, a trip described in the "Official Report of the United States Expedition to Explore the Dead Sea and the Jordan River." The expedition was directed by Lt. W. F. Lynch in 1848.

The broad river valley, which is from 3 to 12 mi. wide, is called in Arabic el-Ghor, "the lowland" (Map II, B-3). Within it is another depression, rimmed by weird-looking grayish marl hills about 100 ft. high called qattarahs, on which nothing grows. The lower depression in which the river flows is called the Zor, "thicket," an appropriate name for it since it contains dense junglelike vegetation in many areas. This thicket was a haven for wild animals in ancient times (Jer 49:19). The river itself is from 90 to 100 ft. wide and 3 to 10 ft. deep.

The settlements which grew up in the Ghor were not found in the Zor but above it, usually on the banks of tributaries of the Jordan. However, only a few places on the western bank were suitable for habitation. One was at the Nahr Jâlûd, which formed the eastern extension of the Valley of Jezreel. On and near its banks were found several important settlements. Another such area was formed by the Wâdī Fâr'ah, which received its water from a spring that lies northeast of Shechem. The 3d place was the Jericho plain, where the Wâdī Qelt joins the Jordan. A copious spring in this area, now called 'Ain es-Sulṭân, provided attractive conditions for a townsite, and a settlement grew up there in the dawn of Palestinian history, as recent excavations have shown. The earliest remains of Tell es-Sulṭân, ancient Jericho, go back farther in remote history than those of any other site ever excavated in Palestine. See Jericho.

The several tributaries that join the Jordan from the east formed small plains at their mouths, with fertile ground, where agriculture was possible. On these, settlements sprang up. The largest of these plains lay immediately northeast of the Dead Sea. Its name, "the plains of Moab" (Num 22:1; etc.), indicates that at some early time in history it must have been occupied by the Moabites.

Biblical passages referring to the Jordan deal mainly with that part of the river between the Sea of Galilee and the Dead Sea. Since no bridges crossed the Jordan in pre-Roman times, the river had to be forded or crossed by boat. In the upper part, north of the mouth of the Jabbok, fords provide easy crossings at a number of places, but in the southern section the current of the Jordan is rapid. Many people have lost their lives in attempts to cross the river in this section. The Israelites crossed the Jordan at the latitude of Jericho, where a miracle enabled them to pass over dry shod (Jos 3:1-17; 4:1-24; Ps 114:3, 5). The Biblical account of this miracle makes it clear that they crossed in the spring, when the Jordan was at flood stage, swelled by the melting snow waters from Mount Hermon. When the priests stepped into the water, the river stopped its flow at Adam, modern *Tell ed-Dâmiyeh,* 22 mi. north of the Dead Sea, and the water south of Adam ran on into the Dead Sea, leaving dry a long stretch of river bed (Jos 3:14-17; 4:15, 16).

Several dammings up by earthquakes at the same place have been recorded in historical times. On the night of Dec. 8, A.D. 1267, a high mound overlooking the river, near *ed-Dâmiyeh,* fell into the stream and dammed it up so that for 16 hours no water was in the river bed south of the natural dam. In the meantime the water north of *ed-Dâmiyeh* flooded the surrounding land, but finally forced a breach in the dam of earth and reclaimed its old river bed. Similar cases are reported to have occurred in 1546 and 1906. Again during the severe earthquake on July 11, 1927, which destroyed much property and many lives, a high cliff at *ed-Dâmiyeh* fell into the river and completely dammed it up, so that for 21½ hours the lower river bed was dry and

273. The river Jordan as seen from the hills of Gilead

people crossed and recrossed it on foot at will (John Garstang, *The Foundations of Bible History* [London, 1931], pp. 136, 137; D. H. Kallner, Amiran, *IEJ* 1 [1950-1951], 229, 236, 245). Some think that for the Israelite crossing under Joshua, God possibly caused an earthquake to produce a landslide to dam up the river at the precise time when the Israelites were ready to cross, thus using, as on other occasions, natural means to perform His miracles. See fig. 5.

Jacob and his family crossed the Jordan probably somewhere near the mouth of the Jabbok (Gen 33:17, 18). The Midianites, pursued by Gideon and his forces, seem to have crossed it north of the Jabbok, near Succoth (Jgs 7:24; 8:4, 5). David, when fleeing before Absalom with a band of faithful followers, crossed the Jordan probably somewhere near Jericho, and this crossing—perhaps by boat—seems to have taken the group all night to accomplish (2 Sa 17:22). Also the crossing of Absalom and his forces is reported, and later that of David on his return to Jerusalem (chs 17:24; 19:15-18, 39). Twice a dry passageway through the Jordan was miraculously prepared in the time of Elijah and Elisha, first to allow the 2 prophets to cross the river, and then for Elisha to recross it (2 Ki 2:5-8, 13-15). The Jordan played a role in the life of Elisha once more when he required Naaman, the Syrian officer, to wash himself 7 times in that river in order to be cleansed from his leprosy (ch 5:10, 14). Jesus Christ was baptized in this river by John (Mt 3:13-16; cf. Jn 3:23). See fig. 268.

Jorim (jō'rĭm). [Gr. *Iōrim* from the Heb. *Yehôram,* "Yahweh is high."] A Judahite in Luke's genealogy of Jesus (Lk 3:29).

Jorkeam (jôr'kē-ăm), KJV **Jorkoam** (jôr'kō-ăm). [Heb. *Yorqo'am.*] Either the son of Raham, of the family of Caleb (1 Chr 2:44), or the name of a place peopled by descendants of Raham. It has not been identified. Some think it to be identical with *Jokdeam.

Jorkoam. *See* Jorkeam.

Josabad. *See* Jozabad, 1.

Josaphat. *See* Jehoshaphat.

Jose. *See* Jesus, 2.

Josech (jō'sĕk). [Gr. *Iōsēch.*] A Judahite appearing in Luke's genealogy of Jesus Christ (Lk 3:26, RSV). The KJV, following a different Greek text, has "Joseph."

Josedech. *See* Jehozadak.

Joseph (jō'zĕf). [Heb. *Yôseph,* "may he add," from the root *yasaph,* "to add," according to Gen 30:24; v 23 seems to indicate that the author also had in mind the similarly sounding verb *'asaph,* "to take away," that is, the reproach of barrenness. Gr. *Iōsēph.*]

1. The son of Jacob, born to his beloved wife Rachel after a long period of barrenness. At his birth his father Jacob had served Laban 14 years, hence was 91 years old (cf. Gen 41:46, 47; 45:6; 47:9); this was 6 years before the family returned to Canaan (chs 30:22-26; 31:41). Because Joseph was the first-born son of his favored wife, Jacob showed favoritism to the boy, especially after Rachel's death. He demonstrated this attitude by providing Joseph with an expensive garment, such as was worn by noble youths (ch 37: 3). The jealousy created by this was increased when Joseph told his brothers 2 dreams in which he had seen all the members of his family, including his parents, doing obeisance to him (vs 4-11). When he was 17 years of age his father sent him to Shechem to visit his brothers, who were pasturing the family's flocks there. Reaching Shechem he found that they had passed on to Dothan, so he sought them there. As soon as they saw him they conspired to kill him, but Reuben, hoping to save him, persuaded the others to throw him into an empty cistern instead. However, when in Reuben's absence a caravan of Ishmaelites and Midianites came along, traveling to Egypt, the other brothers sold him to these traders as a slave. To deceive their father they stained Joseph's garment with the blood of a goat killed for that purpose, and took the bloodstained coat to their father, saying that they had found it. Jacob concluded that Joseph had been torn to pieces by a wild animal (vs 12-33).

On his arrival in Egypt Joseph was sold to Potiphar, an Egyptian captain of the royal bodyguard (Gen 39:1).

Joseph's faithfulness and ability won the confidence of Potiphar so that he was made steward of his master's household. However, his handsomeness created lustful feelings in the heart of his master's wife. When he persistently refused her approaches she accused him of lustful intent. As a result he was imprisoned. Soon, however, he gained the confidence of the jailer through his faithfulness, and obtained a position of trust in the prison. It was there that he was able to interpret the dreams and predict the fate of 2 fellow prisoners, the royal butler and the royal baker (Gen 39:1 to 40:23).

Two years later, some 13 years after Joseph had been sold into slavery, Pharaoh had disturbing dreams which his magicians were unable to explain. Then the royal butler, long since restored to his office, remembered Joseph and told Pharaoh about his own experience with him. Summoned to interpret the dreams to Pharaoh, Joseph told him that Egypt would experience first 7 years of plenty and then 7 years of famine, and counseled the king to store up grain during the first 7 years for the years of want. Seeing Joseph's wisdom, Pharaoh appointed this 30-year-old slave as vizier—the second man in the kingdom—publicly endowing him with all necessary authority (Gen 41:1-46).

Joseph married Asenath, a daughter of the priest of On (Heliopolis), the city in which was located the great temple dedicated to the sun-god Ra. Two sons, Manasseh and Ephraim, were born to Joseph during the 7 years of plenty. Meanwhile he was engaged in storing up foodstuffs for the coming years of famine, when the *Nile would fail the country because of a lack of rainfall in the highlands of Abyssinia and in central Africa. When this drought came, it also affected western Asia and created famine conditions in Canaan. Consequently, Jacob's sons, like other people of Canaan, went to Egypt to purchase grain. They appeared before Joseph, not recognizing in this great official—Egyptian in dress, language, and customs—the brother whom they had sold 20 years before. But Joseph recognized them immediately. Remembering his boyish dreams of long ago, and the jealousy and cruelty of his brothers, he began to test them in various ways. At the same time, the sons of Jacob, thinking of their brother who they supposed was still a slave in Egypt, suffered much anguish and remorse over their mistreatment of him. Finally, on their 2d trip to Egypt at the end of 2 years of famine, he revealed himself to them (Gen 42:1 to 45:8), convinced them of his kind intentions, and sent for his father and the whole family to come down to Egypt. He settled them in Goshen, probably the fertile *Wâdī Ṭumilât,* not far from the Hyksos capital of Egypt —Avaris, Tanis, or *Zoan (Gen 45:9 to 46:30; cf. Ps 78:12, 13). Fearing that his brothers would not be able to withstand the temptations of Egyptian court life, he counseled them to remain *shepherds, following an occupation despised by the Egyptians. This would give them an opportunity to remain separate from the

JOSEPH

pagans and to live together in a section of the country assigned to them (Gen 46:31-34). Pharaoh gave the family a great welcome upon their arrival in Egypt, and granted Jacob an audience.

During the following 5 years of want the country went through hard times, and the Egyptian people were forced to sell all their property, and finally even themselves, to the royal house to obtain food; except for the priests and the temple properties, all land reverted to the Pharaoh, and the occupants thenceforth paid a fifth of the harvest to the king (Gen 47:13-26). Joseph at the same time cared well for his relatives. Shortly before Jacob died, he blessed Joseph's two sons, Ephraim and Manasseh, and adopted them as his own sons; consequently Joseph's descendants formed not one but two tribes. When Jacob passed away he was embalmed according to Egyptian custom and taken to the family sepulcher at Hebron in Canaan for burial. Joseph assured his apprehensive brothers that they would have nothing to fear from him even after their father's death (chs 47:1-12, 27-31; 48:1-20; 49:33; 50:1-21). Joseph reached the age of 110 years, which in Egyptian literature was considered as the perfect age, and before his death charged his descendants to take his bones to Canaan for burial when they should return to the Promised Land (ch 50:22-26). In compliance with his wishes, at the time of the Exodus his embalmed body was taken by the children of Israel to Canaan and buried near Shechem (Ex 13:19; Jos 24:32).

Joseph's 2 sons became the ancestors of 2 large and important tribes, Ephraim and Manasseh, but the name Joseph is frequently used in the OT to denote the combined tribes or the northern kingdom as a whole (Jos 16:1, 4; Jgs 1:22; 1 Ki 11:28; Ps 78:67; Eze 37:16; etc.).

The story of Joseph shows a true Egyptian setting in numerous details, and fits best into the Hyksos period, when the Pharaohs were foreigners, mostly Semitic (see Egypt, V, 6). This is the period to which Joseph belongs, according to Biblical chronology (for the basis of this reckoning, see Chronology, II, 2). In no other time was it more likely that a Semite could occupy a position of honor in Egypt such as Joseph did; the Semitic Hyksos kings would be inclined to have more confidence in officials of kindred race than in any of the subjugated Egyptians, even though they also employed

274. Seti I in his chariot, on the temple wall at Karnak; Joseph probably used such a vehicle

Egyptians as officials, such as "Potiphar, an officer of Pharaoh, the captain of the guard" (RSV). It is noticeable that the Bible calls Potiphar "an Egyptian" (Gen 39:1)—a designation that would seem superfluous and illogical for a high official of a native Egyptian king, but worthy of mention if the king and the ruling class were foreigners. It is evident from the records that the economic change that took place during the Hyksos period can be accounted for by the story of Joseph. During the Middle Kingdom, preceding the Hyksos invasion, Egypt enjoyed a system of private enterprise, and the land was owned by the people as well as by the king and the temple priesthoods. The scanty records surviving from the Hyksos period throw no light on the matter, but in the 18th dynasty, after the expulsion of the Hyksos, we find that all real estate was in the hands of the Pharaoh except the temple properties. The change from private to crown ownership must have taken place during the interval. The story of Joseph explains how all privately owned property had come, during the famine, into the possession of the crown. This new land system would give to the 18th dynasty kings an opportunity to bestow lands and other properties on their veteran soldiers as rewards for faithful service in the war of liberation.

The Egyptian monuments also illustrate many details of the story of Joseph and provide many close parallels to it: A demotic papyrus now in the British Museum, which tells us how prisoners were freed on the anniversary of the accession of Pharaoh, can be compared with Gen 40:20. The Egyptians paid much attention to dreams and believed them to contain divine messages, as is attested by many ancient records (cf. chs 40:8; 41:8); therefore, a professional group of magicians and soothsayers was in great demand to interpret dreams. Before Joseph could appear before the king he had to take time to shave himself, although it was ordered that he should be brought with haste (Gen 41:14). In contrast to the Asiatics, the Egyptians had clean-shaven faces, and the Egyptian story of Sinuhe tells us how Sinuhe, returning to Egypt after a long exile in Asia, first of all shaved and changed his garments, so as to be considered once more a civilized person. Joseph's investiture as vizier, as described in Gen 41:41-44, can be paralleled by literary records from Egypt and by ancient pictures showing the king in the act of placing golden chains with pectorals around the necks of his high courtiers.

From the 13th cent. comes an Egyptian document, the Papyrus D'Orbiney in the British Museum, that contains a "Story of the Two Brothers," who lived together. The older brother's wife made an attempt to seduce the younger brother while her husband was in the field. When the young man failed to submit to her lusts, she became so angry with him that she accused him to her husband of having attempted to rape her. Thereupon the outraged husband immediately set out to kill his younger brother, who, however, was warned through a divine intervention and was able to escape. Later the truth was found out, and the unfaithful wife was killed. The story continues with legendary matter (*ANET* 23-25). Many modern commentators, dating the origin of the Pentateuch in the 1st millennium B.C., think that the story of Joseph in Gen 39 borrowed its theme from the Egyptian "Story of the Two Brothers." However, the 2 stories have only one thing in common: an unfaithful wife attempting unsuccessfully to seduce a young man living in the house, and later accusing him of an attempted rape. Such dramas may have happened frequently in ancient times, as they occur in this modern age, although the object of a seducer usually falls victim. Since Joseph lived many centuries before the Papyrus D'Orbiney was composed, and the "Story of the Two Brothers" has mythological trends, there is no reason to suppose that one story depends upon the other.

2. Father of the spy who represented the tribe of Issachar (Num 13:7).

3. A son of Asaph and head of the 1st of the 24 courses into which David organized the musicians for the sanctuary service (1 Chr 25:2, 9).

4. A Judahite appearing in Luke's genealogy of Jesus Christ (Lk 3:30).

5. A Jew belonging to the family of Bani (RSV "Binnui"); he had married a foreign wife in the time of Ezra (Ezr 10:42).

6. A priest, head of the family of Shebaniah in the time of high priest Joiakim (Neh 12:14).

7. According to the KJV, a Judahite appearing in Luke's genealogy of Jesus Christ (Lk 3:26, KJV). The RSV, following a different Greek text, calls him Josech.

8. Another in Luke's genealogy of Jesus Christ (Lk 3:24).

9. The husband of Mary (Mt 1:16; Lk 3:23), considered by his contemporaries to be the father of Jesus. He seems earlier to have been widowed and apparently had children by a former marriage (*see* Brethren of the Lord). While engaged to Mary he discovered that she was to have a child and decided to put her away without exposing her; but after he was informed in a dream that the child had been miraculously conceived, he married her and brought her child up as his own son (Mt 1:18-25). The birth took place at Bethlehem because Joseph had taken Mary with him from Nazareth, their home town, to Bethlehem in compliance with a census decree that required every individual to register in the town of his ancestors. Since Joseph (as well as Mary) was a member of the tribe of Judah and a descendant of the house of David, he had to fulfill their registration duties at David's birthplace, Bethlehem (Lk 2:1-16). Joseph was also with Mary when the child Jesus was taken to the Temple for the customary presentation, and heard there the predictions of Simeon and Anna (vs 22-38). Before Herod could carry out his cruel murder of the infants at Bethlehem, Joseph was directed in a dream to go to Egypt; hence he took Mary and Jesus to Egypt, returning to Palestine to settle in Nazareth after the death of Herod (Mt 2:13-23). As a faithful Jew he probably went regularly to Jerusalem every year for the great feasts. When Jesus was 12 years old He was taken on the annual pilgrimage to the Passover. It was on this occasion that His parents lost Him, and after a search of 3 days discovered Him in the Temple (Lk 2:41-50). Joseph, a carpenter (Mt 13:55), apparently taught this trade to Jesus (Mk 6:3). Joseph seems to have died before Jesus began His ministry, as seems evident from the fact that it was His mother

and brothers who visited Him (Mt 12:46), and His brothers who attempted to advise Him (Jn 7:3-5); also Jesus' request that the disciple John take care of His mother would hardly have been made if her husband had still been alive (ch 19:26, 27).

10. One of the brothers of Jesus Christ (Mt 13:55, RSV). The KJV, following a different Greek text, calls him Joses (as in Mk 6:3 in both versions).

11. A Jew of the town of Arimathea, a wealthy man who owned a yet-unused rock sepulcher in a garden outside the city of Jerusalem (Mt 27:57, 60; Jn 19:41). He was a member of the Sanhedrin, but had not consented to the resolution condemning Christ, because he was already a secret disciple of the Lord (Mt 27:57; Lk 23:50, 51; Jn 19:38). It was on the day of crucifixion that he, together with Nicodemus, another ruler of the Jews, found the courage to identify himself with the followers of Jesus. Joseph went to Pilate, requested the body of Jesus, and buried Him in his own tomb, which was near the place of crucifixion (Mt 27:58-60; Mk 15:42-46; Lk 23:52, 53; Jn 19:38-41).

12. A Jewish Christian, also called Barsabbas, meaning "son of Sabbas," and surnamed Justus. He had been a follower of Jesus from the beginning of His ministry, and together with Matthias was selected by the apostles as a candidate to replace Judas, who had betrayed the Lord and then committed suicide. Matthias was chosen by lot, and we hear no more of Joseph (Acts 1:21-26). He may have been the brother of "Judas called Barsabbas" (ch 15:22, RSV).

13. The original name of Barnabas (Acts 4:36, RSV). The KJV, following a different Greek text, calls him Joses.

Joses (jō'sēz). [Gr. *Iōsēs*, possibly a Greek form of Joseph. The name is attested in Greek inscriptions.]

1. One of the brothers of Jesus Christ (Mt 13:55; Mk 6:3; KJV). The RSV, following a different Greek text, in Mt 13:55 calls him Joseph.

2. Son of Mary, 5, and brother of Jesus' disciple James the Less (Mt 27:56, KJV; Mk 15:40, 47). In Mt 27:56 the RSV, following a different Greek text, calls him Joseph.

3. The personal name of the apostle Barnabas, who accompanied Paul on his 1st Missionary Journey (Acts 4:36, KJV). The RSV, following a different Greek text, calls him Joseph.

Joshah (jō'shȧ). [Heb. *Yôshah*.] A Simeonite, chief in his family (1 Chr 4:34).

Joshaphat (jŏsh'ȧ-făt), KJV once **Jehoshaphat** (jē-hŏsh'ȧ-făt). [Heb. *Yôshaphaṭ*, shortened form of *Yehôshaphaṭ*, "Jehoshaphat," "Yahweh has judged."]

1. A Mithnite; one of the "mighty men" of David's army (1 Chr 11:43).

2. One of the priests who blew the trumpets before the ark of God when David brought it up to Jerusalem from the house of Obed-edom (1 Chr 15:24).

Joshaviah (jŏsh'ȧ-vī'ȧ). [Heb. *Yôshawyah*.] One of the "mighty men" of David's army (1 Chr 11:46).

Joshbekashah (jŏsh'bē-kā'shȧ). [Heb. *Yoshbeqashah*, meaning uncertain.] A son of Heman, and head of the 17th of the 24 courses into which David organized the musicians for the sanctuary service (1 Chr 25:4, 24).

Josheb-basshebeth. *See* Jashobeam.

Joshibiah (jŏsh'ĭ-bī'ȧ), KJV **Josibiah** (jŏs'ĭ-bī'ȧ). [Heb. *Yôshibyah*, "may Yahweh dwell."] A Simeonite (1 Chr 4:35).

Joshua (jŏsh'ū-ȧ), or **Jeshua** (jĕsh'ū-ȧ), KJV once **Jehoshua** (jē-hŏsh'ū-ȧ), once **Jehoshuah** (jē-hŏsh'ū-ȧ), and once **Hoshea** (hō-shē'ȧ); KJV of NT **Jesus** (jē'zŭs). [Heb. *Yehôshûa'*, "Yahweh is deliverance," or "Yahweh is salvation," transliterated into Aramaic as *Yeshûa'*, and thence into Gr. as *Iēsous*. The name occurs on an ancient Hebrew seal.]

1. A son of Nun of the tribe of Ephraim (Num 13:8, 16). He was Moses' military commander during the wilderness wanderings, and is first mentioned in connection with his victory over the Amalekites a few days before the Hebrews arrived at Mount Sinai (Ex 17:8-16). As Moses' assistant or "minister" he accompanied Moses on the ascent of Mount Sinai (ch 24:13). At Kadesh-barnea, 2 years after the Exodus, Joshua represented the tribe of Ephraim on the expedition to spy out the Promised Land. He and Caleb alone returned with a favorable report (Num 13:8, RSV; 14:6-9; cf. 14:7), and were therefore accorded the privilege of entering Canaan 38 years later (ch 14:30-38). Shortly before his death, Moses publicly inaugurated Joshua as his successor (Num 27:18-23; Deut 1:38; 31:23). When Moses died, Joshua began immediate preparations to enter Canaan (Jos 1:10, 11). He dispatched 2 spies to secure a report on the state of affairs in Jericho (ch 2:1), and when preparations were complete led the people over the Jordan

(Jos 4:10-19). After the capture of Jericho and Ai (chs 6; 8), Joshua met and defeated one coalition of Canaanite kings at Gibeon, near Jerusalem (ch 10), and another at Hazor in the northern part of the country (ch 11). After these preliminary conquests, Joshua set about dividing the land of Canaan among the tribes (chs 13-21), his inheritance, by his own request, being at Timnath-serah in Mount Ephraim (ch 19:50). At the age of 110 he gathered Israel together, counseled them to be faithful to the Lord (ch 24:1-28), and died (vs 29, 30). *See* Hoshea.

2. Owner of the field in Beth-shemesh to which the cattle brought the ark upon its return from Philistia (1 Sa 6:14).

3. A governor of Jerusalem during the reign of King Josiah (2 Ki 23:8).

4. A high priest under Zerubbabel, after the return from Babylonian captivity (Hag 1:12-14; 2:2-4; Zec 3:1-9).

Joshua, Book of. An account of the conquest and settlement of the land of Canaan by the Hebrew people under the leadership of Joshua. In the Hebrew Scriptures Joshua stands as the 1st book of the section called Former Prophets, the other books of this group being Judges, Samuel, and Kings, the whole being part of the 2d division of the OT, called "the Prophets." Commentators and critics are divided as to whether the title of the book designates its author or simply the chief character in the narrative. Critical scholars insist that the book is a composite work by several authors, later compiled by an editor. However, the obvious internal unity of the book makes this conjecture unnecessary and pointless. The further contention that the repeated occurrence of the expression "unto this day" (Jos 5:9; etc.) necessarily indicates a time of writing long after the events recorded in the book, is disproved by the context of ch 6:25. The use of revised place names that were not used until later times (Jos 19:27; cf. 1 Ki 9:13; Jos 15:38; cf. 2 Ki 14:7; etc.) may be attributed to the fact that later copyists substituted names current in their day for the benefit of readers who were unfamiliar with names that had become obsolete. It is generally agreed that the record of Joshua's death in Jos 24:29-33 was written by someone else. The Talmud explains that this was written by Eleazar, the son of Aaron, and that Phinehas appended v 33 (*Baba Bathra* 15a, 15b). Until modern times Jews and Christians alike have acknowledged Joshua as the author of the

book (cf. *Baba Bathra* 14b). The book of Joshua picks up the narrative of Hebrew history at the point where the book of Deuteronomy leaves it. This intimate relationship to the Pentateuch has led to the common practice of considering Joshua as a unit with it, the 6 books being referred to as the Hexateuch.

The book of Joshua opens with Israel's entrance into the Promised Land about 1405 B.C. (*see* Chronology, III). Joshua successfully led the Israelites in the conquest of Canaan, or rather, of at least sufficient portions of it as to make possible the allotment to each tribe of its appointed inheritance, so that all the people might find a permanent place of abode. The land was made up of numerous small kingdoms. Upon 2 or 3 occasions various Canaanite kings joined their armies to halt the progress of the Hebrews, but on each occasion God gave His people victory over their foes. This period of conquest occupied between 6 and 7 years (Jos 14:7-11; cf. Deut. 2:14), and by the close of this time the basic occupation of the land was considered complete (Jos 11:23; 14:5). This did not mean that every part of the land had been brought under Israelite control, but that an area sufficient for the present needs of the tribes had been subdued.

The book may be divided into 3 parts: (1) The conquest of Canaan (Jos 1:1 to 12:24); (2) the partition of the land (chs 13:1 to 22:34); (3) Joshua's farewell address to Israel (chs 23:1 to 24:33). The crossing of the Jordan, including preparations for that great event, occupies the first 4 chapters. Chapters 5 and 6 deal with the fall of Jericho. The preparations included the circumcision of the people and the celebration of the Passover, neither of which had been observed since the departure from Sinai (see ch 5:2-10). In chapters 7 and 8 the preliminary defeat at Ai, the matter of Achan, and the subsequent successful conquest of the city are recorded. Chapters 9 and 10 tell of the treaty with the Gibeonites, and of the Canaanite confederacy against the Gibeonites because of their alliance with the Hebrews, and of Joshua's dramatic victory over them, leaving Israel in effective control of the central mountainous region. A military expedition that brought a large part of the southland under control is reported in ch 10:28-43. The coalition of northern Canaanite kings and the conquest of the north country are related in ch 11:1-15. Further military exploits occupy ch 12. The preliminary conquest of the land now completed, Joshua proceeded to make the tribal allotments (Jos 13 to 19), and set apart certain cities as cities of refuge (ch 20) and others for the Levites (ch 21). Chapter 22 describes the return of the armies of the two and a half tribes to their homes in Transjordan and the misunderstanding that arose between them and their brethren to the west, which was amicably settled. The book closes with Joshua's farewell address to Israel and an account of his death (chs 23; 24).

Josiah (jō-sī′ȧ). [Heb. *Yo'shiyahû* and *Yo'-shiyah,* generally explained to mean "Yahweh heals," though the real meaning of the name is obscure. Gr. *Iōsias.*]

1. The 16th ruler of the kingdom of Judah, who reigned for 31 years (*c.* 639-*c.* 609/08 B.C.). He became king at the age of 8 years, his father Amon having been slain by the royal courtiers (2 Chr 33:21-24; 34:1). In his 12th regnal year, when about 20 years old, he began to purge his country of the high places, destroying Baal altars, Asherah cult images, and other pagan vestiges (ch 34:3-7). His religious activity extended to the territory of the former kingdom of Israel (v 6), the weakness of Assyria during those years being in his favor. It is possible that the Assyrian provinces of Megiddo and Samaria had ceased to function, and that Josiah entered into the political vacuum and established his own authority in that area. Later he was able to choose Megiddo, a city in the heart of the old northern kingdom, to meet Pharaoh Necho's army with his own armed forces.

The greatest event in his life came in his 18th regnal year, when the discovery of a scroll of the Law of Moses in the Temple incited a national religious revival. The message of the scroll, when read to the king, made a deep impression upon him. Convinced that his fathers had not lived according to the divine ordinances, he feared that the curses pronounced by Moses would fall upon him and his kingdom, and consequently sent certain officials to the prophetess Huldah for advice. She confirmed the king's forebodings, but assured him that God would not bring the predicted punishments upon Judah during his lifetime, since he had done everything in his power to live a godly life (2 Ki 22:8-20; 2 Chr 34:14-28). Josiah now doubled his efforts to stamp out idolatry and paganism from the kingdom, and induced the leadership of the country to enter into a solemn covenant with God. He celebrated the Passover in a way it had not been celebrated since the days of Samuel (2 Ki 23:1-25).

As the power of Assyria waned and that of Babylonia increased, Josiah seems to have considered it advantageous to lean toward Babylonia. He may have entered into an agreement with Nabopolassar to assist him, or, without formal agreement, may have felt that the kingdom of Judah would gain only if it supported the Babylonians. It may have been for one of these two reasons that Josiah, in the last year of his reign, attempted to block Pharaoh Necho in his march through Palestine to the north to aid the dying Assyrian power. The Babylonian Chronicle reveals that Egyptian forces had been helping the Assyrians for several years. Since all these Egyptian auxiliary armies had passed through Palestine, Josiah must have made no attempt in the past to prevent them from marching toward the north. Now, however, he determined not to allow the Egyptians to cross his country again. Necho did not wish to fight against Josiah, but was forced into battle with him at Megiddo, where one of the Carmel passes enters the wide Plain of Esdraelon which the Egyptian army had to cross. In this battle Josiah was mortally wounded. He was quickly transported to Jerusalem, where he was buried. The victorious Necho continued his march toward Syria (2 Ki 23:29, 30; 2 Chr 35:20-24). Josiah's death was a major tragedy for the country, and it was sincerely mourned by the people and by the prophet Jeremiah, who composed a Lamentation which has not been preserved (2 Chr 35:24, 25). The religious reformation initiated by Josiah had not had time to become deeply rooted, and so was soon forgotten. Likewise, the political independence that Judah had enjoyed for a short time was irreplaceably lost within weeks after Josiah's death. The rest of the kings of Judah were vassals, subject first to Egypt and then to Babylon.

2. A son of a certain Zephaniah in the days of the prophet Zechariah (Zec 6:10).

Josibiah. *See* Joshibiah.

Josiphiah (jŏs′ĭ-fī′ȧ). [Heb. *Yôsiphyah,* "Yahweh adds."] The father of the Shelomith who returned with Ezra from Babylonia with 160 male members of the family (Ezr 8:10).

Jot. *See* Iota.

Jotbah (jŏt′bȧ). [Heb. *Yoṭbah,* "pleasantness" or "goodness."] The town in which

King Amon's maternal grandfather lived (2 Ki 21:19). It is probably identical with the town called Jotapata by Josephus (*War* iii. 7. 7), now *Khirbet Jefât,* near Cana in Galilee. It is spelled Yotapata on Map XVI, C-3.

Jotbath. See Jotbathah.

Jotbathah (jŏt'bá-thá), KJV once **Jotbath** (jŏt'băth). [Heb. *Yoṭbathah,* "goodness" or "pleasantness."] A desert station of the Israelites, probably situated somewhere in the *Wâdī el-'Arabah,* north of Ezion-geber (Num 33:33, 34; Deut 10:7).

Jotham (jō'thăm), KJV of NT **Joatham** (jō'á-thăm). [Heb. *Yôtham,* "Yahweh is perfect." The name occurs on an ancient Hebrew seal. Gr. *Iōatham.*]

1. The youngest son of the judge Gideon, and the only one of Gideon's 70 sons to escape massacre by Abimelech, their half brother. Later, standing on Mount Gerizim, Jotham foretold the fate of Abimelech and of the Shechemites by the now-famous parable of the trees anointing a bramble as king over them (Jgs 9:1-21).

2. A son of Jahdai, and a descendant of Caleb (2 Chr 2:47).

3. The 11th ruler of the kingdom of Judah, who reigned for 20 years (*c.* 750-*c.* 731 B.C.). In 2 Ki 15:33 and 2 Chr 27:1, 16 regnal years are attributed to him. However, in 2 Ki 15:30 the murder of Pekah is put in his 20th year. This apparent discrepancy can be explained by assuming that he abdicated in favor of his son Ahaz after a reign of 16 years, but lived for at least another 4 years, and that the scribes continued to date events according to his reign. He had a coregency with his father Uzziah as well, taking the throne when his father became a leper (2 Ki 15:5; 2 Chr 26:21). He is described as a good king like his father, although he allowed the people to worship on the high places, as had been done for centuries (2 Ki 15:34, 35; 2 Chr 27:2). He built the high gate of the Temple, repaired the wall at Ophel, south of the Temple, founded cities in the mountainous parts of his country, and erected castles and towers in the forests (2 Ki 15:35; 2 Chr 27:3, 4). He defeated the Ammonites and forced them to pay tribute (2 Chr 27:5). In his reign Pekah of Israel and Rezin of Damascus began an invasion of Judah (2 Ki 15:37), possibly because he did not join them in an alliance against Assyria. He is listed in the genealogy of Jesus Christ as recorded by Matthew (Mt 1:9).

Journey. See Day's Journey; Sabbath Day's Journey.

Journeys of the Israelites. See Exodus; Wilderness Wanderings.

Jozabad (jŏz'á-băd), KJV once **Josabad** (jŏs'á-băd). [Heb. *Yôzabad,* "Yahweh gives."]

1. A warrior from Gederah who joined David at Ziklag (1 Chr 12:4).

2 and 3. Two warriors from Manasseh who joined David at Ziklag (1 Chr 12:20).

4. A Levite who, with others, was in charge of the tithes and offerings in Hezekiah's reign (2 Chr 31:13).

5. A chief of the Levites in the time of King Josiah (2 Chr 35:9).

6. One of the Levites in Jerusalem to whom Ezra delivered the treasures from Babylon (Ezr 8:33).

7. A Levite who was married to a foreign wife in the time of Ezra (Ezr 10:23).

8. A priest who was married to a foreign wife in the time of Ezra (Ezr 10:22).

9. One of the men, probably a Levite, who assisted Ezra in reading the Law to the people (Neh 8:7). He may have been the Levite who was in charge of the outward business of the Temple (ch 11:16). He is possibly identical with Jozabad, 6.

Jozacar (jŏz'á-kär), KJV **Jozachar** (jŏz'á-kär). [Heb. *Yôzakar,* "Yahweh has remembered."] One of the 2 conspirators who slew King Joash of Judah (2 Ki 12:21). Some Hebrew manuscripts read *Yôzabad* instead of *Yôzakar,* a variant spelling that is not surprising, since the Hebrew letters *b* and *k,* as well as *d* and *r,* are very similar in form. This probably forms the basis of the name Zabad given to this assassin in 2 Chr 24:26.

Jozachar. See Jozacar.

Jozadak. See Jehozadak.

Jubal (jōō'băl). [Heb. *Yûbal.*] The younger son of Lamech by his wife Adah. He was the originator of the art of music (Gen 4:19, 21).

Jubilee, KJV **Jubile.** [Heb. *yôbel.*] The 50th year, at the end of 7 sabbatical-year cycles (Lev 25:8, 10), in which sowing and harvesting were forbidden (v 11), all Hebrew slaves were to be freed (v 10), and lands reverted to their original owners (vs 24-28). This last provision prevented a few wealthy men from creating a small group of landowners and a large landless class. Sale of land really would amount to a long-term lease. However, a dwelling in a walled city (except in Levitical cities) was exempt from this provision; its transfer was permanent unless it was redeemed within a year after sale (Lev 25:29-34).

There is difference of opinion as to whether the jubilee year coincided with the 7th sabbatical year in the cycle (that is, the 49th year), which would be the "fiftieth year" (Lev 25:10) by inclusive reckoning, or whether it followed the 49 years. In the latter case there would be 2 consecutive cropless years. There is no record in the Bible, or outside it, of an actual observance of the jubilee; hence the question remains unsettled.

Jucal. *See* Jehucal.

Juda. *See* Joda; Judah.

Judaea. *See* Judea.

Judah (jōō'dá), KJV of NT frequently **Juda** (jōō'dá). [Heb. *Yehúdah*. On the basis of Gen 29:35, the name is usually explained as meaning "let Him (God) be praised," but the etymology is uncertain. The name occurs also on a contract among the non-Biblical documents of the Dead Sea scrolls. In Mt 1:2, 3, KJV, the name appears as Judas. Aramaic *Yehûd*. Gr. *Ioudas*.]

1. The 4th son of Jacob by his wife Leah (Gen 29:32-35). He married a Canaanite girl, Shua, with whom he had become acquainted through a Canaanite friend (ch 38:1, 2). She bore him 3 sons, Er, Onan, and Shelah (vs 3-5). As wife for his son Er he took Tamar, another Canaanite girl (v 6). When Er died childless, Judah gave Tamar to Onan, in harmony with custom of the time (vs 7, 8). When Onan died without leaving an heir (vs 9, 10), Tamar went back to her father's house, having Judah's promise, however, that she would be given to Shelah as soon as he reached the age of maturity (v 11). When Judah failed to keep his word Tamar obtained offspring by deception from Judah himself, and bore him two sons, Perez and Zerah (vs 12-30). Although Judah is revealed to have been morally aberrant in certain respects, yet in many other ways his character seems to have been more exemplary than that of his brothers. He did not take part in Simeon and Levi's massacre of Shechem (ch 34), and it was he who, in an attempt to save Joseph, proposed to his brothers that Joseph be sold rather than murdered (ch 37:26-28). Later, in Egypt, he showed much nobility of character when Joseph, unrecognized by his brothers, wanted to detain Benjamin for having allegedly stolen a silver cup. Judah eloquently pleaded on behalf of

his younger brother, and offered himself as prisoner to Joseph to obtain Benjamin's release (Gen 44). When Jacob and his family migrated to Egypt Judah was chosen to precede the company and announce Jacob's arrival to Joseph (ch 46:28). When Jacob blessed his sons upon his deathbed, he gave Judah the blessings due the first-born (ch 49:8-12), passing over Reuben for his sin of incest (v 4), and Simeon and Levi, because of their murder of the Shechemites (vs 5-7). The prophecies pronounced at that time were later fulfilled. The tribe of Judah became the most important of the tribes of Israel, and Perez (KJV "Pharez"), one of Judah's sons, became the ancestor of David and of the royal house of the southern kingdom (Ruth 4:18-22; 1 Chr 2:3-15; 3:1-6) and of the Lord Jesus, the Saviour of mankind (Mt 1:3-16).

2. A Levite, whose descendant Kadmiel and Kadmiel's sons were prominent in the days of Zerubbabel (Ezr 3:9). He is called Hodaviah in ch 2:40 and Hodevah in Neh 7:43. He is possibly identical with Judah, 3.

3. A Levite who returned from Babylonia with Zerubbabel (Neh 12:8); possibly identical with Judah, 2.

4. A Levite who was married to a foreign wife in the time of Ezra (Ezr 10:23).

5. A Benjamite who was the 2d administrator of Jerusalem in Nehemiah's time (Neh 11:9).

6. A prominent Jew who took part in the dedication of the wall of Jerusalem in Nehemiah's time (Neh 12:34).

Judah, Tribe of, Kingdom of, and **Province of.** [Heb. *Yehúdah:* Aramaic *Yehûd.* The name occurs in cuneiform records as *Yaudu, Yahudu,* and *Yakudu,* and also, in its Aramaic form, in the 5th cent. B.C. Aramaic papyri from Elephantine, as well as on ancient Hebrew coins and jar handles found in Palestine. It was the official name of the Persian province established by Cyrus (Ezr 5:8, RSV).] The term "Judah" in the Bible—apart from the personal name—belongs to 3 stages of Hebrew history: first the tribe descended from one of Jacob's 12 sons, later the kingdom composed principally of that tribe, and finally the repatriated Jewish people after the Exile. Historically this 3d stage was a continuation of the kingdom of Judah composed of whatever remnants of the Hebrew people—now called Jews—lived in Palestine. It was, however, no longer an independent nation, but was under Persian rule.

1. *The Tribe of Judah*. The descendants of Judah, the 4th son of Jacob (Gen 29:32-35; *see* Judah, 1). It was divided into 5 principal families, 3 of which descended from Judah's sons, and 2 from his grandsons (Num 26:19-21; 1 Chr 2:3-6). Nahshon is mentioned as the prince of the tribe of Judah under Moses in the wilderness (Num 1:7; 2:3; 7:12-17; 10:14). Another outstanding leader during the wilderness wandering was Caleb, the son of Jephunneh, who also was the spy representing his tribe (chs 13:6; 34:19). The first census revealed that the tribe had 74,600 men ready to go to war (ch 1:26, 27), and the 2d census showed this number increased to 76,500 (ch 26:22). Judah was the first tribe to take possession of its allotted territory after Joshua's death. With assistance from the tribe of Simeon the men of Judah went into the mountainous country of the southern part of western Palestine, drove the Canaanites from many cities, and occupied these cities and their environs (Jgs 1:1-20).

The territory allotted to Judah lay in the southern portion of Canaan. Jos 15:1-12 describes its borders, stating that the southern border began at the southernmost tip of the Dead Sea. It passed through the Wilderness of Zin, skirted Kadesh-barnea on the south, and then reached the "river of Egypt," the *Wâdī el-'Arîsh*, which it followed to its mouth at the Mediterranean Sea. The eastern border was formed by the Dead Sea. The northern border began at the north end of the Dead Sea, went first to the north, but turned to the west south of Jericho, went up the Ascent of Adummim, probably the *Wâdī Qelt*, and reached En-rogel and the Valley of Hinnom south of Jerusalem. From there it turned to the northwest toward Kiriath-jearim, then toward the southwest to Beth-shemesh, and finally via Jabneh (later Jamnia) to the Mediterranean Sea, which formed the western boundary. Judah, however, never possessed the coastal plain, which was for the most part occupied by the Philistines. Judah's territory was geographically divided into: (1) the hill country (Jos 15:48), densely populated in its western part, but practically uninhabited in the rainless eastern section, which formed the Wilderness of Judah (v 61); (2) the Shephelah, a fertile lowland lying between the hill country and the coastal plain (v 33; cf. 1 Ki 10:21, RSV), in which some of the strongest cities of the country were found; and (3) the Negeb (Jos 10:40, RSV), a barren and almost arid desert land between Beer-sheba and Kadesh-barnea. Although most of Judah's territory was mountainous, it was well adapted to the culture of the vine (cf. Gen 49:10-12), having within its territory the Valley of Eshcol, north of Hebron (Num 13:23, 24), which to the present time produces an excellent type of grape. The Shephelah, on the other hand, was the granary of Judah, and since its possession was of great importance for the state of Judah, its cities were supplied with strong fortifications. Map VI, E/G-1/3.

Judah was the tribe from which the first judge, Othniel, arose, who delivered the nation from the oppression of Cushan-rishathaim, king of Mesopotamia at the beginning of the period of the judges (Jgs 3:8-11). Judah joined the other tribes against Benjamin (ch 20:1, 18) apparently early in the period (see v 28). In a geographical sense Judah, Simeon, and Dan formed a unit, and these tribes were the ones to suffer most from the oppression of the Philistines after that nation became dominant in the 12th cent. B.C. (chs 10:7; 13:1). But Judah seems to have taken little part in the wars of other tribes against the various oppressors that beset Israel during the period of the judges.

When Samuel established the first kingdom, Judah supported Saul. However, the fact that its forces are mentioned separately from those of the other tribes (1 Sa 11:8; 15:4; 17:52) seems to imply that, possibly as the result of historical events not sufficiently known to us, or through geographical isolation, Judah was considered as somewhat different from the other tribes, which seem to have formed a unit. After Saul's death, David, a hero of the tribe of Judah, was made king in Hebron, whereas the northern tribes followed Ishbosheth, Saul's son. This division lasted until Ishbosheth's death 7 years later, when the followers of Saul's house turned to David (2 Sa 2:4; 5:1-3) and made him king over all 12 tribes. For more than 7 decades the kingdom remained under one royal house. David was prudent in moving his capital from Hebron to Jerusalem (ch 5:5), a city that had belonged to no tribe up to that time, and was therefore neutral territory, since tribal jealousy was always present (see ch 19:41-43).

2. *The Kingdom of Judah*. The tribal unity between the south and the north was only artificial (see Map VIII), and

was maintained only as long as rulers with strong personalities like David and Solomon were on the throne. When a weaker king came to the throne after Solomon's death, the northern tribes seceded at once from Judah. With the exception of the priestly tribe of the Levites, which seems for the most part to have moved into the territory of Judah (2 Chr 11:5-14), only the tribe of Benjamin remained with the south (1 Ki 12:1-21). Map IX. From that time on for about 345 years (c. 931 to 586 B.C.), the history of the tribe of Judah is, for the most part, the history of the kingdom of Judah. During this period 19 kings, all descendants of David, and one queen, the wicked Athaliah, reigned over the southern kingdom, which consisted of the territories of Judah and Benjamin, and, for a time, that of Edom. Repeatedly there was war with the northern kingdom (1 Ki 14:30; 15:7, 16; 2 Ki 14:11, 12; 16:5). Occasionally invasions from foreign nations had to be met. The first invader was King Shishak of Egypt in the time of Rehoboam (1 Ki 14:25-28; 2 Chr 12:1-12). Later, in the time of Asa, Zerah the Ethiopian came against Judah (2 Chr 14:9-15), and finally the nation was attacked by Assyria and Babylon (2 Ki 18:14; 24:10; etc.). Under King Jehoram, Edom was permanently lost (2 Chr 21:8-10), with the result that Judah became a rather insignificant state. Subsequent to this Judah owed its survival to the weakness of Egypt, and to the existence of the kingdom of Israel as a buffer state against northern enemies, the Syrians and the Assyrians. During the last years of the kingdom of Israel, Judah under King Ahaz became a vassal state of the Assyrians (2 Ki 16:7-10), and after the fall of the city of Samaria in 723/22 B.C., its northern boundary was adjacent to an Assyrian province (see Map X). During the next hundred years Judah had either to pay a heavy tribute to Assyria or to suffer invasions, as in the time of King Hezekiah (ch 18:13-16). One of its kings, Manasseh, was even carried to Mesopotamia as a hostage and spent some time in prison (2 Chr 33:11-13). See Map XI, C-4. During the time of Assyria's decline after Ashurbanipal's death and until its full destruction shortly after the capture of Nineveh by the Medes and Babylonians, Judah had a period of respite, and under King Josiah extended its authority over some parts of the former kingdom of Israel (ch 34:6, 7). However, Josiah found himself between Egypt, which, un-

der King Necho, aspired to regain its former hold over Palestine, and Babylon, which considered itself the heir of the Assyrian Empire. Josiah evidently chose the side of Babylon, for he lost his life in a battle against Necho (2 Ki 23:29, 30; 2 Chr 35:20-24). During the 2 decades of its existence after Josiah's death, Judah swayed in its allegiance between Egypt and Babylon, saw its territory repeatedly invaded by foreign armies, experienced 3 captures of Jerusalem, its capital, and finally suffered the destruction of its sovereignty and its cities, and witnessed the deportation of the bulk of its population to Babylonia (2 Ki 23:31 to 25:21; 2 Chr 36:1-20). Some of the Jews who were left in the country by the Babylonians migrated to Egypt to escape the wrath of Nebuchadnezzar after some fanatical Jews slew Gedaliah and the Chaldean garrison (2 Ki 25:22-26). It seems that only a small and unimportant group remained.

During the 4 centuries of Judah's history the worship of God was frequently accompanied by the worship of pagan gods for whom shrines and cult places were erected from the time of Solomon to the end of the kingdom (1 Ki 11:4-8; 14:22-24; 2 Ki 21:1-7; etc.). Although the country did not experience the depths of idolatry found in the northern kingdom, Judah was practically a semipagan nation during the period of the kings. Some kings, such as Asa (1 Ki 15:12-14), Jehoshaphat (ch 22:43-46), Hezekiah (2 Ki 18:1-4), Josiah (ch 22:1-20), made serious attempts to stamp out idolatry and pagan cults. These reforms, however, were temporary, and the people lapsed into paganism once more. This was the chief reason for the nation's downfall (2 Chr 36:14-16; Jer 22:6-9; etc.).

3. *The Province of Judah.* The northern tribes lost their identity in exile and merged with the nations among whom they were settled by the Assyrians, but the southern kingdom of Judah and Benjamin retained its national identity during the Babylonian exile. This situation resulted from the leadership of men of strong national and spiritual consciousness, such as Jeremiah, Daniel, and Ezekiel. When Cyrus, the Persian king, gave permission to the Jews to return to Palestine, about 50,000 were at once prepared to go back. Under strong secular and religious leaders they rebuilt their Temple and resumed their political life as a nation under the Persian Empire (see Map

XII, D-5/6). In fact, the Exile had served as a refining process, for the people of Judah discarded paganism and idolatry so that these never again became national sins. During this postexilic period Judah appears in history as a province of the Persian Empire. It retained its old Hebrew name (*Yehûdah*), "Judah."

The capital of the province and the seat of the governor was Jerusalem (Neh 3:7). It was one of the many provinces which belonged to the large satrapy of *'Abar Nahara'*, "Beyond the River" (Map XII, D-5/6), which reached from the Euphrates in the north to Egypt in the south. Its boundaries can be established approximately from the lists of cities given in Ezra and Nehemiah. The northern boundary ran from the Jordan via Jericho and Bethel, which were included in Judean territory, to Ono in the west. The western boundary seems to have skirted the coastal plain and run west of the Shephelah, and the southern boundary began south of Beth-pelet and after passing Beer-sheba ended at the Dead Sea. During the Persian period the province of Judah was administered by a governor appointed by the crown. Jewish governors are known to us. Shesh-bazzar (Ezr 1:8, 11; 5:14), who is identified by many scholars with Zerubbabel (Ezr 3:8; Hag 1:1; etc.), and Nehemiah (Neh 1:1; 5:14) were early Jewish governors. Besides these, unnamed governors are mentioned in ch 5:15 and Mal 1:8, and a Persian governor by the name of Bigvai, who was in office in 407 B.C., appears in the Elephantine papyri. The inhabitants of the province consisted of Judahites, Benjamites, Levites, and members of the other tribes who had made up the former kingdom of Judah and who had been taken captive, and possibly also remnants of the 10 tribes who had earlier gone into captivity (2 Chr 11:1-7; cf. Ezr 2:36-40; 4:1; Neh 11:20; Jer 50:4; Eze 37:15-19; Zec 8:13). After arriving in their homeland in 536 B.C., under the leadership of Zerubbabel, the Jews reoccupied their old cities, rebuilt their houses (Hag 1:4), and completed the Temple in Jerusalem by 515 B.C. (Ezr 5:2; 6:15), in spite of opposition from the surrounding nations. However, the fortifications of Jerusalem were not completed until almost a century after Zerubbabel, under the leadership of Nehemiah (Neh 6:15). In the time of Artaxerxes I the Law of Moses was once more made the law of the land, and Ezra, a scribe, was charged with the reorganization of the province to conform with the new decree (Ezr 7:11-26). During the 2 centuries that the Persian Empire existed the people of Judah seem to have practiced their own religion with little interference from the Persian authorities, although under Artaxerxes II an attempt was made to force the Jews to worship Anahita, a Persian goddess. When the Jews showed hostility to the introduction of this foreign cult, persecution broke out, and many Jews were banished to Hyrcania.

When Alexander the Great destroyed the Persian Empire and founded his own, the Persian province of Judah became part of the Hellenistic world. After Alexander's death Judah fell into the hands of his Hellenistic successors, the Ptolemies, who were followed by the Seleucids. After a brief period of independence and expansion under the Maccabees, it was taken by the Romans, made into a subject kingdom and later given to Herod the Great. After that, the region experienced a checkered history, being either under Herod's descendants or under Roman procurators until its final downfall during the Jewish-Roman wars of the 1st and 2d cent. A.D. For the period from Alexander the Great and on *see* Judea.

Judaism. A rare term that appears only in: (1) Acts 13:43, RSV, in the phrase "devout converts to Judaism," a rendering of the Gr. *sebomenoi prosēlutoï*, literally, "worshiping proselytes" (KJV "religious proselytes"). (2) Gal 1:13, 14, RSV, as a rendering of the Gr. *Ioudaismos*, "Judaism" (KJV "Jews' religion"). In this passage Paul reminded the Galatians of his former extreme zeal for the traditions, laws, and ceremonies of the Jewish religion.

Judas (jōō′das), KJV twice **Juda** (jōō′da). [Gr. *Ioudas*, a transliteration of the Heb. *Yehûdah*, "Judah," a common Jewish name, especially since the days of the patriot Judas Maccabeus, liberator of the Jews from the tyranny of Antiochus Epiphanes (175-164/63 B.C.).]

1. A pre-exilic Judahite appearing in Luke's genealogy of Jesus (Lk 3:30).

2. For Mt 1:2, 3, KJV, *see* Judah, 1.

3. Judas the Galilean, who led a revolt about A.D. 7 when Quirinius, the Roman governor of Syria, to which Judea had been attached the year before, and Coponius, the 1st Roman procurator of Judea, sought, for the first time, to impose a direct Roman

tax upon the Jews (Acts 5:37). Josephus repeatedly mentions Judas and his revolt (*Ant.* xviii. 1. 6; xx. 5. 2; *War* ii. 8. 1; 18. 8; vii. 8. 1). Judas forbade the payment of taxes to the Romans, on the basis that the Jews were God's chosen people and that God had given them the land of Canaan. No foreign power, he contended, had the right to levy taxes upon them, and submission to taxation was no better than slavery. Josephus describes the revolt as a religious war. Judas and his followers were affiliated with the Pharisees, and though the movement failed and its leader was killed, there grew out of it the sect or party of the Zealots. The Zealots are probably to be identified with the Sicarii, or "daggermen," who were chiefly responsible for provoking the Jewish war of A.D. 66-70 that led to the destruction of Jerusalem, the burning of the Temple, and the annihilation of the Jewish nation.

4. Judas Iscariot, a son of Simon Iscariot (Jn 6:71, RSV; cf. ch 13:2, 26), and the disciple who betrayed Jesus. The surname Iscariot distinguishes him from another of the Twelve, Judas the son of James (Lk 6:16; Jn 14:22). The name Iscariot is thought to come from the Heb. *'Ish Qeriyôth*, "man of Kerioth," a city of southern Judah between Beer-sheba and the Dead Sea. The surname probably indicates that Judas was a native of Judea, and if so, the only one of the Twelve not a Galilean. The first mention of Judas is his appointment to be one of the Twelve (Mk 3:19). He may have become a follower of Jesus during the Judean ministry. Apparently a man of some executive ability, Judas became treasurer for the disciples (ch 13:29). That he was not strictly honest in his handling of the common fund is evident from the fact that John calls him a thief (ch 12:6). The seeming deference with which the other disciples treated Judas suggests that they admired him and respected his ability. Approximately 1 year before the betrayal Jesus foretold that one of the Twelve, whom He did not name, would betray Him (ch 6:70, 71). Jesus' mild but direct rebuke to Judas at the feast at Simon's house, the day preceding the Triumphal Entry (see ch 12:12), on account of Judas' protest that the price of Mary's expensive ointment might better have been entrusted to him—"and given to the poor" (Mt 26:6-13; cf. Jn 12:1-8)—was apparently Judas' excuse for making his first contact with the chief priests. He found them assembled together at the

house of Caiaphas, deliberating on what procedure they might take to dispose of Jesus (Mt 26:1-5, 14-16). The "thirty pieces of silver" (v 15) for which Judas conspired to betray his Lord, the traditional price of a slave (see Ex 21:32), would be worth about $12.60 at the current rate for silver. At the Last Supper Jesus gradually revealed to Judas that He knew all about Judas' plot to betray Him. As He washed the disciples' feet Jesus said, "Ye are clean, but not all" (Jn 13:10). Judas must have surmised that Jesus referred to him, but the other disciples had no way of knowing to whom of their number Jesus referred. A little later Jesus made it plain that the betrayer was present in the room, quoting Ps 41:9 cryptically: "He that eateth bread with me hath lifted up his heel against me" (Jn 13:18). When Jesus said, "One of you shall betray me" (Mt 26:21), He spoke in literal terms that could not be misunderstood. A few moments later Jesus identified the betrayer as the one "that dippeth his hand with me in the dish" (v 23). Finally Judas inquired directly, "Master, is it I?" and Jesus replied, "Thou hast said" (v 25). Immediately the betrayer left the upper room, with Jesus' final admonition ringing in his ears, "That thou doest, do quickly" (Jn 13:27). Ever since his first offer to betray Jesus, Judas had been seeking a favorable occasion on which to carry out his perfidious bargain (see Mt 26:16). Doubtless reasoning that with Jesus now inside the city it would be relatively easy for the priests to apprehend Him, Judas went directly from the Last Supper to the Jewish leaders and made final arrangements for the traitorous act. Judas was probably not far away during the trials before the Sanhedrin. When Jesus submitted to the death sentence, he publicly confessed his traitorous act and returned the 30 pieces of silver (ch 27:3, 4), an act that doubtless embarrassed the Jewish leaders greatly. Later, he committed suicide, and the betrayal money was spent for a potter's field (Mt 27:5-10; Acts 1:18, 19).

5. One of the Twelve, a son of James, carefully distinguished from Judas Iscariot (Jn 14:22). He is doubtless to be identified with Lebbaeus Thaddaeus (lĕ-bē′ŭs thă-dē′ŭs) [Gr. *Lebbaios Thaddaios*] (Mt 10:3; Mk 3:18; Lk 6:16; Acts 1:13).

6. A brother of Jesus (Mt 13:55; Mk 6:3), commonly identified as the author of the Epistle of Jude (Jude 1; cf. v 17). *See* Brethren of the Lord; Jude, Epistle of.

7. A Jew of Damascus, with whom Paul lodged for a time after his conversion (Acts 9:10, 11).

8. Judas *Barsabbas, a leader in the church at Jerusalem who, with Silas, was appointed to accompany Barnabas and Paul to Antioch with the letter announcing the decision of the Jerusalem Council respecting Gentile converts (Acts 15:22, 27, 32). He had the prophetic gift and engaged in public ministry (v 32).

Jude (jōōd). [Gr. *Ioudas*, "Judas," a transliteration of the Heb. *Yehûdah*, "Judah."] *See* Judas, 6.

Jude, Epistle of. The last of the General Epistles that appear between Hebrews and the Revelation. It is "general" in the sense that it does not specify any particular individual or church as its recipient, but is addressed to believers everywhere. The writer identifies himself simply as "Jude, the servant of Jesus Christ, and brother of James" (Jude 1). It is generally agreed that the James here referred to is the Lord's brother, later a leader in the church at Jerusalem (see Acts 12:17; 15:13; *see* James, 3). If so, the author of the Epistle of Jude was also a brother of our Lord, since the Gospel writers indicate that Jesus' brothers included a James and a Judas (Mt 13:55; Mk 6:3). Two of the Twelve were named Judas—Judas Iscariot (Mk 3:19), and Judas the son of James (see Jn 14:22)—but the epistle (see Jude 17) seems to indicate that the author was not one of the Twelve. The fact that the author simply identifies himself as "the servant of Jesus Christ" (v 1) may reflect a reluctance to take advantage of a relationship to Jesus.

The epistle provides no direct information as to the circumstances under which it was written or as to the believers to whom it was addressed. It notes, however, that there were disruptive elements at work in the church (Jude 4, 8; etc.). References to certain heretical teachers (Jude 4, 8, 10-13, 16, 18; cf. 2 Pe 3:3) are reminiscent of similar warnings sounded by Peter (cf. 2 Pe 2:1 to 3:3) and John (1 Jn 2:18, 19, 22, 23; 4:1-3; 5:10). This similarity suggests that the Epistle of Jude was written as a warning against the same heretical tendencies—the proto-Gnosticism of Cerinthus and the Docetists. *See* John, Epistles of; John, Gospel of. A considerable portion of the book of Jude (vs 4-18) is very similar to 2 Pe 1 to 3:3; not only the thoughts but in many instances the very same words, some of them being unusual (cf. Jude 4, 16 with 2 Pe 2:1, 3), are used. It would seem that one writer borrowed from the other, or that the two had access to a common source, now unknown. Biblical scholars suggest that Jude may have been the earlier of the two, since it would be difficult to explain why Jude would be writing a letter at all if he had little to say beyond what Peter had written. They conclude that it would be easier to understand why Peter would incorporate some of Jude's thoughts in his epistle along with considerable other material that he added to it. It is often the case that the shorter of 2 similar works proves to be the earlier. However, plausible reasons for the reverse order can be presented, and the matter cannot be settled with certainty. Under any circumstances, the conditions reflected in the epistle existed in the latter half of the 1st cent. A.D.

Jude had originally intended to write an epistle on the general subject of salvation, but learning of the heretical and licentious teachers who were troubling the flock, he decided instead to send a warning against them (Jude 3). So, he unmasks their true character. The libertines of Jude's epistle are doubtless the same persons who held false notions on the character of Christ—the Cerinthian and Docetic heretics. Sensual lusts were indulged openly by the Gnostics, and defended as well. *See* Nicolaitans.

Following his introduction (Jude 1-4), Jude cites historical incidents as a warning against backsliding (vs 5-7). In vs 8-11 he characterizes the defiant attitude of the false teachers of his day, and in vs 12 and 13 sets forth the worthlessness of their course of action. In vs 14-16 he points forward to their certain doom, and in vs 17-19 to the appearance of these licentious teachers as an evidence that it is now "the last time." In his conclusion (vs 20-25) he admonishes the believers to build themselves up in the "most holy faith" and to be patient unto the coming of the Lord.

Judea (jōō-dē′à), KJV **Judaea** (jōō-dē′à). [Gr. *Ioudaia*, an adjectival form from the Aramaic *Yehûday*, " (belonging to) Judah," or " (the land of) Judah." By some accident of translation we find "Judea" in the OT once (Ezr 9:9, RSV) as a rendering of the Heb. *Yehûdah* and once in the KJV (ch 5:8) as a rendering of *Yehûd*, which is the Aramaic equivalent of *Yehûdah*. However, both these terms should be rendered "Judah," which name appears repeatedly in Ezra and Nehemiah (Ezr 1:2, 3; 3:9; Neh 2:5; 6:7; etc.). "Judea" is properly the Latinized form of the Gr. *Ioudaia,* while Judah in Gr. is *Ioudas.*] The term Judea, or Judaea, refers primarily to the area of Palestine south of Samaria occupied by ancient Judah; secondarily, to the whole land of the Jews with varying boundaries. In the NT, Judea most often means the general area south of Samaria (cf. Mt 2:1, 5; Mk 3:7, 8; Acts 9:31; etc.), although it sometimes means more. For instance, we find Herod, who ruled all Palestine, called "king of Judaea" (Lk 1:5).

This article begins more or less arbitrarily at the time of Alexander the Great as being the period when Greek rule and influence—symbolized by the term Judea, which is the Greek name for the country—began. It covers the intertestamental and NT periods. For earlier periods *see* Judah, Tribe of.

1. *The Intertestamental Period.* When Alexander conquered the country bordering the eastern Mediterranean, Jerusalem did not resist; instead, according to Josephus, the high priest received him as an honored guest and as a conqueror foretold in prophecy (*Ant.* xi. 8. 4, 5). Alexander gave favorable terms to the Jews and settled many in his new city of Alexandria. After his death Judea became part of the territory of his successors, and was at first ruled by the Ptolemies of Egypt. However, several times it changed hands between them and the Seleucid rulers of Syria. (See Map XIII, C-3/4.)

The Jews were generally well treated during the first 150 years of Hellenistic rule. Under the Ptolemies, and the earlier Seleucids, they had a large measure of autonomy. Judea was a "Temple state" governed by the high priest, and the Hellenistic ruler was generally satisfied as long as tribute was regularly paid. The Jews were free to retain their own customs and religion, although among the upper classes there was an increasing tendency to adopt the Greek language, dress, and customs. However, a reaction set in when Antiochus IV Epiphanes attempted to Hellenize the Jews by force. In 168 B.C. he commanded them to cease their worship of the Lord and their observance of the Sabbath and of the rite of circumcision, and to participate in heathen sacrifices of unclean beasts offered to Zeus and Dionysus. He had the Temple in Jerusalem dedicated to Zeus, and ordered unclean animals to be sacrificed on its altar. The Sabbath was abolished as well as the reading of the Law, Jewish sacred books were destroyed, and pious Jews loyal to the religion of their fathers were tortured and killed. Jewish resistance finally took the form of the revolt of the Maccabees (Mattathias, his sons, and their followers). The first action against the Syrians was in the nature of guerilla warfare, but under Judas Maccabeus real battles were fought, and extraordinary victories achieved. The fortunes of war changed from time to time, but Judea eventually emerged from this struggle as a free nation. From 143 B.C. it counted itself independent. From 104 B.C. it was an independent kingdom, ruling over a large territory in Palestine, which eventually included Idumea (Edom), Samaria, Galilee, and areas in Transjordan and northeast of the Sea of Galilee (Map XIV). In 63 B.C. Pompey took Jerusalem, and Judea became subject to Rome, and was ruled as a subject kingdom by the last Maccabean rulers. In 40 B.C. the Romans appointed a new native ruler as king of Judea, Herod "the Great," of Idumean ancestry.

2. *New Testament Times.* When Jesus was born, shortly before Herod's death, the kingdom of Judea almost equaled in size that controlled by King David (Map XV). After Herod's death in 4 B.C. the kingdom was divided, and Judea proper and Samaria were placed under his son Archelaus, who received the title ethnarch. When Archelaus was deposed because of mismanagement in A.D. 6, Judea ceased to be governed by native rulers and was placed under Roman provincial administration. After having enjoyed local autonomy under Persian, Hellenistic, and Roman overlords, Judea now came directly under foreign governors—Roman procurators who had their seat in Caesarea. Seven procurators ruled over Judea and Samaria in a period of 35 years, and thoroughly antagonized the Jews. See Map XVI. Then Judea and Samaria were added to the kingdom of a descendant of Herod, Agrippa I, who was ruling in the northeast. He was king over Judea from A.D. 41 to 44. After his death Judea, along with Samaria, again became a province under procurators. Most of the 7 procurators who ruled over the country during the next 22 years were mean and selfish men, whose foolish and unstatesmanlike actions contributed greatly toward provoking the outbreak of the rebellion of A.D. 66. This war resulted

in the destruction of Jerusalem and the Temple by Titus in A.D. 70, and the end of the state of Judea and the Jewish nation as such. *See* Jesus Christ, I, II.

Judge. A public civil officer. Shortly after Israel left Egypt Moses, upon the advice of his father-in-law, Jethro, appointed men to act as judges and rulers over groups of 10, 50, 100, and 1,000—a system roughly similar to our lower civil courts today (Ex 18:13-26). These men were to judge righteously, fearlessly, and without partiality (Deut 1:16, 17). God gave Moses a code of law as the standard by which judgments were to be made (see Ex 20 to 23; Lev 18 to 20; etc.). Upon settling in Canaan the Israelites were to appoint judges and officers for all their towns (Deut 16:18-20; 17:8-12). After the establishment of the kingdom, the king became chief judge in civil affairs (1 Ki 3:9; 7:7; cf. 1 Sa 8:5). David appointed Levites as judges (1 Chr 23:4; 26:29), and Jehoshaphat improved the judicial system in Judah, appointing judges in all fortified cities and establishing a supreme court at Jerusalem, with the chief priest presiding in religious matters and the prince of Judah in civil (2 Chr 19:8, 11).

In a special sense the term "judge" is applied to the magistrates who governed Israel in the period between Joshua and the setting up of the monarchy. The Hebrews borrowed their term for "judge," *shophet*, from the Canaanites. The rulers of Carthage, descendants of the Phoenicians, bore this title for centuries. To the Romans the title was known in the corrupted form *suffes*, plural *suffetes*.

Because of idolatry the Lord permitted enemies to oppress the Israelites (Jgs 2:14). When the people called upon God as a result of their troubles, He raised up judges (v 18) who delivered them and then judged them (ch 2:16; cf. ch 10:2). These judges did not rule in unbroken succession, but appeared sporadically, sometimes contemporaneously in different parts of the country. *See* Chronology, III; History, Biblical, III.

One of the major themes of Psalms is God's function as supreme Judge (Ps 7:8, 11; 9:8; 58:11; 82:1; 96:13). Men often appealed their cases to God when injustice was felt at the hands of men (Ps 35:24; 43:1). That God will be the final judge, and that His judgment will satisfy all the demands of justice, is certain (Eze 33:20; 2 Ti 4:1; Rev 19:2). He has appointed a day in which He will judge the world in righteousness (Acts

17:31). The basis of God's righteous judgment will be, in every case, the evidence from the life of the one judged (Ec 12:14; Lk 19:22; Rom 2:12, 27; 14:10; 2 Cor 5:10; Rev 20:12, 13).

Judges, Book of. The history of the Hebrew people from the death of Joshua, c. 1375 B.C., to the establishment of the monarchy, c. 1050 B.C., a period of approximately 300 years. The book takes its name from the title by which the men who governed Israel during this period were known. These judges were appointed by God (Jgs 3:15; 4:6; 6:12; etc.). Civil and military authority centered in the office of judge, though the book of Judges stresses principally the military leadership of the judges in delivering Israel from foreign bondage. Since their exploits were largely military in character, the term "chieftain" would seem to describe their function more accurately. The need for such leaders arose out of the prevailing apostasy, anarchy, and foreign oppression. The more illustrious of the judges, such as Gideon, Deborah, and Samson, became national heroes.

Ancient Jewish tradition makes Samuel the author of the book (see Babylonian Talmud *Baba Bathra* 14b, 15a). The recurring expression, "In those days there was no king in Israel" (Jgs 17:6), indicates that the book was written after the establishment of the monarchy under Saul. However, it must have been written before David's victory over the Jebusites and his capture of Jerusalem early in his reign (2 Sa 5:6-9; cf. Jgs 19:10, 11).

The occupation of Canaan by the Hebrews was a gradual process (see Jgs 2:3). The preliminary conquest, which was completed in 6 or 7 years after the crossing of the Jordan, brought sufficient land under Hebrew control to provide permanent homes for all and to make possible the tribal apportionment of the land (Jos 7:16, 23). But even after "Joshua took the whole land," and "the land rested from war" (ch 11:23), he told the people that "there remaineth yet very much land to be possessed" (ch 13:1). At first the Hebrews occupied chiefly the mountainous region in the center of the country, while the various Canaanite tribes continued to live in the valleys.

"Israel served the Lord all the days of Joshua, and all the days of the elders that overlived Joshua" (Jos 24:31), but after the passing of the generation that had witnessed the power of God in the crossing of the Jordan and the preliminary conquest of the land, the people adopted the religious customs and practices of the Canaanites. Increasing apostasy was accompanied by a deterioration of civil and social life, to the point where the Hebrews were unable to defend themselves against the surrounding Canaanite tribes, much less extend their conquest. There was no permanent, central government, and except for the guidance of judges who arose from time to time "every man did that which was right in his own eyes" (Jgs 17: 6; 21:25; etc.). Alternate apostasy and servitude, repentance and deliverance, characterize the period of the judges. After suffering for a time at the hands of their heathen neighbors, the Hebrew people would return to the Lord, and He would send someone to deliver them from the foreign yoke. A period of revival would follow, and then the same pattern of apostasy, decline, and oppression would be repeated.

Some of the judges seem to have ruled the entire nation, whereas others served only one tribe or a group of tribes. The record in the book of Judges is largely one of military operations. Separated as the Hebrew tribes were from one another by fortified Canaanite towns, they were exposed to attack, and it was only with difficulty that they could unite their efforts to hold onto the land they had already wrested from the hostile population. Apostasy and idolatry still further weakened the bonds of national unity. The great lesson of the book is that sin and apostasy result in the withdrawal of God's protecting hand, but that true repentance brings deliverance and that righteousness exalts a nation.

The book of Judges falls into 3 main sections. In the 1st (chs 1:1 to 3:6) the author describes the situation at the beginning of the period. He relates the endeavor of the tribes to consolidate their several allotments in Palestine, summarizes the history of the period, and interprets the lessons to be learned from it. In the 2d section the author deals with the period in chronological order (chs 3:7 to 16:31), taking up the successive periods of oppression and the rise of judge after judge to deliver Israel. The more noteworthy of these national heroes were Deborah and Barak, who defeated a northern Canaanite coalition; Gideon, who repelled a Midianite invasion; Jephthah, who defeated the Ammonites; and Samson, who had various adventures with the Philistines. The 3d section (chs 17:1 to

21:25) narrates 2 incidents of the period, doubtless to illustrate what life was like in this period of Hebrew history. *See* names of individual judges.

Judgment. [Heb. generally *mishpaṭ,* "decision," "right," "justice," "ordinance"; Gr. generally *krima,* "judicial sentence," and *krisis,* "act of judging," "execution of a sentence."] A term that may refer variously to the process of judging (Deut 1:17; Is 28:6; Mal 3:5), to the judicial decision (Deut 16:18) or sentence (Rev 17:1), to the decisions of God as expressed in His revealed will (Ps 19:9, KJV), to justice itself (Is 1:17), or to the execution of a sentence previously arrived at (Jer 51: 9; Rev 19:2).

The concept of God's entering into judgment with the inhabitants of earth is frequently presented by Bible writers. Enoch, "the seventh from Adam," pictured the Lord as coming to execute judgment upon all (Jude 14, 15). Isaiah described God as coming with fire to execute judgment (Is 66:15, 16, RSV), and the prophet Jeremiah pictured the awesome time when "the Lord will roar from on high" and enter "into judgment with all flesh" (Jer 25:30, 31, RSV). Daniel foresaw the time when "the judgment was set, and the books were opened" (Dan 7:10), and in mystic language Joel prophesied that God would "sit to judge all the heathen round about" (Joel 3:12; cf. vs 13-16).

Jesus frequently referred to the final judgment. He declared that ancient Sodom and Gomorrah would be treated more leniently in the judgment for refusing the light they had than would the cities of His day that spurned Him (Mt 10:11, 14, 15), and the pagan cities of Tyre and Sidon would receive lesser condemnation in the judgment than Chorazin, Bethsaida, and Capernaum, which rejected Him (Lk 10: 13-15). He asserted that men shall give an account of "every idle word" in the judgment (Mt 12:36; cf. chs 16:27; 24:30, 31; 25:31-46; Mk 8:38; Lk 9:26; etc.).

Paul declared that God has appointed a day in which He will judge the world (Acts 17:31). He preached of coming judgment to Felix with such conviction that the Roman procurator trembled (ch 24:25). He showed that the conviction of a future judgment is found implanted in the human conscience (Rom 1:32; 2:14-16), and that for the wicked the prospect of a future judgment is a fearful thing (Heb 10:26, 27). Peter noted that both evil angels and wicked men are reserved unto judgment (2 Pe 2:4, 9; 3:7; cf. Jude 6). In their judgment the saints are to participate (1 Cor 6:2, 3).

No man can escape the judgment, for all must appear before the "judgment seat of Christ"; and the decision of the judgment is based on "the things done in his body" (2 Cor 5:10; cf. Mt 7:16-20; Rev 20:13). The standard of judgment is the "law of liberty" (Jas 2:12; cf. vs 8-11). God's judgment will be righteous (Rom 2:5; 2 Th 1:5; cf. Gen 18:25; Ps 19:9), decisive, and eternal in consequence (Heb 6:2; 9:27). In the judgment the whole life will be bared before God (Ec 12:13, 14; cf. Lk 12:2). For a discussion of the judgment in its various aspects, see *SDACom* 4:828-830; 7:881-883.

Judgment Hall. *See* Praetorium.

Judith (jōō′dĭth). [Heb. *Yehûdîth*, the feminine form of *Yehûdah*, "Judah."] A daughter of Beeri the Hittite, and one of the wives of Esau (Gen 26:34).

Julia (jōōl′ya). [Gr. *Ioulia*, from Latin *Julia*, a common Roman name, the feminine form of *Julius. This name was borne not only by various prominent women of the Julian house but also by many slaves and freedwomen of the early imperial period.] A Christian woman at Rome to whom Paul sent greetings, possibly the wife or sister of Philologus (Rom 16:15).

Julius (jōōl′yŭs). [Gr. *Ioulios*, from Latin *Julius*, a common Roman name, best known as that of Gaius Julius Caesar, and originally belonging specifically to the Julian gens, or clan.] A centurion of the Augustan Cohort, charged with transporting a group of prisoners to Rome, among whom was the apostle Paul (Acts 27:1). He treated Paul with much kindness and allowed him to go ashore at Sidon to visit his friends (v 3). Although he did not heed Paul's warnings at Crete (v 11), he listened to him later and prevented the sailors from forsaking the ship (vs 31, 32). He also saved Paul at the time of the shipwreck by preventing the guards from killing the prisoners (vs 42, 43).

Jungle of the Jordan. An RSV term referring to the thicket along the banks of the *Jordan. The KJV translates the term rendered "jungle" (*ga'ôn*) "swelling" (Jer 12:5; 49:19; 50:44) and "pride" (Zec 11:3).

Junia. *See* Junias.

Junias (jōō′nĭ-ăs), KJV **Junia** (jōō′nĭ-à). [Gr. *Iounias*, if a masculine name; *Iounia* if a feminine name. *Iounias*, "Junias," is a name otherwise unattested, but may be a contraction of *Junianus*.] A Christian in Rome to whom Paul sent greetings (Rom 16:7). The context suggests that he was a man, hence should be called by the masculine name Junias, as in the RSV. Some commentators, on the basis that a number of Christian households are mentioned in the list of Christian believers in Rom 16 (vs 3, 13, 15), believe that the Christian referred to was the wife of Andronicus, hence should be called by the feminine name Junia (see KJV).

Juniper. *See* Broom.

Jupiter. *See* Zeus.

Jushab-hesed (jōō′shăb-hē′sĕd). [Heb. *Yûshab chesed*, "kindness is returned."] A son of Zerubbabel and descendant of David (1 Chr 3:1, 19, 20).

Justice. In the KJV this term is generally from the Heb. *ṣedeq* or *ṣedaqah*, both of which mean righteousness and are usually so translated. The idea of justice is suggested by the context in certain passages. In the RSV "justice" is generally the translation of the Heb. *mishpaṭ* from *shaphaṭ*, "to judge." *Mishpaṭ* closely approximates the meaning of "justice" as the term is understood today (Gen 18:19; Ex 23:6; Deut 10:18; etc.).

Justification. [Gr. *dikaiōma*, "requirement," "enactment," "righteous deed," "judicial sentence," "declaration of right"; *dikaiōsis*, "justification," "vindication," "acquittal." The verb "justify" is much more frequent than the noun "justification."] As used theologically, the divine act by which God declares a penitent sinner righteous, or regards him as righteous. Justification is the opposite of condemnation (Rom 5:16). Neither term specifies character, but only standing before God. Justification is not a transformation of inherent character; it does not impart righteousness any more than condemnation imparts sinfulness. A man comes under condemnation because of his transgressions, but, as a sinner, he can experience justification only through an act of God. Condemnation is earned, or deserved, but justification cannot be earned—it is a "free [unmerited] gift" (v 16). In justifying the sinner God acquits him, declares him to be righteous, regards him as righteous, and proceeds to treat him as a righteous man. Justification is the act of acquittal and the accompanying declaration that a state of righteousness exists. Charges of wrongdoing are canceled, and the sinner, now justified, is brought into a right relationship with God that Paul describes as being at "peace with God" (Rom 5:1). The state of righteousness to which a sinner attains through justification is imputed (ch 4: 22), that is, counted (v 3) or reckoned (v 4). When God imputes righteousness to a repentant sinner He figuratively places the atonement provided by Christ and the righteousness of Christ to his credit on the books of heaven, and the sinner stands before God as if he had never sinned.

Justification presupposes that God has a perfect standard of right by which He expects created beings to order their lives, and that He requires perfect observance of this standard. Theoretically, God could not legally condemn a man who never violated this standard (Rom 2:13), but the fact is that all have done so (ch 3:10, 23). Divine law—all of God's revealed will concerning man—is thus an expression of His justice, a reflection of His own righteous character as well as the standard of attainment for all created beings.

Justification is *necessary* because "all have sinned, and come short of the glory of God" (Rom 3:23; cf. v 10). Without it, sinners could never be acceptable to God, but would remain in a perpetual state of hostility toward Him. Justification is *possible* because of God's grace, or willingness not to hold sinners accountable for their misdeeds on condition that they accept the righteous provision He has made "for the remission of sins that are past" (vs 24, 25), and by virtue of Christ's righteousness (ch 5:18). The righteous provision is the gift of His Son, "who was delivered for our offences, and was raised again for our justification" (Rom 4:25; 5:16, 18; cf. Jn 3:16). When by faith the sinner accepts the vicarious death of Jesus Christ as the just penalty for his own offenses, God in turn accepts the sinner's faith in lieu of personal righteousness and places the righteousness of Jesus Christ to his credit. Christ's resurrection was fully as essential "for our justification" as was His death upon the cross (see Rom 4:25). Strict justice provides no escape from the penalty for sin, which is death. This is why Christ paid that penalty on the cross. But even as Christ's death on the cross to pay the penalty for sin is a demonstration of divine justice, so the resurrection, which released the Saviour from that penalty, is a demonstration of divine mercy and of God's willingness to transfer the merits of Christ's vicarious death to sinners who are willing to accept the gracious gift. Had Christ remained forever in the tomb, there would be no objective evidence that God can and does justify sinners (Rom 4:24, 25). Thus it is that faith in a risen Lord makes us eligible to, and enables us to accept, justification, by faith in Christ's death. We are "justified by his blood" and "saved by his life" (ch 5:9, 10).

The counterpart, and complement, of God's act of grace in justifying the sinner is the sinner's faith, which reaches out to accept the proffered gift (Rom 5:1, 2). Of himself the sinner can do nothing to attain to justification. His exercise of faith is a confession of inability to attain to a state of righteousness by his own works. God acknowledges his faith and justifies him, and "there is therefore now no condemnation to them which are in Christ Jesus" (ch 8:1).

Justification has both negative and affirmative aspects. It consists first in the forgiveness of sins (Rom 4:5-8), but this is accompanied by a declaration that the pardoned sinner has been restored to divine favor. Paul describes this right relationship as being at "peace with God" (ch 5:1), or "reconciled to God" (v 10). Remorse for sin (Lk 18:13, 14) and a soul-consuming desire to be right with God (Mt 5:6) are prerequisites to justification. Then faith arises to accept the divine provision of grace (Rom 4:4, 5, 16, 24). This right relationship with God bestows upon the repentant sinner his title to the kingdom of heaven. It was thus that Jesus could assure the thief on the cross that he would be with Him in Paradise (Lk 23:43). Justification accords a repentant sinner the *right* to enter the highway of the kingdom and travel there, but it does not provide the *power* to make progress upon it. That power is imparted by the indwelling Christ (Gal 2:20), through the lifelong process of sanctification. From faith in Christ's death the justified sinner is to rise and "*walk* in newness of life" (Rom 6:4, 5). Although justification does not provide him the power to walk along the highway of a new life in Christ Jesus, it does assume this to be his intent. In fact, justification would be futile if he declined to do so, and unless such an experience follows there is no evidence that justification has taken place. The subsequent life attests the reality of justification. Justification and sanctification are 2 steps in salvation. A life in Christ means growth in grace (2 Pe 3:18), a growing up into the full stature of Christ (Eph 4:15).

Justus (jŭs′tŭs). [Gr. *Ioustos,* from Latin *Justus,* "just" or "righteous."]

1. A surname of Joseph, also called Barsabbas, a candidate for the apostleship after the death of Judas (Acts 1:23).

2. A man at Corinth, whose full name was Titius, or Titus, Justus. He was either a proselyte or, more probably, a Gentile who was a friend of the Jewish religion but who had not yet become a full proselyte. His house adjoined the Jewish synagogue, and when the Jews expelled Paul from their house of worship the apostle made the home of Justus the center of his Christian mission (Acts 18:7, 8).

3. A Christian in Rome, whose full name was Jesus Justus. He was â Jewish-Christian fellow worker of Paul, and sent greetings to the church of Colossae (Col 4:11).

Juttah (jŭt′à). [Heb. *Yûṭṭah.*] A town situated in the hill country of Judah, which was assigned to the priests and designated as a city of refuge (Jos 15:55; 21:16); now the village of *Yaṭṭā,* about 4½ mi. south of Hebron (Map XIV, F-3).

K

Kab, KJV **Cab.** [Heb. *qab,* a loan word from the Egyptian *qby.*] A dry and liquid measure. It is mentioned in Jewish documents of the 5th cent. B.C. from Egypt, and frequently in later Jewish literature as being equal to 4 logs. Hence it was 1/18 of an ephah or 1.11 U.S. dry qt. (1.22 liters). In the Bible it is mentioned only in 2 Ki 6:25.

Kabzeel (kăb′zĕ-ĕl). [Heb. *Qabṣe'el,* "God gathers."] A town in the extreme southern part of Judah (Jos 15:21); not identified with certainty. It was the home town of Benaiah, captain of David's guard (2 Sa 23:20; 1 Chr 11:22). It was resettled by the Jews in postexilic times (see Neh 11: 25, where it is called Jekabzeel (jĕ-kăb′zĕ-ĕl) [Heb. *Yeqabṣe'el*].

Kadesh (kā′dĕsh). [Heb. *Qadesh,* "a holy place."]

1. Short form of *Kadesh-barnea.

2. Kadesh on the Orontes, mentioned in the Bible only in 2 Sa 24:6, RSV, as "Kadesh in the land of the Hittites." The Hebrew reads *tachtîm chodshî,* transliterated "Tahtim-hodshi" (tä′tîm-hŏd′shî), in the KJV. However, such a place is unknown; so some scholars accept Lucian's reading, *chettieim kadēs,* and prefer the translation "Kadesh of the Hittites," or "Kadesh in the land of the Hittites." Lucian's reading assumes the Hebrew form *chittîm qadesh.* If "Kadesh of the Hittites" is the correct reading, the strong city of Kadesh on the Orontes is meant, which played a great role in the 2d millennium B.C., its king being then the leader of a coalition of Syrian and Canaanite princes against whom Thutmose III fought his first battle at Megiddo. It was later the scene of the great battle of Ramses II against Muwatallis, king of the Hittites, in which Ramses almost lost his army. The site is now called *Tell Nebī Mend,* 44 mi. south of Hamath in Syria (Map III, C-4). Excavations were conducted there (1921-1922) by a French expedition.

Kadesh-barnea (kā′dĕsh-bär′nĕ-à), frequently **Kadesh** (kā′dĕsh). [Heb. *Qadêsh Barnea‘,* and *Qadesh,* "holy place (of Barnea)."] The name of a fountain, city, or town, and of the surrounding wilderness near the southern border of Judah (Num 20:16; Ps 29:8; Eze 47:19). From other places called Kadesh it is occasionally distinguished by the attribute Barnea (Num 32:8). Its earliest name was En-mishpat, meaning "fountain of judgment" (Gen

275. *'Ain Qedeis,* identified by some as Kadesh-barnea

14:7). It lay apparently on the border between the Wilderness of Zin in the north and the Wilderness of Paran in the south and could therefore legitimately be spoken of as lying in either one of these deserts (Num 13:3, 26; 20:1; 27:14). Deut 1:2 places it 11 days' journey from Mount Sinai by way of Mount Seir, and according to Num 20:16 it lay in the edge of the border of Edom. It was also on the road to Egypt (Gen 16:14; 20:1). In spite of all these geographical data, the site has not been identified definitely. A site called 'Ain Qedeis, 47 mi. southwest of Beer-sheba (Map V, B-6), was discovered by J. Rowlands in 1842. It was rediscovered and identified as Kadesh in 1884 by H. C. Trumbull, and the majority of scholars since then have considered it the site of Kadesh-barnea. However, another site, 'Ain Qudeirât, about 5 mi. to the northwest, is considered by some as the more likely site (see Map V, B-6). In a place near 'Ain Qudeirât Iron Age remains were discovered, showing that this adjacent site was the chief center of that whole area from 1200 B.C. onward.

Kadesh played an important role in the history of southern Palestine. It is first mentioned in the Bible under the name En-mishpat as a place conquered by Chedorlaomer and his confederates (Gen 14:7). Hagar fled into this area (ch 16:7, 14), and Abraham lived in its environs for some time (ch 20:1). The Israelites reached this place in the 2d year of their desert wanderings, and sent out spies to Palestine from there, who returned with gloomy reports. It was there that because of their rebellion they were sentenced to wander in the wilderness for 40 years (Num 13:20, 26; 14:34). After remaining in the wilderness of Kadesh for "many days" (Deut 1:46), they returned to the site of Kadesh in the 1st month, probably of the 40th year of the wandering (Num 20:1). Miriam died there, and Moses and Aaron sinned by smiting a rock to bring forth water, when God had instructed them merely to speak to the rock (vs 1-13). From Kadesh envoys were sent to the king of Edom to request a permit to pass through his country, which was refused (vs 14-21).

Kadmiel (kăd'mĭ-ĕl). [Heb. Qadmî'el, "God is the ancient one."]

1. The ancestral head of a Levite family that returned with Zerubbabel from Babylonia (Ezr 2:40; Neh 7:43).

2. A Jew, probably a Levite, who assisted Zerubbabel in the laying of the

276. 'Ain Qudeirât, the possible site of Kadesh-barnea

foundations of the new Temple in Jerusalem (Ezr 3:9). He probably belonged to the family of Kadmiel, 1.

3. A Levite who assisted Ezra in instructing the people (Neh 9:4, 5), and who set his seal to Nehemiah's covenant (ch 10:9). He probably belonged to the family of Kadmiel, 1.

Kadmonites (kăd'mŏn-īts). [Heb. Qadmonî, "easterners," synonymous with the "children (RSV "people") of the east" referred to repeatedly in the OT (Jgs 6:3, 33; 7:12; 1 Ki 4:30; etc.).] Part of the inhabitants of the land that was promised Abraham's descendants. The name, which appears only once in the Bible (Gen 15:19), may refer to various tribes that occupied Transjordan in the time of Abraham in the same way as the "children of the east," who came with the Midianites into western Palestine in the period of the judges (Jgs 6:3; etc.), constituted various tribes. The Heb. qedem, of which Qadmonî is the gentilic form, is also used in this general sense of the East and its people in the Egyptian story of Sinuhe, which deals with Palestine and Syria in the time of Abraham. See People of the East.

Kain (kān). [Heb. Qayin, "smith," or "spear." The name occurs also in ancient South Arabic inscriptions.]

1. A town in the mountains of Judah (Jos 15:57, KJV "Cain"), now called Khirbet Yaqîn, 3 mi. southeast of Hebron.

2. The name of a tribe (Num 24:22, RSV), also called *Kenite as in the KJV here. The Heb. Qayin occurs also in Jgs 4:11, where, however, both the versions read "Kenite(s)."

Kaiwan (kī-wän'), KJV **Chiun** (kī'ŭn). [Heb. Kîyûn, according to the Masoretic vocalization.] A deity mentioned in Amos 5:26. The name should probably be read Kaywan, which was the Hebrew name of the planet Saturn. The Babylonian form is *Kayawânu* with *Kaywan* as a later Hebrew form, also attested in Arabic. The form *Kîyûn* may have resulted from the Masoretes' supplying the consonants *kywn* with the vowels *i* and *u* contained in *shiqqûṣ*, "a detestable thing." *See* Rephan; Sakkuth.

Kallai (kăl'â-ī). [Heb. *Qallay*, "swift."] A priest of the house of Sallai in the high priest Joiakim's time (Neh 12:12, 20).

Kamon (kā'mŏn), KJV **Camon** (kā'mŏn). [Heb. *Qamôn*.] A place in Gilead where the judge Jair was buried (Jgs 10:5), probably the present *Qamm*, 12 mi. southeast of the southern tip of the Sea of Galilee (Map VI, C-4).

Kanah (kā'nà). [Heb. *Qanah*, "reed."]
1. A brook that formed the boundary between Ephraim and Manasseh (Jos 16:8; 17:9); now identified with *Wâdī Qânah* (Map VI, D-2/3). It rises south of Shechem and later joins the *Nahr 'Aujâ*, better known as *Me-jarkon*, or *Yarkon*.
2. A town on the boundary of Asher (Jos 19:28), mentioned in Egyptian records of Thutmose III as *Qnw* and in the *Amarna Letters as *Qanû*. It is probably the modern *Qânah*, 6 mi. southeast of Tyre (Map VI, B-3).

Kareah (kà-rē'à), KJV once **Careah** (kà-rē'à). [Heb. *Qareach*, "bald." The name occurs in Assyrian inscriptions as *Karhâ* and *Karihi*.] A man whose son Johanan (2 Ki 25:23), along with another son Jonathan, according to Jer 40:8, KJV (*see* Jonathan, 9), came to Gedaliah at Mizpah after the destruction of Jerusalem.

Karka (kär'kà), KJV **Karkaa** (kär'kâ-à). [Heb. *Qarqa'*, "floor," or "bottom."] A town in the south of Judah (Jos 15:3); not identified with certainty.

Karkaa. *See* Karka.

Karkor (kär'kôr). [Heb. *Qarqor*.] A place in Transjordan where Gideon defeated the Midianite kings Zebah and Zalmunna (Jgs 8:10-12); not identified.

Karnaim. [Heb. *Qarnayim*, "2 horns."] A city in Bashan, mentioned in Amos 6:13, RSV (KJV "horns"). In Gen 14:5 it is mentioned in connection with Ashteroth, which was probably situated in its vicinity (*see* Ashteroth-Karnaim). Assyrian records refer to Karnaim as *Qarnini*, and 1 Macc calls it *Carnaim* (1 Macc 5:43). The city has been identified with the conspicuous mound *Sheikh Sa'ad*, about 23 mi. east of the Sea of Galilee in the Hauran (Map VI, C-5). A stele of Ramses II has been found there, which bears a badly worn

hieroglyphic inscription dedicated apparently to a local deity, called *'Adona' Ṣaphôn*, "the lord of the north." Also a well-preserved Hittite lion sculpture belonging to a palace or temple gate (now in the museum in Damascus) comes from this place. These monuments show that Karnaim must have been an important city in the 2d and 1st millenniums B.C. An archeological expedition under B. Hrozny worked there in 1924 for a brief season (*Syria* 5 [1924], 166, 207-209, pl. LII).

Kartah (kär'tà). [Heb. *Qartah*, "city."] A city in the territory of Zebulun, assigned to the Merarite Levites (Jos 21:34); not identified with certainty. Some identify it with *'Athlît* on the coast, south of Carmel.

Kartan (kär'tăn). [Heb. *Qartan*, "city."] A town in the territory of Naphtali, assigned to the Gershonite Levites (Jos 21:32), called Kiriathaim (RSV) and Kirjathaim (KJV) in 1 Chr 6:76 (Heb. *Qiryathayim*). It is identified with *Khirbet el-Qureiyeh*, 15 mi. southeast of Tyre.

Kattath (kăt'ăth). [Heb. *Qaṭṭath*.] A town in the territory of Zebulun (Jos 19:15), identified by some with Kitron (Jgs 1:30) and by others with Kartah (Jos 21:34). It is possibly to be identified with *Khirbet Qoṭeina*, northwest of Megiddo and southwest of Jokneam.

Kedar (kē'dĕr). [Heb. *Qedar*.] A son of Ishmael (Gen 25:13; 1 Chr 1:29), and ancestor of the frequently mentioned Arabic tribe of Kedar. In cuneiform records this tribe is known as *Qidri*, *Qadri*, and *Qidarri*, and in an Aramaic inscription of the 5th cent. as *Qdr*, and by Pliny as *Cedrei*. It was famous for its wealth in flocks (Jer 49:28, 29; Eze 27:21), and its people were famed archers (Is 21:16, 17). It seems that they must have roamed. in the Syrian desert between southern Palestine and Lower Mesopotamia (Map XI, C-4). In Is 60:7 they are referred to in connection with the Arabic tribe of Nebaioth, which is mentioned in cuneiform sources as *Nabâ'ati*, identified by some as Nabataeans. They lived in villages or encampments (ch 42:11), and were ruled by princes (Eze 27:21). A certain Geshem, probably "Geshem the Arab" of Neh 2:19, RSV (called Gashmu in ch 6:6, KJV), is called "King of Kedar" in a votary inscription found in Egypt (*JNES* 15 [1956], 2).

Kedemah (kĕd'ê-mà). [Heb. *Qedmah*, "toward the east."] A son of Ishmael and ancestor of an Arabic tribe bearing the same name (Gen 25:15; 1 Chr 1:31). The "children [RSV "people"] of the east" [Heb. *benê qedem*], so frequently mentioned in the OT (Jgs 6:3, 33; 8:10; 1 Ki 4:30; etc.) and extra-Biblical ancient sources, may be the descendants of this Ishmaelite. *See* People of the East.

Kedemoth (kĕd'ĕ-mŏth). [Heb. *Qedemóth,* "eastern regions."]

1. A wilderness (Deut 2:26) near the headwater of the river Arnon north of Moab.

2. A town in the territory of Reuben (Jos 13:18), assigned to the Merarite Levites (Jos 21:37; 1 Chr 6:79); it may tentatively be identified with *ez-Za'ferân,* 8 mi. southeast of Medeba.

Kedesh (Kē'dĕsh). [Heb. *Qedesh,* "holy place."]

1. A city in the south of Judah (Jos 15:23), to be distinguished from Kadesh-barnea.

2. A Canaanite city captured by Thutmose III and mentioned in his list of conquered Palestinian cities as *Qdsh.* Joshua defeated its king (Jos 12:22), and allotted the city to the tribe of Naphtali (ch 19:37); hence it was also named Kedesh-naphtali (kē'dĕsh-năf'tà-lī; Jgs 4:6), to distinguish it from other towns named Kedesh. Once it is called Kedesh in Galilee (Jos 20:7). It was later assigned to the Gershonite Levites for residence (ch 21:32) and subsequently made a city of refuge (1 Chr 6:76). Kedesh was the home of Barak, and there he and Deborah gathered their forces to fight against Sisera (Jgs 4:6, 9, 10). After Tiglath-pileser III conquered the city he deported its population to Assyria (2 Ki 15:29). It was later the scene of a victory of the Jewish army under Jonathan the Maccabean against the Syrian forces of Demetrius II (1 Macc 11:63, 73). It is now *Tell Qades,* a few miles northwest of the now-drained Lake Huleh (Map VI, B-4).

3. A town in the territory of Issachar, assigned to the Gershonite Levites (1 Chr 6:72); not identified with certainty; called Kishion (kĭsh'ĭ-ŏn) [Heb. *Qishyón*] in Jos 19:20; 21:28 (KJV "Kishon"), the two names being due probably either to a scribal error or to the fact that the town was known by different names in different periods.

Kedesh-naphtali. *See* Kedesh, 2.

Keeper. One who watches, guards, cares for, maintains. Various keepers are mentioned in Scripture: of sheep and cattle (Gen 4:2; 1 Sa 17:20; Gen 46:32, 34, RSV), of doors or thresholds (2 Ki 22:

4; 23:4), of gates (1 Chr 9:19, KJV; Neh 3:29), of women (Est 2:3, KJV), of walls (Song 5:7; RSV "watchmen"), of fields and vineyards (Jer 4:17; Song 8:11), of prisons (Acts 5:23; 12:6, 19; KJV), etc.

Kehelathah (kē'hĕ-lā'thà). [Heb. *Qehelathah,* "assembly."] A station of the Israelites in their wilderness wanderings (Num 33:22, 23); not identified with certainty.

Keilah (kē-ī'là). [Heb. *Qe'ilah.*] A fortified town of the Canaanites, mentioned in the *Amarna Letters as *Qilti.* It was in the Shephelah and belonged to Judah (Jos 15:44). David drove off Philistine raiders from the town when a fugitive from Saul, but could not trust its inhabitants, who he feared would deliver him over to King Saul (1 Sa 23:1-13). The town was repopulated after the Exile, and seems to have stood at the head of a double district (Neh 3:17, 18). It has been identified with *Khirbet Qilā,* 8 mi. northwest of Hebron (Map VI, E-2/3).

In the phrase "Keilah the Garmite" (1 Chr 4:19), Keilah apparently refers to the above-mentioned town, since many of the names in the chapter refer to localities. However, the meaning of "Garmite" in the phrase is unknown.

Kelaiah (kē-lā'yà), or **Kelita** (kĕl'ĭ-tà). [Heb. *Qelayah* and *Qelîta',* meaning uncertain.] A Levite who was married to a foreign wife in the time of Ezra (Ezr 10:23). He, with others, joined Ezra in expounding the Law of God (Neh 8:7). He also set his seal to Nehemiah's covenant (ch 10:10).

Kelita. *See* Kelaiah.

Kemuel (kĕm'ū-ĕl). [Heb. *Qemú'el,* meaning uncertain.]

1. A son of Abraham's brother Nahor, and of Milcah (Gen 22:20, 21).

2. A leader of the tribe of Ephraim, who was a member of the commission in charge of the distribution of the country under Joshua (Num 34:24, 29).

3. A Levite (1 Chr 27:17).

Kenan. *See* Cainan.

Kenath (kē'năth). [Heb. *Qenath,* "possession."] A Canaanite town, mentioned in the *Amarna Letters as *Qanû,* situated on the western slope of the Hauran, and at the extreme northeast of Israelite territory. It was taken by Nobah, a Manassite, who called it after his own name (Num 32:42). However, it seems to have been better known by its former name (1 Chr 2:23). Josephus records a defeat of Herod the Great by the Arabians at this place (*War* i. 19. 2). It has been identified by some with *Qanawât,* about 55 mi. east of the Sea of Galilee (Map VI, C-6), and by others, on the basis of 8 inscriptions, with Kerak, about 13 mi. west of the area of Qanawât.

Kenaz (kē′năz). [Heb. *Qenaz*.]

1. A grandson or descendant of Esau (Gen 36:9, 11) and a chieftain in Mount Seir (v 15). He may have received his name from ruling over the tribe of the Kenizzites, which merged with the Edomites, as can be concluded from the statement that these "chiefs" (KJV "dukes") had their names "according to their families and their dwelling places" (vs 40, 42, RSV).

2. Either the tribe connected with Kenaz, 1, or an individual who was the father of Othniel and possibly the brother of Caleb, son of Jephunneh. The uncertainty stems from the ambiguity of the Hebrew in Jos 15:17 and Jgs 1:13, which speak of Othniel as son of Kenaz, Caleb's brother. (1) If Othniel, and not Kenaz, was the brother of Caleb, then Othniel might be the son of a man called Kenaz (see 1 Chr 4:15), in which case he would appear to be a half brother or a stepbrother of Caleb the son of Jephunneh. Or Othniel might be a son of Kenaz in the sense of a descendant of the tribe; in that case his brother Caleb would be also; and the latter is called a Kenizzite (KJV "Kenezite") in Num 32:12. (2) On the other hand, if it was Kenaz who was the brother of Caleb, then obviously Kenaz was an individual, and Othniel, his son, was a nephew of Caleb.

3. A grandson or descendant of Caleb, the son of Jephunneh. He was probably named after Caleb's relative, or after the old clan to which his family belonged (1 Chr 4:15). *See* Kenaz, 2.

Kenezite. *See* Kenizzites.

Kenites (kē′nīts). [Heb. *Qêni*, "smith."] A tribe or subtribe of Canaan. Their origin is obscure, but they seem to have intermarried with the Midianites, because the father-in-law of Moses is called a Midianite as well as a Kenite (cf. Jgs 1:16 with Num 10:29). The Kenites are mentioned first in the list of peoples whose country was promised to Abraham and his descendants as a possession (Gen 15:18, 19). The oracles of Balaam speak of the Kenites as having their "nest in a rock" (Num 24:21, 22). Since the family of Moses' father-in-law belonged to the Kenites, it seems that they were living in northeastern Sinai and in the *Wâdī 'Arabah,* a rocky, mountainous area. This

area is rich in copper and iron ore, and it is possible that these people were professional and perhaps itinerant smiths. It is not clear whether the name was a professional or a tribal name. Since they were well acquainted with the country through which the Israelites were to travel, Moses was anxious to have them in the camp "instead of eyes" (Num 10: 29-31). This Kenite family joined the Israelites, and after the conquest they settled in the territory of Judah in "the Negeb near Arad," or (KJV) "south of Arad" (Jgs 1:16), which is southeast of Hebron. Possibly they again became mine workers and smiths, because in the Negeb area are also found copper and iron mines, as modern explorations have shown. At least 1 family of the Kenites separated from the main tribe and settled near Kedesh in Naphtali in northern Palestine (ch 4:11). In the time of Saul and David Kenites were found also in the southwestern part of the Negeb, near the Amalekites, but were considered as friendly to the Israelites (1 Sa 15:6; 27: 10; 30:29). The genealogies of Chronicles list them among the tribe of Judah, to which they were apparently reckoned in later times (1 Chr 2:55).

Kenizzites (kē′nĭz-īts), KJV generally **Kenezites** (kē′nĕz-īts). [Heb. *Qenizzî*.] A tribe or subtribe of Canaan. Their origin is obscure. They are mentioned first as the possessors of Canaan in the time of Abraham (Gen 15:19). Caleb, well known from the story of the spies, is called a Kenizzite (KJV "Kenezite") in Num 32: 12, whereas Othniel, who was either his nephew or his younger brother, appears as a "son of Kenaz" (Jos 15:17; Jgs 1:13; 1 Chr 4:13), a designation that possibly refers to a tribe (*see* Kenaz). The Kenizzites are believed to be related also to the *Kenites, who were possibly professional or itinerant smiths. In 1 Chr 4:13, 14, which lists descendants of Kenaz, one is called a father of "Ge-harashim" (RSV), that is, of the "valley of craftsmen" ("Charashim" in the KJV), with the additional remark that "they were craftsmen." Nelson Glueck identifies the "valley of Charashim" or "craftsmen" with the *Wâdī 'Arabah,* which lies between the Dead Sea and the Gulf of Aqabah, and which is full of copper and iron mines, and thus could have served as a center for smiths (*PEQ* 72 [1940], 24; *AASOR* 15 [1934-1935], 26-30). The Kenizzites are mentioned in Gen 15:19 along with the *Kenites, who were smiths.

They also may have merged with the Edomites; at least there is record of an Edomite chieftain known as Kenaz (Gen 36:11, 15, 40-42), a name thought by some to have been derived from his ruling over the Kenizzites.

Kerchiefs. A rendering of the Heb. *mispachôth*, "veils" (Eze 13:18, 21, KJV). These veils were apparently for those who came to consult the false prophetesses who practiced deceptive devices on innocent souls in ancient Israel.

Keren-happuch (kĕr'ĕn-hăp'ŭk). [Heb. *Qeren happûk*, "horn of black eye paint."] The youngest daughter of Job, born to him after his great tribulation (Job 42:14).

Kerioth (kĕr'ĭ-ŏth), KJV once **Kirioth** (kĭr'ĭ-ŏth). [Heb. *Qeriyyôth*, "villages."]

1. A town in the extreme south of the territory of Judah (Jos 15:25); not identified. The translators of the RSV have joined the word "Kerioth" with the following term "Hezron," and render it Kerioth-hezron (kĕr'ĭ-ŏth-hĕz'rŏn). However, not all commentators accept this combination.

2. A town in Moab, which was apparently fortified (Jer 48:24, 41; Amos 2:2). Some consider it as the capital of Moab, and synonymous with Ar. Others suggest identifying it with Kir in Moab. The RSV renders the Hebrew term as "cities" in Jer 48:41.

Kerioth-hezron. *See* Kerioth, 1; Hazor, 3.

Keros (kē'rŏs). [Heb. *Qêros*.] Founder of a family of Nethinim, some of whom returned from Babylonia in the time of Zerubbabel (Ezr 2:1, 44; Neh 7:6, 47).

Kettle. The rendering of: (1) The Heb. *dûd* (1 Sa 2:14), a deep, round-bottomed, handled cooking pot, made either of baked clay or of metal. It was almost spherical in form and had only a small mouth. *Dûd* also means "basket," the same word being used for basket and kettle, apparently because of similarity of shapes. (2) The Heb. *sîr* (Mic 3:3, RSV), a wide-mouthed cooking pot of earthenware or metal. *See* Pot.

Keturah (kĕ-tū'rà). [Heb. *Qeṭûrah*, probably "perfumed."] A wife of Abraham whom the patriarch married after Sarah's death (Gen 25:1). The term "concubine" (1 Chr 1:32) designates her as a secondary wife. She became the mother of 6 sons, Zimran, Jokshan, Medan, Midian, Ishbak, and Shuah (Gen 25:1, 2; 1 Chr 1:32), who became ancestors of Arabian tribes. Abraham did not place them on the same level with Isaac, but gave them

gifts, which were doubtless liberal ones, and sent them to the east country (Gen 25:6).

Key. *See* Bolt.

Kezia. *See* Keziah.

Keziah (kĕ-zī'à), KJV **Kezia** (kĕ-zī'à). [Heb. *Qeṣî'ah*, "cassia."] The 2d of Job's daughters born to him after his trial (Job 42:14).

Keziz. *See* Emek-keziz.

Kibroth-hattaavah (kĭb'rŏth-hă-tā'à-và). [Heb. *Qibrôth Hatta'awah*, "graves of lust."] A station in the wilderness wanderings of the Israelites (Num 33:16, 17) between Mount Sinai and Kadesh; not identified with certainty. Many Israelites who died as a result of a plague that overtook them for lusting after flesh food were buried there (Num 11:18; 35; Deut 9:22).

Kibzaim. *See* Jokmeam.

Kid. A young goat (Gen 37:31). This animal was a favorite article of food (Jgs 13:15; Lk 15:29), and was used for sacrificial offerings (Lev 4:22, 23; Num 15:11; Jgs 13:19, KJV). Boiling a kid in its mother's milk (Ex 23:19; 34:26; Deut 14:21) was prohibited, doubtless because this was a ritual practice of the idolatrous Canaanites, as the religious texts of Ras Shamra show. *See* Goat.

Kidneys. [Heb. *kelayôth*.] The paired glandular, bean-shaped organs in vertebrates serving to excrete urea, uric acid, and other waste products. Most of the passages where the term occurs deal with the kidneys of sacrificial animals that were to be burned upon the altar as an offering of fire unto the Lord (Ex 29:13, 22; Lev 3: 4, 10, 15; etc.). Once human kidneys are mentioned (Job 16:13, RSV). Frequently *kelayôth* is used figuratively of what is innermost in man—the seat of feelings and passions. When used in this sense *kelayôth* is translated "reins" in the KJV and generally "heart" in the RSV.

Kidron (kĭd'rŏn), KJV of NT **Cedron** (sē'drŏn). [Heb. *Qidrôn*; Gr. *Kedrôn*.] A valley or watercourse between Jerusalem and

277. The Kidron Valley, with the southeastern corner of the city wall of Old Jerusalem visible at the upper center

278. The Kidron Valley as seen from the southeastern corner of the city wall of Jerusalem, with the City of David to the right and the village of *Silwán* (Siloam) to the left

the Mount of Olives (Jn 18:1). Several valleys northwest of Jerusalem converge to form the Kidron, which then passes Jerusalem at its eastern side, turns toward the east, south of Jerusalem, and enters the Dead Sea after having traversed the Wilderness of Judah (see 2 Sa 15:23). It is called a brook (Heb. *nachal,* "wadi") in 2 Sa 15:23; 1 Ki 15:13; etc. The "brook" (RSV "valley") of Jn 18:1 is a translation of the Gr. *cheimarros,* with a meaning similar to *nachal.* The valley is now called *Wâdî en-Nâr.* Maps XVII, XVIII; see figs. 259, 277, 278; also figs. 158, 224, 260.

Kinah (kī′nà). [Heb. *Qinah,* "lamentation."] A place in the extreme south of Judah (Jos 15:22); not identified, but probably in the *Wâdî el-Qeini,* running some 15 mi. west of the southwestern shore of the Dead Sea.

Kindred. [Heb. generally *môledeth,* "relationship," "consanguinity," and *mishpachah,* "family," "clan," "circle of relatives"; Gr. *suggeneia,* "relationship," "kinship," *genos,* "descendants (of a common ancestor)," "family," "relatives," *phulē,* "tribe," *patria,* "family," "clan," "relationship."] Relationship, kinship. Where in the KJV "kindred" is the translation of *phulē* (Rev 1:7; 5:9; 7:9; 11:9; 13:7; 14:6) the rendering should be "tribe."

Kine. *See* Cow.

King. [Heb. *melek;* Gr. *basileus.*] A male sovereign in whom is invested supreme authority over a tribe or nation. Generally, rule is for life and succession is on a hereditary basis. That over which he rules is called a kingdom. The kings of ancient heathen nations were often considered as deities or direct descendants of a deity.

The idea of kingship had little empha-

sis in early Hebrew history. Civil authority was centered in the family and the tribe. However, after the Exodus a consciousness of national unity developed. The special covenant relationship set forth God as Israel's supreme ruler and His laws as the basis of government. This form of government has been described as a theocracy. God was their king (cf. Deut 33:1-5). However, the Israelites quickly desired to become "like all the nations" (1 Sa 8:5), as is shown by their request to Gideon that he become their king (Jgs 8:22, 23). Of Samuel they definitely demanded a king, and by doing so rejected God as their king (1 Sa 8:7; cf. 10:19; 12:12, 17, 19). The more worthy kings considered themselves as but deputy kings under God (Ps 5:1, 2; 1 Ki 3:6, 7; 2 Chr 20:5, 6; 2 Ki 19:14-19; etc.), and were willing to be instructed by God's prophets (2 Sa 12:7-15). The less worthy completely ignored the Lord their God and led the nation into moral and spiritual degradation.

The king exercised wide powers and influence in civil, military, and religious affairs. He was regarded as the supreme judicial authority (2 Sa 14:4, 15; 15:2; 1 Ki 3:16-28), possessing the power of life and death (1 Ki 1:51, 52). He was also the leader of his armies (1 Sa 8:20; 1 Ki 12:21-24; 2 Chr 32:2, 3; cf. Gen 14:5; Num 21:23), and entered into military alliances without consulting his people (1 Ki 15:18, 19). Legislative power vested in the kings of heathen nations (Est 3:12, 13; Dan 3:1-6) functioned to a lesser degree in Israel's rulers, for ideally, Israel's laws were given by God. Because of their authority in religious affairs kings were able to lead the entire nation in the service of the true God (2 Sa 6:12; 1 Ki 6:1, 2; 2 Chr 35:1-6) or to use their office and influence to extend the worship of false gods and various vile fertility cults (1 Ki 14:21-24; 16:31-33; 2 Ki 23:12-14). Kings sometimes exercised power in appointment and removal of the priests (1 Ki 2:26, 27), but only rarely and not without protests (2 Chr 13:9). Ordinarily there was a respected line of distinction between the priestly functions and those of the king (1 Sa 13:9-13; Mt 12:3, 4). The sins of kings often brought retribution that involved the entire nation (2 Sa 24:10-15; 21:8-17).

Isaiah 11 presents a beautiful symbolic picture of the kingship and kingdom of Christ, introducing the reader to the deeper and eternal meaning of Christ's

624

claim to be the "King of the Jews" (Mt 27:11; etc.). Jesus possessed the hereditary eligibility to be king of Israel (ch 1: 1-16), but His plea for their loyalty was always based on deeper, spiritual truth that the people failed to comprehend (Jn 6:15; 12:13). Satan recognized Christ's divine royalty, and he tried to take His right away from Him by bribes on the mount of temptation (Mt 4:8-10; Lk 4:5-7). Christ was constantly seeking to lead the people to accept God as their king and to understand the nature of His kingdom (Mt 5:35; 18:23; Lk 22:29, 30). Unfortunately, the Jews failed to recognize Christ as their long-awaited Messiah. They failed to grasp that Christ's rulership was not of the nature of human government (Jn 18:36; Php 3:20, RSV). His kingdom was the spiritual kingdom of grace, one day to be replaced by the kingdom of glory (see *SDACom* 5:295, 296, 318).

Kingdom. A state or monarchy, the head of which is a king. The 1st kingdom mentioned in the Bible is that of Nimrod (Gen 10:9, 10). According to the philosophy of history set forth in the Bible, kingdoms and kings are set up not simply by the will or might of man or the whim of circumstance but by the permission and ordering of God (Dan 2:20, 21; 4:25; cf. 1 Sa 28:17; 2 Chr 1:9). Much of Bible history deals with the kingdom of Israel. God designed that it should function as more than a political unit. It was to be a "kingdom of priests, and an holy nation" (Ex 19:6). God promised to establish the kingdom of David and Solomon forever if the Israelites would cooperate with His plans (2 Sa 7:16; 1 Ki 9:2-9; etc.). But the people failed, and the kingdom was at first divided (1 Ki 12:16, 17, 19), and later the divided kingdoms were carried into captivity (2 Ki 17:22, 23; 24:8-11; 2 Chr 36:15-21). On condition of a belated acceptance of the divine program, God promised to fulfill His promises with respect to the kingdom of David after the return from captivity (Eze 36; 37; cf. Jer 18:7-10). Again the people failed, and the declaration was made concerning them, "The kingdom of God shall be taken from you, and given to a nation bringing forth the fruits thereof" (Mt 21:43; see *SDACom* 4:25-38).

When John the Baptist and Jesus called the Jews to repentance in view of the fact that "the kingdom of heaven is at hand" (Mt 3:2; 4:17), they were presenting to the Jews the opportunity of becoming citizens of the kingdom the Messiah had come to establish. The condition for citizenship was genuine repentance and a thorough conversion (Jn 3:3, 5). The principles that were to control the members of this kingdom were set forth in the Sermon on the Mount and other discourses of Jesus. See *SDACom* 5:295, 296, 318. The Jews' rejection of the Messiah called forth the sorrowful pronouncements recorded in Mt 23:37; Lk 19:42, and the removal of the spiritual status the Jews had held. The new nation to which the "kingdom of God" was given (Mt 21:43) was the Christian church.

This kingdom of God in its present spiritual phase is to culminate in the future kingdom of glory to be set up at Christ's second coming, when He will appear "in his glory, and all the holy angels with him" (Mt 25:31), to take His subjects with Him to heaven (1 Th 4:16, 17; Jn 14:1-3; etc.). At the close of the millennium this kingdom will be established on earth. Its capital will be the New Jerusalem, where Christ will reign "for ever and ever" (Rev 20; 21; cf. 11:15).

Kings, Books of. The history of the Hebrew nation from the crowning of Solomon and the death of David through Solomon's reign and the period of the divided kingdom, to the Babylonian captivity, and beyond, a period of about 400 years. In the ancient Hebrew canon 1st and 2d Kings appeared as 1 book, known as *Melakim,* "Kings." The division into 2 sections goes back to the LXX. In the ancient Hebrew canon the book of Kings stood among the Former Prophets, in the 2d section of the Hebrew Scriptures, which is known as the Prophets. The Former Prophets—Joshua, Judges, Samuel, and Kings—constitute a continuous narrative covering Israelite history from the death of Moses to the Exile. The literary form of the record contained in the books of Kings indicates that the historical data were selected from other sources by an inspired editor, who brought the materials together and arranged them into a unified framework with a specific pattern, and who added inspired comments on the religious and spiritual significance of the events of Hebrew history. He cites as the sources for his information (1) the "book of the acts of Solomon" (1 Ki 11: 41), (2) the "book of the chronicles of the kings of Israel" (ch 14:19) for the northern kingdom to the death of Pekah (2 Ki 15:30, 31), and (3) "the book of the chronicles of the kings of Judah"

(1 Ki 14:29) for the southern kingdom to Jehoiakim's death (2 Ki 24:5, 6). The latter 2 seem at some time, perhaps later, to have been combined into "the book of the kings of Judah and Israel" (cf. 2 Chr 16:11). The editor of Kings repeatedly refers his readers to these other works for further details (cf. 1 Ki 14:19, 29). The historical accuracy of the account preserved in 1st and 2d Kings has been attested beyond question by a remarkable series of archeological discoveries. In accuracy and objectivity this inspired record of the history of God's people is infinitely superior to similar records preserved in Assyria, Babylon, or Egypt. Despite the diversity of the materials brought together from other sources, there is a striking evidence of unity. For instance, a standard formula is used for the beginning and ending of each reign. The reign of each king is evaluated good or evil as compared with previous noteworthy reigns. Characteristic peculiarities of thought and expression that occur throughout point unmistakably to a single person as being responsible for bringing the material together in its present form. According to Jewish tradition (the Talmud, *Baba Bathra* 15a), this compiler was Jeremiah. But whoever the editor was, he had true historical perspective and insight, for although the books are essentially historical in nature, their primary purpose is to point out the lesson that righteousness exalts a nation and that wickedness leads to ruin. The inspired editor traces the growth and decay of the Hebrew kingdom, pointing out the causes of prosperity and adversity and drawing attention to the effect of moral and religious character upon national fortunes (cf. 2 Ki 17). The compiler of Kings is concerned chiefly with the history of the southern kingdom of Judah, but incorporates that of the northern kingdom of Israel, partly as background information and partly to preserve a complete record of the entire nation. At times this procedure involves a measure of repetition. For the kings of Israel the basic pattern usually includes the length of the reign and the time of the king's death. For the kings of Judah the formula includes also the age of each at his accession, the name of his mother, and a reference to his burial. In each case the accession of each monarch is dated in terms of a regnal year of the contemporary ruler of the other kingdom. A noteworthy feature is the basic chronological framework of the books, by which the editor synchronizes the reigns of the kings in the 2 kingdoms. There are difficulties to be overcome in reconciling the figures, and in harmonizing with these non-Biblical chronological data, but the seeming discrepancies are due largely to our lack of information about the technical methods of chronological reckoning in use in Bible times. *See* Chronology, V.

The combined record of 1st and 2d Kings divides logically into 3 major sections: (1) From the death of David to the disruption of the kingdom (1 Ki 1:1 to 11:43). (2) From the disruption to the fall of Samaria and the end of the northern kingdom (1 Ki 12:1 to 2 Ki 17:41). (3) From Hezekiah to the destruction of Jerusalem by Nebuchadnezzar (2 Ki 18:1 to 25:30). For the most part the narrative proceeds in chronological order, and mentions each king in the order of his accession to the throne. Appended to the record is a brief account of the governorship of Gedaliah, whom Nebuchadnezzar left in charge of affairs in Judah after he had destroyed Jerusalem and taken most of the nation into captivity (ch 25:22-26). Brief mention is also made of King Jehoiachin's release from prison a number of years later (vs 27-30).

King's Dale. *See* King's Valley.

King's Friend. [Heb. *re'eh hammelek*, "fellow of the king," or "friend of the king."] An official, probably an adviser and a particularly close confederate of the king (1 Ki 4:5). In 2 Sa 15:37; 16:16 Hushai the Archite is called David's *re'eh*, "friend."

King's Garden. A garden outside of ancient Jerusalem, near "the gate between two walls" (2 Ki 25:4; Jer 39:4; 52:7), and in the vicinity of the Pool of Shelah (KJV "Siloah"), probably the Pool of Siloam (Neh 3:15). The garden was probably watered by the overflow of the pool. The

279. The site of the Biblical "king's garden" (foreground) in the lower Kidron Valley southeast of Jerusalem

king's garden must have been in the lower part of the Kidron Valley, immediately to the north of the well En-rogel, where there are still vegetable gardens (see fig. 279). Map XVII.

King's Highway. *See* Highway.

King's Mother. *See* Queen.

King's Pool. A place mentioned in Neh 2:14, apparently in the southern part of the southeastern hill of Jerusalem, and hence identified by some with the Pool of *Siloam. Others identify it with the Pool of Solomon, which, according to Josephus (*War* v. 4. 2), was probably in the lower Kidron Valley.

King's Valley, KJV **King's Dale.** [Heb. *'emeq hammelek.*] The place where Abraham, after defeating Chedorlaomer and his confederates and rescuing Lot and his family, met the king of Sodom; anciently called Shaveh (shā'vĕ) [Heb. *Shaweh,* "level"; Gen 14:17]. The valley is mentioned in 2 Sa 18:18 as the place where Absalom erected a memorial pillar for himself. Josephus (*Ant.* vii. 10. 3) locates this monument ¼ mi. from Jerusalem; consequently the valley of Shaveh, or "king's dale," is identified with one of the valleys surrounding Jerusalem. Some believe it to be the Kidron Valley.

Kinsmen. In the KJV OT this term is largely restricted to a rendering of a form of the Heb. *ga'al,* "to buy back," "to recover," "to redeem," and most of the references are to Boaz as a near kinsman of Ruth's deceased husband (Ruth 2:20; 3:9, 12; etc.), whose duty it was, in the event of a default of closer relatives, to redeem the childlessness of Ruth by marrying her. In the RSV OT "kinsmen" is much more frequent and is used in the general sense of "relatives," often as the translation of the Heb. *'achim,* meaning brothers, or more distant relatives (KJV in these latter instances usually "brethren"). In the NT "kinsman" generally means "relative," although *suggenēs,* the Greek term thus translated, may be used in the broader sense of "fellow countryman" or "fellow citizen" (see Rom 9:3).

Kir (kĭr). [Heb. *Qir,* "wall," or "city."]
1. The original home of the Aramaeans (Syrians) according to the prophet Amos (Amos 9:7). To Kir, Tiglath-pileser III deported the inhabitants of Damascus after conquering their city in 732 B.C. (2 Ki 16:9; Amos 1:5). Is 22:6 mentions the people of Kir with those of Elam as serving in the Assyrian forces against Judah. The place has not yet been at-

tested in cuneiform records, and remains unidentified.
2. An important city of Moab, mentioned in a parallel construction with Ar in Is 15:1. Some have thought that Ar and Kir are different names for the same city, but this is not probable. *See* Ar. It is more likely that Kir is identical with *Kir-hareseth.

Kir-hareseth (kĭr'hăr'ĕ-sĕth), or **Kir-heres** (kĭr'hē'rĕs), KJV once **Kir-haraseth** (kĭr'hăr'á-sĕth), and once **Kir-haresh** (kĭr'hā'rĕsh). [Heb. *Qir-chareseth, Qir-charasheth, Qir-chares,* and *Qir-chares.*] A fortified city

280. The city of *el-Kerak*, Biblical Kir-hareseth, site of the capital of the Moabites

of Moab, repeatedly mentioned in prophecies concerning that country (Is 16:7, 11; Jer 48:31, 36). At one time the city was besieged by the combined forces of Israel, Judah, and Edom, but was not taken (2 Ki 3:7, 9, 24, 25). It is apparently this city that Isaiah refers to by the simple name Kir (Is 15:1). From 2 Ki 3:8, 21, 24, 25 it is evident that it lay near the southern border of Moab. It has been identified with the impressive city *el-Kerak* (Map VI, F-4), situated 3,700 ft. above sea level on a precipitous hill, connected with the surrounding tableland only on the eastern side. All other sides fall steeply into ravines. Kir-hareseth dominated the great caravan road from Arabia to Damascus. The crusaders who held the city for some time in the 12th cent. built a strong castle at one end and encircled the whole city with impressive fortifications. Tunnels, probably constructed in Roman times, connect the summit with the valleys. Its present population is about 10,000.

Kir-heres. *See* Kir-hareseth.

Kiriathaim (kĭr'ĭ-á-thā'ĭm), KJV 3 times **Kirjathaim** (kĭr'já-thā'ĭm). [Heb. *Qiryathayim,* "twin cities."]

1. An ancient city assigned to the Reubenites after the conquest of Transjordan, and rebuilt by them (Num 32:33, 37; Jos 13:15, 19). It was later held by the Moabites (*see* *Moabite Stone, line 10; cf. Jer 48:1, 23; Eze 25:9). Nearby was Shaveh-kiriathaim (shā'vĕ-kĭr'yá-thā'ĭm) [Heb. *Shaweh-qiryathayim,* "plain of Kiriathaim"], where the Emim were defeated by the Mesopotamian invaders in Abraham's time (Gen 14:5). The city has been identified with *el-Qereiyât,* about 5 mi. northwest of Dibon (Map VI, E-4).

2. Another name for *Kartan (1 Chr 6:76).

Kiriath-arba (kĭr'ĭ-ăth-är'bá), KJV **Kirjath-arba** (kĭr'jăth-är'bá). [Heb. *Qiryath 'arba',* "city of Arba" or "fourfold city."] The original name of Hebron (see Map VI, E-3), given to it probably in honor of its founder, Arba, the father of Anak (Gen 23:2; Jos 14:15; 15:54; 20:7; Jgs 1:10). The name seems to have been applied to Hebron briefly in postexilic times (Neh 11:25).

Kiriath-arim. *See* Kiriath-jearim.

Kiriath-baal. *See* Kiriath-jearim.

Kiriath-huzoth (kĭr'ĭ-ăth-hū'zŏth), KJV **Kirjath-huzoth** (kĭr'jăth-hū'zŏth). [Heb. *Qiryath chuṣôth,* "city of streets."] A city of Moab (Num 22:36, 39); not identified with certainty.

Kiriath-jearim (kĭr'ĭ-ăth-jē'á-rĭm), KJV **Kirjath-jearim** (kĭr'jăth-jē'á-rĭm). [Heb. *Qiryath ye'arîm,* "city of forests."] An old Canaanite city which the Israelites gained through a treaty with its original inhabitants, the Gibeonites (Jos 9:3-17). It was on the border between Benjamin and Judah (chs 15:9; 18:14, 15), and was assigned to Judah (Jos 15:16; Jgs 18:12), although it was also reckoned to Benjamin (Jos 18:28), if Kirjath is an abbreviated form of Kiriath-jearim, as many commentators think. Kiriath-jearim is best known as the place where the ark rested for some 20 years in the time of Samuel, after it had been returned following its capture by the Philistines (1 Sa 5:1; 6:19 to 7:2). It was the home town of the prophet Uriah (KJV "Urijah"), who suffered a martyr's death at the hands of King Jehoiakim (Jer 26:20-23). The city was repopulated after the Exile, being mentioned by Ezra (Ezr 2:25), as Kiriath-arim (kĭr'ĭ-ăth-ā'rĭm), KJV "Kirjath-arim"

(kĭr'jăth-ā'rĭm) [Heb. *Qiryath 'arim*], and by Nehemiah (Neh 7:29). In Jos 15:60; 18:14 it is named (RSV) Kiriath-baal (kĭr'ĭ-ăth-bā'ăl) and (KJV) Kirjath-baal (kĭr'jăth-bā'ăl) [Heb. *Qiryath ba'al,* "city of the master"]. In Jos 15:9, 11; 1 Chr 13:6 it is called Baalah (Heb. *Ba'alah*), and in 2 Sa 6:2 it is named Baale of Judah (KJV), or Baale-judah (Heb. *Ba'alê Yehûdah*). The site is identified with *Tell el-Azhar,* about 7½ mi. west of Jerusalem. Map VI, E-3.

Kiriath-sannah. *See* Debir, 2.

Kiriath-sepher. *See* Debir, 2.

Kirioth. *See* Kerioth, 2.

Kirjath (kĭr'jăth). [Heb. *Qiryath,* "city of." The term appears alone as a place name only once but several times as the first element in compound names.] A town in the territory of Benjamin (Jos 18:28, KJV), identified by many with *Kiriath-jearim (see RSV, LXX).

Kirjathaim. *See* Kiriathaim, 1.

Kirjath-arba. *See* Kiriath-arba.

Kirjath-arim. *See* Kiriath-jearim.

Kirjath-baal. *See* Kiriath-jearim.

Kirjath-huzoth. *See* Kiriath-huzoth.

Kirjath-jearim. *See* Kiriath-jearim.

Kirjath-sannah. *See* Debir, 2.

Kirjath-sepher. *See* Debir, 2.

Kish (kĭsh), KJV of NT **Cis** (sĭs). [Heb. *Qish,* possibly meaning "gift" by analogy with the Akkadian name *Qishu*; Gr. *Kis.*]

1. A Benjamite, son of Jeiel of Gibeon (1 Chr 8:30; 9:35, 36).

2. A Benjamite, father of King Saul. In 1 Sa 9:1 he is said to be a son of Abiel but in 1 Chr 8:33; 9:36, 39, a son of Ner, and a descendant of Jeiel of Gibeon (see Son). According to one interpretation this Kish is identified with Kish, 1.

3. A Merarite Levite in David's time (1 Chr 23:21).

4. A Merarite Levite in Hezekiah's time, who aided in the religious revival (2 Chr 29:12).

5. A Benjamite, an ancestor of Mordecai (Est 2:5).

Kishi (kĭsh'ī). [Heb. *Qishî.*] A Merarite Levite (1 Chr 6:44), called Kushaiah (kŭ-shā'yá) [Heb. *Qûshayahû*] in ch 15:17.

Kishion. *See* Kedesh, 3.

Kishon (kī'shŏn), KJV once **Kison** (kī'sŏn). [Heb. *Qîshôn.*]

1. The most important river of western Palestine, watering the Plain of Esdraelon. Its northern branch springs from the western slopes of Mount Tabor, and several of its southern branches from the western slopes of Mount Gilboa. The

281. The river Kishon and Mount Carmel

various branches meet in the plain north-northeast of Megiddo. The river then flows in a northwesterly direction along the northern foot of the Carmel ridge, entering the Mediterranean at the southeastern corner of the Bay of Acre (Map VI, C-3). Its modern name is *Nahr el-Muqatta'*. The river maintains a year-round flow only for its last 7 mi., receiving here water from numerous springs rising at the base of Mount Carmel, and also from 2 streams coming from the northeast and emptying into the Kishon in the plain of Acre. In the rainy season the stream becomes swollen and can be very dangerous, as Sisera and his chariot forces discovered (Jgs 4:7, 13; 5:21; Ps 83:9). During that season the whole plain is flooded; hence the towns and cities in the area were built on higher ground along the edges of the plain. Some centuries ago the plain became marshy and unhealthful, but it has been properly drained in recent years, so that this area is once more able to support a dense population.

2. For Jos 21:28, KJV, *see* Kedesh, 3.

Kison. *See* Kishon, 1.

Kiss. A common form of salutation used in Oriental lands from early times (Gen 27:26, 27). It was practiced between members of a family, between relatives, and between friends (Gen 29:11; 33:4; 45:14, 15; 48:8-10; 50:1; Ex 4:27; 18:7; Ruth 1:9, 14; 1 Sa 20:41, 42; 2 Sa 19:39; Lk 15:20; Acts 20:37) as a mark of respect or homage (Ps 2:12; Lk 7:37, 38, 45) and as an expression of love (Song 1:2; 8:1). Idols were kissed by their worshipers as a mark of devotion (1 Ki 19:18; Hos 13:2). Because the heavenly bodies were inaccessible, those who worshiped them kissed the hands instead (Job 31:26, 27). Kisses have been used treacherously to disarm or deceive (cf. Prov 27:6). For example, Absalom kissed those who came to him for counsel to draw them away from his father, King David (2 Sa 15:3-6); by kissing Amasa, Joab threw him off guard and easily killed him (ch 20:9, 10); and Judas used a traitorous kiss to betray Jesus to His enemies (Mt 26:48, 49; Mk 14:44, 45; Lk 22:47, 48).

Paul and Peter exhorted the Christian believers to salute one another with a "holy kiss" (Rom 16:16; 1 Cor 16:20; 2 Cor 13:12; 1 Th 5:26; 1 Pe 5:14), referring to a kiss of Christian affection. This custom was apparently practiced only between men and men and women and women (Apostolic Constitutions 2:57; 8:11). In accord with Palestinian convention the kiss was placed upon the beard, cheek, forehead, hands, feet, and possibly also the lips (cf. Prov 24:26). In Ps 85 the revelation of God's salvation is described as reconciling righteousness and peace so that they are figuratively pictured as kissing each other (v 10).

Kite. A rendering of: (1) the Heb. *da'ah* (Lev 11:14, RSV); (2) the Heb. *dayyah* (Is 34:15, RSV); (3) the Heb. *'ayyah* (Lev 11:14, KJV; Deut 14:13). The RSV renders *'ayyah* "falcon" in Lev 11:14; Job 28:7. As we know it today, the kite is a bird of prey belonging to the falcon family, having long, pointed wings and a long, forked tail. This fowl and its kind are unclean (Lev 11:14; Deut 14:13). Driver suggests the saker falcon and the common buzzard for *'ayyah* and the (black) kite for the terms *da'ah* and *dayyah* (Driver, *PEQ* 87 [1955], 20).

Kithlish. *See* Chitlish.

Kitron (kĭt'rŏn). [Heb. *Qitrôn.*] A town in the territory of Zebulun, from which the Canaanites were not expelled (Jgs 1:30); not identified with certainty. Some believe it to be identical with Kattath (Jos 19:15). The site represented as Kitron on Map VI, C-3, is *Tell el-Fâr.*

Kittim (kĭt'ĭm), KJV frequently **Chittim** (kĭt'ĭm). [Heb. *Kittiyim* and *Kittim.*] Descendants of Javan (Gen 10:4; 1 Chr 1:7), identified with the inhabitants of Cyprus, because its ancient capital was named Kition. The inscriptions of Ugarit mention *Kt* as a city or country, and in Phoenician inscriptions *Kty* refers to Cyprus' capital. The *Kittim* of Is 23:1, 12 may refer to Cyprus, because the context implies that it was not far from Tyre and

Sidon. The RSV translates *Kittîm* as Cyprus here and in Jer 2:10 and Eze 27:6. However, the term as used in Dan 11:30 and Num 24:24 seems to have reference, first, to peoples and lands to the west of Israel, and, second, to invaders and destroyers from more distant quarters. In the "War" scroll of the Dead Sea scrolls "Kittim" clearly refers to the Seleucids and Ptolemies, and in the Habakkuk Commentary of the scrolls the term seems to refer to the Romans. One can therefore detect a shift in the application of the term Kittim. Although the term was at first applied to Cyprus, it was later extended to include all the western islands and coastal areas of the Greeks, and finally meant anti-Jewish powers in general, whether they were Greeks or Romans.

Kneading-trough. A container in which dough is mixed in preparation for baking. The term is a rendering of the Heb. *mish'ereth* (Ex 8:3; 12:34; KJV; RSV "kneading bowl"; Deut 28:5, 17, RSV; KJV "store"). The derivation of *mish'ereth* is uncertain (possibly the original was *miś'ereth*), but it is closely related to the Heb. *maśreth*, "a kneading trough" or "kneading pan" (2 Sa 13:9), which in turn is either derived from, or is at least closely related to, *śe'or*, "yeast," "leaven."

Knife. Earliest knives were made of flint (see fig. 178), but most of the later ones were made of bronze or iron. They were used for the slaughtering of animals (Gen 22:6), for performing the rite of circumcision (Jos 5:2, 3), and for many other purposes. Scribes used a penknife to sharpen their *pens (Jer 36:23). In the Palestinian excavations many bronze and some iron knife blades have been found. Their handles, having been made of perishable material, such as wood, have in all cases disappeared.

Knop. *See* Capital, I.

Koa (kō'á). [Heb. *Qôa'*.] A people (Eze 23:23), probably the *Qutû* tribe mentioned in Assyrian inscriptions, living with the *Sutû* tribe east of the Tigris.

Kohath (kō'hăth). [Heb. *Qehath* and *Qohath*.] One of the sons of Levi (Gen 46:11; Ex 6:16-18; Num 3:17; etc.), and the ancestor of the Kohathite Levites, one of the great divisions of the Levites.

Kohathite (kō'hăth-īt). [Heb. *Qehathi* and *Qohathi*.] A member of the large division of Levites descended from Kohath, a son of Levi. This tribal house was subdivided into the families of the Amramites, the Izharites (KJV "Izeharites"), the He-

bronites, and the Uzzielites (Ex 6:18; Num 3:27). Aaron, and consequently all priests, belonged to the Kohathites (Ex 6:20). In the wilderness wanderings the Kohathite Levites camped south of the tabernacle (Num 3:29; see fig. 92), and were in charge of the transport of the sanctuary and its furniture, after the priests had covered these items so that the carriers could transport them without endangering their lives (ch 4:15, 17-20). At the 1st census in the wilderness the number of the Kohathite males from a month upward was 8,600 (ch 3:28), and those from 30 to 50 years of age numbered 2,750 (ch 4:34-37). In the records of the 2d census (ch 26) no figures are given for the various divisions of the Levites. When the country was divided under Joshua, the Kohathite priests received 13 cities for residences in the territories of Judah, Simeon, and Benjamin, whereas the Kohathite Levites received 10 cities in the territories of Ephraim, Dan, and Manasseh (Jos 21:4, 5; 1 Chr 6:61, 66-70).

Kolaiah (kô-lā'yá). [Heb. *Qôlayah,* probably "voice of Yahweh."]
    1. A man whose son Ahab was one of the false prophets in the time of Jeremiah (Jer 29:21).
    2. A Benjamite (Neh 11:7).

Koph. [Heb. *qôph.*] The 19th letter of the Hebrew alphabet, written ק, appearing as the title to the 19th section of Ps 119 in the KJV. *See* Aleph.

Korah (kō'rá), KJV of NT **Core** (kō'rĕ). [Heb. *Qorach*, "bald"; Gr. *Kore.*]
    1. A son of Esau by his wife Oholibamah (Gen 36:5, 14, 18; 1 Chr 1:35).
    2. A son of Eliphaz and grandson of Esau. He was one of the chiefs of the sons of Esau (Gen 36:15, 16).
    3. A son of Hebron, probably also the name of a family in Judah (1 Chr 2:43).
    4. A Kohathite Levite (Num 16:1), known especially for his participation in a rebellion against Moses and Aaron. He resented holding a position lower than his fellow tribesman, Aaron, who had been made high priest. He was joined by Dathan, Abiram, and On, Reubenites, who aspired to be leaders, seeing that they belonged to the tribe descended from the first-born of Jacob. Korah and many of the rebels were destroyed when the ground opened and swallowed them up. An accompanying fire destroyed the priests who had joined them in the rebellion (Num 16:1-49; 26:9-11; 27:3; Jude 11). He is called Kore in 1 Chr 26:19, KJV.

Korahite (kō'rá-īt), KJV 4 times **Korhite** (kôr'hīt), once **Korathite** (kō'răth-īt). [Heb. *Qorchi.*] A descendant of the Korah who was swallowed up in the wilderness for his rebellion (Num 16:32; 26:11); *see* Korah, 4. To the Korahites belonged famous men such as Heman, the singer, and Samuel, the prophet (1 Chr 6:33-38). Heman's descendants were organized into a choir by David for the Temple service (chs 15:17; 16:41, 42; 25:4, 5), and 11 psalms bear the family name in their titles (Ps 42; 44 to 49; 84; 85; 87; 88). Korahites were also employed as gatekeepers for the Temple and as bakers for certain sacrificial cakes (1 Chr 9:19, 31; 26:19).

Korathite. *See* Korahite.

Kore (kō'rě). [Heb. *Qore',* "partridge." The name occurs on an ancient Hebrew ostracon found in archeological excavations of Jerusalem.]

1. For 1 Chr 26:19, KJV, *see* Korah, 4.

2. A Levite of the house of Korah (1 Chr 9:19; 26:1).

3. A Levite, who was in charge of the freewill offerings during the reign of King Hezekiah (2 Chr 31:14).

Korhite. *See* Korahite.

Koz (kŏz), KJV **Coz** (kŏz). [Heb. *Qôṣ,* possibly "thorn."]

1. A Judahite (1 Chr 4:8).

2. For Ezr 2:61; Neh 3:4, 21; 7:63; KJV, *see* Hakkoz.

Kue (kōō'ē). [Heb. *Qeweh* and *Qewe';* Aramaic *Qwh;* cuneiform inscriptions *Qu'e* and *Qâue.*] A country from which Solomon imported horses (1 Ki 10:28, RSV), identified with Cilicia in southeastern Asia Minor. The KJV translators, not recognizing that the Hebrew term appearing in these passages (*miqweh*) really means "from Kue," took it as the name of a product and conjecturally rendered it "linen yarn." See Que on Map XI, B-3/4.

Kushaiah. *See* Kishi.

—— L ——

Laadah (lā'á-dá). [Heb. *La'dah,* meaning uncertain.] A Judahite, and ancestor of (the inhabitants of) Mareshah (1 Chr 4:21).

Laadan. *See* Ladan.

Laban (lā'băn). [Heb. *Laban,* "white."]

1. The son of Bethuel, and grandson of Abraham's brother Nahor. He lived in Haran in Paddan-aram (Gen 24:10, 15; 28:5, 10; 29:4, 5). When Abraham's servant came to Haran and asked for Laban's sister Rebekah as a wife for Isaac, Laban and his father Bethuel consented, especially when they saw the rich presents sent by Abraham (ch 24:28-31, 50-60). The fact that Laban is mentioned before his father (v 50) may indicate that Laban had become head of the household, possibly through incapacity on the part of his father. When Jacob was forced to flee from his brother Esau he found a refuge with his uncle Laban, who owned slaves and large flocks of sheep and goats (chs 29: 16, 24, 29; 31:38). Here Jacob fell in love with Rachel, the younger of Laban's 2 daughters, but having no dowry he worked as shepherd for Laban for 7 years in order to obtain her as his wife (ch 29:15-20). However, Laban fraudulently tricked him into marrying her older

sister Leah first, then gave him Rachel also on condition that he work another 7 years (Gen 29:21-28). Afterward he stayed 6 years longer with Laban, and received sheep and goats in payment for his services (ch 30: 25-43). When Laban and his sons became jealous because of Jacob's rapidly increasing wealth, Jacob left his father-in-law's house and fled toward Canaan with his family and flocks. Laban pursued him and overtook him in Mount Gilead (ch 31:1-23). He intended to force Jacob to return to Paddan-aram, but God forbade him to punish Jacob (v 24). Hence the 2 men concluded a treaty of friendship and then parted, Jacob going on to Canaan, and Laban returning to his home in Haran (chs 31:25 to 32:1). Laban at least paid lip service to Yahweh, the God of Abraham (chs 24:50; 30:27), although he worshiped other gods, for he had figurines of pagan deities (Heb. *teraphim*) in his house (ch 31:30, 32-35; cf. 35:4). He also practiced divination as the Hebrew text of ch 30:27 indicates (see RSV).

2. A place in the wilderness near which Israel camped (Deut 1:1); not identified.

Lace. A rendering of the Heb. *pathil* (Ex 28:28, 37; 39:21, 31), "cord," "string," "line." Blue cords fastened the breastpiece by its rings to the high priest's ephod, and the plate of gold to the miter, or turban.

Lachish (lā′kĭsh). [Heb. *Lakîsh.* The word occurs in the ancient Hebrew ostraca from Lachish (called the Lachish Letters) was *Lksh,* in the *Amarna Letters as *Lakisha* and *Lakisi,* and in the Assyrian inscriptions as *Lakisu.*] An old Canaanite fortress city in the Shephelah. It came under Egyptian control probably in the time of Thutmose III but revolted in the Amarna period, as the Amarna Letters show. When the Israelites invaded the country the king of Lachish joined a coalition under the leadership of the king of Jerusalem, which clashed with the forces of Joshua. In the ensuing battle the king of Lachish was slain, and his city captured (Jos 10:3-35; 12:11) but not destroyed or occupied at that time. It later became a possession of Judah, and King Rehoboam strengthened its fortifications (2 Chr 11:9). King Amaziah sought refuge in Lachish from his conspirators, but was there murdered (2 Ki 14:19; 2 Chr 25:27). Lachish was besieged by Sennacherib of Assyria in Hezekiah's reign, and scenes of its siege, attack, and capture are realistically depicted on stone reliefs found in Sennacherib's palace at Nineveh, which are now in the British Museum (see figs. 284, 428). It was from Lachish that Sennacherib sent a detachment to Jerusalem

282. Lachish according to an artist's conception based on archeological evidence

to demand the surrender of the capital. Although Hezekiah paid a heavy tribute to the king of Assyria, he never surrendered Jerusalem (2 Ki 18:14-17; 19:8; 2 Chr 32:9; Is 36:2; 37:8). When the

prophet Micah charged that Lachish was "the beginning of sin" to Zion and that in her "were found the transgressions of Israel" (Mic 1:13), he may have referred to some pagan cult that the Isra-

283. General view of *Tell ed-Duweir,* the site of ancient Lachish

elites adopted. During the final years of Judah's history Nebuchadnezzar besieged Lachish, which held out after much of the country was devastated by the armies of the Chaldeans (Jer 34:7). Excavations show that the city was destroyed twice by Nebuchadnezzar, first in 597 B.C. and again in 587 or 586 B.C. Lachish was again inhabited by Jews after the Exile (Neh 11:30), although it never regained its former importance.

The city was formerly identified with *Tell el-Ḥesi,* 15 mi. east-northeast of Gaza, the site at which modern scientific methods of excavation started in 1890 when W. M. Flinders Petrie developed in the course of his explorations the science of Palestinian pottery chronology, i.e., a science by means of which the relative age of ruins can be determined from the style of pottery found in them. Later it was recognized that *Tell el-Ḥesi* could not be Lachish, and W. F. Albright identified Lachish as *Tell ed-Duweir* (see fig. 283), 7½ mi. to the northeast of the former place (Map VI, E-2). This identification was virtually proved to be correct in 1935 by the discovery of written documents, called the Lachish Letters, in the ruins of the site. These mention Lachish, apparently as the place to which the letters were addressed.

The excavations of *Tell ed-Duweir* were

carried out from 1933 to 1938 by the Wellcome-Marston Archaeological Research Expedition to the Near East, under the direction of J. L. Starkey, who met an untimely death at the hand of murderers in January, 1938. For some time the work was continued under the direction of O. Tufnell, but it is to be regretted that it was discontinued, although no other Palestinian site has been so fruitful in objects found as Lachish. The excavations showed that the site had been inhabited in what is called the Early Bronze Age, long before Abraham's time. During the Middle Bronze Age (early 2d millennium B.C.) a double wall was erected, to which a deep fosse, or moat, was added by a people identified by the excavators as the Hyksos. After the expulsion of the Hyksos the city came under Egyptian rule. From that time dates a temple whose ruins yielded many cult objects. During the Israelite period, represented by Levels IV-III, the city was surrounded by a new double wall, built probably by Rehoboam (see fig. 282). Destroyed by Sennacherib, the city was rebuilt (Level II) and was again destroyed, this time by Nebuchadnezzar. Level I, dating from the postexilic Persian period, revealed a mansion of a high official, and apparently a cultic building dedicated to the worship of Ahura-Mazda, indications that the city may have had a Persian garrison.

Among the objects discovered during the excavations are a number containing inscriptions. These are most valuable. They can be classified in 2 categories: (1) inscribed objects of the earliest period in the history of alphabetic writing, and (2) inscribed objects of the classical period of ancient Hebrew. The 1st class is represented by a dagger, a bowl, and a ewer, inscribed in proto-Semitic (or Sinaitic) script. This in its semi-pictorial or hieroglyphic form was the forerunner of the Phoenician script (known from the *Moabite Stone) and other pre-exilic inscriptions (see Writing). These objects have been dated by their archeological context as coming from the 16th and 13th cent. B.C., and thus give us some idea of the appearance of alphabetic writing in the time of Moses and in the period of the judges. The 2d class of inscribed objects is represented by the Lachish Letters (see fig. 285). These comprise 21 pieces of broken pottery on which appear communications written in ink; 18 of them were found in 1935 in one of the guardrooms of the city gate, and 3 more came to light in 1938. Since much of the ink has faded away, all the problems of decipherment have not been solved. The letters seem to have been written by an army officer stationed at some distance from Lachish, and were addressed to his superior, apparently the commander of the fortress of Lachish. Their contents and archeological evidence make it certain that they date from the last days of Lachish, shortly before the city fell to Nebuchadnezzar, who destroyed the city in such a terrific conflagration that the clay walls were burned red.

The Lachish Letters are written in the

284. Relief depicting the siege of Lachish by Sennacherib's army

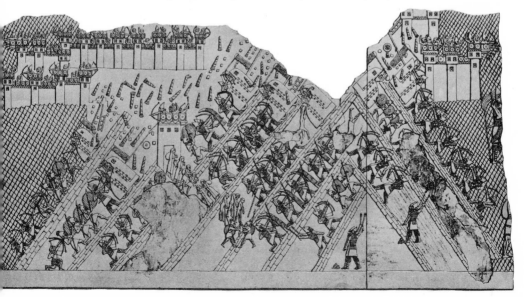

script of the 6th cent. B.C. and in the language of Jeremiah, which is considered classical Hebrew. It is tantalizing to find reference to a prophet in the letters without knowing whether Jeremiah, Uriah, or another of the Biblical prophets of Judah is meant. There are passages that show great similarities to the language of the Bible. For example, Letter VI says: "Behold the words of the pr[inces] are not

285. Lachish Letter IV, from Jeremiah's time; above, obverse; below, reverse

good, (but) to weaken our hands [and to sla]cken the hands of the m[en] who are informed about them." These words should be compared with the accusation directed against Jeremiah recorded in Jer 38:4. Letter IV makes the following statement: "And let (my lord) know that we are watching for the signals of Lachish, according to all the indications which my lord hath given, for we cannot see Azekah." This refers to the time of which Jeremiah speaks, when only two cities besides Jerusalem still held out against Nebuchadnezzar, namely Azekah and Lachish (ch 34:7). Letter IV seems to have been written after Azekah had already fallen and its signals had stopped, but

while Lachish was still uncaptured. The letters show that the writer was a faithful servant of Yahweh, since every letter begins with an appeal to Yahweh, such as the following (in Letter II): "To my lord Yaosh: May Yahweh cause my lord to hear tidings of peace this very day, this very day! Who is thy servant (but) a dog that my lord hath remembered his servant? May Yahweh afflict those who re-[port] an (evil) rumor about which thou art not informed!" (All quotations are taken from *ANET* 322.) The letters contain 22 personal names, of which, 14 are definitely connected with the name Yahweh and one with El (God), but not one of them with a pagan deity. The good results of Josiah's reformation may be reflected in these names.

Among other inscriptional material from Lachish is a seal impression of "Gedaliah, who is over the house" (see fig. 195), apparently the Gedaliah who became governor of Judah after Jerusalem's destruction (2 Ki 25:22-25). Another interesting find—an inscription on stone on the stairway of the Persian mansion of the first 5 letters of the Hebrew alphabet—indicates that the sequence of the letters of the Hebrew alphabet was the same in the 5th cent. B.C. as it is now. This conclusion was confirmed by the later discovery at Ras Shamra of the complete Ugaritic alphabet of the 14th cent. B.C.

Lit.: The official publications: H. Torczyner and others, *Lachish I. The Lachish Letters* (London, 1938); O. Tufnell and others, *Lachish II. The Fosse Temple* (London, 1940); O. Tufnell and others, *Lachish III. The Iron Age* (London, 1953); O. Tufnell and others, *Lachish IV. The Bronze Age* (London, 1958). A brief nontechnical but authoritative report is found in *BA* 1 (1938), 21-32.

Ladan (lā′dăn), KJV **Laadan** (lā′ä-dăn). [Heb. *La'dan.*]

1. A descendant of Ephraim and ancestor of Joshua (1 Chr 7:26).

2. The ancestral head of a division of the Gershonite Levites (1 Chr 23:7-9; 26:21).

Lady. A rendering of: (1) the Heb. *gebereth* (Is 47:5, 7, KJV), "mistress," "lady," a feminine form of *geber*, "a man in his youth, vigor, and full capabilities"; (2) the Heb. *sarah* (Jgs 5:29; Est 1:18), "mistress," "a lady of rank," a feminine form of the Heb. *sar*, *"prince"; (3) the Heb. *shegal*, probably "concubine" (Ps 45:9, RSV); (4) the Gr. *kuria* (2 Jn 1, 5), "lady," "mistress" (*see* Elect Lady).

Lael (lā'ĕl). [Heb. *La'el*, "(belonging) to God."] A man whose son Eliasaph was head of the Gershonites, the division of Levites to whom the care of the tabernacle and the tent was entrusted (Num 3:24-26).

Lahad (lā'hăd). [Heb. *Lahad*, meaning uncertain.] A descendant of Judah through, Shobal (1 Chr 4:2).

Lahai-roi. *See* Beer-lahai-roi.

Lahmam (lä'măm). [Heb. *Lachmam*, in some manuscripts *Lachmas*.] A town in the Shephelah in Judah (Jos 15:40); it is possibly to be identified with *Khirbet el-Lahm*, about 12 mi. northwest of Hebron.

Lahmi (lä'mī). [Heb. *Lachmî*, "my bread."] A Philistine killed by Elhanan, the son of Jair. He was the brother of Goliath the Gittite (1 Chr 20:5). His name does not appear in the parallel text of 2 Sa 21:19. *See* Elhanan, 1; Goliath.

Laish (lā'ĭsh). [Heb. *Layish*, "lion."]

1. A man whose son Palti was given Saul's daughter Michal, David's wife (1 Sa 25:44; 2 Sa 3:15), after David fled from the court of Saul.

2. A Canaanite city in the extreme north of Palestine, renamed Dan when the Danites captured the city (Jgs 18:7-29). It was also called Leshem (lē'shĕm; Jos 19: 47). See Dan, 3. Map VI, B-4.

3. For Is 10:30, KJV, *see* Laishah.

Laishah (lā'ĭ-shà), KJV **Laish** (lā'ĭsh). [Heb. *Layshah*, "lioness."] A place in the territory of Benjamin apparently between Gallim and Anathoth (Is 10:30). It is identified with the present village *el-'Isāwîyeh* northeast of Mount Scopus, the northernmost summit of the Mount of Olives.

Lake of Fire. [Gr. *limnē tou puros*. This expression may be understood as meaning "the lake which is fire."] An expression used by John to describe the place into which in vision he saw cast the beast, the false prophet, the devil, "Death and Hades" (RSV), and all whose names were not found in the book of life (Rev 19: 20; 20:10, 14, 15; 21:8). The casting into the lake represents the destruction of these individuals, powers, and concepts, although torment is also implied (cf. ch 20:10).

John saw the beast and false prophet cast into the lake at the beginning of the millennium in connection with the coming of Christ as a conquering warrior to "smite the nations" and rule them with "a rod of iron" (Rev 19:11-21). The devil, his followers, Death and Hades, he saw

cast in at the close of the *millennium (Rev 20).

Lakkum (lăk'ŭm), KJV **Lakum** (lā'kŭm). [Heb. *Laqqûm*, meaning uncertain.] A town in the territory of Naphtali (Jos 19: 33), probably *Khirbet el-Manṣûrah*, near Anem, which is about 5 mi. southwest of the Sea of Galilee.

Lakum. *See* Lakkum.

Lama. A transliteration through the Greek of the Aramaic *lema'* (Heb. *lammah*), meaning "why." *See* Eloi.

Lamb. [Heb. generally *kebeś*, "a young ram," and *śeh*, "a young lamb (or "kid")"; Gr. *arnion* and *amnos*, "lamb."] Because of its innocence, patience, and harmlessness, a lamb was deemed the most fitting of all animals to represent the promised sin-bearer, the Lamb of God. Thus, the lamb came to play an important part in the ancient sacrificial system, which prefigured the sacrificial ministry of the Saviour. Interchangeably with a kid of the goats (the Heb. *śeh* may mean either) it was one of the principal sacrificial animals, from Eden until sacrifices largely ceased to be offered (Gen 4:4; 22:7; etc.). The 1st unambiguous mention of lambs in Scripture occurs in ch 21:28-31, where Abraham, in order to attest his ownership of the well at Beer-sheba, "the well of the oath," is recorded as giving 7 lambs to Abimelech. The 1st mention of a lamb as a sacrificial animal is in ch 22:7. A yearling lamb or kid (Heb. *śeh*) was prescribed for the Passover (Ex 12:3-5). When the sanctuary ritual was prescribed at Mount Sinai, God ordained that a yearling lamb (Heb. *kebeś*) should be offered as a burnt offering for all Israel every morning and another every evening (Ex 29:38-42; cf. Num 28:4), and on the Sabbath 2 in the morning and 2 at night (Num 28:9, 10). Offerings for special occasions such as the 3 great annual festivals and the Day of Atonement were in addition to the regular lambs of the morning and evening sacrifice. The daily offering of a lamb morning and evening typified the continuing ministry of Jesus Christ on behalf of sinners. Because this was "a continual [daily] burnt offering" (v 3) it came to be known simply as the *tamîd*, literally, the "continual," or "daily." In addition to the daily sacrifice, 7 male yearling lambs were to constitute a part of the special burnt offering for such occasions as the new moon (v 11), for each of the 7 days of the Passover (vs 16, 19, 24), for the Feast of Weeks, or

Pentecost (Num 28:26, 27), for New Year's Day (ch 29:1, 2), and the annual Day of Atonement, 10 days later (vs 7, 8). At the annual Feast of Tabernacles 14 lambs were to be offered each day in addition to the daily sacrifice, for each of the 1st 7 days of the feast, and 7 on the 8th day (vs 12-36). For certain other occasions a male lamb (Lev 9:3; 23:12, 18; Num 6:14; 7:15), a ewe lamb for the common people (Lev 4:27, 28, 32), and either a male or a female lamb for a guilt offering (ch 5:6) or a peace offering (ch 3:6, 7) were specified. In every instance the lamb was to be without blemish in order fitly to represent the perfect character of Jesus Christ (cf. 1 Pe 1:19).

Lamb of God. The title by which John the Baptist introduced Jesus to Israel as the Messiah, the Son of God (Jn 1:29-36). This designation for Christ does not occur in the OT, but the expression was probably based on the words of Is 53:7, "he is brought as a lamb to the slaughter." The title "Lamb of God" presents Jesus as the suffering Messiah and implies that the sacrifices of the OT typified Him as God's appointed sacrifice for sin. Throughout ancient times a lamb—or a kid of the goats (Gen 22:7; Ex 12:3)— was one of the principal sacrificial offerings. The daily burnt offering, a spotless male lamb (Ex 29:39-42), appropriately typified the perpetual ministry of Christ on behalf of sinners. The apostle Paul refers to Christ as "our passover" (1 Cor 5:7), Peter, as "a lamb without blemish and without spot" (1 Pe 1:19), and John, as "the Lamb slain from the foundation of the world" (Rev 13:8). In the Revelation, John designates Christ as the "Lamb" 28 times. *See* Lamb.

Lamech (lā'mĕk). [Heb. *Lemek;* Gr. *Lamech.*]

1. A descendant of Cain and son of Methushael. He was the first polygamist. By his 1st wife, Adah, he had 2 sons, Jabal and Jubal, who became the originators of nomadism and music. By his 2d wife, Zillah, he had a son Tubal-cain, the originator of metal working, and a daughter Naamah, of whom nothing is recorded. Lamech's words to his wives about a tragic event in his life are recorded in poetic form in Hebrew, and have aptly been called the "Song of Lamech." This song constitutes the world's oldest known poetic composition. The somewhat cryptic and ambiguous Hebrew verse allows more than one explanation. Perhaps the meaning is that Lamech would

be ready to repeat his murderous act in case of necessity (Gen 4:18-24).

2. A descendant of Seth and son of Methuselah. When he was 182 years old his son Noah was born. He named the child Noah, meaning "rest," or "comfort," perhaps expecting this son to bring rest for him and his contemporaries from the curse under which the human race lived. He died at the age of 777 years, only a few years before the Flood (Gen 5:25, 28-31).

Lamed. [Heb. *lamed.*] The 12th letter of the Hebrew alphabet, written ל, appearing as the title of the 12th section of Ps 119 in the KJV. *See* Aleph.

Lamentation. *See* Mourning.

Lamentations, Book of. A series of laments composed by the prophet Jeremiah as an elegy upon the fall and destruction of Jerusalem in 586 B.C. Hebrew Bibles title the book by the first word of the elegy, *'êkah,* "how." According to the Talmud the Jews also knew the book as *Qînôth,* "Lamentations." This title the translators of the Septuagint rendered as *Thrēnoi,* to which the Latin Vulgate added the explanatory note "That Is the Lamentations of Jeremiah the Prophet." The English title, "The Lamentations of Jeremiah," is an abbreviation of the Vulgate title. Prior to the rise of modern critical scholarship Jews and Christians alike uniformly attributed the book to the prophet Jeremiah. Modern critics point out that in the ancient Hebrew canon it stands, not in the prophetic section, as would be expected if its author were a prophet, but in the Hagiographa, or Writings, the 3d section of the Hebrew canon. However, certain striking parallels of phraseology and subject matter between the books of Lamentations and Jeremiah point to a common authorship (compare Lam 3:14, 48 with Jer 9:1; 20: 7; Lam 3:52-56 with Jer 12:9; 37:16; 38: 6). Repeated references in Lam 3 (see especially vs 14, 48-57, 61-63) to the personal sufferings of the author correspond with what is known concerning the experiences of Jeremiah.

The prophet Jeremiah bore God's message to Israel prior to and during the early years of the Babylonian captivity. Tender of heart, he sensed keenly the evils of which the nation was guilty, and mourned as God revealed to him the retribution soon to overtake his beloved Jerusalem (see Jer 4:19; 10:20; 13:17; 14:17; etc.). Jeremiah counseled submission to the Babylonian conquerors as a means of avoiding further suffering and disaster (see Jer 27:11-14; 29:4-7), but kings and people alike refused to heed the message. As a result the "yokes of wood," representative of the comparatively light suffering occasioned by the 1st and 2d invasions of Judah by Nebuchadnezzar, were replaced by "yokes of iron" (ch 28:2, 10, 13, 14). This perversity of spirit made inevitable the captivity of practically the entire nation, the desolation of Jerusalem and Judea, and the destruction of the Temple. Only a few of the poorest people of the land were left, scattered about the countryside. Little wonder that Jeremiah is known as "the weeping prophet"—he had more than enough to weep about. In Lamentations he pours forth the sorrow of his heart.

The book is made up of 5 elegiac poems, corresponding to its 5 chapters. The first 4 are written in the *qînah* or elegiac meter characteristic of Hebrew poetry, and the 5th, a prayer rather than an elegy, is in the usual Hebrew poetic meter. Chs 1, 2, 4, 5 each have 22 verses, corresponding with the 22 distinct letters of the Hebrew alphabet, while ch 3 has 66 verses. In chs 1, 2, and 4 the verses are arranged alphabetically, v 1 beginning with the 1st letter of the Hebrew alphabet, v 2 with the 2d, and so on except for small variations in ch 2. In ch 3 the first 3 verses begin with the 1st letter of the alphabet, the next 3 with the 2d letter, and so on to the end. The 5th chapter does not observe an alphabetical arrangement.

Lamp. [Heb. generally *ner*. The related Hebrew word *menôrah*, used to designate the golden "candlestick" in the tabernacle and the Temple, means a *lampstand. The Heb. *lappîd*, also rendered "lamp" in the KJV, is really a torch (Jgs 15:4; Is 62:1; etc.). Two Greek words are used in the NT to designate the lamp, *luchnos* (Mt 5:15; Lk 8:16; etc.), and *lampas*, which is either a torch (Jn 18:3) or a lamp (Mt 25:1, 3, 4, 7, 8). The *phanos* (Jn 18:3) is a lantern, and the *luchnia* (Mt 5:15) a lampstand. *Ner* and *luchnos* are sometimes incorrectly rendered "candle" in the KJV (Job 18:6; Mt 5:15; etc.).]

The Bible does not provide us with a description of a lamp, although it mentions a wick or flax (Is 42:3) and olive oil as fuel (Ex 25:6; 27:20; Mt 25:3, 4). Excavations in Bible lands, however, have unearthed a wealth of ancient lamps from various periods of history. The ancients were buried with lamps in the belief that

286. A series of Palestinian lamps from patriarchal times to the Byzantine period

these would provide light for the dead in the hereafter, so that hardly an ancient Near Eastern tomb is found that does not contain lamps. All early lamps are of clay, but in the 1st millennium B.C. metal lamps came into use. The earliest lamps were merely bowls, the brim of which was pinched at one point. Into the channel thus formed a wick or flax was inserted that conducted the olive or animal oil to the flame. Lamps were made with a deeper pinch in the rim in the course of time; later the rim was turned inward until the vessel was molded with two holes, one in the middle as an intake for oil, and the other, which developed into a spout, for the wick. The earliest lamps had no base, being placed on the floor or in the sand, but later they were made with a base, and eventually with handles. From Hellenistic times on, lamps were decorated with simple designs, later with inscriptions and more elaborate decorations (see fig. 286). Some lamps had more than 1 spout.

Lamps were kept burning day and night in ancient times, for the lamps served not only to give light but also to keep fire at hand. In excavated caves that show signs of ancient habitation, small cut-out niches in the rock walls have been found, in which the ancients placed their lamps to light their primitive places of abode. Such shelves were also found in the walls of houses, in water tunnels, or in any other place that regularly or occasionally needed the light of a lamp. The ancients had also *lampstands on which lamps rested, made of either stone, terra cotta, or metal.

Lampstand, KJV **Candlestick.** [Heb. *menôrah;* Aramaic *nebreshah;* Gr. *luchnia.*] A stand for holding one or more lamps. In the OT such an item of furniture is men-

287. Relief on Titus' Arch of Triumph showing the 7-branched candlestick, the table of showbread, 2 trumpets, and a corner of the Jerusalem Temple

tioned as being used in the *tabernacle (Ex 25:31) and the Temple (1 Ki 7:49), also in a palace (Dan 5:5). NT references to a lampstand are more general. See Lamp. In this article only the lampstand in the sanctuary will be discussed. Since the sources of the light were lamps and not candles, the translation "candlestick" is incorrect. The first lampstand made for the tabernacle was of hammered gold, and consisted of a base and a main shaft from which 6 other branches protruded. It stood on the south side in the first apartment of the tabernacle (Ex 25:31-40; 40:24). The lamps were fed with pure olive oil and burned all night (Ex 27:20, 21; Lev 24:2-4). Josephus says that 3 of the lamps burned also during the day (*Ant.* iii. 8. 3). Solomon replaced the 1 lampstand by 10 in his Temple—5 on each side of the sanctuary (1 Ki 7:49; 2 Chr 4:7). Nebuchadnezzar carried the Temple lampstands to Babylon (Jer 52:19). They were apparently not returned to Jerusalem in Cyrus' time, for Zerubbabel's Temple seems to have contained only one lampstand, which Antiochus IV Epiphanes carried off after he had desecrated the Temple (1 Macc 1:20, 21). Judas Maccabeus had a new one made (ch 4:49), but this one was replaced in Herod's Temple by a much larger one (Jos. *War* vii. 5. 5). This lampstand was captured by the Romans in A.D. 70 and carried in Titus' procession of triumph, as the relief on his triumphal arch shows (see fig. 287). It remained in Rome until the Vandals carried it to Carthage in A.D. 455. Under Belisarius it was taken to Constantinople in 534, and was later sent back to Jerusalem by the emperor Justinian. When the Persians sacked Jerusalem in A.D. 614 it was probably taken to the East. Nothing has been heard of it since.

Since archeology has found no examples of 7-branched lampstands in OT times, but only of lamps consisting of a bowl with 7 spouts for the wicks, many believe that the lampstands of the tabernacle and of Solomon's Temple were in appearance and form quite unlike that of Herod's temple. However, the description in Ex 25:31-37 specifies 7 branches. The 7-branched lampstand became a frequent symbol in later Jewish art on sarcophagi, on tombstones, over the doors of houses, and especially in synagogue decorations, of which the 3d cent. A.D. synagogue of Dura Europus on the Euphrates is one of the earliest examples.

Lance. *See* Spear.

Lancet. *See* Spear.

Landmarks. [Heb. *gebûl* and *gebûlah*, "boundary," "border."] A feature of the terrain, or some man-made device serving to delineate the borders of a farm or other portion of territory. Anciently, boundary markers consisted probably of double furrows plowed between adjacent fields of different owners or of small piles of stones or of pillars. Hereditary property rights were greatly respected in Israel (Deut 19:14; Prov 22:28), and the removal of a neighbor's landmark was regarded as highly reprehensible (Deut 27:17; Hos 5:10).

Language. *See* Tongue.

Lantern. [Gr. *phanos,* originally meaning "torch," but in Koine Greek "lantern."] A lamp enclosed in such a way that it is protected from wind and rain and can be used in the open air. Lanterns were apparently unknown in Palestine until Greek and Roman times. In the excavations of Jericho a lantern of the late Roman period was found. It consists of a clay enclosure in the form of a beehive (9 in. high) with an opening on one side so that a lamp could be inserted. On top of it was a ring that served as handle. The Romans also used lanterns consisting of a metal frame and a cylinder made of some translucent material (bladder, horn) that enclosed a lamp or candle. Lanterns are mentioned in the Bible only once (Jn 18:3). They were carried by some of the soldiers who arrested Jesus in Gethsemane.

Laodicea (là-ŏd'ĭ-sē'à). [Gr. *Laodeikia,* probably "people's court (of justice)," "people's judgment," or "a people adjudged."] An important city of western Asia Minor, belonging to Phrygia. It was situated on the edge of the valley of the river Lycus, a tributary of the Maeander, and lay between mountains that rise to heights of 8,000 and 9,000 ft. (Map XX, B-4). It was

LAODICEA

founded probably by Antiochus II (261-246 B.C.), who named it after Laodice, his sister (see P-W 2:2455) and wife, and populated it with Syrians and Jews transplanted from Babylonia. The city did not gain importance until it became part of the Roman province of Asia, organized in the 2d cent. B.C. It was famous in NT times as a trade center for a glossy black wool and black garments locally manufactured from it, both articles being exported to many countries. Also well known throughout the Eastern world was the medicinal "Phrygian powder" used for the eyes. The city became so wealthy that when it was destroyed in A.D. 60 by an earthquake its citizens, unlike those of other cities who had shared in this misfortune, refused Roman help and rebuilt their city out of their own resources. The city changed hands several times in the succeeding centuries, and was finally destroyed in the 13th cent. by the Turks. Since that time it has lain in ruins, and has served as a quarry for building material for the neighboring city of Denizli. The ruined site, never excavated, bears the name *Eski Hissar,* which means "old castle."

A Christian church existed in the city at the time when the letter of Paul to the Colossians was written (*c.* A.D. 62), but Paul apparently had never been in the city (Col 2:1). It is possible that Epaphras, a native of the neighboring Colossae, was the founder of Christianity in that area (chs 1:7; 4:12). A letter from Paul reached the Laodiceans at the same time that the letter to the Colossians was received (ch 4:16). This letter was probably lost, as were some others of Paul's letters (cf. 1 Cor 5:11). Since the time of Marcion (*c.* A.D. 150) it has frequently been suggested that the letter to the Ephesians is the lost letter to the Laodiceans, because the words "at Ephesus" (Eph 1:1, KJV) are poorly attested by manuscript evidence. See *SDACom* 7:219. An apocryphal letter of Paul's to the Laodiceans from the 4th cent. A.D., existing in a Latin and an Arabic translation, is

289. Ruins of Laodicea

composed of a mixture of passages from Galatians and Ephesians.

One of the 7 letters to the churches in the Revelation is addressed to the church at Laodicea (Rev 3:14-22). The rebukes contained in this letter indicate that the conditions in that church were not good, and the references to wealth, eyesalve, and white raiment are explained by a knowledge of the city's history, its economic importance and pride, and its industrial products. See *SDACom* 7:100-102, 762.

Laodicean (lȧ-ŏd'ĭ-sē'ăn). [Gr. *Laodikeus.*] An inhabitant of *Laodicea (Col 4:16).

Lap. In 2 Ki 4:39; Prov 16:33; Neh 5:13 the translation of Hebrew terms that designate parts, or folds, of a garment, anciently used as receptacles. The "lap" of 2 Ki 4:20, RSV, is literally "knees." The Gr. *kolpos* in Lk 6:38, translated "bosom" in the KJV and "lap" in the RSV, should also be understood as referring to a fold of the garment used as a receptacle.

Lapidoth. *See* Lappidoth.

Lappidoth (lăp'ĭ-dŏth), KJV **Lapidoth** (lăp'ĭ-dŏth). [Heb. *Lappîdôth,* "torches," or

288. Unexcavated rows of seats in the ancient theater at Laodicea

"flashes of lightning."] The husband of the prophetess Deborah (Jgs 4:4).

Lapwing. *See* Hoopoe.

Lasea (la-sē'a). [Gr. *Lasaia*.] A port city on the southern coast of Crete (Map XX, B-3), about 5 mi. from Fair Havens. It is mentioned in Luke's report of Paul's journey to Rome as a prisoner (Acts 27:8).

Lasha (lā'sha). [Heb. *Lesha'*.] An ancient border town of Canaan (Gen 10:19). The site is unknown, but is commonly located in southeastern Palestine because the cities Sodom and Gomorrah are mentioned in connection with it. Jerome's identification of Lasha with the hot springs of Callirrhoë in the *Wâdī Zerqā Mā'în* can hardly be correct, since the valley lies too far north.

Lasharon (la-shā'rŏn). [Heb. *Lashsharôn*.] A Canaanite city or district whose king was defeated by Joshua (Jos 12:18). The Hebrew text allows the passage to be rendered, "the king of Sharon one," making this text refer to the coastal plain of Sharon instead of a particular city. The LXX renders v 18: "the king of Aphek of Sharon."

Last Days. An expression denoting: (1) the remote future; (2) the close of this age, immediately prior to the establishment of the Messianic kingdom. As the context makes evident, "last days" in Gen 49:1, KJV, denotes simply time in the remote future. Another expression, "latter days" (translated from the same Hebrew phrase as "last days"), is often used in this same sense, of the indefinite future (Num 24:14; Deut 4:30; 31:29; Jer 23:20; 30:24; 48:47; Hos 3:5). In an eschatological sense "last day" or "last days" refers to the time immediately preceding the close of this age of earth's history and the inauguration of the Messianic or future age (see Is 2:2; Mic 4:1; Jn 6:39-54; 11:24; 12:48; Acts 2:17; Jas 5:3; 2 Pe 3:3). NT writers apply OT predictions of the last days to their own time (Acts 2:17), or refer to their time as "these last days" (Heb 1:2), and use the equivalent expression "last time" in a similar sense (1 Pe 1:5; 1 Jn 2:18, KJV; Jude 18). It seems that to the NT writers the "last days" of the OT prophets pointed to their own time, since they were living in the period of time between the 1st and 2d advents of Christ, the entire extent of which time they considered the "last days."

Last Supper. *See* Lord's Supper.

Latchet. A translation in the KJV of the

Heb. *serôk* and Gr. *himas,* designating the leather strap that bound the sandal to the foot (Gen 14:23; Is 5:27; Mk 1:7; Lk 3:16; Jn 1:27).

Latin. [Gr. *Rhōmaïsti,* "in Latin," and *Rhōmaïkos,* "Roman," "Latin."] The official language of the Roman government, which ruled Palestine in the time of Christ. Latin became the language not only of all Italy but also of the western provinces, but in spite of the Roman rule over the countries of the eastern Mediterranean for many centuries, the Latin language never replaced Greek in the eastern half of the empire, nor such native languages as Aramaic in Palestine. However, a number of military, administrative, and legal terms found entrance into Greek, and some of them are found as loan words in the Greek text of the NT. For example, the Latin *census,* "census," appears in Greek as *kēnsos,* "tax"; note also *centurio* (Gr. *kenturiōn*), "centurion," KJV "captain"; *assarius* (Gr. *assarion*), a small Roman coin, "farthing" (KJV), or "penny" (RSV); and others. Being the language of the Roman officials, Latin naturally was used, along with Greek and "Hebrew," for the inscription on the cross that described the reason for Christ's crucifixion (Jn 19:20.)

Latrine, KJV **Draught House.** [Heb. *machara'ôth,* changed by the Masoretes to *môsa'ôth.* Both forms are plural and mean "latrine," or "privy," but the first is more archaic.] A privy. One of the first acts of King Jehu of Israel when he came to the throne was to convert the temple of Baal in Samaria into a public latrine (2 Ki 10:27) to make it altogether unclean and contemptible. Public latrines have been excavated in several ancient cities and usually consist of a simple building with a row of holes in stone slabs covering a drain through which water ran.

Latter Rain. *See* Season.

Lattice. A network of crossed laths, screening a window or other opening. Ancient windows were holes in the walls covered with latticework, since window glass was unknown in early times. Three different Hebrew words are used for these lattice windows, and it is not known whether these different words denote differences in appearance, or in the construction of the lattices: (1) *'eshnab* (Jgs 5:28; Prov 7:6), (2) *charakkîm* (pl., Song 2:9), (3) *challôn* (1 Ki 6:4; etc., translated "window"). Another Hebrew word, *sebakah,* also translated "lattice" (2 Ki 1:2), probably designates instead a trellis battlement of the roof.

Laver. [Heb. *kîyôr*, "basin," "laver."] Specifically, the bronze basin in the courtyard of the ancient tabernacle, between the altar of burnt offering and the sanctuary, and later similar but more elaborate water containers in Solomon's Temple (Ex 30:17-21; 1 Ki 7:23-39). The priests used the water for their ritual. They were to wash their hands and feet before ministering at the altar or entering into the sanctuary (Ex 30:17-21; Lev 8:11). These ablutions were symbolic of the concept that God requires absolute cleanness of heart and life on the part of those who approach Him in worship. The bronze laver made at Mount Sinai was cast from the metal mirrors of Israelite women (Ex 38:8). It consisted of 2 parts, a bronze bowl and the bronze pedestal on which it stood (ch 30:18). The "molten sea" and the 10 lavers provided by Solomon for his Temple (1 Ki 7:23-43) served the same purpose as the laver in the sanctuary. Solomon's "molten sea" was for the priests "to wash in," and the 10 smaller lavers were for washing portions of the burnt offerings (2 Chr 4:6). Each of the 10 lavers had its own stand or base, cast separately from the laver, and these bases were equipped with wheels to permit the lavers to be moved about the court as necessary. These bases and that of the "molten sea" were elaborately decorated (1 Ki 7:23-37). Nothing is known of the size or capacity of the laver in the original tabernacle. Figure 290 shows an ancient cult vehicle discovered on Cyprus, which

290. **Mycenaean cult carriage found at Cyprus, probably somewhat similar to the "lavers" of Solomon's Temple**

seems to have served a purpose similar to that of the lavers in Solomon's Temple. For the capacity of Solomon's "molten sea" *see* Sea, Bronze. Each of the 10 smaller, portable "lavers" held 40 "baths," or about 232 gallons (v 38).

Law. [Heb. *tôrah*, "direction," "instruction"; *dath*, "regulation," "law"; Gr. *nomos*, "rule," "principle," "law."] In the Bible, a set of principles or standard of conduct. The usual Hebrew term translated "law" is *tôrah*, a term signifying all the revealed will of God, or any part of it. Unless the context indicates otherwise, "law" in the OT usually denotes the divine "instruction" God had given His people (Gen 26:5; Ex 16:4, 28; Ps 1:2; 19:7; 119:1, 165; Is 1:10; 8:16, 20; etc.). This "law," or written revelation of God's will, made known the divine purpose for the Hebrew people in OT times. To the devout Jew, God's "law" was equivalent to His plan for the salvation of the world. It is in this sense that Isaiah says "the isles shall wait for his law" (Is 42:4). The instructions God imparted to Moses came to be known as "the law of Moses," that is, the instruction given by Moses (Jos 8:31; Neh 8:1; Lk 2:22; 24:44; Acts 28:23; etc.). In view of the fact that the instruction imparted to Moses occupies a major part of the first 5 books of the Bible, commonly known as the Pentateuch, the Jews often referred to the Pentateuch as "the law of Moses" (Lk 24:44; Jn 1:17; cf. Mt 5:17, 18).

In the NT the term "the law" is used with various shades of meaning, and unless these different aspects of "law" are kept in mind, and the context examined to ascertain which shade of meaning the writer is alluding to, the modern reader of the NT is almost certain, at times, to misconstrue what is said about the "law." To a Jewish reader or to one familiar with the Jewish religious system, the different nuances of the word "law" were clear, and a speaker or writer could shift rapidly from one to another without being misunderstood, since the context of his remarks would be sufficient to make his meaning clear. In fact, to the devout Jew all the different shades of meaning implied by the word "law" were, for practical purposes, one, and each blended almost imperceptibly into the other. Furthermore, the Jews did not ordinarily distinguish between moral, ceremonial, civil, and health regulations, since God was the author of them all, and all were binding upon His people. To the mod-

291. The upper part of the Code of Hammurabi. The king is depicted as standing before his god to receive the law from his hand

ern reader, on the other hand, this can all be very confusing. In the NT the word "law" is used in 2 distinct but closely related senses: (1) Scripture as a revelation of the divine will (see Jn 12:34; 15: 24; etc.). In Jewish terminology the word "law" may refer to the Pentateuch, the 5 books of Moses, in contrast with the Prophets and the Writings, or the Hagiographa—the 3 divisions of the OT according to the Hebrew canon (see Lk 24:44). Occasionally they used the expression "law of Moses" when referring to the Pentateuch, but more often simply the word "law" (see Mt 7:12; 11:13; 12:5; 22:40; 23:23; Lk 10:26; 16:16, 17; Jn 1:45; 7:19; 13:15; Rom 5:13, 20; 7; etc.). At times the word "law" is used in connection with the Decalogue, though in some instances "law" may refer specifically to the Pentateuch, of which the Decalogue is an integral part (Mt 22:36-40; Rom 7:7; Jas 2:10-12). (2) The Jewish religious system as a whole, or some particular part of it (Jn 1:17; Acts 18:13, 15; 22:3; Rom 6:

14, 15; Gal 3:19-25; etc.). The Jewish religious system was, of course, based on the revelation of God's will as contained in the OT Scriptures, particularly the Pentateuch. Sometimes the term "law" refers particularly to the ritual law, the characteristic outward feature of the Jewish religious system (Lk 2:22-24; Acts 15: 5, 24; etc.). The expression "works of the law" commonly refers to the requirements of the ritual law, though such law is also spoken of as "the law of the Lord" (Lk 2:23). In Heb 7:12 "law" refers to that part of the Law of Moses dealing with the priesthood.

Obviously, texts referring to "the law" should be used only after the most careful study of the context in order to ascertain the intent of the inspired writer, and with a fine sense of discrimination.

Lawyer. [Gr. *nomikos.*] One versed in the law. Most of the "lawyers" mentioned in the NT were men versed in the Law of Moses and the traditional law of the various rabbinical schools. The term "lawyer" in the NT is almost synonymous with that of *"scribe."* Lawyers are mentioned among those who rejected the message of John the Baptist (Lk 7:30). They showed the same attitude also toward Jesus and sought to catch Him with difficult questions (Mt 22:35; Lk 10:25). On occasion Jesus turned their own weapons against them (Lk 14:3). No wonder that Jesus denounced them, together with the scribes and Pharisees, for placing heavy burdens upon the people without touching such burdens themselves, and for withholding the key to knowledge (ch 11:45, 46, 52). It is not known whether Zenas the lawyer, mentioned in Tit 3:13, was an expert in Mosaic law or in Roman law.

Laying on of hands. An act performed under various circumstances and for various purposes: (1) Presentation of sacrificial animals. The offerer frequently laid his hands upon the animal devoted to sacrifice (Lev 1:2-4; etc.) prior to the slaying (ch 3:1, 2), signifying that the animal was presented as the offerer's substitute. On certain occasions the priests laid their hands upon the animal (Ex 29:9, 10, 19; cf. vs 29, 30; Lev 4:3, 4; 16:21; *see* Atonement, Day of; Azazel). (2) Blessing. Jacob laid his hands upon the heads of Ephraim and Manasseh (Gen 48:14, 20), and Christ laid His hands on children and blessed them (Mk 10:16). (3) Harming or punishing. God said that He would lay His hand upon Egypt to liberate Israel (Ex 7:4). The Jewish leaders "sought to lay hands" on Jesus, but they feared the people (Mt 21:46; Lk 20:19; cf. 22:53). (4) Healing. Christ frequently laid His hands upon those He healed (Mk 6:5; Lk 4:40; 13:13), as did also His disciples (Acts 9:17; cf. Mk 16:18). (5) Ordination to the service of God. The congregation of Israel was directed to lay their hands upon the Levites that that tribe might be set aside for divine service (Num 8:9-11). Paul and Barnabas were consecrated to the ministry by the laying on of hands (Acts 13:2, 3), as also was Timothy (1 Ti 4:14; 2 Ti 1:6). Paul cautioned Timothy to lay hands on no man prematurely (1 Ti 5:22). Heb 6:2 lists the laying on of hands among the elementary doctrines of the Christian church. (6) Bestowal of the Holy Spirit (Acts 8:17; 9:17; 19:6).

Lazarus (lăz′á-rŭs). [Gr. *Lazaros,* from a late Jewish or colloquial abbreviation of the Heb. *'El'azar,* "God has helped."]

1. The name of one of the characters in Christ's parable of the Rich Man and Lazarus (Lk 16:19-31), the only example of Christ's use of a proper name in His parables. Lazarus is pictured as a helpless, diseased beggar who was brought each day and laid at the gate of a certain rich man in hope of finding enough scraps of food from the wealthy man's table to sustain a miserable existence. As he lay there the half-wild scavenger dogs licked at his sores, but the rich man completely ignored him.

Eventually Lazarus died, and later the rich man died also. The parable then represents their respective conditions as being radically reversed. Lazarus was seen by the former rich man as reclining blissfully in *"Abraham's bosom" while he himself was being tormented in *hell. When the rich man appealed to Abraham to send Lazarus to relieve his agonies, Abraham reminded him that he had not aided Lazarus when he had the opportunity. The rich man then requested that Lazarus be sent to warn his still-living brothers, so that they might escape the torments he himself was suffering. Abraham retorted that they had the writings of Moses and the prophets to instruct them, and if they would not heed these, neither would they heed one from the dead.

Tradition names the rich man Dives on the meager grounds that in this parable the Vulgate renders the Gr. *plousios* ("rich") by the corresponding Latin word *dives.*

2. A resident of the village of *Bethany.

He was the brother of *Mary and *Martha, and a beloved friend of Jesus (Jn 11:1-3). He appears in the Bible as the subject of one of Christ's greatest miracles.

According to the narrative, Lazarus was taken ill, and the fact was reported to Jesus, who then was laboring probably in Perea, some 20 mi. or more from Bethany. Instead of hastening to the sick man, as Lazarus' sisters doubtless expected, Jesus lingered for two days, during which time Lazarus died (Jn 11:6, 7). This Jesus permitted "for the glory of God, that the Son of God might be glorified thereby" (v 4); for by the event that followed He was able to prove undeniably to His friends and enemies that He was the Lord of life (vs 25, 26). Jesus and His disciples finally arrived at Bethany, but not until Lazarus had been buried 4 days' (v 17). Accompanied by Mary and Martha and many onlookers, Jesus went to Lazarus' tomb. At His command, after some remonstrance on the part of Martha, the stone covering the opening of the tomb was removed (vs 39-41). Then Jesus, after thanking His Father for hearing Him, called in a loud voice for His dead friend to come forth (vs 41-43). Thereupon the shrouded Lazarus awoke and emerged from the tomb (v 44). This great miracle caused many to believe in Jesus as the Messiah, but it confirmed His enemies in their conviction that they must get rid of Him (vs 45-53). Lazarus, too, was marked for death by Jesus' enemies, for he was a living demonstration of the power of Christ (ch 12:10, 11).

Lazarus was later present at a supper given in Jesus' honor, at which his sister Mary anointed the feet of the Master with precious and costly ointment (Jn 12:1-3).

292. Entrance to the traditional tomb of Lazarus at Bethany

The raising of Lazarus was a contributing factor in the enthusiastic acclaim accorded Jesus by the people of Jerusalem at the Triumphal Entry (Jn 12:12-17).

Lead. [Heb. *'ophereth.*] A heavy pliable metallic element (symbol, Pb), having a specific gravity more than 11 times that of water. Its principal ore, sulphide galena, was found in Egypt, and the rendering of lead was found to be an easy process at an early date. This metal was part of the spoil taken by the Israelites after a battle with the Midianites (Num 31:22), and it is mentioned as a product of Tarshish (Eze 27:12). One interesting use to which it was put was as a filler for inscriptions carved in rock (Job 19:24) to retard corrosion and to increase legibility, as in the inscription of Darius I on the famous Behistun Rock (see fig. 293). The pursuing Egyptian armies "sank

293. The head of Darius I on the Behistun Rock. The incised characters in the inscription over his head were originally filled with lead

as lead" in the waters of the Red Sea (Ex 15:10), a fitting figure of speech, for the ancients used lead weights on their nets as fishermen do today. Both mining and smelting processes are referred to in the Scriptures (Jer 6:29; Eze 22:18, 20).

Leaf. A term used for (1) the foliage of trees (Gen 3:7; 8:11; etc.); (2) columns of a scroll (Jer 36:23, KJV); however, "leaves" in this passage is a misleading translation, for ancient scrolls were not divided into leaves but into columns (*see* Writing Material); (3) a part that slides or is hinged to close a doorway; Solomon's Temple had 2 entrance doors, each consisting of 2 leaves (1 Ki 6:34).

Leah (lē'à). [Heb. *Le'ah,* possibly "cow."] The elder daughter of Laban, who through a deception was given to Jacob in place of Rachel, her younger sister, for whom he had served 7 years. Leah was less attractive than her sister, having "tender" (Heb. *rak,* "weak") eyes (Gen 29:16-26). She became the mother of 6 of Jacob's sons, Reuben, Simeon, Levi, Judah, Issachar, and Zebulun, and of Dinah, a daughter (chs 31-35; 30:17-21). She was buried in the family sepulcher of Machpelah (ch 49:31). In Ruth 4:11 Leah is mentioned equally with Rachel as an honored founder of Israel.

Leannoth. [Heb. *le'annôth,* probably "for singing," or "for afflicting."] A musical term appearing with *Mahalath in the superscription of Ps 88, probably designating the melody to which the psalm was to be sung.

Leasing. [Heb. *kazab,* "lie," "deceit."] An archaic expression (Ps 4:2; 5:6; KJV) meaning "lie."

Leather. The preparation of hides and the *tanning of leather was well known in Bible times. Leather was used for girdles, or belts (2 Ki 1:8; Mt 3:4), footgear (Eze 16:10), the coverings of the tabernacle (Ex 25:5; 26:14), bags to carry water or other liquids, such as wine (Mt 9:17), quivers and helmets, a covering for shields, which were oiled to keep them smooth and shining (Is 21:5; cf. 2 Sa 1:21). Leather was also used as *writing material, and most of the Dead Sea scrolls are of leather. See fig. 244. *Parchment is a refined leather.

Leaven. [Heb. *chameṣ, śe'or;* Gr. *zumē.*] A fermentation-producing substance used to raise doughs of various kinds. The 1st Biblical reference to leaven is found in connection with the institution of the Feast of *Unleavened Bread on the eve of the departure of the Hebrews from Egypt. During this feast no leaven was to be found in their homes (Ex 12:15-20; 13:3-7). No cereal (KJV "meat") offering was to be made with leaven (Lev 2:11); it was to be eaten unleavened in a holy place (ch 6:15-17). The prophet Amos ironically invited the apostate Israelites to offer sacrifices containing leaven (Amos 4:5), a forbidden practice. However, leavened bread was specified for some offerings (Lev 7:13; 23:17). Jesus likened the pervasive qualities of His teachings to the action of leaven upon dough (Mt 13:33; Lk 13:20, 21). He also used leaven to illustrate the permeating influence of the teaching of the Pharisees and Sadducees, and the evil influence of Herod (Mt 16:6, 12; Mk 8:15). Paul, referring to the influence of the Judaizers in their midst, warned the Galatian Christians that "a little leaven [RSV "yeast"] leaveneth the whole lump" (Gal 5:9), and counseled the Corinthians to cleanse out the old leaven and become a new lump (1 Cor 5:6, 7).

Lebana (lĕ-bā′nà), or **Lebanah** (lĕ-bā′nà). [Heb. *Lebanah,* "white."] The ancestral head of a family of Nethinim, or Temple servants, members of which returned from Babylonia with Zerubbabel (Ezr 2: 45; Neh 7:48).

Lebanah. *See* Lebana.

Lebanon (lĕb′à-nŭn). [Heb. *Lebanôn,* "white (mountain)," so called because it is partially covered with snow for the largest part of the year. The name is attested in Ugaritic and Phoenician with the same spelling as the Hebrew, in Akkadian as *Labnana,* and in Hittite as *Lablana.*] The western chain of a double range of mountains. The Lebanons run parallel to the coast of the Mediterranean for about 150 mi. from the Litani (or Leontes) River near Tyre in the south to the *Nahr el-Kebîr* near Latakia in the north. The 2 parallel ranges are separated by a highland valley called the "valley of Lebanon" in the Bible (Jos 11:17; 12:7), in classical times Coele Syria, "Hollow Syria," and in modern times the *Beqā′,* in which the 2 main rivers of Syria flow, the Orontes toward the north and the Litani (Leontes) toward the south.

The Bible seems to apply the term Lebanon to both mountain ranges when it speaks of "the Hivites that dwelt in mount Lebanon," and yet describes them as living in territory ("from mount Baal-hermon unto the entering in of Hamath") that is either on the eastern range or in the valley between (Jgs 3:3; cf. 1 Chr 5: 23). On the other hand, other OT passages give the name *Hermon (also Sirion, Senir) to the southern section of the eastern range and apply Amana to adjacent mountains (Deut 3:8, 9; Song 4:8). Greek authors called the western range

294. A valley in the mountains of Lebanon

Lebanon and the eastern range Anti-Lebanon, names that are still applied to them (Map XIV, A-4/5).

The mountains of the western range are most picturesque, and the elevations of their highest summits run from 8,000 to 10,000 ft. above sea level with passes of 5,000 ft. and more between them. The western slopes of the Lebanon are fertile, and in ancient times were covered with the world-famous cedar trees and firs, or cypresses. Besides these, there are pines and oaks, as well as the following varieties of fruit and nut trees: almond, mulberry, fig, olive, walnut, apricot, pear, pomegranate, and pistachio. Cedars were exported to Egypt from the 3d millennium B.C., and later also to Mesopotamia, Palestine, and other countries. After the Arab conquest so little care was bestowed on the forests that the cedars have practically disappeared from the Lebanon, and wide areas are now denuded of topsoil. The mountains are of limestone and sandstone, and contain many springs that promote the fertility of the mountain slopes. The greatest height of the eastern range, the Anti-Lebanon, is at its southern end, where at its highest point, Mount Hermon, it rises to 9,232 ft. above sea level. The mountains of the Anti-Lebanon, which receive less rain than those of the western range, are more barren and less picturesque. They slope down into the Syrian plateau, which is a steppe in its western part and a desert farther to the east.

The Bible frequently mentions the Lebanon, first of all as the northwestern boundary of the Promised Land (Deut 1:7; 11:24; Jos 1:4; 11:17; 12:7; 13:5), and second as a cedar-producing country. Solomon obtained the beams for his Temple and palace buildings from the Lebanon through Tyre (1 Ki 5:6-10; 2 Chr 2:8-16); and Zerubbabel did likewise for the rebuilding of the Temple after the Exile (Ezr 3:7). Poets and prophets mention the Lebanon for its snow (Jer 18:14), for its wild beasts, such as leopards and lions (2 Ki 14:9; Song 4:8), and for its stately cedars and other trees (2 Ki 19:23; Is 60:13; Zec 11:1, 2) from which the Phoenicians obtained masts and timber for ships (Eze 27:5). See fig. 101.

Lebaoth (lĕ-bā'ŏth). [Heb. *Leba'ôth.*] A town in the south of Judah (Jos 15:32), probably identical with the place called *Beth-lebaoth in ch 19:6.

Lebbaeus. *See* Judas, 5.

Lebo Hamath. *See* Entrance of Hamath.

Lebonah (lĕ-bō'nȧ). [Heb. *Lebônah,* "incense."] A city in the territory of Ephraim, northwest of Shiloh (Jgs 21:19). It is identified with the present *Lubban,* about 10 mi. south of Shechem, on the modern road from Jerusalem to Nablus (Map VI, D-3).

Lecah (lē'kȧ). [Heb. *Lekah.*] Either a man or a town. In 1 Chr 4:21 Er is called the father of Lecah. However, Lecah seems more likely to have been a town in Judah, not identified, than a person, because the passage mentions other towns in a similar context.

Leech, KJV **Horseleach.** [Heb. *'alûqah.*] A blood-sucking annelid worm common to Palestine. It is noted for its insatiable thirst for blood, and this characteristic was apparently in the mind of the author of Proverbs when he said, "The horseleach hath two daughters, crying, Give, give" (Prov 30:15).

Leek. [Heb. *chaṣir,* "greenness."] Usually the Hebrew word denotes grass, but it is generally believed that the leek (*Allium porrum*), a bulbous vegetable resembling the onion, is intended in Num 11:5, one of the more than 20 occurrences of *chaṣir* in the Hebrew Bible. Elsewhere *chaṣir* is generally translated "grass," but here because it appears with words that clearly mean *"onion" and *"garlic," the translation "leek" is adopted. It was for these strong-flavored vegetables that the children of Israel pined when they became tired of a steady diet of honey-flavored manna.

Lees. A rendering of the Heb. *shemarim* (Is 25:6; Jer 48:11; Zep 1:12), "sediment," "dregs," especially of wine. Wines left on the lees gathered strength and flavor from the dregs, but before being served, the wine would be filtered to eliminate the dregs. To "settle on the lees" (Jer 48:11; Zep 1:12) means to be in a state of complacency and in a settled condition that is free from upsetting circumstances.

Legion. [Gr. *legiōn,* or *legeōn,* manuscripts being divided between these readings, from the Latin *legio.*]

1. In non-Biblical Roman usage, a military term for the main division of the Roman army of NT times, a body of troops of about 6,000 men, with a small unit of cavalry. The regular soldiers were Roman citizens, but to each legion a somewhat equal number of auxiliary forces were added, consisting of provincials. Auxiliaries were usually not attached to a legion operating or stationed in their home country. The legion was com-

295. Rock inscription at the *Nahr el-Kelb* in Lebanon records the repairing of the road by the 3d Gallic Legion. However, the name of the legion was later erased after its mutiny

manded by a *legatus* (in Egypt a *prae-fectus*), and was divided into 10 cohorts, and each *cohort (cf. "battalion," Mt 27: 27, RSV; "cohort," Acts 21:31, RSV) was subdivided into 3 maniples, and each maniple into 2 centuries commanded by centurions (Mk 15:39, 44, 45).

2. In a secondary, nonmilitary sense (which had found entrance not only into Greek but also into rabbinical Hebrew), a large host. It is thus used in the NT, re-ferring to a host of angels (Mt 26:53) and to a host of unclean spirits (probably designated in this way to emphasize their number or power), one of whose victims was healed by Jesus (Mk 5:9, 15; Lk 8:30).

Lehabim (lĕ-hā′bĭm). [Heb. *Lehabim,* called *Rbw* (probably pronounced *Lebu*) in Egyptian inscriptions.] A son of, or the descendants of, Mizraim (Gen 10:13; 1 Chr 1:11), from whom presumably de-scended the Libyans of northern Africa. *See* Libya. Map IV, B-4.

Lehem (lē′hĕm). [Heb. *Lechem,* "bread."] A place, apparently in western Palestine (1 Chr 4:22, RSV), not identified, to which certain men of Judah in the time of the early kings returned after having ruled in Moab. In the KJV "lehem" appears as an element of the name, *Jashubi-lehem.

Lehi (lē′hī). [Heb. *Lechi,* "jaw."] The scene of one of Samson's famous exploits, where he killed many Philistines with the jaw-bone of an ass (Jgs 15:9-19). It was later called Ramath-lehi (rā′măth-lē′hī), "Height of Lehi" (v 17). At Lehi, Shammah won a great victory over the Philistines in the time of David (2 Sa 23:11, RSV). The site remains unidentified, but it was evidently on a hill, probably in the Shephelah, in territory invaded by the Philistines when they wished to inflict vengeance on their enemy Samson.

Lemuel (lĕm′û-ĕl). [Heb. *Lemû′el* and *Lemô′el,* "belonging to God."] The name

of a king who composed the poem found in Prov 31. Some take the Hebrew word *maśśa′,* rendered "prophecy" in the KJV (Prov 31:1), as the name of a country, and thus consider Lemuel a king of Massa (RSV). Formerly, Lemuel was generally identified with Solomon, but there is no evidence for or against such identification.

Lending. *See* Loan.

Lentils. [Heb. *'adashim.*] A legume (*Ervum lens*) bearing oblong leaves in pairs, pur-ple-striped white flowers, and lens-shaped wholesome seeds. It is cultivated through-out Palestine (2 Sa 17:28; 23:11). When cooked, the seeds or beans produce a pot-tage (Gen 25:34), or the seeds may even serve as a constituent of poor man's bread (Eze 4:9). Properly prepared and sea-soned, lentils are a tasty dish.

Leopard. [Heb. *namer;* Aramaic *nemar;* and Gr. *pardalis.* The English word "leopard" comes from the Gr. *leopardos,* a combina-tion of *leōn,* "lion," and *pardos,* "pan-ther," since the ancients thought that the leopard was a hybrid between lion and panther.] A large, black-spotted, ferocious member of the cat family inhabiting Af-rica and Southern Asia. It is also found in Palestine but is now almost extinct there. This spotted cat (Jer 13:23), noted for its swiftness (Hab 1:8), apparently lived in ancient times in the Anti-Leba-non Mountains (Song 4:8). According to Isaiah this animal would be in Messiah's kingdom but of course without its ferocity (Is 11:6). In the visions of Daniel and the Revelation leopards appear as symbols of world powers (Dan 7:6; Rev 13:2).

Leper. *See* Leprosy.

Leprosy. [Heb. *sara'ath;* Gr. *lepra.*] A chronic disease, prevalent in certain parts of the world, affecting 1st the skin and then the deeper tissues of the body. The symptoms listed in Lev 13 include a "rising," a "scab," or a "bright spot" (v 2, KJV), described in the RSV as a "swelling or an eruption or a spot." As the disease de-veloped, the hair in the leprous areas turned white, indicating that the disease had become deep seated (v 3). If after 14 days of quarantine the symptoms had not spread, the priest pronounced that the dis-ease was not leprosy (vs 4-6). Some other symptoms were "raw flesh" (v 14), a cer-tain type of infection of a burn (v 24, RSV), and infection of the head or beard, accompanied by thin, yellow hair (vs 29, 30). An analysis of the various symptoms discloses that the term "leprosy" was evi-dently used in a more general sense than dew or fungus, which made the garments and houses unsafe for use by human beings.

In non-Biblical writing the Gr. *lepra* was used to describe what was apparently psoriasis. It has been suggested that Luke, being a physician, probably used the term in that sense (Lk 5:12, 13). Josephus' observations add feasibility to such an identification (*Ant.* iii. 11. 4). He describes lepers by saying merely that they had a misfortune in the color of their skin. He further states that some lepers held important public offices, such as captains of armies (cf. 2 Ki 5:1), and were permitted to enter into holy places and temples.

True leprosy is a fearful thing, and in its advanced stages presents a loathsome sight. The nose, fingers, and toes atrophy and drop off, the eyelids disappear, the sight vanishes, and the sufferer takes on a most dreadful and pathetic appearance. The voice deteriorates and disappears; the breath becomes most foul; the joints are often dislocated or engulfed by the tubercles associated with the disease; and patches of gray, necrotic flesh appear about the body. The hair, nails, teeth, tongue, and palate are often consumed.

According to Levitical instructions lepers were very strictly segregated. The victim was sent away from home (2 Ki 15:5) and society (Num 5:1-4; 12:9-15), he was forbidden to enter any walled city (see 2 Ki 7:3, 4; Lk 17:12), and was not permitted to enter the sanctuary (2 Chr 26:21). He was to wear torn clothes and to let his hair hang loose, and whenever approached by any other person, he was required to cover his lips and cry, "Unclean, unclean" (Lev 13:45, 46).

Leshem. *See* Dan, 3; Laish.

Lethech. [Heb. *lethek;* Ugaritic *lth,* a loan word from the Akkadian *litiktu.*] A dry measure (Hos 3:2, RSV), which according to the Vulgate was a half cor. Since the cor equaled 220 liters, the lethech is 110 liters, or 3.12 bu. U.S. The KJV renders *lethek* "half homer," the homer being equal to the cor.

Letushim (lĕ-tū'shĭm). [Heb. *Leṭûshîm.*] A descendant or descendants of Abraham, by his wife Keturah, in the line of Dedan (Gen 25:3). A tribe by this name has not yet been identified.

Leummim (lĕ-ŭm'ĭm). [Heb. *Le'ummîm.*] A descendant or descendants of Abraham, by his wife Keturah, in the line of Dedan (Gen 25:3). A tribe by this name has not yet been identified.

296. Lepers along a road in former Palestine

it is today. Some have suggested that Lev 13 comprehends 7 different diseases under the general term "leprosy." Most of the symptoms described more closely resemble psoriasis, rather than true leprosy, often called Hansen's disease, although true leprosy is certainly included. *Lepra vulgaris,* one form of psoriasis, is a scaly disease, often beginning with small circular white patches about the knees or elbows, then spreading until these patches meet and become red in the center. The disease eventually covers the back and front of the body and sometimes spreads to the head. Though curable it has a tendency to recur. The "rising" mentioned in v 2 may be similar to the tubercles characteristic of *lepra tuberculoides,* which affects mainly the skin and mucous membranes, or possibly *lepra anaesthetica,* which among other things produces numbness in the peripheral nerves. These 2 last-mentioned diseases and *lepra maculosa,* a disease characterized by spots and streaks, are 3 different manifestations of *elephantiasis graecorum,* or modern leprosy. This disease is considered curable only in its early stages. Even then the "cure" is merely arrested progress of the disease. It must be remembered that medical science as we know it did not exist in Mosaic times; hence the priests would have difficulty differentiating between diseases of similar symptoms. The "leprosy" of clothing (Lev 13:47-59) and of houses (ch 14:34-48), which appeared as red-green streaks, was probably some form of mil-

Levi (lē'vī). [Heb. *Lewî;* Gr. *Leui* and *Leuis,* "joined," or "attached." In Mari a closely related name, *Lawi-ilu,* is found, which means "one attached to the god." In ancient South Arabic inscriptions the terms *lw'* and *lw't* mean "priest" and "priestess" respectively.]

1. The 3d son of Jacob by Leah (Gen 29:34). The only recorded event of Levi's life is his participation in the massacre of Hamor, Shechem, and the rest of the male population of the city of Shechem, in retaliation for Shechem's humiliation of Dinah, Levi's sister (ch 34:25-31). This criminal act of Levi and his full brother Simeon was remembered by Jacob on his deathbed, and his strong disapproval was probably the reason why he passed by these two brothers and gave the blessing of the first-born, which had been forfeited by Reuben, to Judah, the 4th son (ch 29:35). Levi had 3 sons, Gershon (sometimes spelled Gershom), Kohath, and Merari (ch 46:11). He died at the age of 137 years (Ex 6:16). He became the ancestor of the tribe of the *Levites, who were chosen to serve in the sanctuary.

2. The tribe descended from Levi, 1. *See* Levites.

3 and 4. Two Judahites, otherwise unknown, who appear in Luke's genealogy of Christ (Lk 3:24, 29).

5. Another name for the apostle *Matthew (Mt 9:9-13; 10:3; Mk 2:14-17; Lk 5:27-32).

Leviathan (lĕ-vī'á-thǎn). [Heb. *liwyathan,* of which the English term is a transliteration. In Ugaritic *ltn.*] An animal in several poetical and prophetic books (Job, Ps, Is); in Job 41:1-33, Leviathan can easily be recognized as the crocodile. It is described as an animal too powerful to be caught with a fishhook, or killed with a sword, javelin, or harpoon (vs 1, 7, 26). He has "mighty strength" and a "goodly frame" (v 12, RSV); he has a neck, a nose, limbs, nostrils, and a tongue (vs 22, 2, 12, RSV, 20, 1); is covered with scales (vs 15-17). He is ferocious, stretches himself on the mire, stirs up the water, and leaves a wake. All these details fit the crocodile. In order to picture the terror created among those who find themselves suddenly confronted by one of these powerful and extremely dangerous crocodiles, he is figuratively described as breathing forth flame and smoke. The crocodile was found in the rivers of ancient Palestine and Egypt, but has become extinct there now. It is found in the Nile today only in the Sudan.

In the other Bible texts Leviathan seems to be depicted under the figure of a primeval monster, a creature that symbolizes an antidivine power, and therefore is destroyed by God. In Ps 74:14 God is said to have broken "the heads of leviathan in pieces." In Is 27:1 (RSV) Leviathan is called the "fleeing serpent," the "twisting serpent." In ancient Canaanite mythology, as revealed in the texts from Ugarit, Leviathan appears as a 7-headed monster that is also called a "fleeing serpent," the Ugaritic words for "fleeing" and "twisting" being identical with those used in the Hebrew text of v 1. A cylinder seal from *Tell Asmar* in Mesopotamia shows a dragon with 7 heads defeated by 2 heroes. Four of the heads are pictured as subdued, and 3 are shown as still fighting (see fig. 297). The ancient Mesopotamian Creation myth describes a primeval conflict between the gods and a dragon

297. Impression of a cylinder seal found at *Tell Asmar,* showing heroes fighting against a 7-headed dragon

of chaos. The myth seems to indicate that there existed in the heathen world a somewhat corrupted picture of the contest in heaven between Satan, "that old serpent," and God, a contest that preceded the Fall on earth, and ends with the destruction of Satan (Gen 3:15; Rev 12:3, 4, 9). These references to Leviathan in Ps and Is, clothed in poetic imagery, were doubtless generally understood as literary allusions, and were doubtless clearer to their ancient hearers than they are to us.

In Ps 104:26 Leviathan seems to stand for a large sea creature. It is not certain whether this means the crocodile (which lives in rivers and not in the sea) or the whale, nor is it certain what is meant in Job 3:8, where the KJV translates *liwyathan* "mourning." The RSV has the phrase "to rouse up Leviathan." If the author here refers to the mythological Leviathan of the neighboring peoples, he is doing so only to provide a vivid poetic figure of speech.

Levites (lē′vīts). [Heb. *Lewîyim;* Aramaic *Lewaye'* (Q *Lewa'ê*).] The descendants of Levi through his 3 sons, Gershon (or Gershom), Kohath, and Merari, who were the founders of 3 tribal families (Gen 46:11; Ex 6:16; Num 3:17; 1 Chr 6:16-48). Moses and Aaron, famed Levites, belonged to the family of Kohath (Ex 6:16-26). The tribe of Levi was entrusted with the care and service of the tabernacle, and later of the Temple. This privilege was granted them because of the stand they took in connection with the apostasy of the Israelites at Sinai in which all the tribes joined. When Moses descended from the mountain and called for a stand on the side of right, the Levites voluntarily returned to their allegiance to God and showed a zeal for His cause (ch 32:26-29). The result was that God chose this tribe as His special servants to perform the customary religious duties that heretofore had belonged to the first-born, who had, according to patriarchal custom, been considered the priest of each family (Num 3:9, 11-13, 40, 41, 45). In the 1st census in the wilderness it was found that there were 22,000 Levites (v 39), but 22,273 first-born of the other tribes (v 43). The 273 first-born in excess of the number of eligible Levites were redeemed by the payment of 5 shekels apiece, and were thus released from service at the tabernacle (vs 46-51).

As servants of the sanctuary of God, the descendants of Levi were divided into 2 main classes performing distinctly separate functions: (1) the priests, the descendants of Aaron (Deut 33:8-10; Jos 21: 1, 4), acting as mediators between God and men, performing the sacrifices and doing service in the sanctuary building itself (*see* Priests); and (2) the (rest of the) Levites, commissioned to transport the tabernacle in the wilderness on the march, erect it, take care of it when the camp was pitched; and to assist the priests in their duties (Num 1:50-53; 3:6-9, 25-27; 4:1-33; 1 Sa 6:15; 2 Sa 15:24). When the Levites were first appointed as attendants in the tabernacle, it was decided that they should serve from the age of 30 to the age of 50 (Num 4:3). Moses seems to have lowered the age of initiation later from 30 to 25 years (ch 8:24), but it had again been raised to 30 before the time of David (1 Chr 23:3-5), when it was lowered to the age of 20 (vs 24, 27), probably because the more elaborate Temple services needed a larger personnel than the group beginning at the age of 30 pro-

vided. The age of 20 years seems to have continued throughout the OT period as the legal age for priests and Levites to begin their work (2 Chr 31:17; Ezr 3:8). Officiating Levites wore white linen garments on special occasions (1 Chr 15:27; 2 Chr 5:12), but apparently not at all services, because it was not until the time of King Agrippa II (*see* Herod, 7) that the Levites received permission to wear white linen garments at all times like the priests (Jos. *Ant.* xx. 9. 6).

Since the Levites were to devote themselves to the service of the tabernacle, and later of the Temple, they received no territory in Canaan as did the other tribes, but lived from the tithe that all Israelites were required to pay from their income (Num 18:24). However, they were settled throughout the country in cities that were especially assigned to them; 13 cities were given to the priests in the territories of Judah, Simeon, and Benjamin, and 35 cities to the Levites among the other tribes (Jos 21:4-7).

In David's time a great reorganization of the ecclesiastical personnel was carried out, and the Levites were divided into 4 classes: (1) assistants to the priests in their work in the sanctuary, (2) singers and musicians, (3) gatekeepers, and (4) judges and scribes. Each of the first 3 classes, perhaps also the 4th, was divided into 24 courses to perform their service in rotation (1 Chr 24 to 26).

When the united monarchy came to an end with the founding of the northern kingdom of Israel, most Levites found themselves separated from the Temple at Jerusalem. Probably most of these moved south to Judah (2 Chr 11:13-15), but doubtless many remained in their cities and were probably absorbed by the people around them. After the Babylonian exile the number of returning Levites was extremely small in comparison with the number of returning priests. Whereas 4,289 priests who could prove their rights to the priesthood returned from Babylonia with Zerubbabel (Ezr 2:36-39), besides others who could not prove these rights (vs 61, 62), only 341 Levites, singers, and gatekeepers were found in the large company of returning exiles (vs 40-42). And in the time of Ezra only 38 more Levites could be induced to return to Judea after special effort (Ezr 8:15-19; cf. Eze 44:10-14).

The Levites resumed their ecclesiastical duties after the Exile (Ezr 3:8-12; 6:16-20), shared in an occasional apostasy of the people (ch 10:23, 24), but also did a noble work on behalf of God by assisting Ezra in reading and expounding the Law of God (Neh 8:7-13; 9:4, 5). They also assisted Nehemiah in rebuilding part of the city wall (ch 3:17). During the time of Nehemiah's absence from Jerusalem, when the Jews became delinquent in the payment of the tithe, the Levites were forced to neglect the Temple service and make a living by taking up agricultural work. Nehemiah brought them back to Jerusalem and provided for their support (ch 13:10-13).

In the NT the Levites are rarely mentioned; this may or may not indicate that they were still few in number. Christ mentions a Levite in the parable of the Good Samaritan (Lk 10:32), and Levites are spoken of as having been sent by the Jews of Jerusalem to investigate the work of John the Baptist (Jn 1:19). The Biblical record, while stating that "a great company of the priests were obedient to the faith" (Acts 6:7), mentions only one Levite who became a Christian, the apostle Barnabas (ch 4:36).

Levitical Cities. *See* Levites; Priests.

Leviticus, Book of. The 3d book of the Pentateuch, a manual of religious services, consisting primarily of regulations relating to the priesthood, the priestly service, and the sacrificial system. Its Hebrew title is taken from the opening word *Wayyiqra'*, "and (he) called." The Talmud refers to the book as "The Law of the Priests," or "The Law of Sacrifice." The Septuagint calls the book *Leuitikon,* "Levitical (priesthood, or service)." The Vulgate renders this title into Latin as *Leviticus,* whence the English title "Leviticus." From ancient times Jews and Christians unanimously ascribed the book to Moses, whose authorship remained unchallenged until the era of modern critical scholarship. Arguments discounting Moses as the author of the Pentateuch have a conjectural basis only, and are so conflicting as to render the arguments unworthy of the serious attention of conservative Bible scholars. Leviticus belongs, historically, to a period of about 30 days immediately following the erection of the tabernacle at Mount Sinai (Ex 40:17; cf. Num 1:1). This period witnessed the inauguration of the sanctuary service and the implementation of the instruction contained in Leviticus, which was doubtless communicated by the Lord to Moses during this time.

The book of Leviticus deals chiefly with the priesthood and the sanctuary

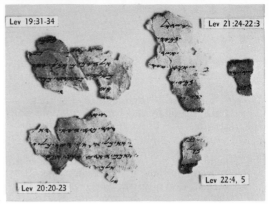

298. Dead Sea scroll fragments of Leviticus from Qumran Cave 1 (*see* Scrolls, Dead Sea)

services. It does not contain all the instruction God gave Israel on these subjects (see Num 3:1 to 9:23; 15:1-41; 18:1 to 19:22; 28:1 to 30:16), but does constitute the fundamental body of revelation and regulation pertaining to them. God ordained the sanctuary services to be an object lesson of the great plan of salvation and of Christ's ministry on behalf of sinners. These services illustrated the means by which the individual sinner might find release from the guilt of sin through repentance. At the end of each year the special service of the Day of Atonement typified the removal of sin from the camp (see Lev 16). Fundamental to the sacrificial system was the concept of the sanctuary as God's dwelling place, and of the reality of His presence in the midst of the camp of the Israelites. Central in the sanctuary service was the type-truth that "it is the blood that maketh an atonement for the soul" (ch 17:11) and that "without shedding of blood is no remission" of sin (Heb 9:22). This truth was implicit in all the blood sacrifices, which prefigured Christ as the Lamb of God (see Is 53:7; Jn 1:29; 1 Cor 5:7) and reflected the vicarious nature of His great sacrifice on the cross (see Is 53:4, 5). Explicit and implicit throughout the Jewish ritual system was the concept of a distinct difference between what was "common" and what was "holy." The sinner was altogether unclean and was unworthy to approach God, but God had graciously provided a means of release from every "uncleanness," which would make it possible for the contrite sinner to enter the divine presence and obtain His blessing. Daily, the various prescribed sacrifices provided a means of "covering" (*see* Atonement), or atoning for, sin and thereby released the sinner from the guilt of sin (Lev 1:1 to 7:38), and the ritual of the annual Day of Atonement "cleansed" the sanctuary itself from the sins typically accumulated there during the course of the year (Lev 16).

The first 7 chapters of Leviticus set forth in detail the basic regulations concerning the different types of sacrifices. Chapters 8 and 9 relate to the consecration of the tabernacle and of the priesthood. The brief historical interlude of ch 10 recounts how 2 of Aaron's sons disregarded God's instruction regarding making a difference between the sacred and the common, and suffered death as a result. All types of personal uncleanness are discussed at length in chs 11 through 15, with a prescribed ritual for release from uncleanness. Chapter 16 deals with the cleansing of the sanctuary, and ch 17 with certain related regulations. Moral and civil regulations occupy chs 18 through 20, and chs 21 through 27 are devoted to a variety of additional regulations pertaining to the priests, the Sabbath, special festivals, and other laws relating to the sanctuary and worship, together with certain laws protecting person and property.

Levy. Generally, a rendering of the Heb. *mas,* "forced labor," or "those levied to forced labor." In 1 Ki 5:13, 14; 9:15; KJV, the reference is to Solomon's drafting of workmen for forced labor in connection with the construction of the Temple. This seems to have been the first time Israelites were drafted for such service, and the system was apparently the cause of much discontent (see 1 Ki 12:4). In 1 Ki 9:21; 2 Chr 8:8; RSV, the reference is to the drafting of non-Israelites ruled by Solomon.

Libations. *See* Sacrifices and Offerings.

Libertines. *See* Freedmen.

Libnah (lĭb′nȧ). [Heb. *Libnah,* "whiteness."]

1. A station in the wilderness wandering of the Israelites (Num 33:20, 21), which is identified by some with the Laban of Deut 1:1.

2. An old Canaanite city, situated in the Shephelah, captured by Joshua (Jos 10:29-31; 12:15). It was allotted to Judah and assigned to the priests as a residence city (Jos 15:42; 21:13; 1 Chr 6:57). In the time of Jehoram, son of Jehoshaphat, Libnah revolted against the kingdom of Judah (2 Ki 8:22; 2 Chr 21:10), but Judah must have later recovered it since it was one of King Hezekiah's cities, being mentioned as one of the major centers of Judah's resistance against the invading Sennacherib of Assyria (2 Ki 19:8; Is 37:8). Libnah was the birthplace of Hamu-

tal, wife of King Josiah (2 Ki 23:31; 24:18; Jer 52:1). It lay probably at the site of Libnah, 21 mi. west of Bethlehem (Map VI, E-2), now known as *Tell eṣ-Ṣâfi.*

Libni (lĭb′nī). [Heb. *Libnî,* "white."]

1. Son of Gershon and grandson of Levi. He was the ancestor of the tribal family of the Libnites (lĭb′nīts) [Heb. *Libnî*] (Ex 6:17; Num 3:18-21; 26:58).

2. Another Levite, the grandson of Merari (1 Chr 6:29).

Libnites. *See* Libni, 1.

Libya (lĭb′ĭ-ȧ) and **Libyans** (lĭb′ĭ-ănz), KJV twice **Lubims** (lū′bĭmz), once **Lubim** (lū′-bĭm). [Heb. *Pûṭ;* Gr. *Libua;* and Heb. *Lûbîm,* once *gibbôrîm Pûṭ* (Jer 46:9).] Libya was the country west of Egypt, and appears in Egyptian texts under the name *Rbw,* which is the linguistic equivalent of Libya. The Libyans, living on the fringe of the desert, were continually casting a longing eye toward the fertile Nile valley, and frequently attempted to invade Egypt. The strongest attempts were made in the 13th and 12th cent., when Merneptah and Ramses III had to meet concerted invasion efforts. They succeeded in defeating the Libyans, and in throwing them back into their desert country. However, when Egypt went into a political and military decline, the Libyans were brought to Egypt in great numbers, and many of them were employed as soldiers in the auxiliary units of the Egyptian army. Shishak I, a Libyan, after having been a general in the Egyptian army for some time, usurped the throne and became the first king of the 22d dynasty, thus founding the Libyan dynasty of Egypt.

The Greeks at one time called all of northern Africa, west of Egypt, Libya, but the name was applied later only to the eastern portion, which lay between Egypt and the Roman province of Africa and extended to the middle of the Greater Syrtis. When the Romans took over the country, they divided it into two parts, "Libya inferior" in the east and "Libya superior" in the west. The former was also called "Marmarica" and the latter "Cyrenaica." Map XIX, E-10/11. Only Cyrenaica was of political and economical importance, since Marmarica was almost wholly desert land. Cyrenaica was united with Crete into one province in 67 B.C. with Cyrene as its capital. Apollonia was its port city. Other important cities were Barca, with its port city of Ptolemais, and Berenice (Map XIX, E-10). Representatives from this province were present on the day of Pentecost, when the Holy Spirit was poured out on the apostles (Acts 2: 10). Also from Cyrene was Simon, whom the Roman soldiers compelled to carry Christ's cross to the place of crucifixion (Mt 27:32), as were some early Christians at Antioch (Acts 11:20; 13:1), as well as some of Stephen's antagonists (ch 6:9).

Libyans. *See* Libya.

Lice. [The translation in the KJV of the Heb. *ken* and *kinnam,* the meanings of which are uncertain.] The Hebrew term designates some kind of vermin, but commentators are divided as to whether "lice," "gnats" (RSV), or "mosquitoes" tormented the Egyptians in the 3d plague (Ex 8:16-18; Ps 105:31).

Lieutenant. *See* Satraps.

Life, Book of. *See* Book of Life.

Lightning. [Heb. *baraq;* Gr. *astrapē.*] The discharge of atmospheric electricity from cloud to cloud or from earth to cloud in a brilliant flash, producing thunder. Lightnings and thunders accompanied the manifestation of God on Mount Sinai (Ex 19:16; 20:18), and lightnings flashed from the throne in John's vision of the Deity (Rev 4:5). Repeatedly Bible writers set forth the phenomenon of lightning as evidence of the power of God (Job 28: 26; 37:3; Ps 77:18; 97:4; 144:6; Jer 51: 16) and speak of lightning as one of God's weapons against the enemies of His people (2 Sa 22:15; Ps 18:14; Zech 9:14). The angel that rolled the stone from Christ's tomb possessed a brilliance similar to that of lightning (Mt 28:3), and the living creatures in Ezekiel's vision darted to and fro like lightning (Eze 1:14). Lightning accompanied the signs revealed under the 7th seal (Rev 8:5), the 7th trumpet (ch 11:19), and the 7th plague (ch 16:18). Jesus declared His return to be a visible event, like a flash of lightning extending across the sky (Mt 24:27).

Lignaloes. *See* Aloes.

Ligure. *See* Jacinth.

Likhi (lĭk'hī). [Heb. *Liqchî.*] A Manassite (1 Chr 7:19).

Lily. [Heb. *shûshan, shûshannah;* Akkadian *sheshanu,* all probably loan words from Egyptian *sshshn* and *sshn,* "lotus flower"; Gr. *krinon.*] The long-stemmed starlike field flower we know as the lily may be only one of many species called lily in the Bible. The lotus, tulip, anemone, autumn crocus, Turk's-cap lily, ranunculus, iris, and gladiolus may all fall within the meanings of the Hebrew and Greek words

299. Anemones of various colors in Palestine, thought to be one kind of "lilies" of the field

translated "lily," different ones perhaps having been thought of by different authors. The "lily" was a common flower of the field (Song 4:5), possessing a lovely fragrance (ch 5:13) and an artistic form, copied in architecture (1 Ki 7:19, 22, 26; 2 Chr 4:5). Of the "lily," Jesus said, "Solomon in all his glory was not arrayed like one of these" (Mt 6:29). See figs. 299, 499.

Lime. [Heb. *śîd,* "plaster," "lime."] A compound of calcium obtained by burning limestone, and used to make mortar, plaster, and whitewash (Is 33:12; Amos 2:1). *Śîd* is translated "plaster" (KJV "plaister") in Deut 27:2, 4.

Line. As used in the KJV this term generally translates Hebrew terms signifying a measuring line, or rule (1 Ki 7:15, 23; Ps 78: 55; KJV; Is 34:17; etc.). Once (2 Cor 10: 16, KJV) it appears as the translation of the Gr. *kanōn,* "rule," "standard," "sphere of action," "sphere of influence." However, in the Corinthian passage the last 2 definitions seem to apply. In the RSV "line," besides signifying measuring line, is also used for lineage (Lev 22:4; literally, "seed"), and for "battle line" (Jgs 20:20, 22; 1 Sa 4:2; etc.).

Linen. A type of cloth made from flax fibers. Flax was raised and processed in Egypt from earliest times (see Gen 41:42; Is 19: 9). The hot, moist lowlands of Palestine were also known for the production of linen. Evidently Rahab was engaged in linen making in Jericho at the time of the Israelites' entry into Palestine (Jos 2: 6). In those areas of the world flax is sown in the fall, usually November. Maturation

300. Fragments of linen in which Dead Sea scrolls were wrapped, found in Qumran Cave 1

requires about 110 days, after which the plants are pulled and the stalks separated from the seed pods. The stalks are then moistened, exposed to the sun for a short period, and submerged in water for about a week and a half. This softens the fibers for crushing prior to separation. After separation they are carded and drawn into thread for weaving.

The majority of references in Exodus come from the Heb. *shesh,* a word probably derived from the Egyptian *shs,* and designating a fine quality of linen cloth. This word was used of the raiment placed upon Joseph by Pharaoh (Gen 41:42), and for the curtains (Ex 26:1) and hangings (ch 27:9, 16, 18) of the sanctuary. It was also used to indicate the linen of the high priest's ephod (ch 28:6), girdle (v 8), and of his coat and miter, or *turban (v 39).

Next in frequency of occurrences is the Heb. *bad.* Some authorities believe that although this word also indicated a fine grade of linen, it was used when quality was not emphasized. The boy "Samuel ministered before the Lord . . . girded with a linen *(bad)* ephod" (1 Sa 2:18), as did the priests slain by Saul at Nob (ch 22: 18). David wore an ephod of this material when he fetched the ark from *Kiriath- jearim (2 Sa 6:14), and the man "which had the writer's inkhorn" seen by Ezekiel in vision was dressed in *bad* (Eze 9:2, 3, 11).

Another general word for linen is the Heb. *pishtah.* It is used when a contrast is made between linen and woolen attire (Lev 13:47, 48, 52, 59; Deut 22:11), but also in a general sense (Jer 13:1; Eze 44: 17, 18). A few other terms are rendered

"linen." In the NT "fine linen" is the rendering of the Gr. *bussos* and *bussinos* (Lk 16:19; Rev 18:16; etc.), loan words from the Heb. *bûṣ.* "Linen cloth" is the rendering of the Gr. *othonion* (Lk 24:12; Jn 19:40; etc.), and of *sindōn* (Mk 14: 51, 52).

Some of the Dead Sea scrolls discovered in 1947 were wrapped in linen cloth (see fig. 300), which when tested proved to be about 1,900 years old. *See* Fine Linen.

Lintel. The horizontal piece of wood or stone at the top of a door, gate, or window frame. The proper Hebrew term for lintel is *mashqôph* (Ex 12:7, 22, 23). The Hebrew word *'ayil* of 1 Ki 6:31, rendered "lintel" in the KJV and the RSV, is considered by some scholars to be a pillar. The same Hebrew word occurs 18 times in Eze, chs 40 and 41, where the KJV renders it "post" and the RSV "jamb." In the KJV of Amos 9:1 and Zep 2:14 "lintel" is a rendering of the Heb. *kaphtôr,* which designates the *capital of a column.

Linus (lī'nŭs). [Gr. *Linos,* a Greek name also appearing in inscriptions.] One of 4 Christians who sent greetings to Timothy (2 Ti 4:21). Irenaeus and Eusebius claim that he became the successor of Paul and Peter as first bishop of the Christian church in Rome. This tradition may be correct, although the fact that he is mentioned 3d in the list of 4 Christians in Paul's letter indicates that he did not occupy any important place in the Christian church at that time.

301. Relief of King Ashurnasirpal hunting lions

Lion. [The Hebrew language had many words for lions (*'arî, 'aryeh, labi', lebiya', shachal*), and two for young lions (*kephir, shachaṣ*). Only one Greek word (*leōn*) for lion occurs in the NT.] The lion, which is mentioned very frequently in the Bible, was found in all parts of Palestine: near the coastal area (Jgs 14:5); in the hilly territory surrounding Bethlehem (1 Sa 17:34), Bethel (1 Ki 13:24), and Samaria (1 Ki

20:36; 2 Ki 17:25), in the Jordan Valley (Jer 49:19; 50:44; Zec 11:3); and in the Lebanon and Hermon mountains (Song 4:8). The lion of Palestine was smaller than the African lion now so well known. L. Koehler thinks that the *'ari* and *'aryeh* designate the African lion and the *labi'* and *lebiya'* the Asiatic lion (*ZDPV* 62 [1939], 122-125). Excellent ancient representations of Palestinian lions have come to light during excavations in Palestine, the best being a basalt relief from the 2d half of the 2d millennium B.C., found at Beth-shean, showing two lions in deadly combat with wild dogs (see fig. 135). The seal of Shema found at Megiddo bears a good representation of a roaring lion (see fig. 258). These animals apparently increased in number when the population of northern Israel diminished after the destruction of Samaria (2 Ki 17:25, 26), but in Roman times only a few lions were left in the country, and since the time of the Crusaders they have been extinct. Many texts show that the lion was well known and greatly feared in ancient times; attacks on human beings are mentioned repeatedly (1 Ki 13:24; 20:36; cf. Prov 22:13; 26:13; Amos 5:19; Jer 5:6; Eze 19:3, 6). But the ordinary prey of lions were wild or domestic animals (1 Sa 17:34; Amos 3:4, 12; Mic 5:8; Nah 2:13). The lion is described as hiding in the thickets (Job 38:40; Jer 4:7; 12:8) during the day (Ps 104:22), as attacking his victim with a roar (Jgs 14:5; Amos 3:4, 8; Is 5:29; 1 Pe 5:8), and carrying it to his den (Nah 2:12). Lions were caught in pits (Eze 19:8). One of Samson's feats of strength was to kill a lion with his bare hands (Jgs 14:5-18). To kill a lion single-handed was a deed of valor (1 Sa 17:34-37; 2 Sa 23:20). The lion was well known as a symbol of strength and courage, either human (Gen 49:9; 2 Sa 1:23) or divine (Job 10:16; Hos 5:14; 11:10; 13:7; Jer 25:38; Rev 5:5).

Litter. A rendering of: (1) The Heb. *miṭṭah* (Song 3:7, RSV), "couch," KJV "bed"; possibly a litter on which persons were carried (see fig. 302). Solomon's couch was guarded by armed men (vs 7, 8). (2) The Heb. *ṣab* (Is 66:20), a wagon fitted with a roof.

302. The carrying chair of Queen Hetep-heres, mother of Khufu, the builder of the Great Pyramid

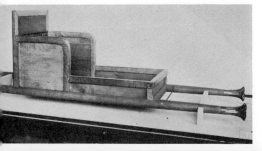

Upon such vehicles the dispersed Jews are pictured as being brought back to Jerusalem. *See* Palanquin.

Little Horn. A symbol in the book of Daniel (chs 7 and 8) for a great foe of God's chosen people. To the Hebrews, originally a pastoral people familiar with the manner in which domestic animals such as rams and bulls used their horns for self-defense and attack, the horn naturally became a symbol of power. Passages that describe the "little horn" and its activities are chs 7:8, 20-26; 8:9-14, 23-26. Parallel passages whose context makes evident that the same power and same developments are being described in literal language are chs 9:26, 27; 11:29-45; 12:1, 6-11. The characteristics ascribed to the little horn in chs 7 and 8, and the activities attributed to it, lead to the conclusion that the 2 visions described the same power in different aspects of its activity and from a slightly different point of view. In each instance the "horn" is "little" when it is first seen on the prophetic stage (ch 7:8; 8:9), but in time it grows to be very great (ch 7:20; 8:9). In ch 7 it comes up "among" (v 8) and "after" (v 24), the 10 horns of the 4th terrible beast (v 7), displacing 3 of the 10 as it rises (vs 8, 20, 24), whereas the little horn of ch 8 comes forth after the "four notable" horns that replaced the "great horn" of the ram have appeared, toward the close of the dominion exercised by the 4 horns "when the transgressors are come to the full" (vs 23, 24). The little horn of ch 7 is said to have "eyes like the eyes of man" (vs 8, 20), and the little horn of ch 8 is said to be "cunning" in its methods of operation (v 25, RSV). The interpretation of the little horn of ch 7 clearly implies that it represents a "king" (v 24), whereas that of ch 8 is specifically declared to represent a "king" (v 23). The horn of ch 7 makes "war with the saints," prevails against them, and wears them out (vs 21, 25); the horn of ch 8 casts down some of the "host," that is, the "holy people," to the ground and stamps upon them (vs 10, 13, 24). With its "mouth that spake very great things" the horn of ch 7 speaks "great words against the most High" and attempts "to change times and laws" ordained by the Most High (vs 20, 25); the horn of ch 8 "magnified himself even to the prince of the host" (v 11), who is described in v 25 as "the Prince of princes"—obviously the Lord—and "cast down the truth to the ground" (v 12). The period of time during which the little horn oppresses "the saints of the most High" is said to be "a time and times and the dividing of time" (Dan 7:25; cf. ch 12:7, "time, times, and an half"). The little horn of ch 8 takes away "the daily sacrifice" and casts down "the place of his sanctuary" (v 11), but after a period called "two thousand and three hundred days" (v 14) the sanctuary is "cleansed" (KJV), or "restored to its rightful state" (RSV). In ch 7 the coming of "the Ancient of days" in judgment deprives the little horn of its power and awards the kingdom to the "saints of the most High" (vs 18, 22, 26, 27). In ch 8, at the close of the specified period of time the sanctuary is "cleansed" of the "transgression of desolation" erected in it by the little horn (vs 13, 14). In ch 9:26, 27 the same power destroys Jerusalem and the Temple, causing "the sacrifice and the oblation to cease" and desolating the sanctuary. In ch 11:30, 31 the same power enters "the glorious land"—Palestine—(vs 16, 41, 45), stands up against "the prince of the covenant" (v 22), pollutes the sanctuary and takes away the daily sacrifice, sets up the desolating abomination (vs 30, 31), and conspires to obliterate the worship of the true God (v 30)—all for "a time, times, and an half" (ch 12:7).

Jews of the 1st cent. B.C. and the 1st cent. A.D. applied the prophecy of the little horn to Antiochus Epiphanes, who in 168 B.C., and for a period of about 3 years, substituted an idol altar for the daily sacrifices at the Temple, and who for some 3½ years cruelly oppressed the Jewish people and sought to obliterate every trace of the Jewish religion (see Josephus *Ant.* x. 11. 7; xii. 5. 3, 4; xii. 7. 6, 7; *War* i. 1. 1, 2; 1 Macc 1:20-64; 4:36-60). During this time the Jewish Scriptures were proscribed and destroyed, and the rites of Judaism were forbidden. During the 1st cent. A.D. some Jewish interpreters began to apply this prophecy to the Romans (see Josephus *Ant.* x. 11. 7). Our Lord Himself applied the parallel prophecy of Dan 11:31 and 12:11 to the Romans (see Mt 24:15-20; cf. Lk 21:20-24), a prediction that was fulfilled in A.D. 70 when the latter destroyed Jerusalem and the Temple and brought the Jewish nation to an end. Some Protestant interpreters have adopted the ancient Jewish interpretation; others have applied the prophecy of the little horn, first to the events of A.D. 70, and second to papal Rome and its counterfeit form of Christianity, to its haughty assumption of divine preroga-

tives, and to its intolerance of all dissent and dissenters and its consistent program of persecuting those who do not consent to its authority. See *SDACom* 4:826-834, 841-843, 866-881.

Little Owl. *See* Owl.

Lizard. Throughout Palestine and the Near East many kinds of lizards are found, and it is extremely difficult to identify the specific kinds designated by the ancient Hebrew words. The English word "lizard" is found once in the KJV of the OT (Lev 11:30), where it is a rendering of the Heb. *leṭa'ah*. However, it is generally recognized that Lev 11:30 mentions 5 different kinds of lizards, and the Heb. *leṭa'ah* has now been identified with one of the geckos (*platydactylus muralis*), a harmless house lizard about 2 inches long, which runs on walls and lives on insects, having received the name gecko from the sound it makes (Bodenheimer, *Animal Life in Palestine* [1935], pp. 194, 195). Other kinds of geckos (*hemidactylus turcicus*) are seen in the 2 Hebrew words *semamith* of Prov 30:28 and *'anaqah* of Lev 11:30 (Bodenheimer, *loc. cit.*). It is said of the *semamith* that it is found in the king's palace and can be taken in the hand. Other commentators see in the *semamith* the spider (thus KJV), and in the *'anaqah* the jerboa, the hedgehog, or a weasel (KJV "ferret"). Another kind of lizard of unknown species is the *koach*, mentioned in Lev 11:30 among the unclean animals that were forbidden as food. The KJV translates the term "chameleon," and the RSV "land crocodile." The 4th animal mentioned in this verse, the *chomeṭ* (RSV "sand lizard," KJV "snail"), is probably another kind of lizard, but exact identification is impossible at the present time. The 5th animal mentioned, the *tinshemeth*, is the "chameleon." In ch 11:29, RSV, "lizard" is a rendering of the Heb. *ṣab*, perhaps the thorn-tailed lizard (KJV "tortoise").

303. A lizard on the rocks at Sela (Petra)

Loaf. [Heb. *kikkar,* literally "round," "oval," *lechem,* "bread"; Gr. *artos,* "bread."] The bread of the Bible was generally round, as the Heb. *kikkar* indicates, and thin, and was usually made of barley (2 Ki 4:42; Jn 6:9; etc.) or wheat, ground into flour (Ps 81:16). *See* Bread. Loaves were generally carried on journeys (1 Sa 10:3) and were probably the basic part of every meal. They were important in certain of the ritual offerings of the children of Israel (Ex 29:23, 24; Lev 23:17). On one occasion Jesus multiplied 5 loaves and 2 fishes to feed more than 5,000 people (Mt 14:17-21; Mk 6:38-44; Lk 9:12-17; Jn 6:5-14), and on another occasion He performed a similar miracle, multiplying 7 loaves and a few fish to feed more than 4,000 people (Mt 15:32-39; Mk 8:1-9).

Lo-ammi (lō-ăm′ĭ). [Heb. *Lo' 'Ammî,* "not my people."] A symbolical name, which, in response to a direct divine command, the prophet Hosea gave to a 2d son of his wife Gomer (Hos 1:8, 9, KJV; the RSV gives the name in translated form, "not my people"). Later Hosea uses the name symbolically of Israel, who in apostasy were not God's people (ch 2:23).

Loan. That which is released to a 2d party for temporary use, which item, or its equivalent, must be returned to its owner. To lend to a brother in time of need was a matter of duty and honor among the ancient Israelites (Deut 15:7-11; 24:10, 11). Contrary to modern practice, God's people were forbidden to collect interest (KJV "usury") on a loan to a poor Israelite (Ex 22:25), but this prohibition was not always heeded (Jer 15:10; Eze 18:13). Collection of interest was permitted when the loan was to a foreigner (Deut 23:20). God found it necessary to place certain safeguards about the unfortunate borrower; for example, a lender could not retain as security an item of clothing the deprivation of which would cause its owner hardship (Ex 22:26, 27; Deut 24:17), or a stone from a grain mill which would make the preparation of food difficult or impossible (Deut 24:6). Sometimes debtors who were unable to meet their obligations were themselves, or their children, sold as slaves (2 Ki 4:1). However, in such cases they were to be required to serve only until the 7th year, or year of release, arrived (Lev 25:39-42; Deut 15:1, 2). In Nehemiah's time a famine compelled many of the poorer Jews in Judah to borrow money on their property and sell their children as servants for food and taxes, so that they were inextricably obligated to their richer countrymen. This situation aroused Nehemiah's ire, and moved him to take strong steps to correct the evil (Neh 5:1-12). There is a possible allusion to Roman law in Christ's parable of the Unmerciful Servant (Mt 18:25), in the creditor's ordering an insolvent debtor to be sold along with his family and property to help liquidate the debt. Christ made reference to the taking of interest in ordinary business without condemning it (Mt 25:27; Lk 19:23).

Lock. *See* Bolt.

Locust. A common insect in Palestine, often bringing a much-dreaded plague, destructive of all vegetation. More than 50 different kinds of locusts are known in that country, and it is not easy to identify correctly the 9 or 10 different OT Hebrew words thought to apply to the insect, which is described in various stages of its development. It is generally agreed that the Biblical locusts belong to the order of *Orthoptera,* under which 4-winged insects are classified, and are of the migratory kind—*Oedipoda migratoria, O. cinerescens,* or *Acridium peregrinum.* The fully developed locust is about 2 or more inches long, and has 4 wings and 6 legs, of which 2 are used only for jumping. It has strong jaws for cutting leaves and blades of grass, enabling it to eat even the bark of twigs and branches of trees (see figs. 174, 175).

Locusts are named as edible in Lev 11:22, and many Orientals eat locusts at the present day, usually in roasted form. They remove the head, legs, wings, and intestines, and eat the fleshy part. Many commentators believe that John the Baptist lived on locusts, whereas others believe that the *akris* of Mt 3:4 and Mk 1:6 refers to the fruit of the locust tree (see *SDACom* 5:303-306). Locusts swept into Egypt by an east wind, probably from Sinai or from the Arabian Desert, were used by God in the 8th plague to torment Pharaoh and the Egyptians when they refused to let the Hebrews leave Egypt (Ex 10:12-19). Plagues of locusts are mentioned frequently in the OT, such as the one that probably devastated Palestine in the time of Joel. In his vivid description (Joel 1:2-7; 2:25) he mentions 4 different kinds; the cutting locust, the swarming locust, the hopping locust, and the destroying locust (ch 1:4, RSV).

As an illustration of a severe locust plague in Palestine, the report of an eyewitness, H. Schneller, director of the Syrian orphanage in Jerusalem, is here presented: "We had a famine in the 2d year of the war [1915] such as we had not experienced in 50 years. The sky was darkened by the gigantic swarms of locusts which covered the whole country, and neither sun nor moon could be seen. All of Palestine was transformed into a desert within a few days. All trees, from their tops to the ground, including the bark, were eaten up clean; our vegetable gardens, cultivated with so much labor, disappeared as by magic. The following spring there crept forth from hundreds of billions of eggs the new brood, which consumed the little that had been left. The result was a terrific famine" (*Evangelisches Sonntagsblatt für Bonn*, April 26, 1925). See figs. 174, 175.

Following is a list of Hebrew words that refer to the locust, either to the adult or its young in different stages of development, with the possible meanings of these words. Since the translators have not been consistent, the Hebrew rather than the English words have been used for classification.

1. *'Arbeh*, rendered "locust" 20 times, and "grasshopper" 4 times in the KJV, and consistently "locust" in the RSV, is the most common word for locust, and is the 1st of the 4 edible kinds listed in Lev 11:22. It is thought that it is the African migratory locust (*Schistocerca gregaria*) in its fully developed winged stage, in which it invades a country in swarms and deposits eggs. This locust is very common in Palestine. Some texts which mention it are Ex 10:4-19; Jgs 6:5; 7:12; 1 Ki 8:37; Jer 46:23; Joel 1:4; etc.

2. *Sol'am*, rendered "bald locust" in Lev 11:22, where it is listed as the 2d of the 4 edible kinds of locusts. It is mentioned only in this text, and it is thought that it may refer to the European migratory locust (*Pachytylus migratorius*).

3. *Chargol*, rendered "cricket" (RSV) and "beetle" (KJV) in Lev 11:22, as the 3d of the 4 edible kinds of the locusts. It is mentioned only in this text. From the meaning of the word in cognate languages the insect has been identified by some with the locust called *Tettigonia vividissima*, a leaping locust.

4. *Chagab*, rendered "locust" once and "grasshopper" 4 times, appears as the last of the 4 edible kinds of locusts in Lev 11:22. Its identification is uncertain, although more than one scholar has suggested that it is the locust called *Stauro-*

304. Locusts in an immature stage crossing a wall, illustrating Joel 2:7

305. The village of Lydda, or Lod

notus maroccanus. Other texts that mention it are: Num 13:33; 2 Chr 7:13; Ec 12:5; Is 40:22.

5. *Gazam,* rendered "palmerworm" in the KJV and "cutting locust," "cutter," and "locust" in the RSV in the 3 texts in which it occurs: Joel 1:4; 2:25; Amos 4:9. It is most probably the locust in the 1st stage of its development, hence wingless, though not a true larva such as a caterpillar. Some see in it the young adult.

6. *Yeleq,* rendered "caterpiller" 3 times and "cankerworm" 6 times in the KJV, and "locust" 3 times, "hopping locust" twice, and "hopper" once in the RSV. It is most probably the creeping, unwinged migratory locust in the last stage of development before it becomes a winged adult. Some have identified it with the newly hatched locust, which can jump but not crawl. It occurs in Ps 105:34; Jer 51:14, 27; Joel 1:4; 2:25; Nah 3:15, 16.

7 and 8. *Geb,* rendered "locust" in Is 33:4, the only place where it occurs; *gobay* and *gôb,* rendered "grasshopper" in the KJV and "locust" in the RSV in Amos 7:1 and Nah 3:17. These are probably terms that stand for "swarms of locusts."

9. *Şelaşal,* rendered "locust" in Deut 28:42. It is probably an insect that makes the sound expressed in its name. Some scholars identify it with the cricket.

10. *Chasîl,* rendered "caterpiller" 6 times in the KJV (1 Ki 8:37; 2 Chr 6:28; Ps 78:46; Is 33:4; Joel 1:4; 2:25). The RSV retains "caterpillar" in all these texts except the last 2, where it reads "destroying locust" and "destroyer." Its identification is uncertain. Bodenheimer (*Animal Life in Palestine,* p. 313) identifies it with the cockroach, whereas the Dutch scientist F. Bruijel (*Bijbel en Natuur* [Kampen, 1939], pp. 182-201) sees it as the fully grown locust at the stage when it leaves Palestine. Others have seen in it the half-grown locust, which can jump and crawl, but not fly (O. R. Sellers, *JAOS* 53 [1933], 405).

Lod (lŏd), or **Lydda** (lĭd′á). [Heb. *Lod;* Gr. *Ludda.* It appears in Egyptian records as *Rtn.*] A city lying in the central part of the fertile coastal plain of Palestine, about 11 mi. southeast of Joppa. Lod and its sister city Ono, with which it is usually named, was built by one or more of the sons of Elpaal of the tribe of Benjamin (1 Chr 8:12). It seems to have played no important role until after the Exile. More than 700 descendants of former inhabitants of Lod, Hadid, and Ono returned from Babylonia (Ezr 2:33; Neh 7:37). In the Hellenistic period the city was called Lydda (1 Macc 11:34), and it appears by that name in the NT as the city in which Peter healed Aeneas (Acts 9:32-35). Lydda was an important city in the 1st cent. and a center of rabbinical learning. Later it became the seat of a Christian bishopric. It is the modern town of *Ludd,* with a population of 12,150 inhabitants, and with an international airport (Maps IX, E-2; XVI, E-2).

Lo-debar (lō′dĕ′bär). [Heb. *Lô Debar* and *Lo' Debar,* meaning uncertain.] A place in Gilead (2 Sa 17:27), where Mephibosheth, son of Jonathan, lived (ch 9:4, 5). It has been identified with *Umm ed-Dabar,* 8 mi. south of the Sea of Galilee. Some identify it with the Debir of Jos 13:26. See Debir, 4.

Lodge. [Heb. *melûnah.*] As used in Is 1:8, a shelter used by a watchman while guarding the ripening fruit against birds or animals. This was probably no more than a crude hut built from branches and mats on poles or in a tree.

Lodging Place. [Heb. *malôn.*] The Hebrew term may apply to any place where the night is spent, whether it provides a shelter or not (Gen 42:27; 43:21; Ex 4:24; Jos 4:3, 8; 2 Ki 19:23; etc.).

Log. [Heb. *log.* The term (spelled *lg*) is attested as a measure in Ugaritic and Aramaic records.] The smallest Hebrew liquid measure (Lev 14:10, 12, 15, 21, 24), which according to Hellenistic Jewish writers was 1/12 of a hin or 1/72 of a bath, or .32 qt. U.S. (.31 liter), or about 1⅓ cups.

Logos. See Word, The.

Loincloth. See Clothing.

Lois (lō′ĭs). [Gr. *Lōis.*] The (probably maternal) grandmother of Timothy. From the context of Paul's words referring to her it seems certain that she was a Jewess by birth or conversion, and that she was presumably, like Eunice, a Christian (2 Ti 1:5; cf. Acts 16:1).

Looking Glass. *See* Mirror.

Loom. A rendering of: (1) The Heb. *'ereg* (Jgs 16:14, RSV). The loom into which Delilah wove Samson's hair, and which he pulled apart, may have been similar to that used by modern Bedouins—a simple device laid out upon the ground by means of stakes. Samson evidently went to sleep near the loom, which permitted Delilah to weave his long hair into it. (2) The Heb. *dallah* (Is 38:12, RSV), incorrectly translated "pining sickness" in the KJV. King Hezekiah, sick to the point of death, bemoaned the fact that his life seemed about to be cut off, as the threads at the end of a web are severed from the loom.

Loops. [Heb. *lula'oth.*] Loops were attached to certain sets of curtains of the tabernacle so that corresponding sets could be fastened together with "clasps" (Ex 26:4, 5, 10, 11; 36:11, 12, 17).

Lord. A number of Hebrew terms are thus translated in the OT, most of them titles of respect or position applied to men, but some of them also to God. A few are used of God exclusively. For example, *'Adôn* is used more than 300 times of earthly lords and masters, but it is also used of God more than 450 times (usually in the form *'Adonay*). The term translated "Lord" most frequently is *YHWH*, the divine name (*see* Yahweh). When translated from this term it is always spelled in capital letters, thus "Lord" in the KJV and RSV. *YHWH* occurs more than 6,800 times in the OT. The abbreviated form *Yah* also occurs a number of times and is also rendered Lord. *YHWH* is, however, not always rendered "Lord," for when *'Adôn*, or *'Adonay*, and *YHWH* appear together, *'Adôn* is translated "Lord" and *YHWH*, "God" (Gen 15:2; ect.).

In the NT the common term for "Lord" is *Kurios*. This term is used of both earthly lords (Mt 27:63; Jn 12:21; "Sir"; etc.) and as a designation of God and of Christ. Often when *Kurios* was used in an address to Christ it was used as a title of respect, without reference to His deity (Mt 8:2, 6, 8; etc.). However, at times the use of the term clearly implied a recognition of His deity (Jn 20:28; Acts 10:36; Rom 6:23; 8:39; 1 Cor 15:31; etc.). *Kurios* was the term used in the LXX for both *'Adôn*, or *'Adonay*, and *YHWH*, hence had a natural connotation of deity to those familiar with the LXX.

Lord of Hosts. *See* Sabaoth.

Lord's Day. [Gr. *kuriakē hēmera*, "Lord's day."] John's identification in Rev 1:10 of the day on which he was "in the Spirit," that is, saw the vision recorded in ch 1. This expression, which in this form occurs nowhere else in Scripture, has been variously interpreted as referring to: (1) the great day of final judgment; (2) an imperial anniversary; (3) Sunday; (4) the 7th-day Sabbath.

1. *As the day of final judgment.* In the OT (see Joel 2:11, 31; Zep 1:14; Mal 4:5) and the NT (1 Th 5:2; 2 Pe 3:10) "the day of the Lord" refers to the time when God will destroy sin and sinners, and deliver His people (*see* Day of the Lord). Advocates of this view point to the fact that the Revelation focuses attention on the great final day of the Lord and events leading up to it. They would translate the Gr. *en tē kuriakē hēmera*, "on the Lord's day," as "concerning the Lord's day." However, the Greek expression translated "the day of the Lord" is always *hēmera [tou] kuriou* (1 Cor 5:5; 2 Cor 1:14; 1 Th 5:2; 2 Pe 3:10). Had it been John's intent to state that his visions concerned events relating to the great "day of the Lord," he might reasonably be expected to employ the usual phraseology employed by Bible writers for that event. However, in Rev 1:1 he has already announced the scope of the visions given to him as relating to "things which must shortly come to pass." In v 9 he identifies himself, gives the place where the visions were received, and accounts for his being there. In logical sequence, v 10 would be expected to provide additional information connected with the giving of the vision, not with its content. Contextual evidence, added to the analogy of Scripture, thus seems to preclude the possibility of applying *kuriakē hēmera* to the great day of the Lord at the close of the gospel age.

2. *As an imperial anniversary.* Imperial Roman pottery and inscriptions dating from NT times show that the adjective *kuriakos* was applied to the "imperial treasury" and the "imperial service," which belonged to the emperor as "lord" of the empire. The emperor was commonly called *kurios*, "lord," in Greek. Consequently, his treasury and service were the "lord's treasury" and the "lord's service." Accordingly, some have suggested that *kuriakē hēmera* denotes an imperial day, perhaps the emperor's birthday or the anniversary of his coronation. How-

ever, no such use of *kuriakē hēmera* has so far been found. Furthermore, 1st-cent. Jews (see Josephus *War* vii. 10. 1) and Christians, at least in the 2d cent. (see *Martyrdom of Polycarp* 8), are known to have refused to call Caesar *kurios,* "lord." It is therefore unlikely that John would have referred to an imperial day as "the Lord's day," especially at a time when he and his fellow Christians were suffering bitter persecution for refusing to worship the emperor as "lord."

3. *As Sunday.* According to this interpretation *kuriakē hēmera* is a Christian designation for the 1st day of the week. However, evidence is completely lacking that Christians of NT times ever used *kuriakē hēmera* to identify Sunday. Conservative Christian scholars agree that John, who wrote the Revelation, also wrote the 4th Gospel at about the same time. In Jn 20:1 he designates Sunday as "the first day of the week," the common title likewise used by all other NT writers. The analogy of Scripture is also against the interpretation of *kuriakē hēmera* as the first day of the week. A candid, contextual examination of NT passages cited in an endeavor to bolster this unscriptural interpretation shows that they have no bearing on the subject.

4. *As the seventh-day Sabbath.* In Mk 2:27, 28 our Lord specifically declares Himself to be "Lord" of the 7th-day Sabbath. In the 4th commandment (Ex 20: 8-11) God specifies the 7th day of the week as His in a special sense: "the seventh day is the sabbath of the Lord thy God" (v 10), and in Is 58:13, 14 He calls it "my holy day." The most logical conclusion is that by the expression "Lord's day" John was identifying the 7th-day Sabbath as the day on which the vision described in Rev 1 was given to him.

Lord's Supper. [Gr. *kuriakon deipnon.*] The meal appointed by Christ (see 1 Cor 11: 20) to replace the Passover for the Christian church. It was instituted in connection with the Passover meal on the eve of the crucifixion (Mt 26:18-20; Mk 14: 12-16; Lk 22:7-13; Jn 13:1). Jesus took some of the bread, which was unleavened (see Lk 22:1; cf. Ex 12:2-8, 15, 17-20; etc.), and, breaking it, passed it to each disciple, saying, "Take, eat: this is my body, which is broken for you: this do in remembrance of me" (1 Cor 11:24; cf. Mt 26:26; Mk 14:22; Lk 22:19). Following this He passed them a cup of wine and directed them all to drink, saying, "This cup is the new testament in my

blood: this do ye, as oft as ye drink it, in remembrance of me" (1 Cor 11:25; cf. Mt 26:27, 28; Mk 14:23, 24; Lk 22:20). The bread and the wine were emblems of the broken body and spilled blood of Christ, and the partaking of these emblems by Christians is an act commemorating the sacrifice of Christ for the salvation of men, and symbolizing the believer's personal appropriation of the benefits of this act, and his personal union with Christ. Christ gave no instructions as to the frequency of the celebration of the Supper. His simple directions were, "as oft as ye drink it" do it "in remembrance of me," adding that each time believers partook of the meal they commemorated His death until His return (1 Cor 11:25, 26). A feast called the love feast was eaten in connection with the Lord's Supper by the early Christians, probably as a memorial of the last Passover eaten by Christ. Certain abuses practiced by some at Corinth during these feasts elicited a rebuke from Paul (vs 20-22, 33, 34). Similarly, Jude referred sharply to those who were "spots" at these love feasts (Jude 12).

Lo-ruhamah (lō'rōo-hä'mä). [Heb. *Lo' Ruchamah,* "not pitied."] A symbolic name given by the prophet Hosea to the daughter of his wife Gomer, commemorating his wife's infidelity to him (Hos 1:6, 8, KJV. In the RSV the name is given in translated form, "Not pitied"). Later he used the name as a symbol for Israel (ch 2:23).

Lot (lŏt). [Heb. *Lôṭ,* etymology uncertain; Gr. *Lōt.*] Son of Abraham's brother Haran (Gen 11:26, 27). Lot went with his grandfather's family from Ur to northern Mesopotamia (v 31). Later he accompanied Abraham to Canaan (ch 12:4, 5), and also to Egypt (ch 13:1). Like his uncle Abraham, Lot had large flocks, and when the shepherds of the 2 families quarreled about the available pasturage, Abraham suggested a separation. Lot agreed and chose the Jordan Valley. Ultimately he selected the prosperous but wicked city of *Sodom as his residence (vs 5-13). When Chedorlaomer and his confederates captured Sodom, Lot and his family were carried away as prisoners, but were rescued by Abraham and then returned to Sodom (ch 14:12, 16). The wickedness of the cities in the area where Lot dwelt became so great that God decided to destroy them. However, since Lot was a righteous man (2 Pe 2:7, RSV), angels were dispatched to rescue him and his family. Appearing in human form, the angels were received in Lot's hospitable home. When the Sodomites attempted to ravish Lot's guests, he considered himself bound, according to the Oriental custom of hospitality, to protect the honor and lives of his guests at any cost—in this case even if it would have meant giving up his own daughters (Gen 19:1-14). The 2 guests admonished him to flee from the city in order to save his life and the lives of his family. However, his sons-in-law, and probably their families, ridiculed his message and refused to leave the doomed city. The next morning, urged by the angels to hasten on, Lot, with his wife and 2 unmarried daughters, fled from the city toward the small town of Zoar. His wife, neglecting to heed the divine instruction, perished during the flight and became a pillar of salt, possibly by being engulfed by falling masses of salt (vs 15-26). Lot and his daughters later fled into the hills, where they lived in a cave. During their stay in the lonely hills east of the Jordan, 2 sons were born to the daughters by incestuous unions with their father. They were called Moab (probably meaning "[seed] from father") and Ben-ammi ("son of kinsman"), and were the ancestors of the Moabites and the Ammonites (vs 31-38). Lot's memory still lingers on in the area of his stay in the modern Arabic name for the Dead Sea, *Baḥr Lûṭ,* the "Sea of Lot."

Lotan (lōʹtăn). [Heb. *Lôṭan.*] One of the sons of Seir the Horite, listed among the dukes or chiefs of the *Horites, or Hurrians (Gen 36:20, 29).

Lots. [Heb. *gôral,* "lot," *chebel,* "rope," "a measuring line"; Gr. *klēros,* "lot," "portion," "share."] Devices employed for ascertaining the will of Deity by the selection of one item from among 2 or more, or for simply making a chance selection. This method was used anciently by the heathen (Est 3:7; 9:24; Jon 1:7; Mt 27:35), and by Hebrews and Christians throughout Bible times. Use of such by believers in the true God is based on the assumption that God will guide in the selection of the alternative that corresponds to His will in the matter. It is evident from Scripture that God approved this method of ascertaining His will, at least for certain purposes and under certain circumstances, as, for instance, the selection of the sacrificial goat for the Day of Atonement (Lev 16:8-10), the tribal assignments in the land of Canaan (Num 26:55; 33:54; 34:13; 36:2, 3), and the detection of Achan's sin (Jos 7:14). After the ascension of our Lord the

apostles cast lots to select a replacement for Judas (Acts 1:26). The casting of lots seems to have been used more as a chance method of assigning certain tasks to priests, Levites, and people after the Captivity, without any apparent intention that the Lord Himself would determine how the lots fell (Neh 10:34).

In view of the fact that the casting of lots has been commonly used by heathen and by unbelievers since time immemorial, and since only when God specifically indicates that this method shall be used can the chance factor be ruled out, intelligent Christians will not employ it or any other haphazard method of attempting to ascertain God's will. The Creator equipped man with intelligence and has set forth the principles upon which to decide the problems and issues of life. It is His purpose that men shall use the intelligence with which He has endowed them to apply these basic principles to the problems that confront them. The Christian has access to prayer, and through it to the personal guidance of the Holy Spirit in directing the use of his mental faculties and enabling him to recognize the leading hand of Providence in the affairs of life. The Creator is honored when men use the facilities He has provided, and only when these are not adequate for meeting a critical situation, or in the case of sincere persons who have not been enlightened, may He reasonably be expected to bless in the use of lots or other chance procedures. But intelligent Christians cannot have confidence in any haphazard method for making the decisions of life, whether great or small. To neglect the facilities God has provided for meeting the problems of life is to dishonor Him, to forfeit His guidance, and to expose oneself to deception (cf. 1 Sa 28:15).

Lot's Wife. A woman otherwise unidentified (Gen 19:15-17). In company with Lot and their 2 unmarried daughters, angels led her forth from the doomed city of Sodom. Apparently resenting the disruption of her comfortable life in Sodom, and wishing to return, she disobeyed the warning not to look back, and was turned into a "pillar of salt" (see v 26). This infraction of the lesser command implied unwillingness to cooperate with the greater command to flee. Christ cited her experience as a warning to those who live in the days immediately preceding the time of His return to earth (see Lk 17:32).

Lotus Plants, or **Lotus Trees.** [Heb. *ṣe'elîm.*] Probably the lotus bush (*Ziziphus lotus*), a small-leaved plant inhabiting dry regions. The plant is mentioned in the description of *behemoth (Job 40:21, 22). The KJV translates *ṣe'elîm* "shady trees."

Love. Several Hebrew and Greek terms are translated "love" in the Bible, conveying several shades of meaning. The OT word generally translated "love" is *'ahabah* and the verb translated "to love" is *'ahab.* These terms comprehend love in its widest scope, from God's love for the righteous (Ps 146:8; etc.), man's love to God (Deut 11:1; Ps 116:1; etc.) and for the things of God (Ps 119:97; etc.), a man's love for his family and friends (Gen 22:2; 24:67; Lev 19:18; etc.), to the illegitimate love born of passion (2 Sa 13:1; 1 Ki 11:1; etc.). The NT has 2 words for love, *agapē,* with its associated verb *agapaō,* "to love," and the verb *phileō,* "to like," "to have affection for," "to love." The associated noun *philia,* "friendship," "love," does not appear in the NT. The Greeks had a 3d word for "love," *erōs,* "love," mostly of the sexual passion, and its associated verb *eraō,* "to love passionately," but these words do not appear in the NT.

Agapē was formerly thought to be a distinctly Christian term, for no example of it in secular Greek sources had been discovered. Now, however, several unquestioned examples of its use outside of early Christian literature have been found. However, the paucity of such examples, and the frequency of *agapē* in Christian literature show that Christians especially adopted this term to describe the higher concept of love revealed in the gospel. God is *agapē* (1 Jn 4:7, 8), and His love and that of Christ for men is represented by the term *agapē* (Rom 5:8; Eph 2:4; 1 Jn 3:1; etc.). *Agapē* also describes the relation between God and Christ (Jn 15:10; 17:26). It is used of human love (Jn 3:35; Rom 12:9; etc.), and is listed as a fruit of the Spirit, being the first of the fruits mentioned (Gal 5:22). The classic definition of *agapē* is found in 1 Cor 13. After listing various spiritual gifts and attainments (ch 12), the apostle notes that love is the "more excellent way" (v 31). Of the abiding qualities of faith, hope, and love, he lists love as the greatest (ch 13:13). In this and several other passages the KJV translates *agapē,* "charity." When the KJV was produced, "charity" did not have the restricted meaning it often has today, and because of its use in this passage it has come to mean "divine love," "love in its perfection."

Phileō, "to love," "to like," "to *kiss," occurs much less frequently than *agapaō.* The love represented by *phileō* is affectionate or sentimental love based more on feelings and emotions than the love represented by *agapaō.* Examples of its usage are Mt 6:5; 10:37; 23:6; Jn 11:3, 36; etc. This kind of love is never commanded in the Bible, for it is more or less spontaneous, as is a parent's love for his child, and a child's love for his parents (Mt 10:37); but the love represented by *agapaō* is commanded (Mt 5:44; Eph 5:25; etc.). This is possible because *agapē* is a principle, and may be described as a love of respect and esteem, a love bringing into play the higher powers of the mind and intelligence. It is this kind of love that the Christian is to exercise even toward his enemies (Mt 5:44). That is, he is to treat his enemies with proper respect, but he is not commanded to have a warm emotional affection toward them, such as would be required of him if he were commanded to show them the love represented by *phileō.*

Love Feast, KJV **Feast of Charity.** [Gr. *agapē,* generally translated "love," but the term was also used for a love feast such as described below.] A common meal eaten by early Christians in connection with their religious services, to foster brotherly love. Apparently in early times the Lord's Supper was generally celebrated with it. The whole service was probably conducted in memory of the last Passover feast that Jesus celebrated with His disciples, at which feast He instituted the Lord's Supper. It was apparently abuses in connection with this feast that Paul rebuked in his letter to the Corinthians (1 Cor 11:17-22). The expression occurs but once (Jude 12), though important textual evidence may be cited for its use also in 2 Pe 2:13.

Loving-kindness. A KJV rendering of the Heb. *chesed* in 30 instances of the 245 occurrences of *chesed* (Ps 17:7; 25:6; 26:3; etc.). Most frequently the KJV translates *chesed* "mercy." It is difficult to find a single English word that adequately defines *chesed.* It has been suggested that "love" comes closer in meaning than any other single term, at least when *chesed* describes the relationship between God and the human family. The RSV has chosen the translation "steadfast love" in 177 instances, for *chesed* seems also to convey the idea of stability and solidarity. See *SDACom* 3:719, 720.

Lowland. *See* Shephelah.

Lubim, Lubims. *See* Libya.

Lucas. *See* Luke.

Lucifer (lū'sĭ-fẽr), RSV **Day Star.** [Heb. *hêlel,* "shining one," "brilliant one," from *halal,* "to flash forth light," "to shine," "to be brilliant." "Lucifer" comes from the Latin, *Lucifer,* "light bearer."] A term appearing in Is 14:12 in a passage in which the Babylonian king seems to appear as a symbol of Satan prior to his being cast out of heaven. Anciently *hêlel* and its equivalent in related languages was commonly applied to the planet Venus when it appeared in unrivaled brilliance as the morning star. At maximum brilliance Venus shines more than 7 times brighter than Sirius, brightest of all the fixed stars. At such times it is visible to the naked eye at noonday, and in a dark, moonless night, casts a shadow of its own. The accompanying phrase "son of the morning," or "son of dawn," was a common expression meaning "morning star." The LXX renders *hêlel* as *heōsphoros,* "morning star," literally "bringer of the dawn," the common Greek designation for Venus as a morning star. A literal rendering of the Hebrew expression translated "Lucifer, son of the morning" would be "shining one, son of dawn." The figurative application of the brilliant planet Venus, brightest of all the heavenly luminaries, to Satan before his fall, when he was next to Christ in power and authority and head of the angelic hosts, is most appropriate as a graphic illustration of the high estate from which Lucifer fell.

Lucius (lū'shĭ-ŭs). [Gr. *Loukios.*]

1. A member of the Christian church of Antioch, a Cyrenian, listed among the Christian prophets and teachers (Acts 13:1); generally identified with Lucius, 2.

2. A Christian whom Paul calls his kinsman (which some interpret to mean his fellow countryman). Being with Paul in Corinth when the letter to the Romans was written, he sent his greetings to the church at Rome (Rom 16:21). He is generally identified with Lucius, 1. The opinion apparently held by Origen, that he was Luke the physician, must be rejected on linguistic grounds, since the 2 names are not spelled the same in the Greek.

Lud (lŭd) and **Ludim** (lū'dĭm). [Heb. *Lûd* and *Lûdim.*]

1. A son of, or a people descended from, Mizraim (Gen 10:13; 1 Chr 1:11).

Some commentators emend the Hebrew term to read "Libyans," but the term appears in different books of the Bible, and in some passages Lubim (the *Libyans, or *Pût*) and Ludim appear as distinct and separate peoples (Jer 46:9; Eze 27:10; 30:5). The LXX, rendering *Lûdim* as "Lydians," makes a plausible identification, but there is no extra-Biblical proof that the Lydians were of Hamitic descent as the Ludim were. They must have migrated from northern Africa at an early stage in their history, for they appear in the plain of Sardis in western Asia Minor before the middle of the 2d millennium B.C. They gradually spread over half of the country, to the great river Halys. During the period of the Hittite empire Lydia was subject to its eastern neighbors, but became independent again after the collapse of the Hittite kingdom (Map XI, B-2/3), and gradually developed into a strong kingdom. It is mentioned frequently in Assyrian records as *Luddu.* It fought against the Medes in the time of Nebuchadnezzar and was conquered by Cyrus the Great in the middle of the 6th cent., becoming at that time part of the Persian Empire. Sardis, its wealthy capital, remained an important city for many centuries and was still a flourishing metropolis in Christian times. In Eze 30:5 the KJV translates *Lûd* "Lydia" (lĭd'ĭ-à), and in Jer 46:5 *Lûdim* "Lydians" (lĭd'ĭ-ăns).

2. A son of, or a people descended from, Shem (Gen 10:22; 1 Chr 1:17). Nothing is known of these Semitic Lydians, but they can probably be identified with the country of *Lubdi,* which is mentioned in ancient cuneiform records as a region lying between the upper Euphrates and Tigris rivers.

Map IV, following a different theory, places the Hamitic Ludim in North Africa (B-2/3), conjecturally, of course; and puts Semitic Lud in Asia Minor (B-4/5).

Ludim. *See* Lud.

Luhith (lū'hĭth). [Heb. *Lûchîth.*] A ruin appearing in the phrase the "ascent [or "going up," or "mounting up"] of Luhith." The ascent was in Moab, presumably south of the river Arnon (Is 15:5; Jer 48:5), but it has not yet been identified with certainty.

Luke (lūk), KJV once **Lucas** (lū'kăs). [Gr. *Loukas,* from the Latin *Lucas,* probably a diminutive form of the Latin *Lucanus* or *Lucius.* The various forms of this name are attested in inscriptions and other ancient texts.] Author of the 3d Gospel and of the book of Acts, a physician, and traveling companion of the apostle Paul. In Col 4:10-14 Paul lists Luke among the Gentile believers who were with him, not with those who were "of the circumcision." Luke is thus believed to have been a Gentile convert to Christianity. Early Christian tradition makes him a native of Antioch in Syria. Luke does not identify himself as the author of the Gospel attributed to him, or of the Acts. However, internal evidence (Lk 1:1-4; cf. Acts 1:1, 2) leaves no doubt of their common authorship. Furthermore, by the use of "we" and "us" in the narrative of Paul's missionary journeys, the author reveals that he was with Paul on his 2d Missionary Journey from Troas to Philippi, on his 3d Journey from Philippi back to Jerusalem, and on the voyage from Caesarea to Rome. He joined Paul in sending greetings from Rome to the Colossian believers (Col 4:14) and to Philemon (Phm 24). He was also with Paul in Rome at the time of his 2d imprisonment (2 Ti 4:11), apparently after all others had forsaken him. Further details of his life are unknown.

Luke, Gospel of. The 3d Synoptic Gospel, traditionally attributed to Luke, the physician (cf. Col 4:14). In the earliest manuscripts the title of this Gospel reads simply, "according to Luke." The ancient and unanimous consensus of Christian tradition points to Luke as the author of the book (see Eusebius *Hist. Eccl.* iii. 4. 6). The famous Muratorian Fragment (c. A.D. 200) attributes the Gospel to Luke the physician, a companion of Paul. Luke nowhere identifies himself as the author, but internal evidence clearly points to him in this role: (1) The introduction to the Gospel of Luke (ch 1: 1-4) and that to the book of Acts (Acts 1:1, 2) leave no doubt concerning their common authorship. Furthermore, both are dedicated to the same individual, a certain Theophilus, and the literary style and diction in both are manifestly the same. (2) The use of the pronouns "we" and "us" in certain passages in Acts (chs 16:10-17; 20:5 to 21:18; 27:1 to 28:16) indicates that the author was with Paul at certain periods of his ministry. He joined Paul at Troas on the 2d Journey and continued with him to Philippi, and on Paul's 3d Journey accompanied him to Jerusalem. It seems, further, that Luke remained in Palestine during the 2 years of Paul's imprisonment at Caesarea. He accompanied Paul on the voyage to Rome

and was with Paul at Rome during the 1st imprisonment (Col 4:14; Phm 24) and later during the 2d imprisonment (2 Ti 4:11), when Paul wrote pathetically, "only Luke is with me."

Conservative scholars generally date the Gospel not later than A.D. 63 because: (1) the writing of the Gospel obviously preceded that of the Acts (see Acts 1:1), and (2) the abrupt ending of the narrative of Acts implies that it was written during Paul's 1st imprisonment in Rome, about A.D. 61-63, and apparently soon after his arrival in the city. The fact that Acts is silent about Paul's trial, release, rearrest, conviction, and execution is generally accepted as evidence that the account was written before these events took place. Luke possibly made use of a probable 2-year stay in Palestine, while Paul was imprisoned at Caesarea, to gather from eyewitnesses (Lk 1-4) materials for his Gospel. According to Col 4:10, 14, Luke and John Mark, author of the 2d Gospel, were in Rome at the same time, and this would have afforded Luke the opportunity for securing further information, which would explain the similarity between extensive passages and the sequence of events followed in their 2 Gospels. These striking similarities have led many to believe that Mark was one of the sources from which Luke drew his information.

Luke addresses his Gospel, as he does the Acts, to a certain "most excellent Theophilus" (Lk 1:3; Acts 1:1), who is otherwise unknown. Because the name Theophilus means "friend of God," some have suggested that it does not refer to any particular individual, but to any person who might be called "friend of God," that is, for Christians in general. However, the title "most excellent" definitely implies that Luke intended an actual person. As the name implies, Theophilus was probably a Gentile convert to Christianity. It has also been suggested, though without any certain factual basis, that, as Luke's patron, Theophilus provided the financial backing for the writing of Luke's 2-volume history of the church. As the introduction to the Acts (ch 1:1, 2) implies, that book takes up the narrative of the early Christian church at the point where the Gospel of Luke lays it down (see Lk 24:50-53). This suggests that Luke's purpose was to write a 2-volume history of the church. In length, Luke contributed about the same amount of material to the NT as Paul, and nearly twice as much as the apostle John. The prologue to Luke's Gospel (Lk 1:1-4) is in splendid literary Koine Greek, the common language of the Greek-speaking Roman world of that day. It is polished, yet gracious and modest, and conforms to the best Greek literary models. This, together with Luke's pains to date events according to the accepted Greek form of the day and his reference to his sources of information, suggests that Luke, who was evidently himself a man of intelligence and culture, addressed himself primarily to the cultured, educated men of his day. In elegance of Greek literary style, the book of Luke stands in the NT next to the book of Hebrews, and in certain particulars reflects the style of the great Greek writers of his time. In v 5 Luke lays aside the literary Koine style with its elegant idiom and turns to a style and form distinctly Hebrew in flavor that is reminiscent of OT narratives such as that about the birth of Samuel.

The prologue also reveals that Luke wrote his Gospel after "many" others had already composed such accounts (ch 1:1). He himself was not an eyewitness to the life and ministry of the Lord, but received much of his information from people who were eyewitnesses (v 2). He had thoroughly investigated all sources of information to which he had access, written and oral alike, and it was his purpose to preserve this record "in order" (v 3). One of his stated objectives in writing was to provide his friend Theophilus, apparently a Gentile convert to Christianity, with a thoroughly reliable account of the life and teachings of Jesus (v 4). There is no way of telling whether Luke includes Matthew and Mark in this reference to the "many" who had already "taken in hand to set forth in order" the facts of the gospel narrative. It is generally believed, however, that the Gospel of Mark, at least, and possibly Matthew, were already in circulation. But "many" clearly implies more than 2, and it would therefore seem that other records of the gospel story, since lost, had already been composed. For the relationship between Luke on the one hand and Matthew and Mark on the other *see* Mark, Gospel of. The fact that Luke does not claim to be an eyewitness himself, but frankly acknowledges his indebtedness to others, speaks well of him as a careful, accurate historian, and implies that, in his case, inspiration is not so much a matter of imparting original information as it is a guarantee of the accuracy of what he records. As a historian he went to the original sources, but he was, as well, an inspired historian. Alone among the Gospel writers, Luke provides a chronological framework correlating the events of Christ's life with the events of contemporary history (see Lk 2:1, 2; 3:1, 2). According to Col 4:14, Luke was a physician as well as a man of letters. Elaborate lists of Luke's supposed medical vocabulary have been compiled. Certain of these, it is true, reflect a physician's training and point of view (compare Lk 4:38; 5:12; 8:43 with the parallel narratives in Matthew and Mark; *see* Gospels, Harmony of). But many of the words and expressions cited as medical terms were also in general use, and their occurrence in the Gospel cannot be taken as absolute proof that the author was a physician.

As already noted, Luke offers his gospel narrative as an accurate, thorough, and systematic presentation of the story of Jesus' life and ministry. Whereas Matthew emphasizes what Jesus taught, and Mark what Jesus did, Luke combines both elements in a more complete and systematic way than either of the other Synoptic writers. His claim to a "perfect understanding of all things from the very first" (Lk 1:3) is no idle boast, since nearly one fourth of the known incidents of the gospel narrative appear only in Luke. Two areas of the life and ministry of Jesus that Luke covers rather fully, but which are mentioned briefly or not at all by the other Gospel writers, are the period of infancy and childhood and the extensive ministry in Samaria and Perea during the 6 months preceding the last Passover (chs 1; 2; 9:51 to 19:10). Luke alone records the circumstances surrounding the birth of John the Baptist (ch 1:5-25, 57-80), the annunciation to Mary and Mary's visit to Elizabeth (ch 1:26-56), the birth of Jesus (ch 2:1-7), the announcement to the shepherds (vs 8-20), the circumcision and presentation in the Temple (vs 21-38), Jesus' 1st Passover visit (vs 41-50), and His youth and young manhood (vs 51, 52). Similarly, Luke alone records Jesus' 1st visit to Nazareth at the beginning of the Galilean ministry, and His rejection there (ch 4:16-30). Were it not for Luke we would have no knowledge whatever of Jesus' extensive ministry in Samaria and Perea (chs 9:51 to 19:10). Perhaps in an endeavor to explain to non-Jewish readers how Jesus could have been rejected by the leaders of His own nation and yet be in truth the promised Messiah, Luke traces Jesus' ancestry back to Adam (Lk 3:23-38), the father of the race, thus implying that He was the Saviour of all men, and not only of the Jews. Matthew, on the other hand, is content to trace Jesus' genealogy back to Abraham and let the matter rest there. Luke also takes a consistent interest in Jesus' personal ministry for non-Jews (see chs 7:1-10; 8:26-39), and he alone records the mission of the Seventy in Samaria (chs 9:51 to 10:20) and relates the parable of the Good Samaritan. In Luke there is scarcely a trace of the Jewish particularism and exclusiveness that may occasionally be detected in Matthew and Mark.

The first 2 chapters are devoted to Jesus' infancy and youth. Like the other Synoptic writers, Luke passes over the early ministry of Jesus from His baptism and the 1st Passover and His ministry in Judea to the 2d Passover. He develops the Galilean ministry, to the 3d Passover, at considerable length (chs 4:14 to 9:17), as do Matthew and Mark. In dealing with the period of Jesus' retirement from public ministry to the Feast of Tabernacles 6 months later, Luke omits a number of incidents that Matthew and Mark record (see Lk 9:18-43). As already mentioned, he deals with the Samarian-

306. Assyrian (left) and Egyptian woman (right) playing the lute

Perean ministry at great length (chs 9: 51 to 19:10), as he also does with the events clustering around the last week of Christ's earthly ministry, at the 4th Passover (chs 19:28 to 23:56). Like the other Gospel writers, he deals, finally, at some length with events of the postresurrection period (ch 24). For the historical background of the Gospel *see* Jesus Christ. For ancient manuscripts of the Gospel of Luke see figs 71, 73.

Lunatick. The translation in the KJV of *selēniazomai,* literally "to be moonstruck,"

from *selēnē,* "moon" (Mt 4:24; 17:15; RSV "[to be an] epileptic"). It was anciently believed that the light of the moon or its periodic changes caused insanity in some people. The English word "lunatick" or "lunatic" comes from Latin *lunaticus,* from *luna,* "moon." In Mt 4:24, KJV, the "lunatick" is distinguished from one who is demon possessed, but a comparison of Mt 17:15 with Mk 9:17 shows that the NT writers apparently saw a close relationship between the two. From the symptoms described in these 2 texts it has been thought that the sufferer there mentioned was a victim of epilepsy, a nervous disease characterized by intermittent seizures, which are accompanied by convulsive contractions of the muscles and by unconsciousness.

Lust. A rendering of various Hebrew and Greek terms, in the NT generally of the Gr. *epithumia,* "desire." *Epithumia* is used both in a good sense (Lk 22:15; Php 1:23; 1 Th 2:17), and in a bad sense (Rom 7:7; 13:14; etc.), the context making clear which sense is intended. "Lust" occurs in the KJV much more frequently than in the RSV, the latter version inclining to the translation "desire," and reserving "lust" largely for sensuous passions or evil lusts generally (Prov 11:6; Is 57:5; Jer 2:24; Rom 1:24; etc.).

Lute. A stringed instrument with a large half-pear-shaped body and a long neck. It is played by plucking the strings. Lutes existed in the ancient world, as pictures, reliefs, and actual instruments found in tombs show (see fig. 306). It is uncertain whether this instrument is mentioned in the Bible. The word appears twice in the RSV, as the rendering of (1) the Heb. *'aśôr* in Ps 92:3, translated "instrument of ten strings" in the KJV, and considered by some scholars to be a "zither," and (2) of the Heb. *nebel* in Ps 150:3, which is translated "psaltery" in the KJV, but which is the harp.

Luz (lŭz). [Heb. *Lûz.*]
1. The earlier name of the city of *Bethel (Gen 28:19; 35:6; Jos 18:13; Jgs 1:23). In Jos 16:2 it is distinguished from Bethel, so that it must be assumed that Bethel developed as a neighboring town while the old city remained in existence for some time and only gradually lost its name.
2. A town in the country of the Hittites, probably in Syria, built by a man from Luz, the later Bethel, in Palestine. For aiding the enemy his life was spared when

the Josephites destroyed his home town. Thereupon he went to the country of the Hittites and built a town which he called Luz after the name of his former home (Jgs 1:22-26). The place has not been identified.

Lycaonia (lĭk′á-ō′nĭ-á). [Gr. *Lukaonia*.] An area in southern Asia Minor, north of Cilicia and Pamphylia. It was a mountainous, semibarren territory whose indigenous population pastured large herds of sheep. The Lycaonians, a wild, independent people, retained a great measure of independence until the Seleucid period. In the 1st cent. B.C. their country was annexed by Amyntas, king of Galatia; and when upon his death his kingdom became a Roman province, Lycaonia became a part of this province. Among its cities were Derbe, Lystra, and Iconium, in which Paul and Barnabas founded Christian churches during their 1st Missionary Journey (Acts 14:6-20). Paul visited the area again during his 2d Missionary Journey (ch 16:1-5), and, as some think, during his 3d (ch 18:23). The Lycaonians spoke a language that Paul and Barnabas could not understand and about which nothing is now known, since no texts in this language have been discovered. Map XX, B-5.

Lycia. (lĭsh′ĭ-á). [Gr. *Lukia*.] A coastal territory in southwestern Asia Minor, a Roman province in NT times. Its land boundaries were formed, in terms of Roman provinces, by Asia, Galatia, and Pamphylia (Map XX, B-4/5). The country is mountainous, and abounds in alpine scenery. Its original population was known to the Greeks as builders of cyclopean walls. About 200 texts written in ancient Lycian, not yet fully understood, are known. In the time when Paul visited Lycia the province was thoroughly Hellenized, as the ruins at ancient sites indicate. It had successively belonged to the Persians, Athens, Alexander, the Ptolemies, the Seleucids, and Rhodes. In 169 B.C. it regained its freedom. It is not certain when it became a Roman province for the first time. It was loyal to Caesar, was then conquered by Brutus, but regained its freedom under Antony. In A.D. 43 it was again a senatorial province under a legate, with Myra as capital. Paul changed ships in two Lycian port cities during his travels, Patara (Acts 21:1, 2) and Myra (ch 27:5, 6).

Lydda. *See* Lod.

Lydia, I (lĭd′ĭ-á). [Gr. *Ludia*. The name occurs in Greek texts and inscriptions.] A woman of Thyatira, a town in the area of the former country of Lydia, II. Possibly Lydia was not her real name, for the Gr. *Ludia* may simply mean "the Lydian (woman)." Thyatira was famous for its dyestuff, and Lydia of Thyatira made her living in Philippi by selling *purple dyes or dyed goods. She was an attendant at the Jewish place of worship, having been sufficiently influenced by the Jewish religion to be called one who "worshipped God," a technical term for converts to Jewry who had not become full proselytes (Acts 16:14). She became one of Paul's earliest converts and his hostess during his stay at Philippi before and after his prison experience (vs 15, 40). Since Lydia may not have been her real name some have suggested that she may have been one of the women who in Php 4:3 are spoken of as having "laboured with" him "in the gospel."

Lydia, II. *See* Lud and Ludim.

Lydians. *See* Lud and Ludim.

Lye. A rendering of: (1) The Heb. *bor* (Job 9:30; Is 1:25; RSV), "potash," "lye." The translators of the KJV, not understanding the meaning of the Hebrew term in these texts, rendered it respectively "never so" and "purely." (2) The Heb. *nether*, "natron" (Jer 2:22, RSV), rendered "nitre" in the KJV. *Bor*, obtained by leaching the ashes of various woods or plants, and *nether* were used in making an equivalent of *soap. The English word "natron" is a loan word from its ancient cognates: Heb. *nether*; Akkadian *nitiru*; Egyptian, *nṯry*.

307. A lyre player of the time of David, as depicted on a vase from Megiddo

308. Hebrew (?) captives with lyres of the time of the Exile, on an Assyrian relief

Lyre, KJV **Harp.** [Heb. *kinnôr;* Aramaic *qîthros.*] The term "lyre" does not appear in the KJV, which translates the 42 occurrences of *kinnôr* in the OT as "harp." However, *kinnôr* is actually a "lyre" and is thus rendered in the RSV, with 2 exceptions (Ps 150:3; Is 23:16). This instrument is one of the most frequently depicted musical instruments of ancient times. Its early use in Palestine is attested by a tomb painting from Beni Hasan, Egypt, about 1900 B.C. (see endsheeet), also by a vase decoration from Megiddo of the time of David (see fig. 307), and a stone relief of Sennacherib from Nineveh, which shows Hebrew (?) captives playing on lyres while guarded by an Assyrian soldier (see fig. 308). On Jewish coins of the 2d cent. A.D. are depicted later forms of Palestinian lyres, with an almost square decorated frame, and a kettle-shaped sounding board below an oval body, on which the lower ends of the strings are fixed.

The lyre seems to have been an instrument of joy and gladness. Its prototype was invented before the Flood (Gen 4: 21). It was found in Laban's household (ch 31:27), was played by David before King Saul (1 Sa 16:16, 23), formed part of the Temple orchestra (1 Chr 15:16, 21, 28; Neh 12:27; etc.), and is frequently mentioned in the Psalms as an instrument used for the praise of God (Ps 149:3; 150: 3; etc.). Ps 137:2 speaks of lyres' being

309. The mound of Lystra from the south

hung on the willows during the Babylonian captivity because the Jews were too despondent to play.

Lysanias (lĭ-sā′nĭ-ăs). [Gr. *Lusanias.*] Tetrarch of Abilene in the 15th year of Tiberius (Lk 3:1). He is mentioned repeatedly by Josephus (*Ant.* xviii. 6. 10; xix. 5. 1; xx. 7. 1), and the name, preceded by the title tetrarch, appears in a Greek inscription discovered at Abila, which lies halfway between Damascus and Baalbek (*Corp. Inscr. Graec.* 4521). Nothing else is known of his ancestry, life, and reign.

Lysias. *See* Claudius Lysias.

Lystra (lĭs′trä). [Gr. *Lustra.*] A city in Lycaonia, which was a section of the Roman province of Galatia. The city was a Roman colony, founded about 6 B.C. It was peopled, by Roman veterans, and its in-

310 Dedication to Augustus by the colony of Lystra

habitants were Roman citizens. The finding of a pedestal with a Latin inscription containing the name *Lustra* identifies Lystra with a site called *Zoldera* (see fig. 310). This site lies about 1 mi. northwest of *Khatyn Serai,* which is 23 mi. in a straight line south-southwest of Iconium, the modern *Konya* (Map XX, B-5). Paul and Barnabas preached there on their 1st Missionary Journey and founded a church. During the course of their ministry there they healed a cripple. As a result the pagan inhabitants of Lystra considered the apostles to be gods and made preparations to offer sacrifices to them. When the apostles refused to accept divine honors, the people were offended. In addition, they were stirred up by the

Jews from Antioch and Iconium so that they became enemies of the apostles. Paul was stoned but recovered from his wounds (Acts 14:6-20; 2 Ti 3:11). He revisited Lystra on his 2d Missionary Journey (Acts 16:1, 2), and possibly also on the 3d journey (ch 18:23). Timothy was probably a native of Lystra (ch 16:1-3).

M

Maacah (mā′å-kå), KJV generally **Maachah** (mā′å-kå), RSV once **Maacath** (mā′å-kăth). [Heb. *Maʻakah* and *Maʻakath,* meaning uncertain.]

1. A son of Nahor, Abraham's brother (Gen 22:24). His descendants may have been the inhabitants of a place and region in Syria called Maachah, or Aram-maacah. *See* Maacah, 10.

2. A wife of Manasseh's son Machir (1 Chr 7:15, 16).

3. The concubine of Caleb the son of Hezron (1 Chr 2:48).

4. The wife of Jeiel (KJV "Jehiel"), in the genealogy of King Saul (1 Chr 8:29; 9:35).

5. Daughter of Talmai, king of Geshur; she became one of David's wives, and mother of Absalom (2 Sa 3:3; 1 Chr 3:2).

6. A man whose son Hanan was one of the "mighty men" of David's army (1 Chr 11:43).

7. A man whose son Shephatiah was chief officer of the Simeonites in David's reign (1 Chr 27:16).

8. The father of Achish, king of Gath, in the reign of Solomon (1 Ki 2:39). *See* Achish.

9. One of the wives of King Rehoboam of Judah (2 Chr 11:20; 1 Ki 15:2), and "daughter" of Absalom—probably granddaughter, since she was the daughter of Uriel (2 Chr 13:2), and Absalom's only daughter was Tamar (2 Sa 14:27; on the loose use of "son" and "daughter," *see* Son). Maacah was the mother of King Abijah (2 Chr 11:20-22), and was influential in the government, especially in religious affairs. She was responsible for the erection of an image for Asherah (ch 15:16, RSV), an offense for which her pious grandson Asa removed her from her position as queen mother. In ch 13:2 she is

called Micaiah (KJV "Michaiah"), probably a variant spelling of Maacah.

10. A place and country in Syria (2 Sa 10:6, 8; also known as Aram-maacah, KJV "Syria-maachah," 1 Chr 19:6, 7). It was near Mount Hermon and near Geshur (Jos 13:11, 13). *See* Aram, 5, d. Its inhabitants may have been descendants of Maachah, Nahor's son. *See* Maacah, 1; Maacathite.

Maacath. *See* Maacah.

Maacathite (må-ăk′å-thīt), KJV **Maachathite** (må-ăk′å-thīt), once **Maachathi** (må-ăk′å-thī). [Heb. *Maʻakathi.*]

1. A native or inhabitant of the Syrian Maacah (*see* Maacah, 1) in the following texts: Deut 3:14; Jos 12:5; 13:11, 13.

2. It is uncertain whether the following texts refer to the sons of someone named Maacah, or to the inhabitants of Beth-maacah, or natives from the Syrian Maacah, as Maacathite, 1: 2 Sa 23:34; 2 Ki 25:23; 1 Chr 4:19; Jer 40:8.

Maachah. *See* Maacah.

Maachathi. *See* Maacathite.

Maachathite. *See* Maacathite.

Maadai (mā′å-dā′ī). [Heb. *Maʻaday,* possibly "Yahweh is a promise."] A member of the family of Bani; he was married to a foreign wife in the time of Ezra (Ezr 10:34).

Maadiah (mā′å-dī′å). [Heb. *Maʻadyah,* possibly "Yahweh is a promise."] A prominent priest who returned from Babylonia with Zerubbabel (Neh 12:5).

Maai (mā-ā′ī). [Heb. *Maʻay.*] A priestly musician who took part in the dedication of the wall of Jerusalem in Nehemiah's time (Neh 12:36).

Maaleh-acrabbim (mā′å-lĕ-å-krăb′īm). [Heb. *Maʻaleh ʻAqrabbim,* "ascent of Akrabbim."] A proper name appearing in the KJV of Jos 15:3. However, the Hebrew should be rendered "ascent of *Akrabbim."

Maarath (mā′ȧ-răth). [Heb. *Ma'arath,* "barren field."] A town in the hill country of Judah (Jos 15:59). It was probably near Hebron, but has not yet been identified with certainty.

Maasai (mā′ȧ-sī), KJV **Maasiai** (mȧ-ăs′ĭ-ī). [Heb. *Ma'say,* a shortened form of *Ma'aseyah,* Maaseiah, "the work of Yahweh."] A priest in Nehemiah's time (1 Chr 9:12), presumably the man called Amashai in Neh 11:13.

Maaseiah (mā′ȧ-sē′yȧ). [Heb. *Ma'aseyahû* and *Ma'aseyah,* "the work of Yahweh." The name is attested on ancient Hebrew seals.]

1. A Levite of the 2d order, who played a harp in the orchestra when the ark was brought from the house of Obed-edom (1 Chr 15:18, 20).

2. A captain who joined the high priest Jehoiada against Queen Athaliah (2 Chr 23:1).

3. An officer in King Uzziah's reign, who kept records of the military men (2 Chr 26:11).

4. A royal prince of Judah who was slain by Zichri, an Ephraimite, during the invasion of King Pekah of Israel (2 Chr 28:6, 7).

5. A governor of Jerusalem in King Josiah's reign (2 Chr 34:8).

6. For Jer 32:12; 51:59, KJV, *see* Mahseiah.

7. Son of Shallum, and doorkeeper of the Temple (Jer 35:4).

8. Father of the false prophet Zedekiah (Jer 29:21).

9. A priest, father of Zephaniah (Jer 21:1; 29:25; 37:3).

10. A member of the family of Pahath-moab; he was married to a foreign wife in the time of Ezra (Ezr 10:30).

11, 12, and 13. Three priests, one a member of the house of the high priest Jeshua, one of the house of Harim, and one of the house of Pashhur, each of whom was married to a foreign wife in the time of Ezra (Ezr 10:18, 21, 22).

14. A Judahite who lived in Jerusalem after the Exile (Neh 11:5), probably identical with Asaiah (1 Chr 9:5). The names are synonymous. *See* Asaiah, 4.

15. A Benjamite whose descendants lived in Jerusalem after the Exile (Neh 11:7).

16. A man whose son Azariah repaired the wall of Jerusalem beside his house in Nehemiah's time (Neh 3:23).

17 and 18. Two priests who took part in the dedication of the wall of Jerusalem in Nehemiah's time (Neh 12:41, 42).

19. A leader who assisted Ezra when the Law was read (Neh 8:4).

20. A Levite or priest who explained the Law to the people in the time of Ezra (Neh 8:7).

21. A chief of the people who set his seal to Nehemiah's covenant (Neh 10:25).

Some of the men listed under 17, 18, 19, and 20 may be identical.

Maasiai. *See* Maasai.

Maath (mā′ăth). [Gr. *Maath,* probably from Heb. *Machath,* with uncertain meaning.] A Judahite appearing in Luke's genealogy of Jesus Christ (Lk 3:26).

Maaz (mā′ăz). [Heb. *Ma'as,* meaning uncertain.] A Judahite of the family of Jerahmeel (1 Chr 2:27).

Maaziah (mā′ȧ-zī′ȧ). [Heb. *Ma'azyah,* and *Ma'azyahu,* "Yahweh is a refuge."]

1. A descendant of Aaron, and ancestral head of the 24th course of the priests as organized by David (1 Chr 24:1, 6, 18).

2. A priest who set his seal to Nehemiah's covenant (Neh 10:8), possibly representing the family of Maaziah, 1.

Macedonia (măs′ē-dō′nĭ-ȧ). [Gr. *Makedonia.*] A country north of Greece (Map XX, A-3), but mostly included in modern Greece. The Macedonians, who were related to the Greeks, were considerably Hellenized by the time of Philip II (known as Philip of Macedon), before whose reign (359-336 B.C.) little is known of Macedonian history. Philip united the various tribes of that area, conquered most of Greece, and left Macedonia a strong national state. His son, Alexander the Great (336-323 B.C.), used Macedonia merely as a starting point for his conquests in the east. With his highly efficient army of Macedonians and Greeks he won an empire that extended from the Adriatic Sea to the Indus River. Both Macedonians and Greeks migrated eastward in the wake of his armies and became the ruling and privileged class, carrying with them Greek language and culture throughout the territories conquered by Alexander. It was this Greco-Macedonian-Oriental empire, known as the Hellenistic world, that was the successor of the Persian Empire, and its Hellenistic culture remained even after its territories were conquered by Rome. *See* Greece, II.

The homeland of Macedonia, as distinguished from the Macedonian Empire, became less important, and after Alexander's death it declined under the rivalry of his successors. At first it was ruled by one or another of the regents for Alexander's half brother, a mental defective, and for Alexander's posthumous son. When the struggle between those who would hold the empire together and those who would divide it was settled in 301 B.C., the bulk of the empire fell apart into 4 kingdoms (later 3). Macedonia became a minor kingdom, holding a fluctuating control over Greece. Soon thereafter it fell to the Antigonid house, which ruled it until Perseus, the last king of that line, was conquered by the Roman general Aemilius Paulus at Pydna in 168 B.C. Macedonia was divided into 4 republics under the protectorate of Rome, with Greece administered separately. Then in 146 B.C. it was made into a Roman province, governed by a proconsul, with Thessalonica as capital.

The eastern section of the country possessed fertile plains around the various rivers flowing into the Thermaic and Strymonian gulfs. This part of the country was peopled predominantly by Greeks, and possessed the most important cities of the province, such as Thessalonica, Philippi, and Apollonia, all lying on the famous military road, the Via Egnatia, which was built by the Romans across Macedonia from Dyrrhachium in the west to Neapolis in the east, and on to Byzantium. The interior, western section of Macedonia, which was mountainous and not very fertile, was sparsely settled by a mixed population. Jewish communities were found in some of the most important cities, and it was in these cities that the apostle Paul carried on his missionary activity and founded Christian churches, namely in Philippi, Thessalonica, and Berea during his 2d Missionary Journey (Acts 16:9 to 17:14). He visited this area repeatedly in later years (Acts 19:21, 22; 20:1-4; 2 Cor 2:13; 7:5; 1 Ti 1:3). Some of Paul's travel companions, Gaius, Aristarchus, Secundus, and Sopater, were Macedonians (Acts 19:29; 20:4). The churches of Macedonia sent financial help to their poor brethren in Jerusalem (Rom 15:26), and also supported Paul in his needs (2 Cor 8:1-5; Php 4:15). Map XX, A-3.

Machbanai. *See* Machbannai.

Machbannai (măk′bȧ-nī), KJV **Machbanai** (măk′bȧ-nī). [Heb. *Makbannay.*] A warrior of the tribe of Gad who joined David at Ziklag (1 Chr 12:13).

Machbenah (măk-bē′nȧ). [Heb. *Makbenah.*] Either a son of Sheva or the name of a

town in Judah. The context seems to favor the latter (1 Chr 2:49). If a town, it is possibly identical with Cabbon (Jos 15:40).

Machi (mā′kī). [Heb. *Maki.*] Father of the spy who represented the tribe of Gad in the wilderness (Num 13:15).

Machir (mā′kĭr). [Heb. *Makir,* "sold."]
1. Manasseh's first-born son (Gen 50:23; Jos 17:1), whose mother was an Aramaean (1 Chr 7:14). He was the founder of the family of the Machirites (mā′kĭr-īts) [Heb. *Makiri*] (Num 26:29). To this family Moses assigned the land which they conquered from the Amorites, and which became known as Gilead, the name of a son of Machir (Num 32:39, 40; Jos 17:1). In the song of Deborah and Barak the name of Machir is used as a synonym for the tribe of Manasseh (Jgs 5:14).
2. A son of Ammiel, living in Lo-debar, east of the Jordan. In his house Jonathan's son Mephibosheth lived before David called him to Jerusalem (2 Sa 9:4, 5). Machir brought provisions to David and his forces during the rebellion of Absalom (ch 17:27-29).

Machirites. *See* Machir, 1.

Machnadebai (măk-năd′ē-bī). [Heb. *Maknadebay.*] A man married to a foreign wife in the time of Ezra (Ezr 10:40).

Machpelah (măk-pē′lȧ). [Heb. *Makpelah,* "double (cave)."] A place near Mamre, consisting of a field with trees on it and a cave at one end of the field. This property, which belonged to Ephron the Hittite (Gen 23:9, 17, 19), was purchased by Abraham, after a series of typical Oriental negotiations, as a family sepulcher (vs 3-20). In this cave were buried Sarah (v 19), Abraham (ch 25:9), Isaac, Rebekah, Leah (ch 49:29-33), and Jacob (ch 50:12, 13). Josephus speaks of monuments dedicated to the patriarchs at Hebron (*War* iv. 9. 7), and from his time on (that is, from the beginning of the Christian Era) there has been an unbroken tradition that the Cave of Machpelah is situated at the spot on which the great mosque at Hebron now stands. This mosque, called *Ḥaram,* the "sacred place," is a fortresslike structure, 197 by 111 ft., with walls of huge blocks of hard limestone. The lower courses of masonry date, at the latest, from the time of Herod, and the upper courses, plastered and whitewashed, from the 14th cent. A.D. (see figs. 3, 216, 311). During the time of the crusaders the building was a Christian church, but since then it has been a

311. The *Ḥaram* of Hebron, covering the Cave of Machpelah, the patriarchal family sepulcher

Moslem mosque, which for a long time was out of bounds for any non-Moslems. In recent years Christians have been permitted to visit the mosque, but not the cave. Inside the mosque, sarcophaguslike cenotaphs, covered with richly embroidered silk tapestries, mark the sites under which the coffins of the patriarchal family are said to be situated. Visitors may look through a small hole in the floor into a little whitewashed room, about 12 ft. square, which is probably the anteroom to the actual cave, but because of the darkness in the room they can see practically nothing. The cave itself has been entered during the last century by only a few non-Moslems—several royal persons, and a British officer in 1917, who entered Hebron and found the mosque deserted just after the Turks and Germans had withdrawn from the city. These people have reported seeing coffins in the cave, but since they were not qualified to evaluate them, it is unknown from what period the coffins date, or whether they contain anything. Although it is extremely doubtful that any remains of the patriarchal period are left in the cave of the *Ḥaram*, the site itself may be authentic. Since it is hardly conceivable that the Jews would have forgotten such an important place as the tomb of Abraham during their historical period in pre-Christian times, many authorities consider the site of the *Ḥaram* at Hebron the true burial place of the patriarchs.

Mad, Madness. These terms are used in several senses: (1) A disordered mind (Deut 28:28; 1 Sa 21:12-15; Zec 12:4; Acts 26:24). (2) The state of being unreasoning because of some foolish obsession, such as Balaam's inordinate greed for wealth (2 Pe 2:15, 16; cf. Ec 1:17; 7:25; etc.). (3) Uncontrolled, passionate anger. Saul of Tarsus carried such feelings toward Christians (Acts 26:11), and the Pharisees felt similar madness against Jesus (Lk 6:11).

Madai (măd′á-ī). [Heb. *Maday*.] A son of Japheth (Gen 10:2; 1 Chr 1:5), and the ancestor of the Medes. *See* Media.

Madian. *See* Midian, 2.

Madmannah (măd-măn′á). [Heb. *Madmannah*, "dunghill."] A place in southern Judah near Ziklag (Jos 15:31); perhaps now *Umm Deimneh*, 10 mi. northeast of Beer-sheba.

Madmen (măd′měn). [Heb. *Madmen*.] A town in Moab (Jer 48:2) identified tentatively with *Khirbet Dimneh*, 8 mi. north of Kerak.

Madmenah (măd-mē′ná). [Heb. *Madmenah*, "dunghill."] A town in the territory of Benjamin (Is 10:31); not identified.

Madon (mā′dŏn). [Heb. *Madôn*, "contention," or "strife."] An old Canaanite city whose king Jobab, allied to Jabin, king of Hazor, fought against the Israelites and was defeated (Jos 11:1-12; 12:19). It has been identified with *Qarn Ḥaṭṭîn*, 5 mi. northwest of Tiberias (Map VI, C-3).

Magadan (măg′á-dăn), KJV **Magdala** (măg′-dá-là). [Gr. *Magadan* and *Magdala*; textual evidence favors the former reading.] A place on the shore of the Sea of Galilee (Mt 15:39); not identified. The parallel passage in Mk 8:10 calls the place Dalmanutha. *Magdala* is derived from the Heb. *Migdal* or Aramaic *Migdela'*. According to the Talmud a Magdala stood on the western shore of the Sea of Galilee near Tiberias and Hammath, less than a Sabbath day's journey from the lake. The place is identified with the village of *Mejdel* (see fig. 312), about 3½ mi. northwest of Tiberias (Map XVI, C-4). However, the reading "Magadan" is to be preferred from a textual point of view.

312. Magdala, on the Sea of Galilee

Magbish (măg'bĭsh). [Heb. *Magbîsh*.] A place in Judah occupied by returned exiles (Ezr 2:30); not conclusively identified.

Magdala. *See* Magadan.

Magdalene (măg'dȧ-lēn). [Gr. *Magdalēnē*, the "one from Magdala."] An attribute borne by one of the Marys, implying that she came from a place called Magdala, probably from the one near the western shore of the Sea of Galilee. *See* Magadan; Mary, 2.

Magdiel (măg'dĭ-ĕl). [Heb. *Magdî'el*, "God is excellence."] One of the chiefs of Edom, descended from Esau (Gen 36:43).

Maggot. [Heb. *rimmah*.] A larva appearing in decaying matter. The term appears twice: (1) Job 25:6, RSV, where man is compared to a maggot, and (2) Is 14:11, RSV, where the prediction is made that the king of Babylon was to lie on a bed of maggots in Sheol.

Magic. The secret art of the magician, sorcerer, enchanter, wizard, or witch. In the practice of magic, rites and formulas are usually used by means of which supernatural forces are believed to become available to the performer of the magic art so that he can bring benefit or harm to people or things. Such arts were widely practiced in the ancient world and were deeply entrenched in Egypt and Babylonia (Gen 41:8; Ex 7:11; Dan 1:20; 2:2; etc.), the 2 most powerful countries of antiquity with which Israel had close connections during several periods of her history. However, magic was also found among the Canaanites and other nations, as is indicated by magic wands, amulets, and other objects used in magic art, found in the excavations of Palestine. From these peoples among whom Israel lived many magical practices were taken over, although the Mosaic law condemned these under pain of death (Lev 20:27; Deut 18:10, 11). In times of stress the Israelites frequently turned to those who practiced magical arts (1 Sa 28:7) and themselves practiced all kinds of magic, as several rebuking statements of the OT prophets indicate (Is 8:19; Eze 13:18, 20; etc.).

In NT times Jewish sorcerers, or magicians, were spread over the whole Greco-Roman world (Acts 8:9-11; 13:6-8; cf. *Juvenal* vi. 542-546; Origen *Against Celsus* iv. 33). Many of Paul's Jewish and Gentile converts in Ephesus had practiced magic arts and possessed expensive handbooks of magic, which they burned after their conversion (Acts 19:18, 19). Paul lists *pharmakeia,* "magic," "sorcery" (KJV "witchcraft") in Gal 5:20, among the chief sins of the flesh, mentioning it immediately after idolatry. *See* Magicians.

Magicians. [Heb. generally *charṭummîm;* Aramaic *charṭummîn*. The English words "magician" and "magic" come from the Greek name *magos,* given to a member of a Median tribe called Magi or Magians (Herod. i. 102), who exercised priestly functions among the Iranian peoples.] Those who, as professionals or amateurs, practice magic. Such people are mentioned in the Bible under different names, such as sorcerers, witches, soothsayers, etc. Magicians were found in great numbers in Egypt (Gen 41:8; Ex 7:11; etc.) and Mesopotamia (Dan 1:20; 2:2; etc.). In the NT 2 Jewish magicians are named, Simon of Samaria (Acts 8:9) and Elymas of Paphos on the island of Cyprus (ch 13: 6, 8). *See* Magic.

Magistrate. A public officer representing and exercising authority in a local district. The term is the rendering of: (1) a form of the Aramaic *shephaṭ* (Ezr 7:25), "to judge"; (2) an obscure Hebrew expression (Jgs 18:7, KJV); (3) the Aramaic *tiphtay* (Dan 3:2, 3, RSV), "police officer," "magistrate"; (4) the Gr. *archōn* (Lk 12:58), "ruler," "magistrate"; (5) the Gr. *stratēgos* (Acts 16:20-38), "praetor," "chief magistrate." The plural form is used of the highest officials of the Roman colony at Philippi. The phrase "to obey magistrates" appears in Tit 3:1, KJV, as a rendering of the Gr. verb *peitharcheō,* which means "to be obedient to one in authority."

Magog (mā'gŏg). [Heb. *Magôg;* Gr. *Magōg.*] The 2d son of Japheth (Gen 10:2), and ancestor of a people not yet identified. In Eze 38:2 and 39:6 Gog, a king of Magog, appears as a cruel enemy of God's people, and in Rev 20:8, 9 "Gog and Magog" are represented as gathered to make war against the "camp of the saints" and "the beloved city." One of the *Amarna Letters written by a 15th cent. Babylonian king to an Egyptian Pharaoh mentions a barbarian land *Gagaia* of the far north, which some have sought to identify with the Biblical Magog. Accordingly, they assume this tribe to have lived somewhere north of the Black Sea, probably in proximity to the descendants of Gomer, a brother of Magog. See *SDACom* 4:704, 705.

Magor-missabib (mā'gŏr-mĭs'ȧ-bĭb). [Heb.

Magôr Missabîb, "terror on every side."]
According to the KJV a name given by
Jeremiah to Pashhur, a priest and chief
officer of the Temple, in a prophecy of
the punishment that awaited him for having ill-treated the prophet (Jer 20:3-6).
The Hebrew phrase is repeatedly used by
Jeremiah but is elsewhere translated (chs
6:25; 20:10; 46:5; 49:29).

Magpiash (măg′pĭ-ăsh). [Heb. *Magpi‘ash.*]
One of the chiefs of the people who set
his seal to Nehemiah's covenant (Neh
10:20).

Magus. *See* Simon, 8.

Mahalab (mā′hȧ-lăb). [Heb. *Machaleb,* a
conjectural emendation of the Heb.
mechebel.] A place near Tyre (Jos 19:29,
RSV). The KJV renders *mechebel* "from
the coast." The reading "Mahalab" finds
support first in the reading of the Codex
Vaticanus of the LXX, and second by the
mention of a place *Mahaliba* together
with Achzib (also mentioned in Jos 19:
29) in Assyrian records. Mahalab has
been identified with *Khirbet el-Mahâlib*
at the mouth of the *Nahr el-Qâsimîyéh,*
northeast of Tyre. See Abel, *Géographie*
2, p. 67. This interpretation of *mechebel*
makes it a city identical with *Ahlab, and
therefore, as some think, also with
*Helbah.

Mahalah. *See* Mahlah, 2.

Mahalaleel. *See* Mahalalel.

Mahalalel (mȧ-hā′lȧ-lĕl), KJV of OT, and
RSV of NT **Mahalaleel** (mȧ-hā′lȧ-lē′ĕl),
KJV of NT **Maleleel** (mȧ-lē′lĕ-ĕl). [Heb.
Mahalal′el, "praise of God"; Gr. *Maleleēl.*]
  1. An antediluvian patriarch in the
line of Seth (Gen 5:12-17; 1 Chr 1:2; Lk
3:37).
  2. A descendant of Judah who lived in
Jerusalem in the time of Nehemiah (Neh
11:4).

Mahalath (mā′hȧ-lăth). [Heb. *Machalath*
and *Macholath,* "sickness" or "weakness."]
  1. A daughter of Ishmael, and one of
the wives of Esau (Gen 28:9); she is also
called Bashemath (ch 36:3, 4, 13, 17).
See Basemath, 2.
  2. A wife of King Rehoboam (2 Chr
11:18).
  3. A term appearing in the titles to Ps
53 and 88, the meaning of which is uncertain. Some suggest that the term signifies that the psalm is to be sung in a
sad, mournful manner.

Mahali. *See* Mahli, 1.

Mahanaim (mā′hȧ-nā′ĭm). [Heb. *Macha-
nayim,* "two camps."] A place in Transjordan given that name by Jacob when 2

groups of angels appeared to him there,
shortly after he had parted from Laban
and before he crossed the Jabbok (Gen
32:2). A city there, on the boundary line
of the territories of the tribes of Gad and
Manasseh (Jos 13:26, 30), was assigned
to the Merarite Levites as a residence city
(Jos 21:38; 1 Chr 6:80). This city was
briefly the capital of northern Israel under Ish-bosheth, Saul's son (2 Sa 2:8, 12,
29), while David ruled at Hebron over
Judah. David used the city as headquarters during the rebellion of Absalom
(2 Sa 17:24, 27; 19:32; 1 Ki 2:7, 8). In
Solomon's reign it was the seat of Ahinadab, one of the royal supply officers (1 Ki
4:14). The site of Mahanaim has not yet
definitely been identified, but may be
Khirbet Mahneh, about 12 mi. northwest
of Jerash (Gerasa). Scholars have proposed several other sites, but none is certain. Map VI, D-4, gives 2 possible sites,
Khirbet Mahneh and *Tell el-Hajjâj.*

Mahaneh-dan (mā′hȧ-nĕ-dăn′). [Heb. *Macha-
neh-dan,* "camp of Dan."] A place west
of Kiriath-jearim (Jgs 18:12), between
Zorah and Eshtaol (ch 13:25), named by
Danite spies who camped there; not
identified.

Maharai (mȧ-hăr′ȧ-ī). [Heb. *Maharay,*
"swift."] A Netophathite, one of David's
"mighty men" (2 Sa 23:28; 1 Chr 11:
30), who was appointed captain for the
10th month (1 Chr 27:13).

Mahath (mā′hăth). [Heb. *Machath,* meaning
uncertain.]
  1. A Kohathite Levite appearing in the
ancestral line of the prophet Samuel (1 Chr
6:33, 35).
  2. A Levite who with others was in
charge of the tithes and freewill offerings
in Hezekiah's time (2 Chr 31:12-14).
  3. A Kohathite Levite (2 Chr 29:12),
probably identical with Mahath, 2.

Mahavite (mā′hȧ-vīt). [Heb. *Machawim,*
meaning unknown.] A name applied to
Eliel, one of David's "mighty men" (1
Chr 11:46).

Mahazioth (mȧ-hā′zĭ-ŏth). [Heb. *Machazi′ôth,*
"visions."] A Levite musician, a descendant of Heman. He was head of the 23d of
the 24 courses of singers organized by
King David for the sacred services (1 Chr
25:4, 30).

Maher-shalal-hashbaz (mā′hēr-shăl′ăl-hăsh′-
băz′). [Heb. *Maher shalal chash baz,* "the
booty hastens, the spoil speeds."] The name
given by the prophet Isaiah to his 2d son.
This name, given by divine direction and
publicly registered and witnessed before

the child's birth, was a prophecy that Damascus and Samaria would soon be conquered by Assyria (Is 8:1-4). This strange procedure was designed to impress the people with the reliability of the prophet's messages upon the fulfillment of the prediction within a year.

Mahlah (mä′là), KJV once **Mahalah** (mà-hä′là). [Heb. *Machlah*, "disease" or "weak."]

1. The eldest of the five daughters of the Manassite Zelophehad (Num 26:33). On the condition that these daughters marry sons of their father's brother, they obtained the right to inherit their father's property, for there was no male heir (chs 27:1; 36:11).

2. A Manassite of the family of Machir (1 Chr 7:18).

Mahli (mä′lī), KJV once **Mahali** (mä′hà-lī). [Heb. *Machli*, "sick" or "weak."]

1. A son of Merari (Ex 6:19; Num 3:20; 1 Chr 6:19), and ancestral head of the Levitical family of the Mahlites (mä′līts) [Heb. *Machlî*] (Num 3:33; 26:58; Ezr 8:18), who were descended from Mahli's grandsons and his granddaughters who intermarried (1 Chr 23:22).

2. A Levite, grandson of Merari, and son of Mushi (1 Chr 6:47; 23:23; 24:30).

Mahlites. *See* Mahli, 1.

Mahlon (mä′lŏn). [Heb. *Machlôn*, "sickness."] The elder son of Elimelech and Naomi, and 1st husband of Ruth (Ruth 1:2, 5; 4:9, 10).

Mahol (mä′hŏl). [Heb. *Machôl*, "dance."] The father of 3 men, Heman, Calcol, and Darda, who were excelled in wisdom only by Solomon (1 Ki 4:31). His origin is unknown.

Mahseiah (mä-sē′yà). [Heb. *Machseyah*, "Yahweh is refuge."] A man whose grandsons were Baruch, Jeremiah's secretary, and Seraiah, royal quartermaster (Jer 32:12; 51:59). His name is rendered Maaseiah in the KJV.

Mail, Coat of. *See* Coat of Mail.

Majesty. A rendering of several Hebrew and 2 Greek words meaning variously "eminence," "dignity," "splendor," "loftiness," "grandeur," "sublimity," "greatness," "majesty." The term "majesty" is most frequently used of God or His work, but it is also used for earthly sovereigns (1 Chr 29:25; Dan 4:30), geographical sites (Is 35:2, RSV), Zion (Lam 1:6, RSV), Israel (Nah 2:2, RSV), and a bull (Deut 33:17, RSV).

Makaz (mä′kăz). [Heb. *Maqaṣ*.] A town near Beth-shemesh, which belonged to the district of "the son of Dekar," one of Solomon's supply officers (1 Ki 4:9); not identified.

Makheloth (măk-hē′lŏth). [Heb. *Maqheloth*, "assemblies."] A camping place in the wilderness wanderings of the Israelites (Num 33:25, 26); not identified.

Makkedah (mă-kē′dà). [Heb. *Maqqedah*, meaning uncertain.] A Canaanite fortress city in the Shephelah. It was taken by Joshua (Jos 10:10-29; 12:16), and its king, who with four other defeated Canaanite kings hid in a cave near the city, was killed. Makkedah was later allotted to Judah (ch 15:41). The site has not yet been definitely identified; some have suggested *Tell Maqdûm,* 7 mi. southeast of *Beit Jibrîn* (Map VI, E-2), but W. F. Albright prefers *Tell eṣ-Ṣâfî,* 7½ mi. northwest of *Beit Jibrîn* (*BASOR* 15 [1924], 9).

Maktesh (măk′tĕsh). [Heb. *Maktesh*, "mortar."] A quarter possibly within or near Jerusalem, inhabited by Canaanite traders (Zep 1:11, KJV). The Targum locates it in the Kidron Valley; others seek it in the northwestern section of the city, or in the northern part of the Tyropoeon Valley, outside of the city wall. The RSV translates the Hebrew term "Mortar."

Malachi (măl′à-kī). [Heb. *Mal'aki,* "my messenger."] Author of the last of "the twelve" or so-called Minor Prophets, the book of Malachi. Possibly the Hebrew name is a contraction for *Mal'akiyah,* "messenger of the Lord." Nothing is known about his life and ministry beyond what his book implies as to the circumstances under which he bore his message. Some have suggested that Malachi was not the name of the author, but simply a title based on ch 3:1; cf. ch 4:5, 6. However, the fact that the other prophetic books carry as their titles the names of their respective authors suggests that Malachi may have been a personal name. *See* Malachi, Book of.

Malachi, Book of. The last of "the twelve" or so-called Minor Prophets, and last also in the section "The Prophets" in the Hebrew Bible. Malachi makes no reference to his personal life nor does he date his ministry as most of the other prophets do, nor is there any reference to him elsewhere in the OT. *See* Malachi. The fact that the prophecy of Malachi appears at the close of the prophetic canon implies that Malachi was the last of the OT prophets. From the chronological data given by Haggai (Hag 1:1) and Zechariah (Zec 1:1), which immediately precede Malachi, it is evident that they wrote after the Babylonian captivity, and it is reasonable to suppose that Malachi bore his message even later than they.

In view of the fact that the abuses Malachi condemns are similar to those that arose during the time of Nehemiah's absence after his first term as governor, it is quite possible that the book of Malachi may be dated to the time preceding Nehemiah's return for his 2d term, about 425 B.C. This would be about a century after the return of the Jews from Babylon under Zerubbabel. The decrees of Cyrus, Darius, and Artaxerxes (see Ezr 6:14) had encouraged many Jews to return to their homeland, where they were re-established as a subject people. The Temple had been rebuilt and the sacrificial services again set in operation, but a sorry state of affairs prevailed, with the people frustrated and discouraged in their attempts to re-establish the nation on a secure basis, and lacking in spiritual life and vigor as well. When Nehemiah, an officer in the Persian court (Neh 2:1-6), learned of the state of affairs in Jerusalem, he requested and was granted leave by King Artaxerxes to visit his brethren there (chs 1:1 to 2:6). Appointed as governor of Judea, Nehemiah served for an unspecified period of time, during which he completed the rebuilding of the wall, reorganized the state, and introduced much-needed religious reforms. At the close of this period he returned to Babylon, but later served a 2d term as governor of Judea, instituting further reforms. It was probably during Nehemiah's absence after his 1st governorship that Malachi bore his prophetic message. In striking contrast with Zechariah's inspiring prophetic outline of the glorious possibilities that lay before the Jews upon their return from Exile, Malachi's prophecy a century later reflects a dismal scene of progressive spiritual declension. He addresses his message to the priests in particular, in their capacity as the spiritual leaders of Israel (Mal 1:6). His stern denunciation of the careless indifference of the priests to the conduct of their sacred duties reflects the sad moral and spiritual state of God's people. Things had come to such a pass that even the priests despised the worship and service of God, and were weary of religion (vs 6, 13), and God, on His part, was weary of their faithlessness and found the Temple services altogether unacceptable (chs 1:10, 13; 2:13, 17). Although for practical purposes the covenant between God and Israel had lapsed by default on their part,

God mercifully sent them this further message to inspire them to return to Him and be faithful until the coming of "the messenger of the covenant" (Mal 3:1), the Messiah, and eventually "the great and dreadful day of the Lord" (ch 4:5) could be fulfilled. Malachi reminded the Jews of their special relationship to God and called upon them to return to Him and once more take up the duties of the covenant relationship.

In 8 addresses the Lord graciously and patiently calls attention to one aspect after another of apostasy, and 8 times the people petulantly deny any fault (see Mal 1:2, 6, 7; 2:13, 14, 17; 3:7, 8, 13, and 14). God's patient endeavor to get the people to recognize and remedy their mistakes, and their progressively vehement denial of any mistakes, constitutes the theme of the book. It may be divided into 2 parts:

(1) The dialogue between God and His people, in which God reveals the nature and extent of their backsliding and apostasy (Mal 1:1 to 3:15). In the first of these 8 encounters between God and His people the Lord protests His everlasting love for His chosen people, but they deny knowledge of any evidence that He loves them (ch 1:2-5). In the 2d encounter (v 6), God declares that instead of the honor a servant owes his master or a son his father, they, particularly the priests, actually despise Him. In injured innocence, the priests reply: "Wherein have we despised thy name?" In the 3d encounter (chs 1:7 to 2:2) God answers their question by accusing them of treating their sacred duties as a common occupation not essentially different from other means of livelihood. The priests callously reply, "Wherein have we polluted thee?" God replies that they have looked upon His service with contempt, as evidenced by the blemished sacrifices they offered Him. "Should I accept this of your hand?" He asks, and then reviews the purpose of His covenant with them (ch 2:5-7) and indicts them for departing from the way themselves and causing many others to stumble (v 8). In the 4th encounter (vs 14-16) God explains that this is the reason why He has made them appear contemptible in the sight of nations around them (v 9) and why He refuses to accept their offerings (v 13). The people think God unfair not to accept their heartless offerings, but God points to the covenant relationship, which they have violated. In the 5th encounter (chs 2:17 to 3:6) God protests that He is weary of their hypocritical profession of loyalty. Petu-

lantly the people reply by asking wherein they have wearied Him, and God points to their blurred sense of right and wrong. God then announces the coming of the Messenger of the covenant and challenges them as to which of them thinks he can survive the day of His coming (Mal 3:1, 2). In the 6th encounter (v 7) God takes note of their apostasy and appeals to the people to return to Him, but like spoiled children they again ask, "Wherein shall we return?" This introduces the 7th encounter (vs 8-12), in which God replies to their previous question by accusing them of robbing Him of the tithes and offerings that are rightfully His. Once more the people deny any guilt, saying, "Wherein have we robbed thee?" Even at this late hour God assures Israel that if they will return to Him He will still open the windows of heaven and bless them. The 8th and last encounter opens with God's protest, "Your words have been stout against me," to which the people reply, "What have we spoken so much against thee?" God answers that they have come to look upon their religious duties as a grievous burden that yields no corresponding "profit" in return. The people thus prove that their spiritual vision is altogether out of focus. Little wonder that with Malachi the voices of the prophets ceased—the people refused to listen, and God left them without the prophetic message.

(2) An epilogue expressing appreciation to the faithful few, and warning that "the proud" and "all that do wickedly" will suffer a just retribution for their sins (Mal 3:16 to 4:6). This section envisions the day of judgment, when God will reward each man according to his works, and, in view of it, admonishes the people to "remember . . . the law of Moses" (ch 4:4). The message closes with the promise that God will send another messenger, the prophet Elijah, "before the coming of the great and dreadful day of the Lord" (v 5).

Malcam (măl′kăm), KJV **Malcham** (măl′-kăm). [Heb. *Malkam,* "their king," or possibly "king."] A Benjamite (1 Chr 8:9).

Malcham.

1. For 1 Chr 8:9, KJV, *see* Malcam.
2. For Zep 1:5, KJV, *see* Milcom.

Malchiah (măl-kī′ă), KJV once **Melchiah** (měl-kī′ă). [Heb. *Malkîyah* and *Malkîyahû,* "Yahweh is my king."]

1. A royal prince into whose cistern (KJV "dungeon") Jeremiah was thrown (Jer 38:6). He is generally considered to be identical with the father of Pashhur (chs 21:1; 38:1).

2. For others named Malchiah in the KJV, *see* Malchijah.

Malchiel (măl′kĭ-ĕl). [Heb. *Malkî'el,* "God is my king." The name occurs in the *Amarna Letters as *Milkili.] A grandson of Asher (Gen 46:17; 1 Chr 7:31), and the ancestral head of the family of the Malchielites (măl′kĭ-ĕl-īts) [Heb. *Malkî'elî*] (Num 26:45).

Malchielites. *See* Malchiel.

Malchijah (măl-kī′jă), KJV frequently **Malchiah** (măl-kī′ă). [Heb. *Malkîyah* "Yahweh is my king." The name occurs in the Jewish Aramaic papyri from Elephantine.]

1. A Levite, descendant of Gershom (1 Chr 6:40).

2. A descendant of Aaron, and ancestral head of the 5th of the 24 courses into which David organized the priests (1 Chr 24:1, 6, 9). Some identify him with Malchijah, 3.

3. A priest whose son Pashhur was the ancestral head of a priestly family of whom 1,247 members returned from Babylonia with Zerubbabel (Neh 11:12; 1 Chr 9:12; Ezr 2:38; Neh 7:41). Some identify him with Malchijah, 2.

4 and 5. According to the KJV, 2 members of the family of Parosh, each of whom had a foreign wife in Ezra's time (Ezr 10:25); however, the RSV has "Hashabiah" for Malchijah, 5, based on 1 Esdras 9:26.

6. A member of the family of Harim who had a foreign wife in Ezra's time (Ezr 10:31) and who, with another Jew, repaired part of the wall of Jerusalem in Nehemiah's time (Neh 3:11).

7. A son of Rechab, and district ruler of Beth-haccerem, who also assisted Nehemiah in rebuilding the wall of Jerusalem (Neh 3:14).

8. A goldsmith who repaired part of Jerusalem's wall in Nehemiah's day (Neh 3:31).

9. A priest who took part in the dedication ceremonies of the wall of Jerusalem (Neh 12:42), possibly identical with Malchijah, 10 and 11.

10. A priest who assisted Ezra in explaining the Law of God to the people (Neh 8:4), possibly identical with Malchijah, 9 and 11.

11. A priest who set his seal to Nehemiah's covenant (Neh 10:3). He may have been identical with Malchijah, 9 and 10.

Malchiram (măl-kī′răm). [Heb. *Malkiram,* "my king is exalted." The name is attested in ancient Hebrew and Phoenician inscriptions, and in cuneiform texts, where it appears as *Milkirâmu.*] A son of King Jeconiah, or Jehoiachin (1 Chr 3:17, 18).

Malchishua (măl'kĭ-shoō'à), KJV twice **Melchishua** (mĕl'kĭ-shoō'à). [Heb. *Malki-shûa'* and *Malkîshûa'*, "my king is noble."] A son of Saul (1 Sa 14:49; 1 Chr 8:33; 9:39), who was killed in the battle of Mount Gilboa (1 Sa 31:2).

Malchus (măl'kŭs). [Gr. *Malchos,* probably from the Heb. *Melek,* "king." The name is attested almost exclusively among non-Jews, especially Nabataean Arabs.] A slave who was a member of the company of soldiers and officers who arrested Jesus. Peter, attempting to defend his Master, cut off Malchus' right ear (Jn 18:3, 10), which Jesus subsequently healed (see Lk 22:49, 50, where the incident is reported, but not the name of the slave).

Malefactor. In the KJV a rendering of: (1) the Gr. *kakopoios* (Jn 18:30), as a substantive, "a criminal," literally, "an evildoer" (RSV); (2) the Gr. *kakourgos* (Lk 23:32, 33, 39; RSV "criminal"), with the same meaning as (1). The English word comes from the Latin *malefacere,* "to do evil."

Maleleel. See Mahalalel.

Mallothi (măl'ŏ-thī). [Heb. *Mallôthi,* "I have proclaimed."] A son of Heman, and head of the 19th of the 24 courses into which David organized the singers for the Temple services (1 Chr 25:4, 26).

Mallow. [Heb. *mallûach.*] It is generally thought that *mallûach* refers to a plant with stubby, sour-tasting leaves, edible but not pleasant to eat, rather than the mallow we know today. Some suggest the saltwort. It was eaten only in case of extreme hunger (Job 30:3, 4). The reading "mallow" in ch 24:24, RSV, is based on the LXX, the Hebrew reading simply "all."

Malluch (măl'ŭk). [Heb. *Mallûk,* "reigning."]

1. A Merarite Levite (1 Chr 6:44).

2. A priest who returned from Babylonia with Zerubbabel (Neh 12:2). He was probably the ancestral head of a family attested in the next generation under the name of Malluchi (măl'ŭ-kī) [Heb. *Mallûkî*] (v 14), translated "Melicu" (mĕl'ĭ-kū) in the KJV.

3 and 4. A member of the family of Bani and one of the family of Harim. They had married foreign wives in Ezra's time (Ezr 10:29, 32).

5 and 6. A priest and one of the "chiefs of the people" who set their seal to Nehemiah's covenant (Neh 10:4, 27).

Malluchi. See Malluch, 2.

Malta (môl'tà), KJV **Melita** (mĕl'ĭ-tà). [Gr. *Melitē.*] A small island in the Mediterranean, with an area of only 91 sq. mi., about 60 mi. south of the southeastern tip of Sicily (Map XX, B-1). It was occupied by Phoenicians and Carthaginians before it came into the possession of Rome in 218 B.C. The Romans made it part of the province of Sicily, but the bulk of its population remained Semitic. That is why they were called "barbarians" by Greek-speaking people (Acts 28:2, 4), that is, people who were neither Roman nor Greek by descent and language, even though they were highly civilized and possessed Roman citizenship. The inhabitants of the island have retained their Semitic Maltese language to the present time. The island was administered by a *princeps municipii,* "chief of the community," attested from an early inscription found on the neighboring island of Gozo. This title corresponds to the term used by Luke in Acts 28:7 who calls Publius "the chief man of the island."

The ship on which Paul was carried as a prisoner, after having been caught in a gale in the Mediterranean, drifted toward Malta and was wrecked there by being grounded on the rocks of the coast (Acts 27:27 to 28:1). Tradition claims this wreck occurred in what is now called St. Paul's Bay (fig. 313) 8 mi. northwest of La Valeta, between the west shore of the bay and the little island of Salmonetta. Paul then spent 3 months on the island (ch 28:11), probably during the winter of A.D. 60-61. The fact that no poisonous snakes are found on Malta now has been taken by some as an indication that the story of Acts 28:3-6 is either untrue or that it happened on another island. However, the fact that the island has been densely populated for many centuries (present population is more than 1/4 million), may be responsible for the complete extinction of all poisonous snakes. Some scholars have

313. St. Paul's Bay at Malta, the traditional scene of Paul's shipwreck

suggested identifying the NT *Melitē* with the island of Meleda, the southernmost of the larger islands of the Dalmatian archipelago, which was called *Melitē* by the Greeks, *Melite* in Latin, and *Mljet* in Slavic. However, the narrative of Paul's continued journey to Rome via Syracuse, Rhegium, and Puteoli makes it very unlikely that he had spent the preceding winter on an island lying off the Dalmatian coast; consequently, the majority of commentators accept the traditional identification of Melita with Malta.

Mammon. A transliteration through the Gr. *mamōnas* of the Aramaic word *mamón*, "wealth," "property" (Lk 16:9, 11). The term appears as a personification in Mt 6:24; Lk 16:13.

Mamre (măm′rĕ). [Heb. *Mamre'*.]

1. An Amorite chief, evidently owner of the site of Mamre, 2, where he lived. He was an ally of Abraham and helped him in pursuing Chedorlaomer and his confederates, in order to recover the captives and spoil carried off by those kings (Gen 14:13, 24).

2. A place near Hebron (Gen 23:19; 35:27), west of Machpelah (ch 23:17). There were trees standing on this property, and both Abraham and Isaac resided

314. The traditional Russian oak of Mamre

there on different occasions (Gen 13:18; 14:13; 18:1; 23:17, 19; 35:27). Josephus (*War* iv. 9. 7) notes that in his time an old terebinth, 6 stadia (⅔ of a mi.) from Hebron, was pointed out as Abraham's tree. In the 4th cent. A.D. another tree was thus identified. This was at a site 2 Roman mi. north of Hebron, the present *Râmet el-Khalîl*, which Constantine enclosed in a basilica. Since the 16th cent. an oak, 1½ mi. west-northwest of modern Hebron, guarded by Russian monks, has been pointed out as marking the true Mamre. This very ancient oak, now held up with steel beams, is centuries old, and its trunk measures 26 ft. around. Both this and the site of Constantine's basilica are probably too far distant from Hebron to be considered the true site of Abraham's Mamre. *Râmet el-Khalîl* was excavated by E. Mader from 1926 to 1928. He found the remains of Constantine's basilica, and also a wall of tremendous stones built by Herod the Great, apparently part of an earlier sanctuary of some kind. In its southwestern corner lay a well near which presumably the oak was located, which in the time of Constantine was considered the tree of Abraham. The pre-Roman history of the site has not yet been clarified. (See E. Mader, *Mambre*, 2 vols. Freiburg im Breisgau, 1957.)

Man of Sin. *See* Antichrist.

Man, Son of. *See* Son of man.

Manaen (măn′á-ĕn). [Gr. *Manaēn,* from the Heb. *Menachem,* "comforter."] A prophet or teacher in the church of Antioch when Paul and Barnabas received the commission for their 1st Missionary Journey. He is called a *suntrophos* of Herod the tetrarch (Acts 13:1), probably Antipas. *Suntrophos* may mean "foster brother," one who had been brought up with Herod (KJV), or "associate," one who was simply a member of Herod's court (RSV). A connection between him and Manahem, an Essene prophet who told Herod the Great that he would obtain the kingdom (Jos. *Ant.* xv. 10. 5), is speculative and without any historical foundation.

Manahath (măn′á-hăth). [Heb. *Manachath,* "resting place."]

1. A son of Shobal the Horite (Gen 36:23; 1 Chr 1:40).

2. A place in Judah, mentioned in the *Amarna Letters as *Manḥate,* to which Benjamites of Geba were carried by some of their fellow tribesmen (1 Chr 8:6); site tentatively identified with the modern *Mâlḥā,* 3 mi. southwest of Jerusalem.

315. Ruin wall of *Rámet el-Khalíl*, the Herodian structure considered to be Mamre in the time of Christ

Manahathites (má-nā'hăth-īts), KJV **Manahethites** (má-nā'hĕth-īts). [Heb. *Manachtî.*] Possibly descendants of a Calebite called Manahath, but more probably the inhabitants of Manahath, a place (1 Chr 2:54). Some think that Menuhoth (v 52, RSV), descendants of another Calebite, should be corrected to Manahathites (see KJV). *See* Menuhoth.

Manahethites. *See* Manahathites.

Manasseh (má-năs'ĕ), KJV of NT **Manasses** (má-năs'ĕz). [Heb. *Menashsheh*, "making to forget"; Gr. *Manassēs*.]

1. The elder son of Joseph, by Asenath, the daughter of Potiphera, priest of On (Gen 41:50, 51). Hence he was half Egyptian, unless the priest of On was one of the Semitic Hyksos, as is possible. When before his death Jacob blessed Manasseh and his brother Ephraim, the old patriarch indicated by crossing his arms and placing his left hand upon Manasseh, that Ephraim, though younger, would become superior (ch 48:8-21). This prophecy was later fulfilled when Manasseh's descendants, though forming an influential tribe in Israel, were surpassed in importance by the tribe descended from Ephraim (*see* Manasseh, 3).

2. A name appearing in Jgs 18:30, KJV, where, however, Moses should be read. The name Manasseh is the result of a modification in the Hebrew consonantal text by the Jewish Masoretes, who inserted an *n* in the name for Moses apparently to obscure the fact that one of Moses' descendants had become the head of an idolatrous priesthood. *See* Jonathan, 1.

3. The tribe which was descended from Joseph's elder son (Jos 16:4). Although their ancestor was only Jacob's grandchild, he and his brother were adopted by Jacob as his own sons (Gen 48:5), and their descendants were always treated by the Israelites as 2 separate tribes, equal to those which descended from Jacob's

other sons. The tribe of Manasseh consisted of 7 tribal families: one was founded by Machir, and the other 6 sprang from Manasseh's grandson Gilead (Gen 50:23; Num 26:28-34; Jos 17:1, 2). In the first census the tribe had 32,200 members ready for war (Num 1:34, 35). A later census gives the number as 52,700 (ch 26:34). Half of the tribe received part of the Transjordan territory conquered under Moses' leadership from the Amorite kings of Heshbon and Bashan. The Manassites were not allowed to occupy it, however, until after they had assisted the other tribes in the conquest of the territories west of the Jordan (ch 32:20-42). The territory allotted to the half tribe of Manasseh in Transjordan covered the northern part of Gilead and all of Bashan (Deut 3:13-15; Jos 13:29-33), an area consisting partly of forest and partly of fertile grain-producing land. The other half tribe had a large territory in Canaan, which was bounded on the south by Ephraim, and on the north by Issachar, Zebulun, and Asher; its southern boundary ran from the Jordan to Taanath-shiloh, near Shechem, and then followed the "brook Kanah" (*Wâdî Qânah*), ending at the Mediterranean (Jos 17:5-10). The fluidity of this boundary is, however, evident from the fact that the tribe of Ephraim possessed cities within the territory of Manasseh (ch 16:9), while at the same time, Manasseh possessed several cities in the territories of Issachar and Asher (Jos 17:11; cf. 1 Chr 7:29). Like the other tribes, the Manassites were not immediately able to expel the Canaanites from many of the fortress cities, but in the course of time made the Canaanites tributary (Jos 17:12, 13; Jgs 1:27, 28). Two Manassite cities in Bashan were assigned to the Levites (Jos 20:8; 21:27; 1 Chr 6:71). The eastern Manassites extended their territory by waging war against the Hagrites and others (1 Chr 5:18-22). The most famous Manassite of Biblical history was Gideon, the hero and judge who delivered Israel from the Midianites (Jgs 6:15). Some members of the tribe of Manasseh joined David at Ziklag (1 Chr 12:19, 20), and 18,000 offered him their service while he was king of Judah in Hebron (1 Chr 12:31; cf. v 37). Manasseh became part of the northern kingdom after the breakup of Solomon's empire, but some Manassites came to Asa of Judah when they saw that the Lord was with him (2 Chr 15:9). Tiglath-pileser III of Assyria carried the bulk of the population into captivity in the 8th cent. B.C. (1 Chr 5:23-26), but some remnants were left in the country, for some members of that tribe attended the Passover of King Hezekiah (2 Chr 30:1, 10, 11, 18), and as the result of the religious revival returned to their territory and destroyed the cult places of their land dedicated to pagan gods (ch 31:1). They also took part in the reform of King Josiah (ch 34:6, 9). The tribe of Manasseh is mentioned in the visions of Ezekiel (ch 48:4) and John (Rev 7:6).

4. The 14th ruler of the kingdom of Judah; he reigned for 55 years (*c.* 696-*c.* 641 B.C.), during part of which he was apparently coregent with his father Hezekiah. He did not follow his father's good example, but was more wicked than any of his predecessors. He re-established the high places, erected an altar to Baal, and made a cult object to Asherah. He worshiped many other gods in the Temple courts, and sacrificed one of his sons by fire. He ignored the prophets' warnings of the consequences of his evildoings and persecuted many followers of the true God, as the statement that he shed much innocent blood obviously indicates (2 Ki 21:1-16; 2 Chr 33:1-10). As a punishment for his wicked deeds God delivered him into the hands of the Assyrian kings. Both Esarhaddon and Ashurbanipal mention Manasseh as having paid tribute to them (*ANET* 291, 294), one king spelling his name *Menasi* and the other *Minsie.* Yet he seems to have been a disloyal vassal, for on one occasion he was taken captive to Babylon—which was at that time part of the Assyrian Empire—by either Esarhaddon or Ashurbanipal. However, he was allowed to return when the Assyrian king apparently became convinced that Manasseh would henceforth be loyal. Although a non-Biblical record of Manasseh's captivity has not yet been found in cuneiform sources, the experience is not without parallels. For example, the Egyptian ruler Necho (I), king of Saïs, was made vassal king of Egypt by Esarhaddon. After Esarhaddon's death Necho rebelled against Assyria, and was taken to Mesopotamia as a prisoner. While there he succeeded in gaining the confidence of Ashurbanipal, who pardoned him and restored him to his throne in Saïs. While captive in Babylon, Manasseh repented, and after his return to Jerusalem he tried to undo his former wickedness by removing idolatry from his kingdom and from the Temple. Yet he did not abolish

the high places, although he allowed worship only of the true God in them. The chronicler records that he engaged in extensive building activity in Jerusalem and that he strengthened the army (2 Chr 33:11-17). After a reign of more years than that of any other Hebrew king, Manasseh died, leaving the throne to his son Amon. He was buried in the garden of his own house (2 Ki 21:18; 2 Chr 33:20).

5. A Jew married to a foreign wife in Ezra's time (Ezr 10:30).

6. Another Jew married to a foreign wife in Ezra's time (Ezr 10:33).

Manasses. *See* Manasseh.

Manassite (ma-năs'īt). [Heb. *Menashshî.*] A member of the tribe of *Manasseh (Deut 4:43; 2 Ki 10:33; 1 Chr 26:32).

Mandrakes. [Heb. *dûda'îm.*] An herb of the belladonna family (*Mandragora officinarum*), bearing an odoriferous applelike or tomatolike fruit. Ancients believed the mandrake possessed qualities that would stimulate sensual desire and encourage fertility. It does produce a narcotic effect, and is known to have been used medicinally in former times. The supposed aphrodisiac value is implied in the Biblical usage (Gen 30:14-16; Song 7:13).

Maneh. *See* Mina.

Manger. [Gr. *phatnē.*] A trough or box holding fodder for animals. Mangers are mentioned in non-Biblical ancient literature,

316. A manger in one of the Israelite stables at Megiddo

and actual stone mangers of stables from the time of Solomon or Ahab have been found at Megiddo (figs. 236, 316). A manger in the stable of Bethlehem in which Joseph and Mary lodged was used as the first bed of the infant Jesus (Lk 2:7, 12, 16). The same word is rendered "stall" in the KJV in ch 13:15, but "manger" in the RSV in harmony with the usage of the word *phatnē* in other texts.

Manna. [Heb. *man,* from Canaanite *manna,* Amorite *mana,* meaning "what?" The phrase "it is manna" (Ex 16:15) should therefore read "what is it?" (see RSV). Such a reading is supported by the subsequent words, "for they wist not what it was." It is probably from this original question that the name *man* was adopted (v 31). Gr. *manna,* "little grain," "granule."] The food God miraculously provided for the Israelites during their wilderness wanderings. It appeared upon the ground in the early morning, "a small round thing, as small as the hoar frost," white, and with the taste of "wafers made with honey" and of "fresh oil" (Ex 16:14, 31; Num 11:8). The giving of the manna tested the Hebrew nation (Ex 16:4) with respect to their faith in, and obedience to, God. The 1st test came in connection with God's instructions that each man gather an omer, or about 2 quarts, each day (v 16), and that he was to leave none for the next day (vs 4, 18, 19). By obeying, the Israelites manifested faith that God would provide for the next day. Some disobeyed and the manna kept over decayed (v 20). The 2d test came with respect to the Sabbath. The Hebrews were instructed to gather enough on the 6th day for that day and the Sabbath (vs 5, 22), for none would be found in the fields on the Sabbath (v 26). A compliance with this command would show their belief that God would miraculously preserve the manna for the Sabbath, which He did (v 24). Some sought for manna on the Sabbath, but found none (v 27). Manna miraculously fed the Israelites until they entered Canaan (Ex 16: 35; Jos 5:12). The fact that manna was found on the ground for 6 days of the week, and none on the Sabbath, attested the true Sabbath day. Moses was directed to preserve a jar of manna for future generations (Ex 16:32-34). It was kept in a golden jar in the ark (Heb 9:4).

Manoah (mȧ-nō'ȧ). [Heb. *Manôach,* "rest."] A Danite, father of Samson (Jgs 13:1-25).

Manservant. See Servant.

Mansion. A rendering of the Gr. *monē* in Jn 14:2, KJV. *Monē* means simply a dwelling place, as did "mansion" when the KJV was translated. The idea of a spacious and pretentious building is not in *monē.*

Manslayer. See Murder.

Mantelet (măn't'l-ĕt). [Heb. *sokek,* precise meaning uncertain.] A movable shelter used by besieging soldiers as a protective shield in their attack movements (Nah 2:5). However, *sokek* may mean "barricade." See fig. 201 for Assyrian soldiers using a mantelet in their attack on Gezer.

Mantle. In the OT the rendering of various Hebrew words. The exact nature of the garments described is in many cases a matter of uncertainty. The "mantle from Shinar" was doubtless a costly decorated garment imported from Babylon (*see* Shinar), such as only royalty and men of opulence could afford. In the NT the term "mantle" appears in the RSV generally as a translation of the Gr. *himation,* an outer garment (Mt 24:18; Mk 10:50; etc.). Once it is the rendering of the Gr. *chitōn* (Mk 14:63), generally an inner vest or undergarment, but here, being used in the plural, perhaps meaning clothes in general. See Clothing. For the mantle of Jgs 4:18, KJV, *see* Rug.

Maoch (mā'ŏk). [Heb. *Ma'ôk,* meaning uncertain.] A Philistine whose son Achish was king of the Philistine city of Gath (1 Sa 27:2). Some think that he is the one called Maacah (Heb. *Ma'akah*) in 1 Ki 2:39 (*see* Achish), but this is unlikely.

Maon (mā'ŏn). [Heb. *Ma'ôn,* "dwelling."]

1. A Judahite, son of Shammai, and ancestor of (the people of) Beth-zur (1 Chr 2:45). Some think that Maon was the ancestor of the inhabitants of Maon, 2, and that Beth-zur was founded by people from Maon.

2. A town in the hill country of Judah (Jos 15:55), the residence of Nabal (1 Sa 25:2, 3), now *Tell Ma'in,* 8 mi. south of Hebron (Map VI, F-3). The area east of Maon, an arid region that slopes down to the Dead Sea, is apparently the "wilderness of Maon," in which David took refuge (ch 23:24).

Maonites (mā'ŏn-īts). [Heb. *Ma'ôn.*] A people who oppressed Israel (Jgs 10:12), probably those elsewhere called Meunites. See Meunim.

Mara (mä'rȧ). [Heb. *Mara',* "bitter."] An appellation chosen by Naomi for herself because of her experience (Ruth 1:20).

Marah (mä'rȧ). [Heb. *Marah,* "bitter."] The name of a bitter spring in the Wilderness of Shur on the route to Sinai, where the

Israelites camped about 3 days after the crossing of the Red Sea. Its bitter, unpalatable waters were miraculously sweetened by Moses to satisfy the murmuring Israelites (Ex 15:23-26; Num 33:8, 9). According to the traditional route to Sinai, the spring is generally identified with 'Ain Hawârah, about 47 mi. southeast of Suez, and about 7 mi. from the shore of the Red Sea (Map V, C-4). Since the soil of this area is rich in soda, the water of the spring is bitter.

317. The oasis of 'Ain Hawârah, the probable site of Marah, on the Sinai Peninsula

Maralah. *See* Mareal.

Maran-atha. [Gr. *maran atha,* a transliteration of the Aramaic *maran 'atha'* " (our) Lord has come." It is possible to divide the forms thus, *marana' tha',* which makes the phrase an imperative, " (our) Lord, come!"] An expression occurring only in 1 Cor 16:22, a transliteration through Greek of an Aramaic phrase. Like many of the Jews of his day, Paul was bilingual, or most likely, multilingual. He spoke both Aramaic, the vernacular of the people of Palestine, and Greek. His letters to the Corinthians, as indeed all of his epistles, were written in the Greek, but his own familiarity (and that of some of his readers) with the Aramaic doubtless accounts for the presence of this foreign phrase. From the transliteration alone it is impossible to tell which of several possible translations of the Aramaic clause is correct. The following have been suggested: "Our Lord has come," "O our Lord, come," "Our Lord cometh." The clause seems to have been used as a Christian watchword with reference to the second coming of Christ (see Php 4:5; Jas 5:8; Rev 1:7; 3:11). The apostle's closing

salutation to the Corinthians, "Maranatha," may then be compared with John the revelator's expression of absolute confidence in the Lord's return at the close of his prophetic messages: "He which testifieth these things saith, Surely I come quickly. Amen. Even so, come, Lord Jesus" (Rev 22:20).

In the KJV "maran-atha" is unfortunately connected with the preceding word "anathema" as though together the 2 created a formula of malediction. The words actually have no necessáry connection.

Marble. [Heb. *shesh, shayish,* loan words from Egyptian *shś,* "alabaster"; Gr. *marmaros.*] A crystalline form of limestone capable of receiving a high degree of polish. Although not widely used in ancient Egypt, marble grew to be a popular structural material in the Greek and Roman eras, as it is today. From Lebanon came red, yellow, and white marble, and from the quarries of Arabia came stones of highest quality. However, *shesh* and *shayish* more probably refer to a noncrystalline form of limestone or to alabaster, rather than to what we usually think of as "marble." This material was gathered by David for the construction of the Temple (1 Chr 29:2), and from it the pillars of the palace at Shushan were made (Est 1:6). Where this word occurs in a description of the bridegroom in Song 5:15, the RSV has "alabaster."

Marcus. *See* John, 4.

Mareal (măr'ē-ăl), KJV **Maralah** (măr'á-lä). [Heb. *Mar'alah.*] A place on the border of Zebulun (Jos 19:11); not identified.

Mareshah (má-rē'shá). [Heb. *Mare'shah,* and *Mareshah.*]

1. A Judahite, father of Hebron (1 Chr 2:42) and son of Laadah (ch 4:21).

2. For 1 Chr 2:42, RSV, *see* Mesha I, 1.

3. A town in the Shephelah (Jos 15:44), fortified by Rehoboam (2 Chr 11:8). In its vicinity must be sought the battlefield of the war between Asa and "Zerah the Ethiopian" (ch 14:9, 10). It became an important city, called Marissa, in the Hellenistic period, and was inhabited by Edomites. The city was sacked by Judas Maccabeus (Jos. *Ant.* xii. 8. 6), repopulated with Jews by John Hyrcanus (*ibid.* xiii. 9. 1; 10. 2), and made a free city by Pompey in 63 B.C. (*ibid.* xiv. 4. 4). It was finally destroyed by the Parthians in 40 B.C. (*ibid.* xiv. 13. 9). The site has been identified with *Tell Sandahannah,* about 1½ mi. south of *Beit Jibrîn* (Eleutheropolis) and 13 mi. northwest of Hebron

(Map XIV, E-2). F. J. Bliss and R. A. S. Macalister excavated the site in 1900 and uncovered large parts of the remains of the Hellenistic city.

Lit.: Bliss and Macalister, *Excavations in Palestine During the Years 1898-1900* (London, 1902).

Marish. A poetic term for "marsh." The word occurs only once (Eze 47:11, KJV), however, the Heb. *gebe'* thus translated may mean "cistern," or "pit," as does its Akkadian cognate, *gubbu*.

Mark. The rendering of several Hebrew and Greek words with different shades of meaning: (1) the Heb. *'ôth,* a distinguishing mark or sign, such as placed on Cain (Gen 4:15; cf. Ex 13:16); (2) the Heb. *maṭarah* and *maṭara',* a mark or target at which one shoots (1 Sa 20:20; Job 16:12 [RSV "target"]; Lam 3:12); (3) the Heb. *miphga',* a target at which one strikes (Job 7:20); (4) the Heb. *taw,* the last letter of the Heb. alphabet, in pre-exilic Hebrew written like a cross (+, see fig. 531), used as a distinguishing mark or brand (Eze 9:4, 6), but also by illiterate people to sign a document in lieu of a signature (cf. Job 31:35, rendered "signature" in the RSV, and mistakenly "desire" in the KJV); (5) the Heb. *qa'aqa'* (Lev 19:28, KJV "mark," RSV *"tattoo"); (6) the Gr. *tupos,* visible marks, used of the nail marks in Jesus' hands (Jn 20:25, KJV "print"); (7) the Gr. *sēmeion,* a distinguishing mark (2 Th 3:17, KJV "token"); (8) the Gr. *skopos,* a goal to be reached (Php 3:14, RSV "goal"); (9) the Gr. *stigma,* a mark or brand put on slaves to indicate ownership (Gal 6:17); (10) the Gr. *charagma,* a mark or stamp engraved, etched, branded, cut or imprinted on documents, coins, animals, and slaves, to designate the issuing authority or the proprietor (Rev 13:16, 17; 14:9, 11; 16:2; 19:20; 20:4).

Mark, Gospel of. The 2d and possibly the earliest of the 4 Gospels. The earliest extant manuscripts bear the simple title "According to Mark." The unanimous testimony of early Christian writers points to John Mark (*see* John, 4) as the author. The right of this Gospel to a place in the NT canon has never been challenged. The fact that it carries the name of so inconspicuous a man as John Mark indirectly attests his authorship, since if the book were a forgery the actual writer would doubtless have selected the name of one of the apostles, as the authors of later spurious gospels and epistles did. Before the middle of the 2d cent. A.D., Papias, a bishop of Hierapolis in Asia Minor and reputed to have been a disciple of John

the apostle, identifies Mark as the author and states that his Gospel is an accurate record of the life and teachings of Jesus as he received it from Peter (see Eusebius *Hist. Eccl.* iii. 39. 15; Loeb ed., vol. 1, p. 297). This accords with Peter's own reference to Mark as his "son" (1 Pe 5:13). Mark's particularly vivid narration of incidents involving Peter tends to confirm Papias' statement that Mark based his Gospel on the apostle Peter's eyewitness reminiscences (Mk 1:36, 40; 2:1-4; 3:5; 5:4-6; 6:39, 40; 7:34; 8:33; 10:21; 11:20; etc.). Though agreeing that Mark is the author of the 2d Gospel, the Church Fathers disagree as to whether he wrote it before or after Peter's death about A.D. 65. Irenaeus of Lyons (*c.* A.D. 185) takes the latter position (*Against Heresies* iii. 1. 1) and Clement of Alexandria (*c.* A.D. 190) the former (Eusebius *op. cit.* vi. 14. 5-7; Loeb ed., vol. 2, pp. 47, 49), which appears the more probable. The Gospel of Mark may thus be dated sometime between A.D. 55 and 70.

The Gospel of Mark was in general use among Christians before the middle of the 2d century. Tatian made use of it in his *Diatessaron,* or *Harmony of the Four Gospels, c.* A.D. 170. Luke, who composed his Gospel about A.D. 63, states that many such accounts, oral and written, were extant in his day, and implies that he had made use of these sources as he wrote (Lk 1:1-3). A careful comparison of the Gospel of Mark with that of Luke reveals extensive passages where the wording is practically identical (Mk 2:10, 11; cf. Lk 5:24; Mt 9:6). A similar situation is seen in a number of extensive, verbally identical passages appearing in the OT (see 2 Sa 22 and Ps 18; 2 Ki 18:13 to 20:19 and Is 36 to 39; 2 Ki 24:18 to 25:21, 27-30 and Jer 52:1-27, 31-34). These passages in the Synoptic Gospels testify to some type of documentary interrelationship under the guidance of the Holy Spirit.

Only 24 verses in the entire Gospel of Mark, constituting about one per cent of the total, are without parallels in Matthew and Luke. If, as Papias reports, Mark's account is based on the reminiscences of Peter, then he did not take it from Matthew or Luke. Also, the fact that Mark's Gospel is the shortest, yet records many events in greater detail than either Matthew or Luke, points to it as basic to Matthew and Luke rather than as a condensation of either of them. Accordingly, then, it seems reasonable to assume that Mark was one of the written sources upon which Matthew and Luke drew, and was thus written before either of them. Additional similarities in material common to Matthew and Luke, but not found in Mark, indicate that they drew upon still another, now-unknown, source besides Mark, commonly referred to as "Q" (an abbreviation of the German word *Quelle,* "source"). It is notable that where Matthew and Luke have materials in common with Mark, the writers all agree on the order in which these materials are presented, which is not true concerning materials which they do not share. Whatever documentary relationship the Synoptic Gospels sustain to one another, however, they remain a divinely inspired record of the life and message of Jesus Christ. The Holy Spirit guided in the selection of materials, safeguarded their handling, and supplemented these by direct revelation wherever necessary.

Mark relates 79 of the approximately 179 separate incidents recorded by all 4 Gospels about the life of Christ, or nearly as many as Matthew, but in less than ⅔ the space. Mark also follows a more nearly chronological order than either Matthew or Luke, and devotes special attention to what Jesus did rather than what He said. Mark devotes nearly ⅔ of his space to narrative, or half again as much as Matthew. For instance, Mark records only one of Christ's major discourses (Mk 13) as compared with 5 in Matthew, and only 6 of some 40 parables. Mark's vocabulary reveals the fact that he wrote with non-Jewish readers in mind, as, for instance, when he transliterates such Latin words as *centuriō,* "centurion" (ch 15:39), *denarius* (ch 6:37, RSV), and *speculator,* "executioner" (ch 6:27) into Greek, the language of culture, instead of using the usual Greek words. This also suggests that the Gospel was intended for Roman readers and comports with the ancient tradition that it was written in Rome. The fact that Mark wrote his Gospel outside of Palestine for non-Palestinian readers is evident from his explanation of such things as Palestinian coinage (ch 12:42), the Passover (ch 14:12), customs of the Pharisees (ch 7:3, 4), and various Aramaic words and expressions (see chs 5:41; 7:34; 15:34), all of which would have been unnecessary for Jewish readers, particularly Palestinian Jews. At the same time, the writer was obviously a Jew who knew Aramaic and who was familiar with the OT, which, however, he quotes generally from the Greek translation. It is written in comparatively simple language, and apparently for nonliterary readers. Although it is the shortest of the Gospels, it is in some respects the most vigorous and colorful of them all. Mark's style is terse, vigorous, incisive, vivid, and picturesque, and he often provides significant details not mentioned by any of the other evangelists.

Like the other Synoptic writers, Mark repeatedly records incidents in which Jesus is represented as seeking to conceal His identity as the Messiah. Upon repeated occasions He forbade men who had been the recipients of His healing power to tell others what He had done for them (Mk 1:43-45; 5:43; 7:36, 37; etc.; cf. Mt 12:16; 17:9). This reluctance of Jesus to discuss His Messiahship or to permit publicity concerning it as reflected in the Synoptic Gospels is sometimes referred to as the Messianic Secret. In striking contrast the Gospel of John from first to last presents Jesus as constantly stressing His deity and Messiahship. As a result, some critical scholars have pointed to this differing emphasis as evidence of conflicting opinions about the mission of Jesus on earth. Unquestionably, there is a difference of emphasis between John and the Synoptics on this score, particularly in areas describing the earlier part of Christ's ministry. It should be remembered, however, that in His day-to-day work Jesus demonstrated His Messiahship by living a faultless life as a man among men and by exercising divine power in meeting the needs of humanity. It was His purpose to present men with visible evidence of His divine nature and to let them form their own conclusions with respect to His identity (see Mt 11:2-6; 3:2; Jn 5:36; 10:25; 15:24). A demonstration of His Messiahship would be more convincing to most people than an outright claim on His part. It is evident, however, that upon certain occasions, as recorded in the Gospel of John, Jesus did come out with the specific claim to deity and Messiahship (Jn 3:11-16; 4:26; 5:17-30, 39-46; 6:35-58; 7:26-30; 8:21-56; 10:30; etc.). It will be noted, however, that not until the closing months of Jesus' ministry, when "he stedfastly set his face to go to Jerusalem," and at the time of His rejection and the close of His public ministry in Galilee (Lk 9:51; Jn 6:51, 62) did Jesus openly declare Himself to be the Messiah in His public ministry. Having presented the evidence, Jesus now challenged the Jewish leaders and people to come to a decision with respect to that evidence.

Mark presents Jesus as a man of action

and takes particular interest in His miracles as evidence of divine power at work on man's behalf, whereas Matthew devotes his major attention to the teachings of Jesus. Unlike Matthew and Luke, Mark says nothing whatever about the infancy, childhood, and youth of Jesus. After a brief introduction, mentioning Jesus' baptism and the beginning of His public ministry (Mk 1:1-13), he passes over the first year and a half of Jesus' public ministry in silence, to take up the Galilean ministry in considerable detail (chs 1:14 to 7:23). He mentions a number of incidents during Jesus' retirement from public ministry for 6 months following the close of the Galilean ministry (chs 7:24 to 9:50), and then gives a brief account of the Samarian-Perean ministry (ch 10). He devotes nearly a third of his Gospel to Jesus' closing ministry in Jerusalem and to events connected with His crucifixion, death, and resurrection (chs 11:1 to 15:47). He mentions also certain postresurrection appearances of Jesus to the disciples (ch 16). For a detailed chronological outline of the events in the book, *see* Gospels, Harmony of.

Mark, John. *See* John, 4.

Market of Appius. *See* Forum of Appius.

Market Place. [Gr. generally *agora*.] Oriental cities of OT times usually did not have specific market places. The free space at the *gate inside the city wall served in most cases not only for the city's court of justice but also as a kind of market place (2 Ki 7:1). However, some cities had bazaars—groups of shops, or streets lined with stalls or shops. The existence of such in Damascus and Samaria is attested (1 Ki 20:34). With the spread of Hellenistic culture market places were introduced into the Orient in the 4th cent. B.C. These were open places, comparable in a certain degree with modern town squares. Their primary function was the selling and purchasing of goods, but they were used also for other purposes. People gathered there (Mt 23:7), listened to orators, or discussed politics and other subjects (Acts 17:17); children sat there or used the market place as a playground (Mt 11:16, 17); and laborers stood around waiting for someone to hire them (ch 20:3). Each city had a superintendent in charge of the market (2 Macc 3:4). Herod Agrippa I held this office in the city of Tiberias before he became king. Ancient market places in Palestine of the Hellenistic period have been excavated in the towns of Marissa and Samaria. These Palestinian market places did not materially differ in layout and general appearance from those of the cities in Greece or western Asia Minor, the homelands of the Hellenistic culture. See figs. 41, 113.

Maroth (mā'rŏth). [Heb. *Marôth*, probably "bitter (fountains)."] A town in Judah (Mic 1:12), believed by some to be identical with Maarath (Jos 15:59), while others have identified it with *Khirbet el-Murrân,* lying to the southwest of *Tell Beit Mirsim,* but both identifications are uncertain.

Marriage. Legal union of a man and woman in partnership with respect to homemaking, bearing and rearing children, and general interdependence and mutual comfort. Marriage was instituted by God, in Eden, before sin entered the world (Gen 2:20-25). God created man male and female (ch 1:27, 28). Adam was first created, then Eve as a "helper fit for him" (ch 2:18, 21-23, RSV). God designed that the marriage relationship should be the means of ennobling both partners and of facilitating the development of mature, unselfish characters on the part of both parents and children. The marriage relationship was to be a permanent arrangement (Mt 19:6), dissolved only by death (Rom 7:2, 3) or by *divorce on certain grounds (Mt 19:3-9). Celibacy is commended only in exceptional cases (Mt 19:10-12; 1 Cor 7:8, 26, 27).

Monogamy (Gen 2:21-24; Mt 19:5) has ever been God's ideal for human marriages, and where polygamous situations existed these were simply tolerated. The most beautiful passages of Scripture relating to marriage give no hint of plurality of wives or husbands (Ps 128:3; Prov 31:10-31; Ec 9:9; etc.). But polygamy was already being practiced as early as the time of Lamech, who had 2 wives (Gen 4:19). The unspeakable conditions that brought on the Flood seem to have been initiated by men's taking a plurality of wives from base physical motives (ch 6:1-3). Abraham attempted by polygamy

318. Bride (right) and bridegroom on their way to the wedding near Mount Sinai

to fulfill God's promise (Gen 16:3, 4). This incident is recorded not as an example to follow but as a demonstration of the sorrowful results that may follow a deviation from God's ideal plan (vs 5, 6). Isaac, the son of promise, had 1 wife (ch 25:20), but Jacob took 2 wives and their maids (chs 29:23-28; 30:4, 9). The Scriptures make no attempt to whitewash the failures of Abraham and Jacob, or of such men as Gideon, Elkanah, Solomon, and Rehoboam in regard to this evil practice (Jgs 8:30, 31; 1 Sa 1:1, 2, 6; 18:27; 25:39, 43; 2 Sa 10:3, 27; 1 Ki 11:1-4; 2 Chr 11:18-21). After the Exile polygamy fell more into disuse.

Among the curbs placed against the worst abuses in marriage in Moses' day were: the prohibition of marriage with those near of kin (Lev 8:6-19), the discouragement of polygamy (Deut 17:17), the prohibition of cruelties in connection with polygamy (Ex 21:7-11; Deut 21:10-17), restrictions against cruel and ungrounded divorce (Deut 22:13-19), rules tending to purity within marriage (Ex 20:14, 17; Lev 20:10; Deut 22:22). Intermarriage with foreigners was discouraged (Ex 34:15, 16; Deut 7:1-4) not for purely ethnic reasons but because of the danger of corruption of the people's faith in Jehovah. The career of Ahab and others witnesses to the evil results of the violation of such prohibitions. Yet through the marriage of an Israelite to Ruth, a Moabitess, came David (Ruth 4:13, 22) and, eventually, Jesus (Mt 1:5-16).

Semitic custom called for the father or other near relatives to choose the bride for a marriageable young man (Gen 21:21; 24; 38:6), a practice still carried out to a great extent in certain Oriental lands. It was customary courtesy also to seek the favor of the girl's father and brothers toward the match (ch 34:11). Dowries to the bride's father were considered proper (chs 24:53; 34:12). Naomi sought out a suitable husband for Ruth (Ruth 3:1, 2). A father could give his daughter in marriage to whomever he wished (Jos 15:16, 17; 1 Sa 18:17; etc.), though her consent might be asked (Gen 24:56, 57). Jacob served Laban for specified periods of time, in return for which Laban gave him Leah and Rachel as wives (Gen 29:18-20, 25, 30).

Marriage serves as a Biblical symbol of the unique relationship between the believer and his Creator (Is 54:5; 62:4, 5; Eph 5:23, 27; etc.). The OT prophets often compared the idolatrous apostasy of the Jews with adulterous behavior by a married person (Is 1:21; Jer 3:1-20; Eze 16:8-22; Hos 2:1-5; 3:1-5). In the NT Christ is represented as the bridegroom, and the body of believers as His bride (Mt 9:15; 2 Cor 11:2; etc.). By thus using the marriage relationship to illustrate the intimate connection between Himself and all who believe in Him, our Lord highly exalted the marriage relationship. He honored it by His presence at the wedding at Cana (Jn 2:1-11). He protected it by affirming God's infinite purpose with respect to the establishment of the home (Mt 19:5), and by declaring the marriage relationship inseparable (vs 3-6). The reunion of the saved of earth with their Saviour is spoken of under the symbol of a wedding feast (Rev 19:7-9).

Mars' Hill. *See* Areopagus.

Marsena (mär-sē′nȧ). [Heb. *Marsena'*, probably a Persian name, but of uncertain etymology.] One of the 7 princes of the Persian Empire (Est 1:14), the chief counselors of Ahasuerus (Xerxes).

Marshal. A rendering of: (1) The Heb. *tiphsar* (Jer 51:27, RSV) from the Akkadian *tupsharru*, "a tablet-writer," "a scribe." Anciently scribes often held positions of relatively great importance, and in this passage a high military officer seems to be implied, perhaps a recruiting officer. (2) The Heb. *sopher* (Jgs 5:14, RSV), "scribe," "high official."

Martha (mär′thȧ). [Gr. *Martha,* from the Aramaic *Marta',* "lady" and "mistress."] The sister of Mary and Lazarus of Bethany (Jn 11:1, 2); she was probably the eldest of the 3, since their home, where Jesus visited repeatedly as a close friend of the family, is called Martha's house (Lk 10:38). A good housekeeper, Martha was greatly concerned about the Master's material needs and His comfort, and requested Jesus to tell her sister Mary to help her in her tasks. Jesus, however, although appreciating her work, told her in kind words that Mary in her craving for spiritual food had made a wise choice (vs 38-42). Both sisters were earnest believers in Christ (Jn 11:21-32). When Jesus attended a supper in the house of Simon the leper at Bethany (Mt 26:6; Mk 14:3), Martha served (Jn 12:2), either as a domestic servant, as some have thought, or as Simon's wife, as others believe, but there is no indication of either in the Biblical narrative.

Martyr. [Gr. *martus,* generally, "witness."] A word appearing 3 times in the KJV (Acts

22:20; Rev 2:13; 17:6), and once in the RSV (Rev 17:6). The word thus translated (*martus*) generally means "witness," but came to mean also one who witnessed unto death. Translators are not agreed as to which of the 34 occurrences of *martus* should be translated "martyr" instead of "witness," the KJV translators selecting 3 occurrences and the RSV translators only 1. Some suggest that the occurrences in Rev 1:5; 3:14 should be included. These passages would then declare Jesus to be a martyr. Early Christians regarded the death of Jesus a martyrdom.

Mary (mâr'ĭ). [Gr. *Maria* and *Mariam,* from the Aramaic *Maryam,* a form of the Heb. *Miryam,* which in turn is probably a Hebrew adaptation of the Egyptian *Mryt,* "the beloved one."]

1. The mother of Jesus (Mt 1:18). That she was of the line of David is suggested in Rom 1:3 (cf. Acts 2:30; 13:23; 2 Ti 2:8). Mary, as well as Joseph, her betrothed, lived at *Nazareth (Lk 1:26; 2: 39), and there the angel Gabriel appeared to her and revealed that she was to be blessed above all women, for upon her was to be bestowed the supreme privilege coveted by women in Israel for many generations; she was to be mother of "the Son of the Highest," "the Son of God" (ch 1:26-35). Mary accepted this honor with humility. It would seem that she went immediately to a city in the hill country of Judea to visit a relative, Elizabeth, who was to be the mother of John the Baptist (vs 39, 40). In Lk 1:36, KJV, Elizabeth is called the cousin of Mary. "Cousin" is the translation of the Gr. *suggenis,* which is a more general term correctly rendered simply "kinswoman" as in the RSV.

Three months later, shortly before the birth of John the Baptist, Mary returned to Nazareth (Lk 1:56). Her marriage to Joseph may have taken place at this time (see Mt 1:18-25).

When the time approached for Jesus to be born, Mary and Joseph found it necessary to go to their ancestral town, Bethlehem, for an "enrollment" (Lk 2: 1-5, RSV), or census (KJV "tax"). In the crowded town they could find accommodation only in a stable, and it was there that Jesus was born (vs 6, 7).

Forty days after the birth of Jesus, Mary brought her first-born to the Temple at Jerusalem, as the ceremonial law required (Lk 2:22-24; cf. Lev 12:1-8; see *SDA-Com* 5:701). On that occasion something of the poignancy of her future experience was revealed to her when Simeon prophesied that "a sword shall pierce through thy own soul also" (Lk 2:34, 35). Shortly after this event Mary and Joseph were warned by an angel to flee to Egypt to protect the life of the Child from the evil designs of King Herod (Mt 2:1-17). After some time they were informed in a dream of the death of Herod, whereupon they returned from Egypt and settled in Nazareth of Galilee (vs 19-23).

When Jesus was twelve, Mary and Joseph took Him to Jerusalem to observe the Passover (Lk 2:41, 42). At that time they lost Jesus. When they reproved Jesus after they had found Him, He explained His actions in words that Mary at the time could not understand (vs 43-51), but she "kept all these things, and pondered them in her heart" as she had done on a previous occasion (vs 8-19).

Mary was present at a marriage feast at Cana of Galilee soon after Jesus entered upon His ministry. There, when need for wine arose, she appealed to Jesus, who in response performed His first public miracle by turning water into wine (Jn 2:1-11). Afterward she, with His disciples and others, accompanied Him to Capernaum (v 12). In Mt 12:46; Mk 3:31, 32; and Lk 8:19, 20, Jesus' mother is mentioned, though not named.

Mary stood near Jesus while He was upon the cross, and Jesus commended her to the keeping of His disciple John, who "from that hour . . . took her unto his own house" (Jn 19:25-27).

The Scriptures have nothing more to say of Mary except that she was present with others of Jesus' disciples who gathered "with one accord in prayer and supplication" previous to the day of Pentecost (Acts 1:14).

Tradition relates that Mary accompanied John to Ephesus many years after the crucifixion, and spent her closing years in that city.

The Bible nowhere justifies an exaltation of Mary such as is found in the Roman Catholic Church. The Bible does not call her the Mother of God, nor is she shown to be a dispenser of grace, but only a receiver of grace, in common with all others. Most of the Catholic teaching regarding her is based upon pagan concepts and apocryphal legend (see *SDACom* 5:680, 681).

2. Mary Magdalene. She is described as accompanying Jesus, with certain other women and His disciples, on a preaching tour (Lk 8:1, 2). Jesus had previously cast 7 devils out of her (Lk 8:2; cf. Mk

16:9). The name Magdalene possibly indicates that she had lived in a town called Magdala (Mt 15:39) on the western side of the Sea of Galilee at the time Jesus cast the devils out of her. The epithet was apparently used to distinguish her from other Marys mentioned in the Gospels. The only context other than the journey mentioned above in which the full name Mary Magdalene occurs is in connection with the crucifixion and resurrection of Jesus. During those events she is described as being with other women beholding the events of the crucifixion (Mt 27:56; Mk 15:40; Jn 19:25); as ascertaining, with another Mary, where Jesus was laid (Mk 15:47); as keeping vigil near the tomb with the same woman (Mt 27:61); as being one of the first at the tomb before or at sunrise on the morning of the resurrection (Mt 28:1; Mk 16:1, 2; Jn 20:1); as being one of the first to inform the disciples of the resurrection (Mt 28:7, 8; Mk 16:9; Lk 24:1-10; Jn 20:18); and as being the first, or among the first, to whom Jesus appeared after His resurrection (Mt 28:1, 5, 6, 9; Mk 16:9; Jn 20:1, 11-17).

She has generally been identified with the "woman . . . which was a sinner," who anointed Jesus' feet (Lk 7:37-50). She has less often been identified with Mary, 3, the sister of Martha and Lazarus, who is recorded as having anointed His feet (Jn 11:1, 2; 12:2, 8). The basis for the latter identification is the similarity of the 2 narratives of the anointing (see *SDACom* 5:764-767).

3. Mary of Bethany. The sister of Martha, who lived in a "certain village" (Lk 10:38). John (Jn 11:1) identifies this village as *Bethany, a place a little less than 2 mi. from Jerusalem on the Jericho Road. It may be concluded from John's account that Lazarus also dwelt with them. Luke records the following incident in connection with a visit of Jesus to their home: Mary is pictured as sitting at Jesus' feet while He talks to her. Martha, on the other hand, busies herself preparing a meal. Exasperated at having been left to toil alone, Martha chides Jesus for permitting Mary to be idle. Jesus gently defends Mary by hinting that she has chosen something of far more lasting value than the mere preparation of a meal (Lk 10:38-42). At the death of her brother Lazarus, Mary expressed her conviction that he would not have died had Jesus been there (Jn 11:32). After Lazarus' resurrec-

tion a feast was made in Jesus' honor, during which Mary anointed His feet (Jn 12:1-8; cf. Mt 26:6; Mk 14:3). For this she was severely criticized by the avaricious Judas, who claimed that the spikenard used to anoint Jesus should have been sold for 300 pence and the proceeds used for the poor. "This he said, not that he cared for the poor; but because he was a thief, and had the bag" (Jn 12:4-6). Jesus responded that she had anointed Him for the day of His burial (v 7). On the identification of this Mary with the one preceding, made by some, *see* Mary, 2.

4. "The other Mary" (Mt 27:61; 28:1). She is described as "sitting over against the sepulchre" with Mary Magdalene immediately after the burial of Christ (ch 27:60, 61), and as accompanying her to the tomb before dawn on the resurrection day (ch 28:1). It is impossible to identify this Mary with any degree of certainty unless she is identical with Mary, 5.

5. "Mary the mother of James the less and of Joses" (Mk 15:40; cf. 15:47; 16:1, where she seems to be named separately, as "Mary the mother of Joses" and "Mary the mother of James"). Matthew also mentions "Mary the mother of James and Joses" (Mt 27:56). On the assumption that "the other Mary" and "Mary the mother of James and Joses" are the same, a comparison of their actions may be made thus: (1) Mary the mother of (James and) Joses lingered with Mary Magdalene at the tomb after the burial of Christ (Mk 15:47), as did also "the other Mary" (Mt 27:61); (2) Mary the mother of James (and Joses) accompanied Mary Magdalene to the sepulcher very early on the resurrection morning (Mk 16:1, 2), as did also "the other Mary" (Mt 28:1); (3) Mary the mother of James (and Joses) and Mary Magdalene were informed by an angel that Jesus had risen, and were instructed to tell the disciples (Mk 16:1-7; Lk 24:1-10); "the other Mary" also had an identical experience with Mary Magdalene (Mt 28:1-8).

It has also been suggested that "the other Mary" is the same as Mary, 6.

6. The wife of Clopas (KJV "Cleophas"). She is described by John (Jn 19:25) as being with Mary Magdalene and Jesus' mother near the cross. If she was Mary, 5, then she and Clopas were the parents of "James the less and of Joses" mentioned in this connection.

7. Mary the mother of John Mark (Acts 12:12). According to the KJV of

Col 4:10 she was the "sister" of Barnabas. The Greek word translated "sister's son" is more properly rendered "cousin" (see RSV). In Acts 12:12 the Christian believers at Jerusalem are described as meeting in her house, praying together for the deliverance of Peter from prison. Because there is no mention of her husband it is concluded that she may have been a widow. She seems to have been a woman of some means.

8. A woman mentioned in Rom 16:6. Nothing is known of her except that she seems to have been a zealous Christian worker in the church at Rome (textual evidence attests the reading "you" instead of "us," thus making the Roman Christians the group among whom she labored).

Maschil. *See* Maskil.

Mash (măsh). [Heb. *Mash*.] The son of Aram (Gen 10:23), and ancestral head of an Aramaean tribe. Probably owing to a scribal error 1 Chr 1:17 has "Meshech" instead, a name that occurs elsewhere as that of a son of Japheth (Gen 10:2). Some seek the Aramaean tribe of Mash at the *Mons Masius,* the modern *Ṭur 'Abdîn,* in northern Mesopotamia (Map IV, B-5/6), whereas others, believing this to be too far north, identify the tribe with a people mentioned in Assyrian inscriptions as living in the desert of Mash on the east side of the Syro-Arabian desert.

Mashal. *See* Mishal.

Maskil (măs′kēl), KJV **Maschil** (măs′kēl). [Heb. *maśkîl.*] A term of uncertain meaning appearing in the superscriptions to Ps 32, 42, 44, 45, 52-55, 74, 78, 88, 89, and 142. Since the Hebrew term comes from the root *śakal,* "to have insight," "to have comprehension," some have conjectured that Maskil indicates poems of a contemplative or didactic nature. Others suggest that Maskil may indicate a type of musical performance.

Mason. A builder in stone. The ancient Egyptians mastered the art of building in stone early in their history, as their monuments, temples, and pyramids reveal. The Hebrews may have been employed in this work when they were slaves in Egypt, although the Bible speaks of them only as brickmakers and bricklayers (Ex 1:11, 14). If they learned the art of masonry in Egypt, they lost it during their long stay in the desert, for archeology reveals that after they occupied Canaan the Hebrews built masonry of poorer and cruder workmanship than that of their predecessors, whose cities they gradually took over. This observation agrees with the Biblical records according to which, as late as the time of King Solomon, Phoenician stonemasons were employed to work with the Hebrew masons in the building of the royal palace and the Temple (1 Ki 5:18). These 10th-cent. masons were able to handle large blocks of stone, as ch 7:10 clearly states. In later building activities Hebrew stonemasons seem to have been able to accomplish without foreign help all that was required of them, for in later references to masons (2 Ki 12:12; 22:6; 2 Chr 24:12; Ezr 3:7) no mention is made of foreign workmen. *See* Brick; Mortar; Plumb Line; Stone.

Masrekah (măs′rĕ-kȧ). [Heb. *Maśreqah.*] An Edomite city, home of the Edomite king Samlah (Gen 36:36; 1 Chr 1:47). The site has not been identified with certainty.

Massa (măs′ȧ). [Heb. *Maśśa′.*] A son of Ishmael and ancestral head of an Arabic tribe (Gen 25:14; 1 Chr 1:30). The exact location of the tribe is unknown, but an Assyrian inscription mentions the tribe of the *Mas′u* in conflict with the people of Nebaioth. The latter lived not far from eastern Palestine, and were also descendants of Ishmael. It is also possible that Agur of Prov 30:1 and King Lemuel of ch 31:1 belonged to this Arabic tribe. The translators of the RSV took the Hebrew term *maśśa′* in this sense, whereas the KJV translators rendered it "prophecy," a meaning which *maśśa′* has in the sense of prophecy being a pronouncement or an oracle.

Massah (măs′ȧ). [Heb. *Massah,* "testing," or "temptation."] The place near Horeb where the children of Israel tempted God by doubting His presence with them when they were in need of water, and where water was produced by Moses' smiting of a rock (Ex 17:7; Ps 95:8, 9, RSV; cf. Deut 6:16; 9:22; 33:8). In Ex 17:7; Deut 33:8; Ps 95:8, 9 the name of Meribah appears along with Massah. However, it is not clear whether the authors of these passages gave both names to the same place or had in mind an additional place near Massah. They may have referred to the Meribah at Kadesh. *See* Meribah, 2.

Master. In the OT the rendering generally of the Heb. *'adôn,* "lord," "master" (Gen 24:9; Ex 21:4; etc.). In the NT several terms, with slightly varying shades of meaning, are rendered "master": (1) *kurios.* "owner," "master," "lord" (Mt 6:24; Rom 14:4; etc.); (2) *kathēgētēs,* "teacher" (Mt

23:10); (3) *epistatēs,* "superintendent," "overseer," "master" (Lk 5:5; 8:24; etc.); this term appears only in Luke and only as a title of Jesus, and is nearly always used by the disciples; (4) *rhabbi* and *rhabbouni, see* Rabbi; (5) *despotēs,* "absolute ruler," "lord," "owner," "master" (1 Ti 6:1, 2; etc.); (6) *kubernētēs,* "steersman," "pilot" (Acts 27:11; RSV "captain"), rendered "shipmaster" in Rev 18: 17; (7) *didaskalos,* "teacher" (Mt 8:19; Mk 4:38; KJV; etc.). In 47 instances the KJV renders *didaskalos* "master," however, in each case the RSV gives the preferred rendering "teacher."

Mathusala. *See* Methuselah.

Matred (mā'trĕd). [Heb. *Matred,* probably "expulsion."] The mother of Mehetabel, and mother-in-law of Hadar, king of Edom (Gen 36:39; 1 Chr 1:50).

Matri. *See* Matrites.

Matrites (mā'trītz), KJV **Matri** (mā'trī). [Heb. *Matrî,* "rainy."] The name of a Benjamite family, to which Saul and his father's house belonged (1 Sa 10:21).

Mattan (măt'ăn). [Heb. *Mattan,* "gift." The name is attested as both a male and female personal name in Phoenician.]

1. A priest of the Baal temple at Jerusalem, slain before the Baal altar when Jehoiada, the high priest, carried out the revolt in which the idolatrous queen Athaliah was slain and the boy Joash placed on the throne (2 Ki 11:18; 2 Chr 23:17). Since Baal worship had come to Israel and Judah from Phoenicia through Jezebel and Athaliah, it is quite possible that Mattan came from Phoenicia, where that name is attested in inscriptions.

2. A man whose son Shephatiah, with others, asked King Zedekiah to put Jeremiah to death (Jer 38:1-4).

Mattanah (măt'à-nà). [Heb. *Mattanah,* "gift."] A camping place in the wilderness wandering of the Israelites, between the Arnon and the plains of Moab (Num 21:18, 19); tentatively identified with *Khirbet el-Medeiyineh,* 11 mi. northeast of Dibon.

Mattaniah (măt'à-nī'à). [Heb. *Mattanyah* and *Mattanyahû,* "gift of Yahweh." The name occurs in cuneiform records as *Mattannu-Yâma,* in the Hebrew Lachish Letters and on ancient Hebrew seals with the Biblical spelling.]

1. A singer, son of Heman, in charge of the 9th of the 24 courses into which David organized the Temple musicians (1 Chr 25:4, 16).

2. A Levite of the family of Asaph, and

a contemporary of King Jehoshaphat (2 Chr 20:14).

3. A Levite, also of the family of Asaph, who assisted King Hezekiah in his reformation (2 Chr 29:13).

4. A king of Judah whose name was changed to Zedekiah when he was appointed king by Nebuchadnezzar (2 Ki 24:17). *See* Zedekiah.

5, 6, 7, 8. Four Jews, one a member of the family of Elam, one of the family of Zattu, one of the family of Pahath-moab, and one of the family of Bani, all of whom had foreign wives in the time of Ezra (Ezr 10:26, 27, 30, 37).

9. A descendant of Asaph and leader of the singers in postexilic times (1 Chr 9:15; Neh 11:17, 22; 12:8).

10. A gatekeeper in the postexilic Temple (Neh 12:25); possibly identical with Mattaniah, 9.

11. Another descendant of Asaph (Neh 12:35). He is possibly identical with Mattaniah, 9.

12. A treasurer in the postexilic Temple (Neh 13:13).

Some of the above mentioned may be identical.

Mattatha (măt'à-thà). [Gr. *Mattatha,* from the Heb. *Mattattah,* "gift."] Grandson of David through Nathan, in Luke's genealogy of Jesus Christ (Lk 3:31).

Mattathah. *See* Mattattah.

Mattathias (măt'à-thī'ăs). [Gr. *Mattathias,* from the Heb. *Mattithyah,* "gift of Yahweh."]

1 and 2. Two Judahites appearing in Luke's genealogy of Jesus Christ (Lk 3: 25, 26).

Mattattah (măt'à-tà), KJV **Mattathah** (măt'-à-thà). [Heb. *Mattattah,* "gift." The name occurs on a contract among the Dead Sea scrolls, and in the form *Mtt* on an ancient Hebrew seal.] A member of the family of Hashum; he had married a foreign wife in the time of Ezra (Ezr 10:33).

Mattenai (măt'ĕ-nā'ī). [Heb. *Mattenay,* a shortened form of *Mattanyah,* "Mattaniah," "gift of Yahweh."]

1. A postexilic priest in the time of the high priest Joiakim (Neh 12:19).

2 and 3. Two Jews, one a member of the family of Hashum and one of the family of Bani, each of whom had a foreign wife in the time of Ezra (Ezr 10:33, 37).

Matthan (măt'thăn). [Gr. *Maththan (Matthan* in TR), from the Heb. *Mattan,* "gift."] A Judahite appearing in Matthew's genealogy of Christ (Mt 1:15).

Matthat (măt'thăt). [Gr. *Matthat* (some

manuscripts *Maththat*), from Heb. *Mattath,* "gift."]

1 and 2. Two Judahites appearing in Luke's genealogy of Christ (Lk 3:24, 29).

Matthew (măth′ū). [Gr. *Matthaios,* probably from the Aramaic *Mattay* or *Matta'y,* "gift of Yahweh."] A publican who became a disciple of Jesus. A comparison of Mt 9:9 with ch 10:3; Mk 2:14; Lk 5:27 clearly identifies Levi and Matthew as one and the same person. Matthew was the son of Alphaeus (Mk 2:14), but probably not the brother of James the son of Alphaeus (Mt 10:3), or the Gospel writers would have mentioned them as brothers, as they do Peter and Andrew, and James and John (Mt 10:2).

Matthew refers to himself as Matthew (ch 9:9); whereas Mark and Luke call him Levi, and Mark identifies him as the son of Alphaeus (Mk 2:14; Lk 5:27). It may be that Jesus assigned h'im the name Matthew at the time of his call to discipleship (cf. Mk 3:16; Jn 1:42). The fact that all 4 lists of the 12 apostles call him Matthew rather than Levi (Mt 10:3; Mk 3:18; Lk 6:15; Acts 1:13) implies that this was his name as a disciple.

Matthew was a "publican," or tax gatherer, stationed at Capernaum (Mt 9:9), probably in the service of Herod Antipas. He had apparently listened with interest to the message proclaimed by Jesus, and when summoned to become a disciple he immediately resigned his occupation. Not long afterward he was appointed as one of the Twelve (ch 10:2, 3). Being a tax collector, Matthew must have had some education and may well have been acquainted with Greek as well as his native Aramaic. At some time subsequent to his call, Matthew made Jesus the guest of honor at a feast to which he invited his former associates at the tax office (see Mk 2:14-17). Matthew's modest reference to himself in connection with the feast (Mt 9:10; cf. Lk 5:29) is reminiscent of the unobtrusive way in which John (Jn 21:24) refers to himself.

The fact that Matthew's Gospel was obviously written for Jews may imply that he devoted his later apostolic ministry to people of his own race. Nothing further is known about his later life or labors.

Matthew, Gospel of. First of the 4 Gospels. It appears in the most ancient of the extant Greek NT manuscripts under the simple title "According to Matthew." Early Christian writers unanimously point to Levi Matthew as its author, and internal evidence indicates that it was written by a Jewish Christian and that his object was to convince his fellow Jews that the Messianic prophecies of the OT had at last met their fulfillment in the person and message of Jesus of Nazareth. It is generally supposed that the Gospel of Matthew was written in Palestine, probably a few years before the fall of Jerusalem to the Roman armies in A.D. 70. Having served as a customs official, probably under Herod Antipas, and thus doubtless accustomed to the preparation of written records (Mt 9:9), Matthew was well qualified to prepare this narrative of the life and teachings of the Lord. About A.D. 140 Papias of Hierapolis in Asia Minor mentions that Matthew wrote such an account (Eusebius *Hist. Eccl.* iii. 39), and half a century later Irenaeus makes a similar comment (*ibid.* v 8). According to these accounts the Gospel of Matthew originally appeared in "Hebrew," that is, in Aramaic, the common language of Palestine. Some have understood these statements as meaning that the Gospel was originally written in Aramaic, and was later translated into Greek. On the basis of present evidence it cannot be determined whether the Gospel as we know it today was originally written in Greek or was the translation of a previous Gospel written in Aramaic.

The following reasons for rejecting the theory of an Aramaic origin of the Gospel of Matthew have been set forth: (1) The Greek text of Matthew does not reveal the characteristics of a translated work. Uniformity of language and style convey the distinct impression that the book was originally written in Greek. Like most of the other NT writers Matthew doubtless thought in Aramaic as he wrote in Greek, and his Greek thus unconsciously reflected certain Aramaic idioms. (2) The great linguistic similarity to the Greek of Mark, in particular, and to a less extent of Luke, seems to preclude the possibility that Matthew could have been a Greek translation of an Aramaic original. For the relationship between Matthew and the other Synoptic Gospels, *see* Mark. (3) The frequent citation of OT passages from the Greek translation. Had Matthew been writing in Aramaic he would have quoted from the Hebrew OT.

Matthew apparently wrote his Gospel with the purpose, as already noted, of convincing Jewish readers that Messianic prophecies of the OT had met their fulfillment in Jesus of Nazareth. This is evident from his frequent citation of relevant OT passages (Mt 1:23; 2:6, 15, 17,

18; 3:3; 12:17-21; 13:35; 26:56; 27:3; etc.). Matthew cites nearly 40 such OT predictions. Furthermore, the book as a whole reflects a strong national consciousness (Mt 2:2; 8:11; 15:24; 19:28; 21:4). The genealogy of Jesus similarly reflects a preoccupation with the Jewish point of view, tracing as it does the human ancestry of our Lord back to. David, the ideal king, and to Abraham, father of the Jewish nation (ch 1:1, 6, 17). Matthew stresses the fact that Jesus was, indeed, "the son of David" (v 1) because the OT repeatedly envisions Messiah as the one who will restore to Israel the glories of his reign (2 Sa 7:12, 13; Ps 132:11; Jer 23:5, 6; cf. Acts 2:29, 30). As a lineal son of David, apparently in direct descent through the royal line, Jesus is eligible to serious consideration as the one to whom the prophets of the OT pointed forward. Matthew's tracing of Jesus' ancestry to Abraham, and no further, implies that Jesus was the one who fulfilled the promises made to Abraham and the fathers (see Gen 12:3; 22:18; cf. Gal 3:16). More than all the other Gospel writers combined, Matthew presents Jesus as the one to whom the types of the OT pointed forward and in whom they found fulfillment. He stresses the fact that Jesus did not come to set aside "the law," but to fulfill it (Mt 5:17); in fact, the entire Sermon on the Mount is an amplification and clarification of principles implicit and explicit in the OT Scriptures—"the law and the prophets." Similarly, Matthew alone quotes Jesus as confirming the authority of the scribes and Pharisees when they "sit in Moses' seat" and as commanding His followers to "observe and do" all that these leaders, sitting "in Moses' seat," bade them to observe (ch 23:2, 3). At the same time, Matthew faithfully records Jesus' denunciations of the Pharisees and their teachings (see chs 5:20; 8:12; 9:11, 13, 34; 12:1, 24, 27; 15:1-9; 16:1-4; 21:43; 23:23).

Like Luke, Matthew stresses the true humanity of Jesus more than do Mark or John, who stress His true divinity. The distinctive characteristic of the 1st Gospel is the completeness with which the author reports the sermons and other discourses of the Saviour. He presents Christ as the master teacher, and gives 6 major discourses, at considerable length, which the other Gospel writers record either briefly or not at all: (1) The Sermon on the Mount, Mt 5-7, (2) the discourse on discipleship, ch 10, (3) the sermon by the Sea, consisting entirely of parables, ch 13,

(4) the discourse on humility and brotherhood, Mt 18, (5) the discourse on hypocrisy, ch 23, and (6) the discourse on Christ's return, chs 24, 25. The other Synoptic writers usually quote Jesus as stating the same truths and using the same illustrations under other circumstances. Much of Jesus' teaching selected by Matthew consists of principles of ethical conduct, in an apparent endeavor to stress the fact that true religion is primarily a matter of how a man treats his fellow men. Though Matthew follows a general chronological pattern, he frequently reports incidents out of what appears to be their true setting and groups them together, often in topical order, by kind (cf. chs 8:2 to 9:8). For instance, in order to read the incidents of Jesus' Galilean ministry, reported in chs 4 to 15, in chronological order it would be necessary to skip back and forth among the chapters as follows: 4, 8, 4, 8, 9, 12, 5-7, 8, 9, 12, 13, 8, 9, 11, 9-10, 13-15. See Gospels, Harmony of. Matthew deviates from chronological sequence more than any of the other Gospel writers. He considers his narrative record chiefly as a framework within which to set the teachings of Jesus. He is not a chronicler, recording events as they occur, but a historian, reflecting upon the significance of those events against the larger background of their setting in the history of the chosen people and God's will for them.

After giving Jesus' human ancestry and relating certain incidents connected with His infancy and childhood (Mt 1, 2), Matthew deals with events immediately preparatory to His ministry—His baptism and temptation in the wilderness (chs 3, 4). Like the other Synoptic writers, he develops the Galilean ministry in considerable detail (chs 4:12 to 15:20). He devotes nearly half of this space to the Sermon on the Mount (chs 5-7), the sermon by the Sea (ch 13), and instruction on methods of evangelism (ch 10). He deals rather fully with the period of Jesus' retirement from public ministry (chs 15:21 to 18:35), and narrates certain incidents in the Samarian-Perean ministry (chs 19:1 to 20:34). Finally, he covers in great detail the events of the week leading up to the crucifixion (chs 21:1 to 27:66), and closes his record with the resurrection of Jesus and His postresurrection appearances (ch 28). For a more complete outline of incidents in the life of Jesus see Gospels, Harmony of.

Matthias (mă-thī′ăs). [Gr. *Maththias* (some manuscripts, *Matthias*), an abbreviated

form of the Heb. *Mattithyah,* "Mattathias," a common name from the Maccabean age onward, meaning "gift of Yahweh."] The disciple chosen by lot to fill
Judas' place (Acts 1:21-26). He had followed Christ since the days of His baptism and had been a witness of His acts
and preachings, although not one of the
12 intimate disciples. Nothing more is
known of his history. Clement of Alexandria identifies him with Zacchaeus, and
others with Barnabas or Nathanael. Eusebius claims that he had been one of the
Seventy sent out by Jesus (Lk 10:1).
Several apocryphal writings, attempting
to supply what the inspired writings
omitted, have made him the central figure
of certain of their stories.

Mattithiah (măt'ĭ-thī'á). [Heb. *Mattithyah*
and *Mattithyahû,* "gift of Yahweh."]

  1. A Korahite Levite in charge of making the flat cakes for the Temple (1 Chr
9:31).

  2. A Levite musician (1 Chr 15:18, 21;
16:5).

  3. A Levite, of the house of Jeduthun,
who was put in charge of the 14th of the
24 courses into which David organized
the Temple musicians (1 Chr 25:3, 21).

  4. A member of the family of Nebo. He
had a foreign wife in the time of Ezra
(Ezr 10:43).

  5. A Levite or priest who stood at Ezra's
right hand while he read the Law of
God (Neh 8:4).

Mattock. An instrument for digging, of the
nature of a pickax. In the RSV it is the
rendering of the Heb. *'eth* (1 Sa 13:20, 21),
which the KJV renders "coulter," but it
is extremely doubtful that any ancient
plows had a coulter. In the KJV "mattock"
appears as the translation of: (1) The
Heb. *machareshah,* which some suggest is
a misspelling of *chermesh,* "sickle," in ch
13:20, since mattocks are mentioned in
the passage by *'eth.* In v 21 *machareshoth,*
rendered "mattocks" in the KJV, is believed to denote plowshares instead. (2)
The Heb. *chereb,* according to the Masoretic tradition, literally "sword" (2 Chr
34:6). The passage in which it occurs is
obscure in the Hebrew. (3) The Heb.
ma'der, "hoe" (Is 7:25).

Maul. *See* Club.

Mazzaroth (măz'á-rŏth). [Heb. *Mazzaroth,*
identified with the planet Venus, the
cluster of stars in Taurus known as the
Hyades, but most often with the constellations of the zodiac.] A feature of the
starry heavens mentioned in Job 38:32,

not certainly identified. A comparison of
Job 38:31, 32 with ch 9:9 suggests that the
celestial object or objects thus designated
may be a constellation or cluster of stars
in the southern skies. If *Mazzaroth* is a
variant of the Heb. *Mazzaloth,* it could be
a designation for the 12 signs of the zodiac
mentioned in 2 Ki 23:5 (KJV "planets";
RSV "constellations"). Mazzaroth, then,
may refer to some of the southern constellations of the zodiac, or possibly to all
of them.

Meadow. A term appearing 3 times in the
KJV (Gen 41:2, 18; Jgs 20:33), but the
Hebrew terms thus translated do not refer
to a grassy plain, but in the Gen passage
to reeds, and in Jgs to "approaches," or
"vicinity." In the RSV the word occurs
twice (Ps 65:13; Zep 2:6), the rendering
of a Hebrew word meaning "pasture
ground."

Meah (mē'á). [Heb. *Me'ah,* "hundred."] The
name of a tower at Jerusalem in the
northern wall between the Sheep Gate
and the tower of Hananeel (Neh 3:1; 12:
39, KJV). Since the Sheep Gate was probably situated at or near the northeastern
corner of Jerusalem, the tower of Meah
was probably part of the fortification of
the castle that overlooked the Temple
from the north and that later formed part
of the castle of Antonia. Instead of "tower
of Meah" the RSV reads "Tower of the
Hundred."

Meal. Grain, ground in mills turned by
hand (see fig. 319) or by animals (*see*

319. A limestone figure of a servant grinding grain,
from *Gizeh*

Mill). The common Hebrew terms thus translated (*qemach; soleth*) are also rendered "flour." The Gr. *aleuron* of Mt 13: 33 and Lk 13:21, rendered "meal," is probably in most cases wheat meal or wheat flour. *See* Flour.

Meal Offering. *See* Sacrifices and Offerings.

Meals. From the evidence available it appears that the early Hebrews did not give special names to their various meals. However, it is clear that they were accustomed, as were their contemporaries, to but 2 regular meals a day (Ex 16:12; 1 Ki 17:6).

Owing to the excessive heat of the late morning and early afternoon, the people of the East found it necessary to rest during this period (2 Sa 4:5) and to work in the early morning (cf. Mt 20:1) and the late evening. Starting for their various places of labor at early morning, farmers, shepherds, and even artisans would take along with them in their girdles or in their donkey sacks an "early snack," consisting of olives, raisins, flat round loaves of bread, goat's-milk cheese, and the like. This was not a true meal, but merely a light lunch to satisfy the appetite until mealtime. There is probably but one reference in the NT to this custom of eating an early lunch (Jn 21:4, 5, 9, 12, 13).

The noon meal was the 1st real meal of the day. For a period varying according to rank and occupation, men and women took time off from their labors at about 10 or 11 A.M., primarily to rest, but also to eat. In the NT this meal is called *ariston* (breakfast). In Joppa, Peter was about to eat at the "sixth hour," that is, 12 noon, when the messengers of Cornelius came for him (Acts 10:9-19). To refrain from this meal was considered "fasting" (Jgs 20:26; 1 Sa 14:24).

The evening meal was the main meal of the day, and was taken about sunset, when the work of the day was over and the laborers had "come in from the field" (Lk 17:7; 24:29, 30), and the whole family was together for the evening. In NT times this was called *deipnon* (supper). It was a *deipnon* at which Mary anointed Jesus' feet (Jn 12:1-3), and Jesus' last meal before His crucifixion was called a *deipnon* (chs 13:2, 4; 21:20). It was this evening meal that Jesus provided for the multitudes (Mk 6:35-44; Lk 9:12-17).

The early Hebrews were most probably in the habit of sitting or squatting on the ground as they partook of their meals, much as the Bedouins or fellahs do today.

The table, in this case, was only slightly elevated above the ground. After the conquest of Canaan, when the people had settled down to agricultural life, the use of seats was adopted (1 Sa 20:5, 24, 25). Later, in keeping with the wealth and luxury of the monarchy, seats were exchanged for couches, and the practice of sitting gave way to that of reclining (Eze 23:41, RSV; Amos 6:4-6). By NT times reclining on couches had seemingly become the universal custom (Jn 13:23). See figs. 320, 362.

Couches were usually placed around tables arranged so as to form 3 sides of a square, the 4th side being left open so that the servants might, without hindrance, carry the various dishes to the table. The couches were designated high-

320. Sketch of a Roman dining arrangement. The arrows represent the diners, generally 3 to a couch, each reclining on the left elbow, leaving the right hand free to reach the table

est, middle, and lowest, in that order, the highest being to the right of the servants as they brought the meal to the table. Christ reproved those who attempted to take the highest positions at wedding feasts (Lk 14:7-11). Ordinarily 3 persons occupied each couch, although occasionally there were more.

Each participant at the meal lay diagonally across his couch with his head toward the table, supporting the upper part of his body by his left elbow, which rested upon a cushion provided for the purpose, and resting his head on or near the breast of the one immediately behind him. He was thus said to "lean upon the bosom" of his neighbor (Jn 13:23; 21:20). The right arm was left free for the handling of food.

Before taking their places at the table the members of the family and guests washed their hands (Mt 15:2; Mk 7:2). This custom was well founded, since each person used his hand to convey the food to his mouth. Generally, there was a single dish on the table from which each person partook. A piece of bread was held between the thumb and fingers and dipped into the common bowl (Mt 26:23; Mk 14:20).

The eating of the meal was preceded by the saying of the grace or blessing (Mt 14:19; 15:36; 26:26; Lk 24:30). At the conclusion of the meal another blessing in the form of a thanksgiving was pronounced, in harmony with Deut 8:10, after which the hands were again washed.

On festive occasions greater ceremony was observed. Guests were invited, a sumptuous repast was prepared, and on the day of the feast a 2d invitation was sent forth as a reminder to those already invited (Mt 22:3, 4). On arrival at the feast the guests were greeted with a kiss (Lk 7:45), and water was provided for the washing of the dusty feet (Gen 18:4; 19:2; Lk 7:44). Guests usually came with head, beard, feet, and sometimes clothes perfumed with ointment; however, occasionally they were anointed on reaching the house of the host (Lk 7:38; Jn 12:3). A steward (KJV "governor," "ruler") directed the meal (Jn 2:8, 9). He acted as the master of ceremonies, tasting the food, regulating its distribution, and directing the program (vs 9, 10). The meal was sometimes brightened with music (Is 5:12), singing (Amos 6:4, 5), dancing (Mt 14:6; Lk 15:25-27), and riddles (Jgs 14:10, 12). Amid these entertainments festivities often lasted several days (v 17).

Mearah (mê-ā'rà). [Heb. *Me'arah*, "cave."] A place near Sidon not occupied by the Israelites in the time of Joshua (Jos 13:4). The site has tentatively been identified with *Mogheiriyeh*, 6 mi. northeast of Sidon.

Measure. A unit of capacity, quantity, or length; used as the rendering of several Hebrew and Greek terms (*see also* Weights and Measures):

(1) The Heb. *se'ah*, a dry measure, 1/3 of an *ephah, the equivalent of 7.33 liters, or 6.66 dry qts. U.S. (Gen 18:6; 1 Sa 25:18; 1 Ki 18:32; 2 Ki 7:1, 16, 18). By NT times the capacity of the *se'ah* had apparently

increased to about 15.5 liters, as attested by an inscribed jar discovered at *Khirbet Qumrân*.

(2) The Heb. *'êphah*, a dry measure (*see* Ephah, II), is rendered "measure" in Deut 25:14, 15; Prov 20:10; and Mic 6:10, but apparently not as a specific unit of measure but of honest values in general.

(3) The Heb. *kor*, a dry measure, transliterated "cor" in Eze 45:14, but translated "measure" in 1 Ki 4:22 and Ezr 7:22; in the KJV also in 1 Ki 5:11; 2 Chr 2:10; 27:5. Its capacity was 10 ephahs, that is, 220 liters, or 6.24 bu. U.S. *See* Cor.

(4) The Gr. *batos* (a transliteration of the Heb. *bath*, but not the same capacity as the OT bath), a Jewish liquid measure, which, according to Josephus (*Ant.* viii. 2. 9), was 72 sextarii; thus it was 39.40 liters, or 10.41 gal. U.S. (Lk 16:6).

(5) The Gr. *koros* (a transliteration of the Heb. *kor*, but not the same capacity as the OT cor), a Jewish dry measure which, according to Josephus (*Ant.* xv. 9. 2), was equivalent to 10 Attic medimni, and thus would equal 525.31 liters, or 14.92 bu. U.S. (Lk 16:7).

(6) The Gr. *saton* (a transliteration of the Heb. *se'ah* but of different capacity), a Jewish dry measure (Mt 13:33; Lk 13:21), which, according to Josephus (*Ant.* ix. 4. 5), was 1½ modii; hence it was equal to 13.13 liters, or 11.92 dry qts., or 1.49 pecks U.S. But if it was equivalent to the *se'ah* in use at *Qumrân* it was 15.5 liters.

(7) The Gr. *choinix*, a Greek dry measure of 2 sextarii, 1.09 liters, or .99 dry qt. capacity (Rev 6:6, KJV; RSV "quart").

Meat. As used in the KJV this word is a rendering of terms meaning food in general (Lev 22:11; 1 Ki 19:6; 1 Ti 4:3; etc.). Where the flesh of animals is specifically intended the KJV uses the translation "flesh" (Num 11:4, 13; Jgs 6:19, 20; etc.). The RSV on the other hand generally uses the word "food" to denote food in general, and "meat" for the flesh of animals.

Meat Market, KJV **Shambles.** [Gr. *makellon*, a transliteration of the Latin *macellum*, "meat market." "Shambles" is an English derivative from the Latin *scamellum*, "little stool" or "bench," used for the butcher's stalls or benches on which meat for sale in the market was placed.] In the excavations of Corinth a commercial building was unearthed north of the basilica on the Lechaeum Road. It showed colonnades and small shops surrounding a paved court. In the late pavement of one of the shops an inscription was found referring to a fish market (fig. 321), but it is uncertain

321. Inscription referring to the fish market (*macellum*, probably the "shambles," or "meat market") of Corinth

whether one shop or the whole building was used for the sale of fish. The word for market in this inscription is the same as that used by Paul in 1 Cor 10:25, and it has been suggested that this building may also have been used for the sale of other meats, and that it could have been in existence when Paul counseled Christians to eat, without raising questions on the ground of conscience, what was sold in the meat market. The building was destroyed by an earthquake in the 6th cent. A.D.

Meat Offering. *See* Sacrifices and Offerings.

Mebunnai (mě-bŭn'ī). [Heb. *Mebunnay*.] One of David's "mighty men" (2 Sa 23: 27). In the list as given in 1 Chr 11:29 the name corresponding to Mebunnai is *Sibbecai.

Mecherathite (mě-kē'răth-īt). [Heb. *Mekerathî*.] Either a descendant of a man named Mecherath, unidentified, or an inhabitant of a place called Mecherah, not known (1 Chr 11:36). It has been suggested that this name is an error for Maacathite (cf. 2 Sa 23:34), but there is nothing to identify the two except their occurrence in corresponding verses.

Meconah (mě-kō'nà), KJV **Mekonah** (mě-kō'nà). [Heb. *Mekonah*.] A town of the postexilic period in the extreme south of Judah, near Ziklag (Neh 11:28); not identified.

Medad (mē'dăd). [Heb. *Mêdad*, probably "beloved." The name occurs in Assyrian as *Mudada*.] One of the 70 elders chosen to assist Moses in his administrative and judicial duties in the wilderness. He and

Eldad were not present for the initiation ceremony at the tabernacle, when the other elders received God's Spirit in a noticeable manner, but the Spirit of God nevertheless came upon them. Joshua was displeased that this manifestation should come without Moses' agency, but Moses reprimanded him by declaring that he wished the Lord would put His Spirit on all His people, so that they all might become prophets (Num 11:24-29).

Medan (mē'dăn). [Heb. *Medan*.] A son of Abraham by Keturah, and ancestral head of a tribe (Gen 25:2; 1 Chr 1:32) which, like that of Midian and others, lived in the eastern desert. No certain identification can be made, but it is possible that the tribe of *Badana*, conquered by Tiglath-pileser III, can be identified with Medan.

Mede (mēd), KJV once **Median** (mē'dǐ-ăn). [Heb. and Aramaic *Maday*; Gr. *Mēdos*.] A native of Media (2 Ki 17:6; 18:11; Est 1:19; Is 13:17; Jer 51:11, 28; Dan 5:28, 31; 9:1; Acts 2:9; etc.). For the relationship between the Medes and the Persians, *see* Media; Persia.

322. Median (left) and Persian soldiers at Persepolis

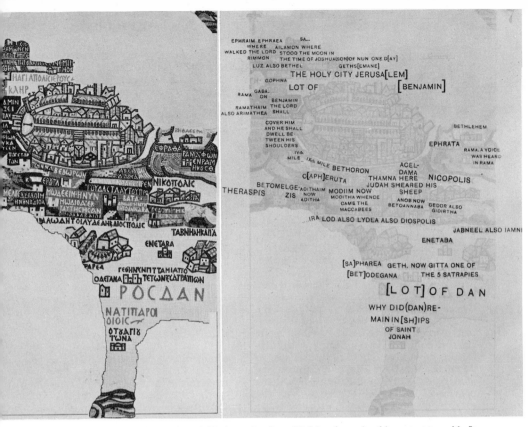

323. Part of the mosaic map of Palestine (left) in a church at Medeba, from the 6th cent. A.D., with Jerusalem in upper center; key to the inscription (right)

Medeba (mĕd′ĕ-bà). [Heb. *Mêdeba′*, spelled *Mhdb′* on the Moabite Stone.] An ancient Moabite town, which the Israelites conquered from King Sihon of Heshbon (Num 2:21-30). It was assigned to the tribe of Reuben (Jos 13:9, 16). In the time of David it was the camping site of the Syrians (*see* Maacah, 11) who came to the help of the Ammonites against Joab's army (1 Chr 19:7, 8). After the disruption of Solomon's kingdom under Rehoboam, Medeba was lost to the Moabites. It was later reconquered by King Omri of Israel, but recaptured by Mesha and fortified by him (*Moabite Stone, lines 7, 8, 29, 30). It played an important role in the Maccabean wars: John, eldest son of Mattathias, was slain there, and because of his death, his brothers Simon and Jonathan took revenge on the town; John Hyrcanus later conquered the town after a siege of about 6 months (1 Macc 9:36-42; Jos. *Ant.* xiii. 1. 2. 4; 9. 1).

The ancient site is covered today by a Christian town, situated about 6 mi. south of Heshbon and 15 mi. southeast of the mouth of the Jordan on the main highway from Amman to Kerak (see Map VI, E-4, where it appears with the modern spelling, *Mâdebā*). Most of the visible ruins date from Byzantine times. In 1896 major remains of a mosaic map of Palestine were discovered in an old Byzantine church there (see fig. 323). It is the oldest map of Palestine in existence, originating probably from the 6th cent. A.D. The original map also contained Syria, the Sinai Peninsula, and Lower Egypt, but large parts were destroyed in the excavations for the building of the new church, before scholars could halt the destruction.

Lit.: M. Avi-Yonah, *The Madaba Mosaic Map* (Jerusalem, 1954).

Media (mē′dĭ-à). [Heb. and Aramaic *Maday*.] A country east of the Zagros Mountains and south of the Caspian Sea (Map XI, B-6). Its inhabitants, the Medes, were a hardy mountain people of Indo-European stock, descendants of Japheth through Madai (Gen 10:2; 1 Chr 1:5). The first reference to them in history dates from the time of Shalmaneser III (859-824 B.C.), and from that time they appear regularly in Assyrian records and are represented as barbaric tribes against whom the Assyrian kings fought repeatedly, but of whom they were able to subjugate only the western tribes. After the fall of Samaria in 723/22 B.C., some of the captured Israelites were deported to the cities of the Medes (2 Ki 17:6; 18:11). Sargon II, Sennacherib, and Esarhaddon of Assyria waged successful wars against the Medes or received tribute from them. Large cuneiform tablets recording treaties between Esarhaddon and local Median princes have recently been discovered at *Nimrûd,* the Biblical Calah. Deioces (*c.* 700 - *c.* 647 B.C.) is said by Herodotus to have united the various Median tribes into a nation, and to have founded *Ecbatana as the capital of the kingdom. His son Phraortes (*c.* 647 - *c.* 625 B.C.) is credited with having subjugated the Persian tribes, but lost his life fighting against Assyria. Cyaxares (*c.* 625 - *c.* 585 B.C.) continued the struggle against the Assyrians and, in company with Nabopolassar of Babylon, made an end to the Assyrian Empire by capturning its capital, Nineveh, in 612 B.C. In the division of the Assyrian Empire the Medes took the mountainous, northern provinces of Assyria, Armenia, and the eastern end of Asia Minor, with the Halys River becoming their western border. The friendship with the Babylonians was sealed by the marriage of Amuhea, the daughter of Cyaxares, to Nebuchadnezzar. In 585 B.C. a battle between the Medes and the Lydians took place which ended when the famous solar eclipse of May 28, 585 B.C., which had been predicted by Thales of Miletus, occurred. A treaty of friendship followed, and the Median crown prince Astyages married a Lydian princess. Under Astyages' rule (*c.* 585 - *c.* 553 B.C.) Cyrus, the Persian vassal king of Anshan, rebelled against his overlord, who may have been also his grandfather, and after some initial setbacks gained Ecbatana and the whole Median Empire. By uniting the Medes with his own Persian tribes Cyrus formed a dual nation and kingdom, the powerful Medo-Persian Empire (*see* Persia).

Median. *See* Mede.

Mediator. [Heb. a form of *lîṣ,* "to be a spokesman"; Gr. *mesitēs,* literally "a go-between," from *mesos,* "middle," and *eimi,* "to go"; thus "mediator," "arbitrator."] A 3d party who mediates between 2 parties with a view to effecting a reconciliation or agreement, either by harmonizing divergent views or interests, or by bringing both parties together in a compact acceptable to each member. The term appears once in the OT (Job 33:23, RSV), where the Hebrew term suggests the idea of a spokesman. In the NT Jesus is set forth as the "one mediator between God and men" (1 Ti 2:5). He represents God to man and man to God in order to effect the salvation of man. This necessitates that the one so designated should have an intimate relationship with both parties, and to this end he should possess the nature and attributes or characteristics of both parties, namely Deity and humanity. Jesus Christ is presented as the only one who is able to fulfill this unique role. As God, He can rightly represent the Deity. As man, He can sympathetically minister in man's behalf. In Heb 8:6; 9:15; 12:24 *mesitēs* seems to be used in the sense of one who acts as a surety, or guarantor. In this particular relation Jesus Christ is presented as the "guarantor" of the "better covenant," that is, the "new covenant."

There is difference of opinion among commentators as to whether the *mesitēs* of Gal 3:19, 20 refers to Moses (most modern exegetes) or to Jesus Christ (Origen, Augustine, most of the Fathers, Calvin). The reference is to the one who mediated when the body of laws was given to Israel at Sinai. By contrast there was no mediator when the promise was made to Abraham. All the obligations were assumed by God.

Medicine. [Heb. *gehah, rephu'ah, terûphah.* These terms primarily mean "healing," and only in a secondary sense designate "means to produce healing," or "medicine."] Any substance taken into or applied upon the body for the purpose of relieving or curing a malady or sickness. Though man was created with perfect mental and physical health, the results of sin were soon evident in the deterioration and malfunction of many body organs. God gave to His people certain health laws which, if followed, would minimize and in many cases obviate the diseases that were overtaking the heathen world (Deut 7:9, 11, 15). The heathen nations, such as Egypt, feeling the heavy curse of disease, early developed their own systems of medicine. Herodotus (iii. 1. 129) speaks of the Persian Cyrus' sending to Egypt for an eye doctor, and there were Egyptian physicians at Susa in Darius' time. We know that midwifery was practiced by the Hebrews in Egypt before the Exodus (Ex 1:15-21). The early Babylonian concern for healing is evidenced in sections of

Hammurabi's Code dealing with doctors' fees and laws against malpractice. Ashurbanipal's library is said to have contained some 800 texts on priestly rites of exorcism and the education of physicians. King Asa, of Judah, consulted the physicians about his foot disease (2 Chr 16: 12). Scattered throughout Scripture we find figurative allusions to the physician and medicine (Prov 17:22; Jer 8:22; 30: 12; Mt 9:12). The trade of the *apothecary was established early in Bible times (Ex 30:25, 35; Neh 3:8; Ec 10:1; etc.). Specific medicines mentioned in Scripture include oil, or ointment (Is 1:6), "oil and wine" (Lk 10:34; cf. 1 Ti 5:23), poultices (2 Ki 20:7), balm of Gilead being especially prized (Jer 8:22). Josephus states that the Essenes experimented with "roots and medicinal stones" for their healing qualities (*War* ii. 8. 6). Mineral springs were widely used medicinally and for hot mineral baths and thermal treatments. The areas around the Dead Sea and the Sea of Galilee are said to have contained several mineral baths that were popular with the ruling class in Palestine during the time of Christ. *See* Disease.

Mediterranean Sea. *See* Great Sea.

Megiddo (mĕ-gĭd'ō), KJV once (Zec 12:11) **Megiddon** (mĕ-gĭd'ŏn). [Heb. *Megiddô* and *Megiddôn*. Spelled *Magiddu* in the *Amarna Letters, *Magidû* in Assyrian texts, and *Mkt(y)* in Egyptian inscriptions.] A strong Canaanite fortress situated at the foot of the Carmel ridge on the northeastern side (Map VI, C-3). Along with the fortress cities of Taanach and Bethshean to the southeast, Megiddo was able to control the whole Plain of Esdraelon, and thus also the trunk roads from Egypt to Syria and Babylonia. It was for this reason that Megiddo played an important role in the history of the New Kingdom of Egypt, when Egypt founded an Asiatic empire. Thutmose III captured the city after a siege in 1482 B.C. The story of its capture is found in a long inscription engraved in the walls of the temple at Karnak in which Thutmose left for

324. The ruin mound of Megiddo

posterity the first detailed battle record of history. The Israelites did not at first conquer the fortress cities of the Plain of Esdraelon (Jos 17:1, 12; Jgs 1:27), and Megiddo remained in Canaanite hands until the 11th cent. B.C., when the Philistines apparently took it over. Not until the reign of David or Solomon did it become a Hebrew city. It was situated in one of Solomon's 12 administrative districts (1 Ki 4:12).

King Shishak of Egypt lists Megiddo among the cities conquered during his military campaign in Palestine. A fragment of his victory monument found in the ruins of the city reveals that he took the city, although, as excavations show, he did not destroy it. About 733 B.C. all Galilee, the Plain of Esdraelon, and the Israelite territories in Transjordan were severed from the kingdom of Israel by Tiglath-pileser III of Assyria, and made into the ·"Province of Megiddo" with Megiddo as resident city of the Assyrian governor (Map XI, C-4). One of these governors, *Ishtu-Adad-aninu,* is known from Assyrian records. The story of Josiah's unsuccessful attempt to stop Pharaoh Necho at Megiddo gives the impression that the city and surrounding area had come into the possession of the kingdom of Judah during Assyria's declining years. The city is not mentioned during the Persian and Hellenistic periods. The Romans built a settlement near there and called it *Legio,* a name still recognizable in the modern village *el-Lejjûn,* lying less than 1 mi. south of Megiddo. The site of ancient Megiddo now bears the name *Tell el-Mutesellim.*

Excavations at Megiddo were carried out by a German pioneering expedition under G. Schumacher from 1903 to 1905, and with more refined methods by an expedition of the University of Chicago under the direction of C. Fisher, P. Guy, and G. Loud from 1925 to 1939. The latter expedition planned to excavate the whole area of the tell (*see* Mound) level by level, but later abandoned this plan as too expensive. Hence, only the 4 upper levels were completely excavated. Of the others only sections were laid bare. In all, 20 levels were discovered in this mound which covered an area of 13 acres. The remains of the city which Thutmose III had conquered in 1482 B.C. were only the 9th level down; this showed that 15th-cent. B.C. Megiddo had already had a long history. The 3 levels above this (VIII-VI from the top) represent the time of Egyptian occupation from the 15th to the 12th cent. B.C. Level V contained poor architectural remains and the typical pottery of the Philistines who seemed to have been in possession during the reign of Saul. Level IV is divided into 2 sublevels by the excavators, IVA (Davidic) and IVB (Solomonic). Recently level IVB has been dated by Y. Yadin in the time of Ahab. Hence in Solomon's or Ahab's time the city was completely rebuilt. New city walls and well-constructed stables for about 500 horses and spacious grounds for 130 chariots were erected. The standard plan of each of the stable units provided entry through double doors from the streets at the ends of the stable units, giving access to a center passageway paved with plaster (see fig. 460). The horses stood on either side of the passageway with their heads toward the center of the building. They were tied to the stone pillars supporting the flat roof. Between the pillars lay hollow stone mangers, 36 in. long (see figs. 236, 316, 460).

The Solomonic level also contained the remains of a fine mansion, probably the residence of the provincial governor, and another building which the excavators believe was the commandant's residence. The northern city gate at this level deserves special mention (fig. 483) because it shows great similarities to the gate buildings described in Ezekiel's vision of

325. Water tunnel at Megiddo, looking east from the well

a temple (Eze 40:20-23). The city seems to have lost its importance shortly after Solomon's time, but revived under Jeroboam II. Level III is attributed to his building activity. This, too, was the city of the Assyrian governor. The next city may have been built by Josiah. After its destruction, Megiddo was no longer a fortress city, but a mere fortified post along the highway, as the excavations of level I show. Between 450 and 350 B.C. the site was finally abandoned.

Among the other important discoveries made during the excavations of Megiddo are: (1) A hoard of exquisite jewelry and a large collection of beautifully carved ivories from the pre-Israelite period, demonstrating the fine artistic taste of the Canaanite craftsmen. (2) An ingenious water system constructed during the pre-Israelite period. From a subterranean spring which lay outside the city's wall a 200-ft.-long tunnel was dug toward the city. This was made accessible to the city by a stairway built in a large vertical well shaft, 83 ft. deep. In this way the people of Megiddo had access to spring water in times of siege. (3) Canaanite temples and many cult objects. (4) A "Shield of David" engraved on a stone block of Solomon's level. (5) Proto-Ionic capitals. See figs. 10, 11, 33, 258, 493.

See Armageddon.

Lit.: Of the German excavations: G. Schumacher, *Tell el-Mutesellim I* (Leipzig, 1908); C. Watzinger, *Tell el-Mutesellim II* (Leipzig, 1929). Of the American excavations, all published at Chicago: C. S. Fisher, *The Excavation of Armageddon* (1929); P. L. O. Guy, *New Light From Armageddon* (1931); H. G. May, *Material Remains of the Megiddo Cult* (1935); R. S. Lamon, *The Megiddo Water System* (1935); P. Guy and R. M. Engberg, *Megiddo Tombs* (1938); R. Lamon and G. M. Shipton, *Megiddo I, Seasons of 1925-1934. Strata I-V* (1939); G. Loud, *Megiddo Ivories* (1939); G. Loud, *Megiddo II, Seasons of 1935-1939* (1948). Good short survey articles are: R. M. Engberg, *BA* 3 (1940), 41-51; 4 (1941), 11-16; G. E. Wright, *BA* 13 (1950), 28-46.

Megiddon. *See* Megiddo.

Mehetabeel. *See* Mehetabel, 2.

Mehetabel (mḗ-hĕt′á-bĕl), KJV once **Mehetabeel** (mḗ-hĕt′á-bēl). [Heb. *Mehêṭab'el,* "God gives benefits."]

1. The wife of Hadar, king of Edom (Gen 36:31, 39; 1 Chr 1:43, 50).

2. The father of Delaiah, 4 (Neh 6:10).

Mehida (mḗ-hī'dȧ). [Heb. *Mechida'*.] The ancestral head of a family of Nethinim, certain members of which returned from Babylonia with Zerubbabel (Ezr 2:1, 52; Neh 7:6, 54).

Mehir (mē'hēr). [Heb. *Mechîr*, "price," or "hire." The name occurs in a similar form in Assyrian as *Maḫur-ili*.] A descendant of Judah (1 Chr 4:1, 11).

Meholathite (mḗ-hō'lȧ-thīt). [Heb. *Mecholathî*.] A native or inhabitant of a place called Meholah (1 Sa 18:19; 2 Sa 21:8), perhaps Abel-meholah, the home of Elisha (1 Ki 19:16).

Mehujael (mḗ-hū'jā-ĕl). [Heb. *Mechîyay'el* (Q *Mechûya'el*), perhaps "smitten of God," or "God gives life."] A great-grandson of Cain, and father of Methushael (Gen 4:18).

Mehuman (mḗ-hū'măn). [Heb. *Mehûman*, probably a Persian name, but of uncertain etymology.] One of the 7 chamberlains of King Ahasuerus (Est 1:10).

Mehunim. *See* Meunim.

Me-jarkon (mē'jär'kŏn). [Heb. *Mê Hayyarqôn*, "green water."] A site in the territory of Dan (Jos 19:40, 46), usually identified with the river that comes from the mountains of Ephraim and enters the Mediterranean Sea about 4 mi. north of Jaffa (Map VI, D-2). At certain times the river water carries a considerable amount of organic soil, which gives it a yellowish color. It is thought that this is responsible for its ancient Hebrew name, meaning "green water." The Arabs call it *Nahr el-'Aujā;* the Israelis, Yarkon (Map XXII, B-2).

Mekonah. *See* Meconah.

Melatiah (mĕl'ȧ-tī'ȧ). [Heb. *Melaṭyah*, "Yahweh delivers."] A Gibeonite who assisted Nehemiah in rebuilding the wall of Jerusalem (Neh 3:7).

Melchi (mĕl'kī). [Gr. *Melchi*, from the Heb. *Malkî*, "my king."] Two Judahites appearing in Luke's genealogy of Jesus Christ (Lk 3:24, 28).

Melchiah. *See* Malchiah, 1.

Melchisedec. *See* Melchizedek.

Melchishua. *See* Malchishua.

Melchizedek (mĕl-kĭz'ĕ-dĕk), KJV of NT **Melchisedec** (mĕl-kĭz'ĕ-dĕk). [Heb. *Malkîṣedeq;* Gr. *Melchizedek*, "my king is righteous" or "my king is righteousness."] The king of Salem, and priest of the most high God who, when Abraham returned from retrieving the captives and spoil carried away by 4 invading kings, met

him, gave him bread and wine and blessed him. On his part Abraham gave him the tithes of all the spoil taken (Gen 14:1, 2, 11-20). The identity of Melchizedek has been much disputed. The Scripture gives little information concerning him. *Salem is most probably an abbreviated form of Jerusalem, as Ps 76:2 indicates. Having been both king of Jerusalem and also priest of the Supreme God of heaven and earth, he is set forth as a type of Christ, who also united the office of king and priest in Himself (Ps 110:2-4; Heb 6:20 to 7:21). See *SDACom* 1:308, 309; 7:439, 440. The statement made in Heb 7:3, that Melchizedek was "without father, without mother, without descent," doubtless means simply that his genealogy was unknown or unrecorded. Such expressions find parallels in extra-Biblical records: (1) Urukagina, one of the early kings of Lagash, said that he had neither father nor mother, but that the god Ningirsu had appointed him as king, by which statement he admitted that he was a usurper and had not inherited his kingship. (2) Abdu-Heba, a king of Jerusalem in the 14th cent., writes in the *Amarna Letters to the Egyptian Pharaoh, "Behold this land of Jerusalem: (It was) not my father (and) not my mother (who) gave (it) to me, (but) the arm of the mighty king (which) gave (it) to me" (*ANET* 488).

Melea (mē'lḗ-ȧ). [Gr. *Melea*, probably from the Heb. *Mele'ah*, "fullness."] A Judahite in Luke's genealogy of Jesus (Lk 3:31).

Melech (mē'lĕk). [Heb. *Melek*, "king."] A descendant of King Saul through Jonathan (1 Chr 8:34, 35; 9:40, 41).

Melicu. *See* Malluch, 2.

Melita. *See* Malta.

Melons. [Heb. *'abaṭṭichîm*.] Most probably the watermelon (*Citrullus vulgaris*), widely cultivated in the Middle East. Its cool refreshment would certainly be missed greatly by a people wandering in the heart of the desert (Num 11:5).

Melzar (mĕl'zär). [Heb. *Melṣar*.] According to the KJV the name of the man put in charge over Daniel and his companions by the chief of the eunuchs (Dan 1:11, 16). However, in Hebrew *melṣar* occurs with the definite article in both passages, which indicates that it is not a personal name. It is most probably the equivalent of the Akkadian *maṣṣāru*, which means "guardian" or "warden." His name is unknown.

Mem. [Heb. *mem*.] The 13th letter of the Hebrew alphabet, written מ, appearing as the title to the 13th section of Ps 119 in the KJV. *See* Aleph.

Memorial. That which reminds of some event, person, etc. Biblical memorials included: the 12 stones from the bed of the Jordan commemorating the parting of that river (Jos 4:3-9); the *Passover feast (Ex 12:12-14; cf. ch 13:7-9); the record of the Amalekite defeat, written down by Moses to remind future generations of the providences of God (ch 17:14; cf. vs 8-13); the 2 stones upon the shoulders of the *ephod of the high priest, and the 12 stones set in the breastplate, upon which were engraved the names of the tribes (ch 28:12, 29; RSV "remembrance"); portions of certain offerings, which were to be burned as a "memorial" to God (Lev 2:2, 9, 16; 5:12; etc.), probably to remind the offerer of God's claims upon him; the observance of the ordinances of the Lord's Supper, which keeps ever before the believer the import of Christ's death, resurrection, and near return (Lk 22:17-19; 1 Cor 11:23-26). Christ predicted that the remembrance of His anointing by a certain woman would serve as a perpetual memorial to her (Mt 26:13; RSV "memory"). The Sabbath is God's specially designated memorial of the relationship between the Creator-God and those loyal to His plan and purpose (Ex 20:8-10; 31:13; Eze 31:16, 17).

Memphis (mĕm'fĭs), KJV generally **Noph** (nŏf). [Heb. *Noph,* once (better) *Moph;* Egyptian *Mn-nfr;* in Assyrian inscriptions *Mempi* and *Mimpi*.] One of the famous capitals of Egypt, whose site lies near the modern city of Cairo, on the western bank of the Nile, a few mi. south of the apex of the Delta (Map V, C-3). Originally it was the name of both the pyramid and the pyramid city of Pepi I at *Saqqârah* (meaning "[Pepi is] remaining beautiful"). Until the founding of Alexandria, Memphis was one of the most important cities in Egypt. As is the case with many

326. Excavations at the site of ancient Memphis

327. The sphinx of Memphis

other ancient cities, little of Memphis has been preserved. Its few remaining ruins lie near the village of *Mit Rahineh.* However, the necropolis, the cemetery of Memphis, with its many pyramids, tomb structures, mortuary temples, and the famous sphinx, spreads for about 25 mi., from *Abu-roâsh* in the north to Dahshur in the south, *Gîzeh* and *Saqqârah* being the most famous sections. Memphis was the royal residence during the Old Kingdom, and was later the capital of Lower Egypt. The city's main temple was dedicated to Ptah, always one of Egypt's most famous deities. Ptah was represented by the sacred bull Apis, that is, a succession of living Apis bulls, each of which was buried after it died in the extensive tomb vaults of the Serapeum at *Saqqârah.* The Memphite teaching about creation was contained in the so-called Monument of Memphite Theology, which is preserved in a copy dating from the 25th dynasty, made from a badly worn manuscript of the Old Kingdom. It makes Ptah the creator god. He was believed to have created the physical world and established world order by means of his heart and tongue, which means through thought and word. The Memphite creation concept is thus higher than that of the earlier Egyptian tradition of creation, according to which the hand and reproductive organ of the creating god is put above the power of the mind. The greatest builder in the later period of the city was Ramses II; also his son Merneptah had a palace in Memphis, as well as Apries (the Biblical Pharaoh Hophra). The city was conquered about 730 B.C. by the Nubian king Piankhi, later by Esarhaddon in 670 B.C., then by Ashurbanipal in 664, and by Cambyses in 525 B.C. Foreigners settled in Memphis from the 7th cent. B.C. on. Among them were Jews who went there after the destruction of Jerusalem (Jer 44:1). The city is frequently mentioned by the prophets (Is 19:13; Jer 2:16; 44:1; 46:14, 19; Eze 30:13; Hos 9:6, where the Hebrew text has *Moph*).

Memucan (mē̆-mū′kăn). [Heb. *Memûkan*, probably a Persian name, but its etymology is uncertain.] One of the 7 princes of the Persian Empire who had free access to the presence of King Ahasuerus (Xerxes) (Est 1:14, 16, 21).

Men of the East. *See* People of the East.

Menahem (mĕn′ȧ-hĕm). [Heb. *Menachem*, "comforter," written *Menihimme* in cuneiform inscriptions. The name occurs also in Egyptian records, on ancient Hebrew seals and an Aramaic ostracon found at Calah.] The 17th king of the northern kingdom of Israel (if Tibni is included in the count), who reigned for 10 years (*c.* 752 - *c.* 742 B.C.). He was probably governor of Tirzah when Shallum, after assassinating Zechariah (probably at Ibleam), made himself king in Samaria. Menahem at once set out for the capital, slew Shallum, and made himself king (2 Ki 15:8-10, 13, 14). To gain Assyrian support for his uncertain position he paid a heavy tribute of 1,000 talents of silver to Tiglath-pileser III (called *Pul in v 19). He raised the money by taxing 60,000 wealthy men of Israel to the amount of 50 shekels each (vs 19, 20). The payment of this tribute is mentioned in a cuneiform display inscription of Tiglath-pileser excavated at Calah (*ANET* 283). King Menahem was evil like his precursors (v 18). At Tiphsah he committed a most atrocious act. The citizens of that place did not want to accept him as king, so he captured the city, killed all the men, and ripped open all pregnant women (v 16).

Menan. *See* Menna.

Mene. One of the words in the inscription that appeared on the wall of King Belshazzar's palace during a feast on the night of Babylon's fall (Dan 5:25). The complete inscription read "mene, mene, tekel, upharsin," which is a transliteration of the Aramaic *mene' mene' teqel ûpharsîn*. *Mene'* is a form of the verb "to number," and means "numbered." *Teqel* is related to a verb meaning "to weigh" and the consonantal Aramaic term may be translated "weighed." The *û* in *ûpharsîn* is an Aramaic conjunction meaning "and," and when detached from *ûpharsîn* the *pharsîn* becomes *parsîn* (RSV "parsin"). *Parsîn* is the plural of *peres* and means "pieces."

The message may thus be interpreted as "numbered, numbered, weighed, pieces." This cryptic communication, even if it could be deciphered, required an interpreter, and Daniel was eventually summoned to interpret the divine message. To *mene'* he gave the interpretation "God hath numbered thy kingdom, and finished it," to *teqel*, "Thou art weighed in the balances, and art found wanting," and to *peres*, "Thy kingdom is divided, and given to the Medes and Persians."

According to the record, the wise men of Babylon could not read the writing (Dan 5:8). The reason is not given, and any explanation is only conjecture. The inscription was apparently in Aramaic, but as noted above, even an understanding of the meaning of the 3 words would not interpret their meaning. See *SDACom* 4:803-805.

Menna (mĕn′ȧ), KJV **Menan** (mē′năn). [Gr. *Menna* (some manuscripts *Maïnan*). The Hebrew equivalent is not known.] A Judahite appearing in Luke's genealogy of Jesus Christ (Lk 3:31).

Menuhoth (mē̆-nū′hŏth). [Heb. *Menuchôth*, "resting places."] A name appearing in the RSV of 1 Chr 2:52 in the phrase "half of the Menuhoth." The reference is obviously to half of the inhabitants of a certain place, which, however, cannot be identified. These inhabitants were Judahites, descended from Caleb through Shobal. Instead of "Menuhoth" the KJV reads "Manahethites," obviously from a comparison with v 54, apparently believing that the other half of the inhabitants of the unidentified place are there described. The Hebrew terms in the 2 verses are from the same root, but are not quite identical, so that the identity of the 2 names cannot be established.

Meonenim (mē̆-ŏn′ē-nĭm). [Heb. *Me'ônenîm*, "soothsayers."] According to the KJV the name of a plain near Shechem (Jgs 9:37). However, the Heb. *'elôn*, translated "plain," properly means a large tree, such as an oak, and thus the name *Me'ônenîm* is that of a tree, not of a plain. The RSV calls it "Diviners' Oak," preferring to translate rather than transliterate *Me'ônenîm*. The site of this tree has not been identified.

Meonothai (mē̆-ŏn′ō-thī). [Heb. *Me'ônothay*, "my habitations."] A Judahite and ancestral head of the inhabitants of Ophrah (1 Chr 4:14).

Mephaath (mĕf′ȧ-ăth). [Heb. *Mêpha'ath*, "splendor."] A town in Transjordan, in the territory of Reuben (Jos 13:15, 18), assigned to the Merarite Levites as one of their residence cities (Jos 21:34, 37; 1 Chr 6:77, 79). Mephaath, with other Reubenite cities, was later occupied by the Moabites and was in their hands in the time of Jeremiah (Jer 48:21). It has been tentatively identified with *Tell ej-Jâwah*, 6½ mi. south of Amman.

Mephibosheth (mĕ-fĭb′ŏ-shĕth). [Heb. *Mephibosheth*, possibly "he who scatters shame."]

1. A son of King Saul by Rizpah, the daughter of Aiah. He was one of those executed at the demand of the Gibeonites as expiation for Saul's crime toward them (2 Sa 21:9).

2. Son of Jonathan. His original name was apparently Merib-baal (mĕr′ĭb-bā′ăl) [Heb. *Meribba'al*, "Baal is an advocate" or "hero of Baal"] (1 Chr 8:34; 9:40). A reaction to Baal-names among the Hebrews probably was the reason why his name was changed to Mephibosheth. He was only 5 years of age when his father and grandfather died in the battle of Gilboa. When the news of this catastrophe reached the court his nurse took him and fled, but during the flight he fell and was lamed for life (2 Sa 4:4). For a time he lived in Transjordan at Lo-debar, but when David learned of his whereabouts he brought him to Jerusalem, and in memory of his friendship to the boy's father made him a member of the official court family. He also restored the estates of Saul and Jonathan to him, placing them under the administration of Ziba, Saul's former steward (ch 9:3-13). During the rebellion of Absalom, Mephibosheth remained in Jerusalem and was accused by Ziba of having joined the rebellion. Consequently David gave Ziba all the property of his master (ch 16:1-4). Upon David's return, Mephibosheth defended his innocence, and half of his property was restored (ch 19:24-30). When seven of Saul's descendants were executed to revenge Saul's unjustified massacre of the Gibeonites, David spared Mephibosheth for the sake of Jonathan (ch 21:7). Mephibosheth had a son, Mica, through whom Saul's family was continued (2 Sa 9:12; 1 Chr 8:34-40; 9:40-44).

Merab (mē′răb). [Heb. *Merab*, meaning uncertain.] The elder daughter of Saul (1 Sa 14:49), promised as wife to David (ch 18:17) but given to Adriel (v 19). The 5 sons of Merab and Adriel were among those given up to the Gibeonites by David to be put to death for Saul's unjustified massacre of some of that people (2 Sa

21:8). The "Michal" of v 8, KJV, should be read "Merab" in harmony with 2 Hebrew manuscripts, Lucian's recension of the LXX, and the Syriac; Michal was childless (ch 6:23).

Meraiah (mē-rā′yȧ). [Heb. *Merayah*, probably "rebellious," or if the first part of the name is a loan word from the Egyptian *mr*, "beloved," the name possibly meant "beloved by Yahweh."] The head of the priestly house of Seraiah in the time of Joiakim (Neh 12:12).

Meraioth (mē-rā′yŏth). [Heb. *Merayôth*, probably "rebellions."]

1. A priest descended from Aaron through Eleazar (1 Chr 6:4-7). He probably did not officiate, since he seems to have lived in the days when the house of Eli, descended from Ithamar, served at the tabernacle.

2. An Aaronic priest, son of Ahitub and probably high priest, who lived not long before the Exile (1 Chr 6:11; Neh 11:11).

3. A priestly house in the days of the high priest Joiakim (Neh 12:15). This Meraioth is considered by some to be a scribal error for Meremoth (v 3). See Meremoth, 1.

Merari (mē-rā′rī). [Heb. *Merari*. The name is probably of Egyptian origin (*Mrry*) and means "beloved."] The 3d and youngest son of Levi (Gen 46:11; Ex 6:16), and ancestor of one of the 3 Levitical families (Num 26:57).

Merarites (mē-rā′rīts). [Heb. *Merari*.] The descendants of Levi's youngest son, Merari, and one of the 3 chief families of the Levites (Num 3:17; 4:29; 26:57; 1 Chr 6:1; 9:14). The family was subdivided into 2 divisions according to the 2 sons of Merari, Mahli and Mushi (Num 3:20, 33). In the wilderness the Merarites camped north (see fig. 92) of the tabernacle (vs 35, 36), and when Israel was on the move this family transported the boards, bars, pillars, sockets, and utensils, for which 4 carts and 8 oxen were provided (chs 4:29-33; 7:8). They performed their service under the direction of Ithamar, the youngest son of Aaron (ch 4:31). At the time the census of chs 3:33, 34; 4:42-45 was taken, the Merarites proved to be the smallest of the Levitical families, having 6,200 males from a month old and upward, of whom 3,200 were from 30 to 60 years of age. During the distribution of Canaan, 12 cities were assigned to the Merarite Levites as residence cities, 4 of which were in the territory of the tribe of Zebulun, 4 in that of Reuben, and 4 in that of Gad (Jos 21:34-40; 1 Chr 6:63, 77-81). One of these, Ramoth-gilead, was a city of refuge (Deut 4:41-43; Jos 20:2, 8, 9). David reorganized the Merarites, along with the rest of the Levites, for the Temple service (1 Chr 23:6, 21-23). Merarite Levites are mentioned as helpers in King Hezekiah's religious reformation (2 Chr 29:12), and as being among the exiles who returned from Babylonia with Ezra in the time of Artaxerxes (Ezr 8:1, 18, 19).

Merathaim (mĕr'à-thā'ĭm). [Heb. *Merathayim*, "double rebellion."] A symbolical name for Babylon used by Jeremiah (Jer 50:21; cf. vs 18, 23). It is thought that this name is an adaptation of *Marratim*, the Akkadian name of a large lagoon in southern Babylonia.

Mercurius. *See* Hermes.

Mercy Seat. [Heb. *kapporeth*, "covering"; Gr. *hilastērion*, "a means (or place) of reconciliation."] The lid, or covering, of the ark of the covenant, beneath which were deposited the tables of the law (Ex 25:17; Deut 10:2). The law and the gospel— divine justice and mercy—were thus closely associated in the ancient sanctuary service. The "mercy seat" was, of course, the literal lid or "covering" for the ark, but *kapporeth* implied much more, as the frequent use of the related verb form *kaphar*, "to cover," meaning "to make atonement" or "to make reconciliation," makes evident. Above the mercy seat appeared the Shekinah glory, the visible token of God's presence among His people (see Heb 8:5). The mercy seat and the tables of law beneath it represented the fundamental principles of God's dealings with His people—justice tempered with mercy. Once a year, on the great Day of Atonement, the high priest entered the Most Holy Place with sacrificial blood, first for himself and then for the people, which he sprinkled before the mercy seat, in the hope that God would accept the vicarious blood of reconciliation as evidence of their confession of sin, and grant them mercy. *See* Atonement, Day of.

Substantiation for the meaning "covering" for *kapporeth* has recently come from Cave 4 at Qumran, by the rendering, in an Aramaic translation of Leviticus, of *kapporeth* as *ksy'*, "covering" (J. T. Milik, *Ten Years of Discovery in the Wilderness of Judaea* [London, 1959], p. 31).

Mered (mē'rĕd). [Heb. *Mered*, "rebellion."] A Judahite who had 2 wives, one a Hebrew, the other the daughter of a Pharaoh (1 Chr 4:17-19).

Meremoth (mĕr'ĕ-mŏth). [Heb. *Meremôth*, "elevations."]

1. One of the leading priests who returned from Babylonia with Zerubbabel (Neh 12:1, 3, 7). In the following generation a priestly house is mentioned in the corresponding position in the list given in vs 12-21 by the name of Meraioth (v 15). It is therefore thought that Meraioth is possibly a variant spelling of Meremoth, which could have occurred through the inadvertent substitution of the letter *y* for *m* in the Hebrew.

2. A priest, son of Uriah, who was in charge of weighing the treasures which Ezra brought from Babylonia (Ezr 8:33, 34). He also assisted Nehemiah in the rebuilding of the wall of Jerusalem by repairing 2 wall sections (Neh 3:4, 21). Possibly identical with Meremoth, 4.

3. A Jew married to a foreign wife in the time of Ezra (Ezr 10:34, 36).

4. A Jew, probably a priest, who set his seal to Nehemiah's covenant (Neh 10:5), possibly identical with Meremoth, 2.

Meres (mē'rēz). [Heb. *Meres*, probably a Persian name, but of uncertain etymology.] One of the 7 princes of the Persian Empire who had free access to King Ahasuerus (Est 1:14).

Meribah (mĕr'ĭ-bà). [Heb. *Meribah*, "strife."]

1. One of 2 names given by Moses to a place near Horeb where the children of Israel murmured against him when in need of water and where, at God's direction, he struck a rock from which, in consequence, water flowed (Ex 17:1-7). It is uncertain whether Deut 33:8 and Ps 95:8 refer to this Meribah or to Meribah, 2. *See* Massah.

2. A place at or near Kadesh-barnea in the Wilderness of Zin, where an incident similar to that in Meribah, 1, occurred. Again water was miraculously produced from a rock, although Moses did not follow God's instruction exactly and as a consequence was not permitted to enter Canaan (Num 20:2-13, 23, 24; 27:12-14; Deut 32:48-51). The waters of this place are mentioned as "waters of Meribah" in Ps 106:32, RSV, and as "the waters of Meribath-kadesh" (mer'ĭ-băth-kā'desh) [Heb. *Meribath Qadesh*, "the strife of Kadesh"] in Eze 47:19 and 48:28, RSV. In his visions Ezekiel refers to this site as the southern limit of the ideal land of restored Israel. It is uncertain whether Deut 33:8 and Ps 95:8 refer to this Meribah or to Meribah, 1.

Meribath-kadesh. *See* Meribah, 2.

Merib-baal. *See* Mephibosheth, 2.

Merodach (mĕ-rō'dăk). [Heb. *Merodak.*] The Babylonian god Marduk (Jer 50:2). *See* Bel.

Merodach-baladan (mĕ-rō'dăk-băl'*a̅*-dăn), KJV once **Berodach-baladan** (bĕ-rō'dăk-băl'*a̅*-dăn). [Heb. *Merodak bal'adan* and *Bero'dak bal'adan;* Akkadian *Marduk-apal-idin,* "Marduk has given a son."] The son of Baladan and for a time king of Babylon. It was he who sent an embassy to Hezekiah congratulating him on his recovery from a mortal disease (2 Ki 20:12-19; Is 39:1-8; cf. 2 Chr 32:31). Merodach-baladan is a well-known figure from Assyrian records. He was a native and chieftain of a Chaldean tribe, called *Bît Yakin,* which lived around the mouth of the Euphrates at the Persian Gulf. Merodach-baladan appears first in the Assyrian annals about 731 B.C., when he paid homage and a great tribute to Tiglath-pileser III of Assyria (Luckenbill, *AR* I, 794). Shortly after the death of Shalmaneser V, Merodach-baladan took Babylon and made himself king, holding the throne for nearly 12 years (approximately 721-709 B.C.), according to the canon of Ptolemy and a Babylonian king list. Sargon II, the successor of Shalmaneser V, had suffered a defeat from the Elamites shortly after his accession to the throne, and was therefore forced to recognize Merodach-baladan as king of Babylon. However, in 709 B.C. Sargon felt strong enough to march against Babylon, and took the city, Merodach-

328. Monument of Merodach-baladan, king of Babylon (left)

baladan having fled. When Sargon fought against *Bît Yakin* a little later, Merodach-baladan was captured, but was restored to his kingship over his native tribe. Merodach-baladan again made himself king of Babylon in 703, using the city of Borsippa as his residence. But he could hold out for only about 9 months, after which he was driven away by Sennacherib, the son and successor of Sargon II. When Sennacherib continued his campaign toward the south against *Bît Yakin,* Merodach-baladan fled to the Elamites and from there organized resistance against the Assyrians. It was probably during this time that he sent his ambassadors to Hezekiah, ostensibly to congratulate him upon his recovery, but more likely with the object of concluding a treaty with him against the Assyrians. To impress the envoys of the ex-Babylonian king with his strength, Hezekiah showed them his arsenal and his financial resources, which action was strongly rebuked by the prophet Isaiah (Is 39:1-8).

Merom (mē'rŏm), **Waters of.** [Heb. *Merôm.*] The site where Joshua defeated Jabin, king of Hazor, and his allies (Jos 11:1-7). For 2 cent. the "waters of Merom" have been identified with Lake Huleh on the upper Jordan (Map XX, A-3), called Lake Semechonitis (Map VI, B-4) by Josephus (*Ant.* v. 5. 1; *War* iv. 1. 1). This lake (now drained) was about 3 mi. long and 2 mi. wide in its northern part, and had a maximum depth of 16 ft. and a surface about 690 ft. above that of the Sea of Galilee, only about 10 mi. south of it. This identification with Lake Huleh was so generally accepted by interpreters that some maps contain the name Merom for Lake Huleh. However, in recent years many scholars have doubted this identification. They have pointed out that Merom, which appears in the list of Palestinian cities conquered by Thutmose III as *Mrm,* is an archaic form for Meron (LXX *Marōn*), a place known today as *Meirôn* in the *Wâdi Meirôn,* 10½ mi. northwest of Capernaum (Map VI, C-3). A powerful spring provides abundant water that flows down through the *Wâdi Meirôn* to the Sea of Galilee. This would identify Joshua's battlefield as the plain in the vicinity of these waters at *Meirôn.*

Meronothite (mĕ-rŏn'ō-thīt). [Heb. *Merono-thî.*] The designation of 2 men, Jehdeiah and Jadon (1 Chr 27:30; Neh 3:7), but a place by the name of Meronoth remains unidentified.

Meroz (mē'rŏz). [Heb. *Merôz*.] A village that was cursed by an angel because it failed to help Israel against Sisera (Jgs 5:23). This curse may imply that the inhabitants allowed Sisera to pass through unmolested, or, as some have suggested, they may have aided him against Israel. Attempts have been made to identify the place, but so far carry no conviction.

Mesech. *See* Meshech.

Mesha, I (mē'shȧ). [Heb. *Mêsha'*, "deliverance."]

1. According to the KJV, a Judahite through Caleb, and ancestor of the inhabitants of Ziph (1 Chr 2:42). The RSV on the basis of the LXX reads Mareshah instead of Mesha.

2. King of Moab, spelled *Msh'* on the Moabite Stone. His father and predecessor, Kemosh-melek, had been made a vassal of Israel when Omri, king of Israel (*c*. 885 - *c*. 874 B.C.), conquered Moab, and he himself, being rich in flocks, paid an annual tribute of 100,000 lambs and the wool of 100,000 rams (2 Ki 3:4). After the death of Ahab (853 B.C.), Mesha renounced his allegiance to Israel (chs 1:1; 3:5). Ahab's son, Joram, or Jehoram, attempted to bring Moab back into subjection after he came to the throne of Israel. He succeeded in winning Jehoshaphat of Judah and an unnamed king of Edom as allies for his campaign (ch 3:6-9). Instead of taking the ordinary invasion route via Gilead, the allied kings planned to attack Moab from the south, marching through Edom south of the Dead Sea. In this dry area their armies suffered from lack of water and almost perished. Elisha, who may have been with the army, was consulted. He ordered that trenches be dug, and predicted that water would be provided. The next morning water rushed down through the valley and filled the trenches. The Lord may have provided the water through a flash flood. Flash floods are known to occur in that country and to come so suddenly that Bedouins encamped in the valleys have been drowned. To the waiting Moabites, the water appeared reddish in the morning sun. They thought that it was colored by blood, and concluded that the confederates had been quarreling among themselves and had turned their swords against one another. They consequently advanced carelessly only to be beaten by the allies. The victorious armies thereupon entered the land of Moab, destroyed its cities, and besieged Kir-haraseth (now *el-Kerak*), into which Mesha had re-

treated with the remnants of his army. Mesha made an attempt to break through the lines of the besiegers, but failed. In desperation he sacrificed his eldest son as a burnt offering upon the wall of Kir-hareseth in full view of friend and foe. The besiegers thereupon gave up their efforts to take the city and returned to their land (vs 8-27). The reason for the lifting of the siege which promised to be successful is not clear. The words "there was great indignation against Israel" (v 27) may be variously interpreted. One suggestion is that the great sacrifice made by Mesha may have aroused the Moabites to such horrified wrath as to give them superhuman strength to defeat the Israelites. Another is that the forces of the allies may have experienced some calamity, such as an outbreak of disease, which they interpreted as a sign of God's displeasure with their campaign. A third is that it was simply from fear that the besiegers relinquished their efforts to take the city. Mesha's own record on the Moabite Stone does not refer to this campaign at all, but restricts its narrative to his rebellion and his successes in occupying territories which had been in the possession of Israel. *See* Moabite Stone.

Shortly afterward, it seems, the Moabites, Ammonites, and Edomites invaded Judah. In response to a cry for help the Lord intervened, causing the enemy nations to destroy one another, and providing King Jehoshaphat of Judah an easy victory (2 Chr 20:22-25).

Mesha, II (mē'shȧ). [Heb. *Mesha'*.] A Benjamite, son of Shaharaim by his wife Hodesh (1 Chr 8:8, 9).

Mesha, III (mē'shȧ). [Heb. *Mêsha'*.] A place in Arabia which marked the boundary of the Arabic Joktan tribes (Gen 10:30); not identified with certainty. Some think it to be *Mesene* at the northwestern end of the Persian Gulf, others tentatively place it elsewhere in Arabia.

Meshach (mē'shăk). [Heb. and Aramaic *Mêshak*.] The Babylonian name of Mishael, one of Daniel's 3 companions (Dan 1:7; 2:49; 3:12-30). All attempts to explain the name, which does not seem to be of Babylonian origin, have so far failed.

Meshech (mē'shĕk), KJV once **Mesech** (mē'sĕk). [Heb. *Meshek*.] A son of Japheth (Gen 10:2; 1 Chr 1:5), and ancestor of a people mentioned by Ezekiel along with the descendants of Tubal, another son of Japheth (Eze 32:26; 38:2, 3; 39:1). They appear as traders in the Tyrian markets in slaves and vessels of bronze

(Eze 27:13). In Ps 120:5 they are mentioned as apparently connected in some way with the people of Kedar. The Assyrian inscriptions mention them from the 12th cent. B.C. on as *Mushku.* They also mention *Tabal,* which is recognized as Tubal. The records of Tiglath-pileser I (1113-1074 B.C.) and Shalmaneser III (859-824 B.C.) show the *Mushku* as a nation situated in northern Mesopotamia. From there they moved to Phrygia in Asia Minor (Map IV, B-5), and while here, under their king Mita, they made war on Sargon II (8th cent. B.C.). Mita was appealed to for help, but in vain, by the last king of Carchemish in his struggle against the Assyrians. After ruling over northern Anatolia for a time, the *Mushku* lost this area, first to the Cimmerians and then to the Lydians. Herodotus calls them *Moschoi,* and their brother nation, *Tubal,* he calls *Tibarēnoi* (Herod. iii. 94; vii. 78; see also Pliny *Hist. Nat.* vi. 4; Strabo xi. 2. 14-17).

For the "Meshech" of 1 Chr 1:17, *see* Mash.

Meshelemiah (mĕ-shĕl'ĕ-mī'ă). [Heb. *Meshelemyah* and *Meshelemyahû,* "Yahweh has recompensed."] The head of a family of Korahite Levites who were gatekeepers at the Temple (1 Chr 9:21, 23; 26:1, 2, 9), called Shelemiah in ch 26:14.

Meshezabeel. *See* Meshezabel.

Meshezabel (mĕ-shĕz'ă-bĕl), KJV **Meshezabeel** (mĕ-shĕz'ă-bēl). [Heb. *Meshêzab'el,* "God delivers."]

1. A man whose grandson Meshullam assisted Nehemiah in rebuilding the wall of Jerusalem (Neh 3:4).

2. A Jew who set his seal to Nehemiah's covenant (Neh 10:21).

3. A man whose son Pethahiah was representative of the people of Judah at the Persian court (Neh 11:24).

Meshillemith. *See* Meshillemoth, 2.

Meshillemoth (mĕ-shĭl'ĕ-mŏth). [Heb. *Meshillemôth,* "restitutions."]

1. An Ephraimite whose son Berechiah used his influence for the release of the Judahite captives brought to Israel by King Pekah's army (2 Chr 28:12-14).

2. A priest of the house of Immer (Neh 11:13), probably the Meshillemith (mĕ-shĭl'ĕ-mĭth) of 1 Chr 9:12.

Meshobab (mĕ-shō'băb). [Heb. *Meshôbab,* "returned," or "converted."] A prince of the tribe of Simeon who joined with other tribal princes and seized the pasture lands of Gedor (1 Chr 4:24, 34-41).

Meshullam (mĕ-shŭl'ăm). [Heb. *Meshullam,*

"recompensed." The name occurs in several ancient Hebrew seal inscriptions.]

1. A Benjamite family head who lived in Jerusalem (1 Chr 8:17, 28).

2. A Gadite enrolled in a genealogy in the days of Jotham of Judah and in the days of King Jeroboam II of Israel (1 Chr 5:13, 17).

3. A man whose grandson Shaphan was a scribe during the reign of King Josiah (2 Ki 22:3, 8).

4. A priest, son of Zadok and father of Hilkiah (1 Chr 9:11; Neh 11:11). He is probably the Shallum of Ezr 7:2 and 1 Chr 6:12, 13. *See* Shallum, 7.

5. A priest of the house of Immer (1 Chr 9:12).

6. A Kohathite Levite, one of the superintendents over the workmen who repaired the Temple in Josiah's time (2 Chr 34:12).

7. A son of Zerubbabel (1 Chr 3:19).

8. A Benjamite, father of Sallu (1 Chr 9:7; Neh 11:7).

9. Another Benjamite, son of Shephatiah (1 Chr 9:8).

10. A chief man among the exiles in Babylonia who helped Ezra to secure some Levites to accompany them to Jerusalem (Ezr 8:16; cf. vs 15, 17-20).

11. One of the Jews who opposed Ezra's method of putting away the foreign wives (Ezr 10:15).

12. A member of the family of Bani. He was married to a foreign wife in the time of Ezra (Ezr 10:29).

13. A son of Berechiah. He assisted Nehemiah in rebuilding the wall of Jerusalem by repairing 2 wall sections (Neh 3:4, 30). His daughter was married to Jehohanan, the son of Tobiah, Nehemiah's enemy (ch 6:18; cf. v 1).

14. A son of Besodeiah. He repaired the Old Gate with Joiada, or Jehoiada, in Nehemiah's time (Neh 3:6).

15. One who stood at the left of Ezra when the Law was read (Neh 8:4).

16 and 17. Two men, chiefs of the people, who set their seals to Nehemiah's covenant (Neh 10:7, 20).

18. A prince of Judah who took part in the dedication of the wall of Jerusalem in the time of Nehemiah (Neh 12:29, 33).

19 and 20. Two heads of families of priests in the days of the high priest.Joiakim. One was of the house of Ezra and the other of the house of Ginnethon (Neh 12:12, 13, 16).

21. A Levite gatekeeper in the days of the high priest Joiakim (Neh 12:25).

Several of the Meshullams who were contemporaries of Nehemiah are possibly identical.

Meshullemeth (mĕ-shŭl′ĕ-mĕth). [Heb. *Meshullemeth*, the feminine form of *Meshullam*, "Meshullam," "restitution."] Wife of King Manasseh of Judah and mother of King Amon (2 Ki 21:19).

Mesobaite. *See* Mezobaite.

Mesopotamia (mĕs′ȯ-pȯ-tā′mĭ-ȧ). [Gr. *Mesopotamia*, "between the rivers." A term taken over from the LXX by the KJV as the rendering of the Heb. *'Aram-Naharayim. See* Aram, 5.] As used subsequent to Alexander the Great's victories in that area, the whole valley of the Euphrates and Tigris, including their tributaries; a territory that was bounded by the Zagros Mountains in the east, the Persian Gulf in the south, the Taurus Mountains in the north, and the desert in the west. However, the Hebrew term *'Aram-Naharayim*, translated "Mesopotamia" in Gen 24:10; Deut 23:4; Jgs 3:8, 10; 1 Chr 19:6, designates no more than Upper Mesopotamia, the region lying between the great bend of the Euphrates, the Khabur River, and the upper Tigris. Hence the rendering "Mesopotamia" in the OT may be misleading. In the NT the name Mesopotamia is used as employed by the Greek and Roman writers, as including the whole country. For example, Stephen places Ur of the Chaldees in Mesopotamia (Acts 7:2). Some inhabitants of Mesopotamia, either Jews or proselytes, were present on the day of Pentecost, when the Holy Spirit was poured out on the apostles (ch 2:9).

Messiah (mĕ-sī′ȧ), KJV of NT Messias (mĕ-sī′ȧs). [Heb. *Mashiach*, "an anointed one," from *mashach*, "to anoint"; Gr. *Messias*, a transliteration of the Hebrew form.] A title of the expected king and deliverer of Israel, appearing only in Dan 9:25, 26, KJV; Jn 1:41; 4:25. Not all scholars accept the Daniel passages as referring to the expected Messiah. However, many conservative Christians regard this passage as a prediction of the time that the Messiah would do His appointed work at the end of the specified period.

The Hebrew term *mashiach* occurs 39 times in the OT and is variously applied to the kings of Israel as the anointed of the Lord (1 Sa 24:6; 2 Sa 19:21; 2 Chr 6:42; etc.); to Cyrus, king of Persia (Is 45:1); to the high priest (Lev 4:3, 5; etc.); and to the expected king and deliverer of Israel (Dan 9:25, 26). The LXX generally

translates this term *Christos,* from *chriō,* "to anoint," hence "an anointed one." It is this term that occurs hundreds of times in the NT, and is transliterated "Christ" (see Jn 1:41). Thus, although the word *Messias,* "Messiah," is extremely rare in the NT, the translated form *Christos,* "Christ," is very frequent. *See* Christ.

Messias. *See* Messiah.

Meteyard. A rendering of the Heb. *middah* (Lev 19:35, KJV), translated "measures of length" in the RSV. Meteyard is an archaic term meaning measuring stick.

Metheg-ammah. *See* Methegh-ammah.

Methegh-ammah (mē′thĕg-ăm′ȧ), KJV **Metheg-ammah** (mē′thĕg-ăm′ȧ). [Heb. *Metheg ha'ammah,* "the bridle of the mother city," or "the bridle of the dwarfs."] An expression occuring in 2 Sa 8:1 in a reference to David's capture of an important city. The parallel text, 1 Chr 18:1, RSV, says that David took "Gath and its villages out of the hand of the Philistines." Hence most commentators believe that the obscure "bridle of the mother city" is a poetical term for Gath, a mother city, or metropolis, of the Philistines. (See W. F. Albright, *IEJ* 4 [1954], 3.)

Methusael. *See* Methushael.

Methuselah (mĕ-thū′zĕ-lȧ), KJV of NT **Mathusala** (mȧ-thū′sȧ-lȧ). [Heb. *Methúshelach;* Gr. *Mathousala,* possibly "man of the javelin."] An antediluvian patriarch of Seth's line. He was son of Enoch and the father of Lamech. His age of 969 years is greater than that recorded of any other man (Gen 5:21-27; Lk 3:37).

Methushael (mĕ-thū′shȧ-ĕl), KJV **Methusael** (mĕ-thū′sȧ-ĕl). [Heb. *Methúsha'el,* "man of God," comparable to the Akkadian *Mutum-ilum.*] One of the descendants of Cain (Gen 4:18).

Meunim (mĕ-ū′nĭm), KJV once **Mehunim** (mĕ-hū′nĭm), or **Meunites** (mĕ-ū′nīts), KJV once **Mehunims** (mĕ-hū′nĭmz). [Heb. *Me'únim.*] An Arabic tribe, south of Judah, near Edom, probably the inhabitants of *Ma'an,* a city about 19 mi. southeast of Petra (Map V, B-7). Some believe that they are mentioned first in the Bible in Jgs 10:12, under the name of Maonites, as an enemy of Israel of long standing. In the days of Jehoshaphat the Meunites joined the Ammonites and Moabites in an unsuccessful attack on Judah (2 Chr 20:1, RSV; see *SDACom* 3:263). They also warred against Uzziah (ch 26:7). A part of the Meunim were exterminated by the Simeonites near Gedor, where they dwelt as strangers in the days of Hezekiah

(1 Chr 4:39-41, RSV; for "Meunim" the KJV here reads "habitations"). Some of the "sons of Meunim," probably prisoners of war, seem to have become Temple servants, and their descendants are mentioned among the exiles returned from Babylonia with Zerubbabel (Ezr 2:50; Neh 7:52). The LXX calls the Meunim *Minaioi,* "Minaeans." If this identification is correct, the Meunim are a northern branch of the South Arabic Minaeans.

Meunites. *See* Meunim.

Mezahab (měz′à-hăb). [Heb. *Mê Zahab,* "waters of gold."] Either the ancestor of Mehetabel, wife of King Hadar of Edom, or a place from which her ancestors originated, which has not, however, been identified (Gen 36:39; 1 Chr 1:50).

Mezobaite (mě-zō′bà-ĭt), KJV **Mesobaite** (mě-sō′bà-ĭt). [Heb. *Meṣobayah,* meaning obscure.] An inhabitant of a town possibly called Mezoba or Mezobai, or a descendant of a man of that name (1 Chr 11:47). Most commentators consider the text in error here.

Miamin. *See* Mijamin.

Mibhar (mĭb′här). [Heb. *Mibchar,* "choice."] One of David's "mighty men," the son of Hagri, according to 1 Chr 11:38. The parallel text in 2 Sa 23:36, however, reads "of Zobah" instead of "Mibhar." The 2 expressions are very similar in Hebrew. Furthermore, instead of "the son of" (1 Chr 11:38), 2 Sa 23:36 reads "Bani," the Hebrew of the 2 expressions again being very similar. The Samuel passage is probably the better reading of the two.

Mibsam (mĭb′săm). [Heb. *Mibsam,* "balsam."]
1. A son of Ishmael and ancestor of an Arabic tribe (Gen 25:13; 1 Chr 1:29); otherwise unknown.
2. A Simeonite (1 Chr 4:25).

Mibzar (mĭb′zär). [Heb. *Mibṣar,* "fortification."] A chief of Edom (Gen 36:42; 1 Chr 1:53).

Mica (mī′kà), KJV **Micha** (mī′kà). [Heb. *Mika'* and *Mikah,* probably either "who is like (Yahweh)?" or "who is like (God)?"]
1. The son of Mephibosheth (Meribbaal), and thus a great-grandson of King Saul (2 Sa 9:12), called Micah in 1 Chr 8:34, 35; 9:40, 41.
2. A Levite who set his seal to Nehemiah's covenant (Neh 10:11).
3. A Levite, descendant of Asaph (1 Chr 9:15; Neh 11:17, 22), called Micah in Neh 11:17, RSV, and 1 Chr 9:15, KJV.

Some consider him identical with Micaiah, 6.

Micah (mī′kà), KJV twice **Michah** (mī′kà). [Heb. *Mikah, Mika', Mikayehû,* probably "who is like Yahweh?"]
1. A Kohathite Levite, a son of Uzziel (1 Chr 23:12, 20; 24:24, 25).
2. An Ephraimite in the time of the judges (Jgs 17:1). He stole 1,100 shekels of silver from his mother, but restored the amount, fearing the curse she had pronounced upon the thief (v 2). She thereupon dedicated the money to the Lord to be made into images. Micah therefore took 200 shekels and had images made, and dedicated one of his sons as a priest for this idolatrous worship (vs 4, 5). However, when an unemployed Levite came to his place he hired him, doubtless considering that a member of that tribe would be more suitable for the office than his son, who was a mere layman (vs 7-13). Some time later Danites, passing by on their way to the north in search of new territory in which to settle, stole Micah's idols and induced the Levite (*see* Jonathan, 1) to accompany them and become the tribe's priest (ch 18:11-21). Hence Micah's idols were carried off to Dan against his protestations (vs 22-26). The Danites built a sanctuary for the "graven image," which existed as long as the tabernacle was in Shiloh, and Jonathan's descendants were priests for the tribe of Dan until the Assyrian captivity (vs 27-31).
3. For 1 Chr 8:34, 35; 9:40, 41, *see* Mica, 1.
4. A descendant of Joel, a Reubenite (1 Chr 5:3-5).
5. A man whose son Abdon was a court official of Josiah (2 Chr 34:20). He is called Micaiah (KJV "Michaiah") in 2 Ki 22:12, where his son is called Achbor.
6. For 1 Chr 9:15; Neh 11:17, 22, *see* Mica, 3.
7. A prophet under the kings Jotham, Ahaz, and Hezekiah (Mic 1:1; Jer 26:18). He was the author of the book that bears his name. *See* Micah, Book of.

Micah, Book of. Sixth of the so-called Minor Prophets. The book is named for the prophet Micah (*see* Micah, 7). Micah identifies himself as "the *Morasthite."* The fact that Micah mentions only Jotham, Ahaz, and Hezekiah, kings of Judah (Mic 1:1), implies that his ministry was confined largely to the southern kingdom, although his message was applicable also to the people of Samaria (see v 1). A comparison of Mic 1:1 with Is 1:1; 6:1;

and Hos 1:1 reveals that Micah's prophetic ministry began shortly after those of Isaiah and Hosea, and that for a number of years he was contemporary with them. Micah's ministry thus fell between about 739 and 686 B.C., probably during the earlier portion of this period. Whereas Hosea bore his message exclusively to the northern kingdom, or nearly so (cf. Hos 4:15; 11:12), and Isaiah to the southern kingdom, especially at Jerusalem (Is 1:1), Micah addressed himself to both. Whereas Isaiah reflects the culture of the capital city, Micah is more a man of the common people and sympathizes with them in their suffering at the hand of oppressive landlords and judges. He has been called the prophet of social justice, since he attacks the wrongs to which the poor were exposed at the hands of heartless aristocrats. His style blends severity with tenderness, sternness with sympathy, boldness with love, simplicity with elegance. Abrupt transitions suggest that the book represents a collection of messages given at various times and places, and brought together without an intention to combine them into one unified message. The direct form of address, particularly the questions he asks of the people (chs 1:5; 2:7; 4:9; 6:3, 6, 7, 10, 11), probably vividly reflects the messages as he originally delivered them in oral form. He frequently employs literary devices such as the metaphor (chs 1:6; 3:2, 3, 6; 4:6-8, 13; 6:10, 11, 14, 15) and paronomasia, or play on words, evident in the Hebrew, as with the place names Aphrah (ch 1:10), Maroth (v 12), Lachish (v 13), Moresheth-gath and Achzib (v 14), and Mareshah (v 15). In ch 7:18 Micah apparently plays on his own name. His familiarity with history is reflected in chs 1:13-15; 5; 6:4, 6, 16; 7:20.

Micah's influence doubtless had a part in the thoroughgoing reforms effected by King Hezekiah, whose father, Ahaz, had gone so far as to set up a heathen altar in the Temple court. Idolatry was rampant throughout Judah, as well as in Israel, and the social injustice against which Micah particularly spoke was the natural result. Even the priests countenanced heathenism in order to retain their popularity with the people. The nobles and wealthier classes had given themselves over to lives of luxury and were unscrupulous and cruel in their dealings with the poorer classes, whom they ground down by excessive exactions and deprived of their legal and moral rights. But, as with most of the OT prophets, Micah's message had a dark

and a bright side. On the one hand he condemned the sins of the people and warned of the result of obstinate persistence in an evil course, and on the other he spoke of the glory and joy of the Messianic kingdom to be established "in the last days" (ch 4:1).

Micah assails the corrupt state of society (Mic 1:1 to 3:12). The "wound" of Judah appears to be "incurable" (ch 1:9), seemingly an allusion to Sennacherib's invasion described at length in Is 36 and 37. The people of Judah are so engrossed in iniquity and the oppression of their fellow countrymen that they lie awake at night devising new means of oppression (Mic 2:1, 2). Accordingly, God promises to "devise an evil" from which they themselves will not be able to escape (v 3). Micah appeals particularly to the leaders and princes of the people, whose responsibility it was to provide justice for all, but who were figuratively eating the very flesh of the common people and flaying them alive instead (ch 3:1-3). False prophets, dishonest judges, and mercenary priests had become the curse of Israel (vs 5-11), and unless the nation repented, Jerusalem would be devastated (v 12). In chs 4:1 to 5:15 Micah turns the page of prophecy to the glorious future when the "mountain of the house of the Lord," which would yet be laid desolate as a result of the sins of the people (ch 3:12), was to be "established in the top of the mountains" in glory and honor (ch 4:1). Israel would then fulfill its Messianic role by converting the nations to the worship of the true God (v 2) and thereby bring peace to the earth (vs 3, 4, 7; cf. ch 5:7, 8). The dominion God had originally planned for His people would be theirs (ch 4:8) when Messiah should come to rule over Israel (ch 5:1-5). In ch 6 Micah returns to the Lord's "controversy with his people" (v 2), and proclaims in plain, simple language what God requires of them—to be fair and kind toward one another, and humble toward God (v 8). Captivity and repentance are foretold in ch 7:1-13 and the prophecy closes with a prayer for reformation and restoration. See Prophet, II.

Micaiah (mī-kā′yá), KJV 7 times **Michaiah** (mī-kā′yá). [Heb. *Mîkayahû, Mîkayehû, Mîkayah,* "who is like Yahweh?"]

1. For 2 Chr 13:2, see Maacah, 9.

2. The son of Imlah, and a prophet in the time of Ahab. When false court prophets assured King Ahab of Israel that he would be successful in his efforts to recover Ramoth-gilead by force of

arms from the Syrians, his ally Jehoshaphat, king of Judah, insisted that a true prophet of Yahweh be summoned, and Micaiah was called. Since he was told to please Ahab, Micaiah at first ironically agreed with the other prophets. Obviously it was clear to his hearers that he did not literally mean what he said, for he was adjured to speak the truth. At this he predicted Ahab's defeat and death at Ramoth-gilead. For this prophecy of doom he was imprisoned (1 Ki 22:4-28; 2 Chr 18:6-27).

3. For 2 Ki 22:12, see Micah, 5.

4. A prince of Judah sent out by King Jehoshaphat to teach the people in the cities of Judah (2 Chr 17:3, 7).

5. A son of Gemariah, and a leading Jew in the reign of Jehoiakim. He reported to the princes of Judah the contents of Jeremiah's prophecies which he had heard Baruch read from a scroll (Jer 36:11-13).

6. A priest, descendant of Asaph. His great-great-grandson Zechariah took part in the dedication of the wall of Jerusalem in Nehemiah's time (Neh 12:35). Some consider him to be identical with Mica, 3.

7. A priest who took part in the dedication of the wall of Jerusalem in Nehemiah's time (Neh 12:41).

Micha. See Mica; Micah, 3.

Michael (mī′kȧ-ĕl). [Heb. *Mîka'el*, "who is like God?"; Gr. *Michaēl*. The name occurs on an Aramaic ostracon found at *Nimrûd*, and in the Dead Sea scrolls.]

1. The archangel (Jude 9). Michael as a heavenly being appears only in apocalyptic passages (Dan 10:13, 21; 12:1; Jude 9; Rev 12:7). In Dan 10:13 he is described as "one of the chief princes" who had come to the help of an angel in his contest with "the prince of the kingdom of Persia." In v 21 he is described as "your prince," and in ch 12:1 as "the great prince" who is the protector and deliverer of Daniel's people. In Rev 12:7 he is mentioned as having fought in heaven with the dragon, that is, Satan (v 9), and the dragon's angels, a fight that ended with the victory of Michael and the expulsion of Satan from heaven. Jude 9 tells of a contest between Michael and the devil for the body of Moses. On this theme the Jews in Christ's time may have had some information, since it is said to be described in the pseudepigraphic Jewish book Assumption of Moses, although this is not in the extant portions of that work. The Targum of Jonathan on Deut

34:6 ascribes to Michael and his angels the burial of Moses. The Jewish literature describes Michael as the highest of the angels, the true representative of God, and identifies him with the "angel of Yahweh" frequently mentioned in the OT as a divine being. It also claims that Michael was the angel who vindicated Israel against Satan's accusations at the heavenly tribunal. See Talmud *Yoma* 37a; Midrash Rabbah, on Gen 18:3; Ex 3:2; 12:29. Many Bible scholars identify Michael with Jesus Christ. See *SDACom* 4:860.

2. A man whose son Sethur was the spy representing the tribe of Asher (Num 13:13).

3 and 4. Two Gadites, one the descendant of the other (1 Chr 5:11, 13, 14).

5. A Gershonite Levite, and ancestor of Asaph (1 Chr 6:40; cf. vs 39, 43).

6. A "chief man" of the tribe of Issachar (1 Chr 7:3).

7. A descendant of Benjamin (1 Chr 8:1, 16).

8. A warrior from the tribe of Manasseh who joined David at Ziklag (1 Chr 12:20).

9. A man whose son Omri was David's chief officer over the territory of Issachar (1 Chr 27:18).

10. A son of King Jehoshaphat of Judah (2 Chr 21:2).

11. A man of the family of Shephatiah, whose son Zebadiah was in charge of 80 men who returned from Babylonia with Ezra (Ezr 8:8).

Michah. See Micah, 1.

Michaiah. See Micaiah; Micah, 5.

Michal (mī′chăl). [Heb. *Mîkal.* This name is commonly interpreted as an abbreviated form of *Mîka'el,* "Michael," meaning "who is like God?" but it is also possible that it is the name of the god Mekal, attested by an inscription found in the excavations of Beth-shean.]

1. King Saul's younger daughter (1 Sa 14:49). When her father discovered that she was in love with David, he schemed to use her affection to destroy the young man. He therefore offered her to David as wife on condition that David kill 100 Philistines, hoping that David would lose his life in the venture. David, however, returned successfully from his raid and was consequently given Michal as wife (ch 18:20-28). When David was forced to flee from the king's wrath, Michal aided him in his flight (ch 19:11-17). Later she was given to another man (ch 25:44).

When Abner approached David and offered to deliver to him the northern tribes ruled by Ish-bosheth, David refused to negotiate until Michal was restored to him (2 Sa 3:12-16). Michal is last mentioned as despising David in her heart, seeing him dancing in public before the ark when it was transferred to Jerusalem (ch 6:15, 16). Feeling that he had debased himself, she rebuked him (vs 20-·22). She died childless (v 23).

2. For 2 Sa 21:8, KJV, see Merab.

Michmas. *See* Michmash.

Michmash (mĭk′măsh), or **Michmas** (mĭk′-măs). [Heb. *Mikmash, Mikmas,* and *Mikmaś.*] A town near Bethel (1 Sa 13:2), "east of Beth-aven" (v 5) and north of Geba (Is 10:28, 29; 1 Sa 14:5, RSV). Detailed information in these verses has made it possible definitely to identify the site with the present village of *Mukhmâs* (Map VI, E-3), 2,020 ft. above sea level on a hill north of the narrow and deep *Wâdī eṣ-Ṣuweinît.* This valley is usually recognized as the "pass of Michmash" (1 Sa 13:23), which leads from the tableland of Ephraim down to Jericho. When held by the Philistines, in the time of King Saul, Michmash became the scene of an unusual act of bravery on the part of Jonathan, who, with his armorbearer, descended from Geba, climbed the steep southern slope of Michmash, and took the Philistines by surprise. A melee followed, ending in their flight (chs 13:5-7, 15, 16;

329. The gorge at Michmash

14:1-23). When Isaiah described the coming attack on Jerusalem by the Assyrians, he mentioned Michmash as one of the cities they would occupy in their march (Is 10:28). Descendants of the former inhabitants of Michmash returned from the Babylonian exile with Zerubbabel (Ezr 2:27; Neh 7:31). It is mentioned as a town inhabited by Benjamites in the postexilic period (Neh 11:31). Jonathan Maccabeus made it his residence in the 2d cent. B.C. (1 Macc 9:73; Jos. *Ant.* xiii. 1. 6). See fig. 329.

Michmethah. *See* Michmethath.

Michmethath (mĭk′mĕ-thăth), KJV **Michmethah** (mĭk′mĕ-thá). [Heb. *Hammikmethath.*] A place on the boundary between Ephraim and Manasseh, east of Shechem (Jos 16:6; 17:7). It has been tentatively identified with either *Khirbet Makhneh el-Fôqā* or the neighboring site of *Khirbet JuleiJil,* 2 mi. southeast of Shechem. E. Danelius now identifies it with the mound *Makhmish,* on the southern bank of the *Wâdī el-Gharbi,* at the northern outskirts of Tel Aviv (*PEQ* 89 [1957], 66, 67).

Michri (mĭk′rī). [Heb. *Mikrî,* meaning uncertain.] A Benjamite (1 Chr 9:7, 8).

Michtam. *See* Miktam.

Middin (mĭd′ĭn). [Heb. *Middîn.*] A town in the Wilderness of Judah (Jos 15:61); identified with *Khirbet Abū Ṭabaq* in the *Buqêʻah,* 4 mi. west-southwest of *Khirbet Qumrân* (Cross and Milik, *BASOR* 142 [1956], 16).

Midian (mĭd′ĭ-ăn), KJV once **Madian** (mā′-dĭ-ăn). [Heb. *Midyan,* "strife"; Gr. *Madiam.*]

1. A son of Abraham by Keturah, and ancestor of the Midianites. His father gave him rich gifts during his lifetime and sent him into the wilderness to prevent him from contesting the inheritance of Isaac (Gen 25:1-6).

2. An area in the north Arabian desert that received its name from the ancestor of the Midianites, Midian. The area cannot easily be defined, but available evidence indicates that it must have included the eastern part of the Sinai Peninsula, the desert east of the Gulf of Aqabah and of Edom, and eastern Moab. In the time of Moses the area east of Mount Horeb was pastureland for the flocks of Jethro, the priest of Midian (Ex 3:1). A district adjacent to Moab, and near Heshbon, the capital of the Amorite king Sihon, was also in the hands of Midianites who had been settled there for

some time (Gen 36:35; Num 22:4; Jos 13:21). There can hardly be any doubt that the desert area between these 2 territories belonged to the Midianites, for they fled that way when Gideon defeated them in the Valley of Jezreel (Jgs 6:33; 7:1), and drove them out of Palestine. This is shown by the fact that in his pursuit Gideon passed Succoth and Jogbehah, which were in Gilead and in the territory of Gad, respectively (ch 8:5, 10, 11). When Joab destroyed the Edomite royal house in the time of David, Hadad, one of the royal princes of Edom, escaped with some courtiers, and found refuge in the adjacent country of Midian (1 Ki 11:14-18).

Midianites (mĭd′ĭ-ăn-īts). [Heb. *Midyan*.] The descendants of Midian, Abraham's son by Keturah (Gen 25:2, 6). They were a people of the desert living in tents and possessing large numbers of camels (Num 10:29-31; Is 60:6; Hab 3:7). Five tribal families descended from Midian (Gen 25:4; cf. Num 31:8). The caravan to which Joseph was sold by his brothers consisted of Ishmaelites and Midianites, who came from Gilead carrying goods to Egypt (Gen 37:25, 28, 36). Moses' father-in-law and brother-in-law were Midianites (Ex 3:1; Num 10:29-31; *see* Reuel). When the Israelites dwelt near the Jordan before crossing into western Palestine, the Midianites joined the Moabites in seducing the Israelites to idolatry and licentiousness. Consequently Moses waged war against them, and slew their 5 kings and many of their people (Num 22:4-6; 25:1-18; 31:1-12). From Jos 13:21 we learn that the Midianite kings had been allies of Sihon, the Amorite king of Heshbon, who had also been defeated by the Israelites under Moses. In the period of the judges the Midianites, the Amalekites, and other eastern people invaded Palestine, and covered the country with their flocks and tents. They oppressed the Israelites for 7 years, appropriating their harvests and bringing great misery upon the population. Finally God raised up Gideon, who, with his small band of brave warriors, routed these oppressors in a battle in the plain of Jezreel. He pursued their remnants deep into their homeland in Transjordan. Their princes, Oreb, Zeeb, Zebah, and Zalmunna, were captured and slain (Jgs 6 to 8; Ps 83:11; Is 9:4; 10:26). Although the Midianites continued to exist, as shown by the fact that they are subsequently occasionally mentioned (Is 60:6; Hab 3:7), they never again became a menace to the Israelites.

Midwife. A woman who assists in childbirth. Midwives are mentioned in the Bible as aiding Rachel in the birth of Benjamin (Gen 35:17) and as helping Tamar in delivering her twins (ch 38:24, 28). Two Hebrew midwives are mentioned by name in Ex 1:15-21 as bravely refusing the demand of the Pharaoh to destroy the Hebrew male babies at birth. Probably in most cases female relatives or friends performed the service of midwives, as is still the custom in the Orient.

Migdal-el (mĭg′dăl-ĕl′). [Heb. *Migdal-'el*, "tower of God."] A city of Naphtali (Jos 19:38), tentatively identified with *Khirbet el-Mejdel*, 4 mi. northwest of Kedesh in Galilee.

Migdal-gad (mĭg′dăl-găd′). [Heb. *Migdal-gad*, "tower of Gad."] A town in the Shephelah of Judah (Jos 15:37), probably to be identified with either *Khirbet el-Mejdeleh*, 5 mi. south of *Beit Jibrin*, or *Tell el-Mejâdil*, 6 mi. southwest of *Tell Beit Mirsim*.

Migdol (mĭg′dŏl). [Heb. *Migdol*, Canaanite-Hebrew term meaning "tower."]

1. A tower near which the Israelites camped when they left Egypt at the time of the Exodus. It was situated near the Red Sea, and near Pi-hahiroth and Baal-zephon (Ex 14:2; Num 33:7). This tower or fortress was probably not a city, but a stronghold that formed part of the fortification system of Egypt's eastern border. However, the precise location of this Migdol, or tower, is not known. Map V, which presents several alternative Exodus routes, based on differing theories, shows a Migdol, but this is the town of Migdol, 2, below, and is not connected with the departure from Egypt except in the northern theory of the Exodus, which is not accepted in this dictionary. *See* Exodus.

2. An Egyptian locality in the northeastern Delta, to which the remnant of Judah fled after the destruction of Jerusalem (Jer 44:1; 46:14). This Migdol and Migdol, 1, may both originally have been part of the eastern border fortification system of Egypt, with Migdol, 1, possibly located near its southern end and Migdol, 2, near the northern limit of the fortified line. This line, which was built by Amenemhet I, is known from Egyptian records by the name "Wall of the Prince." In the *Amarna Letters the city of Migdol, 2, is referred to as *Magdali ina Miṣri* (No.

234:29), "Migdol in Egypt," to distinguish it from other Migdols in Palestine and Syria. It is generally identified with *Magdolus* (now *Tell el-Ḥeir*), a place known from Roman times, lying about 11 mi. south of Pelusium (Map V, B-4). In Eze 29:10 and 30:6 the RSV "from Migdol to Syene" is to be preferred, meaning from the extreme north to the extreme south of Egypt.

Migron (mĭg'rŏn). [Heb. *Migrôn*.]

1. A place where Saul once camped, on the outskirts of Gibeah (1 Sa 14:2); not identified. Some commentators suggest the reading *goren*, "threshing floor," instead of *Migrôn*, "Migron," which in pre-Masoretic Hebrew would have been somewhat similar.

2. A place in the territory of Benjamin, between Aiath and Michmash, on the line of march which the prophet Isaiah describes for the approach of the Assyrian army (Is 10:28); identified either with *Makrûn*, north of Michmash, or with *Tell Miriam*, southwest of Michmash.

Mijamin (mĭj'ă-mĭn), KJV twice **Miamin** (mĭ'ă-mĭn). [Heb. *Mîyamîn*, "from the right hand," that is, "from the side of good luck."]

1. A descendant of Aaron and ancestral head of the 6th of the 24 courses into which David organized the priests (1 Chr 24:1, 9).

2. A chief of the priests who returned from Babylonia with Zerubbabel (Neh 12:5, 7). One generation later, under the high priest Joiakim, a priestly family known by the name of Miniamin is mentioned (vs 12, 17). Miniamin is a variant form of Mijamin. This family may have been descended from Mijamin, 2, or possibly from Mijamin, 1. *See* Miniamin, 2.

3. A member of the family of Parosh. He was married to a foreign wife in the time of Ezra (Ezr 10:25).

4. A priest who set his seal to the covenant of Nehemiah (Neh 10:7). He was possibly the priest Miniamin who took part in the dedication of the wall of Jerusalem (ch 12:41). *See* Miniamin, 3.

Mikloth (mĭk'lŏth). [Heb. *Miqlôth*, "rods."]

1. According to the KJV, chief officer who served in the division of the 2d month in David's army (1 Chr 27:4). The RSV on the basis of the LXX omits this name from the list.

2. The ancestor of a Benjamite family who lived in Jerusalem (1 Chr 8:32; 9: 37, 38).

Mikneiah (mĭk-nē'yă). [Heb. *Miqneyahû*, "property of Yahweh." The name occurs on an ancient Hebrew seal.] A Levite of the 2d order, who was a musician in David's time (1 Chr 15:18, 21).

Miktam, KJV Michtam. [Heb. *miktam*.] A term of uncertain meaning appearing in the superscriptions of Ps 16 and Ps 56-60. One explanation relates the Hebrew term to the Akkadian *katâmu*, "cover," and hence suggests that the psalms so entitled are atonement psalms. Others suggest that Miktam may be a musical title.

Milalai (mĭl'ă-lā'ī). [Heb. *Milalay*, meaning uncertain.] A Levite musician who took part in the dedication of the wall of Jerusalem in the time of Nehemiah (Neh 12:27, 36).

Milcah (mĭl'kă). [Heb. *Milkah*, "queen."]

1. A daughter of Haran, Abraham's brother, and a sister of Lot. She became the wife of Nahor, a brother of her father, and had 8 sons, among whom was Bethuel, the father of Rebekah (Gen 11: 29; cf. v 31; 22:20-23).

2. One of the daughters of the Manassite Zelophehad (Num 26:33; 27:1; 36:11; Jos 17:3).

Milcom (mĭl'kŏm). [Heb. *Milkom*.] The god of the Ammonites (1 Ki 11:5, 33; 2 Ki 23:13). Nothing is known about this god from extra-Biblical sources, although a god *Mlkm* is mentioned in the texts from Ugarit. The name means simply "king" with the familiar termination *om*, and may have been a title rather than a name, similar to the term Baal, which is a title meaning "master" or "lord" applied to many local gods of the Canaanites. "Milcom" should be read in KJV of Jer 49:3; Zep 1:5 instead of "their king" and "Malcham" (măl'kăm), respectively. Some suggest that "Milcom" also be read in 1 Ki 11:7 for "Molech," supposing a final *m* to have dropped from the Hebrew name (see vs 5, 33).

Mildew. [Heb. *yeraqôn*, "paleness."] Not the thin fungus that develops on various objects under damp, dark conditions, but rather a disease that caused plants to become yellow or colorless. This disease is mentioned in the Bible as a curse upon the fields of those who disregarded the word of the Lord (Deut 28:22; Amos 4:9; Hag 2:17). Solomon, in his prayer at the Temple dedication, besought the Lord to deliver from this curse those who prayed to the One in whose name the Temple was erected (1 Ki 8:37; 2 Chr 6:28).

Mile. [Gr. *milion,* a loan word from Latin *mille,* "a thousand."] A Roman measure of length, originally being one thousand paces, but later a fixed measure of 8 *stadia (about 4,855 English ft.), which is the equivalent of about 12/13 English mile (about 1,480 meters). The Roman mile is mentioned in the Bible only in Mt 5:41, where Jesus refers to the custom of Roman soldiers of forcing civilians to carry their baggage for 1 mile, the distance such a coercion was legally permitted. He counseled His hearers to show a cheerful, submissive spirit under such circumstances by volunteering to carry the baggage twice as far as required. The "miles" appearing in RSV of Lk 24:13; Jn 6:19; 11:18 is not a true translation, but the distances given in ancient measures have been computed to English miles.

Miletum. *See* Miletus.

Miletus (mī-lē′tŭs), KJV once **Miletum** (mī-lē′tŭm). [Gr. *Milētos.*] A town on the Carian coast of Asia Minor, about 32 mi. south of Ephesus at the mouth of the Maeander River (Map XX, B-4). It had suffered much at the hands of the Persians, but had recovered from its misfortunes by the time Paul visited it, and had become a trade center of some importance. Extensive excavations have been carried out by German expeditions. The Pergamon Museum in Berlin houses the reconstructed market gate of Miletus originally erected in the 2d cent. B.C. When returning to Jerusalem from his 3d Missionary Journey Paul stopped at Miletus and summoned the church leaders of Ephesus to this port city for a farewell meeting (Acts 20:15-38). Because of the great distance of Miletus from Ephesus, a round trip of more than 70 mi., Paul's ship must have stayed in that port 3 days or more. He visited the city again after his 1st Roman imprisonment and left Trophimus there sick (2 Ti 4:20).

Milk. [Heb. *chalab;* Gr. *gala.*] An item of diet for the people of Bible lands, but not holding as important a place as in our diet today. The word occurs frequently in the expression "a land flowing with milk and honey" (Ex 3:8, 17; etc.). Goats (Prov 27:27), and perhaps also sheep (Deut 32:14, KJV), as well as cattle, supplied milk, although the word "sheep" in the phrase "milk of sheep" in this passage is the rendering of the Heb. *ṣo'n,* meaning "small cattle," such as sheep and goats. The RSV translates *ṣo'n* "flock." Figuratively, "milk" is used to represent the first nutriments of the Word (1 Pe 2:2) for those newborn in the faith, in contrast with the solid food of doctrine that nourishes the experienced Christian (1 Cor 3:2; Heb 5:12).

Mill. A machine for grinding grain into meal and flour, a necessary utensil in every Oriental home. Because of its use in preparation of food the Mosaic law forbade a Hebrew to take a millstone as a pledge (Deut 24:6). The operation of the mills was the work of women (Mt 24:41), female slaves (Ex 11:5; Is 47:2), and prisoners (Jgs 16:21). One of the most familiar sounds in villages and towns was the grinding of mills, accompanied by the chattering of the women and girls operating them, so that the cessation of these sounds was a sign of utter desolation (Jer 25:10; Rev 18:22). The following mills were anciently in use:

1. *Rubbing mills.* Archeological evidence shows that the earliest mills consisted of 2 basalt stones. The nether stone (Heb. *pelach tachtîth*) was a flat oblong

330. Women of Bethlehem grinding wheat in a hand mill in the courtyard of their home

331. A bakery at Pompeii, containing three grain mills (center); the oven to the left contained more than 80 loaves of bread when excavated

rubbing stone, saddle-shaped at the top. The upper millstone (Heb. *pelach rekeb*) was much smaller. It was moved back and forth upon the lower stone, thus crushing the grain between the two. The one working such a mill knelt behind it (Ex 11:5; see fig. 319). It was probably the upper stone of this kind of mill that crushed the skull of King Abimelech (Jgs 9:53).

2. *Rotating hand mills.* It is not certain when these mills, which are still found in the villages of Palestine, came into use. Since they are operated by 2 women, they were evidently in use in Christ's time (Mt 24:41) and probably had been used for several centuries previously. These mills consisted of 2 circular millstones, generally of basalt, about 17 to 19 in. in diameter and 2 to 4 in. thick. The lower one was slightly convex on its upper side and had a wooden peg projecting from its center. The upper millstone was concave on its under side to fit upon the lower stone and had a hole in its center, so that it could revolve around the peg of the nether stone. The grain was poured through the center hole and ground between the 2 stones, the upper of which the 2 women moved back and forth on its axis. The ground

grain emerged over the edge of the lower stone into a cloth spread underneath the mill (see fig. 330).

3. *Commercial mills.* In Roman times large mills for commercial bakeries came into use. Some have been excavated in Roman cities such as Pompeii and Ostia. The lower stone was in the shape of a cone, and had the apex pointing upward. The upper stone was hollowed out to fit the projecting cone. One or more poles inserted in holes in the upper stone permitted it to be rotated (see fig. 331). These mills were turned by slaves, or by animals, such as donkeys. It is to a stone from this type of mill (Gr. *mulos onikos*) and not a hand mill, that Christ referred in Mt 18:6.

Millennium. The word "millennium" does not appear in the Scriptures, but is derived from the Latin *mille annus* and means simply "a thousand years" (Gr. *chilia etē*). The term has been used by the Christian church to designate specifically the 1000-year period of Rev 20, where the expression "thousand years" occurs 6 times in vs 1-7.

Any definition or description of the millennium must be based on Rev 19 and 20, since these are the only passages in the entire Scriptures that deal directly with this subject. Further, an accurate statement of the events connected with this 1000-year period must take into account that these 2 chapters form a continuous narrative, that is, the events presented in ch 20 follow immediately upon those portrayed in ch 19. The sequence of events appears as follows: 1. *Events that precede the millennium.* (1) Christ comes the 2d time. In vivid, symbolic language Christ is pictured as a King riding forth on a white horse to subjugate His enemies and to deliver His faithful followers (ch 19:11-16). (2) The wicked, Christ's enemies, are slain. The beast and false prophet are cast into the lake of fire (v 20) and the "remnant" (v 21) or the "rest" of the wicked are slain. These are the kings, captains, mighty men, and "all men, both free and bond" (v 18). (3) The righteous dead are raised (Rev 20: 4-6, RSV; cf. 1 Cor 15:51, 52; 1 Th 4:15, 16). This resurrection is called "the first resurrection" (Rev 20:5). The resurrected ones, together with the righteous living at the Advent, are then translated "to meet the Lord in the air" (1 Th 4:16). 2. *Conditions during the millennium.* (1) The earth is desolate (Rev 20:3). The destruction of all the wicked, the removal of the saints from the earth, and the fearful convulsions of nature connected with the 7 last plagues (ch 16: 18-21; cf. 6:14) leave the earth a scene of utter desolation. (2) Satan is bound (ch 20:1-3). The binding of the dragon is obviously symbolic of the restriction placed upon Satan's activities. This is indicated by the statement that defines the purpose of his confinement, "that he should deceive the nations no more" (v

3). This is accomplished by the very nature of the situation—the wicked have been slain, and the righteous have been transported to heaven. (3) The righteous reign with Christ in heaven, not upon the earth (Rev 20:4, 6; cf. Jn 14: 1-3; 1 Th 4:17). 3. *Events at the close of the millennium.* (1) The wicked are raised (Rev 20:5). This may be termed the "second resurrection," since there are only 2 main resurrections (cf. Rev 20:6; Jn 5: 28, 29; Acts 24:15) and the resurrection of the righteous is referred to as the "first resurrection" (Rev 20:5, 6). (2) Satan is loosed (v 7). This represents the reverse of the binding of Satan at the beginning of the millennium. As it was the depopulation of the earth that halted his deceptive work, so the repopulation of the earth as a result of the resurrection of the wicked at the end of the thousand years (v 5) will enable Satan again to deceive men. He plans to make an attack upon Christ and His people (vs 8, 9). (3) Christ and the saints return to earth with the New Jerusalem (ch 21:1, 2, 10). (4) Satan and his marshaled forces make an attack on the "beloved city" (ch 20:7-9). (5) The forces of evil are annihilated (vs 9, 10). This is called "the second death" (vs 6, 14). See Death. (6) The earth is purified by fire (2 Pe 3:10, 12), and new heavens and new earth emerge (2 Pe 3:13; Rev 21:1).

Among commentators there is considerable difference of opinion concerning this subject. There are 3 major schools of interpretation: premillennialist, postmillennialist, amillennialist. For a presentation of these particular points of view, see *SDACom* 7:886-887.

THE MILLENNIUM

EVENTS AT THE BEGINNING	"A THOUSAND YEARS" (Rev 20:4)	EVENTS AT THE CLOSE
Christ returns to earth as "King of kings" (Rev 19:11-16; cf. Acts 1:9-11)	Satan remains bound, "that he should deceive the nations no more" (Rev 20:2, 3)	Descent of the saints and the New Jerusalem to earth (Rev 21:2; cf. ch 20:9)
The battle of the great day of God (Rev 19:15, 17-19; cf. chs 16:12-16; 6:14-17)	The earth desolate and depopulated (Rev 20:3, 5; cf. chs 6: 14; 16:17-21)	The second resurrection—of the wicked (Rev 20:5, 6, 8; cf. vs 12, 13)
The wicked slain (Rev 19:19-21)	The saints "reign" with Christ in heaven (Rev 20:4, 6; cf. Jn 14:2, 3; 1 Th 4:17)	Satan "loosed" from his "prison" (Rev 20:3, 7)
Satan "bound" in the "bottomless pit" (Rev 20:1-3)	Judgment given to the saints (Rev 20:4; cf. 1 Cor 6:2, 3)	The battle of Gog and Magog (Rev 20:8, 9)
The "first resurrection"—of the righteous (Rev 20:4-6; cf. 1 Th 4:16)		The "lake of fire"—the "second death" (Rev 20:10-15; 21:8; cf. 2 Pe 3:7, 10, 12)
Ascension of the saints (Rev 20: 4; cf. Jn 14:1-3; 1 Th 4:16, 17)		The earth made new (Rev 21: 1-3; cf. 2 Pe 3:13)

332. Common millet (*Panicum miliaceum*)

Millet. [Heb. *dochan.*] A cereal grass (*Panicum miliaceum* or *Sorghum vulgare*) that is grown extensively in the Middle East, as well as other parts of the world. It is cut for hay in North America. It is an annual grass, attains a height of several feet, and produces large numbers of very small seeds. A bread made from millet would be scarcely palatable, and as such, fits well into the acted parable of Ezekiel (Eze 4:9).

Millo (mĭl′ō). [Heb. *Millô′*, always used with the definite article, meaning primarily "filling," hence a terrace filling. The word later came to mean an artificial elevation, and finally a citadel.]

1. "The house of Millo" (Beth-millo, RSV) at Shechem (Jgs 9:6, 20) was probably a fortress, but some commentators consider it to be the name of a family.

2. Apparently a fortification inside the Jebusite city. It was probably at the northern side of the city where no deep valley provided a natural protection as on the other sides. *See* Jerusalem. It was in existence in David's time, was rebuilt by Solomon, and strengthened by Hezekiah (2 Sa 5:6-9; 1 Ki 9:15, 24; 11:27; 2 Chr 32:2, 5). The house of Millo in which King Joash was slain (2 Ki 12:20) was probably this Jerusalem fortress.

Millstone. *See* Mill.

Mina (mī′nȧ), KJV 4 times **Pound** (pound), once **Maneh** (mā′nĕ). [Heb. *maneh;* Akkadian *manû;* Ugaritic *mn;* Egyptian *mnw;* Aramaic *mene′;* Gr. *mna.*] A weight found in many areas of the ancient East. The Babylonian "mina" weighed 60 shekels, but the Canaanite and Hebrew (1 Ki 10:17; Ezr 2:69; Neh 7:71, 72) "mina" 50 shekels (Eze 45:12, RSV). Metal mina weights in the shape of bulls have been found in Ugarit. They weigh 469 grams, and are thus heavier than the Egyptian mina which weighs between 437 and 439 grams, but lighter than the minas of Babylonia, which weigh between 491 and 505 grams. However, it is certain that the ancient mina was a little heavier than an English pound. If 11.4 grams is taken as the weight for the Palestinian shekel (*see* Shekel), then the mina would weigh 570 grams or 20.1 oz. avoirdupois.

Mingled People. [Heb. *′ereb,* "mixture," "mixed people."] An expression occurring in Jer 25:20, 24; 50:37; Eze 30:5; KJV. In the Jer passages the expression refers perhaps to the foreign mercenaries in the Egyptian and Babylonian armies, and in Eze 30:5 to the Arabs, on the assumption that *′ereb* should be pointed *′arab,* "Arab."

Miniamin (mĭn′yȧ-mĭn). [Heb. *Minyamin,* the longer form of *Mîyamîn,* "Mijamin," "from the right hand." The name occurs in cuneiform records as *Minyamîni, Minyamê,* and *Minyâmen.*]

1. A man in the time of Hezekiah who assisted Kore in distributing the freewill offerings to the Levites (2 Chr 31:14, 15).

2. A priestly family in the time of the high priest Joiakim (Neh 12:12, 17). *See* Mijamin, 2.

3. A priest who took part in the dedication ceremonies for the wall of Jerusalem (Neh 12:41); possibly identical with Mijamin, 4.

Minister. In the OT generally the translation of a form of the Heb. *sharath,* "to serve," which term is applied: (1) to the attendants of a royal court, as in the case of those who served Solomon (1 Ki 10:5; RSV "servants"); (2) to the attendant of a person of high rank or office, in the sense in which Joshua ministered to Moses (Jos 1:1); (3) to the priests and Levites, who were the "ministers of Jehovah" as they served in the sanctuary and the Temple (Eze 44:11; Joel 1:9, 13; etc.); (4) to the angels (Ps 103:21; 104:4).

In the NT the term "minister" is the translation of: (1) The Gr. *hupēretēs,* literally, an "under-rower (from *hupo*, "under," and *eretēs*, "rower") of a galley," and, by extension, "a helper," or "subordinate," acting voluntarily under another's direction, as in the case of the minister (RSV "attendant") of the Nazareth synagogue, who brought to Jesus the scroll of the prophet Isaiah for the scripture reading (Lk 4:20), and John Mark, who ministered to Paul and Barnabas during the 1st Missionary Journey (Acts 13:5). (2) The Gr. *leitourgos*, "one who discharges a public office," "a public servant." This term is used mainly with religious connotations, as in the case of (*a*) Christ as a "minister of the sanctuary" in heaven (Heb 8:2); (*b*) the apostle Paul as an evangelist to the Gentiles (Rom 15:16); (*c*) government officials who, though they do not all act consciously as God's representatives, fulfill certain functions ordained of God so that they are designated as "God's ministers" (ch 13:6). (3) The Gr. *diakonos*, "a servant," not as to standing in society, but as to activity, "an attendant"; as of Timothy (1 Th 3:2), Paul and Apollos (1 Cor 3:5), and Tychicus (Eph 6:21) as gospel ministers. *Diakonos* is also used of a church deacon, but when so used is translated "deacon" (Php 1:1; 1 Ti 3:8, 12). In general, *hupēretēs* refers to a minister in relation to his superior, *leitourgos* in relation to his public responsibilities, and *diakonos* in relation to his work. All 3 terms are employed of ministers of the gospel. (4) The Gr. *dunastēs* (Acts 8:27, RSV), "a court official."

Minni (mǐn′ī). [Heb. *Minnî*.] A kingdom mentioned by Jeremiah in conjunction with Ararat and Ashkenaz in his denunciation of Babylon (Jer 51:27). It is frequently mentioned in Assyrian inscriptions as *Mannâ*, lying east and southeast of Lake Urmiah (Map XI, B-6). Its people were presumably of Indo-European stock. Their capital was *Izirtu*. Their land was frequently invaded by the Assyrians, but was difficult to hold because of its mountainous character. The "Minni" joined the Medes against the Assyrians during the period of Assyria's decline, and were partly responsible for the destruction of Assyria. Since later they belonged to the Persian Empire of Cyrus, they took part in the fight against Babylon, as Jeremiah had implied.

Minnith (mǐn′ǐth). [Heb. *Minnîth*.] A town in the Ammonite territory, which was captured by Jephthah during his campaign against the Ammonites (Jgs 11:32, 33). In Eze 27:17, KJV, it is mentioned as exporting wheat to Tyre. The town has not definitely been identified, but a suggested site appears on Map VI, E-4.

Minstrel. A rendering of: (1) A form of the Heb. *nagan*, "to play upon a stringed instrument." Musicians were frequently hired that their soft music might quiet distraught spirits, and elevate downcast thoughts, gladdening the heart. When troubled by an evil spirit Saul engaged David to fulfill the role of musician in his court (1 Sa 16:14-18, 23), although he is not called a minstrel. When waiting to know the will of God, Elisha called for a minstrel (2 Ki 3:13-15). In Ps 68:25 another form of *nagan* is rendered "players on instruments" (KJV), "minstrels" (RSV). (2) The Gr. *aulētēs* (Mt 9:23, KJV), "one who plays a flute." The "flute players" (RSV) whom Jairus hired were no doubt professional mourners who accompanied the singers and wailing women at funeral processions. Allusions to this practice are found in several passages (2 Chr 35:25; Ec 12:5; Jer 9:17-20; Mt 11:17; Lk 7:32). (3) The Gr. *mousikos* (Rev 18:22, RSV), "a musician."

Mint. [Gr. *hēduosmon*.] Possibly the horsemint (*Mentha sylvestris*), a plant that grows wild on the hills of Syria to this day, or the garden plant *Mentha piperita*, "peppermint." It was among those crops meticulously tithed by the Jews, while weightier matters of the Law were flagrantly neglected (Mt 23:23; Lk 11:42). Mint was used anciently for flavoring in food and as a carminative in medicine.

Miphkad, Gate of. See Muster Gate.

Miracle. [Heb. *′ôth*, "sign," "token," "omen," *môpheth*, "sign," "token," *pele′*, "wonder"; Gr. *dunamis*, "power," "deed of power," "wonder," *sēmeion*, "sign." The English word "miracle" is from the Latin *miraculum*, "an object of wonder," "a wonder," "a wonderful thing," "a strange thing," "a marvel," "a marvelous thing," from *mirari*, "to wonder at," "to be astonished at," "to be amazed at."] A miracle is a supernatural intervention in human affairs that cannot be explained on the basis of known natural laws, or one that would not be expected in the normal course of events. An examination of the miracles performed by our Lord clarifies the nature and purpose of miracles. Jesus never exercised divine power for His own benefit, or merely to satisfy idle curiosity (cf. Mt 16:4; Lk 23:8, 9). Each of His miracles seemed to answer a specific material or physical necessity. By meeting these needs He assured recipient and observer alike of the love, sympathy, and care of their heavenly Father, and simultaneously of His desire and ability to meet their spiritual needs as well. Each miracle illustrated some aspect of spiritual truth (see Mk 2:9-11; Jn 6:11, 12, 27; 9:5-7, 39, 41; 11:23-26, 37, 44), and was calculated to inspire faith in Him as the Son of God (Jn 11:27, 45; 15:24). Again and again Jesus pointed to His "mighty works" as evidence of His Messiahship and divine authority (Mt 11:20-23; Jn 5:36; 10:24, 25, 32, 37, 38; 14:10, 11), and sincerehearted men recognized divinity operating in and through Him (Lk 9:43; 19:37; 24:19; Jn 3:2; 6:14; 9:16, 33). Of the recipients Jesus required faith (see Mt 17:20; Mk 9:23, 24; Jn 4:48, 49), active cooperation (Mt 17:27; Jn 9:7), willingness henceforth to order the life in harmony with the principles of the kingdom of heaven (see Jn 5:14), and acceptance of the obligation to tell others of God's love and power (see Mk 5:19).

Out of 35 recorded miracles of Jesus, 23 were healings; in 3 the dead were raised; 3 provided food or drink, and 2 large catches of fish; the other 4 were: stilling a storm, walking on the water, bringing a curse on a fig tree, and providing tax money.

The power to work miracles is a gift of the Holy Spirit (1 Cor 12:4, 10, 28), not one that a human being can assume or appropriate to himself (see Acts 8:18-22). Jesus promised His disciples that they would do "greater works" than those they had seen Him do (Jn 14:12), not greater in power or value, but in extent and number. The gospel commission carried with it the promise of power to work miracles (see Mk 16:16-18; 1 Cor 12:10), and there is no evidence of a time limit on the promise. The same divine power is available today as in NT times when needed, and the same prerequisite conditions must be met, both by the recipient and by the human agent. Satan also has power to work miracles that closely resemble the true (see Ex 7:11, 22; 8:7, 18; Acts 8:9-11; 2 Th 2:9; Rev 13:14; 19:20). If Satan has the power to bind men in physical infirmity (Lk 13:16), he can also, at times, release them when it suits his purpose. Accordingly, the alert Christian will not fall a prey to satanic deceptions, but will heed the instruction to test, or "try the spirits whether they are of God" (1 Jn 4:1).

Miriam (mĭr′ĭ-ăm). [Heb. *Miryam,* probably a Hebrew adaptation of the Egyptian *Mryt,* "the beloved one." This name later became common, and is found in the Greek form of *Maria* and *Mariam* as the name of several NT women (*see* Mary).]

333. A Jewish ossuary or bone receptacle (above), bearing the inscription (below): "Miriam, the daughter of Simeon"

1. The sister of Aaron and Moses (Ex 15:20; Num 26:59). She watched over the ark containing the infant Moses, which was placed by the river's brink, and negotiated his care (Ex 2:4-9). After the safe crossing of the Red Sea, Miriam, now called a prophetess, led the Israelite women in praise to God for the miraculous deliverance (Ex 15:20, 21; Mic 6:4). Later, with her brother Aaron, she is described as being jealous of Moses' place of leadership. The two voiced their dissatisfaction to Moses, using his marriage to a Cushite woman, by which they probably meant *Zipporah, the Midianitess, as a pretext for their discontent. They also claimed equality with him, stating that God had spoken through them as well as through him. For her rebellion against God's will and His chosen instrument Miriam was punished by leprosy, but was healed after Moses interceded for her (Num 12:1-16; Deut 24:9). She died in Kadesh, and was buried there (Num 20:1).

2. A descendant of Judah (1 Chr 4:17); whether a man or woman, it is not certain.

Mirma. *See* Mirmah.

Mirmah (mûr'mȧ), KJV **Mirma** (mûr'mȧ). [Heb. *Mirmah,* "deceit."] A Benjamite (1 Chr 8:10).

Mirror. Ancient mirrors, many examples of which have been found in excavations of the Near East, especially in Egypt, were made of polished metal, usually an alloy of copper and tin (bronze). Later, silver and golden mirrors came into use. Their shapes were generally round or oval, but some of them were square, and they usually had a handle which, along with the back of the mirror, was often

334. Bronze mirrors from ancient Egypt. On the handle of the mirror on the right is the head of the horned cow-goddess Hathor

decorated (fig. 334). The mirrors which the Hebrew women carried from Egypt were of bronze and provided the material for the laver (Ex 38:8; cf. ch 12:35). Glass mirrors did not come into use until late Roman times; consequently the mirrors mentioned by Paul (1 Cor 13:12; KJV "glass") and James (Jas 1:23; KJV "glass") were probably of metal, hence the RSV rendering "mirror." The reflection in a metallic mirror was inferior to that provided by a modern mirror, as may be seen by Paul's statement that a face could be seen only indistinctly in the mirror (Gr. *esoptron*) with which he was familiar (1 Cor 13:12).

"Glass" appears in the KJV of Is 3:23 as the translation of the Heb. *gillayôn,* a word of uncertain meaning.

Misgab (mĭs'găb). [Heb. *Miśgab,* "secure height," or "refuge."] A place in Moab (Jer 48:1); not identified. The RSV simply translates the Hebrew term as "fortress."

Mishael (mĭsh'ȧ-ĕl). [Heb. *Misha'el,* probably "who belongs to God?"]
1. A Kohathite Levite of the house of Uzziel (Ex 6:22; Lev .10:4).
2. The Hebrew name of one of Daniel's 3 companions, to whom the Babylonians gave the name Meshach (Dan 1:6, 7).
3. One who assisted Ezra when he read the Law to the people (Neh 8:4).

Mishal (mī'shăl), KJV once **Misheal** (mĭsh'ê-ăl). [Heb. *Mish'al.*] A town in the territory of Asher (Jos 19:26), assigned to the Gershonite Levites as a residence city (ch 21:27, 30), called Mashal (mā'shăl) [Heb. *Mashal*] in 1 Chr 6:74. The site has not been identified, but must be sought in the plain of Acco (Acre).

Misham (mī'shăm). [Heb. *Mish'am,* meaning uncertain.] A Benjamite, son of Elpaal (1 Chr 8:12).

Misheal. *See* Mishal.

Mishma (mĭsh'mȧ). [Heb. *Mishma',* meaning uncertain.]
1. The son of Ishmael (Gen 25:13, 14; 1 Chr 1:29, 30) and probably ancestral head of the Arabic tribe, the *Isamme'* of the Assyrian inscriptions.
2. A descendant of Simeon (1 Chr 4:24, 25).

Mishmannah (mĭsh-măn'ȧ). [Heb. *Mishmannah,* "fat," or "tidbit."] A Gadite, one of those who joined David's company at Ziklag (1 Chr 12:1, 8, 10).

Mishraites (mĭsh'rȧ-īts). [Heb. *Mishra'i.*] A family of Kiriath-jearim, belonging to the tribe of Judah (1 Chr 2:3, 53).

Mispar (mĭs'pär), KJV **Mizpar** (mĭz'pär). [Heb. *Mispar,* "number," or "narrative."] One of the leaders of the exiled Jews who returned from Babylonia with Zerubbabel (Ezr 2:1, 2). His name appears in its feminine form, *Mispereth,* "Mispereth" (mĭs'pê-rĕth), in Neh 7:7.

Mispereth. *See* Mispar.

Misrephoth-maim (mĭs'rĕ-fŏth-mā'ĭm). [Heb. *Miśrephôth mayim,* "place of lime burning at the water."] A place near Sidon to which Joshua pursued the kings defeated at the waters of Merom (Jos 11:7, 8). It lay on the border of the land of "the Sidonians" (ch 13:6), and has been identified with *Khirbet el-Musheirefeh,* 11 mi. north of Acco (Acre) on the Phoenician coast, where there are warm springs. Map VI, B-3.

Mist. Water vapor sufficiently concentrated to dim or obstruct the vision. How it forms is known to man, but he cannot control the atmospheric conditions that produce it. Before the Flood the earth was watered not by rain but by a "mist" (Gen 2:6; Heb. *'ed*, over the precise meaning of which there has been much discussion among scholars). A preliminary stage of blindness produces a misting effect over the eyes (Acts 13:11). Spiritual waywardness is likened in Scripture to the vagrancy of mist moved about by unpredictable air currents (2 Pe 2:17), and man's transitory existence is compared to a "mist that appears for a little time and then vanishes" (Jas 4:14, RSV).

Mite. A rendering of the Gr. *lepton* in Mk 12:42; Lk 12:59; 21:2; KJV; (RSV "copper coin," or "copper"). *Lepton* is the smallest Greek coin. Its monetary value was about ⅛ of a cent. Since coins with Greek inscriptions could not be used in the Temple, it is thought that the 2 mites that the poor widow dropped into the box were the smallest Maccabean copper coins issued, which are engraved with Hebrew inscriptions and symbols. *See* Money.

Mithcah. *See* Mithkah.

Mithkah (mĭth′kà), KJV **Mithcah** (mĭth′kà). [Heb. *Mithqah*.] One of the camping places of the Israelites in their wilderness wanderings (Num 33:28, 29); not identified.

Mithnite (mĭth′nĭt). [Heb. *Mithnî*.] A term applied to Joshaphat, one of David's "mighty men" (1 Chr 11:43), suggesting either that he came from a place called Methen, or Mathan, or that his ancestor bore one of these names. These names are otherwise unknown.

Mithredath (mĭth′rĕ-dăth). [Heb. *Mithredath*, a Persian name attested in cuneiform records as *Mitradâti*, meaning "gift of (the Persian god of light) Mithra," and known in classical Greek as *Mithradatēs*.]

1. The treasurer of the Persian Empire under Cyrus. He delivered to the Jews the sacred vessels taken by Nebuchadnezzar from the Temple of Jerusalem (Ezr 1:8).

2. One of the enemies of the Jews (probably in Samaria) who joined others in protesting in a letter to Artaxerxes the rebuilding of the wall of Jerusalem (Ezr 4:7; cf. v 17).

Mitre. Headdress worn by the high priest (Ex 28:4; Lev 8:9; Zec 3:5; KJV; etc.). *See* Turban.

Mitylene (mĭt-ĭ-lē′nē). [Gr. *Mitulēnē*.] The most important city on the island of Lesbos. It played an important role in the Persian period. Paul stopped there while returning to Jerusalem from his 3d Missionary Journey (Acts 20:14, 15). Map XX, B-4.

Mixed Multitude. A rendering of: (1) The Heb. *'ereb* (Ex 12:38), "mixture," "mixed people," in the context the non-Jews who accompanied the Hebrew people in the Exodus from Egypt (cf. Num 11:4-6). Whether these were Egyptians or other Semitic peoples whom the Pharaohs had enslaved is not stated in Scripture. Some may have been the children of Hebrews who had intermarried with the Egyptians. In Neh 13:3 *'ereb* is also used of non-Jews living in Jerusalem during the time of Nehemiah (vs 1-3; cf. vs 4-9). (2) The Heb. *'asaphsuph* (Num 11:4, KJV), "cluster," "collection," and thus in the context "rabble" (RSV). The "mixed multitude" was always first to "murmur," to regret the departure from Egypt, and to lust after its dainties (vs 4, 5).

Mizar (mī′zär). [Heb. *Miṣ'ar*.] A hill or peak east of the Jordan, probably near Mount Hermon (Ps 42:6); not identified.

Mizpah (mĭz′pà), KJV sometimes and RSV once **Mizpeh** (mĭz′pĕ). [Heb. *Miṣpah* and *Miṣpeh*, "watchtower."]

1. A cairn erected by Jacob in the mountains of Gilead as a memorial of the covenant concluded there between Laban and himself, also called Galeed, "heap of witness." The cairn indicated symbolically that God was a watcher between the covenanting parties (Gen 31:45-49). Possibly identical with Mizpah, 2.

2. A town in Gilead, home of the judge Jephthah (Jgs 10:17; 11:34), called "Mizpah" (KJV "Mizpeh") of Gilead (ch 11:29). It was probably identical with Ramath-mizpeh (rā′măth-mĭz′pĕ; Jos 13:24, 26), further known as Ramoth in Gilead (ch 20:8), Ramoth-gilead (1 Ki 22:4), or Ramah (2 Ki 8:28, 29). Ramoth was assigned to the Levites as a city of refuge (Jos 21:38), and was a district capital in Solomon's time (1 Ki 4:13). Israel and Damascus fought bloody battles for possession of this apparently important city (1 Ki 22:3-36; 2 Ki 8:28, 29). It has been identified with *Tell Râmîth*, about 30 mi. east of Beth-shean (Map VI, C-5). If Mizpah in Gilead is not Ramoth-gilead, it remains unidentified. Some have also identified it with Mizpah, 1.

3. A place mentioned in Jos 11:3 as the "land of Mizpah (KJV "Mizpeh")." It is probably identical with "the valley of

Mizpeh" of Jos 11:8. It is usually sought near the southwestern slopes of Mount Hermon (Map VI, B-4), but its exact location has not been ascertained.

335. The ruin mound of *Tell en-Naṣbeh*, probably ancient Mizpah, 4

4. A city of Benjamin in the vicinity of Ramah (Jos 18:21, 26; 1 Ki 15:22). It was sometimes a rallying place for the tribes of Israel (Jgs 20:1-3; 21:1, 5, 8; 1 Sa 7:5, 6; 10:17). King Asa fortified Mizpah and Geba against Israel with the building material Baasha had collected at Ramah to strengthen that city's fortifications (1 Ki 15:21, 22; 2 Chr 16:6). Mizpah was chosen by the Babylonians after the destruction of Jerusalem in 586 B.C. as the administrative seat of the province of Judah and residence city of Gedaliah, their appointed governor (2 Ki 25:21-23; Jer 40:6-10). It was again in-

336. An artist's reconstruction of Mizpah, 4, based on results of the excavation of *Tell en-Naṣbeh*

habited after the Exile, and some of its inhabitants took part in the rebuilding of the wall of Jerusalem under Nehemiah (Neh 3:7, 15, 19). Its location has been the subject of major dispute among schol-

ars. Several sites have been suggested, the 2 main ones being *Nebī-Samwîl*, 4½ mi. northwest of Jerusalem, and *Tell en-Naṣbeh*, 8 mi. north of Jerusalem (figs. 335, 336) on the road to Shechem (Map VI, E-3). The last-mentioned site has probably more in its favor than *Nebī-Samwîl*. It was excavated under the direction of W. F. Badé from 1926 to 1935. A strong Israelite wall (see fig. 193) came to light, also many cisterns. See figs. 335, 336.

Lit.: C. C. McCown and others, *Tell en-Naṣbeh* (Berkeley, Calif.: 1947), 2 vols.

Mizpar. *See* Mispar.

Mizpeh (mĭz'pĕ). [Heb. *Miṣpeh* and *Miṣpah*, "watchtower."]

1. The "valley of Mizpeh" (Jos 11:8), probably identical with the "land of Mizpeh." *See* Mizpah, 3.

2. A city in the Shephelah of Judah, near Lachish (Jos 15:38); not identified.

3. A city in Benjamin, spelled both Mizpah (1 Ki 15:22) and Mizpeh (Jos 18:26). *See* Mizpah, 4.

4. A place in Moab (1 Sa 22:3); not identified.

5. For Jgs 10:17; 11:29, 34; KJV, *see* Mizpah, 2.

6. For Jos 11:3, KJV, *see* Mizpah, 3.

Mizraim (mĭz'rā-ĭm). [Heb. *Miṣrayim*.] The 2d son of Ham (Gen 10:6, 13, KJV) and ancestor of the Egyptians. Since *Mizraim* is the Hebrew term for Egypt the name is thus translated in the RSV. The Hebrew word is dual in form, probably pointing to the 2 countries of Egypt, Lower and Upper Egypt, which were united by the 1st dynasty kings. *See* Egypt.

Mizzah (mĭz'à). [Heb. *Mizzah*.] A descendant of Ishmael and of Esau through a marriage of Ishmael's daughter, Basemath, to Esau. Mizzah became a chief of Edom (Gen 36:2-4, 13, 17; 1 Chr 1:37).

Mnason (nā'sŏn). [Gr. *Mnasōn*, a name attested in many Greek inscriptions.] A native of Cyprus and an early Christian disciple, at whose house Paul was a guest in Jerusalem (Acts 21:16).

Moab (mō'ăb). [Heb. *Mō'ab*, spelled *M'b* on the *Moabite Stone, Ma'aba, Ma'ab,* and *Mu'aba* in cuneiform inscriptions, and *Mĭb* in Egyptian hieroglyphic texts. The name seems to be a combination of *mō* (=*min*), "from," and *'ab*, "father," and thus a reference to the fact that the ancestor of the tribe was born of incest.]

1. Son of Lot's daughter by her own father (Gen 19:30-37).

2. The nation of the Moabites (mō'ăb-ĭts), Moab's descendants. The Moabites

were a brother nation of the Ammonites (Gen 19:37, 38), and both were distantly related to the Israelites, since Lot, the father of Moab, had been Abraham's nephew (ch 12:5).

The tribe developed in southeastern Transjordan, where Lot may have lived after the destruction of Sodom. When it was strong enough it displaced the Emim and occupied their country (Deut 2:9-11) from the brook Zered (*Wâdī el-Ḥesā*), which enters the Dead Sea at its southernmost tip, as far as the "plains of Moab" (Num 22:1), which lay to the northeast of the Dead Sea. However, shortly before the arrival of the Israelites, Sihon, an Amorite king, took from Moab the territory north of the Arnon (*Wâdī el-Môjib*) and established his capital at Heshbon (ch 21:13, 26-30). Moab then extended from the Zered to the Arnon (Map VI, F-4).

When the Israelites came to the southern border of Moab, they requested permission to cross that country, but were refused (Jgs 11:17). Since the Edomites, Moabites, and Ammonites were related to the Israelites, Moses was not permitted to attack them or take any part of their country from them (Deut 2:4, 5, 9, 19). However, Balak, the king of Moab, became alarmed when the Israelites conquered the territory of King Sihon, thus becoming Moab's northern neighbor. Fearing that he could not meet them successfully with force of arms, he hired Balaam, hoping to weaken the Hebrews through curses. By divine intervention these curses were turned into blessings. Following the suggestion of Balaam, the Moabites later seduced the Israelites into licentiousness and idolatry (Num 22-25). Because of this the Moabites were excluded from the congregation of Israel to the 10th generation, and Israel was told to keep aloof from them (Deut 23:3-6; Neh 13:1, 2).

During the early period of the judges the Moabites, under King Eglon, invaded western Canaan, took possession of Jericho, the "city of palms," and oppressed the people of Israel for 18 years. At the end of that period Ehud, a Benjamite, assassinated Eglon in his palace, drove the Moabites back to the east, and delivered his people from the oppression (Jgs 3:12-30). Later in the period of the judges, when a famine raged in western Palestine, Elimelech, a citizen of Bethlehem, moved to Moab, where his 2 sons married Moabite women, Orpah and

Ruth. After the 3 men died, Naomi, Elimelech's wife, and Ruth returned to Bethlehem, where Ruth became the wife of Boaz and subsequently an ancestress of David (Ruth 1-4). Saul had troubles with the Moabites (Map VII, E/F/G-4) and fought a successful war against them (1 Sa 14:47). When David was persecuted by Saul, he found protection for his parents with the king of Moab (ch 22: 3, 4), possibly a distant relative of his ancestress Ruth. However, he fought the Moabites after he became king (2 Sa 8: 2, 11, 12; 1 Chr 18:2, 11), and probably made the country tributary (Map VIII, fig. 4). After the breakup of the united kingdom Moab seems to have taken advantage of Israel's weakness to regain some measure of its independence. However, Omri, a strong king, subjugated Moab once more, and forced the Moab-

337. Bird's-eye view of the mountains of southern Moab

ites to pay a high annual tribute to Israel (*Moabite Stone, lines 4-8; 2 Ki 3:4). After Ahab's death Mesha, king of Moab, rebelled against Israel (2 Ki 1:1; 3:4, 5). Probably shortly after this event, Joram, or Jehoram, of Israel made an attempt to restore his rule over Moab. He induced Jehoshaphat and the unnamed king of Edom to join him in his campaign. Although the allied armies defeated the Moabites in battle, invaded their country, destroyed many cities, and besieged the strong fortress of Kir-hareseth (*Kerak*), they returned to their homeland short of a determinate victory (ch 3:6-27). King Mesha of Moab, apparently at that time, extended his land toward the north and occupied much territory of Israel, as we learn from the Moabite Stone (Map IX, E/F/G-4). Toward the close of Jehoshaphat's reign the Moabites, together with the Ammonites and Edomites, made an invasion of Judah. However, God caused them to destroy one another so that Jehoshaphat, king of Judah, had but to gather the spoil (2 Chr 20:1-30). Moabite bands raided Israel at harvesttime following, and possibly before, the death of Elisha (2 Ki 13:20, RSV). These raids probably illustrate the hostility which the Moabites showed against their Hebrew neighbors. Further invasion of Moabite raiders against Judah is recorded in the reign of King Jehoiakim (ch 24:2). The prophets bitterly denounced this hostile nation (Is 15; 16; 25:10; Jer 9:25, 26; 25:17, 21; 48:1-46; Eze 25:8-11; Amos 2: 1, 2; Zep 2:8-11). However, some of the Jews found a refuge in Moab when their country was devastated by Nebuchadnezzar and returned after the appointment of Gedaliah as governor (Jer 40:11, 12). The Moabites are mentioned in such a conventional and ambiguous way in the postexilic books of the OT that it is difficult to say whether they still existed as a nation or not.

In the Assyrian imperial period, when practically all Syria and Palestine were subjugated by the Assyrians, Moab also became an Assyrian vassal state, and is frequently mentioned in the Assyrian records as paying tribute (Maps X, E/F/G-4; XI, C-4). The following Moabite kings are mentioned by name in the Assyrian records: Under Tiglath-pileser (745-727 B.C.) King *Salamanu* of Moab (*ANET* 282), under Sennacherib (705-681 B.C.) King *Kammusunadbi* (*ANET* 287), under Esarhaddon (681-669 B.C.) and Ashurbanipal (669-627? B.C.) *Musuri* and *Kamashaltu* (*ANET* 291, 294, 298). When Babylonia took over the Assyrian Empire, it incorporated Moab also into its territory (Jos. *Ant.* x. 9. 7). During the time of the Persian rule there was an influx of Arabs into the territory of Moab, with the result that the Moabites eventually lost their identity and merged with Nabataean Arabs, forming part of the Nabataean kingdom in the time of Christ (Map XVI, F-4). After A.D. 105 the former Moabite territory became part of the Roman province of Arabia.

The Moabite religion was polytheistic. The chief god was Chemosh (Jer 48:13), whose name appears on the *Moabite Stone (lines 3, 5, 9, etc.) and in personal names, such as *Kammusunadbi* and *Ka-*

mashaltu, mentioned above. In Num 25: 3 and other passages Baal of Peor is mentioned, presumably as a local Moabite deity. The name of the goddess Ashtar is mentioned on the Moabite Stone, and the *Balu'a* stele discovered at *Balu'a* (Map VI, F-4) shows a god similar to an Egyptian deity. That the Moabites occasionally offered human sacrifices to their gods is attested in 2 Ki 3:27.

The Moabite language was closely related to Hebrew, and had only dialectal variances from Biblical Hebrew, as is shown by the only Moabite inscription known, the Moabite Stone.

Moab (mō'ăb), **City of.** [Heb. *'Ir Mô'ab.*] A city mentioned in Num 22:36 as the place where Balak, king of Moab, met Balaam, who had come to curse Israel. Elsewhere the city is described by terms such as "the city . . . by the river" and "the city . . . in the midst of the [Arnon] river" (Deut 2:36; Jos 13:9, 16; 2 Sa 24: 5). Since the children of Israel apparently approached the city during their desert wandering around Moab, it has usually been sought somewhere at the headwaters of the Arnon River (Map VI, F-4), but no site thus far suggested is certain. Some scholars identify the Ar (*'Ar*) of Num 21:15; Deut 2:18; and Is 15:1 with the "city" (*'Ir*) of Moab.

Moab, Plains of. [Heb. *'arbôth Mô'ab.*] That part of the Jordan Valley that lies between the mountains of Transjordan and the river Jordan northeast of the Dead Sea, opposite Jericho (Num 22:1; 26:3, 63; 31:12; 33:48-50; 35:1; 36:13; Deut 34: 1, 8; Jos 13:32). It received its name probably from the fact that it had been part of Moab before the Amorite king Sihon wrested it from the Moabites (Num 21: 26). Map I, C-2.

Moabite (mō'ăb-īt) **Stone.** A black basalt stele containing 34 lines of a text written in pre-exilic Hebrew script (also called Phoenician) of the 9th cent. B.C. It is the longest historical inscription of ancient Palestine discovered up to the present time in that country. It is composed in the Moabite language, a language closely related to ancient Hebrew, differing from it only in dialectal details. This monument, now in the Louvre, Paris, was discovered in 1868 by the German missionary F. Klein at *Dhîbân* (Biblical Dibon), east of the Dead Sea, where at that time few Europeans could safely travel. He reported his discovery to the Prussian consul Petermann in Jerusalem, who in turn obtained funds from the Berlin Museum to purchase the monument. An agreement was subsequently reached with the people of *Dhîbân* for its purchase. In the meantime, however, Charles Clermont-Ganneau of the French Consulate had heard about the discovery of the stone, and had secured a copy of a few lines of its text, which convinced him of its importance. He therefore also began negotiations with the people across the Jordan to obtain the stone for France. This unfortunate competition between the two Western powers aroused the suspicion of the people of *Dhîbân*. Suspecting that the stone either contained gold or had magical value, they drove the price up, and when Petermann, unhappily, took steps with the Turkish military authorities to force the possessors to surrender the monument according to the agreement, the people of *Dhîbân* decided to destroy it. After first heating it red-hot in a fire they poured cold water on it and thus broke it into many pieces. The pieces were divided among the population and used as charms. Clermont-Ganneau had his agents purchase as many pieces as they could secure. He eventually succeeded in recovering about ⅔ of the monument, and restored it with the help of a rather poor paper squeeze of the inscription made for him by a native before the stone was broken up. See fig. 338.

This monument, which can be dated by its historical contents, comes from the 2d half of the 9th cent. B.C., and is thus of great importance for a study of the Hebrew script and alphabet. It also throws much light on the grammatical and lexical characteristics of the Hebrew language used at that time. Many of its passages and expressions are close parallels to Biblical passages, and it contains the first known non-Biblical text that mentions the name *Yahweh (Jehovah) in the same spelling as in the Hebrew Bible (line 18). It also mentions King Omri of Israel, King Mesha of Moab, and the tribe of Gad, besides numerous Transjordan cities known also from the Bible.

The following translation is an attempt to reproduce the Moabite text as closely as possible. Paragraph divisions are not in the original inscription, but are added in the translation for convenience. The small superior numbers designate the lines, many of which begin in the middle of a word. They are inserted here, since sections of the Moabite Stone are frequently referred to by line in this dic-

tionary. Brackets [ ] indicate a broken text, and words enclosed in them are supplied. Wherever such a break cannot with certainty be reconstructed, dots between the brackets are used. Words enclosed in parentheses ( ) are inserted to clarify the meaning of the text, but these words are no part of the actual inscription. Line 34 is too poorly preserved to allow a sensible translation.

" [1] I am Mesha, son of Kemosh- (Chemosh) [. . .], king of Moab, the D[2]ibonite. My father reigned over Moab 30 years, and I reig[3]ned after my father. And I made this high place for Kemosh in Qorchah [. . .,] for he saved me from all kings and caused me to triumph over all my enemies. Omr[5]i, king of Israel, had oppressed Moab many days, for Kemosh was angry with his la[6]nd. And his son succeeded him, and he also said, 'I will oppress Moab.' In my days he spoke [thus], [7] but I have triumphed over him and his house, and Israel has perished forever. And Omri had occupied the [lan][8]d of Mehedeba, and (Israel) dwelt therein his days and half the days of his son, 40 years, but [9] Kemosh dwelt there in my time.

"And I built Baal-meon, and made a reservoir in it, and buil[t] [10] Qiryathan (Kiriathaim). Now the men of Gad had dwelt in the land of Ataroth from of old,

338. The Moabite Stone

and the king of I¹¹srael had built Ataroth for them, but I fought against the city, took it, and smote all the people ¹²of the city as an intoxication for Kemosh and for Moab. And I brought back from there Orel, its commander (?), dr[ag]¹³ging him before Kemosh in Kerioth, and I settled there the men of Sharon and the m[en] of ¹⁴ Maharath.

"And Kemosh said to me, 'Go, take Nebo from Israel,' and I ¹⁵ went by night, and fought against it from the break of dawn until noon, and to¹⁶ok it and smote all of them, 7,000 men, [boys], women, [girl]s, ¹⁷ and maidservants, for I had devoted it to Ashtar-Kemosh. And I took from there th[e ves]¹⁸sels of *YHWH* (Jehovah) and dragged them before Kemosh. And the king of Israel had built ¹⁹ Yahas, and dwelt therein while he fought against me. But Kemosh drove him out from before me, [and] ²⁰ I took from Moab 200 men, all chiefs, and placed them against Yahas, and I took it ²¹ in order to attach it to Dibon.

"I built Qorchah, the wall of the woods, and the wall ²² of the citadel; I also built its gates and built its towers, and ²³ built the palace, and made both reservoirs for water insi[de] ²⁴ the city. And there was no cistern inside the city of Qorchah. And I said to all the people, 'Make for ²⁵ yourselves each one a cistern in his house.' And I cut timber for Qorchah with prisoner²⁶s of Israel.

"I built Aroer and made the highway in the Arnon. ²⁷ I built Beth-bamoth, for it had been destroyed. I built Beser, for (it lay in) ruins, ²⁸ [with] 50 [me]n of Dibon, for all Dibon was obedient. And I reigned ²⁹ [over] 100 towns which I had added to the land. And I built ³⁰ [Mehed]-eba and Beth-diblathen, and Beth-baal-meon, and I set there the [folds] ³¹ [for the] sheep of the land. And as for Hauronen, there dwelt in it [. . .]. ³² But Kemosh said to me, 'Go down, fight against Hauronen.' And I went down [and] ³³ [took it] and Kemosh [dwelt] in it in my days [. . .]."

The inscription refers to the subjugation of Moab by Omri, and King Mesha's rebellion against Israel's rule at a later time. It deals most certainly with the events mentioned in 2 Ki 1:1; 3:4, 5. Mesha's capture of the cities of Medeba, Nebo, and Jahaz from Israel, and his occupation of Ataroth, formerly inhabited by Gad, probably took place after the unsuccessful campaign of Jehoram and Jehoshaphat against Moab described in ch

3:5-27. Some scholars, however, think that Mesha's hostile actions against these cities preceded the military campaign of Israel and Judah. Certainty concerning the sequence is difficult to arrive at, because the Bible does not mention the events described in the *Moabite Stone, and Mesha is silent about the campaign of Jehoram and Jehoshaphat. Mesha's silence in this respect is understandable since this campaign had devastated his country and had cost the life of his eldest son, whom he had sacrificed on the wall of Kir-hareseth (*el-Kerak*) in order to gain the help of his god Chemosh in a desperate situation. It is of interest to read in lines 14-18 that Mesha had carried away as spoil of war from Nebo some objects of Yahweh (Jehovah), probably cult objects from a high place on which the Israelites, in opposition to God's will, worshiped God in a pagan fashion. Such a high place seems to have been located on top of Mount Nebo, which was hallowed by the memory of Moses' death (Deut 34:1-5). In true barbaric fashion Mesha dragged the cult vessels of Yahweh before his own god Chemosh, and thus intended to humiliate the God of Israel, whose power the Moabites held to be inferior to that of their own god.

Moabites. *See* Moab, 2.

Moadiah (mō'à-dī'à). [Heb. *Mô'adyah,* possibly "Yahweh is one who promises."] A priestly family in the time of the high priest Joiakim (Neh 12:12, 17).

Moat. A rendering of the Heb. *charûs* in Dan 9:25, RSV, perhaps to be equated with the Akkadian *harîsu,* "city-moat." The word *chrs* occurs twice in the Aramaic inscription of Zakir of Hamath with the meaning "moat" (*ANET* 501). The KJV "wall" is probably based on the reading of the Vulgate. Theodotion's Greek version also reads "wall."

Moladah (mŏl'à-dà). [Heb. *Môladah,* "birth," or "origin."] A city situated in the southern part of Judah (Jos 15:21, 26), assigned to Simeon (Jos 19:1, 2; 1 Chr 4:24, 28). It was reinhabited after the Babylonian exile (Neh 11:26). The site has not definitely been identified, but may be *Tell el-Milh,* about 10 mi. southeast of Beer-sheba. Some locate it to the northeast of Beer-sheba (Map VI, F-2).

Mole. The rendering of the Heb. *chapharparah* (Is 2:20, *chapharpar* in the 1QIs^a of the Dead Sea scrolls). The European mole, which belongs to the genus *Talpa,* cannot be meant, for members of that family are not found in Palestine. It is probably the mole rat (*Spalax typhlus*), a rodent larger than the European mole. It has no tail, has only rudimentary eyes, lives on vegetables, chiefly bulbs, and houses underground. J. Aharoni (*Osiris*, 5:463, 464) suggests the shrew-mouse (*Crociduva religiosa*), which was considered sacred in Egypt, and which was mummified there. L. Koehler adopted this view in his *LVTL*, p. 322.

For the mole (Heb. *tinshemeth*) of Lev 11:30, KJV, see Chameleon.

Molech (mō′lĕk), or **Moloch** (mō′lŏk). [Heb. *Molek*; Gr. *Moloch*.] The name of a god to whom human sacrifices were offered; not identified. Originally the name of the god was probably *Melek*, meaning "king," which as an epithet the Hebrews applied also to the true God (see Ps 5:2; 10:16; etc.). If so, it would appear that later Jews, considering it shameful to refer to a pagan god by the same word employed for the true God, changed the pronunciation to *Molek*, taking the vowels *o* and *e* from the Heb. *bosheth*, "shame." Some scholars have denied that such a god was anciently worshiped; however, texts discovered in various places attest that he was. A god *Malkûm* mentioned first in 4 texts from Drehem (late 3d millennium B.C.), appears as *Muluk* in the Mari texts, and as *Malik* in 3 Assyrian texts that equate him with Nergal, the Assyro-Babylonian god of the underworld. A recently discovered text from Ugarit speaks clearly of a "sacrifice for *Mlk*," leaving no doubt that *Mlk* was a god. In the Punic language, which is closely related to Hebrew, *molek* occurs with the meaning "vow" and "pledge." Consequently the expression "to pass through the fire to Molech" has been explained by some scholars to mean "to pass through the fire as the fulfillment of a pledge to a certain god." The word *molek* may have had this meaning in Carthage, but in Biblical usage it seems to be limited to a designation for a pagan god to whom sacrifices, among them human, were offered.

The Mosaic law strongly prohibited devoting one's children to Molech (2 Ki 23:10, KJV; RSV "burn," as an offering), and pronounced the death penalty over any offenders of this law (Lev 18:21; 20:1-5). Yet, the Israelites frequently followed the practice (Jer 7:31; 19:4, 5; 32:35; Eze 16:21; 23:37, 39, KJV). Ahaz and Manasseh burned their children at the high place of Topheth in the Valley of Hinnom, south of Jerusalem (2 Chr 28:

1, 3; 33:1, 6), but the pious king Josiah destroyed this place that it might no longer be used (2 Ki 23:10).

A statement of the prophet Amos (ch 5:26) quoted by Stephen (Acts 7:43) seems to indicate that the Hebrews had at one time possessed a portable sanctuary dedicated to this god Molech. However, some commentators understand the Heb. *sikkûth*, rendered "tabernacle" in the KJV, as a proper name, Sakkuth (RSV). Consequently they substitute different vowels in the term translated "your Moloch" to make it read "your king," thus rendering the whole phrase "Sakkuth your king."

In 1 Ki 11:7 the name Molech should probably be read Milcom (cf. vs 5 and 33). The difference could have arisen by the inadvertent dropping of the final letter *m* from the Hebrew name.

Molid (mō′lĭd). [Heb. *Môlîd*, "begetter."] A Judahite, of the family of Hezron (1 Chr 2:29).

Moloch. *See* Molech.

Molten Sea. *See* Sea, Bronze.

Money. A medium of exchange, issued by authority of a recognized government, representing a fixed value, circulated in modern times either as coins or as paper certificates. The ancient world did not know money of perishable material, such as paper currency, or even metal coins before the end of the 8th cent. B.C. Before that time all payments were made either in produce or in metal, the value of which was determined by weight. Since silver was the most widely used metal of exchange, the Hebrew word *keseph*, "silver," was frequently used with the meaning "money," as were also the Babylonian *kaspu* and the Phoenician *ksp*. Likewise, the terms "to pay" and "to weigh" were both expressed by the same words: Heb. *shaqal* and Akkadian *shaqâlu*. Hence we find Abraham weighing out 400 shekels of silver for the land he bought near Hebron (Gen 23:16), and David paying "600 shekels of gold by weight" for the Jebusite's threshing floor (1 Chr 21:25).

The monetary system in use in Canaan during the 2d millennium B.C. was the Babylonian system, as the *Amarna Letters of the 14th cent. B.C. reveal. Since the OT terms for money values, "shekel" and "mina," are derived from the Babylonian *shiqlu* and *manû*, it is generally assumed that the Israelites also used the Babylonian monetary system rather than the Egyptian, which apparently was not used outside of Egypt, not even by its foreign vassals. On the weight and value of the various units of gold and silver, *see* Mina; Shekel; Talent.

The phrases "piece of money," "piece

339. Jewish shekel, obverse and reverse, of the 1st revolt in Judea, A.D. 66-70 (above), and of the 2d revolt, A.D. 132-135 (below)

of silver," are vague renderings of uncertain Hebrew words denoting certain amounts of precious metal of which the exact equivalent is unknown (Gen 33:19; 1 Sa 2:36). In some passages (Jgs 17:2; 2 Sa 18:11, RSV) the word is supplied and is used in a neutral sense, some weight or unit of money not expressed being implied but not expressed in the Hebrew text. In the RSV footnotes of Gen 33:19; Jos 24:32; Job 42:11 the terms "qesita," "kesita," and "kesitah," respectively, are variant transliterations of the Heb. *qeśiṭah*, translated "piece of money" (KJV once "piece of silver") in the texts. *Qeśiṭah* represents an ancient unit of weight used in making payment. It seems to have fallen into disuse after the conquest of Canaan, since it is never mentioned in later books of the Bible. Its value is unknown. In Mt 26:15 and 27:9 the phrase "piece of silver" stands for a shekel or its equivalent (cf. Zec 11:12); in Lk 15:8, for a drachma.

Coined money was first introduced in Lydia, *c.* 700 B.C. (Herodotus i. 94). From there the process of making metal coins of uniform size and weight spread rapidly to Greece, where the first coins date from before 650 B.C. When Cyrus took Sardis in 547 B.C. and all of Asia Minor became a Persian possession, the Persians adopted coined money and introduced it into all parts of their empire, which com-

prised the whole Near East within a few years after the conquest of Lydia. Gold coins were issued only by the king, but silver coins were issued also by the provincial governments. Darius I introduced the standard gold coin, which was named the *dareikos,* "daric," after him and was worth about $5.00. *See* Darics.

The earliest coined money mentioned in the OT is the Greek "drachma," or "daric," KJV "dram" (Ezr 2:69; Neh 7: 70, 71, 72). A coin imitating the Athenian drachma of the 5th cent. B.C. was discovered at Beth-Zur (fig. 124). Its Hebrew inscription mentions (1) a certain Hezekiah, probably the high priest whom Josephus mentions as a friend of Ptolemy I (*Apion* i. 22), and (2) the name "Judah" as the issuing country. This discovery shows that the Jews used Greek drachmas as silver coins, and even issued them locally during the Persian and early Hellenistic periods. At the same time they also used Persian money such as the daric (Ezr 8:27, RSV). The "drams" of 1 Chr 29:7, KJV (RSV "darics"), is a rendering of the Heb. *'adarkôn.* This term was probably used by the writer of 1 Chr to convert a monetary value of David's time into the currency of his own day.

In *c.* 140 B.C. Antiochus VII issued a decree permitting Simon the Maccabean (143/42-135 B.C.) to coin his own money (1 Macc 15:6). Simon's coins are inscribed in archaic Hebrew characters, and bear as symbols the chalice used for drink offerings in the Temple, the *lûlab,* a bundle of twigs, and the *ethrôg,* a citron, the latter 2 being symbols of the Feast of Tabernacles. On some coins a basket of fruit or a palm tree is depicted. Similar Hebrew coins were issued during the reigns of John Hyrcanus and Aristobulus. Alexander Jannaeus (103-76/75 B.C.), in addition to the Hebrew inscription, had his name and his title of king stamped in Greek on the coins. His successors did likewise. These Maccabean coins, all of copper, were permitted to be used in the Temple in Christ's time, but other money, such as Greek or Roman coins, could not be used but had to be exchanged for these Maccabean coins. This was the reason that money-changers were found in the outer court of the Temple (*see* Moneychanger).

Herod the Great was the first ruler of Judea to use only Greek inscriptions on his coins; however, he avoided offending the religious feelings of his subjects with representations of human figures on his money (fig. 220). All silver and gold coins in use in Palestine were of Greek and Roman origin. Herod's successors, and the Roman procurators who ruled in Palestine for 2 periods (A.D. 6-41, 44-66), issued copper coins of various denominations. Gold coins (the *aureus*, worth 25 denarii) are not specifically mentioned in the NT except perhaps in a general way in Mt 10:9.

The following coins are mentioned in the NT and circulated in Palestine during the ministry of Jesus and of the apostles. They are listed here by their Greek names:

1. *Drachma* (Lk 15:8), a Greek silver coin, called "piece of silver" (KJV), "silver coin" (RSV). It was either a coin from Greece or an imperial coin struck at Antioch in Syria, where drachmas were issued. Its value was about $.105 (on the basis of the coinage value of $.905 per ounce troy).

2. *Statēr* (Mt 17:27), a Greek silver coin, also known as *tetradrachma,* worth 4 drachmas (=about $.42), called "piece of money" (KJV), "shekel" (RSV). These coins were minted at Antioch and were about equal to the former Phoenician shekels. There is slight textual evidence for the reading *"statēr"* in Mt 26:15.

3. *Mna,* "mina," rendered "pound" (Lk 19:13, 16, 18, 20, 24, 25). It was not a coin, but a Greek monetary unit equal to 100 drachmas, with a value of about $10.50. The term is a Semitic loan word.

4. *Talanton,* "talent" (Mt 18:24; 25: 15-28), a Greek monetary unit equal to 60 minas, hence was worth about $630.

5. *Lepton* (Mk 12:42; Lk 12:59; 21:2), KJV "mite," "copper coin," or "copper" (RSV). It was the smallest copper coin in use and was worth about an eighth of a cent.

6. *Assarion,* from the Latin *assarius,* (Mt 10:29; Lk 12:6), rendered "farthing"

2. Tiberius, 14-37

3. Caligula, 37-41

4. Claudius, 41-54

5. Nero, 54-68

1. Augustus, 27 B.C.-A.D. 14

7. Otho, 69

8. Vitellius, 69

10. Vespasian (commemorating reconquest of Judea. Inscription reads: *IVDAEA*)

6. Galba, 68-69

9. Vespasian, 69-79

11. Titus, 79-81

12. Titus (commemorating Jerusalem's capture. Inscription reads: *IVD{AEA} CAP{TA},* "Judea Captured")

13. Domitian, 81-96

14. Nerva, 96-98

15. Trajan, 98-117

340. Roman coins during New Testament times. Numbers 1, 6, 9, and 12 are *dupondii,* numbers 3 and 5 are *assarii,* numbers 2, 4, 7, 8, 10, 11, and 13-15 are *denarii*

(KJV) and "penny" (RSV), a Roman copper coin, worth about one cent (see fig. 340, No. 1). Sixteen of these coins equaled one denarius.

7. *Kodrantēs*, from the Latin *quadrans* (Mt 5:26; Mk 12:42), rendered "farthing" (KJV) and "penny" (RSV), a Roman copper coin worth one fourth of an *assarius*. It was equal to 2 *lepta*, hence was worth about one fourth of a cent.

8. *Dēnarion*, from the Latin *denarius* (Mt 18:28; 20:2, 9, 10, 13; etc.), rendered "penny" (KJV), "denarius" (RSV), the most common silver coin of the Roman Empire (see fig. 340, No. 2). In normal times its worth was about 18 cents, but it became devaluated during the 1st cent. A.D., so that by the time of Nero it was worth only about 8 cents. It was the ordinary daily wage of a laborer. *See* Denarius.

The Jews struck their own coins again during the Roman war of A.D. 66-70, but these coins are not mentioned in the NT; they also minted their own coins during the Roman war of A.D. 132-135 (see fig. 339).

Lit.: F. A. Banks, *Coins of Bible Days,* New York, 1955; A. Reifenberg, "Ancient Jewish Coins," *JPOS* 19 (1941), 59-81, 286-313.

Money-changer. One who changed foreign money of various kinds into Jewish currency, usable as Temple poll tax or as freewill offerings. *See* Money. In the days of Christ and the apostles large numbers of foreign Jews and proselytes annually visited Jerusalem, especially ·during the great feasts, bringing with them their foreign currency unacceptable at the Temple, because only money with Hebrew inscriptions could be presented for offerings; hence the need for money-changers conveniently at hand. During the festal seasons these changers, who ordinarily had their stalls in the city, were admitted to the Temple Court of the Gentiles. Each money-changer sat at a table (Gr. *trapeza,* Mt 21:12; Mk 11:15; Jn 2:15); hence he was called a *trapezitēs* (Mt 25:27). According to the Talmud, for every half shekel he changed he was allowed to take a commission of a *kollubos,* equal to about 12 grains of silver (3 cents). From the name of this commission came the name *kollubistēs* used for the money-changers in Mt 21:12; Mk 11:15; Jn 2:15. On 2 different occasions Jesus became so indignant at the noise, dishonesty, and trading spirit He found among these money-changers in the Temple Court, where quietness should have prevailed, that He overturned their tables, at the same time driving out the cattle dealers who sold sacrificial beasts to the visiting worshipers (Mt 21:12, 13; Jn 2:14-16).

Monster. *See* Dragon.

Month. [Heb. *chodesh, yerach;* Aramaic *yerach;* Gr. *mēn.*] A division of the year derived from the period required by the moon to pass through its 4 phases, as from one new moon to the next. Since the time of the moon's circuit around the earth is neither an exact number of days nor a commensurable part of the year—its synodical revolution, approximately 29½ days—a calendar month must be either a variable or an artificial period.

The Hebrew month was lunar, beginning with the evening on which the crescent moon appeared. The 1st day of the month was called the new moon (see 1 Sa 20:24-27), and was a day of special observances (see Num 10:10; 28:11-15). At first, visual observation was used to determine the appearance of the crescent. If the crescent was seen on the evening following the 29th day of the month, a new month had begun; if not, another day was added so that that particular month had 30 days (a month never had more than 30 days). Later, methods of calculation were devised by which it could be known in advance whether a given month should have 29 or 30 days. Jewish tradition tells of the method of examining at Jerusalem witnesses who claimed to have seen the crescent, to determine whether they had actually seen it or not. It tells also of fire signals that were used to announce the beginning of the new month to the outlying areas.

The Babylonians, like the Greeks, had lunar months. The Egyptian months were 30 days each, with 5 extra days after the 12th month. The Roman months, originally lunar, were changed to the 30, 31, and 28 (29) days that we know today. Modern Jews still use their Biblical months for religious purposes. These months generally alternate between 30 and 29 days, which have been calculated for centuries according to variable but standardized rules, and are no longer dependent on the moon. The Moslems, on the other hand, still depend on the actual sighting of the crescent moon each month for their religious calendar.

Neither the 30-day month implied in the Flood narrative (150 days totaling 5 months; Gen 7:11, 24) nor the 30-day prophetic month (42 months equaling 1260 days; Rev 11:2, 3; *see* Time, 5), has anything to do with the Jewish calendar month. Genesis does not furnish enough information to warrant drawing conclusions as to the sort of calendar Noah might have employed, and the 30-day month of Revelation is prophetic and symbolic, not literal, for no known calendar runs in an unbroken series of 42 30-day months. However, the idea of a theoretical or ideal month of 30 days was logical to the Jews, who called 30 days a "full" month; a 29-day month they spoke of as "hollow," or "deficient." Because of the variability of the moon's motion, lunar months do not invariably alternate 29 and 30 days. Consequently it was impossible for the ancient Jews and Babylonians to predict the exact number of days in a period of months or years ahead. Thus the logical method of reckoning a future period was to count by "full" months, that is, theoretical months, of 30 days each (even as we today sometimes count 30 days to the month in computing interest). The Babylonians did this and quite possibly the Jews did also. Since not even Jewish readers of the book of Revelation could tell exactly how many days were in 42 Jewish months without knowing which months they might be (nor could the Gentiles using the Roman calendar, without taking leap years into account), the most logical method of reckoning a prophecy expressed in months and relating to future time would be by theoretical, rather than calendar, months. And the fact that the 42 months are of 30 days each is clear from the equation with 1,260 days. Further, months in symbolic prophecy are not literal, but symbolic months (which, interpreted by the year-day principle, are each 30 years). *See* Time, 5.

For the names and order of the Jewish calendar months, and the periodical doubling of the 12th month, *see* Year.

Moon. [Heb. *yareach;* Gr. *selēnē.*] The chief luminary ordained by the Creator "to rule the night" (Gen 1:16; Ps 136:9) and to mark off time periods (Gen 1:14, 16). The Hebrew calendar, like that of most ancient nations, was based on the repeated circuit of the moon around the earth as marked off by successive new moons (*see* Month; Year).

In ancient times moon worship was practiced almost universally by the peoples of Mesopotamia, Egypt, and Palestine. In Babylon prognosticators attempted to predict future events on the basis of lunar phases (Is 47:13, RSV). The "crescents"

(RSV) or "round tires like the moon" (KJV) of Is 3:18 were probably associated in some way with moon worship. Toward the close of the divided kingdom the people of Judah adopted moon worship (cf. 2 Ki 21:5; Jer 8:1, 2). Certain idolatrous priests were appointed to burn incense to the moon (2 Ki 23:5). In the time of Job the moon was adored by a kiss of the hand (Job 31:26, 27).

Among the Hebrews the day of the new moon, or the 1st of the month, was set apart as a day for special worship and feasting (1 Sa 20:5). Trumpets were blown to announce the day (Ps 81:3; cf. Num 10:10), ordinary labor was suspended (Amos 8:5), and additional sacrifices were prescribed (Num 28:11-14). The new moon of the 7th month was the civil New Year's Day. *See* Trumpets, Feast of.

Morasthite (mô-răs′thīt). [Heb. *Môrashtî.*] An epithet of the prophet Micah (Mic 1:1; Jer 26:18; KJV), indicating that he was a native or inhabitant of Moresheth-gath. Instead of "the Morasthite" the RSV reads "of Moresheth" (mō′rĕsh-eth), that is, "of Moresheth-gath."

Mordecai (môr′dĕ-kī). [Heb. *Mordokay* and *Mordekay,* from a Babylonian name, *Mardukâ,* borne by several Jews living in the time of Artaxerxes, according to Babylonian cuneiform records.]

1. A leading Jew who returned with Zerubbabel (Ezr 2:2; Neh 7:7).

2. A Benjamite, son or descendant of Jair, son of Shimei, son of Kish (Est 2:5). Mordecai is introduced as a gate official in the palace of Susa (vs 5, 21) who had brought up Hadassah, or Esther, his uncle's daughter (v 7). When King Ahasuerus (Xerxes) deposed Queen Vashti, and a substitute was sought, Esther was chosen to fill the vacancy (vs 8-20). When Mordecai learned of a plot against the king's life, he warned Ahasuerus through

341. The supposed sarcophagi of Queen Esther and Mordecai in the traditional tomb of Esther at Hamadan. See also fig. 165

Esther, and the conspirators were executed (Est 2:21-23). For refusing to bow down to Haman, the prime minister, Mordecai incurred his enmity. Some believe that Mordecai's refusal was due to Haman's possible descent from the former Amalekite kings (see Agagite; Haman). In retaliation Haman plotted to destroy not only him but also the whole Jewish nation, and obtained the king's permission to carry out his plan (ch 3:1-15). When Mordecai learned of this he instructed Esther to speak to the king, which she promised to do after a period of fasting (ch 4:1-17). When Esther saw the king she invited him and Haman to a dinner, and at the dinner repeated the invitation for the following day, deferring presentation of her request until then (ch 5:1-8). Returning home from his first dinner appointment with inflated feelings of the high honor that had been extended to him, Haman became furious when Mordecai, whom he met, refused to honor him. He immediately prepared a gallows, planning to impale Mordecai the next day (vs 9-14). That night the king, unable to sleep, for diversion had the official state chronicles read to him. Therein was found the account of a conspiracy against the king's life which failed because Mordecai, having learned of the plot, informed the king. The king discovered that his faithful servant had not been rewarded. Next morning he asked Haman what to do for a man whom he wished to honor. Thinking that he himself was meant, Haman suggested that the man should be dressed in royal garments and be paraded through the streets on the king's horse. The king accepted the suggestion and ordered Haman himself so to honor Mordecai (ch 6:1-14). During the 2d dinner Esther revealed to the king Haman's plot to wipe out her nation, and received a favorable decision from him. Haman was executed and Mordecai put in his place, and a decree was signed allowing the Jews to avenge themselves upon those who would destroy them (chs 7:1 to 9:16).

During World War II Prof. A. Ungnad found a cuneiform tablet in the Berlin Museum, in which a certain man by the name of *Mardukâ*, the equivalent of Mordecai, is mentioned as one of the state officials in Susa during the reign of Xerxes. His title, *sipîr*, indicates that he was an influential counselor. The discovery of this text has been accepted as welcome proof that Mordecai was a historical

figure, which had been doubted by many scholars. That Mordecai became popular and honored by his people (Est 10:3) is furthermore indicated by the fact that a number of Jews of the next generation bore his name, as the archives of the ancient business house of "Murashu Sons" at Nippur have revealed.

Moreh (mō'rĕ). [Heb. *Môreh*, "teacher."]

1. The name of a large tree or grove of trees at Shechem where Abraham camped after arriving in Canaan from Mesopotamia (Gen 12:6). The name was perhaps given to it because a teacher had lived there in early times. The word translated "plain" in the phrase "plain of Moreh" in the KJV (Heb. *'elôn*) means "a large tree" (RSV "oak"). The word is here probably used in a collective sense with the meaning "a grove of trees," for a later reference to the site in Deut 11: 30, contains the word *'elôn* in the plural. The exact site is not known, but according to the context was near Shechem.

2. A hill in the Valley of Jezreel, north of the spring of Harod (Jgs 7:1), identified with the *Nebî Daḥî*, also called Little Hermon, a hill opposite Gilboa on the northern side of the Valley of Jezreel, and south of Mount Tabor.

Moresheth. See Morasthite.

Moresheth-gath (mō'rĕsh-ĕth-găth'). [Heb. *Môresheth Gath*, "possession of Gath," or "possession of a wine press."] The home of the prophet Micah (Mic 1:1, 14). It is mentioned in connection with several towns of Judah (vs 13-15), in whose vicinity it must have been situated. It has been identified with *Tell ej-Judeideh*, 14 mi. northeast of Hebron, which was excavated in 1899 and 1900 by Bliss and Macalister.
Lit.: F. J. Bliss and R. A. Stewart Macalister, *Excavations in Palestine During the Years 1898-1900* (London, 1902).

Moriah (mŏ-rī'à). [Heb. *Môrîyah*.]

1. An area where Abraham was directed to sacrifice his son Isaac (Gen 22: 2). The name Moriah seems to have been rather uncommon, for it occurs in only one other passage (2 Chr 3:1), where it is used to designate the mountain on which Solomon built the Temple. The "land of Moriah" must therefore have been the mountainous country round about Jerusalem, and Mount Moriah the particular mountain on which the Temple was later built. Josephus calls the mountain on which Isaac's offering took place "the mountain Moriah" (*Ant.* i. 13. 1). The Samaritans, who consider Mount

342. The rock on Mount Moriah, the hill where Abraham offered Isaac, which was also the site of Solomon's altar of burnt offering. The rock is now enclosed by the Dome of the Rock (see fig. 262)

Gerizim the holy mountain of God, place the sacrifice of Isaac on that mountain, and believe that Moriah was Moreh near Shechem; and that it was the site of the first encampment of Abraham in the land of Canaan, where he built an altar to the true God (Gen 12:6, 7). Such an identification, they believe, justifies their separation from Jerusalem, and their right to worship God on Mount Gerizim (see Jn 4:20, 21). It is, of course, entirely without support.

2. The hill where the threshing floor of Ornan, the Jebusite, was situated. David purchased the threshing floor and afterward chose it as the site of the Temple which his son Solomon built (2 Chr 3:1; cf. 2 Sa 24:18). See Moriah, 1. The Temple hill at Jerusalem lay between the Kidron and Tyropoeon valleys, north of the old City of David (see fig. 259), and was about 2,440 ft. above sea level. Its original shape has been obscured by debris and by the tremendous foundations and platform on which the sacred Mohammedan precinct, the *Ḥaram esh-Sherîf*, is located. See Jerusalem.

Morning Watch. *See* Night.

Mortar, I, KJV **Morter.** [Heb. generally *chomer*.] A plastic building material to bind stones or bricks together. Several kinds of mortar are mentioned in the Bible: (1) A mortar consisting of clay and water, with no lime, used by the peasants of the Orient to the present day. It is this that is possibly referred to in Nah 3:14, where an emergency is implied. (2) A mortar consisting of clay, lime, and water, to which ashes and straw were sometimes added. This kind of mortar was widely used in Palestine and Egypt where large quantities of limestone are available. It was used in the building of better-

class houses and public buildings (Ex 1:14; Is 41:25). (3) Bitumen, or "slime" (KJV), was used instead of clay mortar for public buildings in ancient Mesopotamia, inasmuch as this material was readily available in open asphalt wells (Gen 11:3; see fig. 388).

In Jer 42:9 the RSV translates the Heb. *melet,* "mortar" (KJV "clay"), but the type of mortar described is not known. The "morter" of Lev 14:42, 45 (Heb. *'aphar*) literally means "dust," but in these passages "plaster" (see RSV). *See* Whitewash.

Mortar, II. [Heb. *medokah* and *maktesh*.]
1. A strong stone vessel (Num 11:8; Prov 27:22) in which substances such as grains, paint, spices, drugs, and other products were ground by means of a pestle (Heb. *'eli*). Such utensils have been excavated in ancient Palestine. These mortars were usually of basalt and stood on 3 feet.
2. For Zeph 1:11, RSV, *see* Maktesh.

Morter. *See* Mortar, I.

Mortgage. A rendering of the Heb. *'arab* (Neh 5:3), "to give security," used in this passage to mean temporary signing over of property to a lender as evidence of a borrower's intention to repay. Failure to repay the loan ordinarily results in permanent transfer of ownership of the security to the creditor. Certain abuses of the system in postexilic Palestine, in which some were taking advantage of their needy brethren, called forth Nehemiah's wrath and impelled him to take corrective measures (vs 1-5).

Mosaic. [Heb. *riṣephah,* "pavement."] An expression occurring once (Est 1:6, RSV) in a passage describing the mosaic pavement, constructed of various kinds of stone, in the court of the garden of King Ahasuerus' palace in Susa.

Mosera. *See* Moserah.

Moserah (mô-sē'rá), KJV **Mosera** (mô-sē'rá). [Heb. *Môserah.*] A camping place in the wilderness wandering of the Israelites in the vicinity of which Aaron died (Deut 10:6); not identified. In Num 33:37, 38 Aaron is stated to have died at Mount Hor; hence Moserah was evidently near that mountain. Moserah has been identified with the Moseroth (mô-sē'rŏth) [Heb. *Moserôth*] of vs 30, 31.

Moseroth. *See* Moserah.

Moses (mō'zĭz). [Heb. and Aramaic, *Mosheh,* "one drawn out," probably based on the Egyptian *mś* or *mśw,* "child," "son," "the one born of." The Egyptians incorporated the word *mśw,* "mose," into royal names

343. Moses at the burning bush, a wall painting in the 3d cent. synagogue of Dura Europus (see Map XIII, C-5)

such as Ahmose, "the one born of (the moon god) Ah"; Kamose, "the one born of the (deified soul) Ka"; Thutmose, "the one born of (the scribal god) Thoth"; and the common name Ramose (later Ramses), "the one born of (the sun-god) Ra." In everyday life thése names were often abbreviated to "Mose." Similarly, the name Pharaoh's daughter gave Moses may originally have included the name of some Egyptian deity. Since the Egyptians worshiped the Nile, which they deified as "Hapi" (*Ḥ'py*) and commonly called *'Itrw*, later *'Irw*, the princess may have named Moses Hapimose or Irumose, either of which would mean, "the one born of (or "drawn out of") the Nile." When Moses "refused to be called the son of Pharaoh's daughter" (Heb 11:24), he would naturally drop the reference to an Egyptian deity. Gr. *Mōüsēs.*] The deliverer of the Hebrew people from Egyptian bondage, their leader through the wilderness wandering, their great lawgiver, and the author of the Pentateuch.

Moses spent the first 40 years of his life quite likely under the 18th dynasty kings: Thutmose I (*c.* 1525 - *c.* 1508 B.C.), and Thutmose II (*c.* 1508 - *c.* 1504 B.C), and Queen Hatshepsut (*c.* 1504 - *c.* 1482 B.C.), a daughter of Thutmose I and on the basis of the chronology here suggested doubtless the "daughter of Pharaoh" referred to in

Ex 2:5-10. In that case Moses would have witnessed the rise of Egypt to the height of its political power. Under Thutmose III, whose sole reign (*c.* 1482 - *c.* 1450 B.C.) would have fallen in the 40 years during which Moses sojourned in Midian, the Egyptian Empire extended from the Abyssinian highlands in the south to the Euphrates in the northeast. A widespread commerce developed, and riches flowed from foreign lands to support the great projects of the Pharaohs. Cultural life had reached a high level, craftsmanship and architecture were in an advanced state, and astronomy, mathematics, and medical science flourished. Egypt had every reason to boast of its prowess as the most powerful and civilized nation of its time.

Moses was the son of Amram and Jochebed, and a descendant of Levi in the 4th generation (Ex 6:16-20), of the family of Kohath (vs 18-20). His brother Aaron was 3 years older than he (ch 7:7), and he had an older sister, Miriam (ch 15:20; cf. ch 2:6, 7). At Moses' birth the children of Israel had been in Egypt about 135 years (see Gen 12:4; 21:5; 25:26; 47:9; Deut 2:7; 34:7; Acts 7:30; cf. Ex 7:7; 12:40, 41; Gal 3:16, 17). Jacob had been dead for about 118 years (Gen 47:28), and Joseph for about 64 years (ch 50:22; cf. chs 41:46, 47, 54; 45:6; 47:9). On the basis of a 1445 B.C. exodus (*see* Chronology II, 2), Moses was born about 1525 B.C. (cf. Ex 7:7). On this same basis, when the Hebrews entered Egypt the racially related and friendly Hyksos kings ruled the land. However, early in the 16th cent., some 50 or 60 years prior to Moses' birth, the Hyksos were expelled by a native Egyptian dynasty, the 17th. About 1570 B.C. the powerful 18th dynasty arose, one of whose early kings, perhaps Ahmose or Amenhotep I, was probably the "new king over Egypt, which knew not Joseph" mentioned in Ex 1:8. The Hebrews had multiplied rapidly until "the land was filled with them" and they had become "more and mightier" than the Egyptians, or at least the latter so claimed (ch 1:7-9). Because the Hebrews were numerically strong, and because the Egyptians urgently needed cheap labor for their vast building projects, it is little wonder that the kings of this new dynasty instituted a policy of keeping them in subjection at forced labor (vs 10-14). How long prior to Moses' birth the Hebrews were set to work building the "treasure cities, Pithom and Raamses" (v 11) and were made to "serve with rigour" (vs 12-14) is not known. But the more the Egyptians oppressed them "the more they multiplied and grew" (Ex 1:12), and efforts to check the rapid increase in population proved wholly ineffective. At first the Egyptians proposed to grind them down by making their lives "bitter with hard bondage" (v 14), but when this proved unavailing they ordered the Hebrew midwives to kill all male children born to the Hebrews (vs 15, 16). However, the midwives neglected to carry out Pharaoh's orders, giving as their excuse that Hebrew women were more vigorous than Egyptian women and did not need the services of the midwives (v 19). Pharaoh then ordered his own people to take the matter of exterminating the Hebrew male children into their own hands by drowning them in the Nile (v 22). But in view of the many able-bodied men among the Hebrews 80 years later at the Exodus, it would seem that this cruel requirement could not have continued long in force.

At his birth Moses' parents recognized him to be "a goodly child" (Ex 2:2). Their efforts to preserve Moses alive are referred to in Heb 11:23 as an act of faith, implying perhaps an awareness on their part that God had destined him for an important role and would intervene to preserve his life. By putting Moses in an ark of bulrushes and placing him on the bosom of the Nile, Jochebed was complying with the letter of the law that required male children to be offered in sacrifice to the Nile, which the Egyptians worshiped as a god, supposing that its waters had power to impart fertility and guarantee long life. The visit of Pharaoh's daughter to the river "to wash herself" (Ex 2:5) may have been a ritual ablution designed to secure these supposed benefits for herself. The appearance of Moses floating in his little ark of bulrushes as if he were a gift from the Nile god, in answer to her prayers, apparently impressed her as a happy omen. The princess took the child as her own, hiring his own mother as his nurse.

Moses' home training inculcated in him a love for God and some understanding of his life mission (cf. Acts 7:25). Under royal Egyptian tutors and doubtless as a royal prince and heir presumptive to the throne, Moses was instructed in "all the wisdom of the Egyptians" (v 22). From the priests he doubtless mastered Egyptian letters, literature, science, and religion; from army commanders, skill in military leadership, and from other royal officials a knowledge of laws and civil administration. Some have suggested that Moses may have led some military expeditions into foreign lands. As the heir presumptive he was doubtless popular at court, as well as with the army and the common people. His outward appearance, his dress, his speech, his behavior, and his culture may have been completely Egyptian, but he never became an Egyptian at heart. In character, religion, and loyalty he continued to be a Hebrew, as is evident from the incidents related in Ex 2:11-13 (cf. Heb 11:24, 25).

When he was 40 (Acts 7:23)—c. 1485 B.C., while Queen Hatshepsut (see fig. 146) was still reigning—Moses knew that the time had come when he must choose between his Hebrew faith and the throne of Egypt. Inbred loyalty to God (Heb 11:24-26) and an awareness of God's purpose for his life (Acts 7:25) led Moses to cast his lot with his own people and "to suffer affliction" with them rather than "enjoy the pleasures of sin for a season" (Heb 11:25). The fact that he had refused to adopt the Egyptian religion had doubtless aroused misgivings in the minds of his benefactors. Perhaps it was in fear that he might seize the throne, that the priests of Amon in a temple revolution at about this time placed on the throne an illegitimate son of Thutmose II, Hatshepsut's deceased husband, and forced Hatshepsut to accept this young prince as coregent. The new king adopted the throne name of his father and is known in history as Thutmose III. Under such circumstances he would have especially hated Moses, in whom he would see his greatest rival, and thus could have hastened Moses' decision to throw in his lot with his despised countrymen and to attempt to liberate them from Egyptian oppression. Acting rashly, Moses slew an Egyptian taskmaster (Ex 2:11, 12), and by this foolish act he played into the hands of his enemies, perhaps especially Thutmose III, who now would have a legitimate reason to bring Moses to trial and to destroy him. It is quite possible that these were the circumstances that led Moses to flee from Egypt and to find refuge in the land of *Midian to the east (v 15).

Since the Midianites were descendants of Abraham by Keturah (Gen 25:1, 2), Moses was with relatives during his 40 years of sojourn, some of whom still worshiped the true God. Among them was Jethro, a priest of the true God (cf. Ex 18:1, 12, 23). Jethro was also called Reuel (ch 2:16-18), which means "friend of God." Jethro's hospitable reception led Moses to

enter his service, and in course of time his daughter Zipporah became Moses' wife (Ex 2:18-21). Jethro was a man of sound judgment, as is evident from the counsel he later gave his son-in-law (ch 18:12-27). During his 40 years in the lower Sinai Peninsula Moses doubtless became familiar with the geography, resources, and climate of that desert region. Leading Jethro's flocks amid the solemn grandeur of the mountains, he had ample time for reflection upon his past experiences. The 90th psalm, which is attributed to Moses, reflects his thoughts, perhaps toward the close of his sojourn in Midian. If so, the following interpretation seems appropriate: The opening verses of this psalm seem to mirror the mountain solitudes of Sinai and the majesty of God, in contrast with human frailty in general and the great mistakes of his own life (Ps 90:7, 8). Knowing the role Providence had marked out for him (Acts 7:25), Moses doubtless reflected that his impetuous act in slaying the Egyptian had frustrated God's purpose and thwarted the divine plan for his life. He had already passed the mark of "threescore years and ten" and was approaching "fourscore years" (Ps 90:9, 10), but with his great disappointment in mind he prayed that God would teach him to "number" his days that he might apply his heart unto wisdom (v 12). He still had faith in the promises of God to the fathers and hoped for their fulfillment. His thoughts then turned to his suffering brethren in the land of Egypt (vs 13, 14) and he prayed for their deliverance (vs 15, 16). Finally, he pleads with God that the work of his own hands may be established, that his life may not have been altogether in vain (v 17). It was probably about the time of these reflections that God met Moses at the burning bush and commissioned him to return to Egypt to liberate the Hebrews (Ex 3:1-10). Remembering the threat to his own life and sensing his insufficiency for the task (v 11), fearful also that his own people would not accept him and doubtful of his ability to persuade Pharaoh to let Israel go, Moses hesitated to accept the call (vs 11, 13; ch 4:1). But God patiently disposed of these seeming difficulties one by one, and Moses unwillingly

acquiesced (Ex 4:1-19). On the way back to Egypt he met Aaron, whom God had sent out into the wilderness to welcome him, and together they returned to Egypt and met with the elders of Israel (vs 20-31) before approaching the Pharaoh himself (this would have been Amenhotep II according to the chronology suggested above; see fig. 167). Their first audience with Pharaoh (ch 5:1-3) only made the lot of the Hebrews more bitter than it had been before (vs 4-19). Ten plagues fell before Pharaoh changed his mind. With the last of the 10, the death of the first-born, Pharaoh summoned Moses by night and finally ordered the Hebrews to leave Egypt (ch 12:29-32).

Under divine guidance Moses led Israel forth from the land of their servitude (Ex 13:17-22). After a series of crises and providential deliverances, Moses and the Hebrew people arrived at Mount Sinai (ch 19:1, 2). See fig. 448.

On the mount Moses received directly from God instructions for the establishment of the Hebrew nation as a theocracy (Ex 24:9-11; 33:11, 17-23; 34:5-29; etc.), including the basic law of the Ten Commandments, which were also spoken audibly to the entire congregation (ch 20:1-18) and later inscribed upon 2 tables of stone and preserved in the ark (Ex 31:18; 34:1-4; Deut 10:1-5). As spokesman for God, Moses led the people into the covenant relationship which constituted Israel a theocracy (Ex 19:5-8; 24:3-8). God then summoned Moses to meet with Him in the mount (ch 24:12), where He revealed complete plans for the erection of the tabernacle, which was to be His dwelling place as their king (chs 25-31), and at the same time also gave him the 2 tables of the law (ch 31:18). In Moses' absence the people had set up a golden calf, which they were worshiping when Moses returned (ch 32:1-6). Seeing their idolatry, Moses broke the 2 tables of stone (vs 15-19). The Lord had revealed Israel's idolatry to Moses and had proposed to reject Israel and to carry out His purposes through him (vs 7-10), but Moses proved his stature as a leader by graciously interceding in Israel's behalf, and God spared them (vs 11-14). After the people had been duly punished (vs 30-35), Moses once more besought the Lord, who promised, "My presence shall go with thee, and I will give thee rest" (ch 33:12-17). Upon his own request and as a token of God's presence with them, Moses was granted a vision of the divine glory (chs 33:17 to

←

344. Michelangelo's statue of Moses in the church of S. Pietro in Vincoli in Rome

34:9). During a second 40 days in the mount (Ex 34:1, 2, 28; Deut 9:18), Moses received further instructions for the government of Israel and the 2d tables of stone (Ex 34). Upon his descent to camp his face was radiant with divine glory, and the people feared to approach him (vs 29-35). During the remaining months at Sinai the tabernacle was constructed (chs 36-39), and Moses wrote out the instructions God had given him, possibly at this time.

After about a year at Mount Sinai, during which Israel had been constituted a nation, its laws had been codified, the sanctuary had been erected and its services instituted, Israel set out for Canaan (Num 10:11-13). A short time later Miriam and Aaron challenged Moses' leadership (ch 12:1, 2), but the Lord signally vindicated Moses as His appointed spokesman by temporarily inflicting leprosy upon Miriam (vs 4-15). At Kadesh, because of a discouraging report on the land of Canaan, the people rebelled against Moses and proposed to return to Egypt (ch 14: 1-4). This was the 10th rebellion since the departure from Egypt (v 22). Because of their failure the men of that generation were condemned to die in the wilderness (vs 29-35), and for the next 38 years (Deut 2:14) the people encamped at various places in the vicinity of Kadesh-barnea and the northern tip of the Gulf of Aqabah. At Kadesh nearly 38 years later Moses and Aaron sinned, impetuously striking a rock contrary to God's instructions, thereby marring the lesson its miraculous waters were designed to teach. As a result they were denied the privilege of conducting Israel into the Promised Land (Num 20: 7-12). Moses led Israel around the land of Edom in the conquest of Transjordan (vs 14-21), and finally to the last encampment at Shittim, across the Jordan River from Jericho (cf. chs 22:1; 25:1). While encamped there, Moses delivered a series of orations outlining God's providences over the past 40 years, pointing out lessons from these experiences, and repeating the laws God had revealed to him for the people. These 4 orations are recorded in the book of *Deuteronomy. During the encampment at Shittim, Moses ordained Joshua as his successor (Num 27:18-23; Deut 1:38), and shortly before his death took Joshua to the tabernacle to receive his charge from the Lord (Deut 31:14, 23). At the Lord's direction Moses then ascended Mount Nebo, where he viewed the Promised Land (see fig. 349) and died at

the age of 120 years (Deut 32:48-52; 34:7). God buried him nearby (v 6).

Moses' great literary ability is evident from the quantity and great variety of his writings. In Genesis he recounted the history of the world from Creation to the death of Joseph. In Exodus and in parts of Numbers and Deuteronomy he preserved a record of the exodus from Egypt and of the more important events on the way from that country to Canaan. In the last chapters of Exodus he recorded details of the construction of the tabernacle, and in Leviticus he wrote out the regulations governing its sacred services. In Exodus (chs 20-24), Leviticus (chs 18-20; 24:10-23), and parts of Deuteronomy he wrote out the civil laws God had given him for Israel. He was also a skilled poet (see Ex 15:1-19; cf. Ps 90). But Moses was more than a gifted writer; he was one of the great leaders and administrators of all time. Under God's direction he organized Israel as a nation and guided it safely from Egypt to the borders of Canaan. He provided for its civil, judicial, and religious institutions. As a prophet (Deut 18:15) he was the favored recipient of special communications from God for a period of 40 years, and enjoyed privileges no other man has ever known. To no small degree the great achievements of the Hebrew nation were the outgrowth of the character, personality, and consecrated life of Moses, who, above all other leaders, bound its families and tribes together as God's chosen people. Abraham was the father of Israel, but Moses was the founder and lawgiver of the nation. God summoned Moses forth from his resting place (see Jude 9), and later honored him with Elijah on the mount of Transfiguration (Mt 17:3, 4). As lawgiver and leader Moses surpassed all men of antiquity, but despite his superior talents he was "very meek, above all the men which were upon the face of the earth" (Num 12:3).

Most High. A title applied to God, a translation of: (1) The Heb. '*Elyôn*, "most high," "most exalted" (Gen 14:18; 2 Sa 22:14; etc.). This term was also employed by the Canaanites to refer to one of their gods. (2) The Aramaic '*Illay* (Dan 3:26; 4:34; etc.), which occurs also in Palmyrene and Nabataean inscriptions. Nebuchadnezzar did not necessarily mean that he acknowledged the Hebrew God as his own God, but possibly merely as the greatest of all gods. (3) The Gr. *Hupsistos* (Mk 5:7; Acts 7:48; Heb 7:1), "highest," "most high," "most exalted." The Greeks applied this term to *Zeus, the supreme being of their patheon, also to the God of the Jews, when they came into contact with the Jewish religion. *Hupsistos* is the LXX rendering of *'Elyôn*.

Most Holy Place. See Tabernacle; Temple.

Mote. The rendering of the Gr. *karphos* (Mt 7:3-5; Lk 6:41, 42; KJV), translated "speck" in the RSV. The term refers to a small particle of chaff, wood, etc.

Moth. [Heb. *'ash;* Gr. *sēs.*] An insect repeatedly mentioned in the Bible, proverbial for its destruction of clothing (Job 13: 28; Mt 6:19; Jas 5:2). Evidently the clothes moth (*Tinea*) is here meant, which in its larva stage feeds upon wool. Clothes were valuable possessions among the ancients. The Heb. *sas* of Is 51:8, rendered "worm" in the KJV, refers to this moth (RSV) or perhaps to the larva of this moth. Christ admonished His hearers not to store up treasures on earth, where moths destroy, but to lay them up in heaven (Mt 6:19, 20; Lk 12:33).

Mother of Pearl. See Pearl.

Motions. A word appearing once (Rom 7:5, KJV) in the archaic sense of "inclinations," "tendencies," "desires." The phrase rendered "motions of sins" in the KJV is translated "sinful passions" in the RSV.

Mound. Two types of mounds are mentioned in the Bible: (1) A siege mound (2 Sa 20: 15; 2 Ki 19:32; Eze 4:2; etc.; KJV "bank," "mount"), a mound of earth, stones, debris, piled outside city walls upon which the besiegers placed *battering rams to assail the upper, weaker part of the wall, and from which archers shot their arrows into the city. If the city was on a hill (see fig. 284), sloping mounds were erected to gain access to the wall itself. See War. (2) A ruin heap, such as that left by an ancient city that had been destroyed (Jos 11:13; Jer 30:18; 49:2; RSV). When the city was rebuilt the old ruins were leveled off and the new city was built on top of these ruins. Successive destructions and rebuildings resulted in mounds of considerable height. Such a mound is called a *tell* in Arabic, and many such are found in the Near East today. The excavator can recognize the various periods of the city's history by the separate levels, or strata, that he uncovers. For example, the mound of Megiddo (see fig. 324) covers an area of 13 acres, and in it are found 20 levels.

Mount. A rendering of: (1) The Heb. *har,* "mountain," and the Gr. *oros,* "mountain," "hill," in connection with names

such as Mount Sinai (Ex 24:16), Mount Nebo (Deut 34:1), Mount of Olives (Mt 26:30), etc. The KJV also uses the term generally (Gen 31:54; Heb 8:5; etc.), but in such passages the RSV uses the term "mountain." (2) The Heb. *muṣṣab* (Is 29: 3, KJV), translated "siegeworks" in the RSV. (3) The Heb. *solelah,* "mound" (Jer 6:6; 32:24; etc.), translated "siege mound" or "siege walls" in the RSV.

Mount of Assembly, KJV **Mount of the Congregation.** [Heb. *har-mô'ed,* "mountain of assembly."] A place described in Is 14:13, 14 as a mountain upon which the king of Babylon aspired to sit (cf. v 4). The passage is couched in terms of the mythical concepts of the Babylonians, who believed that the gods held their council on a high mountain of the north. The prophecy refers symbolically to Lucifer, or Satan, of whom the Babylonian king was a type. Satan desired to control the councils of heaven and be equal with God. See Armageddon.

Mount of Corruption. See Corruption, Mount of.

Mount of Olives. See Olives, Mount of.

Mount of the Congregation. See Mount of Assembly.

Mountain. [Heb. *har;* Aramaic *ṭûr;* Gr. *oros.*] Eastern and western Palestine, as well as Syria, are mountainous, and the mountains of these areas are frequently mentioned in the Bible. The highest peak is Mount Hermon (over 9,000 ft.), which forms the southernmost peak of the Anti-Lebanon range. In comparison with it the mountains of Palestine are rather low, the highest 3, Mount Ebal, Mount Gerizim, and the Mount of Olives, having altitudes of only about 3,000 ft. The Hebrew poets considered the mountains among God's greatest works (see Ps 65:6; 90:2), and as providing refuge (Jgs 6:2; Ps 11:1). Mountains were used figuratively as symbols of permanence (Deut 33:15; Hab 3:6), stability (Is 54:10), great calamities (Jer 13:16), and insurmountable obstacles (Zec 4:7). See names of specific mountains.

Mountain-sheep, KJV **Chamois.** [Heb. *zemer.*] An animal classified in Deut 14:5 as clean and hence fit for food. The exact identity of *zemer* is uncertain. Both "mountain-sheep" and "chamois" are conjectural translations. The chamois is a goatlike antelope of the mountainous area of Europe and the Caucasus and does not occur in Palestine, hence cannot be referred to.

Mourning. The act and experience of sorrowing and lamenting, especially because of the death of a close friend or relative. In Oriental lands mourning was frequently ostentatious, burdensome, and mechanical. Public evidences that one was in mourning included such acts as replacing the clothing with coarse sackcloth garments (Joel 1:8), neglecting the ordinary habits of cleanliness, such as combing, shaving, bathing (2 Sa 19:24), tearing the mantle and shaving the head (Job 1:20), and sitting in sackcloth and ashes (Job 16:15; cf. 2 Sa 13:31), leaving off ornaments (Ex 33:4), beating the breast (Is 32:12; Neh 2:7; RSV; Lk 23:48), fasting (Ps 35:13), loud weeping (Joel 1:8, 13). Aaron was forbidden to mourn for the death of his rebellious sons, Nadab and Abihu (Lev 10:6). Friends were often joined by professional and sacrilegious mourners (Jer 9:17, 18; Mt 9:23), and Jer 16:7 implies that meals were served. According to Herodotus (ii. 66. 85; iv. 71; viii. 99; ix. 24) similar customs prevailed in Israel's neighboring countries, and certain mourning customs sometimes practiced by Israel (Jer 16:6; 41:5; Mic 1:16) were probably inspired by their pagan neighbors. There seems to have been an idolatrous significance to the custom of shaving the head and cutting the flesh, which customs were forbidden to Israel (Lev 19:27, 28; 21:5; Deut 14:1). The Hebrews mourned 30 days for Moses (Deut 34:8) and 7 days for Saul (1 Sa 31:13). When Jacob died the Egyptians mourned 70 days, and the funeral party mourned an added 7 days at Atad, beyond the Jordan (Gen 50:3, 10). Sorrow for sins is the noblest of all mourning. The prophets repeatedly admonished ancient Israel to mourn for her sins (Jer 4:8; 6:26).

Mouse. [Heb. *'akbar.*] One of the animals listed as unclean, hence forbidden as food (Lev 11:29). The Bible mentions at least one instance when, during a time of apostasy, the restriction was ignored (Is 66: 17). This prohibition applied to all members of the family *Muridae.* A plague of mice caused great damage to the Philistine country when the ark was in Ashdod (1 Sa 6:4, 5, 11, 18). Whether the jerboa or the ordinary field mouse is here meant is not certain. J. Aharoni reported (*ZDPV* 40 [1917], 238) that in 1914, shortly before the harvest season, the area of Ekron, south of Jaffa, was threatened by millions of field mice. The harvest was saved that year by a heavy rain that drowned the mice in their holes.

Moving Things. A rendering of the Heb. *remeś* in Gen 9:3, elsewhere generally translated *"creeping things," but in Gen 9:3 the context requires a more general translation because living creatures in general are intended, such as those man was given permission to eat after the Flood.

Moza (mō'za). [Heb. *Môṣa'*, "going forth."]
1. A Judahite, son of Caleb by his concubine Ephah (1 Chr 2:46).
2. A descendant of Saul through Jonathan (1 Chr 8:33, 36, 37; 9:39, 42, 43).

Mozah (mō'za). [Heb. *Moṣah.*] A town of Benjamin (Jos 18:21, 26), also known as Emmaus, usually identified with *Qalôniyeh,* 4½ mi. northwest of Jerusalem.

Mufflers. A rendering of the Heb. *re'alôth* (Is 3:19), a part of the finery of the women of Israel, probably long, flowing *veils, more delicate and expensive than those of ordinary everyday use. The RSV reads "scarfs."

Mulberry Tree. See Balsam Tree.

Mule. [Heb. *pered* and *pirdah.*] A hybrid between a horse and an ass. Mules unite qualities of both parents, inheriting endurance and sure-footedness from the ass, and strength and courage from the horse. The Hebrews used mules from early times. Since breeding of hybrids was forbidden by law (Lev 19:19), they probably imported them (1 Ki 10:25) as the Tyrians did, who obtained theirs from Togarmah (Eze 27:14). In the time of David the mule was the preferred riding animal (2 Sa 13:29; 18:9), and was used for the coronation of Solomon (1 Ki 1:33). According to a text from Mari, it was more dignified in the 2d millennium for a royal person to ride on a mule than on horseback, but the reason is not stated. This prejudice against horses may still have existed in the time of David. Solomon and Ahab kept both horses and mules (1 Ki 10:25; 18:5). Mules were used to carry heavy burdens (2 Ki 5:17; 1 Chr 12:40). The Jews brought 245 mules with them when they returned from exile in the time of Zerubbabel (Ezr 2:66).

The "mules" of Gen 36:24, KJV, is a translation of the Heb. *yemim,* a word of uncertain meaning (see *SDA Com* 1: 425, 426). The RSV renders the term "hot springs." In Est 8:10, 14 the Heb. *rekesh,* rendered "mules" in the KJV, should rather be translated "horses" (RSV).

Munition. A word appearing in Is 29:7; 33: 16; Nah 2:1; KJV, in its obsolete meaning "fortification," "defense," "rampart."

Muppim (mŭp′ĭm). [Heb. *Muppim*.] A son of Benjamin (Gen 46:21), probably called Shupham, Shephupham, and Shuppim in other OT passages. *See* Shephupham.

Murder. The deliberate killing of a human being. The 1st instance of murder was Cain's slaying of Abel (Gen 4:8), and early in the history of the world the command was given, "Whoso sheddeth man's blood, by man shall his blood be shed: for in the image of God made he man" (ch 9:6). The 6th commandment expressly forbids murder (Ex 20:13; Deut 5:17). Num 35 outlines in some detail the laws governing Israel's handling of the matters of murder and manslaughter. The *avenger of blood had the right to put a murderer to death (v 19), but there were established cities of refuge, where a person might flee for asylum until his case could be tried (vs 11, 12). If the person was proved guilty he was to be delivered to the blood relative of the deceased to be put to death; but if the killing could be shown to have been unintentional he might live in immunity in the city of refuge until the death of the high priest, at which time he could return home in safety (Num 35:15-32; Deut 19). The traditional mercy expected by a wrongdoer who would flee to the altar in the sanctuary and cling to the horns of the altar was not extended to a murderer (Ex 21:14; 1 Ki 2:28-34). As Israel later sank deep in apostasy, human life was considered cheap, and we find Jeremiah (Jer 7:9) listing murder as one of Judah's prime sins. Hosea (Hos 6:9) accused some of the priests' of murder. Christ showed that the commandment prohibiting murder involved more than the outward act, and touched upon the motives (Mt 15:19; 5:19; cf. Mk 7:21). Jesus declared Satan to be "a murderer from the beginning" (Jn 8:44), with the unmistakable implication that those who tried to kill Him were the children of Satan (vs 37, 40, 41).

Murrain. [Heb. *deber*, "plague," "pestilence."] A contagious disease found in cattle (Ex 9:3, KJV), probably some type of ulcerous sore, or a disease similar to the modern anthrax. Elsewhere *deber* is generally translated "pestilence."

Mushi (mū′shī). [Heb. *Mûshî*.] A son of Merari (Ex 6:19; Num 3:20; 1 Chr 6:19; 23:21, 23; 24:26, 30), and ancestral head of the family of Mushites (mū′shīts) [Heb. *Mûshî*] (Num 3:33; 26:58).

Mushites. *See* Mushi.

Music. The art of arranging tones in a pleasing manner, practiced from the beginning of human history. The first musician of whom we have record was Jubal, "the father of all such as handle the harp and organ" (Gen 4:21). There are indications that music was a highly developed art in Egypt and Mesopotamia in 2000 B.C., and thus that it was enjoyed long before that time.

The playing of instruments or singing, or the two combined, was practiced at various occasions, such as feasts (Gen 31: 27; Is 24:7, 8; Lk 15:25), idolatrous celebrations (Ex 32:18, 19), coronations (1 Ki 1:39, 40; 2 Chr 23:13), public mournings (Eze 32:16; Mt 9:23), and for various purposes, such as, to celebrate victories (Ex 15:1-21; 1 Sa 18:6, 7), to praise God (Ps 33:2, 3; 150; etc.), and by wanton women to seduce (see Is 23:15; cf. Prov 7:7-21). David set apart certain persons who were to "prophesy" accompanied by various musical instruments (1 Chr 25:1), and the prophet Elisha used music on one occasion for prophetic inspiration (2 Ki 3:14, 15). The therapeutic effect of music was understood and applied in ancient times (1 Sa 16:14-17, 23).

David, "the sweet psalmist of Israel" (2 Sa 23:1), was a skilled musician (1 Sa 16:18) and a composer of songs (see superscriptions of Ps 69; 109; etc.). When the ark was moved to Jerusalem, David (2 Sa 6:12, 15) appointed musicians to minister before it (1 Chr 15:16; 16:1-6, 42). Later, he organized musicians and singers for the Temple to be built by Solomon. He appointed instrumentalists (ch 23:5) and leaders of music (ch 25:1-7). When the Temple was dedicated a great company of musicians and singers praised the Lord (2 Chr 5:12, 13). Musicians and singers added to the rejoicing when the foundation of Zerubbabel's Temple was laid (Ezr 3:10, 11) and, later, when Jerusalem's repaired walls were dedicated (Neh 12:27, 28, 35, 36, 42). Thus singing played a prominent part in the worship of the Israelites.

Paul exhorted the Ephesian and Colossian Christians to sing "psalms and hymns and spiritual songs" (Eph 5:19; Col 3:16; *see* Hymn). In vision John the revelator saw harpers and heard singing (Rev 5:8, 9; 14:2, 3); among the singers were those who sang "the song of Moses the servant of God, and the song of the Lamb" (ch 15:2, 3). *See* Musical Instruments; Psalms; also names of musical instruments, and of musical terms appearing in the Psalms.

Musical Instruments. Music played a great role in the life of the ancients from earliest history (Gen 4:21), but especially in the religious life of the Hebrews. Many great events were connected with the playing of musical instruments; for example, the celebration of the deliverance from the Egyptians (Ex 15:20), the destruction of the walls of Jericho (Jos 6:16), and the transportation of the ark to Jerusalem by David (2 Sa 6:5). In Solomon's Temple there was an elaborate musical organization, planned by David, consisting of choirs and instrumental orchestras (1 Chr 25). This musical organization was later adopted by the administration of the 2d Temple (Neh 12:41, 42, 46, 47).

The musical instruments of the ancients in general and those of the Hebrews in particular may be divided into 3 general classes:

1. *Percussion instruments:* Castanet, tambourine, timbrel, and triangle.

2. *Stringed instruments:* Harp, lute, lyre, and ten-stringed instruments.

3. *Wind instruments:* Flute, horn, and trumpet.

The majority of these instruments are mentioned in the Bible and are discussed in this dictionary under their individual names. *See* names of these instruments; *see also* Bagpipe; Trigon.

Few musical instruments of the ancient Hebrews have come to light in the excavations—only several pairs of cymbals, some rattles, and the handle of a sistrum. With the exception of a few pictures of lyre players (see figs. 307, 308) there are no portrayals of ancient Palestinian musicians. However, a large number of wall pictures of instrumentalists have been found in the tombs and temples of ancient Egypt, and, to a lesser degree, in Mesopotamia. Furthermore, the dry climate of Egypt has preserved numerous musical instruments, such as lyres and harps, flutes and oboes, trumpets, sistrums, and others. Some musical instruments have also come to light in the excavations of Mesopotamia. Since these instruments did not vary much from country to country, it is justifiable to consider the Hebrew instruments similar in form and construction to those of Egypt and Mesopotamia, the 2 great civilized countries with which the Hebrews had frequent and strong connections. Consequently the archeological material from those countries is used in this dictionary in the description of musical instruments. It must be remembered that some uncertainties still exist in regard to some Biblical terms used for musical instruments. These uncertainties account for the inconsistencies found with regard to the names that are given to such instruments in modern Bible translations.

Lit.: Curt Sachs, *The History of Musical Instruments* (New York, 1940); O. R. Sellers, *BA* 4 (1941), 33-47; J. Wellhausen, *The Book of the Psalms* (New York, 1898), appendix, pp. 217-234; *SDACom* 3: 29-42.

Mustard. [Gr. *sinapi.*] Any plant of the genus *Brassica*. The Biblical variety probably is *Sinapis nigra*, or black mustard. It grows wild in Palestine and is also cultivated for its seeds, which are used as a condiment and are ground up to produce an oil. Although the plant is usually only 3 or 4 ft. tall, it may attain a height of 6 to 12 ft., and thus have sufficient strength to bear up birds. The contrast in the size of the seed and the treelike shrub it produces upon maturing formed the basis for Jesus' parable concerning the growth of the kingdom of heaven (Mt 13:31; Mk 4:31; Lk 13:19) and the smallness of the seed was used by Jesus as an illustration for a lesson on faith (Mt 17:20; Lk 17:6).

Muster (mŭs'tẽr) **Gate,** KJV **Gate Miphkad** (mĭf'kăd). [Heb. *Miphqad*, "enrollment," or "sum."] A gate of Nehemiah's Jerusalem (Neh 3:31). *Miphqad*, rendered "appointed place," appears in Eze 43:21 as a part of the temple area. Commentators have therefore suggested that Muster Gate, or gate of Miphkad, was so named because it led to the particular part of the Temple area to which Ezekiel refers. The context of Neh 3:31 indicates that it was in the northern part of the eastern Temple wall. It was probably close to the present Golden Gate of the Ḥaram esh-Sherîf. Map XVII, II.

Muth-labben. [Heb. *mûth labben.*] A term of uncertain meaning appearing in the superscription of Ps 9. Perhaps the term suggests the melody to which the psalm was to be sung.

Myra (mī'rȧ). [Gr. *Mura.*] A port city of Lycia, 2 mi. inland from the coast on the river *Myros*, after which it was named. It was one of the chief cities of Lycia at the time of the old Lycian confederation, and was the capital of the province of Lycia in Roman times. It was a center of the grain trade. The place, now called *Dembre*, still contains some magnificent ruins of the ancient city. The centurion who took Paul as a prisoner to Rome (*c.* A.D. 60) changed ships at Myra, finding there an Alexandrian vessel that was bound for Italy (Acts 27:5, 6). Map XX, B-5.

Myrrh. [Heb. *loṭ, mor;* Gr. *smurna, muron.*] A pleasant-smelling substance, probably produced by *Balsamodendron myrrha,* a scrubby thick-branched tree, growing in southwest Arabia and in Somaliland. It reaches a height of 6 ft. on the coast, and 15 ft. in the higher elevations (see *JAOS* 78:141ff.), having odoriferous bark through which a gum exudes naturally. A more ready flow can be induced by making an incision in the bark. At first the excretion is oily, but later, by exposure to the air, it hardens into small yellowish or white "tears." Eastern peoples regarded it highly as a perfuming agent and likewise as a medicine.

Myrrh was an ingredient of the holy anointing oil used by the priests (Ex 30: 23-25), and served as a purifying agent for women (Est 2:12). Garments and beds were perfumed with myrrh (Ps 45:8; Prov 7:17), and it is mentioned frequently in Solomon's song of love (Song 1:13; etc.). This fragrant substance was one of the gifts of the Wise Men who came to worship the Christ child (Mt 2:11), and was used somewhat after the fashion of an embalming agent at the time of His death (Jn 19:39, 40). Its medicinal use is implied in Mk 15: 23, where we are told it was offered to Jesus on the cross (*see* Gall). *Loṭ,* translated "myrrh" in Gen 37:25; 43:11, was probably the resinous bark of *Pistacia mutica.* In Jacob's time it was imported by Egypt and considered of sufficient value to be used as a gift to a dignitary. The RSV, following the LXX, reads "myrrh" in 1 Ki 10:25; 2 Chr 9:24; however, the Heb *nesheq* means "armor," "equipment."

Myrtle. [Heb. *hadas.*] Quite likely the evergreen *Myrtus communis,* which bears snow-white flowers bordered with purple and an aromatic fruit from which perfumes are made. In poor soil it may be little more than a scraggly shrub, but it can attain a height of 20 or 30 ft. under ideal conditions. Myrtle branches were used to build booths for the Feast of Tabernacles in postexilic Jerusalem (Neh 8:15). It grows on nearby hills and is now known in all countries bordering the Mediterranean Sea. The myrtle of Scripture is a symbol of God's generosity and of peace and joy (Is 41:19; 55:13). A grove of myrtle trees is the setting for a vision of Zechariah (Zec 1:8-11).

Mysia (mĭsh'ĭ-à). [Gr. *Musia.*] An area in northwestern Asia Minor, bounded on the west and north by the Aegean Sea, the Hellespont, and the Propontis (now called Sea of Marmara), and on the south and east by Lydia, Phrygia, and Bithynia. The Mysians were of Celtic descent and lived as shepherds in the interior of Mysia, with Greeks living along the coast. They played only a small role in history. The Troad was one of the districts of Mysia, and Pergamum was its southernmost city. In NT times it was part of the Roman province of Asia, having fallen to the Romans in 133 B.C. During his 2d Missionary Journey, Paul, accompanied by Silas, passed through this area on his way to Troas, one of Mysia's cities (Acts 16:7, 8). Paul passed through the area twice on his 3d Missionary Journey, once on the way from Ephesus to Macedonia, and again on the return journey to Jerusalem (2 Cor 2:12, 13; Acts 20:6, 13, 14). Map XX, A/B-4.

Mystery. A rendering of: (1) The Aramaic *raz* (Dan 2:18-47; 4:9; RSV), "secret," "mystery," used with reference to Nebuchadnezzar's dreams, which the king and all his wise men could not understand. (2) The Gr. *mustērion.* The pagan Greeks used this term, generally in the plural, for secret rites, secret teachings, religious and political in nature, to be known only to the initiated. In the NT *mustērion* is used of the plans, purposes, and dispensations of God, which the unaided human mind cannot understand. In the Gospels it occurs in only one context, namely, with reference to a question of the disciples concerning a certain parable (Mk 4:10; Lk 8:9) or concerning the use of parables in general (Mt 13:10). In reply Jesus said, "It is given unto you to know the mysteries of the kingdom of heaven, but to them it is not given" (Mt 13:11; cf. Mk 4:11; Lk 8:10; KJV). *Mustērion* occurs most frequently in the Pauline writings (20 times). There the term refers generally to something God wishes to make known to those who are willing to receive His revelations, not something He desires to keep secret (Rom 16:25, 26; Eph 1:9; etc.). "The mystery which hath been hid from ages and from generations" "now is made manifest to his saints" (Col 1:26, KJV). In the Revelation *mustērion* is used of the mysterious things revealed in the book. In chs 1:20; 17:7; cf. v 5 the term seems to be used in the sense of symbolic significance.

Myth. *See* Fable.

N

Naam (nā′ăm). [Heb. *Na'am*, "pleasant."] A son of Caleb the son of Jephunneh (1 Chr 4:15).

Naamah (nā′à-mà). [Heb. *Na'amah*, "pleasant."]

1. A daughter of Lamech by his wife Zillah, and sister of Tubal-cain; a descendant of Cain (Gen 4:22).

2. An Ammonitess, wife of Solomon and mother of King Rehoboam (1 Ki 14:21; 2 Chr 12:13).

3. A town in the Shephelah of Judah (Jos 15:41), tentatively identified with *Khirbet Fered*, near Timnah.

Naaman (nā′à-măn). [Heb. *Na'aman*, "pleasant"; Gr. *Naiman*. The name occurs in Ugaritic as *N'mn*, and in an Egyptian text of the time of Thutmose III as *N'mn3*.]

1. A descendant of Benjamin (Gen 46:21; 1 Chr 8:4), and ancestral head of the Naamites (nā′à-mīts) [Heb. *Na'amî*] (Num 26:40).

2. Another descendant of Benjamin, and son of Ehud (1 Chr 8:6, 7).

3. The commander in chief of the Syrian army under Ben-hadad II, king of Damascus. As a militarist he was successful, and made the Syrian kingdom of Damascus a strong nation (2 Ki 5:1). However, he contracted leprosy, and faced the ruin of his career. In his household was an Israelite slave girl who had been taken captive on one of the Syrian raids into Israel. In her sympathy for her master she expressed the wish that he might be healed by the prophet of Samaria. Presented with the prospect of healing, Naaman took counsel with the king, who at once sent him to Samaria with a letter of recommendation to the king of Israel. When Naaman presented this letter to the court at Samaria, consternation arose, for the incident was considered an excuse to pick a quarrel and begin a war. However, when Elisha heard about the incident he sent word to the king that Naaman should be referred to him. When Naaman and his retinue appeared before Elisha's home, the prophet did not come out to see him; he merely sent word that he should dip 7 times in the Jordan. This was evidently to test Naaman's faith and to humble his pride. Naaman was offended, and proposed to return to Damascus at once, declaring that the rivers *Abana and Pharpar were much better than the muddy Jordan. But finally he was persuaded to give the prophet's prescription a trial. As a result he was healed. He offered Elisha a handsome reward, but the prophet refused to accept anything from him. Elisha's servant Gehazi, however, through deception obtained for himself some of the gifts that Naaman had offered the prophet. This deception cost Gehazi dearly, for as punishment for his sin he became afflicted with Naaman's leprosy (2 Ki 5:1-16, 20-27).

As a result of the miraculous healing Naaman became a believer in Yahweh, the God of Israel, and promised to worship only this God from then on (2 Ki 5:17). He requested 2 mule loads of earth, on which to offer sacrifices to God in Damascus. He explained to the prophet, however, that his position required him to accompany the king to the temple of the god Rimmon, where he would have to bow down before the idol, as the king leaned on his arm. The prophet said to him, "Go in peace" (vs 17-19). This was apparently not the time to urge reform in this matter.

Naamathite (nā′à-mà-thīt). [Heb. *Hanna'amathi*.] A native or inhabitant of Naamah, which was either a town (not the town of Judah of that name) or a country (probably in Arabia). It appears as the designation of Zophar, Job's friend (Job 2:11; 11:1; 20:1; 42:9).

Naamite. *See* Naaman, 1.

Naarah (nā′à-rà), KJV once **Naarath** (nā′à-răth). [Heb. *Na'arah*, "girl."]

1. Wife of Ashhur the ancestor of the inhabitants of Tekoa (1 Chr 4:5, 6).

2. A town on the border of Ephraim between Bethel and Jericho (Jos 16:7), transliterated "Naarath" in the KJV. In 1 Chr 7:28 the town is called "Naaran" (nā′à-răn) [Heb. *Na'aran*]. Josephus records that Herod Archelaus the ethnarch diverted half of the water supply of Neara for the irrigation of the palms at his palace at Jericho (*Ant.* xvii. 13. 1). The town was called Noarah by Eusebius, who located it 5 Roman mi. from Jericho. The site has been identified with *Khirbet el-'Ayâsh*, about 5 mi. northeast of Jericho.

Naarai (nā′a-rī). [Heb. *Na'aray*.] One of David's "mighty men" (1 Chr 11:37), apparently called Paarai in 2 Sa 23:35.

Naaran. *See* Naarah, 2.

Naarath. *See* Naarah, 2.

Naashon. *See* Nahshon.

Naasson. *See* Nahshon.

Nabal (nā′băl). [Heb. *Nabal*, "foolish" or "reckless."] A rich sheep owner who resided in Maon and pastured his flocks around Carmel (1 Sa 25:2, 3), a village on the edge of the Wilderness of Judah. When David lived in that area as a fugitive from the wrath of Saul, he and his armed followers protected Nabal and the residents of the area from marauding raiders or robbers (vs 15, 16). At sheepshearing time, which was a time of feasting, David sent some of his followers to Nabal and asked him for a contribution. Nabal, probably under the influence of strong drink, not only refused but made insulting remarks about David. David became so incensed that he made preparations to attack Nabal and destroy the whole family (vs 4-13). Fortunately, Nabal's understanding wife, Abigail, realized the danger in which her husband's foolish behavior had placed them; she set out at once to meet David with gifts of food, and succeeded in appeasing him. On her return she found her husband strongly intoxicated. When she told him, the next morning, in what danger he had been and what she had done to save him and their belongings, he suffered a stroke and died 10 days later (vs 14-38). Some time later Abigail, whose beauty and prudence had made a deep impression upon David, became one of his wives (1 Sa 25:39-44; 27:3; 2 Sa 2:2; 3:3).

Naboth (nā′bŏth). [Heb. *Nabôth*, probably "elevation."] A citizen of Jezreel who owned a vineyard near the palace of King Ahab in that city (1 Ki 21:1; 2 Ki 9:25). The king desired to acquire it, but Naboth refused to sell the land that he had inherited from his forebears. The sacredness of such an inheritance was so strongly established that under the circumstances the land could not be legally secured so long as Naboth and his sons lived. Ahab's crafty wife Jezebel therefore plotted to put Naboth and his heirs out of the way. She produced false witnesses to accuse them of offenses against the king, and had them executed (1 Ki 21:1-16; 2 Ki 9:26). This heinous crime called down the judgments of God upon the king and his wicked wife (1 Ki 21:17-24),

judgments that found their fulfillment in the course of time (1 Ki 22:34-38; 2 Ki 9:30-37).

Nachon. *See* Nacon.

Nachor. *See* Nahor, 1.

Nacon (nā′kŏn), KJV **Nachon** (nā′kŏn). [Heb. *Nakôn*, "thrust."] The name of the threshing floor (or of its owner) where Uzzah was smitten for touching the ark when David was transporting it to Jerusalem (2 Sa 6:6, 7). It is called Chidon (kī′dŏn) [Heb. *Kîdon*] in 1 Chr 13:9.

Nadab (nā′dăb). [Heb. *Nadab*, "generous."]
1. The eldest of Aaron's four sons (Ex 6:23; Num 3:2). He, his brother Abihu, his father Aaron, and 70 elders were permitted to accompany Moses to a certain height of Mount Sinai (Ex 24:1, 2). He was later dedicated to the priesthood (ch 28:1), but died childless as did his brother Abihu when the 2 offered "strange fire" before God (Lev 10:1-7; Num 3:4). The fact that immediately after this event the command was given forbidding priests to drink alcoholic beverages when they were to serve God (Lev 10:8-11), leads to the conclusion that Nadab and Abihu had committed their offense under the influence of liquor.

2. A Jerahmeelite, descendant of Hezron (1 Chr 2:28, 30).

3. A Benjamite, son of Jeiel (father of Gibeon) and Maacah (1 Chr 8:29, 30; 9:35, 36).

4. Son and successor of Jeroboam I, and the 2d king of the northern kingdom of Israel. He reigned for less than 2 years (*c.* 910-909 B.C.) and followed his father in all his evil ways (1 Ki 15:25, 26). While besieging Gibbethon, which belonged to the Philistines at that time, he was killed by Baasha, who then usurped the throne for himself and afterward exterminated all the relatives of the house of Jeroboam (vs 27-29). This massacre fulfilled Ahijah's prophecy concerning Jeroboam (ch 14:10, 11).

Naggai (năg′ī), KJV **Nagge** (năg′ē). [Gr. *Naggai*.] A Judahite appearing in Luke's genealogy of Jesus Christ (Lk 3:25).

Nagge. *See* Naggai.

Nahalal (nā′ha-lăl), or **Nahalol** (nā′ha-lŏl), KJV once **Nahallal** (na-hăl′ăl). [Heb. *Nahalal* and *Nahalol*, "drinking place (for flocks)."] A Canaanite city, assigned to Zebulun, from which the Canaanites were not driven out at the conquest (Jos 19:15, 16; Jgs 1:30). It was assigned to the Merarite Levites as a residence city (Jos 21:35). The site is possibly to be identified with *Tell en-Nahl,* 8 mi. south of Acco (Map VI, C-3).

Nahaliel (nà-hā'lĭ-ĕl). [Heb. *Nachali'el,* "brook of God."] A camping place in the wanderings of Israel, in the desert near Moab and north of the river Arnon (Num 21:19). It may be either the *Wâdī Wâlâ,* a tributary of the Arnon, or the *Wâdī Zerqā Mā'în,* which enters the Dead Sea about 11 mi. south of its northern shore.

Nahallal. *See* Nahalal.

Nahalol. *See* Nahalal.

Naham (nā'hăm). [Heb. *Nacham,* "he comforts." The name occurs also on ancient Hebrew seals and inscriptions.] A brother-in-law of Hodiah (1 Chr 4:19).

Nahamani (nā'hà-mā'nĭ). [Heb. *Nachamanî,* "he comforts me."] One of the leading Jews who returned with Zerubbabel from Babylonia (Neh 7:7). His name is omitted in the list of Ezr 2:2.

Naharai (nā'hà-rī), KJV once **Nahari** (nā'-hà-rī). [Heb. *Nacharay* and *Nachray,* "snorting."] One of David's "mighty men," armorbearer of Joab; his home was at Beeroth (1 Chr 11:39; 2 Sa 23:37).

Nahari. *See* Naharai.

Nahash (nā'hăsh). [Heb. *Nachash,* "serpent."]

1. Father (or possibly the mother) of Abigail and Zeruiah, sisters of David (2 Sa 17:25; cf. 1 Chr 2:16). Three suggestions have been made as to the identity of Nahash: (1) Nahash was another name for Jesse, (2) Nahash was the wife of Jesse and mother of Abigail, Zeruiah, David, and his brothers (although the name is otherwise known as a man's name), or (3) Nahash was the father of Abigail and Zeruiah who died after his daughters were born; his widow subsequently married Jesse and bore him 8 sons, among them David.

2. A king of the Ammonites, who besieged Jabesh-gilead and as terms of surrender demanded that every man of the city lose his right eye. The inhabitants of the unhappy city requested a week to see whether they could find help before meeting the demands of Nahash. Saul, who had recently become king, came to their rescue and defeated the Ammonites (1 Sa 11:1-11). It was either this king or his son of the same name who showed David some kindness, perhaps during the time that David was persecuted by Saul (2 Sa 10:2). He is possibly identical with Nahash, 3.

3. A man of Rabbath-ammon whose son Shobi helped David when the ex-

iled king stayed in Gilead after his flight from Jerusalem because of Absalom's rebellion (2 Sa 17:27). Since this Nahash was from Rabbah of the Ammonites, he may have been the king of the Ammonites mentioned by that name in 1 Sa 11:1-11 and 2 Sa 10:2. *See* Nahash, 2. On the other hand, he may have been an Israelite living in Rabbah of the Ammonites during that period. It has been suggested that Shobi was the Israelite governor of that city after it had been captured by David (2 Sa 12:29).

Nahath (nā'hăth). [Heb. *Nachath,* "descent," or "rest," "quietness."]

1. A descendant of Esau, and also of Ishmael; he became a chief of Edom (Gen 36:13, 17; cf. vs 3, 4; 1 Chr 1:37).

2. A Kohathite Levite in the ancestral line of Samuel (1 Chr 6:26), apparently identical with Tohu (tō'hū) [Heb. *Tochú*] (1 Sa 1:1), and Toah (tō'à) [Heb. *Tôach*] (1 Chr 6:34).

3. One of the Levites in charge of tithes and offerings in the reign of Hezekiah (2 Chr 31:13).

Nahbi (nä'bĭ). [Heb. *Nachbî,* meaning uncertain.] The spy representing the tribe of Naphtali (Num 13:14).

Nahor (nā'hôr), KJV twice **Nachor** (nā'kôr). [Heb. *Nachôr,* "snorting"; Gr. *Nachōr.* The name occurs in cuneiform records as *Naharan, Niharu,* and *Niharan.*]

1. A son of Serug and grandfather of Abraham (Gen 11:24-26; Lk 3:34).

2. A son of Terah and brother of Abraham (Gen 11:26). Although the fact is not recorded, he probably moved with his father's family from Ur to Haran, or followed them a short time later, for his descendants were later found in the Haran region (chs 24:10, 15; 27:43). He married Milcah, his niece (ch 11:29), and had sons by her (ch 22:21-23) who became ancestors of Aramaean tribes. One of his sons, Bethuel, was the father of Rebekah and Laban (ch 24:15, 29). In addition, Nahor had 4 sons by Reumah, a concubine (ch 22:24). These also seem to have become ancestral heads of tribal units.

The "city of Nahor" (Gen 24:10) was until recently generally thought to be only another name for Haran (see chs 27:43; 28:10). However, cuneiform tablets of the 18th cent. B.C., recently discovered at Mari, and other Middle-Assyrian documents, mention a city in the Haran region by the name of *Til-Nahiri,* in which an Amorite king ruled. Therefore some have concluded that the "city of Nahor" was not the city of Haran itself, but a separate settlement probably founded by Nahor and named after him.

Nahshon (nä'shŏn), KJV once **Naashon** (nā-ăsh'ŏn), KJV of NT **Naasson** (nā-ăs'ŏn). [Heb. *Nachshôn* and Gr. *Naassōn,* "serpent."] A prince of the tribe of Judah in the early wilderness wandering of Israel (Num 1:7; 2:3; 7:12, 17; 10:14). His sister married Aaron (Ex 6:23). He was the ancestor of Boaz, and thus of King David (Ruth 4:20-22; 1 Chr 2:10-12). This placed him in the ancestry of Jesus Christ (Mt 1:4; Lk 3:32, 33).

Nahum (nā'hŭm), KJV of NT **Naum** (nā'ŭm). [Heb. *Nachûm,* "consolation," "the one comforted." The name occurs on an ancient Hebrew seal, on a jar handle, and in Phoenician inscriptions. Gr. *Naoum.*]

1. A prophet of Judah in the 7th cent. B.C., and author of the book that bears his name. He was a native of *Elkosh (Nah 1:1), the location of which is unknown.

2. A name appearing in Luke's genealogy of Jesus Christ (Lk 3:25).

Nahum, Book of. Seventh of the so-called Minor Prophets. Reference in Nah 3:8-10 to the fall of No (Thebes), which was destroyed by Ashurbanipal of Assyria in 663 B.C, suggests that Nahum wrote his book shortly after that date. Nahum foretells the desolation of Nineveh (ch 3: 7), the Assyrian capital, an event that took place in 612 B.C., and his book may therefore be dated between 663 and 612 B.C., perhaps *c.* 640 B.C. The book of Nahum announces the doom of the great Assyrian Empire at the very time when the nation was at the crest of its power (*see* Assyria). Jerusalem and Judah had been suffering repeated Assyrian invasions and had been forced to pay tribute intermittently for ¾ of a century. Assyria appeared invincible, but God prophesied through Nahum that He would break the Assyrian yoke (ch 1:13). This message assured the faithful in Judah that God was still watching over His people and that He would visit justice upon their oppressors. During Ashurbanipal's reign (669-627? B.C.) most of the nations of the Fertile Crescent, from Mesopotamia to Egypt, either were subject to the Assyrians or were under tribute to them. However, before his death, possibly in 627 B.C., the situation had already begun to change. Soon thereafter the empire disintegrated, and Nineveh itself fell in 612 B.C. to the Medes and the Babylonians.

The book of Nahum is concerned exclusively with the coming fate of Nineveh. About a century and a half before Nahum, Jonah went to the city with a call to repentance, and for a time king and people alike humbled themselves before God (Jon 3:5-10). Accordingly, for a time, the city was spared. But the reformation did not last, and Nahum now predicted the imminent destruction of the "bloody city" (Nah 3:1). A century prior to Nahum's time Assyria had been the "rod" of God's anger (Is 10:5) against the northern kingdom, Israel, whose 10 tribes it took captive. A few years later, under Sennacherib, God used the same rod to chasten the people of Jerusalem and Judah (chs 36; 37; cf. 8:7, 8). But by their monumental pride and unabashed cruelty the Assyrians had now filled their cup of iniquity. They were defying the sovereignty of the God of heaven and were abasing the Creator of the universe to a level with idols (ch 36:7, 14-20). Assyria had refused to cooperate with God's purpose for her as a nation and therefore lost her mandate to rule.

The prophecy of Nahum is written in poetic style, its 1st chapter being an alphabetic psalm of unusual form. Although in the text as it has come down to us some letters of the alphabet are missing and others appear out of sequence, it is quite possible that originally the alphabetical arrangement was complete. Each letter of the alphabet introduces a new thought. Thus in v 5 the 1st member of the poetic parallelism, "the mountains quake at him, and the hills melt," begins with the Hebrew letter *he',* while the 2d, "and the earth is burned at his presence, yea, the world, and all that dwell therein," begins with *waw,* the next letter in the Hebrew alphabet.

The prophecy logically falls into 2 parts: (1) an ascription of praise, extolling God as merciful and just, as the ruler of the world and arbiter of national destiny (Nah 1:1-10), and (2) a vivid description of the fall of Nineveh (chs 1:11 to 3:19). Nahum entitles his prophecy "The burden of Nineveh." God takes the enemies of His people to be His own "adversaries" (ch 1:2). Though He is "slow to anger" He will not forever countenance their wickedness (v 3). The forces of nature—the sea, the rivers, the mountains, the earth itself—are subject to His pleasure (vs 4-6). To His own people He is "a strong hold in the day of trouble; and he knoweth them that trust him" (Nah 1:7). When He sets His hand to punish the Assyrians "he will make an utter end," and never again will the Assyrians rise to oppress His people (v 9). For some time God has permitted them to prosper (v 12), but the time is at hand when He will break the Assyrian yoke and restore peace to Judah (vs 13-15). The destroyer is depicted as laying siege to Nineveh, and in irony God summons its garrison to prepare to defend the city (ch 2:1). The shields of the defenders are red, apparently with blood, and the chariots rumble through the streets to the point of attack (vs 3, 4). The warriors stumble at their appointed places on the city wall (v 5), the sluice gates are opened, and the palace is inundated (v 6). As its inhabitants tremble in fear, the invaders rush into the city, and take its spoil (vs 7-10). Ch 3 pictures the horsemen lifting their spears and swords in battle and multitudes falling down slain (ch 3:1-3). God is against Nineveh because of her crimes, her immorality, and her oppression of others (vs 4-6), and therefore lays the city waste (v 7). It is no better than the city of No (Thebes) of Egypt or of other nations that have fallen (vs 7-9). Its people are taken captive or scattered leaderless upon the mountains, and the "shepherds," the leaders of Assyria, are laid to rest in the dust. Nineveh's wound is a mortal one, and "there is no healing" of the bruise it now suffers (vs 10-19).

Nail. The translation of several Hebrew words, one Aramaic, and one Greek word, some of which refer to the nails on fingers and toes (Deut 21:12; Dan 4: 33); others to metal nails used for construction purposes (1 Chr 22:3; 2 Chr 3:9; etc.). Nails were used in the crucifixion of Jesus Christ (Jn 20:25). In Jgs 4:21, 22; 5:26; Ezr 9:8; Is 22:23, 25; Zec 10:4 the KJV uses the rendering "nail" for the Heb. *yathed,* which, however, means "peg," such as a tent peg. For example, the KJV renders *yathed* "pin" in Ex 27:19; 35:18; etc., and "stake" in Is 33:20; 54:2.

Nain (nā'ĭn). [Gr. *Nain.*] A town or village in Galilee where Jesus raised a widow's son to life (Lk 7:11). The place is now a little village called *Nein,* and is situated 5 mi. north of Jezreel (Map XVI, C-3), on a plateau at the foot of the Hill of Moreh, now called Little Hermon. See fig. 472.

Naioth (nā'ŏth). [Heb. *Nayôth* and *Nawyoth,* meaning unknown. The 1st reading is preferred by the Masoretes, whereas the 2d is supported by certain manuscripts of the LXX.] A place "in Ramah," where Samuel and the "sons of the prophets" dwelt, and where David stayed for some time while hiding from Saul (1 Sa 19:18, 19, 22, 23; 20:1). Some have suggested that the Hebrew term may mean "dwelling," in the sense of a "dormitory" in which prophets lived.

Naked. [Heb. generally *'arôm* or *'êrom;* Gr. *gumnos.*] The terms thus translated generally designated an unclothed state (Gen 2:25; 3:7; Job 1:21; Rev 3:17; etc.). It is thought by some that these words may at times have the connotation of being only partly or poorly clad. Such a force, however, would have to be derived from the context in question and not from the meaning of the word itself (see Is 20:2).

Name. [Heb. *shem;* Gr. *onoma.*] The Hebrews, like other ancient Near Eastern peoples, attached great significance to personal names. Their names had a literal meaning sometimes symbolic of the character and personality of the one it designated, and sometimes reflecting the moods or feelings of the one giving the name. Hereditary family names were practically nonexistent in Biblical times. When it was necessary to distinguish between 2 persons with the same name, an epithet was often added that would identify the individual, as in the following examples: Saul of Tarsus, Joseph of Arimathea, Jesus of Nazareth, Elijah the Tishbite, James the son of Alphaeus, Judas the brother of James, etc. Some individuals were called by an additional or alternate name, referred to in the Bible as a "surname" (Acts 10:5, KJV; cf. Mk 3:16, 17). Such names as Abraham, Israel, and Joshua are examples of additional names or names that replaced the former names of the individuals involved.

As to form and structure, Hebrew names followed patterns that seem strange to the modern mind. Frequently the Biblical name was compounded from 2 or more words that might express an abbreviated sentence, as in the following examples: Abidan, "my father is judge"; Ichabod, "the glory is departed"; etc. Occasionally the name consisted of a single word, such as Deborah, "bee"; Barak, "lightning"; Caleb, "dog"; Jonah, "dove"; etc. Often the name was verbal in form: Saul, "asked (of God)" or "lent (to God)"; Nathan, "He (that is, God) has given"; Baruch, "blessed"; etc. Still other Biblical names simply reflected various terms of affection, such as Naomi, "my pleasantness"; Tabitha, "gazelle"; and Samson, possibly "little sun."

Perhaps the most popular type of name among the Israelites was one that contained some reference to the true God. Such a name was often a pious declaration of faith. For example, Elijah means "Yahweh is my God"; other names acknowledged some special blessing received from the Lord, perhaps in the birth of the child thus named. Examples are Nathanael, "God has given"; Berachiah, "Yahweh has blessed"; Hezekiah, "Yahweh has strengthened"; etc. Theophorous names, that is, names containing the name of God, may usually be recognized in the Bible by such prefixes as Jah-, Je-, Jeho- (which are transliterations of abbreviated forms of the divine name; see Yahweh), the suffixes -iah and -jah (also forms of the divine name), the prefixes *El- or El-i, and the suffix -el (transliterations of the abbreviated word for God).

In the NT the name of Jesus is naturally given constant emphasis. Special instruction was given to His parents as to the selection of His name (Mt 1:21, 23); His followers were invited to pray in His name (Jn 16:23, 24); because of His sacrifice, He was given a name above every other name (Php 2:9, 10); salvation is obtained through His name (Acts 2:21; 4:12); whatever His followers do is to be done through His name (Col 3:17); and the early Christians were willing to suffer any humiliation for the sake of that name (cf. Acts 5:41). "Name" in some of these and other passages assumes a wider meaning than that by which a person is known or designated, such as "person," "character," "reputation," "authority"; etc. (see Ex 5:23; 34:5, 6; Deut 7:24; Acts 1: 15; Rev 3:4; etc.).

Naomi (nā-ō'mĭ). [Heb. *Na'omî*, "my pleasantness."] The wife of Elimelech and mother of 2 sons. During a severe famine her family moved from Bethlehem to Moab, where her sons married and where later her husband and sons died. After their death Naomi returned to Bethlehem, taking Ruth, one of her Moabite daughters-in-law, with her. It was through Ruth, who came to fame, that Naomi's name has found a place in the Biblical narrative (Ruth 1-4).

Naphath (nā'făth). [Heb. *Nepheth*, "mountain ridge."] A term occurring in Jos 17:11, RSV, as the name of a place, not identified. The meaning of the Hebrew word in its context is obscure. The KJV renders the term "countries."

Naphath-dor (nā'făth-dôr'), or **Naphoth-dor** (nā'fōth-dôr'). [Heb. *Naphath Dôr, Naphôth Dôr* and *Naphath Do'r,* "mountain ridge of Dor."] Probably one of several mountain spurs that run from Mount Carmel in a southwesterly direction toward the port city of Dor. The Hebrew phrase is rendered variously in the KJV as "borders of Dor," "coast of Dor," and "region of Dor," but is transliterated as a proper name in the RSV (Jos 11:2; 12:23; 1 Ki 4:11).

Naphish (nā'fĭsh), KJV once **Nephish** (nē'-fĭsh). [Heb. *Naphish,* "wealth."] Son of Ishmael (Gen 25:15; 1 Chr 1:31), and ancestor of a tribe with whom the Israelites east of the Jordan came in conflict (1 Chr 5:18-22). It is possible that from the captives made from that tribe originated the Nephisim, Nephusim, or Nephishesim, a family of postexilic Nethinim, or Temple servants. *See* Nephisim.

Naphoth-dor. *See* Naphath-dor.

Naphtali (năf'tà-lī). [Heb. *Naphtalî,* "my wrestling"; Gr. *Nephthalim.*]

1. A son of Jacob and of Rachel's maidservant Bilhah. The name was given him by Rachel to indicate how she had "wrestled" in contest with her sister to obtain a child as a mark of God's favor (Gen 30:7, 8). He was the father of 4 sons and the ancestor of the tribe that bore his name (Gen 46:24; Num 26:48, 49).

2. The tribe (KJV of NT "Nephthalim," nĕf'thà-lĭm, and "Nepthalim," nĕp'-thà-lĭm) of Naphtali, 1. It was divided into 4 great families from the 4 sons of Naphtali, their ancestor (Gen 46:24; Num 26:48, 49). During the years of Israel's wilderness wanderings the tribe encamped north of the tabernacle (see fig. 92), together with the tribes of Dan and Asher (Num 2:25-29). Their prince during those years was Ahira, son of Enan (chs 1:15; 2:29), later Pedahel, son of Ammihud (ch 34:28), and Nahbi, son of Vophsi, was the tribal representative among the 12 spies (ch 13:14). The 1st census in the wilderness showed that there were 53,400 members of the tribe ready for war (ch 2:29, 30), whereas the 2d revealed that their number had decreased to 45,400 (ch 26:50).

The tribe of Naphtali was assigned territory in Galilee. Its eastern boundary was the upper Jordan and lakes Huleh and Galilee. The southern border was formed by the tribes of Issachar and Zebulun, and the western border by the tribe of Asher (Jos 19:32-34). To the north lay the territory of the Phoenicians, and later that of the tribe of Dan. Its area was less than 50 mi. from north to south and between 10 and 20 mi. from west to east. Its soil was fertile and its topography rather mountainous. (See Map VI, B/C-3.) Among its fortified cities were Hazor, Kedesh, Iron, and Beth-anath (Jos 19:35-38). Three cities within its territory, Kedesh, Hammoth-dor, and Kartan, were assigned to the Gershonite Levites as residence cities, with Kedesh being also a city of refuge (Jos 20:7; 21:6, 32; 1 Chr 6:62, 76).

The Naphtalites were not able to drive the Canaanites out of all the fortified cities within the territory allotted to them, but eventually made them tributary (Jgs 1:33). In the records dealing with the period of the judges they are mentioned twice, first as having distinguished themselves in the war against the king of Hazor by jeopardizing "their lives unto the death in the high places of the field" (chs 4:6, 10; 5:18), and second as responding to Gideon's call to assist in the expulsion of the Midianite oppressors (chs 6: 35; 7:23). The tribe is mentioned in the time of David, when 1,000 captains with 37,000 fighting men came to David in Hebron to make him king over all Israel, probably after the death of Ish-bosheth (1 Chr 12:34-38). The leader of the tribe in David's reign was a certain Jeremoth, the son of Azriel (ch 27:19). The supply officer for the tribe in Solomon's time was Ahimaaz, a son-in-law of the king (1 Ki 4:15). Hiram, the great artificer and master workman of Solomon, was a son of a widow from the tribe of Naphtali (ch 7:14).

The tribe was invaded by the Syrians and suffered much under Ben-hadad I of Damascus (1 Ki 15:20; 2 Chr 16:4) in the 9th cent. About a century and a half later many of its inhabitants were deported to Assyria by Tiglath-pileser III (2 Ki 15:29). Isaiah prophesied that "the land of Zebulun and the land of Naphtali" in "Galilee of the nations" would see a great light (Is 9:1, 2). This prophecy was fulfilled in the days of Christ, when His ministry benefited this area more than any other in Palestine (Mt 4:12-16). Famous cities of NT times, such as Capernaum, Chorazin, and Tiberias, lay within the former territory of Naphtali.

In his prophecy of the ideal land of Canaan as it was to have been restored, Ezekiel places Naphtali between Asher and Manasseh (Eze 48:3, 4), and Naphtali is one of the 12 tribes said by John to be sealed by the angel (Rev 7:6).

Naphtuhim (năf-tū′hĭm). [Heb. *Naphtuchîm.*] A people descended from Mizraim, the ancestor of the Egyptians (Gen 10:13; 1 Chr 1:11). Their identity is uncertain. Of the various proposed identifications, the most plausible is the one that refers the name to the inhabitants of the Nile Delta, called in Egyptian *n3 p3 ỉth(w),* probably pronounced *na-patûh,* meaning "people of the Delta." See Map IV, C-5.

Napkin. *See* Handkerchief.

Narcissus (när-sĭs′ŭs). [Gr. *Narkissos,* a name from Greek mythology frequently borne by slaves and freedmen.] The head of a family in Rome, members of which (probably slaves) received special greetings from Paul in his letter to the Romans (Rom 16:11).

Nard. *See* Spikenard.

Nathan (nā′thăn). [Heb. *Nathan,* "He (that is, God) has given"; Gr. *Natham,* variant reading *Nathan.* The name occurs frequently in ancient Hebrew inscriptions, also in South Arabic texts.]

1. A son of Attai, a Jerahmeelite of the tribe of Judah (1 Chr 2:36).

2. A man whose son Igal was one of David's "mighty men" (2 Sa 23:36). He is considered by some to be identical with Nathan, 3.

3. A man whose brother Joel was one of David's "mighty men" (1 Chr 11:38). He was possibly identical with Nathan, 2.

4. An outstanding prophet in David's and Solomon's reigns. It was to him that David submitted his plans to build a temple. At first the prophet approved but a divine message instructed him that not David but his son was to carry out the building of the Temple (2 Sa 7; 1 Chr 17:1-15). Nathan had the unpleasant task of rebuking the king for his sin in the matter of Bathsheba (2 Sa 12:1-15). He and the prophet Gad helped David in the organization of the choirs and musicians for Solomon's Temple (2 Chr 29: 25). His sympathies were apparently for Solomon as David's successor; at least Adonijah and his fellow usurpers did not invite him to the feast during which Adonijah planned to have himself proclaimed king. But Nathan heard of it and acted immediately, informing David of Adonijah's scheme. As a result Solomon was crowned at once. Thus Solomon owed his crown, partly at least, to Nathan's watchfulness and activities (1 Ki 1:8-45). The prophet is also known as a biographer of David and Solomon (1 Chr 29:29; 2 Chr 9:29), and portions of his historical

works are possibly included in those parts of the books of Kings and Chronicles that deal with David and Solomon.

5. The 3d son born to David in Jerusalem (2 Sa 5:14). Through him ran the ancestral line of Jesus Christ according to the genealogy of Luke (Lk 3:31).

6. A man whose son Azariah was a high official of Solomon (1 Ki 4:5). He may be identical with either Nathan, 4 or Nathan, 5.

7. The father of a high-ranking priest (1 Ki 4:5, RSV), Zabud, in Solomon's time; he may be identical with Nathan, 4, if the latter was a Levite.

8. The ancestral head of an important house in Judah (Zec 12:12). It is impossible positively to identify this Nathan.

9. A chief man of the Jews who was with Ezra at the river Ahava in Babylonia (Ezr 8:16).

10. A member of the family of Bani (RSV "Binnui"); he was one of those who had married a foreign wife in the time of Ezra (Ezr 10:39).

Nathanael (nȧ-thăn′ȧ-ĕl). [Gr. *Nathanaēl,* a transliteration of the Heb. *Nethan'el,* "God has given."] A native of Cana in Galilee (Jn 21:2) who through Philip was led to accept Christ. It appeared incredible to him that the Messiah could originate from a town of such low reputation as Nazareth. But his meeting with Jesus quickly dispelled his doubts and he became a disciple of Jesus (ch 1:45-51). The name appears elsewhere in the Gospels only in ch 21:2, where, after the resurrection of Jesus (vs 2-6), Nathanael is mentioned as being associated with Simon Peter and other disciples in the miraculous draught of fishes. Many scholars suggest identifying him with Bartholomew, whose name appears with that of Philip in several Biblical passages (Mt 10:3; Mk 3:18; Lk 6:14; Acts 1:13). Since the Synoptic Gospels mention Bartholomew as one of the Twelve, and that name appears nowhere in the Gospel of John, but that of Nathanael does, as of one who could be one of the Twelve, a good case can be made for the identification of the two men.

For men in the OT bearing the corresponding Hebrew name, *see* Nethanel.

Nathan-melech (nā′thăn-mē′lĕk). [Heb. *Nethan-melek,* "the king has given," or possibly "Molech has given."] An official of the time of Josiah who lived within the Temple compound and occupied a room near which stood the "horses . . . given

to the sun," which Josiah removed (2 Ki 23:11).

Naum. *See* Nahum, 2.

Nave. Hub, that is, the central part of a wheel. However, the Heb. *gab,* thus translated (1 Ki 7:33, KJV), actually means "rim" (cf. Eze 1:18 where the plural form is translated "rings"; RSV "rims").

Nazarene (năz′ȧ-rēn′). [Gr. *Nazōraios* and *Nazarēnos.*]

1. A term used of Christ in Mt 2:23; Mk 14:67, RSV. Since the Matthew passage speaks of Nazareth as Jesus' home town, it seems that the author uses it in the sense of "inhabitant of Nazareth." However, his assertion that this is a fulfillment of a prophecy creates a difficulty in that no such prophecy can be found in the OT. It is, of course, possible that Matthew referred to some inspired prophecy not contained in the sacred canon. Some commentators have interpreted *Nazōraios* as meaning a "Nazirite," but Jesus was not a Nazirite (see Mt 11:19; Lk 7:33, 34; cf. Num 6:2-4). Others think that the Greek term refers to the Messianic prophecy of Is 11:1, which speaks of the *neṣer,* "Branch," and that Nazareth may have derived its name from the root of that word, *naṣar.*

2. A term applied to Christians (Acts 24:5), as the followers of the One who originated from Nazareth, that is, Jesus Christ. It seems to have been used contemptuously.

Nazareth (năz′ȧ-rĕth). [Gr. *Nazara, Nazaret,* and *Nazareth* from a Hebrew or Aramaic word of uncertain form, since the town is not mentioned in the OT, in the writings of Josephus, or in the rabbinical writings of the Jews. This indicates that it must have been a small and insignificant place in pre-Christian times.] The home town of Joseph and Mary, and the childhood home of Jesus (Lk 2:39). There He seems to have spent most of His first 30 years (Lk 2:51, 52; Mt 2:23), and there He preached in the beginning of His public ministry in Galilee (Mt 4:13; Mk 1:9; Lk 4:16-28). As a result He was called "the prophet of Nazareth" (Mt 21:11; cf. Acts 10:38). But His townsmen did not like His preaching and rejected Him twice, and at least once tried to kill Him (Lk 4:28-31; Mt 13:54-58; Mk 6:1-6).

The village standing now at the site of ancient Nazareth is called *en-Nâṣirah.* It is situated in Lower Galilee, immediately to the north of the great Plain of

345. Nazareth

Esdraelon, about 64 mi. north of Jerusalem, and about 17 mi. west of the southern tip of the Sea of Galilee (Map XVI, C-3). It is 1,144 ft. above sea level, and about 920 ft. above the Plain of Esdraelon, in a depression surrounded by hills. This depression is pear-shaped, about 1 mi. across, with the neck of the pear pointing southward and opening by a narrow, winding ravine into the broad Plain of Esdraelon. Since Byzantine times the *Jebel el-Qafsē* has been pointed out as the "brow of the hill" from which the people of Nazareth attempted to push Jesus to His death (Lk 4:16-30). But the traditional site shows no real cliff, as the narrative seems to demand. Therefore, some modern scholars find a more likely site near the Maronite church, where there are several bare scarps from 20 to 50 ft. high. The modern town of Nazareth has recently increased its population from about 10,000 before World War II to 23,000, of which more than 3,000 are Christians. Since there is only one ancient fountain in the town, the so-called Fountain of the Virgin, the tradition claiming that Mary obtained the family's water supply from this fountain is probably correct. See fig. 345.

Of interest is the Inscription of Nazareth, a marble slab containing a Greek text, now preserved in the Louvre in Paris, discovered in Nazareth in 1878. It was in the Froehner collection for many years with its value unrecognized until 1930. The text contains a decree issued by an unnamed Roman emperor prohibiting, under penalty of death, any kind of tomb robbery, including tombs of relatives, or the moving of a body to another place. The date of the inscription is disputed. Some place it in the early years of the imperial period; others in the 2d cent. A.D. It is most improbable that it has any direct connection with the accusation advanced against the disciples of Jesus that they had stolen the body of their Master (Mt 28:12-15), although it throws an interesting light on this event. If it came from a time preceding the crucifixion, it would prove that there was evidently no ground for the accusation, for the authorities would certainly have brought the disciples of Jesus to trial, and the fact that this was not done would show that the rulers of Judea had no hope of proving their case in a public trial with the Roman soldiers as very unreliable witnesses.

NAZARITE

Lit.: F. M. Abel, *RB* 39 (1930), 567-571; R. Tonneau, *RB* 40 (1931), 544-564; S. A. Cook, *QSPEF* 64 (1932), 85-87.

Nazarite. *See* Nazirite.

Nazirite (năz′ĭ-rīt), KJV **Nazarite** (năz′á-rīt). [Heb. *Nazîr,* "separated," "devoted," from a verb meaning "to separate," "to consecrate," "to dedicate," for religious or ceremonial use.] A person who took certain special voluntary and temporary vows dedicating himself to God (see Num 6:2). The one taking the vow continued to live a normal life in society, except that (1) he abstained from all grape products (vs 3, 4); (2) he left his hair uncut (v 5); (3) he refrained from approaching any dead body, to avoid ritual defilement (v 6), and if he accidentally came in contact with a dead body he was to offer specified sacrifices and begin again the whole period of his vow (vs 9-12). A Nazirite was "holy unto the Lord" all the days of his "separation" (v 8). At the close of the specified period he was to appear before the priest with certain prescribed offerings, and to shave his hair and burn it (vs 13-21).

Some, such as Samuel (1 Sa 1:11) and John the Baptist (cf. Lk 1:15), were Nazirites for life. Samson's parents were instructed that he was to be a Nazirite from birth (Jgs 13:5, 7), but he proved notoriously unfaithful to the vow. Amos mentions that certain godless people tempted a group of Nazirites to break their vow of total abstinence from intoxicating drinks (Amos 2:11, 12). Paul took what was apparently a modified form of the Nazirite vow preparatory to his last visit to Jerusalem (Acts 18:18; 21:20-26). There is no recorded instance of a person voluntarily taking the vow for life, since in all instances of a perpetual vow the parents took it on behalf of their children.

Neah (nē′á). [Heb. *Ne‘ah.*] A place on the boundary of the territory of Zebulun (Jos 19:13); not yet identified with certainty.

Neapolis (nē-ăp′ô-lĭs). [Gr. *Neapolis,* "new city," the name of several cities in the ancient world, one of which is mentioned in the NT.] The seaport of Philippi in Macedonia, lying on the Strymonian Gulf, about 10 mi. southeast of Philippi. It was at this point that the Roman highway called the *Via Egnatia* reached the sea after crossing Macedonia from west to east. The site is now called *Kavalla* (Map XX, A-3). It was the first place in Europe touched by Paul. He landed there

346. Harbor and city of *Kavalla,* ancient Neapolis, in Macedonia

on his 2d Missionary Journey, on his way to Macedonia in response to a vision he had at Troas (Acts 16:11). The fact that Paul did not stay in Neapolis but went straight to Philippi was probably due to the absence of a Jewish community there, for Paul's custom was to begin his work in a new area among the Jews before going to the Gentiles. See fig. 346.

Neariah (nē′á-rī′á). [Heb. *Ne‘aryah,* "the boy (that is, servant) of Yahweh."]
1. A Simeonite military leader who fought against the remnant of the Amalekites in the time of King Hezekiah (1 Chr 4:42, 43).
2. A postexilic descendant of David (1 Chr 3:22, 23).

Nebai (nē′bī). [Heb. *Newbay.*] A prominent Jew who set his seal to Nehemiah's covenant (Neh 10:19).

Nebaioth (nē-bā′yŏth), KJV 3 times **Nebajoth** (nē-bā′jŏth). [Heb. *Nebayôth.* The first element is probably the name of the Babylonian god Nabu, the son of Marduk.] A son of Ishmael (Gen 25:13, 16; 28:9; 36:3) and ancestral head of an Arabian tribe rich in flocks (Is 60:7). Since the tribe is mentioned together with Kedar, it is to be sought in the Syrian Desert. In cuneiform records where it is spelled *Nabayâti* or *Niba’âti* it also appears together with Kedar. It is tempting to identify the Nebaioth with the Nabataeans of later time, but such an identification is probably incorrect, since the Nabataeans wrote their name with a *ṭ* and the tribe of Nebaioth with a *t,* 2 Semitic letters that were seldom confused.

Nebajoth. *See* Nebaioth.

Neballat (nē-băl′ăt). [Heb. *Neballaṭ.*] A postexilic town of Benjamin (Neh 11:34), now *Beit Nabala,* 12½ mi. east-southeast of Joppa.

Nebat (nē′băt). [Heb. *Nebaṭ,* "He (that is, God) has seen."] Father of King Jeroboam I of Israel (1 Ki 11:26; etc.).

Nebo (nē'bō). [Heb. *Nebô.*]

1. A Babylonian god, called *Nabû* in Akkadian texts, considered to be the son of Marduk. His chief temple *Ezida* was in Borsippa, now *Birs Nimrûd*, about 12 mi. south-southwest of Babylon. Nabu was worshiped as the god of wisdom, of eloquence, and especially of the art of writing, since he was considered to be the scribe of the universe and the custodian of the tablets of fate of the gods. His image was carried to Babylon during the annual New Year festivities so that he

348. Mount Nebo

(Deut 3:27; 34:1). Nebo lay "over against Jericho," and was one of the loftiest mountaintops. From it much of the country of western and eastern Palestine could be viewed. It was from this summit that Moses saw the land and died without entering Canaan (ch 34:1-8). The height is probably to be identified with the *Jebel Nebã*, about 10 mi. east of the mouth of the river Jordan. However, Christian tradition has clung to *Râs es-Siâghah*, 2,643 ft. above sea level (Map II, C-3), which contains the ruins of a Byzantine church recently excavated. The view from this place is superb. One can see the Dead Sea and can follow its western shore line as far south as En-gedi. Straight to the west lie the barren slopes of the Judean mountains forming the Wilderness of Judea, with the tropical plain of Jericho and the Jordan Valley in the foreground. On the western sky line the Mount of Olives is visible. Toward the north one can see Mount Gerizim, Mount Ebal, and other mountains of Ephraim. In the far-distant north, on clear days it is possible to make out the outlines of the mountains of Gilboa and Tabor at the edge of the Plain of Esdraelon, and sometimes even Mount Hermon's snow-covered head can be seen. Also spread out before one's eyes is the

347. A statue dedicated to Nabu by Bel-tarsi-iluma, found at *Nimrûd*, Biblical Calah

349. View toward western Palestine from Mount Nebo

could enjoy a reunion with his father Marduk. In Is 46:1 Nebo is mentioned together with Bel (Marduk), his father.

2. A summit in the Abarim range (Num 33:47; Deut 32:49; 34:1). The range, or perhaps only its northern part, was apparently also known as Pisgah

land of Gilead and the plain in which the Israelites encamped at the time of Moses' death. Only the view to the east and south is obstructed and this by other mountain ridges. See figs. 348, 349.

3. A town east of the Jordan occupied and fortified by the tribe of Reuben (Num 32:38). The *Moabite Stone (lines 14-16) describes how King Mesha of Moab conquered the town and destroyed the cult place there dedicated to Yahweh. In the time of the prophets Isaiah and Jeremiah the town was still in Moabite hands (Is 15:2; Jer 48:1, 22). It has been tentatively identified with *Khirbet el-Mekhaiyet*, about 2 mi. southeast of *Râs es-Siâghah*.

4. A town in western Palestine, to which certain descendants of its former inhabitants returned from Babylonia with Zerubbabel (Ezr 2:29; Neh 7:33); identified with *Nûbâ* near Aijalon in Judah, 12 mi. northwest of Jerusalem.

Nebuchadnezzar (nĕb'ū-kăd-nĕz'ēr) and **Nebuchadrezzar** (nĕb'ū-kăd-rĕz'ēr). [Heb. *Nebûkadne'ṣṣar* and *Nebûkadre'ṣṣar*, from the Babylonian *Nabû-kudurri-uṣur*, meaning "May (the god) Nabu protect the son," or "May Nabu protect the boundary." In Greek sources the same interchange between *n* and *r* is found in the forms *Nabouchodonosor* and *Nabokodrosoros*; Aramaic, *Nebûkadneṣṣar*. See fig. 81.]

The name of 2 Babylonian kings, of whom only Nebuchadnezzar II, the 2d king of the Neo-Babylonian Empire (605-562 B.C.), played a role in Biblical history. He is especially known for his conquest of Jerusalem and for the rebuilding of Babylon. The many inscriptions of Nebuchadnezzar that have come to light during the last century speak almost exclusively of his building activities at Babylon and other places; only a few historical texts deal with events of his reign. Until recently virtually all historical knowledge about Nebuchadnezzar was obtained from the Bible and Josephus, but the recently discovered tablets of the Babylonian Chronicle covering the first 11 years of his reign are perhaps the harbingers of more to come in the field of historical texts dealing with Nebuchadnezzar's time. He is mentioned first in the Babylonian Chronicle as commander of a separate army during the 19th regnal year of his father Nabopolassar (607 B.C.; an astronomical text establishes beyond doubt the B.C. dating of his regnal years; *see* Chronology, I, 3). Two years later, in the spring of 605 B.C., the ailing Nabo-

polassar stayed behind, and sent Nebuchadnezzar out to fight against the Egyptians, who held the strong city of Carchemish on the upper Euphrates. In the ensuing battle the young crown prince defeated the Egyptians and destroyed Carchemish. Nebuchadnezzar pursued the fleeing Egyptian forces to the district of Hamath and in a 2d battle crushed them completely, then conquered the whole "Hatti land," that is, Syria-Palestine. It must have been on his way southward that he accepted the surrender of Jerusalem and took Jewish hostages, among whom were Daniel and his 3 friends (Dan 1:1-4). Before he reached the border of Egypt, Nebuchadnezzar received the news that his father had died on Abu (Ab) 8 (approximately Aug. 15, 605 B.C.), and hastened home to secure the throne. Josephus, quoting the same story from Berosus, says that he hurried back to Babylon by means of the short desert route, leaving his generals to follow him with the prisoners, including Jews (*Against Apion* i. 135-138). Reaching Babylon, Nebuchadnezzar was able to take the throne without opposition on Ululu (Elul) 1 (approximately Sept. 7). Thereupon he returned to Syria to organize the newly conquered territories. From now on we find Nebuchadnezzar in Syria or Palestine practically every year. However, in 601 B.C. he suffered a defeat or a near defeat from the Egyptians and consequently stayed at home during the next year (600 B.C.) to rebuild his depleted army. The rising power of the Egyptians that led to this defeat was probably the reason that Jehoiakim of Judah risked refusal to pay the annual tribute to Babylon (2 Ki 24:1), thinking that the balance of power had swayed in favor of Egypt. In 599/98 B.C. Nebuchadnezzar's forces went to Syria-Palestine but were engaged in fighting against Arab tribes. Nebuchadnezzar again turned his attention toward Judah the next year. Jehoiakim had died before Nebuchadnezzar arrived and his son Jehoiachin was on the throne. Nebuchadnezzar took the city on Adar 2 (approximately March 16), 597 B.C.; sent Jehoiachin captive to Babylon with 10,000 of his most distinguished citizens (vs 8-15), among whom was the prophet Ezekiel (Eze 1:1, 2; 33:21); and made Jehoiachin's uncle, Zedekiah, king of Judah in Jehoiachin's stead (2 Ki 24:17). When the new king several years later rebelled against Nebuchadnezzar the Babylonians returned and took Jerusalem after a siege

350. A clay prism of Nebuchadnezzar containing a list of his court officials, among whom are some mentioned in the book of Jeremiah

of over 2 years, in the 19th year of Nebuchadnezzar, that is, in the summer of 586 B.C. They destroyed Jerusalem and the Temple and deported the majority of the remaining population to Babylon (2 Ki 25:8-11). Nebuchadnezzar also subjugated Tyre after a siege of 13 years (see Eze 26:1 to 28:19; Jos. *Against Apion* i. 21). A fragmentary inscription mentions a military campaign also against the Pharaoh Amasis of Egypt in Nebuchadnezzar's 37th regnal year (*ANET* 308; see also Jer 42:7-18; Eze 29:17-21).

Dan 1-4 describes the experiences of Daniel under Nebuchadnezzar and tells how the king became acquainted with the Hebrew religion and Daniel's God. The king's mental incapacity for 7 years (ch. 4) is known only from the Bible, since such misfortunes were never recorded by court officials. When Nebuchadnezzar died in 562 B.C. his son Amel-Marduk, the Biblical Evil-Merodach, succeeded him on the throne. For Nebuchadnezzar's extended building activity in his capital city, see Babylon.

Lit.: D. J. Wiseman, *Chronicles of Chaldaean Kings* (London, 1956).

Nebuchadrezzar. See Nebuchadnezzar.

Nebushasban. See Nebushazban.

Nebushazban (nĕb′ū̇-shăz′băn), KJV **Nebushasban** (nĕb′ū̇-shăs′băn). [Heb. *Nebûshaz-ban* from the Akkadian *Nabû-shêzibanni,* "Nabu, save me!" The name is attested in Babylonian inscriptions of the time of Nebuchadnezzar.] The Rabsaris (chief of the eunuchs, or chief of the courtiers) in Nebuchadnezzar's army at the time of the fall of Jerusalem in 586 B.C. (Jer 39:13).

Nebuzaradan (nĕb′ū̇-zär-ā′dăn). [Heb. *Nebûzar'adan,* from the Babylonian *Nabû-zêriddin,* "(The god) Nabu gives offspring."] The commander in chief of Nebuchadnezzar's army that captured Jerusalem in 586 B.C. (2 Ki 25:8, 11, 20; Jer 39:9-13; 40:1; 41:10; 43:6; 52:15, 16, 26, 30). His Hebrew title, *Rab-ṭabbachim* (2 Ki 25:11, 20; etc.), correctly translated "captain of the guard," literally means "chief of the butchers," but had the wider meaning of "chief of the king's bodyguard." Nebuzaradan is probably identical with the officer who is mentioned in a list of Nebuchadnezzar's court officials of *c.* 570 B.C. as "chief baker," which, idiomatically, had the wider meaning of "imperial chancellor" (see fig. 350).

Necho. See Neco.

Nechoh. See Neco.

Neco (nē′kō), KJV **Necho** (nē′kō) and **Nechoh** (nē′kō). [Heb. *Nekoh* and *Nekó;* Egyptian *Nkȝw;* in Assyrian inscriptions *Nikû.*] A Pharaoh of Egypt, generally known as Necho II. He was the son of Psamtik I, the Pharaoh who founded the 26th dynasty of Egypt. Necho reigned from 609 to 594 B.C. He continued the policy of his father, who had aided the hard-pressed remnants of the Assyrians after the fall of Nineveh, considering it in the interest of Egypt to keep alive the Assyrian kingdom of Ashur-uballiṭ as a buffer state between Egypt and Babylonia. It was in 608 B.C., according to the Biblical chronology adopted for this dictionary, that Josiah of Judah attempted to halt Necho's march toward the north, but in the ensuing battle at Megiddo Josiah was mortally wounded (2 Ki 23:29; 2 Chr 35:20, 21-23). After Necho had consolidated his power over Syria and Phoenicia, he summoned Jehoahaz, Josiah's son, to Riblah in Syria, his headquarters, and deposed him after Jehoahaz had reigned only 3 months, made Jehoahaz' brother Jehoiakim king, and laid a heavy tribute upon Judah (2 Ki 23:33-35). In 605 B.C. the Chaldean forces, commanded by the

351. A bowl found at Persepolis, bearing the names and titles of Pharaoh Necho II in Egyptian hieroglyphs

crown prince Nebuchadnezzar, decisively beat Necho at Carchemish and again near Hamath. Egypt at that time escaped an invasion of the Chaldeans only because of the sudden death of Nabopolassar, Nebuchadnezzar's father, which forced Nebuchadnezzar to abandon any plan of invading Egypt at that time. The next clash between Necho and Nebuchadnezzar came in 601 B.C., according to the recently discovered tablets of the Babylonian Chronicle. This battle ended in a defeat or near defeat for Nebuchadnezzar, as may be concluded from the information that his army suffered so great losses that during the next year he could not go on a military campaign, but had to stay in Babylon to reinforce his troops. However, Necho must also have lost heavily because he seems to have been unable to follow up his victory and reoccupy his lost Asiatic possessions. In fact, he ventured no more into the area claimed by the Babylonians (2 Ki 24:7).

Necho sponsored the immigration of Greek colonists, is credited with having spent much energy digging a canal between the Red Sea and the Nile, which remained uncompleted until the time of Darius I, and had Africa circumnavigated by Phoenician sailors. See fig 351.

Necromancy. *See* Familiar Spirit.

Nedabiah (nĕd'á-bī'á). [Heb. *Nedabyah,* "Yahweh has been generous." The name occurs in cuneiform records as *Nadbiyâu.* A similar name, *Nedabel,* "God has been generous," is found on ancient Hebrew seals and on an Aramaic ostracon.] A son of King Jeconiah (Jehoiachin) of Judah (1 Chr 3:18).

Needle. *See* Needle's Eye.

Needle's Eye. This expression, or "eye of a needle" appears 3 times (Mt 19:24; Mk 10:25; Lk 18:25) in a parabolic saying used by Jesus graphically to illustrate "that a rich man shall hardly enter into the kingdom of heaven" (Mt 19:23; Mk 10:23, 24; Lk 18:24). For a correct interpretation of this figure it is necessary to note that Jesus is speaking of human impossibilities (Mt 19:26; Mk 10:27; Lk 18:27). There is, therefore, nothing to be gained by contriving an explanation that attempts to present as possible that which Jesus points out as impossible.

Some have suggested that the expression "needle's eye" refers to one of the small pedestrian gates in the complex of gates to be found at the main entrance to a walled Eastern city. It has been suggested that an unladen camel might, with much pushing and pulling, pass through such a small opening. This explanation implies that Jesus is speaking of difficulties, not impossibilities, but this inference is not in harmony with the whole context. Furthermore, this explanation finds no justification from the language or the traditions of Bible lands. Matthew and Mark use the word for an ordinary sewing or embroidery needle (*rhaphis*), whereas Luke, a physician, employs a medical term (*belonē*), referring to a needle used in surgical operations. The word translated "eye" (Gr. *trēma*) means simply a hole, a perforation, and, in these passages, refers to the tiny eye of a needle through which a thread is passed.

This illustration may have been a current proverb, employed to convey the idea of impossibility. The Koran, written in the 7th cent. A.D., makes reference to the wicked as finding the gates of heaven closed "till a camel shall pass through the eye of a needle." Admittedly the Koran may have borrowed this figure of speech from the NT; nevertheless, the same idea of impossibility is presented in the Koran as is pointed up in the NT passages under consideration.

Others seek to lessen the seeming incongruity of the figure by calling attention to the fact that a few Byzantine manuscripts have *kamilon,* a "rope," or "ship's cable," instead of *kamēlon,* a "camel," or "dromedary." But the evidence in favor of *kamilon,* "rope," is so slight that it hardly seems deserving of serious consideration.

It seems clear that Jesus was trying to

say, in the face of the popular concept that riches were a sign of divine favor, that even as a camel cannot go through a literal needle's eye, so a man who trusts in his riches instead of God cannot enter the kingdom of God. However, Jesus is not saying that it is utterly impossible for a rich man to enter His spiritual kingdom, for He hastens to add that to the man who trusts God "all things are possible" (Mt 19:26).

Neesings. [Heb. *'aṭishoth,* "sneezes."] A rare English word denoting "sneezes," found only in Job 41:18, KJV.

Negeb (nĕg'ĕb), **The.** [Heb. *Negeb,* "dry (land)"; Egyptian *Ngb.*] An expression occurring frequently in the RSV designating the area south of the densely inhabited cultivated land of Palestine (Map II, D-2/3). The KJV generally translates *Negeb* "south." Only certain parts of the Negeb are habitable, because of the scarceness of springs and the small amount of rainfall. However, the numerous ancient ruins found in that area reveal that in pre-Israelite times, when Palestine was controlled by Egypt, a larger population lived there than in later periods. The name is found in Egyptian texts that show the connections between Egypt and this area. The OT distinguishes between the various parts of the Negeb according to the tribes found in them, and talks of the "Negeb of the Cherethites" and the "Negeb of Caleb" (1 Sa 30:14, RSV), the "Negeb of Judah," the "Negeb of the Jerahmeelites," and the "Negeb of the Kenites" (ch 27:10, RSV). Because of the geographical and political disunity of this territory it was an ideal area for raiding tribes, such as the Amalekites or the Edomites, to control the leading caravan routes crossing this region. During the Roman period techniques of water conservation became so refined that certain sections of the Negeb showed as great a fertility as other parts of Palestine, as recent archeological investigations indicate. Centuries of neglect, however, have reconverted the Negeb into a desert with a few oases, such as Kadesh-barnea, a region in which only Bedouins could dwell. During the last few years intensive efforts have been made to recultivate the area, and to make it fruitful and habitable for a sedentary population. Beer-sheba is the most important city of the Negeb, lying at an important crossroad at its northern end. The name is now most often spelled Negev.

Neginoth. [Plural of Heb. *neginah,* "music" (especially of stringed instruments).] A technical term, transliterated from the Hebrew, referring probably to the music of stringed instruments. It appears in the KJV in the superscriptions of Ps 4, 6, 54, 55, 61, 67, 76 (RSV "stringed instruments"). Elsewhere the Hebrew term is rendered "music" (Lam 5:14), "song (s)" (Job 30:9; Ps 69:12), and "stringed instruments" (Hab 3:19; Is 38:20; RSV).

Nehelam. *See* Nehelamite.

Nehelamite (nĕ-hĕl'á-mīt). [Heb. *Nechelamî.*] The appellative of the false prophet Shemaiah (Jer 29:24, 31, 32). The name indicates either that he came from a town named Nehelam (nĕ-hĕl'ăm), which has not been identified, or that he was a descendant of a man by that name. Shemaiah sent letters from Babylonia, where he was an exile, to Jerusalem, complaining about Jeremiah's prophecies. Jeremiah labeled him a false prophet and predicted his death in exile (vs 24-32). The RSV translates *Nechelamî* "of Nehelam."

Nehemiah (nē'hĕ-mī'á). [Heb. *Nechemyah,* "Yahweh has comforted." The name occurs also on an ancient Hebrew seal.]

1. One of the leaders who returned from Babylon with Zerubbabel (Ezr 2:2; Neh 7:7).

2. A ruler of half of the district of Beth-zur. He repaired a section of Jerusalem's wall under Nehemiah's direction (Neh 3:16).

3. A Jew of the postexilic period and son of Hachaliah (Neh 1:1). He was appointed governor of Judea by Artaxerxes I, king of Persia, and distinguished himself as the rebuilder of the city wall of Jerusalem. When first mentioned Nehemiah was serving as a trusted officer at the court of Artaxerxes I, king of Persia, in the 20th year of Artaxerxes' reign (vs 1, 11), or 445/44 B.C. A serious rebellion in Egypt, and more recently a rebellion in the satrapy Beyond the River, to which Judea belonged, had interrupted communications between Susa (Shushan), the Persian capital, and Palestine. Finally a report reached Nehemiah that his countrymen in Jerusalem suffered "great affliction and reproach" and that the city wall had been broken down and the gates burned (vs 1-3). Mourning and fasting for a period of time, Nehemiah was questioned by the king as to the reason for his sad countenance (chs 1:4 to 2:3). Nehemiah took this opportunity to appeal to the king on behalf of his people and, at his request, received a commission to re-

turn to Jerusalem for a specified period of time in order to bring his people whatever help they should require (Neh 2:4-6). Supplied with a royal letter of introduction to the necessary officials authorizing his mission and empowering him to requisition materials necessary for the restoration of the wall, the fortress, and the Temple at Jerusalem (vs 7, 8), Nehemiah journeyed to the satrapy Beyond the River, delivered his royal credentials to the proper authorities, and then went to Jerusalem (vs 9-11). Keeping his plans to himself for the time being, he inspected the walls by night (vs 12-16) and then laid a plan before the leaders at Jerusalem for restoring the wall (vs 17, 18). The work was begun at once, and despite repeated attempts to halt it (chs 4:1-23; 6:1-19), it was completed in a comparatively short time (ch 6:15). In his role as governor, Nehemiah also instituted social reforms, particularly with respect to the oppression of the poor by the rich (ch 5:1-14). He also planned and carried out the repopulation of the city of Jerusalem (chs 7; 11). Assisted by Ezra, who had preceded him to Jerusalem, he carried out a series of religious reforms (chs 8-10), including the public reading of the Law and instruction in it (ch 8). When Nehemiah drew up, and called upon the people to sign, a covenant of reform, leaders, priests, and people entered into a solemn covenant, pledging themselves to the worship of the true God (chs 9; 10). After serving Judah as governor for 12 years (ch 5:14) Nehemiah went back to Susa, but later returned to Jerusalem for a 2d term as governor (ch 13:6, 7). In the interval the people had again lapsed into sin, so that new reform efforts were required.

Nehemiah, Book of. A historical book from the postcaptivity, or restoration, period of Jewish history. In the ancient Hebrew canon the books of Ezra and Nehemiah appeared as one volume, called Ezra. In the LXX this original Ezra was divided into 2 parts entitled 2 and 3 Esdras, with an Apocryphal book of that name appearing as 1 Esdras. Jerome, translator of the Latin Vulgate, gave the separate books the titles Ezra and Nehemiah, whence the division into 2 books in English translations and their respective titles. *See* Ezra, Book of. Ezra and Nehemiah are the historical continuation of Chronicles, since they take up the thread of Jewish history with the restoration from Babylonian captivity. The style and language of Chronicles, Ezra, and Nehemiah strongly suggest a common authorship. The Talmud (*Baba Bathra* 15a) identifies Ezra as the chief author and Nehemiah, a contemporary of Ezra, as the one who completed the work. Nehemiah served as governor at Jerusalem, and Ezra, a priest, as a spiritual leader. For a time their cooperative efforts did much to bring both material and spiritual blessings. In view of the fact that the list of priests and Levites in Neh 12 does not contain names of any who lived after *c.* 400 B.C., it has been conjectured that the book must have been written at approximately that time. Although we are dependent almost exclusively upon Ezra and Nehemiah for our knowledge of postexilic Judea, these books record only the more important events of the period, and there are large gaps where little information is available. Ezra records the successive decrees of Cyrus, Darius, and Artaxerxes. He reports the building of the Temple and its dedication under Darius I, but then skips over nearly 60 years to the decree of 457 B.C., in connection with which he was sent back to Judea by Artaxerxes with far-reaching authority to reorganize the national administration in harmony with the Law of Moses. He relates experiences soon after his return to Jerusalem, but the next recorded event is the coming of Nehemiah several years later.

The decree of 457 B.C. granted the Jews virtual autonomy under Persia. Civil and judicial powers were returned to the local leadership, and the Law of Moses became once more the official law of the land. Except for the payment of taxes the Jews were free to go their own way, but generous royal grants from the treasury of the satrapy Beyond the River were made in return. Ezra's activities during the 13 years before the arrival of Nehemiah are obscure. However, it is known that he went quietly about the work of reform, one feature of which was in regard to mixed marriages (Ezr 9; 10). During this period of time Megabyzos, governor of the province known as Beyond the River, which included Judea, rebelled for a number of years against the king of Persia. The Jews remained loyal to Artaxerxes, but may have been falsely accused by their Samaritan enemies as partisans of Megabyzos. Artaxerxes gave the Samaritans permission to stop the building of the wall of Jerusalem, and they went so far as to destroy parts of the wall and to burn city gates (Ezr 4:21; Neh 1:3). Near the end of 445 B.C. Hanani, the brother of

Nehemiah, and other Jews arrived at the Persian capital, apparently bringing the first news of events in Jerusalem since Megabyzos' rebellion had been quelled.

Though a faithful Jew, Nehemiah had advanced to a position of responsibility in the Persian court. He was apparently well educated and had natural skill as an administrator and organizer. Upon receiving word of the sad state of affairs in Jerusalem, some 12 years after Ezra's return to Jerusalem, Nehemiah was greatly shocked (Neh 1:1-3) and like Daniel (cf. Dan 9:3) fasted and prayed for many days (Neh 1:4-11). About 4 months later (ch 2:1; cf. ch 1:1) Nehemiah was ready with an effective plan for bringing relief to his beleagured and suffering fellow countrymen in Jerusalem. Apparently awaiting a suitable occasion to petition the king (ch 2:1-6), he requested a royal commission that would permit him to go to Jerusalem and restore the fortunes of his people there (v 5). Artaxerxes was favorable to the suggestion and granted Nehemiah letters to the governor of the province Beyond the River to provide him with transportation, timber, and other necessary supplies for the rebuilding of the wall of the city (vs 6-8). Thus equipped with the necessary powers for carrying out his mission, he went to Jerusalem accompanied by a detachment of horsemen and royal army officers (vs 9, 11). After first inspecting the walls of the city by night (vs 12-16), Nehemiah summoned the leaders to rise up and build the wall (vs 17, 18). They responded heartily, and workmen were organized to repair sections of the wall that had been broken down and to rebuild some of the gates (ch 3). When the work of reconstruction became known, the traditional enemies of the Jews in lands bordering on Judea conspired to defeat Nehemiah's purpose. Among these enemies were *Sanballat, governor of Samaria, *Tobiah, a high official or nobleman of Ammon, and *Geshem, a high Arabian official (ch 2:10, 19). But Nehemiah proved himself a capable, fearless, and determined leader. He did not belittle the threat posed by his enemies, but on the other hand he was not unduly disturbed. He simply continued with his work. Throughout the time during which the rebuilding of the wall was in process, these enemies carried forward their attempts to hinder the work, and apparently gave up the idea only when the task was completed after a brief space of 52 days (Neh 6:15). A solemn and impressive ceremony marked the dedication of the wall (ch 12:27-43).

Following the building of the wall, Nehemiah settled down to his work as governor (Neh 5:14). He championed the cause of the oppressed (vs 1-13), repopulated the city (chs 7; 11:1-19), and, in cooperation with Ezra, provided for the religious needs of the people (chs 8-10).

After an absence of unspecified duration at Susa, the Persian capital, Nehemiah returned to Jerusalem for a 2d term as governor (Neh 13:6, 7), during which he instituted certain further reforms (vs 10-31).

Nehiloth. [Heb. *nechîlôth.*] A musical term found only in the title of Ps 5, KJV. The Hebrew word is thought by some to refer to wind instruments (RSV "flutes"), but its real meaning is unknown.

Nehum (nē'hŭm). [Heb. *Nechûm,* "comfort," or "comforted." The name occurs in ancient Hebrew and Phoenician inscriptions.] A leader of the exiles who returned from Babylonia with Zerubbabel (Neh 7:7). He is called Rehum in Ezr 2:2, a variant spelling that probably resulted from the similarity of the postexilic Hebrew letters *n* and *r*.

Nehushta (nē-hŭsh'tà). [Heb. *Nechushta'.*] The wife of King Jehoiakim and mother of Jehoiachin; she was the daughter of Elnathan of Jerusalem (2 Ki 24:8).

Nehushtan (nē-hŭsh'tăn). [Heb. *Nechushtan,* apparently a combination of *nachash,* "serpent," and *nechosheth,* "bronze."] The name given to the bronze serpent that Moses erected in the wilderness (2 Ki 18:4). See Bronze Serpent.

Neiel (nē-ī'ĕl). [Heb. *Ne'î'el.*] A town on the border of Asher (Jos 19:27); identified with *Khirbet Ya'nin,* about 8½ mi. east-southeast of Acco.

Nekeb (nē'kĕb). [Heb. *Neqeb,* "pass."] According to the KJV a place on the boundary of Naphtali (Jos 19:33). However, the name should probably be joined to the preceding name, Adami, as in the RSV. See Adami-nekeb.

Nekoda (nē-kō'dà). [Heb. *Neqôda',* "moor hen." A Babylonian name that occurs in Akkadian as *Niqudu.*]

1. The ancestral head of a family of Temple servants, or Nethinim (Ezr 2:48; Neh 7:50).

2. The ancestor of certain repatriates who could not prove their genealogy (Ezr 2:60; Neh 7:62). Probably the same family as Nekoda, 1.

Nemuel (nĕm′ū-ĕl). [Heb. *Nemû'el.*]
1. A son of Simeon. *See* Jemuel.
2. A Reubenite, brother of the rebels Dathan and Abiram (Num 26:9).

Nemuelites (nĕm′ū-ĕl-īts). [Heb. *Nemû'eli.*] Descendants of Nemuel, 1 (Num 26:12).

Nepheg (nē′fĕg). [Heb. *Nepheg.*]
1. A Kohathite Levite of the house of Izhar, and brother of the rebel Korah (Ex 6:21; cf. Num 16:1).
2. One of the sons of David born in Jerusalem (2 Sa 5:15; 1 Chr 3:7; 14:6).

Nephew. In the KJV, the rendering of several Greek and Hebrew expressions which signify "grandchildren" or "descendants" (Jgs 12:14; Job 18:19; Is 14:22; 1 Ti 5:4)—a meaning which "nephew" also had when the KJV was translated.

Nephilim (nĕf′ĭ-lĭm). A transliteration of the Heb. *Nephilim* (Gen. 6:4; Num 13:33; RSV), the exact meaning of which is uncertain. The Nephilim of Num 13:33 were *giants.

Nephish. *See* Naphish.

Nephishesim. *See* Nephisim.

Nephisim (nĕ-fī′sĭm), or **Nephushesim** (nĕ-fūsh′ĕ-sĭm), KJV **Nephishesim** (nĕ-fīsh′ē-sĭm), or **Nephusim** (nĕ-fū′sĭm). [Heb. *Nephûshesîm* and *Nephîsîm.*] A family of Nethinim, or Temple servants, some of whom returned with Zerubbabel from Babylonia (Ezr 2:50; Neh 7:52). It is possible that their ancestors had originally been captives of the Edomite tribe of *Naphish.

Nephthalim. *See* Naphtali, 2.

Nephtoah (nĕf-tō′à). [Heb. *Nephtôach;* the unvocalized Hebrew of the phrase "Waters of Nephtoah" is *My Nptwch,* which may stand for *Mynptch,* in which the name of the Egyptian king Merneptah may be recognized.] A term appearing in the phrase "spring of the Waters of Nephtoah." The place was on the boundary between Judah and Benjamin (Jos 15:9; 18:15; RSV; the phrase reads slightly differently in the KJV). The spring is usually identified with the spring *Liftā,* 2½ mi. northwest of Jerusalem.

Nephushesim. *See* Nephisim.

Nephusim. *See* Nephisim.

Nepthalim. *See* Naphtali, 2.

Ner (nûr). [Heb. *Ner,* "lamp."]
1. A Benjamite, son of Abiel and father of Abner, Saul's army commander (1 Sa 14:51). According to v 50 either Ner or Abner was Saul's uncle. If Abner was Saul's uncle, Ner was Saul's grandfather and identical with Ner, 2.

2. A Benjamite, son of Jeiel and father of Kish, Saul's father (1 Chr 8:33; 9:35, 36, 39), possibly identical with Ner, 1.

Nereus (nē′rūs). [Gr. *Nēreus,* a Greek sea god. The name was common among Roman slaves and freedmen.] A Christian in Rome to whom Paul sent greetings in his letter to the Romans (Rom 16:15).

Nergal (nûr′gäl). [Heb. and Akkadian *Nergal;* Phoenician *Nrgl.*] A Babylonian deity, the god especially of the underworld and of the realm of the dead. As such he was considered the god of the plague, sicknesses, and of other causes of death, such as war and famine. He was the chief god of Cuth (2 Ki 17:30).

Nergal-sharezer (nûr′găl-shà-rē′zēr). [Heb. *Nergal Śar'eṣer,* from the Babylonian *Nergal-sharri-uṣur,* "may (the god) Nergal protect the king"; the Greek form is *Nēriglisaros.*] The name of 1 or perhaps 2 high officers in Nebuchadnezzar's army (Jer 39:3, 13). In a cuneiform text of Nebuchadnezzar's time (see fig. 350), a sort of court almanac, *Nergal-sharri-uṣur* is called "Prince of *Sin-magir.*" *Sin-magir* was a city and province of Babylonia north of Babylon. This name appears in the shortened form *Samgar* as one element of the compound name Samgar-nebo (săm′gär-nē′bō) [Heb. *Samgar-nebô*] in Jer 39:3. However, *nebô* is properly the first element of the following name. Its misplacement is the result of the Masoretes' misunderstanding of the passage. They mistakenly made Nergal-sharezer's title, *Samgar,* into an element of a personal name. Hence, Jeremiah mentions only "Nergal-sharezer of Sin-magir, Nebo-Sarsechim, the Rabsaris," and "Nergal-sharezer the Rab-mag" (who may possibly be identical with Nergal-sharezer's Sin-magir).

Nergal-sharezer (*Nergal-sharri-uṣur*) is probably the person known from historical sources as Nebuchadnezzar's son-in-law, and as the 4th king of the Neo-Babylonian Empire (560-556 B.C.). He is believed to have seized the throne by a revolution in which his brother-in-law, Amel-Marduk, the Biblical Evil-Merodach, was assassinated. A recently discovered tablet of the Babylonian Chronicle reveals that he carried out a military campaign into Cilicia in his 3d regnal year (557/56 B.C.).

Neri (nē′rī). [Gr. *Nēri* from Heb. *Nerî,* "my lamp," attested on an ancient Hebrew seal inscription.] A Judahite appearing in Luke's genealogy of Jesus Christ (Lk 3:27).

Neriah (nḗ-rī′à). [Heb. *Nerîyah,* and *Nerîyahû,* "Yahweh is my lamp." The name occurs on ancient Hebrew seal inscriptions and in the *Lachish Letters; also in cuneiform documents as *Niriyau.*] The father of Jeremiah's scribe Baruch, and of Seraiah (Jer 32:12; 36:4; 51:59). It is possible that Baruch's father and Seraiah's father are not identical, but merely men of the same name.

Net. A rendering of various Hebrew and Greek words. The Bible refers to nets as: (1) *fishing nets of several types, such as throwing nets and dragnets (see fig. 352); (2) nets used for catching birds (Prov 1:17) or animals (Is 51:20), set with cords and

352. Fishing nets spread out for drying in the small harbor of Tyre

hidden by the wayside (Ps 140:5) to entangle the victim's feet (cf. Job 18:8; Ps 57:6); (3) a metal *network, used as an altar grate (Ex 27:4, 5) or as part of the capitals of the 2 pillars before the Temple (1 Ki 7:17); and (4) figuratively, of that which entraps or victimizes a human being (Ps 9:15; 10:9; 25:15; etc.), of captivity (Eze 12:13; 19:8), and of the kingdom of heaven as gathering in converts "of every kind" (Mt 13:47)—an illustration especially significant to those disciples who had left their nets to become fishers of men (ch 4:19, 20).

Netaim (nḗ-tā′ĭm). [Heb. *Neṭa'îm,* "plantings."] A village of Judah in which potters lived, and where probably (royal) plantings were found (1 Chr 4:23, RSV); identified with *Khirbet en-Nuweiṭi',* 4 mi. north of ancient Moresheth-gath (*Tell ej-Judeideh*).

Nethaneel. *See* Nethanel.

Nethanel (nḗ-thăn′ĕl), KJV **Nethaneel** (nḗ-thăn′ĕ-ĕl). [Heb. *Nethan'el,* "God gives." The name occurs in cuneiform records as *Natan-el.*]

1. The prince of the tribe of Issachar during the early period of the wilderness wanderings of Israel (Num 1:8; 2:5; 7:18, 23; 10:15).

2. The 4th son of Jesse, and David's brother (1 Chr 2:14).

3. A priest who was a trumpeter in the orchestra when the ark was brought to Jerusalem (1 Chr 15:24).

4. A Levite, father of the scribe Shemaiah (1 Chr 24:6).

5. A son of the gatekeeper Obed-edom in David's reign (1 Chr 26:4).

6. A prince of Judah sent out by King Jehoshaphat to teach in the cities of Judah (2 Chr 17:7).

7. A chief of the Levites in the reign of Josiah (2 Chr 35:9).

8. A postexilic priest in the time of the high priest Joiakim (Neh 12:21).

9. A member of the family of Pashhur; he had married a foreign wife in Ezra's time (Ezr 10:22).

10. The son of a priest; he was a trumpeter at the dedication of the wall of Jerusalem (Neh 12:36).

For the NT form of the same name *see* Nathanael.

Nethaniah (nĕth′à-nī′à). [Heb. *Nethanyah* and *Nethanyahû,* "Yahweh gives." The name occurs also on ancient Hebrew seals, and is found in cuneiform texts as *Natanuyâma.*]

1. A son of Asaph, and the head of the 5th of the 24 courses into which David organized the musicians for the Temple (1 Chr 25:2, 12).

2. A Levite who was sent out, with others, by King Jehoshaphat to teach in the cities of Judah (2 Chr 17:8).

3. A man whose son Jehudi was sent by the princes to summon Jeremiah's secretary, Baruch (Jer 36:14).

4. A prince of Judah, whose son Ishmael assassinated Gedaliah (2 Ki 25:23, 25; Jer 40:8, 14, 15; 41:1-3).

Nethinims (nĕth′ĭ-nĭmz). [Heb. *Nethinim,* "the given ones"; Aramaic *Nethinin,* of the same meaning.] A term occurring frequently in postexilic literature, applied to a class of men who were dedicated to the Temple and its service. Since the Heb. *Nethinim* is a plural form, the addition of the "s" to the transliterated name is superfluous. In this article they will be designated simply Nethinim. The RSV renders *Nethinim* "temple servants." From the references in the OT it seems that they were a kind of Temple slave who performed the menial tasks connected with the Temple ceremonies and served the priests and Levites. They were descendants of Canaanites or were prisoners of war, given to the Temple according to an Israelite custom. The first mention of this practice is in Num 31:30, 47, where the record states that Moses gave a number of captured Midianites to the Levites as servants. Later the Gibeonites were made Temple slaves, their special task being to draw water and hew wood (Jos 9:23). More men were added by David and his princes (Ezr 8:20); however, the aliens whom Solomon dedicated as Temple servants apparently retained the designation, "Solomon's servants" (ch 2:55). Several names borne by ancestral heads of the Nethinim, such as Rezin and Sisera, are of foreign derivation (vs 43-54; etc.).

Many Nethinim returned with Zerubbabel from Babylonia after the Exile, although the exact number is not known, since they are numbered with "Solomon's servants" in Ezr 2:58 and Neh 7:60. There were 220 Nethinim who returned with Ezra to Jerusalem about 80 years later (Ezr 8:20). This shows that they had not only become part of the economy of Judah, but considered themselves as belonging to that nation, and that the religion of the Jews had, at least after the Exile, become their religion. This is also obvious from the fact that they joined Nehemiah's covenant, made between the people and God (Neh 10:28, 29). Like other ecclesiastical personnel the Nethinim were exempt from taxes under the Persian administration, and resided in special towns (Ezr 7:24; 2:70). Inside the city of Jerusalem they occupied an area in Ophel, south of the Temple area, opposite the water gate (Neh 3:26).

Netophah (nē-tō′fà). [Heb. *Neṭophah,* "dripping."] A town in Judah, mentioned with Bethlehem and Anathoth (Ezr 2:22, 23; Neh 7:26). Two of David's "mighty men" came from Netophah (2 Sa 23:28, 29), and Netophathites are mentioned among those who supported the administration of Gedaliah, the governor of Judah after the fall of Jerusalem (2 Ki 25:23; Jer 40:8). Fifty-six descendants of former inhabitants of Netophah returned with Zerubbabel from Babylonia after the Exile (Ezr 2:22). Although this town was originally not assigned to the Levites, Levite singers lived in it after the Exile (Neh 12:28). The site has been iden-

tified with *Khirbet Bedd Fâlûḥ,* about 3½ mi. southeast of Bethlehem.

Netophathi. *See* Netophathite.

Netophathite (nē-tŏf′à-thīt), KJV once **Netophathi** (nē-tŏf′à-thī). [Heb. *Neṭôphathî.*] A native or inhabitant of Netophah (1 Chr 2:54; Neh 12:28).

Nettle. [Heb. *charûl; qimmôś.*] One or the other of the Hebrew words rendered "nettle" may be the true nettle (genus *Urtica*). Several species occur in Palestine, and all are characterized by their ability to spring up in neglected farm land and around deserted buildings. The Roman nettle (*U. pilulifera*) is said to have an especially potent sting. Some identify *charûl* with chickling (*Lathyrus ochrus*), and consider *qimmôś* a term for weeds in general. Throughout Scripture these plants are companions of poverty (Job 30:3, 7), slothfulness (Prov 24:31), and desolation (Is 34:13; Hos 9:6; Zep 2:9). *See* Thorns and Thistles.

Network. A rendering of: (1) the Heb. *śebakah;* "grating," "network," used of certain ornamental sections of the capitals of Solomon's bronze pillars (1 Ki 7:18-42); (2) the Heb *ma'aśeh resheth,* "network," used to describe the nature of the grating in the altar of burnt offering in the ancient tabernacle (Ex 27:4; 38:4); (3) the Heb. *chôrai* (Is 19:9, KJV), the exact significance of which in this passage is not clear. It may mean either "white cloth" (RSV "white cotton") or "turn white," that is "the weavers shall turn white (or pale)." The LXX reads *bussos,* "fine linen."

New Earth. [Heb. *'ereṣ chadashah;* Gr. *gē kainē.*] This term occurs twice in the OT (Is 65:17; 66:22) in contexts that describe the blessings that would have been the lot of both the land and the people of Israel had the messages of God through His prophets been heeded. However, Israel failed, and in consequence the literal fulfillment of these promises according to their original intent and detail was rendered impossible. Nevertheless, in principle these prophecies will be fulfilled in the new earth to be inherited by the saints after the *millennium (Rev 20 to 22). See *SDACom* 4:25-38, 332-335.

The expression "new earth" appears twice in the NT (2 Pe 3:13; Rev 21:1). There are 2 Greek words used in the NT that are translated by the one English word, "new." They are: (1) *Neos,* which expresses the idea of newness in respect to time, and may be translated "new," "recent," "young." It is the opposite of *archaios,* "old," "original," "ancient." (2) *Kainos,* which connotes the idea of newness as to form or quality, and may be translated "new," "fresh," "different as to nature." It is opposed to *palaios,* "old," "aged," "worn out," "marred." *Kainos* is the term that is used to describe the "new earth." By their use of *kainos* Peter and John envision not an earth created *ex nihilo,* but the old earth renewed, renovated, and cleansed by fire from all defilement (2 Pe 3:10-13; Rev 21:1).

The descriptions of the "new earth" are few and brief; however, they present a highly desirable scene: a land of peace and security, perfection and happiness, in which sin, death, and pain will be forever banished (2 Pe 3:10-13; Rev 21; 22). Its capital will be the New Jerusalem (Rev 21:2).

New Moon. *See* Month.

New Testament. The collection of 27 short religious writings that constitute the 2d and briefer of the 2 general divisions into which the Christian Bible is divided. The NT is less than ⅓ the length of the OT. It consists of the 4 Gospels, the Acts of the Apostles, a number of letters of Paul, some general epistles, and the Apocalypse. The Gospels are books of faith containing the good news of God's provision for man's salvation through Jesus Christ. They seek to make known the gospel as it is embodied in the person, the work, and the teachings of Jesus Christ. The Acts of the Apostles presents an account of the beginnings of the Christian church. Paul's letters were originally written to specific churches and individuals to meet particular religious needs, but under the inspiration of God they have had abiding value for all Christians in all ages. The same is true of the general epistles of Peter, James, John, and Jude. The book of Revelation, with its symbolism, presents the final victory of Christ and His kingdom over the forces of evil. These books, though written in the 1st cent., have had a message for Christians in every age, and speak with special force today.

The name "Testament" is derived from the Latin *testamentum,* which was erroneously adopted in the Old Latin version as a translation for the Gr. *diathēkē,* employed in the LXX as a rendering for the Heb. *berîth,* "covenant." The germ of the idea of an old and new covenant seems to have been found in Paul's reference to the reading of the old covenant in 2 Cor 3:14, RSV. So far as is known,

the 1st Christian writer to use the designation *Novum Testamentum,* "New Testament," was Tertullian (A.D. 160-230), but its use soon became general.

The majority of NT scholars throughout Christian history have agreed that the original language of the NT was Greek. However, to many of the writers of the NT, Greek was a secondary language, hence a few scholars have advocated that the 4 Gospels and part of Acts were originally written in Aramaic, the native tongue of Jesus and the apostles. But no copies of NT books in Aramaic have survived, and the Semitic flavor that these writings contain can be explained in part, at least, by the Semitic background of the writers and by a conscious imitation, particularly on the part of Luke, of the language of the Septuagint. It was doubtless in the providence of God that the various books of the NT were written in Greek, the international speech of the time.

The kind of Greek in which our NT was written was the subject of considerable debate in the 17th cent. Some scholars in those years argued that the language of the NT was the pure Attic Greek of the classical period. The Hebraists affirmed that it was a Hebraic-Greek, a sort of Jewish-Greek jargon. Still others said it was a special language of the Holy Ghost. Today we know that all of these views were incorrect and that the NT was written in the vernacular *Koinē* Greek of the 1st cent. A.D. This common, or Hellenistic, Greek had become the lingua franca of the Greco-Roman world and was widely used even in Palestine. It was a language based on the late Attic vernacular, but with elements derived from other Greek dialects. Proof of this was derived from a study of the Greek papyri and inscriptions of the period of the NT.

The autographs, that is, the original documents in the authors' own handwritings, have all disappeared. These were written probably on papyrus, a fragile substance (*see* Writing Materials) that could not survive long in damp climates. Of the copies of these autographs only a few from the first 3 cent. have survived. Before the age of printing, copies were laboriously written out, such copies being called manuscripts (Latin *manuscriptum,* "written by hand"). But since there are no perfect copyists, there are no 2 manuscripts of the NT exactly alike. Gradually, through repeated copyings, various mistakes crept into the text of the NT; however, none of so serious a nature as to affect any major doctrine. Where variant readings exist it is the task of the modern scholar to determine if possible the original authentic reading. This is the science of textual criticism.

The earliest printed Greek NT was that incorporated in the Complutensian Polyglot, of which the NT portion was printed in 1514 but not published until 1522. The work was done at Alcalá (Latin *Complutum*) in Spain under the direction of Francisco Jiménez de Cisneros, cardinal archbishop of Toledo, who is more popularly known as Cardinal Ximenes. The first published Greek Testament was edited by Desiderius Erasmus and was published March 1, 1516. Erasmus' edition was based on only a few manuscripts coming from medieval times and therefore contained a late form of the Greek text. Nevertheless, his text, as revised by himself and later by Robert Stephanus, Beza, and the Elzevir brothers, became the *Textus Receptus,* the "Received Text," of the Greek NT until the 19th cent. Upon it the older standard translations of modern Europe are based, such as Luther's and the King James Version.

Since that time many older copies of the Greek text have been discovered, by means of which the text can be restored to a condition much nearer to that of the original autographs than was possible in the 16th cent.

The papyri are the oldest of the Greek manuscripts. Among them are the Chester Beatty Papyri consisting of portions of 3 codices (P^{45}, P^{46}, P^{47}) containing parts of 15 NT books and dating from the 3d cent. (see fig. 215). The oldest existing NT manuscript is the Rylands Papyrus 457 (P^{52}), a scrap (fig. 269) containing parts of Jn 18:31-33, 37, 38, and dating from the first half of the 2d cent. In 1957 and 1958 Prof. Victor Martin of Geneva published a newly discovered papyrus of the Gospel of John dating from about A.D. 200 (P^{66}), also known as Bodmer II. Bodmer VII and VIII contain a manuscript of the 2 epistles of Peter and Jude (P^{72}) dated the 3d cent.

Uncial manuscripts were written in capital letters without separation between words and generally without accents or breathing marks. The great uncials are still our basic source for the reconstruction of the text of the NT. Only some of the more important ones can be mentioned here. *Codex Vaticanus* (B), of the first half of the 4th cent., is regarded

by scholars as probably the oldest fairly complete copy, and the most valuable copy, of the entire Bible (see fig. 71). It has been in the Vatican Library at Rome since before 1481. *Codex Sinaiticus* (א) is a 4th-cent. manuscript discovered by Tischendorf in the monastery of St. Catherine at Sinai (1844-59). This manuscript was purchased by the British Government from Soviet Russia and was transferred to the British Museum in 1933. It contains the whole NT (see fig. 72), also the Epistle of Barnabas and about ⅓ of the Shepherd of Hermas, and about half of the OT. *Codex Alexandrinus* (A), of the early 5th cent., was produced in Egypt. In 1624 it was offered as a gift to King James I of England by the patriarch of Constantinople, but it did not actually reach England until 1627 as a gift to James's successor, Charles I. Originally it contained the whole Bible (see fig. 73) and the 2 Epistles of Clement, but it has suffered a number of mutilations, including the loss of most of Matthew's Gospel and much of 2 Cor. *Codex Ephraemi* (C), a 5th-cent. manuscript now in the Bibliothèque Nationale in Paris, is a palimpsest, that is, a reused manuscript from which the Biblical text had been erased and the sermons of Ephraem written over it in Syriac. It is possible, however, still partly to read the Biblical text. *Codex Bezae* (D), in the library at Cambridge University, is a 5th- or 6th-cent. bilingual Greek-Latin manuscript of the Gospels and Acts in the curious Western type of text. Besides these more important manuscripts, there are the 6th-cent. bilingual manuscript of the Pauline epistles in *Codex Claromontanus* (D_2) with a Western type of text, the Freer Gospels in Washington, D.C. (W), and *Codex Koridethianus* (Θ) of the Gospels, probably from the 9th cent.

Cursive manuscripts date from about the 9th cent. and later. Of these, Minuscule 33 is known as the "Queen of the Cursives," and Family 1 (1-118-131-209) and Family 13 (13-69-124-346) have been subsumed into the Caesarean text.

Originally the books of the Bible were not divided into chapters and verses. Divisions of the books of the NT into various sections were made as early as the 4th cent. Our modern chapter divisions were made in the early 13th cent. by Stephen Langton, then connected with the University of Paris but afterward archbishop of Canterbury. Verse divisions were not made until the age of printing. No Greek manuscript has them. In 1551 Robert

Stephanus, while making a horseback journey from Paris to Lyons, divided his Latin New Testament into 7,959 verses. His object in making the verses was apparently twofold: He was preparing a concordance to the NT which his son Henri finally published in 1594, and hence desired small divisions for ready reference, and he was preparing to publish a NT with the Greek in the center, and Erasmus' Latin translation on one side and Jerome's on the other, the verse divisions of which would afford a ready comparison of the exact words. Henri Stephanus says that his father did the work *inter equitandam,* "while riding," which probably means during intervals on the journey. If the verses were actually made while he was on horseback some of the unfortunate divisions may be due to the jogging of the horse at the wrong place. Stephanus' 4th edition of the Greek NT which appeared in 1551 in 2 small volumes at Geneva was the first to contain the verse divisions. The earliest English NT to have them was William Whittingham's translation of 1557, published at Geneva.

New Year. *See* Trumpets, Feast of; Year.

Neziah (nĕ-zī'à). [Heb. *Neṣiach,* "excellent."] The ancestral head of a family of Temple servants, or Nethinim. Some members of this family returned from Babylonia under the leadership of Zerubbabel (Ezr 2:54; Neh 7:56).

Nezib (nē'zĭb). [Heb. *Neṣib,* "pillar," "garrison."] A town in the Shephelah of Judah (Jos 15:43), now *Khirbet Beit Neṣîb,* 7½ mi. northwest of Hebron.

Nibhaz (nĭb'hăz). [Heb. *Nibchaz.*] A god of the Avvites, a people settled by the Assyrians in the territory of Samaria after the 10 tribes had been carried away into captivity (2 Ki 17:31). Proposed identifications of Nibhaz with some other known deity are inconclusive.

Nibshan (nĭb'shăn). [Heb. *Nibshan.*] A town in the Wilderness of Judah (Jos 15:62), probably now *Khirbet el-Maqâri* in the *Buqê'ah,* 5 mi. southwest of *Khirbet Qumrân* (Cross-Milik, *BASOR* 142 [1956], 16).

Nicanor (nī-kā'nôr). [Gr. *Nikanōr,* "victorious," a frequently occurring Greek name.] One of the 7 men appointed by the church of Jerusalem to look after the Greek-speaking widows and the poor (Acts 6:5).

Nicodemus (nĭk'ô-dē'mŭs). [Gr. *Nikodēmos,* "victor over the people." The name occurs frequently among Greeks and Jews, and is spelled *Naqdêmôn* in its Hebraized form.] A Pharisee and member of the Sanhedrin, who visited Jesus by night for a discussion of His teachings (Jn 3:1-21). He chose the night hour, fearful that if detected he would be ridiculed by his fellow Pharisees, among whom Jesus was decidedly unpopular. Although he was a teacher of Israel and had been interested in the message of Christ, he was ignorant of even the most elementary principles of the kingdom of God as preached by Jesus. However, the interview with Jesus must have made a deep impression on him. Although he did not immediately become a follower of the Lord, the seed sown during that night bore fruit in the course of time. A few months before the crucifixion, when members of the Sanhedrin in one of their meetings denounced Jesus as an impostor, Nicodemus raised his voice in defense of Him, asking whether it was permissible to condemn a man before he was even heard (Jn 7:50-52). After Christ's death on the cross, he openly took his stand on the side of the despised Teacher of Nazareth. He and Joseph of Arimathea, another member of the Sanhedrin, took the body of Jesus from the cross and gave it a decent, though temporary, burial (ch 19:39, 40-42). Christian legend made him the author of the apocryphal work of a late period, *Acts of Pilate.*

Nicolaitanes. *See* Nicolaitans.

Nicolaitans (nĭk'ô-lā'ĭ-tănz), KJV **Nicolaitanes** (nĭc'ô-lā-ī'tănz). [Gr. *Nikolaitai.*] A heretical sect in the apostolic church. This sect is mentioned in the NT only in the letters of John the revelator to the "seven churches which are in Asia." Christ praised the church at Ephesus for "hating" the works of the Nicolaitans (Rev 2:6), and censured the church at Pergamum for accepting some of their teachings.

The earliest extra-Biblical Christian writer to mention this party is Irenaeus (c. A.D. 185), who identifies the Nicolaitans as a Gnostic sect: "John, the disciple of the Lord, preaches this faith [the deity of Christ], and seeks, by the proclamation of the Gospel, to remove that error which by Cerinthus had been disseminated among men, and a long time previously by those termed Nicolaitans, who are an offset of that 'knowledge' falsely so called, that he might confound them, and persuade them that there is but one God, who made all things by His Word" (*Against Heresies* iii. 11. 1; *ANF* vol. 1, p. 426).

There is evidence also of a Gnostic sect in the 3d cent. A.D. bearing the name "Nicolaitans."

Irenaeus (*op. cit.* i. 26. 3), followed by Hippolytus (*The Refutation of All Heresies* vii. 24) and others, presents the theory that this sect originated in the teaching of Nicolas (RSV "Nicolaus"), 1 of the 7 deacons first ordained by the apostles, a "proselyte of Antioch" (Acts 6:1-3, 5). There is no evidence that this tradition is reliable.

The theory has been postulated, based partly on a supposed similarity of the meanings of the names Nicolaus ("conqueror of people") and Balaam (probably "devourer"), that the "doctrine of Balaam" (Rev 2:14) is identical with that of the Nicolaitans (v 15). However, the construction of the passages is against this view.

The doctrine of the Nicolaitans appears to have been a form of antinomianism (see *SDACom* 7:957). Nicolaitans of the 2d cent. seem to have continued and extended the views of the 1st-cent. adherents, holding to the freedom of the flesh, and teaching that the deeds of the flesh had no effect upon the health of the soul and consequently no relation to salvation.

Nicolas. *See* Nicolaus.

Nicolaus (nĭk′ō-lā′ŭs), KJV **Nicolas** (nĭk′ō-lăs). [Gr. *Nikolaos,* "conqueror of the people," a Greek name occurring frequently in the inscriptions.] One of the 7 men appointed by the church of Jerusalem to look after the Greek-speaking widows and the poor (Acts 6:5). He is called a proselyte of Antioch and is the only man in the NT explicitly designated by the term "proselyte."

Nicopolis (nĭ-cŏp′ō-lĭs). [Gr. *Nikopolis,* "city of victory." The name of Greek cities.] The Nicopolis of the NT is probably the city in Epirus, near Actium (Map XX, B-3), which Augustus founded in commemoration of his victory over Antony at Actium in 31 B.C. Under the patronage of the emperor it became a magnificent cultural center with many beautiful buildings, some of them built by Herod the Great (Jos. *Ant.* xvi. 5. 3). Athletic games held every 4 years in honor of the Actian Apollo ranked with the other 4 athletic festivals of Greece. In his letter to Titus (Tit 3:12) Paul stated that he planned to spend the winter at Nicopolis, and requested his younger fellow worker to come there and meet him. Paul

apparently considered Nicopolis a good center from which to evangelize western Greece. It is generally believed that the pastoral epistles, to which the letter to Titus belongs, were written after Paul's 1st Roman imprisonment; hence his stay at Nicopolis must be placed in one of the winters between A.D. 63 and 66, the probable year of his last arrest. The postscript to the letter to Titus in the KJV, stating that the letter was written from Nicopolis in Macedonia, has no historical value, and is not part of the original letter, being found in no early Greek manuscript.

Niger (nī′jẽr). [Gr. *Niger,* from a Latin name meaning "black."] The surname of Symeon, a leader in the early Christian church of Antioch (Acts 13:1). Nothing is known of him except that he was present when the Holy Spirit commissioned Paul and Barnabas to go forth as foreign missionaries (vs 2-4).

Night. The period of darkness between days. In OT times the night was divided into 3 watches; the 1st referred to as "the beginning of the watches" in Lam 2:19, the 2d as "the middle watch" in Jgs 7:19, and the 3d as "the morning watch" (1 Sa 11:11). In NT times the Roman system of 4 night watches was in use (Mk 6:48); these may have been called evening, midnight, cockcrow, and morning (ch 13:35). Sometimes the time of night was designated by hours (Acts 23:23).

Night Hag, KJV **Screech Owl.** [Heb. *lîlîth.*] Because of a similarity between *lîlîth* and *laylah* "night," it has been thought that a nocturnal bird is meant. But the similarity may be incidental. The Hebrew term cannot certainly be identified with a particular bird. "Night hag" is an inexact term, possibly referring to the sooty shearwater, or black hag, a water bird of the Atlantic coast of North America. However, the Biblical bird was at home in deserted buildings (Is 34:14). Driver suggests either the goat-sucker or the night-jar (*PEQ* 91 [1959], 55-58).

Nighthawk. [Heb. *tachmas.*] The Hebrew term cannot be certainly identified with a particular bird. "Nighthawk" (*Caprimulgus europaeus*) is only a conjectural translation. The term appears only in the parallel lists of unclean fowl (Lev 11:16; Deut 14:15). Some think a species of owl is intended. Driver suggests the short-eared owl (*PEQ* 87 [1955], 20).

Nile (nīl). [Heb. *Ye'or,* a transliteration of the Egyptian *ĭtrw,* later *ĭrw,* meaning

353. The Nile River

"river" par excellence.] The great river of Egypt, about 4,000 mi. long, one of the longest rivers on earth. Its sources, consisting of several streams of which the Kagera is the most important, lie in central Africa. These streams flow north and form Lake Victoria. After leaving this lake the river, now called the White Nile (length, 1,560 mi.), receives water from several more streams before it reaches the confluence of another main river at Khartum—the Blue Nile, which up to that point has flowed 1,115 mi. from its source in the highlands of Abyssinia. The last tributary of the Nile is the Atbara, also called the Black Nile, which is 790 mi. long. It joins the main stream about 200 mi. north of Khartum (Map IV, D-5).

Between Khartum and Aswan, the southern border of ancient Egypt, the Nile in its flow of 1,165 mi. tumbles over 6 cataracts, which throughout the history of the Nile country have been formidable barriers to protect Egypt against invasions from the south. The northernmost of these barriers, called the 1st cataract, is formed by a granite ridge 180 mi. in length lying in an east-west direction athwart the river's course at Aswan. From this area red and gray granite has been quarried from the earliest times by the Egyptians for obelisks, steles, columns, and statues.

At Aswan the Nile enters Egypt proper and flows for 748 mi. through the entire length of Egypt from south to north (Map IV, B/C-5; see fig. 353). The width varies from 500 to 1,000 yards. Below Cairo the river divides into several channels, forming a fertile delta. There were 7 main channels in ancient times, but now there are only 2, those emptying at the Rosetta and Damietta mouths of the river (Map V, A-2/3).

The Nile was and is the source of all life to Egypt, a country belonging to the Sahara Desert with practically no rainfall. The river inundates its banks during the summer months and upon receding leaves a layer of rich soil. Thus a fertile strip of land on each side of the Nile has been formed from time immemorial. This narrow ribbon of fertile land (shown in a darker green on Map V), renewed yearly by the Nile, made possible life for Egypt's dense population. The inundation begins at Aswan toward the end of June and in the region of Cairo in the middle of July, reaching its highest level in October. From that time the water level recedes until the lowest level is reached in March. From March the level remains constant until the new inundation begins. The inundations are the result of the following conditions: the White Nile carries a rather constant amount of water throughout the year, since rain falls almost daily in its source area. The Blue Nile and the Atbara, on the other hand, carry a great amount of water only during the time when the highlands of Abyssinia have their rainy season. At that time these rivers become torrential streams whose water rushes from the mountains with great rapidity, carrying with it much of the loose mineral-containing soil of the mountainous country through which it flows. When this madly rushing Blue Nile reaches Khartum, it has so much force that the slowly and evenly flowing water of the White Nile is kept back and dammed up, so that it overflows its banks for a long distance south of Khartum. After a few weeks the force of the Blue Nile, responsible for the initial inundation in Egypt, subsides. By that time the pent-up White Nile has become a mighty stream, pouring its water into the Nile channel with a force equal to that exercised formerly by the Blue Nile, and for several more weeks continues the inundation of Egypt.

Because of the importance of the annual inundation, the Egyptians from very early times kept accurate records of the height of each year's inundation. They also had Nilometers at various places in the country, and a warning system to advise farmers concerning the expected height of the Nile, so that these farmers could take measures to protect themselves if the inundation level should be too high, endangering their dikes, villages, and crops, or could prepare themselves if the level should be too low, in which case they would need additional manual labor to pump water into the fields. If the Nile failed, there was want and hunger, and several periods of famine are recorded. The period of 7 lean years that occurred in Joseph's time (Gen 41:54) is not without historical parallels, for a 7-year period of famine had ravaged Egypt in the 3d dynasty, some centuries before.

Nimrah. See Beth-nimrah.

Nimrim (nĭm′rĭm). [Heb. *Nimrîm,* meaning uncertain.] A place in Moab, well watered and fertile (Is 15:6; Jer 48:34). The name still exists in that of the *Wâdī en-Numeirah,* which flows into the southeastern end of the Dead Sea, and runs parallel to the Zered, about 5 mi. north of that stream. At the source of this wadi is a ruin site called *Numeirah,* probably the site of the ancient Moabite town.

Nimrod (nĭm′rŏd). [Heb. *Nimrod.*] One of the outstanding leaders in the period between Noah and Abraham. He was a son or descendant of Cush, but distinguished himself more than the other sons

354. The ruins of *Birs Nimrûd;* the remains of the temple tower of the ancient city of Borsippa

of Cush mentioned in Gen 10:7, 8, who appear only as ancestral heads of tribes. Nimrod is described as a mighty hunter, a monarch, the founder of the first kingdom on earth, and the builder of several famous cities, such as Babel, Erech (Uruk), Accad, Nineveh, and Calah (vs 8-12). See Map XI, B/C-5/6. In Mic 5:6 Assyria is called the land of Nimrod, and to the present day Nimrod's name clings to ruin sites; for example, the site of ancient Calah in Assyria is now called *Nimrûd,* and that of ancient Borsippa in Babylonia is called *Birs Nimrûd.* It is still unexplained how Nimrod, a Cushite, gained so much influence and power in the Mesopotamian valley, the home of the Semites. See fig. 354.

Nimshi (nĭm′shī). [Heb. *Nimshî,* "ichneumon." The name occurs in Akkadian as *Numushum* and in Ugaritic as *Nmsh.*] The father, that is, grandfather, of Jehu, king

of Israel (1 Ki 19:16; 2 Ki 9:2, 14, 20; 2 Chr 22:7). For the common use of "father" to mean ancestor, see Son.

Nineve. See Nineveh.

Nineveh (nĭn′ĕ-vĕ), KJV of NT once **Nineve** (nĭn′ĕ-vĕ). [Heb. *Nîneweh;* Gr. *Nineuē,* variant reading *Nineui;* Assyrian *Ninua* and *Ninâ;* Hittite *Ninuwa;* the etymology and meaning are uncertain.] A city on the eastern bank of the Tigris, at the mouth of a small tributary now known as the *Khosr,* opposite the present city of Mosul. Map XI, B-5; fig. 355.

The city was founded by Nimrod (Gen 10:11). Excavations have brought to light remains that go back to very ancient times. However, the early history of the city is obscure, because during the first millennium of Assyrian history Nineveh seems to have played only an inferior role, with other cities, such as Asshur and Calah, playing the more important role and serving as capitals of the country. The patron goddess of Nineveh was Ishtar, to whom Manishtusu of Akkad built a temple in the 23d cent. B.C. The cult of Nineveh's Ishtar became very popular among Hurrians and Hittites, and was found as far distant as Egypt. Shalmaneser I (*c.* 1274 - *c.* 1244 B.C.) built the first palace in Nineveh, although retaining the seat of the government in Asshur, about 50 mi. south. Later kings added public buildings to the city and some, such as Ashurnasirpal II (884-859 B.C.) and Shalmaneser III (859-824 B.C.), used Nineveh as their residence city for portions of their reigns. It was probably in the time of Adad-nirari III (810-782 B.C.) that Jonah preached his message of warning in the streets of that city, resulting in temporary repentance and a postponement of the impending doom that had been pronounced over wicked Nineveh (Jon 1-4; cf. 2 Ki 14:25).

However, Nineveh's most glorious period began with Sennacherib (705-681 B.C.). From that time on it remained the undisputed capital of the country until its destruction in 612 B.C. Sennacherib built a great platform within the city and erected his palace on top of it. He built a 2d palace in another part of the city, rebuilt the fortification system and beautified the city's 15 gates, the names of which are known to us through a cuneiform text. His son Esarhaddon (681-669 B.C.) added a new palace, and so did Ashurbanipal (669-627? B.C.), the great lover of books, who installed in his palace the first large private library of which

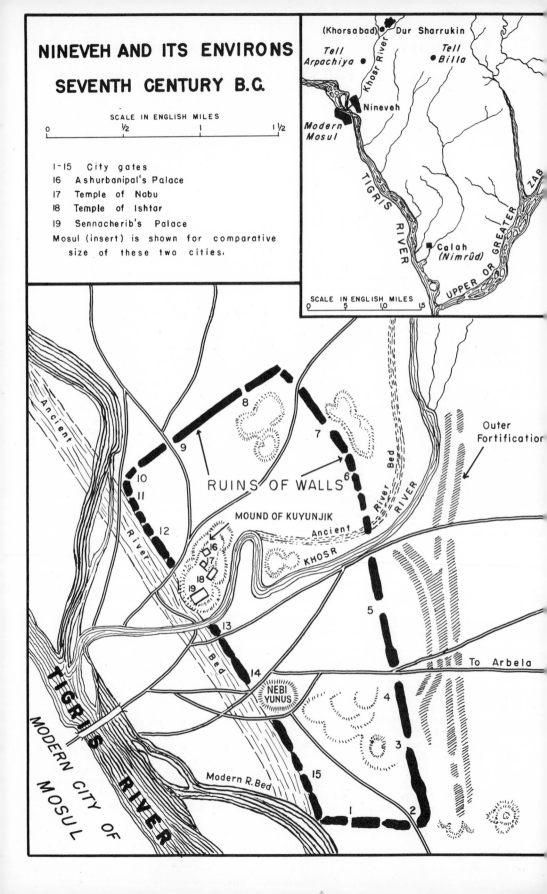

NINEVEH AND ITS ENVIRONS
SEVENTH CENTURY B.C.

SCALE IN ENGLISH MILES

0   ½   1   1½

1-15   City gates
16   Ashurbanipal's Palace
17   Temple of Nabu
18   Temple of Ishtar
19   Sennacherib's Palace

Mosul (insert) is shown for comparative size of these two cities.

(Khorsabad)   Dur Sharrukin
Tell Arpachiya   Tell Billa
Khosr River
Nineveh
Modern Mosul
TIGRIS RIVER
Calah (Nimrûd)
UPPER OR GREATER ZAB

SCALE IN ENGLISH MILES

0   5   10   15

Ancient

8
9
7
10
11
12
RUINS OF WALLS   6
MOUND OF KUYUNJIK
River
Ancient
KHOSR
16
17
18
19
13
Bed
14
NEBI YUNUS
TIGRIS RIVER
MODERN CITY OF MOSUL
Modern R. Bed
15
1
2
3
4
5
To Arbela
River Bed
RIVER
Outer Fortification

we have record (now in the British Museum), and which has given us more information about the ancient world than any other single discovery ever made in Bible lands. Ashurbanipal's successors, Ashur-etil-ilani and Sin-shar-ishkun, were not strong enough to keep the empire intact, and were soon put on the defensive by Nabopolassar, who had made himself king of Babylon in 626 B.C., and by the Medes. In 614 B.C. Asshur fell to the Medes, as did probably also Calah, and 2 years later (612 B.C.) the combined armies of Babylon and of the Medes laid siege to old Nineveh, a city that had seen no hostile foreign armies for centuries. After 3 months the city fell to the attackers, and Sin-shar-ishkun died with his whole palace retinue in the flames of his palace, to which, according to Greek sources, he himself had put the torch.

Thus began to be fulfilled the prophecies of Nahum (Nah 2 and 3) and of Zephaniah (Zep 2:13-15) dealing with Nineveh's doom. The large city not only was completely destroyed, but was actually forgotten in a short time. When Xenophon with his armed forces passed its ruins some 2 cent. later, he could not even learn the real name of the great metropolis that once had flourished there. For many centuries no one knew where Nineveh had been located, although some travelers who visited Assyria in the course of the centuries occasionally made a right guess when they saw the tremendous heaps of ruins across the river from Mosul.

Modern excavations have solved the puzzle of the location of Nineveh. In an effort to discover the site the Frenchman Émile Botta began excavations in 1842 at the mound of ancient Nineveh, but when he found little to reward his efforts, he went to *Khorsabad,* the ancient Dur-Sharrukin, and excavated Sargon's palace city there, thinking that he had discovered Nineveh. Austen Henry Layard began excavating *Nimrûd,* ancient Calah, in 1845, also thinking that he was digging at ol·¹ Nineveh. Both men were mistaken. Only later, when Layard turned his attention to *Kuyunjik,* one of the ruin hills within the confines of the old city of Nineveh, did temples and palaces of Sennacherib and Ashurbanipal in the real city of Nineveh come to light. Layard

and Hormuzd Rassam were the most successful excavators, unearthing untold treasures from the formless heaps of debris and earth. Later Ross, Loftus, and George Smith dug at Nineveh, and in the 20th cent. Budge, King, Thompson, Hutchinson, and Mallowan, thus making possible a book bearing the title *A Century of Exploration at Nineveh* (by R. Campbell Thompson and R. W. Hutchinson [London, 1929]). Yet all work has been confined to *Kuyunjik,* one of the 2 ruin mounds of the ancient city; the other one, the hill of *Nebi Yunus* (see fig. 270), on top of which stands a modern village with a mosque containing what the Moslems believe to be the tomb of the prophet Jonah, hence inviolable, has scarcely been touched by the excavator. It is known that the ruins of the palace of Esarhaddon lie underneath, but they are still inaccessible to the archeologist. One of the original city gates, the Nergal Gate, in the northwest of the old city, has recently been restored and is the only ancient structure still left at Nineveh. Those who wish to see the objects that formerly beautified this marvelous city must go to the museums of Europe, but those who wish to see with their own eyes the literal fulfillment of the prophecies of the OT concerning this metropolis can do so by roaming over the dust heaps of that old city.

The size of ancient Nineveh is known beyond doubt because the city walls are still clearly visible. Their ruins form long, low hills, with gaps where the gates once stood (see fig. 356). The total length of the ancient walls is about $7\frac{1}{2}$ mi. The area of the walled city, roughly triangular in shape, is 1,640 acres (see fig. 355). By allowing about 50 sq. yd. per person, the ancient population inside the walls may be estimated at 160,000; many may have lived outside the walls also. Some have regarded the number of the 120,000 people who "cannot discern between their right hand and their left hand" (Jon 4:11) as meaning small children not yet old enough to know right from left, and have computed that the city would have had at least a population of 600,000. This figure seems to be too large for the known size of the ancient city. It seems better to regard the expression of v 11 as metaphorical, designating the whole population who possessed an imperfect knowledge of good and evil. The statement made in ch 3:3 that "Nineveh was an exceeding great city

355. Map of ancient Nineveh

356. The ruins of the city walls of ancient Nineveh as seen from the east

of three days' journey" probably means that it would take a man 3 days to cover it by going up and down its streets and stopping to preach in enough places to reach all the population within its walls. Also the text stating that "Jonah began to enter into the city a day's journey, and he cried" (Jon 3:4), can hardly mean that he walked for a whole day before he began his work of warning. It may simply be understood as referring to the first day of Jonah's work of preaching his message of repentance. Hence it is not necessary to resort to the supposition that ancient Nineveh included the cities of Dur-sharrukin (now *Khorsabad*), 12 mi. northeast of Nineveh, and Calah (now *Nimrûd*), about 20 mi. south of Nineveh. Those cities were never known as part of Nineveh; they had their own administration, each had its own protective walls, and they were separated by many miles of farmland. But Nineveh was, by ancient standards, a very large city.

Lit.: A. Parrot, *Nineveh and the Old Testament* (New York, 1955).

Ninevite (nĭn′ĕ-vīt). [Gr. *Nineuitēs.*] An inhabitant of Nineveh (Lk 11:30, KJV).

Nisan. [Heb. *Nîsan,* a loan word from the Akkadian *Nisânu.*] The first month of the Hebrew religious year (Est 3:7), called *Abib before the Babylonian exile. It began with the new moon of March or April. See Year.

Nisroch (nĭs′rŏk). [Heb. *Nisrok.*] An Assyrian god in whose temple Sennacherib was murdered by his sons (2 Ki 19:37; Is 37:38). A plausible explanation of the name has not yet been found. Some see in it a composite of Asshur and another divine name, others an intentional corruption of the name Marduk.

Nitre. [Heb. *nether;* Akkadian *nitiru,* loan words from the Egyptian *ntry,* which is the ancestor also of the English term "natron."] "Nitre" means saltpeter, or potassium or sodium nitrate. However, *nether* probably describes a mineral alkali known as natron, found in abundance in Egypt. It is composed largely of bicarbonate of soda

and was used for washing (Jer 2:22; RSV, "lye"). The use of natron with vinegar is as inappropriate and wasteful as the singing of merry songs to one who has a heavy heart, for the chemical reaction between the 2 yields a salt that has the qualities of neither of the 2 original substances (Prov 25:20; the RSV following the LXX has the rendering "wound," assuming that *netheq* should be read instead of *nether*).

No. *See* Thebes.

Noadiah (nō′á-dī′á). [Heb. *Nô'adyah,* "Yahweh has met (me).")]

1. A Levite, a son of Binnui. He was one of the Temple officers to whom Ezra handed over the treasures he had brought from Babylonia (Ezr 8:33).

2. A prophetess who attempted to intimidate Nehemiah (Neh 6:14).

Noah, I (nō′á), KJV of NT frequently **Noe** (nō′ē). [Heb. *Noach,* "rest"; however, in Gen 5:29 the name is explained as though connected in Hebrew with the similar-sounding word *nacham,* "to comfort"; probably a play on words, a device of which the ancients were fond. Gr. *Nōe.*] One of the ancient patriarchs, the 10th in order of descent beginning with Adam (Gen 5:3-29; 1 Chr 1:1-4). His sons belonged to the last generation of the antediluvian period, and Noah through his sons became the progenitor of the whole human race that lived on earth after the Flood. He was the son of Lamech of the lineage of Seth, and like his ancestor Enoch was a man who "walked with God" (Gen 6:9). He was about 480 years of age when God announced the coming Flood to him (ch 6:3; cf. ch 7:6) and gave him instructions to build a ship in which he and his family would be saved (ch 6:13-21). A few years later 3 sons were born to him (ch 5:32), who with their wives were saved in the ark (Gen 7:7, 13; 1 Pe 3:20). That Noah did more than simply build the ark for his family's safety is indicated by the statement in 2 Pe 2:5 that he was "a preacher of righteousness." He must have warned his fellow citizens of the impending catastrophe, but none of that wicked generation responded (cf. 1 Pe 3:20). When the ark was completed the Lord commanded Noah to enter it (Gen 6:22 to 7:5). With Noah also went in clean and unclean animals by pairs (ch 7:2-4, 8, 9, 14-16). God Himself closed the only door into the ark (v 16). Seven days later (v 10) began the *Flood that destroyed all human beings and animals on earth, except those who were in the ark. The ark floated on the Flood waters for 5 months, and then came to rest "upon the mountains of Ararat" (Gen 8:4). After almost 2½ months more the waters had subsided sufficiently to expose the mountaintops (v 5). More than a month later, by means of bird scouts sent out at intervals of 7 days, Noah was able to discover when the earth was dry enough for him to leave the ark. However, he did not abandon the ship until divinely commanded to do so (vs 6-19). Once on the outside he expressed his gratitude to God for his deliverance by building an altar and offering sacrifices. God accepted his offerings and made a covenant with him (chs 8:20 to 9:17).

Some time later Noah planted a vineyard, the first after the Flood, and became drunk with its product, an act that stands in marked contrast with his exemplary life as recorded elsewhere. While in a drunken stupor Noah exposed himself, and Ham, his youngest son, probably also Canaan, Ham's son, seeing his shame, showed disrespect apparently by publishing the fact. The other 2 sons dutifully covered up their father. Because of Ham's disrespectful behavior Noah later pronounced a prophetic curse on Ham's descendants through Canaan, but a blessing on Japheth and Shem (Gen 9:20-27). Nothing more is known of the patriarch, except that he lived another 3½ cent. after the Flood, reaching the age of 950 years (vs 28, 29). Ezekiel lists Noah with Job and Daniel as an example of righteousness (Eze 14:14, 20).

Noah, II (nō′à). [Heb. *No'ah,* meaning uncertain. The name is attested in the ancient Hebrew ostraca from Samaria.] A daughter of Zelophehad of the tribe of Manasseh. She and her sisters obtained the right to inherit their father's property since he left no male heir (Num 26:33; 27:1; 36:11; Jos 17:3).

No-amon. *See* Thebes.

Nob (nŏb). [Heb. *Nob.*] A town of the priests (1 Sa 22:19) in the territory of Benjamin (Neh 11:32), situated, according to Is 10:32, immediately north of Jerusalem. It is now generally agreed that it must have stood on Mount Scopus, the northernmost summit of the Mount of Olives, about 2 mi. northeast of Jerusalem; though some place it at *el-Qu'meh,* a mile north of Scopus. For a time during the reign of Saul, after the destruction of Shiloh, the tabernacle was situated at Nob.

Ahimelech, a descendant of Eli, was high priest there when David, fleeing from Saul, went to Nob and asked for provisions and a sword. Ahimelech, who was ignorant of David's predicament, gave him some of the showbread, and also the sword of Goliath. When this was reported to Saul, the king became so furious that he had Doeg, his Edomite officer, slay all the priests of Nob, with their families (1 Sa 21; 22). Only Abiathar, Ahimelech's son, escaped. Nob was reinhabited after the Exile, as can be seen from Nehemiah's list of resettled cities (Neh 11:32).

Nobah (nō′bà). [Heb. *Nobach,* "barking."]
1. A Manassite who captured the town of Kenath on the western slope of Jebel Hauran, and called it after his own name (Num 32:42).
2. The name which Nobah, 1, a Manasite, gave to the town of *Kenath after its capture (Num 32:42). The new name was not used long. Map VI, C-6.
3. A town in Transjordan mentioned in connection with Jogbehah (Jgs 8:11), a town in the territory of Gad. Some have identified this Nobah, with little justification, with Nobah, 2. The site must still be regarded as unidentified.

Nobleman. A rendering of: (1) The Gr. *eugenēs anthrōpos,* literally, "a wellborn man" (Lk 19:12), one who comes from a wealthy family or from nobility. (2) The Gr. *basilikos,* "a royal one," "royal official" (Jn 4:46, 49), an official from a royal palace or a person of royal blood (the RSV rendering, "official," does not sufficiently stress the royal connections involved).

Nod (nŏd). [Heb. *Nôd,* "wandering," "flight," or "exile."] A land or district east of Eden in the antediluvian period, to which Cain fled from the presence of God (Gen 4:16).

Nodab (nō′dăb). [Heb. *Nôdab.*] A tribe in the Syrian desert, apparently Arab, since it is mentioned with 2 Ishmaelite tribes east of the Jordan, with whom the Israelite tribes of Reuben, Gad, and Manasseh waged a war (1 Chr 5:19).

Noe. *See* Noah, I.

Nogah (nō′gà). [Heb. *Nogah,* "brightness."] A son of David, born in Jerusalem (1 Chr 3:7; 14:6).

Nohah (nō′hà). [Heb. *Nôchah,* "rest."] The 4th son of Benjamin, according to 1 Chr 8:2. He is not mentioned in the list of Benjamin's sons in Gen 46:21, unless he appears there under another name.

Non. *See* Nun.

Noph. *See* Memphis.

Nophah (nō′fȧ). [Heb. *Nophach*.] According to the KJV, a town in Moab (Num 21:30); not identified. The RSV does not render *Nophach* as a proper name.

North. *See* East.

Northeaster. *See* Euroclydon.

Nose, Nostrils. [Heb. generally *'aph*, "nose."] In addition to its usual significance, "nose" (or "nostrils"; the two terms are not distinguished in Hebrew) appears in certain figurative and technical expressions: (1) "Smoke in the nose," as in English, denotes irritation (see Is 65:5). (2) "A *hook in the nose" refers to humiliation, loss of freedom, etc. (3) "To cut off the nose" (see Eze 23:25, RSV) reflects the cruel practice of mutilating prisoners of war. (4) Jewelry or rings "on your nose" (ch 16:12, RSV) pictures an ancient type of ornamentation still practiced by the women of certain Near Eastern tribes. (5) "To put a branch to the nose" (see ch 8:17) refers to some superstitious or pagan practice of uncertain significance.

Nose Jewels. *See* Nose Ring.

Nose Ring. An article of jewelry worn by many women of the East. Abraham's servant placed a ring (Heb. *nezem*) on Rebekah's nose (Gen 24:47, RSV; *see* Earring). Nose rings (KJV "nose jewels") are listed in Is 3:21 among the items that God would remove from "the daughters of Zion" (v 17). Ezekiel mentions this ornament as symbolic among other things of the benefits and honor God bestowed upon Israel (Eze 16:12, RSV). Prov 11:22 states that a beautiful woman without discretion is like a gold ring in a pig's nose. Nose rings are inserted either through the nose septum or through the side of the nose.

Novice. A term that appears only in 1 Ti 3:6, KJV, where it renders the Gr. *neophutos*, literally, "newly planted" (cf. the English derivative "neophyte"). In the context *neophutos* refers either to one who is inexperienced or to one newly converted.

Numbers, Book of. The 4th book of the Pentateuch, called in Hebrew *Bemidbar*, "In the wilderness," the opening word of the book in the Hebrew text. "Numbers" comes from the Latin *Numeri*, its title in the Vulgate, which translated the Septuagint title *Arithmoi*. As one of the 5 books of the Pentateuch, Numbers is traditionally attributed to Moses. Numbers takes up the narrative of Hebrew history at the wilderness of Sinai on the 1st day of the 2d month of the 2d year of the Exodus

(Num 1:1), a month after the account in Exodus closed with the erection of the tabernacle (Ex 40:2, 16). The intervening month was apparently devoted to the inauguration of the sanctuary service as outlined in the book of Leviticus. Numbers traces the experiences of the children of Israel throughout the remaining 38 years of their wilderness wanderings to their last encampment in the plains of Moab, across the river Jordan from Jericho (Num 33:49, 50).

The book opens with a census of the people taken at Sinai and a description of the camp arrangement and the order of march (Num 1; 2; see fig. 92). The Levitical organization is next described in detail, and the duties of the Levites while on the march are given (chs 3; 4). Chapters 5 and 6 pertain to the exclusion of unclean persons from the camp, to certain offerings, and set forth regulations for the Nazirite vow. The sanctuary service is inaugurated (chs 7; 8), and the Passover celebrated (ch 9:1-14). The departure from Mount Sinai and the 1st journey are described in chs 9:15 to 10:36. Chapter 11 recounts the murmuring and rebellion of the people at Taberah and Kibroth-hattaavah. Miriam and Aaron revolt against Moses, but God signally justifies him as the leader of Israel (ch 12). Arriving at Kadesh-barnea, 12 spies are sent to spy out the land of Canaan preparatory to invasion (ch 13), but an unfavorable report leads to rebellion and the decision to return to Egypt (ch 14). This was the 10th occasion on which the people had rebelled, and the Lord ordained that this generation should die in the wilderness, to which He restricted them for the next 38 years. Miscellaneous offerings and regulations are discussed in ch 15. In chs 16 and 17 the revolt led by Korah and his coconspirators against the Aaronic priesthood is described in detail, and also the miracle of the budding of Aaron's rod as an attestation of Aaron's priestly leadership. Chapters 18 and 19 contain further religious regulations. Toward the close of the 40 years in the wilderness the people set out from Kadesh-barnea, one of their chief places of encampment during the 38 years. They make a circuit of the land of Edom preparatory to entering Canaan from the east. Chapter 20 records Edom's insolence in refusing Israel permission to cross its territory and relates the death of Aaron. Deliverance from a plague of fiery serpents and conquest of territory to the east of Jordan are recorded in Num 21. Israel is now encamped on the steppes of Moab east of the Jordan, and in chs 22 to 24 Balak, king of Moab, seeks vainly through Balaam to curse Israel, but through immorality and idolatry is successful in subverting several thousand Israelites (ch 25). A 2d census is taken, showing a slight decrease in population (ch 26). The law of inheritance is modified (ch 27:1-11), and Joshua is appointed as successor of Moses (vs 12-23). Chapters 28 to 31 contain certain additions to the religious laws and report the defeat of Midian. The settlement of the 2½ tribes east of the Jordan is recorded in ch 32. Chapter 33:1-49 lists the camp sites from Egypt to the Jordan. Final arrangements are made for the occupation of Canaan (chs 33; 34), and for Levitical cities and cities of refuge (ch 35). The last chapter (36) deals with the marriage of heiresses who wish to inherit their father's property.

Nun (nŭn), KJV once **Non** (nŏn). [Heb. *Nûn*, "fish," and *Nôn*. The name occurs frequently in Akkadian as *Nûnu, Nunna, Nuniya,* and *Nunâ*.]

1. A man of the tribe of Ephraim (Num 13:8, 16), the father of Moses' successor, Joshua (Ex 33:11; Deut 32:44; 34:9; 1 Chr 7:27).

2. The 14th letter of the Hebrew alphabet, written נ, appearing as the title to the 14th section of Ps 119 in the KJV. *See* Aleph.

Nurse. The rendering of: (1) The Heb. *mêneqeth* (a form of *yanaq*, "to suckle"), a "wet nurse" employed in wealthy homes or by royalty (Ex 2:7; 2 Ki 11:2). Often these remained in the family even after their infant charge grew to maturity (Gen 24:59; 35:8). In Is 49:23, the term is translated "nursing mothers." (2) The Heb. *'omen* (masculine) and *'omeneth* (feminine), "caretakers," those who take care of children (Num 11:12; KJV "nursing father"; Ruth 4:16; 2 Sa 4:4). (3) The Heb. *sokeneth* (a form of *sakan*, "to be of service"), "female nurse" (1 Ki 1: 2, 4, RSV). (4) Gr. *trophos*, "nurse" (1 Th 2:7, RSV), similar to Heb. *'omeneth* in meaning.

Nuts. [Heb. *'egôz; botnah* (sing.).] The dry fruits of certain woody shrubs and trees, having a shell and interior meat. *'Egôz* is the general term (Song 6:11) and *botnah* is the pistachio nut, borne by *Pistacia vera*, a 10- to 30-foot tree with spreading top. The nut maintains a yellowish-green color even when ripe, and is eaten raw or fried with seasoning to form a popular dessert of the Near and Middle East (see Gen 43:11, RSV).

Nympha (nĭm'fà), KJV **Nymphas** (nĭm'făs). [Gr. *Numphas* or *Numpha*, "sacred to the nymphs." Since the name occurs in the Bible only in the accusative form (*Numphan*), it is not certain whether it represents the female name Nympha or the male name Nymphas. Both forms are attested in ancient inscriptions and other texts.] A Christian (whether man or woman is uncertain, see above) at Laodicea or Colossae, to whom Paul sent greetings. The church used his or her house for meetings. The pronouns "his" and "her" are both attested in various ancient manuscripts in the phrase "and the church which is in his ["her"] house" (Col 4:15).

Nymphas. *See* Nympha.

O

Oak. [Heb. *'allôn, 'allah, 'ayil, 'ayyalah, 'elah, 'elôn*.] The Hebrew terms designate a large tree rather than any particular species, among which would be the oak.

Among the oak trees known in Palestine are: the Valonia oak (*Quercus aegilops*), holm oak (*Quercus ilex*), prickly evergreen oak (*Quercus coccifera*), and others. The Hebrew terms doubtless included also the terebinth (*Pistacia terebinthus*). This medium-sized tree has the appearance of an oak in its winter leafless state, but, unlike the oaks, grows more often solitarily than in groves. Because of its size and longevity the terebinth, or turpentine tree, was venerated like the oak in ancient times.

These large, stately trees of the Holy Land were landmarks (1 Ki 13:14; cf. Jos 24:26) and served well as depositaries of wealth (Gen 35:4) and as gravesites (Gen 35:8; 1 Chr 10:12). Under such a tree

Gideon met the angel who directed him to rally Israel against the Midianites (Jgs 6:11, 19), and in the low-hanging branches of such a tree in the forest of Ephraim, Absalom was caught by his head as he rode in battle (2 Sa 18:9, 10, 14).

Oath. [Heb. *'alah,* "execration," "oath," "curse"; *shebû'ah,* "a swearing," "an oath"; Gr. *horkos, horkōmosia,* "oath." "Oath" also appears in verb phrases translating a form of the Heb. *shaba',* "to take an oath," and of the Gr. *anathematizō,* "to bind with an oath."] An appeal to God to attest the truthfulness of a statement, or one's solemn intention to fulfill a promise, implying voluntary submission to divine judgment as the alternative. *Shebû'ah* is probably related to *sheba',* "seven," the sacred number, which occurs frequently in the ritual of an oath. *'Alah* is a stronger word than *shebû'ah* in that it invokes a curse upon the oath breaker (see Neh 10:29; Dan 9:11). This is evident from Num 5:21, where both words occur: "an oath [*shebû'ah*] of cursing [*'alah*]." Both *'alah* (Gen 24:41; 26:28) and *shebû'ah* (Gen 26:3; Deut 7:8; Ps 105:9) are used of an attestation of truth. The oath played a prominent part in lawsuits (Ex 22:11), since, in effect, an oath summoned God as a witness. Accordingly, false swearing or the violation of an oath was considered a gross offense against God (2 Chr 36:13; Eze 17:13), and to swear falsely, invoking the name of God, profaned God's name (Lev 6:3; 19:12). Penalties were prescribed in case of deliberate intent to deceive under oath, and restitution was required (chs 5:1; 6: 1-7). The law strictly forbade false swearing (Ex 20:7; Lev 19:12) or swearing by false gods (Jer 12:16; Amos 8:14), which necessarily implied the reality of the false gods and their ability to intervene in the case. Perjury was rightly considered a most heinous crime because it tended to pervert justice. Under no circumstances might a man "break his word" once he had bound himself by an oath to God, but was required to "do according to all that proceedeth out of his mouth" (Num 30:2; Deut 23:23). Accordingly, it was considered meritorious for a man to stand by a promise as a result of which he later suffered loss (Ps 15:4). Adapting His dealings with man to human understanding and to customs of the day, the Lord bound Himself by an oath to fulfill His promises (Gen 22:16-18; Heb 6:13-20).

An oath was commonly uttered with one hand uplifted to heaven (Gen 14:22, 23; Eze 20:5, 6), or by placing the hand under the thigh of the person to whom the promise was made (Gen 24:2, 3). It was customary to swear by the life of the person addressed (1 Sa 1:26; 2 Ki 2:2), by the life of the king (2 Sa 11:11), by one's own life (Mt 5:36), by heaven—that is, by God Himself— (v 34), and by the Temple, or parts of it (ch 23:16). The formula was often, "God is witness betwixt me and thee" (Gen 31:50), "As the Lord liveth" (Ruth 3:13), or, "The Lord be a true and faithful witness between us" (Jer 42:5).

Our Lord cited the Law of Moses with regard to perjury and the adjuration of promises (Mt 5:33-37), but rejected the elaborate formulas of oath taking common in His day, declaring that a simple Yes or No should carry as much weight. Here Christ is dealing not so much with the judicial oath as with solemn promises made in the course of daily activities. What matters, He says, is the way promises are *kept,* not the way they are *made.* Furthermore, the practice of invoking God's name under certain circumstances implies that a man is free to speak falsely when not under oath. The Bible specifically approves of the judicial oath (Ex 22: 11). Our Lord Himself took such an oath at His trial before the Sanhedrin (Mt 26: 63-65), and the apostle Paul called upon God to witness to the truth of the things he was writing (2 Cor 1:23; 11:31; Gal 1:20).

Obadiah (ō'ba-dī'a). [Heb. *'Obadyah* and *'Obadyahû,* "servant of Yahweh." The name occurs on ancient Hebrew seals and on the Samaria ostraca.]

1. A man of the tribe of Issachar (1 Chr 7:3).

2. A warrior of the tribe of Gad who joined David in the wilderness (1 Chr 12:9).

3. A Zebulunite whose son Ishmaiah was the chief officer of that tribe in David's reign (1 Chr 27:19).

4. A descendant of King Saul through Jonathan (1 Chr 8:38; 9:44).

5. The governor of King Ahab's palace, who is described as a man who feared the Lord. He saved the lives of 100 prophets by hiding them in 2 groups of 50 each in caves (1 Ki 18:3, 4). At the end of the long drought predicted by Elijah, Ahab sent Obadiah to look for pasturage so that the horses and mules of the royal stable might be kept alive. During this search he met Elijah, who sent him to the

king to announce the prophet's arrival (1 Ki 5-16).

6. A prince of Judah whom King Jehoshaphat sent out to teach in the cities of Judah (2 Chr 17:7).

7. A Merarite Levite, one of the overseers of the workmen who repaired the Temple in the reign of King Josiah (2 Chr 34:12).

8. A postexilic descendant of David (1 Chr 3:21).

9. A prophet, and author of the shortest OT book. *See* Obadiah, Book of.

10. A son of Jehiel of the family of Joab; he returned with 218 male members of his family from Babylonia with Ezra (Ezr 8:9).

11. A prominent priest who set his seal to Nehemiah's covenant (Neh 10:5).

12. The head of a Levitical family of gatekeepers (Neh 12:25); possibly identical with Obadiah, 13.

13. A son of Shemaiah of the descendants of Jeduthun (1 Chr 9:16); called Abda in Neh 11:17. He is possibly identical with Obadiah, 12.

Obadiah, Book of. Fourth of the so-called Minor Prophets. The fact that the message concerns Edom, a land to the south of Judah, together with specific references to Judah and Jerusalem (Ob 11, 12, 17, 20, 21), implies that the prophet bore his message to the southern kingdom of Judah. Unlike most of the other prophets, Obadiah does not date his message, and various dates have been suggested, ranging from the 8th to the 6th cent. B.C. The record of the revolt of Edom in the days of King Joram (2 Ki 8:20-22) makes no reference to an Edomite occupation of Jerusalem. However, the similarity of Obadiah's denunciation of Edom (Ob 10-14) to the denunciations of Jeremiah (Jer 49:7-22) and Ezekiel (Eze 25:12-14; 35) seems singularly appropriate to the events of 586 B.C., when Nebuchadnezzar destroyed Jerusalem. According to Ps 137:7 the Edomites approved the destruction of Jerusalem by Nebuchadnezzar and rejoiced over the calamities that overtook Judah.

The literary style of Obadiah is classic and vigorous. His theme is the destruction of Edom because of its violence against the Jews (Ob 10-14). There had been long and bitter warfare between the 2 peoples (2 Sa 8:13, 14; 1 Ki 11:14-22; 2 Chr 20:22; 21:8-10; 25:11, 12; 28:17). At the day of the Lord tables will be reversed, and the people of Edom—blood

relatives of the Jews—will be treated as they have treated others (Ob 15). Their cruelties toward Judah during a time of national crisis will meet a just reward. Then deliverance will come to the house of Jacob, and the kingdom will be restored to its rightful state (vs 17-21).

Obadiah's brief message logically falls into 2 parts: (1) the prediction of doom upon Edom (Ob 1-16) and (2) the triumph and restoration of Israel (vs 17-21). Obadiah first summons the heathen nations to attack Edom (vs 1, 2) because of her pride (vs 3, 4). Edom is to be plundered and her people exterminated (vs 5-9). Her crime has been violence against her brother Jacob, "in the day that the strangers carried away captive his forces, and foreigners entered into his gates, and cast lots upon Jerusalem" (vs 10, 11). Instead of showing mercy the Edomites had laid wait for the Jews as they fled, cutting some of them down and taking others captive (vs 12-14). But the day of the Lord is at hand when the people of Edom will receive their just deserts and "be as though they had not been" (vs 15, 16). That day will bring "deliverance" to "mount Zion," and "the house of Jacob" will inherit the land of Edom (vs 17-20), and the kingdom will then be the Lord's (v 21).

Obal (ō′băl). [Heb. *'Ôbal.*] A son of Joktan, and ancestor of an Arabic tribe (Gen 10:28) called Ebal in 1 Chr 1:22. The name has been recognized in the South Arabic *'Ubal,* the name of a tribe that lived between *Ḥadeida* and *Ṣan'a,* in Yemen.

Obed (ō′bĕd). [Heb. *'Ôbed,* "servant," or "worshiper"; Gr. *Iōbēd.*]

1. A Jerahmeelite (1 Chr 2:37, 38).

2. The son of Ruth and Boaz (Ruth 4:17); he was the father of Jesse, and grandfather of David (Ruth 4:21, 22; 1 Chr 2:12; Mt 1:5; Lk 3:32).

3. One of David's "mighty men" (1 Chr 11:47).

4. A Korahite Levite, a gatekeeper of the family of Obed-edom (1 Chr 26:7).

5. A man whose son Azariah, an army captain, assisted Jehoiada in putting the young prince Joash on the throne (2 Chr 23:1).

Obed-edom (ō′bĕd-ē′dŏm). [Heb. *'Obed-'edôm,* either "Edom is serving" or "servant of Edom." The name is attested also in Punic inscriptions.]

1. A Gittite, thus a native of either the Philistine city of Gath (according to the majority of commentators), Gath-rimmon

in Dan, or Gath-rimmon in Manasseh, the latter 2 cities assigned to the Kohathite Levites. He lived between Kiriath-jearim and Jerusalem, near the spot where Uzzah died for having touched the ark. When this tragedy occurred David did not risk taking the ark on to Jerusalem, but left it in the care of Obed-edom. However, after 3 months, when he saw how the Lord blessed the family of Obed-edom, he moved the ark to Jerusalem and provided a tent for it (2 Sa 6:10-12; 1 Chr 13:13, 14; 15:25).

Some commentators think that this Obed-edom is identical with Obed-edom, 3, who is apparently a Korahite, for the Korahites belonged to the Kohathite Levites (Num 16:1), to whom a town called Gath-rimmon was assigned as a residence city. This view is based partly on a possible connection between 1 Chr 26:5, where reference is made to God's blessing Obed-edom, the Korahite Levite, and 1 Chr 13:14 and 2 Sa 6:11, where the statement is made that Obed-edom, the Gittite, was blessed for having given lodging to the sacred ark.

2. A Levite of the 2d order who was a gatekeeper, and who during the removal of the ark to Jerusalem in David's reign served as a musician, a position he continued to hold in connection with the sanctuary of the ark in Jerusalem (1 Chr 15:18, 21; 16:5).

3. Another Levite who accompanied the ark to Jerusalem in the reign of David (1 Chr 15:24). Like Obed-edom, 2, he was also a gatekeeper in the sanctuary (chs 15:24; 16:38), and was assigned to the south gate in the organization of the Temple personnel at the beginning of the reign of Solomon (ch 26:15). He seems to have been of the family of Korah, of the division of Kohath, and furnished 62 members of his family for service in the sanctuary (vs 1-8). Some identify him with Obed-edom, 1. It was probably a member of this family that was in a responsible position as keeper of the Temple treasures in the time of King Amaziah (2 Chr 25:24).

Obelisks. [Heb. *maṣṣebôth*.] An expression occurring once (Jer 43:13, RSV) in a passage predicting the breaking up of cult objects in the Egyptian "city of the sun" (Heb. *Bêth Shemesh*), which is Heliopolis. *Maṣṣebôth* are stone pillars set up for worship or as monuments. Jeremiah most certainly refers to the many obelisks that in ancient times stood in the great temple of the sun in Heliopolis. One of these obelisks is still found on its orig-

inal site. This 69-foot monolith, bearing an inscription on all 4 sides, was erected by Sesostris I in the 20th cent. B.C. (fig. 360). The accumulation of alluvial soil during the 39 centuries since its construction had buried its lower part, so it has recently been raised and set on a new pedestal. Three of the obelisks that originally stood in the sun temple of Heliopolis have found their way to other countries: (1) the great obelisk that now stands in St. Peter's Square in Rome, which was removed from Egypt by the emperor Caligula and set up in his circus; (2) the so-called Cleopatra's Needle on the bank of the river Thames in London; and (3) its twin, the obelisk that now stands in Central Park in New York City. The 2 last mentioned obelisks, originally erected by Thutmose III in the 15th cent. B.C., as their inscriptions prove, were moved in Roman times to Alexandria, and during the 19th cent. to England and America. Other Egyptian obelisks can be seen in Karnak and Luxor in Upper Egypt, in Paris, Rome (several), and in Istanbul.

Obil (ō'bĭl). [Heb. *'Ôbîl*, "camel driver."] An Ishmaelite who was in charge of King David's camels, probably named after the position he held (1 Chr 27:30).

Oblation. A rendering generally of: (1) the Heb. *minchah,* "offering," in Levitical law "cereal offering" (1 Ki 18:29, 36, RSV; Is 1:13; 19:21; etc.; KJV); (2) the Heb. *qorban,* a general term for "offering," "gift" (Lev. 2:4, 5, 7, etc., KJV); (3) the Heb. *terûmah,* "contribution" (2 Chr 31:14; Is 40:20; etc., KJV). In Eze 45:1-7; 48:8-21 *terûmah* is used for the portion of land contributed for the sanctuary and for the priests (*see* Suburb), an area to be most holy. *See* Sacrifices and Offerings.

Oboth (ō'bŏth). [Heb. *'Oboth,* meaning uncertain.] A place where the Israelites encamped in their wanderings between Kadesh-barnea and Moab (Num 21:10, 11; 33:43, 44), generally identified with the oasis of *'Ain el-Weiba,* about 27 mi. northwest of Petra (Map V, B-7). But some identify it with *'Ain Ḥoṣob,* 14 mi. north-northeast of *'Ain el-Weiba.* Both sites lie on the west side of the *Wâdî 'Arabah.*

Ochran (ŏk'răn), KJV **Ocran** (ŏk'răn). [Heb. *'Okran,* "untouchable."] A man whose son Pagiel was a chieftain of the tribe of Asher (Num 1:13).

Ocran. *See* Ochran.

Oded (ō'dĕd). [Heb. *'Ôded,* meaning uncertain.]

1. A man whose son, the prophet Azariah, encouraged King Asa of Judah (2 Chr 15:1; in v 8 the words "of Azariah the son of" have been supplied in the RSV from the LXX and the Syriac).

2. A prophet of Israel in the reign of Pekah. He protested the enslaving of prisoners taken by the northern kingdom in a war with Judah and secured their release. Not only were they given their liberty, but they were clothed and fed, and the weak among them were provided with transportation (2 Chr 28:9-15).

Offerings. See Sacrifices and Offerings.

Og (ŏg). [Heb. *'Ôg,* meaning uncertain.] The Amorite king of Bashan, whose territory extended from the river Jabbok to Mount Hermon (Deut 3:8, 10; cf. Num 21:23, 24). His residences were in Ashtaroth and Edrei (Jos 12:4, 5; 13:12). He was a remnant of the Rephaim, or "giants," and his large "bedstead" (possibly a sarcophagus) was exhibited in Rabbath-ammon (Deut 3:11). The Israelites under Moses defeated Og in the battle of Edrei, following a victory over his southern neighbor, Sihon, the Amorite king of Heshbon. Og's country was occupied and assigned to the half tribe of Manasseh (Num 21:32-35; Deut 3:13, 14). References by later authors to the conquest of Bashan show that this event was considered one of the high points of Israel's early history (Ps 135: 11; 136:20; Neh 9:22).

Ohad (ō'hăd). [Heb. *'Ohad.*] A son of Simeon (Gen 46:10; Ex 6:15).

Ohel (ō'hĕl). [Heb. *'Ohel,* "tent."] A member of the family of Zerubbabel (1 Chr 3:20).

Oholah (ō-hō'lȧ), KJV **Aholah** (ȧ-hō'lȧ). [Heb. *'Oholah,* either "her tent," or "she has pitched a tent."] A symbolic name of Samaria in the parable of Eze 23:4, 5, 36, 44, which pictures the apostate nation as a wanton harlot.

Oholiab (ō-hō'lĭ-ăb), KJV **Aholiab** (ȧ-hō'lĭ-ăb). [Heb. *'Oholi'ab,* "the father's tent."] A skilled Danite craftsman employed in building the tabernacle (Ex 31:6; 35: 34, 35).

Oholibah (ō-hŏl'ĭ-bȧ), KJV **Aholibah** (ȧ-hŏl'ĭ-bȧ). [Heb. *'Oholibah,* "my tent is in her," or an emphatic form meaning simply "tent."] A poetical name for Jerusalem, referring probably to the fact that God's "tent," or dwelling place, was in that city (Eze 23:1-4; etc.).

Oholibamah (ō-hŏl'ĭ-bā'mȧ), KJV **Aholibamah** (ȧ-hŏl'ĭ-bā'mȧ). [Heb. *'Oholibamah,* "my tent is a high place."]

1. One of Esau's wives (Gen 36:2, 5, 14, 18, 25).

2. Chieftain of an Edomite tribe possibly named after Esau's wife (Gen 36:41; 1 Chr 1:52).

Oil. [Heb. *zayith, shemen, yiṣhar;* Gr. *elaion.*] In ancient Palestine oil was obtained from olives (Lev 24:2), and was used for the preparation of food (cf. 1 Ki 17:12, 13), as fuel for lamps (Ex 25:6; Mt 25:3, 4), as ointment for treating sores and wounds (cf. Is 1:6), and for anointing the body (cf. 2 Sa 12:20; 14:2), a general practice from early times, and still common among primitive peoples. See Anoint. Olive oil was a symbol of prosperity (Deut 32:13; 33:24). The oil placed upon a person anointed at God's direction was apparently symbolic of the endowment of the Holy Spirit (1 Sa 10:1, 6; 16:13). Holy anointing oil (Ex 30:22-25) was used for the consecration of articles used for religious purposes, such as the tabernacle and its furnishings (vs 26-29), and for the consecration of priests (Ex 29:7; 30:30; Lev 8:10-12; etc.). This holy oil was not to be prepared or used for secular purposes (Ex 30:31-33).

The earliest method of production was to press out the oil in an oil press, but oil for the sanctuary lamps was beaten out (Lev 24:2). The berries were carefully cleaned, and all foreign matter was re-

357. A Palestinian oil press operated by a camel

moved. Then they were beaten, and the oil was permitted to seep out. This produced less oil than the other method, but resulted in a superior product.

Usually in the production of pressed oil the ripe olives were crushed in cup holes cut into a rock surface near olive groves (note a possible poetic allusion to this in Job 29:6). Channels led from these cup holes to vats hewn from the rocks, or to jars, into which the oil was collected. Such ancient presses are found in great number throughout Palestine. Another method was to tread the olives in stone vats like grapes. The oldest known real "oil press," discovered in ancient Gezer, comes probably from the 4th cent. B.C. It consisted of a basket into which the crushed olives were put and a stone that was pressed down on the basket by means of a wooden lever with weights hung at the end. The oil dripped from the basket into a container. Oil mills, still used today, were invented in the Greek period. Like grain mills they consist of a lower millstone and an upper one. The nether millstone is a thick, wheellike stone with a depression to hold the berries and a peg fastened in the center. The upper stone is set upright and rolled like a wheel around the depression by means of a beam which serves as an axle and turns around the peg of the lower millstone. Such oil mills are generally operated by animals (see fig. 357).

Oil Press. *See* Oil.

Oil Tree. A literal translation of the Heb. *'eṣ shemen* (Is 41:19, KJV). This tree is thought by some to be the narrow-leaved oleaster, or wild olive (*Elaeagnus hortensis*), a graceful 15- to 20-foot tree common in all parts of Palestine except the Jordan Valley. Its wood is hard and fine grained; its leaves, small and elongated, bluish above and silver below; its flowers small and fragrant. The oil of its fruit is not as useful as olive oil. The wood of *'eṣ shemen* is suitable for carving, and was used in Solomon's Temple for doors, doorposts, and the 2 cherubim (1 Ki 6:23, 31-33). With other trees, it gave its branches for the construction of rustic booths used at the Feast of Tabernacles (Neh 8:15).

Ointment. An unguent usually composed of olive oil and sweet spices, gum resins, or other aromatics, often preserved in alabaster jars (Mt 26:7). These ointments were a much-coveted luxury in Palestine, and were often very expensive (vs 8, 9). They were used variously as cosmetics (Ruth 3:3; Ec 9:8), medicinal salves (Jer 8:22; Rev 3:18), embalming mediums in the preparation of a body for burial (Mk 14:8; Lk 23:56), and in connection with the anointing and consecration rituals of the sanctuary (Ex 30:23-25, 31-33). A person engaged in the preparation of ointments was called a "perfumer" (Ex 30:35; 1 Sa 8:13; Neh 3:8; RSV), or "apothecary," or "confectionary" (KJV).

Old Gate. [Heb. *sha'ar hayeshanah,* possibly "gate of oldness," although the construction of this phrase poses grammatical difficulties. The LXX renders *yeshanah* as a proper name, *Isana,* so that the Hebrew would be read "The Yeshanah Gate."] A gate in the wall of Jerusalem (Neh 3:6; 12:39), which may have taken its name from the city of Jeshanah (2 Chr 13:19), now *Burj el-Isâneh,* northwest of Baal-hazor, about 15 mi. north of Jerusalem. The "Old Gate" is usually identified with the "Corner Gate" of 2 Ki 14:13; Jer 31:38; and Zec 14:10, at the northwest corner of the city wall (Map XVII, II). See fig. 259.

Old Testament. The collection of 39 religious writings which constitute the first and longer of the 2 general divisions into which the Christian Bible is naturally divided. The name "Testament" comes from the Latin *testamentum,* and represents the Gr. *diathēkē,* which is used in the LXX as a rendering for the Heb. *berîth,* "covenant," or "agreement." The OT was the Bible of the Hebrews and is the Bible of Jews today. The number of books in the Hebrew Bible, according to Jewish reckoning, however, was 24, and the OT was divided into 3 sections: the Law (*Tôrah,* our Pentateuch), the Prophets (*Nebî'îm,* Jos, Jgs, Sa, Ki, and the prophets exclusive of Dan), and the Writings (*Kethûbîm,* the rest of the books). *See* Canon. The arrangement of the books in our English Bible is an adaptation from the Latin Vulgate, which in turn was based, at least in part, on the LXX. In our English Bible the 39 books are classified as historical (17 books), poetic (5 books), and prophetic (17 books).

The period of the writing of these books covers about 1,000 years, and perhaps some 30 writers were involved. These books contain the narrative of God's acts in history for man's redemption. They cover the period of sacred history from Creation to the restoration of the Jews after the Babylonian captivity. They do not merely catalogue a series of events, but they interpret these events in the light of God's revelation of Himself to mankind.

The OT was the Bible of Jesus and of His apostles, who used it to teach the Christian religion (Jn 5:39, 45-47; Acts 9: 22; 18:24, 25, 28; 24:14; 26:22, 23; 28:23; etc.). It was not superseded by the New. The NT is only the advancement and unfolding of the Old. The NT assumes the theology of the Old, and declares these writings to be profitable for Christians (Rom 15:4; 2 Ti 3:16, 17; 1 Cor 10:11; 2 Pe 3:1, 2).

The language in which the OT was written was for the most part Hebrew. Two sections of Ezr (Ezr 4:8 to 6:18 and ch 7:12-26), a substantial part of Dan (Dan 2:4b to 7:28), and a single verse in Jer (Jer 10:11) were written in *Aramaic, a Semitic language related to Hebrew, somewhat as modern Italian is to Spanish. Aramaic was an international language widely used in the Near East from about the 6th to the 3d cent. B.C. It became, in fact, the official language of the Persian Empire and was thus the medium of governmental, cultural, and commercial communications. Learned men such as Ezra and Daniel were no doubt at home in both Hebrew and Aramaic.

The Hebrew Bible today is printed in the so-called square characters developed by the Aramaeans. Nearly all the Hebrew manuscripts and fragments of manuscripts of the OT extant today are written in this square script. This includes the ancient copies of Isa and other OT manuscripts among the Dead Sea scrolls and the Nash Papyrus (see figs. 244, 489). Some of these are dated as early as the 3d cent. B.C. The well-known papyri from Elephantine (see fig. 417) and other Aramaic documents of the 5th cent. B.C. are also in this square script. Jesus' saying regarding the perpetuity of the Law (Mt 5:18) presupposes an alphabet in which the *Yod* is the smallest letter, and this is true only of this Aramaic script with its square characters.

Originally, the earliest books of the OT seem to have been written in the Proto-Semitic (or Sinaitic) alphabetic script, which was a semi-hieroglyphic form of writing consisting of some 27 letters. Inscriptions written in that script found at Sinai and Palestine date from the 19th to the 12th cent. B.C. OT books written during the period of the Hebrew kings must have been written in the Phoenician, or pre-exilic Hebrew, alphabet, which is known from inscriptions as early as the

10th and 11th cent. B.C. Some of the monuments exhibiting this script are the Ahiram sarcophagus from Byblos of c. 1000 B.C. (fig. 383), the Gezer calendar from Palestine of c. 950 B.C. (fig. 533), the *Moabite (Mesha) Stone from Dibon of c. 850 B.C. (fig. 338), the Samaria ostraca from Ahab's palace of c. 775 B.C., the *Siloam inscription from Hezekiah's tunnel in Jerusalem of c. 700 B.C. (fig. 445), the *Lachish Letters from c. 587 or 586 B.C. (fig. 285), and some Bible manuscripts found among the Dead Sea scrolls, notably those containing books from the Pentateuch (fig. 298). The postexilic books of the OT were probably written in the Aramaic square script discussed in the preceding paragraph. See Hebrew Language; Writing.

The current text of the Hebrew Bible is known as the Masoretic, or traditional, text (from the Heb. *Masorah,* "tradition"). This text was standardized and preserved by a group of Jewish textual scholars known as the Masoretes, whose main period of activity extended from about the 6th or 7th cent. A.D. to the early part of the 10th cent. These Masoretes devised an elaborate system for safeguarding the text, such as counting verses, words, and even letters in the various books. Jewish scholars also devised systems of vowel signs (known as points) and accentual marks to indicate the proper vocalization in accordance with the traditional pronunciation. At least 3 methods of vowel pointing are known: the Babylonian and Palestinian systems with their supralinear vowel signs, and the Tiberian system written above, within, but largely below the consonants. Eventually the Tiberian system prevailed and is used in the printed Hebrew Bibles of today.

After the Exile the Pentateuch (*Tôrah*) was divided into sections for reading in the synagogue (cf. Acts 13:15; 15:21). Two arrangements were employed: (1) the Palestinian system, according to which the Torah was divided into some 152 weekly sections, called *Sedarîm* (orders, arrangements), requiring some 3 years for the reading of the Pentateuch in worship; (2) the Babylonian, according to which the text was divided into 52 or 54 longer sections, known as *Parashîm,* thus permitting the whole Pentateuch to be read during the course of a year. The Babylonian system finally prevailed, and since the 13th cent. the Jews have universally made it a practice to read the whole Torah during the course of a year in their worship services. This means that a considerable portion of Scripture must be read each week. The 1st pericope, for example, covers Gen 1:1 to 6:8; the 2d, chs 6:9 to 11:32; and the 3d, chs 12:1 to 17:27. These long pericopes were in turn divided into shorter sections or paragraphs technically known as "open" and "closed."

The verse divisions of the OT go back to the time of the Masoretes, though the numbering of the verses is found only from the 16th cent. and later. The Masoretes used the double dot (:), known as the *Sôph-pasûq,* to mark the end of verses. Scholars believe that the division into verses began with the poetic portions of the OT.

The present-day chapter divisions were taken over from the Latin Vulgate, and are credited to Lanfranc, Stephen Langton, and Hugo a Santo Caro. Jewish scholars adopted these divisions for purposes of reference, and they were used in manuscripts from the 13th cent. onward, though the first Hebrew Bible to break up the text into chapters and use the present numbering was Arius Montanus' Hebrew text, with a Latin interlinear translation, in 1571.

The majority of the extant manuscripts of the Hebrew Bible are very late. Before the discovery of the Dead Sea scrolls in 1947 and subsequently, the oldest manuscripts of substantial portions of the Hebrew Bible were no older than the end of the 9th cent. A.D. This is no doubt partially due to the ravages of wars and persecutions, and to the deliberate efforts by the enemies of the Jews to exterminate the Scriptures. Jerusalem was destroyed by the Babylonians in 586 B.C. and by the Romans in A.D. 70. Between these events (*c.* 167 B.C.), Antiochus Epiphanes ordered the destruction of the Scriptures (1 Macc 1:56, 57). In addition, the extreme lateness of the Hebrew manuscripts is in part due to the Jewish practice of disposing of worn-out, defaced, or damaged manuscripts. Such were placed in a genizah, a storeroom connected with the synagogue, and then, when the cupboard was full, buried with an elaborate ceremony.

Our earliest OT manuscript evidence can be classified under 3 headings: (1) The Dead Sea scrolls; (2) manuscripts from the Cairo Genizah; and (3) manuscripts of the Masoretic age.

1. *The Dead Sea Scrolls.* All Biblical books except Est are represented among the discoveries made at *Qumrân* and in the *Wâdî Murabbaʻât.* Most of this material is in fragments, but one book (Isaiah) is extant in a complete copy, and of other books major portions are preserved. They date from the 3d cent. B.C. to the 2d cent. A.D., with the bulk of manuscripts coming from the 1st cent. B.C. and 1st cent. A.D. Of the Pentateuch (*Tôrah*), Deut is represented by fragments of more than 10 copies, and the other books by large fragments. Most of them agree closely with the Masoretic text, although a copy each of Ex, Num, and Deut is related to a Hebrew text underlying the LXX. Of the Former Prophets, an almost complete copy of 1 and 2 Sa has been reconstructed from many fragments. It agrees closely with the LXX. The Latter Prophets are also well represented, especially Isa. Of the Writings, Ps is extant in several fragmentary copies, but one from Qumran Cave 11 is almost complete. The book of Dan is represented by 7 fragmentary manuscripts closely following the Masoretic text. *See* Scrolls, Dead Sea.

2. *Manuscripts From the Cairo Genizah.* In the 19th cent. a forgotten genizah was discovered in the Karaite Synagogue at Cairo, from which a large number of Biblical and extra-Biblical manuscripts have found their way to various institutions in Europe and America, mainly to the Cambridge University, the Bodleian Library at Oxford, and the Leningrad Library. Among the Biblical manuscripts are fragments of the pre-Masoretic age going back to the 6th cent. A.D. There is an important document of Dan (Dan 9:24 to 12:13) of the 7th cent. A.D. Other early documents contain the following passages: Ps 69:28 to 71:2; Is 53:4 to 58:8; Jer 26:19 to 29:31; Eze 13:11 to 16:31. Texts illustrating the various developments of Masoretic pointing throw light on the work of the Masoretes.

3. *Manuscripts of the Masoretic Age.* The earliest manuscript of this period, outside of those of the Cairo Genizah, is one of the Former and Latter Prophets, owned by the Karaite community in Cairo. It was written, according to P. Kahle, by Moses ben Asher in A.D. 895. An equally important manuscript is that of the Pentateuch in the British Museum (Or. 4445), written by Aaron ben Moses ben Asher in the early 10th cent. From the same Jewish scholar comes a complete OT manuscript, formerly owned by the Jewish community in Aleppo, now in Israel. A copy of this manuscript is now in Leningrad (MS. Heb. 19a). It was made by Samuel ben Jacob in

OLIVE

Cairo in A.D. 1009. The oldest Hebrew manuscript that bears an exact date is one of the Latter Prophets in Leningrad (MS. Heb. B3), dated to what is the equivalent of A.D. 916.

The general lateness of the extant manuscripts, however, need not disturb our confidence in the accuracy of the sacred text. The scribes exercised extreme care in the copying of manuscripts, with the result that very little variation is found between earlier and later manuscripts. This fact is demonstrated by the Dead Sea scrolls, which carry our knowledge of the Hebrew Bible back by nearly 1,000 years, and in general, confirm the Masoretic text.

The first printed OT book in Hebrew was a psalter published in 1477. By 1487 all books of the Hebrew OT were available in printed form, and in 1488 the entire OT in Hebrew was published at Soncino, a small place near Milan, Italy. Two more editions appeared before 1500, one in Naples, another one in Brescia. Hence, the Hebrew OT is well represented among the incunabula (books printed before 1500), whereas the Greek NT did not become available in printed form until Erasmus' edition of the NT, which was published in 1516.

Olive. [Heb. generally *zayith;* Gr. generally *elaia.*] The olive tree of the Bible is *Olea europaea,* one of the most valuable trees of the ancient world. In some parts of the Holy Land today the gnarled ash-colored trunk, with its stiff branches and leathery leaves, is the only tree of size to be seen, and picturesque groves are found on the Phoenician plain, the vale of Shechem, and the plains of Gilead and Moreh—to mention but a few prominent locations. It attains a height of from 20 to 40 ft. The evergreen leaves are oblong, or nearly round, and dusty colored, and the flowers are whitish or yellowish. The outer fleshy portion of the black, or violet-blue, fruit yields the highly prized olive *oil. The tree grows slowly and attains a great age. In Oriental minds this tree has been the symbol of prosperity (2 Ki 18:32), strength, and blessing (Ps 52:8; Jer 11:16; Hos 14:6).

Natural or wild trees are worthless commercially unless a cultivated shoot or branch is grafted on, because the wild fruit is small and of no value. The wild stock has marvelous vitality and is almost indestructible, for new shoots appear where the trunk has been cut off and soon a group of 2 to 5 trunks appears where once there was but one tree.

358. Olive grove on Crete

The 1st mention of the olive tree occurs in the story of the Flood. Its leaf was brought back to Noah by the dove he had sent forth (Gen 8:11). Olive groves were part of the spoil the Israelites were promised in Canaan (Deut 6:11). They were commanded to leave some of its fruit on the tree at harvesttime for the poor to glean (ch 24:20). Should the people forsake God, their olive trees would cease yielding or would cast their fruit (Deut 28:40; Hab 3:17). Oliveyards or olive orchards are mentioned frequently (Ex 23:11; Jos 24:13; Jgs 15:5; 1 Sa 8:14). Paul uses the grafting of the olive tree as an illustration of how the Gentiles were to be grafted onto the Jewish stock (Rom 11:16-25).

Olives (ŏl'ĭvz), **Mount of,** or **Olivet** (ŏl'ĭ-vĕt). [Heb. *Ma'aleh Hazzêthim,* "ascent of the olives," and *Har Hazzêthim,* "mount of the olives"; Gr. *Oros tōn Elaiōn;* for "Olivet," *Elaiōn.*] The ridge east of Jerusalem, just across the Kidron ravine. The name appears only twice in the OT (2 Sa 15:30; Zec 14:4), though the ridge is probably meant in Eze 11:23; but the name appears 12 times in the NT. When David fled from Jerusalem during Absalom's rebellion, he crossed the Mount of Olives, worshiping God at the summit (2 Sa 15:30, 32). It was probably on that mountain that Ezekiel saw the glory of the Lord rest (Eze 11:23). Zechariah prophesied that when the Lord would come His feet would stand on the Mount of Olives, which would then split apart, forming a wide valley (Zec 14:4).

During Jesus' visits to Jerusalem He frequently spent the night on the Mount of Olives, probably in Bethany (Lk 21:37; 22:39). He began His celebrated entry into Jerusalem from it (ch 19:37, 38), and on it gave His great sermon on His second coming and on the end of the world (Mt 24:3). The final suffering of Jesus began in a garden on the slope of the Mount of Olives (Mt 26:30, 31), and His ascension to heaven took place from

359. The Mount of Olives as seen from the eastern wall of the Old City of Jerusalem

this memorable mountain (Lk 24:50, 51; Acts 1:9-12).

The Mount of Olives belongs to one of the highest mountains of Palestine, though it is only some 200 ft. higher than the Jerusalem Temple area from which it is separated by the narrow Kidron Valley (see fig. 365). It is in the larger sense rather a mountain ridge, which runs from north to south, having 3 principal summits, in the north "Mount Scopus," in the center *et-Ṭûr*, and in the south the "Mount of Offense." It was on Mount Scopus (2,737 ft.), that Titus in A.D. 70 pitched his camp for the final assault on Jerusalem. Now the British War Cemetery and the former Hebrew University are located there. The central section of this ridge, now called *Jebel eṭ-Ṭûr* (to which most properly belongs the name "Mount of Olives"), lies exactly to the east of the Temple area of Jerusalem, and provides an excellent view over the Holy City and the former Temple compound, now the *Ḥaram esh-Sherif*. The central hill is subdivided into 3 peaks, which from north to south are: (1) Galilee (2,723 ft.), where according to a medieval tradition the disciples stood when the angels appeared to them after the ascension (Acts 1:11); (2) Ascension (2,643 ft.), from which, according to tradition going back to the 4th cent., Jesus rose to heaven; and (3) "the Prophets' hill," which received its name from a number of rock-hewn tombs called "the tombs of the prophets." The southernmost summit of the ridge is the "Mount of Offense" (2,411 ft.), where Solomon is said to have built idolatrous sanctuaries for his pagan wives (1 Ki 11:7, 8). On the "Mount of Ascension," the Mount of Olives proper, a mosque is found at the spot where the emperor Constantine built the first Ascension chapel in the 4th cent. The highest tower on this mount is that of the Russian convent, from the top of which a view in all directions of a large area of Palestine can be obtained, extending from the Mediterranean Sea in the

west to the mountains of Moab in the east, and from the mountains of Samaria in the north to the southern mountains of Judah. On the eastern slopes of the ridge of the Mount of Olives lies the village of Bethany, and on the western side, on the eastern slope of the Kidron Valley, the traditional site of *Gethsemane, with many old olive trees. Large parts of the western slopes are covered with Jewish tombs. See fig. 359; also figs. 198, 199.

Olivet. *See* Olives, Mount of.

Olympas (ō-lĭm′păs). [Gr. *Olumpas,* an abbreviation of a longer Greek name, the first part of which is derived from Olympus, the sacred mountain of Greece. The name is attested in Greek inscriptions.] A Christian believer in the church at Rome to whom Paul sent greetings (Rom 16:15).

Omar (ō-mär). [Heb. *'Ômar,* "the speaking one."] A grandson of Esau through Eliphaz, and a chieftain over one of the Edomite clans (Gen 36:11, 15; 1 Chr 1:36).

Omega. The last letter in the Greek alphabet; used figuratively for "last" or "ending." It appears only in the phrase "Alpha and Omega" (Rev 1:8; 21:6; 22:13). *See* Alpha and Omega.

Omer. [Heb. *'omer.*] A dry measure (Ex 16:16, 18, 32, 33), which was 1/10 the size of an ephah (v 36); this makes it the equivalent of 2.20 liters or 2 qts.

Omri (ŏm′rī). [Heb. *'Omrî;* in cuneiform records *Ḥumri* and *Ḥumria.*]

1. A Benjamite of the family of Becher (1 Chr 7:8).

2. A Judahite of the family of Perez (1 Chr 9:4).

3. Son of Michael, and chief officer over the tribe of Issachar in the time of David (1 Chr 27:18).

4. The 6th king of the northern kingdom of Israel (*c.* 885 - *c.* 874 B.C.) and founder of a strong dynasty that reigned for approximately 44 years (*c.* 885-841 B.C.), one fifth of the duration of the kingdom. Before becoming king, Omri was an army commander of King Elah. He was engaged in fighting against the Philistines at Gibbethon when Zimri, an officer of the chariotry, assassinated Elah and usurped the throne. When this news reached the army it immediately proclaimed Omri king, and marched against Zimri at Tirzah, the capital. Zimri, recognizing that he could not hold the throne against Omri's army, committed suicide. His length of reign was only 7

days (1 Ki 16:8-10, 15-20). However, Omri had to fight for more than 4 years against Tibni, another contender for the throne and one who had a considerable following, before he became sole ruler over Israel.

Omri's reign was of great political importance. He moved the capital to *Samaria (1 Ki 16:24), strategically a much better location than Tirzah. By selecting an entirely uninhabited site that had neither history nor tradition, Omri revealed much political wisdom and did for Israel what David had done for Judah in the selection of Jerusalem. He subjugated Moab as is attested by the *Moabite Stone of King Mesha (see fig. 338). The inscription reads in part: "Omri, king of Israel, had oppressed Moab many days, for Kemosh was angry with his land. . . . And Omri had occupied the land of Mehedeba, and (Israel) dwelt therein his days and half the days of his son, 40 years." That Omri's conquest of Moab was a profitable venture is seen from the tribute that Moab paid to his son Ahab. It amounted, probably annually, to 100,-000 lambs, and the wool of 100,000 rams (2 Ki 3:4). With his Phoenician neighbors Omri established cordial relations, and crowned these relations by marrying his son Ahab to Jezebel, the daughter of Ethbaal, king of Tyre, called "king of the Zidonians" in 1 Ki 16:31, according to ancient usage. The result of this alliance with the Phoenicians was the introduction of the worship of Baal and Asherah into Israel to an extent previously unknown (vs 32, 33).

Not much is known about Omri's relations with the Syrians of Damascus, except that he granted economic concessions to Damascus and allowed Syrian traders to have bazaars in Samaria (1 Ki 20:34, RSV). It is unknown whether this was a purely economic agreement or a concession after a military defeat. There is no evidence of any encounters with the Assyrians, but for the next 150 years the Assyrian records refer to Israel as the "land of Omri," or the "house of Omri." They call even Jehu, the exterminator of the dynasty of Omri, a "son of Omri." Omri's personality, political success, or trading enterprises seem to have gained this fame for him in the eyes of his contemporaries and later generations.

In view of this, Omri must be considered one of the most notable kings of Israel, although the Bible devotes little space to him, noting that he did "evil in the sight of the Lord," even worse "than all who were before him" (1 Ki 16:25, RSV). See fig. 414.

On (ŏn). [Heb. *'Ōn,* as a Hebrew name "power," "strength"; as the name of an Egyptian city, the transliteration of the Egyptian *'Iwnw,* also attested as *'n* in a Phoenician inscription; written *Ûnu* or *Ânu* in cuneiform inscriptions.]

1. A Reubenite who joined in the rebellion of Korah against Moses (Num 16:1).

2. A city in Egypt called *Heliopolis* by the Greeks, the center of sun worship in Lower Egypt. Its few ruins and one remaining obelisk are now found at *el-Maṭarîyeh,* about 6 mi. north of Cairo, adjacent to the modern city of Heliopolis (Map V, B-3). The city had its greatest importance during the Old Kingdom before Ra, the original Egyptian sun-god, was connected with the Upper Egyptian Amon, the city god of Thebes. A large temple at On was dedicated to Ra, and many obelisks, erected in pairs, served as symbols of the rays of the sun. Only one of these obelisks, that of Sesostris I (1971-1928 B.C.), has been preserved and is still standing (69 ft. high) in its original place (see fig. 360). On is mentioned in the Bible in connection with the story of Joseph, whose wife Asenath was the daughter of the (high) priest of On (Gen 41:45, 50; 46:20). Jeremiah mentions the city by a translated name, *Bêth Shemesh,* "house (that is, temple) of the sun" (Jer

360. The only standing obelisk of the sun temple at On (Heliopolis) in Egypt

43:13, KJV; translated "Heliopolis" in the RSV). In Eze 30:17 the Masoretes added vowels to the consonants of the Hebrew name which made it read *'Awen,* "wickedness." This was done probably because of the idolatrous nature of the city and its cult. It is uncertain whether Isaiah mentions it in the phrase translated "city of destruction" (Is 19:18). If the word rendered "destruction," *heres,* is changed to *cheres* (the letters *h* and *ch* are very similar in postexilic Hebrew), then the phrase means "city of the sun" and is thus a reference to On.

In the time of Herodotus (5th cent. B.C.) the city had a flourishing medical and temple school, and the priests of On were highly respected by the Greeks (Herodotus ii. 3). Strabo (1st cent. B.C.), however, claims that the city was no longer inhabited in his time.

Onam (ō'năm). [Heb. *'Ônam,* "strong," or "wealthy."]

1. A Horite (Gen 36:23; 1 Chr 1:40).
2. A Judahite of the family of Jerahmeel (1 Chr 2:26, 28).

Onan (ō'năn). [Heb. *'Ônan,* "strong," or "wealthy."] A son of Judah by Shua, his Canaanite wife. When his brother Er died without leaving children, it became his duty, according to the custom of the country, to marry Tamar, his widowed sister-in-law. He refused to do his duty, acted rashly, and for his sin was killed by the Lord without leaving an heir (Gen 38:2-10; 46:12).

Onesimus (ō-nĕs'ĭ-mŭs). [Gr. *Onēsimos,* "profitable," a meaning that Paul used as a play on words (Phm 11). The name occurs frequently in ancient records, especially as that of slaves.] A slave of Philemon, a Christian of Colossae. Having fled from his master, probably having taken with him some of his master's property (vs 16, 18, 19), he met Paul in Rome and was converted to Christianity. Paul sent the runaway slave back to his master with a letter of recommendation, written in his own handwriting, asking that Philemon receive the once unprofitable Onesimus as a brother (vs 10-19). Onesimus apparently traveled with Tychicus, the carrier of the letter to the Colossians (Col 4:7-9). *See* Philemon.

Onesiphorus (ŏn'ē-sĭf'ō-rŭs). [Gr. *Onēsiphoros,* "carrier of profit." The name is often found in inscriptions.] A Christian, apparently of Ephesus, who was of great help to Paul during his ministry there. During a visit to Rome, Onesiphorus was not afraid to visit Paul in prison, although he thus took the risk of becoming implicated in the charges against the apostle (2 Ti 1:16-18). The fact that Paul sent greetings to, and prayed for, "the house of Onesiphorus" (ch 1:16-18; 4:19) has been interpreted to indicate that Onesiphorus was already dead when Paul's last letter was written.

Onion. [Heb. *baṣal*]. A garden plant, *Allium cepa,* popular as an article of food from ancient times. Little doubt exists that the onions so much missed by the Israelites during the wilderness wanderings (Num 11:5) were what we know today as Egyptian onions, a milder and sweeter variety than is grown in North America. It is said that they may have formed a major part of the diet of the poor, and that the rich used them in flavoring their meat dishes.

Only Begotten. [Gr. *monogenēs,* from *monos,* "only," and *genos,* "kind"; hence, "only one of a kind," "unique."] An expression appearing in the KJV, the rendering of a Greek term that designates an individual as in some way unique or singular, the only person in his particular category. The Greek expression does not contain the idea of "begotten." The RSV consistently translates the term "only" as does the KJV in Lk 7:12; 8:42; 9:38. As a title applied to the Lord, the expression emphasizes Christ's unique relationship to the Father (Jn 3:16, 18; 1 Jn 4:9; cf. Heb 11:17). See *SDACom* 5:902, 903.

Ono (ō'nō). [Heb. *'Ônô,* "vigorous." The name appears in Egyptian records of the time of Thutmose III as *'Inw.*] A Canaanite city in the territory of Benjamin, rebuilt after it came into the hands of Israel, by Shemed, a Benjamite (1 Chr 8:12). Descendants of its pre-exilic inhabitants returned from Babylonia with Zerubbabel (Ezr 2:33; Neh 7:37; 11:35). The "plain of Ono" was chosen by Nehemiah's enemies as the place to meet him (Neh 6:2). Ono has been identified with *Kefr 'Anā,* southeast of Joppa and northwest of Lydda (Map VI, D-2).

Onycha. [Heb. *schecheleth.*] One of 4 basic ingredients of the sacred perfume, or incense, that was to be burned on the golden altar of the tabernacle (Ex 30:34). Some have thought that it may have been derived from the shell of a certain mollusk (stromb, or wing shell, possibly), which when burned gives off a strong fragrance.

Onyx. [Heb. *shoham.*] The onyx of today is a banded form of chalcedony, closely allied to agate and sardonyx, the principal difference being the color of the bands. However, the precious or semiprecious stone represented by *shoham* cannot be identified with certainty. Some believe the carnelian is meant. *Shoham* was found in the antediluvian land of Havilah (Gen 2:12) and in Eden (Eze 28:13). It was the 2d gem in the 4th row of the high priest's breastplate (Ex 39:13), and on 2 of these gems, set upon the shoulder pieces of the priest's ephod, were engraved the names of the 12 tribes of Israel (ch 28:9-12). Job observes that wisdom and understanding are of more value than such a gem as this (Job 28:16).

Ophel (ō'fĕl). [Heb. *'Ophel*, "knoll."]

1. A part of Jerusalem. From Neh 3:26, 27 and several statements of Josephus (*War* ii. 17. 9; v. 4. 1, 2; v. 6. 1; vi. 6. 3) it seems certain that Ophel was part of the eastern hill of Jerusalem, an area immediately south of the Temple. Map XVIII; see figs. 259, 260, 277, 278. King Jotham did some building on the wall of Ophel, and Manasseh increased its height (2 Chr 27:3; 33:14). The Nethinim, or Temple servants, had their residence in this quarter (Neh 3:26; 11:21). The Hebrew term is found in Mic 4:8 as part of "Zion" and is rendered "strong hold" in the KJV and "hill" in the RSV; also in Is 32:14, where it is rendered "forts" in the KJV and "hill" in the RSV, and where its destruction is predicted.

2. An *'ophel* is also mentioned at Samaria (2 Ki 5:24, rendered "tower" in the KJV, "hill" in the RSV), as the place where Gehazi deposited the gifts received from Naaman. King Mesha of Moab says that he built the wall of *'ophel* in one of his cities (*Moabite Stone, line 22, usually rendered "citadel" in English translations).

Ophir (ō'fēr). [Heb. *'Ôphir*.]

1. A descendant or descendants of Joktan (Gen 10:29; 1 Chr 1:23).

2. A land celebrated for its gold (1 Chr 29:4; Job 22:24; 28:16; Ps 45:9; Is 13:12). It is also mentioned in an ancient Hebrew inscription on an ostracon found at *Tell Qasileh.* Solomon sent expeditions to Ophir from Ezion-geber on the Gulf of Aqabah (1 Ki 9:26-28; 10:11). A similar expedition begun by King Jehoshaphat miscarried because his ships were wrecked at Ezion-geber (ch 22:48). The location of Ophir has been much discussed, and India, Elam, South Arabia, East Africa, and South Africa have been suggested. Recent studies have made it plausible that Ophir lay either in southern

Arabia or in Somaliland, which is probably Punt, or even that it included both of these countries. Map IV, D-6.

Ophni (ŏf'nī). [Heb. *'Ophni.*] A town in the territory of Benjamin (Jos 18:24). Some have identified it with the later Gophna, now *Jifnah,* northwest of Bethel, but this identification is uncertain, since the border of Benjamin seems to have been to the south of Bethel.

Ophrah (ŏf'rà). [Heb. *'Ophrah*, "gazelle."]

1. A descendant of Othniel (1 Chr 4:14).

2. A town of Benjamin (Jos 18:23), apparently north of Michmash (see 1 Sa 13:17). On the basis of a statement by Eusebius it is usually identified with *eṭ-Ṭaiyibeh,* 4 mi. northeast of Bethel (Map VI, E-3), although the territory of Benjamin does not seem to have reached so far north. Hence the identification cannot be considered certain.

3. A town in the territory of Manasseh, the home town of the judge Gideon (Jgs 6:11, 15), and his residence during his judgeship. There he built an altar, set up an ephod, and was finally buried (chs 6:24; 8:27, 32). Its site has not been identified, and is sought by some in the vicinity of Shechem and by others in the area of Beth-shean. For a conjectural location, see Map VI, D-3.

Oracle. A communication from God, especially (but not always) in response to a particular appeal for guidance; included are various communications transmitted through dreams, visions, prophetic messages, Urim and Thummim, etc. In the KJV "oracle" is also used for the Most Holy Place of the Temple, as the place where communications from God were at times given. The term appears as the rendering of: (1) The Heb. *dabar,* literally, "word"; translated "oracle" only in 2 Sa 16:23; elsewhere it appears frequently as "saying," "word," "matter," etc. (2) The Heb. *debir,* the Most Holy Place of the Temple (1 Ki 6:5, 16, 19-23; Ps 28:2; etc.; RSV usually "inner sanctuary"). Some object to the translation "oracle" for *debir* because of the implication that the Most Holy Place was a place for the giving of oracles as in heathen temples. (3) The Heb. *maśśa',* "a prophetic utterance," translated "oracle" only in the RSV (2 Ki 9:25; 2 Chr 24:27; Is 13:1; etc.; KJV "burden"). (4) The Heb. *ne'um,* a divinely given "utterance" or "communication"; rendered "oracle" only in the RSV (Num 24:3, 4; 2 Sa 23:1). (5) A form of the

Heb. *nagad,* "to inform," "to give oracles" (Hos 4:12, RSV). (6) The Gr. *logion,* a "saying," or "utterance" (Acts 7:38; Rom 3:2; RSV; etc.).

Orator. A term appearing in the phrase "eloquent orator" (Is 3:3, KJV). However, the Hebrew phrase thus translated (*nebôn lachash*) means "one who is expert in magical charms." In Acts 24:1, KJV, "orator" is a rendering of the Gr. *rhētōr,* "spokesman," "attorney," and signifies a trained public speaker who understood legal terminology and procedures appropriate in a Roman courtroom, and who could make legal or official speeches in behalf of others.

Orchard. *See* Garden.

Ordinance. A legal statute or enactment. The term is a rendering of a number of Hebrew and Greek words which generally refer to a distinct law or regulation of conduct, promulgated by God or by man (Ex 12:14; 2 Chr 35:25; Job 38:33; Eze 46:14; Lk 1:6; Eph 2:15; etc.).

Oreb (ō′rĕb). [Heb. *'Oreb,* "raven."]
1. A Midianite prince captured and slain by the Ephraimites, who pursued him at the command of Gideon and cut off his retreat in the Jordan Valley (Jgs 7:25; 8:3; cf. Ps 83:11).
2. A rock in the Jordan Valley named after the Midianite prince who was slain there (Jgs 7:25; Is 10:26); not identified.

Oren (ō′rĕn). [Heb. *'Oren,* "laurel."] A Jerahmeelite of the tribe of Judah (1 Chr 2:25).

Organ. The KJV rendering of the Heb. *'ûgab,* meaning ***"flute."

Orion (ô-rī′ŏn). [Heb. *kesil,* "insolent one," "fool," "stupid one," "strong one."] A brilliant constellation of the winter sky mentioned in Job 9:9; 38:31; Amos 5:8. In Is 13:10 the same Hebrew word is translated "constellation." In the Targums and the Peshitta *kesil* is rendered "giant." In ancient mythology Orion was a man of great stature and strength, often represented as an ironmonger or hunter who was killed by the goddess Diana and placed in the winter sky as the constellation Orion. Orion stands poised in the sky with his left foot planted in a higher position than his right foot. Defensively, he holds in his left hand a shield, while in his right hand, uplifted above his head, he holds a club. He stands braced for an attack by Taurus, the neighboring constellation of the Bull, ready to deliver that beast a blow on the head. The central "star" in the sword hanging from Orion's

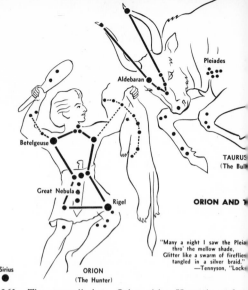

361. The constellations Orion (the Hunter) and Taurus (the Bull). In the latter are the Pleiades

belt is the Great Nebula in Orion, which is composed of a cloud of interstellar gases and dust illuminated by light from neighboring stars.

Ornaments. Articles of adornment, usually considered decorative and sometimes useful, worn about the body or clothing. Isaiah dwelt at length on the ornamentation of the women of Israel of his day as indicative of their unspiritual, haughty, and lustful characters (Is 3:16-24). The custom among the Hebrews had its counterpart (and perhaps its origin) among the Egyptians, Midianites, Syrians, etc. (cf. Ex 3:22; 11:2; Jgs 8:26). Common ornaments included *bracelets, *nose rings, *earrings, finger *rings, *anklets, necklaces (Gen 24:22, 47; Ex 35:22; Jgs 8:24; Song 4:9, RSV; Is 3:18, 21, RSV; Lk 15:22; etc.). Saul's bracelet may have been significant of his rank as king (2 Sa 1:10; for Assyrian royal jewelry see figs. 163, 394). The removal of ornaments implied mourning and reformation (Gen 35:4; Ex 33:6). Paul and Peter admonished that outward ornamentation be replaced by the more valuable adornment of good character and good deeds (1 Ti 2:9, 10; 1 Pe 3:3-5). *See* Jewels, Jewelry.

Ornan. *See* Araunah.

Orpah (ôr′pä). [Heb. *'Orpah,* "stubborn."] A Moabite, the sister-in-law of Ruth. When Naomi, Orpah's widowed mother-in-law, returned to Judah, Orpah was persuaded to remain in Moab, whereas Ruth accompanied Naomi to Bethlehem (Ruth 1:4, 11-19).

Osee. *See* Hosea.

Oshea. *See* Hoshea.

Osnappar (ŏs-năp′ẽr), KJV **Asnapper** (ăs-năp′ẽr). [Aramaic *'Asenappar,* generally believed to be a contraction of the Assyrian *Ashshurbanapli,* " (the god) Asshur is the creator of the son." In the pre-Masoretic Aramaic text of Ezr 4:10, consisting only of consonants, the letters *rb* may have dropped out so that of *'srbnpr* only the letters *'snpr* remained.] One of the Assyrian kings who settled foreign colonists in the territory of Samaria (Ezr 4:10). He is generally identified with Ashurbanipal, who ruled as son and successor of Esarhaddon for about 40 years (669-?627 B.C.). The Assyrian Empire passed the height of her glory during his reign. Not only was he able to hold the far-flung empire together, but he reconquered Egypt, which had rebelled. His conquest and sacking of *Thebes, the glorious capital of Egypt, was considered his greatest triumph. From his victory he carried to Assyria two obelisks and statues of the king of Egypt. Two of these statues have recently been found in fragments in Ashurbanipal's burned palace at *Nebi Yunus,* one of the ruin mounds of ancient Nineveh. Ashurbanipal is best known today as the founder of a great palace library of clay tablets inscribed in cuneiform writing, which was excavated from *Kuyunjik,* another ruin mound inside the area of Nineveh. A great lover of art and literature, Ashurbanipal sent his scribes throughout the country and had the literary treasures of the past copied on many thousands of clay tablets, for his vast library. These tablets now belong to the priceless treasures of the British Museum. Generations of Assyriologists have worked on this library, which has provided us with the bulk of literary information on the ancient Babylonians and Assyrians. See fig. 362.

Ashurbanipal claims that King Manasseh of Judah paid tribute to him. It was probably he (or his father, Esarhaddon) who exiled the rebellious Manasseh temporarily to Babylon (2 Chr 33:11-13).

Signs of a coming breakup of the Assyrian Empire were clearly visible in Ashurbanipal's day, and about two decades after his death the empire collapsed.

Ospray. *See* Osprey.

Osprey, KJV **Ospray.** [Heb. *'ozniyah.*] The osprey (*Pandion haliaetus*) is a large member of the hawk family that feeds on fish, and may be the bird intended by *'ozniyah.* It is widely known throughout the world in coastal areas, and in Palestine is found along the Mediterranean. Some suggest the black vulture, Driver the bearded vulture (*PEQ* 87 [1955], 20). The Mosaic law declared the bird unclean (Lev 11:13; Deut 14:12).

Ossifrage. [Heb. *peres,* possibly from *paras,* "to break."] Because of its habit of carrying bones, snakes, and tortoises to a great height and then dropping them on a stone, on which they will be broken, the ossifrage (*Gypaëtus barbatus*) has been suggested as a likely translation for *peres.* It is also called the lammergeier, or bearded eagle. It is one of the largest of the birds of prey, standing about 3½ ft. high and having a wingspread of about 9 ft. The Scriptures list it among the unclean birds (Lev 11:13; Deut 14:12; in Deut 14:12 the RSV renders *peres* "vulture"). Driver suggests the black vulture (*PEQ* 87 [1955], 20).

Ostraca. *See* Potsherd.

Ostrich. [Heb. *ya'anah, bath ya'anah, renanah, chasîdah.*] A large bird of Africa and the Middle East, the *Struthio camelus.* Its inability to fly is compensated for by its great speed afoot; it can outdistance a man on horseback. The female lays about a dozen 3-pound eggs and places them in a sizable depression in the desert sand which she has scooped out with her pow-

362. Ashurbanipal (probably the Biblical Osnappar) and his queen feasting in their garden

erful two-toed feet. She may leave them during the day, when the heat of the sun incubates them. Her habits are delineated in Job 39:13-18. The ostrich is a bird of seclusion (Job 30:29; Is 13:21; 34:13; RSV), and has a mournful cry (Mic 1:8, RSV). Because of its habit of leaving the nest seemingly unprotected, the ostrich was considered a fit symbol of those who are hardened to sin (Lam 4:3). It is ceremonially unclean (Lev 11:16; Deut 14:15; KJV "owl").

Othni (ŏth′nī). [Heb. '*Othni,* an abbreviated form of '*Othni'el,* *"Othniel."] A Levite gatekeeper appointed by David (1 Chr 26:7).

Othniel (ŏth′nĭ-ĕl). [Heb. '*Othni'el,* meaning uncertain.] A son of Kenaz, and either a younger brother or a nephew of Caleb (Jos 15:17; Jgs 1:13; 1 Chr 4:13). He distinguished himself by capturing the town of Debir (or Kiriath-sepher) in Judah from the Canaanites. As a reward he received Achsah, Caleb's daughter, who had been promised to the conqueror of that city (Jos 15:15-17; Jgs 1:11-13). His bravery was exhibited once more when he defeated Cushan-rishathaim, king of Mesopotamia, who had oppressed the Israelites for 8 years. His victory brought 40 years of peace to his country, and he became the 1st of the *judges (Jgs 3:8-11).

Ouches. A rendering of the Heb. *mishbeṣôth,* meaning: (1) "settings," for the precious stones on the ephod of the high priest (Ex 28:11, 13, 14; 39:6, 7; KJV); (2) ornate fasteners for the cords that suspended the breastplate of the high priest (Ex 28:25; 39:16-18; KJV). The RSV renders *mishbeṣôth* in these occurrences "settings."

Outlandish. An archaic English word meaning "foreign." It occurs only in Neh 13:26, KJV, where it is the rendering of a Hebrew word meaning "foreign."

Oven. [Heb. *tannûr;* Gr. *klibanos.*] Archeological evidence shows that ancient baking ovens varied in form and operation. However, they had one thing in common, namely that their fires were kindled in a hole in the ground. Over the fire in some ovens a convex baking tray was placed. When the tray was hot, a thin layer of dough was spread upon it to form a pancakelike loaf of bread, which during the baking process was turned in order to assure thorough baking (Hos 7:8). In other ovens tapering clay cylinders were placed with their wider openings on the fire. The loaves of bread were then stuck on the heated walls of the oven. Sometimes the loaves were simply placed on the hot ashes or on hot stones (see 1 Ki 19:6). For a later form see fig. 331.

Overseer. A supervisor or superintendent. The word is the rendering of a number of Hebrew terms and one Greek term, which generally refer to various appointed officials of a supervisory nature (2 Chr 2:18; 31:13; Neh 11:9; etc.).

Owl. [Heb. *bath ya'anah,* "ostrich"; *yanshôph* and *yanshûph,* "one that cries"; *kôs; lilith; qippôz.*] A nocturnal bird of unclean habits. Some of the Hebrew words so rendered in the KJV may represent different species of owls. The southern little owl (*Athene glaux*) inhabits wooded areas, ruin heaps, hilltop crags, and oliveyards throughout Palestine, and is probably a satisfactory identification of *kôs,* a bird listed as unclean (Lev 11:17; Deut 14:16) and an inhabitant of waste places (Ps 102:6). *Yanshûph* may be the ibis (Lev 11:17, RSV), or the Egyptian eagle owl (*Bubo ascalaphus*), also unclean and a symbol of desolation (Is 34:11). *Qippôz* may be a small serpent (ASV "dart-snake"). Dead Sea scroll 1QIsᵃ gives a word here (*qippod*) that could be translated "hedgehog," or possibly could mean the short-eared owl, or bustard. In any case, it is a creature of desolate places (v 15). The RSV consistently translates *bath ya'anah* *"ostrich." The *lilith* (KJV "screech owl") is probably a night hag (v 14). Driver suggests that *yanshûph* may represent the screech owl, and *bath ya'anah* the eagle owl (*PEQ* 87 [1955], 20).

Ox. The translation of various Hebrew and Greek words, many of which do not indicate the sex of the animal. Nor do the terms in the case of male beasts distinguish between bulls and castrated animals, though the context often indicates which is meant. Oxen were used in Biblical times as today to pull plows (Deut 22:10; 1 Ki 19:19) or wagons (Num 7:3; 2 Sa 6:3, 6), or to thresh (Deut 25:4; Hos 10:11). An ox was valuable property and the Decalogue prohibited coveting other men's oxen (Ex 20:17). The meat of oxen was eaten (Mt 22:4), since the animal belonged to those declared clean by Mosaic law. The law prohibited yoking an ox with a donkey (Deut 22:10), a custom followed to the present time by many Palestinian farmers (fig. 500), or muzzling a threshing ox (ch 25:4). Oxen were also sacrificial animals (2 Sa 24:22).

Oxgoad. *See* Goad.

Ozem (ō'zĕm). [Heb. *'Oṣem,* "hot-tempered."]
  1. A son of Jesse and brother of David (1 Chr 2:15).
  2. A Jerahmeelite of the tribe of Judah (1 Chr 2:25).

Ozias. *See* Uzziah.

Ozni (ŏz'nī). [Heb. *'Oznî,* "my ear."] Founder of a tribal family of Gad, whose descendants are called Oznites (ŏz'nīts) [Heb. *'Oznî*] (Num 26:16). It is apparently he who is called Ezbon in Gen 46:16.

Oznites. *See* Ozni.

P

Paarai (pā'à-rī). [Heb. *Pa'aray.*] One of David's "mighty men" (2 Sa 23:35), apparently called Naarai in 1 Chr 11:37.

Padan. *See* Paddan-aram.

Padan-aram. *See* Paddan-aram.

Paddan. *See* Paddan-aram.

Paddan-aram (păd'ăn-ā'răm), or **Paddan** (păd'ăn), KJV **Padan-aram** (pā'dăn-ā'răm) or **Padan** (pā'dăn). [Heb. *Paddan 'Aram* and *Paddan.*] The place from which Rebekah, Isaac's wife, came, where Laban dwelt, and where Jacob spent 20 years serving Laban (Gen 25:20; 28:1, 2, 5-7; 31:17, 18; 33:18; 35:9, 26; 46:15). In Hos 12:12, RSV, it is called the land [Heb. *śadeh,* "field"] of Aram." Since Haran was in this area, and Haran means "road," a meaning shared by the Akkadian *padânu,* it has been suggested that Padan-aram might be translated "route of Aram" (R. T. O'Callaghan, *Aram Naharaim* [1948], p. 96). *See* Aram, 5.

Paddle. A term appearing once (Deut 23:13, KJV), the rendering of the Heb. *yathed,* literally, "stake," or "tent peg." Elsewhere, *yathed* is translated "stake" (Is 54:2), "nail" (Jgs 4:21, 22; RSV "peg"), "pin" (Ex 27:19; RSV "peg"), etc.

Padon (pā'dŏn). [Heb. *Padôn,* perhaps "ransom." The name occurs in Ugaritic as *Pdy* and in cuneiform records as *Padî,* the name of the king of Ekron.] The ancestral head of a family of Temple servants, or Nethinim, some members of which returned from Babylonia with Zerubbabel (Ezr 2:1, 2, 44; Neh 7:1, 7, 47).

Pagiel (pā'gǐ-ĕl). [Heb. *Pag'i'el,* "God has met me."] The prince of the tribe of Asher in the wilderness wandering (Num 1:13; 2:27; 7:72-77; 10:26).

Pahath-moab (pā'hăth-mō'ăb). [Heb. *Pachath Mô'ab,* "governor of Moab."]
  1. The ancestral head of a family; he had probably been governor of Moab, perhaps in the time of David. Of his descendants more than 2,800 males returned from Babylonia with Zerubbabel (Ezr 2: 1, 2, 6; Neh 7:6, 7, 11). Another 200 returned with Ezra (Ezr 8:1, 4). Among them were some who had married foreign wives (ch 10:30). One member of this family assisted Nehemiah in rebuilding the wall of Jerusalem (Neh 3:11).
  2. A man who set his seal to Nehemiah's covenant (Neh 10:14), evidently representing the family of Pahath-moab, 1.

Pai. *See* Pau.

Paint. From the earliest times the women of the East have employed cosmetics for the painting of their eyebrows and eyelashes. The few OT references to the practice seem to indicate that it was regarded by the Hebrews as a device unbecoming to women of noble conduct (2 Ki 9:30; Jer 4:30; Eze 23:40). Various dyes were apparently used for this purpose, among them "black mineral powders," such as compounds of antimony. Their use was believed to add beauty and seductive charm (Jer 4:30). House painting with vermilion is mentioned in ch 22:14. Vermilion was probably the red pigment employed in the buildings of the Assyrians (cf. Eze 23:14) and Egyptians, possibly cinnabar, or red clay and oxide of iron.

Palace. [Heb. and Aramaic generally *hêkal;* Ugaritic *hkl,* a loan word by way of the Akkadian *ekallum* from the Sumerian

363. Air view of the great palace of Zimri-Lim at Mari

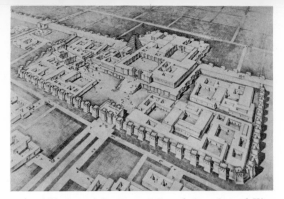

364. An artist's reconstruction of the palace of King Sargon II at *Khorsabad*

E-GAL, "great house." Other Hebrew terms rendered "palace" in the KJV are *bîrah* and *'armôn*, "citadel"; *bayith*, "house"; *harmôn*, meaning unknown; *ṭîrah*, "encampment"; and *'appeden*, from the Old Persian *apadana*, "palatial tents." *Bîthan* is translated "palace" in both KJV and RSV. Aramaic *hêkal* and *bîrah*. Gr. *aulē*, "court," or "palace," and *praitōrion* (KJV only); *see* Praetorium.]

The residence of a king and his entourage, including his family. The buildings were either simple fortresslike structures of modest dimensions, such as King Saul's palace (*see* Gibeah, 2); or the apparently more complex "house of cedar" of King David in Jerusalem (2 Sa 7:1, 2), which was apparently the citadel of the Jebusite city (ch 5:9); or the elaborate structures of King Solomon (1 Ki 7:1).

Excavations of royal cities generally reveal no more than the foundations of ancient palaces. This has been the case at Nineveh, *Khorsabad*, Calah, Mari, and Babylon in Mesopotamia, at Thebes and Amarna in Egypt, and at *Boghazköy*, a Hittite royal city. The only exception is at Persepolis, where many door and window frames of the palace structures of the Persian kings are still standing.

Ancient palaces usually consisted of both private structures, which housed the harem and provided the living quarters of the king, and public buildings, which included a throne hall in which audiences were held or foreign ambassadors were received, a hall in which the king appeared in public for the purpose of judgment or to watch processions. There were generally also a treasury and an armory belonging to the royal precinct, and some of them had a banquet hall.

Although the Bible does not give a clear picture of the ground plans, general appearance, or of the functions of the palace buildings of King Solomon (1 Ki 7:1-9), yet the archeological evidence gathered from many ancient palace ruins helps us to reconstruct these to a limited degree. Thus the purpose of several of the palace buildings of Solomon can be identified with reasonable certainty. Because of his many wives and concubines (1 Ki 11:1-3) he must have had a large harem building. Besides, he built a separate palace for the most honorable of his wives, the Egyptian princess (ch 7:8). This building must have adjoined his private quarters, which probably lay behind the "Hall of Judgment"—a structure of which no details are recorded except that it was finished with cedar (vs 7, 8, RSV). The "Hall of Pillars" may have been the throne room in which ambassadors were received and other ceremonial acts of state performed. It measured 50 by 30 cu., and had a pillared porch with a canopy in front (v 6, RSV). The "House of the Forest of Lebanon," so called because of its 45 pillars of cedarwood, was probably a combined armory and treasury (see ch 10:17, 21, RSV). It was a large building measuring 50 by 100 cu. Whether the 3 rows of 15 pillars stood in 3 parallel rows, or were placed in front of 3 walls around an open court, is not certain (ch 7:2-5). It is also uncertain where the elaborately ornamented throne stood (ch 10:18-20). Since the "House of the Forest of Lebanon" is mentioned preceding and following the description of this throne (vs 17, 21, RSV), some commentators have thought that the throne stood in this building, whereas others place it either in the Judgment Hall or in the Hall of Pillars. The 3 last-mentioned structures, being public buildings, were probably grouped around a rectangular court, the whole precinct of which was surrounded by a wall that separated it from the royal quarters and from the Temple compound. A gate connected the palace and Temple areas (see 2 Chr 23:14, 15; 2 Ki 11:6, 13, 15, 16).

Palal (pā'lăl). [Heb. *Palal*, "he has judged."] A Jew who helped Nehemiah rebuild the wall of Jerusalem (Neh 3:25).

Palanquin. [Heb. *'appiryôn*, probably of Iranian origin. In form it is similar to the Sanskrit *paryaṅka*, and to the Gr. *phoreion*, both terms meaning "litter-bed." In the LXX *phoreion* is employed as the translation of *'appiryôn*. The lexicons suggest the meanings "sedan," *"litter," "palanquin."] A term appearing once (Song 3:9), RSV), apparently as a synonym of the Heb. *miṭṭah* (v 7), "couch," or "bed," translated "litter" (RSV), "bed" (KJV). The "palanquin" of Solomon was made from "wood of Lebanon" and had "posts of silver," a "back of gold," and a "seat of purple" (Song 3:9, 10, RSV).

Palestina. See Palestine.

Palestine (păl′ĕs-tĭn), **Palestina** (păl′ĕs-tī-nả), and **Philistia** (fĭ-lĭs′tĭ-ả). [Heb. *Pelesheth;* Assyrian *Palastu, Pilishta,* and *Pilistu,* the country of the Philistines. The Hebrew term occurs in Ex 15:14; Ps 60:8; 83:7; 87:4; 108:9; Is 14:29, 31; Joel 3:4. In the KJV this term is rendered Palestine once, Palestina 3 times, and Philistia elsewhere. In the RSV it is consistently rendered Philistia.] In modern usage, not *Philistia, but that part of southwestern Asia of which the Mediterranean Sea forms the western boundary, and the Syrian or Arabian Desert the eastern boundary, the Leontes, or Litani, River (*Nahr el-Lîṭânî*) the approximate northern border, and the desert of the Sinai Peninsula the southern one. The familiar name "Palestine" goes back to Greek times when the western nations called the whole land after the Philistines, who occupied part of the coastal region and thus were more familiar to them than were the Israelites in the hinterland. Somehow this name became more popular than any other and is now almost universally used.

However, the name under which the country of Palestine appears most frequently in the OT is "the land of Canaan" (Gen 12:5; etc.), a name it received from its aboriginal population, who were descendants of Ham's son of that name (ch 10:6). However, as used in the OT "Canaan" does not extend to Transjordan, the section east of the Jordan River (Num 34:1, 2, 10-12; 35:9, 14). Egyptian texts and cuneiform records written in Palestine and Syria during the 2d millennium B.C. also use the name "Canaan." To the ancient Egyptians it was known also by other names, one of which, "Hurru" (*Ḫꜣrw*), was derived from the Hurrians (the Biblical Horites), a people that in the patriarchal period spread throughout the civilized world and must have composed a considerable section of the population of ancient Palestine.

I. Size and Importance. The Jordan Valley and its lakes divide Palestine into western and eastern Palestine, or the "land of Canaan" and Transjordan. See Maps I; II; XX, C-5/6. Western Palestine, or Canaan, has an area of approximately 6,000 sq. mi., and eastern Palestine, or Transjordan, about 4,000 sq. mi. Combined, the whole country covers about 10,000 sq. mi., an area that is only slightly larger than the State of Vermont (9,609 sq. mi.). Distances are therefore comparatively short. Bible writers, when speaking of the whole length of the country, frequently used the expression "from Dan to Beer-sheba," since Dan was the northernmost city of Israel and Beer-sheba the southernmost one. The distance in a straight line between the 2 cities was not more than 140 mi. Also a distance of only 30 mi. separates Acre on the Mediterranean from the Sea of Galilee, and only 55 mi. separates Gaza from the Dead Sea. See Maps I; II; XX, C-5/6.

II. Topographical Extremes. There are few places on earth where such a small area shows the extremes in height and depth as does Palestine. Fig. 365 shows 2 cross-sectional views of the country, one at the latitude of the Sea of Galilee and the other at the latitude of Jerusalem. Landing on the coast of Palestine at the foot of Mount Carmel, and proceeding east, a traveler would immediately ascend a steep slope leading up to the Carmel ridge, where the highest point, near its southeast end (not on fig. 365), is 1,800 ft. above sea level. Descending the mountain on its east slopes, he would cross the southern end of the Plain of Acre that is only slightly higher than sea level. Then he would reach the Galilean mountains and would ascend and descend several of them before reaching the Sea of Galilee, about 685 ft. *below* sea level, only about 35 mi. east of his starting point. Having crossed the lake he would meet another steep climb before reaching the top of the Transjordan tableland which rises to a height of 1,700 ft. above the lake within 3 mi.

At the latitude of Jerusalem the contrasts are even more pronounced than in the north. Jerusalem lies less than 40 mi. east of the Mediterranean Sea, but its altitude is about 2,500 ft. Whereas the coastal region enjoys a pleasant and mild climate, Jerusalem experiences great differences in temperatures, with cold winds, high humidity, and occasional snow in the winter. But only 15 mi. to the east of Jerusalem begins the Jordan Valley, where a subtropical climate prevails, where banana trees and date palms grow, and where it is possible to enjoy a swim in the Dead Sea in the midst of winter, when the Mount of Olives lies under snow. Since the summit of the Mount of Olives lies about 2,600 ft. above sea level and the Dead Sea about 1,300 ft. below sea level, the difference in altitude be-

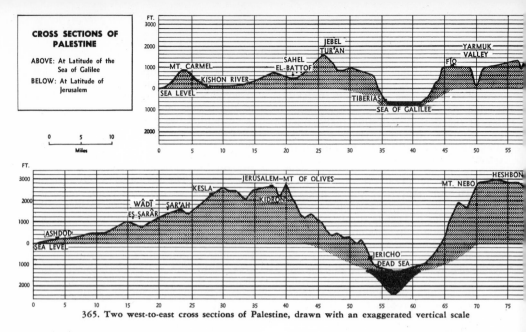

CROSS SECTIONS OF PALESTINE

ABOVE: At Latitude of the Sea of Galilee

BELOW: At Latitude of Jerusalem

0   5   10
Miles

365. Two west-to-east cross sections of Palestine, drawn with an exaggerated vertical scale

tween the 2 points, which are less than 20 mi. apart, is almost 4,000 ft. East of the Dead Sea there is another steep rise to the Transjordan tableland, which lies more than 4,000 ft. above the Dead Sea. Being a semidesert area this tableland shows great extremes in temperatures between day and night, often being very hot in the daytime, but rather cold at night.

III. The Jordan Valley. This valley, its river, and lakes, are discussed separately (*see* Dead Sea; Galilee, Sea of; Jordan), so only a brief statement is here made. The Jordan Valley is known as the deepest rift on earth. The sources of the Jordan lie on the slopes of Mount Hermon, the southernmost mountain of the Anti-Lebanon range. Four feeder rivers meet to form the Jordan, which after a run of 7 mi. reaches 7 ft. above sea level at the former Lake Huleh (Semechonitis), still on the maps but recently drained. Dropping to about 685 ft. below sea level in the next 10 mi., the Jordan enters the Sea of Galilee, which is approximately 13 mi. long and 8 mi. wide. For the next 200 mi. (about 65 mi. in a straight line) the Jordan meanders its way down to the Dead Sea, about 1,286 ft. below sea level. Several important tributaries from the east and some less important ones from the west make some sizable contributions to the Jordan's volume of water. See fig. 272.

IV. Western Palestine—Its Major Divisions. In the mountainous part of western Palestine the geographical divisions are (see Map I) Galilee, the Plain of Esdraelon, Samaria, Judea, including the Shephelah and the Negeb (Israeli *Ne-*

gev), and in the coastal area the plains of Acre and Sharon and the Philistine Plain.

1. *Galilee.* Galilee, lying between the Leontes River (*Nahr el-Liṭânî*) in the north and the Plain of Esdraelon in the south, is an irregular, rugged, hill country. The highest mountain, the *Jebel Jermak* (Map I, B-2), not mentioned in the Bible, rises to 3,934 ft. above sea level. The highest city of Palestine is Ṣafed (Map XVI, C-4), in the heart of Galilee, about 2,790 ft. above sea level. It is not mentioned in the Bible, but Jewish tradition expects the Messiah to come from Ṣafed. In the 1st cent. A.D. Galilee was rather densely populated and, according to Josephus, had 240 settlements. The northern, more mountainous, part was famous for its wealth in olive trees, and the southern portion was rich in grain, so that a 100-fold increase was not unknown (see Mt 13:8). The mountains and hills of southern Galilee have gentler slopes than the northern ones, and the climate there is somewhat milder. Most flourishing was the plain southwest of the Sea of Galilee, where a warm climate and adequate water produced plentiful vegetation.

2. *The Plain of Esdraelon.* This is the widely used Greek name of the large inland plain which in the OT is called "valley of Jezreel" (Jos 17:16; Jgs 6:33). Its modern Arabic name is *Merj Ibn 'Amir.* Its northern boundary is formed by the Galilean mountains, of which the 1,829-ft. Mount Tabor is the most conspicuous peak. In the south the plain is bounded by Mount Gilboa and the Carmel ridge. The plain measures about 20

mi. from northwest to southeast and 14 mi. from northeast to southwest, and has a rich, fertile soil that has been washed down from the mountains of Galilee and Samaria. It is drained by 2 rivers, the *Kishon toward the west, and the Goliath River, the *Nahr Jālûd,* toward the east, where the valley gently drops off toward the Jordan Valley. See fig. 267.

This large depression has been of great strategic importance throughout the country's checkered history. Through this plain ran a vital road from the coast to Transjordan, and every highway that traversed western Palestine from north to south crossed this wide valley. Because of its strategic position it possessed a string of strong fortress cities, of which Jokneam, Megiddo, Taanach, Shunem, Bethshean, and Rehob were the most important. Since their possession meant the control of the most vital crossroads of the country, these cities were coveted by powers that had their eyes on Palestine. The plain around Megiddo became the classic battlefield of the ages, where fought the armies of Egyptian Pharaohs, Hebrew judges and kings, and modern western generals, from Thutmose III of Egypt to General Allenby, Viscount of Megiddo, who won Palestine from the Turkish Empire in 1917.

3. *The Hill Country of Samaria.* Jutting out in a northwesterly direction from the central mountain area of Palestine is the 15-mi. long Carmel ridge. The mountainous area east and south of the Carmel ridge is the hill country of Samaria. Samaria is a later name which the area received from the capital city of the kingdom of Israel. There is no natural topographical border in the south and therefore the political southern border was identified with the country's geographical border. This southern border ran roughly in an east-west direction about 10 mi. north of Jerusalem. Samaria is less rugged than Galilee and contains many pleasant hills and valleys rich in olive groves, vineyards, and fertile fields that have supported a large population. The many valleys anciently formed a network of roads in all directions, and brought the people of Samaria into contact with many other nations, but also exposed them to frequent invasions.

The most famous mountains of Samaria were the twins, Mount *Ebal and Mount *Gerizim, which lie at the geographical center of the country. Because of their central location, the capital city of the northern kingdom was always near one of these mountains, first Shechem, later Tirzah, and finally Samaria.

4. *The Mountains and Wilderness of Judah.* The southern extension of the hill country of Samaria is formed by the mountain ridge of Judah, which runs consistently in a north-south direction until it loses itself in the southland, the Negeb, which begins north of Beer-sheba. The axis of this mountain range lies closer to the Jordan Valley than to the Mediterranean Sea so that ⅔ of the land is found west of the watershed. Most of the western valleys are gentle and wide, and contain fertile soil, whereas the eastern ones are too steep for agricultural use. The only good highway leading through this country from north to south runs on top of the ridge in order to avoid the many valleys and gorges. On this ridge road or close to it lay many of the most important towns and cities of Judah, such as Ramah, Mizpah, Gibeah, Jerusalem, Bethlehem, and Hebron. The western valleys provided good connections with the coast but served also as gateways for attacking armies. Among the more important valleys is that of Rephaim, in which lay the main road from the coast to Jerusalem, a route now followed by the railroad. Another route lay farther to the north and went via Gibeon, Beth-horon, and Lod to Japho. Several similar valleys are also found in the southern section of Judah. In most of them strong and fortified cities were built in ancient times.

The area east of the watershed and west of the Dead Sea and lower Jordan Valley the OT calls the Wilderness of Judah. It is a naked, barren mountain country with deep gorges, narrow valleys, steep hills, practically no watercourses, and very little vegetation (see fig. 523), though there is always some shrubbery and desert grass growing that allows flocks of sheep and goats to find a meager diet. Since the distance from the mountain ridge to the Dead Sea is only about 15 mi. in a straight line, the drop in altitude is tremendous, as much as 4,000 ft., or more than 250 ft. for every mi. This is the reason that water is nowhere conserved, but after every rain rushes torrentially down toward the Dead Sea. In this region (see fig. 100) lived the semimonastic Qumran community, whose literary treasures, known today as the Dead Sea *scrolls, have recently been discovered. During the Jewish-Roman wars of the 1st and 2d cent. A.D. many Jews fled into this area, and, living in caves or on inaccessible

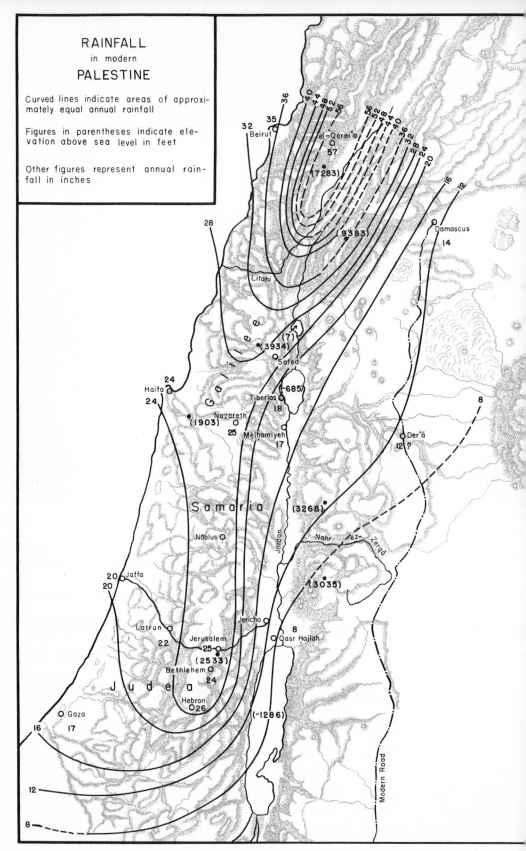

RAINFALL
in modern
PALESTINE

Curved lines indicate areas of approximately equal annual rainfall

Figures in parentheses indicate elevation above sea level in feet

Other figures represent annual rainfall in inches

366. Rainfall in Palestine

mountaintops, held out longer than their compatriots who fought against the Romans in other parts of the country.

5. *The Lowland and the Southland.* The portion of Judah next to the ridge country on the west is called the Shephelah or Lowland. It consists of the broken foot-hills of the Judean plateau. Its wide valleys, good soil, and regular rainfall attracted a large grain-producing farm population, so that the Shephelah became the granary of Judah, although at the same time many vineyards and olive groves covered its hills. To defend this rich area and its hinterland many strongly fortified cities developed in the Shephelah. They were already in existence in the Canaanite period and were later taken over by the Hebrews. Among these were such well-known cities as Lachish, Debir, Socoh, Eglon, Adullam, Libnah, and Azekah.

South of Hebron the hills gradually descend toward the Negeb, the "southland," which, in Biblical terms, began halfway between Hebron and Beer-sheba and extended as far south as Kadesh-barnea, and as far west as the "Brook of Egypt," the *Wâdi el-'Arîsh,* and covered an area of about 4,000 sq. mi. A number of ridges run approximately from east to west in this area, forming steps that lead down from the Judean mountains to the Arabian Desert, and these are natural barriers against traffic in a north-south direction. Because of these barriers caravans going north or south avoided this route and took highways skirting the Negeb. The winter rains cause an abundant vegetation to spring up from fertile soil (Ps 126:4), but the long, dry summers kill every green thing so that the country looks as barren as a desert. Recent explorations in this area have shown that the ancients were very proficient in the conservation of water. They built dams in the valleys and irrigated their terraced fields by means of water saved in reservoirs and cisterns. The ruins of many settlements, churches, and monasteries prove that in times past this country was much more densely populated than it has been during the last 1,000 years. In the modern State of Israel the southern area called the *Negev* in Israeli literature corresponds to (though not exactly coinciding with) the Biblical Negeb. The new state is striving to repopulate this area and hoping, by bringing in irrigation water from the Jordan, to make it once more a fertile country.

6. *The Coastal Plains.* The coast of Palestine, unlike the Phoenician coast, has with one exception no indentations or promontories that make harbors. The only exception is the Carmel ridge and the Bay of Acre, which, however, was always a poor shelter until British engineers built a breakwater running on the bay side of the Carmel headland to provide a safe place for ships at Haifa. The city of Dor, which lay a few mi. south of Carmel, was a port city in Bible times but had no real harbor. The same is true of Japho, which lay halfway between the Carmel ridge and Gaza and was the main port city for Jerusalem. Until modern times it had neither a breakwater nor a harbor, but an irregular line of offshore rocks provided some protection. The ancient ships, small in size, may have entered the mouth of the *Yarkon* River and unloaded their cargo at *Tell Qasileh,* a site north of the *Yarkon,* which has recently been excavated. It may have been this site, not referred to by name in the OT, to which Lebanon timber was brought in the time of King Solomon and of Zerubbabel, and from which it was sent on to Jerusalem (2 Chr 2:16; Ezr 3:7). Also the large city of Gaza in the south of Palestine, which lay 3 mi. inland, had no harbor, and all ancient efforts to build one were without permanent success. Gaza owed its wealth not to any overseas trade but to the fertile country surrounding it, and to the fact that it lay on the main trading route between Egypt and Asia.

Dunes up to 4 mi. wide rise to a height of nearly 150 ft. and bar the coastal plain from the sea. These sand dunes encroach on the fertile land in some areas and also form barriers to the draining of the water of the plain. In the north this action has resulted in the formation of swamps.

The most important section of the coastal plain is the Philistine Plain, an area not held by the Israelites but by the hostile Philistines. It is a rich, level, well-watered plain, originally grassland. Reaching from the *Wâdi Ghazzeh* in the south to the *Nahr Rubîn,* "Reuben's River," in the north (Map I, C-1), this plain is 40 mi. long and approximately 15 mi. wide. The citrus culture, which in modern times has successfully been introduced into this area, demonstrates the fruitfulness of this plain. The control of the principal road from Egypt to Asia gave to any nation that possessed this area wealth and importance. Three of the 5 important Philistine cities, Gaza, Ashkelon, and Ashdod, were among the largest metropolises of Palestine for long periods of its ancient history.

North of the *Nahr Rubîn* was the small Plain of Lydda (Lod), a fertile garden region, the gateway to the area of Jerusalem in the hinterland. This plain, with the exception of the coastal strip on which Japho was located, was usually held by the Israelites, who could ill afford to leave this vital district in the hands of an unfriendly nation. Japho (Jaffa), however, was never under the control of the Hebrews until the Jews of the Maccabean era established themselves in possession of that area.

North of the *Yarkon* begins the Plain of Sharon, which extends as far as the Blue River, the *Nahr ez-Zerqā* (not to be confused with the Jabbok, in central Transjordan, which has the same Arabic name), which reaches the sea near Dor (Map I, B-1). This plain is nearly 40 mi. long, up to 12 mi. wide in the south, but only ⅔ mi. wide in the north. It has fertile soil and is well watered, so that already in antiquity the plain was praised for its fertility. At that time it contained thick forests, "the excellency of Sharon," which the prophets predicted would be turned into a desert (Is 33:9; 35:2). These forests, and the swamps prevailing in some spots, prevented the plain from being densely populated, with the result that cities developed only on the coast. Among them was Dor, and in later times Caesarea.

The coastal strip is interrupted north of Dor by the Carmel ridge (Map II, B-3), north of which lies the Plain of Acco (Acre) extending for about 20 mi. up to *Ras el-Naqûra* (called Rosh Haniqra by the modern Israelis), which marked the modern border between Palestine and Lebanon (Map XXII, A-3). The river Kishon (see fig. 281), coming from the Plain of Esdraelon, crosses the southern part of the Plain of Acco, and in ancient times watered it well, thus enabling it to support a large population, as a number of important tells found in this area indicate. In recent centuries this plain has become marshy, but has now been drained and restored to its former usefulness. A number of small streams coming from the Galilean mountains are important for the agriculture of this coastal region.

The coastal area north of the promontory *Ras el-Naqûra* belongs geographically to Palestine, but has politically been part of Phoenicia since ancient times, and will therefore be excluded here from a discussion of the Palestinian coastal region.

V. The Other Side of the Jordan. Transjordan can be divided into 5 main geographical sections by the following 4 streams: (1) The most northerly one, the river Yarmuk, or Jarmuk (Map I, B-2), not mentioned in the Bible, separating Bashan from Gilead, (2) the Jabbok (*Nahr ez-Zerqā*) in the heart of Gilead (Map I, B-2; see fig. 251), (3) the Arnon (*Wâdi el-Mōjib*), the northern boundary of Moab proper (Map I, C-2; fig. 28), (4) the river Zered (*Wâdi el-Ḥesā*), which forms the border between Moab and Edom (Map I, C/D-2). Since the various people living in this area occasionally extended their influence or were driven back, the names given to the several sections of the Transjordan area defined territories of varying boundaries.

The most northern section is Bashan, called Batanaea in the Greco-Roman period. Its area is roughly identical with the later Hauran (Map I, A/B-3). Its northern boundary cannot well be defined, but it may be considered roughly an east-west line at the latitude of the source of the easternmost stream that forms the Jordan, near the NT city Caesarea Philippi (Map XVI, B-4). The northern part of ancient Bashan is a high tableland, has many volcanoes, and its rocky soil, not suitable for agriculture, provides means for only a nomadic existence (Map II, A-4). The southern part contains an ancient layer of disintegrated lava which has become fertile soil, but it also has some rocky granite areas and many extinct volcanoes. The western part, called Gaulanitis during the Greco-Roman period (Map XVI, B/C-4), is now known as Jaulan. Its highest elevation rises to 4,200 ft. above sea level. The higher portions of the Jaulan provide good pasturage for the large flocks raised there, whereas the lower portions yield rich crops of grain. The eastern portion of the plateau is 2,000-2,500 ft. high, although some mountains are over 6,000 ft. high. Bashan was thickly settled, and was known in Biblical times for its fat cattle and huge oak trees (Amos 4:1; Is 2:13). To the Israelites it was a frontier area which faced constant pressure from the Aramaeans in the north and the Arabs in the east.

The land lying between the rivers Yarmuk and Jabbok is today called 'Ajlûn (Map I, B-2), and covers the area of northern Gilead. Possessing a large number of streams, the *'Ajlûn* is well watered and is suited to sustain a much larger population than Bashan, and consequently played a more prominent role in Israelitic history than its northern neighbor. It also contains forests, which are not plentiful in Palestine. Some sections of the country with its oak woods resemble a Central European landscape. See fig. 205.

The country south of the Jabbok and north of the Zered (Map I, B/C-2) is now called *Belqā*, a name that is believed to be derived from the Moabite king Balak, who played a role in the time of Moses by attempting through Balaam to curse Israel (see Num 22). The northwestern section of the *Belqā* was southern Gilead, whereas the eastern portion of the country was occupied by the Ammonites (Map I, B-2/3). The highest elevation in the northern *Belqā* is "Hosea's Mountain," the *Jebel 'Osha* (Map II, B-3), which is 3,597 ft. high, whereas farther to the south is found Mount Nebo (Map II, C-3), 2,644 ft. high, where Moses died after viewing the Promised Land for the first and last time. In the Ammonite country lay the ancient city Rabbath Ammon, which is now *'Ammân*, the capital of the Hashemite Kingdom of Jordan. Ammon is a level and rolling tableland, whose semiarid character makes it suitable mostly for nomadic dwellers.

The country east of the Dead Sea was the land of Moab. In Moses' time only the southern half of this area was occupied by the Moabites, whereas the northern part, which had already been lost to Moab, was wrested from Amorite settlers by the Israelites. Throughout Israel's history, however, there was a continual struggle between Israel and Moab for that section of the country lying north of the Arnon. Moab is a high tableland with hardly any trees, suited for sheep raising. Its chief stream is the Arnon, which has cut through central Moab and has formed a tremendous canyon which in certain parts is about 4,000 ft. deep. Its bizarre cliffs and colorful rock walls make an unforgettable sight (see figs. 28, 29), and remind the American traveler of the Grand Canyon in Arizona. The southern border of Moab was the Zered (Num 21: 12), now the *Wâdī el-Ḥesā*, another of the many deep valleys of Transjordan.

South of Moab lay the country of the Edomites, which extended to the Gulf of Aqabah. In this country lay the picturesque and strategically well-located city of Sela (later Petra). See fig. 427. This country is a desert, but possesses in its mountains natural resources of copper and iron ore, which were exploited by kings of Judah who possessed Edom. By controlling several trade routes from the desert to Gaza, Egypt, and Phoenicia, and by levying a heavy toll from passing caravans, especially those carrying incense, the inhabitants of this land obtained much income and wealth.

VI. Geology of Palestine. The rocks of Palestine may be classified into 3 general classes: (1) the underlying so-called primitive rocks, including gneiss and schist, penetrated by dikes of granite and other igneous rocks, (2) the sedimentary rocks, and (3) the more recent igneous rocks, of volcanic origin. Lowest among the sedimentary rocks are found the sandstones, varying in texture, color, and content from place to place. Above the sandstones lie the limestones. These are variously classified by strata, but the entire series has been called the cretaceo-nummulitic series. The variation from place to place in color and content of the layers of a given sedimentary rock has been explained on the basis of the changing currents (and hence changing sources of material) occurring at the time of the *Flood. Layers of igneous rock overlie vast areas of the country. Having been extruded by volcanic action through faults and other weak places in the crust, this type covers vast areas of the other rocks.

Palestine's terrain presents the appearance of a generally mountainous, much-disturbed land mass with a predominance of limestone evident in most sections. Along the east coast of the Dead Sea and at many places on the east bank of the Jordan can be seen outcroppings of the Nubian sandstone. The sandstones are also exposed in certain areas on the western slopes of the Anti-Lebanon. The predominating rock formation of the Philistine coastal plain is a calcareous sandstone, the weathering of which has contributed to the extensive sand dunes along the Mediterranean coast line. Wind action drives this sand inland at times, rendering agriculture difficult in areas adjacent to the coast. The rich alluvial soils of areas between the Jordan and the Mediterranean are largely the product of erosion of the highland rocks by rain and stream. The winter rains always add mineral content to the rivers' deposits—so much so that at times marshes are created as streams are blocked in their flow to the sea. The Plain of Gennesaret, the Plain of

Esdraelon, and the coastal areas of the Mediterranean present examples of this action. At many places in the limestone deposits 2 distinct groups can be seen. The strata of the upper group present a relatively solid appearance, but vary in color from white to reddish brown. It is on this solid limestone that the larger buildings of Jerusalem are built. These deposits give to the countryside its characteristic topography of gently rounded hills separated by valleys that occasionally take on the dimensions of a plain. The strata of the lower group of limestone are characteristically dusky in color in the upper layers and full of caverns and other evidences of violence after deposition. The color changes to darker gray with depth, and fossils (especially the remains of marine life) become more abundant. (See Flood, IV.) From the quarries outside the Damascus Gate came the softer limestone used in many of Jerusalem's buildings. In places the limestone hills are crowned with deposits of chalk, evidence of soft deposits once more widespread but now reduced by centuries of erosion. The ravine through which the road descends from Jerusalem to Jericho cuts through a characteristic series of Palestine's limestone deposits. There is much evidence of volcanic activity, which has lifted areas and produced intrusive and outflow activity. Large areas of basalt-type rock are to be found. West of the Jordan they are found mainly in the northern areas. Over the southwestern portion of the Plain of Esdraelon is one such area; another lies to the north of Mount Tabor. East of Jordan, from Damascus to the area south of the Dead Sea, igneous rock—basalt, felsite, etc.—can be found overlying the ever-present limestone of vast areas. There are areas of basalt rock overlying the limestone in various spots along the Jordan, but to the west of the Dead Sea and south of Samaria there is little or no evidence of volcanism in the past. Other remaining evidences of volcanic activity are found in the hot springs of Tiberias and other resorts along the Jordan Valley as far south as the Dead Sea, around which are vast deposits of sulphur, rock salt (fig. 454), and similar chemicals of volcanic origin, mute reminders of the destruction of the cities of the plain (see Gen 19:1-28) in Lot's time. It is probable that there was also some local shifting of the levels at that time.

The great crevasse in which are found the Sea of Galilee, the Jordan River, the Dead Sea, and the *Wâdi el-'Arabah* is the most remarkable feature of Palestine's geology (see Map II). The general elevation of Palestine is considerably above sea level, but much of the Jordan Valley is below the level of the Mediterranean (*see* Dead Sea; Galilee, Sea of; Jordan). At the Dead Sea the water surface averages 1,286 ft. below sea level, and in some places the bottom of that sea is more than 2,600 ft. below sea level. The causes of this great rift have been the subject of much speculation on the part of scientists, but the catastrophic events recorded in Gen 6:11 to 8:19 were doubtless major factors. This fault is of such magnitude that its formation must have been one of the most violent of all geologic actions. It is evident that the valley follows a line of unconformity of the rock strata underlying Palestine. Extending south into central Africa—spanning 1/6 of the earth's circumference—this line can be traced by extensive evidences of faulting all along the Jordan. West of the river (the downthrow side of the fault) the land mass appears to have dropped, whereas to the east those layers deposited earlier are plainly visible in many places. Because this great fault line spans the country, Palestine is ever in danger of earthquake. Many occurrences have been recorded, and doubtlessly many more have occurred but have not been recorded.

The fertile soils of the Jordan Valley result from the erosion of the various rocks of the uplands and the alluvial depositions of the river and its tributaries. The valley itself displays 2 distinct levels, or terraces, in most places, the upper one extending back to the limestone cliffs formed by the rift. Bitumen or asphalt ("slime" of Gen 11:3) is obtained from deep wells or pits in the earth at the southern end of the Dead Sea. Occasional masses of it are found floating on the Dead Sea. This substance, which is the product of great volumes of material buried by the Flood, has since undergone transformation to this form of petroleum.

VII. A Country of Forest, Steppe, and Desert. The visitor to Palestine hardly realizes that this now barren and rocky mountain country was once widely covered with thick forests of oaks and evergreens. Yet not only Egyptian records of ancient travelers are witnesses to this fact but also the modern botanist, whose researches have led him to the conclusion that most of western Palestine and certain sections of Transjordan were covered by forests. Of these forests only meager remnants remain and only in a few places, although great efforts are presently being made to reforest certain parts of the land. In these forests were found evergreen oak, the deciduous oak, and the pine tree. Where the pines grew, dense woods were formed that left no open space for underbrush so that no pasturage was possible.

Practically all of these forests have in the course of time been destroyed. This deforestation is due not only to those nations that settled in Palestine and burned down forests in order to obtain space for agriculture and settlements but also to the many cruel warlords who frequently invaded the country and cut down its forests and orchards alike. Since Palestine is a mountainous country, once the trees were felled or burned, the soil washed off the mountain slopes, exposing limestone rock in large areas. Furthermore, the raising of sheep, and especially of goats, in this area has prevented the regrowth of these forests.

The natural forest areas of Palestine border everywhere on a wide belt of steppe, a grassland with inadequate rainfall to support forests or fruit trees but enough for grass, brush, and some grain production. Where irrigation has brought water into such a steppe area, or where rain water is stored up in cisterns and reservoirs, profuse fertility has resulted, because the composition of the soil in the steppes of Palestine is about the same as in the forest country. This grass belt, of varying width, runs from Gaza via Beer-sheba and along the upper eastern slopes of the Judean mountains as far north as the eastern end of the Plain of Esdraelon. It then crosses the Jordan, and as a narrow strip runs southward east of the Jordan and the Dead Sea through the *Wâdī 'Arabah,* but makes another turn south of Petra. From here on the belt is between 15 and 25 mi. wide and runs west of the Arabian Desert, then encloses the Hauran, which forms a deep pocket of forest country, and finally leaves eastern Palestine in a northerly direction south of Damascus (see fig. 367).

Whatever does not belong to the forest or steppe areas is desert. Such regions are found south of Beer-sheba, and comprise the lower eastern slopes of the Judean mountains, the Jordan Valley, and the country lying east of the areas of sedentary population in Transjordan. These

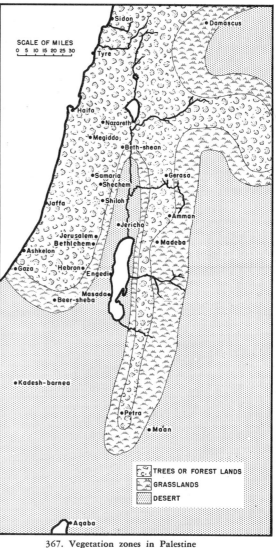

367. **Vegetation zones in Palestine**

regions are generally not level sand areas, but are mostly mountainous. They contain soil capable of producing vegetation if water is accessible, as can be seen around various springs or wells. Jericho is such an oasis in the Jordan Valley, which owes its exuberant fertility to the waters of the *Wâdī Qelt.* Another oasis is En-gedi, on the west side of the Dead Sea (see fig. 157). Its life-giving water comes from a spring that gave its name to the ancient city. The recent discovery of many ruins of ancient towns in the southern Negeb proves that the Palestinian desert areas are capable of supporting a moder-

368. Southern end of the Dead Sea

ately sized population if means could be devised for the proper conservation of water.

Topographical and archeological research has shown that the earliest Palestinians chose the steppe and the oasis for settlements. The excavations of Jericho, for example, have proved that this city was one of the earliest inhabited places in the country. The tropical climate of that area, a good water supply, and the fact that there was no need to clear a forest seemed to make that site an ideal place for a settlement for the earliest colonists. However, when Israel came into Palestine large sections of the forest land had already been cleared and cities founded, supported by the produce of their surrounding fertile countryside. It is quite possible that the Israelites also occupied and cleared wooded lands between the Canaanite cities, and that the woodlands in western and eastern Palestine played an important role in the settlement of the Hebrews in Canaan.

VIII. The Climate of Palestine. Palestine, belonging to the Mediterranean world, shares the climate of that world to a large degree. Yet this climate is varied because of the great differences in altitude, and because of the presence of seas and deserts in close proximity to one another. A difference of about 10,000 ft. in level between the summit of Mount Hermon and Jericho, only 110 mi. apart, is responsible for the fact that plant life similar to that of northern Europe can be found on Mount Hermon and subtropical fruits of the West Indies grow at Jericho. The fauna shows the same diversity as the flora.

Palestine, lying mostly between 31° and 33° north latitude, belongs to the subtropical zone. Its days, therefore, range only between approximately 10 and 14 hours, and extremes in temperature are not frequent, with the exception of the Jordan Valley. The average annual mean temperature in Jaffa, for example, is 67°

PALESTINE

F. and in Jerusalem 63° F. It is seldom hotter than 90° F. even in the summer, and it freezes infrequently. Yet some extremely high and also some low temperatures have occasionally been recorded. The highest recorded temperature for Jerusalem is 112° F. and the lowest 25° F. In Jericho, on the other hand, the temperature is always around 100° F. on summer days, and occasionally may climb to 120° F.

The prevailing winds come from the west. Laden with moisture, they bring the rains in the winter, and even when dry, as in the summer, serve to make high temperatures tolerable. Very tiresome is the hot east wind from the desert, called either sirocco (an Italian word of Arabic origin), or khamsin. It is often accompanied by blinding sand storms. Also the wind from the south can bring a scorching heat in the summer (Lk 12:55). These 2 winds are common in the transitional periods from summer to winter or from winter to summer.

The winter rains are caused by the west winds, which strike the mountains. As the moisture-laden air rises it cools and is forced to shed its moisture in the form of rain on western Palestine up to the mountain ridge. After passing the ridge the air subsides into the hot and deep depression of the Jordan Valley and the Dead Sea. The meeting of cooler air with the hot air in this depression sometimes causes sudden storms of high velocity. However, the cool western winds are warmed here; instead of yielding rain, they absorb any moisture they can find, which is in turn shed on the western slopes of the Transjordan tableland as the air rises again in its course toward the east. It is this simple process that provides rain and fertility to western Palestine by means of water evaporated from the Mediterranean Sea, and rain to western Transjordan by means of additional water evaporated from the Jordan and the Dead Sea. However, this process works only in the winter. There are 2 major factors involved: First, the Palestinian mountains are not lofty enough to give adequate lift to the warmer moisture-laden summer air masses to cool them to the dew point. Second, in summer the polar-front zone, which in winter causes intense and constant on-shore circulation of air, moves northward, thus greatly diminishing the flow of moisture-laden air from the sea in this area.

As a consequence, there are only 2 seasons in Palestine, a dry season in summer and a wet season in winter. However, these 2 seasons of Palestine cannot fully compare with European or North American summers and winters. The summer in Palestine is so dry and hot, with no rain from June to September, that during that time all vegetation withers and the whole country takes on a dead and desertlike appearance. Those who have never been in Palestine in the rainy season, and who see the country for the 1st time at the end of the summer, cannot believe that the land produces anything at all except where permanent irrigation provides the necessary water. Yet a great transformation of the whole country takes place after the rains start. The whole country suddenly comes to life, and out of every crevice of the ground spring up flowers, and the dead brown grass turns lush and green with almost unbelievable speed.

The "early rain" (RSV "autumn rain"), so frequently mentioned in the Bible, comes late in October or in November and softens the soil sufficiently for the farmer to plow and sow his fields. These rains are still comparatively light, but toward the end of December come heavier rains with the greatest rainfall coming usually in January. This water penetrates the soil deeply and causes the crop to grow, but a good harvest still depends on the right amount and the timing of the "latter rain," also frequently mentioned in the Bible (Deut 11:14). These last showers of the season come in March and early April and promote the ripening of the grain. If the last rainy months yield only meager precipitation, a poor harvest may be the result even if the earlier rainfall was good.

In spite of the long dry season Palestine enjoys an amount of rainfall that compares well with that of western Europe or North America. Jerusalem, for example, has an annual average of 52 rainy days, and an annual precipitation of approximately 25 in. However, there are differences even in Jerusalem. Since this city lies on a mountain ridge, the western part of Jerusalem receives 6 in. more rain than the eastern sectors. Jaffa, on the coast, has an annual precipitation of about 20 in., the Jordan Valley about 18 in. in the north, but only 12 in. at Jericho. Beersheba, which lies near the southern desert, receives only 8.8 in. of rain, whereas sections in the northwest of Palestine receive up to 36 in. of rain (see fig. 366).

A godsend in Palestine is the dew that is particularly abundant in the summer. It is brought to western Palestine by moisture-laden air which at night strikes the mountains of western Palestine, and leaves behind its drops of lifesaving liquid in a season when every drop of water is welcome.

Only a small amount of snow falls on Palestine in the winter, and usually only in the mountainous areas, and it causes great hardships and suffering in a country that is not prepared for such emergencies. Heavy snowfalls, however, are occasionally experienced. On Feb. 9, 1920, 3 ft. of snow fell in the course of 1 day in Jerusalem, and snow remained on the ground for a whole week in February, 1950. Even snowfalls in the month of April have been recorded twice in modern history (1870, 1940).

Palestine has had an importance throughout this world's history which is out of proportion to its size or the value of its natural resources. It owes this importance 1st to an exceptionally favorable geographic location, being on the land bridge between 2 great continents, and

369. The rugged pass of En-gedi in the Wilderness of Judah

thus a territory which every great power of antiquity has coveted; 2d, it is the Holy Land of 3 great world religions—Judaism, Christianity, and Islam. Much blood has been spilled for the control of its sacred places and shrines by adherents of all 3 of these great religions.

Pallu (păl′ŭ), KJV once **Phallu** (făl′ōō). [Heb. *Pallu'*, "distinguished."] A son of Reuben (Gen 46:9; Ex 6:14; 1 Chr 5:3), founder of the tribal family of the Palluites (păl′ŭ-īts) [Heb. *Pallu'î*], and ancestor of Dathan and Abiram, who rebelled against Moses (Num 26:5, 8, 9).

Palluites. *See* Pallu.

Palm Tree. [Heb. *tamar, tomer, timmorah;* Gr. *phoinix.*] Scholars generally agree that the palm of the Scriptures is almost always the date palm (*Phoenix dactylifera*), an upright, branchless tree, which held an important place in the economy and daily life of the peoples of Palestine. Under proper cultivation this tree grows to a height of about 60 to 80 ft. and may live and produce until it is 200 years old. Generally, it yields fruit beginning at about its 6th year, attains maturity at 30, and reaches its peak of productivity at the end of its 1st cent. Its long, feathery leaves (called branches in the Bible) die and droop down around the trunk as new leaves grow out, giving the tree a parasol appearance. The dates themselves grow in clusters weighing from 30 to 50 pounds, and constitute a major part of the diet among some Arab tribes. The seeds are ground up for animal feed. The giant leaves of the date palm, from 6 to 10 ft. long, serve many functions in the Palestinian economy—thatch, fencing, matting material, and decoration. The Arabs have a saying that there are as many uses for the date palm as there are days in a year. The trees grow both in dense groves and singly. Much of the Jordan Valley from the shores of Gennesaret to the end of the Dead Sea may once have contained date palm groves, but now there are few of these trees in Palestine except along the maritime plain of Philistia and in the region around Jericho. The near extinction in Palestine of these graceful and important trees has been attributed to a neglect of their cultivation, for they still grow abundantly in other regions of the Near East. See figs. 98, 166, 370.

On their flight from Egypt the Israelites came upon a grove of 70 palm trees at Elim (Ex 15:27; Num 33:9), and they

370. Palm trees at Rephidim on the Sinai Peninsula

later were instructed to use palm leaves in erecting their booths for the Feast of Tabernacles (Lev 23:40; Neh 8:15). Because the tree was so familiar to the Israelites, it was natural that it be employed in architectural designs in Solomon's Temple (1 Ki 6:29, 32, 35) and in the temple of Ezekiel's vision (Eze 40; 41). Jericho was called the "city of palm trees" (Deut 34:3; Jgs 1:16; 3:13; 2 Chr 28:15). Palm fronds were used for various celebrations (Jn 12:13; Rev 7:9; 1 Macc 13:51; 2 Macc 10:7).

Palmerworm. *See* Locust, 5.

Palsy. According to the Greek, paralysis, rather than palsy with its common present-day connotation (Mt 4:24; Mk 2:3; Acts 8:7; etc.).

Palti (păl′tī), KJV once **Phalti** (făl′tī). [Heb. *Palṭî,* an abbreviation of *Palṭî'el,* Paltiel, "He (that is, God) delivered me." The name occurs in Akkadian as *Paliṭu.*]

1. The representative of the tribe of Benjamin among the 12 spies (Num 13:2, 9).

2. Son of Laish to whom Saul gave his daughter Michal, David's wife, after David fled for his life (1 Sa 25:44). Palti was later forced to restore her to David (see 2 Sa 3:14, 15), where the longer name *Paltiel (KJV "Phaltiel," făl′tĭ-ĕl) is used.

Paltiel (păl′tĭ-ĕl). [Heb. *Palṭî'el,* "God delivered me."]

1. The prince of the tribe of Issachar during the wilderness wandering (Num 34:26).

2. For 2 Sa 3:14, 15 see Palti, 2.

Paltite (păl′tīt). [Heb. *Palṭî.*] The appellative of Helez, one of David's "mighty men" (2 Sa 23:26), designating, probably, that he was a native or inhabitant of the city of Beth-pelet in the extreme south of Judah. He is said to have been of Ephraimite descent (1 Chr 27:10). *See* Pelonite.

Pamphylia (păm-fĭl′ĭ-à). [Gr. *Pamphulia*.] A coastal territory in southern Asia Minor, and Roman province in NT times. Bordering countries were Lycia, Pisidia, and Cilicia. At one time the area belonged to the kingdom of Lydia, then passed successively to the Persians, Seleucids, and the kingdom of Pergamum. After Pergamum became a Roman province (133 B.C.) Pamphylia was united with Cilicia for some time. Later it belonged briefly to the kingdom of Amyntas of Galatia. Barnabas and Paul passed through Pamphylia twice during their 1st Missionary Journey (Acts 13:13; 14:24-26; 15:38). At that time it was a Roman province (with Lycia) with a procurator as administrator. Jews from Pamphylia were among the visitors at Jerusalem who witnessed the miracle of Pentecost (ch 2: 5, 10). Map XX, B-5.

Pan. The rendering of various Hebrew words designating different types of pans used for baking and frying. The exact type of utensil described by most of these terms is now uncertain. A few of the utensils involved were probably not pans but kettles, or other cooking ware. The most frequently mentioned is the *machabath,* which seems to have been a large flat pan for baking (Lev 2:5; RSV "griddle"; Eze 4:3; RSV "plate"). The *kîyôr* (1 Sa 2:14) was either a large kettle or a basin. Frequently the KJV translates *kîyôr* "laver" (Ex 30:18; 1 Ki 7:38; etc.). The *sîr* (Ex 27:3) was also a large kettle, and is often rendered "pot" in the KJV (Ex 16: 3; 2 Ki 4:38-41; etc.). Other words rendered "pan" are: *chabath* (1 Chr 9: 31), *marchesheth* (Lev 2:7, KJV "frying-pan"), *maśreth* (2 Sa 13:9), *parûr* (Num 11:8), and *ṣallachath* (2 Chr 35:13).

Pannag (păn′ăg). [Heb. *pannag.*] A kind of food (Eze 27:17); not identified. The KJV simply transliterates the Hebrew term; the RSV conjecturally renders it "early figs."

Paper. A term appearing in 2 Jn 12 as a rendering of the Gr. *chartēs,* a sheet or roll of papyrus. *See* Papyrus; Writing Materials.

Paper Reed. A rendering of the rare Hebrew word *'arah* (Is 19:7, KJV), which some believe refers to open or bare patches of ground (see RSV); others, to some type of reeds or rushes.

Paphos (pā′fŏs). [Gr. *Paphos*.] A city originally a mile inland on the southwestern coast of the island of Cyprus. It gained fame as the seat of the Paphian Aphrodite, the goddess of love—the Greek equivalent of the Phoenician Astarte—who, according to tradition, had sprung there from the sea. The goddess was worshiped under the representation of a conical meteoric stone. According to the Greeks, the temple was founded by the Phoenicians under Cinyras, legendary king of Byblos, a contemporary of Agamemnon. All priests in the temple were considered his descendants. The old city was later superseded by a port town, called New Paphos, situated some 7 mi. distant at the mouth of the Bocarus River. The new city was the seat of the proconsul of Cyprus in Roman times. Its modern name is *Baffo*. Many ruins of NT times are still visible. Barnabas and Paul visited Paphos on their 1st Missionary Journey and had an audience with Sergius Paulus, the proconsul (Acts 13:6-13).

Papyrus (pà-pī′rŭs). [Heb. *gome′*.] A tall plant (*Cyperus papyrus*) once plentiful along the edge of the Nile (Job 8:11; Is 18:2; RSV; the Hebrew term is elsewhere rendered "rush," "bulrush"). See figs. 177, 371. Its fanshaped head appears in Egyptian design and as a symbol of Lower Egypt (see fig. 147). Its stalks, bound in bundles and lashed together, were used to make reed boats (Is 18:2; see fig. 177). The stem was made into a kind of paper (*see* Writing Materials). The term "papyrus" is applied to this material and also (frequently in the plural, papyri) to documents written on it, such as the Nash Papyrus of a Biblical text (see fig. 489) or the Jewish papyri from Elephantine, Egypt, of the time of Nehemiah (*see* Pathros; fig. 417).

371. Papyrus growing in front of the Cairo Museum

Parable. [Heb. *mashal*, "simile," "comparison," "proverbial saying"; **Gr.** generally *parabolē*, "type," "figure," "symbol," "illustration," "parable," literally, "(one thing) thrown alongside (another for comparison)."] The English word "parable" denotes a literary device in which a short narrative, either true or fictitious, illustrates moral or spiritual truth. A parable is an extended simile, in which it is stated or implied that one thing is *like* something else. A parable thus differs from an allegory, which is an extended metaphor, in which one thing is said to *be* another. The statement that the Spirit descended like a dove (Mt 3:16) is a simile, but the story comparing "the kingdom of heaven" with hidden treasure (ch 13:44) is a parable. Similarly, the statement, "Ye *are* the salt of the earth" (ch 5:13), is a metaphor, but Jesus' extended reference to Himself as "the true vine" (Jn 15:1-8) is an allegory. In contrast, a fable is a narrative outside of the world of reality that usually attributes human intelligence, speech, and action to inanimate things or to plants or animals. In the Gospels a parable is generally a narrative "placed alongside" a certain spiritual truth for purposes of comparison. In Biblical usage, however, a "parable" may also be simply any short, pithy statement of truth (see Mk 3:23, 27).

Teaching in parables was popular in Christ's day, but He perfected and used it so extensively and so effectively that it has become identified with His teaching method. His parables were generally based on the common experiences of everyday life, and often on recent incidents or on scenes in view as He spoke. The narrative itself was usually simple and brief and its conclusion so obvious as to involve little uncertainty (see Mt 21:40, 41), though at times it might require explanation (see ch 13:18-23). With Jesus a parable was a bridge by which He led His hearers by a pleasant and familiar path from where they were to where He wanted them to be, from the known to the unknown, from concrete facts to abstract truths, from the seen to the unseen, from the earthly to the heavenly. It was a window through which He invited His hearers to gaze upon vistas of heavenly truth. By His parables Jesus drew men's attention, aroused their interest, and stimulated inquiry. Often, as in the parable of the Two Sons (ch 21:28-31), He imparted unwanted truth, driving home an important message to which His hearers listened patiently and even rendered a verdict against themselves before discovering that it was themselves they were condemning. By His parable teaching Jesus prevented the spies who pursued Him relentlessly from having something with which to accuse Him. It would be difficult to make out a case against Him for simply telling good stories. Parables have the paradoxical quality of revealing truth to those willing to receive it, at the same time concealing it from those who would reject it. Jesus' parables also created in the minds of His hearers lasting impressions that would be renewed and intensified every time the scenes depicted in the parables again came to mind or to view.

The important thing to remember in the interpretation of any parable is to ascertain the lesson the speaker purposed to illustrate by it, and to read no more into it than he intended. Often the explanation accompanies the parable (e.g., Lk 7:41-47; 11:11-13), or is implicit in the context (ch 16:19-31; cf. vs 13-17). The circumstances, persons present, or problem under discussion will often provide the key to interpretation. Before the meaning of a parable in the spiritual realm can become clear, it is frequently necessary to understand the narrative in terms of Oriental customs and modes of thought and expression (Mt 25:1-13; etc.). A parable is a vivid word picture that must be *seen* distinctly before its lesson can be clearly *understood*. In view of the fact that a parable is given to illustrate truth, and usually *one* particular aspect of truth—which is either explicit or implicit in the context—the incidental details of the narrative are important only as they contribute to a clarification of that point of truth, and often serve only to round out the story. These details are not to be assigned a cryptic meaning, nor may they be made the basis for points of doctrine.

Lists of our Lord's parables often differ because not all agree as to which of Jesus' illustrations should be termed parables. Length is one of the important considerations (see Mt 5:14, 15), but some illustrations always considered as parables are very short (see ch 13:44-48). Another factor is whether allegorical illustrations such as Jn 10:1-6; 15:1-8 should, strictly speaking, be counted as parables. Forty of the more important of our Lord's parables are listed, classified, and analyzed in the following table.

Parable	Scripture References	Harmony Entry *	Principles Illustrated
A. Divine Love, Mercy, and Justice			
1. The Pearl of Great Price	Mt 13:45, 46	54	The priceless value of redeeming love. The Saviour in search of men; men seeking for salvation. Cf. No. 11.
2. The Lost Sheep	Mt 18:12-14 Lk 15:3-7	107	God's love for those who know they are lost but know not how to return to Him. His unwillingness that any should perish. Cf. Nos. 3, 4.
3. The Lost Coin	Lk 15:8-10	108	God's love for those who know not that they are lost. Diligence in seeking the lost. Cf. Nos. 2, 4.
4. The Prodigal Son	Lk 15:11-32	109	God's love for those who have wandered from His love. The hardheartedness of man in contrast with the love of God. Cf. Nos. 2, 3.
5. The Barren Fig Tree	Lk 13:6-9	100	The relationship between divine mercy and justice. God's dealings with the Jewish nation. Cf. Nos. 8, 15, 16, 21.
	[See also No. 31]		
B. The Plan of Salvation			
6. The Mustard Seed	Mt 13:31, 32 Mk 4:30-32 Lk 13:18, 19	54	The extensive, quantitative growth of the kingdom of divine grace, the church. God begins in a small way to accomplish great results. Cf. Nos. 9, 19, 20.
7. The Tares	Mt 13:24-30	54	Character decides destiny. The purpose of probationary time; tares do not eventually become wheat. Cf. Nos. 9, 29, 40.
8. The Wicked Husbandmen	Mt 21:33-43 Mk 12:1-12 Lk 20:9-19	135	God's eternal purpose will triumph in spite of man's unfaithfulness. Israel would forfeit its role as the chosen nation. Cf. Nos. 5, 15, 16, 21.
	[See also Nos. 5, 9, 10, 21]		
C. The Reception of Truth			
9. The Sower, the Seed, and the Soils	Mt 13:3-9, 18-23 Mk 4:3-20 Lk 8:5-15	54	The reception of truth by different classes of hearers. Cf. Nos. 6-8, 19.
10. The Great Banquet	Lk 14:16-24	105	The danger of neglecting or rejecting truth. God cannot accept a divided heart. Cf. Nos. 6-8, 21.
11. Hidden Treasure	Mt 13:44	54	The transcendent value of truth and the effort necessary to secure it. Cf. No. 1.

* See Gospels, Harmony of.

Parable	Scripture References	Harmony Entry	Principles Illustrated
12. New Cloth and New Wine	Mt 9:16, 17 Mk 2:21, 22 Lk 5:36-39	59	Truth versus traditionalism. The danger of preconceived opinions.
13. The Two Debtors	Lk 7:41-43	128	Appreciation of, and gratitude for, the love and mercy of God.
14. Building a Tower; A King Going to War	Lk 14:28-33	106	Counting the cost of discipleship.
15. Seven Unclean Spirits	Mt 12:43-45	52	The necessity of a positive attitude toward truth; the unpardonable sin. The condition of the Jewish leaders. Justification incomplete without sanctification. Cf. Nos. 5, 8, 16, 17, 21.
16. The Two Sons	Mt 21:28-32	134	Deeds count, not words; profession without practice is hypocrisy. Cf. Nos. 5, 8, 15, 17, 21.
17. Building on the Rock or on Sand	Mt 7:24-27 Lk 6:47-49	46	The perception of truth not an end in itself but a means to the end of a transformed life. The folly of knowledge without obedience. Cf. Nos. 15, 16, 21, 26.
18. The Rich Fool	Lk 12:16-21	98	The danger of worldly-mindedness; the folly of living for material things.

[See also Nos. 1, 29, 32, 34]

D. The Transformation of Character

Parable	Scripture References	Harmony Entry	Principles Illustrated
19. The Growing Seed	Mk 4:26-29	54	Faith and works: human effort cooperating with infinite power in Christian growth. Cf. Nos. 6, 7, 9, 20.
20. The Leaven	Mt 13:33 Lk 13:20, 21	54	The intensive, qualitative growth of the kingdom of heaven. Power from above is implanted in the heart and transforms the life. Cf. Nos. 6, 9, 19.
21. The Man Without a Wedding Garment	Mt 22:2-14	136	The importance of Christ's righteousness. Cf. Nos. 5-8, 10, 15-17, 25.

[See also Nos. 15, 17, 34]

E. Prayer

Parable	Scripture References	Harmony Entry	Principles Illustrated
22. The Friend Calling at Midnight	Lk 11:5-13	94	Perseverance in prayer. Asking to give to others.
23. The Unjust Judge	Lk 18:1-8	117	Perseverance, earnestness, and confidence in prayer.

[See also No. 25]

F. Humility Versus Pride

Parable	Scripture References	Harmony Entry	Principles Illustrated
24. Choosing Places of Honor	Lk 14:7-11	104	Humility toward one's fellow men; honoring others.
25. The Pharisee and the Publican	Lk 18:9-14	118	Humility before God; the danger of pride and self-righteousness.

[See also No. 38]

G. Utilizing Present Opportunities

Parable	Scripture References	Harmony Entry	Principles Illustrated
26. The Nobleman and the Pounds	Lk 19:11-27	127	The improvement of talents and opportunities. Working while waiting for the kingdom. Faithful service the basis of reward. Cf. Nos. 5, 27, 37.

Parable	Scripture References	Harmony Entry	Principles Illustrated
27. The Talents	Mt 25:14-30	147	Same as No. 26; also, helping others prepare for our Lord's return. Cf. Nos. 26, 34, 37.
28. The Dishonest Steward	Lk 16:1-9	110	The diligent use of present opportunities in preparation for the future life. Cf. Nos. 26, 27.
29. The Rich Man and Lazarus	Lk 16:19-31	111	Eternal destiny is decided in the present life; there is no second probation. The danger of preoccupation with material things. Cf. Nos. 7, 18.

H. The Christian and His Fellow Man

Parable	Scripture References	Harmony Entry	Principles Illustrated
30. The Good Samaritan	Lk 10:30-37	91	True religion consists in active service for others; on this, eternal destiny depends. Contact with suffering humanity frees the soul of selfishness. Cf. No. 39.
31. The Unforgiving Servant	Mt 18:23-35	77	Mercy toward, and forgiveness of, others. Our forgiveness by God contingent on our forgiveness of others. Cf. No. 5.
32. Treasures Old and New	Mt 13:52	54	Familiarity with old truths; alertness for new truth. Adapt truth to the needs of the hearers. Cf. No. 9.
33. The Faithful Steward	Lk 12:42-48	99	Conscientious supervision of the affairs of God's household, the church.

I. Awaiting the Lord's Return

Parable	Scripture References	Harmony Entry	Principles Illustrated
34. The Ten Virgins	Mt 25:1-13	146	Personal preparation for our Lord's return; His coming seemingly delayed. Our need of the Holy Spirit. Cf. Nos. 27, 35, 36.
35. The Watchful Servant	Mk 13:34-37	145	Watching for the Master's return. Cf. Nos. 34, 36.
36. The Watchful Servants; the Vigilant Home Owner	Lk 12:35-40	99	Preparedness for our Lord's sudden return. Living up to the light we have; personal accountability for truth. Cf. Nos. 7, 34, 35.
37. Laborers in the Vineyard	Mt 20:1-16	122	God measures service by the willingness and fidelity with which it is rendered. Rewards are based on our Lord's gracious generosity and on the spirit which motivates our service for Him. Cf. Nos. 8, 26, 27, 38.
38. Unprofitable Servants	Lk 17:7-10	112	Faithfulness to duty. God's claim on all our services. Cf. No. 37.
39. The Sheep and the Goats	Mt 25:31-46	148	The significance of practical religion. The supreme test of the reality of our religion is what it leads us to do for others. Cf. No. 30.

J. The Final Judgment; Eternal Rewards

Parable	Scripture References	Harmony Entry	Principles Illustrated
40. The Dragnet	Mt 13:47-50	54	The final separation of the bad from the good. Not all the wicked eventually become righteous. Cf. Nos. 7, 29.

[See also Nos. 7, 21, 26, 27, 29]

Paradise. [Gr. *paradeisos,* a loan word from the Old Persian *pairidaēza,* "enclosure," "royal park."] A NT expression occurring 3 times (Lk 23:43; 2 Cor 12:4; Rev 2:7). Paul gives the location of Paradise as "the third heaven" (2 Cor 12:2, 3). John pictures it as containing the tree of life (Rev 2:7), a fact that links the NT "paradise" with the OT Garden of Eden. In the LXX the Garden of Eden is called *paradeisos* (Gen 2:8, 15; Eze 31:8). *See* Eden, 2.

Parah (pā′rá). [Heb. *Parah,* "young cow."] A town in the territory of Benjamin (Jos 18:21, 23), identified with *Khirbet el-Fârah,* 7 mi. northeast of Jerusalem.

Paran (pā′răn). [Heb. *Pa'ran.*] A wilderness described as being between Midian and Egypt (1 Ki 11:18) and between Sinai and Canaan (Num 10:12). Kadesh-barnea lay within its confines (ch 13:26) and possibly also Elath on the Red Sea (*see* Elath). The Wilderness of Zin seems to have been part of, or to have overlapped, it (compare Num 13:26 with ch 20:1). Deut 33:2 and Hab 3:3 indicate that it was a mountainous country. These data indicate that the "wilderness of Paran" was that highland desert extending south from Kadesh-barnea to the granite mountains of Sinai. The area is now called *et-Tih.* This highland wilderness rises to an elevation of from 2,000 to 2,500 ft. above sea level (Map V, B/C-6). Ishmael dwelt in this wilderness (Gen 21:21) before his descendants spread into other parts of Arabia, and the children of Israel spent 38 years in this area. It was from this wilderness that the spies were sent out and to which they returned after the conclusion of their mission (Num 13:1-3, 25, 26). David spent some time as a fugitive in this wilderness (1 Sa 25:1).

Parbar (pär′bär). [Heb. *parbar.*] The transliteration of an unidentified Hebrew word which, according to 2 Ki 23:11, where it is translated "suburb" (KJV) and "precinct" (RSV), designates a structure west of, that is behind, the Temple. This structure contained chambers in or near which horses dedicated to the sun were stabled. In 1 Chr 26:18 *parbar* is transliterated by both the RSV and KJV.

Parched Corn. See Parched Grain.

Parched Grain, KJV **Parched Corn.** Roasted grain, a common item of diet in Bible lands (Lev 23:14; Ruth 2:14; 1 Sa 17:17; etc.).

Parchment. [Gr. *membrana* from the Latin *membrana.*] Writing material made of the skin of young animals, mainly lambs and goats, prepared by a more refined method of tanning than that used for the production of ordinary leather. Ancient tradition (Pliny *Hist. Nat.* xiii. 21) claims that the process of making parchment was invented in Pergamum (from Pergamum through the Latin and Old French comes the English "parchment") during the reign of King Eumenes II (197-160/59 B.C.), when King Ptolemy V of Egypt halted the export of papyrus, the most common writing material of antiquity. However, dated parchment documents from the beginning of the 2d cent. B.C. have been discovered in Dura Europus on the Euphrates, showing that parchment was also produced in other countries at an early date. Josephus (*Ant.* xii. 2. 11) describes Hebrew scriptures written on parchment extant in his time, but the Hebrew manuscripts recently discovered at the Dead Sea are written almost exclusively on ordinary leather, with very little parchment represented. Paul possessed parchment manuscripts which he had left in Troas at the time he departed suddenly for Rome. In requesting Timothy to bring them with him Paul used the Latin loan word *membrana,* "skin" (2 Ti 4:13). When the Christian church became rich in the 4th cent., many Bibles for churches were written on parchment codices, and the famous *Bible manuscripts of the 4th and 5th cent., the Codices Sinaiticus, Vaticanus, and Alexandrinus, etc., are of this material. Since parchment was always expensive, old manuscripts were occasionally erased and used for a second time. Such a manuscript is called a "codex rescriptus" or "palimpsest." The best-known palimpsest is the Codex Ephraemi in Paris, which contains sermons of Ephraim the Syrian written over an erased Bible text of the 5th century.

Parents. This term appears only in the NT, the idea being indicated in the OT by expressions such as "father" and "mother" (see Ex 20:12; cf. Eph 6:1). The Hebrew plural for "fathers" includes both fathers and mothers, and often grandparents and other ancestors as well. Various admonitions concerning the duties of parents to their children and children to their parents are given: Children are admonished to obey their parents "in the Lord" (Eph 6:1); parents, in turn, are obligated to provide for their children (2 Cor 12:14), but the children or grandchildren (KJV "nephews") of a widow should learn to care for her (1 Ti 5:4). Jesus prophesied that the time would come when children would betray their believing parents (Mt 10:21; Mk 13:12) and, conversely, parents would deliver their believing children (Lk 21:16). Paul predicted that last-day children would be disobedient to parents (2 Ti 3:2).

Park. A term occurring once (Ec 2:5, RSV) as the rendering of the Heb. *pardes*, "park," "forest," "orchard." *See* Eden, 2; Paradise.

Parlour. A rendering of: (1) the Heb. *'aliyah* (Jgs 3:20, 23-25, KJV), "roof chamber"; (2) the Heb. *lishkah* (1 Sa 9:22, KJV), "hall," apparently a room attached to the high place where sacrificial meals were eaten; (3) the Heb. *cheder* (1 Chr 28:11, KJV), "dark room." The word apparently refers to a private inner chamber in the Temple, as planned by King David.

Parmashta (pär-măsh'tá). [Heb. *Parmashta'*, a Persian name meaning "first," or "greatest."] One of the sons of Haman (Est 9:9).

Parmenas (pär'mē-năs). [Gr. *Parmenas*, a name attested in Greek inscriptions.] One of the 7 appointed to look after the Greek-speaking widows and the poor in general (Acts 6:5). He was probably a Hellenist, that is, a Greek-speaking Jew.

Parnach (pär'năk). [Heb. *Parnak*.] A Zebulunite whose son was chosen to help divide the Promised Land for inheritance (Num 34:18, 25).

Parosh (pā'rŏsh), KJV once **Pharosh** (fā'rŏsh). [Heb. *Par'osh*, "flea." The name is attested on a Phoenician seal and appears as *Puragûsh* on a cuneiform tablet discovered at Taanach.]

1. The ancestral head of a large postexilic family, 2,172 members of which returned with Zerubbabel from Babylonia (Ezr 2:3; Neh 7:8), and another 150 in the time of Ezra (Ezr 8:3). Some members of this family had married foreign wives in the time of Ezra (ch 10:18, 25). One member of this family assisted Nehemiah in the rebuilding of Jerusalem's wall (Neh 3:25).

2. A man who set his seal to Nehemiah's covenant (Neh 10:14).

Parshandatha (pär'shăn-dā'thá). [Heb. *Parshandatha'*, a Persian name of uncertain meaning.] One of the sons of Haman (Est 9:7, 10).

Parsin. *See* Mene.

Parthians (pär'thĭ-ănz). [Gr. *Parthoi*.] A people first appearing in history in the time of the Persian Darius I, when they inhabited a territory in the 16th satrapy (Herodotus iii. 93) of the Persian Empire. This area lay southeast of the Caspian Sea and was bounded by Hyrcania in the north, Media in the west, Carmania in the south, and by several provinces in the east, of which Bactria was the most important (Map XII, C/D-9/10/11). After the conquest of the Persian Empire by Alexander, Parthia became part of his empire. Later it became part of the kingdom of the Seleucids. About 250 B.C. the Parthians revolted under Arsaces I and became an independent state (Map XIII, B/C-7/8), beginning their own era (the Arsacid era) with the year 247 B.C. The successors of Arsaces are generally referred to as Arsacids. Mithridates I (c. 174 - c. 138 B.C.) made tremendous conquests in the east and west and transformed Parthia from a mere kingdom into an empire, which reached from the Indus in the east to the great bend of the Euphrates in the west. Its chief city was Ctesiphon on the Tigris, across the river from Seleucia (Map XIII, C-5). After the breakup of the Seleucid kingdom, the Parthians, whose territories adjoined Roman possessions in eastern Asia Minor and in Syria, became the most formidable foes of the Romans. They frequently clashed with Roman armies, sometimes defeating them severely. The Parthians were never really subdued, although they were occasionally defeated. In 40 B.C. they invaded Asia Minor and Syria. Jerusalem was taken and plundered, and the high priest, Hyrcanus II, and Phasael, the tetrarch of Jerusalem and brother of Herod, were carried away captive. The Parthians placed Antigonus, the last of the Hasmonaeans (40-37 B.C.), on the throne of Judea, but Herod the Great gained control of Palestine in 37 B.C. After a continuation of almost 5 cent., the Parthian kingdom, weakened by luxury and dissipation, was overthrown by the Persians under Ardashir of the family of Sassan (A.D. 226), who founded the Sassanian empire.

The "Parthians" who were present at the outpouring of the Holy Spirit (Acts 2:9) were probably not real Parthians, but Jews who lived in Parthia and who had come as pilgrims to Jerusalem to celebrate the feast of Pentecost.

Partition, Middle Wall of. [Gr. *to mesotoichon tou phragmou*, literally, "the middle wall of the partition," perhaps meaning "the middle wall which is the partition." The RSV translation, "dividing wall of hostility," is partly interpretative.] An expression used metaphorically of the Jewish exclusivism and legalism that separated between Jew and Gentile. Paul asserted that this middle wall of separation was down, through the abolition of the "law of commandments contained in ordinances," and that Jew and Gentile have met at the cross and have been made one (Eph 2:11-15).

This figure may have been derived from the balustrade, or barrier, in the Temple area that separated the lowest and outermost Court of the Gentiles from the more exclusive and inner courts of the Jews, a barrier beyond which no Gentile dared to venture, except on penalty of death (see fig. 487).

Partridge. [Heb. *qore'*, "crier," or "caller."] The Hebrew term is generally identified with the partridge. This game fowl frequents the mountains and hills of Palestine. Two species of partridge occur in the Holy Land, and both may be referred to in the Scriptures. The desert or Hey's sand partridge (*Ammoperdix hayi*) is thought to be the only species occurring in the area where David was when pursued by King Saul as a hunter would pursue a partridge in the mountains (1 Sa 26:20). The chukar partridge (*Caccabis chukar*) is a prominently marked, large bird that is widely distributed in the hills of Palestine. It has been suggested that the people of Jeremiah's time thought that the partridge appropriated eggs or young that were not its own, and so the prophet compares the wealthy man who gathers riches that are not his and is cut down in the midst of his nefarious dealings, to this bird (Jer 17:11). There is, however, some obscurity in the Hebrew text of this passage.

Paruah (pả-rōō'ả). [Heb. *Parûach,* "blooming."] The father of Solomon's supply officer in the territory of Issachar (1 Ki 4: 7, 17).

Parvaim (pär-vā'ĭm). [Heb. *Parwayim.*] The region from which Solomon procured gold for the decoration of the Temple (2 Chr 3:6); not identified. It was possibly in Arabia.

Pasach (pā'săk). [Heb. *Pasak,* meaning uncertain.] An Asherite (1 Chr 7:33).

Pas-dammim. *See* Ephes-dammim.

Paseah (pả-sē'ả), KJV once **Phaseah** (fả-sē'ả). [Heb. *Paseach,* "lame."]
1. A Judahite (1 Chr 4:1, 12).
2. The ancestral head of a family of

Temple servants, or Nethinim, some members of which returned from Babylonia with Zerubbabel (Ezr 2:49; Neh 7: 51). Joiada (KJV "Jehoiada"), a son of Paseah, and presumably of this family, is mentioned in Neh 3:6 as repairing the Old Gate of Jerusalem in Nehemiah's time.

Pashhur (păsh'hẽr), KJV **Pashur** (pash'ẽr). [Heb. *Pashchûr,* apparently from the Egyptian *Psh Ḥr,* "portion of Horus." The name is attested on ancient Hebrew seals.]
1. A prince, the son of Malchiah, and possibly the grandson of King Zedekiah. He was a strong opponent of the prophet Jeremiah (Jer 21:1; 38:1, 4). It is possible that the Malchiah into whose dungeon Jeremiah was thrown after his arrest was Pashhur's father (ch 38:6).
2. A priest, the son of Immer. He put Jeremiah in the stocks overnight because of the messages of doom the prophet had pronounced over the city and the nation (Jer 20:1-3). Jeremiah then predicted Pashhur's captivity (vs 4-6).
3. A man whose son, Gedaliah, was an enemy of Jeremiah (Jer 38:1). This Pashhur, whose father is not named, may be identical with one of the other persons named Pashhur.
4. A priest, son of Malchijah (1 Chr 9: 10, 12); probably not identical with Pashhur, 1, whose companion, not he, is called a priest in Jer 21:1.
5. The ancestral head of a priestly family, 1,247 members of which returned from Babylonia with Zerubbabel (Ezr 2: 2, 38; Neh 7:7, 41). Six members of this family had married foreign wives in the time of Ezra (Ezr 10:22).
6. A priest who set his seal to Nehemiah's covenant (Neh 10:3).

Pashur. *See* Pashhur.

Passages, The. *See* Abarim.

Passengers. A rendering of a form of the Heb. *'abar,* "to pass by," "to pass over" (Prov 9:15; Eze 39:11, 14, 15; KJV). The term is used with the connotation of "wayfarer," "passer-by," or "traveler."

Passion. A term appearing frequently in the RSV (only rarely in the KJV) with its usual meaning of strong emotion or desire (Jas 4:1; 1 Pe 1:14; etc.). Both versions use the term in Acts 1:3 in the obsolete sense of "suffering," as applying to the suffering of Jesus on the cross, or His suffering between the night of the Last Supper and His death, including the agonies of Gethsemane. The word found its way into the English versions through the influence of the Latin Vulgate.

Passover. [Heb. *pesach,* a transliteration either of the Egyptian *p3 šḥ,* "the smiting" (Couroyer, *RB* 62 [1955], 481-496), or of *pashḥu,* a word occurring in the *Amarna Letters describing the results of the formation of a covenant (Mendenhall, *BASOR* 133 [1954], 29). Gr. *pascha.*] The festival instituted at the Exodus to commemorate the night of the Israelites' escape from Egypt, when all the first-born of the Egyptians were slain. Immediately before the departure from Egypt, God instructed Moses that "this month" (Abib, later called Nisan) was to be the 1st month of the year; that on the 10th of this month each family or larger group should set aside a lamb; and that on the 14th they should kill it at evening and eat it that night. Detailed instructions (Ex 12:1-28) were given for this ceremonial meal that was to become an annual observance. The lamb was to be slain by each family, presumably at home, and the blood sprinkled on the lintel and doorposts as a sign that that house should be passed over when the homes of the Egyptians were invaded by sudden death. The lamb, roasted whole, was to be eaten that same night with bitter herbs and unleavened bread; it was to be eaten in haste, the family standing, dressed for travel, with their staffs in their hands. In that same night the plague of death at midnight induced Pharaoh to "thrust out" the Israelites in haste before morning on the 15th (Ex 12:12, 29-33; Num 33: 3; Deut 16:1).

The regulations for the Passover and the succeeding 7-day Feast of Unleavened Bread were repeated in the Levitical law of festivals at Sinai (Lev 23:5-8). Provision was made for a Passover on the 14th of the 2d month for those who were prevented by travel or by ritual uncleanness from participating at the regular time (Num 9:10-13). Later, the Passover was celebrated only at the central sanctuary, eventually at Jerusalem (Deut 16:2, 5, 6). Although only adult males were required to attend (Ex 23:14-17), the families might go voluntarily, as in the case of Joseph, Mary, and the child Jesus (Lk 2:41-43). In the time of Christ the Passover lambs were killed by the priests at the Temple on the afternoon of the 14th, and their owners then took them home for roasting. By that time the procedure was prescribed in detail, including the preliminary ritual search of the house for any remaining bits of leaven, the kind and order of the dishes served at the supper, the number of cups of wine, the hymns, the recital of the Exodus story, and the prayers. The participants no longer girded themselves as for a journey and they ate sitting or reclining instead of standing, since those signs of haste were not appropriate after they were no longer strangers and wanderers but were dwelling in their own land.

Jesus is recorded as attending several Passovers, the last being the occasion upon which He instituted the Lord's Supper (Mt 26:18-30). The word "Passover" came to be used to refer to the whole period from the 14th of the month through the 21st, including the killing of the lamb, the Passover supper, and the whole Feast of Unleavened Bread following; conversely the term "Unleavened Bread" was used of the whole period, including the 14th (Lk 22:1, 7).

Besides being a memorial of the Exodus, the Passover feast, centering around the sacrificed lamb, pointed forward to Christ, "the Lamb of God, which taketh away the sin of the world" (Jn 1:29). Furthermore, instructions given to Moses that no bone of the Passover lamb was to be broken (Ex 12:46; Num 9:12) doubtless found an antitypical fulfillment in the fact that Jesus' bones were not broken (cf. Jn 19:36; Ps 34:20). Paul directly declares Christ to be "our passover [lamb]," "sacrificed for us" (1 Cor 5:7).

Pastor. [Heb. *ro'eh,* a form of the verb *ra'ah,* "to feed," "to graze," "to pasture," "to tend," sheep or cattle; Gr. *poimēn,* "shepherd."] A shepherd; figuratively, a leader, whether civil or spiritual. In Old English the word "pastor" (from a form of the Latin *pascere,* "to pasture," "to feed") was equivalent in meaning to the Anglo-Saxon "shepherd," a herder of sheep. When used literally of a herder of sheep, *ro'eh* is commonly translated "shepherd" (Ex 2:17, 20; etc.).

Patara (păt'á-rá). [Gr. *Patara.*] A Lycian seaport famous for its oracle of the Apollo Patareus. It was situated east of the mouth of the Xanthus, a site now called *Gelemish.* Extensive ruins bear witness to the former greatness of this city. A triumphal arch contains the inscription, "Patara, the capital of the Lycian nation." Paul changed ships in this port city on his voyage to Jerusalem when returning from his 3d Missionary Journey, probably in A.D. 58 (Acts 21:1, 2). Map XX, B-4.

Pathros (păth'rŏs). [Heb. *Pathrôs,* from the Egyptian *Pȝ-tȝ-rśy,* "the southland," called *Paturisi* in cuneiform inscriptions.] A term used by the prophets (Is 11:11; Jer 44:1, 15) as a designation apparently for Upper Egypt (Map XI, D-3). Eze 29:14 points to Pathros as the original home-land of the Egyptians. This agrees with Egyptian tradition, according to which the 1st king, Menes, who united the na-tion, came from the old Upper Egyptian city of This. During the period of the Exile and at least to the end of the 5th cent. B.C., a colony of Jews lived on the Nile island of Elephantine, situated at the 1st cataract and used as a fortress of the southern border of Egypt. Many rec-ords of these Jews, written in Aramaic, have been discovered on this island in modern times. These records, known as the Elephantine papyri, shed much light on the books of Ezra and Nehemiah.

Lit.: E. G. Kraeling, *The Brooklyn Museum Aramaic Papyri* (New Haven, 1953); *SDACom* 3:79-83.

Pathrusim (păth-rōō'sĭm). [Heb. *Pathrusîm.*] The people of *Pathros, or Upper Egypt, descendants of Mizraim, or Egypt (Gen 10:14; 1 Chr 1:12).

Patience. [Gr. *makrothumia,* "patience," "steadfastness," "endurance," "forbear-ance"; *hupomonē,* "patience," "endur-ance," "fortitude," "steadfastness," "per-severance."] Patience is the quality of steadfast endurance, in confident expec-tation of some desired end, despite dif-ficult, discouraging, and disappointing circumstances, and often suffering. The KJV renders *makrothumia* as "longsuffer-ing" (Rom 2:4; 9:22; etc.) and the RSV usually as "patience." NT writers often include patience in the list of Christian graces (Rom 5:3, 4; 2 Cor 6:4; 1 Ti 6:11; 2 Pe 1:6; KJV; 2 Ti 3:10). Patience is based on hope (Rom 8:24, 25; 1 Th 1:3; KJV). In view of the fact that "we must through much tribulation enter into the kingdom of God" (Acts 14:22), and par-ticularly because entrance into the com-ing kingdom of glory involves a pro-longed period of waiting, patience or steadfast endurance becomes a cardinal Christian virtue (see Heb 10:36; Jas 1:3, 4; KJV). Patience ever reminds us that "the sufferings of this present time are not worthy to be compared with the glory which shall be revealed" (Rom 8:18). The term "patience" appears only once in the OT (Prov 25:15, RSV), a render-ing of the Heb. *'orek 'appayim,* "for-bearance."

372. Air view of the island of Patmos

Patmos (păt'mŏs). [Gr. *Patmos.*] A barren, volcanic island in the Aegean Sea, belong-ing to the Sporades. Its coast is greatly indented (fig. 372). The island is about 10 mi. long and 6 mi. across at its widest part. The Romans used it as a penal colony. John, the author of the book of Revelation, was banished to this island (Rev 1:9) in the time of Domitian (*c.* A.D. 95). According to tradition, the cave in which John had his visions is near the monastery of St. John, founded in A.D. 1088 by the monk Christodulus on the authorization of the emperor Alexius Comnenus. An embalmed body, alleged to be that of John, is exhibited there. Map XX, B-4.

373. Seashore at Patmos

Patriarch. [Gr. *patriarchēs,* "first (or fore-most) father"; *patēr,* "father."] Father or ruler of a tribe or family. The patriarchs mentioned in Scripture were the founders of the Jewish race and religion. The term is applied to Abraham (Heb 7:4), the 12 sons of Jacob (Acts 7:8, 9), and David

(Acts 2:29). The heads of families previous to Moses' time, especially the line of godly men given in Gen 5, are often referred to by this title, although not in the Bible. In a patriarchy the right to govern resided first in the founder of the race or tribe and, in succeeding generations, in the *first-born son. During the patriarchal dispensation before the establishment of the theocracy, the head of each family not only governed but also acted as priest of his household.

Patrimony. Property inherited from one's father. The expression occurs once (Deut 18:8) in a passage the Hebrew of which is obscure. The discussion is concerning a Levite moving from one place to another, who at the new abode was to be given an equal share of gifts with the Levites living in the place. He was also permitted to retain the results of the sale of his "patrimony" (vs 6-8), if this is the correct interpretation of the obscure Hebrew passage. When the land of Canaan was divided among the tribes of Israel, the Levites had "no inheritance among their brethren," for the Lord was to be their inheritance (v 2). However, the people were to bring certain gifts to the Levitical priests (vs 3, 4).

Patrobas (păt′rṓ-bás). [Gr. *Patrobas,* a short form of *Patrobios,* "life of the father." The name is attested in Greek inscriptions.] A member of the church in Rome to whom the apostle Paul sent greetings (Rom 16:14).

Pau (pā′ û). [Heb. *Pa'û,* meaning uncertain.] A town in Edom, residence city of King Hadar (Gen 36:39). The name is spelled Pai (pā′ī) [Heb. *Pa'î*] in 1 Chr 1:50, probably by a scribal confusion of the Hebrew letters *w* and *y,* which in ancient manuscripts are almost indistinguishable.

Paul (pôl). [Gr. *Paulos,* from the Latin *Paulus,* a Roman surname meaning "little," or "small."] The great apostle to the Gentiles. He is introduced in the Bible as Saul (Gr. *Saulos,* from the Heb. *Sha'ûl,* "asked [of God]," or "lent [to God]"; Acts 7:58) and is referred to by that name in the narrative of the book of Acts through ch 13:9. There has been considerable speculation as to why, halfway through the book of Acts, Saul is abruptly referred to as Paul, and is called by that name exclusively from that point on, except when he himself relates the story of his conversion (chs 22:7, 13; 26:14). A simple and plausible answer is that he, like others (Acts 1:23; 13:1; Col 4:11;

etc.), had more than one name; in his case a Hebrew name, Saul, and a Grecized Roman name, *Paulos,* or Paul. His Hebrew name was probably commonly used in his home and in his intercourse with Jews. His Greco-Roman name would be in keeping with the Hellenistic influence and environment of the city where he was born, and with his enviable status as a Roman citizen. Later, when he began his work among the Gentiles, it was to his advantage to be known as Paul. It is worthy of note that up to Acts 13 Paul is mentioned only in reference to his contact with the Jews. But in that chapter the record of his activities among the Gentiles begins, as does also the use of his Gentile name, Paul.

I. Paul, the Man.

1. *Background.* By birth, religion, education, and sentiment Paul was a Hebrew; so much so that in spite of his early contacts with Greek and Roman culture and philosophy he could call himself a "Hebrew of the Hebrews" (Php 3:5). He

374. The city wall of Damascus near the traditional spot of Paul's escape from the city. The lower courses of masonry are ancient

was of the tribe of Benjamin (Rom 11:1), and was perhaps a namesake of Saul, the 1st king of Israel, who was also a Benjamite (1 Sa 9:1, 2; Acts 13:21). Little is known of his family. His father was a Roman citizen (Acts 22:28), and probably a Pharisee (ch 23:6). Just how Paul's father gained his Roman citizenship is unknown, but there were certain procedures whereby a prominent Jew in a city such as Tarsus could become a Roman citizen. Assuming that he gained his citizenship through these provisions, we may then also assume that Paul came from a family of some importance. He had at least one sister (ch 23:16). In Rom 16:7, 21 he refers to several men as being his "kinsmen." But this term, a translation of the Gr. *suggeneis,* could mean simply fellow countrymen, so that it is uncertain whether blood relatives are referred to. Paul may have been disowned by his family after he became a Christian (cf. Php 3:8), but if so he does not mention it.

Paul was born in Asia Minor, in the prosperous metropolis of *Tarsus (Acts 21:39; see fig. 475), a city noted for its philosophy, science, education, and culture—a culture in which there was a mingling of Greek, Roman, and Jewish elements. The date of his birth cannot be approximated with any degree of certainty. When he is 1st mentioned in ch 7:58 he is referred to as a "young man" (Gr. *neanias*). However, this broad term, used of men anywhere between the ages of 20 and 40, offers little in ascertaining Paul's age.

According to a tradition from the 2d cent., Paul's family lived originally in Gischala, of Galilee, but were captured by the Romans and taken as slaves to Tarsus about 4 B.C., where they later gained their freedom and Roman citizenship. If this is so, Paul was born after these events, for he was a Roman citizen by birth (Acts 22:28).

2. *Education.* There was probably a synagogue school in Tarsus that Paul attended. In the multilingual city of Tarsus he learned not only Hebrew and the spoken language of his people, *Aramaic (Acts 21:40; 22:2), but also Greek (ch 21:37), and probably Latin. He learned tent-making, probably from his father, by which he later made his living (Acts 18:1, 3; cf. ch 20:34; 1 Cor 4:12; 1 Th 2:9; 2 Th 3:8). He went as a youth to Jerusalem (Acts 26:4) and sat at the feet of the most renowned rabbi and Pharisee of his day, the great Gamaliel (ch 22:3; cf. ch 5:

34). Under his instruction Paul was "taught according to the perfect manner of the law" (Acts 22:3; cf. ch 24:14), and as a result lived "after the most straitest sect" of the Pharisees (ch 26:5). So brilliant a scholar was he, and so ardent for the doctrines and traditions of Judaism, that he went beyond many of his peers in learning and zeal (Gal 1:14); and in his fanatical hatred of the Christians, at least, he outstripped his master, Gamaliel (Acts 8:3; 9:1; cf. 5:34-39). There can be little doubt that he was marked for great things by the leaders of the Jewish nation.

3. *Personal Appearance and Health.* It would appear that, while Paul was intellectually impressive, physically he was not prepossessing. His enemies said of him "his bodily presence is weak, and his speech contemptible" (2 Cor 10:10). Tradition describes him as being short, stooped, and bowlegged. He seems to have suffered from some chronic affliction (2 Cor 12:7-10; Gal 4:13); many believe this was some malady connected with his eyes, basing their conclusion on the facts that he generally dictated his letters (see 2 Th 3:17), that he referred to himself as writing with large letters (Gal 6:11, RSV), and that he mentioned the willingness of the Galatian believers to pluck out their own eyes and give them to him, if it were possible (ch 4:15). Other afflictions have been suggested, but Biblical evidence is insufficient definitely to establish what Paul's "thorn in the flesh" was.

II. Paul, the Convert.

1. *First Contacts With Christianity.* Paul's 1st known contact with Christianity was in connection with the death of Stephen. It has been conjectured that he was one of the Cilicians who, with others, were bested in debate by Stephen (Acts 6:9, 10; cf. ch 21:39). He apparently cast no stones at Stephen, but "was consenting unto his death" (ch 8:1), and watched the garments of the witnesses (ch 7:58). The mob action that resulted in the stoning of Stephen marked the beginning of the 1st period of persecution that ravaged the infant church; and Saul, it seems, was foremost in the persecution. In a fanatical frenzy of hatred against the Christians (ch 26:11), intensified by a pricking conscience (v 14), he dragged them from their houses and thrust them into prison (ch 8:3); he punished them in the synagogues (chs 22:19; 26:11) and gave his consent to their death (chs 22:4; 26:10). Paul carried on this harassment first in Jerusalem (chs 8:1, 3; 26:10), then

followed the scattered believers to other cities and hounded them there "beyond measure" (Acts 8:4; 26:11; Gal 1:13).

2. *Conversion.* It was on one of these persecuting excursions that the course of Paul's life was spectacularly and completely changed. Hearing that there were Christians in Damascus, he sought from the high priest letters—evidently letters of extradition—authorizing him to arrest and bring to Jerusalem any Christian found in that city (Acts 9:1, 2). There are 3 accounts of subsequent experiences on that journey: chs 9:1-9; 22:4-11; 26:9-18. The 1st is in the 3d person; the others in the 1st, recounted by Paul himself, one to a Jewish mob in Jerusalem, the other to King Agrippa and his sister, Bernice. As Paul approached Damascus at midday with a company of men to aid him in his murderous designs, he was suddenly surrounded by a blinding light, brighter than the sun. Paul and his companions fell to the earth (ch 26:14), and a voice, identifying its owner as Jesus of Nazareth, inquired, "Saul, Saul, why persecutest thou me?" adding, "It is hard for thee to kick against the pricks." Paul, overwhelmed by the experience, asked what he was to do, upon which Jesus informed him that he was to become a witness for Him to the Gentiles (vs 16, 17). He was instructed to go into Damascus, where he would receive further information. Meanwhile his amazed and fearful companions, who had arisen from the ground (see ch 9:7), understood nothing of what was taking place, for although they saw the light and heard the words of Jesus, they could not understand what was being said (cf. chs 9:7; 22:9). Rising to his feet, Paul discovered that he was blind.

In that condition Paul was led by his companions to the home of a certain Judas in Damascus, where he stayed 3 days without food or drink (Acts 9:8, 9, 11). While Paul was engaged in prayer, Jesus appeared in vision to one Ananias and directed him to the home of Judas, on the "street which is called Straight," where he would find Paul, who had been given a vision of his coming. Ananias respectfully reminded Jesus of Paul's acts of persecution, but was informed that the erstwhile persecutor had been chosen of God (vs 11-16). Following instructions, Ananias found Paul and laid his hands upon him, whereupon Paul's sight was immediately restored and he received the gift of the Holy Spirit and was baptized (vs 17, 18). See figs. 120, 121.

How long Paul remained in Damascus after this is not known. The record seems to indicate that it was a brief period (Acts 9:19). We know that he associated with the Christians there. Also, true to his character—and to the wonderment of those who knew him—he began to preach in the synagogues the Christ he had once vilified but had recently come to worship (vs 19-21). So powerfully and convincingly did he preach that none could defeat his logic or deny his power (v 22).

3. *Preparation and Early Preaching.* The narrative in Acts omits the next event in Paul's life, but Paul refers to it in the book of Galatians, where he says that following his conversion and his first brief evangelistic venture, he went into Arabia and returned to Damascus (Gal 1:17), before his trip to Jerusalem recorded in Acts 9:26; Gal 1:18. The exact area referred to as "Arabia" is unknown, as is the length of time he remained there. This period of retirement gave him time for meditation upon the great change that had come into his life, solitude in which to re-examine, prayerfully and carefully, the whole foundation of his new convictions in the light of Scripture, and the opportunity to settle for all time his faith in Christ and in His gospel.

Following this apparent time of inaction, Paul once again returned to Damascus (Gal 1:17), from which point the narrative continues in Acts 9. Paul, it would seem, resumed his preaching in the synagogues with the same results as before (v 22). Consequently the Jews laid plans to murder him (vs 23, 24). They were supported in their scheme by the governor of the city, who served under the Arabian ruler *Aretas (2 Cor 11:32, 33). Since Aretas ruled that area probably between A.D. 37 and 39, this event must have occurred somewhere within this period. However, the soldiers, who were watching the gates to prevent Paul's escape from the city, were frustrated in their design, for some of the local believers lowered Paul in a basket from a window of a house built on the city wall, thus enabling him to evade his enemies (Acts 9:25; 2 Cor 11:33). See fig. 374.

4. *Visit to the Apostles at Jerusalem.* With his opportunity for working in Damascus at an end, Paul turned his eyes toward Jerusalem. Three years had now elapsed since his conversion, but up to this time he had had no contact with any of the church leaders (Gal 1:17, 18), which fact he later offered as proof that

his gospel had originated, not with the disciples of Christ, but with Christ Himself (Gal 1:10-12; cf. 1 Cor 15:3-8). His primary reason for going there was to see Peter (Gal 1:18). On arriving in the city he endeavored to join with Peter and the other believers as a Christian brother, but swiftly discovered that 3 years had not sufficed to dim the memory of his previous persecutions, or to remove their fear and suspicion of him (Acts 9:26). The resulting impasse was broken by the Cypriote, *Barnabas, who showed his confidence in Paul's account of his experience by relating it to the others in Paul's presence (v 27).

Paul demonstrated the genuineness of his experience by preaching Jesus in the city of Jerusalem. His incontrovertible logic aroused the ire of certain Hellenistic Jews, who set about to take his life (Acts 9:29). In a later account of his experience (ch 22:17-21), Paul told how God appeared to him in a vision in the Temple, and over his remonstrances directed him to leave Jerusalem, informing him that the Jews would not receive his message, and that he was to be sent to the Gentiles. His brethren immediately accompanied him to the seaport of Caesarea (ch 9:30), about 53 mi. northwest of Jerusalem. There they probably placed him on board ship to ensure his escape from his enemies.

5. *In the Regions of Syria and Cilicia, and Antioch.* From Jerusalem, where he had stayed 15 days (Gal 1:18), Paul went into the regions of "Syria and Cilicia" (v 21). His activities during the next few years are not revealed in Scripture. We may well suppose that he was active in the ministry in Tarsus and the surrounding areas (see Acts 11:25; Gal 1:21-23). It may have been during this period that he had the visions alluded to in 2 Cor 12:2-4. In v 2 he describes it as an experience he had 14 years before the writing of 2 Corinthians. That epistle was written about A.D. 57, which would point to about 43 as the date of the vision. Paul was at Tarsus or the surrounding area from about 38 to 44, which would bring the vision within that period.

Meanwhile, during Paul's stay in Cilicia, Christianity had been progressing in other areas. A growing interest had developed at Antioch in Syria, and Barnabas had been dispatched from Jerusalem to foster it (Acts 11:19-24). Deciding that he needed help, he journeyed to Tarsus, found Paul, and brought him back to Antioch with him (vs 25, 26). Paul and

Barnabas worked together there for a full year, with noteworthy success.

As they labored in Antioch certain ones having the prophetic gift came from Jerusalem (Acts 11:27). One of these, by the name of Agabus, was divinely inspired to predict a worldwide famine (v 28). As a result of this the believers in Antioch determined to send relief to the Christians of Judea. They chose Paul and Barnabas to take the contribution to Judea (vs 29, 30). Upon the fulfillment of their mission, Paul and Barnabas returned to Antioch, taking with them John Mark, a relative of Barnabas (Acts 12:25; cf. Col 4:10).

III. Paul, the Foreign Missionary. While at Antioch the 2d time, Paul received the call that started him upon his great missionary journeys into Asia Minor and Europe, which earned for him the title of "Apostle to the Gentiles." As certain ones of the church "ministered to the Lord, and fasted," they were commanded by the Holy Spirit to set apart Paul and Barnabas for a special work (Acts 13:2). This was done, accompanied by solemn fasting and prayer; then, directed by the Holy Spirit, those apostles set out upon the 1st Missionary Journey, accompanied by John Mark (vs 3, 5).

1. *First Missionary Journey.* Going to Seleucia, which was Antioch's seaport, some 16 mi. from that city, they took ship to the island of Cyprus (Acts 13:4).

(1) *Cyprus.* Landing at Salamis (see fig. 412), on the east coast of Cyprus (Map XX, B-5; follow red line 1 westward), they began to preach in the Jewish synagogues (Acts 13:5), as Paul's custom was (cf. chs 9:20; 17:1, 2; 18:4; etc.). They traversed the island from east to west, and came to the city of Paphos (ch 13:6). Paphos was the headquarters of the Roman proconsul, or *governor, of the island—Sergius Paulus, a man of sense and discernment (v 7). Sergius Paulus was attended by a certain Jew named Bar-Jesus, or Elymas, who was a charlatan and a sorcerer (vs 6, 8). The governor heard of the preaching of Paul and Barnabas and, wishing to hear the gospel, sent for them (v 7). Fearful of losing any influence he might have had over Sergius Paulus, Bar-Jesus opposed the apostles in the presence of the governor (v 8), whereupon Paul (it is here that he is for the 1st time called "Paul"), "filled with the Holy Ghost," fixed his eyes intently upon the sorcerer, bitterly condemned him for misrepresenting and opposing God, and predicted that he

would be temporarily blind. The prediction was instantaneously fulfilled (Acts 13:9-11). This remarkable incident convinced the governor of the truth of the gospel, and he accepted it (v 12).

(2) *Perga*. Following their stay in Paphos, Paul and his group embarked for Perga (Acts 13:13), a city near the coast of Asia Minor, in a northwesterly direction from Paphos. Here John Mark, doubtless discouraged at the hardships and difficulties, left them and returned to Jerusalem (v 13).

(3) *Antioch of Pisidia*. Paul and Barnabas continued on to Pisidian Antioch (Acts 13:14), a city some 100 mi. north of Perga, in the Taurus Mountains. Invited to speak in the synagogue on the Sabbath, Paul preached of the resurrection of Christ (vs 15-41). The sermon made such an impression that he was invited to preach to the Gentiles the following Sabbath (v 42). On this occasion "almost the whole city" came to hear the gospel (v 44). This aroused the jealousy and opposition of the Jews (v 45); thereupon Paul stated that, seeing the Jews spurned salvation, he would preach instead to the Gentiles (vs 46, 47). See fig. 16.

It is not known how long Paul and Barnabas labored in this region. In any case it was long enough for the whole area surrounding the city to learn of the gospel (Acts 13:49). Their success finally aroused the active opposition of the Jews, who succeeded in persuading the magistrates to expel them from the city (v 50).

(4) *Iconium, Lystra, and Derbe*. Some 80 mi. east-southeast of Antioch was Iconium, the next place where Paul and Barnabas labored. Great success attended their efforts (Acts 14:1), and they preached in that city a "long time," their work being accompanied by miraculous attestations of divine favor (v 3). Meanwhile, the Jews who had rejected their message succeeded in turning many Gentiles against Paul and Barnabas, so that 2 factions arose in the city (vs 2, 4). Finally it was planned to use violence against the apostles (v 5). Hearing of this, they fled to "Lystra and Derbe, cities of Lycaonia" (Acts 14:6; cf. Mt 10:23), about 23 mi. south-southwest, and 52 mi. southeast, of Iconium, respectively.

At Lystra Paul healed a man who had been a lifelong cripple (Acts 14:8-10). This miracle led the superstitious Lystrians to conclude—probably from an ancient myth describing the gods Zeus (Jupiter) and Hermes (Mercury) as visiting

that part of the world—that Barnabas and Paul were Zeus and Hermes (Acts 14:11, 12). They prepared to offer sacrifice, and only with great difficulty was Paul able to dissuade them (vs 13-18). See fig. 309.

The apostle's labors in Lystra ended when Jewish enemies from Antioch and Iconium stirred up a mob, which stoned Paul and dragged him outside the city as dead (Acts 14:19). Miraculously preserved, Paul revived and re-entered the city, but departed the next day, accompanied by Barnabas (v 20).

Paul and Barnabas labored next at Derbe, where they probably remained for some time, for they "made many disciples" (Acts 14:20, 21, RSV). See figs. 131, 132.

(5) *Return to Antioch in Syria*. From Derbe they began to retrace their journey back through Lystra, Iconium, and Pisidian Antioch, visiting each church on the way, strengthening the believers and appointing leaders (Acts 14:21-23). They also preached at Perga, where John Mark had deserted them near the beginning of their itinerary (v 25). Doubtless impatient to return to their home base at Antioch, the apostles embarked from the port of Attalia, a few miles from Perga, and sailed to Antioch in Syria (see Map XX, B-5, red line 1 eastward). Arriving there they recounted to the church the story of their success among the Gentiles (vs 25-27). Thus ended the 1st Missionary Journey, which had probably taken about 2 years to accomplish (*c*. A.D. 45-47). Paul remained in Antioch for some time (v 28), during which he no doubt continued to attract many Gentiles to Christianity.

2. *Judaizers and the Jerusalem Council*. A crisis now developed which, if not quickly resolved, could have greatly hindered the spread of Christianity to the Gentiles. A group of Jewish Christians from Judea visited the church at Antioch and began to teach that circumcision and the keeping of the Mosaic law were necessary for salvation (Acts 15:1). Paul and Barnabas, however, held that circumcision was not necessary for the Gentile converts. As a result "no small dissension and disputation" arose between the 2 parties (v 2). Finally the believers at Antioch decided that the matter should be taken to the leaders of the church at Jerusalem, and that Paul and Barnabas and certain others were to go there (v 2). This move may have been suggested by Paul, who later said that he had received a revela-

tion concerning the matter and had gone up with Barnabas and Titus, a Greek convert, to consult the leaders (Gal 2:2, 3).

Arriving at Jerusalem, Paul and his companions were cordially welcomed by the believers (Acts 15:4). They began to recount how God had blessed the work among the Gentiles, but certain Pharisees, members of the church, soon raised the question of the necessity of circumcision and the keeping of the Mosaic law (v 5). Consequently, a council convened to decide the question (v 6). The matter was debated at length, with Peter, Barnabas, and Paul speaking against pressing the ceremonial law upon the Gentiles (vs 7-12). Their view prevailed, and it was ruled that the Gentile converts should not be expected to be circumcised or to keep the Law of Moses. They were, however, told to abstain from pollutions of idols, fornication, things strangled, and blood (vs 13-21).

Their mission successfully completed, Paul and the rest of the delegation from Antioch returned to that city, accompanied by certain brethren commissioned to go with them, carrying with them letters from the Jerusalem church. The outcome of the meeting was favorably received by the Antioch believers (Acts 15:22-31). The Jerusalem Council was held probably in A.D. 49.

Once again Paul and Barnabas took up their work of teaching and preaching in Antioch (Acts 15:35). It is possible that the sequel to the Jerusalem Council, which is related in Gal 2, took place during this time. Peter came to visit the believers at Antioch, and in keeping with the spirit of the council decision he ate with the Gentiles, a practice that was anathema to the Jews. However, when certain Judaizing Christians arrived in the city, Peter, possibly fearing a repetition of the former disputes on the subject of the ceremonial law, discontinued this practice (Gal 2:11, 12). In this compromise he was joined by Barnabas and others (v 13). Learning of this, Paul severely rebuked him in public for his behavior (vs 14-21).

Paul's mind now turned to the churches of Asia Minor. He suggested to Barnabas that they again visit them (Acts 15:36). Barnabas agreed, with the insistence that John Mark also go with them (v 37), but Paul refused on the ground that Mark had failed them before and was not to be depended upon (v 38). This difference of opinion grew into a contention that

caused the 2 to separate; Paul chose a new traveling companion, Silas, and Barnabas took Mark with him and sailed for Cyprus (Acts 15:39).

3. *Second Missionary Journey.* Paul and Silas now began what is termed Paul's 2d Missionary Journey. Traveling overland (see Map XX, B-6/5, red line ② westward), they called upon the churches in Syria and Cilicia (Acts 15:40, 41). Doubtless they visited the believers in Paul's home town of Tarsus, in the latter province. Arriving in the area of Derbe and Lystra, Paul found another traveling companion, *Timothy, a young man of good reputation, whose mother was Jewish and his father Greek (ch 16:1-3).

(1) *Through Phrygia and Galatia.* From Derbe and Lystra Paul and his fellow missionaries "went through the cities," informing the churches of the decisions arrived at by the Jerusalem Council (Acts 16:4). These decrees, declaring that the Gentiles were not required to observe the ceremonial law, doubtless had much to do with the subsequent growth of the church in that region (v 5).

Paul and his companions next traveled "throughout *Phrygia and the region of Galatia" (Acts 16:6). It was at this time, according to the view adopted by this dictionary, that the church to which the Galatian epistle was addressed was established (*see* Galatia). It was consequently during this itinerary into Galatia that Paul was stricken with the "infirmity of the flesh" referred to in Gal 4:13. Paul planned next to do evangelistic work in the area west of Galatia, known at that time as *Asia (Map XX, B-4), but was forbidden to do so by the Holy Spirit (Acts 16: 6). Consequently, he and his companions turned toward Mysia in the northwest, intending to enter the region of Bithynia (Map XX, A-4/5) and preach there, but these plans were also thwarted by the Spirit (v 7). So they bypassed Bithynia and Mysia and continued their journey until they came to the city of Troas (Map XX, B-4), on the shore of the Aegean Sea (v 8).

(2) *The Call to Macedonia.* At Troas Paul's labors were turned to a new and challenging field. In a night vision he was urged by a man of Macedonia to bring the gospel to that country (Acts 16:9). Immediately he and his companions prepared to answer the call, which they recognized as being from God (v 10). Boarding a ship bound for Neapolis in Macedonia (Map XX, A-3), they arrived at

that city on the 2d day (Acts 16:11). From there they went to Philippi (v 12).

(3) *At Philippi*. There was apparently no Jewish synagogue in Philippi (Map XX, A-3), but learning of a certain place for prayer outside the city beside a river, Paul and his company resorted thither on the Sabbath, and Paul preached to a group of women gathered there (Acts 16: 13). As a result, a woman merchant named Lydia, a halfway *proselyte to Judaism, was converted and, with her household, was baptized. Her house then became the headquarters of Paul and his fellow workers (v 14).

Soon an incident occurred that halted Paul's endeavors in Philippi. A young female slave, supposedly possessing certain supernatural abilities which were used to the financial advantage of her masters, began to follow the missionaries, crying out that they were the "servants of the most high God, which shew unto us the way of salvation" (Acts 16:16, 17). The annoyance reached the point where Paul could tolerate it no longer, so in the name of Jesus he cast out the evil spirit that had been controlling her (v 18). Since her supposed oracular abilities were now destroyed, her masters were deprived of the income she had brought to them. Incensed at Paul and Silas, they dragged the 2 before the civil authorities and accused them, as Jews, of teaching things inimical to the laws of Rome (vs 19-21). This was sufficient to stir up the populace and the authorities against them. They were severely flogged and placed in stocks in an inner dungeon of the prison (vs 22-24). See fig. 381.

At midnight, while Paul and Silas were engaged in prayer and hymns of praise, a sudden earthquake shook the prison, threw open the doors, and released the fetters of all the prisoners (Acts 16:25, 26), probably by loosening the chains from the walls to which they were fastened. The prison keeper, awakened by the earthquake and seeing the doors open, concluded that the prisoners, for whom he was apparently responsible with his life, had escaped. He was about to take his own life when the reassuring voice of Paul informed him that not one had escaped (vs 27, 28). Convinced by now that Paul and Silas were men of God, the jailer secured a light and, falling before them, asked how he might be saved. Paul told him of salvation by faith in Christ. Thereupon the jailer took the 2 apostles from the prison, treated their

wounds, set a meal before them, and gathered his family to listen to their instruction. Before morning the jailer and all his family were baptized (Acts 16:29-33).

When morning came the civil authorities sent officers to the prison, asking that Paul and Silas be released (Acts 16:35, 36). But Paul refused to go, stating that he and Silas, as Roman citizens, had been illegally beaten and imprisoned without a fair trial, and that therefore the ones who had unfairly condemned and publicly mistreated them must come and make amends publicly. Upon hearing this the city magistrates apologetically entreated them to leave the prison and the city. After visiting the house of Lydia and the brethren, the 2 men departed from Philippi (vs 37-40).

(4) *To Thessalonica and Beroea*. Paul and his party now journeyed westward (Map XX, A-3, red line ② westward) to the cities of Amphipolis and Apollonia, and finally to *Thessalonica (Acts 17:1). The statement that there was a Jewish synagogue at the latter place implies that there were none at the other cities; this probably explains why they did not stop there. At Thessalonica Paul followed his usual custom of preaching Christ in the synagogue. This he did for 3 successive Sabbaths, with the resultant conversion of some Jews, "of the devout Greeks a great multitude, and of the chief women not a few" (vs 2-4). It would seem that Paul followed his trade of tentmaking in the intervals between the Sabbaths (see Acts 18: 3; 1 Th 2:9; 2 Th 3:8). But now a situation began to develop, the general pattern of which Paul was quite familiar with by this time. Certain of the unbelieving Jews, jealous of the success of Paul, threw the city into an uproar by stirring up a mob against him and his companions. This mob attacked the house of a certain Jason, where Paul and his friends had been staying. Failing to find them there, they dragged Jason and some other believers to the city authorities, accusing them of disturbing the peace and of setting up Jesus as a rival king to Caesar (Acts 17:5-7)—accusations that disturbed the citizens and rulers of Thessalonica. Consequently, Jason and the others were required to pay "security," probably as a guarantee that they would keep the peace, and then were released (v 9), but the tense situation demanded that Paul and Silas leave the city. They traveled by night to Beroea (v 10).

Arriving at *Beroea, Paul once again

resorted to the synagogue, where he preached the gospel to the Jews. The Beroeans proved to be "more noble than those in Thessalonica," in that they were willing to receive the gospel after verifying it from the Scriptures (Acts 17:11). Consequently, a large group, including an unspecified number of Greek women, became Christians (v 12). Meanwhile, word had gone back to Thessalonica of the work of Paul in Beroea, and so, not content with having expelled him from their own city, the Thessalonian Jews determined to drive him from Beroea also. Going to the city, they stirred up the populace against Paul. The believers immediately placed the apostle aboard a ship bound for *Athens (Map XX, B-3, red line ② southward), to which he sailed, accompanied by some Beroean Christians. Silas and Timothy, however, remained at Beroea (vs 13-15).

(5) *In Athens*. It would appear from Acts that Paul had probably not intended to preach in *Athens (Map XX, B-3) but had planned merely to await the coming of his co-workers. However, there is no mention in Acts of Silas and Timothy joining Paul in that city, although 1 Th 3:1-5 suggests that Timothy did go to Athens, but was almost immediately sent by Paul to the church at Thessalonica. In any case the sight of the many idols in Athens provoked him to action. According to one ancient report there were more than 3,000 statues there in Paul's day, the greater number of which were linked with pagan worship. Paul began to preach in the synagogue and in the market place, or agora (see fig. 41). He gained the attention of certain Greek philosophers who, wishing to know more of his teachings, took him to the *Areopagus (Acts 17:16-22), or Mars' Hill, in the civic center of the city (see fig. 25). Paul's address, a portion of which appears in vs 22-31, was masterfully adapted to the thinking of his pagan listeners, but was successful only in causing them to mock him (v 32). He succeeded, however, in winning converts in that city (v 34).

(6) *In Corinth*. Following his experience at Athens, Paul journeyed westward alone to *Corinth (Acts 18:1). (Map XX, B-3.) There he came in contact with Aquila and his wife, Priscilla, Jews who had recently come from Italy subsequent to a decree by the emperor Claudius banning Jews from Rome (v 2). Since these people, like Paul, were tentmakers, he stayed with them and plied his trade (v

3). Paul most probably arrived in Corinth early in A.D. 51; he remained there more than a year and 6 months (Acts 18:11, 18). At first he labored with the Jews in the synagogue (v 4), as was his usual practice when entering a new city. However, when once again the majority of the Jews opposed and reviled him, he turned from them and began to work more directly for the Gentiles (v 6). No longer able to preach in the synagogue, he held his services in a house owned by a worshiper of God (*see* Proselyte), next door to the synagogue (v 7). The gospel bore much fruit in that city, and among the converts was the ruler of the synagogue (v 8; see fig. 468).

Meanwhile Silas and Timothy had arrived with cheering news of the faithfulness of the Thessalonians (Acts 18:5; Th 3:6). These tidings inspired Paul, probably in A.D. 51, to write 1 Thessalonians, his first epistle that has been preserved. This was followed—possibly during late 51 or early 52—by 2 Thessalonians. *See* Thessalonians, Epistles to.

At last, active persecution, that had usually come so quickly in other cities, began to threaten Paul at Corinth also. His Jewish enemies accused him before Gallio, the proconsul of Achaia, of teaching a religion not legally recognized by Rome. However, Gallio drove the accusers away, refusing to become involved in a case that he regarded as a dispute over Jewish, rather than Roman, law. At this the crowd seized the ruler of the synagogue at that time and beat him in the sight of Gallio (Acts 18:12-17). See fig. 113.

After an unspecified period, during which he was apparently able to preach without active opposition, Paul set sail for Syria (Map XX, B-3, red line ② eastward), accompanied by Priscilla and Aquila (Acts 18:18). He tarried briefly in Ephesus, and preached in the synagogue. His message was received with favor by his hearers, who were probably both Gentiles and Jews, and he was invited to remain longer. However, he decided to continue his journey, promising to return if possible. He took ship for Caesarea (Map XX, B-4/5, red line ② south and east), leaving Priscilla and Aquila at Ephesus, doubtless to carry on the work begun there. Landing at Caesarea (see fig. 87) he briefly visited Jerusalem to salute the church, and then went on to Antioch, from which place his missionary journeys had begun (vs 19-22). Thus ended Paul's 2d Missionary Journey, which had lasted about 3 years, probably from some time in A.D. 49 to possibly late in A.D. 52.

4. *Third Missionary Journey*. The length of Paul's stay at Antioch after his 2d Missionary Journey is not known. It is likely that some months, at least, elapsed before he started from there on his 3d Missionary Journey (Map XX, B-6; follow red line ③ westward). He "went over all the country of Galatia and Phrygia," strengthening the churches he had earlier established (Acts 18:23). Having passed through the "upper coasts," he at length arrived at Ephesus (ch 19:1), which was to be his chief center during this itinerary.

(1) *At Ephesus*. In Ephesus (Map XX, B-4) Paul found about 12 men who had evidently been taught by *Apollos, but who had not received a full knowledge of the gospel. These he instructed more fully, and upon being rebaptized they received the Holy Spirit (Acts 19:1-7). For about 3 months Paul preached and reasoned in the synagogue. Then because of opposition he and his converts moved to "the school of one Tyrannus," where Paul held daily meetings (vs 8, 9). This school became his headquarters for "two years," during which "all they which dwelt in Asia" heard the gospel (v 10). Many miracles were wrought (vs 11, 12), and a great number were converted, for "mightily grew the word of God and prevailed" (vs 18-20).

Toward the end of his stay in Ephesus, Paul wrote 1 Corinthians, probably in the spring of A.D. 57 (*see* Corinthians, Epistles to). In that epistle he revealed his plans to visit Corinth via Macedonia after remaining at Ephesus until Pentecost (1 Cor 16:5-8; see Acts 19:21). However, circumstances soon arose that hastened his departure from that city. Opposition that had been building up for some time (see 1 Cor 15:32) came to a head shortly after his letter was dispatched. This happened when a silversmith named Demetrius, probably a prominent member of a guild of manufacturers of shrines in honor of the goddess *Artemis (KJV "Diana"), became greatly concerned over the loss of business occasioned by so many turning to Christianity. He therefore called the craftsmen together and pointed out that Paul's preaching against the worship of idols had affected their business, not only locally but throughout much of the province of Asia. He further pointed out that Paul's preaching was undermining respect for the goddess and her temple, which "all Asia and the world" wor-

shiped (Acts 19:23-27). At this Demetrius' hearers became highly incensed and began shouting, "Great is Diana of the Ephesians." They succeeded in stirring the whole city to indignation. Seeking for someone upon whom to vent their wrath, they dragged 2 of Paul's traveling companions into the theater (see fig. 159). Paul decided to go in also, but was prevented by his disciples and some prominent Ephesian friends (vs 28-31). The mob was finally calmed by the town clerk and dispersed without doing any damage (vs 32-41). After this tumult Paul deemed it advisable to leave Ephesus, where he had spent "three years" (ch 20:1, 31), probably from about A.D. 54 to 57. Taking leave of the believers, he set out for Macedonia. For the possibility of a visit to Corinth during Paul's stay at Ephesus, see *SDACom* 6:835, 836, 922.

(2) *To Macedonia, and to Corinth Again*. Luke's account in Acts 20 passes very quickly over Paul's visit to Macedonia and Achaia, but certain details are supplied by his epistles. He went from Ephesus to Troas (Map XX, B-4, red line ③), where his preaching was favorably received. In Troas the apostle expected to find Titus with a report of the reaction of the Corinthian church to his epistle (1 Cor) sent a short time before, and disappointed at not finding him there, he hurried to Macedonia (Map XX, A-3), with the believers at Corinth weighing heavily upon his heart (2 Cor 2:12, 13; cf. ch 1:9). There he found Titus, and he had encouraging tidings for him from Corinth (ch 7:5-7). Cheered greatly by this report, the apostle wrote 2 Corinthians, in which he promised to visit the Corinthian church (ch 13:1, 2), and dispatched it evidently by Titus (ch 8:6, 16, 17, 23). Paul then went southward (red line ③) into Greece (Acts 20:2) and visited the believers there. While at Corinth for about 3 months he wrote the epistles to the *Romans and the *Galatians (v 3), about A.D. 58.

(3) *Return via Macedonia*. Paul now planned to take ship for Syria, but just about the time for embarkation he learned of a plot by some Jewish enemies to kill him, probably while he was aboard ship. Consequently, he changed his plans and went by way of Macedonia, thus foiling the plot of his would-be murderers (Acts 20:3). He traveled northward, probably by way of Beroea and Thessalonica (Map XX, A-3; retrace red line ③ north and northeast), to Philippi.

While several other companions crossed over to Troas, Paul and Luke remained at Philippi for the Passover and then "after the days of unleavened bread" sailed to join the others (Acts 20:4-6).

(4) *Troas and the Voyage to Palestine.* Paul spent a week at Troas. The evening before his departure a farewell service was held (*see* First Day of the Week). About midnight a young man named Eutychus, who was sitting in an open window of the 3d-story room in which the meeting was being held, went to sleep, fell to the ground below, and was "taken up dead." Hastening down, Paul embraced him and stated that his life was in him, and the youth revived (Acts 20:7-10, 12). Returning to the meeting room, the group celebrated the Lord's Supper, after which Paul conversed with them until dawn. Then he bade them farewell and departed (v 11) for the 20-mi. walk across the peninsula to Assos, to rejoin the ship in which he had been traveling, and which had sailed around the point (Map XX, B-4). Having rejoined his companions in the ship, Paul sailed via Mitylene, Chios, and Samos to Miletus (vs 13-17), some 40 mi. south of Ephesus (Map XX, B-4, red line ③). He had purposely bypassed Ephesus, for a stop there would unquestionably have made impossible his arrival at Jerusalem for Pentecost, which was but a short time away. He sent word to the elders of the Ephesian church to meet him at Miletus. The record of this meeting, during which Paul warned the elders against heresy and exhorted them to faithfulness, is one of the most touching passages of Acts (vs 18-35). Before departing, Paul prayed with his visitors, then bade them a tearful farewell and boarded ship to continue his voyage (vs 36-38). Having at length arrived, via Cos and Rhodes (red line ③ south and east), at Patara, a city on the coast of Lycia, Paul and his companions boarded another ship and eventually reached Tyre (Map XX, C-6; see fig. 515) in Phoenicia (ch 21:1-3). There they found some believers, and remained with them a week. During this time Paul was prophetically warned of the danger of going to Jerusalem. When it was time for him to rejoin his ship, the entire group of believers accompanied him to the shore. Paul's ship stopped next at Ptolemais, where he and those accompanying him spent one day with the brethren, and then continued the journey, probably by foot, to Caesarea. Here they stayed at the home of Philip the evangelist and deacon (Acts 21:4-8; cf. 6:5). At some time during the several days Paul stayed at Caesarea the prophet *Agabus predicted that evil results would follow Paul's visit to Jerusalem. Upon hearing this both those accompanying the apostle and the church at Caesarea pressed him not to go, but he remained inflexible in his decision (ch 21:10-14).

IV. Paul, the Prisoner.

1. *Paul Arrested at Jerusalem.* When Paul and his company arrived at Jerusalem they were gladly received by the Christians there. The report that Paul gave to the leaders of the church regarding the spread of the gospel among the Gentiles caused great rejoicing. However, at the same time the leaders informed Paul that reports were circulating that he was urging the Hellenistic Jewish Christians, as well as the Gentile converts, not to follow circumcision and the other Mosaic laws (Acts 21:15-21). This report was untrue and obviously an invention of his enemies (cf. chs 16:3; 18:18; 24:14; 25:8). Nevertheless, it was suggested that, in order to prove that the accusations were false, Paul should join 4 other Jewish Christians, who were under vows, in performing an act of ceremonial purification in the Temple, thus publicly demonstrating that he had not rejected the Mosaic laws. To this Paul agreed. The period of this vow was almost ended when certain Jews from Asia, probably visitors to Jerusalem for the feast of Pentecost, recognized Paul and stirred up the people against him by falsely accusing him not only of preaching against Jewish customs and institutions but also of having defiled the Temple by bringing Greeks into it (ch 21:22-29). The report of this alleged Temple desecration (see fig. 487) spread rapidly, attracting a crowd to the sacred precincts. Paul was seized and dragged from the Temple by the mob, who intended to kill him. Meanwhile, Claudius Lysias (ch 23:26), the military tribune in command of the Roman garrison, evidently stationed in the adjacent Tower of Antonia overlooking the Temple, heard of the disturbance. He hastily led down soldiers to quell the uproar. Seeing that it was centered around Paul, the commander arrested him and had him fettered. This being done, he inquired who Paul was and what his crime was that had caused such a tumult. Failing to get any satisfactory answer from the mob, he ordered the apostle to be es-

corted to the "castle," or *"barracks," evidently the Tower of Antonia. After being taken with difficulty through the angry crowd, Paul was able to convince the commander that he was not a criminal wanted by the Roman authorities. He was then granted permission to address the mob, which he did from the steps leading to the fortress (Acts 21:30-40; see figs. 485, 486), telling in "Hebrew," that is, in *Aramaic, the story of his life. His audience listened quietly until he told them how God had commissioned him to preach to the Gentiles. At these words the Jews broke into a tumult again and demanded his death. Thereupon the commander, probably not understanding Aramaic and thus not knowing the reason for the sudden outburst, ordered that Paul be examined by scourging. As he was being bound for this purpose Paul disclosed the fact that he was a Roman citizen, and this saved him from torture. The next day Lysias, desiring fully to understand the reason for the disturbance, convened the Sanhedrin and set Paul before them, that the matter might be made clear (ch 22). Paul was in the presence of the Sanhedrin for only a few minutes when it became apparent that he was not to have a fair trial (ch 23:1-5). Thereupon he shrewdly split the *council by stating that he was on trial for his belief, as a Pharisee, in the resurrection of the dead. At this the Sadducees, who did not believe in the resurrection, began to contend with the Pharisees. Thus the Pharisees were forced into the position of defending Paul. So fierce did the contention grow that Lysias, fearing that the apostle would be dismembered in the struggle, sent his soldiers to rescue him and take him to the tower (vs 6-10). That night Paul was given divine assurance that God was leading and that he would witness at Rome, as he had hoped (v 11). The next day his nephew (v 16), who had learned that a group of more than 40 men had taken a vow to assassinate Paul (vs 12-15), came to the tower and informed the apostle, who bade him tell the story to Lysias. The commander, upon learning that he was to be asked to bring Paul before the Sanhedrin the next day in order to give the assassins an opportunity to murder his prisoner, immediately ordered that a strong army escort be prepared to take Paul that very night to *Caesarea (vs 17-24), the Roman capital of Judea.

2. *Hearings at Caesarea*. At Caesarea Paul was turned over to Felix, the governor of Judea, with a letter from Lysias. Felix questioned Paul and then directed that he be confined to the *praetorium until his Jewish accusers should arrive from Jerusalem (Acts 23:25-35). After 5 days Ananias, the high priest, accompanied by certain elders, and Tertullus, a professional orator, appeared and accused Paul of sedition and of profanation of the Temple (ch 24:1-9). After the accused had spoken in his own defense, Felix delayed making a decision until further evidence was available. In the meantime Paul was granted a large measure of freedom (vs 10-23). Some time later he was again brought before Felix and his Jewish wife, *Drusilla. Apparently this hearing was not in the nature of a trial, but merely a pretext to hear what Paul had to say. On this occasion Paul "reasoned of righteousness, temperance, and judgment to come," with the result that Felix' conscience was greatly, but evidently only temporarily, disturbed (vs 24, 25). Following this event, Paul was kept a prisoner for 2 years, until Felix was replaced by Porcius Festus (vs 26, 27). This was about A.D. 60.

Almost as soon as Festus took office the Jews requested that he send Paul to Jerusalem for trial, intending to assassinate him on the way from Caesarea. Festus refused, but invited them to make their charges against the apostle at Caesarea. This they did, making many unproved charges. Festus inquired whether Paul would be willing to stand trial in Jerusalem. Doubtless considering that an order to renew the trial in Jerusalem would be the equivalent to his death sentence, Paul decided to invoke his rights as a Roman citizen, and appealed to Caesar (Nero; *see* Caesar, 4). The appeal was accepted, and Paul awaited transportation to Rome, safely out of reach of his angry countrymen (Acts 25:1-12).

Shortly after this *Herod Agrippa II, king of territories north and east of Judea, came with his sister *Bernice to pay a courtesy visit to Festus, the new governor of Judea. Festus related to them the story of Paul; whereupon Agrippa requested to hear the apostle for himself. The following day Paul was brought before the rulers (Acts 25:13-27), and was given permission to speak. He described his background, his conversion to Christianity, and his experiences of persecution from the Jews. When he told of Jesus and His resurrection from the dead, the pagan Festus declared the apostle to be mad. Nevertheless Paul strongly appealed to the king's convictions, but with no apparent success. Following Paul's defense the rulers decided that the prisoner might have been liberated had he not already appealed to Caesar (Acts 26:1-32).

3. *The Voyage to Rome.* The decision being made to send Paul to Rome (probably in the fall of A.D. 60), he, with other prisoners scheduled for the same journey, was placed in the custody of a centurion named Julius, who was charged with taking them to the capital (Acts 27:1). During this trip Paul had at least 2 Christian companions, Aristarchus (v 2), and Luke, the writer of Acts, as is shown by Luke's frequent use of "we" in the narrative. Soon after departure the vessel stopped at Sidon (Map XX, C-6, red line ④). There Paul, who was well treated by the centurion, was permitted to visit the believers. From Sidon (fig. 442) the ship sailed between the island of Cyprus and the mainland (Map XX, B-5) and finally reached Myra in Lycia (vs 3-5), where the whole company boarded another ship bound for Italy (v 6). This ship then had 276 people aboard (v 37). Putting out to sea from Myra, they evidently encountered strong head winds so that it took several days to sail the less than 200 mi. to Cnidus (see Map XX, B-4). At length the ship reached the island of Crete (B-3/4) and with difficulty sailed to a place called Fair Havens (vs 7, 8). There they spent some time, debating whether, because of the lateness of the season, the voyage should be continued. Paul counseled against doing so, but the shipowner and the captain spoke in favor of it, and the centurion was influenced by the latter. Because Fair Havens was not suitable to winter in, they decided to try to reach Phoenix (Phenice), farther along the coast of Crete (vs 9-12). Consequently, as soon as a suitable wind arose they left Fair Havens and headed toward Phoenix. Shortly afterward, however, a great tempest arose, blowing from the east or east-northeast, which drove the ship before it. When they found temporary shelter under the lee of a small island named Cauda (Clauda), they succeeded in hoisting aboard the ship's boat, which had heretofore been towed. At the same time the sailors, fearing that the ship would founder, fastened ropes completely around its hull for undergirding. They also lowered the gear to check the speed of their drift, for they feared that the ship would be driven upon the Syrtis

(KJV "quicksands"), the treacherous sandbanks off the northern coast of Africa (Acts 27:13-17). Map XX, C-2. On the following day, since the storm continued unabated, it was deemed necessary to lighten the ship by jettisoning some of the cargo (cf. v 38).

The tempest persisted for several days until all hope was abandoned (Acts 27: 20). At about this time Paul was given a vision, in which he was shown that no lives would be lost and that he would have the opportunity of standing before Caesar. He related this experience to his companions, exhorting them to be of good courage (vs 21-26). At last, one night, 2 weeks after the storm struck, the sailors suspected that they were nearing land. Soundings of the depth of the water confirmed this, so that they began to fear that the ship would be driven upon the rocks and destroyed. The sailors anchored the ship, then sought to leave the vessel secretly in the boat. Paul insisted that the crew must remain at their posts if all were to be saved; so the soldiers cut the boat adrift (vs 27-32). While all aboard were waiting for the dawn to decide what further to do, Paul urged them to partake of food, pointing out that they had been "fasting" for 14 days (vs 33, 34). After all had eaten, the anchored ship was further lightened by jettisoning the wheat (v 38). Dawn revealed unfamiliar land with a bay. Into this they decided to try to run the ship. They raised the anchors and endeavored to steer into the bay. Drawing close to land, they were caught by violent crosscurrents, which hurled the ship upon the rocks, where it grounded. The stern was then broken off by the pounding waves. The soldiers, obviously considering that they were responsible for the prisoners with their own lives, now urged that the prisoners be killed lest they escape. However, the centurion, wanting to save Paul, forbade this. Instead he commanded all to attempt to get ashore as best they could, and all on board reached land safely (vs 39-44). The land proved to be the island of Malta (KJV "Melita"), about 560 mi. from their last landfall, the island of Cauda. (For a discussion of this voyage and shipwreck see *SDACom* 6:450-457.) The people of Malta (see fig. 313) treated the castaway group hospitably, and endeavored to care for their needs. Paul, gathering fuel for the fire, was bitten by a viper, whereupon the superstitious Maltese concluded he was some great criminal being punished for his crimes. However, when he suffered no ill effects they decided instead that he must be some god (Acts 28:1-6). Paul and his company were invited to be guests of Publius, the "chief man" of Malta, and stayed with him 3 days (v 7). By the prayers of Paul, Publius' father was healed of *dysentery. When the knowledge of this spread, many others who were sick came and were also healed. These happenings prompted the islanders to heap many gifts upon Paul and those with him. Finally, after spending 3 months on the island (v 11), the shipwrecked company sailed for Rome, probably in the spring of A.D. 61, on an Alexandrian ship that had wintered there (vs 8-11). After stopping for 3 days at Syracuse, on the island now known as Sicily, the ship sailed to Rhegium at the southern tip of Italy, and then continued on to Puteoli, which was about 230 mi. farther northwest (Map XX, A-1). At Puteoli Paul found some Christians—an evidence of the spread of the gospel in Italy (see fig. 395). After a week with them he, with the rest of the travelers, started for Rome. Meanwhile, the report of his arrival in the country had preceded him to that city, so that groups of believers set out to meet him. These met Paul at the Forum of Appius ("Appii forum") and Three Taverns (see figs. 186, 405), about 40 and 30 mi., respectively, from Rome on the Appian Way. Paul was highly gratified and 'encouraged at this welcome (vs 12-15).

4. *First Imprisonment in Rome.* Upon his arrival at Rome, Paul, with the other prisoners, was delivered to "the captain of the guard" (Acts 28:16, KJV), probably the chief of the Praetorian Guard (the imperial guard stationed at Rome) in charge of prisoners who appealed to the emperor. At this time the office was held by Burrus, a man of good principles, one whose restraining influence had helped to curb the emperor Nero's excesses. Paul, presumably on the recommendation of the centurion who had escorted him from Caesarea, was permitted to stay in his own living quarters, being guarded, however, by a soldier (v 16), to whom he was chained (see Acts 28:20; cf. Eph 6:20; Col 4:18). It should be noted, however, that important textual evidence may be cited for the omission of the clause "the centurion delivered the prisoners to the captain of the guard" (see *SDACom* 6:461).

Three days after his arrival in Rome, Paul invited the Jewish elders to visit him. After he had explained to them the reason for his imprisonment they agreed on a time for Paul to expound to them the Christian doctrines. On the appointed day many came to his lodging to hear him as he "testified the kingdom of God." This meeting lasted all day, during which the truths that Paul preached were doubtlessly debated back and forth. At the end of the meeting some believed and some, probably the majority, did not; "they agreed not among themselves." At this Paul quoted from Is 6:9, 10, reproving the unbelieving for refusing to accept the light that had come to them (Acts 28:17-28). The book of Acts and the Bible account of the apostle's life, is rather abruptly ended at this point with the statement that Paul, clearly still a prisoner, was nevertheless able to live for 2 years in his own rented lodging (see fig. 410), obviously under guard, and had visitors to whom he preached Christ (vs 30, 31).

For the rest of the story of Paul's life we must depend upon scant clues found in his various epistles written during and after his 1st imprisonment in Rome, upon statements contained in other early writings, and upon tradition. The epistles of Ephesians, Philippians, Colossians, and Philemon were written during this 1st period in Rome. These epistles reveal that the imprisonment was a trying experience for the aged apostle (Eph 3:1; 6:20; Col 4:18; Phm 1, 9, 10). From Acts 27:2 and Eph 6:21 we know that Luke, Aristarchus, and Tychicus were his companions. He also had with him Mark, Justus, Epaphras, and Demas, possibly for only part time (Col 4:10-12, 14; cf. 2 Ti 4:10). Epaphroditus delivered Paul's epistles to the Philippians (Php 2:25-30). Tychicus carried the letter to the Ephesians (Eph 6: 21, 22) and, accompanied by Onesimus, the letter to the Colossians (Col 4:7-9), and the one to the Christian slaveowner, Philemon. Onesimus, Philemon's slave who had escaped to Rome, seems to have been converted by Paul at Rome (Col 4:9; Phm 10). From Php 4:18 we learn that the Philippians sent gifts to Paul delivered by Epaphroditus.

5. *Acquittal and Subsequent Activities.* At the end of 2 years (probably A.D. 63), Paul was tried at the judgment seat of Nero and released. The epistles written during this period of freedom, 1 Timothy and Titus, show that the apostle once more conducted missionary travels after his release. Clement of Rome (*The First Epistle of Clement to the Corinthians* 5)

says that Paul preached in both East and West. Since the apostle had planned to go to Spain (Rom 15:24, 28), it is possible that he now visited that country. The Muratorian Fragment (c. A.D. 190) states that he did visit Spain. Paul probably also carried out his expressed purpose of visiting Philippi (Php 2:24) and Colossae (Phm 22; cf. Col 4:9; Phm 10). From 1 Ti 1:3 we can conclude that he went to Macedonia and Ephesus. He also apparently visited Crete (Tit 1:5), and possibly Corinth (2 Ti 4:20). He also may have spent a winter (perhaps A.D. 65) at Nicopolis (Tit 3:12), on the western coast of Greece.

6. *Second Imprisonment at Rome, and Death.* The Scripture narrative is silent concerning the events that led to Paul's final arrest. It may well be that the occasion for it came in connection with Nero's cruel persecutions of the Christians at that time. Paul was a prominent leader among them, and therefore a natural target for the sadistic ferocity of the emperor. Nicopolis, Ephesus, and Troas have been suggested as possible places where Paul was seized, with Troas being the most likely (2 Ti 4:13). He was taken to Rome, where he received none of the favors granted him during his former imprisonment. According to tradition he was confined in the Mamertine prison, on the Roman Forum, and was chained (ch 2:9) like a common criminal (see fig. 375). He was forsaken by practically everyone (ch 4:16; cf. vs 11, 20). Paul's last extant epistle, that of 2 Timothy, was written at this time. When it was penned Paul had doubtless already been brought to trial once and had defended himself (vs 16, 17). He seemingly expected a 2d trial shortly and he evidently expected to be sentenced to death (v 6). However, he urged Timothy to put forward every ef-

375. The dungeon of the Mamertine prison in Rome, in which, according to tradition, Paul was held as a prisoner

fort to visit him before his death (2 Ti 4:9, 21). Early Christian authors are unanimous in declaring that Paul died under Nero at Rome. His execution, then, which tradition says was by decapitation somewhere on the Ostian Way, must have taken place at least by A.D. 68, for Nero himself died that year. He was executed probably sometime between A.D. 66 and 68. The apostle's own words in 2 Ti 4:7, 8 offer a fitting epitaph of his life and the purpose of his life: "I have fought a good fight, I have finished my course, I have kept the faith: henceforth there is laid up for me a crown of righteousness, which the Lord, the righteous judge, shall give me at that day: and not to me only, but unto all them also that love his appearing."

Thus died a man of truly pre-eminent abilities and virtues. As a theologian he ranks as perhaps the greatest of all time, having laid much of the foundation upon which Christian dogmatics is built. His elevated concept of Christ has dominated Christianity. He was an able orator (Acts 17:22-31), and a writer of vigorous prose that could sometimes be poetic (1 Cor 13). He was also a great evangelist and organizer. Yet in spite of his many gifts and his high calling, he was a man of great humility (1 Cor 15:9; Eph 3:8), anxious that he should be a burden to none (Acts 20:34; 2 Cor 11:9; 1 Th 2:9; 2 Th 3:8). He was a preacher with a strong sense of duty and destiny (Rom 1:14; 1 Cor 9:16, 17; Gal 1:15, 16). He was versatile (1 Cor 9:19-22; 10:33), optimistic (1 Cor 1:4; 2 Cor 4:16-18; Php 1:3-6; Col 1:3; 1 Th 1:2), courageous (Acts 9:22-29; 13:45, 46; 20:22-24; etc.); he possessed singleness of purpose (1 Cor 2:2; Php 3:13), composure of mind (Php 4:11, 12; 1 Ti 6:6-8), zeal (Acts 22:3; Gal 1:14; Php 3:6), and unfailing faith (Rom 8:28, 38, 39; Gal 2:20; 2 Ti 1:12).

Paulus, Sergius. *See* Sergius Paulus.

Pavement, The. *See* Gabbatha.

Pe. [Heb. *pe'*.] The 17th letter of the Hebrew alphabet, written פ, appearing as the title to the 17th section of Ps 119 in the KJV. *See* Aleph.

Peace Offering. *See* Sacrifices and Offerings.

Peacocks. The rendering of: (1) The Heb. *tukkîyîm* in 1 Ki 10:22; 2 Chr 9:21, an expression designating a certain item brought to Palestine by Solomon's Ophir expeditions. However, the meaning of the Hebrew term is uncertain. For a time it was thought that it was derived from an Indian word, but W. E. Clark has proved this view to be erroneous (*AJSL* 36 [1920], 103-119). Some scholars have suggested that the guinea fowl or other domesticated fowl is meant. Most plausible, however, is the view of W. F. Albright, who sees in *tuki* a loan word from an Egyptian word for a certain kind of monkey (*see* Ape). If *Ophir was not in India, but in eastern Africa, the peacock cannot be meant, for that bird is a native of India and is not known to be found in East Africa. (2) The Heb. *renanim* (Job 39:13, KJV), *"ostrich." See Albright, *AJSL* 37 (1920-21), 144, 145; *Archaeology and the Religion of Israel* (4th ed., 1956), p. 212, n. 16.

Pearl. [Heb. *gabish*, "rock crystal"; Gr. *margarites*, from *margaros*, "pearl oyster."] A highly valued gemlike article formed around a foreign substance between the shell and the mantle of some oysters and certain other mollusks. It grows in size as the creature secretes carbonate of lime and throws membrane around a grain of sand or a parasite, until a round or nearly round object of iridescent white or bluish white is formed. Pearls of fine quality are obtained from the pearl oyster (*Pinctada margaritifera*), which is plentiful in the Persian Gulf and near Ceylon. The Hebrew word translated "pearl" occurs but once in the OT, and means "rock crystal" (Job 28:18). In the NT, however, identification is certain. Jesus warned against casting pearls before swine (Mt 7:6), and compared the kingdom of heaven to a merchant seeking fine pearls (ch 13:45, 46). Paul counseled the women of the church not to adorn themselves with such costly materials as gold and pearls (1 Ti 2:9). John the revelator portrayed Babylon as a woman bedecked with jewelry, including pearls (Rev 17:4; cf. ch 18:12, 16). Each of the 12 gates of the New Jerusalem is described as consisting of a single pearl (ch 21:21). In Est 1:6 the RSV translates the Heb. *dar* "mother-of-pearl," but the exact stone designated by *dar* is uncertain.

Peculiar People. A rendering of: (1) The Heb. *'am segullah* (Deut 14:2; 26:18; KJV), literally, "a people of (that is, constituting God's private) property." It designates Israel as belonging exclusively to God, as being His private property. Elsewhere Israel is said to be His "peculiar treasure" (Ex 19:5; Ps 135:4; KJV). (2) The Gr. *laos eis peripoiesin* (1 Pe 2:9, KJV), literally, "a people unto (God's own) possession." Peter applies this expression to the Christian church.

(3) The Gr. *laos periousios* (Tit 2:14, KJV), "chosen people." The English word "peculiar" properly means "belonging to an individual," "privately owned," "one's own." It is derived from the Latin *peculiaris*, "one's own," "belonging particularly to oneself." The use of "peculiar" to mean "queer," or "eccentric," is colloquial; such a meaning does not belong to these texts.

Pedahel (pĕd'á-hĕl). [Heb. *Pedah'el*, "God has redeemed." The name occurs on an ancient Hebrew seal with the Biblical spelling and in Akkadian as *Padû-ilu*.] A prince of the tribe of Naphtali during the wilderness wanderings (Num 34:28).

Pedahzur (pĕ-dä'zẽr). [Heb. *Pedahṣur*, "the rock has redeemed."] A man whose son Gamaliel was prince of the tribe of Manasseh during the wilderness wanderings (Num 1:10; 2:20; 7:54, 59; 10:23).

Pedaiah (pĕ-dä'yà). [Heb. *Pedayah* and *Pedayahû*, "Yahweh has redeemed." The name occurs also on an ancient Hebrew seal.]

1. A man whose son Joel was chief officer of western Manasseh under David (1 Chr 27:20).

2. A man of Rumah, and the maternal grandfather of Jehoiakim, king of Judah (2 Ki 23:36).

3. A son of King Jeconiah, or Jehoiachin (1 Chr 3:17, 18). He was the father of Zerubbabel according to v 19. Since Zerubbabel is otherwise called the son of Shealtiel (Ezr 3:2; etc.), one of the 2 named as father was probably his legal father and the other his blood father.

4. A member of the postexilic family of Parosh. He was one of those who assisted Nehemiah in rebuilding part of the wall of Jerusalem (Neh 3:25).

5. One who stood at the left of Ezra when he read the Law (Neh 8:4).

6. A Benjamite (Neh 11:7).

7. A Levite treasurer in charge of the tithes, appointed by Nehemiah during his 2d term as governor of Judah (Neh 13:12, 13).

Peel. A rendering of: (1) The Heb. *marat* (Eze 29:18; Is 18:2, 7; KJV), "to pluck," "to pull off," "to make smooth." *Marat* is rendered "pluck off the hair" in Ezr 9:3; Neh 13:25; Is 50:6; KJV. (2) The Heb. *pasal* (Gen 30:37, 38, RSV), "to bark," "to peel" (KJV "pill"). Strictly speaking, "peel" means "to remove the skin," whereas "pill" means "to remove the hair." In Old English this distinction between "peel" and "pill" was not always carefully observed; hence "pilled" in Gen 30:37, 38, KJV.

Pekah (pē'kà). [Heb. *Peqach*, "(God) has opened (the eyes)." In cuneiform records *Paqaḥa*.] The 19th king of Israel, if Tibni is included in the count. He usurped the throne, assassinating Pekahiah, under whom he had served as an army officer.

There are reasons—based on certain Judah-Israel synchronisms in 2 Ki and on dates of the contemporary Assyrian kings mentioned in the Bible—for believing that Pekah did not count his 20 years' reign (2 Ki 15:27) from the time of Pekahiah's death, but that he also included the reigns of his 2 predecessors and called the year in which he killed Pekahiah his 12th year instead of his first. See *SDACom* 2:85, 150. If so, he actually reigned only about 8 years (*c.* 740 B.C. - *c.* 732 B.C.). It is possible that he made a claim to the crown soon after the death of Jeroboam II (*c.* 753 B.C.), or that he made a claim only after his accession to the throne, contending, however, that he had been the legitimate king during the reigns of Menahem and Pekahiah though not actually ruling, or that he actually ruled for some time over part of eastern Israel, before taking the throne over the entire kingdom. He was an ally of Rezin of Damascus, probably in a coalition with several other local kings of western Asia, against Tiglathpileser III, as the Assyrian cuneiform records indicate. Apparently Ahaz of Judah did not join this alliance; and this may have been the reason why Pekah and Rezin planned to invade Judah, dethrone its king, and replace him with the son of Tabeel, probably an Aramaean (Is 7:1, 5, 6). Rezin marched through Transjordan to the Gulf of Aqabah and took Elath, in which the Edomites afterward settled (2 Ki 16:5, 6; this is according to the Hebrew, but the KJV translators assumed that "Edomites" was an error for "Syrians," and the RSV translators assume that "Syria" was an error for "Edom," and also further emend the text). Pekah invaded the kingdom of Judah from the north. In desperation Ahaz, against the advice of Isaiah, sent tribute to Tiglath-pileser III, requesting him to attack the countries of his 2 adversaries. The Assyrian king complied by attacking Damascus (2 Ki 16:7-9). Tiglath-pileser also took from Pekah his territories east of the Jordan (1 Chr 5:26). It may have been at this time that Pekah withdrew from Judah with much spoil and with prisoners who were later allowed to return to their country

when the prophet Oded interceded on their behalf (2 Chr 28:5-21). Tiglathpileser invaded northern Palestine and took it, as well as Israel's territory in Transjordan, from Pekah. He organized these areas into the Assyrian "Province of Megiddo," ruled by an Assyrian governor residing at Megiddo. The Assyrian army then moved on to the country of the Philistines. It was probably while Tiglathpileser was in that area that Hoshea murdered Pekah (2 Ki 15:29, 30), probably with the connivance of Tiglath-pileser III, since that king claims in his inscriptions that he placed Hoshea on the throne.

Pekahiah (pĕk'à-hī'à). [Heb. *Peqachyah*, "Yahweh has opened (the eyes)."] The 18th king of Israel, if Tibni is included in the count. He reigned at Samaria for 2 years (*c.* 742 - *c.* 740 B.C.), but nothing more is known of him except that he was evil like his father, Menahem, and followed the calf worship of Jeroboam I (2 Ki 15:22-24). He was assassinated by Pekah, an army officer, who then usurped the throne for himself (v 25).

Pekod (pē'kŏd). [Heb. *Peqôd*.] A tribe mentioned in connection with Chaldea and Babylon (Jer 50:21), and as part of the Babylonian army (Eze 23:23, 24). This is evidently the tribe mentioned in Assyrian inscriptions as *Puqudu,* whose mountainous territory, adjoining Elam, is referred to as *ḥarri-Piqudu.* Map XI, C-6.

Pelaiah, I (pê-lā'yà). (Heb. *Pela'yah,* "Yahweh has performed a miracle."]

1. A Levite who assisted Ezra in teaching the Law of God to the people (Neh 8:7); possibly identical with Pelaiah, I, 2.

2. A Levite who set his seal to Nehemiah's covenant (Neh 10:10); possibly identical with Pelaiah, I, 1.

Pelaiah, II (pê-lā'yà). [Heb. *Pelayah,* "Yahweh has made a distinction."] A postexilic descendant of David (1 Chr 3:24).

Pelaliah (pĕl'à-lī'à). [Heb. *Pelalyah,* "Yahweh judges."] A postexilic priest (Neh 11:12).

Pelatiah (pĕl'à-tī'à). [Heb. *Pelaṭyah* and *Pelaṭyahû,* "Yahweh is deliverance." The name occurs in cuneiform records as *Palṭiyau.*]

1. A Simeonite captain in a war against the Amalekites (1 Chr 4:42).

2. A prince of Judah living in Jerusalem. In vision Ezekiel, who was living in Babylonia, was shown Pelatiah's wickedness and punishment (Eze 11:1-13).

3. A grandson of Zerubbabel (1 Chr 3:19, 21).

4. A prominent Jew who set his seal to Nehemiah's covenant (Neh 10:22).

Peleg (pē'lĕg), KJV once **Phalec** (fā'lĕk). [Heb. *Peleg*, "division"; Gr. *Phalek*.] A son of Eber and an ancestor of Abraham (Gen 11:16-26). His name had reference to the fact that in his time the earth was divided (ch 10:25). The division referred to is either the general scattering of the descendants of Noah over the earth or the scattering resulting from the confusion of tongues (ch 11:7-9). A city at the mouth of the Khabur in Upper Mesopotamia was called *Paliga,* probably in honor of Peleg, in the same way as other cities in that area commemorated patriarchal names, such as Serug, Terah, Haran, and Nahor.

Pelet (pē'lĕt). [Heb. *Pelet,* "deliverance." The name occurs in Akkadian as *Palitu.*]

1. A man of the house of Caleb (1 Chr 2:42, 47).

2. A Benjamite who joined David at Ziklag (1 Chr 12:1, 3).

Peleth (pē'lĕth). [Heb. *Peleth,* meaning uncertain.]

1. A Reubenite whose son On joined Korah's rebellion against Aaron and Moses (Num 16:1).

2. A Jerahmeelite of the tribe of Judah (1 Chr 2:33).

Pelethites (pĕl'ē-thīts). [Heb. *Pelethi,* seemingly a variant of the Heb. *Pelishti,* "Philistines."] A term designating certain members of David's bodyguard. They and the Cherethites are mentioned together (2 Sa 8:18; 1 Ki 1:38, 44; 1 Chr 18:17), the 2 terms referring most likely to Philistines and Cretans. As foreigners, these mercenary troops would not be concerned with politics or questions of national concern, and would therefore remain loyal to David. This they did during Absalom's rebellion, when many of David's subjects deserted him (2 Sa 15:18-22). Pelethites took part also in the fight against Sheba the son of Bichri, another rebel leader (ch 20:7).

Pelican. [Heb. *qa'ath.*] A large, web-footed bird with a large bill. However, the exact species of bird represented by the Hebrew term is not known, although it has been observed that the pelican is an appropriate symbol of utter loneliness and dejection, as in the psalmist's lament (Ps 102:6, KJV). *Qa'ath* occurs 5 times, and in the KJV is twice translated *"cormorant" (Is 34:11; Zep 2:14) and thrice "pelican" (Lev 11:18; Deut 14:17; Ps 102:6). The RSV retains "pelican" in the Pen-

tateuch, uses "hawk" once (Is 34:11), and twice suggests that the meaning of the Hebrew word is uncertain (Ps 102:6; Zep 2:14). The roseate pelican (*Pelecanus onocrotalus*) frequents rivers, lakes, and marshes of the Holy Land, sometimes perching on trees, with its large bill and pouch resting on its breast, but it would not be expected to occur in wastelands and among ruins (Is 34:11; Zep 2:14) in the manner of owls and vultures. The *qa'ath* is listed among the unclean birds (Lev 11:18; Deut 14:17).

Pelonite (pĕl'ō-nīt). [Heb. *Peloni,* "a certain one," or "such and such a one."] An appellative of Helez (1 Chr 11:27; 27:10) and Ahijah (ch 11:36). Some think that "Pelonite" may be a scribal error for "Paltite" (in pre-Masoretic Hebrew only one letter is involved) on the one hand (2 Sa 23:26), and for "Gilonite" (v 34, KJV) on the other. Others think that the scribe could not make out the words in the manuscript he was copying and therefore called the 2 men simply "such and such a one."

Pelusium. See Sin, II, 2.

Pen. Four terms denoting writing instruments have been rendered "pen" in the Bible: (1) The Heb. *'et,* a stylus of wood or metal with which cuneiform characters were impressed on clay tablets (Ps 45:1; Jer 8:8; 17:1), or a metal graving tool used for cutting letters on stone (Job 19:24). (2) The Heb. *cheret* (Is 8:1), apparently a synonym of *'et,* designating the stylus used by a scribe to write on a tablet. *Cheret* is rendered "characters" in the RSV. (3) The Heb. *shebet,* "staff," but probably correctly rendered "pen" in Jgs 5:14 in the phrase *shebet sopher,* which the RSV translates "marshal's staff." However, there is no evidence that *sopher* ever meant "marshal." (4) The Gr. *kalamos* (3 Jn 13), a "reed pen" used for writing with ink on papyrus. The end of the reed was beaten so that the fibers became loose and resembled a fine brush. This was cut diagonally with a penknife, so that it would produce a thin smooth script. See fig. 424.

Pencil. A rendering of the Heb. *sered* in Is 44:13, RSV, a word of unknown meaning. The context indicates an instrument or some kind of material for marking. Some commentators suggest red chalk, a material widely used by ancient craftsmen for marking purposes.

Pendant. A rendering of: (1) the Heb. *netiphah* (Jgs 8:26; Is 3:19; RSV), an ornament suspended from the ear; (2) the Heb. *'anaq* (Prov 1:9, RSV), "necklace."

Peniel. *See* Penuel, 1.

Peninnah (pĕ-nĭn′à). [Heb. *Peninnah,* "one with rich hair."] One of the 2 wives of Elkanah, Samuel's father (1 Sa 1:2-6).

Penknife. [Heb. *ta'ar sopher.*] A knife used by an ancient scribe to cut his brushlike reed pens so that they would produce a fine neat script on papyrus. A scribal kit for writing on papyrus probably supplied the penknife used to cut up Jeremiah's scroll (Jer 36:23).

Penny. The translation of: (1) The Gr. *kodrantēs,* the equivalent of the Roman *quadrans,* a small bronze coin, 4 of which equaled 1 *as.* The monetary value was about one fourth of a U.S. cent (Mt 5:26; Mk 12:42; KJV "farthing"). (2) The Gr. *assarion,* a diminutive of the Latin *as,* a Roman copper coin, the monetary value of which was about one U.S. cent (Mt 10:29; Lk 12:6; KJV "farthing"). (3) The Gr. *dēnarion,* in the KJV only. *See* Denarius.

Pentateuch. [Gr. *pentateuchos,* "five-volumed," from *penta,* "five," and *teuchos,* originally, a "tool" or "instrument," then "a case" for holding papyrus rolls, and finally a "roll" of writing material.] The 1st 5 books of the OT, Genesis, Exodus, Leviticus, Numbers, and Deuteronomy, the 1st of the 3 divisions of the sacred Hebrew canon of Scriptures. The term was used by Christian writers from about the 2d cent.

I. Designations. The common Hebrew name for these books is *Tôrah,* from the root *yarah,* meaning (in the Hiphil form), to "point out," "show," "direct," or "teach." Hence *Tôrah* denotes "direction," "instruction," "law," or "teaching" (Neh 8:2, 7; etc.). Other OT designations for the Pentateuch in whole or in part are: "the book of the law" (Jos 1:8; 8:34; Neh 8:3), "the book of the law of Moses" (Jos 8:31; 23:6; 2 Ki 14:6; Neh 8:1), "the book of the law of God" (Jos 24:26; Neh 8:18), the "book of the law of the Lord" (2 Chr 17:9; 34:14), the "book of the law of the Lord their God" (Neh 9:3), "the law of the Lord" (1 Chr 16:40; 2 Chr 31:3; 35:26), "the law of God" (Neh 10:28), "God's law" (v 29), and "the law of Moses" (Dan 9:11, 13). In all these instances "law" is a translation of the Hebrew *Tôrah.* The designation "the book of Moses" is also used (Ezr 6:18). These various designations indicate that the Pentateuch was regarded

as a single literary work, and thus emphasize its essential unity. The division into 5 scrolls is very ancient, older than the Septuagint or the Samaritan Pentateuch, and may have been made by the original author. The Jews spoke of the Pentateuch as the "five-fifths of the law."

NT designations of the Pentateuch are "the law" (Mt 12:5; Lk 16:16; Jn 7:19), "the law of Moses" (Lk 2:22; Jn 7:23), "the law of the Lord" (Lk 2:23, 24), and "the book of the law" (Gal 3:10), "the book of Moses" (Mk 12:26). "Law" in these references is a translation of the Gr. *nomos,* the term Greek-speaking Jews used for *Tôrah.*

II. Contents. For the contents of the 5 books of the *Tôrah see* the names of the individual books.

III. Authorship.

1. *The Traditional View.* Until comparatively recent times the Mosaic authorship of the Pentateuch was almost universally accepted by both Jews and Christians. Conservative Biblical scholars today find both external and internal evidence for holding that Moses wrote the first 5 books of the Bible.

(1) *The Testimony of the Pentateuch Itself.* While there is no specific statement claiming Mosaic authorship for the Pentateuch as a whole, there is convincing evidence that it came from the hand of Moses. Some of the legal sections of Exodus, for example, are specifically attributed to Moses. According to Ex 24:4-8, Moses wrote the Book of the Covenant (chs 20 to 23). The laws pertaining to the sanctuary and its services (chs 25 to 31) are presented as personal communications from God to Moses (see chs 25:1, 13, 31; 26:1; 30:11, 17, 22; 31:1, 12; etc.). The account of the erection of the tabernacle (chs 35 to 40) frequently mentions that all was done in harmony with God's personal directions, "as the Lord commanded Moses" (8 times in ch 39). The Song of Deliverance at the Red Sea (ch 15:1-18) is also credited to Moses. The narrative of the victory over Amalek was to be written by him "in a book" (ch 17:14). In all of Exodus, as in the entire Pentateuch exclusive of Genesis, Moses is the central figure and the communicator of the *Tôrah.* In Leviticus the priestly legislation is represented as a direct personal communication from God to Moses. The phrase, "as the Lord commanded Moses," or its equivalent, is found about 30 times, and the giving of the legislation is directly connected with Mount Sinai and

the instrumentality of Moses (Lev 26:46; 27:34). The priestly legislation of Numbers is likewise specifically presented as a direct command from God to Moses (Num 5:1, 5, 11; 6:1; 8:1; 9:1; 10:1; etc.). The itinerary and list of camping places (ch 33) from Egypt to Canaan is declared to have been written by Moses (vs 1, 2). Deuteronomy begins with the statement "These be the words which Moses spake" (Deut 1:1; cf. v 5; 4:5, 14; 29:1). The writing of the Law, it declares, was the work of Moses (ch 31:24), and the song and blessings of chs 32 and 33 are specifically credited to him (chs 31:22, 30; 32:44, 45; 33:1). While there is no specific statement attributing the authorship of Genesis to Moses, that book constitutes an organic part of the Pentateuch. Since Exodus is simply a continuation of Genesis, it seems reasonable to conclude that the same author produced both volumes.

(2) *The Testimony of the Rest of the OT.* Many other books of the OT refer to the Pentateuch as the work of Moses. The most frequent references to Moses and his writings are in the book of Joshua, where the name of Moses occurs more than 50 times. Joshua derived his authority from Moses, and appealed constantly to the Law of Moses (Jos 1:7, 8; 8:31, 32, 34, 35; 23:6). His actions are declared to have been in harmony with the instructions "as the Lord commanded Moses" (chs 11:15, 20; 14:2; etc.). The oppression of the Israelites in the period of the judges was to prove Israel "to know whether they would hearken unto the commandments of the Lord, which he commanded their fathers by the hand of Moses" (Jgs 3:4). David had the ark brought up to Jerusalem on the shoulders of the Levites "as Moses commanded" (1 Chr 15:15), and he charged his son Solomon to observe the regulations "written in the law of Moses" (1 Ki 2:3). Several references to Moses' writings are made in Kings and Chronicles (2 Ki 14: 6; 2 Chr 23:18; 25:4; 34:14; 35:12; cf. 2 Ki 18:6, 12; 21:8; 23:25; 2 Chr 8:13; 30:16). From the Captivity there are references to Moses in Daniel (Dan 9:11-13), and from the period of the restoration there are several references in Ezra, Nehemiah, and Malachi (Ezr 3:2; 6:18; 7:6; Neh 1:7, 8; 8:14; 9:14; 10:29; 13:1; Mal 4:4).

(3) *The Testimony of the NT.* Our Lord made frequent references to the Pentateuch, which He obviously regarded as the writings of Moses (Mt 8:4; 19:7, 8; Mk 1:44; 10:3-5; 12:19; Lk 5:14; 16:29,

31; Jn 5:46, 47). One quotation from Exodus (Ex 3:6) He introduced with the words, "Have ye not read in the book of Moses?" (Mk 12:26). The testimony of the apostles is in harmony with that of Jesus (Acts 3:22; 13:39; 15:5, 21; 26:22; 28:23; Rom 10:5, 19; 1 Cor 9:9; 2 Cor 3:15; Rev 15:3).

(4) *The Testimony of Jewish Tradition.* The Samaritans held that the Pentateuch was the work of Moses. Apocryphal writers held the same view (Ecclus 45:5; 2 Macc 7:30). The same is true of Philo (*Moses* ii. 2) and Josephus (*Against Apion* i. 8). The same position is taken by both the Palestinian and Babylonian Talmuds.

(5) *Internal Evidence.* The story of Joseph in Genesis and the story of Moses in Exodus reveal an author who had an intimate acquaintance with the life and manners of the Egyptians. The use of correct titles for Egyptian officials (Gen 40:2; 41:40), the reflection of Egyptian customs (ch 41:42, 43), the emphasis on dreams and magicians (v 8), and the mummification of Jacob and Joseph (ch 50:2, 26), reveal the Egyptian coloring of the Joseph narrative. Similarly in the Exodus story are found Egyptian words and an accurate picture of Egyptian life and manners. Who else but Moses, who was "learned in all the wisdom of the Egyptians" (Acts 7:22), was qualified to write these narratives? The author of the Pentateuch was also well acquainted with the desert.

2. *The Modern Critical View.* Modern critical scholars, in general, reject the Mosaic authorship of the Pentateuch. The majority of them hold to some form of the documentary hypothesis, which maintains that the Pentateuch is a composite of 4 or 5 documents that date many centuries after the time of Moses. Perhaps the most popular view is the Graf-Wellhausen theory, which finds in the Pentateuch 4 major strands (labeled J, E, D, P) put together by a sort of scissors-and-paste method. According to this view there was: (1) a J document (so called because in it the Tetragrammaton *JHWH* was used as God's name), written by a citizen of the southern kingdom of Judah, *c.* 850 B.C.; (2) an E document (in which God is called *'Elohim*), written *c.* 750 B.C. by a so-called "Elohist" writer, from the northern kingdom of Israel; the 2 were combined as JE by a redactor, or editor, *c.* 650 B.C.; (3) a D document called the Deuteronomic Code, written 621 B.C., but revised

by a later writer; (4) a P document (Priestly Code), consisting of the legal and religious prescriptions of the Pentateuch, produced around 500 to 450 B.C. According to this theory the final editing of the Pentateuch was done *c.* 400 B.C. There are many variations of this general scheme held by critical scholars. Some would add a non-Israelite source, S (from Seir, the supposed place of origin) for the book of Genesis. A number of arguments have been advanced in support of this composite character of the Pentateuch. Only a few can be considered here.

(1) *Variations in the Use of the Divine Names.* There is considerable variation in the OT in the names used for God, particularly in the early chapters of Genesis. For example, *'Elohim* is used uniformly in Gen 1:1 to 2:3, being found 34 times in 34 verses. In the rest of ch 2 and in ch 3 the combination *Yahweh 'Elohim* occurs some 18 times. In ch 4 *Yahweh* by itself is used predominately (10 times). This variation was seized upon by Jean Astruc in 1753 as a clue to the dissection of the book into 2 documents by different authors. Conservative scholars hold that the variation in the use of divine names is no evidence of multiple authorship. They hold that *'Elohim,* which implies "strength," "power," or "ability," is a most appropriate designation for God in the Creation narrative, which is an amazing exhibition of divine power in action, and that *Yahweh* (Jehovah) is God's covenant name (see Ex 6:3, 4). The combination *Yahweh 'Elohim,* they believe, identifies the God of Creation with the God of redemption. They note that in many passages the divine names are used more or less interchangeably and that the Hebrew manuscripts, and such early versions as the LXX, show variations. More recently the well-known Dead Sea scroll of Isaiah (1QIsa) has shown variations from the Masoretic text in the use of the divine names, indicating that copyists at times apparently felt no scruples in substituting one divine name for another (see *SDACom* 5:159, 160). Therefore, it is unsafe to use such differences as pretexts for dissecting the Pentateuch.

(2) *The Supposition That Moses Could Not Have Written the Pentateuch.* Critical scholars in the 19th cent. denied the possibility that Moses could have written a record such as is found in the Pentateuch, since, as they thought, only the complicated hieroglyphic and cuneiform systems of writing, confined to Egypt and Mesopotamia, respectively, were known in Moses' day. The oldest alphabetic writing from Palestine known as late as the 1880's was the *Moabite Stone from the 9th cent. B.C. The discovery of the *Amarna Letters in Egypt in 1887, however, has shown that the cuneiform system was widely used in the 2d millennium B.C. Many of these letters were written by petty rulers in Palestine and Syria to their Egyptian overlords, showing that writing was evidently well known in those regions. After 1916 it became known that Canaanite alphabetic scripts were in use before Moses' day. A whole library of Canaanite literature was found in 1929 at Ras Shamra. It is now known that at least 6 different systems of *writing were used in Palestine before the Hebrew conquest. Among these were the proto-Sinaitic script, believed to be the forerunner of the Hebrew alphabet. Hence, no reputable scholar today would claim that alphabetic writing was unknown in Moses' day.

(3) *Passages of Post-Mosaic Date.* The Pentateuch, it is alleged, contains passages that could not have been written by Moses. The most prominent is the account of Moses' death (Deut 34). But such a post-Mosaic addition is not out of harmony with the integrity and Mosaic authorship of the work as a whole. It is also altogether possible that some revisions and slight changes in wording may have occurred during the process of transmission, along with the insertion of certain later forms of place names.

(4) *The Presence of So-called Doublets.* It is alleged that the Pentateuch contains duplicate stories of the same events, which are often contradictory and involve different people. These, it is asserted, come from different sources. Some claim that there are 2 Creation stories and 2 Flood stories, which they separate arbitrarily by cutting up the narrative piecemeal. Some see as repetitious and conflicting accounts the narratives of the 2 expulsions of Hagar (Gen 16:4-16; 21:9-21), 2 appearances of quail in connection with manna (Ex 16; Num 11), 2 drawings of water from the rock (Ex 17; Num 20), etc. The conservative scholar does not admit that these "doublets" are variant accounts of the same event, but sees in them separate authentic narratives.

(5) *Variations in Style and Diction Indicating Different Documents.* Arguments based on style and diction are always tenuous. They are generally based on opin-

ion, and conclusions are not provable; some authors are known to vary surprisingly in style and vocabulary.

The conservative scholar believes that the acceptance of the popular documentary hypothesis is a serious matter with tremendous philosophical and religious implications, since its acceptance or rejection involves one's view of revelation, inspiration, and the credibility of the Bible.

Pentecost, Feast of. The festival of wheat harvest, called variously the Feast of Weeks (Ex 34:22), of First Fruits (Ex 34:22; Num 28:26), of Harvest (Ex 23:16), and, in NT times, of Pentecost (Acts 2:1). This was one of the 3 festivals at which all Hebrew men were required to "appear before the Lord" (Ex 23:17), that is, they were required to journey to the sanctuary. It was a one-day festival, one of the annual ceremonial sabbaths (Lev 23:21). On it 2 loaves of fine flour, baked with leaven, together with specified animal sacrifices were offered to the Lord (vs 17-20).

The terms "Pentecost" (from a Greek word meaning "fiftieth") and "Feast of Weeks" refer to the date of this feast on the 50th day, inclusive, or 7 weeks from the day of the Wave Sheaf ceremony, which took place on the 2d day of the Feast of *Unleavened Bread, "the morrow after the sabbath" (Lev 23:15, 16). About the time of Christ there was a dispute between certain Pharisees and Sadducees. Some of the latter contended that Pentecost was to be always on the day after a weekly Sabbath because they insisted that the wave sheaf, from which the 7 weeks were counted, should be offered on the day after the *weekly* Sabbath that fell during the Feast of Unleavened Bread (Talmud *Menahoth* 65a). However, the other view prevailed, that the "morrow after the sabbath" meant the 16th of Nisan, the day after the *ceremonial* sabbath that began the Feast of Unleavened Bread following the offering of the Passover lamb on the 14th of Nisan. See *SDA-Com* 1:805.

Penuel (pĕ-nū'ĕl). [Heb. *Penû'el* "face of God."]

1. A place near the river Jabbok in Transjordan where Jacob wrestled with the angel of the Lord, and named after that experience (Gen 32:30, 31). It is called Peniel (pĕ-nī'ĕl) [Heb. *Penî'el*] in v 31. In the time of Gideon it is mentioned as a fortified place with a

tower. Because of its hostility toward his cause, Gideon destroyed it and slew its population (Jgs 8:8, 9, 17). Jeroboam I seems to have rebuilt it (1 Ki 12:25). Shishak of Egypt mentions it in the list of conquered cities of Judah and Israel, spelling it *Pnîr.* Map VI, D-4.

2. A Judahite and ancestor of the inhabitants of Gedor (1 Chr 4:4).

3. A descendant of Benjamin (1 Chr 8:25).

People of the East, KJV sometimes **Children of the East** and **Men of the East.** [Heb. *benê-qedem,* "sons of the East."] A general designation of the tribes, mostly nomadic, which occupied the regions east or northeast of Palestine (Eze 25:4, 10; Jer 49:28). The term is similarly used in the Egyptian story of Sinuhe in the 20th cent. B.C., which shows that it was used in Canaan before the Hebrews adopted it.

Peor (pē'ôr). [Heb. *Pe'ôr.*]

1. A mountain of Moab overlooking the desert (Num 23:28). From its summit Balaam could see the camp of Israel (ch 24:2), evidently at Shittim (ch 25:1). Eusebius and Jerome claim that a mountain in the area still bore this name in the 4th and 5th cent. A.D. However, the name is no longer applied to any place there; hence the mountain has not been identified. While encamped near here the Hebrews were seduced into worshiping the Baal of Peor (chs 25:1-5; 31:16).

2. A pagan deity, worshiped apparently on Mount Peor (Num 25:18; 31:16) otherwise called *Baal-peor (cf. v 5).

Perazim (pĕr'ȧ-zīm). [Heb. *Peraṣîm,* "gaps," "breaches."] A mountain referred to in Is 28:21 as the scene apparently of some well-known event. Perazim is probably identical with *Baal-perazim; hence the event would probably be the battle of David against the Philistines (2 Sa 5:17-20; 1 Chr 14:8-16).

Peres. *See* Mene.

Peresh (pē'rĕsh). [Heb. *Peresh,* "dung."] A Manassite (1 Chr 7:16).

Perez (pē'rĕz), KJV frequently **Pharez** (fā'rĕz), KJV of NT **Phares** (fā'rĕz). [Heb. *Pereṣ,* "breach." The name occurs in Assyrian as *Parṣî;* Gr. *Phares.*] One of the twin sons of Judah (Gen 38:27-29), and ancestor of a tribal family, the Perezites (pē'rĕz-īts), KJV "Pharzites" (fär'zīts) [Heb. *Parṣî*], and of 2 other tribal families, the Hezronites and Hamulites, which took their names from his 2 sons, Hezron and Hamul (Num 26:20, 21; 1

Chr 2:4, 5). Perez was an ancestor of David (Ruth 4:18-22) and is listed in the genealogy of Jesus Christ (Mt 1:3, 6, 16).

Perezites. *See* Perez.

Perez-uzza (pē'rĕz-ŭz'á), or **Perez-uzzah** (pē'rĕz-ŭz'á). [Heb. *Pereṣ 'Uzzah* and *Pereṣ 'Uzza'*, "the breach of Uzzah."] A place near Jerusalem; not identified. It was named by David after Uzzah was smitten there for having touched the ark while it was being conveyed to Jerusalem (2 Sa 6:8; 1 Chr 13:11).

Perez-uzzah. *See* Perez-uzza.

Perfect, Perfection. [Heb. generally *tam* or *tamîm*, "complete," "right," "peaceful," "sound," "wholesome," "blameless"; Gr. generally *teleios*, "complete," "perfect," "full grown," "mature," "fully developed," "having attained its purpose."]

In the OT *tam* signifies completeness, integrity, and sincerity, but always in a relative sense when used of man. A person with a "perfect heart" was a man whose life was completely devoted to the Lord (1 Ki 8:61; 1 Chr 12:38; Is 38:3; KJV). Thus Job was designated as "perfect" (Job 1:1, 8, KJV) despite weaknesses revealed later by adversity (see chs 40:2-5; 42:2-6), showing that his perfection was relative rather than absolute. Similarly, Noah was said to be "perfect" (Gen 6:9, KJV) though later he succumbed to the weakness of the flesh (ch 9:21). Perfection was the ideal God set before Abraham (ch 17:1). The RSV generally translates *tam*, "blameless."

In extra-Biblical Greek literature *teleioi*, "perfect ones" or "mature ones," is used of flawless sacrificial victims, of mature animals, of adult human beings, and of trained, fully qualified professional men. In the NT "perfection" consists essentially in maturity as distinguished from immaturity, as adults differ from children and youth. A mature person is one who has attained the normal limits of stature, strength, and mental power. This concept of maturity is clearly evident in such passages as 1 Cor 2:6; 14:20; Eph 4:13, 14; Php 3:15; Heb 5:14. Paul speaks of himself and his fellow Christians as already perfect (1 Cor 2:6; Php 3:15; KJV), but in almost the same breath makes it evident that there is a sense in which perfection is a goal yet to be attained (Php 3:12). The Christian is to be "perfect" in his finite sphere as God is "perfect" in His infinite completeness (Mt 5:48). Thus a man may be "perfect" before the Lord, but there are ever new heights to which

he may aspire. In this life he never attains to ultimate perfection. A person whose heart and life are wholly devoted to the worship and service of God, that is, to the goal of constant growth in grace and in the knowledge and practice of spiritual truth, and who has gained a measure of experience in cooperating with the Holy Spirit, has attained to Christian perfection (Col 4:12; Jas 3:2). He is no longer a "babe" in Christ, occupied with the rudimentary facts and practices of religion (see Heb 5:12 to 6:2). A perfect man in God's sight is thus one who has reached the degree of development expected of him at any given time. He is a mature Christian fully dedicated to the Lord, and who, though he still has weaknesses to overcome, presses onward toward the mark of the high calling of God in Christ Jesus (Php 3:12-15).

Perfume Boxes. A rendering of the Heb. *bottê hannephesh* (Is 3:20, RSV), "containers of scent," KJV "tablets."

Perfumer. *See* Apothecary.

Perga (pûr'gá). [Gr. *Pergē*.] An important city of Pamphylia, several mi. inland from the Gulf of Pamphylia, on the right bank of the river Cestrus. It was an insignificant city until the Romans made it the capital of the province. Perga was the seat of an Asiatic fertility goddess, Leto, who was assigned functions similar to those of *Artemis of Ephesus, and to whom people referred as the "queen of Perga." The site of the temple of this goddess has not been identified, but the city's theater, which seated 13,000 people, is well preserved, and ruins of other public structures also remain. The apostles Paul and Barnabas visited the city twice during the 1st Missionary Journey, preaching there during their 2d visit (Acts 13:13, 14; 14:25). Map XX, B-5.

Pergamos. *See* Pergamum.

Pergamum (pûr'gá-mum), KJV **Pergamos** (pûr'gá-mŏs). [Gr. *Pergamos* and *Pergamon*,

376. The ruin mound of Pergamum, with the modern city of *Bergama* in the left foreground

PERGAMUM

possibly "citadel," "acropolis"; Latin *Pergamum*.] The old capital of Mysia, a city situated in the Caicus Valley about 15 mi. from the sea, and 3 mi. north of the Caicus River. Its period of greatest importance was during the 3d and 2d cent. B.C., when the Attalids reigned over the kingdom of Pergamum, which comprised much of western Asia Minor. Attalus III willed his kingdom to the Romans, and when he died (133 B.C.) the area was made into the Roman province of Asia with Pergamum as the provincial capital and residence of the proconsul. The acropolis, built on the summit and slopes of a steep hill rising some 1,000 ft. above the plain, contained most of the important public buildings. Among these were the palace of the Attalids, a great theater which rivaled in size that of Ephesus, temples dedicated to Athena and Demeter, and the most marvelous structure of all, the massive altar of Zeus, 127 ft. long, 120 ft. wide, and 40 ft. high. The sculptured stone slabs covering the sides of the altar were masterpieces. The sculpture depicted a war between giants and gods, reflecting the victories of the Pergamese over the Gauls, whom they pushed into central Asia Minor, where the latter became the Galatians of NT fame.

Pergamum was excavated from 1879 to 1886 by Karl Humann, who discovered the Zeus altar and transported its component parts to Berlin, where the whole monument was reconstructed (fig. 377). Recent German excavators concentrated their efforts on the Asclepieion—the compound of Asclepius, the god of healing—in which were found a large school of medicine, a hospital with treatment rooms for the sick, a theater for the entertainment of patients, and a sanctuary of Asclepius. The famous physician Galen received his training in this institution. Pergamum's name has been perpetuated in the word *parchment. Parchment was invented or developed there when Ptolemy V of Egypt (203-181 B.C.) prohibited the export of papyrus scrolls for fear that the large library of Pergamum might soon have more volumes than the library of Alexandria. This resulted in the refining of the tanning process of leather in Pergamum and the development of the excellent writing material that the Greeks called *pergamēne* after that city. A Christian church existed in Pergamum toward the end of the 1st cent. A.D., as is proved by the fact that John addressed a message to it from the island of Patmos (Rev 2:12-17).

377. The ancient altar of Zeus, as reconstructed in the Pergamon-Museum at Berlin

The modern successor of Pergamum is the town of *Bergama*, nestled against the foot of the acropolis hill (fig. 376), with a population of about 20,000.

For the significance of Pergamum as one of the 7 churches of the Revelation see *SDA Com* 7:93-96, 748-750.

Perida (pḗ-rī'dȧ), or **Peruda** (pē-rōō'dȧ). [Heb. *Perîda'* and *Perûda'*, "single," or "unique."] The ancestral head of a family of "Solomon's servants" (Ezr 2:55; Neh 7:57). The difference in the Hebrew names is in the letters *y* and *w*, which in postexilic Hebrew manuscripts are almost indistinguishable.

Perizzites (pĕr'ĭ-zīts). [Heb. *Perizzî*.] One of the pre-Israelite tribes of Canaan, which seems to have occupied an important section of the country, as may be concluded from frequent references to them in the early books of the OT (Gen 13:7; Ex 3:8; Jos 9:1; etc.). However, their identification with people known from secular sources is still very uncertain. They were already in the country in the days of Abraham (Gen 13:7; 15:20), but do not seem to have been a major nation, since they are not listed in the Table of Nations of ch 10. They lived in the mountains of Canaan in Joshua's time (Jos 11:3), particularly in the area that Manasseh and Ephraim later occupied (ch 17:15), but also in sections that Judah later occupied (Jgs 1:4, 5). Many of the Israelites intermarried with them (ch 3:5, 6), but they seem to have retained their identity for centuries, for they are described as being made bondservants by Solomon and as being pressed into his labor corps (1 Ki 9:20, 21; 2 Chr 8:7).

In an effort to identify these people it has been shown that the Heb. *perazî*, "dwellers in open country," and the Heb. *Perizzî*, rendered "Perizzites," are identical terms when unvocalized. Thus it has been suggested that the term "Perizzites" may not refer to an ethnic group at all, but may describe instead a people who did not live in walled cities. Another suggestion is that the Perizzites were a subdivision of the Horites, because a Hurrian (Horite) messenger of King Tushratta, mentioned repeatedly in the *Amarna Letters, bears the name Perizzi.

Persia (pûr'zhá). [Heb. and Aramaic *Paras;* Old Persian *Pārsa;* Babylonian *Parsu;* Late Egyptian *Prs.*] Persia appears first in the annals of history (7th cent. B.C.) as an area on the northeastern coast of the Persian Gulf (Map XII, D/E-9/10), bounded on the east by Carmania, on the north by Media, and on the west by Susiania (Elam). The Persian tribes seem to have centered around Anshan, which has not been definitely identified, but may have been the place later known as "Cyrus' city," now called Pasargadae (Map XII, D-9). Phraortes (*c.* 647 - *c.* 625 B.C.), one of the earliest Median kings known to history, is credited with having subjugated the Persian tribes, and from that time until the time of Cyrus the Great, Persia formed part of the Median kingdom, although the ruler of the Persians continued to bear the title "king of Anshan."

Persian history actually begins with Cyrus the Great (*c.* 553-530 B.C.). Although 4 generations of his royal ancestors are known, no historical records or traditions about their rule have survived. Achaemenes, the great-great-grandfather of Cyrus, as well as an ancestor of Darius through a different line, was considered the founder of the dynasty. Consequently the Persian kings of the ancient empire period are referred to as Achaemenids. On the other hand, the Persian kings who ruled over large parts of the East from A.D. 208 to A.D. 641, are called Sassanians or Sassanids, names derived from that of their family.

Cyrus, whose mother and wife were said to have belonged to the royal house of the Medes, rose up against Astyages, his Median overlord (*c.* 553 B.C.). In spite of some setbacks he succeeded in overthrowing the Median dynasty and in possessing its territory. After consolidating his rule over the whole kingdom he conquered Lydia (547 B.C.) and Babylonia (539 B.C.), in this way becoming the founder of an empire that was greater than any that had previously existed (Map XII). Cyrus was tolerant of other religions, and favored especially people who had been subjugated by the Babylonians, restoring the temples and modes of worship of these people and allowing exiles to return to their homelands.

378. Persian soldiers at Persepolis on a stone relief

Among those who profited by these favorable policies were the Jews, who received permission to return to Palestine and rebuild their Temple in Jerusalem (2 Chr 36:22, 23; Ezr 1:1-11; 6:2-5). *See* Cyrus.

Cambyses (530-522 B.C.), who is not mentioned in the Bible, followed his father on the throne. His major accomplishment was the conquest of Egypt (525 B.C.). He stayed in that country for 3 years and organized the Nile valley into a strong Persian satrapy. However, before he left for Egypt he had his brother Bardiya (called Smerdis, by the Greeks) slain for fear that he might usurp the throne during his absence, since Bardiya was much more popular than he. In 522 B.C., while Cambyses was still in Egypt, Gaumata, a Median Magian, claimed to be Bardiya (Smerdis) and usurped the throne. Cambyses hurried back to Persia, but died on the way home, either by his own hand or as the result of an accident. He left no heir.

Darius, a distant relative, now rose to claim the kingship (522-486 B.C.). He slew Bardiya after that pretender had reigned only about 6 months. However, Darius had to fight several other claimants to the throne before he became the undisputed ruler of the Persian Empire. Once on the throne Darius I proved to be a strong monarch and a great organizer, who ruled over his vast empire (Map XII) with a benevolent and peaceful hand. During the early years of his reign the Jews, who had been hindered in rebuilding the Temple at Jerusalem after the time of Cyrus, finally completed this work without interference under an extremely favorable decree issued by Darius (Ezr 4:24 to 6:15). *See* Darius, 2. Darius' later years were clouded by military disasters in his wars against the Greeks.

Xerxes I (486-465 B.C.), the son of Darius I, was a weak ruler compared with his father, and suffered several heavy defeats in Greece, although he was successful in suppressing revolts in Egypt and Babylonia. He also partly destroyed Babylon after a 2d uprising there against his rule. He thus had a part in fulfilling the prophecies concerning Babylon's fate made long before by Isaiah and Jeremiah (see Is 13:17-22; Jer 50:9-16). In the Bible Xerxes is mentioned by the name of *Ahasuerus.

*Artaxerxes I (465-423 B.C.), Xerxes' son, took the throne upon his father's assassination. He was erratic like his father, and loved pleasure and power but managed to rule for more than 4 decades, largely because of the fact that his brother-in-law, Megabyzos, suppressed an Egyptian rebellion for him, and kept the empire intact. However, Megabyzos himself once rebelled when the perfidy of the king became too much for him. Artaxerxes followed the policy of religious tolerance practiced by his predecessors. Under him Ezra, a scholarly Jew, returned to Jerusalem in 457 B.C. with authority to reorganize the judicial and civil service of the province of Judah according to the Mosaic law (Ezr 7:1, 6, 11-26). Also under him Nehemiah, another Jew, was made governor of Judah and was allowed to refortify Jerusalem (Neh 2:5-8).

Darius II (423-405/04 B.C.) came to the throne after a short interval, during which Xerxes II, possibly also Sogdianus, ruled briefly before being eliminated by force. Darius II is apparently the last Persian ruler mentioned in the OT, being probably the "Darius the Persian" of Neh 12:22, from whose reign we have the last lists of Temple personnel given in the Bible.

Four more rulers followed on the throne of the Achaemenids; Artaxerxes II (405/04-359/58 B.C.), Artaxerxes III (359/58-338/37 B.C.), Arses (338/37-336/35 B.C.), and Darius III (336/35-331 B.C.). During their reigns the empire lost much of its might and territory, including Egypt, while Macedonia arose to challenge Persian rule of the world. In his fight against Alexander the Great, Darius III lost one battle after another, until a few years later the whole empire fell into the hands of the young Macedonian. He himself was killed by his own courtiers as he fled. Thus the 2-cent.-old Persian Empire gave way and was replaced by the Greco-Macedonian world power. *See* Greece, II.

The capitals, or rather royal residences, of the Persian emperors were: (1) Ecbatana (KJV "Achmetha"), the summer residence, situated in the cool highlands of Iran, and (2) Susa (KJV "Shushan"), the winter residence, situated near the head of the Persian Gulf. This place was too hot to be the summer residence, but was pleasantly warm in the winter. (3) Pasargadae, "Cyrus' city," which may be the old capital of Anshan, where Cyrus (and probably also Cambyses) was buried, and the most glorious of all Persian cities. (4) Persepolis, a treasure city with beautiful palaces built in the desert by the Achaemenids. It seems that this place was not used as a residence city for extended periods; however, all rulers from Darius I on had their rock-cut tombs constructed near that city. Neither Pasargadae nor Persepolis is mentioned in the Bible. The first 3 kings of the empire also used Babylon as a residence city.

The Persian religion of the empire period was the most ethical pagan religion ever developed. Its founder was Zarathustra (Zoroaster). His religion knew only one god, Ahura Mazda (or Ormazd), "the wise lord," the main principle of everything good, the wise creator spirit who revealed himself in light and fire. The evil principle was embodied in Angra Mainyu (Ahriman), the chief of all demons, who opposed by evil all that the god of light created. Since man was involved in this fight of the spiritual powers, he had the task of helping to lead the good principle to victory through purity and truth. Every kind of falsehood was despised and to be shunned. By purity Zoroaster understood health, life, strength, honesty, loyalty, agriculture, cattle breeding, protection of useful animals, and destruction of vermin, which were considered to be a creation of the evil one. Defilement was caused by laziness, dishonesty, or by contact with a corpse. Zoroaster thus elevated the code of ethics of his people and educated them to become the bearers of a high moral culture, which spread throughout the empire.

Persian (pûr'zhăn). [Heb. *Paras* and *Paresî;* Aramaic *Paras* and *Parsay.*] An inhabitant of Persia (Neh 12:22; Est 1:19; Dan 5:28; etc.).

Persis (pûr'sĭs). [Gr. *Persis,* "Persian," a typical name of a female slave, frequently attested by inscriptions.] A Christian woman in Rome, to whom Paul sent especially warm greetings in his letter to the Romans (Rom 16:12).

Peruda. *See* Perida.

Pestilence. [Heb. generally *deber;* Gr. *loimos, thanatos.*] An infectious or contagious disease that reaches epidemic proportions. Although this word appears scattered through several OT books (Ex 5:3; Num 14:12; 2 Chr 7:13; Ps 91:3, 6), it is found most often in the writings of the prophets (Jer 21:6; 27:8; Eze 7:15; 28:23; Amos 4:10; etc.) and is there frequently associated with the terms "sword" and "famine," as in the expression "by the sword, and by the famine, and by the pestilence" (Jer 14:12; 21:9; 32:36; Eze 6:11; 12:16; etc.). Human history had so often demonstrated the tragic sequence of the scourges of sword, famine, and pestilence that by the time of Jeremiah and Ezekiel these 3 evils were grouped together in a rather fixed proverbial form. Pestilences were stated by Jesus to be one of the signs of His return (Mt 24:7; Lk 21:11; KJV). In Mt 24:7, RSV, the term "pestilence" is omitted on the basis of textual evidence. In Acts 24:1, 5 the orator Tertullus is recorded as calling Paul "a pestilent fellow" (Gr. *loimos,* literally, "pestilence"). The "pestilence" of Rev 6:8; 18:8; RSV, is a rendering of the Gr. *thanatos,* "death." This translation is adopted doubtless on the basis of the LXX, which at times translates the Heb. *deber,* "pestilence" by *thanatos* (see the LXX of Lev 26:25; Jer 21:6; Eze 5:11).

Pestle. A rendering of the Heb. *'eli* (Prov 27:22), an implement used to pound or pulverize certain products, such as grain, in a mortar. The author of Proverbs states that even though a fool be punished for his folly as severely as grain is crushed by means of a pestle in a mortar, yet he will not learn by his experience.

Peter (pē'tēr). [Gr. *Petros,* "stone," a translation of the Aramaic *Kêpha',* "Cephas," "rock," or "stone." See Jn 1:42.] One of the Twelve, also called Simon (Gr. *Simōn* and *Sumeōn,* from Heb. *Shim'ôn,* "Simeon"), a son of Jona (Jn 1:42), or, on the basis of textual evidence, John (see chs 1: 42; 21:15-17; RSV). Peter's name appears 1st in all 4 NT lists of the Twelve (Mt 10:2; Mk 3:16; Lk 6:14; Acts 1:13). Jesus gave Simon his new name, Peter, when Peter's brother, Andrew, first brought him to Christ (Jn 1:40-42). Peter was thus the 1st Christian convert resulting from what might be called a layman's efforts. His eagerness, earnestness, courage, vigor, and organizing ability apparently earned him a place of leadership among the disciples from the very beginning. He was preeminently a man of action, and his enthusiastic disposition was his outstanding character trait. He was also a man of pronounced extremes, possessing marked virtues and serious defects—seemingly contradictory traits of character that existed side by side. He was usually warmhearted, generous, bold, and daring, but again he might be selfish, boastful, impulsive, or reckless. In a moment of crisis he might prove to be weak, cowardly, and vacillating, and no one could ever be sure which side of his character and personality would prevail.

Peter was a native of *Bethsaida Julias (see Jn 1:44; Jos. *Ant.* xviii. 2. 1), on the northeastern shore of the Sea of Galilee, and was a fisherman by occupation (Mt 4:18). He was married (Mt 8:14; 1 Cor 9:5) and lived with his family at Capernaum, where Jesus, on one occasion, restored Peter's mother-in-law to health (Mt 8:5, 14; Mk 1:29-31; Lk 4:31, 38). Prior to his call by the sea (Lk 5:1-11) Peter had followed Jesus intermittently, returning home from time to time to engage in his former occupation, fishing. He, with James and John, was a member of an inner circle of 3 who were accorded the privilege of accompanying Jesus on special occasions, and in the lists of the 3 he is always named 1st. The 3 recorded occasions on which this special favor was granted were the raising of Jairus' daughter (Mk 5:37), the Transfiguration (Mt 17:1), and Jesus' passion in Gethsemane (Mk 14: 33). Peter often made himself spokesman for all the disciples (see Mt 15:15; 16:16; 26:35; etc.). At Caesarea Philippi he was the first openly to confess Jesus to be the Christ, the Son of God (Mt 16:16), but was also forward in presuming to criticize Jesus (vs 22, 23). At the Last Supper Peter hesitated to have Jesus wash his feet, but when he realized that this act was essential to discipleship he enthusiastically asked for his hands and his head to be washed as well (Jn 13:8, 9). On the night of the betrayal he was foremost in professing loyalty to the Saviour (Mt 26:33), but also the first to deny his Master and confirm his thrice-repeated denial with an oath (vs 69-74). Realizing, too late, what he had done, he "went out, and wept bitterly" (v 75). After the resurrection the first of the 12 to whom Jesus appeared was Peter (Lk 24:34; 1 Cor 15:5), and early one morning when Jesus met with His disciples by the shores of Galilee, Peter was the first ashore to greet his Master (Jn 21:7). Upon this occasion Jesus gave Peter a threefold opportunity to confess his faith and love, and thus to remove any lingering doubt in the minds of his fellow disciples as to his loyalty (vs 15-17). Thereupon Jesus foretold Peter's death as a martyr (vs 18, 19) and a few moments later rebuked his inquisitiveness as to John's fate (vs 21-24).

At Pentecost, fully converted, Peter delivered the great sermon recorded in the 2d chapter of Acts (vs 14-36), an inspired address that led some 3,000 to believe in Jesus as the Messiah (v 41). Together with John, Peter healed the lame man at the Gate Beautiful (ch 3:1-11), and later, surrounded by a throng in the Temple, eloquently testified to the death, resurrection, and power of Christ (vs 12-26). He was arrested for healing the lame man, and when brought before the Sanhedrin for an investigation, he again boldly testified concerning Jesus (ch 4:1-12), and when commanded not to speak further in the name of Jesus, Peter and John declared that they could not "but speak the things" which they had "seen and heard" (vs 19, 20). Peter played a leading part in the collection and distribution of gifts made by the more prosperous Christian believers for their less fortunate brethren (ch 5:1-11). He became known as one through whom divine power operated for the healing of the sick (vs 15, 16). Again Peter and some of the other apostles were imprisoned (vs 17, 18), only to be released by an angel of the Lord and again commanded to preach and teach in the Temple (vs 19, 20). Doing so, they were summoned once more before the high priest (vs 21-27) and reminded of his previous injunction (v 28). As spokesman, Peter declared, "We ought to obey God rather than men" (v 29), and fearlessly witnessed to Christ as the Saviour of Israel (vs 30-32). Peter is next heard of

when, with John, he was sent to Samaria to assist Philip in his successful ministry (Acts 8:14). There he sternly rebuked Simon the sorcerer for proposing to purchase the power of the Holy Spirit for money (vs 18-24). He seems to have engaged in a rather extensive period of evangelism among the Samaritans (v 25). Later, at Lydda, he healed Aeneas, a paralytic (ch 9:32-35). Going on to Joppa, he raised Dorcas from the dead and took up residence at the home of Simon, a tanner (vs 36-43).

While Peter was living in Simon's home the Lord instructed him, by a vision, not to "call any man common or unclean" (Acts 10:9-17, 28). The simultaneous arrival of messengers from Cornelius led him to understand the import of the vision and to accompany the messengers back to Caesarea, where Cornelius and his family were converted through his ministry (vs 19-23, 29-48). Summoned by his brethren at Jerusalem to explain his conduct in associating with Gentiles, Peter defended his course of action as in harmony with the counsel and manifest guidance of the Holy Spirit (ch 11:1-18). About this time Peter was once more imprisoned, but again was miraculously released by an angel (ch 12:1-11). Thereupon he went first to John Mark's home, where the church was praying for his release (vs 12-17), and then left Jerusalem for Caesarea, where he stayed for some time (v 19). At the Jerusalem Council, called to settle the question referred to it by the Gentile church at Antioch as to whether Gentile believers should be required to observe the ritual Jewish law, Peter, recounting his experience with Cornelius (ch 15:6-9), concluded, "Why tempt ye God, to put a yoke upon the neck of the disciples, which neither our fathers nor we were able to bear?" (v 10). When visiting Antioch, Peter, in a moment of overcaution, "withdrew and separated himself, fearing them which were of the circumcision" (Gal 2:11, 12), and was openly rebuked by Paul for his inconsistency (vs 13, 14). Peter labored primarily for his fellow Jews (ch 2:7, 8), and Paul refers to him as one of the "pillars" in the church at Jerusalem (v 9). When Paul first visited Jerusalem after his conversion, he stayed in Peter's home for 15 days (ch 1:18). Some believe that Peter visited Corinth (see 1 Cor 1:12), and that he labored extensively in various parts of Asia Minor (1 Pe 1:1). He glorified God by a martyr's death (cf. Jn 21:18, 19). Peter's 1st epistle was written from the city of Rome (see 1 Pe 5:13, where Babylon is undoubtedly used as a cryptic name for Rome), in which he seems to have labored for awhile shortly before his martyrdom, at about the time Paul sealed his testimony with his blood. According to tradition, he was crucified with his head downward, at Rome, about A.D. 67.

Peter, Epistles of. Two general, or "catholic," epistles. In the earliest Greek manuscripts they are known simply as *Petrou A*, "Of Peter I," and *Petrou B*, "Of Peter II." These epistles are known as "general," or "catholic," epistles because they were addressed, not to an individual person or congregation, but to groups of believers.

Both epistles are of the nature of circular letters addressed to the "strangers scattered throughout Pontus, Galatia, Cappadocia, Asia, and Bithynia" (1 Pe 1:1; cf. 2 Pe 1:1; 3:1). That the 1st epistle was addressed chiefly to Christians of Gentile origin is clear from such passages as 1 Pe 1:14; 2:9, 10; 3:6; and 4:3. That it was probably written from Rome (ch 5:13) indicates a time toward the close of the apostle's life. The epistle also reflects an unfriendly attitude in the Roman Empire toward Christians (see chs 2:12; 4:12-16), which may suggest the time of Nero's persecution, which began in A.D. 64. The 2d epistle may also have been written from Rome. Both may be dated between A.D. 64 and 67.

1 Peter. Ancient Christian tradition unanimously attests Petrine authorship of the 1st epistle. However, modern critics, on the supposed basis that the Greek of 1 Pe is too elegant for a man of Peter's limited educational background, that the theology of the epistle more closely resembles that of Paul than it does that of Peter, that little mention is made of incidents in Christ's life—as would be expected of one so closely associated with Christ as Peter had been—and that Peter is not otherwise known to have been associated in any way with the churches of Asia Minor, have asserted that the apostle could not possibly have been the author of either this or the 2d epistle. On the other hand, it is entirely possible that Silvanus (1 Pe 5:12), who apparently served as Peter's scribe, was responsible for the quality of the Greek in the epistle. The contention that the theology of the epistle does not resemble that of Peter is a matter of opinion, as also that Peter would have had more to say about his experiences with Christ. The latter argu-

ment and the one about Peter's not having been in Asia Minor are no more than assumptions based on silence. The author identifies himself as the apostle Peter (1 Pe 1:1) and there is no valid reason for doubting his claim. Polycarp, a disciple of the apostle John, quotes from the epistle, thus attesting its existence soon after the beginning of the 2d cent. Toward the close of that century Irenaeus and others attribute it to Peter.

1 Peter is a general pastoral epistle imparting counsel on various subjects. Particularly, the apostle would prepare his readers for "the fiery trial" (1 Pe 4:12) that looms ahead, which is already reflected in troublous times. Peter seeks to strengthen their faith, to exhort them to blameless conduct, to give a loyal witness for Christ, and to be prepared to meet their Lord. The introduction (ch 1:1-12) is followed by an exhortation to steadfast Christian living (chs 1:13 to 4:19), in which Peter admonishes his readers to live worthy of the high calling in Christ Jesus (ch 1:13-25), to advance in their knowledge of Christ and in Christian maturity (ch 2:1-8), and to live exemplary lives among the Gentiles (vs 9-18). He also counsels them to be meek under suffering (vs 19-25). He has special advice for servants (v 18), husbands and wives (ch 3:1-7), elders (ch 5:1-4), and younger members of the church (vs 5-9). He encourages believers to unity in the faith (ch 3:8-13). To suffer for Christ is a high privilege with a great reward (vs 14-22). He appeals to the believers to control their fleshly lusts (ch 4:1-6), to be sober and charitable in their lives (vs 7-11), and to be steadfast under persecution (vs 12-19), and counsels church officers and members to be faithful (ch 5:1-9). The conclusion, vs 10-14, consists of a benediction, a doxology, and personal greetings.

2 Peter. Since early Christian times there has been considerable difference of opinion as to the authorship of 2 Peter. Origen, the earliest writer to mention it specifically, expresses doubt as to its authenticity (Eusebius *Hist. Eccl.* vi. 25). Eusebius (*ibid.* iii. 3) wrote that the epistle had not been received as canonical, but that since many considered it useful it was being studied along with other Scriptures. There seem to be no direct quotations from 2 Peter in earliest Christian writings.

Perhaps no other book of the NT has been as emphatically declared postapostolic—and thus spurious—by modern scholars as 2 Peter. They point out that its language and style differ markedly from those of 1 Peter. They note that it gives a special status to the extant epistles of Paul, referring to them as "scripture" (2 Pe 3:15, 16), placing them thus on the same level of inspiration and authority as the OT, and observe that it is incredible that these epistles of Paul should have been collected and have attained to a state equal to that of OT scriptures during Peter's lifetime, especially since Peter and Paul died about the same time. However, the epistle claims to be the writing of Simon Peter, disciple and apostle of Jesus Christ (ch 1:1), and to be his "second epistle" (ch 3:1). The author also claims to have been with Christ upon the mount of Transfiguration (ch 1:17, 18), an occasion on which only Peter, James, and John were present (Mt 17:1). The difference in the style from 1 Peter may be the result of Peter's not having had the help of the same amanuensis he had in writing his 1st epistle (see 1 Pe 5:12). It is most logical to suppose that Peter, an unschooled Palestinian, with Aramaic as his mother tongue, would use a secretary when he wrote in Greek, a language with which he was not entirely familiar, since even Paul, who was fully at home in Greek, commonly used amanuenses. The argument that Paul's epistles could not have been gathered and recognized as "scripture" before Peter's death is only an assumption. In view of the fact that Paul's active ministry covered a period of about 20 years, that Peter was in Rome at the time he wrote his 1st epistle (1 Pe 5: 13), and that Peter and Paul suffered martyrdom about the same time, there is no reason why Paul's epistles could not have attained the status reflected in Peter's statement in 2 Pe 3:15, 16. Paul's active and successful ministry and his explicit claim that he received his gospel by inspiration (see Gal 1:11, 12; 1 Ti 4:1) clearly provide a solid foundation for Peter's statement.

In 1958 an announcement was made of the discovery of a 3d-cent. papyrus containing the general epistles 1 Pe, 2 Pe, and Jude, now in the Bodmer library in Switzerland. This manuscript is a most significant find and is a testimony to the acceptance of these epistles, at least by some, in the 3d cent. It was published in 1959 and is known as Bodmer VII, VIII (P⁷²). For a discussion of certain similarities between 2 Pe and the epistle of Jude, *see* Jude.

Second Peter is a pastoral epistle in which the writer exhorts his readers to continue their growth in grace and in spiritual knowledge, in order that God's purpose in their calling and election may be fulfilled. Following the introduction (2 Pe 1:1-11), he states his purpose in writing as being to establish the believers in present truth and to confirm the gospel message on the basis of his personal experience with Christ and the fulfillment of OT prophecy in Christ (vs 12-21). Chapter 2 consists of a series of stern warnings against false teachers and their deceptive heresies. The last section of the epistle (ch 3:1-18) stresses the coming of Christ and preparation for His appearing. The great day of the Lord is certain (vs 3-10), and in anticipation of that event all should live godly lives (vs 11-18).

Pethahiah (pĕth'á-hī'á). [Heb. *Pethachyah,* "Yahweh opens (the womb)."]

1. A descendant of Aaron, and head of the 19th of the 24 courses into which David organized the priests (1 Chr 24:16).

2. A Levite who had married a foreign wife in the time of Ezra (Ezr 10:18, 23), possibly identical with Pethahiah, 3.

3. A Levite who assisted Ezra in blessing God after the reading of the Law (Neh 9:5), possibly identical with Pethahiah, 2.

4. A Judahite of the family of Zerah. He was an official of the province of Judah representing the Jewish people at the court of the Persian king (Neh 11:24).

Pethor (pē'thôr). [Heb. *Pethôr.*] The home of Balaam near the river Euphrates in Aram (*see* Aram, 5), or northern Mesopotamia (Num 22:5; 23:7; Deut 23:4). The city is mentioned first by Thutmose III (*c.* 1482 - *c.* 1450 B.C.), who lists it with other conquered Syrian cities as *Pdr.* Later Shalmaneser III (859-824 B.C.) conquered the city, which was at that time called *Pitru.* Its site has not yet been located with certainty.

Pethuel (pĕ-thū'ĕl). [Heb. *Pethú'el.*] The father of the prophet Joel (Joel 1:1).

Petra. See Sela.

Peullethai (pĕ-ŭl'ĕ-thī), KJV **Peulthai** (pĕ-ŭl'thī). [Heb. *Pe'ullethay,* probably "reward of Yahweh."] A Levite, the ancestral head of a family of Korahite gatekeepers (1 Chr 26:1, 5).

Peulthai. See Peullethai.

Phalec. See Peleg.

Phallu. See Pallu.

Phalti. See Palti, 2.

Phaltiel. See Palti, 2.

Phanuel (fá-nū'ĕl). [Gr. *Phanouēl,* from Heb. *Penû'el,* "face of God."] An Asherite, the father of the prophetess Anna (Lk 2:36).

Pharaoh (fâr'ō). [Heb. *Par'oh,* a transliteration of the Egyptian *Pr-'3,* "the Great House"; Gr. *Pharaō.*] A term used in Egypt from the time of the Old Kingdom to designate the palace or the court, also as a specific designation for the kings from the 18th dynasty on, the dynasty during which Moses wrote the Pentateuch. (For the royal emblems and throne of an 18th-dynasty Pharaoh, see figs. 422, 501.) These kings each had 3 titles and 2 names. The Egyptians usually used the 1st name, whereas modern Egyptologists and historians use the 2d name. The following Pharaohs are mentioned by name in the OT: *Shishak, *So, *Tirhakah, *Necho, and *Hophra. Several others are designated only by the general term Pharaoh, some of whom cannot be identified; others with varying degrees of certainty:

1. The Pharaoh who took Sarah, Abraham's wife, into his harem and then released her untouched after divine punishments fell upon him (Gen 12:15-20). On the basis of a mid-15th-cent. Exodus (*see* Chronology, II, 2), Abraham, called some 430 years earlier (see SDACom 1: 314, 315, 557), would have lived during the Middle Kingdom; then this Pharaoh would seem to have been one of the 12th-dynasty kings.

2. The Pharaoh who elevated Joseph to the position of vizier of Egypt, and under whom Jacob and his family moved into Egypt (Gen 41-47). This event, 215 years after the call of Abraham (*see* Chronology, II, 2; Exodus), must have happened in the 17th cent. B.C. when the Hyksos ruled over Egypt. It is therefore reasonable to conclude that this Pharaoh was one of the Semitic Hyksos kings. Since the sequence of these kings is not yet known, Joseph's benefactor cannot be identified.

3. The new Pharaoh who "knew not Joseph" (Ex 1:8) was, on the basis of the foregoing, most probably one of the 1st kings of the 18th dynasty, who expelled the Hyksos from Egypt and reestablished national rulership in the country. This would be either Ahmose (*c.* 1570 - *c.* 1546 B.C.), the victor over the Hyksos, or his immediate successor, Amenhotep I (*c.* 1546 - *c.* 1525 B.C.; the 18th-dynasty dates are known only approximately).

4. The Pharaoh who gave the decree to kill the newborn Hebrew male children (Ex 1:15-22). This was most probably Thutmose I (*c.* 1525 - *c.* 1508 B.C.), because the chronological scheme adopted in this dictionary, which places the Exodus in 1445 B.C., when Moses was 80 years old (cf. Acts 7:23, 30), would make 1525 B.C. the year in which Moses was born.

5. The Pharaoh before whom Moses fled to Midian (Ex 2:15); probably Thutmose III, whose sole reign fell into the years *c.* 1482 - *c.* 1450 B.C., but who was already powerful as coregent with his aunt Hatshepsut for some years previously.

6. The Pharaoh of the Exodus (Ex 3: 10), probably Amenhotep II (*c.* 1450 - *c.* 1425 B.C.). See fig. 167.

7. The Pharaoh who received Hadad of Edom in the time of David (1 Ki 11: 14-22), probably either Siamon (*c.* 1004 - *c.* 984 B.C.) or Psusennes II (*c.* 984 - *c.* 950 B.C.) of the 21st dynasty. The Pharaoh who gave his sister to Hadad as wife could have been either the latter or Sheshonk I (Biblical Shishak), the 1st king of the 22d dynasty.

8. The Pharaoh whose daughter Solomon married (1 Ki 3:1; 7:8; 9:16, 24), probably either Siamon (*c.* 1004 - *c.* 984 B.C.) or Psusennes II of Tanis (*c.* 984 - *c.* 950 B.C.), the last two kings of the 21st dynasty.

Lit.: G. Steindorff and K. C. Seele, *When Egypt Ruled the East* (Chicago, 1942); É. Drioton and J. Vandier, *L'Égypte* (Paris, 1946). The latter contains a complete list of the Egyptian kings on pp. 597-602.

Phares. *See* Perez.

Pharez. *See* Perez.

Pharisees. [Gr. *Pharisaioi,* a transliteration of the Heb. *Perûshîm,* "separate ones"; Aramaic *Perîshayya'.*] The conservative religious sect or party of Judaism in intertestamental and NT times. It is supposed that the Pharisees originated as a distinct party in the 2d half of the 2d cent. B.C. However, their origin is somewhat obscure. It seems reasonably certain that they were the successors of the Hasidim (Chasidim or Assideans), "pious ones," who actively supported the early Maccabees in their struggle against the Seleucids. Being strictly orthodox and deeply concerned to preserve the religious purity of their people, they rejected all attempts to introduce Hellenistic practices among the Jews. When the Maccabean rulers began to favor Hellenism, this group of orthodox Jews began to oppose its own government. It is under John Hyrcanus

(135-105/04 B.C.) that the name "Pharisees" first appears in our sources, a name indicating that the Pharisees considered themselves promoters of a separateness from the world and its tendencies. Having become a religio-political party by this time, they actively opposed John Hyrcanus' worldly rule, and even more so that of his son, Alexander Jannaeus (103-76/75 B.C.). The result was a bloody persecution of these zealous religionists and the death of many prominent Pharisees. But it soon became apparent that the influence of the Pharisees over the people grew in spite of adversity. Jannaeus' widow and successor, Alexandra (Salome), sought a reconciliation with the Pharisees, and they became a powerful force in her state. At the time of the civil war between the two brothers Hyrcanus II and Aristobulus II soon after Alexandra's death, the Pharisees supported the former and the *Sadducees the latter. When Palestine came under Roman control (63 B.C.), the Pharisees retained their position as an influential political party and as champions of orthodoxy. When Herod the Great (40-4 B.C.) came into power he was prudent enough not to persecute the Pharisees, for he knew that they had great influence over the people, although the actual number of this sect, about 6,000 (Jos. *Ant.* xvii. 2. 4), was comparatively small. It was during that time that Hillel and Shammai lived, some of the greatest Pharisaic teachers of all time. Their teachings survived in the rabbinical writings of the Mishnah and the Talmud. Pharisees formed 1 of 3 groups in the Sanhedrin, the other 2 being the Sadducees and the Herodians. It was the Pharisaic sect that for several centuries continued to produce the greatest religious leaders among orthodox Jews, and thus exercised more influence on the religious life of its nation than any other force in Jewry.

The place of the Pharisees in NT Jewish life and thought can best be understood when they are contrasted with the other major parties, the *Sadducees. In the religious spectrum of NT Judaism the Sadducees were the liberals. Finding themselves "in the world," they were quite ready and willing to be "of" it as well. The Pharisees, on the other hand, though of necessity they were "in the world," declined to be "of" it. Pharisaism—"separatism"—stressed separation from the world and its defilements. The Essenes not only refused to be "of" the

world but did all within their power to escape from it by leading an ascetic life. Whereas the Pharisees lived apart from the world and looked forward to getting out of it, the Sadducees looked forward to no other world. The eye of the Pharisees was fixed on the future life, and that of the Sadducees on this life, since they entertained no hope of a future life. With the Pharisees, religious interests were uppermost, but secular interests were the dominant concern of the Sadducees. The Pharisees avoided politics and took an interest in political affairs only because they wanted to maintain a separation between the priesthood and political rule. Where the Pharisees avoided civic duties and passively resisted Roman authority, the Sadducees constituted the practical political party, and were willing—things being what they were—to cooperate with the Romans and the Herodians. In fact, they had a strong concern for the secular affairs of the nation and willingly accepted public office. The Pharisees were chiefly of the middle class, whereas the Sadducees were the party of the wealthy aristocracy. The common people belonged to neither sect, but favored the Pharisees (*Ant.* xiii. 10. 6).

The letter and spirit of legalism—of righteousness by one's own works—which, in NT times, came to be identified with Jewish religion, accurately reflected the spirit and teachings of the Pharisees. In their zeal for a strict performance of all religious duties enjoined upon them by the Torah, or "Law of Moses," and by tradition, in the belief that the welfare of the nation depended upon this course of action, the Pharisees tended to overlook the fact that the disposition of the heart was of greater importance than the outward act. Most of the "scribes," or "doctors of the law" (Lk 5:17)—the professional students and expositors of "the law"—were Pharisees. Their business was to interpret and to apply "the law" to every minute detail and circumstance of life. In the time of Christ this ever-increasing mass of regulations was known as "the tradition of the elders" (Mt 15:2). The Pharisees accepted as Scripture most if not all of the OT books that we know today, under 3 divisions (cf. Lk 24:44), whereas the Sadducees rejected all but the 5 books of Moses. Whereas the Pharisees were the conservative, orthodox "fundamentalists" of their day, the Sadducees were the liberal, progressive "modernists." The Pharisees believed that a divine providence ordered the affairs of men, and stressed man's dependence upon God. They conceived of God as a strict Father who watched relentlessly for the least infraction of His will and who was ever ready to visit punishment upon the erring. The Sadducees conceived of God as paying little attention to men and taking little interest in their affairs. They held man to be the arbiter of his own destiny and did not believe in a life after death. The Pharisees believed in the existence of spirits, in the immortality of the soul, in a literal resurrection of the body, and in a future life where men would be rewarded or punished according to their deeds in this life. They believed that at death all men went to Hades, the underworld soul-prison where those who had lived "viciously" in this life would remain forever, but whence those who had lived "virtuously" would escape and "live again" (Jos. *Ant.* xviii. 1. 3). They believed that "all things are done by fate," but that men are nevertheless free to act as they choose (*ibid*).

Though in many respects the teachings of Jesus resembled those of the Pharisees more closely than those of the Sadducees, Jesus was nevertheless involved in a bitter contest with the Pharisees throughout His ministry because of their rigorous adherence to tradition (Mk 7:1-13) and the resulting emphasis on outward action to the practical exclusion of the attitudes and motives of the heart (see Mt 23:4-33). It was precisely this rigorous outward piety in observance of "the Law" as interpreted and applied by their traditions, to the practical neglect of inward piety, also their allowing legalism to become a cloak for sin, that led Jesus to brand the Pharisees as hypocrites (see Mt 23). John the Baptist regarded both the Pharisees and the Sadducees as a "generation of vipers" (ch 3:7), and admonished them to bring forth "fruits" that would testify to a change of heart (v 8). When Jesus came stressing the truth that the motive that prompts the act is of greater importance in the sight of God than the act itself, the Pharisees inevitably plotted to discredit Him in the minds of the people and to silence His message. At one time the Sadducees joined with them to challenge His authority and demand a "sign from heaven" to attest His right to teach (ch 16:1-6); but otherwise it was not until almost at the close of His ministry that the Sadducees took the trouble to attack Him—with a quibble about the resurrec-

tion (Mt 22:23-33). It was the Pharisees who stirred up contention between the disciples of Jesus and those of John (Mt 9:11, 14; cf. Jn 4:1). It was the Pharisees who accused Him of casting out demons by the power of the prince of demons (Mt 9:34; 12:24). It was the Pharisees who took exception to His teaching concerning the uselessness of tradition (ch 15:1, 2, 12). It was the Pharisees who took a leading part in His arrest, conviction, and crucifixion (Mt 27:62; Mk 3:6; Jn 11:47-57; 18:3). Nicodemus was a Pharisee (Jn 3:1), as was Paul and also his teacher Gamaliel (see Acts 5:34; 23:6; 26:5-7).

Pharosh. *See* Parosh, 1.

Pharpar (fär′pär). [Heb. *Parpar,* possibly "haste."] The name of the lesser of the 2 rivers of Damascus, which the Syrian Naaman considered to be superior to the Jordan (2 Ki 5:12). According to local tradition the Pharpar is the *Nahr Taura,* one of the branches of the *Barada. Barada* is the name of the main stream of Damascus, generally identified with the Abana. However, since the *Taura* is not a separate river, but only a branch of the *Barada,* the Pharpar is more likely the *Nahr el-A'waj,* a river formed by several mountain streams from Mount Hermon. After their confluence the *A'waj* flows in an easterly direction about 10 mi. south of Damascus until it reaches the southernmost of the 3 marshy desert lakes about 20 mi. southeast of Damascus. Map IX, B-5.

Pharzite. *See* Perez.

Phaseah. *See* Paseah, 2.

Phebe. *See* Phoebe.

Phenice. *See* Phoenicia; Phoenix.

Phenicia. *See* Phoenicia.

Phichol. *See* Phicol.

Phicol (fī′kŏl), KJV **Phichol** (fī′kŏl). [Heb. *Pikol,* meaning uncertain. The name is attested on an ancient Hebrew seal.] The commander of the army of Abimelech, king of Gerar, who was present when Abraham concluded a treaty with Abimelech. Isaac made a similar treaty with a 2d king named Abimelech, accompanied by a commander named Phicol (Gen 21:22, 32; 26:26), but there is some uncertainty as to whether these 2 Phicols are identical. It has been suggested that in unpointed Hebrew the name be read *pylk* instead of *pykl,* which would make it the equivalent of the Egyptian *p3-Rkw,* "the Lycian" (Albright, *JPOS* 4 [1924], 138, 139). Some commentators suggest that Phicol is a title.

379. Ruins of the ancient city wall of Philadelphia

Philadelphia (fĭl'ȧ-dĕl'fĭ-ȧ). [Gr. *Philadelpheia*, "brotherly love."] An inland city of western Asia Minor, on the river Cogamus, a tributary of the Hermus. It stood at the foot of Mount Tmolus about 25 mi. southeast of Sardis on the road to Colossae (Map XX, B-4). Its founder was Attalus II Philadelphus of Pergamum (*c.* 150 B.C.), who named it Philadelphia, "brotherly love," as an indication of his loyalty to his elder brother, Eumenes II, who had preceded him on the throne of Pergamum. The city was destroyed by the earthquake of A.D. 17 and was rebuilt by Tiberius. Because of its beauty ancient writers referred to the new city as "Little Athens." It changed hands repeatedly in the succeeding centuries. Today it is a small city called *Alashehir,* meaning "the reddish city." Except for parts of the old city wall and of an old church no major ruins are visible above ground. A Christian church existed there before the end of the 1st cent. A.D., as is proved by the fact that John wrote a letter to the church of Philadelphia from the island of Patmos (Rev 3:7-13). This letter contained no rebuke, indicating that the spiritual tone in the church there must have been excellent. For the significance of Philadelphia as one of the 7 churches of the Revelation see *SDACom* 7:99, 100, 757-760.

The Philadelphia appearing on Maps XIV-XVI, E-4, is the Greek name of the OT city of Rabbath-ammon, not called Philadelphia in the Bible.

Philemon (fĭ-lē'mŏn). [Gr. *Philēmōn,* "loving."] A Christian living at Colossae (Phm 2; cf. Col 4:17; Phm 10; cf. Col 1:2), in whose home the believers in that city held their religious services (Phm 2). He was a recipient of one of Paul's letters in which Paul interceded for Onesimus, a runaway slave of Philemon's (*see* Philemon, Epistle to). Paul addresses him as a fellow worker (v 1), and commends him for his kindness to the saints (vs 5-7).

Paul himself had apparently never been at Colossae, at least had never visited this region to labor (see Col 2:1). Philemon may therefore have been converted during Paul's extended period of ministry at Ephesus (see Acts 19:1, 10). It has been suggested that Apphia, mentioned in Phm 2, was Philemon's wife, and Archippus, mentioned in the same verse, his son.

Philemon, Epistle to. A personal letter from the apostle Paul during his 1st imprisonment at Rome, addressed to a Christian living in the city of Colossae, whose name stands as its title. Onesimus was dispatched with this letter to Philemon, in company with Tychicus, who carried the epistles to the churches at Colossae (see Col 4:7-9) and Ephesus (see Eph 6:21, 22). All 3 letters were doubtless written at Rome, probably about A.D. 62.

Onesimus had formerly been a slave of Philemon, but had deserted his master and taken some of his money or possessions (see Phm 16, 18). He had found his way to Rome, doubtless expecting to lose himself among the crowds of that city. While there, Onesimus met Paul, and through him became a believer in Jesus Christ. Paul advised Onesimus to return to his master, and wrote a letter with the express purpose of securing a favorable reception for the returning slave, confident that Philemon would receive Onesimus now as "a brother beloved" (v 16). This little gem of Christian love and tact is unique in Scripture, in that its claim to a place in the sacred canon may be in the fact that it vividly reflects the change that came over one man because of his faith in Christ, and that slave and master are brethren in Christ. It is a simple appeal to Philemon to exercise Christian kindness and mercy toward a slave who had defrauded him. The epistle assures Christians of God's interest in the practical problems that arise when they find their way to Christ, and points the way to a solution to some of them.

After the salutation (Phm 1-3) Paul commends Philemon for his Christian love and faithfulness. With great tact Paul then appeals to Philemon, reminding him that he himself is a debtor to Paul for his faith in Christ, and assumes as a personal obligation any debt that Onesimus still owes Philemon. In verses 21-25 Paul sends his personal greetings to certain believers at Colossae, and ends with his benediction.

Philetus (fĭ-lē'tŭs). [Gr. *Philētos,* "worthy of love."] A Christian heretic who joined *Hymenaeus in teaching that the resurrection was an event of the past (2 Ti 2:16, 17).

Philip (fĭl′ĭp). [Gr. *Philippos,* "fond of horses," "fancier of horses," a frequently occurring Greek name.]

1. Philip the apostle, one of the Twelve (Mk 3:18), native of Bethsaida, the home also of Peter and Andrew (Jn 1:44). He was among the first to be attracted to Jesus as the Messiah (vs 43, 44), and it was he who brought Nathanael to Jesus (vs 45-51). A year and a half later Philip and 11 others received ordination as apostles (Mk 3:13-19). Six months later at the miracle of feeding the 5,000, Jesus, in a question to test Philip's faith, asked him, "Whence shall we buy bread, that these may eat?" (Jn 6:5). Philip's estimate of the amount of bread needed to provide each one of the throng with "a little" stresses the magnitude of the miracle of the loaves and fishes (vs 6, 7). Philip's name does not appear in the gospel record again until Tuesday of the Passion Week, when a group of Greek proselytes who had come to Jerusalem to attend the Passover approached him asking for an interview with Jesus (ch 12:20, 21). Philip first conferred with his fellow townsman Andrew, and the 2 went together to present the request to Jesus (vs 21, 22). During the course of Jesus' discourse concerning His own intimate relationship with the Father, at the close of the Last Supper, Philip requested, "Lord, shew us the Father, and it sufficeth us" (ch 14:8). In reply Jesus emphasized the essential unity of character and purpose that motivated both Father and Son (vs 9, 10). Philip was among the apostles who met together in the upper room after the resurrection, prior to Pentecost (Acts 1:13). This is the last certain reference in the Scriptures to Philip.

2. Philip the evangelist, one of the 7 men chosen by the Jerusalem church to deal with complaints that the Hellenistic Jewish widows were being neglected in the daily distribution of food, etc., carried out in accordance with the communal system adopted by the new church (Acts 6:1-6; cf. 4:32, 34, 35). Previous to this nothing is known of him, although tradition states that he, with Stephen, was one of the Seventy (see Lk 10:1, 17). According to the character requirements specified for the Seven, he was a man "of honest report, full of the Holy Ghost and wisdom" (Acts 6:3).

After the stoning of Stephen, when the believers were forced to leave Jerusalem (Acts 8:2, 4), Philip went to Samaria, where he preached Christ. His preaching was accompanied by miraculous healings and the casting out of devils so that "there was great joy in that city" (vs 5-8). This attracted one Simon the sorcerer (vs 9-11). Impressed by what he saw, Simon was convinced of the superior power of the One whom Philip served, and accepted baptism (v 13). Subsequent events showed that this conversion was only intellectual and partial (vs 18-24). Later, Philip was directed by an angel to go south to Jerusalem to the Gaza road (v 26). Obeying instructions, he saw an Ethiopian eunuch, who was royal treasurer under the queen of Ethiopia, riding from Jerusalem in a chariot, and reading from a scroll of Isaiah. Ordered by the Spirit to approach the chariot, Philip discovered that the eunuch did not understand the passage he was reading, and was invited to explain the prophecy. Philip showed that the passage pointed to Christ. The eunuch, convinced and converted, requested and received baptism of Philip (vs 27-38). Immediately after the baptism "the Spirit of the Lord caught away Philip" (v 39), and he "was found at Azotus" (v 40), near the coast, possibly some 10 or 15 mi. from where he had met the eunuch. From Azotus Philip went to various cities preaching, until he arrived at Caesarea (v 40). Years later, Paul, on his way to Jerusalem toward the end of his 3d Missionary Journey, stayed with Philip in Caesarea. Luke makes note of the fact that Philip "had four daughters, virgins, which did prophesy" (ch 21:8, 9). It is possible that Philip had established his home in this city while he doubtlessly continued to preach in the cities in the area.

3. Philip the tetrarch, a son of Herod the Great. *See* Herod, 4.

4. Another son of Herod the Great. *See* Herod, 5.

Philippi (fĭ-lĭp′ī). [Gr. *Philippoi.*] A city in eastern Macedonia, now called *Filibedjik.* It is situated on a steep hill overlooking the valley of the Gangites River (Map XX, A-3). Its original name, Crenides, meaning "small fountains," was derived from the numerous springs surrounding the hill. The city was founded by Athenians in the 7th cent. B.C., but in 358 or 357 B.C. was captured by Philip II of Macedonia, who rebuilt it as his residence and named it after himself. The gold and silver mines in the neighboring mountains of the Pangaeus ridge gave the city importance. When the Roman commander Aemilius Paulus defeated Perseus, the last Macedonian king, in 168 B.C., Philippi, with the rest of the country, fell to the Romans. The city then became part of the first of the 4 protectorates into which Macedonia was divided. Macedonia became a Roman province in 146 B.C. In 42 B.C. the great battle between Octavian and Antony, the avengers of Caesar, and Brutus and Cassius, his murderers, took place in the vicinity of Philippi. Octavian and Antony were victors and later enlarged the city and elevated it to the status of a colony (*Colonia Julia Philippensis*). Still later it was granted the *ius italicum,* which meant that its citizens received a form of Roman citizenship. Since many Roman veterans had been settled there, about half of its population was of Latin descent in NT times (cf. Acts 16:12, 21); the other half consisted of Macedonians, and some immigrants, such as Jews. The Jews seemed to have formed only a small minority, for they did not have a synagogue in the city (v 13). Although Philippi was not the capital of the province or the district—this honor was given to Amphipolis—the fact that it was a trading center, and that it was favorably situated close to the Via Egnatia, the Roman highway that crossed the whole of Macedonia from west to east, made it the most important city of eastern Macedonia (v 12).

Paul went to Philippi on his 2d Missionary Journey (*c.* A.D. 50) in response to a vision received at Troas (Acts 16: 9-12). He founded a church which became greatly attached to him. It was the only church from which he later accepted financial assistance (Php 1:3-8; 2:25; 4:10-16). He was forced to leave the city because of persecutions (Acts 16:38-40), but undoubtedly visited the church again during his journey from Ephesus to Corinth *c.* A.D. 57 (ch 20:1, 2). The following spring, while on his way to Jerusalem, he

380. Ruins of a basilica at Philippi

spent the Passover season in Philippi (Acts 20:6). While in Rome during his 1st imprisonment there, Paul wrote a letter to the church at Philippi (*see* Philippians, Epistle to the).

Philippians, Epistle to the. A letter written by the apostle Paul, in association with Timothy, to the believers at Philippi in Macedonia (Php 1:1; 2:9). In the earliest extant manuscripts, which go back to the 3d cent., this epistle bears the simple title *Pros Philippēsious,* "to [the] Philippians." In ch 4:15 Paul refers to the occasion when he first labored at Philippi (Acts 16:12-40), and to the liberality of that church in supporting his later labors. The unanimous testimony of early Christian writers leaves no doubt concerning the authenticity of the epistle. About the middle of the 2d cent. Polycarp, in his epistle to the Philippians, wrote concerning Paul that "when absent from you, he wrote you a letter, which, if you carefully study, you will find to be the means of building you up in that faith which has been given you" (Polycarp, *To the Philippians,* ch 3, in *The Ante-Nicene Fathers,* vol. 1, p. 33). Some modern scholars have assigned the letter to Paul's imprisonment at Caesarea, from the spring of about A.D. 58 to the autumn of A.D. 60, but from earliest times—as generally, today—Rome has been considered its place of origin. The apostle's expressed hope of imminent release and of another visit to Philippi (Php 2:24; cf. Phm 22) indicates the 1st of the imprisonments at Rome instead of the 2d, which ended in martyrdom and from which he did not anticipate release (see 2 Ti 4:6-8). Paul's 1st imprisonment began about the spring of A.D. 61 and continued to about the year A.D. 63. His anticipation of release "shortly" (Php 2:24) implies that the epistle was written toward the close of his 1st imprisonment, perhaps late in A.D. 62 or early in A.D. 63.

Because Philippi was the 1st great Eu-

381. The ruins of an ancient prison at Philippi

ropean city to hear Paul proclaim the gospel (see Acts 16:8-12) and because of the personal devotion of its converts to him (Acts 16:14; 2 Cor 11:9; Php 4:14, 15), Paul felt more than usual affection for them (Php 1:3-7). His 1st visit to Philippi took place during the course of his 2d Missionary Journey, about A.D. 50 or 51. His 2d visit was made c. A.D. 57, while on his way from Ephesus to Corinth, and the following spring he celebrated the Passover there (see Acts 20:6). Apparently there had been some tendency toward discord (Php 4:2; cf. ch 2:2), but in no place does Paul reprove the believers in that city for moral corruption or erroneous doctrine, as he did the Corinthians and the Galatians in his letters to them. The epistle reflects joy and thankfulness, and the mutual esteem and fellowship he enjoyed with them. During Paul's imprisonment at Rome they had sent Epaphroditus to convey gifts and to minister to him (chs 2:25; 4:18). Apparently Epaphroditus was entrusted with the epistle upon his return to Philippi (chs 1:26; 2:24). There is no record of a later visit by Paul to Philippi, but he doubtless made such a visit during the 3 years between his release and his 2d imprisonment (A.D. 63-66).

In the epistle to the Philippians Paul addresses the believers as their pastor, giving them spiritual counsel and acknowledging their loving help. He tells of his experience in prison, of the success of his efforts to proclaim the gospel at Rome, and of the attempts of certain misguided persons to undo his work (Php 1:12-17). He tells of joy and peace even in affliction, and takes solace in their sympathy and friendship. He is uncertain of the future, though he anticipates release from prison (vs 19-24). He appreciates the Philippians' gifts and the many evidences of their friendship and solicitude (ch 4: 14-17). Though he is bound in body because of the gospel, his spirit is free, and he declares, "I can do all things through Christ which strengtheneth me" (v 13). The theme of the epistle is joy in Christ through the vicissitudes of life. The words "joy" and "rejoice" fall from his pen again and again. This experience of joy and peace becomes possible through Christ.

Following the introduction (Php 1:1-11), Paul reviews his experiences and shares his feelings (vs 12-26). He exhorts the believers to unity in the faith and to self-denial (chs 1:27 to 2:16). He ex-

plains his plans for the future, of sending Epaphroditus and later Timothy, and of visiting them again himself (Php 2:17-30). He warns against the twin errors of Judaism and materialism—of works versus grace on the one hand and the sensual versus the spiritual mind on the other (chs 3:1 to 4:9). The epistle closes with an acknowledgment of the Philippian gift, certain greetings, and a benediction (ch 4:10-23).

Philistia (fĭ-lĭs'tĭ-à). [Heb. *Pelesheth*. In some passages the KJV renders *Pelesheth* as *"Palestine,"* but "Philistia" in Ps 60: 8; 87:4; 108:9. The RSV uniformly renders *Pelesheth* as "Philistia."] The coastal plain of southwestern Palestine lying southward from Joppa and including Gaza (Map VI, E/F-1/2). The land was fertile, and contained a number of important cities, the 5 largest of which were Gaza, Ashkelon, and Ashdod on or near the coast, and Ekron and Gath in the hinterland.

Philistim. *See* Philistines.

Philistines (fĭ-lĭs'tĭnz). [Heb. *Pelishtî* and *Pelishtîm;* Egyptian *Prst* and *Pwrst* (probably pronounced Pulesati); Assyrian *Palastu, Pilishta,* and *Pilistu.* The name occurs probably also on the Phaestus disk from Crete (the homeland of the Philistines) where in the recently deciphered hieroglyphic script it is spelled Pi-ri-ta (B. Schwartz, *JNES* 18 [1959], 226).] Descendants of the Casluhim, and a brother nation of the Caphtorim (Gen 10:14; KJV for *Pelishtîm,* "Philistim," fĭ-lĭs'tĭm). According to Amos 9:7 they came from Caphtor, which is Crete, and the other islands in its vicinity, and in Jer 47:4, RSV, are described as "the remnant of the coastland of Caphtor." They thus either originally lived on the island of Crete or resided there for some time before moving to Palestine. In fact, they may have been the people who invaded Crete in the middle of the 2d millennium B.C. and destroyed its flourishing native civilization, known as the Minoan culture. Furthermore, Egyptian records and archeological evidence show that they were part of the great movement of Sea Peoples who came from the Greek mainland, from Crete, Sicily, Sardinia, and the islands of the Aegean Sea, and who invaded Asia Minor in the 13th cent. B.C., and destroyed the Hittite Empire and a number of states in Syria. Ramses III (1198-1167 B.C.), in land and sea battles, defeated these Sea Peoples and drove them back to the countries from which they had come. However, the Philistines and some other groups, such as certain Cretans, remained in Palestine and settled in the southern coastal region of that country. Small groups of Philistines had, in fact, lived in this area since the time of the patriarchs, for Abraham and Isaac had dealings with them. However, they were so small and politically insignificant at that time that they were glad to conclude a treaty of friendship with Abraham and Isaac, who were mere nomadic chieftains (Gen 21:32, 34; 26:1, 26-31). But with the arrival of strong Philistine contingents in the time of the judges (12th cent.), the situation changed, and the Philistines became a threat to Israel. The mortuary temple of Ramses III at *Medinet Habu* in western Thebes provides much pictorial information concerning the Philistines. Stone reliefs show them in their feather-decorated helmets—a distinguishing mark of that people (fig. 382) —moving with their families in 4-wheeled wooden ox carts. These carts also were formidable fighting wagons, against which the arrows and spears of the Egyptians were comparatively harmless. The Philistines also possessed iron weapons and exercised a monopoly on the import of iron (cf. 1 Sa 13:19-22), which gave them a military advantage over the native Palestinians, including the Hebrews. After having gained a foothold in the country, they lost no time in using this advantage in an attempt to occupy and control all of Palestine. It was only after many wars that their advance was checked and they were restricted to the coastal area. See Maps VI-X, E-2, etc., for the varying extent of Philistine territory in OT times.

When the Israelites left Egypt they were directed to avoid the way of the Philistines (Ex 13:17, 18), even though at that time the Philistines were not yet a dangerously large group. When a generation later the Israelites invaded Canaan, they did not at first take the cities that later became strongholds of the Philistines (Jos 13:2, 3; cf. Jgs 3:1-3). However, a little later the tribes of Judah took Gaza, Ashkelon, and Ekron (Jgs 1:18). These seem to have been recaptured by the Philistines when they came into the country in force in the 12th cent. B.C., for we do not find them in Israelite hands during Israel's later history. Shamgar, a hero of the period of the judges of whom little is known, distinguished himself by slaying 600 Philistines (ch 3:31). The first

Philistine oppression of the Israelites began shortly after Gideon's rule (Jgs 10:6, 7), probably about the middle of the 12th cent. B.C. Toward the end of that century began another oppression which lasted for 40 years (ch 13:1). During this period Samson's exploits against the Philistines took place. He inflicted great damage and losses upon them, but his undisciplined character led to his ruin and brought no deliverance for Israel (chs 14 to 16). In the midst of this oppression the Philistines defeated the Israelites in the battle at Aphek, captured the ark, and probably at this time destroyed Shiloh (1 Sa 4:1-11). Twenty years later the Israelites rallied under Samuel and smote the Philistines in the battle of Ebenezer, thus freeing the country (ch 7:5-14).

During the time of Saul of Israel the Philistines again extended their control over the hinterland of Palestine. They held Israel in subjection by denying them iron tools and weapons (1 Sa 13:19-21), and by spreading Philistine garrisons throughout the country (chs 10:5; 13:3). Frequent hostilities broke out between the 2 nations (ch 14:52). Despite Jon-

382. Egyptian leading away Philistine prisoners, on the temple wall of *Medinet Habu*

athan's local victories over the Philistines at Geba and Michmash (1 Sa 13:3 to 14:31), they returned and challenged Israel under the leadership of the giant, Goliath. On this occasion they were defeated, losing their champion, whom David slew (ch 17:1-52), but in the course of time several more encounters took place between Saul's forces and those of the Philistines (chs 18:27; 19:8; 23:27, 28). Persecuted by Saul, David went twice to the Philistines to find refuge. On the first occasion he aroused their suspicion, but the next time was able to convince the Philistine king of Gath of his sincerity and usefulness, with the result that he was given the town of Ziklag (chs 21:10-15; 27:1-12). In the meantime the Philistines once more had spread their control to the heart of the Israelite country. The battle of Gilboa ensued, in which the Israelites not only were decisively beaten but also lost their king and royal princes (chs 29:1; 31:1-6). When David became king he succeeded in defeating the Philistines so thoroughly that they ended for a time their attempts to invade the country of their neighbors (2 Sa 3:18; 5:17-25; 8:1; 19:9; 21:15-22; 23:9-17; 1 Chr 11:13, 14; 18:1; 20:4, 5). Hence we find them less frequently mentioned in the later periods of Israel's history.

The northern kingdom of Israel made 2 attempts to capture Gibbethon from the Philistines (1 Ki 15:27; 16:15), and Jehoshaphat of Judah seems to have made some of the Philistines tributary to him (2 Chr 17:11). Under the kings Jehoram and Ahaz the Philistines again invaded the territory of Judah (chs 21:16; 28:18), but Uzziah and Hezekiah carried out successful invasions of Philistine territory (2 Chr 26:1, 6, 7; 2 Ki 18:1, 8). The Assyrians repeatedly invaded and subjugated the Philistines, as Assyrian records indicate. Later the Philistines became part successively of the Babylonian, Persian, and Greco-Macedonian empires, and came under successive Hellenistic rulers. Philistines fought on the side of the Seleucids against the Jews in the period of the Maccabees (1 Macc 3:41). Judas and Jonathan, the Maccabeans, captured Ashdod and Ashkelon and forced Gaza to surrender (chs 5:68; 10:83-89; 11:60-62). Philistine territory, with the exception of Ashkelon, later became part of Herod's kingdom, and as such was inherited by his successors, Archelaus and Agrippa I. (See Maps XIV-XVI.) The Philistines are not mentioned in the NT.

Since the Philistines were bitter enemies of God and His people for many centuries, it is easy to understand why the Hebrew prophets frequently pronounced messages of doom against them (see Is 11:14; Jer 25:15, 16, 20; 47:1-7; Eze 25:15-17; Amos 1:6-8; Ob 19; Zep 2:4, 5; Zec 9:5-7).

The Mediterranean Sea is once called the sea of the Philistines (Ex 23:31).

Philologus (fĭ-lŏl′ȯ-gŭs). [Gr. *Philologos,* "fond of learning." A Greek name appearing frequently in Greek and Latin inscriptions, and borne especially by slaves and freedmen, although it occurs also among nobility and even in the imperial house.] A Christian of the church of Rome to whom Paul sent greetings in the closing chapter of his letter to the Romans (Rom 16:15).

Philosophy. [Gr. *philosophia,* "philosophy," "a devotion to wisdom."] A term occurring only in Col 2:8, where the apostle Paul warns the believers at Colossae to "beware lest any man spoil you through philosophy and vain deceit, after the tradition of men, after the rudiments of the world, and not after Christ." Philosophy is an attempt to arrive at truth through the process of reasoning. Science seeks it by observation and experimentation. Faith relies on a supernatural revelation and upon its observed effect upon those who order their lives according to this revelation. All 3 avenues to truth—philosophy, science, faith—are of divine origin, but all have been perverted by sin. God created the human mind with a capacity for logical thought processes. He formed the natural world and gave it to man for observation and study. He revealed His will to His servants the prophets. Reason, observation, and faith must be used in balance, inasmuch as none of the 3 is adequate, in and of itself, as a complete pathway to truth. When men divorce revelation from philosophy and science in order to leave God out of their thoughts, they become "vain in their imaginations," and their foolish heart is "darkened" (Rom 1:21). When they observe the visible things of the created world but refuse to acknowledge the Creator, to glorify Him as God, and to appreciate His goodness, their reasoning processes become unreliable. Professing themselves to be wise, they become fools (v 22). It is reliance on "philosophy" in this sense, to the exclusion of revealed truth, against which Paul speaks in Col 2:8.

The philosophies of ancient Greece

proposed to solve the problems of the origin, nature, and destiny of man and the natural world by the rational processes, and were thus of a quasi-religious character. Athens was the center of Greek philosophical thought. The 3 great luminaries of ancient Greek philosophy were Socrates, Plato, and Aristotle, who arose successively in the 5th and 4th cent. B.C. within the brief century between the Golden Age of Athens and the rise of Alexander the Great. The systems of Plato and Aristotle greatly influenced Hebrew thought, particularly at Alexandria, where Philo Judaeus, a contemporary of Christ, blended the teachings of Moses and the Greek philosophers into a new system, and attempted to dispose of inconsistencies between the 2 by allegorizing Scripture. Taking reason alone as his source of absolute authority, Aristotle, who served as tutor to Alexander the Great, developed a system of natural philosophy that later dominated the thinking of Christendom down almost to the Reformation. During the early Christian centuries professed Christians attempted to explain the truths of their religion in terms of the Platonic system, thereby laying the foundation for medieval theology, which later developed along Aristotelian lines. During the early part of the 3d cent. B.C., Epicurus and Zeno founded the 2 opposing ethical schools of philosophy known as the *Epicureans and the *Stoics. Teaching that human knowledge is insufficient to arrive at truth with any degree of certainty, the Skeptics held that man attains to happiness when he realizes that he cannot attain to absolute truth and ceases to care about trying to do so.

Phinehas (fĭn′ē-ăs). [Heb. *Pînechas,* from the Egyptian *p3 Nḥsy,* "the Nubian."]

1. Son of Eleazar, grandson of Aaron (Ex 6:25), and high priest (Jgs 20:27, 28). In a time of apostasy he showed his zeal for God, slaying an Israelite offender and a Midianite woman, thus ending a plague that had broken out as a divine punishment. As a reward an everlasting priesthood was promised him and his descendants. His act was not forgotten, being celebrated in the later poetic and historical works of Israel (Num 25:1-18; Ps 106:30; 1 Macc 2:26, 54; Ecclus 45:23-25). In fulfillment of the promise Phinehas' descendants were high priests throughout the OT period with the exception of a short time in which the house of Eli, descendants of Ithamar, held office. Phine-

has accompanied the Israelite army against the Midianites (Num 31:6), and was one of the members of the commission sent by Joshua to Gilead to protest the erection of a separate altar (Jos 22:13-15). When Gibeah's population committed a crime that incurred the wrath of the whole nation, it was Phinehas who inquired of the Lord as to the course Israel should pursue (Jgs 20:27, 28). In the distribution of the country Phinehas received a town in the hill country of Ephraim (Jos 24:33).

2. The younger son of Eli. He and his brother Hophni were priests at the tabernacle at Shiloh when their father was old (1 Sa 1:3). They behaved scandalously, and though twice rebuked by prophetic utterances (chs 2:22-36; 3:11-14), refused to change their conduct, thus bringing a curse upon the family. Nor were they punished or removed from office by their father. Both men lost their lives in the battle at Aphek, and the ark of the covenant, which they had accompanied to the battle, fell into the hands of the Philistines (ch 4:4-11). When the news of this catastrophe reached Phinehas' wife, who was pregnant, the pains of childbirth came upon her and she died giving birth to the child (vs 19-22).

3. Father of a certain Eleazar (Ezr 8:33); probably of the priestly line.

Phlegon (flē′gŏn). [Gr. *Phlegōn,* "burning," a name frequently borne by slaves and freedmen.] A Christian of the church at Rome to whom Paul sent greetings in his letter to the Romans (Rom 16:14).

Phoebe (fē′bē), KJV **Phebe** (fē′bē). [Gr. *Phoibē,* "radiant," or "pure," a name attested in inscriptions.] A deaconess (Gr. *diakonos;* KJV "servant") of the church at Cenchreae, the eastern port of Corinth. When she went to Rome, Paul recommended her to the church there (Rom 16:1, 2). She may have been the carrier of his letter. She is described as having been a "helper" (RSV), or "succourer" (KJV) (Gr. *prostatis*), of many in her home church. *Prostatis* means "patroness," "protectoress." In Athens the term designated the office of someone who represented people without civic rights. Roman law recognized such a patron as the representative of foreigners. If Phoebe held such an office, she must have been a wealthy woman of high society.

Phoenicia (fē-nĭsh′ĭ-à), KJV **Phenicia** (fē-nĭsh′ĭ-à) and **Phenice** (fē′nĭs). [Gr. *Phoinikē.*] A long, narrow strip of coastal ter-

383. Sarcophagus of the Phoenician King Ahiram of Byblos. The king is seated on a sphinx-throne (left). A long Phoenician inscription is carved on the edge of the lid

·ritory between the Mediterranean Sea and the Lebanon Mountains (Map I, A-2). It extended north as far as Arvad (Map XII, D-6), and south as far as the Tyrian Ladder, 14 mi. south of Tyre, although it sometimes extended farther south (Map VI, A/B-3/4, and following maps). In NT times Phoenicia reached as far as Dor, south of the Carmel ridge (Map XVI, A/B/C-2/3/4). In contrast with the Palestinian coast, Phoenicia has good natural harbors formed either by islands lying near the coast, as at Tyre and Arvad, or by bays, as at Byblos and Beirut. The slopes of the Lebanon Mountains were densely wooded with cedars and firs, and thus invited the people along the coast nearby to become shipbuilders and to trade in timber. Hence the Phoenicians became seafarers trading with Egypt, later with Greece, and all other countries around the Mediterranean Sea.

The most important Phoenician cities of antiquity were Byblos (Biblical *Gebal), lying somewhat beyond the sphere of the Palestinians and therefore seldom mentioned in the Bible, and *Sidon and *Tyre, 2 cities that were constantly contending with each other for supremacy. The Phoenicians were *Canaanites (Gen 10:15; Is 23:11), pushed by the Hebrew invasion into the narrow coastal strip which they continued to call *Canaan (Map III, C-4). Through their contact with other nations the Phoenician traders spread the culture of the Orient among the Western peoples. For example, the art of *writing was brought to Greece by the Phoenicians, and the most common *writing material of ancient times, the *papyrus scroll, produced in Egypt,

was distributed through the whole known world by the Phoenicians from Byblos. Consequently, other nations named this writing material after the city from which they received it. Our English words "Bible" and "bibliography," etc., are derived from the same source. The Phoenicians were also colonizers, the most important of their colonies being Carthage in northern Africa, and Tarshish, most probably Tartessus, in southern Spain. Phoenicia's strategic position on the Mediterranean coast, its rich cities, and its importance as the bridge between Asia and Africa made it the object of conquest for the great powers who had an eye on expansion and lust for power. Phoenician cities formed part of the Egyptian Empire in the 18th dynasty. Later they paid tribute to the Assyrians, Babylonians, and Persians. When they refused the demands of invaders they usually resisted valiantly, but were eventually defeated, as was Tyre after a 13-year siege in the time of Nebuchadnezzar, and after a 7-month siege by Alexander. However, the Phoenicians managed to retain their national identity for a long period, and were able to recover from severe catastrophes because of their rich trading connections. After Alexander's death the Phoenicians supported the Seleucids, and later (63 B.C.) became part of the Roman province of Syria.

The name Phoenicia occurs in the Bible only in the NT. The OT refers by name only to various cities of the Phoenician coast (2 Sa 24:6, 7; 1 Ki 17:9), with which the Israelites had profitable connections, as in the time of David and Solomon (2 Sa 5:11; 1 Ki 5:1; 9:11; 10:

858

22), or connections that led to disastrous results, as in the days of Ahab, when a Phoenician princess, Jezebel, introduced Baal and Astarte worship into Israel (see 1 Ki 16:31, 32; 18:19), and almost blotted out the religion of the true God. (*See* Asherah; Baal; Hiram; Jezebel.)

The name Phoenicia is of Greek origin, the Greeks calling the Phoenicians who sold them purple-dyed goods "phoenix-men," from *phoinix,* *"purple." The territory from which these goods came they called *Phoinikē.*

Jesus visited Phoenician territory when He entered the coastal area of Tyre and Sidon (Mt 15:21; Mk 7:24, 31). Some of the Christians who left Jerusalem during the persecution that followed the stoning of Stephen found their way to Phoenicia (KJV "Phenice") and probably founded churches there (Acts 11:19). Paul and Barnabas, passing through this area on their way to Jerusalem after their 1st Missionary Journey, apparently found churches there to which they reported the success of their missionary activities in Asia Minor (ch 15:3). The last time Phoenicia is mentioned in the NT is in connection with the visit of Paul to Tyre on his final journey to Jerusalem (ch 21:2-7).

Phoenix (fē'nĭks), KJV **Phenice** (fē'nĭs). [Gr. *Phoinix.*] A harbor on the southern coast of Crete, doubtless the modern *Lutro,* the only harbor on the southern coast of Crete that provides safe all-year anchorage for ships, and that agrees with the description given in Acts 27:12. The ancient name is perpetuated by the modern *Phinikia,* a town on the plateau, 2,000 ft. above the harbor. It was this harbor that the sailors of the vessel on which Paul was being carried a prisoner to Rome desired to reach, when they recognized that they could not make Rome because of the lateness of the season. Map XX, B-3.

Phrygia (frĭj'ĭ-à). [Gr. *Phrugia.*] A large area in the interior of Asia Minor (Map XX, B-5). The Phrygians were descendants of the Indo-European people who had invaded Asia Minor in the 12th cent. B.C. and had destroyed the Hittite Empire. They founded a kingdom that later comprised the area of Galatia, and parts of Cappadocia and Lycaonia. The kingdom suffered greatly under the invading Cimmerians, but was restored by Lydia. It was finally absorbed into the Persian Empire. It next passed successively into the hands of Alexander, the Seleucids, the Attalids of Pergamum, and

in 133 B.C., Rome. It was administered for some time as a Roman province. Later its territory was divided between the provinces of Asia and Galatia, hence NT passages mentioning Phrygia must be understood as referring to it as an area and not as a political unit.

The country was famous as the homeland of the Phrygian mystery cult. The chief deity was Cybele, the *Magna Mater,* a fertility goddess. She was associated with her son-husband, the sun-god *Sabazius-Attis,* whom the Greeks called Adonis. Every year the death of this god was celebrated with rites of mourning and self-mutilation, and his reappearance was feasted with orgiastic dances and immoral rites in connection with which women offered their bodies in prostitution without losing their civil honors and social standing. Because of these beliefs Phrygians counted their descent from the mother and not from the father. Roman soldiers were influenced by the Phrygian rites, and the Roman Senate fought a losing battle against their introduction into Italy. Phrygian converts were responsible for some of the mystery-cult ideas that entered the churches, and Montanism especially owed much of its peculiar teachings to this cult. Old Phrygian inscriptions from the 7th or 6th cent. B.C. have been discovered, written in a Phrygian alphabetic script; Neo-Phrygian inscriptions from the 1st cent. B.C. are written in Greek.

Many Jews lived in Phrygia from the time Antiochus the Great (223-187 B.C.) settled 2,000 Jewish families from Babylonia in Lydia and Phrygia (Jos. *Ant.* xii. 3. 4). Jews from Phrygia were among those visiting Jerusalem at Pentecost in the year of Christ's death (Acts 2:10). Four of the Phrygian cities are mentioned in the NT: Antioch "in Pisidia," Colossae, Laodicea, and Hierapolis (Acts 13: 14; Col 1:2; 4:13; Rev 3:14). Paul passed through the country apparently stopping at several points en route (Acts 16:6; 18:23).

Phurah. *See* Purah.

Phut. *See* Put.

Phuvah. *See* Puvah.

Phygellus. *See* Phygelus.

Phygelus (fī-jē'lŭs), KJV **Phygellus** (fī-jĕl'ŭs). [Gr. *Phugelos.*] A Christian of Asia who, along with others, deserted Paul during the apostle's last years, possibly for fear of becoming involved in his fate, or for doctrinal reasons (2 Ti 1:15).

Phylactery. [Gr. *phulaktērion*, "means of protection," "amulet." The OT expression on which the idea of phylacteries is based is *ṭôṭaphoth*, "frontlets."]

A term designating a little case containing small strips of parchment upon which certain passages of the Law were written, called *tephillah*, "prayer (strap)," by the Jews. Except on Sabbaths and feast days these cases were fastened daily to the forehead and to the left forearm for the morning prayer. This practice was based on the Jewish belief, dating from at least the 2d cent. B.C., that the words of Ex 13:9; Deut 6:6-8 were to be taken literally. The rabbinical tradition of later times stipulated that Ex 13:1-10, 11-16; Deut 6:4-9; 11:13-21 be used. Several phylacteries, some complete, others fragmentary, were found among the recent discoveries of manuscripts at the Dead Sea. Those of the Qumran area, orginating from before A.D. 70, show deviations in the wording or selection of Biblical passages, while one found in *Wâdī Murabba'ât* dating from the 2d cent. A.D. contains only the passages prescribed by rabbinical tradition. In Christ's time phylacteries were apparently worn in public by Pharisees as signs of their religious zeal, and were made especially wide so that they could easily be seen by others—a practice disapproved by Jesus (Mt 23:5).

Physician. [Heb. *rophe'*, from *rapha'*, "to heal"; Gr. *iatros*, "physician."] A person trained and skilled in the art of healing. Ancient Egyptian physicians were superior to those of any other peoples of the Near East. Several Egyptian medical treatises have been discovered, of which the Edwin Smith Surgical Papyrus and the Ebers Medical Papyrus deserve special mention. These treatises indicate that, from the practical viewpoint, Egyptian

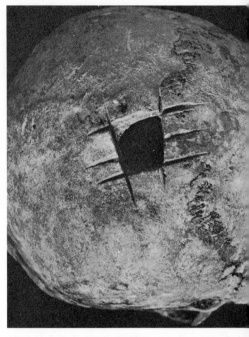

385. A skull found at Lachish, showing a surgical opening

medicine was on a remarkably high level. Herodotus (iii. 1, 129) states that the Persian emperors Cyrus and Darius employed Egyptian physicians. He also states that each Egyptian physician specialized in some one part of the body (ii. 84). They also acted as embalmers (Gen 50:2, 3). The Greeks drew heavily on Egyptian knowledge in this field. Jeremiah (Jer 46:11) seems to imply that although Egypt might produce great physicians, there would be no healing of her own wounds in the day of her visitation. The physicians of Crotona had an enviable reputation among those of ancient Greece; those of Cyrene held second place to them (Herod. iii. 131). Much ancient medical lore was based on superstition and hence was valueless. Amulets of Isis, worn in Egypt, were believed to ward off sickness. The Code of Hammurabi mentions, and regulates, the practice of physicians in Mesopotamia. Ea was the chief Babylonian god of healing; Ishtar was believed to be helpful to women in childbirth; Marduk aided the sick; and Shamash prolonged life. Greek physicians sought the god Asclepius (whose serpent-staff symbol is our present-day symbol of the medical arts). Oracles were commonly consulted on behalf of the sick, and the

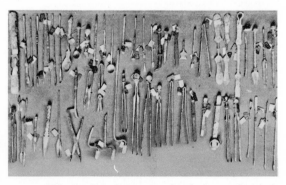

384. Surgical instruments found in a physician's home at Pompeii

use of herbs was widespread. The most famous physician of antiquity is said to have been Galen (c. A.D. 130 - c. 200). He was born in Pergamum and trained in its famed Asclepieion. He studied further at Smyrna, Corinth, and Alexandria, and his influence was felt strongly throughout the Middle Ages. Galen's writings give evidence of some knowledge of the functions of the human body and of certain medicines and therapeutic theatments.

Surgery was performed for the removal of tumors and abscesses. Even successful brain surgeries (trepanations) are attested (see fig. 385). Limbs were skillfully amputated, bones were set, and in Roman times Caesarean sections were performed, that is, in cases of dead or dying mothers. But the ancient surgeons did not have the required knowledge of the function of the internal organs for surgical corrections of vital organs in the abdomen or chest. Israel's prophets were often involved in healing activities (2 Ki 5:10; cf. Jer 8:22), and in a sense, every priest performed some of the functions of a physician (see Lev 12-15). The Levitical law presented a health code greatly superior to like codes of the heathen nations. The authority of the Creator of the human body is expressed in the code, and to the extent that the Jews followed the divine instruction they enjoyed superior mental and physical vigor (see Ex 23:25; Deut 7:15). Christ came as the Great Physician, ministering not only to the spiritual needs of the people but also to the physical (Mt 4:23; 9:12; Mk 2:17; Lk 4:23; 6:17, 18; 8:43; etc.). Luke, the writer of the Gospel of that name and of Acts, and a traveling companion of Paul, was a physician (Col 4:14). *See* Jesus Christ; Medicine; Miracles.

Pibeseth (pī-bē′sĕth). [Heb. *Pi-beseth,* a transliteration of *Pr-Bȝśt.t,* the name of an Egyptian city called Bubastis by the Greeks.] A city in the Delta on the left bank of the most easterly branch of the Nile, about 40 mi. northeast of modern Cairo. The city was inhabited from the 4th dynasty until Roman times. In the time of Sheshonk I (Biblical Shishak), when it was called Bubastis, it became the 2d most important city in the country, and consequently the dynasty founded by Sheshonk is frequently referred to as the Bubastite dynasty. Bubastis possessed a beautiful temple dedicated to the cat-headed goddess Bastet, to which many Egyptians made pilgrimages, and where great feasts were celebrated in honor of the goddess. The city is mentioned in the OT only in Eze 30:17. Its ruins are now called *Tell Basṭa.* See Bubastis on Map V, B-3.

Pick. *See* Harrow.

Piece of Money. *See* Money, 2.

Piece of Silver. *See* Money, 1.

Pigeon. *See* Dove.

Pi-hahiroth (pī′hȧ-hī′rŏth), RSV once **Hahiroth** (hȧ-hī′rŏth). [Heb. *Pi-hachiroth* and *Hachiroth.*] The last stopping place of the Israelites in Egypt before crossing the Red Sea (Ex 14:2, 9; Num 33:7, 8); not identified. The name seems to be the transliteration of an Egyptian term *Pr-Ḥrt,* "temple of *Ḥrt.*" The Egyptian goddess Cheret is known from Egyptian and Syrian inscriptions, but no instance of a city bearing her name has been found in extant Egyptian records (*BASOR* 109 [1948], 16).

Pilate (pī′lȧt). [Gr. *Pilatos,* from Latin *Pilatus,* of uncertain meaning.] Pontius (pŏn′shŭs) Pilatus, Roman procurator (*see* Governor, 2, *c*) of Judea A.D. 26-36. Secular writers do not picture him in a favorable light. Philo says of him that he was "of nature inflexible, and, owing to stubbornness, harsh" (*Embassy to Gaius,* 38). He frequently clashed with the Jews, offending their religious feeling by many stupid acts. Once he had his soldiers march into Jerusalem carrying standards to which images of the emperor were attached. On another occasion he placed gilded shields with the name of the emperor engraved upon them in the former palace of Herod. In both cases he was forced to remove the offensive objects because of the stubborn resistance of the Jews. In the 2d case a direct order from Tiberius in response to a petition sent to Rome by the nobility of Judea compelled him to comply. The Jews were especially shocked when Pilate used money from the Temple treasury to pay for an aqueduct that was being built to bring water into Jerusalem. Their opposition to this misappropriation of sacred money was met with ruthless cruelty. Later Pilate massacred many Samaritans who were foolishly following an impostor who had promised to produce for them sacred gold vessels allegedly hidden by Moses on the top of Mount Gerizim. The Samaritans complained about his needless cruelty to his superior, Vitellius, the legate of Syria, who ordered Pilate to go to Rome and justify his conduct before the emperor.

At the same time Vitellius appointed a new procurator over Judea. Before Pilate arrived in Rome, Tiberius died, but it is said that Pilate was nevertheless banished to Vienne on the Rhone, in the south of Gaul (now France), and that he died a suicide.

The Gospels mention Pilate principally in connection with the trial of Jesus. At that time he was in the midst of his term of office. Knowing that he was extremely unpopular, he was anxious to please the Jews in a matter that cost him nothing, although he realized that the accusations brought against Jesus were false. Other historical events mentioned in the Gospels in connection with his name are in keeping with the character of Pilate as described by the historians of his time. The enmity between him and Herod Antipas (Lk 23:12) can be explained by assuming that the latter may have signed the Jewish petition mentioned above, which was sent to Tiberius, or that Antipas was indignant that Pilate had killed Galilean subjects of his when they were offering sacrifices, presumably in Jerusalem (ch 13:1, 2). The apocryphal Christian literature contains several "Acts of Pilate," but they are all spurious and historically worthless. This is also true of Pilate's alleged report to Tiberius of the condemnation of Jesus, which is clearly a forgery.

Pildash (pĭl'dăsh). [Heb. *Pildash,* "spider."] The son of Abraham's brother, Nahor, by his wife Milcah (Gen 22:20, 22). He was probably the ancestor of an Aramaean tribe.

Pileha. *See* Pilha.

Pilha (pĭl'hä), KJV **Pileha** (pĭl'ê-hä). [Heb. *Pilcha',* "harelip."] A Jew who set his seal to Nehemiah's covenant (Neh 10:1, 24).

Pill. *See* Peel.

Pillar. A number of terms are thus translated, meaning variously:

1. An upright architectural support used in a building to uphold the roof, curtains, etc. (Jgs 16:29; Ex 36:35, 36; etc.). Symbolically pillars are represented as upholding the heavens and the earth (Job 26:11; 1 Sa 2:8); in the NT some apostles are called pillars (Gal 2:9); and the church is called "the pillar . . . of the truth" (1 Ti 3:15).

2. A stone erected as a memorial. Jacob set up a stone pillar to mark the place where God had appeared to him (Gen 28:18), and another as a memorial to a covenant made with Laban (ch 31:45-51).

386. Two standing pillars connected with the high place at Petra

Moses set up 12 pillars as silent witnesses of the conclusion of the covenant made by the 12 tribes with God on Mount Sinai (Ex 24:4). Isaiah predicted that a pillar to the Lord would be erected in Egypt as a sign and witness (Is 19:19, 20).

3. A stone erected for pagan religious purposes. The ancient Canaanites and some other nations erected stones as cult objects for worship in their temples (see fig. 194) and high places (see fig. 200). It is not certain whether these stones (Heb. usually *maṣṣebôth*) represented beams of light and were therefore connected with sun worship or whether they were phallic symbols and thus part of a fertility cult. The Israelites were commanded to destroy these pillars wherever they found them (Ex 23:24; Deut 7:5), and were strictly forbidden to set up pillars in connection with their places of worship (Deut 16:22). These divinely given instructions were not always followed, and the prophets had to denounce Israel and also Judah for worshiping pillars (Hos 3:4; 10:1, 2; Mic 5:13). See fig. 386.

4. Two bronze pillars with ornamental capitals at the entrance of Solomon's Temple. *See* Boaz, 2; Jachin, 3; Temple, I.

Pillow. A rendering of: (1) The Heb. (pl.) *mera'ashôth* (Gen 28:11, 18, KJV). *See* Bolster. (2) The Heb. *kabîr* (1 Sa 19:13, 16), a word of uncertain meaning, in the context signifying something woven or manufactured of goat's hair. (3) The Heb. *keseth* (Eze 13:18, 20), derived from the Akkadian *kasû*, "to bind." The reference is possibly to a charm sewn around some part of the arm or hand. (4) The Gr. *proskephalaion* (Mk 4:38, KJV); perhaps a leather-covered *cushion used on the rower's seat.

Pilot. A rendering of: (1) The Heb. *chobel* (Eze 27:8, 27-29), literally "rope puller," and by extension, "sailor," "steersman"; *chobel* is related to *chebel*, "cord," or "rope," which is derived from *chabal*, "to bind," and is employed by Ezekiel to describe the sailors of ancient Tyre. (2) A form of the Gr. *euthunō*, "to make straight," "to guide in a straight course," hence in the context, one who guides "a ship straightly." To illustrate the far-reaching influence of the tongue, a little member of the body, James calls attention to the fact that a pilot is able to guide large sailing vessels with a very small rudder, even in rough seas (Jas 3:4, RSV).

Piltai (pĭl'tī). [Heb. *Pilṭay*, "deliverance."] The head of the priestly family of Moadiah in the days of the high priest Joiakim (Neh 12:12, 17).

Pim (pĭm). [Heb. *pîm*.] A weight of ⅔ shekel, as attested by actual weight stones found in Palestinian excavations with the word *pym* engraved upon them (see fig. 522). Their actual weight fluctuates between 7.26 and 7.60 grams. The term occurs in 1 Sa 13:21, RSV, but is not found in the KJV, being unknown to the translators of that version, who rendered *pîm* as "file."

Pin. A piece of metal or wood, in the shape of a cylinder or modified cylinder, used for holding separate pieces of material together or for providing a suspension point on which articles may be hung. The "pins" mentioned in connection with the tabernacle (Ex 27:19; 35:18; Num 3:37; KJV) were apparently some form of "pegs" (see RSV). The pin mentioned in Jgs 16:14 was probably the weaver's shuttle with which the woof is beaten into the warp. The word translated *"crisping pins" in Is 3:22, KJV (Heb. *charitim*), should rather be rendered "purses," or "handbags."

Pine. [Heb. *te'ashshûr, tidhar, berôth, 'eṣ shemen.] The Hebrew terms in general represent trees of uncertain identification. *'Eṣ shemen,* translated "pine" in Neh 8:15, KJV, is possibly the wild olive (RSV), sometimes called oleaster. *Te'ashshûr,* translated "pine" in Is 41:19; 60:13; RSV (KJV "box"), is probably the cypress (*Cupressus sempervirens*). "Pine" occurs in these verses also in the KJV as a rendering of *tidhar,* an unknown species of tree (RSV *"plane tree"). *Berôth* occurs in Song 1:17, and is translated "pine" (RSV) and *"fir" (KJV). Some authorities consider *berôth* to be the Phoenician juniper.

Pinnacle. [Gr. *pterugion,* a diminutive of *pterux,* "wing," figuratively the "end," or "edge," of something; Heb. *shemesh.* The English word "pinnacle" is from the Latin *pinnaculum,* a diminutive form of *pinna,* "wing."] In Mt 4:5 and Lk 4:9, probably the pointed roof or peak, or perhaps the edge, of the roof of the Temple, although precisely what part of the Temple structure is designated by this term is not known. Some suggest that it may have been one of the two winglike projections of the Temple of which Josephus speaks in *War* v. 5. 4; others that it was the battlement of the Temple overlooking the Kidron Valley (*Ant.* xv. 11. 5), at the present precipitous southeast corner of the city wall (see figs. 277, 278). In the LXX *pterugion* is used of the fin of a fish (Lev 11:9) and the border of a garment (Num 15:38). In Is 54:12, RSV, "pinnacle" is the rendering of the Heb. *shemesh,* literally, "sun," and in the context may refer to a part of a building reflecting the sun.

Pinon (pī'nŏn). [Heb. *Pinon.*] A descendant of an Edomite chief (Gen 36:41, 43; 1 Chr 1:51, 52).

Pipe. As a musical instrument the translation of: (1) The Heb. *chalîl* (1 Sa 10:5; 1 Ki 1:40; Is 5:12; 30:29; Jer 48:36; KJV). The

387. An Egyptian woman (left) and an Assyrian (right) playing the double flute (oboe)

RSV renders *chalîl* "flute" 4 times and "pipe" once. *Chalîl* most probably refers to a double flute or oboe, a wind instrument consisting of 2 pipes which, to judge from ancient pictures and Egyptian examples, had one mouthpiece. One pipe was held in, and fingered by, each hand. Some of the pipes were cylindrical, others conical. Because the pictures regularly show one hand of the player higher than the other, it has been concluded that 2 tones were produced (fig. 387). The *chalîl* was an instrument of joy, but was apparently not used for Temple music. (2) The Heb. *neqeb* (Eze 28: 13, KJV), a word of unknown meaning. (3) The Heb. *'ûgab* (Gen 4:21; Job 21: 12; 30:31; Ps 150:4), rendered "pipe" (RSV) and "organ" (KJV). See Flute. (4) The Aramaic *mashrôqî,* according to the meaning of cognate words, "reed pipe" (Dan 3:5, 7, 10, 15). (5) The Gr. *aulos.* *See* Flute.

Piram (pī'răm). [Heb. *Pir'am,* "onager," or "wild ass."] The Canaanite king of Jarmuth who was defeated and executed by Joshua (Jos 10:3, 16-27).

Pirathon (pĭr'à-thŏn). [Heb. *Pir'athôn,* "height."] A town in the hill country of the Amalekites, in the territory of Ephraim. It was the home of the judge Abdon (Jgs 12:15), and of Benaiah, a captain of David's army (2 Sa 23:30; 1 Chr 11:31). It is usually identified with *Far'âtā,* about 6 mi. west of Shechem (Map VI, D-3), but this identification is uncertain.

Pirathonite (pĭr'à-thŏn-īt). [Heb. *Pir'athônî.*] An inhabitant of *Pirathon.

Pisgah (pĭz'gà). [Heb. *Pisgah.* The term appears with the definite article, and only in phrases rendered "top of Pisgah," "slopes of Pisgah" in the RSV, and "top of Pisgah," "springs of Pisgah," and *Ashdoth-pisgah in the KJV.] Apparently the northern part of the *Abarim range of mountains, near the northeastern end of the Dead Sea (Deut 34:1; cf. ch 3:17, 27). The Dead Sea was under its slopes (ch 3:17, RSV), and its top overlooked the desert (Num 21:20). Somewhere near its top was the field of Zophim, to which Balak took Baalam (ch 23:14). From the summit of Pisgah, called Mount Nebo, Moses viewed the Promised Land, and there he died (Deut 3:27; 34:1-4). *See* Nebo, 2. In the time of Eusebius the site was still known as *Phasgō,* but the name is no longer used.

Pishon (pī'shŏn), KJV **Pison** (pī'sŏn). [Heb. *Pishôn.*] One of the 4 rivers of Eden (Gen 2:11). Attempts to identify this river are useless, for the surface of the earth was greatly changed during the Flood. The river is said to flow around the land of *Havilah, but this prediluvian country also cannot be identified.

Pisidia (pĭ-sĭd'ĭ-à). [Gr. *Pisidia.*] An area in southern Asia Minor, bounded on the north by Asian Phrygia, on the east by Lycaonia, on the south by Pamphylia, and on the west by Asia. It was a mountainous territory with a fierce, independent population related to the Lycians and Carians. Its inhabitants were able to retain their independence until 25 B.C., when they were subjugated by the Romans and made part of the province of Galatia. "Antioch in Pisidia," which Paul visited twice during his 1st Missionary Journey (Acts 13:13, 14; 14:21, 24), really lay in Phrygia, but was on the border toward Pisidia, hence was called, literally, "Pisidian Antioch" or "Antioch of Pisidia." The Pisidians seem to have spoken an Indo-European language, as indicated by 16 short Pisidian tomb inscriptions, the only witnesses to that language.

Pison. *See* Pishon.

Pispa (pĭs'pà), KJV **Pispah** (pĭs'pà). [Heb. *Pispah.*] An Asherite (1 Chr 7:30, 38).

Pispah. *See* Pispa.

Pistachio Nuts. *See* Nuts.

Pit. A rendering of several Hebrew and Greek terms describing variously a cistern (Gen 37:24), a well (Ps 55:23), a hole in the ground (Ec 10:8), and, in the KJV, the grave or the realm of the dead (Num 16:30, 33; Job 17:16). *See* Grave; Hell.

Pitch. A rendering of: (1) The Heb. *kopher,* "asphalt," a loan word from the Akkadian *kupru.* This substance was used by Noah to daub the ark and thus make it watertight (Gen 6:14). The same substance is described by the Heb. *chemar,* which is rendered "slime" in the KJV and *"bitumen" in the RSV (see fig 388). (2) The Heb. *zepheth,* probably from Akkadian *ṣippatu.* This term describes pitch probably of fir or pine. It designates one of the materials used by Moses' mother to daub the little basket into which she placed her son before entrusting him to the water of the Nile. In Is 34:9 *zepheth* is represented as something fluid and flammable, hence is considered to be an asphaltlike or pitchlike substance, although its real nature is unknown.

388. A brick wall in Babylon showing how pitch (bitumen) was used as mortar

Lit.: R. J. Forbes, *Studies in Ancient Technology,* vol. 1 (Leiden, 1955), pp. 1-120.

Pitcher. [Heb. *kad, gabîa'*; Gr. *keramion.*] A vessel, usually of earthenware, used for oil, wine, or grain, probably in the shape of a *jar. Gideon used pitchers (RSV "jars") in his strategy for defeating the Midianites (Jgs 7:16, 19, 20). In Ec 12:6 death is poetically likened to a pitcher broken at a fountain. Trips to the well with a pitcher were a part of daily life in Bible lands (Gen 24:14; Mk 14:13; Lk 22:10). See fig. 154.

Pithom (pī'thŏm). [Heb. *Pithom,* a transliteration of the Egyptian *Pr-'Itm,* "house (or temple) of (the god) Atum."] An Egyptian store city built by the Hebrew slaves during the period of Egyptian oppression (Ex 1:11). Since 1883, when Édouard Naville carried out excavations at the *Tell el-Maskhûtah* in the *Wâdî Tumilât,* this site has popularly been identified with Pithom. However, Allen Gardiner and W. F. Albright identify Pithom with *Tell 'er-Retâbeh,* about 8 mi. farther west in the same wadi (Map V, B-3/4). In a report of a frontier official written in the late 19th dynasty (end of the 13th cent. B.C.), mention is made of a permit given to "Bedouin tribes of Edom" to pass "the [border] Fortress [of] Merne-Ptah" and go to the "pools of Per-Atum" (Pithom) to keep them and their cattle alive. (See *ANET* 259.)

Pithon (pī'thŏn). [Heb. *Pîthôn.*] A descendant of King Saul through Jonathan (1 Chr 8:33, 35; 9:39, 41).

Plague. [Heb. generally *maggephah* and *makkah;* Gr. *mastix,* "a lashing," "torment," "suffering," and *plēgē,* "blow," "stroke," "wound," "misfortune."] Generally, in Scripture, a divine visitation as punishment for sin, usually a virulent disease or a catastrophe resulting from the unusual operation of the forces of nature, as the 10 plagues upon the land of Egypt (Ex 9:14), the "plague" that

PLAGUE

befell Israel for censuring Moses when God destroyed Korah, Dathan, and Abiram (Num 16:48, 49), or the "plague" that followed the apostasy at Shittim (ch 25:8, 9). The death of the first-born in Egypt is called a "plague" (Heb. *nega'*; Ex 11:1), as is leprosy (repeatedly in Lev 13; 14). The Gr. *mastix* is used of various incurable diseases in such passages as Mk 3:10; Lk 7:21.

The first 9 of the 10 plagues by which God secured Pharaoh's release of His people from Egypt were in the realm of nature: the Nile River turned to blood (Ex 7:17), successive swarms of frogs (ch 8:2), lice (v 16), flies (v 21), disease of cattle (ch 9:3), and of men (v 9), hail (v 18), locusts (ch 10:4), and supernatural darkness (v 21). The miraculous nature of the first 9 visitations consisted chiefly in their unprecedented intensity, and in some instances, at least, their precise timing (see chs 8:29; 9:18; 10:4). The 10th plague occasioned the simultaneous death of the first-born of each family in all Egypt (ch 11:5).

Throughout their history the Hebrew people suffered from various plagues, always in connection with some overt act of disobedience. The 1st of such plagues followed the worship of the golden calf (Ex 32:35). Another fell when the people murmured for flesh food (Num 11:33, 34), and still another at Kadesh-barnea, upon the rebellion that broke out following the evil report of the 10 spies (ch 14:37). More than 14,000 perished in the plague at the insurrection of the rebels Korah, Dathan, and Abiram (ch 16:46-50). Twenty-four thousand similarly died because of idolatry and immorality at Baal-peor (ch 25:9). Centuries later 70,000 perished from a plague when David, in vanity, numbered Israel (2 Sa 24:13-15; cf. v 21).

In Rev (chs 15; 16) 7 great plagues are foretold as falling upon the earth immediately prior to the return of Christ. "In them," says the revelator, "is filled up the wrath of God" (ch 15:1), inasmuch as they are the "judgments" of a righteous God upon perversely impenitent sinners (v 4). As seen in vision, they were administered by the 7 angels whom John saw coming out of the temple of God in heaven (chs 15:5, 6; 16:1). The 1st consisted of a virulent and incurable sore (ch 16:2), while the 2d and 3d rendered the salt and fresh waters of earth, respectively, unusable (vs 3, 4). The 4th and 5th brought intense heat and darkness in

29

865

rapid succession (Rev 16:9-11). The 6th consisted essentially of deception, which resulted in the gathering of the nations for the battle of the great day of God (vs 12-16). Under the 7th plague lightning, hail, and earthquake came upon mankind, and mystical Babylon came before God for judgment (vs 17-21).

Plain. The rendering of: (1) The Heb. *'arabah* (Num 22:1; etc.), the great depression extending through the Jordan Valley, the Dead Sea, and southward from the Dead Sea; *see* Arabah. (2) The Heb. *shephelah,* the lowland to the west of the Judean hills (Jer 17:26; Ob 19; KJV; etc.). This term is frequently transliterated *Shephelah in the RSV. (3) The Heb. *kikkar* (Deut 34:3; etc.), "disk-shaped," "circle," usually referring to the alluvial plain in the vicinity of Jericho to the north of the Dead Sea or a similar region at the south end of the Dead Sea (Gen 13:10, KJV; etc.). (4) The Heb. *mîshôr* (1 Ki 20:23; 2 Chr 26:10; etc.), from *yashar,* "to be level," and thus a "plain" in the more general sense, without reference to any particular locality. (5) The Heb. *'elôn,* translated "plain" (RSV "oak") in Gen 12:6; 13:18; 14:13; KJV; etc., actually means "big tree," the "big trees" of Palestine usually being oaks. (6) The Heb. *'emeq* (Jos 17:16; Jgs 1:19, 34; RSV), "level country." (7) The Heb. *biq'ah* (Gen 11:2; Neh 6:2; etc.), a wide, open valley. (8) The Gr. *topos pedinos* (Lk 6:17, KJV), "level place."

Plaister. An obsolete form of *"plaster" appearing in Deut 27:2, 4, KJV.

Plane (tree). [Heb. *'ermôn,* "plane tree" (Gen 30:37; Eze 31:8), and *tidhar,* a tree of uncertain identification (Is 41:19; 60: 13).] The Oriental plane tree (*Platanus orientalis*) grows 70 to 90 ft. in height and has a trunk up to 40 ft. in circumference. Its wide, deeply cleft leaves and scaling bark give it a resemblance to the sycamore maple. Jacob used stripped plane tree rods, among others, in an attempt to influence the coloring of his livestock's offspring (Gen 30:37). In an allegory Ezekiel (Eze 31:8) implies that the plane tree and also the fir and other cedar trees, imposing as they are, do not equal the great cedar of Lebanon. In the KJV *'ermôn* is translated "chestnut tree," and *tidhar,* "pine (tree)."

Planet. *See* Constellation.

Plaster. Material such as clay, burnt limestone, burnt gypsum, etc., which, when mixed with water, was used as a covering for walls. In Palestine and Syria plaster was frequently made of limestone, a stone common in that area. The Israelites were instructed to plaster large stones and to engrave upon them the law (Deut 27: 2-4). In certain cases of what was apparently some fungus disease infection, a house was to be replastered before reoccupation (Lev 14:37-42). Excavations show that the walls of the large throne room in the Southern Palace of Nebuchadnezzar's Babylon, possibly the scene of Belshazzar's feast, were covered with white plaster made of fine plaster of Paris (see Dan 5:5). *See* Mortar, 1.

Plat. A rendering of the Heb. *chelqah* (2 Ki 9:26, KJV), meaning a plot of ground.

Platter. A rendering of: (1) The Gr. *paropsis* (Mt 23:25, 26; Lk 11:39; KJV), "dish," and so rendered by the RSV. (2) The Gr. *pinax* (Mt 14:8; Mk 6:25; etc.; RSV; Lk 11:39, KJV), "platter," "dish." Originally the *pinax* was a large wooden dish or plate.

Play. This article discusses the term from the point of view of engaging in amusement, sport, or a game, and not from the point of view of "playing" musical instruments (see names of various instruments mentioned in the Bible) or "playing the harlot" or "playing a fool." The Heb. *sha'a'* refers to the playing of a child (Is 11:8). *Sachaq* describes Ishmael's playing or jesting with his younger brother Isaac (Gen 21:9), and the playing of the Israelites at the dedication of the golden calf at Mount Sinai (Ex 32:6). That this latter consisted in singing and dancing is evident from vs 17-19 and from 1 Cor

389. Playing pieces and dice found at *Tell Beit Mirsim,* probably ancient Debir

10:7. Although the playing of social games is not specifically mentioned in the Bible, archeological evidence shows that such games existed in ancient Palestine. The earliest game thus far discovered was found in *Tell Beit Mirsim,* probably Biblical Debir, and dates from about 1600 B.C. It consists of a conical ivory die and 2 sets of playing pieces—5 three-cornered pyramids and 5 little cones, all of faïence (see fig. 389). The game board unfortunately was missing (*BASOR* 39 [1930], 6, 9). See fig. 189.

Pleasant Plants. [Heb. *niṭ'ê na'amanîm.*] These are believed to be the so-called Adonis gardens, or Adonis plantations, spoken of by the Greek writers, or gardens of a similar nature. These gardens consisted of certain grains, such as wheat and barley, or various kinds of vegetables or flowers, planted in baskets and pots and given the kind of attention that would cause them to germinate rapidly. The people believed that they symbolized the magic power of the gods of fertility. Isaiah rebuked the Israelites for forgetting the God of their salvation and turning to these idolatrous practices (Is 17:10).

Pledge. A rendering of several different Hebrew words signifying, in common, any article given as security for a loan (Deut 24:10-13) or for the fulfillment of a promise (Gen 38:17-20). The Law of Moses required that the clothing of a poor man, when taken as a pledge, be returned before sunset (Ex 22:25-27). A widow's garment was never to be taken as a pledge (Deut 24:17). The creditor of a poor Israelite was not permitted to enter a debtor's house and take a pledge article from him by force, but must remain outside and have it brought out to him (vs 10-13).

Pleiades (plē′yȧ-dēz). [Heb. *kîmah.*] The brilliant star cluster in the constellation of Taurus mentioned in Job 9:9 and 38:31. In Amos 5:8 *kîmah* is translated "seven stars" in the KJV and "Pleiades" in the RSV. Traditionally, there are 7 stars in this cluster, but only 6 are normally visible to the unaided eye. Persons with keen eyesight can detect other, fainter stars, particularly with the vision focused slightly to one side. A view of the Pleiades even through a pair of binoculars or a low-power telescope is a sight never to be forgotten. In Job 9:9; 38:31; Amos 5:8 the Pleiades are mentioned together with Orion, doubtless because of adjacent positions in the sky. It has been suggested that "the sweet influences of the Pleiades" (Job 38:31) refers to the force of gravity that holds the individual members of this cluster together in their parallel courses of flight through space.

390. The Pleiades as seen through a telescope

Some take the "sweet influences" to be the conspicuous nebulosity in which the Pleiades are immersed, and which is illuminated like a neon light by the stars themselves. This nebulosity is clearly visible even with a low-power telescope, and on a photographic plate makes the Pleiades an object of unusual beauty. In "Locksley Hall" Tennyson describes the Pleiades as glittering "like a swarm of fireflies in a silver braid."

Plow. Pictures (see fig. 458) and actual models (see fig. 391) of the ancient plow show that it has not changed much in Palestine in the last 4 millenniums. The ancient plows did not turn furrows as do modern plows, but merely scratched the soil to a depth of 3 to 4 in., with the wooden or iron plowshare in the form of a pointed or flat pin. Plowing was done in the autumn (Prov 20:4), and the plow was drawn by oxen (1 Ki 19:19; Job 1:14). The Mosaic law forbade an ox and an ass to be yoked together in plowing (Deut 22:10), a practice still followed in the Near East (see fig. 500). Some an-

391. An ancient Egyptian model of a plowman

cient plows had a funnel attached to the plowshare through which the seed was dropped into the furrow (see fig. 458).

Plumb Line. [Heb. *'anak,* "tin," "lead."] A cord with a weight, the plummet, at one end, used to determine the perpendicular of a structure. Amos represents a plumb line in the hand of the Lord to measure the straightness of Israel (Amos 7:7, 8).

Plummet. A weight fastened to the end of a line, which is then used to determine the perpendicular of a wall, etc. The word is the translation of: (1) the Heb. *mishqaleth* or *mishqoleth* in 2 Ki 21:13 and Is 28:17, a term some believe refers to a device used for horizontal leveling; (2) the Heb. *'eben* (*habbedîl*) in Is 34:11 (KJV "stone") and Zec 4:10.

Pochereth of Zebaim. *See* Pochereth-hazzebaim.

Pochereth-hazzebaim (pŏk'ē-rĕth-hă'zē-bā'ĭm), KJV **Pochereth of Zebaim** (pŏk'ē-rĕth of zē-bā'ĭm). [Heb. *Pokereth Haṣṣebayim,* "pit of the gazelles."] The ancestral head of a family of "Solomon's servants," some members of which returned from Babylonia with Zerubbabel (Ezr 2:55, 57; Neh 7:57, 59).

Poison. A rendering of: (1) The Heb. *chemah,* a word with a wide range of meanings, "heat," "wrath," "venom," "passion," "poison" (Job 6:4; Ps 140:3). (2) The Heb. *ro'sh* and *rôsh* (Job 20:16; etc.). *See* Gall. (3) The Gr. *ios,* "poison," as of the asp, which when absorbed into a living organism results in physical harm and even death. *Ios* is used metaphorically of the evil that proceeds from the organs of speech, the lips (Rom 3:13) and the tongue (Jas 3:8).

Police. *See* Serjeant.

Pollux. *See* Twin Brothers.

Pomegranate. [Heb. *rimmôn.*] A tree (*Punica granatum*) and its fruit, native of southern and southwestern Asia, and cultivated from earliest times in this region as well as along the Mediterranean basin. The tree is most often shrublike, but may attain a height of 12 or 15 ft. The dark-green leaves are oblong-oblanceolate. Occasionally thorns are found on the stems. The flowers, generally brilliant scarlet, grow from a calyx that persists until the fruit is ripe. The tangy pulp of the orange-sized fruit contains a large number of red seeds and is covered by a rind. The tree was cultivated in Palestine (Num 13:23; Deut 8:8; etc.) and Egypt (Num 20:5). Imitation pomegranates were sewn on the hem of the high priest's robe (Ex 28:33, 34; 39:26) and adorned the tops of the pillars Jachin and Boaz at the entrance of Solomon's Temple (1 Ki 7:18, 20). A pleasant and refreshing drink was made from the juice of the fruit (Song 8:2). See fig. 392.

392. Pomegranate tree

Pommel. A rendering of: (1) The Heb. *gullah* (2 Chr 4:12, 13, KJV), "bowl," and thus translated in the parallel passage of 1 Ki 7:41, 42. These passages refer to what were apparently bowllike projections on the capitals of the pillars of Solomon's Temple. (2) The Gr. *hupōpiazō* (1 Cor 9:27, RSV), literally, "to strike under the eye," rendered "keep under" in the KJV. Paul is referring to the severe treatment received in a boxing match, paralleling it with the rigorous self-discipline he practiced.

Pontius. *See* Pilate.

Pontus (pŏn'tŭs). [Gr. *Pontos.*] An area on the northern coast of Asia Minor between the river Halys and Colchis, probably called Pontus after the *Pontus Euxinus,* the Euxine (or Black) Sea. Its importance begins with the founding of a kingdom there in the 4th cent. B.C. Its kings were of Persian descent and most of them bore the name Mithridates. The 6th king of this name was defeated by Pompey in 66 B.C. Some areas of his kingdom were thereupon given to native kings of surrounding territories, and the coastal strip of land was united with Bithynia as a Roman province, which later was made into a senatorial province with a legate as administrator. The most famous governor of this province (called *Bithynia et Pontus*) was Pliny the Younger, who assumed office in A.D. 111. From his pen has come a famous letter to the emperor Trajan (No. 96), in which he explains on what basis he persecuted Christians. This letter gives the earliest extant description of a Christian worship service. Jews living in Pontus attended the feast of Pentecost at Jerusalem in the year of Christ's death, as attested in Acts 2:9. Christian churches were organized in this area at an early date, as shown by Peter's reference to them in his 1st letter (1 Pe 1:1). Pontus was the birthplace of Aquila (Acts 18:2). Map XX, A-4/5.

Pool. The rendering of: (1) the Heb. *'agam* (Ex 8:5; 2 Ki 3:16; etc.), usually designating a collection of stagnant water as in marshes or dry river beds; (2) the Heb. *miqweh,* "pond," a storage tank of water in the open country (Ex 7:19); (3) the Heb. *berekah;* Gr. *kolumbēthra,* a water reservoir, such as is constructed in a city for the storage of water used for bathing, washing, drinking, and cooking. Its water comes from springs, being channeled into the reservoir by aqueducts. The Bible mentions several pools: at Gibeon (2 Sa

2:13); at Hebron (ch 4:12); at Samaria (1 Ki 22:38), which has been excavated; at Heshbon (Song 7:4); and the famous pools of *Siloam and *Bethesda at Jerusalem (Jn 5:2; 9:7).

Poor. The laws given to the Hebrews contained various regulations concerning the poor. God warned His people not to oppress the needy in any way (Ex 22:22-27; cf. Eze 22:7); however, sympathy was not to pervert justice (Ex 23:3; Lev 19:15). The hungry and unfortunate were privileged to pluck and eat in the fields or vineyards of another (Deut 23:24, 25), and gleaning was their accepted right (Lev 19:9, 10; 23:22; Deut 24:10-22). In addition the natural produce of field and vineyard during the *sabbatical year was to be for the needy and for the animals (Ex 23:11; cf. Lev 25:1-7). In cases of the poor who sold their services, they were not to be slaves permanently, but only until the year of *jubilee (Lev 25:39-42); another law provided for release in the 7th year of service (Ex 21:1-6). The rich should lend to the poor even though the 7th year approached, when debts were canceled (Lev 25:35-38; Deut 15:1-10).

Concern for the poor is a vital part of the teachings of Christ (Mt 19:21; Lk 14:13; 18:22). The early Christian church was noted for its generous and unselfish care for the poor (Acts 2:45; 4:32; 11:27-30; 1 Cor 16:1-3; Gal 2:10). The "poor in spirit" (Mt 5:3) are those who are conscious of their spiritual poverty.

Poplar. [Heb. *libneh,* from *laban,* "to be white."] A white-leaved tree large enough to be classed with the oak and terebinth, possibly the white or silver poplar (*Populus alba*). This species of poplar has white wood and its leaves are white and cottony on the underside. Its fast-growing shoots fit well the story of Jacob and Laban's flocks (Gen 30:37), and its height and spreading branches would provide suitable shade for the "high places" of heathen worship (Hos 4:13). Some commentators suggest the storax tree (*Styrax officinalis*). By textual emendation the RSV reads "poplar" in ch 14:5 also.

Poratha (pŏ-rā'thä). [Heb. *Pôratha',* a Persian name of uncertain meaning.] One of the sons of Haman (Est 9:8, 10).

Porch. The rendering of: (1) The Heb. *'êlam* and *'ûlam* (1 Ki 7:6, 12, 19; Eze 8:16), generally translated *"vestibule" in the RSV. (2) The Gr. *pulōn* (Mt 26:71), here the gateway of Caiaphas' residence in Jerusalem. It may have contained a stairway leading into the palace. (3) The Gr. *proaulion* (Mk 14:68, KJV), literally, "forecourt" (RSV "gateway"). (4) The Gr. *stoa* (Jn 5:2; 10:23; Acts 3:11; 5:12; KJV). *See* Portico.

Porcius. *See* Festus.

Porcupine. The rendering of the Heb. *qippôd* in Is 34:11, RSV, translated "bittern" in the KJV. In the 2 other passages where *qippôd* occurs (Is 14:23; Zep 2:14), it is rendered "hedgehog" in the RSV and "bittern" in the KJV. G. R. Driver believes the *qippôd* to be a bustard, a large bird of prey (*PEQ* 87 [1955], 137).

Porphyry. A rendering of the Heb. *bahaṭ* (Est 1:6, RSV), a precious stone of unknown identification.

Port. A term occurring once (Neh 2:13, KJV), a rendering of the Heb. *sha'ar,* "gate." Elsewhere *sha'ar* is almost always rendered **"gate."*

Porter. [Heb. generally *shô'er,* "gatekeeper"; Gr. *thurōros,* "doorkeeper."] A gatekeeper, or doorkeeper. David's organization of the tabernacle service provided 4,000 Levites as porters (RSV "gatekeepers") at the *gate (1 Chr 23:5) to serve in courses (ch 26:1-19). Porters stood guard at the gates of ancient cities (2 Ki 7:10). In NT times doorkeepers were assigned to private houses (Mk 13:34) and to guard the door of a sheepfold (Jn 10:3).

Portico. A rendering of the Gr. *stoa* (Jn 5:2; 10:23; Acts 3:11; 5:12; RSV), translated "porch" in the KJV. This Greek term is a designation for a covered colonnade serving as protection from the sun and rain. Such porticoes were used in Greece for meetings and for market places (see fig. 41). The southern part of the eastern portico of Herod's Temple, called Solomon's Portico, served as a meeting hall (*see* Temple, IV; and fig. 485). The 5 porticos of the Pool of *Bethesda served as halls for the bathers.

Posts. *See* Couriers.

Pot. The rendering of several terms, the most common of which is the Heb. *sîr,* which designates a wide-mouth cooking pot of earthenware or metal (Ex 38:3; 2 Ki 4:38). Pots were used for boiling meat (2 Chr 35:13), preparing a broth (Jgs 6:19), and cooking other foodstuff. Many such vessels, usually broken, have been found in Palestinian excavations.

In Mk 7:4 "pot" is the translation of the Gr. *xestēs,* a liquid measure about 1 sextarius (.58 qt.; .55 liters). Later *xestēs* meant simply "pitcher," "jug," or "pot," and is thus used by Mark.

Potiphar (pŏt′ĭ-fẽr). [Heb. *Pôṭîphar,* a transliteration, as is *Pôṭî Phera'* *"Poti-phera" of the Egyptian *p3-dî-p3-R',* "the one whom the (sun-god) Ra has given." The Egyptian name was discovered in 1935 on a hieroglyphic monument.] An officer of the king of Egypt and captain of the royal bodyguard. Joseph was sold to him as a slave (Gen 37:36; 39:1). The story of how Potiphar's wife unsuccessfully tried to seduce Joseph is well known (ch 39:1-20). Her husband's probably being a eunuch may have had something to do with her unfaithfulness (*see* Eunuch).

Poti-phera (pŏ-tĭf′ẽr-à), KJV **Poti-pherah** (pŏ-tĭf′ẽr-à). [Heb. *Pôṭî Phera',* a transliteration, as is *Pôṭîphar,* *"Potiphar," of the Egyptian name *p3-dî-p3-R',* "the one whom the (sun-god) Ra has given."] The high priest of On (Heliopolis), who was father-in-law of Joseph (Gen 41:45, 50; 46:20).

Poti-pherah. *See* Poti-phera.

Potsherd. [Heb. *chereś.*] A piece of broken pottery. Since pottery breaks easily and its fragments, which are practically worthless, do not disintegrate, potsherds are found strewn on the ground and show up in large quantities in archeological diggings everywhere in the Near East. These potsherds furnish important evidence by which the archeologist may date his finds, for pottery styles were continually changing. Potsherds were used in ancient times as the cheapest form of *writing material. For such inscribed ostraca, see figs. 285, 411. Job scraped himself with a potsherd (Job 2:8), and a potsherd was used to take fire from the hearth or to dip up water from a cistern (Is 30:14).

Potsherd Gate. [Heb. *sha'ar hacharsûth* (Q *hacharsîth*).] A gate in the wall of Jerusalem, rendered erroneously "east gate" in the KJV, but correctly "Potsherd Gate" in the RSV (Jer 19:2). It was probably in the southwestern corner of the old City of David, for it led to the Valley of Hinnom, where wastes and broken pottery were disposed of. Potsherd Gate seems to be another name for Dung Gate (Neh 2:13; 3:14). See Map XVII; fig. 259.

Pottage. [Heb. *nazîd,* "that which is boiled," "that which is stewed," "pottage," from *zîd,* "to stew," "to boil."] A boiled dish of vegetables or herbs (2 Ki 4:38-40; cf. Hag 2:12). The dish for which Esau sold his birthright to Jacob contained red lentils (Gen 25:29-34), and was probably flavored with onions or garlic.

393. A Palestinian potter at his foot-powered wheel

Potter. [Heb. *yôṣer,* "fashioner"; Aramaic *pechar;* Gr. *kerameus.*] One who makes earthenware vessels. The potter's art was apparently invented in Sumeria during the earliest historical period, as archeological evidence indicates, and probably from there spread to all other countries until pottery became the most common possessions of everyone, rich and poor alike. Potters were numerous enough in ancient Palestine to form guilds (see 1 Chr 4:23), and their work is frequently mentioned in the Bible. The potter took the clay from the earth, trod it (Is 41: 25), and then kneaded it into a paste with his hands. A lump of it was put on a wooden wheel (Jer 18:3), and by rotating the wheel by hand or foot the potter could form a vessel according to his taste and pleasure (fig. 393). The ability of the potter was used by Bible writers to illustrate God's sovereignty (Is 45:9; Jer 18:5-12; Rom 9:20-25). The finished product was baked in a furnace, sometimes after the application of glaze-producing paste (Prov 26:23; cf. Ecclus

38:29, 30). The best-preserved ancient pottery shop is that excavated at *Khirbet Qumrân.* It dates from the 1st cent. A.D. and contains the place where the clay was kneaded, the potter's seat, the spot where the wheel stood, and the kiln in which the vessels were baked.

Potter's Field. *See* Akeldama.

Pound. A rendering of: (1) the Heb. *maneh* in the KJV (*see* Mina); (2) the Gr. *litra* (Jn 12:3; 19:39), a unit of weight divided into 12 *unciae,* and equivalent to 327.45 grams, or 11.54 oz. avoirdupois; (3) the Gr. *mna,* "mina" (Lk 19:13, 16; etc.). Although the OT mina (*maneh*) originally meant a unit of weight (see 1 Ki 10:17), and only later a monetary unit (probably so in Ezr 2:69; Neh 7:71, 72), the term *mna* as used in the NT had already for centuries been used as a money value. It was worth 100 drachmas, or about $10.50.

Praetorian Guard. A body of soldiers who attended the emperor and members of his family in Rome and abroad. In Paul's time it consisted of 10 cohorts of 500 soldiers each and was commanded by a tribune. These guardsmen served for 16 years and received 3 times as much pay as legionaries. Their camp was on the edge of the city (see fig. 405). The term occurs once (Php 1:13, RSV), the translation of the Gr. *praitōrion,* rendered "palace" in the KJV. In all other passages the Gr. *praitōrion* refers to the governor's palace or judgment hall (*see* Praetorium). The exact meaning of the Greek term as used by Paul in Php 1:13 is disputed. If the letter to the Philippians was written from Rome, as is most likely, it cannot refer to a palace, which in Rome was not called *praitōrion,* but it could refer either to the Praetorian Guard or to the court of justice, both of which are also designated by the term *praitōrion.*

Praetorium. [Gr. *praitōrion* from the Latin *praetorium,* "pertaining to a praetor." The word originally referred to the headquarters of a praetor or of a general in a camp, but was later applied to the official residence of the governor of a province.] This term is used in the RSV (once in the KJV, Mk 15:16) of the Gospels to refer to the temporary residence of the procurator in Jerusalem during his stay in that city. In this building the trial of Jesus before Pilate was held (Mt 27:27; Mk 15:16; Jn 18:28, 33; 19:9). In Mt and Jn the KJV renders *praitōrion* "common hall" or "judgment hall." It is not certain whether this temporary residence in which the trial was held was Herod's palace, which stood at the site now occupied by the Citadel in the western part of Jerusalem, or whether it was the Tower of Antonia, a palatial fortress also built by Herod north of the Temple. The praetorium of Acts 23:35 refers to the magnificent palace of Herod, built at Caesarea, which was the official residence of the procurators (see Governor, 2, c) of Palestine from A.D. 6 to 41 and from A.D. 44 to 66.

Prayer. [Heb. generally *tephillah*, "prayer," "psalm of praise"; Gr. generally *deēsis*, "entreaty," "prayer," and *proseuchē*, "prayer," "intercession."] Communion with God, consisting usually of praise, gratitude, or entreaty. Prayer presupposes faith that God is, that He hears, that He cares, and that He is "a rewarder of them that diligently seek him" (Heb 11:6). It assumes that a right relation exists between the suppliant and God, or that such a relationship is to be restored. Ideally, prayer is any outgoing of the soul toward God expressing love and appreciation, the desire for divine guidance, the confession of sin, or particular requests. Its purpose is not so much to effect a change in God as to effect one in the suppliant, and to condition the mind and life of the petitioner so that God may accomplish His infinite will in and through him. *Deēsis* usually denotes prayer for particular benefits (Lk 1:13; Rom 10:1; Php 1:19; etc.), while *proseuchē* is prayer in a more general sense (Mt 21:13; Lk 6:12; Acts 1:14; Eph 1:16; 1 Pe 3:7; etc.).

Faith is an essential ingredient of prayer (Mt 21:21, 22). By the parables of the Friend Calling at Midnight (Lk 11:5-13) and the Unjust Judge (ch 18: 1-8), our Lord set forth the importance of persistence, perseverance, and earnestness in prayer. Right home relationships are important, that "prayers be not hindered" (1 Pe 3:7). A forgiving spirit is essential to the forgiveness of one's own sins (Mt 6:14, 15). Humility is likewise an essential ingredient (Lk 18:10, 11). Prayer is to be offered to God in the name of Christ (Jn 14:13, 14). Prayers motivated by selfishness cannot be answered (Jas 4:3), and God declines to heed the prayers of those who deliberately disobey Him, or who purpose to do so (Prov 15:29; 28:9). In view of the fact that prayer reflects consciousness of need and faith in God's power to supply that need, God often accomplishes for us, as a result of prayer, what He might not otherwise do. Some people "have not" because they "ask not" (Jas 4:2).

Prayer is to be simple, and not ostentatious (Mt 6:5-7). An essential for answered prayer is that the petition be in accordance with God's will. The petitioner should pray after Christ's own example, "Nevertheless not as I will, but as thou wilt" (ch 26:39). "If we ask any thing according to his will," we are to have confidence that "he heareth us" (1 Jn 5:14). Too often "we know not what we should pray for as we ought," but "the Spirit itself maketh intercession for us with groanings which cannot be uttered" (Rom 8:26). Special prayer is to be offered for the sick (Jas 5:14, 15). Prayer is to be made with sincerity of heart, in simple faith that in His own good way and time God will provide what is best. He may comply with our requests, or deny them. He may provide something better, or the answer may await a more appropriate time.

As their titles suggest, a number of psalms constitute prayers (Ps 17; 86; 90; 102; etc.). In Christ's intercessory prayer on the night of His betrayal (Jn 17) He prayed for the unity of the disciples and for strength on their part that they might live in the world without being influenced by it (vs 15, 22). The best-known prayer is, of course, the model prayer given by Christ to His disciples—the Lord's Prayer. This prayer is brief, and covers the basic needs and aspirations of the devout believer (Mt 6:9-13).

Precept. [Heb. generally *miṣwah*, "order," "commandment," and *piqqûdîm*, "orders" (always in the plural); Gr. generally *entolē*, "a command," "charge."] A specific command that places the recipient under obligation to obey; usually a divine injunction requiring man's obedience (Ps 119:4; Jer 35:18; Mk 10:5; KJV; Rom 2:26, RSV; etc.). *Piqqûdîm* is rendered "precepts" 21 times in Ps 119, and "statutes" in Ps 19:8, KJV, and "commandments" in Ps 103:18; 111:7; KJV.

Precious Stones. Because of their beauty and rarity precious and semiprecious stones were prized by the peoples of Bible times. In most cases the gems mentioned in the Scriptures are difficult to identify, except where some contextual clue is given, or where archeology has shed some light. *See* names of individual precious stones; also the following table, arranged alphabetically in the 1st column according to the names as they appear in the KJV:

KJV	RSV	Hebrew	Greek
*adamant	adamant	shamir	
*agate	agate	kadkod, shebô	
*amber	(gleaming bronze)	chashmal	
*amethyst	amethyst	'achlamah	amethustos
*beryl	beryl, chrysolite, jewel	tarshish	
"	beryl		bērullos
*carbuncle	carbuncle	bareqath, bareqeth, 'eben 'eqdach	
*chalcedony	*agate		chalkēdōn
chrysolyte	*chrysolite		chrusolithos
chrysoprasus	*chrysoprase		chrusoprasos
*coral	coral	ra'môth	
*crystal	crystal	qerach	krustallos
"	*glass	zekûkith	
*diamond	diamond	shamir	
"	diamond, jasper	yahalom	
*emerald	emerald	nophek	smaragdos
*jacinth	jacinth, sapphire		huakinthos
*jasper	jasper	yashepheh	iaspis
ligure	*jacinth	leshem	
*onyx	onyx	shoham	
*pearl	*crystal	gabîsh	
"	pearl		margaritēs
*ruby	coral, costly stone, jewel, pearl	peninim, peniyim (pl.)	
?	*porphyry	bahat	
*sapphire	sapphire	sappir	sappheiros
sardine (see Sardius)	carnelian (see Sardius)		sardinos, sardion
*sardius	carnelian, sardius	'odem	
*sardonyx	onyx		sardonux
*topaz	topaz	piṭdah	topazion

Predestination. This term does not appear in the Bible, but its verb form, "to predestinate" (Gr. *proorizō*, meaning "to determine beforehand"), occurs in Rom 8:29, 30 and Eph 1:5, 11 (RSV "to predestine," "to destine"). According to Rom 8:28, 29 God predestined all who He knew would accept His salvation "to be conformed to the image of his Son." Such He calls, justifies, and glorifies (v 30). According to Eph 1:4, God made provision that sinners "should be holy and without blame before him in love" through faith in Christ before the creation of this world and the entrance of sin. Such He then "predestinated . . . unto the adoption of children by Jesus Christ to himself, according to the good pleasure of his will" (v 5). Predestination operates within the orbit of God's purpose to "gather together in one all things in Christ, both which are in heaven, and which are on earth," "in the dispensation

of the fulness of times" (Eph 1:10, 11; cf. Jn 1:12).

From these passages some have erroneously assumed that God arbitrarily predestined, or "marked off beforehand," particular individuals to be saved and others to be lost, irrespective of their own choice in the matter, thus arbitrarily imposing the benefits of salvation upon some while denying them to others. Context and the analogy of Scripture demonstrate conclusively the fallacy of this line of reasoning. The Scriptures explicitly teach that God "will have all men to be saved, and to come unto the knowledge of the truth" (1 Ti 2:4), and that He is "not willing that any should perish, but that all should come to repentance" (2 Pe 3:9). Nowhere do the inspired writers state that God has willed that some men should be lost. The idea that God arbitrarily appointed some men to salvation and others to reprobation is a fiction of human invention. That none are excluded from the benefits of salvation is evident from Is 55:1 and Rev 22:17. All who thirst are invited to "take the water of life freely." God has "no pleasure in the death of the wicked," but wills "that the wicked turn from his way and live" (Eze 33:11). The nature of Bible predestination is clearly set forth in Jn 3:16-21, where it is stated that God "loved the world" and gave His Son to be its Saviour —not that He loved certain persons and hated others. Verse 17 states specifically that "God sent not his Son into the world to condemn the world; but that the world through him might be saved." According to Jn 1:12; 3:16 the decisive factor in each individual case is willingness to receive God's only-begotten Son as one's personal Saviour, and to believe in Him. "Whosoever believeth" is eligible to eternal life (ch 3:16). God does not refuse the benefits of salvation to anyone who sincerely chooses the way of life and is willing to comply with His requirements. The way condemnation, or reprobation, comes upon a person is clearly explained in vs 18-21, where the determining factor is said to be the individual response to "the light," that is, to Jesus Christ as "the light of men" (ch 1:4-9). While men remain in an unenlightened state there is no condemnation (see Ps 87:4, 6; Eze 3:18-21; 18:2-32; 33:12-20; Lk 23:34; Jn 15:22; Rom 7:7, 9; 1 Ti 1:13). Only when men deliberately reject truth, clearly spoken to them, do "they have no cloke for their sin" (Jn 15:22). According to ch 3:18, a person who refuses salvation in Christ automatically incurs condemnation, not by some imagined arbitrary act of God, but simply "because he hath not believed in the name of the only begotten Son of God." This thought is emphasized further in v 19, where it is stated that "men loved darkness rather than light, because their deeds were evil." All who choose to cling to their evil ways do so because of their hatred for the light, and avoid it "lest" their "deeds should be reproved" (v 20). Contrariwise, those who seek a better way of life benefit by the sunshine of divine love that melts hard hearts.

The teaching that distorts Bible predestination to mean that God has arbitrarily foreordained certain persons to be saved and others to be lost results from the neglect of the cardinal Bible truth that God has granted to every man the power to settle his own destiny. God never interferes decisively with the free exercise of man's power of choice (see Eze 18:31, 32; 33:11; 2 Pe 3:9). Before the foundation of the world (1 Pe 1:20) He made provision for sinners to be restored to divine favor, and predetermined—foreordained or predestined (Eph 1:4)—that those who accept of this provision should find salvation in Jesus Christ and be restored to sonship. Salvation is offered freely to all, but not all accept the invitation. Salvation is not forced upon man against his will, nor is it denied him contrary to his will. Divine foreknowledge and predestination in no way exclude freedom of choice or render it ineffective, but grant to men the privilege of choosing the way of life eternal. Those who believe in Jesus Christ are justified by their faith in Him, while those who refuse to believe automatically exclude themselves. God has predetermined that those who believe shall be saved and that those who do not believe shall be lost, but He has left it to every man to choose whether to believe or not to believe.

A superficial reading of Rom 9:9-16 and 1 Cor 3:12-15 has led some to the erroneous conclusion that Paul here teaches individual predestination irrespective of personal choice. That such is not the case in either instance becomes evident from a careful reading of the context. In Rom 9:9-16 Paul deals with God's rejection of Esau as the inheritor of the birthright and of His election of Jacob to this sacred office. The context makes evident that the apostle is not here dealing with the matter of personal salvation, but exclusively with the choice of human instruments to be agents of His will on earth. God's rejection of Esau as the inheritor of the birthright did not deny to him the blessings of salvation any more than the later denial of the birthright to Reuben, Jacob's first-born, excluded him from an inheritance in either the earthly or the heavenly Canaan (cf. Gen 49:3, 4). In its context the passage, "It is not of him that willeth, nor of him that runneth, but of God that sheweth mercy" (Rom 9:16), does not refer to the mercies of salvation but to the inheritance of the birthright. Similarly, the passage, "Therefore hath he mercy on whom he will have mercy, and whom he will he hardeneth" (v 18), speaks of Pharaoh as an instrument of the divine will, and does not deal with his personal salvation or reprobation. The sequence based on the illustration of the potter having "power over the clay," to make some vessels to honor and others to dishonor (Rom 9:21-23), is not concerned with the intrinsic character of the respective vessels but of the respective uses to which they are put, some functions being more honorable than others. No potter makes a vessel with the specific intention of destroying it, but he does make different vessels to serve different purposes. A vessel that serves a humble purpose may be as useful and good as one that serves a nobler purpose. In Rom 9 Paul deals with the Jewish nation as God's chosen representative and with their ultimate rejection in preference for the Gentiles (see vs 24-26). Similarly, in 1 Cor 3:12-15 the reward spoken of is for service in the gospel ministry, not for one's personal life as a Christian.

Prefect. A rendering of the Aramaic *segan* (Dan 2:48; 3:2, 3, 27; 6:7; RSV), "prefect," "governor," "overseer."

Preparation. [Gr. *paraskeuē*, "preparation."]
1. The 6th day of the week, the day before the Sabbath (Mt 27:62; Mk 15:42; Lk 23:54; Jn 19:31, 42; Jos. *Ant.* xvi. 6. 2), now called Friday. *Paraskeuē* is the name by which Friday is designated in modern Greek.

2. The day of preparation for the Passover in the phrase *paraskeuē tou pascha* (Jn 19:14). This phrase is probably the equivalent of the Heb. *'ereb happesach*, "the eve of the Passover," a common term in rabbinical literature, designating the 14th of Nisan. John uses the expression apparently with this meaning for the day of Christ's trial before Pilate. For a discussion of the problem of the day of the crucifixion with respect to the day of the Jewish month Nisan, see *SDACom* 5:532, note 1.

Presbytery. [Gr. *presbuterion*, "an assembly of elders," "eldership."] A group or assembly of elders (1 Ti 4:14; RSV "elders"). *Presbuterion* is used in Lk 22:66 and Acts 22:5, in reference to the Jewish Sanhedrin (*see* Council), a body of "elders" (Mt 27:1; 28:12; etc.). The "elders" mentioned in Lk 7:3 were probably the supervisory board of the local Jewish synagogue. The Christian church adopted a plan of local administration similar to that of the Jewish synagogue (1 Ti 5:17; etc.).

Presents. *See* Gifts.

Presidents. [Aramaic *sarekin*, "high officials."] High officials of the Persian Empire (Dan 6:2-7). The Persian "presidents" presided over the affairs of the kingdom, but were not elected "presidents" in the modern sense.

Press. *See* Oil.

Prevent. A term appearing in the KJV in the obsolete sense of "precede," or "go before," as a rendering of the Heb. *qadam,* "to be in front," "to meet," "to go before"; Gr. *prophthanō,* "to come before," "to anticipate," "to do (something) previously"; *phthanō,* "to come before," "to precede," "to reach," "to attain (to something)" (2 Sa 22:19; Mt 17:25; 1 Th 4:15; etc.). Instead of "precede" the RSV reads variously, "confronted" (2 Sa 22: 6), "came upon" (v 19); "receive" (Job 3:12); "come to meet" (ch 30:27); "rise before" (Ps 119:147); "spoke to him first" (Mt 17:25); and "precede" (1 Th 4:15).

Prick. [Heb. *śek,* "thorn," "splinter"; Gr. *kentron,* "goad," "sting."] Any slender, pointed object, such as a thorn or a goad or the sting of an insect. In Acts 26:14, KJV, "pricks" refers to the "goads" (RSV) used to spur beasts of burden on their way, and is used figuratively of the promptings of conscience. *See* Goad.

Pride. An inordinate self-esteem making its possessor blind to weaknesses and dangers, and paving the way for his humiliation and destruction (Prov 11:2; 16:18; 29:23; etc.). It is one of the attitudes that God hates (Prov 8:13). Arrogant pride contributed to the fall of ancient nations (Is 10:12; 13:19; RSV; Jer 13:9; etc.). John listed "the pride of life" as of the world which is about to pass away (1 Jn 2:16, 17). In RSV 1 Cor 15:31; 2 Cor 7:4, 14; Heb 3:6, "pride" is used of legitimate feelings of pleasure and approbation.

Priest. [Heb. *kohen;* Gr. *hiereus.* For "high priest," Heb. *kohen haggadōl,* "great priest," and *kohen haro'sh,* "first priest"; Gr. *archiereus.* The English word is a contracted transliteration of the Latin *presbyter,* in turn from the Gr. *presbuteros,* "elder."] A person duly authorized to minister in sacred things as a mediator between man and God, and to offer sacrifices for the sins of men (Heb 5:1; 8:1-3; cf. v 6). As an institution, the priestly office is based on the assumption that man by nature is out of favor with God, and that therefore he stands in need of a mediator who knows the ways of God and can bring about reconciliation. In Israel, as in other nations of antiquity, the priests formed a distinct class (see Gen 41:45; Ex 2:16; 1 Sa 6:2; Acts 14:13), with the high priest during the monarchy usually standing next in rank, dignity, and influence to the monarch, and occasionally wielding the power behind the throne. The chief role of the Hebrew priesthood was to "offer both gifts and sacrifices for sins" (Heb 5:1; cf. 8:3) in order "to make reconciliation for the sins of the people" (ch 2:17), thereby, in figure, restoring them to divine favor. "Of necessity" a priest must have "somewhat . . . to offer" (ch 8:3), since, figuratively, when God accepted the sacrifice He accepted also with it the plea of the one on whose behalf it was offered.

In addition to administering the sacred ritual the priests were appointed to be the religious teachers of the people (see Lev 10:11; Deut 33:10; Eze 44:23; cf. Ezr 7:25). At the conquest of Canaan they received no tribal inheritance, though they were assigned 13 towns with surrounding pasture and garden lands (Jos 21:10-19; 1 Chr 6:57-60). They were not to engage in any gainful occupation, but were to be supported exclusively by the tithes and certain prescribed offerings (Lev 10:12-15; 23:17-20; Num 18:11, 20; Deut 18:3-5). Even physically defective persons of priestly families, who might not minister at the altar, were entitled to this sustenance (Lev 21:21-23). At least in the time of Ezra the priests were exempted from taxation (Ezr 7:24).

When serving at the sanctuary the common priest was to wear a uniform made of fine linen (Ex 28:40-42). A linen *ephod was the special symbol of the priestly office, but the ephod of the common priest was less elaborate than that worn by the high priest (1 Sa 2:18; 22:18). The high priest's distinctive garb was the blue *robe with bells on the hem, the colorful *ephod with its embroidered girdle and its *breastpiece with the 12 precious stones, or the *Urim and Thummim, and the miter, or *turban, with its gold plate engraved "Holiness to the Lord" (Ex 28:1-39).

From earliest times, prior to the establishment of a regularly organized priesthood, private individuals such as Cain and Abel (Gen 4:3-5) offered sacrifices and thus performed the essential function of a priest (cf. Ex 19:21, 22). Even after the organization of a regular priesthood, individuals offered sacrifices under special circumstances (see Jgs 6:18, 24, 26; 13:16). Throughout patriarchal times the head of the family or tribe usually served as its priest. Thus Noah (Gen 8:

20), Abraham (Gen 22:13), Jacob (ch 35:3), and Job (Job 1:5) served, each as representative priest of his family.

With the establishment of the theocracy at Sinai and the erection of the tabernacle, God appointed the tribe of Levi to its sacred service in place of the firstborn, or head of each family (Num 3:6-13). The tribe of Levi was chosen because of its loyalty at the time of the worship of the golden calf (Ex 32:26-29). Aaron and his sons were set apart to the priestly office, and thenceforth they alone were to serve regularly in this capacity (Num 3:10). The priesthood was hereditary in Aaron's family (Ex 28:1; 40:12-15; Num 16:40; 17; 18:1-8); each of Aaron's male descendants thus automatically became a priest, and served in this capacity unless physically defective (Lev 21:17-21) or temporarily "unclean" (ch 22:3). In Lev 21:10; Num 35:25, 28; etc., Aaron's office is described as that of "high priest," and in Lev 4:3, 5, 16 as that of "anointed" priest. As "the priest" (Ex 31:10) for life, he passed on the right to that sacred office to his eldest qualified descendant. Thus he was succeeded by his son Eleazar (Num 20:28; Deut 10:6), and the latter, in turn, by his son Phinehas (Num 25:11), in whose time the succession to the high priesthood was fixed (vs 12, 13). In a special sense the high priest represented all Israel, and the subordinate priests ministered in his name and as his representatives. The high priest might perform any of the duties required of the common priest, but the right to enter the Holy of Holies on the Day of Atonement was his exclusively (Lev 16:2, 3, 17, 33, 34). See Atonement, Day of.

In David's time the number of priests had so increased that David divided them into 24 courses, or divisions (1 Chr 24; cf. Jos. Ant. vii. 14. 7; Lk 1:5, 9). At least 2 of the great prophets of the OT, Jeremiah (Jer 1:1) and Ezekiel (Eze 1:3), were priests, and probably Zechariah (see Ezr 5:1; cf. Neh 12:16); some think possibly also Haggai.

Not much is known of the activities of the priests during the monarchy after Solomon, although it is evident that they apostatized at times and supported evil kings (Jer 1:18; 2:8, 26; etc.). Yet, a statement made by Ezekiel seems to indicate that they did not fall so deeply into idolatry as did the Levites (Eze 44:10-15). The priests seem to have retained their professional consciousness during the Exile, and thousands could by means of documents prove their status when the Exile ended (Ezr 2:36-39). They were most probably the chief religious leaders during the exile in Babylonia, among them being Ezekiel (Eze 1:3; 8:1; 14:1-4; cf. 2 Chr 17:8, 9; 23:16; 30:27), and they continued this function in the restoration period after the Exile (Neh 8:2; Hag 2: 11, 12). After the return from Babylon only 4 families were at first recognized as legitimately belonging to the priesthood, but the other 20 families eventually succeeded in re-establishing their rights and position, with the result that according to Josephus (*Ant.* vii. 14. 7) in NT times all the 24 courses which had existed in the time of David were again functioning as priests.

Almost nothing is known of the history of the priesthood under the Persians. Under the Ptolemies and early Seleucids the high priest held both religious and civil power, subject to the foreign king. The priestly aristocracy, living from the tithe of the people and receiving other contributions, became wealthy, and consequently sought eagerly to preserve the political status quo of the nation and to prevent any rebellion that might endanger their lucrative position. They embraced Hellenism under the Seleucids. Yet it was a minor priest, Mattathias, who led the revolt against Antiochus Epiphanes' enforcement of Hellenistic paganism; and his sons, the Maccabees, rallied the nation to win independence from the foreign yoke. Jonathan the Maccabean, and after him his brother Simon, though not of a high-priestly family, gained the office, and the Hasmonaean (Maccabean) line became priest-rulers and later priest-kings of Judea. They became increasingly worldly and considerably Hellenized. Though the majority of the people sided with the Pharisees (the party of strict observance of the Law) the priests were leaders of the religio-political party of the Sadducees. That they could maintain their office under such circumstances was due to the fact that the people by tradition and education were accustomed to rendering honor to the holders of high ecclesiastical offices closely connected with the Temple and its services.

When the Romans came they left the Hasmonaean priest-ruler in office, but later set up Herod the Great as vassal king. During the reign of Herod the Great, high priests were appointed by the king, and this custom continued until the destruction of the Temple in A.D. 70. During this period of 106 years (37 B.C. to A.D. 70) not less than 28 high priests held office. Most of them belonged to 5 leading families, and some were extremely mean and unfit for the office they occupied. Even after a high priest was deposed he was usually considered as high priest or chief priest by the people, hence the plural form "chief priests" in the NT (Mt 2:4; 16:21; 20:18; etc.). Though the "chief priests" sought Jesus' death there were many pious priests, such as Zacharias (Lk 1:5, 6), and many of them joined the infant church (Acts 6:7). With the destruction of the Temple in A.D. 70, the Jewish priesthood vanished, never to experience a revival.

The ministry of the Aaronic priesthood was typical only (Heb 8:4, 5), and, in and of itself, had never been truly effective in securing the forgiveness of sins (ch 10:11). Like the sanctuary in which they served, Aaronic priests were only "a figure for the time then present" (ch 9:9). The ritual law of sacrifices could never "make the comers thereunto perfect" (ch 10:1), since "the blood of bulls and of goats" had no power to "take away sins" (v 4). That priesthood was part of the system "imposed" only "until the time of reformation," when Christ Himself should become "an high priest of good things" (ch 9:10, 11). Only by virtue of His sacrificial death, at the close of the Levitical era, when He "put away sin by the sacrifice of himself" (v 26), could the transgressions of OT times be forgiven (v 15). Throughout OT times salvation was provisional, in the sense that it was conditional upon the yet future death of Christ.

Upon the rejection of the Jewish nation as God's chosen people at their rejection and crucifixion of their Messiah (see Mt 21:40-43), God no longer honored the Temple as His "house," and henceforth its services ceased to have meaning in His sight (see ch 23:38). Accordingly, the priesthood was changed (Heb 7:12; cf. vs 15-17; ch 6:20).

Having made one great sacrifice for the sins of all mankind, Christ ascended into heaven and "sat down on the right hand of God" (Heb 10:12), consecrated as our great High Priest and set apart to minister on our behalf in the very presence of the Father (ch 8:1, 2). Only after Christ had offered Himself a sacrifice for sin could He enter upon His special ministry (chs 8:3; 10:12). Only after He Himself had partaken of flesh and blood and been "made like unto his brethren" "in all things" (Heb 2:17), only after He had been "in all points tempted like as we are" and could thus be "touched with the feeling of our infirmities" (ch 4:15; cf. ch 2:14, 18), was He qualified to become "a merciful and faithful high priest in things pertaining to God, to make reconciliation for the sins of the people" (ch 2:17). Upon His ascension, therefore, Christ entered "into heaven itself, now to appear in the presence of God for us" (ch 9:24). "The way into the holiest of all was not yet made manifest, while as the first tabernacle was yet standing" (v 8). Like Aaron, He was "called of God" (ch 5:4) and did not assume the high-priestly office of His own volition (v 5). By an oath (ch 7:21), God ordained Him "an high priest after the order of Melchisedec" (ch 5:10; cf. v 6). Thus the priesthood was "changed" (ch 7:12) from earth to heaven, and "seeing he ever liveth to make intercession" (v 25), His priesthood continues forever (v 24). By virtue of His own perfect sacrifice He "needeth not daily . . . to offer up sacrifice, . . . for this he did once, when he offered up himself" (v 27). His is "a more excellent ministry," since He is "the mediator of a better covenant" (ch 8:6), which in the strict sense of the word came into force only at His death (ch 9:15-17). This is the "new and living way, . . . consecrated for us" following His incarnation, "through the veil, that is to say, his flesh" (ch 10:20). We now have a great High Priest over the household of God (v 21) and are invited to "draw near with a true heart in full assurance of faith" (v 22), to "come boldly unto the throne of grace, that we may obtain mercy, and find grace to help in time of need" (ch 4:16).

Prince. [Heb. generally *śar* and *naśi'*; Aramaic generally *'achashdarpan;* Gr. generally *archōn.*] A male person of rank or authority by reason of relationship in a royal family or by appointment. Abraham was recognized as "a mighty prince" (Gen 23:6). The heads of tribes in Israel were "princes" (Num 1:16; RSV "leaders"). Kings of nations were sometimes referred to as princes (2 Ki 20:5, RSV; Dan 10:13), as were also provincial satraps (Dan 3:2, KJV) and the principal counselors of rulers (Est 1:14; cf. Ezr 7:14).

Among Christ's titles, each of which is significant of some phase of His character or work, are the following: "Prince of Peace" (Is 9:6), "Michael your prince" (Dan 10:21), "the great prince" (ch 12:

1), "the Prince of life" (Acts 3:15). The Bible refers to Satan as the "prince of the power of the air" (Eph 2:2), the "prince of this world" (Jn 12:31; 14:30; 16:11; KJV), "the prince of the devils," or "the prince of demons" (Mt 12:24).

Principality. [Gr. *archē*, "rule," "ruler," "authority."] A term used both of political rulers (Tit 3:1) and of angelic and demonic powers (Rom 8:38; Eph 3:10; 6:12; Col 1:16; etc.). The latter usage may reflect the Jewish designation for one of the orders of angels (see the pseudepigraphical Book of Enoch 61:10). "Principalities" occurs in the OT only in Jer 13:18, KJV, in the rendering of an obscure Hebrew passage.

Prisca. *See* Priscilla.

Priscilla (prĭ-sĭl′ȧ), or **Prisca** (prĭs′kȧ). [Gr. *Priskilla* and *Priska,* the Greek form of a Latin name meaning "old woman," or "revered woman."] Wife of Aquila. The names Aquila and Priscilla are always mentioned together (Acts 18:2, 18, 26; Rom 16:3; 1 Cor 16:19; 2 Ti 4:19). For the history of the couple *see* Aquila.

Prison. A place of confinement for persons awaiting trial or sentenced by a court or ruler. Punishment in ancient pagan nations was characterized by cruelty (see Jgs 1:7; 2 Ki 25:7), and places of incarceration were often designed to deprive prisoners of all comfort. Joseph was fettered for at least part of his imprisonment (Ps 105:17, 18). In the Philistine prison Samson was fettered and forced to do humiliating labor (Jgs 16:21). Jeremiah was placed in a cistern (RSV) where he sank in the mud and was in danger of starving (Jer 38:6, 9). Later, he was taken out and placed "in the court of the prison until the day that Jerusalem was taken" by the Babylonians (v 28). Some of the prophets suffered imprisonment at the hands of rebellious and enraged rulers and people (1 Ki 22:26, 27; 2 Chr 16:10; Mt 14:3; cf. Heb 11:36).

Christ taught His disciples to succor those in prison (Mt 25:36, 39; etc.). The early Christians not infrequently suffered imprisonment not only by pagans but also at the behest of irate Jews (Acts 4:3; 12:1-4; etc.). God sometimes intervened to deliver His servants (chs 5:19; 12:6-10; 16:25-27). Prisoners were sometimes chained to the soldiers appointed to guard them (ch 12:6, 7; cf. 28:16, 20). Paul and Silas were imprisoned in Philippi (ch 16:23, 24), and Paul was later imprisoned for more than 2 years in Caesarea (Acts 23:35; 24:27). In Rome Paul was twice confined: 1st, for 2 years in his own hired house (ch 28:16, 30) and later (cf. 2 Ti 1:8), according to tradition, in a Roman prison. According to tradition both Paul and Peter spent time in the Mamertine prison in Rome, though it is unlikely that Peter as a non-citizen, and of no political importance, would have been held in a place reserved for political prisoners. Followers of Christ were warned that imprisonments would be their lot (Rev 2:10). See figs. 375, 381.

Prochorus (prŏk'ŏ-rŭs). [Gr. *Prochoros,* "leader of dancers."] One of the 7 Christian men of the church at Jerusalem chosen to look after the needs of the Greek-speaking widows and probably of the poor in general (Acts 6:1-5).

Proconsul. *See* Governor, 2, *a.*

Procurator. *See* Governor, 2, *c,*

Prophet. [Heb. *nabî'*, "one called (by God)," or "one who has a vocation (from God)," probably from the cognate Akkadian *nabû,* "to call"; Aramaic *nebî';* Gr. *prophētēs.*]

I. The Prophet and His Work

The prophet is a person supernaturally called and qualified as a spokesman for God. Whereas, in OT times, the priest was the people's representative before God—their spokesman and mediator—the prophet was in a special sense God's official representative to His people on earth. Whereas the priestly office was hereditary, a prophet's appointment came only by divine call. The priest, as mediator of the sacrificial system, led Israel at worship, though his secondary duty was to devote a portion of his time to instructing the people in God's will as already revealed to the prophets, especially Moses. On the other hand, religious instruction was the prophet's primary duty. The priest was concerned largely with the ceremony and ritual of the sanctuary, which centered in public worship, in the mediation of forgiveness of sins, and in the ritual maintenance of right relations between God and His people. The prophet was chiefly a teacher of righteousness, spirituality, and ethical conduct, a moral reformer bearing messages of instruction, counsel, admonition, warning, whose work often included the prediction of future events. In the case of Moses, one of the greatest of the prophets (see Deut 18:15), the prediction of future events was a comparatively minor function.

A prophet first received instruction from the Lord and then conveyed it to the people. These 2 aspects of the prophet's work were reflected in the names by which prophets were known in OT times: seer (*chozeh* or *ro'eh*) and prophet (*nabî'*). The title of seer was more common in the earlier period of Hebrew history (1 Sa 9:9). The term used more frequently in the OT was *nabî'*, "prophet," which designated him as God's spokesman. As a "seer" the prophet discerned God's will, and as "prophet" he conveyed it to others.

In the broad sense of the term there have been prophets ever since the early days of the world. Abraham was specifically called a prophet (Gen 20:7) as was Moses (Deut 18:15). During the period of the judges the prophetic office seems to have languished, and "the word of the Lord was precious [rare] in those days" because "there was no open vision" (1 Sa 3:1). The rise of Samuel the prophet at the close of this period was epoch-making. He was the first "prophet" in the more strict sense of the word, and may be thought of as founder of the prophetic office. He went from place to place as a teacher of Israel (see ch 10:10-13; cf. ch 7:16, 17), and after him, down to the close of OT times, various chosen men spoke to the nation for God, interpreting past and present, exhorting the people to righteousness, and ever pointing their eyes to the glorious future God had marked out for them as a nation. Samuel seems to have founded what have been known as the schools of the prophets. Young men who received training in these schools (ch 19:20) were known as "the sons of the prophets" (see 2 Ki 2:3-5). The 1st such school mentioned was at Ramah (1 Sa 19:18, 20), Samuel's headquarters (ch 7:17). The "sons of the prophets" were not necessarily direct recipients of the prophetic gift, but were divinely called, as are gospel ministers today, to instruct the people in the will and ways of God. The schools of the prophets were a powerful force to restrain the tide of evil that often threatened to submerge the Hebrew people in a flood of idolatry, materialism, and injustice, and provided a barrier against the fast-spreading wave of corruption. These schools provided for the mental and spiritual training of selected young men who were to become the teachers and leaders of the nation.

After Samuel, in the time of the united kingdom of Israel and Judah, there arose such men as Nathan the prophet, Gad the seer (1 Chr 29:29), and Ahijah (2 Chr 9:29). Then, and later under the divided kingdom, there were many prophets. Some (Hosea, Isaiah, etc.) became authors of books preserved in the sacred canon; others (Nathan, Gad, Shemaiah, Iddo, etc.) left no books. Some of the greatest prophets, such as Elijah and Elisha, did not commit their prophetic discourses to writing and are therefore sometimes referred to as "oral prophets." In the Hebrew canon the 4 great historical works of Joshua, Judges, Samuel, and Kings are called the Former Prophets, because prophets were held to be their authors. Though largely historical in nature, these books show also the writers' purpose to preserve a record of God's dealings with Israel as an object lesson for their own and later generations. Isaiah, Jeremiah, Ezekiel, and "The Twelve" —Hosea through Malachi—are called the Latter Prophets. Under the divided kingdom the prophets Hosea, Amos, and Jonah labored chiefly for Israel, the northern kingdom, and the rest chiefly for Judah, the southern kingdom, though some of the latter included the northern kingdom also in their messages.

The Latter Prophets can be divided chronologically into 4 groups: (1) The 8th-cent. prophets, including Jonah, Amos, Hosea, Micah, and Isaiah, roughly in this chronological order. The 8th cent. witnessed the rise of Assyria, and before the century came to a close Assyria had carried the 10 tribes of the northern kingdom into captivity, thus bringing that kingdom to an end. Upon at least 2 occasions it appeared that Judah also was on the verge of being crushed by the Assyrians. The chief role of the 8th-cent. prophets seems to have been, first, to avert if possible the captivity of the northern kingdom by recalling its people to the service and worship of the true God, but also—particularly in the case of Isaiah—to hold the southern kingdom steady through this great time of national crisis. With the death of Isaiah the prophetic gift seems to have lapsed into silence for a half century or more. (2) The 7th-cent. prophets. This century witnessed Assyria at the height of its power, but before its close Assyria had disappeared from the stage of action and the Chaldean, or Neo-Babylonian, Empire had taken its place. During the waning years of Assyrian power and the rise of the Chaldeans, God sent a group of prophets to summon the people of Judah

to a thoroughgoing reformation that would avert the impending Babylonian captivity. Among these prophets were Nahum, Habakkuk, Zephaniah, Jeremiah, and perhaps Joel. (3) The prophets of the period of Babylonian captivity. These were Jeremiah, Ezekiel, Daniel, and possibly Obadiah. The chief aim of the messages of this period was to help Judah understand God's purpose in the Captivity, to inspire hope in eventual restoration, and to lift the eyes of the Jews to the glorious opportunity that awaited them upon return from captivity should they prove faithful to God. Jeremiah delivered his messages to the inhabitants of Jerusalem and Judah preceding and during the beginning of the Captivity, and Ezekiel ministered to the exiles in Babylonia. Daniel was sent to the court of Nebuchadnezzar to communicate God's will to that great monarch and to enlist his cooperation with the divine plan for God's people. (4) The postexilic prophets. These were Haggai, Zechariah, and Malachi, the 1st 2 of whom were instrumental in inspiring the people to arise and rebuild the Temple. Zechariah was also accorded a series of apocalyptic visions depicting the glorious future that awaited Israel during the restoration era if they would be faithful to God (Zec 6:15). About a century after Zechariah came Malachi, and with him the close of the OT prophetic canon (see 1 Macc 4: 46; 9:27; 14:41).

Although the book of Daniel contains some of the greatest prophetic messages to be found anywhere in Scripture, the Hebrew people did not include it in the prophetic section of the canon. In view of the fact that they did include such historical works as Joshua, Judges, Samuel, and Kings in the prophetic section, it is evident that content was not the primary determining factor in their classification of the canonical writings, but the office of the writer (see Canon, I). Thus, Daniel served chiefly as a statesman at the court of Nebuchadnezzar, and although he was the recipient of some of the greatest visions of all time he was not considered a prophet in the same sense as Isaiah, Jeremiah, Ezekiel, Hosea, and others whose lives were devoted exclusively to the prophetic office.

At the dawn of NT times the gift of prophecy was revived, with the inspired utterances of Elizabeth (Lk 1:41-45), Simeon, and Anna (ch 2:25-38). A few years later came John the Baptist in the role of

Elijah (Lk 1:17). Christ declared John to be a prophet and "more than a prophet" (Mt 11:9, 10). Paul listed the prophetic gift as one of the gifts of the Spirit (1 Cor 12:10), and declared it to be one of the greatest of these gifts (ch 14:1, 5). As in OT times, the prophetic gift did not necessarily imply the foretelling of future events, though that aspect of prophecy might be included, but consisted chiefly of exhortation and edification (vs 3, 4).

The call to prophetic office, and the accompanying bestowal of the prophetic gift, were acts of God, as in the case of Isaiah (ch 6:8, 9), Jeremiah (ch 1:5), Ezekiel (ch 2:3-5), and Amos (ch 7:15). Moses received his call at the burning bush (Ex 3:1 to 4:17). Elisha's call to the prophetic office was announced by Elijah (1 Ki 19:19, 20; cf. 2 Ki 2:13, 14). Accompanying the prophetic call was a special endowment qualifying the prophet to speak for God. This call constituted each prophet a "watchman" over the house of Israel (see Eze 33:7), and made the prophet strictly accountable to God for faithfully delivering the messages he was commissioned to bear (vs 3, 6). Having once accepted the prophetic call, a prophet was not free to lay it down at will, as Jeremiah once thought to do (see Jer 20:7-9; cf. 1 Ki 19:9; Jn 1:2-4, 17; 3:2). At times God addressed the prophet in an audible voice (Num 7:89; 1 Sa 3:4), though more commonly in dreams and visions (see Num 12:6; Eze 1:1; Dan 8:2; Mt 1:19). A true prophet taught by the Spirit of God (1 Ki 22:24; 2 Chr 15:1; 24:20; Neh 9:30; Eze 11:5; Joel 2:28; Mic 3:8; Zec 7:12; 1 Pe 1:10, 11) and spoke as he was moved by God's Spirit (2 Pe 1:20, 21). The message he bore was not his own, but God's (see Eze 2:7; 3:4, 10, 11; cf. Num 22:38; 1 Ki 22:14). In certain instances, as with Nathan (2 Sa 7:3) and Samuel (1 Sa 16:6, 7), a prophet's human judgment was overruled by God. For a time Ezekiel was dumb except when bearing a message from the Lord (see Eze 1:2, 3; 3:26, 27; 33:21, 22). This unique experience was a sign to Ezekiel's hearers that whenever he did speak he did so at God's command. In principle, something similar was true of the other prophets also, for no prophecy of Scripture "came by the impulse of man, but men moved by the Holy Spirit spoke from God" (2 Pe 1:21, RSV). Accordingly, we "do well to pay attention" to the messages of the prophets "as to a lamp

shining in a dark place, until the day dawns and the morning star rises" in our hearts (2 Pe 1:19, RSV).

In some instances the prophets themselves found it necessary to inquire and search diligently into the meaning of the words they had spoken (see 1 Pe 1:10, 11). Daniel, for instance, specifically mentions that he did not understand some portions of the messages entrusted to him (see Dan 8:27; 12:8, 9).

The prophets were distinctly aware of the fact that they spoke for God. Commonly they introduced their messages with such expressions as: "Thus saith the Lord" (Is 66:1), "The word that came to Jeremiah from the Lord" (Jer 11:1), "The vision of Isaiah the son of Amoz" (Is 1:1), "Then I looked, and, behold" (Eze 10:1), "I looked, and, behold" (Rev 4:1), "I saw" (ch 5:1). God attested the authority of the men whom He called to the prophetic office by the message they bore (see 1 Sa 3:19-21), by supernatural signs (2 Ki 2:13-15), by the fulfillment of their predictions (Deut 18:22; Jer 28:9), and by the conformity of their teachings to the will of God as already revealed (Deut 13:1-3; Is 8:20). Though they were subject to "like passions" as are other human beings, their lives reflected the high principles to which they bore witness (cf. Jas 5:17). False prophets often arose, as in the days of Ahab (see 1 Ki 22:6; cf. v 22), Jeremiah (see chs 27:14, 15; 28:1, 2, 5-9, 15-17), Ezekiel (ch 13:17), and Micah (ch 3:11). False prophets could be detected by their mercenary motives (ch 3:11), by their willingness to say what people wished to hear (Is 30:10; Mic 2:11), by the failure of their words to come to pass (Deut 18:22), by discrepancies between their messages and those of men already attested as prophets (Deut 13:2, 3; Is 8:20; Jer 27:12-16), by their catering to the wishes of godless people (1 Ki 22:6-8), and by their own evil lives (Mt 7:15-20).

In the same way that a prophet is a spokesman, or messenger, for God, so prophecy is any message spoken for God, at His command. It is a special revelation of the divine mind and will, designed to enable man to cooperate intelligently with the infinite purposes of God, and consists essentially in counsel, guidance, reproof, and warning. Since "God does nothing, without revealing his secret to his servants the prophets" (Amos 3:7, RSV), He expects those who read what the prophets have written to give the most diligent heed thereto. In so doing they are certain to "succeed" (2 Chr 20: 20, RSV). Those who fail to heed the words spoken by a prophet as God's messenger or watchman are personally accountable before God (see Eze 3:17-21; 33:1-9). For the most part, Israel rejected the stirring appeals of the prophets (see Lk 11:47, 48), even as God forewarned Isaiah (Is 6:9-11) and Jeremiah (see Jer 1:8, 17, 19). It was the rejection of the messages of the prophets that brought ruin upon Israel; it led to their refusal to accept their Messiah, and thus to their rejection as a nation.

Much of OT prophecy is written in the form of Hebrew poetry. Literary quality and form generally reflect the personality, education, and emotional state of the prophet. Jeremiah's personality is etched vividly upon the record of his prophetic mission, to the extent that the careful reader comes almost to feel personally acquainted with him (see Jeremiah). Some works, such as those of Isaiah, Joel, and Habakkuk, are of superb literary beauty and reflect a logical development of thought. Unsurpassed in graphic imagery, balanced rhetoric, and picturesque language are such passages as Is 9:1-7; 40:1-8; 52:7 to 53:12; 55; 61:1-3; and Joel 2:1-14. In some works, such as that of Jeremiah, historical events form the mold in which the prophetic messages are cast. Still others seem to be collections of sermons. Some prophets, such as Hosea, reflect strong emotions, and as a result do not lend themselves readily to logical literary analysis. The prophecy of Habakkuk also has a strong emotional appeal, and the prophet depicts his own struggle to understand the revealed will of God, and his reconciliation to it.

At times the prophets dwelt on God's past dealings with Israel (Eze 16; 20; etc.), drawing lessons of importance for the present generation. At other times they dealt with contemporary historical events, pointing out God's purposes and the realization of His will among the nations (for example, Is 36 to 39; most of the book of Jeremiah; many passages in Ezekiel; Dan 1 to 6; the book of Haggai; etc.). Often, and at length, the prophets denounced the sins of Israel (Is 1:2-15; 3:12-15; 9:13; 10:2; Jer 2:5-35; Eze 8:5-16; Hos 5; Amos 8:1-6; the book of Malachi). The prophets constantly stressed the personal responsibility of those who heard their messages to act in accordance with them (Eze 3:17-21; cf.

chs 18:25-32; 33:7-16; etc.). They often called for specific action (Is 1:16-20; Jer 27:1-18; 29:5-13; 38:14-23; 42:1-18; Joel 2:12, 13; Amos 5:4-15; Hag 1:7, 8; Mal 3:10-12; etc.). They faithfully pointed out the rewards of evildoing (Is 2:10-21; 7:17-25; 24; Jer 4; 18:9, 10; 23:9-40; 24; Eze 4; 5; 9; Dan 9:3-14; Hos 5; Joel 1; Amos 7-9; the book of Zep; etc.) and rightdoing (Is 1:18-20; 38; Jer 7:2-7; 17: 20-26; 18:7, 8; Hos 14; Joel 2:12-32; etc.). Often through the prophets God raised the eyes of His people to the glorious future that awaited them as a nation should they cooperate fully with His purpose for them (Is 40-66; Jer 33; Eze 36-48; Mic 4; book of Zechariah; etc.). The climax of the prophetic messages was always the coming of the Messiah and the establishment of the Messianic kingdom (Is 9:1-7; 11: 1-12; 12; 25; 52-66; Dan 2:44; 7:18, 27; Joel 3:9-21; Mic 4:1 to 5:15; etc.).

II. Interpretation of Prophecy

OT prophecies do not always distinguish clearly between what we refer to today as the 1st and 2d advents of Christ, but often deal with these two great events as one, or as one rapidly following the other. Most of the prophetic messages are set forth in literal language, but some are highly figurative or symbolic (Dan 2; 7; 8; Zec 1-6; Rev 6-19; etc.). The element of prediction in prophecy was designed to afford a view of the things of time in the light of eternity, to alert the church for effective action at appropriate times, to facilitate personal preparation for the final crisis, to vindicate God and to leave man without excuse in the day of judgment, and to attest the validity of prophecy as a whole. The many examples of fulfilled prophecies—whether their accomplishment came immediately or in later ages, or whether they were recorded in the Bible or seen in history—serve to establish faith in the inspired Word. God calls attention to His unique power to declare "the end from the beginning" (Is 46:9, 10), and Jesus says, "I have told you before it come to pass, that, when it is come to pass, ye might believe" (Jn 14:29).

At times, because of highly figurative or symbolic language, or because of the difficulty of relating the messages to their historical context, or of the operation of the conditional factor (see Jer 18:7-10) in the forecast of events yet future, or the historical transition from literal Israel to the Christian church, the prophetic books lend themselves more easily to misinterpretation than the historical, poetic, and doctrinal sections of Scripture. Accordingly, the only safe procedure in the interpretation and application of the prophetic messages is a systematic study of, and thorough familiarity with, prophecy as a whole. Only on the basis of such a study is it possible to arrive at sound principles of interpretation. It is first necessary to ascertain precisely what the prophets wrote, under the Spirit's guidance, and what they meant by what they wrote. An exact study of the words and grammatical relationships of a passage is also necessary. At times uncertainty as to the meaning of a passage can be resolved only by reference to the language in which it was originally written. Every sentence must be understood in relation to its larger context. Under no circumstances is it safe to consider a passage without reference to its literary and historical context. Every prophetic message had a meaning for the people to whom it was delivered. One of the first and most important tasks of the interpreter is to ascertain what that meaning was. Only then is it possible to arrive at a valid application of the prophecies to our day. The Bible must be made its own interpreter, that is, Bible passages must be compared with other Bible passages dealing with the same topic.

Generally speaking, the promises and predictions sent through the OT prophets to literal Israel were to have been fulfilled to them on condition of obedience and loyalty. However, they rejected God's plan for them as a nation, and what God purposed to accomplish through Israel of old He will finally accomplish through His spiritual children. (Accordingly, many of God's promises originally made to ancient Israel will be fulfilled in principle to the Christian church.) God's plans and purposes will ultimately prevail (see Is 46:10), though the means and agencies through which this goal is to be achieved may change to meet changed conditions. When an individual or a nation refuses to cooperate with God's expressed purpose, that individual or nation forfeits his role in the divine plan (see Jer 18:6-10; cf. Dan 5:25-28). When, at the crucifixion, the Jews rejected Christ, God took the *kingdom away from them and gave it "to a nation bringing forth the fruits" of the kingdom (Mt 21:41-44; 23:36-38). As the "nation" of which Christ thus spoke, the Christian church replaced Israel in God's plan (see 1 Pe 2:9, 10). The writings of the OT

prophets are fraught with meaning for Christian believers (see Lk 24:25-27, 44; Rom 15:4; 2 Ti 3:16, 17; cf. 1 Cor 10:1-12), but in view of the fact that the Christian church is neither a racial nor a political entity residing in the literal land of Canaan and surrounded by literal enemies such as Assyria, Babylon, and Egypt, many details of the prophecies of the OT are not applicable literally to Christian times. Furthermore, many of the prophecies dealt exclusively with specific historical situations in the long ago. From a reading of the OT prophets the Christian may derive 2 benefits: (1) he may profit from the instruction God gave His people in the long ago by applying its principles to himself and by noting the results of accepting or rejecting that instruction; (2) he can ascertain what predictions, unfulfilled to literal Israel, remain to be fulfilled to God's people today. However, great care must be taken lest unjustified applications be made. He must determine the extent to which a given prophecy is conditional in nature, the extent to which the conditions were fulfilled, and finally whether Inspiration has indicated a later fulfillment. In particular, study must be given to how the transition from literal Israel to the Christian church may affect the fulfillment of the prediction. Only when a later inspired writer reapplies a prophecy to Christian times can a positive reapplication be made.

The record of God's dealings with His people in ages past has been recorded for the benefit of all later generations to the end of time. Under the guidance of the Holy Spirit, messages originally proclaimed by holy men of old to the people of their day become an effective means of disclosing God's will to His church today. Through the ancient prophets it is our privilege to hear His voice speaking distinctly to us in our time. In the inspired utterances of the prophets of old the sincere seeker for truth will find messages of inspiration, comfort, and guidance.

For basic principles of interpretation see SDACom 1:1017-1019; 4:656; and the general index in vol. 7 under "Bible—interpretation" and "Prophetic interpretation." For principles of interpretation of symbolic prophecy see SDACom 4:576, 577. For specific interpretations and fulfillments of the basic symbolic prophecies, which cannot be discussed adequately here without exceeding the scope of this dictionary, see SDACom under the respective Bible texts.

Prophetess. [Heb. *nebî'ah,* "prophetess"; Gr. *prophētis.*] A woman called of God to fulfill the prophetic office. The gift of prophecy was from time to time bestowed upon devout women as well as upon men. Miriam is the 1st woman mentioned in the Bible as honored with this title (Ex 15:20, 21; cf. Num 12:2). Micah names her along with Moses and Aaron as being God's instrument in the Exodus (Mic 6:4). The Israelites resorted to the prophetess Deborah for judgment in the days when Jabin and Sisera oppressed Israel (Jgs 4:4-15). Huldah was a trusted prophetess in the reign of Josiah (2 Ki 22:12-20). Other Bible prophetesses were Anna (Lk 2:36) and the 4 daughters of Philip (Acts 21:8, 9). The term "prophetess" as used in Is 8:3 may simply designate the wife of a *prophet.

Propitiation. *See* Atonement.

Proselyte. [Gr. *prosēlutos,* "proselyte," "convert."] In the NT, Gentile converts to the Jewish religion (Mt 23:15; Acts 2:10; 6:5; 13:43; KJV). By NT times the Jews were dispersed throughout the world, and far more Jews lived outside of, than in, Palestine. There was scarcely a city throughout the civilized world that did not have its Jewish community, whose members were influential in politics and commerce. In some regions of Syria and Babylonia the Jews constituted a majority of the population. Wherever there were 10 or more adult males, a synagogue was established. In comparison with their Gentile neighbors, the Jews of the Dispersion were generally more prosperous, of incomparably superior morality, more admirable in family life, and better educated on the average. These qualities appealed to the more thoughtful of the Gentiles, and as a result they attended the synagogues of the Jews, listened to the reading of their Scriptures, were attracted by their exalted, monotheistic concept of God, and often became converts to the Jewish faith.

Full proselytes were those who had accepted all religious teachings and practices of Jewry, exercised its prescribed washings and baths, and submitted to the rite of circumcision. Yet, even then they became no more than Jews of a 2d order, and only their sons were considered full-fledged Jews. The number of such proselytes was small at all times, mainly because few of the Gentiles were willing to accept circumcision. Only one proselyte is mentioned by name in the NT, "Nico-

las a proselyte from Antioch" (Acts 6:5).

Besides the full proselytes, there were converts from heathenism who formed a more loose connection with Jewry. In later times they were called "proselytes of the gate." In the NT they are called *phoboumenoi ton Theon* "God-fearing ones," *sebomenoi ton Theon,* "God-worshiping ones," or simply *sebomenoi* (Acts 10:2; 13:16, 26; 16:14; 17:17; 18:7; cf. chs 13:50; 17:4). They loved the Jewish nation and religion (Lk 7:5) and financially supported it (Acts 10:2). The more loosely attached visited the synagogue services, refrained from immorality and the eating of unclean meat and blood; those with stronger connection, yet not full proselytes, kept the Sabbath, the Jewish feasts, and observed all ritual regulations. Many of the nobility belonged to the sympathizers with the Jewish religion, especially women. This is attested by the NT (see chs 16:13; 17:4, 12) and other sources. Josephus mentions the emperor Nero's wife Poppaea Sabina as a *theosebēs,* "God-worshiper" (*Ant.* xx. 8. 11).

As Paul went from city to city, he began his preaching at the Jewish synagogue (Acts 13:14), working chiefly for the Jews. Present at these services were Gentile proselytes (v 43), through whom Paul gained access to the Gentile populace (see vs 44, 45). These proselytes to the Jewish faith formed a natural bridge over which Christianity found its way to the Gentile world. Gentile proselytes were present at Jerusalem on the day of Pentecost (ch 2:10).

Proverbs, The. A poetical book consisting of short essays and pithy statements on matters of practical piety. The title "Proverbs" is a translation of the first word of the book in Hebrew, *meshalim,* the singular of which is *mashal,* meaning "simile," "comparison," "proverbial saying," from the root *mashal,* "to be like," "to compare." In a broad sense a proverb is any popular, terse saying. That Solomon was the author of at least the major portion of the book (see chs 25:1; 30:1; 31:1) appears evident from chs 1:1; 10:1; 25:1. But whether he was the original writer of the entire section unequivocally assigned to him, or whether certain portions represent his work as an inspired editor or collector of the wise and true sayings of others, is not stated, nor is this consideration important to the inspiration of the book. According to 1 Ki 4:32, Solomon "spake three thousand proverbs." In view of his great wisdom, given to him as a special blessing from God (see 1 Ki 4:31-34; 10:1-13), he was better qualified than any other known person of OT times to write such a treatise on wisdom.

That Solomon wrote the book of Proverbs during the early years of his reign appears from the fact that it differs markedly from the book of *Ecclesiastes, which he wrote toward the close of his reign, after years of apostasy. The sound and positive principles set forth in the former, contrast sharply with the expressions of disillusionment so often reflected in the latter. The declared purpose of the book of Proverbs is "to know wisdom and instruction" (see ch 1:1-6). Its theme is the exaltation of true wisdom, which Solomon describes as "the fear of the Lord" (chs 1: 7; 9:10). Although, as in the author's own case, true wisdom results from a right relationship with God, the book of Proverbs is not so much a religious treatise as it is a compendium of ethical and moral instruction applied to many practical situations in life. The first 9 chapters constitute a didactic poem in which a father seeks to help his son (see chs 1:8, 15; 2:1; 3:1; 5:1; 6:1; etc.). A new section begins with ch 10, entitled "The proverbs of Solomon" (v 1). This section continues through ch 24. Chapters 22:17 to 24:34 contain a series of moral maxims. Chapters 25 through 29 consist of "proverbs of Solomon, which the men of Hezekiah king of Judah copied out." These would seem to be perhaps proverbs transmitted orally for a time after Solomon's death before being put in writing and later transcribed. A 4th section, ch 30, consists of "the words of Agur the son of Jakeh" (v 1), and the last section, ch 31, is attributed to "king Lemuel." Chapter 31 is an acrostic poem addressed to the ideal, virtuous woman.

Some sections of the book of Proverbs are duplicated in an Egyptian wisdom book, called "The Instruction of Amen-em-Opet," which probably originated in the 7th or 6th cent. B.C. (*ANET* 421-425). Many scholars hold that Amen-em-Opet's work forms the basis of Proverbs, and consider this assumption an argument in favor of assigning a late date to Proverbs. However, the opposite view is more reasonable. Because of his fame for wisdom, Solomon attracted from distant lands important visitors who came to his court to become better acquainted with him. Hence his wisdom literature may have found its way to Egypt, and thus have become the basis of Amen-em-Opet's work

probably 2 cent. after Solomon's death.

Province. [Heb. and Aramaic generally *medînah*, "administrative district," "satrapy," "district of jurisdiction"; Gr. *eparcheia*.] An administrative district ruled over by a prefect or governor. The Babylonians (Dan 2:48, 49; etc.), and later the Persians (Est 1:1, 3; etc.), divided their respective empires into administrative districts under the administration of appointed officials (chs 1:3; 3:12). See Governor, 1. Darius the Great, whose empire extended from India to Ethiopia, divided his empire into 20 satrapies (see Herod. i. 192; iii. 89-94), which in turn were subdivided into smaller units called provinces. In the time of Esther there were 127 provinces (evidently smaller subdivisions) in the Persian Empire (Est 1:1). During the Persian period Judah was a province (Ezr 5:8) that formed part of the satrapy called "Beyond the River" (vs 3, 6); it had its own governors, such as Sheshbazzar and Nehemiah (Ezr 5:14; Neh 5: 14, 15). The provinces of the Roman Empire were of 2 classes, imperial and senatorial. The affairs of the senatorial provinces were administered by the Roman Senate, which appointed a proconsul as governor of each. The senatorial provinces were areas that no longer needed the presence of a Roman army to maintain Roman control. *Achaia (Acts 18: 12) and *Cyprus (ch 13:4; cf. v 7), were senatorial provinces. Imperial provinces were administered directly by the emperor, who appointed a military officer, called a legate, as governor. Imperial provinces—usually recently acquired or frontier areas—supposedly required the presence of an army of occupation. When Archelaus was deposed in A.D. 6, Judea was formally annexed to the imperial province of Syria, and its affairs were administered by an imperial procurator responsible partly to the governor of Syria (*see* Governor, 2, c).

Psalms, The. A collection of sacred hymns appearing in the Hebrew canon as the 1st book in the 3d section known as the *Kethûbîm*, or Writings, which includes the books that appear in the English canon from 1 Chr through Song, with Ruth, Lam, and Dan. In view of the fact that Ps was the first, longest, and most important book in this section, the Jewish people occasionally spoke of the entire section as "Psalms" (see Lk 24:44). In Hebrew the book is called *Tehillîm*, "praises," from *hallal*, "to praise"; in Greek it is called *Psalmoi*, "songs of praise," or "psalms," a translation of the plural of the Heb. *mizmôr,* "a song with instrumental accompaniment," from *zamar,* "to sing with instrumental accompaniment," or simply "to sing" or "to praise." From early times the book has been divided into 5 sections, Book One (Ps 1-41), Book Two (Ps 42-72), Book Three (Ps 73-89), Book Four (Ps 90-106), and Book Five (Ps 107-150). Altogether 8 persons—David, Asaph, Korah, Moses, Heman, Ethan, Solomon, and Jeduthun—are mentioned in the superscriptions to the various psalms as authors, compilers, or musicians. The Hebrew preposition *le,* which precedes these names in the superscriptions, may mean variously "to," "for," "of," "from," etc. In view of the variety of relationships expressed by this Hebrew preposition, it is not always possible to determine whether the person whose name follows is thereby designated as the author, the collector and arranger, the musician for whom it was written, or the one to whom a song was dedicated. These superscriptions or titles appear in the oldest Hebrew texts known. That they were already old at the time the LXX translation was made about the 2d or 3d cent. B.C. is evident from the fact that the translators obviously did not understand a number of the technical musical terms in the superscriptions. Modern critics, who question whether David wrote any of the psalms, challenge the authenticity of these superscriptions. However, because of their great antiquity, because they are included in the oldest extant Hebrew manuscripts, because the oldest known Hebrew lyrics had such superscriptions, and because certain of the superscriptions explain the meaning or historical background of the Psalms, conservative readers of the Bible find no reason for rejecting them. Irrespective of the fact that the expression "of David" may mean either that David wrote the psalm or that it belonged to a collection of psalms arranged by David, the Scriptures clearly represent David as a poet and musician in his own right (1 Sa 16:15-23; 2 Sa 23:1-7; Amos 6:5). He was a man of great faith and deep emotions, which often found expression in poetry and song (2 Sa 1:19-27; 3:33, 34). His intimate acquaintance with nature and "the Law"—the creative and revealed expressions of the divine will—his years of adversity, and his personal devotion to God all qualified him to be the "sweet psalmist of Israel." Furthermore, references and allusions to numerous experiences in his life occur in the psalms and in their superscriptions. The fact that Ps 18 and 105 are repeated in the historical narrative of David (see 2 Sa 22 and 1 Chr 16:7-36, respectively), and are there attributed to him, confirms his authorship of these 2 psalms and implies that he doubtless wrote others. Jesus and various NT writers use David's name when referring to the Psalms (see Mt 22:43-45; Mk 12:36, 37; Lk 20:42-44; Acts 2:14, 25; Rom 4:6-8; 11:9, 10; Heb 4:7). The phrase "of David" occurs in the superscription of 73 psalms—37 times (Ps 3-9; 11-32; 34-41) in Book One, 18 (Ps 51-65; and 68-70) in Book Two, 1 (Ps 86) in Book Three, 2 (Ps 101; 103) in Book Four, and 15 (Ps 108-110, 122, 124, 131, 133, 138-145) in Book Five. The LXX lacks the notation of Davidic authorship in the superscriptions of Ps 122 and 124, but adds it to those of Ps 33, 43, 67, 71, 91, 93-99, 104, 137. The phrase "of Asaph" appears in the superscription of 12 psalms (Ps 50; 73-83). Asaph was a Levite choir leader, musician, and "seer" of the time of David (see 1 Chr 15:19; 16:4-7; 2 Chr 29:30). Of the various groups of Temple singers, only the children of Asaph are mentioned as returning to Jerusalem following the Babylonian captivity (Ezr 2:41). These psalms were either arranged by Asaph or members of his family, or were prepared for their use as the official musicians and singers of the sanctuary. The phrase "for the sons of Korah" appears in the superscription of 11 psalms (Ps 42, 44-49, 84, 85, 87, 88). The sons of Korah and their descendants assisted in the Temple service (cf. Num 26:9-11; 1 Chr 9:19). Thus 96 of the 150 psalms—about ⅔ of the entire collection—are associated with the names of David, Asaph, and Korah. Ps 88 carries the double designation "for the sons of Korah" and "of Heman the Ezrahite." The latter was a Kohathite Levite and a leader of Temple music (see 1 Chr 6:33; 15:17; 16:41, 42). Ps 39; 62; and 77 carry the name of Jeduthun, another leader of Temple music (see 1 Chr 16:41, 42). Inasmuch as the superscriptions of Ps 39 and 62 also carry the name of David, and Ps 77 that of Asaph, it appears likely that these 3 psalms were written for the use of Jeduthun and his fellow Temple musicians. Ps 89 is entitled "Maschil of Ethan the Ezrahite" (see 1 Ki 4:31). The name of Solomon appears in the superscriptions of Ps 72 and 127. Ps 90 is entitled "A Prayer of Moses."

Nearly ⅓ of the total psalms have no superscription and are, accordingly, anonymous. Fifty-five psalms have the phrase, "To the chief Musician" (KJV), or "To the choirmaster" (RSV), possibly suggesting that this group was dedicated or entrusted to the overseer of the choir.

It is evident that the writing of the psalms and their collection and arrangement in the book bearing this title occupied a space of many centuries. There is a period of some 900 years between the writing of Ps 90, which is attributed to Moses, and Ps 137, which describes the Babylonian captivity. With the exception of Ps 137 and certain psalms whose superscriptions refer to specific historical events (Ps 51; 52), there is little clear internal evidence by which to associate particular psalms with known historical events. To a certain extent the diction and grammatical constructions used in a psalm are helpful in assigning it to some particular period of Hebrew history. Modern scholars, who deny the authenticity of the superscriptions, have tended to assign most of the psalms to postexilic times, generally on a supposed basis that diction and phraseology represent a late development in Hebrew literature. However, archeological discoveries in recent decades have demonstrated that many of the words and phrases critical scholars formerly pointed to as evidence of late composition were actually in common use by Canaanite writers a thousand years earlier than the critical scholars once believed possible. Excavations on the site of Ugarit (Ras Shamra), begun in 1929, have unearthed hundreds of clay tablets written in Ugaritic, a Canaanite dialect written in cuneiform and in use about 1400 B.C. Some of these tablets contain texts dealing with the religion of the ancient Canaanites. In this literature many formerly obscure words and phrases that occur in the Psalms appear in a context that clarifies their meaning. A study of this literature confirms the earlier dating implied by the superscriptions, thus invalidating the contentions of modern critics. *The Seventh-day Adventist Bible Commentary* makes extensive use of the information on the Psalms provided by these Ugaritic documents.

The book of Psalms has served Hebrews and Christians with equal effectiveness, for both public worship and private devotion. The chanting of psalms by antiphonal choirs, or by choir and congregation, was a prominent part of worship

in the ancient Temple service, where many of the psalms came to be associated with the great national festivals. Ps 113-118 and 135 were used at the Passover time, Ps 118 at Pentecost, the Feast of Tabernacles, and the Feast of Dedication, Ps 120-134 on the first night of the Feast of Tabernacles, Ps 30 at the Feast of Dedication, Ps 81 at the New Moon, and Ps 29 with the evening sacrifice at the New Moon. Ps 120-134 were probably used as pilgrim psalms (*see* Ascents). After the destruction of the Temple the psalms continued to be used as prayers in the synagogues, Ps 7 for Purim, Ps 12 for the 8th day of the Feast of Tabernacles, Ps 47 for the New Year, Ps 98 and 104 for the New Moon, and Ps 103 and 130 for the Day of Atonement. The great hallels, or praise psalms—Ps 104-106, 111-113, 115-117, 135, and 145-150—were learned by heart and used as congregational expressions of thanksgiving. The psalms still have an honored place in Jewish synagogue ritual, as they do in Christian ritual, whether Roman Catholic, Eastern Orthodox, Anglican, or Evangelical. The dominant theme of the book of Psalms is man's great need and God's gracious provision for meeting that need. Its universal appeal to men of all ages, all nations, and all stations in life is the result of its effective presentation of this great theme. In one way or another it reflects almost every human experience and gives expression to practically every human emotion. It covers the whole range of human experience, from the depths of conscious guilt and self-condemnation to the heights of faith and communion with God. It reflects sorrow, disappointment, sickness, guilt, weakness, and futility, but also joy, satisfaction, recovery from illness, forgiveness of sin, comfort, strength, and trust.

The psalms impart courage in the midst of discouragement, hope in the midst of despair, strength in the midst of weakness, and the certainty of forgiveness in the midst of condemnation. Some psalms take the sinner in secret to the very presence of God, and help him to pour out his own soul alone before God. Seven psalms deal so intimately with the sense of sin and its results that they have been called penitential psalms (Ps 6, 32, 38, 51, 102, 130, and 143), of which Ps 32 and 51 in particular are notable examples of individual confession of sin. Ps 106 expresses national confession of sin. In Ps 42, 43, 60, 74, 79, 89 the writer cries out to God from the depths of disaster, defeat, and conviction of sin. Ps 1, 15, 24, 34, 52, 120, 131, 133 present various aspects of a righteous character. Ps 42, 43, and 63 in particular express intense yearning after God. In others (see Ps 27; 84; 122) the author expresses the blessings of worshiping in the sanctuary. All point to God as man's hope, confidence, strength, and triumph. Many anticipate the coming of Messiah to save His people and to usher in His eternal reign of righteousness. Ps 2, 22, 69, 72, 110 are rich in Messianic overtones. They testify to the Messiah's deity (Ps 45:6; 110:1), Sonship, (Ps 2:7), incarnation (Ps 40:6, 7), priesthood (Ps 110:4), betrayal (Ps 41:9), rejection (Ps 118:22), and His resurrection and ascension (Ps 16:9, 10; 68:18). Ps 46, 61, 62, and 91 present God as our refuge in trouble. The missionary outlook is reflected in Ps 96. Ps 37 and 73 deal with the problem of doubt, and its solution. Ps 16 and 49 reflect faith in the reality of the future life. Ps 8, 19, 29, and 104 deal with various aspects of nature. Ps 68, 79, 105, 106, 114 take as their theme various experiences in Israel's history. Ps 35, 52, 69, 83, 109 are imprecatory, denouncing the enemies of God and His people and bringing down curses upon their heads. Praise is the keynote of Ps 8, 16, 33, 55, 65, 71, 86, 89, 90, 92, 95-100, 103, 104, 107, 142, 143, and 145-150 express praise and adoration. Ps 9, 10, 25, 34, 37, 111, 112, 119, and 145 are alphabetic or acrostic in the Hebrew text, the verses beginning with the letters of the Hebrew alphabet in succession in various arrangements.

Whereas regularly recurring accent and rhyme are the characteristic qualities of most modern English poetry, the rhythm of Hebrew poetry is largely one of recurring thought, and, to a limited extent, of recurring accent. The balanced symmetry of form and sense known as parallelism, variously called "sense rhythm" or "thought rhythm," provides the metrical basis for Hebrew verse. This rhythm of thought can readily be traced in English translations, despite the inevitable loss of a measure of its original artistic beauty. Modern speech translations usually arrange Hebrew poetry in poetic form. Three primary forms of Hebrew parallelism are generally recognized: (1) Synonymous parallelism, in which the basic thought is repeated in different words and images in the 2d line of the couplet, as in Ps 19:8. (2) Antithetical or contrasted parallelism, in which the thought of the first line of the couplet is further explained by its contrast or reversal in the 2d line, as in Ps 1:6. (3) Synthetic, or constructive, parallelism, in which the 2d line of the couplet adds a thought to the first line by way of completion, enlargement, or intensification, as in Ps 14:2. There are, as well, 3 secondary forms of Hebrew parallelism: (1) Emblematic parallelism, an elaborate type of synonymous parallelism in which a figure of speech or image of some kind is used as a basis for developing the thought, as in Ps 129: 5-8. (2) Climactic, or stairlike, parallelism, a vigorous type of synthetic parallelism in which a key word or phrase, or several such words or phrases, are repeated, with the thought being completed at the very end, as in Ps 121:1-4. (3) Introverted parallelism, in which the first and last lines of a series are similar, and enclose a number of lines developing the basic idea, as in Ps 30:8-10. These primary and secondary forms of parallelism are employed with almost infinite variety and ingenuity by the writers of the psalms: as in Ps 144:12-14, where several consecutive lines are synonymous; as in Ps 2:2, where the first 2 lines are synonymous but are supplemented by a 3d that adds a further thought; as in Ps 27:1, where the 1st and 3d, and 2d and 4th lines of a four-line unit are parallel; as in Ps 136:1-3, where there is an accumulation of thought clause by clause throughout the entire poem, with a repeated refrain.

In common with the ancient Egyptian, Assyrian, Babylonian, and Canaanite literatures, Hebrew poetry exhibits a recurring accent, or beat. However, not all Hebrew poetry clearly reflects this feature and even when present the accent may not occur regularly as in conventional English verse. Instead, the accent occurs a given number of times in the line irrespective of the number of syllables. The typical line of Hebrew lyric poetry is divided into 2 parts, with 2 accented syllables in each half. In elegiac and other highly emotional poetry the typical line has 3 accents in the 1st half and 2 accents in the 2d half. This is known as the *qînah* rhythm. Its effect is that of a crescendo of 3 beats followed by a shorter decrescendo of 2 beats. In epic, didactic, and liturgical poetry the typical line tends to show 3 accented syllables in each half. In no case, however, is there any relationship between accented syllables and the number of unaccented syllables. Unfortunately, the accent in Hebrew poetry cannot be preserved in translation and is therefore lost. The Hebrew poem is often broken into a series of strophes or stanzas which indicate transitions of thought within the larger unit. These stanzas may be of equal or nearly equal length (see Ps 1, 42, 43, 119), but are more often unequal. In some psalms (see 42, 43, 46, 57, 67) the transition from one stanza to the next is marked by a refrain.

Certain words or phrases in the superscriptions of many of the psalms are thought to indicate the nature or type of the psalm thus introduced, such as: (1) "Psalm" (Heb. *mizmôr*), in the superscriptions of 57 psalms, a term indicating a song designed to be sung to the accompaniment of stringed instruments. (2) "Song" (Heb. *shir*), in the superscriptions of 30 psalms. (3) "Prayer" (Heb. *tephillah*), in the superscriptions of Ps 17, 86, 90, 102, and 142. (4) "Praise" (Heb. *tehillah*), in the superscription of Ps 145 only. (5) "To teach" (Heb. *lelammed*), in the superscription of Ps 60. (6) "To bring to remembrance" (Heb. *lehazkîr*), in the superscriptions of Ps 38 and 70, an indication that these psalms were intended to be sung during the offering of incense in the morning and evening Temple ritual. (7) "Of praise" (Heb. *lethôdah*), in the superscription of Ps 100, a possible indication of its use at the time of the thank offering.

Other words or phrases in the superscriptions may suggest melodies to accompany the psalms, probably tunes that were well known in the ancient Temple ritual, as, for example, *Gittith. Still others seem to indicate the kind of orchestral instruments used to accompany the singing or chanting of the psalms, such as possibly *Nehiloth. See specific terms. *See also* Selah.

Psaltery. *See* Harp.

Pseudepigrapha. A body of Jewish literature dating from the centuries immediately preceding and following the beginning of the Christian Era. The name, meaning "falsely entitled," comes from the practice of seeking to enhance the authority of many of the books by attributing them to some notable Biblical figure rather than to the real author. Not all of the books classified under this category are pseudonymous, and conversely, some of the pseudonymous books of this period are included among the Apocrypha, for example, the Wisdom of Solomon, Baruch,

and the Letter of Jeremiah. There is no general agreement among scholars as to the specific books to be listed among the pseudepigrapha, but most of the following are usually included:

I. Palestinian Writings

1. *The Book of Jubilees.* A midrashic expansion of Genesis, and of Exodus 1-12, dating from probably the 2d cent. B.C. It was written in Hebrew, but survived in an Ethiopic rendering of a Greek translation. Many fragments of the Hebrew work have been found among the Dead Sea scrolls. The name is derived from its method of dating events according to jubilees of 49 years with their subdivisions. It purports to be a revelation given by "the angel of the presence" to Moses on Sinai (chs 1:29; 2:1). Distinctive Jewish observances are carried back into the patriarchal period.

2. *The Testaments of the Twelve Patriarchs.* A work purporting to be the last words of the 12 sons of Jacob to their children (compare the Blessing of Jacob, Gen 49; and the Blessing of Moses, Deut 33). This work, found in Greek, is considered by many as of Christian origin, and to be based on pseudepigraphical testimonies of the various patriarchs composed by Jews of the 2d or 1st cent. B.C. Aramaic texts of the Testament of Levi and a Hebrew manuscript of a Testament of Naphtali have been discovered among the Dead Sea scrolls, and an Aramaic text of the former has been found in the Cairo Genizah. It teaches the coming of the Messiah from the tribe of Levi, and of Antichrist from the tribe of Dan. *See* Scrolls, Dead Sea.

3. *The Martyrdom of Isaiah.* A traditional Jewish account, preserved in its entirety only in Ethiopic, telling how King Manasseh had Isaiah sawn asunder with a wood saw for predicting the destruction of Jerusalem.

4. *The Paralipomena of Jeremiah.* The name means the "remaining words" of Jeremiah (or, of Baruch). Some scholars think that this work is possibly a Christian production of about the 2d cent. of our era, though the basis of it may be Jewish. According to the Paralipomena, Jeremiah, in obedience to God's command, concealed the Temple's sacred vessels and went to Babylon as an exile before the destruction of Jerusalem by Nebuchadnezzar, while Baruch remained in Jerusalem. Years later Jeremiah, with a group of exiles, returned to Jerusalem. Those of the group who refused to di-

vorce their heathen wives were excluded from Jerusalem, whereupon they founded Samaria. The prophet was finally stoned to death after he had announced redemption through Jesus Christ.

5. *The Lives of the Prophets*. A series of sketches of a legendary nature, biographies, allegedly of OT prophets. The series is preserved in a Greek translation of a Hebrew original, dating probably from the 1st cent. A.D.

6. *The Testament of Job*. A legendary Aramaic Midrash on Job, dating from the 1st cent. B.C., and surviving in Greek. Material from it found its way into the Greek version of the OT after Job 2:9 and 42:18.

7. *The Books of Adam and Eve*. A haggadic amplified account of the fall and the repentance of Adam and Eve. The original (possibly in Aramaic) was most likely composed by a Jew in the 1st cent. A.D., though possibly as late as the 4th cent., and was reworked by Christian hands. In the Greek it is incorrectly named the Apocalypse of Moses.

8. *The Psalms of Solomon*. A Greek translation of 18 Hebrew psalms, composed by Pharisees in the 1st cent. B.C.

9. *The Book of Enoch*. An apocalyptic work, known also as 1 Enoch and Ethiopic Enoch, because it is preserved completely only in Ethiopic, but at least 10 fragmentary manuscripts of this work in Aramaic are among the Dead Sea scrolls. It is the longest of the pseudepigrapha, and is the most important of noncanonical apocalypses. It is a heterogeneous work of several authors, difficult to disentangle, from the 2d and 1st cent. B.C. It consists of a series of alleged revelations to Enoch concerning the origin of evil, the nature and destiny of angels, and includes such eschatological themes as the judgment, the resurrection, and the nature of Gehenna and Paradise. After an introduction giving the purpose of the book and Enoch's survey of the heavens, the 1st obvious division (chs 6-36) traces evil to fallen angels and their lust for the daughters of men. Chapters 37-71 contain the 3 Similitudes of Enoch, the 1st of which introduces, among other things, the future kingdom of God (chs 37-44). In the 2d of these Similitudes (chs 45-57) the superhuman "Son of Man," who is to come to earth as the Messiah, is introduced. Many scholars hold that these "Son of Man" passages have had a great influence on the Gospels in the NT. In the 3d Similitude is pictured the glory of the Messiah and His rulership over the kings of

earth (chs 58-69). However, the absence of the 2d section of Enoch, containing the Similitudes, in the Dead Sea scrolls seems to indicate that they are of a late origin, and must be attributed either to a Jew or to a Christian of the 1st or 2d cent. A.D. Chapters 72-82 deal with the heavenly luminaries. Two dream-visions follow (chs 83-90), one dealing with the Flood, and the other with world history to the founding of the Messiah's kingdom. Next, the work contains Enoch's exhortations, the Apocalypse of Weeks, which divides world history into 10 periods, and, finally, some miscellaneous appendages are added (chs 91-105).

10. *The Assumption of Moses*. A composite Jewish work written in Hebrew or Aramaic early in the 1st cent., but surviving only in part in 2 Latin fragments translated from the lost Greek version. The fragments contain Moses' speech to Joshua predicting the history of Israel, but the account of Moses' death and of his assumption are lost.

11. *The Apocalypse of Baruch*. A composite work describing the capture of Jerusalem by the Babylonians (586 B.C.), and seeking to justify the ways of God in His dealings with Israel. It is known also as the Syriac Baruch because it is preserved in a single manuscript in a Syriac version of the Greek rendering. It was written in the latter half of the 1st cent. A.D. This pseudepigraphic work should not be confused with the apocryphal book called Baruch (*see* Apocrypha, Old Testament, 8).

12. *The Second Book of Esdras*. This apocalyptic work, also known as 4 Esdras or 4 Ezra, is discussed under Apocrypha, to which it is generally counted (see KJV and RSV editions of the Apocrypha), although it is not part of the Catholic canon. *See* Apocrypha, Old Testament, 2.

Recent studies have shown that some of these pseudepigraphical writings, or parts of them, seem to be of Jewish-Christian origin. Even if the Testimony of the 12 Patriarchs, Enoch, Assumption of Moses, Baruch, and 4 Ezra were original Jewish products, there can be little doubt that the extant texts contain some additions and interpolations made by Jewish-Christians of the early 2d cent. A.D.

II. Extra-Palestinian or Alexandrian Writings

1. *The Letter of Aristeas*. An alleged letter of one Aristeas, a court official of Ptolemy II Philadelphus (285-246 B.C.), to a certain Philocrates. This letter, prob-

ably written by an Alexandrian Jew about the 2d cent. B.C., contains a legendary account of the translation of the Jewish Law into Greek (the LXX), possibly inserted by a later editor. According to the letter, Ptolemy, wishing to have a Greek version of the Jewish laws for the Alexandrian library, asked the high priest in Jerusalem to send qualified scholars to make the translation. The high priest responded by sending 72 scholars who are supposed to have completed the work in 72 days.

2. *The Sibylline Oracles.* A collection of oracles which are a mixture of pagan, Jewish, and Christian apocalyptic, partly an adaptation and partly an imitation of the pagan "sibylline books" in hexameter verses like Homer's poems, and dating probably from the 2d cent. B.C. to the 5th cent. A.D., or even later. Originally there were 15 books in the collection; 12 survive (IX, X, and XV are lost).

3. *Third Maccabees.* An account of the frustrating of Ptolemy (IV) Philopator's attempt to enter the Temple (217 B.C.), and the subsequent miraculous thwarting of his plans to massacre the Jews in Alexandria. It was written in Greek not far from 100 B.C. It is found in some manuscripts of the LXX and is favorably regarded by the Syrian church.

4. *Fourth Maccabees.* A Greek philosophical treatise written probably between 63 B.C. and A.D. 38, and directed to the Jews, enjoining the rule of reason over the passions. The Maccabean period is drawn upon for examples of fortitude in suffering to illustrate the theme.

5. *Slavonic Enoch.* Also named 2 Enoch or the Book of the Secrets of Enoch. It is called the Slavonic Enoch because, though written in Greek (probably about the 1st cent.), it has survived only in 2 Slavonic versions. It describes Enoch's guided tour through 7 heavens, and the records of revelations he received from the angel who talked 30 days and nights, and, finally, his exhortations and instructions to his sons before his translation.

6. *Greek Baruch.* Also designated 3 Baruch. Scholars date it as late as the 2d cent. A.D. It records a vision of the 7 heavens, supposedly given to Baruch, the secretary of Jeremiah.

Certain works of a pseudepigraphical nature have been found among the Dead Sea scrolls. These include: (1) an Aramaic work containing a collection of pseudepigraphical material concerning the patriarchs, named by its editors "A Genesis Apocryphon"; (2) a pseudo-Jeremianic work; (3) Psalms of Joshua; (4) A Vision of Amram, the father of Moses; (5) A Prayer of Nabonidus. *See* Scrolls, Dead Sea.

Ptolemais (tŏl'ĕ-mā'ĭs). [Gr. *Ptolemais.*] A city at the northern end of the Acco bay. For its earlier history *see* Acco, which was its former name (Jgs 1:31, RSV). When Palestine belonged to the Ptolemies in the early Hellenistic period, one of them named it Ptolemais, after himself. It was at that time an important seaport of Galilee and Damascus. Paul stopped there on his voyage to Jerusalem while returning from his 3d Missionary Journey (Acts 21:7). The Arabs restored its OT name which the crusaders corrupted to Acre.

Pua. *See* Puvah.

Puah, I. (pū'ă). [Heb. *Pû'ah,* "lass," "girl"; Ugaritic, *Pḡt.*] One of the Hebrew midwives commanded to kill all male Israelite children at their birth, but who disobeyed Pharaoh's command (Ex 1:15).

Puah, II (pū'ă). [Heb. *Pû'ah,* "madder (dye)."]
1. A man of the tribe of Issachar, and father of the judge Tola (Jgs 10:1).
2. For 1 Chr 7:1, *see* Puvah.

Publican, RSV **Tax Collector.** [Gr. *telōnēs,* "tax collector," from *telos,* "tax," and *ōneomai,* "to buy," thus literally, "buyer of taxes"; Latin, *publicanus.*] A proprietary collector of internal revenue for Rome. Instead of collecting taxes directly, through its own officials, the Roman government auctioned off the privilege within a province or a city to a wealthy citizen who paid a stipulated sum, irrespective of how much he was later able to collect, whether more or less. The person thus contracting to collect taxes either subdivided his assigned area among subcontractors, or hired agents for the actual work of collection. The NT "publicans," or "tax collectors," were these agents who actually received the taxes from the people, and they were probably, in nearly every case, Jews. It was expected that each *publicanus* would collect a sufficient additional sum in order to realize a profit. The taxes comprised: (1) the poll or head tax, which was deeply offensive to the Jews in view of the fact that its payment was considered tacit acknowledgment of enslavement to Rome (see Jos. *Ant.* xviii. 1. 1); and (2) the land tax, which was equally offensive, since its payment was considered as an insult to God, whom the Jews regarded as the real owner of the land and the dispenser of its bounties.

It was considered bad enough to pay the Romans taxes, but infinitely worse to assist the Romans in collecting them. Thus the "publicans," who, with a few noteworthy exceptions, were extortioners, and who, with the connivance of Roman soldiers, pressed the traffic for all it could be made to bear, were greatly detested. They were ostracized from society, avoided as far as possible, and seldom seen in the Temple or synagogue (see Mt 11:19; 21:31). A Jew who became a publican was considered a lackey of the hated Romans and a traitor to Israel.

Though recognizing the low moral state of most publicans (cf. Mt 5:46, 47; 18:17), our Lord nevertheless freely associated with them, and thereby incurred the censure of the Jewish authorities (chs 9:10-13; 11:19). The reason He gave for so doing was that He had come for the very purpose of calling sinners like them to repentance (ch 9:13). They appreciated His kindness, and apparently a number of them believed and became His followers (see ch 21:31, 32). In His parable of the Pharisee and the Publican Jesus contrasted the 2 to the advantage of the publican (Lk 18:9-14). One of Jesus' disciples, Levi Matthew, was a publican (Mt 9:9; 10:3). At some time subsequent to his call, Matthew entertained Jesus in his home, with many of his fellow tax collectors present (Mt 9:9, 10; Mk 2:14, 15; Lk 5:27-29). A few days before His crucifixion Jesus befriended Zacchaeus, a Jewish tax collector of Jericho (Lk 19:1-9), who became one of His followers.

Publius (pŭb'lĭ-ŭs). [Gr. *Poplios;* Latin *Publius,* a Roman name attested in inscriptions, among which are some from Malta.] The chief man on the island of Malta, whose father was healed by Paul during the apostle's unplanned stay on the island after his shipwreck while being transported as prisoner to Rome (Acts 28:7, 8). The title "chief man" (Gr. *ho prōtos*) is found in inscriptions on Malta and probably refers to the highest Roman official on the island. *See* Malta.

Pudens (pū'dĕnz). [Gr. *Poudēs,* from Latin *Pudens,* from which the *n* was lost in Greek, as the inscriptions show.] A Roman Christian who sent greetings to Timothy through Paul (2 Ti 4:21). The name was borne by several noblemen in the apostolic age, as inscriptions show, but there is no evidence to link any of these with the Biblical Pudens.

Puhites. *See* Puthites.

394. Relief of King Tiglath-pileser III of Assyria, whose Babylonian name was Pul

Pul (pŭl). [Heb. *Pûl.*]
1. An African place or people (Is 66:19, KJV), mentioned in connection with Tarshish and Lud. Some expositors identify Pul with the island of Philae in Upper Egypt, but the majority of commentators consider Pul a misspelling of *Put (see Eze 27:10).
2. Another name (probably the original) of *Tiglath-pileser III, king of Assyria (1 Chr 5:26). It was formerly thought that Pul and Tiglath-pileser were 2 kings, but the Hebrew permits the following translation in 1 Chr 5:26: "the spirit of Pul, . . . *even* the spirit of Tiglath-pileser." The following phrase, "he carried them away," suggests that only 1 king was involved. Babylonian records show "Pulu" as the equivalent of "Tiglath-pileser."

Pulse. *See* Vegetables.

Punites. *See* Puvah.

Punon (pū'nŏn). [Heb. *Pûnon.*] A station in the wilderness wanderings of the Israelites, which they reached shortly before coming to Moab (Num 33:42, 43). It is identified with *Feinân,* about 25 mi. south of the Dead Sea in the *Wâdî 'Arabah.* Many copper mines active in the time of King Solomon and later have been discovered in its vicinity. Map V, B-7.

Pur. *See* Purim.

Purah (pū'rá), KJV **Phurah** (fū'rá). [Heb. *Purah,* meaning uncertain.] The servant of Gideon (Jgs 7:10, 11).

Purification. Under Levitical law contact with a human corpse, human bones, or a grave (Num 19:11, 13, 16), with the carcass of an unclean animal (Lev 5:2;

11:31, 36, 39), bodily issues from the generative organs (Lev 12:1-5; 15:1-12), and *"leprosy" (chs 13; 14), constituted a person ceremonially unclean (see Uncleanness).

A ceremonially unclean person was barred from the sanctuary or Temple (cf. Lev 12:4; Num 19:13, 20), and might not touch any sacred object for the duration of his uncleanness (cf. Num 19:22). Anyone who touched an unclean person during this time also became unclean and must bathe himself, wash his clothes, and be unclean for the remainder of that day. Then he was clean again "at even" (ch 19:19), that is, "when the sun is down" (Lev 22:6, 7).

Whatever the unclean person might touch similarly became unclean. And anyone who touched what an unclean person had touched was also considered ceremonially unclean for the remainder of that day. For each category of uncleanness a ritual procedure of purification was specified.

1. Purification from uncleanness incurred by contact with a corpse (Num 19). Procedure for the removal of ceremonial defilement incurred from touching a dead body, a bone, or a grave, was as follows: In preparation for the ceremony proper, an unblemished red heifer which had never worn a yoke was taken to the priest, who accompanied the heifer and its master to an appropriate spot outside the camp. The heifer was then slaughtered in the presence of the priest, who dipped his finger into the blood that had been preserved and sprinkled the blood toward the sanctuary 7 times. The whole animal was then burned with fire, into which the priest cast cedarwood, *scarlet material, and hyssop. A ceremonially clean person then gathered up the ashes of the heifer and stored them in a ceremonially clean place outside the camp. The man who slew the heifer and the priest who participated in this ritual thereby became ceremonially unclean, and accordingly were to wash their clothing, bathe, return to camp, and regain ceremonial cleanness at the close of the day. A person ceremonially defiled by contact with a dead body, bone, or grave, remained ceremonially unclean for 7 days. On the 3d and 7th days he was to be sprinkled with water mixed with ashes of the red heifer, by any ceremonially clean person. A bunch of hyssop was used for sprinkling the water. On the 7th day the person defiled by contact with the dead was to bathe, wash his clothes, and regain ceremonial cleanness at the close of the day. The clean person officiating in this rite was to wash his clothes, but continued to be ceremonially unclean for the remainder of the day. The tent and furnishings of the unclean person were likewise to be sprinkled with water containing the ashes of the red heifer, and after 7 days were again considered ceremonially clean. This water is called "water of separation" (KJV) and "water for impurity" (RSV).

A Nazirite defiled by contact with a corpse was likewise to remain unclean for 7 days. But on the 7th day he was to shave his hair, the sign of the vow he had taken, and on the 8th day to present 2 young turtledoves or pigeons, one for a sin offering and the other for a burnt offering, and a lamb for a trespass offering. He forfeited credit for the days of his vow prior to the defilement, and was required to begin the entire period over again (Num 6:9-12).

2. Purification from contact with the carcass of an unclean animal (see Lev 11: 29-31, 39). No ritual was specified for the person thus defiled, but he was to be ceremonially unclean until the close of the day (cf. v 40).

3. Uncleanness incurred by issues from the generative organs (Lev 15). These issues might be either normal or abnormal. A person thus defiled was considered unclean for 7 days from the time that the issue stopped. On the 7th day he was to bathe in running water and wash his clothes. At the close of the day he again became ceremonially clean. On the 8th day he was to present himself at the sanctuary, later the Temple, with two turtledoves or pigeons, one for a sin offering and the other for a burnt offering. Physical contact with someone thus in a state of ceremonial uncleanness, or contact with anything he had touched, rendered another person unclean. The latter, however, was to bathe himself, and he regained ceremonial cleanness at the end of that day.

4. Purification of a mother at childbirth (Lev 12). The mother was to remain ceremonially unclean for 7 days in the case of a male child, and 14 days in the case of a female child, plus 33 additional days for a male child and 66 additional days for a female child. At the close of the specified period of time the mother was to present a lamb for a burnt offering and a turtledove or a pigeon for a

sin offering. If she was poor, only young birds were required, one for a burnt offering and the other for a sin offering (see Lk 2:21-24).

5. *Purification from defilement by leprosy* (Lev 14). When cure from leprosy had been certified, "two birds alive and clean," together with cedarwood, scarlet material, and hyssop, were presented. One bird was killed over an earthen vessel filled with running water and its blood was permitted to drain into the water. The priest then dipped the living bird, the cedarwood, the scarlet material, and the hyssop into the water containing the blood of the bird that had been killed. This water was then sprinkled upon the leprous person 7 times, and following that the living bird was set free. The healed leper was then to wash his clothes, shave off all his hair, bathe, and return to camp, but was forbidden to enter his tent or house for 7 days. On the 8th day he was to present himself at the sanctuary with 2 male lambs, one for a trespass offering and the other for a burnt offering, together with a ewe lamb for a sin offering. He was also to bring a portion of flour mingled with oil for a meal offering, together with an extra container of oil. The trespass offering was slain and waved before the Lord, together with the pot of oil. The priest next touched some of the blood of the trespass offering to the right ear, right thumb, and right great toe of the offerer. He then sprinkled the oil 7 times before the Lord, and touched it also to the healed leper's right ear, thumb, and toe. The remainder of the oil he poured upon the head of the offerer. Finally, he offered the sin offering, and the burnt offering and its accompanying meal offering. In case of poverty, 1 lamb with the oil and flour, would suffice for a trespass offering, and 2 turtledoves or pigeons, one for a sin offering and the other for a burnt offering.

Purim. [Heb. *pûrîm,* "lots."] A feast celebrating the deliverance of the Jews from destruction through the intervention of Queen *Esther. Ahasuerus (Xerxes), the Persian king at that time, had been induced by Haman to decree that on a certain day all Jews in the Persian Empire could be slaughtered and their goods seized. The particular day was chosen by the casting of "Pur, that is the lot" (Est 3:7, RSV). When, at the intervention of Queen Esther (chs 5:1-3; 8:1-7), the king resolved to save the Jews, since he could not revoke the edict because the

laws of the Medes and Persians were unchangeable (Est 1:19; 8:8), he decreed that on the day specified, Adar 13 (ch 3:13), the Jews could fight in self-defense (ch 8:11-13). In the city of Susa they were allowed to avenge themselves on their enemies on the 14th also (ch 9:13-15). This great deliverance and victory was celebrated on the following day and annually thereafter by a festival of thanksgiving on the 14th and 15th of Adar (vs 17-28). The festival was called Purim, "lots," because the date for the execution had been selected by casting lots.

Purple. [Heb. *'argaman,* "purple," "red"; Ugaritic *'rgmn,* a loan word of Anatolian origin; Gr. *porphurous,* "purple (color)," *porphura,* "purple (fabric)," "purple (garment)."] Any color within a vaguely defined range of shades from violet to a deep blue-red. Anciently, crimson was also included (cf. Mt 27:28; Mk 15:17; see Pliny *Hist. Nat.* ix. 61, 62). In antiquity purple dye was obtained from a species of shellfish common in the Mediterranean, the *Murex,* and originally the Gr. *porphura* referred to this animal. Later *porphura* and related terms came to be applied to cloth dyed with purple dye or to a garment made from the cloth. The famous Tyrian purple was derived from 2 species, the *Murex trunculus* and *Murex brandaris.* Murex shells discovered at *Minet el-Beida,* the seaport of ancient Ras Shamra (Ugarit), indicate that purple was produced there from the 2d millennium B.C. Thyatiran purple, in which Lydia dealt (Acts 16:14), was not made from shellfish, but from the madder root, and was a bright red. Purple drapes were used by idolatrous peoples for enshrining their idols (Jer 10:9). Some of the hangings of the tabernacle and the Temple were purple (Ex 25:4; 26:1, 31, 36; 2 Chr 3:14). According to Josephus (*War* v. 5. 4) the purple in the high priest's garments (Ex 28:5, 6, 15, 33; 39:29) represented the sea. The "scarlet" of Dan 5:7 is from the Aramaic *'argewan,* "purple." This was the royal color of antiquity, as evidence from the time of the Persians (Est 8:15; Xenophon *Anabasis* i. 5. 8), the Medes (Xenophon *Cyropaedia* i. 3. 2; ii. 4. 6), and later periods attest. This passage in Daniel indicates that purple was a royal color also in the Neo-Babylonian period, which preceded the Persian period. It was a regal color among ancient Midian kings (Jgs 8:26). Purple was also worn by the rich in NT times (Lk 16:19). The purple (or scarlet) robe put on Jesus by the Roman soldiers (Jn 19:2) was in mockery of His claims that He was a king. Mystical Babylon the great is described as being clothed in purple (Rev 17:4; 18:16).

Purse. A rendering of: (1) The Heb. *kis,* a bag or pouch for the safekeeping of money (Prov 1:14; Is 46:6, RSV). *Kis* is also translated *"bag."* (2) The Gr. *balantion,* "money box," "purse" (Lk 10:4; 12:33; RSV; 22:35, 36). (3) The Gr. *zōnē,* "girdle," or "belt." This was often hollow, and could serve as a purse (Mt 10:9; Mk 6:8; RSV).

Purslane. A rendering of the Heb. *challamûth* (Job 6:6, RSV), probably some plant, but the identification is uncertain. The purslane is a plant of the family Portulacaceae, of usually succulent herbs.

Put (pŭt), KJV twice **Phut** (fŭt). [Heb. *Pûṭ.*] One of the 4 sons of Ham (Gen 10:6; 1 Chr 1:8) and progenitor of a people closely related to Mizraim (RSV "Egypt") and Cush (Ethiopia, or Nubia). This people is mentioned in association with the Libyans, or Lubim (Nah 3:9), Persia and Lud (Eze 27:10), Lud and Ethiopia, or Cush (Jer 46:9; Eze 30:5), and Persia and Cush (Eze 38:5, RSV). The name is generally thought to stand for Libya or the Libyans, and is thus rendered in the LXX as well as in the KJV of Jer 46:9; Eze 38:5. The name is also identified with the Babylonian *Puṭa,* the Elamite *Puṭiyap,* and the Persian *Puṭaya,* in which many scholars see Libya. Egyptologists, however, identify Put with the people of Punt, a country on the African coast of Somaliland and Eritrea, to which the Egyptians sent expeditions to obtain

myrrh trees, leopard skins, ebony, ivory, and other exotic products. Uncertainty thus exists as to the exact identification. Map IV, B-4/5, places Put with a question mark in the Egyptian delta.

Puteoli (pū-tē′ŏ-lĭ). [Gr. *Potioloi,* "fountains," "craters."] A port city near Naples, Italy, now called *Pozzuoli* (fig. 395). It was founded toward the end of the 6th cent. B.C. by Greeks who called it *Dicaearchia.* It is not known when its name was changed to Puteoli. It became a Roman dependency probably in the 4th cent. B.C. and was elevated to the status of a Roman colony in 194 B.C. As the chief port for all of Rome's trade with the Orient it became important, wealthy, and large. Its artificial harbor installations were better than those of any other Italian port city, including Ostia. It had a lighthouse, and a fire brigade. The city was an imperial post-station, and was connected with Rome by a first-class road, the *Via Domitiana,* which joined the *Via Appia* farther to the north. Ruins of the city's amphitheater have survived to the present. Paul landed at Puteoli on his journey to Rome as a prisoner, probably in the early spring of A.D. 61, and spent 7 days there with his fellow believers before going on by land to Rome (Acts 28:13, 14). *See* Paul, IV, 3. Map XX, A-1.

Puthites (pū′thīts), KJV **Puhites** (pū′hīts). [Heb. *Pûthî.*] A family inhabiting the region of Kiriath-jearim (1 Chr 2:53).

Putiel (pū′tĭ-ĕl). [Heb. *Pûṭî′el,* a hybrid name, the first part derived from the Egyptian *p3 dî,* "the one given by," and the 2d from the Heb. *'El,* "God." Thus the name means "the one given by God," which

395. The city of *Pozzuoli,* Biblical Puteoli, with the Bay of Naples in the background

is also one meaning of the name Nathanael.] The father-in-law of Eleazer, Aaron's son (Ex 6:25). Putiel probably received his name in Egypt, where he was born.

Puvah (pū'và), KJV once **Phuvah** (fū'và), and once **Pua** (pū'à). [Heb. *Puwwah,* "madder (dye)."] The second son of Issachar (Gen 46:13) and ancestor of the family of the Punites (pū'nīts) [Heb. *Pûnî*] (Num 26:23), called Puah [Heb. *Pû'ah*] in 1 Chr 7:1.

Pygarg. *See* Ibex.

Pyrrhus (pĭr'ŭs). [Gr. *Purros,* "red," a Greek name occurring frequently in the inscriptions and other ancient records.] A man whose son, Sopater of Beroea, was one of Paul's companions on the apostle's last trip to Jerusalem (Acts 20:4, RSV). The name is not found in the Textus Receptus, and hence is missing in the KJV. However, textual evidence favors its inclusion.

—Q—

Quail. [Heb. *śelaw.*] A Eurasian quail, *Coturnix communis,* similar to the North American bobwhite. It is from 8 to 10 inches in length and belongs to the same order as pheasants, partridges, and grouse. It is a plump bird, generally brown, with buff streaks about the head and back. Once off the ground, it has a rapid flight, but in migration it may tire and fall to the ground, where it is easily captured, even by hand. Ornithologists have reported great migrations of quail from southeastern Europe and southern Russia, across the eastern Mediterranean to North Africa. Twice in their wilderness travels the children of Israel were provided flesh by the descent upon their encampment of thousands of quail, once in the Wilderness of Sin (Ex 16:13; Ps 105:40) and again at Kibroth-hattaavah between Mount Sinai and Kadesh-barnea (Num 11:31. 32).

Quarry. A rendering of: (1) The Heb. *pasîl,* "idol" (Jgs 3:19, 26, KJV), translated "sculptured stone" in the RSV. Elsewhere the KJV translates the term "graven image" or "carved image" and the RSV generally "image" or "carved image" (Deut 7:5; 2 Chr 33:19; etc.). (2) The Heb. *massa',* "quarry" (1 Ki 6:7, RSV). The verb "quarry" appears several times in the RSV (2 Ki 12:12; 22:6; etc.).

Quart. A term appearing once (Rev 6:6, RSV), as the approximate equivalent of the Gr. *choinix,* which equaled 2 sextarii, 1.09 liters, or .99 dry qt. U.S.

Quartermaster. A term appearing once (Jer 51:59, RSV), a rendering of the Heb. *śar menúchah,* literally, "prince of a resting place." The Hebrew expression may designate the official in charge of arranging quarters for the king when he was on a journey. Another suggestion is that Seraiah, the official so designated, may have been the leader of a peace party in Jerusalem. The KJV translates *śar menúchah* "a quiet prince."

Quartus (kwôr'tŭs). [Gr. *Kouartos,* from Latin *quartus,* "fourth."] A Christian of the church of Corinth, who sent greetings to the church of Rome in Paul's letter to the Romans (Rom 16:23).

Quaternion. *See* Squad.

Queen. [Heb. generally *gebirah,* "queen mother," literally "lady," and *malkah;* Aramaic *malkah;* Gr. *basilissa.*] A woman who rules a kingdom or who is the consort of a king (2 Chr 9:1; Est 1:9). The queen of Sheba (1 Ki 10:1-13) and Candace, queen of Ethiopia (Acts 8:27), are examples of legitimate female rulers. Esther and Vashti were Persian queens of the consort type, with probably little official authority with the king (see Est 1:9-22; 2:22; 4:10-16). In the KJV the term "queen" is sometimes used of the queen mother, who was often a woman of influence. King Asa removed his grandmother (*see* Maacah, 10) from her position of influence because she was promoting idolatry (1 Ki 15:13; 2 Chr 15:16). The "queen of the south" (Mt 12:42; Lk 11:31) refers to the queen of Sheba. John speaks of spiritual Babylon's impudent assertion of her queenship (Rev 18:7), and describes her final and complete destruction resulting from her gross sins against God and humanity (vs 2-24).

Queen of Heaven. [Heb. *meleketh hashshamayim.*] A female heathen deity (Jer 7:18;

44:17-19, 25) probably to be identified with the Assyro-Babylonian Ishtar and the Palestinian *Ashtoreth, or Astarte. God denounced the inhabitants of Judah and Jerusalem for their worship of this heathen deity, which they conducted by baking cakes, burning incense, and pouring out libations to her. The worship of the Queen of Heaven was doubtless a part of the worship of various other deities identified with the stars and planets, against which God had repeatedly warned His people (Deut 4:19; 17:2-5; cf. Job 31:26-28).

Queen of Sheba. The Arabian queen who visited Solomon (1 Ki 10:1-10). Tradition places her capital at *Mârib* in Yemen, one of the most forbidden cities of southern Arabia, where spectacular temple ruins, a great river dam, and other structures, besides numerous ancient inscriptions in South Arabic, wait for the exploration and interpretation of the archeologist. An American expedition worked there for a few weeks in 1952 (fig. 432), but it had to abandon its work and all equipment because of the hostility of the local officials. *See* Sheba, I, 1.

Lit.: Wendell Phillips, *Qataban and Sheba* (New York, 1955); R. L. Bowen, *et al., Archaeological Discoveries in South Arabia* (Baltimore, 1958).

Quick, Quicken. Old English words appearing in the KJV with the meanings "alive" and "to make alive" (Num 16:30; Ps 55:15; 71:20; Acts 10:42; Rom 4:17; etc.).

Quicksands. *See* Syrtis.

Quirinius (kwĭ-rĭn′ĭ-ŭs), KJV **Cyrenius** (sĭ-rē′nĭ-ŭs). [Gr. *Kurēnios,* from the Latin *Quirinius.*] A high Roman official, mentioned in Lk 2:2 as *governor of Syria at the time of Jesus' birth. From secular sources the following information is obtained about him: his full name was Publius Sulpicius Quirinius. He seems to have been proconsul of Crete and Cyrene in 15 B.C., in which capacity he defeated the Marmaridae. Between 12 B.C. and A.D. 2 (the exact date is unknown) he subjugated the Homonadenses, who were Cilician brigands in southeastern Asia Minor. From A.D. 6 to 9 he was legate of Syria, during which time he conducted a census in Judea, possibly the one referred to in Acts 5:37. He was married to Aemilia Lepida, a descendant of Sulla and Pompey, and died in A.D. 21. Nothing is known from secular sources about the "first" taxing in Judea under him, which preceded the death of Herod the Great as reported

by Luke (Lk 2:1-5). A fragmentary Latin inscription from Tivoli refers to the legate of Syria without mentioning his name (fig. 396). This inscription has been interpreted by eminent scholars, including

396. One of the Quirinius inscriptions

Mommsen, Ramsay, and Deissmann, as an indication of an earlier governorship of Quirinius over Syria, from 6 to 4 B.C. (See *SDACom* 5:241.)

Quiver. [Heb. *telî;* '*ashpah.*] A case for carrying arrows, usually made of leather (Gen 27:3; Ps 127:5; etc.). A foot soldier usually carried it over the shoulder (see figs. 308, 378), whereas on chariots it was hung at the side (see Is 22:6) for ready accessibility for the archers who fought in the chariot forces (see figs. 274, 304).

R

Raama. *See* Raamah, 1.

Raamah (rā'á-má), RSV once **Raama** (rā'-á-má). [Heb. *Ra'mah* and *Ra'ma'*, "mane of a horse," or "thunder."]

1. Son of Cush and father of Sheba and Dedan (Gen 10:7; 1 Chr 1:9); apparently an ancestor of an Arabic tribe (*see* Raamah, 2).

2. Arabic tribe associated with Sheba, and therefore probably descended from Raamah, 1. The tribe traded spices, gold, and precious stones on the markets of Tyre (Eze 27:22). It has been identified with the Rhammanites, whom the Roman geographer Strabo placed in southwestern Arabia (xv. 4. 24). The tribe is also referred to in a famous ancient South Arabic inscription that ascribes praise to the local deity for saving the Minaeans from attacks of Sheba and Haulan, on the way from *Ma'în* to *Ra'amah*. Map IV, D-6 gives a conjectural location for the tribe of Raamah.

Raamiah. *See* Reelaiah.

Raamses. *See* Rameses, 2.

Rabbah (răb'á), KJV twice **Rabbath** (răb'-ăth). [Heb. *Rabbah*, "the great (city)."]

1. The capital of the Ammonites, a city at the headwaters of the Jabbok in Transjordan (Map VI, E-4). This city is first mentioned as the place where the "iron bedstead" (probably a sarcophagus) of Og, the Amorite king of Bashan, was shown (Deut 3:11). When the Ammonites showed hostility to David and hired the Aramaeans to help them in their war against Israel, David sent his army commander Joab against them. Joab divided his army into 2 parts, placing half of it under command of his brother Abishai, and attacked the enemies separately. His strategy successfully defeated both enemy armies (2 Sa 10:6-14; 1 Chr 19:6-15). In the following year Joab returned to besiege Rabbah. After some time he took the "city of waters," by which is meant, apparently, the lower part of the city which was down by the stream (2 Sa 11: 1; 12:26, 27; 1 Chr 20:1). It was during this siege that Uriah, the husband of Bathsheba, perished (2 Sa 11:2-27). After Joab conquered the lower city he summoned David to complete the conquest of the citadel so that the victory would be connected with his name. David came, took the city, and condemned its population to forced labor (2 Sa 12:27-31; 1 Chr 20:2, 3). Later, however, the Ammonites were apparently allowed to reoccupy their capital (see 2 Sa 17:27). The prophets Jeremiah (Jer 49:2-6) and Ezekiel (Eze 25:5) denounced the city.

Ptolemy II Philadelphus (285-246 B.C.) embellished and Hellenized Rabbah, as a result of which its name was changed to Philadelphia in his honor. In 218 B.C. it was conquered by Antiochus the Great, but in 63 B.C. was taken over by the Romans under Pompey, who made it a member of the Decapolis, a confederation of 10 free Hellenistic cities separated from Jewish rule but under the Romans (Map XV, E-4). The present city, called *'Ammân*, has again come to honor as the capital of the Hashemite Kingdom of Jordan. Excavations of the citadel were conducted

397. An old tower at *'Ammân*, the ancient Rabbah, or Rabbath-ammon

by G. Guidi in 1927 and by R. Bartoccini in 1929. The modern Museum of Transjordan is built on the grounds of the ancient citadel. The lower city in the valley contains impressive ruins from the Hellenistic-Roman period, among them an especially well-preserved theater.

2. A town in the hill country of Judah near Kiriath-jearim (Jos 15:60), probably the *Rubute* of the *Amarna Letters. Its site has not been identified with certainty.

Rabbath. See Rabbah, 1.

Rabbi. [Gr. *rhabbi,* from the Heb. and Aramaic *rabbî,* "my great one," "my master," "my teacher."] A title of respect, by which pupils addressed their teachers. The possessive "my" soon lost its force, and in the NT the word was used as a courteous form of address, generally equivalent to our "sir." It is applied to Christ in Mt 26:25; Mk 14:45; Jn 1:38, 49; 3:2, 26; 4:31; 6:25; 9:2; 11:8; etc., and to John the Baptist in Jn 3:26. Christ counseled His disciples against coveting or using this title (Mt 23:7, 8). In this passage *rhabbi* seems to be used in a more restricted sense, as an honorific title for the scholars and teachers of the Law, with the possible implication that since they were learned in the Law of Moses their interpretations of the religious duties prescribed therein were infallible and thus binding. The author of the 4th Gospel interprets *rhabbi* to mean *didaskalos,* "master," "teacher" (Jn 1:38). Another form of this title was the Gr. *rhabbouni,* a transliteration of the Aramaic *rabbûnî,* which was an even more respectful form of address, and signified "my (great) master." It is applied to Christ in Mk 10:51 and Jn 20:16. In the latter reference it appears as "Rabboni" in the English versions, and is interpreted by the Gr. *didaskalos,* "master," "teacher."

Rabbith (răb'ĭth). [Heb. *Rabbîth.*] A town in the territory of Issachar (Jos 19:20); otherwise unknown.

Rabboni. See Rabbi.

Rabmag (răb'măg). [Heb. *rab-mag.*] The title of Nergal-sharezer, a high Babylonian officer in Nebuchadnezzar's army (Jer 39:3, 13). The exact meaning of the title is unknown, but Rabmag may stand for Akkadian *rab-mûgi,* meaning "great prince," or the *mag* may be an abbreviation of *Sin-magir,* the name of an area, for Nergal-sharezer is mentioned in a Babylonian court almanac of Nebuchadnezzar's time (see fig. 350) as "prince of Sin-magir."

Rabsaris (răb'să-rĭs). [Heb. *rab-saris,* "chief eunuch." The name appears in an Old Aramaic inscription written in 682 B.C. In Assyrian and Babylonian inscriptions the equivalent title *rab shareshi* is found, which means literally "chief (of the) one on the head (of the king)."] The title of a high-ranking courtier in Assyria and Babylonia. One Rabsaris is mentioned in 2 Ki 18:17 as accompanying the expeditionary force sent by Sennacherib from Lachish to Jerusalem in the attempt to conquer that city in 701 B.C. Another Rabsaris accompanied Nebuchadnezzar's army at the time of the capture of Jerusalem in 586 B.C. (Jer 39:3). It is possible that Ashpenaz, the royal courtier mentioned in Dan 1:3, carried the same title, but the Hebrew term there is *rab sarîsim* (*sarîsim* is the plural of *saris*), literally, "chief of eunuchs." He may therefore have been the officer who was placed over the eunuchs of the king, of whom every Oriental potentate employed a great number. This view is supported by the fact that he is called "prince of the eunuchs" (*sar hassarîsim*) in vs 7, 11, and 18.

Rabshakeh (răb'shă-kĕ). [Heb. *rab-shaqeh;* Akkadian *rab-shaqû,* literally, "chief cupbearer."] The title of a high Assyrian court official, also in later times an honorary title used by army commanders and governors. During his Assyrian campaign against Hezekiah (2 Ki 18:17) the Rabshakeh of Sennacherib, associated with the Tartan and the Rabsaris, was in command of an expeditionary force sent against Jerusalem while Sennacherib was at Lachish. Since the Rabshakeh was the spokesman in the discussions with Hezekiah's officials at Jerusalem (vs 19, 26, 27, 37), he seems to have been the head of the expedition. Isaiah does not mention the Tartan and the Rabsaris (Is 36:2, 4, 11-13, 22; 37:4, 8), nor does 2 Ki 19, where the Rabshakeh's return to Sennacherib is recorded (v 8).

Raca. A transliteration of the Gr. *rhaka* (Mt 5:22, KJV), which in turn is a transliteration of the Aramaic *rêqa',* "fool," "emptyhead." *Rêqa'* was an exclamation of strong contempt used by the Jews in the time of Christ (Mt 5:22). The RSV translates the term "You fool."

Racal (rā'căl), KJV **Rachal** (rā'kăl). [Heb. *Rakal.*] A place in Judah to which David sent some of the spoils of Ziklag (1 Sa 30:29); otherwise unknown. The LXX reads "Carmel," which is considered by many commentators as the original reading.

Race. Racing was a sport known to the ancients in both OT and NT times. Best known from ancient literature are the foot and chariot races of the Greeks and Romans, and race courses have been excavated in several sites of the ancient world. Foot races were known to the Hebrews at an early time in their history. The psalmist compares the sun to a strong young man joyfully running a course (Ps 19:5). And Solomon, by observation or participation, knew that the victory in a race does not always come to the swiftest runner, but sometimes to one favored by circumstances and chances (Ec 9:11). The apostle Paul, who, like his readers, was at home in the Greco-Roman world, mentions races repeatedly and compares the Christian life to them. He encourages his readers to exercise self-control like an athlete who trains for a race, and to strive as earnestly for the eternal crown as a runner for a wreath of leaves (1 Cor 9:24-27). At the end of his life he compared his own course to a race successfully run (2 Ti 4:7, RSV). In Heb 12:1, 2 the Christian is said to be compassed with a great crowd of witnesses, such as attended athletic contests. He is told that his training requires much patience, and that he must lay aside everything to obtain his goal, an allusion to the fact that the contestants in Greek foot races (as in other athletic events) took off their garments and ran in the nude in order not to be hampered by anything and thus be hindered from winning.

Rachab. *See* Rahab, I.

Rachal. *See* Racal.

Rachel (rā′chĕl), KJV once **Rahel** (rā′hĕl). [Heb. *Rachel*, "ewe (lamb)"; Gr. *Rachēl*.] Laban's younger daughter, Jacob's 2d wife and the mother of Joseph and Benjamin. Since Laban was Jacob's uncle, on his mother's side, Rachel was Jacob's cousin (cf. Gen 28:2; 29:9, 10). Jacob first met Rachel at the well near Haran upon arriving in Paddan-aram, where he had been sent to find a wife. After chivalrously

398. The so-called tomb of Rachel near Bethlehem

rolling the stone from the well's mouth and watering her flock (Gen 29:10), Jacob greeted Rachel with a kiss and introduced himself (vs 11, 12). Apparently Jacob fell in love with Rachel at first sight, and his affection for her grew to be genuine and deep (v 20). Laban welcomed Jacob into his home (vs 13, 14), and after a month hired him to keep his flocks and herds (v 15; cf. ch 30:31), with the understanding that Rachel was to become Jacob's wife in return for 7 years of service (ch 29:15-19). This procedure was in keeping with the customs of the ancient Orient, which required a prospective husband to make a payment to the bride's father in settlement of the marriage contract (*see* Dowry). Since Jacob had arrived penniless, and was thus unable to pay for his intended bride, it was necessary for him to work for the stipulated price. When the 7 years had passed, Laban surreptitiously substituted Rachel's older sister Leah, and Jacob, the artful deceiver (ch 27), found himself deceived (ch 29:21-25). Under the pretext that custom forbade marrying off a younger daughter before her older sister, Laban proposed to Jacob that the wedding festivities already begun be continued for the nuptial week (cf. Jgs 14:12), at the close of which he would give him Rachel also, in return for another 7 years of service (Gen 29:26, 27, 30). To her great dismay and deep disappointment, "Rachel was barren" (v 31). Leah, on the other hand, gave birth to several children (vs 32-35). Jealous of Leah, Rachel blamed Jacob for her childlessness, and petulantly demanded children of him (ch 30:1), but he reminded her that the matter was in God's hands (v 2). Rachel then gave Jacob her maid Bilhah as a concubine (v 3), in keeping with the ancient Oriental custom whereby a concubine's children became the legal children of the lawful wife. Dan and Naphtali were born to this union (vs 4-8). Upon one occasion Rachel bargained with Leah for mandrakes gathered by her son Reuben (v 14), the mandrake being an herb of the belladonna family thought by people of the Near East to promote fertility. In time "God remembered Rachel," and she gave birth to Joseph (vs 22-24). After 20 years of service (ch 31:38) Jacob surreptitiously left Laban to return to Canaan, with his wives, flocks, and herds (vs 1-18, 20). At the time of departure Rachel stole her father's "images," or household gods (v 19), which were usually small human figurines made of wood, clay, or precious metals, probably hoping that they would promote fertility, which was one of their reputed functions (see fig. 493). When Laban later questioned Jacob, who knew nothing about Rachel's theft of the images, Jacob invited him to search their goods (Gen 31:30-33). Rachel cleverly hid the images, and they were not found (vs 34, 35). Some years later Jacob required that the "strange gods" belonging to members of his household be disposed of, and he "hid them under" an oak in the vicinity of Shechem (ch 35:2-4). It is possible that the "images" of Laban were among them. Several years later, on a journey from Bethel, Rachel gave birth to Benjamin, but died in childbirth and was buried near Ephrath (vs 16-19), where a pillar was built to mark her grave (v 20). The exact location of her grave is not known, but a little chapel has been erected a short distance north of Bethlehem over the traditional site (fig. 398). However, according to 1 Sa 10:2 (cf. Jer 31:15) it seems that she was buried in the vicinity of what later became the border between Benjamin and Judah, a short distance to the north of Jerusalem. The traditional site a mile or more north of the town of Bethlehem would be about 4 mi. from the border of Benjamin. Jacob's deep love for Rachel is reflected in his mention of her many years after her death (Gen 48:7).

Jer 31:15 figuratively represents Rachel (KJV "Rahel") as weeping for her children, the children perhaps being the tribes of Ephraim and Manasseh, sons of her son Joseph, who had been carried into captivity a full century prior to Jeremiah's time, but also, doubtless, the people of Benjamin, her younger son, who were about to be carried into captivity by Nebuchadnezzar. Matthew (ch 2:18) borrows Jeremiah's figure about "Rachel weeping for her children," and applies it to the mourning of the mothers of Bethlehem for their children slain by Herod the Great.

Raddai (răd′ā-ī). [Heb. *Radday,* meaning uncertain.] The 5th son of Jesse, and brother of David (1 Chr 2:14).

Ragau. *See* Reu.

Raguel. *See* Reuel, 2.

Rahab, I (rā′hăb), KJV once **Rachab** (rā′-kăb). [Heb. *Rachab,* "broad"; Gr. *Rhachab* and *Rhaab.*] A harlot whose house stood on the wall of Jericho. She received the Israelite spies and helped them to escape. For this act of kindness the Israelites re-

warded her by sparing her life and the lives of the members of her family when Jericho was destroyed and its population slain (Jos 2:1-24; 6:22-25; Heb 11:31; Jas 2:25). She seems to have become the wife of Salmon and the mother or ancestress of Boaz and thus also an ancestress of King David and of Jesus Christ (Mt 1:5; cf. Ruth 4:21, 22).

Rahab, II (rā′hăb). [Heb. *Rahab,* "storm," or "arrogancy."] A designation of a great power of evil and thus a symbol of Satan (Job 9:13; 26:12; RSV; Ps 89:10; Is 51:9), or a figurative name for Egypt (Ps 87:4; Is 30:7, RSV).

Raham (rā′hăm). [Heb. *Racham,* "he has shown compassion."] A descendant of Judah, of the house of Caleb son of Hezron (1 Chr 2:44).

Rahel. *See* Rachel.

Rain. *See* Palestine, VIII; Season.

Rainbow. [Gr. *iris,* "rainbow."] An arc of color seen in the atmosphere opposite the sun, produced by the refraction of light in droplets of rain. Because rain was not known so long as God's original plan of watering the earth (Gen 2:5, 6) was in operation, a rainbow would not have appeared before "the windows of heaven were opened" in the Flood. Thus it is probable that the first rainbow was seen after the Deluge, when the sun broke through the clouds as Noah sacrificed unto the Lord when he came forth from the ark. God then established the rainbow (called "bow," Heb. *qesheth*) as a covenant sign of the promise that there would never be another flood to destroy all flesh (ch 9:13, 14, 16). Two prophets many centuries apart, Ezekiel and John, described a bow seen in vision around the throne of God (Eze 1:28; Rev 4:3). A rainbow also was seen upon the head of the "mighty angel" that came down from heaven with a little book in his hand (Rev 10:1, 2).

Raisin. [The phrases "bunches of raisins," "clusters of raisins," are a rendering of either the Heb. *ṣimmúqîm,* or the Heb. *'ashîshôth,* meaning "raisin cakes."] The dried fruit of the grapevine. This article of diet was ideal for travelers and armies because it would not spoil easily and because of its concentrated nutritional value (see 1 Sa 25:18; 30:12; 2 Sa 16:1). It was sometimes eaten when there was special occasion for celebration (2 Sa 6:19; 1 Chr 12:40; 16: 3). When Hosea condemned the love of such a delicacy he was doubtless referring to its use in connection with worship of false gods (Hos 3:1). The KJV renders the singular noun *'ashishah* "flagon (of wine)" (2 Sa 6:19; 1 Chr 16:3; Song 2:5; Hos 3:1).

Rakem (rā'kĕm). [Heb. *Reqem,* "variegation."] A descendant of Manasseh (1 Chr 7:16).

Rakkath (răk'ăth). [Heb. *Raqqath,* "narrow place."] A fortified city in the territory of Naphtali (Jos 19:35), tentatively identified with *Tell Eqlāṭiyeh,* about 2 mi. northwest of Tiberias on the shore of the Sea of Galilee (Map VI, C-4).

Rakkon (răk'ŏn). [Heb. *Raqqôn,* "narrow place."] A town in the territory of Dan (Jos 19:46), now *Tell er-Reqqeit,* about 6 mi. north of Joppa on the shore of the Mediterranean Sea.

Ram, I. [Heb. generally *'ayil;* Aramaic *dekar.*] The male sheep, used for food, since it was clean (Gen 31:38), for wool (2 Ki 3:4), and for sacrifice (Gen 15:9; 22:13; Ex 29:1; Lev 5:15; Is 1:11; Mic 6:7). It was offered in burnt offerings (Lev 9:2), and guilt (or trespass) offerings (chs 5:14-16; 6:6), also for a peace offering of the Nazirite (Num 6:14). The Hebrew term is sometimes used as a symbol for a leader or a mighty man (Ex 15:15; Eze 17:13; etc.). In the prophecy of Daniel the ram appears as a symbol of Persia (Dan 8:3, 20). Rams' horns were used as containers for oil (1 Sa 16:1, 13), and as wind instruments for sounding signals for religious and military purposes (Jos 6:4, 5; Jer 4:5; etc.; *see* Trumpet).

Ram, II. [Heb. *Ram;* Gr. *Aram.*]
1. A descendant of Buz, and apparently founder of a family to which Elihu, the friend of Job, belonged (Job 32:2). He should not be identified with the Aram of Gen 22:21, who was not the son of Buz.

2. A Judahite, son of Hezron and brother of Jerahmeel. He was an ancestor of King David and of Jesus Christ (Ruth 4:19; 1 Chr 2:9). He is called Aram in Mt 1:3; Lk 3:33; KJV, but Arni in Lk 3:33, RSV, on the basis of a different Greek text.

3. Another Judahite, a son of Jerahmeel and nephew of Ram, 2 (1 Chr 2:25, 27).

Rama. See Ramah.

Ramah (rā'mä), KJV of NT **Rama** (rā'mä). [Heb. *Ramah,* "height"; Gr. *Rhama.*]
1. A town in the territory of Benjamin (Jos 18:25). Baasha, king of Israel, attempted to fortify it against Judah (1 Ki 15:17, 21, 22; 2 Chr 16:1-6). The Babylonians used Ramah as a collecting cen-

ter for the captives of Judah before transporting them to Babylonia (Jer 40:1). The town was reoccupied after the Exile by descendants of the former inhabitants (Ezr 2:26; Neh 11:33). It has been identified with *er-Râm,* 5½ mi. north of Jerusalem (Map VI, E-3).

2. The town in which Samuel's parents lived and where he later resided and was buried (1 Sa 1:19; 7:17; 25:1; etc.). It is also called Ramathaim-zophim (rā'mà-thā'ĭm-zō'fĭm) [Heb. *Ramathayim ṣôphîm,* "the twin heights of the Zophites"] in ch 1:1; cf. v 19. The site has been widely discussed, and agreement has not been reached among scholars. Some suggest Arimathea (*Rentîs*), others *Beit Rimah,* others Ramah of Benjamin, but its most likely site is *Ramallah,* about 9 mi. north of Jerusalem (Map XXII, C-3). See *SDA Com* 2:458, 459.

3. A town on the border of Asher (Jos 19:29). It is to be identified either with Ramah, 4, of Naphtali (v 36), or with the present *Râmeh,* about 24 mi. southeast by south of Tyre.

4. A fortified city in the territory of Naphtali (Jos 19:36), identified with *er-Râmeh,* about 12½ mi. northwest of Capernaum (Map VI, C-3). It is possibly identical with Ramah, 3.

5. A name used twice for Ramoth-gilead (2 Ki 8:29; 2 Chr 22:6). See Mizpah, 2.

6. A place in the territory of Simeon called "Ramah of the Negeb" (Jos 19:8), KJV "Ramath [rā'măth] of the south." It is probably the "Ramoth of the Negeb" mentioned in 1 Sa 30:27, RSV; KJV "south Ramoth." It has not yet been identified with certainty. Some think that it is identical with *Baalath-beer.

Ramath. See Ramah, 6.

Ramath of the South. See Ramah, 6.

Ramathaim-zophim. See Ramah, 2.

Ramathite (rā'măth-īt). [Heb. *Ramathî.*] A native or inhabitant of Ramah (1 Chr 27:27), but it is impossible to determine which of the 6 cities in Palestine by the name of Ramah is meant.

Ramath-lehi. See Lehi.

Ramath-mizpeh. See Mizpah, 2.

Rameses (răm'ĕ-sēz). [Heb. *Ra'meses,* a transliteration of the Egyptian *R'-mś-św,* meaning "he whom (the sun-god) Ra has begotten." In transliterated cuneiform the name appears as *Riamashêsha.*]
1. The name of an Egyptian Pharaoh, commonly called Ramses, appearing in the name of an area, "the land of Ram-

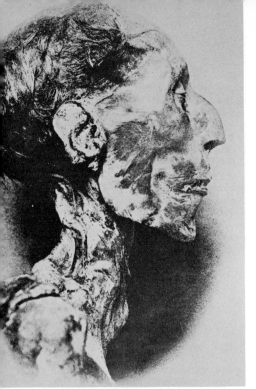

399. The head of the mummy of Pharaoh Ramses II in the Cairo Museum

eses" (Gen 47:11), otherwise called "the country of *Goshen" (v 27). See Rameses, 2.

2. A city built by the Hebrew slaves, called Raamses (rả-ăm'sēz) [Heb. *Ra'ameses*] in Ex 1:11. It was from this city that the Israelites under the leadership of Moses set out for Canaan (Ex 12:37; Num 33:3, 5). Egyptian texts of the 20th dynasty mention a city by the name of *pr-R'mś*, the "House of Ramses," as the residence city of Ramses II. Many Egyptologists identify this with Avaris, the capital of the Hyksos, later called Tanis (Map V, B-3) or *Zoan (Ṣân el-Ḥagar); others identify it with *Qantir*, about 17 mi. southwest of Ṣân el-Ḥagar.

If the Exodus occurred in the 15th cent. B.C. (*see* Chronology II, 2), the names Rameses or Raamses must be considered a modernization of an earlier name, for Ramses II, who gave his name to the city and area, ruled some 200 years later. It would be natural for later scribes to substitute a name in current use for one older and no longer used. For an instance of such a substitution *see* Dan.

Ramiah (rả-mī'ȧ). [Heb. *Ramyah*, "Yahweh is high."] A member of the family of Parosh; he had married a foreign wife in the time of Ezra (Ezr 10:25).

Ramoth (rā'mŏth). [Heb. *Ra'môth* and *Ramoth,* "heights."]

1. A Levite town in Issachar (1 Chr 6:73); *see* Jarmuth, 2.

2. A town in Gilead (Deut 4:43; etc.); *see* Mizpah, 2.

3. A town in the south of Simeon (1 Sa 30:27); *see* Ramah, 6.

4. For Ezr 10:29, KJV, *see* Jeremoth, 8.

Ramoth-gilead. See Mizpah, 2.

Rampart. [Heb. *chel, chêl, meṣûrah,* and *maṣôr.*] A sloping embankment of stone or earth on the outside of a city wall, constructed in such a way at the base as to make it difficult for an enemy to reach the main fortifications of a city (Lam 2:8; Nah 3:8; cf. 2 Sa 20:15; Ps 48:13; Nah 2:1; Zec 9:3; RSV). Cities built in Palestine before the arrival of the Israelites usually had strong ramparts. A portion of the Jebusite ramparts at Jerusalem, built of blocks of stone, has been excavated and is being preserved as a national monument (see fig. 254).

Ranges. A rendering of the Heb. *śederoth* (2 Ki 11:8, 15; 2 Chr 23:14; KJV), an unexplained architectural term, perhaps meaning "row." In 1 Ki 6:9 *śederoth* is translated "boards" (RSV "planks").

Ransom. The rendering of several Hebrew and Greek words meaning variously, "covering," "ransom," "purchase," "ransom price." Moses was instructed that when a national census was taken each one numbered should give a half shekel as "a ransom ["covering"] for his soul" "that there be no plague among them" (Ex 30:12). A ransom price was set to compensate for the life of a person killed by an ox under certain circumstances (ch 21:29, 30). The psalmist stated that no man can ransom (KJV *"redeem") his own soul from the pit (Ps 49:7-9, RSV); only the Lamb of God can purchase us with His own blood (Rev 5:6, 9). Christ came to earth to give His life as a ransom for all (1 Ti 2:6; cf. Mt 20:28; Mk 10:45).

Rapha (rā'fȧ). [Heb. *Rapha',* "He (God) has healed." The name occurs in Assyrian as *Rapâ.*]

1. A son of Benjamin (1 Chr 8:2), probably born in Egypt, since he is not mentioned among Benjamin's sons in Gen 46:21.

2. For 1 Chr 8:37, KJV, *see* Raphah.

Raphah (rā'fȧ), KJV **Rapha** (rā'fȧ). [Heb. *Raphah,* probably a shortened form of *Rephayah,* "Yahweh has healed."] A descendant of King Saul through Jonathan (1 Chr 8:37), called Rephaiah in ch 9:43.

Raphu (rā'fū). [Heb. *Raphû'*, "healed."] A man whose son Palti was the spy who represented the tribe of Benjamin (Num 13:9).

Raven. [Heb. *'oreb;* Gr. *korax.*] A large, glossy-black, iridescent bird, the *Corvus corax.* It resembles the crow but is larger, attaining a length of 26 in. and a weight of 3 lb. The Biblical terms are broad enough to include other black or dusky members of the *Corvidae* family. Noah sent a raven forth from the ark (Gen 8:7), and these voracious birds were miraculously used of God to feed Elijah during a famine (1 Ki 17:4, 6). They are listed as unclean in the Mosaic law (Lev 11:15; Deut 14:14), and are especially mentioned as being the objects of God's care (Job 38:41; Ps 147:9; Lk 12:24). They nest in desolate places (Is 34:11).

Razor. [Heb. *ta'ar* and *môrah.*] A sharp blade, in ancient times usually made of bronze (see fig. 400), for removing the beard or hair (Num 6:5; 8:7, RSV; Jgs 13:5; etc.).

400. An ancient razor of bronze

Reaia. *See* Reaiah, 2.

Reaiah (rē̇-ā'yȧ), KJV once **Reaia** (rē̇-ā'yȧ). [Heb. *Re'ayah,* "Yahweh has seen."]

1. A descendant of Judah, through Shobal (1 Chr 4:2), apparently called Haroeh (hȧ-rō'ĕ) [Heb. *Haro'eh,* "the seeing one"] in ch 2:52.

2. A Reubenite (1 Chr 5:5).

3. The ancestral head of a family of Nethinim, or Temple servants, some members of which returned from Babylonia with Zerubbabel (Ezr 2:47; Neh 7:50).

Reaping. *See* Sickle; see fig. 67.

Reba (rē'bȧ). [Heb. *Reba'.*] One of the 5 Midianite kings who were confederates of the Amorite king Sihon of Heshbon, and who were slain in the war Moses waged against them after they had seduced Israel to licentious idolatry (Num 31:8; Jos 13:21).

Rebecca. *See* Rebekah.

Rebekah (rē̇-bĕk'ȧ), NT **Rebecca** (rē̇-bĕk'ȧ). [Heb. *Ribqah,* meaning uncertain; Gr. *Rhebekka.*] Daughter of Bethuel, Abraham's nephew (Gen 22:23). She lived in Paddan-aram until persuaded by Abraham's servant, who had been sent by his master to seek a wife for Isaac, to accompany him to Canaan to become the wife of Isaac (ch 24:1-67). Finally, 20 years after her marriage, she bore twins, Esau and Jacob (ch 25:19-26). On one occasion when the family dwelt in Gerar, Isaac attempted to pass off Rebekah as his sister (ch 26:6-11), as Abraham his father had done with Sarah many years earlier (ch 12:1-20). Rebekah favored her younger son, Jacob (ch 25:28), and directed him to deceive his blind father so as to obtain the parental blessing that Isaac planned to pronounce upon Esau (ch 27:1-29). Learning that Esau planned to kill his brother for having robbed him of his rights, Rebekah planned Jacob's departure for Paddan-aram and assisted him in his flight (vs 41-46). She seems to have died during the 20 years of Jacob's absence, but the circumstances of her death are not recorded. However, Jacob speaks of his mother as being buried in the Cave of Machpelah (ch 49:31).

Recah (rē'kȧ), KJV **Rechah** (rē'kȧ). [Heb. *Rekah.*] A place in the territory of Judah (1 Chr 4:12); otherwise unknown.

Rechab (rē'kăb). [Heb. *Rekab,* "horseman," "charioteer."]

1. Son of Rimmon (a native of Beeroth), and an army officer under Saul's son Ish-bosheth. He and his brother Baanah murdered Ish-bosheth, and for their treachery were executed by David (2 Sa 4:2-12).

2. A Kenite, who founded a tribe called the Rechabites, and bound his descendants to total abstinence from wine and to a nomadic life (1 Chr 2:55; Jer 35:6). His son or descendant, Jehonadab, or Jonadab, was invited to accompany Jehu to Samaria and witness the new king's zeal for Yahweh in destroying Baal worship (2 Ki 10:15, 16, 23). *See* Rechabites.

3. A man whose son (or descendant ?) Malchijah assisted Nehemiah in rebuilding the wall of Jerusalem (Neh 3:14); possibly, though very unlikely, identical with Rechab, 2.

Rechabites (rĕk′à-bīts). [Heb. *Rekabîm*.] The descendants of Rechab, 2, a Kenite. Obeying the directions of Jonadab, or Jehonadab, son or descendant of Rechab, they abstained from wine and all intoxicating drinks, led a nomadic life in tents, refusing to live in houses, and shunned the possession of fields and vineyards. These regulations were intended to preserve a simplicity of life that had been generally lost in Israel and Judah during the early period of the kings. While in Jerusalem seeking refuge during the invasion of Judah by Nebuchadnezzar, some of the Rechabites were tested by Jeremiah. Finding them true to the regulations of their ancestors, the prophet cited their loyalty as an example worthy of imitation in regard to loyalty toward God (Jer 35: 1-19). Until the recent wholesale migrations to Israel, there were numerous Jews in Syria and Arabia still claiming to be descendants of the Rechabites and to follow their practices to a certain extent. However, a blood relationship to the Biblical Rechabites is uncertain.

Rechah. *See* Recah.

Reconciliation. *See* Atonement.

Recorder. [From a form of the Heb. *zakar,* "to remember."] A high-ranking court official first mentioned in the time of David (2 Sa 8:16; etc.). The recorder was probably the official who issued the king's edicts, took care of his correspondence, and recorded important events. He was one of the officials placed in charge of the Temple repairs in Josiah's reign (2 Chr 34:8).

Red Heifer. *See* Purification, 1.

Red Sea. [Heb. *Yam Sûph,* "sea of reeds." The name "Red Sea" is a literal translation of the Greek term *Eruthra Thalassa,* used in Greek sources (Herod. ii. 8; Jos. *Ant.* ii. 11. 1; 15. 1), and in the LXX and NT as a rendering of the Heb. *Yam Sûph* (Ex 15:4, 22; etc.).] The narrow sea separating the Arabian Peninsula from Africa, divided at its northern end into 2 gulfs separated by the Sinai Peninsula (Map IV, C/D-5/6). The Red Sea from Suez to the Strait of Bab el-Mandeb is about 1,300 mi. long and about 150 mi. wide, but only its 2 northern arms play a role in Biblical history. The western arm, also known by the name of Gulf of Heroonpo-

lis, and now called the Gulf of Suez, is about 180 mi. long, with an average width of about 20 mi. The eastern arm, known as the Gulf of Aqabah, is about 110 mi. long, with an average width of 15 mi. Navigation of the Red Sea was perilous in ancient times because of suddenly rising storms and many hidden coral reefs.

The origin of the names of this sea is not certain. "Red Sea" may come from either the name of a mythological king by the name of Erythras who reigned in that area (Strabo xvi. 3. 5; 4. 20; Pliny *Hist. Nat.* vi. 23), the reddish color of the corals that cover the floor of the sea, the reddish mountains that line its shores, or the Edomite people who lived in an adjacent area (the word Edom means "red"). The Hebrew term meaning "sea of reeds" is equally difficult to explain, for the Red Sea is free of any reeds or sedge. Some have therefore thought that this name originally applied to Lake Timsah or the Bitter Lakes, north of the Gulf of Suez (Map V, B-4), in which reeds are found, and that by extension the name was later transferred to the Red Sea. Others suggest that in very ancient times the Bitter Lakes were connected with the Gulf of Suez, and that the latter received its name "sea of reeds" at the time when its northernmost parts contained reeds. Whatever the correct explanation of the names, it is certain that the Hebrew term *Yam Sûph* and the Greek term *Eruthra Thalassa,* used in the LXX and in the NT, both referred to what is now known as the Red Sea, and not to Lake Timsah or one of the Bitter Lakes as some scholars suggest.

The Red Sea is best known for its connection with the story of the Exodus, as the sea which the Israelites crossed dry shod after the waters had been miraculously divided. The sea that thus provided a way of escape for the hounded Israelites became a watery grave for the Egyptian pursuers (Ex 13:18; 14:21-31; 15:4; etc.). It seems that this crossing took place near the northern end of the Gulf of Suez, although it is difficult to locate the exact spot (*see* Exodus). The Gulf of Aqabah, on the other hand, is evidently the part of the Red Sea referred to in connection with the story of the wilderness wanderings of the Israelites after they had left Mount Sinai (Num 21:4; Deut 1:40; etc.). They touched at Ezion-geber and Elath, 2 places at the northern end of the Gulf of Aqabah (figs. 150, 169), on their way to Transjordan (Deut 2:8; etc.). In Solomon's time Ezion-geber became an important seaport from which the king's naval expeditions departed for the country of Ophir (1 Ki 9:26-28).

Redeem, Redeemer. Generally a rendering of forms of the Heb. *ga'al,* "to ransom," "to buy back," "to recover," and of the Gr. *agorazō,* "to buy," "to purchase," and *lutroō,* "to free by paying a ransom," "to redeem," "to set free," "to rescue." The term "redeem" is used in the sense of: (1) the buying back or ransoming of property or slaves; (2) the release from physical bondage or captivity; (3) the redemption from sin and spiritual bondage. A Hebrew landowner forced, for financial reasons, to sell (actually, lease; *see* Jubilee) his land might redeem it at any time (Lev 25:25). Under certain circumstances produce that would ordinarily be tithe could be redeemed for cash, that is, bought back for personal use (ch 27:31; *see* Tithe). Boaz was willing to redeem the property that had belonged to Naomi's husband (Ruth 4:1-10). God redeemed Israel from Egyptian bondage (Ex 6:6; 2 Sa 7:23; 1 Chr 17:21; etc.) and promised to redeem them from Babylonian captivity (Mic 4:10). God redeems His people from sin (Ps 130:8; Tit 2:14) and the curse (Gal 3:13) and will redeem them from the grave (Hos 13:14; cf. 1 Cor 15:51-54; 1 Th 4:16, 17; etc.). Our redemption is made possible through the sacrifice of Christ (Gal 3:13; 4:4, 5; 1 Pe 1:18, 19; Rev 5:9; etc.).

Reed. [Heb. generally *qaneh,* "reed"; Gr. *kalamos,* "reed," "stalk," "staff."] It is impossible to identify with certainty the various reeds referred to in the Bible. The *Arundo donax,* a stout plant that grows from 8 to 18 ft. tall and has a diameter of from 2 to 3 in. at the base is probably frequently meant. The broken reed which, when leaned upon, splinters and pierces the hand (2 Ki 18:21; Is 36:6) probably is this plant. The reed with which Christ was struck (Mt 27:29, 30), and the reed used when He was offered the drink in the sponge (Mt 27:48; Mk 15:36) may also have been the *Arundo donax. See* Calamus; Flag; Pen.

Reelaiah (rē'ĕl-ā'yȧ). [Heb. *Re'elayah,* "Yahweh has shaken."] One of the leading Jews who accompanied Zerubbabel from Babylonia (Ezr 2:2), apparently identical with Raamiah (rā'ȧ-mī'ȧ) [Heb. *Ra'amyah,* "Yahweh had thundered"] (Neh 7:7).

Refiner. [A form of the Heb. *ṣaraph,* "to smelt," "to refine," "to purify," "to test."] An artisan, whose primary work was to separate the dross from reduced ores. This was accomplished by heating the metal to a liquid state in a crucible (Prov 17:3, RSV) or a *furnace (Eze 22:22), and then, either by oxidation or by adding a flux such as lye (Is 1:25, RSV), removing the foreign substances. Bellows are mentioned among the utensils employed by the refiner (Jer 6:29, RSV), KJV "fining pot" (Prov 17:3; 27:21).

The occupation of the refiner is used figuratively in the OT to illustrate the activity of God as He seeks to remove the dross of iniquity from His people, sometimes finding it necessary to employ the "furnace of affliction" in an endeavor to purify to Himself a holy people (Is 1:25; 48:10; Zec 13:9; Mal 3:2, 3).

Refuge. *See* City of Refuge.

Regem (rē'gĕm). [Heb. *Regem,* meaning uncertain.] A descendant of the Caleb who was a son of Hezron (1 Chr 2:47).

Regem-melech (rē'gĕm-mē'lĕk). [Heb. *Regem Melek,* "Regem is king."] One of a delegation sent by the postexilic inhabitants of Bethel to the priests in Jerusalem with an inquiry about the necessity of further observance of certain fasts (Zec 7:2, 3).

Regeneration. [Gr. *paliggenesia,* "rebirth," "regeneration."] An expression used: (1) of the new birth that accompanies conversion (Tit 3:5); (2) of the renewing of the world at the advent of Christ (Mt 19:28).

Rehabiah (rē'hȧ-bī'ȧ). [Heb. *Rechabyah* and *Rechabyahû,* "Yahweh has enlarged."] Son of Eliezer and grandson of Moses (1 Chr 23:17; 24:21; 26:25).

Rehob (rē'hŏb). [Heb. *Rechob,* "open space," "wide street."]

1. A city in northern Palestine (Num 13:21). *See* Beth-rehob.

2. A boundary town of Asher (Jos 19:28), not yet identified.

3. A Canaanite city in the territory of Asher (Jos 19:30) that must be sought in the plain of Acco, identified by some with *Tell el-Gharbī* (also known as *Tell Berweh*), 6 mi. east of Acco (Albright, *AASOR* II-III [1923], 28). It was assigned to the Levites (Jos 21:31; 1 Chr 6:75). The Israelites could not at first expel the Canaanites from the city (Jgs 1:31). Some have identified this city with Rehob, 2.

4. Father of King Hadadezer of Zobah (2 Sa 8:3, 12).

5. A Levite who set his seal to Nehemiah's covenant (Neh 10:11).

Rehoboam (rē'hō-bō'ăm). KJV of NT **Roboam** (rō-bō'ăm). [Heb. *Rechab'am,* meaning either "the people have been enlarged" or "(the god) *'Am* has enlarged"; Gr. *Rhoboam.*] The son of Solomon by his Ammonite wife Naamah. He began to reign at the age of 41 as the 1st king of the southern kingdom of Judah, after the division (1 Ki 11:43; 14:21), and reigned 17 years (*c.* 931 - *c.* 913 B.C.). At his accession representatives of the nation assembled at Shechem, the most centrally located city of the country, to crown the new king. However, led by Jeroboam, they first demanded that the public burdens be alleviated. Rehoboam, promising to give his answer after 3 days, in the meantime sought counsel of both old and young advisers of the realm. Finally he rejected the counsel of the old men, who urged him to grant the people's justified requests, and accepted the advice of younger men, brought up with him, who advised him to refuse the people's demands. He defied the petitioners by declaring that he would lash them with scorpions instead of with whips as his father had done. The result was that all the northern and eastern tribes of Israel broke with the house of David and made Jeroboam their king. Rehoboam tried to bring the rebellious tribes back by sending Adoniram, the officer over forced labor, to arbitrate. This man, however, apparently because of violent hatred, was immediately killed. Rehoboam, now recognizing the seriousness of the situation, returned to Jerusalem and began at once to make military preparations for war against Jeroboam, to bring the rebellious tribes back by force, and desisted only when the prophet Shemaiah in the name of God forbade the proposed assault (1 Ki 11: 43 to 12:24; 2 Chr 9:31 to 11:4). Nevertheless, there were acts of warfare between the two nations during the later years of Rehoboam's reign (1 Ki 14:30).

In Rehoboam's 5th year Pharaoh Shishak (Sheshonk I, the 1st king of the 22d dynasty of Egypt), took advantage of the division of Solomon's kingdom to invade Palestine in order to rebuild Egypt's lost Asiatic empire. Shishak took many of the fortified cities of Judah, conquered Jerusalem, and carried away the treasures accumulated during the reigns of David and Solomon (1 Ki 14:25-28; 2 Chr 12:1-9). Rehoboam refortified key cities of his country in order to strengthen its defenses against outside dangers (2 Chr 11:5-12).

Rehoboam's character showed that he had inherited both good and bad traits from his father. He obeyed the prophet Shemaiah by refraining from fighting

against Jeroboam (1 Ki 12:24; 2 Chr 11: 4); he humbled himself before God at the time of Shishak's invasion (2 Chr 12:6, 12); he received into his kingdom the priests and Levites who were driven out from the northern kingdom by the introduction of Jeroboam's calf worship at Bethel and Dan (ch 11:11-17). Yet after he had served God for 3 years (v 17), he "did evil" (ch 12:14) by allowing the building of pagan high places, tolerating the practice of immoral rites, and worshiping foreign gods (1 Ki 14:22-24). Rehoboam had 18 wives, 60 concubines, 28 sons, and 60 daughters (2 Chr 11:21).

Rehoboth (rê-hō′bŏth). [Heb. *Rechobóth,* "open spaces," "streets."]

1. A well dug by Isaac in the valley of Gerar, so named because his possession of this well remained uncontested in contrast with the others he had dug (Gen 26:22). Its location has been identified with *Ruheibeh,* about 27 mi. southeast of Raphia (Map VI, F-2).

2. A town "by the river" (Gen 36:37; 1 Chr 1:48). Usually the expression "the river" refers to the Euphrates, and the RSV so translates it in both these verses. There is a *Rahaba* on the left bank of the Euphrates not far from the river *Khâbûr.* However, unless the king of Edom who came from this city was a foreigner, Rehoboth must have been in Edom. "The river" in these passages could refer to the Zered or to some other stream flowing into the Dead Sea. The site is unknown.

3. A place in Assyria. *See* Rehoboth-Ir.

Rehoboth-Ir (rê-hō′bŏth-ĭr). [Heb.. *Rechoboth 'Ir,* "broad places of the city."] According to the RSV a town built by Nimrod in Assyria (Gen 10:11, KJV "the city Rehoboth"), probably *rêbit Ninâ,* "suburb of Nineveh," mentioned in certain cuneiform texts, but it is not known which suburb is meant (F. Delitzsch, *Wo lag das Paradies?* [Leipzig, 1881], pp. 260, 261).

Rehum (rē′hŭm). [Heb. *Rechûm,* "compassionated (by God)." The name occurs in the Aramaic papyri from Elephantine.]

1. An official of the Persian administration (probably of Samaria) who complained to Artaxerxes about the rebuilding of the wall of Jerusalem (Ezr 4:8. 9, 17).

2. One of the leaders of the exiles who returned from Babylonia with Zerubbabel (Ezr 2:2); called Nehum in Neh 7:7 (the letters *n* and *r* are somewhat similar in postexilic Hebrew).

3. One of the leading priests who re-

turned from Babylonia with Zerubbabel (Neh 12:1, 3, 7). In the next generation a priestly house named in the same relative position in the list is spelled Harim in v 15 (probably a transposition of the Hebrew letters *ch* and *r* in the name).

4. A Levite of the family of Bani; he helped Nehemiah to repair the wall of Jerusalem (Neh 3:17).

5. A leading Jew who set his seal to Nehemiah's covenant (Neh 10:25).

Rei (rē'ī). [Heb. *Re'i*, "friend."] One of David's courtiers who did not join in Adonijah's attempt to usurp the throne (1 Ki 1:8).

Reins. [Heb. generally *kelayôth*, "kidneys"; Gr. *nephroi*, "kidneys."] An archaic English word in the KJV meaning "kidneys" or "loins." The ancients considered the kidneys the seat of human emotions (Ps 7:9; 26:2; 73:21; etc.; RSV "heart" or "hearts").

Rekem (rē'kĕm). [Heb. *Reqem*, "variegation."]

1. One of the 5 kings of Midian allied with Sihon, the Amorite king of Heshbon. He was slain by the Israelites in the war against the Midianites after the incident of Baal-peor (Num 31:8; Jos 13:21).

2. A son of Hebron, and a descendant of Caleb son of Hezron (1 Chr 2:43).

3. A town in the territory of Benjamin (Jos 18:27), probably to be identified with *el-Burǧ*, near *en-Nebī-Samwil*.

Release, Year of. *See* Sabbatical Year.

Religion. A rendering of: (1) The Gr. *thrēskeia* (Acts 26:5; Jas 1:26, 27), "worship of God," "religion," from *thrēskeuō*, "to practice religious observances," "to worship." The term denotes reverence or worship, especially such worship as finds expression in ritual acts. In Col 2:18 the KJV translates *thrēskeia*, "worshipping" (RSV "worship"). (2) The Gr. *eusebeia* (1 Ti 3:16; 2 Ti 3:5; RSV), "piety," "godliness," "religion" (KJV "godliness"). (3) The Gr. *theosebeia* (1 Ti 2:10, RSV), "reverence for God," "piety" (KJV "godliness"). (4) In Gal 1:13, 14, KJV, the term *Ioudaismos*, "Judaism," is rendered "Jews' religion."

Remaliah (rĕm'à-lī'à). [Heb. *Remalyahû*, meaning uncertain. The name occurs on an ancient Hebrew seal.] Father of King Pekah of Israel (2 Ki 15:25; Is 7:1, 4, 5; etc.).

Remeth (rē'mĕth). [Heb. *Remeth*, "high place."] A town in the territory of Issachar (Jos 19:21), probably identical with the Levite city of Ramoth (1 Chr 6:73), apparently called also Jarmuth (Jos 21:28, 29). *See* Jarmuth, 2; Ramoth, 1.

Remission. *See* Forgive.

Remmon. *See* Rimmon, 2.

Remmon-methoar. *See* Rimmon, 3.

Remnant. [Heb. chiefly *she'ar* and related terms and *yether*, "what is left over," "what remains," "remainder," "remnant"; Gr. *leimma, kataleimma,* and *loipos,* "what remains," "what is left."] As used in the OT, generally Israelites who survived such calamities as war, captivity, pestilence, and famine, and whom God in mercy spared to continue to be His chosen people (Gen 45:7, RSV; 2 Ki 19:31; Ezr 9:13; etc.). As a result of apostasies the Israelites repeatedly throughout their history suffered major catastrophes that brought their nation to the verge of extinction. Again and again they were "left but a few of [from] many" (see Jer 42:2; cf. Is 10:22). Remembering the true God and turning once more to Him (2 Chr 30:6; Is 10:20; Eze 6:8, 9; etc.), the remnant turned their back on iniquity (cf. Zep 3:13, KJV), and pledged themselves to be loyal to God's commandments (Ezr 9:14; 10:3-12). Accepting anew the responsibilities and privileges of the everlasting covenant, they set themselves to "take root downward," to "bear fruit upward," and to "go forth" declaring His glory among the Gentiles (2 Ki 19:30, 31; Is 37:31, 32; cf. Is 66:19). The "remnant" of OT times was thus the body of God's chosen people in successive generations. Again and again the majority apostatized (cf. Ps 78), but after each apostasy there was a faithful "remnant" that became exclusive heirs to the sacred promises, privileges, and responsibilities of the covenant originally made with Abraham and confirmed at Sinai. God designated this "remnant" as the group to whom He purposed to send the Messiah (Is 11:1; cf. chs 4:2; 53:2), and through whom He proposed to evangelize the heathen (cf. Joel 2:32). In Rom 9 to 11 Paul presents the Christian church as heirs of the promises, privileges, and responsibilities of the everlasting covenant, the successor to Judaism as trustee of God's revealed will, as the corporate representative of His purposes on earth, and as His chosen instrument for the proclamation of the gospel for the salvation of men. In Rom 9:27 Paul applies the term "remnant" to the Jews of his day who, individually, accepted Christ as the Messiah. But now it was as members of the

Christian church, and no longer as Jews, that they had right to this title. In Rom 11:5 Paul speaks of these Christian Jews as "a remnant according to . . . grace." The "remnant" of Rev 12:17 is the group of God's faithful ones, the remnant of that long and worthy line that has survived the fierce onslaughts of Satan down through the history of Christian times, particularly the darkness, persecution, and error of the Middle Ages.

Remphan. *See* Rephan.

Repent, Repentance. [Heb. generally *nacham*, "to be sorry," "to repent," "to comfort oneself"; Gr. generally *metanoeō*, "to change one's mind," "to feel remorse," "to repent," "to be converted," and *metanoia*, "a change of mind," "a turning about," "repentance," "conversion."] As a theological term, the act of forsaking sin, accepting God's gracious gift of salvation, and entering into fellowship with God. True repentance implies a radical change in attitude toward sin and God. It is God's gracious goodness that leads men to repentance (Rom 2:4), working in them "both to will and to do of his good pleasure" (Php 2:13). Repentance is preceded by the conviction of the Holy Spirit, who impresses upon the sinner's heart God's infinite righteousness and the sinner's own lost state (cf. Is 6:5; Acts 2:37). Conviction is followed by contrition, and by an inner acknowledgment of one's need of divine grace, coupled with a spirit of willingness that God shall work out His righteous will in one's life (cf. Ps 34:18; 51:17; Is 57:15; 66:2). Repentance merges into, and reaches its climax in, conversion (Acts 3:19). "Repent" is also used in a nontheological sense of "to change one's mind," "to regret." It is in the sense of regret that God is said to repent (1 Sa 15:11; Jer 18:8; etc.). He cannot change His purpose, but man, being a free moral agent, can change the outworking of God's purpose.

Rephael (rē'fá-ĕl). [Heb. *Repha'el*, "God has healed."] A postexilic gatekeeper of the family of Obed-edom (1 Chr 26:7).

Rephah (rē'fá). [Heb. *Rephach*, "easy (life)."] A descendant of Ephraim and ancestor of Joshua (1 Chr 7:25-27).

Rephaiah (rė-fā'yá). [Heb. *Rephayah*, "Yahweh has healed." The name occurs in Assyrian documents as *Rapaya*.]

1. A descendant of Issachar (1 Chr 7:2).

2. A descendant of King Saul through Jonathan (1 Chr 9:43). The name occurs in 1 Chr 8:37 in the shorter form Raphah (KJV "Rapha").

3. A postexilic descendant of King David (1 Chr 3:21).

4. One of the Simeonite chieftains who defeated the remnants of the Amalekites in Mount Seir and occupied their territory (1 Chr 4:42, 43).

5. One of the district rulers of Jerusalem who assisted Nehemiah in rebuilding the city wall (Neh 3:9).

Rephaim (rĕf'á-ĭm), KJV twice **Rephaims** (rĕf'á-ĭmz). [Heb. *Repha'îm*. This Hebrew term is frequently translated *"giants" in the KJV.] One of the groups of the original inhabitants of Canaan in Transjordan, mentioned first in the time of Abraham (Gen 14:5; 15:20). They lived in the area later occupied by the Moabites and the Ammonites and were called Emims by the Moabites (Deut 2:10, 11), and Zamzummims by the Ammonites (vs 20, 21). In the patriarchal age King Chedorlaomer and his confederates, whose invasion of Transjordan is recorded in Gen 14, subdued them (v 5). Some Rephaim are mentioned by name, such as Og, king of Bashan, who belonged to the remnant of Rephaim, whose "bedstead of iron" (believed rather to have been a sarcophagus of basalt)—was 9 cu. long and 4 cu. wide (Deut 3:11; Jos 12:4, 5; 13:12), and Sippai of Gezer (1 Chr 20:4). These verses show that the Rephaim were taller than most of the other people that were known to the Israelites, and that the translation "giants," found frequently in the KJV, is justified. Commentators suggest that the Rephaim may have built the many megalithic monuments found in Transjordan, especially the "dolmens" on the mountaintops. These last were large tombs built of tremendous slabs of stone in the form of small huts, 4 slabs forming the walls and 1 the roof (see fig. 401). Since not one of these tombs has been found in an undisturbed condition, and no uten-

401. Large stone structure (dolmen) erected by ancient people of Transjordan

sils or pieces of pottery have been recovered from them, it is unknown by whom and at what time these structures were erected.

Rephaim (rĕf'á-ĭm), **Valley of,** KJV twice **Valley of the Giants.** [Heb. *'Emeq-Repha'im.*] A wide valley (Jos 15:8), probably the one running from Jerusalem in a southwesterly direction toward Kiriath-jearim and Beth-shemesh (Map I, C-2), now called the *Baqa'.* It lay on the boundary line between Judah and Benjamin (chs 15:8; 18:16). David twice defeated the Philistines in this valley (2 Sa 5:18-25; 1 Chr 14:9). Rephaim may once have dwelt there, whence probably its name.

Rephaims. *See* Rephaim.

Rephan (rē'făn), KJV **Remphan** (rĕm'făn). [Gr. *Rhephan,* though the manuscripts vary between this and *Rhaiphan, Rhempham, Rhomphan, Rhempha, Rhemphan, Rhompha.*] A star-god worshiped by the ancient Israelites according to Acts 7:43. This verse is a quotation from the LXX of Amos 5:26. The corresponding Hebrew name is *Kywn,* vocalized by the Masoretes as *Kîyûn,* by which probably one of the Babylonian names of Saturn is meant. It has been thought that the Alexandrian translators of the LXX used an Egyptian term for Saturn, but no Egyptian word similar to the Greek term is known.

Rephidim (rĕf'ĭ-dĭm). [Heb. *Rephidim,* "expanses."] A camping place of the Israelites between the Wilderness of Sin and Sinai. There Moses provided water for the whole camp by striking a rock, and there the Amalekites, who attacked the Israelites, were defeated (Ex 17:1, 5, 6, 8-16; 19:2; Num 33:12-15). The exact site is still uncertain. Some scholars identify Rephidim with the *Wâdî Refâyid,* a valley northwest of Jebel Musa (Map V, D-5), but the traditional site is in the *Wâdî Feirân* at the foot of *Jebel Serbal,* a mountain some 25 mi. northwest of the traditional Mount Sinai (Map V, D-5). A hill rising 700 ft. above the valley is pointed out as the eminence on which Moses stood with Aaron and Hur watching the battle and praying for Israel's victory (Ex 17:9-12). In the valley below are some lush gardens, also many ruins from the early centuries of the Christian Era, when a town situated there was the seat of a bishopric. The early Christians identified Rephidim with Paran, whence the name *Feirân.* See figs. 370, 402.

402. The traditional mountain on which Moses, Aaron, and Hur are said to have stood at Rephidim, during the battle of the Israelites with the Amalekites

Reptile. A type of living thing, distinguished from beast, bird, and fish in that it does not walk or run upright on two or four legs, does not fly, and does not propel itself through the water by means of fins. Rather it crawls on its belly or creeps upon short, stubby legs. Modern classification limits reptiles to cold-blooded vertebrates with these characteristics. The Heb. *remeś,* translated "reptile" in 1 Ki 4:33, RSV, is generally rendered *"creeping things," but in the context "reptile" is an allowable translation. In his discourses Solomon revealed his knowledge of these creatures. In the NT "reptile" is a rendering of the Gr. *herpeton.* Reptiles were among the creatures that were shown Peter in a vision (Acts 10:12; 11:6), and are mentioned by both Paul and James in their listings of various types of creatures (Rom 1:23; Jas 3:7).

Rereward. The KJV spelling of "rearward," from Anglo-French *rere-warde,* meaning "rear guard," that is, a company of soldiers assigned to protect the rear of an army on the march (Num 10:25; Jos 6:9, 13; 1 Sa 29:2; Is 52:12; 58:8; KJV).

Resen (rē'sĕn). [Heb. *Resen.*] An early city of Assyria founded by Nimrod (Gen 10:11, 12), situated between Calah and Nineveh on the Tigris; not yet identified.

Reservoir. The translation of the Heb. *miqwah* in Is 22:11, RSV (KJV "ditch"). Reference is made here probably to the Pool of Siloam constructed by King Hezekiah between the southern wall of the City of David and the "second wall" that he erected to the south of it. Some think that the Hebrew term refers to the tunnel the king built to conduct the waters from the old pool at Gihon to the new pool.

Resh. [Heb. *rêsh*.] The 20th letter of the Hebrew alphabet, written ר, appearing as the title to the 20th section of Ps 119 in the KJV. *See* Aleph.

Resheph (rē′shĕf). [Heb. *Resheph*, "flame." The name occurs in ancient secular literature as that of a Canaanite god.] A descendant of Ephraim (1 Chr 7:25).

Rest. A term used variously of: (1) The rest of the Sabbath. After completing the work of Creation, God "rested," that is, He ceased from His work. He did not need to be refreshed, for He "fainteth not, neither is weary" (Is 40:28). The Sabbath thus became a "rest" for man (Ex 16:23; 31:15; 35:2; etc.). (2) The rest God promised the Israelite nation (ch 33:14), outwardly signifying cessation from wandering as a nation without a country, freedom from war (cf. Deut 12:9, 10), and settlement. However, according to Heb 4:3-9, more than physical rest was involved. Joshua gave the nation "rest" (Deut 3:18-20; Jos 21:44; 23:1), but because of rebellion and apostasy (cf. Jgs 2:11, 12; 10:6; 2 Ki 17:9-20; Jer 7:30; Eze 3:7; etc.) the people did not at any period find the spiritual rest God had planned for them (Heb 4:8, 9, RSV). The Israelites were finally excluded as a nation from this "rest" (Heb 4:5, 6; cf. Mt 21:43; etc.). This spiritual rest is available to the Christian church (Heb 4:3, 9-11; cf. v 1). (3) An inward rest of soul, which Christ offers each individual (Mt 11:28, 29). This rest is an experience not dependent on outward conditions but on a supreme trust in Jesus (see Jn 14:17; Php 4:6, 7; etc.). (4) The cessation from persecution the Christian will receive at the second coming of Christ (2 Th 1:6, 7).

Resurrection. [Gr. *anastasis*, "arising," "a resurrection"; *exanastasis*, "arising out of [the grave]"; *egersis*, "a raising," "resurrection."] The restoration of life, together with fullness of being and personality, subsequent to death. The ultimate effect of sin is death (Rom 6:23), and "all have sinned" (ch 3:23). The ultimate effect

of salvation from sin is eternal life (Jn 3:15-17). But once death has occurred, there must be a resurrection from the dead in order that the one who has found release from sin through Jesus Christ may enter upon eternal life. Accordingly, the devout Christian looks forward to the "hope of eternal life" promised "before the world began" (Tit 1:2; cf. ch 3:7). Because it was not explicitly taught in the 5 books of Moses (cf. Jos. *Ant.* xviii. 1. 4), the Sadducees rejected the doctrine of the resurrection (Mt 22:23; Acts 23:8). On the other hand, the Pharisees and the Jews generally believed in "a resurrection of the dead, both of the just and unjust" (Acts 24:15; cf. ch 23:6-8). Whereas the resurrection is implicitly, and at times explicitly, stated in the OT (see Job 14:13-15; 19:25-27; Ps 16:11; 17:15; 49:15; 73:24; Is 26:19; Dan 12:2), it was not until NT times, when the resurrection of Jesus Christ made the doctrine a concrete reality, that teaching on this most important subject became clear and full (1 Cor 15:3-56; 1 Th 4:13-17; Rev 20:4-6, 11-15; cf. Mt 22:23-33; Jn 5:25-29; 11:23-26). Indeed, without the hope of the resurrection the whole fabric of the Christian faith ravels out (see 1 Cor 15:14-19).

Isaiah's declaration, "Thy dead men shall live, together with my dead body shall they arise" (Is 26:19), is the first clear and unambiguous declaration concerning the resurrection as such, though Job, earlier, had looked forward with faith and hope for that great event (Job 14:13-17; 19:25-27). The first explicit statement that some, at least, of the wicked, as well as the righteous, would come forth in the resurrection is found in Dan 12:2. Compared with the NT, however, OT references to the resurrection are comparatively few and brief, doubtless because this great truth was not clearly understood before the resurrection of our Lord had demonstrated the possibility and the reality of the resurrection.

Our Lord ever made the future life, with its reward for rightdoing, prominent in His teaching (Mt 16:27; 25:31-46; Lk 16:19-31; etc.). In addressing a Pharisee, He explained that the reward for a compassionate interest in the needs of one's fellow men would be awarded by God "at the resurrection of the just" (Lk 14:12-14). Speaking to some of the Jewish leaders, He declared that the hour would come "when the dead shall hear the voice of the Son of God: and they that hear shall live" (Jn 5:25). In fact, "all that are in the graves shall hear his voice, and shall come forth; they that have done good, unto the resurrection of life; and they that have done evil, unto the resurrection of damnation" (Jn 5:28, 29).

It was the certainty of Christ's resurrection that brought point and power to the preaching of the gospel (cf. Php 3:10, 11). Peter speaks of "the resurrection of Jesus Christ from the dead" as producing a "lively hope" in believers (1 Pe 1:3). The apostles considered themselves ordained to be witnesses "of his resurrection" (Acts 1:22), and based their teaching of the resurrection of Christ on the Messianic predictions of the OT (ch 2:31). It was their personal knowledge of "the resurrection of the Lord Jesus" that gave "great power" to their witness (ch 4:33). The apostles drew the opposition of the Jewish leaders when they went forth preaching "through Jesus the resurrection from the dead" (v 2). To the philosophical Greeks the idea "of the resurrection of the dead" was nonsense (ch 17:18, 32). When arraigned before the Sanhedrin, Paul declared that it was because of his "hope and resurrection of the dead" that he had been "called in question" before them (ch 23:6; cf. ch 24:21). To the Romans, Paul wrote that Jesus Christ was "declared to be the Son of God with power . . . by the resurrection from the dead" (Rom 1:4). In baptism, he explained, the Christian testifies to his faith in the resurrection of Christ (ch 6:4, 5).

The great NT treatise on the resurrection is found in 1 Cor 15. Here Paul dwells at length upon the certainty of the resurrection and its vital importance in the Christian's belief and faith (vs 1-22), upon the time of the resurrection (v 23), and its manner (vs 35-56). He opens his discussion by enumerating the witnesses to the resurrection of our Lord (vs 4-8), and goes on to show that the gospel of Christ is altogether vain, and the Christian's faith is also vain (v 14), "if Christ be not risen" and "if there be no resurrection of the dead" (vs 14, 13). He predicates the resurrection of the righteous on the prior resurrection of Christ, the one being as certain as the other (vs 13-22). "They that are Christ's," he says, are to "be made alive" "at his coming" (vs 22, 23). He declares the resurrection body to be "a spiritual body" differing in certain essential respects from our present bodies, but nonetheless real (vs 35-44, 49, 50). In vs 51-54 he states that the change from mortality to immortality that

takes place at the resurrection will be instantaneous. John the revelator speaks of the righteous dead coming to life and reigning with Christ for a thousand years (Rev 20:4-6), and of the wicked dead rising at the close of the thousand years (vs 5, 12, 13) to stand in judgment before God (vs 11, 13, 15). See Death; Millennium; Soul.

Reu (rē′ū), KJV of NT **Ragau** (rā′gô). [Heb. *Re'û,* probably "friend." The name occurs in Assyrian texts as *Ra'û;* Gr. *Rhagau.*] A descendant of Eber and an ancestor of Abraham (Gen 11:18-21; 1 Chr 1:25; Lk 3:35). The city of *Rugulihi* in Upper Mesopotamia may have been named in his honor, for several ancient cities in that area bore names commemorating Abraham's ancestors or relatives.

Reuben (rōō′bĕn). [Heb. *Re'ûben,* "behold a son"; Gr. *Rhoubēn.*]

1. The eldest son of Jacob and Leah (Gen 29:31, 32; 35:23; 46:8; 1 Chr 2:1; 5:1). As to his life history, he is mentioned first as finding mandrakes in the field, which Rachel desired (Gen 30:14); next for his immorality with Bilhah (ch 35:22) for which he later lost his father's blessings that would have been due him as the first-born (ch 49:3, 4); third, for his attempt to save Joseph from his murderous brothers by inducing them to throw him into a cistern instead (ch 37:21-29). Although he did not betray his brothers to their father, he was not a partner in their plot against Joseph (ch 42:22). Later, when Jacob feared to send Benjamin to Egypt, Reuben offered 2 of his own sons as guarantees for Benjamin's safety (v 37). On his deathbed Jacob expressed the disappointment that his first-born son's conduct had caused him, and described his character as being unstable as water (ch 49:3, 4). Reuben's sons were Hanoch, Pallu, Hezron, and Carmi (Gen 46:8, 9; Ex 6:14; 1 Chr 5:3).

2. The tribe descended from Jacob's eldest son. It consisted of 4 tribal families, the descendants of Reuben's 4 sons (Num 26:5). In the 1st census 46,500 Reubenites were counted as ready for war (ch 1:20, 21); a later census showed a reduction in strength to 43,730 fighting men (ch 26:7). The tribal prince during the early part of the wilderness wanderings was Elizur, who was also head of the section of that camp where Reubenites, Simeonites, and Gadites pitched their tents (chs 1:5; 2:10-16; 7:30-35; 10:18). The tribe of Reuben was represented among the 12 spies by Shammua, son of Zaccur (ch

13:4). Some prominent members of the tribe—Dathan, Abiram, and On—joined the rebellion of Korah against Moses and Aaron and consequently lost their lives (Num 16:1-50; 26:9, 10; Deut 11:6). After the conquest of the territory of the Amorite kings Sihon of Heshbon and Og of Bashan, the tribes of Reuben and Gad and half of Manasseh requested that these areas be assigned to them, since they had many cattle and found this land suitable for grazing. Moses granted their request on condition that they help their brethren in the conquest of Canaan, west of the Jordan. After the military campaigns were completed under Joshua's leadership, these 2½ tribes returned to their territories in Transjordan (Num 32:1-42; Jos 4:12; 18:7; 22:1-6). When they set up a memorial altar at the Jordan, the other tribes mistook this for a secession from the confederacy, with the result that a civil war was narrowly averted (Jos 22:1-34).

The territory of the Reubenites was bounded on the south by the river Arnon, which formed the northern boundary of Moab; on the east by the Ammonites, and on the west by the Dead Sea and the lower course of the river Jordan. The northern boundary ran from the Jordan, south of Beth-nimrah, to Heshbon (Num 32:36, 37; Jos 13:15-21). Four cities within their territory—Bezer, Jahaz, Kedemoth, and Mephaath, with their suburbs—were assigned as residence cities to the Merarite Levites (Jos 21:7, 36, 37; 1 Chr 6:63, 78, 79), and the 1st of them, Bezer, was at the same time a city of refuge (Jos 20: 8; 1 Chr 6:78). See Map VI, E-4.

The proximity of the Reubenites to the Moabites and Ammonites must have influenced the tribe, for they did not play an important role in the subsequent history of the nation of Israel. They are mentioned in the period of the judges only once, namely in the Song of Deborah and Barak, which rebukes the Reubenites for having failed to assist the western tribes in their struggle against Jabin and Sisera (Jgs 5:15, 16; cf. ch 4:2). With their fellow tribes in Transjordan they at one time waged a successful war against the Hagrites, and occupied their territory until the Assyrian captivity (1 Chr 5:18-22). This success may have compensated for the losses Reuben suffered from the hands of the Moabites, for it is quite obvious (from the towns mentioned in Is 15; 16; and Jer 48; and the *Moabite Stone) that all the territory of Reuben was occupied by the Moabites from the

9th cent. B.C. on (Maps IX, X, E-4). Nothing is learned of the fate of the Reubenites after the loss of their land, although 1 Chr 5:22 indicates that they continued to live in the former territory of the Hagrites until the Exile, so retained their tribal identity at least to the middle of the 8th cent. B.C. It was Tiglath-pileser III (745-727 B.C.) who carried the remnants of the Reubenites into captivity (v 26). From that time on they are not mentioned. Ezekiel allotted Reuben a place in the ideal Canaan as he envisioned it for the future (Eze 48:6, 7), and Reuben is one of the 12 tribes said by John to be sealed by the angel of Rev 7 (v 5).

Reubenites (rōō'bĕn-īts). [Heb. *Re'ûbenî.*] Descendants of Reuben, 1 (Num 26:7; etc.); *see* Reuben, 2.

Reuel (rōō'ĕl), KJV once **Raguel** (rȧ-gū'ĕl). [Heb. *Re'û'el,* "friend of God."]

1. A descendant of Esau and of Ishmael (Gen 36:2-4, 10, 13, 17; 1 Chr 1: 35, 37).

2. Moses' father-in-law (Ex 2:18, 21; Num 10:29). See Jethro.

3. A Benjamite (1 Chr 9:8).

4. A Gadite (Num 2:14). See Deuel.

Reumah (rōō'mȧ). [Heb. *Re'ûmah,* "exalted." The name occurs in Akkadian as *Ra'amu.*] A concubine of Nahor, Abraham's brother (Gen 22:24).

Revelation, The. [Gr. *Apokalupsis,* "apocalypse," "disclosure," "unveiling," "something revealed."] The last book of the NT, to which its author, John, gives the title, "The Revelation of Jesus Christ" (ch 1:1). In the earliest extant Greek manuscripts the title reads simply, *Apokalupsis Iōannou,* "Apocalypse of John," more elaborate titles coming from later centuries. In religious literature the term *apokalupsis* refers to the unveiling of the future, especially through the medium of symbolic prophecy. Daniel and Zechariah are the OT counterparts of the Revelation in the NT. During the intertestamental and early Christian periods, many other non-Biblical apocalyptic treatises were produced by the Jews, the pseudepigraphical works known as First Enoch and the Sibylline Oracles being noteworthy examples of this type of literary activity (*see* Pseudepigrapha). While the Western church accepted the Revelation as Scripture from the very first, for centuries the churches in Egypt, Palestine, and Syria generally rejected its claim to a place in the sacred canon, and it was not until the close of the 4th cent. that the last book of the NT as we know it today was generally accepted in the East. The first Christian writer to refer expressly to the Revelation was Justin Martyr (c. A.D. 140). The first known commentary on it was written about A.D. 170 by Melito of Sardis, the church in his city being one of the churches mentioned in the Apocalypse. Cyprian of Carthage, about the middle of the 3d cent., highly honored the Apocalypse, while Eusebius of Caesarea (died c. A.D. 340) was not sure about its authenticity, but permitted its reading. Gregory of Nazianzus (died A.D. ?389) published a list of NT books omitting the Revelation, as did Cyril of Jerusalem (died A.D. 386). It was not until the "Easter Letter" of Athanasius in A.D. 367 that the 27 books now composing the NT were all mentioned together as canonical.

The author of the Revelation identifies himself simply as "John" (see chs 1:1, 4, 9; 21:2, KJV; 22:8), "your brother" (ch 1:9). Apparently he was so well known that he did not consider it necessary to identify himself further in order to secure the confidence of its intended readers. All Christian writers until the middle of the 3d cent. whose works are extant today and who mention the matter at all, attribute it to John the apostle. Among these writers were Justin Martyr (died c. A.D. 165; *Dialogue With Trypho* 81), Irenaeus (died c. A.D. 202; *Against Heresies* iv. 20. 11; 30. 4; v. 26. 1; 35. 2; etc.), Tertullian (died c. A.D. 240; *The Prescription Against Heretics* 36; *Against Marcion* iii. 14. 3; etc.), Hippolytus (died c. A.D. 235; *Treatise on Christ and Antichrist*, xxxvi), Clement of Alexandria (died c. A.D. 220; *Who Is the Rich Man That Shall Be Saved?* xlii), and Origen (died c. A.D. 254; *Commentary on John* I. 14). Irenaeus (*op. cit.* iii. 3. 4; *ANF*, vol. 1, p. 416) mentions also that the apostle John was living in Ephesus until the days of the emperor Trajan (A.D. 98-117), and Polycrates (died c. A.D. 200) testifies that he was buried there (*Epistle to Victor and the Roman Church Concerning the Day of Keeping the Passover; ANF*, vol. 8, p. 773). These statements coincide with the fact that John addressed himself to Ephesus and the other churches of Asia (Rev 1:4, 11).

However, a certain statement by Papias (died c. A.D. 163), as quoted by the church historian Eusebius (*Hist. Eccl.* iii. 39. 3, 4; Loeb ed., vol. 1, pp. 291, 293), who died c. A.D. 340, has been interpreted to mean that the apostle John died long before the close of the 1st cent. Unfortunately the works of Papias have been lost, and all that is known of what he wrote exists today in highly fragmentary form in quotations preserved by Eusebius and other writers. However, conclusions based on this ambiguous statement of Papias are, at best, highly conjectural. The first serious challenge to Johannine authorship was raised by Dionysius of Alexandria (died c. A.D. 265; see Eusebius *Hist. Eccl.* vii. 24, 25). Because of substantial literary differences between the Revelation and the Gospel of John, he concluded that the 2 works could not have come from one man. For instance, the word *pisteuō*, "to believe," occurs 100 times in the Gospel, and not once in the Revelation; *kosmos*, "world," 79 times in John, and 3 times in the Revelation; *alla*, "but," more than 100 times in John, and only 13 times in the Revelation. In referring to Christ as "the Lamb," the Gospel always uses the word *amnos*, whereas in the Revelation it is consistently *arnion*. Numerous other linguistic differences are also apparent. Dionysius also noted that the Greek of the Gospel is correct and idiomatic, whereas in many places that of the Revelation departs from accepted Greek grammar and syntax. It cannot be denied that the vocabulary and literary style of the Revelation are strikingly different from those of the Gospel According to John. The former exhibits an unusual degree of liberty with the ordinary standards of Greek diction and syntax, whereas the language of the Gospel conforms to good Greek usage. Dionysius also emphasized the fact that whereas in the Revelation the author repeatedly gives his name, the author of the Gospel of John concealed his identity. Furthermore, Eusebius, apparently influenced by Dionysius, interpreted Papias' statement, referred to above, to mean that there were 2 men by the name of John who lived in Asia toward the close of the 1st cent.—the apostle and another called "the presbyter," or elder—and concluded that the latter was the author of the book of Revelation. However, the quotation from Papias may also be taken as identifying this "presbyter" with John the apostle. These criticisms appear to have had a wide influence upon the thinking of the Eastern church in regard to the canonicity of the book. Many modern scholars have followed Dionysius and Eusebius in their conclusion. Certain considerations, however, testify to the fact that the evidence upon which these conclusions were based is not as strong or impressive as might at first appear. Furthermore, there are striking literary parallels between the 2 works that strongly suggest identity of authorship. It must be remembered that Greek was not John's native tongue, and that when called he was most probably an unlettered fisherman. To what extent he later mastered Greek is not known, though the fact that the closing years of his ministry were spent at Ephesus, in a Greek-speaking region, would suggest that he doubtless attained a certain degree of fluency in that language. In writing the Gospel of John, which reflects the deliberate thought and polish of an author quietly at work in his study, John, like Paul and other NT writers, may well have had the services of a Greek amanuensis, or secretary. On the other hand, in the book of Revelation the author explicitly declares that he was on the "isle that is called Patmos" (Rev 1:9), where he would doubtless be forced to rely on his own limited acquaintance with the niceties of the Greek language. Since his native tongue was Aramaic rather than Greek, it is not surprising that the Revelation, though written in Greek, should at many places reflect Semitic idioms and often deviate from the best Greek grammar. The situation under which the Revelation was composed is altogether sufficient to account for the great differences of language and grammatical construction between the two books. To balance the linguistic differences, there are a number of literary parallels. For instance, the Revelation speaks of "the water of life" (chs 21: 6; 22:17), and the Gospel, of "living water" (Jn 4:10; 7:38; cf. Rev 22:17; Jn 7:37). Certain characteristic Johannine expressions that occur in both books but do not occur elsewhere in the NT are *opsis*, "appearance" or "face" (Jn 7:24; 11:44; cf. Rev 1:16); *tērein ton logon*, "keep my saying [or, "word"]" (Jn 8:51, 52, 55; cf. Rev 3:8, 10; etc.); and *onoma autō*, "his name" (Jn 1:6; 3:1; cf. Rev 6: 8). Except in instances where OT symbolism is used, only the Gospel of John (ch 1:29, 36) and the Revelation (ch 5:6; and 28 other times) characterize Christ as the Lamb. Thus, from a strictly scholarly point of view the arguments for the traditional view, making the apostle John author of the Revelation, are fully as reasonable and valid as those that deny his authorship. Inasmuch as Christian writers generally to the middle of the 3d cent.

A.D. attest Johannine authorship, and the challenge to it did not arise until about a century after the book was written, there is strong evidence in favor of the traditional view.

Modern scholarship is divided between assigning the writing of the Revelation to a comparatively early date—usually in the reign of Nero (A.D. 54-68)—or a later date toward the end of the reign of Domitian (A.D. 81-96). Nero was notorious as the first Roman emperor to persecute Christians. Many scholars consider the persecution of the church, reflected at various points in the Revelation (see chs 13; 17), as referring to that of Nero. They also note that his name, Nero Caesar, when spelled in Hebrew consonantal letters (*Nrwn Qsr*) adds up to the mystic number 666 of ch 13:18. Accordingly, a number of outstanding scholars have dated the Revelation in the late 60's or in the 70's of the 1st cent. It should be noted, however, that this line of reasoning depends not on objective evidence but on a subjective interpretation of certain passages in the book. Early Christian writers were almost unanimous in ascribing the writing of the Revelation to the reign of the emperor Domitian. Irenaeus, for instance, declares that it was written "towards the end of Domitian's reign" (*Against Heresies* v. 30. 3; *ANF*, vol. 1, pp. 559, 560). Victorinus (died *c.* A.D. 303) says that John was "condemned to the labour of the mines by Caesar Domitian," and that while there "he saw the Apocalypse" (*Commentary on the Apocalypse,* on ch 10:11; *ANF,* vol. 7, p. 353). Eusebius (*Hist. Eccl.* iii. 20. 8, 9) similarly records that John was sent to the island of Patmos by Domitian, and adds that he was released by Domitian's successor Nerva (A.D. 96-98), after which the apostle returned to Ephesus. Early Christian scholarship thus clearly assigns the writing of the Revelation to the close of Domitian's reign, about A.D. 96.

Domitian (A.D. 81-96) encouraged the cult of emperor worship, but Christians declined to venerate the emperor or to address him by the title "lord," which title they reserved for Jesus Christ alone. When Domitian zealously sought to establish his claim to deity in the minds of the populace and to force his subjects to worship him, he naturally encountered the opposition of the Christians. This situation doubtless constitutes the immediate cause of John's exile to Patmos, and thus of the writing of the Revelation. The church was confronted with the greatest external threat to its existence it had known, and needed a new revelation of Jesus Christ to confirm its faith. Thus the visions accorded John met a specific need in their own time—that of strengthening Christians in their refusal to bow to the emperor, and to reassure them that their Lord, now ascended and standing at the throne of God, would one day reign supreme over the earth.

In 4 successive lines of prophecy the Revelation sets forth the experiences of the church, and events on earth to take place prior to the establishment of the kingdom of Jesus Christ. The book is a revelation of Jesus Christ at work perfecting a people on earth to reflect His flawless character and guiding them through the vicissitudes of history toward the accomplishment of His eternal purpose. The focus of attention is the cataclysmic end of this world and the establishment of a new world. The 4 major divisions, or lines of prophecy, are: (1) the 7 churches (Rev 1-3); (2) the 7 seals (chs 4 to 8:1); (3) the 7 trumpets (chs 8:2 to 11); and (4) the closing events of the great controversy (chs 12-22). Following a brief introduction (ch 1:1-3), John records a series of 7 messages addressed to "the seven churches which are in Asia" (ch 1:4) in which he represents Christ in different aspects of His ministry on their behalf. To each church a message of instruction, warning, and encouragement was addressed, particularly appropriate to its own situation. In view of the fact that in the Revelation the imminent return of Christ is stressed (see chs 1:1, 3; 3:11; 6:11; 12:12; 17:10; 22:6, 7, 12, 20), and because of the nature of the promises made to the 7 churches (see chs 2:7, 10, 11, 17, 26; 3:5, 10, 12, 21), it is evident that John envisioned these messages as relevant to the needs of believers until our Lord's return. Accordingly, the letters to the 7 churches may appropriately be considered as providing guidance, comfort, and strength for the church, not only in John's day but throughout the Christian Era to the very close of time. In the setting of a sublime description of God's throne John introduces a book "sealed with seven seals" (chs 4; 5), prefatory to the prophecy of the 7 seals (chs 6:1 to 8:1). This line of prophecy presents Christ as superintending the affairs of earth and working out all things according to God's will in preparation "for the great day of his wrath" (ch 6:17). The vision of the 7 trumpets (Rev 8:2 to 11:19) presents a series of events that reach a climax when "the kingdoms of this world . . . become the kingdoms of our Lord, and of his Christ" (ch 11:15). Another interlude (chs 10:1 to 11:13) pictures a mighty angel coming down from heaven with "a little book open" that contains a message to be given to "many peoples, and nations, and tongues, and kings" (ch 10:2, 11). Central in the message of this book is "the temple of God, and the altar, and them that worship therein" (ch 11:1), and the work of the "two witnesses" (v 3).

The 4th great line of prophecy (chs 12 to 22) represents the church of God on earth—figuratively "a woman clothed with the sun" and "the remnant of her seed" (ch 12:1, 17)—as enduring severe persecution at the hands of the dragon (vs 13-17), the beast (ch 13:1-8), and "another beast" (vs 11-18). The climactic crisis comes when those who love and serve God are faced with the death decree of ch 13:15-17, which demands their allegiance to the apostate power. This demand for universal allegiance stands in opposition to the messages proclaimed by the 3 angels of ch 14:6-11. Confronted by the threat of ch 13:15-17 and the warning of ch 14:6-11, the inhabitants of earth make the great final decision to be loyal to God or to reject His gracious appeal. God's judgments (chs 15; 16) are then poured out upon those who reject His mercy. The great apostate organization itself, "Babylon the great," is annihilated (ch 18). In heaven there is a paean of victory (ch 19:1-9), and Christ comes forth as King of kings and Lord of lords to defeat the coalition of the kings of the earth who are arrayed against Him (vs 11-21). After a thousand years "the dead, small and great, stand before God" to be "judged . . . according to their works" (ch 20:5, 12). The great judgment scene closes with the lake of fire, in which sin and sinners are destroyed (vs 14, 15). Chapters 21:1 to 22:5 present God's people in the new earth, in God's own presence, reigning "for ever and ever" (ch 22: 5). Verses 6-21 stand as the conclusion to the Apocalypse, which closes with emphasis on the Lord's speedy return (v 20).

Rezeph (rē'zĕf). [Heb. *Reṣeph*.] A city in northern Mesopotamia, mentioned with Gozan, Haran, and the "children of Eden," as places the Assyrians claimed to have conquered (2 Ki 19:12; Is 37:12). Rezeph is probably the *Raṣappa* of the Assyrian inscriptions, which has been identified by some with *Ruṣâfeh,* an oasis northeast of Palmyra (Map XI, B-4), but by E. Forrer (*JBL* 71 [1952], 252) with the modern *Beled Sinjâr* in the *Jebel Sinjâr* (Map XI, B-5).

Rezia. *See* Rizia.

Rezin (rē′zĭn). [Heb. *Reṣín,* probably "brook," from Syriac *raṣṣina'*, a name occurring in Assyrian inscriptions as *Raṣunnu* or *Raḥianu*.]

1. The last king of Damascus (*c.* 750-732 B.C.). He was a tributary of Assyria, according to the Assyrian inscriptions (*ANET* 283). About 734 B.C. he rebelled and with Pekah of Israel undertook a campaign against Ahaz of Judah, possibly because Ahaz had refused to join an alliance against Assyria. He and Pekah planned to depose Ahaz and place a "son of Tabeel" on the throne (Is 7:6; *see* Tabeel). Rezin marched toward the Gulf of Aqabah and took Elath; Pekah made a direct campaign against Judah (2 Ki 16: 5, 6). Ahaz had in the meantime sent messengers to Tiglath-pileser III with a gift and a request to attack the hostile alliance. The Assyrian king gladly complied. He probably turned first against Israel and occupied part of Israel's territory; the Assyrian records for the year 734 mention his attack on the Philistines, who had also fought against Judah. He then invaded the land of Damascus (733), and after besieging the capital city he conquered and destroyed it (732). Rezin lost his life, and the territory of Damascus became an Assyrian province (2 Ki 16:7-9; *ANET* 283).

2. The ancestral head of a family of Temple servants, or Nethinim, some of whom returned from Babylonia with Zerubbabel (Ezr 2:48; Neh 7:50).

Rezon (rē′zŏn). [Heb. *Rezôn,* "high official."] A son of Eliada and a fugitive from Hadadezer, king of Zobah. During David's reign, he organized a band of outlaw troops, seized Damascus (1 Ki 11:23-25), and founded a kingdom that became a formidable enemy of Solomon. If Rezon was the "Hezion" of 1 Ki 15:18, as some think, he became the founder of the dynasty that reigned in that city for more than a century, until Hazael assassinated Ben-hadad II, made himself king, and founded a new dynasty. Rezon's reign may have lasted for about 30 years, probably *c.* 960 - *c.* 930 B.C.

Rhegium (rē′jĭ-ŭm). [Gr. *Rhēgion*.] A city on the southern tip of Italy, guarding the entrance to the Strait of Messina (Map XX, B-2). It was founded originally as a Greek colony and its population was still mainly Greek in imperial times. Its modern name is *Reggio.* Paul touched at Rhegium during his voyage from Malta to Rome (Acts 28:13), probably in the early spring of A.D. 61. His ship stayed there a day before proceeding to Puteoli, probably because the skipper waited for a favorable wind to take him through the dangerous Strait of Messina, where were found the famous rock Scylla and whirlpool Charybdis, feared by all ancient navigators.

Rhesa (rē′sȧ). [Gr. *Rhēsa*.] A son of Zerubbabel, appearing in Luke's genealogy of Jesus Christ (Lk 3:27).

Rhoda (rō′dȧ). [Gr. *Rhodē,* "rose," a frequently occurring Greek name.] A servant girl in the house of Mary, the mother of Mark. She was sent to find out who knocked when Peter, released by an angel from prison, was at the door (Acts 12:12-16). It is unknown whether she belonged to the household of Mary or was a Christian slave of another household who had come for the purpose of praying with the assembled church members on behalf of Peter.

Rhodes (rōdz). [Gr. *Rhodos*.] A fertile island off the southwest coast of Asia Minor, or its capital bearing the same name. The city (see fig. 403), being conveniently situated and possessing a good harbor, be-

403. The entrance to the harbor at Rhodes where the Colossus stood in ancient times

came a shipping center, and in the 3d and 2d cent. B.C. attained prosperity and considerable sea power. Its harbor landmark was the Colossus of Rhodes, a 100-ft. bronze statue of the sun-god Helios, or Apollo, which the Greeks counted among the Seven Wonders of the World. When the eastern Mediterranean area became

Roman in the 2d cent. B.C., Rhodes' trade was ruined, but it remained a free city until the time of Claudius, who placed a Roman garrison there and occupied it for several years. In A.D. 53 Nero induced the Senate to restore its liberty, but Vespasian finally made it part of the Roman province of Asia. Herod the Great favored Rhodes and embellished the city with buildings. Paul passed the island on his voyage to Jerusalem, returning from his 3d Missionary Journey, probably in A.D. 58 (Acts 21:1). Map XX, B-4.

Ribai (rī′bī). [Heb. *Rîbay,* meaning uncertain.] A Benjamite from Gibeah, whose son Ittai, or Ithai, is listed as one of David's "mighty men" (2 Sa 23:29; 1 Chr 11:31).

Ribband. A rendering of the Heb. *pathîl,* "twisted thread," "cord," "rope" (Num 15:38, KJV). The Hebrew people were instructed to wear cords of blue on their garments as a reminder of their duty of obedience to God (v 39).

Riblah (rĭb′lȧ). [Heb. *Riblah.*]

1. A town in the land of Hamath in Syria (2 Ki 23:33; 25:21). It was used as headquarters by Pharaoh Necho II in his military campaign to the north during which he summoned King Jehoahaz of Judah and deposed him after Jehoahaz had reigned only 3 months. He sent the deposed king captive to Egypt, and placed his brother on the throne (ch 23: 33, 34). Riblah was also the headquarters of Nebuchadnezzar during his 3d Palestinian campaign, and there King Zedekiah of Judah was taken after his capture. It was there that Nebuchadnezzar executed all the princes of Judah and put out the captive king's eyes, before carrying him bound to Babylon (2 Ki 25:6, 7, 21, 22; Jer 39:5-7; 52:9-11, 27). Riblah has been identified with the ruin site of *Ribleh,* 36 mi. north by east of *Ba'albek* on the Orontes, a place in a wide plain, suitable for a large military camp (Map XI, C-4).

2. A place on the northern boundary of Palestine, east of Ain (Num 34:11); not identified unless it is the same as Riblah, 1.

Riddle. The terms thus translated (Heb. *chîdah;* Aramaic *'achîdah*) denote variously "enigmatic saying," "ambiguous saying," "riddle," "enigmatic question." The English versions generally use the rendering "riddle" where the context shows that a cryptic saying, the meaning of which is veiled in difficult or symbolic

language and is discernible only by intricate study and shrewd guessing, is intended. Samson apparently followed a common practice when he propounded a riddle to a group of friends at his wedding feast (Jgs 14:12-18). Ezekiel's riddle (Eze 17:2-10) was obviously an attention device, the full and clear explanation of which follows in vs 11-24. In the mythology of various peoples there are records of riddles upon the answer to which hung the fate of those to whom the riddle was propounded.

Rie. *See* Spelt.

Righteousness. [Heb. *ṣedeq* and *ṣedaqah,* "(the) right (thing)," "rightness," "righteousness," "justice," "fairness," "piety"; Gr. *dikaiosunē,* "righteousness," "uprightness," "justice"; *dikaiōma,* "regulation," "requirement," "commandment," "righteous deed."] The state in which a right relationship exists between man and God, within the limits of man's finite comprehension of the divine will and purpose. God's righteousness is absolute, being equivalent to the plenitude and infinite perfection of the divine character. But man has no righteousness whatever of his own. "All our righteousnesses are as filthy rags," wrote Isaiah (Is 64:6), and Paul declared, "in me . . . dwelleth no good thing" (Rom 7:18). Accordingly, whatever righteousness man may have is his by virtue of his relationship with God, and comes from God. The repentant sinner enters into this state of righteousness when by faith he accepts it as God's gracious gift. It was through faith that Abraham attained to righteousness (ch 4:3, 20-23). He was ready to receive with joy whatever God might reveal to him as duty, and to do gladly whatever God should direct.

The state of righteousness into which a repentant sinner enters when justified by faith is spoken of as being at "peace with God" (Rom 5:1). *See* Justification. It was obedience on Christ's part to the righteous requirements of the law that made it possible for Him to justify, or to declare "righteous," those who come to Him by faith (see vs 16-19). By virtue of this right relationship which the Christian enters into, he is enabled to bear "the fruits of righteousness" (Php 1:11; cf. Rom 7:19 to 8:4; Gal 2:20). However, the righteous life that follows justification does not earn merit with God, for no human act can be meritorious in His sight. But without the outward fruits of righteousness (see Gal 5:22, 23) a state of right relationship with God cannot exist in the heart. A faith unaccompanied by the "works" that faith produces "is dead, being alone" (Jas 2:17). It is spurious. *See* Sanctification.

The Jews came to believe that righteousness could be obtained by a punctilious observance of the law. Mechanical conformity to the standard of righteousness prescribed by the law was considered sufficient to make man righteous, apart from faith in God's grace. Prior to his conversion Paul was "blameless" with respect to "the righteousness which is in the law" (Php 3:6). This legal righteousness left no room for the exercise of faith. But "if righteousness come by the law, then Christ is dead in vain," Paul emphatically declares (Gal 2:21). "By the deeds of the law there shall no flesh be justified in his sight" (Rom 3:20).

Rimmon (rĭm′ŏn), KJV once **Remmon** (rĕm′ŏn), RSV once **Rimmono** (rĭm′ō-nō). [Heb. *Rimmôn* and *Rimmônô*, "pomegranate."]

1. A Benjamite whose 2 sons slew Ishbosheth, under whom they served as captains, and took his head to David, expecting a reward from him. Instead they were executed (2 Sa 4:2, 5-12).

2. A town in the south of Judah near Ain (Jos 15:32; 1 Chr 4:32); later the 2 names were joined, resulting in the name En-rimmon (Neh 11:29). En-rimmon belonged first to Judah, but was later transferred to Simeon (Jos 19:1, 7). It is identified with the site of *Khirbet Umm er-Ramāmîn,* about 9 mi. north of Beersheba.

3. A border town of Zebulun assigned to the Merarite Levites (1 Chr 6:77, RSV "Rimmono"). It is mentioned in Jos 19:13, RSV, where the KJV transliterates the Heb. *Rimmôn hammetho'ar* as Remmonmethoar (rĕm′ŏn-mĕth′ō-är). The RSV emends the phrase and translates it "Rimmon it bends." In Jos 21:35 Dimnah is believed by some to stand for Rimmon, *r* having been exchanged for *d*, the 2 letters being similar in postexilic Hebrew scripts. The present village of *Rummâneh,* about 6 mi. north-northeast of Nazareth, has preserved the name and marks the ancient site of Rimmon. Map VI, C-3.

4. The identification of a rock which served as a refuge for about 600 defeated Benjamites until the other tribes readmitted them to their territory several months later (Jgs 20:45-47; 21:13, 14). This rock has been identified with mod-

ern *Rammûn,* 3½ mi. northeast of Bethel (Map VI, E-3). The village lies on the top of a detached limestone eminence, with abrupt ravines on its north, west, and south sides, and with caverns that probably served as living quarters for the refugees.

5. A principal god of the Syrians, to whose worship a temple at Damascus was dedicated (2 Ki 5:18), which is thought to have stood at the place now occupied by the great Omayyad Mosque. Rimmon appears in Mesopotamia as *Ramânu,* "the thunderer," one of the 12 great deities. *Ramânu* was responsible for rain, storm, lightning, and thus partly for fertility. He was identical with Hadad (Adad), a name that appears in the Bible in such proper names as Hadadezer (2 Sa 8:3), and Ben-hadad (1 Ki 15:18). This god was sometimes called *Hadad-rimmon.

Rimmono. *See* Rimmon, 3.

Rimmon-parez. *See* Rimmon-perez.

Rimmon-perez (rĭm′ŏn-pē′rĕz), KJV **Rimmon-parez** (rĭm′ŏn-pā′rĕz). [Heb. *Rimmon Pereṣ,* "pomegranate of the breach."] A camping place in the wilderness during the wanderings of the Israelites (Num 33: 19, 20); not identified.

Ring. The ancients wore rings of various kinds both as ornaments and for use as seals. Among the ornamental rings were the nose ring, Heb. *nezem* (Gen 24:47; Eze 16:12; etc.), and the earring, Heb. *'agîl* (Num 31:50; Eze 16:12), worn by both men and women, as is still the custom in certain Oriental countries. Such rings were made of gold, silver, or bronze as excavations in Palestine have shown. Finger rings were also worn as ornaments, but frequently also served as seals. Signet rings are especially well known from Egypt (Gen 41:42), where they often contain the king's name in hieroglyphic inscriptions. The earliest seal ring found in Palestine which bears an inscription in a Semitic script is a golden ring from the 14th or 13th cent. B.C., found during the excavations of Megiddo (fig. 404). It is uncertain whether the "signet" of Judah (ch 38:18) was a seal

404. Gold ring with a Canaanite inscription (see drawing at right), found at Megiddo

ring hung from the neck by means of a cord, or a perforated cylinder seal, which was customarily so worn (*see* Seal). Inscribed seal rings as well as cylinder seals have been uncovered in Palestinian excavations.

Ringstraked. An archaic spelling of "ringstreaked," meaning marked with circular streaks or bands. The Hebrew word thus translated (*'aqod*) may mean "having a twisted tail" (Gen 30:35, 39, 40; etc.).

Rinnah (rĭn′à). [Heb. *Rinnah,* "shout."] A descendant of Judah (1 Chr 4:20).

Riphath (rī′făth). [Heb. *Rîphath.*] A son (or descendants) of Gomer (Gen 10:3). The name, spelled Diphath (dī′făth) in 1 Chr 1:6, RSV, has not turned up in ancient inscriptions. Josephus (*Ant.* i. 6. 1) identifies the descendants with the Paphlagonians, who lived west of the lower Halys River in Asia Minor and whose chief city was Sinope. Map XIX, C-12.

Rissah (rĭs′à). [Heb. *Rissah,* "sprinkling."] A camping place in the wilderness during the wanderings of the Israelites (Num 33:21, 22); not identified.

Rithmah (rĭth′mà). [Heb. *Rithmah,* "place of the broom."] A camping place in the wilderness during the wanderings of the Israelites (Num 33:18, 19); not identified.

River. As used in the OT, any watercourse, whether large or small. The word is most commonly a rendering of the Heb. *nahar,* "a permanently flowing river." When used with the article, *nahar* often denotes the Euphrates River (see Gen 15:18), and is frequently so rendered by the RSV. However, the term is also used of watercourses of Syria, the Mesopotamian valley, Ethiopia, etc. (2 Ki 5:12; Eze 1:1; Zep 3:10; etc.). Frequently in the KJV "river" is the rendering of the Heb. *ye'or,* which, with few exceptions, signifies the *Nile River or other watercourses in the land of Egypt (Ex 1:22; Zec 10:11). The RSV usually renders the term "Nile." Frequently "river" is the rendering also of the Heb. *nachal,* "wadi" (Lev 11:9, 10; Deut 2:36, 37; etc.), often translated *"brook" (Deut 2:13; 1 Sa 17:40; etc.). *'Ubal,* translated "river" in Dan 8:2, 3, 6, is a canal as is probably also the *yûbal* of Jer 17:8. In the NT "river" is a translation of the Gr. *potamos* (Mk 1:5; Rev 9:14; etc.), "river," "stream."

River, (The). [Heb. *hannahar,* "the river" (Gen 36:37; Ex 23:31; etc.).] The river *Euphrates, unless the name of another river follows. The Euphrates was to the Palestinians "the great river" par excellence (Gen 15:18; Deut 1:7; Jos 1:4). In the RSV *hannahar* is usually rendered "Euphrates," without any indication that the name is not in the Hebrew text.

River of Egypt, I (ē′jĭpt). [Heb. *nachal Miṣrayim,* "brook of Egypt."] The name used in the KJV for the stream that formed the southwestern border of Canaan, also of Judah, and of Solomon's kingdom (Num 34:5; Jos 15:4, 47; 1 Ki 8:65; 2 Ki 24:7; Is 27:12, RSV "Brook of Egypt"). In Assyrian inscriptions it is called *nahal* (*māt*) *Muṣri.* It has been identified with the *Wâdî el-'Arîsh,* which runs north and northwest from the Sinai Peninsula, entering the Mediterranean about 50 mi. southwest of Gaza. It is a seasonal stream and carries water only after heavy rains (Map V, A/B-5/6).

River of Egypt, II (ē′jĭpt). [Heb. *nahar Miṣrayim,* "river of Egypt."] According to some, the Nile, and most probably its eastern channel, the Pelusiac branch. The Hebrew expression occurs only in Gen 15:18, in a passage mentioning the *nahar* of Egypt as the southwestern border of Canaan, which boundary in parallel passages is described as the *nachal* of Egypt, that is, the *Wâdî el-'Arîsh* (*see* River of Egypt, I). It seems logical therefore to conclude that the *nahar* of Egypt in this passage is also this wadi.

Rizia (rĭ-zī′à), KJV **Rezia** (rē-zī′à). [Heb. *Riṣya',* "pleasant."] A descendant of Asher (1 Chr 7:39).

Rizpah (rĭz′pà). [Heb. *Riṣpah,* meaning uncertain.] A concubine of Saul. After Saul's death Ishbosheth accused Abner of taking her, and rebuked him for it, fearing that Abner planned to usurp royal power. Being offended, Abner deserted to David, but then lost his life through the treachery of Joab (2 Sa 3:6-28). During David's reign Rizpah's sons, Armoni and Mephibosheth, were put to death, with 5 other descendants of Saul, to expiate a crime committed by Saul against the Gibeonites. Rizpah watched over their bodies and protected them from beasts and birds until David, upon hearing of her deed of love, had their remains gathered and honorably buried in the family sepulcher of Saul's house (ch 21:1, 8-14).

Road. *See* Highway.

Robber. In the OT the rendering of various Hebrew words denoting a person who takes the property of another by force, as distinguished from a thief, who takes property by stealth. In the NT "robber" is the rendering of: (1) the Gr. *lēstēs* (Jn

10:1; 2 Cor 11:26; etc.), "robber," "bandit," "revolutionary" (*see* Thief); (2) the Gr. *harpax,* "robber," "swindler" (1 Cor 5:10, 11; 6:10; RSV).

Robe. The rendering of several Hebrew and Greek terms, some of which are general expressions for *"clothing." One of them, the Heb. *me'il,* a coat, was apparently sleeveless, worn by people of rank or importance, such as the high priest (Ex 28:4, 31; etc.), a prince (1 Sa 18:4; Eze 26:16), a princess (2 Sa 13:18), a king (1 Sa 24:11; 1 Chr 15:27; etc.), etc. The Gr. *stolē* designates a large flowing robe (Mk 16:5, RSV; Rev 6:11; 7:9; etc.).

Roboam. *See* Rehoboam.

Rock. [Heb. generally *sela',* "crag," "rock," distinguished by its size, height, or elevation, or *ṣûr,* "rock," "large piece of rock"; *sela'* and *ṣûr* are often used synonymously (Num 20:8-11; cf. Deut 8:15); Gr. generally *petra,* "rock," "stone."] With the exception of local outpourings of basalt and an occasional outcropping of calcareous sandstone along the coast, limestone is the only rock of western Palestine (*see* Palestine, VI). There were numerous crags or cliffs (Heb. *sela'*), some of which bore names (see Jgs 15:11; 21:13). This abundance of rocks provided the Bible writers with striking and beautiful imagery. Thus Rock became a name for God, expressing confidence in Him and dependence upon Him (Deut 32:4; cf. 1 Cor 10:4). The psalmist speaks of God as "the rock of my salvation" (Ps 89:26; cf. 62:2, 7; etc.), "the rock of my refuge" (Ps 94:22), and "the rock that is higher than I" (Ps 61:2). Lofty rock formations were sometimes chosen as the location for cities or fortresses. Rocks often provided refuge (Jgs 20:47; 1 Sa 13:6; Jer 48:28; etc.). Our Lord likened a man who heeds His instruction to one who builds his house upon a solid foundation of rock (Mt 7:24). Paul speaks of Christ as a "stumblingstone and rock of offence" for the Jews (Rom 9:33), but One in whom those who believe can trust.

Rock Badger, KJV Coney. [Heb. *shaphan.*] A small relative of the hippopotamus (*Procavia syriaca*), the size of a rabbit. The animal, which is still found in Syria and Palestine, lives in the rocks (Ps 104:18; Prov 30:26; RSV "badger"). Being unclean, it is forbidden as food (Lev 11:5; Deut 14:7). The rock badger is not a real ruminant, but it moves its jaws as if it were chewing the cud. As in the case of the hare, this statement that it chews the cud (Lev 11:5; Deut 14:7) must be considered not as a technical scientific statement but simply as a reference to the outward appearance and to the generally held views about this animal.

Rod. A rendering of various Hebrew words, chiefly *maṭṭeh,* "staff," "rod"; *shebeṭ,* "rod," "scepter"; *maqqel,* "rod," "twig," "staff." *Maṭṭeh* was used of Aaron's rod (Ex 4:2, 4, 17, 20), and of the rods used by God to confirm Aaron's position (Num 17). The *shebeṭ* was evidently a larger rod often used as a weapon (Ex 21:20; 2 Sa 7:14; Ps 2:9). It was used by a shepherd (Ps 23:4) and farmer (Is 28:27) and as an instrument of discipline (Prov 10:13; 13:24; etc.). *Maqqel* is used of the rods Jacob used in his misguided efforts to control reproduction among Laban's flocks and herds (Gen 30:37-41). In the NT "rod" (generally Gr. *rhabdos*) is a symbol of discipline (1 Cor 4:21) and of rulership or retribution (Rev 2:27; 12:5; 19:15). The "rod" of Rev 21:15, 16, RSV (KJV "reed"), is a rendering of the Gr. *kalamos,* "measuring rod."

Rodanim. *See* Dodanim.

Roe. The translation in the KJV of: (1) the Heb. *ya'alah* (Prov 5:19), "a female mountain goat"; (2) the Heb. *ṣebi* or *ṣebiyah* (2 Sa 2:18; Song 4:5; etc.), *"gazelle."

Roebuck. The translation: (1) in the KJV of the Heb. *ṣebi* (Deut 12:15; 14:5), *"gazelle"; (2) in the RSV of the Heb. *yachmûr* (Deut 14:5; 1 Ki 4:23), the Asiatic roebuck (*Cervus capreolus*), which until recent times was found on Mount Carmel and the Lebanon Mountains, a larger animal than the European roebuck. It is dark reddish-brown in the summer, and yellowish-gray in the winter. Its antlers are about 1 ft. long and have 3 points.

Rogelim (rō'gĕ-lĭm). [Heb. *Rogelim,* "spies."] The home of Barzillai in Gilead (2 Sa 17:27; 19:31). It has been tentatively identified by some with *Bersînyā,* about 16 mi. southeast of the Sea of Galilee, though others think that it was farther south, near the place where David crossed the Jordan on his return after the collapse of Absalom's rebellion.

Rohgah (rō'ga). [Heb. *Rôhagah* (Q *Rohgah*).] A descendant of Asher (1 Chr 7:34).

Roll. *See* Scroll.

Romamti-ezer (rŏ-măm'tĭ-ē'zēr). [Heb. *Romamtî 'ezer,* "I have exalted help."] A Levite, son of Heman, and the ancestral head of the last of the 24 courses into which David organized the singers (1 Chr 25:4, 31).

Romans (rō'mănz). [Gr. *Rhōmaioi*.]

1. A general term designating people who represented the Roman government in Palestine (Jn 11:48; Acts 25:16; 28:17).

2. Holders of Roman citizenship. In early Rome the 2 classes then making up the "Roman people" were the patricians (the nobility) and the plebeians (the common people). Citizenship of a 2d degree was enjoyed also by freedmen, whose sons entered into full citizenship if born after the father became free. Roman citizens had the right to vote, to hold office (except that freedmen could not become magistrates or enter into the higher orders), to appeal to the people in capital cases (later to the emperor), to be exempt from shameful punishment, to hold property, and to bear arms. A Roman citizen could be recognized by his name and by the white toga which he wore. At first only people in the city of Rome were citizens; later neighboring tribes were included and still later the people of all Italy, and then residents of various colonies outside of Italy. Citizenship could also be obtained for money or be granted in recognition of valuable services rendered to the state. Finally in A.D. 212 Caracalla made all free inhabitants of the empire citizens.

The apostle Paul was born as a Roman citizen with full rights (Acts 22:28). To be a Roman citizen in the provinces of the empire was equivalent to belonging to the aristocracy. How his family had obtained the *civitas* is unknown, but its possession was useful to him. He embarrassed the magistrates of Philippi by telling them that they had scourged him and Silas although they were Roman citizens; apparently no one had listened to their protestations in the excitement of the previous day (ch 16:37-39). In Jerusalem he refused to submit to questioning under torture (ch 22:25). Paul also appealed to the emperor when he felt that he could not obtain fair treatment in Judea (ch 25:11). This appeal brought him to Rome for the final trial (ch 28:17-19).

Romans, Epistle to the. A letter written by the apostle Paul to the church at Rome. In the earliest Greek manuscripts the title is simply *Pros Rhōmaious*, "To the Romans." That Paul the apostle is the author of this epistle has never been seriously questioned, though some scholars have suggested that ch 16 may have been a separate letter sent to Ephesus instead of a part of the original epistle. However, all the earliest extant manuscripts include ch 16 as an integral part of the epistle. The letter was written apparently from Corinth during Paul's brief stay there on his 3d Missionary Journey (probably during the winter of A.D. 57/58) as appears from the salutations (Rom 16:23; cf. 1 Cor 1:14; 2 Ti 4:20), and from Rom 16:1, where Paul commends Phoebe for her special service to the church at Cenchreae, the eastern seaport of Corinth. Having largely completed his ministry in Greece (ch 15:19, 23) with the establishment of Christian churches in the major cities, Paul was about to return to Palestine, bearing gifts from the Gentile churches to the poor believers in Jerusalem (Rom 15:25, 26; cf. Acts 19:21; 20:3; 24:17; 1 Cor 16:1-5; 2 Cor 8:1-4; 9:1, 2). Upon the completion of his mission, he purposed to extend his labors to the city of Rome and thence westward to Spain (Acts 19:21; Rom 15:24, 28). The Christian faith had already been established in the capital city of the Roman Empire by others, and Paul had an ardent desire to visit the believers there (Rom 1:13; 15:22).

The epistle to the Romans and that addressed to the Galatians deal with the same general subject—righteousness by faith in Christ. But whereas the latter was composed at a time of crisis, when the churches in Galatia were confronted by the teachings of the Judaizing party in the early church (*see* Galatians, Epistle to the), and was thus designed to meet a particular threat, the former deals with the subject in a more systematic, reasoned, and complete way. There is no evidence of any crisis in the city of Rome comparable to that in Galatia. It has been suggested that Paul wrote to the Romans shortly after he had written to the churches in Galatia. The epistle to the Galatians has been called the Magna Charta of Christianity, and the epistle to the Romans, its constitution. Under any circumstances it is obvious that the apostle's mind was full of the issues that had arisen in his many controversies with the Judaizers, since he takes up the basic questions and deals with them against the background of the whole problem of sin and of God's plan to meet the emergency sin created. Accordingly, the theme of the epistle is the universal sinfulness of man and God's universal grace. Paul first proves that all men, Jew and Gentile alike, have sinned and come short of the glory of God (Rom 3:23), and that it is altogether impossible for them in their carnal state to obey God's will (Rom 8:7, 8). He then shows that justification can be obtained only by faith in Jesus Christ (chs 3:22, 24; 8:1-4). Legalistic attempts to attain to righteousness are doomed to failure, since in man "dwelleth no good thing" (ch 7:18).

Following the salutation (Rom 1:1-7), Paul expresses his interest in the believers at Rome and tells of his earnest desire to pay them a visit (vs 8-15). As "debtor" to all Gentiles—since he is in a special sense the apostle to the Gentiles (cf. Gal 2:7, 9)—he feels an obligation to proclaim the gospel "at Rome also" (Rom 1:14, 15). In chs 1:16 to 5:21, he sets forth the doctrine of justification by faith, the topic he announces in ch 1:16, 17. First he sets forth the utter failure of the Gentiles to attain to righteousness, and proves them to be guilty before God (vs 18-32). Then he shows that the Jews, who had enjoyed the great advantage of being custodians of "the oracles of God" (ch 3:1, 2), were equally guilty, and that Jews and Gentiles alike "are all under sin" (v 9). Despite their more favorable opportunity, the Jews have not kept the law themselves (vs 10-24), and "all the world" thus stands "guilty before God" (v 19). "All have sinned, and come short of the glory of God" (v 23). Neither the possession of the written record of God's revealed will, nor the punctilious, mechanical observance of its requirements, gives the Jew a reason for boasting, because men are "justified by faith without the deeds of the law" (v 28). There is no righteousness apart from that given by Jesus Christ (vs 21-32).

By an analysis of Abraham's experiences Paul next proves that even the patriarch attained to righteousness through faith—he "believed God, and it was counted unto him for righteousness" (Rom 4:3; cf. v 22). If, then, Abraham was justified by faith, Paul asks, how much more we for whose offenses Christ was delivered up and for whose justification He was raised again (vs 24, 25)? Paul stresses faith as the basis of Christian experience, since it is through faith that we receive justification and find peace with God (ch 5:1). Whereas formerly we were "enemies" of God, now through faith we have become "reconciled to God by the death of his Son" (vs 10, 11). In vs 12-14 the apostle attributes the presence of sin in the world to Adam, but shows by a parity of reasoning that as the sin of one man brought condemnation upon the world, so the obedience of one—Christ—

brings justification (Rom 5:15-19). He develops the theme that the person who has experienced justification by faith is to serve God "in newness of spirit" (chs 6:1 to 7:6); sin is not to reign in his life, that is, to have dominion over him (ch 6:1, 12, 14), as shown by the rite of baptism, which represents not only death to sin but also a rising to "walk in newness of life" (vs 3-6).

Paul next points out the apparent conflict between the intention to do right and the simple fact that man lacks the power to do so (Rom 7:7-25), a situation that confronts man with a dilemma from which there appears to be no escape (v 24), but "thank God," there is a way of escape (v 25). In ch 8 Paul explains this way of escape, saying that "the law of the Spirit of life" frees a man "from the law of sin and death" (v 2). By virtue of the fact that the Son of God came into the world as man's Saviour and died for his sins, "the righteousness of the law" may now "be fulfilled in us" if we "walk not after the flesh, but after the Spirit" (v 4). Those who are "led by the Spirit of God" are "the sons of God" (v 14), and thus eligible as "heirs of God, and joint-heirs with Christ" (v 17). God is "for us" (v 31), thus "in all these things we are more than conquerors through him that loved us" (v 37), and nothing can separate us from God's infinite love (vs 35, 38, 39).

In view of the fact that justification comes through faith, and not through the punctilious observance of legal requirements, as the Jews thought, the question naturally arises as to Israel's role as God's chosen people (Rom 9-11). God had adopted them as His chosen people and entered into covenant relations with them (ch 9:4), but later rejected them. His election of the chosen people in ancient times may have seemed to be arbitrary (vs 6-23), but "they are not all Israel, which are of Israel" (v 6), and in fact, only "a remnant shall be saved" (v 27). Israel as a nation did not attain to righteousness through the law, simply because they did not seek righteousness by faith, but attempted to find it through "the works of the law" (vs 30-32). Consequently, as a nation they rejected the salvation Paul has already shown to be obtainable only through Christ (vs 32, 33). Turning their backs on Christ, they went "about to establish their own righteousness" and forfeited the gracious provision made available through Him (ch 10:3, 4).

They had a "zeal" for God, "but not according to knowledge" (Rom 10:2). Accordingly, since Israel proved to be "a disobedient and gainsaying people" (v 21), God had no alternative but to reject them. The question is then raised, Did this mean He had utterly and irrevocably deprived the Jews of salvation? In ch 11 the apostle answers by explaining that, like the unproductive branches of an olive tree, they have been "broken off" and Gentile branches grafted in their place (vs 17-22), and that in order to find salvation the people of Israel must be grafted back into the root of the olive tree (v 23). Only "so" can "all Israel . . . be saved" (v 26). God has "concluded" all, Jew and Gentile alike, "in unbelief, that he might have mercy upon all" (v 32).

In Rom 12:1 to 15:13 Paul makes a practical application of the doctrine of righteousness by faith which he has developed in chs 1:16 to 11:36. It means a transformation for the individual Christian (ch 12:1, 2), unity and fellowship among the believers (vs 3-8), and considerate dealings with all men (vs 9-21). It means submission to "the higher powers" (ch 13:1-7), sober living in view of the fact that "now is our salvation nearer than when we believed" (vs 11-14), and forbearance and consideration among Christians (chs 14:1 to 15:13). In his conclusions (chs 15:14 to 16:27) Paul repeats his intention to pay the believers at Rome a visit (ch 15:31, 32), and sends greetings (ch 16:1-16). He warns them against listening to certain false teachers (vs 17-20) and adds greetings from his companions (vs 21-23). Verses 24-27 constitute an apostolic benediction and doxology.

Rome (rōm). [Gr. *Rhōmē;* Latin *Roma.*] An important city of Italy, capital of the Roman Empire until Constantine's reign, and today the capital of Italy. The city is situated in the center of the Italian peninsula some 15 mi. from the coast on the river Tiber. The river allowed seagoing ships to reach Rome, and thus gave the city ready access to the sea. At the same time the sea was far enough away so that the city was protected against direct seaborne attacks. Rome thus occupied a favorable geographical position. Map XIX, C-8.

I. History.

1. *Rome Before Augustus.* Legend attributes the foundation of Rome to the twin brothers Romulus and Remus. The date, according to the prevailing form of the legend, was April 21, 753 B.C. However archeological research seems to indicate that the site was occupied much earlier by groups of Italic people called Latins, with an admixture of Sabines who descended the Tiber valley from the mountains. Settlements were established on several of the 7 hills on which Rome later stood, mainly on the Palatine, Esquiline, Quirinal, and Viminal hills. The inhabitants of the village on the Palatine may have gained predominance over the other settlements under a leader who came down in tradition as Romulus. In any case, the various settlements united into one city called Rome. The valley north of the Palatine and east of the Capitoline became the common market place (Latin *forum*), and was also used as a political and religious center of the new city. As the *Forum Romanum* it remained the center of all political and religious life for many centuries, containing within its confines the seat of the Senate, the foremost temples of the city, the Golden Milestone, from which all roads radiated, and important basilicas (halls of justice or meeting places). As Rome established its supremacy over the neighboring tribes, more and more people moved to the city until it spread over the 7 traditional hills, all lying east of the Tiber: the Palatine, Capitoline, Quirinal, Viminal, Esquiline, Caelian, and Aventine (see fig. 405). Probably for several centuries the city-state of Rome was a kingdom, but little is known of it. There were 7 legendary kings from Romulus to Tarquinius Superbus; the later kings, at least, were Etruscans, from the other side of the Tiber. During this period Rome must have established its power over the neighboring Latins. By about 500 B.C. a revolt of the nobility caused the expulsion of the last king, and subsequently the Etruscans were driven back across the Tiber. The result was a republic which lasted for 5 centuries. Republican Rome was ruled by a Senate and 2 annually elected chief magistrates, called consuls. The 1st period of the republic was marked by struggles between the plebeians and the patricians— the lower classes and the aristocracy— which ended in their reconciliation and the granting of full civil rights to the plebeians, and the conquest and unification of Italy. The sack of Rome by the Gauls in 390 B.C. was a temporary setback but had no lasting adverse influences on the constantly increasing power of the thriving city-state.

After nearly all of Italy had been incorporated into the growing state, Rome moved steadily toward supremacy over the whole Mediterranean. In the west it recognized as its greatest competitor and antagonist Carthage, a strong city-state and sea power in northern Africa, founded by Phoenicians. The struggle against Carthage lasted through 3 wars extending over a century (264-146 B.C.). Rome came close to being permanently defeated and crippled, but it emerged after the 2d Punic War (201 B.C.) as the undisputed victor over Carthage and the possessor of all countries of the western Mediterranean. The wars with Carthage brought about Rome's involvement in the east. Hence we find Roman armies fighting during the 2d and 1st cent. against Macedonia, the Seleucids, the Ptolemies, and other lesser rulers. At first Rome's aim was merely to establish her authority and keep order, but bit by bit, eastern North

Africa, Egypt, Syria, Macedonia, and Greece were absorbed into the empire. But the accumulation of wealth and the increase of power brought social and political tensions in Rome itself, which caused much bloodshed. The dictatorships of Marius and Sulla, and then of that of Caesar, resulted from the fact that the republican form of government, designed for a small state, was not adequate to cope with the problems of an empire. Caesar's murder in 44 B.C. was caused by a resentment of those who feared that he was intending to do away with the Republic and make himself king. Yet a return to the old way of life and rulership was not feasible, and the emperorship of Augustus was finally the natural answer to the demands of the time. In the meantime the empire had continued to expand. Pompey had conquered Syria and Palestine, Caesar had conquered Gaul (now France)

405. A map of ancient Rome

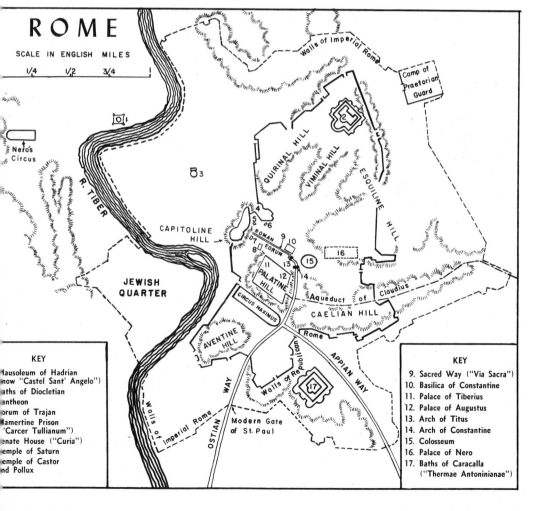

ROME

SCALE IN ENGLISH MILES

1/4   1/2   3/4

Walls of Imperial Rome

Camp of Praetorian Guard

Nero's Circus

R. TIBER

QUIRINAL HILL

VIMINAL HILL

ESQUILINE HILL

CAPITOLINE HILL

ROMAN FORUM

JEWISH QUARTER

PALATINE HILL

CIRCUS MAXIMUS

Aqueduct of Claudius

CAELIAN HILL

Rome

AVENTINE HILL

APPIAN WAY

Walls of Republican Rome

OSTIAN WAY

Modern Gate of St. Paul

Imperial Rome

KEY

Mausoleum of Hadrian (now "Castel Sant' Angelo")
Baths of Diocletian
Pantheon
Forum of Trajan
Mamertine Prison ("Carcer Tullianum")
Senate House ("Curia")
Temple of Saturn
Temple of Castor and Pollux

KEY

9. Sacred Way ("Via Sacra")
10. Basilica of Constantine
11. Palace of Tiberius
12. Palace of Augustus
13. Arch of Titus
14. Arch of Constantine
15. Colosseum
16. Palace of Nero
17. Baths of Caracalla ("Thermae Antoninianae")

and had entered Britain and Germany. In the final struggle for power after Caesar's death Octavian (Augustus) took Egypt and annexed it in 30 B.C.

2. *The Empire From Augustus to Trajan.* Although the empire lasted 5 centuries, only the 1st 2 centuries formed the golden era of Rome; and since only the 1st half of the latter period covers NT history, no more will be included in this brief historical sketch. When Octavian had overcome his opponents and emerged as sole victor, he stabilized the Roman government. On Jan. 13, 27 B.C., he was voted supreme power as imperator by the Assembly and Senate, and was made "Augustus" on Jan. 16. The power of Augustus (see fig. 42), and that of his successors, was based legally on the exercise of the constitutional authority of various magistracies held simultaneously, but his control of the military made every emperor a monarch in fact if not in name. He controlled legislation and practically the whole civil service of the empire. Although the emperor shared his powers with the Senate, this august body eventually came to be a rubber stamp.

The reign of Augustus was marked by a virtual rebuilding of Rome. Many magnificent buildings were erected in the capital and in numerous other cities. Augustus encouraged local government, and secured the frontiers of the empire. The aim of his conquests was to protect his provinces and subject countries rather than to expand his power and territories. Tiberius (A.D. 14-37) followed in the footsteps of his foster father. Although his reign was not free from acts of terror at home, his rule was conscientious and his administration of the provinces good. He did not make new conquests, but concentrated all his efforts on preserving and fostering the peace, and on keeping the empire strong and healthy. Gaius, nicknamed Caligula (A.D. 37-41), was an extravagant and autocratic monarch, but his reign did not last long enough to do any serious harm to the healthy structure of the empire. Claudius' reign (A.D. 41-54) saw greater influence concentrated in the hands of freedmen, many of whom became administrators in the civil service. Several new provinces were added (two Mauretanias, Britain, Lycia, and Thrace). Under Nero (A.D. 54-68) the time of peace temporarily ended for the empire. He was extravagant, tyrannical, and ruthless. He was even accused of having set Rome on fire (A.D. 64). He had to fight against

the Parthians and Armenians, and to suppress conspiracies at home and revolts in Britain, Spain, Gaul, and Judea. Some of these revolts were led by nationals who rebelled against oppressive Roman rule, whereas others were led by Roman administrators or generals who rose up against the emperor. When the hated man was finally overthrown, and died a suicide (A.D. 68), the flames of revolt seemed to engulf the empire. Then, in the year of 4 emperors (A.D. 68-69), which followed, the state survived disaster, chaos, and civil war only because of the constructive work of the earlier empire builders, especially Augustus and Claudius. Galba, Otho, and Vitellius came to the throne in rapid succession, but left the scene of action just as quickly as they came. Only the last of the 4, Vespasian, was able, after his elevation to the throne by his army, to obtain general support (A.D. 69-79). He ended the civil uprisings and brought the foreign wars to successful conclusions, especially the bloody Jewish war that resulted in the destruction of Jerusalem in A.D. 70. He began another era of peace and prosperity that extended beyond the 27 years of his dynasty. Vespasian exercised his authority independently of the Senate, and his economy restored the state finances so that they remained in good condition during the reign of his son Titus (A.D. 79-81) and withstood the expenditures of his other son, Domitian (A.D. 81-96). Nerva (A.D. 96-98) was the 1st of the "five good emperors" whose combined reigns lasted 84 years (A.D. 96-180). Nerva was chosen by the Senate as the "first citizen" and not appointed by the army. Since he found it difficult to control the army, he named a general, Trajan, as his successor and made him virtually coregent. His example of appointing an army officer as successor was followed by the next 3 rulers, and the system seemed to work. Trajan was a firm but tolerant ruler and worked in harmony with the Senate. Under him the empire experienced its greatest extent and prosperity. In his reign (A.D. 97-117), the apostolic era ended, and therefore this discussion will leave the history of Rome for a consideration of conditions in Paul's day.

II. The City of Rome in Paul's Time. The capital of the empire in Paul's day was no longer the comparatively small city that it had been in Republican times. Estimates of the population vary widely, from 800,000 to 1,600,000, for the time of

Augustus. There are too many unknown factors to allow certainty, but the median figure of 1,000,000 is not unreasonable. The old Servian wall, built in the republican era, had enclosed no more than the 7 hills of Rome listed earlier, and the population had long ago spilled over the limits of the old city. It was not until A.D. 271-275 that the wall of Aurelian was built by the emperor whose name it bears, the wall whose course one can still follow through modern Rome for long stretches. See map, fig. 405.

The center of the city of Paul's time was the Forum Romanum with its Sacred Way lined with statues of famous men and gods. There was the traditional tomb of Romulus, Rome's legendary founder, the Senate house (fig. 406), and the temple of Saturn, used as the state treasury in which the tributes of foreign countries and the reserve funds of the empire were stored, also the temple of Castor and Pollux (*see* *Twin Brothers), where weights and measures were tested and metals assayed for coins, and several other temples. Near the Capitol was the Golden Milestone engraved with the distances from Rome to various places on the main Roman roads. On the Palatine Hill (see fig. 513) stood the palaces of Augustus and Tiberius. There also lived Nero until, after the fire of A.D. 64, he extended his new "Golden House" across the southern part of the Esquiline hill. In the Murcia valley, between the Palatine and Aventine hills, was the Circus Maximus, which was built in Republican times, and was rebuilt by Julius Caesar. This great racecourse had space for 320,000 spectators (or 150,000, according to a different estimate). Water was brought into the city through many aqueducts, including 2 constructed by Claudius (completed in A.D. 52), large sections of which are still standing. However, many stately buildings whose impressive ruins are landmarks today did not yet exist in Paul's time: the Colosseum (see fig. 409), built by the Flavian emperors (A.D. 72-80), the triumphal arches of Titus (see fig. 407), Septimus Severus, and Constantine, the large basilica of Constantine, the Forum of Trajan, with the lofty column of that emperor, and the magnificent Thermae (public baths) of Diocletian and Caracalla.

III. Rome and Judea. When the Jews for the first time, during the period of the Maccabees, heard of the conquests of the Romans, they were so impressed that they began to think of entering a

406. Part of the ancient *curia*, the Senate house in Rome, as rebuilt *c.* A.D. 300, preserved by being converted into a church

treaty with them in order to get rid of the Seleucid yoke (1 Macc 1:10; 7:1; 8:1-20). That the first steps to such a treaty were made by the Romans, as 2 Macc 11:34-38 claims, is very doubtful. The initiative was taken by Judas Maccabeus (1 Macc 8:17-32) and his brothers Jonathan (ch 12:1-4, 16) and Simon (ch 14:16-24). John Hyrcanus certainly succeeded in interesting the Romans in his cause, and in making a treaty with them so that he would obtain their protection and help in times of need (cf. ch 15:15-24). Yet the Roman friendship soon changed into guardianship. When the 2 brothers Hyrcanus II and Aristobulus II quarreled about the throne and the office of the high priest, the case was placed before Scaurus, whom Pompey had sent to Syria (65 B.C.), and later before Pompey (63 B.C.). As a result the Romans interfered, conquered Judea and Jerusalem, and put the country under their own control. In 40 B.C. they appointed Herod as a vassal king over the country, and after Herod's death (4 B.C.) divided it into 3 sections among his 3 sons. Nine years later Augustus deposed one of them, Archelaus, and put Roman procurators (*see* Governor, 2, *c*) over his territory, Judea and Samaria. Thenceforth until the outbreak of the Jewish-Roman War in A.D. 66, except when Herod Agrippa I was king of Judea from A.D. 41 to his death in A.D. 44, this territory was administered by Roman procurators. When the Jewish revolt successfully resisted the first efforts of the Roman army of Syria to quell it, Vespasian was sent to continue the campaign. Before victory was complete he was recalled to

Rome, and in A.D. 69 become emperor. His son (later his successor) Titus commanded the siege of Jerusalem and took the city in A.D. 70, though pockets of resistance held out until 73. Titus celebrated his conquest of Judea by striking commemorative coins (see fig. 340, no. 12), and his triumphal arch in Rome (see fig. 407) bears a relief of the captured 7-branched lampstand from the Temple (see fig. 287).

of Rome lying west of the Tiber and of the Tiber island. Caesar favored them, and allowed them to retain their own organization when many other foreign groups were dissolved (Jos. *Ant.* xiv. 10. 8, 17; Suetonius *Div. Julius* 84). Augustus also was favorably disposed toward the Jews and confirmed their privileges. How large the Jewish colony in Rome was at that time can be seen from the fact

407. The Arch of Titus at Rome

IV. The Jews in Rome. Pompey sent Jews to Rome as prisoners after the conquest of Jerusalem (63 B.C.). Yet they were not the first Jews to arrive in Rome, because Cicero says in his defense of Valerius Flaccus (59 B.C.) that he had to speak softly in order not to incite the Jews to rebellion, mentioning also that gold had been sent repeatedly from Rome to Jerusalem (*Pro Flacco* 28). The Jews were especially numerous in the Transtiber (modern Trastevere), a district of the city

that 8,000 Jews joined the envoys from Jerusalem who requested annulment of the will of Herod after his death (Jos. *Ant.* xvii. 11. 1). In A.D. 19, during the reign of Tiberius, the Jews were expelled from Rome because of a financial scandal, but this order was rescinded 12 years later, and there are indications that not all Jews were forced to leave Rome during that time. A 2d expulsion edict was issued by Claudius (cf. Acts 18:2), who first had favored the Jews when he came to the throne. When Paul came to Rome about A.D. 61, he invited the leaders of the Jews to his home in order to explain why he had arrived in the city (Acts 28:17-20). This shows that the Jews had once more returned to Rome. From chs 28:21 and 2:10 it is quite evident that the Jews in Rome had good connections with Jerusalem. When the Jewish war broke out in A.D. 66 a time of great suffering began also for the Jews in foreign lands, among whom were the Jews in Rome.

V. The Origin of the Christian Church in Rome. Nothing reliable is known about the origin of the Christian church in Rome. The tradition making Peter or Paul, or both of them, founders of the Roman church is without foundation; in fact, it is improbable that either Peter or Paul had anything to do with the founding of that church. However, it is possible that the gospel came to Rome through some Jews who had accepted Christianity during the feast of Pentecost in Jerusalem, when so many strangers were converted (Acts 2:10, 41). On the other hand, the fact that the church was large and in excellent spiritual condition (Rom 1:8; 15:14) seems to indicate that it was founded by some prominent Christian missionary. When Claudius expelled all Jews from Rome in A.D. 48/49, only Christians of Gentile descent could remain behind. This may have resulted in a break of connections between the Christian church in Rome and the Jewish community. When Paul arrived in Rome about A.D. 61, the leaders of the Jews knew "concerning this sect" only that it was "everywhere . . . spoken against" (Acts 28:22). Furthermore they revealed no personal knowledge of, or existing antagonism against, the local Christian church.

The apostle Paul had had a long-standing desire to visit Rome, and about A.D. 58 wrote to the Roman Christians that he would visit Rome while passing through Italy on his planned missionary journey to Spain (Acts 19:21; Rom 15:24, 28). However, it was only about 3 years later that he reached Rome, not as a missionary to Spain as he had planned, but as a prisoner on appeal to Nero (Acts 28:16; *see* Paul, IV, 3-6). His 1st stay in the capital lasted about 2 years (*c.* A.D. 61-63). As was his custom, he attempted to make converts among the Jews in Rome, but he had little success (vs 23-29). Apparently from that time on—certainly after A.D. 64—there was enmity between Christians and Jews in the capital. Since the Chris-

tian church was not recognized any longer as a Jewish sect, it lost the privileges it had possessed as long as it was considered to belong to the Jews. In fact, it became an illegal society. This opened the way for persecutions, the first of which to be carried out in an organized way under official sanction in Rome was that by Nero in A.D. 64, when he blamed the Christians for the fire. While in Rome during his 1st Roman imprisonment, Paul wrote the letters to the Ephesians, Colossians, Philemon, and Philippians. After a period of freedom he was rearrested and taken to Rome, and during his 2d Roman imprisonment wrote the 2d letter to Timothy. That he suffered martyrdom in that city is attested by unanimous tradition. Peter also must have reached Rome sometime during Nero's reign, where he, too, lost his life under the cruel hand of that madman. This is also attested by tradition.

VI. Roman Religion. To the superficial observer the Roman religion in the time of the empire may appear to be only slightly different from that of the Greeks. This impression is gained only because the Romans lacked originality in religious matters and therefore borrowed many gods from the Greek pantheon. They produced neither mythology, religious poetry, nor philosophy like the Greeks. The earliest Romans had no personified gods, but believed in divine spirits, powers, or providential workings (*numina*), which were neither male nor female, but these spirits or powers of nature in time developed the attributes of personal deities. The Romans had household gods, Lares and Penates, the spirits of farm, home, and family, who were thought of as protecting the houses, fields, and food supply of the household. They placed great emphasis on magic, especially sympathetic nature magic. The early Roman cult had no need for either temples or statues during its earlier religious history. The king was the priest originally, and it was not until the 6th cent. B.C. that a temple was built for a trinity of gods of the Roman state, Jupiter, Juno, and Minerva, who later became identified with the Greek *Zeus, Hera, and Athena. Religion also became a function of the state. In the Republican era the Romans experienced a great religious change. As they came more and more into contact with other peoples, in Italy and outside, they adopted their religous ideas and forms of worship. Hence, we find temples being built to Demeter, Dionysus, and Persephone, who were worshiped under the Latin names Ceres, Liber, and Proserpina. Later, Diana was taken as representing the Greek *Artemis, and also Venus as standing for Aphrodite. Then also came Apollo, the sun-god. Finally several Oriental deities and their cults were introduced, such as the Phrygian Cybele—the Magna Mater of Anatolia—Bacchus with his orgiastic cult, the Egyptian Isis in the 2d cent. B.C., and Mithras in the 1st cent. B.C.

During the period of Augustus, efforts were made to go back to the primitive Roman religion and its simplicity. These efforts revealed that the better strata of society were not satisfied with the elaborate mythology of the Greeks and the sensual rites of the Oriental religions that had invaded the West. This feeling of religious frustration was partly responsible for the ready acceptance of Christianity by large numbers of the people when it entered the Roman world toward the middle of the 1st cent. A.D. Another new cult influenced by Oriental concepts was introduced in the imperial period—emperor worship. Two years after his death in 44 B.C. Julius Caesar was deified; Augustus, though refusing to accept divine honors during his life in an official way, did not object to being called "god" in the eastern provinces, where various peoples for centuries had considered their kings to be gods. Tiberius likewise refused divine honors at home, but encouraged them in the provinces. Caligula demanded to be treated as a god, and Nero was the first emperor who actually wore the radiate crown, with spikes representing rays of the sun, probably to indicate that he wanted to be considered a protégé of the sun-god Apollo. Domitian had himself addressed as "lord and god." Nothing made it more difficult to be a Christian than the demand of the state to worship the emperor as a god, and most of the later cruel persecutions were waged because Christians came into conflict with official Rome for their refusal to comply with this demand.

VII. Roman City Life. The apostles did most of their missionary work in cities; hence it is of interest to a Bible reader to obtain an idea of Roman city life during the imperial period. The excavations of Pompeii, Ostia, and other Roman cities have given us a vivid picture of the interesting life of a Roman citizen in the apostolic period. The cultural and economic center of every city was the forum or the market, corresponding to a modern town square. At the forum or in its vicinity were found the offices of the magistrates, the chief temples of the city, and many shops, although shops were found throughout the city. In the center of the city was the courthouse, the principal baths, to which people went not only to get clean, but to be entertained, to engage in athletic exercises, and to meet friends and acquaintances. The theater provided plays and musical performances; the amphitheater, or sometimes the circus, or racecourse, saw the bloody games of animals and of gladiators against ferocious wild beasts. Practically all industry and craftsmanship was confined to small workshops, frequently to the houses in which the craftsmen, professionals, or factory owners also lived. Shops generally occupied the ground floor of apartment buildings and sometimes, in smaller houses, the rooms facing the street. Domestic slaves lived in the same house with their masters. All streets were paved with cobblestones, and most had raised footpaths on both sides, with steppingstones on which pedestrians could cross the roadway, which lacked drainage. Carts or wagons were not allowed on the streets during the daytime in the city of Rome. Water was obtained from private wells and from street-corner fountains, to which it was channeled by means of aqueducts and led through the city by means of lead pipes put under the streets. See fig. 410.

Houses were of all sizes and shapes. In earlier Rome, as in smaller towns, the one-family home was the unit, with the rooms facing inward and lighted by roof openings or courts. However, in Paul's day only the wealthy few in the capital could afford to have separate houses such as are well known as the typical Roman dwelling (domus, "house") in such smaller cities as Pompeii and Herculaneum—houses of 1 or 2 floors, with a number of rooms arranged around a courtlike hall called an atrium and around an open court called a peristyle.

The description of an actual private home, the "House of the Surgeon" in Pompeii, will give an idea of a house in which wealthy Romans lived in the time of the apostles (see fig. 408). The street door (A) opens into a narrow vestibule (B) that leads into a reception hall (D, atrium). The atrium roof slopes inward toward an opening in the center that carries the rainwater into a tank (E, impluvium) set into the middle of the floor (from such a tank the water was usually led into a cistern for further use). Opening into both sides of the atrium are small bedrooms (F, cubicula), and at the back of these, 2 opposite alcoves, completely open toward the atrium, called wings (G,

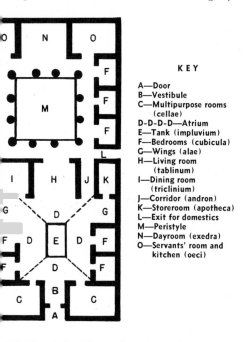

KEY

A—Door
B—Vestibule
C—Multipurpose rooms (cellae)
D-D-D-D—Atrium
E—Tank (impluvium)
F—Bedrooms (cubicula)
G—Wings (alae)
H—Living room (tablinum)
I—Dining room (triclinium)
J—Corridor (andron)
K—Storeroom (apotheca)
L—Exit for domestics
M—Peristyle
N—Dayroom (exedra)
O—Servants' room and kitchen (oeci)

408. Plan of the "House of the Surgeon" at Pompeii, a typical Roman private house of the wealthy class

alae), which were used as rooms for closets or cupboards and boxes in which garments, instruments, and utensils were stored. Here the portrait masks of ancestors were displayed. Opposite the main entrance, and lying between the atrium and the open court (peristyle), is the tablinum (H). This was where the master of the house met his visitors, and it might be called a living room, since family reunions took place there. The tablinum of the surgeon's house (usually closed toward the atrium by a curtain), opens toward the court lying behind it, though in some houses there is a wall, with or without windows, across the back. Next to this room is the dining room, triclinium (I), used during the cold season, opening into the atrium by means of a door. On the other side of the central tablinum is a narrow corridor (J) connecting the atrium with the peristyle. Next to it is a closed storage room (K), also used as a wine cellar (apotheca). The open court (M, peristyle) is surrounded by columns.

This court was a feature that the Romans had adopted from the Greek house, and it usually contained statues, flowers, and shrubbery in its center, hence was a small, well-cultivated house garden. On one side of the peristyle are more bedrooms, also 2 corner rooms for the servants and the kitchen, and between them a room (N), open to the peristyle, the exedra, a room in which meals were taken, or guests were received, in the warm season. Although the house here described is typical for the imperial period, other houses of this type showed great individual varieties. Some had more than one atrium, some had no peristyle, others had several dining rooms, or many rooms for servants, and many had dining rooms or sleeping quarters on a 2d floor. Often outside rooms, fronting on the street, were used as shops.

Roman homes had fewer pieces of furniture than our modern houses. They had beds consisting of wooden rectangular frames on 4 legs, over which interlacing cords were stretched to support a mattress; they had tables, cupboards, shelves, boxes, pottery vessels and dishes, metal vessels and dishes, candlesticks, lamps, and couches, on which the Romans reclined to eat, write, and relax, since they did not sit on chairs to dine (*see* Meals) but reclined around a low table. The walls of such Roman houses were painted with scenes of outside architecture, landscapes, or events of Greek mythology.

409. The Colosseum at Rome

Those who could not afford such houses lived in apartments of various grades, sizes, prices, and degrees of comfort. Poor people might live in 1 or 2 rooms, perhaps behind or over a shop, which

410. Artist's reconstruction, based on archeological evidence, of a Roman apartment house with ground-floor shops. It may well have been in such a building that the Apostle Paul lived for 2 full years "in his own hired dwelling"

would be workrooms and living quarters at the same time. People of small to moderate means lived in apartments in the upper floors of the same buildings. Such a block of apartments and lodgings was called an insula (island) because it was entirely surrounded by the narrow streets. In crowded Rome the bulk of the population lived in such apartment buildings (fig. 410), which rose several stories above the street-level shops. Remains have been found of such a building having as many as 6 or 7 stories. We may imagine Paul, who was not rich but worked with his own hands, as living in his own hired lodgings in a crowded insula in Rome.

Roof. *See* House.

Room.

1. A chamber in a *house (Mt 6:6) or in a temple (2 Ki 10:25); or an apartment in a ship, as in Noah's ark (Gen 6:14).

2. Space of undefined but sufficient extent, as, for example, in the question, "Is there room in your father's house?" (Gen 24;23).

3. Place, position, rank, or status, in a now obsolete sense in the KJV. For example, Archelaus is said to have reigned "in the room of his father" (Mt 2:22); and the Pharisees are accused of loving "the uppermost rooms at feasts" (ch 23:6), meaning "the place of honor at feasts" (RSV).

Rose. [Heb. *chabaṣṣeleth*.] A shrub possessing prickly stems and bearing a sweet-smelling, five-petaled, or double, blossom prized for its beauty and fragrance; also the flower. Whether Bible writers, using *chabaṣṣeleth*, intended any member of the genus *Rosa* cannot be determined. The Hebrew word occurs but twice (Song 2:1; Is 35:1), and in both occurrences is translated "rose" in the KJV. The RSV has "rose" in the text of Song 2:1 but gives "crocus" as a marginal reading, and in Is 35:1 uses "crocus" in the text. Several plants have been suggested: (1) A variety of narcissus (*Narcissus tazetta*) that flourishes in the Plain of Sharon in the spring and on the low-lying hills. Its fragrance makes it a popular blossom. (2) One of the more than 15 varieties of crocus known to the Holy Land, or a similar plant, the colchicum. (3) Asphodel (*Asphodelus microcarpus*), a plant of the lily family. (4) The primrose. Harold N. Moldenke points out that "the 'roses' of the Scriptures . . . are among the most controversial of all Biblical plants. There is no unanimity among commentators regarding any of them" (*Plants of the Bible*, p. 205).

Although traditionally the "rose of Sharon" has been considered an appellation for Christ, the construction of the passage in Song 2:1 indicates this verse to be a statement of the bride. In Is 35:1 *chabaṣṣeleth* is used to picture a land that blooms again after being redeemed from its enemies.

Rosh (rŏsh). [Heb. *Ro'sh,* "head," or "chief."] A son of Benjamin, who went with his father's family to Egypt (Gen 46:21), but seems to have died without leaving issue, since no descendants of his are mentioned in the list of Num 26:38.

Rubies. [Heb. *penînim; penîyîm.*] Precious stones, but the exact identification of the Hebrew term is uncertain. The RSV variously translates it "pearls," "jewels," "costly stones," and "coral." The Oriental ruby is a red variety of corundum, clear and bright. The value of wisdom, of knowledge, or of a virtuous woman is greater than *penînim* (Job 28:18; Prov 3:15; 8:11; 20:15; 31:10). The Nazirites (RSV "princes") were said to be more ruddy of body than rubies (Lam 4:7).

Rudiment. *See* Elements.

Rue. [Gr. *pēganon.*] A cultivated herb (*Ruta graveolens*) highly regarded in ancient times as of medicinal value. The plant's strong odor doubtless gave it the reputation of possessing therapeutic value. The plant, a somewhat shrubby perennial, grows to a height of 2 or 3 ft. and bears yellow flowers and deeply cut bluish-green leaves. According to the Mishnah (*Shebe'ith* 9:1) it was not subject to tithe, but in Christ's time it was meticulously tithed by the Pharisees, while they overlooked the weightier matters of the Law (Lk 11:42).

Rufus (rōō'fŭs). [Gr. *Rhouphos,* the transliteration of Latin *Rufus,* "red," a name occurring frequently in the inscriptions.]
1. Son of the Simon who carried Jesus' cross (Mk 15:21). The Scripture passage implies that he and his brother Alexander were known to the readers of Mark, and hence that they were Christians. It is for this reason that some have identified him with Rufus, 2, though there is no proof of such identity.
2. A member of the Christian church of Rome. Paul sent greetings to him and his mother in his letter to the Romans (Rom 16:13). Some think he is identical with Rufus, 1.

Rug. A rendering of the Heb. *semîkah,* the meaning of which is uncertain (Jgs 4:18, RSV). In the context it may mean either a "tent curtain" separating the women's apartment in a tent, or a tent "rug." Jael used a *semîkah* to conceal Sisera when he sought refuge in her tent following the defeat of his army by Deborah and Barak at the river Kishon in the plains of Megiddo.

Ruhamah (rōō-hä'má). [Heb. *Ruchamah,*

"she has received compassion," "she has obtained pity" (RSV), from *racham,* "to be compassionate."] A cryptic name or expression appearing in Hos 2:1, KJV, a play on the name *Lo-ruhamah (ch 1:6, KJV). The term reflects Hosea's compassion for his household, and in a larger sense, God's compassion for His people Israel.

Ruler. A general term signifying one who exercises authority or official executive guidance over a specific group or body of people, large or small. Joseph was "ruler" in Egypt, and Daniel in Babylon, in the sense of "prime minister" (Gen 45:8; cf. ch 41:41-44; Dan 2:48). The Israelites, during their desert wanderings, had "rulers of thousands, and rulers of hundreds, rulers of fifties, and rulers of tens" (Ex 18:21). The "rulers" before whom Paul and Silas were accused (Acts 16:19) were the magistrates of the city (v 20). The "rulers" before whom Peter and John were arraigned (ch 4:5, 8) were probably the high priests. In ch 23:5 Paul equates the high priest with "the ruler" of the people. Jairus was "a ruler of the synagogue" (Lk 8:41), which probably means he was in charge of public worship. The person in charge of a feast was referred to as the ruler, or governor, of the feast (Jn 2:8, 9, KJV). Micah prophesied (Mic 5:2) of Christ that He would be "ruler in Israel" (cf. Mt 2:5, 6; Jn 7:42). Paul refers to evil angels as the rulers of the spiritual darkness of the world (Eph 6:12).

Rumah (rōō'má). [Heb. *Rûmah,* "high place."] The home of Pedaiah, the maternal grandfather of King Jehoiakim (2 Ki 23:36). Josephus (*Ant.* x. 5. 2) calls it *Abou-mas,* which suggests that it might have been *Arumah (Jgs 9:41), in the neighborhood of Shechem. However, it may have been Rumah in Galilee (Jos. *War* iii. 7. 21), identified with *Khirbet Rûmeh,* about 6 mi. north of Nazareth.

Runnel. A rendering of the Heb. *rahaṭ* (Gen 30:38, 41, RSV), probably a "watering trough" (KJV "gutter").

Rush. *See* Bulrush.

Rust. [Heb. *chel'ah;* Gr. *brōsis,* "eating"; *ios.*] The coating or tarnish that appears on metal surfaces as they oxidize or weather; a symbol of loss and decay. Ezekiel compared Jerusalem to a pot whose rust is "in" it (Eze 24:6, 11-13, RSV). Jesus warned that rust would attack the valuables of those who permit the world to be their treasure house, but treasures laid up in heaven would escape corruption

(Mt 6:19, 20). James predicted the wealth of money hoarders would disintegrate (Jas 5:3).

Ruth (rōōth). [Heb. *Rûth,* meaning uncertain; Gr. *Rhouth.*] A Moabitess, the daughter-in-law of Naomi. She married Mahlon, the son of Elimelech and Naomi, while they were refugees in the land of Moab from a severe famine in Judah, their homeland (Ruth 1:1, 2; 4:10). After a time, during which Elimelech, Mahlon, and Chilion died, Naomi with her 2 widowed daughters-in-law, Ruth and Orpah, set out to return to Bethlehem in the land of Judah (ch 1:6, 7). Orpah was persuaded to remain in Moab, but Ruth, in a supreme act of loyalty and devotion to her mother-in-law, returned with Naomi to Bethlehem (vs 11-18). It is Ruth's unsurpassed spirit of devotion that makes the story recorded in the book of Ruth worth preserving and that doubtless accounts for its inclusion in the sacred canon. Reaching Bethlehem at the time of barley harvest (v 22), probably in early April, Ruth went out into the harvest field to glean, in keeping with the Mosaic law that allotted to the poor whatever the reapers might have missed (Ruth 2: 2, 3; Lev 19:9, 10; 23:22). Ruth's fortune was to glean in a portion of the field belonging to Boaz, a relative of Elimelech, who took special notice of her and extended her special favor because of her fidelity to Naomi and doubtless also because of her own winsome ways. Custom, based on the levirate marriage law (Deut 25:5-10; cf. Ruth 1:11-13), required the nearest kinsman of Mahlon to marry Ruth, so becoming his legal heir and perpetuating Mahlon's family inheritance (see Ruth 4:3, 4, 9). However, the nearest of kin had the privilege of excusing himself if he desired (Deut 25:7-10). In this instance the nearest of kin refused to accept the responsibility (Ruth 4:6), which therefore devolved on Boaz (vs 7, 8), who formally assumed the privileges and responsibilities that fell to him as Elimelech's legal heir, including marriage to Ruth (vs 9, 10). Obed, the grandfather of David (vs 13, 21, 22) and a progenitor of Christ, was born of this union. Ruth is honored by the inclusion of her name in Matthew's genealogy of Jesus Christ (Mt 1:5).

Ruth, Book of. An epic idyl narrating events that occurred during the period of the judges. In the Hebrew canon Ruth appears in the Megilloth, or Five Scrolls, along with Song, Ec, Lam, and

Est. The Megilloth belonged to the 3d division of the *canon, the Hagiographa, or Holy Writings. The opening words of the book—"in the days when the judges ruled" (Ruth 1:1)—imply that it was written sometime after the close of that period of Hebrew history. Critical scholars, both Jewish and Christian, have assigned it to postexilic times, chiefly in view of the fact that it appears in the 3d division of the Hebrew canon—thus implying late composition, it is claimed—and that it contains a number of postexilic Aramaic expressions. These arguments, however, are far from conclusive. It should be remembered that the Hebrew canon in its present form is itself of comparatively late origin, and that therefore the position assigned Ruth in the canon as we now have it is not a conclusive indication of the time of its composition. The presence of certain of the Aramaic words at issue in uncontested, pre-exilic documents proves invalid the contention that these words prove a postexilic date for the book of Ruth. The twin expressions, "in the days when the judges ruled" (ch 1:1) and "in former time" (ch 4:7), cannot be pressed as indicating postexilic origin, since they do no more than denote some point of origin *after* the close of the period of the judges without specifying how *long* after. In view of the fact that the genealogy that concludes the book (vs 18-22) closes with David, it would be reasonable to assume that the book was written about the time his reign began. If certain Aramaic expressions actually prove to belong exclusively to a later time, this may indicate only that the book did not attain final literary form until later. The chronological statements of chs 1:1 and 4:7 may also have been added later to assist later readers in understanding some of the obsolete customs mentioned in the book. The picture of customs, society, and government reflected in the book of Ruth corresponds accurately with what is known from other sources about the period of the judges.

Though rooted in history, the narrative of Ruth is essentially idyllic in quality. Its primary appeal is emotional and inspirational. This is the basis for its inclusion in the sacred canon. As a story of human affection at its best, the story of Ruth is unsurpassed in literature. Her devotion to her mother-in-law was even more impressive in view of the fact that she was a Moabitess, and that her decision to remain with Naomi and to return to Bethlehem meant forsaking her own home, her own people, her own customs, and her former religion for ones that were new and, doubtless in large measure, strange to her. *See* Ruth. In recording the conversion of a Gentile to the Hebrew faith and showing how one not of the stock of Israel became an ancestress of David, Israel's greatest king, the book may also be considered an appeal to the missionary vision of Israel as an encouragement to foster other such conversions. As a narrative of how Naomi and Ruth overcame tragedy in their home, the story also affords encouragement to those who in this modern age pass through similar experiences.

The narrative opens with an explanation of circumstances that brought Naomi and her family to the land of Moab, a brief account of her experiences there, of Ruth's choice to return with her to Bethlehem (Ruth 1). Back in Bethlehem, the narrator explains how Ruth became acquainted with Boaz (ch 2), thus setting the stage for the marriage proposal (ch 3) and the marriage itself (ch 4:1-17). The closing verses of the book (vs 18-22) show Ruth's relationship to the royal ancestors of David.

S

Sabachthani. A transliteration through the Greek of the Aramaic *shebaqtani,* meaning "thou hast forsaken me." (Mt 27:46; Mk 15:34). *See* Eloi.

Sabaoth. A term appearing in Rom 9:29; Jas 5:4; KJV, in the expression "the Lord of sabaoth" (RSV "Lord of hosts"). Sabaoth is a transliteration of the Gr. *sabaōth,* which in turn is a transliteration of the Heb. *ṣeba'ôth,* "hosts," "armies." The expression "Lord of hosts," *Yahweh ṣeba-'ôth,* occurs frequently in the OT as a title of God (1 Sa 1:3, 11; 1 Ki 18:15; etc.).

Sabbath. [Heb. *shabbath,* "Sabbath," "rest (day)," "a cessation," and *shabbathôn,* a variant form of *shabbath,* both from *shabath,* "to cease," "to rest," "to keep Sabbath"; Gr. *sabbaton,* "sabbath."] The weekly day of rest, divinely instituted at the close of Creation week, and observed by the worshipers of God, Jew and Christian alike, throughout Bible times. After God had "finished" creating the earth He "rested on the seventh day from all his work" (Gen 2:1, 2). This *"rest" was not because of weariness or fatigue (Is 40:28), but because the task was complete, and the world perfect (see Gen 1:31). He found that it measured up in every way to His ideal for it, and He ceased His labors because His handiwork could not be improved upon. He then "blessed the seventh day, and sanctified it," as a memorial to the finished work of Creation (ch 2:3). Inasmuch as "the sabbath was made for man" (Mk 2:27)—that is, for man's good—it is logical to conclude that the divine blessing with which the Creator endowed the 7th day of the week was designed to constitute the day a channel of blessing to Adam and Eve. Inasmuch as God also "sanctified" the day (Gen 2:3), or set it apart for holy use, we may be sure that our first parents devoted its sacred hours to such use. That the Creator intended the Sabbath blessing for all men of all time is evident from the declaration that it was "made for man" (Mk 2:27), with the intention that man should use it for holy purposes. Accordingly, the 7th day is a day of rest for all who reckon their descent from Adam and Eve, not for the Jews alone. In fact, there were no Jews until some thousands of years after Creation, and God never intended that they should seek to monopolize the Sabbath.

That our first parents and their descendants must have understood the significance of the 7th day is evident, because: (1) God did not perform the acts of Creation week for His own benefit, but for that of man. Since God's rest on the 7th day was not from weariness, and since that day was an integral part of Creation week, as its title indicates, the conclusion may be drawn that God's blessing and sanctification of the 7th day was also for man's good—particularly his moral and spiritual good. (2) From the dawn of history the 7-day week was known and recognized as a unit of time measurement (see Gen 7:4, 10; 8:10, 12; 29:27). Since the length of the week does not depend upon the movements of any of the heavenly bodies, and since there is no way of accounting for its origin apart from the Creation record of Gen 1 and 2, man's recognition of the 7-day week in those early times must be traced to God's appointment of the 7th day of the week as a day of rest, blessing, and holiness.

The first occurrence of the word Sabbath is in Ex 16:21-30 in connection with the giving of the manna prior to Israel's arrival at Mount Sinai. God stressed the importance of the 7th day of the week as a Sabbath of rest by providing a double supply of manna on the 6th day and none on the 7th. This weekly miracle continued from the 2d month after Israel's departure from Egypt (vs 1, 14, 15) to the 1st month, 40 years later (Jos 5:10-12; cf. Ex 12:2-11; 16:35)—or for more than 2,000 successive weekly Sabbath days.

At Mount Sinai God enjoined the observance of the 7th-day Sabbath in the 4th precept of the Decalogue (Ex 20:8-11). This law He inscribed with His own finger upon tables of stone (Ex 31:18; Deut 9:10) and instructed Moses that it be placed in the ark of the covenant (Deut 10:1-5). The word "remember," with which the Sabbath commandment begins, does not imply that the observance of the 4th commandment is more important than the other 9, for all are of equal importance (see Jas 2:8-11). God's people were to "remember" the Sabbath because "in six days the Lord made heaven and earth, the sea, and all that in them is, and rested the seventh day"—that is, as a memorial of the Creator and Creation. That is why "the Lord blessed the sabbath day, and hallowed it" in the beginning. God knew man's natural tendency would be to become so engrossed with the *things* He had made during the 6 days of Creation week as to forget the *One* who made them, a tendency universally evident since ancient times (see Rom 1:20-25). The OT Scriptures repeatedly distinguish the true God from all false gods on the basis of His creative power, as, for example, Ps 96:5, "the gods of the nations are idols: but the Lord made the heavens." God ordained that man should understand "the invisible things of him . . . even his eternal power and Godhead" through "the things that are made" (Rom 1:20). Accordingly, an all-wise Creator ordained the Sabbath to be a safeguard against forgetting Him and wandering off into idolatry. It was meant to be a blessing to man, not a burden. God specifically declared it to be "a sign" between Him and His people for all time, by which they were ever to remember the true God as their God (Ex 31:13). In addition to its universal import for all men, the Sabbath was of additional significance for Israel as a memorial of God's deliverance, and of rest from the servitude of Egypt (Deut 5:12-15).

In addition to the weekly Sabbath (Lev 23:3) there were 7 annual, ceremonial sabbaths scattered throughout the ritual calendar: the 1st and last days of the Feast of Unleavened Bread (vs 7, 8), Pentecost (v 21), the 1st day of the 7th month (v 24), the Day of Atonement (v 27), and the 1st and last days of the Feast of Tabernacles (vs 32-36). These ceremonial sabbaths might fall upon any day of the week, and sometimes coincided with the weekly Sabbath. Besides the weekly Sabbath and the annual sabbaths, every 7th year was to be a sabbatic year, during which the land was to lie fallow (ch 25:3-7). See Sabbatical Year. Every 50th year was to be proclaimed a year of jubilee, during which all property reverted to its original owner. See Jubilee.

By enjoining cessation from labor, the command to observe the weekly Sabbath provided time for physical rest and spiritual refreshment. The day was not to be spent in idleness, however, for God instructed the people to assemble together for "a holy convocation" (Lev 23:3; cf. Eze 46:3). The pre-eminence of the Sabbath day over the other days of the week was further stressed in the ancient tabernacle and Temple ritual by the offering of an additional lamb (Num 28:9, 19) and by renewing the bread of the Presence (Lev 24:5-8; 1 Chr 9:32). Under the Levitical law the penalty for violation of the Sabbath day was death (Ex 31:14-16), and at least one occasion on which a willful Sabbathbreaker was put to death is on record (Num 15:32-36).

The desecration of the Sabbath day was one of the sins that led to the Babylonian captivity (Jer 17:19-27). Like Jeremiah, the prophet Ezekiel lamented the fact that in his day the Sabbath was, to a large extent, ignored (Eze 20:12-24; 22:8, 26; 23:38). Looking to the future, Isaiah foretold the conversion of the Gentiles and promised a blessing to those of them who should keep the Sabbath (Is 56:2-6; cf. 58:13). After the Captivity the Jews again lapsed into carelessness with regard to the Sabbath, and Nehemiah instituted a reform in its observance (Neh 10:31; 13:15-22).

During the intertestamental period the Pharisees bound the Sabbath about with a multitude of trivial regulations that made the day a burden instead of a blessing. These burdensome regulations, later codified in the Mishnah, constituted a part of the tradition that Jesus so vigorously opposed throughout His ministry (Mt 23:4; Mk 7:1-13). The Mishnah (*Shabbath* 7. 2) lists 39 kinds of labor not to be performed upon the Sabbath day, and there were countless other minute Sabbath regulations. In fact, 2 entire tractates of the Mishnah, *Shabbath* and *'Erubin,* are devoted to various regulations concerning the Sabbath. Forbidden were such acts as tying or loosening a knot, writing as much as 2 letters of the alphabet or erasing in order to make space for 2 letters, lighting a fire or putting one out. The best-known Sabbath regulation concerned the so-called "sabbath day's journey" of about ⅔ of a mile. *See* Sabbath Day's Journey. It was also counted as Sabbathbreaking to look into a mirror fixed on the wall. An egg laid on the Sabbath might be sold to a Gentile, but not eaten, and a Gentile could be hired to light a candle or a fire on the Sabbath. It was counted unlawful to expectorate upon the ground lest thereby a blade of grass be irrigated. It was not permitted to carry a handkerchief on the Sabbath unless one end of it be sewed to one's garment—in which case it was no longer technically a handkerchief but a part of the garment. The rabbis thus emphasized the negative aspect of Sabbath observance —of refraining from certain things—and in so doing magnified the importance of the forms of religion while minimizing its substance. They made the Sabbath an end in itself and bound man in slavery to it. These negative, hairsplitting regulations served effectively to obscure the true purpose of the Sabbath. This rabbinical emphasis on rigid Sabbath observance was at high tide during our Lord's earthly ministry, and at no point did Jesus come into sharper conflict with the leaders of Judaism than on the matter of Sabbath observance. He taught that the Sabbath was made for man's benefit (Mk 2:27, 28), and emphasized the positive aspect of Sabbath observance—the type of activity to which the day should be devoted. Nothing He said or did can be construed as opposed to the Sabbath as set forth in the Ten Commandments or in the Levitical law. His protest was directed exclusively against the abuse the Sabbath day had suffered at the hands of the rabbis, and it was His purpose to set the day free from the burdensome regulations with which

they had hedged it about (see Mt 23:13). It was His own custom to devote the day to attendance at religious services and to religious instruction (Mk 1:21; 3:1; Lk 4:16-27; 13:10), to appropriate social activities (Mk 1:29-31; 2:23; Lk 14:1-3), and to deeds of mercy. Seven of His miracles of healing were performed upon the Sabbath day (Mk 1:21-31; 3:1-5; Lk 13:10-17; 14:1-4; Jn 5:1-15; 9:1-7).

Throughout NT times Christians observed the 7th day of the week as the Sabbath. In view of the great importance the Jews attached to the Sabbath and in the light of the storm of opposition aroused by the Gentile neglect of ritual observances (see Acts 15; Gal 2; 3), any deviation from Sabbath observance as enjoined by the Decalogue, by Paul, or any leaders of apostolic times, would inevitably have aroused a storm of protest similar to that which arose over such regulations as circumcision, eating with Gentiles, and various other ceremonial regulations (see Acts 11:1-3; 15:1, 2; 21:20, 21; Gal 3:1; 4:10; 5:1). It is incredible that contention over the observance of the 7th-day Sabbath, had there been such, would not likewise find mention in the NT. But of such contention the NT writers maintain a profound silence. To the contrary, there is frequent mention that the apostle Paul, as he went about the Gentile world proclaiming the gospel, "went into the synagogue on the sabbath day" (Acts 13:14, 44; 16:13; 17:2; 18:4). It may be argued that he did so because he was sure to find a large gathering there on the Sabbath day. But at the same time the NT is silent concerning *any* Christian religious gatherings on the first day of the week that provide the least hint that Christians attached any particular significance to that day. Among the NT passages sometimes cited in an endeavor to prove observance of the 1st day by the apostolic Christians are Mt 28:1; Acts 20:7; 1 Cor 16:2; Rev 1:10, but upon examination these passages are found to afford no evidence indicating a transfer of sanctity from the 7th to the 1st day of the week, or that the early Christians ever thought of the 1st day as a holy day. *See* First Day of the Week; Lord's Day. The simple fact remains that, from first to last, the Scriptures know of no other day than the 7th day of the week as a weekly holy day of perpetual obligation.

The first mention of the Sabbath in extra-Biblical sources occurs on inscribed potsherds found on the island of Elephan-

411. A piece of broken pottery (ostracon) found at Elephantine. The Aramaic inscription mentions the Sabbath

tine (see fig. 411). These inscriptions of the 5th cent. B.C. were written by Jewish colonists living on that island as mercenaries in Persian employ. In the records of the ancient nations no mention is made of the Sabbath. The Babylonian term *shabatu,* connected by some with the Sabbath, was not a weekly day of rest, but the name given to the day of the full moon, celebrated as a feast once every month. Some have seen traces of the existence of a 7-day week in the special taboos attached to the 7th, 14th, 21st, and 28th days of the month mentioned in early Mesopotamian hemerologies, that is, works that list lucky and unlucky days and contain rules of what should and what should not be done on various days. It is possible that these regulations may reflect some dim recollection of the original week known to the patriarchs. A study of the religious practices among the pagan nations of antiquity shows that polytheism and idolatry erased nearly all knowledge of God and true worship. The pagans learned of the Sabbath from the Jews of the Dispersion. *See* Week.

Sabbath Day's Journey. A term applied in the time of Christ to the distance that a Jew was allowed to travel on the Sabbath without breaking Jewish traditional law. The expression occurs in the Bible only in Acts 1:12, where Luke uses the phrase to indicate the distance between Jerusalem and the Mount of Olives for the information of Theophilus, the recipient of the book of Acts (v 1), who was apparently not familiar with Palestine and Jerusalem. The distance from the eastern wall to the traditional site of ascension on the Mount of Olives is 2,250 ft. in a straight line, but considerably longer in actual travel. The rabbis based their regulations pertaining to the Sabbath day's journey on the prohibition of Ex 16:29, to "let no man go out of his place" on the Sabbath, and ruled that this "place" should extend to a dis-

tance of 2,000 cu. from a man's house. The distance of 2,000 cu. (*c.* 2,916 ft. in NT times) they based partly on Num 35: 5, according to which the area belonging to a Levitical city extended 2,000 cu. from the wall in every direction, and partly on Jos 3:4, according to which the Israelites, when on the march, were required to keep a distance of 2,000 cu. from the ark. This was interpreted to mean that the camp was at that distance from the tabernacle, to which one was naturally allowed to go on the Sabbath. Within the city limits no travel restriction existed, even if a city was very large. Since these restrictions caused the Jews much hardship and many difficulties, the rabbis found a way to extend it from 2,000 to 4,000 cu. This was done by ruling that a "residence" might be established at the end of the first 2,000 cu. previous to the Sabbath by depositing food there. Thus one might travel another 2,000 cu. from that "residence" on the Sabbath.

Sabbatical Year. Every 7th year, during which the Hebrews were commanded to let the land rest, that is, to let the soil lie fallow (Lev 25:1-7). Not even what grew of itself was to be harvested. This was an ancient equivalent of the modern practice of rotating crops, in order to prevent depletion of the soil. The 7th year was also called a "year of release" (Deut 31: 10; cf. 15:1-3), in which the debts of poor Hebrews were to be remitted. Though the Bible mentions no actual observance of a specific sabbatical year, the Jews evidently observed the custom in the time of Alexander the Great and of Julius Caesar, both of whom exempted them from taxes in the sabbatical years (Jos. *Ant.* xi. 8. 6; xiv. 10. 6). Seven "weeks" of years culminated in the *Jubilee.

The sabbatical years evidently ran from Tishri to Tishri, for (1) they were obviously agricultural years, and the agricultural cycle began with plowing in the fall, after the rainy season began; and (2) they ran in series with the jubilee years, which began Tishri 10.

The term "sabbatical year" does not occur in the Bible, but the institution is referred to in the phrases "the sabbath of the land" (Lev 25:6), "then shall the land keep a sabbath" (v 2; cf. ch 26: 34, 35).

Sabeans (sá-bē′ănz). The people of Sheba, Heb. *Sheba'im* (Joel 3:8), as well as those of *Seba, Heb. *Seba'im* (Is 45:14), both Hebrew terms being rendered Sabeans. The Sabeans of Eze 23:42, KJV (Heb.

Sôb'îm K, *Saba'îm* Q), are a people of uncertain identification.

Sabta. *See* Sabtah.

Sabtah (săb'tà), or **Sabta** (săb'tà). [Heb. *Sabtah* and *Sabta'*.] A son of Cush (Gen 10:7; 1 Chr 1:9), and apparently ancestor of an Arabian tribe. Some have identified the tribe with Sabota, the chief city of the South Arabian country of Hadhramaut; others with Ptolemy's *Saphtha* on the Persian Gulf. Definite identification at present is impossible. Map IV, D-6 assigns this tribe to South Arabia.

Sabteca (săb'tĕ-kà), KJV once **Sabtechah** (săb'tĕ-kà) and once **Sabtecha** (săb'tĕ-kà). [Heb. *Sabteka'*.] A son of Cush (Gen 10:7; 1 Chr 1:9), and ancestor of an Arabian tribe, not identified. Map IV, D-5 places this tribe in South Arabia.

Sabtecha. *See* Sabteca.

Sabtechah. *See* Sabteca.

Sacar (sā'kär). [Heb. *Sakar*, "hire."]
1. A Levite, the 4th son of Obed-edom, and a Temple gatekeeper (1 Chr 26:4).
2. For 1 Chr 11:35, KJV, *see* Sacher.

Sacher (sā'kĕr), KJV **Sacar** (sā'kär). [Heb. *Sakar*, "hire," or "wages."] A Hararite, and the father of Ahiam, one of David's "mighty men" (1 Chr 11:35); called Sharar the Hararite in 2 Sa 23:33.

Sachia (sà-kī'à), KJV **Shachia** (shà-kī'à). [Heb. *Sakeyah*, probably "Yahweh looks out."] A Benjamite (1 Chr 8:10).

Sack. [Heb. generally, *'amtachath*, "sack," and *šaq*, "sackcloth," "sack."] With 4 exceptions (1 Sa 9:7; 2 Ki 4:42; RSV; Lev 11:32; Jos 9:4), the Biblical references are all to the bags which held the grain given by Joseph to his brothers in Egypt (Gen 42 to 44). The "sack" of 2 Ki 4:42, RSV, is the result of an emendation. The meaning of the Heb. *ṣiqlôn* is uncertain. In 1 Sa 9:7 "sack" (KJV "vessel") is translated from the Heb. *keli*, literally "vessel," in the context probably a breadbasket.

Sackbut. *See* Trigon.

Sackcloth. [Heb. *šaq*; Gr. *sakkos*, both meaning either "sack," or "sackcloth."] The wearing of sackcloth—a coarse, dark cloth, woven usually of goat's or camel's hair—was a symbol of deep sorrow and mourning (2 Sa 3:31; 2 Ki 19:1, 2). It seems sometimes to have been worn about the loins as a girdle, but may have been worn at times as a loose-fitting sacklike garment covering the greater part of the body (Gen 37:34; 1 Ki 20:31; Is 20:2; etc.). Sometimes the mourner rent his clothing before donning the symbolic

sackcloth, which was in some cases worn next to the body (1 Ki 21:27; 2 Ki 6:30; Is 32:11; etc.). Those wearing the sackcloth of mourning frequently put ashes upon themselves or lay in them (Est 4:1, 3; Is 58:5; Jer 6:26; Jon 3:6; etc.); sometimes they placed earth upon themselves (Neh 9:1). The king of Nineveh wore sackcloth and sat in ashes to symbolize his repentance and fear of coming judgment (Jon 3:6; cf. Job 2:8). Isaiah seems to have worn sackcloth, for a period at least, as a distinctive dress (Is 20:2). Under the 6th seal the sun is described as being "black as sackcloth of hair" (Rev 6:12), the hair doubtless being black *goat's hair. In ch 11:3 "two witnesses" are described as prophesying 1260 days, clothed in sackcloth.

Sacrifices and Offerings. Animals or agricultural products brought to the Lord as an expression of worship, gratitude, or dedication, or for the expiation of sin. The sacrificial system was inaugurated when sin entered the world (see Gen 4:3, 4), and served in subsequent centuries as a reminder that the wages of sin is death and that eternal life can be regained only as a divine gift (Rom 6:23). For many centuries the head of each family was its priest, but at Mount Sinai systematic provision was made for the various types of sacrifices, and eventually all were offered by the priests. In one way or another every sacrifice prefigured the great sacrifice of the "Lamb of God" (Jn 1:29; cf. Is 53:7), and the sin and trespass offerings in particular represented the vicarious sacrifice of Christ, who "was wounded for our transgressions" (Is 53:4, 5; cf. v 6). In and of themselves, the blood sacrifices of OT times never could and never did actually "take away sins" (Heb 10:4, 11), nor could they "make him that did the service perfect, as pertaining to the conscience" (ch 9:9). Christ's perfect sacrifice alone can "purge" the "conscience from dead works" (see vs 11-15). The fundamental truth expressed symbolically by the sacrifices was that "without shedding of blood is no remission" of sin (v 22), and that this shedding of blood is vicarious (Is 53:4, 6). Detailed information on the various sacrifices is given in Leviticus (especially chs 1-7; 16; 23), and in Exodus and Numbers.

The following table summarizes the various types of sacrifices offered by groups or individuals, at set times or for special purposes, and the kind of offering prescribed in each case.

TABLE OF SACRIFICES AND OFFERINGS

	Animals Prescribed*											Nonflesh offerings†	
	Any from flock or herd	Any male from flock or herd	Lamb	Male lamb	Ram	Ewe lamb	Female lamb or goat	He-goat	Bull	Pigeon	Turtledove	Flour	Cakes, wafers, bread
BURNT OFFERING (Purpose: worship, gratitude, dedication)													
Regular													
1. Daily,‡ morning and evening (Ex 29:38-42; Num 28:3-8).				2								✓	
2. Sabbaths (Num 28:9, 10).				2								✓	
3. New moons (Num 28:11-14).				7	1				2			✓	
4. Feast of Unleavened Bread (Num 28:17-25). Daily.				7	1				2			✓	
5. Day of the wave sheaf, Feast of Unleavened Bread (Lev 23:10-14).				1								✓	
6. Feast of Weeks, or Pentecost (Lev 23:15-21; Num 28:26-31).			7	7	3				3			✓	✓
7. New Year's Day: 7th month, 1st day (Num 29:1-6).				7	1				1			✓	
8. Day of Atonement (Lev 16; Num 29:7-11).				7	2				1			✓	
9. Feast of Tabernacles (Num 29:12-34). Daily.§				14	2				13			✓	
10. Octave of Feast of Tabernacles (Num 29:35-38).				7	1				1			✓	
11. As an accessory to sin offering of the congregation (Num 15:22-26); cf. vs 1-10.									1			✓	
Special													
12. As an accessory to sin offering of the poor (Lev 5:7-10).										1 or	1		
13. Dedicatory: at consecration of priests (Ex 29:15-18, 35; Lev 8:18-21).					1								
14. Dedicatory: at consecration of Levites (Num 8:5, 8, 10-12).									1				
15. Expiatory: for accidental violation of the Nazirite vow (Num 6:9-12).										1 or	1		
16. Votive: at completion of the Nazirite vow (Num 6:13-21).			1									✓	
17. Votive: voluntary (Lev 1:3, 10).		1								1 or	1		
18. Cleansing: from a bodily issue (Lev 15:13-15, 25-30).			1 or							1 or	1		
19. Cleansing: at childbirth (Lev 12:6-8).			1 or							1 or	1		
20. Cleansing: from leprosy (Lev 14:1-32).										1 or	1		
SIN OFFERINGS (Purpose: expiation of Godward sins)													
Regular													
21. New moons (Num 28:15).								1					
22. Feast of Unleavened Bread (Num 28:17, 24).								1					
23. Feast of Weeks, or Pentecost (Lev 23:19; Num 28:26-30). Daily.								2					
24. New Year's Day: 7th month, 1st day (Num 29:5).								1					
25. Day of Atonement (Lev 16; Num 29:11). Daily.								2					
26. Feast of Tabernacles (Num 29:12-34). Daily.								1					
27. Octave of Feast of Tabernacles (Num 29:35, 38).								1					

						7			
28. Dedicatory: consecration of priests and altar (Ex 29:14, 35-37; Lev 8:2, 14-17).						7			
29. Dedicatory: consecration of the Levites (Num 8:8-12).						1			
30. Expiatory: accidental violation of the Nazirite vow (Num 6:9-11).									1 or 1
31. Votive: fulfillment of the Nazirite vow (Num 6:13-16).									
32. Expiatory: congregational sin (Lev 4:13-21).				1		1			
33. Expiatory: priest's sin (Lev 4:3-12).						1			
34. Expiatory: ruler's sin (Lev 4:22-26).					1				
35. Expiatory: private individual's sin (Lev 4:27-35; Num 15:27, 28).				1					1 or 1 or ✔
36. Expiatory: private individual's sin: if poor (Lev 5:7, 11, 12).									1 or 1
37. Cleansing: after childbirth (Lev 12:6-8).									1 or 1
38. Cleansing: from a bodily issue (Lev 15:13-15, 28-30).									1 or 1
39. Cleansing: from leprosy (Lev 14:10, 19-22, 30, 31).			1 or						

TRESPASS (GUILT) OFFERING (Purpose: usually for expiation of gross manward sins)

40. Expiatory: for accidental violation of the Nazirite vow (Num 6:9, 12).				1					
41. Expiatory: for perjury, robbery, fraud (Lev 6:2-7).					1				
42. Expiatory: for deception, a rash oath, or uncleanness (Lev 5).				1					
43. Expiatory: ignorant sacrilege (Lev 5:15, 16).				1					
44. Expiatory: violation of a betrothed slave (Lev 19:20-22).									
45. Cleansing: from leprosy (Lev 14:12-18). Lamb plus 1 log of oil.			1						

PEACE OFFERING (Purpose: to express gratitude, good will, brotherhood)

46. At Pentecost, with the bread of the First Fruits (Lev 23:15-20).			2						

47. Freewill, thanksgiving, or votive (Lev 3:1-17; 7:11-36).	✔								✔
48. Dedicatory: at consecration of priests (Ex 29:19-28; Lev 8:22-32).			1						✔
49. Votive: at fulfillment of the Nazirite vow (Num 6:14-20).			1						✔

---

* Animals are listed according to the RSV names, since that version more nearly follows the distinctions in the Hebrew words.

† Cereal offerings, which were always to be accompanied by oil, incense, and salt (Lev 2:1-16), were prescribed, together with drink offerings of wine, for all burnt offerings, those in fulfillment of vows, and peace offerings (Num 15:1-12).

‡ The morning and evening sacrifices were offered every day, and all other burnt offerings for special days were prescribed in *addition to* the regular burnt offerings for that day.

§ The number of bulls was decreased daily by 1.

✔ Number, amount, or description either not given or omitted here for reasons of space.

The OT sacrifices and offerings may be classified variously as to: (1) purpose, (2) offerer, (3) kind.

1. *Purpose.* (1) The "burnt" offering expressed worship, gratitude, and dedication. It represented the unbroken, uninterrupted adoration, worship, and devotion of the entire congregation to the Lord. (2) "Sin" offerings represented the confession of, and atonement for, what have been termed Godward sins, while the "trespass" or "guilt" offering represented the confession of what have been termed manward sins, and restitution for injury or loss, though the precise difference is not always clear. (3) "Peace" offerings expressed gratitude, good will, brotherhood, or the fulfillment of vows.

2. *Offerer.* A distinction was made between sacrifices offered for the entire nation and those for individuals. (1) Those representing the entire congregation included: the *regular* burnt offerings (that is, those offered upon regularly recurring occasions); all regular sin offerings; and those presented for specific instances of sin on the part of the entire congregation; special burnt offerings that were presented with the sin offering for the congregation; the regular peace offering offered with the bread at Pentecost. (2) Those offered by individuals included: all the *special* burnt offerings and sin offerings (those required by specific circumstances), with the exception of the special burnt offerings and sin offerings for congregational sin; all trespass, or guilt, offerings; and all special peace offerings. A ruler's sin offering was more elaborate than that required of the common people, in keeping with his responsible position; the same was true for a priest, for whom there were, in addition, special specified burnt offerings at the time of consecration. Otherwise, all special burnt offerings, sin offerings, and peace offerings, and all trespass offerings were always for individuals.

3. *Kind of offering presented.* Except in the case of a sin offering for a desperately poor person, specific "clean," unblemished animals from the flock or herd, or sometimes pigeons or turtledoves, were prescribed for the various offerings. Some were to be male, others female, and still others either male or female. Of the flock, certain types of lambs and goats were specified, and in some instances a lamb or goat might be used interchangeably. Of the herd, oxen and bullocks were specified. With all burnt offerings, peace offer-

ings, and certain other offerings, were prescribed cereal offerings—sometimes called "meat" (KJV) or "meal" offerings—of grain, flour, or meal, often made into some type of bread. These were accompanied by salt, oil, and incense and by drink offerings, or libations, of wine (Lev 2:2-7, 13; Num 15:4-11). The cereal offerings, after a portion was offered, were generally eaten by the priest or the offerer. Nothing is said about the drink offering; some think that it was at first poured over the sacrifice that it accompanied; Josephus relates that in his time it was poured around the altar (*Ant.* iii. 9. 4).

A regular, or *daily,* burnt offering was offered morning and evening throughout the year, including days when other offerings were prescribed. Additional burnt offerings were required on Sabbaths, on new moons, at the 3 great annual festivals —the Feast of Unleavened Bread, the Feast of Weeks (Pentecost), and the Feast of Tabernacles—and on New Year's Day and the Day of Atonement. Special burnt offerings were offered: with the sin offering for the congregation, at the dedication of priests, with the Nazirite vow, with the sin offering of the poor, for purification from bodily issues, from leprosy, or after childbirth, and by individuals at will or as prescribed to accompany certain other offerings.

Regular sin offerings were specified for the entire congregation at the time of the new moon, on New Year's Day, and the Day of Atonement; and at the 3 great national festivals. Special sin offerings were required: (1) at the dedication of priests and Levites, (2) for the accidental violation of the Nazirite vow and upon the completion of the vow, (3) for congregational sin or (4) that of a priest or ruler, and (5) for individual sins. A sin offering was also required in connection with a bodily issue, at childbirth, or for purification from leprosy.

A trespass (guilt) offering was always individual. It was prescribed for offenses such as perjury, ignorant sacrilege, fraud, theft, and in some cases required restitution and a penalty payment.

Regular peace offerings were required at Pentecost. Special peace offerings were offered in connection with the fulfillment of vows, particularly the Nazirite vow, and at the dedication of priests. Otherwise, peace offerings might be presented by anyone at any time.

A distinction was also observed in the procedure followed in disposing of the various offerings. A burnt offering was always fully consumed upon the altar, and its blood was sprinkled separately upon (in one case, beside) the altar (Lev 1). In the case of a sin offering for a priest or for the congregation the blood was always sprinkled before the veil and placed on the horns of the golden altar (ch 4). Blood from the individual sin offering of a ruler or of the common people was placed on the horns of the altar of burnt offerings. In both instances the remainder of the blood was poured out at the foot of the altar of burnt offerings. Certain specified portions of animals presented for sin offerings were burned on the altar, and the remainder, in the case of the priest or the congregation, was burned outside the camp (ch 4); however, in the case of individual sin offerings for a ruler or one of the common people, the priest was to eat the flesh of the animal (ch 6: 25, 29). Animals presented as trespass offerings were disposed of like those of the sin offering, except that the blood from such animals was sprinkled round about upon the altar instead of being put on the horns of the altar (ch 7:1-7). In the case of animals presented as peace offerings (ch 3) the blood was also sprinkled on the altar round about. Specified portions of the animals were "waved" or "heaved" before the Lord and given to the priest (ch 7:29-34), and the rest was to be eaten by those who presented the peace offerings, in company with their households (Lev 7:11-21; cf. Deut 12:6, 7; 27:7). For sins done with a "high hand," that is, in rebellion against the covenant and its provisions, no sacrifice was provided (Num 15:30).

A sacrifice was presented at the door of the sanctuary, where the offerer laid his hands upon the victim's head, dedicating it to God and making it his own true representative and substitute. He—in later times, the priest—shed its blood and the priest symbolically applied the blood. This was followed by the burning of the sacrifice, or portions of it, or the eating of it as specified in different cases.

The sacrificial system was an educational device adapted to the understanding of the people of that time and was designed to help them develop right concepts concerning the holiness of God, the heinous character of sin, and how they might approach God and become reconciled to Him. But both the OT (Mic 6:6-8) and the NT (Mt 9:13; 12:7) make clear that the sacrifices were subordinate in importance to practical godliness. During the life of Christ on earth the sacrificial system was in full operation, and He sanctioned it (Mt 5:23, 24; 8:4; 23:2, 3; cf. Gal 4:4). He also attested its typical nature (Mt 26:28). Paul similarly speaks of the sacrifices as types of Christ's true sacrifice (1 Cor 5:7; cf. Heb 10:1-11).

Sacrilege. An act of profaning or stealing that which is regarded as sacred. In Rom 2:22, KJV, "commit sacrilege" is a rendering of the Gr. *hierosuleō*, "to rob temples" (see RSV). In Mt 24:15; Mk 13:14; RSV, the Gr. *bdelugma tēs erēmōseōs*, literally, "abomination of desolation," is rendered "desolating sacrilege." In Acts 19:37, RSV, the Gr. *hierosuloi* is rendered "sacrilegious" (KJV "robbers of churches").

Sadducees (săd′ŭ-sēz). [Gr. *Saddoukaioi*, a transliteration of the Heb. Ṣadûqîm, either from the verb ṣadaq, "to be righteous," or from Zadok, a high priest in the time of David (2 Sa 8:17; 15:24), from whom high priests thereafter all claimed descent.] A minority religio-political Jewish party of NT times representing the wealthy, aristocratic, liberal, secular-minded wing of Judaism. Practically nothing is known of their origin or of their early history. In Maccabean times Alexander Jannaeus (103-76/75 B.C.), son of John Hyrcanus I, favored the Sadducees to the extent that he crucified a considerable number of Pharisees. Toward the close of his life, however, he fell out with the Sadducees, and on his deathbed he advised his wife to favor the Pharisees, which she did. After his death the Sadducees took the side of his son Aristobulus II, the younger and abler of the 2 sons, and supported his claim against John Hyrcanus II, his brother. Later, the Sadducees allied themselves with the Herodian party and collaborated with the Romans. They had a strong concern for the secular affairs of the nation, willingly accepted public office, and exerted an influence far beyond that which their numbers would seem to warrant. Under the Romans and the Herods the conduct of the political affairs of the Jews was largely in their hands. In contrast with the Pharisees and the Essenes, who have left us numerous writings, thus providing us with information concerning their beliefs, the Sadducees have left us no works of such a nature. Hence, we are very poorly informed about their views and beliefs, and must base our knowledge mainly on Josephus and the NT. As a religious party the Sadducees prided themselves on their strict interpretation of "the Law"— the 5 books of Moses—which they accepted alone as inspired, and rejected any teaching for which it did not seem to them to provide explicit support (Jos. *Ant.* xiii. 10. 6). This was doubtless the basis for Christ's accusation that they erred, "not knowing the scriptures, nor the power of God" (Mt 22:29). Denying the resurrection, the future life, and the idea of future punishment (Mt 22:23; Acts 23:8; Jos. *Ant.* xviii. 1. 4; *War* ii. 8. 14), they made the secular, material interests of life dominant. They conceived of God as paying little attention to men and taking little interest in their affairs, and of man as the arbiter of his own destiny (*Ant.* xiii. 5. 9; *War* ii. 8. 14). They did not believe in the existence of angels or spirits (Acts 23:8). For a comparison of the Sadducees with the Pharisees, *see* Pharisees.

The Sadducees, as well as the Pharisees, came under the stern denunciation of John the Baptist (Mt 3:7). They joined with the Pharisees in demanding of Christ a sign from heaven (ch 16:1-4), and Jesus warned His disciples against both (vs 6-12). After the ascension the Sadducees joined with the priests in persecuting Peter and John (Acts 4:1-3). Both Pharisees and Sadducees were present at Paul's trial before the Sanhedrin, and the apostle, noting the fact, set them to arguing with one another (ch 23:6-10). A Sadducee high priest was over the Sanhedrin that was responsible for the death of James, the brother of our Lord (Jos. *Ant.* xx. 9. 1), and other Christians. With the destruction of the Temple and the end of the Jewish state in A.D. 70, the Sadducees disappeared as a party.

Sadoc. *See* Zadok, 8.

Saffron. [Heb. *karkôm*.] Probably the saffron crocus, *Crocus sativus*, from which a perfuming agent was made. Solomon compared his bride to a garden in which grew saffron and other beautiful and fragrant plants and trees (Song 4:12-14).

Sakkuth. The rendering of the Heb. *Sikkûth* in Amos 5:26, RSV. The early translators apparently believed that the consonantal Hebrew term *skwt* stood for "booths" (Heb. *sukkôth*) and consequently rendered it *skēnē* (LXX, and thus quoted by Stephen in Acts 7:43) and *tabernaculum*, "tabernacle" (Vulgate), a reading later adopted in the KJV. However, the parallelism with the star-god Kaiwan (KJV "Chiun") in the Amos reference cited,

suggests that *skwt* may represent the Babylonian god *Sakkut*, whose name was applied to the planet Saturn. This identification is accepted in the RSV. The vocalization *Sikkûth* in the Masoretic text is due to the fact that the vowels of the Heb. *shiqqûṣ* (*i* and *û*), "detestable object," were applied to the consonants *skwt*.

Sala. *See* Shelah, I, 1; Salmon, 1.

Salah. *See* Shelah, I, 1.

Salamis (săl′ȧ-mĭs). [Gr. *Salamis*.] The principal Greek city on the island of Cyprus, situated on its east coast. Salamis became the capital of Cyprus in the 5th cent.

412. Ruins at Salamis on Cyprus

B.C., replacing an earlier Mycenaean city at Enkomi. It was the 1st Cypriote city to strike coins, and from these coins a list of its kings can be obtained. In the 4th cent. B.C. Salamis fell to Ptolemy of Egypt, and in 58 B.C. it became a Roman possession. Barnabas and Paul visited the city during the 1st Missionary Journey and preached the gospel in its several synagogues (Acts 13:5), for Salamis had a large Jewish community. Map XX, B-5.

Salathiel. *See* Shealtiel.

Salcah. *See* Salecah.

Salchah. *See* Salecah.

Salecah (săl′ē-kȧ), KJV 3 times **Salcah** (săl′kȧ), and once **Salchah** (săl′kȧ). [Heb. *Salkah*.] A city on the northeastern boundary of the kingdom of Og of Bashan, near Edrei (Deut 3:10; Jos 12: 4, 5; 13:11). It later formed the northern boundary of the territory of Gad (1 Chr 5:11). It is the modern *Salkhad*, east of Bozrah (Map XIV, C/D-6).

Salem (sā′lĕm). [Heb. *Shalem*, "complete," or "peaceful"; Gr. *Salēm*.] The city in which *Melchizedek was king (Gen 14: 18; Heb 7:1, 2) and which, according to a Jewish tradition recorded in an Aramaic scroll from Qumran Cave 1, was Jerusalem. This agrees with Ps 76:2, where Salem is identified with Zion.

Salim (sā′lĭm). [Gr. *Saleim*.] A place near which John the Baptist baptized (Jn 3: 23); not identified with certainty. See Aenon. Map XVI gives 2 conjectural locations; see D-3 and D-4.

Sallai (săl′ȧ-ī). [Heb. *Sallay*, meaning uncertain.]

1. A Benjamite chosen to dwell in Jerusalem in Nehemiah's time (Neh 11:4, 8).

2. A postexilic priestly family (Neh 12:1, 20), possibly descendants of Sallu (v 7). See Sallu, II.

Sallu, I (săl′ū). [Heb. *Sallû′*.] A Benjamite chosen to dwell in Jerusalem in Nehemiah's time (Neh 11:7; 1 Chr 9:7).

Sallu, II (săl′ū). [Heb. *Sallû*.] A postexilic priest (Neh 12:7), possibly an ancestral head of the family called Sallai in v 20. See Sallai, 2.

Salma (săl′mȧ). [Heb. *Śalma′*.]

1. A descendant of Judah through Caleb the son of Hezron, and founder of Bethlehem (1 Chr 2:50, 51, 54). He is evidently not identical with Salma, 2, since the 2 men descended from Judah through different lines.

2. For 1 Chr 2:11 see Salmon, 1.

Salmon (săl′mŏn), or **Salma** (săl′mȧ), RSV once **Sala** (sā′lȧ). [Heb. *Śalmôn, Śalmah,* and *Śalma′;* Gr. *Salmōn, Sala*.]

1. A descendant of Judah through Perez, Hezron, and Ram, and ancestor of David (Ruth 4:18-21; 1 Chr 2:11; Mt 1: 4; Lk 3:32). According to Mt 1:5 he was the husband of Rahab, doubtless the Rahab of Jericho fame.

2. For Ps 68:14, KJV, see Zalmon, 2.

Salmone (săl-mō′nē). [Gr. *Salmōnē*.] The northeastern promontory of the island of Crete, now known by the name Cape Sidero. The ancient name is spelled in different ways in old records: *Samōnion, Salmōnion, Samonium,* etc. The vessel on which Paul traveled to Rome as a prisoner passed this promontory (Acts 27:7). Map XX, B-4.

Salome (sȧ-lō′mē). [Gr. *Salōmē,* a Grecized name formed from Heb. *shalôm,* meaning "peace."]

1. A woman who ministered to Jesus while He was in Galilee, and who followed Him to Jerusalem, thus becoming an eyewitness of the crucifixion (Mk 15: 40, 41). She was apparently the wife of Zebedee, and the mother of James and John (Mk 15:40; cf. Mt 27:56; 4:21). Salome was one of the women who went to Christ's tomb on the resurrection morning with spices to anoint His body (Mk 16:1).

2. The daughter of Herodias, and the girl who was rewarded with the head of John the Baptist for dancing before Herod Antipas (Mt 14:3-11; Mk 6:17-28). Her name is not mentioned in the Bible, but is known from Josephus (*Ant.* xviii. 5. 4). She was later married to her uncle Philip, tetrarch of the northeastern territories mentioned in Lk 3:1.

Salt. [Heb. *melach;* Gr. *halas, hals*.] Sodium chloride, or any one of several related chemical compounds, such as magnesium chloride and calcium chloride. Common salt (sodium chloride), found in sea water and in underground or surface beds, is used in preserving and as a flavoring. In ancient times, when refrigeration and many other modern methods of preserving food were unknown, salt was of even greater value than it is today. An additional enhancement was the ceremonial requirement that it accompany sacrificial offerings (Lev 2:13; Eze 43:24). Newborn babies were rubbed with salt, in the belief that this caused the skin to be drier, firmer, and cleaner (Eze 16:4). Palestine possesses a great natural source of salts at the Dead Sea. Its shores and surrounding hills hold a seemingly limitless supply of poor-quality salt (*see* Salt Pits). Salt gave its name to the sea into which the Jordan River empties (Gen 14:3; Jos 3:16; etc.), to the Valley of Salt, possibly at the south end of the Dead, or Salt, Sea (2 Sa 8:13), and to the City of Salt (Jos 15:62). Captured lands were sometimes sown with salt as a curse (Jgs 9:45). However, when it is used in the right places and in the proper quantity, this substance is of great value. Because of their work and influence Christ compared His disciples to salt (Mt 5:13; cf. Mk 9:50; Lk 14:34). Those who do not pass along the values of the gospel were compared to salt that had lost its flavor (Mt 5:13; Lk 14:35).

Salt, City of. [Heb. *'Ir Hammelach.*] A place in the Wilderness of Judah mentioned in connection with En-gedi (Jos 15:62), a town on the shore of the Dead Sea. In 1938 M. Noth suggested identifying the "City of Salt" with *Khirbet Qumrân* (Map XVI, E-3). Since excavations at *Khirbet Qumrân,* the site of the community that produced the Dead Sea scrolls, have shown that this place was inhabited in OT times, his suggestion has gained in value and recognition (*BASOR* 142 [1956], 16, n. 27). *See* Scrolls, Dead Sea.

Salt Pits. A rendering of the Heb. *mikreh-melach* (Zep 2:9), referring either to salt mines in the *Jebel Usdum,* a mountain ridge at the southwestern shore of the Dead Sea composed of 50 per cent rock salt (see fig. 454), or to the salt flats along the shore where the water has overflowed and evaporated, leaving a salt crust.

Salt Sea. *See* Dead Sea.

Salt, Valley of. [Heb. *Gê'-melach* and *Gê' Hammelach.*] A valley in which David's army slew 18,000 Edomites (2 Sa 8:13; 1 Chr 18:12), and in which King Amaziah of Judah slew another 10,000 Edomites before taking their stronghold, Sela (2 Ki 14:1, 7; 2 Chr 25:11). The valley is now identified by most scholars with the *Wâdī el-Milḥ,* east of Beer-sheba.

Saltwort. *See* Mallow.

Salu (sā'lū). [Heb. *Salû'.*] A Simeonite whose son, Zimri, was slain by Phinehas (Num 25:14).

Salute, Salutation. *See* Greetings.

Samaria (sà-mâr'ĭ-à). [Heb. *Shomerôn,* "look-out"; Assyrian *Samerina,* etc.; Aramaic *Shamerayin;* Gr. *Samareia.* In 1 Ki 16:24 it is stated that the place was named after Shemer, who sold Omri the hill on which the city was built.]

1. The capital city of the kingdom of Israel. It lay 6 mi. northwest of Shechem (Map IX, D-3), and occupied a commanding position on the summit of a round, isolated hill, 1,460 ft. above the Mediterranean Sea, which is visible from the site, and 300 to 400 ft. above the surrounding plain, which is rich in olive groves and grain fields. Its strategic location, and the richness and beauty of the surrounding area, made it a wise choice for a capital. It was built by Omri (*c.* 885 - *c.* 874 b.c.), who bought the hill for 2 talents of silver from Shemer and moved the capital of his kingdom from Tirzah to the new site (1 Ki 16:24). It was one of the few cities founded by the Israelites and it remained Israel's principal city as long as the kingdom existed (*c.* 150 years). It was also the city in which the kings of Israel were buried (1 Ki 16:28, 29; 20: 43; 22:10, 37, 51; 2 Ki 17:1, 6; etc.). Omri, either because of force, or by agreement,

413. Map of the ancient city of Samaria

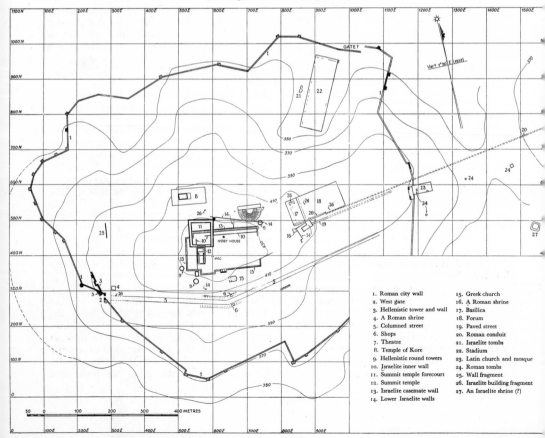

1. Roman city wall	15. Greek church
2. West gate	16. A Roman shrine
3. Hellenistic tower and wall	17. Basilica
4. A Roman shrine	18. Forum
5. Columned street	19. Paved street
6. Shops	20. Roman conduit
7. Theatre	21. Israelite tombs
8. Temple of Kore	22. Stadium
9. Hellenistic round towers	23. Latin church and mosque
10. Israelite inner wall	24. Roman tombs
11. Summit temple forecourt	25. Wall fragment
12. Summit temple	26. Israelite building fragment
13. Israelite casemate wall	27. An Israelite shrine (?)
14. Lower Israelite walls	

SAMARIA

provided market facilities in Samaria for Syrian merchants (1 Ki 20:34, RSV). In Ahab's time the fortifications of the city were already so perfected that the Syrians were unable to conquer it (vs 1-21), and even the Assyrians, great masters though they were in the art of conquest of fortified cities, were able to capture Samaria only after a long siege of 3 years (2 Ki 18:9, 10). When the city finally fell in 723/22 B.C., almost 30,000 citizens were carried away as captives (*ANET* 284, 285). These were replaced by people from Babylonia and Syria (ch 17:24).

From the beginning of its history Samaria was a center of pagan worship and idolatry. Ahab's wife, Jezebel, introduced Baal worship into the city, and a temple and an altar to Baal were erected (1 Ki 16:31, 32). The Asherah cult also found official support from the royal house (ch 18:18, 19). Great moral corruption resulted from this gross idolatry (Hos 4: 1-14). The prophets severely denounced this apostasy (Is 7:9; 8:4; Eze 16:46, 47; 23:4-10, 33; Hos 7:1-7; 8:5, 6; 13:16; Amos 3:9, 10, 12; Mic 1:5-9). The work of Elijah (1 Ki 17; 18), and of his successor Elisha, who seems to have lived in Samaria, should also be mentioned (2 Ki 2:25; 5:3-9; 6:24, 25, 32).

In 722 B.C., after its conquest by either Shalmaneser V or Sargon II, Samaria became the seat of an Assyrian province (Map XI, C-4). When Alexander the Great came to Syria in 333 B.C. he occupied Samaria and made it the seat of a governor. However, Andromachus, the governor he installed, was killed by the Samaritans in 332 or 331 B.C., when Alexander was in Egypt. Consequently, Alexander severely punished the inhabitants of Samaria, transferred them to Shechem, and repeopled the city with Syro-Macedonians. As a result it became one of the first Hellenistic cities in Palestine. About 108 B.C., after a siege of 1 year, John Hyrcanus, the Maccabean king of Judah, conquered Samaria and in an attempt to obliterate all vestiges of its former glory and strength systematically demolished it (Jos. *Ant.* xiii. 10. 2. 3; *War* i. 2. 7). However, the city was soon rebuilt, and when Pompey came to Palestine in 63 B.C. he annexed it to the province of Syria, and Gabinius refortified it (Jos. *Ant.* xiv. 4. 4; 5. 3). Soon thereafter Samaria experienced its most glorious period, when Herod the Great, who there had married his favored wife, Mariamne, and to whom the city was given, rebuilt, refortified, and

414. Remains of a wall of King Omri's time at ancient Samaria

beautified it with magnificent structures, impressive ruins of which are still standing. He also changed its name to *Sebastē*, the feminine form of *sebastos*, "majestic," the Greek equivalent of "Augustus." It has retained its name to the present day, being now called *Sebasṭiyeh.*

In the Christian Era Samaria, or Sebaste, was surpassed in size and importance by Neapolis (now called *Nâblus*), the successor of ancient Shechem, although Sebaste became the seat of a bishop. This bishop's seat was re-established by the Crusaders, and a Greek bishop, now residing in Jerusalem, still takes his title from Sebaste, which is today no more than a village.

Excavations were first carried out by G. Schumacher, G. A. Reisner, D. G. Lyon, and C. S. Fisher for Harvard University from 1908 to 1910. This expedition uncovered the remains of the Herodian forum, a Roman basilica, and a hippodrome. The foundations of the palace of Omri (1 Ki 22:39), with its extensions built by Ahab and Jeroboam II, as well as the pool where palace attendants washed the bloodstained chariot in which Ahab's body was brought home from Ramoth-gilead (v 38), were also excavated. Of great interest were some scores of Hebrew ostraca, probably from the time of Jeroboam II, which contained notes concerning the payment of oil and wine to the royal storehouses, probably constituting payments of taxes. More excavations were carried out from 1931 to 1933 and in 1935 by joint expeditions, in which several scientific institutions cooperated under the direction of J. W. Crowfoot. This further work made it possible to date the earlier discoveries with more precision, and has clarified some archeological and historical problems. The most interesting discoveries of this later expedition include a great number of carved *ivory plaques, probably from Ahab's ivory house (v 39). Some additional Hebrew ostraca also were found.

Lit.: G. A. Reisner and others, *Harvard Excavations at Samaria* (Cambridge, Mass., 1924), 2 vols.; J. W. Jack, *Samaria in Ahab's Time, Harvard Excavations and Their Results* (Edinburgh, 1929); J. W. Crowfoot and others, *Samaria-Sebaste. Reports of the Work of the Joint Expedition in 1931-1933 and of the British Expedition in 1935* (London, 1938, 1942, 1957): vol. I, *The Buildings at Samaria;* vol. II, *Early Ivories From Samaria;* vol. III, *The Objects From Samaria.*

2. The kingdom of Israel, or the territory occupied by the 10 tribes, frequently called Samaria, after its capital city (1 Ki 21:1; 2 Ki 17:24; Jer 31:5). *See* Israel, 3.

3. The province of Samaria. After its conquest by Shalmaneser V or Sargon II, in 723/22 B.C., the city of Samaria became the seat of an Assyrian province. Two of the Assyrian governors who held office during the 7th cent. B.C. are known from cuneiform records—*Nabû-kêna-uṣur* (690 B.C.) and *Nabû-shar-aḥḥêshu* (646 B.C.). Nothing is known concerning its administrative structure as an Assyrian province, but parallels in other parts of the Assyrian Empire make it probable that the administration had only one purpose, and that was to obtain as much tribute in the form of produce as could be squeezed out of the oppressed population.

When the territory of Samaria fell into the hands of the Babylonians and later into the hands of the Persians, its administrative structure probably remained the same, being ruled by a governor in the name of the crown. Such a governor was either a foreigner or a native appointed by the central government. One governor of Samaria in the Persian period was Nehemiah's enemy, *Sanballat, well known from the Bible (Neh 4:1, 2; etc.), and from the Elephantine papyri (*see* Pathros).

During the Hellenistic period Samaria had the status of a province, first as part of Alexander's empire, and later under the rule of Ptolemies and Seleucids, depending upon which of the 2 powers controlled Palestine. When Pompey occupied Palestine for Rome in 63 B.C., the area was placed under the control of the senatorial province of Syria, of which it became a part.

4. The region of Samaria in NT times. When Christ was born, Samaria was part of Herod's kingdom. After Herod's death it was given to his son Archelaus (4 B.C. - A.D. 6), along with Judea and Idumea (Map XVI, D-3). These 3 areas remained a political unit throughout NT times, and were governed by Roman procurators from A.D. 6 to 41, during which time Christ's ministry occurred, and again from A.D. 44 to 66. In the interval, from A.D. 41 to 44, Samaria was part of the kingdom of Agrippa I, who ruled over an area equal in size to that of his grandfather, Herod the Great.

Samaritans (sȧ-măr'ĭ-tănz). [Heb. *Shomeronîm;* Gr. *Samaritai.*] This term occurs only once in the OT (2 Ki 17:29), where it refers to the citizens of the former kingdom of Israel. Later, however, it was applied to the population of the region of which the city of Samaria was the political center, and where there had developed a unique religious and social system. The origin of these Samaritans is described in 2 Ki 17:24-34. After Tiglath-pileser III (745-727 B.C.) and Sargon II (722-705 B.C.) carried the majority of the population of Israel into exile, they settled people from Babylonia, northern Mesopotamia, and Hamath in Syria in the territory of the former kingdom of Israel. These brought their own religion with them, but as a result of mixing with the remaining Israelites they adopted also the religion of Yahweh. This adoption of the new religion was accelerated by catastrophes that the newcomers interpreted as a sign of displeasure of the local deity because not enough attention had been paid to him (Jos. *Ant.* ix. 14. 3). Under Esarhaddon (681-669 B.C.) and Ashurbanipal (669-?627 B.C.), the Biblical Osnapper, new contingents of foreign people were settled in the territory of Samaria (Ezr 4:2, 9, 10).

During the reign of Josiah (*c.* 639 - *c.* 608 B.C.), king of Judah, when Assyria's power was rapidly declining, Josiah was able to extend his authority over the territory of the former kingdom of Israel, which since 722 B.C. had been the Assyrian province of Samaria. Thus when carrying out his religious reformation Josiah traversed not only his own kingdom but also the area of the northern tribes, and destroyed all vestiges of pagan cults and idolatry (2 Chr 34:6, 7). It may have been this work of Josiah that caused the worship of the God of Israel to win out among the Samaritans, and the foreign cults to become more and more suppressed, although the Jews regarded the Samaritan religion as impure. For their Scriptures they adopted the Pentateuch before the Babylonian exile of Judah. Some of the inhabitants of Samaria had the habit of regularly attending divine services at Jerusalem, even after the destruction of the Temple (Jer 41:5; cf. Ezr 4:2).

When the Jews returned from exile (c. 536 B.C.) and began to re-establish their religion, the Samaritans offered to join them, but Zerubbabel, Jeshua, and the other leaders of the Jews, rejected this offer outright (Ezr 4:1-3). They had learned from the admonitions of the prophets that their own national calamity had been the result of their unfaithfulness toward God. Convinced that the Samaritans had a corrupted religion, they wanted to avoid reverting to the errors of pre-exilic times and therefore chose religious and social isolation. As a result of this attitude an increasingly deepening hatred developed between the 2 nations, which was frequently revealed in hostile acts. The Samaritans worked against the returned Jews during their building of the Temple in the time of Cyrus (vs 4, 5), made accusations against them in the time of Ahasuerus (v 6), and actively hindered them during the rebuilding of the wall of Jerusalem in the time of Artaxerxes. They were not satisfied with accusing the Jews of rebellion, but stopped their work evidently by force of arms, burned gates, and destroyed wall sections which had been rebuilt (Ezr 4:7-23; Neh 1:3). Nehemiah describes in detail the efforts that the Samaritans' governor, Sanballat, made to hinder his work, although Nehemiah had been sent by the king and possessed all necessary authority to complete the work of rebuilding the wall of Jerusalem (Neh 2:10, 19, 20; 4:1, 2; 6: 1-14).

Josephus says concerning the Samaritans that they were so insincere that they claimed to be Jews when the Jews were prosperous and respected and when an affinity to them could bring them advantages, but they denied any connection with Jewry when this was to their disadvantage (Ant. ix. 14. 3). After the Samaritans had been rejected by the Jews they built a temple on Mount Gerizim, in which they offered sacrifices according to the Mosaic ritual. It is not quite clear whether this temple was built in the 5th or the 4th cent. B.C. Josephus makes the statement that it was built under *Sanballat in the time of Alexander the Great (Ant. xi. 8. 2). If Josephus, confusing his source data, meant the Sanballat of the time of Nehemiah, then the date would be the 5th cent. If he was referring to another Sanballat in the time of Alexander the Great, then the date would be the 4th cent. Josephus further reports that Jews who came into conflict with their religious authorities turned to the Samaritans (Ant. xi. 8. 7). The contrast between the Jews and Samaritans became especially apparent in the time of Antiochus IV Epiphanes. While the Jews resisted his attempts at Hellenizing them, and suffered severe persecution from the Syrians (2 Macc 6), the Samaritans had their temple on Mount Gerizim dedicated to Zeus (Jupiter), the defender of strangers (2 Macc 6:2). Hence when the Jews regained control of Palestine during the reign of the Maccabees, they turned against the Samaritans, and John Hyrcanus (135-105/4 B.C.) destroyed the temple on Mount Gerizim in 128 B.C. (cf. Jos. Ant. xiii. 9. 1). Yet the place where the temple had stood continued to be used for religious services, and the Samaritans continued to consider it the true place of worship (see Jn 4:20, 21). They still celebrate their Passover feast (figs. 70, 415) on Mount Gerizim, following Mosaic rites, including the slaughter of Passover lambs.

The hatred between Jews and Samaritans had not decreased by the time of the ministry of Jesus on earth. There are several passages in the NT that clearly indicate this (Lk 9:51-54; Jn 4:9; cf. 8: 48). For this reason most pilgrims traveling from Galilee to Jerusalem avoided passing through Samaria, and detoured

415. The Samaritan high priest leading his congregation in prayer at the annual Samaritan Passover ceremony on Mount Gerizim

through Perea instead (cf. Jos. *Ant.* xx. 6. 1). The social and religious isolation of the Samaritans saved them from being swallowed by the Moslem invasion of the 7th cent. and in subsequent times, so that groups of them have survived in the area of *Nâblus* and at some other places in Palestine to the present day.

The religion of the Samaritans did not differ much from that of the Jews in the time of Christ, for with them they accepted the Pentateuch. They also expected a Messiah to come (Jn 4:25). However, their religious beliefs were more liberal than those of the orthodox Jews, especially than those of the Pharisees, and may have been somewhat similar to those of the Sadducees. Christians practiced no discrimination and accepted the Samaritans on an equal basis (Lk 10:29-37; 17:16-18; Jn 4:1-42; Acts 8:5, 6).

Samech. [Heb. *samek.*] The 15th letter of the Hebrew alphabet, written ס, appearing as the title of the 15th section of Ps 119 in the KJV. *See* Aleph.

Samgar-nebo. *See* Nergal-sharezer.

Samlah (săm′lȧ). [Heb. *Šamlah,* "abode" or "garment."] A king of Edom, and native of Masrekah (Gen 36:36, 37; 1 Chr 1:47).

Samos (sā′mŏs). [Gr. *Samos.*] An island in the Aegean Sea, opposite the bay of Ephesus. It became famous in the 6th cent. B.C. under the rule of the tyrant Polycrates, subsequently experiencing varying political fortunes under the Persians and Athenians. Later it came under the influence of Pergamum, and with it fell to the Romans in 133 B.C. However, it was made autonomous in 17 B.C., and this was its status when Paul's ship stopped at the island during his voyage to Jerusalem toward the close of his 3d Missionary Journey (Acts 20:15). Map XX, B-4.

Samothrace (săm′ȯ-thrās), KJV **Samothracia** (săm′ȯ-thrā′shĭ-ȧ). [Gr. *Samothrakē,* "Samos of Thrace."] A mountainous island off the coast of Thrace, hence its name, "Samos of Thrace." It was famous for its pre-Greek mystery cult of the *Cabiri.* The vessel in which Paul sailed from Troas to Neapolis during his 2d Missionary Journey touched at the island (Acts 16:11). Map XX, A-4.

Samothracia. *See* Samothrace.

Samson (săm′s'n). [Heb. *Shimshôn,* meaning uncertain. Some have interpreted the name to be derived from *shemesh,* "sun," with a diminutive ending, thus meaning "little sun"; others have connected it with *shamam,* "to destroy," ex-

plaining the name Samson as meaning "destroyer." Josephus (*Ant.* v. 8. 4) explains the name to mean "the strong one," deriving it from *shamen,* "fat," "robust"; Gr. *Sampsōn.*] A hero of the late period of the judges, who performed feats of superhuman strength during the Philistine oppression of Judah and Dan shortly before Saul became king of Israel. Although Samson is called "judge," he is so different in character and action from the other judges, that he can hardly be compared either with the major judges— Othniel, Ehud, Barak, Gideon, and Jephthah—or with the minor ones—Tola, Jair, Ibzan, Elon, and Abdon.

Samson's birth was predicted to the barren wife of Manoah, by an angel of God who at the same time instructed her as to the nature of his upbringing and work. He was to be a *Nazirite and as such had to live under certain restrictions (Jgs 13). The family of Samson belonged to the tribe of Dan and lived at Zorah (v 2) in the *Shephelah (Map VI, E-2), not far from the territory of the Philistines, hence probably felt the brunt of Philistine oppressive rule. Samson possessed unusual strength with which he was able to perform heroic deeds of extraordinary valor. If his moral character had been commensurate with his strength, God would have used him mightily for the deliverance of His people. As it was, he failed to complete the work God had given him to do, and finally died in captivity and ignominy.

Samson's recorded acts may be divided into 5 episodes, but it should be remembered that neither his whole life nor all his performances of heroism are recorded in the Bible (see Jgs 13:25).

(1). After Samson, under the influence of the Spirit of the Lord, had performed certain unspecified acts of heroism (Jgs 13:25), he fell in love with and married a Philistine girl of Timnah (KJV "Timnath"; Map VI, E-2). At the wedding feast he asked his Philistine guests a riddle based on his experience with a lion he had killed. Their inability to solve the riddle led to a number of complications, the result of which was that Samson thoroughly antagonized the Philistines. Later, his wife was given to another man, and he took revenge by burning some Philistine fields and olive orchards. When they retaliated and burned his wife and her father, he slew many of them (chs 14:1 to 15:8).

(2). Later, Samson found a retreat at the "rock of Etam." While he was there the

Philistines invaded Judah to take vengeance on him. Fearful of the Philistines, 3,000 Judahites went to Samson to deliver him to his enemies, and he agreed to let them hand him over bound. However, when he was brought to the Philistines the Spirit of the Lord came upon him, and, bursting the ropes, he slew 1,000 of them and put the rest to flight. When the slaughter was over he was so thirsty that he feared he would die, but God answered his prayer and miraculously provided water. It was after this experience that he was made judge by his people (Jgs 15:9-20).

(3). The next recorded event reveals him as again a slave of his lower instincts. He went to the Philistine fortress city of Gaza to visit a prostitute, thus placing himself in the hands of his enemies, who determined to have their revenge. However, he left her house at midnight, went to the closed city gate, tore it from its sockets and carried it, with its beams and bar, to the top of a hill that lay in the direction of Hebron (Jgs 16:1-3).

(4). Once more his passions became his master. He fell in love with Delilah, a woman of the valley of Sorek. Seeing this, the Philistines offered her a large sum of money if she would find out for them the secret of Samson's strength. Three attempts to get him into their hands failed because he gave her misleading reasons for his supernatural strength and how he could be weakened. Finally, however, he gave in and revealed to her that his long hair, which was the symbol of his strength, had never been cut. While he was asleep she shaved his hair, and his strength left him. The Philistines captured him, blinded him, and put him in prison in Gaza (Jgs 16:4-21), where he had to grind grain in a *mill, thus doing the humiliating work of a slave.

(5). On the occasion of a great Philistine festival at Gaza when sacrifices were offered to their god Dagon, Samson was brought and publicly exhibited in the temple. The temple was full of people, and about 3,000 more were on the roof. Samson apparently knew the structure, for he had been in Gaza before. Taking hold of 2 central pillars which stood close together and supported the roof, he prayed to God and requested from Him the necessary strength to take revenge for the humiliations suffered at the hands of the Philistines. Using all his strength, he tore the pillars from their foundation with the result that the heavily loaded roof

came down, killing a large number of those on the roof and burying Samson and most of the assembled people in the temple (Jgs 16:22-30). Samson's kindred came, claimed his body, and buried him in his father's tomb near Zorah. He had judged Israel about 20 years (v 31).

In spite of Samson's grave failures the NT lists him among the great heroes of faith (Heb 11:32), possibly because he finally realized his total dependence upon God and called upon Him in his last act of valor. Samson's death should not be considered suicide, but a self-sacrificing act in fulfillment of his calling.

The Samson stories not only give the picture of a chosen instrument of God whose indulgence of weaknesses and passions made it impossible for him to fulfill his calling but also provide valuable information concerning the customs of the judges' period, of which so little is otherwise known. We learn that feasts lasting several days were connected with marriage rites; on occasion at least, riddles were propounded at these feasts; that the father gave his daughter to the bridegroom; and that a rejected wife was given to someone else. This account also throws light on how crimes were punished and prisoners treated.

Samuel (săm′ủ-ĕl), KJV once **Shemuel** (shĕ′-mủ-ĕl). [Heb. *Shemu'el*, meaning uncertain. It has been interpreted as meaning "name of God," but his mother apparently intended it to mean "God has heard," a combination of the verb *shama'* and the noun *'El;* Gr. *Samouēl.*] The 1st of the great prophets of Israel after Moses, being placed side by side with the great lawgiver Moses by Jeremiah (Jer 15:1). His father Elkanah was a Levite of the family of Kohath (1 Chr 6:26, 33, 34) who lived in the territory of Ephraim and therefore was also called an Ephraimite (1 Sa 1:1). His home town was Ramathaim-zophim, also called simply Ramah (chs 1:1, 19; 2:11). This town has been variously identified, but it was most probably at the site of modern *Ramallah* (see *SDACom* 2:458, 459). Elkanah had 2 wives, Hannah and Peninnah. The former was his favorite wife, but she was barren (1 Sa 1:2, 7, 8). After much heart searching and prayer, Hannah vowed that if God would give her a son she would dedicate him to God as a Nazirite. God heard her prayer and she gave birth to a son whom she named Samuel. After he was weaned she took him to the high priest Eli at Shiloh to have him trained in the Lord's service at the tabernacle (1 Sa 1:9-28).

At Shiloh, Samuel lived in a room connected with the sanctuary and in close proximity to the room of the high priest. He was dressed in a simple linen ephod, a garment worn by priests and Levites, and performed simple duties such as opening the doors of the sanctuary in the morning (1 Sa 2:18; 3:1, 3, 4, 15). While he was still a boy, 12 years of age according to Josephus (*Ant.* v. 10. 4), the Lord revealed to him the doom that would overtake Eli's house for the criminal behavior of the high priest's sons, and for the failure of their father to correct them (ch 3:1-18). The Lord appeared to Samuel again at a later time, although the specific message of that revelation is not recorded. The outcome of this was that the whole nation recognized him to be a prophet by the time he had grown to manhood (vs 20, 21). Eventually God's judgment fell on Israel and the house of Eli. His sons were slain in battle, the ark fell into the hands of the Philistines, and the high priest died, possibly of a heart attack, when he heard the news of the disaster (ch 4:1-18). Archeological evidence reveals that Shiloh was destroyed about this time. The Philistines may have done so on this occasion. Shiloh (fig. 436) is never mentioned again as the sanctuary city, but only as a desolate place (Jer 7:12, 14; 26:6), and when the ark was returned to Israel it was left at Kiriath-jearim and kept there for many years (1 Sa 7:1, 2).

Samuel now became a leader, prophet, and judge of Israel. He admonished the people to discard their idols and serve only the true God. At Mizpah, probably modern *Tell en-Naṣbeh,* he gathered the people to make a covenant with God. The Philistines thought that this large gathering was held with hostile intentions, and attacked them. Encouraged and led by Samuel, the Israelites fought valiantly and won a great victory over their enemies, and thus regained their liberty. As long as Samuel was their leader they remained unmolested by the Philistines (1 Sa 7:3-14). He was now undisputed judge of the country. Every year he held court at Gilgal, Bethel, and Mizpah, besides Ramah, his home town (vs 15-17). In his task Samuel apparently was aided by prophets who lived together in communities. These prophets are mentioned for the first time in his days (chs 10:5; 19:20).

As Samuel advanced in years he appointed his 2 sons as additional judges, and placed them in Beer-sheba, at the southernmost border of the country. However, they, unlike their father, were corrupt judges, and the people complained about them. Dissatisfied with the lack of continuity in strong leadership, the Israelites thought that a kingship would be the best solution for their political ills. Hence they requested Samuel to appoint a king over them. Samuel disapproved of this request, even took it as an expression of distrust in his administration. However, the Lord bade him accede to the people's demand, pointing out that, in their desire to exchange their theocratic form of government for that of a kingship, they were not rejecting him, but their higher leader, God Himself. Samuel was instructed to warn them clearly of the disadvantages of their move and the inevitable consequences this change in government would have on all their lives (1 Sa 8:1-22). Following God's directions, Samuel anointed Saul king, at first privately in Ramah, and later in a public ceremony at Mizpah (chs 9; 10). A 3d ceremony was performed at Gilgal after Saul's victory over Nahash, the king of the Ammonites (chs 11:14 to 12:25).

Saul's behavior, however, soon revealed to Samuel that there were reasons for grave concern. The new king began to manifest a spirit of independence and stubborn disobedience with regard to divine leadership. Consequently Samuel was obliged to tell him first that his kingship would not continue (1 Sa 13:8-14), and later that the Lord had taken it from him (ch 15:22-29). Samuel did not see Saul again after that event, although he grieved over him (v 35). Later, Samuel, at God's command, performed the dangerous task of anointing David as king over Israel, although Saul was still in full power (ch 16:1-13). When persecuted by Saul, David sought temporary refuge with Samuel (ch 19:18, 19). Shortly after that the old prophet died, and David went as a fugitive to the southern Wilderness of Judah (ch 25:1).

Samuel's name appears once more in connection with the visit of King Saul to a spirit medium, who illegally practiced her profession at En-dor. Saul certainly knew that such manifestations were the work of the devil, for he had earlier expelled necromancers from the country. Yet he requested the woman to establish contact with the departed Samuel. The spirit that manifested itself to the woman in her séance claimed to be the spirit of Samuel and predicted Saul's death (1 Sa 28:3-19). That the spirit was not that of the dead Samuel is clear from the Scriptures, which teach that there is no consciousness after death, and which condemn necromancy and spiritualism as the work of the devil (see Death).

Samuel was a great man. The NT lists him with the heroes of faith (Heb 11:32). He revealed himself as a political leader, who regained for his people independence and liberty, and who was able to retain it during the long period of his successful administration. He was in communion with God from his childhood and constantly acted according to divine directions. As a judge he was held in high esteem by the people for his impartiality, loyalty, and honesty. As the founder of the kingdom of Israel, he showed humility and prudence by stepping aside when the people demanded a new leader. On the other hand, he was a man who permitted no compromise when the honor of God was at stake, or when a direct command of the Lord had not been carried out. His bloody severity against Agag (1 Sa 15:33) is an illustration of this. Yet, Samuel had a warm heart. He constantly prayed for his people (ch 12:23) and could not cease to love Saul even after he had been forced to reject him as king. Unfortunately, his sons did not follow in his footsteps (ch 8:3).

Samuel, Books of. The historical record of the Hebrew people beginning with the birth of Samuel, the last of the judges, continuing with the establishment of the monarchy under Saul, and covering David's reign practically to its close. In all ancient Hebrew manuscripts 1 and 2 Sa appear as one volume, called Samuel, which in the Hebrew canon stood among the Former Prophets (Jos through 2 Ki, except for Ruth). The Masoretes noted that 1 Sa 28:24 was at the middle of the book as it appeared in the text of their time. The division of Sa into 2 parts was first made by the translators of the LXX about the 3d cent. B.C., under the titles, "First of Kingdoms" and "Second of Kingdoms." In this arrangement 1 and 2 Ki appeared as "Third of Kingdoms" and "Fourth of Kingdoms." In the Latin Vulgate, translated by Jerome near the end of the 4th cent. A.D., the titles were changed to read "Kings" instead of "Kingdoms."

The books of Samuel provide no information as to who their author or authors may have been. According to Jewish tradition Samuel himself composed the first 24 chs of 1 Sa (to the death of the prophet), with the remainder of 1 Sa and all of 2 Sa written by the prophets Nathan and Gad (see 1 Chr 29:29). When the book was divided in Hebrew Bibles in A.D. 1517, and later in English Bibles, the original name "Samuel" was applied to both parts even though his name is not once mentioned in the 2d part. It appears for the last time in 1 Sa 28:20. Doubtless Samuel's name was attached to the whole because his life and ministry dominate the 1st half of the book in its combined form. Irrespective of the question of authorship, this title was appropriate in view of his important role as the last of the judges, as one of the greatest of the prophets, as the evident founder of the schools of the prophets, and as God's appointed agent in the establishment of the Hebrew kingdom. If the combined book represents the continuous work of 1 author, it must have been composed after the death of David (2 Sa 23:1). It seems more reasonable, however, to conclude that 1 Sa and 2 Sa represent composite authorship and that they are the collection of 2 or more narratives, each of which is complete in itself. However this may be, 1 and 2 Sa constitute an inspired record of an important period of Hebrew history.

The LXX varies in some parts from the Masoretic Hebrew text, notably in 1 Sa 17 and 18. That the variant readings go back to a Hebrew recension which differed from that used by the Masoretes and which became the standard Hebrew text has become evident through the discovery of a Sa manuscript among the Dead Sea scrolls. About ⅔ of a scroll of 1 and 2 Sa has been reconstructed from numerous fragments found in Qumran Cave 4. This scroll reveals a close relationship to the LXX. See Scrolls, Dead Sea. See fig. 416.

First Samuel records the transition of Hebrew government from administrative and military "judges" to the united monarchy, which lasted for nearly a cent. (c. 1100 - c. 1011 B.C.), and 2 Sa deals exclusively with the reign of David, about 40 years (c. 1011 - c. 971 B.C.). The somewhat sudden transition from centuries of pure theocracy operating through prophets and judges to the monarchy was a time of difficult adjustment for the Hebrew people. This was followed by the golden age that began with the glorious reign of David. The account of David's last years and death appears in the first 2 chapters of 1 Ki. *See* David; Samuel.

The narrative opens with the birth of

416. The remains of the first 2 columns of a scroll of the book of Samuel found among the Dead Sea scrolls

Samuel, his appointment to serve in the sanctuary, and his call to the prophetic ministry (1 Sa 1:1 to 4:1). When Samuel succeeded Eli in office as priest, judge, and prophet, Israel lay prostrate before the Philistines, but the course of the nation's fortunes soon turned (chs 5-7). Late in Samuel's judgeship, popular demand for a king led to the elevation of Saul to the throne (chs 8-12). The early years of Saul's reign were marked by intermittent war with the Philistines and other neighboring nations (ch 14:47). During this time Saul on two occasions flagrantly disobeyed the explicit instructions of the Lord through the prophet Samuel (chs 13-15). With God's rejection of Saul as king, Samuel secretly anointed David, and the remaining chapters of 1 Sa are largely taken up with Saul's jealous attempts to destroy David (chs 16-27). Finally in a battle between the Philistines and the Israelites, Saul was slain (chs 28-31). Thereupon David became king over Judah, and after about 7½ years of strife the other tribes ac-

knowledged him as king also (2 Sa 1:1 to 5:5). Chapters 5-10 recount the glories of the early years of David's reign, while chs 11-21 are devoted largely to his sin and to family difficulties affecting the throne. Chapters 22-24 form a sort of appendix that contains David's song of thanksgiving, his last words of instruction, and a roster of his mighty men and their exploits. The record closes with his sin in numbering the people of Israel, and its sad result (ch 24).

Sanballat (săn-băl′ăt). [Heb. *Sanballaṭ*; in the Aramaic papyri from Elephantine *Sn'blṭ*; Akkadian *Sin-uballiṭ*, "(the moon-god) Sin has given life."] The governor of Samaria (as revealed by the papyri from Elephantine), a contemporary and enemy of Nehemiah; Nehemiah calls him "the Horonite" (Neh 2:10, 19), but does not mention his official position. It is uncertain whether "Horonite" means that he was a native of one of the 2 Beth-horons in the former territory of Ephraim, whether he was of the city of Horonaim in Moab, or whether he came from the Hauran, in which case he should be called a Hauranite. His pagan name and origin, if from Moab or the Aramaic Hauran, would suggest that Nehemiah called him "Horonite" in contempt rather than address him by his title "governor of Samaria." Sanballat, with the Ammonite Tobiah and the Arabian Geshem, tried by ridicule, intimidation, and threats to prevent Nehemiah from rebuilding the walls of Jerusalem. He accused Nehemiah of rebellion against the Persian government, invited him to the plain of Ono for a conference, planning to have him waylaid and assassinated, and even made preparations for an armed attack upon Jerusalem. However, Nehemiah was equal to the task and fell into none of Sanballat's traps. He took effective measures to defend the city in the event of an attack, which Sanballat under the circumstances did not dare to carry out (chs 2:10, 19, 20; 4:1-5, 7-9, 11-23; 6:1-9, 12-14). Later, when Nehemiah returned to Judah for his 2d term as governor, he found that a grandson of the Jewish high priest Eliashib had married Sanballat's daughter. Recognizing the potential threat to the morale of his people, Nehemiah expelled the couple (ch 13:28).

Sanballat's name appears in a letter of 407 B.C. from the Jews of Elephantine, Egypt (*see* Pathros), written to Bigvai, the Persian governor of Judah. In this letter the Jews requested from Bigvai permission to rebuild their temple, which had been destroyed by Egyptian enemies, and stated that they had written also "to Delaiah and Shelemiah, the sons of Sanballat, governor of Samaria," intimating that they would turn to the Samaritans for help if their present request was not granted by the authorities of Jerusalem (fig. 417). This shows that Sanballat was still alive and apparently in office in 407 B.C., 37 years after Nehemiah had first come to Palestine as governor. However, he seems to have been so old by this time that his 2 sons acted as administrators.

Josephus mentions a Sanballat, calling him a Cuthean whom Darius III (336/35-331 B.C.) had appointed as governor of Samaria, but who had gone over to Alexander after the latter's victory over Darius. Josephus further records that Sanballat's daughter Nicaso was married to Manasseh, brother of the Jewish high priest Jaddua, and that consequently Manasseh was driven from Jerusalem, but was made priest of a temple built on Mount Gerizim by his father-in-law with the permission of Alexander the Great (*Ant.* xi. 7. 2; 8. 2, 4). Regarding the relationship between Josephus' story and the Biblical narrative, scholars have in the past set forth 3 views: (1) that Josephus is in error, (2) that Josephus' story is historically correct, and the book Nehemiah should be corrected accordingly, or (3) that there were 2 Sanballats, one, the Horonite, in Nehemiah's time, and a second one, the Cuthean, 100 years later in the time of the high priest Jaddua and Alexander the Great. The Elephantine papyri have confirmed the Biblical record as correct with regard to the existence of Sanballat in Nehemiah's time, hence view (2) is now largely disregarded. Those who hold view (3) face the difficulty of explaining what seems most unlikely, namely that there were 2 governors of Samaria with the same name reigning 100 years apart, each having a daughter married to a close relative of the high priest of Jerusalem, which led in both cases to the expulsion of the married couple from Judah. Since Josephus' records with regard to Jewish history in the time of Nehemiah contain many historical errors, it seems best to regard his story of Sanballat as being also inaccurate, as expressed in view (1).

Sanctification. [Gr. *hagiasmos,* "holiness," "consecration," "sanctification," from *hagiazō,* "to make holy," "to consecrate," "to sanctify," "to set apart"; equivalent to the Heb. *qadash,* "to separate from common

417. Aramaic papyrus from Elephantine, mentioning the high priest Johanan of Jerusalem (see 2 boxes in 1st line) and Sanballat, the governor of Samaria (see box at bottom)

use."] As a modern theological term sanctification denotes a process of character development, or the result of this process. However, as used in the NT, "sanctification" and "justification" are essentially equivalent terms, the former representing the change of status from sinfulness to holiness, and the latter the change from unrighteousness to righteousness (see Rom 6:19). Thus sanctification is presented as a past act (see 1 Cor 6:11, where "are sanctified" is literally "were sanctified"). See *SDACom* 7:460. This is not to say that the NT writers had nothing to say about "sanctification" in this modern sense, for they discuss it often and at length under such expressions as "follow after righteousness" (1 Ti 6:11), walking "in newness of life" (Rom 6:4), being "transformed" (ch 12:2), "perfecting holiness" (2 Cor 7:1), growing "up into . . . Christ" (Eph 4:15), pressing "toward the mark" (Php 3:12-15), being "built up" in Christ (Col 2:7), becoming "complete in all the will of God" (ch 4: 12), fighting "the good fight of faith" (1 Ti 6:12; cf. v 11), partaking "of the divine nature" (2 Pe 1:4), growing "in grace" (ch 3:18), etc. In justification a man receives the Lord Jesus Christ, and in sanctification he learns to walk in harmony with His will (see Col 2:6, 7), justification taking but a moment, and sanctification requiring a whole lifetime. *See* Justification.

Sanctuary. [Heb. *miqdash,* "sacred place," "sanctuary," *qodesh,* "what is holy," "holy (place)," "holy (things)," both from *qadash,* "to set apart," that is, to separate from common use; Gr. *hagion* (often in the plural), "what is holy," "sanctuary."] A place consecrated to the worship of the true God, especially the *tabernacle erected at Mount Sinai (Ex 25:8; etc.) and the *Temple later constructed on Mount Moriah (2 Chr 3:1; 20:8; etc.).

For the sanctuary services *see* Daily; Priest; Sacrifices and Offerings. See also *SDACom* 4:842-845.

Sand Lizard, KJV **Snail.** [Heb. *chomet.*] There is general agreement that the Hebrew word signifies some type of lizard rather than the snail, but the specific kind is uncertain. The sand lizard is a member of *Scincidae*, lizards characterized by their desert habitat, their light color, and their habit of burrowing rapidly in the sand rather than climbing, as do other lizards. The lizard appears in the list of unclean creatures (Lev 11:30). *See* Lizard.

Sandal. *See* Shoe.

Sanhedrin. *See* Council.

Sansannah (săn-săn′ȧ). [Heb. *Sansannah,* meaning uncertain.] A city in the south of Judah (Jos 15:31), identified with *Khirbet esh-Shamsanîyât,* about 9 mi. northeast of Beer-sheba.

Saph (săf). [Heb. *Saph,* "threshold." The name occurs in Babylonian texts as *Sippê* and *Sippai.*] A Philistine giant, slain by David's hero Sibbecai (2 Sa 21:18). He is called Sippai (sĭp′ī) [Heb. *Sippay*] in 1 Chr 20:4.

Saphir. *See* Shaphir.

Sapphira (să-fī′rȧ). [Gr. *Sapphira,* a transliteration of the Aramaic *Shappîra′,* "beautiful," "fair." The name occurs in both Greek and Aramaic on ossuaries discovered near Jerusalem.] The wife of Ananias, who joined him in selling some property ostensibly for the benefit of the church. She was a willing accomplice with him in the deceptive scheme of holding back a part of the price, while presenting to the apostles the remainder as if it were the whole. Peter denounced this fraudulent behavior, whereupon Sapphira was struck dead, as her husband had been a short time previously (Acts 5:1-11).

Sapphire. A rendering of the Heb. *sappîr,* and of the Gr. *sappheiros,* a semiprecious stone, perhaps what we know today as lapis lazuli: a mixture of several minerals, having an azure-blue color. It was imported from Elam, Media, and Urartu. Some of it had speckles of pyrite. It is this lapis lazuli that is called sapphire by Theophrastus, Pliny, and authors of the Middle Ages. Lapis lazuli was also artificially produced in Assyria and Egypt. The gem of Scripture appeared in the middle of the 2d row of the high priest's breastplate (Ex 28:18; 39:11). When in vision the prophets beheld the throne of God, they selected the rich color of *sappîr* to describe the scene (Ex 24:10; Eze 1:26; 10:1). Both its value and beauty are alluded to in the poetic portions of the Bible (Job 28:16; Song 5:14; Lam 4:7; Eze 28:13), and it is described as the 2d foundation of the New Jerusalem (Rev 21:19). For the translation "sapphire" in ch 9:17, RSV, *see* Jacinth.

Sara. *See* Sarah.

Sarah (sâr′ȧ), or **Sarai** (sā′rī), KJV of NT twice **Sara** (sâr′ȧ). [Heb. *Śarah,* "princess," and *Śaray,* the latter attested in Akkadian as *Saraia;* Gr. *Sarra.*]

1. The wife of Abraham (Gen 11:29) and *daughter of his father, but not of his mother (ch 20:12). She was about 10 years younger than Abraham (ch 17:17), and was therefore about 65 years old when her husband left Haran at the age of 75 (ch 12:4). Shortly after their arrival in Palestine a famine broke out which forced them to go to Egypt to keep their large household alive. Fearing that Sarah's beauty would, in spite of her age, attract the attention of the Egyptians, Abraham pretended she was his sister. Posing now as unmarried, she was taken to Pharaoh's harem. But the king returned her to Abraham when her true status became known, with a rebuke for Abraham's deception and a request that Abraham leave the country (vs 10-20). Abraham did not profit by this experience, but again passed off Sarah as his sister, this time in the country of Abimelech of Gerar (ch 20:1-18). When about 75 years of age (cf. chs 16:16; 17:17) Sarah despaired of ever becoming a mother, and requested her husband to have a child through Hagar, her Egyptian slave. In making this proposal Sarah followed a custom of her native Mesopotamia (see *SDACom* 1:317, 318). The result was the birth of Ishmael (ch 16:1-16). Later, when about 89 years old, Sarah received a definite promise that she would give birth to a son within a year. It was on this occasion that her name, which had hitherto been Sarai, was changed to Sarah. The promise was fulfilled in the birth of Isaac (chs 17:1, 15-22; 18:9-15; 21:1-5). During Isaac's weaning feast Sarah saw Ishmael tormenting Isaac (Gen 21:9; Gal 4:29), whereupon she demanded that Ishmael and Hagar be expelled from the family. At God's direction Abraham reluctantly obeyed (Gen 21:9-14). Nothing more is recorded of Sarah except that

she died at the age of 127 at Kiriath-arba, or Hebron (Gen 23:1, 2). She was buried in the Cave of Machpelah, which Abraham bought after her death as a family sepulcher (vs 19, 20). Isaiah refers to Sarah as the mother of the Israelite nation (Is 51:2), and Paul writes of her as the mother of the child of promise (Rom 4:19; 9:9). Peter mentions her as an example of a good wife (1 Pe 3:6), and in Heb 11:11 she is praised for her faith.

2. For Num 26:46, KJV, *see* Serah.

Sarai. *See* Sarah.

Saraph (sā'răf). [Heb. *Śaraph,* literally, "a burning one," hence, "seraph," or "serpent."] A descendant of Shelah, the son of Judah. He was a ruler in Moab in an unspecified time, possibly as a governor during the period when Moab was ruled by David or Solomon (1 Chr 4:22).

Sardine. *See* Sardius.

Sardis (sär'dĭs). [Gr. *Sardeis.*] The old capital of the Lydian kingdom. It lay on a slope of Mount Tmolus, and was protected on 2 sides by the river Pactolus, a tributary of the Hermus. Map XX, B-4. The original city was built entirely on the hill (see fig. 418), with strong protective walls. Later it was extended to the plain at the foot of the hill. The city appears in history 1st in the 7th cent. B.C., when it was the capital of the Lydian kingdom, the country in which coined money, so important in world economics, was invented. In 547 B.C. Sardis was conquered by Cyrus and its fabulously rich king, Croesus, captured. It then became the capital of a Persian satrapy, from which the Persian wars against Greece were directed. Later the city changed hands several times. It was taken by Alexander, then by Antiochus the Great, and in 190 B.C. was incorporated into the kingdom of Pergamum. When that kingdom became a Roman possession in 133 B.C., Sardis became part of the Roman province of Asia. It was destroyed by an earthquake in A.D. 17, but was rebuilt with the

419. Columns of the great Artemis temple at Sardis, with the ruins of a Christian church at the left

assistance of Tiberius. The final destruction of Sardis came in 1402 when it was conquered by the Mongolians under Timur, or Tamerlane. Nothing remains of its former glory except a few ruins. A nearby village still bears the ancient name in the form of Sart. From 1910 to 1914 excavations were carried out by an American expedition under the direction of H. C. Butler. This expedition excavated the very impressive ruins of a great 4th-cent. B.C. temple dedicated to the mother goddess Cybele, called *Artemis locally in NT times. Two of this temple's 66-ft. columns still stand (see fig. 419). Adjacent to the temple were the ruins of a little Christian church of the 4th cent. A.D. Excavations have been resumed since 1958 under the direction of G. Hanfmann of Harvard University. It is sponsored by the Bollingen Foundation, the American Schools of Oriental Research, and Harvard and Cornell Universities. A Christian church existed in the city before the end of the 1st cent. A.D. as is proved by the letter written by John to the church of Sardis from the island of Patmos (Rev 3:1-6).

418. The ruin mound of ancient Sardis

For the significance of Sardis as one of the 7 churches of the Revelation see *SDACom* 7:97-99, 755-757.

Sardites. *See* Seredites.

Sardius. A rendering of: (1) The Heb. *'odem* (Ex 28:17; 39:10; Eze 28:13; KJV), a precious stone the exact identity of which is uncertain. The Hebrew root indicates that its color was red. This gem was placed in the 1st row of the high priest's breastplate (Ex 28:17; 39:10), and was an adornment of the king of Tyre (Eze 28:12, 13; RSV "carnelian"). (2) The Gr. *sardion* (Rev 21:20, KJV; another form [*sardinos*] with the same meaning is translated "sardine stone" in ch 4:3, KJV), possibly the sard or carnelian. Sard or sardius is a variety of chalcedony and is known in several colors, although the bright-red variety is probably meant here. Carnelian is the transparent red type of chalcedony. However, exact identification is impossible. John describes the One seen by him upon the throne as of the appearance of sardius (ch 4:3; RSV "carnelian"), and notes that this gem constituted one of the foundation stones of the New Jerusalem seen by him in prophetic vision (ch 21:20; RSV "carnelian").

Sardonyx. A rendering of the Gr. *sardonux,* some variety of precious stone, the exact identity of which is uncertain. The 5th foundation stone of the New Jerusalem seen by John was of this stone (Rev 21:20; RSV "onyx").

Sarepta. *See* Zarephath.

Sargon (sär'gŏn). [Heb. *Sargôn;* in Aramaic texts *Śrkn;* Assyrian *Sharru-kên.*] The name of several Mesopotamian kings, of whom only Sargon II (722-705 B.C.) of Assyria (see fig. 420) appears in the Bible. Sargon II is mentioned in the Bible only in Is 20:1, in connection with a campaign against Ashdod. The first Assyrian king's name to be deciphered was that of Sargon II. The decipherment was made in the middle of the 19th cent. when Assyriology was in its infancy, and by it Biblical archeology gained one of its first triumphs, for the name Sargon had been completely unknown except for the one occurrence of it in the book of Isaiah.

Sargon took the throne of Assyria after the death of Shalmaneser V. He was probably a usurper, although he claimed, according to one preserved text, to have been a son of Tiglath-pileser III. He was a powerful king and a great conqueror, and became the founder of the mightiest dynasty of Assyrian rulers, under whom

420. Relief of Sargon II

the empire reached its greatest triumphs. In his later inscriptions he claims to have captured Samaria, and to have deported 27,290 Israelites, and their gods (*ANET* 284-286; *Iraq* 16 [1954], p. 180), probably meaning the golden calves that Jeroboam I had set up at Bethel and Dan. However, from the chronological data of the Bible it seems more likely that Samaria fell shortly before Shalmaneser V's death, when Sargon was still the commander of the army. Nevertheless, Sargon may have been responsible for the transplantation of the population of Samaria to other parts of the empire (2 Ki 17:6), and the initial settlements of colonists from Babylonia, and other places (v 24) in the territory of Samaria. Sargon carried out many military campaigns during his reign of 17 years, but it is unknown whether he fought against King Hezekiah, although he calls himself the subduer of Judah, and claims that that country paid tribute to him (*ANET* 287). He is especially well known as the builder of a new capital city, *Dûr-Sharrukên,* now Khorsabad, about 10 mi. northeast of Nineveh (Map XI, B-5). *Dûr-Sharrukên* was the first Assyrian palace city (fig. 364) excavated. Sargon was succeeded in 705 B.C. by his son Sennacherib.

Sarid (sā'rĭd). [Heb. *Śarîd,* "survivor."] A frontier town of the tribe of Zebulun (Jos 19:10, 12), identified with *Tell Shadûd,* about 4 mi. southwest of Nazareth (Map VI, C-3).

Saron. *See* Sharon, 1.

Sarsechim (sär′sĕ-kĭm). [Heb. *Śar-sekîm*.] The name of a high officer in Nebuchadnezzar's army (Jer 39:3). However, the "nebo" of the preceding word should be included as part of the name, which would then read Nebo-sar-sechim. *Nebô* stands for the Babylonian god *Nabû*, Marduk's son, and the word *śar* for the Babylonian *sharru*, "king." The last part, *sekim*, has not yet been explained satisfactorily. The name remains unattested in Babylonian records.

Saruch. *See* Serug.

Sashes. A rendering of the Heb. *qishshurîm* (Is 3:20, RSV), from *qashar*, "to tie," hence thought to be some form of bands. In the context of the passage it probably refers to ornamental bands (KJV "headbands"). In Jer 2:32 the term is translated "attire."

Satan (sā′tăn). [Heb. *śaṭan*, "adversary," from *śaṭan*, "to cherish animosity"; Gr. *Satan, Satanas*, transliterations of the Hebrew and Aramaic.] The great adversary of God and of man (Rev 12:7-12), otherwise commonly called the devil (Mt 4:10, 11; Rev 12:9), Beelzebub (Mt 12:24), Belial (2 Cor 6:15), the tempter (Mt 4:3), the enemy (ch 13:39), the evil one (cf. ch 13:25), the adversary (1 Pe 5:8), and the deceiver (cf. Rev 12:9). The translators of the LXX generally rendered *śatan* as *diabolos*, "slanderer," "accuser," "devil." Satan's first recorded act on earth was, in the guise of a serpent, to persuade Eve to distrust the goodness of God, to doubt His word, and to reject His authority, and through her, to cause the fall of Adam (Gen 3:1-6; cf. 1 Ti 2:14). He thus enlisted the human race on his side of the great struggle against the divine government, and ever since has occupied himself in snaring, deceiving, beguiling, and seducing mankind (Rom 8:7; 2 Cor 11:3; 2 Ti 2:26; Rev 12:9; etc.). After inciting men to sin (cf. Jn 13:2), he accuses them before God as unworthy of divine mercy (Zec 3:1-4; Rev 12:10). In his role as deceiver he first misrepresents God before man, and then man before God, with the purpose of bringing about eternal estrangement between God and man, and then accuses God before the universe as being to blame for this situation. When he cannot subvert man's loyalty to God, he accuses God of unfairness and seeks to destroy man (see Job 1:6-12, 21, 22; 2:1-9).

Our Lord met Satan in the wilderness, triumphed over him (Mt 4:10, 11), and indicted him as the one actually responsible for human woes (see Lk 13:16; Jn 8:44). Jesus said that He "beheld Satan as lightning fall from heaven" (Lk 10:18; cf. Rev 12:7-12). The Jewish leaders accused Jesus of casting out demons by satanic power, but our Lord showed this reasoning to be fallacious (Mt 12:24-29). Upon one occasion, when Simon Peter sought to divert the Saviour from His appointed mission, our Lord, recognizing Satan's influence on Peter, addressed the latter as if he were Satan (ch 16:21-23). Upon another occasion He warned Peter that Satan desired to gain control of him (Lk 22:31). It was Satan who prompted Judas to sell his Master for 30 pieces of silver (Jn 13:26, 27).

Paul warned his converts against letting Satan get any advantage over them (2 Cor 2:11; cf. 1 Cor 7:5). He also warned that the great Antichrist, the lawless one who was to come, would be carrying out the work of Satan (2 Th 2:3, 4, 9), and cautioned that the great adversary of God and man is able to transform himself into an angel of light (2 Cor 11:14). Satan did all that he could to hinder the great apostle in the work of the ministry (1 Th 2:18, RSV), and was permitted by God to afflict him, in measure (2 Cor 12:7). *See* Devil.

Satraps (sā′trăps). [Heb. *'achashdarpenîm*; Aramaic *'achashdarpenayya'*; in cuneiform (sing.) *aḥshadrapânu* and *shatarpânu*, from Old Persian *khshatrapān*; Gr. *satrapai*, from which the English word satrap is derived.] The highest Persian official over a major division, or "satrapy," of the Persian Empire. The empire was divided into about 20 satrapies (see Map XII), although the number was not always the same. Each of these satrapies was subdivided into provinces. For example, Judah as a province belonged to the satrapy of "Beyond the River," which extended from the Euphrates in the north to Egypt in the south, and which comprised numerous provinces, some of which were governed by native administrators and others by Persians. The satrap was always a Persian of noble birth, in many instances closely related to the king. He functioned as a viceroy, since in his territory he was subordinate to none but the king. The Hebrew term for satraps is found in Ezr 8:36; Est 3:12; 8:9; 9:3 (KJV "lieutenants"), and the Aramaic term in Dan 3:2, 3, 27; 6:1; etc. (KJV "princes"). The RSV correctly renders these terms "satraps" in all these passages.

Satyr. [Heb. *śa'îr,* "hairy (creature)," "hairy (one)," generally rendered "goat," "male goat," or "kid"; in later times a mythical demon supposed to have the appearance of a goat.] The satyrs of Is 13:21; 34:14 were probably wild goats which the prophet foresaw as dancing among the ruins of Babylon and of the cities of Idumea, or Edom. All the other creatures mentioned in the context are literal animals, and it is therefore unlikely that Isaiah was referring to demons in goat-like form. In Lev 17:7 and 2 Chr 11:15 *śa'îrîm* (RSV "satyrs"; KJV "devils") is probably used in reference to objects of idolatrous worship. Gods in the form of he-goats were worshiped by some pagan nations; for example, a temple was dedicated to such a god in Mendes in Egypt.

Saul (sôl). [Heb. *Sha'ûl,* "asked (of God)," or "lent (to God)." The name appears on an ancient Hebrew seal, and in Phoenician, Palmyrene, and Aramaic inscriptions with various spellings. In cuneiform texts it appears as *Saûli.* Gr. *Saoul* and *Saulos.*]

1. For Gen 36:37, 38, KJV, *see* Shaul.

2. The first Hebrew king. He was the son of the Benjamite Kish, whose home town was Gibeah, now *Tell el-Fûl,* about 4 mi. north of Jerusalem. For centuries Israel had been living under a theocratic form of government, being ruled by judges called by God. The last of these, Samuel, had grown old, and his sons did not measure up to the qualities of leadership of their godly father. The people, having become tired of the lack of continuity in strong leadership, thought that a kingship would provide them with a form of government that would cure their political and international ills. Samuel looked upon the popular demand for a king with extreme disfavor, but God directed him to accede to the people's desire, at the same time to make them thoroughly acquainted with the disadvantages and burdens this move would bring upon them (1 Sa 8).

(1) *Saul becomes king.* Shortly after the people's demand for a king, Saul, a young, handsome man of towering stature, was out with a servant searching for some lost asses belonging to his father. After a fruitless search of 3 days the servant suggested that they should consult "the seer," by which he meant Samuel. Although Saul had probably heard of Samuel, he did not know him personally (1 Sa 9:18), and was afraid to approach him without a gift of money (v 7). Mean-while Samuel had received instruction from God that a Benjamite would come to him whom he should anoint as king. When Saul arrived, a specific word came to him that Saul was the man who should rule over God's people. Samuel met him in the gate, assured him that the asses had been found, and invited the surprised Saul to stay for a sacrificial meal. Saul spent the night with Samuel as the prophet's guest, and in the morning Samuel secretly anointed him and prophesied certain experiences that Saul would have on his way home, which took place as predicted. He further directed him to go to Gilgal and wait 7 days for him, at the end of which time he would receive additional instructions. Nothing more is recorded of this particular meeting at Gilgal. Saul told no one of his anointing as king (1 Sa 9:1 to 10:16).

As soon as Samuel knew who the new king was to be he summoned the whole nation to Mizpah, probably the modern *Tell en-Nasbeh,* where lots were cast publicly to confirm Saul as king. When Saul, who had hidden himself but whose place of hiding was discovered, was presented to the people as the Lord's choice, the majority were satisfied. Perhaps the fact that Saul belonged to the smallest tribe facilitated his acceptance. Nevertheless dissenting voices were heard. The young king did not immediately assert his kingship, but went back home (1 Sa 10:17-27), probably to await an opportune occasion when his service and leadership would be needed by the country. He may also have considered it prudent to see whether the opposition against him or against his tribe could peacefully be overcome, and his opponents appeased, before he began his active rule.

The opportunity to show his leadership came soon—according to the LXX (1 Sa 11:1) in about a month. The Israelite town of Jabesh in Gilead was besieged by Nahash, king of the Ammonites, and messengers from Jabesh came to Gibeah telling of the humiliating conditions of surrender demanded by Nahash. Their plea for quick help stirred Saul's soul. He again felt the Spirit coming "mightily" upon him, and driven by compassion for the Gileadites he sent out a nationwide summons to rally behind "Saul and Samuel" for the liberation of Jabesh. As a result 330,000 armed men followed Saul over the Jordan and routed the Ammonites. Having thus given a clear demonstration of his fitness to the throne, Saul was unanimously acclaimed king and solemnly enthroned at Gilgal (1 Sa 11).

(2) *Saul's reign*. Paul gives the total length of Saul's reign as 40 years (Acts 13:21), as does Josephus (*Ant.* vi. 14. 9). However, it is not known how old Saul was when he became king, for the OT verse that originally gave his age when he began to reign (1 Sa 13:1) is now defective (see RSV; *SDACom* 2:506, 507). Nor is it known how much time lay between the events connected with Saul's elevation to the throne and his war with the Philistines recorded in 1 Sa 13. If this interval was brief Saul must have been near 35 years of age at his accession to the throne, because at the time of the battle his son Jonathan was already in charge of one Hebrew army and was a formidable warrior. But if it broke out several years after he came to the throne Saul could have been younger. Because this problem remains unresolved we do not know how long Saul reigned under the tutelage of Samuel.

At the time of his first encounter with the Philistines, Saul had a standing army with 2,000 soldiers under his personal command, stationed at Michmash and the hill country of Bethel, and 1,000 men stationed at Gibeah, the capital (for Saul's stronghold see figs. 202, 421), under the command of Jonathan, the crown prince. Jonathan had defeated a Philistine garrison at neighboring Geba, and knowing that the Philistines would retaliate, Saul called the nation to arms, naming Gilgal as the rallying point because Samuel had promised to meet them. They waited for 7 days, but Samuel did not come, having probably delayed his journey in order to test Saul's and the people's obedience to, and trust in, God. When Saul saw that desertions among his people were increasing and that fear possessed those who remained, he took it upon himself to offer sacrifices that were to be offered only by a priest. Samuel arrived almost immediately and rebuked Saul for his rash act, telling him that because of his disobedience and lack of trust in God his descendants would not occupy the throne (1 Sa 13:2-14). The ensuing war against the Philistines ended in victory. Jonathan by a heroic act of valor put a company of Philistines to flight. This spread terror and panic among the main body of Philistines. Saul took advantage of this situation, led his army into battle, and chased the enemy out of Israelite territory. Saul was evidently a stern disciplinarian, for when Jonathan unwittingly disobeyed his command he was ready to take his son's life. Jonathan's life was saved only upon the demand of the army (1 Sa 13:15 to 14:46).

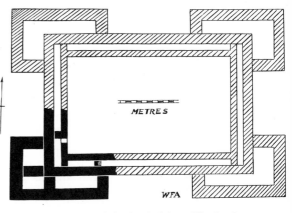

421. Outline plan of Saul's citadel at Gibeah; the part preserved is in solid black

Saul carried out other military campaigns with brilliant results (1 Sa 14:47, 48). During one of these campaigns he committed an act of disobedience that sealed his rejection by God as king. He had been ordered to destroy the Amalekites and their possessions, to fulfill a curse pronounced against them by God for having fought against Israel in the wilderness at Rephidim (Ex 17:8-16). Saul carried out the order, but spared some of the cattle, to sacrifice, as he said, at Gilgal, and their king Agag. For this disobedience to a specific command Samuel declared that God no longer considered him as the legitimate ruler of His people (1 Sa 15). A little later Samuel secretly anointed David the shepherd boy to be the future king of the nation (ch 16:1-13).

(3) *Saul's last years*. God's Spirit departed from Saul when he was rejected as king, and an evil spirit periodically plagued him. In an effort to lift him from his melancholy moods his servants introduced to him young David, who was chosen to play the lyre before the king (1 Sa 16:14-23). At first Saul liked David, but his affection soon changed to jealousy and fear when David, having killed Goliath, and thus secured a victory for the Israelites over the Philistines, was acclaimed by the maidens of Israel as the greatest hero of the nation (chs 17:1 to 18:9). His jealousy led him to attempts on David's life. He tried first to kill him with

his spear, then endeavored to bring about his death in skirmishes with the Philistines (1 Sa 18:10-29). When it became evident that Saul would stop at nothing in his efforts to destroy him, David fled from Saul, left his wife Michal, and was for years a fugitive in different parts of the country, while Saul wasted his time and energy seeking to hunt him down (chs 19 to 27).

Saul's foolish enmity against David deprived Israel of its best army commander and of many valiant soldiers who followed David into exile, and caused him to neglect the defense of his kingdom. The result was a weakening of the nation's defenses and a reinvasion by the Philistines, who this time encamped at Shunem, near the Valley of Jezreel. Saul pitched his camp on the slopes of Mount Gilboa (1 Sa 28:1, 4). The fearful and melancholic king was plagued by forebodings, and went to En-dor to consult a spirit medium. Some time previously he had by divine command expelled all such practitioners from the country, since they were the tools of evil spirits (1 Sa 28:3; cf. Lev 20:27; Deut 18:10-14). Now, however, having been forsaken by God and being possessed by an evil spirit, he felt driven to seek the help of these tools of the devil. He asked that Samuel, who had died some time before, be brought up by the medium, so that the prophet, who during the last years of his life had not communicated with Saul, might advise him. The medium claimed to see an old man coming up, and Saul supposed him to be Samuel. The spirit then predicted that Saul would die the next day (1 Sa 28:5-25). See Death. The battle on the following day went against the Israelites, and 3 sons of Saul were killed and Saul was badly wounded. Seeking to avoid capture by his enemies, Saul asked his armorbearer to kill him. When the man refused, Saul fell upon his sword and ended his own life. Later the Philistines decapitated him and fastened his body and the bodies of his sons on the wall of the city of Beth-shean. They put his armor in their temple of Ashtaroth. However, the citizens of Jabesh, remembering how Saul had saved them from the Ammonites, rescued the mutilated bodies from Beth-shean's wall and gave them an honorable burial at Jabesh (ch 31:1-13).

When the news of Saul's death reached David, he mourned for him and for his friend Jonathan, composing a beautiful elegy (2 Sa 1:17-27). Kingship in Israel

had had a poor beginning. Saul had begun his reign as a magnanimous ruler, but his independent spirit drove him into repeated acts of disobedience, which removed him farther and farther from God, and finally brought him to a sad and shameful end.

3. The name by which the apostle Paul is known in the early part of Acts (Acts 7:58; etc.). See Paul.

Saviour. [Heb. *môshîa'*, "one who delivers," "one who helps," from *yasha'*, "to deliver," "to help"; Gr. *sōtēr*, "savior," "deliverer," "preserver."] Anyone who delivers from danger or saves from grave misfortune (2 Ki 13:5; Neh 9:27). The OT uses the word especially of God as the Deliverer of His people Israel (Ps 106:21; Is 43:3, 11; 63:8; Hos 13:4). The NT similarly refers to God the Father as "Saviour" (Lk 1:47; 1 Ti 1:1; Tit 1:3; etc.), but more particularly to Jesus Christ, who came to "save his people from their sins" (Mt 1:21). The name "Jesus" means "the Lord is salvation." See Jesus.

Saw. [Heb. *megerah* and *maśśôr*.] Discoveries in Egypt show that saws of Bible times consisted of a metal blade, with a wooden handle. The blades were usually of bronze but in later times were made also of iron, and were either bound to their handles by thongs or inserted into them. Metal saws were used for cutting wood and stones (1 Ki 7:9; Is 10:15). Heb 11:37 speaks of faithful martyrs sawn asunder by their persecutors. This refers probably to the prophet Isaiah, who according to Jewish tradition was put to death in this way by the wicked king Manasseh. According to 2 Sa 12:31 David set the captured Ammonites to labor with saws. The parallel passage (1 Chr 20:3) says that David "cut them with saws," but this reading is probably due to some error (see RSV).

Scab. Skin diseases of various kinds are common in Bible lands, and have always been. The exact meaning of several Hebrew expressions translated "scab" (Lev 13:2, 6-8; 14:56; Deut 28:27; KJV; Lev 21:20, RSV; Is 3:17) is not known. It would be difficult to identify each with a specific and accurate designation from the vocabulary of modern medicine.

Scall. See Itch.

Scapegoat. See Azazel.

Scarlet. The color "scarlet" of the Bible was probably a purplish-red shade. In the OT the term is a rendering generally of variations of the Heb. *tôla'ath shanî* (Ex 25:4;

Num 4:8; etc.), "scarlet worm," the worm being the source of the dye. The insect in question is the *Coccus ilicis,* the female of which produces an egg containing a red substance. The dye was obtained from the dried bodies of this insect. The Arabs called this insect *qirmiz,* from which our word "crimson" is derived. Because the female insect appeared somewhat like a berry, the Greeks named it *kokkos;* hence the Gr. *kokkinos* for "scarlet." The color appeared in certain of the hangings of the tabernacle and in parts of the priests' dress (Ex 26:1, 36; 28:5, 33; etc.). Scarlet material was used with other items to sprinkle blood in the ceremony of pronouncing clean a leper's house (Lev 14:49-53), as well as the cured leper himself (vs 1-9). Scarlet was also used in preparing the "water of separation" in the camp of Israel (Num 19:6). Scarlet for dye was considered a luxury item (see 2 Sa 1:24; Rev 18:12, 16), and the wearing of scarlet was a mark of distinction (Dan 5:7, 16, 29). The robe placed in mockery upon Jesus was variously described as scarlet and purple (Mt 27:28; Mk 15:17); however, since certain shades of scarlet and purple blend almost imperceptibly into each other, different observers might well have used 2 terms to describe the same color. The mystic harlot of the Apocalypse is pictured in purple and scarlet array (Rev 17:4).

Scepter, KJV **Sceptre.** The rendering of 2 Hebrew words and 1 Greek word, meaning basically "staff" or "rod." In the hand of a king, judge, or leader, a staff, or rod, became a "scepter" or a symbol of authority. Royal scepters are depicted on ancient sculptures in Egypt and Mesopotamia, and actual royal scepters, very artistically decorated with gold and semiprecious stones, have been discovered in the tomb of King Tutankhamen of Egypt, dating from the 14th cent. B.C. (see fig. 422), and in the royal tombs of Ur which date from the early patriarchal period. Scepters are mentioned in the Bible as emblems of authority in the hands of "God" (Ps 45:6) or of a ruler (Eze 19:11). A golden scepter is mentioned in the hand of the Persian king (Est 4:11; etc.). A reed was put in Christ's hands when He was mocked as king (Mt 27:29).

Sceptre. *See* Scepter.

Sceva (sē'và). [Gr. *Skeuas,* a name attested in Greek inscriptions.] A Jew whose 7 sons, exorcists, Paul encountered at Ephesus. He is called a high priest, or chief priest, an expression difficult to understand in this passage, since he lived in Ephesus and had a Greek name (Acts 19:1, 14).

Schin. [Heb. *shin.*] The 21st letter of the Hebrew alphabet, written ש, appearing as the title of the 21st section of Ps 119 in the KJV. *See* Aleph.

School. A rendering of the Gr. *scholē* (Acts 19:9, KJV). Evidence abounds for the existence of schools in the ancient world. These institutions were found in the principal cities of Mesopotamia and Egypt, and functioned mainly for the training of professional scribes. School buildings have been excavated in several places and texts of students' exercises written on clay tablets or papyrus sheets have been discovered. It is very probable that the Canaanites of pre-Israelitic times had schools, although this has not conclusively been proved. In Shechem a text was found dating from the middle of the 2d millennium B.C. in which a teacher complained to the father of a certain pupil that the tuition had not been paid, and requested payment (W. F. Albright, *BASOR* 86 [1942], 30, 31). Although this teacher may have been a private tutor, the widespread knowledge of the art of writing in Canaan, as attested by archeological evidence, indicates that learning was not limited to a small class (cf. Jgs 8:14, RSV). Hence a justifiable conclusion is that there must have been schools among the Canaanites and probably also among the Hebrews after they took over the country. Passages such as Gen 18:19 and Deut 6:7,

422. Egyptian royal emblems of authority from the tomb of Tutankhamen, in the Cairo Museum

Top: A baton covered with gold

Left: Scepter of gold and blue glass

Right: Flail of gilded wood, green glass, and carnelian

which charge parents to give religious instruction to the members of their households and to their children, do not exclude the possibility of the existence of schools where reading, writing, and other subjects were taught. Samuel founded the schools of the prophets (*see* Prophet, I).

Religious teaching was part of the duties of Levites and priests (Lev 10:11) who lived throughout the country. Sometimes these religious leaders were sent out to teach the Law among the people (2 Chr 17:7-9). It was specifically commanded that the Law be read to all the people every 7 years at the time of the Feast of Tabernacles (Deut 31:10-13). How this was done is described in Neh 8:1-8.

In NT times schools were common throughout Palestine, and all Hebrew boys were required to attend them. Instruction was given in a room attached to the synagogue. It was probably in a schoolroom of the Temple precinct that Joseph and Mary found the child Jesus in a lively discussion with the teachers (Lk 2:46). Wealthy people employed private tutors.

Schools were found in all the large cities and in many villages of the Roman Empire. In many cases slaves were employed as teachers, especially as private tutors. It was a school in Ephesus that Paul used as a meeting hall for 2 years after he had been expelled from the Jewish synagogue (Acts 19:9); the KJV rendering "school" is preferred to the RSV rendering "hall."

Schoolmaster. A rendering of the Gr. *paidagōgos* (Gal 3:24, 25, KJV), "one who leads boys." The *paidagōgos* was not a teacher. That office was designated by the Gr. *didaskalos*, which is clearly distinguished from *paidagōgos* in secular Greek texts. The *paidagōgos* was usually a trusted slave in a Greek household who had the task of watching over the boys of the family. He accompanied them to school, stayed with them in class, corrected them if they misbehaved or used bad language, and was their general guardian. When the children came of age they were free from his supervision. From this it is clear that "schoolmaster" is not the best rendering of *paidagōgos*. The term is more appropriately translated "custodian" (RSV). Paul uses this term as a figure of the "law" which directed and disciplined God's people until the coming of Christ. See *SDACom* 6:961, 962.

Science. A term appearing twice (Dan 1:4; 1 Ti 6:20; KJV), a rendering of the Heb. *madda'*, "knowledge" (RSV "learning"), and the Gr. *gnōsis*, "knowledge," respectively. The Heb. *madda'* is translated "knowledge" in 2 Chr 1:10-12; Dan 1:17; KJV. With the exception of 1 Ti 6:20, KJV; Php 3:8; 1 Pe 3:7; RSV, *gnōsis* is always translated "knowledge." The English word "science" comes from the Latin *scio*, "to know." In Old English it denoted knowledge in the broader sense. The word still retains this broader meaning, but popular usage tends to limit it to a systematic study of the various branches of knowledge about the physical world and universe.

Scorpion. [Heb. *'aqrab;* Gr. *skorpios.*] A small invertebrate of the class *Arachnoidea,* to which the spider belongs, although the scorpion is different from the spider, especially in respect to its lobsterlike claw and its tail by which it stings and poisons. About 8 kinds of scorpions are found in Palestine, living generally in desert regions, resting usually underneath stones. Scorpions are listed in the Bible along with serpents as dangerous creatures (Deut 8:15; cf. Eze 2:6; Lk 10:19; 11:12) whose sting is painful (Rev 9:5, 10).

In 1 Ki 12:11, 14; 2 Chr 10:11, 14 the whips with which Rehoboam threatened to chastise his people are called "scorpions." These whips were probably tipped with sharp points to make the punishment more severe.

Scourge. In the OT the rendering of: (1) the Heb. *nega',* used symbolically of affliction (Ps 89:32; KJV "stripes"), and probably literally of pestilence or plague (Ps 91:10); (2) the Heb. *biqqoreth* (Lev 19:20), "punishment" (RSV "inquiry"); (3) the Heb. *shôt* (Is 10:26; 28:15, 18), "scourge," "whip," used to describe God's punishment of the wicked, and the abuse and slander of the tongue (Job 5:21). The related term *shotet* is used figuratively of the Canaanites as a source of trouble for Israel (Jos 23:13). A scourge or whip was used for administering severe punishment or torture by lashing, usually on the back. The Law of Moses permitted such punishment but set a maximum of 40 stripes (Deut 25:2, 3). In later times the Jews limited the number of stripes to 39 (2 Cor 11:24) to avoid transgressing the Law in case a mistake in counting was made. "Whips" were used in the time of Solomon, among other things to drive unwilling Israelites to their forced labor duties (1 Ki 12:11, 14). Antiochus IV Epiphanes used the scourge in his endeavor to force the Jews to eat swine's flesh (2 Macc 6:30; 7:1). In the time of Christ the Jews allowed beating for transgressions of the ceremonial law, which punishment was not provided for by the Pentateuch. Minor offenses were punished by the synagogue (Mt 10:17; 23:34) and major offenses by the Sanhedrin (Acts 5:40). Beating was done with rods (2 Cor 11:25) or with whips (Gr. *mastiges*, Acts 22:24; Heb 11:36). These whips or lashes consisted of 3 thongs, of which 1 was of ox hide and 2 of ass's hide. The Roman scourge (Gr. *phragellion* from Latin *flagellum*) was a cruel instrument of torture. To its leather lashes were attached pieces of metal or bone to increase the suffering. It was used not only for punishment but also for the extraction of confessions (Acts 22:24). Criminals condemned to be executed were usually scourged (Gr. *phragelloō* from Latin *flagello*) before they were put to death, as was done in the case of Jesus (Mt 27:26; Mk 15:15; Jn 19:1). The victim was stripped to the waist, usually bound to a post with his hands tied together, and the scourge applied to the back with lacerating blows. Eusebius (*Hist. Eccl.* iv. 15) tells us that martyrs of Smyrna, tortured about A.D. 155, were so unmercifully beaten that the veins, muscles, and sinews were exposed, and even the entrails became visible. The Porcian law and the Valerian law provided that Roman citizens could not be scourged (Livy x. 9); and Paul, a Roman citizen, took advantage of this exemption (Acts 22:25-27). This law did not protect slaves or freedmen who were not Roman citizens. Some lawless Roman governors, such as Florus, cared little for the privileges of Roman provincial citizens, and had such citizens scourged in spite of the law (Jos. *War* ii. 14. 9).

Screech Owl. *See* Night Hag.

Screen, KJV generally **Hanging.** [Heb. *masak*, "covering," "screen."] The skillfully woven draperies or curtains at the gate of the tabernacle court (Ex 27:16; 35:17; KJV "hanging"), at the entrance to the tabernacle (chs 26:36, 37; 36:37; 40:5; KJV "hanging"), and between the 2 apartments (Num 3:31, RSV; cf. Ex 39:34; 40:21, KJV "covering").

Scribe. [Heb. *sopher;* Aramaic *saphar;* Gr. *grammateus.*]

1. A professional secretary who sat in the streets, and upon dictation, wrote letters, legal documents, etc., for hire. These scribes are still to be found on the streets

423. A long writing table and bench found at *Khirbet Qumrán,* on which some of the Dead Sea scrolls probably were written

in the Orient. For their equipment *see* Ink; Pen; Writing Materials. Jeremiah employed Baruch, a professional scribe (Jer 36:32), to write his prophecies in a scroll at his dictation (vs 4, 27, 32), and probably also to write the documents of purchase when he bought a field at Anathoth (ch 32:12). See fig. 424.

2. A government official, who either had clerical duties or was a recording minister of state, called "secretary" in the RSV. Several such officers are mentioned by name in the OT, and from the context it is certain that most of them, such as Seraiah in David's time (2 Sa 8:17) and Shebnah, Hezekiah's secretary, who conducted the negotiations with the envoy of King Sennacherib (2 Ki 18:18, 19), held influential and important offices.

3. A man who copied the Law and other books of the Scriptures (Jer 8:8), but more specifically a man who was proficient in teaching and interpreting the Bible. In the modern sense such a man would be called a theologian or a religious scholar. In the NT such a man was sometimes called *nomikos,* "lawyer" (Mt 22:35; Lk 10:25; etc.), or *nomodidaskalos,* "teacher of the law" (Acts 5:34, RSV; 1 Ti 1:7). The first man to bear the title "scribe" in this sense was Ezra, "a ready

scribe in the law of Moses" (Ezr 7:6), who had consecrated himself to study and teach the law of the Lord (v 10). After Ezra's time scribes assumed influential po-

424. Wooden palettes and reed pens of ancient Egyptian scribes

sitions among the Jews as teachers of God's Word. By the time of the Maccabees (2d cent. B.C.) they were recognized as constituting an honored profession (1 Macc 7:12). Some of the most famous scribes of Jewry, such as Hillel, Shammai, and Gamaliel I, lived at the time of Christ's birth and shortly thereafter. They were Pharisees and attempted to adapt the Law of Moses to the times in which they lived, but could not always agree, so different schools of thought developed. The subtle interpretations of the Pharisees were considered by many to be of equal value with the Law of Moses, and Jesus bitterly denounced the sect's hypocrisy and misinterpretation of Scriptures which led the people astray (Mt 15:1, 3; 23:15, 23, 25,

27, 29, 33). Some of the scribes of Christ's day were influential members of the Sanhedrin and shared in the responsibility for His death (Mt 26:57-59; cf. chs 16:21; 27:41). Later some of these men also turned against the apostles and had a hand in their persecution (Acts 4:5; 6: 12). On one occasion a certain scribe expressed his willingness to follow Jesus (Mt 8:19).

Scrip. An archaic word used as a rendering of the Heb. *yalqût* (1 Sa 17:40, KJV; RSV "wallet"), "shepherd's pouch," and the Gr. *pēra* (Mt 10:10; Mk 6:8; Lk 9:3; KJV; etc.; RSV "bag"), "knapsack," "traveler's bag." In 1 Sa 17:40 the terms "shepherd's bag" and "scrip" may be synonymous. Christ instructed His disciples to carry no "scrip" as they went forth preaching (Mt 10:10; Mk 6:8; KJV; etc.).

Scripture. In the OT this expression occurs once, a rendering of the Heb. *kethab* (Dan 10:21, KJV), "a writing" (RSV "book"). The reference appears to be, not to any part of the Bible, but to the plans and purposes of God, which are represented as written in a book. In the NT "scripture" appears frequently, a rendering in every case but one (2 Ti 3:15, KJV) of the Gr. *graphē*, "writing" (Mt 21: 42; Mk 12:24; Rom 15:4; etc.). The term is used exclusively with a sacred meaning, "Holy Scripture," and the reference is generally to the OT writings. The singular may refer either to an individual passage of Scripture (Mk 12:10; Lk 4:21; etc.) or to the Scripture as a whole (Jn 20:9; Acts 8:32; etc.). The plural denotes all scriptures, unless a qualifying word limits the application, as in the phrase "scriptures of the prophets" (Mt 26:56). By implication Peter refers to the epistles of Paul as "scripture" (2 Pe 3:16). Once "scripture" is a rendering of the Gr. *gramma* (2 Ti 3:15, KJV), a general term for "writing," "book," "document." But since *gramma* is qualified by the word *hagios*, "holy," "sacred," the reference is to the sacred writings of the OT.

Scroll, KJV frequently **Roll.** [Heb. *megillah*, *sepher*; Gr. *biblion*, *biblaridion*.] In ancient times literary compositions were written on sheets of leather, parchment, or papyrus (*see* Book; Writing Materials). A single sheet was sufficient for a short communication, but for a lengthy literary work a scroll, or roll, made by joining together a number of sheets of leather or *papyrus in the form of a long strip, was required. For convenience of handling, the strip was rolled on end sticks. The common length of papyrus rolls was about 30 ft., but some were much longer. The longest ever found, the great Harris Papyrus, now in the British Museum, has a length of 133 ft.

These rolls were usually written on one side only, hence the particular remarks of Ezekiel and John, who refer to scrolls written within and without (Eze 2:10; Rev 5:1). The writing was arranged in short columns according to the width of the roll. See fig. 244.

In both OT and NT times the most common form for literary documents was the roll. The codex, or book of leaves fastened together at one edge, is not known to have been used before the 2d cent. A.D.

The Hebrew term translated "roll" in Is 8:1 (*gillayón*) signifies a *tablet.

Scrolls, Dead Sea. The general term given to MSS discovered at various places in the Judean desert, west of the Dead Sea. Most of the MSS were found in caves near *Khirbet Qumrân,* a ruin site near the mouth of the *Wâdī Qumrân,* which runs into the Dead Sea about 9 mi. south of modern Jericho. However, scrolls have also been discovered at other sites; so that the general designation Dead Sea scrolls (DSS) is preferable to the term Qumran scrolls, which properly describes only the MSS coming from the Qumran caves.

1. Discoveries. The oft-told story of the discovery of the first cave containing MSS by a Bedouin boy looking for a lost goat need not be repeated in detail. The discovery of this cave, now labeled Qumran Cave 1, was made probably in the spring of 1947 (though it has recently been claimed that it was made 2 years earlier). This cave yielded 7 leather scrolls, 6 in Hebrew and 1 in Aramaic, some in good condition, others in an extremely poor condition. Four of the scrolls, the book of Isaiah (1QIsª; see fig. 244), a Commentary on Habakkuk (see fig. 207), a Sectarian Rule, and a legendary embellishment of Gen in Aramaic, were bought by Mar Athanasius V. Samuel, the Syrian Metropolitan of the St. Mark's Monastery in the Old City of Jerusalem. They were all in his hands by June, 1947, but for many months his efforts to convince visiting scholars of their antiquity were unsuccessful. In November, 1947, Prof. E. L. Sukenik of the Hebrew University acquired from Bethlehem dealers the other 3 Hebrew scrolls: a poorly preserved MS of Isaiah (1QIsᵇ), one dealing with Rules of a War, and one containing several Psalms

of Thanksgiving. Sukenik recognized their value but made no public announcement until several months later.

The scrolls of the Syrian monastery came to the notice of J. C. Trever, of the American School of Oriental Research in Jerusalem, in February, 1948. He surmised that they were highly valuable, photographed them, and sent sample prints to Dr. W. F. Albright of Johns Hopkins University, who declared them to be genuine ancient documents. In April, 1948, the first news of the discovery of the DSS appeared in the press. In January, 1949, after a careful search, members of the Arab Legion rediscovered the cave. It was then scientifically excavated by R. de Vaux and G. L. Harding in February and March of the same year. Hundreds of fragments of many additional MSS were found, as well as fragments of many jars in which the scrolls had been stored and remnants of the linen in which they had been wrapped. In January, 1949, the 4 scrolls in the St. Mark's Monastery were brought to America by its metropolitan, but in 1954 they were acquired by the State of Israel for $250,000. The 7 scrolls from Cave 1, now on temporary exhibit in the Hebrew University, will later be housed in a building, the Shrine of the Book, to be erected in Israeli Jerusalem. The fragments from Cave 1 are in the Archaeological Museum in Arab Jerusalem. All MS material from Cave 1 is available in published form (see *Lit.* below).

After the Bedouins living in the Judean desert realized the value of the scrolls found in Cave 1, they began a systematic search of all caves throughout the area, and have been responsible for most of the subsequent discoveries. In 1951 they found scroll fragments in caves in the *Wâdī Murabba'ât,* a valley running toward the Dead Sea some 11 mi. south of the *Wâdī Qumrân.* After this new discovery came to the notice of archeologists, scientific excavations were undertaken in 4 caves in that valley early in 1952, and important finds were made, mainly of material originating from the 2d cent. A.D. Cave 2 of the Qumran area was discovered by Bedouins early in 1952, and when this became known a scientific exploration of the whole Qumran area was made. This led to the discovery of Cave 3 in March, 1952. In it two badly corroded copper scrolls were found. In the following summer Bedouins found scrolls in *Khirbet Mird,* Christian monastery ruins about 6 mi. southwest of the Qumran caves. A

Belgian expedition explored these ruins systematically in 1953 and made additional MS discoveries. Between July and August, 1952, various manuscripts came on the market, but their source has not been established. In September, 1952, the highly important Qumran Cave 4 (see fig. 100), adjacent to *Khirbet Qumrân*, was discovered, again by Bedouins. Archeologists learned of it before the Bedouins had had time to clean it out completely. Altogether about 35,000 MS fragments have come from Cave 4. A little later Caves 5 and 6 were found, and in 1955 the excavators of *Khirbet Qumrân* discovered 4 more caves (Caves 7-10), but these contained only a few MS fragments. In January, 1956, the indefatigable Bedouins made another sensational find—Cave 11—which contained, besides fragments, some complete and nearly complete scrolls. In January, 1960, came news reports of the first MS discovery in the Judean desert area belonging to Israel. Among the finds were parts of phylacteries and other materials.

2. *Excavations.* The discovery of Cave 1 near the ruin site of *Khirbet Qumrân* immediately raised the question as to whether there was any connection between the two. Excavations of both sites have proved that there was, and it is now known that the MSS found in the Qumran caves belonged to a community whose members once lived at the *khirbet.* The excavations of the *khirbet* were conducted under the direction of R. de Vaux of the École Biblique at Jerusalem from 1951 to 1956. Enough structural remains were found to enable archeologists to reconstruct the history of the place. Also many objects were discovered in the ruins, among them hundreds of pottery vessels, a long writing table and bench (see fig. 423), 3 inkwells (see fig. 242), various tools, and hundreds of coins, which were especially helpful for dating purposes. The site consisted of several buildings protected by a surrounding wall with a strong tower in the north. Identifiable rooms include a kitchen and a pantry, storerooms, an assembly hall, a scriptorium and a possible library room, a lavatory, a mill, a potter's shop and a smith's shop, and probably also stables. Water was channeled into the site by an aqueduct and was stored in several large and small tanks, most of them rectangular.

Archeological remains show that the site was occupied in the period of the Hebrew kings. Some have identified it with the City of * Salt, mentioned in Jos 15:62.

After the place had lain abandoned for centuries, some modest building activities were resumed under the first Maccabeans in the middle of the 2d cent. B.C. Toward the end of that same century the buildings were enlarged, but were burned to the ground some 60 years later, probably during the Parthian invasion (40-38 B.C.). They were again damaged during the earthquake of 31 B.C. (see fig. 140), mentioned by Josephus (*Ant.* xv. 5. 2). The buildings were then abandoned for more than 25 years, but were rebuilt in the time of Herod Archelaus, and were occupied until about A.D. 68, when they were destroyed by the Romans during the 1st Jewish war. For a few decades the site seems to have served as a fort for a small Roman garrison, but it was again temporarily occupied by Jews during the Bar Cocheba rebellion (A.D. 132-135).

Outside the community center are some thousand graves, of which a representative number have been excavated. They show that with very few exceptions the deceased were men, that none of them was older than 50 years at the time of death, and that no objects were placed in the graves.

In 1958 R. de Vaux conducted excavations also at *'Ain Feshkha,* 2 mi. south of *Khirbet Qumrân.* These revealed that *'Ain Feshkha* had been the farm of the Qumran people and that a large building there excavated had not only served for the storage of agricultural products but also housed a tannery, which probably produced the material for the numerous scrolls found in the various Qumran caves.

3. *The Qumran Community.* Much has been written on the subject of the identity of the community whose members lived in the Qumran area and possessed the DSS. Absolute unanimity among scholars does not exist, but the weight of available evidence strongly favors an identification with the Essenes, a Jewish monastic sect of the time of Christ, referred to by Philo of Alexandria (*Every Good Man Is Free* [Loeb Classical Library, vol. IX], xii, xiii), Pliny (*Hist. Nat.* v. 15. 73), and Josephus (*War* ii. 8. 2, 3). The information provided by these ancient authors agrees closely with that contained in the extra-Biblical DSS, especially in the Rule of the Sect, which deals with their customs and rituals, but also in the Commentary on Habakkuk, which reflects somewhat the history of the sect. If to this literary evidence is added the archeological findings a reasonably complete picture of the ancient Qumran people is obtained.

Members of the community withdrew from the world and lived in ritual purity in an inhospitable desert in the expectation of the end of the world. They had their own farm and workshops, and seem to have been rather independent, having, apparently, few connections with the outside world, although the occurrence of coins in the ruins shows that some measure of trade was carried on. The members of the sect worked, ate, and worshiped together, but lived separately in shelters or caves outside the community center. Their religious duties consisted in daily washings and a rigorous study of the Law. They practiced poverty and surrendered to the administration of the community any means in their possession. This is shown by the fact that objects such as combs, dishes, shoes, and MSS, but no coins, have been found in the caves where the members of the group lived, whereas numerous coins have come to light in the community center, where the funds of the group were probably kept. Members of the sect observed a calendar that differed somewhat from that followed by orthodox Jewry.

Information concerning the history of the Qumran sect is vague. Its spiritual leader, who may also have been its founder, is called the "Teacher of Righteousness." He was persecuted and suffered violence, but the record does not state clearly whether he died a natural death or was killed. His identity is an enigma; scholars disagree as to whether he was any Jew known from history. The same uncertainty exists concerning the "Wicked Priest," a sacrilegious, murderous, despoiling drunkard who came to a bad end, with the "Man of Lie," and the "Preacher of Lie." It seems clear that the early and crucial history of the sect fell within the time of the Maccabees, from the mention of the Syrian kings Antiochus IV? (*'ntykws*), 175-164/63 B.C., and Demetrius III? (*[Dm]trys*), 95-78 B.C., and of the Jewish Queen Alexandria (*Shlmsywn*), 76-67 B.C., and of the Roman governor of Syria, Aemilius (*'mlws*) Scaurus, 62 B.C. At one period, either early in the 1st cent. B.C. or in the 2d half of that same century, the sect seems to have spent some time at Damascus, perhaps as the result of persecutions, and then to have returned to Qumran, where they certainly lived during the last 70 years of their existence. They joined their fellow Jews in the war against the Romans (A.D. 66-70) and perished in it. Before fleeing from Qumran ahead of the advancing Roman armies; they wrapped some of their MSS in linen, put them into jars, and stored them away in Cave 1, but put many others hurriedly into Cave 4. Other MSS were simply left in the caves in which the members had lived.

A Syriac letter written about A.D. 800 tells of the discovery of a cave near Jericho in which Jews found many MSS, which they took to Jerusalem. It has been suggested that the cave in question may have been Qumran Cave 1, for there is evidence that it must originally have contained a much larger number of MSS than those found in it in 1947, which were only the remnants overlooked at an earlier discovery. Karaite Jews of the Middle Ages, who, like the Qumran people, did not follow the rabbinical calendar, seem to have been influenced by writings found in this cave near Jericho. They copied and kept documents originating from the Essenes, such as the Damascus Document, of which two incomplete copies were found in the Cairo Genizah and several fragments in the Qumran caves. In this way some Essene teachings were perpetuated through the Karaites until recent times.

4. *Study and Publication.* A few of the scrolls found in Caves 1 and 11 were well preserved. They are comparatively easy to read and their publication presents few problems. All others were either poorly preserved, thus needing special treatment, or were fragmentary. To this latter class belongs the great bulk of the material—tens of thousands of fragments, varying in size from tiny pieces with only one letter on them to large sheets with more than one column preserved. They must be cleaned, deciphered, and classified, and if possible joined to other fragments of the same MSS. This work can be done only by highly trained and specialized experts. It is a slow process, and requires patience and time. An international team of scholars from England, France, Germany, Poland, and the United States have for years been engaged in this work in a large workroom (the Scrollery) of the Archaeological Museum at Jerusalem. The results of their work will eventually appear in a set of monumental tomes to be published by The Clarendon Press at Oxford, entitled *Discoveries in the Judaean Desert.* Of this series vol. 1, containing the fragments from Cave 1, appeared in 1955, and vol. 2, containing the documents from the caves of the *Wâdî Murabba'ât,* in 1960. At least 8 more volumes in the same series are scheduled to appear in the future.

As might be expected, there was hesitancy in accepting the DSS as ancient when news of them first appeared. That scholars would express doubts was not strange, because for many decades of archeological explorations in Bible Lands not a single ancient Hebrew Bible MS had ever come to light. The destruction of literature such as accompanied persecutions and wars, and the custom of the Jews to destroy any worn-out Hebrew MS for fear that the name of God, which it might contain, would be misused and blasphemed, were believed responsible for this lack. Consequently many voices of skepticism and caution were raised among scholars during the first few years after the discovery of the DSS. However, accumulating evidence has proved the scrolls to be genuine ancient documents. With this practically every scholar agrees. The only apparent exception is S. Zeitlin, the editor of the *Jewish Quarterly Review* (Philadelphia), who from the beginning has fought their acceptance, and who constantly is advancing new arguments to buttress his views.

That the first and most important scrolls were found by Bedouins and not by scholars made it hard to prove their genuineness and antiquity. However, the excavation of Cave 1 by archeologists, and the discovery of scroll fragments by scholars in Caves 3 and 4 and in Caves 7-10, disproved as false any claims that the DSS were the products of modern forgers. Furthermore, the excavations of *Khirbet Qumrân* proved that the owners of the scrolls had lived in that area only up to A.D. 68, had used the same kind of pottery as that found in the caves, and had also employed the same type of script as found on the cave MSS. Moreover, when the linen discovered in Cave 1 was subjected to the Carbon 14 test, its radio-carbon contents dated it to A.D. 33 with a margin of 200 years, showing that the linen could have been produced between 168 B.C. and A.D. 233. To this evidence must be added that of paleography, the study and dating of ancient MSS by the form of their scripts. S. A. Birnbaum, W. F. Albright, J. C. Trever, and F. M. Cross, Jr., have done pioneer work in the field of Hebrew paleography, and their datings of the individual manuscripts are being accepted by an ever-increasing number of scholars. There is now a rather uniform consensus that: (1) all MSS from the Qumran area come from the last 3 cent. of the pre-Christian Era and the 1st cent. of the

Christian Era, (2) that the MSS from the *Wâdî Murabba'ât* and from the Israeli part of the Wilderness of Judah date from the 2d cent. A.D., and (3) that the MSS from *Khirbet Mird* come from later centuries.

5. *The Biblical DSS and Their Importance for Textual Studies.* The discoveries in the Judean desert are usually considered sensational because of the large number of Bible MSS in Hebrew that have come to light in the various caves —MSS that were 1,000 years older than the earliest extant Hebrew codices—and thus provided extensive samplings of the Bible used by Christ and the apostles.

Cave 1 has yielded one complete scroll of Isaiah (1QIsa) and another copy preserving about one third of the same book (1QIsb). In Cave 11 were found an almost complete scroll of Psalms and a comparatively well-preserved scroll of Leviticus. In Cave 4 there were enough fragments of a scroll of Samuel to enable F. M. Cross, Jr., to put together more than two thirds of that book. All other books of the OT (with the exception of Esther, of which nothing has so far been found) are represented, though only in fragmentary form—in some cases (Prov, Chr, and Ezr-Neh) fragments belonging to only 1 MS, in others, fragments of several MSS. The most popular books must have been Deut, Is, the Minor Prophets, and Psalms, because more than 10 MSS have been found of each book. Of Gen, 10 MSS have been discovered; of Ex, 8 MSS; of Num, 7 MSS; and of Dan and Lev, 6 MSS each. These figures show that the members of the Qumran community greatly valued the Scriptures.

Of interest to the Biblical scholar are also the commentaries on various Bible books, discussed under sec. 6, and certain Greek Bible MSS, of great importance to the study of the LXX.

A study of the Biblical DSS reveals that the Masoretic text dates back to at least the beginning of the Christian Era. This was a surprise to many scholars who had thought that the Hebrew Bible text had been subjected to many changes during the Talmudic and Masoretic periods (2d to 10th cent. A.D.). The 1QIsb scroll, for example, contains a text form which is virtually identical with the Masoretic text of our printed Hebrew Bibles. The same can be said of many other texts from Qumran, and the texts from the *Wâdî Murabba'ât*. Even 1QIsa, which contains many scribal errors, orthographic variants, omissions, additions, and corrections, reflects in the main the Masoretic text. *See* Isaiah, Book of.

On the other hand, certain Biblical MSS from Qumran show a great affinity to the LXX and prove that the translators of the LXX in many places followed a Hebrew recension existing in their day, one that differed from that preserved by the Masoretes. For example, Acts 7:14 records that those who went to Egypt with Jacob numbered 75. This number agrees with Gen 46:27 according to the reading of the LXX, but not with the Masoretic text, which gives the number as 70. A Hebrew Gen MS among the Qumran scrolls agrees with the LXX in this instance, and shows that Stephen in his speech before the members of the Sanhedrin in Jerusalem may not have quoted from the LXX, but may have used a Hebrew text that contained readings agreeing with the LXX.

The orthographic and grammatical peculiarities found in some scrolls are of great importance to the student of the Hebrew language, and the scribal forms to the paleographer. A great amount of scholarly literature based on these Biblical MSS has already been produced and it has been predicted that Biblical scholars will work on these texts for generations before all worth-while information has been extracted from them.

6. *Non-Biblical MSS.* The large number of MSS of non-Biblical books that have also come to light in the various Dead Sea caves are important for a correct understanding of the teachings and beliefs of the Qumran sect and throw light on the religious thinking of the Jews in Christ's time. Only an annotated list of some of these MSS is presented here.

(1) COMMENTARIES ON BIBLE BOOKS. An almost complete commentary on Hab, chs 1 and 2, was found in Qumran Cave 1. Only fragments of commentaries on the Ps, Is, Nah, and Mic have been preserved. These works show a peculiar type of scriptural interpretation, applying the words of the prophets to the sect and the time in which it lived, and referring often to the sect's leader, the "Teacher of Righteousness," and to its archantagonist, the "Wicked Priest." The Chaldeans, mentioned in Hab, are explained to be the *Kittim, probably the Romans. Closely related to these works are collections (florilegia) of Biblical passages with accompanying comments.

(2) SECTARIAN RULES. A well-preserved MS, called Manual of Discipline by its first editors, containing the rules according to which the members of the sect were to live. It shows that they were required to conform strictly to the Law of Moses, and mentions various sins and their punishments. It closes with a hymn. A 2-column fragment of another similar MS mentions women and children, thus showing that at least some of the Essenes were married.

(3) ZADOKITE DOCUMENT. Several MSS containing the rules for the members of the sect in the land of Damascus, where they seem to have lived at one time (see sec. 3 above). The first 2 copies of this work came to light in 1896/97 in the Genizah (see sec. 3 above) of a Karaite synagogue at Cairo. Now that further fragmentary copies of it have been found in the Qumran caves, it has become evident that it was originally a document belonging to the Qumran people, apparently one that had come into the hands of the Karaites through a discovery of one of the caves *c.* A.D. 800 (see sec. 3 above).

(4) A RULE OF WAR. A document called by E. L. Sukenik, A War of the Children of Light Against the Children of Darkness, describing a war that the members of the Qumran sect were to fight against the whole wicked world, and outlining the rules for this imaginary warfare. The MS contains also the hymns that were to be sung after the victory was won.

(5) PSALMS OF THANKSGIVING. A collection of about 40 spiritual songs, containing phrases from Is, Jer, and Job but showing also a close relationship with the canonical Psalms. The author, possibly the "Teacher of Righteousness," appears as a persecuted man, also as one who is conscious of his sins, yet is confident that he is filled with the Holy Spirit and that the secrets of God have been revealed to him to enable him to be a guide to his followers.

(6) APOCRYPHA AND PSEUDEPIGRAPHA. Of the former category fragmentary copies of Tobit, Ecclesiasticus, and The Letter of Jeremiah have been found; of the latter, copies of The Book of Jubilees, of Enoch, and of The Testaments of the Twelve Patriarchs. To this class of literature must be assigned also a poorly preserved scroll from Qumran Cave 1, labeled by its modern editors A Genesis Apocryphon. It is a legendary and embellished version of the patriarchal stories. Another work, of which fragments of several MSS have come to light, contains a description of the heavenly Jerusalem. Then there is

a work containing Psalms of Joshua, another describing a Vision of Amram, the father of Moses, and a Prayer of Nabonidus giving thanks to the most high God for healing him from a disease of 7 years' duration.

(7) PHYLACTERIES. *See* Phylactery.

(8) LETTERS AND OSTRACA. Letters were found in the caves of the *Wâdī Murabba'ât,* among which was one written by Bar Cocheba, the leader of the 2d Jewish war (A.D. 132-135). Several ostraca were also found, one from *Khirbet Qumrân.*

(9) CONTRACTS. One of them is a dated marriage contract.

(10) COPPER SCROLL. A strip of copper with a long engraved inscription containing information about the hiding places of great treasures of precious metal and incense. Scholars are divided in their views as to whether this document is a historical record or fiction.

(11) MISCELLANY. To these belong works of a liturgical character, also works of proverbs and wisdom, one dealing with the rotation of the priestly families in service, and horoscopes.

7. *Qumran and the NT.* Scholars differ in their interpretation of the literary and archeological evidence obtained from Qumran, especially with regard to the question of the influence of the DSS on the NT. It is generally recognized that there are many points of contact between the two classes of writings. However, some writers seem to give undue emphasis to them while ignoring or minimizing significant differences between the two. Objective scholarship must recognize both similarities and differences. A hundred years ago Renan set forth the view that "Christianity is an Essenism which has largely succeeded." Some scholars have followed this line of reasoning, and have seen in Jesus merely an unoriginal person who copied the "Teacher of Righteousness." An objective study of the scroll evidence leads to a rejection of such claims, for the work, life, and death of the Teacher of Righteousness in no way resemble the work, life, and death of Jesus Christ, nor does the sect's expected Messiah (actually two Messiahs) show any parallels to Christ and His ministry. Christianity was certainly not born from within Essenism.

However, it must be admitted that the religious ideology of the world in which the Essenes lived exerted certain influences on Christianity. Terms found in the NT that were formerly explained as being Hellenistic in background or purely Christian in origin are now found to have existed in the Jewish literature of Christ's time. Christ and His disciples must have been aware of the existence of the Qumran sect, and may have been familiar with some of their literary products, but there is nothing in the Qumran literature that closely parallels Christ's teachings of salvation, foreshadows His atoning life and death, or comes near the doctrine of grace, and righteousness through faith, so forcefully expounded by Paul. Some have suggested that there were certain connections between the Qumran people and John the Baptist; *see* Jesus Christ, II; John, 1.

Lit.: The literature on the DSS is so extensive that only a few of the most important works are here mentioned:

BIBLIOGRAPHIES have been published by C. Burchard, *Bibliographie zu den Handschriften vom Toten Meer* (Berlin, 1957), and W. S. LaSor, *Bibliography of the Dead Sea Scrolls,* 1948-1957 (Pasadena, Calif., 1958). Continuous bibliographies of current publications now appear regularly in the *Revue de Qumran* (Paris [Éditions Letouzey et Ané], since 1958) a periodical devoted exclusively to the study of the DSS.

GENERAL WORKS: Millar Burrows, *The Dead Sea Scrolls* (New York, 1955); *More Light on the Dead Sea Scrolls* (New York, 1958); Frank M. Cross, Jr., *The Ancient Library of Qumran and Modern Biblical Studies* (Garden City, N.Y., 1958); J. T. Milik, *Ten Years of Discovery in the Wilderness of Judaea* (London, 1959); also articles (since 1948) in the *BA, BASOR, JEOL,* and *PEQ.*

EXCAVATION REPORTS of *Khirbet Qumrân* and *'Ain Feshkha*: R. de Vaux, *RB* 60 (1953), 83-106; 61 (1954), 206-236; 63 (1956), 533-577; 66 (1959), 225-255.

PUBLICATIONS OF TEXTS: (1) Cave 1: Millar Burrows *et al., The Dead Sea Scrolls of St. Mark's Monastery* (2 vols., New Haven, 1950, 1951); E. L. Sukenik, *The Dead Sea Scrolls of the Hebrew University* (Jerusalem, 1955); D. Barthélemy and J. T. Milik, *Discoveries in the Judaean Desert I, Qumran Cave I* (Oxford, 1955); Nahman Avigad and Yigael Yadin, *A Genesis Apocryphon* (Jerusalem, 1956). (2) From other caves, mainly from Cave 4, articles (since 1948) in the *BASOR, JBL, PEQ, RB, Semitica,* and *ZAW.* (3) The latest publication of the Zadokite Document is found in Chaim Rabin, *The Zadokite Documents* (2d ed., Oxford, 1958).

TRANSLATIONS: English translations of

the non-Biblical texts can be found in Millar Burrows, *The Dead Sea Scrolls*, and *More Light on the Dead Sea Scrolls* (see above), and in T. H. Gaster, *The Scriptures of the Dead Sea Sect* (London, 1957).

Scurvy. [Heb. *garab.*] A degenerative disease resulting from dietetic errors. In Lev 21:20; 22:22; KJV; ˙Deut 28:27, RSV, the term is a rendering of the Heb. *garab*, "mange," "scab." It is possibly the same as the Arabic *ǧarab*, a contagious skin disease in which pustules erupt on the skin. The term is used in the KJV in its obsolete sense of "covered or affected with scabs." Whether *garab* ever denotes the degenerative disease known today as scurvy is a matter of conjecture.

Scythian (sĭth′ĭ-ăn). [Gr. *Skuthēs*.] The Scythians were Indo-European nomads who lived in the plains of southern Russia. According to Herodotus (i. 105) they invaded the civilized countries of the Near East in the 7th cent. B.C., clashed with the Medes, whom they defeated, and made plans to invade Egypt. However, Psamtik I of Egypt was able to buy them off with rich gifts while they were still in Palestine. The countries through which they passed were thoroughly devastated, and some commentators think that the prophets Jeremiah (Jer 4-6) and Zephaniah (Zep 1) had the Scythians in mind when they spoke of the devastations caused in Palestine by a certain unnamed nation. However, the foe from "the north" seems rather to refer to Babylon, whose invading forces always entered Judah from the north (cf. Jer 25:9). Beth-shean, a strong city in the eastern part of the Valley of Jezreel, was captured by the Scythians and afterward called Scythopolis, a name it retained for many centuries. The Scythians are nowhere mentioned by name in the OT, and they are mentioned only once in the NT (Col 3:11), where they are classed with barbarians. Map XII, B-4, C-13.

Sea. This term is used variously to describe: (1) The great bodies of water as distinguished from the dry earth (Gen 1:22; Ps 72:8). (2) Specific bodies of water, such as (*a*) the Mediterranean Sea, known in the Bible as the "great sea" (Num 34:6; Jos 9:1), the "uttermost sea" or the "western sea" (Deut 11:24); (*b*) the Dead Sea, known in the Bible as the "salt sea," "east sea," or "sea of the plain" (Num 34:3; Joel 2:20; Deut 3:17); (*c*) the Red Sea (Ex 10:19); (*d*) the Sea of Galilee, also called the Sea of Tiberias and the Sea of Chinnereth (Mt 4:18; Jn 6:1; Num 34:11), etc. (3) Large or important rivers: (*a*) the Nile (Is 19:5, KJV; cf. Nah 3:8); (*b*) the Euphrates (Jer 51:36, 63). (4) The "molten sea" (*see* Sea, Bronze). (5) In symbolic prophecies, peoples and multitudes (Rev 17:15; cf. Dan 7:2-7, 17).

Sea, Bronze, KJV **Brasen Sea.** A large basin of bronze in the Temple of Solomon (2 Ki 25:13; 1 Chr 18:8), also called "molten sea" (1 Ki 7:23; 2 Chr 4:2). The name "sea" (Heb. *yam*), as given to this enormous basin, was not without precedent, for similar ritual basins in Sumerian and Babylonian temples were called AB.ZU (*apsû*), "ocean," in Sumerian, and *tâmtu*, "sea," in Babylonian. Solomon's bronze sea stood in the court between the porch and the altar toward the southeast (1 Ki 7:39). It was one handbreadth thick (about 3½ in.), 5 cu. high (8 ft. 7 in.), and 10 cu. (17 ft. 2 in.) in diameter (vs 23, 26). The capacity is given as 2,000 baths in v 26, but as 3,000 baths in 2 Chr 4:5, the former figure perhaps representing the amount of water normally in the sea, and the latter the total capacity of the sea. If the basin was of hemispherical shape it could hold about 10,000 gallons, which was a little less than 2,000 baths, since a bath was about 5.81 gallons. The basin rested on 12 bronze oxen divided into 4 groups of 3 each. Each group faced 1 of the cardinal points of the compass. The records say nothing of how it was filled or emptied. Its function was to furnish water for the priests' ritual washings (v 6). When King Ahaz was in need of funds, he placed the basin on a stone pedestal, and used the bronze of the oxen to pay tribute (2 Ki 16:17, 18). The Babylonians broke up the basin when they captured Jerusalem and carried the bronze off to Babylon (2 Ki 25:13; Jer 52:17, 20). The basin is not mentioned in Ezekiel's description of the Temple, nor is it mentioned in any description of the postexilic Temple.

Lit.: C. C. Wylie, "On King Solomon's Molten Sea," *BA* 12 (1949), 86-90.

Sea Gull, KJV **Cuckoo,** some editions **Cuckow.** [Heb. *shachaph.*] The Hebrew term represents some unclean bird, but the exact identity of it is uncertain. Terns, gulls, and petrels are common along the shores of the Mediterranean and around the inland bodies of water in Palestine. The *shachaph* of Lev 11:16 and Deut 14:14 may well be one, or all, of these. Driver suggests the long-eared owl (*PEQ* 87 [1955], 20).

425. Lapis lazuli seal given by King Kirikiri to his son Bilalama, found at *Tell Asmar*. To the right, the impression of the seal

Sea Monster. *See* Dragon.

Sea of Glass. [Gr. *thalassa hualinē*.] An expression used by John the revelator to describe a surface he saw in a vision of the heavenly throne (Rev 4:6). The surface, situated "before the throne," appeared like "crystal" (Gr. *krustallos,* "a colorless, transparent mineral," "rock crystal"). In a further vision he saw those who had conquered "the beast" and its "image" and the "number" of its name standing on "the sea of glass" singing the victory song of Moses and the song of the Lamb (ch 15:2, 3). In this vision he describes the sea appearing as if "mingled with fire." This appearance may have been caused by the glory of God being reflected from the crystalline surface of the sea.

Sea of the Arabah. *See* Dead Sea.

Sea of the Plain. *See* Dead Sea.

Seal. A device used to make a distinctive design in clay, wax, etc., indicating authenticity, authority, assurance, completion, inviolability, ratification, etc. The seal was made of metal, stone, etc., and might be a signet ring (fig. 404), or might be cylindrical (fig. 425) or conical in shape. Its design, which might include the owner's name, was peculiar to the owner (see Ex 28:11; Est 8:8). Seals were used in the patriarchal age, and numerous ones have been found in Palestine from that time onward. They were often worn as a finger *ring (Jer 22:24), or on a cord about the neck (Gen 38:18, RSV; *see* Cord). They were used to seal letters, official papers, contracts, scrolls (*see* Book), tombs, etc. (1 Ki 21:8; Est 8:10; Jer 32:9-14; Dan 12:4, 9; Mt 27:66; Rev 5:1). When the clay, or other material upon which the seal was impressed (fig. 426), hardened, an unbroken impression would indicate that the object sealed had not been tampered with. Three clay jar handles excavated at Beth-she-mesh and *Tell Beit Mirsim* (probably Debir) carry the imprint of the stamp seal, "Belonging to Eliakim, steward of Jehoiachin" (fig. 151). This would per-

haps indicate that Nebuchadnezzar had not confiscated Jehoiachin's property when he took him as hostage to Babylon. A seal reading, "Belonging to Gedaliah who is over the house," has been unearthed at Lachish (fig. 195; see Jer 40:9). For other seals and seal impressions see figs. 7, 33, 38, 172, 173, 250, 258, 297.

Daniel was instructed to "seal the book, even to the time of the end" (Dan 12:4); this apparently meant that it would not be understood until the time specified (cf. Rev 10:4). Abraham's circumcision was a "seal of the righteousness which he had by faith" (Rom 4:11, RSV). The Holy Spirit "seals" the believer as God's purchased possession (Eph 1:13, 14; cf. 2 Ti 2:19). Christ spoke of Himself as being

426. Cuneiform tablet of Amurru sealed with a Hittite hieroglyphic stamp seal, found at *Rás Shamra*

sealed by the Father (Jn 6:27). In the book of Revelation the sealing of the 144,-000 "in their foreheads" (ch 7:1-4) signifies their approval by Heaven (ch 14:1, 2). In ch 5 is described a book "sealed with seven seals" which, when opened, graphically portrayed events in the struggle between Christ and Satan (see chs 6:1 to 8:1). For a discussion of the significance of these seals see *SDACom* 7:770-780.

Season. One of the 4 divisions of the natural year, which are marked by the spring and autumnal equinoxes and the summer and winter solstices. The Jews used the term *tequphah*, "circle," referring to the 4 turning points of the year and to the quarters introduced by them. It is not certain, however, whether the Bible uses *tequphah* in this technical sense. The climatic seasons in Palestine are principally the rainy season, which lasts from autumn to spring, and the dry season (*see* Palestine, VIII; table under Year). The first autumn showers, called the "early" (Joel 2:23, RSV; Jas 5:7), or "former," rains (Jer 5:24), are eagerly anticipated to moisten the sun-baked soil to allow for plowing and sowing before the heavy rains of winter. The "latter" rain, at the end of the wet season, matures the grain just before the barley harvest in the spring (Deut 11:14). The spring is the season of green grass and flowers that soon wither under the scorching summer sun. From May through October there is practically no rain, even in the mountainous location of Jerusalem. Most of the streams run dry until the autumn rains return. The Jordan has a flood season in the spring, which is dependent not only on the local rainfall but also on the melting of the snows at its source in the region of Mount Hermon. Spring and summer were the times of the most important military campaigns (1 Chr 20:1) between the rival empires and the city-states that were continually fighting over Syria and Palestine, although on occasion they did not hesitate to fight in the rainy season. We find references in the Bible not only to the agricultural seasons (*see* Year) but also to the stars (possibly the constellations of the zodiac; *see* Mazzaroth) in their season (Job 38:32), to the sun and moon as governing the seasons (Gen 1:14-16; Ps 104:19), to the times of cold and heat (Gen 8:22), with the incongruity of "snow in summer" and "rain in harvest" (Prov 26:1), and to the closed season for navigation as beginning in the autumn (Acts 27:9, 12).

Seba (sē'bá). [Heb. *Seba'*.] A son of Cush (Gen 10:7; 1 Chr 1:9), and ancestor of a people mentioned several times in the OT. Josephus (*Ant.* ii. 10. 2) identifies Seba with the Nubian kingdom of Meroë, whose territory lay between the Blue Nile and Atbara rivers. Since the *Ethiopians had migrated from southern Arabia to Nubia before Josephus wrote his history, his statement may be correct. However, originally the tribe of Seba apparently lived in southern Arabia, for Ps 72:10 pictures Seba as one of the most remote nations of Solomon's time, paying homage to the king. It was presumably to the far south, for Tarshish and Sheba, the other remote points mentioned in the same passage, were in the west and east respectively. In Is 43:3 Seba is referred to as being in close proximity to Ethiopia (Cush), and Is 45:14 speaks about the great stature of its people (*see* Sabeans). It should not be confused with the Cushite tribe of Sheba which lived in the southernmost part of ancient Arabia.

Sebam. *See* Sibmah.

Sebat. *See* Shebat.

Secacah (sě-kā'ká). [Heb. *Sekakah*, "barricade."] A city in the Wilderness of Judah (Jos 15:61), recently identified with *Khirbet es-Samrah*, 5 mi. southwest of *Khirbet Qumrân* in the *Buqê'ah* (*BASOR* 142 [1956], 16).

Sechu. *See* Secu.

Second Coming of Christ. The return of our Lord to this earth in power and glory at the close of the gospel age, to reward men according to their deeds, to establish His eternal, glorious kingdom. The expression "second coming of Christ" itself does not occur in the Bible, but various other terms are used to describe the event. Our Lord repeatedly referred to "the coming of the Son of man" (Mt 24:27, 37, 39; cf. 16:27, 28; Mk 13:26; 14:62; Lk 9: 26; etc.) and of His being "revealed" (Lk 17:30). Paul speaks of "the coming of our Lord Jesus Christ" (1 Th 5:23; etc.), or more simply of "his coming" (2 Th 2:8; etc.) or "his appearing" (2 Ti 4:8). James refers to "the coming of the Lord" (Jas 5:7, 8), and Peter to the "coming of our Lord Jesus Christ" (2 Pe 1:16) and "the coming of the day of God" (ch 3:12). Throughout the NT, reference is made to "that day" (Mt 7:22; 24:36; Lk 10:12; 21:34; 2 Ti 4:8; etc.), "the day" (Rom 13:12; Heb 10:25; etc.), "the day of our Lord" (1 Cor 1:8), "the day of the Lord Jesus" (1 Cor 5:5; 2 Cor 1:14), and "the day of Jesus Christ" (Php 1:6). The doctrine of the 2d coming is not as clearly or extensively set forth in the OT as in the NT, in part because Messiah had not yet come the 1st time and there was no particular need to distinguish between a 1st coming and a 2d coming, but also because the OT prophets describe events the NT associates with the 2d coming of our Lord in terms of the way things would have worked out within the framework of God's original plan for Israel (*see* Chosen People; Prophet, II). Common OT expressions by which reference is made to events associated with the 2d coming of Christ are "the day of the Lord" (Is 2:12; 13:9; etc.), and "that day" (Zec 14:4; etc.). To the OT writers "the day of the Lord" was essentially a day of divine judgment upon the enemies of Israel and of glorious deliverance and exaltation for God's chosen people.

The usual NT terms for the 2d coming of Christ are *parousia*, "presence," "outshining"; *epiphaneia*, "appearance," "appearing"; and *apokalupsis*, "revelation." *Parousia* appears commonly in the papyri for the visit of an emperor or king. It is sometimes used to denote "presence" as opposed to "absence," as in Php 2:12, but more commonly describes "coming" as of Christ (2 Th 2:1), or of men (1 Cor 16:17). *Epiphaneia* occurs often in classical Greek to describe the glorious appearance of the pagan gods. In the NT it is used exclusively for the glorious 1st (2 Ti 1:10) and 2d (1 Ti 6:14; 2 Ti 4:1, 8; Tit 2:13) advents of the Lord Jesus. *Apokalupsis* is used of the "appearing" or "revelation" of Christ at His 2d coming (1 Pe 1:7, 13; cf. ch 4:13).

Implicit and explicit throughout the teachings of our Saviour is the necessity of a 2d advent to complete the work of salvation begun at His 1st advent. The 1st advent witnessed the formal establishment of the kingdom of divine grace, announced first by John the Baptist (Mt 3:2) and later by the Lord (Mk 1:14, 15) and His disciples (Mt 10:7). Throughout His ministry Jesus spoke of His coming in glory as a time when He would "sit upon the throne of his glory" to judge the nations (ch 25:31-46) and "reward every man according to his works" (ch 16:27; etc.); as a time when the dead would "hear the voice of the Son of God: and . . . live" (Jn 5:25-29); as a time when the angels would "gather together his elect from the four winds, from one end of heaven to the other" (Mt 24:30, 31);

and as a time when He would come to receive His own unto Himself (Jn 14:1-3). Prior to His ascension Jesus entrusted His disciples with the gospel commission (Mt 28:19, 20). Time would be needed to carry out this commission but with its completion the gospel age would come to a close (ch 24:14). As to the nature of His 2d coming, Christ said, "I go" and "I will come again" (Jn 14:3). Similarly, at His ascension 2 angels not only assured the apostles that "this same Jesus" would return but also promised that He would "come in like manner" as they had "seen him go into heaven" (Acts 1:11). Upon His return "every eye shall see him" (Rev 1:7; cf. Mt 24:30). When the Lord descends from heaven "the dead in Christ shall rise first: then we which are alive and remain shall be caught up together with them in the clouds, to meet the Lord in the air: and so shall we ever be with the Lord" (1 Th 4:16, 17). Immortality will be bestowed upon the living and the resurrected righteous, "in a moment, in the twinkling of an eye," when "the dead shall be raised incorruptible, and we shall be changed" (1 Cor 15:52). The 2d coming of Christ is the great climactic event that brings this age of earth's history to a close and that marks the transition to the ceaseless ages of eternity. The glorious appearing of Jesus Christ is the "blessed hope" toward which the Christian looks forward in this life (Tit 2:13) as a time when he will be united forever with his Lord (Jn 14:2, 3; 1 Th 4:17). Then he will be called to enter upon immortality, with its infinite joy in the presence of God (Rev 21:1-5), to "inherit the kingdom prepared" for him "from the foundation of the world" (Mt 25:34), and to "reign for ever and ever" (Rev 22:1-5).

Second Death. A term appearing 4 times in the Bible (Rev 2:11; 20:6, 14; 21:8), describing the death suffered by the wicked at the close of the 1000 years (ch 20:2, 3, 4, 6, 7), or *millennium. At the beginning of the millennium the wicked are struck down at the presence of Christ (ch 19:11, 16-21). At the end of the millennium they, together with all the wicked of previous ages, are resurrected (Rev 20:5; Jn 5:28, 29; Acts 24:15). They then join in a final act of defiance against God, at which fire flashes from heaven and consumes them (Rev 20:8, 9). This is the second death (v 14). The Bible teaches that this second death is not an endless fiery torment but total destruction (Mt 10:28). *See* Death; Hell; Soul; Spirit. The righteous are shielded from the second death (Rev 2:11), which is reserved for the fearful, unbelieving, abominable, murderers, fornicators, sorcerers, idolaters, and liars (ch 21:8; cf. ch 20:15).

Second Quarter. [Heb. *mishneh*, "second."] A section in ancient Jerusalem (2 Ki 22: 14; 2 Chr 34:22; Zep 1:10; RSV). Its exact location is uncertain, but it is believed to have been the area enclosed by the 2d wall, built by Manasseh (2 Chr 33:14). The translation "college" in 2 Ki 22:14; 2 Chr 34:22; KJV, appears to have been based upon an assumed connection between the Heb. *mishneh*, "second," and the later Heb. *mishnah*, "instruction."

Second Sabbath After the First. [Gr. *sabbaton deuteroprōton*, literally, "a second-first Sabbath."] An expression occurring once (Lk 6:1, KJV). There is considerable doubt as to the genuineness of this reading. A. T. Robertson speaks of it as a "curious reading" and "undoubtedly spurious." In describing how it may possibly have entered into Western and Syrian (Byzantine) MSS he says: "A possible explanation is that a scribe wrote 'first' (*prōtoi*) on the margin because of the sabbath miracle in ch 6:6-11. Then another scribe recalled ch 4:31 where a sabbath is mentioned and wrote 'second' (*deuteroi*) also on·the margin. Finally a third scribe combined the two in the word *deuteroprōtoi* that is not found elsewhere" (*Word Pictures in the New Testament*, vol. 2, p. 80). Alexander Souter remarks concerning *deuteroprōtos*, "a ghost-word which has crept into the text of many authorities at Lk. vi I, by mistake" (*A Pocket Lexicon to the Greek New Testament*, p. 60).

In attempting to interpret the expression some have conjectured that (*a*) it may have meant the 2d Sabbath after the Passover; or (*b*) the 1st Sabbath of a 2d year in a sabbatical year series; or (*c*) the 2d Sabbath in a series of Sabbaths in the ritual calendar; or (*d*) that it simply distinguishes the Sabbath in this passage from the Sabbaths mentioned earlier in Lk 4:16, 31. None of these explanations are satisfactory. *Deuteroprōtos* does not occur elsewhere in the Bible or in secular Greek literature. On this count alone it is very difficult to know its intended significance. Robertson has well said, "If it were genuine, we should not know what it means" (*loc. cit.*).

Secretary. *See* Scribe.

Sect. A rendering of the Gr. *hairesis*, "sect," "party," "faction," "opinion," "dogma," "heresy," appropriately translated "sect" or "party" in Acts 5:17; 15:5; 24:5, 14; 26:5; 28:22. The following sects or parties are mentioned: Sadducees, Pharisees, and Nazarenes, or Christians.

Secu (sē'kū), KJV **Sechu** (sē'kū). [Heb. *Śekû*.] A place where Saul stopped on his way from Gibeah, his capital, to Ramah, Samuel's residence, in search of David (1 Sa 19:22). The site has not been identified.

Secundus (sĕ-kŭn'dŭs). [Gr. *Sekoundos*, from Latin *secundus*, "second," attested in Greek and Latin inscriptions, among which is one from Thessalonica.] A Christian from Thessalonica, who accompanied Paul on his last journey to Jerusalem (Acts 20:4). He probably represented his home church in the delivery of the collection to the church of Jerusalem.

Seedtime. *See* Year.

Seer. *See* Prophet.

Seethe. [Heb. *bashal*, "to ripen," "to boil."] An expression occurring in Ex 16:23; 23: 19; 29:31; 2 Ki 4:38; KJV; etc., used with the archaic meaning "to boil," "to stew."

Segub (sē'gŭb). [Heb. *Śegûb*, "exalted." The name occurs in Aramaic documents as *Śgb*.]

1. The father of Jair, and a descendant of Judah (1 Chr 2:21, 22).

2. The youngest son of Hiel; he perished when his father set up the gates of the rebuilt city of Jericho (1 Ki 16:34). This occurred in fulfillment of a curse pronounced by Joshua (Jos 6:26), but it is not clear whether he was slain by God or sacrificed by his father to appease the wrath of God.

Seir (sē'ĭr). [Heb. *Śe'îr*, "hairy." The name is attested in Egyptian as *S'r*, in Akkadian as *Sa'arri*, and in the *Amarna Letters as *Shêri*.]

1. A mountainous land (Gen 32:3), also the name of its inhabitants (Eze 25: 8, KJV). The area, known also as Mount Seir (ch 35:15), reached from near the southern end of the Dead Sea almost to the Gulf of Aqabah, and lay east of the depression known as the *Wâdī 'Arabah* (Map V, B-7). This land is mentioned also in extra-Biblical records, first in an *Amarna letter written from Jerusalem (*ANET* 488), then by Ramses III as a land whose people he had destroyed, and then by Ashurbanipal of Assyria, in whose list it follows the Hauran and Moab (*ANET* 298). The inhabitants of this mountain range in the time of Abraham

were Horites (Gen 14:6), that is, Hurrians. Esau made this area his home (ch 32:3), and his descendants dispossessed the Horites (Deut 2:12; Jos 24:4). The name Seir is therefore also used in later times as synonymous with *Edom (Eze 35).

2. A mountain ridge on the northern border of Judah (Map II, C-3), near Kiriath-jearim (Jos 15:10). The place named *Saris*, near Chesalon, may preserve the ancient name.

Seirah (sē-ī'rȧ), KJV **Seirath** (sē-ī'răth). [Heb. *Śeʻîrah*, "hairy" (a feminine form).] A place in the hill country of Ephraim to which Ehud, the judge, escaped after having assassinated Eglon, the Moabite king (Jgs 3:26); not identified with certainty. From there Ehud rallied the Israelites to fight against their oppressors (vs 27-29).

Seirath. *See* Seirah.

Sela (sē'lȧ), KJV once **Selah** (sē'lȧ). [Heb. *Selaʻ*, "rock."] An Edomite city identified by some with the modern *Selaʻ* near Bozrah, but generally, and probably correctly, identified with the rock-city of Petra (Gr. *Petra*, "rock," equivalent to the Heb.

Selaʻ), which is located in the heart of Mount Seir, about halfway between the Dead Sea and the Gulf of Aqabah (Map V, B-7). The Hebrew term, frequent in the Bible, is probably a proper name referring to this city in the following 6 passages: 2 Ki 14:7; 2 Chr 25:12; Is 16:1; 42:11; Jer 49:16; Ob 3; and possibly also in Jgs 1:36. However, the translators have not always felt free to translate it as such, and in some of these passages render it "rock." In the time of Moses the Edomite capital was probably at Bozrah, but Sela seems to have been the capital in the time of the kings of Judah. Jeremiah's (Jer 49:16) and Obadiah's (Ob 3, 4) descriptions of the Edomites having built their nests like eagles in the clefts of the rocks fit the situation of Petra exactly, for the terrain there is an irregular valley of trapezoidal shape surrounded on all sides by lofty cliffs, with only a few narrow gorges leading into this area. This natural defense made the city almost impregnable. Archeological remains of the Edomite period have been found only on top of

427. The rock *Umm el-Bayyárah*, ancient Sela (at Petra), on which the capital of the Edomites was situated

Umm el-Bayyârah, a towering mountain inside the area of Petra, whose summit is a plateau extremely difficult to reach (see fig. 427). This was probably the place conquered by King Amaziah of Judah and renamed Joktheel (2 Ki 14:7). Probably about 300 B.C. the Arabic Nabataeans drove the Edomites to the west, and occupied Petra, their mountain fortress. Under the Nabataeans, who became rich by controlling the caravan routes between southern Arabia and Egypt and other countries in the north and west, Petra was converted into a splendid city. Many structures, such as temples, houses, tombs, and a theater, were cut out of the solid rock, and others were built in the open spaces between the cliffs. More than a thousand ancient structures of Petra, mostly those cut from the rocks, have survived and are found in varying stages of preservation. The variegated colors of the rock—red, brown, purple, yellow—give to Petra a picturesqueness unequaled anywhere. The kingdom of the Nabataeans came to an end in A.D. 105 when Petra was conquered by the Romans, and its territory made into the province of Arabia Petraea. Gradually it lost its importance, and was eventually deserted after the decline of the caravan routes. It was forgotten for centuries by the Western world, until rediscovered by Burckhardt in 1812. This place is one of the most interesting of the ancient Near Eastern sites, and a great attraction to tourists, although its isolation and its distance from the beaten paths make a visit to it difficult.

For remains from the Nabataean period of Petra see figs. 227, 386, 431.

Selah. [Heb. *selah,* derivation and meaning uncertain.]

1. A term, apparently musical, that occurs 71 times in Ps and 3 times in Hab (ch 3:3, 9, 13). It has been suggested that the term may have indicated a raising of the voice, a pause or interlude, or a change of voices. "Selah" should not be pronounced when psalms are read orally.

2. For 2 Ki 14:7, KJV, *see* Sela.

Sela-hammahlekoth (sē'lȧ-hȧ-mä'lĕ-kŏth). [Heb. *Sela' Hammachleqôth,* usually considered to mean "rock of divisions," but "rock of smoothness," or "rock of escapes," has also been suggested.] A rock in the Wilderness of Maon where Saul pursued David (1 Sa 23:25-28, KJV). The RSV translates the Hebrew term as, "the Rock of Escape." It has been identified with the *Wâdî el-Malâqi,* a deep, narrow gorge near the Judean Carmel, where the incident recorded in 1 Sa 23:25, 26 must have taken place. While Saul and his men were on one side of the gorge, David and his followers were on the other side. They could see each other, and were even close enough to speak to each other, but Saul would have had to make a long and arduous detour to reach David.

Seled (sē'lĕd). [Heb. *Seled.*] A man of Judah descended from Jerahmeel (1 Chr 2:30).

Seleucia (sĕ-lū'shĭ-ȧ). [Gr. *Seleukeia.*] The name of numerous cities in the ancient Near East, most of which were named after Seleucus I Nicator (312-280 B.C.). The Bible mentions the port city of Antioch in Syria only (Acts 13:4). This Seleucia was situated 5 mi. north of the mouth of the Orontes River and about 16 mi. northwest of Antioch (Map XX, B-6). About 245 B.C. this city was captured by Ptolemy III of Egypt, but was recovered by Antiochus III of Syria in 219. It issued its own coinage from Antiochus IV's reign, and was given its freedom in 108. The Roman conqueror, Pompey, confirmed this freedom in 63 B.C. as a reward for the city's resistance to Tigranes of Armenia against whom the Romans had fought. The city then became a station of the imperial fleet in the East, since the magnificent harbor installations made it suitable for that purpose. It now bears the name *Selûqiyeh.*

Self-control. *See* Temperance.

Sem. *See* Shem.

Semachiah (sĕm'ȧ-kī'ȧ). [Heb. *Semakyahû,* "Yahweh has sustained." The name occurs also in the *Lachish Letters.* A comparable name, *Samakuyam,* occurs in cuneiform.] A Levite, descendant of the gatekeeper Obed-edom (1 Chr 26:7).

Semei. *See* Semein.

Semein (sĕm'ĕ-ĭn), KJV **Semei** (sĕm'ĕ-ī). [Gr. *Semeïn,* from Heb. *Shim'i.*] A Judahite appearing in Luke's genealogy of Jesus Christ (Lk 3:26).

Senaah. *See* Hassenaah.

Seneh (sē'nĕ). [Heb. *Seneh,* "thorn."] One of 2 sharp rocks in the pass at Michmash, between which Jonathan climbed up when he overcame the Philistine garrison (1 Sa 14:4, 5). It is one of the cliffs in the *Wâdî eṣ-Ṣuweinît* (see fig. 329), but which one is uncertain. *Qurnet Khallet el-Haiy* has been suggested as most likely.

Senir. *See* Hermon.

Sennacherib (sĕ-năk'ēr-ĭb). [Heb. *Sancherib;* in Aramaic texts *Šnchryb* and *Snch'ryb;* Assyrian *Sin-aḥḥê-eriba,* meaning "may (the god) Sin increase my brothers."] An As-

428. Assyrian relief showing King Sennacherib on his throne before Lachish in Palestine during the siege of the city

SENNACHERIB

syrian king who succeeded his father Sargon II in 705 B.C. and ruled for 25 years (705-681 B.C.). He is best remembered in secular history for his senseless destruction of Babylon in 689 B.C. and in the Bible for the catastrophe that overtook his army at Jerusalem shortly afterward. On Sennacherib's accession Merodach-Baladan, former king of Babylon, attempted to throw off the Assyrian yoke, but he and his Elamite ally were defeated. Sennacherib's next major campaign was carried out in the west in 701 B.C., where a revolt in Syria and Palestine demanded his attention. First he captured a number of Phoenician cities, and then marched against the center of rebellion in Palestine, the Philistine cities and the kingdom of Judah. Sennacherib claims to have taken 46 fortified cities from Hezekiah of Judah, besides many villages, and to have carried off 200,150 captives (the Assyriologist A. Ungnad believes that the number should be read 2,150), besides tremendous amounts of spoil. His siege of Lachish, probably the strongest fortress city of Judah with the exception of Jerusalem, is mentioned in the Bible (2 Ki 18:14, 17; 19:8) and also depicted by Sennacherib on long stone reliefs (see figs. 284, 428, 502). Jerusalem was besieged for a time by an Assyrian army, but was not taken (ch 18:17). So Sennacherib could claim only that he had made Hezekiah "a prisoner in Jerusalem, his royal residence, like a bird in a cage. I surrounded him with earthwork in order to molest those who were leaving the city's gate" (*ANET* 288). Since his attention was urgently needed in the east, Sennacherib

had to be satisfied with receiving a heavy tribute from Hezekiah, which is mentioned in the Bible and in the Assyrian king's records (2 Ki 18:14-16; *ANET* 288). The detailed Assyrian version of this campaign, inscribed on well-preserved clay prisms (*ANET* 287, 288), agrees in all major points with the Biblical records, although it shows differences in details. See fig. 223.

During the next 10 years Sennacherib was kept busy mainly with affairs in Babylonia and Elam. Finally he became so weary of the frequent rebellions of Babylon that he destroyed the city ruthlessly and thoroughly, and even flooded the whole area by diverting the Euphrates, in order to transform the surrounding land into a marsh and thus prevent the city's resurrection. Shortly afterward he must have carried out another military campaign against Hezekiah, because 2 Ki 19:9 mentions an attempt of Tirhakah, the Nubian king of Egypt, to aid Hezekiah during a campaign of Sennacherib. Since *Tirhakah did not leave Nubia, his homeland, until about 689 B.C., when he became coregent with his brother at the age of 20, this campaign cannot be dated earlier. Therefore it must be concluded that the Biblical records of chs 18-20 and parallel passages deal with 2 distinct campaigns and not with one as a cursory reading of the narrative seems to indicate. It must have been during this later campaign that Sennacherib's army suffered the disastrous loss recorded in ch 19:35, when it was smitten by an angel during the siege of Jerusalem. Although the Assyrian records naturally are silent about this disaster, it was not forgotten among the ancient nations, as is proved by a story of the Greek historian Herodotus. While visiting Egypt more than 200 years after Sennacherib's death Herodotus was told that when the Assyrian king advanced against Egypt, immense numbers of mice ate the bowstrings of his army so that the soldiers fled in panic. Since the mice were considered the bearers of bubonic plague, it is generally believed that the story implies an outbreak of this disease in the army of the Assyrians. There is little reason to doubt that this was the Egyptian version of the catastrophe recorded in v 35. *See* Hezekiah.

In his homeland Sennacherib was known as the great rebuilder of Nineveh, which in his time became the most beautiful and glorious city of antiquity. He also built an aqueduct which brought water to Nineveh and its surrounding area from the eastern mountains some 30 mi. away. The Gomer River was spanned by an arched causeway 1,000 ft. long, possibly the first permanent stone bridge of history. In 681 B.C. Sennacherib was murdered by his 2 sons, Adrammelech and Sharezer, who were perhaps jealous of their brother Esarhaddon, the crown prince (2 Ki 19:37; 2 Chr 32:21). Although this murder is referred to in several contemporary texts (*ANET* 288-290, 302), all references to it are so vague and ambiguous that a detailed historical reconstruction of the event is still impossible. The murderers did not succeed in usurping the throne, but were driven out by Esarhaddon, who succeeded his father.

Lit.: E. G. Kraeling, *JAOS* 53 (1933), 335-346; A. Ungnad, *ZAW* 59 (1942-43), 199-202; W. F. Albright, *BASOR* 130 (1953), 8, 9.

Senuah. See Hassenuah, 2.

Seorim (sĕ-ō'rĭm). [Heb. *Še'orîm,* "barley."] A descendant of Aaron, and ancestral head of the 4th of the 24 courses into which David organized the priests (1 Chr 24:8).

Separate Place. [Heb. *gizrah,* from *gazar,* "to cut," hence, "a space cut off."] The space at the west end of Ezekiel's ideal temple, between the temple and "the building" (Eze 41:12-15; 42:1, 10, 13; KJV), and probably also the space along the north and south of the temple. In these passages the RSV renders *gizrah* "temple yard" or "yard." *Gizrah* appears in Lam 4:7, where the KJV translates it "polishing"; RSV "form." Its meaning in the Lam passage is uncertain.

Sephar (sē'fär). [Heb. *Sephar,* "numbering."] A place in southern Arabia which formed the limit of the territory of the Joktanites (Gen 10:29, 30). It has been identified by some with *Zafâr* in South Arabia, but this identification is uncertain.

Sepharad (sĕ-fā'răd). [Heb. *Sepharad.*] The residence of exiles from Jerusalem (Ob 20). It has been identified with the *Sparda* of Persian cuneiform texts (Kent, *Old Persian,* p. 210), which is Sardis, the capital of the Lydians (Map XII, C-4). A more likely identification is *Shaparda* in southwestern Media, mentioned in a text of Sargon II (Luckenbill, *AR* II, 76).

Sepharvaim (sĕf'är-vā'ĭm). [Heb. *Sepharwayim.*] A city from which the Assyrians deported inhabitants to Samaria (2 Ki 17:24, 31). Because it is mentioned with 2 Babylonian cities, Babylon and Cuthah,

many have identified it with Sippar, which lies on the eastern side of the Euphrates, 35 mi. northwest of Babylon (Map XI, C-5). However, Sepharvaim is listed immediately after Hamath in Syria; thus it could also be identified with *Shabarain* of the Assyrian inscriptions, a city not yet definitely located, although it seems to have been between Hamath and Damascus (W. F. Albright, *Archaeology and the Religion of Israel,* 2d ed. [Baltimore, 1946], p. 220, n. 116).

Sepharvites (sē'fär-vīts). [Heb. *Sepharwîm.*] The inhabitants of *Sepharvaim (2 Ki 17:31).

Sepulchre. A burial vault. In the KJV the word is a rendering of the Heb. *qeber* and *qebûrah,* and of the Gr. *mnēma, mnēmeion,* and *taphos;* in the RSV only of the Heb. *qeber* (Gen 23:6; Neh 2:3, 5; Ps 5:9; Is 14:19) and of the Gr. *taphos* (Mt 27:61, 64, 66; 28:1). The context shows that these terms are synonymous and simply mean "tomb." They do not indicate architectural differences. See Burial.

Sepulchres of the Kings. See Tombs of the Kings.

Serah (sē'rá), KJV once **Sarah** (sâr'á). [Heb. *Serach,* attested in Akkadian as *Surhu.*] A daughter of Asher (Gen 46:17; Num 26:46; 1 Chr 7:30).

Seraiah (sĕ-rā'yá). [Heb. *Serayah* and *Serayahû,* "Yahweh contends," or "Yahweh rules." The name occurs also on an ancient Hebrew seal.]

1. A son of Kenaz of the tribe of Judah (1 Chr 4:13, 14).

2. A secretary (KJV "scribe") of David (2 Sa 8:17), possibly identical with Sheva (ch 20:25), Shisha (1 Ki 4:3), and Shavsha (1 Chr 18:16). See Shavsha.

3. A Simeonite (1 Chr 4:35).

4. An officer ordered by King Jehoiakim to arrest Baruch and Jeremiah (Jer 36:26).

5. A chief priest in the time of King Zedekiah. He was taken to Riblah and executed by Nebuchadnezzar (2 Ki 25:18-21; Jer 52:24-27); his son Jehozadak went to Babylonia into captivity (1 Chr 6:14, 15). Seraiah's grandson, Jeshua, returned to Jerusalem with Zerubbabel and was the 1st high priest of the new Temple (Ezr 3:2). Ezra, the scribe, also was a descendant of this same Seraiah (ch 7:1; *see* Son).

6. The son of Neriah (Jer 51:59), presumably brother of Baruch (cf. ch 43:3). He was a quartermaster (the rendering "quiet prince" in the KJV is incorrect)

who accompanied King Zedekiah on a trip to Babylon in the 4th year of the king's reign. This trip was probably made by Zedekiah to assure Nebuchadnezzar of his loyalty, or possibly, as some have speculated, to be present at the dedication of the golden image in the plain of Dura (Dan 3). Seraiah carried with him a copy of Jeremiah's prophecy against Babylon (Jer 51:60, 61).

7. A son of Tanhumeth, the Netophathite; he was a captain of one of Zedekiah's army units. Having escaped capture by Nebuchadnezzar he came to Gedaliah at Mizpah and, with other officers, submitted to him (2 Ki 25:23; Jer 40:8).

8. One of the leading Jews who returned with Zerubbabel from Babylonia (Ezr 2:2), probably the Azariah of Neh 7:7; possibly identical with Seraiah, 9.

9. A priest who returned with Zerubbabel from Babylonia (Neh 12:1, 7). His name was perpetuated as that of a priestly family (v 12). He is possibly identical with Seraiah, 8.

10. A priest who set his seal to Nehemiah's covenant (Neh 10:2). He may have represented the family of Seraiah, 9, and may possibly be identical with Seraiah, 11.

11. A priest, son of Hilkiah and ruler of the Temple in Nehemiah's time (Neh 11:11), possibly identical with Seraiah, 10.

Seraphim. [Heb. *śeraphím,* plural of *śaraph,* "serpent," "seraph," "burning one," from *śaraph,* "to burn."] Celestial beings seen in vision before God's throne by the prophet Isaiah (Is 6:2, 6). Each had 6 wings, with 1 pair covering its face, with a 2d pair covering its feet, and with a 3d pair used for flying. Isaiah heard the seraphs chanting, "Holy, holy, holy, is the Lord of hosts: the whole earth is full of his glory" (v 3). Upon Isaiah's confession of sin, one of the seraphs took a burning coal from the altar and with it touched the prophet's lips, indicating purification from iniquity (vs 5-7). The Bible provides no further clue as to the identity of these beings. The Heb. adjective *śaraph* is rendered "fiery" in Num 21:6 in a description of the serpents that attacked the Israelites in the wilderness. In v 8 the "serpent" Moses made is called in Heb. *śaraph,* which in Is 14:29 and 30:6 is translated "fiery . . . serpent" (RSV "serpent"). Inasmuch as the root word, *śaraph,* denotes burning (see Ex 32:20; Lev 13:55; 1 Ki 13:2), it would appear that when *śaraph* is applied to a serpent it refers, not to its form, as a serpent, but either to its fiery sting or the resulting inflammation, or possibly to its brilliant appearance. Similarly, when used of celestial beings before the throne of God, it probably denotes the effulgent glory ra-

429. A six-winged seraph on a stone slab from *Tell Haláf*

diating from them. In Is 6 the designation "seraphim" may be associated with the fact that one *śaraph* became an agent for administering symbolic purification by fire (vs 6, 7). The words and deeds of the seraphim of ch 6 show them to be intelligent beings who honor God and minister to Him. Whether the seraphim have 6 literal wings each or whether these were merely a symbolic feature employed for purposes of the vision, is not certain. For a pagan equivalent of a six-winged seraph see fig. 429.

Sered (sē'rĕd). [Heb. *Sered,* attested in Ugarit as *Srd.*] A son of Zebulun (Gen 46:14), and ancestral head of the family of the *Seredites.

Seredites (sē'rĕd-īts), KJV **Sardites** (sär'dīts). [Heb. *Sardi.*] Descendants of *Sered (Num 26:26).

Sergius Paulus (sûr'jĭ-ŭs pô'lŭs). [Gr. *Sergios Paulos.*] Proconsul of Cyprus at the time of Paul's 1st Missionary Journey (*c.* A.D. 45-

47). Paul presented the gospel to him, but in this was opposed by Elymas, a magician. The signal manifestation of divine disfavor that overtook Elymas convinced the governor, and he "believed" (Acts 13: 7-12). The name of Sergius is mentioned by Pliny (*Hist. Nat.* ii. 90. 97, 112), and a Latin inscription (*CIL* VI, 31, 545) mentions an L. Sergius Paulus who has been identified by Mommsen with the proconsul of ch 13. On the basis of this inscription his term of office has been dated in A.D. 46/47 or 49/50. An inscription found at Soloi on the northern coast of Cyprus mentions a "Paulus proconsul."

Serjeant. [Gr. *rhabdouchos,* "lictor," originally "staff bearer." *Rhabdoi* probably actually refers to the fasces, or bundle of sticks with an ax blade projecting, carried by the lictors.] An attendant of a Roman *magistrate (Acts 16:35, 38; RSV "police") who carried fasces as a symbol of office. The Philippian magistrates sent "serjeants" to inform the jailer that Paul and Silas were to be released from prison (Acts 16: 35-40).

Sermon on the Mount, The. One of the major discourses of our Lord, delivered on a Galilean hillside, in which He epitomized the nature, purpose, and principles of the kingdom of divine grace He had come to establish (Mt 5-7). Jesus had recently returned from His first evangelistic tour through the towns and villages of Galilee announcing "the kingdom" (ch 4:23), and had appointed the Twelve to be apostles of the kingdom (Mk 3:13-19; Lk 6:12-16). This sermon was addressed to them in particular, but many other followers and listeners were present. The Sermon on the Mount may be thought of as our Lord's inaugural address as Ruler of the kingdom of divine grace, or as the constitution of that kingdom. In this discourse He sets forth the requirements for entering the kingdom, the character expected of its citizens, and their privileges and responsibilities, in a more comprehensive way than upon any other recorded occasion. It is a delineation of life in the new spiritual society Jesus came to establish, and the principles set forth cover the entire scope of man's duty toward God and toward his fellow men. In the sermon our Lord repeatedly quotes from "the law, or the prophets" (see Mt 5:17-22, 27, 38; cf. Ex 21:24; etc.), thus enriching the spiritual insight of His hearers and making a practical application of OT principles to His new kingdom of righteousness. True religion, He points out, controls motives and attitudes as well as the resulting words and deeds, since it is possible to have the form of religion and of right living without the heart and life being sincerely dedicated to God or without having the real interests of one's fellow men at heart.

The Sermon on the Mount might well be entitled "Responsibilities and Privileges of Citizens in the Kingdom of Heaven." Mt 5 delineates the character motivated by love for one's fellow men as the goal of citizenship, and reaches its climax in an appeal to be "perfect" even as God Himself is perfect (v 48). Chapter 6 deals with incentives to right living and exemplary citizenship and closes with a challenge to make the kingdom of heaven first in one's life (v 33). Chapter 7 is devoted to certain specific privileges and responsibilities of citizenship and ends with a call to decisive action respecting the claims of the kingdom upon those who hear (vs 24-27). The sermon opens with a gracious explanation of how one may become a citizen of the kingdom (ch 5:3-12) and defines a citizen as a living representative of its principles (vs 13-16). What these principles are is discussed in greater detail in vs 17-48. Our Lord then continues, stressing the importance of right motives in worship, service, and human relations (ch 6:1-18), and of complete trust in God's goodness for the needs of this life (vs 25-34). Our relations with one another are to be a living expression of the golden rule (ch 7:1-12). Strict obedience and self-discipline are the test of discipleship (vs 13-23). In closing, Jesus makes an urgent appeal to His hearers to translate these principles into practice in the daily life (vs 24-27).

Serpent. There are about 35 kinds of serpents in Palestine, some of which are extremely poisonous. Nine different Hebrew and 4 different Greek words are used in the Bible to designate various types of serpents. Some of these terms are generic, designating serpents in general; others are specific, naming such serpents as cobras, vipers, adders, etc. Unfortunately, none can be identified with certainty.

Serpents live among stones (Amos 5: 19) and rocks (Prov 30:19), or in the warm sand of the desert. Some seek wet areas, such as the vicinity of wells, which probably explains why the Semites named many of their wells after snakes. The serpents were feared for their poison, and were represented frequently as the tools of God's wrath (Num 21:6; Deut

32:24; Jer 8:17). They are set forth as symbols of dishonesty, stealthiness, and slander (Gen 49:17; Ps 140:3), cunning evil (Mt 3:7; 23:33), effects of intoxication (Prov 23:32), but also of wisdom (Mt 10:16). Satan used a serpent to bring about the fall of man (Gen 3; 2 Cor 11:3); hence he is sometimes referred to as a serpent (Rev 12:9; 20:2; etc.).

Snake charmers of the type mentioned in the Bible (Ps 58:4; Ec 10:11; Jer 8:17; Jas 3:7) are still found in Egypt, Palestine, and India. They are able to paralyze even the most venomous serpent by applying pressure to its neck so that it becomes rigid. It has been suggested that the Egyptian magicians used such paralyzed snakes to counterfeit Moses' miracle (Ex 7:12).

The following names are used in the Bible for serpents: (1) the Heb. *nachash,* a frequently used generic term which, when referring to a reptile, is always translated "serpent" in the KJV; (2) the Heb. *tannin,* also used in the generic sense to mean "serpent" (Ex 7:9, 10, 12; Deut 32:33, KJV "dragon"; Ps 91:13, KJV "dragon"); (3) the Heb. *pethen,* rendered "asp" and "adder" (Deut 32:33; Job 20:14, 16; Ps 58:4; 91:13; Is 11:8), and representing a very fierce and poisonous snake, perhaps the cobra, of which certain kinds are found in Palestine; (4) the Heb. *shephiphon* (Gen 49:17), rendered "adder" (KJV) and "viper" (RSV), usually understood to mean a horned snake; (5) the Heb. *'akshûb* (Ps 140:3),

rendered "adder" (KJV), "viper" (RSV), apparently another form of horned serpent; (6) the Heb. *sepha',* and (7) *siph-'oni,* 2 words, rendered "adder" and "cockatrice" in the KJV, and "adder" in the RSV (Prov 23:32; Is 11:8; 14:29; 59:5; Jer 8:17), representing some kind of poisonous snake; (8) the Heb. *'eph'eh,* rendered "viper" (Job 20:16; Is 30:6; 59:5), another poisonous serpent of unknown species; (9) the Heb. *śaraph* in the combination *śaraph me'ôpheph* rendered "flying serpent" (Is 14:29; 30:6); likewise the combination *nachash śaraph* is translated "fiery serpent" in Num 21:6 and Deut 8:15, but the kind of snake referred to is uncertain. In addition, a form of the Heb. *zachal* (Deut 32:24), rendered "serpents" in the KJV and "crawling things" in the RSV, refers to some form of snake.

The most common NT word for snake is the Gr. *ophis,* which is used 14 times (Mt 7:10; Jn 3:14; Rev 12:9; etc.). The Gr. *echidna* is found 5 times and is uniformly rendered "viper" (Mt 3:7; 12:34; 23:33; Lk 3:7; Acts 28:3). *Aspis,* "asp," occurs once (Rom 3:13). The Gr. *herpeton* is used in the general sense of "reptile" (Acts 10:12; 11:6; Rom 1:23).

It has been argued that the ancients believed that serpents ate dust and that this mistaken view was rooted in the predictive curse pronounced by God that the serpent would eat dust (Gen 3:14). The recently recovered literature of the ancient world has revealed, however, that the ancients understood such statements

430. A serpent stele (left) found at *Tell Beit Mirsim,* ancient Debir; drawing (right) facilitates recognition of details

431. Snake monument at Petra

figuratively, for they accompanied their strong curses by the statement that the cursed one would have to eat dust (see *SDACom* 1:232).

Serpents were objects of worship in the Canaanite religion, though it is uncertain whether these creatures were considered to be gods. Steles have been discovered at several places in Palestine and Syria that show individuals, probably gods, around whom serpents are wound (see fig. 430). Some gods and goddesses were depicted holding snakes in their hands (see fig. 429). Serpent monuments, such as the one at Petra (see fig. 431), were certainly erected as objects of worship. When the Israelites imitated pagan serpent worship by making the bronze serpent of Moses into an idol, the pious king Hezekiah destroyed it (Num 21:8, 9; 2 Ki 18:4).

Serpent, Brasen. *See* Bronze Serpent.

Serug (sē'rŭg), KJV once **Saruch** (sā'rŭk). [Heb. *Serûg;* Gr. *Serouch,* meaning uncertain.] Son of Reu, and father of Nahor in the ancestral line of Abraham (Gen 11:20-23; 1 Chr 1:26; Lk 3:35). The city of *Sarugi* near Haran is believed to have been named after him.

Servant. [Heb. generally *na'ar,* "youth" or "young man"; *'ebed,* "slave," "servant," "subject," "minister"; Gr. generally *doulos,* "slave," "servant"; *diakonos,* "servant," "helper," "deacon"; *oiketēs,* "domestic servant"; *pais,* "boy," "youth," "servant," "slave," "child."] A person who renders service, voluntary or involuntary, to another person. The term may denote court officials as servants of their king (Gen 41:10; Ex 7:10, 20; etc.), or persons in any subordinate relationship to another (Dan 1:12, 13). When politely ad-dressing a superior, an inferior would often refer to himself as a servant of the superior, thus expressing submission (Gen 50:18; 2 Ki 1:13; Lk 2:29; Acts 4:29). Those who worship and serve the true God as His subjects are called His servants (Gen 19:19; 1 Sa 3:10; Rev 1:1; 22:6), and especially His chosen representatives and spokesmen (1 Ki 8:56; 2 Ki 9:7; Dan 9:6). Paul commonly referred to himself as a "servant," or "slave," of Jesus Christ (Rom 1:1; Php 1:1; Tit 1:1; etc.).

Of particular interest is the expression "my servant" or its equivalent in Is 41-66, where it occurs frequently of Israel as God's "servant," the one whom He has "chosen" (ch 41:8, 9). Isaiah envisions the nation in its role under the covenant relationship, particularly with reference to God's purpose for it following the Babylonian captivity (v 9). As His "witnesses" (ch 43:10) they were to know and understand God's will in order that they might testify of Him to the nations round about. God would pour out His Spirit upon them to enable them to do so effectively (ch 44:1-3). The Lord would redeem His "servant" Jacob from Babylon, restore them to their own land (ch 65:9), bless them (vs 13-15), and be glorified among them (ch 49:3). If they would prove faithful to Him He would defend them against their enemies (cf. ch 54:15-17).

In a special sense Messiah Himself was to be the "servant" of the Lord, to complete the spiritual restoration and glorification of Israel (Is 42:1-4). He is the suffering servant of chs 52:13 to 53:12. As Israel bears witness to the nations, many come to worship and serve the true God, also becoming His "servants" (ch 56:6). Modern Jewish expositors usually attribute all comment about the Lord's "servant" in chs 41-66 to Israel as God's chosen people. Older Jewish expositors, however —the Targum of Isaiah, for instance— commonly applied chs 52:13 to 53:12 to the Messiah. The majority of the learned Jewish scholars who contributed to the Midrash applied this passage to the future Messiah.

Seth (sĕth), KJV once **Sheth** (shĕth). [Heb. *Sheth;* Gr. *Sēth,* "appointed," or "substituted."] The 3d son of Adam, born after Abel (whose substitute he became) was murdered (Gen 4:25; 5:3). Seth became the father of Enosh (KJV "Enos"), and the progenitor of the godly line of men (see ch 6:2). He died at the age of 912 years (ch 5:8).

Sethur (sē'thĕr). [Heb. *Sethûr,* "hidden." The feminine form of this name (*Strh*) occurs on an ancient Hebrew seal.] The representative of the tribe of Asher among the 12 spies (Num 13:13).

Settle. A term appearing as a noun in Eze 43:14, 17, 20; 45:19; KJV, as a rendering of the Heb. *'azarah,* probably in these passages meaning "ledge" (RSV).

Seven. [Heb. and Aramaic *sheba';* Gr. *hepta.*] Pre-eminently the sacred number among both the Hebrews and other peoples of the ancient East, and also to some extent in remote lands such as India, China, Central Europe, and the British Isles. This usage was particularly strong among Semitic peoples, in ancient Babylonia, and in regions that came under Babylonian influence. The cuneiform texts indicate that the Babylonians regarded 7 as the number of totality or completeness. The origin of the concept that sacredness is attached to the number 7 is shrouded in the mists of antiquity. The widespread recognition attached to the number 7 implies that the concept was already well known and firmly established in the thinking of people before the dispersion of the races, and there is every reason to believe that it originated with the 7 days of Creation week. No other plausible explanation has been made. The creation of the earth in 7 days, the 7 great luminaries of the solar system, visible to the unaided eye—the sun, the moon, and the planets Mercury, Venus, Mars, Jupiter, and Saturn—and the successive phases of the moon approximately every 7 days were phenomena from which men may have inferred that God recognized the number 7 as belonging especially to Him. Particularly impressive was the fact that He had blessed the 7th day and hallowed it, the 7th portion of time, as a sacred season set apart in token of divine favor, good will, and blessing toward man. *See* Sabbath.

The number 7 recurs repeatedly in the ancient Jewish ritual service. Every 7th day was holy (Ex 20:8-11). There were the 7 days of Unleavened Bread (ch 34:18) and 7 days of the Feast of Tabernacles (Lev 23:34). Every 7th year was a sabbatical year (Ex 21:2). The 1st day of the 7th month was a sabbath day (Lev 23:24). There was a sevenfold sprinkling of blood on the Day of Atonement (ch 16:14, 19), as well as upon other occasions such as the purification of a leper or a leprous house (ch 14:7, 16, 27, 51). Seven days of ritual seclusion were required in cases of real or suspected uncleanness through leprosy or contact with a corpse, or for other reasons (Lev 13:2, 4, 22, 26; etc.). Circumcision took place after 7 days (ch 12:3; cf. v 2). A sacrificial animal must be at least 7 days old (Ex 22:30). The consecration of the priests was to be repeated each day over a 7-day period (ch 29:35). The lampstand in the sanctuary was equipped with 7 lights (Num 8:2). There are, as well, numerous historical instances in which the number 7 seems to have played a symbolic part (see especially Gen 29:20; 33:3; 41:53; Num 23:1, 14, 29; Jos 6:8; cf. 1 Ki 18:43; Dan 3:19; 4:16, 23, 25, 32). Of particular interest is the use of the number 7 in the book of Revelation. Here we find 7 churches (Rev 1:4), 7 golden candlesticks (v 12), 7 stars, or angels (vs 16, 20), 7 lamps of fire (ch 4:5), 7 Spirits of God (chs 1:4; 3:1; 4:5), a book with 7 seals (ch 5:1), a lamb with 7 horns and 7 eyes (v 6), 7 angels with 7 trumpets (ch 8:2), 7 thunders (ch 10:3), 7 heads, 7 crowns (chs 12:3; 13:1; cf. 17:3), 7 angels having 7 last plagues (ch 15:1, 7).

Special significance seems also to have attached to various multiples of 7. Thus the Passover fell on the 14th day of the 1st month (Ex 12:6; cf. v 16). Fourteen lambs were offered on each of the 7 days of the Feast of Tabernacles (Num 29:13, 15-32). Matthew's genealogy of Christ is arranged in 3 groups of 14 each (Mt 1:17). The number 49, or 7 times 7, figures in the computation of Pentecost as the 50th day from the 2d day of Unleavened Bread (Lev 23:15). Two successive years of jubilee were separated by 49 (ch 25:8). There are many instances of the use of the number 70, or 7 multiplied by 10 (Ex 1:5; 15:27; 24:1; Jgs 1:7; 8:30; 2 Ki 10:1; 2 Chr 29:32; Ps 90:10; Eze 8:11; Dan 9:24; Lk 10:1, 17). See also the use of the number 490 (70 times 7), as in Ezr 8:35; Dan 9:25; Mt 18:22. The half of 7 is also significant, in Dan 7:25; 9:27; 12:7; Rev 11:2; 13:5. The number 7 in its varied uses in the Bible expresses fullness or completeness.

Seven Stars. *See* Pleiades.

Seventh Year. *See* Sabbatical Year.

Shaalabbin. *See* Shaalbim.

Shaalbim (shȧ-ǎl'bĭm), or **Shaalabbin** (shā'ȧ-lǎb'ĭn). [Heb. *Sha'albim* and *Sha'alabbin,* "fox."] A Canaanite town assigned to the tribe of Dan (Jos 19:42). It was not occupied by the Israelites for a long time (Jgs 1:35; 1 Ki 4:9). It has been identified with *Selbît,* 8 mi. southeast of Lydda.

Shaalbonite (shā'ăl-bō'nīt). [Heb. *Sha'alboni.*] The designation of an inhabitant of either a place called Shaalbon, not identified, or, more probably, the city of *Shaalbim (2 Sa 23:32; 1 Chr 11:33).

Shaalim (shā'ȧ-lĭm), KJV **Shalim** (shā'lĭm). [Heb. *Sha'alim,* "hollow hands."] A district through which Saul passed in search of his father's asses (1 Sa 9:4). Some think that it is a shortened form of *Sha'albim,* whereas others identify it with *Shual (ch 13:17), north of Michmash.

Shaaph (shā'ăf). [Heb. *Sha'aph,* "balsam."]
1. A son of "Caleb the son of Hezron," by his concubine Maacah. He became the ancestor of (the inhabitants of) Madmannah (1 Chr 2:49; cf. v 18).
2. A descendant of Caleb, son of Hezron (1 Chr 2:47).

Shaaraim (shā'ȧ-rā'ĭm), KJV once **Sharaim** (shȧ-rā'ĭm). [Heb. *Sha'arayim,* "two gates."]
1. A town in the Shephelah of Judah (Jos 15:36), near Philistine territory (1 Sa 17:52); not identified.
2. A town in the territory of Simeon (1 Chr 4:31), probably identical with the *Sharuhen of Jos 19:6.

Shaashgaz (shā-ăsh'găz). [Heb. *Sha'ashgaz,* a Persian name of uncertain etymology.] The chamberlain to whom Esther was entrusted (Est 2:14).

Shabbethai (shăb'ĕ-thī). [Heb. *Shabbethay,* "born on the Sabbath," a name attested in cuneiform inscriptions as *Shabbatai,* and in Nabataean and Palmyrene inscriptions as *Shbty.*] An influential Levite in the days of Ezra and Nehemiah, who opposed Ezra's method of dealing with mixed marriages (Ezr 10:15, RSV). He was presumably the one who assisted Ezra in teaching the Law, and who was in charge of the outside work of the Temple (Neh 8:7; 11:16).

Shachia. *See* Sachia.

Shadow of Death. [Heb. *ṣalmaweth,* "darkness," perhaps from *ṣel,* "a shadow," and *maweth,* "death."] An expression appearing 18 times in the KJV OT, but only once in the RSV (Ps 23:4). The term occurs 10 times in the book of Job (chs 3:5; 16:16; etc.), and is used poetically for thick darkness (ch 3:5), as descriptive of Sheol (ch 10:21; etc.), and of deep distress (ch 12:22; etc.). The idea of intense darkness, whether literal or figurative, and thus of suffering, sorrow, and privation seems to be implicit in the expression. The RSV generally translates *ṣalmaweth* "deep darkness."

Shadrach (shā'drăk). [Heb. *Shadrak.*] The name given by the Babylonians to Hananiah, one of Daniel's 3 Jewish companions (Dan 1:7; 2:49; 3:12-30). The name is inexplicable in Babylonian. Some think it to be a corruption of *Marduk,* the name of the chief Babylonian god, whereas others try to explain it with the help of Sumerian words. Still others suggest that it was the name of the Elamite god *Shutruk,* but it is difficult to explain why the Babylonians should have employed an Elamite name.

Shaft. *See* Spear.

Shage. *See* Shagee.

Shagee (shā'gē), KJV **Shage** (shā'gē). [Heb. *Shage',* meaning uncertain.] A Hararite, the father of one of David's "mighty men" (1 Chr 11:34).

Shahar. *See* Aijeleth Shahar.

Shaharaim (shā'hȧ-rā'ĭm). [Heb. *Shacharayim,* "double dawn," or "(born at the hour of) dawn."] A Benjamite who had many descendants (1 Chr 8:8).

Shahazimah. *See* Shahazumah.

Shahazumah (shā'hȧ-zoō'mȧ), KJV **Shahazimah** (shā'hȧ-zī'mȧ). [Heb. *Shachaṣûmah* (Q *Shachaṣimah*), "high place."] A border town of Issachar between Tabor and the Jordan (Jos 19:22); not identified with certainty.

Shalem (shā'lĕm). [Heb. *Shalem,* "peace."] A city near Shechem, according to the ancient versions which the KJV follows (Gen 33:18). However, the Hebrew term is here probably an adverb meaning "peacefully," or "safely" (see RSV).

Shalim. *See* Shaalim.

Shalisha (shȧ-lī'shȧ). [Heb. *Shalishah,* "third part."] A district in the hill country of Ephraim through which Saul passed while searching for his father's asses (1 Sa 9:4). It is sought northeast of Lydda, but has not yet been identified.

Shallecheth (shăl'ĕ-kĕth). [Heb. *Shalleketh,* "casting out."] The name of a gate of Solomon's Temple. It seems to have been located on the western side of the court (1 Chr 26:16). *See* Temple, I.

Shallum (shăl'ŭm), KJV once **Shallun** (shăl'ŭn). [Heb. *Shallûm* and *Shallûn,* "recompense." The name occurs frequently on ancient Hebrew seals and in other texts.]
1. A son of Naphtali (1 Chr 7:13).
2. A descendant of Simeon (1 Chr 4:25).
3. A descendant of Judah (1 Chr 2:40, 41).
4. A gatekeeper and head of a family

of gatekeepers, or porters, at the Temple at Jerusalem (1 Chr 9:17, 19, 31; Ezr 2:42; Neh 7:45).

5. The 16th king of Israel (if Tibni is included in the count), who reigned at Samaria 1 month (*c.* 752 B.C.), after murdering Zachariah, the last king of the dynasty of Jehu. Shallum was in turn assassinated by Menahem, who succeeded him on the throne (2 Ki 15:8-15).

6. A man whose son Jehizkiah was an official of Samaria in the time of King Pekah (2 Chr 28:12).

7. An ancestor of Ezra, and a high priest before the Exile (Ezr 7:2; 1 Chr 6:12, 13). He is called Meshullam in 1 Chr 9:11.

8. The husband of the prophetess Huldah (2 Ki 22:14; 2 Chr 34:22).

9. Uncle of Jeremiah, and the father of Hanameel (Jer 32:7, 8).

10. Fourth son and successor of Josiah. He took the throne name Jehoahaz (1 Chr 3:15; Jer 22:11; 2 Ki 23:30).

11. A gatekeeper of the Temple who in the time of Ezra had married a foreign wife (Ezr 10:24).

12. A citizen of Judah who in the time of Ezra had married a foreign wife (Ezr 10:42).

13. A ruler of half the district of Jerusalem. He, with his daughters, repaired a sector of the wall of Jerusalem in Nehemiah's time (Neh 3:12).

14. Ruler of the district of Mizpah in the time of Nehemiah. He repaired the Fountain Gate of Jerusalem and the wall of the Pool of Shelah (Neh 3:15). He is called Shallun in the KJV.

Shallun. *See* Shallum, 14.

Shalmai (shăl'mī), RSV once **Shamlai** (shăm'lī). [Heb. *Šalmay* and *Shamlay.* In the consonantal Hebrew the 2 names are identical except for the transposition of 2 letters.] The ancestral head of a family of Nethinim, or Temple servants, some of whom returned from Babylonia with Zerubbabel after the Captivity (Ezr 2:46; Neh 7:48).

Shalman (shăl'măn). [Heb. *Shalman.*] The name of the destroyer of Beth-arbel (Hos 10:14), who has not been definitely identified. The following suggestions have been made as to his identity: (1) that he is Shalmaneser V (Shalman being a shortened form of Shalmaneser), who took Galilee and destroyed Arbela, now *Khirbet Irbid* (*see* Beth-arbel); (2) that he is the Shallum who murdered Zachariah, the son of Jeroboam II (*see* Shallum, 5). This interpretation is supported by the

LXX, which for Beth-arbel reads "the house of Jeroboam"; (3) that he is *Salamanu,* a Moabite king in the time of Tiglath-pileser III (745-727 B.C.), who could have destroyed Beth-arbel (Map VI, C-4), although we have no record of his doing so.

Shalmaneser (shăl'măn-ē'zẽr). [Heb. *Shalman'eser;* Assyrian *Shulmânu-asharid,* "(the god) Shulman is superior."] Name of 5 Assyrian kings, of whom I, II, and IV played no role in Biblical history and are therefore not discussed in this article.

1. Shalmaneser III (859-824 B.C.), a son of Ashurnasirpal II. He was a great warrior and the first Assyrian king to come in contact with Israel. In his first year he waged an aggressive war in northern Syria, causing several kings of Syria and Palestine to form a league to meet his menace. Twelve kings in all joined the league whom Shalmaneser met in his 6th year (853 B.C.) at Qarqar in central Syria. The allied armies were led by Ben-hadad of Damascus and the king of Hamath. Ahab of Israel furnished 10,000 foot soldiers and 2,000 chariots, about half of all the chariots of the allied armies. Shalmaneser claims to have won a victory, but the truthfulness of his claim is doubted, because he returned at once to Assyria, and therefore must have been weakened. He returned after 5 years, but was again stopped by the allies, and again during the following campaign. However, he was finally able to break the power of the league in his 14th year (845 B.C.), and in his 18th year (841 B.C.) he defeated King Hazael of Damascus at Mount Hermon. The kings of Tyre and Sidon, as well as King Jehu of Israel, paid tribute and at once became Assyrian vassals. On the famous Black Obelisk, found in 1845 by Henry Layard at Nimrud, and now in the British Museum, the payment of Jehu's tribute is depicted in sculpture. On the 2d of the 5 rows of relief King Jehu is seen kissing the ground at the feet of Shalmaneser and offering him, as tribute, bars and vessels of precious metals, which are carried by Israelite courtiers (see fig. 255, also fig. 246).

2. Shalmaneser V (727-722 B.C.), son and successor of Tiglath-pileser III. Hardly any contemporary records of this king have survived, and our knowledge of the events of his brief reign depends mainly on the Bible (2 Ki 17:3; 18:9) and Josephus (*Ant.* ix. 14). Early in his reign he carried out a campaign against the Phoenicians. At this time King Hoshea of

Israel assured Shalmaneser of his loyalty, but later, trusting in So of Egypt, rebelled against his Assyrian overlord. Shalmaneser marched into Israel and began the 3-year siege of Samaria which ended with the destruction of the city, the deportation of its population, and the cessation of the kingdom of Israel (2 Ki 17:3-6). Although Sargon II, the successor of Shalmaneser, claimed later to have conquered Samaria in his 1st regnal year, the chronological data of the Bible seem to indicate that Samaria fell shortly before Shalmaneser's death, in 723/22 B.C.

Shama (shā′mȧ). [Heb. *Shamaʿ*, "he hears."] A son of Hotham the Aroerite, and one of David's "mighty men" (1 Chr 11:44).

Shamariah. *See* Shemariah, 2.

Shambles. *See* Meat Market.

Shamed. *See* Shemed.

Shamer. *See* Shemer, 1 and 2.

Shamgar (shăm′gär). [Heb. *Shamgar,* probably a Hurrian name, such as *Shimgari,* " (the god) Shimike has given," attested in cuneiform texts.] A son of Anath (Jgs 3:31). To judge from his name, Shamgar may have been a Hurrian, but his father's name is Semitic (there was a Canaanite goddess named Anath), so that the conclusion is valid that Shamgar's father was a Canaanite or even an Israelite. Shamgar fought against the Philistines and slew 600 of them singlehanded. His efforts delivered Israel from the Philistines, and made the highways, which had been controlled by the Philistines, safe for the Hebrews to travel (chs 3:31; 5:6). He is not called a judge, and no indication is given that he was considered a judge by the Israelites whom he delivered from oppression.

Shamhuth (shăm′hŭth). [Heb. *Shamhûth,* " (born at the time of a) horrible event."] An Izrahite, David's captain for the 5th month (1 Chr 27:8), possibly identical with Shammah (2 Sa 23:25) and Shammoth (1 Chr 11:27).

Shamir (shā′mēr). [Heb. *Shamîr,* "thorn," or "emery."]

1. A Levite of the sons of Micah (1 Chr 24:24).

2. A town in the hill country of Judah (Jos 15:48), identified with *Khirbet Sômerah,* about 13 mi. west-southwest of Hebron.

3. A town in the hill country of Ephraim, the home of the judge Tola (Jgs 10:1, 2). It has not yet been identified, unless it is Samaria, as the LXX (Codex Alexandrinus) suggests.

Shamlai. *See* Shalmai.

Shamma (shăm′ȧ). [Heb. *Shammaʾ,* "horror."] A descendant of Asher (1 Chr 7:37).

Shammah (shăm′ȧ). [Heb. *Shammah,* "horror." The name attested in Assyrian as *Shamâ.*]

1. A son of Reuel (Gen 36:13; 1 Chr 1:37), and thus a descendant of both Esau and Ishmael (Gen 36:3, 4). He became an Edomite chief (v 17).

2. The 3d son of Jesse and brother of David (1 Sa 16:9; 17:13), also called Shimea. *See* Shimeah, 1.

3. One of David's first 3 "mighty men," a son of Agee the Hararite (2 Sa 23:11).

4. A Harodite, one of David's 30 "mighty men" (2 Sa 23:25), possibly identical with Shamhuth the Izrahite (1 Chr 27:8), and with Shammoth (shăm′ŏth) [Heb. *Shammôth*] the Harorite (ch 11:27).

Shammai (shăm′ȧ-ī). [Heb. *Shammay,* meaning uncertain.]

1. A descendant of Jerahmeel of the tribe of Judah (1 Chr 2:26, 28, 32).

2. A descendant of Caleb, son of Hezron, of the tribe of Judah (1 Chr 2:42, 44).

3. A descendant of Caleb, son of Jephunneh, of the tribe of Judah (1 Chr 4:17).

Shammoth. *See* Shammah, 4.

Shammua (shă-mū′ȧ), KJV once **Shammuah** (shă-mū′ȧ). [Heb. *Shammûaʿ,* "heard (by God)."]

1. The representative of the tribe of Reuben among the 12 spies (Num 13:4).

2. A son of David, born in Jerusalem (2 Sa 5:13, 14; 1 Chr 14:3, 4), called Shimea (a name synonymous with Shammua) in 1 Chr 3:5.

3. The head of a family of priests in the time of Joiakim (Neh 12:12, 18).

4. A Levite descended from Jeduthun (Neh 11:17).

Shammuah. *See* Shammua, 2.

Shamsherai (shăm′shĕ-rī). [Heb. *Shamsheray.*] A descendant of Benjamin (1 Chr 8:1, 26).

Shapham (shā′făm). [Heb. *Shapham.*] A descendant of Gad (1 Chr 5:11, 12).

Shaphan (shā′făn). [Heb. *Shaphan,* "rock badger." The name occurs also in a Phoenician inscription.] A royal scribe, or secretary, in the reign of Josiah. When the book of the Law was found in the Temple, Hilkiah, the high priest, gave it to Shaphan, who, after he had read it, read it also to the king. He, with others, was sent by the king to Huldah, the prophetess, to inquire about the will of God (2 Ki 22:3-14; 2 Chr 34:15-20).

The name Shaphan appears also as the father of a number of men of the next generation: Ahikam (2 Ki 22:12; 2 Chr 34:20; Jer 26:24; 39:14), Elasah (Jer 29:3), Gemariah (ch 36:10), Jaazaniah (Eze 8:11), and through Ahikam as grandfather of Gedaliah (2 Ki 25:22; etc.). It is impossible to determine whether only one Shaphan was the father of all these, and, if so, whether he was the secretary of Josiah.

Shaphat (shā'făt). [Heb. *Shaphaṭ*, "he has judged," a name attested in an ancient Hebrew seal inscription, and in a Phoenician inscription.]
1. The representative of the tribe of Simeon among the 12 spies (Num 13:5).
2. A Gadite who lived in Bashan (1 Chr 5:11, 12).
3. The overseer of David's cattle in the valley (1 Chr 27:29).
4. The father of Elisha the prophet (1 Ki 19:16, 19).
5. One of the postexilic descendants of David (1 Chr 3:1, 22).

Shapher. *See* Shepher.

Shaphir (shā'fēr), KJV **Saphir** (sā'fēr). [Heb. *Shaphîr*, "beautiful."] A town mentioned by Micah (Mic 1:11), tentatively identified with *Khirbet el-Kôm*, about 8 mi. west-northwest of Hebron.

Sharai (shá-rā'ī). [Heb. *Sharay*, meaning uncertain.] An Israelite who married a foreign wife in the time of Ezra (Ezr 10:40).

Sharaim. *See* Shaaraim, 1.

Sharar (shā'rēr). [Heb. *Sharar*, "firm."] A man whose son Ahiam was one of David's "mighty men" (2 Sa 23:8, 33), called Sacher (KJV "Sacar") in 1 Chr 11:35.

Sharezer (shá-rē'zēr), KJV once **Sherezer** (shĕ-rē'zēr). [Heb. *Śar'eṣer;* Akkadian *Shar-uṣur*, "protect the king." The Dead Sea Isaiah scroll (1QIsᵃ) spells the name *śr'wṣr* (the Masoretic text has *śr'ṣr*), indicating by the additional consonant *w* the correct pronunciation of the Akkadian name.]
1. A son of Sennacherib. He and his brother Adrammelech assassinated their father, but neither of them gained the throne, and both escaped to Armenia (2 Ki 19:37; Is 37:38).
2. A man sent with a companion from Bethel (RSV) to the priests, evidently at Jerusalem (Zec 7:2), to inquire whether the fasts of the 5th month (v 3), observed to mourn the destruction of Jerusalem by Nebuchadnezzar, should be continued now that the city was being rebuilt. The fact that this postexilic Israelite had an

Akkadian name indicates that he was born in Mesopotamia.

Sharon (shăr'ŭn), KJV once **Saron** (sā'rŏn). [Heb. *Sharôn*, "plain"; Gr. *Sarōn;* Phoenician *Shrn;* Egyptian *S3rn3*.]
1. An undulating coastal plain of Palestine, between Joppa and the Carmel ridge (Map II, B-2), which has a length of about 50 mi. and a width varying from 6 to 12 mi. The area is fertile (see Is 35:2) and suitable for pasturing (1 Chr 27:29; Is 65:10). However, sand dunes along the coast have been encroaching upon the fertile land, with the result that the cultivable area is now smaller than in ancient times. Many people of that area accepted the Christian faith after the healing of a palsy-stricken man in Lydda by Peter (Acts 9:35).
2. A region east of the Jordan (1 Chr 5:16); not identified with certainty. Some believe it to be the highland between the Arnon and Heshbon; others think the name is a scribal error for Sirion (Heb. *Śiryôn*), which is Mount Hermon. The 2 names are practically identical in unpointed Hebrew.

Sharonite (shăr'ŭn-īt). [Heb. *Sharônî*.] The appellative of Shitrai, a herdsman of David's in the Plain of Sharon (1 Chr 27:29).

Sharuhen (shá-rōō'hĕn). [Heb. *Sharûchen*, Egyptian *Sh3rh3n*.] A city assigned to Simeon (Jos 19:6), probably identical with Shilhim (ch 15:32), and the Shaaraim of 1 Chr 4:31. It is the city which, according to Egyptian records of the 18th dynasty, the Hyksos made their headquarters after they were expelled from Egypt. The records also state that Pharaoh Ahmose, conqueror of the Hyksos, besieged the city for 3 years, at the end of which he conquered it and drove the Hyksos to the north (*ANET* 233). It has been identified with *Tell el-Fâr'ah*, 14 mi. east of Raphia (Map VI, F-1). Sir Flinders Petrie directed excavations there from 1927 to 1929, but identified *Tell el-Fâr'ah* erroneously with Beth-pelet.

Lit.: Flinders Petrie, *et al.*, *Beth-pelet* (London: British School of Archaeology in Egypt, 1930, 1932), 2 vols. W. F. Albright, *BASOR* 33 (1929), 7.

Shashai (shā'shī). [Heb. *Shashay*, meaning uncertain. The name occurs in cuneiform inscriptions as *Shashî*.] An Israelite married to a foreign wife in Ezra's time (Ezr 10:40).

Shashak (shā'shăk). [Heb. *Shashaq*.] A descendant of Benjamin and father of Iphdeiah and Penuel (1 Chr 8:1, 14, 25).

Shaul (shā'ŭl), KJV twice **Saul** (sôl). [Heb. *Sha'ûl*, "asked for." The name occurs in Phoenician inscriptions, and as *Saûli* in cuneiform documents.]

1. A king of Edom, originating from Rehoboth on the Euphrates (Gen 36:37; 1 Chr 1:48).

2. A son of Simeon by a Canaanite woman (Gen 46:10; Ex 6:15; 1 Chr 4:24), and founder of a tribal family, the Shaulites (shā'ŭl-īts) [Heb. *Sha'ûlî*] (Num 26: 12, 13).

3. A Kohathite Levite (1 Chr 6:24), considered by some to be identical with Joel, an ancestor of Samuel (v 36). *See* Joel, 1.

Shaulites. *See* Shaul, 2.

Shave, Shaving. [Heb. usually *galach*, "to shave"; Gr. *xuraō*, "to shave."] Shaving was required in the priestly diagnosis of certain skin diseases (Lev 13:33), and in the rite of purification from leprosy (ch 14:8, 9). God forbade His people to shave off the corners of their beards (ch 21:5), probably because of the idolatrous connotations of the act. Among the ancients the shaving of the head was a sign of mourning (Job 1:20; cf. Deut 21:12). At the expiration of a Nazirite vow or in case of ritual defilement during the period of the vow, the Nazirite was to shave his whole head (Num 6:9, 18; cf. Acts 21:24). Otherwise, he was forbidden to use a razor while subject to the vow (Num 6:5). At one time Hanun, king of the Ammonites, cut off half of the beards of the Israelites whom David had sent to him as emissaries of peace—a supreme insult (2 Sa 10:4; 1 Chr 19:4). Isaiah spoke of the forthcoming Assyrian invasion of Palestine as a figurative razor drawn by God over the land (Is 7:20). *See* Razor.

Shaveh. *See* King's Valley.

Shaveh Kiriathaim. *See* Kiriathaim.

Shavsha (shăv'shả). [Heb. *Shawsha'*, probably an Aramaic name, meaning uncertain.] A scribe, or secretary, of David (1 Chr 18:16), and, according to his name, probably an Aramaean. The handling of state papers may have necessitated the employment of a foreigner who was in command of several languages. In 1 Ki 4:3 two of Solomon's scribes are called sons of Shisha (Heb. *Shisha'*), possibly identical with Shavsha. The difference in spelling in consonantal Hebrew consists only in the substitution of a *y* for a *w*, 2 letters practically indistinguishable in postexilic Hebrew manuscripts. He is possibly identical also with Sheva

(2 Sa 20:25), an abbreviated form of Shavsha, and with Seraiah (ch 8:17; *see* Seraiah, 2). If he is identical with Seraiah it would indicate that at some time he had adopted a Hebrew name.

Sheal (shē'ăl). [Heb. *She'al*, "asking."] A member of the family of Bani. He was among those who were married to foreign wives in the time of Ezra (Ezr 10:29).

Shealtiel (shḗ-ăl'tĭ-ĕl), KJV 3 times **Salathiel** (sȧ-lā'thĭ-ĕl). [Heb. and Aramaic *She'alti'el*, "I have asked God." The name is attested in cuneiform records as *Salti-ilu;* Gr. *Salathiēl.*] Son of Jeconiah (Jehoiachin) of Judah (Mt 1:12), and father of *Zerubbabel (Ezr 3:2, 8; 5:2; Neh 12:1; Hag 1:1, 12, 14; 2:2, 23). But Lk 3:27 says that Shealtiel was the son of Neri, of the line of David through Nathan. This apparent discrepancy has been explained by assuming that one of Jeconiah's descendants, perhaps a son, died childless, and that Neri married the widow and Shealtiel was born to this union. Neri would thus be the blood father (Lk), but Jeconiah a legal ancestor (Mt). *See* Genealogy; Father.

Sheariah (shē'ȧ-rī'ȧ). [Heb. *She'aryah*, "gate of Yahweh."] A descendant of King Saul through Jonathan (1 Chr 8:38; 9:44).

Shearing House. *See* Beth-eked of the Shepherds.

Shearjashub (shē'är-jȧ'shŭb). [Heb. *She'ar yashûb*, "A remnant shall return."] One of Isaiah's sons whose name was intended to be a reminder of the certainty of a prophecy pronounced by his father (Is 7:3; cf. 10:20, 21).

Sheba, I (shē'bȧ). [Heb. *Sheba'*, in ancient South Arabic *Sb'*.]

1. A son of Raamah, grandson of Cush (Gen 10:7; 1 Chr 1:9), and an ancestor of an Arabic tribe known as the Sabeans. In OT times the descendants of Sheba appear as a wealthy nation, trading in gold, incense, and precious stones (Ps 72: 10; Is 60:6; Jer 6:20; Eze 27:22; 38:13). Although there have been conflicting claims for Ethiopia and Arabia as the home of the queen of Sheba, it is now generally held that it was a queen of this Arabian Sheba, in the area now called Yemen, who made a visit to Solomon (1 Ki 10:1-13). The Sabeans were one of the most important peoples of all Arabia. A wealth of inscriptions, many still unpublished, bear witness to their religion, history, and culture. They built large dams and an extensive irrigation system, which made their country the most fertile in an-

432. Excavating the Moon temple at *Marib*, the ancient capital of the queen of Sheba

cient Arabia. This is why it was known in classical times as *Arabia Felix,* "Happy Arabia." The neglect and eventual destruction of these dams brought about the gradual eclipse of the Sabeans as a nation. The Sabean capital lay at the site of modern *Marib,* which contains many well-preserved ruins. A brief and very successful excavation was carried out there in 1951. See R. L. Bowen, *Archaeological Discoveries in South Arabia* (Baltimore, 1958), pp. 215-286. This Arabic tribe should not be confused with the Cushite tribe of Seba which lived farther to the north in Arabia.

2. A son of Joktan, and thus a descendant of Shem (Gen 10:28; 1 Chr 1:20, 22). In contrast to the Sabeans of South Arabia, the Joktanite Sabeans are probably the *Saba* of northern Arabia mentioned in the inscriptions of Tiglath-pileser III (745-727 B.C.) and Sargon II (722-705 B.C.) as allies of the *Aribi* (*ANET* 283, 286).

3. A son of Jokshan, and grandson of Abraham (Gen 25:3; 1 Chr 1:32). He was probably the ancestor of a tribe that dwelt in Arabia of which nothing is known.

Sheba, II (shē′bà). [Heb. *Sheba‘,* "oath," or "seven."]

1. A Benjamite who, after the collapse of Absalom's rebellion, led a revolt against David and tried to separate the 10 tribes from Judah. David's army under Joab's direction besieged him in Abel, in northern Israel. When the inhabitants of Abel saw that the revolt had failed they slew Sheba and threw his head over the wall to Joab (2 Sa 20:1-22).

2. A descendant of Gad (1 Chr 5:13).

3. A town in Simeon (Jos 19:2). There is some uncertainty about its site. Some think that on the basis of the LXX it is identical with *Shema, 5; others, that it is an abbreviated form of Beer-sheba.

Sheba, Queen of. *See* Queen of Sheba.

Shebah. *See* Shibah.

Shebam. *See* Sibmah.

Shebaniah (shĕb′à-nī′à). [Heb. *Shebanyah* and *Shebanyahû,* meaning uncertain. The name is attested on an ancient Hebrew seal, and is similar to the Akkadian name *Shubunu-yâma.*]

1. A Levite Temple musician in the reign of David (1 Chr 15:24).

2. The ancestor of a priestly family represented by a priest named Joseph in the days of the high priest Joiakim (Neh 12:14). Some identify him with the Shecaniah of v 3. *See* Shecaniah, 3.

3. A priest who set his seal to Nehemiah's covenant (Neh 10:4), possibly representing the family of Shebaniah, 2.

4. A Levite who assisted in the reading of the Law in Nehemiah's time (Neh 9:4, 5), probably identical with either Shebaniah, 5 or Shebaniah, 6.

5 and 6. Two Levites who set their seals to Nehemiah's covenant (Neh 10: 10, 12); one was probably identical with Shebaniah, 4.

Shebarim (shĕb′à-rīm). [Heb. *Shebarîm,* "quarries."] A locality now unidentified, probably a quarry near Ai (Jos 7:5).

Shebat (shĕ-bät′), KJV **Sebat** (sē′băt). [Heb. *Shebat,* a loan word from the Akkadian *Shabâṭu.*] The 11th month of the Jewish religious year (Zec 1:7). It began at the new moon of January or February. *See* Year.

Sheber (shē′bĕr). [Heb. *Sheber,* meaning uncertain.] A son of Caleb (son of Hezron), by his concubine Maacah (1 Chr 2:48).

Shebna (shĕb′nà), RSV twice **Shebnah** (shĕb′nà). [Heb. *Shebna′* and *Shebnah,* probably a shortened form of Shebaniah. The name is attested on an ancient Hebrew seal and on an inscribed jar handle.] Hezekiah's high palace official, and steward, or treasurer (Is 22:15), who negotiated with the Rabshakeh when Sennacherib demanded the surrender of Jerusalem (2 Ki 18:18, 26, 37; 19:2; etc.). Isaiah reproved him for making for himself a rock-hewn sepulcher and predicted that he would die in a distant land (Is 22:15-19). The palace official had probably been selfishly thinking of himself when the nation was in peril. In 1870 C. Clermont-Ganneau discovered 2 Hebrew inscriptions, 1 above and 1 at the side of a door of an ancient tomb in the village of *Silwan,* overlooking the Kidron Valley. The inscriptions, which are now in the British Museum, were so weathered that for a long time all attempts at decipherment ended in failure, but N. Avigad finally succeeded in deciphering them. One inscription reads: [1] "This is [the sepulchre of . . .]yahu who is over the house. There is no silver and gold here, [2] but [his bones] and the bones of his slave-wife with him. Cursed be the man [3] who will open this!"

The 2d inscription reads merely: " (Tomb-)chamber in the side of the rock. . . ." Although the name of the owner of the tomb unfortunately is broken, the paleography of the characters makes it certain that the inscriptions were cut in the rock in the time of Hezekiah, and the title of the tomb owner, "the one who is over the house," is the same as that borne by Shebna, so that an identification with the Biblical Shebna is possible and has been generally accepted by scholars (N. Avigad, *IEJ* 3 [1953], 137-152; 5 [1955], 163-166). Since the 1st of the 2 inscriptions is the second-largest Hebrew stone inscription of the period of the kings of Judah, it is of some importance to scholars and Biblical historians, as it is also of interest, to be able to identify with reasonable certainty the actual tomb that was the object of one of Isaiah's prophecies.

Shebnah. *See* Shebna.

Shebuel (shĕ-bū'ĕl), or **Shubael** (shoō'bȧ-ĕl). [Heb. *Shebû'el* and *Shûba'el*. If the 2d term, which is supported by the LXX, is correct, the meaning is "Return, O God!"]

1. A grandson of Moses, and ancestor of a family of Gershonite Levites (1 Chr 23:16; 26:24; 24:20).

2. A son of Heman, and the ancestor of a family of singers (1 Chr 25:4, 20).

Shecaniah (shĕk'ȧ-nī'ȧ), KJV frequently **Shechaniah** (shĕk'ȧ-nī'ȧ). [Heb. *Shekanyah* and *Shekanyahû,* "Yahweh has established His dwelling."]

1. A descendant of Aaron, and ancestral head of a family that became the 10th of the 24 courses into which David organized the priests for service in the Temple (1 Chr 24:11).

2. A distributor of the freewill offerings for the priests in Hezekiah's time (2 Chr 31:15).

3. A chief priest who returned from Babylonia with Zerubbabel (Neh 12:3, 7). Some think that he is identical with the ancestor of a family of priests of the next generation called Shebaniah in v 14, since in postexilic Hebrew the letters *b* and *k* were very similar. *See* Shebaniah, 2.

4. The head of a family descended from David (1 Chr 3:21, 22; Ezr 8:3, 5).

5. A son of Jehiel of the "sons of Elam." He became the spokesman of those who had taken foreign wives but repented of their action and expressed willingness to put them away (Ezr 10:2, 3). However, he does not seem to have been involved in this sin himself, since his name does not appear among the members of the family of Elam who put their wives away (v 26).

6. A man whose son, Shemaiah, assisted Nehemiah in rebuilding the wall of Jerusalem (Neh 3:29).

7. The father-in-law of Tobiah the Ammonite (Neh 6:17, 18).

Shechaniah. *See* Shecaniah.

Shechem (shē'kĕm), KJV once **Sichem** (sī'kĕm). [Heb. *Shekem,* "shoulder." The personal name is attested in inscriptions of Palmyra and South Arabia; Gr. *Suchem.*]

1. The son of Hamor, a Hivite prince of the city of Shechem. He fell in love with Dinah, Jacob's daughter, dishonored her, and took her to his house. Desiring to marry her, he agreed to submit to the act of circumcision with all the citizens of Shechem, a condition placed before them by Dinah's brothers for giving him their consent to the marriage. When the victims were indisposed by the postoperative effects, Simeon and Levi treacherously attacked the city and put to death all the men of Shechem, including the young prince (Gen 33:18 to 34:31).

2. A son of Gilead, and ancestral head of a tribal family, the Shechemites (Num 26:31; Jos 17:2).

3. A son of Shemida of the tribe of Manasseh (1 Chr 7:19).

4. A fortified Canaanite city in central Palestine, in the vicinity of which Abraham pitched his 1st camp and erected his 1st altar to God after arriving in Canaan (Gen 12:6, 7). Egyptian texts (*ANET*

433. The mound of *Balâṭah*, ancient Shechem, in the middle of the pass between Mount Gerizim (left) and Mount Ebal (right)

230) report a military campaign of the Pharaoh Sesostris III (1880-1840 B.C.) against Shechem, spelled *Skmm* in the texts, which must have taken place during the time of Abraham's sojourning in Canaan. Jacob settled in the vicinity of Shechem after his return from Paddan-aram, and bought a piece of land there where Joseph was later buried (Gen 33: 18, 19; Jos 24:32). While Jacob sojourned at Shechem his sons Simeon and Levi massacred the male population of Shechem in revenge for the defiling of their sister Dinah (Gen 34:25-29). Jacob condemned this action and, fearing reprisals from the surrounding people, moved to another part of the country (chs 34:30; 35:3, 5; 49:5-7). However, not long after, the sons of Jacob apparently felt that it was safe to return to that area, for they pastured their father's flocks near Shechem (ch 37:12, 13).

During the invasion of Canaan by the Israelites (c. 1400 B.C.) Shechem is not mentioned among the conquered cities, but the fact that the Israelites could hold a great rally on the slopes of Mount Ebal and Mount Gerizim (Jos 8:30, 33), where Shechem was located, shows that the city was either friendly to the Israelites or awe-stricken by Israelite victories so that it did not molest them. An *Amarna letter written by the king of Jerusalem a few years later states that Shechem (written *Shakmi*) had been given to the Habiru (*ANET* 489), by which the *Hebrews may be meant. In the distribution of the country among the Israelite tribes Shechem seems to have been assigned to Manasseh, but lay close to the border of Ephraim (ch 17:7). It was furthermore assigned as residence city of the Kohathite Levites and a city of refuge

(Jos 20:7; 21:21). Joshua's farewell address was delivered while the nation was gathered at Shechem (ch 24:1).

In the period of the judges Shechem had a temple dedicated to Baal-berith (Jgs 8:33; 9:4). The city was the home of Abimelech, a son of Gideon by his concubine. After his father's death Abimelech, assisted by the Shechemites, made himself king, but later his fellow citizens turned against him, whereupon he retaliated by destroying their city (ch 9:1-7, 23-57). Shechem again became important in the period of the kings. It was there that the 10 tribes of Israel rejected Rehoboam, Solomon's son, as king and crowned Jeroboam instead (1 Ki 12:1-19). The new king fortified the city and used it for some time as his capital (v 25). It seems to have lost its importance later when Samaria, only 7 mi. to the northwest of Shechem, became the capital of the country. The Samaria ostraca (*see* Potsherd) mention Shechem as paying taxes to the royal storehouse, and the prophet Jeremiah mentions it as inhabited after the destruction of the kingdoms of Israel and Judah (Jer 41:5).

During the Hellenistic period it became the chief city of the Samaritans (Jos. *Ant.* xi. 8. 6). It was captured by John Hyrcanus (*ibid.* xiii. 9. 1). Flavius Vespasian passed a night at Shechem during the Jewish War (Jos. *War* iv. 8. 1), and when the city was rebuilt after that war, it was named Flavia Neapolis after him. The latter name has been retained in the form of *Nâblus*, for that of the present-day town, which has a population of about 25,000, mostly Moslems, and a small Samaritan community of about 200 people.

OT Shechem lay at the eastern exit of

the narrow valley between the mountains Ebal and Gerizim (Map VI, D-3) at a site now called *Balâṭah*. Neapolis, or *Nâblus*, the later successor of Shechem, lies on the watershed 1 mi. to the west of the old Shechem, at an altitude of 1,870 ft. above sea level, and occupies parts of the slopes of the 2 adjacent mountains Ebal and Gerizim.

Balâṭah, OT Shechem, was excavated first by the Germans under the direction of E. Sellin and G. Welter in 1913-1914, 1926, 1928, 1931, and 1934, and since 1956 by an American expedition under the direction of G. Ernest Wright. The 1st expedition carried on its work in an unscientific and haphazard way, and excavated parts of the tremendous fortifications of the city (including the wall pictured in fig. 519), the northwestern gate, and a large structure which has been interpreted as a temple. The excavators were fortunate in finding 2 cuneiform tablets and a proto-Semitic alphabetic inscription. The American expedition excavated the eastern gate in the ancient city wall (see fig. 434), and in other areas checked the levels of occupation and cleared up the archeological history of the site. During the 1st season of the American excavations a coin dating from *c.* 500 B.C. was discovered, the earliest coin ever found in Palestine.

Lit.: W. Harrelson, *et al.,* "Shechem, 'Navel of the Land,'" *BA* 20 (1957), 1-32; H. C. Kee and L. E. Toombs, "The Second Season of Excavation at Biblical Shechem," *ibid.,* 81-105.

434. The east gate of ancient Shechem excavated

Shechemites (shĕ′kĕm-īts). [Heb. *Shikmî.*] Descendants of *Shechem, 2 (Num 26:31).

Shedeur (shĕd′ê-ēr). [Heb. *Shedê′ûr,* "Shadai is light."] A Reubenite (Num 1:5; etc.).

Sheep. [Heb. *rachel, śeh,* and *ṣo′n;* Gr. *probaton* and *probation.*] The most common sheep of Palestine, the *Ovis laticaudata,* differs from that of northern countries in its loosely hanging ears, and its broad, fat tail, which weighs from 10 to 15 lb., even 20 lb. or more. Female animals have no horns. The fat tail (Heb. *'alyah,* KJV "rump") is regarded as a special delicacy among the Arabs. The sacrificial laws specified that it was to be burned (Lev 3:9; 7:3; 8:25; 9:19). The wool is usually white (Ps 147:16; Is 1:18; Dan 7:9), but that of some sheep is black or a deep brown in color (Gen 30:32, 33), and was used for making garments (Job 31:19, 20). Both rams and female sheep were prescribed for sacrifices (Ex 29:3; Lev 4:32; 5:6; 8:18; etc.). Sheep-shearing time was a feast of joy (see Gen 38:12; 1 Sa 25:4-8). The sheep was considered to be a stupid, timid, defenseless animal, patient in sufferings (Ps 119:176; Is 53:6, 7; Jer 11:19; Mt 9:36). God's people are frequently likened to sheep (Ps 78:52; 95:7; Mt 10:6, 16; Jn 10:1-6; 1 Pe 2:25; etc.).

Sheep Gate. [Heb. *sha'ar haṣṣo′n.*] A gate (Neh 3:1, 32; 12:39; Jn 5:2, RSV) in the north wall of Nehemiah's Jerusalem, apparently at the eastern end. See Maps XVII, XVIII, also fig. 259. It is probable that there was a sheep market in the vicinity giving the gate its name (see Jn 5:2; KJV; however, the word translated "sheep market" should probably be rendered "sheep gate"). Since the northern wall of Jerusalem in the time of the kings and of Nehemiah was also probably the northern wall of the Temple area, it is possible that the Sheep Gate was identical with the "upper [KJV "high"] gate," or "Gate of Benjamin" (2 Ki 15:35; 2 Chr 23:20; 27:3; Jer 20:2; 37:13; Eze 9:2; Zec 14:10), and that the name Sheep Gate was a name given to it in the postexilic period.

Sheep Market. A rendering of the Gr. *probatikos* (Jn 5:2, KJV), literally, "belonging to sheep" (RSV "sheep gate"). Although it is reasonable to assume that there was a sheep market in Jerusalem, where sheep were sold especially for sacrificial purposes, the reference of v 2 seems to be rather to the *Sheep Gate.

Sheepcote. A term appearing in the KJV as a rendering of: (1) the Heb. *naweh* (2 Sa 7:8; 1 Chr 17:7), "place for pasture"; (2) the Heb. *gidrath haṣṣo'n* (1 Sa 24:3), "stone sheepfold." The term "cotes" appears in 2 Chr 32:28, KJV, in the expression "cotes for flocks," as a rendering of the Heb. *'awerôth,* "pens," "stalls." *See* Sheepfold.

Sheepfold. An enclosure to protect sheep and goats from inclement weather, from marauders, and from wild animals such as jackals and hyenas. For the wandering nomad a sheepfold was, and still is, no more than a hastily erected enclosure of thorny bushes and shrubbery, but under sedentary conditions permanent folds were built (Num 32:16). These consisted of stone walls, sometimes topped with branches of thorny shrubs. Inside were shelters to protect the animals from the cold and rain of winter. Several shepherds could use one fold, and Lk 2:8, 15, 20 seems to indicate that this was the case with the shepherds to whom the angels announced the birth of the Messiah. The enclosing wall had only one gate (Jn 10:1), which was guarded by the shepherds, who took turns as watchmen. When a shepherd left the fold in the morning his own sheep would separate from the others and would follow him (vs 2-5). In the mountainous areas of Palestine large caves abound which have been used as sheepfolds since ancient times (cf. 1 Sa 24:3). These required only a short wall with gate to complete the enclosure and hence were very popular with shepherds.

Sheerah (shē'ē-rȧ), KJV **Sherah** (shē'rȧ). [Heb. *She'erah,* "kinswoman."] A daughter or granddaughter of Ephraim; she built Upper and Lower Beth-horon, and the now-unidentified town Uzzen-sheerah (1 Chr 7:24).

Sheet. A rendering of: (1) The Heb. *sadîn,* "a garment," "a wrap" (Jgs 14:12, 13; RSV "linen garment"). Possibly a large rectangular piece of linen wrapped loosely about the body by day, and used as a wrap by night, is meant. Thirty such linen garments figured in the riddle Samson put to his guests at a nuptial feast. (2) The Gr. *othonē,* "linen cloth," "sheet." In vision Peter saw "a great sheet" containing all manner of unclean creatures (Acts 10:11; 11:5).

Shehariah (shē'hȧ-rī'ȧ). [Heb. *Shecharyah,* meaning uncertain.] A descendant of Benjamin (1 Chr 8:26).

Shekel. [Heb. *sheqel;* Aramaic *teqel;* Ugaritic *ṯql;* Akkadian *shiqlu.*] A weight used for metals (Gen 24:22). The shekel was used as a recognized standard in financial trans-

actions in the early period of the ancient world before coined money was introduced in the 7th cent. B.C. So far no inscribed shekel weight has been found in Palestinian excavations, and uninscribed shekel weights that have come to light vary in weight from about 10.2 to 12 grams. A weight found at *Tell Beit Mirsim* equaling 8 minas (= 400 shekels) weighed 4,565 grams, giving the weight for the shekel as 11.4 grams (176.85 grains); see *AASOR* 21/22 (1943), 76-78. This seems to represent a good average weight for the uninscribed Palestinian shekel weights, and has been taken as the basis for the computation of the other OT weights: bekah, gerah, mina, pim, and talent. In Mt 17:27, RSV "shekel" is a rendering of the Gr *statēr,* a Greek silver coin (*see* Money, 2).

Shelah, I (shē'lȧ), KJV frequently **Salah** (sā'lȧ) and once **Sala** (sā'lȧ). [Heb. *Shelach;* Gr. *Sala,* "javelin."]

1. A son or grandson of Arpachshad, or Arphaxad (Gen 10:24; 11:12-15; 1 Chr 1:18; Lk 3:35), one of the postdiluvian ancestors of Abraham.

2. A pool in Jerusalem (Neh 3:15, RSV; KJV "Silvah"), better known as Pool of *Siloam.

Shelah, II (shē'lȧ). [Heb. *Shelah,* "petition."] The 3d son of Judah by Shua, his Canaanite wife (Gen 38:2, 5, 11, 14, 26), and ancestral head of the Shelanites (Num 26:20).

Shelanites (shē'lȧn-īts). [Heb. *Shelanî.*] Descendants of Shelah, II (Num 26:20).

Shelemiah (shĕl'ē-mī'ȧ). [Heb. *Shelemyah* and *Shelemyahû,* "Yahweh has completed," "Yahweh has kept peace," or "Yahweh has recompensed." The name occurs in the ancient Hebrew *Lachish Letters and on seals in the spellings of the Bible, and in a similar form (*Shalamyâma*) in Akkadian.]

1. A Levite gatekeeper appointed in David's time (1 Chr 26:13, 14), called *Meshelemiah in chs 9:21 and 26:1, 9.

2. Son of Cushi (Jer 36:14).

3. Son of Abdeel, and a royal officer commanded by King Jehoiakim to arrest Jeremiah and Baruch (Jer 36:26).

4. A man whose son Irijah arrested Jeremiah in the gate of Jerusalem and accused him of desertion to the Babylonians (Jer 37:13).

5. A man whose son Jucal was one of the princes who stood up against Jeremiah (Jer 38:1, 4).

6 and 7. Two men who were married to foreign wives in the time of Ezra (Ezr 10:39, 41).

8. Father of the Hananiah who assisted Nehemiah in rebuilding the wall of Jerusalem (Neh 3:30), possibly identical with Shelemiah, 9.

9. A priest, appointed as treasurer by Nehemiah to distribute the tithe among the Levites (Neh 13:13), possibly identical with Shelemiah, 8.

Sheleph (shē′lĕf). [Heb. *Sheleph,* "ancestor," or "brother-in-law."] A son of Joktan (Gen 10:26; 1 Chr 1:20), and ancestor of an Arabic tribe. Two Yemenite tribes near Aden bear the names *es-Salif* and *es-Suláf,* which names may go back to the Biblical Sheleph. The unidentified Arabic people, the *Salapenes,* mentioned by Ptolemy, may also be descendants of Sheleph.

Shelesh (shē′lĕsh). [Heb. *Shelesh,* "triad."] A descendant of Asher (1 Chr 7:35).

Shelomi (shĕ-lō′mī). [Heb. *Shelomî,* "peaceful," or "perfect."] An Asherite whose son Ahihud was tribal prince in the latter part of the wilderness wanderings (Num 34:27).

Shelomith (shĕ-lō′mĭth). [Heb. *Shelomîth,* the feminine form of *Shelomî,* "peaceful," or "perfect."]

1. A Danite woman, mother of the Israelite who was executed in the wilderness for blaspheming the name of the Lord (Lev 24:11).

2. A Gershonite Levite (1 Chr 23:9, KJV). The RSV, following the pre-Masoretic text, calls him Shelomoth (shĕ-lō′mŏth) [Heb. *Shelomôth*].

3. A Kohathite Levite (1 Chr 23:18; cf. v 12); called Shelomoth (cf. Shelomith, 2) in ch 24:22.

4. A descendant of Moses through Eliezer. He and his brethren were appointed by David over the dedicated treasures (1 Chr 26:25, 26, 28, KJV). The RSV, following the pre-Masoretic text, calls him Shelomoth (cf. Shelomith, 2).

5. A son of King Rehoboam (2 Chr 11:20).

6. A descendant of Bani according to the RSV of Ezr 8:10, which is based on the LXX. He led 160 male members of the family of Bani from Babylonia to Jerusalem with Ezra. His father's name was Josiphiah.

7. A daughter of Zerubbabel (1 Chr 3:19).

Shelomoth. *See* Shelomith, 2, 3, 4.

Shelumiel (shĕ-lū′mĭ-ĕl). [Heb. *Shelumî'el,* "God is my peace." The name is attested on an ancient Hebrew seal as *Shlm'l.*] The prince of the tribe of Simeon early in the wilderness wanderings (Num 1:6; 2:12; 7:36, 41; 10:19).

Shem (shĕm), KJV of NT **Sem** (sĕm). [Heb. *Shem,* "name," or "renown." The name is attested in Phoenician inscriptions; Gr. *Sēm.*] A son of Noah, apparently the 2d oldest, for Ham was the youngest (Gen 10:1; cf. ch 9:24), and Japheth seems to have been 2 years older, having been born apparently when Noah had reached the age of 500 years (ch 7:6; cf. ch 5:32), whereas Shem was born 98 years before the Flood, when his father was 502 years old (ch 11:10; cf. ch 7:6). Consequently the rendering "Japheth the elder" in ch 10:21, KJV, seems to be better than that of the RSV, which declares Shem to be the elder brother of Japheth. Shem, his wife, his parents, and his 2 brothers and their wives went into the ark and were saved from the Flood (ch 7:7). In the post-Flood period Shem is mentioned with his brother Japheth as endeavoring to protect their drunken father's honor following a shameful act by Ham. For this Shem received a special blessing (ch 9:20-27). Shem became the progenitor of the Semitic race to which the Babylonians, Assyrians, Aramaeans, Arabs, and Hebrews belonged (ch 10:21-32). Some scholars believe that the Sumerians were also descendants of Shem. The Hebrews were the descendants of Shem's son Arpachshad or Arphaxad, who was born 2 years after the Flood (ch 11:10-26). Shem died at the age of 600 years (vs 10, 11). He is mentioned in the genealogy of Christ (Lk 3:36).

Shema (shē′mȧ). [Heb. *Shema',* "he has heard." The name occurs on ancient Hebrew seals.]

1. A Judahite, son of Hebron (1 Chr 2:43, 44).

2. A descendant of Reuben (1 Chr 5:8).

3. A Benjamite (1 Chr 8:13).

4. One of Ezra's assistants at the public reading of the Law (Neh 8:4).

5. A town in the extreme south of Judah (Jos 15:26); identified by some with the Jeshua of Neh 11:26, by others with Sheba, II, 3.

Shemaah (shĕ-mā′ȧ). [Heb. *Shema'ah,* "report," or "fame."] A Benjamite of Gibeah. His sons, Ahiezer and Joash, joined David at Ziklag and served him as warriors (1 Chr 12:1, 3).

Shemaiah (shĕ-mā′yȧ). [Heb. *Shema'yah* and *Shema'yahû,* "Yahweh has heard." The name is attested on an ancient Hebrew seal.]

1. A Simeonite (1 Chr 4:37).

2. A descendant of Reuben (1 Chr 5:4).

3. A Levite, chief of 200 of his brethren, who took part in the ceremonies connected with the transport of the ark to Zion in David's time (1 Chr 15:8, 11).

4. A Levite scribe who recorded the organization of the priests into 24 courses in the time of David (1 Chr 24:6).

5. A son of Obed-edom; he and his sons formed a family of gatekeepers of the sanctuary of the Lord (1 Chr 26:4, 6-8).

6. A prophet who counseled Rehoboam against trying to keep the 10 tribes in his kingdom by force of arms (1 Ki 12:22-24; 2 Chr 11:2-4). During the invasion of Shishak he was instrumental in causing Rehoboam and the princes of Judah to repent of their sins by pointing out that this catastrophe had come as the result of sins (2 Chr 12:5-8). He is mentioned as a chronicler of Rehoboam (v 15).

7. A Levite sent by King Jehoshaphat to teach the Law in the cities of Judah (2 Chr 17:8, 9).

8. A Levite who helped to cleanse the Temple in Hezekiah's reign (2 Chr 29:14).

9. A Levite distributor of the freewill offerings in the cities of the priests in the reign of Hezekiah (2 Chr 31:15).

10. A chief Levite in the reign of Josiah who generously donated animals for the Passover service (2 Chr 35:9).

11. The father of the prophet Uriah (Jer 26:20).

12. A man whose son Delaiah was one of the princes to whom Baruch read Jeremiah's scroll (Jer 36:12).

13. A Nehelamite, a false prophet among the exiles in Babylonia who prophesied a speedy return from captivity. He wrote to Zephaniah, the priest in charge of the Temple in Jerusalem, complaining that Jeremiah had prophesied a long exile, and demanding that he rebuke the prophet. When Jeremiah heard about it he foretold that Shemaiah would leave no posterity to see the return from exile (Jer 29:24-32).

14. A chief priest who returned with Zerubbabel from Babylonia (Neh 12:6, 7), and ancestor of a family that bore his name in another generation (v 18).

15. A son of Adonikam, and one of the leaders of the exiles who returned from Babylonia with Ezra (Ezr 8:13).

16. A leading exile sent by Ezra to persuade Levites to join those who returned to Jerusalem with Ezra (Ezr 8:16); possibly identical with Shemaiah, 15.

17 and 18. Two men, 1 a member of the priestly family of Harim and the other a member of the lay family of Harim, who had married foreign wives in the time of Ezra (Ezr 10:21, 31).

19. A son of Shecaniah, and a postexilic descendant of David (1 Chr 3:22; cf. v 1).

20. A Levite (1 Chr 9:16), probably the Shammua of Neh 11:17.

21. The ancestor of 1 of the trumpeters who took part in the dedication of the wall of Jerusalem (Neh 12:35).

22. A keeper of the east gate who assisted Nehemiah in rebuilding the wall of Jerusalem (Neh 3:29).

23. A Levite of the family of Bunni; one of those in charge of the outside work of the Temple (Neh 11:15; 1 Chr 9:14).

24. A false prophet, son of Delaiah. Being in the pay of Sanballat and Tobiah, he sought to intimidate Nehemiah by advising him to seek protection from assassination in the sanctuary. Shemaiah shut himself up in his house as though fearing for his own life also (Neh 6:10-13).

25, 26, and 27. Three men who took part in the dedication of the wall of Jerusalem (Neh 12:34, 36, 42).

28. A priest who set his seal to Nehemiah's covenant (Neh 10:8).

Shemariah (shĕm'ȧ-rī'ȧ), KJV once **Shamariah** (shăm'ȧ-rī'ȧ). [Heb. *Shemaryah* and *Shemaryahû,* "Yahweh has guarded." The name is attested on ancient Hebrew seals and on the Samaria ostraca.]

1. A Benjamite warrior who joined David at Ziklag (1 Chr 12:5).

2. A son of King Rehoboam (2 Chr 11:18, 19).

3 and 4. Two men who were married to foreign wives in the time of Ezra (Ezr 10:32, 41).

Shemeber (shĕm-ē'bẽr). [Heb. *Shem'eber.*] The king of Zeboiim, one of the 5 cities of the Plain, defeated by Chedorlaomer and his confederates in the days of Abraham (Gen 14:2, 8, 10).

Shemed (shē'mĕd), KJV **Shamed** (shā'mĕd). [Heb. *Shemed.*] A Benjamite who rebuilt Ono and Lod, with their dependent villages (1 Chr 8:12).

Shemer (shē'mẽr), KJV twice **Shamer** (shā'-mẽr). [Heb. *Shemer,* "watchman." The name is attested on an ancient Hebrew seal impression.]

1. A Merarite Levite (1 Chr 6:46).

2. A descendant of Asher (1 Chr 7:34), called Shomer in v 32.

3. The owner of the hill of Samaria, which Omri bought and on which he built his capital (1 Ki 16:24).

Shemida (shĕ-mī'dȧ), KJV once **Shemidah** (shĕ-mī'dȧ). [Heb. *Shemidaʻ*, "my name (or posterity) has known." The name is attested on ancient Hebrew seals and the Samaria ostraca.] A son of Gilead, and ancestral head of a Manassite tribal family, the Semidaites (Num 26:32; Jos 17:2).

Shemidah. *See* Shemida.

Shemidaites (shĕ-mī'dȧ-īts). [Heb. *Shemidaʻi.*] Descendants of *Shemida (Num 26:32).

Sheminith (shĕm'ĭ-nĭth). [Heb. *sheminith.*] A term appearing in 1 Chr 15:21 and in the superscriptions of Ps 6 and 12, thought for a long time to be the name of a musical instrument not yet identified. However, most scholars now agree that it refers to a melody or a style of singing.

Shemiramoth (shĕ-mĭr'ȧ-mŏth). [Heb. *Shemîramôth*, "name of heights," regarded by some as parallel with the name of the Assyrian queen *Sammurâmat.*]
1. A Levite musician in the time of David (1 Chr 15:18, 20; 16:5).
2. A Levite who was appointed by Jehoshaphat to teach the Law (2 Chr 17:7-9).

Shemuel (shĕ-mū'ĕl). [Heb. *Shemûʼel*, possibly, "name of God." The same Hebrew name is commonly rendered "Samuel."]
1. A Simeonite leader appointed to serve on the commission that divided the land among the tribes (Num 34:20).
2. An Issacharite (1 Chr 7:2).
3. The prophet *Samuel (1 Chr 6:33, KJV).

Shen (shĕn). [Heb. *Shen*, "tooth."] A landmark in the vicinity of which Samuel set up a stone as a memorial of the battle against the Philistines (1 Sa 7:12, KJV). No place of this name is known. The RSV, on the basis of the LXX, reads *Jeshanah, a place mentioned in 2 Chr 13:19.

Shenazar. *See* Shenazzar.

Shenazzar (shĕ-năz'är), KJV **Shenazar** (shĕ-nā'zär). [Heb. *Shenʼaṣṣar*; Akkadian *Sin-uṣur*, "O (moon-god) Sin, protect!"] One of Jeconiah's (Jehoiachin's) sons (1 Chr 3:18). The name, being of Babylonian origin, was probably given him in exile.

Shenir. *See* Hermon.

Sheol. *See* Hell.

Shepham (shē'făm). [Heb. *Shepham.*] A place on the northeastern border of Canaan (Num 34:10, 11); not identified.

Shephathiah. *See* Shephatiah, 4.

Shephatiah (shĕf'ȧ-tī'ȧ), KJV once **Shephathiah** (shĕf'ȧ-thī'ȧ). [Heb. *Shephaṭyah* and *Shephaṭyahû*, "Yahweh has judged." The name is attested on an ancient Hebrew seal.]

1. A Haruphite warrior of the tribe of Benjamin who joined David at Ziklag (1 Chr 12:5).
2. A son of David by his wife Abital (2 Sa 3:4; 1 Chr 3:3).
3. The chief officer over the tribe of Simeon in the reign of David (1 Chr 27:16).
4. The father of a Benjamite who lived at Jerusalem (1 Chr 9:8), called Shephathiah in the KJV.
5. A son of Jehoshaphat (2 Chr 21:2).
6. A prince of Judah who counseled King Zedekiah to put Jeremiah to death for the prophet's allegedly discouraging the defenders of Jerusalem during the siege of that city by Nebuchadnezzar (Jer 38:1, 4).
7. The ancestor of a family of Judah who lived in Jerusalem (Neh 11:4).
8. The ancestral head of a family, of which 372 members returned from Babylonia with Zerubbabel (Ezr 2:4; Neh 7:9), and another 81 with Ezra (Ezr 8:8).
9. The ancestral head of a family of "Solomon's servants," some members of which returned from Babylonia with Zerubbabel (Ezr 2:57; Neh 7:59).

Shephelah (shĕf-ē'lȧ). [Heb. *Shephelah.*] The rolling country between the central mountain range of Palestine and the coastal plain. In the RSV the Hebrew term is sometimes transliterated and sometimes rendered "lowland." The KJV translates the term variously as "vale," "the valley," "the low country," "the plain." The Shephelah has hills that rise to heights of from 500 to 800 ft., with a few higher summits. It is separated from the mountainous hinterland by a series of valleys that run from north to south from Aijalon to near Beer-sheba. Several wide and fertile valleys lead from the mountains of Judah toward the coast. The area is rich in olives and grain, and many important Biblical cities, such as Beth-shemesh, Gezer, Eglon, Lachish, Libnah, Gath, and Azekah, were situated there. The area was assigned to Judah (Jos 15:12), but parts were given to the tribes of Simeon (ch 19:9) and Dan (vs 40, 41; cf. ch 15:33). Map I, C-1. The ancient Hebrew name has been restored to the area in modern Israel.

Shepher (shē'fēr), KJV **Shapher** (shā'fēr). [Heb. *Shepher*, "beautiful."] A mountain in the wilderness at which the Israelites encamped during their wanderings (Num 33:23, 24); not identified.

Shepherd. [Heb. generally *roʻeh*, a form of the verb *raʻah*, "to feed," "to graze," "to pasture." When ro'eh is combined with miqneh, "cattle," the resultant phrase designates a herdsman (KJV "herdman"). See below. Gr. poimēn, "shepherd."] A keeper of sheep. The occupation of shepherd is as old as the human race. Abel was a shepherd (Gen 4:4), Abraham, Isaac, Jacob, and Job kept sheep (Gen 12:16; 26:12-14; 30:31-43; Job 1:3), and Jacob's sons (Gen 37:12), Moses (Ex 3:1), David (1 Chr 17:7), and Amos (Amos 7:14, 15) were shepherds.

Shepherds were often nomadic or seminomadic, for it was necessary to move from place to place to find adequate water and pasturage for their flocks (Gen 4:20; 13:2-6, 11, 18). Some had permanent facilities and lived in towns (Num 32:16, 24). In such cases the sheep were led to pasture in the morning and brought back to the *sheepfold in the evening (cf. Jn 10:1-4). Besides finding water and pasturage for his flocks (Ps 23:2) and providing shelter for them, the shepherd had to protect his sheep from thieves and from wild animals such as wolves, lions, and bears (Gen 31:39; 1 Sa 17:34, 36; Jn 10:12). He also had to keep the helpless animals from scattering and being lost (Lk 15:4). The shepherd became so well known to his sheep that his call was the only one to which they would respond (Jn 10:3-5). The hired shepherd was held responsible for the welfare of his sheep (cf. Gen 31:39) but, according to the ancient laws of Mesopotamia, could be charged only for that which was lost through neglect. A hireling might not have the courage or the concern to protect his charges in dangerous circumstances (Jn 10:12, 13).

The shepherd was variously equipped with a rod or staff (Lev 27:32; 1 Sa 17: 40; Ps 23:4; Mic 7:14), a *sling, a bag for food, and one for his slingstones (1 Sa 17:40). He also had a tent for protection

435. An emaciated herdsman leading oxen, on a tomb wall from Meir, Egypt

from the weather (Song 1:8; Is 38:12).

The figurative use of "shepherd" is common in the Bible. People without proper leadership were likened to sheep without a shepherd (Num 27:16, 17; 1 Ki 22:17; Eze 34:1-6; Mt 9:36; 26:31; Mk 6: 34; etc.). Isaiah prophesied that Cyrus the Great would be God's "shepherd" to bring the Jews from captivity (Is 44: 28). The prophets Isaiah, Ezekiel, and Zechariah sharply reproved the leaders of Israel, who were like false shepherds, unperceptive, greedy, who led their charges astray, and even took advantage of them and killed them (Is 56:11; Eze 34:2-10; Zec 11:3-8). Bible writers refer to the Lord as a Shepherd who gently and faithfully leads and cares for His "sheep" (Ps 23; 80:1; Is 40:11; Eze 34:11, 12). Jesus described Himself as the Good Shepherd who would give His life for His sheep (Jn 10:11-15). In Heb 13:20 He is called the "great shepherd of the sheep." Peter likens his readers (1 Pe 2:25) to sheep who had been straying but had returned to Christ, "the Shepherd." He also calls Christ "the chief Shepherd," who, when He appears, will reward the faithful undershepherds with an unfading crown of glory (ch 5:1-4). At his second coming Christ will separate the righteous from the wicked as a shepherd separates the sheep from the goats (Mt 25:32). See Pastor.

Herdsmen, or keepers of cattle, are designated by the Heb. ro'ê miqneh, or 'anshê miqneh. They are mentioned less frequently than the shepherds, because cattle have always been less numerous in the Near East than flocks of sheep and goats. Abraham, Lot, and Isaac had herdsmen (Gen 13:7, 8; 26:20), and Joseph introduced his brothers to Pharaoh as "keepers of cattle" ('anshê miqneh; ch 46:32, RSV). The Egyptians are described in v 34 as considering shepherds an abomination. This contempt of shepherds seems to have been especially strong toward herdsmen, for they frequently appear in ancient Egyptian paintings and reliefs as miserable creatures, dirty and unshaven, naked and half starved, and often either deformed or lame (fig. 435). The Bible mentions also the herdsmen of Kings Saul and David (1 Sa 21:7; 1 Chr 27:29), and notes that the prophet Amos was a herdsman (Amos 7:14). The NT mentions the "herdsmen" (Gr. boskontes, a form of the verb boskō, "to feed," "to pasture") of swine belonging to the Gadarenes (Mt 8:33, RSV), and observes that the prodigal son of the parable was employed in this profession for some time (Lk 15:15, 16).

Shephi (shē′fī), or **Shepho** (shē′fō). [Heb. *Shephî* and *Shephô*, meaning uncertain.] A son of Shobal and a descendant of Seir the Horite. He was probably the ancestor of a tribal family (Gen 36:23; 1 Chr 1:38, 40).

Shepho. *See* Shephi.

Shephupham. *See* Shephuphan.

Shephuphan (shē̆-fū′făn), or **Shephupham** (shē̆-fū′făm), KJV for the latter **Shupham** (shoo′făm). [Heb. *Shephûphan* and *Shephûpham.*] A son or descendant of Benjamin, and ancestral head of the Shuphamites (shoo′făm-īts) [Heb. *Shûphamî*] (Num 26:39), apparently called Muppim in Gen 46:21, and Shuppim in 1 Chr 7: 12, 15. The variant names are the result of an exchange of the letters *m* and *sh,* which were very similar in pre-exilic Hebrew.

Sherah. *See* Sheerah.

Sherebiah (shĕr′ĕ-bī′å). [Heb. *Sherebyah,* "Yahweh has parched." The name is attested in Babylonian records as *Ishribi-yâma.*]
  1. A Levite who came from Babylonia with Zerubbabel (Neh 12:8).
  2. A Levite who returned with 18 kinsmen from Babylonia with Ezra (Ezr 8: 18). He is most probably identical with the Sherebiah of v·24, who, with others, was entrusted by Ezra with the gifts to be carried to Jerusalem. Although v 24 appears to call him a priest, the Hebrew can be interpreted to mean that he and the other Levites were chosen in addition to the 12 priests. He is possibly identical with one or more of Sherebiah,·3-5.
  3. A Levite who assisted Ezra in reading the Law to the people (Neh 8:7). He took part in the confession of sins after the Feast of Tabernacles (ch 9:4). He is possibly identical with one or more of Sherebiah, 2, 4, and 5.
  4. A Levite who set his seal to Nehemiah's covenant (Neh 10:12), possibly identical with one or more of Sherebiah, 2, 3, and 5.
  5. A Levite musician in Nehemiah's time (Neh 12:24), probably identical with one or more of Sherebiah, 2-4.

Sheresh (shē′rĕsh). [Heb. *Sheresh,* "root."] A descendant of Manasseh (1 Chr 7:16).

Sherezer. *See* Sharezer, 2.

Sheriff. A rendering of the Aramaic *tiphtay* (Dan 3:2, 3; RSV "magistrate"), "sheriff," "police officer." Nebuchadnezzar summoned the sheriffs of his kingdom, with

other officials, to the plain of Dura to worship his golden image (Dan 3:1-7).

Sheshach (shē′shăk). [Heb. *Sheshak, Shshk* in unpointed Hebrew.] A name for Babylon (Jer 25:26; 51:41; KJV), and so translated in those passages in the RSV. It has been explained as either (1) a transliteration of *Shish-ku,* a name of Babylon in late king lists, or (2) a cipher according to a device known as atbash in which the letters of a word are replaced by those standing in the equivalent place in the alphabet, counted from the end. The name Babel in Hebrew consists of the consonants *b b l,* the 2d and 12th letters in the Hebrew alphabet. If the 2d letter from the end, *sh,* is substituted for the 2 *b*'s, and the 12th letter from the end, *k,* is substituted for *l,* one gets the cipher *shshk* in unpointed pre-Masoretic Hebrew. Until recently the 2d explanation was questionable, since it was not known whether the sequence of the Hebrew alphabet was the same in the time of Jeremiah as it is now. However, lists of alphabets of the 14th cent. B.C. have been discovered in Ras Shamra, which show that the sequence of the Hebrew characters has been virtually unchanged from early times. *See* Writing. Hence, no valid reason exists for rejecting the interpretation that *Sheshak* is a cipher for Babel.

Sheshai (shē′shī). [Heb. *Sheshay,* meaning uncertain. The name seems to be identical with the Hurrian *Sheshwaya.*] A son or descendant of Anak, possibly also a clan name of a family of the Anakim at Hebron (Num 13:22), driven out by Caleb (Jos 15:14; Jgs 1:10).

Sheshan (shē′shăn). [Heb. *Sheshan,* meaning uncertain.] A Jerahmeelite of the tribe of Judah. He had no sons, and gave one of his daughters to an Egyptian slave as wife (1 Chr 2:31, 34, 35).

Sheshbazzar (shĕsh-băz′ĕr). [Heb. and Aramaic *Sheshbaṣṣar,* possibly a transliteration of the Babylonian *Shamash-abal-uṣur,* "O sun (-god), protect the son!"] A prince of Judah to whom the sacred vessels were delivered. He was made the 1st governor of the province of Judah by Cyrus, and laid the foundation of the Temple (Ezr 1:8, 11; 5:14, 16). Since his functions are identical with those of *Zerubbabel, and since he was active in the same period, it is plausible to assume that Sheshbazzar is another name for Zerubbabel. However, some commentators do not equate the two, and believe that Sheshbazzar was made governor first, and that he was soon replaced by Zerubbabel.

Sheth (shĕth). [Heb. *Sheth*, "substitute."]

1. The 3d son of Adam (1 Chr 1:1, KJV), otherwise rendered *Seth.

2. An ancient name for Moab, with which it stands in poetic parallel in Num 24:17. The name is attested in the Egyptian execration texts of the 18th cent. B.C. as *Shwtw* (*BASOR* 83 [1941], 34).

Shethar (shē′thär). [Heb. *Shethar*, a Persian name, meaning uncertain.] One of the 7 princes of Persia who had free access to the king (Est 1:14).

Shethar-bozenai (shē′thär-bŏz′ē-nī), KJV **Shethar-boznai** (shē′thär-bŏz′nī). [Aramaic *Shethar bōzenay*, probably the equivalent of the Old Iranian *Shêthrabûzana*, which appears in cuneiform documents as *Shatabarzana* and *Ushtabuzana*.] Apparently the secretary of Tattenai, the deputy satrap. With Tattenai and others he visited Jerusalem during the reign of Darius I, when the Temple was being built, and sent a written report of the visit to the court (Ezr 5:3, 6; 6:6, 13).

Shethar-boznai. *See* Shethar-bozenai.

Sheva (shē′va). [Heb. *Shewa′*, "vanity."]

1. A Judahite, descendant of Caleb the son of Hezron. The inhabitants of Machbena and Gibea were his descendants (1 Chr 2:49).

2. David's secretary (2 Sa 20:25). *See* Shavsha.

Shewbread. *See* Showbread.

Shibah (shī′ba), KJV **Shebah** (shē′ba). [Heb. *Shib′ah*, "oath."] A well near Beer-sheba, dug by Isaac's servants. The name "oath" was given to it because when the well was dug Abimelech and Isaac entered into a covenant under oath (Gen 26:33). These circumstances gave the name of Beersheba, "well of the oath," to the adjacent town.

Shibboleth. [Heb. *shibboleth*, "an ear of grain," "a bunch of twigs."] A word pronounced *shibboleth* by the Gileadites and *sibboleth* by the Ephraimites, and used by the former to identify the latter at a ford across the Jordan River (Jgs 12:6). Ephraimites, betrayed thus by their failure to pronounce the word as the Gileadites did, were slain.

Shibmah. *See* Sibmah.

Shicron. *See* Shikkeron.

Shield. Egyptian pictures show that the Syrians and Hittites used flat, oblong shields covered with leather. The Mitannians, Philistines, and Assyrians are depicted with round shields, although the Assyrians used also a long curved shield.

The Hebrews had 2 kinds of shields, a small round one, Heb. *magen* (2 Chr 14:8; Neh 4:16; etc.), and a long one, Heb. *ṣinnah* (1 Chr 12:8; 2 Chr 25:5; etc.). The Heb. *magen* is generally translated "shield." The Heb. *ṣinnah* is generally rendered "shield" in the RSV, but the KJV translates it "shield," "buckler," and "target." A shield was ordinarily made of wood, with a hide stretched over it to which oil was applied (2 Sa 1:21; Is 21:5) to keep it pliable. During marches it was protected by a cover (Is 22:6). Prominent warriors had shield bearers (1 Sa 17:7, 41). The bronze (RSV) shields of 1 Ki 14:27 were probably only partly that metal. Some shields were covered with gold leaf for decorative purposes (ch 10:17). The Assyrian relief of Lachish shows the Jewish defenders of that city with small round shields. For various kinds of shields see figs. 19, 210, 232, 284.

Shiggaion (shǐ-gā′yŏn). [Heb. *shiggayôn*, possibly "dirge."] A term occurring in the title of Ps 7 and in the plural, Shigionoth (shĭg′ĭ-ō′nŏth) [Heb. *shigyonôth*], in Habakkuk's prayer (Hab 3:1). The idea of "dirge" is suggested by the cognate Akkadian word *shegû*.

Shigionoth. *See* Shiggaion.

Shihon. *See* Shion.

Shihor (shī′hôr), KJV generally **Sihor** (sī′hôr). [Heb. *Shîchôr, Shichôr,* and *Shichor;* Egyptian *sh Ḥr*, "lake of Horus." The Egyptian name refers to part of the Bubastite Pelusiac branch of the Nile (Gardiner, *JEA* 5 [1918], 251, 252).] A term of uncertain application appearing in Jos 13:3; 1 Chr 13:5; Is 23:3; Jer 2:18, KJV. It is variously thought to be: (1) a portion of the Nile (cf. Jer 2:18, RSV); (2) the *Wâdī el-′Arîsh,* otherwise called the "Brook of Egypt"; (3) a body of water, unidentified, in the eastern border of Egypt.

Shihor-libnath (shī′hôr-lĭb′năth). [Heb. *Shichôr Libnath.*] A river on the southern border of Asher (Jos 19:26). It is commonly identified with the *Nahr ez-Zerqa,* south of the Carmel. Some believe the Hebrew terms designate 2 different sites.

Shikkeron (shĭk′ē-rŏn), KJV **Shicron** (shĭk′-rŏn). [Heb. *Shikkarôn,* "drunkenness."] A town on the northern border of Judah (Jos 15:11); not identified with certainty.

Shilhi (shĭl′hī). [Heb. *Shilchî,* meaning uncertain.] The maternal grandfather of King Jehoshaphat of Judah (1 Ki 22:42; 2 Chr 20:31).

Shilhim (shĭl′hĭm). [Heb. *Shilchim,* of uncertain meaning.] A city in the southwest of Judah (Jos 15:32); probably identical with *Sharuhen (ch 19:6).

Shillem (shĭl′ĕm). [Heb. *Shillem,* "He (that is, God) has made compensation." The name is attested on an ancient Hebrew seal.] A son of Naphtali (Gen 46:24), and ancestor of a tribal family, the Shillemites (Num 26:49). He is called Shallum in 1 Chr 7:13.

Shillemites (shĭl′ĕm-īts). [Heb. *Shillemi.*] Descendants of *Shillem (Num 26:49).

Shiloah. *See* Siloam.

Shiloh, I (shī′lō). [Heb. *Shiloh* and *Shilô.*] A town about 10 mi. north of Bethel and 3 mi. southeast of Lebonah, east of the main road leading from Jerusalem to Shechem (Map VI, D-3). Its modern name is *Seilûn.* Excavations have shown that the city was in existence some time before the Hebrew conquest. It is not known how it came into the hands of the Israelites, who held it from Joshua's time until it was destroyed by the Philistines 300 years later. At Shiloh the tabernacle was erected (Jos 18:1), the land was distributed (vs 8-10), and while the Israelites were encamped there, Joshua died (ch 24:1, 29). Judges 21:19-24 mentions an annual "feast of the Lord" celebrated at Shiloh, with dances performed by girls. Toward the end of the period of the judges Eli officiated at Shiloh as high priest, and under his tutelage the prophet Samuel grew to manhood (1 Sa 1-3). It was during this time that the Philistines captured the ark in the battle of Aphek (ch 4:1-11), and probably destroyed Shiloh, as may be concluded from the fact that the ark was not taken back to Shiloh when the Philistines returned it to the Israelites (chs 6: 21 to 7:2). Excavations have shown that Shiloh was destroyed about 1100 B.C., a date that agrees with the Biblical chronology, according to which the ark was taken about half a century before Saul's coronation. The city remained mainly in ruins for many centuries, and Jeremiah seems to have known it only in a ruined condition (Jer 7:12, 14; 26:6, 9). However, it seems to have had some inhabitants, for it was the home of the prophet Ahijah in the time of Jeroboam I (1 Ki 14:2, 4) and also of certain men who were murdered at Mizpah on their way to Jerusalem to bring offerings to the ruined Temple in Jeremiah's time (Jer 41:5). Shiloh became an inhabited town again in the Hellenistic period and continued to be inhabited to Byzantine times. A Danish expedition under the direction of H. Kjaer and A. Schmidt excavated parts of the ancient city in the years from 1926 to 1932.

Lit.: H. Kjaer, *PEFQS* 59 (1927), 202-213; 63 (1931), 71-88; *JPOS* 10 (1930), 87-174; W. F. Albright, *AJA* 39 (1935), 143, 144.

Shiloh, II (shī′lō). [Heb. *Shîloh* (Q *Shilô*).] A term found in Gen 49:10, understood by many commentators to be an appellation for the Messiah. The name has been understood as meaning variously, "offspring," "the one sent out," "he to whom it (the sceptre) belongs," "the rest giver," "peace giver." The name appears in a prophecy of Jacob stating that "the sceptre" would not depart from the tribe of Judah, nor a "ruler's staff from between his feet" (RSV), until Shiloh should come. This has been interpreted to mean that the Jewish nation would have national rulers until the time for the appearance of the Messiah. In explaining the fulfillment it has been pointed out that even when Judah was a subject state it had a measure of local autonomy, and was for the most part governed by Jewish

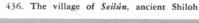
436. The village of *Seilûn,* ancient Shiloh

administrators. These were governors such as Zerubbabel, Ezra, and Nehemiah under the Persians, high priests under the Ptolemies and Seleucids, and later the native Hasmonaean priest-kings, under whom Judah was temporarily independent. Then the Romans replaced the Hasmonaeans with the local king Herod the Great, who was of Idumean descent but Jewish by religion. Finally in A.D. 6 Archelaus, Herod's successor in Judea, was deposed, and Judea for the 1st time became a mere province, administered directly by a Roman governor. By this time Christ had been born.

Shiloni. *See* Shilonite, 2.

Shilonite (shī'lō-nīt). [Heb. *Shiloni*.]
1. A native of the town of Shiloh (1 Ki 11:29; 12:15; 15:29; 1 Chr 9:5; 2 Chr 9:29).
2. The ancestor of an inhabitant of Jerusalem (Neh 11:5, RSV; KJV "Shiloni," shĭ-lō'nī). It is usually thought that he was a descendant of Shelah, Judah's son, father of "the Shelanites" (Num 26:20).

Shilshah (shĭl'sha). [Heb. *Shilshah*, "triad."] A descendant of Asher (1 Chr 7:30, 37).

Shimea (shĭm'ē-a). [Heb. *Shim'a'*, "He (God) has heard." The name occurs in Phoenician and proto-Semitic (Sinaitic) inscriptions.]
1. A Merarite Levite (1 Chr 6:30).
2. A Gershonite Levite (1 Chr 6:39-43).
3. A son of David (1 Chr 3:5); called Shammua in 2 Sa 5:14.

Shimeah (shĭm'ē-a). [Heb. *Shim'ah*, "He (God) has heard."]
1. A son of Jesse and brother of David (2 Sa 13:3, 32), called Shimea (Heb. *Shim'a'*) in 1 Chr 20:7, Shimei (Heb. *Shim'i*) in 2 Sa 21:21, RSV, Shammah (Heb. *Shammah*) in 1 Sa 16:9 and 17:13, and Shimma (shĭm'a) [Heb. *Shim'a'*] in 1 Chr 2:13, KJV.
2. For 1 Chr 8:32 *see* Shimeam.

Shimeam (shĭm'ē-ăm). [Heb. *Shim'am*.] A Benjamite (1 Chr 9:38), called Shimeah (Heb. *Shim'ah*) in ch 8:32.

Shimeath (shĭm'ē-ăth). [Heb. *Shim'ath*, "report."] An Ammonitess, the mother of one of the assassins of King Joash of Judah (2 Ki 12:21; 2 Chr 24:26).

Shimeathites (shĭm'ē-ăth-īts). [Heb. *Shim'athim*.] A family of scribes of Kenite descent through "Hemath, the father of the house of Rechab" (1 Chr 2:55).

Shimei (shĭm'ē-ī), KJV once **Shimi** (shĭm'ī), once **Shimhi** (shĭm'hī), and once **Shimeah** (shĭm'ē-a). [Heb. *Shim'i*, probably a short-

ened form of *Shema'yah*, Shemaiah, "Yahweh has heard."]
1. The 2d son of Gershon, and a grandson of Levi. He became the ancestral head of a subdivision of the tribal family of Gershon (Ex 6:17; Num 3:18; 1 Chr 23:7), the Shimeites (shĭm'ē-īts) [Heb. *Shim'i*] (Num 3:21; KJV "Shimites," shĭm'īts; Zec 12:13; KJV "family of Shimei").
2. A descendant of Simeon and father of 16 sons and 6 daughters (1 Chr 4:26, 27).
3. A Merarite Levite (1 Chr 6:29).
4. A Gershonite Levite (1 Chr 6:42).
5. A Benjamite chief (1 Chr 8:21); called Shema in v 13.
6. A Gershonite Levite (1 Chr 23:9).
7. A descendant of Reuben (1 Chr 5:4).
8. A Levite, the head of the 10th of the 24 courses into which David organized the musicians for Solomon's Temple (1 Chr 25:17). He was a son apparently of Jeduthun (v 3), although his name does not appear among the sons of Jeduthun in the Hebrew text, having been inadvertently omitted as shown by the fact that Jeduthun is said to have 6 sons but only 5 are listed. The name is supplied in the RSV, an inclusion supported by the LXX and by 1 Hebrew manuscript.
9. A Ramathite, who was in charge of the vineyards of David (1 Chr 27:27).
10. A son of Gera, of the house of Saul. He considered David a usurper to the throne, and when David fled before Absalom he vented his disdain by crude cursing, apparently thinking David to have been permanently dethroned (2 Sa 16:5-13). When David triumphantly returned, Shimei professed repentance and was spared by the generous king (ch 19:18-23). Solomon, however, had him executed for a later act of disobedience (1 Ki 2:8, 9, 36-46).
11. One of David's officers who remained faithful during the usurpation of Adonijah (1 Ki 1:8); possibly identical with Shimei, 13.
12. A brother of David (2 Sa 21:21); called Shimeah (Heb. Q *Shim'ah*) in the KJV.
13. Son of Ela; he was Solomon's supply officer in the territory of Benjamin (1 Ki 4:18); possibly identical with Shimei, 11.
14. A Levite of the sons of Heman; he assisted in the cleansing of the Temple in Hezekiah's reign (2 Chr 29:14, 15); possibly identical with Shimei, 15.
15. A Levite, who acted as assistant superintendent of the Temple treasury

under Hezekiah (2 Chr 31:12); possibly identical with Shimei, 14.

16. A Benjamite, ancestor of Mordecai (Est 2:5).

17. A brother of Zerubbabel (1 Chr 3:19).

18, 19, and 20. Three men who had married foreign wives in the time of Ezra (Ezr 10:23, 33, 38).

Shimeites. *See* Shimei, 1.

Shimeon (shĭm′ē-ŭn). [Heb. *Shim‛ôn*, "hearkening (of prayer)," or "answering (of prayer)." The name is found on a Hebrew contract among the Dead Sea scrolls.] A member of the family of Harim; he had married a foreign wife in the time of Ezra (Ezr 10:31).

Shimhi. *See* Shimei, 5.

Shimi. *See* Shimei, 1.

Shimma. *See* Shimeah, 1.

Shimon (shī′mŏn). [Heb. *Shîmôn*. The name occurs in Assyrian as *Simânu*.] The head of a family of Judah (1 Chr 4:20).

Shimrath (shĭm′răth). [Heb. *Shimrath*, "watching," or "guarding."] A descendant of Benjamin (1 Chr 8:1, 21).

Shimri (shĭm′rī), KJV once **Simri** (sĭm′rī). [Heb. *Shimrî*, "He (God) has watched."]

1. A descendant of Simeon (1 Chr 4:24, 37).

2. A man whose son Jediael was one of David's "mighty men" (1 Chr 11:45).

3. A Merarite Levite, and head of a family of gatekeepers (1 Chr 26:10); called Simri in the KJV.

4. A Levite who helped to cleanse the Temple in the reign of Hezekiah (2 Chr 29:13).

Shimrith (shĭm′rĭth). [Heb. *Shimrîth*, "vigilant."] A Moabitess, the mother of one of the assassins of King Joash (2 Chr 24:26); called Shomer in 2 Ki 12:21.

Shimrom. *See* Shimron, 1.

Shimron (shĭm′rŏn), KJV once **Shimrom** (shĭm′rom). [Heb. *Shimrôn*, "watching."]

1. A son of Issachar (Gen 46:13), and ancestral head of a tribal family, the Shimronites (shĭm′rŏn-īts) [Heb. *Shimroni*] (Num 26:24). He is called Shimrom in 1 Chr 7:1, KJV.

2. A Canaanite city in the north of Palestine, mentioned in an Egyptian text as *Sh₃m‛rwn₃*. It joined the confederacy formed by King Jabin of Hazor to stem the advance of the Israelites into Galilee under Joshua (Jos 11:1). The city was afterward assigned to the tribe of Zebulun (ch 19:15), but it is not known when it was occupied by the Israelites. The site has not yet been identified with cer-

tainty, but some scholars place it near Japhia (Map VI, C-3).

Shimronites. *See* Shimron, 1.

Shimron-meron (shĭm′rŏn-mē′rŏn). [Heb. *Shimrôn Mer′ôn*.] A Canaanite town of western Palestine, whose king was defeated by Joshua (Jos 12:20). It is possible that the Hebrew terms stand for 2 towns. On the other hand, Shimron-meron may be the full name of Shimron, 2. Map VI, B-3 gives a conjectural location, based on the idea that Shimron-meron is not identical with *Shimron, 2.

Shimshai (shĭm′shī). [Aramaic *Shimshay*, "my sun." The name occurs in cuneiform records as *Samsaya*.] A Persian official, a scribe, or secretary, who with others sent a complaint to Artaxerxes regarding the rebuilding of the wall of Jerusalem by the Jews (Ezr 4:8, 9, 17, 23).

Shinab (shī′năb). [Heb. *Shin′ab*, "(the god) Sin is (his) father." The name occurs in Akkadian as *Sin-abushu*.] The king of Admah, one of the 5 cities of the Plain defeated by the confederacy of Chedorlaomer in the time of Abraham (Gen 14:2, 8-10).

Shinar (shī′när). [Heb. *Shin′ar*.]

1. The country of Babylonia, since the Babylonian cities Babel, Erech, Accad, and Calneh, two of which are well known, are said to be located in it (Gen 10:10; 11:2). There can also be little doubt that the Shinar of Dan 1:2 and Zec 5:11 must be identified with Babylonia, but it is uncertain whether Is 11:11 refers to Babylonia or to one of the Shinars mentioned under Shinar, 2. In cuneiform records this name has not yet been found as a designation for Babylonia.

2. The country over which Amraphel, one of the kings who invaded Transjordan in the days of Abraham, reigned (Gen 14:1, 9). Many commentators have in the past identified the Shinar of *Amraphel with Babylonia, but the discovery that other ancient countries were named Shinar has made this identification doubtful. Cuneiform texts mention a *Shanḫara* as an area in northern Mesopotamia west of Nineveh, which has been identified with the mountainous land today called *Jebel Singar*. On the other hand, the *Amarna Letters mention a kingdom of *Shanḫar* (No. 35, line 49), which, according to J. A. Knudtzon (*Die El-Amarna-Tafeln* [Leipzig, 1915], pp. 1081, 1082) and F. M. Th. de Liagre Böhl (*Opera Minora* [Groningen, 1953], p. 45) must have been in northern Syria. Amraphel's kingdom

is probably to be identified with this latter kingdom.

Shion (shī'ŏn), KJV **Shihon** (shī'hŏn). [Heb. *Shī'ōn*, meaning uncertain.] A town in the territory of Issachar (Jos 19:19); not identified with certainty.

Ship. The Hebrews, living during most of their history in the interior of Palestine, were not a seafaring people, though at various periods they did engage in maritime enterprises. In the period of the judges Dan and Asher were rebuked for conducting their seagoing or fishing projects when their help was required to save their kindred tribes from enslavement (Jgs 5:17). Solomon built ships to send expeditions to Ophir and Tarshish, but engaged Phoenician shipbuilders and sailors (2 Chr 8:17, 18; 9:21). King Jehoshaphat attempted to imitate Solomon's maritime venture, but his ships were broken up in the Gulf of Aqabah (1 Ki 22:48). It is possible that King Uzziah (Azariah) also carried out maritime operations from Ezion-geber or Elath (2 Ki 14:22; 2 Chr 26:2; cf. Is 2:6, 16). Bible writers frequently refer to the ships of other nations and their overseas trade (Prov 31:14; Eze 27:4-9; Acts 28:11; etc.). When Jonah attempted to flee from Palestine to distant Tarshish he embarked at Joppa, but on a foreign ship (Jon 1:3, 5, 9). The apostle Paul doubtless employed ships of many nationalities for his extended traveling. In 2 Cor 11:25, 26 he tells of having experienced 3 shipwrecks, and frequent "perils of waters [RSV "rivers"]" and "perils in the sea." Luke, who accompanied Paul on his voyage to Rome, has furnished a detailed and instructive report of that trip and its mishaps (Acts 27). From this description it is evident that Paul was an experienced sea traveler, who could give valuable advice, which unfortunately was not always heeded (Acts 27:9-11, 30-34).

The ships used by Jesus and His disciples on the Sea of Galilee (Mt 8:23, 24; 9:1; 13:2; etc.) were ordinary fishing boats, probably similar to those found there today, which usually have one mast for a sail but are also provided with oars, which are always carried along.

Although the Bible contains practically nothing concerning the appearance and constructional details of the ships it mentions, much information is available from other ancient sources. Pictures of ships have been found drawn or painted on Egyptian tomb walls, sculptured on stone in temples, carved on sarcophagi (fig.

437. Phoenician merchant ship depicted on an ancient stone sarcophagus

437) or on monuments, and in later times, engraved on coins. The dry climate of Egypt has also preserved ancient models of river boats and seagoing vessels (see fig. 77), and actual size ceremonial vessels such as the sun boats of King Khufu recently discovered at Gizeh.

Since from earliest times rivers were main arteries of traffic in the ancient world, the Nile in Egypt, as well as the 2 rivers of the Mesopotamian valley, swarmed with river boats. In Egypt river boats were built of bundles of reeds, or of pieces of wood "sewn" together with leather. Some of them were of sufficient size to transport large amounts of cargo, even big blocks of stone for monuments or building purposes. Passenger ships had cabins and flat decks. Some were constructed to function as kitchen boats, or butcher boats, and these would accompany state officials on their inspection tours. The Egyptians also built seagoing ships that made voyages along the coast to Gaza in Palestine, to Byblos in Phoenicia, and to the islands of Cyprus and Crete. Ships built in the Red Sea were dispatched to Punt (probably Somaliland in eastern Africa). They were constructed of wood, with masts made from fir trees from the Lebanon. The sterns and prows of these ships turned sharply upward. Mattings stretched along the sides added to the comfort of the voyagers and protected the cargo by breaking the force of the wind and spray. Rafts of timber supported on inflated skins have also been used for the transportation of cargo and people from ancient times to the present day. The typical river boats of Mesopotamia were of circular basketwork calked with bitumen like the modern *guffahs*, their direct descendants (fig. 225). Wooden boats shaped like those of other countries were also used. The Mesopotamians also built high-prowed and high-sterned seagoing vessels, with which they made connections with coastal places of Persia, India, southern Arabia, and with Egypt via the Red Sea, as early Egyptian pictures show.

The most experienced shipbuilders of pre-Roman times, however, seem to have been the Phoenicians. Their ships plied between all ports of the Mediterranean. They maintained connections between the East and the West, exchanging the raw products of Spain, Anatolia, Italy, and other countries for papyrus and linen from Egypt, finished metal products or woolen cloth from Mesopotamia, and oil and wine from Palestine and Syria. Their ships were therefore large freighters by ancient standards, although they would look small in comparison with modern ships. Eze 27:5-9 describes the Tyrian merchant vessel built of wooden planks and calked, having a mast, linen sails, awnings, and oars of oak. The description also mentions rowers (KJV "mariners"), and pilots.

The "ships of Tarshish" (1 Ki 10:22; Is 2:16; etc.) were formerly thought to have been the name of seaworthy vessels that could sail as far as Tartessus in Spain. However, Albright has suggested that the term means "ore-carrying vessels," or "refinery ships," carrying copper or iron ores from mining countries to smelter cities such as Ezion-geber. *See* Tarshish.

In Roman times the shipbuilding industry was able to supply vessels of formidable size for merchant or military fleets. The ship that carried Paul to Rome conveyed 276 persons in addition to a cargo of wheat (Acts 27:37, 38). Josephus once traveled on a ship that carried 600 persons (*Life* 3). Lucian describes a 2d-cent. Alexandrian wheat ship, the *Isis,* which was 180 ft. long and 45 ft. wide. It had a displacement of probably more than

1,000 tons, but this ship was exceptionally large. According to Luke's description Paul's ship had a foresail, which could be raised and lowered (Acts 27:40). This implies that the ship had at least 2 masts—foremast and mainmast. It was steered by "rudders"—customarily 2 large oars—and carried 4 anchors in the stern. The ship also towed a little boat that could be hoisted on deck by means of ropes or davits (vs 30-32). It was also equipped to take soundings (v 28), and was manned by a crew that worked under the direction of a master and the owner of the ship (v 11). To secure the ship in the gale and prevent it from foundering, ropes or chains were put around it for undergirding (v 17). A ship generally had a sign or symbol of some god by which it was known. This was either carved or painted on the sides of the prow (ch 28:11).

Roman war galleys, which are not mentioned in the Bible, were propelled by numerous oars, and were built long, slender, and light, with sharp beaks on their prows for ramming.

Shiphi (shī'fī). [Heb. *Shiph'i,* "abundant." The name occurs in Assyrian texts as *Shapi'.*] A descendant of Simeon (1 Chr 4:37).

Shiphmite (shĭf'mīt). [Heb. *Shiphmi.*] The designation of Zabdi, showing him to be a native or inhabitant of either Shepham or Siphmoth (1 Chr 27:27). *See* Zabdi, 3.

Shiphrah (shĭf'rȧ). [Heb. *Shiphrah,* "beauty." The term appears as *Shpr* in an Egyptian text as the name of a Semite female slave (Albright, *JAOS* 74 [1954], 229).] One of the 2 Hebrew midwives in Egypt who were ordered to kill the Hebrew male babies, but did not carry out the royal command (Ex 1:15).

Shiphtan (shĭf'tăn). [Heb. *Shiphtan,* "judgment."] An Ephraimite whose son Kemuel was a member of the group commissioned to divide the land among the tribes (Num 34:17, 24).

Shisha (shī'shȧ). [Heb. *Shisha'.*] A man whose 2 sons were scribes in the reign of Solomon (1 Ki 4:3). *See* Shavsha.

Shishak (shī'shăk). [Heb. *Shûshaq* (Q *Shishaq*), a transliteration of the Egyptian *Shshk* or *Shshnk,* better known by its Grecized form Sheshonk.] The founder of the 22d dynasty (Libyan) of Egypt, who attempted to re-establish the Asiatic empire that had been lost since the time of the Ramessides (*see* Egypt V, 10). He began to reign *c.* 950 B.C. but dared no conquests during Solomon's reign, although he harbored Solomon's enemies or rebels as guests (1 Ki 11:40, cf. vs 17-22). But when upon the death of Solomon the Hebrew kingdom split into 2 factions, he took advantage of the unsettled state of affairs in Palestine, and invaded the country in the 5th year of King Rehoboam of Judah (*c.* 926/25 B.C.). The Biblical records mention only the invasion of Judah and the conquest of Jerusalem, from which city Shishak carried away the treasures of Solomon (1 Ki 14:25, 26; 2 Chr 12:2-9), but Shishak's victory relief carved on the temple wall at Karnak (fig. 438) mentions more than 100 cities captured from Judah and Israel, among them Megiddo. His conquest of Megiddo in the northern kingdom has been confirmed by the discovery in excavations of the city of a fragment of a victory stele. However, his campaign was not much more than a raid, and the internal restless conditions in Egypt did not allow him to follow up his foreign conquests. In the tomb of one of Shishak's grandsons, discovered by P. Montet at Tanis, a golden bracelet was discovered, inscribed with the name of Shishak (fig. 80). It is intriguing to consider that it is quite possible, though there is no evidence, that this bracelet was made of gold

that had been taken from the treasures of Solomon. Shishak's tomb has not yet been found.

Shitrai (shĭt′rī). [Heb. *Shiṭray.*] A Sharonite who was in charge of David's herds in the region of Sharon (1 Chr 27:29).

Shittah. [Heb. *shiṭṭah*, "acacia"; plural *shiṭṭîm*, transliterated in the KJV as "shittim."] Any one of several species of the genus *Acacia* which grow in Bible lands, all of which are capable of surviving in arid regions where little else can grow. In the desert the acacia is small, twisted, and weatherworn, but under favorable conditions the tree may attain a height of 15-25 ft. Its branches bear strong, slender white thorns, and the fruit is a narrow bow-shaped pod. The wood itself is hard, close-grained, and durable, and hence is especially well suited for cabinetwork. It was used extensively in the construction of the tabernacle and its furniture (Ex 25; 26; 27; 30; 37; etc.). See fig. 439.

Shittim (shĭt′ĭm). [Heb. *Shiṭṭîm*, "acacias."]
1. The last camping site of the Israelites before reaching the Jordan (Jos 2:1; 3:1), called Abel-shittim (ā′bĕl-shĭt′ĭm) [Heb. *'Abel hashshiṭṭîm*, "meadow of the acacias"] in Num 33:49. The incidents of *Balaam and of Baal-peor occurred at this camping site (Mic 6:5; cf. Num 25:1). The identification of the site is still doubtful. Some suggest *Tell el-*

438. The list of Palestinian cities conquered by Pharaoh Shishak, on the temple wall at Karnak. Inset (right) is an enlargement of the portion enclosed in white line on the left

439. Shittim (acacia) tree at En-gedi in Palestine

Kefrein, 5 mi. east of the river Jordan, opposite Jericho; others *Tell el-Ḥam-mâm,* 7 mi. east of the Jordan (Map VI, E-4). See Abel, *Géographie* II, 234; Nelson Glueck, *BASOR* 91 (1943), 13-18.

2. A valley that was apparently well known for its dryness and sterility (Joel 3:18), but where acacias grew, as its name indicates. It has not been identified, but the lower Kidron Valley, which passes the east side of Jerusalem, has been suggested.

Shittim Wood. *See* Shittah.

Shiza (shī′zà). [Heb. *Shîza′.*] A Reubenite whose son Adina was one of David's "mighty men" (1 Chr 11:42).

Shoa (shō′à). [Heb. *Shôa',* "noble."] A people mentioned with the Babylonians, Chaldeans, and Assyrians (Eze 23:23). They are possibly the *Sutû,* mentioned in the *Amarna Letters as nomads in the Syrian desert, and in the Assyrian inscriptions as a people living east of the Tigris, and as allies of the Aramaeans in constant wars against the Assyrians.

Shobab (shō′băb). [Heb. *Shôbab,* "rebellious."]
1. A son of the Hezronite Caleb of the tribe of Judah (1 Chr 2:18).
2. A son of David, born at Jerusalem (2 Sa 5:13, 14; 1 Chr 3:5; 14:4).

Shobach (shō′băk). [Heb. *Shôbak,* meaning uncertain.] A captain of Hadadezer, or Hadarezer, king of Zobah. He led the Syrian forces against David, but was defeated and slain at Helam in Transjordan (2 Sa 10:16, 18). He is called Shophach (shō′făk) [Heb. *Shôphak*] in 1 Chr 19:16, 18.

Shobai (shō′bī). [Heb. *Shobay,* meaning uncertain. The name occurs on an ancient Hebrew seal.] A Levite and ancestral head of a family of gatekeepers, some of whom returned from Babylonia with Zerubba-

bel after the Captivity (Ezr 2:42; Neh 7:45).

Shobal (shō′băl). [Heb. *Shôbal.*]
1. A son of Seir the Horite, and probably the ancestral head of a tribe (Gen 36:20, 23; 1 Chr 1:38, 40). He is also listed among the Horite chiefs (Gen 36:29).
2. A son of Hur, and the ancestor of (the inhabitants of) Kiriath-jearim (1 Chr 2:50, 52; cf. 4:1, 2, 4).

Shobek (shō′běk). [Heb. *Shôbeq,* meaning uncertain.] A Jew who set his seal to Nehemiah's covenant (Neh 10:24).

Shobi (shō′bī). [Heb. *Shobi,* meaning uncertain. The name occurs on an ancient Hebrew seal.] A son of Nahash of Rabbah of the Ammonites, who with others furnished David with food and other necessities at the time of Absalom's rebellion (2 Sa 17:27-29). It is uncertain whether Shobi was the son of the Ammonite king or of a Hebrew resident in Rabbah, possibly the Hebrew governor installed there after the conquest of the city several years earlier.

Shocho. *See* Socoh, 1.

Shochoh. *See* Socoh, 1.

Shoco. *See* Socoh, 1.

Shoe. [Heb. generally *na'al;* Gr. *hupodēma.*] Shoes in Bible times were usually sandals of leather or of twisted reed, consisting of soles fastened to the feet by means of thongs (KJV "latchets"), or straps (Heb. *śerôk;* Gr. *himas;* Gen 14:23; Is 5:27; Mk 1:7; Lk 3:16; Jn 1:27). Examples of both types of sandals have been found in ancient Egyptian tombs (see fig. 440). Some footgear seems to have been of the moccasin type, that is, the shoes were heelless and covered the feet entirely. Such shoes

440. Papyrus sandals of King Tutankhamen in the Cairo Museum

are depicted in an ancient Egyptian painting at Beni Hasan, which shows Palestinian women with such shoes, but the men with sandals (see end sheet). Women's shoes made of leather are mentioned by Ezekiel (Eze 16:10). Some people, however, seem to have had no shoes if we can trust the Egyptian monuments, which show most Syrians and Palestinians barefooted. The Bible narratives give the impression that most people wore shoes, at least outdoors, from patriarchal times onward; apparently they did not wear them during meals (cf. Lk 7:38), and they removed them before entering a sacred precinct or standing on holy ground (Ex 3:5; Jos 5:15). The priests apparently wore no shoes in the Temple service, for none are mentioned in the description of the priestly garments. Captives were deprived of shoes as part of their plight (Is 20:2). Mourners did not wear them (2 Sa 15:30; Eze 24:17, 23). During the early history of Israel it was customary to give a shoe to the one with whom an agreement in matters of exchange or redemption was made (Ruth 4:7, 8). The Mosaic law required that a man's shoe be taken from him as one of the symbolic acts of insult he had to endure if he refused to take his deceased brother's wife (Deut 25:9, 10).

For the high laced boots of the Assyrian soldiers see Boot.

Shoham (shō′hăm). [Heb. *Shoham*, perhaps "carnelian."] A Merarite Levite (1 Chr 24:27).

Shomer (shō′mēr). [Heb. *Shômer*, "guard."]
1. A descendant of Asher (1 Chr 7:32); called Shemer (KJV "Shamer") in v 34.
2. For 2 Ki 12:21, see Shimrith.

Shophach. See Shobach.

Shophan. See Atroth-Shophan.

Shoshannim [Heb. *shôshannîm*, plural of *shûshan*, *"lily."] A term occurring in the titles of Ps 45 and 69, KJV (RSV "lilies"), and in the phrase "Shoshannim-Eduth" in the title to Ps 80, KJV. The term is obscure, but perhaps suggests the title of a popular religious melody.

Shoshannim-Eduth. See Shoshannim.

Shovel. The OT mentions 2 kinds of shovels: (1) The Heb. *ya‘îm* (plural), bronze tools used in the tabernacle (Ex 27:3; 38:3; Num 4:14) and in the Temple (1 Ki 7:40, 45; 2 Ki 25:14; etc.), probably for the purpose of placing coals on, and removing the ashes from, the altar. A bronze shovel, 22 in. long, apparently used for a similar purpose, has been found in the excavations of Megiddo. It consists of a long thin handle and a rectangular scoop. (2) The Heb. *rachath* (Is 30:24), an agricultural shovel much larger than the one mentioned under (1), used for winnowing.

Showbread, KJV Shewbread. [Heb. *ma‘areketh*, "layer (bread)," *ma‘areketh lechem*, and *lechem hamma‘areketh*, "layer bread," *lechem happanîm*, "bread of the presence"; Gr. *artoi tēs prostheseōs*, "loaves to set before (God)."] Unleavened bread displayed continually upon the table of showbread in the holy place of the *sanctuary (Ex 25:30; Lev 24:5-8; 1 Ki 7:48). The 12 loaves, or cakes, of showbread, which were replaced each Sabbath. The loaves that were removed, being considered holy, were eaten by the priests in the "holy place" (Lev 24:5-9). These 12 loaves constituted a perpetual thank offering to God from the 12 tribes for the blessings of life they received daily from Him. In ch 24:5-7 specific instructions are given for the preparation and use of the showbread. Each cake was made of about 4 quarts of fine flour, such as was used in a "cereal offering" (ch 2:1, RSV) and, in certain cases, as sin offerings (ch 5:11). The record is not explicit as to whether the bread was leavened, but Josephus states that leaven was not used (*Ant.* iii. 6. 6). Certain of the Kohathite Levites prepared and arranged the cakes (1 Chr 9:32). In Solomon's Temple there were "tables of shewbread," presumably ten (1 Chr 28:16; cf. 2 Chr 4:8, 19), although elsewhere we find the singular "table" (1 Ki 7:48). Perhaps they were thought of as one; possibly at a later time there was only one (see 2 Chr 13:11; 29:18). For the location of the table see fig. 471.

Shrine. A boxlike enclosure or small building in which the image or symbol of a god is kept. The word "shrine" is found in the KJV only as the rendering of the Gr. *naos* in Acts 19:24, where the reference is to a small silver object, probably a replica of the temple of Artemis at Ephesus, sold to visiting worshipers of that goddess. In the RSV, "shrine" is also the rendering of: (1) The Heb. *bêth 'elohîm* (Jgs 17:5), referring to the place set up by Micah for the worship of his images. The term is translated literally "house of gods" in the KJV. (2) The Heb. *bêth habbamôth* (2 Ki 17:29, 32; 23:19), literally "the houses of the high places." (3) The Heb. *bamah* (Eze 16:16), literally "high place." (4) The Gr. *esōteron* (Heb 6:19), literally "the innermost," or "the (place) more within."

Shroud. [Heb. *choresh,* "a wooded place."] A term appearing in Eze 31:3, KJV, used in the Old English sense of "shelter," or "covering," such as that provided by a wooded thicket.

Shua, I (shoo'à), KJV twice **Shuah** (shoo'à). [Heb. *Shúa‘*, "noble."] A Canaanite whose daughter became Judah's wife and the mother of his sons Er, Onan, and Shelah (Gen 38:2, 12; 1 Chr 2:3). She is called Bath-shua in 1 Chr 2:3, RSV.

Shua, II (shoo'à). [Heb. *Shú‘a’*.] An Asherite woman (1 Chr 7:32).

Shuah (shoo'à). [Heb. *Shúach*.]
1. A son of Abraham by Keturah (Gen 25:2; 1 Chr 1:32), and ancestor of the tribe of the Shuhites (shoo'hīts) [Heb. *Shúchí*] (Job 2:11; etc.). The name has been identified by some with the Assyrian *Súhu,* a district (spelled Sukhu on Map XI, C-5) below the mouth of the *Khábúr* River on the Middle Euphrates.
2. For Gen 38:2, 12, KJV, *see* Shua, I.
3. For 1 Chr 4:11, KJV, *see* Shuhah.

Shual (shoo'àl). [Heb. *Shú‘al,* "fox." The name occurs also on an ancient Hebrew seal.]
1. A descendant of Asher (1 Chr 7:36).
2. A district north of Michmash, near Ophrah (1 Sa 13:17).

Shubael. *See* Shebuel.

Shuhah (shoo'hà), KJV **Shuah** (shoo'à). [Heb. *Shúchah,* probably "pit."] A descendant of Judah (1 Chr 4:11).

Shuham (shoo'hăm). [Heb. *Shúcham.*] The son of Dan, and ancestral head of a tribal family, the Shuhamites (shoo'hăm-īts) [Heb. *Shúchamí*] (Num 26:42, 43). He is called Hushim [Heb. *Chushím*] in Gen 46:23, which is the result of a transposition of 2 letters of the Hebrew name.

Shuhamites. *See* Shuham.

Shuhite. *See* Shuah, 1; Bildad.

Shulamite. *See* Shulammite.

Shulammite (shoo'lăm-īt), KJV **Shulamite** (shoo'lăm-īt). [Heb. *Shúlammíth.*] A native of Shulem, by which probably "Shunem" is meant, as may be concluded from the fact that the town of * Shunem was known as Shulem in the time of Eusebius (4th cent. A.D.), and today bears the name *Sôlem.* The term is found in the Song of Solomon (ch 6:13) as the designation of a young woman. It has been suggested that Solomon used the term because the women of that town were noted for their beauty (cf. 1 Ki 1:3).

Shumathites (shoo'măth-īts). [Heb. *Shumathí.*] One of the families of Kiriath-jearim (1 Chr 2:53).

Shunammite (shoo'năm-īt). [Heb. *Shúnammíth,* a native (woman) or inhabitant of Shunem.]
1. The appellative of Abishag, David's nurse (1 Ki 1:3, 15; 2:17, 21, 22).

2. The designation of a wealthy woman of Shunem who showed great kindness to the prophet Elisha. As a reward he promised her that God would give her a son. Later when the boy died Elisha raised him to life (2 Ki 4:8-37). At a later date the Shunammite left Israel because of a famine. During her absence her property was seized, but was returned by special order of the king, who was influenced in his decision by the story of her experiences with Elisha (ch 8:1-6).

Shunem (shoo'něm). [Heb. *Shúnem.*] A Canaanite city, mentioned in the Egyptian records of Thutmose III as *Shnm,* and in the *Amarna Letters as *Shunama.* The city was assigned to Issachar (Jos 19:18). The Philistines encamped there before the battle of Gilboa, which ended in the death of Saul (1 Sa 28:4). It was the home town of the young woman who nursed David during his last days (1 Ki 1:3), and of the wealthy woman who offered hospitality to Elisha (2 Ki 4:8-37). The site is now

441. The village of *Sôlem,* ancient Shunem

known as *Sôlem,* and lies 7 mi. east of Megiddo (Map VI, C-3).

Shuni (shoo'nī). [Heb. *Shúní.*] A son of Gad (Gen 46:16), and ancestral head of a tribal family, the Shunites (shoo'nīts) [Heb. *Shúní*] (Num 26:15).

Shunites. *See* Shuni.

Shupham. *See* Shephuphan.

Shuphamites. *See* Shephuphan.

Shuppim (shŭp'ĭm). [Heb. *Shuppim,* meaning unknown.]

1. A Benjamite (1 Chr 7:12, 15). *See* Shephuphan.

2. A Levite gatekeeper (1 Chr 26:16).

Shur (shōōr). [Heb. *Shûr,* "wall."] A desert area on the northeastern border of Egypt (1 Sa 15:7; 27:8), where the angel found Hagar (Gen 16:7). Between this area and Kadesh, Abraham dwelt (ch 20:1). The Ishmaelites later occupied the territory adjacent to Shur (ch 25:18). The Israelites entered the territory after crossing the Red Sea (Ex 15:22). It seems to have received its name from the border fortifications built by the Egyptians across the Isthmus of Suez to protect Egypt from the intrusion of Asiatics. This fortification system, called "the wall of the princes" in the Egyptian texts, existed at least as early as the 20th cent. B.C. Map V, B-5.

Shushan. *See* Susa.

Shuthalhites. *See* Shuthelah, 1.

Shuthelah (shōō-thē'lá). [Heb. *Shûthelach,* meaning uncertain.]

1. A son of Ephraim, and a tribal ancestor of the Shuthelahites (shōō-thē'lá-hīts), KJV Shuthalhites (shōō-thăl'hīts) [Heb. *Shuthalchî*] (Num 26:35, 36; 1 Chr 7:20).

2. A later Ephraimite (1 Chr 7:21).

Shuthelahites. *See* Shuthelah, 1.

Shuttle. *See* Weaving.

Sia. *See* Siaha.

Siaha (sī'á-há), or **Sia** (sī'á). [Heb. *Si'aha'* and *Si'a',* meaning uncertain.] The ancestral head of a family of Nethinim, or Temple servants, some of whom returned from Babylonia (Ezr 2:44; Neh 7:47).

Sibbecai (sĭb'ē-kī), KJV twice **Sibbechai** (sĭb'ē-kā'ī). [Heb. *Sibbekay.*] A Hushathite, one of David's "mighty men" (1 Chr 11: 29), who gained fame by slaying a gigantic Philistine named Saph (2 Sa 21:18; 1 Chr 20:4), and became captain of the division of David's army that served in the 8th month (1 Chr 27:11). He is called Mebunnai in 2 Sa 23:27.

Sibbechai. *See* Sibbecai.

Sibboleth. *See* Shibboleth.

Sibmah (sĭb'má), KJV once **Shibmah** (shĭb'má). [Heb. *Sibmah.*] A town of Transjordan assigned to the tribe of Reuben (Num 32:38; Jos 13:19); called Sebam (sē'băm), KJV "Shebam" (shē'băm) [Heb. *Sebam*] in Num 32:3. It afterward fell to the Moabites, during whose occu-

pancy it seems to have become celebrated for its vines (Is 16:8, 9; Jer 48:32). The site is sought near Heshbon, but has not been identified with certainty.

Sibraim (sĭb-rā'ĭm). [Heb. *Sibrayim,* meaning uncertain.] A place on the northern boundary of Ezekiel's ideal Canaan (Eze 47:16); identification uncertain.

Sichem. *See* Shechem.

Sickle. [Heb. *chermesh, maggal;* Gr. *drepanon.*] A curved, knifelike agricultural tool used for cutting grain (Deut 16:9; 23:25; etc.). The earliest archeological specimens of the sickle consist of a curved wooden handle into which flint blades were inserted. Later the sickle had a bronze or iron blade and a wooden handle, and differed little in appearance from modern sickles. The reading "sickle" (1 Sa 13:20, RSV) is based on the LXX, the Hebrew reading "plowshare" twice here.

Siddim, Vale of. *See* Siddim, Valley of.

Siddim (sĭd'ĭm), **Valley of,** KJV **Siddim, Vale of.** [Heb. *Siddîm.*] A valley apparently identified with the Dead Sea in Gen 14:3. In v 10 this valley is said to have been full of "slimepits" (that is, asphalt or bitumen pits). Asphalt is found in Palestine only in the Dead Sea, where it arises from the bottom of the southern part of the sea and floats to the shore in large chunks. This is the main reason why the Vale of Siddim is sought in this part of the Dead Sea, south of the peninsula *el-Lisán,* "the Tongue," where the water has an average depth of only 16 ft., in contrast with the northern section, where the depth exceeds 1,000 ft. As late as Roman times the section at the Tongue was still shallow enough to be forded, but the water level of the Dead Sea has constantly risen and covered large areas in the south.

Sidon (sī'dŏn), KJV OT usually **Zidon** (zī'dŏn). [Heb. *Sîdôn.* The name appears as *Sidunu* in the *Amarna Letters and Akkadian records, *Dydwn3* in Egyptian records, and *Sdn* in Phoenician inscriptions; Gr. *Sidōn.*] A Phoenician port city situated on a small promontory jutting out into the Mediterranean Sea about 23 mi. north of Tyre, and about as far south of Beirut (Map VI, A-3; fig. 442). It marked the northern limit of Canaan (Gen 10:19). In the 2d millennium B.C. Sidon was the leading city of the Phoenicians, and consequently "Sidonian" became a general term for "Phoenician." However, it lost its supremacy to Tyre toward the end of that millennium. Sidon appears for the 1st time in secular records in the Amarna period

442. Air view of the harbor and city of Sidon, on the Phoenician coast

(14th cent. B.C.) as an Egyptian possession. According to these records Zimreda, Sidon's king, notified the Egyptian Pharaoh that Aziru, the Amorite ruler, threatened Egypt's sovereignty over the city.

When the Israelites settled in Canaan, Sidon was assigned to Asher, but it was never occupied by the Israelites (Jos 19:28; Jgs 1:31). However, during the period of the judges the people of Israel adopted the idolatrous worship of the gods of the Sidonians along with that of the heathen deities of other nations (Jgs 10:6). Also during that period the Sidonians oppressed the Israelites (v 12). The Sidonian divinities, including *Baal and *Ashtoreth, were again worshiped in Israel in the period of the kings (1 Ki 11:5, 33; 16:31; 2 Ki 23:13), during which time Sidon was subordinate to Tyre (Jos. *Ant.* ix. 14. 2).

In 701 B.C. Sidon submitted to Sennacherib of Assyria (*ANET* 287), but rebelled in the time of Esarhaddon and as a result was conquered and destroyed in 678 B.C. Esarhaddon rebuilt the city and called it "Esarhaddon's castle" (*ANET* 290). However, Assyria, in turn, vanished

after a short time, whereupon Sidon, under its old name, made a political comeback and once more became an important city. Jeremiah predicted its subjugation by Nebuchadnezzar, king of Babylon (Jer 27:3, 6), but no historical records concerning the fulfillment of this prophecy have so far come to light. Ezekiel denounced the city for its hostility toward Israel (Eze 28:21-23), and Joel claimed that the Sidonians had spoiled Jerusalem of its treasures and sold its inhabitants for slaves (Joel 3:4-6). It is not known to which time these statements refer.

When Cambyses, the 2d king of the Persian Empire, marched against Egypt, Sidon submitted to him (526 B.C.). The Sidonians later proved themselves great friends of the Persians and were consequently given the Plain of Sharon as a reward for their loyalty (*ANET* 505). When the Jews returned from exile, Zerubbabel procured cedars for the new Temple from the Sidonians (Ezr 3:7). Sidon rebelled against Artaxerxes III in 351 B.C., but was reconquered and once more destroyed. After it was rebuilt it became part of Alexander the Great's Hellenistic empire in 333 B.C. Upon his death it was inherited by his successors. When Pompey conquered the Seleucid possessions in Syria and Phoenicia for the Romans in the 1st cent. B.C., Sidon became a Roman possession and, like Tyre, enjoyed the right of a "free city." This was probably the status of Sidon in the time of Christ.

Of the ancient kings of Sidon the following are known by name from various records: Zimreda in the 14th cent. B.C. (*Amarna Letters), Tubalu in the time of Sennacherib, 701 B.C., Abdimilkutte in the 7th cent. B.C. in the time of Esarhaddon, Tabnit and Eshmunazar, *c.* 450 B.C. (from sarcophagi), and Tennes in the time of Artaxerxes III in the 4th cent. B.C.

People of Sidon came to Galilee and listened to the preaching of Jesus (Mk 3:8; Lk 6:17). On one occasion Jesus visited the region of Sidon (Mt 15:21; Mk 7:24, 31). King Agrippa I of Judea had certain grievances against Tyre and Sidon, but their administrators appeased him with the help of one of his intimate courtiers (Acts 12:20). There was apparently a Christian church in Sidon when Paul passed through this port city as a prisoner on his way to Rome about A.D. 60, for he was allowed to visit his (Christian) friends there (ch 27:3). In subsequent centuries several battles were fought at Sidon, especially in the time of the crusaders. The most conspicuous ruin of Sidon, the Tower of Sagette, dates from the time of the crusaders.

The modern town of Saida has a population of about 40,000, the majority of whom are Moslems. In the ancient necropolis have been found several Hellenistic sarcophagi, among them the sarcophagus of King *Eshmun'azar,* now in the Louvre in Paris, bearing a long Phoenician inscription of the 5th cent. B.C. (see its translation in *ANET* 505; see fig. 532), and the sarcophagus of Tabnit, another king of the 5th cent. B.C., whose remains were still in the coffin (now in the Museum of the Ancient Orient at Istanbul).

Sidonians (sĭ-dŏ′nĭ-ăns), KJV frequently **Zidonians** (zĭ-dŏ′nĭ-ănz). [Heb. *Sidonim.*] Primarily the natives or inhabitants of Sidon, but later used as a general term for Phoenicians (Deut 3:9; Jgs 3:3; 18:7; etc.). This latter usage is evident in 1 Ki 16:31, RSV, where *Ethbaal, who was a king of Tyre, is referred to as "king of the Sidonians." Similarly, Hiram, known as a king of Tyre, is referred to in a Phoenician inscription discovered on Cyprus as "king of the Sidonians."

Siege. *See* Battering Ram; Mound.

Siege Mound. *See* Mound.

Sieve. [Heb. *kebarah, naphah.*] A utensil with openings permitting smaller particles to fall through while the larger ones are retained. The term is used figuratively, once (Is 30:28) of "vanity," that is, "nothingness" (RSV "destruction," that is, that which leads to nothingness), and once (Amos 9:9) in a figure of speech illustrating the separation of sinners from Israel.

Sign. [Heb. generally *'ôth,* "distinguishing mark," "sign"; Gr. *sēmeion,* "sign," "miracle."] A distinguishing mark, a reminder, a token, sometimes of a miraculous nature, often given to confirm an inspired message or divine authority, or to warn or encourage to cooperation with the divine will. At Creation God decreed that the solar luminaries were to serve "for signs, and for seasons" (Gen 1:14), perhaps meaning in part that divine omens would be portrayed in them, but also that they would be useful for telling directions, as in navigation, and for measuring time (*see* Day; Month; Season; Year).

The sign of the *rainbow was given as a reminder that a universal flood would not again occur (Gen 9:12-17, RSV). As a sign of divine leadership God assured Moses that the Israelites would worship at the mountain where he received his call (Ex 3:12, RSV). The plague of flies that

came upon the Egyptians but not the Israelites was a "sign" distinguishing God's people from the Egyptians (Ex 8:20-24). The blood upon the houses of the Hebrews during the 1st Passover was a sign distinguishing the homes to be passed over (ch 12:13, RSV). God commanded the Israelites to bind His statutes, for a sign, or reminder, upon their hands and between their eyes (Deut 6:8; 11:18), a command taken literally by the Jews (see Mt 23:5). Korah and those with him were swallowed by the earth as a "sign," or "warning" (RSV), to others (Num 26:10). Gideon and King Hezekiah received supernatural signs of the Lord to assure them that His word was dependable (see Jgs 6:17-21; Is 38:5-8). Jonathan recognized the challenge of the Philistine garrison as a good omen given by God (1 Sa 14:9-15). Certain signs were given as proof of a prophet's commission (Ex 4:30, 31; 1 Sa 2:34; cf. ch 3:20; see Is 20:2-4).

The shepherds were able to recognize the Christ child by the fact that He was "wrapped in swaddling clothes, lying in a manger" (Lk 2:12). Christ enumerated certain "signs" or omens of His second coming (Mt 24:3; Mk 13:4; Lk 21:7). *See* Last Days. Paul stated that the "signs of a true apostle" (2 Cor 12:12, RSV), as manifested in himself, were in "patience, in signs, and wonders, and mighty deeds." The term "sign" is sometimes used to mean *"miracle" (see Ex 4:8, 9; Deut 4:34; Jer 32:21; cf. Num 14:22). The Jews desired a miraculous sign from Christ (Mt 12:38; Mk 8:11; Lk 11:16; etc.) as proof of His divinity, ignoring His many miracles attesting that fact. Ancient Israel was cautioned regarding false signs (Deut 13:1-3; etc.) and Christ and Paul warned of the deceptive signs of Satan that would occur in the last days (Mt 24:24; Mk 13:22; 2 Th 2:9).

Signet. *See* Seal.

Sihon (sī′hŏn). [Heb. *Sichon.*] An Amorite king in the Transjordan region whose kingdom reached from the Jabbok to the Arnon. His capital was Heshbon. He conquered his territory from the Moabites (Num 21:26-30), and also subjugated certain Midianite tribes, for 5 Midianite princes were his vassals (Jos 13:21). When the Israelites appeared on his border they requested permission to pass through this territory on their way to Canaan. Sihon refused and came against Israel with an army instead. In the ensuing battle of Jahaz the Amorites were defeated, Sihon was slain, and all his territory was taken over by the Israelites (Num 21:21-32; Deut 2:26-36; Jgs 11:22; Ps 135:4, 10-12). They pitched their camp in the midst of Sihon's former kingdom before advancing against the king of Bashan (Num 22:1). Because the territory captured from Sihon was good pastureland, the tribes of Reuben and Gad requested it, and were assigned that area as a possession by Moses (ch 32:1-38).

Sihor. *See* Shihor.

Silas (sī′lȧs). [Gr. *Silas,* probably from the Aramaic *She'ila',* equivalent to the Heb. *Sha'ûl,* "Saul." The name Silas occurs in Josephus' writings and in Greek inscriptions. Its Latin form, also attested by inscriptions, is *Silvanus,* of which the NT Greek form is *Silouanos.*] A Roman citizen (Acts 16:37, 38), a companion of Paul during the 2d Missionary Journey (chs 15:40 to 18:22). Since a comparison of Acts 18:5 with 2 Cor 1:19 shows that he was also called Silvanus (sĭl-vā′nŭs), he was doubtless the Silvanus of 1 Th 1:1; 2 Th 1:1; 1 Pe 5:12. He was a leader in the church (Acts 15:22) and a prophet (v 32). After the Jerusalem Council he, with Judas Barsabas, was chosen to go with Paul and Barnabas to convey letters from the Council to the Gentile members in "Antioch and Syria and Cilicia" explaining the decisions reached by the Council (vs 22, 23). Arriving at Antioch, Silas and the others delivered their messages, and Silas and Judas, being prophets, exhorted and strengthened the church there (vs 30-32). Later Silas was chosen by Paul to accompany him on his 2d Missionary Journey (vs 40, 41). At Philippi, Silas and Paul were arrested, flogged, and thrown into prison (ch 16:17-24). An earthquake brought about their release, and their Roman citizenship elicited an apology from the magistrates (vs 25-40). Later Silas and Paul went to Thessalonica and to Beroea (ch 17:1-10). Silas remained there with Timothy while Paul continued on to Athens (vs 14, 15). Later Silas and Timothy joined Paul at Corinth and spent some time preaching (cf. Acts 18:5; 2 Cor 1:19). Nothing is known of Silas' later life unless, as probably indicated by Acts 18:5 and 2 Cor 1:19, he was the secretary who wrote down Peter's 1st epistle (1 Pe 5:12).

Silk. A fabric woven from the delicate thread prepared from the fibers produced by the silkworm, a mulberry-feeding caterpillar. It is highly probable that the Hebrews, at least from the time of their commercial enterprises under Solomon, were acquainted with, and made use of, silk, although there is no unquestioned reference to it in the OT. It is not certain that the Heb. *meshî,* rendered "silk" in Eze 16:10, 13, actually refers to that material. The Heb. *shesh,* rendered "silk" in Prov 31:22, KJV, should be translated "fine linen" (RSV). To the Greeks silk became known as *sērikon,* that is, "pertaining to the Seres," a people thought by some to be the Chinese. This term, *sērikon,* is accurately rendered "silk" (Rev 18:12), and appears in the list of various articles of merchandise handled by the merchants of Babylon.

Silla (sĭl′ȧ). [Heb. *Silla'.*] A place near Jerusalem (2 Ki 12:20); not identified.

Siloah. *See* Siloam.

Siloam (sĭ-lō′ăm), or **Shiloah** (shĭ-lō′ȧ), KJV once **Siloah** (sĭ-lō′ȧ), RSV once **Shelah** (shē′lȧ). [Heb. *Shiloach,* from *shalach,* "to send," and *Shelach;* Gr. *Silōam.*] A pool fed by an aqueduct leading from the *Gihon spring. It is called Siloam in Jn 9:7, and Shelah (KJV "Siloah") in Neh 3:15. The pool was situated, according to Jo-

443. The Pool of Siloam at Jerusalem

444. The Siloam tunnel, at the spot where the work-men met as they tunneled from each end

sephus (*War* v. 4. 1, 2), in the southern part of Jerusalem, where a pool 58 x 18 ft., called *Birket Silwân*, is still found (fig. 443). It receives its water from the Virgin's Well in the Kidron Valley through a rock-hewn tunnel 1,749 ft. long, about 2 ft. wide, and between 5 and 15 ft. high (Map XVII, XVIII, fig. 259). It is generally believed that the tunnel (fig. 444) and the original pool were constructed by King Hezekiah (2 Ki 20:20; 2 Chr 32:30).

In 1880 a Hebrew inscription of 6 lines was discovered (fig. 445) on the wall of the tunnel, about 20 ft. from its exit at the pool. It describes the process of tunnel digging and gives some valuable information concerning its measurements:

"[. . . when] (the tunnel) was driven through. And this was the way in which it was cut through:—While [. . .] (were) still [. . .] axe (s), each man toward his fellow, and while there were still three cubits to be cut through, [there was heard] the voice of a man calling to his fellow, for there was *an overlap* in the rock on the right [and on the left]. And when the tunnel was driven through, the quarrymen hewed (the rock), each man toward his fellow, axe against axe; and the water flowed from the spring toward the reservoir for 1,200 cubits, and the height of the rock above the head (s) of the quarrymen was 100 cubits" (W. F. Albright, *ANET* 321).

The tower of Siloam mentioned in Lk 13:4 was probably a structure standing near the Pool of Siloam.

Silvanus. *See* Silas.

Silver. [Heb. *keseph;* Aramaic *kesaph;* Gr. *arguros* and *argurion*.] A white metallic element, mined since ancient times and used for various ornamental and utilitarian purposes. *Tarshish is mentioned as a source for silver (Jer 10:9; Eze 27:12). Egyptian texts mention Assyria, Syria, Mitanni, and the land of the Hittites as countries from which they obtained silver, and it was probably imported into

445. The Siloam inscription from Hezekiah's time, now in a museum in Istanbul

Palestine, where it does not occur, from the same countries. It is found occasionally in a native, almost pure state, but is usually found mixed, sometimes generously, with gold. After being mined (Job 28:1, RSV), it is purified from dross in a furnace (Ps 12:6; Prov 17:3; 25:4; Eze 22:22). Its first mention in the Bible relates it to wealth (Gen 13:2), and along with other precious materials it served many purposes in the building of the tabernacle (Ex 26:19; 27:10; 38:10; etc.) and was used in the Temple built by Solomon (2 Chr 2:7, 14; 9:24; etc.). Although the Jews did not mint coins until after the Exile, silver served as a medium of exchange from the days of Abraham (Gen 20:16; 37:28; etc.). Jewelry (Gen 24:53; Song 1:11), household objects (Gen 44:2), crowns (Zec 6:11), and idols (Ps 115:4; Acts 19:24) were made of silver.

Silver Coin. See Money, 1.

Silverling. A rendering of the Heb. *keseph* (Is 7:23, KJV), literally, "silver" (RSV "shekel of silver"). A piece of silver, or shekel, is doubtless intended.

Simeon (sim′ē-ŭn). [Heb. *Shim'ôn,* "hearkening (of prayer)," or "answering (of prayer)." The name is attested in a Heb. contract among the Dead Sea scrolls, in an inscription on a Jewish ossuary (see fig. 446), and in Nabataean and Palmyrene inscriptions. Gr. *Sumeōn.*]

446. Inscription on a Jewish ossuary (bone receptacle) mentioning "Simeon Barsaba"

1. The second son of Leah and Jacob (Gen 29:33). He and his brother Levi massacred the men of Shechem in revenge for the humiliation of their sister Dinah (ch 34:25-31). Simeon was selected by Joseph to be kept bound in prison as security until the other brothers returned with Benjamin (ch 42:24). Simeon had 6 sons, of whom 5 became ancestors of tribal families (Gen 46:10; Num 26:12-14; 1 Chr 4:24). When Jacob on his deathbed blessed his sons he condemned Simeon's and Levi's cruelty and predicted that their descendants would become divided and scattered in Israel (Gen 49:5-7).

2. The tribe descended from Simeon, 1. The tribe was strong at the time of the

Exodus, numbering 59,300 fighting men (Num 1:23; 2:13), but it suffered such heavy losses in subsequent years that a 2d census some years later listed only 22,-200 (ch 26:12-14). The tribal leader during the early wilderness wandering was Shelumiel, son of Zurishaddai (ch 1:6; 2:12; 7:36, 41; 10:19), and later, Shemuel, son of Ammihud (ch 34:20). Shaphat, son of Hori, represented the tribe among the spies (ch 13:5). It seems strange that in the blessings of Moses (Deut 33) no mention is made of Simeon. It is not known whether the omission was intentional on the part of Moses or whether some scribe later inadvertently omitted it.

When the 12 tribes gathered at the mountains of Ebal and Gerizim, the tribe of Simeon stood on the slopes of Mount Gerizim, pronouncing the blessings of the Lord (Deut 27:12). When the country was distributed by lot, the tribe of Simeon, which apparently had become one of the most insignificant, was given land within the southern part of the territory of Judah (Map VI, F-2), in which some important cities were located, such as Beer-sheba, Ziklag, and Hormah (Jos 19:1-9). Subsequently the Simeonites joined Judah in their wars against the Canaanites (Jgs 1:1, 3, 17). They seem eventually to have been absorbed by Judah, and hardly ever played a role as a separate tribe, although they did not entirely lose their identity, for in the time of Hezekiah they are reported to have defeated the people of Ham and the Meunim who dwelt in the valley of Gedor, and to have occupied their territory (1 Chr 4:24, 39-41). About the same time some 500 Simeonites exterminated the remnants of the Amalekites and took over their land (vs 42, 43). The tribe was envisioned by Ezekiel in the ideal Israel in Canaan (Eze 48:24, 25, 33), and by John among those sealed by the angel of Revelation 7 (v 7).

3. A pious man who waited for the salvation of Israel. Having received the promise from the Holy Spirit that he would not die until he had seen the Messiah, he was present at the Temple when Joseph and Mary were there to present the infant Jesus to the Lord according to Hebrew law. Simeon recognized in Him the Christ and made predictions concerning the Child and His mother, at the same time expressing his willingness to die now that his most fervent desire had been fulfilled (Lk 2:25-35).

4. For Acts 15:14, KJV, *see* Peter.

5. For Lk 3:30, KJV, *see* Symeon, 1.

6. For Acts 13:1, KJV, *see* Symeon, 3.

Simeonites (sĭm'ē-ŭn-īts). [Heb. *Shim'oni*.] Members of the tribe descended from Simeon, 1.

Simon (sī'mŭn). [Gr. *Simōn*, probably like *Sumeōn* (*see* Simeon), a transliteration of the Heb. *Shim'ôn*, "hearkening (of prayer)." The name occurs also in inscriptions.]

1. Simon Peter. *See* Peter.

2. Simon the *Cananaean (KJV "Canaanite"), or *Zealot (Mt 10:4; Mk 3:18; Lk 6:15; Acts 1:13), one of Jesus' disciples. The Bible says nothing of him beyond naming him as one of the Twelve. There is a tradition that he labored in North Africa, and that he was martyred in Palestine during the reign of Domitian, a persecutor of the Christians.

3. Simon, the brother of Jesus (Mt 13:55; Mk 6:3). For his relationship to Jesus *see* Brethren of the Lord.

4. Simon the leper, a resident of Bethany (Mt 26:6; Mk 14:3). The term "leper" suggests that he had suffered from leprosy but had recovered, doubtless healed by Jesus, for he would otherwise have been an outcast. While Jesus was a guest at Simon's home a woman anointed Him with a precious ointment (Mt 26:6-13; Mk 14:3-9). A similar account of a woman's anointing of Jesus calls the host, Simon, a Pharisee (Lk 7:36, 39, 40). Many commentators regard this as a separate incident, and thus make this Pharisee another Simon. For reasons for identifying the two see *SDACom* 5:764-767.

5. Simon the Pharisee. *See* Simon, 4.

6. Simon of Cyrene (Mt 27:32; Mk 15:21; Lk 23:26), the man who was forced to bear Jesus' cross. Mark records that he was "coming out of the country" at the time, and that he was the father of Alexander and Rufus.

7. Judas Iscariot's father (Jn 6:71; 13:2, 26).

8. Simon the *sorcerer (Acts 8:9-24), usually called Simon Magus (mā'gŭs), the 2d element coming from the Gr. *magos*, "magician." According to Justin Martyr he was born at Gitto, a village of Samaria (*First Apology* 26). Simon's first contact with Christianity seems to have been on the occasion of Philip the evangelist's laboring in Samaria (Acts 8:5). Simon, who is described as one who deceived the people of Samaria by performing so-called miracles, which earned for him the title "the great power of God" (v 10), was probably actually of a class of Jews who traded on the superstition and

credulity of the heathen. When Simon heard the gospel of Christ preached by Philip he believed and was baptized, although in the light of later events there is doubt that he was converted. The "miracles and signs" Philip performed amazed him (Acts 8:13), so that when he later discovered that the power to do these things came through the receiving of the Holy Spirit, he offered to buy the gift from Peter (vs 18, 19). Peter thereupon severely rebuked him (vs 20-23). Simon asked for prayer that no punishment befall him (v 24). Simon became a central figure in certain literature of the early centuries, being described as a precursor of the Gnostic heretics, and as a teacher whose system was to a large degree founded on angelology, astrology, and an unbounded belief in his own "divine" powers. In the so-called *Recognitions of Clement* and the *Clementine Homilies* he is depicted as disputing and performing miracles in opposition to Peter, in both of which he is worsted by the apostle.

9. Simon the *tanner (Acts 9:43), a resident of Joppa who was the host of Peter for "many days." While staying at his house, which was "by the sea side" (ch 10:6), Peter had the vision of the sheet let down from heaven (vs 9-16), and was called to visit Cornelius (vs 17-22).

Simon Magus. *See* Simon, 8.

Simple. In the OT a rendering generally of the Heb. *pethî*, "inexperienced, innocent, unsuspecting"; "one who can be easily influenced either for good or for bad, and sometimes one who is, in addition, morally weak." For example, in Ps 19:7 a "simple" person is one without experience but who is able to learn and can profit by instruction. The simple young man of Prov 7:7 was lacking in good sense (see chs 8:5; 14:15). In the NT "simple" appears twice, once in Rom 16:18, KJV, as the rendering of the Gr. *akakos*, "innocent," "guileless," and once in v 19, KJV, as the rendering of the Gr. *akeraios*, "pure," "innocent."

Simri. *See* Shimri, 3.

Sin, I. [Heb. generally *chatta'th* and related terms, "fault," "sin," from *chata'*, "to miss (a mark)," "to fall short," "to do wrong," "to offend," "to be culpable," "to commit a sin"; Gr. chiefly *hamartia*, "a missing (of the mark)," "sin."] Any deviation from the known will of God, either of neglect to do what He has specifically commanded or of doing what He has specifically forbidden. Sin originated with Lucifer as the result of inordinate pride in the beauty and wisdom God had given him (see Eze 28:17), and of an overweening desire and jealousy for what God had not given him (Is 14:12-14). Sin entered this earth when Satan persuaded Adam and Eve to take that which God had reserved for Himself, under the subterfuge that they might thereby attain to a superior state of wisdom (Gen 3:1-6). Thus, "by one man sin entered into the world," and as a result "all have sinned" (Rom 5:12). "By one man's disobedience many were made sinners" (v 19). "Sin is the transgression of the law" (1 Jn 3:4) even as "love is the fulfilling of the law" (Rom 13:10)—that is, "law" in the sense of all of God's revealed will, and especially the Decalogue, which epitomizes all that God requires of man (see Ec 12:13, 14). Where there is no "law"—that is, where there is no divine revelation of God's will—there is no sin or transgression (Rom 4:15). Our Lord declared, "If I had not come and spoken unto them, they had not had sin," but once the will of God is known, men "have no cloke for their sin" (Jn 15:22). The prophet summed up God's requirements in the admonition, "To do justly, and to love mercy, and to walk humbly with thy God" (Mic 6:8), that is, to be fair and kind toward one's fellow men and to maintain a humble spirit before God. Sin is any failure to attain to this high standard. "The wages of sin is death" (Rom 6:23).

There are many synonyms of "sin," such as "evil" (Heb. generally ra'; Gr. generally forms of kakos) and "iniquity" (Heb. generally 'awen, "wickedness," 1 Sa 15:23; etc., and 'awon, "intentional transgression," "guilt," Gen 15:16; etc.; Gr. generally adikia, "unrighteousness," Lk 13:27, etc., and anomia, "lawlessness," Mt 7:23; etc.).

Sin, II (sĭn). [Heb. Sîn.]

1. A wilderness through which the Israelites passed on their way from Egypt to Mount Sinai (Ex 16:1; 17:1; Num 33:11, 12), lying between Elim and Rephidim. Two tracts of desert have traditionally been identified with this Wilderness of Sin: (1) Debbet er-Ramleh, which lies near Serābîṭ el-Khâdem, the center of the ancient Egyptian turquoise mines in the interior of the Sinai Peninsula (Map V, C-5), and (2) the plain of el-Merkhâh on the western coast of the peninsula between Abu Zeneimeh and the Wâdî Feirân (Map V, C/D-5). Map V, B-5, gives another location conjecturally, according to the "northern route" theory. If the 1st

447. The Wilderness of Sin (*Debbet er-Ramleh*) on the Sinai Peninsula

identification is correct, the Israelites left the coast of what is now the Gulf of Suez at the mouth of the Wâdî Baba and followed it to the interior of the Sinai Peninsula, but if the 2d identification is correct, they continued their wandering along the coast until they reached the Wâdî Feirân, and then turned inland through that wadi.

2. A city and fortress of Egypt (Eze 30:15, 16, KJV), generally recognized as the city of Swn, Pelusium (pĕ-lū'shĭ-ŭm), a frontier city of Lower Egypt. This identification was first made by Jerome in the Vulgate in contradistinction to the tradition reflected in the LXX that the city of Saïs was meant. Pelusium was strongly fortified and rightly considered as the key to Egypt, and as its "strength" (v 15). The city lies close to the sea, and though not definitely identified, is believed to be the ruins of Tell el-Farāma, some 13 mi. east of the Suez Canal. Map V, A-4.

Sin Offering. See Sacrifices and Offerings.

Sina. See Sinai.

Sinai (sī'nī), KJV of NT twice **Sina** (sī'nà). [Heb. Sînay, meaning uncertain, although the name may be connected with Sin, the Babylonian moon-god. Gr. Sina.]

1. The mountain from which God spoke the Decalogue; also called Horeb (hō'rĕb) [Heb. Choreb], the meaning of which is also uncertain (Deut 1:2, 6, 19; 4:10, 15; 5:2; 9:8; cf. Ex 19:11, 18, 20, 23; 24:

16; 31:18; 34:2, 4, 29, 32; Lev 7:38; etc.). The children of Israel reached the mountain of Sinai by way of Marah, Elim, and Rephidim in the 3d month of their travel from Egypt (Ex 15:23, 27; 16:1; 17:1; 19:1, 2). It lay at a distance of 11 days' journey from Kadesh-barnea (Deut 1:2). "Before" the mountain was a wilderness large enough for the camp of Israel (Ex 19:2). Christian tradition has consistently located this mountain in the interior of the Sinai Peninsula, but 2 mountains there have been identified as Mount Sinai. A tradition going back to Eusebius (4th cent. A.D.) states *Jebel Serbal* to be the mountain of lawgiving. This mountain is a solitary and impressive prominence, 6,791 ft. high, south of the *Wâdī Feirân* (usually identified with Rephidim). However, there is no plain in its vicinity that would have allowed an encampment of any considerable size. The 2d tradition, going back to the time of Justinian (6th cent. A.D.), identifies Sinai with *Jebel Mûsā*, the southeastern crest of a 2-peaked granite mountain. The northwestern peak, the *Ras es̱-Ṣafṣafeh*, has an altitude of 6,540 ft., and the southeastern, the *Jebel Mûsā*, an altitude of about 7,363 ft. In front of the *Ras es̱-Ṣafṣafeh* is a wide plain called *er-Râhah*,

from which the mount is clearly seen and upon which a large camp could be situated. There is no plain near the other sides of the mountain ridge suitable for a large-sized camp. Also *Jebel Mûsā's* summit is visible from only a limited area. Modern visitors who climb both peaks and compare the geography with the description given in the Pentateuch usually are inclined to identify *Ras es̱-Ṣafṣafeh* with Mount Sinai, and can hardly understand why *Jebel Mûsā* has had this honor for so many centuries. See fig. 448.

In a valley (*Wâdī ed-Deir*) adjoining *Jebel Mûsā,* lies the famous monastery of St. Catherine, founded by the emperor Justinian in A.D. 527 in honor of St. Catherine, a Christian martyr who was tortured on the wheel and beheaded in Alexandria in A.D. 307. This place near Mount Sinai was selected for the monastery because tradition claimed that angels had carried her body to the summit of *Jebel Katherin,* a lofty mountain 8,576 ft. high, 2¼ mi. southwest of *Jebel Mûsā.* The monastery (fig. 449), staffed by Greek monks, has one of the finest libraries of the East. It was there that Tischendorf in 1844 and 1859 discovered the Codex Sinaiticus, one of the oldest Bible manuscripts extant (4th cent. A.D.). See fig. 72.

448. *Ras es̱-Ṣafṣafeh,* the probable mount of lawgiving

Some scholars, thinking that the giving of the law as described in the Pentateuch (Ex 19:18) was accompanied by volcanic activities, object to the identification of Mount Sinai with any mountain within the confines of the Sinai Peninsula, on the ground that there are no volcanoes there. They point instead to an area in Midian, east of the Gulf of Aqabah, where volcanoes that have erupted in historical times can be found. However, there is no necessity for the divine manifestations connected with the giving of the Decalogue to be explained in terms of a volcanic eruption. God was not bound to use a volcano to manifest Himself in smoke and fire on top of a mountain. Other scholars, with no convincing arguments in favor of their views, attempt to locate Mount Sinai near Kadesh, or in Mount Seir south of the Dead Sea. This dictionary holds that *Ras eṣ-Ṣafṣafeh* has more to recommend it as the true Mount Sinai than any other proposed mountain in southwestern Asia.

2. The wilderness before Mount Sinai in which the Israelites camped when they received the Law and built the tabernacle (Ex 19:1, 2; Num 1:1, 19; 3:4, 14; etc.). It is most probably the plain *er-Râḥah* (*see* Sinai, 1), 2 mi. long and about 1 mi. wide, north of *Ras eṣ-Ṣafṣafeh*.

Sinim. *See* Syene, II.

Sinites (sī′nīts). [Heb. *Sînî.*] A Canaanite people of Phoenicia (Gen 10:17; 1 Chr 1:15), who lived in and about the city of *Siannu*. Tiglath-pileser III (8th cent. B.C.) mentions this city along with other tributary Phoenician vassals. The exact location of *Siannu* is unknown.

Sion. *See* Hermon; Zion.

Siphmoth (sĭf′mŏth). [Heb. *Śiphmôth.*] A town in southern Judah to which David sent a part of the spoils taken from the Amalekites (1 Sa 30:28); not identified.

Sippai. *See* Saph.

Sirah (sī′rȧ). [Heb. *Sirah,* appearing with the article.] A well (RSV "cistern"), according to Josephus (*Ant.* vii. 1. 5) 20 stades from Hebron. Abner was at this well when he was treacherously recalled to Hebron by Joab and slain (2 Sa 3:26). It has been identified with the *'Ain Sārah,* 1½ mi. northwest of Hebron.

Sirion. *See* Hermon.

Sisamai. *See* Sismai.

Sisera (sĭs′ẽr-ȧ). [Heb. *Sîsera',* etymology and meaning unknown.]

1. The commander of the army of Jabin, the Canaanite king of Hazor, whom

449. The monastery of St. Catherine, as seen from the slopes of Mount Sinai

Deborah and Barak defeated in a battle at the river Kishon. Fleeing from the field of battle, and seeking a temporary hiding place, he turned to the tent of Heber, a Kenite who hitherto had lived in peace with the Canaanites. Jael, Heber's wife, invited him in and slew him in his sleep (Jgs 4:2-7, 12-22; 5:20-30; 1 Sa 12:9; Ps 83:9, 10).

2. The ancestor of a class of Nethinim, or Temple servants, in the postexilic period (Ezr 2:53; Neh 7:55), possibly descendants of prisoners taken by Deborah and Barak at the battle of the Kishon.

Sismai (sĭs′mī), KJV **Sisamai** (sĭs′ȧ-mī). [Heb. *Sismay,* containing the word *Ssm,* the name of a Semitic deity attested in Ugaritic and Phoenician inscriptions.] A Judahite of the family of Hezron (1 Chr 2:40).

Sister. [Heb. *'achôth,* "sister," feminine of *'ach,* "brother"; Gr. *adelphē,* "sister."] A term used to describe the relationship of one female person to one or more other persons born of the same parents (Gen 4:22; Jn 11:1; etc.); of a female to one who has one parent common with her, such as Sarah, who was Abraham's half sister on their father's side (Gen 20:12); of a female to one of the same family or tribe (ch 24:59, 60), or to one of the same nation (Num 25:17, 18). Figuratively "sister" is used of the relationship of the nations of Judah and Israel (Jer 3:7; Eze 23:4). "Sister" is used of a woman of the same faith (Rom 16:1; 1 Cor 7:15; etc.). The term "elect sister" (2 Jn 13) may refer either to the actual sister of the "elect lady" (v 1) or to a sister church (*see* Elect Lady).

Sistrum. *See* Castanets.

Sith. [Heb. *'im,* "if," "suppose," "though."] An archaic word meaning "though" or "since," appearing in Eze 35:6, KJV.

Sithri (sĭth'rī), KJV **Zithri** (zĭth'rī). [Heb. *Sithrî,* "my hiding place (is Yahweh)." The name occurs in the Aramaic papyri from Elephantine.] A Levite of the house of Kohath (Ex 6:22).

Sitnah (sĭt'nà). [Heb. *Śiṭnah,* "enmity," or "accusation." The name comes from the same Hebrew root as the name "Satan."] One of the wells dug by Isaac in the vicinity of the Philistine city of Gerar, whose inhabitants disputed his right to it (Gen 26:21). The site is uncertain.

Sivan (sĕ-vän'). [Heb. *Sîwan,* a loan word from Akkadian *Simânu.*] The 3d month of the Jewish religious *year (Est 8:9); it begins at the new moon of May or June.

Skirt. A rendering of several Hebrew words, chiefly *kanaph,* "skirt," literally "wing," denoting the loose, flowing, outer garment typical of Oriental lands. The word "skirt" is sometimes used in a euphemistic sense, as in Deut 22:30; 27:20.

Skull, Place of the. *See* Golgotha.

Slaughter, Valley of. *See* Topheth.

Slave. [Heb. generally *'ebed,* "slave"; Gr. generally *doulos,* "slave."] A person who is considered the property of another, and is completely under his control. This term appears many times in the RSV, but only twice in the KJV, once in Jer 2:14, where it is a supplied word, and once in Rev 18:13 as a rendering of the Gr. *sōma,* "body." In both instances the term is suggested by the context. The RSV also renders *sōma* as "slave" in Rev 18:13. *'Ebed* and *doulos,* which are frequently translated "slave" in the RSV (Gen 9:25; Mt 8:9; etc.), are usually rendered "servant," or "bondman" by the KJV.

The practice of keeping slaves goes back to very early times. Abraham, in accordance with the times, kept slaves (Gen 15:3, RSV); Joseph was a slave (Ps 105: 17, RSV), and Israel was a nation of slaves

in Egypt (see Deut 16:12; 24:18, 22; RSV; etc.). Slaves were common in Mesopotamia, where they could be bought for about 40 shekels; hence many of its citizens kept slaves for household and agricultural work. In Egypt, however, slaves were much less numerous, being owned chiefly by the rich, but also at times by war veterans who were given slaves as a reward for valor. A slave might be acquired by war (cf. 2 Ki 5:2), he might be bought (Ex 12:44), sometimes for debt (2 Ki 4: 1; cf. Lev 25:39), he might be born into slavery in his master's household (Gen 15:3, RSV), or inherited (Lev 25:46). A Hebrew slave could be required to serve for only 6 years (Ex 21:2), a law not always observed (Jer 34:8-11, RSV). When a slave was released, a slave wife given him by his master, as well as children born in slavery, remained the property of the master (Ex 21:2-4). The slave might, however, voluntarily choose perpetual slavery, in which case the master bored his ear through with an awl as a sign of servitude (vs 5, 6). It was possible for a talented slave to rise to a position of importance (Prov 17:2; cf. Ps 105: 17-21; Gen 41:42-44). A slave owner was punished for killing a slave (Ex 21:20), and a slave was to be freed in certain cases of maiming (v 26). An escaped slave was not to be forcibly returned to his master (Deut 23:15, RSV). Sometimes a man sold his daughter as a slave (Ex 21:7) to be made a concubine, or secondary wife. According to Herodotus this was a regular practice among the Thracians. Solomon made slaves of the surviving Canaanites of the land (1 Ki 9:21, RSV), but not of the Israelites (v 22).

Under early Roman law the slave was at the absolute mercy of his master, for life or death. He could not appeal to the civil court, he could own no property, but was subject to the slightest whim of his owner. As a result many slaves suffered untold hardship. On one occasion when a Roman senator was murdered by a slave, his death was revenged by the slaying of all the 400 slaves of his *familia,* or household. However, some owners treated their slaves with great consideration (cf. Lk 7:2, RSV). Apparently there were Christians in Paul's day who owned slaves (see Eph 6:5, 9, RSV). *Onesimus (Phm 10-16, RSV) was a runaway slave whom Paul converted in Rome and sent back to his master in Colossae. The Christian slave was advised not to be cast down at his physical bondage; spiritually he was free (1 Cor 7:20-22, RSV; cf. 1 Ti 6:1, 2). In God's sight a slave's soul is as precious as a freeman's (Gal 3:28, RSV).

The term "slave" is used in the NT mostly in a figurative sense. The sinner is a slave to the sin he commits, for it controls him (Jn 8:34; Rom 6:17; Gal 4:3; Tit 3:3; cf. Rom 6:16, RSV; etc.). A religion based on ceremonies and legalism is a religion of spiritual slavery (cf. Gal 4:9-11, 21-23; 5:1-4; RSV; etc.). Paul referred to himself as a slave of Christ (Rom 1:1), not in the sense of bondage, but of voluntary choice and love. Only the one who is a "slave" of Christ is truly free (Jn 8:34-36; cf. 1 Cor 7:22; Gal 5:1; etc.).

The OT recognition and regulation of slavery must be understood against the background of the immaturity of the Hebrews and the low level of the entrenched paganism surrounding them. God dealt leniently with His people in times of ignorance. But this raises the question as to why Christianity did not abolish slavery outright. Jesus laid down a new rule with respect to divorce and remarriage to supersede that found in the Mosaic law, which had been adapted to "the hardness of your hearts" (Mt 19:8; Mk 10:5), but gave no new regulation concerning slavery. Does it follow, then, that Jesus approved of slavery because in the NT we find no "Moses said unto you . . . but I say unto you" on that subject also? By no means.

We are not told specifically why Jesus remained silent on the subject of slavery or polygamy, or why Paul sent Onesimus back to his master with a request, not a command, to receive the runaway slave "not now as a servant [slave], but above a servant, a brother beloved" (Phm 16). But it is clear that Jesus laid down principles which, if applied, would result in the abolition of social evils through the regeneration of the individuals composing society. Simply observing the golden rule would prevent the enslavement of human beings.

Those who find fault with the early church for not making a frontal attack on the social evils of the time, such as slavery, the exposure of unwanted infants, and other widespread evils, should consider that the function of the gospel is primarily to cure the malady of sin. Once the cure has been effected, the symptoms will disappear. Further, if the infant church had attacked the social system as such, it would never have had time or strength to do anything else, and it would probably have been completely crushed in the process.

Slavery. *See* Slave.

Sledge. *See* Threshing.

Slime. *See* Pitch.

Sling. A weapon consisting of a piece of leather or strong cloth with a string attached to each end, or with the mate-

450. Palestinian shepherd boy with a sling

451. Copper-smelting furnace at *Khirbet Jariyeh*, in ancient Edom

rial itself narrowed into the form of strings, used by practically all nations of antiquity. In use the sling was doubled and held by the ends of the strings, a stone was inserted in the loop, and the sling was whirled around the head several times; one string was then released so that the stone was projected with great force (fig. 450). Smooth, round, ball-like sling-stones have been found in practically all excavated sites. The sling was standard equipment of the shepherd, such as David (1 Sa 17:40); it was also a weapon in the hand of the soldier (Jgs 20:16; 2 Ki 3:25; 2 Chr 26:14). On the Assyrian relief of the capture of Lachish a Hebrew soldier is shown on a tower swinging a sling (fig. 284). The Jews used slings as late as the Roman war of the 1st cent. A.D. (Jos. *War* ii. 17. 5; iv. 1. 3).

Sluice. A term appearing in Is 19:10, KJV, denoting a pent-up body of water. However, the Hebrew word thus translated (*śeker*) means "hire" (see RSV). The KJV translation is based on the Jewish Targums and the Latin Vulgate.

Smelt. A rendering of the Heb. *yaṣaq* (Job 28:2, RSV), "to pour (liquid)," or "to cast (metal)," rendered "molten" in the KJV, and the Heb. *ṣaraph* (Is 1:25, RSV), translated "purge" in the KJV. Job 28:1-11 describes in poetic language the various operations of gold, iron, and copper mining, mentioning the smelting of copper from the ore in v 2. In the *Wâdī 'Arabah* (Map II, D-3) and in the *Negeb* (Map II, D-2/3) several copper and iron mines of the period of the Hebrew kings have been discovered by Nelson Glueck. Mining shafts (fig. 83) show how the ancient miners extracted the ore, which was then roasted in primitive furnaces built near the mines (fig. 451). Large heaps of slag (cf. Is 1:25) are witnesses to the extent of the operations of those mines. The extracted metal, which was still impure after this initial smelting, was shipped to *Ezion-geber at the Gulf of Aqabah, where it was further smelted (fig. 170) and formed into various domestic, industrial, or military objects.

Smith. A rendering of: (1) The Heb. *charash*, "artisan," "smith," where the context indicates that a metal worker or craftsman who worked in iron or bronze is involved. The smiths were the weapon-makers in Israel (1 Sa 13:19), and the artisans who cast and molded idols (Is 44: 10, 12). (2) The Heb. *masger* (2 Ki 24: 14, 16; Jer 24:1; 29:2), the exact meaning of which is uncertain. Perhaps a builder of bulwarks and trenches is meant. (3) A form of the Heb. *ṣaraph* (Prov 25:4, RSV), "to smelt." *See* Goldsmith; Kenites; Kenizzites.

Smyrna (smûr'nà). [Gr. *Smurna*, traditionally explained as meaning "myrrh," but scholars doubt that this was the original meaning.] One of the most important cities of western Asia Minor. It was founded by Aeolian Greeks, but it later became an Ionian city and was incorporated into the Ionian confederation. Smyrna was one of 7 cities that claimed to be the birthplace of Homer. After its destruction by the Lydians in the 6th cent. B.C., it remained a place of little importance for some time, until its ideal location was recognized by Alexander, who ordered its rebuilding. The city was rebuilt by Lysimachus according to Alexander's plans (301-281 B.C.). It thereafter grew quickly, becoming one of the richest coastal cities of Asia Minor. In 133 B.C. Smyrna became part of the Roman province of Asia, and in the imperial period was one of the strongest centers of the emperor cult in Asia Minor. A Christian church existed there by the end of the 1st cent., as is evident from the fact that the book of Revelation, written by John probably about A.D. 96, contains a letter to the Smyrna church (Rev 2:8-11). The spirituality of that church must have been excellent at that time, for the letter contains no rebuke of any kind, whereas, with the exception of the church at Philadelphia, the other churches addressed at this time were all censured. The Smyrna church may have come into existence through the efforts of Paul, who spent 3 years in nearby Ephesus (Acts 20:31). In A.D. 169 Polycarp, bishop of Smyrna, was burned at the stake near the stadium of the city. Smyrna was destroyed several times by earthquakes and wars, but because of its favorable location on a protected bay, it always recovered itself. Today, under the name *Izmir*, it has a population of about 230,000, and is thus the 3d largest city of Turkey. Map XX, B-4. See figs. 110, 452, 453.

452. View over modern Smyrna and its bay from the Citadel

For the significance of Smyrna as one of the 7 churches of the Revelation see *SDACom* 7:91-93, 745-748.

Snail. A rendering of: (1) The Heb. *chomeṭ* (Lev 11:30, KJV), some kind of unclean animal, perhaps a reptile, but not precisely identified. Some scholars think *chomeṭ* may designate a type of *lizard (RSV "sand lizard"). (2) The Heb. *shabbelûl* (Ps 58:8), according to tradition a shell-less land snail.

Snow. [Heb. *sheleg;* Aramaic *telag;* Gr. *chiōn.*] A form of precipitation, more frequent in temperate and polar regions than in the Bible lands. Snow falls occasionally in the hill country of Palestine, though in most places it remains on the ground for no more than a few hours. Snow fell twice in Jerusalem (1870 and 1940) as late as April. On Feb. 9, 1920, Jerusalem experienced an exceedingly heavy snowfall of 3 ft. 3 in. within 24 hours. Snow remained on the ground in Jerusalem for one week in February, 1950. In the mountains of Lebanon it gathers to a considerable depth in the ravines, remaining until nearly the end of summer. Mount Hermon wears a perpetual cap of snow. Snow is listed among God's mysteries (Job 38:22). It is seldom referred to in a historical sense (2 Sa 23:20; 1 Chr 11:22). It is used as symbolic of purity and whiteness (Ps 51:7; Lam 4:7; Dan 7:9; Mt 28:3).

Snuffers. A rendering of: (1) the Heb. *mezammerôth* (1 Ki 7:50; 2 Ki 12:13; 25:14; 2 Chr 4:22; Jer 52:18), and (2) the Heb. *melqachayim* (Ex 25:38, RSV; 37:23; Num 4:9, RSV), instruments used in the tabernacle and the Temple to snuff out the lights of the "candlestick." Their exact form is unknown, but it is usually thought that the *mezammerôth* were spoonlike metal tongs, which could be placed over the spouts of the lamps, thus snuffing out the light by shutting off the oxygen. The *melqachayim* seem to have been scissorlike or tweezerlike instruments, performing the same function.

So (sō). [Heb. *Sô',* although according to available evidence *Siwe'* would be a preferred pronunciation.] A king of Egypt in the 24th dynasty who entered into an alliance with King Hoshea of Israel against Shalmaneser V of Assyria (2 Ki 17:4). Nothing is known concerning this king from Egyptian records; however, a mummy-formed figurine in the Berlin

453. Ruins of the ancient forum of Smyrna

Museum, a so-called *ushebti*, contains a royal cartouche with the name *Śbw*, revealing that there must have been a king by that name in Egypt, probably a local Delta prince. He is referred to in the Assyrian inscription of King Sargon II as *Sib'e*, the *turtânu* of Egypt, who in 720 B.C. joined with Ḥanunu, king of Gaza, and fought against Sargon at Raphia, south of Gaza (*ANET* 285; this identification is questioned by R. Borger, *JNES* 19 [1960], 49-53). The identification of So with the Ethiopian king Shabaka of the 25th Egyptian dynasty is philologically indefensible.

Soap. [Heb. *borîth*, related to *barar*, "to cleanse," "to purify."] The Hebrew word is a general term referring to almost any substance that has cleansing properties, such as "lye," "alkali," "potash." Soap in the present sense of the word was probably not known in OT times. In Jer 2:22; Mal 3:2 *borîth* may refer to a vegetable alkali, or some kind of potash.

Sober, Sobriety. A rendering of: (1) Forms of the Gr. *sōphroneō*, "to be of a sound mind," "to be reasonable," "to be self-controlled." Paul admonishes the Romans "to think soberly" (Rom 12:3), that is, to use good judgment, and Titus, to "live soberly" (Tit 2:12), or in harmony with the dictates of a sound mind. He counsels the women in the church to live with "sobriety," or in keeping with what would be considered good feminine judgment (1 Ti 2:9, 15, KJV). Peter urges believers to be "sober" (1 Pe 4:7), that is, to take a sane, Christian attitude toward the circumstances and problems of life. (2) The Gr. *nēphalios* (1 Ti 3:2, 11; Tit 2:2), "temperate," "sober" (RSV "temperate"). (3) The verb phrase "be sober" (1 Pe 1:13) is a rendering of the Gr. *nēphō*, "to be self-possessed."

Socho. See Socoh, 2.

Sochoh. See Socoh, 3.

Socket. A rendering of: (1) The Heb. *'eden* (Ex 26:19-37; etc.), usually translated "base" in the RSV (except in ch 38:12, where the KJV rendering "socket" is used). The *'eden* is the designation of the metal bases made for the tabernacle pillars on which the curtains of the court were hung, and of the bases for the boards, or frames, which formed the walls of the holy place and Most Holy Place. (2) The Heb. *qaneh* (Job 31:22, RSV), "arm socket" or "bone of the upper arm" (KJV "bone"). (3) The Heb. *chor* (Zec 14:12, RSV), "eye socket" (KJV "holes"). (4) The Heb. *poth* (1 Ki 7:50, RSV),

probably meaning "front," rendered "hinge" in the KJV, and *pethach* in the parallel text (2 Chr 4:22, RSV), rendered "entry" in the KJV. *Pethach* is probably a scribal error for *poth*.

Soco. See Socoh, 1, 2, and 3.

Socoh (sō′kō), RSV 3 times **Soco** (sō′kō), KJV once **Socho** (sō′kō), once **Shoco** (shō′kō), once **Shocho** (shō′kō), once **Shochoh** (shō′kō), and once **Sochoh** (sō′kō). [Heb. *Śôkô, Śôkoh*, "hedge of thorns."]
1. A city of Judah in the Shephelah (Jos 15:35). The Philistines pitched their camp to the northwest of this city when their champion, Goliath, challenged Israel (1 Sa 17:1). Rehoboam strengthened its fortifications (2 Chr 11:7), but it was captured by the Philistines in the time of King Ahaz of Judah (ch 28:18). It has been identified with *Khirbet ʿAbbâd*, about 14 mi. west-southwest of Bethlehem (Map VI, E-2).
2. A city in the hill country of Judah (Jos 15:48; 1 Chr 4:18), identified with *Khirbet Shuweikeh*, 10 mi. south-southwest of Hebron. It is probably this Socoh that is spelled *Śwkh* on many inscribed jar handles found in Palestinian excavations. It was most probably a royal manufacturing center of standardized jars.
3. A place 10 mi. west-northwest of Samaria (1 Ki 4:10), now *esh-Shuweikeh* (Map VIII, D-3).

Sodering. See Soldering.

Sodi (sō′dī). [Heb. *Sôdî*, "my intimate counsel (is Yahweh)." The name occurs also in Ugaritic and Palmyrene texts.] The father of the spy representing the tribe of Zebulun (Num 13:10).

Sodom (sŏd′ŭm), KJV of NT once **Sodoma** (sŏd′ŏ-mȧ). [Heb. *Sedom*, spelled *Swdm* and *Swdwm* in the Dead Sea scrolls; Gr. *Sodoma*.] A city in the plain of the Jordan (Gen 10:19; 13:10), usually mentioned with Gomorrah. It was one of the 5 cities defeated by Chedorlaomer and his confederates in the time of Abraham (ch 14:8-11). Lot dwelt there but escaped with 2 of his daughters as the only survivors when it and the other "cities of the plain" (ch 19:29) were destroyed by a fire from heaven because of the wickedness of their inhabitants. Some suggest that for this destruction God may have used natural means ready at hand—natural oil and gases that could, when ignited by fire

---

→

454. Rock salt formations on the slopes of the *Jebel Usdum*, Mount of Sodom

from heaven, shower burning asphalt and sulphur upon the doomed cities (Gen 18: 20; 19:24-29; Deut 29:23; Is 1:9, 10; 3:9; 13:19; Jer 49:17, 18; 50:35, 40; Lam 4:6; Eze 16:46-56; Amos 4:11; Zep 2:9; Mt 10: 15; 11:24; Lk 10:12; 17:29; Rom 9:29; 2 Pe 2:6; Jude 7). In the book of Revelation Sodom is used as a symbol for a sinful city (ch 11:8; *SDACom* 7:803).

The sites of Sodom and its neighboring cities are unknown. Some scholars seek them north of the Dead Sea, and present 2 arguments: (1) Gen 13:10 indicates that these cities, lying in the Jordan Valley, could be seen from the vicinity of Bethel (cf. v 3), and (2) since Chedorlaomer and his confederates, coming from the south, fought against Sodom and its allies after having reached Hazezon-tamar, that is, En-gedi (ch 14:7, 8), and since En-gedi lies midway up the western shore of the Dead Sea, Sodom must have been located to the north of it, hence at the northern end of the Dead Sea. However, neither conclusion is required by the Scripture passages cited.

Other scholars seek these cities underneath the waters of the southern end of the Dead Sea. Arguments for this view are more numerous and weighty: (1) The "vale of Siddim" in which these cities were located is identified with the "salt sea" in Gen 14:3. The northern ⅔ of the present Dead Sea reaches a depth of 1,328 ft., and must have existed as early as Abraham's time, but the depth of the southern part nowhere exceeds 16 ft. Submerged trees show that part of this area was dry

455. Submerged forest in the Dead Sea near *Jebel Usdum*, "Mount of Sodom"

in relatively modern times (fig. 455), and accurate measurements have shown that the level of the sea has been steadily rising during the last cent. (2) Asphalt is found at the southern end of the Dead Sea, while the Vale of Siddim is said to have been "full of slimepits," RSV "bitumin pits" (Gen 14:10). Bitumen, or asphalt, still erupts from the bottom of the southern part of the Dead Sea and floats to the shore. (3) Statements made by classical authors, Diodorus Siculus (ii. 48. 7-9), Strabo (*Geogr.* xvi. 2. 42-44), Tacitus (*Hist.* v. 6. 7), and Josephus (*War* iv. 8. 4), describe an area south of the Dead Sea (presumably now covered by its rising water) as scorched by a fiery catastrophe that destroyed several cities whose burned remains were still visible in their day. Foul gases are said to emerge from fissures of the ground. Compare Deut 29:23. (4) Geologists have found oil and natural gases in the ground at the southern end of the Dead Sea, which is at the same time an area frequently disturbed by earthquakes, hence furnished all the conditions for the catastrophe described in the Bible, if God used natural means in the destruction of the cities (see above). Furthermore, *Jebel Usdum,* the "Mount of Sodom," at the southwestern shore of the Dead Sea, consists of 50 per cent rock salt (see fig. 454). Some have conjectured that in an upheaval during the destruction of Sodom some of this salt may have been dislodged and may have buried Lot's wife, piling over her to form a "pillar of salt" (Gen 19:26). (The place where the Israelis have a potash extraction plant, on the southwestern shore, has been named Sodom, but it has no connection with the ancient Sodom.) (5) A number of streams enter the southern part of the Dead Sea from the east, in a region that is still very fertile, and it is reasonable to believe that the whole valley now forming the southernmost part of the Dead Sea was once that exceptionally fertile plain, one fitting the Bible description which compares the land with the Garden of Eden and the Nile valley (ch 13:10). (6) Kyle and Albright, in their exploration of the region lying southeast of the Dead Sea, found no ancient ruins of cities, but discovered an elaborate place of worship on a hillside with remains dating from before 1800 B.C. This site, *Bâb edh-Dhrâ',* evidently was a place where the annual festivals of a large population were held. The cities in which this population once lived must have been in the area now covered by the waters of the

Dead Sea. (7) Zoar, one of the 5 cities of the plain (Gen 14:2), was at the southern end of the Dead Sea (Map XVI, F-3) in the time of Christ (Jos. *War* iv. 8. 4).

Lit.: F. G. Clapp, *AJA* 40 (1936), 323-344; J. P. Harland, *BA* 5 (1942), 17-32; 6 (1943), 41-54; W. F. Albright, *BASOR* 14 (1924), 3-9.

Sodoma. *See* Sodom.

Sodomite. *See* Cult Prostitute.

Soft Raiment. [Gr. *malakon* (Mt 11:8) and *malakon himation* (Lk 7:25).] Raiment worn by the fastidious and wealthy, in contrast to the coarse garments worn by the poor.

Sojourner. *See* Stranger.

Soldering, KJV **Sodering.** A rendering of the Heb. *debeq,* in the context referring to some process of binding of metals (Is 41:7). *Debeq* comes from the related verb *dabaq,* "to cling," "to cleave to."

Solemn Assembly. A rendering of the Heb. *'aṣarah* and *'aṣereth,* from the root *'aṣar,* "to detain," "to restrain" (except once, Zep 3:18, KJV, from *mô'ed,* "appointed times"), in the sense of halting all work for the purpose of convening an assembly. The term is used in connection with the 8th day of the Feast of Tabernacles (Lev 23:33-36; Num 29:35; Neh 8:15, 16), and the 7th day of Unleavened Bread (Deut 16:8); also of the 8th day of the dedication of the Temple by Solomon (2 Chr 7:9). King Jehu ordered a "solemn assembly for Baal" that he might destroy all the adherents of that god in Israel (2 Ki 10:20). Because of their cynical and unspiritual ritualism, God found the solemn assemblies and other religious feasts and practices of Judah and Israel sacrilegious and an abomination (Is 1:13).

Solomon (sŏl'ô-mŭn). [Heb. *Shelomoh,* "peaceable." The name is attested in Hebrew on an ancient jar handle. It appears in Moabite as *Shlmn,* in Akkadian as *Shalamânu.* Among the Arabs it is known as *Suleimân;* Gr. *Solomōn.*] The son of David and Bathsheba (2 Sa 12:24; 1 Chr 3:5), and the 3d and last king of united Israel, who reigned from *c.* 971 to *c.* 931 B.C. In one passage he is called Jedidiah, "beloved of Yahweh" (2 Sa 12:25). This was possibly his personal name and Solomon his throne name; or the reverse may have been true.

I. Accession. Solomon was made king shortly before his father's death, and owed his crown to the watchfulness of the prophet Nathan. Hearing that Solomon's older brother Adonijah, supported by Joab, was to be proclaimed king, the prophet appealed to David through Bathsheba for quick action. In response Solomon, supported by Zadok the priest, Benaiah, a high military officer, and David's bodyguard, was immediately proclaimed king. This prompt action brought a quick end to Adonijah's conspiracy (1 Ki 1:5-40). After David's death Solomon executed his most violent opponents. The less violent he discharged from their office or banished or placed under surveillance (ch 2). About the same time he married an Egyptian princess (ch 3:1), probably a daughter of one of the last kings of the 21st dynasty. During a visit to Gibeon, where the tabernacle of the Lord was at that time, he had a dream in which God asked him to make his desires known, and promised that they would be granted. In response Solomon requested wisdom, which so pleased God that wealth and honor were promised him in addition to the requested wisdom (1 Ki 3:4-15; 2 Chr 1:3-13). His wisdom was later put to a test when he was asked to arbitrate a quarrel between 2 women over the possession of a baby (1 Ki 3:16-28). The judgment pronounced in this case became proverbial, and made such an impression on the ancients that it became an art motif in the ancient world (see fig. 456).

II. Reign. Solomon's relations with other countries during his 40-year reign were generally good. Through his marriage with the Egyptian princess he came into possession of the city of Gezer, which had remained in Canaanite hands up to that time (1 Ki 9:16). He waged only one war, that against Hamath-zobah, to make his northern possessions more secure (2 Chr 8:3). With Phoenicia he concluded a trade agreement (1 Ki 5:1-12). Apparently he also had good relations with other neighboring nations, such as Ammon, Moab, Edom, and the Hittite city-states of northern Syria, countries from which he imported women for his harem (chs 11:1; 14:21). He had contact even with distant Sheba in South Arabia (ch 10:1-13). He built the caravan city of *Tadmor in the desert (2 Chr 8:4), and carried on a flourishing trade with many surrounding nations, buying horses in Kue (Cilicia), and importing chariots from Egypt, which he then exported to princes from northern regions (1 Ki 10:28, 29, RSV).

He also organized chariot forces as part of his army and built strong garrison cities, among which Hazor, Megiddo, and Gezer are specially mentioned (1 Ki 9: 19; 10:26). The excavations at *Megiddo uncovered large stables of either Solomon's or Ahab's time (fig. 460), and a gate structure belonging to the time of Solomon (fig. 483) that corresponds in size and layout to the Temple gates described by Ezekiel. Other gates of identical style have been excavated at the Solomonic level of Hazor (fig. 482) and Gezer.

Explorations carried out by Nelson Glueck in Edom have discovered the copper and iron mines exploited by Solomon, and a metal refinery and production center at Ezion-geber on the Gulf of Aqabah, containing 2 rows of smelters (fig. 170), doubtless used by him. Ezion-geber was also the port from which Solomon's ships, partly manned by Phoenician crews, sailed to Ophir, probably Somaliland in eastern Africa, and brought back gold. His "ships of Tarshish" (*see* Tarshish, 2) brought monkeys, ivory, peacocks, etc. (1 Ki 9:26-28; 10:11, 22; Jos. *Ant*. viii. 7. 2).

Solomon divided Israel into 12 administrative provinces, which did not in every case correspond with tribal boundaries. They were administered by an able corps of officers, some of whom were bound to the king by marriage ties (1 Ki 4:1-19). For his extensive building enterprises Solomon initiated a system of forced labor, which became very unpopular in the course of time (chs 5:13-16; 9:

15, 20, 23). Besides his workmen, he also drafted an immense number of Israelites for his infantry, chariotry, and horsemen (1 Ki 9:22).

III. Building Activity in Jerusalem. For many years Solomon's main attention was directed toward the beautification of his capital. His father David, who was not permitted to build a temple, had amassed much building material for such a structure (1 Chr 29:2-8; cf. ch 17:4), and had bought a site north of "David's City," the old Mount Moriah. Solomon's building activities in Jerusalem lasted 20 years, 7 years of which were spent in building the magnificent Temple which brought him great fame (1 Ki 6:37, 38), and 13 years in erecting the palace buildings (ch 7:1). Solomon's architect and some of his builders were from Tyre. The Phoenicians also supplied him with material for the buildings and furnishings (chs 5:1-18; 7:13, 14). New walls were erected for the widely extended city area (ch 9:15), although it is not known whether Solomon's Jerusalem included any part of the city which in later times lay west of the Tyropoeon Valley, or whether his city was confined to the 2 eastern hills—the southeastern hill on which the City of David stood, also called Zion, and the northeastern hill, or Temple Hill. Solomon also carried out building activities at Millo (chs 9:15, 24; 11:27), which was probably a special fortress, mentioned in the time of David (2

456. Mural painting from Pompeii, depicting the judgment of Solomon

Sa 5:9), at the northern side of the old City of David. See fig. 259.

IV. Failure. Solomon was an Oriental monarch who loved luxury, and who unfortunately followed in many of the ways of Oriental despots. Outstanding among his mistakes was his taking many foreign wives. These brought about disloyalty toward God, which in turn resulted in the breakup of his empire after his death. To accommodate these women he erected pagan sanctuaries and shrines and he himself occasionally worshiped at them (1 Ki 11:1-13). Another mistake Solomon made was to tax the people heavily over an extended period. His forced-labor program was especially unpopular and became the most visible cause of the breakup of the kingdom immediately following his death (ch 12:4-16).

One of Solomon's enemies was Hadad of Edom, who had fled to Egypt after David's victory over the Edomites but returned to Edom in Solomon's time (1 Ki 11:14-22, 25b). Another adversary was Rezon, an Aramaean leader of a band of outlaws, who made himself master of *Damascus and founded a dynasty there. He caused Solomon even more trouble than Hadad (vs 23-25). The most dangerous of Solomon's internal opponents was Jeroboam, an Ephraimite overseer of a group of builders employed at the construction project at Millo in Jerusalem. Because of Solomon's apostasy God had promised Jeroboam the greater part of the kingdom. Jeroboam thereupon made an unwise move, with the result that Solomon sought to kill him. But Jeroboam fled to Egypt, where he remained until Solomon's death, after which he returned to become the spokesman of the dissatisfied workmen of the realm and king over the northern tribes (vs 26-40; ch 12:2, 3).

V. Religious Life and Literary Activity. Solomon began his reign as a deeply spiritual leader of his nation, one who desired nothing so much as wisdom adequately to serve God and the interests of his people (1 Ki 3:3-9). His prayer and his counsel to the people at the dedication of the Temple show that he stood close to God (ch 8:22-61). However, his wealth and luxury, but especially his many wives, corrupted him so that he finally became an idolater (ch 11:3-8). In later life he regretted the follies of his way, as statements he made in Ecclesiastes reveal (chs 1:1, 12-17; 2:1-11).

Solomon was known especially for his extraordinary wisdom, the fame of which reached far beyond the national boundaries (1 Ki 4:29-34), and which excelled even that of the traditionally wise Egyptians (v 30) of whom much wisdom literature has been preserved. The 2 books that bear his name as author—Proverbs and Song of Solomon—and the book of Ecclesiastes, which does not bear his name but is traditionally attributed to him because ch 1:1 sets forth the author as "the son of David, king in Jerusalem," have preserved for all times some of his wise utterances and inspired philosophy. The fact that certain sayings contained in Proverbs find close parallels in the Egyptian "Instruction of Amen-em-Opet" (*ANET* 421-425) has frequently been held to prove that the author of Proverbs borrowed from Amen-em-Opet. However, this cannot be true because Solomon lived in the 10th cent. b.c., whereas Amen-em-Opet's instruction dates from the 8th to the 6th cent. b.c. Hence, it is more likely that Solomon's proverbs found their way to Egypt, and were re-edited and rephrased by Amen-em-Opet into the form in which they have come to us in their Egyptian edition.

Solomon's Portico. A covered colonnade of 2 corridors at the eastern side of the outer court of the Temple of Christ's time. It stood on an artificial embankment (Jos. *Ant.* xx. 9. 7; *War* v. 5. 1) overlooking the Kidron Valley, and seems therefore to have been at the southern portion of the eastern side (fig. 485), as a topographical study of the Temple area suggests. This portico, or porch (KJV), was the scene of an incident in Christ's life (Jn 10:23), and is twice mentioned as a place where the apostles preached the gospel (Acts 3:11, 12; 5:12).

Solomon's Servants. The ancestors of a group of exiles who returned under Zerubbabel (Ezr 2:55, 58; Neh 7:57, 60), and later dwelt in the cities of Judah (Neh 11:3). Since they are mentioned with the *Nethinim, who were Temple servants, they would seem to have been descendants of aliens whom Solomon had pressed into servitude for the Temple (1 Ki 9:20, 21).

Son. [Heb. *ben;* Aramaic *bar;* Gr. *huios.*] A term with a much wider meaning in the language of the OT than in modern usage, and this wider meaning is also reflected in Semitic idioms used in the Greek of the NT. Following are the varied meanings of "son":

1. A male child of the 1st generation (Gen 16:15; etc.).

2. A grandson; for example Jehu, who

was a son of Jehoshaphat and a grandson of Nimshi (2 Ki 9:2), is also called a "son of Nimshi" (v 20). Compare the same usage for "daughter" (ch 8:18; cf. v 26, KJV).

3. A descendant of some famous ancestor, regardless of the number of generations. For example Joseph, the reputed father of Jesus Christ, was called a "son of David" though he lived 10 cent. later (Mt 1:20).

4. An adopted male child (Ex 2:10).

5. A kindly form of address of an older man to a younger friend, student, or companion (1 Sa 26:17, 21, 25; 2 Sa 18:22; 1 Ti 1:18; 2 Ti 2:1).

6. The members of a tribe or group of people (Neh 12:23). In many passages this use is not apparent in the English translations. For example, for "Edomites" in Ps 137:7, RSV (KJV "children of Edom"), the Hebrew text has literally "sons of Edom"; and for "Grecians" in Joel 3:6, KJV (RSV "Greeks"), the Hebrew text has "sons of Javan" (cf. "daughters of Israel," Jgs 11:40). In many instances of this type the plural "sons" includes women and girls.

7. A member of a professional group or guild, for example, "sons of the prophets" (1 Ki 20:35; 2 Ki 2:3), or the "sons of the singers" (Neh 12:28).

8. Inhabitant, as of a city, as the "sons of Zion" (Lam 4:2); "of Jericho" (Ezr 2:34); cf. "daughters" (Is 3:16; Jer 49:3; Lk 23:28). As under 6, "sons" may include women and girls.

9. A possessor of a quality, as a "son of peace" (Lk 10:6).

10. A faithful follower, as in "sons of God" (Gen 6:2).

11. Heavenly beings, created by God; evidently angels (Job 1:6; 2:1).

12. A product of spiritual birth, or adoption; Christians become "sons" and "daughters" of God through faith (Rom 8:14, 15, 23; 2 Cor 6:18; etc.).

Son of David. *See* Jesus Christ.

Son of God. As applied to Jesus Christ, a Messianic title stressing His deity, comparable with the title "Son of man," which stresses His humanity. Like the many other names and titles accorded Him in Scripture, the title "Son of God" accommodates to human minds and understanding an important aspect of His work for our salvation. In view of the broad range of meanings latent in the word "son," as used by the Hebrew people and the Bible writers (*see* Son), it is not possible arbitrarily to circumscribe

the expression "Son of God" within the narrow limits implied by the English word "son." Whether or not the title is in any sense an appropriate description of the absolute and eternal relationship between Son and Father, is a matter on which Scripture is silent. Obviously, it does not connote a generic relationship comparable in any way to the usual human father-son relationship, and accordingly it is necessary to understand it in some sense other than a strictly literal one. A clue to the implied meaning may occur in the expression "only begotten" (Gr. *monogenēs*), which characterizes Christ as having a "unique" relationship with the Father (Jn 1:14; *see* Only Begotten). Properly understood of Christ's unique status as *the* Son of God, *monogenēs* distinguishes between Him and all others who, through faith in Him, are given "power to become the sons of God" (v 12) and who are specifically declared to be "born . . . of God" (v 13). Christ is, and always has been, very "God" (v 1), and by virtue of this fact we have been granted the privilege of *becoming* "the sons of God."

A further aspect of the meaning implied by the term "son of God" is set forth in Col 1:15, where He is said to be "the image of the invisible God"; in Heb 1:3, where He is declared to be "the express image of his person"; in Php 2:6, where it is stated that, prior to the Incarnation, He was "in the form of God" and "equal with God." The expression is thus an affirmation of the absolute and unqualified deity of Jesus. At the annunciation the angel Gabriel declared to the virgin Mary that by virtue of the overshadowing power of the Holy Ghost her Son was to be "called the Son of God" (Lk 1:35). Here the angel plainly attributes the title "Son of God" to the unique union of Deity with humanity at the incarnation of our Lord. Paul stated that Jesus was "declared to be the Son of God with power, according to the spirit of holiness, by the resurrection from the dead" (Rom 1:4).

The Synoptic Gospels never quote Jesus as applying the title "Son of God" to Himself, though when others use it of Him He accepts it in such a way as to acknowledge it (see Mt 4:3, 4; 8:29; 14:33; 26:63, 64; 27:40, 43). Only in Jn is Jesus recorded as thus using it (see chs 5:25; 9:35; 10:36; 11:4). At His birth (Lk 1:35; cf. Mt 1:23), His baptism (Mt 3:17), and again at the Transfiguration the Father acknowledged Jesus as His Son (Mt 17:5). This Father and Son relationship is both explicit and implicit in many statements by our Lord Himself (see Mt 11:27; Lk 10:21; Jn 5:18-23; 10:30; 14:28; etc.). Jesus' claim to being the Son of God incurred the implacable hatred of the Jews, who protested that He thereby made "himself equal with God" (Jn 5:18) and, indeed, made Himself out to *be* God (ch 10:33). Eventually, His own clear statement of this claim led to His condemnation and crucifixion (Mt 26:63-66; Lk 22: 67-71).

During His earthly ministry our Saviour voluntarily surrendered the prerogatives, though not the nature, of deity, and assumed the limitations of human nature, thereby subordinating Himself to the Father (see Ps 40:8; Mt 26:39; Jn 3:16; 4: 34; 5:30; 12:49; 14:10; 17:4, 8; 2 Cor 8:9; Php 2:7, 8; Heb 2:9), even as we are to be subject to Him. He said, "My Father is greater than I" (Jn 14:28), and "the Son can do nothing of himself" (ch 5:19). His use of the title "Son of God" thus clearly links this title to His incarnation and earthly ministry, giving meaning to the expression.

Son of Man. As used frequently in the OT, a Hebrew idiomatic expression meaning "man," that is, a human being. In this sense it is used nearly 100 times in the book of Eze (chs 2:1, 3, 6, 8; 3:1, 3; etc.) as the form of address used by the Lord when speaking to Ezekiel in vision. In Dan 7:13, 14, "Son of man" occurs in a description of a being seen by Daniel in vision, whom conservative scholars generally identify with the Messiah. Here, as later in the Gospels, the Messiah is identified as a human being. The expression "one like the Son of man" in this passage is probably to be understood in the sense, "one who appeared to be a human being," or "one in human form," or "one like a human being." In Jewish apocalyptic literature the "son of man" is primarily a heavenly being who would appear at the last day as judge.

"Son of man" was our Lord's favorite designation for Himself, occurring more than 80 times in the Gospels. The title stresses the reality of His human nature, even as the companion title, "Son of God," affirms His deity. Others never addressed Jesus by the title "Son of man." Jesus was "Son of man," not only in the strictly historical sense (cf. Lk 1:31-35; Rom 1:3, 4; Gal 4:4) but in a higher sense as well. The title designates Him as

the incarnate Christ (see Jn 1:14; Php 2: 6-8) and bears mute witness to the miracle whereby Creator and creature were united in one divine-human person, deity being identified with humanity in order that humanity might be made over again into the divine image. A somewhat less challenging and provocative title than "Son of God," "Son of man" nevertheless also had clear Messianic overtones. As used by our Lord, it was doubtless reminiscent of Dan 7:13, 14, where "the Son of man" receives His everlasting dominion. In at least 2 instances (Mt 24:30; 26:64) His use of the term seems clearly to reflect the scene depicted in Dan 7, in part, perhaps, purposely to lead men to think of Him as the One spoken of by Daniel the prophet. When haled before the Sanhedrin, Jesus declared that He had been given "authority to execute judgment . . . because he is the Son of man" (Jn 5:27), thus associating the title with the judgment scene of Dan 7. Later He told His disciples that when, as Son of man, He should "come in his glory" He would "sit upon the throne of his glory"—in judgment, as the following verses make evident (Mt 25:31).

In a sense, the title "Son of man" half concealed His claim to Messiahship, since according to Hebrew usage it could be interpreted as meaning simply "man." But on the other hand it also half revealed His claim to Messiahship, in view of the OT usage of the term already mentioned. The question raised in the minds of His hearers by the title became evident from the occasion about 4 days before the crucifixion when they directly inquired, "Who is this Son of man?" (Jn 12:34). That the disciples themselves understood the relationship between the titles "Son of man" and "Son of God" is clear from the encounter at Caesarea Philippi when Jesus asked them, "Whom do men say that I the Son of man am? . . . Whom say ye that I am?" and Peter replied, "Thou art the Christ, the Son of the living God" (Mt 16:13-16). The title "Son of man" assures us that the Son of God indeed came to live on earth as a man among men in order that He might die as a man for His fellow men. "The Son of man came not to be ministered unto, but to minister, and to give his life a ransom for many" (Mk 10:45).

Song. [Heb. generally *shîr*; Gr. *ōdē*, from which we derive the English word "ode."] A composition conveying some theme or burden expressed in poetic form and frequently set to music. Song played a significant part in the secular and religious life of the Israelites (see Gen 31:27; Is 38:20; cf. Eph 5:19), providing emotional outlet for varied feelings (Ps 69:12, 30; Jas 5:13; etc.). Praise and thanksgiving, as well as deep sorrow, were voiced in song (Num 21:17, 18; Ps 92; 96; 98; 137:1-6; etc.), and national heroes were subject matter for songs of praise (1 Sa 18:6, 7; etc.). The word "song" occurs most frequently in the book of Psalms.

Song of Solomon, The. Last of the 5 poetical books of the OT in the English canon, and one of the Megilloth, or Five Scrolls, of the Hebrew canon. The Five Scrolls constitute the 2d section of the *Ketûbîm*, or Hagiographa, the 3d division of the Hebrew canon. The Hebrew title, *Shîr Hashshîrîm,* "the song of songs" (Song 1:1), may mean the greatest or sweetest of all songs in the same way that "King of kings" means "supreme king." The name Canticles, sometimes given to the book, is derived from the title in the Latin Vulgate, *Canticum Canticorum.* Its right to a place in the sacred canon was debated as late as NT times, and it is of interest to note that the NT never quotes from it or alludes to it. The book claims Solomon as its author, and in view of the fact that he is known to have composed 1,005 "songs" (1 Ki 4:32) there is no reason why he could not have written "the song of songs, which is Solomon's" (Song 1:1). The fluent vocabulary and graceful literary style of the poem are such as would be expected of a writer in the time of Solomon, the Hebrew golden age. The author was evidently familiar with the geography of Palestine in Solomon's time, and the glory and pomp of Israel's golden age are fresh in the writer's mind. The writer's obvious knowledge of plants, animals, products of the soil, and foreign imports accords with what is said about Solomon in 1 Ki 4:33; 9:26-28; 10:24-29; etc. The similarity of the Song with passages in the book of Proverbs is an additional indication of Solomonic authorship (Song 4:5; cf. Prov 5:19; Song 4:11; cf. Prov 5:3; Song 4:14; cf. Prov 7:17; Song 4:15; cf. Prov 5:15; Song 5:6; cf. Prov 1:28; Song 6:9; cf. Prov 31:28; Song 8:6, 7; cf. Prov 6:34, 35). These observations tend to confirm the claim made by the book that it came from Solomon himself.

The writer implies that he had 60 queens and 80 concubines (Song 6:8), but the Shulammite maid, whose marriage the Song celebrates, surpasses them all (Song 6:9, 13). Solomon's harem later increased to 700 wives and 300 concubines (1 Ki 11:1, 3); therefore, Solomon evidently composed the Song during the early part of his reign. "Shulammite" is probably equivalent to Shunammite, as suggested by the LXX (see 1 Ki 1:3). Shunem was a town in the territory of Issachar (Jos 19:17, 18), some 7 mi. east of Megiddo (cf. 2 Ki 4:8-37). Several speakers appear in the Song, though where each enters is not always clear, especially in the English translation, which does not give the gender of the speakers as does the Hebrew. In view of the difficulty, even in the Hebrew text, of tracing the logical connection between the different parts of the poem, some have considered the Song to be an anthology of love songs, perhaps by different authors, rather than a single work by one author writing with a unified plan. However, the unity of the book seems indicated by the fact that Solomon's name is prominent throughout (Song 1:1, 5; 3:7, 9, 11; 8:11, 12), and by the recurrence of similar words, illustrations, and figures throughout (ch 2:16; cf. ch 6:3; ch 2:5; cf. ch 5:8). Furthermore, the bride's family—her mother and brothers—are consistently mentioned, but never her father (see chs 1:6; 3:4; 8:2).

In poetic form the Song is an idyl with a simple plot—Solomon's love for a country girl of northern Palestine, whom he married, not for political advantage, but out of genuine love. Most modern critics and commentators favor an outline that recognizes 3 principal characters—Solomon, the Shulammite maid, and her shepherd lover. Various theories have been advanced as to the nature and sequence of the various parts of the poem. According to one view, the Shulammite maid successfully resists the king's attentions and remains true to her country lover. According to another and more probable view, the poem celebrates Solomon's marriage to the Shulammite maid after he had won her affections. Solomon brings the maid to Jerusalem to woo her, the wedding takes place, and is followed by mutual expressions of admiration and love, first by the bride and then by the groom (Song 1:2 to 2:7). Upon a later joyous occasion king and bride reminisce about their betrothal and marriage (chs 2:8 to 5:1). For some unexplained reason, perhaps an unhappy dream (ch 5:2), estrangement enters between the royal couple, but love is restored and the king again idolizes his bride (chs 5:2 to 6:9).

The supreme beauty of the Shulammite stands forth in contrast with that of the other young women of Jerusalem, and Solomon is enraptured by her (Song 7:6-9). Eventually, king and bride return to her home in the northern part of Palestine, and a dialogue takes place between the king, his bride, and her brothers (chs 7: 10 to 8:14).

From a modern Occidental point of view it may be difficult to account for the Song of Songs' finding a place in the sacred canon. For centuries, apparently, even many Jews were not certain that it deserved a place alongside the other inspired works, though the Jews have generally interpreted it as a spiritual allegory of God's love for ancient Israel. The allegorical pattern of interpretation was followed by Hippolytus of Rome in the 3d cent. A.D., and Origen, who lived in Palestine and is known as the father of the allegorical method of the interpretation of Scripture. According to Origen, the king represents Christ, and the Shulammite maid His church, or perhaps individuals within the church—a spiritual relationship that recurs frequently in the NT (Eph 5:25-33; Rev 19:7-9; 21:9; etc.). However, careful students of Scripture generally look upon the allegorical method of interpretation with caution, in view of the fact that this method almost inevitably lends itself to the fanciful opinions of the interpreter. A safe approach to the interpretation of the Song of Songs would seem to be to consider it simply as what it purports to be—a poetic narrative commemorating Solomon's love for a lovely country maid—and to consider that it found a place in the sacred canon by virtue of its exalted idealization of marriage as ordained by the Creator, albeit with a rich Oriental fervor that tends to puzzle the Western reader. It is possible, however, to draw lessons of spiritual value from the book without necessarily considering these lessons as the intent of Inspiration in the composition and canonization of the book.

Sons of God. There is no reason for supposing that the expression "sons of God" in Gen 6:2 refers to others than human beings, as some have proposed, although the expression was so interpreted in preChristian times. The Bible knows nothing about mythical deities having intercourse with human beings—an idea found in various ancient pagan religions. The context (chs 5; 6) deals exclusively with human beings, and clearly implies that the "sons of God" were simply the Godfearing descendants of Adam, whose genealogy is given in Gen 5, and the "daughters of men" were worldly young women from families where God was not honored. The statement of ch 6:2, 3 lays a background for the declaration of v 5, that "the wickedness of man was great in the earth" prior to the Flood.

In Job 1:6; 2:1; 38:7 the expression clearly refers to supernatural beings, evidently angels.

The designation "sons of God" for those who submit to being made over into the likeness of His perfect character is the logical counterpart of the designation "Father" as applied to God throughout the Scriptures. Begotten of God (Jas 1: 18) and "born again . . . by the word of God" (1 Pe 1:23), they have received Christ, have believed on His name (Jn 1:12, 13), and have experienced the new birth of ch 3:3-8. By the mediation of God's indwelling Spirit they have become partakers of the divine nature (ch 6:48-51; cf. 15:4, 5) and resemble Him in character (1 Jn 3:9; 4:7; 5:4). This resemblance is not yet perfect (Php 3:12-16), but will be complete at the appearance of the Lord Jesus in glory (1 Jn 3: 2, 3). His love enfolds all mankind (Jn 3: 16; cf. Mt 5:45), but in a special sense He is solicitous of the interests and needs of His adopted sons and daughters who acknowledge Him as Father (see Mt 6:25-34; Rom 8:15; Gal 4:6).

Sons of the East. *See* People of the East.

Sons of the Prophets. *See* Prophet.

Soothsayer. One claiming to possess the special gift of accurately determining the destiny and predicting the future of individuals and nations. By recourse to various occult arts they made their computations, divinations, and subtle prognostications.

In the OT "soothsayer" is the translation of: (1) a form of the Aramaic *gezar* (Dan 2:27; 4:7; 5:7, 11, KJV), "to decide (destiny)," "to determine (destiny)," hence "astrologers"; (2) a form of the Heb. *'anan* (Deut 18:10, 14, RSV; Is 2:6; Mic 5:12), "to make appear," "to raise spirits," "to practice soothsaying"; (3) a form of the Heb. *qasam* (Jos 13:22), "to practice divination."

In the NT the form "soothsaying" is found in Acts 16:16 as a translation of the Gr. *manteuomai*, "to divine," "to practice soothsaying." This term consistently appears in the LXX to describe the work of a lying prophet (Deut 18:10; 1 Sa 28:8; Eze 13:6), and is to be understood in this sense in Acts 16:16. The careful avoidance of *manteuomai,* "to divine," and the frequent use of *prophēteuō,* "to prophesy," by the NT writers in describing the work of God's representatives is significant.

Sop. A rendering of the Gr. *psōmion* (Jn 13:26, 27, 30, KJV), "a (small) piece of bread" (RSV "morsel"). From ancient times it has been a mark of favor among Orientals for a host to dip a morsel in the central dish and to present the morsel to a guest. However, in Eastern lands even today a man will avoid so much as eating at a table with a person he wishes to take advantage of. Judas' action in accepting the "sop" marked him as being beyond the pale of respectability.

Sopater (sō'pá-tẽr). [Gr. *Sōpatros,* "of good parentage."] The son of Pyrrhus (Acts 20:4, RSV), of Beroea in Macedonia. He accompanied Paul from Greece to Asia on his return trip from his 3d Missionary Journey.

Sope. An archaic spelling of "soap" appearing in certain editions of the KJV (Jer 2:22; Mal 3:2). *See* Soap.

Sophereth (sõ-fẽ'rĕth), RSV once **Hassophereth** (hăs' õ-phē'rĕth). [Heb. *Sophereth* and *Hassophereth,* " (female) scribe."] The ancestral head of a family of Solomon's servants, some members of which returned from Babylonia with Zerubbabel (Ezr 2:55; Neh 7:57).

Sorcerer. [Heb. generally a form of *kashaph,* "to practice sorcery"; Gr. *pharmakeus, pharmakos,* and *magos,* "magician."] One who uses witchcraft or employs powers gained from the assistance and control of evil spirits, though in some instances certain terms thus translated may refer to one possessing a knowledge of chemistry and physics that enable him to give demonstrations that the ignorant would regard as supernatural feats. Sorcerers are mentioned as being active in Egypt (Ex 7:11), Babylon (Dan 2:2; cf. Is 47:9; etc.), Israel (2 Ki 9:22, RSV), Judah (2 Chr 33:1, 6, RSV; Jer 27:1, 9), and among the Jews in Nehemiah's time (Mal 3:5; see *SDACom* 4:1121). In Egypt sorcerers counterfeited Moses' miracles before Pharaoh (Ex 7:11; etc.). In Israel those who practiced sorcery were condemned to death (see Ex 22:18, RSV; cf. Lev 20:6, 27; Deut 18:9-12). A certain Simon practiced sorcery (KJV), or magic (RSV), in Samaria (Acts 8:4-11), as did

also Elymas in Paphos on the island of Cyprus (Acts 13:6, 8). God classifies sorcery with the vilest of sins (Gal 5:20, RSV) and promises to those who practice it ultimate destruction in the lake of fire (Rev 21:8).

Sorcery. *See* Sorcerer.

Sorek (sō'rĕk). [Heb. *Śôreq.*] The valley where Delilah, the mistress of Samson, lived (Jgs 16:4). It has usually been identified with the *Wâdī eṣ-Ṣarâr,* which begins about 13 mi. west of Jerusalem and winds in a northwesterly direction toward the sea. The ruin site *Khirbet Sûrîq,* situated on the north slope of the valley, has preserved the ancient name, and thus indicates that Sorek must have been situated in that vicinity.

Sosipater (sõ-sĭp'á-tẽr). [Gr. *Sōsipatros,* "saving the father."] A Christian of Greece who sent greetings through Paul to Rome; possibly a relative of the apostle (Rom 16:21).

Sosthenes (sŏs'thĕ-nēz). [Gr. *Sōsthenēs,* "of sound strength."]

1. The head of the synagogue at Corinth when Paul was accused before Gallio. When Gallio refused to condemn Paul, Sosthenes was maltreated by either his own people or the Greek public (Acts 18:17), possibly because he had done poorly as an accuser.

2. A Christian whose name appears in 1 Cor 1:1 as being the joint sender with Paul of that epistle. He may be identical with Sosthenes, 1, and if so he must have been converted after the events described in Acts 18. According to later Christian tradition he was one of the Seventy.

Sotai (sō'tī). [Heb. *Sôṭay,* meaning uncertain.] The ancestral head of one of the families of Solomon's servants (Ezr 2:55; Neh 7:57).

Soul. [Heb. generally *nephesh,* "breath," "life," "person," "emotions," "appetites," from *naphash,* "to breathe"; Gr. *psuchē,* "breath," "life," "life principle," "living creature," "person," "the affections," "the feelings."] The terms thus translated have a variety of meanings. In its first occurrence (Gen 2:7), the Heb. *nephesh* denotes man, who was given existence when the divine spark of life was injected into a physical body formed from the dust of the ground. Similarly, a new soul comes into existence whenever a child is born, each "soul" being a new unit of life uniquely different, and separate, from other similar units. This quality of individuality in each living being, which constitutes it a unique entity, seems to be the idea emphasized by the Hebrew term *nephesh*. When used in this sense *nephesh* is not a part of the person; it *is* the person, and, in many instances, is translated "person" (see Gen 14:21; Num 5:6; Deut 10:22; cf. Ps 3:2) or "self" (Lev 11:43; 1 Ki 19:4; Is 46:2; etc.). On the other hand, expressions such as "my soul," "your soul," "his soul," etc., are generally idioms for the personal pronouns "I," "me," "you," "he," etc. (see Gen 12:13; Lev 11: 43, 44; 19:8; Jos 23:11; Ps 3:2; Jer 37:9; etc.). In more than 100 of 755 occurrences in the OT the KJV translates *nephesh* as "life" (Gen 9:4, 5; 1 Sa 19:5; Job 2:4, 6; Ps 31:13; etc.). Often *nephesh* refers to desires, appetites, or passions (cf. Deut 23:24; Prov 23:2; Ec 6:7), and is sometimes translated "appetite" (Prov 23:2; Ec 6:7). It may refer to the seat of the affections (Gen 34:3; Song 1:7; etc.), and at times it represents the volitional part of man, as when translated "pleasure" (KJV) in Deut 23:24; Ps 105:22; Jer 34: 16. In Num 31:19 the *nephesh* (translated "person") is "killed," and in Jgs 16:30 (translated "me") it dies. In Num 5:2 ("the dead") and ch 9:6 ("dead body") it refers to a corpse (cf. Lev 19:28; Num 9:7, 10).

The usage of the Greek word *psuchē* in the NT is similar to that of *nephesh* in the OT. It is used of animal life as well as human life (Rev 16:3). In the KJV it is translated 40 times simply as "life" or "lives" (see Mt 2:20; 6:25; 16:25; etc.). In some instances it is used to mean simply "people" (see Acts 7:14; 27:37; Rom 13:1; 1 Pe 3:20; etc.), and in others it is equivalent to the personal pronoun (see Mt 12:18; 2 Cor 12:15; etc.). Sometimes it refers to the emotions (Mk 14:34; Lk 2:35), to the mind (Acts 14:2; Php 1:27), or to the heart (Eph 6:6).

The idea that a "soul" can have sentient existence apart from the body, or that it possesses an immortal essence, is wholly foreign to the Bible. This nonscriptural idea originated in the ancient pagan religious and philosophical systems of Greece and Egypt, and finds no support in the inspired writings. There is nothing in the words translated "soul" or in their usage in the Bible that even remotely implies a conscious entity that survives the body after death, or that attributes immortality to it. In fact, the NT specifically teaches that the soul (*psuchē*) is destroyed along with the body in "hell" (Mt 10:28).

South. *See* East.

457. Relief (right) on the Tower of the Winds at Athens, representing the South Wind

South Wind. [Heb. *darôm;* Gr. *notos.*] The south wind in Palestine was the dreaded hot wind, now called khamsin or sirocco (a name sometimes given also to a hot east or southeast wind), which brings an unbearable heat from the Arabian Desert (Job 37:17; Lk 12:55). The south wind of Acts 27:13 and 28:13 was really a southwest wind, favorable for ships sailing on the Mediterranean in a westerly or northwesterly direction. An ancient waterclock tower at Athens has sculptured symbols depicting the 8 winds known to the Greeks. The south wind, designated by the Greek inscription *notos,* is there symbolized by a young man with a water vessel (fig. 457), because the south wind brought rain to Greece.

Sowing. Early Mesopotamian pictures of plows and plowmen show a sowing funnel attached to the plow (see fig. 458), through which seed was dropped into the furrows during plowing. Even when seeding by hand the Near Eastern sower often laid his seed in rows (Is 28:25), although he sometimes sowed broadcast (Mt 13: 3-8). It is probable that the ancient farmer made a difference between early and late seeding as the farmer does today. Shortly after the 1st rain has sufficiently softened the ground to allow plowing, barley is

458. Black basalt memorial stone depicting a plow with a sowing funnel

sown, and then wheat, usually in November or December. Later in January and February millet, sesame, melons, cucumbers, etc., are sown. The Mosaic law did not allow the sowing of mixed seed (Lev 19:19; Deut 22:9).

Spain (spān). [Gr. *Spania;* Latin *Hispania.*] A geographical name for the southwestern peninsula of western Europe, not excluding what is now Portugal. The Phoenicians founded colonies in Spain in OT times (*see* Tarshish) to exploit its rich silver and tin mines. Spain later became a possession of Carthage and played an important role in the Punic wars. After Rome's victory over the Carthaginians the eastern part of Spain, which was the only section of the peninsula civilized at that time, became a Roman possession. During the succeeding 2 centuries the northern and western sections were subjugated, and finally the whole peninsula was Romanized. The country was strongly influenced by Roman culture and language, and became almost a copy of Italy. Paul planned to do missionary work in Spain (Rom 15:24), but shortly after he announced his plans he was arrested and then spent about 5 years in the prisons of Caesarea and Rome; hence it is uncertain whether he ever reached that country. Clement of Rome, writing from Italy to Corinth *c.* A.D. 95, stated that Paul had "reached the bounds of the west," an expression that gives the impression that he had Spain in mind. The first explicit claim of Paul's visit to Spain is found in the Muratorian fragment written in the 2d half of the 2d cent. A.D. If Paul went to Spain after his release from the 1st

imprisonment, his activity in that country must have been of short duration, for it is known that he spent some time in the east. A visit to Spain, if such was made, would have taken place in the interval between his 2 Roman imprisonments, during the years from *c.* A.D. 63 to 67. Map XIX, C/D-4/5/6.

Span. A rendering of Heb. *zereth* from Egyptian *ḏr.t* (Ex 28:16; 39:9; 1 Sa 17:4; Is 40:12; Eze 43:13), a unit of length equal to 3 handbreadths or ½ cu., hence according to the values adopted in this dictionary either 10.3 in. (26.16 cm.) long, if the Egyptian cubit is used, or 8.75 in. (22.23 cm.) long if a 17.5-in. cubit based on the Siloam tunnel is used. The term rendered "span long" in Lam 2:20, KJV (*ṭippuchîm*), probably means instead "perfect physical condition." The expression "span of life" (Mt 6:27; Lk 12:25; RSV) is the rendering of the Gr. *hēlikia,* which may refer either to "age," "time of life," or to "stature."

Sparrow. [Heb. *ṣippôr;* Gr. *strouthion.*] The Hebrew term is a general word for "bird," which would include the sparrow (Ps 102:7, KJV; Prov 26:2, RSV; Ps 84:3). The term describes both the house sparrow (*Passer domesticus*) and the tree sparrow (*Passer montanus*), as well as finches, blackbirds, and thrushes. The gregarious and ever-present starling or the house sparrow may be the species intended by the psalmist as the one that frequents the sanctuary (Ps 84:3), and the blue thrush, notably a solitary bird, has been suggested as that referred to in Ps 102:7. The Greek term describes small birds, especially the sparrow, which had almost no commercial value, so served Christ well in His illustration of the value of a human being (Mt 10:29, 31; Lk 12: 6, 7).

Spear. A weapon used for thrusting or hurling (1 Sa 13:22; 17:7; Jn 19:34; etc.). It consisted of a wooden shaft ending in

459. Two spearheads found in Palestine

a metal spearhead. The weapon was formed either by forcing the spearhead into the shaft or by placing the shaft in a socket in the spearhead. The term is generally a rendering of: (1) The Heb. *cha-*

nith (1 Sa 26:7; Job 39:23; etc.), which is erroneously translated "javelin" in a few passages in the KJV. (2) The Heb. *romach* (Jgs 5:8; Neh 4:13; etc.), "lance," usually rendered "spear," translated "lancet" in 1 Ki 18:28, KJV, but correctly "lance" in the RSV. This was a much longer weapon than the *chanith*, and was used only for thrusting. The *romach* is described in the "War" document of the Dead Sea scrolls as being 7 cu. long with a point ½ cu. long. (3) The Gr. *logchē* (Jn 19:34), probably a long Roman spear. It was used by a Roman soldier at the cross to pierce the side of Jesus.

Spearmen. The rendering of the Gr. *dexiolaboi* (Acts 23:23), in its context designating Roman soldiers of some kind. The word does not occur outside the NT, but is explained in a work of the 7th cent. A.D. to designate a lightly armed soldier, but the source gives no further details. Various scholars explain the term to mean lightly armed auxiliary soldiers who did not belong to a legion, members of the governor's bodyguard, or soldiers handling a sling with the right hand. The rendering "spearmen" follows the Vulgate, in which the Gr. *dexiolaboi* is translated *lancearii*, "lancers."

Speckled Bird. A rendering of the Heb. *'ayiṭ ṣabûa'*, meaning a bird of prey, apparently mottled. According to Driver *'ayiṭ* represents a class of birds which, from an etymology of the word, may be designated screamers (*PEQ* 87 [1955], 5). God bemoaned the fact that His people were like a bird of prey that was the object of attack by enemies (Jer 12:9).

Spelt, KJV **Fitches** and **Rie.** [Heb. *kussemeth*, "spelt."] A hard-grained, inferior variety of wheat (*Triticum spelta*), grown extensively in early times, and still in southern Germany. It will thrive in soil wholly unfit for wheat. As a late cereal grain it was not destroyed by the plague of hail (Ex 9:32). Its sowing and its use as an ingredient of an inferior kind of bread are mentioned in the Bible (Is 28:25; Eze 4:9).

Spice. A rendering of: (1) The Heb. *neko'th* (Gen 43:11, KJV; RSV "gum"). This term has been associated with tragacanth gum derived from the tragacanth shrub (*Astragalus gummifer*), a dwarf shrubby plant, 1 or 2 ft. tall, which exudes a scentless gum from its stem and branches, and with labdanum, the resin of various species of the rockrose (genus *Cistus*).

(2) The Heb. *sam* (Ex 30:34; 37:29; KJV), "paste," "perfume." This term may refer to the various ingredents of incenses and perfumes, such as stacte, onycha, and galbanum. (3) The Heb. *bośem, beśem,* and *baśam* (Ex 30:23; Song 4:14; etc.), "perfumes" in general. (4) The Gr. *arōma* (Mk 16:1; Jn 19:40; etc.), a collective term for perfumes and spices. (5) The Gr. *amōmon* (Rev 18:13, RSV), an Indian spice plant. *Amōmon* is not in the Textus Receptus, hence its translation does not appear in the KJV. Spices were used for seasoning food, for making cosmetics, and in the preparation of bodies for burial. They were highly valued by all ancient nations. A lucrative trade was conducted in spices, and the ancient spice routes became most important highways. Spices appear early in the Biblical record as an article of trade (Gen 43:11, KJV), and were used in the preparation of the anointing oil and the incense of the tabernacle service (Ex 35:8). Caravans bearing spices and other precious cargo traversed the Holy Land throughout OT times (1 Ki 10:2; Eze 27:21, 22). These sweet-smelling substances were prepared for the embalming of our Lord (Lk 23:56; 24:1; etc.).

Spice Merchant. This expression occurs only in 1 Ki 10:15, KJV, where it is the translation of a form of the Heb. *rakal*, "to trade," "to traffic," hence "a trader," "a merchant."

Spicery. *See* Gum.

Spider. [Heb. *'akkabîsh*.] A member of the order Araneida, class of *Arachnida*, mentioned in the Bible for its cobwebs, which are a symbol of something that is worthless and vain (Job 8:14; Is 59:5, 6). Palestine has several hundred different kinds of spiders. The Heb. *śemamîth* of Prov 30:28, rendered "spider" in the KJV, is actually a *lizard.

Spikenard. [Heb. *nerd*, "nard," a word of Indo-European origin; Gr. *nardos pistikē*, "pure nard."] A powerful perfume extracted from a Himalayan plant of the Valerian family, *Nardostachys jatamansi*, which grows at an elevation of 11,000 to 17,000 ft. Its roots and stem provide the essence, a very expensive item of commerce from early times. It was customary for ointment of spikenard to be kept in sealed alabaster containers and brought forth only on very special occasions or for the wealthy (Song 1:12; 4:13, 14; RSV "nard"). The fragrant spikenard with which Mary anointed the feet of Jesus represented almost a year's wages for a laboring man of the time (Jn 12:3; RSV "pure nard").

Spin. [Heb. *ṭawah,* "to spin"; Gr. *nēthō,* "to spin."] The references to spinning in the Scriptures are surprisingly few even though the art must have been widely practiced by the women of Palestine. In Ex 35:25, 26 mention is made of the work of the "wise hearted" women who spun blue, purple, scarlet, fine linen, and goat's hair for the furnishing of the tabernacle. The only other OT allusion to this craft (Prov 31:19) refers to the instruments employed, namely the distaff and the spindle, instruments that have continued in vogue for hand spinning even to this day. The word translated "spindle" (Heb. *kishôr*) in the KJV more probably refers to the "distaff," to which the women would reach forth with their hands as they spun the thread from the flax or wool, etc., tied to it. The word rendered "distaff" (Heb. *pelek*) is more accurately construed as "spindle," it being more probable that the women would hold the spindle, since by rotating it the fibers were twisted into a thread. Albright considers both terms, *kishôr* and *pelek,* synonyms for the spinning whorl (W. F. Albright, *Archaeology and the Religion of Israel,* p. 216, n. 63). In the NT "spin" occurs only in Mt 6:28; Lk 12:27.

Spirit. [Heb. and Aramaic *rûach,* "breath," "wind," "vital element," "mind"; Gr. *pneuma,* "breath," "wind," "spirit."] The divine energy, or life principle, that animates human beings. Whereas the Hebrew word *nephesh,* "soul," denotes individuality, or personality (*see* Soul), *rûach,* "spirit," refers to the energizing spark of life essential to individual existence. *Rûach* occurs 377 times in the OT, and most frequently is translated "spirit," "wind," or "breath" (Gen 8:1; etc.). It is also used to denote vitality (Jgs 15:19), courage (Jos 2:11), temper or anger (Jgs 8:3), disposition (Is 54:6), moral character (Eze 11:19), and the seat of the emotions (1 Sa 1:15). In the sense of breath, the *rûach* of men is identical with the *rûach* of animals (Ec 3:19). The *rûach* of man leaves the body at death (Ps 146:4) and returns to God (Ec 12:7; cf. Job 34:14). *Rûach* is used frequently of the Spirit of God, as in Is 63:10. Never in the OT, with respect to man, does *rûach* denote an intelligent entity capable of sentient existence apart from a physical body.

The NT equivalent of *rûach* is *pneuma,* "spirit," from *pneō,* "to blow," or "to breathe." As with *rûach,* there is nothing inherent in the word *pneuma* denoting an entity in man capable of conscious existence apart from the body, nor does NT usage with respect to man in any way imply such a concept. In such passages as Rom 8:15; 1 Cor 4:21; 2 Ti 1:7; 1 Jn 4:6 *pneuma* denotes "mood," "attitude," or "state of feeling." It is also used of various aspects of the personality, as in Gal 6:1; Rom 12:11; etc. As with *rûach,* the *pneuma* is yielded to the Lord at death (Lk 23:46; Acts 7:59). Like *rûach,* *pneuma* is also used of the Spirit of God (1 Cor 2:11, 14; Eph 4:30; Heb 2:4; 1 Pe 1:12; 2 Pe 1:21; etc.).

Spirit, Holy. *See* Holy Spirit.

Spirit of Divination. *See* Divination.

Spiritual Body. *See* Resurrection.

Spiritual Gifts. Special spiritual endowments bestowed by the Holy Spirit upon the various members of the church (1 Cor 12: 1, 4), for the "common good" (v 7, RSV). These gifts were provided in a special way after Jesus' ascension (Eph 4:8, 11), and were to continue until the church should reach the stage of development desired by God (vs 12, 13). Spiritual gifts are enumerated as being: (1) "the word of wisdom" (1 Cor 12:8), or "the utterance of wisdom" (RSV), meaning the gift of wisdom and the ability to communicate that wisdom to others; (2) "the word of knowledge" (v 8), or "the utterance of knowledge" (RSV), meaning the ability to understand spiritual truths and to present them to others; (3) faith (v 9), not the ordinary faith which all Christians have, but the special spiritual gift of faith, which enables the recipient to do exceptional things for God; (4) gifts of healing (v 9); (5) the working of *mir-acles (v 10); (6) prophecy (v 10; *see* Prophet); (7) discerning of spirits (v 10), or the ability to distinguish between spirits (RSV), the gift that would help to detect the false prophets and false manifestations; (8) divers, or various, kinds of tongues (v 10), see *SDACom* 6:795, 796; (9) interpretation of tongues (v 10), to make intelligible what was spoken in a tongue (ch 14:13-28). Paul encouraged believers to desire spiritual gifts for the purpose of building up the church (vs 1, 12).

Spit, Spitting. Anciently, spitting on or before a person was an expression of extreme contempt (Num 12:14; Job 30:10). A man refusing to enter into levirate marriage was to suffer indignity by having his face spit upon by the woman he refused (Deut 25:5-9). Isaiah prophesied (Is 50:6) of the Messiah that He would have His face spit upon (see Mt 26:67; 27:30; Mk 14:65; Lk 18:32; etc.). Christ used saliva in several of His healing miracles (Jn 9:6; Mk 7:33; 8:23).

Sponge, KJV **Spunge.** [Gr. *spoggos.*] An object of porous and elastic consistency used to hold quantities of liquid; the skeleton of certain marine animals. The 3 occurrences of the word (Mt 27:48; Mk 15:36; Jn 19:29) are all in connection with the vinegar-filled sponge offered to Christ as a deadening agent as He hung upon the cross.

Spoon. A rendering of the Heb. *kaph* (Ex 25:29; Num 7:84; KJV; etc.), literally, "hand." It is generally believed that, as used in these passages, where the KJV renders *kaph* "spoon," the reference is to some kind of flat bowl or dish (RSV). Numerous bowls have been found in the excavations of Palestine and Syria with a hand carved on the back, thus explaining the name "hand" (Wright, *BA* 4 [1941], 30).

Spring. [Heb. generally *'ayin,* also frequently rendered "fountain."] Palestine is plentifully supplied with springs. They rise usually under a bank or a rock ledge on the slope of a hill, and on such hills ancient cities were most often built. Many cities made provision for reaching the springs through subterranean tunnels and shafts without leaving the protection of the city walls. Some of the ancient springs became famous, such as the Gihon in the Kidron Valley, the place of Solomon's coronation (1 Ki 1:33, 34). Of special importance were springs in the desert (Gen 16:7). Where there were no springs men were dependent on *wells and *cisterns. The route of the Israelites after leaving Egypt was at first conditioned by the location of springs and wells (Ex 15:23-25, 27). Springs were not always distinguished from wells, as a comparison of Gen 16:7 and v 14 shows (*see* Beer-lahai-roi). Many cities were named after springs, such as En-gedi, En-dor, En-rimmon, En-shemesh, etc., the "En" being a transliteration of *'ên,* a form of the Heb. *'ayin,* "spring." See figs. 154, 157, 204.

Sprinkle. *See* Sacrifices and Offerings.

Spunge. *See* Sponge.

Squad, KJV **Quaternion.** [Gr. *tetradion.*] A group of 4 soldiers (Acts 12:4). The KJV term is a Latin loan word meaning 4 persons or things. Four squads, or quaternions, 16 soldiers in all, were ordered to guard Peter in prison in Jerusalem. Each of these squads was evidently responsible for guarding the prisoner for one watch of 3 hours. During the night when Peter was freed, 2 of the soldiers were with the prisoner in his cell, while the other 2 stood guard outside the door (Acts 12:6). There was apparently 1 squad of 4 placed to guard Jesus at the cross, as may be concluded from the report that the soldiers at the cross divided His garment into 4 parts (Jn 19:23).

Stable. *See* Stall.

Stachys (stā'kĭs). [Gr. *Stachus,* "ear of grain," a name attested in Greek inscriptions.] A Christian in Rome whom Paul called "my beloved," and to whom he sent greetings (Rom 16:9).

Stacte. [Heb. *nataph.*] A sweet gum or resin, the exudation of a certain plant, not certainly identified, but possibly the storax shrub (*Styrax officinalis*), a small stiff-branched plant sometimes growing to 20 ft. in height. A highly perfumed gum may be obtained from it by making incisions in the branches. This product, however, is not the liquid storax of commerce. Some suggest opobalsamum, a resinous juice also called the *balm of Gilead, still others the gum of *Pistacia lentiscus.* Stacte was one of the ingredients of the perfume used in the tabernacle (Ex 30:34).

Stadia. [Gr. *stadia,* sing., *stadion.*] A stadium is a linear measurement of 600 Greek ft., 625 Roman ft., and about 606 English ft., which is about 54 ft. short of an English furlong (it is translated "furlong" consistently in the KJV; Lk 24:13; Jn 6:19; 11:18; Rev 14:20; 21:16). "Furlongs" occurs in the RSV only once (Mt 14:24), where *stadia* represents a variant reading. In 3 instances (Lk 24:13; Jn 6:19; 11:18) the RSV computes the *stadia* to their equivalents in English miles. In 2 others (Rev 14:20; 21:16) it renders the word "stadia."

Staff. The rendering of several Hebrew words meaning variously "stick," "shaft," "carrying pole," "rod," "support," "bar," "scepter," and of the Gr. *rhabdos,* "staff," "stick," "scepter." Anciently travelers took staffs with them on their journeys (cf. Gen 32:10; Mk 6:8) for support or for protection from robbers and wild animals. Staffs were sometimes used as weapons (2 Sa 23:21). The old used them for support (Zec 8:4; Heb 11:21). A staff (Heb. *matteh,* "staff," "rod") was used in threshing certain crops (Is 28:27). The term "staff of bread" (Lev 26:26; Eze 4: 16; 5:16; etc.) doubtless refers to bread as the most important item of diet. The southern kingdom of Judah, toward the end of its existence, depended upon Egypt for military help against its enemies, but that nation proved to be only a "staff of this broken reed" that could give no support (Is 36:6; see 2 Ki 18:21; Eze 29:6). See Club.

Stall. A covered-in shelter for the housing and feeding of domestic animals. In Palestine the "stall" is frequently part of the owner's house (see fig. 241). "Stall" is a rendering of: (1) the Heb. *'urawóth* (pl.) with variant spellings, stalls for horses and cattle (1 Ki 4:26; 2 Chr 9:25; 32:28); (2) the Heb. *marbeq,* "fattening stall" (Amos 6: 4; Mal 4:2); (3) the Heb. *repheth,* enclosures for sheep and goats (Hab 3:17); (4) the Gr. *phatnē,* "manger," "crib," "stall" (Lk 13:15, KJV). Fig. 460 is a model of a horse stable excavated at Megiddo. See also fig. 236.

460. Model (restoration) of the Israelite stables at Megiddo

Stallion. A rendering of: (1) The Heb. *'abbîr,* "powerful," "stallion," "bull" (Jer 8:16; 47:3; 50:11; RSV). The KJV renders *'abbîr* "strong one" and "strong" in chs 8:16; 47:3, respectively, and "bull" in ch 50:11. (2) The Heb. *sûs,* "horse" (ch 5:8, RSV).

Standard. See Banner.

Star. [Heb. *kôkab;* Gr. *astēr; astron.*] Heavenly bodies attracted the attention of the ancients, and their movements, their number, and their apparent groupings became the subject of much study and discussion. When mankind lost sight of God's creatorship they came to consider the stars as objects of veneration rather than evidence of divine omnipotence. Around the superstitions of hea-

then peoples concerning the stars there grew up the pseudo science of astrology, which taught that heavenly bodies had an influence not only on the natural world but also upon human affairs. *Astrologers during some eras held positions of great importance in the royal courts (Dan 2: 2). The astronomers of Babylonia, Assyria, and Egypt charted the boundaries of the constellations, and assigned the 12 constellations in the plane of the ecliptic to be 12 signs of the zodiac. They established calendars, and predicted eclipses with amazing accuracy. The heathen nations surrounding Israel in Palestine included the stars (as well as the sun and moon) in their pantheon, and in their apostasy both Israel and Judah worshiped the host of heaven (2 Ki 17:16; 21: 3; cf. Deut 4:19). God referred to the numberless stars to illustrate to Abraham the limitless blessings and innumerable offspring the patriarch would have (Gen 15:5; 22:17). Job mentions certain constellations in his portrayal of God's power (Job 9:9; 38:31, 32; *see* names of individual constellations), and other Bible writers recognized that the stars are under His power (Is 13:10; Jer 31:35) and were objects of His creation (Ps 8:3, 4; 19:1). For the "seven stars" of Amos 5:8, KJV, *see* Pleiades. For the "Day Star" of Is 14: 12, RSV, *see* Lucifer. The "day star" of 2 Pe 1:19, KJV (Gr. *phōsphoros,* RSV "morning star"), is believed to designate the planet Venus.

Stargazers. [Heb. *chozîm bakkôkabîm.*] Astrologers who, by their watching of the stars and planets, purported to be able to foretell future events. God pronounced judgment against the Babylonian stargazers (Is 47:13, 14, KJV).

Star-god. The designation of the deity *Kaiwan (Amos 5:26, RSV).

Statute. [Heb. generally *choq,* "something prescribed," "an obligation," "statute," from *chaqaq,* "to enact," "to decree," "to command," and *chuqqah,* "something prescribed," "statute," "regulation," "prescription."] A specific, fixed requirement, usually a divine decree as in Ex 27:21; 29: 28; Lev 6:18; Deut 8:11; etc.

Stealing. See Robber.

Steel. Iron to which, by special process, carbon, up to 1.7%, has been added. The word occurs 4 times in the KJV, a rendering of the Heb *nechûshah* and *nechosheth* (2 Sa 22:35; Job 20:24; Ps 18:34; Jer 15:12), "copper" or "bronze." It is doubtful that steel is mentioned in the

STEPHANAS

Bible. Some suggest that the Heb. *pela-doth* (Nah 2:3), rendered "torches" on the basis of the meaning of similar words in the cognate languages, Syriac and Arabic, may designate "steel." The earliest steel object ever discovered is a blade of an ax dating from the 14th cent. B.C. found at Ugarit.

Stephanas (stĕf'á-năs). [Gr. *Stephanas*, probably a shortened form of *Stephanēphoros*, "crown bearer." The name is attested also in Greek inscriptions.] The head of a family that comprised Paul's 1st converts in Greece (Achaia), and whose members the apostle, against his usual practice, had personally baptized (1 Cor 1:16; 16:15). With Achaicus and Fortunatus, Stephanas had come to Ephesus with messages from the Corinthian church (ch 16:17). He possibly took 1 Corinthians back to his home church of Corinth.

Stephen (stē'vĕn). [Gr. *Stephanos*, "coronet," "wreath of victory," a common name in ancient inscriptions.] The first Christian martyr. His Greek name suggests a Hellenistic background. Tradition says that he and Philip were among the Seventy sent out by Jesus (see Lk 10:1-17). The 1st mention of Stephen is in Acts 6:5, where he is named as one of the 7 men chosen by the Jerusalem church and ordained to supervise the daily distribution of food to its poor members (vs 1-6), in accordance with the communal system adopted by the new church (ch 4:32, 34, 35). The men in this office were to be "of honest report, full of the Holy Ghost and wisdom" (ch 6:3).

Stephen is next mentioned as performing miracles and doing other great acts as a consequence of his faith and the power bestowed upon him by the Holy Spirit (Acts 6:8). The success that attended his labors and the power with which he preached the gospel stirred the antagonism of certain men "who belonged to the synagogue of the Freedmen (as it was called), and of the Cyrenians, and of the Alexandrians, and of those from Cilicia and Asia" (v 9, RSV). These men were apparently devout Jews of the Dispersion, who had come from the various countries mentioned to worship at Jerusalem. Concluding from Stephen's preaching that he was propagating ideas calculated to lessen the importance of the Temple and the customs of Moses (vs 13, 14), they sought first to weaken his influence and nullify his preaching by disputing with him. However, his logic and spiritual insight, and the power which attended his

461. Stephen's Gate at Jerusalem

preaching, overcame all their arguments (Acts 6:10). Having failed in this strategy, they instigated certain ones to accuse him of blasphemy (v 11). This aroused the indignation of the people and rulers; he was arrested and arraigned before the *council (v 12). He was there confronted with charges of having spoken against the Temple and the Law, and of having taught that Jesus would destroy the Temple (chs 6:13-15; 7:1). In his defense Stephen presented a résumé of the history of God's chosen people, beginning with Abraham (ch 7:2), and endeavored to show that the Hebrews had consistently rejected God's leadership and had now rejected His Messiah.

Sensing, evidently by the reaction of his listeners, that his defense had failed and that his enemies were determined to take his life, Stephen abruptly ended his line of reasoning and began a severe indictment of his accusers (Acts 7:51-53). Finally, as his enemies manifested hottest anger (v 54), he, "being full of the Holy Ghost," was given a vision of Jesus at God's right hand (v 55). He described this vision to his audience, who stopped their ears at what they considered blasphemy, dragged him out of the city, and stoned him (vs 56-58). "And devout men carried Stephen to his burial, and made great lamentation over him" (ch 8:2). Stephen's death, which took place only a few years after the earthly life of Jesus, began the first wave of persecution to overtake the church. The believers were forced to leave Jerusalem, and thus the seed of the gospel of Jesus Christ was spread farther afield (v 1).

Steward. A man employed to manage and be responsible for the care of the property or business affairs of another. Several Hebrew and Greek terms are thus translated, and various stewards are mentioned. Joseph had a steward over his house (Gen 43:19; 44:4). Shebna was steward during Hezekiah's reign (Is 22:15, RSV; cf. 2 Ki 18:37; 19:2). A steward was appointed over Daniel and his companions in Babylon (Dan 1:11, 16, RSV). In the NT Chuza is mentioned as Herod's steward (Lk 8:3). Stewards played a part in the parables of Jesus (Mt 20:8; Lk 12:42; 16:1-9). Stewardship is given a spiritual application in the NT. The Christian minister acts as God's steward (Tit 1:7), and is a steward of the "mysteries of God" (1 Cor 4:1, 2), and of the "manifold grace of Christ" (1 Pe 4:10). He is responsible to God for his treatment of, and attitude toward, those in darkness about him.

Stewardship. See Steward.

Stocks. "Stock" is used as meaning: (1) a stump, a piece of wood (Job 14:8; Is 44:19; Jer 2:27; Hos 4:12; KJV; etc.), or the stubble of grass or wheat (Is 40:24, KJV); (2) lineage, family line, human offspring (Lev 25:47, KJV; Eze 44:22, RSV; Acts 13:26; Php 3:5; KJV). "Stocks" are a wooden structure containing holes into which the arms or legs of a prisoner might be locked as a method of punishment (Job 13:27; Jer 20:2; Acts 16:24; etc.).

Stoic (stō′ĭk), KJV **Stoick** (stō′ĭk). [Gr. *Stoïkos*.] An adherent of Stoicism, a Greco-Roman philosophy, prominent in the Mediterranean world in NT times. Paul met Stoic philosophers in the market place at Athens, and his disputations with them and with the Epicurean philosophers led to the famous address at the Areopagus (Acts 17:16-21). Stoic philosophy took its name from the *Stoa Poikilē*, the painted porch at the agora (market place) in Athens, where Zeno, its founder, taught for about half a century, beginning *c.* 300 B.C. It was a Hellenistic rather than a Hellenic philosophy. Zeno was a native of Citium in Cyprus, a Greek city with a Phoenician element, and was probably of Semitic extraction. His immediate successors at the head of the school, Cleanthes and Chrysippus, also came from the East. Of the early heads of the school, not one was an Athenian, and 5 came from the Semitic fringe of the Greek world. Stoicism owes much to the East. Its moral earnestness breathes the East's religious atmosphere. It was, in fact, the offspring of the union between the religious consciousness of the Orient and the classical culture of the West. Three of the most prominent Stoics were the slave Epictetus, the Roman philosopher Seneca, and the emperor Marcus Aurelius.

Stoicism may be described as a materialistic pantheism. According to it everything is material, even God, the human soul, and all the qualities of things. The universe is permeated and controlled by a world-soul, or rational force, which is God. Man is not only made in the rational image of God, but has within him a spark of deity. By virtue of this spark he is a child of God.

The primary interests of Stoicism were practical and ethical rather than speculative. The chief end of existence, according to it, is virtuous living. Stoic teachers laid great stress on living in conformity with nature. Seneca declared: "We have a habit of saying that the highest good is to live according to nature." For the Stoic this meant to find a rational way of life in conformity to the divine will. Whatever happens beyond the power of man is due, they taught, to the divine will. It must therefore be accepted with equanimity. Regardless of what happened to him, the Stoic endeavored to allow nothing to disturb his tranquillity. He sought to be indifferent to both pleasure and pain. To achieve a life of virtue he practiced rigid self-discipline, and subjected himself to a daily self-examination. Four cardinal virtues of Stoicism were wisdom, justice, courage, and soberness or temperance. Stoicism regarded suicide as honorable.

Stoicism taught an elementary concept of world unity and brotherhood. Since all rational beings are under the same world-law, all men are brothers. Class distinctions, it held, were artificial barriers to be removed by religion rather than social revolution.

The allegorical method of interpretation used by the Stoics and other philosophers in explaining the Greek myths was adopted by Philo in the interpretation of the OT, and had a great influence on Christian interpreters of Scripture.

Stomacher. A rendering of the Heb. *pethigil* (Is 3:24), "garment of fine material and work" (RSV "rich robe"). Isaiah prophesied that instead of these luxurious garments the "daughters of Zion" would be wearing sackcloth.

Stone. [Heb. and Aramaic generally *'eben;* Gr. generally *lithos*.] Stones were used in ancient times as a building material, and in countries where building timber was scarce stonemasons were of greater importance than carpenters. Monuments, temples, altars, public buildings, and homes of the upper classes were constructed of stone (see Ex 20:25; Lev 14:40; 2 Sa 18:18; 1 Ki 5:18; 2 Ki 22:6;

2 Chr 16:6; etc.). The stonemasons of Egypt developed the skill of constructing their buildings without mortar, depending on friction and the weight of the structure for cohesion. It is a source of amazement to modern engineers how stones of such tremendous size as are seen in the ruins of Egypt, Syria, and Judea could have been so accurately hewed, and transported from the quarries to the building sites (see Mk 13:1). A farmer opening up new land for cultivation in Palestine had first to clear it of stones (Is 5:2). Stones were used to build walls for vineyards (cf. Prov 24:30, 31) and sheepfolds. Stone cairns or pillars were erected as memorials to commemorate notable events (Gen 28:18; 35:14; Jos 4:9; 1 Sa 7: 12), and as a token of a treaty (Gen 31: 46, 47). In addition, stones were used for the construction of aqueducts, reservoirs, and bridges. Single stones were used to close up the mouths of wells (ch 29:2), to cover or mark graves (Jos 7:26; 2 Sa 18:17; Mt 27:60; Jn 11:38), and for guideposts along the highways (cf. Jer 31:21). The heathen worshiped stones (Is 37:19; Eze 20:32; etc.). Meteorites were especially venerated as having fallen from heaven. The most common kinds of stone in Palestine are limestone and sandstone. *See* Palestine, VI. Stone is used figuratively of the carnal heart (Eze 11:19), of the people of God (1 Pe 2:5), and of Christ (Lk 20:17; 1 Pe 2:6-8; etc.), and symbolically of the kingdom of God (Dan 2:34, 44, 45). *See* names of individual precious stones.

Stones, Precious. *See* Precious Stones.

Stoning. Stoning is first mentioned in Ex 8:26, where Moses expressed the fear that if the Israelites sacrificed in Egypt the Egyptians would stone them. However, there is no record of such mode of punishment in Egypt as a means of inflicting the death penalty. It is known that stoning was practiced in later times among the Persians, Macedonians, and Greeks. The Israelites were commanded to stone those guilty of idolatry (Lev 20:2; Deut 13:6-10; 17:2-5), unchastity (Deut 22:20-24), or blasphemy (Lev 24:11-16; cf. 1 Ki 21:9-13). Before a person might be stoned there must be at least 2 or 3 witnesses, who were to cast the first stones, then all the people were to join in the casting of stones (Deut 17:5-7). The Mishnah (*Sanhedrin* 6:4) describes in detail the later procedure followed in stoning: "The place of stoning was twice a man's height. One of the witnesses

pushed him by the hips, [so that] he was overturned on his heart. He was then turned on his back. If that caused his death, he had fulfilled [his duty]; but if not, the second witness took the stone and threw it on his chest. If he died thereby, he had done [his duty]; but if not, he [the criminal] was stoned by all Israel, for it is written: The hand of the witnesses shall be first upon him to put him to death, and afterwards the hand of all the people [Deut 17:7]," (Soncino ed. of the Talmud, p. 295). Achan was stoned for appropriating certain materials contrary to God's instructions (Jos 7:25, 26; cf. ch 6:18, 19). The Jews attempted to stone Christ for alleged blasphemy on at least 2 occasions (Jn 8:59; 10:31-33). Stephen was charged with blasphemy and stoned (Acts 7:57-59). Paul was stoned once in Asia Minor (Acts 14:19; cf. 2 Cor 11:25), and was in danger of being stoned on other occasions (cf. Acts 14:5, 6).

Stool. *See* Birthstool.

Store Cities. [Heb. *miskenôth,* "storage places."] Cities built with facilities for storing large supplies of grain and other supplies, such as the cities of *Pithom and *Rameses in Egypt (Ex 1:11, RSV; KJV "treasure cities"). At 2 temples of ancient Thebes dating from the 19th and 20th dynasties, the Ramesseum and the temple at *Medînet Habu,* many vaulted store chambers of brick have been excavated. From ancient reliefs and paintings it is known that grain bins had openings only at the top, which were reached by a ramp. The grain was poured in and extracted through these openings. Many large grain bins of the Persian period, measuring 20 to 33 ft. in diameter, have been excavated in *Tell Jemmeh* near Gaza, showing that this city—not yet definitely identified—was an important store city in the time of Ezra and Nehemiah. Solomon built store cities (1 Ki 9:19; 2 Chr 8:4). Such cities were apparently conveniently situated in various parts of the country (see 2 Chr 16:4; 17:12).

Storehouse. *See* Granary.

Stork. [Heb. *chasîdah,* "stork," "heron."] The *Ciconia alba,* a large yet graceful white and black bird related to the heron. The stork is a migratory bird (Jer 8:7), nesting in populated areas of Palestine, Syria, and the whole of Europe, and wintering in central and southern Africa, and is known for its attention to its young. Its red bill and glossy black wings contrast with its pure-white plumage. Its food consists of fish, small reptiles, garbage, and other waste. It is listed as unclean (Lev 11:19; Deut 14:18), and is said to nest in fir trees (Ps 104:17). Another species of stork, *Ciconia nigra*, is common around the Dead Sea valley, where it nests in the trees. G. R. Driver suggests that both the stork and the heron may be represented by the Hebrew term *chasîdah* (*PEQ* 87 [1955], 17).

Storm. Storms of a destructive nature were known to the ancients and are frequently mentioned in the Bible (Ps 107:25-29; Is 25:4; etc.). Recent meteorological observations have explained why seasoned fishermen such as Christ's disciples, who were well acquainted with the Sea of Galilee, would be overtaken by these dangerous

462. Storm on the Sea of Galilee

storms. The Sea of Galilee lies about 685 ft. below sea level and is bounded on the east and west by mountains more than 1,000 ft. above sea level. Down these, strong winds, dangerous to boats on the lake, descend, usually with no advance signs. Sometimes during summer afternoons gusts of 40 to 50 mi. an hour are experienced. In the winter the southwesterly wind sometimes blows with gale force over the lake. The most dangerous wind of all is the east wind, descending on the lake in the winter from the Hauran plateau. These winds, which are experienced rather frequently, come very suddenly, and are accompanied by gusts of great velocity during this season of the year. See figs. 190, 462.

Lit.: M. Nun, *IEJ* 2 (1952), 196, 197.

Stove. A covered-in heating unit in which the heat is produced by burning wood

or other similar fuels, and on which the pots of water or food were placed for heating or cooking. The term occurs but once (Lev 11:35, RSV), a rendering of the Heb. *kîrayim,* a dual form probably from the noun *kîr,* a "small hearth." The dual form probably denotes that it supported 2 pots.

Straight, Street Called. *See* Damascus.

Strakes. A term in Gen 30:37, KJV (Heb. *peṣalôth*), referring to the peeled streaks (RSV), or stripes, made by Jacob on the boughs or rods used when breeding Laban's flocks and herds. In Lev 14:37, KJV, "strakes" (Heb. *sheqaʿarûroth*) refers to hollow depressions or "spots" (RSV) in the wall of a dwelling presumed to be affected by *leprosy.

Stranger. [Heb. generally *ger,* "foreign resident," *zar,* "one who is strange" or "different," or "who does not belong to the community," *nekar* and *nokrî,* "foreigner" or "alien," from *nakar,* "to act as a stranger," "to disguise oneself"; Gr. generally *xenos,* "strange," "foreign," "alien," and *allotrios,* "strange," "not one's own," "belonging to another."]

In the OT a stranger, or sojourner, as the RSV frequently reads, is usually one who, because of some misfortune such as war, famine, plague, or some criminal act, has been constrained to leave his original place of residence, or tribe, and to seek shelter elsewhere (cf. Gen 15:13; Ex 2:22; 20:10; 23:9; Lev 25:47; etc.). In ancient times, when travel and change of residence were much less common than now, only the most unusual circumstances would lead a person to leave his own people and live elsewhere, and consequently a stranger might be regarded with suspicion. During the reign of Solomon there were 153,600 strangers in Israel (2 Chr 2:17). If the "stranger" needed assistance and protection the Israelites, according to Mosaic law, were to help him (see Lev 19:33, 34; Deut 10:18, 19). If poor, he was to enjoy the same privileges as the Hebrew poor (Deut 24:19, 20), but if a bond slave he could not go free in the year of jubilee like a Hebrew slave (Lev 25:45, 46). The stranger was not a full citizen, but nevertheless enjoyed certain inalienable rights (Ex 22:21; 23:9). The Hebrews themselves had been strangers in the land of Egypt and were therefore to pity and to avoid oppressing the sojourner among them (ch 23:9). The stranger was subject to the laws of the land (Lev 16:29; 17:10; 18:26; 20:2; 24:16), but could not join in certain religious rites unless he was circumcised and was thus regarded as an Israelite (Ex 12:43-49). In others he was free to participate (Lev 17:8, 15; Num 15:14, 29; 19:10; 35:15; Deut 16:11-14). The Ammonites and Moabites were not to be admitted to citizenship even by circumcision (Deut 23:3). In certain cases of ritual uncleanness the stranger was to obtain purification by the same rites required of the Hebrews (Lev 17:15; Num 19:10).

The technical, legal connotation of the word "stranger" in the OT does not carry over into NT usage. In the NT the word is used in a more general sense. In Acts 2:10 the "strangers of Rome" were "Jews and proselytes," or simply "visitors from Rome" (RSV), at Jerusalem. The "strangers" of 1 Pe 1:1 apparently refers to Jews as well as Gentiles residing abroad, or outside of Palestine. In Eph 2:12, 19 the "strangers" are non-Jews. Otherwise, usually, a "stranger" is simply a person with whom one is unacquainted (Mt 25:35, 38, 43, 44; 27:7; Jn 10:5). See Foreigner.

Straw. [Heb. *mathben, teben.*] The hollow stalk and husks left from grain after threshing; stubble is that portion of the stalk left above the ground after mowing or harvesting. Straw was used as fodder for animals (see Gen 24:25, 32; Jgs 19:19; 1 Ki 4:28; Is 11:7; 65:25). The Egyptians used chopped straw in the making of bricks (cf. Ex 5:7, 12, 16), a device that increased the strength of the bricks threefold, as modern experiments have shown. This added strength was due partly to the presence of the straw stalks themselves and partly to the chemical reaction of decaying vegetable matter upon the brick mixture. An additional burden was placed upon the captive Israelites when, after a time, they were required to provide their own straw for brickmaking.

Stream. *See* River.

Street. There was no systematic street system in ancient cities prior to the Hellenistic period, with the possible exception of a few large cities such as Babylon. The Palestinian and Syrian cities had narrow streets (Jos. *Ant.* xx. 5. 3; *War* ii. 14. 9; 15. 5; vi. 8. 5) which ran through the city in circuitous courses. A straight street was such an exception that one such in *Damascus was named "Straight" (Acts 9:11; see fig. 121). Few streets were wide enough to allow vehicles to be driven through (see Jer 17:25; Nah 2:4), and many hardly allowed 2 beasts of burden to pass each other. Since the rooms of

houses opened toward a central court, the streets were usually flanked on both sides by blank walls broken only by doors. Shops had their fronts open to the street. Merchants dealing in the same kind of merchandise or artisans in the same trade usually lived in the same street (*see* Bazaars), hence names such as "bakers' street" (Jer 37:21). Street corners were centers of display and gathering places (Mt 6:5; cf. Lk 13:26). Near city gates the streets were usually wider and in some cases became open spaces (*see* Gate). There was no street cleaning in Palestinian cities, and garbage thrown in the street was disposed of by the dogs that roamed about at will (Ex 22:31; Ps 59:6, 14, 15). Palestinian city streets were not paved. Herod Agrippa II gave Jerusalem its 1st recorded paved street (Jos. *Ant.* xx. 9. 7), following an example of Herod the Great, his great-grandfather, who had paid for paving one of the principal streets in Antioch (Jos. *Ant.* xvi. 5. 3). There was no street lighting at night, but at least certain cities had "watchmen that went about the city" (Song 3:3; 5:7; cf. Ps 127:1).

Stripes. *See* Scourge.

Strong Drink. [Heb. *shekar,* related to the Akkadian *shikaru,* "beer"; Gr. *sikera,* from the Aramaic *shikra'* with the same meaning as the Heb. *shekar.*] An alcoholic beverage, usually beer (Lev 10:9; Num 6:3; Deut 29:6; etc.). The *Amarna Letters reveal that beer was part of the rations that the Palestinian princes were required to furnish for Egyptian soldiers (55, 10-13; 324, 10-14; 325, 15-19). Beer was widely used, by poor and rich alike, throughout the ancient Orient. Pictures of beer brewing and drinking have been found in Egypt (fig. 463), and ancient texts describing the techniques of brewing have been discovered in Mesopotamia.

Though information concerning Palestinian beermaking has not yet come to light, the method was probably not too different, for emmer and barley, 2 of the principal grains used in making beer (occasionally also figs) in Egypt and Mesopotamia, were found in Palestine. Mesopotamian cuneiform texts reveal that the ancients had several (16) kinds of beer, among them dark, light, young, and lager. These beers were made of barley, dehusked emmer, and barley malt. The barley was first malted, and the dehusked emmer shredded. The malt was then bruised and, with the shredded grain, baked into beer breads. Wort was then made in the mash vats from the beer breads. Whether this was done by boiling or by pouring hot water over the breads is not known. Since a malt extract was obtained, it appears that the mash was boiled. Nothing

463. Egyptian relief depicting the production of beer

is said in available documents about the refining of the wort, nor of the process and time of fermentation, nor how it was drawn off into the lager vats. Boiled-down wort was sometimes called "honey beer," and could be kept for a long time. Before use it was mixed with water and allowed to ferment. Is 5:22 seems to speak of this kind of beer, also called "mixed beer." Priests were prohibited by the Mosaic law from using *shekar* when they were about to enter the sanctuary (Lev 10:9), and rulers were warned against its use (Prov 31:4, 5). Prov 20:1 declares that all who drink it are "not wise," and Isaiah pronounced a woe over imbibers (Is 5:11, 22). "Strong drink" was also forbidden to the dedicated Nazirite (Num 6:3), and was especially forbidden to Samson (Jgs 13:4, 7, 14) and to John the Baptist (Lk 1:15). The Israelites had no opportunity to use strong drink during their 40 years of desert wandering (Deut 29:6), but were permitted to spend

money "for wine, or for strong drink" for use at a feast which followed the delivery of tithe (Deut 14:22, 26; see *SDACom* 1: 1002, 1003). The permission to "give strong drink unto him that is ready to perish" (Prov 31:6) was obviously not a recommendation of it as a beverage, but probably a reference to the custom of giving a stupefying alcoholic beverage to criminals before execution (*Sanhedrin* 43a; cf. Mt 27:34). Isaiah speaks of seeing priests and prophets drunk from *shekar* (Is 28:7; 56:12). That the Jews used beer in post-Biblical times, and probably earlier, can be concluded from the prohibition found in the Mishnah (*Pesahim* 3. 1) of drinking beer during the Passover season. The reason given is that beer was made of fermented grain, and so partook of the nature of leaven. The "Passover papyrus" from Elephantine from the time of Darius II also seemed to require the Jews at that place to abstain from the drinking of beer during the Passover feast (Cowley, *Aramaic Papyri of the Fifth Century B.C.* [Oxford, 1923], No. 21, line 7).

Strong Hold. *See* Fortifications.

Stud. In the KJV a rendering of the Heb. *nequddah* (Song 1:11), a decorative device, probably beads. In the RSV "royal stud" is a rendering of the Heb. *rammak* (Est 8:10; KJV "dromedary"), a word of uncertain meaning. The latter part of the verse in which *rammak* occurs is obscure in the Hebrew.

Stuff. In the KJV a rendering generally of the Heb. *keli,* "vessel," "receptacle," "utensil," "furniture," "implement," "instrument," "weapon," etc., thus, portable property, usually household possessions (Gen 31:37; 45:20; Ex 22:7; Neh 13:8; etc.). *Keli* is variously rendered by the RSV as "goods" (Gen 31:37), "stuff" (Jos 7:11), "baggage" (Eze 12:3), etc., according to the context. In the RSV "stuff" is rarely used in the above sense (Jos 7: 11) but occurs chiefly in the phrase "scarlet stuff," meaning "scarlet fabric" (Ex 25:4; 26:1; etc.).

Stumbling Block. [Heb. generally *mikshôl,* "obstacle," "stumbling block"; Gr. *proskomma,* "stumbling," "offense," "obstacle," "hindrance"; *skandalon,* "trap," "temptation," "enticement," "whatever gives offense," literally, "the trigger that springs a trap."] Whatever causes one to stumble or fall, whether literally (Lev 19: 14) or, as the term is commonly used, figuratively (Is 57:14, KJV; Jer 6:21; Eze 3:20; 14:3-7). Among the spiritual stumbling blocks in Israel's pathway were silver and gold (Eze 7:19) and the iniquity of their idolatry (ch 14:3). In the NT the expression is always used in the figurative sense. For instance, Christian liberty was not to be made a stumbling block in the way of inexperienced Christians (1 Cor 8:9). Christ was a "stumblingblock," or "stumblingstone," for the Jews who refused to accept Him as the Messiah (see Rom 9:32, 33; 1 Cor 1:23; 1 Pe 2:8).

Suah (sū'à). [Heb. *Sûach*, "rubbish"; Old Babylonian *Suḥum*.] A descendant of Asher (1 Chr 7:36).

Subtil, Subtilty. A KJV rendering of several Hebrew words denoting generally intellectual cleverness, whether in a good sense (Prov 1:4) or a bad sense (Gen 3: 1; 27:35; Prov 7:10), and of 2 Greek words: (1) *dolos*, "deceit," "cunning," "treachery," used of Judas' betrayal of Christ (Mt 26:4), and of the "deceit" (RSV) of Elymas the sorcerer (Acts 13: 10), and (2) *panourgia*, "craftiness," "trickery," used of the serpent's "cunning" (RSV) in beguiling Eve (2 Cor 11:3).

Suburbs. [Heb. generally *migrash*, "pasture ground," "untilled ground," from *garash*, "to drive out."] The open countryside beyond the walls of a city, to which cattle could be driven for grazing or where gardens could be cultivated (Num 35:2; Jos 14:4; Eze 48:17; KJV; etc.). "Suburbs" is thus equivalent to the English word "common," an open space for the common use of the community. The RSV renders *migrash* by such terms as "common land" (Lev 25:34), "pasture land" (Num 35: 2), and "open country" (Eze 48:15).

In Ezekiel's vision of the future division of the restored land of Palestine, a central area around the temple is set apart as an "oblation" (Eze 48:10, KJV), or "holy portion" of land (RSV), 25,000 cu. square (see fig. 464), with lands for the prince on each side of it. The part of the "oblation" not assigned to the priests and Levites was a strip 5,000 by 25,000 cu. for the city and for "suburbs" (KJV), or "open country" (RSV), evidently farmlands for the city (Eze 48:15; see vs 8-21).

Sucathites (sū'kăth-īts), KJV **Suchathites** (sū'kăth-īts). [Heb. *Śukathîm*.] One of 3 families of scribes living at Jabez; related to the later Rechabites (1 Chr 2:55).

Succoth (sŭk'ŏth). [Heb. *Sukkôth*, "booths," or "huts."]

1. A place near the Jabbok, where Jacob camped for some time on his return to Canaan from Paddan-aram. It received its name from the booths the patriarch built there for his cattle (Gen 33:17). By the time the Israelites invaded Canaan, Succoth had grown to a city and belonged to the territory of Sihon, king of Heshbon. After the conquest it was assigned to the tribe of Gad (Jos 13:27). The city was severely punished by Gideon for refusing him help in his struggle against the Midianites (Jgs 8:5-16). It lay near Zarethan in the Jordan Valley, in the vicinity of which were the foundries where Solomon cast various implements for the Temple (1 Ki 7:45, 46; 2 Chr 4:16, 17). It is probably mentioned on Pharaoh Shishak's victory relief (fig. 438) as one of the cities (No. 55) conquered during his Palestine campaign (Mazar, *VT, Supplement* 4 [1957], 60, 61). It has been identified with *Tell Deir'allā*, north of the lower Jabbok, near the point where that stream turns sharply southward toward the Jordan (Map VI, D-4).

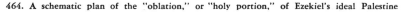

464. A schematic plan of the "oblation," or "holy portion," of Ezekiel's ideal Palestine

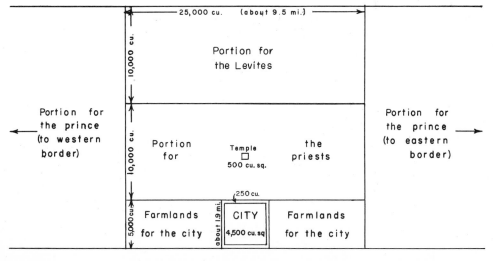

2. The 1st camping place of the Israelites after leaving Rameses on the way out of Egypt (Ex 12:37; 13:20; Num 33: 5, 6). It is usually identified with the Egyptian border town of Theku (*Ṯkw*), identified with *Tell el-Maskhûṭah* in the *Wâdî Ṭumilât* (Map V, B-4).

Succoth-benoth (sŭk'ŏth-bē'nŏth). [Heb. *Sukkôth Benôth*.] An idol set up in the province of Samaria by Babylonian colonists (2 Ki 17:30); not identified with certainty. The name has been interpreted (by Rawlinson, Schrader, Šanda) as a corrupt form of the name of the Babylonian goddess *Ṣarpanitu,* the consort of Marduk, or (by Friedrich Delitzsch) as standing for *sakkut binûtu,* "judge of the universe," a title of Marduk, Babylon's chief god. The 2d part of the name has recently been found in an Aramaic papyrus from Hermopolis West, spelled *Bnt,* as that of a deity of Syene (E. Kraeling, *The Brooklyn Museum Aramaic Papyri* [New Haven, Conn., 1953], p. 86,· n. 9).

Suchathites. *See* Sucathites.

Sukkiim (sŭk'ĭ-ĭm), KJV **Sukkiims** (sŭk'ĭ-ĭmz). [Heb. *Sukkîyim.*] One of the peoples composing the army of Shishak, king of Egypt, during his invasion of Palestine in the time of King Rehoboam (2 Chr 12:3). Sukkiim are mentioned in connection with the Libyans (Lubims) and the Ethiopians, and thus were probably African. It is thought that the *Sky'* mentioned in an Aramaic document from Elephantine are to be identified with the Sukkiim.

Sukkiims. *See* Sukkiim.

Sun. [Heb. generally *shemesh;* Aramaic *shemash;* Gr. *hēlios.*] The nearest star, the body about which the earth and the planets revolve. It was set to rule the day on the fourth day of Creation, while the moon, the lesser light, was to rule the night (Gen 1:16-19). The rising and setting of the sun furnish the most easily observable natural points for marking off the day. Between sunrise and sunset the Hebrews recognized at least 3 periods marked by the sun, the morning hour when the sun became hot (1 Sa 11:9; Neh 7:3); noon (2 Sa 4:5); and the cool of the day (Gen 3:8). Preserved by God and subject to His laws (Jer 31:35; Ps 104: 19), the sun is spoken of poetically as dwelling in a tent in the heavens and as coming forth in the morning as a bridegroom from his chamber (Ps 19:4-6).

On one occasion God intervened in the course of nature to give additional daylight while Israel was pursuing its enemies (Jos 10:12-14). Whether the rotation of the earth was halted, or light refracted, or some other means was used to perform the miracle, we do not know.

Many ancient nations worshiped the sun personified as one or more of their gods, but God warned His people against sun worship, an idolatry with which they came in contact in Egypt and among the heathen nations of Canaan and Syria. Despite the warnings Israel followed after these heathen sun-gods (2 Ki 21:5; 23:5, 11). For symbols of sun-gods see the Hittite sun symbol on an altar (fig. 12), an Assyrian sun symbol (fig. 255, center), and an Egyptian winged sun disk on a gate (fig. 495).

Superscription. [Gr. *epigraphē,* literally, "an overwriting," thus "an inscription," "a title."] A term appearing in the KJV for: (1) The inscription on coins. Roman coins bore the likeness of the emperor and were inscribed with the emperor's name and title (Mt 22:20; Mk 12:16; Lk 20:24, RSV "inscription"). See fig. 340. Jewish coins, on the other hand, carried the images of olive trees, palm trees, and other symbols, but no images of men (fig. 339), the trees being, as they reasoned, more in keeping with the 2d commandment. (2) The inscription borne by criminals. In the Roman Empire this inscription, called *titlos* (Gr.), *titulus* (Latin), contained the criminal's name, residence, and offense. The writers of the 4 Gospels state that, in the case of the crucifixion of Christ, the title was attached to the cross. Matthew (ch 27:37) refers to it as an "accusation," whereas Mark (ch 15: 26) and Luke (ch 23:38) call it a "superscription." In John the technical term "title" appears. The superscription "written over" Christ was trilingual, being written in (*a*) Aramaic (called Hebrew in the NT), the language of the country, (*b*) Greek, the universally understood language of the empire, and (*c*) Latin, the official language of the Roman administration (Jn 19:20). The wording of the superscriptions as given by the various writers varies somewhat, the fullest title being that given by John (v 19). This variation, rather than arguing against, supports the authenticity of the Gospel narratives (see *SDACom* 5:306, Note 2).

Suph (sōof). [Heb. *Sûph,* "reed."] According to Deut 1:1, RSV, a place near which Moses delivered his farewell speech. The site is unknown, but some identify it with *Khirbet Sûfa,* 3¾ mi. south-southeast of *Mâdebâ.* Others think it is identical with *Suphah (Num 21:14, RSV). Still others assume, as the translators of the KJV probably did, that in both these passages the word *yam* has been lost from the Hebrew text and that the full name should read *Yam Sûph,* "Red Sea," particularly in these cases the Gulf of Aqabah.

Suphah (sōō'fȧ). [Heb. *Sûphah,* "reed."] According to the RSV of Num 21:14, a place in Moab, possibly identical with *Suph (Deut 1:1, RSV). The KJV considers *Sûphah* a corrupt form of *Yam Sûph,* "Red Sea."

Supper. *See* Dinner; Lord's Supper; Meals.

Sur (sûr), **Gate.** [Heb. *sha'ar Sûr,* meaning uncertain.] A gate either of the Temple or of a palace building at Jerusalem (2 Ki 11:6); not identified. It is apparently the one called "gate of the foundation" (*sha'ar Hayesôd*) in 2 Chr 23:5.

Surety. One who pledges himself to fulfill an obligation assumed by another in case of failure or default of the debtor; the guarantee or security (Gen 43:8, 9). Solomon warned that one becoming surety for a friend or stranger was in a grave position from which he should diligently seek release (Prov 6:1-5; cf. 11:15). In ch 20:16 the possible meaning is that if you must do business with one who has unwisely become guarantor for a stranger, be sure of your own pledge from him. In Heb 7:22, the only place where "surety" appears in the NT, Jesus is stated to be the "surety," or pledge, of the

"better testament," that is, the "new covenant," based on better promises (Heb 8:6).

Surfeiting. [Gr. *kraipalē,* "carousing," "intoxication," "drunken headache," "hangover," "dizziness," "staggering."] One of the dangers against which Christ warned His disciples, especially in anticipation of His own return to earth (Lk 21:34; RSV "dissipation"). Greek medical writers used *kraipalē* to describe the nausea and stupor that follow a drunken debauch.

Surname. *See* Name.

Susa (sōō'sȧ), KJV **Shushan** (shōō'shăn). [Heb. *Shûshan;* Elamite *Shushân;* Akkadian *Shushan;* Old Persian *Çûshâ.*] The illustrious capital of the Elamites and later one of the capitals of the Persian Empire, called Susa by the Greek historians and Shushan by the Hebrews. The city had a long history, being referred to from the 3d millennium B.C. in the records of Mesopotamia. Susa was situated on the river Ulai (Dan 8:2), and was about 100 mi. north of the Persian Gulf (Map XII, D-8). It was conquered *c.* 645 B.C. by Ashurbanipal, and some of its inhabitants were carried to Samaria (Ezr 4:9). During the time of the Neo-Babylonian Empire Susa was in the hands of the Chaldean kings. It was later taken over by Cyrus, the founder of the Persian Empire and conqueror of Babylon. Darius I began great building operations at

465. Site of the ancient festival hall of Susa in which Xerxes must have held his banquet. Castlelike building in the background is headquarters of the archeological expedition

Susa and erected a beautiful palace with a large apadana (festival hall). The city shared the honor of being capital with Babylon and Ecbatana (Achmetha). Susa was the scene of events described in the book of Esther in the time of King Ahasuerus (Xerxes). Nehemiah served in the city as cupbearer of Artaxerxes I (Neh 1: 1). When Alexander the Great came to Susa in 331 B.C. vast treasures which generations of Persian kings had amassed fell into his hands. The ancient site is now completely abandoned and contains tremendous mounds of debris covering several square miles. The modern town located at the foot of these mounds bears the name *Shush*. Excavations were started on the mounds in 1851 by Loftus, and since 1884 have been carried out intermittently by French expeditions with extremely rewarding results. In the palace of the Persian period beautifully colored tiled wall decorations were found which are now in the Louvre in Paris. The discoveries in the palace and the apadana showed that only a man intimately acquainted with these places could have written the book of Esther. One of the greatest finds made on the site was the Code of Hammurabi, discovered there in 1901-1902. It had been brought to Susa anciently from Babylon as a spoil of war by an Elamite king. See figs. 291, 465.

Susanchites (sū-săn′kīts). [Aramaic *Shûshankaye′*.] The inhabitants of *Susa, the old capital of Elam, who had been deported to Samaria, probably by Ashurbanipal, who destroyed Susa *c.* 645 B.C. (Ezr 4:9). The term is rendered "men of Susa" in the RSV.

Susanna (sū-zăn′à). [Gr. *Sousanna* from Heb. *Shûshannah*, "lily."] A woman who supported Jesus' work with her means (Lk 8:3).

Susi (sū′sī). [Heb. *Sûsi*, "my horse (?)."] A man whose son Gaddi represented the tribe of Manasseh among the 12 spies (Num 13:11).

Swaddling Band. A band of cloth used for wrapping a newborn child. The term is used poetically in Job 38:9 of darkness enclosing the earth at Creation. Jesus was wrapped in swaddling clothes at His birth (Lk 2:7, 12).

Swallow. A nearly black songbird, somewhat larger than the English sparrow, with long tapered wings and forked tail, abundant in Palestine from early spring until the approach of winter. The swift, an unrelated but similar bird, may be intended in some of the Biblical references. The term "swallow" is a rendering of: (1) The Heb. *derôr* (Ps 84:3; Prov 26:2), probably the swallow. In Ps 84:3 this bird is mentioned as building its nest at the altars of God, and in Prov 26:2 reference is made to its flight. (2) The Heb. *'agûr* (Is 38:14; Jer 8:7; KJV), translated "crane" in the RSV. G. R. Driver favors an identification with the wryneck (*PEQ* 87 [1955], 132). In Is 38:14 reference is made to the plaintive cry of this bird, and in Jer 8:7 its migratory instincts are alluded to. (3) The Heb. *sîs* or *sûs* (Is 38:14; Jer 8:7; KJV), rendered "crane" in KJV, which Driver identifies with the swift (*ibid.*, 131).

Swan. [Heb. *tinshemeth*.] The Hebrew term describes an unclean bird (Lev 11:18; Deut 14:16), but there is considerable uncertainty about its identity. Quite likely the swan, a graceful white water bird, is not meant. Some suggest the purple gallinule (*Porphyrio caeruleus*), others the glossy ibis (*Ibis falcinellus*), still others the water hen (RSV). G. R. Driver suggests that *tinshemeth* be identified with the little owl, one of the most widely distributed owls in Palestine (*PEQ* 87 [1955], 15).

Swearing. *See* Oath.

Sweet Cane. [Heb. *qaneh*, once with *ṭôb*, "good," "sweet."] Generally identified with the sweet calamus, grown in India and South Arabia. The plant was crushed to yield a fragrant essence. It was used in connection with sacrifices (Is 43:24; Jer 6:20).

Swine. [Heb. *chazîr*; Gr. *choiros*.] A domestic animal widely used for food in the ancient world, but prohibited as unclean in Lev 11:7; Deut 14:8. The Jews were not alone in their abhorrence of pork. Pliny says that the Arabs did not raise swine (*Hist. Nat.* viii. 78) and this is true of the Moslem Arabs to the present day. The swine was also considered unclean by the ancient Egyptians from early times. Herodotus reports that an Egyptian would immediately wash himself after accidentally touching swine, that no swineherd was allowed to enter a temple, and that it was practically impossible for one of such a vocation to find a wife outside the circle of his profession (ii. 47). Because the Jews generally kept themselves aloof from swine, the animal is mentioned only rarely in the Bible (Prov 11:22; Mt 7:6; Lk 15:15; 2 Pe 2:22; etc.). That in times of apostasy even Jews ate pork is attested by Isaiah (Is 65:4; 66:

17). The extent to which strict Jews detested the use of pork was demonstrated in the time of the Maccabees, when the demand of Antiochus IV Epiphanes that the Jews eat pork to demonstrate their loyalty to him was met with stubborn refusal, some choosing death rather than compliance with the demand (2 Macc 6:18 to 7:42). After the liberation from Antiochus' tyranny, the keeping of swine in Judea—a practice probably introduced by Greek immigrants, who were great pork eaters—was officially prohibited by John Hyrcanus. The large herd of swine which Christ allowed to perish in the country of the Gadarenes (Mt 8:30-32) may not have belonged to Jews, since the incident occurred in the *Decapolis, where the majority of the population consisted of Hellenized non-Jews. To become a swineherd was for a Jew a great abasement; and the prodigal son took up that line of work only as a last resort (Lk 15:15).

Sword. Anciently the principal weapon for close hand-to-hand fighting (1 Sa 17:51; 31:4; 2 Sa 2:16; Mt 26:51), consisting of a blade of bronze or (later) iron, and a hilt (Jgs 3:22), which was usually attached to the blade by rivets.

466. A curved sword found in Palestine

The Egyptians distinguished between the long sword (*sf.t*) and the short (*ḥrp*) sword. Among the Babylonians only one term for sword (*namṣůru*) is known, which, as is the case with the Heb. *chereb*, seems almost exclusively to represent a dagger. Hence many scholars think that the Hebrews had no long sword. They estimate that their longest daggers did not exceed about 16 in. in length. The sword was carried in a sheath (1 Sa 17:51; Jer 47:6) and was worn in a girdle on the thigh (Ex 32:27; 2 Sa 20:8). Apparently it was usually worn at the left side (Jgs 3:16; cf. vs 15, 21).

The frequently occurring expression "edge of the sword" (Jos 10:28; etc.) is literally "mouth of the sword." This expression is now explained on the basis of the hilts' being molded or shaped in the form of heads of wild animals, from whose mouths the blades emerged (T. J. Meek, *BASOR* 122 [1951], 31-33). This would also explain the figure of the sword de-

vouring (2 Sa 11:25; Nah 3:15; etc.). Compare also the symbolism of Rev 1:16; 2:16; 19:15. "Sword" is frequently used synonymously for war (Lev 26:25, 33; etc.) or for punishment in various forms (Jer 12:12; etc.).

In the NT the terms *romphaia* and *machaira* are used to designate the sword. *Romphaia* originally designated a large, wide sword used by barbaric tribes, but was used in NT times as a synonym for *machaira,* the common Greek designation for any large sword (Mt 26:47, 55; Rev 1:16; 2:12; etc.). Roman foot soldiers generally wore the sword on the left side, and cavalrymen on the right (Jos. *War* iii. 5. 5).

Sycamine Tree. [Gr. *sukaminos.*] The black mulberry (*Morus nigra*), widely cultivated throughout Palestine for its fruit. Jesus mentioned the tree in His discourse on faith (Lk 17:6).

Sycamore. [Heb. *shiqmah;* Gr. *sukomorea.*] The sycamore fig or fig mulberry (*Ficus sycomorus*), a vigorous wide-spreading tree plentiful in Bible times in the Shephelah of Judah (1 Ki 10:27; 1 Chr 27:28; 2 Chr 1:15; 9:27). It grew also in the Jordan Valley as well as in Egypt (Ps 78:47). This evergreen has gnarled and twisted main branches that fork outward in all directions near the ground, and it bears a fruit similar to the common fig but inferior in size and quality. Nevertheless, it serves as food, especially among the poorer classes. In Palestine the sycamore tree was closely connected with the rites of nature worshipers, against which the Hebrew prophets so often warned.

The prophet Amos was a "dresser" (RSV) of sycamore trees (Amos 7:14). His work was doubtless that of puncturing the nearly ripened fruit in order to ensure ripening and edibility. Zacchaeus climbed into the low branches of a sycamore tree to watch Jesus pass (Lk 19:4).

467. A Palestinian sycamore fig tree

This tree must not be confused with our sycamore.

Sychar (sī′kär). [Gr. *Suchar.*] A town of Samaria situated near Jacob's Well (Jn 4: 5). Some consider Sychar to be a corruption of Shechem, and identify it with *Tell Balâṭah,* the site of ancient Shechem (Map XVI, D-3). Most commentators, however, identify it with the modern village of *Askar* at the eastern foot of Mount Ebal, ⅝ mi. north of Jacob's Well. However, no ancient remains have so far been found at *Askar.* See fig. 196.

Syene, I (sī-ē′nê). [Heb. *Seweneh;* Egyptian *Swn.*] The southernmost city of ancient Egypt (Eze 29:10; 30:6), now known as Aswan. It lay at the 1st cataract and was the southern border fortress of ancient Egypt. The phrase "from Migdol to Syene" (RSV) means all of Egypt from the extreme north to the extreme south. At Aswan is the famous Nile island of Elephantine, on which a colony of Jewish mercenaries lived during the Babylonian exile and at least until the end of the 5th cent. B.C. Map XI, E-3. *See* Pathros.

Syene, II (sī-ē′nê), KJV **Sinim** (sī′nĭm). [Heb. *Sînîm.*] A remote area from which Jewish exiles were to return to their homeland (Is 49:12). Commentators have frequently identified it with China, especially with the *Ch'in* dynasty that reigned over China in the 3d cent. B.C. This identification has generally been abandoned in favor of *Syene, I, since it is known that a large colony of Jewish mercenaries lived there during the time of the Exile and at least to the end of the 5th cent. B.C. The Dead Sea scroll 1QIsa reads *Swnyym* (*Seweniyim*), "people of *Seweni,*" which definitely favors an identification with Syene. The LXX reads Persia. Other identifications, such as Sinai, the Wilderness of Sin, Phoenicia, and the northern Arabian Desert, have been proposed, but none of these can be established.

Symeon (sĭm′ê-ŭn), KJV **Simeon** (sĭm′ê-ŭn). [Gr. *Sumeōn,* from Heb. *Shim'ôn,* "hearing."]

1. A Judahite appearing in Luke's genealogy of Jesus Christ (Lk 3:30).

2. For Acts 15:14, RSV, *see* Peter.

3. A Christian prophet and/or teacher at Antioch at the time of the appointment of Saul and Barnabas for foreign mission service. He was also known by his Latin name Niger, meaning "black," suggesting that he may have been of African stock (Acts 13:1).

Synagogue. [Gr. *sunagōgē,* "place of assembly," "congregation." The word appears once in the OT (Ps 74:8, KJV) as the rendering of the Heb. *mô'ed,* "meeting place."] A Jewish place of worship presided over by a local board of elders. The

468. Inscription of "[Syna]gogue of the Hebr[ews]" found at Corinth

synagogue is thought to have come into existence during the Babylonian exile, when the Temple at Jerusalem lay in ruins. Tradition names the prophet Ezekiel as its founder. Some time after the return from Captivity synagogues were established in the towns of Judea and in Alexandria, Antioch of Syria, Rome, and in virtually every other important city of the Roman Empire (see Acts 15:21). To establish a synagogue there had to be 10 adult Jewish males to constitute its board of elders or "rulers." In Palestine there were synagogues both for native Jews and for Jews of the Dispersion who had returned to the land of their fathers. Thus, in NT times there was at Jerusalem a synagogue of the Libertines (ch 6:9; RSV "Freedmen"), probably Jews or their descendants who had at one time been taken captive by the Romans and later set free. Paul found Jewish synagogues not only at Corinth, Ephesus, and Thessalonica, but in more remote places such as Salamis on the island of Cyprus, Antioch in Pisidia, Iconium, and Beroea in Greece. See figs. 95, 106, 468.

Whereas the Temple and its ritual were under the control of the priests, the synagogue was under the direction of Jewish laymen. Sacrifices were never offered at the synagogue. At first it was chiefly a place for the reading and exposition of the Law, but in time a more elaborate service developed and eventually it served also as a school and as a court for the administration of justice as defined by the Mosaic law (see Mk 13:9). In NT times many more Jews lived outside of, than in, Palestine, and the synagogue in each Jewish community served to preserve the religion, culture, and racial consciousness of the Jews. The affairs of the synagogue and of the community it served were under the supervision of the board of elders (see Lk 7:3-5), the chief officer being known as the "ruler" (Mk 5:22; Lk 8:49; 13:14). His duty was to provide for its services and to appoint suitable men from the congregation to pray, to read, and to exhort. There was a lesser officer known as a *chazzan,* equivalent to a deacon, to whom were entrusted the humbler duties such as removing the rolls of the Law and the Prophets from the ark and returning them, and inflicting corporal punishment.

Ruins of synagogues, some of them dating from early Christian centuries, may be observed at various sites in Palestine, notably at *Tell Ḥûm,* usually identified as Capernaum (fig. 95), and Chorazin. The earliest synagogue inscription extant is that of Theodotus (fig. 187), of which a translation is found in the article Freedmen. A most interesting synagogue was discovered during the excavations of Dura Europus (Map XIII, C-5). It dates to the 3d cent. A.D. and is well preserved. Its interior walls were covered with colored paintings of OT scenes (see figs. 2, 127, 171, 343). The remains of the building have been moved and the synagogue has been reconstructed in the museum at Damascus. Some synagogues were elaborately ornamented with devices such as a scroll of vine leaves and a bunch of grapes—Israel's national symbol—the 7-branched candlestick, a paschal lamb, the pot of manna, and many other objects and scenes from the OT Scriptures. In later times certain pagan symbols found their way into synagogue ornamentations. The main room of the synagogue contained a reading desk, a seat for the exhorter, and a chest, or ark, that contained the rolls of the Law and the Prophets. There were usually benches for the wealthier members of the congregation (see Jas 2:2, 3), those near the reader's desk being considered the "chief seats" (see Mt 23:6). The women sat apart, probably in the gallery. Attendance was required on Sabbaths and feast days.

By modern standards the synagogue service was long. A typical service consisted of 5 parts in the following order: (1) The recitation in unison of the *shema',* a confession of faith based chiefly on such passages as Deut 6:4-9; 11:13-21; Num 15:37-41. Before and after the *shema'* a member of the congregation stood before the ark of the Law to offer, in the name of all, a sevenfold prayer, each part of which was confirmed by an "Amen" from the congregation. Between the 6th and 7th sections of this prayer, priests, if present, ascended the platform of the ark, lifted their hands, and pronounced in unison the Aaronic blessing (Lev 9:22; Num 6:23-27). (2) The *parashah,* or reading of the appointed section of the Law. Reverence required that the scroll containing the Law—the 5 books of Moses—be unrolled behind a curtain, out of sight of the congregation. In NT times, and later, there was a regular 3-year cycle, during which the Law was read through in 3 years, a definite portion being specified for each Sabbath. Each Sabbath's portion was divided into 7 parts of at least 3 verses each. A different member of the congregation was called upon to read each of these subdivisions, and it was considered an act of merit and privilege to participate in the service. Anyone who made the least mistake was immediately replaced by someone else. A verse-by-verse translation was made into Aramaic, the language of the common people, by another person in order to avoid the possibility that the translation should be mistaken for the actual text of Scripture. (3) The *haphṭarah,* or reading from the Prophets. Whereas the scroll of the Law was mounted on 2 rollers, that of the Prophets, which was considered less sacred, had but one and might be unrolled in the sight of the congregation. There is no evidence that a cycle for the reading of the Prophets had been established in the time of Christ, although this was probably the case. The scroll was probably handed by the ruler of the synagogue to the one appointed, who then apparently selected the passage to be read (cf. Lk 4:17). Later a particular section from the Prophets was chosen to accompany each assigned portion of the Law. The one who read from the Prophets was called the "dismisser," in view of the fact that this, together with accompanying remarks and exhortation, constituted the closing part of the main section of the service. (4) The *derashah,* or "investigation," "study," a sermon either by the one reading from the Prophets or by another member of the congregation. While those who read from the Law and the Prophets stood, the one who gave the sermon sat in a special seat near the lectern, or reading desk, known as "Moses' seat" (see Mt 23:2). His remarks were usually based on the reading of the Prophets, but might be based also on that from the Law. Visitors were often honored by being invited to deliver the sermon. This privilege Paul often utilized as an opportunity to preach the gospel (see Acts 13:14-16; 14:1; 17:1, 2, 10, 11; 18:4; 19:8). (5) The benediction, which was pronounced by a priest, if one was present; otherwise a prayer was offered. In some synagogues the singing of psalms was introduced into the service.

Lit.: E. L. Sukenik, *Ancient Synagogues in Palestine and Greece* (London, 1934); Carl H. Kraeling *et al., The Synagogue* in "The Excavations at Dura-Europos," Final Report VIII, Part I (New Haven, 1956).

Synagogue of the Libertines. See Synagogue.

Syntyche (sĭn'tĭ-chē). [Gr. *Suntuchē,* "fortunate," a Greek female name occurring frequently in inscriptions.] A woman in the Christian church at Philippi (Php 4:2).

Syracuse (sĭr'a̯-kūs). [Gr. *Surakousai.*] The most important city of Sicily, lying on the eastern coast of the island. Historical records claim that Corinthian and Dorian Greeks expelled Phoenician settlers from there, and in 734 B.C. founded one of the most important Greek colonies in the West. In 413 B.C. the people of Syracuse defeated an Athenian navy and destroyed 200 of its vessels. In 212 B.C. the city was taken by the Romans. The emperors gave it self-government and embellished it with magnificent buildings, some large ruins of which are still there today. Paul spent 3 days there during his voyage to Rome as a prisoner (Acts 28:12), probably in the spring of A.D. 61. Map XX, B-2.

Syria (sĭr'ĭ-a̯). [Heb. *'Aram;* Gr. *Suria.* Syria, a loan word from Greek, is an abbreviated form of "Assyria."] A name used first in ancient times by Herodotus as a term, not for Assyria, but for a country bounded on the north by the Taurus Mountains in Asia Minor, on the east by the Syrian desert, on the south by Palestine, and on the west by the Mediterranean Sea. For the history of OT Syria *see* Aram, 5; Damascus.

In the NT Syria is a designation for the Roman province of Syria (Lk 2:2; Acts 15:23, 41; 18:18; 20:3; 21:3; Gal 1:21), which was organized after Pompey's conquest of the remnant of the Seleucid kingdom in 64 B.C. The Seleucid Empire, which is well known because of its wars with the Jews under the Maccabees, had been brought to an end early in the 1st cent. B.C. by Tigranes, the Parthian king

469. A Syrian depicted in color on a glazed tile from *Medinet Habu,* Egypt

of Armenia. However, the Roman Lucullus defeated Tigranes, and Pompey occupied Syria in 64 B.C. It was then made a senatorial province administered by a *legatus,* or legate (*see* Governor, 2, *b*) sent by the Roman Senate, and later into an imperial province administered by a deputy sent by the emperor. It is not entirely clear to what area the Syria of Mt 4:24 refers (see *SDACom* 5:319-320). Palestine was under the province of Syria during part of the NT period and after A.D. 70. Map XIX, E-13.

Syriack. *See* Aramaic.

Syrian (sĭr'ĭ-ăn). [Heb. *'Aram, 'Arammî;* Akkadian *Aramu;* Gr. *Suros.*] The designation for the people of Syria (2 Sa 8:5; Lk 4:27; etc.). *See* Aram, 5; Aramaic; Damascus; Syria.

Syrophoenician (sī'rṓ-fē-nĭsh'ăn), KJV **Syrophenician** (sī'rṓ-fē-nĭsh'ăn). [Gr. *Surophoinikissa.*] An inhabitant (the Greek is feminine) of the Phoenician coast, which belonged to the Roman imperial province of Syria in NT times. The word was used to distinguish the Syrian Phoenicians from the Libyphoenicians who lived around Carthage. Mark uses this term (Mk 7:26) for a woman whom Matthew calls "a woman of Canaan" (Mt 15:22).

Syrtis, KJV **Quicksands.** [Gr. *Surtis.*] One of the 2 gulfs lying between Tunisia and Cyrenaica, which were greatly feared by ancient sailors because of their many sand bars and surfs. The Greater Syrtis (*Syrtis Major*), which is the southeastern one, is about 265 mi. wide and is very shallow and full of sand bars. It is now called the Gulf of Sidra. The Lesser Syrtis (*Syrtis Minor*) is about 70 mi. wide, and is dangerous to navigate because of difficult winds, treacherous tides, and many sand bars. Its modern name is Gulf of Gabès. The sailors on Paul's ship were successful in preventing their vessel from being driven on the Syrtis (Acts 27:17), by which the eastern or Greater Syrtis is probably meant, since the Lesser Syrtis lies at a considerable distance to the southwest of Malta.

T

Taanach (tā'à-năk), KJV once **Tanach** (tā'năk). [Heb. *Ta'anak;* in the *Amarna Letters it is spelled *Tâhnuka,* and in Egyptian records *T'nk.* The ruin hill *Tell Ta'annak* still bears the ancient name.] An old Canaanite fortress city in the southern part of the Plain of Esdraelon, about 5 mi. southeast of Megiddo, mentioned in the records of Thutmose III (1482-1450 B.C.) and in the *Amarna Letters (*c.* 1400 B.C.). Taanach was not occupied by the Israelites in Joshua's time (Jgs 1:27) although its king was among those defeated by Joshua and listed in Jos 12:21. During the period of the judges the Hebrews, under Deborah and Barak, fought against Jabin and Sisera in the immediate vicinity of the city (Jgs 5:19). Although Taanach lay in the territory of Issachar or Asher, it was held by Manasseh (Jos 17:11; 1 Chr 7:29). In Solomon's time it belonged to the rich district that was administered by Baana, including Megiddo, Beth-shean, and other towns (1 Ki 4:12). After that time it is not mentioned again in the OT.

An Austrian expedition under the direction of Ernst Sellin partly excavated Taanach from 1901 to 1904. Since modern archeological techniques were still in their infancy, the scientific results were negligible, although the excavations proved that Taanach was inhabited throughout the 2d millennium B.C. Among the noteworthy discoveries made by Sellin were 12 cuneiform tablets which had belonged to the archive of a local ruler in the 15th cent. B.C., an incense altar from the 12th cent.

470. House ruins in ancient Taanach

B.C. decorated with mythological creatures, and a cylinder seal carrying one text in cuneiform characters and another in Egyptian hieroglyphs. Some ruins not correctly interpreted by Sellin were later found by P. Guy to be the remains of Israelite stables like those found at Megiddo. Map VI, C-3. For house ruins see fig. 470.

Lit.: Excavation reports: E. Sellin, *Tell Ta'annek* (Vienna, 1904); Sellin, *Eine Nachlese auf dem Tell Ta'annek* (Vienna, 1906); P. Guy, *New Light From Armageddon* (Chicago, 1931), p. 44. On the cuneiform tablets see W. F. Albright, *BASOR* 94 (1944), 12-27.

Taanath-shiloh (tā'à-năth-shī'lō). [Heb. *Ta'anath Shiloh*, meaning uncertain.] A place on the border between Ephraim and Manasseh (Jos 16:6), identified with *Khirbet Ta'nah el-Fôqā*, about 7 mi. southeast of Shechem. Map VI, D-3.

Tabbaoth (tă-bā'ŏth). [Heb. *Ṭabba'ôth*, "rings."] The ancestral head of a family of Nethinim, or Temple servants, who returned from Babylonia with Zerubbabel (Ezr 2:43; Neh 7:46).

Tabbath (tăb'ăth). [Heb. *Ṭabbath*.] A place in the Jordan Valley where the Midianites fled from Gideon (Jgs 7:22). It has been identified with *Râs Abū Tâbât*, 3½ mi. east of the Jordan at the latitude of Samaria.

Tabeal. *See* Tabeel, 1.

Tabeel (tā'bĕ-ĕl), KJV once **Tabeal** (tā'-bĕ-ăl). [Heb. *Ṭabe'el*, "good is God" (but *Ṭabe'al* means "good for nothing").]

1. Either the father or the native country of the man whom Rezin of Damascus and Pekah of Israel planned to put on the throne of Judah (Is 7:6). The view that Tabeel is a place has been fortified by the reference to a country in Syria by that name (spelled *Ṭâbilâya*) in an Assyrian document (see Albright, *BASOR* 140 [1955], 34).

2. Apparently an official in the Persian province of Samaria who with others complained to Artaxerxes about the building of the wall of Jerusalem by the Jews (Ezr 4:7). His Semitic name, attested in Assyrian as *Ṭâb-ilu*, may indicate that he was not of Persian descent.

Taberah (tăb'ĕ-rà). [Heb. *Tab'erah*, "burning."] A place in the wilderness where a fire broke out in the Israelite camp as the result of their murmuring, and was quenched only after the intercession of Moses (Num 11:1-3; Deut 9:22); not identified.

Tabering. A rendering of a form of the

Heb. *taphaph* (Nah 2:7, KJV), "to drum," "to beat." The maidens of Nineveh are pictured as beating their breasts because of the downfall of the city.

Tabernacle. [Heb. generally *'ohel*, "tent," and *mishkan*, "dwelling place," from *shakan*, "to dwell"; Gr. generally *skēnē*, "tent," "booth," "lodging," "dwelling place."] Any tent or temporary dwelling place, especially the tabernacle erected by Moses at Mount Sinai, God's sacred dwelling place (Ex 25:8, 9) and the center of Hebrew worship for more than 4 cent. Under the theocracy God was Israel's Supreme Ruler, and in the Most Holy Place of the tabernacle abode the visible glory symbolic of the Divine Presence (chs 25:22; 40:34, 35), sometimes called Shekinah, which, however, is a rabbinical term and is not found in the Bible. *Mishkan*, "dwelling place," designates the *'ohel*, "tent," as the residence of the glorious "abiding Presence." The visible glory hovered above the mercy seat of the ark between the 2 cherubim (ch 25:22). The tabernacle was constructed in accordance with the "pattern" God revealed to Moses on Mount Sinai (Ex 25:9-40; cf. Heb 8:5; 9:23). The bulkier materials, such as the wood and the animal skins used in its construction, were obtainable in the vicinity of Sinai. The precious metals—the gold, silver, and brass—and the linen had obviously been brought by the people from Egypt (Ex 35:21-29; cf. 3:22; 12:35, 36). A tabulation of the various materials used in the construction of the tabernacle shows that it represented a considerable investment. The candlestick, or lampstand, with its lamps and utensils, was made from a talent of gold, which would have a market value of somewhat over $30,000 today. Approximately 6 months were required for the construction of the tabernacle, and it was carried on during the last half of the 1st year after the departure from Egypt (chs 19:1; 24:18; 34:28; 40:2).

The tabernacle proper was a quadrangular tent, 30 cu. long by 10 cu. wide and 10 cu. high (*see* Cubit). The over-all dimensions are not precisely stated in the Exodus account, but are computed from the specifications given for the curtains and the boards, or frames, used in the walls of the tabernacle and from the corresponding but larger dimensions of Solomon's Temple (1 Ki 6:2; see fig. 471). The tent was divided into 2 apartments, the 1st being known as "the holy place" (Ex 28:29), and the 2d as "the most holy [place]" (Ex 26:33). The latter was a cube,

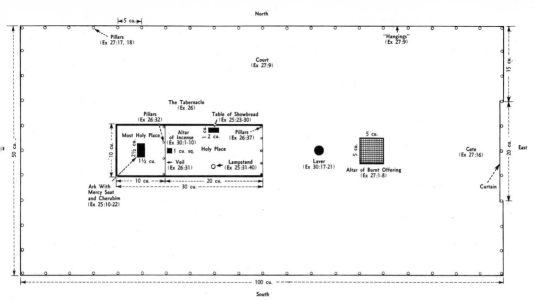

471. Scale drawing of the plan of the tabernacle, its court, and its furnishings

10 cu. on a side, and the holy place 10 cu. by 20 cu. The tabernacle was surrounded by a courtyard 50 cu. wide and 100 cu. long, enclosed by linen hangings 5 cu. high (see Ex 27:18). This curtain-wall was suspended from 60 "pillars," probably of acacia wood (cf. ch 26:37) filleted with silver and resting in "brass" (that is, *bronze) sockets. At the middle of the east end of the court was the entrance, which was formed by a separate curtain 20 cu. in length (see ch 27:9-17). In the eastern half of the court, near the entrance, were the altar of burnt offering (vs 1-8) and the laver (ch 30:17-21). The tabernacle proper occupied a central position in the western half of the court. Its entrance likewise faced eastward. This portal consisted of a linen curtain suspended from 5 pillars of shittim (acacia) wood, which were overlaid with gold and ‛rested in brass (bronze) sockets (ch 26:36, 37). Within the holy place, to the right (or north) as one entered, was the table for the "shewbread," or bread of the Presence. This table was made of acacia wood overlaid with gold (ch 25:23-30). To the left (or south) was the 7-branched candlestick (actually a lampstand), which was made, together with its lamps and utensils, from a talent of pure gold (vs 31-40). Before the veil that divided the holy place from the Most Holy Place—but considered as belonging to the latter (Heb 9:3, 4)—was the altar of incense, also made of acacia wood overlaid with pure gold (Ex 30:1-10). Entrance into the Most Holy Place was through an elaborately embroidered linen curtain sus-

pended from 4 "pillars" (Ex 26:31-33). The only object within the Most Holy Place was the ark of the covenant, a chest made of acacia wood overlaid with pure gold, covered with a lid known as the "mercy seat," and surmounted on either end by a golden cherub (ch 25:10-22). The tabernacle structure consisted of a wooden framework and a threefold tent covering (ch 26:1-37). There were 48 acacia boards, or frames, each 10 cu. long by 1½ cu. broad, overlaid with gold. These were held in place by tenons and anchored in silver sockets, 2 to a board, and bound together laterally by transverse wooden bars, 5 on each side. The innermost covering, which constituted walls and ceiling and was draped over these upright boards, was made of linen cloth skillfully embroidered with cherubim in blue, purple, and scarlet (vs 1-6). Outside of this linen curtain was another, of goat's hair, in 11 sections, each 30 cu. by 4 cu. Over this covering of goat's hair was a 3d, or outer, tent (v 14) made of rams' skins from the flock, and another kind of leather, *"badgers' skins" (KJV), "goatskins" (RSV). Into the courtyard came the priests and the Levites, as duty required, to conduct the services and to supply its needs. Members of the congregation also, apparently, entered within the gate of the court to present their sacrifices and to confess their sins.

During the original conquest of Canaan the tabernacle remained at Gilgal—the initial camp in Canaan and Joshua's headquarters—near Jericho (Jos 4:19,

20; 5:9, 10; 10:43; 14:6). With the completion of the conquest the tabernacle was moved to Shiloh, where it remained through the period of the judges (Jos 18:1; 1 Sa 1:3) until the capture of the ark by the Philistines; then Shiloh was evidently destroyed and ceased to be a center of worship (1 Sa 4:3, 11, 21, 22; Ps 78:60-64; cf. Jer 7:12-14; 26:6, 9). During the reign of Saul the tabernacle was at Nob (1 Sa 21:1, 6), and during a considerable part of David's reign and until the dedication of Solomon's Temple it was at Gibeon (1 Chr 16:39; 21:29; 2 Chr 1:3-6). With the erection of the latter the tabernacle was brought, along with the ark and the sacred vessels, to the new structure (1 Ki 8:4; 2 Chr 5:5).

For further information on the various parts of the sanctuary *see* names of structural parts and of equipment and furnishings. For the priestly ministration and various services conducted in the sanctuary *see* Priest; Sacrifices and Offerings; Temple.

Tabernacles. *See* Booths.

Tabernacles, Feast of. The joyous festival celebrating the ingathering at the end of the harvest, particularly of the grain, olive, and grape harvests (RSV generally "feast of booths"). This feast began on the 15th of the 7th month (*Ethanim, or Tishri), and lasted 7 days, beginning with a ceremonial sabbath, and followed by an additional day, also a sabbath (Lev 23:33-36). Although it came 2 weeks after the end of the civil calendar year, it was actually the celebration of the close of the agricultural year, and was referred to as "the feast of ingathering . . . in the end of the year" (Ex 23:16). The term "tabernacles," or "booths" (Heb. *sukkôth*), refers to the custom of living during the feast in booths made of branches, commemorative of the wilderness wanderings (Lev 23:34-43). It was one of the 3 festivals that all Hebrew males were required to attend (Ex 23:14-17; Deut 16:16). Jesus is recorded as attending a Feast of Tabernacles (Jn 7:2, 14).

Special sacrifices, in addition to the regular daily sacrifice, were prescribed for each day of the feast, there being 13 bullocks, 2 rams, and 14 male lambs for a burnt offering on the 1st day, and 1 additional kid for a sin offering. Each day thereafter the number of bullocks was reduced by 1 until, on the last day, the offering was 7 bullocks, 2 rams, and 14 male lambs for a burnt offering, and the kid for a sin offering (see Lev 23:34-43; Num 29:

12-34; Deut 16:13-15). Every 7th year at the Feast of Tabernacles, "in the solemnity of the year of release"—the sabbatical year during which there was no sowing and harvest—the Law of Moses was read publicly (Deut 31:9-13).

With the passing of the centuries, especially after the return from Babylonian captivity, an elaborate ritual was developed for the celebration of the feast. Going up to the Temple at the morning hour of worship, the people, carrying branches of willow in their hands, marched joyfully around the altar of burnt offering once each day and 7 times on the 7th day (Mishnah *Sukkah* 4. 5; Jos. *Ant.* iii. 10. 4; xiii. 13. 5; cf. 2 Macc 10:6, 7). Also daily, in connection with the morning sacrifices, a priest brought to the Temple a vessel filled with the water that flows from the Gihon spring on the slopes of the Kidron Valley to the Pool of Siloam, to the chanting of the words of Is 12:3: "Therefore with joy shall ye draw water out of the wells of salvation." Mixed with sacrificial wine, and to the accompaniment of instrumental music and the singing of psalms, this water was poured out beside the altar into a conduit through which it flowed down to the Kidron Valley, a ceremonial reminder of the prophecy of Eze 47. It was during this festival, apparently in reference to the custom of pouring out a libation of water (Mishnah *Sukkah* 4. 1, 9), that Jesus stood up and offered Himself as the water of life, saying, "If any man thirst, let him come unto me, and drink" (Jn 7:37). At nighttime, atop 2 lofty pillars erected in the Court of the Women, immense lamps were lighted which cast their glow over the courts of the Temple and beyond its walls into the city, while on the steps of the Temple court Levites sang psalms accompanied by instrumental music. Jews living in foreign lands, who were unable to make the pilgrimage to Jerusalem, celebrated the feast in their local synagogues.

Tabitha (tăb′ĭ-thà). [Gr. *Tabitha*, a transliteration of the Aramaic *Ṭebîtha'* or *Ṭabyetha'*, "gazelle."] A Christian woman of Joppa (Acts 9:36-43). *See* Dorcas.

Table. *See* Tablet.

Tablet. The rendering of 2 Hebrew terms and 2 Greek words denoting *writing materials: (1) The Heb. *gillayôn* (Is 8:1, RSV; KJV "roll"), indicating an object with a smooth surface. Galling (*Bibl. Reallexikon*, col. 464) and Driver (*Semitic Writing* [London, 2d ed., 1954], 80) believe that *gillayôn* denotes the "blank surface or unwritten space on material suitable for writing," in the Is passage probably a sheet of papyrus or leather. In Mishnaic Hebrew, *gillayôn* designates the blank margin of a page. (2) The Heb. *lûach,* "tablet" (Ex 24:12; etc.), used of the stone tablets of the Decalogue, and (3) the Gr. *pinakidion,* "writing tablet," frequently wooden tablets, generally covered with wax, into which writing was engraved by means of a stylus. Such tablets are referred to in Is 30:8 (KJV "table") and Lk 1:63 (KJV "table"). Prov 3:3; 7:3; Jer 17:1 mention figuratively the "tablet" (KJV "table") of the heart. (4) The Gr. *plax,* a broad slab or table, used of the tables of stone (Heb 9:4), and of the tables, or tablets of the heart (2 Cor 3:3).

Tabor (tā'bẽr). [Heb. *Tabôr.*]

1. A mountain on the boundary of Issachar (Jos 19:22; some think this verse refers to the town; *see* Tabor, 2), referred to as an inland mountain by Jeremiah (Jer 46:18), and mentioned by the psalmist along with Mount Hermon (Ps 89: 12), although it is much smaller than the majestic Hermon (see fig. 472). It was the rallying place of the forces of Naphtali and Zebulun before the battle against Sisera (Jgs 4:6, 12, 14). The mountain is detached and lies about 5 mi. southeast of Nazareth and about 12 mi. west of the southern end of the Sea of Galilee. It rises to 1,829 ft. above sea level (Map I, B-3). The Arabs call it *Jebel eṭ-Ṭôr* (or *Jabal aṭ-Ṭûr*), a name they also give to Sinai, Gerizim, and the Mount of Olives. Its slopes are covered with fruit trees (olive and fig trees) and timber (oak and terebinth), and its summit affords a good view of the whole Valley of Jezreel and Mount Carmel. Early Christian tradition made Mount Tabor the mount of Transfiguration, with the result that ecclesiastical buildings were erected on it from time to time in commemoration of that event. However, in Christ's time there was a town on the summit which Josephus fortified in the days of the first Jewish-Roman war (Jos. *Life* 37); therefore it is unlikely that this mountaintop was a place "apart," as described in Mk 9:2; cf. Mt 17:1.

2. A town in the territory of Zebulun assigned to the Merarite Levites (1 Chr 6: 77). It may be the place mentioned in Jos 19:22 if that is not the mount by that name (*see* Tabor, 1). It is possibly correctly identified with the village of *Debûriyeh,* which lies west of Mount Tabor on the ridge that connects this mount with the hill of Nazareth.

3. An oak (not "plain" as in the KJV) which Saul passed by on his way home from Ramah to Gibeah (1 Sa 10:3). Its site has not been identified, but it seems to have been in the territory of Benjamin.

Tabret. The translation in the KJV of: (1) The Heb. *toph* (Gen 31:27; 1 Sa 10:5; 18: 6; etc.), translated "tambourine" or "timbrel" in the RSV. Authorities on ancient musical instruments agree that the *toph* was a hand drum, made of a wooden hoop and very probably 2 skins. It was beaten by the hands, and must have made a kind of tom-tom sound. It was played mostly by women, and used as an accompaniment to singing and dancing, to accentuate the beat (fig. 505). See *SDACom* 3:30. (2) The Heb. *topheth* (Job 17:6), actually meaning "spitting," from the root *tûph,* "to spit." The translation "tabret" comes from confusing *topheth* with *toph,* a "hand drum."

Tabrimmon (tăb'rĭm-ŏn), KJV **Tabrimon** (tăb'rĭ-mŏn). [Heb. *Tabrimmon,* "(the god) Rimmon is good."] Father of Benhadad (I), king of Damascus (1 Ki 15: 18). His name has been deciphered on the Melkarth stele of Ben-hadad, now in

472. Mount Tabor, with Nain in the foreground

Aleppo (Albright, *BASOR* 87 [1942], 25). See fig. 58.

Tabrimon. *See* Tabrimmon.

Taches. An archaic word describing the fasteners or "clasps" (RSV) holding together the hangings of the Mosaic tabernacle (Ex 26:6, 11).

Tachmonite. *See* Tahchemonite.

Tackle, KJV **Tackling.** A rendering of: (1) the Heb. *chebel* (Is 33:23), "rope," "cord," "line," "tackle"; (2) the Gr. *skeuē* (Acts 27:19), a collective noun denoting "gear," "equipment," "tackling" of a ship.

Tackling. *See* Tackle.

Tadmor (tăd′môr). [Heb. *Tadmor;* Palmyrene *Tdmr* and *Tdmwr;* Akkadian *Tadmurium, Tâdmer,* and *Tadmar.* The name is possibly derived from *tamar,* "palm tree."] An oasis in the Syrian desert, about 130 mi. northeast of Damascus and 90 mi. south of the Great Bend of the Euphrates. It is mentioned 1st in the Assyrian texts from Cappadocia in the 19th cent. B.C., again in the Mari texts (*c.* 1700 B.C.), and then by Tiglath-pileser I (*c.* 1100 B.C.). Solomon came into possession

of Tadmor and fortified it (2 Chr 8:4), probably to protect his caravan route, since Tadmor was an important stopping place for caravans traveling between Mesopotamia and Syria. The reading "Tadmor" in 1 Ki 9:18, KJV, is based on Masoretic tradition. The Hebrew reads *Tamor* and is rendered "Tamar" in the RSV. Perhaps *Tamar, 5, is meant. See *SDA-Com* 2:776.

In Roman times Tadmor, then known by its Greek name Palmyra, reached its greatest importance. It became a wealthy and highly cultured caravan city with temples, aqueducts, and beautiful mansions. Its isolation strengthened its security, and under its king, Odenathus (d. A.D. 267), and his famous widow, Zenobia, it became an independent kingdom with possessions in many countries. But in A.D. 273 the emperor Aurelian personally directed a military campaign against Palmyra and destroyed it. Palmyra never regained its importance, and is now merely a village, called *Tudmur.* Nearby are the magnificent ruins (figs. 473, 535) that make Palmyra an archeological show place. Map XIX, E-13.

473. Ruins at Tadmor, later known as Palmyra

Tahan (tā'hăn). [Heb. *Tachan,* meaning uncertain.]

1. A son of Ephraim and head of the tribal family of Tahanites (tā'hăn-īts) [Heb. *Tachani*] (Num 26:35); he was probably identical with Tahath, 1 (1 Chr 7:20).

2. A later descendant of Ephraim (1 Chr 7:25).

Tahanites. *See* Tahan, 1.

Tahapanes. *See* Tahpanhes.

Tahash (tā'hăsh), KJV **Thahash** (thā'hăsh). [Heb. *Tachash,* "porpoise."] A son of Nahor by his concubine Reumah (Gen 22:24), and probably the head of an Aramaean clan.

Tahath (tā'hăth). [Heb. *Tachath,* "(that which is) underneath," or "compensation."]

1 and 2. Two descendants of Ephraim (1 Chr 7:20), the 1st of whom may be identical with Tahan, 1.

3. A Korahite Levite, an ancestor of Samuel (1 Chr 6:24, 37).

4. A camping place in the wilderness journey of the Israelites (Num 33:26, 27); not identified.

Tahchemonite (tä'kĕ-mŏ-nīt), KJV **Tachmonite** (tăk'mŏ-nīt). [Heb. *Tachkemoni.*] The designation of one of David's "mighty men" (2 Sa 23:8). In 1 Chr 11:11 he is called a Hachmonite (Heb. *Chakmoni*). It is usually thought that the *t* in *Tachkemoni* is a mistake for the article *h.* The 2 letters are similar in postexilic Hebrew.

Tahpanhes (tä'păn-hēz), or **Tehaphnehes** (tĕ-hăf'nĕ-hēz), KJV once **Tahapanes** (tà-hăp'à-nēz). [Heb. *Tachpanches* and *Techaphneches;* Egyptian *T3-ht-(n)-p3-nhsy,* "the fortress of the Negro."] A city in Egypt to which the remnant left in Judah by Nebuchadnezzar fled after the murder of Gedaliah (Jer 43:5-9; 44:1). In ch 2:16, RSV, it is mentioned, together with Memphis, and in Eze 30:14-18 it is listed among several Egyptian cities. Because the LXX calls it *Taphnas,* it has been identified with the harbor city of Daphnae, now *Tell Defneh* (Map V, B-3), in the eastern Delta, a city dedicated to the cult of the god Baal-zephon, the patron deity of the sailors. Some scholars, however, identify Tahpanhes with the area lying between Tanis and *Qanṭîr.*

Tahpenes (tä'pĕ-nēz). [Heb. *Tachpenês,* perhaps a transliteration of Egyptian *T3-hnt-p3-nsw,* "she whom the king protects" (Albright, *BASOR* 140 [1955], 32).] An otherwise unidentified queen of Egypt, whose sister was given to the Edomite prince Hadad (1 Ki 11:19, 20) in the time of Solomon; her husband must have been one of the last kings of the 21st dynasty.

Tahrea. *See* Tarea.

Tahtim-hodshi. *See* Kadesh, 2.

Tale. In Ex 5:8, 18; 1 Chr 9:28; KJV, a word used with the archaic meaning of "a count," "enumeration," translating Hebrew terms meaning "measurement," "proportion," "fixed quantity," "number."

Talebearer. A rendering of: (1) a form of the Heb. *ragan* (Prov 18:8; 26:20, 22; KJV), "to grumble," "to slander"; (2) the Heb. *rakil* (Lev 19:16; Prov 11:13; 20:19; KJV), "slanderer."

Talent. [Heb. *kikkar;* Aramaic *kakkar;* Ugaritic *kkr,* "disk," from the shape of a talent, a metal disk with a hole in the center; Gr. *talanton.*] A unit of weight or money. The Babylonian talent consisted of 3,600 shekels; but the Hebrew talent, in conformity with the Canaanite talent, consisted of only 3,000 shekels (see Ex 38:25-27). Its weight was 965.37 oz. troy (34.2 kilogr., or 75.39 lb. av.) and its monetary value in gold $33,804.00, in silver $874.20, and in bronze probably about $23.00.

From the parable of the Talents, in which servants received talents according to their abilities to make profitable investments with them (Mt 25:14-30), the English figurative use of the word "talent" is derived. In Rev 16:21 the phrase "about the weight of a talent" is a rendering of the Gr. *hōs talantiaia,* literally "as weighing a talent" (RSV "heavy as a hundredweight"). The NT talent has been variously estimated as weighing from about 58 to 80 lb. *See* Money, 4.

Talitha. A term appearing in Mk 5:41 in the expression "Talitha *cumi,*" as a transliteration of the Gr. *talitha,* which in turn is a transliteration of the Aramaic *ṭalyetha'* or *ṭelitha',* "girl," "maiden." "Talitha cumi" means "Maiden, arise."

Talmai (tăl'mī). [Heb. *Talmay,* probably a Hurrian (Horite) name like *Talmiana,* meaning "great." The name occurs in Nabataean inscriptions as *Tlmy, Tlmw,* and *Tlm.*]

1. One of the descendants of Anak (Num 13:22). The clan was expelled from Hebron by Caleb the son of Jephunneh (Jos 15:14; Jgs 1:10).

2. A king of Geshur, whose daughter Maacah became one of David's wives and the mother of Absalom (2 Sa 3:3; 13:37; 1 Chr 3:2).

Talmon (tăl'mŏn). [Heb. *Ṭalmôn,* meaning uncertain.] The head of a Levite family of gatekeepers (1 Chr 9:17; Ezr 2:40, 42; Neh 7:45; 11:19; 12:25).

Tamah. *See* Temah.

Tamar (tā'mēr), KJV of NT **Thamar** (thā'-mär). [Heb. *Tamar,* "date palm"; Gr. *Thamar.*]

1. A daughter-in-law of Judah. After being widowed she became the mother of 2 of Judah's sons, Perez and Zerah, and thus the ancestress of 2 tribal families of Judah (Gen 38:6-30; Ruth 4:12; 1 Chr 2: 4; Mt 1:3).

2. A beautiful daughter of David, who was violated by her half brother Amnon. Absalom, a full brother of Tamar, avenged the crime by slaying Amnon (2 Sa 13:1-32; 1 Chr 3:9).

3. The daughter of Absalom, probably named after his sister (2 Sa 14:27).

4. A place near the southeastern corner of Palestine (Eze 47:19; 48:28). It must be sought in the vicinity of the southern end of the Dead Sea, but has not been identified with certainty.

5. A place in the wilderness, fortified by Solomon (1 Ki 9:18, RSV); possibly identical with Tamar, 4. The KJV, however, reads *Tadmor, in harmony with the Jewish Masoretes.

Tamarisk Tree. [Heb. *'eshel.*] A small hardwood tree of the desert, having minute evergreen leaves. The largest species (*Tamarix articulata*) grows no higher than 30 ft. The tree provides valuable shade, and promise of rest and survival in the most forbidding areas, to which it is well suited by having leaves that lose little moisture by transpiration. Abraham planted a tamarisk tree in Beer-sheba (Gen 21:33; KJV "grove"); King Saul rested beneath one during his pursuit of David, and he and his sons were buried together under a tamarisk tree (1 Sa 22: 6; 31:13; KJV "tree").

Tambourine. *See* Tabret.

Tammuz (tăm'ŭz). [Heb. *Tammúz;* Babylonian *Dumuzi, Du'ûzu,* and *Dúzu.*] A god of Sumerian origin whose worship was spread throughout the ancient world. He was the god of pastures and flocks, the heavenly shepherd, who died annually and rose to new life every year after Ishtar, his wife and sister, descended into the nether world and brought him up again. The Tammuz feast was one of the most widely celebrated festivals among the ancient Semites. In Ezekiel's time the Tammuz cult had found entrance into Judah, and Hebrew women were weeping for that god at the Temple gates (Eze 8:14);

hence they must have performed the religious rites connected with his annual death. The myth of Tammuz and Ishtar, described in many Babylonian texts and praised in songs, was known in Phoenicia as that of Adonis, and thence it was carried to Greece and Rome, and found its expression there in the form of the myth of Venus and Adonis.

The 4th Babylonian month was named after him, and after the Captivity, when the Jews adopted the Babylonian month names (*see* Nisan), it became the name also of the 4th month of the Jewish religious year. It began at the new moon of June or July. *See* Year.

Tanach. *See* Taanach.

Tanhumeth (tăn-hū'mĕth). [Heb. *Tanchumeth,* "consolation." The name occurs on an ancient jar handle.] A Netophathite, whose son Seraiah was one of the captains of Zedekiah's army who joined Gedaliah at Mizpah after the fall of Jerusalem (2 Ki 25:23; Jer 40:8).

474. Goatskin tannery at Hebron

Tanner. [Gr. *burseus,* "tanner."] One engaged in the processing of animal hides for various uses. Peter lodged "many days" in the home of a tanner named Simon, in Joppa, during the course of which he restored Dorcas to life and was prompted by a vision to visit Cornelius the centurion (Acts 9:43; see vs 36-41; chs 10 to 11:18). Simon's house was by the seaside (ch 10:6), where abundant water was available for the tanning process. Skins were treated with an application of lime, etc., to loosen the hair, then hair and fat were removed by soaking the skin in a solution made from oak bark, the juice of a certain acid-bearing plant, *Periploca secamine*, etc. They were then dried for 2 or 3 days, after which they were submitted to various other solutions intended to cure the leather and make it pliable. See fig. 474.

Tapestry. A term appearing in Prov 7:16; 31:22, in the phrase "coverings of tapestry," which is a rendering of the Heb. *marbaddim*, "coverlets," from *rabad*, "to bind," "to prepare." The exact nature of the coverings or coverlets is a matter of conjecture.

Taphath (tā'făth). [Heb. *Taphath*, meaning uncertain.] A daughter of Solomon, and wife of Ben-abinadab, one of Solomon's governors (1 Ki 4:11).

Tappuah (tăp-pū'ä). [Heb. *Tappûach*, "apple."]

1. A son of Hebron and descendant of Caleb, son of Hezron (1 Chr 2:43).

2. A town in the Shephelah in Judah (Jos 15:34); site unidentified.

3. An old Canaanite city, defeated by Joshua (Jos 12:17), which later belonged to Manasseh (ch 17:8). Since it lay on the border between Manasseh and Ephraim it could also be counted to Ephraim (chs 16:8; 17:7, 8). It is also called En-Tappuah (ĕn-tăp'ū-ä), "spring of Tappuah" (ch 17:7). According to the RSV it was Tappuah (KJV "Tiphsah") that was sacked by Menahem (2 Ki 15:16). It is identified with *Sheikh Abū Zarad*, about 9 mi. south of Shechem (Map VI, D-3).

Tarah. See Terah, 2.

Taralah (tär'å-lä). [Heb. *Tar'alah*.] A town in Benjamin (Jos 18:27); site unidentified.

Tarea (tā'rĕ-ä), or **Tahrea** (tä'rĕ-ä). [Heb. *Ta'rea'* and *Tachrea'*, meaning uncertain.] A descendant of Saul through Jonathan (1 Chr 8:35; 9:41).

Tares. [Gr. *zizania*, "darnel," probably a Semitic loan word.] The true tare is a vetch easily distinguishable from wheat. The tares (RSV "weeds") of Scripture are possibly the bearded darnel (*Lolium temulentum*), a common Palestinian grass growing about 2 ft. tall, which in its early stages of growth is indistinguishable from wheat. If the seeds of the plant are eaten they produce violent nausea, convulsions, and sometimes death. It is believed that it is not the seed itself, but a fungus associated with the seed, that is poisonous. Jesus used this plant in one of His parables (Mt 13:25-40).

Target. The erroneous rendering in the KJV of: (1) the Heb. *kîdôn*, "javelin," in 1 Sa 17:6; and (2) the Heb. *ṣinnah*, "shield," in 1 Ki 10:16; 2 Chr 9:15; 14:8 (RSV "bucklers"). The RSV uses "target" once (Job 16:12), as the translation of the Heb. *maṭṭarah*, translated "mark" in the KJV. *Maṭṭarah* is translated "mark" in both versions in 1 Sa 20:20.

Tarpelites (tär'pĕl-īts). [Aramaic *Tarpelaye'*.] Probably a class of Persian "officials" (RSV), whose exact function is unknown, since the word occurs nowhere outside the Bible in extant sources (Ezr 4:9).

Tarshish (tär'shĭsh), KJV sometimes **Tharshish** (thär'shĭsh). [Heb. *Tarshish*, a Phoenician term, derived from an Akkadian word meaning "smelting plant," "refinery." The name was given to localities in which the Phoenicians had mining operations, as in southeastern Spain, in Tunisia, and on the island of Sardinia.]

1. A descendant or descendants of Javan (Gen 10:4; 1 Chr 1:7). This Tarshish is generally connected with the *Tartessus* in Spain, known to classical writers (Herod. iv. 152), a region lying around the middle and lower Baetis (the modern Guadalquivir) River (Map IV, B-1). This identification is probably correct, for when Jonah went to the port of Joppa and embarked on a ship bound for Tarshish, it was his object to flee to a faraway country (Jon 1:3), and Tarshish in Spain, at the opposite end of the Mediterranean, would be such a place. According to Is 60:9 and 66:19 it was a distant land. According to the prophets Jeremiah and Ezekiel, silver (Jer 10:9), iron, tin, and lead (Eze 27:12) were obtained from Tarshish, by which they most probably meant *Tartessus* of Spain. However, 2 Chr 9:21 may refer to a metal-producing area at Ophir, unless the verse is to be read like its parallel passage in 1 Ki 10:22, in which Tarshish is the name of Solomon's ships (*see* Tarshish, 2).

2. "Ships of Tarshish" is an expression that has generally been explained to mean large, seagoing ships which were capable of sailing as far as Spain. Recently it has been suggested that the term

should probably be translated as "refinery fleet," designating ships that brought metal from refineries to the market places of the world (W. F. Albright, *BASOR* 83 [1941], 21, 22). In some OT passages where these ships are mentioned the Phoenicians are the owners or the sailors of such ships (Is 23:1, 14; Eze 27:25), or cooperate with the Israelites in joint enterprises (1 Ki 10:22; 2 Chr 9:21). Other passages where these ships are mentioned are 1 Ki 22:48; Ps 48:7; Is 2:16.

3. A Benjamite, son of Bilhan (1 Chr 7:10).

4. The name of one of the 7 highest princes of the Persian Empire in the time of Ahasuerus (Xerxes) (Est 1:14). As applied to him the name seems to be Persian, but the etymology of the word is uncertain.

Tarsus (tär′sŭs). [Gr. *Tarsos*.] The chief city of Cilicia, founded by Phoenicians, situated on both banks of the Cydnus River about 12 mi. from the sea, on the important trade route between Syria and western Asia Minor (Map XX, B-5). It is mentioned on the Black Obelisk of Shalmaneser III (859-824 B.C.). In the 7th cent. B.C. it became the capital of an independent kingdom, and later the capital of a Persian satrapy, or province. During the period of the Seleucids it lost much of its Oriental character, because many Greeks settled there. In this period was founded the philosophical school of Tarsus, which in Paul's time was rivaled only by those of Athens and Alexandria. Antiochus IV Epiphanes greatly embellished the city, which temporarily adopted the name of "Antioch on the Cydnus," but later reverted to its old name of Tarsus. Pompey annexed it for Rome in 64 B.C., and Antony granted it freedom and immunity. In 22 B.C. it became the capital of the Roman province of Cilicia. Augustus raised it to the dignity of a metropolis. After that the city became ardent in its emperor worship. The native god of the city was *Baal-Tarz*, "lord of Tarsus," who came to be identified with the Greek Zeus. He is always portrayed as accompanied by a youthful god, Sandon, who was identified with Heracles. Although the city was destroyed several times, it was never permanently deserted. The modern town, lying several ft. above the ruined remains of the ancient city, is located entirely on the western riverbank. Famous men who haled from Tarsus were: Athenodorus the Stoic, the teacher of Augustus; Nestor the Platonist, the teacher of Marcellus; the physician Dioscorides;

the Stoics Antipater and Archedemus; and the greatest, as far as Christians are concerned, the apostle Paul (Acts 9:11; 21:39; 22:3). At least once after his conversion Paul revisited Tarsus, and may have been engaged in missionary work there (Acts 9:30; 11:25; cf. Gal 1:21).

475. Roman gateway in west wall of Tarsus

Tartak (tär′tăk). [Heb. *Tartaq*.] An otherwise unknown god of the Avvites, worshiped in Samaria (2 Ki 17:31).

Tartan (tär′tăn). [Heb. *tartan;* Assyrian *tartânnu* and *turtânu*.] The title of the Assyrian commander in chief, which could perhaps best be translated "field marshal." One tartan is mentioned in Is 20:1 as the military leader (RSV "commander in chief") of an expedition of Sargon II against Ashdod, probably carried out in 711 B.C. A tartan accompanied Sennacherib's army on an expedition against Jerusalem in 701 B.C. (2 Ki 18:17).

Taskmaster. [Heb. generally a form of *nagaś,* "to exact (tribute)," "to oppress."] In Ex 1:11; 3:7; 5:6-14, taskmasters are the minor Egyptian officials who made the life of the Hebrew slaves bitter. In Job 3:18; Is 60:17 *noges* is rendered "taskmaster" by the RSV, and "oppressor" and "exactor," respectively, by the KJV. "Taskmaster" is a supplied term in 1 Ki 12:18; 2 Chr 10:18; RSV, suggested by the context.

Tatnai. *See* Tattenai.

Tattenai (tăt′ĕ-nī), KJV **Tatnai** (tăt′nī). [Aramaic *Tattenay*.] A governor of the Persian satrapy, or province, of "Beyond the River" (Ezr 5:3, 6; 6:6, 13), which comprised all the areas lying between the river Euphrates and Egypt. Until recently it was thought that *Tattenay* was the

Aramaic form of *Ushtani,* who was known from historical records to have been the satrap of the 2 satrapies "Babylonia" and "Beyond the River" in the time of Darius I, during whose reign the Temple at Jerusalem was rebuilt and Tattenai visited Judah. A recently discovered cuneiform tablet, however, provides the information that *"Tattanni,* governor of *Ebir-nâri,"* acted as Ushtani's deputy in the west, since the 2 satrapies were too large for 1 man to administer efficiently. The cuneiform tablet mentioning Tattenai uses as his title the word "governor," *pâḥatu,* a cognate of *pechah,* used in the Bible to designate his office. Tattenai came to Jerusalem to investigate the activities of the Jews, probably because accusations made by their enemies had reached his ears. He showed himself an impartial and broad-minded Persian official, giving his king an unbiased report of his findings and requesting instructions so as to know how to act in the best interests of all concerned (Ezr 5:3-17).

Lit.: Albert T. Olmstead, *JNES* 3 (1944), 46.

Tattoo. Tatooing is the practice of indelibly marking the skin by pricking it and planting dyestuff in skin openings thus produced. The Heb. *qaʻaqaʻ* has the meaning "tattoo" in Mishnaic Hebrew, and probably also in Lev 19:28 where it is thus rendered in the RSV (KJV "print"). Tattooing was practiced in ancient times by the Libyans and probably by the earliest Egyptians (A. Erman and H. Ranke, *Aegypten und aegyptisches Leben im Altertum* [Tübingen, 1923], p. 257, n. 1).

Tau. [Heb. *taw.*] The 22d and last letter of the Hebrew alphabet, written ת, appearing as the title of the last section of Ps 119 in the KJV. *See* Aleph.

Taunt. That which is said to anger or wound a person; ridicule, derision. The term, both as a verb and as a noun, occurs only in the OT, and is the rendering of several Hebrew terms more or less synonymous. Most of the references are to the taunts directed against God's people by their enemies (Ps 44:13; 79:4; Jer 24:9; 44:8; RSV; etc.).

Taverns, The Three. *See* Three Taverns.

Taxes. Money, produce, or property paid to the governing power as required by law. Moses required of the Israelites a tax to be used for the tabernacle (2 Chr 24:6, RSV; cf. Ex 30:13-16; Lev 27:2-8). The paying of this tax had lapsed, but King Joash revived the practice (2 Chr 24:8-

10, RSV). According to Josephus the Jews paid this tax into a treasury (*Ant.* xviii. 9. 1) even when they were captives in Babylon. King Jehoiakim of Judah taxed his people in order to pay tribute to Pharaoh Necho (2 Ki 23:35). Psamtik I (663-609 B.C.), of Egypt, received an income tax of 20 per cent from the population, but left priests and soldiers exempt. In the Persian system taxation was partly in produce, such as wheat, wine, oil, and salt (see Ezr 7:21, 22), and every province was required to remit to the royal court the choicest portion of its produce. The Jews of the Persian province of Judah paid heavy taxes to their rulers in Nehemiah's day (cf. Neh 9:37), and many of them had to mortgage property or borrow money to pay taxes (ch 5:4, RSV). During the feast celebrating Esther's elevation to be queen of Persia the king canceled the taxes of the provinces (Est 2:18, RSV).

The "taxing" of Lk 2:2, KJV, is a rendering of the Gr. *apographē,* "registration," "census." Doubtless the registration of names and of property was also the basis for the levy of a property tax. Levi Matthew, a Jewish tax collector (*see* Publican) under Roman appointment, was called by Christ to be a disciple (Mt 9:9; Mk 2:14; Lk 5:27). Christ disapproved the general practice of extorting amounts above the official tax (see Lk 3: 12, 13), yet earned the reputation of "a friend of tax collectors" (Mt 11:19, RSV; cf. ch 9:10-13). When asked whether it was lawful to pay taxes (see RSV) to Caesar, Jesus endorsed the practice, but used the opportunity to enjoin the fulfillment of obligations toward God, thus setting forth the Christian's separate duties to church and to state (ch 22:17-22).

Tebah (tē'bȧ). [Heb. *Ṭebach,* "(born at the time of a) slaughter."] A son of Nahor by his concubine Reumah (Gen 22:24), and probably the founder of an Aramaean clan.

Tebaliah (tĕb'ȧ-lī'ȧ). [Heb. *Ṭebalyahû,* probably "Yahweh has immersed (= purified)."] A son of the Merarite Levite Hosah (1 Chr 26:11).

Tebeth (tē'bĕth). [Heb. *Ṭebeth,* a loan word from the Akkadian *Ṭebîtu.*] The 10th month of the Jewish religious year (Est 2: 16); it began at the new moon of December or January. *See* Year.

Tehaphnehes. *See* Tahpanhes.

Tehinnah (tē-hĭn'ȧ). [Heb. *Techinnah,* "supplication."] A descendant of Judah and ancestor of (the inhabitants of) Irnahash (1 Chr 4:12).

Teil Tree. A term occurring once (Is 6:13, KJV), a rendering of the Heb. *'elah*, a large tree, without the exact species being necessarily indicated (RSV *"terebinth"). The teil is of the genus *Tilia*, but no member of this group, to which the linden belongs, occurs in Palestine. *'Elah* is generally translated "oak."

Tekel. *See* Mene.

Tekoa (tĕ-kō'á), KJV 3 times **Tekoah** (tĕ-kō'á). [Heb. *Teqôa'*, "blowing (of alarm)."] A town of Judah, the home of Ira, one of David's "mighty men" (2 Sa 23:26), of the "wise woman" employed by Joab to persuade David to bring the banished Absalom back (ch 14:2-20), and of the

476. The wilderness near Tekoa

prophet Amos (Amos 1:1). King Rehoboam fortified it (2 Chr 11:6). The citizens of Tekoa helped Nehemiah to rebuild the wall of Jerusalem, whereas their nobles refused to do so (Neh 3:5, 27). The city was situated on a hill in the wilderness of Tekoa (2 Chr 20:20) at an

altitude of 2,700 ft. above sea level, a point from which can be seen Bethlehem, about 5 mi. to the north, the Mount of Olives, the Dead Sea, and the mountains of Moab. The present village is called *Tequ'* (Map VIII, E-3).

Tekoah. *See* Tekoa.

Tekoite (tĕ-kō'īt). [Heb. *Teqô'î*.] A native or inhabitant of Tekoa (2 Sa 23:26, KJV).

Tel-abib (tĕl'ā'bīb). [Heb. *Tel 'Abîb*, "heap of grain."] A place in Babylonia in the vicinity of the canal *Chebar, where exiles from Judah dwelt (Eze 3:15). It is most likely that the name *Tel 'Abîb* is a Hebrew modification of *til-abûbi*, meaning "mound of the Flood," a name given by the Babylonians to every ruin mound on which a city had formerly been situated.

Telah (tē'lá). [Heb. *Telach*, "fracture."] A descendant of Ephraim (1 Chr 7:25).

Telaim (tē-lā'īm). [Heb. *Tela'im*, meaning uncertain.] A place in the south of Judah where Saul mustered his army before marching against the Amalekites (1 Sa 15:4). Some identify it with the Telem of Jos 15:24, but its location is uncertain.

Tel-assar (tĕl-ăs'ēr), KJV once **Thelasar** (thē-lā'sēr). [Heb. *Tela'ssar* and *Telassar*.] An area where the people of Eden dwelt (2 Ki 19:12; Is 37:12). The area of *Bit-Adini* (Beth-eden) lay near the middle Euphrates (Map XI, B-4), where *Til Ashûri*, "hill of Ashur," mentioned in inscriptions of Tiglath-pileser III, was situated (Luckenbill, *AR* I, 278, 291).

Telem (tē'lĕm). [Heb. *Telem*.]

1. A gatekeeper who had married a foreign wife in the time of Ezra's reform (Ezr 10:24).

2. A place in the south of Judah (Jos 15:24); equated by some with Telaim of 1 Sa 15:4, but not identified with certainty.

Tel-haresha. *See* Tel-harsha.

Tel-harsa. *See* Tel-harsha.

Tel-harsha (tĕl'här'shá), KJV **Tel-harsa** (tĕl'här'sá) and **Tel-haresha** (tĕl'há-rē'shá). [Heb. *Tel Charsha'*, meaning uncertain.] A place in Babylonia from which certain exiles returned to Judah who could not prove their Hebrew citizenship (Ezr 2:59; Neh 7:61). The site has not been identified.

Tel-melah (tĕl'mē'lá). [Heb. *Tel Melach*, "hill of salt."] A place in Babylonia from which exiles returned to Judah who could not prove their Hebrew citizenship (Ezr 2:59; Neh 7:61); site unidentified.

Tema (tē'má). [Heb. *Têma'*; in cuneiform

inscriptions *Têmâ* and *Têmâ'*, in an Aramaic text *Tymn*.]

1. A descendant or descendants of Ishmael (Gen 25:15; 1 Chr 1:30).

2. A locality in Arabia (Is 21:14; Jer 25:23) whose caravans were well known (Job 6:19). It is a fertile oasis, now called *Teimâ*, about 260 mi. southeast of Aqabah, in northwestern Arabia. Lying on the caravan route between the incense- and myrrh-exporting countries of southern Arabia and the northern regions (Egypt and Palestine-Syria), it was an important stopping place. It is mentioned frequently in Assyrian and Babylonian records, and became especially famous in the 6th cent. when Nabonidus, the last king of Babylonia, went to Tema early in his reign, leaving his son Belshazzar as coruler in Babylon. He spent about 10 years at Tema and built up the city with the intention of making it a rival to Babylon in beauty. Map XI, D-4.

Lit.: R. P. Dougherty, *Nabonidus and Belshazzar* (1929); C. J. Gadd, *Anatolian Studies* 8 (1958), 35-92.

Temah (tē'ma), KJV **Tamah** (tā'ma) and **Thamah** (thā'ma). [Heb. *Temach*.] The ancestral head of a family of Nethinim, or Temple servants, some of whom returned with Zerubbabel from Babylonia (Ezr 2:53; Neh 7:55).

Teman (tē'măn). [Heb. *Têman*, "on the right hand," or "southern."] A grandson of Esau (Gen 36:11), and the district inhabited by the tribe descended from him (Jer 49:20; Amos 1:12; Ob 9; Hab 3:3). It probably lay in the northern part of Edom (Eze 25:13). One of the kings of Edom was from Teman (Gen 36:34), and one of Job's friends may have been from there (Job 2:11). The Temanites were famous for their wisdom (Jer 49:7). Two conjectural locations are indicated on Map V, B-7.

Temani. *See* Temanite.

Temanite (tē'măn-īt), KJV once **Temani** (tĕm'a-nī). [Heb. *Têmanî*.] A native of Teman (Gen 36:34; 1 Chr 1:45). However, it is not certain whether Eliphaz, called a Temanite (Job 2:11; 4:1; etc.), was from Teman or from Tema.

Temeni (tĕm'ĕ-nī). [Heb. *Têmenî*.] One of the sons of Ashhur of the tribe of Judah (1 Chr 4:6).

Temper. As used in the KJV, the rendering of several Hebrew terms and 1 Greek word meaning variously "to mix," "to blend," "to sprinkle." These terms are rendered by the RSV as "mixed" (Ex 29:2), "blended" (ch 30:35), "moisten" (Eze 26:14), and "adjusted" (1 Cor 12:24). In the RSV "temper" appears twice (Prov 14:17, 29) in the sense of disposition or frame of mind.

Temperance, Temperate. [Gr. *egkrateia*, "self-control"; *egkrateuomai*, "to exercise self-control"; *egkratēs*, "self-controlled"; and *sōphrōn*, "prudent" or "self-controlled."] Terms appearing in the KJV with the archaic meanings of "self-control" and "self-controlled." Self-control is one of the important Christian graces (Gal 5:23; 2 Pe 1:6; etc.). It is essential to victory in the Christian race, as it is in an athletic contest (1 Cor 9:25).

Temple. A rendering of: (1) Hebrew and Aramaic *hêkal* (a loan word from Sumero-Akkadian *ekallu*, borrowed from the Sumerian E-GAL, "palace," "temple," literally "great house"), used also of the tabernacle at Shiloh (1 Sa 1:9; 3:3), and of God's heavenly abode (2 Sa 22:7). (2) The Heb. *bayith*, "house," "temple," used for God's Temple (2 Chr 35:20), also for a pagan temple (1 Chr 10:10). In many passages where *bayith* is rendered "house," reference is to a temple, either that of a pagan deity (Jgs 9:46; 2 Ki 10:21; etc.) or the Temple of God in Jerusalem (1 Ki 6:2-10; etc.). A temple was considered primarily a dwelling place of the deity, and

477. Models of foundations of 2 temples at Beth-shean of the 13th and 12th cent. B.C.

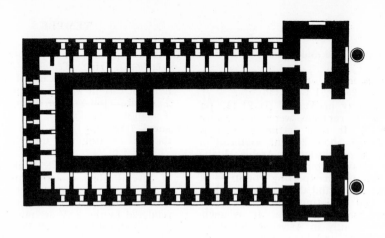

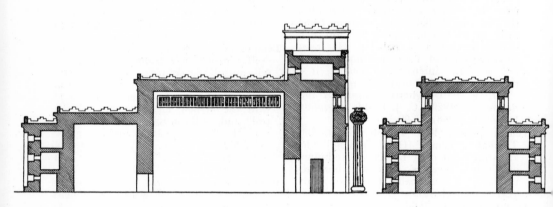

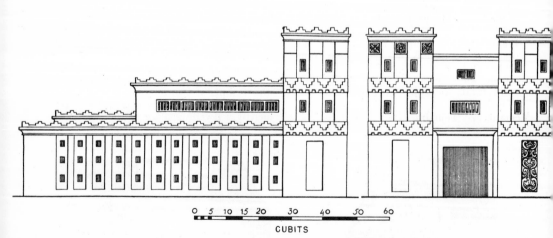

478. The Temple of Solomon (according to L.-Hugues Vincent and A.-M. Steve)

Top: Ground plan of the Temple building. Center, left: East-west section. Center, right: Cross section through the sanctuary. Bottom: Side and front elevations

1070

only secondarily a place of worship. (3) Gr. *hieron* (Mt 4:5; 12:5, 6; etc.). (4) Gr. *naos* (ch 23:16; etc.). Strictly speaking, *hieron* applies to the whole Temple complex, with all its auxiliary buildings and courts, whereas *naos* designates the sacred shrine or the Temple building, consisting of the "holy place" and the "most holy [place]."

All ancient nations built temples to their gods. Some of them were elaborate structures, covering many acres of land, and consisted of magnificent buildings and courts. One of the largest well-preserved ruined temples is the great temple of *Amon at Thebes in Upper Egypt (see figs. 147, 148. For remains of other temples see figs. 25, 40, 41, 44, 46, 112, 146, 162, 194, 432, 513, 516, 535). In the region of Palestine no temple ruins from pre-Roman times have survived above ground, but several earlier ones have been excavated. They reveal that most of the pre-Israelite temples in Canaan consisted of 3 main rooms: (1) an anteroom through which the worshiper or priest had to pass before he could enter; (2) the sanctuary in which he presented his sacrifices, prayed, or performed other religious duties; (3) beyond this, usually on a raised level, the most holy place containing a pedestal on which the image of the god stood. The temple of Dagon at Ashdod, to which the Philistines took the captured ark of God (1 Sa 5:2-4), was probably a structure like those excavated at Beth-shean (for ground plans, see fig. 477). Also, the temple of the god El-berith (KJV "Berith") at Shechem (Jgs 9:46), or of Baal at Samaria (2 Ki 10: 21), may not have differed from those excavated at various places in Palestine and Syria.

Although the OT says very little about the pagan temples of Canaan, it gives detailed descriptions of the Temple of Solomon and of the ideal temple of Ezekiel's vision, and also some information about Zerubbabel's Temple. Herod's Temple, the scene of Christ's ministry, is described in detail in the writings of Josephus and in the Mishnah.

I. The Temple of Solomon. David had originally planned to build the Temple at Jerusalem (2 Sa 7:1-3), and when he was not permitted to erect it (vs 5, 6), he amassed during his lifetime a tremendous amount of building material and precious metal (1 Chr 22:2-16) which, together with detailed plans (ch 28:11, 12), he gave to his son Solomon, charging him with

carrying out the project. David had already bought the Temple site, the threshing floor of Araunah (1 Chr 21:25 to 22: 1), on what had formerly been called Mount *Moriah, the scene of the offering of Isaac.

479. The rock on which Solomon's altar of burnt offering is believed to have stood at Jerusalem

Although the OT gives a detailed description of the Temple building and its furniture, some terms are obscure, and consequently, most conjectural reconstructions made before the accumulation of archeological evidence concerning the building methods, techniques, and architectural details of Solomon's time are incorrect. Much more is now known, but uncertainties with regard to some of the details remain, as the following discussion will show.

The northeastern hill of Jerusalem, on which Solomon erected the Temple and most probably the palace structures, is irregularly shaped; and doubtless a great deal of time, expense, and effort was expended to provide first a level platform on which the various buildings could be erected (see fig. 259). This accounts to some extent for the long span of time— 20 years (1 Ki 9:10)—required to build

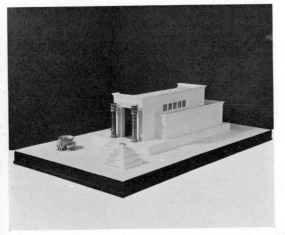

480. The Howland-Garber model of Solomon's Temple

the Temple and the palaces. Examples of such artificial platforms are plentiful in the Near East, the most famous of which are those of Persepolis and Pasargadae in Persia, and of the great Sun temple at Baalbek in the Lebanon. In fact, the present platform of the Temple area at Jeru-

481. The approximate site of the Most Holy Place (foreground) in the Temple building at Jerusalem

salem, now a Moslem sacred precinct (see fig. 260), gives a good idea of the platform erected by King Solomon, although the present structure consists of Herodian and later masonry. Some of the subter-

ranean vaults in the present platform structure at Jerusalem are used as cisterns, and Solomon's platform most likely contained similar cisterns for the storage of rain water, for Jerusalem has always suffered from a shortage of water.

The Temple and its auxiliary buildings were erected in 7 years (1 Ki 6:37, 38). Besides the sanctuary structure, the Temple precinct (fig. 478) contained 2 courts (2 Ki 23:12): (1) a "great court" (2 Chr 4:9) to which everyone had access, and (2) an "inner court" (1 Ki 6:36)—also called "the court of the priests" (2 Chr 4:9) and the "upper court" (Jer 36:10)— which was mainly the domain of priests and Levites. Nothing is said concerning their size or shape. The Bible mentions a number of gates that seem to have given access to the Temple area, but it does not specify which of them led into the outer court and which from the outer court into the inner one, nor does it give their exact locations. The gates mentioned by name are: (1) the "king's gate" (1 Chr 9:18), on the east side, (2) the "new gate" (Jer 26:10; 36:10), probably on the south side, (3) the upper Benjamin Gate (ch 20:2), probably on the north side, (4) the "higher gate," built by Jotham (2 Ki 15:35), probably in the north wall and possibly identical with the upper Benjamin Gate (Jer 20:2), (5) another "higher gate" connecting the Temple precinct with the palace area (2 Chr 23:20), hence probably on the south side, and (6) the gate of Shallecheth on the west side (1 Chr 26:16). Nothing is known of the wall of the outer court; it was apparently—in the north and east, at least—the outer wall of the city. The wall of the inner court was lightly built and consisted of 3 courses of stone with 1 course of cedar beams laid in the walls (1 Ki 6:36), an unusual method of building attested in Hittite ruins excavated in northern Syria, and in structures at Megiddo erected in Solomon's time.

The Temple had a length of 60 cu., a width of 20 cu., and a height of 30 cu. These measures most probably apply to the interior. It is not known whether the builders employed the common cu. or the longer royal cu. The building, which faced east, consisted of (1) a vestibule or porch, 20 cu. wide and 10 cu. deep; (2) the "holy place," 20 cu. wide and 40 cu. long; and (3) the "Holy of Holies" or "most holy [place]," which was 20 cu. in each direction, hence a perfect cube (1 Ki 6:2, 3, 16, 17, 20). See fig. 481.

The walls were of stone cut to size in quarries (1 Ki 6:7), and the ceiling was of beams and planks of cedar (v 9). The walls were covered with cedarwood, and the floor with cypress wood (v 15). The whole interior was carved with figures of cherubim, palm trees, and flowers, and overlaid with gold (1 Ki 6:18, 20-22, 29, 30, 32, 35; 2 Chr 3:7). Underneath the roof were series of windows with recessed frames (1 Ki 6:4, RSV), perhaps with latticework that gave access to the sunlight.

The partition between the holy place and the Most Holy Place was of cedar boards overlaid with gold, with a door consisting of 2 leaves of olivewood and decorated with cherubim, palm trees, and flowers, and covered with gold (1 Ki 6:31, 32). A gold chain was hung in front of the partition, evidently to support a curtain patterned after that which had been in the tabernacle (1 Ki 6:21; 2 Chr 3:14). It is uncertain whether the Most Holy Place lay on the same level as the holy place, or at an elevation to be reached by a stairway. Some scholars think that the lower height given for the smaller room, 20 cu. against 30 for the holy place, indicates that its floor level was 10 cu. higher, with the same roof level for both (see fig. 480), thus following the pattern of temples excavated elsewhere, which frequently show the innermost part of the sanctuary on a higher level than the other rooms. Other scholars, believing that the floors of all rooms lay on the same level and that the part of the roof covering the Most Holy Place lay 10 cu. lower than the rest of the roof, or that there may have been upper chambers between the ceiling of the Most Holy Place and the roof, find in 1 Chr 28:11 and 2 Chr 3:9 some support for such a view. See fig. 478.

Against the outside walls of the sanctuary on the north, west, and south were built 3 stories of small chambers that were probably used as offices for administration officials, and as storerooms (1 Ki 6:5-10). Many scholars believe that the front of the Temple had either 2 high monumental towers or a pylonlike entrance. The monumental towers find some basis in 2 Chr 3:4, which speaks of the height of the vestibule, or porch, as 120 cu. If this figure is correct, only high towers can be meant. In front of the Temple stood 2 bronze pillars with richly decorated capitals, each 18 cu. high (1 Ki 7:15-22; 2 Chr 3:15-17). Their names,

*Boaz and *Jachin, may have been the initial words of Hebrew inscriptions carved in the pillars. Archeological evidence shows such freestanding pillars as

482. A gate of Solomon's time at Hazor (lower left), closely corresponding to the temple gates described by Ezekiel and probably those of Solomon's Temple

a common feature of Phoenician temples.

In the Most Holy Place stood the ark with its lid (called "mercy seat"). This was the original ark made at Mount Sinai under the direction of Moses. It was can-

483. Artist's reconstruction of the Solomonic gate at Megiddo. The inner part (upper center) corresponds in layout and size to the temple gates described by Ezekiel, and probably to those of Solomon's Temple

opied by the extended wings of 2 large gold-overlaid cherubim that were new products of Solomon's artisans (1 Ki 6:23-28). In the holy place, but belonging to the inner sanctuary, was the golden

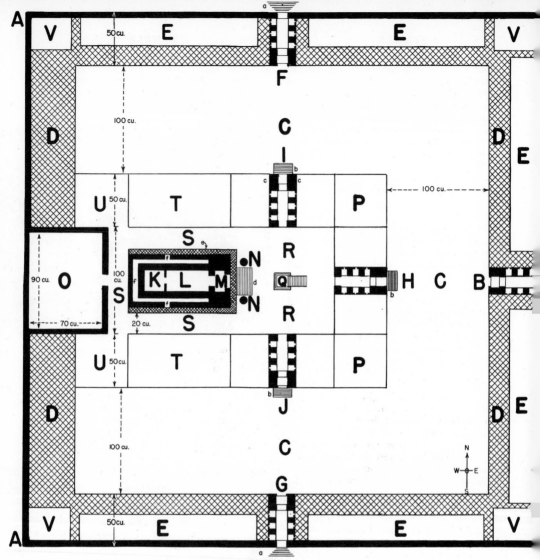

484. Plan of Ezekiel's temple

NOTE: This is not a detailed plan of the temple area, but an attempt to reproduce diagrammatically the measurements of the Bible text. No effort is made to imitate certain structural details often found in excavations, such as the projection of the gatehouses beyond the face of the wall. Some recent scholars, because of the massiveness of ancient walls, have suggested placing vestibules lengthwise rather than crosswise, consequently combining the other dimensions differently. Where the text is not detailed or not clearly understood, this plan shows general locations, or indicates a building in outline (for example, E, P, T, U).

A. Wall of outer court—Eze 40:5; 42:16-20
B. East outer gate—40:6-16
C. Outer court—40:17, 20, 31, 34, 37; 42:1, 3, 7-9, 14
D. Pavement—40:17, 18
E, E, E, E, E, E. Thirty chambers—40:17
F. North outer gate structure—40:20-23
G. South outer gate structure—40:24-27
H. East inner gate structure—40:32-34
I. North inner gate structure—40:35-38
J. South inner gate structure—40:28-31
K. Most Holy Place—41:3, 4
L. Holy place—41:1, 2, 5
M. Porch of the house—40:48
N, N. Pillars—40:49

O. Building—41:12-15
P, P. Chambers for priests—40:44-46
Q. Altar—40:47; 43:13-18
R. Inner court—40:28, 44, 47
S, S, S. Separate place—41:10, 12-15
T, T. Three-story chambers for the priests—42:1-14
U, U. Priests' kitchens—46:19, 20
V, V, V, V. People's cooking chambers—46:21-24
a, a, a. Seven steps to outer gate—40:22, 26
b, b, b. Eight steps to inner gate—40:31, 34, 37
c, c. Tables for killing sacrifices—40:39-43
d. Temple steps—40:49
e. Platform—41:8, 9, 11
f. Series of side chambers—41:5-9, 11

1074

altar of incense (1 Ki 6:20, 22; ch 7:48); 10 lampstands instead of the one in the tabernacle (ch 7:49); and "tables" of showbread (1 Chr 28:16; 2 Chr 4:18, 19; 13: 11). In the inner court stood the large bronze altar of burnt offering (1 Ki 8: 64; 2 Ki 16:14), 4 times the length and width of that which had served in the tabernacle (2 Chr 4:1; cf. Ex 27:1); also the large bronze sea, or tank, standing on the backs of 12 cast-bronze oxen, and 10 movable lavers (1 Ki 7:23-39). *See* names of specific items.

Solomon's Temple was repaired several times (2 Ki 12:5-14; 22:5-7) and stood for about 400 years. It was destroyed by Nebuchadnezzar's army in 586 B.C.; the pillars and the sea were broken up and the bronze taken to Babylon, along with all the other metal vessels (ch 25:9-17).

II. The Temple of Ezekiel. The temple described in Eze 40:1 to 43:27 was seen by the prophet in vision, and it is not clear whether or to what extent Zerubbabel built his Temple according to its plans and specifications, or whether the vision temple merely represented a plan for a temple that was to have served a restored, obedient people—a plan never realized because the people did not meet God's expectations and requirements (*see* Chosen People; Prophet, II).

It has been recognized for a long time that in its essential features Ezekiel's temple was patterned like Solomon's Temple, and recently discovered archeological evidence indicates that Ezekiel's gates, described in great detail, almost exactly matched gates built by Solomon's architects at Megiddo, Hazor, and Gezer (see figs. 482, 483). C. G. Howie (*BASOR* 117 [1950], 13-19) was the first to recognize that the layout and measurements given by Ezekiel for the east gate of his temple in all essential features agreed with a city gate of Megiddo, excavated in the Solomonic level of that city. In 1957 Y. Yadin discovered an identical city gate during the excavations at Hazor in the Solomonic level, which indicated that it had been planned by the same architect who had been responsible for the Megiddo gate. Recently Yadin showed that a Solomonic gate of about the same dimensions had been uncovered during excavations of Gezer many years ago, although its true character had not been fully recognized, partly because of its poor preservation and the imperfect archeological methods employed at that time (Y. Yadin, *IEJ* 8 [1958], 80-86; G. E. Wright, *BA* 21

[1958], 103, 104). These discoveries show that the description of either Solomon's Temple or of Ezekiel's ideal structure can be used to clarify structural and architectural details of the other.

Since Ezekiel's temple never existed in reality, only a brief summary of its essential features will be given here (see fig. 484). Its main feature is the perfect symmetry prevailing throughout. The whole precinct, 500 cu. square, faces the east. It consists of an outer court surrounded by a wall broken by 3 identical gates, one in the north wall, one in the east wall, and one in the south wall. A number of structures serve as partitions between the outer and inner courts, and 3 gates identical to those already mentioned are located opposite the outer gates and give access to the inner court. In this court stands a large altar of sacrifice, of which exact dimensions are given, and the temple structure itself, built on a raised platform and reached by steps in front of the vestibule. The temple consists of a (presumably towered) vestibule, the holy place, and the Most Holy Place (all having measurements approximately like those given for Solomon's Temple), surrounded by side chambers in 3 stories on the north, west, and south sides of the building. In front of the temple are 2 freestanding pillars. For all further details see fig. 484, also the descriptions of the attempts at reconstructing the plan of Ezekiel's temple, and differing interpretations of his description in Bible commentaries, especially *SDACom* 4:712-726.

III. The Temple of Zerubbabel. The postexilic Temple at Jerusalem was built with the permission of Cyrus. According to the royal grant it was to have a breadth of 60 cu. and a height of 60 cu., but its length is not mentioned in the preserved document (Ezr 6:3). The building was begun in the 2d year after the return of the exiles from Babylon, but the builders encountered so much opposition from enemies in their homeland that the work soon came to a virtual stop and remained interrupted until the reign of Darius I. In the 2d year of his reign the prophets Haggai and Zechariah encouraged Zerubbabel, the governor, and Joshua, the high priest, to make another effort to rebuild the Temple. They responded, and with the enthusiastic support of the whole nation and the good will of the Persian officials and of the king himself, the new Temple, usually referred to as the Second Temple, was finished, along with its auxiliary structures, in a period of about 4½ years, from 520 to 515 B.C. (Ezr 3:8 to 4:5; 4:24 to 6:15). See Map XVII, I.

The dimensions of this Temple are unknown, although it is reasonable to assume that the general outline of Solomon's Temple was followed. The buildings were less lavishly decorated, and those who had seen the old Temple wept in sorrow over the simpler layout when no more was seen than the foundation stones (Ezr 3:12; cf. Hag 2:3). The fact that it took the Jews about 2 years less time to build the new Temple was due not only to its poorer construction but also to the existence of the old Solomonic platform (see above), large parts of which could probably be utilized after some repair work. Since the building of such a platform must have consumed much time, effort, and money, a rebuilding of the superstructures on the same site could certainly profit from whatever was left of the substructures of the former Temple precincts.

For the construction of the Temple cedarwood was obtained from the Lebanon Mountains (Ezr 3:7), and precious metals for decorations were provided by freewill offerings of the people and the leaders (chs 1:6; 2:68, 69). Many of the vessels of the former Temple, taken to Babylon by Nebuchadnezzar's army (ch 1:7-11), were returned by Cyrus to the Jewish officials, and were taken back to Jerusalem. The Temple building was, as before, divided into a holy place and the Holy of Holies, perhaps by a wall as before, but at least by a curtain (1 Macc 1:22). The interior walls were covered with gold.

The Most Holy Place was empty (Tacitus *Hist.* v. 9; Cicero *Pro Flacco* 28), because the ark of God and the cherubim had disappeared at the time of Nebuchadnezzar's conquest of Jerusalem in 586 B.C. The Jews have preserved a tradition that Jeremiah and some of his followers had hidden the ark in a cave (see *SDA-Com* 4:484, 485). After their return from the Exile all efforts to recover this sacred emblem were fruitless, and to the present day have been without success. In the holy place stood the golden altar of incense, one lampstand, and one table of showbread (1 Macc 1:21, 22). Various passages indicate that offices and miscellaneous storerooms were attached to the Temple building, or were situated in buildings surrounding the courts (Ezr 10:6; Neh 10:37-39; 12:44; 13:4; 1 Macc 4:38). Mention is also made of the courts of

the Temple (Neh 8:16; 13:7; Jos. *Ant.* xiv. 16. 2). In the inner court stood, as before, an altar of sacrifice (Ezr 7:17), this time built of stone and not of bronze like that in Solomon's Temple (1 Macc 4:44-47). Also in this court was a "sea," probably of bronze (Ecclus 50:3). Access to the Temple area was obtained through gates (Neh 6:10; 1 Macc 4:38) whose number and location are not known.

It appears that the religious rites of the Mosaic law were performed uninterruptedly during the Persian period and also during the 1st 150 years of the Hellenistic domination of Palestine. Alexander the Great is said to have visited the Temple (Jos. *Ant.* xi. 8. 5), as did at least 2 of the Ptolemies (Ptolemy III, Jos. *Against Apion* ii. 48; Ptolemy IV, 3 Macc 1:9, 10). Antiochus IV Epiphanes desecrated the Temple in 168 B.C. by erecting an altar dedicated to Jupiter Olympius in the Temple court and sacrificing swine on it. He stole the sacred furniture from the holy place and removed all Temple treasures (Jos. *Ant.* xii. 5. 4; 1 Macc 1:21-23). However, the Temple was repaired, refurnished, and rededicated in 165 B.C., after the Maccabean forces took Jerusalem (1 Macc 4:43-59). The Feast of Dedication (Jn 10:22) originated at that time. When Pompey conquered Jerusalem in 63 B.C. the Temple was spared any damage (Jos. *Ant.* xiv. 4. 4), but it was later pillaged by Crassus (*ibid.* 7. 1). It may have suffered some further damage in the conquest of Jerusalem by Herod in 37 B.C. (*ibid.* 16. 2, 3). By this time the Temple, being now about 500 years old, needed a thorough overhauling or rebuilding, and Herod decided to build a new Temple which would exceed in splendor and beauty every other structure in the country (see Mt 24:1; cf. Lk 21:5).

IV. The Temple of Herod. When Herod announced his intention of building a new Temple, the Jews feared he would tear down the old one and then fail to rebuild it. Consequently, Herod devised a method of reconstruction by which the old was demolished only as the new construction progressed; it appeared at the different stages as if he were doing nothing but repairing the older structures, while in reality a completely new complex of buildings was erected without interrupting the services. He first rebuilt the Temple proper. This work was begun in 20/19 B.C. and lasted 18 months. He had all building material finished to size before it was brought to the Temple area, and employed only priests to work on the inner Temple structure. After that was finished, most of the outer buildings, including the cloisters, were completed during the next 8 years, but the work of decoration and embellishment went on until the procuratorship of Albinus (c. A.D. 62-64), immediately before the outbreak of the Jewish war (Jos. *Ant.* xv. 11; *War* v. 5). Since building activities were still going on during Christ's ministry, it is understandable that the Jews said the Temple had been in building for 46 years (Jn 2:20). It was this Temple of Herod in which Jesus was dedicated as an infant, in whose halls He met the teachers of the Law as a boy of 12 years, and from whose outer court He drove away the money-changers. Its halls saw Him, and later His apostles, teach and preach, and at one of its beautifully decorated gates Peter and John healed a crippled man. The whole Temple with all its buildings was destroyed by fire during the capture of Jerusalem by the forces of Titus in A.D. 70. Although strict orders had been given to spare it, a soldier threw a torch in the sanctuary and set it on fire. Thus was destroyed one of the most beautiful buildings of its time (Jos. *War* vi. 4).

Although the Temple built by Herod the Great was actually a new structure, the Jews always referred to it as still the Second Temple, considering his work no more than a repair and remodeling. Because of the Jews' hatred for him, the orthodox Jewish writings, like the Mishnah, which gives detailed descriptions of this Temple, never mention the name of its builder. From the descriptions of Josephus (*Ant.* xv. 11; *War* v. 5) and of the Mishnah (*Middoth*), and from the archeological evidence of the present site, a fairly good idea of the Temple precinct of Herod can be obtained. The following description is based on these sources (see figs. 485, 486).

The old Temple area was enlarged to twice its former size, including also the palace grounds of Solomon's time. Archeological investigations show that the present Moslem enclosure, the *Ḥaram esh-Sheriƒ*, almost exactly covers Herod's Temple area, and large parts of the present walls rest on foundations or wall stumps of Herod's time (Map XVIII; see fig. 485). This outer wall surrounded the Court of the Gentiles, to which everyone had access. Covered colonnades, usually called porches (porticoes, cloisters), ran

around the inner portion of the enclosure wall. They were constructed after the pattern of the Greek *stoae,* colonnaded halls that flanked the agora (market place) of every Greek city (fig. 41). The southern portico, called the Royal Porch, had 162 gigantic columns arranged in 4 rows, thus forming 3 corridors—the middle one being higher and wider than those on each side. All other porticoes surrounding the outer court had 3 rows of columns. The southern portion of the eastern portico was called Solomon's Porch (Jn 10:23; Acts 3:11; 5:12).

Eight gates gave access to this outer court. One, the Shushan Gate, lay on the east side, at the site of the present Golden Gate (P in fig. 485), and one in the north (O in fig. 485). The 2 southern gates, called Huldah gates, gave access to the Temple court from the lower part of the city through stairways that ended inside. All other porticoes surrounding the gates, still visible in the preserved wall portions, show that one had 2 doors and the other 3 doors (I^2 and I^3 in fig. 485). The western wall was broken by 4 gates, of which the southernmost (K in fig. 485) was a small portal reached through stairways from the bottom of the Tyropoeon Valley, which flanked the western wall. Another gate (L in fig. 485) was reached via a bridge that spanned the valley. A portion of this bridge is still preserved, now known as Wilson's Arch, although the whole valley has been filled up with debris. Not much is known about the 2 other western gates (M and N in fig. 485). A bridge which in ancient times crossed the Tyropoeon Valley at the southwestern corner of the outer wall (remains are now known as Robinson's Arch, T in fig. 485), also seems to have provided an entrance to the Temple precinct, but this entrance is not attested in the ancient literature. At the northwestern corner (H in fig. 485) were stairways which led up to the Castle, or Barracks, of Antonia, which was located on a rock platform higher than the Temple court. It had been built by John Hyrcanus at the site of the old citadel, called *birah* by Nehemiah (ch 2:8). Herod had enlarged it and transformed it into a fortified palace (*see* Barracks).

In the center of the whole enclosure was the sacred precinct, on a higher level than the large outer court, reached from the north, east, and south sides by flights of 14 steps each. Outside this terrace was a wall, 3 cu. high, surmounted by pillars, with entrances to the sacred enclosure at

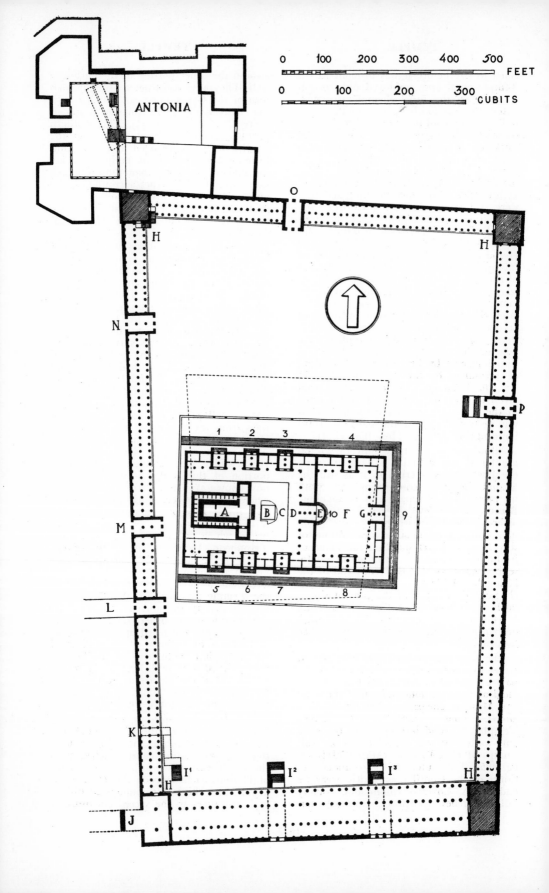

ANTONIA

FEET

CUBITS

O

H H

N

P

M

L

1 2 3 4

A B C D E 10 F G 9

5 6 7 8

K

I¹ I² I³ H

H

J

9 places exactly in front of the 9 gates of the inner wall (1-9 in fig. 485). Warning tablets inscribed in Greek and Latin contained the following text: "No stranger (=non-Jew) is to enter within the balustrade and enclosure around the Temple. Whoever is caught will be responsible to himself for his death, which will ensue." One such tablet with a complete Greek inscription was found by Charles Clermont-Ganneau in 1871; it is now in a museum at Istanbul (fig. 487). Part of a 2d one, discovered in street-building operations at Jerusalem in 1935, is now in the Jerusalem Archaeological Museum (*QDAP* 6 [1936], 1-3). The apostle Paul was accused of having brought a Gentile within this wall, and thus of having transgressed this ordinance, when he was arrested in the Temple (Acts 21:28, 29).

Upon the terrace stood the inner wall, 25 cu. high, which separated the inner courts from the outer one, and also the sanctuary proper from the world. Access to the inner courts was obtained through 9 gates, of which one was in the east and 4 each on the north and south sides (1-9 in fig. 485). Against the inner side of this wall were built storage chambers and offices opening onto colonnades. The eastern portion, or about one third of the whole sacred area, was separated from the rest by a wall. It was the Court of the Women (F in fig. 485), so called because Jewish women and children had access to this court. The "treasury," a place mentioned as the scene of Christ's teaching in the Temple (Jn 8:20), lay within the Court of the Women. The name is applicable either to the colonnade around the court, in which were located the contribution boxes, called "trumpets" because of their shape, or to those rooms in which gifts and offerings were deposited. One large gate lay between this Court of the Women and the next one, which lay on a higher level. Fifteen steps, semicircular in form, led to this great gate, which was 40 cu. wide and 50 cu. high (E in fig. 485). It is not certain whether this gate or the one that led into the Court of the Women from the outer

court was the Beautiful Gate (Acts 3:2), where Peter healed a crippled beggar (*see* Beautiful Gate).

The western portion of the sacred enclosure contained the Court of the Priests (C in fig. 485), next to the Temple building. Around it on 3 sides was the Court of Israel, also called Court of Man (D in fig. 485), to which all Jewish men had access. The 2 courts were separated from each other by a wall about 1 cu. high. Within the Court of Israel was a series of storage chambers, and also the hall in which the Sanhedrin, or Supreme Court (see Acts 5:21), had its sittings.

The Court of the Priests (C in fig. 485) contained the altar of sacrifice and the "sea" of bronze. Only priests were allowed to enter this court, except that Jews were permitted to enter and come before the altar for the presentation of their offerings. The altar of unhewn stone was, according to the Mishnah, 15 cu. high and 32 cu. square at its base, with a ramp leading up. However, these measures can hardly be correct. It is generally believed that this altar of sacrifice stood at the spot now covered by the Moslem Dome of the Rock, often erroneously called the Mosque of Omar (see figs. 259, 260, 262, 342, 479). Underneath this rock is a cave to which access can be gained by means of a stairway. There was a hole through which the priests could drop into the cave the discarded parts of the sacrificial victims, as well as the ashes and bones, which could then be removed from the cave during the night, so that the worshipers in the Temple area would not be offended by the odor of this waste material (see fig. 479).

Twelve steps led up from the Court of the Priests to the vestibule of the Temple building. This vestibule was 100 cu. high, 100 cu. broad, and 20 cu. deep, containing spiral staircases in its side wings. The monumental portal was 70 cu. high and 25 cu. wide, without doors, so that the great doorway to the sanctuary itself was visible from the outside. This doorway contained 2 golden doors, 55 cu. high and 16 cu. wide, opening into the holy place (A in fig. 485), which was the same size (40 x 20 cu.) as that of Solomon's Temple, except that it was 60 cu. high (instead of 30). It contained the usual equipment: a golden altar of incense, a table of showbread, and a lampstand. The Most Holy Place, which was empty, was separated from the larger room (according to the Mishnah *Yoma* 5. 1)

---

485. Plan of Herod's Temple and its enclosure, with the Castle of Antonia in the upper left corner (according to L.-Hugues Vincent and A.-M. Steve). Explanation of letters and figures is found in the text; *see* Temple, IV

486. Schick's model of Herod's Temple at Jerusalem, showing the Tower of Antonia (upper left corner)

by two parallel curtains. The rending of this partition at the death of Christ (Mt 27: 51; Heb 6:19; 10:20) gave proof that the shadow service of the sacrificial system had come to an end.

Attached to the north, west, and south

487. A Greek inscription, from Herod's Temple balustrade, forbidding Gentiles to enter the sacred area of the Temple

sides of the Temple building were side chambers in 3 stories, like those in Solomon's Temple.

Temple Keeper. A rendering of the Gr. *neōkoros* (Acts 19:35, RSV), "temple keeper," "temple guardian" (KJV "worshipper"). The passage designates Ephesus as the guardian of the temple of *Artemis, or Diana. The term occurs in a Greek inscription discovered at Priene in a sense similar to that of the NT by calling a certain "Megabyzos the *neōkoros* of the Artemis which is in Ephesus."

Temple Servants. *See* Nethinims.

Temptation. [Heb. *massah,* "proving," "trial," "test"; Gr. generally *peirasmos,* "test," "trial," "temptation," "enticement."] The terms thus translated generally describe any situation that confronts a person with a test of character. In Deut 4:34; 7:19; 29:3, *massah* is used of testing with a view to strengthening character. In Lk 4:13 the devil tempts, or tests, Christ with the intention of breaking His will to obey God. Elsewhere in the NT, generally speaking, "temptation" refers to any trying experience that might conceivably weaken a person's hold on God but which, patiently endured, strengthens faith and character. Thus the Christian is to "count it all joy" when he falls "into divers temptations" (Jas 1:2), that is, when he encounters difficulties that test the reality of his Christian experience. The RSV frequently translates *peirasmos,* "trials," and in Heb 3:8, "testing." In Ps 95:8 the RSV transliterates *massah* as a proper name, Massah.

The site of Jesus' temptation in the wilderness (Mt 4:1; Lk 4:1), and of the mountain to the top of which the devil took Jesus (Mt 4:8) has not been revealed. Fig. 488 shows one of the conjectured spots.

488. The so-called mount of temptation in the Wilderness of Judah near Jericho

Ten. [Heb. *'eśer, 'aśarah;* Aramaic *'aśar* and *'aśrah;* Gr. *deka.*] A significant number that recurs frequently throughout the Bible. There were 10 patriarchs before the Flood (Gen 5), and 10 after the Flood, down to and including Abraham (ch 11:10-26). For the sake of 10 righteous persons the Lord would have spared Sodom (ch 18:32). There were 10 plagues on the land of Egypt (Ex 7:17; 8:2, 16, 21; 9:3, 9, 18; 10:4, 21; 11:5). There were 10 commandments (ch 20:2-17). The number 10 occurs frequently in the parables of our Lord, there being 10 virgins (Mt 25:1), 10 pieces of silver (Lk 15:8), and 10 servants entrusted with 10 pounds (ch 19:13), the most able of whom was appointed over 10 cities (v 17). In symbolic vision there were 10 days of tribulation predicted for the Smyrna church (Rev 2:10), 10 horns upon the beasts of Dan 7:7; Rev 13:1; 17:3, and upon the dragon of Rev 12:3. Ten also seems to be used as a round number, meaning "many times" (Gen 31:7; Neh 4:12; Dan 1:20; etc.). The *tithe was one tenth of the income.

Ten Commandments. The law recorded in Ex 20:2-17, also called the Decalogue, which sums up what God requires of man, and defines his duty toward God and toward his fellow men (cf. Mt 22:34-40). The principles enunciated by the Ten Commandments are eternal, for they are based upon the character of God, but the form in which these principles were uttered at Sinai was adapted to the understanding and instruction of men in their state of sinfulness and natural nonconformity to the divine will. The 10 commands of the Decalogue have the unique distinction of being the only words addressed audibly by God to the entire congregation of Israel (see Ex 20:1, 18, 19; Deut 4:10-13; 5:22). All of the other laws and regulations God ordained at that time were communicated through Moses as an intermediary (see Ex 20:19-22; Deut 4:14; 6:1). Subsequent to the oral delivery of the law God inscribed these 10 commands upon 2 tables of stone which He gave to Moses to be preserved in the ark (Ex 31:18; 32:19; 34:1-4; Deut 5:22; 10:1-5). Moses' original account of the law as proclaimed by God, and later engraved upon the tables of stone, gives the Decalogue in the wording of Ex 20:1-17. Later Moses repeated the law in oral form with slight variations in wording (Deut 5:6-21). The only noteworthy difference in this repetition of the law is the reason assigned for the observance of the 7th-day Sabbath—deliverance from Egyptian bondage, in place of the creation of the world in 6 days, as in the original form. The many civil regulations enacted at Mount Sinai were an application of the principles of the 2d table of the Decalogue to the society and needs of the Jewish people. The ceremonial law, which sets forth a divinely ordained system of worship appropriate to the period of earth's history when that law was given, was an extension and development of the principles enunciated in the Decalogue particularly with respect to man's relationship to his God.

In the time of Christ the Jews arranged and numbered the 10 commands of the Decalogue as most Protestants do today (see Jos. *Ant.* iii. 5. 5). The arrangement and enumeration followed by the Roman Catholic Church, dividing the 10th, on covetousness, is that adopted by St. Augustine, who preferred, of the two then-existing methods, the one combining the 1st and 2d commands and dividing the 10th. He thus assigned 3 commands to the 1st table of the Decalogue, and 7 to the 2d. One of his reasons for adopting this arrangement was to have the symbolic numbers 3, 7, and 10 in the Decalogue.

The 1st command enjoins monotheism, or the exclusive worship of the one true God, *Yahweh, in contrast with polytheism, or the worship of many gods. The 2d command forbids idolatry of all kinds, that is, attempts to worship the invisible God through visible forms (cf. Hos 8:6; Col 1:15-17). The 3d command forbids

489. The Nash Papyrus of about 100 B.C., containing the Ten Commandments

all irreverence, especially the needless mention of God's name in ordinary conversation, and perjury accompanied by an invocation of the divine name. The 4th command enjoins the observance of the Sabbath and identifies the true God as Creator of heaven and earth. By keeping the Sabbath men were to remember Him as such, and they would thus be protected against all false worship. The 5th command enjoins respect and submission to parents as God's appointed agents for the transmission of His revealed will to succeeding generations (see Deut 4:9; 6: 7). The 6th command protects life as sacred. The 7th command enjoins purity and thus safeguards the marital relationship in order that the home may realize its divinely appointed objectives. The 8th command safeguards property. The 9th command safeguards truth and protects against perjury. The 10th command goes to the root of all human relationships by

providing that man shall not covet that which belongs to another, much less deprive him of it by force.

A fragmentary papyrus sheet, the famed Nash Papyrus, contains the Decalogue in the form presented in Deut 5, together with the "Shema," a quotation of Deut 6:1. This famous Hebrew document, originating in the 1st cent B.C., is now in Cambridge, England. Up to the discovery of the Dead Sea scrolls it was the earliest Hebrew document containing any part of the Bible (fig. 489).

Tender Eyed. An expression appearing in Gen 29:17, KJV, describing Leah's eyes. The Heb. *rak*, here translated "tender," is generally understood to mean "weak," "sensitive," "delicate," a meaning supported by the LXX. The condition of Leah's eyes was probably the reason that Jacob was not attracted to her.

Ten-stringed Harp. [Heb. *nebel 'aśôr.*] In 2 texts (Ps 33:2; 144:9) the Heb. *nebel*, "harp," is modified by the word *'aśôr*, "ten," and the phrase is rendered "harp of ten strings" and "ten-stringed harp" in the RSV and "instrument of ten strings" in the KJV. In Ps 92:3 *'aśôr* alone appears as the name of a musical instrument, and is rendered "lute" in the RSV and "instrument of ten strings" in the KJV. Since lutes in all pictorial representations in Egypt and Mesopotamia are shown to be so narrow that they could not accommodate more than 2 or 3 strings, it has been suggested that this instrument was rather a zither. The zither was known to the Phoenicians, the neighbors of the Israelites. Two such 10-stringed zithers are depicted in the hands of 2 women on an ivory jewel case found at *Nimrûd* (fig.

490. Syrian women of the 8th cent. B.C., playing zithers

490). Also in a strange illustrated letter attributed to Jerome, the translator of the Bible into Latin, a 10-stringed Phoenician zither is depicted under the title *psalterium decachordum* (fig. 491), to which is given the explanation, "It has ten strings, as it is written: I shall praise you on the ten-stringed psaltery" (Curt Sachs, *The History of Musical Instruments* [New York, 1940], p. 118).

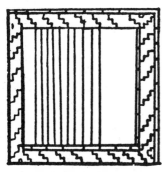

491. Phoenician ten-stringed zither, according to Jerome

Tent. [Heb. *'ohel;* Ugaritic *'hl;* Gr. *skēnē.*] Tents were used by the patriarchs during their sojourn in Palestine (Gen 12:8) and by the Israelites during their wandering in the wilderness and during their early history in Canaan (Ex 16:16; Jos 7:21-24). Their tents were either round, having one central pole, or flat and oblong with several poles. The covering (Heb. *yeri'ah*) was usually made of cloth woven of black goat's hair (Song 1:5), such as the Bedouins still use in Palestine, but may also have been made of animal hides, as were the coverings of the tabernacle (Ex 26:14). The tent coverings had wooden rings sewn on them, to which tent cords (Heb. *mêth- arîm*) were connected. These cords were then tightly drawn around tent pins (Heb. *yethedoth*) driven into the ground (Is 54:2). See figs. 20, 492.

Tent of Meeting. *See* Tabernacle.

Tent of the Testimony. *See* Tabernacle.

Tenth. *See* Tithe.

Tentmaker. [Gr. *skēnopoios.*] One who fabricated tents of skin or cloth of goat's hair (Acts 18:3). The art of tentmaking was practiced from earliest times (cf. Gen 4:20; 12:8; 25:27; etc.). Aquila, Priscilla, and Paul were tentmakers (Acts 18:1-3). Both the city of Tarsus, Paul's home town, and the province of Pontus, from which Aquila came, were noted for their good-quality goat's-hair fabrics, which were much in demand for tents and sails. *See* Tent.

Terah (tē'rá), KJV twice **Tarah** (tā'rá), KJV of NT **Thara** (thā'rá). [Heb. *Terach,* probably "ibex" as the Akkadian *turâḫu;* Gr. *Thara.*]

1. The father of Abraham, Nahor, and Haran. After having lived some time in Ur of the Chaldees, he migrated with his family to Haran, where he died at the age of 205 years (Gen 11:24-32; 1 Chr 1:26; Lk 3:34). He had served other gods than Yahweh (Jos 24:2), probably the moon-god, since both Ur and Haran were centers of moon worship. The ancient city *Til-sha-Turâḫi,* located in the neighborhood of Haran, may have been named after him.

2. A wilderness camping place of the Israelites (Num 33:27, 28); not identified.

Teraphim. [Heb. *teraphîm,* literally "the perishing ones," or "the decaying ones."] A contemptuous designation for idols or images of divine beings. The Hebrew term is used in a collective sense and can stand for a single object or for several. In the KJV *teraphîm* is rendered "idol," "image," or "idolatry," or is transliterated. In the RSV it is translated "idolatry" (1 Sa 15:23), "household gods" (Gen 31:19, 34, 35), and "image" (1 Sa 19:13, 16), and transliterated "teraphim" (Jgs 17:5; 18:14, 17, 18, 20; 2 Ki 23:24; Eze 21:21; Hos 3:4; Zec 10:2). The context of the various passages shows that the word usually designates images of various sizes, representing heathen gods. The teraphim ("household gods," RSV) that Rachel stole from her father and hid under her camel's saddle (Gen 31:34, 35) were evidently small figurines, such as have turned up in great number in excavations of practically every ancient site of the Near East. The most numerous of the excavated little figurines are nude goddesses (fig. 493), many of them grossly accentuating the sex fea-

492. Bedouin tent of goat's-hair cloth in Palestine

tures. It is generally believed that they were thought to promote fertility; most heathen women may have worn them on their bodies as amulets or fertility charms. Some teraphim must have been much

493. A household goddess (mother goddess) from Megiddo

larger than figurines, as is evident from the fact that Michal, David's first wife, had one in her home large enough to represent her husband (1 Sa 19:13). Such large teraphim have not yet been discovered in the excavations of Palestine. According to Eze 21:21, teraphim were consulted to learn what course of action one should take, although Zec 10:2 declares that their counsel amounts to nonsense. Documents found at Nuzi, in Mesopotamia, indicate that in the patriarchal age the possession of the family's household gods, such as Laban had, guaranteed to

their holder the title to his father's properties (*ANET* 219, 220). This was probably the chief reason why Laban was so anxious to retrieve them after they had been lost (Gen 31:30, 33-35). The Mesopotamian laws decreed capital punishment for the theft of divine property (Code of Hammurabi, sec. 6; *ANET* 166), and the validity of this law was recognized by Jacob in his declaration that whoever had Laban's gods should die (ch 31:32). He seems to have learned later that these and other gods were in the possession of his wives, hence demanded their surrender and buried them (ch 35:2-4). During the period of the judges Micah set up teraphim and other idols in his house and arranged for their worship (Jgs 17:4, 5). These cult objects, later carried to Dan, probably formed the nucleus of the idolatrous worship that existed there for centuries (ch 18: 14, 30, 31). Samuel declared Saul's sin of stubbornness to be as idolatry (Heb. *teraphîm;* 1 Sa 15:23). Hosea denounced the use of teraphim in the northern kingdom of Israel (Hos 3:4). Josiah destroyed them wherever he could find them in his work of reformation (2 Ki 23:24), but Zec 10:2 suggests that some were possibly found among the Jews as late as the postexilic period.

Terebinth. A term appearing twice (Is 6:13; Hos 4:13; RSV), a rendering of the Heb. *'elah,* a large tree, but the species is not indicated. The terebinth is a common and venerated tree of stately lines and proportions (*Pistacia terebinthus* var. *palaestina*).

Teresh (tē'rĕsh). [Heb. *Teresh,* a Persian name of uncertain meaning.] One of the 2 eunuchs whose plan to assassinate King Ahasuerus was frustrated by Mordecai. For their plot on the king's life Teresh and his accomplice were executed (Est 2: 21-23; 6:2).

Tertius (tûr'shĭ-ŭs). [Gr. *Tertios,* from Latin *tertius,* "third."] The scribe who wrote Paul's letter to the Romans, and included his own greetings to the church in Rome (Rom 16:22).

Tertullus (tēr-tŭl'ŭs). [Gr. *Tertullos,* from Latin *Tertullus,* diminutive of *Tertius.* The name occurs frequently in Greek and ·Latin inscriptions.] A professional advocate employed by the Jewish authorities of Jerusalem to plead their case against Paul at the court of the procurator Felix at Caesarea (Acts 24:1-8). Since the name is very common, Tertullus' nationality cannot be ascertained. His rhetoric shows that he was a professional.

Testament. A KJV term, a rendering of the Gr. *diathēkē*, "last will and testament," "compact," "covenant," "contract." In Heb 9:16, 17 *diathēkē* clearly means "last will and testament" (RSV "will"), but elsewhere in the NT it is equivalent to "covenant," in the sense of an agreement between 2 parties; or to be more exact, in the sense of a compact between a superior (God) and an inferior (man), in which the former stipulates the conditions and the latter promises compliance. *See* Covenant. The terms "old testament" and "new testament" mean specifically "old covenant" and "new covenant," that is, the divine provision for man's salvation in OT and NT times (see Heb 8:6-10, 13). For the use of these terms to apply to the two parts of the Bible, *see* New Testament; Old Testament.

Teth. [Heb. *têth*.] The 9th letter of the Hebrew alphabet, written ﬞ, appearing as the title of the 9th section of Ps 119 in the KJV. *See* Aleph.

Tetrarch. [Gr. *tetraarchēs*, "ruler over a fourth part."] Originally the administrator of a 4th part of a certain territory. The term was introduced by Philip of Macedonia in Thessaly in the 4th cent. B.C. Later it became the title for a petty prince of a small territory. It was used in this way by the Romans, who granted it to native princes in Asia Minor and Syria whose territories were not large enough to be called kingdoms. The NT mentions 3 rulers with this title: Herod (Antipas) (Mt 14:1; Lk 3:1, 19; Acts 13:1), Philip, and Lysanias (Lk 3:1).

Tetter. A term appearing once (Lev 13:39, RSV), a rendering of the Heb. *bohaq*, "a harmless eruption of the skin." In appearance the tetter was somewhat similar to a spot of leprosy, but could be distinguished. The KJV translates *bohaq*, "freckled spot."

Thaddaeus. *See* Judas, 5.

Thahash. *See* Tahash.

Thamah. *See* Temah.

Thamar. *See* Tamar.

Thank Offering. *See* Sacrifices and Offerings.

Thara. *See* Terah, 1.

Tharshish. *See* Tarshish.

Theater, KJV **Theatre.** [Gr. *theatron*, related to the verb *theaomai*, "to behold."] This term appears only with reference to the theater at Ephesus (Acts 19:29, 31), for a description of which *see* Ephesus. Paul employs the Greek term in a meta-

494. The great ancient theater at Pergamum

phorical sense in 1 Cor 4:9, where he speaks of the apostles as being a "spectacle [*theatron*] to the world." See figs. 159, 288, 494.

Theatre. *See* Theater.

Thebes (thēbz), KJV **No** (nō). [Heb. *No'* from the Egyptian *Nîwt* (*'Imn*), "the city (of Amon)."] The famous Upper Egyptian capital of Egypt (Map XI, D-3). The Egyptians referred to it simply by the name "city," as the Romans frequently called Rome merely *urbs*, "the city." The Greeks named the city Thebes after a city of the same name in central Greece. Although Thebes was not always the royal residence, it was the official capital of Egypt during the New Kingdom for several centuries. It was probably the largest city of antiquity, exceeding in size famous metropolises such as Nineveh and Babylon. Homer speaks of it as the city of a hundred gates (*Iliad* ix. 381). When it became the capital of an empire in the 16th cent. B.C., its local ram-headed god, *Amon, became the chief god of Egypt, and the high priest of Amon became so powerful that he was 2d only to the king. Generations of kings built on the Amon temple there (now known as the temple of Karnak) until it became the largest temple ever known, covering many acres of ground. Even in its destroyed state it is still impressive. When the "Ethiopian" kings conquered Egypt in the 8th cent. B.C. Thebes did not suffer, since these Nubian rulers, who were also worshipers of Amon, retained Thebes as capital. But the city was destroyed in the 2d Assyrian invasion of Egypt by Ashurbanipal in 663 B.C. The Hebrew prophet Nahum declared shortly afterward that this destruction of Thebes was a type of the destruction Nineveh would suffer (Nah 3:8). Yet, Thebes recovered from this catastro-

495. A Ptolemaic gate, with the temple of Khonsu in the background, at Karnak, a portion of ancient Thebes

phe to a certain degree and again became a city of some importance, until finally it was completely destroyed by the Roman prefect, Cornelius Gallus, for its participation in a revolt against oppressive taxation in 30/29 B.C. Besides Nahum, the prophets Jeremiah (ch 46:25) and Ezekiel (ch 30:14, 15) mention this city.

The ruins of Thebes are located on both sides of the Nile. At the sites of the modern villages of Karnak and Luxor stand the magnificent remains of the great Amon temple with its subsidiary temples dedicated to Mut and Khonsu, and of a temple by Ramses II. In western Thebes are, among other ruins, those of the mortuary temple of Queen Hatshepsut at *Deir el-Baḥri*, of Ramses II (the Ramesseum), and of Ramses III at *Medinet Habu*, the best-preserved temple of pre-Hellenistic Egypt. West of these temples are the Valleys of the Tombs of the Kings and Queens in which numerous rock-cut tombs are found, the burial places of the illustrious monarchs of the empire period. See figs. 146-148, 168, 495.

Thebez (thē′bĕz). [Heb. *Tebeṣ*, meaning uncertain.] A city near Shechem, which Abimelech captured, but its fortress within the city held out, and Abimelech lost his life while besieging it, felled by a stone that a woman hurled down from a parapet (Jgs 9:50-55; 2 Sa 11:21). It has been identified with the large village of *Ṭūbâṣ*, about 10 mi. northeast of Shechem (Map VI, D-3).

Theft. See Robber.

Thelasar. See Tel-assar.

Theophilus (thē-ŏf′ĭ-lŭs). [Gr. *Theophilos,* "loved by God," or "friend of God," a name attested as borne by Gentiles and Jews.] A nobleman, possibly some high official, to whom Luke addressed his Gospel and the book of Acts (Lk 1:1-4; Acts 1:1). It is unknown whether Theophilus was a Christian at that time or was merely interested in Christianity. According to early Christian tradition he was from Antioch in Syria.

Thessalonians, Epistles to. Two letters by the apostle Paul addressed to Christian believers at Thessalonica, in Macedonia; probably the earliest of Paul's preserved epistles. In the earliest Greek manuscripts these 2 epistles bear the simple titles *Pros Thessalonikeis A,* "To [the] Thessalonians I," and *Pros Thessalonikeis B,* "To [the] Thessalonians II." No serious challenge has arisen with respect to the fact of the Pauline authorship of the epistles. The famous Muratorian Canon (*c.* A.D. 170) includes 1 and 2 Th among Paul's letters. Early church writers who discuss the matter, such as Irenaeus, Clement of Alexandria, and Tertullian—all of whom lived at the close of the 2d cent. and in the first part of the 3d—attributed them to Paul. The style of both epistles is wholly in keeping with what is known about him from his other epistles and from the record in Acts, and modern scholars are in general agreement that he was their author. About A.D. 150 Polycarp and Justin Martyr both seem to make reference to passages found in the epistles.

The apostle Paul first proclaimed the gospel at *Thessalonica during the course of his 2d Missionary Journey, probably late in A.D. 50 or early the following year (*see* Chronology, IX, 7). On 3 successive Sabbaths Paul preached in the synagogue from the OT Scriptures, proving Jesus Christ to be the Messiah for whom the Jewish people had been looking (Acts 17: 2, 3). Some Jews and a large number of Greek proselytes accepted Paul's message (v 4), and these believers he organized into a church. The church there seems to have been largely Gentile in composition (see 1 Th 1:9; cf. 4:5). Furious at his success, doubtless, especially in making Gentile converts (see 1 Th 2:16), the unbelieving Jews raised a riot against him, charging him with sedition and compelling him to leave the city (Acts 17:5-10). Going on to Beroea, Paul was pursued by the unbelieving Jews of Thessalonica (vs 10, 13); he was forced to depart from that city also, but he left Silas and Timothy there (v 14). He went on to Athens, but had no sooner arrived than he sent for Silas and Timothy to join him there (v 15). From 1 Th 3:1, 2 it appears that he sent Timothy back from Athens to Thessalonica to give further instruction to the believers there; when Silas and Timothy rejoined Paul he had already gone on to Corinth (Acts 18:1, 5; cf. 1 Th 3:1-6). Soon after Timothy's return from Thessalonica to Corinth Paul wrote the 1st of the Thessalonian letters (1 Th 1:1; 2:17; 3:6-10). Paul earnestly longed to return to Thessalonica himself, but was hindered by Satan (ch 2:17, 18). When the bearer of the 1st epistle returned from Thessalonica and Paul learned that certain of his statements relative to the imminence of the 2d Advent were being misunderstood and misapplied by some in the church, he addressed the 2d epistle to them, clarifying these and other points of doctrine. The 2d epistle was written

probably a few months after the first, while Paul was still busily engaged in establishing the Corinthian church.

The earnestness and zeal with which the Thessalonian believers had adopted the Christian faith is reflected in Paul's gracious words of commendation to them in 1 Th 1:1-4. He treasures the memory of their strong faith and their zealous labors of love, which testified to their patient hope in Christ. With ardent love the apostle cherished the new converts as a nurse does the children under her care, and was "affectionately desirous" of them (ch 2:7, 8). He had, indeed, imparted to them his own soul (v 8), laboring night and day on their behalf (v 9). The bonds of affection that bound him to the Thessalonian believers were deep and enduring. He repeatedly mentions the persecution they endured, particularly at the hands of unbelieving Jews (see 1 Th 1:6; 2:14·16; cf. Acts 17:5, 6).

There were, nevertheless, certain tendencies among the believers at Thessalonica that called for reproof and further instruction with respect both to certain points of doctrine and to practical Christian living. For example, some were neglecting their daily work and depending upon others for support, apparently misled

496. The walls of Thessalonike, ancient Thessalonica

by a fanatical anticipation of the near coming of Christ. Paul commanded such to earn their livelihood with their own hands (1 Th 4:11, 12; cf. 2 Th 3:11, 12). Either there was some laxness in morals (1 Th 4:3-5) and carelessness in business dealings (vs 6-9), or else Paul, mindful of their heathen background, warned them against lowering their new standards. The apostle's hasty departure from Thessalonica had evidently interrupted his instruction of them; certainly they had erroneous ideas regarding the return of Christ and the resurrection; some were now grieving over loved ones whom they had laid to rest since Paul's departure who had apparently expected to live until the coming of Jesus (v 13). This afforded him an opportunity to write what has proved to be one of the two most glorious NT passages that breathe joyous assurance in the resurrection (1 Th 4:14-18; cf. 1 Cor 15).

In his 2d letter to Thessalonica the apostle continues his instruction about the day of judgment (2 Th 1:5-10). On the basis of something Paul had told them either while still in Thessalonica or in his 1st epistle, or from statements in some of the spurious epistles, the believers there had concluded that the day of Christ was even then at hand (ch 2:2). In order to clear up this misconception Paul enters upon a somewhat extended discourse concerning the great apostasy that is to precede Christ's return (vs 3-11). He repeats his former counsel to those who were living in idleness (ch 3:6-12). The stubbornness of some members of this group is reflected in v 14. If they persist in their obdurate course the rest of the believers are to have nothing to do with them. Such misguided ones, however, are not to be treated as enemies but to be warned as brothers (v 15).

The two Thessalonian letters may be summarized as follows: After a brief salutation (1 Th 1:1), Paul reviews his ministry to the Thessalonians and his relations with them in times past (chs 1:2 to 3:13). He greatly appreciates their fellowship in the gospel (ch 1:2-10), looks back with joy upon his ministry among them (ch 2:1-16) and regrets that he has had no further opportunity to visit them (vs 17-20). Instead he has sent Timothy in his place, and explains the purpose and the result of Timothy's visit (ch 3:1-13). The remainder of the epistle (chs 4:1 to 5:28) consists of instructions and exhortations on sanctification and on broth-erly love (ch 4:1-10), on diligence in self-support (vs 10-12), on the resurrection (vs 13-18), and on the time of Christ's coming (ch 5:1-11). The epistle closes with a series of admonitions to faithfulness and godly living (vs 12-22), with a prayer for their spiritual welfare, and with greetings (vs 23-28). In his 2d epistle, Paul commends the Thessalonians for their growth in faith and brotherly love and for their patient endurance in the midst of persecution (2 Th 1:1-4). From tribulation he turns their thoughts forward to the return of the Lord and to the glorification of Christ in His saints (vs 5-12). He goes on to instruction regarding the Antichrist, the "man of sin," whose rebellion and revelation must precede the 2d Advent, and warns against fanaticism regarding the time of Christ's coming (ch 2:1-12), in view of which he admonishes them to stand fast in the faith (vs 13-17). In ch 3 he requests their prayers, expresses confidence in them, and exhorts them to exemplary living (vs 1-15). The epistle closes with a prayer, with his personal greetings, and with a benediction (vs 16-18).

Thessalonica (thĕs'á-lō-nī'ká). [Gr. *Thessalonikē*.] A city of eastern Macedonia, the modern Thessalonike. Its original name was Thermae, "hot springs," but when Cassander, one of the successors of Alexander the Great, made it his capital in 315 B.C., he changed the name from Thermae to Thessalonica in honor of his wife, Alexander's sister. The city experienced its greatest expansion under the Romans, into whose hands it fell after the battle of Pydna in 168 B.C. When the province of Macedonia was organized in 146 B.C., Thessalonica became the provincial capital as well as the capital of the 2d district of the 4 into which the province was divided. After the battle at Philippi (42 B.C.), Thessalonica was made a free city, administered by magistrates called *politarchai*, "rulers of the city," in Acts 17:8, an expression attested also by a Greek inscription on the arch in Thessalonike (fig. 497). It was an important commercial city and military station on the *Via Egnatia* (Egnatian Way), which crossed the whole of Macedonia from west to east. Paul came to Thessalonica from Philippi during his 2d Missionary Journey. Beginning his preaching in the synagogue, he had little success among the Jewish community, but was able to found a church before persecution drove him out of this city (Acts 17:1-9). Notwithstanding

497. The Arch of Galerius in Thessalonike, ancient Thessalonica

persecutions this church, which seems to have been composed mainly of Gentile Christians (1 Th 1:9), grew into a strong Christian community (vs 4-8). Paul made a 2d visit, and possibly a 3d, to Thessalonica during his 3d Missionary Journey (Acts 20:1-6). Two of his extant letters are addressed to this church, and 2 of his travel companions, Aristarchus and Secundus, came from Thessalonica (chs 20:4; 27:2). The city has never lost its importance through the centuries, and at the present time has a population of 310,-000. Map XX, A-3.

Theudas (thū′dås). [Gr. *Theudas*, meaning uncertain, although the name is attested in Greek inscriptions.] A rebel leader referred to by Gamaliel in his speech before the Sanhedrin. He claimed "to be somebody" and found 400 followers, but he perished and his movement failed. Gamaliel also mentioned a 2d rebellion led by Judas, a Galilean in the days of "the census" (Acts 5:36, 37, RSV). The 2d event took place under Coponius' procuratorship (A.D. 6 - c. 10), as recorded by Josephus (*Ant.* xviii. 1. 1; *War* ii. 8.

1). Hence, the uprising of Theudas must have been earlier, for the rebellion of Judas occurred "after" that of Theudas (Acts 5:37).

A difficulty is presented in that Josephus (*Ant.* xx. 5. 1) relates a story about a Theudas who, in the days of the procurator Fadus (A.D. 44 - c. 46), claimed to be a prophet and led a multitude to the Jordan River, which he promised to divide. Soldiers sent against him by Fadus dispersed his followers and killed Theudas. However, Gamaliel made the speech recorded by Luke before A.D. 40. Commentators are divided in their interpretations of the difficulties involved, some asserting that Luke made an erroneous statement, others that Josephus was in error. However, Josephus is known to have erred occasionally in his historical records, whereas Luke's accuracy as a historian has been confirmed by recent archeological discoveries. It is, of course, possible that there were actually 2 rebels bearing the same name active in Judea, for Josephus speaks of several rebellions in the last years of Herod the Great and of later times without giving the name of the leaders in each instance (see *Ant.* xvii. 10. 4, 8).

Thief. [Heb. *gannab*, "thief"; Gr. *kleptēs*, "thief"; *lēstēs*, "robber," "revolutionary."] One who steals that which belongs to another; especially one who creeps up secretly to perform such an act. Under the theocracy an apprehended thief was required to replace a stolen ox fivefold and a stolen sheep fourfold if the animal had been disposed of (Ex 22:1). If the animal was retrieved, then the thief was to pay double (v 4). If not capable of making restitution he was himself to be sold into servitude until the debt was paid (v 3). No guilt was incurred if one killed a burglar in one's house at night, but there was "bloodguilt" on the householder who killed him in daylight (vs 2, 3, RSV). Judas was a thief (Jn 12:6). Christ taught that His second advent would come as stealthily to the unaware as a thief approaches a house (Lk 12:39, 40). Unregenerate thieves are among those who will not have eternal life (1 Cor 6:10). In a number of instances the KJV has rendered *lēstēs* as "thief" (Mt 21:13; 26: 55; 27:38, 44; Mk 11:17; 14:48; 15:27; Lk 10:30, 36; 19:46; 22:52). However, *lēstēs* more appropriately describes a robber, highwayman, bandit.

Thigh. [Heb. generally *yarek*, "hip," "thigh," "loin"; *shôq*, "knee," "thigh"; Aramaic *yarkah*, "hip," "thigh," "loin"; Gr. *mēros*, "thigh."] The upper leg from knee to hip. *Yarek* is also translated "loins," as in Gen 46:26; Ex 1:5; KJV; cf. Num 5:21-27, where it refers to the reproductive organs. The Heb. *shôq* is usually rendered "thigh" by the RSV and "shoulder" by the KJV (cf. Lev 7:32, 34; 10:15; etc.). The custom of placing the hand "under" the thigh of a person to whom a solemn oath was taken, as in Gen 24:2, was equivalent to a promise of loyalty to his wishes with respect to which the oath was taken—as surely as the latter lived, and in case of death, to his posterity.

Thimnathah. *See* Timnah, 1.

Thistle. *See* Thorns and Thistles.

Thomas (tŏm'ăs). [Gr. *Thōmas*, a transliteration of the Aramaic *Te'ôma'*, "twin."] One of the 12 apostles, called Didymus (Gr. *Didumos*), also meaning "twin" (Jn 11:16; 20:24; 21:2). Except for his call among the Twelve, which is recorded by Matthew (ch 10:3), Mark (ch 3:18), and Luke (ch 6:15), the only incidents in which he appears in the gospel narrative

are related by John: When Jesus, upon being summoned by Mary and Martha, proposed to return to Judea, Thomas said to his fellow disciples, "Let us also go, that we may die with him" (Jn 11:16). Twice during the weeks preceding this incident the Jews at Jerusalem had taken up stones to kill Jesus (chs 8:59; 10:31), and Thomas feared that another visit to Jerusalem could only result in death for both Jesus and His followers. On the night of the betrayal, as Jesus sought to explain His coming passion, death, resurrection, and ascension (chs 13:31 to 14: 4) Thomas protested, "Lord, we know not whither thou goest; and how can we know the way?" (ch 14:5), obviously not understanding the import of his Master's remarks. Thomas was not present when Jesus first appeared to the disciples in the upper room after the resurrection, and refused to believe the report of his fellows except he too should have the opportunity of confirming it to his own sat-

498. Globe thistle in Palestine

isfaction (Jn 20:24, 25). A week later, when Jesus again appeared, Thomas was present (v 26), and the risen Lord invited him to touch His wounded hands and side. Thomas exclaimed in reply, "My Lord and my God" (v 28), whereupon Jesus said to him: "Blessed are they that have not seen, and yet have believed" (v 29). To be sure, the unwillingness of Thomas to credit hearsay reports about the resurrection actually provides us with confirmatory evidence that it was, indeed, a historical fact. But on the other hand, Jesus gently rebuked his slowness to believe, for if belief in that great event were to be limited to eyewitnesses, none but those who saw Christ in His risen form could be expected to believe the report. Still later, Thomas was one of a group of disciples to whom Christ appeared on the shores of Galilee (Jn 21:1, 2), and he is named with the other 10 disciples in the upper room after the ascension (Acts 1:13). These incidents from the life of Thomas characterize him as one ardently devoted to his Lord (Jn 11), as slow to comprehend unfamiliar truth (ch 14)—though perhaps no slower than his fellow disciples—and as one who was slow to credit the word of others (ch 20). The latter experience has given rise to the popular expression "doubting Thomas." According to one tradition Thomas labored in Parthia and Persia and died at Edessa. According to another tradition the apostle Thomas went to India and was martyred there. This latter tradition appears in the apocryphal Acts of Thomas, a Gnostic-type work dating from the 2d cent. and of dubious value. A place near Madras, India, is called St. Thomas' Mount. An ancient Christian community in southern India known as the "Thomas Christians" traces its origin to the apostle, but whether the Thomas associated with the early days of Christianity in India was indeed the apostle or some other early Christian by the same name is not known.

For the apocryphal Gospel of Thomas see Apocryphal Books (NT), I, 5.

Thorns and **Thistles.** Many of the terms translated "thorns" or "thistles" are probably generic, referring to any one of several varieties of thistles, of which perhaps more than 100 grow in Palestine, to say nothing of numerous kinds of thorny plants, shrubs, and small trees. Palestine has been called "a land of thorns." About a dozen Hebrew and 3 Greek words are used in the Bible to designate these vari-

499. A "lily" (white anemone) among the thorns

ous plants. Although exact identification is impossible, we may assume that Bible writers referred at various times to the true star-thistle (*Centaurea calcitrapa*), dwarf centaury (*C. verutum*), Iberian centaury (*C. iberica*), and lady's-thistle (*Silybum marianum*). Among the thorn plants known to be indigenous to Palestine are the box thorn (*Lycium europaeum*), the bramble (*Rubus discolor*), and the hawthorns (*Crataegus azarolus, C. monogyna, C. orientalis*). The thorny burnet (*Poterium spinosum*), the thorny caper (*Capparis spinosa*), and the Jimson weed (*Datura stramonium*) may be included. A specific plant, the caltrop (*Tribulus terrestris*), may be intended where the Heb. *dardar* and the Gr. *tribolos* appear.

The presence of such plants and bushes may be considered a fulfillment of the curse of God after man's fall (Gen 3:18) and after Israel's persistent waywardness (Hos 2:6; 9:6). They constituted a continual fire hazard (Ex 22:6; Ps 118:12) in the field, but served as useful fuel (Ec 7:

6). Symbolically these plants represented annoyances, or infirmities (Num 33:55; Jos 23:13; 2 Cor 12:7), or spiritual obstacles (Mk 4:7; cf. v 18). The Master wore a plaited crown of thorny branches (Mt 27:29; Mk 15:17; Jn 19:2, 5), perhaps *Zizyphus spina-christi*, a species of lotus tree with soft, pliant branches, the leaves of which resembled the ivy with which victorious generals were crowned, or the *Paliurus spina-christi*, a shrub which grows up to 9 ft. tall and bears long, sharp thorns. *See* Nettle.

Three Taverns. [Gr. *Treis Tabernai*, a transliteration of the Latin name *Tres Tabernae*.] A small post station on the *Via Appia*, probably about 30 mi. southeast of Rome, north of the Forum of Appius (*Appii Forum*), apparently named from some taverns found there. It was the 2d place in Italy where Paul met brethren on his way to the capital. Christians from Rome had heard of his arrival in Italy, and had traveled to the Three Taverns to meet him and to accompany him to Rome (Acts 28:15). Map XX, A-1.

Threshing. [Heb. generally *dûsh*, "to tread on," "to thresh"; Gr. *aloaō*, "to thresh."] Threshing of the various kinds of grain was done in the "threshing season" (Heb.

dayish), which in Palestine lasts from May to early September (cf. Lev 26:5). Some commodities, such as fitch (RSV "dill") and cummin, and also small quantities of grain were beaten with a stick or flail (Is 28:27; Jgs 6:11; Ruth 2:17) to separate the grain from the husk and straw. However, most threshing was done on a threshing floor (Heb. *goren*), which belonged either to one owner (2 Sa 24:18, 24), or, more commonly, to a whole community. Such a threshing floor was usually situated outside the village on a flat piece of ground, about 50 ft. in diameter; if in uneven terrain, it was artificially built up. It was usually placed where the west wind had easy access, for a wind was needed for the *winnowing which always followed the threshing. During the threshing season owners of the grain used to sleep at the floor or in its vicinity to prevent stealing (cf. Ruth 3:2).

Threshing was performed in two ways, either by driving animals (mainly oxen) round and round on the grain to tread it (Hos 10:11; Deut 25:4), or by having them pull threshing sledges or carts over the grain. Both of these methods are still widely used in the Near East. Although pictures of the ancient threshing instru-

500. Threshing at Sarepta (Zarephath) with a threshing sledge drawn by an ox and a donkey

ments have not been preserved, there can be little doubt that they were very similar to those still in use. The OT mentions two kinds of threshing sledges, the *môrag* (2 Sa 24:22; 1 Chr 21:23; Is 41:15) and the *charûs* (Job 41:22 [v 30 in English versions]; Is 28:27; 41:15; Amos 1:3). The *môrag* is probably an instrument made of heavy planks curved upward at the front, with sharp pieces of stone or of metal attached to the bottom. The *charûs* is associated with cart wheels in Is 28:27, and it is therefore assumed that it describes the threshing cart, such as is used to the present day in Egypt and in the lowlands of Palestine. It consists of a wooden frame with 2 or 3 axles to which toothed wheels are attached. The sharp stones of the *môrag* or the wheels of the *charûs* cut into the grain as they are pulled over it, and separate the kernels from the straw. The animals that do the pulling are often led by a boy, and a man stands on the sledge and with his weight presses it down on the grain (see fig. 500). The Mosaic law forbade the muzzling of the threshing oxen, a practice greedy owners may have been guilty of (Deut 25: 4). It also prohibited the use of 2 animals of different species for work at the same plow and perhaps other agricultural instruments as well (ch 22:10), a practice still widely observed in the Near East (see fig. 500). In symbolic terms the punishment inflicted on Gilead by the invading Syrians is described as a threshing with "sledges of iron" (Amos 1:3, RSV).

Threshold. [Heb. generally *saph* and *miphtan.*] The sill of a door, consisting of a piece of timber or stone which lies under a door. Being the 1st part of a house on which someone would step upon entering, the threshold has often been considered as the symbol of the entrance itself. It is probably for this reason that the gatekeepers of the Temple and of the royal palace are frequently referred to as "keepers of the threshold" (2 Ki 22:4; cf. Est 2:21; 6:2; RSV; etc.). When the image of Dagon in the temple at Ashdod fell from its pedestal during the ark's stay there, and the idol's broken hands were found lying on the threshold of Dagon's temple, the Philistines, being superstitious avoided stepping on the threshold of that building, but from that time on stepped over it when entering the temple (1 Sa 5: 4, 5). Zephaniah may have had a similar pagan practice in mind when he condemned people who leap "over the threshold" (Zep 1:9, RSV).

Thresholds of the Gates. The KJV rendering of the Heb. *'asuppê hashshe'arîm* in Neh 12:25. Actually, storage rooms are meant, in which property of the Temple was kept, hence the RSV rendering, "storehouses of the gates." These particular rooms were situated apparently near the Temple gates, as the phrase "of the gates" indicates.

501. Throne of Tutankhamen in the Cairo Museum. It is made of wood overlaid with gold, and inlaid with gold, silver, faïence, and colored glass. In foreground is the footstool decorated with figures of captive enemies

Throne. [Heb. *kisse'*; Aramaic *korse'*, "seat," "throne"; Gr. *thronos.*] A chair occupied by one in supreme authority, most often a royal chair of state. Elaborate ornate thrones of ancient Oriental kings are depicted in Egyptian and Assyrian paintings and reliefs. A portable throne of Sennacherib appears on the Lachish reliefs (figs. 428 and 502). For a throne of Darius of Persia, see fig. 6. The tomb of Tutankhamen has provided us with actual royal thrones and footstools which are made of wood, richly ornamented and overlaid with gold (fig. 501).

The thrones mentioned in the Bible were occupied by kings and also by judges (Ex 11:5; etc.; Ps 122:5; etc.). Some were

502. Sennacherib, king of Assyria, on his throne

portable like that of Sennacherib, as were those used by Ahab and Jehoshaphat when they discussed their planned military campaign against Ramoth-gilead (1 Ki 22:10). Solomon's throne seems to have compared favorably with the most luxurious thrones of contemporary monarchs, as may be deduced from the description given of it in the Bible. It was elevated on 6 steps, with 2 lions on each step, was overlaid with gold and probably had inlays of *ivory (1 Ki 10:18-20; 2 Chr 9:17-19), hence may have been similar to the thrones of the Egyptian kings.

The throne denotes royal power, and is frequently used in that sense in the Scrip-

tures as representing (1) the royal power of an earthly monarch (2 Sa 3:10), of God (Ps 47:8), of the Messiah (Lk 1:32), and (2) the authority of Christ's disciples in judgment (Mt 19:28; cf. Rev 20:4).

Thummim. *See* Urim and Thummim.

Thunder. [Heb. generally *qôl*, "sound," "noise," "thunder," or *ra'am*, "thunder"; Gr. *brontē*, "thunder."] The noise produced by lightning. A thunderstorm with its accompanying racing black clouds, lightning, pouring rain, and sometimes hail was an exceptional event in the summer, or dry season, of Palestine (Prov 26:1; *see* Year). Hence when a thunderstorm arose at harvesttime as a result of Samuel's prayer it was recognized as an evidence of God's great displeasure (1 Sa 12:17, 18). Such incidents as this and the Lord's presence atop Mount Sinai (Ex 19:16) led Israel to associate the majesty and wrath of God with thunder (2 Sa 22:14, 15; Job 37:2-5). Because of their evil temper two of Christ's disciples, John and James, were called "sons of thunder" (Mk 3:17).

Thyatira (thī'á-tī'rá). [Gr. *Thuateira*.] A city of Lydia, on the road between Pergamum and Sardis on the Lycus River, a tributary of the Hermus. It was refounded by Seleucus I between 301 and 281 B.C. as a Macedonian military colony, but developed into an important center of trade and industry. The town gained fame from its guilds of weavers and dyers of wool and linen textiles, also for its leather works, and for being a production center of metal objects. Lydia, Paul's first convert in Philippi, was a merchant of purple (bright red, from madder-root dye)

503. Stone sarcophagus at *Akhisar,* ancient Thyatira. Greek inscription mentions Thyatira

goods from Thyatira (Acts 16:14), and probably had been a member of the dyers' guild of that city. A Christian church existed in the city before the end of the 1st cent. A.D., as is proved by the letter written by John to Thyatira from the island of Patmos (Rev 2:18-28). The modern city of *Akhisar* is built on the site of ancient Thyatira. Few remains of its ancient structures or other reminders of its history are still visible. Map XX, B-4; see fig. 503.

For the significance of Thyatira as one of the 7 churches of the Revelation, see *SDACom* 7:96, 97, 750-752.

Thyine. [Gr. *thuïnos.*] Thyine wood is often identified with a tree of the cypress family, variously called *Callitris quadrivalvis, Tetraclinis articulata,* and *Thuya articulata.* The tree seldom grows to more than 30 ft. in height and has a durable, dark-colored, fragrant wood that takes a high polish. The ancient Greeks and Romans prized the wood and used it for various ornamental purposes and for cabinetwork. It was commonly said to be worth its weight in gold. A nearly transparent resin called sandarac exudes from the tree and is used in making varnish and incense. Some have suggested that "thyine wood" is the same as the **"almug" of 1 Ki 10: 11, 12, etc.; others, that it represents the citron tree, a small evergreen about 10 ft. tall. Thyine (RSV "scented") wood was a highly valued item of trade of mystical Babylon (Rev 18:12).

Tiberias (tī-bē′rĭ-ăs). [Gr. *Tiberias.*] A city on the western shore of the Sea of Galilee, founded by Herod Antipas between A.D. 17 and 22, and named after the emperor Tiberius (see fig. 504). After its founding the capital of Galilee was moved from Sepphoris to Tiberias (Jos. *Ant.* xviii. 2. 3; *War* ii. 9. 1). Since the city had been built on the site of an old cemetery, the better-class Jews considered Tiberias ceremonially unclean and avoided living there. Consequently, most of the citizens were foreigners or Galileans forcibly settled there. In the NT Tiberias is mentioned only once (Jn 6:23), although twice the Sea of Galilee is called "sea of Tiberias" (chs 6:1; 21:1). In A.D. 61 Nero gave Tiberias as a gift to Herod Agrippa II. During the Jewish war it was fortified by Josephus, the commander of Galilee (Jos. *Life* 8; *War* ii. 20. 6). After the 2d Jewish war (A.D. 132-135), when Jerusalem was destroyed, and Jews were not permitted to return to their former capital, the Sanhedrin lifted its ban on Ti-

504. Old city of Tiberias

berias, and made that city its seat. It has been suggested that the warm springs of Tiberias may have influenced their decision. Henceforth Tiberias became the most important center of Jewish learning for many centuries. It was here that Jewish oral tradition, the Mishnah, was put into writing (*c.* A.D. 200), later also most of the Talmud, and finally, it was in Tiberias that the system of vowel pointing was developed that was eventually adopted by all Jews, bringing their vowelless script to perfection. Tiberias, now called *Ṭabarîyeh,* is a town with a population totaling more than 12,000 (Map XVI, C-4).

Tiberias, Sea of. *See* Galilee, Sea of.

Tiberius Caesar (tī-bē′rĭ-ŭs sē′zẽr). [Gr. *Tiberios Kaisar,* a transliteration of Latin *Tiberius Caesar.*] Roman emperor from A.D. 14 to 37 (*see* Caesar, 2). He was born in 42 B.C. and was adopted by Augustus in A.D. 4, and later entrusted with equal authority with Augustus in the provinces. He succeeded to the throne after his foster father's death in A.D. 14, and through military ability and administrative skill perpetuated the prosperous era of the empire initiated by Augustus. Yet he was suspicious and ruthless, and as a result his morose retirement to the island of Capri gave rise to gossip about his supposed debaucheries, but he was actually austere. John the Baptist and Jesus Christ began and completed their ministries under Tiberius (see Lk 3:1). Several references to "Caesar" in the Gospels (Mt 22:17; Lk 23:2; Jn 19:12, 15) refer to Tiberius without naming him. Pilate was apparently afraid of him (Jn 19:12, 13), since the emperor's last years were filled with executions. When Herod Antipas founded a new city on the western shore of the Sea of Galilee he called it Tiberias, in honor of the emperor.

Tibhath (tĭb′hăth). [Heb. *Ṭibchath.*] A city of Hadadezer of Aram-zobah (1 Chr 18: 8), probably that called Betah in 2 Sa 8: 8. The *Amarna Letters mention a place *Tubiḫi,* and the topographical lists of Thutmose III mention a place *Dbḥ* in Syria, which may refer to the Biblical Tibhath. The site has not been identified.

Tibni (tĭb′nī). [Heb. *Tibnî,* "strawman."] Son of Ginath; he was for several years (*c.* 885 - *c.* 880 B.C.) recognized by a section of the people as king of Israel while another section followed Omri. However, he died in an unspecified manner, and Omri became sole ruler in Israel (1 Ki 16:21, 22).

Tidal (tī′dăl). [Heb. *Tid′al.*] King of nations (RSV "Goiim"), who with Chedorlaomer invaded Transjordan in the time of Abraham (Gen 14:1, 9). For a long time this king's name was identified with that of Tudhaliyas, a name borne by several Hittite kings, the 1st of whom ruled from his capital, *Kussar, c.* 1700 B.C. Although it is impossible to identify the Tidal of Gen 14 with a known Hittite king, it seems possible that an early Hittite, or proto-Hittite, king (*see* Hittites) bore that name. His title "king of nations" gives no clue as to the identity of the country over which he ruled. However, there are parallels to this title in the Mari texts, where the word *gâ′um* means "group," or "gang." This suggests the possibility that Tidal was king not over an established kingdom, but over a nomadic tribe with no fixed habitations. Since the Hittites poured into Anatolia and into the Fertile Crescent at the time of Abraham, Tidal, if he were a Hittite, could have been appropriately designated "King of a group of people." (F. M. Th. de Liagre Böhl, *Opera Minora* [Groningen, 1953], p. 47; R. de Vaux, *RB* 55 [1948], 333, 334.)

Tiglath-pileser (tĭg′lăth-pī-lē′zēr), or **Tilgath-pilneser** (tĭl′găth-pĭl-nē′zēr). [Heb. *Tiglath Pil′eser* and *Tilgath-pilne′eser;* Assyrian *Tukulti-apil-Esharra,* meaning "my trust is the son of Esharra (that is, the god Ninib)."] The name of 3 Assyrian kings, of whom only the last played a role in Biblical history. Hence, only Tiglath-pileser III (745-727 B.C.) will be discussed here. He is twice designated *Pul in the Bible (1 Chr 5:26; cf. 2 Ki 15:19), which may have been his original name. That Pul and Tiglath-pileser III designate the same king can be clearly demonstrated: Where Ptolemy's canon mentions Poros as king of Babylon, the Babylonian king list has Pulu, and the Babylonian Chronicle

calls the king of that time Tiglath-pileser. Tiglath-pileser III (fig. 394) was a usurper who seems to have taken a throne name already made famous by great kings of the past. He was an ambitious king and his accomplishments prove that he was worthy of the famous name he bore, for he became one of the greatest kings of the empire period. He extended his power in all directions, and campaigned frequently in Syria and Palestine. King Menahem of Israel paid him tribute (2 Ki 15:19) that the Assyrian king might help to confirm him in the kingship. This tribute is mentioned in the display inscription found in Tiglath-pileser's palace at Calah (*ANET* 283), as well as a tribute of "Azriau from Iuda," believed to be King Azariah of Judah, which payment is not mentioned in the Bible (*ANET* 282). During the reign of King Pekah of Israel Tiglath-pileser received a request from King Ahaz of Judah to come to his aid against Pekah and Rezin of Damascus. This request was accompanied by a large tribute (ch 16:7, 8), which is mentioned in building inscriptions of Tiglath-pileser. The Assyrian king complied with Ahaz' request and invaded Israel, taking from it all its northern territories and its possessions in Transjordan (ch 15:29), which he incorporated into the Assyrian Empire. He also captured and destroyed Damascus and killed its king, Rezin (ch 16:9). When King Pekah of Israel was assassinated by Hoshea (ch 15:30), Tiglath-pileser was campaigning in southwestern Palestine, and had probably given his approval to the murder, since he claimed to have placed Hoshea on the throne (*ANET* 284). Tiglath-pileser was the 1st king to introduce wholesale transplantations of subjugated nations to other countries in order to uproot them, kill their nationalistic spirit and sentiments, and destroy old loyalties, in this way to facilitate his reign over his conquered peoples (see fig. 37).

Tigris. *See* Hiddekel.

Tikvah (tĭk′vȧ). [Heb. *Tiqwah,* "hope."]

1. The father-in-law of Huldah, the prophetess (2 Ki 22:14). In 2 Chr 34:22 he is called Tokhath (tŏk′hăth) in the RSV, and Tikvath (tĭk′văth) in the KJV; Heb. *Toqhath.*

2. A man whose son Jahzeiah opposed Ezra's method of reforming the mixed marriages among the Jews (Ezr 10:15).

Tikvath. *See* Tikvah, 1.

Tile. A rendering of: (1) the Heb. *lebenah* (Eze 4:1, KJV), *"brick"; (2) the Gr. *keramos* (Lk 5:19), "clay," "roof tile." The paralytic was let down through the "tiling" into the presence of Jesus. If the incident occurred in the house of a native Palestinian, the *keramos* would represent simply the clay used to cover the flat roof. Tiles were used in Greek and Roman houses, perhaps also by certain aliens in Palestine.

Tilgath-pilneser. *See* Tiglath-pileser.

Tilon (tī'lŏn). [Heb. *Tîlôn.*] A Judahite (1 Chr 4:20).

Timaeus (tī-mē'ŭs). [Gr. *Timaios; see* Bartimaeus.] The father of the blind beggar of Jericho (Mk 10:46).

Timbrel. The rendering in the RSV in 8 passages of the Heb. *toph* (Ex 15:20; Jgs 11:34; 1 Sa 18:6; etc.), "hand drum." *See* Tabret; also *SDACom* 3:30, 31.

505. Egyptian women playing hand drums

Time. Statements of time in the Bible employ various words with various meanings.

1. Time as duration: "in process of time" (Gen 4:3; Jgs 11:4); "the time that David dwelt in the country" (1 Sa 27:7).

2. Time as measured: *see* Day; Even; Hour; Month; Night; Week; Year. For ancient methods of reckoning time, *see* Age; Chronology, I.

3. A specific time: "at the time of the evening" (Gen 24:11); "Pharaoh . . . hath passed the time appointed" (Jer 46:17).

4. A period or season: "the time came that the saints possessed the kingdom" (Dan 7:22); "in time of temptation" (Lk 8:13); "now is the accepted time" (2 Cor 6:2). For historical periods of time *see* Chronology.

5. Prophetic time: Prophetic time periods are sometimes literal, such as the 70-year captivity predicted by Jeremiah, and sometimes nonliteral, as in figurative, or symbolic, prophecies. In the figurative prophecies, that is, those in which representations such as beasts, horns, etc., stand for something different from the symbol itself, we would also expect the time periods to be nonliteral. From Num 14:34 and Eze 4:6 the principle has been deduced that a symbolic day represents a literal year. Thus prophetic periods such as the 1260 days are to be interpreted as 1260 actual years.

We find in prophecy other time words besides "day"; for example, one time prophecy mentions "an hour, and a day, and a month, and a year" (Rev 9:15). An hour is obviously the 24th part of a day. The key as to the number of days to assign to a prophetic month or year lies in the use of the word "time" in several related prophecies (Dan 7:25; 11:13; Heb 12:7; Rev 12:14; etc.).

A "time" in prophecy seems to be equivalent to a "year." This is shown by a comparison of time periods in the book of Revelation, where 3½ times are equated with 1260 days (ch 12:6, 14) and forty-two months also are equated with 1260 days (ch 11:2, 3). Therefore 3½ "times" are the same period as 42 months (which would be 3½ twelve-month years). Further, from the total of 1260 days for this period it can be computed that one "time," or year, has 360 days, and that the 42 months have 30 days each.

Now, a year of 12 thirty-day months, totaling 360 days, does not belong to any known calendar of Bible times. Therefore the question arises, Why would such an unusual scheme be used in prophecy? Possibly for the reason that in a lunar calendar such as was used by the Jews, Babylonians, and others, no one could predict the exact number of days in any future series of months or years without knowing not only what specific calendar they were to be reckoned in but also what specific months or years were involved. The year could be either a common lunar year of 354 days (with a day's variation, depending on the moon) or a "leap" year of 384 days or thereabouts, when an extra month was added to correct the difference between 12 lunar months and the true *year. Even an Egyptian, whose 365-day calendar had 12 thirty-day months and 5 extra days at the end of each year, could not tell exactly how many days were included in 3½ years unless he knew whether the interval embraced 3 or 4 of the extra 5-day periods. Thus 3½ calendar years, or 42 months, would not represent a precise period of time to Jewish readers unless the calendar was specified.

The year, then, in symbolic prophecy is a period of 360 symbolic days. A symbolic day in prophecy, it has been noted, is an actual year when translated into literal time. (Some expositors of prophecy have been confused because they forgot that the 30-day month and 360 years are not actual calendar years, and have tried to reckon the 1260 symbolic days, for example, by 1260 x 360 literal days rather than 1260 actual years.) Now what is an actual, literal year? It is obviously a true solar, or seasonal, year; even the variable lunar calendar such as that used by both Daniel and John, or by the Jews to this day, is kept, through "leap" years, in step with the seasonal year, so that 1260 Jewish years total 1260 natural years. The prophetic, symbolic year (or time), reckoned on the theoretical 30-day month and 360-day year, is not real, but theoretical; but the symbolic day represents an *actual* year, and an actual year is not 360 days but the true solar year of approximately 365¼ days. So 3½ years in symbolic prophecy are 1260 symbolic days, which in turn represent 1260 full, natural years; a "time," or year, in symbolic prophecy represents 360 symbolic days, which in turn represent 360 true, or solar, years.

Timna (tĭm'nȧ), KJV twice **Timnah** (tĭm'nȧ). [Heb. *Timna'*.]

1. A daughter of Seir and sister of Lotan (Gen 36:20, 22; 1 Chr 1:38, 39). She became the concubine of Eliphaz, the eldest son of Esau, and the mother of Amalek (Gen 36:12).

2. A chieftain of Edom (Gen 36:40; 1 Chr 1:51); called Timnah in the KJV. The capital of Qataban in southern Arabia bears the name *Timna'*. The name of this city may go back to a tribal name received from this Biblical Timna.

Timnah (tĭm'nȧ), KJV 8 times **Timnath** (tĭm'năth), once **Thimnathah** (thĭm'nȧthȧ). [Heb. *Timnah*, "assigned portion."]

1. A town on the western border of Judah, near Beth-shemesh (Jos 15:10), but assigned to the tribe of Dan (ch 19:43). In the time of Samson it was apparently in the hands of the Philistines (Jgs 14:1, 2, 5). It seems to have been returned to Israelite possession, probably in David's time, for 2 Chr 28:18 states that it was again captured by the Philistines in the reign of King Ahaz of Judah. Timnah was

formerly identified with *Khirbet Tibnah*, 2½ mi. southwest of Beth-shemesh, but it is more likely the site of *Tell el-Baṭâshi*, 3 mi. northwest of *Khirbet Tibnah* (Y. Aharoni, *PEQ* 90 [1958], 27-31). Map VI, E-2.

2. A town in the hill country of Judah, near a certain Gibeah (Jos 15:57). It is probably the Timnah near Adullam and Enaim where Judah went in order to shear his sheep (Gen 38:12-14). It has been identified with *Tibnah*, about 9 mi. west-southwest of Bethlehem.

3. For Gen 36:40; 1 Chr 1:51; KJV, *see* Timna, 2.

Timnath. *See* Timnah, 1, 2.

Timnath-heres. *See* Timnath-serah.

Timnath-serah (tĭm'nȧth-sē'rȧ). [Heb. *Timnath-serach*, "extra portion," "luxuriant portion," or "portion that protrudes (over a bluff or a cliff)."] A place in the hill country of Ephraim, which was assigned to Joshua, and was the place of his burial (Jos 19:50; 24:30). In Jgs 2:9 the name appears as Timnath-heres (tĭm'nȧth-hē'rēz), Heb. *Timnath-cheres*, "portion of the sun." The word *serach* here seems to have been accidentally written backward. Timnath-serah has been identified with *Khirbet Tibneh*, about 12 mi. northeast of Lydda. The traditional tombs of Joshua and Caleb are shown there today. Map VI, D-3.

Timnite (tĭm'nīt). [Heb. *Timni*.] A citizen, or inhabitant, of Timnah, 1 (Jgs 15:6).

Timon (tī'mŏn). [Gr. *Timōn*, "worthy," a name which appears frequently in inscriptions.] One of the 7 men chosen in the early church at Jerusalem to carry out social work among the Hellenistic church members (Acts 6:5).

Timotheus. *See* Timothy.

Timothy (tĭm'ȯ-thĭ), KJV frequently **Timotheus** (tĭ-mŏth'ē-ŭs). [Gr. *Timotheos*, "one who reverences God," "one who worships God," "one who honors God." The name occurs frequently in Greek inscriptions.] A convert of, traveling companion of, and assistant to, the apostle Paul. Timothy is mentioned first in connection with Paul's visit to Lystra on his 2d Missionary Journey, about A.D. 49 (*see* Chronology, IX, 7), when Timothy was already a Christian believer (Acts 16:1). Apparently he and members of the family had been converted by Paul upon the occasion of Paul's 1st visit to that city (Acts 14:8-18; cf. 1 Ti 1:2; 2 Ti 1:1, 5). Timothy was half Jewish, for his mother was a Jewess, but his father a "Greek" (Acts 16: 1), that is, a non-Jew. He had been well trained in religious matters by his godly mother, Eunice, and his pious grandmother, Lois (Acts 16:1; 2 Ti 1:5), who had taught him the OT Scriptures (2 Ti 3:15), but his father seems to have objected to his being circumcised (see Acts 16:3). As a Christian young man, Timothy had already earned an excellent reputation among the believers at Lystra and nearby Iconium (v 2), and seeing in him a promising worker for God, Paul decided to associate Timothy with himself as an apprentice missionary. "Because of the Jews which were in those quarters," Paul circumcised the half-Jew Timothy (vs 1, 3), in order to forestall unnecessary controversy on this point (v 3). Timothy accompanied Paul as he revisited the churches of that area (vs 4, 5), as he penetrated into "Phrygia and the region of Galatia" (v 6), as he went to Troas (vs 8, 9), and as he carried the gospel to the great Macedonian cities of Philippi, Thessalonica, and Beroea (chs 16:9 to 17:14). When Paul was unexpectedly forced to flee from Beroea for Athens he left Timothy and Silas there (ch 17:14), but no sooner had he arrived in Athens than he sent for them to join him again (vs 15, 16). Paul immediately sent Timothy back to Thessalonica with the purpose to strengthen the new believers in that city (1 Th 3:1, 2), and Silas and Timothy did not actually rejoin Paul in his labors until later at Corinth (Acts 18:5; see 1 Th 1:1; 3:6; 2 Th 1:1). Timothy may have remained in Greece when Paul returned to Jerusalem the following year.

We next hear of Timothy 4 or 5 years later, during the course of Paul's 3 years of ministry in Ephesus, whence Paul sent him across the Aegean Sea to settle problems that had arisen in the church at Corinth (1 Cor 4:17), a mission that seems not to have been altogether successful, as may be concluded from the severe tone of the latter part of 2 Cor (see Corinthians, Epistles to; cf. 1 Cor 16:10). Luke mentions the fact that Timothy and Erastus were sent to Macedonia (Acts 19:21, 22). Paul followed a little later (2 Cor 1:1), and they were together in Corinth (see Rom 16:21), probably during the winter of A.D. 57-58. In the following spring Paul, Timothy, and others began the return journey to Jerusalem, thus bringing Paul's 3d Missionary Journey to a close (Acts 20:4). It is not known whether Timothy was with Paul during the apostle's imprisonment at Jerusalem and Caesarea and on his journey to

Rome. We next hear of Timothy during the 1st imprisonment at Rome (about A.D. 61-63), probably toward its close when Paul mentions him, among other companions, in his epistles written during that imprisonment (Php 1:1; 2:19-23; Col 1:1; Phm 1). During the interval between Paul's 1st and 2d imprisonments (about A.D. 63-66), Paul addressed his 1st Epistle to Timothy, possibly about A.D. 64. When Paul went into Macedonia (1 Ti 1:3), he asked Timothy to stay at Ephesus, apparently as pastor of the Ephesian church; the epistle contains instructions addressed to him in that capacity. But about A.D. 66 Paul was again arrested and taken to Rome, and toward the close of his 2d imprisonment there he wrote Timothy a 2d time, urgently appealing to him to come to him soon (2 Ti 4:9) since his other companions had been dispatched on missions to one place or another and one, at least, had forsaken him (vs 10-13). At his first hearing Paul had stood alone (v 16), and now, surmising that he would soon be executed (vs 6-8), he longed for the fellowship of his "dearly beloved son" Timothy (ch 1:2). Timothy is mentioned in Heb 13:23 as having been set at liberty, but nothing is otherwise known of the imprisonment here alluded to.

Timothy, Epistles to. Two letters by the apostle Paul to Timothy, his "own son in the faith" (1 Ti 1:2), his "dearly beloved son" (2 Ti 1:2). Together with Titus, these epistles are known as the Pastoral Epistles, since they were written to counsel and instruct younger ministers with respect to the administration of local church affairs. In the earliest Greek manuscripts the titles of these 2 letters are simply *Pros Timotheon A*, "To Timothy I," and *Pros Timotheon B*, "To Timothy II." Generally speaking, early Christian writers from the very first considered these epistles as authentically Pauline. Clement of Rome, toward the end of the 1st cent., and Polycarp, during the middle of the 2d cent., use language that may imply familiarity with these letters; and Irenaeus, Tertullian, and others toward its close, attested the genuineness of the epistles, quoting from them as Scripture and attributing them to the apostle; the Muratorian Canon (c. A.D. 170) lists them with Paul's letters. Many modern critics, however, reject Paul's authorship, chiefly (1) because of the difficulty of finding any place to fit such historical allusions as those of 1 Ti 1:3; 2 Ti 4:20; Tit 3:12 into his life as recorded in the book of Acts and elsewhere in his uncontested epistles; (2) because of the relatively advanced stage of church organization reflected in the epistles, to which these scholars feel the churches could not possibly have attained during Paul's lifetime; (3) because in some instances they take the warning against "oppositions [Gr. *antitheseis*] of science falsely so called" (1 Ti 6:20) to be an allusion to a heretical work called *Antitheses,* written about the middle of the 2d cent. by Marcion, many of whose views resembled those of the Gnostics; (4) because the vocabulary and style of the Pastoral Epistles differ considerably from those of Paul's uncontested epistles, there being a considerable number of words that do not occur elsewhere in his uncontested epistles.

It is true that conclusive objective evidence of Pauline authorship is not as strong as with several of the other epistles attributed to him, nevertheless, a careful examination of these objections shows them to be highly subjective and without substantial proof: (1) It is freely granted that the historical allusions in the Pastoral Epistles do not fit into the record of Paul's life in the book of Acts (for example, 1 Ti 1:3; cf. Acts 18:19-21; 19:22; 20:4; 2 Cor 1:1). However, the objection disappears if it be granted that these letters were written after the end of the period covered by the book of Acts, which breaks off abruptly with Paul in prison at Rome for 2 full years (Acts 28:30), probably A.D. 61-63, without indicating the outcome of his appeal to the Roman emperor. In the prison epistles (Ephesians, Philippians, Colossians, and Philemon), which are generally considered to have been written during the latter part of his 1st imprisonment, he clearly anticipates imminent release (see Php 2:24; Phm 22). Thus, writing to the Philippians, he expresses hope that he will be able to visit them shortly (Php 2:24). There is ample evidence in the Pastoral Epistles that during the interval between his 1st and 2d imprisonments Paul traveled widely, visiting Christian communities in Asia Minor, Macedonia, and Greece (1 Ti 1:3; 2 Ti 4:13, 20; Tit 1:5), and possibly even going as far as Spain (see Rom 15:24, 28). Certain passages clearly indicate persons not mentioned before, places Paul had recently visited and other circumstances that do not accord with the records of his life prior to the 1st imprisonment (see 2 Ti 1:15-17; 4:6, 9, 13, 16, 17, 20, 21; Tit 1:5; 3:12). Accordingly, there is good

reason to believe that these letters were written during the interval between Paul's 1st imprisonment and his execution. (2) The opinion that the rather fully developed church organization reflected in the Pastoral Epistles indicates a period of time well beyond the lifetime of Paul lacks historical confirmation. (3) Recent archeological discoveries, notably those of the Dead Sea scrolls, and of a Gnostic library at Nag Hammadi (Chenoboskion) in Egypt, show that Gnostic teachings were already well developed in the 1st cent. (4) The argument based on the differences in vocabulary and style between the Pastoral Epistles and those more generally attributed to Paul loses much of its weight when it is observed that the subject matter of these epistles—various aspects of church organization and administration —is scarcely touched upon in the other epistles. Furthermore, many of the churches Paul established had now been in operation for 15 or 20 years. It is only natural to expect that they would have grown considerably in membership and that a more complex organization would have become necessary. Also, early Christian church organization generally followed the existing pattern of that of the Jewish synagogue. The fact that persons named in the Pastoral Epistles (see 2 Ti 4:10, 13, 19, 21; Tit 3:12, 13) do not appear elsewhere in Paul's letters is further evidence that these epistles come from a later period of the apostle's career. It is inconceivable that a later writer would have been so naive as intentionally to introduce persons not mentioned elsewhere by Paul, yet attempt to attribute the epistles to him.

The 1st Epistle to Timothy was written probably toward the close of the interval between Paul's 1st and 2d imprisonments (*c.* A.D. 63-66), since he had evidently been at liberty for some time and had been visiting churches in the vicinity of the Aegean Sea. He had recently departed from Ephesus, leaving Timothy in charge of the church there. The 2d Epistle to Timothy was written about A.D. 66, toward the close of Paul's 2d imprisonment, probably not long before his death, after one trial (2 Ti 4:16, 17) and while he awaited the death sentence (vs 6-9). The apostle had recently been at Troas, where his 2d arrest would seem to have taken place (v 13).

In 1 and 2 Ti, Paul counsels Timothy to conduct himself in a manner acceptable to God and for the building up of the flock God had entrusted to his care. These exhortations to vigorous leadership may imply that Timothy was a man of mild temperament and less aggressive than Paul thought he should be. In 2 Ti, realizing that his own end was near, Paul sought further to strengthen his younger co-worker's faith by a recital of his own example and warned against certain heresies, urging the younger worker to hold firm to the Inspired Word and to remain faithful.

These 2 epistles may be summarized as follows: Following the salutation (1 Ti 1:1, 2) Paul first charges Timothy to rebuke teachers of perverted doctrine (vs 3-20) and develops the concept of Christianity as a universal religion (ch 2). Next, he sets forth the character qualifications of bishops (ch 3:1-7) and deacons (vs 8-13), and contrasts the true gospel (vs 14-16) with counterfeits (ch 4:1-5). Then follows a series of practical suggestions on effective ministry. Timothy is to concentrate on sound doctrine, to avoid speculation, and to be a living example of the message he proclaims (vs 6-16). He is to guard his relationship with various specified groups of church members (chs 5:1-25; 6:17-19). In the final section Paul treats of Christian masters and slaves (ch 6:1, 2), of heretical teachers (vs 3-5), of worldly riches (vs 6-10, 17-19), and of Timothy's responsibility to provide a living pattern of character (vs 11-16). The letter closes with a personal charge to Timothy (vs 20, 21). In the 2d epistle Paul greets his "beloved son" in the faith, fondly reviewing his own affection for him (2 Ti 1:1-5). He exhorts Timothy to be faithful, to give a good account of his responsibility as a minister, and to stand courageously for the gospel message (vs 6-18). In ch 2:1-6 Paul elaborates on the traits of an ideal minister, and then dwells upon the content of the message Timothy should preach and the way in which he should proclaim it (vs 7-26). He then warns of perilous times to come, and points to the Scriptures as a safeguard against error (ch 3:1-17). The 4th chapter has been called Paul's "last will and testament." In it he challenges Timothy to take up the torch of truth that he must soon lay down (ch 4:1-22).

Tin. [Heb. *bedil*, "tin."] A soft, bluish-white metallic chemical element obtained by smelting, known and used from pre-Exodus times, especially in the form of its alloy *bronze (copper and tin). It was exported from Tarshish (Eze 27:12).

Very little if any tin is native to Palestine; consequently tin found in that country probably came from *Tarshish or from India.

Tiphsah (tǐf'sä). [Heb. *Tiphsach*, "ford."]
1. A city on the extreme northeastern boundary of Solomon's kingdom (1 Ki 4:24), generally identified with Thapsacus, a city above the confluence of the Balikh on the right bank of the middle Euphrates, which guarded an important crossing of that river toward northern Syria (Map XI, C-6). Cyrus the Younger and Alexander used this ford to transfer their armies over the river.
2. A place near Tirzah (see Tirzah, 2), destroyed by Menahem after he had killed Shallum of Israel and taken the throne (2 Ki 15:14, 16). The site has not been identified. Many scholars, following the Greek version of Lucian, read Tappuah. See Tappuah, 3.

Tiras (tī'răs). [Heb. *Tiras*.] A son of Japheth (Gen 10:2; 1 Chr 1:5) and probably ancestor of the Tyrsenians who lived on the western Asia Minor coast (Map IV, B-4), where they were notorious as pirates. Herodotus calls them *Tursēnoi* (i. 57. 94). They are mentioned in Egyptian inscriptions of the late 13th cent. B.C. under the name Turusha (*Twrwsh3*), as one of the Peoples of the Sea who invaded Syria and Palestine on their way down the Mediterranean coast to Egypt.

Tirathites (tī'răth-īts). [Heb. *Tir'athim*.] A family of scribes that lived at Jabez (1 Chr 2:55). It is not known whether the name is derived from a locality or from an ancestor.

Tire. A rendering of the Heb. *pe'er* (Eze 24:17, 23, KJV), "headdress," "turban" (RSV). For its use in Is 3:18, KJV, see Crescents.

Tirhakah (tûr'há-kä). [Heb. *Tirhaqah*; Egyptian *T3hrq*, generally transliterated Taharka. The name is spelled *Tarqû* in Assyrian texts.] The 3d king of the 25th, or Ethiopian, dynasty of Egypt. He lived in Nubia until the age of 20 years, when his brother Shabataka, the king of Egypt, sent for him to join him in the government as a coregent. Tirhakah relates that he entered Egypt about 690 B.C. for the 1st time (see fig. 506). After the death of Shabataka in 684 B.C., Tirhakah reigned alone until 664 B.C. In 2 Ki 19:9 and Is 37:9 Tirhakah is mentioned in connection with an invasion of Judah by *Sennacherib. These verses speak of his approach with an army to fight against Sennacherib. Many formerly believed that this was at the time of Sennacherib's campaign of 701 B.C., of which the Assyrian king has left us long and detailed records. However, Tirhakah was only about 9 years of age at that time, and had not yet come to Egypt from Nubia,

506. Inscribed stele of Taharka (Biblical Tirhakah), dated in the 6th year of his reign; it tells the story of his accession to the throne

his homeland; therefore it seems that the campaign which proved so disastrous to Sennacherib (2 Ki 19:35) must have taken place after Tirhakah began his coregency, and therefore some time after 690 B.C., but before the death of *Hezekiah, which appears to have occurred about 686 B.C. When Esarhaddon, Sennacherib's son, invaded Egypt in 670 B.C., Tirhakah was defeated and driven back to Nubia (see fig. 163).

Lit.: W. F. Albright, *BASOR* 130 (1953), 4-11; G. Schmidt, *Kush* 6 (1958), 121-129.

Tirhanah (tûr'há-nä). [Heb. *Tirchanah.*] A son of Caleb, the Hezronite, by Maacah, his concubine (1 Chr 2:48).

Tiria (tĭr'ĭ-á). [Heb. *Tireya',* meaning unknown. The name has a parallel in the Babylonian *Tirayâma.*] A descendant of Judah (1 Chr 4:16).

Tirshatha. See Governor, 1.

Tirzah (tûr'zá). [Heb. *Tirṣah,* "pleasure."]

1. The youngest daughter of Zelophehad of the tribe of Manasseh. Zelophehad left no male heir, so the inheritance went to his daughters (Num 26:33; 27:1; 36:11; Jos 17:3-6).

2. A city renowned for its beauty (Song 6:4). Joshua captured it from the Canaanites (Jos 12:24), but it did not come into prominence until the time of the Hebrew kings when Jeroboam made it his royal residence and the capital of the northern kingdom (1 Ki 14:17). It kept this position until Omri built Samaria and moved the capital there (chs 15:21, 33; 16:6, 8, 9, 15, 17, 23, 24). However, Tirzah remained an important city (2 Ki 15:14, 16). It has tentatively been identified with *Tell el-Fâr'ah,* about 7 mi. northeast of Nablus. Excavations at this site carried out intermittently since 1946 under the direction of R. de Vaux have shown that *Tell el-Fâr'ah's* ancient history agrees with that of Tirzah, but no evidence has come to light to confirm the identification. Map VI, D-3, gives 2 alternative locations for Tirzah, both conjectural: *Tell el-Fâr'ah,* northeast of Shechem, and *Jemma'in,* southwest of Shechem. The latter of these sites is the less probable. See R. de Vaux, *PEQ* 88 (1956), 125-140.

Tishbite (tĭsh'bīt). [Heb. *Tishbî.*] The appellative of Elijah (1 Ki 21:17, 28; 2 Ki 1: 3, 8; 9:36), "of the inhabitants of Gilead" (1 Ki 17:1; the RSV, following the LXX, has "of Tishbe in Gilead"). The most probable interpretation of this term is that Tishbe (tĭsh'bĕ), Tishbih, or Tishbeh is the name of a locality rather than of a family. On evidence from ancient Jewish and Christian writers Tishbe is usually identified with *Lisdib* (also called *el-Istib*), whose ruins lie about 13 mi. northwest of Gerasa. Elijah's name still lingers there, for the ruins of a Christian church and convent at this locality are called *Mâr Ilyâs.*

Tithe. [Heb. *ma'aser,* "tenth part," "tithe"; Gr. *dekatē,* "tenth," "tithe."] The 10th part of one's increase, which God claims as His (Lev 27:30). Tithing in one form or another was practiced among various peoples of antiquity for both secular and religious purposes, and by worshipers of the true God at a very early time. Having sinned, man was sentenced to earn his livelihood by the sweat of his face (Gen 3: 17-19), and there was danger that he would come to say in his heart, "My power and the might of mine hand hath gotten me this wealth" (Deut 8:17), whereas in reality it was God who had given him the power to get it (Deut 8:18). Accordingly, when the Israelites were about to enter Canaan, God warned them that when they should attain to some degree of prosperity they should beware lest they forget Him (Deut 8:7-11; cf. Rom 1:19-21). By paying tithe man acknowledges that he is a steward of God, the owner of all things. God does not need man's financial support, for "the world" is His, "and the fulness thereof" (Ps 50:10-12). But man, particularly in his sinful state, stands in urgent and constant need of a reminder that God is the source of "every good gift and every perfect gift" (Jas 1:17). Even prior to the entrance of sin the danger of forgetfulness was latent in man's character, and as a test God forbade man to eat of the tree of knowledge of good and evil (Gen 2:17), claiming it as His own. By complying with this command Adam and Eve were to acknowledge God's proprietorship of the beautiful home that had been entrusted to their care. God gave Adam dominion over the world and over all forms of life upon it (ch 1:28), but withheld from him the use of this one tree as a token of His own ownership of all. By not eating the fruit of this tree Adam acknowledged God's ownership, even as the setting aside of the tenth part of one's income testifies to the same eternal truth.

That the principle of tithe paying was early understood by those who worshiped the true God is evidenced by the fact that Abraham paid tithe to Melchizedek as a priest of the most high God (Gen 14:18-20), who, in blessing Abraham, called him servant "of the most high God, possessor of heaven and earth" (v 19).

Jacob promised to devote "the tenth" unto God (Gen 28:22). The practice of tithing was incorporated into the Levitical code at Mount Sinai, when God explained to Moses that "all the tithe of the land . . . is holy unto the Lord" (Lev 27:30), and "the tithe of the herd, or of the flock" as well (v 32). The provision was made that "if a man . . . redeem ought of his tithes, he shall add thereto the fifth part" (v 31). Some have interpreted this as allowing a temporary withholding of the tithe for personal use, subject to the payment of a 20 per cent penalty when eventually the tithe is paid. The context, however, makes clear that such was not the intent of this proviso (cf. v 33). This gracious provision, that permitted a man to *exchange*—never to *withhold*—one kind of seed "of the land, or of the fruit of the tree" (Lev 27:30), if he needed it, for example, for seed for the next crop, was designed to avoid inflicting hardship upon the farmer. There was no need for the same exemption in the case of animals from the flock or from the herd (vs 32, 33).

Under the Levitical system God ordained that the tithes of Israel were to be devoted to the support of the Levites (Num 18:24) in view of the fact that they had received no tribal allotment in order that they might devote their time to ministering at the Temple and instructing the people in the law of the Lord (Num 18:21; cf. 1 Cor 9:13; Deut 25:4). The Levites, in turn, paid a tithe of what they received from the people (Num 18:26-28). The tithe of Deut 14:23-29 (cf. ch 12:5-11, 17-19), consisting of the products of the soil, flock, and herd, which might be eaten "before the Lord" in company with Levites, the poor, and other invited guests, was apparently a 2d tithe. The tithe was to be reckoned annually (ch 14:22). Those who lived at a great distance from the Temple and would encounter difficulty in paying their tithe in kind, were to change it into money (vs 24, 25). Provision was made that every 3d year the tithe be used for the Levites and the poor (Deut 14:28; cf. Amos 4:4, KJV). Slackness in the payment of tithe led Hezekiah to urge the people not to neglect their duty (2 Chr 31:4-12). Their response was so hearty that it was necessary to prepare additional storage space at the Temple for the tithes that were brought in (vs 10, 11). The Second Temple was likewise provided with storehouses for the tithe (Neh 10:38; 13:10-14; cf. Mal 3:10). The prophet Malachi rebuked Israel's tendency toward carelessness in the payment of the tithe (Mal 3:8-11). To withhold the tithe, he said, is to rob God, and to incur a curse. Contrariwise, upon those who faithfully pay the tithe God promises to open "the windows of heaven, and pour . . . out a blessing, that there shall not be room enough to receive it" (v 10).

The command to pay tithe is not explicitly restated by any of the NT writers. But in view of the fact that Abraham, as a matter of course, paid tithe centuries before the formulation of the Levitical code, and that the principle of tithe paying was implicit even before man sinned, it is evident that the principle and practice of tithe paying existed long before the Levitical system came into being, and was not peculiar to it. Therefore, the obligation to pay tithe was not automatically waived when the Levitical code became inoperative at the cross. Our Lord's admonition in Mt 23:23 constitutes tacit approval, though not an explicit command, for tithe paying. Neither Christ nor any NT writer in the least relaxes the obligation to pay tithe. Jesus clearly was not against tithing as such, but against the hypocritical spirit of scribe and Pharisee, whose religion consisted chiefly in the scrupulous observance of the outward forms of the Law, in this case the law of the tithes. The principle of tithe paying is also tacitly approved by the writer of the book of Hebrews (see ch 7:8).

Titius (tĭsh'ŭs). [Gr. *Titios,* probably a transliteration of the Latin *Titius.* Both names, the Greek as well as the Latin, occur in inscriptions of the apostolic age.] A Jewish proselyte of Corinth surnamed Justus (Acts 18:7, RSV), in whose home, adjoining the Jewish synagogue, Paul made his headquarters after the Jews rejected his message. The KJV, following the Textus Receptus, calls him simply Justus.

Title. In 2 Ki 23:17, KJV, an archaic rendering of the Heb. *ṣiyûn,* "mark," "signpost" (RSV "monument"); in Jn 19:19, 20 it is a rendering of the Gr. *titlos,* "inscription," "notice." The latter passage refers to Pilate's inscription upon the cross written in Hebrew, Greek, and Latin, "Jesus of Nazareth the King of the Jews."

Tittle. [Gr. *keraia,* literally "a little horn."] As used in Mt 5:18 and Lk 16:17, a projection or hook as part of a letter, a serif (RSV "dot"). Not even so minute a part as one of these little projections was to pass from the Law till all be fulfilled.

Titus (tī'tŭs). [Gr. *Titos,* a transliteration of the Latin *Titus.* Both the Greek and the Latin forms of the name were common during the apostolic age.] An intimate friend, traveling companion, and assistant of the apostle Paul. His name occurs in the NT only in the epistles of Paul to the Corinthians (2 Cor 2:13; etc.), the Galatians (Gal 2:1, 3), Timothy (2 Ti 4:10), and Titus (Tit 1:4). Paul considered Titus his "own son after the common faith" (v 4)—evidently because he was one of his own converts. That Titus was a Gentile is indicated by Paul's refusal to circumcise him in order to appease overzealous Jewish Christians at Jerusalem—perhaps on the occasion when he visited that city as a member of the Antioch delegation to the council held to resolve the issue of Gentile converts (Gal 2:1-5; cf. Acts 15). Possibly he was a native of Antioch. In any case, he was apparently a member of the Gentile church in that city (Gal 2:1) and probably accepted Christianity during Paul's early ministry there. When some in the Corinthian church turned against Paul, about A.D. 57, he sent Titus to effect a reconciliation. Paul's anxiety for the success of this mission is evident from his perplexity at not meeting Titus at Troas as planned (2 Cor 2:12, 13; 7:6, 13, 14). A little later he met Titus in Macedonia, joyfully received his glowing report of success (ch 7:6, 7, 13, 14), and sent him back to Corinth with the 2d Epistle to the Corinthians (ch 8:6, 17, 18, 23), and to supervise the collection of funds for the poor at Jerusalem (chs 8:23 to 9:5). Several years later, apparently not long before his 2d imprisonment in Rome, Paul wrote the Epistle to Titus. He had left Titus on the island of Crete to organize the churches there and to instruct the believers more thoroughly (Tit 1:4, 5). In his letter he summoned Titus to meet him in *Nicopolis (ch 3:12). The last we hear of Titus is shortly before Paul's death, when, in a letter to Timothy, Paul says that he had sent Titus on a mission to Dalmatia (2 Ti 4:10).

Titus, Epistle to. A letter addressed by Paul to Titus, whom the apostle had left on the island of Crete to supervise the organization of churches there (Tit 1:5). In the oldest extant Greek manuscripts the title of this epistle is simply *Pros Titon,* "To Titus." Modern critical scholarship generally questions the authenticity of this epistle, as it does the Pauline authorship of the epistles to Timothy. For a discussion of this problem *see* Timothy, Epistles to. Together with 1st and 2d Timothy, Titus belongs to a group of letters known as the Pastoral Epistles. Apparently the epistle was written during the interval between Paul's 1st- and 2d imprisonments, probably about A.D. 65 or 66 (*see* Paul, IV, 5; Timothy, Epistles to). Paul instructed Titus to meet him at Nicopolis (Tit 3:12) in northwestern Greece, where he planned to labor during the coming winter. The letter to Titus seems to have been written after the 1st letter to Timothy. The invitation to Titus to meet him at Nicopolis doubtless implies that when Paul left Crete (v 12) he had gone into Greece. If he had already visited Macedonia, and probably Ephesus (1 Ti 1:3), he probably went, after writing to Titus, to Corinth, Miletus, and Troas (see 2 Ti 4:13, 20).

The subject matter of Titus is similar to that of Timothy. The epistle consists chiefly of instructions to Titus with respect to his conduct and to the administration of church affairs. Apparently the Christian churches on Crete had not yet been fully organized or firmly established, and were in need of further instruction to place them on a sound, permanent basis. False teachers, perhaps half-converted Jews, were laying great emphasis on myths, genealogies, and the Law of Moses (Tit 1:10-14; 3:9). Paul counsels a more thorough form of church organization in order to safeguard the believers against the inroads of these false teachers, and outlines the qualifications of church elders (ch 1:5-9).

After the salutation (Tit 1:1-4), Paul discusses the ordination of these elders (vs 5-10), and proceeds to instruct Titus on how to check the activities of the false teachers (vs 10-16). He discusses the need of exemplary living on the part of all church members, including especially Titus himself as a minister of the gospel (ch 2:1-10). Anticipation of the advent of Christ should prove an incentive to the development of this excellency of character (vs 11-15). Also, certain civic responsibilities devolve upon the Christian (ch 3:1-3). Paul then explains the means by which Christians are enabled to live exemplary lives (ch 3:4-7), and ends his discussion by reiterating the fact that Christians are to be known by their good works and by avoiding unprofitable activities (vs 8-11). The epistle closes with personal remarks and an apostolic benediction (Tit 1:12-15).

Tizite (tī'zīt). [Heb. *Tiṣî.*] A designation of Joha, one of David's "mighty men" (1 Chr 11:45). However, it is not known whether the term designates his family relationship or citizenship.

Toah. *See* Nahath, 2.

Tob (tŏb). [Heb. *Ṭôb,* "good."] A land to which Jephthah fled when his brothers expelled him (Jgs 11:3, 5); not identified with certainty. It appears in Thutmose III's list of Palestinian cities as a place in Transjordan named *Tby,* and in the *Amarna Letters as *Ṭubu.* Some seek it east of Mount Hermon; others identify it with *eṭ-Ṭaiyibeh,* about 40 mi. east-south-east of the Sea of Galilee. The OT Tob seems to be the *Toubion* of 1 Macc 5:13 and its inhabitants the *Toubianoi,* "Toubiani" mentioned in 2 Macc 12:17, whom the 2d passage locates as 750 stadia, or 86 mi. (variant 500 stadia = 57 mi.), from Chasphor (*Khisfîn*), which would be east even of the Hauran. The "Ish-tob" of 2 Sa 10:6, KJV, should rather be read, with the RSV, "men of Tob," and therefore also refers to this land.

Tobadonijah (tŏb'ăd'ô-nī'jà). [Heb. *Ṭôb 'Adôniyah,* "my Lord Yahweh is good."] One of the Levites appointed by King Jehoshaphat to teach the Law in the cities of Judah (2 Chr 17:8).

Tobiah (tô-bī'à). [Heb. *Tobiyah,* "Yahweh is good." The name occurs on ancient Hebrew jar handles. It is also found incised twice in the rocks at 'Arâq el-Emîr (*see* Tobiah, 2), and in cuneiform is spelled *Ṭâbiya.*]

507. Part of the ruins of Tobiah's family castle at *'Arâq el-Emîr* in Transjordan

1. The ancestral head of a family who returned with Zerubbabel to Jerusalem after the Exile, whose members could not prove their Hebrew nationality (Ezr 2:60; Neh 7:62).

2. An Ammonite official of a noble family, possibly of half-Jewish descent. He, Sanballat, the governor of Samaria, and Geshem, the prince of Qedar in Arabia, were strong enemies of Nehemiah, actively engaged in frustrating the work of rebuilding the wall of Jerusalem (Neh 2:10, 19; 4:3, 7; 6:1, 12, 14). Tobiah was related by marriage to prominent families in Jerusalem (ch 6:17-19), and after Nehemiah's departure was given a room in one of the outer Temple buildings. When Nehemiah returned to Jerusalem after an absence of several years, and found Tobiah in the Temple precincts, he immediately expelled him (ch 13:4-8). Tobiah's family evidently continued to play an important role in the affairs of Transjordan, and sometimes in those of Judah. Impressive ruins of their estate are still visible at 'Arâq el-Emîr, 14½ mi. west-southwest of Amman, close to the modern road from Jericho to Amman. See fig. 507.

Lit.: C. C. McCown, *BA* 20 (1957), 63-76; B. Mazar, *IEJ* 7 (1957), 137-145, 229-238. See Map XIV, D/E-4.

Tobijah (tō-bī′jà). [Heb. *Ṭôbiyah* and *Ṭôbiyahû*, "Yahweh is good." The name occurs in the form *Tbyhw* in the *Lachish Letters.]

1. One of the Levites appointed by King Jehoshaphat to teach the Law in the cities of Judah (2 Chr 17:8).

2. One of the Jewish exiles from whom Zechariah, the prophet, received silver and gold to make a crown (KJV "crowns") for Joshua, the high priest (Zec 6:10, 11, 14).

Tochen (tō′kĕn). [Heb. *Token,* "measurement."] A town near Rimmon (En-rimmon) in the territory of Simeon (1 Chr 4:32); not identified.

Togarmah (tō-gär′mà). [Heb. *Togarmah;* in a Hittite text *Tegarama* and *Takarama;* Akkadian *Tilgarimmu.*] The ancestor of a people descended from Gomer (Gen 10:3; 1 Chr 1:6), mentioned in Hittite and Assyrian texts as living in the northern Taurus Mountains (see Map IV, B-5/6). Sennacherib seems to locate them in central Asia Minor. He, as well as his father, Sargon, claims to have conquered their country. The Armenians trace their genealogy back to Haik, the son of *Torgom,* and may therefore be descendants of

Togarmah. Ezekiel states that mules and horses were brought to the markets of Phoenicia from "the house of Togarmah" (Eze 27:14; RSV "Beth-togarmah"), which in ch 38:6 appears as an ally of Magog.

Tohu. *See* Nahath, 2.

Toi. *See* Tou.

Tokhath. *See* Tikvah, 1.

Tola (tō′là). [Heb. *Tôla',* "crimson."]

1. A son of Issachar, and ancestral head of the Tolaites (tō′là-īts) [Heb. *Tôla'î*], a tribal family of Issachar (Gen 46:13; Num 26:23; 1 Chr 7:1, 2).

2. One of the so-called minor judges, who judged Israel for 23 years. Little is known of him, for the record simply states that he was a son of Puah, of the tribe of Issachar, and that he lived and died at Shamir, in the hill country of Ephraim (Jgs 10:1, 2).

Tolad. *See* Eltolad.

Tolaites. *See* Tola, 1.

Tomb. *See* Sepulcher.

Tombs of the Kings, KJV Sepulchres of the Kings. The royal burying place in the City of David, the place where David was buried (1 Ki 2:10; cf. 2 Chr 26:23). "The sepulchres of David" were near the Pool of Siloam (Neh 3:15, 16). David, Solomon, and, following the division of the kingdom, all the kings of Judah to Hezekiah were buried in the City of David, but not all in the royal sepulchers. Some were not admitted there: Jehoram (2 Chr 21:20), Joash (ch 24:24, 25), Uzziah (ch 26:23), and Ahaz (ch 28:27). Others had their own separate tombs prepared: Asa (ch 16:14), Hezekiah (ch 32:33, RSV). Manasseh and Amon were buried in the garden of Uzza in Jerusalem (2 Ki 21:18, 25, 26). The last 4 kings of Judah were not buried in Jerusalem: Jehoahaz died in Egypt (ch 23:34), Jehoiakim did not receive a proper burial (Jer 22:19; 36:30; Jos. *Ant.* x. 6. 3), and Jehoiachin (see 2 Ki 25:27-30) and Zedekiah (Jer 52:10, 11) died in Babylon.

In NT times the tomb of David was pointed out as being on the southern end of the western hill in Jerusalem, but this is obviously erroneous in the light of the OT passages quoted above, because the western hill was still outside of the city in the time of David, and possibly did not become part of Jerusalem until Hellenistic times. The reference to David's sepulcher in Acts 2:29 may have been to the traditional tomb mentioned by Josephus (*Ant.* vii. 15. 3). He claims that John Hyrcanus opened the sepulcher of David and extracted large treasures from it (*Ant.* xiii. 8. 4). He also states that Herod intended to do the same, entered the tomb, took away the furniture of gold, but upon approaching the bodies of David and Solomon became frightened and therefore desisted from a further violation of the tombs of the kings; instead he honored them by erecting a glistening white monument (*ibid.* xvi. 7. 1). Although there is still much uncertainty about the site of the royal tombs, it is quite possible that in the excavations of the southeastern hill some of these tombs have been unearthed. Several cavelike subterranean structures have come to light, although they had been despoiled of their contents in ancient times and contained no evidence for identification.

Tongs. See Snuffers.

Tongue. [Heb. generally *lashôn,* "tongue"; Aramaic *lishshan;* Gr. generally *glōssa.*] The muscular organ in the mouth serving as a speech organ in man; a spoken language. Using tongue as a metonym for speech the Bible has much to say of its power for good and evil (see Job 5:21; Ps 10:7; 35:28; 51:14; 57:4; Rom 3:13; Jas 3:2-13; etc.). The gift of tongues, one of the miraculous gifts of the Holy Spirit promised to the early church (Mk 16:17), was bestowed at Pentecost in the form of tongues of fire (Acts 2:1-4). This gift enabled the apostles to speak the message to people of foreign-language groups (ch 2:6-12; cf. ch 10:46). As bestowed upon the Corinthian believers, the gift functioned to provide personal edification. But the gift was used for public display, and Paul found it necessary to counsel and reprove the Corinthian church members in regard to their misuse of it (1 Cor 12; 14). For tongue meaning language *see* Aramaic Language; Greek Language; Hebrew Language.

Topaz. [Heb. *piṭdah;* Gr. *topazion.*] A yellow-colored, more or less transparent precious stone. However, the term thus translated in the OT probably describes the gold-colored chrysolite. It was the 2d stone in the 1st row of the high priest's breastplate (Ex 28:17; 39:10), and appears in a similar list of gems adorning the covering of the prince of Tyre (Eze 28:13). Its value cannot be compared to wisdom (Job 28:19). John the revelator lists topaz as the 9th foundation of the New Jerusalem, mentioning also chrysolite, (Rev 21:20). The ancients obtained chrysolite mainly from the Red Sea island of *Zabarqad* (called *Topazus insula*

by Pliny, *Hist. Nat.* xxxvii. 9), which lies off the Egyptian coast, about 34 mi. east of *Râs Benas.* Some chrysolite may have been imported from India and Ethiopia.

Tophel (tō'fĕl). [Heb. *Tophel.*] A camping place of Israel in the wilderness (Deut 1:1); generally identified with *eṭ-Ṭafîleh,* about 16 mi. southeast of the southern tip of the Dead Sea (Map V, B-7), but the identification is probably erroneous.

Tophet. See Topheth.

Topheth (tō'fĕth), KJV generally **Tophet** (tō'fĕt). [Heb. *Topheth.* The Hebrew word in the Masoretic pronunciation is the result of assigning to the consonants *t-ph-th* the vowels of *bosheth,* "shame," giving to the word the meaning of "spitting," or "place of abhorrence." However, most commentators believe that the word is based on the Aramaic root *t-ph-t,* "to burn," and that it therefore means "fireplace."] The place in the Hinnom Valley where in the time of certain kings of Judah human sacrifices, especially infants, were offered by burning them to Molech (2 Ki 23:10; Jer 7:31). Isaiah, using highly figurative language, uses Topheth as a symbol of the destruction of an Assyrian king (Is 30:33), and Jeremiah prophesied that this particular place would become a place of slaughter so that the whole valley in which Topheth had been located would be called the valley of slaughter (Jer 7:31, 32; 19:6) and would be defiled (ch 19:13).

Torch. [Heb. *lappîd;* Gr. *lampas.*] A source of light produced by burning resinous wood, a bundle of reed, or twisted tow soaked with oil, grease, or pitch. Ancient torches have not yet been found in excavations, but the Assyrian relief depicting the conquest of Lachish shows torches being thrown upon the Assyrian soldiers by the Hebrew defenders of Lachish (fig. 284). These torches look like bundles of twigs bound together. Torches are frequently mentioned in the Bible (Nah 2:4; Zec 12:6; Jn 18:3; Rev 8:10, RSV; etc.). The Heb. *lappîd* is frequently rendered "lamp" in the KJV (Gen 15:17; Jgs 7:16, 20; etc.).

Tortoise. See Lizard.

Tou (tō'oō), or **Toi** (tō'ī). [Heb. *To'i* and *To'û,* in cuneiform texts *Tûi, Tuḫi.*] A king of Hamath, probably a Hittite, who congratulated David for his victory over their common enemy, the Syrian king Hadadezer of Zobah, and sent presents to David, thus recognizing David's supremacy (2 Sa 8:9-12; 1 Chr 18:9-11).

Tow. A rendering of: (1) The Heb. *ne'oreth,* "the material shaken off from flax when beaten," "tow," from the verb *na'ar,* "to shake," "to shake out." A string of tow is easily snapped when it touches fire (Jgs 16:9), and its flammability makes it a suitable figure for destruction by fire (Is 1:31). (2) The Heb. *pishtah,* "flax," in ch 43:17, KJV, where *pishtah* refers to a flax wick.

Tower. A structure built for height, generally considerably higher than its width or diameter. Several Hebrew words and one Greek word (*purgos*) are rendered tower. The most common Hebrew term is *migdal.* Towers in ancient times were not erected for ornamental purposes, as are modern church towers, nor for the pleasure of viewing the scenery from a vantage point; they were mostly watchtowers, and

508. A watchtower near *Taibeh,* in the hill country of Ephraim

served defensive purposes, either for fortifying cities (2 Chr 14:7), protecting vineyards from intruders (Is 5:2; Mt 21:33; fig. 508), or defending shepherds and caravan routes from desert raiders (2 Chr 26:10). Ruins of many Nabataean towers can still be seen on the border of the desert in Transjordan. Towers usually formed part of every city fortification, flanking the gates (v 9) and standing at intervals in the walls (Neh 3:1; see fig. 336). They served as lookouts for watchmen (2 Ki 9:17), as vantage points from which missiles were hurled on attacking enemies (2 Chr 26:15), and places of refuge for citizens when a city wall was breached (Jgs 9:51, 52). The stone reliefs of Sennacherib

depicting the siege and fall of Lachish show the defenders on the towers of their city wall hurling stones and fiery torches on the attacking Assyrians, and shooting arrows at them (fig. 284).

Tower of Babel. *See* Babel.

Tower of David. [Heb. *migdal Dawîd.*] Probably one of the additions to Jerusalem's fortifications built by David (Song 4:4). It must have been part of David's city that was limited to the southeastern hill (*see* David, City of; Jerusalem, I). During the excavations of Jerusalem, conducted under the direction of Macalister and Duncan, part of a Jebusite bastion was uncovered into which a tower of Davidic or Solomonic origin had been incorporated, giving us some idea of a typical tower of David's time (see fig. 254). The present "Tower of David" near the Jaffa Gate (see fig. 263) has really no right to that name. Its lower courses belong to the tower of Phasael, one of 3 built by Herod the Great as part of his palace and left standing by Titus as a memorial of the city's fortifications when he ruthlessly destroyed Jerusalem in A.D. 70 (Jos. *War* v. 4. 3).

Tower of Eder. *See* Eder, 1.

Tower of Hananeel. *See* Hananel.

Tower of Hananel. *See* Hananel.

Tower of Lebanon. [Heb. *migdal Hallebanôn.*] A tower mentioned in Song 7:4. It is not known whether an actual locality or tower in the Lebanon Mountains or elsewhere by that name existed. Since it is mentioned only in a poetic simile, it was possibly an imaginary structure, whose name suggested beauty, loftiness, and prominence, with which the poet compared the nose of his beloved.

Tower of Meah. *See* Meah.

Tower of Penuel. *See* Penuel, 1.

Tower of Shechem. [Heb. *migdal Shekem.*] A fortress in the general area of Shechem. However, it probably did not form part of the actual city of Shechem (Jgs 9:46-49). It has been variously identified with the ruins of *Khirbet en-Naṣrallah,* near the village of *Sâlim,* 3 miles east of *Balâṭah,* the site of ancient Shechem (Map XVI, D-3), or with *Tell Sufar* at the western exit of the pass between the mountains of Ebal and Gerizim.

Tower of Siloam. *See* Siloam.

Tower of Syene. A rendering of the Heb. *migdol Seweneh* in Eze 29:10 and 30:6, KJV. However, *migdol* should probably be considered as a proper noun, in which case it would denote a north-Egyptian city, elsewhere attested (*see* Migdol, 2). The RSV reading "from Migdol to Syene" is to be preferred over that of the KJV "from the tower of Syene." See Syene, I.

Tower of the Furnaces, RSV once **Tower of the Ovens.** [Heb. *migdal hattannúrîm.*] The name of a tower in the western wall of Jerusalem during Nehemiah's time (Neh 3:11; 12:38). Some have located it outside the city and have connected it with city bakeries. This interpretation must be rejected, because vital industries, such as bakeries, were always placed within the fortification system of any ancient city. Most scholars therefore consider it a part of the western wall. A study of Nehemiah's description of Jerusalem's walls (chs 2: 13-15; 3:1-13; 12:31-40) shows that the Tower of the Furnaces stood between the Ephraim Gate and the Valley Gate, hence somewhere in the center of Jerusalem's western wall (see fig. 259).

Town Clerk. [Gr. *grammateus,* "secretary," "clerk."] A prominent public official in the city of Ephesus (Acts 19:35). The designation *grammateus* implies that he supervised the city archives and was responsible for drawing up and announcing official decrees. The skill and authority he demonstrated in quelling the riot against Paul implies that he was a man of considerable administrative authority (vs 35-41). Coins and inscriptions found in various sites of Asia Minor frequently mention the *grammateus* of cities, thus attesting his high office.

Trachonitis (trăk'ô-nī'tĭs). [Gr. *Trachōnitis,* "rough region," or "hilly region"; also called *Trachōn* by Josephus.] Part of the tetrarchy of Herod the Great's son, Philip, who ruled over all the northeastern territories of Palestine from 4 B.C. to A.D. 33/34 (Lk 3:1). The area, now called the *Lejā* (Map XVI, B/C-5/6), is a rugged, inaccessible, and lava-covered plateau, about 370 sq. mi. in extent, lying south of Damascus, and north of the Hauran. Anciently its population was mixed and consisted mainly of non-Jews. See Jos. *Ant.* xv. 10. 3; xvii. 2. 1 and 2; Strabo xvi. 2. 20.

Tradition. [Gr. *paradosis,* "tradition," literally, "(instruction) handed over," that is, from one person to another or from one generation to the next.] In the Gospels the accumulated body of oral interpretation of the OT, particularly the Law of Moses, as given by the scribes. It was called Halakah in Jewish literature. Later this body of oral tradition was written down and preserved in the Mishnah and the Talmud (see *SDACom* 5:96-100). The Pharisees referred to this body of teaching as "the tradition of the elders" (Mt 15:2), and Jesus called it "your tradition" (vs 3, 6), or the "tradition of men," meaning that it originated with man and not with God (Mk 7:8). While enjoining upon His own disciples the strict observance of the laws of Moses (Mt 23:2, 3), our Lord again and again declared worse than useless the great mass of human interpretation whose effect was to frustrate or at least obscure "the commandment of God" (cf. Mk 7:1-9). The fundamental error of "the tradition of the elders" was that it blinded men to the need for a religion that springs from the heart and made the observance of certain outward forms the essential qualification for salvation and acceptance with God.

In the epistles "tradition" is used also (cf. Gal 1:14) of Paul's teachings (1 Cor 11:2, RSV; 2 Th 2:15; 3:6). There was also in NT times the authentic tradition of the testimony of eyewitnesses to the acts and teachings of Jesus (see Lk 1:2 where "delivered" is a rendering of the Gr. *paradidōmi,* the verb form corresponding to the noun *paradosis,* "tradition"). Compare Heb 2:3, 4.

Trance. [Gr. *ekstasis,* literally, "a standing out," and by extension, "any displacement, especially that of the mind." The English word "ecstasy" is derived directly from *ekstasis.*] A condition of the mind in which normal consciousness, with its attendant perception of the natural environment, is suspended and the mental processes are predisposed to the communications of a supernatural power. This term is used with reference to the experience of Peter (Acts 10:10; 11:5) and Paul (ch 22:17). "Trance" occurs in Num 24:4, 16, KJV, but, as the italics indicate, it is a supplied word, there being no corresponding Hebrew word in the text.

Translate, Translation. [Heb. *'abar,* "to pass over"; Gr. *methistēmi, metatithēmi,* "to transfer," "to convey from one place to another," "to remove"; *metathesis,* "a removal," "a change," "a transformation."] Terms referring to the transfer of a thing or a person from one place to another. The English word "translate" is from the Latin *translatus,* which, though from a different root, was used as a past participle of *transfero,* "to transfer." The term is used of the transfer of the kingdom of Israel from Saul to David (2 Sa 3:10,

KJV). In Col 1:13, KJV, it is used figuratively of the transfer of the converted Christian from the kingdom of this world to the kingdom of Christ, that is, to the kingdom of divine grace in this life. In Heb 11:5, KJV, it refers to the translation of Enoch from this earth to heaven.

Treasure City. See Pithom.

Trees. See Flora and Fauna; Forest; Palestine, VII.

Trench. The rendering of: (1) The Heb. *te'alah* (1 Ki 18:32, 35, 38), a ditch dug in the ground, used of the ditch dug by Elijah on Mount Carmel around his altar. (2) The Heb. *chêl* (2 Sa 20:15, KJV), meaning uncertain. The term is translated "rampart" in the RSV. (3) The Heb. *ma'gal* (1 Sa 17:20; 26:5, 7, KJV), "round encampment," rendered "encampment" in the RSV. (4) The Gr. *charax* (Lk 19:43), "palisade wall," rendered "bank" in the RSV.

Trespass. [Heb. *'asham,* "offense," "guilt"; *'ashmah,* "guiltiness," "guilt"; *ma'al,* "unfaithfulness," "a dereliction of duty"; *pesha',* "rebellion," "revolt," "guilt"; Gr. *paraptōma,* "false step," "transgression," "sin," "trespass."] The act of going beyond one's own rights so as to infringe upon the rights of another; any violation of the civil or moral law. Usually the "trespass" was "against the Lord" (Num 5:6, KJV), though at times against one's fellow man (Gen 31:36; 50:17; KJV). Certain offenses required a "trespass," or "guilt," offering (Lev 5:6, 7). Jesus counseled that when an offender confessed to trespassing against another, the offended person was required to forgive (Mt 6:14; cf. Eph 4:32; Col 3:13), thus effecting reconciliation.

Trespass Offering. See Sacrifices and Offerings.

Tribute. In general, forced contributions of money, goods, or labor to be made at stated times by a subject people to the ruler by whom they are conquered and under whose suzerainty they live. Moses instructed Israel (Deut 20:11) concerning the placing of other nations under "tribute" (the Heb. *mas,* "forced labor," is commonly rendered "tribute" in the KJV, Gen 49:15; Jgs 1:28; 1 Ki 4:6; etc.). A "tribute" of the spoil captured by the army was to be given to the Lord (Num 31:28-30). The Israelites paid tribute at various times to Moab (Jgs 3:15, RSV), Egypt (2 Ki 23:33; 2 Chr 36:3; RSV), Assyria (2 Ki 17:3; 2 Chr 28:21; RSV), and Persia (Est 10:1; etc.). Taxes were always heaviest in times of emergency, for the military campaigns of kings and emperors were financed by subject peoples. Xerxes (Ahasuerus) king of Persia distinguished himself as a great raiser of tribute (see Est 10:1). His disastrous campaign against Greece necessitated increased burdens on those he ruled (see Dan 11:2). In Ezra's time the Jews were still under tribute to Persia (Ezr 4:13). Paul counseled Christians to pay *phoros,* "tribute," "taxes," to the civil government (Rom 13:6, 7). See figs. 246, 509.

Trigon. [Aramaic *śabbeka'* and *sabbeka'.*] A triangular, 4-stringed instrument with a bright tone, played in Nebuchadnezzar's orchestra at the dedication of the golden image (Dan 3:7, 10, 15). The term is erroneously rendered "sackbut" in the KJV. The sackbut is a medieval wind instrument, not known to the ancients. The *śabbeka'* appears in Greek as *sambukē* and in Latin as *sambuca.* However, according to Lidzbarski the trigon was not of Western origin (*Ephemeris* 2 [1908], 137). The Greeks and Romans took over the name, along with the instrument, from the Phoenicians, a fact attested by Strabo, who says that the word is of "barbarian" origin (*Geography* x. 3. 17).

Troas (trō'ăs). [Gr. *Trōas.*] Originally the name of a district east of the Hellespont in western Mysia, in which the famous Troy of Homer's *Iliad* was located. The NT Troas was a city (Map XX, B-4) founded by Antigonus, one of Alexander's generals, not far from the site of ancient Troy, and given the name Antigonia. After his death the name was changed to Alexandria by his opponent, Lysimachus, king of Thrace. In order to avoid confusion with Alexandria of Egypt, its official name became Alexandria Troas. Augustus made it a colony, and later emperors embellished the city with magnificent buildings. Extensive ruins, among which are baths, a theater,

509. Tribute brought to Shalmaneser III by people of Carchemish, portrayed on the bronze gates from *Balawat*

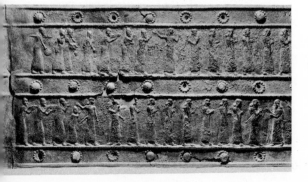

an aqueduct, and a temple, still bear witness to its former glory. It was at this seaport, on the main route between western Asia and Macedonia, that Paul on his 1st visit to Troas, during his 2d Missionary Journey, received the divine call to labor in Europe (Acts 16:8-10). He passed through the city twice during his 3d Missionary Journey (2 Cor 2:12; Acts 20:6). On the 2d occasion he remained 1 week with the Troas church, of which he probably was the founder. He was in the city again after his 1st Roman imprisonment, and may have been arrested there, for he seems to have left the city in such a hurry that he had no opportunity to take his cloak and books with him (2 Ti 4:13).

Trogyllium (trŏ-jĭl'ĭ-ŭm). [Gr. *Trōgullion*.] A town and promontory on the west coast of Asia Minor, lying opposite the island of Samos (Map XX, B-4). The narrow strait separating Samos and Trogyllium was the site of the famous sea battle between the Persians and the Greeks in 479 B.C., which ended in the destruction of the Persian navy. Paul may have spent at least a night at this place on his voyage to Jerusalem returning from his 3d Missionary Journey (Acts 20:15, KJV), although important textual evidence may be cited for the omission of the clause "and tarried at Trogyllium," hence its absence in the RSV. An anchorage at that place is still called St. Paul's Port.

Troop. *See* Fortune.

Trophimus (trŏf'ĭ-mŭs). [Gr. *Trophimos*, "nourishing." The name occurs also in Greek inscriptions.] A Gentile Christian of Ephesus, who, with Tychicus, represented the churches of Asia in the presentation of a gift to the Jerusalem church (Acts 20:4). The Jews falsely accused Paul of having taken him into the inner Temple precincts, and thus started the tumult that led to Paul's imprisonment (ch 21:29). He is mentioned again in Paul's last letter (2 Ti 4:20), as having been left sick at Miletus.

Trucebreaker. A rendering of the Gr. *aspondos*, "irreconcilable" (2 Ti 3:3; RSV "implacable"). The text describes the last-day condition of men (v 1).

Trumpet. A rendering of: (1) The Heb. *shôphar* (Ex 19:16; Lev 25:9; Jos 6:4; Jgs 3:27; etc.), a ram's horn used as a signaling instrument. *See* Horn. (2) The Heb. *yôbel*, "ram," usually connected with the Heb. *qeren* or *shôphar*, meaning "ram's horn," but it occurs once alone (Ex 19:

13) with the meaning "ram's (horn)." Since the *yôbel* horn was blown to open the 50th year, the name of that year became "the year of *yôbel*," translated "year of jubilee" (*see* Jubilee). (3) The Heb.

510. Egyptian army trumpeters as depicted on the walls of the temple of Ramses III at *Medinet Habu*

chaṣoṣerah (Num 10:2, 10; 1 Chr 13:8; etc.). This trumpet is made of metal in contrast to the one made of a ram's horn. Those mentioned in Num 10:1, 2 were made, according to divine instruction, "of a whole piece," the phrase probably meaning "of hammered work" (RSV), of 1 sheet of metal (cf. fig. 511). This in-

511. Copper and silver trumpets of Tutankhamen, in the Cairo Museum

strument is, with one exception (Hos 5:8), referred to in the plural, and is depicted on coins (fig. 512) and on the relief of the Arch of Titus in pairs (fig. 287). It therefore seems reasonable to conclude that 2 horns were played either simultaneously or alternately, and possibly each on a different note. These trumpets were used for alarm (Num 10:9), and also in religious services (2 Chr 5:12, 13; etc.). See *SDACom* 3:40, 41. (4) The Heb. *taqôa'* (Eze 7:14); of uncertain meaning. (5) The Gr. *salpigx*. This instrument was used in war (1 Cor 14:8; fig. 510); it is mentioned in the description of the second advent of Christ (Mt 24: 31), and of the resurrection of the dead (1 Cor 15:52). Seven great visions of Revelation are introduced by the sound of trumpets (Rev 8:2, 6-8, 10, 12; 9:1, 13; 11:15), and heavenly voices heard by John sounded to him like trumpets (chs 1:10; 4:1). See figs. 510, 511, 512.

512. Trumpets, as shown on a Jewish coin of the 2d cent. A.D.

Trumpets, Feast of. A feast celebrated on the 1st day of the 7th month (Ethanim, or Tishri), the beginning of the civil *year. This 1st day fell on the "new moon" of September or October. This month was always numbered the 7th (see Lev 23:24), according to God's instructions to Moses to begin the year with the Passover month of Abib (Nisan), as the first month (see Ex 12:2); yet the year was still reckoned as beginning with Tishri for civil matters. Tishri 1 was marked by extra sacrifices in addition to the new-moon sacrifices of the other months (Num 29:1-6). It was a ceremonial sabbath, and was celebrated by the blowing of trumpets (Lev 23:24, 25). The tradition of the Jews is that on New Year's Day (celebrated to this day as Rosh Hashana) everyone is judged for his deeds of the past year, but that one's doom is not settled until the 10th, on the Day of Atonement, apparently after 9 days of grace (Talmud *Rosh Hashanah,* 16a).

Tryphaena (trī-fē′na), KJV **Tryphena** (trī-fē′na). [Gr. *Truphaina,* "luxuriant." The name occurs in Greek inscriptions, and was borne by an Egyptian Jewess and by a queen of Thrace.] A Christian woman in Rome to whom Paul sent greetings, commending her for her zealous work in the Lord (Rom 16:12). Since she is mentioned with Tryphosa, and has a similar name, many commentators suppose that the 2 women are sisters.

Tryphena. *See* Tryphaena.

Tryphosa (trī-fō′sa). [Gr. *Truphōsa,* "luxuriant." The name occurs in Greek and Latin inscriptions.] A Christian woman in Rome to whom Paul sent greetings, commending her for her zealous work in the Lord (Rom 16:12). She may have been a sister of *Tryphaena.

Tubal (tū′bǎl). [Heb. *Tubal.*] A son of Japheth (Gen 10:2; 1 Chr 1:5), and ancestor of the Tibarenians mentioned by Herodotus (iii. 94), called *Tabal* in Assyrian texts. This people is mentioned first in the 12th cent. B.C. as allied with the Muski (Meshech) and Kaski in an attempt to conquer northeastern Mesopotamia. Tabal is mentioned as a country for the 1st time in the 9th cent B.C., and in the 8th cent. as situated in southern Cappadocia. The Tabaleans later were pushed into Armenia, where Greek authors of the classical period came in contact with them. They are mentioned together with Javan by Isaiah (Is 66:19), and with Javan and Meshech by Ezekiel, who describes them as trading in slaves and metal vessels in the markets of Tyre (Eze 27:13; cf. 32:26). In chs 38:2, 3; 39: 1 Gog is described as their prince. Map IV, B-5.

Tubal-cain (tū′bǎl-kān′). [Heb. *Tûbal Qayin,* "Tubal, the smith," or "Tubal of Cain's (descendants)."] A son of Lamech and Zillah, and a descendant of Cain. He was the 1st metal worker of the antediluvian world (Gen 4:22).

Tunic. *See* Clothing.

Turban. [Heb. *miṣnepheth, ṣaniph,* and *ṣeniphah,* "turban"; all 3 terms being derived from the same verb, *ṣanaph,* "to wrap around"; *tebulim,* "turban," "that which is wound about"; *pe'er,* "headdress."] An Oriental headdress formed by binding a length of linen (Ex 28:39, RSV) or other material around the head. Although usually worn by men (Job 29: 14, RSV), it is also listed with the dress of women (Is 3:23, RSV). The royal turban, a badge of kingship, was donned by the princes of Israel (Eze 21:26, RSV). The high priest wore a turban (Lev 8:9; 16:4; Zec 3:5; RSV), to which was attached, with a "lace of blue," the inscription "Holiness to the Lord" (Ex 28: 36-38; 39:30, 31). Describing the garments of the high priest, Josephus says: "Upon his head he wears a cap without a peak. . . . It is . . . so fashioned as to resemble a coronet, consisting of a band of woven linen thickly compressed; for it is wound round and round and stitched repeatedly" (*Ant.* iii. 7. 3). Some turbans were fashioned with considerable style (Eze 23:15, RSV). "Turban" is also used in a metaphorical sense in Job 29:14, RSV. The term does not occur in the KJV, which variously renders the Hebrew terms "mitre," "diadem," "tire," "hood," "bonnet," "attire."

Turtle. *See* Turtledove.

Turtledove, KJV 4 times **Turtle.** [Heb. *tôr;* Gr. *trugōn.*] A small variety of pigeon, 3 species of which occur in Palestine—the common turtledove (*Turtur vulgaris*), the collared turtledove (*Turtur risorius*), and the palm turtledove (*Turtur senegalensis*). It is noted in Scripture for its arrival from the south as a harbinger of spring (Song 2:11, 12; Jer 8:7). The Lord directed that those who could not afford the larger animals for sacrifices could bring "two turtledoves" (Lev 5:7; 14:22; Lk 2:24). These birds were among the creatures Abraham offered upon entering into covenant agreement with God (Gen 15:9).

Tutor. *See* Guardian.

Twin Brothers, KJV **Castor and Pollux** (kăs'tẽr and pŏl'ŭks). [Gr. *Dioskouroi.*] Twin hero-divinities in Greek and Roman mythology, sons of Leda. According to different legends their father was either Zeus or a king of Sparta, Tyndareus, or, in a 3d legend, Tyndareus was the father of Castor, and Zeus the father of Pollux. Castor was a master of horses and chariots and was killed in a fight. Pollux was a prize fighter who chose to share his immortality with his brother. They were worshiped under the name *Dioscuri* (Latin), or *Dioskouroi* (Greek). They were also considered as the tutelary divinities of sailors. It is not certain whether the ship on which Paul traveled from Malta to Italy carried the name *Dioskouroi* or had the images of the Twin Brothers ornamenting its prow (Acts 28:11). To Castor and Pollux was dedicated one of the most famous temples of Rome, built in the early Republican period and repeatedly restored during the empire. It stands in the Roman Forum on the spot where, according to the local tradition, the *Dioscuri* had appeared in the form of two young horsemen and announced the victory of the Roman army over the Tarquins and Tusculans at Lake Regillus (*c.* 449 B.C.). Three columns of this temple are still standing (see fig. 513).

Tychicus (tĭk'ĭ-kŭs). [Gr. *Tuchikos,* "happy."] A Christian, probably Gentile, who, with Trophimus, represented the church of Asia when a gift was presented to the Jerusalem church (Acts 20:4). He was with Paul in Rome during the apostle's 1st imprisonment and was the bearer of Paul's letters to the Colossians and Ephesians (Col 4:7; Eph 6:21), who were told that Tychicus could give them additional informa-

513. The three remaining columns of the temple of Castor and Pollux in the Roman Forum, with the Palatine Hill in the background

tion concerning Paul's condition. It was probably he whom Paul sent to Crete (Tit 3:12). Later he was sent to Ephesus (2 Ti 4:12). Paul characterized him as a beloved brother and faithful minister in the Lord (Col 4:7).

Tyrannus (tĭ-răn'ŭs). [Gr. *Turannos,* "an absolute ruler," or "tyrant." The name occurs in Greek inscriptions.] An Ephesian who was probably a teacher of rhetoric, philosophy, or other subjects. He owned a school building which he made available to Paul for meetings after the apostle had been expelled from the Jewish synagogue (Acts 19:9). Whether he was a Jew, or a visitor of the synagogue who had become impressed by Paul's teachings, or a mere stranger who had a hall for rent, is not known. According to the 6th-cent. Codex Bezae and a few other manuscripts, Paul taught in Tyrannus' school "from the 5th to the 10th hour," hence followed the custom of the philosophers of his time.

Tyre (tīr), KJV frequently **Tyrus** (tī'rŭs). [Heb. *Ṣor,* "rock"; Phoenician and Ugaritic *Ṣr;* Akkadian *Ṣurru;* Egyptian *Ḏꜣyr;* Gr. *Turos.*] An important Phoenician port city of antiquity, about 23 mi. south of Sidon (Map VI, B-3). It was situated

514. Map of Tyre and environs

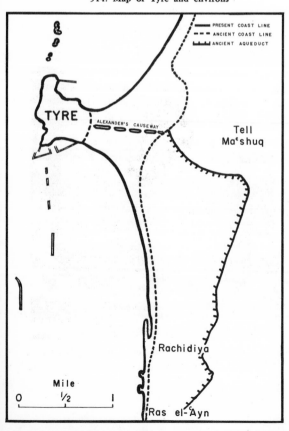

first on the mainland and used the island off the coast for harbor installations. The mainland city was called *Ushu* in cuneiform records, *Palaityros* by the Greeks. Repeatedly the population of Tyre sought refuge on the rock island, containing about 140 acres, and eventually made it their exclusive place of habitation.

The origin of Tyre is unknown. Although it was regarded as a city of great antiquity (Is 23:7; Jos. *Ant.* viii. 3. 1), Sidon seems to have been more important in the beginning, being mentioned in the earliest Biblical records without Tyre (Gen 10:15; 49:13). When Herodotus visited Tyre, about 450 B.C., he was told by the priests of Melkarth that their city was 2,300 years old (ii. 44), but this may have been an unfounded tradition. The city is mentioned for the first time in Egyptian records (the Execration Texts) of the 19th cent. B.C., and later in the *Amarna Letters, which reveal that its king Abimilki was a vassal of Egypt as were all other Syrian and Palestinian princes in the 14th cent. B.C. Shortly afterward it regained its independence, was later reconquered by Pharaoh Seti I, but was lost again by Egypt, probably during the reign of Ramses II. By the Bible writers it was known as a fortress from the time of Joshua on (Jos 19:29; 2 Sa 24:7). It was not assigned to any tribe, and at no time belonged to Israel.

Tyre's king Hiram had friendly relations with David and Solomon, and furnished both kings building material and craftsmen for the erection of their palaces and the Temple (2 Sa 5:11; 1 Ki 5:1-6; 9:10-14; 1 Chr 14:1; 2 Chr 2:3-16). Experienced sailors of Tyre also helped Solomon carry out his maritime expeditions to Ophir and Tarshish (1 Ki 9:26-28; 10:22). These friendly relations were continued, at least for a time, even after the breakup of the kingdom, to which the marriage of Prince Ahab of Israel to Jezebel, a Tyrian princess, bears witness (ch 16:31; *see* Ethbaal). About that time colonists from Tyre founded Carthage on the Tunisian coast. In the course of time Carthage grew so powerful that it became a serious rival of Rome, and almost overpowered it.

The Tyrian rulers, being merchant princes, were not interested in warfare (Is 23:8); they traded with all countries around the Mediterranean Sea, and later in lands beyond that sea. Their main products were purple dyes, glassware, and metal objects, but they also traded in

TYRE

slaves (Eze 27:13; Amos 1:9; Joel 3:5, 6) —among them Hebrews—and products of other countries. Their wealth aroused the jealousy of war-loving nations and repeatedly involved them in undesired wars. When the Assyrians appeared in Syria in the 9th cent. B.C., Tyre was able to buy itself off from Ashurnasirpal II (884-859 B.C.) by paying tribute (*ANET* 276b). His son Shalmaneser III (859-824 B.C.), Adad-nirari III (810-782 B.C.), and Tiglath-pileser III (745-727 B.C.) report that they also received tribute from Tyre (*ANET* 280b, 281b, 283a). According to Josephus (*Ant.* ix. 14. 2), Shalmaneser V (727-722 B.C.), of whom so far no cuneiform records have been found, conquered mainland Tyre and laid siege to the island without being able to capture it. Other attempts to conquer the island were made by Sennacherib (705-681 B.C.), Esarhaddon (681-669 B.C.), and Ashurbanipal (669-?627 B.C.). Sennacherib and Ashurbanipal were satisfied with conquering mainland Tyre (= *Ushû*, *ANET* 287b, 300b), but Esarhaddon claims to have reduced the island (*ANET* 290a). See fig. 163. Another great test came when Nebuchadnezzar besieged the island city for 13 years without success (Jos. *Against Apion* i. 21), although he got mainland Tyre into his hands. The prophecies of Ezekiel deal with this unsuccessful siege (Eze 26:1-14; 29:18). Finally a compromise was reached, when Nebuchadnezzar allowed Tyre to retain its kingship and a semi-independent status with a Babylonian high commissioner, who had the duty to see that tribute commensurate with the income of the subject nation was regularly paid into the treasury of the Babylonians.

Mainland Tyre seems not to have been rebuilt at that time, but the island city continued to flourish during the Persian period, and apparently enjoyed a great measure of independence. When that city, relying on its isolation and impregnability, refused to submit to Alexander after the battle of Issus (333 B.C.), he besieged the city. He built a mole from the mainland to the island by using debris of the old city, thus fulfilling Ezekiel's prophecy of ch 26:12. Seven months after reaching Tyre he made a concerted attack in which his land army advancing over the newly built mole was joined by amphibious forces, landing from all sides on the shores of the island. The city was captured and destroyed, its nobles slain, and the remnants of its citizens sold into

515. Remains of the ancient quay walls in the sea at Tyre

slavery. Although the city recovered from its downfall, it never regained its old glory. In 198 B.C. it was incorporated into the Seleucid kingdom, but later received a measure of independence, which was respected when Pompey took Syria in the 1st cent. B.C.

Christ visited the region of Tyre during His Galilean ministry (Mt 15:21-28; Mk 7:24-31), and people from Tyre were occasionally found among His hearers (Mk 3:8; Lk 6:17). A Christian church existed in the apostolic period in this city, which was visited by Paul when he returned to Jerusalem from his 3d Missionary Journey (Acts 21:3-6). Tyre was conquered by the Crusaders in A.D. 1124, but was lost in A.D. 1291 to the Saracens, who destroyed it almost completely. Since that time only a small settlement of Moslems has lived there with a few Christians. Their houses stand partly on the northern section of the old island and partly on the causeway of Alexander which through the accretions of sand on both sides has been so enlarged in width that it is now almost 1/2 mi. wide (fig. 514). The modern name of the town is *Ṣûr*. Its population numbers about 12,000. Its visible ruins date from the Byzantine period, but excavations have uncovered Roman and earlier remains. Part of the western coast has been battered by the sea, and in the water the remains of ancient structures can be seen, as well as many ancient columns and other stone blocks. The little modern fishing harbor (see fig. 352) on the north side of the former island is located at the site of the ancient Sidonian harbor. Of the so-called Egyptian harbor in the south, half submerged breakwaters and quays are still visible. See fig. 515.

Tyrus. See Tyre.

Tzaddi. [Heb. *ṣadê.*] The 18th letter of the Hebrew alphabet, written צ, appearing as the title of the 18th section of Ps 119 in the KJV. *See* Aleph.

U

Ucal (ū'kăl). [Heb. *'Ukal*, meaning uncertain.] An obscure word in Prov 30:1. The Masoretes regarded it as the name of an individual. If they were correct, Ucal is one of 2 sons or pupils to whom Agur addressed his instructions.

Uel (ū'ĕl). [Heb. *'Ū'el*, possibly "desire of God."] A descendant of Bani; he had married a foreign wife in the time of Ezra (Ezr 10:34).

Ulai (ū'lī). [Heb. *'Ūlay*.] A river at Susa, on the banks of which Daniel saw the vision of the he-goat and the ram (Dan 8:2, 16). Although it is mentioned in Assyrian inscriptions as *Ulâ*, its identification is uncertain. Pliny (vi. 135) locates Susa on the Eulaeus (the modern *Karûn*), but Herodotus (i. 188; v. 49. 52) and Strabo (xv. 728) place it on the Choaspes (the modern *Kerkha*). Some scholars think that the Ulai was an artificial canal connecting the Choaspes and the Coprates, the main streams of that region.

Ulam (ū'lăm). [Heb. *'Ūlam*, meaning uncertain.]

1. A Manassite (1 Chr 7:16, 17).

2. A Benjamite descendant of Saul through Jonathan; he was the ancestor of a family of famous archers (1 Chr 8:39, 40).

Ulla (ŭl'ā). [Heb. *'Ulla'*, meaning unknown.] A descendant of Asher (1 Chr 7:39).

Ummah (ŭm'ā). [Heb. *'Ummah*, "juxtaposition."] A place in the territory of Asher (Jos 19:30); not identified, unless, as some think, *'Ummah* is a scribal mistake for *Acco.

Umpire. See Daysman.

Uncircumcised. See Circumcision.

Uncle. A rendering of Heb. *dôd*, which is twice translated "father's brother" in the KJV. It sometimes means literally that, for example, Aaron's uncle Uzziel (Lev 10:4) was the brother of his father Amram (Ex 6:18, 20); Zedekiah was Jehoiachin's uncle (2 Ki 24:17; cf. 24:6; 1 Chr 3:15). However, in OT usage *dôd* can refer to some other kinsman on the father's side (probably because *"brother" could mean the father's more distant relative); it apparently is equivalent to "distant cousins," members of the same tribe, in Num 36:11 (cf. vs 8, 12).

Unclean Animals. [The expression "unclean" is a rendering generally of the Heb. *tame'*, "(ceremonially) polluted," "defiled," "unclean," and the Gr. *akathartos*, "impure," "defiled," "unclean."] Animals declared by the Law of Moses to be unfit for either food or sacrifice. The purpose in distinguishing certain animals as clean and others as unclean was apparently twofold—dietary and religious. Whether the distinction between clean and unclean animals was based exclusively on their habits and on the unwholesomeness of their flesh as food is not altogether certain, but the fact remains that from very early times—centuries before the giving of the Mosaic law—the distinction was clearly recognized (see Gen 7:2, 3; 8:20). Generally speaking at least, animals designated as clean are herbivorous in diet and comparatively gentle in disposition, whereas birds and animals listed as unclean are carnivorous. With quadrupeds and sea animals the distinction between clean and unclean is clear. An animal is clean if it parts the hoof, is clovenfooted, and chews the cud (Lev 11:3, 8, 26). To be clean, a creature of the water must have both fins and scales (vs 9-12). For the various kinds of fowl no basic rule is stated. There is only an enumeration of the unclean fowl (Lev 11:13-20; cf. Deut 14:12-18). Because it flies, the bat is included among the birds (Lev 11:19; Deut 14:18). Of insects, the locust, bald locust, cricket (RSV), and grasshopper are listed as clean; others are unclean (Lev 11:20-23). All small creeping animals are declared to be unclean (vs 29, 30, 41, 42). A man who incurred uncleanness by contact with an unclean creature was required to wash his clothes and to remain unclean for the rest of the day (vs 24-28, 31, 32, 39, 40; ch 17:15). By contact with an unclean creature any earthen vessel, food, water, seed grain, or clothing also became unclean (ch 11:32-38).

In a number of instances the animal designated by the Hebrew terms is uncertain. *See* names of specific animals. For a list of the animals mentioned in the Bible *see* Flora and Fauna.

Unclean Spirit. [Gr. *pneuma akatharton*.] A common NT designation for evil spirits that at times took possession of human beings (see Mt 12:43; Mk 1:23, 26; etc.). Otherwise they are called unclean devils or unclean demons (Lk 4:33), devils or demons (Mt 9:33), or simply "spirits" (Mk 9:20). Twice (Mk 9:25; Rev 18:2) the KJV translates *pneuma akatharton* "foul spirit." There are a number of instances in which a miracle of our Lord involved the casting out of an unclean spirit or demon (see Mk 1:21-28; Mt 9: 32-34; 12:22-32; Mk 5:1-20; Mt 15:21-28; Mk 9:14-29). The disciples received power to cast out unclean spirits (Mt 10: 1). See Demon.

Uncleanness. [Heb. generally *tame'*, and related words, "(ceremonial) uncleanness"; Gr. generally *akatharsia*, "uncleanness," "impurity."] Defilement that might be physical, moral, or ceremonial, though in the OT chiefly the last (see Lev 5:2; 7:19; 10:10; etc.). God's purpose in having a person declared unclean because of certain acts, whether voluntary or involuntary, was to teach His people the distinction between the holy and the unholy, and between the clean and the unclean (cf. ch 10:10), a distinction that all must recognize in order to serve God acceptably. Contact with a human corpse (Num 19:11-22) made a person unclean for 7 days (v 11). The one thus defiled was to purify himself on the 3d day and to become clean on the 7th day (v 12). Anyone who ignored this provision was to be "cut off from Israel" (v 13). Furthermore, everything in a tent in which a man died was to be unclean for 7 days (v 14). Leprosy also rendered a man unclean (Lev 13:45, 46), and special regulations prescribed the manner in which a person cured of leprosy might become clean (ch 14:1-32). A 3d, and less serious, occasion for uncleanness was the normal or abnormal issues from the generative organs (ch 15), including "uncleanness" at childbirth (ch 12). Contact with the carcass of any unclean animal, or with that of any clean animal not slain for food, also incurred uncleanness (ch 11:24-40). In the NT "uncleanness" is used of immorality, unnatural vices, and sexual sins (Rom 1:24, KJV; Eph 4:19; Col 3:5, KJV; 1 Th 4:7; etc.).

Unction. *See* Anoint.

Undergird. *See* Ship.

Undersetter. [Heb. *katheph*, "shoulder," "support."] In the context of 1 Ki 7:30, 34, KJV, one of the supports at the 4 corners of the portable stands used for the lavers of Solomon's Temple.

Undertake. A word used in Is 38:14, KJV, in the archaic sense of "to be a guarantee." The Hebrew word thus translated (*'arab*) means "to become surety for."

Unicorn. In the KJV the rendering of the Heb. *re'em* (Num 23:22; Is 34:7; etc.), translated "wild ox" in the RSV. The translators of the KJV, possibly following the LXX, may have had the legendary unicorn in mind. This legend may have originated from art reliefs depicting bulls from the side, so that only the horn in the foreground was visible. That the *re'em* had more than a single horn is clear from Deut 33:17, which speaks of the horns of the *re'em*, where *re'em* is singular, not plural, as the KJV translators rendered it. From the Akkadian cognate *rimu* it is now certain that the term refers to the wild ox (*Bos primigenius*) which roamed in Syria in ancient times. Tiglath-pileser I (1113-1074 B.C.) hunted this beast in Syria, and Shalmaneser III (859-824 B.C.) depicts one of these animals on the famous Black Obelisk among tribute received from Musri. The wild ox is now extinct in the Near East. The strength of this animal and of its horns is mentioned in the OT (Num 24:8; Deut 33:17; Ps 22:21; 92:10), and the book of Job refers to the impossibility of taming this strong animal for work (Job 39:9-11).

Unleavened Bread, Feast of. The 7-day festival connected with the Passover (Lev 23: 5-8), and sometimes considered as included in it (Lk 22:1, 7). The original instructions for the observance of the Passover supper included the prohibition of leaven, or yeast, in the houses of the Hebrews from the evening of Nisan 14 (the day when the Passover lamb was killed) to the evening of the 21st (Ex 12: 8, 18-20). Later the custom arose of making a search to be sure all leaven was removed on the 14th. The day after the Passover, the 15th, was the 1st day of the Feast of Unleavened Bread, and was a festival sabbath, a day of rest and "holy convocation," or assembly (*see* Sabbath); then the next day ("the morrow after the sabbath"), the 16th, came the ceremony of waving a sheaf of grain—the first fruits of barley—that marked the beginning of the harvest season (Lev 23:10-14). It was this requirement of the "wave sheaf" that made the Jews adjust their calendar so as to keep their lunar year in line with the seasons (*see* Year). The last day of Unleavened Bread, the 21st of the month, was, like the 15th, a ceremonial sabbath (vs 7, 8).

Unni (ŭn′ī). [Heb. *'Unnî*, meaning uncertain.]

1. A Levite of the 2d order, appointed by David as one of the musicians (1 Chr 15:18, 20).

2. For Neh 12:9, KJV, *see* Unno.

Unno (ŭn′ō), KJV **Unni** (ŭn′ī). [Heb. *'Unnô* (Q *'Unnî*), meaning uncertain.] A Levite of the time of Zerubbabel (Neh 12:9).

Unpardonable Sin. An expression not appearing in the Bible, but based on certain passages such as Mt 12:31, where Christ teaches that "blasphemy against the Holy Ghost shall not be forgiven unto men" (Mt 12:31; cf. Lk 12:10). This assertion was made in response to a statement by certain Pharisees who, after witnessing a healing performed by Jesus, said that He "cast out devils . . . by Beelzebub the prince of the devils" (Mt 12:22-24; Mk 3:22-30). The Pharisees had expressed this sentiment on another occasion (Mt 9:34). This attitude was taken in the face of undeniable evidence given them of His divine power: the holiness of His life, which they could but recognize and which they later tacitly admitted (cf. Jn 8:46), His supernatural healing of the sick (Mt 8:14-17; Mk 1:29-34; Lk 4:38-40; etc.), His casting out of devils (Mt 9:32, 33; Mk 1:21-28), and His raising of the dead (Lk 7:11-17). However, by refusing to admit Christ's divinity, and by actively opposing Him (cf. Mk 3:2, 6; Lk 5:21; Jn 5:16; etc.), they had placed themselves in such a position that they were forced to explain His works on some other grounds than divine, and hence assigned to Satan the work of God, and thereby closed their minds to the evidence of the Holy Spirit (cf. Mt 12:25-29). The Holy Spirit impresses truth upon the mind and heart (cf. Jn 14:17; 16:13) and convicts of sin (ch 16:8). But although God is "longsuffering, and of great mercy" (Num 14:18), "not willing that any should perish, but that all should come to repentance" (2 Pe 3:9), His Spirit will not labor with the obdurate heart indefinitely (Gen 6:3). If truth is persistently resisted and refused, the Spirit's promptings cease to be heard and the soul is left in terrible darkness. This is possibly the condition to which Paul referred when he described certain consciences as being "seared with a hot iron" (1 Ti 4:2). For a man guilty of the sin against the Holy Ghost probation has closed and there is for him "no more sacrifice for sins, but a certain fearful looking for of judgment" (Heb 10:26, 27; cf. Jude 12, 13). This was the fearful condition of King Saul (1 Sa 16:14; cf. 28:6), Esau (Heb 12:16, 17), and Judas (see Jn 17:12), as it will be the condition of all the finally impenitent (Rev 22:11a). Paul solemnly warned his readers not to "quench" (Gr. *sbennumi*, "to extinguish," "to put out," "to stifle," "to suppress") the Holy Spirit (1 Th 5:19), "whereby ye are sealed unto the day of redemption" (Eph 4:30).

Unquenchable Fire. [Gr. *pur asbestos*, "inextinguishable fire."] An expression denoting the means by which the final destruction of the wicked is accomplished (Mt 3:12; Mk 9:43, RSV; Lk 3:17). The expression does not denote fire that will never go out, but only fire that cannot be *put* out—by any human means. The words used by John the Baptist in Mt 3:12 appear to be based on the prediction of Mal 3:1-3; 4:1. The fire of ch 4:1 apparently goes out when it has completed its work of destruction (cf. v 3). Jude pointed to the ancient cities of Sodom and Gomorrah as "an example, suffering the vengeance of eternal fire" (Jude 7; cf. 2 Pe 2:6), yet the fire that consumed those wicked cities, having completed its task, went out long ago. They are not burning today and have not been for more than 3,500 years, but the Bible cites them as an illustration of what the fires of the last great day will be like. Far from conveying the idea of a fire that burns eternally and in which the wicked are endlessly tormented, the Scriptures emphasize the fact that the wicked are to be burned up so completely that no trace of them will be left. *See* Death; Hell.

Upharsin. *See* Mene.

Uphaz (ū′făz). [Heb. *'Ûphaz*.] A place or land mentioned in Jer 10:9; Dan 10:5 as a source for gold; otherwise unidentified. Since no such place name is attested anywhere else, some commentators believe that *'Ûphaz* is a scribal error either for *'Ôphir*, "Ophir," a well-known gold-producing area, or for *ûphaz*, meaning "and pure gold."

Upper Gate, KJV **Higher Gate,** or **High Gate.** [Heb. *sha'ar 'elyôn*.] A gate of the Temple, location uncertain. It was built by King Jotham of Judah (2 Ki 15:35; 2 Chr 27:3). Some scholars are inclined to locate it in the northern Temple wall (cf. Eze 9:2), since the ground is higher there than in the south. Some have also identified it with the "upper Benjamin Gate" (RSV) of the Temple (Jer 20:2), but the location of that gate is also uncertain.

516. The temple tower of Ur in its present condition

However, the "upper gate" mentioned in 2 Chr 23:20 seems to have been a gate connecting the Temple precinct with the palace area south of it, and probably has to be distinguished from the "upper gate" of the Temple.

Ur (ûr). [Heb. *'Ûr*, "light," when used as a personal name. When used as the name of the city of Ur it is a transliteration of the Akkadian *Uru*.]

1. An ancient Sumerian city in Lower Mesopotamia, called "Ur of the Chaldees" in the Bible, since the Chaldeans lived in that area. Abraham's family lived there before migrating to Haran (Gen 11:28, 31; 15:7; Neh 9:7). Its site is the modern *el-Muqaiyar*, about 150 mi. southeast of old Babylon, and about 150 mi. northwest of the Persian Gulf. Anciently the Persian Gulf was much closer to Ur than now, for the gulf shore has been constantly silting in (Map III, C-6). The city was an important seat of the moon-god Sin (Sumerian, *Nannar*), and a center of culture, learning, and trade. Before the time of Abraham it had been the capital of the powerful 3d dynasty of Ur, whose kings ruled over all Lower Mesopotamia. Excavations carried out from 1922 to 1934 under the direction of Sir Leonard Woolley cleared the *ziggurat* (temple tower) from its debris, and left it standing as one of the most impressive ancient monuments of Iraq. Besides this, the palace of the kings of Ur, temples, residential sections, and royal tombs were excavated, and a great number of unusual archeological objects were found, which have greatly increased our knowledge of the history, culture, and religion of ancient Mesopotamia. See figs. 217, 238, 516, 517.

Lit.: Sir Charles Leonard Woolley, *Excavations at Ur* (London, 1954).

2. A man whose son, Eliphal, was one of David's "mighty men" (1 Chr 11:35).

Urbane. *See* Urbanus.

Urbanus (ûr-bā'nŭs), KJV **Urbane** (ûr'bān). [Gr. *Ourbanos*, from Latin *Urbanus*, "polite," or "polished." The name occurs in Greek and Latin inscriptions.] A Christian of Rome to whom Paul sent greetings (Rom 16:9).

Uri (ū'rī). [Heb. *'Ûrî*, probably an abbreviation of *'Ûrîyah*, "Uriah," "Yahweh is my light."]

1. Father of the chief craftsman of the tabernacle in Moses' time, Bezalel (Ex 31:2; 35:30; 38:22; etc.).

2. Father of Solomon's supply officer Geber (1 Ki 4:19).

3. A Temple gatekeeper who had a foreign wife in Ezra's time (Ezr 10:24).

Uriah (û-rī'ȧ), KJV 6 times **Urijah** (û-rī'jȧ), KJV of NT **Urias** (û-rī'ȧs). [Heb. *'Ûrîyah* and *'Ûrîyahû*, "Yahweh is my light." The name occurs in Hebrew on a postexilic seal found at Jericho. In cuneiform writing it appears as *Uriaia*. Gr. *Ourias*.]

1. A Hittite soldier, one of David's "mighty men" (2 Sa 23:39; 1 Chr 11:41). Either his name was Hebrew, or *'Ûrîyah* was the Hebrew rendering of the frequently occurring Hurrian name *Ariya*. David committed adultery with Uriah's wife while her husband was taking part in the siege of Rabbah of the Ammonites. In order to hide his crime David had Uriah placed in the front lines in a position where he would be killed in action. His scheme worked, and after Uriah's death David took Uriah's wife (2 Sa 11:1-27). He is called Urias in Mt 1:6, KJV.

2. A priest who witnessed to a certain document for the prophet Isaiah (Is 8:2), possibly identical with *Urijah, 1.

3. A prophet of Kiriath-jearim, a son of Shemaiah. He predicted Jerusalem's doom in the time of King Jehoiakim. The king became so incensed that he plotted to kill Uriah. The prophet fled to Egypt, but was extradited, brought back to Judah, and executed (Jer 26:20-23). He is called Urijah in the KJV.

4. A priest and father of the Meremoth who helped rebuild Jerusalem in Nehemiah's time (Ezr 8:33; Neh 3:4, 21).

517. Well-preserved courtyard and houses of ancient Ur of the Chaldees

5. An assistant of Ezra when the Law was read to the people (Neh 8:4).

Urias. See Uriah, 1.

Uriel (ū'rĭ-ĕl). [Heb. *'Ûrî'el*, "God is my light." The name occurs in Assyrian texts as *Ilu-urri*.]

1. A Kohathite Levite who assisted David in bringing the ark from the house of Obed-edom to Jerusalem (1 Chr 6:24; 15:5, 11).

2. A man of Gibeah, whose daughter Micaiah was King Abijah's mother (2 Chr 13:2).

Urijah (ū-rī'ja). [Heb. *'Ûrîyah* and *'Ûrîyahû*, "Yahweh is my light."]

1. The high priest in the reign of King Ahaz. He was directed by the king to make an altar (probably Assyrian) like the one Ahaz had seen at Damascus when he went to pay his respects to Tiglath-pileser III—an altar that then took the place of Solomon's altar of burnt offering (2 Ki 16:10-16). Urijah is regarded by some to be one of the witnesses to Isaiah's document (Is 8:2). See Uriah, 2.

2. For Jer 26:20-23, KJV, see Uriah, 3.

3. For Neh 3:4, 21, KJV, see Uriah, 4.

4. For Neh 8:4, KJV, see Uriah, 5.

Urim and Thummim. [Heb. *'ûrîm* and *tummîm*, literally, "lights" and "perfection." The 2 Hebrew terms begin with the 1st and last letters of the alphabet, respectively.] Two objects attached to the breastplate worn by the high priest upon the *ephod (Ex 28:30; Lev 8:8). The word "urim" is used alone twice (Num 27:21; 1 Sa 28:6). The high priest used these 2 objects to ascertain the will of God in doubtful matters involving the welfare of the nation, usually when requested by its leaders (cf. Num 27:21; 1 Sa 22:10). The Bible does not make clear the means by which these objects certified the divine will (see *SDACom* 1:648, 649). After God had rejected Saul as king He refused to answer him by this method (1 Sa 28:6). Ezr 2:63; Neh 7:65 indicate that God did not communicate through the Urim and Thummim immediately following the Exile, and there is no record of their later use.

Usury. See Loan.

Uthai (ū'thī). [Heb. *'Ûthay*, meaning uncertain. The name occurs in a Nabataean inscription.]

1. A Judahite living in Jerusalem; his father's name was Ammihud (1 Chr 9:4).

2. A member of the family of Bigvai; he returned from exile with Ezra, together with 71 others of his family (Ezr 8:14).

Uz (ŭz), KJV once **Huz** (hŭz). [Heb. *'Ûṣ*, meaning unknown.]

1. The eldest son of Aram, and grandson of Shem (Gen 10:22, 23). In 1 Chr 1:17 he is called a "son" of Shem. "Son" is here used for "grandson," as is frequently the case in the Bible. See Son. Uz was probably the ancestor of a tribal Aramaean family.

2. The eldest son of Nahor, Abraham's brother. His mother was Milcah (Gen 22:21). He is called Huz in the KJV.

3. One of the sons of Dishan, a Horite of Edom (Gen 36:28; 1 Chr 1:42).

4. The land of Uz, the home of Job (Job 1:1). It is uncertain whether its name came from any of the 3 individuals by the name of Uz mentioned in the OT (see Uz, 1 to 3). If the author of Job wrote the book from the viewpoint of a Palestinian, the land of Uz must have been situated east of Palestine (v 3), and since it was within striking distance of the Sabeans and Chaldeans (vs 15, 17), it seems to have been part of the Arabian Desert. Jeremiah mentions its kings after having spoken of the king and princes of Egypt, and before he mentions the kings of the Philistines (Jer 25:19, 20), but this sequence is hardly proof that Uz lay between Egypt and the Philistine country. The author of Lamentations (Lam 4:21) seems to imply that Uz was part of the land of Edom. Josephus reflects a tradition that places Uz in the country of Damascus (*Ant.* i. 6. 4), whereas at least 2 of the friends of Job, Eliphaz and Shophar (Job 2:11) came from places that, as far as they can be located, were near Edom or Midian. Uz is apparently mentioned once in an Assyrian inscription as *Uṣṣâ*, but without any indication of where it was. While Uz cannot definitely be identified with any known locality, it seems to have lain near the Syrian desert or in northern Arabia, and not far from Edom.

Uzai (ū'zī). [Heb. *'Ûzay*, meaning uncertain.] A man whose son Palal helped rebuild Jerusalem's wall in Nehemiah's time (Neh 3:25).

Uzal (ū'zăl). [Heb. *'Ûzal;* ancient South Arabic *Azâl* and *Izâl.*] One of the sons of Joktan (Gen 10:27; 1 Chr 1:21), and probably ancestor of an Arabian tribe from which wine was procured (Eze 27:19, RSV). According to Arabic tradition, *'Ûzal* in pre-Islamic times was the name of the city Ṣan'â, the present capital of Yemen. The change from *'Ûzal* to Ṣan'â was made after the Abyssinian occupation in the 6th cent. A.D.

Uzza (ŭz'à). [Heb. '*Uzza*', meaning uncertain, but the name is found on an ancient Hebrew seal, on an inscribed *potsherd from *Nimrûd,* and in a Phoenician inscription.]

1. A Benjamite (1 Chr 8:7).

2. The ancestral head of a family of Nethinim, or Temple servants, some of whom returned with Zerubbabel to Jerusalem (Ezr 2:49; Neh 7:51).

3. A man after whom a garden in or near Jerusalem, in which Kings Manasseh and Ammon were buried, was named (2 Ki 21:18, 26); probably its owner.

4. For 2 Sa 6:3-11; 1 Chr 13:7-14, KJV, *see* Uzzah, 1.

5. For 1 Chr 6:29, KJV, *see* Uzzah, 2.

Uzzah (ŭz'à), KJV frequently **Uzza** (ŭz'à). [Heb. '*Uzzah* and '*Uzza*', meaning uncertain.]

1. One of the drivers of the cart upon which David transferred the ark to Jerusalem. When he saw the oxen stumble, he put forth his hand to support the ark, but was smitten by the Lord for touching the sacred emblem, which no layman was allowed to touch (2 Sa 6:3-11; 1 Chr 13:7-14; cf. Num 4:15).

2. A Merarite Levite (1 Chr 6:29).

Uzzen-sheerah (ŭz'ĕn-shē'ĕ-rà), KJV **Uzzen-sherah** (ŭz'ĕn-shē'rà). [Heb. '*Uzzen She-'erah*.] A town near the 2 Beth-horons; not identified. It was founded by Sheerah, an Ephraimite woman (1 Chr 7:24).

Uzzen-sherah. *See* Uzzen-sheerah.

Uzzi (ŭz'ī). [Heb. '*Uzzi*, a shortened form of '*Uzziyah*, "Uzziah," "Yahweh is my strength."]

1. A man of Issachar and ancestral head of a tribal family (1 Chr 7:2, 3).

2. A priest, an ancestor of Ezra (1 Chr 6:5, 6, 51; Ezr 7:4).

3. A Benjamite and ancestral head of a tribal family (1 Chr 7:7).

4. A Benjamite whose descendants lived in Jerusalem (1 Chr 9:8).

5. A Levite of the family of Bani; he was overseer of the postexilic Levites in Jerusalem (Neh 11:22).

6. A priest, and head of the house of Jedaiah (Neh 12:19), possibly identical with Uzzi, 7.

7. A priest who took part in the dedication of the wall of Jerusalem under Nehemiah (Neh 12:42), possibly identical with Uzzi, 6.

Uzzia (ŭ-zī'à). [Heb. '*Uzziya*', "Yahweh is my strength," a variant form of '*Uzziyah*, "Uzziah."] One of David's "mighty men," from the town of Ashtaroth (1 Chr 11:44).

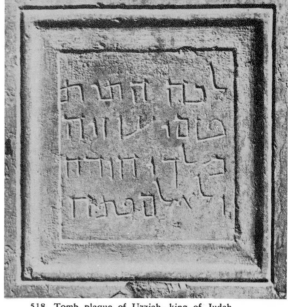

518. Tomb plaque of Uzziah, king of Judah

Uzziah (ŭ-zī'à), KJV of NT **Ozias** (ō-zī'ăs). [Heb. '*Uzziyahû*, and '*Uzziyah*, "Yahweh is my strength"; Gr. *Ozias*.]

1. A Kohathite Levite (1 Chr 6:24).

2. The father of David's storekeeper Jonathan (1 Chr 27:25).

3. The 10th ruler of the kingdom of Judah, who reigned for 52 years (c. 790-c. 739 B.C.). He was also called Azariah. This was probably his original name and Uzziah his throne name (2 Ki 15:1; cf. 2 Chr 26:1). Uzziah seems to have been elevated to the position of coregent with his father after his father Amaziah suffered a serious defeat by Jehoash of Israel. This conclusion can be drawn not only from an interpretation of the chronological data given in the Bible but also from the remark that "he [Azariah] built Elath, . . . after that the king [Amaziah] slept with his fathers" (2 Ki 14:22; 2 Chr 26:2). Apparently his sole reign did not begin until the 27th year (c. 767 B.C.) of Jeroboam II's reign (2 Ki 15:1), so that the coregency seems to have lasted for about 24 years. Uzziah is known for rebuilding Judah's army, promoting his country's agriculture, and reorganizing its defenses (2 Chr 26:9-15). He was also responsible for restoring his nation's military fame by a number of victories over Philistine cities and Arabian tribes, and by forcing the Ammonites to pay tribute to him (vs 6-8). He is described as a good king, although he tolerated the worship of other gods on the high places (2 Ki 15:3, 4; 2 Chr 26:4, 5). Finally, however, his success and power led him to presume to enter the Temple in order to exercise priestly

functions by offering incense. The high priest Azariah and 80 priests protested against this presumption, and God punished the king with incurable leprosy. From that time until his death he lived as a leper in a separate house, while his son Jotham reigned as coregent (2 Ki 15:5; 2 Chr 26:16-21). During Uzziah's reign the prophets Amos, Hosea, and Isaiah began their ministry (Amos 1:1; Hos 1:1; Is 1:1). A severe earthquake occurred in his time (Amos 1:1; Zec 14:5). Dr. E. L. Sukenik found a stone tablet in the Russian Archeological Museum on the Mount of Olives in 1931 with the following Aramaic inscription: "Hither were brought the bones of Uzziah king of Judah—do not open!" (see fig. 518). Since this inscription dates from about the time of Christ, it shows that in the beginning of the Christian Era the king's original tomb, apparently still known to the people at Jerusalem, had been disturbed, and that his bones had been moved to a new resting place, where this tablet seems to have been set up. (W. F. Albright, *BASOR* 44 [1931], 8-10; E. L. Sukenik, *QSPEF* 63 [1931], 217-221.)

4. A priest, a son of Harim; he had a foreign wife in Ezra's time (Ezr 10:21).

5. A Judahite, of the family of Perez (Neh 11:4).

Uzziel (ŭ-zī′ĕl). [Heb. *'Uzzî'el*, "God is my strength." The name occurs in Assyrian inscriptions as *Azilu*.]

1. The ancestral head of the Uzzielites, a division of Kohathite Levites (Ex 6:18, 22; Num 3:19, 27, 30). He was Aaron's uncle (Lev 10:4). Amminadab and 112 members of the clan were organized by David to assist in the transfer of the ark to Jerusalem (1 Chr 15:10).

2. Son of Bela, and head of a Benjamite family (1 Chr 7:7).

3. One of the chief musicians in David's time (1 Chr 25:4); called Azarel in v 18.

4. A Levite engaged in the work of reform carried out by King Hezekiah (2 Chr 29:14).

5. One of the leaders of a band of Simeonite warriors who carried out a raid against the Amalekites in the reign of Hezekiah (1 Chr 4:41-43).

6. A goldsmith who helped Nehemiah repair the wall of Jerusalem (Neh 3:8).

Uzzielites (ŭ-zī′ĕl-īts). [Heb. *'Ozzî'elî*.] The descendants of *Uzziel, 1.

V

Vagabond. A word appearing in verb phrases translating: (1) The Heb. *nûd*, "to be homeless," that is, without a fixed place of abode. The curse pronounced upon Cain sentenced him to be a homeless person (Gen 4:12, 14). (2) The Heb. *nûa'*, "to be unstable," "to be homeless." Homelessness was the fate of the children of the wicked (Ps 109: 10). In Prov 6:11, RSV, "vagabond" is a rendering of a form of the Heb. *halak*, "to go," and in Acts 19:13, KJV, a form of the Gr. *perierchomai*, "to go from place to place."

Vail. *See* Veil.

Vaizatha (vī-zä′thȧ), KJV **Vajezatha** (vȧ-jĕz′ȧ-thȧ). [Heb. *Wayzatha'*, a Persian name meaning probably "son of maturity."] One of Haman's sons (Est 9:9).

Vajezatha. *See* Vaizatha.

Valley of Charashim. *See* Ge-harashim.

Valley of Decision. [Heb. *'emeq hecharûṣ*, "valley of decision," "valley of determina-

tion."] A figurative expression in Joel 3:14 for the great day of judgment at the end of the world when God utters His voice from Zion and when the heavens and the earth shake (v 16). The "decision" here referred to is that of God as judge (see vs 2, 12), and not that of the people, who are being judged. It is God who determines the fate of the wicked. Since *charûṣ* may mean "threshing instrument," as in Amos 1:3; Is 28:27; etc., the Hebrew expression may also be understood as meaning "valley of threshing." In this sense God threshes the heathen in His anger (Hab 3:12; cf. Rev 14:14-20).

Valley of Hinnom. *See* Hinnom, Valley of.

Valley of Keziz. *See* Emek-keziz.

Valley of Rephaim. *See* Rephaim, Valley of.

Valley of Shaveh. *See* King's Valley.

Valley of the Giants. *See* Rephaim, Valley of.

Vaniah (vȧ-nī′ȧ). [Heb. *Wanyah*, probably a Persian name, but of uncertain meaning.] A member of the family of Bani;

he had married a foreign wife in the time of Ezra (Ezr 10:36).

Vashni. *See* Joel, 2.

Vashti (văsh′tī). [Heb. *Washti,* an Old Persian name meaning "the desired one," or "the best one."] The queen of the Persian king Ahasuerus (Xerxes). When asked to show herself to the king's guests she refused, and was therefore deposed (Est 1:3 to 2:4). Secular sources know the name of only one wife of Xerxes, Amestris, whom the king had married before he ascended the throne. Vashti may have been one of Xerxes' other wives, unknown from extra-Biblical sources.

Vat. *See* Wine.

Vau. [Heb. *waw.*] The 6th letter of the Hebrew alphabet, written ו, appearing as the title of the 6th section of Ps 119 in the KJV. *See* Aleph.

Vegetables. [Heb. *zero'im,* "plants," "vegetables"; *yaraq,* "greens," "vegetables"; Gr. *lachana,* "garden herbs," "vegetables."] A term appearing in the RSV: (1) in a reference to the cultivation and irrigation methods of Egypt as compared to the natural verdure of Palestine (Deut 11:10; KJV "herbs"); (2) in the account of Ahab's attempt to acquire Naboth's vineyard for a vegetable garden (1 Ki 21:2; KJV "herbs"); (3) in the account of the Hebrew children's request for a diet of vegetables (Dan 1:12, 16; KJV "pulse"); (4) as specifying the diet of the overscrupulous Christian (Rom 14:2; KJV "herbs").

Veil, KJV frequently **Vail.** In general a covering, wrapping, sometimes a curtain. Rebekah "took a vail, and covered herself" when she met her bridegroom (Gen 24:64, 65). However, according to pictorial representations women of that period apparently did not, like the later Moslems, habitually veil their faces (see picture on end sheet). Paul counseled the Corinthian believing women that they were not to pray or prophesy with their heads uncovered (1 Cor 11:5, RSV "unveiled"). According to the custom of that period a Roman or Greek lady when in public covered her head with a veil or scarf, or a fold of her garment, whereas female slaves and women of the lower classes customarily went about bareheaded.

Separating the holy place and the Most Holy Place (Ex 26:31-35) was a veil made of blue, purple, and scarlet material (v 31), with figures of cherubim, representative of the angels about God's throne. The veil in the ancient tabernacle, and

later the Temple, veiled the presence of God from the priest as he stood before it ministering the sacrificial blood and burning incense upon the golden altar day by day throughout the year (see Lev 4:6; *see also* Sacrifices and Offerings). This was as close as anyone could approach the Divine Presence, except on the Day of Atonement (ch 16:2, 12, 15, 16; cf. ch 21:21-23; *see* Atonement, Day of). Because of its proximity to the ark of the testimony the veil was sometimes called "the vail of the testimony" (ch 24:3), or "the vail, which is before the testimony" (Ex 27:21). When transported from one place to another, the ark was draped with this veil (Num 4:5). At the time of Christ's death the corresponding veil in the Herodian Temple was rent from top to bottom (Mt 27:51; etc.).

In the LXX the veil separating the two apartments of the ancient sanctuary was called *katapetasma,* a name given also to the curtain at the door of the tabernacle; hence, apparently, the designation "second veil" for the inner curtain in Heb 9:3.

Heb 10:20 speaks of our Lord's ascension to heaven in the likeness of humanity as consecrating "a new and living way . . . through the veil, that is . . . , his flesh," by which we are enabled to "draw near with a true heart in full assurance of faith" (vs 20, 22), entering into the Divine Presence through faith. The Christian's hope, the apostle further declares, enters "into that within the veil; whither the forerunner is for us entered, even Jesus" (ch 6:19, 20).

Venison. *See* Game.

Vermilion. [Heb. *shashar,* "red ocher," "red color," "minium" "vermilion."] The paint used in the royal house of Jehoiakim (Jer 22:14), probably in an effort to emulate the architectural splendor of the Egyptian palaces of Pharaoh Necho, who put him on the throne (2 Ki 23:34). This paint was probably the same as the red pigment (possibly cinnabar or red clay and oxide of iron) employed in Assyria (Eze 23:14).

Versions. Translations of the Hebrew (and Aramaic) text of the OT, or Greek text of the NT, as a whole or in part, into vernacular languages. Manuscripts of the ancient versions of the Bible are used by scholars as one of the sources for the reconstruction of the original text of both the OT and the NT. Four ancient versions of the Hebrew OT have been preserved: the Greek Septuagint, the Syriac Peshitta, the Aramaic Targums (paraphrases), and the Latin Vulgate. These, together with the Hebrew manuscripts and the Samaritan Pentateuch, constitute our chief sources in the study of the text of the OT. Such other versions as the Old Latin, Coptic, Ethiopic, Gothic, Armenian, Arabic, Georgian, and Slavonic, are translations of the Septuagint. For the NT the most important of the ancient versions are the Latin, the Syriac, and the Coptic. The testimony of the Armenian, the Georgian, the Ethiopic, and the Gothic, is, however, of great value in the study of the NT text.

I. Ancient Old Testament Versions.

1. *The Samaritan Pentateuch.* Properly speaking, the Samaritan Pentateuch is not a translation or version, but an independent Hebrew text written in a modified form of the old Semitic alphabet and transmitted independently since the days of the Samaritan schism. It is therefore a check on the errors and corruptions that may have crept into the Hebrew text of the Pentateuch through its numerous copyings before the age of printing. Its value is lessened by the obscurity that surrounds the history of its text, and by the lateness of its manuscripts, none of which is known to be older than the 10th cent. A.D. The Samaritan Pentateuch differs from the Hebrew Masoretic text in about 6,000 instances, but the vast majority of the differences are of trifling import, many of them being simply variations in spelling and grammar. Some of the important variations, which reflect Samaritan ideals of religion and ritual, were doubtless introduced by the Samaritans to advance their views. In some 1,900 instances the Samaritan text agrees with the Septuagint where the latter differs from the Masoretic Hebrew. In such instances its testimony is regarded as important.

2. *The Septuagint.* The most important and the oldest of the ancient translations of the OT was the Septuagint (abbreviated LXX). With the exception of the epoch-making Dead Sea *scrolls, the oldest known manuscripts of the OT are copies of this Greek translation. The LXX is therefore of great importance from both a textual and a historical viewpoint. The apocryphal Letter of Aristeas, purported to be written by Aristeas to his brother Philocrates during the reign of Ptolemy II Philadelphus (285-246 B.C.), gives an account of the translation of the Pentateuch which is now largely discredited. According to this story the version was made by 70, or more strictly, 72, Jewish scholars in Alexandria, under the direction of the librarian, Demetrius Phalereus, hence the name "Seventy" (LXX) or Septuagint. Actually the LXX was the work of many different hands, as is evident from the variations in style and method, and was not completed until *c.* 150 B.C.

According to the Letter of Aristeas the translation was made because the Scriptures were regarded as worthy of a place in the royal library. Scholars today think that this cultural interest is an insufficient reason for its production, and that the real purpose for it was to meet the religious needs of the Greek-speaking Jews in Alexandria. Perhaps an added incentive in its production was the desire of these Jews to demonstrate the superiority of their religion, and thus to make a missionary appeal to the Greek world.

The version is of great value both textually and historically. Since it was made before the Christian Era it is an aid in recovering a pre-Masoretic text. The LXX prepared the way for Christian mission work and became the first Christian Bible. It was the OT of Paul and the early church, and many of the quotations of the OT in the NT are cited from it. It molded the religious vocabulary of the NT. It was the version from which other important translations were made. Semitic scholars have also found it helpful in the study of Hebrew morphology and grammar.

The 2 best-known manuscripts of the LXX are Greek Bibles dating from about the middle of the 4th cent. A.D., Codex Vaticanus (B) and Codex Sinaiticus (ℵ). From the 1st half of the 5th cent. comes the Codex Alexandrinus (A). Also from the 5th cent. is the Codex Ephraemi (C), a palimpsest. All in all there are extant about 30 uncials, some rather fragmentary; more than 1,500 minuscules, which are in general of a later date than the uncials; and some 30 lectionaries, containing the text of the LXX. Older than these are the papyri. The Chester Beatty Biblical Papyri include parts of 8 distinct manuscripts of the LXX, ranging in date from the 2d to the 4th cent. A.D. and representing 8 books of the OT. There are also the John H. Scheide Papyrus leaves of Ezekiel, from the 1st half of the 3d cent., the Freer manuscript of the Minor Prophets from the latter part of the 3d cent., and 2 fragments of the book of Deuteronomy (John Rylands Library,

Papyrus Greek 458; Papyrus Fouad 266) which date from about the middle of the 2d cent. B.C. Some LXX fragments were discovered in Qumran Cave 4, assigned to the 1st cent. B.C. A fragmentary copy of the Minor Prophets in Greek, assigned to the end of the 1st cent. A.D., came to light in a cave of the *Wâdî Mura-ba'at* in 1952. It is a recension of the LXX.

3. *Rival Greek Versions and Recensions.* After the LXX became the Bible of the Christian church, it came, in the process of time, to be repudiated by the Jews. In theological disputes with the Jews, the Christians sometimes used the LXX in ways which the Jews regarded as invalid proof. Furthermore, the text of the LXX was at times at variance with the standard Hebrew. After the destruction of Jerusalem there developed among the Jewish scholars a so-called atomistic exegesis, which regarded the Scriptures as the embodiment of God's will in all its parts and in every word, even in every letter. The LXX, not agreeing in all parts with the accepted Hebrew text, was completely repudiated and branded as the work of Satan. In the 2d cent. A.D. several other Greek translations were made in an attempt to meet the need of a faithful rendering of the Hebrew text acceptable to the Jewish community for use by Greek-speaking Jews.

(1) *Aquila.* The first of these was made probably somewhere between A.D. 130 and 150 by Aquila, a proselyte to Judaism from Sinope in Pontus, who, according to Jerome, was a pupil of Rabbi Akiba between A.D. 95 and 135. It was a slavishly literal and pedantic rendering, fully in keeping with the spirit of Akiba and his school. It carried the principle of literal accuracy to the point of absurdity and unintelligibility. It sought to render every word and every particle faithfully and consistently.

(2) *Theodotion.* The version of Theodotion, described by some as a Jewish proselyte, by others as an Ebionite Christian, was made between A.D. 180 and 192. Its style and character is very similar to that of the LXX. Many scholars regard it simply as a revision of the LXX to bring it into harmony with the received Hebrew text. It gained much popularity among the Christians. Its version of the book of Dan was incorporated into LXX Bibles in place of the original. The result was that the true LXX translation of Dan was known only from 1 late Greek manuscript and 1 version in Syriac until portions

of it were discovered among the Chester Beatty Papyri.

(3) *Symmachus.* This version, produced between *c.* A.D. 170 and 200, was designed to be not only accurate but in good literary Greek. According to nearly all ancient authorities Symmachus was an Ebionite; on the other hand Epiphanius said that he was a Samaritan convert to Judaism.

(4) *The Hexapla and Recensions of the LXX.* In the 1st half of the 3d cent., Origen made use of Aquila, Symmachus, and Theodotion in his effort to save the LXX by bringing it into line with the Hebrew text of his day. About the year 245 he and his associates, working at Caesarea in Palestine, completed a sixfold version of the OT known as the Hexapla. It was a stupendous task that required the diligent labor of nearly a quarter of a century. In parallel columns Origen presented (*a*) the Hebrew text, (*b*) a transliteration of the Hebrew into Greek letters, (*c*) the version of Aquila, (*d*) the version of Symmachus, (*e*) the Septuagint in his own revised text, (*f*) the version of Theodotion. When the LXX disagreed with the Hebrew text it was brought into harmony with it by the use of the other Greek versions and diacritical markings. While his work was done in good faith with a desire to arrest the corruptions due to repeated copyings, the actual result was increased confusion in the LXX text. The colossal size of this sixfold OT precluded its reproduction as a whole. At the beginning of the 4th cent. Eusebius of Caesarea and his friend Pamphilus copied and circulated the 5th column (the revised LXX text) of the Hexapla separate from the rest, with Origen's critical notations. Since the critical marks were meaningless apart from the rest of the Hexapla, the natural tendency with repeated copyings in time was to write the text without these critical symbols. The result for the textual criticism of the LXX has been disastrous, for without these marks the additions made by Origen appear as genuine and original parts of the LXX text. The problem of securing a pre-Hexaplaric text has therefore been a source of great perplexity to the textual scholar.

Two other recensions of the LXX made in the 4th cent. are known: (*a*) that of Hesychius, used in Alexandria and elsewhere in Egypt, and (*b*) that of Lucian of Samosata, which was used throughout Asia Minor from Antioch to Constantinople. Little is known concerning Hesychius, and the identification of the text of his revision is still involved in uncertainty. Lucian carefully revised the LXX with the aid of manuscripts both of the Hebrew and of the LXX, which contained frequent readings intrinsically superior to those we possess. These readings make the Lucianic recension of great importance for the textual criticism of the OT. Many of the alterations made by Lucian in the LXX, however, do not point to a different Hebrew reading; they are merely grammatical and stylistic changes in the literary form, made under the influence of the Atticist reaction.

4. *The Aramaic Targums.* In postexilic Judaism, Aramaic displaced Hebrew as the vernacular language (*see* Aramaic), and it became necessary to accompany the reading of the Hebrew text with an interpretation in Aramaic. Such interpretations or translations, which were originally oral, were called Targums, and the translator was spoken of as a *turgeman* or *meturgeman.* The Targums combined real translation with free paraphrase and explanatory material. In the course of time they became somewhat standardized and already were committed to writing in the pre-Christian era, as some copies found among the Dead Sea *scrolls show. Three Targums of the Pentateuch are known: (1) the Targum of Onkelos, or the Babylonian Targum, which is for the most part a strictly literal and simple translation; (2) the Old Palestinian Targum, often spoken of as the Fragmentary Targum; (3) and the Jerusalem Targum (pseudo-Jonathan). The official Targum of the Prophets is attributed to Jonathan ben Uzziel, a pupil of Hillel in the 1st cent. A.D. It paraphrases more freely than does Onkelos. The Targums on the Hagiographa are comparatively late. The value of the Targums for the textual criticism of the OT is freely recognized, but this value is qualified by their introduction of explanations and alterations. However, used critically their witness is of considerable value. Moreover, they are a rich storehouse of Jewish religious thought and exegesis. The Palestinian Targum, in particular, has been regarded also as a source for the recovery of the Aramaic language Jesus spoke.

5. *Syriac Versions.* Syriac, often termed Eastern Aramaic, was the language of Christians in Syria and Mesopotamia. There are several translations of the NT into Syriac, but only 2 of the OT.

(1) *The Peshitta,* that is, the "simple" (translation). This version has had such a complex literary history that its origin has long been a matter of debate. As far back as it can be traced, it has been a Christian version, since it contains the NT as well as the OT, and the extant copies of it have come from Christian hands. Yet the OT shows such a strong Jewish influence that many scholars hold that it was, at least in part, of Jewish origin, though some explain it as of Jewish-Christian origin. It may have been produced at Edessa, though Kahle states that it came from the region of Adiabene, lying east of the Tigris, where King Isates and his mother Helena became Jewish proselytes in the 1st cent. A.D. There are passages in the OT that are little more than transliterations of western Aramaic Targums into the Syriac script. While the text agrees in the main with the Masoretic Hebrew, it seems to have been revised on the basis of the LXX. Originally this Syriac version lacked Chr, Ezr, Neh, and Est, as well as the Apocrypha, all of which were added at a later date. The most valuable Syriac manuscript is the Codex Ambrosianus from about the 6th cent., now in Milan. A manuscript of Gen, Ex, Num, and Deut, from the monastery of St. Mary Deipara in Egypt, bears a date corresponding to A.D. 464, and is thus the oldest copy of the Bible in any language bearing a definite date.

(2) *The Syro-Hexaplar* version is a rendering of the 5th column of Origen's Hexapla into Syriac by Bishop Paul of Tella in A.D. 616-617. Since the translation was very literal and included Origen's critical marks, it is our chief authority for reconstructing the revised Septuagint text of the Hexapla.

6. *Latin Versions.*

(1) *The Old Latin.* The Latin rendering of the Bible probably originated in North Africa as early as A.D. 150. It is even possible that the Christians of North Africa adopted a translation of the OT from Latin-speaking Jews. Tertullian (*c.* A.D. 160 - *c.* 230) knew the Old Latin Bible at least in part, and Cyprian (*c.* 200-258), bishop of Carthage, quotes frequently from both Testaments of this Bible. Only fragments of the Old Latin of the OT have survived. Several of the Apocryphal books were incorporated unrevised into the Vulgate. As for the rest of the Bible, scholars have been able to piece together manuscript fragments covering a considerable portion of the OT. These,

together with quotations in the early Latin Fathers, are our sources for the reconstruction of the Old Latin text of the OT. Scholars distinguish 2 types of text: the African and the European. The Old Latin of the OT was made from the Greek LXX, and its chief value today is as an aid in recovering the text of the LXX as it was before Origen's revision of it.

(2) *The Vulgate.* The official Latin version was produced by Jerome in response to the request of Pope Damasus (A.D. 382) for a revision of the Old Latin Bible. Jerome made 3 revisions of the Psalms. The 1st of these, based on the LXX, is known as the Roman Psalter (A.D. 384), because it was officially adopted by Pope Damasus for use in the churches in Rome and Italy. It still remains in official use in St. Peter's in Rome, as well as in Milan. A more thorough revision followed *c.* A.D. 387 on the basis of the Hexapla. This revision, because it was first adopted in Gaul, became known as the Gallican Psalter. It is still embodied in the Vulgate. The 3d version, known as the Hebrew Psalter, because it was a new rendering of the original Hebrew, never achieved popularity or general usage, though some manuscripts of the Vulgate contain it, generally in parallel columns with the Gallican. Jerome then spent several years in making a new translation of the rest of the OT books directly from the Hebrew. This translation, which is called the Vulgate, or "common" version, became the Bible of Western Christendom and is still the official Bible of the Roman Catholic Church. In the study of the OT text its value is qualified by its freedom of rendering, and by its late date. It was produced after the Hebrew text had been standardized substantially as it is today.

In all there is a total of some 8,000 manuscripts of the Vulgate extant in Europe. Perhaps the most highly regarded manuscript is Codex Amiatinus, copied in England about the beginning of the 8th cent., carried as a gift to the pope, but now located in Florence. The 1st printed edition of the Vulgate was Gutenberg's (see fig. 74 for a facsimile of the first page of Genesis from the copy in the Library of Congress). The official Bible of the Catholic Church has been a revision of the Sixtine Bible of Pope Sixtus V, known as the Clementine Bible because revised and reissued under Pope Clement VIII. A new critical edition, however, is now being prepared by scholars of the Benedictine order.

7. *Other Eastern Versions.*

(1) *Coptic Version.* Coptic, the language of Egypt in the early Christian period, consists of several dialects. The most important of these, so far as Bible versions are concerned, are the Sahidic (derived from the Arabic name for Upper Egypt, *es-Sa'id*) and the Bohairic (from the Arabic name for Lower or Coastland Egypt, *Boḥeireh*). The Sahidic translation was probably made about the 3d cent., and was current in Upper (Southern) Egypt. The Bohairic is to be dated sometime between the 3d and the 5th cent., probably the 4th, and was current in Lower (Northern) Egypt. The Bohairic became the official version of the Coptic Church. In both versions the OT was translated from the LXX.

(2) *The Ethiopic Version.* This version, variously dated between the 5th and the 7th cent., was a translation of the Greek. The oldest manuscripts of this version extant today are from the 13th cent.

(3) *The Gothic Version.* This version, representing the 1st written literature of the Goths, was made from the Lucianic recension of the LXX by Ulfilas about the middle of the 4th cent. Only a few fragments of the OT are extant today.

(4) *The Armenian Version.* A translation made for the Christians of eastern Asia Minor from the LXX about A.D. 400, after the invention of the Armenian alphabet. The version shows definite influence from the Syriac Peshitta.

(5) *The Georgian Version.* A version made in the 5th or 6th cent., probably from the Greek LXX with some reference to the Syriac. The whole Bible is preserved in a manuscript of 2 volumes in the Iberian Monastery on Mount Athos.

(6) *The Slavonic Version.* A version of the 9th cent. attributed to 2 brothers, Cyril and Methodius. Some of the books were translated from the Greek, some from the Hebrew, and others from the Vulgate.

(7) *The Arabic Version.* The Pentateuch and Joshua of this version were made by Saadya the Gaon (892-942) on the basis of the Hebrew. The rest of the OT books were apparently translated from the Peshitta and the Septuagint.

II. Ancient New Testament Versions.

1. *Latin New Testaments.*

(1) *The Old Latin.* The Old Latin translation of the NT was produced

about the latter half of the 2d cent. A.D., probably, though not certainly, in North Africa, where there was a flourishing church centering in Carthage. Since this version takes us back within 2 or 3 generations of the actual writing of the NT books, it is an exceedingly important witness to the primitive text of the NT. It is one of the chief witnesses to the Western type of text. About 50 manuscripts and fragments of the Old Latin NT survive. None of these contains the entire NT. However, these manuscripts, together with quotations in the Latin Fathers, contain almost the complete NT. On the basis of the patristic quotations the manuscripts are divided into 3 types: the African, used by Cyprian, the European, found in a 2d-cent. Latin translation of Irenaeus' works, and the Italian, found in the writings of Augustine. Many scholars, however, dispute the existence of the Italian. A number of the Old Latin manuscripts go back to the 4th and the 5th cent., and are very important.

(2) *The Vulgate.* The Vulgate NT is a rather conservative revision of the Old Latin on the basis of some ancient Greek manuscripts. Jerome completed the revision of the Gospels in 384, and the rest subsequently. Whether Jerome did all the work is a matter of uncertainty. The new version was not immediately accepted with enthusiasm, but it won its way gradually. It was not until about the 7th cent. that the Vulgate was supreme. In the meantime the text of the Old Latin and the Vulgate had suffered an intermixture which has added to the complexity of their literary history. Several attempts were made during the Middle Ages to preserve the true text of the Vulgate: by Cassiodorus (d. *c.* 583), by Alcuin, under Charlemagne (8th cent.), and by Theodulf (9th cent.). At the Council of Trent, 1546, the Vulgate was officially recognized as the standard text of the Roman Catholic Church. It was the Bible of Western Europe for 1,000 years, and was the basis of the earliest English translations.

2. *Syriac New Testaments.*

(1) *The Diatessaron.* The earliest Syriac translation of the NT was in the form of a fusion of the 4 Gospels into one continuous narrative of the life and teachings of Jesus. This Diatessaron was produced *c.* A.D. 170 by Tatian, a gifted and powerful Oriental personality, who had studied under Justin Martyr at Rome. His work was in time so com-

pletely displaced by the "Gospel of the Separated" (see (2) below) that it has survived only in translations such as 2 Arabic manuscripts, 1 of which is in the Vatican Library, an Armenian commentary on it by Ephraem, and a 14-line Greek fragment found at Dura Europus in 1933.

(2) *The Old Syriac Gospels.* Although there may have been an Old Syriac version of all, or most, of the NT books, only the Gospels have been recovered. This version, called The Gospel of the Separated (that is, the 4 separate Gospels), was probably made *c.* A.D. 200. It is extant in 2 forms: (*a*) the "Curetonian," consisting of some 80 leaves of a 5th-cent. manuscript coming from the monastery of St. Mary Deipara in the Nitrian Desert of Egypt, and edited by Dr. William Cureton in 1842; (*b*) the "Sinaitic," represented by a palimpsest manuscript a half century older than the Curetonian, found at St. Catherine's Monastery at Mount Sinai by Mrs. A. S. Lewis and her sister, Mrs. A. D. Gibson, in 1892. These 2 manuscripts are highly significant witnesses to the early text of the Gospels.

(3) *The Peshitta.* The NT of the Peshitta (the "simple," or "common," version) is usually credited to Bishop Rabbula of Edessa (A.D. 411-435), who revised the divergent copies of the Old Syriac in accord with the current Byzantine Greek text. This version, which was in use in the Syriac church from the 5th cent. onward, is represented by about 250 manuscripts, some 15 of which date from the 5th and 6th cent. It lacked 2 Pe, 2 and 3 Jn, Jude, and the Apocalypse.

(4) *The Philoxenian and Harkleian Version.* A revision of the Peshitta was made in 508 by Philoxenus, bishop of Mabug. This, in turn, was revised by Thomas of Harkel (Heraclea) in A.D. 616, on the basis of Greek manuscripts from Alexandria. While the Philoxenian is free and idiomatic, the Harkleian is extremely literal.

(5) *The Palestinian Syriac.* There is a Syriac version known only in fragmentary form, largely through lectionaries, which in language is closely related to Western or Jewish Aramaic, the language Jesus is believed to have used. The version was probably made in Antioch not later than the 6th cent. and probably earlier.

3. *Coptic New Testaments.* Of some 5 known Coptic versions, the most important are the Sahidic and the Bohairic.

(1) *The Sahidic.* This version is the older version and was used in Southern (Upper) Egypt. It was formerly designated Thebaic, after the city of Thebes. Only fragments of this version are extant, but these fragments are of sufficient quantity to reconstruct the major part of the NT. The earliest manuscripts originate from the 4th cent. A.D.

(2) *The Bohairic.* This version was current in Northern (Lower) Egypt and eventually replaced the other dialects. It is the Coptic used to this day in the church services, and the complete NT has been preserved in it. Both the Sahidic and Bohairic versions of the NT contain principally an Alexandrian type of text, similar to a text such as is found in the Codex Vaticanus.

4. *Other Eastern Versions of the New Testament.*

(1) *The Armenian New Testament.* This version, made in the 1st part of the 5th cent., is noted for its accuracy and literary beauty. Scholars are still divided on the question of whether it was made from the Syriac or the Greek, and the ancient Armenian traditions are themselves divided on the matter. Recent studies have convinced some scholars that, as far as the Gospels are concerned, there was an Armenian translation earlier than the standard one, and that this translation was based on the Old Syriac Gospels. The Armenian version of the NT is regarded as an important witness to the Caesarean type of text. The oldest known manuscript of this version is dated 887. Some of the most beautifully illuminated manuscripts known are Armenian.

(2) *The Old Georgian New Testament.* This version is closely related to the Armenian, and, in fact, has been regarded as a translation of it. If so, the Armenian version on which it is based would be a form not now in our possession. The Georgian is another important witness to the Caesarean type of text.

(3) *The Ethiopic New Testament.* This version was produced probably around A.D. 600. The current text of the version was made from the Greek, but some scholars have found traces of an earlier form of it based allegedly on the Old Syriac. The manuscripts are late, the earliest being from the 13th cent., and the majority between the 16th and 18th cent. These late manuscripts have been influenced by an Arabic version.

(4) *The Gothic New Testament.* This version was made directly from a Greek text of the Byzantine type by Ulfilas *c.* A.D. 350. Since the version is almost slavishly literal it is valuable for recovering its Greek original. The most famous of the Gothic manuscripts is Codex Argenteus, a 5th or 6th cent. Gospel manuscript on purple vellum of Bohemian origin, which is now in Uppsala, Sweden.

III. English Versions.

1. *Anglo-Saxon Versions.* The metrical paraphrases of Biblical narratives by Caedmon in the 7th cent. constitute the earliest attempt to translate the Bible into Anglo-Saxon. Partial translations followed, such as Aldhelm's rendering of the Psalms (7th cent.), Bede's translation of John (8th cent.), and Egbert's version of the Gospels. But the earliest translations of the Gospels into Anglo-Saxon which have survived are in the form of word-for-word interlinear glosses of Latin manuscripts. These are represented by the Lindisfarne Gospels, which have a Latin text written about 700, and an interlinear translation in Anglo-Saxon of about 950, and the Rushworth Gospels, which have glosses of a slightly later date. The West Saxon Gospels of the 10th cent. are the earliest copies of an independent translation in Anglo-Saxon, separate from a Latin text. After the Norman Conquest (1066) brought in a new language, there was linguistic fusion and confusion, but in the 13th cent., after the Norman-English combination emerged, Orm produced a metrical version of the church service, including parts of the Gospels and Acts, known today as The Ormulum. In the same century a metrical translation of the Psalter appeared, which is extant in several copies; before 1350 there was also a prose version in the dialect of West Midlands, sometimes attributed to William of Shoreham; and a version with a verse-by-verse commentary by Richard Rolle, a hermit living at Hampole in Yorkshire.

2. *The Wyclif Bible, c. 1382.* The 1st complete Bible in the English language was produced under the influence and direction of John Wyclif. Just how much of the work of translation was done by Wyclif himself we have no way of knowing. It is quite certain that most of the OT was produced by an ardent friend and supporter of Wyclif at Oxford, Nicholas of Hereford. The Wyclif Bible was a translation of the Latin Vulgate, not of the Hebrew, Aramaic, and Greek. Since it was made before the invention of printing, it circulated in manuscript

form. The version has come down to us in 2 editions, represented by about 170 copies. Less than 30 copies represent the original form, and the remainder a revised edition produced shortly after Wyclif's death, in 1388 or later, by one of Wyclif's closest friends, most probably John Purvey. The Wyclif Bible helped to mold the language of the English Bible. We owe to it such expressions as "strait gate," "make whole," "compass sea and land," "son of perdition," and "enter thou into the joy of thy lord."

3. *The Tyndale New Testament, 1525.* The 1st printed English New Testament was translated by William Tyndale directly from Erasmus' Greek text as published in 1516 and revised in 1522. Tyndale's translation was made in Hamburg, but was published in Worms. As subordinate aids Tyndale made use of the Vulgate, the Latin translation of Erasmus, and Luther's German version. More than any other man Tyndale molded the language of our English Bible. Practically nine tenths of the language of the King James Version of the NT is Tyndale's. He deserves the credit for much of its beauty and dignity. Tyndale discarded many of the cherished ecclesiastical terms such as "priest," "church," "charity," "penance," etc. He made a revision of his New Testament in 1534 and again in 1535. His labors, however, were not confined to the NT. In 1530 there was published at Marburg a translation of the Pentateuch he had made from the Hebrew. This was followed by a translation of Jonah in 1531. It is also believed that during his imprisonment he made a translation of the OT books from Joshua to Chronicles, which was not published till after his death, having been left with his friend, John Rogers. In October 1536 Tyndale was strangled and burned as he cried, "Lord, open the King of England's eyes." To William Tyndale the King James Version is largely indebted for its character, form, and style. See fig. 75.

4. *Miles Coverdale's Bible, 1535.* Coverdale's was the 1st complete printed English Bible. The printer and place of publication are unknown; it was probably printed at Marburg. According to the title page Coverdale translated this Bible "out of Douche [German] and Latyn in to Englishe." The NT was simply a revision of Tyndale's, in which many of the beloved ecclesiastical terms were restored. In the OT, use was probably made of Tyndale's Pentateuch, and the remainder

was translated from Luther's German and the Zürich Bible of 1529, the Vulgate, and the Latin text of Pagninus. It was dedicated to Henry VIII and was apparently sponsored by Thomas Cromwell. The revised edition of 1537 asserted that it was "set forth with the king's most gracious license." This was the year after Tyndale's martyrdom. The Coverdale Bible is especially noteworthy as the 1st English Bible to separate the Apocrypha from the OT. In earlier versions these Apocryphal books were interspersed among the books of the OT. Coverdale segregated them under the heading: "Apocripha, the bokes and treatises which amonge the fathers of olde are not rekened to be of like authorite with the other bokes of the byble, nether are they founde in the Canon of the Hebrue." In all later versions the example of Coverdale was followed, or the Apocrypha was omitted.

5. *The "Thomas Matthew" Bible, 1537.* The 1st licensed English Bible was a revision produced by John Rogers, a disciple of Tyndale, and was probably printed at Antwerp. Through the efforts of Cromwell and Cranmer, permission for its public sale was secured from Henry VIII. The actual translation was taken largely from the published and unpublished works of Tyndale, including his NT of 1535, and his rendering of the OT books from Gen through 2 Chr. The remainder of the OT and the Apocryphal books were a revision of Coverdale's Bible. In order to hide the actual sources of this version, Rogers placed the name "Thomas Matthew" on the title page.

6. *Taverner's Bible, 1539.* An independent revision of Matthew's Bible by Richard Taverner, the 1st English Bible to be completely printed in England.

7. *The Great (or Cranmer's) Bible, 1539.* Coverdale's revision of the Thomas Matthew Bible was the 1st English Bible authorized by the King of England and by Parliament for use in the Church of England. It was prepared by Coverdale at the request of Thomas Cromwell. Coverdale revised the OT in accordance with Sebastian Münster's Latin version of 1535, and the NT with reference to the Vulgate and the Latin version of Erasmus. The name "Great" Bible is derived from its large size. The pages measured 15 by 10 in. It is called Cranmer's Bible because of the preface written by Cranmer, who was then the Archbishop of Canterbury. The printing was begun in Paris and finished in London. Cromwell ordered that every church in

England was to have a copy in a convenient place. The Book of Common Prayer still makes use of the Psalms from this version.

8. *The Geneva Bible; NT 1557, OT 1560.* The scholarly revision by Protestant refugees in Switzerland during Mary's reign, under the leadership of William Whittingham. It was the 1st version printed in Roman type. Not only was it the most scholarly English version that had thus appeared, but it was in a handy quarto size. It became the popular household Bible for ¾ of a century. It had a strong influence upon the King James Version, and was also the 1st complete English Bible to have verse divisions.

9. *The Bishops' Bible, 1568.* The 2d authorized English Bible, a revision of the Great Bible by a group of scholars that included a number of bishops. It showed considerable borrowings from the Geneva Bible, including the division into verses. The version was of uneven quality because of the lack of consultation between the revisers, and became the occasion and the basis of the later revision known as the King James Version. It immediately superseded the Great Bible in the churches, but never displaced the Geneva Bible in the homes of the people.

10. *The Rheims-Douai Version; Rheims NT 1582, Douai OT 1609-10.* The popularity of the Protestant English Bibles resulted in a Roman Catholic translation of the Latin Vulgate. The title page speaks of it as "The Holie Bible, Faithfully Translated into English out of the Authentical Latin." The translation is so literal as to be stilted and at times unintelligible. Nevertheless, it influenced the revisers of the King James Version, especially in words of Latin derivation.

11. *The King James (or "Authorized") Version, 1611.* A revision of the Bishops' Bible, by a large group of scholars, made at the request of King James I, (hence the name, now abbreviated to KJV). A long and scholarly preface by Miles Smith set forth the purpose and principles employed in the translation. Unfortunately this preface, entitled "The Translators to the Reader," is not now generally printed in the King James Bible. It states the purpose of the new version in these words: "Truly (good Christian Reader) we never thought from the beginning, that we should need to make a new Translation, nor yet to make of a bad one a good one, . . . but to make a good one better, or out of many good ones, one principal good one, not justly to be excepted against; that hath been our endeavour, that our mark." This goal the translators achieved. They produced a scholarly and adequate rendering of the then-known Hebrew and Greek texts in an English style known for its beauty, dignity, and charm. The influence of this version on the religious life and literature of the English-speaking peoples is incalculable. It is often spoken of as the Authorized Version, though there is no record of any order or decree by either Parliament or the King authorizing its use in the churches, as the title page implies. The King James Version was revised in minor details a number of times in the 17th and 18th cent. The generally accepted current form of the version is substantially the revision of 1769.

12. *The English Revised Version; NT 1881, OT 1885.* The phenomenal discovery of new manuscripts in the centuries that followed the production of the KJV gave rise to a new, radical revision, as scholars now had a more ancient text of the Greek NT from which to make their translation. Also a better understanding of Hebrew resulted in a clearer rendering of the OT. The result was the Revised Version. An effort was also made to eliminate obsolete words and archaisms. The paragraphing of the text by verses was superseded by a division into sense units or paragraphs. The version, however, lacked the literary charm of the King James Version.

13. *The American Standard Version, 1901.* An American edition of the Revised Version incorporating the readings and renderings preferred by the American Committee of Revision but not accepted by the British revisers, also containing further changes.

14. *The Revised Standard Version; NT 1946, OT 1952.* The newest revision by an American committee of scholars, embodying the latest in Biblical scholarship, and presenting God's Word in the American English of today. Its translators state in the preface: "That Word must not be disguised in phrases that are no longer clear, or hidden under words that have changed or lost their meaning. It must stand forth in language that is direct and plain and meaningful to people today."

15. *Jewish Versions.* Several translations of the OT into English by Jewish scholars have been made, such as the version by Abraham Benisch (1851), that by Isaac Leeser (1853), and the *Jewish Fam-*

ily Bible by Michael Friedlander. But the generally accepted version used by English-speaking Jews was produced by the Jewish Publication Society of America. The translation was done by a board of American Jewish scholars under the leadership of Max L. Margolis. It was published in 1917 under the title *The Holy Scriptures According to the Masoretic Text—A New Translation.*

16. *Roman Catholic Versions.* Several important Catholic translations have appeared in addition to revisions of the Rheims-Douai Version. The following may be mentioned: *The Westminster Version of the Sacred Scriptures,* begun in 1913 and completed in 1935, the Confraternity revision of the Challoner-Rheims translation in 1941, and the Ronald A. Knox rendering, of which the NT appeared in 1945 and the OT in 1949.

17. *Some Private and Modern Speech Translations.*

(1) *The Fenton Version, 1883-1903.* Ferrar Fenton was a London businessman who devoted many years of his life to fulfill a youthful resolve "to establish the authenticity of the Sacred Scriptures as revealed from Him to Man, by making them intelligible, through the use of modern English, to my countrymen. . . ." In 1883 he published his translation of Paul's epistles, in 1895 his NT, and in 1903 *The Holy Bible in Modern English.*

(2) *The Twentieth Century New Testament, 1898-1901.* A new translation of the NT said to have been inspired by a mother's desire to have a version her children could understand. It was produced from the Greek text of Westcott and Hort by an anonymous group of about 20 American scholars. The "tentative edition" was published in 3 parts in 1898, 1900, and 1901. The text was then thoroughly revised and published as a permanent edition in 1904.

(3) *Moffatt Bibles.* James Moffatt produced 2 entirely distinct translations. In 1901 at Edinburgh he published *The Historical New Testament; being the literature of the New Testament arranged in the order of its literary growth and according to the dates of the documents,* in which he followed the critical literary theories of his time. In 1913 appeared his brilliant and stimulating *The New Testament: A New Translation,* a rendering of Von Soden's Greek text in the modern colloquial English of Britain. In 1924 he added *The Old Testament: A New Translation,* and in 1935 he published his revised and final edition of the complete Moffatt Bible.

(4) *Weymouth's New Testament.* Richard Francis Weymouth prepared a dignified but free and idiomatic translation into everyday English of his *Resultant Greek Testament* (1892) with special attention to the Greek tenses. Because of Weymouth's illness the version was edited and partly revised by E. Hampden-Cook, and published as *The New Testament in Modern Speech* in 1903. An American edition, "newly revised by James Alexander Robertson" was published in Boston in 1929.

(5) *The Smith-Goodspeed Bible.* In 1923 Edgar J. Goodspeed published *The New Testament: An American Translation,* in the simple, common language of everyday life in America. He used as his basis the Greek text of Westcott and Hort, with some variations. In 1927 appeared a companion volume, *The Old Testament: An American Translation,* the work of T. J. Meek, Leroy Waterman, A. R. Gordon, and J. M. Powis Smith, who also acted as editor. These were combined in 1931 as *The Bible: An American Translation,* and in 1939, with the addition of Goodspeed's version of the Apocrypha, as *The Complete Bible.*

(6) *The Riverside New Testament.* A sort of eclectic rendering of Nestle's Greek text by W. G. Ballantine, who confesses his indebtedness to other modern versions. It was published as the *Riverside New Testament* in 1923, and revised in 1934.

(7) *Centenary Translation of the New Testament.* A version to commemorate the first 100 years of service by the American Baptist Publication Society, published by Mrs. Helen Barrett Montgomery in 1924 in Philadelphia. Many of her colloquial paragraph and chapter headings are striking, such as "Play the Game," "A 'Close-up' of Sin," "Paul's Swan Song," and "Orchestrate Your Virtues."

(8) *The Williams New Testament.* Charles B. Williams, a professor of Greek, in 1937 (Boston) published *The New Testament, A New Translation in the Language of the People* in which he gave special attention to the rendering of the Greek tenses. The version was reprinted in Chicago in 1950.

(9) *The Berkeley Version.* A version produced by Gerrit Verkuyl who, in the translation of his NT, based chiefly on Tischendorf's 8th edition of the Greek text, aimed to produce "a translation less interpretative than Moffatt's, more cul-

tured in language than Goodspeed's, more American than Weymouth's, and freer from the King James Version than the Revised Standard" (*The Bible Translator,* Vol. II, No. 2, p. 81, April, 1951). Verkuyl also edited the OT, and in 1959 *The Holy Bible: The Berkeley Version in Modern English* appeared (named for Verkuyl's home, Berkeley, California).

(10) *The Bible in Basic English.* A version prepared by a committee under S. H. Hooke of the University of London. In 1941 the New Testament was produced using about 1,000 words, of which 850 are Basic English, 50 are special Bible words, and 100 others are words giving most help in reading English prose. The whole Bible appeared in 1949.

(11) *Phillips' Translation.* A work by an Anglican priest, J. B. Phillips, a remarkable modern speech version in flowing language, based on Souter's Greek text. In 1947 he published his *Letters to Young Churches,* in 1952, *The Gospels,* in 1955, *The Young Church in Action* [Acts], and in 1958, *The New Testament in Modern English.* The version is fresh and challenging though at times a bit free, as in phrases such as "dear old Stachys" (Rom 16:9), and "Give one another a hearty handshake all round for my sake" (v 16).

(12) *The Rieu Gospels.* E. V. Rieu, editor of the Penguin Classics, in 1952 translated *The Four Gospels, A New Translation from the Greek,* which is included in the Penguin series.

(13) *The New Testament: A New Translation in Plain English.* A version by Charles Kingsley Williams, published in London in 1952. The translator makes good the title; the translation is in simplified English, the vocabulary containing only about 2,000 words.

Vestibule. A rendering of: (1) The Heb. *'ûlam* (1 Chr 28:11; 2 Chr 3:4; RSV), translated "porch" in the KJV, and in the RSV of 1 Ki 7:6; Eze 8:16. The RSV renders *'ûlam* "hall" (1 Ki 7:6-8) when it describes the structures that formed part of the Temple and of a palace of Solomon. These were probably vestibules that had 3 sides and a roof, but which were open at the front, except for pillars to support the roof. (2) The Heb. *misderôn* (Jgs 3:23), a word of uncertain meaning, rendered "porch" in the KJV. (3) The Heb. *'êlam* with variations of spelling (Eze 40:16, 22, RSV; etc.), "porch," or "vestibule," rendered "arch" in the KJV. (4) The Heb. *'ayil* (Eze 40:37, 38, RSV),

translated "posts" in these passages in the KJV. The exact meaning of the Hebrew term is uncertain. Probably pillars are meant.

Vestment. *See* Clothing.

Vesture. *See* Clothing.

Vial. *See* Basin.

Village. The rendering of the following terms: (1) the Heb. *chaṣer,* "enclosure" (Gen 25:16, RSV; Is 42:11), a settlement of nomadic people; (2) the Heb. *kaphar,* "village," as the modern Arabic term *kafr* indicates (1 Chr 27:25; Neh 6:2); (3) the Heb. *banôth,* the plural of *bath,* "daughter," with the meaning of "dependency (of a town or city)" (Num 21:25, 32; 32:42; 2 Chr 28:18); and (4) the Gr. *kōmē* (Mt 9:35; 14:15; etc.). In contrast to cities or towns, which were walled, villages were usually unprotected settlements. However, *chaṣer,* which means "enclosure," indicates that the type of settlement described by this term had some kind of protective hedge or wall. In some cases the term may refer to an encampment rather than to a village. In other cases a type of village may be meant in which the houses are connected by their side walls and surround a square or a rectangular place. Such villages are found in the Near East today. The houses open toward this central open place and the whole village has one entrance, an opening between two houses, which can be bolted and locked. The inhabitants of open villages always looked to a neighboring city or town as their haven of refuge in times of need. For this reason villages are usually considered dependencies of walled cities or towns, and are never mentioned by name in the OT, nor in any other way than in the plural. The NT does not make a sharp distinction between cities and villages, and we find both terms applied to Bethlehem (Lk 2:4; Jn 7:42; RSV) and Bethsaida (Lk 9:10; Mk 8:22, 23; RSV).

Vine. [Heb. generally *gephen;* Gr. *ampelos.*] Specifically the common grapevine (*Vitis vinifera*). References to the planting, tending, pruning, and harvesting of the grape in the Scriptures are abundant. The cultivation of the grapevine is mentioned early (Gen 9:20). The appearance of the grapevine, as it is grown in the Holy Land, is much like that of a small tree, with a stem up to 1½ ft. in diameter. The branches, which may be left on the ground or allowed to entwine themselves about a supporting trellis, bear clusters of fruit that weigh from 10 to 12 pounds. The size of the clusters has frequently amazed travelers in Palestine, where vineyards have always abounded. See figs. 164, 436.

A rather complete description of the stages by which a family grew and tended its vines is found in the parable of Is 5:1-6, and in the figures and parables of Christ (Mt 20:1-16; 21:28-31; Mk 12:1-9; Jn 15:1-6). To the Hebrews a vineyard was a most valued possession, and to be promised the fruits of the vine forever was a symbol of security, prosperity, and reward (Is 65:21).

Terracing was sometimes done, so that vineyards could be placed on hillsides or hilltops (cf. Is 5:1; Joel 3:18). Around the plot was a stone fence to keep out marauding animals (Num 22:24; Ps 80:8-13; Prov 24:30, 31; Song 2:15; Is 5:5), and a watchtower was provided for a watchman whose duty it was to protect the crop (Mt 21:33). See fig. 508.

The vine provided the prophets and teachers of Bible times with many illustrations for various spiritual lessons. To dwell under one's fig tree or vine symbolized contentment, peace, and plenty (Zec 3:10). Israel was compared to the grapevine transplanted from Egypt (Ps 80:8-16). The rebellious Hebrews were likened to a good vine that had degenerated (Jer 2:21). Christ pictured Himself as the vine, with His disciples as the branches, which were expected to bear much fruit (Jn 15:1-8). *See* Wine.

Vine of Sodom. A rendering of Heb. *gephen Sedom* (Deut 32:32), possibly the trailing plant colocynth (*Citrullus colocynthis*) belonging to the families of melons, and which, according to Moldenke (*Plants of the Bible*, p. 79), who quotes Tristram, "has long, straggling tendrils or runners like the vine, with a fruit fair to look at, but nauseous beyond description to the taste, and, when fully ripe, merely a quantity of dusty powder with the seeds, inside its beautiful orange rind." *See* Gourd.

Vinegar. [Heb. *chomeṣ;* Gr. *oxos.*] Sour wine, wine vinegar, or in general, liquids or sauce used as a relish, in which acetous fermentation has occurred. "Vinegar of wine" and "vinegar of strong drink" were forbidden to Nazirites (Num 6:3). The statement in Ps 69:21, "in my thirst they gave me vinegar to drink," is shown to have had a fulfillment in connection with the suffering of Christ on the cross as recorded in Mt 27:48; Mk 15:36; Lk 23:36; Jn 19:28-30. In Mt 27:34 textual evidence favors the reading *oinos,* "wine" (RSV), rather than *oxos,* "vinegar." Roman soldiers are said to have drunk a thin, sour wine called, in Latin, *acetum,* "vinegar," "sour wine."

Vineyard. *See* Vine.

Vineyards, Plain of the. *See* Abel-keramim.

Viol. The rendering of the Heb. *nebel* in Is 5:12; 14:11; Amos 5:23; 6:5; KJV. Elsewhere when a musical instrument is described, the KJV translates *nebel* "psaltery" (1 Sa 10:5; 2 Sa 6:5; etc.). However, *nebel* is a harp, a musical instrument which pictorial evidence shows was in common use in Egypt and Mesopotamia from early times. Preserved harps have been discovered in the royal tombs of Ur, and in ancient Egyptian tombs. *See* Harp. The stringed instrument called a viol is not attested before the Middle Ages.

Viper. A rendering of: (1) The Heb. *'eph'eh,* "a poisonous snake." It was found in the south country (Is 30:6), was deadly (Job 20:16), and was a type of reptile that hatched from eggs (Is 59:5). (2) The Heb. *shephiphon* (Gen 49:17, RSV), a serpent of uncertain identification. (3) The Heb. *'akshûb* (Ps 140:3, RSV), perhaps the horned viper, *Cerastes cornutus.* (4) The Gr. *echidna,* probably the common viper (*Vipera communis*). Christ called the Jewish leaders a "generation of vipers" (Mt 3:7; 12:34; 23:33; Lk 3:7). Paul was bitten by a viper on the island of Malta after his shipwreck on the journey to Rome (Acts 28:3).

Vision. [Heb. generally *chazôn* and related words, "vision," or *mar'eh* and related words, "appearance," "sight," "vision"; Gr. *optasia,* "vision"; *horama,* "vision"; *horasis,* "appearance," "vision."] A supernatural means by which God communicates His will to His servants the prophets (Is 1:1; etc.). *Chazôn* is a more general term descriptive of any divine communication, whatever form it may take, whereas *mar'eh* refers specifically to visions in which the prophet sees enacted before him a representation of truths God wills to impart to His people. A vision may come in waking moments (Dan 10:7; Acts 9:3, 7), by day (Acts 10:3) or night (Gen 46:2), or it may come as a dream (Num 12:6). The Bible makes no sharp distinction between visions and dreams, except possibly that dreams come during hours of slumber. In vision the prophet becomes oblivious of his natural surroundings and the Spirit of God so controls the sensory areas of his brain that the prophet seems literally to see, hear, and feel what is presented to him in vision. A vision may contain instruction for God's people, or reveal facts about the future that will enable God's people to live more intelligently in the present. In vision the *prophet sometimes seems to be transported over considerable distances (see Eze 3:12-15; 8:3; 40:2; cf. 2 Cor 12:2-4).

Vophsi (vŏf'sī). [Heb. *Wophsi,* meaning unknown.] The father of the spy, Nahbi, who represented the tribe of Naphtali (Num 13:14).

Votive Offerings. *See* Sacrifices and Offerings.

Vow. [Heb. generally *neder,* "vow"; Gr. generally *euchē,* "prayer," "vow."] An obligation voluntarily assumed, either in appreciation for a divine blessing already received or in anticipation of one. Frequently it reflected a realization of need for special dependence upon God. Nowhere does God command people to take vows, but He does require that a vow, once made, be fulfilled (Num 30:2; Ps 76:11; Ec 5:4, 5). In taking a vow a man might devote property or persons—himself or members of his family—to God. Jacob vowed to pay tithe to God on condition that God would keep him and bring him safely back to the land of his fathers (Gen 28:20-22). Persons vowed to God and not redeemed became attached to the sanctuary (1 Sa 1:11, 24, 28). Persons vowed to the Lord might be redeemed upon the payment of stipulated sums of money (Lev 27:2-8; cf. 2 Ki 12: 4). A clean beast might not be redeemed (Lev 27:9, 10), but an unclean beast could be redeemed (vs 11-13). A house or field could be devoted to the Lord (vs 14-16). The house might be redeemed by adding the usual fifth to the price, but somewhat different regulations applied to redeeming the field (vs 17-24). There were also vows of abstinence, like that taken by the Rechabites, who refrained

from drinking wine (see Jer 35). The Nazirite vow, which was considered the highest type of vow, might be either temporary or permanent. *See* Nazirite. Only in special instances, as with Samson (Jgs 13:5, 7), Samuel (1 Sa 1:11), and John the Baptist (Lk 1:15; cf. ch 7:33), was the Nazirite vow obligatory and permanent. Upon at least one occasion the apostle Paul also took a temporary Nazirite vow (Acts 18:18; cf. ch 21:23). In certain instances a man had a right to annul a vow taken by an unmarried daughter or by his wife (Num 30:3-16). The vow of Jephthah, a judge of Israel, is a classic example of a rash vow (see Jgs 11:30-40).

Vulture. The rendering of: (1) The Heb. *'ayyah* (Job 28:7, KJV), probably the falcon (see RSV), since the context suggests a bird of keen sight, and the Falconidae are noted for their sharp sight. (2) The Heb. *da'ah* or *dayyah* (Lev 11: 14; Deut 14:13; Is 34:15; KJV), probably the *kite (RSV). (3) The Heb. *nesher* (Prov 30:17; Lam 4:19; Hos 8:1; RSV; KJV "eagle"). This term is generally rendered "eagle" by both the KJV and RSV, but probably at times refers to allied birds such as the vulture. (4) The Heb. *qa'ath* (Ps 102:6; Zep 2:14; RSV), a bird of uncertain species, possibly a species of owl. (5) The Heb. *racham* (Lev 11:18, RSV; KJV "gier eagle"), a term appearing only in this passage, variously identified as the pelican, sea eagle, osprey, and vulture. (6) The Heb. *peres* (Deut. 14:12, RSV), a bird of uncertain species, perhaps a kind of vulture (KJV "ossifrage"). *See also* Carrion Vulture. G. R. Driver, in a study of Biblical birds of prey, identifies the various Hebrew names rendered "vulture" with: (1) common buzzard or falcon, (2) black kite, (3) griffon vulture or (golden) eagle, (4) scops owl, (5) osprey, and (6) black vulture (*PEQ* 87 [1955], 8-20).

Wafer. A rendering of: (1) The Heb. *raqiq.* A thin cake of bread. Unleavened wafers were used ceremonially in connection with the consecration of priests (Ex 29:2, 23; Lev 8:26), certain offerings (Lev 2: 4; 7:12), and the offerings made at the

fulfillment of Nazirite vows (Num 6:15, 19). (2) The Heb. *ṣappichith* (Ex 16: 31), "a flat cake."

Wages. A workman's or servant's pay, received in return for services rendered. The Biblical writers employ the term "wages" both literally (Gen 30:28; Ex 2: 9) and figuratively (Rom 6:23; Jn 4:36). As to the literal they make mention of 2 main methods of payment: (1) in kind (Gen 29:15, 20; 31:7, 41), and (2) by money (Ex 2:9; Mt 20:2). The Law of Moses required that wages be paid each evening (Lev 19:13; Deut 24:14, 15), and the Scriptures vigorously denounce the withholding of wages due (Jer 22:13; Mal 3:5). The only reference to the rate of wages paid is found in Mt 20:2, where the laborer's pay per day is set at one *dēnarion* (the Roman *denarius,* a silver coin worth from 8 to 18 cents, depending upon the precise period in the 1st cent. A.D.). *Dēnarion* is translated "penny" (KJV) and *"denarius" (RSV). See fig. 340.

Wagon. Generally a rendering of the Heb. *'agalah,* frequently translated "cart." The vehicles that Joseph sent to Canaan to assist his father's family in their move to Egypt (Gen 45:19, 21, 27; 46:5) were probably two-wheeled carts. *See* Cart. Six covered wagons, each drawn by 2 oxen, were used in the wilderness wanderings for the transport of the tabernacle (Num 7:3-8). The "wagon" of Eze 23:24, KJV, is a rendering of the Heb. *rekeb,* translated "chariot" in the RSV. The "wagon" of Eze 23:24; 26:10; RSV, is a rendering of the Heb. *galgal,* literally, "wheel."

Waheb (wā'hĕb). [Heb. *Waheb.*] A place near the river Arnon (Num 21:14, RSV); not identified. The KJV, not regarding the Hebrew term as a proper noun, renders it "what he did."

Wall. [Hebrew for the wall of a town or city, generally *chômah;* Gr. *teichos.*] Ancient towns and cities were surrounded by *fortification systems usually consisting of walls of stone, bricks, or packed earth.

The earliest walls found so far in Palestine are those in the lowest levels of Jericho, constructed of stone masonry in a period before pottery was invented. Walls of the Early Bronze Age (3d millennium B.C.), such as those in Ai, *Tell el-Fâr'ah* (probably Tirzah) and Megiddo, were formidable structures ranging from 25 to 30 ft. in thickness. They consisted of 2 parallel stone walls and a core of earth and gravel between them.

During the Middle Bronze Age (*c.* 2000 - *c.* 1500 B.C.) new forms of fortifications were developed, which may be divided into 3 types: (1) A sloping rampart, consisting of a stone foundation built of several layers of large blocks of irregularly cut stones set in a shallow trench (fig. 519), on top of which a brick wall was erected. The lower part was plastered with hard-packed clay or lime plaster, to make a scaling of the wall difficult, if not impossible. Such walls have been found at Shechem and Jericho. (2) An outer moat and a wall. The moat of *Tell el-'Ajjûl* was 20 ft. deep on the outer side and had a slope of 35 degrees up toward the city wall. (3) Massive sloping ramparts of packed earth, known as the Hyksos fortifications. They usually surrounded rectangular camps large enough to accommodate sizable chariot forces, which were introduced into the Near East at that time. Examples of these fortifications are the walls of *Qaṭna* in Syria, Ashkelon in southern Palestine, and *Tell el-Yehūdîyeh* in Lower Egypt.

During the Late Bronze Age (*c.* 1500-1200 B.C.) the Canaanites further improved city walls by adding strong towers and monumental gate structures several towers in depth (*see* Gate; Tower). The blocks of stone used during this period were usually larger than those used before, and in some instances (Beth-shean) double walls were erected in casemate style, that is, the 2 parallel walls were connected with cross walls forming small rooms.

519. The lower part of the ancient city wall of Shechem

WALL

The Israelites were much impressed by the strong walls of the Canaanites (Num 13:28), but during the early period of their history in Palestine made no attempts to build fortified cities for themselves. Apparently they were satisfied to live in camps as they had done during their wilderness wanderings, and they left the strong cities in the hands of the Canaanites (Jgs 1:21, 27-33). Gradually, however, the Israelites took over some of these cities and began to imitate the building techniques of the Canaanites; yet archeological evidence shows that their building methods were at first much inferior to those employed by their predecessors, as, for example, the poorly constructed little castle of Saul at Gibeah clearly shows. But they improved rapidly, and the walls of Solomon are rather good. Examples of Solomonic fortifications have come to light at Megiddo and Eziongeber. Strong city walls were built also during the divided kingdoms. For example, the wall of *Tell en-Naṣbeh* has an average thickness of 13 ft. and strong towers at regular intervals (*see* Mizpah, 4; see also figs. 193, 336). The Israelite wall surrounding Lachish also shows great strength and fine workmanship. See figs. 282, 284.

The Persian period, during which postexilic Judaism rebuilt its political structure, has left us very few examples of city walls. Nehemiah rebuilt Jerusalem's wall during that time, but the Bible describes only the course of that wall (Neh 3) and says nothing of the techniques employed. More is known of fortifications of the Hellenistic period, examples of which have been preserved at Samaria with its strong round tower, at Bethzur, and at the strong castle of the Tobiads in Transjordan. From the early Herodian period, in which walls of tremendous strength were erected, sizable samples have survived, such as the Wailing Wall in Jerusalem (fig. 520). A large part of the tower now called David's Tower (fig. 263), also ruined walls at Masada, Machaerus and elsewhere.

The present wall that surrounds the socalled Old City of Jerusalem was built by Suleiman the Magnificent in the 16th cent. A.D., who used much building material of ancient structures for its construction, as every visitor can easily see. Although this structure is not ancient, it probably does not differ greatly in appearance from the city walls of the time of Christ. See figs. 260, 277, 461.

520. The Wailing Wall at Jerusalem, remains of the outer wall of Herod's Temple

Lit.: A.-G. Barrois, *Manuel d'archéologie biblique* I (1939), 127-212; M. Burrows, *What Mean These Stones?* (New Haven, 1941), pp. 136-156.

Wallet. *See* Scrip.

War. It is necessary to distinguish between the offensive or defensive wars waged by Israel under a theocratic form of government and the wars waged under the monarchy. When Israel was ruled by a divine government, under such leaders as Moses, or judges such as Gideon, or prophets such as Samuel, wars were a religious matter. They were the Lord's wars (Ex 17:16; Num 21:14; 1 Sa 18:17; 25:28), and Israel's enemies were God's enemies (Jgs 5:23, 31). Wars were carried out upon God's explicit command (ch 6:14). It is for this reason that the warriors had to keep themselves ceremonially pure (1 Sa 21:4-6; cf. 2 Sa 11:11), for the Lord Himself led His devoted armies (Is 13:3; Deut 20:4), and His presence was in the camp (Num 14:42; Deut 23:14; 1 Sa 4:7). The Lord is called Israel's banner (Ex 17:15), its shield and sword (Deut 33:29), a warrior (Ex 15:3), and the one who strikes His enemies with terror (Ex 23:27, 28; Jos 10:10, 11; 24:12). Divine regulations were given even with regard to exemptions from military duty. Those who had built a home but had not dedicated it, were not to go to war, as well as those who had planted a vineyard but had not yet eaten of its fruit, or who were engaged to a woman but had not married her, or who were fainthearted (Deut 20:5-9). If no explicit command had been given, the Israelites consulted God's will before engaging in aggressive war (Jgs 20:23, 27, 28). When threatened by a war which they had not sought, they prayed to God for divine help (1 Sa 7:8, 9).

Under the monarchy wars were waged by Saul and David, as in the theocratic period, in obedience to God's command (1 Sa 15:2, 3; 2 Sa 5:22-25). But such occasions were exceptions, and most recorded wars were undertaken either to extend the nation's territory (2 Sa 8:1-14), to recover lost areas or cities (1 Ki 22:3, 4), to defend the country (ch 20:1-22), or to prevent a foreign king from passing through the territory of Palestine for a military campaign (2 Chr 35:20-22). A formal declaration of war occasionally preceded a campaign (2 Ki 14:8-11), and sometimes notice of an impending war was given to an enemy nation to frighten it or to induce it to advance a peaceful solution to the difficulties existing between the 2 nations (Jgs 11:12-28; 1 Sa 11:1-3; 1 Ki 20:1-12). In most cases, however, wars were started by surprising the enemy without giving him any advance notice (Gen 14:15; Jos 8:2-7; Jgs 7:16-22; 2 Sa 5:23, 24). Military campaigns usually began in the spring (2 Sa 11:1), after the wet season had ended. Camping in the open was then possible and the ground was hard enough for movements of large armies and battle operations. Frequently spies were sent out to obtain military intelligence about the enemy's weaknesses (Num 13:17; Jos 2:1; Jgs 7:9-11; 1 Sa 26:4). Occasionally persons from the enemy's camp or city were picked up, through whom important information was obtained (Jgs 8:14; 1 Sa 30:11-15).

On the battles and the military strategies followed during campaigns, see Array; Battering Ram; Battle; Mound.

Ancient wars were usually waged with great cruelty. Captured cities were generally destroyed, and their inhabitants slaughtered or taken captive and made slaves (2 Ki 15:16; 2 Chr 25:11, 12). Attempts were sometimes made to buy off an attacking force by paying a heavy tribute, although such attempts were seldom successful, for they whetted the appetite of the attacker and disclosed that the attacked nation felt itself too weak for a successful defensive war (1 Ki 20:2-9; 2 Ki 18:13-16). The victorious nation celebrated its victory with song and dance (2 Chr 20:26-28). The conquered nation was either subjugated and garrisoned (2 Sa 8:13, 14) or required to pay a heavy annual tribute (2 Ki 3:4). See Army.

In the NT "war" is often used in a figurative sense. James speaks of human passions that war in the Christian's members (ch 4:1). Paul notes that the Christian war is fought not with material, but with spiritual, weapons (2 Cor 10:3-5; Eph 6:11-17).

Peter urges his readers to separate themselves from all carnal desires and practices, which "war against the soul" (1 Pe 2:11). Paul exhorted Timothy to "war a good warfare" in his ministry (1 Ti 1:18).

Wardrobe. A rendering of: (1) The Heb. *begadîm* (2 Ki 22:14; 2 Chr 34:22), "cloaks," "garments," "coverings." Shallum is mentioned as being in charge of either the royal wardrobe or the vestments of the priests. (2) The Heb. *meltachah* (2 Ki 10:22; Jer 38:11; RSV) "wardrobe." However, in the latter text *meltachah* is an emended reading for *'el-tachath,* meaning literally "to under."

Wars of the Lord. A lost book, part of which is quoted in Num 21:14, 15, and possibly also in vs 17, 18, and 27-30. It has been conjectured that this book is the same as the book of Jasher (Jos 10:13; 2 Sa 1:18).

Washing. *See* Bathing.

Watch. *See* Night.

Watchman. [Heb. generally forms of *ṣaphah, naṣar,* and *shamar.*] A sentinel appointed to guard a specified area against predators, thieves, etc., to watch for messengers, and to give the alarm in case enemy forces approach or threaten attack. Watchmen were stationed on city walls (2 Sa 18:24; 2 Ki 9:17-20), in wilderness watchtowers, and on hilltops (2 Chr 20:24; Jer 31:6), and functioned also as street watchmen or patrols (Song 3:3; 5:7). The term is used figuratively of the spiritual and secular leaders (Is 56:10), Ezekiel being especially so named (Eze 3:17; 33:1-9). *See also* Night.

Water. *See* Cistern; Conduit; Pool; Siloam; Spring; Well.

Water for Impurity. *See* Purification, I.

Water of Bitterness, KJV **Bitter Water.** [Heb. *mê hammarîm,* literally, "water of bitternesses."] Water employed in a symbolic ritual to adjudicate the unwitnessed charge of adultery brought by a man against his wife (Num 5:11-31), in compliance with the Mosaic law known as "the law of jealousy" (v 29). When a man suspected his wife of marital infidelity he was to bring her to the priest, together with the specified offering of barley meal known as "an offering of jealousy" (v 15). The priest first set the woman in the presence of the Lord. He then took "holy water," apparently from the laver in the courtyard, and mingled with it dust from the floor of the sanctuary, loosed her hair, and placed the barley meal offering in her hands. Holding the "bitter water"—the "holy water" mingled with dust—in his hand, the priest placed her under oath, to the effect that if she were innocent the "bitter water" would have no effect upon her but that if guilty the Lord would make her "thigh to rot" and her "belly to swell" (Num 5:22). The woman then responded, confirming the oath as uttered by the priest, and the priest recorded the oath in a book, washed off the record thus made into the water of bitterness, and ·gave it to the woman to drink. The priest next presented the barley meal offering before the Lord and offered it upon the altar. The result of the test was left in the hands of the Lord, the curse either remaining inoperative or rendering the woman sterile.

Water of Separation. *See* Purification, I.

Waterpot. *See* Jar; Pitcher.

Waters of Merom. *See* Merom, Waters of.

Waters of Strife. *See* Meribah.

Waterspout. A rendering in Ps 42:7, KJV, of the Heb. *ṣinnôr*, the precise meaning of which is uncertain. The LXX reads *katarraktēs*, "waterfall," "cataract," a suitable meaning in the context.

Wave Offering. *See* Sacrifices and Offerings.

Wax. [Heb. *dônag*.] Beeswax, the only wax known to have been used in ancient Egypt and doubtless in the surrounding countries. It was used in ancient times as an adhesive, as a base for colors in painting, and for coating writing tablets, in shipbuilding, and in mummification. The fearful heart melts like wax before the enemy (Ps 22:14) and the power of God is said to melt the earth and the wicked as though they were wax (Ps 68:2; 97:5; Mic 1:4).

Way. *See* Highway and Road.

Waymark. [Heb. *ṣiyyûn*, "signpost," "road mark," such as a heap of stones, "monument."] A term occurring once (Jer 31:21) designating a road mark. However, *ṣiyyûn* occurs also in Eze 39:15, where it means "signpost," and in 2 Ki 23:17, where it means "gravestone."

Wealth. The possession of riches is not in itself sinful (see Ec 5:19), as evidenced by the fact that such outstanding Bible characters as Abraham, Job, and Nicodemus were wealthy. However, the possession of wealth is accompanied by great peril to one's salvation (Mt 19:23), particularly if the wealth be amassed by oppressing others or if the heart be set upon it. Our Lord did not censure the wealthy, but did give considerable instruction about the right use of material possessions. See the parables of the Talents (ch

25:14-30), the Rich Fool (Lk 12:16-21), the Dishonest Steward (ch 16:1-9), and the Pounds (ch 19:11-27).

Weapons. *See* names of weapons: Arrow; Battering Ram; Bow; Chariot; Club; Dagger; Javelin; Sling; Spear; Sword.

Weasel. [Heb. *choled*, "digger," or "creeper," from the verb *chalad*, meaning "to dig" in Middle Hebrew and "to creep" in Syriac.] An unclean animal, mentioned in Lev 11:29. The rendering "weasel" is based on the LXX and the Vulgate. This interpretation is also supported by a description in the Talmud of an animal called *chuldah*, a word derived from the same root as the Biblical *choled*. Some scholars, however, on the basis of an Arabic cognate word, think it means "mole."

Weaving. The manufacture of cloth from threads of any of a number of plant or animal fibers. Egypt had a highly developed textile industry. Weaving was an established art long before the arrival of Jacob's sons there (see Gen 37:3; 41:42). The Egyptians developed great skill in weaving, and some of their material was so fine that a woman's dress made from it could be drawn through a finger ring. Weaving in that country seems to have been done mostly by men (see Herod. ii. 35). Among the Jews the women are

521. Ancient Egyptian model showing weavers with a loom

most often mentioned as the weavers and needleworkers (2 Ki 23:7; Prov 31:22, 24; cf. Acts 9:39). The men who wove material for the tabernacle and robes, etc., for the priests (Ex 35:35; 39:22, 27), probably learned much of the art during their stay in Egypt. Coarse-textured fabrics, such as those of goat's and camel's hair, were commonly used for clothing, tents, etc. (Ex 26:7; Mt 3:4). Cotton appears to have been a relatively latecomer to the loom, appearing as late as the Greek Empire. Weaving was done on looms of various types. One type was laid out horizontally on the ground (*see* Loom). Another was arranged upright with the warp fastened to a lower beam, passed over an upper beam, and held taut by being fastened to a peg in the ground or by being weighted with stones. The woof threads were carried at right angles to the warp by the shuttle to which the thread was attached. It was by variations in span and by the working in of different-colored woof threads that the design or pattern was woven into the cloth. After each crossing of the shuttle a wooden transverse member was struck against the woof to keep the threads in close proximity. Loom parts have been excavated in several Palestinian sites, and dyeing vats have been found at *Tell Beit Mirsim,* probably Debir. Tunics woven in one piece were worn by the priest (Jos. *Ant.* iii. 7. 4); Jesus wore a coat that was "without seam" (Jn 19:23). *See* Beam; Distaff; Loom; Spin.

Wedding. *See* Marriage.

Week. The cycle of 7 days ending with the Sabbath. The week, unlike the day and the year, does not exist as a cycle in nature, but was divinely designated, first by God's resting on and sanctifying the Sabbath at the close of Creation (Gen 2:1-3), then by the miracle of the manna (Ex 16:15-27), and finally by the 4th commandment on the tables of stone given at Sinai (ch 20:8-11). For 40 years the giving of the manna every day except "the holy sabbath unto the Lord" (ch 16:23) marked off each week for the Hebrews. The week was known by the patriarchs (see Gen 29:27, 28; cf. chs 7:10; 8:10, 12), although it may have been largely forgotten during the period of enslavement in Egypt. After Sinai there was no opportunity to lose count of the week; even after the manna ceased at the time of the entrance into Canaan, the sanctuary services, with their extra offerings on the Sabbath (Num 28:9, 10) and the changing

of the showbread each week (Lev 24:5-9), would have kept the reckoning straight—even if it were possible for a whole nation to miss count, which is a possibility not worth considering. By their observance of the Sabbath through the centuries the Hebrew people preserved the week. In Jesus' time the record is that His followers "rested the sabbath day according to the commandment" (Lk 23:56) on the day before "the first day of the week" (ch 24:1). Jesus Himself kept the Sabbath and declared Himself Lord of it (Mk 2:28).

The Biblical week came down to us through the Jews. Some have held that certain Babylonian taboos on the 7th, 14th, etc., of the month indicate a Babylonian origin of the week, but this series was not a continuous 7-day cycle. The Greeks had 10-day periods in the month, and the Romans an 8-day market-day cycle, but the pagans had no 7-day week until the development of the planetary week from the Chaldean astrology of the Hellenistic period.

It was in this period, between OT and NT times, that the days were named for the 7 planets (the 5 visible planets plus the sun and moon). The more generally accepted explanation for such a naming (one given by Dio Cassius, fl. *c.* A.D. 200) is that the hours of the day were ruled successively by the planets in their supposed astronomical order, beginning with the outermost: Saturn, Jupiter, Mars, Sun, Venus, Mercury, Moon. The day of Saturn was the one on which the 1st hour was ruled by Saturn, the 2d by Jupiter, and so on. Saturn ruled again in the 8th, 15th, and 22d hours, then Mars in the 24th. Thus the 1st hour of the next day would be the Sun's; hence Saturn's day would be followed by Sunday, and so on. The day sequence ran: Saturn, Sun, Moon, Mars, Mercury, Jupiter, Venus (see Dio Cassius, *Roman History* xxvii. 19; cf. ch 16 in which Dio equates the Jews' Sabbath with Saturn's day).

The astrological week, used unofficially in Italy as early as Augustus, was soon spread over the empire along with Mithraism, an eastern sun cult popular among Roman soldiers. By the worshipers of Mithra "each day in the week, the Planet to which the day was sacred was invoked in a fixed spot in the crypt; and Sunday, over which the Sun presided, was especially holy" (Franz Cumont, *The Mysteries of Mithra,* p. 167).

The week was 1st given legal recognition in the Roman civil calendar when Constantine, the 1st "Christian" emperor, added to the pagan idea of a Sun's day the Christian idea of a weekly *rest* day and made laws enforcing rest on Sunday, "the venerable day of the Sun." The Roman astrological names are still current in the European languages derived from Latin. Translated into Germanic names of the equivalent gods, these names have come down into present-day English. The use of the week has spread to the far-flung nations of the world, through missionary activity and through the adoption of the Julian-Gregorian calendar for business dealings with the West.

The present weekly cycle is the same, without any interruption, as was that of the 1st cent. Many think mistakenly that "time has been lost" through calendar changes, but there has been only one revision since Julius Caesar instituted our calendar in 45 B.C. The Julian year averaged 365¼ days, by the addition of a 366th day to every 4th year. But Caesar's astronomers had reckoned the solar year 11 minutes too long, and every 4 centuries had 3 leap years too many, thus causing the calendar to shift 3 days out of step with seasons. By the 1500's the spring equinox fell on March 11. The popes were concerned about Easter because in A.D. 325 it had been dated with reference to March 21 as the equinox. In order to restore Easter to where it had been in 325, Pope Gregory XIII, on the advice of astronomers, decreed in 1582 that the day after the 4th of October should be called, not the 5th, but the 15th; and he provided for fewer leap years in the future to prevent further shifting of the calendar. The 10 "dropped" days were not lost, for they had already been used as 10 extra leap-year days. England and her colonies did not accept the pope's revision until 1752, after the error had reached 11 days. Other countries adopted it at various times, but through it all the days of the week kept the same sequence. The calendar reform changed the day of the *month,* not the week. *The Catholic Encyclopedia* says of Pope Gregory's revision: "It is to be noted that in the Christian period the order of the days of the week has never been interrupted. Thus, when Gregory XIII reformed the calendar in 1582, Thursday, 4 October, was followed by Friday, 15 October. So in England in 1752, Wednesday, 2 September, was followed by Thursday, 14 September" (Article "Chronology," 3:740).

Weeks, Feast of. *See* Pentecost, Feast of.

522. Inscribed weights found at Beth-zur. The two upper weights (inscribed: *nṣf*) weigh 9.54 and 9.8 grams, respectively. The one at the lower left (inscribed: *py[m]*) weighs 7.18 grams. The one on the lower right (inscribed: *bq'*, "beka") weighs 5.8 grams

Weights and Measures. Biblical weights and measures, discussed separately under their various names, are also tabulated here. The metric and U.S. equivalents are approximate only, because the ancient source information is sometimes scanty and often conflicting. There are differences in corresponding units between one country and another (as there are today between the U.S. and British quarts), and between one period and another. Furthermore, the actual ancient cubit rules, measuring vessels, or weights that have been discovered differ among themselves, owing to the lack of a centralized and widely enforced official standard. The values here given are based on the best information obtainable, and sometimes on an average of several values derived from surviving linear measures, vessels, or weights. The decimals in the equivalent values in the tables give an impression of exactness that does not actually exist. However, the approximations are close enough to be useful. The table on the following page lists all units of measures and weights mentioned in the Bible, with their metric and U.S. equivalents.

Lit.: Of the large number of articles and books dealing with weights and measures only a few recent survey articles are here listed: A. Segrè, *JBL* 64 (1945), 357-375; A.-G. Barrois, *Manuel d'archéologie biblique,* II (Paris, 1953), 243-258; *The Interpreter's Bible,* vol. 1 (New York, 1952), pp. 153-157; J. Trinquet, *Dictionaire de la Bible, Supplément,* vol. 5 (Paris, 1957), cols. 1212-1250; J. T. Milik, *Biblica* 40 (1959), 985-991.

TABLES OF WEIGHTS AND MEASURES

		Ancient	Metric	U.S. Equivalent

1. Weights

In the OT:

		Ancient	Metric	U.S. Equivalent
Gerah	(Heb. *gerah,* see Ex 30:13)	1/20 shekel	.57 gram	.02 oz. av.
Beka; KJV, bekah	(Heb. *beqa',* see Ex 38:26)	½ "	5.7 grams	.20 "
Pim	(Heb. *pim,* see 1 Sa 13:21, RSV)	⅔ "	7.6 "	.27 "
Shekel	(Heb. *sheqel,* see Ex 30:13)		11.4 "	.40 "
Mina; KJV, maneh, pound	(Heb. *maneh,* see Eze 45:12)	50 shekels	570 "	20.10 "
Talent	(Heb. *kikkar,* see Ex 38:25)	3,000 "	34.20 kilogr.	75.39 lb. av.

In the NT:

		Ancient	Metric	U.S. Equivalent
Pound	(Gr. *litra,* see Jn 12:3)	12 unciae (ounces)	327.45 grams	11.54 oz. av.

2. Linear Measures

In the OT:

			(Egyptian)	(Time of Hezekiah)	(Egyptian)	(Time of Hezekiah)
Finger	(Heb. *'esba',* see Jer 52:21)	1/24 cubit	2.18 cm.	1.85 cm.	.86 in.	.73 in.
Handbreadth	(Heb. *tephach, tophach,* see 1 Ki 7:26)	1/6 "	8.72 "	7.41 "	3.43 "	2.92 "
Span	(Heb. *zereth,* see Ex 28:16)	½ "	26.16 "	22.23 "	10.30 "	8.75 "
Cubit	(Heb. *'ammah,* see Gen 6:16; *gomed,* see Jgs 3:16)		52.32 "	44.45 "	20.60 "	17.50 "

In the NT:

		Ancient	Metric	U.S. Equivalent
Cubit	(Gr. *pēchus,* see Mt 6:27)		44.45 cm.	17.5 in.
Fathom	(Gr. *orguia,* see Acts 27:28)	about 4 cubits	about 1.78 m.	about 5.83 ft.
Stadium and Furlong	(Gr. *stadion,* see Rev 14:20; Mt 14:24)	⅛ Roman mi.	185.00 "	606.5 "
Mile (Roman)	(Gr. *milion,* only once, in Mt 5:41)		1,480 "	about 4,855 "

3. Measures of Area

Only the acre (Heb. *ṣemed,* Is 5:10; Heb. *ma'anah,* 1 Sa 14:14) is mentioned in the Bible as a unit of area, and its size is uncertain.

4. Dry Measures

In the OT:

		Ancient	Metric	U.S. Equivalent
Kab; KJV, Cab	(Heb. *qab,* see 2 Ki 6:25)	1/18 ephah	1.22 liters	1.11 dry qt.
Omer	(Heb. *'omer,* see Ex 16:36)	1/10 "	2.20 "	2.00 " "
Measure	(Heb. *se'ah,* see 2 Ki 7:1)	⅓ "	7.33 "	6.66 " "
Ephah	(Heb. *'ēphah,* see Ex 16:36)	1/10 homer	22.00 "	2.50 pecks
Lethech; KJV, half homer	(Heb. *lethek,* see Hos 3:2)	½ "	110.00 "	3.12 bu.
Homer	(Heb. *chomer,* see Hos 3:2)	10 ephahs	220.00 "	6.24 "
Cor	(Heb. *kor,* see Eze 45:14)	10 "	220.00 "	6.24 "

In the NT:

		Ancient	Metric	U.S. Equivalent
Quart; KJV, measure	(Gr. *choinix,* see Rev 6:6)	2 sextarii	1.09 "	.99 dry qt.
Bushel	(Gr. *modios,* see Mt 5:15)	16 "	8.76 "	7.95 " "
Measure	(Gr. *saton,* see Mt 13:33)	24 "	13.13 "	11.92 " "
Measure	(Gr. *koros,* see Lk 16:7)	10 medimni	525.31 "	14.92 bu.

5. Liquid Measures

In the OT:

		Ancient	Metric	U.S. Equivalent
Log	(Heb. *log,* see Lev 14:10)	1/72 bath	.31 "	.32 qt.
Hin	(Heb. *hin,* see Ex 29:40)	1/6 "	3.67 "	3.87 "
Bath	(Heb. *bath,* see 1 Ki 7:26)	1/10 homer	22.00 "	5.81 gal.
Cor	(Heb. *kor,* see Eze 45:14)	10 baths	220.00 "	58.12 "

In the NT:

		Ancient	Metric	U.S. Equivalent
Pot	(Gr. *xestēs,* see Mk 7:4)	1 sextarius	.55 "	.58 qt.
Measure	(Gr. *batos,* see Lk 16:6)	72 sextarii	39.40 "	10.41 gal.
(Ten) gallons; KJV, firkin	(Gr. *metrētēs,* see Jn 2:6)		about 39.00 "	about 10.00 "

Well. In present-day ordinary usage, a hole dug (or bored) into the ground to reach a supply of subterranean water, in contrast with a *cistern, which might be similar in appearance to a well, but serves to collect rain water, or with a spring that flows naturally. Sometimes the Bible uses the terms "well" and *"spring" interchangeably, because some wells were fed by subterranean springs (Gen 16:7; cf. v 14). "A well of springing water" is mentioned (ch 26:19), probably a well that had opened a strong-flowing spring. The Hebrew term generally and correctly rendered "well" is *be'er.* Other Hebrew and Greek terms occasionally rendered "well" are: (1) the Heb. *bôr,* actually a "pit," or "cistern," rendered "well" in Deut 6:11; 1 Sa 19:22; 2 Sa 3:26; etc.; KJV, and in 1 Sa 19:22; 2 Sa 23:15, 16; 1 Chr 11:17, 18; RSV; (2) the Heb *ma'yan,* "spring," or "fountain" (Jos 18:15; 2 Ki 3:19; etc.; KJV); (3) the Heb. *maqôr,* "source" (Prov 10:11, KJV); (4) the Heb. *'ayin,* "spring" (Gen 24:13, 16, 29; etc.; KJV; Neh 2:13, RSV); (5) the Gr. *pēgē* and *phrear,* used synonymously in Jn 4:6, 11, 12 as designations for Jacob's well near Sychar.

Wells are important sources of water in a relatively dry land such as Palestine, and especially in its more arid areas such as the Negeb or the desert of Judea. Quarrels for the possession of wells, such as described in Gen 21:25 and ch 26:18-22, may frequently have happened. Many ancient localities were named from wells, such as Beer-elim, Beeroth, Beer-sheba and others. Some wells were very deep, *Jacob's Well at Sychar (Jn 4:11) being 75 ft. deep now and deeper in antiquity. The mouth of a well was usually covered by a flat stone (Gen 29:2, 3) to prevent man or beast from falling into it. Water from it was dipped with a jar, attached to a rope if the well was deep. Figuratively, a "well" symbolizes a beloved woman (Song 4:15), and a wife (Prov 5:15), while an adventuress is compared to a "narrow well" (Prov 23:27, RSV).

Wen. An indolent encysted tumor. The Hebrew term thus translated in Lev 22:22 (*yabbeleth*) probably means "wart," although the RSV translates it "discharge." A *yabbeleth* was one of the defects that disqualified an animal from being used as a sacrifice.

West. *See* East.

Western Sea. *See* Great Sea.

Whale. A rendering of: (1) The Heb. *tannim* (Eze 32:2, KJV; RSV "dragon").

Perhaps in the context of the passage the crocodile is intended. (2) The Heb. *tannin* (Gen 1:21; Job 7:12; KJV), "sea monster," a general term for large sea animals. (3) The Gr. *kētos* (Mt 12:40), "sea monster," like *tannin,* a word of general meaning.

Wheat. [Heb. generally *chiṭṭah;* Aramaic *chinṭah;* Gr. *sitos.*] A familiar and basic grain grown in Bible lands from earliest times (Gen 30:14), particularly in Egypt (Ex 9:32), which was known as the granary of the Mediterranean region. The wheat of the ancients was both spelt and emmer, having smaller kernels than our modern wheat, and having also a bitter taste. The sweet, large-kerneled wheat of modern times was unknown in Bible times.

Many of the lands of the Middle East were known in ancient times as wheat-producing areas, but they were subject to devastating droughts that brought on widespread famine (Gen 12:10; 41:57). In Palestine the wheat was sown after the autumn rains began, and was harvested in April, May, or June, depending upon both the climate and the soil. The wheat harvest, celebrated by the Feast of Weeks (*see* Pentecost) 50 days after the Feast of Unleavened Bread, was followed by *threshing and *winnowing. The grain was made into flour for *bread (Ex 29:2); like other grains it was roasted (Lev 2:14, 16; Ruth 2:14) or crushed, and used for food. Wheat played a large part in cereal offerings (KJV "meat offerings").

Wheel. [Heb. generally *'ôphan* and *galgal.* The wheel consisted of the *gab,* "rim," the *chishshuqîm,* "spokes," the *chishshur,* "hub," and the *yad,* "axle."] The wheel was first simply a wooden disk on an axle. From Sumer, where it apparently was invented, it spread over the whole ancient world and found varied uses.

1. Chariot wheels (Ex 14:25). When the Hyksos introduced the chariot into Egypt, light 6-spoked wheels were produced (fig. 103). The chariot wheels of the Canaanites and those of the Hebrews were probably not much different. Some wheels had 8 spokes (*see* Chariot); see fig. 19.

2. Wheels for the *lavers of Solomon's Temple; these were made of bronze and had bronze axles (1 Ki 7:30-33).

3. Cart wheels for threshing; figuratively used of troubles (Is 28:27; cf. Prov 20:26). See fig. 393.

4. The wheel of the *potter, a wooden disk on which clay vessels were formed (Jer 18:3; etc.).

523. The Wilderness of Judea on the way from Jerusalem to Jericho

5. Wheels in connection with cisterns (Ec 12:6); evidently ropes were run over them to lift buckets.

6. Symbolic wheels, seen by Ezekiel and Daniel in vision (Eze 10:9-17; Dan 7:9).

Whitewash. Usually a liquid consisting of lime and water used for whitening walls, etc. The walls of the houses of common people were not whitewashed in ancient times as we understand that process today. Their houses were simply covered with mortar or mud inside and outside. Better-class people covered the walls of their homes with a white plaster, or had the plaster whitewashed or painted. "White-wash" appears in the Bible in phrases that are renderings of the following terms: (1) the Heb. *ṭaphal*, "to coat," "to cover," "to smear," "to soil" (Job 13:4, RSV); (2) the Heb. *ṭûach taphel*, "to daub with white-wash" (KJV "untempered morter"), that is, to apply any kind of plaster; the Hebrew expression does not imply a white color (Eze 13:10, 11, 14, 15; 22:28); (3) the Gr. *koniaō*, a true equivalent of the English "whitewash," and used in this sense in non-Biblical secular Greek sources. In one discourse Jesus referred to tomb structures whose whitewashed (KJV "whited") outer appearance concealed their rotten contents (Mt 23:27). Paul called the high priest Ananias a "whitewashed" (KJV "whited")

wall (Acts 23:3). The priestly robes, symbolic of holiness, served but to lend an appearance of sanctity to an evil heart.

Whore. *See* Harlot.

Widow. [Heb. generally *'almanah;* Gr. *chēra,* "a bereaved one."] The lot of the widow in ancient times was often difficult (see Lk 21:2-4), especially in heathen lands, where various superstitious stigmas attached to widowhood. Judaism and Christianity have done much to bring respect, sympathy, fellowship, and sustenance to those bereaved of their husbands (Deut 14:29; 16:11, 14; 27:19; Mk 12:40; Acts 6:1; 1 Ti 5:3-8; Jas 1:27). The Mosaic law offered protection to widows, who were frequently exploited (Ps 94:6; Is 1:23; Eze 22:7; Mal 3:5; etc.). They were not to be afflicted (Ex 22:22; cf. Deut 27:19). Their clothing could not be confiscated as security for debt (Deut 24:17), they shared the benefits of the 3d-year *tithe (ch 26:12), and *gleaning was one of their prerogatives (ch 24:19-21). It was customary for a widow to wear special garments by which she would be recognized as a widow (Gen 38:14, 19; cf. Judith 10:3, 4). The brother of the dead husband of a childless widow was supposed to take her as wife to assure continuance of his brother's line (see Gen 38:7-9; Ruth 4:1-10). The high priest could not marry a widow (Lev 21:10, 14; cf. Eze 44:22).

Wife. *See* Marriage.

Wild Ass. *See* Ass, 1.

Wild Beast. *See* Beast.

Wild Bull. *See* Antelope.

Wild Goat. *See* Goat, Wild.

Wild Ox. *See* Unicorn.

Wilderness or **Desert.** Renderings of various Hebrew words, chiefly of *midbar*, "wilderness," "pasturage," and *'arabah*, "arid region," "desert"; also, of the Gr. *erēmos*, "wilderness," "grassland," "desert." None of these words refer to a sandy wasteland exclusively, but in general to an uncultivated and uninhabited region where wild animals roam. The Wilderness (*midbar*) of Judea (fig. 523) is an arid region, mostly hilly, between the central range of mountains and the Dead Sea and lower Jordan Valley (Jgs 1:16). Sometimes *'arabah* denotes the plain of the Jordan and Dead Sea, which extended for many miles south of the Dead Sea (*see* Arabah).

Wilderness Wandering. When the Israelites left Egypt at the time of the *Exodus they passed through the Red Sea, probably at the northern end of the Gulf of Suez, and then went to Mount Sinai, where they received the Law and built the tabernacle.

They spent almost a year there, after which they were to move into Canaan and occupy the land (Num 10:11, 12; 13: 1-3). However, the rebellion at Kadeshbarnea, after the report of the 12 spies, compelled God to change the program, so that the nation spent 38 more years in the desert (Deut 2:4) until a new generation had grown up, to whom God entrusted the conquest of Canaan. These 38 years are usually referred to as the wilderness wandering, but the 1st year of the Exodus and the last year before their arrival at the Promised Land were also spent for the most part in the wilderness, and these sections will also be included in the discussion presented here (Num 14:26-35; Deut 2:14). The table below lists the events that are dated in years of the 40-year period of wandering.

I. Physical Features of the Area of Wandering. The region where the Israelites wandered lies in the Sinai Peninsula and the semi-arid land between the Sinai area and Palestine. This territory, whose physical features vary greatly, can be divided into 4 areas:

1. The northern and northwestern sand belt, consisting of a coastal strip between Philistia and Egypt, extending in the west toward the Gulf of Suez; an area

Dated Events of the Forty Years in the Wilderness

	Month	Day	Year
Passover observed (Ex 12:2, 6)	1st	14th	(1st)
Departure from Egypt (Num 33:3)	1st	15th	(1st)
Manna given in Wilderness of Sin (Ex 16:1)	2d	15th	(1st)
Arrival at Sinai (Ex 19:1)	3d	—	(1st)
(Moses' two 40-day periods on the mountain—Ex 24:18; 34:28)			
(Making of tabernacle and equipment)			
Tabernacle erected (Ex 40:1, 2, 17)	1	1	2d
Passover enjoined (Num 9:1, 2)	1	—	2d
Passover observed (Num 9:5), evidently first time since Exodus (cf. vs 6-14)	1	14	—
Numbering of men directed (Num 1:1)	2	1	2d
Departure from Sinai (Num 10:11), nearly a year after arrival	2	20	2d
(Spies sent out in time of first ripe grapes, i.e., late summer—Num 13:17-20)			
(Return of spies to Kadesh 40 days later; Israel sentenced to 40 years' wandering—Num 13:25, 26; 14:33, 34)			
From Kadesh to crossing of Zered, 38 years (Deut 2:14)			
Death of Miriam at Kadesh (Num 20:1)	1	—	(40th?)
Death of Aaron on Mount Hor (Num 33:38)	5	1	40th
Israel at Zered (Num 21:12) after Aaron's death (cf. Num 20:27-29; 21:4-11)	(6?)	—	(40th)
(Moses' death; 30-day mourning—Deut 34:7, 8)	(12?)	—	(40th)
Crossing of Jordan and encampment before Jericho (Jos 4:19)	1	10	(41st)
Passover kept in Promised Land (Jos 5:10)	(1)	14	(41st)
Manna ceases (Jos 5:11, 12) on 40th anniversary of the Exodus	(1)	15	(41st)

with an approximate width of 30 to 40 mi. The "way of the land of the Philistines" (Ex 13:17), a road that was used by the ancient Egyptian armies for their campaigns against Palestine and Syria, as well as by caravans and couriers, passed through this area. It was probably this "way" that was traveled by Abraham, Joseph, and Jacob when they moved into Egypt. This sandy region, which followed the Mediterranean coast, turned south before it reached the Nile Delta, and formed a strip about 10 mi. wide from the Mediterranean to the Gulf of Suez, skirting that gulf's eastern shore for about 50 mi. This strip was the western part of the "wilderness of Shur" (ch 15:22), which extended in an easterly direction into the northern part of the interior tableland, described under 2. (Map V, C-4 to B-5.) This sandy region is practically without any vegetation, and consists of undulating sand dunes in which armies and caravans can move only with difficulty.

2. The great tableland of limestone covering the northern half of the Sinai Peninsula and the area north of it up to the sandy belt described under 1. This area, which on the average is about 2,000 to 2,500 ft. high, slopes down toward the north, becomes a mountainous area in the northeast, and is girdled on the other sides by mountains (called *Jebel et-Tîh*) from 4,000 to 5,000 ft. high (Map V, B/C-5/6). The central part of this tableland is drained toward the Mediterranean Sea, principally by the *Wâdī el-'Arîsh* (Map V, B-6), the Biblical "river [or brook] of Egypt" (Num 34:5; Jos 15:4; etc.) and its tributaries, but also by other wadies of lesser importance. The region is gravelly and almost barren, but some vegetation is found in the wadies, especially in the rainy season, which is in winter. The whole area contains few springs, and whatever water is found is usually brackish, except for some wells and springs in the eastern portion bordering on the *Wâdī el-'Arabah* (Map V, B-7), and in the area of Kadesh-barnea. In the northern part of this great tableland is the "wilderness of Shur" (Ex 15:22), through which passed the "way to Shur" between Beer-sheba in Palestine and Egypt (Gen 16:7). The northeastern section was apparently called the Wilderness of Zin and the larger, southern part, the Wilderness of Paran, though these terms are not clearly defined in Biblical usage (Num 10:12; 13:26; 1 Sa 25:1). It was in this large tableland that the Is-

raelites spent most of the 38 years, and they remembered it as "that great and terrible wilderness" (Deut 1:19).

3. The sandstone belt that crosses the Sinai Peninsula south of the *Jebel et-Tîh*. It extends almost from the Gulf of Suez (Red Sea) to the Gulf of Aqabah, and separates the tableland of the north from the granite mountains of the south. This belt is mountainous and rich in minerals, and it was here that the Egyptians had their copper and turquoise mines (Map V, D-5). The mountains are very picturesque and colorful, but rugged, and the narrow plains and wadies between the mountain ranges are sandy. The Wilderness of Sin and the historical sites of *Rephidim and Hazeroth were probably located in this belt (Map V, D-5).

4. The granite mountains in the heart of the Sinai Peninsula, to which the traditional Mount *Sinai belongs. Majestic peaks, from 6,000 to 7,000 ft. high, make this region one of awesome grandeur.

II. The Route of the Israelites Through the Wilderness. The accompanying table lists 56 different places and areas from Goshen in Egypt to the eastern border of Palestine, mentioned in the Pentateuch. The first 5 are discussed in the article on the Exodus. Of the remaining 51 only a few have been identified with reasonable or almost absolute certainty. Geographical sites definitely identified are, No. 39, *Ezion-geber on the Gulf of Aqabah (Map V, C-6); No. 49, the river *Arnon, now the *Wâdī Môjib* (Map V, A-7); and No. 55, Dibon-gad, now *Dhîbân* (Map VI, E-4). Sites whose identification is reasonably certain are: Nos. 20 and 41, *Kadesh-barnea, which is either *'Ain Qedeis* or the neighboring *'Ain Qudeirat* (Map V, B-6); No. 45, *Punon, now *Feinân*, 30 mi. south of the Dead Sea (Map V, B-7); and No. 57, *Abarim, the mountain range *esh-Shefa*, of which No. 58, *Pisgah, and Mount Nebo (Map II, C-3) formed a part. These sites, whose identification is more or less certain, make it possible to follow the Israelites on their route during the latter part of their wilderness wanderings. If one also accepts with most conservative students of the Bible the location of the mount of lawgiving in the Sinai Peninsula, the route of the Israelites can be followed in great sweeps from Egypt to Palestine, although most of the sites mentioned in connection with their wilderness wanderings cannot be identified. *See* names of the sites mentioned in the accompanying table.

The following tabulation lists the places where the Israelites camped on the way through the wilderness to Canaan: (1) according to the narrative in Exodus and Numbers; (2) according to the summary of the itinerary as recorded in Numbers 33; (3) according to scattered references to these places in Moses' final messages to Israel given in Deuteronomy:

NARRATIVE IN EX-NUM		ITINERARY IN NUM 33		INCIDENTAL MENTION IN DEUT	
From Goshen to Sinai					
1. Rameses	Ex 12:37	1. Rameses	v 3	1.	
2. Succoth	12:37; 13:20	2. Succoth	v 5	2.	
3. Etham	13:20	3. Etham	v 6	3.	
4. Pi-hahiroth	14:2	4. Pi-hahiroth	v 7	4.	
5. The sea	14:9, 22, 29	5. The sea	v 8	5. The Red Sea	11:4
6. Wilderness of Shur	15:22	6. Wilderness of Etham	v 8	6.	
7. Marah	15:23	7. Marah	v 8	7.	
8. Elim	15:27; 16:1	8. Elim	v 9	8.	
9.		9. Red Sea	v 10	9.	
10. Wilderness of Sin	16:1	10. Wilderness of Sin	v 11	10.	
11.		11. Dophkah	v 12	11.	
12.		12. Alush	v 13	12.	
13. Rephidim	17:1; 19:2	13. Rephidim	v 14	13. (Rephidim	25:17; cf. Ex 17:8)
13a. Massah and Meribah	17:8	13a.		13a. Massah	6:16
14. Wilderness of Sinai	19:1, 2	14. Wilderness of Sinai	v 15	14. Horeb	4:10; 5:2
From Sinai to Kadesh-barnea					
15. Wilderness of Paran	Num 10:12	15.		15. Paran	1:1
16. Taberah	11:1-3	16.		16.	
17. Kibroth-hattaavah	11:34	17. Kibroth-hattaavah	v 16	17.	
18. Hazeroth	11:35	18. Hazeroth	v 17	18. Hazeroth	1:1
19. Wilderness of Paran	12:16	19.		19.	
20. Kadesh (barnea)	13:26	20.		20. Kadesh-barnea	1:2, 19
38 Years in the Area of Kadesh-barnea					
21.		21. Rithmah	v 18	21.	
22.		22. Rimmon-perez	v 19	22.	
23.		23. Libnah	v 20	23. Laban?	1:1
24.		24. Rissah	v 21	24.	
25.		25. Kehelathah	v 22	25.	
26.		26. Mount Shepher	v 23	26.	
27.		27. Haradah	v 24	27.	
28.		28. Makheloth	v 25	28.	
29.		29. Tahath	v 26	29.	
30.		30. Terah	v 27	30.	
31.		31. Mithkah	v 28	31.	
32.		32. Hashmonah	v 29	32.	
33.		33. Moseroth	v 30	33.	
34.		34. Bene-jaakan	v 31	34. Beeroth Bene-Jaakan	
35.		35.		35. Moserah	10:6
36.		36. Hor-haggidgad	v 32	36. Gudgodah	10:7
37.		37. Jotbathah	v 33	37. Jotbathah	10:7
38.		38. Abronah	v 34	38.	
39.		39. Ezion-geber	v 35	39.	
40. Wilderness of Zin (Kadesh)	20:1	40. Wilderness of Zin (Kadesh)	v 36	40.	

NARRATIVE IN EX-NUM		ITINERARY IN NUM 33		INCIDENTAL MENTION IN DEUT	
From Kadesh-barnea to the Jordan					
41. Kadesh (barnea)	Num 20:1-14	41. Kadesh	v 36	41. Kadesh	1:46
42. Mount Hor	20:22	42. Mount Hor	v 37	42. Mount Hor	32:50
43. Red Sea	21:4	43.		43. Red Sea	1:40
44.		44. Zalmonah	v 41	44.	
45.		45. Punon	v 42	45.	
46. Oboth	21:10	46. Oboth	v 43	46.	
47. Iye-abarim	21:11	47. Iye-abarim	v 44	47.	
48. Valley of Zered	21:12	48.		48. Brook Zered	2:13
49. Arnon	21:13	49.		49.	
50. Beer	21:16	50.		50.	
51. Mattanah	21:18	51.		51.	
52. Nahaliel	21:19	52.		52.	
53. Bamoth	21:19	53.		53.	
54. Valley in Moab	21:20	54.		54.	
55.		55. Dibon-gad	v 45	55.	
56.		56. Almon-diblathaim	v 46	56.	
57.		57. Abarim	v 47	57. Abarim	32:48
58. Pisgah	21:20	58.		58. Pisgah	34:1
59. Plains of Moab by the Jordan	26:3	59. Plains of Moab by Jordan (from Beth-jeshimoth to Abel-shittim)	v 48 v 49	59. Beyond the Jordan in the land of Moab	1:5

1. *From Goshen to Sinai.* The whole journey took about 2 months. For the first 5 sites *see* Exodus. After the Israelites crossed the Red Sea, they marched along the sandy coast region of the Gulf of Suez, called the Wilderness of Shur, past the oases of Marah and Elim, then went through the sandstone mountains, the Wilderness of Sin, to Rephidim, traditionally identified with the *Wâdî Feiran* (Map V, D-5), until they reached Mount Sinai, probably *Râs eṣ-Ṣafṣafeh*, where they encamped in the plain *er-Râha* and other valleys surrounding the mount of lawgiving (Map V, D-5/6).

2. *From Sinai to Kadesh-barnea.* After having spent about a year at Sinai, the Israelites moved on toward the north until they reached Kadesh-barnea, from where the spies were sent to Canaan, and where the people rebelled after the return of the spies. The abortive attempt to conquer Canaan was also made from Kadesh (Num 13:1 to 14:45).

3. *Thirty-eight years in the area of Kadesh-barnea.* Of the 20 sites mentioned in the list dealing with the itinerary of the Israelites during the longest period of their wilderness wanderings, not more than 1 or 2 can be identified with even some semblance of probability. They must for the greatest part be sought in the limestone tableland, the Wilderness of Paran, and in the *Jebel et-Tîh.* During the 38 years that the Israelites spent in this region most of the adults who rebelled at Kadesh-barnea died.

4. *From Kadesh-barnea to the Jordan.* During the last year of their wanderings the Israelites passed several sites that are identifiable. Aaron died at Mount Hor, not far from the border of Edom (Num 33:37-39). After this event the Israelites detoured around Edom, crossed the Brook Zered (probably the *Wâdî el-Ḥesâ*), and later the Arnon, then, after having passed through eastern Moab, reached the territory of the Amorite king of Heshbon. Their last camp before entering Canaan was pitched in the Plains of Moab (see Map I, C-2) near the Jordan not far from Jericho (ch 26:3).

Willow. A rendering of: (1) The Heb. *'arabah* (Job 40:22; Is 15:7; etc.), a tree mentioned in connection with water. Its branches were used to construct booths for the Feast of Tabernacles (Lev 23:40). It has been variously identified with such trees as the poplar (*Populus euphratica*), and certain of the genus *Salix*, or willows. Some have identified *'arabah* with the *Salix babylonica*, or weeping willow (Ps 137:2), but certain authorities hold that this tree, which is of Chinese or Japanese origin, was not introduced into Bible lands early enough to be mentioned. (2)

The Heb. *ṣaphṣaphah* (Eze 17:5), which can be identified with reasonable certainty with the *Salix safsaf*, or Palestine willow.

Willows, Brook of the. [Heb. *nachal ha'arabîm,* "brook of the poplars," or "brook of the willows."] A watercourse in Moab (Is 15:7). Some have identified it with the lower course of the *Wâdî el-Ḥesā,* which formed the boundary between Moab and Edom; others identify it with the *Wâdî Gharbeh,* the southernmost tributary of the Jordan, formed by the confluence of the *Wâdî Kefrein* and the *Wâdî Ḥesbân.*

Wimple. A rendering of the Heb. *miṭpachath,* "cloak," probably a large shawl worn over the tunic (Is 3:22, KJV). The term occurs in a list of the finery used by some women in Palestine; (RSV) "cloaks." The Dead Sea scroll 1QIsa omits the Hebrew term. *Miṭpachath* occurs also in Ruth 3:15, where it is rendered "vail" (KJV), "mantle" (RSV).

Wind. [Heb. and Aramaic generally *rûach,* "air," "wind," "breath," "spirit"; Gr. generally *anemos,* "wind," and *pneuma,* "wind," "spirit."] To the inhabitant of Bible lands "wind" meant both the torture of heat, drought, and sandstorm (Gen 41:6; Is 21:1; Jer 4:11; Eze 19:2; Hos 13:15; Lk 12:55; etc.) and the cooling relief of life-giving rains (Prov 25:23, RSV; cf. 1 Ki 18:43-45). A "strong east wind" was used of God to open the Red Sea (Ex 14:21). Trade via ocean routes was dependent on the winds for motive power. Symbolically the "four winds" represented the 4 main points of the compass (Dan 8:8; Mk 13:27; Rev 7:1). Winds were used as symbols of war's destruction (Jer 18:17), of the uncertainty of life (Job 7:7; Ps 78:39), and of the irresistible judgments that overtake the wicked (Job 21:18; Prov 10:25). The word is used metaphorically of vain and empty things (Jer 5:13). It sometimes indicates activity or energy of some form, the particular form to be determined by the context (see Jer 49:36; Eze 37:9-14; Dan 7:2; 11:4). God sometimes chose to impress His messages through the whirlwind (Eze 1:4). The whirlwind also symbolized the swiftness or fury of an army (Jer 4:13; Hab 3:14), destruction (Prov 1:27; Is 40:24; etc.) and the personal, visible intervention of God in human affairs (Is 66:15). The manifestation of the Holy Spirit on the day of Pentecost was described as the "rush of a mighty wind" (Acts 2:2, RSV). Jesus used the intangible nature of the wind to illustrate the working of the Holy Spirit (Jn 3:8). *See* East Wind; Euroclydon; South Wind.

Window. In the East the window usually took the form of a rectangular aperture in the wall of a building (Gen 26:8; 1 Ki 6:4; Jer 22:14), which, when necessary, as in the case of privacy from the gaze of neighbors and protection against the cold of winter, was closed in by means of a movable shutter (Gen 8:6; 2 Ki 13:17; Dan 6:10) or a lattice (Jgs 5:28; 2 Ki 1:2; Prov 7:6, RSV; Song 2:9). A window on the ground floor was commonly set high in the wall and probably in Biblical times, as today, securely barred. In the more elaborate homes of the upper class most windows faced the courtyard.

Wine. [Heb. generally *yayin* or *tîrôsh;* Aramaic *chamar;* Gr. generally *oinos.*] Juice of grapes, *yayin* being the usual word for wine fully aged and thus intoxicating (Gen 14:18; Lev 10:9; 23:13; etc.), and *tîrôsh* standing in many passages for fresh grape juice or for wine not fully aged but already intoxicating (Gen 27:37; Num 18:12; Deut 12:17; Jgs 9:13; Prov 3:10; Hos 4:11; etc.). Both terms are rendered *oinos* in the LXX. The Palestinian vintage season varied from June, in the hot Jordan Valley, to August along the coastal plains, and September in the hills and mountains. This was the great holiday season of the year, and the joy of the vintage was proverbial (Is 16:10; 48:33; etc.). The ruins of many ancient wine presses may be seen in Palestine today. Usually there were 2 excavations, which might be either rectangular or circular, hewn in the rock to a depth of 2 or 3 ft., with one higher than the other and the 2 connected by a conduit (see ch 5:2). The grapes were crushed in the wider and shallower upper vat, and the juice flowed down through the conduit to the lower vat (see Neh 13:15; Job 24:11; Is

524. The "king's winepresses," near Jerusalem

16:10; Jer 25:30; 48:33), from which it was removed into jars (Hag 2:16).

Aaron and his sons, the priests, were strictly forbidden to drink either wine or *strong drink when they went into the tabernacle to minister before the Lord (Lev 10:9). Nazirites were likewise forbidden to use wine while under the vow (Num 6:3, 20; cf. Jgs 13:4-7). The Rechabites lived a noteworthy example of permanent abstinence from wine, adhering strictly to the command of their ancestor, Jonadab, to refrain from it (Jer 35:2, 5, 6, 8, 14). The book of Proverbs is replete with warnings against indulgence in wine and strong drink (see chs 20:1; 21:17; 23:30, 31; 31:4; etc.). Wine mocks those who use it (ch 20:1), and rewards them with woe, sorrow, strife, and wounds without cause (ch 23:29, 30). "At the last it biteth like a serpent, and stingeth like an adder" (v 32). The prophet Isaiah declared, "Woe unto them that are mighty to drink wine, and men of strength to mingle strong drink" (Is 5:22). Daniel and his compatriots set a worthy example by refusing to drink of the king's wine (Dan 1:5, 8, 10-16). When fasting later in life, Daniel abstained from "flesh" and "wine" (ch 10:3). *See* Drunkenness.

The usual NT word for wine, whether fermented or unfermented, is *oinos*. Jesus likened His revolutionary teaching to new wine, which would burst the old bottles of tradition (Mt 9:17). Paul warned believers against drunkenness (Eph 5:18), and ruled that deacons should not be "addicted to much wine" (1 Ti 3:8, RSV). For the relief of a digestive ailment he recommended "a little wine" to Timothy (1 Ti 5:23). He counseled Titus that the older women should not be "slaves to drink" (Tit 2:3, RSV).

Figuratively, Jeremiah speaks of the Lord as giving "the wine cup of this fury" to the heathen nations to drink (Jer 25:15, 16). In the Revelation, Babylon the great is figuratively represented as making "all nations drink of the wine of the wrath of her fornication" (Rev 14: 8; cf. v 10; ch 17:2; 18:3). In retribution Babylon is given the cup of the wine of the wrath of God to drink (ch 16:19), and Christ is pictured as treading the wine press of the fierceness of His wrath (ch 19:15).

Winebibber. A person who drinks excessively of alcoholic beverages, a drunkard. The author of Proverbs counseled against associating with winebibbers (Prov 23:20, KJV), "for the drunkard . . . shall come

to poverty" (Prov 23:21). Because Christ ate and drank with "publicans and sinners" He was accused of being a winebibber (Mt 11:19; Lk 7:34; RSV "drunkard").

Winepress. *See* Wine.

Wineskin. *See* Bottle.

Winevat. *See* Wine.

Winnowing. The separation of the chaff from the grain by means of the wind after the husk is loosened by the preliminary process of threshing. Most ancient and modern threshing floors in the Near East are situated on elevated places, so that as the threshed-out grain is thrown high in the air by means of a shovel or a fork (Is 30:24), the wind blows the chaff away (ch 41:16) and the purified grain falls to the ground in a heap (fig. 525). Winnowing in Palestine is usually done in the eve-

525. Winnowing at *el-Ḥuṣn*, in Transjordan

ning, when the wind has the most favorable velocity. In a long windless spell large fans plied by helpers may supply the artificial wind for winnowing.

Winter. *See* Palestine.

Wisdom. [Heb. and Aramaic usually *chokmah*, "skill," "wisdom"; Gr. usually *sophia*, "wisdom."] A quality of sound judgment developed by experience, observation, and reflection. Wisdom is a function of the trained mind, which Bible writers set forth as coming from the Lord (Job 28:20, 23, 27; Ps 111:10) and which they connect with obedience to His commands (Ps 37:30, 31; Prov 2:1, 2). Of the canonical books, Job, Proverbs, and Ecclesiastes belong to what is commonly called the "wisdom literature." "The price of wisdom," says Job, "is above rubies" (Job 28:18). "The fear of the Lord," he declares, "is wisdom; and to depart from evil is understanding" (v 28). As in Job's case, true wisdom enables a man to face the vicissitudes of life with equanimity. Only as he looked to God and trusted in Him could Job wisely relate himself to the disappointments and difficulties of life. David similarly looked to God for instruction in wisdom (Ps 51:6). A psalm attributed to Moses appeals to God to teach men to number their days, that they may apply their hearts unto wisdom (Ps 90:12). Here, as in Job 12:12, wisdom is seen as being developed by experiences through which the Lord leads those who fear Him. Solomon's declared objective in writing out his proverbs was that his people might "know wisdom and instruction" (Prov 1:2). In the early chapters of the book of Proverbs he personifies wisdom (see ch 3:16-18; etc.). "Wisdom is the principal thing," he says; "therefore get wisdom: and with all thy getting get understanding" (ch 4:7). The book of Ecclesiastes summarizes the wisdom that came to Solomon after many years of dissipation, during which his moral sensibilities were blunted, his conscience seared, and his judgment perverted. Toward the close of his life conscience finally awakened and Solomon began to see folly in its true light, realizing that he had come to be "an old and foolish king" who would "no more be admonished" (Ec 4:13). The time was drawing near when he must die, and he found no pleasure in reflecting upon his wasted life (ch 12:1). Sincerely repentant, he sought to retrace his wayward steps, and chastened in spirit he turned, weary and thirsty, from earth's broken cisterns to drink once more of the fountain of life. He came to realize the folly of his course, and in the book of Ecclesiastes sought to lift a voice of warning to save others from the bitter experiences through which he himself had passed, hoping thereby to counteract as best he could the baleful influence of his own earlier example.

In the NT *sophia* is used with much the same meaning as *chokmah*. It describes both the wisdom of the world (1 Cor 1:22; 3:19) and the wisdom of God (Rom 11:33; 1 Cor 2:7). Sometimes the two are contrasted (1 Cor 1:21; Jas 3:13-17). Christ is declared to be the "wisdom of God" (1 Cor 1:24), in that His words and life manifested divine wisdom, and in that the salvation coming through Him demonstrates God's wisdom in ordaining the manner in which men might be redeemed. Paul preached "the wisdom of God in a mystery" (ch 2:6, 7)—the marvelous and profound plan of salvation, which even the angels cannot fully grasp (cf. 1 Pe 1:12). Those who need wisdom to meet conditions beyond their capacity or control may ask God in faith to supply the need, and it will be supplied (Jas 1:5, 6).

Wise Men. Specifically, the "wise men from the east" who brought gifts to Jesus (Mt 2:1; cf. vs 7, 16). The term translated "wise men" (*magoi*) originally denoted an ancient priestly class among the Medians (and later the Persians). The term came to mean one adept in the "sciences" of astrology, etc. A legend, which has no basis in any known fact, states that there were 3 wise men named Gaspar, Balthasar, and Melchior, who brought gifts to Jesus; the number was probably derived from their 3 gifts—gold, frankincense, and myrrh (see ch 2:11). The Wise Men were doubtless acquainted with the Jewish belief in a coming Messiah, a belief known to many in the East (see *SDACom* 5:59-62), and were sincere seekers after the true God.

Witch. A rendering of forms of the Heb. *kashaph*, "to practice sorcery" (Ex 22:18; Deut 18:10; KJV), generally rendered *"sorcerer," or "sorceress."

Witchcraft. *See* Sorcerer.

Withs. A term appearing in Jgs 16:7-9, KJV, as a rendering of the Heb. *yetharim*, "fresh, moist sinews (of cattle)"; in the context it is the material used by Delilah to bind Samson. The RSV here translates the term "bowstrings."

Witness. [Heb. generally *'ed*; Gr. *martus, marturia*.] One who can testify to the facts bearing on any specific question, because he has observed directly; also the attestation of the fact or facts involved. Sometimes inanimate objects, such as cairns, altars, pillars, were erected as witness of an agreement or as a reminder of some event or obligation (Gen 31:44-48; Jos 22:26, 27; 24:26, 27; Is 19:19, 20). The Mosaic law required 2 or 3 witnesses in cases involving capital punishment (Num 35:30; Deut 17:6; Heb 10:28; etc.), as a safeguard against false witnessing. When a person was condemned the witnesses took first action in administering punishment (Deut 13:9; cf. Acts 7:58). False witnessing was strictly forbidden by the 9th commandment (Ex 20:16; cf. Lk 18:20), and a person found guilty of such an act was to receive the punishment he sought to bring upon another (Deut 19:16-19). Witnesses were called upon to confirm various legal transactions (Ruth

4:9, 10; Is 8:2; Jer 32:8-11). The apostles were witnesses of the resurrection and of the gospel, and bore their testimony with assurance (Acts 1:8; 2:32; 3:15; 10: 39; 1 Pe 5:1; cf. Lk 24:48; etc.). Paul was especially called and fitted to be a witness for Christ (Acts 22:14, 15; 26:12-16). Jesus is called "the faithful and true witness" (Rev 3:14; ch 1:5). In certain usages the Gr. *martus* came to have the connotation of *"martyr," and is so rendered in the KJV in Acts 22:20; Rev 2:13; 17:6; the RSV has "martyr" in Rev 17:6.

Wizard. [Heb. *yidde'oni*, from *yada'*, "to know," "to observe," hence a "knowing one."] A man reputed to have special knowledge concerning the unseen world gained by supposedly consulting the dead (Is 8:19). Wizards were found in Egypt (ch 19:3). God abominated men who practiced this devilish art (Lev 19:31; 20: 6; Deut 18:11), and the Hebrew nation was forbidden to tolerate them, and was to put them to death (Lev 20:27). Kings Saul and Josiah rid their kingdoms of wizards (1 Sa 28:3; 2 Ki 23:24), but Manasseh tolerated and consulted them (2 Ki 21:6; 2 Chr 33:6). *See* Divination; Familiar Spirit; Magic; Sorcerer.

Wolf. [Heb. *ze'eb*; Gr. *lukos*.] A variety of *Canis lupus*, the wolf of Europe and Asia, although the Palestinian wolf is somewhat lighter in color. It is a fierce wild animal (Hab 1:8) that lies between the rocks or in the desert during the day (Jer 5:6), and attacks herds of small cattle at night (Zep 3:3; Jn 10:12). Although the lion has become extinct in Palestine, the wolf is still found in some parts of Transjordan. Benjamin was compared to a wolf because of the martial qualities of the tribe (Gen 49:27), but otherwise we find wolves used as symbols of enemies and wicked men (Eze 22:27; Mt 7:15; 10: 16; Lk 10:3; Jn 10:12; Acts 20:29). Isaiah predicts peace between wolf and lamb (Is 11:6; 65:25) in the restored earth.

Wood. *See* Forest; *also* names of specific trees (see list under Flora and Fauna).

Wool. *See* Sheep; Spin; Weaving.

Word, The. [Gr. *ho logos*, "saying," "utterance," "speech," "narrative," "account," "treatise." The term stresses the systematic, meaningful arrangement of the thoughts expressed in words, rather than primarily the words themselves.] A designation for Christ, characterizing Him as the incarnate expression of the character, mind, and will of God, and used in this sense only by John (Jn 1:1, 14; Rev 19:13).

Jesus Christ was God's thought made visible, audible, and intelligible to human beings, particularly with respect to His infinite purpose that all men should find salvation (see 1 Ti 2:4). In the LXX *logos* is commonly used of both the creative (Ps 33:6; cf. Gen 1:3, 6, 9; etc.) and communicative (Jer 1:4; Eze 1:3; Amos 3:1; etc.) expressions of the divine mind and will. Doubtless these OT uses of *logos* were in the mind of John as he wrote his Gospel and epistles. Creation was an expression of the divine will and purpose; and revelation, as embodied in the OT Scriptures, was an even more exact and meaningful expression of that will and purpose. Now (Jn 1:14) God sent Christ into the world as the supreme and perfect revelation of Himself to the human race.

World. [Heb. generally *tebel*, "the habitable world"; Gr. generally *aiōn*, "age," "time," "aeon," "world"; *kosmos*, literally "adorning," and then "world," denoting sometimes humanity, sometimes the planet of the earth itself, and sometimes the sum total of everything here and now, "the (orderly) universe"; *oikoumenē*, "the inhabited earth," "mankind," "the civilized world," especially the Roman Empire.] Generally speaking, the known world of Bible times was limited to lands bordering on the Mediterranean Sea, the Black Sea, the Persian Gulf, and the Red Sea. In earlier OT times the known world was limited to an area within an approximate radius of 750 miles from Palestine, consisting of the Euphrates and Nile valleys, together with Syria and Palestine. With the passing of time the horizon of the known world gradually extended until it included what is known today as the Middle East, North Africa, and Southern Europe, a region that centers on the Mediterranean (literally, "middle of the land," "inland") Sea. In greatest extent from east to west the known world of the OT extended from India (Est 1:1) on the east to the land of Tarshish (Jon 1:3) on the west, and from Scythia on the north (Col 3:11; cf. Eze 39:1) to Ethiopia (Est 1:1) on the south, a distance of about 1,500 mi. east and west by about 1,500 mi. north and south. By NT times the borders of the Roman Empire included part of the British Isles and Germany. There was some limited knowledge of regions beyond these boundaries, but little contact with these areas.

Of the NT words translated "world," *aiōn*, "age," considers the world from the viewpoint of time, as in Mt 12:32; 13:22;

24:3; 28:20; Mk 4:19; etc. and is rendered "age" in Eph 2:7; Col 1:26. *Kosmos,* on the other hand, considers the world from the viewpoint of its orderly arrangement in space, as in Mt 4:8; Rom 1:8, 20; etc. In the NT *kosmos* also often stands for the ungodly multitude, alien and hostile to God, or for worldly interests that lead one away from God as in 1 Jn 2:15. *Oikoumenē* refers specifically to the "inhabited world," that is, to the world from the viewpoint of its suitability as a home for the human race, at times to the human race itself (see Mt 24:14; Lk 2:1; 4: 5; etc.), and often to the Greco-Roman world as distinct from the barbarian regions beyond its borders.

Worm. Small invertebrate animals that have boneless, limbless bodies consisting of a number of movable joints. Several Hebrew and Greek words designating various kinds of worms are found in the Bible, although the same word may be used for more than one kind of worm or maggot. The following terms are thus translated:

1. The Heb. *tôla'ath, tôle'ah, tôla'.* In Ex 16:20 the maggot found in putrid manna is described; and in Is 14:11 and 66:24, maggots feeding on corpses. In Deut 28:39 and perhaps also in Jon 4:7 the vine weevil (*Cochylis ambiguella*) is probably referred to, known also as the vine borer, which destroys vines by boring into their stems. Some think v 7 refers to a snail. In Job 25:6; Ps 22:6; Is 41: 14 man, as weak and despised, is compared with a worm—not necessarily of any particular kind.

2. The Heb. *rimmah,* the maggot, which lives on putrid food (Ex 16:24) and corpses (Job 21:26; 24:20; Is 14:11), and which sometimes feeds on wounds (Job 7:5). Feeble man is compared with it (ch 25:6).

3. The Heb. *sas* (Is 51:8), a *moth.

4. The Heb. *zachal* (Mic 7:17, KJV), a verb form meaning "creeping." The RSV renders it "crawling things."

5. The Gr. *skōlex,* "worm," or "maggot." It is found in Mk 9:46, where it refers to worms that feed on corpses. In Acts 12:23 the related adjective, *skōlēkobrōtos,* "eaten by worms," is used in the description of the intestinal worm disease that caused the death of King Herod Agrippa.

Wormwood. [Heb. *la'anah;* Gr. *apsinthos.*] A bitter and poisonous plant, probably one of the large composite genus *Artemisia,* several varieties of which occur in Palestine. They are woody plants with a strong aromatic odor and bitter taste (Prov 5:4). The undiluted juice is noxious (Rev 8:10, 11). Bible writers follow the Oriental custom of symbolizing calamity, sorrow, and disappointment with plants of this nature (Jer 9:15; Lam 3: 19). In Deut 29:18, the Heb. *la'anah* is rendered "hemlock" (RSV) and "wormwood" (KJV), whereas in Amos 6:12 the term is rendered "wormwood" (RSV) and "hemlock" (KJV).

Worship. [Heb. generally a form of *shachah,* "to bow down," "to worship"; Gr. generally *latreuō,* "to serve," especially with respect to the outward forms of worship, and *proskuneō,* "to do obeisance," "to prostrate oneself," "to reverence."] The attitude of humility, reverence, honor, devotion, and adoration that properly mark the relationship of created beings to their Creator, especially in His presence. The Bible teaches that such worship is due to the one true God alone (Ex 20:1-3; 34:14; Mt 4:10; Acts 10:25, 26; Rev 19:10). Angels, though divine beings, are not properly objects of worship (Rev 19:10). Strict monotheism is to characterize the worship of those who honor the true God, the Creator of heaven and earth (Deut 6:4, 5). Furthermore, in view of the fact that God is "spirit" (Jn 4:23, 24, RSV), man is forbidden to worship Him through material representations (Deut 4:12, 15-18).

Writing. Cultures can exist and flourish without writing, but there is no civilization without the art of writing. All ancient civilizations had systems of writing: Sumeria, Babylonia, Assyria, Egypt, Phoenicia, Canaan, Crete, the Hittites, and others. This article discusses briefly only the scripts of Mesopotamia and Egypt, to provide the background for the development of the alphabetic scripts of the Hebrews and Greeks in which the Bible was written.

I. Scripts and Their Development

1. *Cuneiform.* Because the earliest written documents ever discovered come from Sumeria, the Sumerians are considered the inventors of the first script—a script described as cuneiform writing. Its characters are composed of groups of straight, short lines impressed with a stylus on soft clay tablets. Since the point of the stylus made a wider impression at one end of each mark, thus forming wedge-shaped signs, this script is called cuneiform writing, from the Latin *cuneus,* "wedge." The earliest tablets, from Uruk, show that

the first attempts at writing were mere pictures drawn or impressed in the clay; there were 891 different pictures or characters on the preserved tablets. The tablets from *Fara,* coming from a somewhat later period, show the signs in a more stereotyped form, and their number reduced to 800. By the time of Sargon of Akkad there were 600, and in the 2d millennium B.C., when this system of writing was fully developed, about 350. Originally every character was a word-sign representing an idea (sheep, grain, house, etc.), but gradually symbols were used to stand for syllables (*ma, am, tu, ut,* etc.). In the course of time, most characters received syllabic values, although some word-signs remained in use, especially for very common words such as "man," "king," "son," "city," etc. The lines ran from the top to the bottom in the earliest inscriptions (see fig. 291), but later from left to right (see fig. 528).

When the Semites conquered Mesopotamia, they also adopted the Sumerian cuneiform writing. The form of the individual characters was slightly changed in the course of time, and those used by the Babylonians also differed somewhat from those employed by the Assyrians, but all syllabic cuneiform scripts are basically the same (see figs. 181, 223, 350, 528). The

526. The Rosetta Stone, the inscription that provided the key to the decipherment of the Egyptian language and scripts

Sumerian cuneiform script was taken over also by the neighboring Elamites in the east, then by the Hittites (fig. 426) in Anatolia, and by the Urartians in the Armenian mountains. During the 2d millennium B.C. the Babylonian cuneiform script and language were used in practically all diplomatic international correspondence of the ancient Near East, even by the Egyptian court in dealing with its vassals in Palestine and Syria (fig. 13).

In the syllabic cuneiform script, which expresses the vowel sounds of its words as well as the consonants, the pronunciation is clearly indicated, as is not the case with the consonantal scripts (for example, Egyptian, Canaanite, and pre-Masoretic Hebrew) which were written without vowels. Therefore, any Egyptian or Canaanite names or words found written in cuneiform have their vowels expressed and therefore can be pronounced. Thus cuneiform records are often valuable in the study of these other languages.

Alphabetic cuneiform scripts were developed in 2 widely separated countries. These did not employ the Sumerian or Babylonian characters, but independent symbols, although the idea of writing in clay by means of a stylus was borrowed from the peoples of Mesopotamia. One was the alphabetic script of Ugarit (*Râs Shamra*) consisting of 30 consonantal characters. This script was apparently in use for only a brief period (15th-14th cent. B.C.), and spread little from Ugarit, where it was developed, although 2 brief texts in the Ugaritic script have been found in Palestine (see fig. 529). The 2d alphabetic cuneiform script was developed by the Achaemenid Persians in the 6th cent. B.C. It consisted of 36 (semi-) alphabetic characters and a few additional word-signs and other symbols. The Persian script, the simplest of all cuneiform writings known in the early 19th cent., was the first of the various cuneiform systems deciphered. G. F. Grotefend made the first successful attempt at reading this ancient Persian script in 1802. Henry C. Rawlinson succeeded later in deciphering the Persian, Babylonian, and Elamite scripts by means of trilingual inscriptions from Persepolis and the Behistun Rock (see fig. 293).

2. *Egyptian Hieroglyphs.* The term "hieroglyphs," meaning literally "sacred engraved characters," is the Greek name given to the pictorial script of the Egyptians used on the monuments (fig. 527). The Egyptians probably received from

527. Hieroglyphic inscription at Abydos, containing a list of Egyptian kings. For other hieroglyphic inscriptions see figs. 235, 245, 438

tian texts written in the native script date from the 3d cent. A.D. After that time knowledge concerning it was completely lost until it was resurrected when J. Fr. Champollion in 1822 deciphered the trilingual Rosetta Stone, found in 1799 (see fig. 526).

3. *Alphabetic Writing.* It is quite certain that the Egyptian hieroglyphic script forms the basis of the alphabetic proto-Semitic (also called proto-Sinaitic) script, and that the basic development from a purely ideographic and syllabic script to an alphabet took place during the first half of the 2d millennium B.C. However, the exact date is still disputed, as well as the area in which the invention was made. Either Phoenicia, southern Palestine, or the Sinai Peninsula may have been the scene of this epoch-making invention. There is evidence that experiments with various forms of writing developed at several places, and it is possible that there was a coordination of effort after a workable script had been developed in one of the areas mentioned. Without prejudice to the other areas in matter of priority, the development of the alphabetic script is discussed here as if it were established that it took place on the Sinai Peninsula (see fig. 530).

528. Cuneiform tablet bearing a list of Assyrian kings (SDAS Assyrian King List)

the Sumerians the idea of writing by means of pictures, although they developed an entirely independent script. The earliest hieroglyphic inscriptions date from the beginning of Egyptian history, the 1st dynasty. Within a few centuries, when it was fully developed, it consisted of about 750 characters, which represented either whole words (king, house, woman, etc.), single consonants (*b*, *p*, *m*, etc.), or combinations of consonants (*mn*, *nt*, *pr*, etc.), but no vowels. Almost every word received one or more "determinatives" to indicate to the reader whether the word was an abstract noun, an individual, an animal, a building, a name, etc. There was no fixed direction of writing; the texts could run from left to right, from right to left, or from the top to the bottom. The direction can always easily be recognized, since the heads of men or animals depicted as hieroglyphs look toward the beginning of the line.

Besides the hieroglyphic script there was developed in early times a cursive script, written with a reed pen on papyrus, which the Greeks called hieratic. From the 7th cent. B.C. on, a simplified script, demotic, came into being, used especially for common documents such as letters, bills, and notes. The latest Egyp-

529. Clay tablet inscribed with the complete Ugaritic alphabet, found at *Rás Shamra*

In 1905 Flinders Petrie explored the turquoise mines at *Serābīṭ el-Khâdem,* where the ancient Egyptians had left a temple dedicated to Hathor as well as numerous hieroglyphic inscriptions from the 3d dynasty to the 20th dynasty. He discovered several stone inscriptions written in a hieroglyphic script whose characters were similar to the Egyptian hieroglyphs, though poorly executed, but which were not Egyptian (fig. 530). Since only about 22 characters were used, Petrie recognized the script as alphabetic and also suggested that it may have been employed by Semites. The Egyptologist Alan Gardiner succeeded in making the first successful decipherment of a word in these texts in 1915 (published in 1916), when he correctly read the name *Ba'alath* and identified about 10 of the 22 signs in which the texts were written. He recognized the script as an alphabetic form of picture writing in a Semitic language. New discoveries have increased the number of extant proto-Sinaitic inscriptions to about 25, to which can be added another 11 or 12 written in the same script, found at various places in Palestine. Scholars who followed Gardiner and who have contributed to our understanding of these texts and their history are A. Cowley, K. Sethe, H. Grimme, R. Butin, and notably W. F. Albright. The texts can now be considered as virtually deciphered, although there is room for doubt with regard to some of the readings because of the brevity of most of these inscriptions. This is also the reason that some scholars are still doubtful about the claim that these inscriptions have actually been successfully deciphered.

The great advance of this script over all existing ones was the invention and application of the acrophonic principle, which means that the picture of an object was used to represent not the object depicted, but only the initial consonant of the name of that object. For example,

in Egyptian hieroglyphs a wavy line represents water, and "water" in the various Semitic languages is expressed by words whose initial consonant is *m: mayim* (Hebrew), *my* and *mym* (Ugaritic), *mu* (Akkadian), etc. Hence, the wavy line, an Egyptian hieroglyphic character which stood for water, was used to represent only one isolated consonant, namely the 1st of the word for water. The Table of Alphabetic Scripts (fig. 531) shows the various proto-Sinaitic symbols in col. 1, a description of the symbols in col. 2, and their consonantal value as far as they are recognizable in col. 12. This table reveals that the drawing of the head of an ox, called *'aleph* in Hebrew, became the character for the Semitic consonant ', now written ℵ (*see* Aleph); that the outline of a simple house, in Hebrew called *bayith* (or in another form *bêth*) became the character *b;* and that the picture of a serpent, Heb. *nachash,* provided the character *n,* etc.

In the course of time these hieroglyphic signs became more stereotyped and cursive and by the 9th cent. B.C. had the form shown in col. 3 on the Table of Alphabetic Scripts (fig. 531), as they appear in the long inscription of King Mesha on the *Moabite Stone (fig. 338). This script,

530. A proto-Semitic stone inscription from the Sinai Peninsula

known as Phoenician or paleo-Hebrew, was used for several centuries throughout Palestine and Syria, as many stone inscriptions (figs. 445, 532, 553) and papyrus texts show. By Jeremiah's time it had reached the form indicated in col. 4,

531. A table of alphabetic scripts

Sign	Description of Sign [1]	Paleo-Hebrew (Phoenician) Moabite Stone 9th Cent. B.C.	Paleo-Hebrew (Phoenician) Lachish Letters 6th Cent. B.C.	Samaritan	Greek Old 8th Cent. B.C.	Greek Late	Name of Character	Square Hebrew Dead Sea Scrolls 1st Cent. B.C. [2]	Square Hebrew Modern Print [2]	Name of Character	Transliteration except of Greek characters	Ugaritic Characters	Ugaritic Transliteration [3]
1	2	3	4	5	6	7	8	9	10	11	12	13	14
	oxhead					A	alpha			'aleph	'		'
	house					B	bēta			bêth	b		b
						Γ	gamma			gimel	g		g
	double loop												ḥ
	fish				Δ	Δ	delta			daleth	d		d
	man praying					E	epsilon			he'	h		h
										waw	w		w
	?				I	Z	zēta			zayin	z		z
	fence ?				B	H	ēta			chêth	ch		ḥ
	?					Θ	thēta			têth	ṭ		ṭ
	?					I	iōta			yôd	y		y
	palm of hand				K	K	kappa			kaph	k		k
													sh
	oxgoad				Λ	Λ	lambda			lamed	l		l
	water				M	M	mu			mem	m		m
													ž
	serpent				N	N	nu			nûn	n		n
	blossom												ẓ
	?					Ξ	xi			samek	s		s
	eye				o	O	omicron			'ayin	'		'
	throw stick					Π	pi			pe'	p		p
	?									ṣadê	ṣ		ṣ
	?									qôph	q		q
	human head					P	rhō			rêsh	r		r
	bow					Σ	sigma			śin	ś		t
	?									shîn	sh		ṭ
	?												ǧ
	mark of cross				T	T	tau			taw	t		t
													'i
													'u
													ṣ
						Υ	upsilon						
						Φ	phi						
						X	chi						
						Ψ	psi						
						Ω	ōmega						

[1] According to W. F. Albright, *The Archaeology of Palestine* (1949), p. 192.
[2] Where there are two characters on the same line, the 2d is the form used at the end of the word.
[3] In general, this transliteration scheme follows the system of C. H. Gordon, *Orientalia* 19 (1950), 375.

which are the characters as they appear on the Lachish Letters (fig. 285) written shortly before the conquest of Judah and Jerusalem by King Nebuchadnezzar. This script with slight variations was retained by the Samaritans, and all their Bible manuscripts are written in it. The Samaritan script is shown in col. 5 of fig. 531.

Greek tradition claims that Cadmus, a legendary prince of Tyre, introduced the Phoenician alphabet to Greece. That the Greek alphabet is derived from the Phoenician script is obvious by a comparison of col. 6, showing the Greek characters as they appear in inscriptions of the 8th cent. B.C., with the Phoenician characters of the 9th cent. B.C. in col. 3. Also the sequence of the letters is the same in both systems. The Greeks immensely improved the usefulness of the alphabet by introducing letters to express the vowels. Since they had no use in their Indo-European language for certain signs, like 'aleph or 'ayin, representing purely Semitic sounds, they used these characters to represent the vowels a and o respectively. They also invented 5 additional signs which they added to the alphabet at the end. Since that time no major improvement of the alphabetic script has been made for more than 2,500 years. For examples see figs. 71-73, 187, 191, 215, 264, 269, 468, 487. Latin script—used in all the languages of western Europe, including English—is an adaptation of Greek, as is the Cyrillic alphabet used in Russia. For Latin inscriptions see figs. 161, 221, 295, 321, 396.

Among the Aramaeans, who also adopted the Phoenician script, the individual characters experienced more drastic changes in appearance than among the Greeks, and by about 500 B.C. had developed into forms in which the original characters can hardly be recognized. Because the Jews have become its principal users, and many of its characters have the appearance of squares, this form of writing is now called Hebrew square script. The Elephantine papyri of the 5th cent. B.C. (fig. 417) and other Aramaic texts on papyri, leather (fig. 207), and stone (fig. 518) from that period give us samples of the square script. Col. 9 of fig. 531 shows the Hebrew characters as they appear on the Dead Sea Isaiah scrolls from about 100 B.C. Col. 10, containing modern Hebrew type, shows that the Hebrew script has hardly changed during the last 2,000 years (see figs. 207, 244, 416, 489).

A most interesting discovery, made in 1949, illustrates the great antiquity of the

alphabet. A small tablet found at Ugarit (see fig. 529) contained a list of all 30 characters of the Ugaritic alphabet in the sequence in which the scribes of that city had memorized them. To the great amazement of all scholars concerned, the tablet revealed that the sequence of all the characters, except one, that are common to Ugaritic and Hebrew is the same as in the Hebrew alphabet. The only exception is the letter sh, which occupies a place in the Ugaritic series other than that in the Hebrew list of characters. Four of the Ugaritic characters (ḥ, ž, ẓ, ġ) are found at various places in the list (see cols. 13 and 14 of fig. 531). They existed also in the proto-Siniatic script, but were lost in the course of time, and therefore do not appear in later Phoenician or Hebrew writing, although ġ remained in Hebrew pronunciation, as some old place names

532. The sarcophagus of Eshmunazar, king of Sidon, bearing a long Phoenician inscription

show; for example, the city of Gaza is written with an initial 'ayin, but pronounced with a ġayin (that is, Gaza, not 'Aza). Three characters peculiar to Ugaritic were added at the end of the list. Since the tablet in question originates from the 14th cent. B.C., it reveals that at that early date alphabetic script had already become so widely used throughout Palestine, Phoenicia, and Syria that the sequence of its letters was in the same form in Ugarit (in northern Syria) as in Palestine. It might be mentioned in this connection that the first 5 letters of the Hebrew alphabet were scratched on a stairway found at ancient Lachish. This was done in the 9th or 8th cent. B.C. according to paleographic evidence.

Lit.: W. F. Albright, *BASOR* 110 [1948], 6-22; 118 [1950], 12-14; 119 [1950], 23-24; E. A. Speiser, *BASOR* 121 [1951], 17-21. In the footnotes of these articles references can be found to most of the pertinent literature on the progressive development of alphabetic writing.

II. Writing Among the Hebrews and by the Authors of the Bible. It is evident from the foregoing brief survey that various writing systems were in use when the patriarchs lived and when the Biblical authors wrote their books. If Abraham and his family could read and write —which is possible—they must have known the cuneiform script, because that was the system of writing used in the country from which they came, and the script employed for official purposes in Canaan, the country to which they migrated. If the patriarchs possessed the genealogical lists of Gen 5 and 11 in written documents, such records most probably had the form of cuneiform tablets.

Moses, however, did not use clay tablets, but scrolls, called "books" (Ex 17:14; Num 5:23), which were of papyrus. This was the cheapest writing material of his time in Egypt, and that country culturally dominated the surrounding countries, including Sinai, where Moses spent so many years of his life. But which script did he use? Several writing systems were in use in his time, and he may have been familiar with several of them, since he had been trained "in all the wisdom of the Egyptians" (Acts 7:22). Hence it is reasonable to assume that he knew how to write in both hieroglyphic script and cuneiform characters, the latter being the international mode of writing used also by the Egyptian scribes of his time. Furthermore, when he came to Sinai, if not before, he must have become acquainted with the simple alphabetic script of the Canaanites used on that peninsula.

It seems, then, to have been in the provi-

dence of God that this simplest of all writing systems ever discovered had been invented shortly before Moses received the divine order to write the history and laws of his people for the instruction of future generations (Ex 17:14; cf. 24:4). If he had used either the cumbersome hieroglyphic script of the Egyptians or the difficult cuneiform writing of the Babylonians, his writings, unless translated, could never have become a people's book, and would probably have become no more than a piece of literature read and understood by only a few learned men. However, alphabetic writing existed in the time of Moses among the people of Canaan, and was employed in Sinai, the area in which he spent so many years as a shepherd for his Midianite father-in-law. It is therefore reasonable to assume that Moses used this alphabetic script, which because of its simplicity gradually developed into the universally used scripts of the ancient Mediterranean world. There is evidence that in the 2d millennium B.C. literacy was more common in Syria and Palestine than in Egypt or Babylonia, and that many ordinary people mastered the art of writing. This statement can be supported by many evidences. For example, in the time of Gideon (*c.* 1200 B.C.) a boy encountered by chance outside a city was able to write down the names of the 77 officials of his city (Jgs 8:14). Also archeological finds reveal that many simple folk made efforts to practice writing. For example, the Gezer Calendar, which was produced in the 10th cent. B.C., is a crude piece of stone on which someone, probably a peasant, rudely scratched a record of the agricultural activities of the various months of the year (see fig. 533).

That Moses was not the only literate individual among the Hebrews can be learned from such passages as Num 5:23, which indicates that the priests of his time could read and write, and Jos 24:26, which attests Joshua's ability to write. Other men and women of the Bible who are mentioned as writing are Samuel (1 Sa 10:25), David (2 Sa 11:14), Queen Jezebel (1 Ki 21:8, 9), King Jehu (2 Ki 10:1), and many others, among whom are some authors of the prophetic books of the OT. Also the art of engraving among the Hebrews is attested as being practiced during their early history; names were engraved on precious stones and metal plates (Ex 39:14, 30). Many other OT and NT passages show that the art of writing was a common possession of many people, and most authors of Bible books were apparently able to write. Even those who used scribes to write their messages did so not necessarily because of illiteracy but for other reasons. Jeremiah used a scribe (Jer 36:4), but was able to sign a document and write out a message (chs 32:10; 51:60).

In NT times the art of reading and writing was widespread. Elementary *schools for boys existed in many places, although a greater emphasis was placed on reading than on writing. The excavations at *Khirbet Qumrân* have brought to light a long table made of plaster, and a bench (see fig. 423) and 2 inkwells (see fig. 242). These are believed to have belonged to a scriptorium in which manuscripts were prepared. The hundreds of Dead Sea *scrolls found in the Qumran caves, most of them in fragmentary condition, show that among the members of the small Qumran community were industrious scribes. The result of their productivity and zeal was an amazingly large library consisting of Bible manuscripts and other religious literature. The preservation of much of this rich material gives us some idea of the wealth of Jewish literature that must have existed in the time of Christ. Many similar centers of scribal activities and book collections may have existed in Palestine, especially in Jerusalem and other big cities.

The NT sheds light on the writing activities of some of its authors, especially on those of Paul. It is not known whether Jesus ever wrote out any of His messages, nor do we know that He left any written documents in the hands of His disciples. The only record of His writing is in connection with the story of the adulterous woman, which describes Him as writing with His finger on the ground (Jn 8:6, 8). Paul was an industrious letter writer, but he generally employed scribes to write his letters (Rom 16:22). However, the letter addressed to Philemon (Phm 19) and at least a part of the letter to the Galatians (Gal 6:11) he himself wrote. It is possible that bad eyesight (*see* Paul, I, 3) made it difficult for him to write, and that therefore he wrote with unusually large characters (v 11, RSV). Letters written by his secretaries he signed personally (1 Cor 16: 21; Col 4:18; 2 Th 3:17), to give them the stamp of genuineness. To what extent the authors of the other books of the NT employed secretarial help is not known. A statement in 1 Pe 5:12 notes that Peter's first epistle was written by Silvanus, who acted as the author's scribe. Differences in style and vocabulary between the Revelation and the Gospel of John have been explained by assuming that the apostle used scribes for his Gospel, but that in the penal colony on the island of Patmos he wrote the book of Revelation without the help of an amanuensis (see Rev 1:19; 2:1, 8; 10:4; etc.). Perhaps 3 John was also written personally by its author (v 13).

Writing Case, KJV Inkhorn. A rendering of the Heb. *qeseth hassopher* (Eze 9:2, 3, 11). *Qeseth* is a loan word from Egyptian *gśty,* "a scribe's palette." This was usually an oblong piece of wood, ivory, or ebony holding several reed pens and having 2 cup holes in which the black ink and red ink were mixed and prepared (see fig. 424). Inkwells of burned clay and bronze were found in the scriptorium of *Khirbet Qumrân,* one of which still contained desiccated carbon ink (see fig. 242).

Writing Materials. A variety of writing material was used in the ancient world. The people of the Mesopotamian valley invented the clay tablet very early in their history. The cuneiform characters (*see* Writing, I, 1) were impressed in wet clay by means of a stylus and the tablet was then allowed to dry or was baked (see fig. 528). This type of writing spread widely throughout the ancient world, and was also used by the Palestinian princes in the 14th cent. B.C. in their correspondence with one another and with their Egyptian overlord. However, there is no clear evidence of the use of clay tablets by the Bible writers. Inscriptions were also engraved on stone for display purposes (Job 19:24), and several Hebrew stone inscriptions have been found (see fig. 445).

In Egypt papyrus was invented as writing material. Sheets of papyrus were made from narrow strips of the stem of the *papyrus plant, laid in 2 layers, one lengthwise and the other crosswise. These were then glued, pressed, hammered, and rubbed smooth. The sheets were glued end to end into long rolls, and writing was entered in columns by means of pen and carbon ink. Papyrus scrolls were used from the 3d millennium B.C. in Egypt, and in the course of time became the common writing material of the ancients, not only in Egypt but throughout the Mediterranean area. See figs. 22, 50, 424.

Another widely used writing material was leather, attested at least from the 15th cent. B.C. on. In Pergamum, Asia Minor, a refining process was later developed by which parchment was produced, the finest writing material ever invented. Since leather and parchment were more expensive than papyrus, they were used only for important documents or books. It is not known whether the authors of the Old and New Testaments used papyrus or leather scrolls for their original manuscripts. The oldest extant OT Hebrew manuscripts, the Dead Sea *scrolls, are with few exceptions written on leather, probably chosen for its durability (see fig. 244). But the earliest NT manuscripts—the Rylands Papyrus 457 (fig. 269), Papyrus Bodmer II, the Chester Beatty Papyri, etc. —are of papyrus (fig. 215). This is probably because of the poverty of the early Christian church. It was not until the 4th cent. A.D., when the church became recognized by the state and grew in wealth, that parchment manuscripts made their appearance—the Codex Vaticanus, Codex Sinaiticus, etc. (see figs. 71-73).

Notes and short messages were written with a stylus on slatelike wooden tablets, which were covered with wax; such tablets have been found in Calah, Assyria, and in Pompeii, Italy (see Is 30:8; Lk 1:63). Tablets were not suitable for long treatises such as the books of the Bible.

The same can be said of another rather common writing material—potsherds, or broken pieces of pottery. Since they were everywhere available and cost nothing, they were widely used for brief memoranda, notes, letters, receipts, and other documents of everyday occurrence. Such inscribed potsherds are designated by the Greek term *ostraca* (singular, *ostracon*). Since they are practically indestructible they have been preserved in the humid soil of Palestine where most other writing materials have perished long ago. More than 60 ostraca were found in the ruins of the storehouses of the kings of Israel at Samaria. They are a tax collector's records of oil and wine received by the royal house. At Lachish 21 ostraca were found, most of them letters by a military officer during the last days of Judah's existence (fig. 285). Other valuable ostraca from OT times have been discovered at Jerusalem, *Tell Qasîleh*, Beth-shemesh, *Qumrân*, and on the Nile island of Elephantine. On several ostraca from Elephantine occurs the earliest mention of the Sabbath outside the Bible (fig. 411). The many Greek ostraca and papyri of NT times found in Egypt are especially helpful for a better understanding of the Koine Greek in which the NT was written.

Y

Yahweh (yä′wĕ). [Heb. *YHWH*.] A conjectural transliteration of the sacred name by which God instructed that Israel was to know Him, to distinguish Him from all false gods (see Ex 3:13-15). In consonantal Hebrew the name was written *YHWH*, which, according to *LVTL*, occurs about 6,823 times in the OT, these 4 letters being commonly known as the Tetragrammaton. Because of the sacredness attached to *YHWH*, and the fear of profaning it, the Hebrew people gradually ceased to take this word on their lips, and sometimes left a blank space where it would normally have been written. Although conclusive documentary evidence to confirm the vocalization *Yahweh* is lacking, scholars are now rather generally in agreement that this was the original pronunciation. When an ancient Hebrew reader came to the word *YHWH* he would read *'Adônay*, or simply *'Adôn*, "Lord." As a result, the vowels originally used in pronouncing these 4 consonants were lost. Accordingly, when, about the 7th or 8th cent. A.D., the Masoretes came to the 4 Hebrew consonants *YHWH* they added the vowels of the word *'Adônay*. Unaware of this Jewish custom, English translators of the Bible from the 12th cent. on rendered the word *YHWH* with the accompanying vowels of *'Adônay* as "Jehovah," and pronounced it accordingly (see KJV of Ex 6:3; Ps 83:18; Is 12:2; etc.). The KJV translators usually rendered *YHWH* as Lord, and *'Adônay* usually as *Lord. *YHWH* is generally believed to be a form of the verb *hayah*, "to be," in which case it would mean, "the Eternal One," "the Existent One," "the Self-existing One," "the Self-sufficient One," "the One who lives eternally." The particular divine attribute stressed by this title is that of self-existence and faithfulness, pointing to the Lord as the living God, the Source of life, in contrast with the gods of the heathen that had no existence apart from the imagination of their worshipers (see Is 41:23-29; 44:6-20).

Yard. An English measure of length, equaling 3 ft., or 36 in. (.9144 m.). The term occurs in Jn 21:8, RSV, in the phrase "about 100 yards" (KJV "200 cubits"). The KJV, following the Greek literally, states that the distance between Peter's ship and the shore after the miraculous catch of fish was 200 cubits. This distance is converted to "about a hundred yards" in the RSV. Since the cubit in NT times was about 17.5 in. long, 100 yards (3,600 in.) are only 100 in. longer than 200 cubits (3,500 in.).

Yarn. *See* Kue.

Year. The natural year, marked by the 4 seasons, is measured by the sun, and represents the period required for 1 revolution of the earth around the sun (now known to be 365 days, 5 hours, 48 minutes, 45.51 seconds, or 365.2422 days). A calendar year is divided into months, which are based on, or at least derived from, the moon's phases, which repeat themselves each time the moon revolves once around the earth. The interval from one new moon to the next is about 29½ days, or a little less than 1/12 of a year: consequently there can never be an exact number of lunar months in a true year. There are at least 12 new moons in every year of our calendar, but frequently there are 13 (when the first comes early in January).

A number of different calendars have been devised to measure the year in terms of months in such a manner as to adjust the difference between the cycles of the sun and of the moon. The Moslem religious calendar to this day uses only the common lunar year of 12 lunar months, entirely disregarding the solar, or seasonal, year. Since 12 lunar months run about 11 days shorter (354 or 355 days) than the solar year, the uncorrected lunar year of the Moslems shifts in 3 years more than a month earlier in relation to the seasons. For example, the Moslem New Year came on our Nov. 3 in 1948, on Oct. 24 in 1949, on Oct. 13 in 1950, and on Oct. 2 in 1951 (a month earlier than in 1948); and by 1959 it had shifted back to July 7. The ancient Egyptians, on the other hand, disregarded the moon. They divided their year into 12 months of 30 days each, with 5 extra days at the end to make up 365 days, which they originally supposed to be the exact solar year, but which they later discovered to be about ¼ of a day short. Thus the Egyptian New

Year's Day shifted 1 day earlier in relation to the seasons every 4 years.

If Moses, trained in "all the wisdom of the Egyptians" (Acts 7:22), had adopted for the Israelites the Egyptian calendar, their months would have gradually lost step with the seasons; for example, by the time of David the Passover would have moved from the spring, in which it was instituted (*see* Abib), to midwinter. But the brief and simple directions given to the Israelites at the Exodus, rules that required no technical astronomical knowledge, were sufficient to keep the Hebrew year from wandering away from the seasons. It was easy enough to count 12 months by the new moon; and one simple adjustment, which was implicit in the law of the Festivals, served to keep the variation within the compass of one month.

The following instructions affected the calendar: (1) The 1st month in the year was to be the month in which the Israelites left Egypt (Ex 12:2). (2) The ceremony of the wave sheaf in connection with the Feast of Unleavened Bread, which followed the Passover in the middle of the 1st month (Ex 23:15; Lev 23:5, 6; Deut 16:1-8), was to mark the beginning of the (barley) harvest (Lev 23:5-14), and should precede by 49 days (50, inclusive) the festival that was to mark the first fruits of the wheat harvest (Lev 23: 15-21; Deut 16:9, 10), a festival called the Feast of Weeks (Ex 34:22), later *Pentecost (Acts 2:1; 20:16; 1 Cor 16:8). The Bible mentions no method for ascertaining the precise time for these feasts with respect to the seasons, but quite possibly the earlier Hebrews followed the same custom described in later Jewish tradition: If in the 12th month (Adar) it was evident from the condition of the barley crop at Jerusalem that the middle of the next month would be too early for a wave sheaf of ripe barley, the announcement was made that the month after Adar would be called a 2d Adar (or Veadar); in that case the 1st month, Nisan, would be postponed until the following new moon. This insertion of what was actually a 13th month, though always regarded as a duplicate 12th, was eventually observed to occur on an average of 7 times in 19 years. Thus methods of computation were developed by which the extra month could be known in advance. It is not known when computation replaced simple observation in determining which new moon was to begin the 1st month. After Biblical times, however, when the

Jews were scattered from Jerusalem, they depended on a method of calculation by 19-year cycles so that Jews in all parts of the world could know the length of the year in advance and could have a uniform calendar. According to this system the 13-month years were, and are, always the 3d, 6th, 8th, 11th, 14th, 17th, and 19th of each cycle, and the months were arranged in a varied but standardized sequence of 30 and 29 days.

As long as the Temple stood, however, the year was keyed to the barley harvest, and the months to the crescent moon. Since the 1st appearance of the crescent each month comes at a variable interval after the astronomical "new moon" (called conjunction), and since we do not know the ancient system, if one then existed, we cannot today translate Biblical Jewish dates into our calendar with absolute certainty and must allow for a possible error of a day, and at times of a month.

The Hebrews always numbered their months beginning with Abib (Nisan) in the spring, in harmony with the system of festivals outlined in the Levitical law. But for civil purposes they began the year in the autumn with the 7th month, Ethanim, or Tishri. Thus we speak of a *religious* (or ecclesiastical, or sacred) year and a *civil* year. The latter seems to have been known before the new numbering of the months was introduced at the Exodus, for the Feast of Ingathering (or Tabernacles) in the 7th month is spoken of as coming at "the end of the year" (Ex 23: 16; cf. 34:22). The beginning of the jubilee years was to be announced on the 10th of the 7th month; and the feast called the Blowing of Trumpets, on the 1st of the 7th month (Lev 23:24), is what the Jews still call Rosh Hashana, or New Year's Day.

For dating purposes the Hebrews did not number their years in one long series, as we number the years from 1 to 1960 and on, in our Christian Era (*see* Chronology, I, 1). Their numbering during the period of the kings began again in the reign of each king; for example: "in the fourth year of Solomon's reign over Israel, in the month of Ziv" (1 Ki 6:1, RSV). There are distinct indications that Solomon and the kings of Judah reckoned their reigns in civil calendar years, beginning with Tishri, the 7th month, in the autumn. Nehemiah, who put Chislev (the 9th month) before Nisan (the 1st month) in the 20th year of Artaxerxes

(Neh 1:1; 2:1), was evidently using the Jewish civil year in reckoning the reign of that Persian king, even though Artaxerxes himself reckoned his years, by the Babylonian-Persian calendar, as beginning in the spring. (Thus during half of each year the Jewish and Babylonian reg-

533. The Gezer Calendar listing the farmer's activities for each month, written in a crude handwriting in the 10th cent. B.C.

nal numbering of the same king could differ by one year.) However, the indications are that in the period between the Testaments, including the reign of Herod, the years of the reign were reckoned by the Jewish religious year, beginning with Nisan, in the spring. Thus when we speak of the Hebrew or Jewish year we must consider that there was more than one way of reckoning the year.

See Season. For an outline of the months, festivals, and seasons of the year see the following table.

HEBREW MONTHS, FESTIVALS, AND SEASONS

LUNAR MONTHS	BEGIN AT NEW MOON OF	LUNAR MONTH DATES	FESTIVALS	APPROXIMATE AGRICULTURAL SEASONS
1. Abib (Nisan)* Ex 23:15 (Neh 2:1)	March or April	1	New Moon. Beginning of Religious Year	Latter rains Joel 2:23
		10	Passover lamb selected. Ex 12:3	
		14	PASSOVER killed "in the evening"; eaten "that night," beginning of 15th. Ex 12:6-8	
		15†	UNLEAVENED BREAD begins. Lev 23:6, 7	
		16	Wave sheaf offered. Lev 23:10-14	Barley harvest; new crop may be eaten
		21	Last day of Unleavened Bread. Lev 23:8	Beginning of dry season
2. Zif [Iyyar] 1 Ki 6:1	April or May	1	New Moon	
		14	Passover for those unclean in 1st month. Num 9:10, 11	Wheat ripe in lowlands
3. (Sivan) (Est 8:9)	May or June	1	New Moon	Early figs
		6	PENTECOST, or Feast of Weeks. Wave loaves offered, 50th day from Nisan 16. Lev 23:15-21	Hot weather Wheat harvest, general
4. [Tammuz]	June or July	1	New Moon	Wheat harvest in mountains First grapes
5. [Ab]	July or Aug.	1	New Moon	Olives in lowlands
6. (Elul) (Neh 6:15)	Aug. or Sept.	1	New Moon	Dates, figs Vintage
7. Ethanim [Tishri] 1 Ki 8:2	Sept. or Oct.	1	BLOWING OF TRUMPETS, Rosh Hashana, or New Year. Lev 23: 24, 25. Beginning of civil year	
		10	DAY OF ATONEMENT, or Yom Kippur. Lev 23:27-32; Lev 16	
		15-21	FEAST OF INGATHERING or Tabernacles. Lev 23:34-43	End of harvest
		22	Holy convocation. Lev 23:36, 39; Num 29:12, 35	Former or early rains Plowing begins
8. Bul [Marhesh-van or Heshvan] 1 Ki 6:38	Oct. or Nov.	1	New Moon	Barley and wheat sown
9. (Chisleu or Chislev) (Neh 1:1)	Nov. or Dec.	1	New Moon	Winter rains Occasional snow
10. (Tebeth) (Est 2:16)	Dec. or Jan.	1	New Moon	Lowlands green
11. (Shebat) (Zec 1:7)	Jan. or Feb.	1	New Moon	
12. (Adar) (Est 3:7)	Feb. or March	1 (14, 15	New Moon (Purim. Est 9:21-28)	Oranges ripe in lowlands Barley ripe at Jericho
[13. Second Adar, c. 7 times in 19 years.]	March	14, 15	(Purim in c. 7 out of 19 years.)	

---

* The first day of Abib always came in our March or April, and coincided with the new moon. Similarly, the month of Zif began in April or May. The other months of the Hebrew calendar follow the same pattern.
† Annual ceremonial sabbaths (cf. Col 2:16, 17) in italics.
( ) Postexilic month names or festivals, and the corresponding texts.
[ ] Postexilic months not mentioned in the Bible.

Year of Jubilee. *See* Jubilee.

Year, Sabbatical. *See* Sabbatical Year.

Yeast. *See* Leaven.

Yiron (yī′rŏn). [Heb. *Yir′ôn*.] A fortified city in the territory of Naphtali (Jos 19:38, RSV), called Iron (ī′rŏn) in KJV. It has been identified with the present village of *Yārûn*, 10 mi. northwest of Hazor.

Yoke. [Heb. generally *'ol*, "yoke"; Gr. generally *zugos*, "yoke."] A ferrule around a prisoner's neck, to which the hands were tied, also a shaped piece of wood placed upon the necks of beasts of burden, by means of which loads were pulled. The type of yoke that was commonly used probably consisted of a piece of straight wood with "bars" at the ends (Lev 26:13; Eze 34:27; RSV), fastened by means of "bands" around the animal's neck (cf. Jer 2:20, RSV). The yoke is used as a symbol of bondage (Gen 27:40; Lev 26:13; Deut 28:48; 1 Ki 12:4; etc.). Jeremiah was instructed to wear yokes and thus warn of impending captivity (Jer 27:1-7). Jesus invited His followers to take His "yoke," which was "easy" (Mt 11:29, 30). Paul likened the legalism into which the Galatians were slipping to a "yoke of bondage" (Gal 5:1), and spoke of one of his fellow laborers as a "true yokefellow" (Php 4:3). He warned Christians not to be "unequally yoked" with unbelievers (2 Cor 6:14).

Z

Zaanaim. *See* Zaanannim.

Zaanan (zā′á-năn). [Heb. *Ṣa'anan*.] A town near Lachish (Mic 1:11); possibly identical with Zenan.

Zaanannim (zā′á-năn′ĭm), KJV once Zaanaim (zā′á-nā′ĭm). [Heb. *Ṣa'ananním* and *Ṣa'annayim* (Q *Ṣa'anannim*).] A place on the northeastern border of the territory of Naphtali (Jos 19:33), near Kedesh (Jgs 4:11). The "oak" mentioned in these passages in the RSV was probably a famous terebinth. The site is unidentified.

Zaavan (zā′á-văn), KJV once Zavan (zā′văn). [Heb. *Za'awan*, "terror," if the name is Semitic, but it is more probably of Hurrian origin.] A son of the Horite (Hurrian) Ezer (Gen 36:27; 1 Chr 1:42).

Zabad (zā′băd). [Heb. *Zabad*, "He (God) bestows."]

1. A descendant of Ephraim, of the family of Shuthelah (1 Chr 7:21).

2. A son of Nathan and grandson of Jarha, the Egyptian servant of Sheshan, a Jerahmeelite of Judah (1 Chr 2:36).

3. One of the "mighty men" of David (1 Chr 11:41).

4. Another name for *Jozacar (2 Chr 24:26).

5, 6, and 7. Three men of Ezra's time who had married foreign wives (Ezr 10:27, 33, 43).

Zabbai (zăb′á-ī). [Heb. *Zabbay*, meaning uncertain. The name occurs also in South Arabic and Palmyrene inscriptions; in cuneiform texts it is spelled *Zabbai*.]

1. A member of the family of Bebai; he had a foreign wife in Ezra's time (Ezr 10:28); possibly identical with Zabbai, 2.

2. A man whose son Baruch helped Nehemiah to rebuild the wall of Jerusalem (Neh 3:20); possibly identical with Zabbai, 1.

Zabbud. *See* Zakkur.

Zabdi (zăb′dī). [Heb. *Zabdí*, "my gift," or, if a shortened form of *Zabdí'el*, "gift of God." The name occurs in the Aramaic documents from Elephantine as *Zbdy*, and in cuneiform texts as *Zabdi*.]

1. A Judahite, ancestor of Achan (Jos 7:1, 17, 18); called Zimri in 1 Chr 2:6.

2. A son of Shimei, of the tribe of Benjamin (1 Chr 8:19, 21).

3. The overseer of David's vineyards (1 Chr 27:27).

4. A son of Asaph, and the ancestral head of a family of Levite singers (Neh 11:17); possibly identical with Zaccur, 4, and Zichri, 5.

Zabdiel (zăb′dĭ-ĕl). [Heb. *Zabdí'el*, "a gift of God." The name occurs in a South Arabic inscription as *Zbd'l*, and in cuneiform as *Zabdi-ilu*.]

1. The father of David's divisional commander for the 1st month (1 Chr 27:2).

2. A Temple overseer in the time of Nehemiah (Neh 11:14).

Zabud (zā′bŭd). [Heb. *Zabúd*, "given (by God)," or "bestowed."] A priest, and confidential minister of Solomon (1 Ki 4:5).

Zabulon. *See* Zebulun.

Zaccai (zăk′á-ī). [Heb. *Zakkay,* meaning uncertain.] The ancestral head of a family of which 760 men returned with Zerubbabel to Judah (Ezr 2:9; Neh 7:14).

Zacchaeus (ză-kē′ŭs). [Gr. *Zakchaios,* from the Heb. *Zakkay.*] A Jewish tax collector at Jericho, who, when Jesus passed through the city, made special efforts to see Him. Jesus recognized in him an honest soul, stayed with him in his home, and converted him (Lk 19:1-10).

Zacchur. *See* Zaccur, 2.

Zaccur (zăk′ûr), KJV once **Zacchur** (zăk′ûr). [Heb. *Zakkûr,* "remembered (by God)." The name occurs on ancient Hebrew seals and in the Aramaic documents of Elephantine as *Zkr,* and in cuneiform texts as *Zakurum.*]
1. The father of the Reubenite spy Shammua (Num 13:4).
2. A Simeonite (1 Chr 4:25, 26).
3. A Merarite Levite (1 Chr 24:27).
4. A Levite, a son of Asaph. He was placed by David over a group of singers (1 Chr 25:2, 10; cf. Neh 12:35). He is possibly identical with Zabdi, 4, and Zichri, 5.
5. A son of Imri, and helper in rebuilding Jerusalem's walls (Neh 3:2).
6. A Levite who set his seal to Nehemiah's covenant (Neh 10:12); possibly identical with Zaccur, 7.
7. A Levite whose son Hanan was assistant to the Temple treasurers appointed by Nehemiah (Neh 13:13); possibly identical with Zaccur, 6.

Zachariah. *See* Zechariah, 14.

Zacharias. *See* Zechariah, 12, 32.

Zacher. *See* Zechariah, 1.

Zadok (zā′dŏk), KJV of NT **Sadoc** (sā′dŏk). [Heb. *Ṣadôq,* "righteous." The name occurs on an ancient Hebrew jar handle. Gr. *Sadōk.*]
1. One of the 2 chief priests during David's reign. He was a descendant of Aaron through Eleazar (1 Chr 24:3), and was the son of Ahitub (2 Sa 8:17). He was with the chief men of the northern tribes who came to Hebron to invite David to become king over the whole nation (1 Chr 12:23, 28). He and Abiathar, who had been David's chief priest while David was still a fugitive from Saul, shared their rights and duties as equals (2 Sa 17:15; 19:11; 20:25). When Absalom rebelled, the 2 priests wished to join David and follow him into exile, but David asked them to remain in Jerusalem (ch 15:24, 29). After his victory over Absalom David

sent them to induce the elders of Judah to invite him back to the capital (2 Sa 19:11). Near the close of David's reign the 2 men differed over the successor to the throne. Abiathar supported Adonijah's abortive attempt to grasp the throne. Zadok remained faithful to David, and he and the prophet Nathan succeeded in having Solomon crowned before Adonijah's effort was successful (1 Ki 1:7, 8, 32-45). As a result of his action Abiathar was deposed from the priesthood by Solomon and sent to his home at Anathoth (ch 2:26, 27), and Zadok became sole high priest (v 35) and continued in that role until his death.
2. A priest and descendant of Zadok, 1, and an ancestor of Ezra (1 Chr 6:12; 9:11; Ezr 7:2; Neh 11:11; however, it is possible that not all these passages refer to the same individual).
3. The maternal grandfather of King Jotham of Judah (2 Ki 15:33).
4. A son of Baana; he aided Nehemiah in the rebuilding of the wall of Jerusalem (Neh 3:4); possibly identical with Zadok, 6.
5. A son of Immer; he aided Nehemiah in the rebuilding of the wall of Jerusalem (Neh 3:29); perhaps identical with Zadok, 7.
6. A leading Jew who set his seal to Nehemiah's covenant (Neh 10:21); possibly identical with Zadok, 4.
7. A scribe whom Nehemiah appointed Temple treasurer (Neh 13:13); possibly identical with Zadok, 5.
8. A Judahite (KJV "Sadoc") appearing in Matthew's genealogy of Jesus Christ (Mt 1:14).

Zaham (zā′hăm). [Heb. *Zaham,* "loathing."] A son of King Rehoboam of Judah (2 Chr 11:19).

Zain. [Heb. *zayin.*] The 7th letter of the Hebrew alphabet, written ז, appearing as the title of the 7th section of Ps 119 in the KJV. *See* Aleph.

Zair (zā′ĭr). [Heb. *Ṣa'ir,* "little."] A place either in southern Judah (some identify it with Zior) or in the land of Edom. The army of Joram of Judah camped at Zair before a battle with Edom (2 Ki 8:21).

Zakkur (zăk′ûr), KJV **Zabbud** (zăb′ŭd). [Heb. *Zabbûd* (Q *Zakkûr*). *Zakkûr* means "remembered (by God)."] One of the leaders of the family of Bigvai. He returned with Ezra to Jerusalem with 70 male members of his family (Ezr 8:14).

Zalaph (zā′lăf). [Heb. *Ṣalaph,* "caper plant."] A man whose son Hanun helped Nehemiah to repair the walls of Jerusalem (Neh 3:30).

Zalmon (zăl′mŏn), KJV once **Salmon** (sal′-mŏn). [Heb. Ṣalmôn, meaning uncertain.]

1. One of David's "mighty men" (2 Sa 23:28), called Ilai in 1 Chr 11:29.

2. A mountain near Shechem (Jgs 9:48), possibly one of the peaks of Mount Gerizim; possibly the same as Zalmon, 3.

3. An unknown locality (Ps 68:14), possibly the same as Zalmon, 2.

Zalmonah (zăl-mō′nȧ). [Heb. Ṣalmonah, meaning uncertain.] A camping place of the Israelites in the wilderness, between Mount Hor and Punon, evidently somewhere in the *Arabah (Num 33:41, 42).

Zalmunna (zăl-mŭn′ȧ). [Heb. Ṣalmunna‘, either "shadow (= protection) is withheld" or "(the god) Ṣalm (= Saturn) rules."] A Midianite king captured and slain by Gideon (Jgs 8:5-21; Ps 83:11).

Zamzummims (zăm-zŭm′ĭmz). [Heb. Zamzum-mîm.] The name given by the Ammonites to the Rephaim, whose country they occupied and whom they had replaced (Deut 2:20). Their name has not been satisfactorily explained nor identified from secular sources. They are possibly identical with the *Zuzim of Gen 14:5.

Zanoah (zȧ-nō′ȧ). [Heb. Zanôach, "repugnance."]

1. A town in the Shephelah in Judah (Jos 15:34), apparently founded by Jekuthiel (1 Chr 4:18). It was resettled after the Exile (Neh 11:30), and its citizens repaired the Valley Gate at Jerusalem (ch 3:13). It has been identified with Khirbet Zānû‘, about 2 mi. south-southeast of Beth-shemesh.

2. A town in the hill country of Judah (Jos 15:56), which has tentatively been identified with Khirbet Zanûtā, about 12 mi. southwest of Hebron (Abel, Géographie II, 489). Map VI, F-3.

Zaphenath-paneah (zăf′ĕ-năth-pȧ-nē′ȧ), KJV **Zaphnath-paaneah** (zăf′năth-pā′ȧ-nē′ȧ). [Heb. Ṣaphenath pa‘neach.] An Egyptian name given by Pharaoh to Joseph when he was appointed food commissioner of Egypt (Gen 41:45). The name has not been found in ancient Egyptian texts. The most plausible interpretation is that of Spiegelberg, who sets forth the view that it stands for the Egyptian Dd-p3-ntr-iw.f-‘nḫ, "the god speaks and he lives."

Zaphnath-paaneah. See Zaphenath-paneah.

Zaphon (zā′fŏn). [Heb. Ṣaphôn, "north."] A city in the Jordan Valley, mentioned in the *Amarna Letters as Ṣapuna. It was assigned to Gad after its capture (Jos 13:27; Jgs 12:1, RSV). Because of a clue in the Talmud it has usually been identified with Tell ‘Ammatā, north of the Jabbok at the mouth of the Wâdī Râjeb, but N. Glueck identifies it plausibly with Tell el-Qôs, less than ½ mi. northeast of Tell ‘Ammatā (BASOR 90 [1943], 20, 21). Map VI, D-4.

Zara. See Zerah, 3.

Zarah. See Zerah, 3.

Zareah. See Zorah.

Zareathite. See Zorathite.

Zared. See Zered.

Zarephath (zăr′ĕ-făth), KJV of NT **Sarepta** (sȧ-rĕp′tȧ). [Heb. Ṣarephath; cuneiform records Ṣariptu; Egyptian texts D3rptî; Gr. Sarepta.] A Phoenician town, about 14 mi.

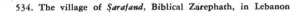

534. The village of Ṣarafand, Biblical Zarephath, in Lebanon

north of Tyre, now a village called *Sarafand* (Map IX, B-3). Since it lay on the coastal road in Phoenicia, it saw many armies pass by, and is therefore occasionally mentioned in ancient records, but it never became an important city. It is mentioned in the Bible as the town where Elijah was entertained during a severe famine by a poor widow whose son he later raised from the dead as a reward for her unselfishness (1 Ki 17:8-24; "Sarepta" in Lk 4:26). Obadiah envisioned the boundary of restored Israel at Zarephath (Ob 20). See figs. 500, 534.

Zaretan. *See* Zarethan.

Zarethan (zăr′ĕ-thăn), KJV **Zaretan** (zăr′ĕ-tăn), **Zartanah** (zär-tā′na), and **Zarthan** (zär′thăn). [Heb. *Ṣarethan.*] A place in the Jordan Valley, apparently east of the river near Adam (Jos 3:16). King Solomon had his foundries in the clay ground near there (1 Ki 7:46). It is apparently this site that is called Zeredah [Heb. *Ṣeredah*] in 2 Chr 4:17, RSV. In 1 Ki 4:12 it seems to be placed farther north, near Beth-shean below Jezreel. Hence identification is difficult, and the proposals made by certain scholars are rejected by others. N. Glueck tentatively identifies it with *Tell es-Saʿîdîyeh,* about 1 mi. east of the Jordan and west of Jerash (Map VI, D-4). N. Glueck, *BASOR* 90 (1943), 6-8.

Zareth-shahar. *See* Zereth-shahar.

Zarhite. *See* Zerahite.

Zartanah. *See* Zarethan.

Zarthan. *See* Zarethan.

Zatthu. *See* Zattu.

Zattu (zăt′û), KJV once **Zatthu** (zăt′thū). [Heb. *Zattûʾ,* meaning uncertain.] The ancestral head of a family of which 945 members returned with Zerubbabel to Jerusalem (Ezr 2:8; 845 in Neh 7:13). Six of his descendants were married to foreign wives in the time of Ezra (Ezr 10: 27), and probably 1 representative of the family set his seal to Nehemiah's covenant (Neh 10:14).

Zavan. *See* Zaavan.

Zaza (zā′za). [Heb. *Zazaʾ,* meaning uncertain, although the name occurs in Akkadian as *Zazâ.*] A man of the family of Jerahmeel of the tribe of Judah (1 Chr 2:33).

Zealot, KJV **Zelotes.** [Gr. *Zēlōtēs,* "the zealous one." *Zēlōtēs* appears several times in a commendable sense of "zealous," or "eager," in the NT (Acts 21:20; 22:3; Gal 1: 14; etc.).] A term used to distinguish Simon, one of the 12 disciples of Jesus

Christ (Lk 6:15; Acts 1:13), from Simon Peter. The Zealots in the time of the Jewish war of A.D. 66-70 were members of a nationalistic Jewish party that rose, according to Josephus, from Judas of Gamala, in opposition to the census taken under Quirinius in A.D. 6 (Jos. *Ant.* xviii. 1. 1, 6; *War* ii. 8. 1), and became fanatical resistance fighters against the Romans, but in the end were no more than assassins, and therefore were called Sicarii, "daggermen" (Jos. *War* iv. 3. 9; vii. 8. 1). Some think that "zealot" in Jesus' time meant a member of this party; others hold that it was not yet a party name, but rather a general designation for those who were extremely zealous for the observance of the Law, without necessarily denoting any specific organized group. If this Simon, before he became a disciple, belonged to the party later known as the Zealots, he could hardly have remained a member of it after he began to work with Jesus as one of His intimate followers. In the lists of disciples given by Mark and Matthew (Mk 3:18; Mt 10:4; RSV) Simon is called the *Cananaean, from the Aramaic equivalent term for Zealot.

Zebadiah (zĕb′a-dī′a). [Heb. *Zebadyah* and *Zebadyahû,* "Yahweh has given," or "Yahweh has bestowed."]

1 and 2. Two Benjamites, descendants respectively of Beriah and Elpaal (1 Chr 8:15-18).

3. A Benjamite from Gedor who joined David at Ziklag (1 Chr 12:7).

4. A Korahite Levite, the 3d son of Meshelemiah, and one of the gatekeepers of the sanctuary (1 Chr 26:2).

5. A nephew of Joab, and one of the commanders, assigned for the 4th month (1 Chr 27:7).

6. One of the Levites sent out by King Jehoshaphat to teach the Law in the cities of Judah (2 Chr 17:8).

7. Son of Ishmael, and a prince of Judah, appointed by King Jehoshaphat to judge civil or criminal cases in the court at Jerusalem (2 Chr 19:11).

8. A member of the family of Shephatiah. He, with 80 male members of that family, returned with Ezra to Jerusalem (Ezr 8:8).

9. A priest of the family of Immer; he had married a foreign wife in the time of Ezra (Ezr 10:20).

Zebah (zē′ba). [Heb. *Zebach,* "(born on the day of) sacrifice."] One of the 2 Midianite kings captured and slain by Gideon (Jgs 8:5-21; Ps 83:11).

Zebaim. *See* Pochereth-hazzebaim.

Zebedee (zĕb′ĕ-dē). [Gr. *Zebedaios,* the Greek form of either Zebedaiah, Heb. *Zebadyah,* "Yahweh bestows," or Zabdi, Heb. *Zabdi,* "my gift."] A Galilean fisherman, the father of the apostles James and John (Mt 4:21, 22; Mk 1:19, 20). His wife seems to have been Salome (Mk 15:40, 41; cf. Mt 27:56).

Zebidah (zē-bī′dȧ), KJV **Zebudah** (zē-bū′dȧ). [Heb. *Zebidah* (Q *Zebûdah*), "given," or "bestowed."] The daughter of Pedaiah of Rumah, and mother of King Jehoiakim of Judah (2 Ki 23:36).

Zebina (zē-bī′nȧ). [Heb. *Zebina',* an Aramaic name meaning "purchased." The name occurs in cuneiform records as *Zabinu.*] One of the members of the family of Nebo; he had married a foreign wife in the time of Ezra (Ezr 10:43).

Zeboiim (zē-boi′ĭm), KJV 3 times **Zeboim** (zē-bō′ĭm), [Heb. *Ṣebo'îm, Ṣeboyim,* and *Ṣeboyyim,* "gazelles."] A Canaanite city, which, with 4 other "cities of the plain" (Gen 10:19; cf. ch 13:12; KJV), revolted against the rule of Chedorlaomer (ch 14:2-9). God later destroyed it along with Sodom, Gomorrah, and Admah (Deut 29:23; cf. Gen 19:24, 25; Hos 11:8). Its site has not been identified, and most probably should be sought underneath the waters of the southern part of the Dead Sea. *See* Sodom.

Zeboim (zē-bō′ĭm). [Heb. *Ṣebo'îm,* "hyenas."]
1. A valley in Benjamin, between Michmash and the wilderness to the east (1 Sa 13:16-18). It has been identified with the *Wâdī Abū Dabā',* a tributary of the *Wâdī Qelt,* through which the ancient road from Jerusalem to Jericho led.
2. A town in Benjamin, near Hadid, occupied by Benjamites after the Exile (Neh 11:34). It seems to be this town that is mentioned in the *Amarna Letters as *Ṣabuma,* but its location is uncertain.
3. For Gen 10:19; Deut 29:23; Hos 11:8; KJV, *see* Zeboiim.

Zebudah. *See* Zebidah.

Zebul (zē′bŭl). [Heb. *Zebul,* "prince," or "exalted."] The governor of Shechem, who remained loyal to Abimelech in the rebellion of Gaal, and held the city until Abimelech came and put an end to Gaal's revolt (Jgs 9:28-45).

Zebulonite. *See* Zebulunite.

Zebulun (zĕb′ů-lŭn), KJV of NT **Zabulon** (zăb′ů-lŏn). [Heb. *Zebûlûn,* "exalted," or "habitation"; Old Babylonian *Ziblanum;* Egyptian *Tb3wnw;* Ugaritic *Zbln;* Gr. *Zaboulōn.*]

1. The 6th son of Jacob by Leah (Gen 30:19, 20). He had 3 sons: Sered, Elon, and Jahleel (ch 46:14). When Jacob blessed his sons he predicted that Zebulun's descendants would live near the sea in the northern part of Palestine toward Sidon (ch 49:13).

2. The tribe descended from Zebulun, 1. It was divided into 3 tribal families, whose ancestors were Zebulun's 3 sons (Num 26:26, 27). During the early wilderness wandering the tribe was led by Eliab, son of Helon (chs 1:9; 10:16), and later by Elizaphan, son of Parnach (ch 34:25). Gaddiel, son of Sodi, represented Zebulun among the spies (ch 13:10). During the 1st census 57,400 fighting men were registered (ch 1:30, 31), and at the 2d census, 60,500 (ch 26:27). After the tribes entered Canaan and gathered before the mountains of Ebal and Gerizim, the Zebulunites stood with 5 other tribes on Mount Ebal and pronounced the curses that would descend on the people in the case of transgressions (Deut 27:13; cf. Jos 8:32-35).

When the country was distributed by lot among the 12 tribes, Zebulun received territory in the center of southern Galilee. The territory was bounded on the east and north by Naphtali, on the south by Issachar and Manasseh, and on the west by Asher (Jos 19:10-16). No major cities were found in this area, but it was strategically located, controlling the east-west highway that ran through the Valley of Jezreel (Map VI, C-3), and its soil was fertile.

The tribe of Zebulun played an important role in the war of liberation led by Barak and Deborah to throw off the oppressive yoke of Jabin of Hazor (Jgs 4:6-10; 5:14-18). It also played an important part in Gideon's war against the Midianites (ch 6:35). Elon, one of the minor judges, was a Zebulunite (ch 12:11, 12). When the northern tribes went to Hebron and invited David to become ruler over the whole kingdom, Zebulun was represented by the impressive number of 50,000 warriors (1 Chr 12:33, 40). David's governor for Zebulun's territory was Ishmaiah, son of Obadiah (ch 27:19). With the other northern tribes it seceded from Judah and fell into idolatry. It suffered much in the wars with the Syrians and Assyrians, but Isaiah prophesied a glorious compensation through the Messianic light that would shine in its territory (Is 9:1, 2). This prophecy was fulfilled when Jesus Christ grew up in the midst of its territory and conducted much of His ministry there (Mt 4:12-16). A number of Zebulunites followed the invitation of King Hezekiah and celebrated the Passover in Jerusalem (2 Chr 30:10, 11, 18). There are no further historical references to the tribe. Ezekiel includes the tribe of Zebulun among the 12 tribes of his ideal Israel (Eze 48:33), and the tribe is mentioned in connection with the vision of the sealing of the 144,000 (Rev 7:8).

Zebulunite (zĕb′ù-lŭn-īt), KJV twice **Zebulonite** (zĕb′ù-lŭn-īt). [Heb. *Zebûloni.*] A member of the tribe of Zebulun (Num 26:27; Jgs 12:11, 12).

Zechariah (zĕk′á-rī′á), KJV 4 times **Zachariah** (zăk′á-rī′á); KJV of NT **Zacharias** (zăk′á-rī′ăs). [Heb. *Zekaryah* and *Zekaryahû,* "Yahweh has remembered." The name occurs on an ancient Hebrew seal and on an inscribed weight. Aramaic *Zekaryah.* Gr. *Zacharias.*]

1. A Benjamite of Gibeon, a son of Jeiel (1 Chr 9:35, 37). His shorter name Zecher (zē′kēr), KJV Zacher (zā′kēr), appears in ch 8:31.

2. A descendant of Reuben and a chief of the tribe (1 Chr 5:7).

3. A son of Meshelemiah, a Kohathite Levite; he served as gatekeeper at the sanctuary in David's time (1 Chr 9:21, 22; 26:2), and was a shrewd counselor of the king (ch 26:2, 14).

4. A Levite of the 2d order employed by David, first for the transfer of the ark to Jerusalem (1 Chr 15:18, 20) and later for the service before the ark of the Lord (ch 16:5); possibly identical with Zechariah, 6.

5. A priest who blew the trumpet when the ark was transferred to Jerusalem in the reign of David (1 Chr 15:24).

6. A son of Isshiah, a Kohathite Levite of the time of David (1 Chr 24:25); possibly identical with Zechariah, 4.

7. A Merarite Levite, a son of Hosah; he was employed by David as gatekeeper (1 Chr 26:10, 11).

8. A man whose son, Iddo, was leader of the Manassites of Gilead in the reign of David (1 Chr 27:21).

9. A Gershonite Levite of the family of Asaph, and a son of Benaiah. His son Jahaziel encouraged King Jehoshaphat to fight against Moab (2 Chr 20:14, 15).

10. One of the princes appointed by King Jehoshaphat to teach the Law in the cities of Judah (2 Chr 17:7).

11. A son of King Jehoshaphat of Judah (2 Chr 21:2).

12. A son of Jehoiada, and the high priest in the reign of King Joash of Judah. When a general apostasy of the people occurred after the death of his father Jehoiada, Zechariah was moved by the Spirit of God to rebuke the nation for its transgressions. This aroused such a resentment in certain circles, and so angered the king, who had probably been personally censured, that he had him stoned in the court of the Temple (2 Chr 24:20-22).

This is doubtless the Zechariah referred to centuries afterward in the famous statement of Christ about the righteous blood shed on earth "from the blood of Abel unto the blood of Zacharias, which perished between the altar and the temple" (Lk 11:50, 51). Zechariah, son of Jehoiada, is the only person by that name mentioned in the Bible who was slain in the Temple. Abel's death is recorded in the first book of the Scripture, and Zechariah's martyrdom in the last book (Chronicles) of the Hebrew Bible; hence the words of Christ "from" and "to" were intended to cover the sweep of OT Scripture history. That Zechariah is called the son of Barachiah (KJV "Barachias") in the parallel passage of Mt 23:35 poses a problem, for the well-known prophet Zechariah (*see* Zechariah, 20), who lived and worked after the Exile in the time of Zerubbabel, was a son of *Berechiah. Some explain this difficulty by concluding that the words "the son of Barachiah" in Mt 23:35 are not part of Christ's statement but the mistaken addition of a later scribe, who thought of the prophet when copying this passage. However, this is not the only possible explanation. In Hebrew, "son" often means grandson or descendant; the martyr Zechariah might have been called the *son of both Jehoiada and Barachiah if he was the grandson or descendant in the line of both of them.

13. An adviser of King Uzziah of Judah; his counsel brought Uzziah prosperity as long as the king followed the counselor's advice (2 Chr 26:5).

14. The 15th king of the northern kingdom of Israel, if Tibni is included in the count; called Zachariah in the KJV. He was the son of Jeroboam II, and with him ended the dynasty of Jehu (see 2 Ki 10:30), when he was assassinated at Ibleam by Shallum after a brief reign that lasted only 6 months *c.* 753-752 B.C. (chs 14:29; 15:8-12).

15. The maternal grandfather of King

Hezekiah of Judah (2 Ki 18:1, 2; 2 Chr 29:1); called Zechariah in 2 Chr 29:1, KJV.

16. Son of Jeberechiah. He was one of the witnesses to a tablet written by Isaiah (Is 8:2).

17. A Levite of the house of Asaph; he aided King Hezekiah in cleansing the Temple (2 Chr 29:13).

18. A Kohathite Levite, overseer of the workmen who repaired the Temple in the reign of King Josiah (2 Chr 34:12).

19. A chief officer of the Temple, probably a priest, in the reign of King Josiah (2 Chr 35:8).

20. A prophet, a son of Berechiah, and grandson of Iddo (Ezr 5:1; Zec 1:1); author of the book of Zechariah. His first recorded message was given in the 2d regnal year (520/519 B.C.) of Darius I (Zec 1:1). He was presumably born in Babylonia. Like Jeremiah and Ezekiel he was most likely prophet and priest at the same time. This is concluded from the fact that he belonged to the house of Iddo, and a leading priest named Iddo returned with Zerubbabel (Neh 12:1, 4). It is also possible that the Zechariah who was the head of the priestly house of Iddo in the days of the high priest Joiakim (v 16) was a descendant of the prophet Zechariah. The book of Zechariah contains messages directed to Zerubbabel, the political head of the nation, Joshua, the high priest, and to the people as a whole, but little information about the prophet himself. With the prophet Haggai, Zechariah was instrumental in stirring up the returned Jews to resume activity in restoring the Temple and to finish the building (Ezr 5:1, 2).

21. A member of the family of Parosh. He returned to Jerusalem under Ezra's leadership, accompanied by 150 male members of his family (Ezr 8:3).

22. A member of the family of Bebai. He returned to Jerusalem in Ezra's time accompanied by 28 male members of his family (Ezr 8:11).

23. One of the prominent men sent out by Ezra to induce Levites and Temple servants to return with him to Jerusalem (Ezr 8:16).

24. A member of the family of Elam; he had married a foreign wife in Ezra's time (Ezr 10:26).

25. A leading Levite or priest, who assisted Ezra in the reading of the Law (Neh 8:4).

26. A Levite, son of Jonathan, of the house of Asaph. He led a group of musicians during the dedication of the wall of Jerusalem in Nehemiah's time (Neh 12:35, 36).

27. A priest who blew a trumpet at the dedication of the wall of Jerusalem in Nehemiah's time (Neh 12:41).

28. A man of Judah, son of the Shilonite, or Shiloni (Neh 11:5).

29. A son of Amariah of the Judahite family of Perez (Neh 11:4).

30. A priest, son of Pashhur and father of Amzi (Neh 11:12).

31. A priest, head of the house of Iddo in the days of the high priest Joiakim (Neh 12:16); possibly a descendant of Zechariah, 20, the prophet.

32. The father of John the Baptist (Lk 3:2), a priest who belonged to the division of Abijah (KJV "Abia"; see Abijah, 8) and lived in a city in the hill country of Judea with his wife, Elizabeth (ch 1: 5, 39, 40). He and his wife are described as an aged, childless couple, who "were both righteous before God, walking in all the commandments and ordinances of the Lord blameless" (vs 6, 7).

At one time when the course, or division, to which Zechariah belonged was performing the Temple services, he was chosen by lot to burn incense (Lk 1:9). As he was discharging his duties in the Temple, with a large crowd worshiping outside (v 10), the angel Gabriel suddenly appeared to him, standing by the altar of incense (vs 11, 19). Naturally Zechariah was fearful, but was reassured by the angel, who informed him that his prayers were about to be answered; he was to have a son, who was to be named John (vs 12, 13). The child was to partake of no intoxicants, and would be full of the Holy Spirit from birth. His special work would be to "make ready a people prepared for the Lord" (v 17). Zechariah expressed doubt as to the possibility of this, seeing that he and his wife were so old (v 18), whereupon Gabriel informed him that he would be dumb until the prediction should be fulfilled (v 20). Emerging from the Temple, Zechariah indicated to the waiting people the reason for his delay (vs 21, 22). His period of ministration completed, he returned to his home (v 23), and continued mute until after the birth of the child.

When the baby was to be circumcised, relatives and neighbors decided that he should be named after his father, but the still-dumb Zechariah wrote on a tablet that his name should be John (vs 59-63). At this, his tongue was immediately loosed "and he spake, and praised God" (Lk 1: 64), and prophesied of the work of his son, who would be called "the prophet of the Highest" (vs 67-79). As a result of this experience, which became well known over much of Judea, many were cognizant of John and wondered what destiny was in store for him (vs 65, 66).

Zechariah, Book of. Next to the last of the so-called Minor Prophets, or "the Twelve," as they are known, according to Jewish classification. The title of the book gives the name of its author (Zec 1:1; *see* Zechariah, 20). Zechariah, who was probably a Levite and also a priest, returned with Zerubbabel from Babylon in 536 B.C. (see Neh 12:16; cf. Ezr 5:1; Zec 1:1). His prophetic ministry began in the 2d year of Darius the Great (Zec 1:1), that is, 520/19 B.C., about 16 years after the first return from the Babylonian captivity. The last chronological notation in the book is the 4th year of Darius (ch 7:1), 518/17 B.C., but it is almost certain that Zechariah lived to see the completion of the Temple in 515 B.C., in the 6th year of the same reign (Ezr 6:15). He was contemporary with the prophet Haggai (Hag 1:1; Zec 1:1).

Upon the decree of Cyrus about 50,000 Jewish exiles had returned to Judea under the leadership of *Zerubbabel (see Ezr 1:8; 2:1, 2, 64, 65). Shortly after their return they laid the foundation for the Second Temple (ch 3:1-10), and some progress was made during the remainder of Cyrus' reign (535-530 B.C.) and the reign of Cambyses (530-522), despite enemies who sought to halt the work (ch 4:5). Eventually work virtually ceased, owing mainly to the continued opposition and hindrance of the Samaritans (vs 1-5). The reign of the false Smerdis, Cambyses' successor (522), was too brief to affect the work for long, and Darius I, the legitimate successor to the throne, who slew Smerdis, gave specific permission to proceed. But even before his official decree reactivating Cyrus' original decree authorizing the rebuilding of the Temple (chs 5:3 to 6:13), the people, encouraged by the prophets Haggai and Zechariah, had enthusiastically set to work again (see Hag 1:2, 12-15; Zec 1:1; Ezr 5:1) and were prospered by God (Hag 2:5, 15, 18, 19). The work went forward rapidly until the Temple was completed in the 6th year of Darius (Ezr 6:15). Zechariah's prophetic messages were delivered during this final period of reconstruction (520-518), their purpose

being to inspire hope in the glorious possibilities that lay before the Jews upon their return from captivity on condition of their obedience.

Following the Captivity, God had promised to renew His covenant with Israel (Eze 36:21-27, 34, 38; cf. Jer 31:10-38; Zec 1:12-17; 2:12), and offered to bestow its accompanying blessings (Jer 33: 4, 6-26; Eze 36:8-15). All that He had promised might yet come to pass *if* His people would only cooperate (Zec 6:15; cf. Is 54:7; Eze 36:11; 43:10, 11; Mic 6: 8; Zec 10:6), and the prospective golden era would have reached its climax with the coming of Messiah. But like the messages of the prophets before him, Zechariah's forecast of Jerusalem's glorious future was conditional upon Israel's cooperation (Zec 6:15; cf. Jer 18:6-10), and her failure as a nation to measure up to God's minimum requirements was clearly evident a century later in the days of Malachi (see Mal 1:6, 7, 12, 13; 2:2, 13, 14, 17; 3:7, 13; etc.).

Zechariah's prophecies may be summarized as follows: The first of Zechariah's 3 messages consists of a series of 8 apocalyptic visions (Zec 1:1 to 6:15) which depict symbolically the complete restoration of the chosen people and reach a climax in the Messiah's advent. The 2d message (chs 7:1 to 8:23) constitutes a reproof for sin and an appeal for righteousness. The 3d message (chs 9:1 to 14:21) depicts the closing events of history in terms of God's original plan for Israel, including a glorious deliverance from all their enemies.

In the introduction (Zec 1:1-6) the Lord appeals to His people, "Turn ye unto me, . . . and I will turn unto you" (v 3). He appeals to them not to follow the evil example of their fathers, to whom, in captivity, had been fulfilled the curses invoked in the Law of Moses for disobedience (Zec 1:4-6; cf. Dan 9:11, 12). In the first of the series of 8 apocalyptic visions (Zec 1:7-17) Zechariah sees a man seated upon a red horse in a grove of myrtle trees and behind him other horses. The question is asked of the Lord, "How long wilt thou not have mercy on Jerusalem?" (v 12), and the Lord answers that He is "jealous for Jerusalem and for Zion with a great jealousy," that He is "very sore displeased with the heathen" who have so oppressed His people (vs 14, 15). Now He has returned to Jerusalem with mercy and the Temple will be rebuilt (vs 16, 17). In the 2d vision the work of the nations that have oppressed Jerusalem is symbolized by 4 "horns," and the means the Lord proposes to use to repair the damage done, by 4 "carpenters," who are to "cast out the horns of the Gentiles" (see Zec 1:18-21). In the 3d vision Zechariah sees a man with a measuring line (ch 2:1-13) who sets out to "measure Jerusalem" (v 2), laying plans for its restoration. The city is to be inhabited again (v 4), and the Lord Himself will protect it against all enemies (vs 5-9). He will "dwell in the midst" of it (v 10), and "many nations shall be joined to the Lord in that day" (v 11). The 4th vision (ch 3) depicts Joshua, the high priest, in his role as representative of the returned Jews, standing before the angel of the Lord with "filthy garments." Satan accuses him before God as unworthy. The Lord rebukes Satan and promises Joshua—and thus his people— a "change of raiment" (vs 2-4) if they will walk in His ways and honor Him (v 7). Then Messiah, "the Branch," will come, and Israel will dwell in safety (vs 8-10). In the 5th vision (ch 4) Zechariah sees a golden lampstand with 2 olive trees beside it providing oil for the lamps. Accompanying this vision is God's message to Zerubbabel that His glorious purpose for His people is to be accomplished "not by might, nor by power, but by my spirit" (v 6). The time of Zerubbabel is "a day of small things," but a great future lies before the people. In the 6th vision (ch 5:1-4) Zechariah sees "a flying roll," or "curse," that will enter into the house of everyone who fails to measure up to the divine standard. This flying roll represents the revealed will of God to His people, particularly His moral law (see v 4). The 7th vision (vs 5-11) depicts the manner in which God proposes to dispose of the sinners of vs 1-5. Zechariah sees an ephah (that is, a container of the capacity of an *ephah) with a cover of lead, and a woman inside; this, he is told, represents the "wickedness" (v 8) of unrepentant Jews, which is symbolically carried back to the land of Shinar (to Babylonia). In the 8th vision (ch 6:1-8) Zechariah sees 4 chariots pulled by 4 kinds of horses. These, he is told, are "the four spirits of the heavens" (v 5) that go "to and fro through the earth" (v 7) to superintend the working out of God's purpose for Israel. God will not leave His people until He has accomplished for them all that He purposed to do. In the conclusion of the 1st section of the book, Zechariah is instructed to place symbolic crowns upon the head of Joshua, the high priest, as a proclamation of the coming of the Branch, the Messiah (Zec 6:11, 12), who was to be a royal priest (v 13). In His day men shall come from "far off" to "build in the temple of the Lord" (v 15). The joyous future depicted in these symbolic visions would all "come to pass," said the prophet, if only the people would "diligently obey the voice of the Lord your God" (v 15).

In the 2d message (Zec 7; 8) the prophet first denounces certain hypocritical religious practices, and declares that what the Lord desires of His people is justice and mercy, "every man to his brother" (ch 7:9), which is the essence of true religion. For want of this, God had permitted His people to go into exile (v 14) and to languish in Babylon for 70 years. But He is still "jealous for Zion" (ch 8:1) and will carry out His purpose for it (v 3). He will return to Jerusalem, bring His people from the land of exile, cause them to dwell safely there, and reconstitute them as His chosen people (vs 7, 8). Therefore, He says, "let your hands be strong" (v 9)—strong in moral character (vs 16, 17), strong to "love the truth" (v 19). If they do so, the nations of earth will "go speedily . . . to seek the Lord of hosts in Jerusalem" (vs 21, 22). From all parts of the earth people will join the Jews, saying, "We will go with you: for we have heard that God is with you" (v 23).

The 3d and last message is divided into 2 sections, each of which Zechariah refers to as a "burden," or "oracle," a solemn message (Zec 9:1; 12:1). In the first of these God proposes to overthrow Judah's enemies, turn their people to Himself, and set up Messiah's kingdom (ch 9). He will refresh His people (ch 10:1), and it will be "as though I had not cast them off" (v 6; cf. vs 8-12)—that is, into captivity. Chapter 11 constitutes a solemn warning to the false "shepherds," or leaders, who have led astray the people under their care.

The 2d "burden" (Zec 12-14) outlines the closing events of history as they would have come to pass had Israel proved faithful (see ch 6:15). The picture presented is comparable to Ezekiel's battle of Gog and Magog (Eze 38; 39), and these 2 passages form the prophetic basis for the picture of the last great battles to be fought at the close of time, at Armageddon (Rev 16:12-16) and the battle of

Gog and Magog after the millennium (Rev 20:8, 9). As Zechariah depicts the scene: "all the people of the earth" lay siege to Jerusalem (Zec 12:2, 3), but the Lord defends its inhabitants (v 8) and destroys "all the nations that come against Jerusalem" (v 9). During the course of these events the people apparently pierce their Messiah-deliverer but, realizing what they have done, mourn bitterly (vs 10, 11). Nevertheless, "in that day" a fountain is "opened to the house of David and to the inhabitants of Jerusalem for sin and for uncleanness" (ch 13:1), and God cleanses the land of idols and false prophets (vs 2, 3). Messiah having been "wounded in the house" of His presumed "friends" (v 6), the people are scattered as a result (v 7). Two thirds in all the land are "cut off and die" but the 3d part is brought "through the fire," "refined," and is evermore to be God's people (vs 8, 9). They are the ones to whom the "fountain" of v 1 is opened for cleansing from sin and uncleanness. Then the Lord goes forth to "fight against those nations" (ch 14:1-3) that attack Jerusalem, and descends to the Mount of Olives, which splits apart and makes a great valley (v 4). In that day living waters go forth from Jerusalem (Zec 14:8; cf. Eze 47), the Lord is "king over all the earth" (Zec 14:9), and Jerusalem is "safely inhabited" (v 11). The means by which God disposes of those among the nations who have rejected His gracious invitation to unite with His chosen people, and who fought against Jerusalem, is depicted in vs 12-14, 17-19. Eventually "every one that is left of all the nations which came against Jerusalem shall even go up from year to year to worship the King, the Lord of hosts" (v 16).

On the conditional nature of the prophecies made to ancient Israel as the chosen people, to which Zechariah calls attention (Zec 6:15), and on the degree of their application to the people of God in the last times, after unfaithful Israel forfeited the fulfillment of the promises, see Chosen People; Prophet, II.

Zecher. See Zechariah, 1.

Zedad (zē'dăd). [Heb. Ṣadad.] A place on the northern boundary of the Promised Land (Num 34:8; Eze 47:15); identified with Ṣadâd, about 70 mi. northeast of Damascus.

Zedekiah (zĕd'ĕ-kī'á), KJV once **Zidkijah** (zĭd-kī'já). [Heb. Ṣidqiyah and Ṣidqiyahû, "Yahweh is righteousness," or "righteousness is Yahweh." It is probably this name

that occurs in Assyrian records as Ṣidqaia.]

1. Son of Chenaanah, and one of King Ahab's 400 court prophets. He encouraged Ahab to march against the Syrians and to reconquer Ramoth-gilead, and struck the face of Micaiah, the prophet of the Lord, when Micaiah prophesied misfortune (1 Ki 22:6, 11-25).

2. Son of Maaseiah, and a false prophet among the exiles in Babylon. Jeremiah predicted that Nebuchadnezzar would roast him in the fire (Jer 29:21-23), presumably for treasonous activities.

3. Son of Hananiah, and a prince of Judah during the reign of Jehoiakim (Jer 36:12).

4. The 20th and last ruler of the southern kingdom of Judah, who reigned for 11 years (597-586 B.C.). His original name was Mattaniah, but Nebuchadnezzar changed it to Zedekiah when he appointed him king in place of his nephew Jehoiachin (2 Ki 24:17; 1 Chr 3:15). In 2 Chr 36:9, 10 he is called Jehoiachin's brother, meaning "kinsman," as the word *"brother" is sometimes used in the Bible. His appointment to the kingship after the capture of Jerusalem and the deportation of Jehoiachin by Nebuchadnezzar in 597 B.C. is also referred to in recently discovered tablets of the Babylonian Chronicle, although his name is not mentioned in the record (see Jehoiachin).

Zedekiah had a weak character. Though he was occasionally inclined to follow Jeremiah (Jer 38:14-26), he did not have the moral strength to withstand the pressure of the people around him. He tolerated the pollution of the Temple and gross injustice throughout the nation (2 Chr 36:14; Jer 21:11, 12; 34:8-11). A strong anti-Babylonian party exercised much pressure upon him to shake off the foreign yoke, and envoys from the surrounding nations were found in Jerusalem, probably to plot against Nebuchadnezzar (Jer 27:1-22). Zedekiah tried to withstand them for a while. Once he sent envoys to Babylonia, presumably with tribute and assurances of his loyalty to Nebuchadnezzar, and in his 4th regnal year he went to Babylon himself, probably for the same purpose (chs 29:3; 51:59). It is possible, though purely conjectural, that this visit may have been connected with the dedication of the great image erected in the plain of Dura (Dan 3). Zedekiah finally succumbed to the pressure of the anti-Babylonians among his citizens, and trusting in the help of Egypt, rebelled against Nebuchadnezzar. The result of this faithlessness was an invasion of Judah by Nebuchadnezzar, which ended in the 3d capture of Jerusalem in 20 years, the city's total destruction, the end of the kingdom of Judah, and the deportation of the greater part of the citizens of Judah (2 Ki 24:18-20; 25:1-21; 2 Chr 36:13-21).

The final siege was begun on the 10th day of the 10th month in the 9th regnal year of Zedekiah (Jer 52:4), most likely on approximately Jan. 15, 588 B.C. Once it was temporarily lifted when an Egyptian army attempted to bring relief (ch 37:5). After a long siege, during which appalling famine conditions prevailed in the city, the Babylonians broke through the walls on the 9th day of the 4th month of Zedekiah's 11th year, the 19th year of Nebuchadnezzar (ch 52:5, 6; cf. v 12), approximately July 19, 586 B.C. In the ensuing confusion Zedekiah was able to escape from Jerusalem. However, the Chaldeans learned of his escape, pursued him, and captured him near Jericho. He was then taken to Nebuchadnezzar, who had made Riblah in central Syria his headquarters. After his sons were killed in his sight, Nebuchadnezzar put his eyes out, and transported him to Babylon in chains, where he remained a prisoner until he died (2 Ki 25:1-7; Jer 39:1-7; 52: 1-11).

5. The son of Jeconiah, or Jehoiachin (1 Chr 3:16). Some commentators believe that "son" is used here in the sense of successor. *See* Son.

6. A prominent leader of postexilic Judah who set his seal to Nehemiah's covenant as the 1st representative of the people after the governor (Neh 10:1, RSV); called Zidkijah in the KJV.

Zeeb (zē'ĕb). [Heb. *Ze'eb*, "jackal," "wolf."] A Midianite prince captured by the Ephraimites during Gideon's war of liberation and slain at a wine press which from that time was called by his name (Jgs 7:25).

Zela (zē'lȧ), KJV **Zelah** (zē'lȧ). [Heb. *Sela'*, "rib," "side."] A town in the territory of Benjamin (Jos 18:28), where the bones of Saul and Jonathan were buried (2 Sa 21:14); not identified.

Zelah. *See* Zela.

Zelek (zē'lĕk). [Heb. *Seleq*, "an outcry."] An Ammonite warrior who was one of David's "mighty men" (2 Sa 23:37; 1 Chr 11:39).

Zelophehad (zė-lō'fė-hăd). [Heb. *Selophchad*,

"shadow of fear," that is, a dreadful shadow.] A Manassite of the family of Gilead. He died leaving no sons but 5 daughters (Num 26:33). This was the occasion for legislation giving daughters the rights of inheritance in special cases (ch 27:1-8). This law was later extended to include the provision that if such daughters married, it must be within their own tribe, in order to prevent the loss of property from the tribe (ch 36:1-12). The possessions of Zelophehad's family lay in Transjordan (Jos 17:3-6).

Zelotes. *See* Zealot.

Zelzah (zĕl'zȧ). [Heb. *Selsach*.] A place near Rachel's tomb in the territory of Benjamin (1 Sa 10:2). The site has not been identified.

Zemaraim (zĕm'ȧ-rā'ĭm). [Heb. *Semarayim*, possibly "double peak."]

1. A town in the territory of Benjamin (Jos 18:22), tentatively identified with *Râs ez-Zeimara*, on a hilltop between *eṭ-Ṭaiyibeh* and *Rammûn*, about 4½ mi. northeast of Bethel.

2. A mountain in Ephraim, from the top of which King Abijah of Judah addressed the 10 tribes of Israel before fighting against them (2 Chr 13:4). Its location is unknown. Some because of the name seek it near Zemaraim, 1. However, since one of these lay in Benjamin and the other in Ephraim, they could be adjacent only if they were near the common borderline, which is possible but not certain.

Zemarite (zĕm'ȧ-rīt). [Heb. *Semari*.] A member of a tribe descended from Canaan (Gen 10:18; 1 Chr 1:16). The Zemarites were probably the inhabitants of a town on the coast of Phoenicia, called *Simirra* in Assyrian inscriptions, *Sumur* in the *Amarna Letters, and *D³m³r* in Egyptian hieroglyphic records. Its site has not yet been identified with certainty (see Thomsen, *AfO* 13 [1939-41], 173a). Thutmose III conquered the city for Egypt in the 15th cent. B.C., but it was lost in the Amarna period. Seti I captured it again in the latter part of the 14th cent. B.C. During the period of the Assyrian supremacy *Simirra*, like other Phoenician cities, became tributary to Tiglath-pileser III and his successors. It is apparently this town that is referred to by the conjectural rendering Zemer (zē'mĕr) [Heb. *Semer*] in Eze 27:8, RSV, where the Masoretic text reads *Sôr*, "Tyre."

Zemer. *See* Zemarite.

Zemira. *See* Zemirah.

Zemirah (zĕ-mī'rȧ), KJV **Zemira** (zĕ-mī'rȧ). [Heb. *Zemîrah*, probably "praised."] A son of Becher, a Benjamite (1 Chr 7:8).

Zenan (zē'năn). [Heb. *Ṣenan,* meaning uncertain.] A place in the Shephelah of Judah (Jos 15:37); not identified. It may be identical with Zaanan (Mic 1:11).

Zenas (zē'nȧs). [Gr. *Zēnas.* The name occurs in this form in a Greek inscription, and may be a short form of *Zēnodōros,* "gift of Zeus."] A Christian lawyer who was traveling with Apollos in Crete when Paul sent his letter to Titus. Paul requested Titus to help them on their journey and to see that they lacked nothing (Tit 3:13).

Zephaniah (zĕf'ȧ-nī'ȧ). [Heb. *Ṣephanyah* and *Ṣephanyahû,* "Yahweh has concealed," or "Yahweh has protected." The name occurs also on an ancient Hebrew jar handle.]

1. A Kohathite Levite, son of Tahath (1 Chr 6:36-38).

2. A son of Maaseiah and 2d priest under the high priest Seraiah in the reign of King Zedekiah (2 Ki 25:18; Jer 52:24). He carried messages between the king and the prophet Jeremiah (Jer 21:1; 37:3). Once he received a letter from Shemaiah, a false prophet in Babylon, suggesting that Jeremiah be punished for discouraging the people (ch 29:24-29). After the Babylonians captured Jerusalem Zephaniah with other leaders of the Jews was taken to Riblah in Syria and executed by Nebuchadnezzar (2 Ki 25:18-21).

3. A Jew in the home of whose son, Josiah, Zechariah was instructed to make certain memorial crowns (Zec 6:9-14).

4. A prophet in the days of King Josiah, and author of the book of Zephaniah. He was descended from Hezekiah (KJV "Hizkiah"), and thus was probably of royal blood (Zep 1:1), as commentators generally agree. A prince of royal blood could more easily and effectively denounce the sins of the nobility and princes (ch 1:8). Although Zephaniah has left us a short book of prophecies, he provides no information about himself other than that found in v 1, and we know nothing about his life since he is mentioned nowhere else in the Bible.

Zephaniah, Book of. Ninth of the so-called Minor Prophets, or "the twelve," as they are known according to Jewish classification. The title of the book gives the name of its author (Zep 1:1). *See* Zephaniah, 4. Nothing is known of this prophet aside from what he tells about himself. Apparently (v 1) he came from a distinguished family that could trace its an-cestry to King Hezekiah (KJV *"Hizkiah"). The prophet dates his message during the reign of Josiah, king of Judah (*c.* 639 - *c.* 608 B.C.). Since he predicts the overthrow of Assyria and the destruction of Nineveh (Zep 2:13), events that occurred late in the 7th cent. B.C., it appears that his ministry fell during the early part of Josiah's reign. Possibly he was contemporary with the prophet Habakkuk, and if so he may have had part in the great reformation of that period.

The terrible events soon to befall Judah and Jerusalem in connection with the Babylonian captivity Zephaniah presents as "the great day of the Lord," which he declares "is near, and hasteth greatly" (Zep 1:14). He predicts that during the repeated Babylonian invasions of Judah the entire land will be consumed (v 2), for God will stretch out His hand upon Judah and Jerusalem and cut off those who worship idols (vs 4-6). He will "punish the princes, and the king's children," and all those whose lives have been marked by "violence and deceit" (vs 8, 9), and all who "say in their heart, The Lord will not do good, neither will he do evil" (v 12). The prophet therefore summons all the "meek of the earth" among his people to repent and to "seek righteousness, seek meekness," in order that they may "be hid in the day of the Lord's anger" (ch 2:3). His gaze next turns to the surrounding nations of Palestine, who "for their pride" have "magnified themselves against the people of the Lord of hosts" (v 10). They, too, will suffer, as will the people of Ethiopia and Assyria (vs 12-15). Zephaniah then pronounces a stern woe upon the leaders at Jerusalem for betraying their sacred trust and refusing to receive correction (ch 3:1-4), but promises that if they "wait" upon the Lord He will gather the other nations and pour His "indignation" upon them instead, and "all the earth shall be devoured with the fire" of His "jealousy" (v 8). Then all men will "call upon the name of the Lord" and "serve him with one consent" (v 9); the "remnant of Israel" who survive will "not do iniquity, nor speak lies" (v 13), nor will they "see evil any more" (v 15). The prophecy closes with a glowing picture of the prosperity that will follow this genuine reformation (vs 16-20).

On the failure of Israel to fulfill their destiny after the return from captivity, and the significance of these prophecies, *see* Chosen People; Prophet, II.

Zephath (zē'făth). [Heb. *Ṣephath,* meaning uncertain.] A Canaanite city in the extreme south of Judah, assigned to the tribe of Simeon (*see* Hormah). The Simeonites conquered the city with the help of Judah and changed its name to Hormah (Jgs 1:17). Its site has not been identified with certainty.

Zephathah (zĕf'á-thá). [Heb. *Ṣephathah,* meaning uncertain.] A valley near Mareshah, where King Asa of Judah smote the army of Zerah the Ethiopian (2 Chr 14: 10). It has not been identified with certainty. It may be the *Wâdī Zeitā,* which has its beginning 2 mi. north of Mareshah, now *Tell Sandaḥannah,* and continues in a northwesterly direction toward the Mediterranean.

Zephi (zē'fī), or **Zepho** (zē'fō). [Heb. *Ṣephî* and *Ṣephô,* meaning uncertain. The name occurs in Assyrian as *Ṣupû.*] A son of Eliphaz and grandson of Esau. He became chief of an Edomite tribal family (Gen 36:11, 15; 1 Chr 1:36). The difference in the spelling of the name is evidently due to the similarities of the Hebrew letters *yod* and *waw* in postexilic Hebrew script.

Zepho. *See* Zephi.

Zephon (zē'fŏn), or **Ziphion** (zĭf'ĭ-ŏn). [Heb. *Ṣephôn* and *Ṣiphyôn,* "lookout."] A son of Gad, and ancestral head of a tribal family, the Zephonites (zē'fŏn-īts) [Heb. *Ṣephônî*] (Gen 46:16; Num 26:15). The difference in the spelling of the name may be due to the accidental dropping of the *yod* in Num 26:15.

Zephonites. *See* Zephon.

Zer (zûr). [Heb. *Ṣer,* possibly "rock."] A town in the territory of Naphtali (Jos 19:35); not identified.

Zerah (zē'rá), KJV twice **Zarah** (zā'rá), KJV of NT **Zara** (zā'rá). [Heb. *Zerach,* "dawning," "shining." The name is found in cuneiform records as one element of *Zarḥi-ilu.* Gr. *Zara.*]

1. A chieftain of Edom, descendant of Esau and his wife Bashemath (Gen 36: 13, 17; 1 Chr 1:37).

2. The father of a king of Edom (Gen 36:33; 1 Chr 1:44).

3. One of the twins borne to Judah by Tamar, and the ancestor of a tribal branch of Judah known as Zerahites (Gen 38:12-30; 46:12; Num 26:20; cf. Jos 7:1, 17).

4. A son of Simeon, and ancestor of a family called Zerahites (Num 26:13; 1 Chr 4:24). He is called Zohar in Gen 46:10; Ex 6:15.

5. A Levite of the family of Gershom,

and an ancestor of the musician Asaph (1 Chr 6:21, 41).

6. An "Ethiopian," or Cushite, who attacked King Asa of Judah with a great host, but was defeated in the battle at Mareshah (2 Chr 14:9-15; 16:8). This Zerah has not yet been identified. Some commentators tried to identify him with Pharaoh Osorkon I of the 22d dynasty of Egypt, but this identification is untenable and is no longer held. Since Cushites were found not only in eastern Africa but also in western Arabia (Gen 10:7; cf. 2 Chr 21:16), Zerah seems to have come from that area rather than from Egypt. In South Arabic inscriptions a personal name *Dariḥ,* the equivalent of Heb. *Zerach,* is attested.

Zerahiah (zĕr'á-hī'á). [Heb. *Zerachyah,* "Yahweh has dawned," or "Yahweh shines forth."]

1. A son of Uzzi in direct descent from Aaron, and one of the ancestors of Ezra (1 Chr 6:6, 51; Ezr 7:4).

2. A member of the family of Pahathmoab; his son Eliehoenai returned to Jerusalem under Ezra's leadership, accompanied by 200 male members of the family (Ezr 8:4).

Zerahite (zē'rá-hīt), KJV **Zarhite** (zär'hīt). [Heb. *Zarchî.*]

1. The descendants of Zerah, son of Judah (Num 26:20; Jos 7:17; 1 Chr 27: 11, 13). *See* Zerah, 3. They were also called *Ezrahites.

2. The descendants of Zerah, son of Simeon (Num 26:13). *See* Zerah, 4.

Zered (zē'rĕd), KJV once **Zared** (zā'rĕd). [Heb. *Zered.*] A river that formed the ancient boundary between Edom and Moab. The crossing of this river by the Israelites 38 years after they left Mount Sinai, marked the end of their wilderness wanderings (Num 21:12; Deut 2:13, 14). It has been identified with the *Wâdī el-Ḥesā,* the southernmost of the 4 main streams of Transjordan. After flowing through a deep canyon this wadi enters the Dead Sea near its southeastern corner (Map II, D-3).

Zereda. *See* Zeredah.

Zeredah (zĕr'ĕ-dá), KJV **Zereda** (zĕr'ĕ-dá) and **Zeredathah** (zĕr'ĕ-dā'thá). [Heb. *Ṣeredah.*] The birthplace of Jeroboam I, the 1st king of the northern kingdom of Israel (1 Ki 11:26). It has been identified with *Deir Ghassâneh,* about 11 mi. west of Shiloh. At that site a well, called *'Ain Ṣerêdah,* still bears the ancient name (Albright, *BASOR* 11 [1923], 5, 6).

The Zeredah (KJV "Zeredathah") of 2 Chr 4:17, in the Jordan Valley, where Solomon's metal work was done for the Temple, should probably be read *Zarethan.

Zeredathah. See Zeredah.

Zererah (zĕr'ĕ-ra), KJV **Zererath** (zĕr'ĕ-răth). [Heb. Ṣererah.] A town in the Jordan Valley (Jgs 7:22), usually considered to be the same as *Zarethan (1 Ki 4:12, RSV).

Zererath. See Zererah.

Zeresh (zē'rĕsh). [Heb. Zeresh, a Persian name of uncertain meaning.] The wife of Haman (Est 5:10, 14; 6:13).

Zereth (zē'rĕth). [Heb. Ṣereth, meaning uncertain.] A son of Ashhur by his wife Helah (1 Chr 4:5, 7).

Zereth-shahar (zē'rĕth-shā'här), KJV **Zareth-shahar** (zā'rĕth-shā'här). [Heb. Ṣereth hashshachar, "Sereth of the dawn."] A town in the territory of Reuben; not identified. It was situated on a hill in a valley, apparently the Jordan Valley (Jos 13:19).

Zeri (zē'rī), or **Izri** (ĭz'rī). [Heb. Ṣerî and Yiṣrî, meaning uncertain.] A Levite musician, a son of Jeduthun (1 Chr 25:3, 11). The difference in spelling may be the result of the accidental dropping of the initial yod, the smallest letter of the Hebrew alphabet, from Yiṣrî, "Izri."

Zeror (zē'rôr). [Heb. Ṣerôr, "bag," or "pebble."] A Benjamite, and an ancestor of Saul (1 Sa 9:1).

Zeruah (zĕ-rōō'a). [Heb. Ṣerû'ah, "skin-diseased."] The mother of King Jeroboam I (1 Ki 11:26).

Zerubbabel (zĕ-rŭb'a-bĕl), KJV of NT **Zorobabel** (zŏ-rŏb'a-bĕl). [Heb. and Aramaic Zerubbabel, from the Babylonian name Zêr-Babili, "offspring of Babylon"; Gr. Zorobabel.] A son of Pedaiah and grandson of King Jehoiachin of Judah (1 Chr 3:17-19). In all other texts where his "father" is mentioned he is called a son of Shealtiel, who was Pedaiah's brother (Ezr 3:2, 8; 5:2; Neh 12:1; Hag 1:1, 12, 14; 2:2, 23; Mt 1:12; Lk 3:27). This apparent discrepancy can best be solved by the assumption either (1) that one of the 2 brothers died childless, upon which his wife was taken by the remaining brother according to the law of levirate marriages (Deut 25:5-10), and Zerubbabel, the son of that union, bore the name of the 1st husband of the mother although the 2d was his real father; or (2) that at the real father's death the boy was brought up by his uncle and was counted as the "son" of his foster father (for an example of an adoptive son see Ex 2:10; cf. Gen 48:5).

When after the conquest of Babylon in 539 B.C., Cyrus, king of Persia, adopted the policy of allowing nations deported by the Babylonians to return to their homelands, he granted this privilege also to the Jews, and appointed a certain Sheshbazzar, a prince of Judah, as governor over the province of Judah. To him he entrusted the vessels of Solomon's Temple that Nebuchadnezzar had carried to Babylon, to be returned to Jerusalem (Ezr 1:8, 11; 5:14). The fact that all other records tell us that Zerubbabel was the leader of the returning exiles leads to the conclusion that Sheshbazzar and Zerubbabel were 2 names borne by the same individual (Ezr 2:1; Neh 7:7; 12:1).

Zerubbabel and Jeshua, the high priest, were the leaders of the large group of people—about 50,000—who returned from Babylon to their homeland. Ten other leaders aided them in their work (Ezr 2: 1, 2, 64, 65; Neh 7:7, 66, 67). After arriving in Jerusalem, probably in the summer of 536 B.C., Zerubbabel and other leaders reinstituted the daily sacrificial service; they set up the altar of burnt offering and celebrated the Feast of Tabernacles (Ezr 3:1-6). Having done this Zerubbabel began to make preparations for the rebuilding of the Temple, and laid its foundations in the following spring (vs 7-13). However, various hostile acts on the part of Judah's neighbors frustrated his efforts and halted the work until the 2d year of Darius (520/19 B.C.; ch 4:1-5, 24).

After Darius I overcame his adversaries and ascended the throne of Persia, stability returned to the empire and conditions became more favorable for a resumption of the work on the Temple. At the same time the prophets Haggai and Zechariah rose up and urged Zerubbabel and Jeshua to resume the work, promising them the help and blessing of God if they would obey (Hag 2:1-9; Zec 8:9; etc.). These leaders accepted the challenge, and with the help of a willing nation, the tolerant and helpful attitude of the Persian authorities, and the encouraging messages of the prophets of God, the work progressed and was brought to a successful completion in the 6th year of Darius (Ezr 5:1 to 6:15; Hag 1; 2; Zec 4: 6-10), in the spring of 515 B.C. Since the 2d Temple was built under the leadership of Zerubbabel it is frequently called "Zerubbabel's Temple."

Zerubbabel was the first governor of postexilic Judah. He was appointed *c.* 537 B.C., and was still in office in 515 B.C., at the time of the Temple dedication (Zec 4:9, 10; cf. Ezr 6:15). Thus he held office for more than 20 years. It was fitting that the 1st postexilic ruler of the country and the rebuilder of the Temple should be a representative of the Davidic royal line, and one who also was in the direct line of ancestry of Jesus Christ (Mt 1:6, 12, 13; Lk 3:27, 31).

Zeruiah (zĕr'ŏŏ-i'à). [Heb. *Ṣerûyah*, "perfumed with mastic."] One of David's sisters (1 Chr 2:16). However, according to 2 Sa 17:25, she was a sister of Abigail, a daughter of Nahash. She was thus a half sister either of Abigail or of David, for David's father was Jesse. She was the mother of Joab, Abishai, and Asahel, 3 great warriors of David's army (1 Sa 26: 6; 2 Sa 2:13, 18; 3:39; etc.).

Zetham (zē'thăm). [Heb. *Zetham,* probably "olive trees."] Either a son or a brother of Jehiel (or Jehieli), a Gershonite Levite (1 Chr 23:8; 26:22).

Zethan (zē'thăn). [Heb. *Zêthan,* "one working with olive trees."] A son of Bilhan, a Benjamite (1 Chr 7:10).

Zethar (zē'thär). [Heb. *Zethar,* a Persian name probably meaning "killer" or "victor."] One of the chamberlains at the court of Ahasuerus (Est 1:10).

Zeus (zōŏs), KJV **Jupiter** (jōŏ'pĭ-tẽr). [Gr. *Zeus.*] The highest god of the Greek pantheon; equated by the Romans to their chief god Jupiter. The main temple of Zeus was at Olympia in Elis, Greece. When Hellenistic culture and religion spread to the Eastern world, many temples were dedicated to Zeus in other lands (see fig. 377). In his efforts to Hellenize Judea, Antiochus IV Epiphanes dedicated the Temple at Jerusalem to the Olympian Zeus, and the Samaritans named their temple on Mount Gerizim for Zeus. In the Greco-Roman period the oasis city of Palmyra (Tadmor) worshiped as its patron god the Babylonian Bel, and Hellenized him into Zeus-Belos (see fig. 535; cf. fig. 473). Many other existing sanctuaries in Syria (see fig. 44) and Palestine adopted Zeus as their patron deity. The people of Lystra took Barnabas for Zeus and Paul for Hermes (the Roman god Mercury) when Paul healed a crippled man (Acts 14:12). In describing the incident Luke mentions a priest of Zeus,

and a temple "in front of the city" dedicated to him (Acts 14:13, RSV). Although the remains of ancient temples of Zeus have been discovered in many ruined cities of Asia Minor, the Zeus temple of Lystra is

535. Colonnade surrounding the court of the great temple of Bel (Aramaic, Baal) built in A.D. 32 at Palmyra (Tadmor). To the Hellenized Palmyrenes, Bel had become known as Zeus-Belos

not mentioned in extra-Biblical records, and its site has not yet been found. In Acts 19:35, KJV, "Jupiter" occurs in the phrase translating the Gr. *diopetēs,* which means literally "fallen from Zeus," or in a wider sense "fallen from heaven."

Zia (zī'à). [Heb. *Zîa',* probably "the trembler."] A descendant of Gad (1 Chr 5:13).

Ziba (zī'bà). [Heb. *Ṣiba',* meaning uncertain.] A servant of King Saul (2 Sa 9:2); a freedman, according to Josephus (*Ant.* vii. 5. 5). In David's time he had a large family of 15 sons and had 20 servants of his own (chs 9:10; 19:17). When David restored Saul's former property to Mephibosheth, Jonathan's son, he put Ziba in charge of it, requiring him to administer it with his sons and slaves (2 Sa 9: 7, 9-11).

When David was forced to flee from Jerusalem during the rebellion of Absalom, Ziba met him on the eastern slope of the Mount of Olives and presented him with 2 asses loaded with provisions. Upon inquiry he told the king that Mephibosheth had stayed behind hoping that Saul's former kingdom would now be restored to him. Hearing this, David immediately transferred Mephibosheth's estates to Ziba (2 Sa 16:1-4). When the king returned to Judah after victory over Absalom, Ziba, with his sons and slaves, was there to welcome him at the Jordan (ch 19:17), but this time David was also met by Mephibosheth, who proclaimed his loyalty to David by his dirty and unkempt appearance, a manifestation of mourning over the king's departure and humiliations. He claimed that he had wanted to accompany the king on his flight, and had ordered Ziba to saddle an ass for him, but that Ziba had disobeyed him, and in addition had slandered him before the king. Apparently David was not completely convinced of Mephibosheth's claims of loyalty, or he would have punished Ziba. He resolved the situation by ordering that half of the former estate of Saul should be returned to Mephibosheth, whereas the other half should remain in the hands of Ziba (vs 24-30).

Zibeon (zĭb′ĕ-ŭn). [Heb. *Ṣib'ôn*, "hyena," according to the meaning of a similar name in the cognate Arabic.]

1. A Hivite whose granddaughter became one of Esau's wives (Gen 36:2, 14).

2. A Horite chieftain, the son of Seir (Gen 36:20, 24, 29; 1 Chr 1:38, 40). Most commentators believe that 1 and 2 are identical and either emend the "Hivite" in Gen 36:2 to "Horite," or think that the Hivite Zibeon migrated to Mount Seir and thus became a Horite.

Zibia (zĭb′ĭ-à). [Heb. *Ṣibya'*, "gazelle."] A Benjamite, son of Shaharaim, and head of a tribal family (1 Chr 8:9).

Zibiah (zĭb′ĭ-à). [Heb. *Ṣibyah*, "female gazelle."] A woman of Beer-sheba, the mother of King Joash of Judah (2 Ki 12: 1; 2 Chr 24:1).

Zichri (zĭk′rī). [Heb. *Zikri*, "my remembrance," or if a shortened form of *Zecharyah*, "Zechariah," " (Yahweh) remembers me."]

1. A son of Izhar, a Kohathite Levite (Ex 6:21).

2. A son of Shimei, a Benjamite (1 Chr 8:19-21).

3. A son of Shashak, a Benjamite (1 Chr 8:23-25).

4. A son of Jeroham, a Benjamite (1 Chr 8:27).

5. A descendant of Asaph, a Levite (1 Chr 9:15); possibly identical with Zabdi, 4, and Zaccur, 4.

6. A Levite, descendant of Eliezer, Moses' son (1 Chr 26:25).

7. The father of Eliezer of the tribe of Reuben (1 Chr 27:16).

8. A man whose son Amasiah was a commander in the army of Jehoshaphat (2 Chr 17:16); possibly identical with Zichri, 9.

9. A man whose son Elishaphat, a commander in the army of Queen Athaliah of Judah, aided Jehoiada in overthrowing the queen (2 Chr 23:1-15); possibly identical with Zichri, 8.

10. A "mighty man of Ephraim" in the army of King Pekah of Israel. In a war against Judah he killed Maaseiah, a royal prince, Azrikam, the commander of the palace, and Elkanah, the highest officer of the government of King Asa of Judah (2 Chr 28:7).

11. A man whose son Joel was an overseer of the Benjamites under Nehemiah (Neh 11:9).

12. A postexilic priest, head of the family of Abijah in the days of the high priest Joiakim (Neh 12:17).

Ziddim (zĭd′ĭm). [Heb. *Ṣiddim*, "sides."] A fortified city in the territory of Naphtali (Jos 19:35). On the basis of the Talmud, it is usually identified with *Ḥaṭṭîn*, about 5½ mi. northwest of Tiberias.

Zidkijah. *See* Zedekiah, 6.

Zidon. *See* Sidon.

Zidonians. *See* Sidonians.

Zif. *See* Ziv.

Ziha (zī′hà). [Heb. *Ṣicha'*, meaning uncertain, although the name occurred among the Jews of Elephantine as *Ṣch'*, and in cuneiform records as *Ṣiḫâ*.]

1. The ancestral head of a family of Nethinim, or Temple servants, some of whom returned with Zerubbabel to Jerusalem (Ezr 2:43; Neh 7:46).

2. One of the overseers of a group of Nethinim in the time of Nehemiah (Neh 11:21).

Ziklag (zĭk′lăg). [Heb. *Ṣiqlag*.] A city in the southwestern territory of Judah (Jos 15: 31), assigned to the tribe of Simeon (Jos

19:5; 1 Chr 4:30). The Simeonites apparently did not occupy it for some time, for it was still in the hands of the Philistines in the time of Saul. King Achish of Gath gave it to David, when David became his vassal (1 Sa 27:6; 1 Chr 12:1-20). From that time on it was considered a property of the kings of Judah (1 Sa 27: 6). The Amalekites captured and burned it while David followed the Philistines during their last campaign against Saul. When David returned and found his residence city destroyed and the inhabitants taken away, he pursued the Amalekites and recovered the captives and the spoil (ch 30:1-20). It is mentioned again in the postexilic period, as a city of Judah (Neh 11:28). Ziklag has been identified with *Tell el-Khuweilfeh,* about 10 mi. north-northeast of Beer-sheba (Map VII, F-2), but this identification is not certain.

Zillah (zĭl′á). [Heb. *Ṣillah,* "shadow."] An antediluvian woman, one of Lamech's 2 wives, and the mother of Tubal-cain (Gen 4:19-23).

Zillethai (zĭl′ě-thī), KJV **Zilthai** (zĭl′thī). [Heb. *Ṣillethay,* possibly " (Yahweh is) a shadow (that is, protection)."]

1. A son of Shimei, a Benjamite (1 Chr 8:20).

2. A chief over 1,000 Manassites who joined David at Ziklag (1 Chr 12:20).

Zilpah (zĭl′pá). [Heb. *Zilpah,* probably "(woman with) a short nose."] A maidservant of Laban, given to his daughter Leah when she married Jacob (Gen 29:24). Following the example of her sister Rachel, Leah gave Zilpah to her husband as a concubine to obtain more sons through her. Zilpah became the mother of Gad and of Asher (chs 30:3, 9-13; 35:26; 46: 16-18).

Zilthai. See Zillethai.

Zimmah (zĭm′á). [Heb. *Zimmah,* probably "device." The name occurs in Akkadian as *Zimmâ.*]

1. A Gershonite Levite, an ancestor of Asaph (1 Chr 6:20, 42, 43).

2. A Gershonite Levite whose son Joah helped cleanse the Temple in the reign of Hezekiah (2 Chr 29:12). If Joah is taken to be a son in the sense of "descendant," this Zimmah might conceivably be identical with Zimmah, 1.

Zimran (zĭm′răn). [Heb. *Zimran,* meaning uncertain.] A son of Abraham by Keturah, and probably the ancestor of an Arabic tribe (Gen 25:2; 1 Chr 1:32). The name has been recognized in *Zambran,* a town west of Mecca (Ptol. vi. 7. 5) and in

Zamareni, an Arabian tribe (Pliny *Hist. Nat.* vi. 32).

Zimri (zĭm′rī). [Heb. *Zimri,* meaning uncertain. Some take it to mean "my praise"; others consider it an abbreviated form of *Zimriyah,* "my praise is Yahweh," a name found inscribed on an ancient Hebrew seal.]

1. A Judahite, son of Zerah, and ancestor of Achan (1 Chr 2:6), otherwise called Zabdi (Jos 7:1, 17, 18).

2. A Simeonite leader who brought a Midianite woman into his tent when the Israelites defected at Shittim. He was slain by Phinehas, a grandson of Aaron (Num 25:14; cf. vs 1-9).

3. A descendant of King Saul through Jonathan (1 Chr 8:36; 9:42).

4. The 5th king of the northern kingdom of Israel, who reigned only 7 days (c. 885 B.C.). He was commander of one half of King Elah's chariot forces when he plotted against the king and slew him at Tirzah. He usurped the throne and exterminated the whole house of his predecessor, thus fulfilling a prophecy made to Baasha by the prophet Jehu (1 Ki 16: 9-15). When the news of Zimri's acts reached the army that was besieging Gibbethon at that time, they proclaimed the commander, Omri, king by acclamation, and at once marched against Zimri at Tirzah. The city was taken after a short siege, and Zimri committed suicide by burning the palace over him (vs 15-18). Some commentators have identified him with Zimri, 3, thinking that he tried to bring the kingdom back to the house of Saul.

5. A people or country not yet identified (Jer 25:25). Some connect the name with Zimran, Abraham's eldest son by Keturah (Gen 25:1, 2), and seek the people or country in the Arabian Desert southeast of Palestine. Others consider Zimri a cryptic name for Elam.

Zin (zĭn). [Heb. *Ṣin.*] A wilderness, named perhaps after a locality by that name (Num 34:4; cf. Jos 15:3). The Wilderness of Zin (Map VI, G-2/3) lay beyond the southern boundary of Judah (Num 34:3; Jos 15:1), and had Kadesh-barnea within its confines (Num 20:1; 27:14; 33: 36; Deut 32:51). However, the southern part of the Wilderness of Zin, in which Kadesh was located (see Map V, B-6/7), was occasionally reckoned as part of the Wilderness of Paran (Num 13:26); consequently its southern extent cannot be ascertained exactly.

Zina. See Zizah.

Zion (zī'ŭn), KJV frequently **Sion** (sī'ŭn). [Heb. *Ṣiyôn,* meaning uncertain, possibly "sign post"; Gr. *Siōn.*] Originally the name of the southeastern hill of the later city of Jerusalem, the hill on which was situated the old Jebusite fortress that David conquered and renamed the City of David (2 Sa 5:7; 1 Ki 8:1). This hill lay between the valleys of Kidron and Tyropoeon, and south of the later Temple hill. When David transferred the ark into his new capital, Zion became the name especially of the place where God dwelt. Consequently the name Zion was used to refer to the northeastern hill after Solomon had built his Temple there and moved the ark into it (Is 2:3; 8:18; etc.). Occasionally, however, the name Zion seems to be applied to the whole city (chs 33: 20; 60:14), or even to the whole nation of Israel (Is 40:9; Zec 9:13). The city of Jerusalem with her inhabitants is also called the children, sons or daughters (daughter), of Zion (Ps 48:11, 12; Is 1:8; 10:32; Joel 2:23; Zec 9:13; etc.). The church of the NT, the legitimate successor of the OT people of God, is described as having come to "mount Sion" (Heb 12:22, 23; cf. 1 Pe 2:5, 6), and finally this name is given to the place on which John saw the 144,000 stand with the "Lamb" (Rev 14:1).

Unfortunately the name Zion has been attributed erroneously to the southwestern hill of Jerusalem ("Upper City," Map XVIII) since the Middle Ages. This application of the name must be attributed to medieval tradition. The Jews based this on Josephus' description of the city walls, and the Christians on the location of the church Sancta Sion, which was built on the traditional site of the Cenaculum, the room of Christ's Last Supper, and which therefore remained the center of Christian activities in Jerusalem for a long time. The excavations of the last 75 years have proved, however, that the City of David was confined to the southeastern hill, and that the southwestern hill apparently was not part of the city until Hellenistic times. See fig. 230, hill at left. For the original Zion *see* David, City of; see figs. 259, 260, 278.

Zior (zī'ôr). [Heb. *Ṣi'or,* "little."] A town in the hill country of Judah, near Hebron (Jos 15:54), tentatively identified with the village of *Sa'îr,* about 5 mi. northeast of Hebron (Abel, *Géographie* II, 464).

Ziph (zīf). [Heb. *Ẓiph.* The term occurs as a place name on inscribed ancient jar handles found in Palestine.]

1. A city in the hill country of Judah (Jos 15:55), apparently settled by descendants of Caleb, son of Hezron (1 Chr 2:42). It was situated near a wilderness (1 Sa 23:14, 15). David took refuge there when fleeing from Saul, but the people of Ziph, probably fearing that they would share the fate of the priests at Nob, betrayed him to Saul (chs 23:14, 15, 19-24; 26:1, 2). Rehoboam fortified the city (2 Chr 11:8). It has been identified with *Tell Zif,* about 4 mi. southeast of Hebron (Map VI, F-3).

2. A town in the extreme south of Judah (Jos 15:24), identified with *ez-Zeifeh,* 15 mi. west of the southwestern tip of the Dead Sea.

3. A Judahite (1 Chr 4:16).

Ziphah (zī'fà). [Heb. *Ẓiphah.* The name occurs in ancient South Arabic as *Zypt.*] A son of Jehallelel of Judah (1 Chr 4:16).

Ziphims. *See* Ziphites.

Ziphion. *See* Zephon.

Ziphites (zīf'īts), KJV once **Ziphims** (zīf'ĭmz). [Heb. *Ziphîm.*] Natives or inhabitants of Ziph, 1 (1 Sa 23:19; 26:1; Ps 54, title).

Ziphron (zīf'rŏn). [Heb. *Ziphrôn.*] A place on the northern border of the Promised Land (Num 34:9); not identified with certainty.

Zippor (zīp'ôr). [Heb. *Ṣippôr,* "bird."] The name is attested in Egyptian as *Ḏpwr.*] The father of King Balak of Moab (Num 22:2, 4, 10, 16; Jos 24:9; Jgs 11:25).

Zipporah (zī-pō'rà). [Heb. *Ṣipporah,* "female bird." The name is attested in Palmyrene as *Ṣpr'.*] Daughter of Jethro, priest of Midian, and wife of Moses (Ex 2:21; 3: 1). She traveled with Moses toward Egypt after he had received his commission to deliver Israel, and on the way circumcised her son (ch 4:18-26). Some time before Moses' negotiations with Pharaoh concerning the Israelites' departure from Egypt, she and her 2 sons were evidently sent away to her father for their safety (ch 18:2, 3). After the departure of Israel from Egypt, Jethro brought them back to Moses while the Israelites encamped at "the mountain of God" (ch 18:1-6, RSV). In Num 12:1, 2, Moses' wife is called a "Cushite" woman (*see* Ethiopia). This appellation was not unlikely to be applied to a Midianite, for Midian was a part of northwestern Arabia where some Cushite tribes lived. Then again this appellation might have been given to her because her complexion may have been darker than that of most Israelites. Some commentators think that Num 12:1, 2 does not refer to Zipporah but to another wife of Moses, but there is no evidence whatever that Moses had more than one wife.

Zithri. *See* Sithri.

Ziv (zĭv), KJV **Zif** (zĭf). [Heb. *Ziw,* Phoenician *Zyb.*] The 2d month of the Hebrew religious year (1 Ki 6:1, 37), called Iyyar after the Babylonian exile. It began at the new moon of April or May, and was considered the "month of blossoms." *See* Year.

Ziz (zĭz). [Heb. *Ṣîṣ,* "blossom," or "ornament."] An "ascent" leading toward the wilderness of Tekoa (2 Chr 20:16, 20) by which the Moabites, Ammonites, and Meunites advanced from En-gedi (vs 1, 2, RSV) to attack Judah in the reign of Jehoshaphat. It has been identified with *Wâdî Ḥaṣâṣah,* leading from Tekoa toward the Dead Sea, reaching it about 6 mi. north of En-gedi.

Ziza (zī′zȧ). [Heb. *Zizaʾ,* meaning uncertain.]
1. Son of Shiphi, a Simeonite prince (1 Chr 4:37, 38).
2. A son of Rehoboam by Maacah (2 Chr 11:20).

Zizah (zī′zȧ). [Heb. *Zizah,* meaning uncertain.] A son of Shimei, and a descendant of Gershom (1 Chr 23:11), called Zina (zī′nȧ) [Heb. *Zinaʾ*] in v 10.

Zoan (zō′ăn). [Heb. *Ṣoʿan;* Egyptian hieroglyphs *Ḏʿnt;* cuneiform records *Ṣaʾanu* and *Ṣiʾinu;* Gr. *Tanis.*] An ancient Egyptian city in the eastern Delta, built 7 years later than Hebrón in Palestine (Num 13:22), better known by its Greek name Tanis. It appears under the name Avaris in the records of the 6th Egyptian dynasty. In the 12th dynasty Avaris was made a fortress guarding the northeastern approach to Egypt. The Hyksos made it their capital and the experiences of Joseph probably took place there. It remained in ruins for some time after the expulsion of the Hyksos, but underwent another period of greatness under Ramses II, who made it a center of Seth worship, and established it as his capital city, calling it after himself. It is mentioned by this name (with the variant spelling Raamses) in Ex 1:11 as one of the cities in which the Israelites were employed as slave laborers. (For the explanation that this was a later modernization of the name in this text and others, *see* Rameses.) Later, it was given the name Zoan. Ps 78:12, 43 indicates that the area around Zoan was the center of the miracles wrought by Moses. The Pharaoh of his time may have deemed it wise to stay close to Goshen, the home of the Israelites, during this period of crisis, although Zoan was not the capital city under the 18th dynasty. The city was later the capital of the 21st and 22d dynasty kings (*c.* 1085 - *c.* 750 B.C.), from which period some undisturbed tombs have recently been discovered in the ruins of Zoan. It was still an important city in the 8th cent., when Isaiah accused the princes of Zoan and Memphis (Noph) of being fools and giving foolish counsel to Pharaoh (Is 19:11, 13; cf. also ch 30:4). The city was soon afterward captured by the Assyrians under Ashurbanipal (*ANET* 294b). It still existed as an important city 100 years later, in the days of Ezekiel's exile (Eze 30:14), who predicted its destruction. It is now a ruined site called *Ṣân el-Ḥagar* (Map V, B-3). Excavations intermittently carried out there during the last cent. by A. Mariette and W. M. Fl. Petrie, and recently by P. Montet, have been very successful, despite the city's location in the humid Delta where the chemically active soil has prevented any perishable material from escaping destruction. Hyksos statues, many remains of buildings erected by Ramses II, and untouched royal tombs have been discovered. A very interesting but somewhat

536. Excavating the Stele of the Year 400 at Biblical Zoan, now *Ṣân el-Ḥagar*

enigmatic inscription on what is called Stele of the Year 400, erected about the time of the accession of Ramses I (*c.* 1320 B.C.), commemorates the 400th year reckoned either from the founding of the city under the Hyksos or from another important event, now unknown, in its history (fig. 536).

Lit.: P. Montet, *Le drame d'Avaris* (Paris, 1940); Montet, *Douze années de fouilles dans une capitale oubliée du Delta égyptien* (Paris, 1942); Montet, *Les énigmes de Tanis* (Paris, 1952).

Zoar (zō'ẽr). [Heb. *Ṣo'ar*, "small."] A city, also known as Bela, apparently the smallest of the 5 cities of the valley of Siddim (Gen 13:10; 14:2, 8; 19:20, 22). When Sodom and its sister cities were destroyed, Lot interceded for Zoar and fled to it, living with his daughters in a cave near Zoar (ch 19:20-23, 30). In the description of the land of Canaan shown to Moses on Mount Nebo, Zoar is apparently the most southern city of the land, as Dan, which lay north of Lake Huleh, was the most northern one (Deut 34:1-3). From Is 15:5 and Jer 48:34 it is reasonable to assume that it lay in the land of Moab. Josephus placed it in Arabia (*War* iv. 8. 4), and Eusebius located the Dead Sea between "Zoara" and Jericho (*Onomasticon* 261). On the mosaic map of Palestine at Medeba, dating from about the 6th cent. A.D., Zoar is placed at the southeastern corner of the Dead Sea. One Arab writer of the Middle Ages located it in the land of Edom and another placed it near the southern end of the Dead Sea. It is assumed by most authorities that the site is now covered by the rising waters of the southern part of the Dead Sea. Map VI, F-3 shows Zoar at a site known as Zoara in the time of Josephus (see Map XVI, F-3); the name may have been transferred to a later town founded in the vicinity of the place where the original Zoar was believed to have been.

Zoba. *See* Aram 5, e.

Zobah. *See* Aram 5, e.

Zobebah (zō-bē'bȧ). [Heb. *Ṣobebah*, meaning uncertain.] A son of Koz of Judah (1 Chr 4:8).

Zohar (zō'här). [Heb. *Ṣochar*, "yellowish-red." The name occurs in South Arabic inscriptions.]

1. A Hittite whose son Ephron sold the cave of Machpelah to Abraham (Gen 23:8; 25:8, 9).

2. A son of Simeon and ancestral head of a tribal family (Gen 46:10; Ex 6:15). The spelling Zerah in Num 26:13 and 1 Chr 4:24 is apparently due to a transposition of the Hebrew letters *ch* and *r*. *See* Zerah, 4.

Zoheleth (zō'hĕ-lĕth). [Heb. *Zocheleth,* formerly interpreted to mean "serpent," now "gliding."] The name of a stone in the vicinity of En-rogel at the mouth of the Hinnom Valley near which Adonijah offered a sacrifice when he planned to make himself king (1 Ki 1:9, KJV). The RSV designates it "Serpent's Stone." The stone, which has not been identified with any known locality, may have been an old Jebusite place of sacrifice.

Zoheth (zō'hĕth). [Heb. *Zôcheth,* meaning uncertain.] A son of Ishi of Judah (1 Chr 4:20).

Zophah (zō'fȧ). [Heb. *Ṣôphach,* probably "(bellied) jar."] A son of Heler (KJV "Helem"), of the tribe of Asher (1 Chr 7:35, 36).

Zophai. *See* Zuph, 1.

Zophar (zō'fẽr). [Heb. *Ṣôphar,* probably "chirper," or "twitter."] One of Job's friends, a Naamathite (Job 2:11; 11:1; 20:1; 42:9).

Zophim (zō'fĭm). [Heb. *Ṣophim,* "watchmen."] A field on Mount Pisgah to which Balak took Balaam, and from which one of Balaam's oracles was pronounced (Num 23:14); not identified with certainty.

Zorah (zō'rȧ), KJV once **Zoreah** (zō'rĕ-ȧ), once **Zareah** (zā'rĕ-ȧ). [Heb. *Ṣor'ah,* "disease."] A city mentioned in the *Amarna Letters as *Ṣarḥa.* It lay in the Shephelah of Judah (Jos 15:33), but was inhabited by Danites (ch 19:41). Samson's parents lived there, and he was born there (Jgs 13:2) and later buried in its vicinity (ch 16:31). Some of the 5 spies who went out in search of new land for Dan came from Zorah, also some of the Danites who, after the favorable report of the spies, migrated to the north and settled at Laish, subsequently called Dan (ch 18:2, 8, 11, 27-29). Zorah was fortified by Rehoboam (2 Chr 11:10), and is mentioned among the places inhabited by Judahites in the postexilic period (Neh 11:29). It has been identified with *Ṣar'ah,* about 15 mi. west of Jerusalem (Map VI, E-2), on the northern side of the *Wâdī eṣ-Ṣarâr,* the ancient Valley of Sorek.

Zorathite (zō'răth-īt), KJV once **Zareathite** (zā'rĕ-ăth-īt). [Heb. *Ṣor'athi.*] A native or inhabitant of Zorah (1 Chr 2:53; 4:2).

Zoreah. *See* Zorah.

Zorite (zō'rīt). [Heb. *Ṣor'i.*] A native or inhabitant probably of Zorah or of some unidentified place (1 Chr 2:54).

Zorobabel. *See* Zerubbabel.

Zuar (zū'ẽr). [Heb. *Ṣû'ar,* "small."] Father of Nethaneel, a man of Issachar (Num 1:8).

Nethaneel was the leader of his tribe during the wilderness wanderings (Num 2:5; 7:18, 23; 10:15).

Zuph (zŭf). [Heb. *Ṣûph,* "honeycomb."]

1. Son of Elkanah, a Kohathite Levite, and ancestor of Samuel the prophet (1 Sa 1:1; 1 Chr 6:35), called Zophai (zō'fī) [Heb. *Ṣôphay*] in 1 Chr 6:26.

2. An area beyond the territory of Benjamin, where Saul sought the lost asses of his father (1 Sa 9:5). It probably received its name from the Zuphites living there. It must be sought near Ramathaim-zophim, but its exact location has not been ascertained.

Zur (zûr). [Heb. *Ṣûr,* "rock."]

1. A Midianite chieftain, whose daughter Cozbi seduced a Hebrew man to licentious idolatry and was consequently slain by Phinehas (Num 25:15; cf. v 6). Zur, being probably an ally or vassal of Sihon, the Amorite king of Heshbon, was killed in a war waged by Moses against the Midianites for their hostility toward Israel (Num 25:7, 8, 15, 18; 31:8; Jos 13:21).

2. A son of Jeiel, a Benjamite (1 Chr 8:29, 30; 9:35, 36).

Zuriel (zū'rĭ-ĕl). [Heb. *Ṣûri'el,* "God is my rock." The name occurs in the Mari texts as *Ṣura-ilu.*] The son of Abihail, and chief over the tribal family of the Merarite Levites (Num 3:35).

Zurishaddai (zū'rĭ-shăd'ī). [Heb. *Ṣûrishadday,* "Shaddai (the Almighty) is my rock."] A Simeonite whose son, Shelumiel, was the leader of his tribe during the wilderness wanderings (Num 1:6; 2:12; 7:36, 41; 10:19).

Zuzim (zū'zĭm), KJV **Zuzims** (zū'zĭmz). [Heb. *Zûzîm.*] A people in Transjordan who occupied an area called Ham. They were defeated by Chedorlaomer and his confederates in the time of Abraham (Gen 14:5). Nothing is known about these people from any other source, but it is possible that they are the Rephaim whom the Ammonites replaced, and who were called by the latter the Zamzummins (Deut 2:20).

Zuzims. *See* Zuzim.

ATLAS

Index to Maps

NOTE: The index below is for the color maps that follow, though maps appearing in the body of this dictionary are also included, but by title only. The place names are indexed exactly as they appear on the maps, except that italics and diacritical marks have been ignored. Inasmuch as the color maps were purchased from another publisher, there are, in some cases, differences between the content of the color maps and that of the Dictionary—differences in spelling, transliteration, dates appearing under some map titles, or identification of ancient sites. The Dictionary article will often explain these differences when referring to the maps, and thus supplement this index as a guide to the use of the maps.

In certain cases, where the identification of a Biblical site is uncertain or subject to a difference of scholarly opinion, the identification made on these maps may differ from that adopted for the Dictionary article. Especially is this true of certain Exodus sites, such as Baal-zephon and the Wilderness of Sin, which are located on Map V on the basis of theories of the Exodus that differ from the one presented in this dictionary. In such cases the Dictionary article dealing with these geographical sites should be consulted.

Each place name in the index is followed by one or more map references (such as XIV, A-5) or by a cross reference to the heading under which these map references will be found. For example, in the first column below, the heading "Acre" is followed by the cross reference: "See under Acco." An analysis of the entry "Acco" shows that in addition to the map references for Acco, two names with their map references are indented below it, namely "Acre" and "Ptolemais." This type of grouping signifies that these three names refer to the same place. Sometimes these indented names show simply variations in spelling. In the case of Acco the city had different names at different times, that is, it was called Acco in OT times, Ptolemais in NT times, and has been called Acre since the Crusades. Certain anachronisms are found because for convenience of printing an almost identical set of place names was used for Maps VI-X; the same holds true for Maps XIV-XVI. However, in general the place names are correct for the periods indicated in the respective map titles.

Aaqraba: XXII, A-4
Abana R.: VI-X, A-5; XIV-XVI, B-5
Abar Nahara: XII, D-6
Abasan: XXII, C-2
Abdeh: V, B-6
Abel-beth-maacah: VI-X, B-4
Abel-Keramim: VI-X, E-4
Abel-meholah: VI-X, D-4
Abel-shittim: V, A-7; VI-X, E-4
Abila (in northern Transjordan): XIV-XVI, C-4
Abila (in the Anti-Lebanon): XIV-XVI, A-5
Abila (near the lower Jordan): XIV-XVI, E-4
Abilene: XIV-XVI, A-4
Abu Habba. See under Sippar
Abu Shahrein. See under Eridu
Abu Simbel: IV, C-4
Abu Zeneimeh: V, C-4
Abukir: V, A-1
Abusir: V, C-3
Abydos: XI, D-3
Abydus: XIII, A-2
Abyssinia: IV, E-6
Acco: II, B-3; III, C-3; VI-X, C-2; XI, C-3; XII, D-5; XIV-XVI, C-3
Acre: XXII, B-3
Ptolemais: XIII-XVI, C-3; XX, C-5
Achaea: XII, C-3
Achaia: XIX, D-10; XX, B-3
Achshaph: VI-X, C-3
Achzib: III, inset; VI-X, B-3; XI, C-4; XIV-XVI, B-3
Ekdippa: XIV-XVI, B-3
Acre. See under Acco
Acre, Bay of: XXII, B-2
Actium: XIX, D-10; XX, B-3
Adana: XI, B-4
Aden: IV, D-6
Aden, Gulf of: IV, D-6
Adhem, el, R.: XI, C-5
Adora. See under Adoraim

Adoraim: VI, VIII-X, E-2; VII, E-3
Adora: XIV-XVI, F-3
Dura: XXII, C-3
Adramyttium: XX, B-4
Adria, Sea of: XX, B-2
Adriatic Sea: XIX, C-8; XX, A-2
Adullam: VI, VIII-X, E-3; VII, E-2
Aegean Sea: XI, XIII, B-1; XIX, D-10; XX, B-3
Aegyptus. See under Egypt
Aelana: XIX, F-13
Elath (modern): XXII, E-2
Aenon: XIV-XVI, D-3
Aenus: XIII, A-2
Aenus R.: XIX, B-8
Aetna, Mt.: XX, B-1
Aetolia: XII, C-3; XX, B-3
Affuleh: XXI, inset
Afula: XXI, B-3
Africa (Roman province): XIX, E-8
Afula. See under Affuleh
Agerud. XXII, D-2
Agrigentum: XIX, D-8; XX, B-1
Agrippias. See under Anthedon
Ahhiyawa: III, B-2
Ahlab: VI-X, B-3
Ahmetha: XII, D-8
Ecbatana: III, XI, XIII, C-6; XII, D-8
Hamadan: III, XI, C-6
Ai: VI-X, E-3
et Tell: XXI, inset
Aijalon: III, inset; VI, E-2; VII-X, E-3
Aila: V, C-7; XIII, D-3
Ain el Akhdar: V, D-6
Ain el Weibeh. See under Oboth
Ain Feshkha: XIV-XVI, E-3
Ain Hawwarah. See under Marah
Ain Hudherah. See under Hazeroth
Ain Karim: XIV-XVI, E-3
Ain Qadeis: XXII, D-2
Ain Qedeis: V, B-6
Ain Quedeirat. See under Kadesh-barnea
Aina, el: XXII, D-3

Aiy. See under Iye-Abarim
Ajlun (district): I, B-2
Ajlun (town): XXII, B-3
Akkad: III, C-6
Akkaron. See under Ekron
Akrabatta: XIV-XVI, D-3
Aqraba XXII, B-3
Akrabbim, Ascent of: VI-X, G-3
Maale Aqrabim (Scorpion Pass): XXII, D-3
Aksum: IV, D-5
Alaca Huyuk: III, XXI, A-4
Alalakh: III, B-4
Tell Atshana: XXI, B-4
Alarodians: XII, C-7
Alashia. See under Cyprus
Albis R.: XIX, A-8
Aleppo. See under Khalab
Alexandria (in Egypt): V, A-1; XIII, C-2; XIX, E-11; XX, C-4
Alexandria (in Syria): XIII, B-4; XX, B-6
Alexandrium: XIV-XVI, D-3
Alishar. See under Alishar Huyuk
Alishar Huyuk: XXI, B-4
Alishar: III, B-4
Almon: VI-X, E-3
Amalekites: V, B-6
Amanus Mts.: XX, B-6
Amardi: XIII, B-6
Amarna, Tell el. See under Ekhet Aton
Amasia: XII, B-6; XIX, C-13; XX, A-6
Amastris: XIX, C-12
Amathus: XIV-XVI, D-4
Amida: XII, C-7; XIII, B-5; XIX, D-14
Amisia R.: XIX, A-7
Amisus: XIII, A-4; XIX, C-13; XX, A-6
Amman. See under Rabbath Ammon
Ammon: I, B-3; VI-X, D-5; XI, C-4

1189

Danuvius R. *See under* Danube R.
Daphnae. *See under* Tahpanhes
Dascylium: XII, B-5
Dead Sea: I, C-2; II, C-3; III, C-4
and inset; V, A-7; VI-X, XIV-XVI, E-3; XIII, C-4; XXII, C-3
Asphalt Lake: VI-X, XIV-XVI, F-3
Salt Sea: V, A-7
Debir: V, A-7; VI-X, F-2; VI-X, F-3
Tell Beit Mirsim: XXI, inset
Decapolis: XV, XVI, C-4
Dedan: IV, C-5; XI, XIII, D-4
el Ela: IV, C-5; XI, XIII, D-4
Deir Abu Said: XXII, B-3
Deir el Balah: XXII, C-2
Delos: XX, B-4
Delphi: XII, C-3; XX, B-3
Demavend, Mt.: XI, B-7
Der: III, C-5
Dera. *See under* Edrei
Derbe: XX, B-5
Derbent: XII, B-8
Dhahab: V, D-6
Dhahiriya: XXII, C-2
Dhalal, Jebel: V, D-5
Dhiban. *See under* Dibon
Dibon: VI-X, XIV-XVI, E-4; XI, C-4
Dhiban: XXI, inset; XXII, C-3
Diklah: IV, C-6
Dilbat: XI, C-5
Dilmun: III, D-7
Bahrain: III, XI, XXI, D-7; IV, C-7
Tylos Island: XII, E-9
Dion (in Macedonia): XX, A-3
Dion (in Transjordan): XIII, C-4; XIV-XVI, C-5
Diospolis. *See under* Lod
Diyala R.: XI, XIII, C-6
Dizful: III, XI, C-6
Dodanim: IV, B-4
Rodanim: IV, B-4
Dok: XIV-XVI, E-3
Dophkah: V, C-5
Dor: I, B-1; III, XI, C-3 and inset; XII, D-5
Dora: XIV-XVI, C-2
et Tanturah: XXI, inset
Dora. *See under* Dor
Dorylaeum: XIII, B-2; XIX, D-11; XX, B-4
Dothan: VI-X, XIV-XVI, D-3
Tell Dothan: XXI, inset
Drangiana: XII, D-11
Sakastan: XII, D-11
Sistan: XII, D-11
Zaranga: XII, D-11
Dravus R.: XIX, B-9
Drilon R.: XIX, C-10
Dumah: XI, D-4
ej-Jauf: XI, D-4
Dur Kurigalzu: III, C-5
Aqarquf: III, XXI, C-5
Dura. *See under* Adoraim
Dura-Europus: XIII, C-5
Durius R.: XIX, C-4
Durocortorum: XIX, B-6
Dur-Sargon: XI, B-5
Khorsabad: XI, XXI, B-5
Dyrr(h)achium: XIX, C-9; XX, A-2

Ebal, Mt.: II, B-3; VI-X, XIV-XVI, D-3
Eber: IV, B-5
Eburacum: XIX, A-5
Ecbatana. *See under* Ahmetha
Edessa: XII, C-6; XIII, B-4; XIX, D-13
Urhai: XII, C-6
Edfu: XI, E-3
Edom: I, D-2; V, B-7; VI-X, G-4; XI, C-4
Seir, Mt.: II, C-3; V, B-7
Edrei: VI-X, C-5
Dera: VI-X, C-5; XXII, B-4
Eglon: VI-X, E-2
Tell el Hesi: XXI, inset
Egnatian Way: XX, A-3
Egra: XIII, D-4

Egypt: V, B-2; XI, XIII, D-3; XII, E-5; XX, D-5; XXI, C-2; XXII, D-1
Aegyptus: XIX, F-12
Magan: III, D-3
Misru: III, D-3
Mizraim: IV, C-5
Mudraya: XII, E-5
Ein Gev: XXII, B-3
Ein Harod: XXII, B-3
Ein Netafim: XXII, E-2
ej. *See* next part of name, under J
Ekallate: III, B-5
Ekdippa. *See under* Achzib
Ekhet Aton: III, D-3; V, E-3
Tell el Amarna: III, XI, D-3; V, E-3
Ekron: VI-X, XIV-XVI, E-2; XI, C-4
Akkaron: XIV, E-2
el. *See* next part of name
Ela, el. *See under* Dedan
Elam: III, XI, C-6; IV, B-6
Elymais: XIII, C-6
Khuzistan: XII, D-8
Susiana: XII, D-8; XIII, C-6
Uwaga: XII, D-8
Elath (ancient): V, C-7; XII, E-6
Aqaba(h): V, C-7; XXII, E-3
Elath (modern). *See under* Aelana
Elburz Mts.: XI, B-7
Elealeh: VI-X, E-4
Elephantine: IV, inset; XI, E-3
Yeb: XI, E-3
Eleutheropolis: XIV-XVI, E-2
Beit Guvrin: XXII, C-2
Beit Jibrin: I, C-1
Beth Gubrin: XIV-XVI, E-2
Elim: V, C-4
Elisha: IV, B-3
Eltekeh: VI-X, E-2
Elusa: XIV-XVI, F-2
Elymais. *See under* Elam
Emerita Augusta: XIX, D-4
Emesa: XIII, C-4; XX, C-6
Homs: XI, C-4; XX, C-6
Emmaus: XIV-XVI, E-2
Nicopolis: XIV-XVI, E-2
en Nakhl. *See* Qalat en Nakhl
En Noweibeh: V, D-6
En-dor: VI-X, C-3
En-gannim: VI-X, D-3
En-gedi: V, A-7; VI-X, XIV-XVI, F-3
en-Nuqra: I, B-3
Ephah: XI, D-4
Ephesus: XI, XIII, XXI, B-2; XII, C-4; XIX, D-11; XX, B-4
Ephraim (in Ephraim): VI-X, D-3; XIV-XVI, E-3
Aphairema: XIV, E-3
Ephron: VI-X, D-3
et Taiyiba: XXII, C-3
Ophrah: VI-X, E-3
Ephraim (in Transjordan): VI-X, C-4
Ephron: VI-X, C-4
Ephraim (tribe): I, B-2; VI, D-3
Ephron (in Ephraim). *See under* Ephraim (in Ephraim)
Ephron (in Transjordan). *See under* Ephraim (in Transjordan)
Epidaurum: XIX, C-9
Epirus: XII, B-2; XIX, D-10; XX, A-3
er. *See* following part of name
Erech: III, XI, XIII, C-6; IV, B-6
Orchöe: XII, D-8; XIII, C-5
Uruk: XI, C-5; XII, D-8
Warka: XI, XXI, C-6
Eridu: III, XI, C-6
Abu Shahrein: XXI, C-6
Eritrea: IV, D-6
Erivan: XI, A-5
Erweis el Ebeirig: V, D-6
Erythraean Sea: XII, F-11
Erzerum: XI, A-5
es. *See* following part of name
Esdraelon, Plain of: I, B-2; II, B-3; XIV-XVI, C-3
Eshnunna: III, C-6
Tell Asmar: XXI, C-6
Eshtaol: VI, VIII-X, E-3; VII, E-2
Eshtemoa: VI-X, F-3

Essebon. *See under* Heshbon.
Etam: V, A-6; VI-X, E-3
Eth Thuwaneh: V, B-7
Etham: V, B-4 (see note, p. 1189)
el Kantara: III, C-3
Sile: V, B-4
Tr: III, C-3; V, B-4
Ethiopia: IV, D-5 and inset; XII, F-5; XIII, E-3
Cush: IV, C-5; XI, E-3; XII, F-5
Kusiya: XII, F-5
Meluhha: III, XI, E-3
Nubia: III, E-3
"Ethiopians": XII, E-10
Etruscan Sea: XX, B-1
Euboea: XX, B-3
Eulaeus R. *See under* Ulai R.
Eumenia: XX, B-4
Euphrates R.: III, XI, XIII, XXI, C-5; IV, B-6; XII, D-7; XIX, E-14
Ufratu: XII, D-7
Euphrates, Road to the: XX, B-5
Europe: IV, inset
Europus: XIII, B-7
Exodus, lands of (13th cent. B.C.): V
Ezion-geber: II, E-2; V, C-6; XI, D-4
Tell el Kheleifeh: XXI, D-4; V, C-6
Ezraa: XXII, B-4

Fadak: XI, D-5
Fair Havens: XX, C-3
Faiyum: V, C-2
Fandaqumiya: XXII, B-3
Faqus: V, B-3
Fara: XXI, C-6
Faran, Jebel. *See under* Paran, Mt.
Feinan. *See under* Punon
Fiq: XXII, B-3
Formiae: XX, A-1
Forum of Appius: XX, A-1
Frank Mt. *See under* Herodium
Frisii: XIX, A-7
Fundi: XX, A-1

Gaash, Mt.: VI-X, E-3
Gaba: XIV-XVI, C-3
Gabae: XII, D-9
Gabai: XIII, C-7 (is not Aspadana)
Gabai. *See under* Gabae
Gad: VI, D-4
Gadara: XIII-XVI, C-4
Gades: XIX, D-4
Gador: XIV-XVI, D-4
Galatia: XIII, B-3; XIX, C-12; XX, B-5
Galatian Pontus: XX, A-6
Galilee: I, A-2 and B-2; XIV-XVI, C-3; XX, C-6; XXII, B-3
Galilee, Sea of: I, B-2; II, B-3; III, inset; VI-X, XIV-XVI, C-4; XXII, B-3
Gallaecia et Asturia: XIX, C-4
Gallia: XIX, B-6
Gamala: XIV-XVI, C-4
Gandara: XII, D-13
Gangra: XI, A-3; XX, A-5
Gari: III, C-4
Gath: VI-X, E-2
Gath-heper: VI-X, C-3
Gaudos: XX, B-1
Gaugamela: XII, C-7
Gaulanitis: XIV-XVI, C-4
Jaulan: I, B-2
Gaza: I, C-1; II, C-2; III, inset; V, A-6; VI-X, XIV-XVI, E-1; XI, XIII, C-3; XII, D-5; XIX, E-12; XX, C-5; XXII, C-2
Ghazzeh: XXI, inset
Gaza Area: XXII, C-2
Geba: VI-X, E-3
Gebel (mountain). *See* other part of name
Gedrosia: XII, E-11
Maka: XII, E-11
Genua: XIX, C-7
Geraia: R. XXII, D-2
Gerar: VI-X, F-2

Gerasa: XIV-XVI, D-4
  Jerash: I, B-3; VI-X, D-4; XXI, C-4; XXII, B-3
Gerizim, Mt.: II, B-3; VI-X, XIV-XVI, D-3
Germania (non-Roman): XIX, A-8
Germania (Roman): XIX, A-6
Gerrha: XI, D-6; XII, E-8; XIII, D-6
Gesher Haziv: XXII, A-2
Geshur: VI-X, C-4
Gezer: III, inset; VI-X, XIV-XVI, E-2
Ghabia, el, R.: XXII, E-1
Ghadyan, el: V, C-7
Ghazna: XII, D-12
Ghazzeh. See under Gaza
Ghor, el: I, B-2; II, B-3
Gibbethon: VI-X, E-2
Gibeah: VI-X, E-3
  Tell el Ful: XXI, inset
Gibeon: VI-X, E-3
  ej Jib: XXI, inset
Gilboa, Mt.: XIV-XVI, D-3
Gilead (city): VI-X, E-4
Gilead (district): I, B-2; VI-X, D-4; XI, C-4
Gilgal: VI-X, E-4
Gilgal-goiim: VI-X, D-2
Gimirrai: XI, B-3
Ginesar: I, B-2
Ginnaia: XIV-XVI, D-3
Girgashites: IV, B-5
Girsu: III, C-6
Gischala: XIV-XVI, B-3
  Gush Khalab: XIV-XVI, B-3
Gitta: XIV-XVI, D-3
Gizeh: V, C-3
Golan: VI-X, C-4
Gomer: IV, A-5
Gophna. See under Gophnah
Gophnah: VI-X, E-3
  Gophna: XIV-XVI, E-3
Gordion: XI, B-3; XIII, B-3
  Gordium: XII, C-5; XIII, B-3
Gordium. See under Gordion
Gordyene: XII, C-7; XIX, D-14
Goshen (in Egypt): III, C-3; V, B-3
  Wadi Tumilat: III, C-3
Goshen (in Judah): VI-X, F-2
Gozan: XI, B-5
  Guzana: XI, B-5
  Tell Halaf: III, XI, XXI, B-5
Granicus R.: XX, A-4
Great Sea: VI-X, XIV-XVI, A-2
  Inner Sea: XX, C-3
  Mediterranean Sea: I, A-1; II, B-1; III, C-2; IV, B-3; V, A-3; XI, XIII, XXI, C-2; XII, D-4; XIX, D-6; XXII, B-1
  Phoenician Sea: XX, C-5
  Greater (Upper) Zab R.: III, XI, XIII, B-5
Greece: XXI, A-1
Gurgum (district): XI, B-4
Gurgum (town): XI, B-4
Gush Khalab. See under Gischala
Gutium: III, B-6
Guzana. See under Gozan

ha Arava. See under Wadi el Arabah
Hadera: XXII, B-2
Hadrach: XI, B-4
Hadrumetum: XIX, D-8
Hafire, el, R.: XXII, C-4
Haifa: I, B-1; XXII, B-2
Hail: XI, XIII, D-5
Hala el Bedr: V, E-7
Halah: XI, B-5
Halak, Mt.: II, D-2; V, B-6; VI-X, G-2
Halal, Gebel: XXII, D-1
Haleb. See under Khalab
Halhul: VI-X, E-3; XXII, C-3
Halicarnassus: XI, XIII, B-2; XII, C-4; XIX, D-11
Halys R.: III, XI, XIII, B-3; IV, B-5; XII, B-5; XIX, D-12; XX, A-5; XXI, B-3; XXI, B-4
Hama. See under Hamath
Hamadan. See under Ahmetha
Hamath: III, XI, B-4
  Hama: XXI, B-4
  Hamathites: IV, B-5

Hammeh, el: XXI, inset
Hanesh. See under Heracleopolis Magna
Hanita: XXII, A-3
Hannathon: VI-X, C-3
Haradah: V, C-6 or C-7
Haraiva. See under Aria
Haran: III, XI, B-4; XII, C-6
Harauwatish. See under Arachosia
Harir, Nahr el: XXII, B-4
Harod (spring): VI, VIII-X, C-3; VII, D-3
Harosheth-ha-goiim: VI-X, C-2
Harra el Awarez: V, E-7
Harra er Raha: V, E-7
Harun, Jebel. See under Hor, Mt.
Hasa, el. See under Zered, Brook
Hatra: XIX, D-14; XXI, B-5
Hauran (district): I, B-3; see also Hauran, Jebel
Hauran, Jebel: V-X, XIV-XVI, C-6; XI, C-4
Havilah: IV, C-6
Havvoth-Jair: VI-X, C-4
Hazarmaveth: IV, D-7
Hazeroth: V, D-6
  Ain Hudherah: V, D-6
Hazor: III, C-4 and inset; VI-X, XIV-XVI, B-4
Hebron: I, C-2; III, C-4 and inset; V, A-7; VI-X, XIV-XVI, E-3; XII, D-6; XXII, C-3
  Kiriath-arba: VI-X, E-3
Hebrus R.: XIII, A-2; XIX, C-11
Hecatompylos: XII, C-10
  Hecatompylus: XIII, B-8
Helal, Jebel: II, D-1; V, B-6
Helbon: XIV-XVI, A-5
  Chalybon: XIV-XVI, A-5
Helkath: VI-X, C-3
Hellas: XIII, B-1
Hellenistic World (185 B.C.): XIII
Hellespont: XX, B-4
Hellespontians: XII, B-4
  Khuza: XII, B-4
Hepher: VI-X, D-2
Heraclea (in Macedonia): XX, A-3
Heraclea (on the Black Sea): XX, A-5
Heracleopolis Magna: V, C-3
  Hanesh: V, C-3; XI, D-3
  Heracleopolis: XI, D-3; XII, E-4; XIX, F-11
Heracleopolis Parva: V, C-3
Hermon, Mt.: I, A-2; II, A-3; VI-X, XIV-XVI, B-4; XI, C-4
Hermopolis: V, E-2; XI, XIII, D-3; XIX, F-12
Hermus R.: XIII, B-2; XIX, D-11; XX, B-4
Herodium: XIV-XVI, E-3
  Frank Mountain: II, C-3
Heroonpolis. See under Pithom
Heroonpolis, Gulf of: V, D-5
Herzliya: XXII, B-2
Hesa, el. See under Zered, Brook
Heshbon: V, A-7; VI-X, XIV-XVI, E-4; XI, C-4
  Essebon: XIV, E-3
Heth: IV, B-5
Hierapolis: XX, B-4
Hindukush. See under Paropamisus
Hindush. See under India
Hippo Regius: XIX, D-7
Hippos: XIV-XVI, C-4
Hismeh, el: V, C-7
Hispalis: XIX, D-4
Hispania: XIX, C-5
Hissarlik. See under Troy
Hit. See under Is
Hivites: IV, B-5
Holon: XXII, B-2
Holwan: XI, C-6
Homs. See under Emesa
Hor, Mt.: V, B-7
  Jebel Harun: V, B-7
Horeb: V, D-6
  el Khrob: V, D-6
Hormah: V, A-6; VI-X, F-2
Hul: IV, B-5

Huldah: XXII, C-2
Huleh. See under Semechonitis
Humeima, el: XXII, E-3
Husn, el: XXII, B-3
Hypanis R.: XII, A-7; XIX, B-11
Hyrcania: XII, C-9; XIII, B-7
  Warkana: XII, C-9
Hyrcanium: XIV-XVI, E-3

Iaxartes R.: XII, B-12
  Silis R.: XII, B-12
Iberus R.: XIX, C-5
Ibleam: VI-X, D-3
Iconium: XII, C-5; XIII, B-3; XIX, D-12; XX, B-5
Icosium: XIX, D-6
Ida, Mt.: XX, B-4
Idna: XXII, C-2
Idumaea: I, C-1; XIV-XVI, F-2; XX, C-5
Ijon: VI-X, B-4
Ilici: XIX, D-5
Ilion. See under Troy
Illyria. See under Illyricum
Illyricum: XX, A-3
  Illyria: IV, inset; XII, B-2
Imbros: XX, A-4
Ina: XIV-XVI, B-4
India: IV, inset; XII, E-12
  Hindush, Sind: XII, E-12
Indus R.: IV, inset; XII, E-12
Inner Sea. See under Great Sea
Ionian Sea: XIX, D-9; XX, B-2
Ionians: XII, C-4
Ipsus: XIII, B-3
Iran: XXI, C-7
Iraq: XXI, C-5
Irbid. See under Beth-arbel
Iris R.: XI, XIII, A-4; XX, A-6
Is: XI, C-5; XII, D-7
  Hit: XI, XI, C-5; XII, D-7
Isana: XV, D-3
  Jeshana XV, D-3
Isaur(ian) Pisidia: XX, B-5
Isfahan. See under Aspadana
Ishkuza. See under Scythians
Isin: III, C-5
Isles of the Sea (satrapy): XII, C-4
Ismailieh: V, B-4
Ispahan. See under Aspadana
Israel (ancient): VIII, D-3; IX, D-3
Israel (modern): XXI, C-3 and inset; XXII, C-2
Issachar: VI, C-3
Issatis: XIII, C-7
Issus: XII, C-6; XIII, B-4; XX, B-6
Ister R.: XII, B-3
  Istros R.: IV, inset
Istros R. See under Ister R.
Itabyrion: XIV, C-3
Ituraea (in Lebanon): I, A-2; XIV-XVI, A-4
Ituraea (near Hermon): XIV-XVI, B-4

Jabal Mubarak: XXII, E-3
Jabbok R.: I, B-2; II, B-3; VI-X, XIV-XVI, D-4
  Zerka R.: XXII, B-3
Jabesh: VI-X, D-4
Jabneel. See under Jabneh
Jabneh: VI-X, E-2
  Jabneel: VI-X, E-2 (not different site from Jabneh)
Jamnia: XIV-XVI, E-2
Jaffa. See under Japho
Jamnia. See under Jabneh
Janoah: VI-X, D-3
Japha: XIV-XVI, C-3
Japhia: VI-X, C-3
Japho: I, B-1; VI-X, D-2; XII, D-5; XXII, B-2
  Jaffa: XXII, B-2
  Joppa: II, B-2; III, inset; XI, XIII, C-3; XIV-XVI, D-2; XX, C-5
  ·Joppe: XIX, E-12

1193

Jarmuk R.: I, B-2
Jarmuth: VI-X, E-3
Jathrib: XIII, E-3
Jattir: VI-X, F-3
Jauf, ej. *See under* Dumah
Jaulan. *See under* Gaulanitis
Javan: IV, B-4
Jazer: VI-X, E-4
Jebel (mountain). *See* last part of name
Jebeil. *See under* Byblos
Jebusites: IV, B-5
Jedur. *See under* Ituraea (near Hermon)
Jehud: VI-X, D-2
Jemdet Nasr: XXI, C-6
Jemma. *See under* Yehem
Jemmain. *See under* Tirzah
Jenin: XXII, B-3
Jerabis. *See under* Carchemish
Jerash. *See under* Gerasa
Jerasus R.: XIX, B-11
Jericho: I, C-2; V, A-7; VI-X, XIV-XVI, E-3; XXII, C-3
Tell es Sultan: XXI, inset
Jermak, Jebel: I, B-2
Jerusalem: I, C-2; II, C-3; III, C-4 and inset; V, A-7; VI-X, XIV-XVI, E-3; XII, D-6; XIII, C-3; XIX, E-13; XX, C-6; XXI, C-4 and inset; XXII, C-3
Jerusalem (city maps): XVII, XVIII; fig. 259
Jeshana. *See under* Isana
Jezreel: VI-X, C-3
Jezreel, Plain of: VI-X, C-3
Jib, ej: *See under* Gibeon
Jibal, ej: I, D-2
Jidda: IV, C-5
Jiza: XXII, C-3
Jobab: IV, D-7
Jodephath. *See under* Yotapata
Jogbehah: VI-X, D-4
Joktan: IV, C-6
Joppa. *See under* Japho
Joppe. *See under* Japho
Jordan (state): XXI, C-4 and inset; XXII, D-3
Jordan R.: I, B-2; II, B-3; III, inset; VI-X; XIV-XVI, E-4; XXII, B-3
Joseph (tribes): VI, D-3
Judaea. *See under* Judah
Judah: VI-X, E-2; XI, C-4
Judaea: I, C-2; XIV-XVI, E-3; XX, C-5
Yehud: XII, D-5
Judah, Kingdom of: IX, X
Judah, Wilderness of: I, C-2
Judean Hills: XXII, C-3
Julias. *See under* Bethsaida
Jurf ed Durawish: XXII, D-3
Juttah: V, A-7; XIV-XVI, F-3

Kab, el: XI, D-3
Kabul: XII, D-12
Kadesh (on the Orontes): III, C-4
Kinza: III, C-4
Tell Nebi Mind: XXI, C-4
Kadesh-barnea: II, D-2; III, C-3; V, B-6
Ain Qudeirat: V, B-6
Kanah: VI-X, XIV-XVI, B-3
Qana: XXII, A-3
Kanan, Jebel: II, B-3; XIV-XVI, C-4
Kanata: XIV-XVI, C-5
Kanatha: XIV-XVI, C-6
Kandahar: XII, D-12
Kanesh: III, B-4
Kultepe: III, XXI, B-4
Kantara, el. *See under* Etham
Kaptaru. *See under* Crete
Kar Tukulti-Ninurta: XI, B-5
Karabel, Mt.: III, B-2
Karatepe: III, XI, XXI, B-4
Karduniash: III, C-6
Karim Shahir: XXI, B-6
Karkiya. *See under* Caria
Karkur: XXII, B-3
Karnaim: III, C-4; VI-X, C-5; XI, C-4
Cheikh Saad: XXII, B-3

Karnion: XIV, C-5
Sheikh Saad: VI-X, C-5; XXI, C-4
Karnak. *See under* No Amon
Karnion. *See under* Karnaim
Karun R. *See under* Ulai R.
Kashka: III, A-4
Katerin, Jebel: V, D-6
Katpatuka. *See under* Cappadocia
Kedar: XI, C-4
Kedesh: VI-X, XIV-XVI, B-3
Kefr Birim: XIV-XVI, B-4
Keilah: III, inset; VI, VIII-X, E-3; VII, E-2
Kelishin Pass: XI, B-6
Kenath. *See under* Nobah
Kenaz: VI-X, F-3
Kenites: V, B-6; VI-X, F-3
Kerak, el. *See under* Kir-haresheth
Kerkha R.: XI, C-6
Kerkuk. *See under* Arrapkha
Kermanshah: III, C-6
Kesarya. *See under* Caesarea (in Palestine)
Keykavus Kaleh: III, B-4
Kfar Ata: XXII, B-3
Kfar Blum: XXII, A-3
Kfar Sava: XXII, B-2
Kfar Vitkin: XXII, B-2
Khabab: XXII, A-4
Khabur R.: III, XI, B-5
Khadattu: XI, B-4
Arslan Tash: III, XI, XXI, B-4
Khafajeh: III, XXI, C-6
Khaibar: XI, D-4
Khalab: III, B-4
Aleppo: III, XI, B-4; XX, B-6
Beroea: XIII, B-4; XX, B-6
Haleb: XII, C-6
Khalman: XI, B-4
Khalpa: III, B-4
Khalasa, el: V, A-6
Khalman. *See under* Khalab
Khalpa. *See under* Khalab
Khan ez Zebib: XXII, C-4
Khan Yunis: XXII, C-2
Khanigalbat. *See under* Mitanni
Kharput: XI, B-4
Kharuf, Jebel: II, D-2
Khatti: III, B-3
Khattusha: III, B-3
Boghazköi: III, XI, B-3; XXI, B-4
Khayasha: III, B-4
Khilaku. *See under* Cilicia
Khindan: XI, C-5
Khirbet et Tubeiqah. *See under* Beth-zur
Khirbet Fahl. *See under* Pella (in Transjordan)
Khirbet Kerak. *See under* Philoteria
Khirbet Qumran: XIV-XVI, E-4; XXI, inset
Khisfin: XXII, B-3
Khochniye: XXII, A-3
Khorsabad. *See under* Dur-Sargon
Khrob, el. *See under* Horeb
Khurri: III, B-5
Khuza. *See under* Hellespontians
Khuzistan. *See under* Elam
Khwarizm. *See under* Chorasmia
Kinakhi. *See under* Canaan
Kinza. *See under* Kadesh (on the Orontes)
Kir Moab. *See under* Kir-haresheth
Kir-haresheth: VI-X, F-4; XI, C-4
el Kerak: V, A-7; VI-X, XIV-XVI, F-4; XXII, C-3
Kir Moab: XIV-XVI, F-4
Kiriathaim: VI-X, E-4
Kiriath-arba. *See under* Hebron
Kiriath-jearim: VI-X, E-3
Kish: III, XI, C-5
el Oheimir: XXI, C-5
Kishon R.: I, B-2; II, B-3; VI-X, XIV-XVI, C-3; XXII, B-3
Kition (city): XI, C-3; XII, D-5; XX, C-5
Kition (island). *See under* Cyprus
Kitron: VI-X, C-3
Kizzuwatna: III, B-3
Klysma: V, C-4
Suez: V, C-4; XI, C-3
Kokab: XIV-XVI, B-5

Komana (in Anti-Taurus Mts.): XI, B-4
Komana (near Black Sea). *See under* Comana
Koptos: XI, D-3
Koraea: XIV-XVI, D-3
Korakesion: XX, B-5
Korasion: XX, B-5
Korykos: XX, B-5
Koyunjik. *See under* Nineveh
Kültepe. *See under* Kanesh
Kummukh: XI, B-4
Kuntilla, (el): V, C-6; XXII, E-2
Kurnub: V, A-6; XIV-XVI, F-3
Kusiya. *See under* Ethiopia
Kuwait: XI, D-6
Kuweit, el: XIII, D-6
Kyros R. *See under* Cyrus R.

Lachish: III, E-2; VI-X, E-2
Tell ed Duweir: XXI, inset
Laish. *See under* Dan (city)
Laodicea (in "Asia"): XX, B-4
Laodicea (in Galatia): XX, B-5
Laodicea (in Syria): XIII, B-4; XIX, D-12; XX, B-6
Laqe: XI, B-4
Laranda: XX, B-5
Larissa: XIII, B-1; XIX, D-10; XX, B-3
Larsa: III, XI, C-6
Senkereh: XXI, C-6
Lasea: XX, B-4
Latrun: XXII, C-3
Lauriacum: XIX, B-9
Lebanon (modern): XXI, C-3; XXII, A-2
Lebanon Mts.: I, A-2; XI, C-4; XIV-XVI, A-4; XX, C-6
Lebonah: VI-X, XIV-XVI, D-3
Lechaeum: XX, B-3
Legio. *See under* Megiddo
Lehabim: IV, B-4
Leja: I, B-3; VI-X, B-6; XIV-XVI, C-5
Lemnos: XX, B-3
Leontes R.: I, A-2; II, A-3; VI-X, XIV-XVI, B-3
Leontopolis: XX, C-5
Leptis Magna: XIX, E-9
Lesbos: XIII, B-2; XX, B-4
Lesser (Lower) Zab R.: III, XIII, B-5; XI, B-6
Libba: XIV, E-4
Libnah: VI-X, E-2
Tell es-Safi: XXI, inset
Libya: IV, inset; XIII, C-2; XIX, E-11
Putiya: XII, D-4
Liger R.: XIX, B-5
Lilybaeum: XX, B-1
Limassol: XX, C-5
Lisan, el: I, C-2
Lisht: V, C-3
Livias. *See under* Beth-haram
Lod: III, inset; VI-X, E-2; XXII, C-2
Diospolis: XIV-XVI, E-2
Lydda: XIV-XVI, E-2; XX, C-5; XXII, C-3
Londinium: XIX, A-5
Lower Zab R.: *See* Lesser Zab R.
Lucus Augusti: XIX, C-4
Lud: IV, B-5
Ludim: IV, B-2
Lugdunensis, Gallia: XIX, B-6
Lugdunum: XIX, B-6
Lugdunum Batavorum: XIX, A-6
Lukka. *See under* Lycia
Luristan: III, C-6; XII, D-8
Lusitania: XIX, D-4
Luxor. *See under* No Amon
Lycaonia: XIX, D-12
Lycaonia, Galatian: XX, B-5
Lycaonia, Antiochian: XX, B-5
Lycia: XI, XIII, B-2; XII, C-4; XIX, D-11; XX, B-4
Lukka: III, B-2
Lycian Sea: XX, B-4
Lycus R. (in Phoenicia): VI-X, XIV-XVI, A-4
Lycus R. (in Pontus): XI, A-4; XIX, D-13; XX, A-6
Lydda. *See under* Lod

Lydia: XI, B-3; XII, C-4; XX, B-4
Lydian Kingdom: XI, B-3
Lystra: XX, B-5

Maad: XXII, B-3
Maale Aqrabim. *See under* Akrabbim, Ascent of
Maan: II, D-3; V, B-7; XI, C-4; XXII, D-3
Mabartha: XIV-XVI, D-3
   Nablus: XIV-XVI, D-3; XXII, B-3
Macedonia: XII, B-3; XIII, A-1; XIX, C-10; XX, A-3
Macestus R.: XX, B-4
Machaerus: XIV-XVI, E-4
Maciya: XII, D-3
Mada. *See under* Media
Madai. *See under* Media
Madeba: I, C-2; VI-X, XIV-XVI, E-4; XX, C-3
Madiama: XIX, F-13
Madian: V, D-6
   el Bed: V, D-7
Madon: VI-X, C-3
Maeander R.: XI, XIII, B-2; XX, B-4
Mafraq: XXII, B-4
Magan. *See under* Egypt
Magdala: XIV-XVI, C-3
   Migdal: XXII, B-3
   Tarichaea: XIV-XVI, C-3
Maghara, Jebel: V, B-5
Magharah: V, D-5
Magnesia: XI, XIII, B-2; XX, B-4
Magog: IV, B-6
Mahanaim: VI-X, D-4
Mahra: IV, D-7
Maka. *See under* Gedrosia
Makkedah: VI-X, E-2
Malaca: XIX, D-5
Malea, Cape: XX, B-3
Malta. *See* Melita
Mamshath: VI-X, F-2
Manasseh: VI, C-5, D-3
Mannai: IV, B-6
   Minni: XI, B-6
Maon: VI-X, F-3
Maqrah, Jebel: V, B-6
Maracanda: XII, C-12
   Samarkand: XII, C-12
Marah: V, C-4
   Ain Hawwarah: V, C-4
Mardin: XI, B-5
Marea: XI, C-2; XII, D-4
Mareotis, Lake: V, A-2
Margiana: XII, B-10
   Margush: XII, C-10
Margush. *See under* Margiana
Mari: III, XI, C-5
   Tell Hariri: XXI, C-5
Marisus R.: XIX, B-10
Marmarica: XIX, E-10
Masada: XIV-XVI, F-3
Masash el Sirr: XXII, D-1
Masdash Abu Khuf: XXII, E-1
Mash: IV, B-5
Masius, Mons (mt.): IV, B-6
Massaade: XXII, A-3
Massawa: IV, D-5
Massilia: XIX, C-7
Matala Cape: XX, C-3
Matiane: XII, C-7
Mauretania Caesariensis: XIX, D-5
Mauretania Tingitana: XIX, D-4
Mazaca: XIII, B-4; XIX, D-12; XX, B-6
   Mazaka: XII, C-6
Mazaka. *See under* Mazaca
Mazar (el) (in Egypt): V, B-5; XXII, C-1
Mazar (in Jordan): XXII, C-3
Mecca: IV, C-6
Medain Salih: XI, D-4
Medhbeh, Kh(irbet): V, A-6
Media: IV, inset; XI, B-6; XII, C-8
   Mada: XII, C-8
   Madai: VI-X, B-6
   Media (Seleucid): XIII, C-7
Media Atropatene: XIII, B-6
Medina: IV, C-6; XI, E-4
Mediolanium: XIX, B-7

Mediterranean Sea. *See under* Great Sea
Megara: XIII, B-1; XX, B-3
Megiddo: III, inset; VI-X, C-3
   Legio: XIV-XVI, C-3
   Tell el Mutesellim: XXI, inset
Meiron. *See under* Merom
Me-jarkon (R.): VI-X, D-2
   Yarkon R.: XXII, B-2
Melid: XI, B-4
   Melite: XII, C-6
   Melitene: XIII, B-4; XIX, D-13
Melita: XIX, D-8
   Malta: XIX, B-1
Melite. *See under* Melid
Melitene. *See under* Melid
Melos: XX, B-3
Meluhha. *See under* Ethiopia
Memphis: III, D-3; V, XI, C-3; XII, E-5; XIII, D-3; XIX, F-12
   Moph: XI, D-2
   Noph: V, C-3; XI, D-3
Mendes: V, A-3
Mendesic Mouth (Nile): V, A-4
Menzaleh, Lake: V, A-3
Menzil, el: XXII, C-4
Merkhah, el: V, D-5
Merom: VI, VII, VIII, X, C-3; IX, B-3
   Meiron: XIV-XVI, C-3
Mersin: XXI, B-2
Merv: XII, C-11
Mesene: IV, B-6; XII, D-8
Meshech: IV, B-5
   Moschians: XII, B-7
   Mushki: XI, B-3
Mesopotamia: XIX, E-14
Messana: XIX, D-8
Messara, Gulf of: XX, B-3
Messina: XX, B-2
Mesta: XI, B-6
Metropolis: XX, B-4
Metulla: XXII, A-3
Michmash: VI-X, XIV-XVI, E-3
Midas, Tomb of: XI, B-3
Midian: V, D-7
Migdal. *See under* Magdala
Migdal Ashqelon. *See under* Ashkelon
Migdol: III, XI, C-3; V, B-4 (see note, p. 1189)
   Tell el Her: III, C-3; V, B-4
Miletus: III, C-4; XIII, XXI, B-2; XIX, D-11; XX, B-4
Minius R.: XIX, C-4
Minni. *See under* Mannai
Minnith: VI-X, E-4
Mishrifeh, el. *See under* Qatna
Misrephoth-maim: VI-X, B-2
Misru. *See under* Egypt
Mitanni: III, B-4
   Khanigalbat: III, B-4; XI, B-5
Mizpah: XIV-XVI, E-3
   Tell en Nasbeh: XXI, inset
Mizpeh (in Gilead): VI-X, D-4
Mizpeh (near Hermon): VI-X, B-4
Mizraim. *See under* Egypt
Moab: I, C-2; V, A-7; VI-X, F-4; XI, C-4
Moabitis: XIV-XVI, F-4
Moab, Plain of: I, C-2
Moabitis. *See under* Moab
Modein: XIV-XVI, E-3
Moeris, Lake: V, C-2
Moesia: XIX, C-10
Mogontiacum: XIX, B-7
Mohammediyeh Qatieh: V, A-4
Mojib, el, R. *See under* Arnon R.
Mokha: V, D-7
Moladah: VI-X, F-2
Moledet: XXII, B-3
Mons Casius. *See* Baal-Zephon
Moph. *See under* Memphis
Mopsuestia: XI, XIII, B-4; XX, B-6
Moschians. *See under* Meshech
Mosella R.: XIX, B-7
Mosul: XII, C-7; XIII, B-5
Moyat Yerga: XXII, E-1
Mubarak, Jabal: XXII, E-3
Mudraya. *See under* Egypt
Muhhazzi: III, inset
Mukish: III, B-4

Muluchath R.: XIX, E-5
Muqayyar, el. *See under* Ur
Mursa: XIX, B-9
Musa, Jebel. *See under* Sinai, Mt.
Musasir: XI, B-6
Mushki. *See under* Meshech
Musri: XI, B-4
Mycenae: III, B-1
Mygdonia: XIII, B-5
Myra: XX, B-5
Myriandros: XII, C-6
   Myriandus: XIII, B-4
Myriandus. *See under* Myriandros
Mysia: XII, C-4; XX, B-4
Mytilene: XX, B-4

Nabataeans: XIII, C-4; XIV-XVI, F-4; XIX, E-13; XX, C-6
Nablus. *See under* Mabartha
Nahalol: VI-X, C-3
Naharaim: III, B-5
Nahariya: XXII, A-3
Nahr. *See* last part of name
Nain: XIV-XVI, C-3
Nakhl, (Qalat) en: V, C-5; XI, C-3
Naoua: XXII, B-4
Napata: IV, D-5
Naphtali: VI, C-3
Naphtuhim: IV, C-5
Naqb Ashtar: XXII, E-3
Naqb el Emreikheh: V, D-6
Naqb el Mirad: V, C-6
Naqura: XXII, A-3
   Tyrian Ladder: I, A-2; VI-X, B-3; XIV-XVI, B-3
Narbata: XIV, D-3
   Arbatta: XIV, D-3
Narbo: XIX, C-6
Narbonensis, Gallia: XIX, C-6
Natanya: XXII, B-2
Nations, Table of (Gen 10): IV
Naucratis: V, B-2; XIII, XXI, C-3; XIX, E-11
Nazareth: I, B-2; XIV-XVI, C-3; XXII, B-3
Nazianzos: XX, B-5
Nazla: XXII, C-2
Neapolis (in Italy): XIX, C-8; XX, A-1
Neapolis (in Macedonia): XX, A-3
Nebi Samwil: I, C-2
Nebo, Mt.: II, C-3; V, A-7; VI-X, XIV-XVI, E-4
Nefud: IV, B-5; XI, D-5
Negeb: I, C-1; II, D-2; VI-X, F-2
   Negev: XXII, D-2
Negev. *See under* Negeb
Nejd: XI, D-5
Nejran: IV, D-6
Nekhl: XXII, E-1
Nemrud Dagh: XI, XIII, XXI, B-4
Neqb Shtar: V, C-7
Nerab: XXI, B-4
Nerane: XXII, A-3
Nesher: XXII, B-3
Nessana: XIV-XVI, G-1
   Auja el Hafir: VI-X, XIV-XVI, G-1; XXI, C-3
   el Auja: V, B-6; XXII, D-2
Ni. *See* No Amon
Nicaea: XX, A-4
Nicer R.: XIX, B-7
Nicomedia: XIII, A-3; XIX, C-11; XX, A-5
Nicopolis (in Greece): XX, B-3
Nicopolis (in Judea). *See under* Emmaus
Nicopolis (in Thrace): XIX, C-11
Nihawend: III, C-6
Nile, Blue R.: IV, D-5
Nile Cataracts: IV, C-5
Nile R.: XI, XIII, D-3; IV, C-5 and inset; V, C-3; XII, E-5
   Nilus R.: XIX, F-12
   Yeor R.: XI, D-3
   Ytr: XI, D-3
Nile R., mouths of:
   Damietta: V, A-3
   Mendesic: V, A-4
   Pelusiac: V, A-4
   Phatnitic: V, A-3
   Rosetta: V, A-2
   Sebennytic: V, A-2
   Tanitic: V, A-4

Nile, White R.: IV, D-5
Nimrud. *See under* Calah
Nineveh: III, XI, B-5; IV, B-6
  Koyunjik: XXI, B-5
  Nineveh (city map) fig. 355
Nippur: III, XI, C-5
  Nuffar: XXI, C-5
Nisaea: XII, C-11
Nisibis: III, XI, XIII, B-5; XII,
  C-7; XIX, D-14
Nisir, Mt.: III, XI, B-6
  Pir Omar Gudrun: III, B-6
Niya: III, B-4
No Amon, Ni: XI, D-3
  Karnak and Luxor: XI, D-3
  Thebae: XIII, D-3; XIX, F-12
  Thebes: III, XI, D-3; IV, inset;
    XII, E-5
Nobah: VI-X, C-6
  Kenath: VI-X, C-6
Noph. *See under* Memphis
Noricum: XIX, B-8
Nubia. *See under* Ethiopia
Nuffar. *See under* Nippur
Nukhasse: III, B-4
Numidia: XIX, D-7
Nuqra, en-: I, B-3
Nuzi: III, B-5
Nvalat: XXII, C-3

Obal: IV, D-6
Oboth: V, B-7
  Ain el Weibeh: V, B-7
Oea: XIX, E-8; XX, C-1
  Tripoli: XX, C-1
Oheimir, el. *See under* Kish
Olbia: XIX, B-12
Olisipo: XIX, D-3
Olympus, Mt.: XX, A-3
Oman: IV, C-7
Oman, Gulf of: IV, C-7
On: III, C-2; V, B-3
  Heliopolis: III, XIII, C-3; IV,
    inset; V, B-3; XII, D-5; XIX,
    E-12; XX, C-5
Ono: VI-X, D-2
Ophir: IV, D-6
Ophrah (in Ephraim). *See under*
  Ephraim (in Ephraim)
Ophrah (near Megiddo): VI-X, C-3
Ophrah (Tirzah): VI-X, D-3
Opis: XII, D-7
Orchoë. *See under* Erech
Orda: XIV-XVI, F-2
Orontes R.: XI, XIII, B-4
Osha, Jebel: I, B-2; II, B-3; VI-X,
  D-4
Ossa, Mt.: XX, B-3
Ostia: XX, A-1
Ostrakine: V, A-5
Ouadi ed Dahab: XXII, B-4
Ouadi ez Zedr: XXII, B-4
Oxyrhynchus: V, XIII, D-2

Padus R.: XIX, B-7
Pahel. *See under* Pella (in Transjordan)
Palegawra: XXI, B-6
Palestine: XX, C-6; XXII, D-3
Palestine, maps of:
  12th and 11th cent. B.C.: VI
  1000 B.C.: VII
  10th cent: B.C.: VIII
  c. 850 B.C.: IX
  after the fall of the northern king-
    dom: X
  Maccabean period: XIV
  37-4 B.C.: XV
  A.D. 28: XVI
  today: XXII
  geographic regions (ancient and
    modern): I
  physiographic map: II
  rainfall: fig. 366
  roads (ancient): fig. 229
  vegetation, ancient zones of: fig.
    367
Palmyra. *See under* Tadmor
Palus Maeotis: XIX, B-13
Pamir: XII, C-13
Pamphylia: XI, XIII, B-3; XII, C-
  5; XIX, D-12; XX, B-5
Pamphylian Sea: XX, B-5
Paneas: XIII, C-4
  Baniyas: XXII, A-3

Caesarea Philippi: XIV-XVI, B-4;
  XX, C-6
Pannonia: XIX, B-9
Panormus: XIX, D-8; XX, B-1
Panticapaeum: XII, A-6
Paphlagonia: XII, B-5; XIII, A-3;
  XIX, C-12; XX, A-5
Paphos: XIII, C-3; XX, C-5
Paraetacene: XIII, C-7
Paraetonium: XIII, C-2
Paran (wilderness): V, C-6
Paran, Mt.: V, B-6
  Jebel Faran: V, B-6
Pardess Hanna: XXII, B-2
Paropamisus: XII, C-13
  Hindukush: XII, D-13
Parsa (city): XII, E-9
  Persepolis: XII, E-9; XIII, XXI,
    D-7
Parsa (district). *See under* Persis
Parthava. *See under* Parthia
Parthia: XII, C-10; XIII, C-7
  Parthava: XII, D-10
Pasargadae: XII, D-9; XXI, D-7
Patara: XX, B-4
Patavium: XIX, B-8
Pathros. *See under* Pathrusim
Pathrusim: IV, C-5
  Pathros: III, D-3
Patmos: XX, B-4
Patrae: XIX, D-10; XX, B-3
Pattala: XII, E-12
Paul's journeys: XX
Pax Julia: XIX, D-4
Pazarli: XXI, A-4
Pekod: XI, C-6
  Pukudu: XI, C-6
Peleg: IV, B-6
Pelion, Mt.: XX, B-3
Pella (in Macedonia): XIII, A-1;
  XIX, C-10; XX, A-3
Pella (in Transjordan): XIV-XVI,
  D-4
  Khirbet Fahl: XXI, inset
  Pahel: III, inset; VI-X, XIV-
    XVI, D-4
Pelusiac Mouth (Nile): V, A-4
Pelusium: V, A-4; XI, D-5; XIII,
  C-3; XIX, E-12; XX, C-5
  Sin: V, A-4; XI, C-3
Penuel: VI-X, D-4
Peraea: I, B-2; XV, XVI, E-4
Perga: XX, B-5
Pergamum (city): XI, XIII, XXI,
  B-2; XII, C-4; XIX, D-11; XX,
  B-4
Pergamum (kingdom): XIII, B-3
Perinthus: XX, A-4
Persepolis. *See under* Parsa (city)
Persepolis Gate: XII, D-9
Persia: IV, inset, XII. *See also*
  Iran; Persis
Persian Empire: XII
Persian Gulf: III, XI, XIII, XXI,
  D-7; IV, C-7; XII, E-9
Persis: XII, E-9; XIII, D-7
  Parsa: XII, E-9
Pessinus: XX, B-5
Petah Tiqva: XXII, B-2
Petra: V, B-7; XI, XIII, XXI,
  C-4; XIX, E-13; XX, C-6;
  XXII, D-3
Rekem: V, B-7; XI, C-3
Pharpar R.: VI-X, XIV-XVI, B-5
Pharsalus: XX, B-3
Phasaelis: XIV-XVI, D-3
Phasis: XII, B-7
Phatnitic Mouth (Nile): V, A-3
Phiala, Lake: II, A-3
  Birket Ran: II, A-3
Philadelphia (in Asia Minor): XX,
  B-4
Philadelphia (in Transjordan). *See*
  under Rabbath Ammon
Philippi: XIII, A-1; XIX, C-10;
  XX, A-3
Philippopolis: XII, B-4; XIII, A-2;
  XIX, C-10
Philistia: I, C-1
Philistines: IV, B-5; VI-X, E-2
Philoteria: XIV-XVI, C-4
  Beth Yerah: VI-X, XIV-XVI,
    C-4
  Khirbet Kerak: XXI, inset
Phocis: XII, C-3

Phoenice. *See* Phoenicia
Phoenicia(ns): I, A-2; VI-X, XIV-
  XVI, B-3; XX, C-6
  Phoenice: XIX, E-12
Phoenician Sea. *See under* Great
  Sea
Phoenix: XX, B-3
Phrygia: XII, C-5; XIX, D-11
  Asian Phrygia: XX, B-5
  Galatian Phrygia: XX, B-5
  Phrygian Kingdom: XI, A-3
Pir Omar Gudrun. *See under* Nisir,
  Mt.
Pirathon: VI-X, D-3
Pisae: XIX, C-8
Pisidia: XII, C-5; XIII, B-3; XIX,
  D-12; XX, B-5
Pithom: III, C-3; V, B-3
  Heroonpolis: V, B-3; XIII, C-3
  Tell Ertabeh: V, B-3
Podandus: XX, B-6
Polemon, Kingdom of: XX, B-6
Pompeii: XX, A-1
Pontus: XI, A-3; XIII, A-4; XIX,
  C-13; XX, A-5
Pontus Euxinus. *See* Black Sea
Priene: XX, B-4; XXI, B-2
Propontis: XI, XIII, A-2; XX, A-4
Prymnessus: XX, B-4
Pteria: XX, A-5
Ptolemaic Empire: XIII, C-3
Ptolemais (in Egypt): XIII, D-3;
  XIX, E-10
Ptolemais (in Palestine). *See under*
  Acco
Punon: V, B-7
  Feinan: V, B-7
Puqudu. *See under* Pekod
Put: IV, B-4
Puteoli: XX, A-1
Putiya. *See under* Libya
Pydna: XX, A-3
Pyramids: V, C-2
Pyramos R.: XIX, D-13; XX, B-6
Pyretus R.: XIX, B-11

Qabatiya: XXII, B-3
Qala Sherqat. *See* Asshur (city)
Qalat ed Daba: XXII, C-4
Qalat el Hasa: XXII, D-4
Qalat el Mudauwara: XXII, E-4
Qalat en Nakhl: V, C-5; XI, C-3
Qalat ez Zerga: XXII, B-4
Qalqiliya: XXII, B-3
Qana. *See under* Kanah
Qantir: III, C-3
Qasr el Azraq: XI, C-4
Qatar: XXI, D-7
Qatna: III, C-4
  el Mishrifeh: XXI, C-4
Qatrani, el: XXII, C-4
Qebu, el, R.: XXII, D-4
Qiryat Anavim: XXII, C-3
Qiryat Hayim: XXII, B-2
Qoseimeh: V, B-6
Qudeirat, Ain. *See under* Kadesh-
  barnea
Que. *See under* Cilicia
Qum: XXI, C-7
Quneitra(h), el: VI-X, B-5; XXII,
  A-3
Qusaima: XXII, D-2
Quweira, el: XXII, E-3

Raamah: IV, D-6
Raamses. *See under* Zoan
Rabbah. *See* Rabbath Ammon
Rabbath Ammon: II, C-4; VI-X,
  XIV-XVI, E-5
  Amman: I, C-3; XXII, C-3
  Philadelphia: XIII, C-4; XIV-
    XVI, E-5
Rabbath Moab: VI-X, F-4
Raetia: XIX, B-7
Rafah. *See under* Raphia
Raga: XII, C-9
Ray: XXI, B-7
Rhagae: III, B-7
Ragaba: XIV-XVI, D-4
Rakkath: VI-X, C-3
Ram(m), Jebel: II, XXII, E-3; V,
  C-7; XI, D-4
Rama, er. *See under* Ramah (in
  Galilee)

Ramah (in Benjamin): VI-X, XIV-
XVI, E-3
Ramah (in Galilee): VI-X, C-3
er Rama, XXII, B-3
Ramallah: I, C-2; XXII, C-3
Ramat Gan: XXII, B-2
Ramle: XXII, C-2
Ramon, Mt.: XXII, D-2
Ramoth-gilead: VI-X, C-5
Raphana: XIV-XVI, C-5
Raphia: III, E-2; V, A-6; XI, XIII,
C-3; XIV-XVI, F-1; XX, C-5
Rafah: XXII, E-1
Ras el Abyad: XI, E-4; XII, F-6
Ras el Ain: XI, B-5
Ras esh Shamra. *See under* Ugarit
Ras Mohammed: V, E-6
Ras Safsafeh. *See under* Sinai, Mt.
Rasappa: XI, B-5
Ravenna: XIX, C-8
Ray. *See under* Raga
Red Sea: IV, C-5 and inset; V,
E-6; XI, XIII, D-4
Arabian Gulf: XII, F-6; XIX,
F-13
Regina Castra: XIX, B-8
Rehob: III, inset; VI-X, D-3
Rehoboth: V, A-6; VI-X, F-2
Rehovot: XXII, C-2
Rekem. *See under* Petra
Remeth: VI-X, C-4
Remtha, er: XX, B-4
Rephaim, Plain of: I, C-2
Rephidim: V, D-5
Retenu: III, C-3
Reuben: VI, E-4
Revivim: XXII, C-2
Rezeph: XI, B-4
Rhagae. *See under* Raga
Rhazale: XXII, B-4
Rhegium: XIX, D-9; XX, B-2
Rhenus R.: XIX, A-7
Rhinocorura. *See under* Arza
Rhodanus R.: XIX, C-7
Rhodes (city): XII, C-4; XIII,
B-2; XX, B-4
Rhodes (island): XII, C-4; XIII,
B-2; XX, B-4
Rhodus (island):·XIX, D-11
Rhodus. *See under* Rhodes (island)
Rhyndacus R.: XX, B-4
Riblah: XI, C-4
Rihab: VI-X, D-5
Rimmon (in Galilee): VI-X, C-3
Rimmon (near Bethel): VI-X, E-3
Riphath: IV, A-5
Rishon-le-Zion: XXII, C-2
Rithmah: V, C-7
Rodanim. *See under* Dodanim
Roman Empire (1st cent. A.D.):
XIX
Rome: XX, A-1
Roma: XIX, C-8
Rome (city map): fig. 405
Rosetta (town): V, A-2
Rosetta Mouth (Nile): V, A-2
Rosh Pina: XXII, B-3
Ruba el Khali: IV, C-6
Rubin, Nahr: I, C-1; II, C-2
Ruweiha: XXII, D-3

Sabkhet el Bardawil. *See under*
Sirbonis, Lake
Sabrata: XIX, E-8
Sabta: IV, D-6
Sabteca: IV, D-6
Safed: XIV-XVI, B-4
Safad: XXII, B-3
Safiye, es: XXII, C-3
Sagartians: XII, D-9
Asagarta: XII, D-9
Sais: XI, C-3; XII, D-5; XX, C-5
Sajur R.: III, B-4
Saka: *See under* Scythians
Sakastan. *See under* Drangiana
Saktshegözu: XXI, B-4
Salamis (on Cyprus): XII, C-5;
XIII, B-3; XIX, D-12; XX,
B-5
Saldae: XIX, D-6
Salecah: XIV-XVI, D-6
Salfit: XXII, B-3
Salhieh: V, B-3
Salim: XIV-XVI, D-3 or D-4
Salkhad: XIV-XVI, D-6

Salmone, Cape: XX, B-4
Salonae: XIX, C-9
Salt, es: VI-X, XIV-XVI, D-4;
XXII, B-3
Salt Sea. *See under* Dead Sea
Samal: XI, B-4
Sinjirli: XXI, B-4
Samaria (city): I, B-2; VI-X, XIV-
XVI, D-3; XI, D-5; XIII, C-3;
XX, C-6
Samaria (city map): fig. 413
Sebaste: XV, XVI, D-3
Sebastiyeh: XXI, inset
Samaria (district): I, B-2; XI, C-4;
XIV-XVI, D-3
Samarkand. *See under* Maracanda
Sammonium: XX, B-4
Samos: XX, B-4
Samosata: XI, XIII, B-4; XII, C-6
Samothrace: XX, A-4
Samu: XXII, C-3
San. *See under* Zoan
Sana: IV, D-6
Sanamein, es: XXII, A-4
Sangarius R.: XI, XIII, A-3; XX,
A-5
Sanamein, es: XXII, A-4
Saqqara: V, C-3
Sardinia: XIX, C-7
Sardis: III, XI, XIII, XXI, B-2; IV,
D-2; XII, C-4; XIX, D-11; XX,
B-4
Sepharad: XII, C-4
Sparda: XII, C-4
Sarepta. *See under* Zarephath
Sarid: VI-X, C-3
Saripul: III, C-6
Sarmatia: XIX, A-10
Saros R.: XX, B-6
Saspeires: XII, B-7
Sattagydians: XII, E-13
Thatagush: XII, E-13
Saudi Arabia: XXI, D-5; XXII,
E-3
Savus R.: XIX, B-9
Saxones: XIX, A-7
Sbeita, es: V, B-6
Scallabis: XIX, D-4
Scenae: XIV-XVI, D-4
Schedia: XX, C-5
Scorpion Pass. *See under* Akrabbim,
Ascent of
Scrolls Caves: XIV-XVI, E-3
Scythians: IV, inset; XII, A-4
Amyrgian Scythians: XII, C-13
Ishkuza Scythians: XII, B-5
Pointed Helmet Scythians: XII,
B-13
Saka: XII, A-4
Saka Haumavarga: XII, B-13
Saka Tigrakhauda: XII, B-13
Scythopolis: XIV-XVI, C-3
Sdom: XXII, C-2
Sdot Yam. *See under* Caesarea (in
Palestine)
Sealand: XI, C-6
Seba: IV, D-5
Sebaste. *See under* Samaria (city)
Sebastiyeh. *See under* Samaria (city)
Sebastopolis: XX, A-6
Sebennytos: V, B-2
Sebka, es-: I, C-2; II, D-3
Seffuriyeh: XXI, inset
Segovia: XIX, C-5
Sehab: XXII, C-4
Seilun. *See under* Shiloh
Seir, Mt.: II, C-3; V, B-7. *See also*
Edom
Seleucia (in Babylonia): XIII, C-5;
XIX, E-14
Seleucia (in Cilicia): XIII, B-3;
XX, B-5
Seleucia (in Transjordan): XIV-
XVI, C-4
Seleucia Pieria (in Syria): XIII,
B-3; XX, B-6
Seleucid Empire: XIII, B-5
Seleucis: XIII, B-4
Selinus: XIX, D-12; XX, B-5
Semechonitis, Lake: I, A-2; II,
A-3; VI-X, XIV-XVI, B-4
Huleh, Lake: XXII, A-3
Senkereh. *See under* Larsa
Sepharad. *See under* Sardis

Sepphoris: XIV-XVI, C-3
Sequana R.: XIX, B-6
Serabit el Khadem: V, C-5; XI,
D-3
Serbal, Jebel: V, D-5
Sewen. *See under* Syene
Shamiramalti: III, B-5
Shammar, Jebel: XI, D-5
Shankhar. *See under* Sinjar, Jebel
Shapur: XXI, D-7
Sharon, Plain of: I, B-1; II, B-2;
VI-X, XIV-XVI, D-2
Sharuhen: III, inset; VI-X, F-1
Tell el Farah: XXI, inset
Shasu: III, C-3
Shatt el Hai: XI, C-6
Sheba: IV, D-6
Shechem: I, B-2; III, C-4 and
inset; VI-X, XIV-XVI, D-3
Balatah: XXI, inset
Sheikh Saad. *See under* Karnaim
Sheikh Zuweid: XXI, C-3
Sheleph: IV, D-6
Shephelah: I, C-1
Shfaram: XXII, B-3
Shihan, Jebel: II, C-3; VI-X, F-4
Shiloh: VI-X, D-3
Seilun: XXI, inset
Shimron: VI-X, C-3
Shimron-meron: VI-X, B-3
Shiraz: IV, C-7; XII, E-9
Shobek: V, B-7; XXII, D-3
Shomer, Jebel Umm: V, D-6
Shuah: XI, C-5
Sukhu: XI, C-5
Shunem: VI-X, XIV-XVI, C-3
Shurem [Shunem]: III, inset
Shupria: XI, B-5
Shur, Wilderness of: V, B-5
Shurem. *See under* Shunem
Shush. *See under* Susa
Shushan. *See under* Susa
Shusht el Maghara: XXII, D-1
Sicily: XX, B-1
Sicilia: XIX, D-8
Sicyon: XX, B-3
Side: XIII, B-3; XX, B-5
Sidon: I, A-2; II, VI-X, XIV-XVI,
A-3; III, C-4; XI, XIII, C-3;
XII, D-5; XIX, E-13; XX, C-5
Sidonians: IV, B-5
Siir: XXII, C-3
Sile. *See under* Etham
Silis R. *See under* Iaxartes R.
Simeon: VI, F-2
Simonias: XIV-XVI, C-3
Sin (in Egypt). *See under* Pelu-
sium
Sin, Wilderness of: V, B-5 (see
note, p. 1189)
Sinai, Mt.: V, D-6; XI, D-3
Jebel Musa: V, D-6
or
Ras Safsafeh: V, D-5
Sinai Peninsula: IV, C-5; XXII, E-1
Sind. *See under* India
Sinites: IV, B-5
Sinjar, Jebel: XI, B-5
Shankhar: III, B-5
Sinjirli. *See under* Samal
Sinope: IV, D-2; XI, XIII, A-4;
XII, B-6; XIX, C-13; XX, A-6
Sippar: III, XI, C-5; XII, D-7
Abu Habba: XXI, C-5
Sipylos, Mt.: III, B-2
Sipylus, Mt.: XI, B-2; XX, B-4
Sirbonis, Lake: V, A-5
Sabkhet el Bardawil: XXII, C-1
Sirmium: XIX, B-10
Sistan. *See under* Drangiana
Siwa. *See under* Ammonium
Siyalk: XXI, C-7
Skudra: XII, B-4
Sminthium, Cape: XX, B-4
Smyrna: III, XI, XIII, B-2; XIX,
D-11; XX, B-4
Socoh (in Judah): VI-X, E-2
Socoh (in Manasseh): VI-X, D-3
Socotra: IV, D-7
Sogdiana: XII, C-12
Suguda: XII, C-12
Soli (in Cilicia): XIII, B-3
Soli (on Cyprus): XIII, B-3
Soloi: XX, B-5
Soviet Union: XXI, A-5

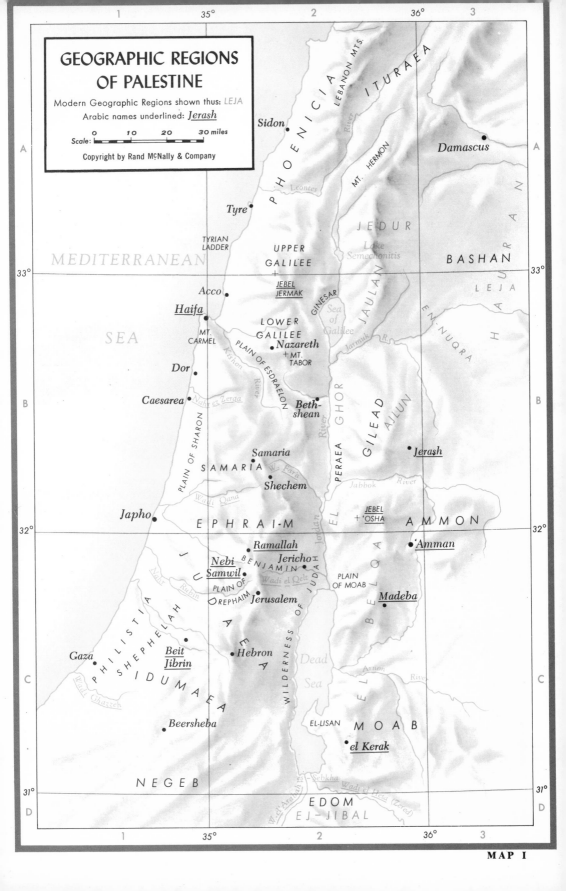

GEOGRAPHIC REGIONS
OF PALESTINE

Modern Geographic Regions shown thus: LEJA

Arabic names underlined: *Jerash*

Scale: 0 10 20 30 miles

Copyright by Rand McNally & Company

MAP I

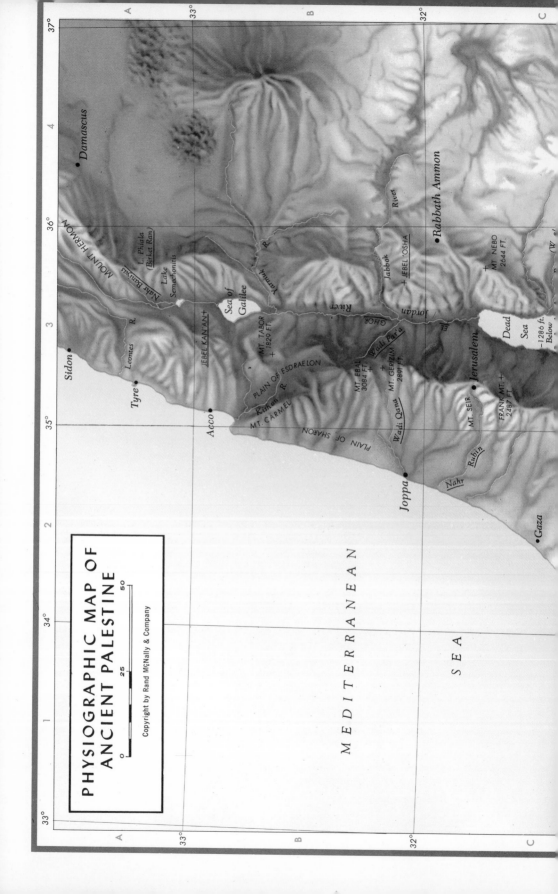

PHYSIOGRAPHIC MAP OF ANCIENT PALESTINE

Copyright by Rand McNally & Company

0   25   50

• Damascus

MOUNT HERMON

L. Phiala
(Birket Ram)

Lake
Semechonitis

Nahr Banias

Sidon •

Leontes R.

JEBEL KAN'AN+

Sea of
Galilee

MT. TABOR
+ 1829 FT.

R.

Yarmuk

Tyre •

PLAIN OF ESDRAELON

Kishon R.

MT. CARMEL

Jabbok   River

+ JEBEL 'OSHA

Jordan

GHOR

El

River

Rabbath Ammon •

MT. NEBO
+ 2644 FT.

Acco •

Wadi Far'a

MT. EBAL +
3084 FT.

+ MT. GERIZIM
2891 FT.

Wadi Qana

PLAIN OF SHARON

Jerusalem •

MT. SEIR •

FRANK MT. +
2487 FT.

Dead
Sea

-1286 ft.
Below

Joppa •

Nahr   Rubin

Gaza •

M E D I T E R R A N E A N

S E A

33°   34°   1   35°   2   36°   3   37°   4

A   33°

B   32°

C

MAP II

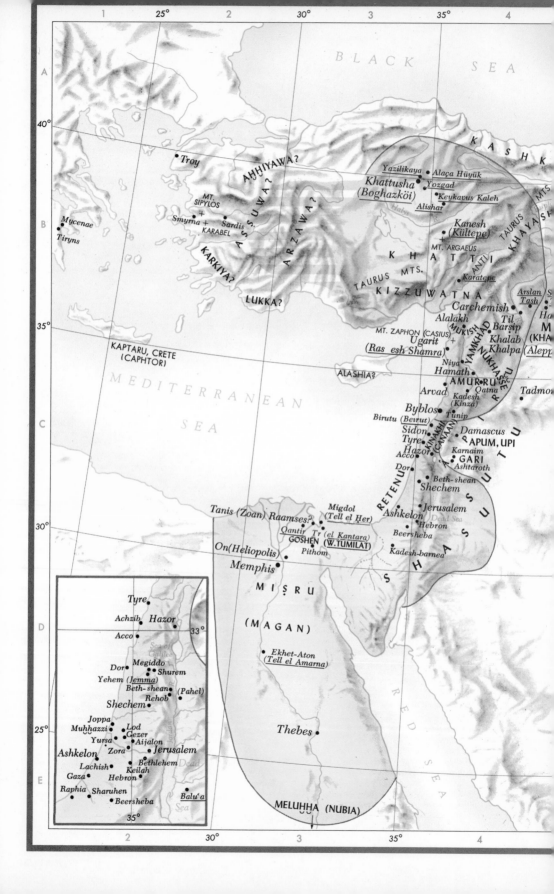

Main map labels

BLACK SEA

40°

A

Troy

AHHIYAWA?

MT. SIPYLÒS
Smyrna + Sardis
KARABEL

Mycenae
Tiryns

B

KARKIYA?

ASSUWA?

ARZAWA?

LUKKA?

Yazilikaya · Alaça Hüyük
Khattusha · Yozgad
(Boghazköi) · Keykavus Kaleh
Alishar

Kanesh
(Kültepe)

MT. ARGAEUS

KHATTI

Karatepe

KIZZUWATNA

TAURUS MTS.

35°

KAPTARU, CRETE
(CAPHTOR)

MT. ZAPHON (CASIUS)

Ugarit
(Ras esh Shamra)

ALASHIA?

MEDITERRANEAN

SEA

KASHK

TAURUS MTS.
ANTI
KHAYASH

Carchemish
Alalakh · Til
Barsip
MUKISH · Khalab
YAMKHAD · Khalpa
NUKHASSE

Niya
Hamath

AMURRU

Arvad · Kadesh
(Kinza)
Qatna

Byblos · Tunip
Birutu (Beirut)
Sidon · KINAKHI
Tyre · CANAAN
Hazor

Acco · Karnaim
GARI
Ashtaroth

Dor · Beth-shean
Shechem

Jerusalem
Ashkelon · Hebron
Beersheba

Kadesh-barnea

Arslan
Tash

Ha

M
(KHA
Alepp

Tadmor

Damascus
APUM, UPI

RETENU

SUTU

C

30°

Tanis (Zoan) Raamses?
Qantir Tr (el Kantara)
GOSHEN (W. TUMILAT)
Pithom

On (Heliopolis)

Memphis

MISRU

(MAGAN)

Migdol
(Tell el Her)

Ekhet-Aton
(Tell el Amarna)

SHASU

D

RED

Thebes

SEA

MELUHHA (NUBIA)

Inset map (lower left)

Tyre

Achzib · Hazor

Acco

33°

Sea of
Galilee

Dor · Megiddo
Shurem
Yehem (Jemma)
Beth-shean
Rehob (Pahel)

Shechem

Joppa
Muhhazzi · Lod
Yursa · Gezer
Zora · Aijalon
Jerusalem

Ashkelon
Lachish · Bethlehem
Gaza · Hebron · Keilah

Raphia · Sharuhen
Beersheba

Balu'a

Dead
Sea

35°

Grid numbers and coordinates

25° · 30° · 35°

1 · 2 · 3 · 4

40° · 35° · 30°

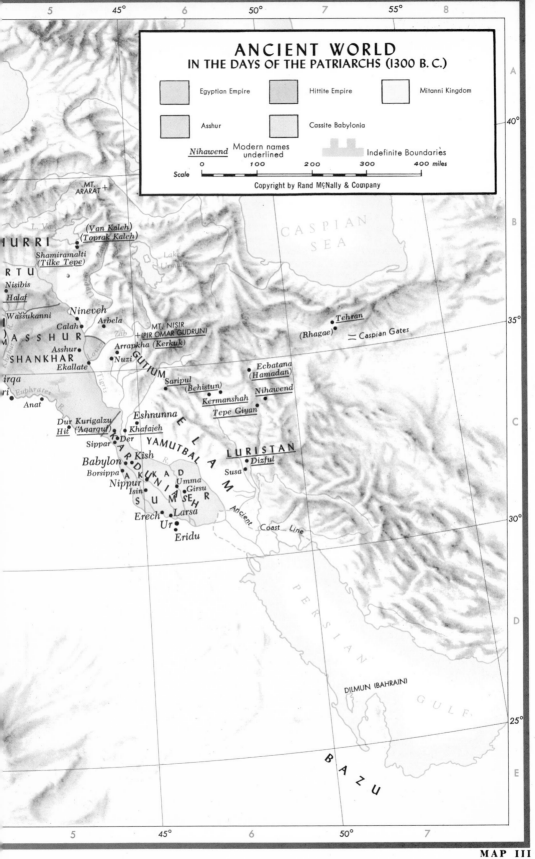

ANCIENT WORLD
IN THE DAYS OF THE PATRIARCHS (1300 B.C.)

☐ Egyptian Empire	☐ Hittite Empire	☐ Mitanni Kingdom
☐ Asshur	☐ Cassite Babylonia	

Nihawend   Modern names
underlined

Indefinite Boundaries

Scale   0   100   200   300   400 miles

Copyright by Rand McNally & Company

MT.
ARARAT +

L. Van

(*Van Kaleh*)
(*Toprak Kaleh*)

Shamiramalti
(*Tilke Tepe*)

HURRI

RTU

Nisibis
Halaf

Lake
Urmia

CASPIAN
SEA

Wassukanni

Nineveh

Arbela

MASSHUR

Calah

MT. NISIR
+(PIR OMAR GUDRUNI)

Tehran

35°

Asshur
SHANKHAR

Arrapkha (*Kerkuk*)

Nuzi

GUTIUM

(*Rhagae*)

— Caspian Gates

Ekallate

Saripul
(*Behistun*)

Ecbatana
(*Hamadan*)

irqa

Euphrates R.

Anat

Tigris R.

Kermanshah

Nihawend

Tepe Giyan

ri

Dur Kurigalzu
Hit (*Aqarquf*)

Eshnunna

Khafajeh

E
L
A
M

Sippar

Der

YAMUTBAL

LURISTAN

Babylon
Borsippa

Kish

A
K
K
A
D

Dizful

Nippur
Isin

Umma
Girsu

Susa

S U M
S E
E R

Ancient

Erech
Ur

Larsa

Eridu

Coast Line

30°

PERSIAN

DILMUN (BAHRAIN)

GULF

25°

B A Z U

MAP III

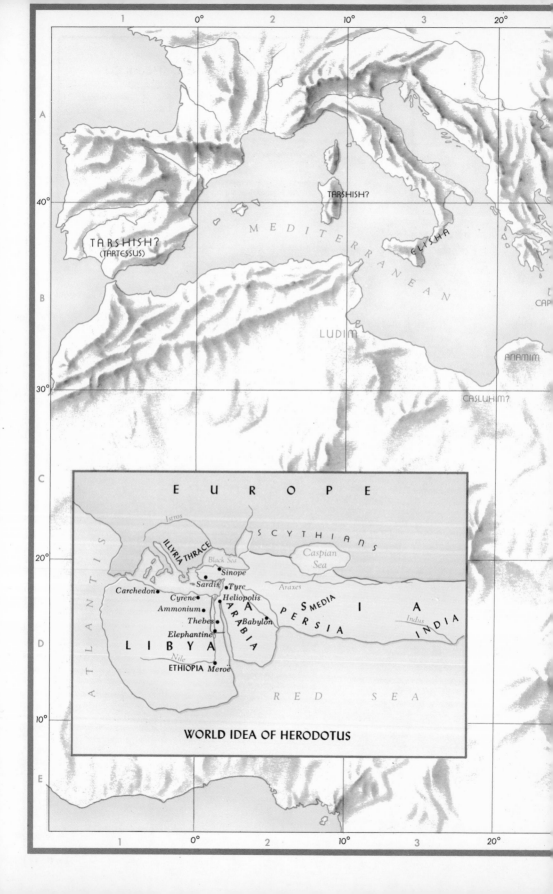

TARSHISH?

TARSHISH?
(TARTESSUS)

M E D I T E R R A N E A N

ELISHA

CAP

LUDIM

ANAMIM

CASLUHIM?

E U R O P E

Istros

ILLYRIA THRACE

S C Y T H I A N S

Black Sea

Caspian Sea

●Sinope

Sardis

Araxes

Carchedon●

Cyrene● ●Tyre

●*Heliopolis*

Ammonium

Thebes

ARABIA

PERSIA

MEDIA

Indus

INDIA

ATLANTIS

Elephantine

LIBYA

Nile

ETHIOPIA *Meroë*

R E D   S E A

WORLD IDEA OF HERODOTUS

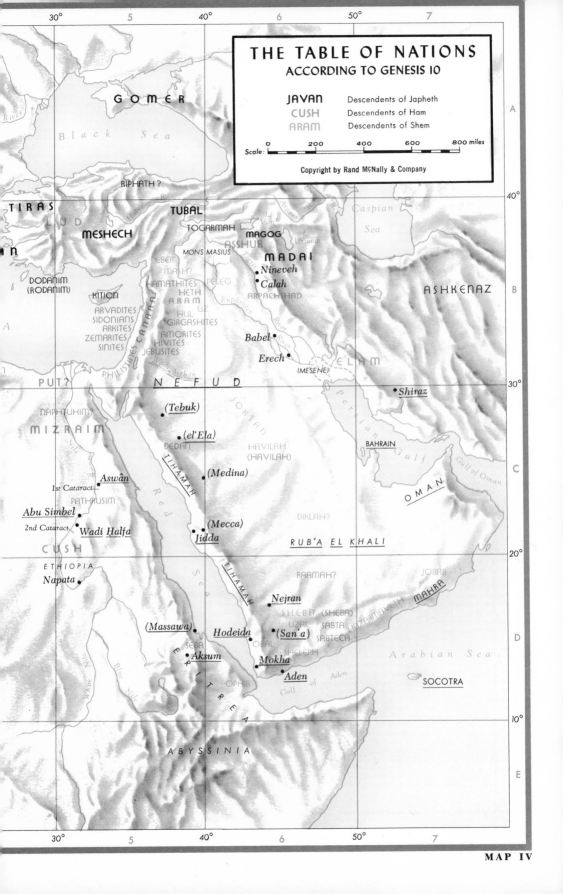

THE TABLE OF NATIONS
ACCORDING TO GENESIS 10

JAVAN — Descendents of Japheth
CUSH — Descendents of Ham
ARAM — Descendents of Shem

Scale: 0 — 200 — 400 — 600 — 800 miles

Copyright by Rand McNally & Company

River

GOMER

Black Sea

TIRAS

RIPHATH ?

LUD

TUBAL

MESHECH

TOGARMAH

MONS MASIUS

ASSHUR

MAGOG

MADAI

Caspian Sea

Van

Urumiah

DODANIM
(RODANIM)

A

KITION

EBER
MASH?
HAMATHITES
HETH
ARAM
HUL
GIRGASHITES
AMORITES
HIVITES
JEBUSITES

ARVADITES
SIDONIANS
ARKITES
ZEMARITES
SINITES

PELEG

UZ

ARPACHSHAD

Euphrates

Nineveh
Calah

ASHKENAZ

B

PHILISTINES CANAAN

Wadi Sirhan

Babel
Erech

(MESENE)

ELAM

PUT?

NEFUD

Shiraz

30°

NAPHTUHIM?

MIZRAIM

(Tebuk)

(el'Ela)

DEDAN

JOKTAN

HAVILAH
(HAVILAH)

BAHRAIN

Persian Gulf

Gulf of Oman

C

1st Cataract

Aswân

PATHRUSIM

(Medina)

TIHAMA

Red

OMAN

Abu Simbel

2nd Cataract Wadi Halfa

(Mecca)

Jidda

DIKLAH?

RUB'A EL KHALI

20°

CUSH

ETHIOPIA

Napata

Sea

TIHAMA

RAAMAH?

SHEBA (SHEBA)
UZAL
OBAL
SABTA
SHELEPH
SABTECA

JOBAB

MAHRA

Nejran

Arabian Sea

(Massawa)

Hodeida

(San'a)

SEBA

Aksum

ERITREA

Mokha

OPHIR

Aden

Gulf

of Aden

SOCOTRA

White Nile

Blue Nile

ABYSSINIA

MAP IV

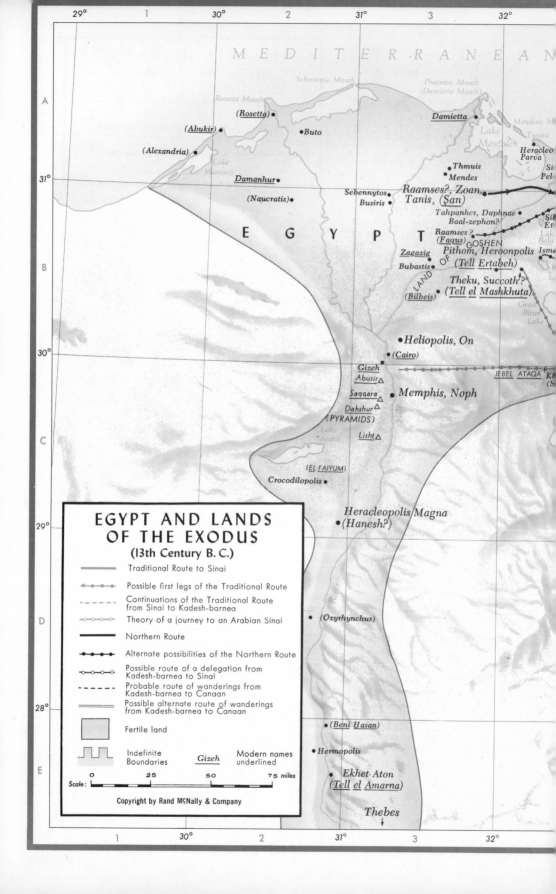

EGYPT AND LANDS
OF THE EXODUS
(13th Century B.C.)

Traditional Route to Sinai

Possible first legs of the Traditional Route

Continuations of the Traditional Route
from Sinai to Kadesh-barnea

Theory of a journey to an Arabian Sinai

Northern Route

Alternate possibilities of the Northern Route

Possible route of a delegation from
Kadesh-barnea to Sinai

Probable route of wanderings from
Kadesh-barnea to Canaan

Possible alternate route of wanderings
from Kadesh-barnea to Canaan

Fertile land

Indefinite
Boundaries   *Gizeh*   Modern names
                                 underlined

Scale: 0   25   50   75 miles

Copyright by Rand McNally & Company

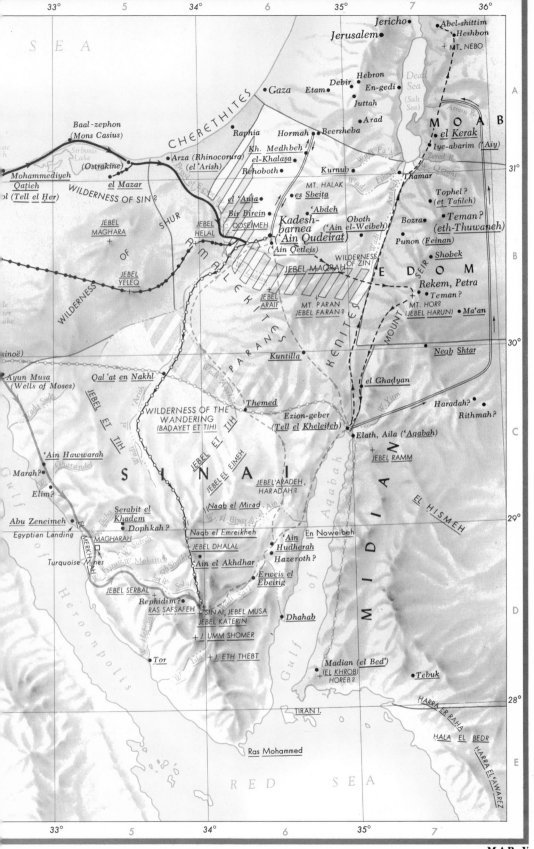

MAP V

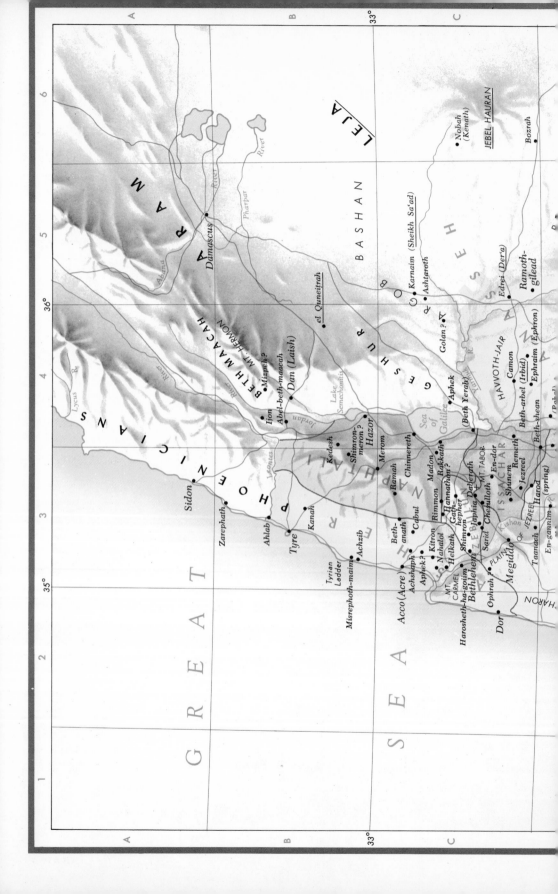

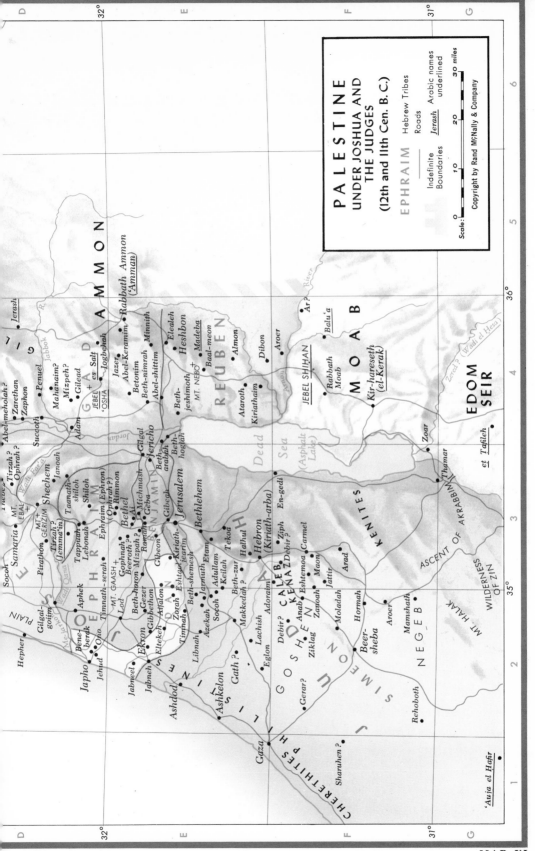

PALESTINE
UNDER JOSHUA AND
THE JUDGES
(12th and 11th Cen. B. C.)

EPHRAIM   Hebrew Tribes
           Roads
Jerash   Arabic names
           underlined

Indefinite
Boundaries

Copyright by Rand McNally & Company

Scale: 0   10   20   30 miles

MAP VI

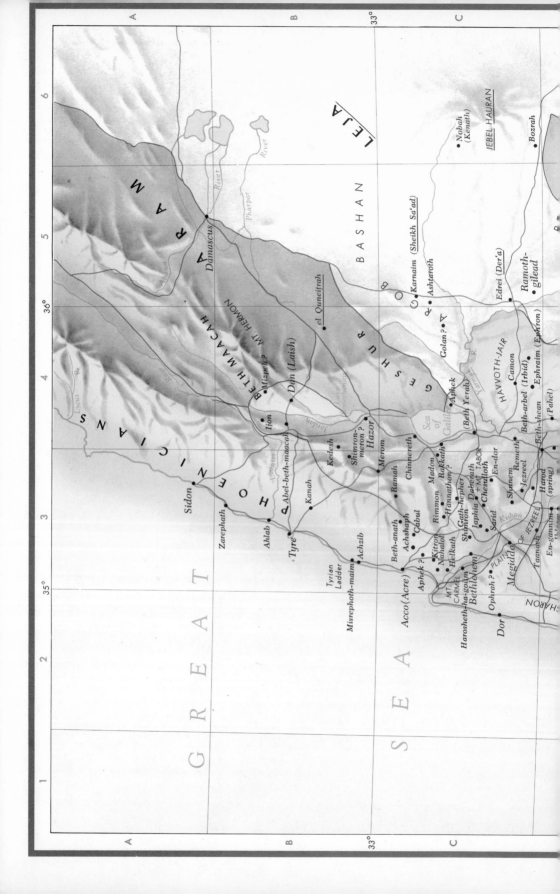

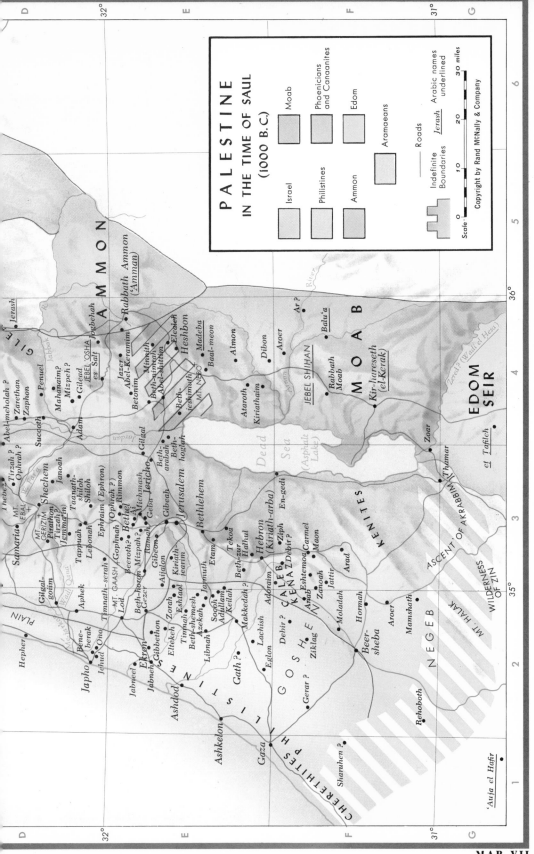

PALESTINE
IN THE TIME OF SAUL
(1000 B.C.)

Israel
Moab
Philistines
Phoenicians and Cananites
Ammon
Edom
Aramaeans

Roads
Indefinite Boundaries
Jerash Arabic names underlined

Scale 0   10   20   30 miles

Copyright by Rand McNally & Company

MAP VII

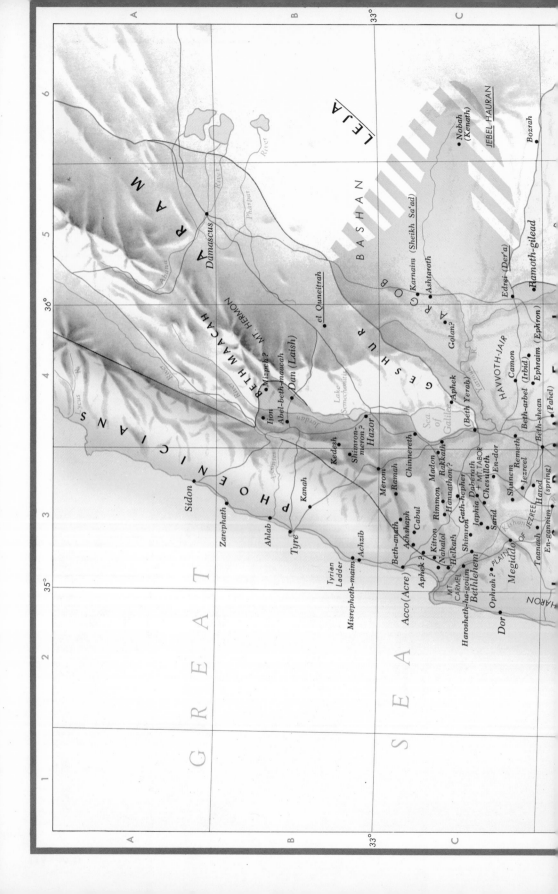

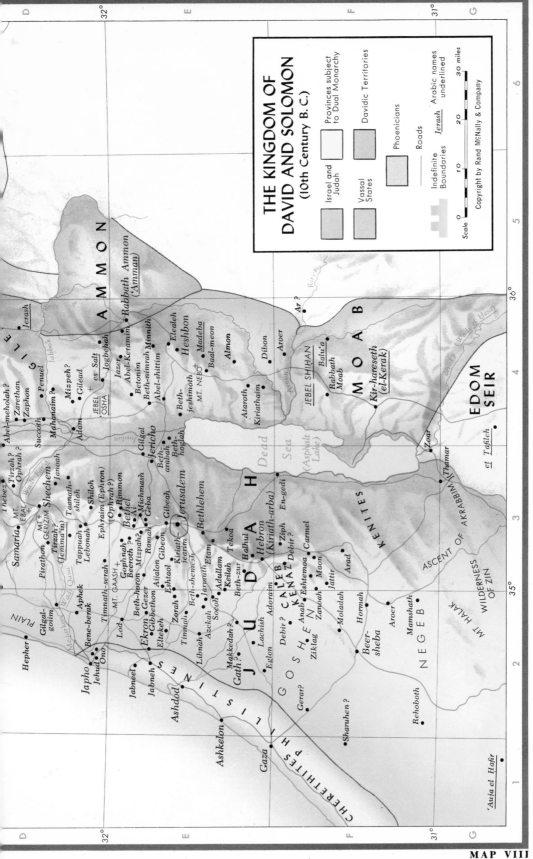

THE KINGDOM OF
DAVID AND SOLOMON
(10th Century B.C.)

Israel and Judah

Vassal States

Provinces subject to Dual Monarchy

Davidic Territories

Phoenicians

Indefinite Boundaries

Roads

Jerash   Arabic names underlined

Scale   0   10   20   30 miles

Copyright by Rand McNally & Company

AMMON

Rabbath Ammon (Amman)

GILEAD

Jerash

Abel-meholah?
Zarethan
Zaphon
Penuel
Tirzah?
Ophrah?
Succoth
Mizpeh?
Gilead
Mahanaim?
Adam
JEBEL OSHA

Jabesh?
es Salt
Jogbehah
Jazer
Abel-Keramim
Betonim
Beth-nimrah
Minnith
Abel-shittim
Beth-jeshimoth
MT. NEBO
Elealeh
Heshbon
Madeba
Baal-meon
Almon
Ataroth
Kiriathaim
Dibon
Aroer

Ar?

MOAB

JEBEL SHIHAN
Rabbath Moab
Balu'a
Kir-hareseth (el-Kerak)

EDOM
SEIR

Thebez
Tirzah?
MT. EBAL
Samaria
MT. GERIZIM
Shechem
Pirathon
Tirzah?
(Jemma'in)
Taanath-shiloh
Janoah
Tappuah?
Lebonah
Shiloh
Ephraim (Ophrah?)

Aphek
MT. GAASH
Timnath-serah
Gophnah
Beeroth?
Beth-horon
Ramah
Ajalon
Gibeon
Gibeah
Jerusalem
Geba
Michmash
Ai
Bethel
Rimmon
Gilgal
Jericho
Beth-hoglah
Beth-arabah
Beth-shemesh
Kiriath-jearim

Dead   Sea
(Asphalt Lake)

Zoar
et Tafileh
Thamar

Gilgal-goiim
Bene-berak
Jehud-Ono
Japho
Lod
Ekron
Gezer
Gibbethon
Eltekeh
Zorah
Eshtaol
Beth-shemesh
Jarmuth
Adullam
Keilah
Beth-zur
Halhul
Hebron (Kiriath-arba)
Tekoa
Bethlehem
Etam
Gophnah

Ashdod
Jabneel
Jabneh
Timnah
Makkedah?
Gath?
Azekah
Sofoh
Libnah
Adoraim
Lachish
Eglon
Debir?
Anab
Debir?
Ziph
Carmel
Maon
Eshtemoa
Zanoah
Jattir
Arad
En-gedi

JUDAH
CALEB
KENAZ
GOSHEN

KENITES

Ashkelon
Gaza

CHERETHITES   PHILISTINES

Gerar?
Ziklag
Sharuhen?
Gath?
Moladah
Hormah
Beer-sheba

Aroer
Mamshath
Rehoboth

NEGEB

MT HALAK
WILDERNESS OF ZIN
ASCENT OF AKRABBIM

Hepher
PLAIN

'Auja el Hafir

MAP VIII

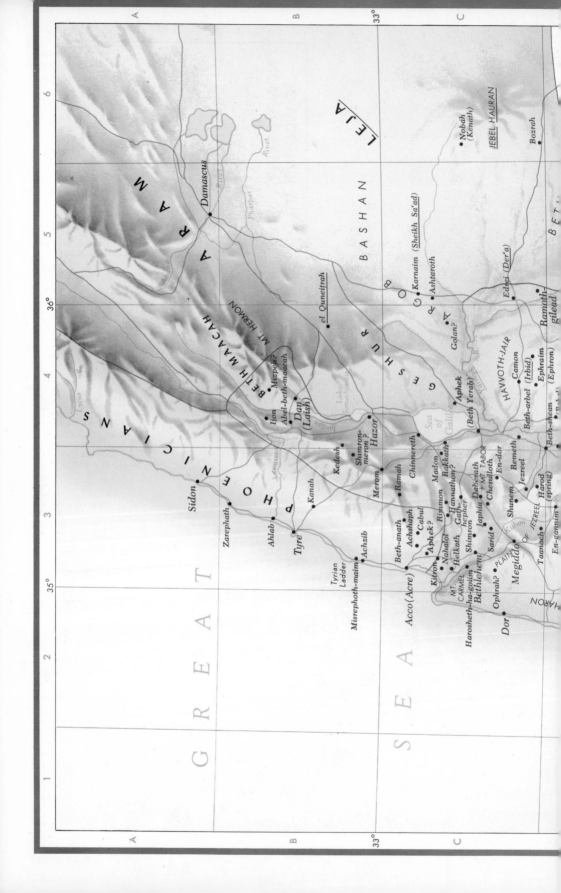

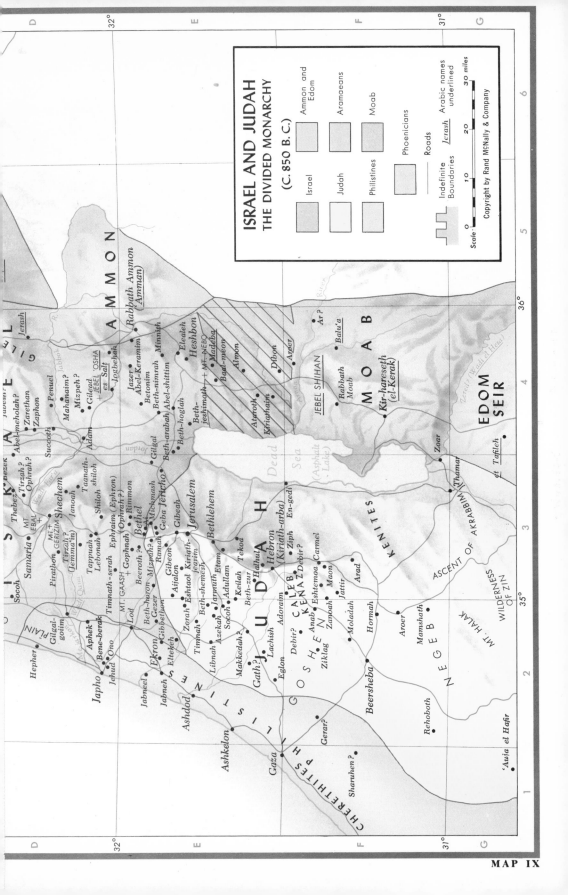

ISRAEL AND JUDAH
THE DIVIDED MONARCHY
(C. 850 B.C.)

Israel	Ammon and Edom	
Judah	Aramaeans	
Philistines	Moab	
	Phoenicians	

Roads

Jerash Arabic names underlined

Indefinite Boundaries

Scale: 0 10 20 30 miles

Copyright by Rand McNally & Company

ISRAEL

GILEAD

AMMON

Jerash

Jabbok R.

Jabesh?

Penuel

Mahanaim?

Mizpeh?

Abel-meholah?

Zarethan

Zaphon

Gilead

+ JEBEL 'OSHA
es Salt

Jogbehah?

Jazer

Rabbath Ammon
(*Amman*)

Abel-keramim

Betonim

Abel-shittim

Beth-nimrah

Minnith

Elealeh

Heshbon

+ MT. NEBO

Madeba

Baal-meon

Almon

Dibon

Aroer

Ar?

Balu'a

MOAB

JEBEL SHIHAN

Rabbath
Moab

Kir-hareseth
(*el-Kerak*)

Zoar

EDOM
SEIR

et *Tafileh*

Thamar

Thebez

MT.
EBAL

Tirzah?
Ophrah?

GERIZIM

MT.

Samaria

Pirathon?

Tappuah

Shechem
(*Tenna'in*)

Tirzah?

Janoah

Shiloh

Lebonah

Timnath-serah

Ephraim (Ophrah?)

Taanath-
shiloh

Succoth

Adam

Zaphon

Jordan R.

Gilgal

Beth-arabah

Beth-shittim

Ataroth

Kiriathaim

Beth-
jeshimoth

Dead Sea
(Asphalt
Lake)

Hepher

Aphek

Bene-berak

Japho

Jehud Ono

Lod

MT. GAASH

Beeroth?

Mizpeh?

Bethel

Rimmon

Michmash

Geba

Gibeon

Ramah

Gibeah

Jericho

Gilgal

Ai?

Jerusalem

Bethlehem

Tekoa

Beth-zur

Hebron
(*Kiriath-arba*)
Hadhul

Ziph

Debir?

Carmel

Maon

En-gedi

KENITES

Beth-horon

Gezer

Gibbethon

Aijalon

Eshtaol

Kiriath-
jearim

Zorah

Beth-shemesh

Jarmuth

Etam

Adullam

Keilah

Beth-zur

JUDAH

Adoraim

CALEB

KENAZ

Anab

Debir?

Eshtemoa

Jattir

Arad

Socoh

Timnah

Azekah

Libnah

Makkedah?

Lachish

Eglon

Gath?

GOSHEN

Debir?

Ziklag

Zanoah

Moladah

Hormah

Aroer

Mamshath

NEGEB

Beersheba

Rehoboth

Gerar?

Gaza

Ashkelon

Ashdod

Jabneel

Jabneh

Ekron

Eltekeh

PHILISTINES

CHERETHITES

Sharuhen?

'Auja el Hafir

ASCENT OF AKRABBIM

WILDERNESS
OF ZIN

MT. HALAK

SHUR

PLAIN

Gilgal-
goiim

Socoh

MAP IX

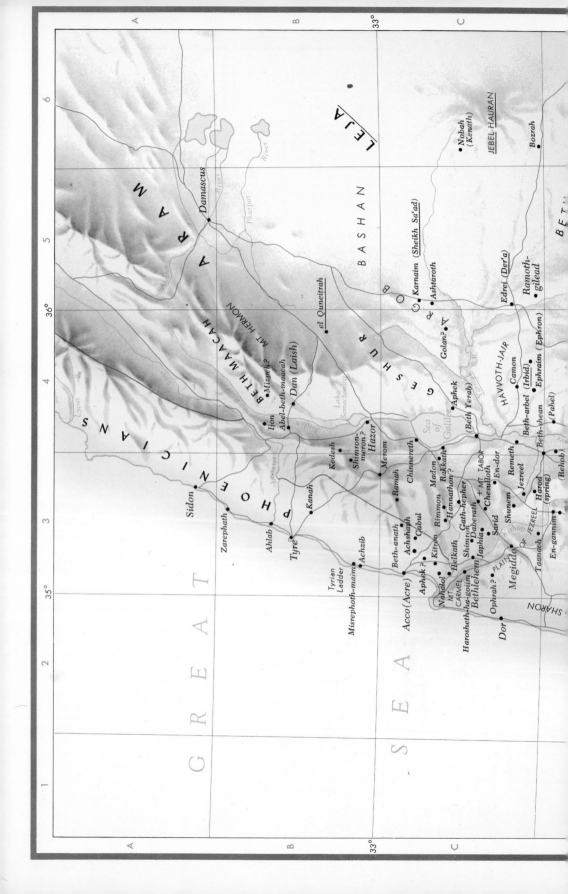

A
B
33°
C

6

LEJA

JEBEL HAURAN

Nobah
(Kenath)

Bozrah

A R A M

5

Damascus

River

Phalpar

Abana

B A S H A N

Karnaim (Sheikh Sa'ad)

Ashtaroth

Edrei (Der'a)

Ramoth-gilead

BETH

O
B

R

36°

el Quneitrah

MT. HERMON

Golan?

Aphek

HAVVOTH-JAIR

Camon

Beth-arbel (Irbid)

Ephraim (Ephron)

G E S H U R

4

B E T H M A A C A H

Mizpeh?

Dan (Laish)

Ijon

Abel-beth-maacah

Hazor

Merom

Shimron-meron?

Lake Semachonitis

Jordan

Sea of Galilee

(Beth Yerah)

Yarmuk R.

Pahel

Beth-shean

Rehob

P H O E N I C I A N S

Kedesh

Chinnereth

Madon

Rakkath

Hannathon?

+ MT. TABOR

Chesulloth

En-dor

Remeth

Jezreel

Harod (spring)

Ramah

Rimmon

Litani

Kanah

Leontes

Sidon

Zarephath

Ahlab

Tyre

Achzib

Beth-anath

Achshaph

Gabul

Kitron

Gath-hepher

Shimron

Daberath

Sarid

Shunem

Taanach

En-gannim

3

MT. HERMON

Leontes

Tyrian
Ladder

Misrephoth-maim

Acco (Acre)

Aphek?

Nahalol

MT. CARMEL

Helkath

Harosheth-ha-goiim

Bethlehem

Japhia

Ophrah?

Dor

PLAIN OF JEZREEL

Megiddo

Kishon

SHARON

35°

G R E A T

S E A

2

Lycus R.

33°

A
B
C

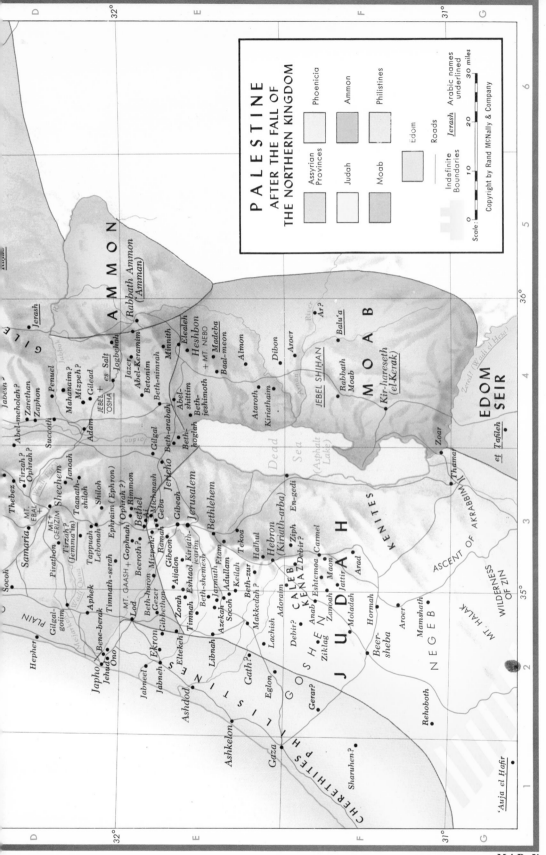

PALESTINE
AFTER THE FALL OF
THE NORTHERN KINGDOM

Assyrian Provinces

Phoenicia

Judah

Ammon

Moab

Philistines

Edom

Roads

Indefinite Boundaries

Jerash Arabic names underlined

Copyright by Rand McNally & Company

Scale: 0 10 20 30 miles

MAP X

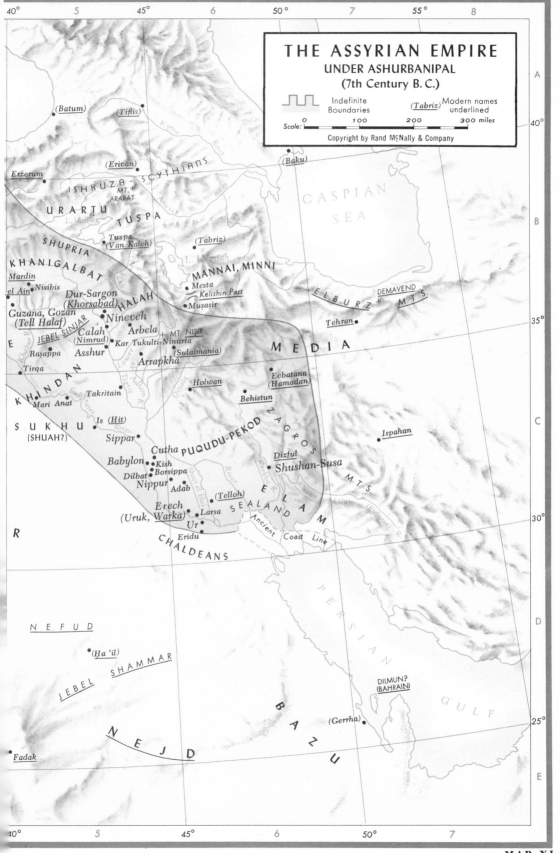

THE ASSYRIAN EMPIRE
UNDER ASHURBANIPAL
(7th Century B.C.)

Indefinite Boundaries

(*Tabriz*) Modern names underlined

Scale: 0   100   200   300 miles

Copyright by Rand McNally & Company

40° 5 45° 6 50° 7 55° 8

(*Batum*) (*Tiflis*)

Erzerum

(*Erivan*) SCYTHIANS (*Baku*)

ISHKUZA MT. ARARAT

URARTU TUSPA CASPIAN SEA

SHUPRIA L. Van

KHANIGALBAT Tuspa (*Van Kaleh*) (*Tabriz*)

Mardin el Ain Nisibis L. Urmiah MANNAI, MINNI DEMAVEND

Dur-Sargon (*Khorsabad*) HALAH Mesta Kelishin Pass ELBURZ MTS.

Guzana, Gozan (*Tell Halaf*) Nineveh Muşaşir *Tehran*

Raşappa Calah (*Nimrud*) Arbela MT. NIŞIR MEDIA

JEBEL SINJAR Kar Tukulti-Ninurta (*Sulaimania*)

Tirqa Asshur Arrapkha *Holwan* Ecbatana (*Hamadan*)

KHINDAN Takritain *Behistun* ZAGROS

Mari Anat *Ispahan*

SUKHU (SHUAH?) Is (*Hit*) PUQUDU-PEKOD Dizful

Sippar Shushan-Susa

Cutha ELAM MTS.

Babylon Kish

Dilbat Borsippa SEALAND

Nippur Adab

Erech (Uruk, *Warka*) (*Telloh*) Larsa Ancient Coast Line

Ur Eridu

CHALDEANS

NEFUD

(*Ha'il*)

JEBEL SHAMMAR PERSIAN

BAZU DILMUN? (BAHRAIN) GULF

NEJD (*Gerrha*)

Fadak

MAP XI

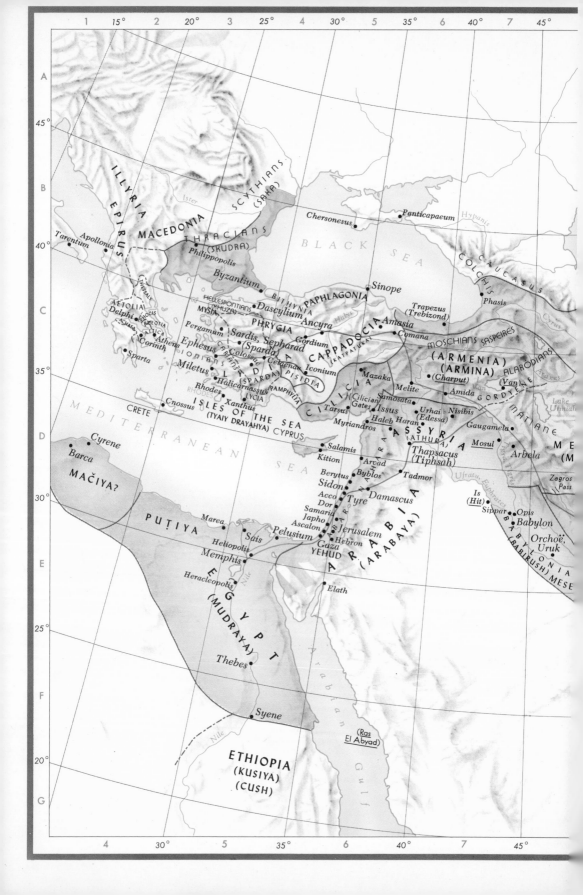

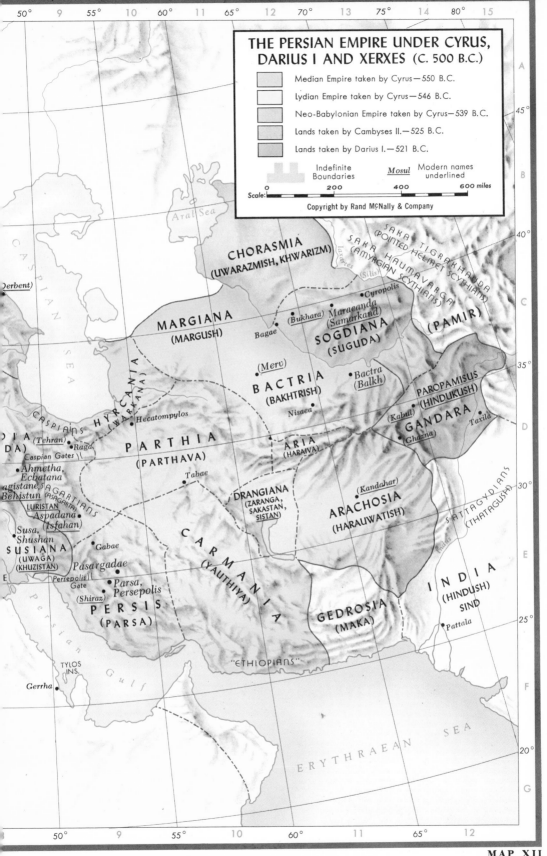

THE PERSIAN EMPIRE UNDER CYRUS, DARIUS I AND XERXES (C. 500 B.C.)

Median Empire taken by Cyrus—550 B.C.

Lydian Empire taken by Cyrus—546 B.C.

Neo-Babylonian Empire taken by Cyrus—539 B.C.

Lands taken by Cambyses II.—525 B.C.

Lands taken by Darius I.—521 B.C.

Indefinite Boundaries

Mosul Modern names underlined

Scale: 0   200   400   600 miles

Copyright by Rand McNally & Company

Aral Sea

CHORASMIA (UWARAZMISH, KHWARIZM)

SAKA TIGRAKHAUDA (POINTED HELMET SCYTHIANS)

SAKA HAUMAVARGA (AMYRGIAN SCYTHIANS)

(*Jaxartes*) (*Silis*)

Derbent)

MARGIANA (MARGUSH)

•Cyropolis

(*Bukhara*) •Maracanda (*Samarkand*)

Bagae

SOGDIANA (SUGUDA)

(PAMIR)

(*Merv*)

BACTRIA (BAKHTRISH)

•Bactra (*Balkh*)

PAROPAMISUS (HINDUKUSH)

HYRCANIA (WARKANA)

•Hecatompylos

Nisaea

(*Kabul*) GANDARA

(*Ghazna*) •Taxila

DIA (DA)

•(*Tehran*) •Raga

PARTHIA (PARTHAVA)

ARIA (HARAIVA)

•Tabae

•Ahmetha, Echbatana agistane, (*Isfahan*) Behistun

SAGARTIANS (ASAGARTA)

DRANGIANA (ZARANGA, SAKASTAN, SISTAN)

(*Kandahar*)

ARACHOSIA (HARAUWATISH)

SATTAGYDIANS (THATAGUSH)

LURISTAN Aspadana• (*Isfahan*)

•Susa, Shushan

SUSIANA (UWAGA) (KHUZISTAN)

•Gabae

Pasargadae

CARMANIA (YAUTHIYA)

INDIA (HINDUSH) SIND

Persepolis• Gate

•Parsa, Persepolis

(*Shiraz*)

PERSIS (PARSA)

GEDROSIA (MAKA)

•Pattala

TYLOS INS.

"ETHIOPIANS"

•Gerrha

ERYTHRAEAN SEA

MAP XII

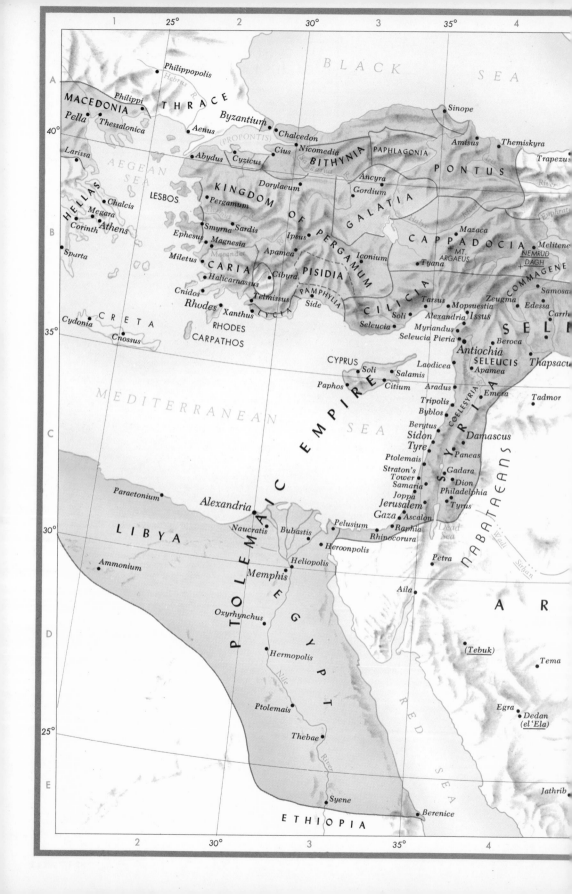

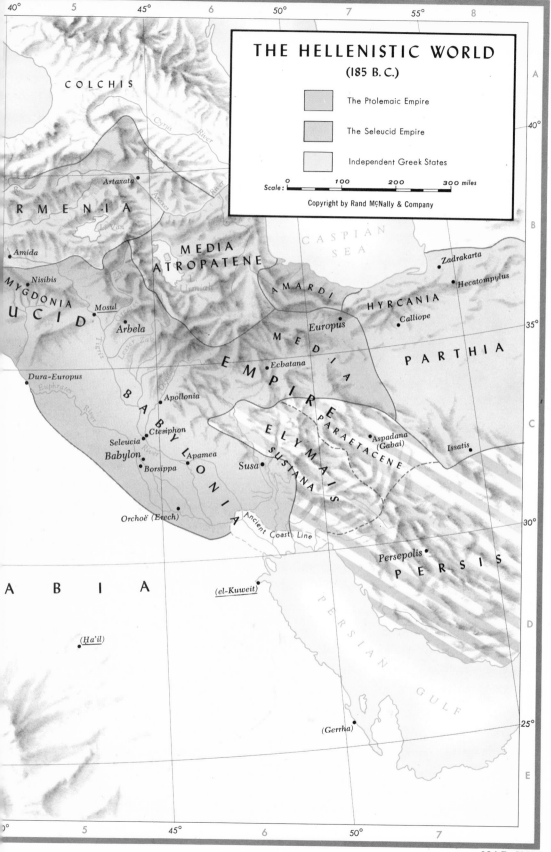

THE HELLENISTIC WORLD
(185 B.C.)

The Ptolemaic Empire

The Seleucid Empire

Independent Greek States

Scale: 0 100 200 300 miles

Copyright by Rand McNally & Company

COLCHIS

Artaxata

ARMENIA

Amida

Nisibis

MYGDONIA

UCID

Mosul

Arbela

MEDIA ATROPATENE

L. Van

Urmia L.

Cyrus River

Araxes River

CASPIAN SEA

Zadrakarta

Hecatompylus

AMARDI

HYRCANIA

Calliope

Europus

MEDIA

Ecbatana

PARTHIA

EMPIRE

Dura-Europus

Euphrates River

BABYLONIA

Apollonia

Seleucia *Ctesiphon*

Babylon *Apamea*

Borsippa

Susa

SUSIANA

ELYMAIS

PARAETACENE

Aspadana (Gabai)

Issatis

Tigris *Lesser Zab*

Orchoë (Erech)

Ancient Coast Line

Persepolis

PERSIS

ABIA

(el-Kuweit)

(Ha'il)

PERSIAN GULF

(Gerrha)

MAP XIII

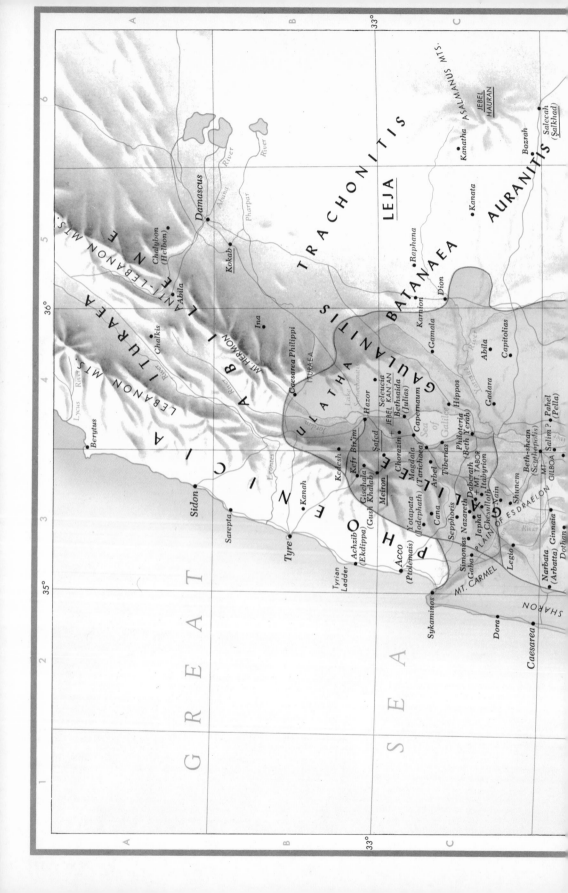

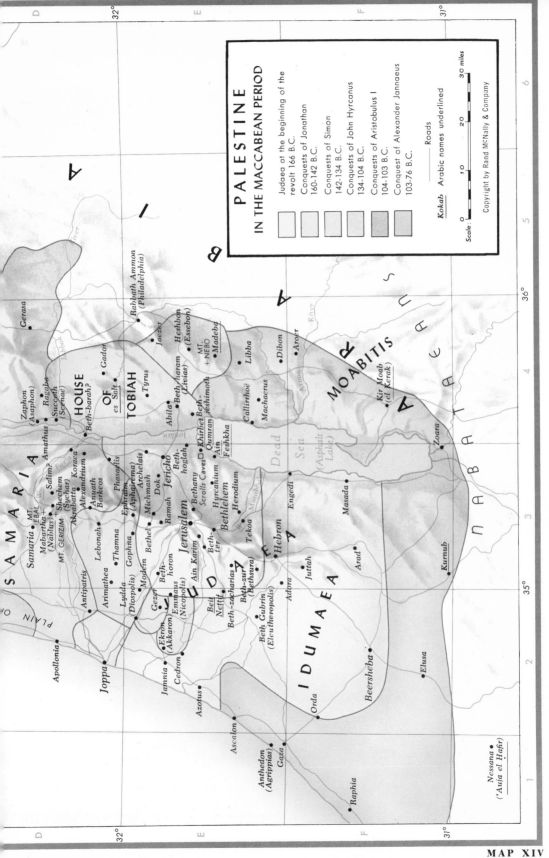

PALESTINE
IN THE MACCABEAN PERIOD

Judaea at the beginning of the
revolt 166 B.C.

Conquests of Jonathan
160-142 B.C.

Conquests of Simon
142-134 B.C.

Conquests of John Hyrcanus
134-104 B.C.

Conquests of Aristobulus I
104-103 B.C.

Conquest of Alexander Jannaeus
103-76 B.C.

Roads

Kokab Arabic names underlined

Scale: 0   10   20   30 miles

Copyright by Rand McNally & Company

Gerasa

Rabbath Ammon
(Philadelphia)

Jaezer

Heshbon
(Essebon)

MT.
+ NEBO
Madeba

Libba

Dibon
Aroer

River

Zaphon
(Asophon)
Raqaba
Succoth
Seznae?

HOUSE

Gador
Beth-barah?

OF
es Salt

Tyrus

TOBIAH

Beth-haram
(Livias)
Beth-
jeshimoth

Khirbet
Qumran
Ain
Feshkha

MOABITIS

Kir Moab
(el Kerak)

Callirrhoë

Machaerus

Dead
Sea
(Asphalt
Lake)

Zoara

SAMARIA

Samaria
MT.
EBAL +
Mabartha +
(Nablus)
MT. GERIZIM +
Akrabatta

Salim? Amathus
Shechem
(Sychar)

Koraca
Alexandrium

Abila

Asaphon)

PLAIN OF

Apollonia

Antipatris

Lydda
(Diospolis)

Arimathea

Thamna

Lebonah

Gophna

Bethel

Anuath
Borkeos

Ephraim
(Aphairema)
Archelais
Michmash
Ramah

Phasaelis
Dok
Jericho
Beth-
hoglah

Bethany
Scrolls Caves

Hyrcanium

Herodium

Joppa

Jamnia

Cedron

Ekron
(Akkaron)
Emmaus
(Nicopolis)

Gezer

Beth-
horon
Ain Karim

Modein

JERUSALEM

Beth-
ter

Bethlehem
Tekoa

Azotus

Beit
Nettif

Beth-zacharias
Beth-zur
(Bethsura)

Adora
Juttah

Hebron

JUDAEA

Engedi

Masada

Ascalon

Beth Gubrin
(Eleutheropolis)

Adora

Orda

Arad

Anthedon
(Agrippias)
Gaza

IDUMAEA

Beersheba

Elusa

Kurnub

NABATAEAN

Raphia

Nessana
('Auja el Hafir)

MAP XIV

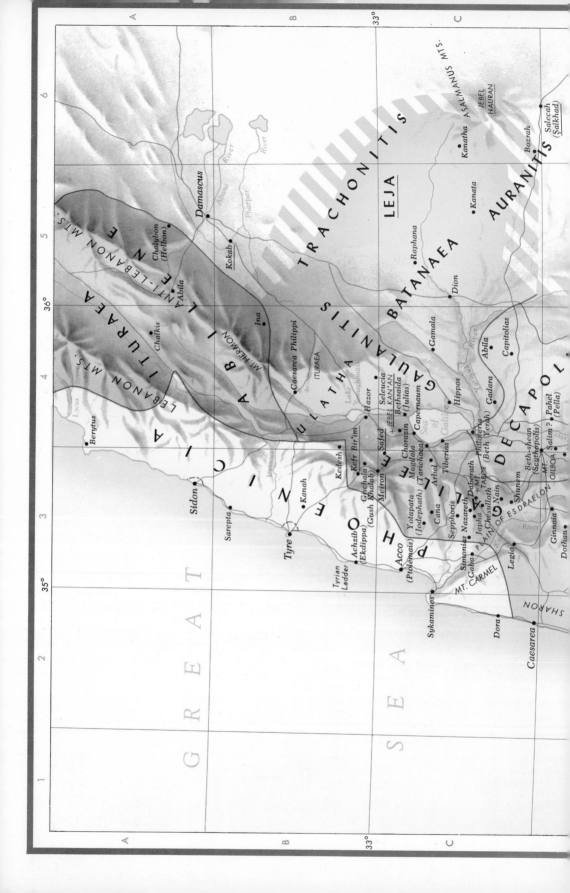

PALESTINE
UNDER HEROD THE GREAT (37-4 B.C.)

Herod	Phoenicia (Syria)
Decapolis	Ituraea

Roads

Kokab Arabic names underlined

Indefinite Boundaries

Scale: 0 — 10 — 20 — 30 miles

Copyright by Rand McNally & Company

Map labels (selection):

Gerasa · Rabbath Ammon (Philadelphia) · Ragaba · Zaphon (Asaphon) · Succoth (Scenae) · Beth-barah? · es Salt · Tyrus · Gador · Jaezer · Heshbon · MT. NEBO · Madeba · Dibon · Aroer

PERAEA · Abila · Beth-haram (Livias) · Beth-jeshimoth · Callirrhoë · Machaerus · MOABITIS · Kir Moab (el Kerak)

SAMARIA · Samaria (Sebaste) · MT. EBAL · Mabartha (Nablus) · MT. GERIZIM · Shechem (Sychar) · Akrabatta · Korea · Alexandrium · Anuath Borkeos · Phasaelis · Archelais · Khirbet Qumran · Ain Feshkha · Scrolls Caves

Apollonia · PLAIN OF SHARON · Antipatris · Arimathea · Thamna · Lydda (Diospolis) · Lebonah · Isana (Jeshana) · Gophna · Bethel · Michmush · Dok · Jericho · Beth-hoglah · Bethany · Hyrcanium · Herodium

Joppa · Ekron · Gezer · Modein · Beth-horon · Emmaus (Nicopolis) · Beit Nettif · Ain Karim · Jerusalem · Ramah · Ephraim · Bethlehem · Tekoa · Beth-zur · Hebron

Jamnia · Azotus · Ascalon · Anthedon (Agrippias) · Gaza · Orda · Beth Gubrin (Eleutheropolis) · Adora · Juttah · Arad · Engedi · Masada · Kurnub

JUDAEA · IDUMAEA · Beersheba · Elusa · Raphia · Nessana ('Auja el Hafir)

Dead Sea (Asphalt Lake) · Zoara · NABATAEA

Jordan River · Jabbok · Wadi Fara

MAP XV

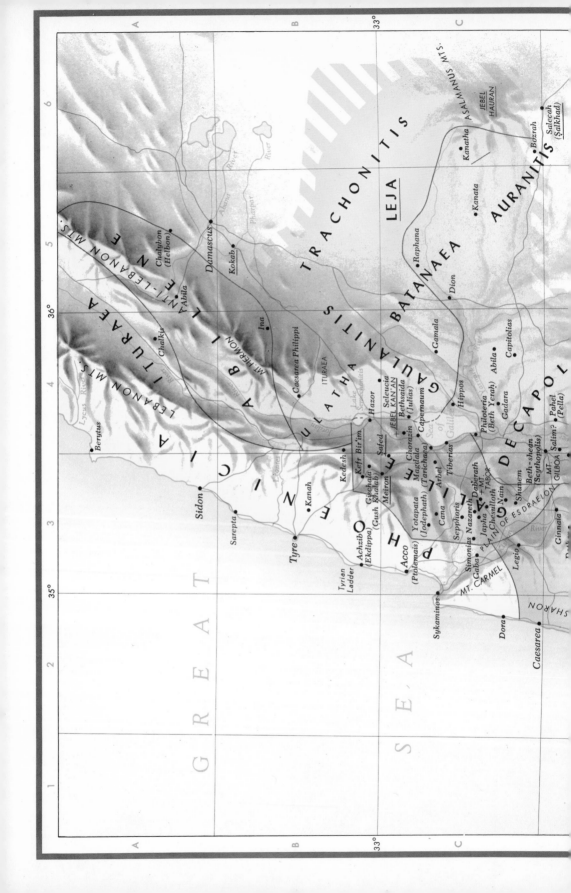

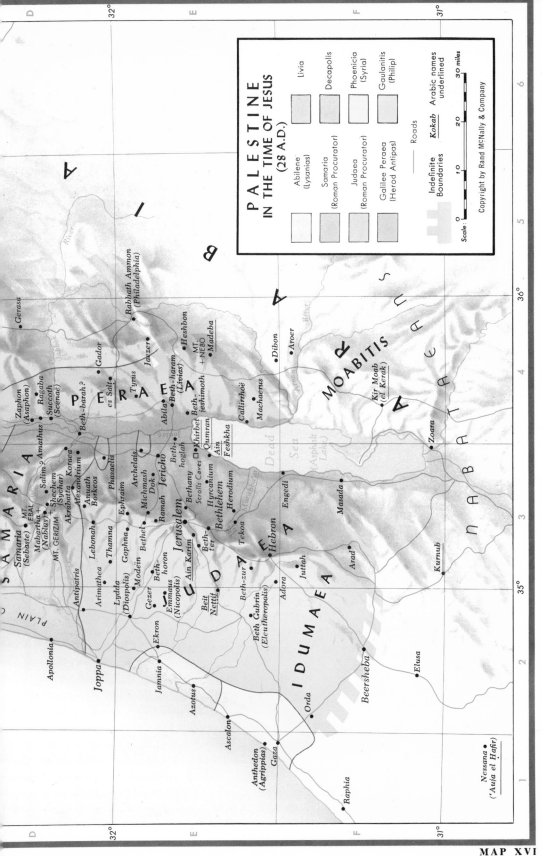

PALESTINE
IN THE TIME OF JESUS
(28 A.D.)

Abilene
(Lysanias)

Samaria
(Roman Procurator)

Judaea
(Roman Procurator)

Galilee Peraea
(Herod Antipas)

Livia

Decapolis

Phoenicia
(Syria)

Gaulanitis
(Philip)

Indefinite
Boundaries

Roads

Kokab   Arabic names
underlined

Scale   0   10   20   30 miles

Copyright by Rand McNally & Company

MAP XVI

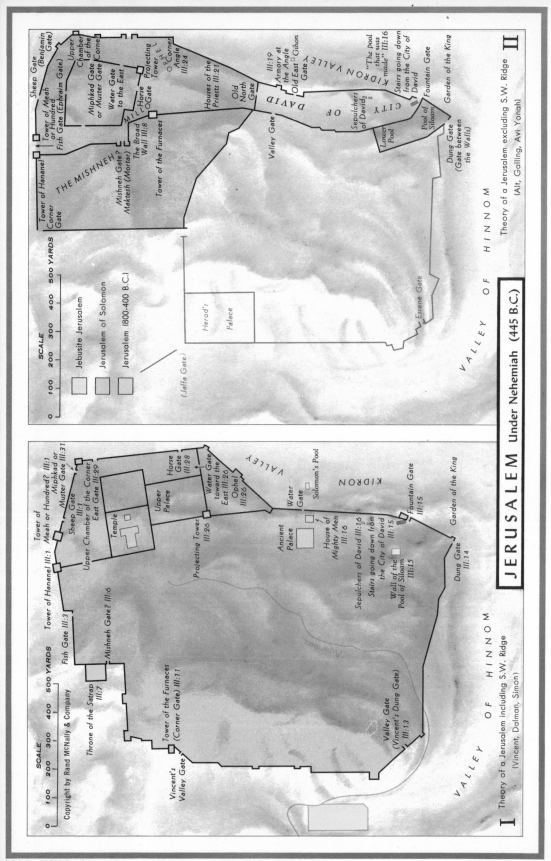

JERUSALEM Under Nehemiah (445 B.C.)

II Theory of a Jerusalem excluding S.W. Ridge
(Alt, Galling, Avi Yonah)

Map II labels:

Sheep Gate (Benjamin Gate)
Tower of Meah or Hundred
Fish Gate (Ephraim Gate)
Upper Chamber of the Corner
Miphkad Gate or Muster Gate
Water Gate to the East
Horse Gate
Projecting Tower
Corner Angle III:24
Houses of the Priests III:21
Old North Gate
Armory at the Angle III:19
Old East Gihon Gate
"The pool that was made" III:16
Stairs going down from the City of David
Fountain Gate
Garden of the King
Sepulchers of David
Lower Pool
Pool of Siloam
Dung Gate (Gate between the Walls)

Tower of Hananel
Corner Gate
THE MISHNEH
Mishneh Gate? Maktesh (Mortar)
The Broad Wall III:8
Tower of the Furnaces
MILL HILL

CITY OF DAVID
KIDRON VALLEY
Valley Gate

Herod's Palace
(Jaffa Gate)
Essene Gate

VALLEY OF HINNOM

SCALE
0   100   200   300   400   500 YARDS

Jebusite Jerusalem
Jerusalem of Solomon
Jerusalem (800–400 B.C.)

I Theory of a Jerusalem including S.W. Ridge
(Vincent, Dalman, Simon)

Map I labels:

Tower of Meah or Hundred? III:1
Miphkad or Muster Gate III:31
Sheep Gate III:1
Upper Chamber of the Corner
Tower of Hananel III:1
East Gate III:29
Temple
Horse Gate III:28
Upper Palace
Water Gate toward the East III:26
Ophel III:26
Water Gate
Solomon's Pool
KIDRON VALLEY
Fish Gate III:3
Mishneh Gate? III:6
Throne of the Satrap III:7
Tower of the Furnaces (Corner Gate) III:11
Projecting Tower III:26
Ancient Palace
House of Mighty Men III:16
Sepulchers of David III:16
Stairs going down from the City of David
Wall of the Pool of Siloam III:15
Fountain Gate III:15
Garden of the King
Dung Gate III:14
Vincent's Valley Gate
Valley Gate (Vincent's Dung Gate) III:13

VALLEY OF HINNOM

Copyright by Rand McNally & Company

SCALE
0   100   200   300   400   500 YARDS

MAP XVII

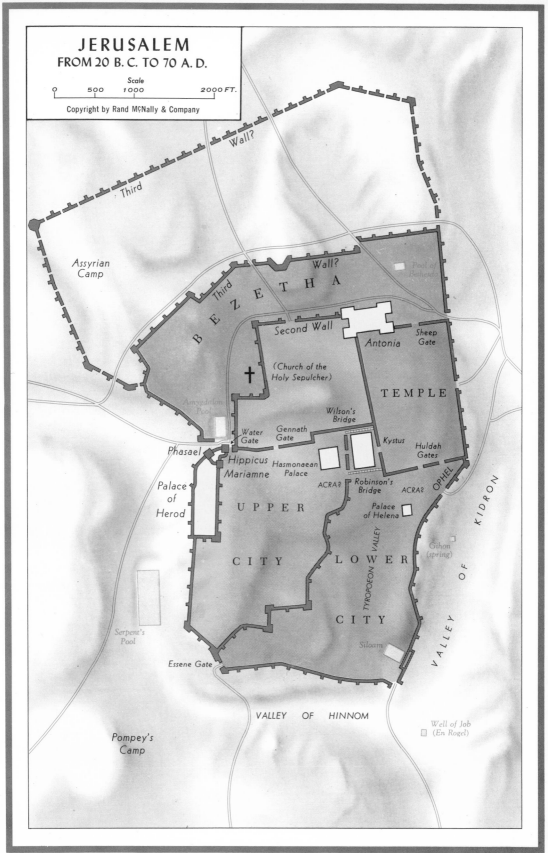

JERUSALEM
FROM 20 B.C. TO 70 A.D.

Scale
0   500   1000   2000 FT.

Copyright by Rand McNally & Company

Assyrian
Camp

Third

Wall?

Third

B E Z E T H A

Wall?

Second Wall

Antonia

Sheep
Gate

TEMPLE

(Church of the
Holy Sepulcher)

Pool of
Bethesda

Amygdalon
Pool

Water
Gate

Gennath
Gate

Wilson's
Bridge

Kystus

Huldah
Gates

Phasael

Hippicus
Mariamne

Hasmonaean
Palace

ACRA?

Robinson's
Bridge

ACRA?

OPHEL

Palace
of
Herod

UPPER

CITY

Palace
of Helena

Gihon
(spring)

VALLEY   OF   KIDRON

LOWER

CITY

TYROPOEON   VALLEY

Serpent's
Pool

Siloam

Essene Gate

VALLEY   OF   HINNOM

Pompey's
Camp

Well of Job
(En Rogel)

MAP XVIII

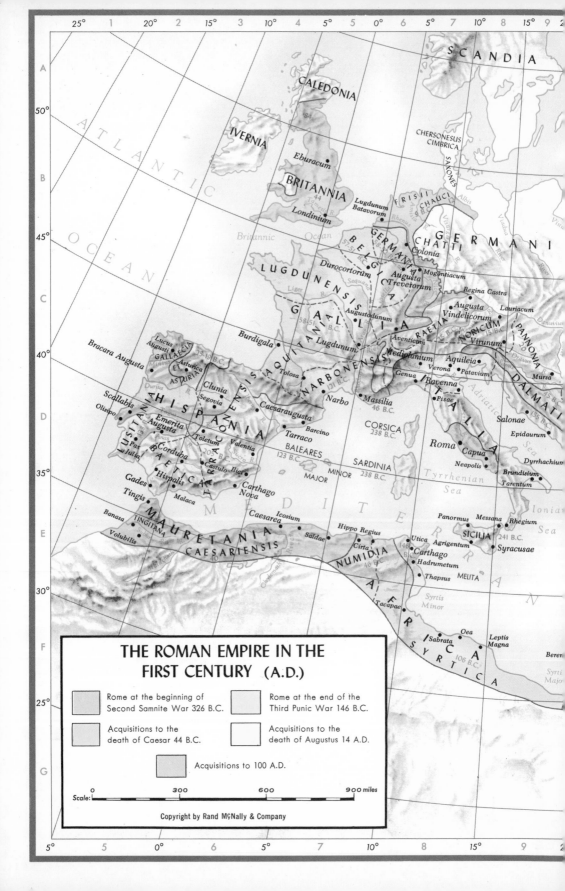

THE ROMAN EMPIRE IN THE FIRST CENTURY (A.D.)

Rome at the beginning of Second Samnite War 326 B.C.

Rome at the end of the Third Punic War 146 B.C.

Acquisitions to the death of Caesar 44 B.C.

Acquisitions to the death of Augustus 14 A.D.

Acquisitions to 100 A.D.

Scale: 0   300   600   900 miles

Copyright by Rand McNally & Company

SCANDIA

CALEDONIA

IVERNIA

BRITANNIA
Eburacum
Londinium

ATLANTIC OCEAN

Britannic Ocean

CHERSONESUS CIMBRICA
SAXONES

GERMANI
CHAUCI
FRISII
CHATTI
Colonia
Mogontiacum
Regina Castra
Lauriacum

Lugdunum Batavorum

BELGICA
GERMANIA
Durocortorum
Augusta Trevetorum

LUGDUNENSIS
GALLIA
Augustodunum
Lugdunum
Aventicum
RAETIA
Augusta Vindelicorum
NORICUM
Virunum
PANNONIA

Burdigala

AQUITANIA
NARBONENSIS

Bracara Augusta
Lucus Augusti
GALLAECIA
Asturica
ASTURIA
Clunia
Segovia
Caesaraugusta
Tolosa
Narbo
Massilia 46 B.C.
Mediolanium
Verona
Patavium
Genua
Ravenna
Pisae
Aquileia
ITALIA
DALMATIA
Mursa
Salonae
Epidaurum

HISPANIA
Scallabis
Olisipo
Emerita Augusta
LUSITANIA
Pax Julia
Corduba
BAETICA
Hispalis
Gades
Tingis
Malaca

TARRACONENSIS
Barcino
Tarraco
BALEARES
MAJOR
MINOR 123 B.C.
CORSICA 238 B.C.
SARDINIA 238 B.C.
Toletum
Valentia
Castulo
Iliei
Carthago Nova

Roma
Capua
Neapolis
Tyrrhenian Sea
Dyrrhachium
Brundisium
Tarentum

Caesarea
Icosium
Saldae
Banasa
Volubilis
TINGITANA
MAURETANIA CAESARIENSIS

Panormus
Messana
Rhegium
SICILIA
Agrigentum
Syracusae
241 B.C.
Ionian Sea

Hippo Regius
Utica
Cirta
Carthago
Hadrumetum
Thapsus
MELITA
NUMIDIA

Tacapae

AFRICA
SYRTICA

Sabrata
Oea
Leptis Magna
106 B.C.
Berer

Syrtis Minor

Syrti Maj

MEDITERRANEAN

MAP XIX

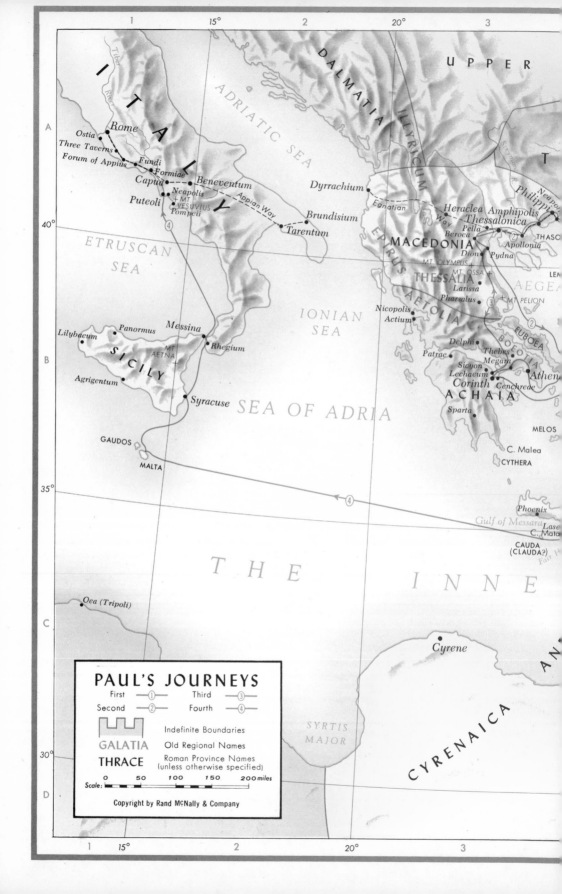

Map labels

1   15°   2   20°   3

ITALY

DALMATIA

UPPER

ADRIATIC SEA

ILLYRICUM

A

Ostia
Rome
Three Taverns
Forum of Appius
Fundi
Formiae
Capua   Beneventum
Neapolis   Appian Way
MT.
Puteoli   VESUVIUS
Pompeii

Dyrrachium

Egnatian
Way
Heraclea   Amphipolis
Thessalonica
Pella
Beroea
Apollonia
THASO
Dion   Pydna

T

Philippi

Neapol

40°

Appian Way

Brundisium

Tarentum

MACEDONIA

MT. OLYMPUS
MT. OSSA

THESSALI

LEM

ETRUSCAN
SEA

EPIRUS

AETOLIA

Larissa
Pharsalus

MT. PELION

AEGE

Nicopolis
Actium

IONIAN
SEA

EUBOEA

Delphi
Patrae

BOEOTIA
Thebes
Megara
Sicyon
Lechaeum
Corinth   Cenchreae
ACHAIA

Athen

B

Lilybaeum

Panormus

Messina
MT.
AETNA

SICILY

Rhegium

Agrigentum

Syracuse

SEA OF ADRIA

Sparta

MELOS

C. Malea
CYTHERA

GAUDOS

MALTA

35°

Phoenix
Gulf of Messara   Lase
C. Mata

CAUDA
(CLAUDA?)

Oea (Tripoli)

THE

INNE

C

Cyrene

SYRTIS
MAJOR

CYRENAICA

AN

PAUL'S JOURNEYS

First	①	Third	③
Second	②	Fourth	④

Indefinite Boundaries

GALATIA   Old Regional Names

THRACE   Roman Province Names
(unless otherwise specified)

Scale: 0   50   100   150   200 miles

Copyright by Rand McNally & Company

30°

D

1   15°   2   20°   3

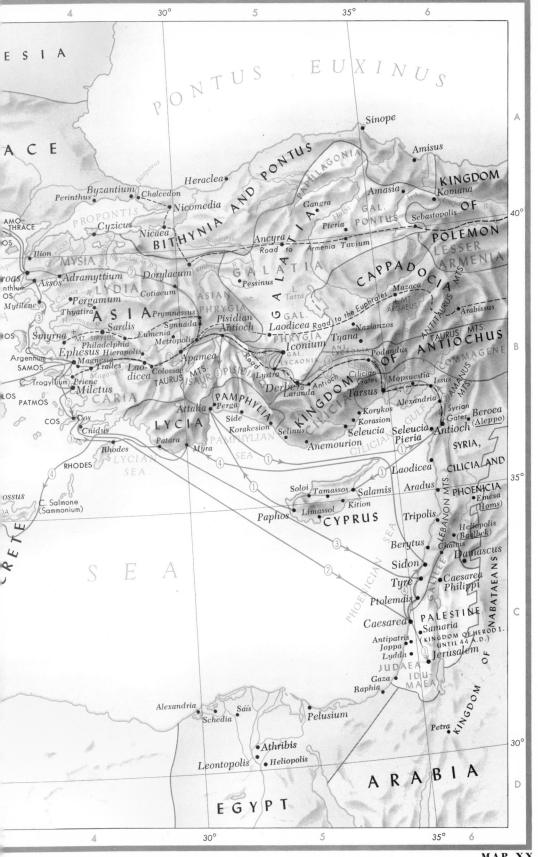

PONTUS EUXINUS

ESIA

ACE

THRACE

4 **30°** **5** **35°** **6**

Sinope — A

Amisus

Heraclea

KINGDOM

Perinthus Byzantium Chalcedon

Komana

PROPONTIS Nicomedia

PAPHLAGONIA Amasia

AMO- Cyzicus Nicaea

THRACE

Gangra GAL.

OS Ilion

BITHYNIA AND PONTUS Pteria PONTUS Sebastopolis — 40°

Ancyra Armenia Tavium

OF

Road to POLEMON

MYSIA Dorylaeum LESSER

roas Assos Adramyttium Cotiaeum GALATIA ARMENIA

R LYDIA ASIAN

OS Pergamum PHRYGIA CAPPADOCIA Arabissus

Mytilene Thyatira Prymnessus Mazaca

A ASIA Synnada G. GAL. MT.

Sardis Eumenia Pisidian Laodicea ARGAEUS ANTITAURUS MTS.

Philadelphia Metropolis Antioch PHRYGIA Nazianzos TAURUS MTS.

Smyrna MT. SIPYLUS Iconium Tyana OF COMMAGENE

Argennum Ephesus Hierapolis GAL. Podandus KINGDOM AMANUS

SAMOS Magnesia Apamea LYCAONIA Cilician ANTIOCHUS

C. Trogyllium Tralles Lao- ANT. Antioch Gates Mopsuestia MTS.

Priene dicea Colossae LYCAONIA Derbe Tarsus Alexandria Issus

PATMOS Miletus TAURUS MTS. Lystra Laranda Alexandria Syrian Beroea

ISAUR PISID CILICIAN Gates (Aleppo)

CARIA PAMPHYLIA KINGDOM Seleucia Syrian Antioch

COS Cos Attalia Perga Pieria Gates

Cnidus Side Korykos SYRIA,

Rhodes Korakesion Selinus Korasion CILICIA AND

RHODES Patara Anemourion Seleucia Laodicea PHOENICIA

Myra PAMPHYLIAN Pieria — 35°

ossus LYCIAN SEA Aradus Emesa

C. Salmone SEA Soloi Tamassos Salamis Tripolis (Homs)

(Sammonium) Limassol Kition CYPRUS Heliopolis

Paphos (Baalbek)

Berytus Chalcis Damascus

SEA Sidon GALILEE Caesarea

Tyre Philippi

Ptolemais

CRETE Caesarea PALESTINE

Samaria (KINGDOM OF HEROD I.

Antipatris UNTIL 44 A.D.)

Joppa Jerusalem

Lydda JUDAEA KINGDOM

IDU-

Gaza MAEA

Raphia

Alexandria Saïs Petra

Schedia Pelusium — 30°

KINGDOM OF NABATAEANS

Athribis

Leontopolis Heliopolis D

ARABIA

EGYPT

4 **30°** **5** **35°** **6**

MAP XX

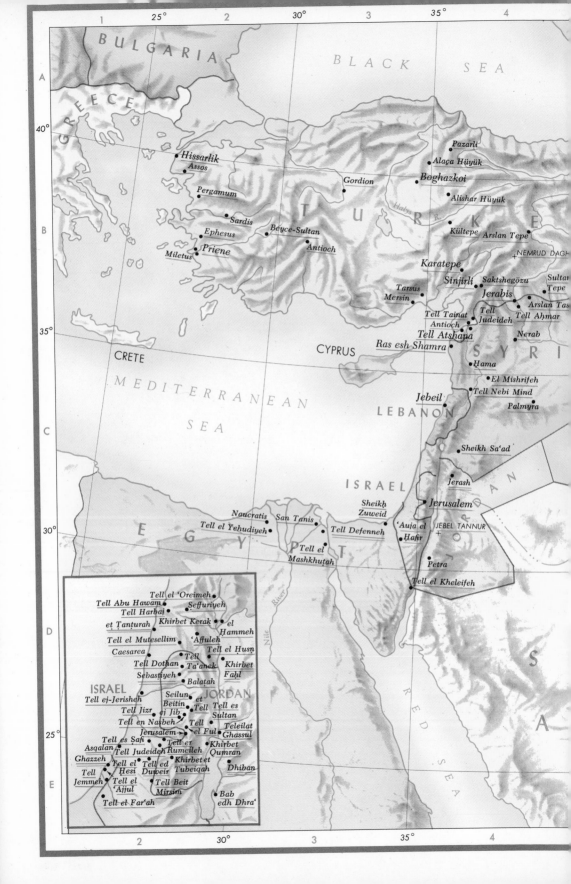

Map coordinates top: 1 · 25° · 2 · 30° · 3 · 35° · 4

BULGARIA

BLACK SEA

GREECE

A

40°

Hissarlik
Assos

Pergamum

Pazarli
Alaça Hüyük

Boghazkoi

Alishar Hüyük

Gordion

B

Sardis

Ephesus
Beyce-Sultan
Priene
Miletus
Antioch

TURKEY

Kültepe
Arslan Tepe

NEMRUD DAGH

Karatepe

Sinjirli
Saktshegözu
Sultan
Tepe

Tarsus
Mersin
Jerabis

Arslan Tash

Tell Tainat
Antioch
Tell
Judeideh
Tell Aḥmar

35°

Tell Atshana
Ras esh Shamra
Nerab

CYPRUS

SYRIA

Ḥama

CRETE

El Mishrifeh
Tell Nebi Mind
Palmyra

MEDITERRANEAN

Jebeil

LEBANON

SEA

Sheikh Saʿad

C

Jerash

ISRAEL

Jerusalem

JORDAN

Sheikh
Zuweid

Naucratis
San Tanis
Tell Defenneh
ʿAuja el
Ḥafir
JEBEL TANNUR

30°

Tell el Yehudiyeh

EGYPT
Tell el
Mashkhuṭah

Petra

Tell el Kheleifeh

D

Nile River

RED SEA

Inset map (ISRAEL / JORDAN):

Tell el ʿOreimeh
Tell Abu Hawam
Seffuriyeh
Tell Harbaj
Khirbet Kerak
el
Ḥammeh
et Tanṭurah
Tell el Mutesellim
ʿAffuleh
Caesarea
Tell el Husn
Tell Dothan
Tell
Taʿaneck
Khirbet
Fahl
Sebastiyeh
Balatah
ISRAEL
Seilun
et
Tell ej-Jerisheh
Beitin
Tell
Tell es
Sultan
Tell Jizr
ej Jib
JORDAN
Tell en Nasbeh
Tell
el Ful
Teleilat
Ghassul
Jerusalem
Asqalan
Tell es Safi
Tell er
Rumeileh
Khirbet
Qumran
Ghazzeh
Tell Judeideh
Tell el
Duweir
Khirbet
Tubeiqah
Dhiban
Tell
Hesi
Tell ed
Tell Beit
Mirsim
Tell el
Jemmeh
ʿAjjul
Bab
edh Dhra'
Tell el Farʿah

Bottom coordinates: 2 · 30° · 3 · 35° · 4

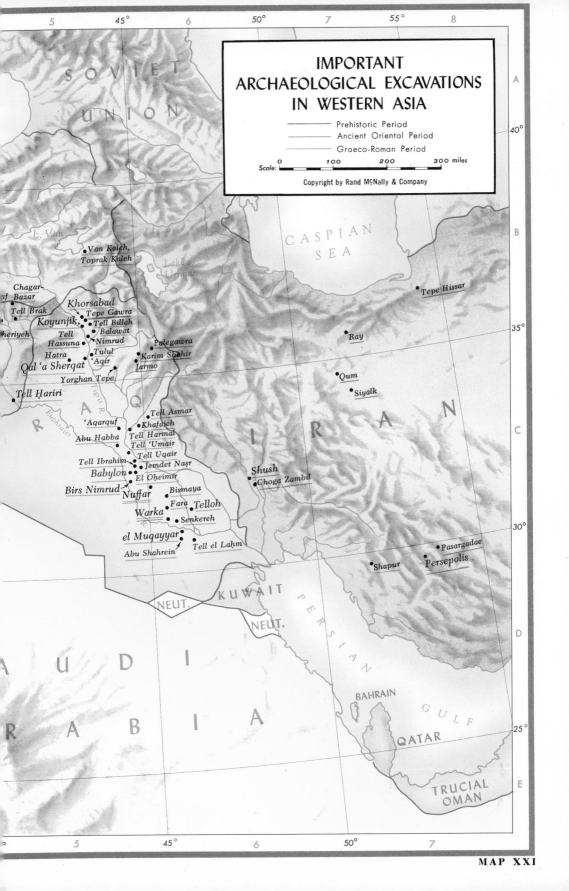

IMPORTANT
ARCHAEOLOGICAL EXCAVATIONS
IN WESTERN ASIA

Prehistoric Period
Ancient Oriental Period
Graeco-Roman Period

Scale: 0   100   200   300 miles

Copyright by Rand McNally & Company

SOVIET UNION

L. Van

Van Kaleh,
Toprak Kaleh

Lake Urmia

CASPIAN SEA

Tepe Hissar

Chagar-
af Bazar
Tell Brak
Khorsabad
heriyeh
Koyunjik
Tepe Gawra
Tell Billah
Tell
Hassuna
Balawat
Nimrud
Hatra
Tulul
Aqir
Qal 'a Sherqat
Yorghan Tepe
Palegawra
Karim Shahir
Jarmo

Ray

Qum
Siyalk

Tell Hariri

IRAQ

Euphrates

Tigris R.

'Aqarquf
Tell Asmar
Khafajeh
Abu Habba
Tell Harmal
Tell 'Umair
Tell Uqair
Tell Ibrahim
Jemdet Nasr
Babylon
El Oheimir
Birs Nimrud
Nuffar
Bismaya
Fara Telloh
Warka
Senkereh
el Muqayyar
Abu Shahrein
Tell el Lahm

IRAN

Shush
Choga Zambil

Pasargadae

Persepolis

Shapur

KUWAIT

NEUT.

NEUT.

PERSIAN

AUDI

RABIA

SAUDI ARABIA

BAHRAIN

GULF

QATAR

TRUCIAL
OMAN

MAP XXI

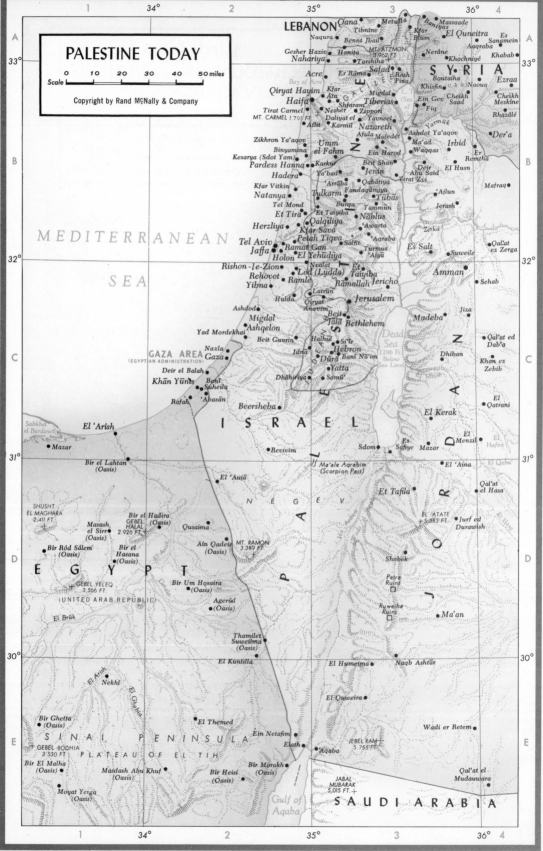

PALESTINE TODAY

Scale 0 10 20 30 40 50 miles

Copyright by Rand McNally & Company

MAP XXII